THE STATESMAN'S YEAR-BOOK

1978–1979

Man hat behauptet, die Welt werde durch Zahlen regiert: das aber weiss ich, dass die Zahlen uns belehren, ob sie gut oder schlecht regiert werde.

GOETHE

Editors

Frederick Martin	1864–1883
Sir John Scott-Keltie	1883–1926
Mortimer Epstein	1911/27–1946
S. H. Steinberg	1946–1969
John Paxton	1963/1969–

THE STATESMAN'S YEAR-BOOK

STATISTICAL AND HISTORICAL ANNUAL
OF THE STATES OF THE WORLD
FOR THE YEAR

1978–1979

EDITED BY

JOHN PAXTON

ST. MARTIN'S PRESS
NEW YORK

First published in 1864
115th edition 1978

For information, write:
ST. MARTIN'S PRESS, INC.
175 Fifth Ave., New York, N.Y. 10010

Printed in Great Britain by
RICHARD CLAY (THE CHAUCER PRESS) LTD.
Bungay Suffolk

Library of Congress Catalog Card Number 4–3776

ISBN: 0-312-76091-4

This edition published United States of America 1978

PREFACE

The Statesman's Year-Book has been published annually since 1864 and in this the 115th edition some fundamental changes have taken place. The editor has aimed at even easier access to facts and has divided it into two parts, as was the 1864 edition. The first deals with international organizations and the second with the states of the world in an A–Z sequence. Countries have also been re-arranged in a more logical order and he hopes that the new format will be appreciated by users. The editor always welcomes constructive and informed criticism, indeed, without the help of hundreds of correspondents all over the world The Statesman's Year-Book would not be celebrating its 115th edition nor would it be found on the shelves of the majority of libraries of the world.

The whole of the volume has been re-set this year and the editor is particularly grateful to the small army of proof-readers who have read the million words four times. This year particular praise should go to Richard Clay (The Chaucer Press) Ltd who have printed The Statesman's Year-Book since 1892 and for this edition have used photographic typesetting producing characters in complete page form on film for conversion to printing plates—printed web-offset. The kindness and consideration of the directors and staff of Richard Clay has considerably lightened the editor's load.

This year three maps are provided; one showing Guatemala and Belize, another giving details of the Treaties recently signed and ratified by the Government of the Republic of Panama and the US Government. The third is a specially drawn map showing World Desertification.

A companion volume, The Statesman's Year-Book World Gazetteer, is available for those who wish to have more detail about individual towns and cities.

J.P.

The Statesman's Year-Book Office,
The Macmillan Press Ltd,
Little Essex Street,
London, WC2R 3LF

WEIGHTS AND MEASURES

On 1 Jan. 1960 following an agreement between the standards laboratories of Great Britain, Canada, Australia, New Zealand, South Africa and the USA, an international yard and an international pound (avoirdupois) came into existence. 1 yard = 91·44 centimetres; 1 lb. = 453·59237 grammes.

The abbreviation 'm.' signifies 'million(s)' and tonnes implies metric tons.

Length		Dry Measure	
Centimetre	0·394 inch	Litre	0·91 quart
Metre	1·094 yards	Hectolitre	2·75 bushels
Kilometre	0·621 mile	**Weight—Avoirdupois**	
		Gramme	15·42 grains
Liquid Measure		Kilogramme	2·205 pounds
Litre	1·76 pints	Quintal (= 100 kg)	220·46 pounds
Hectolitre	22 gallons	Tonne (= 1,000 kg)	0·984 long ton; 1·102 short tons
Surface Measure		**Weight—Troy**	
Square metre	10·76 sq. feet	Gramme	15·43 grains
Hectare	2·47 acres	Kilogramme	32·15 ounces; 2·68 pounds
Square kilometre	0·386 sq. mile		

BRITISH WEIGHTS AND MEASURES

Length		Weight	
1 foot	0·305 metre	1 ounce (= 437·2 grains)	28·350 grammes
1 yard	0·914 metre	1 lb. (= 7,000 grains)	453·6 grammes
1 mile (= 1,760 yds)	1·609 kilometres	1 cwt. (= 112 lb.)	50·802 kilogrammes
		1 long ton (= 2,240 lb.)	1·016 tonnes
		1 short ton (= 2,000 lb.)	0·907 tonne
Surface Measure		**Liquid Measure**	
1 sq. foot	9·290 sq. decimetres	1 pint	0·568 litre
1 sq. yard	0·836 sq. metre	1 gallon	4·546 litres
1 acre	0·405 hectare	1 quarter	2·909 hectolitres
1 sq. mile	2·590 sq. kilometres		

CONTENTS

Comparative Statistical Tables

Part I: International Organizations

The United Nations

Other International Organizations

Part II: Countries of the World, A–Z

WHEAT

Countries	Area (1,000 hectares) Average 1961–65	1973	1974	1975	1976	Production (1,000 tonnes) Average 1961–65	1973	1974	1975	1976
Algeria	1,969	2,347	2,000	2,100	2,300	1,254	1,158	1,091	1,848	2,200
Argentina	4,916	3,958	4,233	5,271	7,175	7,541	6,560	5,970	8,570	11,200
Australia[1]	6,726	8,956	8,308	8,552	8,900	8,222	11,902	11,357	11,980	12,000
Bulgaria[1, 2]	1,222	934	861	819	793*	2,213	3,258	2,911	2,771	3,100
Canada	11,145	9,575	8,934	9,487	11,141	15,364	16,159	13,295	17,078	23,523
Chile[1]	753	534	571	686	698	1,082	747	939	1,002	850
China[1]	25,175	28,700	29,000	30,001	31,001	22,230	36,001	37,001	41,003	43,003
Czechoslovakia[2]	735	1,230	1,267	1,176	1,270	1,779	4,646	5,059	4,202	4,640
Egypt[1]	557	525	575	586	586	1,459	1,838	1,884	2,033	1,960
France	4,265	3,960	4,140	3,876	4,279	12,495	17,850	19,100	15,013	16,089
Germany, Fed. Rep. of[2]	1,391	1,603	1,631	1,569	1,632	4,607	7,134	7,761	7,014	6,702
Greece	1,193	841	916	920	920*	1,765	1,659	2,153	2,140	2,351*
Hungary[1, 3]	1,083	1,294	1,325	1,251	1,325	2,020	4,502	4,971	4,007	5,138
India	13,402	19,464	18,583	18,010	20,112	11,191	24,735	21,778	24,104	28,336
Iran	3,580	5,100	5,200	5,600	5,200	2,873	4,600	4,700	5,483	6,000
Iraq	1,210	1,156	1,633	1,408	1,499	849	957	1,339	845	1,312
Italy	4,398	3,590	3,712	3,545	3,552	8,857	8,920	9,695	9,610	9,528
Japan[1]	572	75	83	90	89	1,332	202	232	241	222
Morocco	1,578	2,039	1,917	1,691	1,911	1,336	1,574	1,853	1,575	2,190
Pakistan[1]	4,984	5,971	6,113	5,812	6,111	4,152	7,443	7,629	7,673	8,636
Poland[1]	1,516	1,962	2,002	1,842	1,832	2,988	5,807	6,408	5,207	5,741*
Portugal	688	442	470	466	567	550	517	546	611	680
Romania[1]	2,966	2,359	2,396	2,351	2,388*	4,321	5,489	5,007	4,862	6,730*
S. Africa, Republic of	1,197	1,480	1,450	1,460	1,460	840	1,871	1,596	1,792	2,060
Spain[2]	4,161	3,151	3,164	2,658	2,772	4,365	3,966	4,535	4,302	4,176
Tunisia	1,002	1,140	1,070	1,065	1,189	495	690	755	976	919*
Turkey[2]	7,959	8,915	8,808	9,309	8,600*	8,585	10,080	11,080	14,830	16,500
USSR[1]	66,622	63,155	59,676	61,985	59,462	64,207	109,784	83,913	66,224	96,900
UK	870	1,146	1,233	1,035	1,231	3,520	5,003	6,132	4,488	4,773
USA	19,432	21,800	26,552	28,182	28,661	33,040	46,408	48,885	58,102	58,444
Yugoslavia[2]	2,006	1,697	1,843	1,615	1,724	3,599	4,751	6,283	4,405	5,980
World total	210,474	221,431	222,834	228,356	235,302	254,399	376,700	360,341	355,824	417,478

* Unofficial figures. [1] Sown area. [2] Includes spelt. [3] Field crops and other crops.

RYE

Countries	Area (1,000 hectares) Average 1961–65	1973	1974	1975	1976	Production (1,000 tonnes) Average 1961–65	1973	1974	1975	1976
Argentina	548	656	375	300	437*	422	613	306	273	330
Austria	180	123	123	119	120	393	400	415	347	410
Belgium	39	17	13	9	16*	120	63	54	33	50*
Bulgaria[1]	58	15	15	17	15	58	19	21	18	20
Canada	275	256	341	320	323	319	363	480	523	561
Czechoslovakia[2]	429	224	218	190	185	897	690	671	530	530*
Denmark	131	42	46	49	73	380	140	168	163	236
Finland	93	52	73	38	65	141	124	134	81	178
France	235	122	116	111	114	367	327	312	301	283
German Demo. Rep.	820	646	637	593	650	1,741	1,699	1,949	1,563	1,400
Germany, Fed. Rep. of	1,138	739	708	624	663	3,031	2,576	2,560	2,125	2,100
Hungary[1, 3]	253	107	106	104	93	271	178	177	147	156
Italy	53	18	17	17	17	87	38	37	37	35
Netherlands	107	31	22	18	21	312	105	78	63	65
Poland[1]	4,563	3,416	3,138	2,792	2,934*	7,466	8,268	7,882	6,270	6,914*
Portugal	311	207	210	210	198	177	134	143	145	147
Romania[1]	88	33	32*	41*	40*	95	39*	42*	52*	49*
Spain	442	268	249	228	226	385	252	254	241	209
Sweden	56	95	109	97	121	142	324	440	331	418
Turkey	689	610	600	565	560*	734	690	560	750	900
USSR[1]	16,300	7,012	9,810	8,010	9,035	15,093	10,759	15,223	9,064	12,000
USA	670	418	363	329	325	828	667	490	454	423
Yugoslavia	163	96	91	84	76	169	118	120	98	105
World total	27,838	15,335	17,527	14,979	16,431	33,833	28,738	32,659	23,739	27,660

* Unofficial figures. [1] Sown area. [2] In cludes mixture of wheat and rye. [3] Field crops and other crops.

BARLEY

Countries	Area (1,000 hectares) Average 1961–65	1973	1974	1975	1976	Production (1,000 tonnes) Average 1961–65	1973	1974	1975	1976
Algeria	810	786	618*	855	800	476	374	331	743	600
Argentina	547	502	369	439	500*	679	732	430	523	760
Australia[1]	873	1,894	1,826	2,328	2,300	978	2,398	2,513	3,178	2,840*
Bulgaria[1]	336	458	477	575	530	694	1,368	1,636	1,699	1,800
Canada	2,315	4,839	4,775	4,468	4,339	3,860	10,223	8,802	9,520	10,303
Czechoslovakia	682	871	860	973	850	1,556	2,962	3,375	3,114	3,100
Denmark	912	1,445	1,437	1,443	1,471	3,506	5,432	5,967	5,156	4,767
France	2,353	2,799	2,712	2,779	2,734	6,594	10,948	9,972	9,336	8,280
German Demo. Rep.	438	692	779	929	850	1,291	2,848	3,422	3,681	3,300
Germany, Fed. Rep. of	1,150	1,671	1,665	1,756	1,735	3,462	6,622	7,048	6,970	6,487
Hungary[1, 2]	518	291	272	257	228*	970	874	899	701	746
India	2,998	2,449	2,650	2,885	2,941	2,590	2,379	2,371	3,135	3,196
Iran	1,000	1,314	1,280	1,532	1,480	792	923	863	1,438	1,487
Iraq	920	464	519	567	576	851	462	533	437	579
Japan[1]	554	78	78	78	80	1,380	216	233	221	210
Korea, South[1]	896	816	704	711	711*	1,419	1,778	1,388	1,700	1,759*
Mexico	219	262	179	286	315*	175	392	271	440	460*
Morocco	1,627	2,041	1,998	1,844	2,130	1,316	1,257	2,389	1,587	2,862
Peru[1]	180	185*	187*	187*	185*	185	165*	168*	168*	165*
Poland[1]	704	1,083	1,230	1,335	1,210*	1,368	3,158	3,909	3,638	3,608*
Romania[1]	237	315	403	442	410*	415	730	917	952	1,220*
Spain	1,420	2,773	3,027	3,262	3,240	1,959	4,402	5,404	6,728	5,163
Syria	740	914	697	1,011	1,172	649	102	656	596	1,059
Tunisia	507	400	390	335	350	145	210	171	260	230*
Turkey	2,791	2,405	2,575	2,588	2,700*	3,447	2,900	3,330	4,500	5,100
USSR[1]	18,296	29,387	31,079	32,548	34,258	20,318	55,044	54,208	35,808	69,500*
UK	1,858	2,267	2,216	2,345	2,182	6,668	9,006	9,140	8,513	7,793
USA	4,509	4,231	3,306	3,539	3,407	8,676	9,180	6,622	8,360	8,215
Yugoslavia	369	328	330	360	293	557	676	794	703	653
World total	68,011	87,854	87,773	92,100	93,446	99,686	169,417	170,286	156,591	189,654

* Unofficial figures. [1] Sown areas. [2] Field crops and other crops.

OATS

Countries	Area (1,000 hectares) Average 1961–65	1973	1974	1975	1976	Production (1,000 tonnes) Average 1961–65	1973	1974	1975	1976
Argentina	538	395	282	338	423*	676	561	327	433	530
Australia	1,380	1,182	897	987	1,080	1,172	1,107	874	1,141*	1,190*
Austria	147	94	92	101	95	322	284	290	306	283
Belgium	116	62	59	70	48	389	250	269	257	145*
Canada	3,626	2,711	2,471	2,411	2,471	6,075	5,041	3,929	4,467	4,961
China	2,100	2,700	2,750	2,800	2,900	1,690	2,700	2,800	3,000	3,000
Czechoslovakia[2]	416	272	221	221	190	792	740	687	591	580
Denmark	192	129	122	111	95	713	444	472	367	267
Finland	463	528	550	572	551	828	1,169	1,113	1,450	1,573
France	1,250	693	666	641	652	2,583	2,208	2,059	1,898	1,424
German Demo. Rep.	319	238	222	243	240	850	806	922	780	600
Germany, Fed. Rep. of	758	821	851	920	856	2,185	3,045	3,482	3,445	2,497
Hungary[1, 2]	93	40	37	45	39	108	72	85	92	86
Irish Republic	131	50	44	50	37*	357	162	157	168	123*
Italy	398	238	236	239	236	545	419	462	506	440
Netherlands	111	30	33	34	25	421	134	163	158	103
Poland[1]	1,548	1,271	1,182	1,291	1,115*	2,641	3,221	3,244	2,920	2,696*
Portugal	273	157	171	207	189	87	79	99	121	133
Romania[1]	150	105	85	70	67*	154	102	91	57	48*
Spain	534	472	475	457	454	447	425	559	609	505
Sweden	480	474	436	464	460	1,304	1,209	1,686	1,345	1,281
Turkey	406	279	275	260	270*	495	380	380	390	400*
USSR[1]	7,311	11,887	11,567	12,107	11,237	6,052	17,516	15,302	12,495	17,000
UK	539	281	255	232	235	1,531	1,080	955	795	806
USA	8,567	5,692	5,344	5,507	5,015	13,848	9,680	8,909	9,546	8,164
World total	33,400	32,145	30,599	31,723	30,244	47,813	54,369	51,034	49,010	50,373

* Unofficial figures. [1] Sown area. [2] Includes mixture of oats and barley. [3] Field crops and other crops.

MAIZE

Countries	Area (1,000 hectares) Average 1961–65	1973	1974	1975	1976	Production (1,000 tonnes) Average 1961–65	1973	1974	1975	1976
Argentina	2,836	3,662	3,486	3,070	2,766	4,984	9,700	9,900	7,700	5,855
Brazil	7,814	9,908	10,294	10,473	11,122	10,112	14,109	16,285	16,354	17,929
Bulgaria	632	623	523	652	605	1,601	2,565	1,626	2,822	2,900
China	9,178	10,631	10,839	11,050	11,548	22,756	30,384	31,107	33,138	34,114
Colombia	747	710	650	657	648*	826	824	775	800	884*
Egypt	678	696	738	769	739*	1,913	2,508	2,641	2,781	2,710*
France	914	1,942	1,907	1,966	1,425	2,760	10,692	8,885	8,163	5,477
Ghana	210	405	425	320	360*	202	438	486	343	395*
Greece	167	167	131	125	132*	241	585	459	468	551*
Hungary	1,281	1,500	1,497	1,413	1,407*	3,350	6,025	6,333	7,215*	5,200*
India	4,630	6,015	5,863	5,996	6,200	4,593	5,804	5,559	7,036	6,500
Indonesia	2,870	3,433	2,648	2,444	2,600	2,804	3,690	3,011	2,638	2,532*
Italy	1,108	890	890	897	909	3,633	5,089	5,043	5,326	5,082
Mexico	6,960	6,965	6,139	6,694	7,000	7,369	8,556	7,784	8,459	8,945
Morocco	442	446	447	492	430	352	217	389	371	430
Pakistan	492	633	614	620	601	513	768	747	802	711*
Peru	337	430	320	370*	400*	490	616	472	625*	670*
Philippines	1,978	2,763	2,929	3,126	3,260*	1,305	2,289	2,414	2,697	2,710*
Portugal	492	372	360	392	352	560	509	486	506	357
Rhodesia	396	400*	500*	475*	475*	833*	617*	1,700*	1,400*	1,400*
Romania	3,308	2,957	2,963	3,305	3,401*	5,853	7,397	7,440	9,241	11,700*
S. Africa, Republic of	4,186	3,611	6,500	5,700	5,700	5,229	4,160	11,105	9,140	7,312
Spain	471	523	501	488	442	1,101	2,038	1,993	1,792	1,543
Turkey	674	617	620	597	600*	950	1,100	1,200	1,200	1,230*
USSR[1]	5,887	4,031	3,955	2,652	3,303	13,122	13,216	12,104	7,328	10,300
USA	22,933	25,047	26,449	27,203	28,767	95,561	143,435	118,461	147,251	157,893
Venezuela	441	439	462	506	480*	477	454	554	653	532*
Yugoslavia	2,474	2,377	2,256	2,363	2,372	5,618	8,253	8,031	9,389	9,112
World total	99,682	110,218	113,671	113,858	118,054	216,381	311,212	293,233	324,670	334,014

* Unofficial figures. [1] For dry grain only.

RICE (Paddy)

Countries	Area (1,000 hectares) Average 1961–65	1973	1974	1975	1976	Production (1,000 tonnes) Average 1961–65	1973	1974	1975	1976
Bangladesh	8,955	9,878	9,792	10,329	10,000	15,034	17,863	16,930	19,143	18,500
Brazil	3,809	4,795	4,164	5,279	6,588	6,123	7,167	6,483	7,538	9,560
Burma	4,741	4,879	4,884	5,069	5,180*	7,786	8,602	8,583	9,221	9,400*
China	30,953	34,724	35,278	35,390	35,391	86,038	111,954	115,213	116,267	116,570
Egypt	348	419	442	442	484*	1,845	2,274	2,242	2,423	2,530*
India	35,626	38,285	37,888	39,688	38,600	52,733	66,077	59,368	74,186	70,500
Indonesia	7,036	8,404	8,537	8,765	8,800	12,393	21,500	22,473	22,570	22,950
Iran	292	380	400	400	430	851	1,334	1,380*	1,615*	1,500
Iraq	86	64	31	30	50	138	157	69	61	163
Italy	121	190	188	174	180	612	1,045	1,047	1,009	976
Japan	3,281	2,622	2,724	2,764	2,779	16,444	15,778	15,964	17,097	15,292
Kampuchea, Democratic	2,284	811	555	1,050	1,400	2,461	1,050	635	1,500	1,800
Korea, South	1,169	1,182	1,205	1,218	1,215	4,809	5,854	6,178	6,485	7,250
Madagascar	843	1,055	1,134	1,066	1,050	1,563	1,730	1,844	1,874	1,814
Malaysia	535	739*	740	767	738	1,140	1,967	2,093	2,013	1,908
Mexico	137	150	173	196	155*	314	451	469	510	450*
Pakistan	1,287	1,512	1,604	1,710	1,699	1,824	3,682	3,470	3,926	3,942
Philippines	3,147	3,437	3,539	3,579	3,562*	3,957	5,594	5,660	6,217	6,439*
Sierra Leone	273	351	370	380	390	336*	479	524*	547*	580
Spain	62	61	61	62	65	386	386	367	379	392
Sri Lanka	505	571	797	597	635	967	1,312	1,603	1,154	1,253
Thailand	6,348	7,743	7,333	8,383	8,200	11,267	14,898	13,386	15,300	14,900
USSR	158	462	495	500	524	390	1,765	1,913	2,009	2,100*
USA	705	878	1,026	1,134	1,012	3,084	4,208	5,098	5,805	5,308
Vietnam	4,813	5,030	5,112	5,310	5,300	9,629	11,125	11,023	12,000	12,000*
World total	123,602	135,490	135,798	142,085	142,248	253,180	323,163	320,083	348,570	345,386

* Unofficial figures.

MILLET

Countries	Area (1,000 hectares) Average 1961–65	1973	1974	1975	1976	Production (1,000 tonnes) Average 1961–65	1973	1974	1975	1976
Argentina	158	198	208	194	231	186	227	229	200	294
Australia	28	27	40	22	25	29	26	35	22	35
Cameroon	454	459	404	430	430	413	321	366	386	390
Chad	1,193	832	851	850	900	895	464	559	523	533
Egypt	201	205	211	205	206*	723	853	825	775	800*
Ghana	109	192	222	200*	215*	68	109	154	122*	71*
India	18,638	20,860	18,215	18,784	20,500	7,728	11,557	7,021	10,148	9,600
Korea, South	140	37	32	27	27	70	31	30	26	26
Mali	1,132	1,200	1,250	1,121	1,244	782	525	600	696	804
Niger	1,340	2,000	2,230	2,200	2,532	524	627	883	634	1,195
Nigeria	4,324	4,500	4,900	5,000	5,000	2,615	2,350	3,000	3,200	3,200
Pakistan	835	733	545	624	696	394	352	265	308	350
Poland	27	14	13	12	10*	32	17	13	9	8
Rhodesia[1]	416	390	390	390	390	240	220	220	220	220
Senegal	956	1,100	1,154	963	955	483	514	795	621	555
Sri Lanka	28	32	41	48	41	19	21	24	26	20
Sudan	523	1,052	1,132	1,111	1,200	303	268	434	432	450
Syria	57	22	26	31	30	46	13	14	24	25
Togo	230	202	191	200	199	99	147	101	120	119
Turkey	47	38	30	25	25	60	33	40	40	40
Uganda	535	650	510	567	508	444	651	571	482	650
USSR	3,773	2,850	2,970	2,774	2,999	2,639	4,416	2,907	1,125	4,500
Upper Volta	728	720	850	911	911	300	253	370	383	370
Zaïre	53	78	86	70	70	40	64	70	41*	42*
World total	66,622	70,703	69,412	69,280	72,808	38,159	48,994	45,407	46,580	51,461

* Unofficial figures. [1] On farms and estates.

SORGHUM

Countries	Area (1,000 hectares) Average 1961–65	1973	1974	1975	1976	Production (1,000 tonnes) Average 1961–65	1973	1974	1975	1976
Argentina	856	2,282	2,324	1,938	1,834	1,359	5,159	6,074	5,000	5,200*
Australia	154	697	540	511	504	228	1,018	1,061	901	1,120*
El Salvador	97	119	127	132	125*	91	156	131	175	164
Ethiopia[1, 2]	1,041	1,150	1,100	748	770	831	1,000	800	658	863
Ghana	158	184	215	208*	210*	104	167	176	137*	81*
Honduras	42	30*	55	56	57*	51	42*	39	53	47
India	18,155	16,716	16,189	16,101	16,000	8,848	9,097	10,414	9,525	8,700
Mexico	205	1,185	1,153	1,116	1,180*	452	3,182	3,183	2,843	3,350*
Morocco	120	54	71	58	49	74	52	88	75	19
Niger	464	448	542	600	633	306	126	219	254	308
Nigeria	5,237	5,300*	5,645*	5,795*	5,940	4,204	2,968*	3,500*	3,590*	3,680*
Pakistan	529	589	445	476	523	261	378	266	281	325*
Rwanda	100	131	134	133	135	134	142	121	144	140
Saudi Arabia	115	135	138	140	140	167	175	200	200	200
Sudan	1,400	1,822	2,343	2,596	2,600	1,256	1,638	1,702	2,026	1,800
Uganda	302	287	367	311	359	276	416	546	467	538
USA	4,909	6,415	5,615	6,280	6,020	13,912	23,623	15,983	19,307	18,382
Upper Volta	999	1,037	1,200	1,138	1,138	514	481	705	738	717
World total	38,313	42,838	42,406	43,768	43,929	35,779	54,461	50,487	52,097	51,812

* Unofficial figures. [1] Includes teff. [2] Unspecified millet and sorghum.

CENTRIFUGAL RAW SUGAR

(in 1,000 tonnes)

Countries	*Average 1961–65*	*1970*	*1972*	*1973*	*1974*	*1975*	*1976*
Argentina	971	979	1,303	1,638	1,530	1,353	1,565*
Australia [1]	1,801	2,514	2,835	2,527	2,849	2,933*	3,400*
Barbados [2]	176	157	113*	118*	113*	101*	106*
Brazil	3,786	5,447	6,289	6,943	6,986*	6,180*	7,340*
Canada	144	107	125	117	101	133	163
China	2,430	3,657	4,035	4,117	4,327	4,287	4,552
Cuba	5,254	7,559	4,688	5,350*	6,044*	6,432*	5,700*
Czechoslovakia	931	763*	753*	714*	750*	800*	680*
Dominican Rep.	798	1,015	1,201*	1,193*	1,230	1,234*	1,250*
Egypt	357	491*	593	651*	611*	550*	626*
France	2,034	2,696	2,984	3,170	2,947	3,230*	2,957*
Fiji [1]	266	361	303	301	273	272	298*
German Demo. Rep.	603	490*	637	548*	655*	665*	560*
Germany, Fed. Rep. of	1,737	2,056	2,214	2,453	2,439	2,534	2,736*
Guyana	312	316	320	270	345	311	343*
India [3]	2,976	4,663	3,806	4,209	4,292	5,211	4,630*
Indonesia [4]	664	713	889	820	1,137*	1,126*	1,149*
Italy	1,053	1,202	1,280	1,149	1,012	1,442	1,630
Jamaica	472	376	379	331	372	361	368*
Mauritius [4]	591	576	686	718	697	468	690
Mexico	1,738	2,365*	2,526	2,821	2,834	2,713*	2,750*
Pakistan [3]	152	680	399	470	661	547	641*
Peru	791	773	922	914	1,021	990	950
Philippines	1,515	1,926	1,859	2,245	2,534	2,471	2,735
Poland	1,532	1,505	1,826	1,817	1,589	1,699	1,801*
Puerto Rico	896	413	268	229	261	271	279
S. Africa, Rep. of	1,080	1,399	1,915	1,732	1,883	1,801	2,042
Spain	514	795	832	816	597	917	1,346*
Sweden	247	220	293	264	302	277	302*
Trinidad	234	221	235	184	186	163*	205*
USSR	7,659	9,293*	8,315*	9,538*	7,800*	7,700*	9,100*
UK	875	984	964	1,046	622	697*	760*
USA [5]	4,561	5,277	5,773	5,215	4,924	6,308	6,187
World total	57,001	74,189	74,251	77,627	77,409	80,900	86,393

[1] 94° net titre. [2] Includes the sugar equivalent of fancy molasses. [3] Includes sugar (raw value) refined from gur. [4] Tel quel. [5] Includes Hawaii.

* Unofficial figures.

WORLD ESTIMATED CRUDE OIL PRODUCTION[1]

(in 1,000 tonnes)

	1960	*1970*	*1976*	*1977*
North America				
USA	384,080	533,677	454,963	462,830
Canada	27,480	69,954	70,774	73,000
Caribbean Area				
Venezuela	148,690	193,209	118,926	116,450
Trinidad	6,075	7,225	10,992	11,850
Colombia	8,100	11,071	7,567	7,580
Other Latin America				
Mexico	14,125	21,877	44,474	51,700
Argentina	9,160	19,969	20,195	21,800
Brazil	4,050	8,009	8,704	8,050
Ecuador	390	191	9,020	8,640
Peru	2,680	3,450	3,708	3,940
Bolivia	450	1,128	1,888	1,860
Chile	990	1,620	1,086	930
Middle East				
Saudi Arabia	61,090	176,851	428,800	453,160
Iran	52,065	191,663	293,951	276,410
Iraq	47,480	76,600	112,010	110,950
Kuwait	81,860	137,397	109,134	94,320
Abu Dhabi	—	33,288	76,534	79,700
Qatar	8,210	17,257	23,520	21,410
Oman	—	17,169	18,105	16,880
Dubai	—	4,306	15,291	15,550
Egypt	3,600	16,404	16,600	22,000
Syria	—	4,350	9,976	8,890
Turkey	350	3,461	2,568	2,560
Bahrain	2,250	3,834	2,880	2,780
Sharjah	—	—	1,807	1,370
Africa				
Nigeria	880	53,420	102,302	104,280
Libya	—	159,201	91,859	100,110
Algeria	8,630	47,253	50,100	47,290
Gabon	850	5,460	11,251	11,220
Angola	70	5,066	6,281	8,150
Tunisia	—	4,151	3,712	4,230
Congo	—	—	2,002	1,840
Zaïre	—	—	916	1,000

[1] Excluding small-scale production in Afghánistán, Bangladesh, Cuba, Guatemala, Israel, Mongolia, Morocco, New Zealand, Taiwan and Thailand.

WORLD ESTIMATED CRUDE OIL PRODUCTION
(*contd.*)

(in 1,000 tonnes)

	1960	*1970*	*1976*	*1977*
Western Europe				
UK	90	84	12,036	40,100
Norway	—	—	13,718	13,590
Germany, Fed. Rep. of	5,560	7,536	5,526	5,450
Austria	2,440	2,798	1,931	1,890
Spain	—	156	1,982	1,630
Netherlands	1,920	1,919	1,546	1,610
France	2,260	2,308	1,058	1,050
Italy	1,990	1,408	1,123	990
Denmark	—	—	213	500
Far East				
Indonesia	20,560	42,102	74,822	83,200
Australia	—	8,292	19,617	20,300
Brunei	4,690	6,916	11,033	10,300
India	440	6,809	8,623	9,600
Malaysia	—	—	8,024	9,150
Burma	530	750	1,160	1,210
Japan	510	750	579	620
Pakistan	360	486	341	500
USSR and Eastern Europe				
USSR	148,000	352,667	520,000	551,500
Romania	11,500	13,377	14,800	14,800
Yugoslavia	1,040	2,854	3,880	3,900
Albania	600	1,199	1,860	1,900
Hungary	1,215	1,937	2,141	2,200
Poland	195	424	455	400
German Dem. Rep.	—	60	200	200
Bulgaria	200	334	120	120
Czechoslovakia	140	203	131	130
China	5,000	20,000	87,000	95,500
World Total	1,090,080	2,336,153	2,925,815	3,025,070

TERRITORIAL SEA LIMITS (IN MILES)

State	*Territorial Sea*	*Jurisdiction over fisheries (measured from the baseline of the territorial sea)*
Albania	15 (1976)	—
Algeria	12 (1963)	—
Angola	20 (1975)	200 (1975) (economic zone)
Argentina	200 (1966)	—
Australia	3 (1878)	12 (1967)
Bahamas	12 (1977)	200 (1977)
Bahrain	3	—
Bangladesh	12 (1974)	200 (1974) (economic zone)
Barbados	3	—
Belgium	3	200 (1977)
Benin	200 (1976)	—
Brazil	200 (1970)	—
Bulgaria	12 (1951)	—
Burma	12 (1968)	200 (1977)
Cameroon	50 (1974)	—
Canada	12 (1970)	200 (1977)
Cape Verde	100 (1975)	—
Chile	3	200 (1952)
China	12 (1958)	—
Colombia	12 (1970)	—
Comoro Islands	12 (1976)	200 (1976) (economic zone)
Congo	30 (1971)	—
Costa Rica	12 (1972)	200 (1972) (patrimonial sea)
Cuba	12 (1977)	200 (1977)
Cyprus	12 (1964)	—
Denmark (including Faroe Islands and Greenland)	3 (1966)	200 (1977)
Djibouti	12 (1971)	—
Dominican Republic	12 (1977)	200 (1977)
Ecuador	200 (1966)	—
Egypt	12 (1958)	—
El Salvador	200 (1950)	—
Equatorial Guinea	12 (1970)	—
Ethiopia	12 (1953)	—
Fiji	12 (1976)	—
Finland	4 (1956)	12 (1975)
France	12 (1971)	200 (1977) (economic zone; North Sea and Atlantic)
Gabon	100 (1972)	—
Gambia	50 (1971)	200 (1977)
German Democratic Republic	3	—
Germany, Federal Republic of	In accordance with international law	200 (1977)
Ghana	200 (1977)	—
Greece	6 (1936)	—
Grenada	3 (1878)	—
Guatemala	12 (1934)	200 (1976)
Guinea	200 (1975)	—
Guinea-Bissau	150 (1974)	—
Guyana	12 (1977)	200 (1977)
Haiti	12 (1972)	200 (1977)

TERRITORIAL SEA LIMITS (IN MILES)—*contd.*

State	*Territorial Sea*	*Jurisdiction over fisheries (measured from the baseline of the territorial sea)*
Honduras	12 (1965)	200 (1951)
Iceland	—	200 (1975)
India	12	200 (1977) (economic zone)
Indonesia	12 (1957)[1]	—
Iran	12 (1959)	[2]
Iraq	12 (1958)	—
Irish Republic	3 (1959)	200 (1977)
Israel	6 (1956)	—
Italy	12 (1974)	—
Ivory Coast	12 (1977)	200 (1977)
Jamaica	12 (1971)	—
Japan	12 (1977)	200 (1977)[2]
Jordan	3 (1943)	—
Kampuchea, Democratic	12 (1969)	—
Kenya	12 (1969)	—
Korea (North)	12 (1967)	200 (1977)
Korea (South)	—	20–200 (1952–54)
Kuwait	12 (1967)	—
Lebanon	—	6 (1921)
Liberia	200 (1976)	—
Libya	12 (1959)	—
Madagascar	50 (1973)	—
Malaysia	12 (1969)	—
Maldive, Republic of	3–55[3]	100–150[3]
Malta	6 (1971)	20 (1975)
Mauritania	30 (1972)	—
Mauritius	12 (1970)	200 (1977)
Mexico	12 (1969)	200 (1976) (economic zone)
Monaco	12	—
Morocco	12 (1973)	70 (1973)[4]
Mozambique	12 (1976)	200 (1976) (economic zone)
Nauru	12 (1971)	—
Netherlands	3 (1889)	200 (1977)
New Zealand	12 (1977)	200 (1977)
Nicaragua	—	200 (1965)
Nigeria	30 (1971)	—
Norway	4 (1812)	200 (1977)
Oman	12 (1972)	200 (1977)
Pakistan	12 (1966)	200 (1976)
Panama	200 (1967)	—
Papua New Guinea	12 (1977)	200 (1977)
Peru	200 (1947)[5]	200[5]
Philippines	[6]	[6]

[1] The territorial sea of Indonesia is measured by straight lines surrounding the archipelago.

[2] Outer limits of the superjacent waters of the continental shelf. 50 miles in the Sea of Oman (1973).

[3] Territorial limits and fishing zones defined by geographical co-ordinates at estimated mileage given.

[4] Six miles for Strait of Gibraltar.

[5] Sovereignty and jurisdiction over the sea, its soil and subsoil up to 200 miles (1947).

[6] The territorial sea of the Philippines is determined by straight base-lines joining appropriate points of the outermost islands forming the Philippine archipelago in accordance with Treaties of 1898, 1900 and 1930 (1961).

TERRITORIAL SEA LIMITS (IN MILES)—*contd.*

State	*Territorial Sea*	*Jurisdiction over fisheries (measured from the baseline of the territorial sea)*
Poland	3 (1932)	Up to limits of shelf (1977)
Portugal	12 (1977)	200 (1977)
Qatar	3	[1]
Romania	12 (1951)	—
São Tomé	6	12
Saudi Arabia	12 (1958)	[1]
Senegal	150 (1976)	200 (1976)
Seychelles	12 (1977)	200 (1977)
Sierra Leone	200 (1971)	—
Singapore	3 (1878)	—
Somalia	200 (1973)	—
South Africa, Republic of	12 (1977)	200 (1977)
Spain	12 (1977)	—
Sri Lanka	12 (1971)	—
Sudan	12 (1960)	—
Surinam	3	12
Sweden	4 (1779)	200 (1978)
Syria	12 (1964)	—
Tanzania	50 (1973)	—
Thailand	12 (1966)	—
Togo	200 (1977)	—
Tonga	[2]	—
Trinidad and Tobago	12 (1969)	—
Tunisia	12 (1973)	—
Turkey	6 (1964)	12 (1964)
USSR	12 (1909)	200 (1977)
United Arab Emirates	3[3]	—
UK	3 (1878)	200 (1977)
USA	3 (1793)	200 (1977) (fishery conservation zone)
Uruguay	200 (1969)	—
Venezuela	12 (1956)	—
Vietnam	12 (1977)	200 (1977)
Western Samoa	3	6
Yemen, Peoples Dem. Rep. of	12 (1970)	18
Yemen, Republic of	12 (1967)	—
Yugoslavia	10 (1965)	—
Zaïre	12 (1974)	—

[1] Outer limits of the superjacent waters of the continental shelf (1974).
[2] Territorial limits defined by geographical co-ordinates (173–177° W. and 15–23° 30′ S.) (1887).
[3] Sharjah, 12 miles.

The table above, reproduced from a survey prepared by the FAO of the UN shows: (*a*) the territorial sea limit, and (*b*) jurisdiction over fisheries.

Books of Reference

Buzan, B., *Seabed Politics*. New York, 1976
Churchill, R., Simmonds, K. R., and Welch, J. (eds.), *New Directions in the Law of the Sea*. London, 1973
Janis, M. W., *Sea Power and the Law of the Sea*. Lexington, 1977
Luard, E., *The Control of the Sea-Bed*. London, 1974

WORLD TOP FIFTY BANKS

Bank	*Balance sheet total (US$1,000)*	*Balance date*
Bankamerica Corporation	75,607,894	June 1977
Citicorp	64,281,504	Dec. 1976
Chase Manhattan Corporation	44,718,551	Dec. 1976
Deutsche Bank	44,425,986	Dec. 1976
Credit Lyonnais	40,993,058	Dec. 1976
Banque Nationale de Paris	40,153,992	Dec. 1976
Dai-Ichi Kangyo Bank	40,047,116	Mar. 1977
Banco do Brasil	38,926,700	Dec. 1976
Dresdner Bank	35,623,428	Dec. 1976
Fuji Bank	34,820,505	Mar. 1977
Sumitomo Bank	34,690,523	Mar. 1977
Mitsubishi Bank	33,322,449	Mar. 1977
Sanwa Bank	32,644,002	Mar. 1977
Barclays Bank Group	32,457,689	Dec. 1976
Manufacturers Hanover Corporation	32,075,419	June 1977
Société Générale	32,070,912	Dec. 1976
Bank Handlowy w Warszawie	30,969,274	Dec. 1976
Westdeutsche Landesbank Girozentrale	30,654,017	Dec. 1976
Sal. Openheim Jr. & Cie	30,146,975	Dec. 1976
J. P. Morgan & Co.	30,136,534	June 1977
Industrial Bank of Japan	28,987,364	Mar. 1977
National Westminster Bank Group	28,677,673	Dec. 1976
Royal Bank of Canada	28,623,622	Oct. 1976
Chemical New York Corporation	27,757,363	June 1977
Daiwa Bank	26,813,031	Mar. 1977
Commerzbank	26,708,934	Dec. 1976
Canadian Imperial Bank of Commerce	25,934,863	Oct. 1976
Tokai Bank	25,190,798	Mar. 1977
Banca Nazionale del Lavoro	24,506,333	Dec. 1976
Bayerische Vereinsbank	23,955,635	Dec. 1976
Bank of Tokyo	23,504,169	Mar. 1977
Mitsui Trust and Banking Company	23,356,777	Mar. 1977
Mitsubishi Trust and Banking Corporation	23,356,772	Mar. 1977
Mitsui Bank	23,350,969	Sept. 1976
Taiyo Kobe Bank	23,201,969	Mar. 1977
Continental Illinois Corporation	23,025,239	June 1977
Algemene Bank Nederland	22,631,617	Dec. 1976
Long-Term Credit Bank of Japan	22,561,921	Mar. 1977
Consorzio di Credito per le Opere Pubbliche	22,532,386	Dec. 1976
Bankers Trust New York Corporation	22,160,309	June 1977
Sumitomo Trust and Banking Company	21,757,991	Mar. 1977
Swiss Bank Corporation	21,564,943	Dec. 1976
Union Bank of Switzerland	21,521,675	Dec. 1976
First Chicago Corporation	21,432,627	June 1977
Centrale Rabobank	20,587,627	Dec. 1976
Amsterdam-Rotterdam Bank	20,414,625	Dec. 1976
Bank of Montreal	20,199,323	Oct. 1976
Midland Bank Group	19,896,895	Dec. 1976
Lloyds Bank Group	19,803,871	Dec. 1976
Bayerische Hypotheken- und Wechsel-Bank	19,449,106	Dec. 1976

ADDENDA

FEDERAL REPUBLIC OF GERMANY. Werner Maihofer, Minister of the Interior, resigned on 7 June 1978.

ITALY. President Giovanni Leone resigned on 15 June 1978. Amintore Fanfani acting as Head of State until Presidential elections.

JORDAN. On 8 June 1978 King Hussein announced that his youngest son, Prince Ali, will become Crown Prince when Prince Hassan succeeds to the throne. King Hussein married Elizabeth Halabi (now Queen Nur) on 15 June.

MALAYSIA. General elections are to be held on 8 July 1978.

DENMARK. From 1 July 1978 the Danish Prime Minister, Anker Joergensen, took over the portfolio of Foreign Affairs.

PAKISTAN. Lieut.-Gen. Mohammad Akbar Khan, Ambassador to London, died in June 1978.

YEMEN ARAB REPUBLIC. The President of the Republic was assassinated on 25 June 1978.

DOMINICAN REPUBLIC. On 26 May 1978 Antonio Guzman was confirmed as the successful winner of the Presidential elections thus ending the 12-year rule of Joaquín Balaguer.

PART I

INTERNATIONAL ORGANIZATIONS

THE UNITED NATIONS

The United Nations is an association of states which have pledged themselves, through signing the Charter, to maintain international peace and security and to co-operate in establishing political, economic and social conditions under which this task can be securely achieved. Nothing contained in the Charter authorizes the organization to intervene in matters which are essentially within the domestic jurisdiction of any state.

The United Nations Charter originated from proposals agreed upon at discussions held at Dumbarton Oaks (Washington, D.C.) between the USSR, US and UK from 21 Aug. to 28 Sept., and between US, UK and China from 29 Sept. to 7 Oct. 1944. These proposals were laid before the United Nations Conference on International Organization, held at San Francisco from 25 April to 26 June 1945, and (after amendments had been made to the original proposals) the Charter of the United Nations was signed on 26 June 1945 by the delegates of 50 countries. Ratification of all the signatures had been received by 31 Dec. 1945. (For the complete text of the Charter *see* THE STATESMAN'S YEAR-BOOK, 1946, pp. xxi–xxxii.)

The United Nations formally came into existence on 24 Oct. 1945, with the deposit of the requisite number of ratifications of the Charter with the US Department of State. The official languages of the United Nations are Chinese, English, French, Russian and Spanish; the working languages are English, French and (in the General Assembly) Arabic, Chinese, Spanish and Russian.

The headquarters of the United Nations is in New York City, USA.

Flag: United Nations blue with UN emblem in white in the centre.

Membership. Membership is open to all peace-loving states whose admission will be effected by the General Assembly upon recommendation of the Security Council.

The table on pp. 12–15 shows the member states of the United Nations and their participation in the Related Agencies, and those non-member states which have been admitted to certain Related Agencies.

The Principal Organs of the United Nations are: 1. The General Assembly. 2. The Security Council. 3. The Economic and Social Council. 4. The Trusteeship Council. 5. The International Court of Justice. 6. The Secretariat.

1. **The General Assembly** consists of all the members of the United Nations. Each member is entitled to be represented at its meetings by 5 delegates and 5 alternate delegates, but has only 1 vote. The General Assembly meets regularly once a year, commencing on the third Tuesday in Sept.; the session normally lasts until mid-December and is resumed for some weeks in the new year if this is required. Special sessions may be convoked by the Secretary-General if requested by the Security Council, by a majority of the members of the United Nations or by 1 member concurred with by the majority of the members. The General Assembly elects its President for each session.

The first regular session was held in London from 10 Jan. to 14 Feb. and in New York from 23 Oct. to 16 Dec. 1946.

Special sessions have been held, on Palestine, in 1947, 1948, 1963 and 1967; emergency sessions on the Middle East and on Hungary in 1956, on Lebanon in 1958, on the Congo in 1960, on South West Africa and the Middle East in 1967, on raw materials and development in 1974, on International Economic Co-operation in 1975.

The work of the General Assembly is divided between 6 Main Committees and the Special Political Committee, on each of which every member has the right to be represented by 1 delegate. I. Political Security. II. Economic and Financial. III. Social, Humanitarian and Cultural. IV. Trust and Non-Self-Governing Territories. V. Administrative and Budgetary. VI. Legal.

In addition there is a General Committee charged with the task of co-ordinating the proceedings of the Assembly and its Committees; and a Credentials Committee which verifies the credentials of the delegates. The General Committee consists of 25 members, comprising the President of the General Assembly, its 17 Vice-Presidents and the Chairmen of the 7 Main Committees. The Credentials Committee consists of 9 members, elected at the beginning of each session of the General Assembly. The Assembly has 2 standing committees—an Advisory Committee on Administrative and Budgetary Questions, and a Committee on Contributions. The General Assembly establishes subsidiary and *ad hoc* bodies when necessary to deal with specific matters. These include: Special Committee on Peace-keeping Operations (33 members), Commission on Human Rights (32 members), Commission for the unification and rehabilitation of Korea (7 members), Committee on the peaceful uses of outer space (28 members), Conciliation Commission for Palestine (3 members), Conference of the Committee on Disarmament (26 members), International Law Commission (25 members), Scientific Committee on the effects of atomic radiation (15 members), Special Committee on the implementation of the declaration on the granting of independence to colonial countries and peoples (24 members), Special Committee on the policies of Apartheid of the Government of the Republic of South Africa (11 members), UN High Commissioner for Refugees, UN Relief and Works Agency for Palestine Refugees in the Near East, Peace Observation Commission (14 members), UN Commission on International Trade Law (29 members) and Committee on the Peaceful Uses of Sea-bed and Ocean Floor Beyond the Limits of National Jurisdiction (91 members), Governing Council for Environmental Programmes (54 members).

The General Assembly may discuss any matters within the scope of the Charter, and, with the exception of any situation or dispute on the agenda of the Security Council, may make recommendations on any such questions or matters. For decisions on important questions a two-thirds majority is required, on other questions a simple majority of members present and voting. In addition, the Assembly at its fifth session, in 1950, decided that if the Security Council, because of lack of unanimity of the permanent members, fails to exercise its primary responsibility for the maintenance of international peace and security in any case where there appears to be a threat to the peace, breach of the peace or act of aggression, the General Assembly shall consider the matter immediately with a view to making appropriate recommendations to members for collective measures, including in the case of a breach of the peace or act of aggression the use of armed force when necessary, to maintain or restore international peace and security.

The General Assembly receives and considers reports from the other organs of the United Nations, including the Security Council. The Secretary-General makes an annual report to it on the work of the Organization.

2. **The Security Council** consists of 15 members, each of which has 1 representative and 1 vote. There are 5 permanent and 10 non-permanent members elected for a 2-year term by a two-thirds majority of the General Assembly.

Retiring members are not eligible for immediate re-election. Any other member of the United Nations will be invited to participate without vote in the discussion of questions specially affecting its interests.

The Security Council bears the primary responsibility for the maintenance of peace and security. It is also responsible for the functions of the UN in trust territories classed as 'strategic areas'. Decisions on procedural questions are made by an affirmative vote of 9 members. On all other matters the affirmative vote of 9 members must include the concurring votes of all permanent members (in practice, however, an abstention by a permanent member is not considered a veto), subject to the provision that when the Security Council is considering methods for the peaceful settlement of a dispute, parties to the dispute abstain from voting.

For the maintenance of international peace and security the Security Council can, in accordance with special agreements to be concluded, call on armed forces, assistance and facilities of the member states. It is assisted by a Military Staff Committee consisting of the Chiefs of Staff of the permanent members of the Security Council or their representatives.

The Presidency of the Security Council is held for 1 month in rotation by the member states in the English alphabetical order of their names.

The Security Council functions continuously. Its members are permanently represented at the seat of the organization, but it may meet at any place that will best facilitate its work.

The Council has 2 standing committees, of Experts and on the Admission of New Members. In addition, from time to time, it establishes *ad hoc* committees and commissions such as the Truce Supervision Organization in Palestine. It has also appointed a Representative for India and Pakistan.

Permanent Members: China, France, USSR, UK, USA.
Non-Permanent Members: Canada, Federal Republic of Germany, India, Mauritius, Venezuela (until 31 Dec. 1978); Bolivia, Czechoslovakia, Gabon, Kuwait, Nigeria (until 31 Dec. 1979).

3. **The Economic and Social Council** is responsible under the General Assembly for carrying out the functions of the United Nations with regard to international economic, social, cultural, educational, health and related matters.

By Jan. 1963, 14 specialized inter-governmental agencies working in these fields had been brought into relationship with the United Nations. The Economic and Social Council may also make arrangements for consultation with international non-governmental organizations and, after consultation with the member concerned, with national organizations; by Dec. 1965, 141 non-governmental organizations had been granted consultative status and a further 219 were on the register.

The Economic and Social Council consists of 1 delegate each of 54 Member States elected by a two-thirds majority of the General Assembly. Nine are elected each year for a 3-year term. Retiring members are eligible for immediate re-election. Each member has 1 vote. Decisions are made by a majority of the members present and voting.

The Council nominally holds 2 sessions a year, and special sessions may be held if required. The President is elected for 1 year and is eligible for immediate re-election.

The Economic and Social Council has the following commissions:

Regional Economic Commissions: ECE (Economic Commission for Europe); ESCAP (Economic and Social Commission for Asia and the Pacific. Bangkok); ECLA (Economic Commission for Latin America. Santiago, Chile); ECA (Economic Commission for Africa. Addis Ababa). ECWA (Economic Commission for Western Asia. Beirut). These Commissions have been established to enable the nations of the major regions of the world to co-operate on common problems and also to produce economic information.

(1) Six functional Statistical Commissions; with subcommission on Statistical Sampling. (2) Commission on Human Rights; with subcommission on Prevention of Discrimination and Protection of Minorities; (3) Social Development Commission; (4) Commission on the Status of Women; (5) Commission on Narcotic Drugs; (6) Population Commission.

The Economic and Social Council has the following standing committees: The Economic Committee, Social Committee, Co-ordination Committee, Committee on Non-Governmental Organizations, Interim Committee on Programme of Conferences, Committee for Industrial Development, Advisory Committee on the Application of Science and Technology to Development, Committee on Housing, Building and Planning.

Other special bodies are the Permanent Central Opium Board, the Drug Supervisory Body, the Interim Co-ordinating Committee for International Commodity Arrangements and the Administrative Committee on Co-ordination to ensure (1) the most effective implementation of the agreements entered into between the United Nations and the specialized agencies and (2) co-ordination of activities.

Membership: Argentina, Cameroon, Central African Empire, China, Dominican Republic, Finland, Hungary, India, Japan, Lesotho, Malta, Romania, Sweden, Tanzania, Trinidad and Tobago, United Arab Emirates, USSR, UK, USA (until 31 Dec. 1980); other members: Columbia, Iran, Iraq, Italy, Jamaica, Mauritania, Mexico, Netherlands, New Zealand, Philippines, Poland, Rwanda, Somalia, Sudan, Syria, Ukraine, Upper Volta (until 31 Dec. 1979); Afghánistán, Algeria, Austria, Bangladesh, Bolivia, Brazil, Cuba, France, Federal Republic of Germany, Greece, Malaysia, Nigeria, Portugal, Togo, Tunisia, Uganda, Venezuela, Yugoslavia (until 31 Dec. 1978).

4. **The Trusteeship Council.** The Charter provides for an international trusteeship system to safeguard the interests of the inhabitants of territories which are not yet fully self-governing and which may be placed thereunder by individual trusteeship agreements. These are called trust territories.

By 1968 all, except 2, trust territories had become independent or joined independent countries.

The Trusteeship Council consists of the 1 member administering trust territories: USA; the permanent members of the Security Council that are not administering trust territories: China, France, USSR and UK. Decisions of the Council are made by a majority of the members present and voting, each member having 1 vote. The Council holds one regular session each year, and special sessions if required.

5. **The International Court of Justice** was created by an international treaty, the Statute of the Court, which forms an integral part of the United Nations Charter. All members of the United Nations are *ipso facto* parties to the Statute of the Court.

The Court is composed of independent judges, elected regardless of their nationality, who possess the qualifications required in their countries for appointment to the highest judicial offices, or are jurisconsuls of recognized competence in international law. There are 15 judges, no 2 of whom may be nationals of the same state. They are elected by the Security Council and the General Assembly of the United Nations sitting independently. Candidates are chosen from a list of persons nominated by the national groups in the Permanent Court of Arbitration established by the Hague Conventions of 1899 and 1907. In the case of members of the United Nations not represented in the Permanent Court of Arbitration, candidates are nominated by national groups appointed for the purpose by their governments. The judges are elected for a 9-year term and are eligible for immediate re-election. When engaged on business of the Court, they enjoy diplomatic privileges and immunities.

The Court elects its own President and Vice-Presidents for 3 years and remains permanently in session, except for judicial vacations. The full court of 15 judges normally sits, but a quorum of 9 judges is sufficient to constitute the Court. It may form chambers of 3 or more judges for dealing with particular categories of cases, and forms annually a chamber of 5 judges to hear and determine, at the request of the parties, cases by summary procedures.

Competence and Jurisdiction. Only states may be parties in cases before the Court, which is open to the states parties to its Statute. The conditions under which the Court will be open to other states are laid down by the Security Council. The Court exercises its jurisdiction in all cases which the parties refer to it and in all matters provided for in the Charter, or in treaties and conventions in force. Disputes concerning the jurisdiction of the Court are settled by the Court's own decision.

The Court may apply in its decision: (*a*) international conventions; (*b*) international custom; (*c*) the general principles of law recognized by civilized nations; and (*d*) as subsidiary means for the determination of the rules of law, judicial decisions and the teachings of highly qualified publicists. If the parties agree, the Court may decide a case *ex aequo et bono*. The Court may also give an advisory opinion on any legal question to any organ of the United Nations or its agencies.

Procedure. The official languages of the Court are French and English. At the request of any party the Court will authorize the use of another language by this party. All questions are decided by a majority of the judges present. If the votes are equal, the President has a casting vote. The judgment is final and without appeal, but a revision may be applied for within 10 years from the date of the judgment on the ground of a new decisive factor. Unless otherwise decided by the Court, each party bears its own costs.

Judges. The judges of the Court, elected by the Security Council and the General Assembly, are as follows: (1) To serve until 5 Feb. 1979; Frederico de Castro (Spain), Louis Ignacio-Pinto (Benin), C. Dillard (USA), Eduardo Jimenez de Aréchaga (Uruguay), Platon D. Morozov (USSR). (2) To serve until 5 Feb. 1982: André Gros (France), Isaac Forster (Senegal), Sir Humphrey Waldock (UK), Nagendra Singh (India), José Maria Ruda (Argentina). (3) To serve until 5 Feb. 1985: Manfred Lachs (Poland), Taslim Olawale Elias (Nigeria), Hermann Mosler (Federal Republic of Germany), Shigeru Oda (Japan), Salah E. Dine Tarazi (Syria).

'National' Judges. If there is no judge on the bench of the nationality of the parties to the dispute, each party has the right to choose a judge. Such judges shall take part in the decision on terms of complete equality with their colleagues.

The Court has its seat at The Hague, but may sit and exercise its functions elsewhere whenever it considers this desirable. The expenses of the Court are borne by the United Nations.

Registrar: Stanislas Aquarone (Australia).

Year-Book of the International Court of Justice. The Hague, 1950 ff.

6. **The Secretariat** is composed of the Secretary-General, who is the chief administrative officer of the organization, and an international staff appointed by him under regulations established by the General Assembly. However, the Secretary-General, the High Commissioner for Refugees and the Managing Director of the Fund are appointed by the General Assembly. The first Secretary-General was Trygve Lie (Norway), 1946–53; the second, Dag Hammarskjöld (Sweden), 1953–61; the third, U. Thant (Burma), 1961–71.

The Secretary-General acts as chief administrative officer in all meetings of the General Assembly, the Security Council, the Economic and Social Council and the Trusteeship Council.

Secretary-General: Kurt Waldheim (Austria), appointed 1 Jan. 1972.

The Secretary-General is assisted by 11 Under-Secretaries-General and 5 Assistant Secretaries-General.

The *UN Development Programme*, created on 22 Nov. 1965, is an amalgamation of the programme of Technical Assistance and the Special Fund. *Administrator:* Bradford Morse (USA).

The *UN Conference on Trade and Development* was established by the General Assembly on 30 Dec. 1964. It comprises those states which are members of the UN, its specialized agencies or the International Atomic Energy Agency. Its permanent organ, the Trade and Development Board (55 members), meets twice a year. Its 4 subsidiary organs meet annually: these are the Committees on Commodities, Manufactures, Shipping, and Invisibles and Financing Related to Trade. The first UNCTAD was held in Geneva in 1964, the second in New Delhi in 1968 and the third in Santiago (Chile) 1972. *Secretary-General:* Gamani Corea (Sri Lanka, appointed May 1974). *Headquarters:* Geneva, Switzerland.

The *UN Industrial Organization* (UNIDO) has worked as an autonomous body with the UN to promote industrialization and co-ordinate activities undertaken by the UN family in this field since 1967. Principal body is the 45-member Industrial Development Board, which formulates UNIDO's policy and its programme of activities. UNIDO tries to help the urgent need of developing countries to accelerate their promotional and operational activities and supports them by relevant studies and research. *Executive Director:* Abderraham Khane (Algeria). *Headquarters:* Rathausplatz 2, Vienna, Austria.

Office of the United Nations High Commissioner for Refugees (UNHCR) was established by the UN General Assembly with effect from 1 Jan. 1951, originally for 3 years. Since 1954, its mandate has been renewed for 5-year periods. Under General Assembly resolution 32/67 adopted in Nov. 1977 the Office was prolonged until 31 Dec. 1983.

The task of UNHCR is of a purely humanitarian and non-political character.

The main functions of the Office of the High Commissioner are to provide international protection for refugees, to seek permanent solutions to their problems through voluntary repatriation, resettlement in other countries or integration into the country of present residence. UNHCR may also be called upon to provide emergency relief and supplementary aid where necessary.

UNHCR concerns itself with refugees who have been determined to come within its mandate under the Statute, and with persons in analogous circumstances whom it assists under the terms of the good offices resolutions adopted by the General Assembly.

The High Commissioner is elected by the General Assembly and follows policy directives given him by the General Assembly or the Economic and Social Council. He reports to the Third Committee of the General Assembly (Social and Humanitarian Affairs), through the Economic and Social Council. The Executive Committee of the High Commissioner's Programme gives the High Commissioner guidance in respect of material assistance programmes and advises him at his request in the exercise of his functions under the Statute. It meets normally once a year at Geneva. It includes representatives of 31 states, members and non-members of the UN. Its annual sessions are normally held in October in Geneva. In recent years it has been customary for the High Commissioner to invite representatives of member states to meet with him informally at least once between sessions to keep them abreast of important developments.

International protection is the primary function of UNHCR. Its main objective is to promote and safeguard the rights and interests of refugees. In so doing UNHCR devotes special attention to promoting a generous policy of asylum on the part of governments and seeks to improve the status of refugees in their country of residence. It also helps them to cease to be refugees through the acquisition of the nationality of their country of residence when voluntary repatriation is not applicable. UNHCR pursues its objectives in the field of protection by encouraging the conclusion of intergovernmental legal instruments in favour of refugees, by supervising the implementation of their provisions and by encouraging governments to adopt legislation and administrative procedures for the benefit of refugees. The main instrument in this field is the 1951 Convention Relating to the Status of Refugees. It prescribes a minimum standard of treatment for refugees in such important matters as employment, social security and freedom of movement, and provides for the issuance, by contracting states, of travel documents in lieu of national passports. The most important provision of the Convention is embodied in Article 33 which forbids the return of a refugee to a country where his life or liberty would be in danger because of persecution for reasons of race, religion, nationality or political opinion (*refoulement*).

A protocol relating to the status of refugees came into force in 1967 and had the effect of extending the provisions of the 1951 Convention (which applies to persons who have become refugees as a result of events prior to that date) to new groups of refugees.

In 1977, Djibouti became party to both instruments. The 69 parties to the 1951 Convention and the 64 to the 1967 Protocol represent less than half the UN membership.

In 1977, as in the two preceding years, the High Commissioner was prompted to make reference both in the Sub-Committee of the Whole Executive Committee on Protection and at the General Assembly to condemn abuses in the treatment of refugees, including *refoulement*, kidnapping and illegal detention. In some cases, these acts were found to have been perpetrated by governments that had acceded to the instruments noted above.

At the close of its discussions, the Executive Committee *inter alia* expressed its grave concern that in a number of cases the basic rights of refugees had still not been respected and called on governments to co-operate in a spirit of international solidarity with the High Commissioner in the performance of its functions.

A conference of plenipotentiaries was held in Geneva from 10 Jan. to 4 Feb. 1977 'to adopt a Convention on Territorial Asylum'. This would, from the standpoint of UNHCR, strengthen significantly the legal basis for granting asylum by ruling out, in a legally binding instrument, measures such as rejection at the frontier, thus supplementing the 1967 Declaration on Territorial Asylum, which has no legally binding force, and the 1951 Convention relating to the Status of Refugees, which does not expressly deal with the question of asylum. At the conclusion of its first session, the Conference noted that it had been unable to draft a Convention within the allocated time. It nevertheless considered that efforts should continue and recommended that the General Assembly at its 32nd session consider convening a further session at an appropriate time.

Commitments under General Programmes of material assistance (the former UNHCR annual programme and the \$2m. Emergency Fund) came to \$22·5m., of which nearly \$10m. were for refugees in Africa. Other major assistance programmes were undertaken in Latin America, where commitments in 1977 amounted to nearly \$6m., mainly for Chilean refugees admitted temporarily to Argentina and Peru. As in previous years, the High Commissioner made repeated appeals to governments to provide resettlement opportunities for these refugees. In addition, in response to new refugee situations, programmes were begun in Djibouti and Gabon. The financial target for UNHCR General Programmes in 1978 totals \$35·2m.

The major Special Programme entrusted to UNHCR during 1977 arose from developments in Southern Africa. Considerable numbers of students from Namibia, South Africa and Southern Rhodesia (Zimbabwe) sought refuge in Botswana, Lesotho, Swaziland and Tanzania. The Secretary-General, after receiving the report of a UN Special Mission, designated the High Commissioner co-ordinator of assistance from the UN system to student refugees. Subsequently, the High Commissioner appealed to all states members of the UN system to contribute towards a \$16m. assistance programme and asked members of the Organization of African Unity to provide school places to give refugees an opportunity to continue their education.

Total commitments under Special Programmes in 1977 amounted to nearly \$76m., of which the largest part, \$23·3m., was for repatriation and resettlement of refugees and displaced persons in Angola. At the request of the Secretary-General, the High Commissioner had been appointed in 1976 as co-ordinator for one year of the UN Programme of Humanitarian Assistance to Angola. By mid-1977, some 38,000 tonnes of food and more than three-quarters of the financial target of \$32·5m. were pledged or contributed towards the programme. Arrangements were made by the Government and operational partners in the UN system to evolve a smooth transition as the High Commissioner withdraws from his co-ordinating role.

The High Commissioner also continued, at the request of the Secretary-General, to assist with the problem of the Sahrawis in Algeria.

Financial requirements for 1977 were sharply reduced in Indo-China. The 'return to villages' resettlement and rehabilitation programme in the Lao People's Democratic Republic was virtually completed. In Vietnam, UNHCR continued, at the request of the Government, to provide assistance in 1977 under a \$7m. programme for specific needs or completion or consolidation of the projects undertaken.

In Thailand, the influx from neighbouring countries continued and by Nov. UNHCR was supporting some 30,000 displaced persons, mostly Lao of hill-tribe origin, notwithstanding the resettlement abroad of some 40,000 persons, mainly in France and USA.

Throughout 1977, the number of persons from Vietnam arriving in small boats at ports around the South China Sea or rescued at sea by passing ships and taken to first ports of call continued to grow rapidly. Some 15,700 persons arrived in 1977, bringing the total number of arrivals since 1975 to more than 19,000. More than 60% arrived in Malaysia and Thailand, 24% in Indonesia, Japan and the Philippines, and the remainder in Hong Kong, Singapore and other parts of South

East Asia, or ports of call outside the area. UNHCR intervened actively in requesting governments to allow them to land at least temporarily (often guaranteeing care and maintenance during their stay) and urged countries to accept them for permanent resettlement. The High Commissioner also endeavoured to encourage shipping companies to provide assistance when called upon by asylum-seekers in fragile or unseaworthy craft and to alleviate their suffering in accordance with the Convention for the Unification of Certain Rules of Law relating to Assistance and Salvage at Sea, signed at Brussels in 1910.

In its on-going capacity as co-ordinator of United Nations humanitarian assistance in Cyprus, UNHCR in 1977 channelled some $18m. in aid for displaced persons throughout Cyprus for food, medicine, temporary accommodation and agriculture.

Headquarters: Palais des Nations, Geneva, Switzerland.
UK Office: 36 Westminster Palace Gardens, London, SW1.
High Commissioner: Poul Hartling (Denmark).
Deputy High Commissioner: Charles H. Mace (USA).

UNHCR reports. Geneva, 1966 ff.
UNHCR Bulletin. Geneva, 1968–74.
UNHCR Tabloids. Geneva, 1974 ff.
Forty Years of International Assistance to Refugees. Geneva, 1962
The Red Cross and the Refugees. Geneva, 1963
A Mandate to Protect and Assist Refugees. Geneva, 1971
The Refugee Problem Isn't Hopeless Unless You Think So. Geneva, 1975
Habitat: Refugees in Human Settlements. Geneva, 1976

The United Nations Relief and Works Agency for Palestine Refugees in the Near East (UNRWA) was established by the General Assembly in Dec. 1949. It is supported by private contributions and by governmental pledges made each year at the General Assembly. UNRWA's operations, direct relief, long-term rehabilitation and vocational training, cover the Gaza Strip, Jordan, Lebanon and Syria, where over 1m. refugees were living before the war of June 1967.

Headquarters: Elias Abu Ata Building, Jabal el Husein, Amman, Jordan.
Commissioner-General: Thomas W. McElhiney (USA).

The Children's Fund (UNICEF), established by the General Assembly on 11 Dec. 1946, functions under the supervision of the Economic and Social Council. It assists child health, nutrition and welfare programmes in 116 countries and territories. Its work is financed through voluntary contributions from governments and donations from the public.

Estimated income 1973 (including contributions for special emergencies), $95·8m.

Headquarters: United Nations Headquarters, New York City.
Executive Director: Henry R. Labouisse (USA).

The Budget of the United Nations. The financial year coincides with the calendar year; accountancy is in US$. Budget for 1978–79, $985,913,300.

Membership and percentage scale of contributions to UN budget, 1978:

Afghánistán	0·02	Botswana	0·02	Congo	0·02
Albania	0·02	Brazil	1·04	Comoros	0·02
Algeria	0·10	Bulgaria	0·13	Costa Rica	0·02
Argentina	0·83	Burma	0·02	Cuba	0·13
Australia	1·52	Burundi	0·02	Cyprus	0·02
Austria	0·63	Byelorussia	0·40	Czechoslovakia	0·87
Bahamas	0·02	Cameroon	0·02	Denmark	0·63
Bahrain	0·02	Canada	2·96	Djibouti	0·02
Bangladesh	0·04	Cape Verde	0·02	Dominican Republic	0·02
Barbados	0·02	Central African Rep.	0·02	Ecuador	0·02
Belgium	1·07	Chad	0·02	Egypt	0·08
Benin	0·02	Chile	0·09	El Salvador	0·02
Bhután	0·02	China	5·50	Equatorial Guinea	0·02
Bolivia	0·02	Colombia	0·11	Ethiopia	0·02

Fiji	0·02	Liberia	0·02	Saudi Arabia	0·24
Finland	0·41	Libya	0·17	Senegal	0·02
France	5·66	Luxembourg	0·04	Sierra Leone	0·02
Gabon	0·02	Madagascar	0·02	Singapore	0·08
Gambia	0·02	Malawi	0·02	Somalia	0·02
Germany, Demo. Rep.	1·35	Malaysia	0·09	South Africa, Rep. of	0·40
Germany, Federal Rep.	7·74	Maldive, Republic of	0·02	Southern Yemen	0·02
Ghana	0·02	Mali	0·02	Spain	1·53
Grenada	0·02	Malta	0·02	Sri Lanka	0·02
Greece	0·39	Mauritania	0·02	Sudan	0·02
Guatemala	0·02	Mauritius	0·02	Surinam	0·02
Guinea	0·02	Mexico	0·78	Swaziland	0·02
Guinea-Bissau	0·02	Mongolia	0·02	Sweden	1·20
Guyana	0·02	Morocco	0·05	Syria	0·02
Haiti	0·02	Mozambique	0·02	Tanzania	0·02
Honduras	0·02	Nepál	0·02	Thailand	0·10
Hungary	0·34	Netherlands	1·38	Togo	0·02
Iceland	0·02	New Zealand	0·28	Trinidad and Tobago	0·02
India	1·70	Nicaragua	0·02	Tunisia	0·02
Indonesia	0·14	Niger	0·02	Turkey	0·30
Iran	0·43	Nigeria	0·13	Uganda	0·02
Iraq	0·10	Norway	0·43	Ukraine	1·50
Irish Republic	0·15	Oman	0·02	USSR	11·33
Israel	0·24	Pakistan	0·06	United Arab Emirates	0·08
Italy	3·30	Panama	0·02	UK	4·44
Ivory Coast	0·02	Papua New Guinea	0·02	USA	25·00
Jamaica	0·02	Paraguay	0·02	Upper Volta	0·02
Japan	8·66	Peru	0·06	Uruguay	0·04
Jordan	0·02	Philippines	0·10	Venezuela	0·40
Kampuchea, Demo.	0·02	Poland	1·40	Yemen	0·02
Kenya	0·02	Portugal	0·20	Vietnam	0·02
Kuwait	0·16	Qatar	0·02	Yugoslavia	0·38
Laos	0·02	Romania	0·26	Zaïre	0·02
Lebanon	0·03	Rwanda	0·02	Zambia	0·02
Lesotho	0·02	São Tomé	0·02		

Books of Reference

Yearbook of the United Nations. New York, 1947 ff. Annual
United Nations Chronicle. Monthly
Monthly Bulletin of Statistics
General Assembly: Official Records; Resolutions
Reports of the Secretary-General of the United Nations on the Work of the Organization. 1946 ff.
Documents of the United Nations Conference on International Organization, San Francisco, 1945. 16 vols.
Charter of the United Nations and Statute of the International Court of Justice. Text in English, French, Chinese, Russian and Spanish.
Repertory of Practice of UN's Organs. 5 vols. New York, 1955
Official Records of the Security Council, the Economic and Social Council, Trusteeship Council and the Disarmament Commission
Demographic Yearbook, 1948 ff. New York, 1969
Everyman's United Nations. 7th ed. New York, 1958 ff. Annual
Statistical Yearbook. New York, 1947 ff.
Yearbook of International Statistics. New York, 1950 ff.
World Economic Survey. New York, 1947 ff.
Economic Survey of Asia and the Far East. New York, 1946 ff.
Economic Survey of Latin America. New York, 1948 ff.
Economic Survey of Europe. New York, 1948 ff.
Economic Survey of Africa. New York, 1960 ff.
Bailey, S. D., *The General Assembly*. London, 1960
Boyd, A., *Fifteen Men and a Powder Keg*. London, 1971
Foote, W., *Dag Hammarskjold—Servant of Peace*. London, 1962
Forsythe, D., *United Nations Peacemaking: The Conciliation Commission for Palestine*. Johns Hopkins Univ. Press, 1973
Hiscocks, R., *The Security Council: A Study in Adolescence*. New York, 1974
Lie, Trygve, *In the Cause of Peace*. London, 1954

Luard, E., *The United Nations in a New Era.* London, 1972
Nicholas, H. G., *The United Nations as a Political Institution.* OUP, 1959
Ogley, R., *The United Nations and East–West Relations.* Univ. of Sussex, 1972
Richards, J. H., *International Economic Institutions.* London, 1970
Rikhye, I. J., Harbottle, M., Egge, B., *The Thin Blue Line.* London, 1974
Symonds, R., and Carder, M., *The United Nations and the Population Question.* London, 1973
Thant, U., *Towards World Peace.* New York, 1964
Urquhart, B., *Hammarskjold.* London, 1973
Walters, F. P., *A History of the League of Nations.* 2 vols. London, 1952
Winton, H. N. M. (comp. and ed.), *Man and the Environment. A Bibliography of Selected Publications of the United Nations System 1946–1971.* New York, 1972
Witthauer, K., *Die Bevölkerung der Erde: Verteilung und Dynamik.* Gotha, 1958.—*Distribution and Dynamics Relating to World Population.* Gotha, 1969
Her Majesty's Stationery Office. *Sectional List 23* (currently revised) and *International Organizations Publications* contain a full list of publications on UN and Specialized Agencies, issued by HMSO.

London Information Centre. 14–15 Stratford Place, W1N 9AF.

AGENCIES IN RELATIONSHIP WITH THE UN

(as in 1977)

	IAEA	ILO	FAO	UNESCO	WHO	BANK & FUND	ICAO	UPU	ITU	WMO	IFC	IMCO	GATT
Afghánistán	*	*	*	*	*	*	*	*	*	*	*	—	—
Albania	*	—	*	*	*	—	—	*	*	*	—	—	—
Algeria	*	*	*	*	*	*	*	*	*	*	—	*	—
Angola	—	*	—	*	*	—	—	—	*	—	—	—	—
Argentina	*	*	*	*	*	*	*	*	*	*	*	*	*
Australia	*	*	*	*	*	*	*	*	*	*	*	*	*
Austria	*	*	*	*	*	*	*	*	*	*	*	*	*
Bahamas	—	*	*	—	*	*	*	*	*	*	—	*	—
Bahrain	—	—	*	*	*	*	*	*	*	—	—	*	—
Bangladesh	*	*	*	*	*	*	*	*	*	*	*	*	*
Barbados	—	*	*	*	*	*	*	*	*	*	—	*	*
Belgium	*	*	*	*	*	*	*	*	*	*	*	*	*
Benin	—	*	*	*	*	*	*	*	*	*	—	—	*
Bhután	—	—	—	—	—	—	—	*	—	—	—	—	—
Bolivia	*	*	*	*	*	*	*	*	*	*	*	—	—
Botswana	—	—	*	*	*	*	—	*	*	*	—	—	—
Brazil	*	*	*	*	*	*	*	*	*	*	*	*	*
Bulgaria	*	*	*	*	*	—	*	*	*	*	—	*	—
Burma	*	*	*	*	*	*	*	*	*	*	*	*	*
Burundi	—	*	*	*	*	*	*	*	*	*	—	—	*
Byelorussia	*	*	—	*	*	—	—	*	*	*	—	—	—
Cameroon	*	*	*	*	*	*	*	*	*	*	*	*	*
Canada	*	*	*	*	*	*	*	*	*	*	*	*	*
Cape Verde	—	—	*	—	*	—	—	—	*	*	—	*	—
Central African Rep.	—	*	*	*	*	*	*	*	*	*	—	—	*
Chad	—	*	*	*	*	*	*	*	*	*	—	—	*
Chile	*	*	*	*	*	*	*	*	*	*	*	*	*
China	—	—	*	*	*	—	*	*	*	*	—	*	—
Colombia	*	*	*	*	*	*	*	*	*	*	*	*	—
Comoros	—	—	—	—	*	—	—	—	*	—	—	—	—
Congo	—	*	*	*	*	*	*	*	*	*	—	*	*
Costa Rica	*	*	*	*	*	*	*	*	*	*	*	—	—
Cuba	*	*	*	*	*	—	*	*	*	*	—	*	*

See notes on pp. 14–15.

	IAEA	ILO	FAO	UNESCO	WHO	BANK & FUND	ICAO	UPU	ITU	WMO	IFC	IMCO	GATT
Cyprus	*	*	*	*	*	*	*	*	*	*	*	*	*
Czechoslovakia	*	*	*	*	*	—	*	*	*	*	—	*	*
Denmark	*	*	*	*	*	*	*	*	*	*	*	*	*
Dominican Rep.	*	*	*	*	*	*	*	*	*	*	*	*	*
Ecuador	*	*	*	*	*	*	*	*	*	*	*	*	—
Egypt	*	*	*	*	*	*	*	*	*	*	*	*	*
El Salvador	*	*	*	*	*	*	*	*	*	*	*	—	—
Equatorial Guinea	—	—	—	—	—	*	*	*	*	—	—	*	—
Ethiopia	*	*	*	*	*	*	*	*	*	*	*	*	—
Fiji	—	*	*	—	*	*	*	*	*	—	—	—	—
Finland	*	*	*	*	*	*	*	*	*	*	*	*	*
France	*	*	*	*	*	*	*	*	*	*	*	*	*
Gabon	*	*	*	*	*	*	*	*	*	*	*	*	*
Gambia	—	—	*	*	*	*	—	*	*	—	—	—	*
German Democratic Republic	*	*	—	*	*	—	—	*	*	*	—	*	—
Germany, Federal Republic of	*	*	*	*	*	*	*	*	*	*	*	*	*
Ghana	*	*	*	*	*	*	*	*	*	*	*	*	*
Greece	*	*	*	*	*	*	*	*	*	*	*	*	*
Grenada	—	—	*	*	*	*	—	—	—	—	*	—	—
Guatemala	*	*	*	*	*	*	*	*	*	*	*	—	—
Guinea	—	*	*	*	*	*	*	*	*	*	—	*	—
Guinea-Bissau	—	—	*	*	*	—	—	*	*	—	—	—	—
Guyana	—	*	*	*	*	*	*	*	*	*	*	—	*
Haiti	*	*	*	*	*	*	*	*	*	*	*	*	*
Holy See	*	—	—	—	—	—	—	*	*	—	—	—	—
Honduras	—	*	*	*	*	*	*	*	*	*	*	*	—
Hungary	*	*	*	*	*	—	*	*	*	*	—	*	*
Iceland	*	*	*	*	*	*	*	*	*	*	*	*	*
India	*	*	*	*	*	*	*	*	*	*	*	*	*
Indonesia	*	*	*	*	*	*	*	*	*	*	*	*	*
Iran	*	*	*	*	*	*	*	*	*	*	*	*	—
Iraq	*	*	*	*	*	*	*	*	*	*	*	*	—
Irish Republic	*	*	*	*	*	*	*	*	*	*	*	*	*
Israel	*	*	*	*	*	*	*	*	*	*	*	*	*
Italy	*	*	*	*	*	*	*	*	*	*	*	*	*
Ivory Coast	*	*	*	*	*	*	*	*	*	*	*	*	*
Jamaica	*	*	*	*	*	*	*	*	*	*	*	*	*
Japan	*	*	*	*	*	*	*	*	*	*	*	*	*
Jordan	*	*	*	*	*	*	*	*	*	*	*	*	—
Kampuchea, Demo.	*	*	*	*	*	*	*	*	*	*	—	*	*
Kenya	*	*	*	*	*	*	*	*	*	*	*	*	*
Korea, Rep. of	*	—	—	*	*	—	—	*	*	*	—	—	—
Kuwait	*	*	*	*	*	*	*	*	*	*	*	*	*
Laos	—	*	*	*	*	*	*	*	*	*	—	—	—
Lebanon	*	*	*	*	*	*	*	*	*	*	*	*	—
Lesotho	—	—	*	*	*	*	*	*	*	—	*	—	—
Liberia	*	*	*	*	*	*	*	*	*	*	*	*	—
Libya	*	*	*	*	*	*	*	*	*	*	*	*	—
Liechtenstein	*	—	—	—	—	—	—	*	*	—	—	—	—
Luxembourg	*	*	*	*	*	*	*	*	*	*	*	—	*
Madagascar	*	*	*	*	*	*	*	*	*	*	*	*	*
Malawi	—	*	*	*	*	*	*	*	*	*	*	—	*
Malaysia	*	*	*	*	*	*	*	*	*	*	*	*	*
Maldive Is.	—	—	*	—	*	—	*	*	*	—	—	*	—
Mali	*	*	*	*	*	*	*	*	*	*	—	—	—
Malta	—	*	*	*	*	—	*	*	*	—	—	*	*
Mauritania	—	*	*	*	*	*	*	*	*	*	*	*	*
Mauritius	*	*	*	*	*	*	*	*	*	*	*	—	*
Mexico	*	*	*	*	*	*	*	*	*	*	*	*	—
Monaco	*	—	—	*	*	—	—	*	*	—	—	—	—
Mongolia	*	*	*	*	*	—	—	*	*	*	—	—	—
Morocco	*	*	*	*	*	*	*	*	*	*	*	*	—

	IAEA	ILO	FAO	UNESCO	WHO	BANK & FUND	ICAO	UPU	ITU	WMO	IFC	IMCO	GATT
Mozambique	—	*	—	—	*	—	—	—	*	—	—	—	—
Nauru	—	—	—	—	—	—	*	*	*	—	—	—	—
Nepál	—	*	*	*	*	*	*	*	*	*	*	—	—
Netherlands	*	*	*	*	*	*	*	*	*	*	*	*	*
New Zealand	*	*	*	*	*	*	*	*	*	*	*	*	*
Nicaragua	—	*	*	*	*	*	*	*	*	*	*	—	*
Niger	*	*	*	*	*	*	*	*	*	*	—	—	*
Nigeria	*	*	*	*	*	*	*	*	*	*	*	*	*
Norway	*	*	*	*	*	*	*	*	*	*	*	*	*
Oman	—	—	*	*	*	*	*	*	*	*	*	*	—
Pakistan	*	*	*	*	*	*	*	*	*	*	*	*	*
Panama	*	*	*	*	*	*	*	*	*	*	*	*	—
Papua New Guinea	*	*	*	—	*	*	—	—	*	*	*	—	—
Paraguay	*	*	*	*	*	*	*	*	*	*	*	—	—
Peru	*	*	*	*	*	*	*	*	*	*	*	*	*
Philippines	*	*	*	*	*	*	*	*	*	*	*	*	—
Poland	*	*	*	*	*	—	*	*	*	*	—	*	*
Portugal	*	*	*	*	*	*	*	*	*	*	*	—	*
Qatar	*	*	*	*	*	*	*	*	*	*	—	—	—
Romania	*	*	*	*	*	*	*	*	*	*	—	*	*
Rwanda	—	*	*	*	*	*	*	*	*	*	*	—	*
San Marino	—	—	—	*	—	—	—	*	—	—	—	—	—
São Tomé	—	—	—	—	*	—	—	—	*	—	—	—	—
Saudi Arabia	*	*	*	*	*	*	*	*	*	*	*	*	—
Senegal	*	*	*	*	*	*	*	*	*	*	*	*	*
Sierra Leone	*	*	*	*	*	*	*	*	*	*	*	*	*
Singapore	*	*	—	*	*	*	*	*	*	*	*	*	*
Somalia	—	*	*	*	*	*	*	*	*	*	*	—	—
South Africa, Rep. of	*	—	—	—	*	*	*	*	*	*	*	—	*
Southern Yemen	—	*	*	*	*	*	*	*	*	*	—	—	—
Spain	*	*	*	*	*	*	*	*	*	*	*	*	*
Sri Lanka	*	*	*	*	*	*	*	*	*	*	*	*	*
Sudan	*	*	*	*	*	*	*	*	*	*	*	*	—
Surinam	—	*	*	—	*	—	—	—	*	—	—	*	—
Swaziland	—	*	*	—	*	*	*	*	*	—	*	—	—
Sweden	*	*	*	*	*	*	*	*	*	*	*	*	*
Switzerland	*	*	*	*	*	—	*	*	*	*	—	*	*
Syria	*	*	*	*	*	*	*	*	*	*	*	*	—
Tanzania	*	*	*	*	*	*	*	*	*	*	*	*	*
Thailand	*	*	*	*	*	*	*	*	*	*	*	*	—
Togo	—	*	*	*	*	*	*	*	*	*	*	—	*
Tonga	—	—	—	—	*	—	—	*	*	—	—	—	—
Trinidad	—	*	*	*	*	*	*	*	*	*	*	*	*
Tunisia	*	*	*	*	*	*	*	*	*	*	*	*	—
Turkey	*	*	*	*	*	*	*	*	*	*	*	*	*
Uganda	*	*	*	*	*	*	*	*	*	*	*	—	*
Ukraine	*	*	—	*	*	—	—	*	*	*	—	—	—
USSR	*	*	—	*	*	—	*	*	*	*	—	*	—
United Arab Emir.	*	*	*	*	*	*	*	*	*	—	—	—	—
UK	*	*	*	*	*	*	*	*	*	*	*	*	*
USA	*	—	*	*	*	*	*	*	*	*	*	*	*
Upper Volta	—	*	*	*	*	*	*	*	*	*	*	—	*
Uruguay	*	*	*	*	*	*	*	*	*	*	*	*	*
Venezuela	*	*	*	*	*	*	*	*	*	*	*	*	—
Vietnam	*	*	*	*	*	*	*	*	*	*	*	—	—
Western Samoa	—	—	—	—	*	*	—	—	—	—	*	—	—
Yemen	—	*	*	*	*	*	*	*	*	*	*	—	—
Yugoslavia	*	*	*	*	*	*	*	*	—	*	*	*	*
Zaïre	*	*	*	*	*	*	*	*	*	*	*	*	*
Zambia	*	*	*	*	*	*	*	*	*	*	*	—	—

UNESCO has 3 associate members: the British Eastern Caribbean Group, Namibia and Papua New Guinea.

WHO has 3 associate members: Rhodesia, Papua New Guinea and Namibia.

The 153 members of UPU include the following not listed in the table: Netherlands Antilles and Surinam, Overseas Territories for the international relations of which the Government of the United Kingdom of Great Britain and Northern Ireland is responsible, Spanish Territory in Africa, the whole of the Territories of United States of America, including the Trust Territory of the Pacific Islands, and the Territories represented by the French Office of Overseas Posts and Telecommunications.

The 146 members of ITU include the following not listed in the table: Group Territories represented by the French Overseas Post and Telecommunication Agency, Overseas Territories for the international relations of which the Government of the United Kingdom of Great Britain and Northern Ireland is responsible. Portuguese Overseas Province, Rhodesia, the Spanish Province in Africa, and the Territories of the United States of America. ITU has 1 associate member: Papua New Guinea.

The 138 members of WHO include 123 Member States listed in the table and the following 13 members not listed in the table which maintain their own meteorological service: British Caribbean Territories, Comoro Islands, French Polynesia, the French Territory of the Afars and Issas, Hong Kong, Netherlands Antilles, New Caledonia, Portuguese East Africa, Portuguese West Africa, St Pierre and Miquelon, Rhodesia and Surinam.

The 76 members of IMCO include 1 associate member: Hong Kong.

GATT: The 83 contracting parties to GATT include Rhodesia. In addition there are 2 countries—Tunisia and the Philippines—which have provisionally acceded to the Agreement, and 14 countries—Algeria, Bahrain, Botswana, Cambodia, Equatorial Guinea, Fiji, Lesotho, Maldives, Mali, Qatar, Southern Yemen, Swaziland, Tonga and Zambia—to whose territories GATT had been applied before independence and which now as independent states maintain a *de facto* application of the GATT pending final decisions as to their future commercial policy.

In ICAO, USSR membership includes Byelorussia and the Ukraine.

INTERNATIONAL ATOMIC ENERGY AGENCY (IAEA)

Origin. The International Atomic Energy Agency came into existence on 29 July 1957. Its statute had been approved on 26 Oct. 1956, at an international conference held at UN Headquarters, New York. A relationship agreement links it with the United Nations. The IAEA had 110 member states in 1977.

Functions. (1) To accelerate and enlarge the contribution of atomic energy to peace, health and prosperity throughout the world, and (2) to ensure that assistance provided by it or at its request or under its supervision or control is not used in such a way as to further any military purpose.

The IAEA gives advice and technical assistance to developing countries on nuclear power development (provides a series of training courses on nuclear power project planning), on health and safety, and on radioactive waste management, on legal aspects of the use of atomic energy, and on prospecting for and exploiting nuclear raw materials; in addition it promotes the use of radiation and isotopes in agriculture, industry, medicine and hydrology through expert services, training courses and fellowships, grants of equipment and supplies, research contracts, scientific meetings and publications. Since 1958 the Agency has provided technical assistance totalling $77m., consisting of the services of 2,900 experts, 6,300 fellowships, equipment worth $25m. not including research contracts. The IAEA has research laboratories in Austria and Monaco. At Trieste, the International Centre for Theoretical Physics was established in 1964 which is now operated jointly by UNESCO and IAEA.

The IAEA applies safeguards in 28 States pursuant to NPT and in 20 States under other agreements to 87 power plants, 25 conversion and fuel fabrication plants, 1 enrichment plant, 3 reprocessing plants, 11 pilot fuel fabrication plants, 3 pilot reprocessing plants, 170 research reactors and critical facilities, 12 sub-critical facilities, 43 research and development facilities and 198 separative storage and other locations. The above figures include facilities safeguarded under the agreement with the European Atomic Energy Community and its non-nuclear-weapons States.

Organization. The Statute provides for an annual General Conference, a Board of Governors of 34 members and a staff headed by a Director-General.

Headquarters: Kärntnerring 11, A1010 Vienna, Austria.
Director-General: Sigvard Eklund (Sweden).

INTERNATIONAL LABOUR ORGANISATION (ILO)

Origin. The ILO, established in 1919 as an autonomous part of the League of Nations, is an intergovernmental agency with a tripartite structure, in which representatives of governments, employers and workers participate. It seeks through international action to improve labour conditions, raise living standards and promote productive employment. In 1946 the ILO was recognized by the United Nations as a specialized agency. In 1969 it was awarded the Nobel Peace Prize. In 1977 it numbered 134 members.

Functions. One of the ILO's principal functions is the formulation of international standards in the form of International Labour Conventions and Recommendations. Member countries are required to submit Conventions to their competent national authorities with a view to ratification. If a country ratifies a Convention it agrees to bring its laws into line with its terms and to report periodically how these regulations are being applied. More than 4,131 ratifications of 149 Conventions had been deposited by the end of 1977. Machinery is available to ascertain whether Conventions thus ratified are effectively applied.

Recommendations do not require ratification, but member states are obliged to consider them with a view to giving effect to their provisions by legislation or other action. By the end of 1977 the International Labour Conference had adopted 157 recommendations.

Organization. The ILO consists of the International Labour Conference, the Governing Body and the International Labour Office.

The Conference is the supreme deliberative organ of the ILO; it meets annually at Geneva. National delegations are composed of 2 government delegates, 1 employers' delegate and 1 workers' delegate.

The Governing Body, elected by the Conference, is the executive council. It is composed of 28 government members, 14 workers' members and 14 employers' members.

Ten governments hold permanent seats on the Governing Body because of their industrial importance, namely, Canada, China, Federal Republic of Germany, France, India, Italy, Japan, USSR, UK and until 5 Nov. 1977, USA, which withdrew from membership on that date. The remaining 18 government seats were, at the end of 1977, held by Australia, Brazil, Guinea, Hungary, Iran, Kuwait, Liberia, Mexico, Norway, Pakistan, Panama, Somalia, Sudan, Togo, Trinidad and Tobago, Venezuela, Yugoslavia and Zaïre.

The Office serves as secretariat, operational headquarters, research centre and publishing house.

The ILO budget for 1978–79 was $169m but was later revised because of the withdrawal of USA from the Organization to $132·4m.

Activities. In addition to its research and advisory activities, the ILO extends technical co-operation to governments under its regular budget and under the UN Development Programme and Funds-in-Trust in the fields of employment promotion, human resources development (including vocational and management training), development of social institutions, small-scale industries, rural development social security, industrial safety and hygiene, productivity, etc. Technical co-operation also includes expert missions and a fellowship programme. Some $52m. was spent on technical co-operation in 1977. Projects were in progress in over 100 countries and nearly 1,000 experts involved.

Major emphasis is being given during the UN Second Development Decade to the ILO's World Employment Programme, launched in 1969 with the purpose of stimulating national and international efforts to increase the volume of productive employment, and so to counter the problem of rising unemployment in developing countries. Employment strategy missions were carried out under the Programme in Colombia, Iran, Kenya, Sri Lanka, the Philippines and the Dominican Republic. The work of these missions was complemented by an ILO programme of research designed to provide policy-makers with the information to promote employment. A World Employment Conference was held in June 1976. The International Labour Conference (Geneva, June 1977) set new international standards for protection against air pollution, noise and vibration in the working environment, and on the employment and working conditions of nurses.

In 1960 the ILO established in Geneva the International Institute for Labour Studies. The Institute specializes in advanced education and research on social and labour policy. It brings together for group study experienced persons from all parts of the world—government administrators, trade-union officials, industrial experts, management, university and other specialists.

A training institution was opened by the ILO in Turin, Italy, in 1965—the International Centre for Advanced Technical and Vocational Training. The Centre provides opportunities for technical, vocational and management training for individuals who have advanced beyond the facilities available in their own countries. Courses are geared particularly to the needs of developing countries.

Headquarters: International Labour Office, CH-1211 Geneva 22, Switzerland.
Director-General: Francis Blanchard (France).
Chairman of the Governing Body: Joseph Morris (Canada).
London Branch Office: 87 New Bond St., W1.

There are also branch and area offices in Abidjan, Algiers, Ankara, Beirut, Bonn, Buenos Aires, Cairo, Dakar, Dar es Salaam, Islamabad, Lagos, Lusaka, Manila, Mexico City, Moscow, New Delhi, Ottawa, Paris, Port-of-Spain, Rio de Janeiro, Rome, San José (Costa Rica), Suva (Fiji), Tōkyō, Washington and Yaoundé. There are regional offices in Addis Ababa (for Africa), Bangkok (for Asia) and Lima (for the Americas).

Publications. Regular periodicals in English, French and Spanish include the *International Labour Review* (bi-monthly); *Legislative Series* (bimonthly); *Bulletin of Labour Statistics* (quarterly); *Official Bulletin* (quarterly); the *Year Book of Labour Statistics*; a number of research studies and manuals including: *Adapting Working Hours to Modern Needs. Agrarian Reform and Rural Poverty. Egypt, 1952–75. Dust Control in Working Environment (Silicosis). Ergonomics in Industry, Agriculture and Forestry. Poverty and Landlessness in Rural Asia. Safety and Health in Dock Work. Social and Labour Practices of Multinational Enterprises in Petroleum Industry. Social and Labour Practices of some US-based Multinationals in the Metal Trades. Technologies for Basic Needs. Tenure of Trade Union Office.* All 1977.

FOOD AND AGRICULTURE ORGANIZATION OF THE UNITED NATIONS (FAO)

Origin. The UN Conference on Food and Agriculture in May 1943, at Hot Springs, Virginia, set up an Interim Commission in Washington in July 1943 to plan the Organization, which came into being on 16 Oct. 1945.

Functions. FAO gives international support to national programmes to increase the efficiency of agriculture, forestry and fisheries, and to improve the conditions of the people engaged in relevant activities.

FAO keeps world food and agricultural conditions under continuous review and supplies member governments with facts and figures, appraisals and forecasts relating to trends in the world agricultural situation and on production, trade and consumption.

The FAO Conference meets every 2 years. At its 19th session held in Nov. 1977, it admitted 8 new States: Angola, the Comoros, the Democratic People's Republic of Korea, Djibouti, Mozambique, South West Africa (Namibia), São Tomé and Principe, and the Seychelles.

The Conference reviewed progress made towards the achievement of the objectives defined at its 1975 session as essential for ensuring international agricultural adjustment. Policy guidelines laid down at that time called for an increase of at least 4% per annum in developing countries' food production to enable them to meet their peoples' growing demand for food and improve their nutritional standards. The total flow of financial and other resources into agricultural production needed to be greatly increased, especially for expansion and diversification of production in developing countries. It was suggested that national policies of developing countries provide appropriate incentives for farmers, while developed countries were urged to use their resources rationally, consider the needs and interests of developing countries and take into account the requirements of world food security. Two years have elapsed, and the 1977 Conference found that performance with respect to these guidelines had moved in the right direction, but at a disappointingly slow pace.

Although food production and food stocks increased in 1977, the world made insufficient progress towards overcoming the longstanding problems of agricultural development, trade in commodities and the assurance of adequate food supplies. Such was the consensus of opinion at the Conference, which also warned that 'the situation remains fragile'.

Cereal stocks were 60% higher than in 1973–74 and were expected to reach 160m. tons (not including China and USSR for which no information was available) by the end of the 1977–78 crop season. This represented 18% annual food consumption thus providing a degree of world food security.

After large increases in 1974 and 1975, total official commitments of external assistance to agriculture are estimated to have fallen by 7% in real terms in 1976. Commitments in 1976 were less than half the estimated annual requirements of the developing countries, the gap amounting to almost $5,000m. The establishment of the International Fund for Agricultural Development (IFAD) is not likely to offset more than a relatively small part of this gap.

Aid given in the form of food increased during the year and would rise to 9·6m. tonnes during 1977–78. This was still below the 10m. tonne target set by the World Food Conference.

The FAO Conference found that little or no progress had been made towards the eradication of hunger and malnutrition, and it believed that the high level of stocks in part reflected the inability of both countries and individuals to purchase adequate supplies of food.

FAO provides secretariat services for the exchange of information and for co-operative action in its field of concern. More than 1,600 experts are assigned to field projects in developing countries. Through co-operative arrangements with private and public lending institutions, such as the World Bank, it helps to mobilize capital backing to programmes of development. With the UN, FAO sponsors the World Food Programme, which uses food and cash pledged by member countries for economic and social development projects and for alleviating distress during emergencies. Through the Freedom from Hunger/Action for Development Programme, which is conducted by some 100 national committees, FAO arouses concern over the gravity and extent of the world food situation and mobilizes public support for programmes to improve the quality of life of rural communities.

Organization. FAO's programme and overall policy are approved by a Conference (composed of one representative of each of the 144 member nations) and interim supervision is given by a Council (consisting of 49 nations elected by the Conference). The work of the Organization is carried out by an international staff led by a Director-General.

Budget for 1978–79: $211·35m.

Headquarters: Viale delle Terme di Caracalla, Rome, Italy.
Director-General: Dr Edouard Saouma (Lebanon).

FAO publications include: FAO Books in Print 1976–77: The State of Food and Agriculture (annual), 1974 ff.; *Animal Health Yearbook* (annual), 1957 ff.; *Production Yearbook* (annual), 1947 ff.; *Trade Yearbook* (annual), 1947 ff.; *FAO Commodity Review* (annual), 1961 ff.; *Yearbook of Forest Products Statistics* (annual), 1947 ff.; *Yearbook of Fishery Statistics* (in two volumes). *Ceres* (bimonthly). *Annual Fertilizer Review. World Grain Trade Statistics. Exports by Source and Destination* (annual). *Food and Nutrition* (quarterly).

UNITED NATIONS EDUCATIONAL, SCIENTIFIC AND CULTURAL ORGANIZATION (UNESCO)

Origin. A Conference for the establishment of an Educational, Scientific and Cultural Organization of the United Nations was convened by the Government of the UK in association with the Government of France, and met in London, 1–16 Nov. 1945. UNESCO came into being on 4 Nov. 1946.

Functions. The purpose of UNESCO is to contribute to peace and security by promoting collaboration among the nations through education, science and culture in order to further universal respect for justice, for the rule of law and for the human rights and fundamental freedoms which are affirmed for the peoples of the world, without distinction of race, sex, language or religion, by the Charter of the United Nations. The UNESCO budget for 1969 was $42,095,750.

Activities. The education programme has three main objectives: the extension of education; the improvement of education; and education for living in a world community.

To train teachers specialized in the techniques of fundamental education UNESCO is helping to establish regional and national training centres. A centre for Latin America was opened in Mexico in 1951, one for the Arab States was set up in Egypt in 1953. UNESCO seeks to promote the progressive application of the right to free and compulsory education for all and to improve the quality of education everywhere.

In the natural sciences, UNESCO seeks to promote international scientific co-operation, such as the International Hydrological Decade which began in 1965. It encourages scientific research designed to improve the living conditions of mankind. Science co-operation offices have been set up in Montevideo, Cairo, New Delhi and Jakarta.

In its mass communication work, UNESCO endeavours, by disseminating information, carrying out research and providing advice, to increase the scope and quality of press, film and radio services throughout the world.

Organization. The organs of UNESCO are a General Conference (composed of representatives from each member state), an Executive Board (consisting of 34 government representatives elected by the General Conference) and a Secretariat. UNESCO had 125 members and 3 associate members in 1969.

National commissions act as liaison groups between UNESCO and the educational, scientific and cultural life of their own countries.

Budget for 1972: $51·98m.

Headquarters: UNESCO House, 9 Place de Fontenoy, Paris (7ème).
Director-General: Amadou Mahtar M'Bow (Senegal).

Periodicals. Museum (quarterly, English and French); *International Social Science Journal* (quarterly, English and French); *Impact of Science on Society* (quarterly, English and French); *Unesco Courier* (monthly, English, French and Spanish); *Fundamental and Adult Education Bulletin* (quarterly, English, French and Spanish); *Copyright Bulletin* (twice-yearly, English and French); *Unesco Chronicle* (monthly, English, French and Spanish); *Unesco Bulletin for Libraries* (monthly, English, French and Spanish).

WORLD HEALTH ORGANIZATION (WHO)

Origin. An International Conference, convened by the UN Economic and Social Council, to consider a single health organization resulted in the adoption on 22 July 1946 of the constitution of the World Health Organization. This constitution came into force on 7 April 1948.

Structure. The principal organs of WHO are the World Health Assembly, the Executive Board and the Secretariat. Each of the 150 member states and the 2 Associate Members (1977) has the right to be represented at the Assembly, which meets annually usually in Geneva, Switzerland. The 30-member Executive Board is composed of technically qualified health experts designated by as many member states elected by the Assembly. The Secretariat consists of technical and administrative staff headed by a Director-General. Health activities in member countries are carried out through regional organizations which have been established in Africa (regional office, Brazzaville), South-East Asia (New Delhi), Europe (Copenhagen), Eastern Mediterranean (Alexandria) and Western Pacific (Manila). The Pan American Sanitary Bureau in Washington serves as the Regional Office of WHO for the Americas.

Functions. WHO's objective, as stated in the first article of the Constitution is 'the attainment by all peoples of the highest possible level of health'. As the directing and co-ordinating authority on international health it establishes and maintains collaboration with the UN, specialized agencies, government health administrations, professional and other groups concerned with health. The Constitution also directs WHO to assist governments to strengthen their health services, to stimulate and advance work to eradicate diseases, to promote maternal and child health, mental health, medical research and the prevention of accidents; to improve standards of teaching and training in the health professions, and of nutrition, housing, sanitation, working conditions and other aspects of environmental health. The Organization also is empowered to propose conventions, agreements and regulations and make recommendations about international health matters; to revise the international nomenclature of diseases, causes of death and public health practices; to develop, establish and promote international standards concerning foods, biological, pharmaceutical and similar substances.

Methods of work. Co-operation in country projects is undertaken only on the request of the government concerned, through the 6 regional offices of the Organization. Worldwide technical services are made available by headquarters. Expert committees whose members are chosen from the 45 advisory panels of experts meet to advise the Director-General on a given subject. Scientific groups and consultative meetings are called for similar purposes. To further the education of all levels of health personnel of all categories, seminars, technical conferences and training courses are organized and advisors, consultants and lecturers are provided. WHO awards fellowships for study to nationals of member countries (the cumulative total had reached more than 56,300 by the end of 1976).

Activities. In communication disease control, the certification of eradication of smallpox in Bangladesh in Dec. 1977 was a major event. This meant that the virulent, classical form of the disease, *variola major* no longer exists in the world. Efforts to eradicate *variola minor*, a milder form of the disease, continued in the Horn of Africa particularly in Somalia, where cases were still being recorded in the last quarter of 1977.

The worldwide spread of influenza is kept under surveillance through a global network of laboratories constantly on the look-out for any variations in the influenza virus. Programmes in malaria, cholera, tuberculosis, leprosy, etc. are supported through assistance in planning of campaigns as well as field and laboratory research. Water supply and wastes disposal projects are promoted and advice given on soil, water and food pollution. Safety levels are set for food additives and contaminants.

WHO co-operates with member countries in building up their health services to ensure that primary health care reaches the maximum number of people. The World Health Assembly has adopted the goal of 'Health for all by the year 2000'. Development of health manpower remains a top priority, with particular emphasis on basing the training of health workers on the needs of the community they are to serve and on the local social, cultural and economic conditions.

In programmes relating to non-communicable diseases, such as cardiovascular diseases and cancer, research figures prominently. Work in cancer is carried out both at the International Agency for Research on Cancer at Lyons in the field of environmental biology, and in a number of WHO collaborating centres which are concerned with clinical studies, classification and cancer control services. The medical research programme of WHO is based on a world-wide network of collaborating centres and on advisory committees on medical research established in its 6 regions. A number of countries are being helped to develop an effective organization of mental health services. In pharmacology and toxicology work is geared to ensuring the availability of effective and safe drugs

Headquarters: 1211 Geneva 27. *Regional Offices:* Alexandria, Brazzaville, Copenhagen, Manila, New Delhi, Washington.

Director-General: Dr Halfdan T. Mahler (Denmark).

Basic Documents. 27th ed., 1977 (English, French, Russian, Spanish)
Handbook of Resolutions and Decisions. Vol. I, 1973 and Vol. II, 1977 (Arabic, English, French, Russian, Spanish).
Official Records, 1947 ff. (English, French, Russian, Spanish; 242 vols. to 1977)
WHO Chronicle (monthly from 1947; Chinese, English, French, Russian and Spanish)

Bulletin of WHO (quarterly, 1947–51; monthly, from 1952; English, French and Russian)
International Digest of Health Legislation (quarterly, from 1948; English and French)
World Health, the Magazine of WHO. 1957 ff. (10 issues a year; Arabic, English, French, German, Italian, Persian, Portuguese, Russian and Spanish)
WHO Technical Report Series, 1950 ff. (English, French, Russian, Spanish)
WHO Monograph Series, 1951 ff. (English, French, Russian, Spanish)
Public Health Papers, 1959 ff. (English, French, Russian, Spanish)
World Health Statistics Annual (from 1939; English, French and Russian)
World Health Statistics Report (monthly, 1947–76 then quarterly; English and French)
Weekly Epidemiological Record (from 1926; English and French)
Publications of the WHO, 1947–57; a bibliography (1958).—*1958–62* (1965).—*1963–67* (1969).—*1968–72* (1974)
World Directories:
Dental Schools, 1963 (1967); *Medical Schools, 1970* (1973); *Post-Basic and Post-Graduate Schools of Nursing* (1965); *Schools of Pharmacy, 1963* (1966); *Schools of Public Health, 1971* (1972); *Venereal Disease Treatment Centres at Ports* (1972); *Veterinary Schools, 1971* (1973). *Schools for Medical Assistants, 1973* (1976)
Medical Research Programme of WHO, 1964–68 (1969; English, French, Russian, Spanish)
Specifications for the Quality Control of Pharmaceutical Preparations International Pharmacopoeia (2nd ed. 1967; English, French, Russian, Spanish).—Supplement 1971
Manual of the International Statistical Classification of Diseases, Injuries and Causes of Death. 9th rev. (1977; English, French, Russian, Spanish)
The First Ten Years of the World Health Organization (1958; English, French, Russian, Spanish)
The Second Ten Years of the World Health Organization, 1958–1967 (1968; English, French, Spanish)
Report on the World Health Situation. 1959 ff. (English, French, Russian, Spanish); every 4 years. Fifth report 1969–72 (1975)

INTERNATIONAL MONETARY FUND (IMF)

The international Monetary Fund was established on 27 Dec. 1945 as an independent international organization; its relationship with the UN is defined in an agreement of mutual co-operation which came into force on 15 Nov. 1947. The first amendment to the Fund's articles creating the special drawing right (SDR) took effect on 28 July 1969 and the second amendment took effect on 1 April 1978 which increases the power of the managing director of the IMF to supervise national exchange rate policies.

The Fund is authorized under its Articles of Agreement to supplement its resources by borrowing. In Jan. 1962, a 4-year agreement was concluded with 10 industrial members (Belgium, Canada, France, Federal Republic of Germany, Italy, Japan, Netherlands, Sweden, UK, USA) who undertook to lend the Fund up to $6,000m. in their own currencies, if this should be needed to forestall or cope with an impairment of the international monetary system. These agreements, extended in 1965 until 1970, for a further 5 years in 1970, were again renewed in 1974 for a 5-year period from 24 Oct. 1975, were used to finance drawings made by the UK in 1964, 1965, 1968 and 1969, and by France in 1969 and 1970. By Aug. 1971 all such borrowings had been repaid in full to the Fund.

Purposes: To promote international monetary co-operation, the expansion of international trade and exchange stability; to assist in the removal of exchange restrictions and the establishment of a multilateral system of payments; and to alleviate any serious disequilibrium in members' international balance of payments by making the resources of the Fund available to them under adequate safeguards.

Activities. Each member of the Fund undertakes to establish and maintain an agreed par value for its currency, and to consult the Fund on any change in excess of 10% of the initial parity. Countries retaining exchange controls are required to hold annual consultations with the Fund regarding the restrictions in use, the balance of payments justification for them, and the possibilities for their removal. The Fund makes its foreign exchange resources available, under proper safeguards, to its members to meet short-term or medium-term payments difficulties. The Fund also supplements, as and when needed, the existing reserve assets of participants in the Special Drawing Account. The first allocation of special drawing rights was made on 1 Jan. 1970, in a total amount equivalent to $3,500m. The second allocation, on 1 Jan. 1971, was equivalent to $2,900m. and the third, on 1 Jan. 1972, was equivalent to $2,900m.

Following serious monetary disturbances in 1971, a Report on Reform of the International Monetary System was submitted to the Board of Governors at the 1972 annual meeting. During the meeting the Committee on Reform of the International Monetary System and Related Issues, generally known as the Committee of Twenty, held its first session, with the mandate to advise and report to the Board on all aspects of the international monetary system, including proposals for any amendments of the Articles of Agreement. The Committee of Twenty ceased to exist after submitting its final report in 1974. An Interim Committee of the Board of Governors on the International Monetary System and a Joint Ministerial Committee of the Boards of Governors of the World Bank and the Fund on the Transfer of Real Resources to Developing Countries (Development Committee) were established and held their meetings in Jan. 1975.

Organization. The highest authority in the Fund is exercised by the Board of Governors on which each member government is represented. Normally the Governors meet once a year, although the Governors may take votes by mail or other means between annual meetings. The Board of Governors has delegated many of its powers to the executive directors in Washington, of whom there are 20, 5 appointed by the 5 members with the largest quotas and the other 15 elected by groups of countries. Each appointed director has voting power proportionate to the quota of the government he represents, while each elected director casts all the votes of the countries which elected him. The 5 appointed executive directors represent the US, UK, France, Federal Republic of Germany, and Japan.

The managing director is selected by the executive directors; he presides as chairman at their meetings, but may not vote except in case of a tie. His term is for 5 years, but may be extended or terminated at the discretion of the executive directors. He is responsible for the ordinary business of the Fund, under general control of the executive directors, and supervises a staff of 1,400.

Headquarters: 19th & H St. NW, Washington, D.C., 20431. Offices in Paris and Geneva.

Managing Director: H. Johannes Witteveen (Netherlands).

Publications. Summary Proceedings of Annual Meetings of the Board of Governors.—Annual Report of the Executive Directors.—Financial Statement (quarterly).—*Schedule of Par Values.—International Financial Statistics* (monthly).—*IMF Survey* (bi-monthly).—*Balance of Payments Yearbook.* Washington, 1949 ff.—*IMF Staff Papers* (three times a year). Washington, from Feb. 1950.—*Annual Report on Exchange Restrictions.* Washington, 1950 ff.—*Finance and Development.* Washington, from June 1964 (quarterly).—*Direction of Trade* (monthly).

de Vries, M. G., *The International Monetary Fund 1966–1971.* Washington D.C., 1976

INTERNATIONAL BANK FOR RECONSTRUCTION AND DEVELOPMENT

Conceived at the Bretton Woods Conference, July 1944, the Bank began operations in June 1946. Its purpose is to provide funds and technical assistance to facilitate economic development in its poorer member countries.

The Bank obtains its funds from the following sources: Capital subscribed by member countries; sales of its own securities; sales of parts of its loans; repayments; and net earnings. The subscribed capital of the Bank amounted to $30,869m. at 30 June 1977. 10% of this amount is paid-in while the remainder is subject to call if needed to meet the Bank's obligations. Borrowing in the market had reached $29,515m. by 30 June 1977, of which $18,478m. was outstanding, and sales of portions of Bank loans from portfolio had totalled $2,742m. The Bank is self-supporting. Its net earnings for year ending 30 June 1977 amounted to $209m.; in addition, the Bank had reserves of $2,026m.

By 30 June 1977 the Bank had made 1,453 loans totalling $38,610m. in 98 of its 129 member countries. Excluding loans of $550m. to its affiliate, the International Finance Corporation (IFC), its lending had been for the following purposes:

Agriculture, $6,780m.; education, $1,224m.; industry, $7,666m.; non-project, $1,855m.; population, $120m.; electric power, $8,455m.; telecommunications, $934m.; tourism, $247m.; transportation, $9,588m.; urbanization, $368m.; water supply and sewerage, $1,344m., and technical assistance, $31m.

In order to eliminate wasteful overlapping of development assistance and to ensure that the funds available are used to the best possible effect, the Bank has organized consortia or consultative groups of aid-giving nations for the following countries: Bangladesh, Bolivia, Burma, Colombia, Egypt, Ethiopia, India, Korea, Morocco, Nepál, Pakistan, Peru, the Philippines, Sri Lanka, the Sudan, Thailand, Tunisia, Zaïre and East Africa (Kenya, Uganda, Tanzania). The Bank furnishes a wide variety of technical assistance. It acts as executing agency for a number of pre-investment surveys financed by the UN Development Programme. Resident missions have been established in 21 developing member countries as well as 3 regional missions in East and West Africa and Thailand primarily to assist in the preparation of projects. The Bank helps member countries to identify and prepare projects for the development of agriculture, education and water supply by drawing on the expertise of the FAO, WHO, UNIDO and UNESCO through its co-operative agreements with these organizations. The Bank maintains a staff college, the Economic Development Institute in Washington, D.C., for senior officials of the member countries.

To help the poorest member countries the INTERNATIONAL DEVELOPMENT ASSOCIATION (IDA) was established in 1960. IDA grants development credits on a long-term, interest-free basis. By 30 June 1977 IDA had extended 666 credits to 69 countries, totalling $11,397m. for the same general purpose as bank loans. IDA's primary lending resources have been the subscriptions and supplementary contributions of member countries, chiefly its 21 wealthiest. The World Bank has made grants to IDA out of its net income; the Association also has a small flow of net income of its own.

Headquarters: 1818 H St., NW, Washington, D.C., 20433, USA. *European office:* 66 avenue d'Iéna, 75116 Paris, France. *London office:* New Zealand House, SW1. *Tōkyō office:* Kokusai Building, 1–1, Marunouchi 3-chome, Chiyoda-ku, Tōkyō 100, Japan.

President: Robert S. McNamara (USA).

Publications. Annual Reports. 1946 ff.—*Summary Proceedings of Annual Meetings.* 1947 ff.—*The World Bank Group.* 1971.—*The World Bank Atlas.* 1967 ff.—*The World Bank, IDA and IFC Policies and Operations.* 1971 ff.—*Catalog of Publications,* 1977.—IDA, 1977.

INTERNATIONAL FINANCE CORPORATION (IFC)

The Corporation, an affiliate of the World Bank, was established in July 1956. Paid-in capital at 30 June 1977 was $108·3m., subscribed by 106 member countries. In addition, it has a general reserve of $87·3m. IFC supplements the activities of the World Bank by encouraging the growth of productive private enterprises in less developed member countries. Chiefly, IFC makes investments in the form of subscriptions to the share capital of privately owned companies, or long-term loans, or both. The Corporation will help finance new ventures, and it will also assist established enterprises to expand, improve or diversify their operations.

At 30 June 1976 IFC has made commitments, amounting to $1,712m., in 62 countries. The total amount of loans and equity which IFC had sold or agreed to sell to other investors as of that date was $515·6m. Standby and underwriting commitments totalled $55·4m.

President: Robert S. McNamara (USA).

Executive Vice-President: Moeen A. Qureshi (Pakistan).

Publications. IFC, What it is.—*Annual Reports.* 1956 ff.—*General Policies.* 1976.—*IFC in Latin America.* 1974.—*IFC in Africa.* 1976.—*IFC in Asia.* 1975.

INTERNATIONAL CIVIL AVIATION ORGANIZATION (ICAO)

Origin. The Convention providing for the establishment of the International Civil Aviation Organization was drawn up by the International Civil Aviation

Conference held in Chicago from 1 Nov. to 7 Dec. 1944. A Provisional International Civil Aviation Organization (PICAO) operated for 20 months until the formal establishment of ICAO on 4 April 1947.

The Convention on International Civil Aviation superseded the provisions of the Paris Convention of 1919, which established the International Commission for Air Navigation (ICAN), and the Pan American Convention on Air Navigation drawn up at Havana in 1928.

Functions. It assists international civil aviation by establishing technical standards for safety and efficiency of air navigation and promoting simpler procedures at borders; develops regional plans for ground facilities and services needed for international flying; disseminates air-transport statistics and prepares studies on aviation economics; fosters the development of air law conventions. As part of the UN Development Programme it provides technical assistance to States in developing civil aviation programmes.

Organization. The principal organs of ICAO are an Assembly, consisting of all members of the Organization, and a Council, which is comprised of 30 states elected by the Assembly, for 3 years, and meets in virtually continuous session. In electing these states, the Assembly must give adequate representation to: (1) member states of major importance in air transport; (2) those member states not otherwise included which make the largest contribution to the provision of facilities for the international civil air navigation; (3) those member states not otherwise included whose election will ensure that all major geographical areas of the world are represented. The main subsidiary bodies are: the Air Navigation Commission, composed of 15 members appointed by the Council; Air Transport Committee, open to council members; and the Legal Committee, on which all members of ICAO may be represented. There are 141 members.

Budget for 1976: $19,101,000.

Headquarters: International Aviation Building, 1000 Sherbrooke St West, Montreal, Quebec, Canada H3A 2R2.

President: Dr Assad Kotaite (Lebanon).

Secretary-General: Yves Lambert (France).

UNIVERSAL POSTAL UNION (UPU)

Origin. The UPU was established on 1 July 1875, when the Universal Postal Convention adopted by the Postal Congress of Berne on 9 Oct. 1874 came into force. The UPU was known at first as the General Postal Union, its name being changed at the Congress of Paris in 1878. In Oct 1974 there were 154 member countries.

Functions. The aim of the UPU is to assure the organization and perfection of the various postal services and to promote, in this field, the development of international collaboration. To this end, the members of UPU are united in a single postal territory for the reciprocal exchange of correspondence.

Organization. The UPU is composed of a Universal Postal Congress, which usually meets every 5 years, a permanent Executive Council consisting of 40 members, a consultative Committee, which consists of 35 members elected on a geographical basis by each Congress, and an International Bureau, which functions as the permanent secretariat.

Since 1 July 1948 the Union has been governed by the revised Convention adopted by the twelfth Congress in Paris on 5 July 1947.

Budget for 1976: $4·26m.

Headquarters: Weltpoststrasse 4, 3000, Berne 15, Switzerland.

Director-General: Mohamed Ibrahim Sobhi (Egypt).

Publications. Documents of the Lausanne Congress 1974. Bern, 1975.—*Universal Postal Convention: Paris, 5 July, 1948.* (Cmd. 7435).—*The Postal Union* (monthly, Arabic, Chinese, English, French, German, Spanish, Russian).—*The UPU: Its Foundation and Development.* Bern, 1959.

INTERNATIONAL TELECOMMUNICATION UNION (ITU)

Origin. The International Telegraph Union, founded in Paris in 1865, and the International Radiotelegraph Union, founded in Berlin in 1906, were merged by the Madrid Convention of 1932 to form the International Telecommunication Union. ITU came into being on 1 Jan. 1934. The ITU has been governed since 1 Jan. 1975 by the revised International Telecommunication Convention adopted on 23 Oct. 1973.

Functions. The ITU: (1) allocates radio frequencies and registers radio-frequency assignments; (2) seeks to establish the lowest rates possible, consistent with efficient service and taking into account the necessity for keeping the independent financial administration of telecommunication on a sound basis; (3) promotes the adoption of measures for ensuring the safety of life through telecommunication; and (4) makes studies and recommendations and collects and publishes information for the benefit of its members.

Organization. The ITU consists of the Plenipotentiary Conference, Administrative Conferences, the Administrative Council of 36 members, the General Secretariat, the International Frequency Registration Board, and 2 international consultative committees (radio, telephone and telegraph).

Budget for 1975: $62·32m.

Headquarters: Place des Nations, Geneva, Switzerland.
Secretary-General: Mohamed Mili (Tunisia).
Deputy Secretary-General: Richard E. Butler (Australia).

Publications. International Convention on Telecommunications, Malaga-Torremolinos, 1973.—*Yearbook of Common Carrier Telecommunication Statistics (1964–73),* 1975.—*Telecommunication Journal* (monthly).—*Radio Regulations.* 1971.

WORLD METEOROLOGICAL ORGANIZATION (WMO)

Origin. A Conference of Directors of the International Meteorological Organization (set up in 1873), meeting in Washington in 1947, adopted a Convention creating the World Meteorological Organization. The WMO Convention became effective on 23 March 1950, and WMO was formally established on 19 March 1951, when the first session of its Congress was convened in Paris. An agreement to bring WMO into relationship with the United Nations was approved by this Congress and came into force on 21 Dec. 1951 with its approval by the General Assembly of the United Nations.

Functions. (1) To facilitate world-wide co-operation in the establishment of networks of stations for the making of meteorological observations as well as hydrological or other geophysical observations related to meteorology, and to promote the establishment and maintenance of meteorological centres charged with the provision of meteorological and related services; (2) to promote the establishment and maintenance of systems for the rapid exchange of meteorological and related information; (3) to promote standardization of meteorological and related observations and to ensure the uniform publication of observations and statistics; (4) to further the application of meteorology to aviation, shipping, water problems, agriculture and other human activities; (5) to promote activities in operational hydrology and to further close co-operation between meteorological and hydrological services; and (6) to encourage research and training in meteorology and, as appropriate, to assist in co-ordinating the international aspects of such research and training.

Organization. WMO is an inter-governmental organization of 135 member states and 9 member territories responsible for the operation of their own meteorological services. Constituent bodies of WMO are the World Meteorological Congress which meets every 4 years, the executive commitee composed of 24 members elected in their personal capacity and including the President and 3 Vice-Presidents of the Organization, 6 regional associations of members and 8 technical commissions established by the Congress. A permanent secretariat is maintained in Geneva.

Budget for 1977: $10,353,900.

Headquarters: 41 Avenue Giuseppe Motta, Geneva, Switzerland.
Secretary-General: David A. Davies (UK).

Publications. WMO Bulletin. 1952 ff.—*Meteorological Services of the World.* 1971.—*Publications of the World Meteorological Organization, 1951–1975.*

INTER-GOVERNMENTAL MARITIME CONSULTATIVE ORGANIZATION (IMCO)

Origin. IMCO was established as a specialized agency of the UN by a convention drawn up at the UN Maritime Conference held at Geneva in Feb./March 1948. The Convention became effective on 17 March 1958 when it had been ratified by 21 countries, including 7 with at least 1m. gross tons of shipping each. IMCO started operations in Jan. 1959.

Functions. To facilitate co-operation among governments on technical matters affecting merchant shipping, especially concerning safety at sea; to prevent and control marine pollution caused by ships; to encourage abolition of discriminatory and restrictive practices affecting merchant shipping. IMCO is responsible for convening international maritime conferences and for drafting international maritime conventions.

Organization. IMCO had 103 members (and 1 associate member) in 1978. The Assembly, composed of all member states, normally meets every 2 years. The Council of 24 member states acts as governing body between Assembly sessions. The Maritime Safety Committee deals with all technical questions. It can establish specialized sub-committees to deal with specific problems. The Marine Environment Protection Committee, Legal Committee, Facilitation Committee and Committee on Technical Co-operation are open to all IMCO members. The Secretariat is composed of international civil servants.

IMCO is depositary authority for the International Convention for the Safety of Life at Sea, 1960, and the Regulations for Preventing Collisions at Sea, 1948 and 1960; the International Convention for the Prevention of Pollution of the Sea by Oil, 1954, as amended in 1962; the Convention on Facilitation of International Maritime Traffic, 1965; the International Convention on Load Lines, 1966; the International Convention on Tonnage Measurement of Ships, 1969; the International Convention relating to Intervention on the High Seas in cases of Oil Pollution Casualties 1969; the International Convention on Civil Liability for Oil Pollution Damage, 1969; Convention on International Compensation Fund for Oil Pollution Damage, 1971; Convention on International Regulations for Preventing Collisions at Sea, 1972; the International Convention for Safe Containers, 1973; the International Convention on Prevention of Pollution from Ships, 1973; the International Convention for the Safety of Life at Sea, 1974; Athens Convention relating to the Carriage of Passengers and their Luggage by Sea, 1974; Convention of the International Maritime Satellite Organization, 1976; Convention on Limitation of Maritime Claims, 1976; Torremolinos International Convention for the Safety of Shipping Vessels, 1977.

Headquarters: 101 Piccadilly, London, W1V 0AE.
Secretary-General: C. P. Srivastava (India).
Secretary, Maritime Safety Committee: Capt. G. Kostylev (USSR).

IMCO, What it is, What it does. 1974
Imco News.

GENERAL AGREEMENT ON TARIFFS AND TRADE (GATT)

Origin. The General Agreement on Tariffs and Trade was negotiated in 1947 and entered into force on 1 Jan. 1948. Its 23 original signatories were members of a Preparatory Committee appointed by the UN Economic and Social Council to draft the charter for a proposed International Trade Organization. Since this charter was never ratified, the General Agreement, intended as an interim arrangement, has instead remained as the only international instrument laying down trade rules accepted by countries responsible for most of the world's trade. In Dec. 1977 there were 83 contracting parties, with a further 28 countries participating under special arrangements.

Functions. GATT functions both as a multilateral treaty that lays down a common code of conduct in international trade and trade relations and as a forum for negotiation and consultation to overcome trade problems and reduce trade barriers. Key provisions of the Agreement guarantee most-favoured-nation treatment (exceptions being granted to customs unions and free trade areas, and for certain preferences in favour of developing countries), require that protection be given to domestic industry only through tariffs, provide for negotiations to reduce tariffs (which are then 'bound' against subsequent increase) and other trade distortions and lay down principles (particularly in Part IV of the Agreement, added in 1965) to assist the trade of developing countries. The Agreement also provides for consultation on, and settlement of, disputes, for 'waivers' (the grant of authorization, when warranted, to derogate from specific GATT obligations) and for emergency action in defined circumstances.

Six major trade negotiations, most recently the highly successful Kennedy Round of 1964–67, took place in GATT up to 1973. In Sept. 1973 a Ministerial conference in Tōkyō launched new negotiations of unprecedented scope, in which some 98 countries are engaged. The negotiations are guided by the Tōkyō Declaration, which provides that the negotiations shall cover tariffs, non-tariff barriers and other measures which impede or distort international trade in industrial and agricultural products, including tropical products and raw materials and, in particular, products of export interest to developing countries and measures affecting their exports. The negotiations are based on the principles of mutual advantage, mutual commitment and overall reciprocity (*i.e.*, that the totality of concessions made by each developed country should balance those received) with the joint aim of achieving an overall balance of advantage at the highest possible level. In addition, special terms have been agreed upon for the participation of developing countries, as well as specific aims for the negotiations as regards their trade. A firm technical basis for the negotiations is provided by a comprehensive work programme undertaken in GATT since 1967.

To assist the trade of developing countries, GATT established in 1964 the International Trade Centre (since 1968 operated jointly with the UN Conference on Trade and Development) to provide information and training on export markets and marketing techniques. Other GATT action in favour of developing countries includes training courses on trade policy questions.

Budget for 1978: Sw. Frs. 38·5m.

Headquarters: Centre William Rappard, 154 rue de Lausanne, 1211, Geneva 21, Switzerland.

Director-General: Olivier Long (Switzerland).

Publications. Basic Instruments and Selected Documents. 4 vols and 23 supplements 1952–77.—*International Trade* [i.e., annual review], 1952 ff. Annually from 1953.—*GATT, What It Is, What It Does* (1977).—*GATT Activities*, 1960 ff. Annually from 1972.—*GATT Studies in International Trade.* 1971 ff. (irregular series).

Casadio, G. P., *Transatlantic Trade: USA–EEC Confrontation in the GATT Negotiations.* Farnborough, 1973

Dam, K. W., *The GATT: Law and International Economic Organization.* Chicago and London, 1970

Golt, S., *The GATT Negotiations, 1973–75: A Guide to the Issues.* London, 1974

Hudec, R. E., *The GATT Legal System and World Trade Diplomacy.* New York, 1975

Jackson, J. H. *World Trade and the Law of GATT: A Legal Analysis of the General Agreement on Tariffs and Trade.* New York, 1969

THE INTERNATIONAL NARCOTICS CONTROL BOARD (INCB)

Origin. The INCB was established by the Single Convention on Narcotic Drugs, 1961, and assumed the functions of the Permanent Central Board and the Drug Supervisory Body, which were themselves treaty organs created by the narcotics Conventions of 1925 and 1931 respectively. The 1961 Convention came into force on 13 Dec. 1964. The INCB entered upon its duties on 2 March 1968. Its functions and membership were enlarged by the 1972 Protocol amending the 1961 Convention.

Functions. The functions of the Board under the Treaties are to work with governments to ensure that the aims of the drug control treaties are not seriously endangered by reason of the failure of any country or territory to carry out the provisions of such treaties; to limit the cultivation, production, manufacture and use of drugs to an adequate amount required for medical and scientific purposes; to prevent the illicit cultivation, production and manufacture of, and illicit trafficking in and use of, drugs; to ensure the availability of drugs for medical and scientific purposes; to encourage universal co-operation in the field of drug control. The 1971 Convention on Psychotropic Substances broadens the scope of the Board's activities to include the supervision of national control over these substances.

Organization. The INCB is composed of 13 members, elected by the Economic and Social Council in their individual capacities and not as representatives of governments, who, by their competence, impartiality and disinterestedness, will command general confidence. During its sessions held at least twice a year, the Board reviews the drug situation throughout the world and supervises the implementation of the various drug control treaties. The INCB is assisted by a permanent secretariat which is in continuous dialogue with national authorities. Information received from over 170 governments is analysed by the secretariat and submitted for the Board's attention during its sessions.

Headquarters: Palais des Nations, Geneva, Switzerland.
President: Professor Paul Reuter.
Secretary: Stephan Stepczyński.

Publications. Report of the International Narcotics Control Board. 1968 ff.—*Estimated World Requirements of Narcotic Drugs and Estimates of World Production of Opium.* With supplements. 1969 ff.—*Statistics on Narcotic Drugs and Maximum Levels of Opium Stocks.* 1967 ff.—*Comparative Statement of Estimates and Statistics on Narcotic Drugs.* 1967 ff.—*List of Narcotic Drugs under International Control.* 1968 ff.

WORLD INTELLECTUAL PROPERTY ORGANIZATION (WIPO)

Origin. The Convention establishing WIPO was signed at Stockholm in 1967 by 51 countries, and entered into force in April 1970. In Dec. 1974 WIPO became a specialized agency of the UNO.

Objectives. The objectives of WIPO are to promote the protection of intellectual property throughout the world through co-operation among States and, where appropriate, in collaboration with any other international organization, and to ensure administrative co-operation among the Unions established by various treaties for the protection of intellectual property. The Convention provides expressly for the encouragement of the conclusion of international agreements designed to promote the protection of intellectual property, and for the provision of legal-technical assistance at the request of States.

Intellectual property includes the rights relating to: literary, artistic and scientific works; performances of performing artists, phonograms and broadcasts; inventions in all fields of human endeavour; scientific discoveries; industrial designs; trademarks, service marks and commercial names and designations; protection against unfair competition and all other rights resulting from intellectual activity in the industrial, scientific, literary or artistic fields.

Functions. Among its other functions, WIPO performs the administrative tasks of certain international treaties dealing with various subjects of intellectual property, assembles and disseminates information concerning the protection of intellectual property, carries out and promotes studies in this field, publishes the results of such studies, and maintains services, including registration and publication services, facilitating the international protection of intellectual property.

WIPO performs the administrative tasks conferred by the Paris Convention for the Protection of Industrial Property, by various Special Agreements made within the framework of the Paris Convention and by the Berne Convention for the Protection of Literary and Artistic Works. The Special Agreements referred to, and currently in force, are: Madrid Agreement for the Repression of False or Deceptive Indications of Source on Goods, Madrid Agreement concerning the International

Registration of Marks, The Hague Agreement concerning the International Deposit of Industrial Designs, Nice Agreement concerning the International Classification of Goods and Services for the Purposes of the Registration of Marks, Lisbon Agreement for the Protection of Appellations of Origin and their International Registration, Locarno Agreement Establishing an International Classification for Industrial Designs, Strasbourg Agreement concerning the International Patent Classification. Other special agreements in the industrial property field, to be administered by WIPO when they come into force, are: Patent Co-operation Treaty, Trademark Registration Treaty, Vienna Agreement for the Protection of Type Faces and their International Deposit and the Protocol to that Agreement, and Vienna Agreement Establishing an International Classification of the Figurative Elements of Marks. In the field of neighbouring rights, the International Convention for the Protection of Performers, Producers of Phonograms and Broadcasting Organizations administered by WIPO, the International Labour Organization and Unesco. There are also the Convention for the Protection of Producers of Phonograms Against Unauthorized Duplication of their Phonograms, which is administered by WIPO and the Convention Relating to the Distribution of Programmes carrying Signals Transmitted by Satellite.

WIPO also provides the Secretariat for ICIREPAT (Paris Union Committee for International Co-operation in Information Retrieval among Patent Offices). The objective of ICIREPAT is to promote international co-operation in the field of the storage and retrieval of technical information particularly in connexion with the searching or examination of applications for patents, inventors' certificates, or similar titles. 'Storage and retrieval of technical information' are understood in their widest sense and include all supporting operations and all activities facilitating them, including in particular: abstracting, indexing, classification, translation, standardization of the form of documents and of search tools, processing of documents, communication and exchange of documents.

So far as its administrative functions are concerned, WIPO is a continuation of the United International Bureaux for the Protection of Intellectual Property (BIRPI), which, under the supervisory authority of the Government of the Swiss Confederation, has provided the International Bureau of the Unions established by the Paris and Berne Conventions since the end of the 19th century. As long as there are States members of the Paris or Berne Unions which have not become members of WIPO, the International Bureau and the Director-General of WIPO function as BIRPI, and its Director, respectively.

Technical Assistance. The legal-technical assistance programme of WIPO is intended to assist developing countries in the improvement of their intellectual property systems in order to support their national and regional plans for economic development. The methods used include expert advice on the modernization of laws and on the building of appropriate governmental institutions, including the training of staff, together with the stimulation of industrial research and development activities by assisting in the flow of scientific and technical information.

The International Bureau of WIPO will act also as the International Bureau of the Patent Co-operation Treaty (PCT), which was signed by 35 countries in 1970 but is not expected to enter into force for a few years. The PCT contains provisions relating to technical assistance on a larger scale than that likely to be provided for in the WIPO programme, and calls for the conclusion of agreements between the International Bureau and international financing organizations concerned with development. Before the entry into force of the PCT, an Interim Committee, consisting of all signatory countries, has been authorized to put the technical assistance programme into effect. WIPO will also act as the International Bureau of the Trademarks Registration Treaty (TRT) which was signed by 14 countries in 1973 and is not yet in force.

Membership in WIPO is open to any State which is a member of the Unions and to other States which are members of the organizations of the United Nations system, are party to the Statute of the International Court of Justice, or are invited to join by the General Assembly of WIPO. Membership of the Unions is open to any State. The total combined membership of the WIPO and of Unions on 1 Jan. 1977, including 6 States not members of either of the Unions, was 100 States.

WIPO member States: Algeria, Australia, Austria, Bahamas, Belgium, Benin, Brazil, Bulgaria, Burundi, Byelorussian SSR, Cameroon, Canada, Chad, Chile, Congo, Cuba, Czechoslovakia, Denmark, Egypt, Federal Republic of Germany, Fiji, Finland, France, Gabon, German Democratic Republic, Ghana, Greece, Hungary, India, Iraq, Irish Republic, Israel, Ivory Coast, Japan, Jordan, Kenya, Korea (North), Libya, Liechtenstein, Luxembourg, Malawi, Mauritania, Mauritius, Mexico, Monaco, Morocco, Netherlands, Niger, Norway, Poland, Portugal, Qatar, Romania, Senegal, Republic of South Africa, Spain, Sudan, Surinam, Sweden, Switzerland, Togo, Tunisia, Uganda, Ukrainian SSR, USSR, United Arab Emirates, UK, USA, Upper Volta, Vatican, Yugoslavia, Zaïre. (73 States.)

Paris Union: Algeria, Argentina, Australia, Austria, Bahamas, Belgium, Benin, Brazil, Bulgaria, Cameroon, Canada, Central African Empire, Chad, Congo, Cuba, Cyprus, Czechoslovakia, Denmark, Dominican Republic, Egypt, Federal Republic of Germany, Finland, France, Gabon, German Democratic Republic, Greece, Haiti, Hungary, Iceland, Indonesia, Iran, Iraq, Irish Republic, Israel, Italy, Ivory Coast, Japan, Jordan, Kenya, Lebanon, Libya, Liechtenstein, Luxembourg, Madagascar, Malawi, Malta, Mauritania, Mauritius, Mexico, Monaco, Morocco, Netherlands, New Zealand, Niger, Nigeria, Norway, Philippines, Poland, Portugal, Rhodesia, Romania, San Marino, Senegal, Republic of South Africa, Spain, Sri Lanka, Surinam, Sweden, Switzerland, Syria, Tanzania, Togo, Trinidad and Tobago, Tunisia, Turkey, Uganda, USSR, UK, USA, Upper Volta, Uruguay, Vatican, Vietnam, Yugoslavia, Zaïre, Zambia. (88 States.)

Berne Union: Argentina, Australia, Austria, Bahamas, Belgium, Benin, Brazil, Bulgaria, Cameroon, Canada, Chad, Chile, Congo, Cyprus, Czechoslovakia, Denmark, Fiji, Finland, France, Gabon, German Democratic Republic, Federal Republic of Germany, Greece, Hungary, Iceland, India, Irish Republic, Israel, Italy, Ivory Coast, Japan, Lebanon, Libya, Liechtenstein, Luxembourg, Madagascar, Mali, Malta, Mauritania, Mexico, Monaco, Morocco, Netherlands, New Zealand, Niger, Norway, Pakistan, Philippines, Poland, Portugal, Romania, Senegal, Republic of South Africa, Spain, Sri Lanka, Surinam, Sweden, Switzerland, Thailand, Togo, Tunisia, Turkey, UK, Upper Volta, Uruguay, Vatican, Yugoslavia, Zaïre. (68 States.)

Organization. The bodies of WIPO are: The *General Assembly*, consisting of all States members of WIPO which are members of any of the Unions. Among its other functions, the General Assembly appoints and gives instructions to the Director-General, reviews and approves his reports and adopts the triennial budget of expenses common to the Unions. The *Conference*, consisting of all States members of WIPO whether or not they are members of any of the Unions. Among its other functions, the Conference adopts its triennial budget and establishes the triennial programme of legal-technical assistance. The *Co-ordination Committee*, consisting of the States members of WIPO which are members of the Executive Committees of the Paris or Berne Unions. Among its other functions, the Co-ordination Committee establishes the annual budgets and programmes on the basis of the triennial budgets adopted by the General Assembly and the Conference.

In addition, the Paris and Berne Unions have Assemblies and Executive Committees, with functions similar to those of the WIPO bodies in respect of the triennial and annual budgets and programmes of the Unions. Each Union holds conferences at irregular intervals to revise its Convention.

Principal publications. Industrial Property (monthly, in English and French).—*Copyright* (monthly, in English and French).—*La Propriedad Intelectual* (quarterly, in Spanish).—*Les Marques internationales* (monthly, in French).—*Manuals and Brochures of Conventions and Agreements.*—*Collections of Laws and Treaties.*—*Model Laws for Developing Countries on Inventions, on Marks Trade Names and Acts of Unfair Competition on Designs on Copyright and on Neighbouring Rights* (in English, French and Spanish).—*Guide to the Application of the Paris Convention, by Professor G. H. C. Bodenhausen* (in English, French and German).

Headquarters: 32, chemin des Colombettes, 1211 Geneva 20, Switzerland.
Director-General: Arpad Bogch (USA).

INTERNATIONAL UNION FOR THE PROTECTION OF NEW VARIETIES OF PLANTS (UPOV)

The Director-General of WIPO is also the Secretary-General of the International Union for the Protection of New Varieties of Plants (Upov) whose headquarters are at the same address.

Origin. The Convention establishing Upov was signed in Paris in 1961 and entered into force in 1968. Upov began its operation in Oct. 1969 upon the appointment of its first Secretary-General.

Functions. The purpose of the Convention for the Protection of New Plant Varieties is to recognize and secure to the breeder of a new plant variety certain rights in the member States, in particular to ensure that he receives a fair remuneration for his work. The effect of the rights of the breeder is that his prior authorization shall be necessary for the production of propagating material of his protected variety for the purpose of sale. Before protection is granted the new variety is subject to examination for novelty (distinctness from other varieties), stability and homogeneity and must have received a denomination. In some cases (regarding certain species) the Convention provides for national treatment of breeders belonging to the member States. In other cases (regarding other species) protection is granted to breeders from other member States on the basis of reciprocity concerning the species in question. Upov assists member States in the promotion of international co-operation concerning the examination of new plant varieties and the naming of such varieties.

THE COMMONWEALTH

Constitution. The Commonwealth is a free association of sovereign independent nations, numbering 36 at the end of 1976. There is no charter, treaty or constitution; the association is expressed in co-operation, consultation and mutual assistance for which the Commonwealth Secretariat is the central co-ordinating organization.

The Commonwealth was first defined by the Imperial Conference of 1926 as a group of 'autonomous communites within the British Empire, equal in status, in no way subordinate one to another in any aspect of their domestic or foreign affairs, though united by a common allegiance to the Crown, and freely associated as members of the British Commonwealth of Nations'. The basis of the association changed from one owing allegiance to a common Crown, and the modern Commonwealth was born, in 1949 when the member countries accepted India's intention of becoming a republic at the same time continuing 'her full membership of the Commonwealth of Nations and her acceptance of the King as the symbol of the free association of its independent member nations and as such the Head of the Commonwealth'. There are now (1978) 11 Queen's realms, 21 republics, and 5 other monarchies in the Commonwealth. All have acknowledged the Queen symbolically as Head of the Commonwealth. For the Queen's titles in the Commonwealth *see* United Kingdom.

A number of territories, formerly under British jurisdiction or mandate did not join the Commonwealth on independence: Egypt, Iraq, Transjordan, Burma, Palestine, Sudan, British Somaliland, South Cameroons, the Maldive Islands and Aden. Two countries, the Republic of South Africa in 1961 and Pakistan in 1972, have left the Commonwealth.

Nauru is a special member, with the right to participate in all functional Commonwealth meetings and activities but not to attend meetings of Commonwealth Heads of Government.

Member States. The following are the member countries, with their dates of independence, and, were appropriate, the date on which they became republics: *United Kingdom*; *Canada* 1 July 1867; *Australia* 1 Jan. 1901; *New Zealand* 26 Sept. 1907;

India 15 Aug. 1947 and became a Republic on 26 Jan. 1950; *Sri Lanka* 4 Feb. 1948 (Republic on 22 May 1972); *Ghana* 6 March 1957 (Republic on 1 July 1960); *Malaysia* 31 Aug. 1957 as Federation of Malaya, 16 Sept. 1963 as Federation of Malaysia; *Cyprus* 16 Aug. 1960 (Republic on independence); *Nigeria* 1 Oct. 1960 (Republic on 1 Oct. 1963); *Sierra Leone* 27 April 1961 (Republic 19 April 1971); *Tanzania*—Tanganyika 9 Dec. 1961 (Republic 9 Dec. 1962), Zanzibar 10 Dec. 1963 (Republic on independence), United Republic of Tanganyika and Zanzibar 26 April 1964, renamed Tanzania 29 Oct. 1964; *Western Samoa* 1 Jan. 1962; *Jamaica* 6 Aug. 1962; *Trinidad and Tobago* 31 Aug. 1962 (Republic on 1 Aug. 1976); *Uganda* 9 Oct. 1962 (Republic 8 Sept. 1967, second republic 25 Jan. 1971); *Kenya* 12 Dec. 1963 (Republic on 12 Dec. 1964); *Malawi* 6 July 1964 (Republic on 6 July 1966); *Malta* 21 Sept. 1964 (Republic on 13 Dec. 1974); *Zambia* 24 Oct. 1964 (Republic on independence); *The Gambia* 18 Feb. 1965 (Republic on 24 April 1970); *Singapore* 16 Sept. 1963 as a state in the Federation of Malaysia, 9 Aug. 1965 as an independent state and republic not part of Malaysia; *Guyana* 26 May 1966 (Republic on 23 Feb. 1970); *Botswana* 30 Sept. 1966 (Republic on independence); *Lesotho* 4 Oct. 1966; *Barbados* 30 Nov. 1966; *Nauru* 31 Jan. 1968 (Republic on independence); *Mauritius* 12 March 1968; *Swaziland* 6 Sept. 1968; *Tonga* 4 June 1970; *Fiji* 10 Oct. 1970; *Bangladesh* seceded from Pakistan 16 Dec. 1971, recognized by United Kingdom 4 Feb. 1972; *Bahamas* 10 July 1973; *Grenada* 7 Feb. 1974; *Papua New Guinea* 16 Sept. 1975; *Seychelles* 29 June 1976 (Republic on independence).

Associated States. The Caribbean islands of Antigua, St Christopher–Nevis–Anguilla, Dominica, Grenada and St Lucia entered into a new form of association with Britain in Feb. 1967. St Vincent became an associated state on 27 Oct. 1969. Each has control of its internal affairs, with the right to amend its own constitution (including the power to end the associated status and declare itself independent). Britain continues to be responsible for external affairs and defence. Grenada became independent, within the Commonwealth, on 7 Feb. 1974. *See below* for Anguilla.

Dependent Territories. Territories dependent on Great Britain comprise dependent territories, a protectorate and a Condominium. A dependent territory is a territory belonging by settlement, conquest or annexation to the British Crown. A protectorate is a territory not formally annexed but in which, by treaty, grant and other lawful means the Crown has power and jurisdiction.

United Kingdom dependencies administered through the Foreign and Commonwealth Office comprise, in the Far East: Hong Kong (dependent territory); in the Indian Ocean: British Indian Ocean Territory; in the Mediterranean: Gibraltar (dependent territory); in the Atlantic Ocean: Bermuda, Falkland Islands and dependencies, South Georgia and South Sandwich Islands (dependent territory), British Antarctic Territory (dependent territory), St Helena and dependencies of Ascension and Tristan da Cunha (dependent territory); in the Caribbean: Belize, Montserrat, British Virgin Islands, Cayman Islands, Turks and Caicos Islands (dependent territories); in the Western Pacific: Solomon Islands (protectorate), Gilbert Islands, Tuvalu, Pitcairn (dependent territories), New Hebrides (Anglo-French Condominium).

British Government Department. With effect from 17 Oct. 1968, the Secretary of State for Foreign and Commonwealth Affairs is responsible for the conduct of relations with members of the Commonwealth as well as with foreign countries, and for the administration of British dependent territories.

The island of *Anguilla*, although technically part of the Associated State of *St Kitts–Nevis–Anguilla*, is administered as a dependent territory and now has its own Constitution and Ministerial form of Government. The Anguilla (Constitution) Order 1976 (made under the Anguilla Act 1971) came into operation on 10 Feb. 1976. Provision is made in the constitution for a Legislative Assembly, comprising 7 elected members, 2 nominated members and 3 *ex-officio* members, and for an Executive Council comprising the Chief Minister, 2 other Ministers and 2 *ex-officio* members. The constitution provides for the Executive authority of Anguilla to be exercised by HM Commissioner. The constitution of St Kitts–Nevis–Anguilla now no longer applies in and in relation to Anguilla.

While constitutional responsibility to Parliament for the government of the dependent territories rests with the Secretary of State for Foreign and Commonwealth Affairs, the administration of the territories is carried out by the Governments of the territories themselves.

Brunei is a sovereign state in treaty relationship with Great Britain, whereby Great Britain is responsible for the conduct of external affairs and has a consultative responsibility for defence. It has never been a dependent territory, and in 1971 ceased to be a protected state. The relationship between Great Britain and Brunei was under review in Jan. 1978.

Commonwealth Secretariat. The Commonwealth Secretariat is an international body at the service of all 36 member countries. It provides the central organization for joint consultation and co-operation in many fields. It was established in 1965 by Commonwealth Heads of Government and has consultative status at the UN General Assembly.

The Secretariat disseminates information on matters of common concern, organizes and services meetings and conferences, co-ordinates many Commonwealth activities, and provides expert technical assistance for economic and social development through the multilateral Commonwealth Fund for Technical Co-operation. The Secretariat is organized in divisions and sections which correspond to its main areas of operation: International affairs, economic affairs, food production and rural development, youth, education, information, applied studies in government, science and technology, law and health. Within this structure the Secretariat organizes the biennial meetings of Commonwealth Heads of Government, annual meetings of Finance Ministers of member countries, and regular meetings of Ministers of Education, Law, Health, and others as appropriate.

To emphasize the multilateral nature of the association, meetings are held in different cities and regions within the Commonwealth. Heads of Government decided that the Secretariat should work from London as it has the widest range of communications of any Commonwealth city, as well as the largest assembly of diplomatic missions.

The Commonwealth Secretary-General, who has access to Heads of Government, is the head of the Secretariat which is staffed by officers from member countries and financed by contributions from member governments.

Headquarters: Marlborough House, Pall Mall, London, SW1Y 5HX.
Secretary-General: Shridath S. Ramphal (Guyana).

Books of Reference

Year-Book of the Commonwealth. HMSO, 1976
The Cambridge History of the British Empire. 8 vols. CUP, 1929 ff.
Economic Survey of the Colonial Territories. 7 vols. HMSO, 1952 ff.
Ball, M., *The Open Commonwealth.* Duke Univ. Press, 1971
Bradley, K. (ed.), *The Living Commonwealth.* London, 1961
Burns, Sir Alan, *In Defence of Colonies.* London, 1957
Crick, W. F. (ed.), *Commonwealth Banking Systems.* OUP, 1965
Grierson, E., *The Imperial Dream.* London, 1972
Griffiths, Sir P., *Empire into Commonwealth.* London, 1969
Hailey, Lord, *An African Survey.* Rev. ed. Oxford, 1957.—*Native Administration in the British African Territories.* 5 vols. HMSO, 1951 ff.
Hall, H. D., *Commonwealth: A History of the British Commonwealth.* London and New York, 1971
Ingram, D. T., *The Commonwealth at Work.* London, 1969.—*The Imperfect Commonwealth.* London, 1977
Jeffries, Sir C., *The Colonial Office.* London, 1956
Keeton, G. W. (ed.), *The British Commonwealth: Its Laws and Constitutions.* 9 vols. London, 1951 ff.
Kuczynski, R. R., *Demographic Survey of the British Colonial Empire.* 3 vols. London, New York, Toronto, 1948–53
Mansergh, N., *The Commonwealth Experience.* London, 1969
Maxwell, W. H. and L. F., *A Legal Bibliography of the British Commonwealth of Nations.* 2nd ed. London, 1956

Miller, J. D. B., *Survey of Commonwealth Affairs*. London, 1974
Morris, J., *Heaven's Command: An Imperial Progress*. London, 1973.
Patterson, A. D., *Handbook of Commonwealth Organizations*. London, 1965
Roberts-Wray, K., *Commonwealth and Colonial Law*. London, 1966
Wade, E. C. S., and Phillips, G. G., *Constitutional Law: An Outline of the Law and Practice of the Constitution, Including Central and Local Government and the Constitutional Relations of the British Commonwealth and Empire*. 8th ed. London, 1970
Walker, A., *The Modern Commonwealth*. London, 1976.—*A New Look at the Commonwealth*. Oxford, 1977
Wheare, K. C., *The Statute of Westminster and Dominion Status*. 5th ed. Oxford, 1953.—*Constitutional Structure of the Commonwealth*. Oxford, 1960
Wiseman, V. H., *The Cabinet in the Commonwealth*. London, 1958.

WORLD COUNCIL OF CHURCHES

The World Council of Churches was formally constituted on 23 Aug. 1948, at Amsterdam, by an assembly representing 147 churches from 44 countries. In 1978 the member churches numbered 293, from over 100 countries and territories.

The basis of membership (1975) states: 'The World Council of Churches is a fellowship of Churches which confess the Lord Jesus Christ as God and Saviour according to the Scriptures and therefore seek to fulfil together their common calling to the glory of the one God, Father, Son and Holy Spirit.' Membership is open to Churches which express their agreement with this basis and satisfy such criteria as the Assembly or Central Committee may prescribe. Today 271 Churches of Protestant, Anglican, Orthodox and Old Catholic Confessions belong to this fellowship.

The movements which joined together to form the World Council were:

(*a*) *Co-operation in oversea missionary work* by the non-Roman Catholic Churches. The World Missionary Conference held in Edinburgh, Scotland, in 1910 was followed in 1921 by the establishment of the *International Missionary Council*. In 1961 this Council became the Commission and Division of World Mission and Evangelism of the World Council.

(*b*) *The Faith and Order Movement* was founded through the initiative of Charles Brent, Bishop of the Protestant Episcopal Church of the USA in the Philippines. This movement has held world conferences at Lausanne in 1927, Edinburgh in 1937, Lund in 1952, Montreal in 1963 and the Commission on Faith and Order met in Accra, Ghana in 1973.

(*c*) *The Life and Work Movement* was founded largely under the leadership of Archbishop Nathan Söderblom of Uppsala. World conferences were held in Stockholm in 1925, at Oxford in 1937 and in Geneva in 1966. The Department on Church and Society promotes common Christian study and action on social, political and economic problems of the present time.

On 13 May 1938 at Utrecht a provisional committee was appointed to prepare for the formation of a World Council of Churches. It was under the chairmanship of William Temple, then Archbishop of York.

A new structure of the World Council was approved by the Central Committee at its meeting in Addis Ababa, Ethiopia, in Jan. 1971.

Assembly. The governing body of the World Council, consisting of delegates specially appointed by the member Churches. It meets every 6 or 7 years to frame policy and to consider some main theme. The Assembly has no legislative powers and depends for the implementation of its decisions upon the action of the member Churches. Assemblies have been held in Amsterdam (1948), Evanston (1954), New Delhi (1961), Uppsala (1968), and Nairobi (1975).

Presidents. Hon. President: The Rev. Dr W. A. Visser't Hooft. *Presidium:* Mrs Justice A. R. Jiagge (Ghana), Prof. José Miguez-Bonino (Argentina), His Eminence Nikodium (USSR), Dr T. B. Simatupang (Indonesia), Most Rev. Olof Sundby (Sweden), Dr Cynthia Wedel (USA).

Central Committee. This is appointed by each Assembly to carry out its policies and decisions. It consists of 130 members chosen from among Assembly delegates. It meets once a year.

Executive Committee. This consists of 26 members chosen by the Central Committee from its own membership, to prepare its work, carry out its decisions and supervise the WCC between meetings of the Central Committee. It meets twice a year.

Officers of the Central and Executive Committees: *Moderator:* The Most Rev. Edward W. Scott (Canada). *Vice-Moderators:* His Holiness. Karekin II (Lebanon); Jean Skuse (Australia). *General Secretary:* The Rev. Dr Philip A. Potter. *Deputy General Secretaries:* The Rev. Dr Alan A. Brash, Dr Konrad Raiser.

Office: P.O. Box 66, 150 route de Ferney, 1211 Geneva 20, Switzerland.

The British Council of Churches, which is an associated national council of the World Council, acts as agent for the WCC in the UK.

Member Churches. The following is a list of the Member Churches:

Argentina. Iglésia Evangélica del Rio de la Plata; Iglésia Evangélica Metodista Argentina.

Australia. Church of England in Australia; Churches of Christ in Australia; Uniting Church in Australia; Presbyterian Church of Australia.

Austria. Alt-katholische Kirche Österreichs; Evangelische Kirche A.B. in Österreich.

Bangladesh. Bangladesh Baptiste Sangha.

Belgium. Eglise Protestante de Belgique; Eglise Réformée de Belgique.

Benin. Eglise Protestante Méthodiste au Benin–Togo.

Brazil. Igreja Episcopal do Brasil; Igreja Evangélica de Confissão Lutherana no Brasil; Igreja Evangélica Pentecostal 'O Brasil para Cristo'; Igreja Metodista do Brasil; Igreja Reformada Latino Americana.

Bulgaria. Eglise Orthodoxe Bulgare.

Burma. Burma Baptist Convention; Church of the Province of Burma.

Cameroon. Eglise évangélique du Cameroun; Eglise presbytérienne camérounaise; Presbyterian Church in Cameroun; Union des Eglises baptistes du Cameroun.

Canada. Anglican Church of Canada; Canadian Yearly Meeting of the Society of Friends; Christian Church (Disciples of Christ); Evangelical Lutheran Church of Canada; Presbyterian Church in Canada; United Church of Canada.

Central Africa. Church of the Province of Central Africa.

Chile. Iglesia Evangélica Luterana en Chile; Iglesia Pentecostal de Chile; Mision Iglesia Pentecostal.

China. China Baptist Council; Chung-Hua Chi-Tu Chiao-Hui; Chung Hua Sheng Kung Hui; Hua Pei Kung Lu Hui.

Congo (People's Republic of the). Eglise Evangélique du Congo.

Cook Islands. Cook Islands Christian Church.

Cyprus. Church of Cyprus.

Czechoslovakia. Českobratrská cirkev evangelická; Československá cirkev husitská; Pravoslavná církev v ČSSR; Ref. krest. církev na Slovensku; Slezká církev evangelická a.v.; Slovenská evanjelická církev a.v. v ČSSR.

Denmark. Det danske Baptistsamfund; Den evangelisk-lutherske Folkekirke i Danmark.

East Africa. Presbyterian Church of East Africa.

Egypt. Coptic Orthodox Church; Evangelical Church—The Synod of the Nile; Greek Orthodox Patriarchate of Alexandria.

Ethiopia. Ethiopia Orthodox Church.

Finland. Suomen Evankelis-Luterilainen Kirkko.

France. Eglise de la Confession d'Augsbourg d'Alsace et de Lorraine; Eglise Evangélique Luthérienne de France; Eglise Réformée d'Alsace et de Lorraine; Eglise Réformée de France.

Gabon. Eglise Evangélique du Gabon.

German Democratic Republic. Bund der Evangelischen Kirchen in der Deutschen Demokratischen Republik; Evangelische Brüder-Unität (Distrikt Herrnhut); Gemeindeverband der Alt-Katholischen Kirche in der Deutschen Demokratischen Republik.

Federal Republic of Germany. Katholisches Bistum der Alt-Katholiken in Deutschland; Evangelische Brüder-Unität; Evangelische Kirche in Deutschland: Vereinigung der Deutschen Mennonitengemeinden.

Ghana. Evangelical Presbyterian Church; Methodist Church, Ghana; Presbyterian Church of Ghana.

Greece. Ekklesia tes Ellados; Hellenike Evangelike Ekklesia.

Hong Kong. Church of Christ in China. The Hong Kong Council.

Hungary. Magyarországi Baptista Egyház; Magyarországi Evangélikus Egyház; Magyarországi Reformatus Egyház.

Iceland. Evangelical Lutheran Church of Iceland.

India. Church of North India; Church of South India; United Evangelical Lutheran Churches in India; Mar Thoma Syrian Church of Malabar; Orthodox Syrian Church Catholicate of the East; Samavesam of Telugu Baptist Churches.

Indonesia. Gereja Masehi Injeli Sangihe Talaud; Gereja Batak Karo Protestan; Gereja-Gereja Kristen Java; Gereja Kalimantan Evangelis; Gereja Kristen Jawi Wetan; Gereja Kristen Injili Di Irian Jaya; Gereja Kristen Indonesia; Gereja Kristen Pasundan; Gereja Kristen Sulawesi Tengah; Gereja Masehi Injili Minahasa, Gereja Masehi Injili Di Timor; Gereja Protestan Di Indonesia; Gereja Protestan Maluku; Gereja Kristen Protestan Simalungen; Gereja Toraja; Huria Kristen Indonesia; Banua Nihá Keriso Protestan Nias.

Iran. Synod of the Evangelical Church of Iran.

Italy. Chiesa Evangelica Internazionale; Chiesa Evangelica Metodista d'Italia; Chiesa Evangelica Valdese.

Jamaica. Moravian Church in Jamaica; United Church of Jamaica and Grand Cayman.

Japan. Japanese Orthodox Church: Nippon Kirisuto Kyodan; Nippon Sei Ko Kai.

Jerusalem. Greek Orthodox Patriarchate of Jerusalem.

Kenya. Church of the Province of Kenya; Methodist Church in Kenya.

Korea. Korean Methodist Church; Presbyterian Church in the Republic of Korea; Presbyterian Church in Korea.

Lebanon. Armenian Apostolic Church; Union of the Armenian Evangelical Churches in the Near East.

Lesotho. Lesotho Evangelical Church.

Liberia. Lutheran Church in Liberia.

Madagascar. Eglise de Jésus Christ à Madagascar; Eglise Luthérienne Malgache.

Malaysia. Methodist Church in Malaysia.

Mexico. Iglesia Metodista de México.

Netherlands. Algemene Doopsgezinde Sociëteit; Evangelische Lutherse Kerk; De Gereformeerde Kerken in Nederland; Nederlandse Hervormde Kerk; Oud-Katholieke Kerk van Nederland; Remonstrantse Broederschap.

New Caledonia. Eglise Evangélique en Nouvelle Calédonie et aux Iles Loyauté.

New Hebrides. Presbyterian Church of the New Hebrides.

New Zealand. Associated Churches of Christ in New Zealand; Baptist Union of New Zealand; Church of the Province of New Zealand; Methodist Church of New Zealand; Presbyterian Church of New Zealand.

Nigeria. Methodist Church, Nigeria; Nigerian Baptist Convention; Presbyterian Church of Nigeria.

Norway. Den Norske Kirke.

Pakistan. Church of Pakistan: United Presbyterian Church of Pakistan.

Philippines. Iglesia Evangelica Metodista en las Islas Filipinas; Iglesia Filipina Independiente; United Church of Christ in the Philippines.

Poland. Autocephalic Orthodox Church in Poland: Kosciola Ewangelicko-Augsburskiego w PRL; Kosciola Polskokatolickiego w PRL; Staro-Katolickiego Kosicola Mariatowitow w PRL.

Romania. Biserica Evangelica Dupa Confesiunea Dela Augsburg; Biserica Ortodoxa Romana; Biserica Reformata Din Romania; Evangelical Synodal Presbyterial Church of the Augsburg Confession in the Socialist Republic of Romania.

Samoa. Congregational Christian Church in Samoa.

Sierra Leone. Methodist Church Sierra Leone.

South Africa, Republic of. Bantu Presbyterian Church of South Africa; Church of the Province of South Africa; Evangelical Lutheran Church in Southern Africa (South-Eastern Region); Methodist Church of South Africa; Moravian Church in South Africa (Eastern Province); Moravian Church in South Africa (Western Cape Province); Presbyterian Church of Southern Africa; United Congregational Church of Southern Africa.

Sri Lanka. Church of Ceylon; Methodist Church.

Spain. Iglesia Evangélica Española.

Sweden. Svenska Kyrkan; Svenska Missionsförbundet.

Switzerland. Christkatholische Kirche der Schweiz; Schweizerischer Evangelischer Kirchenbund.

Syria. National Evangelical Synod of Syria and Lebanon; Patriarcat Grec-Orthodoxe d'Antioche et de tout l'Orient; Syrian Orthodox Patriarchate of Antioch and All the East.

Tahiti. Eglise évangélique de Polynésie française.

Tanzania. Church of the Province of Tanzania; Evangelical Lutheran Church in Tanzania.

Thailand. Church of Christ in Thailand.

Togo. Eglise Evangélique du Togo.

Trinidad. Presbyterian Church in Trinidad and Grenada.

Turkey. Ecumenical Patriarchate of Constantinople

Uganda. Church of Uganda, Rwanda and Burundi.

Union of Soviet Socialist Republics. Eglise apostolique arménienne; Eesti Evangeeliumi Luteri usu Kirik; Georgian Orthodox Church; Latvijas Evangeliska-Luteriska Baznica; Russian Orthodox Church; Union of Evangelical Christian Baptists of USSR.

United Kingdom and Republic of Ireland. Baptist Union of Great Britain and Ireland; Church of England; Churches of Christ in Great Britain and Ireland; Methodist Church; Moravian Union; Salvation Army; United Reformed Church of England and Wales; Church of Ireland; Methodist Church in Ireland; Presbyterian Church in Ireland; Church of Scotland; Congregational Union of Scotland; Episcopal Church in Scotland; United Free Church of Scotland; Church in Wales; Presbyterian Church of Wales; Union of Welsh Independents.

United States of America. African Methodist Episcopal Church; African Methodist Episcopal Zion Church; American Baptist Churches in the USA; American Lutheran Church; Antiochian Orthodox Christian Archdiocese; Christian Church (Disciples of Christ); Christian Methodist Episcopal Church; Church of the Brethren; Episcopal Church; Hungarian Reformed Church in America; Lutheran Church in America; Moravian Church in America (Northern Province); Moravian Church in America (Southern Province); National Baptist Convention of America; National Baptist Convention, USA, Inc.; National Council of Community Churches; Orthodox Church in America; Polish National Catholic Church of America; Presbyterian Church in the United States; Reformed Church in America; Friends General Conference; Friends United Meeting; United Church of Christ; United Methodist Church; United Presbyterian Church in the United States.

West Africa. Church of the Province of West Africa.

West Indies. Church in the Province of the West Indies; Methodist Church in the Caribbean and the Americas; Moravian Church, Eastern West Indies Province.

Yugoslavia. Reformatska Crke u SFRJ; Serbian Orthodox Church; Slovenská ev. -kr. a.v. cirkev v. Juhuslávii.

Zaïre, Republic of. Eglise du Christ au Zaïre (Disciples of Christ); Eglise du Christ au Zaïre (Community of Christ the Light); Eglise du Christ au Zaïre (Mennonite Community in Zaïre); Eglise du Christ sur la Terre par le Prophète Simon Kimbangu; Eglise évangélique du Zaïre; Eglise Presbyterienne au Zaïre.

Zambia. United Churches of Zambia.

Other churches. Eesti Evangeeliumi Luteri Usu Kirik; Latvijas Evangeliska Luteriska Baznica.

Associate Member Churches: Eglise Protestante d'Algérie (Algeria); Iglesia Evangélica Luterana Unida (Argentina); Iglesia Evangélica Metodista en Bolivia (Bolivia); Eglise Protestante Africaine (Cameroon); Iglesia Metodista de Chile (Chile); Iglesia Metodista en Cuba; Iglesia Presbiteriana-Reformada en Cuba (Cuba); Bengal–Orissa–Bihar Baptist Convention (India); Korean Christian Church in Japan (Japan); Presbytery of Liberia (Liberia); Protestantse Kerk van de Nederlandse Antillen (Netherlands Antilles); Iglesia Metodista del Peru (Peru); Igreja Evangélica Presbiteriana de Portugal; Igreja Lusitana Catolica Apostolica Evangélica (Portugal); Iglesia Española Reformada Episcopal (Spain); Presbyterian Church in the Sudan (Sudan); Eglise du Christ au Zaïre (Church of Christ in Zaïre).

Books of Reference

Official Reports: The First [. . . etc.] *Assembly* (London, 1948, 1955, 1962, Geneva, 1968)
New Delhi to Uppsala 1961–68, Geneva, 1968
Official Reports of the Faith and Order Conferences at Lausanne 1927, Edinburgh 1937, Lund 1952, Montreal 1963, Meeting of Faith and Order Commission, Louvain 1971, Accra 1974.
Official Reports of the Life and Work Conferences at Stockholm 1925 and Oxford 1937; World Conference on Church and Society 1966
Minutes of the Central Committee. Geneva, 1949 to date
Fey, H. E., *The Ecumenical Advance, 1948–68.* London, 1970
Goodall, N., *The Ecumenical Movement.* 3rd ed. OUP, 1966.—*Ecumenical Progress, 1961–1971*, OUP, 1972
Paton, D. M., *Breaking Barriers—Nairobi 1975.* London, 1976

INTERNATIONAL TRADE UNIONISM

International trade-union co-operation is organized through the three major 'Internationals', the democratic International Confederation of Free Trade Unions

(ICFTU), the Communist-directed World Federation of Trade Unions (WFTU) and the World Confederation of Labour (WCL). In addition, federations of specific trades or industries protect their special interests by organizing on an international level and are associated to a varying degree with their corresponding 'Internationals'. The International Trade Secretariats (ITS) are completely autonomous but seek to co-ordinate their policies and activities with those of the ICFTU; the International Trade Federations (ITFs) are very closely integrated with the WCL; the Trade Union Internationals (TUIs) are completely subservient to WFTU.

Levinson, C., *International Trade Unionism*. London, 1972

History. The first general trade-union International, the International Federation of Trade Unions (IFTU), was set up in 1913, but no real achievement was possible until its post-war reconstitution in 1919. Some trade-union movements, seeking to implement the social precepts of the Christian faith, established the International Federation of Christian Trade Unions (IFCTU) in 1920. The name was changed to the World Confederation of Labour in 1968.

During the Second World War moves to establish universal trade unionism resulted in the formation of the World Federation of Trade Unions (WFTU) in 1945. The Christian trade unions refused to join the new association and reconstituted the IFCTU. Attempts by the Communists to impose their own ideology within the WFTU led to the eventual secession of the democratic elements, which reconstituted themselves in the ICFTU in 1949.

EUROPEAN TRADE UNION CONFEDERATION. In Feb. 1973 the European Trade Union Confederation was formed by trade unionists in 15 Western European countries to deal with questions of interest to European working people arising inside and outside the EEC. All the founding organizations were ICFTU affiliates but subsequently they accepted into membership European WCL affiliates, the Irish Congress of Trade Unions and the Italian Communist trade union centre (CGIL) and other national organizations. The membership now exceeds 38m. from 31 centres in 18 countries.

INTERNATIONAL CONFEDERATION OF FREE TRADE UNIONS. The first congress of ICFTU was held in London in Dec. 1949. The constitution as amended provides for co-operation with the United Nations and the International Labour Organization and for regional organizations to promote free trade unionism, especially in less-developed countries.

Organization. The Congress meets every 3 years. It elects the Executive Board of 29 members nominated on an area basis for a 3-year period; the Board meets at least twice a year. Various committees cover policy *vis-à-vis* such problems as those connected with Atomic Energy and also the administration of the International Solidarity Fund. There are joint ICFTU–ITS Committees for co-ordinating activities and also for women workers' problems. Headquarters: 37–41, rue Montagne aux Herbes Potagères, Brussels 1000, Belgium.

General Secretary: Otto Kersten.

Regional organizations exist in America, office in Mexico City; Asia, office in New Delhi.

Membership. The total membership in 1977 was about 56m. The biggest groups were the British Trades Union Congress (11m.), the Federal German Deutscher Gewerkschaftsbund (7·4m.), the Confederazione Italiana Sindacati Lavoratori (2·1m.), the Swedish Landsorganisationen (1·9m.), the Canadian Labour Congress (1·3m.), the Österreichischer Gewerkschaftsbund (1·6m.), the Belgian General Federation of Labour (900,000), the Indian National Trade Union Congress (3·3m.), and the French Confédération Générale du Travail Force Ouvrière (900,000). Brazilian Confederacao Nacional dos Trabalhadores no Comercio (2·5m.), Australian Council of Trade Unions (1·3m.), Japanese Confederation of Labour, Domei (1·3m.).

The American Federation of Labor and Congress of Industrial Organizations disaffiliated in Feb. 1969.

Publications (in 4 languages). *Free Labour World* (monthly); *ICFTU Bulletin* (bi-monthly); *Press and Radio Service* (weekly); *International Trade Union News* (fortnightly).

THE WORLD FEDERATION OF TRADE UNIONS. The WFTU formally came into existence on 3 Oct. 1945, representing trade-union organizations in more than 50 countries of the world, both Communist and non-Communist, excluding Federal Republic of Germany and Japan, as well as a number of lesser and colonial territories. Representation from the USA was limited to the Congress of Industrial Organizations, as the American Federation of Labor declined to participate.

In Jan. 1949 the British, USA and Netherlands trade unions withdrew from WFTU, which had come under complete Communist control; and by June 1951 all non-Communist trade-unions, including the Yugoslavian Federation, had left WFTU.

Organization. The Congress meets every 4 years. In between, the General Council, of 134 members (including deputies), is the governing body, meeting (in theory) at least once a year. The Bureau controls the activities of WFTU between meetings of the General Council; it consists of the President, the General Secretary and members from different continents, the total number being decided at each Congress. The Bureau is elected by the General Council.

General Secretary: Pierre Gensous (France).

Membership. A total membership of 150m. is claimed. The biggest groups are the Soviet All-Union Central Council of Trade Unions (90m.), the German Democratic Republic Free German Trade Union Federation (7·5m.), the Polish Central Council of Trade Unions (7m.), the Czechoslovak Central Council of Trade Unions (5·5m.), the Italian General Confederation of Labour (GCIL, 3·5m.), the Romanian General Confederation of Labour (3·5m.), the Hungarian Central Council of Trade Unions (3m.) and the French Confederation of Labour (CGT, 2·5m.).

Publications. World Trade Union Movement (monthly, in 11 languages); *Trade Union Press* (fortnightly, in 6 languages).

WORLD CONFEDERATION OF LABOUR. The first congress of the International Federation of Christian Trade Unions (IFCTU), as the WCL was then called, met in 1920; but a large proportion of its 3·4m. members were in Italy and Germany, where affiliated unions were suppressed by the Fascist and Nazi régimes, and in 1940 IFCTU went out of existence. It was reconstituted in 1945, and declined to merge with WFTU and, later, with ICFTU. The policy of IFCTU was based on the papal encyclicals *Rerum novarum* (1891) and *Quadragesimo anno* (1931), but in 1968, when the Federation became the WCL, it was broadened to include other concepts. The WCL now has Protestant, Buddhist and Moslem members as well as its mainly Roman Catholic members.

Organization. The WCL is organized on a federative basis which leaves wide discretion to its autonomous constituent unions. Its governing body is the Congress, which meets every 4 years. The Congress appoints (or re-appoints) the Secretary-General at each 4-yearly meeting. The General Council which meets at least once a year, is composed of the members of the Confederal Board (at least 22 members, elected by the Congress) and representatives of national confederations, international trade federations, and trade union organizations where there is no confederation affiliated to the WCL. The Confederal Board is responsible for the general leadership of the WCL, in accordance with the decisions and directives of the Council and Congress. Headquarters: 50 rue Joseph II, Brussels 1040, Belgium.

Secretary-General: Jan Kulakowski.

There are regional organizations in Latin America (office in Caracas), Africa (office in Banjul, Gambia) and Asia (office in Manila). There is also a liaison centre in Montreal.

Membership. A total membership of 15m. in about 90 countries is claimed. The biggest groups are the French Democratic Confederation of Labour (800,000), the Confederation of Christian Trade Unions of Belgium (1·1m.), the Netherlands Catholic Workers' Movement (340,000).

Publication. Labour Press and Information (11 each year, in 5 languages).

EUROPEAN ORGANIZATIONS

	OECD	*NATO*	*WEU*	*C of E*	*ECSC, EEC, Euratom*	*EFTA*	*Warsaw Pact*	*Comecon*
Albania	—	—	—	—	—	—	*	*[1]
Austria	*	—	—	*	—	*	—	—
Belgium	*	*	*	*	*	—	—	—
Bulgaria	—	—	—	—	—	—	*	*
Cyprus	—	—	—	*	—	—	—	—
Czechosolovakia	—	—	—	—	—	—	*	*
Denmark	*	*	—	*	*	—	—	—
Finland	—	—	—	—	—	o	—	—
France	*	*	*	*	*	—	—	—
German Dem. Rep.	—	—	—	—	—	—	*	*
Fed. Rep. of Germany	*	*	*	*	*	—	—	—
Greece	*	*	—	—	o	—	—	—
Hungary	—	—	—	—	—	—	*	*
Iceland	*	*	—	*	—	*	—	—
Irish Republic	*	—	—	*	*	—	—	—
Italy	*	*	*	*	*	—	—	—
Luxembourg	*	*	*	*	*	—	—	—
Malta	—	—	—	*	—	—	—	—
Netherlands	*	*	*	*	*	—	—	—
Norway	*	*	—	*	—	*	—	—
Poland	—	—	—	—	—	—	*	*
Portugal	*	*	—	—	—	*	—	—
Romania	—	—	—	—	—	—	*	*
Spain	*	—	—	—	—	—	—	—
Sweden	*	—	—	*	—	*	—	—
Switzerland	*	—	—	—	—	*	—	—
Turkey	*	*	—	*	o	—	—	—
USSR	—	—	—	—	—	—	*	*
UK	*	*	*	*	*	—	—	—
Yugoslavia	o	—	—	—	—	—	—	—
Canada	*	*	—	—	—	—	—	—
Mongolia	—	—	—	—	—	—	—	*
USA	*	*	—	—	—	—	—	—

* = member. o = associate. — = non-member. [1] Resigned in Dec. 1962.

ORGANISATION FOR ECONOMIC CO-OPERATION AND DEVELOPMENT (OECD)

History and Membership. On 30 Sept. 1961 the Organisation for European Economic Co-operation (OEEC), after a history of 14 years (*see* THE STATESMAN'S YEAR-BOOK, 1961, p. 32), was replaced by the Organisation for Economic Co-operation and Development. The change of title marks the Organisation's altered status and functions: with the accession of Canada and USA as full members it ceased to be a purely European body; while at the same time it added development aid to the list of its other activities. The member countries are now Australia, Austria,

Belgium, Canada, Denmark, Federal Republic of Germany, Finland, France, Greece, Iceland, Irish Republic, Italy, Japan, Luxembourg, the Netherlands, New Zealand, Norway, Portugal, Spain, Sweden, Switzerland, Turkey, UK and USA. Yugoslavia participates in the Organisation's activities with a special status. The Commission of the European Communities generally takes part in OECD's work.

Objectives. To promote economic and social welfare throughout the OECD area by assisting its member governments in the formulation of policies designed to this end and by co-ordinating these policies; and to stimulate and harmonize its members' aid efforts in favour of developing countries.

Organs. The supreme body of the Organisation is the Council composed of one representative for each member country. It meets either at Permanent Representative level (about once a week) under the Chairmanship of the Secretary-General, or at Ministerial level (usually once a year) under the Chairmanship of a Minister elected annually. Decisions and Recommendations are adopted by mutual agreement of all members of the Council.

The Council is assisted by an Executive Committee composed of 14 members of the Council designated annually by the latter. The major part of the Organisation's work is, however, prepared and carried out in numerous specialized committees and working parties, of which there exist over 100. Thus, the Organisation comprises Committees for Economic Policy; Economic and Development Review; Development Assistance (DAC); Trade; Invisible Transactions; Financial Markets; Fiscal Affairs; Restrictive Business Practices; Consumer Policy; Tourism; Maritime Transport; International Investment and Multinational Enterprises; Energy Policy; Industry; Scientific and Technological Policy; Education; Manpower and Social Affairs; Environment; Agriculture; Fisheries, etc. Moreover, High-Level Groups have been established on: Commodities and Economic Relations between Member Countries and Developing Countries.

Five autonomous or semi-autonomous bodies also belong to the Organisation: the International Energy Agency (IEA); the Nuclear Energy Agency (NEA); the Development Centre; and the Centre for Educational Research and Innovation (CERI).

The Council, the committees and the other bodies are serviced by an international Secretariat headed by the Secretary-General of the Organisation.

Chairman of the Council (ministerial): Elected annually.
Chairman of the Council (official level): The Secretary-General.
Chairman of the Executive Committee: T. Hirahara (Japan).
Secretary-General: Emile van Lennep (Netherlands).
Deputy Secretaries-General: Charles G. Wootton (USA), Gérard Eldin (France).
Headquarters: Château de la Muette, 2, rue André Pascal, 75775 Paris Cedex 16, France.

Activities of OECD in 1972. 1973
Convention on the Organisation for Economic Co-operation and Development. 1960
The OECD Observer. Bi-monthly, from 1962
The OECD Economic Outlook. 1966 ff.
OEEC/OECD Economic Surveys of Member Countries. 1954 ff.
European Nuclear Energy Agency, Activity Report. 1959–71
The Flow of Financial Resources to Countries in Course of Economic Development. 1960 ff.
Development Assistance Efforts and Policies. 1962 ff.

NORTH ATLANTIC TREATY ORGANIZATION (NATO)

On 28 April 1948 the Canadian Secretary of State for External Affairs broached the idea of a 'security league' of the free nations, in extension of the Brussels Treaty of 17 March 1948. The United States Senate, on 11 June, recommended 'the association of the United States with such regional and other collective arrangements as are based on continuous self-help and mutual aid, and as affect its national security'. Detailed proposals were subsequently worked out between the Brussels Treaty powers, the USA and Canada.

On 4 April 1949 the foreign ministers of Belgium, Canada, Denmark, France, Iceland, Italy, Luxembourg, the Netherlands, Norway, Portugal, the UK and the USA met in Washington and signed a treaty, the main clauses of which read as follows:

Article 1. The parties undertake, as set forth in the Charter of the United Nations, to settle any international disputes in which they may be involved by peaceful means in such a manner that international peace and security and justice are not endangered, and to refrain in their international relations from the threat or use of force in any manner inconsistent with the purposes of the United Nations.

Article 2. The parties will contribute toward the further development of peaceful and friendly international relations by strengthening their free institutions, by bringing about a better understanding of the principles upon which these institutions are founded, and by promoting conditions of stability and well-being. They will seek to eliminate conflict in their international economic policies and will encourage economic collaboration between any or all of them.

Article 3. In order more effectively to achieve the objectives of this treaty, the parties, separately and jointly by means of continuous and effective self-help and mutual aid, will maintain and develop their individual and collective capacity to resist armed attack.

Article 4. The parties will consult together whenever, in the opinion of any of them, the territorial integrity, political independence or security of any of the parties is threatened.

Article 5. The parties agree that an armed attack against one or more of them in Europe or North America shall be considered an attack against them all and consequently they agree that, if such an armed attack occurs, each of them, in exercise of the right of individual or collective self-defence recognized by article 51 of the Charter of the United Nations, will assist the party or parties so attacked by taking forthwith, individually and in concert with the other parties, such action as it deems necessary, including the use of armed force, to restore and maintain the security of the North Atlantic area. Any such armed attack and all measures taken as a result thereof shall immediately be reported to the Security Council. Such measures shall be terminated when the Security Council has taken the measures necessary to restore and maintain international peace and security.

Article 6. For the purpose of Article 5 an armed attack on one or more of the parties is deemed to include an armed attack (*i*) on the territory of any of the parties in Europe or North America, on the Algerian Departments of France,* on the territory of Turkey or on the islands under the jurisdiction of any of the parties in the North Atlantic area north of the Tropic of Cancer; (*ii*) on the forces, vessels or aircraft of any of the parties, when in or over these territories or any other area in Europe in which occupation forces of any of the parties were stationed on the date when the treaty entered into force or the Mediterranean Sea or the North Atlantic area north of the Tropic of Cancer.†

Article 8. Each party declares that none of the international engagements now in force between it and any other of the parties or any third state is in conflict with the provisions of this treaty, and undertakes not to enter into any international engagement in conflict with this treaty.

Article 10. The parties may, by unanimous agreement, invite any other European state in a position to further the principles of this treaty and to contribute to the security of the North Atlantic area to accede to this treaty. Any state so invited may become a party to the treaty by depositing its instrument of accession with the government of the United States of America. The government of the United States of America will inform each of the parties of the deposit of each such instrument of accession.

Article 12. After the treaty has been in force for 10 years, or at any time thereafter, the parties shall, if any of them so requests, consult together for the purpose of reviewing the treaty, having regard for the factors then affecting peace and security in the North Atlantic area, including the development or universal as well as regional arrangements under the Charter of the United Nations for the maintenance of international peace and security.

Article 13. After the treaty has been in force for 20 years, any party may cease to be a party one year after its notice of denunciation has been given to the government of the United States of America, which will inform the governments of the other parties of the deposit of each notice of denunciation.

* The relevant clauses of the treaty have become inapplicable to the Republic of Algeria as from 3 July 1962.

† This Article was modified as a result of the accession of Greece and Turkey to the treaty.

The treaty came into force on 24 Aug. 1949. Greece and Turkey were admitted as parties to the treaty in 1951 (effective Feb. 1952), the Federal Republic of Germany in Oct. 1954 (effective 5 May 1955).

As reorganized by the Council at its session in Lisbon in Feb. 1952, the structure of NATO is as follows:

The *Council*, the principal body of the organization, 'charged with the responsibility of considering all matters concerning the implementation of the provisions of the Treaty', incorporates the Council and the Defence Committee originally envisaged. The Council is a Council of Governments, on which NATO nations are normally represented by their Minister for Foreign Affairs and/or the Minister of Defence, or by other competent Ministers, especially those responsible for financial and economic affairs. The Council normally meets at ministerial level two or three times a year.

Each member government appoints a *Permanent Representative* to represent it on the Council when its ministerial representatives are not present. Each Permanent Representative also heads a national delegation of advisers and experts. The Permanent Representatives meet once or twice a week and can be called together at short notice at any time.

In carrying out its role, the Council is assisted by a number of committees, some of a permanent nature, some temporary. Like the Council, the membership of each committee is made up of national representatives. They study questions submitted to them by the Council for recommendation. The work of the Committees has a direct bearing on the activities of the International Secretariat.

The Political Committee, charged with preparing the political agenda for the Council, dates from 1957 as does the Economic Committee, which studies and reports to the Council on economic issues of special interest to the Alliance. In 1963 a Defence Planning Committee was established as the civilian co-ordinating body for the defence plans of member countries. Since France's withdrawal in 1966 from NATO military organizations, this Committee is composed of the Permanent Representatives of the 18 countries which take part in NATO's integrated common defence. Like the Council, it also meets at ministerial level. And at the Ministerial meeting in Dec. 1966 two bodies for nuclear planning were established: the Nuclear Defence Affairs Committee and a Nuclear Planning Group of 7–8 members.

Among other important Committees are: the Science Committee and the Infrastructure Committee, whose varied tasks are directly linked to fundamental and applied research; the Senior Civil Emergency Planning Committee; the Committee for European Airspace Co-ordination; the Committee for Pipelines; the Committee for Information and Cultural Relations; and the Civil and Military Budget Committees, who carefully supervise the expenditures of NATO funds for the maintenance of the International Secretariat and military headquarters. In Nov. 1969 the Council established a Committee on the Challenges of Modern Society to consider problems of the human environment. This new Committee examines methods of improving the exchange of views and experience among the Allied countries in the task of creating a better environment for their societies.

More recently, the old Armaments Committee has been replaced by the Conference of National Armaments Directors.

Headquarters: 1110 Brussels, Belgium.
Secretary-General: Joseph Luns (Netherlands), appointed Oct. 1971.
Flag: Dark blue with a white compass rose of 4 points in the centre.

The Secretary-General takes the chair at all Council meetings, except at the opening and closing of Ministerial sessions, when he gives way to the Council President. The office of President is held annually by the Foreign Minister of one of the Treaty countries.

The *Military Committee* is responsible for making recommendations to the Council/Defence Planning Committee on military matters and for supplying guidance to the Allied Commanders. Composed of the Chiefs-of-Staff of all member countries except France and Iceland (which has no military forces), the Committee is assisted by an integrated International Military Staff. It meets at Chiefs-of-Staff level at least twice a year but remains in permanent session at the level of national military representatives. Liaison between the Military Committee and the French High Command is effected through the French Mission to the Military Committee. The permanent chairman of the Military Committee is elected by the Chiefs-of-Staff for a period of 2–3 years. The present chairman is Gen. Herman F. Zeiner Gundersen (Norway), appointed April 1977.

The strategic area covered by the North Atlantic Treaty is divided, taking account of geographical and political factors among three commands: The Atlantic Ocean Command, the European Command and the Channel Command. Defence plans for the North American area are developed by the Canada–US Regional Planning Group.

The NATO commanders are responsible for the development of defence plans for their respective areas, for the determination of force requirements and for the deployment and exercise of the forces under their command.

The *Allied Command Europe* (ACE) covers the area extending from the North Cape to the Mediterranean and from the Atlantic to the eastern border of Turkey, excluding the UK and Portugal, the defence of which does not fall under any one major NATO Command. The European area, which is subdivided into a number of subordinate commands, is under the Supreme Allied Commander Europe (SACEUR) whose Headquarters, near Mons in Belgium, are known as SHAPE (Supreme Headquarters Allied Powers Europe).

SACEUR has also under his orders the ACE Mobile Force, composed of both land and air force units from different member countries, which can be ready for action at very short notice in any threatened area and in particular on the northern and southern flanks of ACE. The present SACEUR is Gen. Alexander M. Haig, Jr (US), appointed Dec. 1974.

Under the Supreme Allied Commander Atlantic (SACLANT) the *Atlantic Command* extends from the North Pole to the Tropic of Cancer and from the coastal waters of North America to those of Europe and Africa, but excludes the Channel and the British Isles. SACLANT, who would have the primary task in wartime of ensuring the security of the sea lanes in the whole Atlantic area, is an operational rather than an administrative commander. Under his orders is the Standing Naval Force Atlantic (STANAVFORLANT) which is a permanent international squadron of ships drawn from NATO Navies which normally operate in the Atlantic.

The present SACLANT, whose Headquarters are in Norfolk (USA), is Admiral Isaac C. Kidd (US), appointed May 1975.

The *Channel Command* covers the English Channel and the southern North Sea. Under the Allied Commander-in-Chief Channel (CINCHAN) its mission is to control and protect merchant shipping in the area, co-operating with SACEUR in the air defence of the Channel. The forces earmarked to the Command in emergency are predominantly naval but include maritime air forces. CINCHAN has also under his command the NATO Standing Naval Force Channel (STANAVFORCHAN) a permanent mine counter measures force comprising ships drawn from the navies of Belgium, the Netherlands and the UK. The present CINCHAN, with Headquarters at Northwood (UK), is Admiral Sir Henry Leach (UK), appointed Oct. 1977.

The *Canada–US Regional Planning Group*, which covers the North American area, develops and recommends to the Military Committee plans for the defence of this area. It meets alternately in Washington and Ottawa.

The NATO Handbook.—NATO: Facts and Figures.—The NATO Review (bi-monthly).—*Aspect of NATO.—NATO Pocket Guide.—Why NATO pamphlet.—NATO and the Warsaw Pact.—The Challenges of Modern Society.*

WESTERN EUROPEAN UNION

On 17 March 1948 a 50-year treaty 'for collaboration in economic, social and cultural matters and for collective self-defence' was signed in Brussels by the Foreign Ministers of the UK, France, the Netherlands, Belgium and Luxembourg. (*See* THE STATESMAN'S YEAR-BOOK, 1954, pp. 32 f.)

On 20 Dec. 1950 the functions of the Western Union defence organization were transferred to the North Atlantic Treaty command and the Western Union command ceased to exist.

After the rejection by France of the European Defence Community on 30 Aug. 1954 a conference was held in London from 28 Sept. to 3 Oct. 1954, attended by Belgium, Canada, France, the Federal Republic of Germany, Italy, Luxembourg, the Netherlands, the UK and the USA, at which it was decided to invite the Federal Republic of Germany and Italy to accede to the Brussels Treaty, to end the occupation of Western Germany and to invite the latter to accede to the North Atlantic Treaty; the Federal Republic agreed that it would voluntarily limit its arms production, and provision was made for the setting up of an agency to control the armaments of the 7 Brussels Treaty powers; the UK undertook not to withdraw from the Continent her 4 divisions and the Tactical Air Force assigned to the Supreme Allied Commander against the wishes of a majority, *i.e.*, 4 of the Brussels Treaty powers, except in the event of an acute overseas emergency.

At a Conference of Ministers held in Paris from 20 to 23 Oct. 1954 these decisions were put into effect. The Union was formally inaugurated on 6 May 1955.

The *Council of WEU* consists of the Foreign Ministers of the 7 powers or their representatives. An *Assembly*, composed of the WEU delegates to the Consultative Assembly of the Council of Europe, meets twice a year, usually in Paris. An *Agency for the Control of Armaments* and a *Standing Armaments Committee* have been set up in Paris. The social and cultural activities were transferred to the Council of Europe on 1 June 1960.

After the breakdown of the negotiations for Britain's entry into the Common Market in 1963 the 6 EEC countries proposed to the UK that the WEU Council (the Six and the UK) should meet every 3 months 'to take stock of the political and economic situation in Europe'. The UK welcomed this proposal, and regular meetings took place. Following the re-opening of negotiations in 1970 which led to the signing of the Treaty of Accession in Jan. 1972 this arrangement has been reviewed.

Headquarters: 9 Grosvenor Place, London, SW1.
Secretary-General: Edouard F. T. Longerstaey.

COUNCIL OF EUROPE

In 1948 the 'Congress of Europe', bringing together at The Hague nearly 1,000 influential Europeans from 26 countries, called for the creation of a united Europe, including a European Assembly. This proposal, examined first by the Ministerial Council of the Brussels Treaty Organization, then by a conference of ambassadors, was at the origin of the Council of Europe. The Statute of the Council was signed at London on 5 May 1949 and came into force 2 months later. The founder members were Belgium, Denmark, France, the Irish Republic, Italy, Luxembourg, the Netherlands, Norway, Sweden and the United Kingdom. Turkey and Greece joined in 1949, Iceland in 1950, the Federal Republic of Germany in 1951 (having been an associate since 1950), Austria in 1956, Cyprus in 1961, Switzerland in 1963, Malta in 1965, Portugal in 1976 and Spain in 1977.

Membership is limited to European States which 'accept the principles of the rule of law and of the enjoyment by all persons within [their] jurisdiction of human rights and fundamental freedoms'. The Statute provides for both withdrawal (Art. 7) and suspension (Arts. 8 and 9). Greece withdrew from the Council in Dec. 1969 and rejoined in Nov. 1974.

Structure. Under the Statute two organs were set up: an inter-governmental *Committee of* [*Foreign*] *Ministers* with powers of decision and of recommendation to governments, and an inter-parliamentary deliberative body, the *Parliamentary Assembly*—both of which are served by the Secretariat. In addition, a large number of committees of experts have been established, two of them, the Council for Cultural Co-operation and the Committee on Legal Co-operation, having a measure of autonomy; on municipal matters the Committee of Ministers receives recommendations from the European Local Authorities Conference.

The Committee of Ministers meets usually twice a year, their deputies 10 times a year.

The Parliamentary Assembly normally consists of 154 parliamentarians elected or appointed by their national parliaments (Austria 6, Belgium 7, Cyprus 3, Denmark 5, France 18, Federal Republic of Germany 18, Greece 7, Iceland 3, Irish Republic 4, Italy 18, Luxembourg 3, Malta 3, Netherlands 7, Norway 5, Portugal 7, Spain 10, Sweden 6, Switzerland 6, Turkey 10, UK 18); it meets 3 times a year for approximately a week. For domestic reasons Cyprus is not at present represented in the Assembly. The work of the Assembly is prepared by parliamentary committees.

The *Joint Committee*, consisting of the Committee of Ministers and representatives of the Assembly, harmonizes relations between the two organs.

The European Convention on Human Rights, signed in 1950, set up special machinery to guarantee internationally fundamental rights and freedoms. A *European Commission* investigates alleged violations of the Convention submitted to it either by States or, in most cases, by individuals. Its findings can then be examined by the *European Court of Human Rights* (set up in 1959), whose obligatory jurisdiction has been recognized by 13 States, or by the Committee of Ministers, empowered to take binding decisions by two-thirds majority vote.

For questions of national refugees and over-population, a Special Representative has been appointed, responsible to the governments collectively. In 1956 the Resettlement Fund for National Refugees and Over-Population was created on the initiative of the special representative. Fourteen countries are members of this Fund, allocating loans for almost US$300m.

The European Youth Centre was set up in 1970. The European Youth Foundation is administered by the Secretary-General of the Council of Europe.

Aims and Achievements. Art. 1 of the Statute states that the Council's aim is 'to achieve a greater unity between its members for the purpose of safeguarding and realising the ideals and principles which are their common heritage and facilitating their economic and social progress'; 'this aim shall be pursued . . . by discussion of questions of common concern and by agreements and common action'. The only limitation is provided by Art. 1 (*d*), which excludes 'matters relating to national defence'.

It has been the task of the Assembly to propose action to bring European countries closer together, to keep under constant review the progress made and to voice the views of European public opinion on the main political and economic questions of the day. The Ministers' role is to translate the Assembly's recommendations into action, particularly as regards lowering the barriers between the European countries, harmonizing their legislation or introducing where possible common European laws, abolishing discrimination on grounds of nationality and undertaking certain tasks on a joint European basis.

The Committee of Ministers periodically reviews the programme of activities of the Council of Europe. It comprises projects for co-operation between member governments in economic, legal, social, public health, environmental, and educational and scientific matters.

About 96 conventions have been concluded, covering such matters as social security, patents, extradition, medical treatment, training of nurses, equivalence of degrees and diplomas, innkeepers' liability, compulsory motor insurance, the protection of television broadcasts, adoption of children, transportation of animals and *au pair* placement. A *Social Charter* sets out the social and economic rights which all member governments agree to guarantee to their citizens.

The official languages are English and French.

Chairman of the Committee of Ministers: (held in rotation).
President of the Parliamentary Assembly: Karl Czernetz (Austria).
President of the European Court of Human Rights: Prof. Giorgio Balladore Pallieri (Italy).
President of the European Commission of Human Rights: James E. S. Fawcett (UK).
Secretary-General: Georg Kahn-Ackermann (Federal Republic of Germany).
Headquarters: Palais de l'Europe, 67006, Strasbourg, CEDEX, France.
Flag: Dark blue with a ring of 12 gold stars in the centre.

European Yearbook. The Hague, from 1955
Forward in Europe. Strasbourg, from 1959, 4 times a year
Guide to the Council of Europe. Strasbourg, 1977
Manual of the Council of Europe. London, 1970
Yearbook on the Convention on Human Rights. Strasbourg, from 1958
Nova, F., *Contemporary European Governments.* Dublin, 1965
P.E.P., *European Organisations.* 2nd ed. London, 1966
Cook, C., and Paxton, J., *European Political Facts, 1918–73.* London, 1975
Robertson, A. H., *The Council of Europe.* 2nd ed. London, 1961.—*European Institutions.* 2nd ed. London, 1966

EUROPEAN COMMUNITIES

Six countries of western Europe—Belgium, France, Federal Republic of Germany, Italy, Luxembourg and the Netherlands—first established 3 communities with the aims of gradually integrating their economies and of moving towards political unity: the European Coal and Steel Community (ECSC), the European Economic Community (EEC) and the European Atomic Energy Community (EAEC or Euratom).

Up to 1 July 1967 the 3 Communities, though legally separate under their constituent treaties, had some institutions in common. On that day they merged their 3 executives in one Commission of the European Communities and also their 3 councils. This was the first step towards the complete merger of the 3 communities under a new single treaty.

On 30 June 1970 membership negotiations began between the Six and UK, Denmark, Irish Republic and Norway. On 22 Jan. 1972 those 4 countries signed the Treaty of Accession to the Community. In Nov. 1972 a Norwegian referendum rejected entry, but on 1 Jan. 1973 UK, Irish Republic and Denmark became full members.

The *Commission* consists of 13 members appointed by the member states to serve for 4 years; the President and 5 Vice-Presidents serve for 2 years. The Commission acts independently in the interests of the Community as a whole. Its task is the implementation of the Treaties, and in this it has the right of both initiative and execution: it proposes to the Council of Ministers the methods by which the aims of the Treaties can be achieved, and is then responsible for carrying them through.

President: Roy Harris Jenkins.
Address: 200 rue de la Loi, 1049, Brussels.

The *Council of Ministers* consists of Ministers from the 9 national governments and represents the national as opposed to the Community interests. It is the body which has the power of decision in the Community. Under the Treaties many of its decisions are taken to be by qualified majority vote; since the 'Luxembourg Compromise' of 1966 majority voting has been used for minor matters only. In addition, at a meeting held in Dec. 1974, the Heads of Government decided, in the interest of political co-operation, to meet 3 times a year as the *European Council.*

Address: 170 rue de la Loi, 1048, Brussels.

The *European Parliament* consists of 198 members delegated by the 9 national Parliaments. The EEC Treaty provides for the direct election of its members, and on 20 Sept. 1976 the Council of Ministers agreed that direct elections should be held, if possible in May or June 1978 for an enlarged Parliament of 410 seats. The Parliament has to be consulted over the annual budgets of the 3 Communities and a wide range of other matters. It can dismiss the Commission on a motion of censure approved by a two-thirds majority. As part of the decision in 1970 to provide the Community with its own independent financial resources, the Parliament has been given more control over the administrative budget consisting of non-mandatory expenditure, *i.e.*, expenditure not arising directly from the Treaty or from regulations made under it. The budgetary power of the Parliament was reviewed in 1973 and has been enlarged.

President: Emilio Colombo.
Address: Centre Européan du Kirchberg, Luxembourg.

Annuaire—Manuel de l'Assemblée Parlementaire Européenne. Annual, from 1959

The *Court of Justice* is composed of 9 judges and 3 advocates-general, is responsible for the adjudication of disputes arising out of the application of the treaties, and its findings are enforceable in all member countries.

President: Hans Kutscher.
Address: Kirchberg, Luxembourg.

Receuil de la Jurisprudence de la Cour. From 1954
Bebr, G., *Judicial Control of the European Communities.* London, 1962

The *Economic and Social Committee* has an advisory role and consists of 144 representatives, employers, trade unions, consumers, etc. The *Consultative Committee*, of 84 members, performs a similar role for the ECSC.

EUROPEAN ECONOMIC COMMUNITY

E.E.C. or COMMON MARKET. The EEC came into being on 1 Jan. 1958, based on the treaty signed in Rome on 25 March 1957, by Belgium, France, Federal Republic of Germany, Luxembourg, Italy and the Netherlands. UK, the Irish Republic and Denmark became members on 1 Jan. 1973.

The Customs Union. The Treaty required the achievement of a complete customs union between the 6 countries over a transitional period of 12 to 15 years. This was achieved 18 months ahead of the 12-year schedule when, on 1 July 1968, customs duties on trade between the Six were removed. The customs tariffs of the 3 new member countries were phased out by stages, ending on 1 July 1977. From that date the Nine offered a Common Customs Tariff (CCT) to third industrial countries, while goods traded by the UK, the Irish Republic and Denmark and other EEC members became free of customs duties and other import and export charges.

The Economic Union. Work is progressing on common transport and external trade policies and the co-ordination of financial, commercial, economic and social policies. The Treaty forbids agreements or practices which restrict, prevent or distort fair competition, and the Commission has powers to prevent such agreements that flout the Treaty except where EEC Regulations specify exceptions.

At the Paris 'summit' of Oct. 1972 the Nine affirmed the aim of 'Economic Union' by the end of 1980 and to increase their collaboration in the fields of scientific research and advanced technology. The summit also laid the bases for environmental and social action programmes, and a regional policy and fund. However, the economic recession that followed the OPEC raising of oil prices in 1973 destroyed any hope of achieving economic union by the target date.

The Common Agricultural Policy (*CAP*). The basic features of a common policy in agriculture were first adopted in Jan. 1962. The aims are greater efficiency in production, stable market conditions, a fair return for farmers and reasonable prices for consumers. The two essential principles are common price levels and the replacement of national systems of protection by a Community system whose most characteristic feature is a method of variable levies on imports of certain farm products. The common marketing arrangements for all major items were operative by July 1968. Management committees of national experts advise the Commission on the various products. A European Guidance and Guarantee Fund has also been established to finance the common policy. Various measures have been introduced at a Community level to help the modernization of farms and to assist older farmers who wish to give up farming their land. The 3 new member countries were gradually integrated into the CAP over a 5-year period ending on 31 Dec. 1977. In 1975, the Community completed a review of the CAP, concluding that, while it required adjustments, its basic principles remained sound.

Community Resources. Originally the EEC budget was financed entirely from direct contributions by member states. From 1 Jan. 1978, however, the Community budget has been financed by its 'own resources' collected from customs duties, agricultural levies and a uniform assessment of up to 1% of value-added tax. In 1975, in response to a British request for re-negotiation, machinery was established to compensate any member state paying an undue proportion of the budget.

External Relations. In 1961, UK, the Irish Republic, Norway and Denmark opened negotiations for membership but these were broken off at the insistence of France in 1963. A fresh attempt in 1967 failed for the same reason.

After the retirement of President de Gaulle, and particularly after The Hague 'summit' meeting of the Six, it became clear that renewed efforts might succeed and on 30 June 1970 successful negotiations began. The basis of the agreement was that the principles of the 1957 treaty remain intact and the great majority of the regulations made in it would continue to apply to the new Community of Nine.

The Community has trade and co-operation agreements of varying kinds with over 40 countries, excluding the special arrangement with 52 developing countries from Africa, the Caribbean and the Pacific (ACP states) under the Lomé Convention. At the end of 1977 trade talks started with China and there were preliminary discussions with Comecon countries. On 1 July 1977 internal tariffs on manufactured goods between the Community and 7 EFTA countries were abolished.

The Lomé Convention replaced the earlier Yaoundé Conventions with Associated States following the accession of the new member countries and, apart from Asia, covers nearly all developing countries in the Commonwealth. The Convention provides for duty-free entry or concessionary tariffs on a wide range of goods from the ACP countries and through STABEX offers a system to stabilize the export earnings of developing countries covered by the Convention.

It is becoming common practice for the European Commission to negotiate with third countries on trade agreements on behalf of the Nine, and for the President of the Council to speak for the Community in international *fora*, such as the UN. The Council has taken a common stance on the Middle East, South Africa and Portugal.

Following the advent of the Junta in Greece, negotiations for her to join the Community were suspended. With the restoration of democratic governments in Greece, Portugal and Spain, all three countries have applied for Community membership. Negotiations on enlargement began in 1978.

As a first step towards the creation of a political union, the Six agreed, in 1970, to hold twice-yearly consultations on foreign policy; since then 'political co-operation' meetings of foreign ministers have increased in frequency. In Dec. 1975, Leo Tindemans submitted a report on 'European Union' which had been requested at a meeting in Dec. 1974.

General Report on the Activities of the Community (annual, from 1958).—*Bulletin of the EEC* (monthly).—*Bulletin Général de Statistiques* (monthly).—*Statistique Mensuelle du Commerce Extérieur* (monthly).—*Graphiques et Notes Rapides sur la conjoncture de la Communauté* (monthly, from 1959).

European Community (monthly), obtainable from the UK office of the Commission of the European Communities, 20 Kensington Palace Gdns, London, W8 4QQ

Balfour, C., *Industrial Relations in the Common Market*. London, 1972

Bellamy, C., and Child, G. D., *Common Market Law of Competition*. London, 1973
Böhning, W. R., *The Migration of Workers in the United Kingdom and the European Community*. New York, OUP, 1972
Butler, D. and Kitzinger, U., *The 1975 Referendum*. London, 1976
Calmann, J. (ed.), *The Rome Treaty: The Common Market Explained*. London, 1967
Coffey, P., *The External Economic Relations of the E.E.C.* London, 1976
Cocks, Sir Barnett, *The European Parliament*. HMSO, 1973
Dyas, G. P., and Thanheiser, H. T., *The Emerging European Enterprise*. London, 1976
Goodhart, P., *Full-hearted Consent*. London, 1976
Hallstein, W., *Europe in the Making*. London, 1973
Kitzinger, U., *Diplomacy and Persuasion: How Britain Joined the Common Market*. London, 1972
Love, J., *Jane's Major Companies of Europe 1976*. London, 1976
Mally, G., *The European Community in Perspective*. Lexington, Mass., 1973
Marx, E., and Kendall, W., *Unions in Europe: A Guide to Organised Labour in the Six*. Univ. of Sussex, 1971
Mathijsen, P. S. R. F., *A Guide to European Community Law*. London, New York, 1972
Mayne, R., *The Recovery of Europe*. London, 1970
Mowat, R. C., *Creating the European Community*. London, 1973
Parry, A., and Hardy, S., *EEC Law*. London, 1973
Paxton, J., *The Developing Common Market*. London, 1976.—*A Dictionary of the European Economic Community*. London, 1977
Prag, D., and Nicholson, E. D., *Businessman's Guide to the Common Market*. London, 1973
Pryce, R., *The Politics of the European Community*. London, 1973
Spinelli, A., *The European Adventure*. London, 1972
Thomas, H., *Europe: The Radical Challenge*. New York, 1973
Wallace, H., *National Governments and the European Communities*. London, 1973
Walsh, A. E., and Paxton, J., *Trade in the Common Market Countries*. London, 1965.—*Trade and Industrial Resources of the Common Market and EFTA Countries*. London, 1970.—*Competition Policy*. London, 1975
Warnecke, S. J. (ed.), *The European Community in the 1970's*. New York, 1972

EUROPEAN COAL AND STEEL COMMUNITY. The ECSC came into being on 10 Aug. 1952 following the ratification of a treaty signed in Paris on 18 April 1951. The original suggestion for it was made in the Schuman Plan on 9 May 1950, which proposed the pooling of Franco-German coal and steel production in a Community open to other western European countries as a first step towards a United States of Europe. (*See* map in THE STATESMAN'S YEAR-BOOK, 1958.) UK, the Irish Republic and Denmark joined the ECSC as full members on 1 Jan. 1973.

Until 1 July 1967 the *High Authority* was the executive body of the ECSC and consisted of 8 members appointed by the 6 governments plus one co-opted member. After the merger of the Executives its power passed to the single European Commission which is now responsible for the execution of the ECSC Treaty.

The Common Market for Coal and Steel. A common market for coal, iron ore and scrap was established on 10 Feb. 1953, for steel on 1 May 1953 and for special steels on 1 Aug. 1954. A harmonized external tariff on steel is now at around 9%. Rules for fair competition have been established; currency restrictions, the dual-pricing system (under which prices for export and home-consumed coal and steel varied) and discriminatory transport rates based upon nationality have been abolished within the Community.

To meet the changing circumstances in the two industries, and especially to ensure that the contraction of the coal industry occurs without social or economic dislocation, there are ECSC readaption, retraining and other schemes to which the Commission makes grants. In 1973–76 these amounted to 97·8m. units of account towards readaption and retraining 98,700 workers throughout the Community.

A Common Energy Policy. Of the various forms of energy, coal falls within the competence of the ECSC, nuclear energy within that of Euratom, and all others with that of the EEC. The 1972 Paris summit set up the goal of a common energy policy; the post-1974 energy crisis has intensified the need for ensuring supplies.

General Report of the High Authority (annual, from 1953).—*Bulletin Statistique* (bi-monthly from 1952).—*Investment Report* (annual, from 1956).—*Financial Report* (annual, from 1956).—*Journal Officiel de la CECA* (1952–58).—*Journal Officiel des Communautés Européennes* (from 1958).—*European Community* (monthly, from 1963)

Diebold, W., *The Schuman Plan; A Study in Economic Co-operation, 1950–59.* New York, 1959
Lister, L., *Europe's Coal and Steel Community.* New York, 1960
Meade, J. E. (ed.), *Case Studies in European Economic Union.* Oxford, 1962
Schuman, R., *Pour l'Europe.* Paris, 1963

EUROPEAN ATOMIC ENERGY COMMUNITY (EURATOM). Euratom came into being on 1 Jan. 1958 following the ratification of a treaty signed in Rome on 25 March 1957. Its task is to promote a common effort between its 6 members in the development of nuclear energy for peaceful purposes. It is in no way concerned with the military uses of nuclear energy; indeed, the member governments are forbidden under the treaty to use nuclear materials obtained from or through the Community in national military programmes.

The execution of the treaty now rests with the *European Commission*, which is advised by a *Scientific and Technical Committee* (27 members) and the *Economic and Social Committee* (144 members). Major decisions are taken by the *Council of Ministers*, which is common also to the EEC.

Euratom supplements and co-ordinates research undertaken by the member states, pools scientific information and promotes the training of scientists and technicians. It promotes research (*a*) through its own research centres at Ispra, Italy (concentrating on the Orgel heavy-water reactor), at Geel, Belgium (the Central Nuclear Measurements Bureau), at Karlsruhe, Germany (the European Transuranium Institute) and at Petten, Netherlands (a general-purpose research establishment); (*b*) by contracting specific tasks to national centres or firms, and by 'association contracts' under which it contributes finance and personnel to joint teams; (*c*) by joining international projects such as the European Nuclear Energy Agency project at Winfrith Heath, England (the Dragon reactor).

Euratom has its own large Information and Documentation Centre, has set up a radioisotope information bureau and has worked out a Community policy on ownership of patents resulting from nuclear research. It has laid down basic standards for health protection throughout the Community, and worked out an insurance convention for large-scale atomic risks.

A common market for all nuclear materials and equipment came into force, and external tariffs were suspended, on 1 Jan. 1959. Since 1966 Euratom has been growing steadily less effective though attempts are still made to rationalize the research centres' operations, and co-ordinate them with national efforts.

International Links. An agreement was signed with the US Atomic Energy Commission in Nov. 1958 and widened in 1964. UK, the Irish Republic and Denmark joined Euratom on 1 Jan. 1973.

General Report on the Activities of the Community (annual, from 1958).—*Euratom Bulletin* (quarterly, from Jan. 1962)

EUROPEAN FREE TRADE ASSOCIATION (EFTA)

The European Free Trade Association has 6 member countries: Austria, Iceland, Norway, Portugal, Sweden and Switzerland. A seventh country, Finland, is an associate member. The Stockholm Convention establishing the Association entered into force on 3 May 1960 and Finland became associated on 27 March 1961. Iceland joined EFTA on 1 March 1970 and was immediately granted duty-free entry for industrial goods exported to EFTA countries, while being given 10 years to abolish her own existing protective duties. Two founder members of EFTA, the UK and Denmark, left EFTA on 31 Dec. 1972 to join the EEC.

When the Association was created it had three objectives: to achieve free trade in industrial products between member countries, to assist in the creation of a single market embracing the countries of Western Europe, and to contribute to the expansion of world trade in general.

The first objective was achieved on 31 Dec. 1966, when virtually all inter-EFTA tariffs were removed. This was 3 years earlier than originally planned. Finland removed her remaining EFTA tariffs a year later on 31 Dec. 1967. The achievement of free trade made EFTA the world's first completed free-trade area, and intra-EFTA trade more than doubled in the period 1959–68.

The fulfilment of the second aim was secured in 1972. On 22 Jan. 1972 the UK and Denmark signed the Treaty of Accession to the EEC whereby they became members of the enlarged Community from 1 Jan. 1973. On 22 July 1972, 5 other EFTA countries, Austria, Iceland, Portugal, Sweden and Switzerland signed Free Trade Agreements with the enlarged EEC. A similar agreement negotiated with Finland was signed on 5 Oct. 1973. Norway, whose intention of joining the EEC was reversed following a referendum, signed a similar agreement on 14 May 1973. Through these agreements virtually complete free trade in industrial goods was achieved in 16 Western European countries from 1 July 1977.

The third objective was to contribute to the expansion of world trade. In 1959 trade between the countries then in EFTA amounted to US$759m. and total exports were US$6,852m. In 1976 the respective figures were US$10,258m. and US$58,248m.

EFTA tariff treatment applies to those industrial products which are of EFTA origin, and these are traded freely between member countries. Each EFTA country remains free, however, to impose its own rates of duty on products entering from outside the EFTA area.

Generally, agricultural products do not come under the provisions for free trade, but bilateral agreements have been negotiated to increase trade in these products.

The operation of the Convention is the responsibility of a Council assisted by a small secretariat. Each EFTA country holds the chairmanship of the Council for 6 months.

Secretary-General: Charles Müller (Switzerland).

Headquarters: 9–11 Rue de Varembé, 1211 Geneva 20, Switzerland.

Convention Establishing the European Free Trade Association (new ed. 1977)
EFTA Bulletin (Nine issues a year)
EFTA Structure, Rules and Operation
EFTA What it is, What it does

COUNCIL FOR MUTUAL ECONOMIC ASSISTANCE[1]

Membership. Founder members were USSR, Bulgaria, Czechoslovakia, Hungary, Poland and Romania. Later admissions were Albania (1949; ceased participation 1961), Cuba (1972), German Democratic Republic (1950), Mongolia (1962). In 1964 Yugoslavia concluded an agreement with CMEA whereby Yugoslavia would participate in the work of some CMEA bodies (at present 21). Angola, Laos, North Korea and Vietnam participate in various bodies as observers. There are co-operation agreements with Finland, Iraq and Mexico.

The Charter. The charter consists of a preamble and 18 articles. Extracts (in the language of the official English version) are as follows:

Article 1. Aims and Principles: 1 'The purpose of the Council is to facilitate, by uniting and co-ordinating the efforts of its member countries, the planned development of the national economy, acceleration of economic and technical progress in these countries, a rise in the level of industrialization in countries with less developed industries, uninterrupted growth of labour productivity and a steady advance of the welfare of the peoples. 2 The Council is based on the principles of the sovereign equality of all member countries.'

Article 2. Membership 'open to other countries which subscribe to the purposes and principles of the Council'.

Article 3. Functions and Powers to (a) 'organize all-round ... co-operation of member coun-

[1] *Abbreviations and Foreign Names.* CMEA is the official abbreviation. Other unofficial abbreviations are COMECON and CEMA. The working language of the organization is Russian. The Russian form is *Sovet Ekonomicheskoi Vzaimopomoshchi* (SEV).

tries in the most rational use of natural resources and acceleration of the development of their productive forces'; (b) 'foster the improvement of the international socialist division of labour by co-ordinating national economic development plans, and the specialization and co-operation of production in member countries'; (c) to assist in . . . carrying out joint measures for the development of industry and agriculture . . . transport . . . principal capital investments . . . [and] trade'.

Article 4. Recommendations and Decisions '. . . shall be adopted only with the consent of the interested member countries.'

The Structure. The supreme authority is the 'Session' of all members held (usually annually) in members' capitals in rotation under the chairmanship of the head of the delegation of the host country; all members must be present, and decisions must be unanimous. Delegations are usually led by prime ministers.

The *Executive Committee* is made up of one representative from each member state of deputy premier rank. It meets at least once every 3 months.

The administrative organ is the *Secretariat.*

Headquarters: Prospekt Kalinina, 56, Moscow, G-205.
Secretary: N. V. Faddeev (appointed 1958).

There is a *Committee for Co-operation in the Field of Planning* and a *Committee for Scientific and Technical Co-operation* set up in 1971 and a *Committee for Material and Technical Supply* set up in 1974. There are *Permanent Commissions* on: Statistics, Foreign Trade, Currency and Finance, Electricity, Peaceful Uses of Atomic Energy, Geology, Coal Industry, Oil and Gas Industry, Chemical Industry, Iron and Steel Industry, Non-Ferrous Metals Industry, Engineering Industry, Radio Engineering and Electronics Industries, Light Industry, Food Industry, Agriculture, Construction, Transport, Posts and Telecommunications, Standardization, Civil Aviation, Public Health.

There are seven *Standing Conferences:* for Legal Problems; of Ministers of Internal Trade; of Chiefs of Water Resources Authorities; of Chiefs of Patent Authorities; of Chiefs of Pricing Authorities; of Chiefs of Labour Authorities, and of Representatives of Freight and Shipping Organizations.

There are three semi-autonomous bodies within Comecon: The Institute of Standardization, The Bureau for the Co-ordination of Ship Freighting and The International Institute of Economic Problems of World Socialist System.

In 1976 there were 27 technical and economic agencies associated with Comecon.

Also associated with Comecon are:

The **International Bank for Economic Co-operation** was founded in 1963 with a capital of 300m. roubles and started operating on 1 Jan. 1964. It undertakes multilateral settlements in 'transferable roubles' (*i.e.*, used for intra-Comecon clearing accounts only) and advances credits to finance trading and other operations. The transferable *rouble* is a unit of account: gold content 0·987412 gramme.

The **International Investments Bank** was founded in 1970 and went into operation on 1 Jan. 1971 with a capital of 1,000m. roubles (70% transferable and 30% convertible or in gold).

Charter of the Council for Mutual Economic Assistance. Moscow, 1976
Council for Mutual Economic Assistance: Twenty-five Years. Moscow, 1974
Comprehensive Programme for the Further Extension and Improvement of Co-operation and the Development of Socialist Economic Integration by the CMEA-member Countries. Moscow, 1971 (The official English-language version. This document also frequently referred to as the *Complex Programme*, etc.)
Ekonommicheskoe Sotrudnichestvo Stran-Chlenov SEV. Moscow, 6 a year
Purposes, Principles, Structure, Activities. Moscow, 1975
Statistical Year Book of CMEA Member Countries. Moscow, annual
Survey of CMEA Activities. Moscow, annual
Bautina, N. V., *CMEA Today: from Economic Co-operation to Economic Integration.* Moscow, 1975
Faddeev, N. V., *Soviet Ekonomicheskoi Vzaimopomoshchi, 1949–1974.* Moscow, 1974
Lascelles, D., *Comecon to 1980.* London, 1976
Mellor, R. E. H., *COMECON: A Challenge to the West.* New York, 1971

Shaeffer, H. W., *Comecon and the Politics of Integration.* New York and London, 1972
Szawlowski, R., *The System of the International Organizations of the Communist Countries.* Leyden, 1976
van Brabant, J. M. P., *Essays on Planning, Trade and Integration in Eastern Europe.* Rotterdam Univ. Press, 1974
Wilczynski, J., *Technology in Comecon.* London, 1974

COLOMBO PLAN

The Colombo Plan was established for co-operative economic development in south and south-east Asia in 1951 as a result of a meeting of Commonwealth foreign ministers held in 1950. It seeks to improve the living standards of the people of the area by reviewing development plans and co-ordinating development assistance. Aid to member countries is negotiated and administered bilaterally. Membership comprises 21 developing countries within the region: Afghánistán, Bangladesh, Bhután, Burma, Fiji, India, Indonesia, Iran, Kampuchea, Republic of Korea, Laos, Malaysia, Republic of the Maldives, Nepál, Pakistan, Papua New Guinea, Philippines, Singapore, Sri Lanka, Thailand and Vietnam; and 6 non-regional members: Australia, Canada, Japan, New Zealand, UK and USA.

The annual meetings of the Consultative Committee are also attended by observers from major international and regional organizations concerned with development.

Technical Co-operation. The Colombo Plan has no permanent secretariat. A small Bureau, set up in Colombo in 1951, operates under the supervision of a Council for Technical Co-operation in South and South-East Asia, representing member governments. An information unit has been attached to the Bureau since 1953. The Colombo Plan Staff College for Technician Education was established at Singapore in 1974. The Council publishes its own annual report.

During 1976, 4,642 experts were assigned to countries of the region, and 6,936 training places were provided. Most training is given outside the region, but the Bureau has increasingly urged members to make more use of training facilities available within the region, by adequate arrangements for the exchange of students.

External Aid. The net bilateral Official Development Assistance flows to countries of the region provided by Australia, Canada, New Zealand and UK during 1976 was US$761·21m. Information on Japan and USA not available. In addition there is substantial private investment from countries outside the region. In 1976 UK bilateral aid amounted to US$242m., bringing the total since 1950 to US$3,377m. Of the total expenditure in 1976, US27m. was on technical co-operation, bringing the total of such expenditure since 1950 to US279m.

The Colombo Plan (Cmd. 8080). HMSO, 1950; reprinted 1952.—*Annual Report.* HMSO, 1952 to 1971 followed by Colombo Plan Bureaux, Sri Lanka, 1972 to date
Reports of the Council for Technical Co-operation. HMSO annually until 1966–67 followed by the Colombo Plan Bureau, Sri Lanka, 1967–68 to date

ASSOCIATION OF SOUTHEAST ASIAN NATIONS (ASEAN)

History and Membership. The organization was formed on 7 Aug. 1967 and replaced the Association of South East Asia (ASA) which had been formed by Malaysia, the Philippines and Thailand in 1961. The present members of ASEAN are Indonesia, Malaysia, the Philippines, Singapore and Thailand.

Objectives. The main objectives are to accelerate economic growth, social progress and cultural development, to promote active collaboration and mutual assistance in matters of common interest, to ensure the stability of the South East Asian region and to maintain close co-operation with existing international and regional organizations with similar aims. Principal projects include programmes aiming at the relaxation or elimination of restrictions on free trade, joint research programmes, and various cultural exchanges.

Organs. The organization consists of a ministerial conference of the foreign ministers of the member states held annually in the capital of each country in turn, a standing committee which meets in Singapore between ministerial meetings for consultations when necessary. There are also several specialized permanent committees to consider matters relating to communications, science and technology, transport, food production, and commerce and industry. Each capital has a national ASEAN secretariat, and a central secretariat has now been established in Jakarta in Indonesia. The post of secretary-general revolves among member states in alphabetical order every 2 years. Heads of bureaux remain in office for 3 years.

Secretary-General: Umarjadi Njotowijono (Indonesia).

CENTRAL TREATY ORGANIZATION (CENTO)

A pact of mutual defence was signed in Baghdad by Turkey and Iraq on 24 Feb. 1955. It was joined by the UK (4 April), Pakistan (23 Sept.) and Iran (3 Nov.). The USA became a full member of the economic and counter-subversion committees in April 1956, of the military committee in March 1957 and of the scientific council in May 1961, and is represented at the council meetings by observers. Bilateral defence agreements between the USA and Turkey, Iran and Pakistan were signed in Ankara on 5 March 1959.

Iraq ceased to participate in the activities of the Pact countries after the revolution in July 1958 and formally withdrew on 24 March 1959.

Headquarters were transferred from Baghdad to Ankara in Oct. 1958. On 21 Aug. 1959 the name of the organization was changed from Baghdad Pact to Central Treaty Organization (CENTO).

Acting Secretary-General: Sirdar Hasan Mahmud (Pakistan).

The Council. The permanent governing body of CENTO is the Council of Ministers which lays down policy and provide for continuous consultation on political and economic questions as well as military matters.

The main clauses of the Pact may be summarized as follows:

1. Consistent with Art. 51 of the UN Charter, the contracting parties will co-operate for their security and defence. This co-operation may form the subject of special agreements.

3. The contracting parties undertake to refrain from any interference in each other's internal affairs. They will settle any dispute between themselves in a peaceful way in accordance with UN Charter.

4. The contracting parties declare that the dispositions of the Pact are not in contradiction with any of the international obligations contracted by either of them with any third state. They undertake not to enter into any international obligations incompatible with the Pact.

5. The Pact shall be open for accession to any member state of the Arab League or any other state actively concerned with the security and peace of this region, and which is fully recognized by the contracting parties.

7. This Pact remains in force for a period of 5 years, renewable for other 5-year periods. Any party may withdraw by notifying the other parties 6 months before the expiration of any of the above-mentioned periods.

The economic development programmes include:

Road Links: Pakistan–Iran road link joining Karachi, Lasbela, Quetta, Nok Kundi, Zahedan, Kerman and Kashan. Pakistan–Iran road link joining Lasbela, Pishin and Chahbahar. Turkey–Iran road link joining Iskenderun–Bağilişi, Serow, Rezaiyeh and Tábriz–Tehrán main road at Zanjan.

Rail Links: Turkey–Iran rail link (including a ferry across Lake Van) joining Muş, Tatvan, Khoy and Sharafkhaneh completed in Sept. 1971. Muş–Tatvan section completed 1964. Iran–Pakistan rail link joining Zarand to Zahedan and Quetta under construction and is due to be completed in 1980.

See map in THE STATESMAN'S YEAR-BOOK, 1970–71.

Port Development: Development of the ports of Trabzon and Iskenderun has been completed.

Airway: CENTO Airway; US and UK have contributed considerable amounts towards improved navigational and other aids for regional air traffic. Now completed.

Telecommunications: High-frequency radio telecommunication links between London and key regional stations, *i.e.*, Istanbul, Ankara, Tehrán and Karachi. First stage completed in 1964; in full operation 1968. Ankara–Tehrán–Karachi microwave links project involving 88 relay stations and 13 air navigation stations opened 1965, completed 1966.

In addition, research is being undertaken into health, science, agriculture and mineral development. Technical assistance is also undertaken and industrial development projects are under consideration.

ORGANIZATION OF AMERICAN STATES

On 14 April 1890 representatives of the American republics, meeting in Washington at the First International Conference of American States, established an 'International Union of American Republics' and, as its central office, a 'Commercial Bureau of American Republics', which later became the Pan American Union. This international organization's object was to foster mutual understanding and co-operation among the nations of the western hemisphere. Since that time, successive inter-American conferences have greatly broadened the scope of work of the organization.

This led to the adoption on 30 April 1948 by the Ninth International Conference of American States, at Bogotá, Colombia, of the Charter of the Organization of American States. This co-ordinated the work of all the former independent official entities in the inter-American system and defined their mutual relationships. The purposes of the OAS are to achieve an order of peace and justice, promote American solidarity, strengthen collaboration among the member states and defend their sovereignty, territorial integrity and independence. The OAS is a regional organization of the United Nations for the maintenance of peace and security.

Membership is on a basis of absolute equality. Each country has one vote in the Council of the Organization and its organs. The member countries are: Argentina, Barbados, Bolivia, Brazil, Chile, Colombia, Costa Rica, Dominican Republic, Ecuador, El Salvador, Grenada, Guatemala, Haiti, Honduras, Jamaica, Mexico, Nicaragua, Panama, Paraguay, Peru, Surinam, Trinidad and Tobago, USA, Uruguay, Venezuela.

The OAS has been concerned increasingly in recent years with programmes to promote Latin American economic and social development. The OAS provides specialized training for thousands of Latin Americans each year in a wide variety of development-related fields. It also carries out several missions projects each year in response to requests from member governments.

On 27 Feb. 1967 the Third Special Inter-American Conference in Buenos Aires approved the Protocol of Amendment to the Charter of the OAS, which contained new standards for inter-American co-operation and a number of structural changes in the Organization.

On 14 April 1967 the Declaration of the Presidents of America, signed in Punta del Este, Uruguay, expressed the commitment of the American chiefs of state to promote Latin American economic integration; to join in efforts to increase substantially Latin American foreign-trade earnings; to modernize the living conditions of the rural population and raise agricultural productivity; and to expand programmes in education, science, technology and health.

On 22 Feb. 1968, in the Resolution of Maracay, the Inter-American Cultural Council launched new regional programmes for educational development and for scientific and technological development.

On 27 Feb. 1970, by ratification of more than the mandatory two-thirds of the OAS member states, the Protocol of Buenos Aires, modifying the 1948 Charter, entered into effect.

Under the amended Charter, the OAS accomplishes its purposes by means of:

(*a*) The *General Assembly*, which meets annually in various countries of the member states.

(*b*) The *Meeting of Consultation of Ministers of Foreign Affairs*, held to consider problems of an urgent nature and of common interest.

(*c*) Three councils of equal rank: the *Permanent Council*, which replaces the old OAS Council; the *Inter-American Economic and Social Council*; and the *Inter-American Council for Education, Science and Culture*. Functions are to direct and co-ordinate work in the areas of their competence and render the governments such specialized services as they may request. Each council is composed of 1 representative from each member state, appointed by his government.

(*d*) The *Inter-American Juridical Committee* which acts as an advisory body to the OAS on juridical matters and promotes the development and codification of international law. Eleven jurists, elected every 4 years by the General Assembly, represent all the American States.

(*e*) The *Inter-American Commission on Human Rights* which oversees the observance and protection of human rights. Six members represent all the OAS member states.

(*f*) The *General Secretariat* is the central and permanent organ of the OAS.

(*g*) The *Specialized Conferences*, meeting to deal with special technical matters or to develop specific aspects of inter-American co-operation.

(*h*) The *Specialized Organizations*, intergovernmental organizations established by multilateral agreements to discharge specific functions in their respective fields of action, such as women's affairs, agriculture, child welfare, Indian affairs, geography and history, and health.

Secretary-General: Alejandro Orfila (Argentina).
Assistant Secretary-General: Jorge Zelaya-Coronado (Guatemala)

The Secretary-General and the Assistant Secretary-General are elected by the General Assembly for 5-year terms. The General Assembly approves the annual budget for the Organization, which is financed by quotas contributed by the member governments.

General Secretariat: Washington, D.C., 20006, USA.
Flag: Light blue with the OAS seal in colour in the centre.

Books of Reference

Publications of the OAS General Secretariat include:

Charter of the Organization of American States. 1948.—*As Amended by the Protocol of Buenos Aires in 1967*
Americas. Illustrated monthly, from 1949. (Spanish, Portuguese and English edition)
Organization of American States, a Handbook. Rev. ed. 1977
Organization of American States. Directory. Quarterly, from 1951
Report on the Tenth Inter-American Conference, Caracas 1954. 1955
Inter-American Review of Bibliography. Quarterly, from 1951
Annual Report of the Secretary-General
Status of Inter-American Treaties and Conventions. Annual
The Alliance for Progress: The Charter of Punta del Este. 1962
Human Rights in the American States. 1960
Report of Inter-American Commission on Human Rights. From 1970

Publications on Latin America (*see also* the bibliographical notes appended to each country):

Revenue, Expenditure and Public Debts of the Latin American Republics. Division of Financial Information, US Department of Commerce. Annual
Fortnightly [from July 1960 also *Quarterly*] *Review of Business and Economic Conditions in South*

and Central America. Bank of London and South America. London, 1935–66; restyled *B.O.L.S.A. Review*, from Jan. 1967
Boundaries of the Latin American Republics: An Annotated List of Documents, 1493–1943. Department of State, Office of the Geographer. Washington, 1944
Latin America: An Introduction to the Basic Books in English. 2nd. ed. Hispanic & Luso-Brazilian Councils, London, 1966
Baerresen, D. W., and others, *Latin American Trade Patterns*. Washington, D.C., 1965
Bailey, H. M., and Nasatir, A. P., *Latin America: The Development of its Civilization*. London, 1960
Burgin, M. (ed.), *Handbook of Latin American Studies*. Gainesville, Fla., 1935 ff.
Calvert, P., *Latin America: Internal Conflict and International Peace*. London, 1969
Davies, H. (ed.), *The South American Handbook*. London, 1924 to date
Ferguson, J. M., *Latin America: The Balance of Race Redressed*. OUP, 1961
Hirschman, Albert O., *Latin American Issues:* [11] *Essays and Comments*. New York, 1961
Humphreys, R. A., *Latin American History: A guide to the Literature in English*. London, 1958
James, P. E., *Latin America*. 3rd ed. New York, 1959
Karnes, T. L., *The Future of Union: Central America 1824–1960*. Univ. of N. Carolina, Chapel Hill, 1961
Munro, D. G., *The Latin American Republics; A History*. London, 1961
Nehemkis, P., *Latin America: Myth and Reality*. New York, 1964
Pendle, G., *A History of Latin America*. Rev. ed. Harmondsworth, 1967
Plaza, G., *The Organization of American States: Instrument for Hemispheric Development*. Washington, 1969.—*Latin America Today and Tomorrow*. Washington, 1971
Steward, J. H. (ed.), *Handbook of the South American Indian*. 7 vols. Washington, 1946–59
Szulc, T., *Winds of Revolution*. New York, 1965
Thomas, A. V. W. and A. J., *The Organization of American States*. Southern Methodist Univ. Press, 1963
Ureña, P. H., *A Concise History of Latin American Culture*. London, 1966
Worcester, D. E., and Schaeffer, W. G., *The Growth and Culture of Latin America*. OUP, 1956

LATIN AMERICAN ECONOMIC GROUPINGS

The Economic Commission for Latin America, an organ of the United Nations, with headquarters in Santiago, Chile, has facilitated the co-operation of two groups of countries concerning production, tariffs and trade.

Latin American Free Trade Association was concluded in Montevideo on 18 Feb. 1961 by Argentina, Brazil, Chile, Mexico, Paraguay, Peru and Uruguay. Colombia (3 Oct. 1961), Ecuador (20 Oct. 1961) and Venezuela (1 Sept. 1966) have joined the ALALC/LAFTA Treaty. The permanent secretariat is at Montevideo, where the 17th conference took place 8–25 Nov. 1977.

Central American Common Market (ODECA). On 13 Dec. 1960, at Managua, El Salvador, Guatemala, Honduras and Nicaragua concluded a general treaty on Central American integration; a protocol on the equalization of import duties and charges; and an agreement establishing the Central American Bank for Economic Integration. Costa Rica acceded in 1962 and in Sept. 1963 ratified the charter of the Banco Centroamericano de Integración Económica (in Tegucigalpa), whose capital was thereupon increased to US$20m.

The San Salvador Charter, signed on 14 Dec. 1962, expanded these provisions, envisaging permanent political, economic, educational, defence, etc., councils. The permanent secretariat is at Guatemala City.

Total intra-ODECA trade increased from US$8·6m. in 1960 to US$176m. in 1966. Total USA investments in the area are about $400m.

The Andean Group (*Grupo Andino*). On 26 May 1969 an agreement was signed by Bolivia, Chile, Colombia, Ecuador and Peru creating the Andean Group. Venezuela was initially actively involved but did not sign the agreement. The Group signed a further agreement on 31 Dec. 1970 on common regulations controlling foreign investments. Under the Cartagena Agreement of 1975 the development of an integrated petrochemical industry in each of the member countries was established.

Sistema Económico Latinoamericano (SELA) was created by 25 countries (not including USA) meeting at Panama, 17 Oct. 1975. Its Permanent Secretary is Jaime Moncayo, former Finance Minister of Ecuador. It held an 'extraordinary' technical meeting at Caracas, 5 Jan. 1976, to prepare for other activities, such as UNCTAD, at Nairobi in May 1976.

British Bulletin of Publications on Latin America, the West Indies, Portugal and Spain. London, from June 1949 (half-yearly)
Hispanic and Luso-Brazilian Councils, Portuguese and Spanish Dictionaries. London, 1971
Instruments of Economic Integration in Latin America and the Caribbean. New York, 1975
Libre Comercio. Revista oficial de la Associación de Empresarios participantes de la ALALC. Montevideo, from June 1964 (monthly)
Committee on Latin America (COLA), *Latin American Economic and Social Serials.* London, 1969
Dell, S., *A Latin American Common Market.* OUP, 1966
Einaudi, L., R. (ed.), *Beyond Cuba: Latin America Takes Charge of its Future.* New York, 1974
Furtado, C., *Economic Development of Latin America.* London, 1970
Griffin, K., *Financing Development of Latin America.* London, 1971
Jaguaribe, H., *Political Development: A General Theory and a Latin American Case Study.* New York, 1973
Milenky, E. S., *The Politics of Regional Organization in Latin America. The Latin American Free Trade Association.* New York, 1973
Morawetz, D., *The Andean Group: A Case Study in Economic Integration Among Developing Countries.* MIT Press, 1974
Sánchez-Albornoz, N., *The Population of Latin America: A History.* Univ. of Calif. Press, 1974
UN Economic Commission for Latin America. *The Latin America Economy.* Washington. Annual
van Niekerk, A. E., *Populism and Political Development in Latin America.* Rotterdam Univ. Press, 1974

CARIBBEAN COMMUNITY (CARICOM)

Establishment and Functions. The Treaty establishing the Caribbean Community, including the Caribbean Common Market, and the Agreement establishing the Common External Tariff for the Caribbean Common Market, was signed by the Prime Ministers of Barbados, Guyana, Jamaica and Trinidad and Tobago at Chaguaramas, Trinidad, on 4 July 1973, and entered into force on 1 Aug. 1973. Six less developed countries of CARIFTA signed the Treaty of Chaguaramas on 17 April 1974. They were Belize, Dominica, Grenada, St Lucia, St Vincent and Montserrat, and the Treaty came into effect for those countries on 1 May 1974. Antigua acceded to Membership on 4 July 1974 and on 26 July the Associated State of St Kitts–Nevis–Anguilla signed the Treaty of Chaguaramas in Kingston, Jamaica and became a member of the Caribbean Community.

The Caribbean Community has 3 areas of activity: economic integration (that is, the Caribbean Common Market which replaces CARIFTA); co-operation in non-economic areas and the operation of certain common services; and co-ordination of foreign policies of independent member states.

The Caribbean Common Market provides for the establishment of a Common External Tariff, a common protective policy and the progressive co-ordination of external trade policies; the adoption of a scheme for the harmonization of fiscal incentives to industry; double taxation arrangements among member countries; the co-ordination of economic policies and development planning; and a special regime for the less developed countries of the community.

Membership: Antigua, Barbados, Belize, Dominica, Grenada, Guyana, Jamaica, Montserrat, St Kitts–Nevis–Anguilla, St Lucia, St Vincent and Trinidad and Tobago.

Structure: The *Heads of Government Conference* is the principal organ of the Community, and its primary responsibility is to determine the policy of the Community. It is the final authority of the Community and the Common Market, and for the conclusion of treaties and relationships between the Community and international organizations and States. It is responsible for financial arrangements for meeting the expenses of the Community.

The *Common Market Council* is the principal organ of the Common Market and shall consist of a Minister of Government designated by each member state. Decisions in both the Conference and the Council are in the main taken on the basis of unanimity.

The *Secretariat*, successor to the Commonwealth Caribbean Regional Secretariat, is the principal administrative organ of the Community and of the Common Market. The Secretary-General is appointed by the Conference on the recommendation of the Council for a term not exceeding 5 years and may be reappointed. The Secretary-General shall act in that capacity in all meetings of the Conference, the Council, and of the institutions of the Community.

Institutions of the Community, established by the Heads of Government Conference, are: Conference of Ministers responsible for Health; Standing Committees of Ministers responsible for Education, Industry, Labour, Foreign Affairs, Finance, Agriculture, and Mines, respectively.

Associate Institutions: East Caribbean Common Market Council of Ministers; West Indies Associated States Council of Ministers; Caribbean Development Bank; Caribbean Examinations Council; Caribbean Investment Corporation; Council of Legal Education; Caribbean Meteorological Council; Regional Transport Council; University of the West Indies; University of Guyana.

Acting Secretary-General: Joseph A. Tyndall.
Headquarters: Bank of Guyana Building, P.O. Box 607, Georgetown, Guyana.

The language of the Community is English.

THE ARAB LEAGUE

Origin. The formation of the League of Arab States in 1945 was largely inspired by the Arab awakening of the 19th century. This movement sought to re-create and reintegrate the Arab community which, though for 400 years a part of the Ottoman Empire, had preserved its identity as a separate national group held together by memories of a common past, a common religion and a common language, as well as by the consciousness of being part of a common cultural heritage. The leaders of the Arab movement in the 19th century and of the Arab revolt against Turkey in the First World War sought to achieve these aims through secession from the Ottoman Empire into a united and independent Arab state comprising all the Arab countries in Asia. However the 1919 peace settlement divided the Arab world in Asia (with the exception of Saudi Arabia and the Yemen) into British and French spheres of influence and established in them a number of separate states and administrations (Syria, Lebanon, Iraq, Jordan and Palestine) under temporary mandatory control.

By 1943, however, 7 of these countries had substantially achieved their independence. An Arab conference therefore met in Alexandria in the autumn of 1944; it formulated the 'Alexandria Protocol', which delineated the outlines of the Arab League. It was found that neither a unitary state nor a federation could be achieved, but only a league of sovereign states. A covenant, establishing such a league, was signed in Cairo on 22 March 1945 by the representatives of Egypt, Iraq, Saudi Arabia, Syria, Lebanon, Jordan and Yemen. Membership, in 1976, also included Algeria, Bahrain, Kuwait, Libya, Mauritania, Morocco, Oman, Qatar, Somalia, Sudan, Tunisia, the United Arab Emirates, and Yemen Peoples Democratic Republic.

Organization. The machinery of the League consists of a Council, a number of Special Committees and a Permanent Secretariat. On the Council each state has one vote. The Council may meet in any of the Arab capitals. Its functions include mediation in any dispute between any of the League states or a League state and a country outside the League. The Council has a Political Committee consisting of the Foreign Ministers of the Arab states.

The Permanent Secretariat of the League, under a Secretary-General (who enjoys, along with his senior colleagues, full diplomatic status), has its seat in Cairo.

The League considers itself a regional organization within the framework of the United Nations at which its secretary-general is an observer.

Secretary-General: Mahmoud Riad (Egypt).

Flag: Dark green with the seal of the Arab League in white in the centre.

Arab Common Market. The Arab Common Market came into operation on 1 Jan. 1965. The agreement, reached in April 1964 and open to all the Arab League states, has been signed by Iraq, Jordan, Syria and Egypt. The agreement provides for the abolition of customs duties on agricultural products and natural resources within 5 years, by reducing tariffs at an annual rate of 20%. Customs duties on industrial products are to be reduced by 10% annually. The agreement also provides for the free movement of capital and labour between member countries, the establishment of common external tariffs, the co-ordination of economical development and the framing of a common foreign economic policy.

Books of Reference

Atlas of the Arab World and the Middle East. London and New York, 1960
Oxford Regional Economic Atlas: The Middle East and North Africa. OUP, 1960
Glubb, Sir John, *Britain and the Arabs.* London, 1956
Gomaa, A. M., *The Foundation of the League of Arab States.* London, 1977
Macdonald, R. W., *The League of Arab States.* Princeton Univ. Press, 1965

EAST AFRICAN COMMUNITY

Organization. On 9 Dec. 1961, with the achievement of full independence by Tanganyika, the East Africa High Commission, which had, since 1947, been administering services of an inter-territorial nature for Kenya, Uganda and Tanganyika, was re-organized under the name of the East African Common Services Organization. On 6 June 1967 the heads of state of Kenya, Tanzania and Uganda signed a treaty in Kampala, which transformed and expanded the EACSO into the East African Community. This was inaugurated on 1 Dec. 1967. The Treaty was under review in 1978 and in 1977 Kenya stated that it was withdrawing from membership.

The Community has its headquarters in Arusha, Tanzania. The Community Headquarters consists of: Finance and Administration Secretariat; Common Market and Economic Affairs Secretariat; Communications, Research and Social Services Secretariat. Office of the Secretary-General and the E.A. Legislative Assembly. Chambers of the Council to the Community. Office of the Auditor-General.

Secretary-General: E. M. I. Mtei.

Flag: Horizontally dark green over light blue, with across the centre 7 unequal stripes of white, black, green, yellow, green, red, white; in the canton 3 red stars.

There are 5 councils: the Common Market Council, the Communications Council, the Economic Consultative and Planning Council, the Finance Council, and the Research and Social Council. Each of these consists of the 3 East African Ministers plus a varying number of national Ministers (one from each country in the Finance Council, 3 from each country in the other Councils).

To legislate for all Community matters there is an East African Legislative Assembly, with 9 members appointed from each country, together with the East African Ministers and Deputy Ministers, the Secretary-General, the Counsel to the Community and a Chairman.

The 4 Corporations within the Community, that is, the E.A. Railways Corporation; the E.A. Harbours Corporation; the E.A. Posts and Telecommunications

Corporation; and the E.A. Airways Corporation, conduct their business according to commercial principles, and are controlled by a Board of Directors.

The treaty also includes a transfer tax system to protect from undue competition young industries in the less-developed member countries in the common market.

The E.A. Development Bank established under the Treaty, gives financial and technical aid to industries within the Community.

Currency. Tanzania introduced its own currency on 14 June 1966, Uganda on 14 Aug. 1966 and Kenya on 14 Sept. 1966 and later replaced the coins of the East African Currency Board by their own issues. The standard coin is the East African shilling of 100 cents (20 shillings = 1 East African £). The paper currency in general use consists, of 5, 10, 20, 50 and 100-shilling notes.

Communications. See map of the roads, railways, ports and airports in THE STATESMAN'S YEAR-BOOK, 1964–65.

Revenue, 1975, from railways, inland waterways and road services, Sh.755·2m.; from harbours, Sh.775·7m. Expenditure (excluding contribution to renewals fund), 1975, on railways, Sh.934·5m.; on harbours, Sh.524·5m.

Roads. Road services operate in Uganda over approximately 370 miles connecting Kampala with Masindi, and Pakwach, the railhead on the Nile with Arua. Road services in Tanzania over approximately 2,000 miles serve the Southern Highlands from the Central (Dar es Salaam–Kigoma) line. A railway link between the Tanga and Central lines, completed in 1963, replaces the road services north of the Central line, with the exception of the Arusha–Dodoma passenger service.

Railways. The railways comprise 3,663 route miles of single metre-gauge track. Main lines: Mombasa–Kasese, 1,036 miles; Dar es Salaam–Kigoma, 779 miles; Tanga–Moshi–Arusha, 272 miles. Principal branch lines: Nakuru–Kisumu, 131 miles; Nairobi–Nanyuki, 145 miles; Tororo–Pakwach, 313 miles; Vol–Kahe, 94 miles; Tabora–Mwanza, 236 miles; Mnyusi–Ruvu, 117 miles. Minor branch lines: Gilgil–Thomson's Falls, 48 miles: Rongai–Solai, 27 miles; Leseru–Kitale, 41 miles; Busembatia–Jinja *via* Mbulamuti, 93 miles; Kisumu–Butere, 43 miles; Port Bell–Kampala, 6 miles: Kilosa–Mikumi, 44 miles; Kaliua–Mpanda, 131 miles; Konza–Magadi, 91 miles. The 3 ft 6 in. gauge Tan–Zam railway linking Dar es Salaam with Kapiri Mposhi, in Zambia, was opened in Oct. 1975. Its administration is entirely separate from that of East African Railways.

In 1971, 5,912,611 tons of goods and 5·99m. passengers were carried by the railway.

Shipping. The principal harbours are: Mombasa (Kilindini) in Kenya; Tanga, Dar es Salaam and Mtwara in Tanzania. Kilindini has 17 deep-water berths, bulk oil jetty and lighterage quays. There are 11 deep-water berths at Dar es Salaam and 2 at Mtwara.

Steamer services are operated on lakes Victoria and Tanganyika.

Aviation. East African Airways in 1975 had a revenue of Sh.734·1m. showing a net profit of Sh.36·7m. Total expenditure amounted to Sh.697·4m. Passengers carried in 1975 amounted to 705,282, representing an increase of 8·3% over 1974. The load factor was 52·4% which was slightly below that achieved in 1974. The E.A. directorate of civil aviation, a common service and member of ICAO, is responsible for the safety of all civil aircraft in the E.A. flight information region. In Dec. 1976 it was recommended that East African Airways should be dissolved.

Posts and Telecommunications. The East African Posts and Telecommunications Corporation operates as a self-contained service with its own capital account. Capital assets (1974), Sh.1,018·38m. The net revenue earned during 1974 was Sh.65,329,620m. On 31 Dec. 1974 there were 1,291 post offices. East African External Communications Ltd operate the overseas telegraph and telephone services and a radio-telephone service.

Books of Reference

Statistical Information: The East African Statistical Department is responsible for the collection, analysis and publication of economic statistics relating to East Africa. The department was set up originally as the Statistical Section of the Conference of the East African Governors in 1943 and is situated in Nairobi, Kenya (P.O. Box 30462).

Statistics relating to the individual territories are the responsibility of the appropriate government departments, as follows: TANZANIA: The Government Statistician, Central Statistical Bureau, P.O. Box 796, Dar es Salaam.—UGANDA: The Government Statistician, Ministry of Planning and Economic Development, P.O. Box 13, Entebbe.—KENYA: The Chief Statistician, Ministry of Economic Planning and Development, P.O. Box 30266, Nairobi.

The East African Statistical Department issues a quarterly Economic and Statistical Review, and each territorial office an annual statistical abstract, in addition to other economic and statistical reports.

Annual Reports and Accounts, 1972. E.A. Harbours Corp.
Annual Report and Accounts, 1972. E.A. Posts and Telecommunications Corp. Kampala, 1969
Hill, M. F., *Permanent Way: The Story of the Kenya and Uganda Railway.* E.A. Railways and Harbours, 1950
Russell, E. W., *The Natural Resources of East Africa.* Nairobi, 1962

ORGANIZATION OF AFRICAN UNITY

On 25 May 1963 the heads of state or government of 30 African countries, at a conference in Addis Ababa, signed a charter establishing an 'Organization of African Unity' (*Organisation de l'Unité Africaine*).

Its chief objects are the furtherance of African unity and solidarity; the co-ordination of the political, economic, cultural, health, scientific and defence policies and the elimination of colonialism in Africa.

The organs of the Organization are: (1) the conference of the heads of state or government; (2) the council of foreign ministers; (3) the general secretariat; (4) a commission of mediation, conciliation and arbitration. Arabic, French and English are recognized as official languages.

Chairman: President Omar Bongo (Gabon).

Headquarters: Addis Ababa.

Flag: Horizontally green, white, green, with the white fimbriated yellow, and the seal of the OAU in the centre.

DANUBE COMMISSION

The Danube Commission was constituted in 1949 based on the Convention regarding the regime of navigation on the Danube, which was signed in Belgrade on 18 Aug. 1948. The Belgrade Convention reaffirmed that navigation on the Danube from Ulm to the Black Sea, with access to the sea by the Sulina Canal, is equally free and open to the nationals, merchant shipping and merchandise of all states as to harbour and navigation fees as well as conditions of merchant navigation.

The Danube Commission is composed of representatives from the countries on the Danube (1 for each of these countries), namely, Austria, Bulgaria, Hungary, Romania, Czechoslovakia, USSR and Yugoslavia. Since 1957, representatives of the Ministry of Transport from the Federal Republic of Germany have attended the meetings of the Commission as guests of the Secretariat.

The responsibilities of the Danube Commission are to check that the provisions of the Convention are carried out, to establish a uniform buoying system on all the Danube's navigable waterways and to establish the basic regulations for navigation on the river. The Commission co-ordinates the regulations for river, customs and sanitation control as well as the hydrometeorological service and collects statistical data concerning navigation on the Danube.

The Danube Commission enjoys legal status. It has its own seal and flag. The members of the Commission and elected officers enjoy diplomatic immunity. The Commission's official buildings, archives and documents are inviolable. French and Russian are the official languages of the Commission.

Since 1954 the headquarters of the Commission have been in Budapest.

Flag: Blue, with a red strip fimbriated white along the bottom edge, and the initials of the Commission within a wreath in the canton—Latin letters on obverse Cyrillic on reverse.

Books of Reference

Danube Commission's publications include: *Summary Records and Documents Adopted by the Sessions of the Danube Commission. Rules of Procedure of the Danube Commission. Basic Regulations for Navigation on the Danube. Reports on the Maintenance of the Navigability of the Danube. Guidebook for Sailors. Hydrological Yearbooks. Statistical Yearbooks. Mileage Chart of the Danube. Ice Control on the Danube. Collection of Internal Laws Concerning Navigation on the Danube. Collection of International Agreements Relating to Navigation on the Danube. Radio-Codes for Navigation on the Danube.*

PART II

COUNTRIES OF THE WORLD

A–Z

AFGHÁNISTÁN

Capital: Kábul
Population: 19·58m. (1976)
GNP per capita: US$160 (1976)

Doulat i Jumhouri ye Afghánistán

HISTORY. A military *coup* on 17 July 1973 overthrew the monarchy of King Záhir Shàh. The *coup* was led by the King's cousin and brother-in-law Mohammad Daoud who declared a Republic. King Záhir abdicated on 24 Aug. 1973. This was followed by a *coup* on 27 April 1978 in which President Daoud was killed.

AREA AND POPULATION. Afghánistán is situated between parallels 29° and 38° 35′ N. lat., and 60° 50′ and 71° 50′ E. long., with a long narrow strip extending to 75° E. long. (Wákhán). For the boundaries, *see* THE STATESMAN'S YEAR-BOOK, 1925, pp. 654–55.

A new boundary agreement with the Soviet Union was signed in Moscow in June 1946; a joint commission completed the demarcation in Sept. 1948.

A border treaty with China was signed in 1963; the frontier was demarcated in 1964.

The area is 250,000 sq. miles (657,500 sq. km). Population, according to the (1976) Afghan estimate, is 19·58m., of which some 2·5m. are nomadic tribes. Birth rate (1970) 39 per 1,000 live births; death rate 16 per 1,000.

Estimate (1976), Kábul 377,715 (metropolitan area, 587,643). Estimates of population of other municipalities are: Kandahár, 115,000; Herát, 62,000; Gardez, 46,000; Jalálábád, 44,000; Mazár-i-Sharif, 40,000.

The main ethnic group are the Pashtuns. Other ethnic groups include the Tajiks, the Hazaras, the Turkomans and the Uzbeks.

CONSTITUTION AND GOVERNMENT. The 1964 Constitution was abolished by Presidential decree in 1973 and on 14 Feb. 1977 a new Constitution was adopted by the *Loya-Jirgah* (Grand Assembly). The military leaders of the *coup* with some senior civilians form the 'Central Committee of the Republic', a body of uncertain membership and responsibilities which approved the ministerial appointments announced on 1 Aug. 1973. Ministers appointed after the 1978 *coup* were as follows:

President: Nur Muhammad Tarakki.

Vice-President and Deputy Prime Minister: Babrak Karmal. *Deputy Prime Minister responsible for Foreign Affairs:* Hafizullah Amir.

National flag: Three horizontal stripes of black, red, green, with the green of double width; in the canton the national emblem in gold.

The official languages are Pushtu and Dari (Persian).

DEFENCE

Army. The Army is based on selective conscription with a regular cadre of officers and n.c.o.s. An agreed figure of conscripts is chosen in each province under local arrangements. A proportion of conscripts is drafted into the Labour Corps (employed mainly on public works). Call-up begins at the age of 20, and is for 2 years (1 year for conscript officers). Reserve liability is up to the age of 42. There is a reserve of officers.

The peace-time strength of the Army is about 90,000. Reserves, 150,000. It is organized in 3 armoured and 10 infantry divisions. Equipment is almost entirely Russian and includes T-54 and T-34 tanks and surface-to-air missiles. Transport is mainly mechanized.

The Army has the following training establishments: a military academy (formed 1932), a school for each principal arm, a technical school, an n.c.o.s' school and a military high school (Kábul), which takes boys from the age of 10, and from which the regular element in the armed forces is mainly drawn. Selected officers receive training abroad, chiefly in USSR but also in India; a few go to USA, France and Egypt.

Air Force. The Air Force, which is Russian-equipped, has about 260 aircraft and 10,000 officers and men. There are 2 squadrons of Su-7 attack aircraft, 3 squadrons of supersonic MiG-21 interceptors (about 50 aircraft), 5 squadrons of MiG-17s (about 80 aircraft), 3 bomber squadrons each with about 10 twin-jet Il-28s, a transport wing with about 20 piston-engined An-2s and Il-14s, 30 Mi-8 and Mi-4 helicopters and 1 or 2 turboprop Il-18s, and Yak-11, Yak-18 and MiG-15UTI trainers. The main fighter station is Bagram, with facilities for the largest jet airliners and bombers. A Russian-built bomber station was completed at Shindand in 1963. There is a training station at Mazar-i-Sharif and an air academy at Sherpur with about 400 cadets. Large numbers of 'Guideline' surface-to-air missiles are operational in Afghánistán.

Gendarmerie. The *gendarmerie*, about 30,000 strong, is administered by the Ministry of the Interior.

INTERNATIONAL RELATIONS

Membership. Afghánistán is a member of UN and of the Colombo Plan.

ECONOMY

Planning. The first two 5-year plans ran 1956–61 and 1962–67. The third plan (1967–72) envisaged expenditures of Afs. 33,000m. (compared with actual expenditures of 25,000m. during the second plan), but was never approved by Parliament. It was later tacitly abandoned, although some of the projects mentioned in the plan were implemented. The Minister of Planning then prepared a series of 1-year rolling plans but abandoned these in favour of a third 7-year plan which was in preparation in 1976.

Budget. The revenue and expenditure for years ending 20 March (in 1m. afgháni):

	1970	*1971*	*1972*	*1973*	*1974*
Revenue	6,796	6,269	6,751	7,622	7,017
Expenditure	7,419	8,175	7,149	8,295	6,531

Currency. The monetary system is on the silver standard. The unit is the *afgháni*, weighing 10 grammes of silver 0·900 fine, which is subdivided into 100 *puls*. Rates of exchange fluctuate round Afs. 77 = £1; Afs. 43 = US$1.

Banking. The Afghan State Bank (*Da Afghánistán Bánk*) is the largest of the 3 main banks and also undertakes the functions of a central bank, holding the exclusive right of note issue. Total assets of the 3 main banks on 21 Sept. 1967 were: Da Afghánistán Bánk, Afs. 28,074·4m.; Pashtany Tejaraty Bánk, Afs. 1,070·46m.; Bánk-i-Milli, Afs. 1,410·29m.

Weights and Measures. Weights and measures used in Kábul are: Weights: 1 *khurd* = 0·244 lb.; 1 *pao* = 0·974 lb.; 1 *charak* = 3·896 lb.; 1 *sere* = 16 lb.; 1 *kharwár* = 1,280 lb. or 16 maunds of 80 lb. each. Long measure: 1 yard or *gaz* = 40 in. The metric system is in common use by the bigger cloth merchants in Kábul. Square measures: 1 *jaríb* = 60 × 60 kábuli yd or $\frac{1}{2}$ acre; 1 *kulbá* = 40 jaríbs (area in which $2\frac{1}{2}$ kharwárs of seed can be sown); 1 jaríb yd = 29 in.

Local weights and measures are in use at Kandahár, Herát and Jaláálábád.

ENERGY AND NATURAL RESOURCES

Minerals. Mineral resources are scattered and little developed. Coal is mined at Karkar in Pul-i-Khumri, Ishpushta near Doshi, north of Kábul and Dara-i-Suf south of Mazar (total production, 1967–68, 151,000 tonnes). Natural gas is found in northern Afghánistán around Shiberghan and Sar-i-Pol; this is now being piped to the USSR, and 57,700m. cu. metres are to be supplied by 1985. Rich, but as yet unexploited, deposits of iron ore exist in the Hajigak hills about 100 miles west of Kábul; beryllium has been found in the Kunar valley and barite in Bamian province. Other deposits include gold; silver (now unexploited, in the Panjshir valley); lapis lazuli (in Badakhshán); asbestos; mica, sulphur (near Maimana); chrome (in the Logar valley and near Herát); and copper (in the north).

Agriculture. Although the greater part of Afghánistán is more or less mountainous and a good deal of the country is too dry and rocky for successful cultivation, there are many fertile plains and valleys, which, with the assistance of irrigation from small rivers or wells, yield very satisfactory crops of fruit, vegetables and cereals. It is estimated that there are 14m. hectares of cultivable land in the country, of which 7,844,000 hectares are being cultivated (5·34m. hectares of this being irrigated land). Afghánistán is virtually self-supporting in foodstuffs (including wheat in 1973), apart from sugar. The castor-oil plant, madder and the asafœtida plant abound. Fruit forms a staple food (with bread) of many people throughout the year, both in the fresh and preserved state, and in the latter condition is exported in great quantities. The fat-tailed sheep furnish the principal meat diet, and the grease of the tail is a substitute for butter. Wool (annual production, about 10,000 tonnes, of which about 7,000 tonnes are exported) and skins provide material for warm apparel and one of the more important articles of export. Persian lambskins (Karakuls) are one of the chief exports.

Cotton production, 1975–76, was estimated at 140,000 tonnes; wheat, 2·75m.; barley, 380,000; maize, 770,000; rice, 420,000.

Livestock (1976): Cattle, 3·68m.; horses, 370,000; sheep, 18m.; goats, 2·35m.; poultry, 10m.

INDUSTRY AND TRADE

Industry. At Kábul there are factories for the manufacture of cotton and woollen textiles, leather, boots, marble-ware, furniture, glass, bicycles, prefabricated houses and plastics. A large machine shop has been constructed and equipped by the Russians, with a capability of manufacturing motor spares. There is a wool factory and there are several cotton-ginning plants; a small cotton factory at Jabal-us-Seráj and a larger one at Pul-i-Khumri. A cotton-seed oil extraction plant has been built in Lashkargah by a British firm which also has a contract for the construction of 4 factories in the north which became operative in 1972. Germans have built and equipped a large modern cotton textile factory at Gulbahar, and another has been built and equipped by the Chinese at Bagram. A large cotton plant has recently been completed in the north at Balkh.

An ordnance factory manufactures arms and ammunition, boots and clothing, etc. for the Army. There is a beet sugar plant at Baghlan (equipped with British machinery) and a fruit-canning factory in Kandahár. Hydro-electric plants have been constructed at Sarobi, Nangarhár, Naghlu, Mahipár, Pul-i-Khumri and Kandahár; more hydro and thermal plants are under construction.

Government agencies, such as the Ministry of Mines and Industries and the Ministry of Commerce, are actively engaged in the establishment of new industrial enterprises, many of which are assisted by long-term foreign loans. Industries include hydro-electric projects, cement, coalmining, cotton textiles, small vehicle assembly plants, fruit canning, carpet making, leather tanning, footwear manufacture, sugar manufacture, preparation of hides and skins, and building. Most of these are relatively small and, with the exception of hides and skins, carpets and fruits, do not meet domestic requirements. The Government encourages foreign investment in Afghan industries; a new domestic and foreign productive investment law was introduced in 1967, under which about 100 new industries have been established. A new foreign and domestic private investment law was introduced in 1974 for the encouragement of local industries but the conditions were not as attractive as the early law. The law states that foreign ownership should be limited to a maximum of 49%. The Ministry of Planning is responsible for general policy and for co-ordinating the establishment of new industries.

Commerce. Trade is supervised by the Government through the Ministries of Commerce and Finance and the Da Afghánistán Bánk. The Association of Afghan Chambers of Commerce works in close liaison with the Ministry of Commerce. Afghánistán follows liberal trading policies so far as the balance-of-payments position will allow. The Government monopoly controls the import of petrol and oil, sugar, cigarettes and tobacco, motor vehicles and consignment goods from bilateral trading countries. Bilateral trade agreements exist between Afghánistán and the USSR, Czechoslovakia, Poland, China, India, Canada, Iran and Pakistan. These agreements are reviewed annually. Transit agreements have been reached with Pakistan (Karachi being the most important port for the transit of Afghan imports and exports), the USSR, Turkey and Iran.

In the year ended 20 March 1975 Afghan imports (c.i.f.), including loan and grant imports, totalled Afs. 9,406m. and exports (f.o.b) Afs 7,801m.

Afghánistán's largest customers during this period were USSR, India, UK, Pakistan, USA, Czechoslovakia and Federal Republic of Germany, and the largest suppliers were USSR, Japan, India, USA, Federal Republic of Germany, UK and Pakistan. Main export commodities were karakul skins (US$13·1m.), raw cotton (US$5·6m.), dried fruit and nuts (US$19·5m.), fresh fruit (US$8·9m.) and natural gas (US$12·1m.). Main items imported were petroleum products (US$3·6m.), textiles (US$9·3m.), tea (US$9·3m.).

Total trade between Afghánistán and UK (in £1,000 sterling, British Department of Trade returns):

	1973	*1974*	*1975*	*1976*	*1977*
Imports to UK	11,592	12,887	8,645	18,508	21,865
Exports and re-exports from UK	2,905	3,345	4,541	7,577	11,427

Tourism. In 1974 over 96,000 tourists visited the country.

COMMUNICATIONS

Roads. There were in 1978 over 2,500 km of asphalted road. The Americans have asphalted the Kandahár–Chaman and Kábul–Torkham roads. The Russians have constructed a road and tunnel through the Salang pass (over 11,000 ft) which was opened in Sept. 1964 and cuts 120 miles off the old road from Kábul to the north; they have continued this road to Kunduz and Sherkhan Bandar (Qizil Qala) on the Oxus. In addition, the Americans in 1966 completed the road between Kábul and Kandahár and the Russians have constructed a concrete road betwen Kandahár and Herát. In 1968 the Americans completed an asphalt road from Herát to the Iranian frontier at Islam Qala. With Soviet assistance a metalled road from Pul-i-Khumri to Mazar-i-Sharif was completed in 1969 and Mazar-i-Sharif to Shiberghan in 1971.

Railways. There are no railways in the country. Government approval has been given to plans drawn up by French consultants for a 1,815 km network of 1,435 mm gauge linking Kábul with Kandahár and Herát, connecting with the Iranian and Pakistani networks.

Aviation. On 29 June 1956 Afghánistán signed an agreement with the USA for the development of civil aviation, including the construction of the international airport at Kandahár, comprising a loan of $5m. and a grant of $9·56m. Kábul airport has been expanded with Russian assistance. New runways at Kábul and Kandahár airports have been completed. Provincial all-weather airports have been constructed at Herát, Qunduz, Jalálábád and Mazar.

Ariana Afghan Airlines (a national airline) operates regular services to Tehran, Istanbul, Frankfurt, Rome, London, New Delhi, Tashkent and Moscow.

Bakhtar Afghan Airlines (the domestic national airline) began operations on 8 Feb. 1968 and regularly serves the main internal airfields and the remoter airfields at Bamian, Chakcharan, Lashkargah, Faizabad, Khost, Maimana, Neemroz and Taleqan.

Shipping. There are practically no navigable rivers in Afghánistán, and timber is the only article of commerce conveyed by water, floated down the Kunar and Kábul rivers from Chitral on rafts. A port has been built at Qizil Qala on the Oxus; barge traffic is increasing on the Oxus. Three river ports on the Amu Darya have been built at Sherkhan Bandar, Tashguzar and Hayratan, linked by road to Kábul.

Post and Broadcasting. Telephones, installed in most of the large towns, numbered 20,960 in 1972. There is telegraphic communication between all the larger towns and between Kábul and Kandahár and Peshawar and Chaman. A wireless installation connects Kábul with Europe, Bombay, the Far East, America and other parts of the world. Kábul Radio broadcasts in Pushtu, Persian, Urdu, English, French, Russian and German. The first TV colour transmissions in Kábul are due in mid-1978. The telecommunication system is being expanded slowly, mainly with German assistance.

JUSTICE, RELIGION, EDUCATION AND WELFARE

Justice. Until 1965 Afghánistán was ruled on the basis of Shariat or Islamic law.

Religion. The predominant religion is Islam, mostly of the Sunni sect, though there is a minority of about 1m. Shiah Moslems.

Education. The number of elementary schools is rapidly increasing, but secondary schools exist only in Kábul and provincial capitals. Both elementary and secondary education are free. There are several teacher-training institutions in Kábul and a few elsewhere; UNESCO is supporting a 30-year expansion programme. Technical, art, commercial and medical schools exist for higher education. The Kábul University was founded in 1932 and has 9 faculties (medicine, science, agriculture, engineering, law and political science, letters, economics, theology, pharmacology). The University of Nangarhar in Jalálábád, founded in 1963, has at present only a faculty of medicine. A Polytechnic in Kábul was completed in 1968.

In 1963 the Prime Minister stated that illiteracy was over 90%.

Health. In 1971 there were 971 doctors and 2,479 hospital beds.

DIPLOMATIC REPRESENTATIVES

OF AFGHÁNISTÁN IN GREAT BRITAIN
(31 Prince's Gate, London, SW7 1QQ)

Ambassador: Abdul Rhaman Pazhwak (accredited 1 March 1977).

OF GREAT BRITAIN IN AFGHÁNISTÁN
(Karte Parwan, Kábul)

Ambassador: K. R. Crook.

OF AFGHÁNISTÁN IN THE USA (2341 Wyoming Ave., NW, Washington, D.C., 20008)

Ambassador: Dr Abdul Wahid Karim.

OF THE USA IN AFGHÁNISTÁN
(Wazir Akbar Khan Mina, Kábul)

Ambassador: Theodore L. Eliot, Jr.

OF AFGHÁNISTÁN TO THE UNITED NATIONS

Ambassador: (Vacant).

Books of Reference

Afghanistan Republic Annual, 1976
Dupree, L., *Afghanistan*. Princeton Univ. Press, 1974
Fraser-Tytler, Sir W. K., *Afghanistan*. Rev. ed. OUP, 1967

Gilbertson, G. W., *Pakkhto Idiom Dictionary*. 2 vols. London, 1932
Gregorian, V., *The Emergence of Modern Afghanistan*. Stamford, 1970
Griffiths, J. C., *Afghanistan*. New York, 1967
Humlum, J., *La Géographie de l'Afghanistan*. Copenhagen, 1959
Klimburg, M., *Afghanistan*. Vienna, 1966
Mele, P. F., *Afghanistan*. Florence, 1966
Newell, R. S., *The Politics of Afghanistan*. Cornell Univ. Press, 1972
Wilber, D. N. (ed.), *Afghanistan*. 2nd ed. New Haven, 1962.—(ed.), *Afghanistan, A Bibliography*. 2nd ed. New Haven, 1963

ALBANIA

Republika Popullore Socialiste e Shqipërisë

Capital: Tirana
Population: 2·43m. (1976)
GNP per capita: US$540 (1976)

HISTORY. After the death of George Kastriota—known as Skanderbeg—in 1467 Albania passed under Turkish suzerainty until 1912. Albanian independence was proclaimed at Vlonë on 28 Nov. 1912, and the London conference of ambassadors decided upon its frontiers and nominated as its ruler Prince William of Wied, who arrived at Durrës (Durazzo) on 7 March 1914, but on 3 Sept. 1914 left the country, which fell into a state of anarchy. By the secret Pact of London of 26 April 1915 provision was made for the partition of Albania; but this arrangement was repudiated on 3 June 1917, when the Italian C.-in-C. in Albania proclaimed at Gjirokastër the independence of Albania. In Jan. 1925 a republic was proclaimed and on 1 Sept. 1928 a monarchy. Ahmed Beg Zogu, President since 31 Jan. 1925, reigned as King Zog till April 1939, when, on the occupation of the country by the Italians, he fled to England. After the liberation he was deposed *in absentia* on 2 Jan. 1946. During the years 1939–44 the country was overrun by Italians and Germans. The official Albanian date of the liberation is 29 Nov. 1944.

On 10 Nov. 1945 the British, US and USSR Governments recognized the Provisional Government under Gen. Enver Hoxha, on the understanding that it would hold free elections. The elections of 2 Dec. 1945 resulted in a Communist-controlled assembly, which on 11 Jan. 1946 proclaimed Albania a republic.

In 1946 Great Britain and the USA broke off relations with Albania and vetoed its admission to the United Nations. Albania was finally admitted on 15 Dec. 1955, the USA abstaining from voting.

Because of Albania's Stalinist and pro-Chinese attitudes diplomatic relations with USSR were broken off in 1961. In 1977 Albania terminated its special relationship with China by making ideological attacks on the post-Mao Chinese leadership's foreign policy.

AREA AND POPULATION. The area of the country is 28,748 sq. km (11,101 sq. miles). By the peace treaty Italy restored the island of Sazan (Saseno) to Albania. At the census of 2 Oct. 1960 the population was 1,626,315 (51·3% males, 30·9% urban). Population in 1976, 2,432,000; 34% urban; density, 80 per sq. km). The capital is Tirana (1976 population in 1,000), (192·3); other large towns are Shkodër (Shkodra, Scutari) (62·5), Durrës (Durrsi, Durazzo) (61), Vlorë (Vlona, Vlonë, Vlora, Valona) (58·4), Korçë (Korça, Koritza) (50·7). Other towns (1971): Elbasan (48), Berat (26), Fier (23), Kavajë (18), Lushnjë (18), Gjirokastër (Argyrocastro) (17), Qytet Stalin (formerly Kuçovë) (14).

There is a small Greek minority (1977 estimate, 50,000).

Vital statistics, 1975 (per 1,000): Births, 29·4; deaths, 6·7; marriages (1974), 7·9; divorces (1969), 0·8. Natural increase, 22·6. Life expectancy in 1974 was 69 years.

The country is administratively divided into 26 districts (*rreth*, pl. *rrethët*) (*see* map in THE STATESMAN'S YEAR-BOOK, 1962. N.B. The district of Ersekë has been renamed Kolonjë). Districts are subdivided into *lokaliteteve*.

Districts	*Area (sq. km)*	*Population (in 1,000) (1973)*	*Districts*	*Area (sq. km)*	*Population (in 1,000) (1973)*
Berat	1,026	124·3	Fier	1,191	171·5
Dibrë	1,569	106·8	Gramsh	695	29·4
Durrës	859	182·4	Gjirokastër	1,137	53·5
Elbasan	1,466	154·7	Kolonjë	805	19·2

Districts	Area (sq. km)	Population (in 1,000) (1973)	Districts	Area (sq. km)	Population (in 1,000) (1973)
Korcë	2,181	175·4	Pogradec	725	49·3
Krujë	607	75·6	Pukë	969	32·8
Kukës	1,564	71·4	Sarandë	1,097	66·5
Lezhë	479	40·5	Skrapar	775	30·8
Librazhd	1,013	48·5	Shkodër	2,528	178·5
Lushnjë	712	94·1	Tepelenë	817	37·8
Mat	1,028	53·5	Tirana	1,222	272·0
Mirditë	698	29·4	Tropojë	1,043	30·5
Përmet	930	31·7	Vlorë	1,609	133·5

The districts are for the greater part named after their capitals; exceptions: Tropojë, chief town, Bajram Curri; Mat, Burrel; Mirditë, Rrëshen; Skrapar, Çorovodë.

The Albanian language is divided into two dialects—Gheg, north of the river Shkumbi, and Tosk in the south. Many places therefore have two forms of name: Vlonë (Gheg), Vlorë (Tosk), etc., and many are known also by an Italian name, *e.g.*, Valona. Since 1945 the official language has been based on Tosk.

CONSTITUTION AND GOVERNMENT. The political structure derived from the Constitution of 14 March 1946 as amended in 1950, 1955, 1960 and 1963. In Dec. 1976 a new Constitution was adopted, by which Albania became a 'Socialist People's Republic'. The supreme legislative body is the single-chamber People's Assembly of 270 deputies, which meets twice a year, and delegates its day-to-day functions to a Presidium composed of a chairman, 3 deputy chairmen, a secretary and 10 members. Election to the People's Assembly is by universal suffrage (at 18) every 4 years.

In the elections of 6 Oct. 1974 it was claimed that 1,248,528 of the electorate of 1,248,530 voted for the 270 candidates on the single list of the Albanian Democratic Front. (There were 2 spoiled papers.)

The government consists of a prime minister (Chairman of the Council of Ministers), 4 deputy prime ministers, 13 ministers and the chairman of the State Planning Commission.

Effective rule is exercised by the Albanian Labour (*i.e.*, Communist) Party, founded 8 Nov. 1941, whose governing body is the Politburo.

In 1971 the Party had 68,858 full and 18,127 candidate members (women, 22%; workers, 36%; peasants, 30%; professional and managerial, 34%).

Titular Head of State: Chairman of the Presidium of the People's Assembly: Haxhi Lleshi, elected July 1953. In March 1977 the chief Party and Government posts were filled as follows: The 12 full members of the Politburo:

First Secretary of the Central Committee of the Party: Enver Hoxha. *Chairman of the Council of Ministers and Minister of Defence:* Mehmet Shehu. Adil Çarçani,[1] Spiro Koleka, Kadri Hazbiu (*Minister of the Interior*), Pali Miska,[2] Haki Toska (*Minister of Finance*); Manush Myftiu, Mrs Rita Marko. *Secretaries of the Central Committee:* Hysni Kapo, Ramiz Alia, Prokop Muran. Candidate members: Lenka Cuko; Simon Stefani; Pilo Peristeri. Not in the Politburo: *Foreign Minister:* Nesti Nase. *Minister of Foreign Trade:* Nedin Hoxha. *Minister of Agriculture:* Mrs Themi Thomal. *Chairman, State Planning Commission:* Petro Dode.

[1] First Deputy Chairman, Council of Ministers. [2] Deputy Chairman, Council of Ministers.

Local Government is carried out by People's Councils at village, *lokalitet*, town and district level. Councillors are elected for 3 years.

National flag: Red, with a black double-headed eagle and a red, gold-edged 5-pointed star above it. *Mercantile flag:* red, black, red (horizontal) with a red yellow-edged star in the centre.

National anthem: Rreth Flamurit te per bashkuar (The flag that united us in the struggle).

DEFENCE. Albania withdrew from the Warsaw Pact in 1968 in protest against the invasion of Czechoslovakia.

Ranks were abolished in March 1966 and political commissars re-introduced.

Army. Army service is 2 years. Strength in 1976, 36,000 in 8 infantry and 1 armoured brigade, with about 100 T-34, T-54 and T-59 tanks. Security police ('SSSh') had a strength of 13,000, divided into 4 security battalions, and 5 battalions of frontier-guards.

Navy. The Navy consists of 4 submarines, 2 fleet minesweepers, 4 patrol vessels, 6 inshore minesweepers, 42 torpedo boats, 4 fast gunboats, 10 minesweeping boats, 1 degaussing ship, 4 oilers and 20 small auxiliaries and service tenders. Navy personnel (1977) 3,000 officers and ratings, including 300 coastal frontier guards. Service for ratings is 3 years. There are naval bases at Durrës and Vlorë.

Air Force. The Air Force, controlled by the Army, has about 100 combat aircraft and 8,000 officers and men. There are about 6 fighter squadrons of Chinese-built MiG-21s and MiG-19s and 2 ground attack squadrons of MiG-15s and MiG-17s. Transport and training types include 4 Il-14s, Mi-4 helicopters, Yak-11s, Yak-18s and MiG-15UTIs.

INTERNATIONAL RELATIONS

Membership. Albania is a member of UN.

Aid. In 1975 trade and aid agreements up to 1980 were signed with China.

ECONOMY

Planning. For the first four 5-year plans *see* THE STATESMAN'S YEAR-BOOK, 1976–77. The fifth covered 1971–75, during which it is claimed that national income increased by 38%, industrial production by 52% and agricultural production by 33%. The sixth 5-year plan is running from 1976 to 1980. Target increases: national income, 38%; industrial production, 41%; agricultural, 37%. Emphasis is laid on industrial expansion, especially in the oil, mining and chemical industries. Some economic leaders were sacked in 1975 and 1976, and it was stated that economic policy is founded on 'the revolutionary principle of self-reliance'.

Budget. Budget figures for 1976: Revenue, 7,300m. leks (6,400m. leks from enterprises and agricultural co-operatives); expenditure, 6,300m. leks (national economy, 4,500m. leks).

Currency. The monetary unit is the *lek* of 100 *qintars.* It replaced the Albanian gold franc (*franc ar*) in July 1947. In Aug. 1965 a new *lek* was introduced: 10 old *leks* = 1 new *lek*. In 1976, US$1 = 4·14 *leks* (official rate), 10·25 *leks* (tourist rate).

Banking. The National Bank of Albania was founded in 1925 with Italian aid. In 1970 savings deposits amounted to 572m. leks. In 1970 the Agricultural Bank was set up as a credit institution for agricultural co-operatives.

Weights and Measures. The metric system is in force.

ENERGY AND NATURAL RESOURCES

Electricity. There are 6 hydro-electric power plants operational and one under construction. Electric power production in 1973 was 1,603m. kwh., of which 1,127m. was hydro-electric.

Oil. The oil industry is being rapidly expanded. Output in 1973: Crude, 2,107,000 tonnes; refined, 1,596,000 tonnes. Refining capacity in 1970 was over 1m. tonnes. Oil is produced chiefly at Qytet Stalin which a pipeline connects to the port of Vlonë. Natural gas is extracted.

Minerals. The mineral wealth of Albania is considerable but is only recently being developed. In 1971 there were 8 coal, 7 chromium (1974 output 502,300 tonnes) and 6 copper mines. Ferro-nickel ores are mined and output is increasing. In 1969 extensive coal deposits were discovered at Valias, near Tirana. There is no bituminous coal. Salt is extracted near Vlonë and bitumen mined at Selenicë. Production in tonnes (1973): Chrome ore, 611,000; copper ore, 435,000; ferro-nickel ore, 384,000; brown coal, 811,000; phosphate, 110,000; nitrogenous fertilizer, 106,000; bitumen (1964), 242,000; cement (1965), 133,600.

Agriculture. The country for the greater part is rugged, wild and mountainous, the exceptions being along the Adriatic littoral and the Korçë (Koritza) Basin, which are fertile. In 1973 a programme of land reclamation and anti-erosion measures was instituted. In 1970 arable land comprised 599,000 hectares and pasture 623,000 hectares. 283,200 hectares were irrigated.

Land is held by the State (largely forests and non-agricultural), state farms (33 in 1970 holding 100,700 hectares of arable land) and co-operatives (459 in 1973 holding 500,900 hectares). Co-operatives are divided into 'advanced' and 'ordinary'. A pension plan for collective farmers was enacted in 1972. Tractors in 1973 numbered 13,936 (in 15-h.p. units).

The yield of the main crops in 1973 was (in 1,000 tonnes): Grain, 572; cotton, 20; tobacco, 15; potatoes, 81; sugar-beet, 162; maize, 255; fruits, 53; rice, 15; beans, 11; sunflower seeds, 19; grapes, 65.

Livestock, 1964: Cattle, 427,100; sheep, 1,682,200; goats, 1,199,300; pigs, 146,600; (1963) horses and mules, 122,100; poultry, 1·69m.

Forestry. 47% of the territory of Albania is forest land, of which 38% is oak forest, 26% elm and 18% pine and birch. Timber reserves reach 44·5m. cu. metres. In 1967 forests covered 1,242,100 hectares; 6,784 hectares were afforested, 10,000 hectares improved in 1967.

Fisheries. The catch in 1964 was 3,600 tonnes.

INDUSTRY AND TRADE

Industry. All industry is nationalized down to the smallest workshop. Output is small, and the principal industries are agricultural product processing, textiles, oil products and cement. Chemical and engineering industries are being built up. The metallurgical combine at Elbasan is being extended.

Labour. In 1973, 462,900 persons worked in the socialist sector of the national economy, of whom 34·7% were employed in industry. In 1976, 46% of wage-earners were women. Minimum wages may not fall below one-third of maximum. Monthly salaries over 900 leks were reduced in 1976 by 14–20%, in a campaign against 'degenerate elements and privileged groups'.

Commerce. In 1969, 70% of Albania's trade was with China and 25% with other communist countries (nothing to USSR). Italy is Albania's biggest non-communist trading partner. The establishment of joint companies with, and the acceptance of credits from, capitalist firms is forbidden by the Albanian constitution.

Exports include crude oil, bitumen, chrome ore, copper wire, tobacco, fruit and vegetables. In 1971, 56% of exports were finished or semi-finished goods.

Total trade between Albania and UK (British Department of Trade returns, in £1,000 sterling):

	1972	*1973*	*1974*	*1975*	*1976*	*1977*
Imports to UK	12	58	135	117	40	61
Exports and re-exports from UK	47	35	845	644	127	222

COMMUNICATIONS

Roads. There were, in 1960, 3,100 km of roads suitable for motor traffic. The mountain districts of the north are still mostly inaccessible for wheeled vehicles, and communications are still by means of pack ponies or donkeys. Registered motor vehicles in 1960: Cars, 1,900; lorries and buses, 3,400. Road traffic carried 8·6m. passengers in 1970; goods carried, 34m. tonnes.

Railways. All railways, except the short narrow-gauge line Selenicë–Vlonë, have been built since 1947. Total length, in 1975, was 201 km. They comprise the lines Durrës–Tirana, Durrës–Kavajë–Pegin–Elbasan, Vlonë–Memaliaj and Vlonë–Milot. In 1974 a railway was opened from Elbasan to the iron mines at Pishkash and a line is under construction from Fier to Balkh. Goods carried in 1970 amounted to 2,324,000 tonnes; passengers, 6m.

Aviation. There are regular scheduled flights from Tirana (Rinas Airport) to

Belgrade, Bucharest, Budapest, East Berlin and Peking. Olympic Airways operate a weekly flight from Athens to Tirana.

Shipping. The ports are Shëngjin (San Giovanni di Medua), Durrës (Durazzo), Vlonë (Valona) and Sarandë (Santi Quaranta). 567,000 tonnes of freight were carried in 1970. Albania has ocean-going ships capable of reaching Shanghai.

Post and Broadcasting. Number of post and telegraph offices (1970), 292; telephones (1963), 10,150. There are 17 broadcasting stations, including Tirana and Korçë. Radio Tirana operates a foreign service in 18 languages and since 1971 has relayed parts of the Radio Peking service for Europe. Radio receiving sets (1973), 170,000; television sets, 3,000. Regular television broadcasting began in 1971.

Cinemas and Theatres (1973). There were 105 cinemas with an attendance of 7·9m. and 27 theatres with an attendance of 1·6m.

Newspapers. In 1972 there were 22 newspapers with an annual circulation of 59m. The Party paper is *Zëri i Popullit* (Voice of the People) (daily circulation, 95,000).

JUSTICE, RELIGION, EDUCATION AND WELFARE

Justice is administered by People's Courts. Judges of the Supreme Court are elected by the People's Assembly for 4-year terms. The Office of the Procurator-General oversees the administration of justice. In 1966 the Ministry of Justice was incorporated into the Ministry of the Interior. In 1968 tribunals were set up in towns and villages to try minor crimes which had previously been dealt with by courts.

Religion. Albania is constitutionally an atheist state. In 1967 the Government closed all mosques and churches. For details of the situation before 1967 *see* THE STATESMAN'S YEAR-BOOK, 1969–70. The population had been mainly Moslem.

Education. Primary education is free and compulsory in 8-year schools from 7 to 15 years. Secondary education is available in 12-year (general), technical–professional or lower vocational schools. Periods of productive work and military service are intermingled with full-time education. There were, in 1973–74, 1,615 kindergartens with 52,899 pupils and 2,790 teachers; 1,470 primary schools with 569,600 pupils and 22,686 teachers; 39 secondary schools with 32,900 pupils; 116 technical–professional schools with 69,700 pupils (the last two categories had 3,990 teachers taken together); and (in 1969–70) 36 institutes of higher education with 36,525 students and 941 teachers, including a university in Tirana (founded 1957), a polytechnic, an agricultural college, a medical school, 5 teachers' training colleges and an institute of science. In 1969–70 there were 382 teachers and 12,783 full-time students at Tirana University. An Albanian Academy was founded in 1973.

Health. Medical services are free. In 1970 there were 15,100 hospital beds. In 1974 there was 1 doctor per 850 inhabitants.

DIPLOMATIC REPRESENTATIVE

OF ALBANIA TO THE UNITED NATIONS

Ambassador: Abdi Baleta.

Books of Reference

Vjetari Statistikor (Statistical Yearbook). Tirana, irregular, from 1959
30 vjet Shqipëri socialiste (statistical handbook). Tirana, 1974
History of the Labor Party of Albania. Tirana, 1971
Frasheri, K., *History of Albania.* Tirana, 1965
Logoreci, A., *The Albanians: Europe's Forgotten Survivors.* London, 1977
Mann, S. E., *An Historical Albanian–English Dictionary.* London 1948.—*An English–Albanian Dictionary.* CUP, 1957
Marmullaku, R., *Albania and the Albanians.* London, 1975
Pano, N. C., *The People's Republic of Albania.* Baltimore, 1968
Pollo, S. *et. al.*, *Histoire de l'Albanie des Origines à Nos Jours.* Roanne, 1974

ALGERIA

Capital: Algiers
Population: 17m. (1977)
GNP per capita: US$990 (1976)

El Djemhouria El Djazaïria Eddemokratia Echaabia—République Algérienne Démocratique et Populaire

HISTORY. On 1 Nov. 1954 the National Liberation Front (FLN) went over to open warfare against the French administration and armed forces.

On 19 Sept. 1958 a free Algerian government was formed in Cairo with Ferhat Abbas as provisional President of the National Assembly.

A referendum was held in Metropolitan France and Algeria on 6–8 Jan. 1961 to decide on Algerian self-determination as proposed by President de Gaulle. His proposals were approved by 15,200,073 against 4,996,474 votes in Metropolitan France, and by 1,749,969 against 767,546 votes in Algeria. In Metropolitan France 20·2m. out of 27·2m registered voters went to the polls; in Algeria 2·5m. out of 4·5m. registered voters.

Long delayed by the terrorism, in Metropolitan France as well as Algeria, of a secret organization (OAS) led by anti-Gaullist officers, a cease-fire agreement was concluded between the French Government and the representatives of the Algerian Nationalists on 18 March 1962; but OAS terror acts continued for some months.

On 7 April a provisional executive of 12 members was set up, under the chairmanship of Abderrhaman Farès.

On 8 April 1962 a referendum in Metropolitan France approved the Algerian settlement with 17,505,473 (90·7%) against 1,794,553 (9·3%) and 1,102,477 invalid votes; 6,580,772 voters abstained. On 1 July 1962, 5,975,581 Algerians voted in favour of, 16,534 against the settlement.

AREA AND POPULATION. Algeria (2,381,745 sq. km) is divided into 15 departments. Population (census 1966) 12,102,000; estimate (1977) 17m.

There are 31 departments: Adrar, Alger, Annaba, Batna, Bechar, Bejaia, Biskra, Blida, Bouira, Constantine, Djelfa, El Asnam, Guelma, Jijel, Laghouat, Mascara, Médéa, Mostaganem, Ouahran (Oran), Ouargla, Oum Bouaghi, Saida, Sétif, Sidi-Bel-Abbès, Skikda, Tamanrasset, Tébessa, Tiaret, Tizi-Ouzou, Tlemcen and M'Sila (Bou Saada).

The chief towns (estimates, 1974) are as follows: Algiers, 1,503,720; Oran, 485,139; Constantine, 350,183; Annaba, 313,174; Tizi-Ouzou, 223,702; Blida, 158,947; Sétif, 157,065; Sidi-Bel-Abbès, 151,148; Skikda, 127,968; Batna, 115,138; Tlemcen, 115,054; Al Asnam, 114,327; Boufarif, 109,234; Bejaia, 103,996; Médéa, 102,336; Mostaganem, 101,780.

CONSTITUTION AND GOVERNMENT. On 3 July 1962 President de Gaulle proclaimed Algeria independent and handed over sovereign power.

On 25 Sept. the National Assembly met and elected Ferhat Abbas President of the Assembly and Ben Bella President of the Council of Ministers.

A national referendum held on 15 Sept. 1963 elected Ben Bella, the only candidate, as President of the new Democratic People's Republic of Algeria.

The Government was overthrown by a junta of army officers which, on 19 June 1965, established a Revolutionary Council under Col. Houari Boumédienne.

Elections to the National People's Assembly took place on 25 Feb. 1977. This was the first election since the *coup* of 1965. The 261 members of the Assembly were elected for a 5-year term and 78·5% of the electorate voted.

President of the Republic, President of the Council of the Revolution, President of the Council of Ministers and Minister of Defence: Houari Boumédienne. (The President was elected for a further 6-year term in Dec. 1976.)

Foreign Affairs: Abdelaziz Bonteflika.

National flag: Vertically green and white, a red crescent and star over all in the centre.

The official language is Arabic, French being the principal foreign language.

DEFENCE

Army. The Army in 1977 had a strength of 67,000 men, organized in 1 armoured and 4 motorized brigades, 3 tank battalions, 1 parachute and 50 independent battalions. Equipment includes Soviet T-34 and T-54–55 tanks.

Navy. The Navy consists of 2 fleet minesweepers, 6 coastal escorts, 9 missile boats, 10 torpedo boats acquired from the USSR between 1963 and 1966, 1 torpedo recovery vessel, 1 survey ship, 2 fishery protection craft and 1 harbour tug. Naval personnel, 1977: 300 officers and cadets and 3,500 ratings.

The French naval base of Mers el Kebir was taken over by the Algerian army and navy in Feb. 1968.

Air Force. Five MiG-15 jet-fighters were delivered in 1962 as the nucleus of an Algerian Air Force. Since then many more aircraft of Soviet design have followed, and the Air Force now has about 175 combat aircraft and 4,000 personnel. Training and technical assistance are given by Egypt and the Soviet Union. There are 3 squadrons (each 12 aircraft) of supersonic MiG-21Fs, 4 squadrons (each 12–16 aircraft) of MiG-17 fighter-bombers, at least 1 squadron of Su-7 attack fighters, 2 squadrons (each nominally 10 aircraft) of Il-28 twin-jet bombers, 1 squadron of four-turboprop An-12 and Il-18 transports, 6 F.27 Friendship and 4 Beech King Air twin-turboprop transports, a wing of 4 Mi-6, 5 Mi-8, about 40 Mi-4, 5 Puma and 6 Hughes 269 helicopters, and training units equipped with Yak-11s, CM.170 Magister armed jet counter-insurgency/trainers (26), 3 Beech Queen Air twin-engine/instrument trainers, and MiG-15s and -15UTIs. Surface-to-air missile units have Soviet-built 'Guidelines'.

INTERNATIONAL RELATIONS

Membership. Algeria is a member of UN, OAU, the Arab League, OAPEC, OPEC and the Maghreb Organization.

ECONOMY

Planning. The second 4-year development plan (1974–77) envisaged investment of DA 110,000m. A third development plan (1978–81) is in preparation.

Currency. The Algerian *dinar* (DA) is at par with the new French franc. There are in circulation bank-notes of DA 5, 10, 50, 100 and 500 and coins of 1, 2, 5, 20 and 50 centimes and DA 1. Money in circulation in Dec. 1974, DA 23,431m.

Budget. The budget (including extraordinary budget) was as follows in calendar years (in 1m. DA):

	1971	*1972*	*1973*	*1974*	*1975*
Revenue	6,919	9,178	11,067	23,438	25,053
Expenditure	6,941	8,197	9,694	12,539	19,136

Banking. The Banque Centrale d'Algérie is the government emission bank. Other banks operating in Algeria are Banque National d'Algérie, Crédit Populaire d'Algérie, Banque Extérieure d'Algérie, Caisse Algérienne de Développement, Banque Algérienne de Développement.

Weights and Measures. The metric system is in use.

ENERGY AND NATURAL RESOURCES

Electricity. Production of energy in 1972 totalled 2,013m. kwh.

Oil. Two large oilfields went into production in 1957 around Edjélé and Hassi Messaoud and in 1959 at El Gassi. In 1960 about 200 wells were productive. Natural gas was discovered at Djebel Berga in 1954 and at Hassi-R'Mel in 1956. Oil pipelines from Edjélé to Skirra (Tunisia) and from Hassi Messaoud to Bougie, and a gas pipeline from Hassi Messaoud *via* Hassi-R'Mel to Mostaganem–Oran–Algiers, have been completed. Oil production in 1974, 79m. tonnes. Oil revenue in 1972, DA 3,200m. Production of natural gas in 1971 was 13,426m. cu. metres.

Minerals. Algeria possesses deposits of iron, zinc, lead, mercury, copper and antimony. Kaolin, marble and onyx, salt (110,000 tonnes in 1957) and coal are also found. Mineral output in 1972 (1,000 tonnes): Ferrous metals, 3,275; lead, 8·7; zinc, 30; iron pyrites, 27·4 (1971); phosphates, 489.

Agriculture. There exists a small area of highly fertile plains and valleys near the coast, mainly owned by self-management committees and some Europeans, which is cultivated scientifically, and where profitable returns are obtained from vineyards, cereals, etc. Self-management groups supplied 60% of revenue from agriculture in 1970, and held 80% of cultivated land. The greater part of Algeria is of limited value for agricultural purposes. In the northern portion the mountains are generally better adapted to grazing and forestry than agriculture, and a large portion of the native population is quite poor. In spite of the many excellent roads built by the Government, a considerable area of the mountainous region is without adequate means of communication and is accessible only with difficulty. There were an estimated 16·3m. hectares of agricultural land in 1970–71, of which 6·4m. hectares were arable; 292,000 hectares under vine and 35·3m. hectares pastures and brushlands.

The chief crops in 1971–72 were (in 1,000 tonnes): Wheat, 13,174; barley, 3,718; wine, 9,247; olive oil, 228; dates, 1,749.

Livestock, 1976: 156,000 horses, 644,000 mules and asses, 1,281,000 cattle, 8,886,000 sheep, 2·4m. goats and 157,000 camels.

Forestry. The greater part of the state forests are mere brushwood, but there are very large areas covered with cork-oak trees, Aleppo pine, evergreen oak and cedar. The dwarf-palm is grown on the plains, alfa on the table-land. Timber is cut for firewood, also for industrial purposes, for railway sleepers, telegraph poles, etc., and for bark for tanning. Considerable portions of the forest area are also leased for tillage, or for pasturage for cattle and sheep.

Fisheries. There are extensive fisheries for sardines, anchovies, sprats, tunny fish, etc., and also shellfish. In 1972, 557 boats and 3,391 fishermen were employed in fishing. Fish taken in 1972 amounted to 5,386 tonnes of white and shell fish and 22,952 tonnes of blue fish (sardines, anchovy, etc.).

INDUSTRY AND TRADE

Industry. The main industries are iron and steel and fertilizers.

Commerce. The foreign trade of Algeria was as follows (in DA 1m.):

	1973	*1974*	*1975*	*1976*
Imports	8,908	16,514	21,959	21,069
Exports	7,479	19,241	17,535	21,067

The value of petroleum exports almost trebled between 1973 and 1974 although the volume declined by 6% to 45m. tonnes. Crude oil and refined products accounted for 92% of exports in 1974. In 1972, 61·4% of imports and 57·8% of exports were with EEC, of which 30·2% and 23·3% were with France.

Total trade between UK and Algeria (British Department of Trade returns, in £1,000 sterling):

	1972	*1973*	*1974*	*1975*	*1976*	*1977*
Imports to UK	22,944	45,694	36,168	87,490	80,228	49,762
Exports and re-exports from UK	33,773	37,868	54,723	78,681	101,834	98,655

Tourism. In 1972 nearly 200,000 tourists visited Algeria.

COMMUNICATIONS

Roads. There were in 1970, 18,649 km of national highway. Work began in 1969 on the Algerian section (240 miles) of the Trans-Sahara highway. Motor vehicles in 1968 included 115,192 passenger cars and 68,000 commercial vehicles.

Railways. In 1976 there were 3,837 km of railway open for traffic, of which 2,657 km are of standard gauge (299 km electrified) and 1,180 km of narrow gauge. In 1974 the railways carried 7·9m. passengers and 3·7m. tonnes of freight.

Aviation. There are 65 airfields controlled by government and 135 owned by petroleum companies. Air Algeria serves the main Algerian cities, and an international network. Algeria is also served by Swissair, Royal Air Maroc, United Arab Airline, Tunis Air, SABENA, Aeroflot, Interflug, Alitalia and Air France. In 1971 the airports handled 1·4m. passengers and 6·5m. tonnes of freight.

Shipping. In 1970, 50m. tonnes of goods were handled at Algerian ports.

A state shipping line, Compagnie Nationale Algérienne de Navigation, was formed in Jan. 1964 and possesses 7 vessels and also charters others.

Post and Broadcasting. There were, in 1969, 862 post offices; number of telephones (1977), 266,470, of which 102,350 were in Algiers and 25,920 in Oran. In 1974 there were some 3·5m. radio receivers and 500,000 TV licences issued.

Post office savings accounts on 31 Dec. 1971 numbered 314,807, with a total balance of DA 12,000m.

Newspapers (1977). There were 4 daily newspapers, 1 in French and 3 in Arabic, with a combined circulation of 250,000.

JUSTICE, RELIGION, EDUCATION AND WELFARE

Justice. There are appeal courts at Algiers, Constantine and Oran; and in the *arrondissements* are 17 courts of first instance. There are also commercial courts and justices of the peace with extensive powers. Criminal justice is organized as in France. The Supreme Court is at the same time Council of State and High Court of Appeal.

Religion. The overwhelming part of the population are Moslems. The Roman Catholic Church has an archbishop and 2 bishops, with some 400 officiating clergymen. Jews number about 150,000. There are 13 Protestant pastors and 6 Jewish rabbis sharing in government grants.

Education. About 57% of children attended school in 1970. Primary schools had 3,614,000 pupils in 1977; secondary schools had 332,318 pupils including 105,239 girls. The University of Algiers had 60,000 students in 1977. A university in Oran opened in 1967 and others are now open at Constantine and Annaba. There are also university centres at Tlemcen, Tizi-Ouzou, Setif, Batna and Tiaret.

Four-year Plan expenditure on education (1973–77) is 9,947m. DA; with 587m. DA for training and technical institutes, this forms 12% of total Plan investment.

Health. There were in 1966 148 general and 13 specialized hospitals with together 42,722 beds (39,073 beds in 1969); in 1969 there were 1,700 doctors, 222 dentists, 265 pharmacists. There were 1,225 dispensaries and consulting rooms, 308 health centres and 49 specializing centres for tuberculosis, venereal disease and trachoma. There were 18 hospitals built between 1965 and 1969. National disease prevention campaigns are carried out mainly against tuberculosis (by BCG vaccination), trachoma, malnutrition and malaria.

DIPLOMATIC REPRESENTATIVES

OF ALGERIA IN GREAT BRITAIN
(6 Hyde Park Gate, London, SW7 5EW)

Ambassador: Lakhdar Brahimi.

OF GREAT BRITAIN IN ALGERIA (Résidence Casiopée,
7 Chemin des Glycines, Algiers)

Ambassador: R. S. Faber.

OF ALGERIA IN THE USA (2118 Kalorama Rd, NW, Washington, D.C., 20008)

Ambassador: Abdelaziz Maoui.

OF THE USA IN ALGERIA (4 Chemin Cheikh Bachir Brahimi, Algiers)

Ambassador: Ulric St. Clair Haynes, Jr.

OF ALGERIA TO THE UNITED NATIONS

Ambassador: (Vacant).

Books of Reference

Statistical Information: The Service de Statistique Générale (12, rue Bab-Azoun, Alger) publishes the annual *Statistique Générale de l'Algérie, Documents statistiques sur le commerce de Algérie* (from 1902). *Tableaux de l'économie algérienne* (1960).

Cornet, P., *Le Pétrole Saharien.* Paris, 1961
Gordon, D. C., *The Passing of French Algeria.* OUP, 1965
Horne, A., *A Savage War of Peace: Algeria 1954–1962.* London, 1977
Ministère de l'Information et de la Culture, *La Révolution Algérienne: Réalités et Perspectives,* Algiers, 1972.—*Dix années de réalisations 19 juin 1965–19 juin 1975.* Algiers, 1976.
L'Algérie en Chiffres. Algiers, 1972
Le Rumeur, G., *Le Sahara avant le pétrole.* Paris, 1961
Thé, B. de, *Essai de bibliographie du Sahara Français.* Paris, 1961
Verlaque, C., *Le Sahara pétrolier.* Paris, 1964
Verlet, B., *Sahara.* Paris, 1960
Verneuil, H., *Sahara.* Paris, 1960

ANDORRA

Capital: Andorra-la-Vielle
Population: 30,700 (1977)

Les Vallées d'Andorre—Valls d'Andorra

HISTORY AND CONSTITUTION. The political status of Andorra was regulated by the *Paréage* of 1278 which placed Andorra under the joint suzerainty of the Comte de Foix and of the Bishop of Urgel. The rights vested in the house of Foix passed by marriage to that of Béarn and, on the accession of Henri IV, to the French crown. The sovereignty is exercised jointly by the President of the French Republic and the Bishop of Urgel.

The co-princes are represented in Andorra by the '*Viguier français*' and the '*Viguier Episcopal*'. Each co-prince has set up a Permanent Delegation for Andorran affairs; the Prefect of the Eastern Pyrenees is the French Permanent Delegate.

The valleys pay every second year a due of 960 francs to France and 460 pesetas to the bishop.

A 'General Council of the Valleys' submits motions and proposals to the Permanent Delegations. Its 24 members are elected for 4 years; half of the council is renewed every 2 years.

The council nominates a First Syndic (*Syndic Procureur Général*) and a Second Syndic from outside its members.

National flag: Three vertical strips of blue, yellow, red, with the arms of Andorra in the centre.

AREA AND POPULATION. The co-principality of Andorra is situated in the eastern Pyrenees on the French–Spanish border. The country consists of gorges, narrow valleys and defiles, surrounded by high mountain peaks varying between 1,880 and 3,000 metres. Its maximum length is 30 km and its width 20 km; it has an area of 465 sq. km (190 sq. miles) and a population of (1977) 30,700, scattered in 6 villages.

Catalan is the spoken language.

ECONOMY

Currency. French and Spanish currency are both in use.

Tourism. Tourism is the main industry, and over 3m. people visited Andorra in 1974.

COMMUNICATIONS

Roads. A good road connects the Spanish and French frontiers by way of Sant Julià, Andorre-la-Vieille, les Escaldes, Encamp, Canillo and Soldeu: it crosses the Col d'Envalira (2,400 metres). Another road connects Andorre-la-Vieille with La Massana and Ordino. Motor vehicles (1974) 15,000.

Aviation. The nearest airport is at Barcelona.

Post and Broadcasting. Radio Andorra and Sud Radio are private commercial broadcasting companies. Number of receivers (1973), 6,000.

JUSTICE. Judicial power is exercised in civil matters in the first instance, according to the plaintiff's choice, by either the *Bayle Français* or the *Bayle Episcopal*, who are nominated by the respective co-princes. The judge of appeal is appointed alternately by each co-prince; the third instance (*Tercera Sala*) is either the supreme court of Andorra at Perpignan or the ecclesiastical court of the Bishop at Urgel.

Criminal justice is administered by the *Corts* consisting of the 2 Viguiers, the judge of appeal, 2 *rahonadors* elected by the general council of the valleys, a general attorney and a deputy attorney nominated for 5 years alternatively by each of the co-principalities, adjudicating several times a year. The accused may be assisted by a barrister.

RELIGION. The prevailing religious denomination is Roman Catholic.

Books of Reference

Brutails, *La Coutume d'Andorre*. Paris, 1904
Corts Peyret, *J., Geografia e Historia de Andorra*. Barcelona, 1945
Llobet, S., *El medio y la vida en Andorra*. Barcelona, 1947
Vidally Guitart, J. M., *Institutiones politicas y sociales de Andorra*. Madrid, 1949

ANGOLA

Capital: Luanda
Population: 5·67m. (1970)
GNP per capita: US$330 (1976)

HISTORY. Angola, with a coastline of over 1,000 miles, is separated from the Congo by the boundaries assigned by the convention of 12 May 1886; from Zaïre by those fixed by the convention of 22 July 1927; from Rhodesia in accordance with the convention of 11 June 1891, and from South West Africa in accordance with that of 30 Dec. 1886. The Congo region was discovered by the Portuguese in 1482, and the first settlers arrived there in 1491. Luanda was founded in 1575. It was taken by the Dutch in 1641 and occupied by them until 1648.

AREA AND POPULATION. Angola is bounded by Zaïre on the north and north-east, Zambia on the east, Botswana and South West Africa on the south and the Atlantic ocean on the west. The area is 1,246,700 sq. km (481,351 sq. miles). Angola is divided into 16 districts: Cabinda, Zaïre, Uíge, Luanda, Cuanza Norte, Cuanza Sul, Malange, Lunda, Benguela, Huamba, Bié, Moxico, Chuando-Cubango, Moçâmedes, Huíla and Cunene. The important towns are S. Paulo de Luanda (capital), Benguela, Moçâmedes, Lobito, Lubango, Malange and Huambo. The population at census, 1970, was 5,673,046, of whom 300,000 were white. There were (1978) about 40,000 whites in Angola.

CONSTITUTION AND GOVERNMENT. On 15 Jan. 1975 the 3 Angolan liberation groups signed an agreement under which Angola became independent on 11 Nov. 1975. Following the capture of most of the strategic towns in the north and south of Angola by the liberation movement, *Movimento Popular de Libertação de Angola* (MPLA), which was supported by the USSR, assumed effective military control of Angola by Feb. 1976. The People's Republic of Angola was proclaimed in Nov. 1975. The two retreating liberation movements, *Frente Nacional de Libertação de Angola* (FNLA) and *União Nacional para a Independêcia Total de Angola* (UNITA) announced that they would wage guerrilla warfare from the bush.

President: Dr Agostino Neto.

The Cabinet at 7 Jan. 1978 was as follows:

Prime Minister: Lopo Fortunato Ferreira do Nascimento.

First Deputy Prime Minister: José Eduardo dos Santos. *Second Deputy Prime Minister:* Cdr Carlos Rocha Dilolua. *Third Deputy Prime Minister:* Cdr Pedro de Castro dos Santos van Dunen. *Defence:* Cdr Iko Teles Carreira. *Foreign Affairs:* Paulo Teixeira Jorge. *Justice:* Dr Diogenes de Assis Boavida. *Education and Culture:* Ambrosio Lucoque. *Health:* Coelho da Cruz. *Finance:* Maj. Saidi Vieira Dias Mingas. *Internal Trade:* David Aires Machado. *External Trade:* Bemvindo Rafael Pitra. *Industry:* Maj. Alberto do Carmo Bent Ribeiro. *Transport:* Fernado Faustino Muteka. *Fisheries:* Antonio da Costa Lopes da Camera. *Housing and Construction:* Manuel Resende de Oliveira. *Agriculture:* Carlos Fernandes. *Labour and Social Security:* Nogueira Silva Saude.

Flag: Horizontally red over black, with a star and an arc of cogwheel crossed by a machete, all yellow over all in the centre.

DEFENCE

Army. The Army has 1 armed, 9 infantry, 1 commando and 1 air defence regiments. Total strength (1977): 30,000.

Navy. There are 13 patrol boats and 5 landing craft. Naval personnel in 1977: 700.

Air Force. The Angolan Republic Air Force (FAPA) was formed in 1976. Combat equipment is mainly of Soviet origin, comprising about 15 MiG-21 and 10 MiG-17 fighters and 3 MiG-15UTI two-seat trainers, supplemented possibly by 3 Fiat G.91R-4 fighter-bombers donated by Portugal at the time of 1975 withdrawal. FAPA also has at least 3 An-26 and 3 C-47 transports, 2 Turbo-Porter liaison aircraft and 20 Alouette III helicopters, plus a variety of obsolete combat aircraft, transports and trainers left in Angola by Portugal, some of which may be refurbished for use.

INTERNATIONAL RELATIONS

Membership. Angola is a member of UN and OAU.

Aid. About 3,500 Cuban technicians and workers were in Angola in 1977.

ECONOMY

Budget. In 1974 the budget envisaged an expenditure of 19,475,000 contos, and public debt, 9,066,000 contos.

Currency. The currency is the *kwanza* divided into 100 *lwei.*

Banking. Banking is under state control and the main bank is Banco National de Angola

Weights and Measures. The metric system is in force.

NATURAL RESOURCES

Oil. Total production 1974, 10m. tonnes (1976, 8m.)

Minerals. The country possesses valuable diamond deposits. Production of diamonds during 1973 totalled 2,124,719 carats (1974, 1·94m.; 1975, 750,000). Production (1973) of iron ore, 6,052,194 tonnes; salt, 96,717 tonnes.

Agriculture. The principal crops are coffee, maize, sugar, palm-oil and palm kernels. Other products are cotton, wheat, tobacco, cacao, sisal and wax. Livestock (1976): 3m. cattle, 200,000 sheep, 900,000 goats, 400,000 pigs.

COMMERCE. Imports 1973, 13,269m. (1974: 17,000m.) contos; exports, 1973, 19,158m. (1974: 34,000m.) contos. The chief imports are textiles, transport equipment, foodstuffs, pig-iron and steel; chief exports are coffee, diamonds, sisal, iron ore, fish, maize, crude oil, palm-oil. Coffee exports were valued at 5,162m. contos in 1973.

Total trade between Angola and UK for calendar years (British Department of Trade returns, in £1,000 sterling):

	1974	*1975*	*1976*	*1977*
Imports to UK	41,646	6,694	5,464	5,506
Exports and re-exports from UK	21,456	14,082	7,306	10,501

COMMUNICATIONS

Roads. There were, in 1973, 72,323 km of roads.

Railways. The length of railways open for traffic in 1972 was 3,049 km. The Benguela Railway runs from Lobito to the Zaïre border at Dilolo where it connects with the National Railways of Zaïre. Other lines link Luanda with Malange; Gunza with Gabela; and Moçâmedes with Menongue. In 1972 Angola's railways carried 2,495,000 passengers and 7,878,000 tonnes of freight.

Aviation. Regular air service is maintained by the Divisão de Transportes Aéreos from Luanda to: (South) Moçâmedes *via* Lobito and Sá da Bandeira, with connexions to Porto Alexandre and Lucira; (east) Vila Luso *via* Cela, Nova Lisboa and Silva Porto; (north) Pointe Noire (Congo) *via* Cabinda; and to Kinshasa; (east) Portugália *via* Malange and Henrique de Carvalho; (south) Vila Pereira d'Eça *via* Nova Lisboa, Lubango and Rocadas; Windhoek *via* Lubango.

Shipping. In 1973, 6,500 vessels of 16,256,322 net tons entered Angolan ports.

Post and Broadcasting. Angola is connected by cable with east, west and south African telegraph systems. There were, in 1973, 1,808 km of telegraph lines, 77 telephone stations (with 37,086 instruments), 162 telegraph stations and 31 wireless stations.

Emissora Oficial de Angola is the largest of the 18 stations operating on medium- and short-waves. *Emissora Oficial* transmits 3 programmes as well as operating 2 regional stations.

Four regional stations are under construction. Number of receivers (1974): 110,000.

Cinemas. There were, in 1972, 47 cinemas with a seating capacity of 35,142.

Newspaper. The national daily newspaper is *Jornal de Angola.*

RELIGION, EDUCATION AND WELFARE

Religion. Article 7 of the Constitution of the People's Republic of Angola states that: 'The People's Republic of Angola is a lay state, where there is a complete separation of religious institutions from the state. All religions will be respected and the State will give protection to churches and religious places and objects so long as they accept the laws of the state'.

There are considerable numbers of Christians, both Catholic and Protestant, but the majority of the population is animist.

Education. For primary education there were (1977) 25,000 primary school teachers with 1,026,291 pupils. There were 105,363 pupils at secondary level and 1,109 university students.

Health. In 1971 there were 523 doctors and 15,000 hospital beds.

DIPLOMATIC REPRESENTATIVES

The British Consul-General and his staff have been withdrawn. The British Government recognized the People's Republic of Angola on 18 Feb. 1976 and an ambassador will be appointed in 1978.

OF ANGOLA TO THE UNITED NATIONS

Ambassador: Elisio de Figueiredo.

Books of Reference

Anuário Estatístico de Angola. Luanda, from 1897
How to Invest in Angola. Luanda, 1963
Araújo, A. Correia de, *Aspectos do desenvolvimento económico e social de Angola.* Lisbon, 1964
Bahia dos Santos, F., *Angola.* Lisbon, 1954
Davidson, B., *Growing from Grass Roots.* London, 1974.—*In the Eye of the Storm.* London, 1972
Dias, G. de Sousa, *Os portugueses em Angola.* Lisbon, 1959
Egerton, F. C. C., *Angola in Perspective.* London, 1957
Wheeler, D. L., and Pélissier, R., *Angola.* London, 1971
Zirka, A. K., *Angola Libre? Paris, 1975*

ARGENTINA

República Argentina

Capital: Buenos Aires
Population: 25·06m. (1977)
GNP per capita: US$1,550 (1976)

HISTORY. In 1515 Juan Díaz de Solís discovered the Río de La Plata. In 1534 Pedro de Mendoza was sent by the King of Spain to take charge of the 'Gobernación y Capitanía de las tierras del Río de La Plata', and in Feb. 1536 he founded the city of the 'Puerto de Santa María del Buen Aire'. In 1810 the population rose against Spanish rule, and in 1816 Argentina proclaimed its independence. Civil wars and anarchy followed until, in 1853, stable government was established.

AREA AND POPULATION. The Argentine Republic is bounded in the north by Bolivia, in the north-east by Paraguay, in the east by Brazil, Uruguay and the Atlantic Ocean and the west by Chile. The republic consists of 22 provinces, 1 federal district, and the National Territories of Tierra del Fuego, the Antarctic and the South Atlantic Islands (census of 1960 and census of 1970) as follows:

Provinces	*Area: sq. km, 1960*	*Population: census, 1960 (1,000)*	*Population: census, 1970 (1,000)*	*Pop. per sq. km, 1965*
Litoral				
Federal Capital (Buenos Aires)	200	3,040	2,906	17,061·0
Buenos Aires (La Plata)	307,804	7,139	8,788	24·2
Corrientes	88,199	559	574	6·75
Entre Ríos (Paraná)	76,216	825	821	11·7
Chaco (Resistencia)	99,633	559	562	6·3
Santa Fé	133,007	1,928	2,122	15·7
Formosa	72,066	189	232	2·8
Misiones (Posadas)	29,801	415	447	14·9
Norte				
Jujuy	53,219	253	306	5·1
Salta	154,775	435	507	3·0
Santiago del Estero	135,254	489	507	3·9
Tucumán	22,524	818	781	39·2
Centro				
Córdoba	168,766	1,829	2,087	11·8
La Pampa (Santa Rosa)	143,440	161	169	1·2
San Luis	76,748	180	183	2·5
Andina				
Catamarca	99,818	179	172	1·9
La Rioja	92,331	133	137	1·6
Mendoza	150,839	869	979	6·25
San Juan	86,137	370	391	4·65
Neuquén	94,078	116	164	1·4
Patagonia				
Chubut (Rawson)	224,686	151	195	0·73
Río Negro (Viedma)	203,013	203	263	1·1
Santa Cruz (R. Gallegos)	243,943	55	83	0·16
Tierra del Fuego (Ushuaia)	20,912	7	14	0·38
Grand total	2,777,815[1]	20,900[2]	23,390	8·3

[1] Total area claimed was 2,808,602 sq. km (1,084,120 sq. miles).

[2] The official census including the 'Antarctic Sector', and stated to comprise the 'Malvinas' (Falklands), South Orcadas (Orkneys), South Georgias, South Sandwich Islands and the 'sovereign territories of Argentina in the Antarctic': population, 3,300.

Estimated registered voters, 31 Dec. 1966, were 6·37m. men and 6·31m. women; total, 12·68m. (1973 total, 14m.). In 1970 the urban population, *i.e.*, in communities of 2,000 or more inhabitants, was 72% of the total; 36% of the inhabitants lived in greater Buenos Aires; of the national total, 11,617,000 were men and 11,773,000 women; foreign born, 2,180,918. Estimated population, June 1974, 25·05m.

The population is overwhelmingly European in origin (principally from Italy and Spain) with little mixture with the aborigines. The dwindling Indian population is estimated at from 20,000 to 30,000. Immigration was, under the Perón Constitution, restricted to white persons, exception being made for the relatives of non-white persons (Japanese, etc.) already resident. An agreement signed in Buenos Aires on 19 Oct. 1964 provided for immigration of French subjects formerly resident in North Africa.

Movement of population:

	Births	*Deaths*	*Immigrants*	*Emigrants*
1964	496,256	193,141	905,644	878,385
1965	481,814	196,467	966,081	939,571
1966	479,396	194,450	967,700	959,200
1967	480,459	195,224	1,038,000	1,008,900
1968	...	...	1,136,900	1,116,400

In 1970 births were 20·9 (per 1,000 population); deaths, 8·4; migrations, 1·2.

The population of the capital, Buenos Aires (census 1970), was 2,972,453; and, in 1,000: Rosario, 807; Córdoba, 791; Mendoza, 471; La Plata, 391; Tucumán, 366; Santa Fé, 245; Bahía Blanca, 182; Paraná, 128.

Canals, S., *Poblaciones Indígenas de la Argentina.* Buenos Aires, 1953
Serrano, A., *Los Aborígenes Argentinos.* Buenos Aires, 1947
Censo nacional de poblacion, familias y viviendas—1970. National Institute of Statistics and Census. Buenos Aires, 1970

CONSTITUTION AND GOVERNMENT. Until 16 March 1949 the Constitution of the Argentine Republic was that of 1853, with modifications of 1860, 1866 and 1898. On the date mentioned a new constitution drafted by the Perón government and passed by the Constitutional Convention elected 5 Dec. 1948 came into force giving the Government great powers over the national economy. At a National Constituent Assembly held in Santa Fé Sept.–Nov. 1957 it was decided to revert to the 1853 constitution as amended up to 1898; thereafter the President and Vice-President were to be elected through electoral colleges by popular vote for 6-year terms. The President was not to be immediately re-elected. The Vice-President was to preside over the Senate. The President would be Commander-in-Chief of the Armed Services and would make appointments to all civil services and Judicial Offices. The President would be responsible with the Cabinet for the Executive. Both President and Vice-President must be Roman Catholic and of Argentine birth.

A law of 11 July 1975 provided that, should the Presidency become vacant, the president of the Senate should assume the office, but Congress should meet within 48 hours to choose a new president from among senators, deputies and provincial governors; he would serve the remainder of the interrupted term.

The National Congress consisted of a Senate and House of Deputies: the Senate with 2 representatives from the capital and each province (with a total of 46 seats), elected by popular vote for 9 years (one-third retiring every 3 years). The House of Deputies was to have 192 seats, each deputy being elected for 4 years and half the seats renewable each 2 years. The 2 Chambers meet annually from 30 Sept. to 2 May. Since 1912 voting has been free, secret and obligatory. Women were enfranchised on 9 Sept. 1947; beginning with the presidential election on 11 Nov. 1951, all women 18 years of age or older must vote. Equal suffrage was confirmed by a revisionary law of Aug. 1961.

The military leaders supported by the Navy and Air Force staged a coup d'état on 27 June 1966, and the temporary Revolutionary Junta of the Commanders-in-Chief of the three Armed Services deposed Dr Illia and his Government elected in 1963. A former Commander-in-Chief of the Army, Lieut.-Gen. Onganía, was appointed President and the Junta dissolved. The previous Constitution remained in force in so far as it was consistent with the statutes and objectives of the Revolution.

In Aug. 1967 a law was promulgated decreeing the registration of communists and excluding them from holding any public office, any position in employers' and workers' trade unions, and any teaching post in state and private schools.

The following is a list of Presidents from 1946 onwards:

Gen. Juan Domingo Perón. 4 June 1946–22 Sept. 1955. (Deposed.)
Gen. Eduardo Lonardi. 23 Sept.–13 Nov. 1955. (Deposed.)
Gen. Pedro Aramburu. 13 Nov. 1955–30 April 1958.
Dr Arturo Frondizi. 23 Feb. 1958–29 March 1962. (Deposed.)
Dr José Maria Guido. 29 March 1962–12 Oct. 1963.
Dr Arturo Illia. 12 Oct. 1963–June 1966. (Deposed.)
Gen. Juan Carlos Ongania. 29 June 1966–8 June 1970. (Deposed.)
Brig.-Gen. Robert Marcelo Levingston. 18 June 1970–22 March 1971. (Deposed.)
Gen. Alejandro Agustin Lanusse. 26 March 1971–May 1973.
Dr Hector Cámpora. 27 May 1973–13 July 1973.
Gen. Juan Domingo Perón. 12 Oct. 1973–1 July 1974.
Maria Estela (Isabel) Martinez Perón. 1 July 1974 (*a.i.* from 29 June 1974)–23 March 1976. (Deposed.)

On 24 March 1976 President Maria Estela Perón was deposed by a military junta consisting of Gen. Jorge Rafael Videla (who assumed the Presidency on 29 March), Adm. Emilio Massera and Brig. Orlando Agosti.

President of the Republic: Gen. Jorge Rafael Videla (re-appointed 1978).

The Secretaryships of State for War, Navy and Air Force have been assumed by the commanders-in-chief of the Services.

After the general election of 11 March 1973 the distribution of seats in the National Congress was: Frente Justicialista de Liberación (Fréjuli), 145; Union Civica Radical (UCR), 51; Alianza Popular Federalista, 20; Alianza Popular Revolucionaria, 12; others, 15.

National flag: Three horizontal stripes of light blue, white and light blue, with the gold Sun of May in the centre.

National anthem: Oid, mortales, el grito sagrado Libertad (words by V. López y Planes, 1813; tune by J. Blas Parera).

Local Government. From 1958 until the June 1966 Revolution, apart from the period March 1962 to Oct. 1963, the governors were elected for terms of either 3 or 4 years. The Provinces elected their own Legislature and have control over their own internal affairs. After the Revolution of June 1966 the governors were appointed by the President and are responsible to him.

Ravignani, Emilio, *Asambleas Constituyentes Argentinas*. 6 vols. Buenos Aires, 1939

DEFENCE

Army. The Army is a National Militia, service in which is compulsory for all citizens from their 20th to their 45th year. Naturalized citizens are exempt for a period of 10 years. For the first 10 years the men belong to the 'active' Army, or first line. After completing 10 years in the first line the men pass to the National Guard, and serve in it for another 10 years, finishing their service with 5 years in the Territorial Guard; the latter is mobilized only in case of war. The period of continuous service, or training in the ranks with the permanent forces, is for 1 year for the Army or Air Force, and 14 months for the Navy. The reservists can be called out for training periodically.

The territory of the republic is divided into 5 military districts for administrative purposes. The Army is organized in 4 army corps; it consists of 2 motorized and 2 infantry brigades, 3 mountain brigades, 1 airborne brigade, 2 mechanized brigades and 2 air defence regiments.

In 1976 the Army was 83,500 strong, of whom 60,000 were National Service men and the remainder, an officer corps of 5,000 and 15,000 n.c.o.s, all of whom were career regulars.

The trained reserve numbers about 250,000, of whom 200,000 belong to the National Guard and 50,000 to the Territorial Guard.

Navy. Principal ships of the Argentine Navy:

Completed	*Name*	*Standard displacement Tons*	*Armour Belt In.*	*Armour Guns In.*	*Principal armament*	*Torpedo tubes*	*Shaft horse-power*	*Speed Knots*
			Aircraft Carrier[1]					
1945	Veinicinco de Mayo[2]	15,892	—	—	21 aircraft (capacity): light A.A.	—	40,000	24·0
			Cruisers					
1939	General Belgrano[3]	10,800	4	3–5	15 6-in., 8 5-in.	—	100,000	32·5
1939	Nueve de Julio[3]	10,500	4	3–5	15 6-in., 8 5-in.	—	100,000	32·5

[1] The aircraft carrier *Independencia*, ex-*Warrior*, purchased from the UK in 1958 was withdrawn from service in 1971.

[2] Ex-*Karel Doorman*, purchased from the Netherlands, 1968, ex-*Venerable*, from UK, 1948.

[3] Ex-*Phoenix* and ex-*Bloise*, purchased from the USA in 1951. The cruiser *La Argentina* was stricken from the list in 1975.

There are also 2 new German-built submarines, 2 old *ex*-US submarines, 2 new British-built destroyers (Type 42), 8 old *ex*-US destroyers, 2 small frigates, 1 corvette (*ex*-fleet minesweeper), 4 coastal minesweepers, 2 minehunters, 9 patrol vessels (armed ocean tugs), 2 missile boats, 2 fast patrol vessels, 2 torpedo boats, 5 patrol craft, 5 survey ships, 2 survey launches, 1 training ship, 2 transports, 3 oilers, 1 dock landing ship, 5 landing ships, 35 minor landing craft, 1 icebreaker, 9 auxiliary vessels and service craft and 14 tugs.

The new construction programme includes 2 more Type 209 patrol submarines, 6 Type 21 fast frigates, 1 oceanographic ship, 1 hydrographic survey vessel and an icebreaker.

The active personnel of the Navy in 1977 comprised 32,900 (2,890 officers and 30,010 men, including 12,000 conscripts, who serve 14 months). There is a marine corps of 6,000 including coast artillery, a naval school and a school of mechanics.

The Naval Aviation Service, formed on 17 Oct. 1919, has some 2,000 personnel, in 4 wings. Aircraft acquired in recent years include 16 A-4Q Skyhawk attack bombers, 12 Aermacchi M.B.326 light jet armed trainers, 4 P-2H Neptune and 6 S-2A Tracker anti-submarine aircraft, navalized Harvard trainers, and 30 North American armed T-28s bought from France, of which only the last 3 types can be launched from the Argentine aircraft carrier with existing equipment; various training, transport and general purpose aircraft, including helicopters.

Air Force. The Air Force, founded on 10 Aug. 1912 and autonomous since 4 Jan. 1945, is organized into Air Operations, Air Regions, Materiel and Personnel Commands. Air Operations Command, responsible for all operational flying, is made up of 6 (increasing to 8) air brigades, each with 2 to 4 squadrons, usually operating from a single base. No. I Air Brigade is a military air transport service, with responsibility also for LADE (state airline) operations into areas of Argentina not served by civilian companies. Its equipment includes 7 C-130E/H Hercules and 9 F.27 Friendship/Troopship turboprop transports, 5 twin-turbofan F.28 Fellowship freighters, 6 C-47s, 5 Twin Otters, 15 Guarani IIs, the Presidential Boeing 707-320B, twin-turboprop HS 748, and many older or smaller types. No. II Air Brigade has 9 Canberra twin-jet bombers and 2 Canberra trainers; a photographic squadron with Guarani IIs, and twin-engined Huanquero armed trainer and reconnaissance aircraft; and a squadron of IA 58 Pucara twin-turboprop COIN aircraft. No. IV Air Brigade comprises 3 ground attack squadrons equipped with about 25 A-4 P Skyhawks and 30 Paris light jet combat and liaison aircraft. No. V Air Brigade comprises only 2 squadrons, with a total of about 50 A-4P Skyhawk strike aircraft. No. VII Air Brigade has 1 squadron with 14 armed Hughes 500M and 6 Bell UH-1 helicopters. No. VIII Air Brigade has 1 squadron with 12 Mirage

IIIE fighter-bombers and 2 Mirage IIID trainers. Also in current service are Sikorsky S-61N and S-61R and SA 315B Lama helicopters, and HU-16B Albatross amphibians for search and rescue. There is a flying school at Córdoba, equipped with piston-engined T-34 Mentors and Paris jets. Total strength of the Air Force is about 17,000 personnel and 375 aircraft.

INTERNATIONAL RELATIONS

Membership. Argentina is a member of UN, OAS and LAFTA.

ECONOMY

Budget. The financial year commences on 1 Nov. Budget estimates of total receipts in 1973 were 34,438m. pesos, including 7,048m. from customs and ports and 6,005m. from interest and revenue; expenditure (1972) totalled 14,894m. on current account and 8,602m. on capital account.

Currency. The monetary system is on a gold-exchange standard, the unit for foreign transactions being, nominally, the *peso oro* (gold peso) and for domestic transactions, the *peso moneda nacional* (paper peso), legal tender for all domestic debts.

The gold peso weighs 1·6129 grammes of gold 0·900 fine; it is divided into 100 *centavos*, but gold is not in circulation. Circulation consists chiefly of paper notes (issued since 1897) ranging from 10,000 down to 50 pesos. The coins actually circulating, 1968, were steel–nickel, 25, 10, 5, 1 peso and 50 centavos. The government in 1970 introduced a 'new peso', equivalent to 100 of the present units of currency.

Due to constant inflation, the international value of the peso has fallen steadily. In Oct. 1955 it was 18 to US$1; in Dec. 1965 it was officially 189 to US$1. The buying and selling of foreign exchange is now controlled, and with certain minor exceptions may only be through authorized institutions. In Oct. 1975 the rate of exchange was officially 37·50 new pesos to US$1.

Monetary circulation 592,495m. pesos on 31 Dec. 1976. Gold and foreign-exchange reserves were equal to 18,550m. new pesos.

Banking. A law promulgated 25 March 1946 nationalized the Central Bank (established in 1935), originally as an autonomous institution, but later, in Oct. 1949, placed under the Minister of Finance, who became president. Six decree-laws of Oct. 1957 have brought back a greater elasticity to the structure, especially as regards the deposits and loans of the private banks, which have regained their autonomy. The Central Bank continues the normal functions of a national institution.

On 31 July 1948 there were 44 banks, each with capital of 1m. paper pesos or over (including the Banco de la Nación, with 36% of the total assets of the banking system), consisting of 9 provincial banks, 25 domestic banks and 10 foreign banks, all of which are shareholders in the Central Bank. The Banco de la Nación (founded in 1891) has 306 branches and agencies, including one at Asunción, Paraguay. In March 1974 the Government nationalized 7 foreign banks, including subsidiaries of the Citibank and the Banco de Santander. There are 5 Stock Exchanges.

Weights and Measures. Since 1 Jan. 1887 the use of the metric system has been compulsory.

ENERGY AND NATURAL RESOURCES

Electricity. Electric power production (1972) was 25,319 kwh.

Oil. Crude oil production (1974) 24·02m. cu. metres.

Minerals. Mining is of mainly local importance. Since 1954 it has been under state control. Argentina produced 472,300 tonnes of washed coal in 1968 (Río Turbio, with reserves of 300m. tonnes). Gold, silver and copper are worked in Catamarca, where there are also 2 tin-mines, and gold and copper in San Juan, La Rioja and the south-western territories. Iron ore (102,000 tonnes in 1972), tungsten, beryllium, mica, uranium (25 tonnes in 1972), lead (39,900 tonnes in 1972), barites, zinc (43,500 tonnes in 1972), tin (1·8m. tonnes in 1972), manganese and limestone are produced.

Agriculture. Argentina has an area of about 670,251,000 acres, of which about 41%

is pasture land, 32% woodland and 11% (73·73m. acres) cultivated. It was estimated (1966) that 30m. hectares were cultivated by the country's 110,600 tractors.

Argentina's wealth is based on agriculture and livestock. With about 53m. cattle she ranks fourth (eclipsed by India, 160m.; USA, 96m., and USSR, 70m.), but as an exporter of raw meat (excluding Denmark's exceptional trade in bacon) she has long led the world (pre-war average, 662,000 tonnes). In 1972 production amounted to 2·58m. tonnes carcase weight.

The livestock estimate (1972) showed: Cattle, 52·3m.; sheep, 40m.; pigs, 4·5m.; horses, 3·5m. The Province of Buenos Aires has 38% of the cattle. Wool production, 1972, was 194,000 tonnes.

Wheat production usually exceeds 6m. tonnes (1973, provisional, 7·6m.), ahead of Australia but behind Canada and US. Other cereals and linseed are important.

Crop statistics with area (in 1,000 hectares) and production (in 1,000 tonnes) are shown as follows:

	1974–75		*1975–76*[1]		*1976–77*[1]	
	Area	*Output*	*Area*	*Output*	*Area*	*Output*
Wheat	5,183	5,970	5,753	8,570	7,192	11,000
Linseed	520	381	471	377	722	617
Maize	3,871	7,700	3,696	5,855	2,980	8,300
Oats	1,201	327	1,342	433	1,471	530
Barley	950	323	977	422	962	650
Rye	2,370	306	2,408	273	2,300	330
Sunflower seed	1,196	732	1,411	1,085	1,460	900
Sugar-cane	348	15,600	351	14,310	356	14,500

[1] Provisional.

The total grain and meat exports, in tonnes:

	Wheat	*Maize*	*Barley*	*Meat*
1975	1,758,087	3,882,906	9,942	166,525
1976	3,154,590	3,079,965	16,297	364,424
1977[1]	4,156,493	1,817,163	34,953	150,337

[1] Provisional.

Argentina's meat exports are calculated in terms of actual weight; not 'carcase weight', as is the international practice.

Cotton, potatoes, vine, tobacco, citrus fruit, olives, rice, soya, and yerba maté (Paraguayan tea) are also cultivated. There are 36 cane-sugar mills and 1 beet-sugar factory; production, 1974, 1·49m. tonnes. Potato harvest, 1971–72, amounted to 327,900 tonnes. The area under tobacco, 1971–72, was 66,700 hectares; output 73,700 tonnes.

Before the Second World War the country was the largest grower and shipper of linseed (flaxseed), but, preferring to convert it into oil, exported virtually none from 1946 until April 1950, when export was resumed. Sunflower seed, first grown by Russian immigrants in 1900, now furnishes the country's most popular edible oil. There are more than 10m. olive trees, of which 48% are in Mendoza. 496,000 tonnes of groundnuts were produced in 1974 (mainly in Córdoba). Argentina is the world's largest source of tannin.

Flour-milling ranks second to refrigeration. In 1972 Argentine mills produced 427,000 tonnes of flour.

Fisheries. Fish landings in 1973 amounted to 276,400 tonnes. On 5 Jan. 1968 a government decree extended Argentina's territorial waters to 200 miles offshore. Fishing by foreign vessels inside this limit up to 12 miles from the coast would be granted.

INDUSTRY AND TRADE

Industry. Cotton yarn produced in 1972 amounted to 88,800 tonnes; mixed cotton yarn, 75,900; rayon, acetate and man-made fibre yarns, 52,150; wood pulp (1971), 206,000; paper and board (1971), 678,000; sulphuric acid, 242,000; caustic soda, 123,000; nitrogenous fertilizers, 38,000; plastics and resins, 146,000; fuel oils, 14·68m.; motor spirit, 4·5m. Cement output, 1972, was 5·5m. tonnes; pig-iron and ferro-alloys was 849,000 tonnes; crude steel, 2·15m. tonnes. Electric power production, 1972, was 25,319m. kwh.

In Aug. 1974 the Government nationalized all distribution outlets of fuel and gas.

Trade Unions. According to the 1965 national census of workers' associations there are 502 trade unions with a total of nearly 1,764,700 paying members. Of these unions 240 are connected with manufacturing industries, 5 with construction, 36 with gas, water, electricity and sanitary services, 70 with commerce, 62 with transport, storage and communications and 117 with other services. The majority of these unions are affiliated to the General Confederation of Labour. The economically active population was estimated at the end of 1964 to total 8,422,700, of which 6,623,700 were males and 1,799,000 females. The main groups are agriculture and fishing (19%), manufacturing industries (20%), commerce (12%) and other services (28%).

Legal status which confers authority to negotiate wage agreements and other privileges is granted by the Secretary of Labour (Ministry of Economy and Labour) to one union in each industry or activity. The minimum wage law provides for a twice-yearly adjustment of the minimum wage to take account of cost-of-living changes. On 1 May 1966 the minimum monthly wage for a family consisting of a man, wife and 2 children was fixed at 22,500 pesos and that for a single man at 15,750 pesos.

The Trade Union Law was revised by decree in 1966. Political activity within the unions is prohibited, finances are placed under government supervision and all strikes must be decided by a two-thirds majority obtained by secret ballot.

Commerce. Import values include charges for carriage, insurance and freight; export values are on a f.o.b. basis. Real values of foreign trade (in US$1m.), exclusive of coin and bullion:

	1967	*1968*	*1969*	*1970*	*1971*	*1972*	*1973*	*1974*
Imports	1,096	1,169	1,576	1,694	1,868	1,905	2,235	3,570
Exports	1,465	1,368	1,612	1,773	1,740	1,941	3,266	4,005

Principal imports, 1973	*US$1m.*	*Principal exports, 1973*	*US$1m.*
Vegetable products	183·5	Animals and animal products	712·3
Mineral products	211·5	Vegetable products	985·7
Chemical products	298·6	Animal and vegetable oils	138·3
Paper manufactures	115·7	Food, drink, tobacco	468·4
Wood manufactures	56·6	Mineral products	12·7
Base metals	548·6	Chemical products	84·8
Machinery and electrical equipment	475·1	Hides and skins	152·5
Transport equipment	111·0	Textiles	213·4

Trade by countries in market values (in US$1m.):

Imports from	*1972*	*1973*	*Exports to*	*1972*	*1973*
Brazil	175·0	205·2	Brazil	186·8	309·5
France	77·6	67·8	Belgium	47·9	77·9
Germany, Fed. Rep. of	246·4	239·2	France	118·5	122·8
Italy	122·6	165·7	Germany, Fed. Rep. of	225·6	265·4
Japan	142·8	256·4	Italy	251·6	404·9
Netherlands	52·6	44·8	Japan	57·5	134·9
UK	129·4	104·4	Netherlands	115·6	215·4
USA	385·4	476·8	UK	169·9	214·0
Venezuela	32·2	23·0	USA	184·8	252·9

Total trade between Argentina and UK (British Department of Trade returns, in £1,000 sterling):

	1972	*1973*	*1974*	*1975*	*1976*	*1977*
Imports to UK	76,537	106,132	98,467	53,461	90,113	120,040
Exports and re-exports from UK	51,429	41,732	49,204	67,796	63,356	130,271

Tourism. In 1974, 955,000 tourists visited Argentina, contributing about US$110m. to the economy.

COMMUNICATIONS

Roads. In 1974 there were 309,086 km of national and provincial highways. The 4 main roads constituting Argentina's portion of the Pan-American Highway were opened to traffic in 1942. In 1974 there were 2·56m. cars and 994,000 lorries and buses.

Railways. A rationalization plan was implemented in 1977 with the aim of making stringent staff economies and closing at least 10,000 km of uneconomic route. A basic network of trunk routes is to be modernized to carry bulk freight and fast passenger trains between major cities. The amalgamation brought together 7 government railways (mostly small) with 8,347 miles (and some 12% of the aggregate revenue), 3 French-owned railways (2,660 miles and 7% of the revenue) and 8 British-owned railways (15,561 miles and 80% of the revenue). Legal formalities were completed on 5 May 1949. The present system comprises 6 railways with a total route-km of 39,782 (metre, 4 ft 8½ in. and 5 ft 6 in. gauges).

Aviation. Commercial airlines flew a total of 26m. km in 1972, carrying 607,000 passengers. Lines operating international flights to and from Buenos Aires include BUA, Aerolíneas Argentinas, Air France, Iberia, Alitalia, KLM, Swissair, SAS, Canadian Pacific Airlines, Lufthansa and PANAM.

Shipping. The merchant fleet, 31 Dec. 1973 (registered with Lloyd's), consisted of 1,453,000 GRT; traffic during 1971: vessels of 13·27m. GRT entered ports; 14m. tonnes of goods were unloaded and 10·6m. tonnes were loaded.

The state-owned ocean and river fleet (1963) included 216 vessels of over 1,000 GRT which totalled 1,200,061 GRT.

Post and Broadcasting. In 1949 the telephone service was nationalized; instruments numbered 2,469,250 in 1976. Privately owned exchanges operated 122,005 instruments. There were, in 1945, 4,382 post offices. There are (1964) 90 broadcasting stations and 10 television stations with 5·2m. viewers. Cable service to other Latin-American countries and US is provided by All-America Cables.

Cinemas (1972). Cinemas number 1,650, with seating capacity of 611,400.

Newspapers (1972). Daily newspapers numbered 162 with an aggregate daily circulation of 3,677,000. The largest circulation daily and 9 other newspapers have been closed since May 1974.

JUSTICE, RELIGION, EDUCATION AND WELFARE

Justice. Justice is administered by federal and provincial courts. The former deal only with cases of a national character, or in which different provinces or inhabitants of different provinces are parties. The chief federal court is the Supreme Court, with 5 judges at Buenos Aires. Other federal courts are the appeal courts, at Buenos Aires, Bahía Blanca, La Plata, Córdoba, Mendoza, Tucumán and Resistencia. Each province has its own judicial system, with a Supreme Court (generally so designated) and several minor chambers. Trial by jury is established by the Constitution for criminal cases, but never practised, except occasionally in the provinces of Buenos Aires and Córdoba.

The death penalty was re-introduced in 1976 for the killing of government, military police and judicial officials, and for participation in terrorist activities.

The police force is centralized under the Federal Security Council.

Religion. The Roman Catholic religion is supported by the State.

In 1888, civil marriage was established in the republic. Divorce was made legal in Dec. 1954 but ceased to be so by a decree of 1 March 1956.

The Department of Worship is under the Ministry of Foreign Affairs. The tax exemption enjoyed by some religious establishments has been derogated. There are at present 2 Cardinal-Archbishops, 11 Archbishops and 46 bishops. The clergy has 10 seminaries. On 10 Oct. 1966 Argentina returned to the Vatican the right to appoint bishops and archbishops, who had been nominated by the Argentine Government since 1853.

Education. Education is free (subsidized by the central and provincial governments), secular and compulsory for children from 6 to 14 years of age. In 1970 the pre-primary schools had 11,639 teachers and 223,251 pupils; primary schools had 175,929 teachers and 3,385,790 pupils; secondary schools had 132,721 teachers and 974,826 pupils; higher schools had 22,477 teachers and 274,634 pupils. Recurring expenditure on education for the year was 1·6m. pesos, capital expenditure 166,820 pesos. This represented 14% of public expenditure, and 61% of that was spent in salaries.

There are national universities at Córdoba (founded 1613), with, 1966, 47,000 students; Buenos Aires (1821), with 81,000 students; La Plata (1897), with 57,000 students; Tucumán (1914), with 8,000 students; the National University of the Litoral, in Santa Fé, with branches in Rosario (1920), and in Corrientes (1920), with 15,000 students; the National University of Cuyo, with 14,700 students, and that of the North-East, with 4,300 students. In 1956 the Technological Institute in Bahía Blanca was raised to the status of 'Universidad del Sur'; (1968) 7,000 students. Since 29 July 1966 these formerly autonomous institutions are under the authority of the Ministry of Education.

Health. Free medical attention is obtainable from public hospitals. Many trade unions provide medical, dental and maternity services for their members and dependants. Welfare services are scanty in places distant from urban centres. A Ministry of Social Welfare was set up in 1966. In 1971 there were 2,864 hospitals with 133,847 beds.

DIPLOMATIC REPRESENTATIVES

OF ARGENTINA IN GREAT BRITAIN (9 Wilton Crescent, London, SW1X 8RP)

Ambassador: (Vacant).

OF GREAT BRITAIN IN ARGENTINA (Luis Agote 2412/52, Buenos Aires)

Ambassador: (Vacant).

OF ARGENTINA IN THE USA (1600 New Hampshire Ave., NW, Washington, DC., 20009)

Ambassador: Jorge A. Aja Espil.

OF THE USA IN ARGENTINA (Saramiento 663, Buenos Aires)

Ambassador: Raul H. Castro.

OF ARGENTINA TO THE UNITED NATIONS

Ambassador: Dr Enrique Jorge Ros.

Books of Reference

Boletin del comercio exterio Argentino y estadísticas económicas retrospectivas. Annual
Anuario de comercio exterior de la República Argentina. Annual
Economic Review, Banco de la Nación. Buenos Aires
Síntesis Estadística Mensual. Dirección General de Estadistica. Buenos Aires, 1947 ff.
Boletín Internacional de Bibliografía Argentina. Ministry of Foreign Relations. Buenos Aires. Monthly
Geografía de la República Argentino. Ed. by the Sociedad Argentina de Estudios Geográficos. 7 vols. Buenos Aires, 1945–53
Argentine Economic Policy. Buenos Aires, 1967
Bridges, E. L., *Uttermost Part of the Earth* [*Tierra del Fuego*]. New York, 1949
Daus, F. A., *Geografía de la Argentina.* 2 vols. Buenos Aires, 1946–53
Ferns, H. S., *Britain and Argentina in the 19th Century.* OUP, 1960.—*The Argentine Republic 1516–1971.* Newton Abbot, 1973
Ferrer. A., *Argentina.* New York, 1969
Pendle, G., *Argentina.* R. Inst. of Int. Affairs. 3rd augmented ed., 1963

Romero, José Luis, *A History of Argentine Political Thought*. Stanford and OUP, 1963
Santillán, Diego A. de (ed.), *Gran Enciclopedia Argentina*. 9 vols. 1956–64
Tornquist, Ernesto, & Co. Ltd., *Business Conditions in Argentina*. Buenos Aires, from 1916; monthly from Jan. 1968

AUSTRALIA

Capital: Canberra
Population: 13·5m. (1976)
GNP per capita: US$6,100 (1976)

HISTORY. On 1 Jan. 1901 New South Wales, Victoria, Queensland, South Australia, Western Australia and Tasmania were federated under the name of the 'Commonwealth of Australia', the designation of 'colonies' being at the same time changed into that of 'states'—except in the case of Northern Territory, which was transferred from South Australia to the Commonwealth as a 'territory' on 1 Jan. 1911.

In 1911 the Commonwealth acquired from the State of New South Wales the Canberra site for the Australian capital. Building operations were begun in 1923 and Parliament was opened at Canberra on 9 May 1927 by HRH the Duke of York (afterwards King George VI). A further area at Jervis Bay was acquired in 1915.

Territories under the administration of Australia in Jan. 1977, but not included in it, comprise Norfolk Island, the territory of Ashmore and Cartier Islands, and the Australian Antarctic Territory (24 Aug. 1936), comprising all the islands and territory other than Adélie Land, situated south of 60° S. lat. and between 160° and 45° E. long.

The British Government transferred sovereignty in the Heard Island and McDonald Islands to the Australian Government on 26 Dec. 1947. Cocos (Keeling) Islands on 23 Nov. 1955 and Christmas Island on 1 Oct. 1958 were also transferred to Australian jurisdiction.

AREA AND POPULATION. Area and population, Census 30 June 1976:

States and Territories (capitals in brackets)	*Area (sq. km)*	*Males*	*Females*	*Total*	*Per 100 sq. km*
New South Wales (Sydney)	801,600	2,380,172	2,396,931	4,777,103	595
Victoria (Melbourne)	227,600	1,814,786	1,832,195	3,646,981	1,602
Queensland (Brisbane)	1,727,200	1,024,611	1,012,586	2,037,197	117
South Australia (Adelaide)	984,000	620,162	624,594	1,244,756	126
Western Australia (Perth)	2,525,500	581,177	563,680	1,144,857	45
Tasmania (Hobart)	67,800	201,512	201,354	402,866	594
Northern Territory (Darwin)	1,346,200	52,443	44,647	97,090	7
Aust. Cap. Terr. (Canberra)	2,400	100,103	97,519	197,622	8,234
Total	7,682,300	6,774,966	6,773,506	13,548,472	176

Population of major cities and towns, Census 30 June 1976:

Statistical division	*State*	*Persons*	*City*	*State*	*Persons*
Sydney	NSW	3,021,299	Gold Coast	Qld	105,777
Melbourne	Vic.	2,603,578	Toowoomba	Qld	63,956
Brisbane	Qld	957,710	Launceston	Tas.	63,386
Adelaide	SA	900,379	Ballarat	Vic.	60,737
Perth	WA	805,489	Bendigo	Vic.	50,169
Newcastle[1]	NSW	362,980	Rockhampton	Qld	50,132
Canberra[1]	ACT	215,461	Greater Darwin	NT	41,374
Wollongong[1]	NSW	211,122	Cairns	Qld	39,305
Hobart	Tas.	162,059	Whyalla	SA	33,426
Geelong[1]	Vic.	131,643	Wagga Wagga	NSW	32,984
Townsville[2]	Qld	88,386	Mt.Isa	Qld	25,377

[1] Statistical district. [2] City.

The number of occupied dwellings in Australia (at 1976 census) was 4,166,601, distributed as follows: New South Wales, 1,500,017; Victoria, 1,127,623; Queensland, 603,586; South Australia, 392,761; Western Australia, 339,448; Tasmania, 122,567; Northern Territory, 23,553; Australian Capital Territory,

57,046. There were also 429,501 unoccupied dwellings. Total completed new dwellings numbered 129,000 in 1976–77.

Vital statistics for 1975:

States and Territories	*Marriages*	*Divorces*[1]	*Births*	*Deaths*	*Infant deaths*
New South Wales	36,958	10,737	80,919	40,499	...
Victoria	27,706	5,683	61,897	29,499	806
Queensland	15,230	2,689	36,403	16,421	547
South Australia	9,843	1,819	19,986	9,947	222
Western Australia	9,026	2,241	20,338	7,972	271
Tasmania	3,242	591	6,982	3,339	128
Northern Territory	406	87	2,118	610	58
Aust. Cap. Terr.	1,462	460	4,370	736	62
Total	103,873	24,307	233,013	109,023	...
Rate[2]	7·67	17·95	17·21	8·05	...

[1] Includes nullities of marriages and judicial separations.
[2] Rate per 1,000 mean population.

Foreign-born residents (1971); UK and Irish Republic, 1,088,210; Italy, 289,476; Greece, 160,200; Yugoslavia, 129,816; Germany (Fed. Rep. and Dem. Rep.), 110,811; Netherlands, 99,295; New Zealand, 80,466; Poland, 59,700; Malta, 53,681. Total, 2,579,318.

Overseas arrivals during 1976 numbered 1,641,636 and departures 1,602,156. Of these 141,504 were long-term and permanent arrivals and 115,890 were long-term and permanent departures. Of these 58,317 came to Australia intending to settle. There were 26,733 Australian residents departing permanently.

Australian Bureau of Statistics, *Demography Bulletin.* Canberra, 1911 to date
First Report on the Progress and Assimilation of Migrant Children in Australia. Commonwealth Immigration Advisory Council. Canberra, 1960
Coleman, P. (ed.), *Australian Civilization: A Symposium.* Melbourne, 1962
Conference on Immigration Research, *The Study of Immigrants in Australia.* Canberra, 1960
Elkin, A. P., *The Australian Aborigines.* 5th ed. Sydney, 1961
Price, C. A., *Southern Europeans in Australia.* Melbourne, 1963
Zubrzycki, J., *Immigrants in Australia.* Melborne, 1960.—*Statistical Supplement.* Canberra, 1960

CONSTITUTION AND GOVERNMENT. *Federal Government:* Under the Australian Constitution legislative power in Australia is vested in a Federal Parliament, consisting of the Queen, represented by a Governor-General, a Senate and a House of Representatives. Under the terms of the constitution there must be a session of parliament at least once a year.

The Senate comprises 64 Senators (10 for each State voting as one electorate and as from Aug. 1974, 2 Senators respectively for the Australian Capital Territory and the Northern Territory) chosen for 6 years. In general, the Senate is renewed to the extent of one-half every 3 years, but in case of prolonged disagreement with the House of Representatives, it, together with the House of Representatives, may be dissolved, and an entirely new Senate elected. The House of Representatives consists, as nearly as practicable, of twice as many Members as there are Senators, the numbers chosen in the several States being in proportion to population as shown by the latest statistics, but not less than 5 for any original State. The numerical size of the House after the election in 1975 was 127, including the Members for Northern Territory and the Australian Capital Territory. The Northern Territory has been represented by 1 Member in the House of Representatives since 1922, and the Australian Capital Territory by 1 Member since 1949 and 2 Members since May 1974. The Member for the Australian Capital Territory was given full voting rights as from the Parliament elected in Nov. 1966. The Member for the Northern Territory was given full voting rights in 1968. The House of Representatives continues for 3 years from the date of its first meeting, unless sooner dissolved. Every Senator or Member of the House of Representatives must be a British subject, be of full age, possess electoral qualifications and have resided for 3 years within Australia. The franchise for both Houses is the same and is based on universal (males and females aged 18 years) suffrage. Compulsory voting was introduced in 1925. If a Member of a State Parliament wishes to be a candidate in a federal election, he must first resign his State seat.

Executive power in Australia is vested in the Governor-General, who is advised by an Executive Council. This is presided over by the Governor-General, and its members hold office at his pleasure. All Ministers of State are members of the Executive Council under summons. A record of proceedings of meetings is kept by the Secretary to the Council. At Executive Council meetings the decisions of the Cabinet are (where necessary) given legal form, appointments made, resignations accepted, proclamations, regulations and the like made.

The policy of a ministry is, in practice, determined by the Ministers of State meeting without the Governor-General under the chairmanship of the Prime Minister. This group, known as the Cabinet, does not form part of the legal mechanism of government; its meetings are private and deliberative; the actual ministers of the day are alone present; no records of the meetings are made public, and the decisions taken have, in themselves, no legal effect.

From Jan. 1956 the composition of the Ministry consisted of a Cabinet including a limited number of Ministers, and a group of Ministers not in the Cabinet who could be invited to attend Cabinet meetings whenever matters affecting their departments are being considered. In Dec. 1972 all members of the Ministry became Cabinet members.

The current Ministry of the Liberal–National Country Party Coalition Government comprises a Cabinet of 14 senior Ministers and another 13 Ministers who attend meetings of Cabinet when required.

The legislative powers of the Federal Parliament embrace trade and commerce, shipping, etc.; finance, banking, currency, etc.; defence; external affairs; postal, telegraph and like services; census and statistics; weights and measures; copyright; railways; conciliation and arbitration in industrial disputes extending beyond the limits of any one State; social services (an amendment of the Constitution in 1946 specifying, in addition to the existing provision for invalid and old-age pensions, the provision of maternity allowances, widows' pensions, child endowment, unemployment, pharmaceutical, sickness and hospital benefits, medical and dental services, etc.). The Senate may not originate or amend money bills; and disagreement with the House of Representatives may result in dissolution or, in the last resort, a joint sitting of the two Houses. No religion may be established by the Commonwealth. The Federal Parliament has limited and enumerated powers, the several State parliaments retaining the residuary power of government over their respective territories. If a State law is inconsistent with a Commonwealth law, the latter prevails.

The Constitution also provides for the admission or creation of new States. Proposed laws for the alteration of the Constitution must be submitted to the electors, and they can be enacted only if approved by a majority of the States and by a majority of all the electors voting.

The 31st Parliament was elected on 13 Dec. 1977.

House of Representatives (as at 1 Jan. 1978): Liberal Party, 67; National Country Party of Australia, 19; Australian Labor Party, 38; total, 124.

Senate (as at 16 Jan. 1978): Liberal Party, 27; National Country Party of Australia, 8; Australian Labor Party, 27; Australian Democrats, 1; Independent, 1; total, 64.

Governor-General: Sir Zelman Cowen, GCMG (sworn in 8 Dec. 1977).

The following is a list of Governors-General of the Commonwealth:

Earl of Hopetoun	1901–02	HRH the Duke of Gloucester	1945–47
Lord Tennyson	1902–04	Sir William McKell	1947–53
Lord Northcote	1904–08	Viscount Slim	1953–60
Earl of Dudley	1908–11	Viscount Dunrossil	1960–61
Lord Denman	1911–14	Viscount De Lisle	1961–65
Viscount Novar	1914–20	Lord Casey	1965–69
Lord Forster	1920–25	Sir Paul Hasluck	1969–74
Lord Stonehaven	1925–31	Sir John Kerr	1974–77
Sir Isaac Isaacs	1931–36	Sir Zelman Cowen	1977–
Earl Gowrie	1936–45		

National flag: The British Blue Ensign with a large star of 7 points beneath the Union Flag, and in the fly 5 stars of the Southern Cross, all in white.

The Liberal–National Country Party Coalition (constituted Dec. 1975) was at 20 Dec. 1977:

Prime Minister: Rt. Hon. Malcolm Fraser, CH (L).
Deputy Prime Minister, Trade and Resources: Douglas Anthony (NCP).
Industry and Commerce: Phillip Lynch (L).
Primary Industry: Ian Sinclair (NCP).
Administrative Services: Reginald Withers (L).
Employment and Industrial Relations: Anthony Street (L).
Transport: Peter Nixon (NCP).
Treasurer: John Howard (L).
Education: John Carrick (L).
Foreign Affairs: Andrew Peacock (L).
Defence: James Killen (L).
Social Security: Margaret Guilfoyle (L).
Finance: Eric Robinson (L).
Aboriginal Affairs: Ivan Viner (L).
Health: Ralph Hunt (NCP).
Immigration and Ethnic Affairs: Michael MacKellar (L).
Northern Territory: Evan Adermann (NCP).
Construction: John McLeay (L).
National Development: Kevin Newman (L).
Science: James Webster (NCP).
Posts and Telecommunications: Anthony Staley (L).
Attorney-General: Peter Durack (L).
Productivity: Ian MacPhee (L).
Business and Consumer Affairs: Walter Fife (L).
Special Trade Representations: Victor Garland (L).
Environment, Housing and Community Development: Raymond Groom (L).
Home Affairs and Capital Territory: Robert Ellicott (L).
Veterans' Affairs: Glenister Sheil (NCP).

The Acts of the Parliament of the Commonwealth of Australia Passed from 1901 to 1973. 12 vols. Annual volumes, 1974 to date
Parliamentary Handbook of the Commonwealth of Australia. Canberra, 1915 to date
Commonwealth of Australia Directory [until 1960: *Federal Guide*]. *Prime Minister's Department.* Canberra, 1924 to date
Butler, D., *The Canberra Model: Essays on Australian Government.* Melbourne and London, 1974
Crisp, L. F., *Australian National Government.* 3rd ed. Melbourne and London, 1975
Davis, S. R., *The Government of the Australian States.* London, 1960
Else-Mitchell, R., *Essays on the Australian Constitution.* 2nd ed. Sydney, 1961
Hughes, C. A., and Graham, B. D., *A Handbook of Australian Government and Politics.* Canberra, 1968
Odgers, J. R., *Australian Senate Practice.* 4th ed. Canberra, 1971
Paton, Sir George (ed.), *The Commonwealth of Australia: its Laws and Constitution.* London, 1952
Sawer, G., *Australian Federal Politics and Law 1901–1929, 1929–1949.* 2 vols. Melbourne, 1974.—*Australian Government To-day.* 11th ed. Melbourne, 1973
Spann, R. N. (ed.), *Public Administration in Australia.* 3rd ed. Sydney, 1973
Wynes, W. A., *Executive and Judicial Powers in Australia.* 5th ed. Sydney, 1976

State Government: In each of the 6 States (New South Wales, Victoria, Queensland, South Australia, Western Australia, Tasmania) there is a State government whose constitution, powers and laws continue, subject to changes embodied in the Australian Constitution and subsequent alterations and agreements, as they were before federation. The system of government is basically the same as that described above for the Commonwealth—*i.e.*, the Sovereign, her representative (in this case a Governor), an upper and lower house of Parliament (except in Queensland, where the upper house was abolished in 1922), a cabinet led by the Premier and an Executive Council. Among the more important functions of the State governments are those relating to education, health, hospitals and charities, law, order and public safety, business undertakings such as railways and tramways, and public utilities such as water supply and sewerage. In the domains of education, hospitals, justice, the police, penal establishments, and railway and tramway operation, State government activity predominates. Care of the public health and recreative facilities are shared with local government authorities and the Federal Government, social services other than those referred to above are now primarily the concern of the Federal Government, and the operation of public utilities is shared with local and semi-government authorities.

Other activities of State government relate to lands and surveys, agriculture, forestry and public works, including roads (the latter shared with local and semi-government authorities).

Local Government. The system of municipal government is broadly the same throughout Australia, although local government legislation is a State matter.

Each State is sub-divided into areas known variously as municipalities, cities, boroughs, towns, shires or district councils, totalling about 900. Within these areas the management of road, street and bridge construction, health, sanitary and garbage services, water supply and sewerage, and electric light and gas undertakings, hospitals, fire brigades, tramways and omnibus services and harbours is generally part of the functions of elected aldermen and councillors. The scope of their duties, however, differs considerably, for in all States the State Government, either directly or through semi-government authorities, also carries out some or all of these types of services.

In some instances, *e.g.*, in New South Wales, a number of local government authorities combine to conduct a public undertaking such as the supply of water or electricity.

DEFENCE. Under legislation passed by the Australian Parliament in Sept. 1975 and which came into force 9 Feb. 1976, the Minister for Defence has responsibility for the general control and administration of the Defence Force. The legislation also provides for the appointment, by the Governor-General, of a Chief of Defence Force Staff to command the whole of the Defence Force and, under the Chief of Defence Force Staff, a Chief of Naval Staff to command the Navy, a Chief of the General Staff to command the Army, and a Chief of the Air Staff to command the Air Force. The administration of the Defence Force has been placed jointly with the Chief of Defence Force Staff and the Secretary of the Department of Defence. In addition, the legislation makes provision for the powers of command and administration of the Defence Force to be subject to the directions of the Minister. These arrangements have resulted in the abolition of the Naval, Military and Air Boards.

The creation of a unified Department of Defence has led to the distribution of the functions of policy advice, policy direction on behalf of the Minister, and management, to: (*a*) A group of 5 functional organizations consisting of Strategic Policy and Force Development; Supply and Support; Resources and Financial Programmes; Defence Manpower; and Organization and Management Services (responsible in the main to the Secretary of the Department of Defence but responsive, where appropriate, to the Chief of Defence Force Staff and the individual Chiefs of Staff); (*b*) the joint Service organization under the Chief of Defence Force Staff comprising the Military Plans and Operations Staff, the Surgeon-General, and the Judge Advocate-General; and (*c*) the single Service Organizations under each Chief of Staff.

In addition there are 3 specialist organizations dealing with Defence Science and Technology, Intelligence and Natural Disasters respectively. There is also a Defence Force Ombudsman.

Army. Overall organization and financial control of the Australian Army is vested in the Chief of General Staff. Under the Defence Force Re-organisation Act, which received the Royal Assent on 9 Sept. 1975, the Military Board, which was previously the controlling body of the Army, was abolished. The Act became effective on 1 Feb. 1976. A functional command structure. Headquarters

Field Force Command, Headquarters Logistic Command, and Headquarters Training Command, with Headquarters in military districts, was introduced in 1973.

The strength of the Army was 31,424 at 30 June 1976. There is emphasis in the field force organization on the combat element and high-priority logistic units to meet the requirements for limited war with light air-portable formations. The Field Force is organized on the divisional structure, on the basis of 6 battalions organized in 3 task forces of 2 battalions each with combat and logistic support.

There is a volunteer Regular Army Emergency Reserve of 413 former members of the Regular Army, and the strength of the Citizens Military Forces is 19,961.

Training for commissioned rank is carried out at the Royal Military College and the Officer Cadet School. The Royal Military College was established in Canberra in 1911, to train young men from Australia and New Zealand for the Regular Armies of those two countries. The college, which is affiliated with the University of New South Wales, accepts young men between the ages of 17 and 20 who are qualified to enter university. The course covers 4 years and leads to the award of the university's degrees of Bachelor of Arts in Military Studies and Bachelor of Science in Military Studies.

The Officer Cadet School was established at Portsea, Victoria, in 1952. The course there takes 11 months.

High staff and command training is, in the main, carried out at the Australian Staff College, Queenscliff, Victoria.

Expenditure on Army capital equipment was $A51·6m. in 1971–72, $A73m. in 1972–73, $A25·53m. in 1973–74, $A21·35m. in 1974–75.

Navy. The overall control of the Royal Australian Navy is vested in the Chief of Naval Staff assisted by the Deputy Chief of Naval Staff with the Chief of Naval Personnel, the Chief of Naval Technical Services, the Chief of Naval Material, and the Special Deputy (Navy Office). Under the Defence Re-organisation Act effective from 1 Feb. 1976 the Naval Board was abolished. The operation and administration of the Fleet is the responsibility of the Flag Officer Commanding HM Australian Fleet.

Aircraft carrier of the Royal Australian Navy:

Completed	*Name*	*Standard displacement, tons*	*Principal armament*	*Shaft-horse-power*	*Speed, knots*
1955	Melbourne (*ex*-Majestic)[1]	16,000	12 40-mm AA	40,000	24

[1] Sister ship *Sydney* (ex-*Terrible*), completed as an aircraft carrier in 1949, converted to a fast military transport in 1961, officially announced for disposal on 20 July 1973, left Sydney for shipbreakers on 23 Dec. 1975.

There are also 6 British-built 'Oberon' class submarines, *Onslow*, *Otway*, *Ovens* and *Oxley* (completed in 1967–69) and *Orion* and *Otama* (completed in 1977–78), 3 US-built guided-missile destroyers, *Brisbane*, *Hobart* and *Perth* (completed in 1965–68), 3 'Daring' class destroyers, *Vampire*, *Vendetta* and *Duchess*,[1] 6 destroyer escorts or 'Type 12' fast anti-submarine frigates, 4 oceanographic research and survey ships, 2 minehunters, 1 minesweeper, a destroyer tender, 12 patrol craft, 6 landing craft, 1 fleet oiler, 14 auxiliary vessels, 8 service craft and 55 workboats, etc. An oceanographic research ship is being built in Australia. Three so-called 'light destroyers' (DDL) with a displacement of 4,200 tons, a length of 425 ft and gas turbines giving a speed of 30 knots were scheduled to be built by Williamstown naval dockyard, but in Aug. 1973 the then Minister for Defence, announced that this decision by previous Government was deferred; the Navy would not proceed with construction of the fast combat support ship *Protector* (fleet replenishment ship of 20,270 tons carrying 2 helicopters); and the training ship *Anzac* ('Battle' class destroyer) would be paid off (left Sydney on 30 Dec. 1975 for shipbreakers in Hong Kong). In Aug. 1974 the Minister for Defence signed for the purchase of 2

[1] On loan from the Royal Navy from 1964 to 1972 when she was purchased outright for conversion to training purposes completed in 1974.

'patrol frigates' of 3,500 tons with a length of 445 ft to be completed in US shipyards in 1981–82. In Aug. 1975 the Minister for Defence announced plans to provide a replacement fleet tanker for HMAS *Supply* in 1980 and the acquisition of replacement patrol craft towards the end of the decade.

Naval dockyards are at Garden Island, Sydney, and Williamstown, Victoria. Naval shipbuilding is carried out at Williamstown, at Cockatoo Dock and Engineering Company, Sydney, or by private contract. The main repair base and store depots are at Sydney.

The main training establishments are HMAS *Cerberus* in Victoria, HMAS *Watson*, HMAS *Penguin* and HMAS *Nirimba* at Sydney, HMAS *Albatross* (Naval Air Station) at Nowra, NSW, and HMAS *Creswell* (Royal Australian Naval College) at Jervis Bay, ACT. Training for junior recruits is carried out at HMAS *Leeuwin* in Fremantle, WA, and Reserve training in naval establishments in all capital cities.

The Fleet Air Arm was established in 1948. In Dec. 1977 it had 63 (12 destroyed by fire) aircraft and 1,750 personnel and consisted of 6 squadrons the operational elements of which were 1 Skyhawk, 1 Tracker and 1 Wessex squadrons embarked in HMAS *Melbourne*. The Wessex helicopters are being replaced by Sea King helicopters in the anti-submarine warfare role. Six Trackers and other aircraft are on order to replace those lost.

The serving strength in Dec. 1977 totalled 16,000 personnel including 880 WRANS but excluding maritime units of the Papua New Guinea Defence Force.

Navy estimates 1974–75, $A375,014,000; 1975–76, $A391,791,000; 1976–77, $A428,879,000; 1977–78, $A539,808,000.

Air Force. The Royal Australian Air Force was established as a separate service on 31 March 1921. It is commanded by the Chief of Defence Force Staff, who administers all armed forces in conjunction with the Secretary of the Department of Defence, delegating operational command of the RAAF to the Chief of Air Staff.

Operational Command, with Headquarters near Sydney, is responsible for operational training and operational activities within Australia; while Support Command, with Headquarters in Melbourne, is responsible for recruitment, basic training, supply and major maintenance. Support Command also supervises RAAF units based outside Australia.

Flying establishment comprises 16 squadrons, of which 2 are equipped with F-111C strike/reconnaissance aircraft. Of the others, 1 is equipped with Canberras for target flying and photographic duties, 3 with missile-armed Mirage III-O Mach-2 fighters, 2 with Orion maritime reconnaissance aircraft, 1 with Boeing Vertol CH-47C medium-lift helicopters, and 2 with Iroquois helicopters. There are 5 transport squadrons, 2 with Hercules turboprop transports, 2 with Caribou STOL transports, and a special transport squadron equipped with BAC One-Eleven, Mystère 20 and HS 748 aircraft. Training aircraft include piston-engined Airtrainers, built in New Zealand, and Aermacchi MB 326H jets for pilot training, and HS 748 aircraft for navigation and air electronics training.

At 1 July 1975 the strength of the RAAF was as follows: Permanent Air Force, 21,546; Citizen Air Force, 417; General Reserve, 6,962; Emergency Force, 137.

Long, G. (ed.), *Australia in the War of 1939–45.* 22 vols. Canberra, 1952 ff.
Millar, T. B., *Australia's Defence.* Melbourne Univ. Press, 1965

INTERNATIONAL RELATIONS

Membership. Australia is a member of the UN, the Commonwealth, OECD, Colombo Plan and SEATO.

ECONOMY

Budget. In 1929, under a financial agreement between the Australian Government and States, approved by a referendum, the Australian Government took over all State debts existing on 30 June 1927 and agreed to pay $A15·17m. a year for 58 years towards the interest charges thereon, and to make substantial contributions towards a sinking fund to extinguish existing debts in 58 years and future debts in 53 years. The Australian

Government arranges all borrowing for both Australian Government and States through a loan council consisting of representatives of Australian Government and State governments. Since 1942 the Australian Government alone has levied taxes on incomes. In return for vacating this field of taxation, the States are reimbursed by a grant from the Australian Government out of revenue received.

Receipts and Financing Transactions for years ending 30 June (in $A1m.):

	1973–74	*1974–75*	*1975–76*	*1976–77*
Receipts:				
Income taxes	7,498	10,141	11,813	13,941
Estate duty	66	64	76	76
Gift duty	10	16	10	11
Customs duties	604	841	1,044	1,273
Excise duties	1,555	1,729	2,331	2,485
Sales tax	969	1,154	1,408	1,650
Primary production taxes	64	143	116	159
Broadcasting listeners' and television viewers' licences	68	19	...	...
Stevedoring industry charge	19	22	37	47
Payroll tax	7	14	17	19
Other taxes, fees, fines, etc.	21	22	31	38
Total taxes, fees, fines	10,881	14,165	16,883	19,699
Income from public enterprises	283	246	434	656
Property income	87	88	116	147
Total receipts	11,287	14,545	17,488	20,573
Financing Transactions:	621	2,816	3,953	3,522
Total funds available	11,908	17,360	21,441	24,095
Outlay:				
General public services	998	1,308	1,481	1,629
Defence	1,306	1,610	1,853	2,182
Education	331	553	599	715
University	240	544	616	708
Primary and Secondary	291	577	691	802
Total education	862	1,674	1,906	2,225
Health				
Hospital and clinical services	405	580	1,658	1,446
Other	536	696	1,285	1,093
Total health	941	1,276	2,943	2,539
Social security and welfare				
Care of and assistance to				
Aged persons	1,187	1,683	2,247	2,576
Incapacitated and handicapped persons	242	338	474	587
Ex-servicemen	383	505	599	695
Families and children	276	313	406	1,199
Other	402	860	1,286	1,298
Total social security, etc.	2,490	3,699	5,012	6,355
Housing and community amenities	466	1,028	939	740
Recreation and culture	158	233	252	258
Economic services				
Agriculture, forestry and fishing	336	566	210	214
Mining, manufacturing and construction	140	206	176	87
Transport and communication	1,194	1,531	1,700	1,770
Other	248	406	415	539
Total economic services	1,918	2,709	2,501	2,610
Other purposes	2,769	3,824	4,553	5,556
Total Outlay	11,908	17,360	21,441	24,095

The following table shows Government securities on issue on account of the Commonwealth Government and States, at 30 June 1977:

Currency in which repayable	*Australian Government*	*States*	*Total*
Australian Dollar ($A1,000)	9,448,355	11,971,365	21,419,720
Sterling (£1,000)	45,718	48,149	93,867
United States Dollar (US$1,000)	1,057,683	46,392	1,104,075
Canadian Dollar (Can.$1,000)	1,663	8,621	10,284
Swiss Francs (SW.F.1,000)	599,869	—	599,869
Netherlands Guilders (fl.1,000)	102,380	10,954	113,334
Deutsche Marks (DM 1,000)	1,078,469	—	1,078,469
European Units of Account (EUA1,000)	13,000	—	13,000
Japanese Yen (Yen 1m.)	10,000	—	10,000
Total ($A1,000 equivalents)[1]	11,191,762	12,098,548	23,290,310

[1] Converted at rate of exchange ruling at 30 June 1977.

Debt per head of population at 30 June 1977 was $A1,665, while the annual interest charge amounted to $A116 per head.

States: The following table presents a summary of the receipts and outlay of State and local authorities during 1975–76 (in $A1m.).

Receipts and Financing Transactions	*NSW*	*Vic.*	*Qld*	*SA*	*WA*	*Tas.*	*All States*
Taxes, fees, fines, etc.	1,766	1,309	515	361	325	106	4,382
Income from public enterprises	121	114	71	54	51	28	439
Grants from Commonwealth Government	2,299	1,762	1,153	773	773	336	7,094
Advances from Commonwealth Government	451	355	190	187	116	74	1,373
All other	443	440	204	44	101	30	1,265
Total funds available	5,080	3,980	2,133	1,419	1,366	574	14,553
Outlay							
Final consumption expenditure	2,500	1,989	1,031	714	743	285	7,263
Interest paid	411	401	215	134	115	68	1,345
Gross fixed capital expenditure on new assets	1,822	1,279	783	462	454	201	5,001
All other	347	311	104	109	54	20	944
Total outlay	5,080	3,980	2,133	1,419	1,366	574	14,553

Finance (5 parts), Australian Bureau of Statistics, Canberra, 1907–1962/63
Australian National Accounts. Australian Bureau of Statistics. 1953–54 to date
Public Authority Finance, No. 1. Australian Bureau of Statistics, 1972
Public Authority Finance: Federal Authorities. Australian Bureau of Statistics, 1962–63 to date
Public Authority Finance: State and Local Authorities. Australian Bureau of Statistics, 1971–72 to date.
Public Authority Finance: Public Authority Estimates 1976–77. Australian Bureau of Statistics, 1976
National Income and Expenditure. Australian Bureau of Statistics. Canberra, 1946 to date
Australia's *Committee of Economic Enquiry.* Report. Canberra, 1965
Treasury Information Bulletin (and Supplements). Canberra Treasury Dept., 1956 to date (quarterly)
Arndt, H. W. (ed.), *The Australian Economy.* Melbourne, 1963
Campbell, W. J., *Australian State Public Finance.* Sydney, 1954
Karmel, P. H., *The Structure of the Australian Economy.* Melbourne, 1962
Maxwell, J. A., *Commonwealth–State Financial Arrangements in Australia.* Melbourne Univ. Press
Ratchford, B. U., *Public Expenditure in Australia.* Durham, N.C., 1959

Currency. On 14 Feb. 1966 Australia adopted a system of decimal currency. The new currency unit, the dollar ($) is divided into 100 cents. The transition period ended on 31 July 1967. Decimal system notes have been issued in denominations of $1, 2, 5, 10, 20 and 50. Coins have been issued in denominations of 50, 20, 10, 5 and 2 cents and 1 cent.

Australian notes, issued by the note-issue department of the Reserve Bank, are legal tender throughout Australia. The total value of notes in circulation on 29 June 1977 was $A3,290·8m., of which $A2,912·8m. were held by the public. Coins are minted by the Royal Australian Mint and distributed by the Reserve Bank.

Banking. The banking system in Australia comprises:

(*a*) The Reserve Bank of Australia. This is the central bank which in addition to its central banking business (including the note-issue department) provides special financing facilities through the rural credits department for the processing, manufacture and marketing of primary produce.

(*b*) Seven major trading banks: (i) The Commonwealth Trading Bank of Australia; (ii) 6 private trading banks: The Australia and New Zealand Banking Group Ltd, The Bank of Adelaide, the Bank of New South Wales, The Commercial Bank of Australia Ltd, The Commercial Banking Company of Sydney Ltd and The National Bank of Australasia Ltd.

(*c*) Other trading banks: (i) 3 State Government banks—The Rural Bank of New South Wales, the State Bank of South Australia, and the Rural and Industries Bank of Western Australia; (ii) one joint stock bank—The Bank of Queensland Ltd, formerly The Brisbane Permanent Building and Banking Co. Ltd, which has specialized business in one district only; (iii) branches of 2 overseas banks—the Bank of New Zealand and the Banque Nationale de Paris, which are mainly concerned with financing trade, etc., between Australia and overseas countries.

(*d*) The Commonwealth Development Bank of Australia.

(*e*) Savings Banks.

(*f*) The Australian Resources Development Bank Ltd opened on 29 March 1968. Its main objective is to assist Australian enterprises in the development of Australia's natural resources, through direct loans and equity investment or by refinancing loans made by trading banks. The bank is jointly owned by the 7 major Australian trading banks.

The Reserve Bank's functions and responsibilities derive from the Reserve Bank Act 1959 and the Banking Act 1959, which came into effect in 1960. They had their origins, however, in the development of the central banking role of the Commonwealth Bank, which was established in 1911 as a Government savings and trading bank.

Control of the Australian note issue was transferred from the Commonwealth Treasury to a Notes Board in 1920 and, in 1924, to the Bank. The Commonwealth Bank Act 1945 formally constituted the Bank as a central bank, and these powers were carried through into the 1959 Act establishing the Reserve Bank.

The Acts of 1959 provided for: (i) the separation of the central bank from the Commonwealth group of banking institutions and its reconstitution as the Reserve Bank of Australia; (ii) the establishment of an entirely separate Commonwealth Banking Corporation, with responsibilities for the non-central-banking elements that had developed from within the original Commonwealth Bank—namely the Commonwealth Trading Bank, the Commonwealth Savings Bank and the Commonwealth Development Bank, the latter being basically an amalgamation of the Mortgage Bank and Industrial Finance Department of the Commonwealth Bank.

At 30 June 1977 the capital of the Reserve Bank totalled $A49·4m. and reserve funds (including a special reserve for IMF special drawing rights) $A239·3m. The capital was distributed as follows: Central banking business, $A40m.; rural credits department, $A9·4m. Reserve funds held were: Central banking business, $A5·6m.; rural credits department, $A15·6m. Profits for the year ended 30 June 1977 (including all departments) amounted to $A128·4m.

Particulars as at 30 June 1976 for the banks under the control of the Commonwealth Banking Corporation: Commonwealth Trading Bank, capital, $A14·9m.; reserve fund, $A35·3m.; profits for the year, $A8·3m. Commonwealth Development Bank, capital, $A61·7m.; reserve fund, $A41·6m.; profits for the year, $3·6m. Commonwealth Savings Bank, reserve fund, $A64·2m.; profits for the year, $A24·1m.

At 30 June 1976 the 13 trading banks operating in Australia provided full banking facilities at 4,958 branches and 1,143 agencies all over Australia.

The weekly average of deposits in Australia with all trading banks (under (*b*) and (*c*) above) during June 1977 amounted to $A19,095·8m.; the average of advances made by the banks was $A13,985·3m.; the average of total assets was $A23,130·2m.

At 30 June 1976, 13 savings banks were operating in Australia. These are the Commonwealth Savings Bank with branches throughout Australia; 7 private savings banks being wholly owned subsidiaries of the 6 private trading banks and operating, with certain exceptions, in all States and Territories; the State Savings Banks in Victoria and South Australia; the Rural and Industries Bank of Western Australia, and 2 Trustee Savings Banks in Tasmania. At 30 June 1976 these savings banks provided savings facilities at 5,572 branches and 13,586 agencies throughout Australia. At end of June 1977 they held deposits in Australia amounting to $A16,371·8m.

In 1977 there were 49 companies registered under the Life Insurance Act, 1945, transacting life insurance business in Australia; in addition there were 2 State government institutions. During 1976–77 premiums received were $A1,563·6m. and claims, etc., paid were $A1,004m.

The following table is a summary of banking and insurance business (in $A1,000) in the several States of the Commonwealth:

Particulars	*NSW*	*Vic.*	*Q'ld*	*SA*	*WA*	*Tas.*	*Australia (including A.C.T. and N.T.)*
All trading banks:[1]							
Fixed deposits	5,087,349	2,747,869	1,661,927	840,317	784,083	197,938	11,457,168
Current deposits	3,146,370	2,049,530	1,050,666	460,565	603,406	149,254	7,630,941
Advances	6,136,930	3,451,326	1,678,170	1,149,413	1,009,645	228,945	13,982,807
Savings bank deposits[2]	4,803,155	5,977,532	2,148,693	1,780,841	960,548	477,134	16,365,260
Life insurance:[3]							
New policies issued (sum insured)							
Ordinary	1,853,863	2,544,432	1,456,295	823,485	881,965	227,748	10,096,363
Superannuation	391,907	2,272,975	641,507	404,288	385,359	124,739	8,318,019
Industrial	61,530	42,243	42,073	19,710	14,970	2,969	187,008
Policies existing[2] (sum insured)							
Ordinary	9,813,208	12,378,039	7,244,305	4,333,602	4,201,850	1,213,350	47,572,049
Superannuation	1,461,448	8,023,309	2,128,722	1,479,731	1,250,316	472,512	27,685,489
Industrial	573,535	440,735	274,911	164,057	114,881	31,207	1,625,860

[1] Weekly averages for June 1977. [2] At June 1977. [3] Year ended 30 June 1977.

Treasury Information Bulletin. Department of the Treasury. Canberra, 1956 to date (quarterly)
Reserve Bank of Australia. *Statistical Bulletin.* Sydney, 1937 to date (monthly)
Arndt, H. W., and Harris, C. P., *The Australian Trading Banks.* 3rd ed. Melbourne, 1965
Gifford, J. L. K., Wood, J. V., and Reitsma, A. J., *Australian Banking.* 4th ed. Brisbane, 1960

Weights and Measures. Conversion to the metric system is in progress.

ENERGY AND NATURAL RESOURCES

Electricity. Total production 1976–77, 82,522m. kwh.

Minerals. The mineral output was valued at the mine as follows (in $A1,000)[1]:

Mineral	*1974–75*	*1975–76*
Copper[2]	170,253	162,123
Gold[2]	43,147	43,745
Iron ore	613,169	674,515
Lead[2]	135,129	128,122
Rutile	53,674	71,750
Tungsten	11,385	15,497
Zinc[2]	140,824	134,940
Black coal	874,879	1,211,199
Brown coal[2]	40,556	48,346
Petroleum	446,298	513,155
Total (value of minerals and construction materials)	3,304,012	3,864,189

[1] The values in this table include the value of materials used in process of production, whereas those in preceding and subsequent tables exclude these values to show net value.
[2] Value of all minerals containing the metal shown as the principal content.
[3] Excludes value of brown coal used in making briquettes.

Gold production (1,000 grammes), in 1971–72, 23,253; 1972–73, 20,002; 1973–74, 16,271; 1974–75, 15,153; 1975–76, 16,901.

Black coal (1,000 tonnes) mined in 1971–72, 53,549; 1972–73, 59,755; 1973–74, 59,344; 1974–75, 70,142; 1975–76, 69,269.

Agriculture. At 30 June 1975, of a total Australian area of 768m. hectares, 421m. hectares (54·7%) were leased or licenced Crown lands, 248m. hectares (32·3%) were occupied by the Crown or reserved, unreserved or unoccupied; private lands formed the remainder, of which 77m. hectares (10%) were alienated and 23m. hectares (3%) were in the process of alienation.

Area and yield of the principal crops in 1975–76:

Crops	*Total area (1,000 hectares)*	*Total yield (1,000 tonnes)*
Wheat (grain)	8,555	11,982
Oats (grain)	988	1,141
Barley (grain)	2,329	3,179
Maize (grain)	47	131
Hay	230	738
Potatoes (ordinary)	34	696
Sugar-cane (for crushing)	257	21,958
Vineyards	63[1]	709
		(1,000 litres)
Wine made (1974–75)	...	352,708
Orchards and fruit gardens	100	...

[1] Bearing area.

The following summary shows the production and gross value of the most important items or classes of production, classified by States:

Production, 1975–76	*NSW*	*Vic.*	*Q'ld*	*SA*	*WA*	*Tas.*	*Aust.*[1]
Area of crops (1,000 hectares)	4,285	1,852	2,010	2,116	4,208	61	14,540
Production of wheat (1,000 tonnes)	4,310	1,578	830	1,139	4,122	2	11,982
Total wool production (1,000m. tons)	240·3	137·9	66·3	105·6	183·6	20	754·3
Factory butter (1,000 kg)	10,323	107,731	10,965	3,302	4,552	10,762	147,635
Non-processed cheese (1,000 kg)	12,478	52,252	12,809	19,073	2,763	13,332	112,617
All meat (tonnes, carcase weight)							
1975–76	746,804	748,362	556,961	174,247	270,361	82,528	2,601,960
1976–77[2]	798,516	718,494	596,222	190,011	270,212	78,824	2,669,220
Total Agriculture (value $A1m.) 1975–76	1,817·7	1,258·5	1,276·0	678·6	995·9	140·3	6,183·7

[1] Includes Northern Territory and Australian Capital Territory.
[2] Preliminary, subject to revision.

Livestock (in 1,000) at 31 March 1976:

	NSW	*Vic.*	*Q'ld*	*SA*	*WA*	*Tas.*	*N. Terr.*	*ACT*	*Australia*
Cattle	9,138	5,868	11,347	1,891	2,654	909	1,603	23	33,434
Sheep	53,200	25,395	13,599	17,279	34,771	4,249	1	148	148,643
Pigs	709	393	409	326	260	70	7	...	2,173

Forestry. At 31 March 1975 there were 565,000 hectares of coniferous plantations. Roundwood production is more than 2·6m. cu. metres per annum.

INDUSTRY AND TRADE

Industry. Statistics of the manufacturing industries in Australia in 1975–76: Number of establishments, 27,523; workers employed, 1,200,766; salaries and wages paid, $A9,745m.; value-added, $A16,946m. (excludes small single-establishment enterprises).

Estimated gross value (in $A1,000) of the products of Australia:

Products	*1970–71*	*1971–72*	*1972–73*	*1973–74*	*1974–75*
Crops	1,477,425	1,585,084	1,569,723	2,846,096	3,172,291
Livestock slaughterings and other disposals	1,012,755	1,134,384	1,542,166	1,695,956	1,026,110
Livestock products	1,083,163	1,237,122	1,834,035	1,859,020	1,662,656
Forestry, fishing and hunting	224,555	253,138	282,907	325,344	334,258
Mining and quarrying	1,582,632	1,790,460	1,998,615	2,461,320	3,304,637

Labour. The majority of wage and salary earners in Australia have their minimum wages and conditions of work prescribed in awards of industrial arbitration authorities established under federal and State legislation. However, in some States, some conditions of work (*e.g.*, normal weekly hours of work, long-service leave, annual leave) are set down in State legislation. Practically all employees in Australia have a standard working week of 40 hours or less; paid annual leave of at least 4 weeks; and paid long-service leave (*i.e.*, leave granted to workers who remain with one employer over an extended period of time) of at least 13 weeks after 15 years' continuous service. For most occupations equal pay for males and females has been granted.

In addition to the minimum rates of pay for a standard working week prescribed in awards of industrial arbitration authorities, many wage-earners are in receipt of over-award pay and payments for overtime. At the end of Oct. 1976 it was estimated that the average weekly earnings of adult males (other than managerial, professional and higher supervisory staff) in full-time private and government employment was $A187.60 and average weekly hours 40·7.

Employees in all States are covered by workers' compensation legislation and industrial arbitration award provisions provide for compensation for work injuries.

During 1976 industrial disputes involving stoppages of work of 10 man-days or more accounted for 3,799,200 working days lost. In these disputes 2,189,900 workers were involved. Stoppages over the national health scheme (Medibank) in all States and Territories in June and July, resulted in a loss of 2,057,500 working days (55% of the total).

The following table shows estimates (in 1,000) of the civilian population, by employment status. The estimates are based on results of the quarterly population survey, carried out by personal interview at a sample of dwellings throughout Australia.

	May 1973	*May 1974*	*May 1975*[1]	*May 1976*[1]	*May 1977*[1]
In the labour force	5,676·1	5,845·3	5,963·0	6,088·1	6,198·0
Employed	5,575·8	5,750·1	5,710·6	5,840·6	5,883·8
Unemployed	100·3	95·2	252·2	247·6	314·2
Not in the labour force	3,665·8	3,669·0	3,749·2	3,781·3	3,916·9
Civilian population aged 15 years and over	9,341·9	9,514·3	9,712·3	9,869·4	10,107·8

[1] Definitions of labour force, unemployed and not in labour force were revised in Feb. 1975.

The following table shows estimates (in 1,000) of the civilian wage and salary earners in Australia classified by industry (excluding defence forces, and employees in agriculture and private domestic service):

Industry[1]	*June 1974*	*June 1975*	*June 1976*	*June 1977*
Forestry, fishing and hunting[2]	14·9	15·9	14·9	14·8
Mining	76·8	80·8	78·5	79·0
Manufacturing	1,331·4	1,204·8	1,196·9	1,156·2
Electricity, gas and water	99·5	101·1	100·5	102·1
Construction	404·7	411·5[3]	371·0	361·0
Wholesale and retail trade	969·2	955·7	968·4	968·9

[1] Australian Standard Industrial Classification. Some Division totals include industries not specified separately.

[2] Excludes ASIC Sub-divisions 01 (Agriculture) and 02 (Services to agriculture).

[3] Affected by industrial dispute.

Industry[1]	*June 1974*	*June 1975*	*June 1976*	*June 1977*
Transport and storage	255·3	255·5	250·8	249·3
Communication	101·2	102·5	101·1	100·1
Finance, insurance, real estate and business services	387·9	379·5	380·3	385·0
Public administration and defence[2]	219·0	243·5	243·5	246·1
Community services	681·0	727·4	761·0	792·4
Health	283·4	301·5	316·9	331·4
Education, libraries, museums, and galleries	267·2	293·7	308·3	323·7
Entertainment, recreation, restaurants, hotels and personal services[3]	265·7	274·5	272·3	271·3
Total	4,806·5	4,752·7[4]	4,739·1	4,726·2

[1] Australian Standard Industrial Classification. Some Division totals include industries not specified separately.
[2] Excludes members of the permanent defence forces.
[3] Excludes ASIC Sub-division 94 Private households employing staff.
[4] Affected by industrial dispute.

The following table shows the number of unemployed persons and job vacancies registered with the Commonwealth Employment Service and the number of persons in receipt of unemployment benefit:

	June 1973	*June 1974*	*June 1975*	*June 1976*	*June 1977*
Registered unemployed	81,376	78,827	245,975	265,251	332,793
Registered job vacancies	54,508	62,180	25,517	19,194	19,129
Unemployment benefit recipients	37,945	32,009	160,748	188,423	253,809[1]

[1] July 1977.

Trade Unions. At the end of 1976 there were 282 trade unions in existence in Australia with a reported membership of 2,792,000. Over 57% of wage and salary earners were estimated to be members of unions. In 1976 there were 29 unions with fewer than 100 members and 9 unions with 80,000 or more members. Many of the larger trade unions are affiliated with central labour organizations, the oldest being the Australian Council of Trade Unions formed in 1927. Other central labour organizations have as affiliates Public Service associations, and salaried and professional associations.

Labour Statistics. Australian Bureau of Statistics. Canberra, 1977
Foenander, O. de R., *Better Employment Relations and Other Essays in Labour*. Sydney, 1954.—*Industrial Conciliation and Arbitration in Australia*. Sydney, 1959.—*Trade Unionism in Australia*. Sydney, 1962.—*Shop Stewards and Shop Committees*. Melbourne Univ. Press, 1965
Isaac, J. E., *Trends in Australian Industrial Relations*. Melbourne, 1962
O'Dea, R., *Industrial Relations in Australia*. Sydney, 1965
Perlman, M., *Judges in Industry*. Melbourne, 1954
Portus, J. H., *The Development of Australian Trade Union Law*. Melbourne, 1958
Sykes, E. I., *Strike Law in Australia*. Sydney, 1960
Walker, K. F., *Industrial Relations in Australia*. Cambridge, Mass., 1956

Commerce. Throughout Australia there are uniform customs duties, and trade between the States is free. For 1975–76 the gross revenue collected from customs duties amounted to $A958·6m. and from excise to $A2,318·5m. For 1976–77 the gross revenue collected from customs duties amounted to $A1,181·6m. and from excise to $A2,520·1m.

Value of the total imports and exports for years ending 30 June, in $A1,000:

		Exports (excluding ships' and aircraft stores)		
	Imports	*Australian produce*	*Re-exports*	*Total*
1973–74	6,085,004	6,707,055	207,340	6,914,395
1974–75	8,083,099	8,404,387	268,375	8,672,762
1975–76[1]	8,240,187	9,300,773	299,974	9,600,748

[1] Preliminary, subject to revision.

The Australian customs tariff provides for preferences to goods produced in and shipped from certain specified countries such as UK, Canada, New Zealand and Ireland. Preferences occur as a result of reciprocal trade agreements between Australia and these countries. Australia also has bilateral agreements with a number of other countries guaranteeing reciprocal treatment in matters of trade.

The Australia–New Zealand free-trade agreement came into force on 1 Jan. 1966 in certain scheduled goods.

In addition, Australia is a signatory to the multilateral General Agreement on Tariffs and Trade (GATT).

Principal commodities exported to and imported from Australia (in $A1,000) in 1976–77[1]:

	Exports	*Imports*
Live animals	60,386	17,337
Meat	885,815	3,330
Dairy products	199,210	19,525
Fish	136,430	109,996
Cereals	1,349,707	12,492
Fruit and vegetables	110,468	73,635
Sugar, etc., and honey	654,814	11,100
Coffee, tea, etc.	21,831	184,718
Food for animals	47,584	10,986
Miscellaneous food	7,226	11,823
Beverages	15,877	52,282
Tobacco	5,502	47,008
Hides, skins, etc.	247,717	2,080
Oil-seeds, nuts, kernels	4,360	7,151
Crude rubber	1,281	44,399
Wood, timber and cork	9,561	143,814
Pulp and waste paper	347	66,872
Textile fibres and their waste	1,489,880	65,126
Crude fertilizers and minerals	52,589	102,324
Metalliferous ores and metal scrap	1,623,026	13,563
Crude animal and vegetable materials, n.e.s.	27,710	25,386
Coal, coke and briquettes	1,291,607	1,740
Petroleum and products	205,798	993,843
Petroleum gases	...	128
Animal oils and fats	68,398	432
Fixed vegetable oils and fats	1,209	48,177
Animal and vegetable oils and fats	5,387	5,034
Chemicals	621,053	357,150
Mineral tar, crude chemicals, from coal, etc.	5,178	4,339
Dyeing, tanning and colouring materials	14,664	53,933
Medicinal and pharmaceutical products	44,051	101,725
Essential oils and perfumes, etc.	15,168	39,673
Fertilizers, manufactured	305	21,055
Explosives and pyrotechnic products	2,886	7,447

	Exports	*Imports*
Plastic materials	30,922	225,337
Chemical materials and products, n.e.s.	47,782	114,628
Leather manufactures, n.e.s.	19,755	18,471
Rubber manufactures, n.e.s.	6,220	138,888
Wood and cork manufactures (except furniture)	83,569	59,198
Paper and paperboard	19,679	281,959
Textile yarn, fabrics, etc.	31,373	639,897
Non-metallic mineral manufactures, n.e.s.	60,655	222,952
Iron and steel	435,002	216,300
Non-ferrous metals	595,376	47,233
Manufactures of metal, n.e.s.	90,381	266,029
Machinery (except electric)	235,887	1,706,216
Electric machinery	106,977	999,315
Transport equipment	140,096	1,274,061
Sanitary, etc., fixtures and fittings	3,177	24,700
Furniture	2,254	53,623
Travel goods and handbags	482	30,293
Clothing	12,526	242,232
Footwear, gaiters, etc.	1,159	74,262
Professional and scientific instruments; photographic and optical goods, watches and clocks	63,269	348,369
Miscellaneous manufactured articles, n.e.s.	57,319	580,498
Commodities and transactions of merchandise trade, not elsewhere classified	213,801	105,141
Total merchandise trade	11,484,688	10,329,225
Commodities and transactions not included in merchandise trade	162,668	81,122
Total recorded trade	11,647,356	10,410,347

[1] Preliminary.

Total trade (in $A1,000) with the more important countries, according to origin (imports) and consignment (exports):

From or to	Imports 1975–76	Imports 1976–77[1]	Exports 1975–76	Exports 1976–77[1]
Belgium-Luxembourg	69,969	83,821	125,262	149,793
Canada	204,080	292,203	243,617	280,171
China	68,942	103,151	219,791	184,685
Egypt	92	121	162,754	144,970
France	138,766	170,763	206,781	372,631
Germany (Fed. Republic of)	543,618	715,324	294,518	381,744
Hong Kong	216,512	254,287	147,392	189,157
India	50,053	70,586	71,498	201,342
Indonesia	24,535	50,174	161,331	180,508
Iran	83,582	103,657	89,296	150,310
Italy	192,230	265,815	209,644	340,038
Japan	1,609,559	2,149,722	3,192,131	3,955,786
Kuwait	125,817	197,211	34,674	47,631
Malaysia	82,116	113,522	172,735	224,266
Netherlands	129,258	158,818	175,566	178,499
New Zealand	250,510	319,598	455,297	579,456
Pakistan	5,968	6,836	22,552	23,140
Papua New Guinea	36,399	80,277	174,719	189,907
Saudi Arabia	236,020	281,655	39,539	54,237
Singapore	160,319	196,290	185,334	183,503
Sri Lanka	11,744	17,426	35,487	21,368
Sweden	166,982	203,938	57,405	57,869
Switzerland	105,352	127,198	7,861	11,628
USSR	3,719	5,795	372,783	346,730
UK	1,108,680	1,136,191	406,982	528,589
USA	1,655,802	2,161,630	968,322	1,009,381

[1] Preliminary.

Imports and exports for particular States, 1976–77[1] ($A1,000):

States, etc.	Imports	Exports	States, etc.	Imports	Exports
New South Wales	4,278,062	2,809,391	Tasmania	94,622	338,501
Victoria	3,665,911	2,216,017	Northern Territory	72,341	169,733
Queensland	838,098	2,813,720	Aust. Cap. Terr.	4,799	1,843
South Australia	630,955	789,716			
Western Australia	829,414	2,597,481	Total	10,410,347	11,647,356

In this table the value of goods sent from one state to another for transhipment abroad has been included in the State from which the goods were finally dispatched.

[1] Preliminary, subject to revision.

Total trade between UK and Australia (British Department of Trade returns, in £1,000 sterling):

	1973	1974	1975	1976	1977
Imports to UK	340,762	311,460	279,518	394,300	
Exports and re-exports from UK	404,086	599,489	631,278	687,756	

Overseas Trade. Australian Bureau of Statistics. Canberra, 1906 to date

Tourism. During 1976, 531,868 overseas visitors arrived in Australia intending to stay for less than 12 months, and international tourism receipts were $A250m.

Australian Bureau of Statistics, Canberra: *Rural Industries*. 1962–63 to date.—*Manufacturing Establishments: Details of Operations*. 1968–69 to date.—*Non-rural Primary Industries*. 1967–68 and 1968–69.—*Value of Production*. 1964–65 to 1968–69.—*Manufacturing Industry*. 1963–64 to 1967–68.—*Manufacturing Commodities*. 1963–64 and 1964–65.—*Building and Construction*. 1964–65 to date

Quarterly Review of Agricultural Economics. Bureau of Agricultural Economics. Canberra, 1948 to date

Atlas of Australian Resources. Department of National Development. Canberra, 1953–60

Developments in Australian Manufacturing Industry. Department of Trade, Melbourne, 1954–55 to date (annual)

The Australian Mineral Industry Review. Department of National Development—Bureau of Mineral Resources, Geology and Geophysics. Canberra, 1948 to date

Australian Economy. Department of the Treasury. Canberra, 1956 to date

Australasian Institute of Mining and Metallurgy. *Proceedings: New Series*. Melbourne, 1912 to date

Barnard, J. A. (ed.), *The Simple Fleece: Studies in the Australian Wool Industry.* Melbourne, 1962.
Beattie, W. A., *A Survey of the Beef-cattle Industry of Australia.* Melbourne, 1956
James, W., *Wine in Australia.* 3rd ed. Melbourne, 1962
Roughley, T. C., *Fish and Fisheries of Australia.* Rev. ed. Sydney, 1961
Shann, E. O. G., *An Economic History of Australia.* London, 1948
Shaw, A. G. L., *Economic Development of Australia.* 4th ed. Melbourne, 1960
Wadham, Sir Samuel, Kent Wilson, R., and Wood, J., *Land Utilisation in Australia.* 3rd ed. Melbourne, 1957

COMMUNICATIONS

Roads. The length of roads in Australia for general traffic is about 864,000 km, of which approximately 212,000 is sealed, 209,000 of macadam and similar composition and 443,000 of cleared or natural surface or formed only.

At 30 Sept. 1976, 6,635,600 motor vehicles, including 5·12m. cars and station wagons, 708,000 utilities and panelvans, 516,300 truck type vehicles and buses and 292,300 motor cycles, were registered in Australia. The revenue derived from registration fees and motor tax for the year 1974–75 was $A287·7m., drivers' and riders' licences, $A44m., and miscellaneous, $A120·5m. New vehicles registered in 1976–77 numbered 447,102 cars and station wagons, 87,952 utilities and panelvans, 46,759 truck type vehicles and buses and 50,320 motor cycles.

Railways. Government railways for the year ended 30 June 1976:

System	*Route-km open*	*Revenue train-km run, 1,000*	*Passenger journeys,[1] 1,000*	*Goods and livestock carried,[1] 1,000 tonnes*	*Gross earnings,[2] $A1,000*	*Working expenses,[2] $A1,000*
State:						
New South Wales	9,755	54,943	159,872	31,234	318,763	472,188
Victoria	6,653	33,818	109,669	10,803	147,292	271,940
Queensland	9,844	30,813	34,278	33,118	230,492	265,662
South Australia	3,894	10,304	12,672	6,139	49,688	91,352
Western Australia	6,163	12,856	351	17,647	130,850	118,607
Tasmania	849	1,748	151	1,610	8,048	22,087
National:						
Trans-Australian	1,857	4,220	159	1,555	44,553	64,279[4,5] (all National systems)
Central Australia	1,219	1,252	13	1,997	9,179	
North Australia	511	88	...	42	618	
Aust. Cap. Terr.	8	36	47	210	268	
Total all systems	40,753	150,078	317,213	104,355	939,751	1,306,115

[1] Intersystem traffic is included in the total for each system over which it passes.
[2] Excluding government grants. [3] Excludes interest payments.
[4] Includes provision of reserves for depreciation. [5] Not available separately.

The State railway gauges are: New South Wales, 1,435 mm; Victoria, 1,600 mm (325 km 1,435 mm and 14 km 762 mm); Queensland, 1,067 mm (111 km 1,435 mm and 48 km 610 mm); South Australia, 1,600 mm for 2,513 km, 398 km 1,435 mm and the rest 1,067 mm; West Australia, 1,365 km, 1,435 mm and the rest 1,067 mm, and Tasmania, 1,067 mm. Of the Australian National Railways, the gauge of the Trans-Australian and Australian Capital Territory is 1,435 mm, for the Central Australia 1,067 mm for 869 km and 1,435 mm for 350 km and for North Australia, 1,067 mm. Under various Commonwealth–State standardization agreements Brisbane, Sydney and Melbourne are linked by a standard 1,435 mm gauge line and Sydney is linked with Perth, *via* Broken Hill to Port Pirie (South Australia), from Port Pirie to Kalgoorlie (Western Australia) and from Kalgoorlie to Perth. The overall length of the Sydney–Perth railway is 3,961 km. The Central Australia railway extends as far north as Alice Springs (1,067 mm gauge from Maree to Alice Springs).

Aviation. Civil flying in Australia and Territories is subject to legislative control by the Australian Government. The administration of the Air Navigation Act and

Regulations is a function of the Air Transport Group under the Minister of Transport.

Operations of regular internal air services in Australia include flights of all Australian-owned airlines, except Qantas Airways, within Australia. During 1975–76 hours flown numbered 274,985. The total distance flown was 136m. km. Paying passengers carried numbered 9,415,747; weight of goods carried was 107,038 tonnes, and gross weight of mail was 9,878 tonnes.

During 1975–76 hours flown by Australian regular overseas services numbered 92,798; km flown, 64m.; paying passengers, 1,453,219; freight, 33,477 tonnes; mail, 2,967 tonnes.

Expenditure by the Australian Government on air transport for the year 1976–77 was $A174m. (including $A10·1m. on capital works).

At 30 June 1977 there were 368 licensed aerodromes and 83 governmental aerodromes in Australia, excluding Papua New Guinea.

Shipping. As at 30 June 1976 the Australian merchant marine (vessels of 200 tons gross and over) consisted of 77 coastal vessels of 1,113,950 tons gross and 16 overseas vessels of 233,861 tons gross.

Entrances and clearances of vessels (with cargo and in ballast) engaged in overseas trade:

	Entrances		*Clearances*	
	No.	*Net tons*	*No.*	*Net tons*
1973–74	5,975	72,041,746	5,909	71,462,297
1974–75	6,230	80,313,404	6,254	80,304,793
1975–76	5,772	75,001,819	5,824	75,399,334

The following summary shows shipping activity by States, 1975–76:

Particulars	*NSW*	*Vic.*	*Q'ld*	*SA*	*WA*	*Tas.*	*NT*	*Aust.*
Entrances of overseas vessels direct:								
Number	1,405	647	1,052	294	2,019	163	192	5,772
Net tonnage (1,000 tonnes)	14,279	4,970	13,072	2,539	35,730	2,457	1,956	75,002
Overseas cargo:								
Discharged 1,000 tonnes	6,193	2,964	2,188	2,556	4,781	281	756	19,718
Discharged 1,000 cu. metres	2,212	3,516	627	376	409	17	13	7,170
Loaded 1,000 tonnes	20,536	6,049	28,521	4,571	88,510	3,969	3,977	156,133
Loaded 1,000 cu. metres	875	718	269	285	313	27	...	2,488
Interstate cargo:								
Shipped 1,000 tonnes	3,091	9,844	1,692	4,103	8,064	1,168	280	28,241
Shipped 1,000 cu. metres	237	1,151	47	17	51	1,413	20	2,937

Post and Broadcasting. Business, year ended 30 June 1975. Number of post offices, 6,068. Earnings: Postal, $A302m.; telecommunications, $A1,068·6m.; total, $A1,370·6m. Working expenses: Postal, $A352·7m.; telecommunications, $A799·8m.; total, $A1,152·5m. Interest: Postal, $A13·9m.; telecommunications, $A173·7m.

At 30 June 1975, 5,772 telephone exchanges with 3,539,020 services and 5,266,845 instruments, were in operation.

Wireless broadcasting stations are in operation in all State capitals and in other regional areas throughout Australia. The National Broadcasting Service is provided by the Australian Broadcasting Commission, which at 30 June 1975 operated 85 medium-wave and 6 high-frequency stations and 10 high-frequency stations for overseas services. In addition, 118 medium-wave commercial broadcasting stations were operating.

The Overseas Telecommunications Commission, established in Aug. 1946, is responsible for all overseas services by cable, radio, telephone, including radio telephone services with ships at sea.

Television services are conducted in each State and the Australian Capital Territory by the National Television Service and by the Commercial Television Service. There were 84 national television stations and 48 commercial television stations in operation at 30 June 1975.

Cinemas (1971). There were 976 cinemas including 241 drive-in cinemas, with a total seating capacity of about 478,000.

Newspapers (1976). There was 1 national newspaper (average daily circulation 188,000) and 14 metropolitan daily newspapers in Australia with a combined daily circulation of 3·6m. Of these, 3 papers published in Melbourne accounted for 1·3m. and 4 published in Sydney for 1·2m.

Australian Transport 1974–75. Annual Report. Department of Transport, Canberra
Australian Transport. Sydney, Institute of Transport, 1937 to date (quarterly)
Brogden, S., *The History of Australian Aviation.* Melbourne, 1960

JUSTICE, RELIGION, EDUCATION AND WELFARE

Justice. The judicial power of Australia is vested in the High Court of Australia (the Federal Supreme Court), in the Federal Courts created by Parliament (the Federal Court of Australia, the Family Court of Australia, the Federal Court of Bankruptcy and the Australian Industrial Court) and in the State Courts invested by Parliament with Federal jurisdiction.

High Court. The High Court consists of a Chief Justice and 6 other Justices, appointed by the Governor-General in Council. The Constitution confers on the High Court original jurisdiction, *inter alia,* in all matters arising under treaties or affecting consuls or other foreign representatives, matters between the States of the Commonwealth, matters to which the Commonwealth is a party and matters between residents of different States. Parliament may make laws conferring original jurisdiction on the High Court, *inter alia,* in matters arising under the Constitution or under any laws made by Federal Parliament. It has in fact conferred jurisdiction on the High Court in matters arising under the Constitution and in matters arising under certain laws made by Parliament.

The High Court may hear and determine appeals from its own Justices exercising original jurisdiction, from any other Federal Court, from a Court exercising Federal jurisdiction and from the Supreme Courts of the States. It also has jurisdiction to hear and determine appeals from the Supreme Courts of the Territories. No appeal from the High Court to the Privy Council is permitted on questions as to the limits *inter se* of the constitutional powers of the States or the Commonwealth and the States except on the certificate of the High Court. No appeal to the Privy Council, whether special or otherwise, is permitted from a decision of Federal Courts (not being the High Court) or of the Supreme Court of a Territory. Appeal from the High Court to the Privy Council by special leave of the Privy Council is possible only in a matter in which the decision of the High Court was a decision that (*a*) was given on appeal from a decision of a Supreme Court of a State given otherwise than in the exercise of Federal jurisdiction and (*b*) did not involve the interpretation of the Constitution, a law made by the Federal Parliament or an instrument (including an ordinance, rule, regulation or by-law) made under a law made by the Parliament.

Other Federal Courts. Four other Federal courts, which have been created to exercise special jurisdiction, are the Federal Court of Australia, the Family Court of Australia, the Australian Industrial Court (*see below*) and the Federal Court of Bankruptcy. The Federal Court of Australia, which was established in 1977 to exercise jurisdiction in a number of matters that were previously invested in either the High Court, the Australian Industrial Court, the Federal Court of Bankruptcy or State and Territory Supreme Courts, exercises both original and appellate jurisdiction. The Federal Court will ultimately take overall the original jurisdiction now conferred on the Australian Industrial Court and the Federal Court of Bankruptcy, as well as exercising jurisdiction under other Acts, and will also act as a court of appeal from State and Territory courts in relation to Federal matters. Appeal from the Federal Court to the High Court of Australia will be by way of special leave only. The State Supreme Courts have also been invested with Federal jurisdiction in bankruptcy.

State Courts. The general Federal jurisdiction of the State Courts extends, subject to certain restrictions and exceptions, to all matters in which the High Court has jurisdiction or in which jurisdiction may be conferred upon it. In matters of non-Federal jurisdiction appeal is still possible, as a matter of law, from the State Courts direct to the Privy Council.

Industrial Tribunals. The chief industrial tribunals of Australia are at present the Australian Industrial Court, constituted by judges, and the Australian Conciliation and Arbitration Commission, constituted by presidential members (with the status of judges) and commissioners. The Australian Industrial Court deals with questions of law, the judicial interpretation of awards, imposition of penalties, etc. The Commission's functions include settling industrial disputes, making awards, determining the standard hours of work, wage fixation, etc.

Australian Digest of Reported Decisions of the Australian Courts and of Australian Appeals to the Privy Council. 2nd ed. Sydney, Law Book Co. 1963—Supplements 1964 ff.
Baalman, J., *Outline of Law in Australia.* 3rd ed. Sydney, 1969
Benjafield, D. G., and Whitmore, H., *Principles of Australian Administrative Law.* 3rd ed. Sydney, 1966
Cowen, Z., *Federal Jurisdiction in Australia.* Melbourne, 1959
Fleming, J. G., *The Law of Torts.* 5th ed. Sydney, 1977
Gunn, J. A. L., *Australian Income Tax Law and Practice.* 9th ed. by F. C. Bock and E. F. Mannix, Sydney, 1969, and *Butterworth's Taxation Service* to date
Howard, C., *Criminal Law.* 3rd ed. Sydney, 1975
Joske, P. E., *Matrimonial Causes and Marriage and Practice of in Australia and New Zealand.* 2 vols. 5th ed. Sydney, 1969
Mills, C. P., and Sorrell, G. H., *Federal Industrial Law. (Nolan and Cohen.)* 5th ed. Sydney, 1975
O'Connell, D. P. (ed.), *International Law in Australia.* Sydney, 1966
Paterson, W. E., and Ednie, H. H., *Australian Company Law.* 2nd ed. Sydney, 1976, and *Butterworth's Company Service* to date
Wynes, A., *Legislative, Executive and Judicial Powers in Australia.* 5th ed. Sydney, 1976
Yorston, R. K., and Fortescue, E. E., *Australian Mercantile Law.* 14th ed. Sydney, 1971

Religion. Under the constitution the Commonwealth cannot make any law to establish any religion, to impose any religious observance or to prohibit the free exercise of any religion, nor can it require a religious test as qualification for office or public trust under the Commonwealth. The figures in the table refer to those religions with the largest number of adherents at the census of 1971. The census question on religion was not obligatory, however.

Religion	*Persons*	*Religion*	*Persons*
Christian		Non-Christian	
Baptist	175,969	Hebrew	62,208
Brethren	22,963	Muslim	22,311
Catholic, Roman [1]	1,529,232	Other	14,404
Catholic [1]	1,913,402		
Churches of Christ	97,423	Total Non-Christian	98,923
Church of England	3,953,204		
Congregational	68,159	Indefinite	29,413
Jehovah's Witness	35,752	No religion	855,676
Orthodox	338,632	No reply	781,247
Lutheran	196,847		
Methodist	1,099,019	Grand Total	12,755,638
Presbyterian	1,028,581		
Salvation Army	65,831		
Seventh-day Adventist	41,617		
Protestant (undefined)	243,602		
Other (including Christian undefined)	180,546		
Total Christian	10,990,379		

[1] As stated in individual census schedules.

Education. Under the federal constitution education is a responsibility of the six State Governments, which administer their own systems of primary, secondary and technical education through government departments responsible to State Ministers. In each State, except New South Wales and South Australia, a single Education Department is responsible for these three levels of education. In New South Wales and South Australia the Education Department concentrates on primary and secondary education and a separate department is responsible solely for technical and further education.

The Commonwealth Government provides education services in the Australian

Capital Territory, the Northern Territory, Norfolk Island, Christmas Island and the Cocos (Keeling) Islands. The Commonwealth Government also has special responsibilities for student assistance, international relations in education and for supplementing the general educational provisions to meet the special needs of the Aboriginal people and migrants.

The Australian constitution empowers the Commonwealth Government to make grants to the States and to place conditions upon such grants. This power has been used to provide financial assistance to the States specifically for educational purposes. There are two national Education Commissions which advise the Commonwealth Government on the needs of educational institutions throughout Australia for the purpose of financial assistance. The Schools Commission, established in 1973, advises on the provision of financial assistance to the States for government and non-government schools. The Tertiary Education Commission, which was established in 1977 to replace three former commissions (the Universities Commission, the Commission on Advanced Education and the Technical and Further Education Commission), advises on the provision to the States of total funding for universities and colleges of advanced education and of supplementary financial assistance for their institutions of technical and further education.

School attendance is compulsory throughout Australia between the ages of 6 and 15 years, at either a government school or a recognized non-government educational institution. In all States and Territories the opportunity for 4-year-olds to attend pre-schools, either government or voluntary organizations, is becoming more widely available. Government schools are usually co-educational and comprehensive. Non-government schools are usually single-sex and operated by religious denominations. Tuition is free at government schools, but fees are normally charged at non-government schools.

The following is a summary for 1976 of primary and secondary school education:

	Schools		*Teachers*[1]		*Pupils*[2]	
States and Territories	*Government*	*Non-government*	*Government schools*	*Non-government schools*	*Government schools*	*Non-government schools*
New South Wales	2,225	791	42,374	10,367	799,737	218,435
Victoria	2,164	586	37,612	9,628	624,707	201,083
Queensland	1,209	331	18,162	4,068	334,313	91,713
South Australia	625	147	13,427	1,989	233,614	39,299
Western Australia	640	187	10,345	2,199	203,898	44,393
Tasmania	250	61	4,241	720	79,696	14,008
Northern Territory	115	11	1,195	146	21,830	3,009
Aust. Cap. Terr.	78	24	2,312	600	37,636	12,879
	7,306	2,138	129,668	29,717	2,335,431	624,819

[1] Full-time teachers plus the full-time equivalent of part-time teaching.
[2] Enrolment first week in August.

Post-secondary education takes place at institutions of technical and further education, colleges of advanced education and universities. Education in post-secondary institutions has been free since 1974. The majority of institutions of technical and further education are operated by State authorities and offer vocational and personal-interest courses to students, most of whom are part-time and employed. Universities and colleges of advanced education are autonomous institutions, the colleges tending to offer courses which have a more applied emphasis and are more vocationally oriented than university courses.

Universities and colleges of advanced education at 30 April 1976:

	Universities			*Colleges of advanced education*		
States and Territory	*Number*	*Students*	*Staff*[1]	*Number*	*Students*	*Staff*[1]
New South Wales	6	60,245	4,584	25	31,132	2,099
Victoria	3	38,387	2,729	32	50,085	3,646
Queensland	3	20,904	1,517	10	14,517	1,061

[1] Full-time teaching staff plus the full-time equivalent of part-time teaching staff.

States and Territory	*Universities* Number	Students	Staff[1]	*Colleges of advanced education* Number	Students	Staff[1]
South Australia	2	13,493	1,098	8	14,560	975
Western Australia	2	11,293	833	6	17,133	1,070
Tasmania	1	3,536	309	1	2,642	222
Aust. Cap. Terr.	1	6,102	432	1	4,545	273
	18	153,960	11,502	83	134,614	9,346

[1] Full-time teaching staff plus the full-time equivalent of part-time teaching staff.

In 1975 there were 180 principal institutions of technical and further education with 679 associated branches, annexes and centres. Full-time teaching staff numbered 9,302 and there were 671,013 enrolments.

Teacher education usually takes place in colleges of advanced education, though a substantial number of secondary teachers and a few primary teachers receive their pre-service education in a university. Government school teachers are recruited by the State departments of education, and in the Australian Capital Territory and the Northern Territory by the Commonwealth Teaching Service. Non-government schools recruit their own teachers.

The Commonwealth Government provides a number of schemes of assistance for students to facilitate access to education. The Secondary Allowances Scheme aims to help parents with a limited income to keep their children at school for the final 2 years of secondary education. The Tertiary Education Assistance Scheme is a means-tested scheme to assist students enrolled for full-time study in approved courses at post-secondary institutions. Allowances are also available for post-graduate study and overseas study. Aboriginal students are eligible for assistance under the Aboriginal Secondary Grants Scheme and the Aboriginal Study Grants Scheme. The States also offer various schemes of assistance, principally at the primary and secondary levels.

There are a number of bodies at the national level which have an important co-ordinating, planning or funding role. The major ones are: the Australian Education Council, comprising the Commonwealth and State Ministers of Education, the Conference of Directors-General of Education and the Curriculum Development Centre.

Total expenditure on education in Australia in 1975–76 was estimated at $A4,388m., of which $A3,607m. was current expenditure. Direct expenditure on education by public authorities was $A4,083m. including $A272m. by Federal authorities. In addition, the Commonwealth Government spent $A173m. on scholarships and other grants to persons and non-government organizations, and $A1,461m. in grants to the States for specific educational purposes. Total direct expenditure by State and local authorities amounted to $A3,811m., and a further $A235m. was paid in scholarships, etc.

Austin, A. G., *Australian Education 1788–1900*. Melbourne, 1961
Commonwealth Education Directory. Canberra, 1976
Directory of Tertiary Courses 1977. Canberra, 1976
Education in Australia. Canberra, 1977
Jones, P. E., *Education in Australia*. Melbourne, 1974
Primary and Secondary Schooling in Australia. Canberra, 1977
Schools Commission, *Report for 1977–79 Triennium*. Canberra, 1976
Tertiary Education Commission, *Recommendations for 1978*. Canberra, 1977

Social Security. The National Welfare Fund finances all Australian Government social and health benefits except Medibank, repatriation and certain other payments primarily of a capital nature. Total expenditure from the Fund during 1976–77 was $A6,355m.

The following summarizes the rates and conditions of the major benefits provided at June 1977. For expenditure on these benefits during 1976–77, *see* table on p. 105.

Age and invalid pensions—men 65 years of age or more and women 60 years of age or more may receive an age pension. Persons 16 years of age or more who are permanently blind or permanently incapacitated for work to the extent of at least 85% may receive an invalid pension. To be paid a pension, a person must have lived in Australia for a specified period and, unless permanently blind or over 70 years of age, also satisfy an income test. The maximum rates are $A47.10 a week in the case of the 'standard' rate pension, and in the case of the 'married' rate pension, $A78.50 a week ($A39.25 each). These amounts are subject to income tax. Additional amounts, subject to an income test, are paid to pensioners with dependent children. Pensions, free of the income test, are paid to permanently blind persons and to persons 70 years of age and over. Supplementary assistance of up to $A5 a week may be paid to a pensioner paying rent or for lodging. Supplementary assistance and additional pension for children are not taxable.

Widows' pensions—widows, divorcees, certain deserted wives, women who have been the dependant of a man for 3 years immediately prior to his death and women whose husbands are in mental hospitals or prison may, if they satisfy a residence requirement and a means test, receive a widow's pension. Such women with at least one dependent child may be paid a pension of up to $A47.10 a week plus a mother's allowance of $A4 a week ($A6 if she has an invalid child requiring full-time care or a child under 6 years) plus $A7.50 a week for each child. Widows, divorcees, etc., without a child and who are 50 years of age or more (as well as certain younger widows), may be paid a pension of up to $A47.10 a week. Persons who pay rent may also receive supplementary assistance of up to $A5 a week. Pensions, but not mothers' allowances, additional pension for children or supplementary assistance, are subject to income tax.

Supporting mothers' benefit—unmarried mothers and mothers who are deserted *de facto* wives, *de facto* wives of prisoners and separated wives ineligible for widow's pension may, if they satisfy a residence requirement and a means test, receive supporting mother's benefit. It is payable at the same rate as the widow's pension payable to a widow with one or more children in her care and is subject to the same income test.

Maternity allowance—is paid without income test in respect of every eligible child born in Australia. The rates are $A30 where there are no other children under 16 years; $A32 where there are 1 or 2 other children under 16; $A35 where there are 3 or more other children under 16; in addition $A10 is paid for each additional child born at a birth.

Family allowance—is paid without income test to families with children under 16 years or eligible student children aged 16 years or more but under 25 years. It is not subject to income tax. Weekly rates payable are: 1 child, $A3.50; 2 children, $A8.50; 3 children, $A14.50; 4 children, $A20.50; an additional $A7 for each additional child after the fourth. For each child or eligible student in an approved institution, the rate is $A5 per week.

Handicapped child's allowance—payable to parents or guardians of severely physically or mentally handicapped children in the family home and needing constant care and attention. The allowance is $A15 per week and is free of income test.

Double orphan's pension—the guardian of a child under 16 years of age or of a full-time student under 21, both of whose parents are dead, or one of whose parents is dead and the whereabouts of the other parent unknown, may receive double orphan's pension of $A11 a week. The payment is not subject to an income test.

Unemployment and sickness benefits—are paid, subject to an income test, to persons between the ages of 16 and 65 (males) and 16 and 60 (females) who are temporarily unemployed, or temporarily incapacitated and thereby suffer loss of income. The maximum rates of benefit are $A47.10 (single) and $A78.50 (married). To be granted benefit a person must have resided in Australia for at least 12 months preceding his claim or intend to reside permanently in Australia. For unemployment benefit purposes unemployment must not be due to direct participation in a strike.

Hospital benefits. $A2 per day is paid for each qualified patient insured with a registered hospital benefits organization and receiving treatment in a public or approved private hospital. Where the patient is uninsured the benefit is 80c. per day. However, if a patient is treated free of charge, $A2 is paid to the hospital. Public hospitals are paid $A5 per day for treating persons covered by the pensioner medical service.

Nursing home benefits. $A3.50 per day is paid for each qualified patient in an approved nursing home and a supplementary benefit of $A3 per day is paid in respect of patients who require and receive intensive nursing home care. As from 1 Jan. 1973, an additional benefit is paid for patients covered by the pensioner medical service. The maximum daily rates of benefit vary among the States.

Nursing home deficit financing. As from 1 Jan. 1975 deficit financing of nursing homes run by religious and charitable and similar non-profit organizations is available under the Nursing Home Assistance Act. This is an alternative form of nursing home financing to the payment of nursing home benefits for patients in these types of nursing homes.

Medical benefits. The Australian Government subsidizes the payment of medical expenses of persons insured with a registered medical benefits organization.

Subsidized health benefits. Free health insurance is provided for persons receiving unemployment and sickness benefits, for migrants during their first 2 months in Australia, and for families with weekly incomes not exceeding $A80.50. Partial assistance in meeting insurance contributions is available to families with weekly incomes not exceeding $A92.50.

Pensioner medical service. Eligible pensioners and their dependants receive free general practitioner medical services, free pharmaceuticals, free public ward treatment in public hospitals and additional nursing home benefits.

Domiciliary nursing care benefit. As from 7 March 1973, $A14 a week is paid as an incentive for people to care for sick and frail aged people, 65 years or more, who are in need of continual nursing care and supervision in the home environment. In addition, the benefit enables people to meet the extra cost involved in caring for the aged person in the home.

Pharmaceutical benefits—a comprehensive range of drugs and medicinal preparations is available. In general, a fee of $A1.50 is charged for each prescription. However, persons enrolled in the subsidized health benefits scheme pay 75c. per prescription and pensioners are supplied free of charge.

Tuberculosis campaign—this provides for diagnosis, treatment, after-care and allowances to sufferers and their dependants. The Australian Government meets additional maintenance costs and provides all approved capital expenditure.

Service pensions—are paid, subject to a means test, to veterans on the grounds of: (*a*) age, (*b*) permanent unemployability and (*c*) pulmonary tuberculosis. Wives of service pensioners are also eligible provided that they do not receive pensions from the Department of Social Security. Service pensioners who are aged 70 years or more are not subject to the means test.

Disability pensions—are not subject to a means test and may be paid to veterans who have incurred incapacity as a result of service, and their dependants. Expenditure on disability pensions during 1974–75 was $A315m. and on service pensions $A155m.

The total numbers of pensions, etc., in force at 30 June 1975 were: Age and invalid pensions, 1,266,009; child endowment (number of endowed children), 4,283,516; widows' pensions, 120,791; unemployment, sickness and special, 191,827; disability pensions, 514,367; and service pensions, 121,726. Maternity allowances (number granted during 1974–75), 238,512.

Department of Territories, *Progress Towards Assimilation.* Canberra, 1958
Bilton, J., *The Royal Flying Doctor Service of Australia.* Sydney, 1961
Henderson, R., *People in Poverty.* Melbourne, 1970
Kewley, T. H., *Social Security in Australia.* Sydney University Press, 1965
Scott, D., *Leisure: A Social Enquiry into Leisure Activities and Needs in an Australian Housing Estate.* Melbourne, 1962
Stoller, A. (ed.), *The Family Today.* Melbourne, 1962.—*Growing Old: Problems of Old Age in the Australian Community.* Melbourne, 1960

DIPLOMATIC REPRESENTATIVES

OF AUSTRALIA IN GREAT BRITAIN (Australia House, Strand, London, WC2B 4LA)

High Commissioner: The Hon. Gordon Freeth.

OF GREAT BRITAIN IN AUSTRALIA (Commonwealth Ave., Canberra)

High Commissioner: Sir Donald Tebbitt, KCMG.

OF AUSTRALIA IN THE USA (1601 Massachusetts Ave, NW, Washington, D.C., 20036)

Ambassador: A. P. Renouf, OBE.

OF THE USA IN AUSTRALIA (Moonah Pl., Canberra)

Ambassador: Philip H. Alston, Jr.

OF AUSTRALIA TO THE UNITED NATIONS

Ambassador: R. L. Harry, OBE.

Books of Reference

Statistical Information: The Australian Bureau of Statistics (Cameron Offices, Belconnen, A.C.T., 2616) was established in 1906. All the activities of the Bureau are covered by the Census and Statistics Act, which confers authority to collect information and contains secrecy provisions to ensure that individual particulars obtained are not divulged. Under the provisions of the Statistics (Arrangements with States) Act which became law on 12 May 1956, the statistical services of all the States have been integrated with the Australian Bureau. An outline of the development of statistics in Australia is published in the *Official Year Book*, No. 51, 1965. *Australian Statistician:* Dr R. J. Cameron.

The principal publications of the Bureau are:

Official Year Book of Australia. 1907 to date
Pocket Compendium of Australian Statistics. 1913 to date
Monthly Review of Business Statistics. Oct. 1937 to date
Digest of Current Economic Statistics. Aug. 1959 to date
Catalogue of Publications, 1977

Other Official Publications

Atlas of Australian Resources. Dept. of National Development, Melbourne, 1955 ff.
Climatological Atlas of Australia. Bureau of Meteorology. Melbourne, 1940
Norfolk Island—Annual Report. Government of New South Wales and Commonwealth of Australia. From 1896
Cocos (Keeling) Islands—Annual Report. Dept. of Administrative Services, Canberra
Christmas Island—Annual Report. Dept. of Administrative Services, Canberra. From 1958
Australian Books: Select List of Works About or Published in Australia. National Library of Australia, Canberra, 1934 to date
Australian National Bibliography. Canberra, 1936 to date
Historical Records of Australia. 34 vols. National Library, Canberra, 1914–25
Australia: Official Handbook. Dept. of the Capital Territory, Canberra, 1961 to date
Australian Foreign Affairs Record. Dept. of Foreign Affairs, Canberra, 1936 to date

Non-Official Publications

Australian Treaty List. Dept. of Foreign Affairs, Canberra, consolidated volume from Federation to 1970 with supplements to date
Documents on Australian Foreign Policy 1937–49. Vol. 1: 1937–38, Vol. 2: 1939, Vol. 3 in preparation. Dept. of Foreign Affairs, Canberra
Diplomatic List. Dept. of Foreign Affairs, Canberra. 1949 to date
Consular and Trade Representatives. Dept. of Foreign Affairs, Canberra. 1936 to date
Australian Quarterly: A Quarterly Review of Australian Affairs. Sydney, 1929 to date
Australian National Travel Association. *Australian Tourist Guide.* Melbourne, 1960
Barnes, V. S. (ed.), *The Modern Encyclopædia of Australia and New Zealand.* Sydney, 1965
Butler, D., *The Canberra Model: Essays on Australian Government.* London, 1974
Chisholm, A. H. (ed.), *Australian Encyclopædia.* 10 vols. Sydney, 1962

Clark, C. M. H. (ed.), *Select Documents in Australian History, 1788–1900*. 2 vols. Sydney, 1950–55
Ferguson, Sir John, *Bibliography of Australia, 1784–1850*. 4 vols. Sydney, 1941–55; vol. 5 (1851–1900), Part 1, 1963. Parts 2 and 3 in preparation
Grant, B., *The Crisis of Loyalty: A Study of Australian Foreign Policy*. Sydney, 1972
Greenwood, G. (ed.), *Australia, A Political and Social History*. 3rd ed. Sydney, 1960.—(ed.), *Australia in World Affairs, 1950–55*. Melbourne, 1957
Hancock, Sir Keith, *Australia*. Brisbane, 1961
Horne, D., *The Australian People*. Sydney, 1972
Menzies, Sir Robert, *Speech is of Time*. London, 1958
Moore, T. I. (ed.), *A Book of Australia*. London, 1961
Noble, N. S. (ed.), *The Australian Environment*. 3rd ed. Melbourne, 1960
Serle, P., *Dictionary of Australian Biography*. 2 vols. Sydney, 1949
Spate, O. H. K., *Australia*. London, 1968
Taylor, T. G., *Australia: A Study of Warm Environments and their Effect on British Settlement*. 7th ed. London, 1959
Who's Who in Australia. Melbourne, 1906 to date

National Library: The National Library, Canberra, A.C.T. *Director-General:* Dr G. Chandler.

AUSTRALIAN TERRITORIES

AUSTRALIAN ANTARCTIC TERRITORY

An Imperial Order in Council of 7 Feb. 1933 placed under Australian authority all the islands and territories other than Adélie Land situated south of 60° S. lat. and lying between 160° E. long. and 45° E. long. The Order came into force with a Proclamation issued by the Governor-General on 24 Aug. 1936 after the passage of the Australian Antarctic Territory Acceptance Act 1933. The boundaries of Adélie Land were definitively fixed by a French Decree of 1 April 1938 as the islands and territories south of 60° S. lat. lying between 136° E. long. and 142° E. long. The Australian Antarctic Territory Act 1954 declared that the laws in force in the Australian Capital Territory are, so far as they are applicable and are not inconsistent with any ordinance made under the Act, in force in the Australian Antarctic Territory.

In 1968 responsibility for the administration of this Act was transferred from the Minister for External Affairs to the Minister for Supply; in 1972 responsibility was transferred to the Minister for Science.

On 13 Feb. 1954 the Australian National Antarctic Research Expeditions (ANARE) established a base on MacRobertson Land at lat. 67° 36′ S. and long. 62° 52′ E. The base was named Mawson in honour of the late Sir Douglas Mawson. Meteorological and other scientific research is conducted at Mawson, which is the centre for coastal and inland survey expeditions.

A second Australian scientific research station was established on the coast of Princess Elizabeth Land on 13 Jan. 1957 at lat. 68° 34′ 36″ S. and long. 77° 58′ 36″ E. The station was named Davis in honour of Capt. John King Davis, Mawson's second-in-command on 2 expeditions. The station was temporarily closed down in Jan. 1965 and re-opened in Feb. 1969.

In Feb. 1959 the Australian Government accepted from the US Government custody of Wilkes Station, which was established by the US on 16 Jan. 1957 on the Budd Coast of Wilkes Land, at lat. 66° 15′ S. and long. 110° 32′ E. The station was named in honour of Lieut. Charles Wilkes, who commanded the 1838–40 US expedition to the area, and was closed in Feb. 1969. Operations were transferred to the new station, Casey. Construction commenced on Casey station in Jan. 1965 and was continued, mainly during summer visits, until Feb. 1969, when it was opened. The station, specially designed to withstand blizzard winds and prevent inundation by snow, is situated 2·4 km south of Wilkes at lat. 66° 17′ S. and long. 110° 32′ E. It was named after Lord Casey, Governor-General of Australia 1965–69. ANARE have also operated a station, since March 1948, at Macquarie Island, about 1,370 km south-east of Hobart. Macquarie Island is a dependency of the State of Tasmania.

On 1 Dec. 1959 Australia signed the Antarctic Treaty with Argentina, Belgium, Chile, France, Japan, New Zealand, Norway, South Africa, the USSR, the UK and the USA. Poland, Czechoslovakia, German Democratic Republic, Netherlands, Romania, Brazil and Denmark have subsequently acceded to the Treaty. The Treaty reserves the Antarctic area south of 60° S. lat. for peaceful purposes, provides for international co-operation in scientific investigation and research, and preserves, for the duration of the Treaty, the *status quo* with regard to territorial sovereignty, rights and claims. The Treaty entered into force on 23 June 1961. Since then the Antarctic Treaty powers have held several consultative meetings.

COCOS (KEELING) ISLANDS. The Cocos (Keeling) Islands, 2 separate atolls comprising some 27 small coral islands with a total area of about 14·2 sq. km, are situated in the Indian Ocean in 12° 05′ S. lat. and 96° 53′ E. long. They lie some 2,770 km north-west of Perth and 3,685 km west of Darwin, while Colombo is 2,255 km to the north-west of the group.

The islands were discovered in 1609 by Capt. William Keeling of the East India Company. The islands were uninhabited until 1826, when the first settlement was established on the main atoll by an Englishman, Alexander Hare, who left the islands in 1831. In the meantime a second settlement was formed on the main atoll by John Clunies Ross, a Scottish seaman and adventurer, who landed with several boat-loads of Malay seamen. In 1857 the islands were annexed to the Crown; in 1878 responsibility was transferred from the Colonial Office to the Government of Ceylon, and in 1886 to the Government of the Straits Settlement. By indenture in 1886 Queen Victoria granted the land comprised in the islands to George Clunies Ross and his heirs in perpetuity (with certain rights reserved to the Crown). The head of the family had semi-official status as resident magistrate and representative of the Government. In 1903 the islands were incorporated in the Settlement of Singapore and in 1942–46 temporarily placed under the Governor of Ceylon. In 1946 a Resident Administrator, responsible to the Governor of Singapore, was appointed.

On 23 Nov. 1955 the Cocos Islands were placed under the authority of the Australian Government, which accepted them under the Cocos (Keeling) Islands Act, 1955, as the Territory of Cocos (Keeling) Islands. An Administrator, appointed by the Governor-General, is the Government's representative in the Territory and is responsible to the Minister for Home Affairs.

The main islands are West Island (the largest, about 10 km from north to south), on which is an airport and most of the European community; Home Island, the headquarters of the Clunies Ross Estate which employs and houses the Cocos Malay community; Direction Island; South Island and Horsburgh Island. North Keeling Island, which forms part of the Territory, lies about 24 km to the north of the group and has no inhabitants. Main settlements are on West Island and Home Island.

The airport on West Island is maintained and controlled by the Department of Home Affairs. Until April 1967 it was a re-fuelling point for aircraft on the service between Australia and South Africa.

The population of the Territory at 30 June 1977 was 444, distributed between Home Island (319) and West Island (125).

The group of atolls is low-lying, flat and thickly covered by coconut palms, and surrounds a lagoon in which ships drawing up to 7 metres may be anchored, but which is extremely difficult for navigation. Copra exports (1977) 171 tonnes.

The climate is equable and pleasant, being usually under the influence of the south-east trade winds for about three-quarters of the year. However, the winds vary at times, and meteorological reports from the Territory are particularly valuable for those engaged in forecasting for the eastern Indian Ocean. The temperature varies between 21° and 32° C., the rainfall is moderate and there are occasional violent storms.

The Cocos (Keeling) Islands Act 1955–1975 is the basis of the Territory's administrative, legislative and judicial systems. The laws of the Colony of Singapore which were in force in the islands immediately before the transfer have, with certain exceptions, been continued in force. They can be amended, repealed or substituted by ordinances made by the Governor-General.

Administrator: C. I. Buffett, MBE.

CHRISTMAS ISLAND is in the Indian Ocean, lat. 10° 25′ 22″ S., long. 105° 39′ 59″ E. It lies 360 km S., 8° E. of Java Head, and 417 km N. 79° E. from Cocos Islands, 1,310 km from Singapore and 2,623 km from Fremantle. Area about 135 sq. km. The climate is moderate. The island was formally annexed on 6 June 1888, placed under the administration of the Governor of the Straits Settlements in 1889, and incorporated with the Settlement of Singapore in 1900. Sovereignty was transferred to the Australian Government on 1 Oct. 1958. The population (estimate, 1977), 3,255 (Europeans, 378; Chinese, 1,839; Malays, 956 and 82 others).

The legislative, judicial and administrative systems are regulated by the Christmas Island Act, 1958–73, which is administered by the Minister for Home Affairs with an Administrator, responsible for the local administration. The laws of Singapore which were in force before the transfer have been continued but can be amended, repealed or substituted by ordinances made by the Governor-General.

Extraction and export of rock phosphate and phosphate dust is the island's only industry. In Dec. 1948 Australia and New Zealand bought the lease rights of the Christmas Island Phosphate Co. and set up the Christmas Island Phosphate Commission, for which the British Phosphate Commissioners act as managing agents. The export of phosphate rock during 1976–77 was 995,650 tonnes, which is shipped to Australia and New Zealand; in addition, about 123,260 tonnes of phosphate dust was shipped to Singapore, Malaysia and Indonesia.

There is direct radio communication with Australia and Singapore. Regular air charter flights commenced in 1974 to Australia.

At 30 June 1977 there were 557 pupils at primary and secondary schools. There is also a technical education centre with some 520 students.

Medical, dental and hospital services are provided free of charge by the British Phosphate Commission.

Administrator: F. C. Boyle.

AUSTRALIAN CAPITAL TERRITORY

HISTORY. The area, now the Australian Capital Territory, was first visited by white men in 1820 and settlement commenced in 1824. Until its selection as the seat of government it was a quiet pastoral and agricultural community.

AREA AND POPULATION. The area of the Australian Capital Territory is 2,432 sq. km (including Jervis Bay area). The population at 30 June 1977 was 209,000. Previous census population:

	Males	*Females*	*Total*
1911	992	722	1,714
1921	1,567	1,005	2,572
1933	4,805	4,142	8,947
1947	9,092	7,813	16,905
1954	16,229	14,086	30,315
1961	30,858	27,970	58,828
1966	49,991	46,041	96,032
1971	73,589	70,474	144,063
1976	100,103	97,519	197,622

(Figures before 1961 exclude particulars of full-blood Aborigines.)

CONSTITUTION AND GOVERNMENT. The constitution of Australia provided (Sec. 125) that the seat of government should be selected by parliament and that it should be within New South Wales but at least 161 km from Sydney. The present area was surrendered by New South Wales and accepted by the Australian Government from 1 Jan. 1911. In 1915 an additional 73 sq. km at Jervis Bay was transferred from New South Wales to the Commonwealth. In 1911 an international competition was held for the city plan. The plan chosen was that of W. Burley Griffin, of Chicago. Construction was delayed by the First World War, and it was not until 1927 that, with the transfer of parliament and certain departments, Canberra became in fact the seat of government. Most Commonwealth Government departments now have their headquarters in Canberra.

The general administration of the Territory is in the hands of the Minister for the Capital Territory, but certain specific services are undertaken by other Australian Government Departments and Authorities. Since Sept. 1974 the Minister has been advised on matters of local concern by the ACT Legislative Assembly consisting of 18 elected members. Prior to that date this function was performed by an Advisory Council consisting of both nominated and elected members.

The Australian Capital Territory Representation (House of Representatives) Act, 1973, provided for the representation of residents of the Territory by 2 elected members in the House of Representatives. The Senate (Representation of Territories) Act 1973 provided for the election of 2 Senators from the Territory. Elections took place in Dec. 1975.

FINANCE. The receipts and outlay of the Australian Capital Territory cover the transactions of the Commonwealth Government in the Consolidated Revenue and other funds. They also include details of the ACT public corporations.

Receipts and outlay ($A1,000) for years ended 30 June:

	Receipts	*Outlay* *Capital*	*Current*	*Total*
1973	31,000	60,000	68,000	128,000
1974	36,000	117,000	85,000	202,000
1975	41,000	175,000	127,000	302,000
1976	56,000	199,000	170,000	369,000

The chief sources of receipts in 1975–76 were taxes, fees and fines, $A32m.; and interest and rent, $A17m. Capital outlay comprised gross capital formation, $A170m., and advances to other sectors, $A29m.

PRODUCTION. The Territory is predominantly pastoral. Livestock, 31 March 1977: 19,000 cattle, 124,000 sheep. A considerable amount of reafforestation (mostly pine) has been undertaken, the total area of commercial plantations at 31 Dec. 1976 being 13,600 hectares. There is no secondary industry of any importance.

EDUCATION. In 1974 education in government schools became the direct responsibility of the Commonwealth Government. A School's Authority has been established to administer the Australian Capital Territory government school system. There are 62 government primary and infants schools, including 1 in the Jervis Bay area, with a total enrolment (Aug. 1977) of 24,731 pupils. Secondary education is provided at 15 secondary schools and 5 secondary colleges with an enrolment, at Aug. 1977, of 14,192 pupils. Pre-school education is provided at 69 centres with a total enrolment of 4,782 (Aug. 1977). There are also 27 non-government schools, 9 of which provide secondary education; total enrolment (Aug. 1977) 13,811. The Canberra Technical College and Bruce College of Technical and Further Education with a total enrolment of about 11,000 in 1977 provide training for apprentices and journeymen and also offer commercial and special courses.

The Canberra School of Music, opened in 1965, had about 340 students in 1977.

The Canberra College of Advanced Education commenced operation in 1970. Courses are available in the schools of administrative studies, applied science, computing studies, liberal studies and teacher education. Enrolments (1977) 4,705.

The Australian National University is situated in Canberra (*see* p. 119).

Books of Reference

A.C.T. Statistical Summary. Australian Bureau of Statistics. From 1960
Annual Report. National Capital Development Commission. From 1958
Tomorrow's Canberra. National Capital Development Commission, 1970
Wigmore, L., *Canberra: A History of Australia's National Capital.* 2nd ed. Canberra, 1971

NORFOLK ISLAND. 29° 04′ S. lat, 167° 57′ E. long., area 3,451 hectares, population, approximately 1,600. The island was formerly part of the colony of New South Wales and then of Van Diemen's Land. It has been a distinct settlement since 1856, under the jurisdiction of the state of New South Wales; and finally by the passage of the Norfolk Island Act 1913, it was accepted as a Territory of the Australian Government. Norfolk Island Council consists of the Administrator and 8 elected members. The Council may consider and advise the Administrator on any matter affecting the peace, order and government of the territory, and is consulted on legislative and financial matters.

The island is very picturesque and has a delightful climate. Primary production is not fully adequate for local needs and foodstuffs are imported from New Zealand and Australia, mainly for the tourist trade. Tourism is the major industry. The island has many links with Australia's early penal days and the descendants of the *Bounty* mutineers are residents. In 1976–77 imports ($A3·2m. from Australia) totalled $A6·9m. and exports $A0·8m. A programme of forestry development is being carried out.

Administrator: D. V. O'Leary, VRD.

HEARD AND McDONALD ISLANDS. These islands, about 2,500 miles south-west of Fremantle, were transferred from UK to Australian control as from 26 Dec. 1947. Heard Island is about 43 km long and 21 km wide; Shag Island is about 8 km north of Heard. The total area is 412 sq. km (159 sq. miles). The McDonald Islands are 42 km to the west of Heard.

NORTHERN TERRITORY

HISTORY. The Northern Territory, after forming part of New South Wales, was annexed on 6 July 1863 to South Australia and in 1901 entered the Commonwealth as a corporate part of South Australia. The Commonwealth Constitution Act of 1900 made provision for the surrender to the Commonwealth of any territory by any state, and under this provision an agreement was entered into on 7 Dec. 1907 for the transfer of the Northern Territory to the Commonwealth, and it formally passed under the control of the Commonwealth Government on 1 Jan. 1911.

AREA AND POPULATION. The Northern Territory is bounded by the 26th parallel of S. lat. and 129° and 138° E. long. Its total area is 1,346,200 sq. km. On 30 June 1973 the area held under freehold title was 74,000 hectares; 80,570,800 hectares were held under leasehold; 2,350,600 hectares were held under various licences; 25,242,900 hectares were reserved for public purposes and for the benefit of Aboriginals; and 26,381,700 hectares were unalienated. Land rent collected for the year 1975–76 amounted to $A288,564. The coastline is about 6,200 km in length, the principal port being Darwin. The greater part of the interior consists of a tableland rising gradually from the coast to a height of about 700 metres. On this tableland there are large areas of excellent pasturage. The southern part of the Territory is generally sandy and has a small rainfall, but water may be obtained by means of sub-artesian bores. The climate is tropical, but varies considerably over the whole Territory.

In the coastal region, there are two main climatic divisions—the wet season, Nov. to April, and the dry season, May to Oct. Farther south the climate is of a continental type, showing a great variation between the hottest and coldest months.

The census population, excluding full-blood Aboriginals, was as follows:

	Europeans	*Total*		*Europeans*	*Total*
1881	667	3,451	1947	9,116	10,868
1901	782	4,811	1954	14,031	16,469
1911	1,418	3,310	1961	23,599	27,095
1921	2,458	3,867	1966	33,784	37,433
1933	3,306	4,850	1971	—	86,390

The census population, including Aboriginals, was 97,090 as at June 1976; the population of Darwin urban area was 42,818. After the cyclone, 'Tracy', that devastated Darwin on 25 Dec. 1974, the population of Darwin fell to 11,000.

CONSTITUTION AND GOVERNMENT. On 1 Feb. 1927 the Northern Territory was divided for administrative purposes into two parts, North Australia and Central Australia, the dividing line being the 20th parallel of S. lat. Each part was under a Government Resident, with headquarters at Darwin and Alice Springs respectively. This division was effected under the authority of the Northern Territory Act, 1926, which also provided for a North Australia Commission, the powers of which extended to matters relating to the development of North Australia, and also to the administration of Crown lands throughout North Australia and Central Australia. The Northern Australia Act, 1926, was repealed as from 12 June 1931 by the Northern Territory (Administration) Act, 1931. The North Australia Commission was abolished, and the whole of the Northern Territory was again placed under the control of an Administrator. The Administrator remains the head of government in the Territory. His residence is in Darwin, and he is responsible to the federal Executive Council through the Minister of State for the Northern Territory. The administration of the Territory is divided between various federal departments.

The Legislative Council for the Northern Territory was set up by an amendment to the Northern Territory (Administration) Act in 1947. The Council was reconstituted in 1959 by a further amendment to the Act to consist of the Administrator, 6 official members, 3 appointed non-official members and 8 elected members. In 1965 an amendment provided for the withdrawal of the Administrator and the election of a Council President from among the elected members. The council was again reconstituted in 1968 to consist of 6 official and 11 elected members with effect from the elections for the Council held in Oct. 1968. In 1974 the Legislative Council was replaced by a fully-elected, 19-member Legislative Assembly, as a step towards self-government for the Territory. The presiding officer of the new Assembly is known as the Speaker.

All Ordinances passed by the Assembly are presented to the Administrator for assent. The Administrator must reserve certain Ordinances for the Governor-General's pleasure. Others he may assent to, withhold assent, reserve for the Governor-General's pleasure or return to the Assembly with amendments that he recommends. The Governor-General may assent to an Ordinance, withhold assent to whole or part of an Ordinance, or return it to the Administrator with amendments he recommends. He may also disallow in whole or part any Ordinance the Administrator has assented to. An Administrator's Council was set up in 1959 to advise the Administrator on any matter referred to it by the Administrator or in accordance with any Ordinance. In 1976 the Northern Territory (Administration) Act was amended to replace the Administrator's Council with an Executive Council of 5 members of the Legislative Council with the designation Executive Member. The Northern Territory elects one member to the House of Representatives who has full voting rights, and is represented by 2 Senators in the Senate. In Dec. 1973 the

Northern Territory Administration was replaced by the Department of the Northern Territory.

Administrator: J. A. England.

FINANCE. The revenue and expenditure (in $A1,000) for years ended 30 June covering the transactions of the Northern Territory Department were as follows:

	1971–72	*1972–73*	*1973–74*	*1974–75*	*1975–76*
Revenue	18,051	20,876	22,506	31,947	22,290
Expenditure	130,005	143,328	110,625	205,174	302,687

The chief sources of revenue for 1975–76 were: Electricity supply, $A5·2m.; rents and rates, $A4·8m. Capital expenditure (excluding business undertakings) amounted to $A55·3m.

NATURAL RESOURCES, INDUSTRY AND TRADE

Minerals. The mining industry is the Northern Territory's main industry. The main minerals produced are bauxite ore, manganese ore, copper, gold and bismuth ore. The value of all mineral production in 1974–75 was $A139·5m.

In the Gove area of Arnhem Land a bauxite/alumina project has been completed. Development costs were in excess of $A310m. Exports of bauxite commenced in June 1971 and the alumina plant commenced operation at a capacity of 500,000 tonnes per annum in July 1972. The plant expanded to a capacity of 1m. tonnes per annum by July 1973 and by July 1974 the capacity had risen to 1·6m. tonnes per annum.

During 1974–75, 4,177,981 tonnes of bauxite ore were produced, 2,375,977 tonnes of this went into the alumina plant, where 921,310 tonnes of alumina were produced from it. The balance of the bauxite ore was exported to Europe (49%), Japan (47%) and the USA (4%).

Manganese ore is produced on Groote Eylandt. Northern Territory production in 1974–75 was 3m. tonnes. The ore is shipped to Tasmania, Japan, Europe and the USA.

Shipments of iron ore from Frances Creek through the port of Darwin ceased in Dec. 1975, after the bulk loading facilities at the wharf had been badly damaged by cyclone 'Tracy'.

Mines in the Tennant Creek area are the principal producers of gold, copper and bismuth in the Northern Territory. In 1974–75 the Northern Territory production of these minerals was bismuth concentrate, 1,168 tonnes; copper, 8,893 tonnes; silver, 1,876,974 grammes; and gold, 4,891,781 grammes.

In the Alligator River region 240 km east of Darwin, rich deposits of uranium have been discovered at Nabarlek, Jabiru (Ranger), Koongarra and Jabiluka. This area is considered to be a uranium province of world importance.

The possibilities for the development of the oil deposits of the Palm Valley and Mereenie Fields are still under investigation. In the interim the recoverable reserves at Mereenie are estimated to be 60m. bbls of crude oil and 300,000m. cu. metres of natural gas.

Agriculture. General agriculture is conducted on a small scale in the Northern Territory. Small quantities of fruit, vegetables, eggs, dairy produce, poultry and pasture are produced. Seeds were produced in areas adjacent to the principal population centres. The total gross value of agricultural production for 1975–76 was $A1·5m. However the beef cattle industry is the main rural activity in the Northern Territory, and production depends almost entirely on export markets. Due to the depressed state of the industry brought about by restricted meat export markets, the value of beef production for the year 1975–76 was only $A19·8m. Buffalo production realized $A500,000. A recent development has been an increase in the export of live cattle and buffalo to overseas countries which has provided alternative markets to producers.

Despite the depressed state of the industry, the accelerated eradication programme for tuberculosis and brucellosis is progressing satisfactorily and compensation payments are now extended to include cattle slaughtered as brucellosis reactors.

Livestock (30 June 1976): 1·5m. cattle; 2,000 sheep; 300,000 buffalo; 2,500 breeding sows.

Forestry. A forest development programme which commenced in 1970 has continued the multiple use management of Northern Territory forested areas; this programme included a softwood programme of 400 hectares per year, the introduction of additional suitable tree species in both arid and higher rainfall areas, conservation and management of native forests for production and recreational purposes, survey and assessment of resources, fire control activities and the creation of training opportunities for Aboriginals in forestry and allied saw-milling activities.

Local production of sawn timber, mainly Cypress pine, amounted to 870 cu. metres of pine in 1975–76. This was supplemented by 35,500 cu. metres of timber imported from interstate and overseas.

Local production of treated poles and rails amounted to 115 cu. metres. Only 280 hectares of plantation were established during the year because of complications arising from cyclone 'Tracy'.

During 1975–76 the Forestry Section of the Department of the Northern Territory redeveloped parks and open-space areas on behalf of the Darwin Reconstruction Commission.

Fisheries. The fishing industry is second only to beef cattle in Northern Territory primary industries. During 1974–75 the industry employed over 600 people and used vessels and equipment worth in excess of $A24m. The major fishery is prawning, and for 1974–75 over 1,100 tonnes (processed weight) of prawns were exported. This represented 15% of the total Australian prawn exports and was valued at $A3·14m.

The other main fishery in the Territory is scale fish, particularly Barramundi (Giant Perch). Total scale fish production for 1974–75 was 781 tonnes live weight, valued at $A613,000.

A major review of Northern Territory fisheries was carried out between 1973 and 1975 with assistance of a consultant resource economist and the final report contains several specific recommendations designed to increase the economic stability of fisheries.

Industry. In 1974–75 value added in the manufacturing industry, from 67 factories (with 4 or more persons employed) was $A47,798,000. 2,305 persons were employed in these factories.

Tourism. Prior to cyclone 'Tracy' the industry had been experiencing growth rates in the order of 12% per annum. There has been some fall off in visitor flow since. The most recent visitor figures available show approximately 113,000 people visiting the Territory, including 12,000 overseas visitors. Of these, 70,670 visited the Alice Springs region and 64,200 visited Darwin.

National Parks and Reserves. About 43,000 sq. km have been set aside as wildlife sanctuaries under the Wildlife Conservation and Control Ordinance. They are controlled by the Chief Inspector of Wildlife who is an officer of the Department of the Northern Territory. 236,000 sq. km of Aboriginal reserves are also wild-life protected areas.

The Northern Territory Reserves Board administers some 37 national parks and reserves covering an area of over 249,926 hectares. The Board is responsible under the National Parks and Gardens Ordinance for the care, control and management of these reserves, and its functions include the preservation and protection of natural and historical features and the encouragement of public use and enjoyment of land set aside in such reserves.

COMMUNICATIONS

Roads. There are now 4,846 km of sealed road within the Northern Territory. They include three major interstate links: the Stuart Highway from Darwin to the South Australian border, the Barkly Highway, Tennant Creek to Mt. Isa, 447 km of which is in the Northern Territory, and the Victoria Highway, Katherine to the Western

Australian border, a distance of 452 km. In addition to this there are 1,440 km of gravel roads, 4,400 km of formed roads and 9,250 km of unformed roads or tracks, totalling approximately 20,000 km of roads within the Northern Territory.

Railways. Services ceased from 20 June 1976 on the narrow-gauge railway from Darwin to Larrimah (510 km).

Alice Springs is connected by a narrow-gauge (869 km) and standard-gauge railway (342 km) through Port Augusta to the Australian rail network. A standard-gauge railway is currently being constructed on a completely new alignment from Tarcoola on the Trans-Australian line to Alice Springs. Completion of the new line is expected by 1981.

Aviation. Darwin is the first port of arrival in Australia for some aircraft from Europe and Asia. There are regular inland services connecting Darwin with all the State capitals and many inland towns.

Shipping. Regular freight shipping services connect Darwin with Western Australia, the eastern States and overseas. Passenger vessels also call at Darwin at irregular intervals.

The ports of Melville Bay (Gove) and Milner Bay (Groote Eylandt) are connected with Darwin, the eastern States and overseas by regular shipping freight services.

The island and coastal communities around the coast are provided with regular freight barge services from Darwin. Some of these communities also receive a barge freight-transhipment service out of a Brisbane vessel which calls at Melville and Milner Bays, where the transhipment is effected.

TERRITORY OF ASHMORE AND CARTIER ISLANDS. By Imperial Order in Council of 23 July 1931, Ashmore Islands (known as Middle, East and West Islands) and Cartier Island, situated in the Indian Ocean, some 320 km off the north-west coast of Australia, were placed under the authority of the Commonwealth.

Under the Ashmore and Cartier Islands Acceptance Act, 1933, the islands were accepted by the Commonwealth under the name of the Territory of Ashmore and Cartier Islands, and the effective date was proclaimed by the Governor-General to be 10 May 1934. It was the intention that the Territory should be administered by the State of Western Australia, but owing to administrative difficulties the Territory was annexed to and deemed to form part of the Northern Territory of Australia (by amendment to the Act in 1938) and all the laws of the Northern Territory, as far as they are applicable, apply to the Territory of Ashmore and Cartier Islands. The islands are uninhabited.

An automatic weather station on West Ashmore Island (completed in Sept. 1962) supplies the Commonwealth Meteorological Bureau with regular reports.

Periodic visits are made to the islands by ships of the Royal Australian Navy, and aircraft of the Royal Australian Air Force make aerial surveys of the islands and neighbouring waters.

Books of Reference

The Northern Territory: Annual Report. Dept. of Territories, Canberra, from 1911. Dept. of the Interior, Canberra, from 1966–67. Dept. of Northern Territory, from 1972

Australian Territories, Dept. of Territories, Canberra, 1960 to 1973. Dept. of Special Minister of State, Canberra, 1973–75. Department of Administrative Services, 1976

Northern Territory Statistical Summary. Australian Bureau of Statistics, Canberra, from 1960

Prospects of Agriculture in the Northern Territory. Dept. of Territories, Canberra, 1961

Northern Territory Scientific Liaison Conference, Darwin, 1961, *Conference Papers.* Melbourne, 1961

Holmes, J. M., *Australia's Open North.* Sydney, 1963

Lockwood, D. W., *Fair Dinkum.* London, 1960

Polisheck, N., *Life on the Daly River.* London, 1961

NEW SOUTH WALES

HISTORY. New South Wales became a British possession in 1770; the first settlement was established at Port Jackson in 1788; a partially elective Council was established in 1843, and responsible government in 1856. New South Wales federated with the other Australian states to form the Commonwealth of Australia in 1901.

AREA AND POPULATION. New South Wales is situated between the 28th and 38th parallels of S. lat. and 141st and 154th meridians of E. long., and comprises 309,433 sq. miles (801,428 sq. km), inclusive of Lord Howe Island, 6 sq. miles (17 sq. km), but exclusive of the Australian Capital Territory (911 sq. miles, 2,359 sq. km) at Canberra and 28 sq. miles (73 sq. km), at Jervis Bay.

Lord Howe Island, 31° 33′ 4″ S., 159° 4′ 26″ E., a dependency of New South Wales, situated about 702 km north-east of Sydney; area, 1,656 hectares, of which only about 120 hectares are arable; population (30 June 1976), 244. The island, which was discovered in 1788, is of volcanic origin. Mount Gower, the highest point, reaches a height of 852 metres.

A Board at Sydney and an elected Island Committee manage the affairs of the island and supervise the Kentia palm-seed industry.

Census population (includes full-blood aboriginals from 1966):

	Males	*Females*	*Persons*	*Population per sq. km*	*Average annual increase % since previous census*
1881	410,211	339,614	749,825	1	4·07
1891	609,666	517,471	1,127,137	1	4·16
1901	710,264	645,091	1,355,355	2	1·86
1911	857,698	789,036	1,646,734	2	1·97
1921	1,071,501	1,028,870	2,100,371	3	2·46
1933	1,318,471	1,282,376	2,600,847	3	1·76
1947	1,492,211	1,492,627	2,984,838	4	0·99
1954	1,720,860	1,702,669	3,423,529	4	1·98
1966	2,126,652	2,111,249	4,237,901	5	1·58
1971	2,307,210	2,293,970	4,601,180	6	1·66
1976	2,380,172	2,396,931	4,777,103	6	0·75

At 30 June 1976 the census population of New South Wales was 4,777,103, Sydney (Statistical Division), 3,021,299; Newcastle (Statistical District), 362,980; Wollongong (Statistical District), 211,122. Population of principal country municipalities: Wagga Wagga, 34,301; Albury, 32,942; Tamworth, 29,385; Broken Hill, 27,643; Orange, 25,499; Lismore, 22,080; Goulburn, 21,735; Dubbo, 20,149; Armidale, 19,709; Queanbeyan, 18,920; Bathurst, 18,589; Grafton, 16,514; Port Macquarie, 13,495; Taree, 12,912; Lithgow, 12,343; Inverell, 9,432.

Vital statistics for calendar years:

	Live births	*Marriages*	*Divorces*	*Deaths (excluding still-births)*	*Infantile mortality per 1,000 live births*	*Estimated net migration*
1973	87,332	40,722	7,396	41,122	17·1	– 5,300
1974	86,162	39,327	7,117	43,999	16·6	22,932
1975	80,918	36,958	10,723	40,497	15·2	–24,500
1976	78,492	38,486	22,872	42,122	14·7	800

The annual rates per 1,000 of the population in 1976 were: Births, 15·97; deaths, 8·57; marriages, 7·83.

CONSTITUTION AND GOVERNMENT. Within the State there are three levels of government: the Australian Government, with authority derived from a written constitution; the State Government with residual powers; the local government authorities with powers based upon a State Act of Parliament, operating within incorporated areas extending over seven-eighths of the State.

The constitution of New South Wales is drawn from several diverse sources; certain Imperial statutes such as the Colonial Laws Validity Act (1865) and the Commonwealth of Australia Constitution Act (1900); the Australian States Constitution Act (1907); the Letters Patent and the Instructions to the Governor; an element of inherited English law; amendments to the Commonwealth of Australia Constitution Act; the State Constitution Act and certain other State Statutes; numerous legal decisions; and a large amount of English and local convention.

The Parliament of New South Wales may legislate for the peace, welfare and good government of the State in all matters not specifically reserved to the Australian Government.

The State Legislature consists of the Sovereign, represented by the Governor, and two Houses of Parliament, the Legislative Council (upper house) and the Legislative Assembly (lower house).

The Legislative Council consists of 60 members elected jointly by both Houses of Parliament for a term of 12 years. Fifteen members retire every third year.

The President has an annual salary (1977) of $A26,140; the Chairman of Committees, $A15,760; the Leader of the Opposition, $A11,620; the Deputy Leader of the Opposition and Government and Opposition Whips, $A11,100 each. An annual expense allowance paid to the President, $A4,425; and for the other positions mentioned above, $A4,350 each. Other members who are not Ministers receive an annual salary of $A9,540 and an annual expense allowance of $A3,540. All members, other than Ministers, receive a living-away-from-home allowance of $A42 per day if they live outside the metropolitan area.

The Legislative Assembly has 99 members elected for a period of 3 years. Voting is compulsory. British subjects above 18 years of age, having resided 6 months in Australia, 3 months in the State and 1 month in any one electoral district, are eligible for enrolment as electors. Women were enfranchised in 1902. Salaries are adjusted annually, and those given are for 1977.

The Speaker of the Legislative Assembly receives a salary of $A35,990; the Leader of the Opposition, $A35,990; the Chairman of Committees, $A25,910; the Deputy Leader of the Opposition, $A25,910; Government and Opposition Whips, $A24,140 each. The Speaker also receives an expense allowance of $A5,000; the Leader of the Opposition, $A4,900; the Chairman of Committees, $A2,750; the Deputy Leader of the Opposition, $A2,750; Government and Opposition Whips, $A1,300 each, and the Country Party Whip, $A1,300. Members who are not Ministers receive an annual salary of $A20,660. All members receive an annual electoral allowance ranging from $A6,300 to $A9,900 according to the location of their constituencies.

The Legislative Assembly, elected on 1 May 1976, consisted in Oct. 1977 of the following parties: Labor, 50; Liberal and Country Party, 48; Independent, 1.

The executive is in the hands of a Governor, appointed by the Crown, and an Executive Council consisting of members of the Cabinet. Ministers receive the following annual salaries: Premier, $A45,860; Deputy Premier, $A41,030; the Leader of the Government in the Legislative Council, $A41,530; other Ministers, $A38,550. Ministers also receive an expense allowance (Premier, $A10,700; Deputy Premier, $A5,350; other Ministers, $A5,000 each). Ministers who are members of the Legislative Assembly receive an electoral allowance ranging from $A6,300 to $A9,900 according to the location of their constituency.

Governor: Sir Roden Cutler, VC, KCMG, KCVO, CBE, KStJ (sworn in 20 Jan. 1966).

The Labor Party Cabinet, in Oct. 1977, was constituted as follows:

Premier: The Hon. N. K. Wran, QC, MLA.

Deputy Premier, Minister for Public Works and Minister for Ports: The Hon. L. J. Ferguson, MLA. *Treasurer:* The Hon. J. B. Renshaw, MLA. *Minister for Transport and Minister for Highways:* The Hon. P. F. Cox, MLA. *Attorney-General:* The Hon. F. J. Walker, LLM, MLA. *Minister for Industrial Relations, Minister for Mines and Minister for Energy:* The Hon. P. D. Hills, MLA. *Minister for Planning and Environment and Vice-President of the Executive Council:* The Hon. D. P. Landa,

LLB, MLC. *Minister for Decentralization and Development and Minister for Primary Industries:* The Hon. Donald Day, MLA. *Minister for Education:* The Hon. E. L. Bedford, BA, MLA. *Minister for Local Government:* The Hon. H. F. Jensen, MLA. *Minister for Lands:* The Hon. W. F. Crabtree, MLA. *Minister for Health:* The Hon. K. J. Stewart, MLA. *Minister for Consumer Affairs and Minister for Co-operative Societies:* The Hon. S. D. Einfield, MLA. *Minister of Justice and Minister for Housing:* The Hon. R. J. Mulock, LLB, MLA. *Minister for Sport and Recreation and Minister for Tourism:* The Hon. K. G. Booth, MLA. *Minister for Conservation and Minister for Water Resources:* The Hon. A. R. L. Gordon, MLA. *Minister for Youth and Community Services:* The Hon. R. F. Jackson, MLA. *Minister for Services and Minister Assisting the Premier:* The Hon. W. H. Haigh, MLA.

Agent-General in London: Sir Davis Hughes (66 Strand, WC2N 5LZ).

Local Government. A system of local government extends over most of the State, including the whole of the Eastern and Central land divisions and more than two-thirds of the sparsely populated Western division. At 30 June 1977 there were 82 municipalities, and 127 corporate bodies called shires. A number of the municipalities and shires have combined to form 52 county councils, which administer electricity or water supply undertakings or render other services of common benefit.

ECONOMY

Budget. State revenue and expenditure (in $A1,000) for financial years ending 30 June:

Service	*1973–74*	*1974–75*	*1975–76*	*1976–77*
Revenue				
Governmental	1,536,005	2,071,442	2,496,151	2,888,929
Business undertakings	347,674	385,843	418,268	465,729
Total[1]	1,878,509	2,452,089	2,909,110	3,354,658
Working Expenditure				
Governmental	1,269,607	1,764,248	2,100,993	2,368,117
Business undertakings	447,096	532,034	594,247	718,244
Debt Charges	183,520	...	220,128	268,754
Total[1]	1,895,052	2,492,634	2,910,059	3,355,115

[1] Net of inter-fund transfers.

State Government revenue in 1976–77 included (in $A1,000) receipts from the Australian Government of 1,302,110; namely, towards public debt charges, 5,835; general financial assistance, 1,133,400; health, etc., 30,356; education, 112,229; other purposes, 20,290 (including 12,729 for relief of national disasters). State Government expenditure in 1976–77 included (in $A1,000) expenditure on education, 1,012,921; health etc., 449,470; law, order, and public safety, 284,376; state resources, 226,663, and social amelioration, 103,709. Revenue of business undertakings (in $A1,000) comprised railways, 358,286; omnibuses, 40,513, and harbour services, 66,930. Provision for debt redemption included in debt charges was (in $A1,000), 29,234 in 1973–74, 30,217 in 1974–75, 35,182 in 1975–76 and 45,819 in 1976–77.

In terms of the financial agreement between the Australian and State Governments, the Australian Government has assumed responsibility for debts of the Australian States, and contributes towards the interest thereon and sinking funds established for redemption of the debts. Loans for the States are raised by the Australian Government in accordance with decisions of the Australian Loan Council.

Public Debt. The public debt of New South Wales at 30 June 1977 (overseas loans converted to Australian currency equivalent at current rates of exchange) comprised the following (in $A1,000): Repayable in Australia, 3,904,051; in London, 34,158; in New York, 17,299; in Canada, 2,290; in Netherlands, 1,254. Interest payments of 1976–77 amounted (in $A1,000) to 295,711, of which 2,975 was in respect of the external debt. The Australian Government contributed 5,835 towards the public debt charges. Contributions to the sinking fund for New South Wales debt, 54,615, included 10,506 contributed by the Australian Government, and the cost of securities redeemed to the year was 53,248.

Since the institution of the sinking fund in 1928 contributions have totalled $A845·74m. ($A181·02m. by the Australian Government), and redemptions at cost $A841·88m.

Banking. There were 10 trading banks operating in New South Wales at 30 June 1977, including the Commonwealth Trading Bank and Rural Bank (Government banks) and 1 New Zealand bank. The trading bank business is transacted chiefly by the Commonwealth Trading Bank and 6 private banks, all of which have their head offices in Australia. At 30 June 1977 the 10 banks operated 1,858 branches and 286 agencies in New South Wales.

The weekly average amount of deposits held in New South Wales by the 10 banks was $A8,233·7m. in June 1977, consisting of $A5,544·3m. bearing interest and $A2,689·4m. not bearing interest. Bank advances, overdrafts, bills discounted, etc., amounted to $A6,137m. A statement of other assets and liabilities of the banks in New South Wales is of little significance, as banking business is conducted on an Australia-wide basis.

Savings bank deposits at the end of June 1977 amounted to $A4,803·3m., representing $A974 per head of population.

ENERGY AND NATURAL RESOURCES

Minerals. New South Wales contains extensive mineral deposits. The most important minerals mined are: Coal (which accounts for 65% of the value of the State's mineral production); silver–lead–zinc (13%); construction materials (sand, gravel, stone, etc., 9%); and mineral sands (rutile, zircon etc., 7%). At 30 June 1976, there were 465 mining establishments employing 24,654 persons. During 1975–76, wages and salaries paid were $A291m., and value added was $A734m. Mine production of coal and metallic minerals (gross content) is shown below:

	1972–74	*1973–4*	*1974–75*	*1975–76*
Antimony (tonnes)	1,583	1,446	1,682	1,678
Cadmium (tonnes)	1,066	852	1,019	961
Coal (tonnes)	38,060,049	36,631,776	42,482,172	40,934,666
Cobalt (tonnes)	107	92	116	103
Copper (tonnes)	15,336	14,187	13,535	12,034
Gold (grammes)	301,746	259,438	335,486	481,790
Lead (tonnes)	239,773	216,940	256,608	225,808
Silver (grammes)	282,236,611	265,281,938	290,085,729	260,868,772
Sulphur (tonnes)	217,979	181,075	225,073	203,878
Tin (tonnes)	2,998	2,234	1,854	1,464
Titanium (tonnes)	213,571	184,066	183,698	192,789
Zinc (tonnes)	306,823	246,576	301,838	271,658
Zircon (tonnes)	240,074	175,,,428	187,957	183,585

The value of output in mining and quarrying in 1975–76 was $A976,775,154.

Land settlement. The total area of land alienated, virtually alienated or in process of alienation from the Crown on 30 June 1976 was 28,178,651 hectares, exclusive of the Australian Capital Territory; 40,363,186 hectares (including 30,109,646 hectares of the Western Division) were held under perpetual lease from the Crown; 2,766,263 hectares under the Crown leasehold tenures, and the total area of land neither alienated nor leased (including roads, reserves for public purposes, etc.) was 8,834,681 hectares.

Agriculture. The area under cultivation in New South Wales during 3 years (ended 31 March) and the principal crops (in tonnes) produced were as follows:

	1974	*1975*	*1976*
Hectares under cultivation	5,042,182	4,384,965	4,544,750
Value (farm) of all crops	$A669m.	$A683m.	$A745m.

Principal crops		1974 Hectares	1974 Produce	1975 Hectares	1975 Produce	1976 Hectares	1976 Produce
Wheat	Grain	2,882,971	3,961,525	2,646,336	3,808,658	2,774,081	4,310,465
	Hay	19,469	52,620	15,338	42,713	13,430	37,462
Maize	Grain	17,950	47,916	22,177	59,628	17,419	50,624
Barley	Grain	385,580	447,915	326,596	407,553	486,033	697,376
	Hay	2,055	4,961	1,591	3,239	1,287	2,887
Oats	Grain	404,828	327,219	269,913	293,068	289,563	349,902
	Hay	26,820	72,852	19,305	50,982	20,322	59,176
Potatoes		8,502	124,586	9,302	117,901	8,331	117,875
Lucerne (hay)		149,264	693,193	101,114	465,806	103,893	445,104
Tobacco		837	1,252	873	1,369	861	1,047
Rice		65,442	403,446	72,925	376,232	72,150	408,267
Cotton		31,020	58,806	27,511	82,110	23,861	66,153

In 1975–76, 11,010 hectares of sugar-cane were cut for crushing, the yield being 889,677 tonnes. The total area under grapes was 14,603 (including 1,442 not bearing) hectares; the production of table grapes was 4,939 tonnes; of wine, 50,626,409 litres; of dried vine fruits, 8,844 tonnes.

In 1975–76, 5,370 hectares of banana plantations; yield from 4,875 hectares, 55,289 tonnes; there were 186 hectares of passion fruit, pineapples, berries, etc.

At 31 March 1976 the State had 53m. sheep and lambs, 9,138,000 cattle and 708,800 pigs. The production of wool in 1975–76 was 217·2m. kg (greasy). In the year ended 30 June 1976 production of butter was 10,323,469 kg; cheese, 12,418,420 kg, and bacon and ham, 21,344,000 kg.

Forestry. The estimated forest area of Crown and private lands is 16·2m. hectares. The total area of State forests amounts to 3·3m hectares, and 372,000 hectares have been set apart as timber reserves.

The revenue from royalties, licences, etc., amounted in the year ended June 1976 to $A12,266,000.

At 30 June 1976 there were 682 saw-mills, employing 6,663 persons. The value of forestry production for 1975–76 was $A56·4m.

INDUSTRY AND TRADE

Industry. Approximately 27% of the civilian work force in New South Wales is employed in manufacturing industries.

A very wide range of manufacturing activities is undertaken in the Sydney area, and there are large iron and steel works and associated metal fabrication works in operation in proximity to the coalfields at Newcastle and Port Kembla.

The following table shows a preliminary summary of manufacturing industries' statistics for 1975–76:

Industry	Establishments[1] (No.)	Employment[2] Males (No.)	Employment[2] Females (No.)	Wages and salaries[3] ($A1m.)	Value added ($A1m.)
Food, beverages and tobacco	1,054	46,548	16,889	520·6	913·4
Textiles	247	7,041	5,992	96·7	168·6
Clothing and footwear	961	6,136	22,974	179·0	280·7
Wood, wood products and furniture	1,327	21,886	3,904	181·5	328·8
Paper and paper products, printing	1,125	26,207	10,450	309·3	529·1
Chemical, petroleum and coal products	429	20,069	9,471	275·8	645·3
Non-metallic mineral products	541	16,507	2,122	175·3	298·3
Basic metal products	212	51,099	3,723	488·2	867·0
Fabricated metal products	1,553	30,340	8,457	302·4	515·4
Transport equipment	400	35,344	4,078	328·1	480·6
Other machinery and equipment	1,644	55,635	22,099	615·7	1,004·1
Miscellaneous manufacturing	836	16,510	10,246	197·6	340·0
Total manufacturing	10,329	333,397	120,406	3,608·5	6,371·4

[1] Operating at 30 June 1976. Excludes single-establishment manufacturing enterprises with less than 4 persons employed.

[2] Persons employed—average over whole year, including working proprietors.

[3] Excludes drawings by working proprietors.

Some of the principal articles manufactured in 1976–77 were:

Article	*Quantity*	*Article*	*Quantity*
Flour (1,000 tonnes)	491	Gas (town) (1m.)	16,326
Footwear (1,000 prs)	5,192	Raw steel (1,000 tonnes)	6,441
Cloth: cotton, wool, rayon, synthetic (1,000 sq. metres)	57,553	Cars, etc.[1] (1,000)	66
		Claybricks (1m.)	655
Pig-iron (1,000 tonnes)	5,408	Electricity (1m. kwh.)	31,793

[1] Finished and partly finished motor vehicles, excluding trucks.

During 1976–77 the value of all building jobs commenced in New South Wales was $A1,648m. (of which jobs valued at $A354m. were being built for government ownership), jobs completed were valued at $A1,781m. ($A439m. for government ownership), and jobs under construction at the end of the period were valued at $A1,465m. ($A596m. for government ownership).

Labour. Two systems of industrial arbitration and conciliation for the adjustment of industrial relations between employers and employees are in operation—the State system which operates within the territorial limits of the State, and the Commonwealth system, which applies to industrial disputes extending beyond State borders.

The industrial tribunals are authorized to fix minimum rates of wages and other conditions of employment. Their awards may be enforced by law, as may be industrial agreements between employers and organizations of employees, when registered.

The principal State tribunal is the Industrial Commission, composed of judges. The Commission is empowered to exercise all the arbitration and conciliation powers conferred on subsidiary tribunals, and has in addition authority to determine any widely defined 'industrial matter', to adjudicate in case of illegal strikes and lockouts, etc., to investigate union ballots when irregularities are alleged and to hear appeals from subsidiary tribunals. Subsidiary tribunals are Conciliation Committees for various industries, each having an equal number representing employers and employees and a Conciliation Commissioner as chairman.

The chief industrial tribunals of the Commonwealth are the Industrial Court, composed of judges, and the Australian Conciliation and Arbitration Commission, composed of presidential members, and commissioners.

State awards and agreements prescribe a basic wage and, for each industry, margins assessed on skill, etc. Since May 1974, the State Industrial Commission has also specified a minimum wage in line with Commonwealth Awards. In Aug. 1977, the minimum wage payable in Sydney for a full week's work by an adult male or female was $A111.40 under both State and Commonwealth awards.

A standard working week of 40 hours is prescribed for employees in most industries. Overtime is permitted under prescribed conditions.

Trade Unions. Registration of trade unions is effected under the New South Wales Trade Union Act, 1881–1972, which follows substantially the Trade Union Acts of 1871 and 1876 of England. Registration confers a quasi-corporate existence with power to hold property, to sue and be sued, etc., and the various classes of employees covered by the union are required to be prescribed by the constitution of the union. For the purpose of bringing an industry under the review of the State industrial tribunals, or participating in proceedings relating to disputes before federal tribunals, employees and employers must be registered as industrial unions, under State or Federal industrial legislation respectively.

Commerce. The external commerce of New South Wales, exclusive of interstate trade, is included in the statement of the commerce of Australia (*see* pp. 111–13). The overseas commerce of the State is given in $A1,000 ending 30 June:

	Imports	*Exports*[1]		*Imports*	*Exports*[1]
1971–72	1,764,770	1,204,938	1974–75	3,494,781	1,979,005
1972–73	1,810,086	1,420,990	1975–76	3,451,189	2,253,660
1973–74	2,590,179	1,513,684	1976–77	4,278,062	2,809,391

[1] Includes non-Australian produce ($A152m. in 1976–77).

The main exports from New South Wales of Australian produce are coal (22·2%), wool (13·2%), wheat (11%), iron and steel (10·3%), machinery and transport equipment (6·7%), meat (5·3%), chemicals (3·8%), non-ferrous metals (3·5%). Principal imports are machinery and transport equipment (36·1%), chemicals (10·2%), textiles (6·1%), petroleum and petroleum products (5·5%), precision instruments and apparatus (4·6%).

Principal destinations of all exports from New South Wales are Japan (26·4%), EEC countries (18·7%), New Zealand (8·3%), USA (5·8%), Papua New Guinea (3·2%), USSR (2·5%). Major sources of supply are EEC countries (25%), USA (22·6%), Japan (21·1%), Federal Republic of Germany (6%) and New Zealand (3·4%).

COMMUNICATIONS

Roads. There are 209,271 km of roads and streets in New South Wales, comprising 436 km cement concrete, 6,230 km bituminous concrete, 60,212 km other bitumen surface, 65,499 km gravel, 41,920 km earth formed and 34,974 km natural surface. The bridge across Sydney Harbour is one of the largest arch bridges in the world.

The principal omnibus services in Sydney and Newcastle are the property of the State Government.

The number of registered motor vehicles (excluding tractors and trailers) on 30 June 1977 was 2,252,200, including 1,752,100 cars and station wagons, 136,900 utilities, 114,300 panel vans, 141,500 trucks, 11,600 buses and 95,800 motor cycles.

Railways. On 30 June 1977, 9,755 km of government railway were open. The earnings in 1976–77 were $A352m.; the working expenses, $A554m.; the number of passengers carried, 180m. Also open for traffic are 324 km of Victorian Government railways which extend over the border; 68 km of private railways (mainly in mining districts) and 8 km of Australian Government-owned track.

Aviation. Sydney is the major airport in New South Wales and Australia's principal international air terminal. During the year ended 30 June 1976 aircraft movement at Sydney totalled 104,900. Passengers totalled 4,788,086 on domestic services and 1,722,596 on international services. Freight handled on domestic and international services was 46,544 tonnes and 52,537 tonnes respectively.

Shipping. The vessels engaged in the interstate and overseas trade which entered the ports of New South Wales in 1975–76 numbered 3,489; net tonnage, 29,295,110; the clearances were 3,502 vessels, 29,470,317 tons. Sydney Harbour is the principal port of Australia. The number of vessels, coastal, interstate and overseas, which entered in 1975–76 was 2,409; net tonnage, 15·6m.

JUSTICE, RELIGION, EDUCATION AND WELFARE

Justice. Legal processes may be carried on in Lower or Magistrates Courts, or in the Higher Courts presided over by judges. There is also an appellate jurisdiction. Persons charged with the more serious crimes must be tried before the Higher Courts.

Children's Courts have been established with the object of removing children as far as possible from the atmosphere of a public court. There are also a number of tribunals exercising special jurisdiction, *e.g.*, the Industrial Commission and the Workers' Compensation Commission.

In 1976 there were 2,511 distinct persons convicted at the Higher Courts. During 1975–76, 8,408 persons were received into prisons under sentence and there were 3,222 persons (including 81 females) held under sentence in prison on 30 June 1976.

Religion. There is no established church in New South Wales, and freedom of worship is accorded to all.

The following table shows the statistics of the religious denominations in New South Wales at the census, and of ministers of religion registered for the celebration of marriages, in 1971:

Denomination	*Ministers*	*Adherents*	*Denomination*	*Ministers*	*Adherents*
Church of England	888	1,639,316	Churches of Christ	79	14,353
Roman Catholic	1,588	1,319,250[1]	Orthodox	56	129,178
Presbyterian	359	352,107	Seventh Day Adventist	147	16,183
Methodist	363	302,856	Hebrew	23	25,971
Baptist	242	59,541	Others	291	668,014[2]
Congregational	76	20,902			
Lutheran	42	33,776			
Salvation Army	216	19,733	Total	4,370	4,601,180

[1] Includes 789,030 'Catholics undefined'.

[2] Includes 253,631 'no religion' and 265,494 'religion not stated' (this is not a compulsory question in the census schedule).

Education. The State maintains a system of primary and secondary education, and attendance at school is compulsory from 6 to 15 years of age. In all state schools education is free. Private schools are subject to State inspection.

In Aug. 1976 there were 2,225 state schools, comprising 1,706 primary and infant schools, 73 combined primary and secondary schools, 338 secondary schools and 108 special-purpose schools. In Aug. 1976 the effective enrolment was 799,737 children, comprising 496,095 receiving primary instruction and 303,642 receiving secondary instruction. There were, in 1976, 41,800 full-time teachers.

In Aug. 1976 there were 791 private schools with 9,612 full-time teachers and an effective enrolment of 218,435 pupils, of which 619 were Roman Catholic schools, having 7,482 teachers and 185,118 scholars. Church of England schools numbered 33 with 812 teachers and 13,851 scholars; other denominational schools, 42; teachers, 703; pupils, 11,413; non-denominational schools, 97; teachers, 615, and scholars, 8,053.

The University of Sydney, founded in 1850, in 1976 had 17,358 students (including 6,883 women). There are 6 colleges providing residential facilities at the university. The principal government training college for teachers is situated in the university grounds.

The University of New England at Armidale, previously affiliated with the University of Sydney, was incorporated on 1 Feb. 1954, and in 1976 had 7,883 students (including 3,304 women).

The University of New South Wales was established by the State Government in 1949. Enrolments in 1976 numbered 18,378 (including 5,170 women). There are 7 colleges providing residential facilities at the university. The University of Newcastle, previously affiliated with the University of New South Wales, was granted autonomy from 1 Jan. 1965, and in 1976 had 4,501 students (including 1,510 women). The University of Wollongong, also previously associated with the University of New South Wales, became autonomous on 1 Jan. 1975, and in 1976 had 2,268 students (including 585 women). The Macquarie University in Sydney, established on 12 June 1964, in 1976 had 9,857 students (including 4,457 women).

Colleges of Advanced Education were first established in 1971 to provide tertiary training with a vocational emphasis. In 1976 there were 31,132 students (including 11,146 part-time students) enrolled at 25 colleges.

Post-school technical and further education is provided at State technical colleges, principally in the evening. Students enrolled in 1976 totalled 226,337 (including 13,807 correspondence students).

State government expenditure (including loan expenditure) on education in 1975–76 was $A902·8m.

Social Welfare. The Australian Government makes provision for social benefits, such as age and invalid pensions, widows' pensions, child endowment, health benefits, maternity allowances, and unemployment and sickness benefits.

The number of age and invalid pensions current in New South Wales on 30 June 1977 was: Age, 442,863 (males, 140,774; females, 302,089); invalid, 82,486 (males, 54,017; females, 28,469). Expenditure for the year ended 30 June 1977 was $A913m. for age pensions and $A208,807,000 for invalid pensions.

Australian Government widows' pensions current in New South Wales at 30 June 1977 numbered 52,383, the expenditure for 1976–77, $A138,398,000.

At 30 June 1977 persons in receipt of a wife's pension numbered 25,726 and expenditure during 1976–77 amounted to $A49,803,000.

Under the new Family Allowance scheme, which commenced on 15 June 1976, payments to families and approved institutions for children under 16 years and full-time students under 25 years (1,469,088 such children or students) during 1976–77 amounted to $A349,532,000.

During the year 1976–77, 77,616 maternity allowances amounting to $A2·45m. were paid in New South Wales.

Unemployment, sickness and special benefits commenced on 1 July 1945. During the year 1976–77 claims totalling $A338·96m. were paid in New South Wales. At 30 June 1977 unemployment benefit was being paid to 108,617 persons, and sickness and special benefits to 14,971 persons.

Direct State social welfare services are limited, for the most part, to the assistance of persons not eligible for Australian Government benefit and the provision of certain forms of assistance not available from the Australian Government. The State also subsidizes many approved services for indigent persons. During 1976–77, expenditure on social amelioration and war obligations was $A138,303,000.

Books of Reference

Statistical Information: The NSW Government Statistician's Office was established in 1886, and in 1957 was integrated with the Commonwealth Bureau of Census and Statistics (now called the Australian Bureau of Statistics). *Deputy Commonwealth Statistician and Government Statistician of NSW:* D. W. Maitland. Its principal publications are:

Official Year Book of New South Wales (1886/87–1900/01 under the title *Wealth and Progress of NSW*): latest issue, 1974
New South Wales Handbook of Local Statistics. Latest issue, 1977
New South Wales Principal Subject Bulletins (previously published under the title *Statistical Register*, since 1858); latest issue of separate bulletins, 1975–76 and 1976
New South Wales Pocket Year Book. Published since 1913; latest issue, 1977
Monthly Summary of Business Statistics. Published since May 1931
New South Wales in Brief. 1977
Major Economic Indicators. Latest issue Sept. 1977

New South Wales Dept. of Tourism, *New South Wales—Australia.* Sydney, 1974
New South Wales Dept. of Decentralization and Development, *New South Wales Handbook for Industrialists.* 1977
State Planning Authority, *Sydney Region: Outline Plan.* Sydney, 1968
State Planning Authority, *Hunter Region, Growth and Change: Prelude to a Plan.* Sydney, 1972
New South Wales Planning and Environment Commission, *Gosford-Wyong: Structure Plan.* Sydney, 1975
State Planning Authority, *The New Cities of Campbeltown, Camden, Appin: Structure Plan.* Sydney, 1973

State Library: The State Library of NSW, Macquarie St., Sydney. *State Librarian*: R. F. Doust, BA, M.Lib, FLAA.

QUEENSLAND

AREA AND POPULATION. Queensland comprises the whole north-eastern portion of the Australian continent, including the adjacent islands in the Pacific Ocean and in the Gulf of Carpentaria. Estimated area 1,728,000 sq. km.

The increase in the population as shown by the censuses since 1901 has been as follows:

	Population at census date			*Intercensal increase*	
Year	*Males*	*Females*	*Total*	*Numerical*	*Rare per annum %*
1901	277,003	221,126	498,129	—	—
1911	329,506	276,307	605,813	107,684	1·98
1921	398,969	357,003	755,972	150,159	2·24
1933	497,217	450,317	947,534	191,562	1·86
1947	567,471	538,944	1,106,415	158,881	1·11
1954	676,252	642,007	1,318,259	211,844	2·53
1961	774,579	744,249	1,518,828	200,569	2·04

Year	Population at census date			Intercensal increase	
	Males	Females	Total	Numerical	Rate per annum %
1966	849,390[1]	824,934[1]	1,674,324[1]	144,857	1·84
1971	921,665[1]	905,400[1]	1,827,065[1]	152,741[1]	1·76[1]
1976	1,024,611[1]	1,012,586[1]	2,037,197[1]	210,132[1]	2·20[1]

[1] Including Aboriginals

Preliminary statistics on birthplaces from the 1976 census are as follows: Australia, 1,723,531 (84·6%); UK, 131,448 (6·5%); other countries, 127,389 (6·3%); not stated, 54,829 (2·7%).

Vital statistics (including Aboriginals) for calendar years:

	Total births	Marriages	Divorces	Deaths
1974	37,852	16,086	1,844	18,128
1975	36,403	15,262	2,689	16,421
1976	35,243	16,711	9,631	17,239

The annual rates per 1,000 population in 1976 were: Marriages, 7·9; births, 16·7; deaths, 8·2. The infant death rate was 15·2 per 1,000 births.

Brisbane, the capital, had on 30 June 1976 a population of 985,920 (Statistical Division). The populations of the other chief towns at the same date were: Gold Coast, 87,510; Townsville, 80,365; Toowoomba, 66,436; Rockhampton, 51,133; Cairns, 34,857; Bundaberg, 30,456; Mount Isa, 26,536; Maryborough, 21,527; Mackay, 20,224; Gladstone, 18,948; Gympie, 11,205.

CONSTITUTION AND GOVERNMENT. Queensland, formerly a portion of New South Wales, was formed into a separate colony in 1859, and responsible government was conferred. The power of making laws and imposing taxes is vested in a Parliament of one House—the Legislative Assembly, which comprises 82 members, returned from 4 electoral zones for 3 years, elected for single-member constituencies at compulsory ballot. Members are entitled to $A24,190 per annum, with individual electorate allowances for travelling, postage, etc., of from $A6,000 to $A15,000.

At the general election of 12 Nov. 1977 there were 1,209,494 persons registered as qualified to vote under the Elections Act 1915–1976. This Act provides franchise for all males and females, 18 years of age and over, qualified by 6 months' residence in Australia and 3 months in the electoral district.

The Legislative Assembly, following the elections of 12 Nov. 1977, was composed of the following parties: National, 35; Liberal, 24; Australian Labor, 23; total, 82.

Governor of Queensland: Cmde Sir James Maxwell Ramsay, CBE, DSC (assumed office April 1977).

The Executive Council of Ministers, at 16 Dec. 1977, consists of the following members:

Premier: Johannes Bjelke-Petersen (National).

Treasurer: William Edward Knox (Liberal). *Mines, Energy and Police:* Ronald Ernest Camm (National). *Labour Relations:* Frederick Alexander Campbell (Liberal). *Welfare:* John Desmond Herbert (Liberal). *Primary Industries:* Victor Bruce Sullivan (National). *Maritime Services and Tourism:* Allen Maxwell Hodges (National). *Lands, Forestry and Water Resources:* Neville Thomas Eric Hewitt (National). *Local Government and Main Roads:* Russell James Hinze (National). *Culture, National Parks and Recreation:* Thomas Guy Newbery (National). *Transport:* Kenneth Burgoyne Tomkins (National). *Health:* Llewellyn Roy Edwards (Liberal). *Education:* Valmond James Bird (National). *Industry and Administrative Services:* Norman Edward Lee (Liberal). *Works and Housing:* Claude Alfred Wharton (National). *Justice and Attorney-General:* William Daniel Lickiss (Liberal). *Survey and Valuation:* John Ward Greenwood (Liberal). *Aboriginal and Island Affairs:* Charles Robert Porter (Liberal).

Each Minister has a salary of $A39,750, the Premier receives $A50,520, the Deputy Premier, $A43,320, and the Leader of the Opposition, $A34,300.

Agent-General in London: W. A. R. Rae (392 Strand, WC2)

Local Government. Provision is made for local government by the subdivision of the State into cities, towns and shires. These are under the management of aldermen or councillors, who are elected by all persons 18 years and over. Local Authorities are charged with the control of all matters of a parochial nature, such as sewerage, cleansing and sanitary services, health services, domestic water supplies, and roads and bridges within their allotted areas. In addition to Government grants and subsidies, Local Authority revenue is derived from general rates, paid by landowners on the unimproved capital value of land, and by charging for some specific services. Loans for most capital works are raised subject to the provisions of the Australian Loan Council. Shires are mostly rural districts although most contain some urban centres not classed officially as towns.

The number and area of these subdivisions, together with the receipts and expenditure (including receipts and expenditure from loans) for the year ended 30 June 1975, were:

	No.	*Area in sq. km*	*Receipts,*[1] *$A1,000*	*Expenditure,*[1] *$A1,000*	*Rateable values, $A1,000*
City of Brisbane	1	1,220	233,629	227,308	879,586
Other Cities	14	42,405	122,310	130,168	666,250
Towns	4	585	12,519	13,896	25,724
Shires	112	1,682,155	207,380	209,704	1,101,148
Total	131	1,726,000	575,838	581,077	2,672,708

[1] These columns include receipts from loans and loan subsidies of $A141·9m.; expenditures from loans and loan subsidies of $A152·5m.; and the operating receipts and expenditures of business undertakings (principally water supply, sewerage, electricity and transport) which were $A193m. and $A197·6m. respectively.

ECONOMY

Budget. Revenue and expenditure of the Consolidated Revenue Fund of Queensland during 5 years ending 30 June (in $A1,000):

	1973–74	*1974–75*	*1975–76*	*1976–77*	*1977–78*[1]
Revenue	853,676	1,112,866	1,349,513	1,610,538	1,806,549
Expenditure	855,184	1,121,218	1,348,799	1,611,555	1,806,152

[1] Estimates.

Total funds available to the Queensland Government in 1974–75 were $A1,378·9m., of which Taxation and Australian Government grants amounted to $A1,167·2m. Expenditure from these funds included: Education, $A445·6m.; economic services (roads, electricity, etc.), $A386·4m.; health, $A173m.

Revenue and expenditure of Australian Government departments on account of Queensland are not included.

Debt. The gross public debt of the State amounted, on 30 June 1976, to $A1,642m. The debt was domiciled as follows (in $A1,000): Australia, 1,628,434; UK, 9,444; USA, 1,555; Canada, 450; Netherlands, 235; other European countries, 1,589. The annual interest charge on the public debt at 30 June 1976 was $A117·1m.

Banking. There were 9 trading banks operating in Queensland at 30 June 1976, including the Commonwealth Trading Bank of Australia, the 6 larger Australian trading banks, a Queensland bank with head office in Brisbane and the Banque Nationale de Paris. The Commonwealth Trading Bank had 139 branches and 65 agencies; the private banks had 635 branches and 109 agencies in the State. Queensland deposits of all trading banks, including the Commonwealth Trading Bank of Australia, amounted to $A2,335·5m.; and loans, advances and bills discounted in Queensland were $A1,483·3m. At 30 June 1976 savings bank business was conducted in Queensland by 7 banks, the Commonwealth Savings Bank with 161 branches and 1,300 agencies, and 6 private banks with 623 branches and 1,218 agencies. Depositors' balances amounted to $A1,940·3m. in 2·70m. accounts.

ENERGY AND NATURAL RESOURCES

Electricity. The State Electricity Commission, established in 1938 and under a single Commissioner since 1948, co-ordinates the electricity industry in Queensland. Electricity generated by the principal stations in the year ended 30 June 1976 was 8,501m. kwh. Natural gas is being used for electric generation at Roma. Black coal was used to generate 90% of the power; hydro-electric stations generated 9%.

Minerals. Principal minerals produced during 1975–76 were: Copper, 156,566 tonnes; coal, 24,182,000 tonnes; lead, 151,000 tonnes; zinc, 132,000 tonnes; silver, 380,867 kg; tin, 1,692 tonnes; gold, 1,329 kg; bauxite, 8,831,000 tonnes; mineral sands concentrates, 229,000 tonnes. Value of output, at the mine, was $A988,583,000. The chief mines are Mount Isa (copper, silver, lead, zinc), Weipa (bauxite), Mount Morgan (copper, gold), Moreton and Bowen Basin (coal), and Greenvale (nickel).

Land Settlement. Of the total area of the State, 12·7m. hectares had been alienated at 31 Dec. 1975; in process of alienation, under deferred payment system, were 17·19m. hectares, leaving 142·96m. hectares, still the property of the Crown, or 82·7% of the total area. A large proportion of the area is leased for pastoral purposes (96·9m. hectares at 31 Dec. 1975).

In the western portion of the State water is comparatively easily found by sinking artesian bores. At 30 June 1976, 3,363 such bores had been drilled, of which 2,287 were flowing.

Agriculture. Livestock on farms and stations at 31 March 1976 numbered 11,347,000 cattle, 13,599,000 sheep and 409,000 pigs. The wool production (greasy) was, in 1975–76, 66·3m. kg, valued at $A90·6m. The total area under crops during 1975–76 was 2,074,118 hectares, 185,924 hectares were irrigated in 1975–76, the principal crops so watered being sugar-cane, fodder crops, vegetables, cereals, tobacco, cotton and fruit.

Crop	*Area (hectares)* 1974–75	1975–76	*Yield (tonnes)*[1] 1974–75	1975–76
Sugar-cane, crushed	243,231	245,795	19,421,069	21,068,863
Wheat	488,500	576,152	692,090	829,998
Maize	28,675	28,720	71,769	78,261
Sorghum	328,886	338,988	634,120	739,896
Barley	156,319	236,229	297,268	419,090
Oats	25,406	11,910	28,457	13,033
Potatoes	6,068	6,020	107,587	99,771
Pumpkins	4,314	4,075	30,319	26,383
Tomatoes	2,422	2,430	32,133	30,564
Peanuts	23,742	26,916	31,323	35,336
Tobacco	4,424	4,580	8,007	8,198
Apples[1]	4,126	4,120	38,344	24,514
Grapes[1]	1,308	1,300	5,811	5,888
Citrus[1]	2,229	2,223	40,711	41,365
Bananas[1]	1,794	1,833	31,621	36,398
Pineapples[1]	3,801	3,773	110,118	102,666
Green fodder[2]	340,951	301,645	...	...
Hay (all kinds)	48,697	40,359	258,472	209,346
Cotton (raw)	7,386	5,966	6,396	4,985

[1] Bearing area only. [2] Excluding lucerne.

Forestry. A considerable area consists of natural forest, eucalyptus, pine and cabinet woods being the timbers mostly in evidence; a large quantity of ornamental woods are utilized by cabinet makers. The amount of native timber processed in 1975–76 was (in cu. metres): Softwoods, 426,712; hardwoods, brushwoods and scrubwoods, 653,405. Forest and timber reservations total 3,973,000 hectares (30 June 1976);

areas for national parks, 1,153,000 hectares. The State Forest Service had planted 101,000 hectares for reforestation and had treated 427,000 hectares for natural regeneration by June 1976. Thinnings from State reforestation areas are used for hardboard and paper pulp.

INDUSTRY AND TRADE

Industry. Approximately one-third of the secondary production of the State is from works processing primary products, the most important being sugar-mills, meat works, butter factories and saw-mills. There are 30 cane-crushing mills, 3 oil refineries, 1 alumina refinery, 2 sugar refineries, 46 meat works (including bacon factories) producing largely for export, 19 butter factories and many saw-mills and plywood and veneer mills. Other industries include engineering works, railway workshops, copper and nickel refining, rubber, cement, cardboard and building board manufacture, ammonia and fertilizer works and the production of various items of food, clothing and vehicles, chiefly for local use. In 1975–76 there were 3,129 establishments, with 4 or more workers, employing 91,372 males and 21,703 females, and providing goods and services worth $A4,572m. The value of production (value added in manufacture) was $A1,814m.

The gross value of Queensland primary production, excluding mining (in $A1,000) during 1975–76 amounted to 1,322,566, which included crops, 851,854; livestock disposals, 243,151; livestock products, 180,968; forestry, 28,647; fishing, 17,137; hunting, 810.

Labour. Of the total population of 2m., 883,300 were in employment in May 1976, 133,500 in manufacturing. Industrial wages and conditions are controlled partly by Federal and partly by State authorities. A State Industrial Commission is empowered to determine all industrial matters in relation to employers and employees, and to fix minimum wage-rates and other conditions of employment. An Industrial Court hears appeals and decides points of industrial law. The Australian Industrial Court and Conciliation and Arbitration Commission are superior within their jurisdictions. In Queensland most employees (62%) work under State awards; 26% under Federal awards.

Rates of wages for each occupation are prescribed by these courts. The minimum weighted average award wage for adult males was $A147.57 and for adult females $A135.82, at 30 June 1977, while average weekly earnings (including overtime, etc.) were $A184.50 per employed male unit. (Average earnings are calculated on a unit basis, as earnings are not available separately for males and females.) A standard working week of 40 hours is prescribed for most awards.

Trade Unions. Unions both of employees and employers must be registered with the State or Australian Commission. There were 75 employees' and 41 employers' unions registered with the State Commission at 31 Dec. 1976, the former comprising 348,451 and the latter 37,565 members.

Commerce. The overseas commerce of Queensland is included in the statement of the commerce of Australia (*see* pp. 111–13).

Total value of the direct overseas imports and exports of Queensland (in $A1,000) f.o.b. port of shipment for both imports and exports:

	1970–71	*1971–72*	*1972–73*	*1973–74*	*1974–75*	*1975–76*
Imports	321,638	270,484	311,448	542,646	580,051	634,893
Exports	789,180	980,954	1,305,569	1,360,701	2,007,775	2,322,021

In 1975–76 interstate exports totalled $A727m. and imports $A1,674m. The chief exports overseas are minerals, meat (preserved or frozen), sugar, coal, wool, chemicals (including alumina), cereal grains and machinery and transport equipment. Principal imports are machinery, motor vehicles, chemicals, textiles, paper and paper board materials, articles of rubber including tyres and tubes, and iron and steel. Chief sources of imports in 1975–76 went Japan ($A159m.), USA ($A147·8m), UK ($A65·2m.); exports went chiefly to Japan ($A969·3m.), USA ($A353·2m.), Canada ($A155·7m.).

COMMUNICATIONS

Roads. At 30 June 1976 there were 188,895 km of road; of these, 132,522 km were formed roads, of which 71,274 km were surfaced with concrete, bitumen or macadam.

At 30 Sept. 1976 motor vehicles registered in Queensland totalled 1,023,000, comprising 722,900 cars and station wagons, 122,500 vans, 3,700 buses, 101,100 trucks and 72,800 motor cycles.

Railways. Practically all the railways are owned by the State Government. Total length of line at 30 June 1976 was 9,844 km. In 1975–76, 34,278,000 passengers and 33·1m. tonnes of goods and livestock were carried.

Aviation. Queensland is well served with a network of air services, with overseas and interstate connexions. Subsidiary companies provide planes for taxi and charter work, and the Flying Doctor Service operates throughout western Queensland.

Shipping. In 1975–76, 3,052 vessels totalling 28·7m. net tons entered Queensland ports. Cargo discharged was 5·48m. tonnes and 0·65m. cu. metres, and cargo shipped was 30·2m. tonnes and 0·32m. cu. metres.

Broadcasting. At 30 June 1976, 48 broadcasting and 43 television stations were in operation throughout Queensland.

JUSTICE, RELIGION, EDUCATION AND WELFARE

Justice. Justice is administered by a Supreme Court, district courts, magistrates' courts and children's courts. The Supreme Court comprises a Chief Justice, a senior puisne judge and 12 puisne judges; the district court, 19 district court judges. Stipendiary magistrates preside over the lower courts, except in the smaller centres, where justices of the peace officiate. A parole board may recommend prisoners for release.

The total number of persons convicted of serious offences by the superior courts in 1975–76 was 1,966; the summary convictions in lower courts (including cases of bail estreated and committals to higher courts for sentence or trial) numbered 117,222. There were, at 30 June 1976, 5 prisons, 2 gaols for short-term prisoners, 2 prison farms conducted on the honour system and 1 prison for mentally-ill prisoners, with 1,536 male and 30 female prisoners. The total police force, including policewomen and 6 native trackers, was 4,040 at 30 June 1976.

Religion. There is no State Church. Membership, census 1971: Church of England, 544,432; Roman Catholic, 231,808; Catholic (not further defined), 235,395; Presbyterian, 192,079; Methodist, 182,887; Lutheran, 45,228; Baptist, 28,329; Orthodox, 15,554; Congregational, 9,627; other Christian, 96,472; Hebrew, 1,491; all others (including not stated and no religion), 243,763.

Education. Education is compulsory between the ages of 6 and 15 years. Education is free in State primary and high schools. Expenditure on education, including Loan Fund for 1975–76, net of certain receipts, was $A536·4m. At Aug. 1976 there were 1,086 state primary schools (including 13 native schools administered by the Department of Aboriginal and Islanders Advancement, 43 special schools and 1 correspondence school), with 10,967 teachers and enrolment of 227,288 scholars. Secondary education was provided during 1976 by 121 state high schools, 1 special school, 1 correspondence school and 100 secondary departments attached to state primary and special schools, with 7,195 teachers, the enrolment being 110,693 scholars, and by 8 subsidized grammar schools (4 for boys, 3 for girls, 1 mixed), with 260 teachers and an enrolment of 4,306 secondary and 36 primary pupils. There were, in addition, 323 other, mostly church, schools with 4,243 teachers and an enrolment of 87,371 children.

In 1976, tertiary level course enrolments at colleges of advanced education, including teachers' colleges, and technical colleges were 10,719 full-time and 4,865 part-time. Non-tertiary (vocational, post-secondary) level course enrolments at these establishments and rural training schools numbered 2,842 full-time and 33,232 part-time, including correspondence and apprenticeship students. Full-time teaching staff at the Queensland University and Griffith University at Brisbane and the James Cook University at Townsville comprised, at 30 April 1976, 290 professors, associate professors and readers, 745 senior lecturers, lecturers and teaching registrars; 396 assistant lecturers, demonstrators, tutors and teaching fellows. Students enrolled numbered 20,904. There are 7 denominational and 3 undenominational residential colleges attached to the Queensland University in Brisbane with 4 denominational residential colleges and 1 undenominational hall of residence at the University in Townsville.

Social Welfare. Public hospitals are maintained by State and Australian Government endowment, supplemented by fees from patients not in public wards. From 1 Oct. 1976, health insurance became compulsory. Persons may either pay a health insurance levy on personal income tax or contribute to a registered health insurance organization to obtain medical and hospital cover. Welfare institutions for aged people, and for orphans and the blind, deaf and dumb, and homes for other handicapped persons are also maintained or assisted by the State. A maternal and child welfare service is provided throughout the State. Age, invalid, widows' and disability (war) pensions, maternity allowances, family allowances, and unemployment and sickness benefits are paid by the Australian Government. Age pensioners in the State at 30 June 1976 numbered 175,603; invalid pensioners, 29,856; disability pensioners, 80,689 (including dependants). Maternity allowance was paid to 33,195 mothers during 1975–76.

There were 17,262 widows' pensions current at 30 June 1976, and at the same date family allowances were being paid to 285,785 families in respect of 611,785 children under 16 years. In addition, 27,100 families received endowment for 30,500 student children aged 16–21.

Housing. In 1976–77, 24,036 new dwellings were completed and 7,371 were being built at 30 June 1977. The Queensland Housing Commission, financed by State and Australian Government loans, builds dwellings for sale and for rental. Building and co-operative housing societies are assisted by State and Australian Government loans.

Books of Reference

Statistical Information: The Statistical Office (345, Ann St., Brisbane) was set up in 1859. *Deputy Commonwealth Statistician:* O. M. May. A *Queensland Official Year Book* was issued in 1901, the annual *ABC of Queensland Statistics* from 1905 to 1936 with exception of 1918 and 1922. Present publications include: *Queensland Year Book*. Annual, from 1937 (omitting 1942, 1943, 1944).—*Queensland Pocket Year Book*. Annual from 1950.—*Monthly Summary of Queensland Statistics*. From Jan. 1961.

Australian and New Zealand Association for the Advancement of Science, *Introducing Queensland*. Brisbane, 1961
Queensland Department of Agriculture and Stock, *The Queensland Agricultural and Pastoral Handbook*. 2 vols. Brisbane, 1962
Australian Sugar Year Book. Brisbane, from 1941
Bolton, G. C., *A Thousand Miles Away! A History of North Queensland to 1920*. Brisbane, 1963
Cilento, R., and Lack, C., *Triumph in the Tropics*. Brisbane, 1959
Greenwood, G., and Laverty, J., *Brisbane 1859–1959*. Sydney, 1959
Greenwood, R. H., *Queensland, City, Coast and Country*. London, 1959
Lack, C., *Queensland, Daughter of the Sun*. Brisbane, 1959.—*Three Decades of Queensland Political History*. Brisbane, 1962.

State Library: The State Library of Queensland, William St., Brisbane. *State Librarian: S. L.* Ryan.

SOUTH AUSTRALIA

AREA AND POPULATION. The total area of South Australia is 380,070 sq. miles (984,375 sq. km). The settled part is divided into counties and hundreds. There are 49 counties proclaimed, covering 23m. hectares, of which 19m. hectares are occupied. Outside this area there are extensive pastoral districts, covering 76m. hectares, 51m. of which are under pastoral leases.

Census population (exclusive of full-blood Aboriginals before 1966):

	Males	Females	Total		Males	Females	Total
1891	161,920	153,292	315,212	1947	320,031	326,042	646,073
1901	180,485	177,861	358,346	1961	490,225	479,115	969,340
1911	207,358	201,200	408,558	1966	550,196	544,788	1,094,984
1921	248,267	246,893	495,160	1971	586,051	587,656	1,173,707
1933	290,962	289,987	580,949	1976[1]	620,099	624,546	1,244,645

[1] Preliminary.

The number of Aboriginals (as reported on Census schedules) in the State at the census of 30 June 1971 was 7,140.

Vital statistics for calendar years:

	Births	Marriages	Divorces	Deaths
1974	20,181	10,769	1,561	10,236
1975	19,986	9,843	1,819	9,947
1976	18,947	10,902	...	9,999

The infant mortality rate in 1976 was 14·6 per 1,000 live births.

CONSTITUTION AND GOVERNMENT. South Australia was formed into a British province by letters patent of Feb. 1836, and a partially elective Legislative Council was established in 1851. The present constitution bears date 24 Oct. 1856. It vests the legislative power in an elected Parliament, consisting of a Legislative Council and a House of Assembly. The former is composed of 22 members. Every 3 years half the members retire, and the resulting vacancies are filled at a general election on the basis of proportional representation with the State as one multi-member electorate. The qualifications of an elector are, to be a natural born or naturalized British subject of at least 18 years of age and to have lived continuously in Australia for at least 6 months, in South Australia for at least 3 months and in the sub-division for which he is enrolled for at least 1 month. War service may substitute for residential qualifications in some cases. By the Constitution Act Amendment Act, 1894, the franchise was extended to women, who voted for the first time at the general election of 25 April 1896. The qualifications for election as a member of both Houses are the same as for an elector. Certain persons are ineligible for election to either House.

The House of Assembly consists of 47 members elected for 3 years, representing single electorates. Election of members of both Houses takes place by preferential secret ballot. Voting is compulsory for those on the Electoral Roll.

The House of Assembly, elected on 17 Sept. 1977, consists of the following members: Australian Labor Party, 27; Liberal Party of Australia, 18; Australian Democrats, 1; National Country Party, 1. The Legislative Council consists of 11 Liberal Party of Australia and 10 Labor members.

Each member of Parliament receives $A18,730 per annum with allowances of $A2,750–5,900 according to location of electorate, a free pass over government railways and superannuation rights. Electors enrolled (Aug. 1977) numbered 818,341.

The executive power is vested in a Governor appointed by the Crown and an Executive Council, consisting of the Governor and the Ministers of the Crown. The Governor has the power to dissolve the House of Assembly but not the Legislative Council unless that Chamber has twice consecutively with an election intervening defeated the same or substantially the same Bill passed in the House of Assembly by an absolute majority.

Governor: Keith D. Seaman, OBE (sworn in 1 Sept. 1977).

The South Australian Labor Ministry, at 6 Oct. 1977 was as follows:

Premier, Treasurer and Minister of Immigration and Ethnic Affairs: Donald Allan Dunstan, QC, MP.

Deputy Premier, Minister of Works, Minister for the Environment and Minister of Marine: James Desmond Corcoran, MP. *Minister of Mines and Energy and Minister for Planning:* Hugh Richard Hudson, MP. *Minister of Health and Minister assisting the Deputy Premier:* Donald Hubert Louis Banfield, MLC. *Minister of Transport and of Local Government:* Geoffrey Thomas Virgo, MP. *Minister of Lands, Minister of Irrigation, Minister of Repatriation and Minister of Tourism, Recreation and Sport:* Thomas Mannix Casey, MLC. *Minister of Education:* Donald Jack Hopgood, MP. *Minister of Agriculture, Minister of Forests and Minister of Fisheries:* Brian Alfred Chatterton, MLC. *Minister of Labour and Industry:* John David Wright, MP. *Minister of Community Welfare:* Ronald George Payne, MP. *Attorney-General and Minister of Prices and Consumer Affairs:* Peter Duncan, MP. *Chief Secretary and Minister assisting the Premier:* Donald William Simmons, MP.

The provision for the payment of Ministers is $A421,430. They are jointly and individually responsible to the legislature for all their official acts, as in the UK.

Agent-General in London: W. M. Scriven (50 Strand, WC2).

Local Government. The closely settled part of the State (mainly near the sea-coast and the river Murray) is incorporated into local government areas, and sub-divided into district councils (rural areas only), municipal corporations (mainly metropolitan, but including larger country towns) and cities (more densely populated areas with a qualification of 15,000 residents in the Adelaide metropolitan area, and 10,000 in the country). The main functions of councils are the construction and maintenance of roads and bridges. Other functions include health, welfare, recreation and garbage disposal.

The number and area of the sub-divisions, together with revenue expenditure (in $A1,000) for the year ended 30 June 1975, were:

	No.	*Area (1,000 hectares)*	*Roads and bridges*	*Health and recreation*	*All other*	*Total expenditure*
Adelaide statistical division	31	232·1	18,768	13,397	29,713	61,878
Other municipal corporations and district councils	106	14,752·6	15,552	5,640	13,523	34,715
Total	137	14,984·7	34,320	19,038	43,235	96,593

ECONOMY

Budget. Revenue and expenditure (in $A1,000) for years ended 30 June:

	1973	*1974*	*1975*	*1976*	*1977*	*1978*[1]
Revenue	520,866	641,967	828,985	1,036,985	1,174,025	1,171,004
Expenditure	524,777	645,368	820,601	1,034,698	1,183,180	1,189,418

[1] Estimates.

The public debt of the State amounted, on 30 June 1977, to $A1,495·7m. representing $A1,171 per head of the population.

Banking. There were 8 trading banks at 30 June 1977, including the Commonwealth and State Government Banks. In 1976–77 their average deposits were $A1,353·5m. and average advances $A1,026·22m.

The 8 savings banks on 30 June 1977 had deposits amounting to $A1,780·8m. or $A1,404 per head of population.

NATURAL RESOURCES

Minerals. The value of minerals produced in 1974–75 was $A125·98m. The principal minerals produced are iron ore, copper, gypsum, salt, talc, clays, limestone, dolomite and sub-bituminous coal.

Agriculture. Of the total area of South Australia (984,375 sq. km), 69,170 sq. km were alienated, 601,064 sq. km were held under lease and 314,100 sq. km were unoccupied. Area under cultivation, at 31 March 1977, was 58,300 sq. km.

Soil Conservation. Under the direction of special officers in the Department of Agriculture and Fisheries, determined efforts are made to deal with the problems of erosion and soil conservation. Included in the programme are the planting of cereal rye, perennial rye and other grasses to check sand drifts; contour-furrowing and contour banking; contour planting with vines and fruit trees and several water-diversion schemes.

Irrigation. In 1975–76, 77,894 hectares were under irrigated culture, being used as follows: Vineyards, 18,387; orchards, 13,132; vegetables, 5,601, and other crops and pasture, 40,774. Most of these areas are along the river Murray.

Gross value of production (in $A1,000), 1976–77: Crops, 338,279; livestock slaughtering, 178,848; livestock products, 199,862; forestry, fishing and hunting, 49,113. Total gross value, 766,102; local value (*i.e.*, less marketing costs), 703,274.

	1975–76		*1976–77*	
Chief crops	*Hectares*	*Tonnes*	*Hectares*	*Tonnes*
Wheat	958,453	1,138,959	839,115	831,866
Barley	832,058	1,094,353	855,414	889,124
Oats	119,037	107,273	116,708	90,294
Hay	159,068	506,129	164,343	511,609
Vines	...	213,863,000[1]	...	229,973,000[1]

[1] Litres of wine.

Fruit culture is extensively carried on, and in 1974–75, 6,800 tonnes of dried fruit and 218,000 tonnes of fresh fruit were produced. Other products, in addition to all kinds of root crops and vegetables, are grass seeds and oil seeds. Livestock, March 1977: 1,607,800 cattle, 15,132,200 sheep and 316,500 pigs. In 1976–77, 198,442 tonnes of wool and 354·9m. litres of milk were produced.

INDUSTRY AND TRADE

Industry. The turnover for manufacturing industries for 1975–76 was $A3,460·6m. The following statistics for 1975–76 are not comparable with factory statistics for years prior to 1968–69.

Industry sub-division	*Establishments (No.)*	*Persons employed (No.)*	*Wages and salaries ($A1,000)*	*Turnover ($A1,000)*	*Value added ($A1,000)*
Food, beverages and tobacco	384	17,914	128,909	637,055	252,930
Textiles, clothing and footwear	116	6,830	43,132	145,325	67,058
Wood, wood products and furniture	337	8,940	61,804	258,281	113,023
Paper and paper products, printing	194	7,224	57,601	211,183	102,900
Chemical, petroleum and coal products	59	2,721	25,138	122,430	51,061
Non-metallic mineral products	147	4,213	35,404	163,094	78,496
Basic metal products	49	9,978	83,698	372,268	135,738
Fabricated metal products	367	8,846	61,547	249,245	115,791
Transport equipment	143	24,647	195,399	718,203	285,366
Other machinery and equipment	315	19,088	139,551	450,340	218,012
Miscellaneous manufacturing	176	5,704	39,400	133,180	65,311
Total	2,287	116,105	871,583	3,460,603	1,485,686

Practically all forms of secondary industry are to be found, the most important being smelting, motor-body building, shipbuilding, saw-milling and the manufacture of household appliances, agricultural machinery, industrial chemicals and chemical fertilizers.

Labour. Two systems of industrial arbitration and conciliation for the adjustment of industrial relations between employers and employees are in operation—the State system, which operates when industrial disputes are confined to the territorial limits of the State, and the Federal system, which applies when disputes involve other parts of Australia as well as South Australia.

The industrial tribunals are authorized to fix minimum rates of wages and other conditions of employment, and their awards may be enforced by law. Industrial agreements between employers and organizations of employees, when registered, may be enforced in the same manner as awards. The Commission fixed the minimum wage in Aug. 1977 at $A110.10.

Commerce. The commerce of South Australia, exclusive of inter-state trade, is comprised in the statement of the commerce of Australia given under the heading of the Commonwealth, *see* pp. 111–13.

Overseas imports and exports in $A1,000 (year ending 30 June):

	1971–72	*1972–73*	*1973–74*	*1974–75*	*1975–76*	*1976–77*
Imports	189,748	199,978	313,915	482,077	501,476	630,955
Exports	394,064	521,720	662,881	764,410	685,029	789,716

Principal exports in 1976–77 were (in $A1,000): Wool, 172,539 (91m. kg); lead, 58,063 (137,228 tonnes); wheat, 77,900 (637,000 tonnes); barley, 88,119 (835,600 tonnes); beef, lamb and mutton, 34,561 (47,900 tonnes); iron and steel, blooms billets, sheet bars and roughly forged pieces, 55,621 (512,137 tonnes).

Principal imports in 1976–77 were (in $A1,000): Machinery, 127,983; transport equipment, 99,472; petrol and products, 156,542.

In 1976–77 the leading suppliers of imports were (in $A1m.): Japan (140), Saudi Arabia (126·1), USA (84·2), UK (53·6); main exports went to Japan (168·3), USSR (60·6), Federal Republic of Germany (45·4), New Zealand (42·1), UK (40·3), Iran (33·7) and USA (33).

COMMUNICATIONS

Roads. At 30 June 1976, of the roads customarily used by the public, there were 2,666 km of national roads, 10,898 km of arterial roads and 86,877 km of local roads, totalling 100,441 km. Lengths of road classified by surface were as follows: Sealed, 17,843 km; unsealed, 21,180 km; formed, 24,392 km; natural, 37,026 km. Costs of construction and maintenance are shared by the State and Commonwealth governments and by the councils of the local areas. Motor vehicles registered at 30 June 1977 include 444,992 cars, 74,009 station wagons, 114,288 commercial vehicles and 31,039 cycles.

Railways. There were (1976) 6,034 km of railway, including the South Australian portion of the Transcontinental Railway from Port Pirie in South Australia to Kalgoorlie in Western Australia, which, in connexion with various State lines, completes a through rail connexion between Brisbane on the north-east coast and Fremantle on the west coast. It also includes the South Australian portion of the Australian National Railways from Port Augusta to the Northern Territory and private railways from Iron Knob to Whyalla and Coffin Bay to Port Lincoln but excludes the line between Cockburn and Broken Hill. In the year ending 30 June 1976 the State-controlled sections carried 12,672,027 passengers and 6·2m. tonnes of freight.

Aviation. For the year ended 30 June 1976 there were 1,454,917 passengers and 16,390 tonnes of freight handled at Adelaide, South Australia's principal airport. On 30 June 1976 there were 9 government and 20 licensed aerodromes.

Shipping. There are several good harbours, of which Port Adelaide is the principal one. In 1975–76, 1,219 vessels (exceeding 200 NRT) of 7,758,763 net tonnage entered South Australian ports direct from interstate or overseas.

Post and Broadcasting. Postal, telephone and telegraph facilities are available at 771 offices. Telephone services connected totalled 334,948 on 30 June 1976; on 30 June 1976 there were 19 radio and 11 television stations.

JUSTICE, RELIGION, EDUCATION AND WELFARE

Justice. There is a Supreme Court, which incorporates admiralty, civil, criminal, matrimonial and testamentary jurisdiction; district criminal courts, which have jurisdiction in many indictable offences; local courts and courts of summary jurisdiction. Circuit courts are held at several places. Bankruptcy jurisdiction is administered by the State Court of Insolvency at Adelaide which is invested with jurisdiction by the

Federal Bankruptcy Act. During the year ending 30 June 1976 there were 351 sequestrations and schemes under the Bankruptcy Act; 1,107 adults convicted for felonies and misdemeanours in the higher courts in 1976 and 104,402 in the courts of summary jurisdiction in 1974–75. The total number of persons in gaols on 30 June 1976 was 706, of whom 594 were prisoners under sentence.

Religion. At the census of 1971 the religious distribution of the population (as reported on Census schedules) was as follows: Church of England, 286,754; Roman Catholic and Catholic (so described), 242,166; Methodist, 215,328; Lutheran, 62,641; Presbyterian, 39,920; other Christians, 155,067; non-Christian, 3,183; indefinite, 3,751; no religion, 95,874; no reply, 69,023.

Education. Education is secular and is compulsory to the age of 15. Primary, secondary and technical education at government schools is free. In 1976 there were 625 government schools, comprising 436 primary, 51 primary and secondary, 104 secondary schools and 34 special schools. There were 233,614 full-time students. The Department of Further Education is responsible for technical, adult and vocational education. In 1976 there were 5 metropolitan and 6 country community colleges, 11 metropolitan and 7 country colleges of further education, a college of external studies and a migrant education centre. Advanced education, including teacher education, is provided by 8 colleges of advanced education and tertiary education by 2 universities. There were 147 non-government schools and colleges, most of which are associated with religious denominations (39,299 students) and 446 children's services centres with a total enrolment of 24,755 pre-school children.

Social Welfare. Age, invalidity, war, etc., pensions are paid by the Commonwealth Government. The number of pensioners in South Australia at 30 June 1976 was: Disability and service, 59,536; age, 112,917; invalid, 17,312. There are schemes for maternity allowances, family allowances, widows, unemployment and sickness and hospital and pharmaceutical benefits. The total amount paid during 1975–76 was $A404·07m.

Books of Reference

Statistical Information: The State branch of the Australian Bureau of Statistics is in Prudential Building, 195 North Terrace, Adelaide (GPO Box 2272). *Deputy Commonwealth Statistician:* B. E. Leonard. Although the first printed statistical publication was the *Statistics of South Australia, 1854* with the title altered to *Statistical Register* in 1859, there is a written volume for each year back to 1838. These contain simple records of trade, demography, production, etc. and were prepared only for the use of the Colonial Office; one copy was retained in the State.

The publications of the State branch include the *South Australian Year Book*, the *Pocket Year Book of South Australia* and a duplicated *Monthly Summary of Statistics*, a duplicated quarterly bulletin of building constructions, duplicated quarterly bulletin of trade statistics and approximately 30 special duplicated bulletins issued each year as particulars of various sections of statistics become available.

Best, R. J. (ed.), *Introducing South Australia.* Cambridge, 1959
Centenary History of South Australia. Royal Geographical Society of Australasia. Adelaide, 1936
Crowley, F. K., *South Australian History: A Survey for Research Students.* Adelaide, 1965
Finlayson, H. H., *The Red Centre: Man and Beast in the Heart of Australia.* 2nd ed. Sydney, 1952
Gibbs, R. M., *A History of South Australia.* Adelaide, 1969
Madigan, C. T., *Central Australia.* 2nd ed. Melbourne, 1944
Mincham, H., *The Story of the Flinders Ranges.* Rev. ed. Adelaide, 1965

State Library: The State Library of S.A., North Terrace, Adelaide. *State Librarian:* R. K. Olding, BEc., FLAA.

TASMANIA

HISTORY. Abel Janzoon Tasman discovered Van Diemen's Land (Tasmania) on 24 Nov. 1642. The island became a British settlement in 1803 as a dependency of

New South Wales; in 1825 its connexion with New South Wales was terminated; in 1851 a partially elective Legislative Council was established, and in 1856 responsible government came into operation. On 1 Jan. 1901 Tasmania was federated with the other Australian states into the Commonwealth of Australia.

AREA AND POPULATION. Area (including islands) 68,330 sq. km, or 6·83m. hectares, of which 6,441,000 hectares form the area of the main island. The population at 10 consecutive censuses was:

	Population	*Increase % per annum*		*Population*	*Increase % per annum*
1901	172,475	1·64	1954	308,752	2·65
1911	191,211	1·04	1961	350,340	1·82
1921	213,780	1·12	1966	371,436	1·18
1933	227,599	0·52	1971	391,813[1]	1·07
1947	257,078	0·87	1976	407,363[1]	0·78

[1] Adjusted for over-enumeration.

The census population on 30 June 1976 consisted of 201,503 males and 201,341 females. At the census of 30 June 1971, 5·8% were natives of the British Isles, 3·3% natives of other European countries and 90·1% natives of Australia and New Zealand, almost exclusively of European ancestry. The last Tasmanian Aboriginal died in 1876.

Vital statistics for calendar years:

	Marriages	*Divorces*[1]	*Births*	*Deaths*	*Natural increase*
1973	3,395	443	7,326	3,347	3,979
1974	3,567	535	7,398	3,484	3,914
1975	3,206	591	6,981	3,340	3,641
1976	3,477	1,782	6,702	3,389	3,313

[1] Family Court came into operation during 1976.

CONSTITUTION AND GOVERNMENT. Parliament consists of the Governor, the Legislative Council and the House of Assembly. The Council has 19 members, elected by adults with 6 months' residence. Members sit for 6 years, 3 retiring annually and 4 every sixth year. There is no power to dissolve the Council. Vacancies are filled by by-elections. The House of Assembly has 35 members; the current term for the House of Assembly is 4 years. Members of both Houses are paid a salary of $A20,625 (1977–78), plus an electorate allowance, according to the division represented. The annual allowance payable is calculated as a percentage of basic salary. The amounts vary from $A2,269 (11%) to $A7,219 (35%). Women received the right to vote in 1903. Proportional representation was adopted in 1907, the method now being the single transferable vote in 7-member constituencies. Casual vacancies in the House of Assembly are determined by a transfer of the preference of the vacating member's ballot papers to consenting candidates who were unsuccessful at the last general election.

A Minister must have a seat in one of the two Houses; only one of the present Ministers is a member of the Legislative Council.

In addition to the salary paid to Ministers as members of either House, the following allowances are payable: Premier, in conjunction with a ministerial office, $A25,781 plus entertainment allowance $A2,475; Deputy Premier, in conjunction with a ministerial office, $A17,531; other Ministers, $A14,438. The Leader of the Opposition in the House of Assembly receives an allowance of $A14,438. The holders of some other offices receive allowances ranging from $A1,238 to $A6,875.

At the election on 11 Dec. 1976, 18 Labor and 17 Liberal members were returned to the House of Assembly.

The Legislative Council is predominantly independent without formal party allegiance; 2 members are Labor-endorsed.

Governor: Sir Stanley Burbury, KBE.

The Labor Party Cabinet is composed as follows:

Premier, Treasurer and Minister for Planning and Development: W. A. Neilson.

Deputy Premier, Industrial Relations and Health: D. A. Lowe. *Attorney-General, Police, and Emergency Services:* B. K. Miller. *Education, Recreation and the Arts:* N. L. C. Batt. *Tourism and the Environment:* M. T. C. Barnard. *Resources and Energy:* G. D. Chisholm. *Main Roads, Transport and Local Government:* D. J. Baldock. *Primary Industries:* E. W. Barnard. *Housing and Construction, and Minister assisting the Premier:* H. N. Holgate.

Agent-General in London: R. R. Neville.
Official Secretary: C. Langbant (485/9 Strand, WC2).

Local Government. For the purposes of local government, the State is divided into 49 municipal areas comprising the cities of Hobart, Launceston and Glenorchy and 46 municipalities. The cities and municipalities are managed by elected aldermen and councillors respectively with reference to local matters such as sanitation and health services, domestic water supplies and roads and bridges within each particular area. The chief source of revenue is rates (based on improved values) levied on owners of property.

Tasmanian Islands. Three inhabited Tasmanian islands (Bruny, King and Flinders) are organized as municipalities. Nearly 1,600 km south-east lies Macquarie Island, part of the State, and used only as an Australian research base and meteorological station.

ECONOMY

Budget. The revenue is derived chiefly from taxation (payroll tax, motor, land, stamp and death duties), and from grants and reimbursements from the Australian Government. Customs, excise, sales and income tax are levied by the Australian Government, which makes grants to Tasmania for both revenue and capital purposes. Australian Government grants to Tasmania in 1976–77 totalled $A368m. These included Financial Assistance Grants, $A149m.; Specific purpose payments, $A149m.; and Capital Grants, $A32m.

Specific purpose payments are mainly used to provide essential services such as housing, roads and schools, while Financial Assistance Grants have been paid since 1942 to compensate the State for the loss of income tax to the federal government.

Consolidated Revenue Fund receipts and expenditure, in $A1,000, for financial years ending 30 June:

	1971–72	*1972–73*	*1973–74*	*1974–75*	*1975–76*	*1976–77*
Revenue	157,782	181,866	206,947	268,522	322,091	396,617
Expenditure	160,237	185,998	210,097	282,065	317,947	395,033

The public debt at current exchange rates amounted to $A811m. at 30 June 1977.

In 1976–77 State taxation receipts amounted to $A85·1m., of which pay-roll tax provided $A35·2m.; motor vehicles, $A11m.; death duties, $A6·5m.; land tax, $A3·8m., and stamp duties, $A17·7m.

Banking. Trading bank activity in Tasmania is divided between 6 private banks and the Commonwealth Bank of Australia. For the month of June 1977 liabilities represented by depositors' balances averaged $A347m. and assets represented by advances, $A229m. The 9 savings banks operating in Tasmania are the Commonwealth Savings Bank, 2 trustee savings banks and 6 private savings banks operated by trading banks. At 30 June 1977 total savings bank deposits were $A477m.

ENERGY AND NATURAL RESOURCES

Electricity. Tasmania has plentiful supplies of hydro-electric power because of assured rainfall and high level water storages (natural and artificial). The Hydro-Electric Commission, Tasmania's sole commercial supplier of electricity, has been surveying water power resources of the State for many years and it is estimated that about 3m. kw. can be economically developed. By early 1977, 1,492,000 kw. of generating plant was in commission. In 1976 the peak loading was 943,400 kw. Completion of Gordon River Scheme, Stage 1, will bring the generating capacity to 1·75m. kw.

during 1977. The major construction project is the Gordon River scheme involving the construction of Australia's largest artificial water storage (combined area of the 2 lakes will be over 1,000 sq. km) and one of the nation's largest dams. Water will be carried from the Lake Gordon storage by a near vertical shaft to the power station 186 metres underground, which is designed to be operated by remote control from Hobart, 160 km away. Generator capacity of the Gordon River (Stage 1) scheme will be 288,000 kw.

Minerals. The assayed content of principal metallic minerals contained in locally produced concentrates for 1975–76 was (in tonnes): Zinc, 67,318; iron, 1,463,044; copper, 25,061; lead, 19,542; tin, 5,870; gold, 1,598 kg; silver, 75,515 kg. Coal production (1975–76), 176,352 tonnes.

Primary Industries. The estimated gross value of recorded production from agriculture in 1975–76 was (in $A1,000): Crops, 43,988; livestock slaughterings and other disposals, 33,928; livestock products, 63,880; total gross value, 141,796. Estimated gross value of production in forestry, fisheries and hunting was $A54·2m.

Agriculture. The area occupied by the 8,214 holdings in 1975–76 totalled 2,459,256 hectares, of which 995,194 were devoted to crops and sown pasture. The following table shows the area and production, in tonnes, of the principal crops:

	1973–74		*1974–75*		*1975–76*[1]	
	Hectares	*Production*	*Hectares*	*Production*	*Hectares*	*Production*
Wheat	2,521	3,510	1,535	2,282	1,644	1,728
Barley	11,121	23,790	12,020	27,266	11,475	18,389
Oats	9,173	8,247	6,069	5,496	3,924	3,497
Peas (blue)	587	1,027		2,171	209	261
Green peas, ex-			969			
shell	4,761	17,157	4,651	21,081	5,538	20,688
Potatoes	3,127	62,866	4,143	95,610	3,354	95,614
Hay	91,924	461,459	80,483	384,257	71,567	327,239
Hops (bearing) (dry)	703	1,949	662	1,439	513	1,129

[1] Not strictly comparable with previous years; as from 1975–76 a new definition of rural holdings excludes small 'non-commercial' holdings. The effect on agricultural statistics is minimal.

Livestock at 31 March 1976: Sheep, 4·2m.; cattle, 909,232; pigs, 69,773.

Wool produced during 1975–76 was 20m. kg, valued at $A28m. In 1975–76 butter production was 10,762 tonnes; cheese, 13,332 tonnes.

Forestry. Indigenous forests cover a considerable part of the State, and the sawmilling industry is very important. Production of sawn timber in 1976–77 was 368,160 cu. metres. Almost 1m. cu. metres of logs were used for milling in 1976–77 and a further 2·9m. cu. metres were used for chipping, grinding or flaking. Newsprint and paper are produced from native hardwoods, principally eucalypts.

INDUSTRY AND TRADE

Industry. The most important manufactures for export are refined metals, newsprint and other paper manufactures, pigments, woollen goods, fruit pulp and jam, confectionery, butter, preserved and dried vegetables, sawn timber, iron ore pellets and processed fish products. The electrolytic-zinc works at Risdon near Hobart treat large quantities of local and imported ore, and produce zinc, sulphuric acid, superphosphate, sulphate of ammonia, cadmium and other by-products. At George Town, large-scale plants produce refined aluminium and manganese alloys. During 1976–77, 3m. tonnes (green weight) of woodchips were produced. In 1975–76 the number of manufacturing establishments employing 4 or more persons was 668; employment, 27,785; wages and salaries (excluding proprietors drawings), $A217m.; turnover, $A1,031m.; value added, $A456m.

Labour. The Commonwealth Industrial Court (judicial powers) and Commonwealth Conciliation and Arbitration Commission (arbitral powers) have jurisdiction over federal unions, *i.e.*, with interstate membership. The Arbitration Commission abolished the concept of the basic wage in June 1967 and made an award in terms of total wage; in June 1969 it adopted the principle of equal pay for equal work for females. The Commission adopted wage indexation in principle in May 1975 as a result of the national wage case. The Commission decided to sit quarterly to consider the national wage pending a firm decision on wage indexation. Quarterly percentage wage increases were subsequently granted in line with the increase in the consumer price index during the March, June, Sept. and Dec. quarters, 1975 and the Sept. quarter, 1976. Increases, based on the consumer price index, were granted for the March, June and Dec. quarters, 1976, and March and June quarters, 1977, but not to the full extent of the increase in the index.

Most Tasmanian employees not covered by federal awards operate under State Industrial Boards established for the various trades by resolution of Parliament or proclamation of the Governor. Each Board consists of a Chairman appointed by the Governor with equal representation of employers and employees. The Boards have authority over minimum rates for wages or piece work, number of working hours for which the wage is payable, conditions of apprenticeship, annual leave and adjustment of wage and piece-work rates. Industrial Boards follow to a large extent the wage rates fixed by the Conciliation and Arbitration Commission; from Oct. 1968 to May 1977 they followed the quantum of increase in the minimum wage fixed by the Australian Commission but did not abolish the basic wage concept.

Commerce. Trade by sea and air in $A1m. for years ending 30 June:

	1971–72	*1972–73*	*1973–74*	*1974–75*	*1975–76*
Imports	341·9	356·1	451·8	529·5	607·6
Exports	510·9	570·2	698·7	637·8	728·3

In 1975–76 imports by sea and air from other Australian states totalled (in $A1m.) 531; from Japan, 12; from New Zealand, 10; from USA, 10; from UK, 9; from Canada, 8; from other countries, 27. Exports to other Australian states amounted to (in $A1m.) 478; to Japan, 111; to USA, 34; to Indonesia, 12; to UK, 11; to Thailand, 9; to other countries, 74.

Principal imports, 1975–76, in $A1m.: New motor vehicles, 70; machinery, 66; petroleum products, 65; food, 57; ores and concentrates, 43; clothing, 31. Principal exports: Food, 117; ores and concentrates, 93; refined zinc, 75; textiles, yarns and fabrics, 42; woodchips, 36; greasy wool, 31; timber, 26; and confectionery, aluminium, newsprint, fine writing and printing papers, woodpulp for paper-making, calcium carbide, Portland cement, ferro-manganese and titanium oxides.

Tourism. In 1976–77 a total of 505,000 persons entered Tasmania. It is estimated that of this total 350,000 were visitors to the State and 220,000 of these were tourists.

COMMUNICATIONS

Roads. The total road length is about 21,000 km, consisting of a classified road system of 3,600 km maintained by the State Department of Main Roads, and the remainder maintained by local government authorities, the Forestry Commission and the Hydro-Electric Commission. Motor vehicles registered at 31 Dec. 1976 comprised 164,200 cars, 38,800 commercial vehicles and 6,400 motor cycles.

Railways. There is an 849-km network of 1,067-mm gauge lines linking Hobart and Launceston with coastal and country areas, formerly operated by Tasmanian Government Railways but since 1 July 1975 worked by the Australian National Railways Commission. Earnings in 1975–76 were $A8m. and expenditure $A22·1m.

Aviation. Regular daily passenger and freight air services connect the south, north and north-west of the State with the mainland of Australia. Statistics of regular air transport services for the year 1975–76 are as follows: Kilometres flown, 11m.; passengers carried, 903,920; freight carried, 20,772 tonnes; mail carried, 328 tonnes.

Shipping. The most important development has been the introduction of roll-on roll-off freighters, allowing door-to-door delivery between Tasmanian and mainland ports.

For railways, posts and telegraphs, *see* COMMONWEALTH OF AUSTRALIA, pp. 114–15.

JUSTICE, RELIGION, EDUCATION AND WELFARE

Justice. The Supreme Court of Tasmania, with civil, criminal, ecclesiastical, admiralty and matrimonial jurisdiction, established by Royal Charter on 13 Oct. 1823, is a superior court of record, with both original and appellate jurisdiction, and consists of a Chief Justice and 5 puisne judges. There are also inferior civil courts with limited jurisdiction, licensing courts, mining courts, courts of petty sessions and coroners' courts.

During the year 1975, 34,788 persons were summarily convicted in lower courts (21,488 for traffic offences) and 347 persons were convicted in the Supreme Court. The total police force on 30 June 1976 was 1,004. There was one gaol, with 297 inmates at the end of June 1976.

Religion. There is no State Church. At the census of 1971 the following numbers of adherents of the principal religions were recorded:

Church of England	169,089	Churches of Christ	2,500
Roman Catholic	77,250	Other religions	24,490
Methodist	42,173	Not stated [1]	45,457
Presbyterian	17,281		
Baptist	8,039	Total	390,413
Congregational	4,134		

[1] Includes 993 whose religion was indefinite and 20,221 who stated 'no religion'.

Education. Education is controlled by the State and is free, secular and compulsory between the ages of 6 and 16. At 1 Aug. 1976 government schools had a total enrolment of 81,182 pupils, including 30,183 at secondary level; private schools had a total enrolment of 14,431 pupils, including 6,221 at secondary level.

The University of Tasmania, established 1890, had 294 full-time teachers with 3,536 students in 1976.

Social Welfare. Old Age, Invalid, War Service and Widows' Pensions are paid by the Australian Government. The number of pensioners in Tasmania on 30 June 1976 was: Age, 35,594; invalid, 6,091; war, 20,046; widows, 4,209. Benefit payments totalled $A100·5m.

Books of Reference

Statistical Information: The State Government Statistical Office (Commonwealth Government Centre, Hobart), established in 1877, became in 1924 the Tasmanian Office of the Australian Bureau of Statistics, but continues to serve State statistical needs as required. *Deputy Commonwealth Statistician and Government Statistician:* R. Lakin.

Main publications: *Annual Statistical Bulletins* (*e.g., Demography, Agricultural Industry, Finance, Manufacturing Establishments* etc.).—*Pocket Year Book of Tasmania.* Annual (from 1913).—*Tasmanian Year Book.* Annual (from 1967).—*Monthly Summary of Statistics* (from July 1945).

Directorate of Industrial Development and Trade, *A Survey of Recent Developments in the Tasmanian Economy.* Hobart. Annual
Angus, M., *The World of Olegas Truchanas.* Hobart, 1975
Clark, C. I., *The Parliament of Tasmania.* Hobart, 1947
Davies, J. L. (ed.), *Atlas of Tasmania.* Hobart, 1965
Green, F. C. (ed.), *A Century of Responsible Government.* Hobart, 1956
Mercury-Walch Pty. Ltd, *The Tasmanian Almanac.* Hobart. Annual
Townsley, W. A., *Government of Tasmania.* Melbourne, 1974
Wettenhall, R. L., *A Guide to Tasmanian Government Administration.* Hobart, 1968

State Library: The State Library of Tasmania, Hobart. *Librarian:* W. L. Brown, FLA, ALAA.

VICTORIA

AREA AND POPULATION. The State has an area of 227,600 sq. km, and a census population of 3,746,000 at 30 June 1976. Estimate (1977) 3,782,000

The population of the Melbourne Statistical Division at 30 June 1976 was

2,672,200 or 71·3% of the population of the State. The population of each Statistical District in Victoria was: Ballarat, 70,490; Bendigo, 56,800; Geelong, 135,560; Morwell, 16,750; Shepparton-Mooroopna, 32,090.

The census population (exclusive of full-blood aboriginals prior to 1961) was:

Date of census enumeration	*Population*			*On previous census*	
	Males	*Females*	*Total*	*Numerical increase*	*Increase %*
3 April 1881	451,623	409,943	861,566	131,368	17·99
5 April 1891	598,222	541,866	1,140,088	278,522	32·33
31 March 1901	603,720	597,350	1,201,070	60,982	5·35
3 April 1911	655,591	659,960	1,315,551	114,481	9·53
4 April 1921	754,724	776,556	1,531,280	215,729	16·40
30 June 1933	903,244	917,017	1,820,261	288,981	18·87
30 June 1947	1,013,867	1,040,834	2,054,701	234,440	12·88
30 June 1954	1,231,099	1,221,242	2,452,341	397,640	19·35
30 June 1961	1,474,536	1,455,830	2,930,366	478,025	19·49
30 June 1966	1,614,240	1,605,977	3,220,217	289,851	9·89
30 June 1971	1,760,651	1,759,706	3,520,357	300,140	9·32
30 June 1976	1,870,097	1,875,884	3,745,981	225,625	6·41

The population of urban Melbourne (capital city) on 30 June 1976 was 2,480,670. The population of urban Geelong was 122,080; urban Ballarat, 60,737; urban Bendigo, 50,169. Other urban centres: Shepparton-Mooroopna, 25,848; Wangaratta, 20,195; Warrnambool, 20,195; Moe-Yallourn, 18,710; Morwell, 16,094; Traralgon, 15,089; Mildura, 14,417. Other urban centres (1971 population): Werribee, 12,872; Horsham, 11,045; Sale, 10,436; Colac, 10,362; Hamilton, 9,673; Bairnsdale, 8,552; Ararat, 8,312; Benalla, 8,255; Portland, 8,216; Swan Hill, 7,712; Castlemaine, 7,699; Maryborough, 7,472; Warragul, 7,101.

Vital statistics for calendar years:

	Births	*Marriages*	*Divorces*	*Deaths*
1974	66,201	29,708	4,450	30,875
1975	61,897	27,806	5,663	29,499
1976	60,667	28,760	13,759	30,753
1977	59,524	27,563	...	29,483

The annual rates per 1,000 of the population in 1977 were: Marriages, 7·29; births, 15·74; deaths, 7·8; infant deaths, 10·92 per 1,000 births.

CONSTITUTION AND GOVERNMENT. Victoria, formerly a portion of New South Wales, was, in 1851, proclaimed a separate colony, with a partially elective Legislative Council. In 1855 responsible government was conferred, the legislative power being vested in a parliament of two Houses, the Legislative Council and the Legislative Assembly. At present the Council consists of 40 members who are elected for 6 years, one-half retiring every third year. The Assembly consists of 81 members, elected for 3 years from the date of its first meeting unless sooner dissolved by the Governor. Members and electors of both Houses must be adult natural born or naturalized British subjects. Women are fully enfranchised. No property qualification is required, but judges may not be members of either House. Single voting (one elector one vote) and compulsory preferential voting apply to Council and Assembly elections. Enrolment of Council and Assembly electors is compulsory. The Council may not initiate or amend money bills, but may suggest amendments in such bills other than amendments which would increase any charge. Any Minister, with the consent of the House of which he is not a member, may sit and speak in that House to explain a bill relating to the department administered by him, but may not vote in that House. A bill shall not become law unless passed by both Houses, except that, in the event of a continued disagreement between the two Houses as to a bill passed by the Assembly, other than certain constitutional bills, the Governor having dissolved the Assembly may subsequently dissolve the Council, and if the disagreement still continues he may convene a joint sitting of the members of the Council and the Assembly; if at such joint sitting the bill in dispute is passed by an absolute majority of all members it shall become law.

Private members of both Houses receive salaries of $A23,869 per annum, additional allowances rising from $A5,225 to $A7,035 (outer country), and a living-away-from-home allowance of $A35 for each day of attendance for each member (not being a responsible Minister or a metropolitan member).

Members holding the following offices receive the salaries and allowances specified: The President of the Council, $A41,771 salary and $A2,626 expense allowance; the Speaker of the Assembly, $A41,771 salary and $A2,626 expense allowance; the Chairman of Committees of the Council, $A31,507 salary and $A955 expense allowance; the Chairman of Committees of the Assembly, $A31,507 salary and $A955 expense allowance; the Leader of the Opposition in the Assembly, $A41,771 salary and $A4,297 expense allowance; the Deputy Leader of the Opposition in the Assembly, $A31,507 salary and $A2,626 expense allowance; the Leader of the Third Party, $A31,507 salary and $A1,432 expense allowance; a member of either House who is the Parliamentary Secretary of the Cabinet, $A31,507 salary and $A1,432 expense allowance; the Government Whip in the Assembly, $A28,165 salary; the Whip of any recognized Party which consists of at least 12 members of Parliament, of which Party no member is a responsible Minister, $A26,495 salary. All members have free passes over the Victorian Railways; country members are also entitled to certain allowances for air travel.

The Legislative Assembly, elected on 20 March 1976, is composed as follows: Liberal Party, 52; Labor Party, 21; National Party, 7; Independent Labor, 1.

Governor: Sir Henry Winneke, KCMG, OBE.

In the exercise of the executive power the Governor is advised by a Cabinet of responsible Ministers. Section 50 of the Constitution Act 1975 provides that the number of responsible Ministers shall not at any one time exceed 18, of whom not more than 6 may sit in the Legislative Council. No responsible Minister may hold office for more than 3 months unless he is or becomes a member of the Council or the Assembly.

Responsible Ministers receive the following amounts: The Premier, $A47,738 salary and $A10,025 expense allowance and, if he usually resides more than 80 km from the Melbourne Post Office and maintains an additional residence within 15 km of the Melbourne Post Office, he receives a residential allowance of $A3,660; the Deputy Premier, $A44,758 salary and $A5,012 expense allowance; 16 other responsible Ministers, $A41,771 salary and $A4,297 expense allowance. Each responsible Minister receives, when travelling on business of the State, a travelling allowance. The President, Speaker, Parliamentary Secretary of the Cabinet, Leader and Deputy Leader of the Opposition in the Assembly, and the leader of any recognized party (other than the Opposition) consisting of at least 12 members of Parliament, of which party no member is a responsible Minister, also receives a travelling allowance when travelling on official business. Members of Committees receive attendance fees and certain travelling expenses when on Committee duties.

The Liberal Party Government (first appointed 7 June 1955) is as follows:

Premier, Treasurer and Minister of the Arts: R. J. Hamer, ED, MLA.

Education: L. H. S. Thompson, CMG, MLA. *Minerals and Energy:* J. C. M. Balfour, MLA. *Conservation, Lands, and Soldier Settlement:* W. A. Borthwick, MLA. *Transport:* J. A. Rafferty, MLA. *Agriculture:* I. W. Smith, MLA. *Public Works:* R. C. Dunstan, DSO, MLA. *Special Education:* A. H. Scanlon, MLA. *Social Welfare, and Youth, Sport and Recreation:* B. J. Dixon, MLA. *Labour and Industry, and Consumer Affairs:* R. R. C. Maclellan, MLA. *Immigration and Ethnic Affairs, and Assistant Minister of Health:* W. Jona, MLA. *Housing and Planning:* G. P. Hayes, MLA. *Chief Secretary:* V. O. Dickie, MLC. *Local Government and Federal Affairs:* A. J. Hunt, MLC. *Health:* W. V. Houghton, MLC. *Water Supply and Forests:* F. J. Granter, MLC. *State Development and Decentralization, and Tourism:* D. G. Crozier, MLC. *Attorney-General:* Haddon Storey, QC, MLC. *Parliamentary Secretary of the Cabinet:* J. H. Ramsay, MLA.

Agent-General in Great Britain: J. F. Rossiter (Victoria House, Melbourne Place, WC2).

Local Government. With the exception of Yallourn Works area (26·96 sq. km) and the unincorporated areas—French Island (168 sq. km), Lady Julia Percy Island (2·64 sq. km), the Bass Strait Islands and part of Gippsland Lakes (335 sq. km) and Tower Hill Lake Reserve (5·91 sq. km), the State is divided (at 30 June 1976) into 211 municipal districts, namely 65 cities, 6 towns, 7 boroughs and 133 shires. The constitution of cities, towns, boroughs and shires is based on statutory requirements concerning population, rate revenue and net annual value of rateable property.

ECONOMY

Budget. The receipts and payments (in $A1,000) of the Consolidated Fund in the years shown (ended 30 June) were:

	1973–74	*1974–75*	*1975–76*	*1976–77*	*1977–78*[1]
Receipts	1,610,923	2,114,416	2,568,197	2,955,620	3,282,800
Payments	1,610,923	2,114,416	2,568,197	2,955,620	3,282,800

[1] Estimates.

The principal receipt items (in $A1,000) during 1975–76 were: Taxation, 1,594,445 (including Commonwealth Government reimbursement, 706,389, but excluding 155,182 paid to special funds); railways, 146,943; other Commonwealth Government payments, 281,784, and mining royalties, 43,334. The principal heads of expenditure were: Interest and public debt charges (including railways), 205,775; railways, 273,561; education, 707,278; health, hospitals and charities, 336,219.

The amount raised by taxation (exclusive of taxes collected by the Commonwealth Government or paid to special funds but inclusive of the Commonwealth Government reimbursements under the uniform taxation scheme), as shown in the above paragraph, was approximately $A431.40 per head of population.

The public debt of Victoria (in $A1m.) on 30 June 1976 was 2,834. During the year ending 30 June 1976, an amount of 417 was expended from loan funds. Of this amount, 135 was spent on education, 32 on railways, 32 on water supply, irrigation and drainage, 65 on protection of the environment (including sewerage), 14 on electricity supply, 8 on forestry, 44 on health services, 12 on agricultural, pastoral, etc., services, 15 on culture and recreation, 12 on law, order and public safety, 15 on legislature and general administration and 33 on all other purposes. In addition to the public debt noted above, Victoria had other liabilities due to the Commonwealth Government at 30 June 1976. These included 785·1 advances for housing, 12·1 special assistance loans for soldier settlement, 62·2 advance for sewerage. 46·2 for rural and dairy reconstruction, 47·8 for growth centres and 23·7 for land acquisition.

Banking. On 30 June 1977 there were 6·66m. operative accounts (excluding school bank accounts) in savings banks in Victoria. The total credit due to depositors amounted to $A5,978m., made up of State Savings Bank, $A2,849m.; Commonwealth Savings Bank, $A1,242m.; private savings banks, $A1,886m.

The weekly average of deposits and advances of trading banks operating in Victoria during June 1977 were as follows: Deposits, not bearing interest, $A1,755m.; deposits, bearing interest, $A3,042m.; total deposits, $A4,797m.; loans, advances, and bills discounted, $A3,451m. The weekly average of debits to customers' accounts (excluding debits to Commonwealth and State Government accounts at City branches in State capitals) for the same period totalled $A5,209m.

ENERGY AND NATURAL RESOURCES

Electricity. All electricity in this State for public supply is generated by the largest electricity supply authority in Australia—the State Electricity Commission of Victoria. Its supply network serves over 99% of the entire Victorian population and some New South Wales municipalities as well as irrigation settlements bordering the Murray River.

The major base load generating stations are located in the Latrobe Valley on top of a large brown coal field with estimated geological reserves of 114,000m. tonnes. Burning raw brown coal on site and with an installed generating capacity of

3,016,000 kw., these stations produce over 85% of Victoria's electricity. The chief one is Hazelwood, which was completed in 1971 with a capacity of 1·6m. kw. The total installed generating capacity of all thermal stations in Victoria is 3,342,000 kw. including the base load stations in the Latrobe Valley and smaller ones in Melbourne, and some provincial cities.

The total installed capacity of the Commission's system at 30 June 1977 was 4,745,000 kw.; it includes Victoria's share of about one-third (1,059,000 kw. at 30 June 1977) of the Snowy Mountains hydro-electric scheme in New South Wales and its half share (25,000 kw.) of the Hume hydro-electric station, shared with New South Wales. Excluding the Snowy and Hume schemes in New South Wales the installed hydro-electric capacity totalled 318,500 kw. at 30 June 1977, with Kiewa (3 stations totalling 183,600 kw.) being the chief undertaking.

Total power generated and purchased in 1976–77 was 19,727 gwh.

Oil and Natural Gas. Crude oil in commercially recoverable quantities was first discovered by the Esso/BHP partnership in 1967 in 2 large fields offshore in East Gippsland in Bass Strait between 65 and 80 km from land. These fields, Halibut and Kingfish, with 4 smaller fields since discovered—Barracouta, Mackerel, Tuna and Flounder, have been assessed as containing initial recoverable reserves of 1,928m. bbls of treated crude oil. Total production since 1969 from the 3 producing fields to the end of June 1977 has amounted to 837m. bbls, leaving a balance of recoverable reserves of 1,091m. bbls.

Gippsland crude now supplies approximately 69% of Australia's refinery requirements, and during 1977 a total of 162·5m. bbls were produced from the 3 fields. Halibut, Kingfish and Barracouta. Depletion of production from the 2 major fields, Kingfish and Halibut and the smaller Barracouta field, is now expected to occur in the mid-1980s.

Natural gas was discovered offshore in East Gippsland in 1965. The initial recoverable reserves of treated gas are 7,763,000m. cu. ft. Reserves are sufficient for 30 years. Following an extensive development and distribution programme, natural gas was first connected to homes and industry in Victoria in April 1969. All gas consumers in Melbourne, Geelong, Ballarat, Bendigo, Shepparton, Euroa, Benalla, Wangaratta, Wodonga, Albury and a number of towns near Melbourne, in the Latrobe Valley and in East Gippsland, are now using natural gas. At 30 June 1977 a total of 711,857 consumers were being supplied with it. During the period 1 July 1976 to 30 June 1977 a total volume of 3,157·3m. cu. metres of gas was consumed in Victoria, including commercial sales and plant usage.

Natural gas and crude oil are conveyed from the producing fields to a large treatment plant at Longford in East Gippsland from where both hydrocarbons are distributed by a network of transmission lines to tank farms and city gate distribution points.

The crude oil is then distributed to refineries in Victoria by pipeline and to other States by seagoing tankers. Natural gas is distributed to residential and industrial consumers through pipelines comprising some 1,684 km of high-pressure lines and over 13,700 km of transfer, direct high-pressure and reticulation lines.

Liquefied petroleum gas is now being produced after extraction of the propane and butane fractions from the untreated oil and gas; about 1·2m. tonnes a year is exported by Esso and BHP, mainly to Japan.

Brown Coal. Major deposits of brown coal are located in the Central Gippsland region and comprise approximately 94% of the total reserves in Victoria. In the Latrobe Valley section of this region the thick brown coal seams underlie an area from 10–30 km wide and extend over a length of approximately 70 km from Yallourn in the west to the south of Sale in the east. Small fields have also been found at Stradbroke in the ranges on the southern flank of the Valley and in the Gelliondale–Welshpool area near the coast. On a geological basis the brown coal reserves in Central Gippsland are estimated to be in the order of 114,000 megatonnes, of which about 67,000 megatonnes are proven and the remaining 47,000 megatonnes are inferred.

About 54% of the reserves occur in areas where the overburden over the uppermost seam is less than 30·5 metres while 95% is in areas with less than 91·4 metres of overburden. The current primary use of these reserves is to fuel the major base load electricity generating stations located at Morwell and Yallourn, and larger cuts have been opened for this purpose at these localities.

Land Settlement. Of the total area of Victoria (22·76m. hectares), 13,818,931 hectares on 30 June 1976 were either alienated or in process of alienation. The remainder (8,941,069) constituted Crown land as follows: Perpetual leases, grazing and other leases and licences, 2,423,955; reservations including forest and timber reserves, water, catchment and drainage purposes, national parks, wildlife reserves, water frontages and other reserves, 3,170,367; unoccupied and unreserved including areas set aside for roads, 3,346,747. Rural holdings at 31 March 1976 numbered 58,468.

Agriculture. The following table shows the area under the principal crops and the produce of each for 3 seasons (in 1,000 units):

	Total crop area	*Wheat*		*Oats*		*Barley*		*Potatoes*		*Hay*	
Season	*Hectares*	*Hectares*	*Tonnes*	*Hectares*	*Tonnes*	*Hectares*	*Tonnes*	*Hectares*	*Tonnes*	*Hectares*	*Tonnes*
1973–74	1,980	1,258	1,490	271	233	222	285	12	254	626	2,967
1974–75	1,775	1,141	2,091	198	186	243	319	13	283	506	2,017
1975–76	1,851	1,073	1,579	243	436	344	445	11	244	488	1,852

In 1975–76 there were 22,347 hectares of vines, yielding 60,869 tonnes of grapes for wine-making, 52,025 tonnes of dried fruit and 8,199 tonnes of table grapes. Green fodder covered 46,574 hectares, and orchards and vegetables, including potatoes and onions, occupied 48,596 hectares.

At March 1976 there were in the State 5·86m. head of cattle, 25,395,140 sheep and 392,834 pigs. In 1975–76, 748,362 tonnes of fresh meat was produced. The wool produced in the season 1975–76 amounted to 111m. kg, valued at $A174m. The quantity of butter produced in 1975–76 was 108m. kg.

The gross value of Victorian primary production (rural and non-rural) in 1975–76 was $A1,327m.

Minerals. The recorded production of certain metals and minerals raised in Victoria for the year 1975–76 was: Gold, 119,000 grammes, value $A343,000; coal, brown, 26·7m. tonnes, value $A48·3m.

INDUSTRY AND TRADE

Industry. From the 1975–76 Census of Manufacturing Establishments onwards only a limited range of data—employment and wages and salaries—has been collected from single-establishment manufacturing enterprises with less than 4 persons employed. This procedure significantly reduces the statistical reporting obligations of small businesses. Data in respect of the larger manufacturers provides reliable information for the evaluation of trends in the manufacturing sector of the economy. The following data relates to manufacturing establishments owned by multi-establishment enterprises, and single-establishment manufacturing enterprises with 4 or more persons employed.

The total number of manufacturing establishments in Victoria in 1975–76 (figures for 1974–75 in brackets) was 8,893 (8,924). Persons employed, including working proprietors, on the last pay day in June were males 292,079 (302,234) and females 125,507 (130,617). Salaries and wages paid were $A3,295m. ($A2,961m.), excluding drawings of working proprietors. The cost of purchases, transfers in, and selected expenses was $A7,571m. ($A7,031m.) and sales, transfers out and other operating revenue were $A13,249m. ($A11,729m.).

The preceding figures exclude gas and electricity producing and distributing establishments. In terms of persons employed the most important manufacturing activities were: Basic and fabricated metal products including transport equipment, other machinery and equipment, 171,580 (181,293); textiles, clothing and footwear, 73,433 (72,128); food, beverages and tobacco, 59,464 (60,848).

Trade Unions. There were 164 trade unions with a total membership of 717,900 operating in Victoria in Dec. 1976.

Commerce. The commerce of Victoria, exclusive of inter-state trade, is included in the statement of the commerce of Australia, *see* pp. 111–13.

The total value of the overseas imports and exports of Victoria, including bullion and specie but excluding inter-state trade, was as follows (in $A1,000):

	1971–72	*1972–73*	*1973–74*	*1974–75*	*1975–76*	*1976–77*
Imports	1,431,076	1,472,602	2,155,759	2,793,411	2,875,772	3,665,911
Exports	1,139,731	1,495,373	1,593,640	1,696,828	1,820,081	2,216,017

The chief exports in 1976–77 were: Wool, petroleum products and gases, meat, dairy products, wheat, non-electric machinery, hides and skins, fruits, motor vehicles and parts.

COMMUNICATIONS

Roads. At 30 June 1976 there were 159,560 km of road open for general traffic consisting of 56,693 km of bituminous seal, etc., 45,845 km of waterbound macadam, gravel, etc., 28,060 km formed, but not paved, and 28,962 km not formed. The number of registered motor vehicles (other than tractors) at 30 Sept. 1976 was 1,821,900.

Railways. All the railways are the property of the State and are under the management of a 7-member governing board, appointed by, and responsible to, the Victorian Government.

At 30 June 1976, 6,654 km of government railway were open. The total liability of the State for railways, construction, etc., to this date was $A607m. During the year 1975–76 the gross revenue amounted to $A147,449,945 and the total working expenses to $A272,395,050. 109,669,067 passengers, 10,446,669 tonnes of freight and 356,023 tonnes of livestock were carried.

Aviation. During the year ended 31 Dec. 1975 there were 79,224 aircraft movements at Melbourne (Tullamarine) airport. Passengers totalled 4·1m. on domestic flights (international, 551,626). Freight handled, 55,366 tonnes, domestic flights (12,277 international).

JUSTICE, RELIGION, EDUCATION AND WELFARE

Justice. There is a Supreme Court with a Chief Justice and 19 puisne judges. There are magistrates' courts, county courts, a court of licensing, and a bankruptcy court.

Criminal statistics for 1973: 342,758 convictions (in addition approximately for 204,000 driving and traffic offences) in magistrates' courts; 1,841 convicted persons in higher (judges') courts.

There are 11 gaols in Victoria. At 30 June 1976 there were confined in these prisons, 1,488 males and 35 females.

Religion. There is no State Church in Victoria, and no State assistance has been given to religion since 1875. At the date of the 1971 census the following were the enumerated numbers of each of the principal religions: Catholic, Roman,[1] 408,864; Catholic,[1] 594,962; Church of England, 892,568; Methodist, 256,058; Presbyterian, 364,338; Protestant (undefined), 113,351; other Christian, 350,503; Hebrew, 30,117; other non-Christians, 12,156; indefinite, 7,792; no religion, 256,430; no reply, 215,212.

[1] So described on individual census schedules.

Education. Education establishments in Victoria consist of 3 universities, established under special Acts and opened in 1855, 1961 and 1967; Colleges of Advanced Education; government schools (primary, primary-secondary, secondary and junior technical, senior technical schools or colleges), and non-government schools.

The University of Melbourne, founded in 1853, had, in 1976, 16,087 students (including 5,816 females) and 1,398 teaching and research staff.

Monash University, founded in 1958 in an eastern suburb of Melbourne, had, in 1976, 13,751 students (including 5,326 females) and 1,108 teaching and research staff.

La Trobe University, founded in 1964 in a northern suburb of Melbourne, had

8,549 students (including 3,781 females) and 540 teaching and research staff in 1976.

Primary education of children of the ages of 6 to 15 years inclusive is free, secular and compulsory. At 1 Aug. 1976 there were 1,720 government primary schools and 46 special schools with 17,433 full-time and 1,377 part-time teachers and an enrolment of 377,429 pupils; 23 government primary-secondary schools had 503 full-time and 88 part-time teachers and an enrolment of 7,207 pupils. There were also 375 government secondary schools, including junior technical schools and high schools with 16,074 full-time and 5,068 part-time teachers and an enrolment of 240,071 pupils. In 1976 there were also 103 senior technical schools. The total expenditure in 1975–76 was $A826m.

Non-government Schools. There were at 1 Aug. 1976, 586 non-government schools, excluding commercial colleges, with 8,888 full-time and 1,835 part-time teachers and 201,083 pupils enrolled. Of these schools, 473 were Roman Catholic.

Social Services. Victoria was the first State of Australia to make a statutory provision for the payment of Age Pensions. The Act providing for the payment of such pensions came into operation on 18 Jan. 1901, and continued until 1 July 1909, when the Australian Invalid and Old Age Pension Act came into force. The Social Services Consolidation Act, which came into operation on 1 July 1947, repealed the various legislative enactments relating to age (previously old-age) and invalid pensions, maternity allowances, child endowment, and unemployment, and sickness benefits and while following in general the Acts repealed, considerably liberalized many of their provisions: it has since been amended. On 30 June 1976 there were 316,950 age and 42,044 invalid pensioners in Victoria, and the amount paid in pensions, including payments to wives of invalid pensioners, during 1975–76 was $A667·76m.

The number of disability pensions (members of the forces and their dependants) payable in Victoria on 30 June 1976 was 129,851, and the number of service pensions was 36,298. The amount paid in war and service pensions by the Commonwealth Government during 1975–76 was $A144·59m.

During the year ended 30 June 1976 maternity allowances were granted to 62,197 mothers in the State, the total amount paid in allowances during the year being $A1·95m.

Under the Australian Unemployment and Sickness Benefit Act 1944, there were 54,625 persons receiving benefits at June 1976 (excluding migrants in accommodation centres) and the amount paid in benefits totalled $A158·6m. in the year ended 30 June 1976.

The number of widows' pensions in force in Victoria at 30 June 1976 was 36,664, and the total amount paid in allowances during the year was $A90·5m.

The number of family allowances in force in Victoria at 30 June 1976 was 1,181,798 (including students), representing 528,017 endowed families. In addition (in 1976), endowment was being paid in respect of 4,302 children who were being maintained in approved institutions. The total amount paid in endowment in Victoria during the year ended 30 June 1976 was $A73·91m.

State Housing. The various State housing authorities were consolidated under the control of the Ministry of Housing early in 1973. The authorities include the Housing Commission, the Teacher Housing Authority, the Co-operative Housing Registry, and the Decentralised Industry Housing Authority which was established in April 1973 to provide housing for key personnel of industries in the country. The Co-operative Housing Registry administers distribution of finance to the co-operative building societies from loan moneys advanced by the Commonwealth Government.

The Housing Commission is controlled by a Commission of 5 full-time members appointed under the Housing Act. The Housing Commission was established in 1938 and its activities are now spread throughout the State. Since its inception to 30 June 1975, 353 estates have been developed by the Commission and 81,792 dwelling units provided thereon. In addition at 30 June 1976, 2,635 dwellings were under construction. About 62% of the units built in 1975–76 were built in country towns, particularly where industries are established. Expenditure on land purchase, development and dwelling construction to 30 June 1976 was $A855m. Rental charges for the year were $A42,030,704, against which $A3,172,000 was allowed in rent rebates to tenants on low incomes, including pensioners.

Books of Reference

Statistical Information: Australian Bureau of Statistics (Commonwealth Banks Building, corner of Elizabeth and Flinders Streets, Melbourne, 3000). *Deputy Commonwealth Statistician:* N. Bowden, B.Ec.

Victorian Year Book. (Annually since 1873)
Victorian Pocket Year Book. (Annually since 1956)
Victorian Statistical Register. (Annually from 1854 to 1916)
Victorian Monthly Statistical Review (from Jan. 1960)

Victoria: The First Century. Official History of Victoria. Melbourne, 1934
Grant, J., and Serle, G. *The Melbourne Scene 1803–1956.* Melbourne Univ. Press, 1956
Pratt, A., *The Centenary History of Victoria.* Melbourne, 1934
Saunders, D. (ed.), *Historic Buildings of Victoria.* Melbourne, 1966

State Library: The State Library of Victoria, Swanston St., Melbourne, 3000. *State Librarian:* K. A. R. Horn, BA, Mus.B(NZ), ANZLA.

WESTERN AUSTRALIA

HISTORY. In 1791 Vancouver, in the *Discovery*, took formal possession of the country about King George Sound. In 1826 the Government of New South Wales sent 20 convicts and a detachment of soldiers to King George Sound and formed a settlement then called Frederickstown. In 1827 Captain (afterwards Sir) James Stirling surveyed the coast from King George Sound to the Swan River, and in May 1829 Captain (afterwards Sir) Charles Fremantle took possession of the territory. In June 1829 Captain Stirling, newly appointed Lieut.-Governor, founded the colony now known as the State of Western Australia. On 1 Jan. 1901 Western Australia became one of the 6 federated States within the Commonwealth of Australia.

AREA AND POPULATION. Western Australia lies between 113° 09′ and 129° E. long. and 13° 44′ and 35° 08′ S. lat.; its area is 2,525,500 sq. km.

The enumerated population at each census from 1921 was as follows[1]:

	Males	Females	Total		Males	Females	Total
1921	177,278	155,454	332,732	1961	375,452	361,177	736,629
1933	233,937	204,915	438,852	1966	432,569	415,531	848,100
1947	258,076	244,404	502,480	1971	529,066	501,403	1,030,469
1954	330,358	309,413	639,771	1976	581,177	563,680	1,144,857

[1] 1961 and earlier exclude full-blood Aboriginals; from 1966 figures refer to total population (*i.e.*, including Aboriginals).

Of the census population in 1976, 806,408 were born in Australia. Married persons numbered 516,120 (259,975 males and 256,145 females); widowers, 8,948; widows, 33,278; divorced, 8,823 males and 10,169 females; never married, 229,106 males and 243,824 females. The number of males under 21 was 231,444 and of females 219,699.

Perth, the capital, had a population of 805,747 at the census of 1976. Of this, the area administered by the City of Perth had a population of 87,598 while the population in the area for which the City of Fremantle is responsible (which includes the chief port of the State) was 23,497.

Principal towns outside the metropolitan area, with estimated population at 30 June 1976: Bunbury, 19,513; Kalgoorlie–Boulder, 19,041; Geraldton, 18,773; Albany, 13,696; Port Hedland, 11,144; Mandurah, 7,050; Northam, 6,866; Collie, 6,771; Busselton, 5,550; Carnarvon, 5,341; Esperance, 5,262; Narrogin, 4,812.

Vital statistics for calendar years[1]:

	Births	Ex-nuptial births	Marriages	Divorces	Deaths
1974	20,207	2,352	9,295	1,761	7,778
1975	20,338	2,527	9,026	2,240	7,972
1976	20,670	2,621	9,518	4,816	7,740

[1] Including Aboriginals.

CONSTITUTION AND GOVERNMENT. In 1870 partially representative government was instituted, and in 1890 the administration was vested in the Governor, a Legislative Council and a Legislative Assembly. The Legislative Council was, in the first instance, nominated by the Governor, but it was provided that in the event of the population of the colony reaching 60,000, it should be elective. In 1893 this limit of population being reached, the Colonial Parliament amended the Constitution accordingly.

The Legislative Council consists of 32 members, 2 members representing each of the 16 electoral provinces. Each member is elected for a term of 6 years, one-half of the members retiring every 3 years.

There are 55 members of the Legislative Assembly, each member representing one of the 55 electoral districts of the State. Members are elected for the duration of the Parliament, normally 3 years. The qualifications applying to candidates and electors are identical for the Legislative Council and the Legislative Assembly. A candidate must have resided in Western Australia for a minimum of 12 months, be at least 18 years of age and free from legal incapacity, be a British subject, and be enrolled, or qualified for enrolment, as an elector. A judge of the Supreme Court, the Sheriff of Western Australia, an undischarged bankrupt or a debtor against whose estate there is a subsisting order in bankruptcy may not be elected to Parliament. No person may hold office as a member of the Legislative Assembly and the Legislative Council at the same time. An elector must be at least 18 years of age, be a British subject free from legal incapacity, must have resided in the Commonwealth of Australia for 6 and in Western Australia for 3 months continuously and in the electoral district for which he claims enrolment for a continuous period of 1 month immediately preceding the date of his claim. Enrolment is compulsory for all qualified persons except Aboriginal natives of Australia, who are entitled but not required to enrol. Voting at elections is on the preferential system and is compulsory for all enrolled persons.

Ordinary members of the legislature are paid a salary of $A20,816 a year, with an additional electorate allowance, ranging from $A4,800 to $A10,500 according to location of electorate. Members are entitled to free travel on Western Australian government railways and on the Metropolitan (Perth) Passenger Transport Trust omnibus and ferry services, and, by arrangement, once every year on government railways in other States. All members of Parliament contribute to superannuation benefits.

The Premier receives a salary, including an electorate allowance, of $A48,707, the Deputy Premier $A43,187, the Leader of the Government in the Legislative Council $A44,527, and all other Ministers $A38,667–42,717 according to location of electorate.

The Legislative Assembly, elected on 19 Feb. 1977, is composed as follows: Australian Labor Party, 22; Liberal Party, 27; National Country Party, 6. The Legislative Council, one-half of which was elected on the same day, is composed of 10 Australian Labor Party, 18 Liberal Party, 4 National Country Party.

Governor: Air Chief Marshal Sir Wallace Kyle, GCB, KCVO, CBE, DSO, DFC, KStJ.

The Liberal–National Country Party coalition Cabinet was, at 30 June 1977:

Premier, Treasurer, Minister Co-ordinating Economic and Regional Development: Sir Charles Walter Michael Court, OBE, MLA.

Deputy Premier, Chief Secretary, Minister for Police and Traffic, and Minister for Regional Administration and the North-West: Desmond Henry O'Neil, MLA. *Minister for Agriculture:* Richard Charles Old, MLA. *Minister for Fisheries and Wildlife, Tourism, Conservation and the Environment, and Leader of the Government in the Legislative Council:* Graham Charles MacKinnon, MLC. *Minister for Works, Water Supplies, and Housing:* Raymond James O'Connor, MLA. *Minister for Labour and Industry, Consumer Affairs, and Immigration:* William Leonard Grayden, MLA. *Attorney-General, and Minister for Federal Affairs:* Ian George Medcalf, ED, QC, MLC. *Minister for Education, Cultural Affairs, and Recreation:* Peter Vernon Jones, MLA. *Minister for Industrial Development, Mines, and Fuel and Energy:* Andrew Mensaros, MLA. *Minister for Local Government, and Urban Development and Town Planning:* Edgar Cyril Rushton, MLA. *Minister for Health, and Community Welfare:* Keith Alan Ridge, MLA. *Minister for Transport:* David John Wordsworth, MLC. *Minister for Lands and Forests:* Margaret June Craig, MLA.

Agent-General in London: J. A. Richards (Western Australia House, 115 Strand, WC2R 0AJ).

Local Government. The only unincorporated area in mainland Western Australia is King's Park, a public reserve of about 403 hectares in Perth. Including the lord-mayoralty of Perth there were 7 cities (all in the metropolitan area), 15 towns and 116 shires at 30 June 1977. The executive body in each of these districts is normally an elective council, presided over by a mayor (city and town) or a president (shire), but in certain circumstances it may be a commissioner appointed by the Governor. Their functions include road construction and repair, the provision of parks and recreation grounds, the administration of building controls and local services such as health and, in some country districts, traffic. Finance is derived largely from rates levied on property owners as well as charges for services and government grants (mainly for road construction).

ECONOMY

Budget. The revenue and expenditure (in $A) of Western Australia in years ended 30 June, are given as follows:

	1975	*1976*	*1977*	*1978*[1]
Revenue	734,239,941	950,861,398	1,144,540,956	1,329,903,000
Expenditure	743,373,039	950,267,621	1,141,112,364	1,329,903,000

[1] Estimates.

Main items of revenue in 1976–77: Railways ($A124,721,627), taxation ($A241,663,856), lands, timber and mining ($A63,879,482), public utilities other than railways ($A17,030,368), from Commonwealth Funds ($A582,743,646). Western Australia had a net loan liability of $A1,158,503,784 on 30 June 1977, the charge for the year being $A93,807,518.

Banking. There are 9 trading banks in Western Australia including the Commonwealth Trading Bank and The Rural and Industries Bank of Western Australia. In June quarter, 1977, the average of customers' balances was $A1,413·4m. and average advances $A991·9m.

At 30 June 1977, the 8 savings banks held deposits of $A960·5m., in 1,466,200 accounts.

ENERGY AND NATURAL RESOURCES

Minerals. The mining industry has been for many years of considerable significance in the Western Australian economy. Until the mid-1960s the major mineral produced was gold. However, in recent years gold has been displaced by iron ore, crude oil, bauxite and nickel concentrates in terms of value.

The total ex-mine value of minerals from mining and quarrying in the State in 1975–76 was $A995,672,000. Principal minerals produced in 1975–76 were: Iron ore, 86,092,000 tonnes, value $A619·8m.; crude oil, 12,413,000 bbls, value $A29,363,000; gold bullion, 10,091,000 grammes, value $A27,156,000; construction materials (excluding sand and gravel), value $A18,856,000; mineral sands, 1,061,000 tonnes, value, $A47,035,000; black coal, 2,157,000 tonnes, value $A17,613,000; salt, 4,512,000 tonnes, value $A24·4m.; tin concentrates, 940 tonnes, value $A3,178,000;

nickel concentrates, 472,000 tonnes; bauxite, 8,743,000 tonnes, and natural gas, 836·7m. cu. metres.

Land Settlement. Up to 31 Dec. 1976, of the entire area of the State (252·55m. hectares) 15,503,838 hectares had been alienated; on that date 3,182,398 hectares were in process of alienation; the area alienated and in process of alienation thus amounting to 18,686,236 hectares. There were in force leases comprising an area of 100,032,723 hectares, of which 96,061,291 hectares were pastoral, 1,211,607 hectares were timber, 114,168 hectares mining leases, 12,575 hectares miners' homestead leases and 2,653,082 hectares for reserves, residential lots, special and perpetual leases.

Agriculture.

Crop	*1974–75* *Hectares*	*1974–75* *Production*	*1975–76* *Hectares*	*1975–76* *Production*
Wheat (tonnes)	2,809,883	3,277,071	3,171,289	4,122,011
Oats (tonnes)	262,347	249,526	319,877	385,670
Barley (tonnes)	386,998	329,056	418,985	505,002
Hay (tonnes)	163,623	508,361	163,329	536,477
Potatoes (tonnes)	2,356	67,450	2,308	68,033
Apples (bu.)	4,477	2,730,724	4,163	2,672,096
Pears (bu.)	385	241,516	376	255,757
Oranges (bu.)	1,376	371,993	1,189	374,899
Currants, raisins and sultanas (tonnes, dried)	1,068	1,198	—	1,067,799

Irrigation has been established by the Government along the south-western coastal plain and in the north of the State. Reservoirs with an aggregate capacity of 6,137m. cu. metres provided irrigation water for 18,884 hectares in 6 districts during 1975–76.

The livestock at 31 March 1976 consisted of 2,654,499 cattle, 34,770,722 sheep and 259,851 pigs.

The wool clip in 1975–76 was 173,987 tonnes; the exports for 1975–76, greasy wool, 140,581 tonnes; degreased wool, 12,667 tonnes.

Forestry. The area of State forests and timber reserves at 30 June 1976 was 1,988,648 hectares; 1975–76 production of sawn timber was 388,210 cu. metres, principally Jarrah and Karri hardwoods.

Value of Primary Production. The estimated gross value of Western Australian primary production (excluding mining) during 1975–76 was as follows: Crops, $A596·24m.; livestock slaughterings and other disposals, $A113,605,000; livestock products, $A286,788,000; forestry, fisheries and hunting, $A74,607,000.

INDUSTRY AND TRADE

Industry. Up to the early 1950s most of the factories in Western Australia were small and medium sized establishments supplying the local market and carrying out some processing of the State's primary products for export. Development of heavy industry and large-scale operations since the early 1950s has been associated with the establishment of a large oil refinery at Kwinana in 1954 which provided the basis for an integrated industrial complex adjacent to Perth; more recent developments have been associated with the processing of the State's vast deposits of iron ore, nickel, bauxite and mineral sands.

The following table shows a summary of manufacturing industry statistics for 1975–76[1]:

Industry sub-division	*Number of establishments operating at 30 June*	*Persons employed*[2]	*Wages and salaries $A1,000*	*Turnover $A1,000*	*Value added $A1,000*
Food, beverages and tobacco	312	14,301	105,450	535,862	195,336
Textiles	28	651	4,544	18,694	8,320
Clothing and footwear	57	1,544	8,163	18,044	11,030

[1] Excludes single establishment enterprises with less than 4 persons employed.
[2] Annual average. Includes working proprietors.

Industry sub-division	Number of establishments operating at 30 June	Persons employed[1]	Wages and salaries $A1,000	Turnover $A1,000	Value added $A1,000
Wood, wood products and furniture	397	7,832	50,948	175,389	92,531
Paper and paper products, printing	154	5,404	40,805	119,238	65,146
Chemical, petroleum and coal products	63	3,062	29,628	203,290	78,134
Non-metallic mineral products	165	4,766	40,593	185,062	88,959
Basic metal products	37	6,203	64,002	612,119	131,510
Fabricated metal products	345	8,039	58,744	238,473	107,263
Transport equipment	136	5,289	40,883	103,963	54,340
Other machinery and equipment	230	6,917	52,499	173,949	89,855
Miscellaneous manufacturing	127	1,914	12,405	47,432	21,855
Total	2,051	65,922	508,664	2,431,515	944,279

[1] Annual average. Includes working proprietors.

Labour. The Industrial Arbitration Act Amendment Act (No. 2), 1963, which came into operation on 1 Feb. 1964, abolished the Court of Arbitration and established The Western Australian Industrial Commission and the Western Australian Industrial Appeal Court.

The Commission consists of a Chief Industrial Commissioner and 6 other Commissioners. A Commissioner sitting or acting alone constitutes the Commission and may exercise all its powers and jurisdiction, except that which is reserved to the Commission in court session. The Commission in court session is constituted by not less than 3 Commissioners sitting or acting together; in addition to other functions, it hears and determines appeals from decisions of a single Commissioner.

Working conditions in the State are governed by decisions of the Commission, which is also empowered to declare a State basic wage, subject to regular review, and to determine wage rates, including a minimum wage, for all awards under its jurisdiction. The minimum weekly wage rates (for a full week's work) in operation at 30 Sept. 1977 were $A111.40 for adult males and $A108.60 for adult females.

The Western Australian Industrial Appeal Court consists of 3 judges, one of whom is president of the court. An appeal lies to the court from any decision of the Commission or the Commission in court session, but only on the ground that such decision is erroneous in law or in excess of jurisdiction.

Under the Act unions and associations of employees and of employers may be registered and the Act confers upon these bodies the right of approaching the Commission in connexion with industrial disputes. There were 80 employees' and 15 employers' bodies registered at 30 June 1977; the former comprising 185,186 and the latter 2,021 members.

Commerce. The external commerce of Western Australia, exclusive of interstate trade, is comprised in the statement of the commerce of Australia given under the heading of the Commonwealth, *see* pp. 111–13.

The total value of the imports and exports, including interstate trade in 5 years (30 June) is, in $A, as follows:

	1971–72	*1972–73*	*1973–74*	*1974–75*	*1975–76*[2]
Imports	1,071,050,510	1,013,446,826	1,308,271,585	1,711,926,586	2,056,164,926
Exports[1]	1,084,981,575	1,313,686,247	1,612,266,691	2,098,693,882	2,377,438,805

[1] Excluding ships' stores. [2] Excludes interstate value of horses.

Selected exports (in $A) for 1975–76: Iron ore, 772,198,619; wheat, 375,897,285; wool and other animal hair, 232,081,653; petroleum and petroleum products, 65,602,124; iron and steel, 60,764,771; mutton and lamb, 34,008,817; beef and veal, 32,693,346; barley, 31,740,053; transport equipment, 31,553,720; rock lobster tails, 27,776,853; salt, 22,607,024; gold bullion, 19,335,122; oats, 16,177,853; live sheep and lambs, 14,436,436; hides and skins, 13,728,351; furniture, 13,328,194; prawns, 11,927,039; wood, timber and cork, 9,830,451; tallow, 9,493,900; apples, 4,226,146; pig meat, 3,696,293.

Selected imports in 1975–76 (in $A): Machinery, 429,624,766; transport equipment, 303,625,610; petroleum and petroleum products, 238,257,041; textiles and apparel, 178,656,228; food, 130,666,793; iron and steel, 100,662,203; beverages and tobacco, 47,235,211; rubber and rubber manufactures, 46,564,509; paper, paper-board, 43,600,105.

The chief countries exporting to Western Australia were (in $A): Japan, 113,827,437; USA, 78,780,488; Kuwait, 66,124,584; UK, 60,391,889; Iran, 53,912,823; Singapore, 37,216,352. Western Australian exports (in $A) went chiefly to: Japan, 926,363,295; USA, 162,544,502; Federal Republic of Germany, 104,004,717; China, excluding Taiwan, 86,875,394; Egypt, 79,946,358; USSR, 69,118,348.

COMMUNICATIONS

Roads. At 30 June 1976 there were 109,185 km of prepared and formed roads in Western Australia, namely, 31,797 km of bituminous surface, 31,579 other constructed surfaces and 45,808 formed but not metalled or otherwise prepared. In addition, there are approximately 52,794 km unprepared except for clearing which are used for general traffic.

New motor vehicles registered in Western Australia during the year ended 30 June 1977 were 65,612.

Railways. At 30 June 1976 the State had 6,163 km of State government railway and 730 km of Commonwealth line, the latter being the western portion of the Trans-Australian line (Kalgoolrie–Port Pirie), which links the State railway system to those of the other States of the Commonwealth. At 30 June 1976, mining companies operated 1,178 km of private railways for the transport of ore to ports on the north-west coast.

Aviation. An extensive system of regular air services operates in Western Australia for the transport of passengers, freight and mail. During the year ended 30 June 1976, Perth Airport handled a total of 14,623 aircraft movements, 12,443 tonnes of freight and 814,382 passengers on domestic and international services.

Shipping. In 1975–76, the number, net tonnage of vessels entering and cargo shipped at major ports were as follows: Port of Fremantle, 1,318 vessels of 10·8m. net tonnage, shipped 8·4m. tonnes plus 310,000 cu. metres of cargo; Dampier, 540 vessels of 12·6m. net tonnage, shipped 34m. tonnes plus 57 cu. metres of cargo; Port Hedland, 561 vessels of 13m. net tonnage, shipped 36·1m. tonnes plus 5,000 cu. metres of cargo; Port Walcott, 171 vessels of 5m. net tonnage, shipped 11·1m. tonnes plus 3,000 cu. metres of cargo.

Post and Broadcasting. Postal, telephone and telegraph facilities are afforded at 540 offices. An additional 40 offices provide only telephone and telegraph facilities. Telephones connected totalled 436,033 at 30 June 1976.

There were 31 wireless broadcasting and 21 television stations in operation at 30 June 1977.

JUSTICE, RELIGION, EDUCATION AND WELFARE

Justice. In Western Australia justice is administered by a Supreme Court, consisting of a Chief Justice and 6 puisne judges at 31 Dec. 1976, a District Court comprising a chairman of judges and 5 district court judges and magistrates' courts exercising both civil and criminal jurisdiction. The lower courts are presided over by justices of the peace, except in the more important centres, where the court is constituted by a stipendiary magistrate. There are special magistrates' courts for juvenile offenders.

Offences against law	*1971*	*1972*	*1973*	*1974*	*1975*
Charges [1]	102,570	104,001	112,736	122,316	127,813
Lower Court convictions [2]	93,548	95,673	101,972	109,411	111,478
Higher Court convictions	755	1,081	654	680	880

[1] In the case of concurrent offences each offence is included.
[2] Includes convictions for traffic offences: 40,388 in 1971, 41,255 in 1972; 46,468 in 1973; 52,607 in 1974; 59,852 in 1975. In addition, small fines were imposed for minor traffic offences as follows: 1971, 176,994; 1972, 200,723; 1973, 211,913; 1974, 271,266; 1975, 265,096.

The total number of admissions to prison for penal imprisonment in the year ended 30 June 1977 was 3,903. Inmates at 30 June 1977 numbered 989 males and 43 females.

Religion. There is no State Church, and freedom of worship is accorded to all. At the census, 30 June 1971, the principal denominations were: Church of England, 362,759; Roman Catholic, 174,792; Catholic (not further defined), 93,198; Methodist, 85,283; Presbyterian, 48,367; Churches of Christ, 13,436; Orthodox, 13,491; Baptist, 13,345; Congregational, 8,258; Lutheran, 6,998; Salvation Army, 6,070; Seventh-day Adventist, 4,819; other Christian, 39,062; Hebrew, 3,102; all other, including not stated and no religion, 157,489.

Education. School attendance is compulsory from the age of 6 until the end of the year in which the child attains 15 years. Pre-school education is provided by a kindergarten system partly financed from government subsidy. In 1977 there were 648 government primary and secondary schools providing free education to 211,988 pupils and 188 non-government primary and secondary schools providing education, for which fees are charged, to 44,899 pupils.

Technical education is available at a number of technical colleges, schools and centres, which are staffed and controlled by the Education Department.

In 1977 the full-time teaching and research staff of the University of Western Australia was 639 and the number of students enrolled was 9,865. Murdoch University, which commenced operations in 1974, enrolled 1,908 students in 1977. Full-time teaching and research staff numbered 136.

Tertiary education is also offered by the Western Australian Institute of Technology and 5 other colleges of advanced education.

State Government expenditure from consolidated revenue on education, including financial assistance to the Universities, during the year ended 30 June 1977, amounted to $A277,848,460.

Social Welfare. At 30 June 1977 there were 47 general hospitals and 7 nursing homes maintained wholly by public funds and 51 general hospitals and 9 nursing homes partly assisted therefrom. In addition, there are numerous private hospitals. Government mental health services comprise 4 approved hospitals, 17 clinics, 3 rehabilitation units, 16 units concerned with the intellectually handicapped, 2 after-care hostels and 1 in-patient unit for children.

The Department for Community Welfare centres and facilities include 2 reception homes for the temporary care and assessment of children, a secure remand and assessment centre, a secure training centre for delinquent boys, a treatment and rehabilitation centre for girls, a long-term residential treatment centre for emotionally disturbed boys and girls, a day centre for problem school children and 9 residential centres for children requiring specialized care. The Department also runs a training centre, in a farm-like setting, for less delinquent boys who do not require placement in a closed or secure centre.

There are 17 metropolitan and 14 country hostels provided for the care of children of Aboriginal descent who attend secondary school or work.

Through the Department, the State Government makes financial assistance available to people in necessitous circumstances.

At 30 June 1977, 1,645 families were receiving assistance.

Age, invalid, widows' and war and service pensions are paid by the Australian Government. The number of pensioners in Western Australia at 30 June 1977 was: Age, 86,470; invalid, 13,263; widows, 10,691; and war and service pensioners, 54,797.

Housing. The State Housing Commission was established in Jan. 1947 to replace the Workers' Homes Board created in 1912. The objects of the Commission are 'the improvement of existing housing conditions' and 'the provision of adequate and suitable housing accommodation for persons of limited means and certain other persons not otherwise adequately housed'. The Commission provided 957 new dwelling units for sale and for rental in 1976–77. During the same period 15,155 new houses and 6,152 new other dwellings were completed throughout the State.

Books of Reference

Statistical Information: The State Government Statistician's Office was established in 1897 and now functions as the Western Australian Office of the Australian Bureau of Statistics (1–3 St

George's Tce, Perth). *Deputy Commonwealth Statistician and Government Statistician:* W. M. Bartlett. Its principal publications are: *Statistical Register of Western Australia* (annual, from 1896 to 1967–68). *Statistics of Western Australia* (annual from 1968–69). *Western Australian Year Book* (new series, from 1957). *Western Australian Pocket Year Book* (from 1919). *Quarterly Statistical Abstract* (from 1917).

Battye, J. S., *Western Australia: A History from its Discovery to the Inauguration of the Commonwealth.* Oxford, 1924.—*The Cyclopedia of Western Australia.* Adelaide, Vol. 1 (1912), Vol. 2 (1913)

Crowley, F. K., *A Short History of Western Australia.* Melbourne, 1959.—*Australia's Western Third.* London, 1960

Crowley, F. K., and De Garis, B. K., *A Short History of Western Australia.* Melbourne, 1969

Gentilli, J., *Atlas of Western Australian Agriculture.* Perth, 1941

Kerr, Alex, *The South-West Region of Western Australia.* Perth, 1965.—*Australia's North-West.* Perth, 1967

Stephenson, G., and Hepburn, J. A., *Plan for the Metropolitan Region: Perth and Fremantle.* Perth, 1955

The Metropolitan Region Planning Authority, *The Corridor Plan for Perth.* Perth, 1970

State Library: The State Library of Western Australia, Perth. *State Librarian:* R. C. Sharman, FLAA.

AUSTRIA

Republik Österreich

Capital: Vienna
Population: 7·46m. (1971)
GNP per capita: US$5,330 (1976)

HISTORY. On 27 April 1945 a provisional government restored the Republic of Austria and was recognized by the Allied Control Council on 20 Oct. 1945.

AREA AND POPULATION. For the boundaries of Austria according to the Treaty of St Germain, signed in Sept. 1919, *see* THE STATESMAN'S YEAR-BOOK, 1920, pp. 674–75.

Federal States	*Area, sq. km*	*Population (census 12 May 1971)*	*Percentage of population*	*Population per sq. km*
Vienna (Wien)	415	1,614,841	21·7	3,897
Lower Austria (Niederösterreich)	19,171	1,414,161	19·0	74
Burgenland	3,966	272,119	3·6	69
Upper Austria (Oberösterreich)	11,979	1,223,444	16·4	102
Salzburg	7,154	401,766	5·4	56
Styria (Steiermark)	16,387	1,192,100	16·0	73
Carinthia (Kärnten)	9,533	525,728	7·0	55
Tirol	12,647	540,771	7·3	43
Vorarlberg	2,601	271,473	3·6	104
Total	83,853[1]	7,456,403	100·0	89

[1] 32,375 sq. miles.

Vital statistics for calendar years:

	Live births	*Still births*	*Deaths*[1]	*Marriages*	*Divorces*	*Emigration Austrians*	*Emigration Others*
1973	98,041	877	92,768	49,430	9,972	561	4,105
1974	97,430	828	94,324	49,296	10,638	534	3,012
1975	93,757	791	96,041	46,542	10,763	233	1,787
1976	87,446	683	95,140	45,767	11,168	29	1,186

[1] Excluding still births.

The population of the principal towns (excluding Vienna), according to the census of 12 May 1971 (area, 1 Jan. 1976) was as follows:

Graz	248,500	Steyr	40,578	Bregenz	22,839	Braunau am Inn	16,432
Linz	202,874	Leoben	35,153	Baden	22,631	Bruck an der Mur	16,359
Salzburg	128,845	Wiener Neustadt	34,774	Klosterneuburg	21,912	Ternitz	16,352
Innsbruck	115,197	Dornbirn	33,810	Amstetten	21,692	Lustenau	15,239
Klagenfurt	82,512	Wolfsberg	29,002	Feldkirch	21,214		
Villach	50,993	Kapfenberg	26,001	Traun	20,843		
St Pölten	50,144	Krems a.d.D.	23,409	Mödling	18,712		
Wels	47,279						

CONSTITUTION AND GOVERNMENT. Austria recovered its sovereignty and independence on 27 July 1955 by the coming into force of the Austrian State Treaty between the UK, the USA, the USSR and France on the one part and the Republic of Austria on the other part (signed on 15 May).

On 12 March 1938 Austria was forcibly absorbed in the German Reich until it was liberated by the American, British, French and Soviet armies in spring 1945. Already in the Moscow Declaration of Oct. 1943, the UK, the USA and the USSR had resolved upon the re-establishment of a free and independent Austria.

On 27 April 1945 Dr Karl Renner set up a provisional government which restored the Republic of Austria in the spirit of the Constitution of 1920/29, and was recognized by the Four-Power Allied Control Council on 20 Oct. 1945. The last occupation forces left Austria in Oct. 1955.

President of the Republic: Dr Rudolf Kirchschläger, former Minister of Foreign Affairs, elected on 23 June 1974 by 2,392,367 votes against 2,238,470 cast for Dr Alois Lugger.

On 5 Oct. 1975 the elections were held for the National Assembly, which returned 93 Socialists, 80 People's Party, 10 Freedom Party.

From 1 Jan. 1971 the number of members of the National Council was increased from 165 to 183. The government of the Socialist Party which was formed in Oct. 1971 was composed Nov. 1977 as follows:

Chancellor: Dr Bruno Kreisky.

Vice-Chancellor and Finance: Dr Hannes Androsch. *Social Welfare:* Dr Gerhard Weiszenberg. *Foreign Affairs:* Dr Willibald Pahr. *Interior:* Eric Lanc. *Agriculture and Forestry:* Dip. Ing. Günther Haider; Albin Schober (*Minister of State*). *Transport:* Karl Lausecker. *Justice:* Dr Christian Broda. *Education and the Arts:* Dr Fred Sinowatz. *Trade, Commerce and Industry:* Dr Josef Staribacher. *Defence:* Otto Rösch. *Construction and Technology:* Josef Moser. *Science and Research:* Dr Hertha Firnberg. *Health and Environment:* Dr Ingrid Leodolter. *Federal Chancellory:* Dr Adolf Nussbaumer (*Minister of State*). *Family Policy:* Elfriede Karl (*Minister of State*); Franz Löschnak (*Minister of State*).

The Federal Council (*Bundesrat*) which represents the federal provinces has 58 members and (1977) the Socialist Party had 29 members and the People's Party 29. The *Nationalrat* and *Bundesrat* together form the National Assembly.

National flag: Three horizontal stripes of red, white, red.

National anthem: Land der Berge, Land am Strome (words by Paula Preradovic; tune by W. A. Mozart).

The official language is German.

Local Government. The Republic of Austria comprises 9 Federal States (Vienna, Lower Austria, Upper Austria, Salzburg, Styria, Carinthia, Tirol, Vorarlberg, Burgenland). There is in every province an elected Provincial Assembly.

Every commune has a Council, which chooses one of its number to be head of the Commune (burgomaster) and a committee for the administration and execution of its resolutions.

Adamovich, L., *Grundrisz des österreichischen Verfassungsrechts.* 8th ed. Vienna, 1953

DEFENCE. The supreme command is vested in the Federal President; operational control is exercised by the Minister of Defence.

Army. The Army is in a state of reorganization. When complete, it will consist of an alert force (*Bereitshaftruppe*) of 1,500 regulars and a militia (*Landwehr*) of 6-month conscripts and reservists. The country is divided into 2 corps areas, I (Graz) and II (Salzburg). The aim is to deploy 6 alert brigades, 4 armoured, 2 infantry and 8 *Landwehr* brigades of local defence battalions and companies. Strength (1977) 33,000 (conscripts, 18,000).

Air Force. The Air Force is an integral part of army command and comprises a fighter-bomber wing (2 squadrons) with 37 Saab-105Oe jet light attack aircraft and 2 Flight Regiments. Flight Regiment 1 has a transport/support wing with 22 Agusta-Bell 204B and 2 heavy-duty Sikorsky S-65Oe helicopters; a wing of 20 Alouette III helicopters for liaison, search and rescue; and a wing equipped with 12 armed Kiowa and 13 JetRanger helicopters for general duties. Fixed-wing types in service with Flight Regiment 1 include 2 Skyvan and 12 Swiss-built Turbo-Porter transports, and Cessna O-1 Bird-Dogs operated for army support. Pilot training by Flight Regiment 2 begins on 15 Saab Safir piston-engined basic trainers and continues on either Saab-105Oe jet aircraft or JetRanger helicopters. Personnel strength 4,300, with about 140 aircraft.

INTERNATIONAL RELATIONS

Membership. Austria is a member of UN and EFTA.

External debt. The external debt was (1977) 120·9m. schilling.

ECONOMY

Budget. The budget for calendar years provided revenue and expenditure (ordinary and extraordinary) as follows (in 1m. schilling):

	1970	*1971*	*1972*	*1973*	*1974*	*1975*	*1976*
Revenue	94,366	104,824	120,209	128,315	148,598	168,116	179,361
Expenditure	101,584	112,567	127,889	141,151	167,133	184,442	215,419

Currency. The Austrian unit of currency is the *schilling* of 100 *groschen*. The rate of exchange in Oct. 1976, £1 = 29·08 *schilling*, US$1 = 16·25 *schilling*. Exchange rates since 24 Aug. 1971 have been floating.

Banking. The National Bank of Austria, opened on 2 Jan. 1923, was taken over by the German Reichsbank on 17 March 1938. It was re-established on 3 July 1945. At 31 Dec. 1976 foreign exchange amounted to 50,995m. and note circulation to 58,863m. schilling. The balance-sheet showed assets and liabilities of 107,558m. schilling.

Weights and Measures. The metric system of weights and measures is in use.

ENERGY AND NATURAL RESOURCES

Electricity. Electric current produced (1m. kwh.): 1975, 35,205; 1976, 35,332.

Oil. The commercial production of petroleum began in the early 1930s. Production of crude oil (in tonnes): 1960, 2,448,391; 1965, 2,854,544; 1971, 2,798,237; 1975, 2,036,797; 1976, 1,930,848.

Minerals. The mineral production (in tonnes) was as follows:

	1975	*1976*		*1975*	*1976*
Lignite	3,397,404	3,214,598	Raw magnesite[1]	1,265,849	926,540
Iron ore	3,833,000	3,784,000	Pig-iron	3,005,788	3,318,060
Lead and zinc ore[1]	390,513	417,985	Raw steel	4,068,017	4,477,215
Copper ore[1]	153,620	98,425	Rolled steel	2,856,982	3,370,934

[1] Including recovery from slag.

Austria is one of the world's largest sources of high-grade graphite. Production, which averaged 20,000 tonnes yearly from 1929 to 1944, dropped to 246 in 1946, but rose to 102,237 in 1964, and fell again to 23,992 in 1970, 17,211 in 1973, 29,550 in 1974, 30,586 in 1975 and 33,057 in 1976.

Agriculture. In 1976 the total area sown amounted to 1,471,189 hectares.

The chief products (area in hectares, yield in tonnes) were as follows:

	1974		*1975*		*1976*	
	Area	*Yield*	*Area*	*Yield*	*Area*	*Yield*
Wheat	269,131	1,101,762	269,567	945,188	289,326	1,233,520
Rye	122,836	414,527	118,745	347,099	119,676	410,409
Barley	319,256	1,237,869	315,472	1,006,242	324,507	1,286,583
Oats	91,834	290,093	101,045	305,987	94,747	282,725
Potatoes	82,304	1,996,305	69,101	1,578,687	73,312	1,746,023

Production of raw sugar in 1949, 66,700; 1955, 219,300; 1960, 308,000; refined sugar: 1970, 298,000; 1975, 470,862; 1976, 383,000 tonnes.

Livestock (1976): Cattle, 2,502,422; pigs, 3,877,586; sheep, 174,323; goats, 40,299; horses, 41,416, poultry, 13,597,764.

FORESTRY. Felled timber, in cu. metres: 1960, 10,015,925; 1968, 9,635,001; 1969, 10,468,757; 1970, 11,122,896; 1971, 10,595,873; 1972, 10,153,360; 1973, 9,713,886; 1974, 10,023,540; 1975, 9,598,917; 1976, 11,579,586.

Land- und forstwirtschaftliche Betriebszählung 1970. 10 vols. Vienna, Statistisches Zentralamt

INDUSTRY AND TRADE

Industry. On 26 July 1946 the Austrian parliament passed a government bill, nationalizing some 70 industrial concerns. As from 17 Sept. 1946 ownership of the 3 largest commercial banks, most oil-producing and refining companies and the principal firms in the following industries devolved upon the Austrian state: River navigation; coal extraction; non-ferrous mining and refining; iron-ore mining; pig-iron and steel production; manufacture of iron and steel products, including structural material, machinery, railroad equipment and repairs, and shipbuilding; electrical machinery and appliances. Six companies supplying electric power were nationalized in accordance with a law of 26 March 1947.

According to the Census of Industrial Establishments 1976 (average), there were 6,761 establishments employing 629,189 persons, producing a gross output of 359·4m. schillings and value added of 57·6m. schillings.

GDP *per capita* (1976) US$5,407.

Commerce. Imports and exports are as follows (excluding precious metals):

	Imports			*Exports*		
	1974	*1975*	*1976*	*1974*	*1975*	*1976*
Quantity (1,000 tonnes)	30,401	26,879	30,701	11,154	10,428	11,956
Value (1m. sch.)	168,281	163,376	206,081	133,356	135,884	152,114

The total trade between UK and Austria (British Department of Trade returns, in £1,000 sterling):

	1973	*1974*	*1975*	*1976*	*1977*
Imports to UK	178,228	203,659	204,115	232,436	268,630
Exports and re-exports from UK	136,709	153,139	164,320	212,352	251,923

Statistik des Aussenhandels [from 1964: *Der Aussenhandel*] *Österreichs*. Vienna, Statistisches Zentralamt. Annually 1949–50; quarterly from 1951

Tourism. Tourism is an important industry. In 1976, 21,694 hotels and boarding-houses had a total of 624,606 beds available; 11,598,273 foreigners visited Austria; of these 384,010 came from the UK and 514,496 from the USA.

COMMUNICATIONS

Roads. On 1 Jan. 1977 federal roads had a total length of 10,140 km, 743·2 km autobahn; provincial roads, 23,060 km. On 31 Dec. 1976 there were registered 2,919,324 motor vehicles, including 1,828,050 passenger cars, 150,990 lorries, 299,968 tractors and 138,939 trailers.

Railways. Austrian railways have been nationalized since before the First World War. Length of track (Dec. 1976), 5,858 km, of which 2,728 km were electrified. Twenty private railways have a total length of 636 km. Passengers in 1976 numbered 130m., plus 38m. in suburban transport.

Aviation. Austria has 6 airports in Vienna (Schwechat), Linz, Salzburg, Graz, Klagenfurt and Innsbruck. In 1976, 44,498 aircraft arrived and departed at Austrian airports on scheduled flights.

Shipping. Austria has no sea frontiers, but the Danube is an important waterway. Goods traffic (in tonnes): 6,120,536 in 1973; 5,963,016 in 1974; 6,088,694 in 1975; 5,436,735 in 1976. Coal and coke, mineral oil products and iron ore comprise in bulk more than two-thirds of these cargoes. The Danube Steamship Co. (DDSG) is the main Austrian shipping company.

Post and Broadcasting. All postal, telegraph and telephone services are run by the State. On 1 Jan. 1977 there were 2,281,251 telephones.

Österreichischer Rundfunk transmits 4 programmes, including a 24 hours overseas service. There is also regional and local broadcasting. All broadcasting is financed by licence payments and advertisements. There were 2·1m. registered listeners in Aug. 1976. Television was inaugurated in autumn 1955 and 2 programmes are transmitted, both in colour.

Cinemas (1976). There were 536 cinemas.

Newspapers (1976). There were 30 daily newspapers (6 of them in Vienna) with a combined circulation of 2,436,300.

JUSTICE, RELIGION, EDUCATION AND WELFARE

Justice. The Supreme Court of Justice (*Oberster Gerichtshof*) in Vienna is the highest court in the land. Besides there are 4 higher provincial courts (*Oberlandesgerichte*), 20 provincial and district courts (*Landes- und Kreisgerichte*) and 228 local courts (*Bezirksgerichte*).

Religion. In 1971 there were 6,540,294 Roman Catholics (87·7%), 446,307 Protestants (6%), 111,558 others (1·5%), 320,031 without religious allegiance (4·3%) and 38,213 (0·5%) unknown. The Roman Catholic Church has 2 archbishoprics and 7 bishoprics.

Education (1976–77). There were in Austria 5,573 elementary and special schools with 55,321 teachers and 949,256 pupils. Of all kinds of secondary schools there were 935 with 325,760 pupils.

There were also 88 commercial academies with 20,783 students and 2,994 teachers. There were 152 schools of technical and industrial training (including schools of hotel management and catering) with 3,826 teachers and 38,951 pupils; 28 schools of women's professions (secondary level) with 7,497 pupils; 8 training colleges of social workers with 625 pupils. 138 trade schools had 28,626 pupils.

Austria has 12 universities and 6 colleges of arts maintained by the State: Universities at Vienna (2,947 teachers, 30,629 students), Graz (944 teachers, 11,242 students), Innsbruck (1,275 teachers, 10,968 students) and Salzburg (921 teachers, 5,982 students). There are also technical universities at Vienna (1,001 teachers, 7,697 students) and Graz (586 teachers, 4,389 students), a mining university at Leoben (212 teachers, 868 students), an agricultural university at Vienna (254 teachers, 1,550 students), a veterinary university at Vienna (156 teachers, 947 students), a commercial university at Vienna (204 teachers, 6,226 students), a university for social and economic sciences at Linz (363 teachers, 3,379 students) and a university for educational sciences at Klagenfurt (86 teachers, 636 students). There is an academy of fine arts at Vienna (127 teachers, 595 students), a college of applied arts at Vienna (131 teachers, 631 students), 3 colleges of music and dramatic art at Vienna (351 teachers, 2,077 students), Salzburg (164 teachers, 850 students) and Graz (202 teachers, 742 students); the college for industrial design at Linz (77 teachers, 207 students).

Health. In 1976 there were 17,576 doctors, 299 hospitals and 80,871 hospital beds.

DIPLOMATIC REPRESENTATIVES

OF AUSTRIA IN GREAT BRITAIN (18 Belgrave Mews West, London, SW1X 8HU)

Ambassador: Dr Kurt Enderl (accredited 4 Feb. 1975).

OF GREAT BRITAIN IN AUSTRIA (Reisnerstrasse, 40, 1030 Vienna)

Ambassador: H. T. Morgan, CMG.

OF AUSTRIA IN THE USA (2343 Massachussetts Ave., NW, Washington, D.C., 20008)

Ambassador: Karl Herbert Schober.

OF THE USA IN AUSTRIA (IX Boltzmangasse, 16, A-1091 Vienna)

Ambassador: Milton A. Wolf.

OF AUSTRIA TO THE UNITED NATIONS

Ambassador: Dr Peter Jankowitsch.

Books of Reference

Statistical Information: The Austrian Central Statistical Office was founded in 1863. *Address:* Neue Burg, Heldenplatz, A-1014 Vienna. *President:* Dr Lothar Bosse. Main publications:

Statistisches Handbuch für die Republik Österreich. New Series from 1950. Annually
Statistische Nachrichten. Monthly
Beiträge zur österreichischen Statistik (435 vols.)
Ergebnisse der nichtlandwirtschaftlichen Betriebszählung, 1964. 1971
Ergebnisse der Volkszählung vom 12 Mai 1971
Ergebnisse der Häuser- und Wohnungszählung vom 12 Mai 1971
HA-Taschenbuch 75. Annually from 1971
Republic of Austria 1945–1975. Vienna, 1976

Barker, E., *Austria 1918–1972*. London, 1973
Bobek, H. (ed.), *Atlas der Republik Österreich*. 3 vols. Vienna, 1961 ff.
Östereich Lexikon. Wien-München, 1966
Scheidl, L. G., and Lechleitner, H., *Österreich–Land, Volk, Wirtschaft*. Vienna, 1967
Steiner, K., *Politics in Austria*. Boston, 1972

National Library: Osterreichische Nationalbibliothek, Vienna. *Librarian:* Dr Rudolf Fiedler.

THE COMMONWEALTH OF THE BAHAMAS

Capital: Nassau
Population: 218,000 (1977)
GNP per capita: US$3,310 (1976)

HISTORY. The Bahamas were discovered by Colombus in 1492 but the Spanish did not make a permanent settlement. British settlers arrived in the 17th century and it was occupied by Britain, except for a short period in the 18th century, until it gained independence.

AREA AND POPULATION. The Commonwealth of the Bahamas consists of 700 islands and more than 1,000 cays off the S.E. coast of Florida. They are the surface protuberances of two oceanic banks, the Little Bahama Bank and the Great Bahama Bank. Land area, 5,353 sq. miles (13,864 sq. km). The total rainfall (New Providence) in 1972 was 48·57 in.; highest in July (10·01 in.). Average winter temperature, 69·9° F. (21·1° C.); average summer temperature, 82·8° F. (28·2° C.).

Principal islands with census population in 1970: New Providence (101,503, containing capital, Nassau), Abaco (6,501), Harbour Island and Spanish Wells (3,221), Grand Bahama (25,859), Cat Island (2,657), Long Island (3,861), Mayaguana (581), Eleuthera (6,247), Exuma (3,767), San Salvador or Watling's Island (776), Acklin's Island (936), Crooked Island (689), Inagua (1,109), Andros (8,845), Bimini (1,503), Ragged Island (208).

Census population, 1970, 168,812. Estimate (1977) 218,000. Vital statistics, 1974: Births, 4,401; deaths, 1,186 (excluding still-births); marriages, 1,233 (1972).

CONSTITUTION AND GOVERNMENT. Internal self-government with cabinet responsibility was introduced 7 Jan. 1964.

Qualification for membership of the House of Assembly, under the 1973 Independence Constitution requires that a member shall be a citizen of the Bahamas of the age of 21 years or upwards, and shall have been ordinarily resident in the Bahamas for a period of not less than 1 year immediately before the date of his nomination for election. The Representation of the People's Act provides for adult suffrage. Women are eligible for election to the House of Assembly.

The Constitution of the Commonwealth of the Bahamas establishes the Bahamas as a free and democratic sovereign state. The constitution is the supreme law of the Bahamas and where any other law is inconsistent with it, the Constitution shall prevail and the other law shall, to the extent of the inconsistency be void.

The Constitution created the office of Governor-General, the holder of which is appointed by Her Majesty. There is a Senate of 16 members, 9 appointed by the Governor-General on the advice of the Prime Minister, 4 appointed by the Governor-General on the advice of the Leader of the Opposition and 3 appointed by the Governor-General on advice of the Prime Minister after consultation with the Leader of the Opposition. The House of Assembly consists of 38 members. The life of a Parliament is 5 years, but it may be prorogued or dissolved at any time by the Governor-General on the advice of the Prime Minister.

At the elections of 19 July 1977 the Progressive Liberal Party obtained 30 seats, the Bahamas Democratic Party 5 seats and the Free National Movement 2 seats.

Independence from Britain took place on 10 July 1973.

Governor-General: Sir Milo B. Butler, GCMG, GCVO.

Prime Minister and Minister of Economic Affairs: Rt. Hon. Lynden O. Pindling.

National flag: Three horizontal stripes of aquamarine, gold, aquamarine, with a black triangle on the hoist.

INTERNATIONAL RELATIONS

Membership. The Commonwealth of the Bahamas is a member of UN, the Commonwealth and an ACP state of EEC.

ECONOMY

Budget (in B$):

	1975	*1976*	*1977*
Revenue	133,884,360	147,992,031	152,155,721
Expenditure	131,393,880	147,903,879	156,251,650

Currency. A decimal system of currency was introduced in 1966. Bahamian $1.75 = £1 sterling (Jan. 1977). Notes: $0.50, 1, 3, 5, 10, 20, 50, 100; coins: 1, 5, 10, 15, 25, 50 cents, $1, 2, 5. Sterling currency has been withdrawn. American currency is generally accepted.

Bank of England and Canadian notes are not accepted, except at the banks from travellers from the UK.

Banking. The Central Bank of the Bahamas was established in June 1974 with assets (Dec. 1976) B$68·69m. and capital and reserves of B$12·38m. The Royal Bank of Canada, the Bank of Nova Scotia, Barclays Bank International, Canadian Imperial Bank of Commerce, the Bank of London and Montreal, Chase Manhattan Bank, Citibank, E. D. Sassoon Banking Co., Butlers Bank, Commonwealth Industrial Bank, International Bank of Washington and the Mercantile Bank of the Bahamas have branches in Nassau. The Royal Bank of Canada, Bank of Nova Scotia, Chase Manhattan Bank and Barclays Bank International have branches on several other islands.

On 10 Aug. 1977 there were 270 institutions licensed to carry on banking and/or trust business under the Banks and Trust Companies Regulations Act. There were 7 trust companies designated by the Exchange Control Department to act as custodians and dealers in foreign securities.

Post office savings bank, 30 June 1972, depositors, 34,831; balance due (30 June 1971), B$2,633,711.

Weights and Measures. The UK (Imperial) system is in force.

ENERGY AND NATURAL RESOURCES

Electricity. Electricity for lighting and power is available in New Providence, Grand Bahama and the Family Islands. Total units generated in New Providence in 1975–76, 314,646,000 kwh. Total number of consumers is 34,626.

Agriculture. There are about 200,000 acres of agricultural land mainly on Abaco, Andros and Grand Bahama.

Livestock (1974): Cattle, 4,000; Sheep, 28,000; goats, 16,000; poultry, 729,000.

INDUSTRY AND TRADE

Industry. Several light industries have been established on Grand Bahama and New Providence in response to special encouragement legislation, these include garment manufacturing, ice, furniture, purified water, plastic containers, perfumes, industrial gases, jewellery and others. Larger industrial activities in the Bahamas include oil refining, oil transshipment, manufacture of alcoholic beverages, pharmaceuticals, aragonite mining, solar salt production and manufacture of steel piping. Two industrial sites, one in New Providence and the other in Grand Bahama, have been developed as part of the industrialization programme.

Commerce. The principal exports in 1975 were salt, crawfish, pulp-wood, cement, rum, aragonite, hormones and petroleum products.

The principal imports in 1974 were: Food, drink and tobacco, raw materials and articles mainly unmanufactured, articles wholly or mainly manufactured, animals not for food.

Imports and exports (excluding bullion and specie) for 6 calendar years in B$:

	Imports	*Exports*		*Imports*	*Exports*
1970	337,484,425	89,602,000	1973	764,260,752	529,743,304
1971	511,320,891	266,552,401	1974	1,908,377,389	1,443,585,764
1972	484,867,873	301,401,104	1975	2,696,903,595	2,508,332,684

The Bahamas became affiliated with CARIFTA (now CARICOM) in 1968.

Trade with UK, in £1,000 sterling (British Department of Trade returns):

	1972	*1973*	*1974*	*1975*	*1976*	*1977*
Imports to UK	4,248	19,253	10,552	9,851	15,094	13,960
Exports and re-exports from UK	8,854	8,164	8,548	7,698	7,801	21,995

Tourism. Tourism is the most important industry in the Bahamas. It accounts for more than 50% of government revenue and employment. In 1975 there were 1,380,855 foreign arrivals in the Bahamas.

COMMUNICATIONS

Roads. There are 240 miles of paved roads in New Providence, and 426 miles in Grand Bahama. The other major islands have 400 miles of motorable roads. In 1976, 48,928 motor vehicles were registered. There are no railroads.

Aviation. Nassau international airport is located on the island of New Providence, about 10 miles from the city of Nassau. There is another international airport at Freeport. Scheduled flights—British Airways: daily from New York (twice daily from Dec. to April); twice weekly from Bermuda; once weekly from Jamaica. PANAM: daily from New York; 4 times daily from Miami. Air Canada: daily from Toronto, Montreal and Jamaica. Eastern Airlines: daily from Tampa, West Palm Beach and Fort Lauderdale; 6 times daily from Miami; once weekly from Jacksonville *via* West End, Grand Bahama. There are numerous domestic schedules to the Family Islands. Bahamasair provides commercial and charter services to the Family Islands and Florida. There are 52 airstrips on the various Family Islands and numerous water alighting areas. During 1976, 476,649 passengers landed at Nassau and 15,065 aircraft arrivals. At Freeport in 1976, 333,817 passengers landed from 10,746 aircraft arrivals.

Shipping. The total tonnage of ships entering ports in 1975 was approximately 11·2m., which included 599 cruise ships, 632 freighters and 30 naval vessels. There are cargo services with UK, USA and Canada and passenger services with UK, USA, the West Indies and South America.

Telecommunications. In the island of New Providence an automatic telephone system of the latest type is in operation, together with an extensive system of underground cables. The total number of telephones in use at 1 Jan. 1977 was 58,033, 132 radio-telephone channels provide service *via* the USA to any part of the world. In 1971 direct dialling was introduced to the USA and in 1973 to Canada. All the important islands are connected with Nassau by means of radio-telegraphy, and in most cases radio-telephony is also available. Connexion through Nassau to the UK, the USA, Canada and Central America can be provided. Radio-teletype to Bermuda and Florida and ship-shore radio-telephone services are also available. Radio-teletype service is provided from Nassau to Freeport and West End in Grand Bahama. The Bahamas broadcasting station operates on 1,540 and 1,240 kc.

JUSTICE, EDUCATION AND WELFARE

Justice (1973). 7,538 cases (traffic, 3,746; criminal, 1,693; civil, 1,185; domestic, 914) were dealt with in the magistrates' court, and civil, 844; divorce, 173 in the Supreme Court in 1974. The strength of the police force (1973) was 932 officers and other ranks.

Education. Education is under the jurisdiction of the Ministry of Education and Culture. 224 schools exist, and of these, 182 (with 47,039 pupils) are fully maintained by Government and 42 (with 12,966 pupils) are independent schools. There are 28 government-owned schools in New Providence and 144 on the Family Islands. 18

independent schools are located on New Providence and 14 on the Family Islands. Free education is available in ministry schools in New Providence and the Family Islands. Courses lead to the Bahamas Junior Certificate and the General Certificate of Education (GCE).

Independent schools provide education at primary, secondary and higher levels. Several schools of continuing education offer secretarial and academic courses. The Government-operated Princess Margaret Hospital offers a nursing course at two levels. The College of the Bahamas was established in 1974. It provides a 2- or 3-year programme leading to an associate degree in any of the 7 academic divisions. Several college degree programmes are offered in conjunction with the University of the West Indies and the University of Miami. The Hotel Training College offers a wide range of subjects up to middle management level in aspects of hotel work. Enrolment in this institution includes Bahamian as well as regional and international students.

Health. In 1976 there was a government general hospital in Nassau (460 beds) and 1 in Freeport (50). Grand Bahama has 4 clinics, 3 staffed by district medical officers and 1 by a nurse and the Family Islands have about 50 health centres. There are 2 private hospitals. Medical treatment is provided for smaller islands by a flying doctor service. There are 128 doctors, 410 nurses, 22 midwives and 21 dentists.

DIPLOMATIC REPRESENTATIVES

OF THE BAHAMAS IN GREAT BRITAIN (39 Pall Mall, London, SW1Y 5JG)

High Commissioner: R. F. Anthony Roberts.

OF GREAT BRITAIN IN THE BAHAMAS (Bitco Bldg., East St., Nassau)

High Commissioner: Peter Mennell, CMG, MBE.

OF THE BAHAMAS IN THE USA (600 New Hampshire Ave., NW, Washington, D.C., 20037)

Ambassador: Livingston Basil Johnson.

OF THE USA IN THE BAHAMAS (Queen St., Nassau)

Ambassador: William B. Schwartz, Jr.

OF THE BAHAMAS TO THE UNITED NATIONS

Ambassador: Livingston Basil Johnson.

Books of Reference

Annual Report, 1968–69. HMSO, 1969
Bahamas Handbook and Businessman's Annual, 1973
Commonwealth of the Bahamas, Statistical Abstract, 1970–71. Nassau, 1972
Albury, P., *The Story of the Bahamas.* London, 1975
Craton, M. A., *A History of the Bahamas.* London, 1962

Library: Nassau Public Library.

BAHRAIN

Capital: Manama
Population: 275,549 (1978)
GNP per capita: US$2,410 (1976)

HISTORY. Treaties with Britain of 1882 and 1892 were replaced by a treaty of friendship which was signed on 15 Aug. 1971. Under the earlier treaties Britain had been responsible for Bahrain's defence and foreign relations. On the same day Bahrain declared its independence.

AREA AND POPULATION. The Bahrain islands form an archipelago in the Arabian Gulf, between the Qatar peninsula and the mainland of Saudi Arabia. The total area is about 255 sq. miles. Bahrain ('Two Seas'), largest island, is 30 miles long and 10 miles wide. Muharraq, to the north-east, 4 miles long and 1 mile wide, is connected with Bahrain by a causeway, nearly 1·5 miles long, carrying a motor road. Other islands are Sitra, to the east, 3 miles long and 1 mile wide; Umm An-Nassan, to the west, $3\frac{1}{2}$ miles by $2\frac{1}{2}$ miles; Jidda, also to the west, 1 mile by $\frac{1}{2}$ mile, the Hawar group off Qatar and several islets, some uninhabited. From Sitra oil pipelines and a causeway carrying a road extend out to sea for 3 miles to a deep-water anchorage. The islands are low lying, the highest ground being a hill in the centre of Bahrain, 450 ft high.

The population in 1971 (census) was 216,815. Estimate (1978) 275,549. The majority of the people are Moslem Arabs.

Manama, the capital of the state and the commercial centre, is situated at the northern end of the largest island and extends for $1\frac{1}{2}$ miles along the shore. It has a population of 82,345 (1971 census). Estimate (1978) 114,030. Electricity from the government power-station in Manama supplies light and power in Manama, Muharraq (48,161, 1978 estimate), Hidd (6,725), Rifa'a (13,696) and Isa Town (9,573) and the villages. Water is obtained from artesian wells, and there is a piped supply in Manama, Muharraq, Isa Town, Rifa'a and most villages.

CONSTITUTION AND GOVERNMENT. A Constituent Assembly met in Dec. 1972 to draft a Constitution and this was published in 1973. A National Assembly with a proposed 4-year life met for the first time in 1973 but was dissolved at the end of 1975. Bahrain is administered by a cabinet, which was formed in 1971 to succeed the Council of State.

Reigning Amir: The ruling family, the Al Khalifa, an Arab dynasty, who have been in power since 1782. The present Amir, HH Shaikh Isa bin Sulman Al-Khalifa (born 1933) succeeded on 2 Nov. 1961. *Heir Apparent and Minister of Defence:* Shaikh Hamed bin Isa Al-Khalifa.

Prime Minister: Shaikh Khalifa bin Sulman Al-Khalifa.

Defence: Shaikh Hamed bin Isa Al-Khalifa. *Transport:* Ibrahim Mohammed Hassan Homaidan. *Housing:* Shaikh Khalid bin Abdulla Al-Khalifa. *Information:* Tariq Abdulrahman Almoayyed. *Education:* Shaikh Abdul Aziz bin Mohammed Al-Khalifa. *Justice:* Shaikh Abdullah bin Khalid Al-Khalifa. *Health:* Dr Ali Fakhro. *Labour and Social Affairs:* Shaikh Isa bin Mohammed bin Abdullah Al-Khalifa. *Works, Power and Water:* Majid Jawad Al Jishi. *Interior:* Shaikh Mohammed bin Khalifa Al-Khalifa. *Foreign Affairs:* Shaikh Mohammed bin Mubarak Al-Khalifa. *Finance:* Ebrahim Abdul-Karim. *Development and Industry:* Yusuf Ahmed Al-Shirawi. *Commerce and Agriculture:* Habib Kassem. *Minister of State for Cabinet Affairs:* Jawad Salim Al-Arrayed. *Minister of State for Legal Affairs:* Dr Hussain Al Baharna.

Flag: Red, with white serrated vertical strip on hoist.

DEFENCE

Army. The Army consists of 1 infantry battalion and 1 armoured car squadron with a personnel strength of 2,300 (1977).

Air Force. Initial equipment comprises a number of Agusta-Bell helicopters, funded by Saudi Arabia.

INTERNATIONAL RELATIONS

Membership. Bahrain is a member of UN, the Arab League and OAPEC.

ECONOMY

Budget. The revenue of the state is derived from oil royalties and from customs duties, which are 10% *ad valorem* for luxury goods and 5% for essential goods. The exceptions are liquor (75%) and tobacco (15%). Total revenues in 1973, BD 32·5m.; 1974, BD 53m.; 1975, BD 134m.; 1976, BD 181m.; 1977, BD 249m.

On 2 Jan. 1958 Manama was declared a free transit port and the former 2% transit duty was abolished, but storage charges are levied.

Reserves were BD 200m. in Dec. 1977.

Currency. The Bahrain *dinar* is divided into 1,000 *fils*. The Bahrain currency board issues notes of 10, 5, 1, ½ and ¼ *dinars* and 100 *fils*, and coins of 100, 50, 25 and 5 *fils*. £1 = BD 0·760 in Jan. 1978.

Banking. Banking facilities are provided by the National Bank of Bahrain, the Bank of Bahrain and Kuwait and branches of the Chartered Bank, the British Bank of the Middle East, the Arab Bank, Habib Bank (Overseas), United Bank, Citibank, Banque du Caire, Chase Manhattan, National & Grindlays Bank, Bank Melli, Alemene Bank, Bank Saderet, Continental Bank of Chicago, Bank of Paris, National Bank of Abu Dhabi and the Rafidain Bank.

Weights and Measures. British and US standard weights and measures are understood. The following local weights are in use: 1 *tola* = 180 grains = 11·641 grammes; 39 *tolas* = 1 *ratl* (lb.) = 0·454 kg; 4 *ratls* = 1 *Ruba'* (4 lb.) = 1·816 kg; 15 *Ruba'as* = 1 *Maund* (56 lb.) = 54·424 kg. The metric system for weighing was adopted in 1978

OIL. In 1931 oil was discovered. Operations are being conducted by the Bahrain Petroleum Company, registered in Canada but owned by US interests, under a concession granted by the Shaikh. Production of oil in 1975 was 61,120 bbls per day. A large oil refinery on Bahrain Island, besides treating crude oil produced locally, also processes oil from Saudi Arabia transported by pipeline. Refinery throughput in 1977 was 260,913 bbls daily.

In 1975 the Bahrain Government assumed a direct 60% interest in the Bahrain oilfield and related crude oil facilities of BAPCO. Bahrain's gas reserves are 100% government-owned.

Under the terms of the agreement signed between Bahrain and Saudi Arabia in 1958, Bahrain will receive 25% of the profits on any oil produced in the Abu Saafa area of sea between Bahrain and Saudi Arabia. Aramco, which is responsible for the development of this field, began production in 1966.

INDUSTRY AND TRADE

Industry. Bahrain is being developed as a major manufacturing state, the first important enterprise being the Aluminium Bahrain Smelter, which is operated by a company whose shareholders include the Bahrain Government and British, Swedish, Federal German and US interests. The aluminium operation is the largest non-oil industry in the Gulf. Ancillary industries developed around aluminium smelting include the production of aluminium powder. Other projects at present under consideration include the further development of marine industries.

In addition to the traditional minor industries such as boat-building, weaving, pottery, etc., other modern industries have developed, which include the manufacture of building materials, soft drinks, drinking straws, paper bags, woollen garments, plastic and other consumer goods. There is also an important fishing industry and a fairly large farming community. The most important crops are dates and vegetables, and there is also poultry farming.

The pearling industry for which Bahrain used to be famous has considerably declined. Only about 10 boats visit the pearl banks each year, as compared with the 600–1,000 that were employed 30 years ago.

Commerce. In 1976 imports totalled BD 385·7m.; exports and re-exports, non-oil, BD 136·6m. Chief imports were manufactured goods, machinery and transport equipment, food and live animals, chemicals.

Exports and re-exports (in BD 1,000) went to: Japan, 25,700; Saudi Arabia, 68,200.

Import of arms and ammunition and telecommunication equipment is subject to special permission; the sale of alcoholic liquor is restricted and the import of cultured pearls is forbidden.

Total trade between Bahrain and UK (British Department of Trade returns, in £1,000 sterling):

	1973	*1974*	*1975*	*1976*	*1977*
Imports to UK	15,811	20,345	17,849	30,146	13,673
Exports and re-exports from UK	24,338	33,694	60,947	89,628	113,777

COMMUNICATIONS

Aviation. The airport, situated at Muharraq, can take the largest aircraft. Gulf Air, Middle East Airlines, Pakistan International Airways, Qantas, Kuwait Airways, Air India International, Singapore Airlines, UTA, Saudi Arabian Airlines, KLM, Iran Airways, Egyptair, Alia, Cyprus Airways, Ethiopian Airlines and Sudan Airways also operate to and from Bahrain. Bahrain International Airport is the Arabian Gulf's main air communication centre. In 1976 the first scheduled Concorde landed in Bahrain.

Shipping. Bahrain's traditional position as the entrepôt of the Southern Gulf has been supplemented by the development of Mina Sulman—the new modern harbour—as a free transit and industrial area. Local and international companies have developed industries in this area, which is also used as a storage centre for firms selling elsewhere in the Gulf. The facilities offered by Mina Sulman include engineering and ship repairing yards; the Basrec slipway is probably the largest between Rotterdam and Hong Kong.

A large drydock to take tankers of up to 500,000 DWT is being built in Bahrain under the auspices of the Organization of Arab Petroleum Exporting Countries. The Arab Shipbuilding and Repair Yard (ASRY) was being constructed in 1977.

Post and Broadcasting. There were, at Sept. 1976, 33,276 telephones, not counting 1,959 telephones on the oil company exchange. There is a state-operated radio station and television.

EDUCATION. There were, in 1976, 112 state schools for boys and girls with 2,826 teachers and 61,201 pupils. Four boys' secondary schools have a commercial studies section. There are 2 boys' technical schools at secondary level, with 718 pupils. In addition there are 7 private schools. The Men's Teacher Training College (established 1966) and the Women's Teacher Training College (established 1967) give 2-year courses. Approximately 1,000 Bahrainis have graduated from universities abroad. The Gulf Technical College opened in Bahrain in Sept. 1968.

HEALTH. There is a free medical service for all residents of Bahrain. There are 19 government hospitals and health centres with 926 beds, an American mission hospital and an oil company hospital.

DIPLOMATIC REPRESENTATIVES

OF BAHRAIN IN GREAT BRITAIN (98 Gloucester Rd, London, SW7 4AU)

Ambassador: Ali Ebrahim Al-Mahroos (accredited 20 Feb. 1976).

OF GREAT BRITAIN IN BAHRAIN (Government Road North, Manama)

Ambassador: E. F. Given, CMG.

OF BAHRAIN IN THE USA (2600 Virginia Ave., NW, Washington D.C., 20037)

Ambassador: Abdulaziz Abdulrahman Buali.

OF THE USA IN BAHRAIN (Shaikh Isa Road, Manama)

Ambassador: W. Tyler Cluverius, IV.

OF BAHRAIN TO THE UNITED NATIONS

Ambassador: Dr Salman Mohamed Al Saffar

Books of Reference

Statistical and General Information: Ministry of Information, P.O. Box 253, Manama.

Belgrave, J. H. D., *Welcome to Bahrain.* 9th ed. Manama, 1975

BANGLADESH

Capital: Dacca
Population: 76·82m. (1975)
GNP per capita: US$110 (1976)

People's Republic of Bangladesh

HISTORY. The state was formerly the Eastern Province of Pakistan. In Dec. 1970 Sheikh Mujibur Rahman's Awami League Party gained 167 seats out of 300 at the Pakistan general election and immediately made known their wish for greater independence for the then Eastern Province. Martial law was imposed following disturbances in Dacca, and civil war developed in March 1971. The war ended in Dec. 1971 and Bangladesh was proclaimed an independent state.

EVENTS. On 30 May 1977 a referendum was held to ascertain public confidence in Maj.-Gen. Ziaur Rahman as head of the government. The result was officially given as: 33,609,869 votes cast (85% of the electorate); 33,234,752 for Maj.-Gen. Ziaur Rahman; 375,117 against. A general election has been promised for Dec. 1978.

AREA AND POPULATION. Bangladesh is bounded west and north-west by West Bengal (India), north by Assam and Meghalaya (India), east by Assam, Tripura (India) and Burma, south by the Bay of Bengal. The area is 55,598 sq. miles (144,020 sq. km); population (1974 census), 71,316,517 (36,949,033 male, 34,367,484 female), an increase of 40·27% since 1961. Population estimate, 1975, 76,815,000 (37,071,740 male, 34,407,331 (female). The capital is Dacca (population, 1,310,972 in 1974) and its ports are Chittagong (416,733) and Khulna (437,304). Other large cities are Narayanganj (176,459), Rajshahi (132,909) and Barisal (98,127). There are 19 districts:

	Area (sq. km)	*Population 1974*
Dinajpur	6,757	2,572,000
Rangpur	9,593	5,427,709
Bogra	3,890	2,224,328
Rajshahi	9,464	4,265,763
Pabna	4,861	2,809,000
Rajshahi division	*34,565*	*17,298,000*
Tangail	3,370	2,072,000
Mymensingh	13,105	7,562,471
Dacca	7,464	7,607,499
Faridpur	6,977	4,047,324
Dacca division	*30,916*	*21,289,294*
Kushtia	3,551	1,882,290
Jessore	6,597	3,314,000
Khulna	12,049	3,551,772
Bakerganj	6,757	3,906,305
Patuakhali	4,224	1,488,593
Khulna division	*33,178*	*14,142,960*
Sylhet	12,393	4,712,910
Comilla	6,718	5,808,935
Noakhali	4,804	3,231,000
Chittagong	7,006	4,324,487
Chittagong Hill Tracts	13,191	508,131
Chittagong division	*44,112*	*18,585,463*

The language is Bengali.

GOVERNMENT AND CONSTITUTION. Bangladesh is a republic. The Constitution came into force on 16 Dec. 1972 and provided for a parliamentary democracy. On 25 Jan. 1975 Sheikh Mujibur Rahman took on the office of President, with an advisory Parliament. All political parties were abolished, and replaced by the new Bangladesh Krishak Sramik Awami League. On 15 Aug. 1975 Sheikh Mujibur Rahman and his family were killed; martial law was introduced on 20 Aug. and political parties were banned (including the new BKSAL) on 30 Aug. A. Mohammad Sayem was installed as President. Elections to parliament were promised for Feb. 1977 but postponed indefinitely in 1976. Political parties were made legal once again and requested to apply for registration in Aug. 1976.

On 29 Nov, 1976 Maj.-Gen. Ziaur Rahman became Chief Martial Law Administrator, with the Chiefs of Naval and Air Staff as his deputies. On 21 April 1977 President Sayem resigned and Maj.-Gen. Ziaur Rahman was sworn in as President. On 22 April 1977 the constitution of 1972 was amended to establish 'absolute trust and faith in Allah' as the first fundamental principle of state and to provide for a Supreme Judicial Council which would prescribe a code of conduct for judges and advise the President.

Parliament has one chamber of 300 members directly elected every 5 years by citizens over 18. For the first 10 years there will be 15 extra women members elected by Parliament. The judiciary is independent of the executive.

The Government was in Oct. 1977 composed as follows:

President and Chief Martial Law Administrator: Maj.-Gen. Ziaur Rahman.

Vice-President: Mr Justice Abdus Sattar.

President's Council. Finance, Defence, Cabinet Affairs and Home Affairs: Maj.-Gen. Ziaur Rahman. *Law and Parliamentary Affairs:* Abdus Sattar. *Chief of Naval Staff and Deputy Chief Martial Law Administrator, Communications, Water Resources, Flood Control and Power:* Rear-Adm. M. H. Khan. *Chief of Air Staff and Deputy Chief Martial Law Administrator, Civil Aviation and Tourism:* Air Vice Marshal A. G. Mahmud. *Land Administration, Local Self-Government, Rural Development and Co-operatives:* K. A. Huq. *Planning:* M. H. Huda. *Public Works and Urban Development:* M. A. Rashid. *Population Control and Family Planning:* M. Ibrahim. *Relief and Rehabilitation:* Benita Roy. *Health, Labour and Social Welfare:* M. M. Huq. *Agriculture:* Azizul Huq. *Education, Sports and Cultural Affairs:* S. A. Ahsan. *Textiles:* M. Ahmed. *Industries:* J. Uddin. *Petroleum and Mineral Resources:* A. H. Khan. *Food:* A. M. Khan. *Jute:* S. M. Shafiul Azam. *Foreign Affairs:* M. Shamsul Huq. *Commerce:* M. Saifur Rahman. *Information and Broadcasting:* S. H. Chowdhury.

National flag: Bottle green with a red disc in the centre.

National anthem: Amar Sonar Bangla, ami tomay bhalobashi (My golden Bengal, I love you). Words by Rabindranath Tagore.

DEFENCE

Army. There are 5 infantry brigades with 17 battalions and 1 tank regiment, 3 artillery regiments, 3 engineer battalions and supporting arms. Strength, 59,000. There are 20,000 paramilitary militia volunteers. By an ordnance of 5 Oct. 1975 the Rakkhi Bahini militiamen were incorporated into the Army and the body disbanded.

Navy. The Navy was formed in 1972 under Cdr Nurul Huq (trained in the Royal Naval Engineering College, Manadon, and served in the Pakistan Navy as an engineer) appointed as Chief of Naval Staff at the end of March. He was relieved by Cmdre (now Rear-Adm.) M. Hussain Khan in Nov. 1973. Naval bases are at Chittagong (handed over by India on 14 Feb. 1972), Kulna and Dacca.

The composition of the Navy had been planned to be gunboats and possibly destroyers and frigates purchased abroad. The established strength in 1977 comprised 1 frigate, 2 *ex*-Indian 150-ton patrol craft, 2 *ex*-Yugoslav 200-ton patrol vessels, 3 indigenously built 70-ton river gunboats and 1 training ship of 710 tons. On 10 Dec. 1976 HMS *Llandaff*, an aircraft direction frigate of the British 'Cathedral' class, displacing 2,408 tons full load, was transferred from the Royal Navy to the Bangladesh Navy at the Royal Albert Docks in London and was renamed BNS *Umar Farooq*, thus becoming Bangladesh's biggest warship.

The manpower of the Navy at the end of 1977 was 3,500, comprising 200 officers and 3,300 ratings.

Air Force. Initial combat equipment of the Air Wing of the Defence Forces comprised a few Sabre 6 jet fighters salvaged from former Pakistan Air Force units. These were superseded in 1973 by a squadron of about 11 MiG–21MFs. Other aircraft in service include 2 MiG-21 two-seat trainers, 1 An-24, and 3 An-26 turboprop transports, 1 DC-6 piston-engined transport, about 19 Mi-8, Bell 212 and Alouette III helicopters and some light aircraft, including Otters. Personnel strength, 3,000.

INTERNATIONAL RELATIONS

Membership. Bangladesh is a member of the UN and all its related agencies and of the Colombo Plan.

External Debt. In June 1975 the World Bank agreed that Bangladesh might purchase currencies up to 62·5m. Special Drawing Rights (about US$75m.). By previous agreements SDR62·5m. were granted in 1972, SDR31·2m. in 1974 and SDR51·5m. under an 'oil-facility' scheme.

Treaties. Bangladesh signed an economic and technical co-operation agreement with China on 4 Jan. 1977. The amended constitution of 1977 states that Bangladesh seeks fraternal relations with Moslem countries based on Islamic solidarity.

ECONOMY

Planning. Proposed outlay for the 5-year plan 1974–79 is Tk.44,550m., of which Tk.39,520m. is allocated to the public sector. Tk.10,670m. is allocated to agriculture, rural development, co-operatives and flood control; the aim is 36% increase in rice and wheat production, 26% in jute. Tk.8,770m. is for industry. Tk.6,080m. for communications and transport, Tk.3,160m. for education, Tk.700m. for family planning. Grants from IDA have been allocated to an irrigation project on the Halda and Ichamati rivers, training rural development officers and the development of fertilizer plants. The development budget for 1977–78 was Tk.11,506·5m., of which Tk.1,814·7m. was for transport, Tk.1,513·3m. for agriculture, Tk.1,480·2m. for industries, Tk.1,352·9m. for flood control and water resources and Tk.1,253·6m. for power.

The second 5-year plan will be launched in 1980, as part of a 20-year perspective plan. There will be a 2-year interim plan 1978–80, with an envisaged investment of Tk.36,700m. mainly for rural development.

Budget. Details were as follows for the financial year 1977–78 (Tk.1m.):

Expenditure	*9,063·10*	Receipts	*11,566·10*
Defence	1,624·10	Duties and Taxes	8,573·50
Education	1,138·10	Land Revenue	300·40
Health	376·80	Nationalized Banks	228·30

Money supply (June 1977) stood at Tk.9,695m. and foreign exchange reserves at Tk.4,561·6m.

Currency. A new currency, the *Taka*, was floated in 1976 (Tk.26·7 = £1 on 18 Jan. 1977).

Banking. The former private banking system, except for foreign banks, has been nationalized. Currency in circulation, mid-1977, was Tk.9,691·1m.

Weights and Measures. Imperial measures are in use. Weight is in the *seer* (1 *seer* = 2 lb.); the *maund* (1 *maund* = 40 *seers*) and the ton.

ENERGY AND NATURAL RESOURCES

Electricity. There is a hydro-electric power station at Kaptai on Karnafulli and other power stations at Siddhirganj (80 mw), Ashuganj (120). Ghorasal (110), Shahjibazar (1,000), Khulna (60) and Bheramara (40). Installed capacity for electric power (1976) 755,000 kw (of which 80,000 kw are from hydro-electric plants). Production (1975), 1,378m. kwh., of which 355m. kwh. are hydro-electricity.

Water. On 5 Nov. 1977 India and Bangladesh signed an agreement on sharing the water of the river Ganges. The flow will be monitored daily at the Farakka barrage and two other points. A joint rivers commission is studying how to increase the flow.

Oil. Supplies have been located in the Bay of Bengal.

Gas. Natural gas from Titas is piped to Dacca; drilling is in progress at other sites. Production (1974) 850m. cu. metres.

Minerals. Coal has been found at Jamalpur (about 700m. tons). Other minerals include salt (750,000 tonnes in 1975), limestone, white clay, glass sand. The Rajshahi area has known reserves of deep lying coal.

Agriculture. Agriculture contributes 58·8% of GDP and employs about 75% of the population; 64% of the total area is under cultivation; 80% of that is under rice and 9% under jute. Cultivable waste is about 1·5m. acres. Rice is the most important food crop, production in 1976–77, 11·7m. tonnes. Other crops in 1975 (1,000 tonnes): Barley, 16; groundnuts, 32; potatoes (1974), 731; wheat, 117; tobacco, 40·4; tea, 29·3. There were 2,250 tractors in use in 1974.

Livestock in 1975 (1,000): Poultry, 35,054; cattle, 27,418; goats, 11,938; sheep, 753; horses, 43 (FAO estimate).

Bangladesh produces about 50% of the world production of raw jute which is the principal foreign exchange earner. Production, 1976–77 (estimate), 4·7m. bales.

Forestry. The total area under forests is 9,000 sq. miles, of which 4,480 sq. miles are Reserved Forests. The output of timber in 1975 was 15·9m. cu. metres of roundwood (broad-leaved timber) and 410,000 cu. metres of sawn wood. Among minor forest products are 76·5m. stems of bamboos, 415,000 canes, 6,500 maunds of honey annually.

Fisheries. Being bounded on the south by the Bay of Bengal and having numerous rivers, streams, khals and bils, the state is pre-eminently a fish-producing area and possesses great possibilities for the manufacture of various oils and fish products. Fish production, 1975, 640,000 tonnes.

INDUSTRY AND TRADE

Industry. Out of the existing industries, the textile-mills, sugar factories, match factories, glass works, hosiery factories, a paper-mill, jute-mills, aluminium works and a cement factory, with a capacity of 2m. tons per annum, are the most prominent. Refinery distillation capacity, 1·68m. tonnes. There is a steel mill at Chittagong with a capacity of 250,000 ingot-tons per annum. There is also a newsprint factory, a fertilizer factory, a shipyard and a dockyard. Production in 1976–77 (1,000 tons): Jute textiles, 489; steel ingots, 193; fertilizer, 338; woven cotton fabric, 68m. yd; cotton yarn, 82·4m. lb.; sugar, 139. In 1975 (1,000 tonnes): Residual fuel oil, 306; kerosene, 178; distillate fuel oils, 124; naphtha, 49; motor spirit, 44; cement, 128.

Labour. In 1974–75, 1,417 firms (employing more than 10 people) had 293,200 paid employees earning Tk.1,298·7m.; value added, Tk.3,781m.

Commerce. The main export commodities are jute, hide, skins, leather and tea. Bangladesh has resumed trade with Pakistan. In 1976–77 exports were valued at Tk.7,114m., of which Tk.5,018m. was from jute and jute products. Principal imports are machinery, transport equipment, food grains, mineral fuels, chemicals, drugs, medicines and consumer goods.

Value of trade (April–March) in US$1m.:

	1973–74	*1974–75*	*1975–76*
Exports	331	378	314
Imports	866	1,156	881

Total trade with UK (British Department of Trade returns, in £1,000 sterling):

	1974	*1975*	*1976*	*1977*
Imports to UK	15,511	8,916	23,646	25,001
Exports and re-exports from UK	11,542	15,111	28,635	30,627

Tourism. In 1975 there were 63,847 visitors to Bangladesh. They spent the equivalent of US$3m.

COMMUNICATIONS

Roads. The State is backward in the matter of road communications, but there are some 2,500 miles of paved and 2,000 miles of unpaved road. In 1972 there were 31·7m. passenger vehicles and 24·8m. commercial vehicles.

Railways. There are 1,786 miles of railways (1977) of metre (1,187) and broad gauge. In 1975–76 the railways carried 3·5m. tonnes and 94·2m. passengers.

Aviation. Bangladesh Biman (Bangladesh Airways) has domestic flights from Dacca and international services to Calcutta, Kathmandu, Bombay, Dubai, Abu Dhabi, Jeddah, Bangkok, Singapore and London. Pakistan International Airlines resumed regular weekly flights to Dacca in Dec. 1976.

Shipping. Bangladesh possesses important natural advantages in her navigable channels which give valuable service in carrying produce by 5,000 miles of cheap water routes. There are 3 principal waterways, the Padma, Brahmaputra and Meghna. These are freely used by inland steam vessels, which serve areas where railways cannot be economically constructed. The Bangladesh Shipping Corporation owns 21 ships including a 93,000-ton oil tanker (*Banglar Noor*) and a passenger vessel (*Hizbul Bahar*). The Corporation has the capacity to carry 20% of imports and 12% of exports.

Post and Broadcasting. There were 80,100 telephones in 1976. Dacca and Islamabad were linked by telephone in Oct. 1976 and a second telephone circuit was agreed on 11 April 1977. International communications are by satellite, Chittagong being linked to the Indian Ocean Intelsat IV satellite.

Newspapers. In Nov. 1976 there were 17 daily newspapers, 60 weeklies, 4 fortnightlies, 40 monthlies and 80 quarterly periodicals. Most papers are published in Dacca. The Government has set up a paper (*Dainik Barta-at Rajshahi*) to stimulate a regional press. Most papers are privately owned. Press censorship and restrictions of 1975 were removed by the Newspaper (Annulment of Declaration) Repeal Ordinance of June 1976. There is a Press Institute.

JUSTICE, RELIGION, EDUCATION AND WELFARE

Justice. The amended constitution in 1977 set up a Supreme Judicial Council to establish a code of conduct for Supreme Court and High Court judges, who may be removed from office by the President on the Council's recommendation.

Religion. Islam is the official religion, about 80% of the people being Muslim and the rest Hindus, Buddhists and Christians.

Education. The compulsory primary education scheme has been replaced by model primary education. The Government has dissolved the District School Boards and taken over school administration. In 1974 there were 38,000 primary schools, 9,084 secondary schools and about 600 intermediate and degree colleges. There were 6 universities including those at Dacca, Rajshahi, Mymensingh and Chittagong (founded 1964); one university is for engineering and one for agriculture. There are 6 teacher-training colleges, 48 primary training institutes, 22 polytechnics and 35 vocational institutes.

Health. In 1977 there were 1 mental and 2 tuberculosis hospitals, 8 medical colleges and nursing training centres which train about 1,200 nurses annually. In 1977 the number of beds was 14,000.

DIPLOMATIC REPRESENTATIVES

OF BANGLADESH IN GREAT BRITAIN
(28 Queen's Gate, London, SW7)

High Commissioner: A. R. S. Doha (accredited 15 Feb. 1978)

OF GREAT BRITAIN IN BANGLADESH
(D.I.T. Bldgs., Dilkhusha, Dacca, 2)

High Commissioner: F. S. Miles.

OF BANGLADESH IN THE USA
(3421 Massachusetts Ave., NW, Washington, D.C., 20007)

Ambassador: Mustafizur Rahman Siddiqui.

OF THE USA IN BANGLADESH
(Adamjee Court, Montijheel, Dacca)

Ambassador: David T. Schneider.

OF BANGLADESH TO THE UNITED NATIONS

Ambassador: Khwaja Mohammed Kaiser.

Books of Reference

Bangladesh Bureau of Statistics, *Statistical Digests*
Bangladesh Planning Commission, *The First Five Year Plan*
Chen, L. C. (ed.), *Disaster in Bangladesh. Health Crisis in a Developing Nation*. OUP, 1973
Chowdhury, R., *The Genesis of Bangladesh*. London, 1972
Kamal, K. A., *Sheikh Mujibur Rahman*. 2nd ed. Dacca, 1970
Kashyap, S. C. (ed.), *Bangla Desh: Background and Perspectives*. New Delhi, 1971
Khan, A. R., *The Economy of Bangladesh*. London, 1972
Robinson, E. A. G., and Griffin, K. (ed.), *The Economic Development of Bangladesh*. London, 1974

BARBADOS

Capital: Bridgetown
Population: 258,000 (1976)
GNP per capita: US$1,550 (1976)

HISTORY. Barbados was occupied by the British in 1627 and during its colonial history never changed hands. Full internal self-government was attained in 1961. Barbados became an independent sovereign state within the Commonwealth on 30 Nov. 1966.

AREA AND POPULATION. Barbados lies to the east of the Windward Islands. Area 166 sq. miles (430 sq. km). The hot and rainy seasons last from June to December, and the average rainfall is 56 in. per year. In 1976 the estimated population was 258,500. Births, 4,593; deaths 2,266. Bridgetown is the principal city: population, 8,789, and its suburbs, 88,097.

CONSTITUTION AND GOVERNMENT. The Legislature consists of the Governor-General, a Senate and a House of Assembly. The Senate comprises 21 members appointed by the Governor-General, 12 being appointed on the advice of the Prime Minister, 2 on the advice of the leader of the opposition and 7 in the Governor-General's discretion. The House of Assembly comprises 24 members elected every 5 years. In 1963 the voting age was reduced to 18.

The Privy Council is appointed by the Governor-General after consultation with the Prime Minister. It consists of 12 members and the Governor-General as chairman. It advises the Governor-General in the exercise of the royal prerogative of mercy and in the exercise of his disciplinary powers over members of the public and police services.

In the general election of Sept. 1976 the Barbados Labour Party held 17 seats and the Democratic Labour Party 7 seats.

Governor-General: Sir Deighton Ward, GCMG, CVO.

The cabinet, appointed on 8 Sept. 1976, was:

Prime Minister, Finance and Planning: Rt Hon. J. M. G. M. Adams, PC.

Caribbean Affairs, External Trade, Industry and Tourism: Bernard St John. *Labour and Community Service:* Lionel Craig. *Attorney-General and External Affairs:* Henry Forde. *Agriculture, Food and Consumer Affairs:* Charles Bolden. *Health and National Insurance:* Billie Miller. *Housing and Land, Leader of the Senate:* Ronald Mapp. *Communications and Works:* Lloyd Braithwaite. *Education and Culture:* Louis Tull.

National flag: Three vertical strips of blue, gold, blue, with a black trident in the centre.

INTERNATIONAL RELATIONS

Membership. Barbados is a member of UN, OAS, CARICOM, the Commonwealth and an ACP state of EEC.

ECONOMY

Budget. The fiscal year runs from 1 April to 31 March; accounts in BD$

	1973–74	*1974–75*	*1975–76*	*1976–77*
Revenue	130,084,800	164,200,945	203,041,202	216,804,579
Expenditure	142,549,532	181,424,449	189,929,820	225,082,713
Public debt	148,300,000	187,600,000	213,700,000	271,200,000

Currency. The monetary unit is the Barbardos dollar (BD$) divided into 100 cents.

Banking. Ten main banks operate in Barbados including Barclays Bank International, the Royal Bank of Canada, Canadian Imperial Bank of Commerce, the Bank of Nova Scotia, the Bank of America, Chase Manhattan Bank, First National Bank of Chicago and Citibank. The Government Savings Bank on 31 Dec. 1974 had 45,819 depositors and deposits of BD$22·2m.

Barbados is headquarters for the Caribbean Development Bank. It is a member of the Caribbean Common Market (CARICOM). The Barbados Development Bank opened on 15 April 1969 and Barbados became a member of the Inter-American Development Bank on 19 March 1969.

NATURAL RESOURCES

Agriculture. Of the total area of 106,240 acres, about 54,932 acres are arable land. The land is intensely cultivated, and sugar-cane occupies 64,000 acres, 39,178 were reaped in 1977. The agricultural sector accounted for 14·4% of GDP in 1970 (1946, 45%; 1967, 24%). In 1976, 4,342 persons were employed on sugar estates and 498 in sugar factories. In 1977, 117,911 tons of sugar were produced. There are 12 sugar factories, 1 syrup plant and a rum distillery in production.

Livestock (1976): Cattle, 23,000; sheep, 49,000; goats, 25,000; pigs, 37,000; poultry, 375,000.

Fisheries. There are about 544 powered boats and many men and women are employed during the flying-fish season. Large numbers of these boats are laid up from July to Oct. The annual catch is about 2,240 tons.

INDUSTRY AND TRADE

Industry. Industries operating in Barbados in 1976 numbered about 170 and ranged from the manufacture of processed food to small specialized products such as garment manufacturing, furniture and household appliances, electrical components, plastic products and electronic parts.

Commerce. Total trade for fiscal years (1 April–31 March) in BD$:

	1971–72	*1972–73*	*1973–74*	*1974–75*
Imports[1]	243,685,000	270,435,700	351,860,288	416,526,000
Exports[1]	76,847,248	86,011,440	115,728,000	179,593,000

[1] Exclusive of bullion and specie.

In 1972 the principal imports were: Machinery all kinds, $36,360,339; motor vehicles, $17,171,378; petroleum and petroleum products, $14,795,025; cotton and rayon piece-goods, $10,359,271; meat (fresh chilled, frozen), $11,482,702; clothing, $8,179,320; animal feeds, $6,651,121; medicinal and pharmaceutical products, $5,627,862; lumber, $5,395,011; milk and cream, $5,034,507; meat (canned and not canned), $4,888,331.

The principal domestic exports in 1974 were: Sugar, $25,184,000; clothing, $18·29m.; electrical goods, $8,769,000; molasses and syrup, $7,769,000; other food and beverages, $6,198,000; rum, $4,974,000; chemicals, $4,866,000; lard and margarine, $2,278,000; other manufactures, $16,375,000.

Total trade with UK (British Department of Trade returns, in £1,000 sterling):

	1973	*1974*	*1975*	*1976*	*1977*
Imports from UK	8,601	9,733	14,797	1,639	5,239
Exports and re-exports to UK	14,123	14,499	17,184	19,141	24,713

Tourism. In 1976, 224,314 visitors came to Barbados, including 54,854 from USA, 38,070 from the CARICOM countries, 24,802 from UK, 23,005 from Canada and 28,203 from other countries. Tourism contributes 10·3% of GDP.

COMMUNICATIONS

Roads. There are 1,020 miles of road open to traffic, of which 840 miles are all-weather roads. On 30 June 1973 there were 28,410 motor vehicles, including 22,339 cars and 235 buses.

Aviation. There is an international airport at Seawell, Christ Church, Barbados, served by British Airways, BWIA, Leeward Islands Air Transport, PANAM, Air Canada, SAS, International Caribbean Airways and Eastern Airlines, Cubana Airlines, Venezuelan Airlines. In 1976, 360,170 passengers arrived by air; 217,729 were in transit.

Shipping. A deep-water harbour opened in 1961 at Bridgetown provides 8 berths for ships 500–600 ft in length, including one specially designed for bulk sugar loading. The number of merchant vessels entering in 1972 was 1,381 of 4,067,500 net tons.

Post and Telephone. There is a general post office in Bridgetown and 13 branches on the island. In Aug. 1974 there were 25,706 exchange lines and 39,445 stations in service.

Cinemas. There were (1977) 6 cinemas with a seating capacity of 5,040, and 2 drive-in cinemas for 600 cars.

Newspapers. In 1977 there was 1 daily newspaper (average daily circulation 25,642 and 35,746 on Sundays) and 1 bi-weekly (circulation 48,418).

JUSTICE, RELIGION, EDUCATION AND WELFARE

Justice. Justice is administered by the Supreme Court and by magistrates' courts. All have both civil and criminal jurisdiction. There is a Chief Justice and 3 puisne judges of the Supreme Court and 8 magistrates.

Religion. The majority (about 70%) of the population are Anglicans, the remainder mainly Methodists, Moravians and Roman Catholics.

Education. In 1976 children in primary schools numbered 32,264; in 20 secondary schools, 22,629; in 18 approved secondary schools, 6,904. There are 19 government-aided independent schools with 7,506 pupils and a number of independent schools for which no accurate figures are available. As from Jan. 1962 tuition fees were abolished for children at all government secondary schools.

In 1963 Erdiston College became one of the constituent Colleges of the University of the West Indies Institute of Education. The College of Arts and Sciences of the University of the West Indies in Barbados was opened in Sept. 1963 and Cave Hill campus in 1967. In 1973–74, 942 students attended. Education at this College is free for Barbadians. However, students in the Faculty of Law are required to pay a fee. A Community College for higher education at pre-university level was opened in 1969. In 1973–74, 1,517 students attended the S. J. Prescod Polytechnic which was opened in Nov. 1969 to give training in, among other things, construction, electrical and engineering trades. In 1972–73, 74 government scholars, bursars and exhibitioners were attending universities overseas. Government expenditure on education during 1974–75 is estimated at BD$37,984,086.

Health. In 1972 there were 2,220 hospital beds and (1973) 160 doctors.

DIPLOMATIC REPRESENTATIVES

OF BARBADOS IN GREAT BRITAIN
(6 Upper Belgrave St., London, SW1X 8AZ)

High Commissioner: C. B. Williams, OBE.

OF GREAT BRITAIN IN BARBADOS
(147/9 Roebuck St., Bridgetown)

High Commissioner: J. S. Arthur.

OF BARBADOS IN THE USA
(2144 Wyoming Ave, NW, Washington, D.C. 20008)

Ambassador: Oliver H. Jackman

OF THE USA IN BARBADOS (P.O. Box 302, Bridgetown)
Ambassador: Frank V. Ortiz, Jr.

OF BARBADOS TO THE UNITED NATIONS
Ambassador: Dr Donald G. Blockman

Books of Reference

Statistical Information: The Barbados Statistical Service (NIS Bldg, Fairchild St., St Michael) produces selected monthly statistics and annual abstracts. *Government Statistician:* Keith Padmore.

Barbados Economic Survey, 1970
Barbados Development Plan, 1969–72
Chandler, M. J., *A Guide to Records in Barbados.* University of the West Indies, 1965
Hoyos, F. A., *Barbados, Our Island Home.* London, 1970.—*Barbados: A History from the Amerindians to Independence.* London, 1978
Starkey, O. P., *Commercial Geography of Barbados.* Indiana Univ. Press, 1961

Library: The Barbados Public Library, Bridgetown, *Librarian:* Chalmer St Hill, BA.

BELGIUM

Capital: Brussels
Population: 9·8m. (1976)
GNP per capita: US$6,780 (1976)

Royaume de Belgique—Koninkrijk België

HISTORY. The kingdom of Belgium formed itself into an independent state in 1830, having from 1815 been part of the Netherlands. The secession was decreed on 4 Oct. 1830 by a provisional government, established in consequence of a revolution which broke out at Brussels, on 25 Aug. 1830. A National Congress elected Prince Leopold of Saxe-Coburg King of the Belgians on 4 June 1831; he ascended the throne 21 July 1831.

By the Treaty of London, 15 Nov. 1831, the neutrality of Belgium was guaranteed by Austria, Russia, Great Britain and Prussia. It was not until after the signing of the Treaty of London, 19 April 1839, which established peace between King Leopold I and the King of the Netherlands, that all the states of Europe recognized the kingdom of Belgium. In the Treaty of Versailles (28 June 1919) it is stated that as the treaties of 1839 'no longer conform to the requirements of the situation', these are abrogated and will be replaced by other treaties.

AREA AND POPULATION. Belgium is bounded north by the Netherlands, north-west by the North Sea, west and south by France, east by Federal Republic of Germany and Luxembourg. Belgium has an area of 30,513 sq. km (11,778 sq. miles). The Belgium exclave of Baarle–Hertog in the Netherlands has an area of 7 sq. km, and a population (31 Dec. 1976) of 1,076 males and 1,014 females.

By an agreement, 23 Sept. 1956, the frontier with Germany was slightly readjusted.

Census	*Population*	*Increase % per annum*	*Census*	*Population*	*Increase % per annum*
1900	6,693,548	1·03	1947	8,512,195	0·36
1910	7,423,784	1·09	1961	9,189,741	0·52
1920	7,465,782	0·06	1970	9,650,944	0·55
1930	8,092,004	0·84			

Provinces	*Provincial capitals*	*Area (hectares)*	*Estimated population (31 Dec.)* 1970[1]	1974	1975	1976
Antwerp (Anvers)	Antwerp	286,058	1,533,249	1,555,186	1,559,269	1,562,775
Brabant	Brussels	337,080	2,176,373	2,211,456	2,220,088	2,223,168
Flanders West	Bruges	373,397	1,054,429	1,069,844	1,071,604	1,073,407
Flanders East	Ghent	298,164	1,310,117	1,323,504	1,325,419	1,325,221
Hainaut	Mons	378,983	1,317,453	1,322,626	1,321,846	1,318,303
Liège	Liège	387,628	1,008,905	1,010,523	1,019,266	1,016,510
Limbourg	Hasselt	242,219	652,547	678,592	685,576	692,127
Luxembourg	Arlon	441,847	217,310	219,111	219,642	219,746
Namur	Namur	366,025	380,561	388,477	390,442	392,045
Total		3,051,395	9,650,944	9,788,248	9,813,152	9,823,302

[1] Census.

In 1976 there were 4,808,465 males and 5,014,837 females.

Foreigners numbered 851,601 on 31 Dec. 1976.

Vital statistics for calendar years:

	Births	*Deaths*	*Marriages*	*Divorces*	*Immigration*	*Emigration*
1972	134,437	116,743	74,584	7,972	62,474	42,665
1973	129,425	118,313	72,797	8,512	64,250	40,448
1974	123,155	116,039	73,363	10,355	71,866	40,808
1975	119,273	119,273	72,869	11,245	69,886	40,151
1976	120,472	118,765	71,093	12,925	58,724	56,921

	1973	*1974*	*1975*
Illegitimate births	3,879	3,777	3,730
Of the total births including still-born	*129,424*	*123,674*	*119,693*
Boys	66,576	63,595	61,574
Girls	62,848	60,079	58,119

The most important towns, with estimated population on 31 Dec. 1976:

Brussels and suburbs[1]	1,042,052	Hasselt	40,446
Antwerp (Anvers)	206,786	Seraing	40,276
Ghent (Gand)	139,812	Roeselare (Roulers)	39,157
Liège (Luik)	135,347	Tournhout	37,958
Brugge (Bruges)	119,351	Mouscron (Moeskroen)	37,200
Deurne	80,427	Hoboken	34,097
Oostende (Ostende)	71,446	Tournai (Doornik)	32,821
Mechelen (Malines)	64,185	Vilvoorde (Vilvorde)	32,768
Mons (Bergen)	61,566	Verviers	30,895
Genk	61,156	Namur (Namen)	30,845
St Niklaas (St Nicolas)	48,680	Herstal	28,808
Berchem	47,752	Leuven (Louvain)	28,755
Borgerhout	46,079	Jumet	28,055
Aalst (Alost)	44,677	Lier (Lierre)	27,834
Wilryck	44,040	Lokeren	27,110
Kortrijk (Courtrai)	42,810	Ronse (Renaix)	24,622
Merksem	41,458	Charleroi	21,307

[1] The suburbs comprise 18 distinct communes, viz., Anderlecht, Etterbeek, Forest Ixelles, Jette, Koekelberg, Molenbeek St Jean, St Gilles, St Josse-ten-Noode, Schaerbeek, Uccle, Woluwe-St Lambert, Auderghem, Watermael-Boitsfort, Woluwe-St Pierre, Berchem, Ste Agathe, Evere and Ganshoren.

KING. Baudouin, born 7 Sept. 1930, succeeded his father, Leopold III, on 17 July 1951, when he took the oath on the constitution before the two Chambers: married on 15 Dec. 1960 to Fabiola de Mora y Aragón, daughter of the Conde de Mora and Marqués de Casa Riera.

Father of the King. Leopold III, born 3 Nov. 1901, son of the late King Albert (died 17 Feb. 1934) and of Queen Elisabeth, Duchess of Bavaria (died 23 Nov. 1965); married (1) on 4 Nov. 1926 to Princess Astrid of Sweden, died 29 Aug. 1935, and (2) on 11 Sept. (civil marriage, 6 Dec.) 1941, to Mlle Mary Lilian Baels, Princess de Rethy, daughter of Hendrik Baels, formerly Minister of Agriculture. Leopold III succeeded to the throne on 23 Feb. 1934; on 20 Sept. 1944 parliament elected Prince Charles, Count of Flanders, Leopold's brother as Regent of the Kingdom. The Regency ended on 22 July 1950; but King Leopold delegated his powers to Prince Baudouin on 11 Aug. 1950, and abdicated on 16 July 1951.

Brother and Sister of the King. (1) Josephine Charlotte, Princess of Belgium, born 11 Oct. 1927; married to Prince Jean of Luxembourg, 9 April 1953; (2) Albert, Prince of Liège, born 6 June 1934; married to Paola Ruffo di Calabria, 2 July 1959; *offspring:* Prince Philippe, born 15 April 1960; Princess Astrid, born 5 June 1962; Prince Laurent, born 19 Oct. 1963. *Half-brother and half-sisters of the King*. Prince Alexandre, born 18 July 1942; Princess Marie Christine, born 6 Feb. 1951; Princess Maria-Esmeralda, born 30 Sept. 1956.

Uncle and Aunt of the King. (1) Prince Charles, Count of Flanders, born 10 Oct. 1903. (2) Princess Marie-José, born 4 Aug. 1906, married to Prince Umberto (King Umberto II of Italy in 1946) on 8 Jan. 1930.

BELGIAN SOVEREIGNS

Leopold I	1831–65	Leopold III	1934–44, 1950–51
Leopold II	1865–1909	Regency	1944–50
Albert	1909–34	Baudouin	1951–

CONSTITUTION AND GOVERNMENT. According to the constitution of 1831, Belgium is a constitutional, representative and hereditary monarchy. The legislative power is vested in the King, the Senate and the Chamber of Representatives. The royal succession is in direct male line in the order of primogeniture.

By marriage without the King's consent, however, the right of succession is forfeited, but may be restored by the King with the consent of the two Chambers. No act of the King can have effect unless countersigned by one of his Ministers, who thus becomes responsible for it. The King convokes, prorogues and dissolves the Chambers. In default of male heirs, the King may nominate his successor with the consent of the Chambers. If the successor be under 18 years of age the two Chambers meet together for the purpose of nominating a regent during the minority.

National flag: Three vertical strips of black, yellow, red.
National anthem: Après des siècles d'esclavage (La Brabançonne; words by Jenneval, 1830; tune by F. van Campenhout, 1930).

French, Dutch and German are official languages.
Those sections of the Belgian Constitution which regulate the organization of the legislative power were revised in Oct. 1921. For both Senate and Chamber all elections are held on the principle of universal suffrage.
The Senate consists of members elected for 4 years, partly directly and partly indirectly. The number elected directly is equal to half the number of members of the Chamber of Representatives. The constituent body is similar to that which elects deputies to the Chamber; the minimum age of electors is 21 years, and the minimum length of residence required is 6 months. Women were given the suffrage at parliamentary elections on 24 March 1948.
In the direct elections of members both the Senate and Chamber of Representatives the principle of proportional representation was introduced by law of 29 Dec. 1899.
Senators are elected indirectly by the provincial councils, on the basis of 1 for 200,000 inhabitants. Every addition of 125,000 inhabitants gives the right to 1 senator more. Each provincial council elects at least 3 senators. There are at present 48 provincial senators. No one, during 2 years preceding the election, must have been a member of the council appointing him. Senators are elected by the Senate itself in the proportion of half the preceding category. The senators belonging to these two latter categories are also elected by the method of proportional representation. All senators must be at least 40 years of age. They receive 900,000 francs per annum. Sons of the King, or failing these, Belgian princes of the reigning branch of the royal family, are by right senators at the age of 18, but have no voice in the deliberations till the age of 25 years; this prerogative is hardly ever used.
The members of the Chamber of Representatives are elected by the electoral body. Their number, at present 212 (law of 3 April 1965), is proportional to the population, and cannot exceed one for every 40,000 inhabitants. They sit for 4 years. Deputies must be not less than 25 years of age, and resident in Belgium.
Each deputy has an annual allowance of 900,000 francs. Senators and deputies have also free railway passes.
The Senate and Chamber meet annually in October and must sit for at least 40 days; but the King has the power of convoking extraordinary sessions and of dissolving them either simultaneously or separately. In the latter case a new election must take place within 40 days and a meeting of the chambers within 2 months.
An adjournment cannot be made for a period exceeding 1 month without the consent of the Chambers.
Parties in the Senate, at 17 April 1977. Christian Social, 70, Socialist, 52; Freedom and Progress, 26; Front Democrate francophone and Rassemblement Wallon, 15; Flemish People's Union, 17; Communist, 1.
Parties in the Chamber elected 17 April 1977: Christian Social, 80; Socialists, 61; Freedom and Progress, 33; Flemish People's Union, 20; Front Democrate francophone and Rassemblement Wallon, 15; Communist, 2.
Legislation on 'preparatory regionalization' was enacted in July 1974 which would establish 3 administrative regions.
The Executive Government, sworn in on 3 June 1977, was composed as follows:

Prime Minister: Léo Tindemans.
Defence: Paul Vanden Boeynants. *Finance:* G. Geens. *Foreign Affairs:* H. Simonet. *Public Health and the Environment:* L. Dhoore. *Social Security:* Alfred

Califice. *Justice:* R. van Elslande. *Foreign Trade:* H. de Bruyne. *Interior:* H. Boel. *Labour:* G. Spitaels. *Agriculture and Middle Classes:* Antoine Humblet. *Communications:* Jos Chabert. *Education (National):* J. Ramaekers, J. Michel. *Public Works and Walloon Affairs:* G. Mathot. *Economic Affairs:* W. Claes. *Culture (Dutch) and Fleming Affairs:* Rita De Backer-Van Ocken. *Culture (French):* J.-M. Dehousse. *Public Affairs:* L. Hurez. *Co-operation for Development:* L. Outers. *Posts, Telegraphs and Telephones, and Brussels Affairs:* L. Defosset. *Pensions:* J. Wynickx. *Scientific Policy:* A. Vandkerckhove. There are also 7 Secretaries of State.

Local Government. The 9 provinces and 589 communes of Belgium have a large measure of autonomous government. According to the law of 15 April 1920, changed by the law of 1 July 1969, all Belgians over 18 years of age without distinction of sex, who have been domiciled for at least 6 months, have the right to vote in communal elections. Proportional representation is applied to the communal elections, and communal councils are to be renewed every 6 years. In each commune there is a college composed of the burgomaster as the president and a certain number of aldermen.

DEFENCE. A military and technical agreement signed by Belgium and the Netherlands on 10 May 1948 provides for standardization of equipment, co-ordination of training methods and contacts between the staffs of the military colleges.

Army. According to the Military Law of 30 April 1962, the Belgian Army is recruited by annual calls to the colours and by voluntary enlistments.

Compulsory service lasts 8 or 10 months for private soldiers, 13 months for voluntary reserve officers and 15 for the paracommando regiment. Duration of military obligation is 8 years for most soldiers called for compulsory service.

The Army comprises as major units 1 armoured and 3 mechanized brigades (3 of which are deployed as the Belgian divisions in the Belgian corps area in the Federal Republic of Germany) and 1 paracommando regiment. There are also 3 reconnaissance and 2 motorized battalions. Total strength about 64,000 (including medical services). *Gendarmerie*, 15,000.

Navy. The naval forces include 4 new frigates (the first fully designed by the Belgian Navy and built in Belgian yards) of 2,304 tons full load (and armed with guided missiles as well as guns, torpedoes, anti-submarine mortars and rocket launchers) built in 1974–78, 7 ocean minesweepers–minehunters, 2 command and logistic support ships, 9 coastal minesweepers, 14 inshore minesweepers, 2 research ships, 6 river patrol boats, 6 tugs and 6 miscellaneous craft. Naval personnel in 1977 totalled 4,460 officers and ratings.

The naval air arm comprises 1 S58 search and rescue helicopter and 3 Alouette III general utility helicopters.

Air Force. The Air Force has a strength of about 20,000 personnel and more than 300 aircraft in 10 operational squadrons and support and training units. There is 1 all-weather fighter wing (2 squadrons) of F-104G Starfighters; 1 fighter-bomber wing (2 squadrons) of F-104G Starfighters; 2 tactical wings with 3 squadrons of Mirage 5Bs, including Mirage 5BD two-seat trainers, and 1 squadron of Mirage 5BR photo-reconnaissance aircraft; and 1 wing (2 squadrons) equipped with 12 C-130H Hercules turboprop transports, 2 Boeing 727 jets, 2 light twin-jet Falcons, 3 HS 748 twin-turboprop transports and 6 Swearingen Merlin III light turboprop transports. Two wings, based in Germany, have Nike surface-to-air missiles. All but one transport squadron are assigned to NATO. Other types in service include Sea King Mk 48 search and rescue helicopters, and SIAI-Marchetti SF.260M, Magister and T-33A training aircraft. 12 twin-engined Islanders and light helicopters are operated by the Army. Alpha Jet advanced trainers have been ordered for service from 1979, and F-16 air superiority fighters to re-equip F-104G units.

INTERNATIONAL RELATIONS

Membership. Belgium is a member of UN, EEC, Beneleux Economic Union, Council of Europe, NATO, OECD and WEU.

ECONOMY

Budget. Revenue and expenditure for calendar years (in 1m. francs):

	1972	*1973*	*1974*	*1975*	*1976*	*1977*[1]
Receipts						
Ordinary	366,557	410,676	490,065	587,879	664,269	802,028
Extraordinary	80,705	91,973	86,420	95,434	111,394	1,107
Total	447,262	502,649	576,485	683,313	775,663	803,135
Expenditure						
Ordinary	370,953	422,924	497,504	626,908	716,470	793,539
Extraordinary	65,882	67,977	78,695	73,074	77,114	102,758
Total	436,835	490,901	576,199	699,982	793,584	896,297

[1] Budget estimates.

On 30 June 1977 the Belgian public debt consisted of (in 1m. francs): Internal debt consolidated, 919,743; short and middle terms, 212,572, at sight, 83,573. External debt, 3,672.

Currency. The *franc*, containing 0·01826 gramme of fine gold, is the unit of currency.

No gold has been minted since 1882 (save only 5m. francs struck in 1914). New silver coins of 100 francs have been issued since 15 Oct. 1948.

The official rate of exchange in July 1977 was US$1 = 35·53 francs; £1 = 61·20 francs.

Banking. The bank of issue in Belgium is the National Bank, instituted in 1850. It is the cashier of the State, and is authorized to carry on the usual banking operations. The note circulation on 31 Dec. 1976 amounted to 307,197m. francs. The articles of association of the National Bank of Belgium were modified on 13 Sept. 1948 so as to strengthen public control.

The savings banks are mainly operated by the Caisse Générale d'Epargne et de Retraite and by the private savings banks. The Caisse Générale d'Epargne et de Retraite is an autonomous institution with legally regulated functions; operating under the supervision of the Minister of Finance. It co-operates with the Belgian postal service, thus obviating any need of a postal-savings system. The savings deposits and savings bonds of the Caisse d'Epargne amounted to 369,007m. francs on 31 Dec. 1976. The private savings banks, whose liabilities expressed in savings accounts and bonds amounted to 352,259m. francs on 31 Dec. 1976, are controlled by the 'Commission bancaire'.

Weights and Measures. The metric system is in force.

Baudhuin, Fernand, *Histoire économique de la Belgique, 1914–39*. Brussels. 1944.—*L'économie belge sous l'occupation 1940–44*. Brussels, 1945

Van Houtte, J. A., *Esquisse d'une histoire économique de la Belgique*. Louvain, 1943

ENERGY AND NATURAL RESOURCES

Electricity. The production of electricity (1m. kwh.) amounted to 39,121 in 1973; 40,764 in 1974; 38,974 in 1975; 31,435 in 1976.

Gas. Production of gas (in 1m. cu. metres) 997 in 1973; 1,003 in 1974; 699 in 1975; 1,286 in 1976.

Minerals. Output (in tonnes) for 5 calendar years:

	1972	*1973*	*1974*	*1975*	*1976*
Coal	10,499,869	8,841,770	8,110,976	7,478,703	7,237,738
Briquettes	495,979	455,884	416,783	268,730	165,930
Coke	7,239,202	7,774,070	8,050,411	5,727,825	6,216,084
Cast iron	11,777,253	12,655,110	13,019,635	9,068,719	9,864,755
Wrought steel	14,537,082	15,526,666	16,230,483	11,587,172	12,149,321
Finished steel	10,728,068	11,443,179	12,162,402	7,909,684	8,470,509

Agriculture. Of the total area of 3,050,708 hectares, there were, in 1976, 1,469,058 hectares under cultivation, of which 420,616 were under cereals, 27,440 vegetables, 108,605 industrial plants, 109,019 root crops, 734,832 pastures and meadows.

Chief crops	*Area in hectares* 1974	1975	1976	*Produce in tonnes* 1974	1975	1976
Wheat	190,332	176,382	195,297	1,004,122	676,649	890,933
Barley	149,324	122,799	139,389	699,023	426,130	609,890
Oats	59,458	70,297	48,406	222,373	227,763	128,759
Rye	13,229	9,123	15,584	46,303	28,554	47,531
Potatoes	40,201	36,088	37,672	1,459,830	1,049,195	714,096
Beet (sugar)	105,091	119,639	96,220	4,465,323	4,913,193	4,600,284
Beet (fodder)	26,817	26,617	24,315	2,325,231	2,493,462	2,196,359
Tobacco	495	489	460	1,504	1,584	1,397

On 1 Dec. 1976 there were 31,498 farm horses and 17,964 other horses, 2,822,770 cattle (including 986,326 milch cows), 82,003 sheep, 6,394 goats and 4,813,287 pigs.

Forestry. In 1970 the forest area covered 19·7% of the land surface. In 1970, 2·85 cu. metres of timber were felled.

Fisheries. The total quantity of fish landed amounted to 34,464 tons valued at 1,374m. francs in 1976. The fishing fleet had a total tonnage of 24,044 gross tons at 31 Dec. 1976.

Buttgenbach, H., *Les Minéraux de Belgique et du Congo Belge.* Liège, 1947

INDUSTRY AND TRADE

Industry. In 1976 there were 19 sugar factories, output 137,634 tonnes of raw sugar; 4 sugar refineries, output 214,936 tonnes; 13 distilleries, output 488,448 hectolitres of potable and industrial alcohol; 174 breweries, output 14,543,796 hectolitres of beer; margarine factories, output 145,313 tonnes; match factories, output (1973) 43,631m. matches.

Six trusts control the greater part of Belgian industry: the Société Générale (founded in 1822) owns about 40% of coal, 50% of steel, 65% of non-ferrous metals and 35% of electricity; Brufina-Confinindus operates in steel, coal, electricity and heavy engineering; the Groupe Solvay rules the chemical industry; the Groupe Copée has interests in steel and coal; Empain controls tramways and electrical equipment; the Banque Lambert owns petroleum firms and their accessories.

Sabbe, E., *Histoire de l'industrie linière en Belgique.* Brussels, 1945

Commerce. By the convention concluded at Brussels on 25 July 1921 between Belgium and Luxembourg and ratified on 5 March 1922 an economic union was formed by the two countries, and the customs frontier between them was abolished on 1 May 1922. Dissolved in Aug. 1940, the union was re-established on 1 May 1945.

On 14 March 1947, in execution of an agreement signed in London on 5 Sept. 1944, there was concluded a customs union between Belgium and Luxembourg, on the one hand, and the Netherlands, on the other. The union came into force on 1 Jan. 1948, and is now known as the Benelux Economic Union. A joint tariff has been adopted and import duties are no longer levied at the Netherlands frontier, but import licences may still be required. A full economic union of the three countries came into operation on 1 Nov. 1960.

Benelux information is supplied by the Secrétariat Général de l'Union Douanière Néerlando-Belgo-Luxembourgeoise, Rue de la Régence, 39, 1000 Brussels. It publishes *Benelux. Bulletin Trimestriel de Statistique; Statistisch Kwartaalbericht* (1955 ff.).

Trade by principal countries (in 1,000 Belgian francs):

	Imports from 1974	1975	1976[1]	*Exports to* 1974	1975	1976[1]
France	199,862,926	196,759,000	222,162,514	219,701,339	202,073,473	265,820,093
USA	75,469,264	71,748,409	83,617,799	61,619,340	43,106,002	44,915,911
UK	66,823,435	70,155,301	92,076,267	59,339,617	68,395,045	76,328,297
Netherlands	191,684,861	192,306,738	235,340,050	188,777,562	181,156,928	214,412,409
German Dem. Rep.	2,528,226	2,989,842	3,632,788	2,286,192	2,755,316	2,928,559
Germany, Fed. Rep.	257,315,222	248,443,387	307,432,560	236,480,557	235,401,734	294,044,509

[1] Provisional.

	Imports from			Exports to		
	1974	*1975*	*1976*[1]	*1974*	*1975*	*1976*[1]
Argentina	4,596,170	3,299,283	4,994,133	2,335,133	3,032,969	1,027,469
Italy	43,423,392	44,004,210	52,100,424	49,256,209	42,548,974	59,919,262
Switzerland	18,910,388	25,496,360	21,318,588	22,777,291	17,364,126	22,058,091
Zaïre	29,032,152	16,212,321	23,679,870	7,173,529	5,809,674	5,066,272
Denmark	5,473,340	5,490,890	6,136,839	12,405,540	13,633,039	18,145,772
USSR	10,537,995	11,028,308	11,590,191	14,307,909	12,811,867	11,425,599
India	2,287,225	1,964,840	3,836,476	3,689,628	5,736,411	5,814,225
Rep. of S. Africa	9,829,955	8,154,202	9,609,985	5,800,552	5,408,732	4,406,042
Canada	10,498,765	11,654,844	14,128,705	5,955,101	4,613,418	4,627,610
Brazil	6,703,384	5,964,057	7,248,467	11,921,481	7,065,317	5,111,556
Australia	5,513,866	5,554,166	8,074,496	3,818,689	2,906,549	3,651,720

[1] Provisional.

Imports and exports for 6 calendar years (in 1,000 Belgian francs):

	Imports	*Exports*		*Imports*	*Exports*
1970	568,114,922	580,467,451	1974	1,160,684,663	1,099,824,920
1972	686,919,829	707,862,740	1975	1,130,944,557	1,056,879,476
1973	852,639,796	570,244,933	1976	1,363,470,342	1,264,813,843

The total trade between UK and Belgium was as follows (British Department of Trade returns, in £1,000 sterling):

	1973	*1974*[1]	*1975*[1]	*1976*[1]	*1977*[1]
Imports to UK	434,297	729,561	951,501	1,300,229	1,682,511
Exports and re-exports from UK	612,165	837,766	920,473	1,401,243	1,837,119

[1] Including Luxembourg.

Principal Belgian–Luxembourg exports to UK in 1976 (tonnes; francs): Textiles (38,313; 4,680m.); metals (530,348; 9,665m.); chemical and pharmaceutical products (355,175; 5,662m.); precious stones and manufactures thereof (291; 10,996m.).

Principal Belgian–Luxembourg imports from the UK in 1976 (tonnes; francs): Machinery and electrical apparatus (69,148; 11,378m.); vehicles, chiefly motor cars, and aircraft (184,396; 14,085m.); textiles (29,027; 3,489m.); precious stones (89; 30,037m.); base metals and manufactures thereof (145,780; 4,619m.).

COMMUNICATIONS

Roads. The total length of the roads in Belgium on 31 Dec. 1975 was as follows: State roads (including 1,051 km of motorway), 11,958 km; provincial roads, 1,394 km. The majority of roads are metalled. Number of motor vehicles in Belgium, 1 Aug. 1976, 3,273,438, including 2,737,989 passenger cars, 19,854 buses, 237,325 lorries, 36,397 non-agricultural tractors, 110,438 agricultural tractors, 99,888 motor cycles and 31,547 special vehicles.

Railways. The main Belgian lines were a State enterprise from their inception in 1834. In 1926 the 'Société Nationale des Chemins de Fer Belges' (SNCB) was formed to take over the railways. The State is sole holder of the ordinary shares of SNCB, which carry the majority vote at General Meetings. The State also retains a control over fares, freight rates, borrowing and the construction of new lines, and appoints the Board of the company. The length of railway operated on 31 Dec. 1976 was 3,998 km. Revenue (1976), 34,482m. francs; expenditure, 36,577m. francs.

Aviation. The national Belgian airline SABENA (Société anonyme belge d'exploitation de la navigation aérienne) was set up in 1923. Its capital is 750m. francs. In addition to its European network, SABENA operates different routes to North and South America, to North, Central and South Africa and to the Near, the Middle and the Far East. In 1976 its airfleet comprised 31 aircraft. In 1976 SABENA flew 52m. km, carrying 1,681,982 revenue passengers, 316·67m. ton-km of freight and 9·13m. ton-km of mail.

Shipping.[1] On 1 Jan. 1977 the Belgian merchant fleet was composed of 91 vessels of 1,410,403 tons. There were 38 shipping companies, of which the most important

[1] Belgian shipping returns are given in the official 'Moorsom tons', which may be converted into net tons by deducting 19·85% from the Moorsom total.

were the Compagnie Maritime Belge, with 27 ships, and the Belgian Fruit Lines, SA, with 6 ships.

The navigation at the port of Antwerp in 1976 was as follows: Number of vessels entered, 17,711; tonnage, 66,343,697. Number of vessels cleared, 17,730; tonnage, 66,076,987.

The total length of navigable waterways (rivers and canals) was 1,573·7 km in 1976.

Post and Broadcasting. On 31 Dec. 1975 there were 1,836 post offices. The gross revenue of the post office in the year 1975 amounted to 11,834m. francs.

A régie of telegraphs and telephones for running the services on business lines was created in 1930. Telegraph offices for dispatching and receiving wires numbered 106; for dispatching only, 138. Receipts for 1975 were 2,491,455,979 francs; expenditure, 2,838,597,948 francs.

In 1975 the telephone service comprised 609 exchanges, connecting 5,189 public telephone stations and 1,849,960 subscribers. Number of telephones, 1 Jan. 1976, 2,776,882. Receipts in 1975, 19,365·16m. francs; expenditure, 19,724·14m. francs.

Radiodiffusion-Télévision Belge–Belgische Radio en Televisie is a public service broadcasting on medium- and short-waves and on FM. There are 3 programmes in each network including regional broadcasts. The short-wave service is mainly intended for Africa and it is broadcast in French, Dutch, English and Spanish languages. RTB broadcasts a TV programme in French and BRT in Dutch. The programmes are financed by state grants in aids. Colour programmes are broadcast by PAL system. Number of receivers (1978), radio, 4·04m.; TV, 2·65m. (including 1·82m. colour sets).

Cinemas (1976). There were 558 cinemas, with a seating capacity of 253,239.

Newspapers. (1977). There are 41 daily newspapers (some of them only regional or local editions of larger dailies), of which 25 are in French, 15 in Dutch and 1 in German.

JUSTICE, RELIGION, EDUCATION AND WELFARE

Justice. Judges are appointed for life. There is a court of cassation, 5 courts of appeal, and assize courts for political and criminal cases. There are 26 judicial districts, each with a court of first instance. In each of the 222 cantons is a justice and judge of the peace. There are, besides, various special tribunals. There is trial by jury in assize courts.

Religion. Of the inhabitants professing a religion the majority are Roman Catholic, but no inquiry as to the profession of faith is now made at the censuses. There are, however, statistics concerning the clergy, and according to these there were in 1976: Roman Catholic higher clergy, 128; inferior clergy, 6,944; Protestant pastors, 71; Anglican Church, 10 chaplains; Jews (rabbis and ministers), 25. The State does not interfere in any way with the internal affairs of any church. There is full religious liberty, and part of the income of the ministers of all denominations is paid by the State.

There are 8 Roman Catholic dioceses subdivided into 261 deaneries.

Estimated number of Protestants, 24,000; of Jews, 35,000.

The Protestant (Evangelical) Church is under a synod. There is also a Central Jewish Consistory, a Central Committee of the Anglican Church and a Free Protestant Church.

Education. On 8 Nov. 1962/2 Aug. 1963 a linguistic frontier was fixed between the Dutch-speaking, French-speaking and German-speaking parts of Belgium. In the north, Flemish is recognized as the official language, in the south, French, and along the eastern border, German. The city and *arrondissement* of Brussels are bilingual. The percentage of the population in the Flemish, French, German and bilingual regions was 56·6, 32·1, 0·7, 10·6 on 31 Dec. 1976. (*See* map in THE STATESMAN'S YEAR-BOOK, 1967–68.)

Higher Education (1975–76). Higher education is given in state universities: Ghent (11,482 students), Liège (8,918 students), Mons (1,228 students), the Polytechnic Faculty in Mons (587 students), the Antwerp State University Centre (1,581 students), the Gemblours Faculty of Agronomical Sciences (499 students), the Royal

Military School in Brussels (524 students) and in the private universities: Catholic University of Louvain (33,525 students), the Free University of Brussels (16,369), University Institution Antwerp (1,150 students), St Ignatius Antwerp (2,386 students), Our Lady of Peace in Namur (2,622 students), Catholic University Faculty in Mons (579 students), St Lewis in Brussels (1,154 students), the Limbourg University Centre (699 students) and the Protestant Faculty of Theology in Brussels (87 students). The total number of students in university colleges, faculties and institutes was 83,360.

There are 5 royal academies of fine arts and 5 royal conservatoires at Brussels, Liège, Ghent, Antwerp and Mons.

Secondary Education. 1,134 (1970–71) middle schools and 3,937 (1970–71) technical schools had a total of 275,630 (1976–77) pupils in the general classes and 313,873 in the technical classes in the traditional system and 241,245 pupils in the new system.

Elementary Education. There were 8,380 (1971–72) primary schools, with 935,804 pupils in 1976–77 and 5,443 (1971–72) infant schools, with 428,419 pupils in 1976–77.

Normal Schools. There were 56 (1971–72) schools for training secondary teachers (10,060 students) in 1975–76; 96 for training elementary teachers (5,410 students), 91 technical normal schools in 1971–72 with (1975–76) 2,126 students and 45 normal infant schools with 977 students.

Health. In 1975 there were 18,506 physicians (including 412 dentists), 2,273 other dentists, 7,688 pharmacists and (1970) 3,593 midwives. Hospital beds numbered 87,457 in 1975.

Social Security. Social security is based on the law of Dec. 1944. It applies to all workers subject to an employment contract, and is administered by the Central National Office of Social Security (ONSS), which collects from employers and employees all contributions referring to family allowances, health insurance, old age insurance, holidays and unemployment. These sums are distributed by the Central Office to the various institutions concerned with these benefits. Insurance against unemployment is organized through a common fund, which also undertakes to retrain the unemployed for another employment while providing for their families. Since 1944 further laws have increased allowances, made fresh provisions for housing (1945), injuries while working, professional illnesses, etc. (1948).

Apart from private charity, the poor are assisted by the communes through the agency of the *Centre Public d'Aide Sociale* in French-speaking parts of the country and *Openbaar Centrum voor Maatschappelijk Welzijn* in Dutch-speaking areas. Provisions of a national character have been made for looking after war orphans and men disabled in the war. Certain other establishments, either state or provincial, provide for the needs of the deaf-mutes and the blind, and of children who are placed under the control of the courts. Provision is also made for repressing begging and providing shelter for the homeless.

DIPLOMATIC REPRESENTATIVES

OF BELGIUM IN GREAT BRITAIN (103 Eaton Sq., London, SW1W 9AB)

Ambassador: Robert Vaes, KCMG (accredited 17 Feb. 1977).

OF GREAT BRITAIN IN BELGIUM (Britannia Hse., rue Joseph II 28, 1040 Brussels)

Ambassador: Sir David Muirhead, KCMG, CVO.

OF BELGIUM IN THE USA (3330 Garfield St., NW, Washington, D.C., 20008)

Ambassador: Willy van Cauwenberg.

OF THE USA IN BELGIUM (Blvd. du Régent 27, 1000 Brussels)

Ambassador: Anne Cox Chambers.

OF BELGIUM TO THE UNITED NATIONS

Ambassador: André Ernemann.

Books of Reference

Statistical Information: The Institut National de Statistique (44 rue de Louvain, Brussels) was set up on 24 Jan. 1831, under the designation of Bureau de Statistique Générale; after several changes, it received its present name on 2 May 1946. *Director-General:* Dr P. van Landeghem. *Main publications:*

Bulletin du Commerce Extérieur
Bulletin de Statistique. Monthly
Annuaire Statistique de la Belgique (from 1870).—*Annuaire statistique de poche* (from 1965)
Statistiques Agricoles. Monthly
Recensement général de la population au 31 déc. 1970. 13 vols.
Recensement de l'agriculture au 15 mai 1970. 3 vols.
Recensement de l'industrie et du commerce au 31 déc. 1970. 3 vols.

Almanach royal officiel. Annual. Brussels
L'économie belge. Ministère des Affaires Economiques. Annual (from 1947)
Meynaud, J. (ed.), *La Décision politique en Belgique*. Paris, 1965
Raeymaker, O. de, *Belgie's international Beleid, 1919–39*. Brussels, 1945
Van Kalken, Frans, *Histoire de Belgique*. Brussels, 1944.—*Entre deux guerres: Esquisses de la vie politique en Belgique de 1918–1940*. Brussels, 1945

BELIZE

Capital: Belmopan
Population: 150,000 (1975)

HISTORY. The early settlement of the territory was probably effected by British woodcutters about 1638; from that date to 1798, in spite of armed opposition from the Spaniards, settlers held their own and prospered. In 1780 the Home Government appointed a superintendent, and in 1862 the settlement was declared a colony, subordinate to Jamaica. It became an independent colony in 1884. Self-government was attained in 1964.

AREA AND POPULATION. Belize is bounded north by Mexico, west by Guatemala and south and east by the Caribbean sea. Area, 22,963 sq. km. There are 6 districts:

	Sq. km	*Population census, 1970*		*Sq. km*	*Population census 1970*
Corozal	1,860	15,504	Cayo	5,338	16,034
Belize	4,204	49,661	Stann Creek	2,176	13,044
Orange Walk	4,737	16,666	Toledo	4,649	8,954

Total population (census, 1970) 119,863. Estimate, 1975, 150,000. Voters on the roll numbered 33,737 in 1974. In 1974 the birth rate per 1,000 was 38 and the death rate 5·2; infantile mortality 33·3 per 1,000 births; there were 779 marriages and 19 divorces.

Main city, Belize City; population, census 1970, 39,257. Estimate, 1975, 45,000. Following the severe hurricane which struck the territory on 31 Oct. 1961 the capital Belmopan (population, 1974, 4,000) has been moved to a new site 50 miles inland; construction began in Jan. 1967 and it became the seat of government on 3 Aug. 1970.

See map in this edition of THE STATESMAN'S YEAR-BOOK.

CONSTITUTION AND GOVERNMENT. Under the constitution, which came into force on 1 Jan. 1964, Belize, formerly British Honduras has a 2-chamber legislature, with a ministerial system and cabinet responsibility. The House of Representatives consists of 18 members elected by universal suffrage. The Senate consists of 8 members, 5 of whom are appointed on the advice of the Premier, 2 on the advice of the Leader of the Opposition and 1 by the Governor.

State of parties at Oct. 1976: People's United Party 13 and the United Democratic Party 5 seats.

The Governor retains responsibility for defence, external affairs, internal security, the safeguarding of conditions of service of public officers, and over finance 'so long as the Government of Belize is in receipt of budgetary aid from the British Government'.

Governor and C.-in-C.: Peter Donovan McEntee, OBE.

Premier and Minister of Finance: George Price.

Flag: Blue with the arms of the Colony surrounded by a green garland on a white disc in the centre; flown in conjunction with the Union Flag.

ECONOMY

Budget. Revenue and expenditure (in $B) for calendar years:

	1972	*1973*	*1974*	*1975*	*1976*	*1977*
Revenue	29,845,986	35,888,502	40,164,477	49,500,000	68,911,795	92,611,862
Expenditure	29,845,986	35,888,502	40,164,477	49,500,000	68,911,795	92,611,862

Debt, 31 Dec. 1975, $B18·3m.; sinking fund, $B1·4m.

Currency. There was (31 Dec. 1974) a paper currency of $B8,704,000 in government notes of $B50, 25 and 10, and a subsidiary mixed metal coinage of 1-, 5-, 10-, 25- and 50-cent pieces whose issues amount to $B896,000.

Banking. The Royal Bank of Canada took over the business of the local bank in 1912; it has 8 branches. There are 6 government savings banks; depositors, about 10,000; deposits, $B60·2m. on 31 Dec. 1975.

Barclays Bank International have 7 branches, Bank of Nova Scotia have 5 branches and Atlantic Bank 3 branches.

NATURAL RESOURCES

Agriculture. The main agricultural export is sugar, followed by citrus fruit, chiefly grapefruit and oranges, whole, canned, juice and concentrates. Citrus production, 1976, 1,335,643 boxes. Sugar production in 1977 was 92,000 tons. Banana production began in 1973, and first shipments began in 1974; exports, 1976, 425,000 boxes. [Ed. note: Box of grapefruit, 80 lb., oranges, 90 lb., bananas, 40 lb.]

Livestock (1976): Cattle, 46,000; sheep, 3,000; pigs, 18,000; poultry, 321,000.

Forestry. 2,964 sq. miles, 49% of the total land area, are under forests which include mahogany, cedar, Santa Maria, pine and rosewood, and many secondary hardwoods of known or probable market value, as well as woods suitable for pulp production. Exports of forest produce in 1975 amounted to $B3m.

Fisheries. Food and game fish are plentiful, and domestic consumption is heavy. The total exported in 1976 was valued at $B6·5m. Turtles—Hawksbill, Loggerhead and Green—are plentiful but as yet are not exported.

LABOUR. The labour market alternates between full employment, often accompanied by local shortages in the citrus and sugar-cane harvesting (Jan.–July), and under-employment during the wet season (Aug.–Dec.), aggravated by the seasonal nature of the major industries.

COMMERCE. In 1975 total imports amounted to $B153·8m. Total domestic exports, $B130m. The principal domestic exports were timber, sugar, fish products and citrus fruit.

Total trade between Belize and UK (British Department of Trade returns, in £1,000 sterling):

	1972	*1973*	*1974*	*1975*	*1976*	*1977*
Imports to UK	2,613	2,736	4,975	11,154	9,156	13,300
Exports and re-exports from UK	3,835	3,778	4,218	6,469	7,346	8,129

COMMUNICATIONS

Aviation. In 1975, 137,548 passengers and 9·25m. lb. of freight arrived and departed on international flights.

Shipping (1974). Registered shipping, 15 sailing vessels, 1,340 net tons, and 397 motor vessels, 446,234 net tons.

Post. Telephone lines connect Belize City with Corozal Town and Consejo on the coast, Orange Walk Town on New River, San Antonio on the Rio Hondo and other stations in the north, San Ignacio and Benque Viejo Towns in the west, Stann Creek and Punta Gorda Towns and other points in the south. Number of telephones (1977), 5,556. The government-operated telecommunication services were taken over by Cable and Wireless Ltd in 1962, which installed an automatic telephone service in 1963 and also operates a radio-telephone service. The Belize Telecommunication Authority has instituted a country-wide fully automatic telephone dialling facility. There are 6 post offices and 44 rural sub-post offices.

Cinemas (1975). There were 18 cinemas with seating capacity of 10,000.

Newspapers (1974). There was 1 bi-weekly newspaper with a combined circulation of 5,000 and 3 weekly.

JUSTICE, EDUCATION AND WELFARE

Justice The police force contained (1974) 31 officers, 375 n.c.o.s and constables and 14 women constables.

Education In 1975, 6 government, 181 grant-aided and 12 private primary schools had a total enrolment of 33,000 pupils; 21 secondary schools, 5,000 pupils; a government technical high school, 350 pupils; 2 government junior colleges, 600 pupils. All aided schools, except the government technical high school, are under the management of Christian bodies. Three colleges for post-secondary education had 580 students.

Health. In 1972 there were 41 doctors and 641 hospital beds.

Books of Reference

Annual Report, 1972. Government Printer, Belize City, 1974
Abstract of Statistics 1975. Government Printer, Belize City, 1976
UN Economic Report. 1963. Ministry of Finance and Development, 1964
Anderson, A. H., *Brief Sketch of the British Honduras.* 7th ed. Belize, 1958
Bianchi, W. J., *Belize: The Controversy Between Guatemala and Great Britain.* New York, 1959
Dobson, D., *A History of Belize.* Belize, 1973
Floyd, B., *Focus on Honduras.* Univ. of West Indies, Jamaica, 1970
Grant, C. H., *The Making of Modern Belize.* CUP, 1976
Romney, D. H., (ed.), *Land in British Honduras.* HMSO, 1959
Waddell, D. A. G., *British Honduras: A Historical and Contemporary Survey.* OUP, 1961

BENIN

Capital: Porto Novo
Population: 3·2m. (1976)
GNP per capita: US$130 (1976)

République Populaire du Benin

AREA AND POPULATION. The People's Republic of Benin is bounded east by Nigeria, north by Niger and Upper Volta and west by Togo. The area is 112,600 sq. km, and the population, in 1976, 3·2m. The seat of government is Porto Novo (104,000 inhabitants); the chief port and business centre is Cotonou (178,000); other important towns are Abomey, Ouidah and Parakou. There are 6 administrative districts: Atakora, Borgou, Zou, Ouémé, Atlantique and Mono.

CONSTITUTION AND GOVERNMENT. The People's Republic of Benin, formerly the Republic of Dahomey, became independent on 1 Aug. 1960, after having been a territory of French West Africa from 1904. The Republic was admitted to the UN on 20 Sept. 1960.

In the fifth *coup* since independence Maj. Kerecou took over the government on 26 Oct. 1972. The ruling political party is the Benin People's Revolutionary Party. In May 1977 President Kerecou announced that discussions and a new Constitution were about to begin.

President, Prime Minister, Minister of Planning and Defence: Lieut.-Col. Mathieu Kerecou.

Minister of Foreign Affairs: Maj. Michel Aladaye.

National flag: Green with a red star in the canton.

DEFENCE.

Army. The Army consists of 2 infantry battalions and support units; strength, 2,100.

Air Force. The Air Force has a strength of about 150 officers and men, 4 C-47 transports, 1 Cessna Skymaster, 1 Aero Commander 500, 2 Broussard communications aircraft and an Alouette II helicopter.

INTERNATIONAL RELATIONS

Membership. Benin is a member of UN, OAU and is an ACP country of EEC.

ECONOMY

Budget. The ordinary budget for 1976 balanced at 16,080m. francs CFA.

Currency. The monetary unit is the franc CFA (*Communauté financière africaine*), which is divided into 100 centimes.

AGRICULTURE. The population is mainly agricultural, growing maize (200,800 tonnes in 1973), millet (7,000 tons in 1973) and groundnuts (35,000 tons in 1973). In 1976 there were 800,000 cattle, 1·7m. sheep and goats, 400,000 pigs, 6,000 horses, 1,000 donkeys. The forests contain oil palms, which have been profitably utilized. These furnish the chief exports—kernels and oil. Cotton cultivation has been successfully introduced in the north; coffee cultivation has given good results in the southern districts.

TRADE. Imports in 1973, 24,859m. francs CFA; exports, 9,794m. francs CFA. The principal imports in 1971 (in 1m. francs CFA): Clothing and footwear, 2,143;

chemicals, 1,904, motor vehicles and parts, 1,430; machinery, 1,382. The principal exports were: Palm-oil, 3,127; cocoa beans, 2,807; cotton lint, 2,304.

Total trade between Benin and UK (British Department of Trade returns, in £1,000 sterling):

	1973	*1974*	*1975*	*1976*	*1977*
Imports to UK	54	458	183	2,814	3,057
Exports and re-exports from UK	2,032	3,605	7,144	6,860	10,045

COMMUNICATIONS

Roads. There are 6,937 km of roads in 1972. There were 13,000 motor cars in 1971.

Railways. Railways (metre-gauge) connect Cotonou with Parakou (438 km); Pahou–Segboroué on Lake Aheme (34 km); Cotonou–Pobé (107 km).

Aviation. In 1970, 15,697 passengers and 799 tonnes of freight and 129 tonnes of mail were dealt with at Cotonou airport.

Shipping. In 1971, 755 vessels of 2,076,000 net tons entered the port of Cotonou.

Post. There were, in 1975, 9,624 telephones. A telegraph line connects Cotonou with Abomey, Togo, Niger and Senegal.

EDUCATION. There were, in 1972, 186,000 pupils in primary schools, 27,000 in secondary schools, 2,000 in technical schools.

DIPLOMATIC REPRESENTATIVES

OF BENIN IN GREAT BRITAIN

Ambassador: Yaya Mede-Moussa (resides in Paris).

OF GREAT BRITAIN IN BENIN

Ambassador: J. R. Williams, CMG (resides in Lagos).

OF BENIN IN THE USA (2737 Cathedral Ave., NW, Washington, D.C., 20008)

Ambassador: Thomas Setondji Boya.

OF THE USA IN BENIN (Rue Caporal Anami Bernard, Cotonou)

Ambassador: W. Kenneth Thompson.

OF BENIN TO THE UNITED NATIONS

Ambassador: Thomas S. Boya.

Book of Reference

Ronen, D., *Dahomey: Between Tradition and Modernity.* Cornell Univ. Press, 1975

BERMUDA

Capital: Hamilton
Population: 53,500 (1976)

HISTORY. The Spaniards visited the islands in 1515, but, according to a 17th-century French cartographer, they were discovered in 1503 by Juan Bermudez, after whom they were named. No settlement was made, and they were uninhabited until a party of colonists under Sir George Somers was wrecked there in 1609. A company was formed for the 'Plantation of the Somers' Islands', as they were called at first, and in 1684 the Crown took over the government.

AREA AND POPULATION. Bermuda consists of a group of some 150 small islands (about 20 inhabited), situated in the western Atlantic (32° 18′ N. lat., 64° 46′ W. long.); the nearest point of the mainland, about 570 miles distant, is Cape Hatteras, N.C., and 690 miles from New York; noted for its climate and scenery; a favourite resort for Americans.

The area is 20·59 sq. miles (53·3 sq. km), of which 2·3 sq. miles were leased in 1941 for 99 years to the US Government for naval and air bases. The civil population (*i.e.*, excluding British and American military, naval and air force personnel) in 1976 was estimated at 53,500.

Chief town, Hamilton; population, about 3,000.

In 1976 there were 856 live births, 509 marriages and 384 deaths; infantile mortality rate was 23·4 per 1,000 live births.

CONSTITUTION AND GOVERNMENT. Bermuda is a colony with representative government. Under the constitution of 8 June 1968 the Governor, appointed by the Crown, is normally bound to accept the advice of the Cabinet in matters other than external affairs, defence, internal security and the police, for which he retains special responsibility. The Cabinet is appointed from among members of the bicameral legislature, on the recommendation of the Premier. The Legislative Council, of whom one or two members may serve on Cabinet, consists of 11 members; 5 are appointed in the discretion of the Governor, 4 on the recommendation of the Premier and 2 on the recommendation of the Opposition Leader. The 40 members of the House of Assembly are elected 2 from each of 20 constituencies under full universal, adult suffrage. The general election on 18 May 1976 resulted in the return of 26 members of the United Bermuda Party and 14 members of the Progressive Labour Party. A by-election was held on 21 Sept. 1976 resulting in a total of 25 members of the United Bermuda Party and 15 members of the Progressive Labour Party.

Governor: The Hon. Sir Peter Ramsbotham, GCMG, KCVO.
Premier: John David Gibbons.
Flag: The British Red Ensign with the badge of the Colony in the fly.

DEFENCE. The Bermuda Regiment had 350 men in 1978.

ECONOMY

Budget. Revenue and expenditure in $B for years ending 31 March:

	1971–72	*1972–73*	*1973–74*	*1974–75*	*1975–76*
Revenue	35,657,048	50,207,362	56,083,823	60,488,675	65,381,918
Expenditure	32,968,623	48,393,205	54,096,231	62,187,728	62,911,334

Expenditure in $B (excluding capital items) was earmarked as follows:

	1970	*1973–74*	*1974–75*	*1975–76*
Agriculture and fisheries	1,421,979	1,589,622	1,996,501	2,319,550
Tourism and trade development	3,197,399	4,335,332	4,892,910	5,366,300
Education	7,454,638	9,345,933	10,869,980	13,166,845
Hospital grant	1,968,000	5,102,990	6,567,000	6,407,255

	1970	*1973–74*	*1974–75*	*1975–76*
Police	2,142,059	3,832,342	5,256,575	5,906,350
Prisons	791,463	1,539,051	2,063,464	2,351,730
Post office	1,284,726	1,737,184	2,073,110	2,259,590
Health and welfare	3,000,536	3,090,395	2,931,448	3,373,775
Public transportation	1,403,627	1,631,936	2,111,869	2,630,230
Public works	4,924,783	5,385,224	5,112,196	6,942,820
Civil aviation	1,130,893	688,001	829,451	928,740

Chief sources of revenue in 1976 were: Company duties, \$28·5m.; land tax, \$5·7m.; employment tax, \$5·56m.; motor vehicles and other licences, \$3,694,010; hospital tax, \$2·6m.; companies tax, \$2,566,150; passenger tax, \$1·9m.; stamp duties, \$1·75m.

Public debt, as at 31 March 1977, exceeded \$17m.

Currency. Decimal currency based on a Bermuda dollar of 100 cents was introduced on 6 Feb. 1970. In Nov. 1975 £1 = 2·07 Bermuda dollars and US\$1 = 1 Bermuda dollar. The Bermuda Monetary Authority issues notes in denominations of \$50, \$20, \$10, \$5 and \$1, and coins in values of 50c, 25c, 10c, 5c and 1c.

Banking. There are 4 banks, the Bank of Bermuda, Ltd, the Bank of N. T. Butterfield and Son, Ltd, the Bermuda National Bank, Ltd, and the Bermuda Provident Bank, Ltd.

Weights and Measures. British, except that US instead of Imperial fluid measures are used.

AGRICULTURE. The chief products are concentrated essences, plants, bananas, citrus fruit, lilies, potatoes and other kitchen-garden vegetables. In 1975, 700 acres were under cultivation, 1·5% of the work force are engaged in agriculture, fishing and horticulture.

Livestock (1976): Cattle, 1,000; pigs, 1,000; poultry, 74,000.

TRADE UNIONS. Legislation providing for trade unions was enacted in Oct. 1946, and there are 10 trade unions with a total membership (1976) of 8,082.

COMMERCE. Imports and exports in \$B:

	1973	*1974*	*1975*	*1976*
Imports	123,000,000	155,000,000	144,000,000	165,000,000
Exports	30,000,000	34,000,000	34,000,000	47,000,000

The visible adverse balance of trade is more than compensated for by invisible exports, including tourism.

Imports in 1975 from USA, \$69·1m.; UK, \$25·2m.; Canada, \$11·6m.; Venezuela, \$7m.; Netherlands West Indies, \$4·3m.; New Zealand, \$2·9m.; France, \$2·7m.; Netherlands, \$2·5m.; Federal Republic of Germany, \$2·3m.; Japan, \$2·3m.; Italy, \$1·9m. Exports in 1971 to UK, \$373,382; USA, \$141,886; Canada, \$111,693.

In 1971 the principal imports were fresh meat (\$12·2m.), petroleum products (\$11·3m.), clothing (\$10·9m.), electric machinery (\$10·5m.), transport equipment (\$7·3m.); the principal local exports, concentrated essences (\$603,288), beauty preparations (\$130,561).

Total trade between Bermuda and UK, in £1,000 sterling (British Department of Trade returns):

	1972	*1973*	*1974*	*1975*	*1976*	*1977*
Imports to UK	5,889	5,947	4,154	3,179	3,065	5,780
Exports and re-exports from UK	10,358	12,797	14,371	17,927	14,396	19,686

TOURISM. In 1976, 558,874 tourists visited Bermuda. Tourism represents 44% of GDP.

COMMUNICATIONS

Roads. In 1948 the railway service was discontinued and a government-operated bus service introduced.

Between 1908 and Aug. 1946 the use of motor vehicles, with the exception of ambulances, fire engines and other essential services, was prohibited. With the passing of the Motor Car Act in 1946, the use of motor vehicles, subject to certain limitations on size and horse-power, became lawful. In 1971, 10,842 private cars, 672 public passenger vehicles, 1,888 lorries and trucks, 24,066 auto-cycles and 867 miscellaneous motor vehicles were registered.

Aviation. American Airlines, Delta Airlines and Eastern Airlines maintain regular services between Bermuda and the USA. British Airways also have regular flights through Bermuda linking London with Mexico and the Caribbean. Air Canada Airlines call at Bermuda on their service between Canada, Barbados, Antigua and Trinidad; they also operate services between Bermuda, Toronto, Montreal and Halifax.

Shipping. The registered shipping consisted (1975) of 9 steam vessels, 35 sailing vessels and 162 motor vessels with a total gross tonnage of 1,502,490. In 1975 the gross tonnage of 630 vessels entered and cleared was 5,684,766 tons.

Post and Broadcasting (1977). There are 15 post offices. The telephone company is privately owned and operated 34,872 telephones in 1974. Cables connect the islands with the USA, Halifax (N.S.) and Tortola, providing connexion with the world.

Radio and television broadcasting is commercial.

Cinemas. There were (1974) 4 cinemas with a seating capacity of 2,260.

JUSTICE, EDUCATION AND WELFARE

Justice. There are 4 magistrates' courts, a Supreme Court and a court of appeal. The police had a strength of 380 in 1976.

Education. Education is compulsory between the ages of 5 and 16, and government assistance is given by the payment of grants, and, where necessary, of school fees. Free elementary education was introduced on 1 May 1949 and free secondary education in Sept. 1965. In 1976, there were 10 government nurseries (398 pupils), 6 special units for the handicapped (224 pupils), 18 government primary schools (5,510 pupils), 9 government secondary schools (3,950 pupils), the Bermuda College (621 pupils). Four private schools accommodated an additional 2,000 pupils of all ages. Total enrolment was 12,696 pupils.

Health. In 1970 there were 70 doctors.

Books of Reference

Annual Report, 1971. HMSO, 1972
Bermuda Historical Quarterly. 1944 ff.
Baron, S., *Your Guide to Bermuda*. London, 1965
Bell, E. Y., *Beautiful Bermuda*. 10th ed. New York and Bermuda, 1947
Dyer, H. T., *The Next 20 Years: A Report on the Development Plans for Bermuda*. Hamilton, 1963
Wilkinson H. C., *Bermuda from Sail to Steam*. OUP, 1973
Zuill, W. S., *The Story of Bermuda and Her People*. London, 1973

National Library: The Bermuda Library, Hamilton. *Head Librarian:* Mrs M. Skiffington.

BHUTÁN

Druk-yul

Capital: Thimphu
Population: 1·1m. (1974)
GNP per capita: US$70 (1976)

HISTORY. In 1774 the East India Company concluded a treaty with the ruler of Bhután. Under a treaty signed in Nov. 1865 the Bhután Government was granted an annual subsidy. By an amending treaty concluded in Jan. 1910 the British Government undertook to exercise no interference in the internal affairs of Bhután, and the Bhután Government agreed to be guided by the advice of the British Government in regard to its external relations.

The Government of India concluded a fresh treaty with Bhután on 8 Aug. 1949. Under this treaty the Government of Bhután continues to be guided by the Government of India in regard to its external relations, and the Government of India have undertaken not to interfere in the internal administration of Bhután. The subsidy paid to Bhután has been increased to Rs 500,000, and the Government of India agreed to retrocede to Bhután an area of about 32 sq. miles in the territory known as Dewangiri, which was annexed in 1865.

AREA AND POPULATION. Bhután is situated in the eastern Himalayas, between 26° 45′ and 28° N. lat. and between 89° and 92° E. long., bordered on the north and east by Tibet and India, on the west by Sikkim and on the south by India. Extreme length from east to west 190 miles: extreme breadth 90 miles. Area about 18,000 sq. miles (46,600 sq. km); population estimated at approximately 1·1m. (1974). The capital is at Thimphu. The official language is Dzongkha, which belongs to the Tibeto-Burman group of languages.

KING. Jigme Singye Wangchuk, succeeded his father Jigme Dorji Wangchuk who died 21 July 1972.

GOVERNMENT. In 1907 the Tongsa Penlop (the governor of the province of Tongsa in eastern Bhután), Sir Ugyen Wangchuk, GCIE, KCSI, was elected as the first hereditary Maharaja of Bhután. The Bhutanese title is Druk Gyalpo, but his successor is now addressed as King of Bhután. From Oct. 1969 the absolute monarchy was changed to a form of 'democratic monarchy'.

National flag: Diagonally orange over dark red, over all in the centre a white dragon.

DEFENCE. Bhután has an army of about 4,000 men, trained by Indian officers.

ECONOMY

Planning. The Government of Bhután has drawn up four 5-year development plans (1961–65, 1966–70, 1971–76, 1976–81), with the active co-operation and financial support of the Government of India. Educational facilities are being expanded and medical facilities are being provided. Forest and mineral wealth is to be exploited. About 1,300 km of new roads have been built.

Budget. The budget for 1973–74 envisaged expenditure of N46m. and revenue of N21m.

Currency. Paper currency has been introduced, known as the *Ngultrum.* Silver currency is known as *Tikchung.* Indian currency is also legal tender.

Banking. The Bank of Bhután was established in 1968. The headquarters are at

Phuntsholing with branches at Thimphu, Chimakothi, Samdrup Jongkhar and Geylegphug.

ENERGY AND NATURAL RESOURCES

Electricity. In 1974 construction work began on the Chukha hydro-electric project at a cost of US$92m.

Minerals. Large deposits of limestone, marble, dolomite, graphite, lead, copper, slate, coal, talc and gypsum have been found.

Agriculture. The chief products are rice, millet, wheat, barley, maize, cardomom, oranges, apples, handloom cloth, timber and yaks. Extensive and valuable forests abound.

Livestock (1976): Horses, 19,000; asses, 17,000; cattle, 198,000; pigs, 56,000; sheep, 39,000; poultry, 102,000.

COMMERCE. Trade with India is considerable but timber, cardomom and liquor are also exported to the Middle East, Singapore and Western Europe. Bhután imported from the UK in 1975 goods valued at £8,000.

TOURISM. The country has been opened for tourism since 1974 and it is now (1978) the largest source of foreign exchange.

COMMUNICATIONS

Roads. In 1974 there were about 1,500 km of roads.

Post. A modern postal system was introduced in 1962. There are 2 general post offices and 49 other offices. In 1974 there were 480 km of telephone lines and 7 automatic exchanges.

RELIGION, EDUCATION AND WELFARE

Religion. The majority of the people are Mahayana Buddhists of the Drukpa sub-sect of the Karyud School which was first introduced from Tibet during the 12th century.

Education. In 1974 there were 93 state schools with 13,410 pupils including 2 technical schools with 400 students. Many students are receiving training under the Colombo Plan in Australia, New Zealand, Japan, Singapore and UK.

Health. There were (1974) 6 general hospitals, 45 dispensaries, 4 leprosy hospitals and 1 mobile hospital. Beds totalled 300 and there were 25 doctors and 51 nurses.

DIPLOMATIC RELATIONS. The Government of Bhután is in diplomatic relations with Bangladesh and India at ambassadorial level.

Books of Reference

Facts about Bhutan. Kalimpong, 1974
Coelho, V. H., *Sikkim and Bhutan*. New Delhi, 1970
Karan, P. P., *Bhutan: A Physical and Cultural Geography*. Univ. of Kentucky Press, 1967
Karan, P. P., and Jenkins, W. M., *The Himalayan Kingdoms*. Princeton Univ. Press, 1963
Ronaldshay, the Earl of, *Lands of the Thunderbolt*. 2nd ed. London, 1931

BOLIVIA

Capital: La Paz
Population: 4·7m. (1976)
GNP per capita: US$390 (1976)

República de Bolivia

HISTORY. Until 1884, when Bolivia was defeated by Chile, she had a strip bordering on the Pacific which contains extensive nitrate beds and at that time the port of Cobija (which no longer exists). She lost this area to Chile; but in Sept. 1953 Chile declared Arica a free port and, although it is no longer a free port for Bolivian imports, Bolivia still has certain privileges.

AREA AND POPULATION. Boliva is a landlocked state with an area of some 424,160 sq. miles (1,098,580 sq. km). In the series of disastrous wars in the 19th and early 20th centuries its territorial losses to each of 5 neighbouring nations reduced its area from an estimated 1·16m. sq. miles.

The following table shows the area and population of the departments (the capitals of each are given in brackets):

Departments	*Area (sq. km)*	*Census Aug.–Sept. 1950*	*Estimated 1975*	*Per sq. km 1975*
La Paz (La Paz)	133,985	948,446	1,769,800	12·50
Cochabamba (Cochabamba)	55,631	490,475	915,300	15·57
Potosí (Potosí)	118,218	534,399	997,300	7·98
Santa Cruz (Santa Cruz)	370,621	286,145	533,900	1·36
Chuquisaca (Sucre)	51,524	282,980	527,900	9·69
Tarija (Tarija)	37,623	126,752	236,600	5·95
Oruro (Oruro)	53,588	210,260	392,500	6·93
Beni (Trinidad)	213,564	119,770	228,600	0·99
Pando (Cobija)	63,827	19,804	36,900	0·55
Total	1,098,581	3,019,031[1]	5,638,800	4·85

[1] An official estimate allowing for under-enumeration; the total actually recorded was 2,704,165.

Total population (census 1976) 4,687,718.

Population (census 1976) of the principal towns: La Paz, 654,700; Santa Cruz, 237,000; Cochabamba 194,000; Potosí, 77,000; Sucre, 63,000; Tarija, 38,500.

Crude birth rate, 1968, 42 per 1,000 population; crude death rate (1976), 17·96; crude marriage rate (1958); 4; infantile mortality, 174·73 (1976) per 1,000 live births.

The language of the educated classes is Spanish, that of the majority of Indians, Aymará (25·2%) or Quechua (34·4%).

CONSTITUTION AND GOVERNMENT. The Republic of Bolivia was proclaimed on 6 Aug. 1825; its first constitution was adopted on 19 Nov. 1826.

La Paz is the actual capital and seat of the Government, but Sucre is the legal capital and the seat of the judiciary.

National flag: Three horizontal stripes of red, yellow, green, with the arms of Bolivia in the centre.

National anthem: Bolivianos, el hado propicio (words by I. de Sanjinés; tune by B. Vincenti).

The following is a list of presidents since 1931 and the date on which they took office:

Dr Daniel Salamanca, 5 March 1931 (resigned Nov. 1934).
Luis Tejada Sorzano, 27 Nov. 1934 (deposed 17 May 1936).
Col. José David Toro, 17 May 1936 (deposed 13 July 1937).
Lieut.-Gen. German Busch, 13 July 1937 (committed suicide 23 Aug. 1939).
Gen. Carlos Quintanilla (provisional), 23 Aug. 1939–12 March 1940.
Gen. Enrique Peñaranda, 12 March 1940 (deposed 20 Dec. 1943).
Maj. Gualberto Villaroel, 20 Dec. 1943 (deposed and lynched 21 July 1946).
Dr Néstor Guillén (27 July–1 Aug. 1946, provisional).
Chief Justice Monje Gutiérrez (15 Aug. 1946–9 March 1947).
Dr Enrique Hertzog (10 March 1947–23 Oct. 1949).
Dr Mamerto Urriolangoitia (24 Oct. 1949–15 May 1951).
Gen. Hugo Ballivián Rojas (15 May 1951–8 April 1952).
Dr Victor Paz Estenssoro (16 April 1952–6 Aug. 1956).
Dr Hernán Siles Zuazo (6 Aug. 1956–6 Aug. 1960).
Dr Victor Paz Estenssoro (6 Aug. 1960–4 Nov. 1964, deposed).
Gen. René Barrientos Ortuño, 4 Nov. 1964–26 May 1965 (Head of Military Junta).
Gen. René Barrientos Ortuño and Gen. Alfredo Ovando Candia (joint Presidents), 26 May 1965–Jan. 1966.
Gen. Alfredo Ovando Candia, Jan. 1966–6 Aug. 1966.
Gen. René Barrientos Ortuño (Constitutional President killed in air accident), 6 Aug. 1966–27 April 1969.
Dr Luis Adolfo Siles Salinas (deposed), 27 April 1969–26 Sept. 1969.
Gen. Alfredo Ovando Candia, 26 Sept. 1969–6 Oct. 1970.
Gen. Juan José Torres, 7 Oct. 1970–21 Aug. 1971
Gen. Hugo Banzer Suarez, 21 Aug. 1971.

On 7 Oct. 1970 Gen. Juan José Torres proclaimed himself President after an abortive military *coup* had overthrown President Alfredo Ovando Candia. For details of political history 1964–70, *see* THE STATESMAN'S YEAR-BOOK, 1973–74. Gen. Torres was overthrown by a nationalist, military and civilian *coup* by Gen. Banzer Suarez in Aug. 1971. Elections were to be held in Aug. 1975 but are to be held in 1978. President Banzer Suarez stated on 2 Dec. 1977 that he would not stand for a further term.

The Cabinet consists of the President and 19 Ministers of State.

President: Gen. Hugo Banzer Suarez.
Minister of Foreign Affairs: Gen. Oscar Andriázola Valda.

The Republic is divided into 9 departments, established in Jan. 1826, with 98 provinces administered by sub-prefects, and 1,272 cantons administered by corregidores. The supreme authority in each department is vested in a prefect appointed by the President.

DEFENCE. Bolivia is divided into 8 military districts, with divisional headquarters in Viacha, Oruro, Villa Montes, Camiri, Roboré, Riberalta, Santa Cruz, Cochabamba; regional HQ are located at La Paz, Sucre, Tarija, Potosí, Trinidad and Cobija.

Army. The law of 1943 provided for a permanent force of 15,000 men, including the police force and the frontier carabineers, but the standing army in 1977 numbered 17,000 men. Military service is compulsory for all males from the 19th to the 49th year. The Army consists of 14 infantry regiments, 2 motorized regiments, 3 artillery regiments, a paratroop regiment (CITE) and 3 ranger battalions specially trained in anti-guerrilla warfare.

Air Force. The Air Force, established in 1923, has 3 ground attack/operational training squadrons, equipped with 18 Brazilian-built MB 326GB and 16 Canadian-built T-33 armed jet trainers, about 7 modernized Cavalier F-51D Mustang piston-engined fighters supplied under MAP and a few T-28 armed trainers, plus 9 Hughes 500M armed light observation helicopters for counter-insurgency operations. Other types in service include Brazilian T-23 Uirapuru and Fokker S-11, and American T-41 primary trainers, T-6 armed trainers, at least 1 Electra four-turboprop transport, 5 Israeli-built Arava twin-turboprop light transports, 3 Convair 580 twin-turboprop transports, 2 C-130H Hercules, 10 C-47 piston-engined transports with which a military airline service is operated and some light aircraft. Personnel strength is about 6,000.

INTERNATIONAL RELATIONS

Membership. Bolivia is a member of UN, OAS, LAFTA and the Andean Group.

External Debt. The external debt was US$1,418m., Dec. 1976.

ECONOMY

Budget. The foreign-exchange revenue is derived mainly from sales of tin and other non-ferrous metals (furnishing about 55% of export revenue in 1976), but oil and gas produced 30% of export revenue in 1976. Revenue and expenditures in 1m. *pesos bolivianos* balanced as follows: 1967, 860·4; 1968, 1,224·7; 1969, 1,265·3. In 1975 expenditure exceeded income by 142·6. Aid from USA in 1971 was about US$20·2m. The external debt amounted to US$1,650m. in 1976.

Currency. On 1 Jan. 1963 the *peso boliviano* ($b.) was introduced. Current exchange rates are $b.20·4 = US$1 and $b.35 = £1.

Money in circulation at the end of Oct. 1970 totalled 1,396m. *pesos bolivianos.*

Banking. The Banco Central de Bolivia was established in 1911 as Banco de la Nacion Boliviana and re-organized in 1928. The Bank was nationalized in 1939. In 1945 the Banco Central de Bolivia was divided into two independent departments, the Banking Department and the Monetary Department. The latter has the sole power of note issue and must maintain a legal reserve equal to the amount of notes in circulation; 50% of such reserve must be in gold and foreign exchange and 50% in securities. At 31 Dec. 1974 the Bank's gross gold and foreign exchange reserves amounted to US$180m. and Bolivia's net gold and reserves stood at US$121m. The country also has a stand-by agreement of up to US$45·3m. with the International Monetary Fund.

There are Argentine, Brazilian, Peruvian, US and domestic banks.

Weights and Measures. The metric system of weights and measures is used by the administration and prescribed by law, but the old Spanish system is also employed.

ENERGY AND NATURAL RESOURCES

Electricity. Electric power production is expanding. Installed capacity was estimated at 345,800 kw. at the end of 1974. Consumption during 1974 amounted to 967·2m. kwh. Hydro-electric production amounted to 747·5m. kwh.

Oil and Gas. There are petroleum and natural gas deposits in the Santa Cruz–Camiri areas. A pipeline for crude oil connects Caranda (Santa Cruz) with the Pacific coast at Arica (Chile) and a natural gas pipeline to Argentina was inaugurated in May 1972. Bolivia is self-sufficient in petroleum products. All production, refining and internal distribution is now in the hands of *Yacimientos Petroliferos Fiscales Bolivianos* (the State Petroleum Organization), the Bolivian Gulf Oil Company having been nationalized on 17 Oct. 1969. Total production of crude oil in 1977 amounted to 37,000 bbls. Production of natural gas in 1974 was 4,081m. cu. metres. There are 16 foreign consortia currently exploring for hydrocarbons.

Minerals. Mining is the most important industry, accounting for about 55% of the foreign-exchange earnings. About half the mineral mined is tin. Tin mines are at altitudes of from 12,000 to 18,000 ft, where few except native Indians can stand the conditions; transport is costly. Bolivian tin is extracted by shaft-mining, frequently very deep; the ore yields only 3·5% or less of tin and is very refractory; tin is exported in concentrates called *barrilla*, through Pacific ports for refining. A twin dredger has been installed by Grace & Co. to exploit alluvial deposits and another dredger is operated by COMSUR. Total tin production in 1974 was 28,933 tonnes.

A decree of 31 Oct. 1952 nationalized the mining companies of the Patiño, Hochschild and Aramayo groups, which were responsible for about 60% of Bolivia's mineral output. Provisional compensation proposed was: Patiño, US$7·5m.; Hochschild, US$9·25m.; Aramayo, US$4,976,324. Agreements were concluded during 1953 for the gradual payment of compensation on a sliding scale based on prices received for Bolivian tin abroad, but a final settlement has still to be negotiated. The state industry is being run by the *Corporación Minera de Bolivia* (COMIBOL) employing about 23,000 in mining and administrative capacities.

Alluvial gold deposits in the Alto Beni region are being exploited. Co-operative mines at Tipuani produce over 100 kg of gold per month.

One foreign concern is exploring for uranium and the Bolivian Government hopes that more companies will follow. Large deposits of salt are found near Lake Poopó and in the south of Bolivia.

Agriculture. The extensive and still largely undeveloped region east of the Andes comprises about three-quarters of the entire area of the country, and since the agrarian reform of 1952 sugar-cane, rice and cotton have been grown in this *Oriente* in increasing abundance, reaching self-sufficiency in all these products. Output in tonnes in 1974 was: Sugar-cane, 153,607; rice, 75,384; coffee, 13,870; maize, 276,660; potatoes, 748,480; wheat, 62,500, and cotton (lint), 26,700.

In 1976 there were some 2·9m. head of cattle, mostly in the Santa Cruz and Beni departments; some are exported to Peru. The public lands of the state have an area of about 245,000 sq. miles, of which 104,000 sq. miles are reserved for special colonization. The National Agrarian Reform Service reported in Nov. 1969 that since May 1965 it had distributed 5·5m. hectares of land in 323,046 properties.

A colony of Jewish refugees was established in 1940 at Buena Tierra, 60 miles east of La Paz and, more recently, Japanese and Okinawan settlements in the region of Santa Cruz. The Bolivian Development Corporation has a programme for relief of over-population on the barren altiplano and in 1964 resettled 1,217 families in tropical areas.

Forestry. Tropical forests with woods ranging from the 'iron tree' to the light *palo de balsa* are beginning to be exploited. In 1962 the Forestry Service announced proved reserves of 46·3m. hectares, plus a similar amount available for immediate development.

Rubber exports in 1974 earned US$1·9m.

INDUSTRY AND TRADE

Industry. There are few industrial establishments and the country relies on imports for the supply of many consumer goods. However a new investment law passed in 1971 provides incentives and protection for new investment, both foreign and domestic, and for reinvestment in various fields including manufacturing industry, mining, agriculture, construction and tourism. The new law of hydrocarbons encourages foreign participation in developing the petroleum and natural gas resources of the State.

GDP *per capita* (1976) US$640.

Labour. The Ministry of Planning estimated economically active population in 1970 at 1·48m., of whom 1m. were employed in agriculture, 118,300 in industrial manufacture, 35,100 in construction, 74,000 in commerce and finance, 65,000 in central and local government, 47,800 in mining and 41,900 in transport. The ban on trade unions, imposed in 1974, was lifted in 1978.

Commerce. The value of imports and exports in US$1,000 has been as follows:

	1971	*1972*	*1973*	*1974*	*1975*	*1976*
Imports	171,000	189,000	249,500	471,200	510,000	536,000
Exports	212,000	254,000	336,400	627,500	449,000	545,000

Tin ore remains the principal export. Total exports, 1976, of minerals, in concentrates, ingots or solder, were valued at US$378·5m.

Bolivia having no seaport, imports and exports pass chiefly through the ports of Arica and Antofagasta in Chile, Mollendo-Matarani in Peru, through La Quiaca on the Bolivian–Argentine border and through river-ports on the rivers flowing into the Amazon. The chief imports are lard, flour, cooking oil, iron and steel products, mining machinery, motor vehicles, pharmaceuticals, paper products and textiles.

Total trade between UK and Bolivia for 5 years (British Department of Trade returns, in £1,000 sterling):

	1973	*1974*	*1975*	*1976*	*1977*
Imports to UK	19,964	9,684	19,007	24,510	37,333
Exports and re-exports from UK	2,205	4,316	5,279	9,995	12,049

COMMUNICATIONS

Roads. A highway, 808 km long, runs from Cochabamba to the lowland farming region of Santa Cruz. La Paz and Oruro are also connected by a metalled road. Of other main highways (unmetalled) there is one from La Paz through Guaqui into Peru, another from La Paz, *via* Oruro, Potosí, Tarija and Bermejo, into Argentina, with branches to Cochabamba, Sucre and Camiri, passable throughout the year except at the height of the rainy season, and others from Villazón to Villa Montes *via* Tarija, passable during the dry season. The total length of the road system is 37,075 km (1975). Motor vehicles registered in 1972, 68,311.

Railways. The total length of railway open in 1975 was 3,579 km. On 1 Nov. 1974 the State Railway Authority was set up to run all lines in the Western system except the Guaqui–La Paz Railway (owned by the Peruvian Corporation); and also the Corumbá–Santa Cruz line, which until 1964 was administered by a Brazilian–Bolivian Mixed Commission. The new 500-km line Santa Cruz–Yacuiba is administered by an Argentine–Bolivian Mixed Commission. Access to the Pacific is by lines to Antofagasta—of which the Chilean section is owned by the Antofagasta (Chili) and Bolivia Railway Co.—and Arica, and to Mollendo in Peru *via* Guaqui and Arequipa. The Bolivian and Peruvian sections are separated by Lake Titicaca (12,506 ft) which is crossed by steamer. Another railway from Santa Cruz to Trinidad Beni is being built.

Aviation. The national airline is Lloyd Aéreo Boliviano; in 1974 a total of 12,883 hours were flown, carrying 430,518 passengers. The airline runs regular services between La Paz and Lima, São Paulo, Buenos Aires, Miami, Caracas, Salta and Arica as well as many internal services. Braniff International Airways runs regular flights between La Paz, Lima, Buenos Aires, Santiago and Asunción, linking Bolivia (*via* Lima) to the USA. Lufthansa links Bolivia with Europe.

Shipping. Traffic on Lake Titicaca between Guaqui and Puno is carried on by the steamers of the Peruvian Corporation. About 12,000 miles of rivers, in 4 main systems (Beni, Pilcomayo, Titicaca–Desaguadero, Mamoré), are open to navigation by light-draught vessels.

Post and Broadcasting. In Bolivia there were, in 1974, 418 post offices, of these, 205 provided telegraph and telephone services together with a further 245 offices for telegraph and telephone service only. There is telephone service in the towns of La Paz, Cochabamba, Oruro, Sucre, Potosí, Santa Cruz, Tarija and Trinidad with 88,200 telephones. There are about 85 broadcasting stations, of which 7 are state-owned. There is a commercial government television service and a service provided by the National Council for Higher Education.

Newspapers. There are 7 daily newspapers in La Paz, and 2 in Cochabamba. Several other towns have regular newspapers devoted to local news, but most of them appear only a few times a week. An economic monthly journal *Revista Econimica* is produced in Santa Cruz.

JUSTICE, RELIGION, EDUCATION AND WELFARE

Justice. Justice is administered by the Supreme Court, superior district courts (of 5 or 7 judges) and courts of local justice. The Supreme Court, with headquarters at Sucre, is divided into two sections, civil and criminal, of 5 justices each, with the Chief Justice presiding over both. Members of the Supreme Court are chosen on a two-thirds vote of Congress. They nominate the district judges and largely administer the judiciary budget.

Religion. The Roman Catholic is the recognized religion of the state; the free exercise of other forms of worship is permitted. The Catholic Church is under a cardinal (in Sucre), an archbishop (in La Paz), 6 bishops (Cochabamba, Santa Cruz, Oruro, Potosí, Riberalta and Tarija) and vicars apostolic (titular bishops resident in Cueva, Trinidad, San Ignacio de Velasco, Riberalta and Rurrenabaque). Protestants numbered 43,135 in 1962.

By a law of 11 Oct. 1911 all marriages must be celebrated by the civil authorities. Divorce is permitted by a law enacted on 15 April 1932.

Education. Primary instruction is free and obligatory between the ages of 6 and 14 years. Estimates for 1974 show that 989,858 children between 6 and 14 years attended school. All illiterates between 15 and 50 years are obliged to attend literacy classes and in 1977 this represented 40% of the population.

At Sucre, Oruro, Potosí, Cochabamba, Santa Cruz, Tarija, Trinidad and La Paz are universities; La Paz is the most important of them while the San Francisco Xavier University at Sucre is one of the oldest in America, having been founded in 1624.

Health. In 1972 there were 2,143 doctors.

DIPLOMATIC REPRESENTATIVES

OF BOLIVIA IN GREAT BRITAIN (106 Eaton Sq., London, SW1W 9AD)

Ambassador: Gen. Rogelio Miranda Baldivia.

OF GREAT BRITAIN IN BOLIVIA (Avenida Arce 2732–2745, La Paz)

Ambassador: A. C. Buxton, CMG.

OF BOLIVIA IN THE USA (1625 Massachusetts Ave, NW, Washington, D.C. 20036)

Chargé d'Affaires: Juan L. Cariaga.

OF THE USA IN BOLIVIA (Banco Popular Del Peru Bldg, La Paz)

Ambassador: Paul H. Boeker.

OF BOLIVIA TO THE UNITED NATIONS

Ambassador: Dr Mario R. Gutierrez.

Books of Reference

There is a weekly official gazette.

Anuario Geográfico y Estadístico de la República de Bolivia
Anuario del Comercia Exterior de Bolivia
Boletín Mensual de Información Estadistica
Constitución Politica del Estado. La Paz, 1961
Fifer, J. V., *Bolivia: Land, Location and Politics Since 1825.* CUP, 1972
Guillermo, L., *A History of the Bolivian Labour Movement 1848–1971.* CUP, 1977
Osborne, H., *Bolivia: A Land Divided.* R. Inst. of Int. Affairs, 3rd ed. 1964.—*Indians of the Andes*, London, 1952
Pardo Valle, N., *Poligrafía de Bolivia.* La Paz, 1966
Zondag, *The Bolivian Economy, 1952–65.* New York, 1966

BOTSWANA

Capital: Gaborone
Population: 630,379 (1971)
GNP per capita: US$410 (1976)

HISTORY. In 1885 the territory was declared to be within the British sphere; in 1889 it was included in the sphere of the British South Africa Company, but was never administered by the company; in 1890 a Resident Commissioner was appointed, and in 1895, on the annexation of the Crown Colony of British Bechuanaland to the Cape of Good Hope, the British Government was in favour of transferring the Protectorate to the BSA Company, but the three major chiefs of the Bakwena, the Bangwaketse and the Bamangwato went to England to protest against this proposal, and agreement was reached that their country should remain a British Protectorate if they ceded a strip of land on the eastern side of the country for railway construction. This railway was built in 1896–97.

On 30 Sept. 1966 the Bechuanaland Protectorate became an independent and sovereign member of the Commonwealth under the name of the Republic of Botswana.

AREA AND POPULATION. Botswana comprises the territory lying between the Molopo River on the south and the Zambezi on the north, and extending from the Transvaal Province and Rhodesia on the east to South-West Africa on the west. The climate is on the whole sub-tropical and the atmosphere throughout the year is very dry. Area about 222,000 sq. miles (575,000 sq. km); population, according to the census of 1971, is 630,379. The most important tribes are the Bamangwato (216,058), under Chief Ian Khama; the Bakgatla (31,150), under Chief Linchwe II; the Bakwena (62,251), under Chief Bonewamang P. Sechele; the Bangwaketse (71,289), under Chief Seepapitso IV; the Batawana (42,347), under Chief Letsholathebe; the Bamalete (13,861), under Regent Kelemogile Mokgosi (brother of the late Chief Mokgosi, who died in 1966); the Batlokwa (3,711), under Acting Chief Kema Gaborone; the Barolong (10,662), under Chief Besele.

The main business centres (with estimated population, 1976) are Gaborone (37,300), Francistown (25,000), Selebi-Pikwe (23,200) and Lobatse (15,500). The largest villages are Serowe (15,723), Mahalapye (12,056), Kanye (10,664), Maun (9,614), Molepolole (9,448), Ramotswa (7,991) and Mochudi (6,945).

The seat of government is at Gaborone.

CONSTITUTION AND GOVERNMENT. The constitution of the Republic is based on the constitution which came into effect in March 1965, with some minor alterations.

The executive rests with the President of the Republic who is responsible to the National Assembly.

The National Assembly consists of 36 members (32 elected by universal suffrage, 4 nominated by the President and the Attorney-General *ex-officio*). The third general election, held on 26 Oct. 1974, returned 27 members of the Botswana Democratic Party, 2 Botswana People's Party, 2 Botswana National Front and 1 Botswana Independence Party.

The President is an *ex-officio* member of the Assembly. If the President is already a member of the National Assembly, a by-election will be held in the constituency of that member.

There is also a House of Chiefs to advise the Government. It consists of the Chiefs of the 8 principal tribes and 4 members elected by and from among the sub-chiefs in 4 districts.

President of the Republic: Sir Seretse Khama, KBE.

Vice-President and Minister of Finance and Development Planning: Dr Q. K. J. Masire, JP. *External Affairs:* A. M. Mogwe. *Public Service, Information and Broadcasting:* D. K. Kwelagobe. *Mineral Resources and Water Affairs:* Dr G. K. T.

Chiepe. *Agriculture:* E. S. Masisi. *Works and Communications:* J. G. Haskins, OBE. *Education:* K. P. Morake. *Home Affairs:* P. Mmusi. *Health:* L. Seretse. *Local Government and Lands:* L. Makgekgenene. *Commerce and Industry:* M. P. K. Nwako.

Local Government. Local government is carried out by 9 district councils and 4 town councils. Revenue is obtained mainly from local income tax, levied on all inhabitants in the area; from rates in the towns and from central government subventions in the districts.

National flag: Light blue with a horizontal black stripe, edged white, across the centre.

DEFENCE

Army. A small defence force has been created.

Air Force. Initial equipment includes 3 Britten-Norman Defender armed light transports for border patrol, counter-insurgency and casualty evacuation duties.

INTERNATIONAL RELATIONS

Membership. Botswana is a member of UN, OAU, the Commonwealth and is an ACP state of EEC.

ECONOMY

Planning. The National Development Plan 1970–75 envisaged a total capital expenditure of R95,246. The 1973–78 plan aims at a higher rate of economic growth, rural development and fuller employment. It forecast total development of R215·3m. A new 'roll-over' plan for 1976–81 was published in 1976.

Budget. Revenue and expenditure (in Rand) for financial years ending 31 March:

Recurrent Budget:	*1975–76*[1]	*1976–77*[1]	*1977–78*[1]
Revenue	72,700,000	79,868,425	138,719,290
Expenditure	46,600,000	46,767,205	65,798,610
Development Budget:			
Expenditure	33,000,000	...	...

[1] Estimate.

Chief items of revenue, 1973–74: Taxes and duties, R8,906,000; customs and excise, R20,941,000; posts and telegraphs, R2,041,000; government property, R4,613,000; licences, R684,000.

Chief items of expenditure, 1973–74: Education, R2·5m.; medical, R2m.; works and communication, R4·8m.; agriculture, R3·1m.; development, R60·5m.

Public debt, on 31 March 1972, amounted to R33,904,210.

Currency. The currency was formerly the South African Rand but in Oct. 1976 a new currency, the *pula*, was introduced (P1·517 = £1 sterling in Dec. 1977).

Banking. The Standard Bank Ltd and Barclays Bank International have branches in Francistown, Lobatse, Mahalapye, Maun and Gaborone and about 46 agencies throughout the country.

A government-financed National Development Bank was founded in 1964 and had assets of R2·3m. on 30 Sept. 1972.

The post office savings bank has deposits of about R455,000 from 11,000 depositors in mid-1972.

NATURAL RESOURCES

Minerals. The revenue from the diamond mine at Orapa (production started in 1971, 821,914 carats; 1972, over 2m.) and the nickel–copper complex at Selebi-Pikwe (production started in 1974) will become considerably larger than that of agricultural exports. An open-pit coalmine has been developed at Morupule, close to Serowe in the Central District of Botswana.

Mineral resources in north-east Botswana are being investigated, including salt and soda ash on the Sua Pan of the Makgadikgadi Salt Pans, nickel–copper at Selkirk and Phoenix, copper south of Maun and close to Ghanzi, and coal at Mmamabula.

Production of manganese (1973), was 340 tonnes; semi-precious stones (1975), 65,000 kg; diamonds (1975), export value P31·9m.; coal (1975) 68,639 tonnes; copper–nickel matté (1975), 16,513 tonnes.

Agriculture. Cattle-rearing and dairying are the chief industries but the country is more a pastoral than an agricultural one, crops depending entirely upon the rainfall. However, increasing numbers of boreholes are being established where underground supply is adequate. In 1975 a reform of land ownership, which allows for more modern land use, was announced.

The abattoir at Lobatse, opened in Oct. 1954, is of great importance to the country's economy. In 1976 the number of cattle was 2·8m.; goats, 1·4m.; sheep, 400,000; poultry, 295,000.

LABOUR. In 1973, 13·7% of the wage-earners were employed in agriculture, 17·9% in construction, 22·6% in central government, 2·6% in commerce and finance, 5·3% in manufacturing and 8% in mining and quarrying.

COMMERCE. Chief items of import in 1973: Cereals (R4·03m.), sugar (R1·88m.), petroleum products (R6·07m.), iron and steel products (R8·68m.), machinery (R14·75m.), transport equipment (R13·47m.). Chief items of export in 1973: Carcases (R4·22m.), boneless beef (R27·13m.), small stock (R72,738), edible offal (R1·23m.), compound offal (R448,281), hides and skins (R1·46m.) and by-products (R1·18m.). Total export from the abattoir (1973), R36,491,260. Mineral exports in 1973 totalled R23·23m.

Botswana is a member of the South African customs union with Lesotho, the Republic of South Africa and Swaziland.

Total trade between Botswana and UK (British Department of Trade returns, in £1,000 sterling):

	1973	*1974*	*1975*	*1976*	*1977*
Imports to UK	12,204	2,532	10,606	24,935	39,843
Exports and re-exports from UK	748	1,322	1,388	1,333	3,017

TOURISM. The infrastructure for tourism is being developed and will allow for over 50,000 tourists from 1975.

COMMUNICATIONS

Roads. There are 8,000 km of roads, all of which are maintained by the Ministry of Works and Communications. In 1973 there were 9,427 registered motor vehicles.

Aviation. There are 3 airports. Regular international flights are flown by Zambia Airways, Air Botswana and SAA into Gaborone.

Post and Broadcasting. The telegraph, telephone and railway (630·4 km) lines from Cape Town to Rhodesia traverse Botswana. Wireless communication has been established between headquarters at Gaborone and various district offices and police stations. There are 39 post offices and 42 agencies. There were 7,947 telephones installed in 1976.

JUSTICE, EDUCATION AND WELFARE

Justice. The Botswana Court of Appeal succeeded the Court of Appeal for Basutoland, Bechuanaland and Swaziland, which was established in 1954. It has jurisdiction in respect of criminal and civil appeals emanating from the High Court of Botswana. Further appeal lies in certain circumstances to the Judicial Committee of the Privy Council.

The High Court for Botswana succeeded the High Court for Bechuanaland, which was established in 1938. It has jurisdiction in all criminal and civil causes and proceedings. Subordinate courts and African courts are in each of the 12 administrative districts.

Police. The police force consists of 157 officers and subordinate officers, 183 n.c.o.s and 919 other ranks.

Education (1975). There were 323 primary, 15 secondary, 15 governmental aided, 14 private secondary and continuation, 26 vocational training schools and 3 teacher-training colleges. The great majority of the primary schools and the junior secondary schools are controlled, under the Chief Education Officer, by school committees with district-council and mission representatives. Three secondary schools and the homecraft centre are run by missions with Government support; Moeng College by a governing council; the remaining schools by the Government. District-council schools are financed by district-council treasuries and assisted with grants from the Central Government. Enrolment in primary schools in 1975 was 116,293; government secondary, 8,434; private secondary, 3,664; vocational, 1,699; in teacher-training colleges, 489. University students on the Botswana campus of the University of Botswana and Swaziland 289 and university students abroad numbered 218. Total recurrent expenditure on education was R6,155,589 for the year ended 31 March 1974 and capital expenditure (1975) R5,592,903.

In 1971, an estimated 20% of the total population were literate. In 1975, 71% of children of primary school age were receiving instruction.

The national language is Setwsana, the official language English.

Welfare (1975). There were 11 general hospitals, a maternity centre, a mental home, 7 health centres, 68 clinics and 177 health posts. Total number of beds, 1,871. There were 42 registered medical practitioners, 2 dentists, 222 practising registered nurses and 150 enrolled nurses. The health facilities are the concern of central and local government, medical missions, mining companies and voluntary organizations. Government expenditure on medical services, P5m. for the year ended 31 March 1975.

DIPLOMATIC REPRESENTATIVES

OF BOTSWANA IN GREAT BRITAIN
(162 Buckingham Palace Rd., London, SW1)

High Commissioner: Aloysius William Kgarebe (accredited 21 March 1978).

OF GREAT BRITAIN IN BOTSWANA (Private Bag 23, Gaborone)

High Commissioner: W. Turner, CMG.

OF BOTSWANA IN THE USA
(4301 Connecticut Ave., NW, Washington, D.C., 20008)

Ambassador: Bias Mookodi.

OF THE USA IN BOTSWANA (P.O. Box 90, Gaborone)

Ambassador: Donald R. Norland.

OF BOTSWANA TO THE UNITED NATIONS

Ambassador: Dr Thomas Tlou.

Books of Reference

Statistical Information: The Chief Information Officer, P.O. Box 51, Gaborone, Botswana publishes *Facts About Botswana*, the monthly *Kutlwano* and *The Botswana Daily News*.

Annual Report, 1965. HMSO, 1966
Botswana: Resources and Development. Pretoria, 1970
Report on the Population Census, 1971. Government Printer, 1972
Report of the Economic Survey Mission. HMSO, 1960
Selwyn, P., *Industries in the Southern African Periphery*. London, 1975
Sillery, A., *Botswana: A Short Political History*. London, 1974
Young, B. A., *Bechuanaland*. HMSO, 1966

BRAZIL

Capital: Brasília
Population: 110·1m. (1976)
GNP per capita: US$1,140 (1976)

República Federativa do Brasil

HISTORY. Brazil was discovered on 22 April 1500 by the Portuguese Admiral Pedro Alvares Cabral, and thus became a Portuguese settlement; in 1815 the colony was declared 'a kingdom', and on 13 May 1822 Dom Pedro, eldest surviving son of King João of Portugal, was chosen 'Perpetual Defender' of Brazil by a National Congress. He proclaimed the independence of the country on 7 Sept. 1822, and was chosen 'Constitutional Emperor and Perpetual Defender' on 12 Oct. 1822. He resigned in 1831 and, 9 years later, his 14-year-old son Pedro became the second Emperor of Brazil.

AREA AND POPULATION. Brazil is bounded east by the Atlantic and on its north-west and southern borders by all the South American countries except Chile and Ecuador. Population as at 1 Sept. 1970 (census) and July 1976 (estimate):

State and Capital	*Area (sq. km)*	*Census 1970*	*Estimate 1976*
North	3,581,180	3,603,860	4,347,400
Rondônia[1] (Pôrto Velho[2])	243,044	111,064	147,000
Acre (Rio Branco)	152,589	215,299	256,400
Amazonas[3] (Manaus)	1,564,445	955,235	1,120,100
Roraima (Boa Vista[2])	230,104	40,885	49,700
Pará (Bélem)[4]	1,250,722	2,167,018	2,626,100
Amapá (Macapá[2])	140,276	114,359	148,100
North-east	1,548,672	28,111,927	32,822,600
Maranhão (São Luis)	328,663	2,992,686	3,399,000
Piaul (Teresina)[7]	250,934	1,680,573	2,047,900
Ceará (Fortaleza)[7]	150,630	4,361,603	5,257,700
Rio Grande do Norte (Natal)	53,015	1,550,244	1,913,300
Paraíba (João Pessoa)	56,372	2,382,617	2,729,200
Pernambuco (Recife)[11]	98,281	5,160,640	5,994,700
Alagoas (Maceió)	27,731	1,588,109	1,828,700
Fernando de Noronha[5,6]	26	1,241	...
Sergipe (Aracajú)	21,994	900,744	1,011,500
Bahia (Salvador)	561,026	7,493,470	8,640,600
South-east:[8]	924,934	39,853,498	46,486,600
Minas Gerais (Belo Horizonte)	587,172	11,487,415	12,764,000
Espírito Santo[9] (Vitória)	45,597	1,599,333	1,750,300
Rio de Janeiro (Rio de Janeiro)[13]	42,912 1,356	4,742,884 4,251,918	10,704,200
São Paulo (São Paulo)	247,898	17,771,948	21,268,100
South	577,723	16,496,493	19,865,200
Paraná (Curitiba)	199,554	6,929,868	8,791,400
Santa Catarina (Florianópolis)	95,985	2,901,734	3,450,700
Rio Grande do Sul (Pórto Alegre)	282,184	6,664,891	7,623,100
Central West	1,879,455	5,073,259	6,601,700
Mato Grosso (Cuiabá)	1,231,549	1,597,090	2,097,300
Goiás (Goiânia)[12]	642,092	2,938,677	4,504,400
Distrito Federal (Brasília)	5,814	537,492	...
Total	8,511,965[10]	93,139,037	110,123,500

Density of census population, 1970, was about 11 per sq. km.

The 1970 census showed 46,331,343 males and 46,807,694 females. The urban and suburban population comprised 36·2% in 1950, 45·1% in 1960 and 55·9% in 1970.

The language is Portuguese.

The new capital, Brasília, was inaugurated 21 April 1960. The federal district (5,814 sq. km) was detached from the west-central state of Goiás, about 1,000 km north-west of Rio de Janeiro.

In 1970 the census population of the principal cities was: São Paulo, 5,924,615; Rio de Janeiro, 4,251,918; Belo Horizonte, 1,235,030; Recife, 1,060,701; Salvador, 1,007,195; Pôrto Alegre, 885,545; Fortaleza, 857,980; Nova Iguaçu, 727,140; Belém, 633,374; Curitiba, 609,026; Brasília, 537,492; Duque de Caxias, 431,397; Santa Andre, 418,826; Goiânia, 380,773; Manaus, 311,622.

The number of immigrants, between 1820 and 1953 was over 5m., but it is estimated that only one-half remained. Immigrants in recent years have numbered:

	1972	*1973*	*1974*	*1975*
Portuguese	1,095	581	426	959
Japanese	472	25	75	111
Spanish	470	225	244	410
Italian	535	402	478	1,356
Others	6,195	4,698	5,543	8,730
Total	8,767	5,931	6,766	11,566

Pierson, D., *Negroes in Brazil.* Chicago, 1942.—*Survey of Literature on Brazil of Sociological Significance.* Cambridge, Mass., 1945

Ramos, A., *The Negro in Brazil.* Washington, 1939.—*Las Poblaciones del Brazil.* Mexico City, 1945

CONSTITUTION AND GOVERNMENT. On 15 Nov. 1889 Dom Pedro II (1825–91) was dethroned by a revolution, and Brazil declared a republic.

Presidents since the establishment of the republic:

Marshal Deodoro da Fonseca, 15 Nov. 1889–23 Nov. 1891 (resigned).

Marshal Floriano Peixoto (Acting), 23 Nov. 1891–15 Nov. 1894.

Dr Prudente de Moraes Barros, 15 Nov. 1894–15 Nov. 1898.

Dr Manuel Ferraz de Campos Salles, 15 Nov. 1898–15 Nov. 1902.

Dr Francisco da Paula Rodrigues Alves, 15 Nov. 1902–15 Nov. 1906.

Dr Affonso Penna, 15 Nov. 1906–14 June 1909 (died).

Dr Nilo Peçanha (Acting), 14 June 1909–15 Nov. 1910.

Marshal Hermes da Fonseca, 15 Nov. 1910–15 Nov. 1914.

Dr Wenceslau Braz, 15 Nov. 1914–15 Nov. 1918.

Dr Francisco da Paula Rodrigues Alves.[1]

Dr Delphim Moreira (Acting), 15 Nov. 1918–28 July 1919.

Dr Epitácio da Silva Pessoa, 28 July 1919–15 Nov. 1922.

[1] Owing to illness did not take office; died 16 Jan. 1919.

---

[1] The name 'Território Federal do Guaporé' was changed to 'Território Federal de Rondônia' on 17 Feb. 1956.

[2] Raised to the status of territorial capitals in 1943; previously, Pôrto Velho and Boa Vista belonged to the state of Amazonas and Macapá to the state of Pará.

[3] Excluding 2,680 sq. km in dispute with the state of Pará.

[4] Includes an area of 2,680 sq. km to be demarcated between states of Amazonas and Pará.

[5] Including 8 sq. km of islets.

[6] Territory created in 1942.

[7] A region of 2,614 sq. km is to be delimited between the states of Piauí and Ceará.

[8] Including 10,153 sq. km and population figures of 160,072 and 384,297 respectively for 1950 and 1960 corresponding to the Região da Serra dos Aimorés. Territory in dispute between Minas Gerais and Espírito Santo and subsequently separated from both. Dispute settled 1963.

[9] Including the islands of Trindade and Martim Vaz.

[10] 3,286,000 sq. miles.

[11] Including Fernando de Noronha territory.

[12] Including federal district.

[13] According to Complementary Law no. 20 of 1 July 1974, the States of Rio de Janeiro and Guanabara were consolidated, since 15 March 1975, into a single political unit, the State of Rio de Janeiro with the City of Rio de Janeiro as its capital city.

Dr Arthur Bernardes, 15 Nov. 1922–15 Nov. 1926.
Dr Washington Luiz Pereira de Souza, 15 Nov. 1926–25 Oct. 1930 (deposed).
Dr Getúlio Dornelles Vargas, 26 Oct. 1930–29 Oct. 1945 (resigned).
Dr José Linhares (Provisional President), 30 Oct. 1945–31 Jan. 1946.
Gen. Eurico Gaspar Dutra, 31 Jan. 1946–31 Jan. 1951.
Dr Getúlio Dornelles Vargas, 31 Jan. 1951–died 24 Aug. 1954.
Dr João Café Filho, 24 Aug. 1954–8 Nov. 1955 (resigned).
Carlos Coimbra da Luz (Acting), 8 Nov. 1955–11 Nov. 1955 (deposed).
Nereu Ramos (Acting), 11 Nov. 1955–31 Jan. 1956.
Juscelino Kubitschek, 31 Jan. 1956–31 Jan. 1961.
Jânio da Silva Quadros, 31 Jan. 1961–25 Aug. 1961 (resigned).
João Belchior Marques Goulart, 7 Sept. 1961–31 March 1964 (deposed).
Marshal Humberto de A. Castelo Branco, 15 April 1964–15 March 1967.
Marshal Artur da Costa e Silva, 15 March 1967–31 Aug. 1969 (resigned).
Gen. Emilio Garrastazu Medici, 30 Oct. 1969–15 March 1974.

On 24 Jan. 1967 both houses of Congress in joint session approved the new constitution and press law which came into force on 15 March. An amendment to the constitution, which came into force on 30 Oct. 1969, was issued on 17 Oct. The present constitution provides for the indirect election of the President and Vice-President by an electoral college, comprising the members of Congress and delegates from the state legislatures; it grants powers to the President to issue decree-laws on matters connected with the economy and national security; it gives the President authority to intervene in any of the 22 states without consultation with Congress and the right to declare a state of siege and to rule by decree. President and Vice-President are elected for a 6-year term and are not immediately re-eligible. The Senate elected for 8 years, the rs.

The name of the country was changed from 'United States of Brazil' to 'Brazil' and later to 'República Federativa do Brasil'.

Freedom of speech and press are not absolute: war propaganda, the teaching of 'subversive doctrines' and the dissemination of race or class prejudices are banned, as also are political parties opposed to democracy, the existing multi-party system or to 'fundamental human rights' which include the right to own private property. The Supreme Electoral Court on 7 May 1947 declared the Communist Party illegal.

The Institutional Act No. 5 issued on 13 Dec. 1968 was incorporated into the new constitution through an amendment on 17 Oct. 1969. This gives the President power to cancel citizens' political rights for periods of 10 years. The Congress renewed its session on 22 Oct. 1969 and elections were held on 15 Nov. 1970 and Nov. 1974.

Voting is compulsory for men and women between the ages of 18 and 65 and optional for persons over 65. Enlisted men and illiterates (who comprise about 40% of the adult population) may not vote.

President of the Republic: Gen. Ernesto Geisel, assumed office 15 March 1974.
Vice-President: Adalberto Pereira dos Santos.
Minister of Foreign Affairs: Antônio Francisco Azeredo da Silveira.

There are Secretaries of State at the head of the following Ministries: Finance; Justice; Interior; Foreign Affairs; Transport; Communications; Agriculture; Labour; Education and Culture; Health; Industry and Commerce; Mines and Power; Welfare and Social Security; and the Ministries of Army, Marine and Air.

National flag: Green, with yellow lozenge enclosing a blue sphere, with 22 white stars, of which 5 form the southern cross, and the motto *Ordem e Progresso.*

National anthem: Ouviram do Ipiranga (words by J. O. Duque Estrada; tune by F. M. da Silva).

Local Government. Brazil consists of 21 states, 4 federal territories (Rondônia, Roraima, Amapá, Fernando de Noronha) and 1 federal district. Each state has its distinct administrative, legislative and judicial authorities, its own constitution and laws, which must, however, agree with the constitutional principles of the Union. The states may unite or split or form new states. Taxes on interstate commerce, levied by individual states, are prohibited. The governors and members of the legislatures are elected, but magistrates are appointed and are not removable from office save by judicial sentence. Rio de Janeiro and Guanabara became one state in 1975.

The National Congress issued a decree and, in Oct. 1977, the President of Republic enacted the law by which the State of Mato Grosso was divided in 2 distinct states: the now established State of Mato Grosso do Sul to be installed on 1 Jan. 1979, when its first governor will take office, and the State of Mato Grosso.

DEFENCE

Army. Under the constitution military service is compulsory for every Brazilian man from 21 years of age to 45. The terms of service are 9 years (from the 21st to the 30th years of age) in the Army 'first line' (1 in the ranks, the rest in the reserve) and 14 years (from the 30th to the 45th years of age) in the army 'second line' (7 in the 'second line' and 7 in the reserve of the same). The men in the Territorial Army also have an annual training of 2 to 4 weeks. The army is organized in 7 divisions, each with up to 4 armoured, mechanized or motorized infantry brigades; 7 other infantry and 1 parachute brigades; total strength, 170,000.

Navy. The principal ships[2] of the Brazilian Navy are as follows:

Completed	*Name*	*Standard displacement Tons*	*Armour Belt In.*	*Armour Guns In.*	*Principal armament*	*Torpedo tubes*	*Shaft horse-power*	*Speed Knots*
				Aircraft Carrier				
1945	Minas Gerais[1]	15,890	—	—	10 40-mm. AA	—	40,000	24

[1] Ex-*Vengeance*, purchased from Great Britain in 1956.

[2] The 10,000-ton cruiser *Tamandaré* (ex-*St. Louis*), of the 'St. Louis' class purchased from USA in 1951 was offered for sale in 1975. The cruiser *Barroso* (ex-*Philadelphia*) of the 'Brooklyn' class, also transferred in 1951, was listed for disposal in 1973.

There are also 9 diesel-powered submarines (2 new built in Britain and 7 old *ex*-US), 4 new destroyer leaders (or large frigates), the *Constituição, Defensoza, Liberal* and *Niteroi*, built in Britain, 12 old *ex*-US destroyers, 10 fleet tug type corvettes, 6 coastal minesweepers, 1 river monitor, 5 river patrol ships, 6 coastal gunboats, 1 submarine rescue ship, 2 tank landing ships, 4 transports, 2 oilers, 1 repair ship, 6 survey ships, 11 survey launches, 10 small river patrol boats, 48 minor landing craft, 2 buoy tenders (*ex*-coastal minesweepers) and 3 tugs. There are also 3 floating docks.

The new construction programme includes 1 submarine (being built in Britain), 2 more guided-missile destroyer leaders, the *Independencia* and *Uniao* of the 'Niteroi' class, and 2 coastal minesweepers.

Projected ships include 1 helicopter carrier, 3 anti-aircraft frigates, 6 to 12 corvettes, 4 coastal patrol craft, 1 replenishment oiler, 18 minor landing craft, 1 survey ship and 3 tugs.

Naval bases are at Rio de Janeiro, Aratu (Bahia), Belém, Natal, Recife, Salvador, with a river base at Ladario.

The Fleet Air Arm was formed on 26 Jan. 1965. Aircraft obtained from the USA for service on the carrier include 6 Sikorsky SH-3D and 5-SH-34J helicopters and 5 S-2A Tracker anti-submarine aircraft, the latter being operated by the Air Force (to be replaced by Navy S-2E Grumman Trackers). Three Wasp light anti-submarine helicopters were obtained from Britain in 1965, and have been followed by 7 turbine-powered Whirlwind Srs. 3s and 6 American-built Fairchild Hiller FH 1100 light observation helicopters. Nine Westland Lynx WC 13 helicopters are being provided for the destroyer leader/frigates of the 'Niteroi' class.

The active personnel in 1977 was 46,000 (3,900 officers and 42,100 men), including marines and auxiliary corps.

Air Force. The Air Force, formed in 1918, has been independent of the Army and Navy since 1941. It is organized in 6 zones, centred on Belém, Recife, Rio de Janeiro, São Paulo, Porto Alegre and Brasília. The 1a ALADA (air defence wing) has 11 Mirage IIIE fighters and 4 Mirage IIID trainers, integrated with Roland mobile short-range surface-to-air missile systems deployed by the Army, and a radar/communications/computer network. One fighter group has 2 squadrons of F-5E Tiger II supersonic fighter-bombers and two-seat F-5Bs; 2 others operate AT-26 (Aermacchi MB 326G) Xavante light jet attack/trainers, licence-built in Brazil. Counter-insurgency squadrons are equipped with AT-26 Xavantes for reconnaissance and attack, and with Neiva Regente lightplanes, Universal armed piston-engined trainers, and UH-1D/H Iroquois and armed JetRanger helicopters for liaison and observation. There is an ASW group of S-2A/E Trackers for shore-based and carrier-based operations; 3 air-sea rescue units operate RC-130E Hercules reconnaissance transports, HU-16 Albatross amphibians and UH-1D Iroquois helicopters respectively; currently entering service for maritime duties is the EMB-111 coastal patrol aircraft developed from the Brazilian-designed Bandeirante twin-turboprop transport. Equipment of transport units includes 1 group of C-130E/H Hercules transports and KC-130H Hercules tankers; 1 group made up of a squadron of HS 748 and C-95 Bandeirante turboprop transports and a second squadron of HS 748s with large freight doors; 1 troop-carrier group with DHC-5 Buffaloes; and 6 independent squadrons with Bandeirantes and Buffaloes. The VIP transport group has 2 Boeing 737s, 8 HS 125 twin-jet light transports, some Bandeirantes, 5 Embraer Xingu twin-turboprop pressurized transports and 6 JettRanger helicopters. Training is performed primarily on locally-built Aerotec T-23 Uirapuru *ab initio* trainers, T-25 Universal basic trainers, and AT-26 Xavante armed jet basic trainers.

Personnel strength about 43,000, with more than 600 aircraft of all types.

INTERNATIONAL RELATIONS

Membership. Brazil is a member of UN, OAS and LAFTA.

ECONOMY

Budget. Receipts and expenditures for the federal government (excluding states, federal district and municipalities) for calendar years have been as follows in 1m. Cr$ (paper):

	1972[2]	*1973*[2]	*1974*[1,2]	*1975*[1,2]	*1976*[1,2]	*1977*[1,2]
Revenue	39,420	52,726	58,556	113,396	189,377	287,541
Expenditure	38,198	50,767	58,556	113,396	189,377	287,541

[1] Estimates. [2] Cr$1m.

Chief items of revenue were estimated in 1976 as follows (in 1,000 Cr$): Taxes, 116,365,700; government property, 546,423. Principal items of expenditure: Finance, 2,567,660; communication, 3,612,676; army, 6,795,000; education, 8,351,037; navy, 5,189,013; aviation, 6,194,137; transport, 47,291,037.

The foreign debt (including states and municipalities) of Brazil on 30 June 1975 amounted to US$19,500m. Internal funded federal and states debt, 31 Dec. 1974, was Cr$32,949m. and 1975, was Cr$60,100m.

Currency. On 15 May 1970 the *cruzeiro* (Cr$) became the monetary unit, equivalent to 1 *new cruzeiro*; it is divided into 100 *centavos*. The exchange rate was in 1977 US$1 = Cr$13; £1 = Cr$18·67.

Banking. The Bank of Brazil (founded in 1808 and reorganized in 1906, with an authorized capital of NCr$60m. from 1967) is not a central bank of issue but a closely controlled commercial bank; it had 962 branches in 1975 throughout the republic. On 31 Dec. 1975 deposits were Cr$71,956·8m.

On 31 Dec. 1964 the Banco Central da República do Brasil was founded.

The country's note circulation, 31 Dec. 1974 was Cr$20,807m. and 1975, Cr$31,031m. Since Sept. 1939 gold and dollar supply has risen from US$40m. to US$420m., of which the government's gold was US$288m. in May 1961.

Banking institutions numbered 106, with 8,544 agencies in Dec. 1975. All banks had on 31 Dec. 1975 deposits of Cr$277,902·9m. and loans of Cr$303,572·6m. Foreign banks had total assets of Cr$3,213,390·2m. in 1975.

Weights and Measures. The metric system has been in use in all official departments since 1862. It was made compulsory in 1872, but the ancient measures are still partly employed in remote districts. They are: *libra* = 1·012 lb. avoirdupois;

arroba = 32·98 lb.; *quintal* = 129·54 lb.; *alqueire* (of Roi) = 1 Imperial bushel, or 40 litres; *oitava* = 55·34 grains.

ENERGY AND NATURAL RESOURCES

Electricity. Brazil's potential capacity for electric power production is estimated at 55m. kw., one of the largest in the world. Production in 1974, 71,468,641 mwh. Consumption, 1975, 66m. mwh. Of the total capital invested in industrial concerns (US$1,779,786,350), 49% was foreign-owned.

Oil. The entire petroleum industry was placed under federal control in April 1938; there are, 1974, 12 refineries. The country imports substantial amounts (40,563,000 tonnes in 1976) to supplement its total production. Crude oil output, 1976, 8,481,000 tonnes.

Minerals. Brazil is the only source of high-grade quartz crystal in commercial quantities; exports in 1975, 2,042 tonnes. It is an important source of industrial diamonds (exports, 1974, 2,417 grammes); the second largest western producer of chrome ore (reserves of 4m. tonnes; output, 1974, 424,339 tonnes; 1973, 327,461 tonnes); fifth in the output of mica (81 tonnes in 1974); third in zirconium, 2,518 tonnes in 1974; she is the largest producer of beryllium, output (1974) 43 tonnes; graphite (1974), 28,625 tonnes; titanium ore (1974), 6,743 tonnes, and magnesite (1974), 365,661 tonnes. Along the coasts of the states of Rio de Janeiro, Espírito Santo and Bahia are found monazite sands containing thorium; reserves are estimated at 100,000 tons. Manganese ores of high content are important (reserves in the Amapá region alone are estimated at 10m. tonnes); output, 1974, 2,800,239 tonnes. Output of tungsten ore, 1974, totalled 1,641 tonnes. Mine production of lead (1974) 304,125, (1973) 324,122 tonnes. Asbestos production (1974) 818,768, (1975) 1,051,309 tonnes. Coal deposits exist in Rio Grande do Sul, Santa Catarina, Paraná and Sâo Paulo. Total reserves are estimated at 5,000m. tonnes; output (1975), 6·31m. tonnes.

Iron is found chiefly in Minas Gerais, notably the Cauê Peak at Itabira. The Government is now opening up what is believed to be one of the richest iron-ore deposits in the world, with estimated reserves of 35,000m. tonnes, of which half rival the Swedish ores in iron content (about 68·5%) and have lower silica and phosphorus contents. Total output of iron ore, 1974, mainly from the Cia. Vale do Rio Doce mine at Itabira, was (1975) 108,162,444 tonnes. The National Iron and Steel Co. at Volta Redonda, State of Rio de Janeiro, furnishes a substantial part of Brazil's steel. Brazil's total output: Pig-iron (1975) 7,052,665 tonnes, (1974) 5,846,014 tonnes; ingots castings (1975) 8,308,046 tonnes. (1974) 7,502,473 tonnes.

Production of aluminium was started in Minas Gerais in 1945; output of bauxite, 1974, 858,457 tonnes; 1973, 849,218 tonnes. Exports of barytes, 1974, was 46 tonnes. There were no exports of barytes, 1975 and 1976. Cement output, 1975, was 16,737,458 tonnes; 1974, 14,919,644 tonnes. Output of phosphate rock, 1968, was 648,793 tonnes, plus 582,703 tonnes of apatite.

Gold is found in practically every state, though large-scale mining is confined to a single mine in Minas Gerais; the production in 1974, was 5,864 kg. Silver output, 1974, 16,378 kg. Salt output (1975), 2,145,345 tonnes. Diamond districts are Diamantina Grão Mogol, Chapada Diamantina, Bagagem, Goiás and Mato Grosso; output in 1972 was 99,087 carats.

AGRICULTURE. 44·07% of Brazil's population is rural, and 75% of her foreign exchange derives from agricultural exports. Production (in tonnes):

	1974	*1975*[1]		*1974*	*1975*[1]
Bananas	6,974,380	7,080,880	Oranges	6,232,128	6,333,307
Beans	2,238,012	2,270,747	Potatoes	1,672,508	1,668,874
Castor beans	573,135	352,577	Sweet potatoes	. . .	. . .
Cocoa	164,616	281,766	Rice	6,482,920	7,537,589
Coffee	3,220,000	2,526,328	Sisal	293,021	314,254
Cotton, raw	1,958,758	1,750,556	Soya	7,876,209	9,892,299
Jute	31,554	41,426	Sugar-cane	96,412,043	91,386,073
Maize	16,284,713	16,353,645	Tobacco	304,095	287,121
Mandioca	24,714,631	25,811,981	Wheat	2,858,530	1,787,850

[1] Preliminary.

The 4 states of São Paulo, Paraná, Espírito Santo and Minas Gerais are the principal districts for coffee-growing. Large plantations or fazendas with more than 100,000 trees are the rule. Output, 1974, from 2,269,738 hectares, 3·22m. tonnes; exports (1975), 781,990 tonnes. Between 1962 and 1966 about 1,650m. coffee trees were destroyed.

Export of cocoa was nationalized in May 1943, but in 1952 reverted to private enterprise. Bahia furnishes 90% of the output; in 1974 total output was 164,616 tonnes from 416,175 hectares. Two crops a year are grown. The US takes one-half of the crop. Castor-bean output usually exceeds 250,000 tonnes; output, 1973, 448,863 tonnes (1974, 573,135) from 496,026 hectares.

Tobacco output was 304,095 tonnes in 1974. In 1976, 101,161 tonnes were exported.

Sugar production, 1974, was 96,412,043 tonnes. Exports in 1975, 1·73m. tonnes.

Brazil now ranks second only to the US in production of oranges, output 1973, 4,930m. tonnes; 1974, 6,232m.; 1975, 6,333m. Output of bananas, 1973, 7,071,540 tonnes; 1974, 6,974,380; 1975, 7,080,880. Cotton lint and seed, estimate 1970, 2,426,963 tonnes. Exports of cotton, 1976, 5,579 tonnes; 1975, 107,202. Brazil formerly furnished only 10% of her own requirements in wheat (average output, 1934–38, 144,000 tonnes); output, 1973, 2,031,538 tonnes; 1974, 2,858,530; 1975, 1,787,850; imports, 63,165 tonnes in 1975. Rice is important; output (rough rice), 1975, was 7,537,589 tonnes.

Rubber is another natural product of the country, chiefly in the states of Acre, Amazonas and Pará. Output, 1975, 149,196 tonnes (gross weight); peak reached in 1912 (when rubber realized US$3 a lb.) was 42,510 gross tons. Output of tyres in local factories has risen from 421,765 units (tyres and tubes) in 1940 to 40,486,936 in 1974. Brazilian consumption of rubber in 1975, was 263,510 tonnes. Brazil is the chief source of carnaúba wax, used for electric insulation and gramophone records, exporting 7,320 tonnes in 1975. Caroá fibre is grown as a substitute for Indian jute; production, 1970, 1,463 tonnes. Jute output, 1975, 41,426 tonnes. Plantations of tung trees established in 1930 (4m. trees in 1946) are beginning to yield tung oils in commercial quantities; output of tung, 1973, 7,763 tonnes.

Livestock (in 1,000): 1974, 92,495 cattle, 34,191 swine, 18,877 sheep, 7,172 goats, 5,215 horses, 1,566 asses and 1,756 mules. In 1975, 8·5m. cattle, 7·2m. swine, 1·1m. sheep and lambs, 400,000 goats, 256·9m. poultry and rabbits were slaughtered for meat.

Fisheries. The fishing industry totalled a fleet of 154,695 vessels in 1968; the catch in 1974 was 815,720 tonnes.

In 1971 the sovereignty over territorial waters, including fishing rights, was extended to 200 miles.

INDUSTRY AND TRADE

Industry. The most important manufacturing industry in Brazil is the weaving industry, which employs about 14% of all industrial workers; nearly 52% of the factories are in São Paulo and the remaining 48% in other states. Output of cotton textiles, 1974, was 818,499m. metres of cloth. Exports of cotton piece-goods, 1974, were 19,806 tonnes and 1975, 20,950 tonnes. Rayon yarn output, 1970, was 42,183 tonnes. In all, about 650 textile-mills are working. Local production and assembly of vehicles, including automobiles (920,834 in 1975) and tractors (59,851 in 1975), is steadily increasing. Fiat are planning to build a factory at Betim.

A paper-mill, reported to be the largest pulp-and-paper mill in South America, is at Monte Alegre, Paraná. Brazil's output of paper, 1975, was 1,688,323 tonnes.

Foreign investment is encouraged by special tax holidays for companies locating in certain regions. There is also a 10-year tax holiday for hotel and tourist investments and export profits tax exemption.

GDP *per capita* (1973) US$768.

Commerce. In 1957 Brazil modernized her 20-year-old tariff (at present duties are levied mainly on volume and not on values) in order to protect her infant industries and to increase government revenue. Her present tariffs furnish 12% of the

Government's revenue (*see* under GATT). She ratified the Treaty of Montevideo on 3 Feb. 1961 (*see* LAFTA).

Imports and exports for calendar years in Cr$1,000:

	1972	*1973*	*1974*	*1975*	*1976*
Imports	28,060,426	37,916,357	94,655,153	107,671,765	...
Exports	23,588,387	37,827,974	53,768,654	68,773,057	107,105,989

Converted into US$1m., these trade figures were:

	1973	*1974*	*1975*	*1976*	*1977*
Imports	6,192·0	12,641	12,210	12,347	11,999
Exports	6,199·2	7,951	8,670	10,128	12,139

Exports in 1975, 92·9m. tonnes; 1976, 89·7m. Imports in 1975, 52·8m. tonnes; 1976, 61·5m. tonnes.

Principal imports in 1975 were (in US$1m.): Fuel and lubricants, 3,100; machinery and vehicles, 3,934; chemicals, 1,442; wheat, 331.

Principal exports in 1975 were (in US$1m.): Sugar, 770; coffee, 855; iron ore, 921; cotton, 98; pinewood, 63.

Of exports (in US$1m.) in 1975, USA took 1,316·9; Netherlands, 561·7; Germany (Fed. Rep.), 701·8; Japan, 671·9; Argentina, 383·1; Italy, 360·2; UK, 340·1; France, 247·9. Of 1975 imports, USA furnished 3,074·8; Germany (Fed. Rep.), 1,337·2; Japan, 1,105·2; UK, 330·9; Argentina, 238·7.

Total trade between UK and Brazil (according to British Department of Trade returns, in £1,000 sterling):

	1972	*1973*	*1974*	*1975*	*1976*	*1977*
Imports to UK	86,256	157,432	195,409	174,883	239,491	300,576
Exports and re-exports from UK	84,159	111,835	142,973	160,890	174,286	245,405

COMMUNICATIONS

Roads. There are (1974) 1,344,374 km of highways. In 1974 Brazil had 4,560,047 motor vehicles, including 3,795,002 passenger cars and 765,045 freight cars. 920,834 motor vehicles of all types were produced in 1975.

Railways. Public railways are operated by two administrations, the Federal Railways (RFFSA) formed in 1957 and São Paulo Railways (FEPASA) formed in 1971, which is confined to the state of São Paulo. RFFSA has a route-length of 24,491 km in 1975 and FEPASA 5,295 km in 1975. Principal gauges are metre and 1,600 mm. The share of the freight market declined to a low of 15% in 1967, but subsequent heavy government investment in reconstruction and new lines, coupled with a policy of forcing bulk commodities on to rail, had raised the share to over 20% in 1974. Continued investment in new wagons, electrification, gauge-conversion, and 'export corridor' routes to the ports will further improve this figure by 1981, and some 6,000 km of new construction is planned up to the year 2000. Except in the urban areas of Rio de Janeiro and São Paulo, passenger traffic moving by rail is negligible. Traffic moved by RFFSA in 1975 amounted to 19,800m. ton-km of freight and 216m. suburban passengers, and total numbers 243m. passengers. FEPSA also has a substantial investment programme underway.

There are several important independent freight railways, including the Vitoria à Minas (782 km) and the Amapa (194 km). São Paulo has a rapid transit railway, and a similar system is under construction in Rio de Janeiro.

Aviation. Twenty-five companies (20 foreign) furnish air-mail and passenger services. In 1974 passengers numbered 6,241,757; freight carried amounted to 110,647 tonnes; mail 3,962 tonnes.

Shipping. Inland waterways, mostly rivers, are open to navigation over some 21,944 miles. Rio de Janeiro and Santos are the 2 leading ports; there are 13 other large ports. Bolivia and Paraguay have been given free ports at Santos. During 1975, 6,919 vessels entered the ports of Rio de Janeiro and Santos.

The Lloyd Brasileiro is owned and operated by the Government; its fleet comprised (1974), 43 vessels of 401,399 gross tons. Brazilian shipping, 1974 (registered with Lloyds) amounted to 665 vessels of 4,109,843 DWT. Petrobrás, the government oil monopoly, took over the government tanker fleet of 26 vessels in 1958; total tanker fleet in 1974 was 97 vessels of 2,090,315 DWT.

Post and Broadcasting. Of the telegraph system of the country, about half, including all interstate lines, is under control of the Government. There were 2,647 telegraph offices in 1975. Telephone instruments in use, 1977, were 3,987,072. In 1974 there were 977 broadcasting and 75 television stations.

Cinemas (1974). Cinemas numbered 2,619.

Newspapers (1974). There were 284 daily newspapers with a daily circulation of 1·3m. Foreigners and corporations (except political parties) are not allowed to own or control newspapers or wireless stations. The press law of 1967 prohibits anonymous journalism and the publication of material defamatory to the armed forces and other public institutions.

JUSTICE, RELIGION, EDUCATION AND WELFARE

Justice. There is a supreme federal Court of Justice at Brasília. It has 11 judges; all are appointed by the President with the approval of the Senate. There are also federal courts in each state and the federal district and in the Territories, as well as 'electoral courts' to protect the elections, and labour tribunals. Justice is administered in the states in accordance with state law, by state courts, but in Brasília federal justice is administered. Judges are appointed for life. There are also 3,074 magistrates and 5,634 justices of the peace. Divorce laws were approved by the National Congress on 28 June 1977; however, they are not yet (1978) in force and are awaiting the supplementary rules for their regulation. The death penalty was reintroduced in Sept. 1969.

Religion. The population is overwhelmingly Roman Catholic (91% at the census, 1970). In 1889 connexion between Church and State was abolished; it was restored by the 1934 constitution, but again abolished in 1946. In 1970 (census) Catholics numbered 85,472,022; Protestants, 4,814,728, and Spiritualists, 1,178,293.

Education. Elementary education is compulsory. In 1970 (census) there were 47,864,531 persons 5 years of age or over who could read and write; this was 60·33% of that age group; 50·9% of the literates were men.

There were, in 1974, 180,915 first degree school units, with 19,286,611 pupils; 10,885 second degree units, with 1,681,728 pupils.

The Government undertakes to provide, in part, for higher or university instruction, but some institutions are maintained by the states, and some by private associations, while primary schools are chiefly maintained and supervised, either by the states or by the municipalities and private initiative. There are 57 official universities, including the University of Rio de Janeiro (founded on 7 Sept. 1920), the University of Bahia (founded in 1946), the University of Recife (1946), the University of Paraná (1946), the Rural University (1948, State of Rio de Janeiro), the University of São Paulo (1934), the University of Minas Gerais (1927), the University of Rio Grande do Sul (1934) and the University of Brasília (1960). There are also 10 Catholic universities in Rio de Janeiro (1946), São Paulo (1946), Rio Grande do Sul (1948), Pernambuco (1951), Minas Gerais (1958), Bahia, Paraná, Campinas, Petrópolis and Pelotas. Students in 1974 totalled 937,593.

Health. In 1974 there were 800 government and 3,941 private hospitals and 62,743 physicians.

DIPLOMATIC REPRESENTATIVES

OF BRAZIL IN GREAT BRITAIN (32 Green St., London, W1Y 4AT)

Ambassador: Roberto de Oliveira Campos, GCVO (accredited 6 March 1975).

OF GREAT BRITAIN IN BRAZIL (Ave. das Nacões, Lote 8, Brasília, D.F.)
Ambassador: Sir Norman Statham, KCMG, CVO.

OF BRAZIL IN THE USA (3006 Massachusetts Ave., NW, Washington, D.C., 20008)
Ambassador: João Baptista Pinheiro.

OF THE USA IN BRAZIL (Ave das Nocões, Lote 3, Brasília, D.F.)
Ambassador: John Hugh Crimmins.

OF BRAZIL TO THE UNITED NATIONS
Ambassador: Sérgio Corrêa Da Costa.

Books of Reference

Anuário Estatístico do Brazil. Instituto Brasileiro de Estatística. Rio de Janeiro
Atlas do Brasil. Instituto Brasileiro de Geografia. 2nd ed. Rio de Janeiro, 1959
Brazil Up to Date. Instituto Brasileiro de Estatística. Rio de Janeiro, 1955
Bulletin of the British Chamber of Commerce in Brazil. Rio de Janeiro. Monthly
Azevedo, Aroldo de. *Geografia do Brazil.* 2 vols. Rio. 1960
Banco do Brasil, *Boletim Trimestral.* Brasília, D.F. From 1966
Burns, E. B., *A History of Brazil.* New York, 1971
Calogeras, João Pandiá, *A History of Brazil.* Chapel Hill, North Carolina, 1939
Camacho, J. A., *Brazil.* R. Inst. of Int. Affairs. 2nd ed. 1954
Campbell, G., *Brazil Struggles for Development.* London, 1973
Castro, J. de, *Géographie de la faim.* Paris, 1949
Cowell, A., *The Tribe that Hides from Man.* London, 1973
Delgado de Carvalho, C. M., *Historia Diplomatica do Brazil.* Rio, 1961
Fiechter, G.-A., *Brazil since 1964: Modernisation under a Military Regime.* London, 1975
Furtado, C., *The Economic Growth of Brazil.* Univ. of California Press and CUP, 1963
Hanbury-Tenison, R., *A Question of Survival for the Indians of Brazil.* London, 1973
Hill L. F. (ed.), *Brazil.* Univ. of California Press and London, 1948
Leff, N. H., *Economic Policy-Making and Development in Brazil, 1947–64.* New York and London, 1968
Moraes, R. Borba de. *Bibliographia Brasiliana (1504–1900).* 2 vols. 1958
Raine, P. *Brazil: Awakening Giant.* Washington, 1974
Roiter, F., *Brazil.* London, 1971
Saunders, J., *Modern Brazil: New Patterns and Developments.* Univ. of Florida Press, 1971
Schuh, G. E., and Alves, E. R., *The Agricultural Development of Brazil.* New York, 1970
Skidmore, T. E., *Politics in Brazil, 1930–1964.* OUP, 1967.—*Black into White: Race and Nationality in Brazilian Thought.* OUP, 1975
Smirh, P. B., *Oil and Politics in Modern Brazil.* Toronto, 1975
Smith, T. Lynn, *Brazil; People and Institutions.* Rev. ed. Baton Rouge, 1954.—(Ed.) *Brasil: Portrait of Half a Continent.* Gainesville, Fla., 1951.—*Brazilian Society.* Univ. of New Mexico Press, 1975
Wellington, R. A., *The Brazilians.* Newton Abbot, 1974

National Library: Biblioteca Nacional Avenida Rio Branco 219–39, Rio de Janeiro, G.B. *Director:* Janice de Mello Montemor.

BRUNEI

Capital: Bandar Seri Begawan
Population: 177 080 (1976)

HISTORY. The Sultanate of Brunei was a powerful state in the early 16th century, with authority over the whole of the island of Borneo and some parts of the Sulu Islands and the Philippines. At the end of the 16th century its power had begun to decline and various cessions were made to Great Britain, the Rajah of Sarawak and the British North Borneo Company in the 19th century to combat piracy and anarchy. By the middle of the 19th century the State had been reduced to its present limits.

In 1847 the Sultan of Brunei entered into a treaty with Great Britain for the furtherance of commercial relations and the suppression of piracy, and in 1888, by a further treaty, the State was placed under the protection of Great Britain. Brunei was the only former British dependency inhabited by a Malay people that did not join the Federation of Malaysia in 1963.

AREA AND POPULATION. Brunei, on the north-west coast of Borneo, is bounded on all sides by Sarawak territory, which splits the State into two separate parts. Area, about 2,226 sq. miles (5,800 sq. km), with a coastline of about 100 miles. Estimated population in mid-1976 was 177,080. The capital is Bandar Seri Begawan, 9 miles from the mouth of Brunei River. The climate is of tropical marine type, hot and moist, with cool nights.

CONSTITUTION AND GOVERNMENT. On 29 Sept. 1959 the Sultan promulgated a constitution. There is a Privy Council, an Executive and a Legislative Council. On 6 Jan. 1965 the constitution was amended to provide for general elections to the Legislative Council; at the same time the Executive Council was renamed Council of Ministers. The Legislative Council consists of 20 members and a Speaker appointed by the Sultan. The Council of Ministers is presided over by the Sultan and consists of 6 *ex-officio* members and 4 other members, all of whom except one are members of the Legislative Council. The Mentri Besar, who is one of the *ex-officio* members of the Legislative Council and the Council of Ministers, is responsible to the Sultan for the exercise of executive authority in the State. A new agreement was signed with UK in Nov. 1971.

The official language is Malay, but English may be used for all official purposes. The official religion is Islam.

Sultan of Brunei: The 28th Sultan abdicated on 4 Oct. 1967 in favour of his son, who was installed on the 5th as Sultan Hassanal Bolkiah Muizzaddin Waddaulah, DK, PSSUB, DPKG, DPKT, PSPNB, PSNB, PSLJ, SPMB, PANB, GCMG, DK (Kelantan), DK (Johore), and was crowned on 1 Aug. 1968.

General Adviser to H.H. The Sultan: The Most Honourable, Pehin Orang Kaya Setia Bakti Di-Raja Dato Laila Utama Isa bin Pehin Dato Perdana Mentri Dato Laila Utama Haji Ibrahim, DK, SPMB, DSNB, CVO, OBE, PHBS, PJK.

Flag: Yellow, with 2 diagonal strips of white over black.

DEFENCE

Army. The Royal Brunei Malay Regiment, whose strength as at 31 Dec. 1975 was approximately 96 officers and 1,800 other ranks is expanding and being provided with modern sophisticated weapons and equipment. A second battalion was formed in May 1975. All members of the regiment are now armed with the modern automatic rifles M16, while the 7·62 SLR are held in reserve and form the main equipment of the 7 platoons of the Brunei Cadet Corps from the 7 colleges in Brunei.

A battalion of the British Brigade of Gurkhas is stationed in Brunei and financed by the Sultan.

Navy. The Navy flotilla of the Royal Brunei Malay Regiment comprises 1 fast missile craft (built by Vosper-Thornycroft (UK)), 6 coastal patrol boats (built by Vosper-Thornycroft (Singapore)), 3 riverine patrol launches, 2 landing craft and 24 fast assault boats. Personnel in 1978 numbered 300 (25 officers and 275 ratings).

Air Wing. The Air Wing of the Royal Brunei Malay Regiment was formed in 1965 with 3 helicopters for communications and casualty evacuation duties. Current equipment includes 3 Bell 205A Iroquois, 4 Bell 206A/B JetRanger and 4 Bell 212 helicopters, and a twin-turboprop Hawker Siddeley 748 transport used also for VIP passenger and search and rescue duties. Seconded RAF pilots are being supplemented and replaced by Brunei personnel.

Police. Establishment provides over 1,000 officers and men (1976). In addition, there is a small auxiliary force mostly employed on static guard duties.

ECONOMY

Planning. A third Five-Year National Development Plan was announced in 1974 to develop the economic, social and cultural life of the people.

Budget. In 1975 the actual revenue was B$1,564,338,393 and expenditure was $370,872,742 (excluding expenditure from development fund of $88m.). The main sources of revenue were: Duties, $17,835,382; taxes, $1,056,134,659; royalties, $195,170,853; interest etc., $271,634,019. The main heads of expenditure were: Security and defence, $119,717,831; health, $14,976,397; public works, $25,097,633; religious affairs, $9,687,728.

The estimated revenue for 1976 was $1,600,122,800 and expenditure $480,489,400 and the contribution to the development fund was $136,762,300.

Currency. The currency is the Brunei Dollar with a par value of US cents 35·46.

ENERGY AND NATURAL RESOURCES

Oil. The Seria oilfield, discovered in 1929, has passed its peak production. The high level of crude oil production is maintained through the increase of offshore oilfields production, which exceeds onshore oilfields production. Production is about 192,000 bbls a day. The crude oil is exported directly, and only a small amount is refined at Seria for domestic uses.

Forestry. Most of the interior is under forest, containing large potential supplies of serviceable timber.

INDUSTRY AND TRADE

Industry. Brunei depends primarily on its oil industry, which employs 7% of the entire working population. Crude oil accounts for 78% of the total value of the exports and re-exports. The second main export is liquefied natural gas, which contributes 17% and petroleum products 4%. Other minor products are rubber, jelutong, buffalo and pepper. Local industries include boat-building, cloth weaving and the manufacture of brass- and silver-ware.

COMMERCE. In 1975 imports totalled B$648,856,700; exports, B$2,494,805,900. Total trade with UK (British Department of Trade returns, in £1,000 sterling):

	1972	*1973*	*1974*	*1975*	*1976*	*1977*
Imports to UK	67	150	1,986	618	343	454
Exports and re-exports from UK	1,952	2,550	5,113	9,642	14,640	17,429

COMMUNICATIONS

Roads. The State has about 781 miles of road, of which 340 miles are bituminous surfaced. The main road connects Bandar Seri Begawan with Kuala Belait and Seria. Considerable work is being undertaken for development of secondary roads. The number of motor vehicles (1975) was 27,858.

Aviation. Singapore Airlines and MSA provide daily services linking Sarawak, Brunei and Sabah and West Malaysia and Singapore. Cathay Pacific Airways operates two services weekly linking Brunei with Hong Kong. British Airways provides a weekly service between Brunei and UK. The Malaysia Air Charter Ltd and other operators provide chartered services both in Brunei and East Malaysia. Royal Brunei Airlines began operating in 1975; it has flights to Hong Kong, Manila, Kuching and Kota Kinabalu as well as daily flights to Singapore.

Shipping. Regular shipping services operate from Singapore, Hong Kong, and from ports in Sarawak and Sabah to Bandar Seri Begawan. The Straits Steamship Company carries passengers in some of its ships operating between Singapore and Bandar Seri Begawan. The Government of Brunei operates a passenger ferry service between Bandar Seri Begawan and Labuan, Sabah, 6 days a week.

Post and Broadcasting. There were 7 post offices and a telephone network (9,607 telephones) linking the main centres in 1975. Radio Brunei is operated by the Department of Radio and Television and operates on medium- and short-waves in Malay, Iban, Dusun, English and Chinese. Number of radio receivers, 29,119.

A final feasibility report has been completed on the establishment of a satellite communications earth station primarily to improve long-distance external communication.

EDUCATION (1975). Free education in the Malay language is provided in government primary schools (17,329 pupils) and 7 government secondary schools (4,139 pupils). Free education in English was provided in 16 government preparatory schools (6,424 pupils) and 7 government secondary schools (6,845 pupils). Teacher-training was provided in 2 government teachers' colleges, in both Malay and English for 601 students. Seven unassisted Mission schools provided education in English at kindergarten, primary and secondary level for a total of 5,178 pupils; 8 unassisted Chinese schools provided education in Chinese at the same three levels for a total of 5,263 pupils. One private kindergarten and primary school, administered by the Brunei Shell Petroleum Company, provided education in either English or Dutch for a total of 258 pupils, and there was also one private vocational school administered by the Brunei Shell Petroleum Company (140 artisan-trainees). Two government vocational schools provided full training courses to 197 students in the engineering and building trades.

Recurrent expenditure on education in 1975 was B$43·1m.; capital expenditure, B$6·9m.

DIPLOMATIC REPRESENTATIVE

OF GREAT BRITAIN IN BRUNEI (Jalan Residency, Bandar Seri Begawan)

High Commissioner: J. A. Davidson, OBE.

BULGARIA

Capital: Sofia
Population: 8·73m. (1975)
GNP per capita: US$2,310 (1976)

Narodna Republika Bulgaria

HISTORY. The Bulgarian state was founded in 681, but fell under Turkish rule in 1396. By the Treaty of Berlin, which followed the Russo-Turkish war of 1878, the Principality of Bulgaria and the Autonomous Province of Eastern Rumelia, both under Turkish suzerainty, were constituted. In 1885 Rumelia was reunited with Bulgaria. On 5 Oct. 1908 Bulgaria declared her independence of Turkey. *Rulers:* Prince Alexander I of Battenberg, 1879–86; Prince (after 1908, Tsar) Ferdinand, 1887–1918 (abdicated); Tsar Boris III, 1918–43; Tsar Simeon II, lost his throne as a result of a referendum held on 8 Sept. 1946 (3,801,160 votes for a republic, 197,176 for the monarchy, 119,168 invalid).

In 1941 Bulgaria signed the Three Power Pact and the Anti-Comintern Pact. In 1944 Bulgaria asked the UK and the USA for an armistice. The USSR declared war on Bulgaria on 5 Sept. 1944. The Fatherland Front government (established 9 Sept.) asked the USSR for an armistice, which was signed on 28 Oct. 1944 by the USSR, the UK and the USA. The peace treaty was signed in Paris on 10 Feb. 1947.

AREA AND POPULATION. On 8 Sept. 1940 by the treaty of Craiova, Romania ceded to Bulgaria the Southern Dobrudja, fixing the new frontier on the 1912 line.

In April 1941 Bulgaria occupied the Yugoslav part of Macedonia, and the Greek districts of Western Thrace, Eastern Macedonia, Florina and Castoria. The peace treaty of 1947 restored the frontiers as on 1 Jan. 1941.

The area of Bulgaria is 110,911·5 sq. km (42,823 sq. miles) and is bounded in the north by Romania, east by the Black Sea, south by Turkey and Greece and west by Yugoslavia.

The country is divided into 28 provinces (*okrŭg*, plur. *okrŭzi*). Area and population in 1975:

Province	*Area (sq. km)*	*Pop. 1,000*	*Province*	*Area (sq. km)*	*Pop. 1,000*	*Province*	*Area (sq. km)*	*Pop. 1,000*
Blagoevgrad	6,464	324	Pleven	4,184	359	Sofia (City)	1,038	1,066
Burgas	7,604	421	Plovdiv	5,591	721	Stara Zagora	4,902	390
Gabrovo	2,068	176	Razgrad	2,645	204	Tolbukhin	4,689	250
Khaskovo	4,029	293	Russe	2,624	294	Tŭrgovishte	2,754	179
Kŭrdzhali	4,020	288	Shumen	3,374	254	Varna	3,820	430
Kyustendil	3,002	199	Silistra	2,876	177	Veliko Tŭrnovo	4,690	350
Lovech	4,129	217	Sliven	3,729	238	Vidin	3,110	179
Mikhailovgrad	3,585	236	Smolyan	3,518	163	Vratsa	4,186	312
Pazardzhik	4,379	314	Sofia	7,385	321	Yambol	4,162	207
Pernik	2,355	175						

The population at the census of 1 Dec. 1965 was 8,227,866 (males, 4,114,167; urban, 3,822,824). Population on 31 Dec. 1975 was 8·73m. (4·4m. males; 5·1m. urban). Population density 78·5 per sq. km.

Ethnic minorities are estimated to total 1·2m. The language estimates are: Bulgarian 88%, Turkish 8·6%. The remainder include Gipsies, Jews, Romanians and Armenians. Some Turks have been repatriated.

Population of principal towns (1975): Sofia, 965,728; Plovdiv, 309,242; Varna, 251,588; Russe, 163,012; Burgas, 144,000; Stara Zagora, 112,200; Pleven, 108,180; Sliven, 90,000; Gabrovo, 90,000; Pernik, 87,432; Tolbukhin, 86,184; Shumen, 84,321; Yambol, 75,861; Khaskovo, 75,031; Pazardzhik, 67,911.

Vital statistics, 1975: Live births, 144,918; deaths, 89,919; marriages, 75,078; divorces, 11,030; crude birth rate, 16·6 per 1,000 population; crude death rate, 10·3; infant mortality, 22·9 per 1,000; growth rate, 7·4.

Expectation of life in 1977 was 69 years.

CONSTITUTION AND GOVERNMENT. A People's Republic was proclaimed by the National Assembly on 15 Sept. 1946, and the existing 'Tŭrnovo' Constitution of 1879 was replaced by the 'Dimitrov' Constitution in 1947. This was in turn replaced by a new constitution on 18 May 1971. This provides for a single-chamber National Assembly (*Narodno Sŭbranie*). The highest permanently operating organ of the state is the Council of State which consists of a chairman, 2 first vice-chairmen, 4 vice-chairmen, a secretary and 17 members; it is elected by the National Assembly from its members. Supreme power is vested in the National Assembly, which consists of 400 deputies elected from areas of equal population by direct, secret and universal suffrage (everybody at age of 18 being eligible to vote and hold office) for a term of 5 years; it is to meet at least three times every year. The National Assembly also elects the Council of State and the ministers who are responsible to it.

A general election was held on 27 Oct. 1946. The Fatherland Front, composed of the Workers (Communist), Agrarian, Socialist and Zveno Parties, and non-party independents, obtained 364 seats (277 of which went to the Communists) and the opposition 101. On 26 Aug. 1947 the oppositional Agrarian Union was dissolved; its leader, Nikola Petkov, was sentenced to death and hanged on 23 Sept. The Socialist Party was merged with the Workers' Party in Aug. 1948, and the Zveno Party dissolved itself.

The Fatherland Front was transformed, in Feb. 1948, into a unified mass organization with individual memberships. Inside the Fatherland Front, there remain two political parties, the Bulgarian Communist Party and the Bulgarian People's Agrarian Union. Petŭr Tanchev (*1st Vice-Chairman, Council of State*) is Secretary of the Agrarian Union and Pencho Kubadinski Chairman of the Fatherland Front's National Council.

In 1976 the membership of the Communist Party was 788,221 (41% workers, 23% peasants); Young Communist League, 1·3m.; Agrarian Union, 120,000; Fatherland Front, 3,770,080.

At the elections of 30 June 1976, 99·99% of the electorate voted, and 99·92% of the votes were cast for the 400 candidates (79 women) of the Fatherland Front; there were no other candidates. The list comprised 272 Communists, 100 Agrarians and 28 independents. The President of the National Assembly is Vladimir Bonev.

There is no constitutional single Head of State, but Todor Zhivkov (*Chairman of the Council of State, 1st Secretary of the Communist Party*), performs some of the functions of a Head of State.

The highest policy-making and executive body of the Bulgarian Communist Party is its Politburo, consisting of 12 full members and 4 candidate members. The Politburo is elected by and from the Central Committee.

The Politburo was in April 1978 composed as follows: FULL MEMBERS: Todor Zhivkov, Gen. Ivan Mihailov, Stanko Todorov (*Chairman, Council of Ministers, i.e., Prime Minister*), Pencho Kubadinski (*Deputy Chairman, Council of Ministers*), Tano Tsolov (*1st Deputy Chairman, Council of Ministers*), Tsola Dragoicheva, Grisha Filipov (*Secretary, Central Committee*), Aleksandŭr Lilov (*Secretary, Central Committee*), Gen. Dobri Dzhurov (*Defence Minister*), Petŭr Mladenov (*Foreign Minister*), Ognian Doinov. CANDIDATE MEMBERS: Krustiŭ Trichkov (*1st Deputy Chairman, Council of Ministers, Chairman, Committee of State Control*), Peko Takov (*Deputy Chairman, Council of State*), Todor Stoichev, Drazha Vŭlcheva.

Ministers not in the Politburo include: Kiril Zarev (*Deputy Chairman, Council of Ministers, Chairman, State Planning Committee*), Khristo Khristov (*Foreign Trade*), Dimitŭr Stoyanov (*Internal Affairs*), Belcho Belchev (*Finance*).

In May 1967 a second 20-year treaty of friendship, co-operation and mutual assistance with the Soviet Union was signed.

National flag: Three horizontal stripes of white, green, red, with the national emblem in the canton.

National anthem: An arrangement of Mila Rodino (Dear Fatherland), a popular patriotic song, was declared the national anthem in 1964.

Local Government. People's Councils at province and commune level are elected for terms of 30 months, to deal with all economic, social and cultural problems of their area. They also supervise the management of state and publicly owned enterprises. The Council's executive organs are Permanent Committees. In 1977 the People's Councils had a total membership of 55,393.

DEFENCE. There is a compulsory service of 2 years in the Army and Air Force (3 years in the Navy).

Army. In 1975 the Army had a strength of 120,000 men, organized in 8 motorized and 5 tank divisions, not at full strength. There are 3 Army Commands (Military Regions), Sofia, Plovdiv, Sliven. Tanks, mainly T-34s and some T-54s and T-55s, numbered 2,250. Security police numbered 45,000 (5 brigades of border guards, 8 regiments of security forces).

Navy. The Navy consists of 2 *ex*-Soviet 'R' class submarines, 2 *ex*-Soviet 'Riga' class frigates, 3 *ex*-Soviet 'Poti' class corvettes, 4 *ex*-Soviet 'Osa' class missile boats, 6 patrol vessels, 8 torpedo boats, 2 fleet minesweepers, 4 coastal minesweepers, 2 inshore minesweepers, 24 minesweeping service boats, 20 landing craft, and 10 auxiliaries, 3 oilers, 2 survey ships, 2 salvage craft and 5 tugs. Personnel, 1977, was 10,000 officers and ratings.

Air Force. The large tactical Air Force has about 250 Soviet-built combat aircraft and 25,000 personnel. There are 4 squadrons of MiG-21s; about 12 squadrons of fighter/ground attack MiG-27s, MiG-17s and MiG-19s; 3 reconnaissance squadrons of MiG-21s and MiG-15s; a total of about 12 Tu-134, Il-14 and An-24 transport aircraft; 30 Mi-4, 30 Mi-2 and a few Mi-8 helicopters; and L-29 Delfin, MiG-15UT1 and MiG-21UT1 trainers. Soviet-built 'Guideline' and 'Goa' surface-to-air missiles have also been supplied to Bulgaria.

INTERNATIONAL RELATIONS

Membership. Bulgaria is a member of UN, Comecon and the Warsaw Pact.

External Debt. Agreements of 1955 and 1963 settled outstanding financial claims by the UK and USA respectively.

ECONOMY

Planning. State economic planning started in 1947. After 1964 there was a limited decentralization in planning, culminating in the economic reform of 1 Jan. 1969. Some local planning, profitability and consumer demand have been admitted, although central price regulation has been retained. The economy has been reconstructed into large trusts for each industry, each responsible for its own foreign trade.

For the first five 5-year plans *see* THE STATESMAN'S YEAR-BOOK for 1976–77. The sixth 5-year plan ran from 1971 to 1975, emphasis being laid on the engineering, metallurgical, electronic, shipbuilding and chemical industries. The national income annual growth rate averaged 8%. The seventh 5-year plan (1976–80) envisages a rise in national income of 9%, and in industrial production of 55%.

There is a long-term perspective plan up to 1990.

Budget. The revenue and expenditure of Bulgaria for calendar years were as follows (in 1m. leva):

	1967	*1968*	*1969*	*1970*	*1971*	*1972*	*1973*	*1974*	*1975*
Revenue	4,083	4,504	5,227	5,723	6,184	6,355	7,055	8,060	9,157
Expenditure	4,051	4,426	5,158	5,650	6,063	6,261	7,036	8,044	9,139

Of the 1975 revenue 6,675m. leva came from national economy. 1975 expenditure was: Investments, 4,725m. leva; social and education, 2,861m.; administration, 171m.

Currency. The unit of currency is the *lev* (pl. *leva*) divided into 100 *stotinki* (sing. *stotinka*). It has been linked to the Soviet rouble since May 1952. A new *lev*, equalling 10 old leva, was introduced on 1 Jan. 1962. The parity (clearing value) is 1 rouble = 1·30 leva. The official rate of exchange (Nov. 1976) was £1 = 1·58 leva;

US$1 = 0·96 leva. Rate of exchange for non-commercial transactions: £1 = 2·40 leva; US$1 = 1·65 leva.

Banking. In 1947 banks were nationalized and the National Bank gained autonomy, freeing it from responsibility for state debts. In 1969 the banking system was reorganized. The National Bank became the central bank and was made responsible for issuing currency. It also plays an important part in the management of the economy: its chairman has ministerial rank. There is also a Foreign Trade Bank and a State Savings Bank.

In 1975, 8·92m. depositors had savings totalling 5,962m. leva. The State Savings Bank has advanced personal loans up to 500 leva at 3·5% interest to some 500,000 users. Interest on deposits is from 1% to 3%.

Weights and Measures. The metric system is in general use. On 1 April 1916 the Gregorian calendar came into force in Bulgaria.

ENERGY AND NATURAL RESOURCES

Electricity. A joint Romanian–Bulgarian hydro-electric station is being built on the Danube at Turnu-Magurele-Nikopol.

Oil and Natural Gas. Oil is extracted in the Balchik district on the Black Sea, in an area 100 km north of Varna and at Dolni Dubnik near Pleven. Crude oil production was 122,000 tonnes in 1975. There are refineries at Burgas (annual capacity 5m. tonnes) and Dolni Dubnik (7m. tonnes). 111m. cu. metres of natural gas were produced in 1975.

Minerals. Ore production in 1,000 tonnes in 1973: Copper, 53; lead, 100; zinc, 80; (1974) manganese, 9·6; iron, 846. 21m. tonnes of lignite and 29m. tonnes of hard coal were mined in 1975. 89 tonnes of salt were extracted in 1975.

Agriculture. In 1975 cultivated agricultural land covered 5,955,100 hectares, of which 4,739,900 hectares are arable.

Collectivization was completed by 1958. The United Central Co-operative Union co-ordinates the activities of collective farms and consumer co-operatives. Size of private plots (maximum, 0·5 hectare; in mountainous areas, 1 hectare) is based on the number of members of a household. The total area of private plots in 1975 was 569,200 hectares. There were, in 1975, 281 co-operative farms and 91 state farms. There were 66 machine-tractor stations. 136,551 tractors (in 15-h.p. units) were in use and 22,562 combine harvesters. Collective and state farms are being incorporated into 'agricultural-industrial complexes'. There were 162 of these in 1975 with 4,090,900 hectares.

In 1975, 26 irrigation systems and 125 dams irrigated 1,128,000 hectares.

Yield in 1975 (in 1,000 tonnes): Wheat, 2,771; rye, 18; maize 2,822; barley, 1,699; oats, 56; sunflower seed, 426; unginned cotton, 32; tobacco, 141; tomatoes, 569; potatoes, 318; grapes, 789. Bulgaria is the world's principal supplier of attar of roses; annual production, 1,200 kg.

Other products (in 1,000 tonnes) in 1975: Meat, 659; wool, 34; sugar, 316; 1,845m. eggs were produced and 1,749m. litres of milk.

Livestock (1976): 133,000 horses, 1·6m. cattle, including 670,000 milch cows, 10m. sheep, 3·8m. pigs and 38m. poultry.

Forestry. The forest area, 1975, was 3·8m. hectares, of which 1m. coniferous. 62,174 hectares were afforested in 1975. 5·8m. cu. metres of timber were cut in 1973.

Fisheries. The catch of sea fish was 151,324 tonnes in 1975.

INDUSTRY AND TRADE

Industry. All industry was nationalized in 1947.

Industrial production	*1970*	*1971*	*1972*	*1973*	*1974*	*1975*
Electricity (1m. kwh.)	19,513	21,016	22,271	21,952	22,800	25,232
Crude steel (1,000 tonnes)	1,800	1,947	2,121	2,246	2,188	2,265
Pig-iron (1,000 tonnes)	1,251	1,378	1,562	1,610	1,528	1,565
Cement (1,000 tonnes)	3,668	3,880	3,914	4,178	4,298	4,400
Sulphuric acid (1,000 tonnes)	502	514	513	561	761	853

In 1975 there were also produced (in 1,000 tonnes): Coke, 1,364; rolled steel, 2,495; artificial fertilizers, 2,574; calcinated soda, 1,009; cotton fabrics, 372m. sq. metres; silk fabrics, 31m. metres.

Trade Unions. Trade unions had 3,323,600 members in 1976. The phased introduction of a 42½-hour 5-day working week commenced in 1968. In 1973 the minimum wage was fixed at 80 leva per month. The average wage (excluding peasantry) was 146 leva per month in 1975. Retiring age is 60 for men and 55 for women. The labour force (excluding peasantry) in 1975 was 3,676,632 (1,744,307 female), of whom 1,297,432 worked in industry, 316,818 in building and 819,165 in agriculture and forestry.

Commerce. Foreign trade is controlled by the Ministry of Foreign Trade. Bulgarian trade has developed as follows (in 1m. leva):

	1970	*1971*	*1972*	*1973*	*1974*	*1975*
Imports	2,142·3	2,479·9	2,772·2	3,171·7	4,154	5,155
Exports	2,344·5	2,553·3	2,837·0	3,200·7	3,723	4,467

Main exports are food products, tobacco, non-ferrous metals, cast iron, leather articles, textiles and (to Communist countries) machinery.

79% of Bulgaria's trade is with the Communist countries (54% with USSR). Agreements with USSR envisage the co-ordination of the Soviet and Bulgarian 5-year plans in the spirit of 'socialist internationalism'. Bulgaria imports oil, natural gas, steel, cellulose and timber, and exports food products, clothing and electronic components. Italy is Bulgaria's biggest non-Communist export market, Federal Republic of Germany her major non-Communist supplier.

Trade deficit with the West was some US$2,000m. in 1976.

Total trade between UK and Bulgaria (British Department of Trade returns, in £1,000 sterling):

	1973	*1974*	*1975*	*1976*	*1977*
Imports to UK	9,339	13,549	7,412	11,210	11,863
Exports and re-exports from UK	13,146	18,049	23,601	23,048	24,961

Western firms may open offices in Bulgaria, by arrangement with one of the 13 'Interpred' agencies.

The first Anglo-Bulgarian long-term trade agreement was signed in 1970. The Anglo-Bulgarian Joint Commission held its first meeting in March 1973. On 13 May 1974 Bulgaria and the UK signed a 10-year economic, scientific and technological co-operation agreement.

COMMUNICATIONS

Roads. In 1975 there were 31,434 km of roads, including 7,683 km of first-class roads. 724m. tonnes of freight and 1,853m. passengers were carried.

Railways. In 1976 Bulgaria had 4,045 km of standard gauge railway, including 1,326 km electrified. 105m. passengers and 78m. tons of freight were carried in 1975.

Aviation. BALKAN (Bulgarian Airlines) operates internal flights from Sofia (airport: Vrazhdebna) to Burgas, Khaskovo, Pleven, Plovdiv, Russe, Silistra, Stara Zagora, Tŭrgovishte, Veliko Tŭrnovo, Varna, Vidin and Yambol and international flights to Algiers, Amsterdam, Athens, Baghdad, Bratislava, Belgrade, Benghazi, Berlin, Brussels, Bucharest, Budapest, Cairo, Casablanca, Copenhagen, Damascus, Frankfurt, Istanbul, London, Madrid, Moscow, Nicosia, Paris, Prague, Rome, Stockholm, Tunis, Vienna, Warsaw and Zürich. In 1972 BALKAN had 234 planes and in 1975 it carried 2·1m. passengers and 16,321 tonnes of freight. British Airways opened a service from London to Sofia in 1970.

Shipping. Ports, shipping and shipbuilding are controlled by the Bulgarian United Shipping and Shipbuilding Corporation. The mercantile marine in 1972 possessed 33 passenger vessels and 110 cargo vessels and tankers with a total loading capacity of 875,380 DWT. Burgas is a fishing and oil-port open to tankers of

20,000 tons. Varna is the other important port; its shipyards were re-equipped in 1969. In 1975, 905,000 passengers and 19·3m. metric tons of cargo were carried.

Post and Broadcasting. In 1975 there were 2,686 post offices, 777,127 telephones, 40 broadcasting stations and 11 television stations. Radio Sofia, the government broadcasting station, is transmitting 2 programmes on medium- and short-waves. There is also a special tourist service, broadcast *via* the Varna II transmitter on 1,124 kHz. Advertisements are broadcast for half an hour a day. Bulgaria participates in the East European TV link 'Intervision'. Colour programmes by SECAM system. Radio receiving sets, 2,270, 917; television sets, 1,507,650.

Cinemas and Theatres (1975). There were 35 theatres, 11 puppet theatres, 6 opera houses, 1 operetta house and 3,633 cinemas. 445 films were made (20 full-length).

Newspapers and Books. In 1975 there were 14 dailies with a circulation of 2·08m. The Party newspaper is *Rabotnicheskoto Delo* ('The Workers' Cause') with a circulation of 697,931 in 1974. 3,900 book titles were published in 1975.

JUSTICE, RELIGION, EDUCATION AND WELFARE

Justice. The Constitution of 1971 provides for the election (and recall) of the judges by the people and, for the Supreme Court, by the National Assembly. The lower courts include lay assessors as well as professional judges. There are a Supreme Court, 28 provincial courts (including Sofia), 105 regional courts and 'Comrades' Courts' for minor offences.

New Family and Penal Codes were approved by the National Assembly in April 1968. The maximum term of imprisonment is now 20 years except for 'exceptionally dangerous crimes' which carry the death penalty.

The Prosecutor General, elected by the National Assembly for 5 years and subordinate to it alone, exercises supreme control over the correct observance of the law by all government bodies, officials and citizens. He appoints and discharges all Prosecutors of every grade. Prosecutors are independent of judges and Government.

Religion. 'The traditional church of the Bulgarian people' (as it is officially described), is that of the Eastern Orthodox Church. It was disestablished under the 1947 Constitution. On 10 May 1953 the Bulgarian Patriarchate was revived and Metropolitan Kiril was elected the first Bulgarian Patriarch since 1393. Upon the death of Kiril Metropolitan Maksim of Lovech was enthroned as the new Patriarch in July 1971. The seat of the Patriarch is at Sofia. There are 11 dioceses, each under a Metropolitan, 10 bishops, 2,600 parishes and 1,500 priests. In 1976 there were 3,720 churches, 500 chapels and some 20 monasteries and nunneries.

The Constitution provides for freedom of conscience and belief but forbids propaganda against the Government. The State provides 17% of Church funds.

Churches may not maintain schools or colleges, except theological seminaries, or organize youth movements.

In 1976 there were some 50,000 Roman Catholics in 3 bishoprics with 40 priests and 30 churches, and 16,000 Protestants with 101 churches and 265 priests. There were 80,000 Moslems under a Grand Mufti and 6 regional mufti boards with 1,180 mosques.

Education. Education is free, and compulsory for children between the ages of 7 and 16. The gradual introduction of unified secondary polytechnical schools offering compulsory education for all children from the ages of 7 to 17 was begun in 1973–74. Complete literacy is claimed. Schools are classified according to which years of schooling they offer: Elementary (1–4), primary (1–7), preparatory (5–8), secondary (9–11), complete secondary (1–11).

Educational statistics for 1975–76: 7,550 kindergartens (392,625 children, 24,137 teachers); 942 elementary schools; 2,408 primary schools; 69 preparatory schools; 128 secondary schools; 200 complete secondary schools. Numbers of teachers and pupils: School years 1 to 4, 20,142 and 495,645; 5 to 8, 28,303 and 486,658; 9 to 11, 7,637 and 116,586. There were also 8 vocational-technical schools (180 teachers, 9,708 students), 307 technical colleges (9,245 teachers, 136,566 students), 28 post-secondary institutions (982 teachers, 19,779 students) and 24 institutes of higher education (11,248 teachers, 106,055 students). There are 3 universities: the Kliment Ohrid University in Sofia (founded 1888) had 1,154 teachers and 13,299 students (in 1975–76); the Kirill i Metodii University in Veliko Tŭrnovo (founded 1971) had 203 teachers and 5,046 students; the Paisi Hilendarski University in Plovdiv (founded 1972) had 215 teachers and 5,046 students.

The Academy of Sciences (founded 1869) and other research bodies had 167 institutes in 1974.

Social Welfare. Retirement and disablement pensions and temporary sick pay are calculated as a percentage of previous wages (respectively 55–80%, 35–100%, 69–90%) and according to the nature of the employment.

Monthly family allowances for children under 16: 5 leva for 1 child, 20 leva for 2 children and 35 leva for 3 children.

In 1975, 1·89m. persons received pensions totalling 571·4m. leva including 720,000 retirement pensions.

All medical services are free. In 1975 there were 183 hospitals with 67,220 beds, and 18,770 doctors.

DIPLOMATIC REPRESENTATIVES

OF BULGARIA IN GREAT BRITAIN
(12 Queen's Gate Gdns, London, SW7 5NA)

Ambassador: Vladimir Velchev.

OF GREAT BRITAIN IN BULGARIA
(Blvd. Marshal Tolbukhin 65–67, Sofia)

Ambassador: J. C. Cloake, CMG.

OF BULGARIA IN THE USA (2100–16th St., NW, Washington, D.C., 20009)

Ambassador: Konstantin N. Grigorov.

OF THE USA IN BULGARIA (1 Stamboliiski Blvd., Sofia)

Ambassador: Raymond L. Garthoff.

OF BULGARIA TO THE UNITED NATIONS

Ambassador: Dr Alexander Yankov.

Books of Reference

Kratka Bŭlgarska Entsiklopediia (Short Bulgarian Encyclopaedia), 5 vols. Sofia, 1963–69
Statisticheski Godishnik (Statistical Yearbook). Sofia from 1956
Constitution of the People's Republic of Bulgaria. Sofia, 1971
Atanasova, T., *et al.*, *Bulgarian–English Dictionary.* Sofia, 1975
Brown, J. F., *Bulgarian under Communist Rule.* London, 1970
Dobrin, B., *Bulgarian Economic Development Since World War II.* New York, 1973
Feiwel, G. R., *Growth and Reforms in Centrally Planned Economies: the Lessons of the Bulgarian Experience.* New York, 1977
Markov, M., *System of Social Administration in Bulgaria.* Sofia, 1969
Oren, N., *Communism Administered: Agrarianism and Communism in Bulgaria.* Baltimore, 1973
Pundeff, M. V., *Bulgaria: A Bibliographic Guide.* Library of Congress, 1965
Spasov, B., *La Bulgarie.* Paris, 1973
Todorov, N., and others, *Bulgaria: Historical and Geographical Outline.* Sofia, 1965
Zhivkov, T., *Modern Bulgaria: Problems and Tasks in Building an Advanced Socialist Society,* New York, 1974

BURMA

Capital: Rangoon
Population: 28·89m. (1973)
GNP per capita: US$120 (1976)

Pyidaungsu Socialist Thammada Myanma Naingngandaw

HISTORY. The Union of Burma came formally into existence on 4 Jan. 1948 and became the Socialist Republic of the Union of Burma in 1974. In 1948 Sir Hubert Rance, the last British Governor, handed over authority to Sao Shwe Thaike, the first President of the Burmese Republic, and Parliament ratified the treaty with Great Britain providing for the independence of Burma as a country not within His Britannic Majesty's dominions and not entitled to His Britannic Majesty's protection. This treaty was signed in London on 17 Oct. 1947 and enacted by the British Parliament on 10 Dec. 1947.

For the history of Burma's connexion with Great Britain *see* THE STATESMAN'S YEAR-BOOK, 1950, p. 836.

AREA AND POPULATION. Burma is bounded east by China, Laos and Thailand, west by the Indian Ocean, Bangladesh and India. The total area of the Union is 261,789 sq. miles (678,000 sq. km). Some small rectifications of the border with China were agreed upon in 1960 and with Pakistan in 1964. The population in March 1973 was estimated at 28·89m. The leading towns are: Rangoon, the capital (1973), 3,662,312; Mandalay, 417,266; Bassein, 355,588; Henzada, 283,658; Pegu, 254,761, Myingyan, 220,129; Moulmein, 202,967; Prome, 148,123; Akyab, 143,215; Tavoy, 101,536.

	Area in sq. km.	*Population (1,000) 1969 estimates*	*Chief town*
Kachin State	87,808	687	Myitkyina
Sagaing Division	99,150	2,933	Sagaing
Mandalay Division	34,253	3,172	Mandalay
Shan State	158,222	2,725	Taunggyi
Magwe Division	44,799	2,760	Yenangyaung
Chin Hills Special Division	36,009	354	Falam
Arakan Division	36,762	1,847	Sittwe
Irrawaddy Division	35,167	4,264	Bassein
Pegu Division	50,305	3,689	Pegu
Rangoon Division		1,785	Rangoon
Kayah State	11,670	113	Loikaw
Kawthoolei State	28,726	795	Pa-an
Tenasserim Division	55,159	1,856	Moulmein
	678,030	26,980	

The Burmese belong to the Tibeto-Chinese (or Tibeto-Burman) family.

CONSTITUTION. From Independence Day until 1962 Burma was a parliamentary democracy, having 2 houses, the Chamber of Deputies and the Chamber of Nationalities. The latter comprised 125 members, 62 of whom represented the central unit, 63 the states and special areas. The Chamber of Deputies had twice as many members. Both were elected for 4 years. The Head of State was the President, elected for a 5-year term, by both Chambers of Parliament in joint session.

On 29 Oct. 1958 Gen. Ne Win, the Army Chief of Staff, became prime minister of a caretaker government. The elections to the lower house, held in Feb. 1960, gave the Pyidaungsu (Union) Party, led by U Nu, 161 out of 250 seats. On 2 March 1962 Gen. Ne Win overthrew the government of U Nu and replaced it by a

Revolutionary Council. Parliament and the state councils were dissolved; the latter were reformed as 'state supreme councils' under appointed chairmen.

A new Constitution was approved by referendum in Dec. 1973. On 2 March 1974 military rule ended and Burma became a one-party socialist republic. Elections to the People's Assembly took place in Jan. and Feb. 1974. U Ne Win became President under the new Constitution and in Jan 1978 his term of office was extended for 4 years.

On 3 March 1978 the Assembly elected a Council of Ministers:

Prime Minister: U Maung Maung Kha.

Planning and Finance: U Tun Tin. *Foreign Affairs:* Brig.-Gen. Myint Maung. *Defence:* Maj.-Gen. Kyaw Htin. *Home and Religious Affairs:* Col. Sein Lwin. *Mines:* Col. Than Tin. *Construction:* Brig.-Gen. Hla Tun. *Agriculture and Forests:* U Ye Gaung. *Industry:* Col. Tint Swe; Col. Maung Cho. *Transport and Communications:* U Sein Lwin. *Co-operatives:* Col. Sein Tun. *Health:* Col. Win Maung. *Education:* Dr Khin Maung Win. *Trade:* U Hla Aye. *Information:* U Mya Maung. *Labour and Social Welfare:* U Mahn San Myat Shwe. *Culture:* U Aye Maung.

As from 22 April 1972, military ranks were dropped by most of the Revolutionary Council Members. From 15 March 1972, the entire governmental system was re-organized, with the Secretariat in Rangoon being abolished and with re-organized Security and Administrative Committees composed of officials and political representatives becoming the directing authority at central and regional levels.

National flag: Red with a blue canton bearing 2 ears of rice within a cog-wheel and a ring of 14 stars, all in white.

Language: The official language is Burmese; the use of English is permitted.

DEFENCE

Army. The strength of the Army (1977) was 153,000. The Army is organized into 9 regional commands comprising approximately 84 infantry battalions. Three operational divisions are directly under the Ministry of Defence and contain 5 armoured and 112 infantry battalions.

Navy. The Navy includes 1 frigate, 1 escort minesweeper (both *ex*-British), 2 escort patrol vessels (*es*-USA PCE and MSF types), 3 support gunboats (*ex*-landing craft), 13 coastal gunboats, 20 river gunboats, 35 small river patrol craft, 1 support ship, 2 survey vessels, 9 landing craft and 4 auxiliaries. Personnel in 1977: 300 officers and 9,000 ratings, including reserves and 800 marines.

Air Force. The Air Force is intended primarily for internal security duties. Its primary combat force comprises about 5 T-33A jet fighter/trainers supplied under MAP. Training is done with piston-engined SIAI-Marchetti SF.260Ms, and jet-powered T-37Cs and T-33s, which also carry light armament for security operations. Transport and second-line units are equipped with small numbers of C-47, Otter and Beech D18 aircraft, and Japanese-built Bell 47 (H-13), Bell UH-1, H-43B Huskie and Alouette III helicopters. Personnel about 7,500.

INTERNATIONAL RELATIONS

Membership. Burma is a member of the UN and Colombo Plan.

Aid. In Dec. 1957 Burma received a US loan of $5·4m. to reclaim land in the delta, in 1960 a £30m. loan from China to set up specified projects. In Aug. 1971 Japan extended a loan of US$10m. for offshore oil exploration. A commodity loan of 4,620m. yen was provided as well as a loan of 7,000m. yen. The International Development Association also granted a loan of US$33m. for rehabilitation of the railways and waterways.

Long-term loans amounting to K.149·2m. and short-term loans amounting to K.133·6m. were taken during 1971–72, mainly from Japan, followed by Federal Republic of Germany, USA and Czechoslovakia.

A loan of DM 42m. was given by Federal Republic of Germany in 1974 for a machine-tool factory and a sheet-glass manufacturing plant, and a further loan of DM 6m. for a natural gas liquefying plant. DM 75m. was also given as capital aid and DM 26·5m. in the form of technical assistance grants. A loan of DM 24·48m. was also given in Jan. 1975 for the establishment of a soda ash factory and formaldehyde plant. The International Development Association approved loans of US$17m. and US$24m. for promoting agricultural production and to rehabilitate and improve timber extraction operations. The Asian Development Bank approved loans of US$9·8m. and US$6·5m. for the fishing industry and the rice products industry. In 1975 the UNDP granted aids of US$2·21m. for offshore oil exploration and US$1·01m. for civil aviation telecommunications, while US$35m. was approved towards the second country programme for Burma covering the years 1974–78. A third commodity loan of 6,500m. yen was pledged by Japan while aid of 700m. yen was granted for the construction of a biochemical research centre. Britain also gave a grant of £2m. for the purchase of equipment spare parts and a further £1·9m. for onshore oil exploration.

ECONOMY

Planning. In 1968, 168 industrial concerns in Rangoon and Mandalay were nationalized followed by a further 69 on 1 Jan. 1972.

Budget. The budget estimates (in K.1m.) for fiscal years 1 Oct.–30 Sept. until 1973–74 and then 1 April–31 March were as follows:

	1970–71	*1971–72*	*1972–73*	*1973–74*[1]	*1974–75*	*1975–76*
Revenue	8,841	8,962	8,734	4,901	10,652	14,472
Expenditure	9,359	9,633	9,702	5,718	11,797	14,713

[1] From 1974 the fiscal year ended on 31 March. The figures shown for 1973–74 represent a supplementary budget to cover the interim 6 months period.

The largest items, in 1975–76, of revenue were customs (K.307·2m.) and income tax (K.616·4m.); of expenditure, industries (K.285m.); transport and communication (K.656m.); economic activities (K.5,167m.); trade (K.4,761m.).

The internal public debt was K.4,823m. at the end of Sept. 1974.

Currency. The currency unit is now the *kyat* divided into 100 *pyas.* There are notes of *kyat* 25, 20, 10, 5 and 1, and coins of *kyat* 1; *pyas* 50, 25, 10, 5 and 1.

Currency in circulation at 30 Sept. 1974 was valued at K.3,839m.

Banking. The Union of Burma Bank is being reconstituted into 4 banks and an insurance corporation with effect from 1 April under the 1975 Bank Law and the 1975 Insurance Law.

The banks being formed in reconstitution are the Union of Burma Bank, the Myanma Economic Bank, the Myanma Foreign Trade Bank and the Myanma Agricultural Bank and the corporation is the Myanma Insurance Corporation. Work now being carried out by the Union of Burma Bank will be continued by the 4 banks and the Corporation.

ENERGY AND NATURAL RESOURCES

Electricity. In 1974–75 the total installed capacity of power plants was 359,620 kw.; total units generated, 779m. kwh.

Minerals. Production in 1974–75: Crude oil, 7·63m. bbls; silver, 730,000 oz.; zinc, 7,000 tons; copper matte, 140 tons; refined lead, 8,700 tons; nickel speiss, 72 tons; antimony, 1,050 tons; lead ore, 2,452 tons; tin, 719 tons; tungsten, 414 tons; tin tungsten-scheelite, 600 tons.

Agriculture. By the end of 1958, 3,346,911 acres had been distributed among peasant proprietors under the Land Nationalization Scheme. The Revolutionary Government has given top priority to the development of agriculture.

Acreage (1,000) and production (1,000 tonnes) of principal crops:

	1972–73		1973–74		1974–75	
	Acreage	*Production*	*Acreage*	*Production*	*Acreage*	*Production*
Rice, rough	12,034	7,241	12,569	8,466	12,776	8,446
Maize	235	55	228	61	223	59
Pulses	1,861	265	1,852	333	1,787	312
Sesamum	2,256	69	2,651	166	2,636	98
Sugar-cane	292	2,000	275	1,715	227	1,185
Cotton	532	43	530	40	538	45
Groundnuts	1,563	377	1,612	452	1,671	459

Paddy crop in 1973–74 was 8·58m. tons.

Livestock (1976): Oxen, 7·3m.; buffaloes, 1·7m.

In 1974–75 the area irrigated by government-controlled irrigation works was 2,440,075 acres.

Forestry. The area of reserved forests in 1974–75 was 37,655 sq. miles. On 1 June 1948 the Government took over one-third of the concessions held by European and indigenous lessees. On 1 Feb. 1949 the European lessees surrendered their concessions. The takeover payments amounted to K.73·45 lakhs.

Teak extracted in 1971–72, 291,247 tons (1,209 lakhs); 1972–73, 307,436 tons; 1973–74, 345,000 tons; 1974–75, 250,000 tons. Hardwood, 1971–72, 1,038,416 tons (982 lakhs); 1972–73, 1,007,035 tons; 1973–74, 1,035,000 tons; 1974–75, 858,000 tons. 2,780 elephants are at work on extraction.

INDUSTRY AND TRADE

Trade Unions. Labour disputes are dealt with by the government labour sub-committees.

Commerce. All foreign trade is handled by the government trading organizations.

Imports and exports (in K. lakhs) for the fiscal years 1 Oct.–30 Sept.:

	1970–71	*1971–72*	*1972–73*	*1973–74*[1]	*1974–75*[2]
Imports	5,342	9,214	7,042	2,921	6,897
Exports	5,691	6,860	6,356	3,941	8,778

[1] 1 Oct.–31 March. [2] 1 April–31 March.

Exports of milled rice and rice products, K.3,359 lakhs. Exports of raw rubber amounted to 6,000 tons; raw jute, 71,000 tons, and pulses, 47,000 tons in 1974–75.

Trade between Burma and UK (British Department of Trade returns, in £1,000 sterling):

	1972	*1973*	*1974*	*1975*	*1976*	*1977*
Imports to UK	5,901	6,979	4,099	2,510	2,711	3,652
Exports and re-exports from UK	6,937	3,767	4,366	6,221	7,044	12,314

Tourism. There were 15,600 tourists in 1974.

COMMUNICATIONS

Roads. Burma had 2,452 miles of arterial highways and 11,194 miles of other roads (including roads in the various states and divisions) in 1974–75.

Railways. The Burma Railway system is entirely of metre gauge (3 ft 3⅜ in.) and its main lines run from Rangoon to Prome (161 miles) to the north-west and Rangoon to Mandalay (386 miles) towards the north, extending to Myitkyina farther north (723 miles from Rangoon). Branch lines extend from Letpadan to Tharrawaw (24 miles) on the west, the delta lines from Henzada to Bassein (82 miles) and Henzada to Kyangin (65 miles). In the Tenasserim Division, the lines are Pegu to Martaban (122 miles)—for Moulmein by bridge—and the Moulmein South to Ye (89 miles), and from Nyaunglebin into Madauk (11 miles). Then there are the branch lines from Pyinmana to Kyeeni (163 miles), from Thazi to Myingyan (70 miles), from Mandalay to Madaya (17 miles) and from Ywataung to Alon (71 miles). The Northern and Southern Shan States hill sections connect with the main lines at Myohaung and Thazi. The Ava bridge across the Irrawaddy at Sagaing permits through traffic from Rangoon to Myitkyina (723 miles).

In 1974–75 the railway carried 248·18m. freight-ton-mileage and 1,979·39m. passenger-mileage.

Aviation. Union of Burma Airways started its internal service in Sept. 1948 and its external service in Nov. 1950. International services were in 1963 maintained between Rangoon and Bangkok and Calcutta. The routes were extended to Hong Kong in 1969 and to Dacca and Káthmándu in 1970. There were, in 1971, 43 civil aerodromes and landing grounds. In 1974–75 the total freight-ton-mileage was 2,172,000 and the passenger-mileage, 114·86m.

Shipping. Burma has 60 miles of navigable canals. The Irrawaddy is navigable up to Myitkyina, 900 miles from the sea, and its tributary, the Chindwin, is navigable for 390 miles. The Irrawaddy delta has nearly 2,000 miles of navigable water. The Salween, the Attaran and the G'yne provide about 250 miles of navigable waters around Moulmein. The Inland Water Transport Board runs services from Bhamo to Myitkyina. The Burma Five Star Line Ltd operates coastal steamer services to the major ports in Burma, India, East Pakistan, Malaya, Japan, Europe and UK.

The port of Rangoon in 1974–75 handled 1·19m. tons of seaborne trade.

Post and Broadcasting. There were 1,094 post offices in 1975. Number of telephones was 31,456 in 1977, of which about 22,140 are in Rangoon.

There are 283 telegraph offices, and the internal system of communication is chiefly by wireless. Radio telephone or direct wireless telegraph links exist with most Asian countries, USA, USSR, UK, Denmark, Switzerland, Australia, Canada and Italy.

Cinemas. In 1971 there were about 418 cinemas.

Newspapers. In 1978 there were 7 daily newspapers.

JUSTICE, RELIGION, EDUCATION AND WELFARE

Justice. The Chief Court has supervision over all courts in the Union. It is presided over by the Chief Justice and other judges. Its present name was revived in March 1972 having been called Chief Court since 1962. All lower courts are now replaced by People's Courts formed with ordinary citizens to preside over trials, aided by former judges and magistrates acting as law officers.

Religion. The Revolutionary Government, having repealed the amendment of 1961 which made Buddhism the state religion, recognizes 'the right of everyone freely to profess and practise his religion'.

Education. After the attainment of independence the Government has adopted a centralized system of control of schools which are graded as primary, middle and high school. The medium of instruction in all schools is Burmese; English is taught as a compulsory second language in secondary schools.

Education is free in the primary, junior secondary and vocational schools; fees are charged in senior secondary schools and universities.

In 1974–75 there were 571 state high schools with 182,848 pupils, 1,202 state middle schools with 762,871 pupils and 19,399 state primary schools with 3,449,552 pupils; the total teaching staff was 100,414.

On 1 April 1965 the Government nationalized 129 of the 883 registered private schools, including all the major high schools.

The Higher Education Law 1964 has decentralized the University of Rangoon. Beside the Arts and Science University, there are independent degree-giving institutes of engineering, education, medicine, agriculture, economics and commerce, and veterinary sciences. In 1974–75 students numbered 61,154. The University of Mandalay (with 7,639 students) has been similarly decentralized. A foreign-languages institute in Rangoon has about 800 students learning French, German, Russian, Japanese, Chinese and Italian.

There are intermediate colleges at Taunggyi, Magwe, Akyab and Myitkyina, and degree colleges at Moulmein and Bassein, and several technical and agricultural institutes at higher and middle level. 3,703 middle and primary school teachers were being trained in 15 training colleges in 1974–75.

A correspondence course for universities and colleges was introduced in 1976.

Health. In 1973 there were 4,400 doctors and 25,000 hospital beds.

DIPLOMATIC REPRESENTATIVES

OF BURMA IN GREAT BRITAIN (19A Charles St., London, W1X 8ER)

Ambassador: U Kyi Maung (accredited 10 May 1978).

OF GREAT BRITAIN IN BURMA
(80 Strand Rd., Rangoon)

Ambassador: C. L. Booth.

OF BURMA IN THE USA (2300 S St., NW,
Washington, D.C., 20008)

Ambassador: U Tin Lat.

OF THE USA IN BURMA
(581 Merchant St., Rangoon)

Ambassador: Maurice D. Bean.

OF BURMA TO THE UNITED NATIONS

Ambassador: U Maung Maung Gyee.

Books of Reference

Statistical Information: A Central Statistical Office is organized as a department of the Ministry of National Planning.

Burma: Treaty between the Government of the United Kingdom and the Provisional Government of Burma. (Treaty Series No. 16, 1948.) HMSO, 1948
Cornyn, W. S., and Musgrave, J. K., *Burmese Glossary.* New York, 1958
Furnivall, J. S., *A Governance of Modern Burma.* New York, 1960
Lehman, F. K., *The Structure of Chin Society.* Univ. of Illinois Press, 1963
Maung, M., *Burma in the Family of Nations.* Amsterdam, 1956
Smith, D. E., *Religion and Politics in Burma.* Princeton Univ. Press, 1965
Stewart, J. A., and Dunn, C. W., *Burmese–English Dictionary.* London, 1940 ff.
Tinker, H., *The Union of Burma.* OUP, 1957
Trager, F. N., *Burma: From Kingdom to Republic.* London, 1966
Woodman, D., *The Making of Burma.* London, 1962

BURUNDI

Capital: Bujumbura
Population: 3·9m. (1977)
GNP per capita: US$120 (1976)

HISTORY. Tradition recounts the establishment of a Tutsi kingdom under successive Mwamis as early as the 16th century. German military occupation in 1890 incorporated the territory into German East Africa. From 1919 Burundi formed part of Ruanda-Urundi administered by the Belgians, first as a League of Nations mandate and then as a United Nations trust territory. Elections supervised by the United Nations in Sept. 1961 resulted in a large majority for the Unité et Progrès National party (UPRONA). Internal self-government was granted on 1 Jan. 1962, followed by independence on 1 July 1962. An agreement, signed with Rwanda under United Nations auspices at Addis Ababa in April 1962, provided for a monetary and customs union. This union and all organizations operated jointly by the two governments were dissolved by 30 Sept. 1964.

On 8 July 1966 Prince Charles Ndizeye deposed his father Mwami Mwambutsa IV, suspended the constitution and made Capt. Michel Micombero Prime Minister. On 1 Sept. Prince Charles was enthroned as Mwami Ntare V. On 28 Nov., while the Mwami was attending a Head of States Conference in Kinshasa (Congo), Micombero declared Burundi a republic with himself as president.

On 31 March 1972 Prince Charles returned to Burundi from Uganda and was placed under house arrest. On 29 April 1972 President Micombero dissolved the Council of Ministers and took full power; that night heavy fighting broke out between rebels from both Burundi and neighbouring countries, and the ruling Tutsi, apparently with the intention of destroying the Tutsi hegemony. Prince Charles was killed during the fighting and it was estimated that up to 120,000 were killed. On 14 July 1972 President Micombero reinstated a Government with a Prime Minister. On 1 Nov. 1976 President Micombero was deposed by the Army. A Supreme Military Council of the Armed Forces was established which appointed Col. Jean-Baptiste Bagaza president.

AREA AND POPULATION. Burundi extends from lat. $2\frac{1}{2}°$ to $4\frac{1}{2}°$ S. and long. 29° to 31° E., and has an area of 27,834 sq km (10,759 sq. miles). It lies astride the main Nile–Congo dividing crest (6,000–7,000 ft) bounded on the west by the narrow plain of the Ruzizi River and Lake Tanganyika (2,534 ft). The interior is a broken plateau at an average height of about 5,000 ft, sloping eastwards down to Tanzania and the valley of the Maragarazi River. The southernmost tributary of the Nile system, the Luvironza, rises in the south of the country.

The Ruzizi plain has an average temperature of 23° C. (73° F.), the Nile–Congo crest of 17·3° C. (63° F.), the central plateau of 20° C. (68° F.). The long dry season lasts from June to August, the long rainy season from February to May. The annual rainfall at Bujumbura is 31 in., on the Nile–Congo crest 57 in.

The population at the last census in 1959 was 2,213,280; but was probably over 3·9m. in 1977. There are three ethnic groups—Hutu (Bantu, forming the great majority): Tutsi (Nilotic, less than 15%); Twa (pygmoids, less than 1%). There are some 3,500 Europeans and 1,500 Asians. In 1974 some 49,000 Tutsi refugees from Rwanda were living in Burundi.

Bujumbura, the capital, has about 100,000 inhabitants. Kitega (10,000 inhabitants) was formerly the royal residence.

CONSTITUTION AND GOVERNMENT. Burundi remains a republic under the new military government but the activities of the Uprona party have been suspended. The Supreme Military Council of 30 members is headed by the President as is its 11 member Executive Committee. The President is responsible to the Supreme Military Council and the government is responsible to him. The government has a Prime Minister, 14 other ministers and 3 Secretaries of State.

President of the Republic: Col. Jean-Baptiste Bagaza.
Prime Minister: Lieut.-Col. Edward Nzambimana.

The administrative divisions are: 8 provinces, each under a military governor (Bujumbura, Bubanza, Muramvya, Ngozi, Gitega, Muhinga, Ruyigi and Bururi); 18 arrondissements; and 78 communes.

Flag: White diagonal cross dividing triangles of red and green, in the centre a white disc bearing 3 red green-bordered 6-pointed stars.

DEFENCE. The national armed forces totals 7,000 (there are also about 2,000 in paramilitary units) and includes a small naval flotilla and air force flight of 2 C-47 pistoned-engined transports.

INTERNATIONAL RELATIONS

Membership. Burundi is a member of UN and OAU and is an ACP state of EEC.

Aid. Economic and technical assistance is provided substantially by Belgium and to a smaller degree by the EEC and the UN. Foreign aid (1973, in 1m. Burundi francs): Belgium, 636; EEC, 567; UN, 314; France, 180; Federal Republic of Germany, 39. Aid from all sources 1965–75 totalled 11,000m. Burundi francs.

ECONOMY

Planning. In the second 5-year plan, 1973–77, priority was given to agriculture with investment in rural development being 39% of the total budget.

Budget. The revised 1976 budget envisaged receipts of 4,200m. Burundi francs, and expenditure of 3,100m. Burundi francs. Main expenditure (1976, in Burundi francs): Education, 814m.; defence, 800m.; public health, 224m.; public works, 316m.; agriculture, 147m. Development budget: Receipt, 1,492m., and expenditure, 1,890·5m.

Currency. The currency is administered by the Bank of the Republic of Burundi. The rate was 153 Burundi francs = £1 in Jan. 1977. The rate for the US$1 was fixed at 90 in May 1976.

Weights and Measures. The metric system operates.

ENERGY AND NATURAL RESOURCES

Electricity. Electricity generation capacity was 6 mw in 1976.

Minerals. There is some incipient mining activity and a recent discovery of large nickel deposits as yet unexploited of some 280m. tonnes. Production (in tonnes): Basthenaesite (150, 1975), cassiterite (74, 1975), kaolin (150, 1973) and gold. Total mineral exports (1973), 29m. Burundi francs.

Agriculture. The main economic activity and the main source of employment of the country is subsistence agriculture, which accounts for well over half of the gross national product. Beans, kassava, maize, sweet potatoes, groundnuts, peas, sorghum and bananas are grown according to the climate and the region.

The main cash crop is coffee, of which about 93% is arabica. A coffee board (OCIBU) manages the grading and export of the crop. In 1975–76, 15,000 tonnes of arabica and 2,000 tonnes of robusta were produced. The average crop 1963–73 was 21,000 tonnes. Cotton production is falling; 1,421 tonnes 1975–76 (7,426, 1968). Plantations of good-quality tea are being developed. Production (1975) 787 tonnes, of which 583 tonnes were exported mainly to Canada and UK.

Cattle play an important traditional role, and there were about 800,000 head in 1976. The quality is poor, but efforts are being made to improve it. There are some 1m. goats and sheep and 46,000 pigs.

Fisheries. There is a small commercial fishing industry on Lake Tanganyika which produced 7,941 tonnes in 1973 and is undergoing further development.

Tourism. Tourism is developing and there were 13,000 visitors Jan.–June 1976.

INDUSTRY AND TRADE

Industry. Industrial development is rudimentary. In Bujumbura there are plants for the processing of coffee and by-products of cotton, a brewery, cement works, a textile factory, a soap factory, a shoe factory and small metal workshops.

Commerce. The total value of exports in 1975 was 2,513m., re-exports, 29m. Burundi francs and of imports, 4,856m. Burundi francs. Main exports in 1975 were coffee (88·8%), tea, cotton and hides (9%). Sources of imports in 1974 were EEC, 51·3%, of which Benelux, 22·6%, Federal Republic of Germany, 11·1%, France, 8·8%; USA, 5·2%; UK, 4·7%. Principal imports were cottons and cotton goods, motor vehicles, synthetic textiles, flour and petrol products.

Trade of Burundi with the UK (British Department of Trade returns, in £1,000 sterling):

	1972	*1973*	*1974*	*1975*	*1976*	*1977*
Imports to UK	699	1,116	590	476	993	1,817
Exports and re-exports from UK	238	464	964	1,003	844	1,645

JUSTICE, RELIGION, EDUCATION AND WELFARE

Justice. There is a Supreme Court, an appeal court and a *tribunal de première instance* at Bujumbura.

Religion. Over half the population is Roman Catholic; there is a Roman Catholic archbishop and 3 bishops. The Anglican Missions under a bishop fall within the archdiocese of Uganda.

Education. In 1970–71 the number of children in primary schools was 175,600, 7,892 pupils were receiving secondary education and 2,031 were receiving craft and technical training. The university of Bujumbura has over 400 students.

The local language is Kirundi, a Bantu language. French is also an official language. Kiswahili is spoken in the commercial centres.

Health. In 1974 there were about 70 doctors and over 4,000 hospital beds.

COMMUNICATIONS

Roads. There is a comprehensive interior road network of 6,400 km connecting with Rwanda, Congo and Tanzania but only 300 km are macadamized and travelling can be difficult in the rainy season.

Aviation. Bujumbura has an airport of international standard and there are regular services to Europe, Zaïre and East Africa. Average air passengers (1968–73) 28,000.

Shipping. These are lake services from Bujumbura to Kigoma (Tanzania). The main route for exports and imports is *via* Kigoma, and thence by rail to Dar es Salaam.

DIPLOMATIC REPRESENTATIVES

OF BURUNDI IN GREAT BRITAIN

Ambassador: Jérôme Ntungumburanye (resides in Brussels).

OF GREAT BRITAIN IN BURUNDI

Ambassador: A. E. Donald (resides in Kinshasa).

OF BURUNDI IN THE USA (2717 Connecticut Ave., NW, Washington, D.C., 20009)

Ambassador: Laurent Nzeyimana.

OF THE USA IN BURUNDI (Chausée Prince Louis Rwagasore, Bujumbura)

Ambassador: David E. Mark.

OF BURUNDI TO THE UNITED NATIONS

Ambassador: Artémon Simbananiye.

Books of Reference

Ruanda-Urundi [Engl. ed.]. Office of Information for the Congo, Brussels, 1960
Lemarchand, R., *Rwanda and Burundi*. London, 1970
Melady, T. P., *Burundi: The Tragic Years*. Maryknoll, New York, 1974
Mpozapara, G., *La République du Burundi*. Paris, 1971

CAMEROON

République Unie du Cameroun

Capital: Yaoundé
Population: 7·5m. (1976)
GNP per capita: US$290 (1976)

HISTORY. The former German colony of Kamerun was occupied by French and British troops in 1916. The greater portion of the territory (432,000 sq. km) was in 1919 placed under French administration, excluding the territory ceded to Germany in 1911, which reverted to French Equatorial Africa. The portion under French trusteeship was granted full internal autonomy on 1 Jan. 1959 and complete independence was proclaimed on 1 Jan. 1960.

The portion assigned to Great Britain (89,270 sq. km) consisted of 2 parts. A plebiscite held in Feb. 1961 in the northern part decided in favour of joining the Federation of Nigeria with 145,265 votes for and 97,654 against joining the Cameroon Republic. The Southern Cameroons held a plebiscite in Feb. 1961 and decided by 135,830 votes against some 97,654 to join the Cameroon Republic.

On 1 Oct. 1961 the former British trusteeship territory of Southern Cameroons and the Cameroon Republic combined in the Federal Republic of Cameroon.

On 20 May 1972, as the result of a national referendum, the creation of a unitary, bilingual and pluricultural state, as The United Republic of Cameroon was overwhelmingly approved and came into force on 2 June 1972. French and English are the 2 official languages.

AREA AND POPULATION. Cameroon is bounded west by the Bight of Bonny, north-west by Nigeria and north-east by Chad with Lake Chad at its northern tip. The total area is about 474,000 sq. km; its population was (census 1976) 7·5m. Chief towns (1975): Yaoundé (population 274,399); Douala (485,797), Foumban (59,701), Maroua (46,077), Bafoussam (45,998), Garoua (36,661) and Victoria (31,222). Cameroon is divided into 7 administrative provinces.

CONSTITUTION AND GOVERNMENT. The constitution provides for a President as chief of state and commander of the armed forces, who is elected for a 5-year term, and a cabinet whose members must not be members of parliament.

The National Assembly, elected by universal adult suffrage, consists of 120 representatives. General elections took place on 18 May 1973 and all seats were won by the *Union National Camerounaise*.

The capital is Yaoundé and the country is divided into 6 provinces.

President: Ahmadou Ahidjo (re-elected for fourth 5-year term on 5 April 1975).
Prime Minister: Paul Biya.
National flag: Three vertical strips of green, red, yellow, with a gold star in the centre.

DEFENCE

Army. The Army consists of 4 infantry battalions and support units; total strength, 5,500.

Air Force. The Air Force has 2 C-130H Hercules turboprop transports, 2 HS.748 twin-turboprop freight transports, 2 Caribou STOL transports, 4 C-47s, 1 Flamant, 1 Dornier Do 28 and a Queen Air for transport and communications duties, 4 Broussard liaison aircraft, 4 Magister jet basic trainers, 4 Alouette II helicopters, 1 Alouette III helicopter, and a twin-engined Puma helicopter for VIP and transport duties. Personnel total about 300.

INTERNATIONAL RELATIONS

Membership. Cameroon is a member of UN, OAU and is an ACP state of EEC.

ECONOMY

Budget. The budget for 1976–77 balanced at 128,000m. francs CFA.

Currency. The unit of currency is the franc CFA.

Banking. At 31 Dec. 1960 savings banks had 22,248 depositors with 335m. francs CFA to their credit. The main banks are Banque Internationale pour l'Afrique Occidentale, Société Camerounaise de Banque, Société Générale de Banques au Cameroun and Cameroon Bank. Most of the banks operate in all the large cities and towns throughout the United Republic.

AGRICULTURE. Production (1974, in tonnes): Cocoa, 110,000; coffee, 31,000; bananas, 900,000; cotton, 45,300; rubber, 13,900.

Livestock (1976): 2·1m. cattle, 1·6m. sheep, 1·63m. goats, 400,000 pigs.

INDUSTRY AND TRADE

Industry. There are factories producing shoes, soap, oil, food products, cigarettes. aluminium. Foreign investment is encouraged by, depending on the type of company, various tax exemptions and deductions and import duty exemption on equipment, materials and machinery.

Commerce. Imports and exports in 1,000 francs CFA were as follows:

	1971	*1973*	*1974*	*1975*
Imports	69,880	67,720	104,900	128,103
Exports	60,152	81,800	114,900	102,087

In 1974 the main trade was with France, other EEC countries and USA.

Trade with UK (British Department of Trade returns, in £1,000 sterling):

	1973	*1974*	*1975*	*1976*	*1977*
Imports to UK	2,417	3,043	5,377	8,991	12,237
Exports and re-exports from UK	4,315	6,253	7,730	8,089	20,702

Tourism. There were an estimated 10,000 foreign visitors in 1976.

COMMUNICATIONS

Roads. There were (1977) 2,155 km of tarred roads, 9,284 km earth roads and 15,482 km of secondary roads.

Railways. Cameroon Railways (1,173 km in 1977) link Douala with Nkongsamba and Ngaoundére, with branches M'Banga–Kumba and Makak–M'Balmayo.

Shipping. Important ports are Douala, Tiko and Bota.

Post and Broadcasting. There were (1957) 86 post offices and 6 postal agencies; telephone lines, 2,677 km; telephones (1974), 21,881; radio stations, 36.

EDUCATION (1969). There were 3,372 public primary schools with 800,000 pupils and 50,000 pupils in secondary schools. The University of Yaoundé had (1972) 2,370 students and 131 teachers.

DIPLOMATIC REPRESENTATIVES

OF THE UNITED REPUBLIC OF CAMEROON IN GREAT BRITAIN
(84 Holland Pk., London, W11 3SB)

Ambassador: Vincent Paul-Thomas Pondi (accredited 23 Feb. 1978).

OF GREAT BRITAIN IN THE UNITED REPUBLIC OF CAMEROON
(Le Concorde, Ave. J. F. Kennedy, BP 547, Yaoundé)

Ambassador: A. E. Saunders, CMG, OBE.

OF THE UNITED REPUBLIC OF CAMEROON IN THE USA
(2349 Massachusetts Ave., NW, Washington, D.C., 20008)

Ambassador: Benoit Bindzi.

OF THE USA IN THE UNITED REPUBLIC OF CAMEROON
(Rue Nachtigal, BP 817, Yaoundé)

Ambassador: Mabel M. Smythe.

OF THE UNITED REPUBLIC OF CAMEROON
TO THE UNITED NATIONS

Ambassador: Ferdinand Léopold Oyono.

Books of Reference

Statistical Information: The Service de la Statistique Générale, at Douala, set up in 1945, publishes a monthly bulletin (from Nov. 1950)

Ardener, E. (and others), *Plantation and Village in the Cameroons: Economic and Social Studies.* OUP, 1960

Le Vine, V. T., *The Cameroon Federal Republic.* Cornell Univ. Press, 1971

CANADA

Capital: Ottawa
Population: 23m. (1976)
GNP per capita: US$7,510 (1976)

HISTORY. The territories which now constitute Canada came under British power at various times by settlement, conquest or cession. Nova Scotia was occupied in 1628 by settlement at Port Royal, was ceded back to France in 1632 and was finally ceded by France in 1713, by the Treaty of Utrecht; the Hudson's Bay Company's charter, conferring rights over all the territory draining into Hudson Bay, was granted in 1670; Canada, with all its dependencies, including New Brunswick and Prince Edward Island, was formally ceded to Great Britain by France in 1763; Vancouver Island was acknowledged to be British by the Oregon Boundary Treaty of 1846, and British Columbia was established as a separate colony in 1858. As originally constituted, Canada was composed of Upper and Lower Canada (now Ontario and Quebec), Nova Scotia and New Brunswick. They were united under an Act of the Imperial Parliament, 'The British North America Act, 1867', which came into operation on 1 July 1867 by royal proclamation. The Act provides that the constitution of Canada shall be 'similar in principle to that of the United Kingdom'; that the executive authority shall be vested in the Sovereign, and carried on in his name by a Governor-General and Privy Council; and that the legislative power shall be exercised by a Parliament of two Houses, called the 'Senate' and the 'House of Commons'. The present position of Canada in the British Commonwealth of Nations was defined at the Imperial Conference of 1926.

On 30 June 1931 the British House of Commons approved the enactment of the Statute of Westminster freeing the Provinces as well as the Dominion from the operation of the Colonial Laws Validity Act, and thus removing what legal limitations existed as regards Canada's legislative autonomy. A joint address of the Senate and the House of Commons was sent to the Governor-General for transmission to London on 10 July 1931. The statute received the royal assent on 12 Dec. 1931.

Provision was made in the British North America Act for the admission of British Columbia, Prince Edward Island, Newfoundland, Rupert's Land and North-western Territory into the Union. In 1869 Rupert's Land, or the Northwest Territories, was purchased from the Hudson's Bay Company. On 15 July 1870, Rupert's Land and the North-western Territory were annexed to Canada and named the North West Territories, Canada having agreed to pay the Hudson's Bay Company in cash and land for its relinquishing of claims to the territory. By the same action the Province of Manitoba was created from a small portion of this territory and they were admitted into the Confederation on 15 July 1870. On 20 July 1871 the province of British Columbia was admitted, and Prince Edward Island on 1 July 1873. The provinces of Alberta and Saskatchewan were formed from the provisional districts of Alberta, Athabaska, Assiniboia and Saskatchewan and originally parts of the North-West Territories and admitted on 1 Sept. 1905. Newfoundland formally joined Canada as its tenth province on 31 March 1949. In Feb. 1931 Norway formally recognized the Canadian title to the Sverdrup group of Arctic islands. Canada thus holds sovereignty in the whole Arctic sector north of the Canadian mainland.

EVENTS. A USSR military satellite powered by a small nuclear powerpack fell to earth over north-west Canada on 24 Jan. 1978.

AREA AND POPULATION. Population of the area now included in Canada:

1851	2,436,297	1901	5,371,315	1951	14,009,429
1861	3,229,633	1911	7,206,643	1961	18,238,247
1871	3,689,257	1921	8,787,949	1971	21,568,311 [2]
1881	4,324,810	1931	10,376,786 [1]	1976	22,992,604
1891	4,833,239	1941	11,506,655 [1]		

[1] From 1951 figures include Newfoundland. [2] Census, preliminary.

Population (estimated), 1 April 1977, was 23·2m.

Areas of the provinces, etc. (in sq. km) and population at recent censuses:

Province	*Land area*	*Fresh water area*	*Total land and fresh water area*	*Population, 1966*	*Population, 1971*	*Population, 1976*
Newfoundland	370,485	34,032	404,517	493,396	522,104	557,725
Prince Edward Island	5,657	—	5,657	108,535	111,641	118,229
Nova Scotia	52,841	2,650	55,491	756,039	788,960	828,571
New Brunswick	72,092	1,344	73,436	616,788	634,557	677,250
Quebec	1,356,791	183,889	1,540,680	5,780,845	6,027,764	6,234,445
Ontario	891,194	177,388	1,068,582	6,960,870	7,703,106	8,264,465
Manitoba	548,495	101,592	650,087	963,066	988,247	1,021,506
Saskatchewan	570,269	81,631	651,900	955,344	926,242	921,323
Alberta	644,389	16,796	661,185	1,463,203	1,627,874	1,838,037
British Columbia	930,528	18,068	948,596	1,873,674	2,184,621	2,466,608
Yukon	531,844	4,481	536,325	14,382	18,388	21,836
Northwest Territories	3,246,390	133,294	3,379,684	28,738	34,807	42,609
Total	9,220,975	755,165	9,976,140	20,014,880	21,568,311	22,992,604

Of the total population in 1971, 18,272,780 were Canadian born, 933,040 other British born and 2,362,490 foreign born, 309,640 of the latter being USA born.

The population born outside Canada in the provinces was in the following ratio (%): Newfoundland, 1·7; Prince Edward Island, 3·3; Nova Scotia, 4·7; New Brunswick, 3·7; Quebec, 7·8; Ontario, 22·2; Manitoba, 15·3; Saskatchewan, 12; Alberta, 17·3; British Columbia, 22·7.

In 1971, figures for the population, according to origin, were:

British Isles		Polish	316,430	Belgian	51,135
English	6,245,970	Hebrew	296,945	Chinese	118,815
Scottish	1,720,390	Indian and Eskimo	312,760	Austrian	42,120
Irish	1,581,730	Italian	730,820	Romanian	27,375
Other	76,030	Norwegian	179,290	Icelandic	27,905
Total, British	9,624,115	Swedish	101,870	Japanese	37,260
French	6,180,120	Russian	64,425	Yugoslav	104,955
German	1,317,200	Czech and Slovak	81,870	Negro	34,445
Ukrainian	580,660	Hungarian	131,890	Greek	124,475
Netherlands	425,945	Finnish	59,215	Lithuanian	24,535
		Danish	75,725	Not stated	171,645

The native Indian population numbered 282,762 in 1975 and the Eskimo population was 17,550 in 1971.

Populations of Census Metropolitan Areas (CMA) and Cities (proper), 1976 census:

	CMA	*City proper*		*CMA*	*City proper*
Toronto	2,803,101	633,318	Halifax	267,991	117,882
Montreal	2,802,485	1,080,546	Windsor	247,582	196,526
Vancouver	1,166,348	410,188	Victoria	218,250	62,551
Ottawa	693,288	304,462	Sudbury	157,030	97,604
Winnipeg	578,217	560,874	Regina	151,191	149,593
Edmonton	554,228	461,361	St John's	143,390	86,576
Quebec	542,158	177,082	Oshawa	135,196	107,023
Hamilton	529,371	312,003	Saskatoon	133,750	133,750
Calgary	469,917	469,917	Chicoutimi-Jonquiere	128,643	—
St Catharines-Niagara	301,921	—	Chicoutimi	—	57,371
St Catharines	—	123,351	Jonquiere	—	60,691
Niagara Falls	—	69,423	Thunder Bay	119,253	111,476
Kitchener	272,158	131,870	Saint John	112,974	85,956
London	270,383	240,392			

The total 'urban' population of Canada in 1976 (preliminary) was 17,353,640, against 16,403,505 in 1971.

While the registration of births, marriages and deaths is under provincial control, the statistics are compiled on a uniform system by Statistics Canada.

The following table gives the results for 1975, preliminary:

Province	Living births Number	Living births Per 1,000 population	Marriages Number	Marriages Per 1,000 population	Deaths Number	Deaths Per 1,000 population
Newfoundland	11,243	20·4	4,313	7·8	3,219	5·9
Prince Edward Island	1,928	16·2	936	7·9	1,057	8·9
Nova Scotia	13,119	16·0	7,059	8·6	6,799	8·3
New Brunswick	11,775	17·4	5,945	8·8	5,150	7·6
Quebec	93,000[1]	15·0[1]	50,377	8·1	43,414	7·0
Ontario	125,708	15·3	72,209	8·8	60,604	7·4
Manitoba	17,144	16·8	8,915	8·8	8,385	8·2
Saskatchewan	15,260	16·6	8,066	8·8	7,672	8·4
Alberta	31,618	17·9	17,520	9·9	11,397	6·4
British Columbia	36,277	14·8	21,824	8·9	19,151	7·8
Yukon Territory	408	19·6	201	9·7	112	5·4
N.W. Territories	1,171	31·0	220	5·8	216	5·7
	358,621	15·7	197,585	8·7	167,176	7·3

[1] Estimated.

Immigrant arrivals by country of last permanent residence:

Country	1972	1973	1974	1975	1976
England	12,520	19,979	28,828	27,761	16,759
Northern Ireland	2,048	2,263	2,391	1,977	1,536
Scotland	3,270	4,038	6,259	4,182	2,343
Wales	323	662	931	1,031	890
Lesser isles	36	31	47	27	20
Total, British Isles	18,197	26,973	38,456	34,978	21,548
Australia	1,694	2,096	2,022	1,654	1,387
France	2,742	3,586	4,232	3,891	3,251
Germany, Fed. Rep. of	2,025	2,564	3,619	3,469	2,672
Greece	4,016	5,833	5,632	4,062	2,487
Hong Kong	6,297	14,662	12,704	11,132	10,725
India	5,049	9,203	12,868	10,144	6,733
Irish Republic	936	1,129	1,292	1,098	639
Italy	4,608	5,468	5,226	5,078	4,530
Japan	718	1,105	859	635	498
Lebanon	996	1,325	1,762	1,506	7,161
Netherlands	1,471	1,898	2,103	1,448	1,359
Pakistan	1,190	2,285	2,315	2,165	2,173
Philippines	3,946	6,757	9,564	7,364	5,939
Poland	1,321	1,261	945	809	903
Portugal	8,737	13,483	16,333	8,547	5,344
South Africa, Rep. of	440	766	1,154	1,567	1,611
Switzerland	778	953	1,336	1,272	1,192
USA	22,618	25,242	26,541	20,155	17,315
Yugoslavia	2,047	2,873	3,200	2,932	1,741
Total, all countries	122,006	184,200	218,456	187,881	149,429

Blishen, B. R. (ed.), *Canadian Society; Sociological Perspectives.* 3rd ed. Toronto, 1965
Brunet, M., *La présence anglaise et les Canadiens.* Montreal, 1958
Card, B. Y., *Trends and Change in Canadian Society: Their Challege to Canadian Youth.* Toronto, 1968
Clark, S. D., *Urbanism and the Changing Canadian Society.* 2nd ed. Toronto, 1970.—*The Developing Canadian Community.* 2nd ed. Toronto, 1968
Cowan, H. I., *British Emigration to British North America, The First Hundred Years.* Rev. ed. Toronto, 1961
Dawe, A., *Profiles of a Nation: Canadian Themes and Styles.* Toronto, 1970
Department of the Secretary of State, *The Canadian Family Tree.* Ottawa, 1967
Garigue, P., *La Vie familiale des Canadiens français.* Montreal, 1962
Iglauer, E., *The New People: The Eskimo's Journey in Our Time.* New York, 1966
James, S., *Urban Canada.* Toronto, 1969
Jenness, D., *The Indians of Canada.* 5th ed. Ottawa, 1960
Park, J., *The Culture of Contemporary Canada.* Toronto, 1970
Porter, J., *The Vertical Mosaic.* Toronto, 1965

Rosenberg, S. E., *The Jewish Community in Canada: A History*. Toronto, 1970
Wade, M., *The French Canadians, 1760–1967*. 2 vols. 2nd ed. Toronto and London, 1968

CONSTITUTION AND GOVERNMENT. The members of the Senate are appointed until age 75 by summons of the Governor-General under the Great Seal of Canada. Members appointed before 2 June 1965 may remain in office for life. The Senate consists of 104 senators, namely, 24 from Ontario, 24 from Quebec, 10 from Nova Scotia, 10 from New Brunswick, 4 from Prince Edward Island, 6 from Manitoba, 6 from British Columbia, 6 from Alberta, 6 from Saskatchewan, 6 from Newfoundland, 1 from the Yukon Territory and 1 from the Northwest Territories. Each senator must be at least 30 years of age, a born or naturalized subject of the Queen and must reside in the province for which he is appointed and his total net worth must be at least $4,000. The House of Commons is elected by the people, for 5 years, unless sooner dissolved. Women have the vote and are eligible. From 1867 to the election of 1945 representation was based on Quebec having 65 seats and the other provinces the same proportion of 65 which their population had to the population of Quebec. In the General Election of 1949 readjustments were based on the population of all the provinces taken as a whole. Generally speaking, this format for representation has prevailed in all subsequent elections with readjustments made after each decennial census. However, on 31 Dec. 1974, the law was changed so that it has reverted somewhat to the type of system that had prevailed initially. That is to say, Quebec is to be assigned a fixed number of seats in the House of Commons and the representation of the other provinces calculated by a quotient which reflects this fact.

The thirtieth Parliament, elected on 8 July 1974, comprises 264 members and the provincial and territorial representation are: Ontario, 88; Quebec, 74; Nova Scotia, 11; New Brunswick, 10; Manitoba, 13; British Columbia, 23; Prince Edward Island, 4; Saskatchewan, 13; Alberta, 19; Newfoundland, 7; Yukon Territory, 1; Northwest Territories, 1.

State of parties in the Senate (Oct. 1977): Liberals, 72; Progressive Conservatives, 15; Independent, 2; Social Credit, 1; Independent Liberal, 1; Vacant, 13; total 104.

State of the parties in the House of Commons (Oct. 1977): Liberals, 141; Progressive Conservatives, 92; Social Credit, 10; New Democratic Party, 16; Independent, 1; Vacant, 4; total, 264.

The following is a list of Governors-General of Canada:

Viscount Monck	1867–1868	Viscount Byng of Vimy	1921–1926
Lord Lisgar	1868–1872	Viscount Willingdon	1926–1931
Earl of Dufferin	1872–1878	Earl of Bessborough	1931–1935
Marquess of Lorne	1878–1883	Lord Tweedsmuir	1935–1940
Marquess of Lansdowne	1883–1888	Earl of Athlone	1940–1946
Lord Stanley of Preston	1888–1893	Field-Marshal Viscount Alexander of Tunis	1946–1952
Earl of Aberdeen	1893–1898	Vincent Massey	1952–1959
Earl of Minto	1898–1904	Georges Philias Vanier	1959–1967
Earl Grey	1904–1911	Roland Michener	1967–1974
HRH the Duke of Connaught	1911–1916		
Duke of Devonshire	1916–1921		

Governor-General: The Rt Hon. Jules Léger (sworn in Jan. 1974).

National flag: Vertically red, white, red with the white of double width and bearing a stylized red maple leaf.

The office and appointment of the Governor-General are regulated by letters patent, signed by the King on 8 Sept. 1947, which came into force on 1 Oct. 1947. In 1977 the Queen approved the transfer to the Governor-General functions discharged by the Sovereign. He is assisted in his functions, under the provisions of the Act of 1867, by a Privy Council composed of Cabinet Ministers.

The following is the list of the Liberal Cabinet in Nov. 1977, in order of precedence, which in Canada attaches generally rather to the person than to the office:

Prime Minister: Rt Hon. Pierre Elliott Trudeau.
Deputy Prime Minister and President of the Privy Council: Allan MacEachen.
Finance: Jean Chrétien.
Labour: John Munro.
Justice and Attorney-General: Stanley Basford.

External Affairs: Don Jamieson.
Treasury Board: Robert Andras.
Transport: Otto Lang.
Supply and Services: Jean-Pierre Goyer.
Energy, Mines and Resources: Alastair Gillespie.
Agriculture: Eugene Whelan.
Consumer and Corporate Affairs: Warren Allmand.
Indian Affairs and Northern Development: Hugh Faulkner.
Urban Affairs: André Ouellet.
Veterans Affairs: Daniel MacDonald.
Federal–Provincial Relations: Marc Lalonde.
Communications: Jeanne Sauvé.
Government Leader in the Senate: Ray Perrault.
National Defence: Barnett Danson.
Public Works, and Science and Technology: Judd Buchanan.
Fisheries and the Environment: Roméo LeBlanc.
Regional Economic Expansion: Marcel Lessard.
Employment and Immigration: Jack Cullen.
Minister of State responsible for Environment: Leonard Marchand.
Secretary of State: John Roberts.
National Health and Welfare: Monique Bégin.
Postmaster-General: Jean-Jacques Blais.
Solicitor-General: Francis Fox.
Minister of State responsible for Small Businesses: Tony Abbott.
Minister of State responsible for Fitness and Amateur Sport: Iona Campagnolo.
National Revenue: Joseph-Philippe Guay.
Industry, Trade and Commerce: John Horner.
Minister of State responsible for Multiculturalism: Norman Cafik.

The sessional allowance of members of the Senate and House of Commons is $25,600 per annum. Senators receive an additional annual tax-free expense allowance of $5,600 and members of the House of Commons $11,300–$15,175. The Leader of the Government in the Senate and the Opposition Leader in the Senate receive additional remuneration of $20,000 and $8,500 respectively. The remuneration of the Prime Minister is $33,300, a cabinet minister and Leader of the Opposition $20,000, a minister without portfolio $7,500, in addition to the sessional and expense allowances they receive as members of Parliament. Each minister and the Leader of the Opposition is also entitled to a $2,000 motor vehicle allowance. The speaker of the Senate receives a salary of $12,500 and the Speaker of the House of Commons a salary of $20,000; each is allowed $3,000 in lieu of residence. An allowance of $5,600 is given to the leader of a party with 12 or more members in the House of Commons, other than the Prime Minister and Leader of the Opposition, and to the chief Government and Opposition whips. Parliamentary Secretaries receive an additional annual allowance of $5,600.

An Act to provide retiring allowances, on a contributory basis, to members of the House of Commons was given the Royal Assent on 4 July 1952. This Act was amended in July 1963; a member can now opt for a reduced retiring allowance in favour of an additional allowance for the widow; and provision has been made for retiring allowance for former Prime Ministers and their widows.

The Canadian Parliamentary Guide. Annual. Ottawa
Report of the Royal Commission on Dominion–Provincial Relations, Canada 1867–1939. 3 vols. Ottawa, 1940
Bissonnette, B., *Essai sur constitution du Canada*. Montreal, 1963
Cheffins, R. I., *The Constitutional Process in Canada*. Toronto, 1969
Clokie, H. McD., *Canadian Government and Politics*. New rev. ed. Toronto, 1950
Corry, J. A., *Democratic Government and Politics*. 3rd ed. Toronto, 1959
Dawson, R. M., *Democratic Government in Canada*. Rev. ed. Toronto, 1957
Eayrs, J. G., *The Art of the Possible: Government and Foreign Policy in Canada*. Toronto, 1961
Eggleston, W., *Road to Nationhood: A Chronicle of Dominion–Provincial Relations*. Toronto, 1946.—*Canada at Work*. Montreal, 1953
Henderson, G. F. (ed.), *Federal Royal Commissions in Canada, 1867–1966: A Checklist*. Toronto, 1967

Hutchinson, B., *Mr. Prime Minister, 1867–1964.* Toronto, 1964
Information Canada, *Organization of the Government of Canada.* Loose-leaf service. Ottawa, 1970
Kennedy, W. F. M., *Statutes, Treaties and Documents of the Canadian Constitution, 1713–1929.* Toronto, 1930
Kernaghan, N. (ed.), *Bureaucracy in Canadian Government, Selected Readings.* Toronto, 1969
Kunz, F. A., *The Modern Senate of Canada, 1925–63.* Toronto, 1965
Lamontagne, M., *Le Fédéralisme canadien.* Quebec, 1954
Laskin, B., *Canadian Constitution Laws.* 2nd ed. Toronto, 1960
Lower, A. R. M. (and others), *Evolving Canadian Federation.* Duke Univ. Press, Durham, NC, 1958
McWhinney, E., *Comparative Federation; States' Rights and National Power.* Toronto, 1962
Martin, C. B., *Foundations of Canadian Nationhood.* Toronto, 1955
Morton, W. L., *The Kingdom of Canada; A General History From Earliest Times.* Toronto, 1969
Olmsted, R. A., *Decisions of the Judicial Committee of the Privy Council Relating to the British North America Act, 1867, and the Canadian Constitution, 1867–1954.* Ottawa, Queens' Printer, 1954.
Ricker, J. C., *How Are We Governed?* Toronto, 1961
Russell, P. H. (ed.), *Leading Constitutional Decisions; Cases on the British North America Act.* Toronto, 1968
Saywell, J. T., *The Office of Lieutenant-Governor.* Toronto, 1957
Stanley, F. G., *A Short History of the Canadian Constitution.* Toronto, 1969
Trudeau, P. E., *Federalism and the French Canadians.* London, 1968
Varcoe, F. P., *The Distribution of Legislative Power in Canada.* Toronto, 1954
Ward, N., *The Public Purse: A Study in Canadian Democracy.* Toronto, 1962
Willms, A. (ed.), *Public Administration in Canada.* Toronto, 1862

DEFENCE. The Minister of National Defence has the control and management of the Canadian Forces, the Defence Research Board and all matters relating to national defence establishments and works for the defence of Canada. He is the Minister responsible for presenting before the Cabinet, matters of major defence policy for which Cabinet direction is required. Until Oct. 1973, he was responsible for the Canada Emergency Measures Organization which was renamed the 'National Emergency Planning Establishment' effective 1 April 1974, and given wider responsibilities for the co-ordination of civil emergency planning. The new organization will remain, for administrative purposes, within the Department but will report to the Privy Council Office. The Minister will continue to be responsible for certain civil emergency powers, duties and functions. The Deputy Minister is the senior public servant in the Department and the principal civilian adviser to the Minister on all departmental affairs. He is responsible to ensure that all policy direction emanating from the Government is reflected in the administration of the Department and in military plans and operations. The Chief of the Defence Staff is the senior military adviser to the Minister and is charged with the control and administration of the Canadian Forces. He is responsible for the effective conduct of military operations and the readiness of the Canadian Forces to meet the commitments assigned to the Department by the Government. The Defence Research Board is responsible for advice to the Minister of National Defence on scientific matters relating to defence and for evaluating the contribution of science and technology to the achievement of defence objectives. Within National Defence Headquarters, the Deputy Minister and the Chief of the Defence Staff have reporting to them, the Vice Chief of the Defence Staff, 4 assistant deputy ministers as well as the Judge Advocate General, Director General Information and Director General Departmental Administrative Services.

Command Structure. The Canadian forces are organized on a functional basis to reflect the major commitments assigned by the Government. All forces devoted to a primary mission are grouped under a single commander who is assigned sufficient resources to discharge his responsibilities. Specifically, the Canadian forces are formed into 7 major entities reporting to the Chief of the Defence Staff. These are as follows:

1. *Mobile Command* provides units trained and equipped to support the United Nations or other peacekeeping operations; provides ground forces for the protection of Canadian territory; maintains combat formations in Canada for support of

overseas commitments. It is comprised of 3 airportable combat groups in Canada; the United Nations force in Cyprus; the Canadian Airborne Regiment, and 1 combat training centre. The Militia and Air Reserve components are also controlled by Mobile Command.

2. *Maritime Command.* All maritime sea forces on the Atlantic and Pacific coasts are under the Commander, Maritime Command, with headquarters in Halifax, Nova Scotia. The Maritime Commander (Pacific), who is the Deputy Commander, has his headquarters in Esquimalt, British Columbia. Maritime Command is to defend Canada against attack from the sea; provide anti-submarine defence in support of NATO; provide sea transport in support of Mobile Command. Composition of the maritime forces includes 24 destroyer-escorts, 3 supply ships, 4 submarines, 6 small support and training vessels. There are 16 naval reserve units in major Canadian cities which form an essential component of Maritime Command.

3. *Air Command.* On 2 Sept. 1975, the aviation units administered by Mobile Command and Maritime Command were withdrawn and allocated to a newly-formed Air Command, which now controls all Canadian military aviation units through a single senior commander. Air Command responsibilities include maintenance of operationally-ready regular and reserve air forces to meet Canada's sovereignty requirements, participation with the USA in the air defence of North America through NORAD, and support of overseas commitments including NATO responsibilities in Europe and elsewhere. It is organized in 4 operational groups: Air Defence Group, Maritime Air Group, Air Transport Group and 10 Tactical Air Group; has reinforcement and training responsibilities to 1 Canadian Air Group (1 CAG) in Europe; and exercises command and control over Air Training Schools and the Air Reserve.

Air Defence Group, through NORAD, has entire responsibility for control of Canadian airspace. It comprises 3 squadrons of CF-101 Voodoo all-weather interceptors, armed with nuclear and conventional missiles; an electronic warfare squadron with CF-100 Mk. 5 and T-33A aircraft and 2 operational training squadrons with Voodoos; eastern and western control centres and a trans-continental radar chain, integrated in NORAD through the semi-automatic ground environment (SAGE) network.

Maritime Air Group's primary responsibilities include coastal and anti-pollution patrol, fishery protection and Arctic surveillance. Its equipment includes 4 squadrons of Argus and 1 of Tracker maritime patrol aircraft, and 2 ASW helicopter squadrons with CH-124 Sea Kings.

4. *Training Command* plans and conducts all recruit and individual trades and classification training that is common to more than one command. The Command is also responsible for the Prairie Region, one of 6 military regions into which Canada is divided. The Command headquarters is in Winnipeg and the 9 bases within the Command are located in 7 provinces. A total of 24,239 students attended one or more of 1,258 courses conducted by the Command during 1973.

5. *Canadian Forces Communications Command* (*CFCC*) manages, operates and maintains strategic communications for the Canadian Forces and, in the event of emergencies, for the federal and provincial governments. The Command also provides points for interconnecting strategic and tactical networks and CFCC manages, operates and maintains the major DND automatic data processing centres.

6. *The Reserves* are composed of the Naval Reserve, the Militia and the Air Reserve.

Canadian Armed Forces expenditures amounted to $3,396m. in 1976–77. Estimates for 1977–78 were $3,794m. Strength of the Regular Forces on 31 March 1977 was 78,535.

7. *Canadian Forces Europe.* The Canadian Forces allocated to support NATO in Europe are part of Canadian Forces Europe. The land element is No. 4 Canadian Mechanized Brigade Group operationally responsible to the Central Army Group. The air element, No. 1 Canadian Air Group, consisting of 3 CF-104 Starfighter squadrons, is operationally assigned to No. 4 Allied Tactical Air Force. These ele-

ments are located in the Baden-Baden area of Federal Republic of Germany and are supported administratively by CFB Europe at Lahr.

Police Forces. The police forces of Canada are organized in three groups: (1) the federal force, which is the Royal Canadian Mounted Police; (2) provincial police forces—the Provinces of Ontario and Quebec have their own provincial police forces, but all other provinces engage the services of the Royal Canadian Mounted Police to perform parallel functions within their borders, and (3) municipal police forces—each urban centre of reasonable size maintains its own police force or engages the services of the provincial police, under contract, to attend to police matters.

In addition, the Canadian National Railways, the Canadian Pacific Railway Company and the National Harbours Board have their own police forces.

Royal Canadian Mounted Police. It was organized in 1873 as the North West Mounted Police, to provide police protection in the unsettled portions of the northwest. In 1904 the title 'Royal' was given to the force. In 1920 the Dominion Police was amalgamated with it and the name was changed to the Royal Canadian Mounted Police. The headquarters was moved from Regina to Ottawa, and the force may now be called upon to perform duties in any portion of Canada. In 1928 the Royal Canadian Mounted Police absorbed the Saskatchewan Provincial Police, and in 1932 the Provincial Police Forces of Alberta, Manitoba, New Brunswick, Nova Scotia and Prince Edward Island. During 1932 the Force also assumed the administration of the Preventive Service Branch of the Department of National Revenue. In Aug. 1950 the Royal Canadian Mounted Police absorbed the Newfoundland Rangers and selected members of the Newfoundland Constabulary whose duties are outside the City of St John's. The British Columbia Provincial Police were also absorbed by the Royal Canadian Mounted Police in 1950. The Force is under the jurisdiction of the Solicitor-General of Canada.

Recruits receive 6 months of basic training at the Royal Canadian Mounted Police Academy at Regina. This is followed by a further 6 months of supervised on-the-job training.

In March 1977 the Force had a total strength of 18,198, including regular members, civilian members and public servants. It maintained 4,874 motor vehicles, 69 police service dogs and 151 horses.

The Force has 13 divisions actively engaged in law enforcement, 1 Headquarters Division and 2 training divisions. In addition it maintains a Marine Services and Air Services with headquarters at Ottawa. The Marine Services is comprised of 13 patrol vessels and 307 smaller craft which operate on the east and west coasts, the Great Lakes and the St Lawrence River. The Air Directorate has stations throughout Canada and maintains 27 aircraft.

Canada's Army in Korea. Dept. of National Defence. Ottawa, 1956

Dornbusch, C. E., *The Canadian Army 1855–1958; Regimental Histories.* Cornwailville, N.Y., 1959

Eayrs, J., *In Defence of Canada.* 2 vols. Toronto, 1965

Feasby, W. R. (ed.), *Official History of the Canadian Medical Services, 1939–45.* 2 vols. Dept. of National Defence. Ottawa, 1953–56

Goodspeed, D. J., *A History of the Defence Research Board of Canada.* Defence Research Board. Ottawa, 1958

Roberts, L., *There Shall Be Wings: A History of the Royal Canadian Air Force.* Toronto, 1960

Schull, J., *The Far Distant Ships: An Official Account of Canadian Naval Operations in the Second World War.* Ottawa, Queen's Printer, 1952

Stacy, C. P., *Six Years of War: Official History of the Canadian Army.* 3 vols. Ottawa, Queen's Printer, 1955–60

Stanley, G. F. G., *Canada's Soldiers; The Military History of an Unmilitary People.* Rev. ed. Toronto, 1960

Swettenham, J., *Canada and the First World War.* Toronto, 1970

Tucker, G. N., *The Naval Service of Canada: Its Official History.* 2 vols. Ottawa, Queen's Printer, 1952

INTERNATIONAL RELATIONS

Membership. Canada is a member of UN, the Commonwealth, OECD, NATO and Colombo Plan.

ECONOMY

Budget. Budgetary revenue and expenditure of the Government of Canada for years ended 31 March (in Canadian $1m.):

	1972–73	*1973–74*	*1974–75*	*1975–76*	*1976–77*
Revenue	16,602	19,383	24,909	29,956	32,640
Expenditure	16,116	20,056	26,055	33,978	38,941

Budgetary revenue, 1976–77 (in Canadian $1m.):

Income tax, personal	14,620	Other tax revenue	2,047
Income tax, corporation	5,377	Return on investment	2,493
Sales and other excise taxes	5,014	Net postal revenue	615
Import duties	2,097	Other non-tax revenue	377

Details of budgetary expenditure, year ended 31 March 1977 (in Canadian $1m.):

Agriculture	630	National Revenue	447
Atomic Energy	196	Parliament	73
Auditor-General	14	Post Office	1,103
Canadian Broadcasting Corporation	408	Privy Council	33
Communications	51	Public Works	683
Consumer and Corporate Affairs	62	Regional Economic Expansion	495
Energy, Mines and Resources	1,149	Royal Canadian Mounted Police	420
Environment, Dept. of the	485	Science and Technology (including National Research Council)	241
External Affairs	730	Secretary of State	1,163
Finance	8,319	Solicitor-General	265
Governor-General and Lieutenant-Governors	3	Statistics Canada	143
Indian Affairs and Northern Development	1,003	Supply and Services	115
Industry, Trade and Commerce	628	Transport	1,313
Justice	85	Treasury Board	193
Labour	32	Urban Affairs (including Central Mortgage and Housing Corporation)	625
Manpower and Immigration	2,770	Veterans Affairs	748
National Defence	3,365		
National Health and Welfare	10,951		

On 31 March 1977 the net debt was $29,597m.

Canadian Tax Foundation. *The National Finances: An Analysis of the Revenues and Expenditures of the Government of Canada.* Toronto. Annual

Perry, J. H., *Taxation in Canada.* 3rd ed. rev. Toronto, 1961.—*Taxes, Tariffs and Subsidies.* Toronto, 1955

Robinson, A. J. (ed.), *Public Finance, Selected Readings.* Toronto, 1968

Currency. The denominations of money in the currency of Canada are dollars and cents. The cent is one-hundredth part of a dollar. Subsidiary coins of the denominations of 1, 5, 10, 25 and 50 cents and $1 are in use. The monetary standard is gold of 900 millesimal fineness (23·22 grains of pure gold equal to 1 gold dollar). The Currency Act provides for gold coins in the denominations of $5, $10 and $20, which are legal tender. The British and US gold coins are also legal tender, at the par rate of exchange. The legal equivalent of the British sovereign is $4.86⅔.

The Bank of Canada has the sole right to issue paper money for circulation in Canada. Restrictions introduced by the 1944 revisions of the Bank Act cancelled the right of chartered banks to issue or re-issue notes after 1 Jan. 1945; and in Jan. 1950 the chartered banks' liability for such of their notes as then remained outstanding was transferred to the Bank of Canada in return for payment of a like sum to the Bank of Canada. On 31 May 1970 the Canadian dollar which was stabilized at 92·50 US cents was allowed to fluctuate. The value of the US$ in Canadian funds was 107·74 cents in Oct. 1977.

The Bank of Canada issues notes, which are legal tender, in denominations of $1, $2, $5, $10, $20, $50, $100, $500 and $1,000. Under the terms of the Bank of Canada Act, the bank is required to sell gold in bars of 400 oz. to any person tendering legal tender. This obligation is at the present time suspended by Order-in-Council. The exportation of gold from Canada is prohibited except by licence issued by the Minister of Finance to the Bank of Canada or a chartered bank.

The Ottawa Mint was established in 1908 as a branch of the Royal Mint, in pursuance of the Ottawa Mint Act, 1901. In Dec. 1931 control of the Mint was passed over to the Canadian Government, and since that time has operated as the Royal Canadian Mint. The Mint issues silver, nickel, bronze and steel coins for circulation in Canada. In 1967, in celebration of Canada's Centennial of Confederation, a $20 gold piece was minted, the first gold coin struck since 1919. In 1935, on the occasion of His Majesty's Silver Jubilee, the Royal Canadian Mint issued the first Canadian silver dollars. Commemorative dollars were also issued in 1939 on the occasion of the visit of King George VI and Queen Elizabeth to Canada; in 1949, when Newfoundland became the tenth Province of Canada; in 1958, the one-hundredth anniversary of the establishment of the Colony of British Columbia; in 1964, the centennial of the Charlottetown and Quebec Conferences which paved the way to confederation. The silver dollar bearing the design of the canoe manned by an Indian and a Voyageur has been issued in the years 1935–38, 1945–48, 1950–57, 1959–63, 1965, 1966 and 1972. For centennial year the Canada goose replaced the usual canoe design on the silver dollar. Because of a world-wide shortage of silver, the Government, in Aug. 1967, authorized the Mint to change the metal content of the 25-cent and 10-cent coins. Commencing in Sept. 1968, the 10-cent, 50-cent and $1 coins were minted in pure nickel.

Gold refining is one of the principal activities of the Mint. In 1975, 1,371,965 troy oz. of rough bullion were received for treatment, containing 1,079,022 oz. of fine gold and 161,766 oz. of fine silver. Coin issued: Bronze, $6,247,200; nickel, $60,937,915; silver, $58,203,873.

Banking. Commercial banks in Canada are known as chartered banks and are incorporated under the terms of the Bank Act, which imposes strict conditions as to capital, notes in circulation, returns to the Dominion Government, types of lending operations and other matters. In July 1977 there were in operation 11 chartered banks incorporated under the provisions of the Bank Act, with 7,276 branches and sub-agencies in Canada and 277 branches and sub-agencies in other countries. The Bank Act is subject to revision by Parliament every 10 years; latest revision 1967. Bank charters expire every 10 years and are renewed at each decennial revision of the Bank Act. The chartered banks make detailed monthly and yearly returns to the Minister of Finance and are subject to periodic inspection by the Inspector-General of Banks, an official appointed by the Government.

The following are some particulars of the 11 chartered banks at 31 Aug. 1977: Capital paid up, $403m.; rest account, $2,942·7m.; Canadian currency deposits, $31,950·9m.; foreign currency deposits, $44,209·1m.; liabilities to the public, $136,864·5m.; total assets, $140,210·2m. Cheques cashed at the clearing-house centres of Canada for 1976 amounted to $2,406,649·7m.

The Bank of Canada Act, passed on 3 July 1934, provided for the establishment of a central bank for the Dominion. This bank commenced operations on 11 March 1935 with a paid-up capital of $5m. By reason of certain changes introduced into the composition of stockholders of the bank (for which *see* THE STATESMAN'S YEAR-BOOK, 1944, pp. 322–23), the Minister of Finance on behalf of Canada is the sole registered owner of the capital stock of the bank. The revised Bank Act, which came into force on 1 May 1967, requires the chartered banks, beginning Feb. 1968, to maintain a statutory cash ratio of 12% on demand deposits and 4% on other deposits, in the form of reserves with and notes on the Bank of Canada. A secondary reserve of 7% in treasury bills, government bonds, etc., is also required. All gold held in Canada by the chartered banks was transferred to the Bank of Canada along with the gold held by the Government as reserve against Dominion notes outstanding at the time of the commencement of operations of the Bank of Canada. The liability of the Dominion notes outstanding at the commencement of business of the Bank of Canada was assumed by the bank. The following are some of the particulars of the Bank of Canada as at 31 Oct. 1977: Notes in circulation, $7,913·8m.; chartered bank deposits, $3,498·9m.; total liabilities, $12,503m.; investments, $11,144·8m.

In Aug. 1944 the Industrial Development Bank, a subsidiary of the Bank of Canada, was set up for the purpose of providing credit in the post-war period to small industrial establishments. The statement of assets and liabilities of the Industrial Bank for the fiscal year ended 30 Sept. 1975 showed outstanding loans and investments of $1,175·2m. The authorized, issued and paid-up capital at this date amounted to $78m. The year ending 30 Sept. 1975 was the last year of operation of the Industrial Development Bank. During its existence from 1 Nov. 1944 to 30 Sept. 1975, the Industrial Development Bank authorized 65,000 loans for $3,000m. to more than 48,000 businesses in Canada. It is succeeded by the Crown corporation, the Federal Business Development Bank, which was proclaimed in force on 2 Oct. 1975. In the year ending 31 March 1977, the Federal Business Development Bank authorized 9,311 loans for a total of $424,076,000.

Binhammer, H. H., *Money, Banking and the Canadian Financial System.* Toronto, 1968
Boreham, G. F., and others, *Money and Banking: Analysis and Policy in a Canadian Context.* Toronto, 1969
Cairns, James P. (ed.), *Canadian Banking and Monetary Policy: Recent Readings.* Toronto, 1965
O'Brien, J. H., and Lerner, G., *Canadian Money and Banking.* 2nd ed. Toronto, 1969

Weights and Measures. The legal weights and measures are the Imperial yard, pound avoirdupois, gallon and bushel; but the hundredweight is declared to be 100 lb. and the ton 2,000 lb. avoirdupois, as in the USA. The Metric Commission, established in June 1971, advises on Canada's conversion to the metric system.

ENERGY AND NATURAL RESOURCES

Electricity. The installed capacity on 31 Dec. 1975 was 61,351,995 kw., of which 61% was hydro power and 39% thermal. Utilities accounted for 89% of the generating capacity and 90% of the net generation in 1975. The total net electric energy generated in 1975 was 273,392·3m. kwh. In 1975 gross revenue from 7,910,268 customers was $3,113·55m.

Oil and Natural Gas. With the discovery of large oilfields in Alberta, the production of petroleum became a major Canadian industry. The Interprovincial Pipeline, Canada's longest oil pipeline, moving crude oil from Edmonton, Alberta, to Montreal, Quebec, has a length in Canada of 3,605 miles. Total pipeline mileage, including mileage of American subsidiaries, is 5,996 miles. The pipeline serves Canadian refineries from Edmonton to Montreal and many in the USA. Another pipeline, Trans-Mountain, extends from Edmonton to Vancouver with a Canadian length of 825 miles and an overall length, including American mileage, of 889 miles. Eight refineries, 4 in Canada and 4 in Washington State, are served by the pipeline. At the end of 1976 Canada's oil pipeline system had 20,424 miles of line in operation. Net oil deliveries in 1976 were 905,269,808 bbls. The Trans-Canada natural gas line is the longest in the world (5,721 miles in 1976). It brings natural gas from the Alberta–Saskatchewan border across the prairies, through northern Ontario to Toronto, then eastward to Montreal. Natural gas pipeline mileage totalled about 82,876 miles in 1976. Net deliveries of natural gas into the pipelines in 1976 was 2,478,024m. cu. ft.

Minerals. Alberta, Ontario, British Columbia, Quebec and Saskatchewan are the chief mining provinces. The total value of the mineral produced in 1976 was $15,392,839,000. The principal minerals produced in 1976 were as follows:

Metallics	*Quantity (1,000)*	*Value ($1,000)*
Copper (lb.)	1,647,141	1,126,156
Nickel (lb.)	578,693	1,232,143
Zinc (lb.)	2,292,118	862,296
Iron ore (tons)	62,721	1,241,263
Gold (troy oz.)	1,686	207,796
Lead (lb.)	571,175	129,388
Silver (troy oz.)	40,887	175,128
Iron, remelt (tons)	...	65,086
Molybdenum (lb.)	31,780	91,873
Total metallics	...	5,241,151

	Quantity (1,000)	Value ($1,000)
Non-metallics		
Asbestos (tons)	1,707	445,523
Potash (K_2O) (tons)	5,650	361,442
Titanium dioxide (tons)	...	74,410
Salt (tons)	6,338	75,691
Sulphur, elemental (tons)	4,166	63,339
Gypsum (tons)	6,240	22,906
Total non-metallics	...	1,142,516
Fuels		
Crude petroleum (bbls)	489,610	4,128,458
Natural gas (mcf)	3,067,367	2,466,621
Natural gas by-products (bbls)	104,053	794,325
Coal (tons)	27,900	604,000
Total fuels	...	7,993,404
Structural materials		
Cement (tons)	10,858	339,159
Sand and gravel (tons)	273,000	320,800
Stone (tons)	96,100	209,600
Clay products (bricks, tiles, etc.)	...	92,110
Lime (tons)	2,012	54,099
Total structural materials	...	1,015,768

Value (in Canadian $1,000) of mineral production by provinces:

Provinces	1975	1976	Provinces	1975	1976
Newfoundland	550,879	756,007	Saskatchewan	861,606	908,554
Pr. Ed. Island	1,787	1,700	Alberta	5,737,474	6,995,572
Nova Scotia	101,399	117,201	British Columbia	1,296,801	1,421,096
New Brunswick	231,628	255,057	Yukon Territory	230,150	131,069
Quebec	1,239,929	1,521,321	N.W. Territories	206,349	213,100
Ontario	2,350,006	2,594,042			
Manitoba	529,619	478,120	Total	13,337,627	15,392,839

Agriculture. Though the manufacturing industries now predominate, agriculture is still very important to the Canadian economy. It contributes between 7 and 10% of the net value of production and in 1976 accounted for over 11% of the value of commodities exported.

It is estimated that about 35% of the total land area is forested; according to the census of 1976, 259,338 sq. miles (7·2% of the total land area) is classed as occupied agricultural land. Grain growing, dairy farming, fruit farming, ranching and fur farming are all carried on successfully.

The following table shows the estimated value of agricultural production for 1976, in $1,000 Canadian:

Field crops	5,984,374[1]	Poultry meat	483,956	Potatoes	208,665
Livestock on farms	4,063,666	Eggs	297,292	Fruit	127,023[2]
Milk and cream	1,580,893	Tobacco	181,998	Maple products	17,079
Butter, creamery	279,329[2]	Vegetables	222,039[3]	Honey	25,085

[1] 1974. [2] 1975. [3] Excluding potatoes.

Number of occupied farms (census of 1976) was 300,118.

Field Crops. In 1974, 64,247,000 acres were under principal field crops with an estimated total value of $5,984,374,000. The most valuable field crops are wheat, tame hay, oats, barley, potatoes, corn for grain, flaxseed, mixed grains, rapeseed, fodder corn, soybeans and sugar-beet. The estimated acreage and yield of the principal field crops, by provinces, 1976 were:

Provinces	Wheat 1,000 acres	Wheat 1,000 bu.	Tame hay 1,000 acres	Tame hay 1,000 tons	Oats 1,000 acres	Oats 1,000 bu.
Prince Edward Island	10	469	130	244	47	3,158
Nova Scotia	4	170	152	319	17	901
New Brunswick	5	180	156	298	51	2,193
Quebec	90	2,529	2,700	5,211	620	24,304
Ontario	530	24,978	2,700	6,750	400	16,520
Manitoba	3,800	103,000	1,300	2,400	1,250	61,000
Saskatchewan	17,400	548,000	1,950	3,000	1,850	103,000
Alberta	5,600	182,000	3,300	5,400	1,800	106,000
British Columbia	90	3,000	625	1,700	70	4,600
Total, Canada	27,529	864,326	13,013	25,322	6,105	321,676

Provinces	Barley 1,000 acres	Barley 1,000 bu.	Potatoes 1,000 acres	Potatoes 1,000 cwt	Corn for Grain 1,000 acres	Corn for Grain 1,000 bu.
Prince Edward Island	25	1,475	53	13,853	—	—
Nova Scotia	7	343	4	616	—	—
New Brunswick	9	354	58	11,838	—	—
Quebec	60	2,268	52	8,622	135	10,719
Ontario	350	14,805	49	11,700	1,520	133,000
Manitoba	1,550	65,000	37	4,500	14	950
Saskatchewan	3,000	135,000	2	550	—	—
Alberta	5,500	245,000	17	3,800	—	—
British Columbia	220	9,000	12	2,750	—	—
Total, Canada	10,721	473,245	284	58,229	1,669	144,669

Provinces	Flaxseed 1,000 acres	Flaxseed 1,000 bu.	Mixed grains 1,000 acres	Mixed grains 1,000 bu.	Rapeseed 1,000 acres	Rapeseed 1,000 bu.
Prince Edward Island	—	—	81	5,365	—	—
Nova Scotia	—	—	10	560	—	—
New Brunswick	—	—	6	258	—	—
Quebec	—	—	125	5,425	—	—
Ontario	—	—	800	38,400	—	—
Manitoba	550	6,300	200	8,100	250	4,500
Saskatchewan	225	3,800	160	7,300	850	19,400
Alberta	100	1,600	350	17,500	850	16,500
British Columbia	—	—	5	250	35	600
Total, Canada	875	11,700	1,737	83,158	1,985	41,000

Provinces	Fodder corn 1,000 acres	Fodder corn 1,000 tons	Soybeans 1,000 acres	Soybeans 1,000 bu.	Sugar-beet 1,000 acres	Sugar-beet 1,000 tons
Prince Edward Island	9	140	—	—	—	—
Nova Scotia	15	215	—	—	—	—
New Brunswick	10	135	—	—	—	—
Quebec	200	2,850	—	—	7	117
Ontario	750	9,675	370	9,250	—	—
Manitoba	35	300	—	—	31	386
Saskatchewan	—	—	—	—	—	—
Alberta	—	—	—	—	41	774
British Columbia	20	350	—	—	—	—
Total, Canada	1,039	13,665	370	9,250	79	1,277

Livestock. In parts of Saskatchewan and Alberta stockraising is still carried on as a primary industry, but the livestock industry of the country at large is mainly a subsidiary of mixed farming. The following table shows the numbers of livestock (in 1,000) by provinces in July 1977:

Provinces	Milch cows	Other cattle	Sheep and lambs	Swine	Poultry[1]
Prince Edward Island	25	80	7	82	
Nova Scotia	39	99	40	77	1,753
New Brunswick	31	85	12	43	
Quebec	785	915	43	1,866	4,061
Ontario	647	2,423	131	2,056	9,546
Manitoba	94	1,,282	19	650	2,626
Saskatchewan	77	2,863	77	500	1,210
Alberta	155	4,316	160	910	2,506
British Columbia	82	630	44	60	2,934
Total 1976	1,946	13,209	563	5,826	25,332[2]
Total 1977	1,935	12,693	533	6,244	25,025[2]

[1] Hens and pullets only. [2] Including hens and pullets in Newfoundland.

Net production of farm eggs in 1963, 417·2m. doz. ($160,178,000); 1967, 434·7m. doz. ($153·3m.); 1968, 444·6m. doz. ($168·2m.); 1969, 464m. doz. ($199·5m.); 1970, 490·7m. doz. ($183·7m.); 1971, 489·7m. doz. ($161·4m.); 1972, 468·4m. doz. ($173·9m.); 1973, 461·7m. doz. ($255·3m.); 1974, 459·5m. doz. ($283·9m.); 1975, 448·1m. doz. ($274·5m.); 1976, 437·1m. doz. ($297·3m.).

Wool production (in 1m. lb.), 1960, 7·8; 1965, 5·8; 1966, 5; 1967, 3·8; 1968, 3·5; 1969, 3·5; 1970, 3·5; 1971, 3·6; 1972, 3·4; 1973, 3·2; 1974, 3·2; 1975, 3·1; 1976, 2·7.

Dairying. The dairy industry has shown a marked tendency towards centralization; the number of establishments decreased between 1961 and 1975 from 1,720 to 519 (69·8%), whereas the number of employees has decreased only 12·5%. Production, 1976: Creamery butter, 251·3m. lb.; factory cheese, 276·7m. lb.; milk, 16,941·9m. lb.

Fruit Farming. The value of fruit production by provinces in 1975 was (in $1,000): Ontario, 58,820; British Columbia, 39,060; Quebec, 15,012; Nova Scotia, 7,301; New Brunswick, 2,328; Newfoundland, 869; Prince Edward Island, 682. Total apple production in Canada in 1975 was 20,884,000 bu.

Tobacco. The production in 1976 of tobacco, which is practically confined to Ontario and Quebec, was estimated at 180m. lb. and valued at $182m.

Forestry. The total area of land covered by forests is estimated at 1,259,192 sq. miles, of which 53% is suitable for regular harvest.

Lumber production (in 1,000 bd ft) 1967, 9,962,480; 1968, 10,754,523; 1969, 11,100,357; 1970, 10,711,645; 1971, 12,030,735; 1972, 13,279,062; 1973, 14,751,564; 1974, 12,973,302.

The volume of lumber shipments in 1974 was 13,136,632,000 bd ft valued at $1,877,695,000. Pulp production was 20·5m. tons in 1973 and 21·7m. tons in 1974. In 1974 mill shipments of newsprint amounted to 9·72m. tons valued at $1,878,534,000.

Fur Trade. In 1975–76 (year ended 30 June), 4,500,531 pelts valued at $53,942,714, were taken. In wild-life pelt production muskrat led in total value, followed by beaver, wolf, seal and lynx. The most important animal raised on fur farms is mink, with 99% of the total production. The value of pelts from fur farms in 1975–76 was $19,774,861, of which mink accounted for $19,425,356. There were, in 1975, 447 fur farms, of which 54 reported fox and 393 mink.

Fisheries. During 1975, landings in Canadian commercial fisheries reached 1,935·1m. lb. The landed value was $290·7m. and the estimated market value was $713m. The landed value of principal fish in 1975 was (in $1,000): Lobster, 48,378; salmon, 46,913; cod, 33,678; herring, 27,065; scallops, 25,708; halibut, 12,119; fresh-water fish, 20,048.

Canadian Mines Handbook. Annual. Toronto, from 1931

Caves, R. E., and Holton, R. H., *The Canadian Economy: Prospect and Retrospect*. Harvard Univ. Press, 1959

Innis, H. A., *The Fur Trade in Canada*. Rev. ed. Toronto Univ. Press, 1956.—*The Cod Fisheries*. Rev. ed. Toronto, 1954

LeBourdais, D. M., *Metals and Men: The Story of Canadian Mining*. Toronto, 1957.—*Canada and the Atomic Revolution*. Toronto, 1959

Lougheed, W. F., *Secondary Manufacturing Industry in the Canadian Economy*. Toronto, 1961
Rea, K. J., *The Political Economy of the Canadian North; An Interpretation of the Course of Development in the Northern Territories of Canada*. Toronto, 1968
Robinson, J. L., *Resources of the Canadian Shield*. Toronto, 1969
Scott, Anthony, *Natural Resources: The Economics of Conservation*. Toronto, 1955
Stovel, J. A., *Canada in the World Economy*. Harvard Univ. Press, 1959
Strange, H. G. L., *A Short History of Prairie Agriculture*. Winnipeg, 1954
Wilson, G. W., and others, *Canada: An Appraisal of Its Needs and Resources*. Toronto, 1965

INDUSTRY AND TRADE

Industry. Industry groups ranked by value of shipments, 1975:

Industry	*Production workers*	*Wages ($1,000)*	*Cost of materials ($1,000)*	*Value of shipments ($1,000)*
Food and beverages	145,357	1,396,422	11,325,767	16,492,290
Transportation equipment	120,844	1,446,500	7,636,173	11,195,043
Paper and allied industries	95,794	1,054,795	3,346,680	7,131,614
Primary metals	90,169	1,119,159	3,641,157	6,682,356
Metal fabricating	117,115	1,241,607	3,056,214	6,217,314
Petroleum and coal products	7,877	122,267	5,108,677	5,953,330
Chemical and chemical prods.	42,576	462,724	2,566,268	5,107,353
Electrical products	82,711	776,409	2,190,236	4,605,972
Wood industries	81,598	846,248	2,098,283	3,802,635
Machinery	63,392	695,580	1,999,276	3,731,625
Printing, publishing and allied industries	55,044	587,431	1,016,868	2,897,471
Non-metallic products	42,158	471,534	974,686	2,569,385
Textiles	56,450	435,869	1,344,492	2,439,005
Clothing	89,347	573,274	1,201,314	2,306,619
Rubber and plastics	39,473	355,806	972,106	1,955,825
Miscellaneous manufacturing	48,804	381,486	917,059	1,942,966
Furniture and fixtures	41,460	329,384	642,136	1,363,703
Tobacco products	6,540	71,806	1,506,963	831,522
Knitting mills	21,567	141,853	323,764	624,490
Leather industries	23,440	158,242	308,751	619,191
All Industries	1,272,071	12,672,053	51,177,275	88,462,370

Labour. In Sept. 1977 the industrial distribution of the employed was estimated as follows (in 1,000): Manufacturing, 1,951; service, 2,720; trade, 1,715; agriculture, 514; other primary industries, 255; construction, 695; transportation, communication and other utilities, 826; finance, insurance and real estate, 542; public administration, 687; total employed, 9,906; unemployed, 798.

About 37% of Canada's non-agricultural paid workers belong to trade unions, which had 2·88m. members in Jan. 1975. About 71% of the organized workers are members of unions affiliated with the Canadian Labour Congress, and more than 6% are in affiliates of another central body, the Confederation of National Trade Unions. Over 1m. of the union members were in international unions, which have branches both in Canada and the US and in most cases belong to central labour organizations in both countries.

It is generally established by legislation, both federal and provincial, that a trade union to which the majority of employees in a unit suitable for collective bargaining belong, is given certain rights and duties. An employer is required to meet and negotiate with such a trade union to determine wage-rates and other working conditions of his employees. The employer, the trade union and the employees affected are bound by the resulting agreement. If an impasse is reached in negotiation conciliation services provided by the appropriate government board is available. Generally, work stoppages may not take place until an established conciliation procedure has been carried out and are prohibited while an agreement is in effect. Almost 28% of the workers affected by collective agreements are in the manufacturing industry.

Freedom of association is a civil right in Canada, and under common law workers are at liberty to join unions and participate in their activities. This right has also been guaranteed by statutes which make it an offence to interfere with freedom of association.

Certain specific minimum standards in regard to working conditions are set by law, for the most part by provincial labour legislation. Minimum wages, maximum hours of work or an overtime rate of pay after a specified number of hours, minimum weekly rest periods and annual vacations with pay are established for the majority of workers.

Workmen injured in the course of employment or disabled by industrial disease are required to receive compensation under workmen's compensation laws which apply to most employees except agricultural workers. Benefits during the period of disability for work are set by law at a proportion (now 75%) of the workman's average earnings, subject to a maximum established in each province. Benefits (which also include monthly allowances to dependants in the case of the death of a workman caused by an accident or disease arising out of his employment) are paid out of an accident fund administered by a government board in each province. The fund is made up of contributions from employers according to an annual assessment rate, varying from a few cents to several dollars per $100 of payroll according to the hazards of the industry.

Dept. of Labour, *Working Conditions in Canadian Industry*. Annual. Ottawa
Cameron, J. C., *The Status of Trade Unions in Canada*. Kingston, 1960
Carrothers, A. W. R., *Labour Arbitration in Canada*. Toronto, 1961
Woods, H. D., *Labour Policy and Labour Economics in Canada*. Toronto, 1962

COMMERCE. In the past the custom tariff of Canada has been protective, with a preferential tariff in favour of the UK, the Dominions, a number of Crown Colonies, and the Irish and South African Republics. At the Imperial Economic Conference of 1932, held in Ottawa, the UK developed further the policy of preferential tariffs to the Dominions, and on the part of the latter there was a general lowering of the existing tariffs against certain lines of UK manufacturers. Canada is one of the signatories of the General Agreement on Tariffs and Trade (GATT) and of the Kennedy Round agreements.

Imports for home consumption and domestic exports (in $1,000 Canadian) for calendar years (merchandise only):

	Imports	*Exports*		*Imports*	*Exports*
1960	5,842,695	5,255,575	1973	23,323,493	24,836,870
1970	13,951,903	16,820,098	1974	31,692,121	31,674,495
1971	15,611,271	17,803,523	1975	34,635,513	32,325,043
1972	18,736,066	19,977,198	1976	37,390,942	37,212,853

Exports (domestic) by countries in 1976 (in $1,000 Canadian):

African Commonwealth Countries (not elsewhere specified)	98	Leeward and Windward Islands	11,654
Australia	359,067	Malaysia	30,460
Bahamas	15,207	Malawi	1,765
Bahrain	1,474	Malta	2,282
Bangladesh	37,398	Mauritius and Dependencies	610
Barbados	13,633	New Zealand	56,241
Belize	1,850	Nigeria	32,259
Bermuda	17,459	Pakistan	33,562
Britain	1,826,797	Qatar	4,193
British Oceania	62	Sierra Leone	168
Cyprus	2,393	Singapore	31,781
Falkland Islands	164	South Africa, Republic of	95,771
Fiji	1,139	Sri Lanka	14,421
Gambia	204	Tanzania	9,038
Ghana	19,109	Trinidad and Tobago	37,480
Gibraltar	3,158	Uganda	318
Guyana	11,283	Zambia	25,568
Hong Kong	58,608	Afghánistán	1,495
India	152,926	Albania	145
Irish Republic	30,658	Algeria	93,236
Jamaica	41,921	Angola	756
Kenya	8,967	Argentina	46,446

Austria	20,339	Lebanon	3,042
Belgium and Luxembourg	472,154	Liberia	3,020
Benin	1,622	Libya	9,474
Bolivia	3,731	Madagascar	1,157
Brazil	327,588	Mauritania	809
Bulgaria	5,709	Mexico	212,903
Burma	3,954	Morocco	2,737
Cambodia–Laos	1	Mozambique	6,375
Cameroon Republic	2,782	Netherlands	442,327
Chile	13,609	Netherlands Antilles	4,133
China	195,819	Nicaragua	4,777
Colombia	59,298	Norway	151,605
Costa Rica	16,947	Panama	17,686
Cuba	3,258,387	Paraguay	320
Czechoslovakia	17,431	Peru	49,266
Denmark	30,803	Philippines	51,598
Dominican Republic	21,795	Poland	123,956
Ecuador	24,064	Portugal	18,828
Egypt (UAR)	34,810	Portuguese Africa	319
El Salvador	9,285	Portuguese Asia	1
Ethiopia	6,331	Puerto Rico	57,552
Finland	16,724	Romania	37,449
France	393,464	Saudi Arabia	106,321
French Africa	3,597	Senegal	1,799
French Guiana	394	Somalia	1,135
French Oceania	1,670	Spain	126,601
French West Indies	1,960	Spanish Africa	102
Gabon	2,417	St Pierre and Miquelon	13,628
German Democratic Rep.	46,001	Sudan	3,064
Germany, Fed. Rep. of	694,778	Surinam	3,147
Greece	32,049	Sweden	100,102
Greenland	1,689	Switzerland	84,052
Guatemala	21,823	Syria	12,959
Guinea	531	Taiwan	41,417
Haiti, Republic of	17,399	Thailand	38,228
Honduras	13,166	Togo	10,925
Hungary	5,858	Tunisia	18,829
Iceland	1,085	Turkey	62,973
Indonesia	76,017	USSR	535,224
Iran	143,838	United Arab Emirates	11,242
Iraq	35,631	USA	25,122,901
Israel	55,840	US Oceania	1,134
Italy	547,917	US Virgin Islands	901
Ivory Coast	6,344	Uruguay	6,548
Japan	2,386,190	Venezuela	355,317
Jordan	5,614	Vietnam (South)	171
Korea, North	9,536	Yemen	2,858
Korea, South	116,663	Yugoslavia	16,483
Kuwait	22,282	Zaïre	15,277

Imports (for consumption) by countries in 1976 (in $1,000 Canadian):

African Commonwealth Countries (not elsewhere specified)	123	India	66,724
Australia	340,836	Irish Republic	25,582
Bahamas	11,663	Jamaica	14,790
Bahrain	1	Kenya	14,632
Bangladesh	8,585	Leeward and Windward Islands	555
Barbados	5,229	Malaysia	48,428
Belize	1,900	Malawi	115
Bermuda	1,871	Malta	797
Britain	1,153,318	Mauritius and Dependencies	1,512
British Oceania	...	New Zealand	74,091
Cyprus	211	Nigeria	155,860
Fiji	475	Pakistan	10,104
Ghana	4,161	Rhodesia	12
Gibraltar	28	Sierra Leone	1,454
Guyana	5,410	Singapore	77,445
Hong Kong	285,181	South Africa, Republic of	159,136
		Sri Lanka	12,084

Tanzania	9,601	Ivory Coast	7,255
Trinidad and Tobago	21,285	Japan	1,523,727
Uganda	1,654	Korea, North	2,271
Zambia	125	Korea, South	303,251
		Kuwait	22,439
Afghánistán	216	Lebanon	446
Albania	...	Liberia	1,284
Algeria	65,420	Libya	104,840
Angola	1,075	Madagascar	2,776
Argentina	21,020	Mauritania	...
Austria	59,086	Mexico	146,350
Belgium and Luxembourg	124,660	Morocco	2,768
Benin	...	Mozambique	1,511
Bolivia	4,520	Netherlands	181,179
Brazil	160,777	Netherlands Antilles	7,101
Bulgaria	2,181	Nicaragua	13,326
Burma	21	Norway	133,470
Cambodia–Laos	18	Panama	5,412
Cameroon Republic	5,369	Paraguay	2,539
Chile	33,373	Peru	15,410
China	88,309	Philippines	31,329
Colombia	41,211	Poland	45,057
Costa Rica	24,120	Portugal	22,366
Cuba	60,527	Portuguese Africa	278
Czechoslovakia	40,399	Portuguese Asia	859
Denmark	75,949	Puerto Rico	38,316
Dominican Republic	28,769	Romania	24,185
Ecuador	30,296	Saudi Arabia	481,614
Egypt (UAR)	10,309	Senegal	76
El Salvador	9,619	Somalia	...
Ethiopia	1,558	Spain	105,825
Finland	34,354	Spanish Africa	36
France	437,721	St Pierre-Miquelon	136
French Africa	9,378	Sudan	534
French Guiana	...	Surinam	9,720
French Oceania	80	Sweden	262,232
French West Indies	126	Switzerland	162,923
Gabon	61,676	Syria	50
German Democratic Rep.	5,065	Taiwan	292,061
Germany, Fed. Rep. of	817,855	Thailand	9,071
Greece	29,370	Togo	16
Greenland	461	Tunisia	59
Guatemala	17,075	Turkey	5,874
Guinea	7,948	USSR	55,235
Haiti, Republic of	2,253	United Arab Emirates	61,995
Honduras	17,266	USA	25,661,677
Hungary	15,917	US Virgin Islands	50
Iceland	765	Uruguay	3,704
Indonesia	18,204	Venezuela	1,295,110
Iran	695,426	Vietnam, South	27
Iraq	133,643	Yemen	201,715
Israel	38,396	Yugoslavia	17,599
Italy	365,369	Zaïre	11,607

Leading imports into Canada in 1976 (in $1m. Canadian):

Transportation equipment	10,224	Outerwear	604
Fabricated materials, inedible	6,199	Fruit	592
Other equipment and tools	4,174	Meat and fish	546
Crude petroleum	3,272	Coal	544
Special industry machinery	1,903	Non-ferrous metals	485
Chemicals	1,679	Metal ores, concentrates and scrap	429
Agricultural machinery and tractors	1,323	Photographic materials	409
General-purpose machinery	1,313	Coffee, cocoa, tea	341
Textiles	839	Vegetables	269
Wood and paper	740	Raw sugar	254
Iron and steel	722		

Principal exports (Canadian produce) in 1976 (in $1m. Canadian):

Transportation equipment	8,871	Other equipment and tools	826
Wood and paper	6,408	Meat and fish	715
Metal ores, concentrates and scrap	2,501	Coal	561
Crude petroleum	2,288	Petroleum and coal products	557
Non-ferrous metals	2,133	Barley	542
Wheat	1,705	Agricultural machinery and tractors	538
Natural gas	1,616	Asbestos	471
Chemicals	1,359	Telecommunication and related equipment	395
Industrial machinery	877		
Iron and steel	831	Other cereals	320

The following figures are from the British Department of Trade returns (in £1,000 sterling):

	1973	*1974*	*1975*	*1976*	*1977*
Imports to UK	735,574	982,464	855,778	1,159,651	1,222,871
Exports and re-exports from UK	413,811	488,186	538,298	628,470	712,662

Royal Commission on Canada's Economic Prospects. Report. Ottawa, 1957
Cockfield, Brown & Co., *Canada's Economic Future: Digests of 127 Submissions to the Royal Commission on Canada's Economic Prospects.* Toronto, 1957
Easterbrook, W. T., *Canadian Economic History.* Toronto, 1956
Litvak, I., and Mallen, B., *Marketing in Canada: Recent Readings.* Toronto, 1964
Mahatoo, W. H., *Marketing Research in Canada.* Toronto, 1968
Newman, D., and Newman, J. P., *Canadian Business Handbook.* Toronto, 1964
Officer, L. H. (ed.), *Canadian Economic Problems and Policies.* Toronto, 1970
Shea, A. A., *Canada 1980.* Toronto, 1960
Wilkinson, B. W., *Canada's International Trade: An Analysis of Recent Trends and Patterns.* Toronto, 1968

Tourism. The number of visitors to Canada in 1975 was 35,909,797 (1976, 33,808,232). In 1975, 34,582,241 come from USA (1976, 32,230,902).

COMMUNICATIONS

Roads. The total highway mileage in Canada in 1973 was 526,136. Of this total 419,780 miles were surfaced and 106,356 miles improved and other earth roads. Expenditure (1973) on roads, bridges, ferries, etc., reached a total of \$3,118·1m. Federal and provincial governments supplied \$2,183m., with the remainder contributed by municipal and other sources. Federal expenditures were chiefly devoted towards the upkeep of national-park roadways and nationally owned bridges and ferries, although for the 'Mackenzie Highway' from Grimshaw, Alberta, to Hay River, Northwest Territories, the Federal Government paid about 68% of the total cost. In general, however, highways are provincially controlled and maintained, and the responsibility of assisting municipalities and townships falls directly on the provinces.

The Alaska Highway is part of the Canadian highway system. For the Trans-Canada Highway *see* map in THE STATESMAN'S YEAR-BOOK, 1962.

Registered motor vehicles totalled 11,442,643 in 1975; they included 8,870,307 passenger cars and taxis, 2,240,989 commercial vehicles and 331,347 motor cycles.

Urban Transit. In 1976 urban transit systems (motor bus, trolley coach, street car and subway operations) carried 1,188,312,192 fare passengers 338,039,996 vehicle-miles for an operating revenue of \$371,195,880. Intercity and rural bus operations carried 32,354,550 fare passengers 120,028,667 vehicle-miles, earning revenues of \$122,906,692.

Railways. The total mileage of railways in Canada on 31 Dec. 1975 was 43,941. The total track mileage, including route duplicate, yardtrack and sidings, was 60,045.

Canada has 2 great trans-continental systems: the Canadian National Railway system (CN), a government-owned body which operates 23,315 miles of the total first maintrack, and the Canadian Pacific Limited (CP Rail), a joint-stock corporation with first maintrack totalling 16,328 miles (July 1977). From 1 April 1978, a government funded organization known as Via Rail took over passenger services formerly operated by CP and CN.

Selected statistics of Canadian railways for 1976: Passengers carried 23,636,253; revenue freight, 138,511,349,551 ton-miles; freight revenue, \$2,629,965,514; total railway operating revenues, \$3,192,484,532.

Aviation. Civil aviation in Canada is under the jurisdication of the federal government. The technical and administrative aspects are supervised by the Administrator of Air Transportation, while the economic functions are assigned to the Canadian Transportation Commission.

Landings and take-offs controlled by the Department of Transport's 58 towers totalled 6,462,685 in 1976.

In 1976 Canadian airlines carried 20,584,529 passengers, flying 20,359m. revenue-passenger-miles and 534·4m. ton-miles of freight. Operating revenue was $1,991·3m.; operating expenditure, $1,935·9m.

Shipping. The registered shipping on 31 Dec. 1976, including vessels for inland navigation, totalled 31,953 with a gross tonnage of 4,374,923. The sea-going and coasting vessels that entered Canadian ports during the year ending 31 Dec. 1975 were as follows: Foreign service vessels, 20,225 of 115,591,697 tons. Coasting service vessels, 46,867 of 83,731,925 tons.

The major canals in Canada are those of the St Lawrence–Great Lakes waterway with their 7 locks, providing navigation for vessels of 25·75-ft draught from Montreal to Lake Ontario; the Welland Canal by-passing the Niagara River between Lake Ontario and Lake Erie with its 8 locks; and the Sault Ste Marie Canal and lock between Lake Huron and Lake Superior. These 16 locks overcome a drop of 582 ft from the head of the lakes to Montreal. The St Lawrence Seaway was opened to navigation on 1 April 1959 (*see* map in THE STATESMAN'S YEAR-BOOK, 1957). In 1976, 6,932 vessels passed through the St Lawrence Seaway carrying 71,843,204 cargo tons of freight, chiefly grain, iron, fuel oil and coal. The total value of capital assets was $779,030,408 at 31 March 1977.

Coast Guard. The Canadian Coast Guard (formed in 1962) is responsible to the Minister of Transport. In 1976 it comprised 6 heavy icebreakers; a heavy icebreaker/cable repair vessel; 8 medium icebreakers/aids tenders; 11 light icebreakers/aids tenders; 9 aid tenders; 4 special shallow draft vessels; 2 ocean weather ships; a northern supply vessel; 30 search and rescue vessels (all types and sizes); 2 hovercraft and 30 helicopters.

Post. On 31 March 1976 there were 8,506 postal facilities in operation and 5·6m. points of call were served. Rural and suburban services numbered 4,986. Gross revenue was $568·2m.; gross expenditure, $1,114·4m. for the fiscal year 1975–76.

There were 767,609 miles of telegraph wire in Canada in 1975 (including external cable landed in Canada). There were 77·7m. miles of telephone wire and 13,165,000 telephones on 31 Dec. 1975 (57·2 per 100 population).

Broadcasting. There were 421 standard broadcast band stations operating in Canada at 31 March 1977, of which 53 were Canadian Broadcasting Corporation stations and 368 were privately owned stations and CBC affiliates. In addition, there were 8 short-wave stations, 3 of which were CBC and 5 privately owned, together with 137 CBC and 139 privately owned frequency-modulation stations. Of the 834 television stations, 340 were owned by the CBC, 19 were privately owned and 259 were CBC affiliates. Radio and television licence fees were abolished in 1953.

Wireless 'beam' stations are operated at Montreal for direct communications with Great Britain and Australia, and a station at Louisburg, N.S., provides a long-distance service to ships.

Cinemas (1975). There were 1,173 cinemas with a seating capacity of 666,591 and 315 drive-in theatres with a capacity of 148,531 cars.

Newspapers (1975). There were 116 daily newspapers, of which 103 are in English and 13 in French.

JUSTICE, RELIGION, EDUCATION AND WELFARE

Justice. There is a Supreme Court in Ottawa, having general appellate jurisdiction in civil and criminal cases throughout Canada. There is an Exchequer Court, which is also a Court of Admiralty. There is a Superior Court in each province and county courts, with limited jurisdiction, in most of the provinces, all the judges in these courts being appointed by the Governor-General. Police, magistrates and justices of the peace are appointed by the provincial governments.

For the year ended 31 Dec. 1972, 55,541 adults were charged and 45,614 convicted of indictable offences.

Canadian Legal and Directory. Toronto. Annual
Anger, W. H., and Anger, H. D., *A Digest of Canadian Law*. 19th ed. Toronto, 1967
Gosse, R., *The Law on Competition in Canada*. Toronto, 1962
Houlden, L. W., *Bankruptcy Law of Canada*. Toronto, 1960
McRuer, J. D., *The Evolution of the Judicial Process*. Toronto, 1957
McWhinney, E., *Canadian Jurisprudence: Civil Law and Common Law*. Toronto, 1958
O'Connor, A. R. M., *An Analysis of and a Guide to the New Criminal Code*. Toronto, 1955

Religion. Membership of the leading denominations in 1971:

Province	*Roman Catholic*	*United Church of Canada*	*Anglican Church of Canada*	*Presbyterian*	*Lutheran*
Newfoundland	190,960	101,805	144,445	3,055	515
Prince Edward Island	51,215	27,830	6,905	13,050	95
Nova Scotia	286,320	162,885	135,695	40,380	11,570
New Brunswick	331,290	85,185	69,260	13,155	1,875
Quebec	5,226,150	176,825	181,875	51,785	23,845
Ontario	2,568,695	1,682,820	1,220,535	540,035	267,225
Manitoba	242,855	256,560	123,015	30,825	64,735
Saskatchewan	258,630	274,285	87,210	20,805	90,850
Alberta	391,390	456,925	170,230	57,185	133,045
British Columbia	408,330	537,565	386,670	100,940	120,335
Yukon	4,670	3,110	4,645	690	925
Northwest Territories	14,385	3,005	12,685	445	725
Total, Canada	9,974,895	3,768,805	2,543,175	872,330	715,740

Other denominations: Baptist, 667,245; Greek Orthodox, 316,605; Jewish, 276,025; Ukrainian (Greek) Catholic, 227,730; Pentecostal, 220,390; Mennonite, 168,150; other, 1,817,220.

Boon, T. C. B., *The Anglican Church from the Bay to the Rockies*. Toronto, 1962
Clark, S. D., *Church and Sect in Canada*. Toronto, 1968
Walsh, H. H., *The Christian Church in Canada*. Toronto, 1956
Wilson, D. J., *The Church Grows in Canada*. Toronto, 1966

Education. By the British North American Act each provincial government is responsible for its education system. While each system differs from the others in particulars, the general plan is similar for all provinces. Separate elementary and secondary schools for minority groups, mainly Roman Catholic, are found in most provinces. Though administration of the schools in Newfoundland has a denominational basis, they are not exclusive and a number are non-denominational. In general, education is free to the end of the secondary level. The principal sources of revenue are provincial government grants and direct taxation for school purposes. Except in Quebec the number of private schools is small; their enrolment was less than 4% of the total in elementary and secondary grades.

The federal government operates schools for Indians and Eskimos with an enrolment in 1975–76 of 37,466. An additional 37,012 attend non-federal schools.

In 1976–77, 382,060 full-time regular students were enrolled in 69 degree-granting institutions, other than purely theological institutions. In 1975–76 some 153,079 enrolled in arts and science, 24,155 in engineering, 26,883 in commercial business administration, 7,612 in medicine, 8,775 in law, 87,153 in other faculties. Another 102,861 or more students were enrolled in part-time courses.

The following statistics give information, for 1976–77, about all elementary and secondary schools, public, federal and private:

Province	*Schools*	*Teachers*	*Pupils*
Newfoundland	726	7,489	158,096
Prince Edward Island	75	1,458	27,978
Nova Scotia	628	11,030	203,850
New Brunswick	516	7,922	164,543
Quebec	2,878	72,472	1,398,621

Province	Schools	Teachers	Pupils
Ontario	5,001	96,508	2,040,037
Manitoba	846	12,157	240,989
Saskatchewan	1,064	11,138	226,744
Alberta	1,422	22,007	451,425
British Columbia	1,801	27,210	562,135
Yukon	23	260	4,866
Northwest Territories	70	675	12,916
National Defence (overseas)	11	295	4,382
Total	15,061	270,621	5,496,582

Association of Canadian Universities & Colleges. *Canadian Universities & Colleges*. Ottawa. Annual
Craik, W. A., *History of Canadian Journalism*. 2 vols. Toronto, 1959
Harris, R. S., and Trembley, A., *A Bibliography of Higher Education in Canada*. Toronto and Quebec, 1960
Harrison, J. F. C., *Learning and Living, 1790–1960; A Study in the History of the English Adult Education Movement*. Toronto, 1961
Hodgetts, J. W., *Higher Education in a Changing Canada*. Toronto, 1966
Katz, Joseph, *Elementary Education in Canada*. Toronto, 1961
Wilson, J. D., and others, *Canadian Education: A History*. Toronto, 1970

Health. Canada achieves national health insurance through a series of interlocking provincial plans which qualify the provinces for federal financial support if they meet the minimum criteria of the federal legislation with respect to comprehensiveness of coverage with regard to services, universality of coverage with regard to people, accessibility to services uninhibited by excessive user charges, portability of benefits and non-profit administration by a public agency. The federal contributions to the provinces cover about 50% of the provincial costs for the insured services of the national Hospital Insurance and Medical Care Programmes. (In the health field the federal government also furnishes the provinces with *per capita* cash contributions towards the cost of extended health care services; *e.g.*, nursing home care, certain home care services, but the provinces do not need to meet the programme criteria described above with respect to these latter contributions.)

The Canadian approach to the development of a national health programme has been to progressively provide major segments of personal health care on a publicly financed basis to virtually the whole population, and this is achieved with the co-operation of the provinces, which exercise the primary constitutional prerogative in health matters.

The insurance programmes are designed to ensure that all residents of Canada have access to needed medical and hospital care on a prepaid basis. The insured services of the Hospital Insurance Programme, which commenced in 1958, include in-patient care (including necessary drugs, diagnostic tests, etc.), as well as elective out-patient services that vary somewhat from province to province. Complementing the protection of the Hospital Insurance Programme is the Medical Care Programme, inaugurated in 1968, which covers all medically required services rendered by medical practitioners no matter where the services are rendered, and certain surgical–dental procedures undertaken by dental surgeons in hospital. All 10 provinces and the 2 northern territories are participating in both programmes, which provide health insurance coverage for over 99% of the population (or over 23m. people).

The approach taken by Canada is one of state-sponsored health insurance. Accordingly, the advent of the programmes produced little change in the ownership of hospitals, almost all of which are owned by non-governmental non-profit corporations, and the rights and privileges of private medical practice. Patients are free to choose their own general practitioners and/or specialists without losing their insured benefits (there is a minor exception in Quebec involving only a few physicians). Except for 0·5% of the population whose care is provided for under other legislation (such as serving members of the Canadian Armed Forces), all residents are eligible, regardless of whether they are in the work force. Benefits are available without upper limit so long as they are medically necessary. Benefits are also portable during any temporary absence from Canada anywhere in the world—subject to any limitation a province may impose upon treatment electively sought outside the particular province without prior approval, though such a restriction does not pertain to emergency care.

In addition to the benefits qualifying for federal contributions, provinces are free to provide additional benefits at their own discretion. Most provinces provide such benefits, which cover a variety of services (*e.g.*, optometric care, children's dental programme, drug benefits) depending upon the province. Most provinces fund their portion of health insurance costs out of general provincial revenues. Three provinces levy premiums which meet part of the provincial costs, 1 province imposes a special income-tax surcharge and a levy on employers, and 1 province utilizes part of its sales tax revenues for this purpose. Two provinces have nominal co-charges for short-term hospital care. Three provinces have charges for long-term hospital care geared, approximately, to the room and board portion of the OAS–GIS payments mentioned under Social Welfare.

Social Welfare. The Department of Health and Welfare administers a number of social security programmes. Most notable among them, as welfare programmes, are the Family Allowances programme, introduced in 1945 and amended in 1974; the Old Age Security programme, introduced in 1952 and to which were added the Guaranteed Income Supplement in 1966 and the Spouse's Allowance in 1974; and the Canada Pension Plan which came into being in 1966. Social assistance and services programmes which are provided by the provinces and territories are cost-shared by the federal government under the Canada Assistance Plan, which was introduced in 1966.

The 1974 federal Family Allowances Act provides for the payment of a monthly Family Allowance ($23.89 in 1977) on behalf of a dependent child under the age of 18. This allowance is paid to a parent who is a resident of Canada, who wholly or substantially maintains the child and who is either a Canadian citizen, a landed immigrant or a non-immigrant admitted to Canada for a period of not less than 1 year, during which time his or her income is subject to Canadian Income Tax. Benefits are also paid under certain prescribed circumstances to Canadian citizens living abroad. A Special Allowance is paid on behalf of a child under the age of 18 who is maintained by a welfare agency, a government department or an institution. In some cases, payment is made directly to a foster parent.

The Family Allowances Act provides for the escalation of benefits, in January of each year, based on the Consumer Price Index. It also specifies that a provincial legislature may vary the monthly federal rate payable within that province subject to the fulfilment of stipulated conditions. Only the provinces of Alberta and Quebec have exercised this option.

Generally speaking, the Canada Pension Plan and the Quebec Pension Plan are an integral part of Canada's social security system, serving as the vehicle whereby millions of members of the Canadian labour force acquire and retain, during their productive years, protection for themselves and their families against loss of income due to retirement, disability or death, regardless of where their employment may take them in Canada and, under certain circumstances, outside Canada.

The Canada Pension Plan does not operate in Quebec because the province exercised its constitutional prerogative to establish a similar provincial pension plan to operate in lieu of CPP.

The Plans cover employed members of the labour force between the ages of 18 and 70, with a small number of exceptions (*e.g.*, a person working for his/her spouse, and members of certain religious sects who have opted out of the Plans). Both plans are funded through direct contributions and interest on the investment of excess funds. Contributions are deductible for income-tax purposes, while benefits are taxable and are adjusted annually to fully reflect increases in the Consumer Price Index.

The Old Age Security (OAS) pension is payable to persons 65 years of age and over who satisfy the residence requirements stipulated in the Old Age Security Act. The amount payable, whether full or partial, is also governed by stipulated conditions, as is the payment of an OAS pension to a recipient who absents himself from Canada. OAS pensioners with little or no income apart from OAS may, upon application, receive a full or partial supplement known as the Guaranteed Income Supplement (GIS). Entitlement is normally based on the pensioner's income in the preceding year, calculated in accordance with the Income Tax Act. The spouse of an OAS pensioner, aged 60 to 64, meeting the same residence requirements as those stipulated for OAS, may be eligible for a full or partial Spouse's Allowances (SA). As of July 1977, SA is payable, upon application, if the annual combined income of the couple is less than $6,816. This is subject to an income test which does not include the OAS pension, the Guaranteed Income Supplement or the Spouse's Allowance.

The OAS pension is taxable; GIS and SA are not taxable. However, they must be included in computing the net income of a dependant for income-tax purposes. OAS, GIS and SA are subject to an increase every January, April, July and October to reflect increases in the Consumer Price Index.

Under the Canada Assistance Plan, the federal government pays 50% of the cost, to the provinces, of assistance to persons in need; welfare services provided to persons who are in need or likely to become in need if they do not receive such services (welfare services means services having as their object the lessening, removal or prevention of the causes and effects of poverty, child neglect or dependence on public assistance); and work activity projects which are designed to improve the employability of persons who have unusual difficulty in finding or retaining jobs or in undertaking job training.

In addition to persons in need as defined in the Plan, federal contributions may be made towards agency costs of providing welfare services to persons who are likely to become in need, if such services are not provided. The amount of federal subsidy is dependent on the proportion of eligible persons as determined by the use of an income test or a pre-determined income level for different sized families. 'Need' is defined by each province and is determined by the 'budget deficit' method, that is, the difference between an applicant's requirements and his income and resources. The rates of assistance payable are also determined by provincial authorities and are non-taxable. No systematic indexation exists; however, provinces do adjust social assistance rates from time to time in accordance with certain economic indicators. Quebec social assistance rates are indexed at the beginning of each year by the rate of change in the Quebec Pension Index.

In 1975 the Unemployment Insurance Commission marked its 35th anniversary. Since its inception it has provided about 40m. unemployed Canadian workers with more than $15,000m. in income replacement.

DIPLOMATIC REPRESENTATIVES

OF CANADA IN GREAT BRITAIN
(Canada House, Trafalgar Sq., London, SW1Y 5BJ)

High Commissioner: Paul Martin, PC, QC.

OF GREAT BRITAIN IN CANADA
(80 Elgin St., Ottawa, K1P 5K7)

High Commissioner: Sir John Ford.

OF CANADA IN USA
(1746 Massachusetts Ave., NW, Washington, D.C., 20036)

Ambassador: Peter M. Towe.

OF THE USA IN CANADA (100 Wellington St., Ottawa)

Ambassador: Thomas O. Enders.

OF CANADA TO THE UNITED NATIONS

Ambassador: William H. Barton.

Books of Reference

Statistical Information: Statistics Canada, Ottawa, has been the official central statistical organization for Canada since 1918. The Bureau, which reports to Parliament through the Minister of Industry, Trade and Commerce, serves as the statistical agency for federal government departments; co-ordinates the statistics of the provincial governments along national lines; and channels all Canadian statistical data to internal organizations. *Statistician Chief of Canada:* Dr Peter G. Kirkham.

Publications of Statistics Canada are classified as periodical (issued more frequently than once a year), annual, biennial and occasional publications. The occasional publications frequently supplement the annual reports and usually contain historical information. A complete list is contained in the 1976–77 edition of the Statistics Canada catalogue and supplements, available on request. Official publications include:

The Canada Year Book. Annual, from 1905
Canada, Official Handbook. Annual, from 1930
Atlas and Gazetteer of Canada. Dept. of Energy, Mines and Resources Branch. Ottawa, 1969
Canadian Statistical Review. Monthly, with weekly supplements, from 1948
Canadiana; A List of Publications of Canadian Interest. National Library, Ottawa. Monthly, with annual cumulation. 1951 ff.
1966 Census of Canada. Ottawa, 1967
1976 Census of Canada. Ottawa, 1977
Tenth Decennial Census of Canada, 1961. Ottawa, 1962
Eleventh Decennial Census of Canada, 1971. Ottawa, 1972

Cambridge History of the British Empire. Vol. VI. Canada and Newfoundland. Cambridge, 1930
Canadian Almanac and Directory. Toronto. Annual.
Canadian Annual Review. Annual, from 1960
Canadian Dictionary: French–English. Toronto, 1970
Canadian Who's Who. 11th ed. Toronto, 1969
National Reference Book on Canadian Business Personalities. 11th ed. Montreal, 1969
Bohne, H. (ed.), *Canadian Books in Print, 1970.* Toronto, 1970
Brebner, J. B., *North Atlantic Triangle: The Interplay of Canada, the United States and Great Britain.* New York, 1958
Brown, G. W. (ed.), *Dictionary of Canadian Biography*, Vol. I. Univ. of Toronto Press, 1966
Bruchési, Jean, *L'Histoire du Canada.* 6th ed. Montreal, 1951.—*Canada, réalités d'hier et d'aujourd'hui.* Montreal, 1954.—*Le Canada.* Paris, 1952
Brunet, M., and others. *Histoire du Canada par les textes.* Montreal, 1952
Camu, P., Weeks, E. P., and Sametz, Z. W., *Economic Geography of Canada.* London, 1965
Careless, J. M. S., *Canada, A Story of Challege.* Ref. ed. Toronto, 1963
Careless, J., and Brown, R. C. (ed.), *The Canadians, 1867–1967.* Toronto, 1967
Cook, R., *French-Canadian Nationalism; An Anthology.* Toronto, 1970.—*The Maple Leaf Forever; Essays on Nationalism and Politics in Canada.* Toronto, 1971
Creighton, Donald G., *Dominion of the North: A History of Canada.* New ed. Toronto, 1957.—*The Empire of the St Lawrence.* Toronto, 1956.—*Canada's First Century.* Toronto, 1970.—*Towards the Discovery of Canada.* Toronto, 1974
Dictionnaire Bélisle de la Langue Française au Canada; dictionnaire oxford. 1970
Dictionnaire canadien; français–anglais–français. Toronto, 1962
Encyclopedia Canadiana. 10 vols. Rev. ed. Ottawa, 1967
Fortin, J.-A., *Biographies canadiennes-françaises.* 16th ed. Montreal, 1952
Garneau, F. X., *Histoire du Canada.* 8th ed. Montreal, 1944–45
Glazebrook, G. P. de T., *A History of Canadian External Relations.* Toronto, 1950
Hardy, W. G., *From Sea to Sea; Canada, 1850–1920: The Road to Nationhood.* Toronto, 1960
Hawkins, F., *Canada and Immigration.* Montreal and London, 1972
Hockin, T. A., *Government in Canada.* London, 1976
Keenleyside, H. L., *Canada and the United States.* Rev. ed. New York, 1952
Kerr, D. G. G., *Historical Atlas of Canada.* Toronto, 1960
Lefebvre, F. J., *Le Canada, l'Amérique-géographique, historique, biographique, littéraire; supplément du Larousse canadien complet.* Montreal, 1954
Lower, A. R. M., *Colony to Nation: A History of Canada.* 4th ed. Toronto, 1964
Lumsden, I. (ed.), *Close the 49th Parallel, etc.; The Americanization of Canada.* Toronto, 1970
Mallory, J. R., *The Structure of Canadian Government.* Toronto, 1971
McInnis, E., *Canada: A Political and Social History.* Rev. ed. Toronto, 1959
MacLennan, Hugh, *Seven Rivers of Canada: the Mackenzie, the St Lawrence, the Ottawa, the Red, the Saskatchewan, the Fraser, the St John.* Toronto, 1961
Moir, J., and Saunders, R., *Northern Destiny: A History of Canada.* Toronto, 1970
Morton, W. L., *The Kingdom of Canada; A General History from Earliest Times.* Toronto, 1969

Putnam, D. F., Canadian Regions. A Geography of Canada. 2nd ed. Toronto, 1954.—*Canada: A Regional Analysis.* Toronto, 1970
Ross, M. M., *Our Sense of Identity; A Book of Canadian Essays.* Torontc, 1954
Sandwell, B. R., *La Nation canadienne.* Monaco, 1954
Tanghe, R., *Bibliogrraphy of Canadian Bibliographies.* Toronto, 1962
Urquhart, M. C., and Buckley, K. A. H. (ed.), *Historical Statistics of Canada.* Toronto, 1965
Wallace, W. (ed.), *Macmillan Dictionary of Canadian Biography.* Toronto, 1963
Warkentor, J. (ed.), *Canada; A Geographical Interpretation.* Toronto, 1968
Wilson, G. W., and others, *Canada: An Appraisal of Its Need and Resources.* New York, 1965

National Library: The National Library of Canada, Ottawa, Ontario. *Librarian:* J. Guy Sylvestre.

CANADIAN PROVINCES

The 10 provinces have each a separate parliament and administration, with a Lieut.-Governor, appointed by the Governor-General in Council at the head of the executive. They have full powers to regulate their own local affairs and dispose of their revenues, provided only they do not interfere with the action and policy of the central administration. Among the subjects assigned exclusively to the provincial legislatures are: the amendment of the provincial constitution, except as regards the office of the Lieut.-Governor; property and civil rights; direct taxation for revenue purposes; borrowing; management and sale of Crown lands; provincial hospitals, reformatories, etc.; shop, saloon, tavern, auctioneer and other licences for local or provincial purposes; local works and undertakings, except lines of ships, railways, canals, telegraphs, etc., extending beyond the province or connecting with other provinces, and excepting also such works as the Dominion Parliament declares are for the general good; marriages, administration of justice within the province; education.

Local Government. Under the terms of the British North America Act the provinces are given full powers over local government. All local government institutions are, therefore, supervised by the provinces, and are incorporated and function under provincial acts.

The acts under which municipalities operate vary from province to province. A municipal corporation is usually administered by an elected council headed by a mayor or reeve, whose powers to administer affairs and to raise funds by taxation and other methods are set forth in provincial laws, as is the scope of its obligations to, and on behalf of, the citizens. Similarly, the types of municipal corporations, their official designations and the requirements for their incorporation vary between provinces. The following table sets out the classifications as at 1 Jan. 1974.

Type and size of group	*Nfld.*	*PEI*	*NS*	*NB*	*Que.*	*Ont.*	*Man.*
Type:							
Regional municipalities	—	—	—	—	75	40	—
Metropolitan and regional municipalities [1]	—	—	—	—	3	11	—
Counties and regional districts	—	—	—	—	72	29	—
Unitary municipalities	114	33	65	111	1,577	815	183
Cities	2	1	3	6	68	43[2]	5
Towns	112[3]	8	38	20	204	146	33
Villages	—	24	—	85	270	130	39
Rural municipalities [4]	—	—	24	—	1,035	496	106
Quasi-municipalities [5]	163	—	—	—	—	14	19
Total	277	33	65	111	1,652	869	202
Population size group (1971 census):							
Unitary municipalities—							
Over 100,000	—	—	1	—	3	14	1
50,000 to 99,999	1	—	2	1	10	12	—
10,000 to 49,999	1	1	16	6	72	65	3
Under 10,000	112	32	46	104	1,492	724	179
Total	114	33	65	111	1,577	815	183

For notes see end of table.

Type and size of group	*Sask.*	*Alta.*	*BC*	*YT*	*NWT*	*Canada*
Type:						
Regional municipalities	—	—	28	—	—	143
Metropolitan and regional municipalities [1]	—	—	—	—	—	14
Counties and regional districts	—	—	28	—	—	129
Unitary municipalities	784	327	139	3	7	4,158
Cities	11	9	32	2	1	183
Towns	131	102	11	1	3	809
Villages	350	168	59	—	3	1,128
Rural municipalities [4]	292	48	37	—	—	2,038
Quasi-municipalities [5]	9	22	—	5	7	239
Total	793	349	167	8	14	4,540
Population size group (1971 census):						
Unitary municipalities—						
Over 100,000	2	2	2	—	—	25
50,000 to 99,999	—	—	6	—	—	32
10,000 to 49,999	5	12	29	1	—	211
Under 10,000	777	313	102	2	7	3,890
Total	784	327	139	3	7	4,158

[1] Includes urban communities in Quebec; and Metropolitan Toronto, regional municipalities and the district municipality in Ontario.
[2] Includes the 5 boroughs of Metropolitan Toronto.
[3] Includes 8 rural districts.
[4] Includes municipalities in Nova Scotia; parishes, townships, united townships and municipalities in Quebec; townships in Ontario; rural municipalities in Manitoba and Saskatchewan; municipal districts and counties in Alberta; and districts in British Columbia.
[5] Includes local government communities, local improvement districts and the metropolitan area in Newfoundland; improvement districts in Ontario and Alberta; local government districts in Manitoba; local improvement districts in Saskatchewan and the Yukon Territory; and hamlets in the Northwest Territories.

ALBERTA

HISTORY. The southern half of the province of Alberta was part of Rupert's land which was granted by royal charter in 1670 to the Hudson's Bay Company. The intervention by the North West Company in the fur trade after 1783 led to the establishment of trading posts. In 1869 Rupert's land was transferred from the Hudson's Bay Company (which had absorbed its rival in 1821) to the new Dominion, and in the following year this land was combined with the former Crown land of the North Western Territories to form the Northwest Territories.

In 1882 'Alberta' first appeared as a provisional 'district', consisting of the southern half of the present province. In 1905 the Athabasca district to the north was added when provincial status was granted to Alberta.

Four parties have held office: the Liberals 1905–21; the United Farmers 1921–35; Social Credit 1935–71, and Progressive Conservative since Sept. 1971. The stable political climate created by these parties has eased Alberta's transition from an agrarian to an industrial society.

AREA AND POPULATION. The area of the province is 255,285 sq. miles; 248,800 sq. miles being land area and 6,485 sq. miles water area. The population (census, 1 June 1976) was 1,838,037; the urban population, centres of 1,000 or over, was 1,381,000 and the rural 457,000. Population of the principal cities (1 June 1976): Calgary, 469,917; Edmonton, 461,361; Lethbridge, 46,752; Medicine Hat, 32,811; Red Deer, 32,184; St Albert, 24,129, and Grande Prairie, 17,626.

Vital statistics, *see* pp. 259–60.
Religion, *see* p. 279.

CONSTITUTION AND GOVERNMENT. The constitution of Alberta is contained in the British North America Act of 1867, and amending Acts; also in the

Alberta Act of 1905, passed by the parliament of the Dominion of Canada, which created the province out of the then Northwest Territories. All the provisions of the British North America Act, except those with respect to school lands and the public domain, were made to apply to Alberta as they apply to the older provinces of Canada. On 1 Oct. 1930 the natural resources were transferred from the Dominion to provincial government control The province is represented by 6 members in the Senate and 19 in the House of Commons of Canada.

The executive is vested nominally in the Lieut-Governor, who is appointed by the federal government, but actually in the Executive Council or the Cabinet of the legislature. Legislative power is vested in the Assembly in the name of the Queen.

Members of the Legislative Assembly are elected by the universal vote of adults over the age of 18 years.

There are 75 members in the legislature (elected 26 March 1975): 69 Progressive Conservative, 4 Social Credit, 1 New Democratic Party, 1 Independent.

Lieut.-Governor: His Hon. Ralph G. Steinhauer (sworn in 2 July 1974).
Flag: Blue with the shield of the province in the centre.

The members of the Ministry (all Progressive Conservative) are as follows:

Premier, President of Executive Council: Hon. Peter Lougheed.
Transport and Deputy Premier: Hon. Dr Hugh M. Horner. *Energy and Natural Resources:* Hon. Donald R. Getty. *Federal and Intergovernmental Affairs and Government House Leader:* Hon. Louis D. Hyndman. *Provincial Treasurer:* Hon. C. Mervin Leitch. *Attorney-General:* Hon. James L. Foster. *Labour:* Hon. Neil S. Crawford. *Social Services and Community Health:* Hon. W. Helen Hunley. *Hospitals and Medical Care:* Hon. Gordon T. W. Miniely. *Housing and Public Works:* Hon. William J. Yurko. *Environment:* Hon. David J. Russell. *Agriculture:* Hon. Marvin E. Moore. *Advanced Education and Manpower:* Hon. Dr Albert E. Hohol. *Education:* Hon. Julian G. J. Koziak. *Solicitor-General:* Hon. Roy A. Farran. *Business Development and Tourism:* Hon. Robert W. Dowling. *Utilities and Telephones:* Hon. Dr Allan A. Warrack. *Government Services and Culture:* Hon. Horst A. Schmid. *Recreation, Parks and Wildlife:* Hon. J. Allen Adair. *Consumer and Corporate Affairs:* Hon. Graham L. Harle. *Municipal Affairs:* Hon. Dick Johnston. *Without Portfolio:* Hon. Stewart A. McCrae; Hon. Dallas W. Schmidt; Hon. Robert J. Bogle (*responsible for Native Affairs*).

Local Government. The local government units are City, Town, New Town, Village, Summer Village, County and Municipal District.

There are 11 cities in Alberta, namely: Edmonton, Calgary, Lethbridge, Wetaskiwin, Red Deer, Medicine Hat, Drumheller, Camrose, Lloydminster, Grande Prairie and St Albert. These cities operate under the Municipal Government Act. The governing body consists of a mayor and a council of from 6 to 20 members. A city can be incorporated by order of the Lieut.-Governor-in-Council. A population of 10,000 is required.

There are no limits of area specified in the statutes for any of the different local government units. The population requirement for a Town as specified in the Municipal Government Act is 1,000 people, and the area at incorporation is that of the original village.

A Village must contain 75 separate and occupied dwellings. The Municipal Government Act requires each dwelling to have been occupied continuously for a period of at least 6 months. A Summer Village must contain 50 separate dwellings.

A rural County area is an area incorporated through an order of the Lieut.-Governor-in-Council under the provisions of the County Act. One board of councillors deal with both municipal and school affairs.

A rural Municipal District is an area which has been incorporated under the Municipal Government Act. In Municipal Districts separate boards control municipal and school affairs.

Areas not incorporated as counties or Municipal Districts are termed Improvement Districts or Special Area. Sparsely populated, such districts are administered and taxed by the Department of Municipal Affairs of the provincial government. There are no requirements as to the minimum number of residents of a County or Municipal District.

FINANCE. The budgetary revenue and expenditure (in Canadian $) for years ending 31 March were as follows:

	1973–74	*1974–75*	*1975–76*	*1976–77*[1]	*1977–78*[1]
Revenue	1,747,673,536	2,172,100,000	2,646,800,000[2]	3,134,000,000[2]	3,577,000,000[2]
Expenditure	1,504,000,260	2,083,226,000	2,720,700,000	3,011,300,000	3,329,100,000

[1] Estimates. [2] Excludes funds allocated to Alberta Heritage Savings Trust Fund.

The net funded debt of the province on 31 March 1973 amounted to $244,378,725, and the unfunded debt to $122,119,661; total net funded debt and unfunded debt, $366,498,386.

Income *per capita* (1976), $6,775.

ENERGY AND NATURAL RESOURCES

Oil. In 1976, 414m. bbls of crude oil and condensate were produced with a gross sales value of $3,531m. Alberta produced 85% of Canada's oil output in 1976. Production of natural gas by-products was 101m. bbls, valued at $772m.

Major deposits of oil sands are found in areas totalling 19,000 sq. miles in northern and eastern Alberta. The ultimate remaining recoverable reserves of synthetic crude oil from the oil sands are estimated at 250,000m. bbls.

One recovery plant, situated 25 miles north of Fort McMurray, began production in 1967. The deposit being used as sufficiently close to the surface to permit strip mining. A second plant, that will produce 125,000 bbls per day of synthetic crude oil, is scheduled to begin production in 1978.

Gas. Natural gas is found in abundance in numerous localities. In 1976, 2,601,000m. cu. ft valued at $2,302·2m. were produced.

Minerals. In 1976 the ultimate remaining recoverable coal resources of Alberta were estimated at 93,500m. tons; the proved remaining recoverable reserves were estimated at 12,650m. tons.

Value of total mineral production in 1976, $6,996m.

Agriculture. Of the surveyed area of the province (about 85m. acres) approximately 70m. acres may be classed as capable of agricultural development. Up to the present, however, only 40% of this area has been brought under cultivation.

For particulars of agricultural production and livestock, *see under* CANADA. Farmers' total gross income in 1975 was $2,036·87m. Farm cash receipts in 1976 totalled $1,822,578,000, of which crops contributed $911m.; livestock and products, $891m., and other sources, $21m.

Forestry. Alberta has an estimated net merchantable volume of 59,900,875m. cu. ft of timber comprised of 23,798,365m. cu. ft of hardwood and 36,102,510m. cu. ft of softwood. In 1976, over 525m. bd ft of timber were produced; the value of forest produce was $89m.

Fisheries. The lakes of the province abound in whitefish, pike and tullibee. Commercial catches are marketed through the Freshwater Fish Marketing Corporation which was inaugurated in May 1969 as the result of an agreement between the federal government and the provinces for the buying and exporting of freshwater fish. Value of fish marketed in year ending 31 March 1977 was $2,165,000.

INDUSTRY. The leading manufacturing industries are food and beverages, petroleum refining, metal fabricating, wood industries, primary metal, chemical and chemical products and non-metallic mineral products industries. There were in 1975 approximately 1,821 manufacturing establishments, in which were employed about 64,678 persons, who earned in salaries and wages $741m.

Manufacturing shipments had a total value of $4,726·5m. in 1975. Chief among these shipments were: Food and beverages, $1,684m.; petroleum and coal products, $700m.; metal fabricating, $288m.; chemicals and chemical products, $281m.; wood, $260m.; primary metals, $324m.; non-metallic mineral products, $231m.

Total retail sales (1976, estimate) $5,289·7m.

COMMUNICATIONS

Roads. In 1976 there were 89,830 miles of roads and highways, including 58,683 miles gravelled and 6,906 miles paved.

In March 1977 there were 1,320,657 motor vehicles registered, including 763,430 passenger cars, 351,070 public and commercial vehicles, 170,483 trailers and 29,084 motor cycles.

Railways. In Dec. 1976 the length of main railway lines was 6,810 miles. A rail rapid transit network is under construction (1977) in Edmonton.

Post and Telecommunications. Alberta's modern telephone system is owned and operated by the provincial government, except in the city of Edmonton and some rural lines. There were 1,226,170 telephones in service by 31 March 1977.

JUSTICE AND EDUCATION

Justice. The Supreme Judicial authority of the province is the Supreme Court, which consists of the Appellate and Trial divisions. Judges of the Supreme Court are appointed by the Dominion Government and hold office until retirement at the age of 75. There are courts of lesser jurisdiction in both civil and criminal matters. District courts have full jurisdiction over civil proceedings. A Provincial Court which has jurisdiction in civil matters up to $500 is presided over by provincially appointed magistrates. Juvenile Courts have power to try boys 16 and under and girls 18 years of age and under for offences against the Juvenile Deliquents Act.

The jurisdiction of all criminal courts in Alberta is enacted in the provisions of the Criminal Code. The system of procedure in civil and criminal cases conforms as nearly as possible to the English system.

Education. Schools of all grades are included under the term of public school (including those in the separate school system which are publicly supported). The same board of trustees control the schools from kindergarten to university entrance. In 1976–77 there were 423,273 pupils enrolled in elementary, junior high schools and high schools. The University of Alberta (in Edmonton), organized in 1907, had, in 1976–77, 20,019 full-time students. The University of Calgary, formerly part of the University of Alberta and autonomous from April 1966, had in 1976–77, 10,864 full-time students. The University of Lethbridge, organized in 1966, had in 1976–77, 1,483 full-time students. The full-time enrolment at Alberta's 6 public colleges totalled 7,370 students in 1976–77.

Books of Reference

Statistical Information: The Alberta Bureau of Statistics (Dept. of Treasury, Edmonton), which was established in 1939, collects, compiles and distributes information relative to Alberta. *Director:* Harvey W. Ford. Among its publications are: *Alberta Statistical Review* (Annual).—*Alberta Statistical Review* (Monthly).—*Alberta Economic Accounts* (Annual).—*Alberta Salary and Wage Rate Survey* (Annual).—*Alberta Working Conditions and Fringe Benefit Plans Survey* (Occasional).—*Retail and Service Trade Statistics, Alberta* (Annual).—*Alberta Fact Sheet* (Annual).—*Alberta Petroleum Statistics* (Occasional).—*Principal Manufacturing Statistics, Alberta* (Annual).

Hardy, W. G., *Alberta Golden Jubilee Anthology.* Toronto, 1955
Irving, J. A., *The Social Credit Movement in Alberta.* Toronto, 1959
Kroetsch, R., *Alberta.* Toronto, 1968
Macpherson, C. B., *Democracy in Alberta*, 2nd ed. Toronto, 1962
Nesbitt, L. D., *Tides in the West* [history of the Alberta Wheat Pool]. Saskatoon, 1962

BRITISH COLUMBIA

AREA AND POPULATION. British Columbia has an area of 366,255 sq. miles. The capital is Victoria. The province is bordered westerly by the Pacific Ocean and Alaska Panhandle, northerly by the Yukon and Northwest Territories, easterly by the Province of Alberta and southerly by the USA along the 49th parallel. A chain of islands, the largest of which are Vancouver Island and the Queen Charlotte Islands, affords protection to the mainland coast.

The June 1976 census population was 2,406,212.

The principal cities and their populations (1976) are as follows: Greater Vancouver, 1,056,894; Greater Victoria, 224,566. 1976 census populations: Prince George, 58,292; Kamloops, 57,241; Kelowna, 50,111; Nanaimo, 39,655; Penticton, 21,017; Port Alberni, 19,304; Vernon, 17,162; Prince Rupert, 14,247; Cranbrook, 13,310; Dawson Creek, 10,316.

Vital statistics, *see* pp. 259–60.

Religion, *see* p. 279.

CONSTITUTION AND GOVERNMENT. British Columbia (then known as New Caledonia) originally formed part of the Hudson's Bay Company's concession. In 1849 Vancouver Island and in 1858 British Columbia were constituted Crown Colonies; in 1866 the two colonies amalgamated. The British North America Act of 1867 provided for eventual admission into Canadian Confederation, and on 20 July 1871 British Columbia became the sixth province of the Dominion.

British Columbia has a unicameral legislature of 55 elected members. Government policy is determined by the Executive Council responsible to the Legislature. The Lieutenant-Governor is appointed by the Governor-General of Canada, usually for a term of 5 years, and is the head of the executive government of the province.

Lieut.-Governor: The Hon. Walter Stewart Owen, QC, LLD.

Flag: A banner of the arms, *i.e.*, blue and white wavy stripes charged with a setting sun in gold, across the top of a Union Flag with a gold coronet in the centre.

The Legislative Assembly is elected for a maximum term of 5 years. Every male or female Canadian citizen 18 years and over, having resided a minimum of 6 months in the province, duly registered, is entitled to vote. Representation of the parties as of 7 March 1978: New Democratic Party, 18; Social Credit, 35; Liberal, 1; Progressive Conservative, 1; total, 55.

The province is represented in the Federal Parliament by 23 members in the House of Commons, and 6 Senators.

The Executive Council was in Dec. 1976 composed as follows:

Premier and President of the Council: William R. Bennett.

Provincial Secretary and Tourism: Grace M. McCarthy. *Finance:* Evan M. Wolfe. *Attorney-General:* Garde B. Gardom. *Mines and Petroleum Resources:* James R. Chabot. *Forests:* Thomas M. Waterland. *Labour:* Robert A. Williams. *Education:* Patrick L. McGeer. *Energy, Transport and Communications:* Jack Davis. *Municipal Affairs and Housing:* Hugh A. Curtis. *Agriculture:* James J. Hewitt. *Economic Development:* Donald M. Phillips. *Highways and Public Works:* Alexander V. Fraser. *Health:* Robert McClelland. *Human Resources:* William N. Vander Zalm. *Environment:* James A. Nielsen. *Consumer and Corporate Affairs:* Rafe Mair. *Speaker of the House:* D. Ed Smith.

Agent-General in London: Lawrence James Wallace (British Columbia House, 1 Regent St., London, SW1Y 4NS).

Local Government. Vancouver City was incorporated by statute and operates under the provisions of the Vancouver Charter of 1953 and amendments. This is the only incorporated area in British Columbia not operating under the provisions of the Municipal Act. Under this Act municipalities are divided into the following classes: (*a*) a village with a population between 500 and 2,500, governed by a council consisting of a mayor and 4 aldermen; (*b*) a town with a population between 2,500 and 5,000, governed by a council consisting of a mayor and 4 aldermen; (*c*) a city where the population exceeds 5,000 governed by a council consisting of a mayor and 6 or 8 aldermen depending on population; (*d*) a district where the area exceeds 2,000 acres and the average density is less than 2 persons per acre, governed by a council consisting of a mayor and 6 or 8 aldermen depending on population.

There are two other forms of local government: the regional district covering a number of areas both incorporated and unincorporated, governed by a board of directors; and the improvement district governed by a board of 3 trustees.

Revenue for municipal services is derived mainly from real-property taxation, although additional revenue is derived from licence fees, business taxes, fines, public utility projects and grants-in-aid from the provincial government.

ECONOMY

Budget. Current provincial revenue and expenditure, including all capital expenditures, in Canadian $ for fiscal years ending 31 March:

	1973–74	*1974–75*	*1975–76*	*1976–77*
Revenue	2,108,879,721	2,625,723,749	2,927,721,575	3,618,905,867
Expenditure	2,095,948,226	2,639,271,176	3,377,907,818	3,542,776,137

The main sources of current revenue are the income taxes, sales and fuel taxes, contributions from the federal government, and privileges, licences and natural resources taxes and royalties.

The main items of expenditure in 1976–77 are as follows: Education, $870·4m.; highways and ferries, $373·6m.; health and social services, $1,385·5m.; general government, $154·3m.; natural resources and primary industry, $212·8m.

Banking. Cheques cashed (in $1,000): 1972, 78,726,888; 1973, 101,995,925; 1974, 133,447,000; 1975, 163,993,000; 1976, 194,272,000.

ENERGY AND NATURAL RESOURCES

Electricity. Electric power consumption in 1976 totalled an estimated 36·4m. kwh.

Minerals. Copper, coal, natural gas, crude oil, molybdenum and zinc are the most important minerals produced. The 1977 total value of mineral production was estimated at $1,800m. Total value of fuels produced in 1977 was estimated at $907·3m.

Agriculture. Only 6·5m. acres or 2·8% of the total land area is arable or potentially arable. Farm cash receipts, in 1977, reached $493·6m.

Forestry. About 56% of British Columbia's land is forest land, with 118m. acres bearing commercial forest. Over 95% of the forest area is owned or administered by the provincial government. The total cut from forests in 1976 was 2,455m. cu. ft.

Fisheries. In 1977 fish landings totalled 381·5m. lb. and were valued at $134·2m.

INDUSTRY AND TRADE

Industry. The selling value of factory shipments from all manufacturing industries reached an estimated $10,229·3m. in 1977.

Commerce. Exports through British Columbia customs ports during 1976 totalled $7,437·1m. in value, while imports amounted to $3,056·7m.

Principal export commodity groups (1976): Forest products, $2,330·3m.; coal, crude petroleum and natural gas, $2,131m.; metal refinery and mine products, $653m.; grain and cereal products, $922·8m.; fish products, $161·4m. About 40% of exports through British Columbia customs ports are products from other provinces, primarily grains, potash and fuels from the Prairie Provinces. USA is the largest market for products exported through British Columbia customs ports ($3,097·2m. in 1976) followed by Japan ($2,029·4m.) and the EEC ($1,043·5m.).

COMMUNICATIONS

Roads. At 31 July 1976 there were 32,167 miles of provincial highway in the Province.

Railways. The province is served by two transcontinental railways, the Canadian Pacific Railway and the Canadian National Railway. British Columbia is also served by the publicly owned British Columbia Railway, the Railway Freight Service of the B.C. Hydro and Power Authority, the Northern Alberta Railways Company and the Burlington Northern Inc. Their combined route-mileage of mainline track, totals 5,194 miles. In addition, 5 American railways interchange with Canadian railways at southern border points or connect by railway barge.

Aviation. International airports are located at Vancouver and Victoria. Daily inter-provincial and intraprovincial flights serve all main population centres. Small public and private airstrips are located throughout the province.

Shipping. The major ports are Vancouver, New Westminster, Victoria, Nanaimo and Prince Rupert. The volume of foreign shipping loaded (1976) was 36·1m. tons.

The British Columbia Ferries connect Vancouver Island with the Mainland and also provide service to other coastal points. Service by other ferry systems is also provided between Vancouver Island and the USA. The Alaska State Ferries connect Prince Rupert with centres in Alaska.

Post and Broadcasting. The British Columbia Telephone Company had (1976) 1,543,310 telephones in service. There are 9 television stations and 91 radio stations in the Province.

EDUCATION (1975–76). Education, free up to Grade XII levels, is financed jointly from municipal and provincial government revenues. Attendance is compulsory from the age of 6 to 15. There were 542,688 pupils enrolled in public schools.

Higher education (1975–6) is provided at the University of British Columbia at Vancouver (founded 1908), 30,652 students; the University of Victoria (1963), 9,452 students; Simon Fraser University (1965), Burnaby, 9,942 students; Notre Dame University (1963), Nelson, 695 students; Selkirk College (1966), Castlegar, 796 students; Vancouver Community College (1964), 6,129 students; Okanagan Community College (1968), Kelowna, 1,818 students; Capilano Community College (1970), Vancouver, 3,273 students; Malaspina Community College (1969), Nanaimo, 1,935 students; New Caledonia Community College (1969), Prince George, 1,243 students; Cariboo Community College (1970), Kamloops, 1,341 students; Douglas College (1970), New Westminster, 3,981 students; Camosun College (1971), Victoria, 1,956 students; Fraser Valley Community College (1974), Abbotsford, 789 students; East Kootenays Community College (1975), Castlegar, 296 students; Northern Lights Community College (1975), Dawson Creek, 93 students; North Island Community College (1975), Campbell River, 290 students; North West Community College (1975), Terrace, 318 students; British Columbia Institute of Technology (1964), Burnaby, 8,567 students.

HEALTH. The Government operates a hospital insurance scheme giving universal coverage after a qualifying period of 3 months' residence in the province. The province has come under a national medicare scheme which is partially subsidized by the provincial government and partially by the federal government.

Books of Reference

Statistical Information: Information Services (Ministry of Economic Development, Hon. Don Phillips—Minister, Parliament Buildings, Victoria, B.C.), collects, compiles and distributes information relative to the Province.

Publications include *Monthly Bulletin of Business Activity*; *Summary of Economic Activity* (annual); *Manufacturers' Directory*; *Regional and Industrial Studies*; *B.C. Market News, External Trade Report*; *B.C. Facts and Statistics*.

Department of Finance, *British Columbia Financial and Economic Review*. Victoria, B.C. (annual)

Fifteenth British Columbia Natural Resources Conference, *Inventory of the Natural Resources of British Columbia*, 1964

Haig-Brown, R. L., *Living Land: An Account of the Natural Resources of British Columbia*. Toronto, 1961

MANITOBA

AREA AND POPULATION. The area of the province is 251,000 sq. miles (652,218 sq. km), of which 211,775 sq. miles are land and about 39,200 sq. miles water. From north to south it is 761 miles and the widest point is 493 miles.

The population (Dec. 1975 estimate) was 1,018,000. Population of the principal cities (1975): Winnipeg (capital), 553,000; Brandon, 32,475; Thompson, 20,625; Portage la Prairie, 13,300; Flin Flon, 9,600.

Vital statistics, *see* pp. 259–60.

Religion, *see* p. 279.

CONSTITUTION AND GOVERNMENT. Manitoba was known as the Red River Settlement before its entry into the Dominion in 1870. The provincial government is administered by a Lieut.-Governor and a legislative assembly of 57 members elected for 5 years. Women were enfranchised in 1916. The Electoral Division Act, 1955, created 57 single-member constituencies and abolished the transferable vote. The Electoral Divisions Act, 1969, created 29 rural electoral divisions, and 28 urban electoral divisions. The province is represented by 6 members in the Senate and 13 in the House of Commons of Canada.

Lieut.-Governor: Francis L. Jobin (sworn in 15 March 1976).

Flag: The British Red Ensign with the shield of the province in the fly.

State of parties in the Legislative Assembly (elected 11 Oct. 1977): Progressive Conservative, 33; New Democratic Party, 23; Liberals, 1.

The members of the Progressive Conservative Ministry are as follows (Oct. 1977):

President of Executive Council, Minister of Dominion–Provincial Relations: Sterling R. Lyon, QC.

Finance, Minister charged with administration of Manitoba Hydro Act: Donald W. Craik. *Consumer, Corporate and Internal Services, Co-operative Development, Minister responsible for Manitoba Telephone System and Communications and for administration of Manitoba Lotteries Act:* Edward R. McGill. *Without portfolio:* Warner H. Jorgenson. *Health and Social Development, Minister responsible for Corrections and Rehabilitation:* Louis R. Sherman. *Without portfolio:* Sidney J. Spivak, QC. *Public Works, Minister responsible for Manitoba Public Insurance Corporation:* Harry J. Enns. *Without portfolio, Minister responsible for Manitoba Housing and Renewal Corporation:* John F. Johnston. *Agriculture:* James E. Downey. *Education, Minister of Continuing Education and Manpower:* Keith A. Cosens. *Attorney-General, Keeper of the Great Seal, Municipal Affairs, Urban Affairs, Minister responsible for administration of Liquor Control Act:* Gerald W. J. Mercier. *Industry and Commerce, Tourism, Recreation and Cultural Affairs, Minister responsible for administration of Manitoba Development Corporation Act:* Robert D. Banman. *Labour, Minister responsible for Civil Service Act, the Civil Service Superannuation Act, the Public Servants Insurance Act and the Pensions Benefits Act:* Norma L. Price. *Northern Resources and Northern Affairs:* Ken MacMaster. *Mines, Resources and Environmental Management:* Alan B. Ransom.

Local Government. Rural Manitoba is organized into rural municipalities which vary widely in size. Some have only 4 townships (a township is 6 miles square), while the largest has 22 townships. The province has 105 rural municipalities, as well as 33 incorporated towns, 40 incorporated villages and 5 incorporated cities.

Revisions to the City of Winnipeg Act came into effect with the municipal elections held in Oct. 1977, when the number of wards and councillors was reduced from 50 to 29. Members of the central council also sit on 'community committees' which represent the wards they serve. These ward committees are advised by non-elected residents of the area on provision of municipal services within the community committee jurisdiction. Taxing powers and overall budgeting rest with the central council. The mayor is elected at the same time as the councillors in a city-wide vote.

On 1 Jan. 1972, the cities and towns comprising the metropolitan area of Winnipeg were amalgamated to form the City of Winnipeg. A mayor and council are elected to a central government, but councillors also sit on 'community committees' which represent the areas or wards they serve. These committees are advised by non-elected residents of the area on provision of municipal services within the community committee jurisdiction. Taxing powers and overall budgeting rest with the central council.

Since Jan. 1945, 19 Local Government Districts have been formed in the less densely populated areas of the province. They are administered by a provincially appointed person, who acts on the advice of locally elected advisory committees.

In the extreme north, many communities have locally elected councils, while others are administered directly by the Department of Northern Affairs. This department provides most of the funding in all these northern settlements.

FINANCE. Revenue and expenditure (current account) for fiscal years ending 31 March (in Canada $):

	1973–74	*1974–75*	*1975–76*	*1976–77*[1]	*1977–78*[1]
Revenue	694,600,400	834,490,800	1,020,996,000	1,163,656,100	1,158,007,500
Expenditure	696,965,500	834,368,500	1,027,369,000	1,176,490,100	1,183,100,500

[1] Estimates.

ENERGY AND NATURAL RESOURCES

Electricity. The total generating capacity of Manitoba's power stations is 2·9m. kw. The Manitoba Hydro system, owned by the province, provides most of this power, while the city-owned Winnipeg Hydro provides about 185,000 kw. The systems have about 283,000 consumers and consumption was 9,100m. kwh in 1976.

Oil. Crude oil production in 1976 was valued at $33m. for the 3·9m. bbls produced.

Minerals. Total value of minerals in 1976 was about $480m. Principal minerals mined are nickel, zinc, copper, and small quantities of gold and silver. Manitoba has the world's largest deposits of caesium ore and also produces tantalite concentrates.

Agriculture. Rich farmland is the main primary resource, although the area of Manitoba in farms is only about 14% of the total land area. In 1976 the total value of agricultural production in Manitoba was $1,052m., with $716m. from crops, $328m. from livestock and about $8m. from the sale of other products including furs, hides and honey.

Forestry. About 50% of the land area is wooded, of which 53,700 sq. miles is productive forest land. Value of forest production in 1975 was $55·3m.

Fur Trade. Value of fur production to the trapper was $4m. in 1975–76, with the value of all furs exported from the wild $18m.

Fisheries. From 22,000 sq. miles of rivers and lakes fisheries production was about $6·7m. in 1976. Whitefish, sauger, pickerel, pike, trout and perch are the principal varieties of fish caught.

INDUSTRY AND TRADE

Industry. Manufacturing, the largest industry in the province, encompasses almost every major industrial activity in Canada. Estimated output (1976) $2,643m. Manufacturing employed about 53,000 persons, paying $566m. in salaries and wages in 1975. Due to the agricultural base of the province, the food and beverage group of industries is by far the largest, accounting for about 32% of the total value. The next largest segments are machinery at about 10%, transportation equipment and metal fabricating at 5% and clothing at about 4%.

Trade. Products grown and manufactured in Manitoba find ready markets in other areas of Canada, in the USA, particularly the upper midwest region, and in other countries. Export shipments from Manitoba in 1976 were valued at more than $500m., with about 65% going to the US. Of these, about 5% are raw materials, 33% wheat and unmilled grains, and 50% manufacture products.

Tourism. In 1976, Canadian, US and Manitoba tourists contributed about $112m. to the economy.

COMMUNICATIONS

Roads. Highways and provincial roads had a total mileage of 11,681 in 1976.

Railways. In 1976 the province had 4,892 miles of railway, not including industrial track, yards and sidings.

Aviation. A total of 34 licensed commercial air carriers operate from bases in Manitoba, as well as major national and international airlines.

Post. About 99% of the province's 600,000 (estimate) telephones are now dial-operated.

EDUCATION. Education is controlled through locally elected school divisions, with about 80% of the financing provided through the province. There are about 226,000 children enrolled in the province's elementary and secondary schools. The University of Manitoba, founded in 1877, in Winnipeg, has a regular student enrolment of about 14,000; the University of Winnipeg, over 3,000; and Brandon University, 1,000, during the 1977–78 year. Expenditures on education in the 1977 fiscal year are $340m.

Books of Reference

General Information: Inquiries may be addressed to the Information Services Branch, Room 29, Legislative Building, Winnipeg, R3C OV8

The Department of Industry and Commerce publishes: *The Economy of Manitoba*
The Department of Agriculture publishes: *Year Book of Manitoba Agriculture.*
Information Services Branch publishes: *Manitoba Facts.*
Tenth Census of Canada: Manitoba. Statistics Canada, 1971.

NEW BRUNSWICK

HISTORY. Touched by Jacques Cartier in 1534, New Brunswick was first explored by Samuel de Champlain in 1604. It was ceded by the French in the Treaty of Utrecht in 1713 and became a permanent British possession in 1763. It was separated from Nova Scotia and became a province in June 1784, as a result of the great influx of United Empire Loyalists. Responsible government came into being in 1848, and consisted of an executive council, a legislative council (later abolished) and a House of Assembly.

AREA AND POPULATION. The area of the province is 28,354 sq. miles (72,000 sq. km), of which 27,835 sq. miles are land area. The population (census 1976) was 677,250. Of the total population about 58% are of British origin, 37% French and the remainder are principally of Netherlands, German and Scandinavian descent, and in 1978 there were about 4,000 Indians. Census population of urban centres: Saint John, 106,916; Moncton, 80,093; Fredericton (capital), 44,972; Bathurst, 16,195; Edmundston, 12,553; Campbellton, 9,241.

Vital statistics, *see* p. 259–60.
Religion, *see* p. 279.

CONSTITUTION AND GOVERNMENT. The government is vested in a Lieut.-Governor and a Legislative Assembly of 58 members on a constituency basis. A simultaneous translation system is used in the assembly. Any Canadian subject of full age and 6 months' residence is entitled to vote. As a result of the provincial election held on 18 Nov. 1974 and subsequent by-elections, the Assembly is composed of 33 Progressive Conservatives and 25 Liberals. The province has 10 members in the Canadian Senate and 10 members in the federal House of Commons.

Lieut.-Governor: Hedard J. Robichaud (appointed 8 Oct. 1971).

Flag: A banner of the Arms, *i.e.*, yellow charged with a black heraldic ship on wavy lines of blue and white; across the top a red band with a gold lion.

The members of the Progressive Conservative Ministry are as follows (Feb. 1978):

Premier: Richard B. Hatfield.

Agriculture and Rural Development: Malcolm MacLeod. *Commerce and Development:* Gerald S. Merrithew. *Education:* Charles Gallagher. *Fisheries:* Omer Leger. *Finance and Environment:* Ferdinand Dubé. *Health:* Brenda Robertson. *Justice and Provincial Secretary:* Rodman Logan. *Labour and Manpower:* Lawrence Garvie. *Municipal Affairs:* Horace Smith. *Natural Resources:* Roland Boudreau. *New Brunswick Electric Power Commission:* G. W. N. Cockburn. *Social Services:* Leslie Hull. *Supply and Services:* Harold Fanjoy. *Tourism:* Leland McGaw. *Transportation:* Wilfred Bishop. *Treasury Board:* Jean-Maurice Simard. *Youth, Recreation and Cultural Resources:* Jean-Pierre Ouellet.

Local Government. Under the reforms introduced in 1967 the province has assumed complete administrative and financial responsibility for education, health, welfare and administration of justice. Local government is now restricted to provision of services of a strictly local nature. Under the new municipal structure, units include existing and new cities, towns and villages. Counties have disappeared as municipal units. Areas with limited populations have become local service districts. The former local improvement districts have become towns, villages or local service districts depending on their size.

FINANCE. The ordinary budget (in Canadian $) is shown as follows (financial years ended 31 March):

	1973	*1974*	*1975*	*1976*	*1977*
Gross revenue	535,907,818	642,934,583	739,537,015	996,200,000	986,731,000
Gross expenditure	509,917,557	578,679,204	685,209,458	963,800,000	1,012,239,000

Funded debt and capital loans outstanding (exclusive of Treasury Bills) as of 31 March 1977 was $976·6m. Sinking funds held by the province at 31 March 1977, $197·7m. The ordinary budget excludes capital spending.

ENERGY AND NATURAL RESOURCES

Electricity. Hydro-electric and thermal power plants of the New Brunswick Electric Power Commission had a combined capacity of 1,332,484 kw. in 1977. This includes four 100,000 kw. generating units now in operation at the Mactaquac hydro-electric development near Fredericton. Two of the three 300,000 kw. units are in operation at Lorneville near Saint John. The 650,000 kw. nuclear plant at Point Lepreau will be completed in 1980 and plans include two 100,000 kw. units at Mactaquac and a 200,000 kw. unit at Dalhousie. The Commission is interconnected with the neighbouring provinces of Nova Scotia and Quebec and the state of Maine, USA. Hook-up permits exchange of power including large blocks from Churchill Falls in Labrador through Hydro-Quebec as well as with the state of Maine, USA.

Minerals. A considerable variety of metals, industrial minerals, fuels and structural materials occur in the province. These include zinc, lead, copper, cadmium, bismuth, nickel, gold, silver, cobalt, tungsten, tin, molybdenum, antimony, potash, salt, glauberite, limestone, dolomite, gypsum, oil, gas, coal, uranium, oil shale, sand, gravel, clay, peat, diatomite and marl. Not all have been explored sufficiently. 60% of the value of minerals produced in 1975, which totalled $251m., was attributed to zinc produced from 3 mines in the Bathurst–Newcastle area: Brunswick Mining and Smelting, Heath Steele and Nigadoo River Mines Ltd. New Brunswick is now the second largest producer of zinc in Canada. A lead smelter, fertilizer plant and port facilities have been constructed at Belledune. Numerous other discoveries have been made in the area and 4 deposits are now in the final stages of exploration. Canada's only primary antimony producer is located at Lake George, near Fredericton, and a large low-grade tungsten–molybdenum–bismuth deposit is being developed at Mount Pleasant. Exploration is also in process near Sussex and Salt Springs, where potash and salt occurrences have been found. Limestone and gypsum are quarried at Havelock and Hillsborough and small quantities of oil and natural gas are produced from the Stoney Creek Field south of Moncton. Coal is mined at Grand Lake and exploration is underway for other deposits of this important energy resource.

Agriculture. The total area under crops is estimated at 322,000 acres, exclusive of improved pasture land (115,000 acres). Farms numbered 3,244 and averaged 306 acres each (census 1976). Mixed farming is common throughout the province. Dairy farming is centred around the larger urban areas, and is located mainly along the Saint John River Valley and in the south-eastern sections of the province. For particulars of agricultural production and livestock, *see under* CANADA, pp. 270–72. Farm cash receipts in 1976 were approximately $110m.

Forestry. New Brunswick contains some 15·3m. acres of productive forest lands, of which 7·3m. acres is Crown-owned. The combined value of primary and secondary forest production was about $794m. in 1974, including logging wood and paper and allied industries, which accounted for about $628m. In 1975 some 95 sawmills shipped timber valued at about $74·9m. Timber-using plants employ about 10,150 men. Practically all forest products are exported from the province's numerous ports and harbours near which the mills are located or sent by road or rail to the USA.

Fisheries. Commercial fishing is one of the most important basic industries of the province. Over 35 commercial species of fish and shellfish are landed, of which lobster, herring, tuna, crabs and groundfish are the most valuable. More than 5,000 fishermen and 7,000 plant workers are employed in 64 fish processing plants; the gross income of fishermen in 1975 was approximately $25m., and the total market value of fish products was approximately $116·3m.

INDUSTRY. There are about 1,000 manufacturing establishments, employing about 29,000 persons. New Brunswick's location, with deep-water harbours open throughout the year and container facilities at Saint John, makes it ideal for exporting. Industries include food and beverages, paper and allied industries, timber products. About 25% of the industrial labour force work in Saint John.

TOURISM. In 1977, 4·1m. tourists visited the province.

COMMUNICATIONS

Roads. There are about 1,400 miles of arterial highways and 1,300 miles of collector roads, 95% of which are hard-surfaced. Over 10,000 miles of local roads provide access to most areas in the province. The main highway system, including 380 miles of the Trans-Canada Highway, links the province with the principal roads in Quebec and Nova Scotia, as well as the Interstate Highway System in the eastern seaboard states of the USA. Passenger vehicles, 31 March 1976, numbered 218,919; commercial vehicles, 60,497; motor cycles, 9,656.

Railways. New Brunswick is served by main lines of both Canadian Pacific and Canadian National railways.

Post and Broadcasting. On 31 Oct. 1976 the New Brunswick Telephone Co. Ltd had 332,090 telephones in service. The province is served by 14 radio stations. Ten are privately owned and 4 owned by the Canadian Broadcasting Corporation. One station broadcasts in the French language, 1 is bilingual and the CBC International Service broadcasts in several languages from its station at Sackville. The province is serviced by 3 television stations, 1 of which broadcasts in French.

Newspapers. New Brunswick had (1978) 6 daily newspapers, 1 in French, and 19 weekly newspapers, 5 in French or bilingual.

EDUCATION. Public education is free and non-sectarian. There are 4 universities. The University of New Brunswick at Fredericton (founded 13 Dec. 1785 by the Loyalists, elevated to university status in 1823, reorganized as the University of New Brunswick in 1859) had 5,400 students at the Fredericton campus and 495 students at the Saint John campus (Dec. 1976); Mount Allison University at Sackville had 1,362 students; the University of Moncton at Moncton, 2,593 students; St Thomas University at Frederiction, 769 students.

On 1 Nov. 1976 there were 752 students enrolled in 3 technical schools and 3,058 students enrolled in 5 regular trade schools.

There were, in Sept. 1976, 162,819 pupils and 7,708 teachers in school buildings (Grades 1–12). Large new regional schools are absorbing numbers of small country schools; there are 33 school districts.

Books of Reference

Industrial Information: Dept. of Commerce and Development, Fredericton.

New Brunswick and Its People. Fredericton, 1962

Department of Commerce and Development, *Annual Report.* Fredericton, 1973.—*New Brunswick in Profile.* Fredericton

NEWFOUNDLAND AND LABRADOR

HISTORY. Archaeological finds at L'Anse-au-Meadow in northern Newfoundland suggest that the Vikings had established a colony there at about A.D. 1000. Newfoundland was discovered by John Cabot 24 June 1497, and was soon frequented in the summer months by the Portuguese, Spanish and French for its fisheries. It was formally occupied in Aug. 1583 by Sir Humphrey Gilbert on behalf of the English Crown, but various attempts to colonize the island remained unsuccessful. Although British sovereignty was recognized in 1713 by the Treaty of Utrecht, disputes over fishing rights with the French were not finally settled till 1904.

By the Anglo-French Convention of 1904, France renounced her exclusive fishing rights along part of the coast, granted under the Treaty of Utrecht, but retained sovereignty of the offshore islands of St Pierre and Miquelon.

AREA AND POPULATION. Area, 156,185 sq. miles (383,300 sq. km). In March 1927 the Privy Council decided the boundary between Canada and Newfoundland in Labrador. This area, now part of the Province of Newfoundland and Labrador, is 112,826 sq. miles. The coastline is extremely irregular. Bays, fiords and inlets are numerous and there are many good harbours with deep water close to shore. The coast is rugged with bold rocky cliffs from 200 to 400 ft high; in the Bay of Islands some of the islands rise 500 ft, with the adjacent shore 1,000 ft above tide level. The interior is a plateau of moderate elevation and the chief relief features trend north-east and south-west. Long Range, the most notable of these, begins at Cape Ray and extends north-east for 200 miles; the highest peak reaching 2,673 ft. Approximately one-third of the area is covered by water. Grand Lake, the largest body of water, has an area of about 200 sq. miles. The principal rivers flow towards the north-east. On the borders of the lakes and water-courses good land is generally found, particularly in the valleys of the Terra Nova River, the Gander River, the Exploits River and the Humber River, which are also heavily timbered.

Census population, 1976, was 557,725.

The capital of Newfoundland is the City of St John's (143,390, metropolitan area). The only other city is Corner Brook (25,198); important towns are Labrador City (12,012), Stephenville (10,284), Gander (9,301), Grand Falls (8,729), Happy Valley–Goose Bay (8,075), Windsor (6,349), Channel-Port aux Basques (6,187), Carbonear (5,026), Wabana (4,824), Bonavista (4,299), Wabush City (3,769).

Vital statistics, *see* pp. 259–60.

Religion, *see* p. 279.

CONSTITUTION AND GOVERNMENT. Until 1832 Newfoundland was ruled by the Governor under instructions from the Colonial Office. In that year a Legislature was brought into existence, but the Governor and his Executive Council were not responsible to it. Under the constitution of 1855, which lasted until its suspension in 1934, the government was administered by the Governor appointed by the Crown with an Executive Council responsible to the House of Assembly of 27 elected members and a Legislative Council of 24 members nominated for life by the Governor in Council. Women were enfranchised in 1925. At the Imperial Conference of 1917 Newfoundland was constituted as a Dominion.

In 1933 the financial situation had become so critical that the Government of Newfoundland asked the Government of the UK to appoint a Royal Commission to investigate conditions. On the strength of their recommendations, the parliamentary form of government was suspended and Government by Commission was inaugurated on 16 Feb. 1934.

A National Convention, elected in 1946, made, in 1948, recommendations to H.M. Government in Great Britain as to the possible forms of future government to be submitted to the people at a national referendum. Two referenda were held. In the first referendum (June 1948) the three forms of government submitted to the people were: commission of government for 5 years, confederation with Canada and responsible government as it existed in 1933. No one form of government received a clear majority of the votes polled, and commission of government, receiving the fewest votes, was eliminated. In the second referendum (July 1948) confederation with Canada received 78,408 and responsible government 71,464 votes.

In the Canadian Senate on 18 Feb. 1949 Royal assent was given to the terms of union of Newfoundland and Labrador with Canada, and on 23 March 1949, in the House of Lords, London, Royal assent was given to an amendment to the British North America Act made necessary by the inclusion of Newfoundland and Labrador as the tenth Province of Canada.

Under the terms of union of Newfoundland and Labrador with Canada, which was signed at Ottawa on 11 Dec. 1948, the constitution of the Legislature of Newfoundland and Labrador as it existed immediately prior to 16 Feb. 1934 shall, subject to the terms of the British North America Acts, 1867 to 1946, continue as the constitution of the Legislature of the Province of Newfoundland and Labrador until altered under the authority of the said Acts.

The franchise was in 1965 extended to all male and female residents who have attained the age of 19 years and are otherwise qualified as electors.

The House of Assembly (Amendment) Act, 1974, established 51 electoral districts and 51 members of the Legislature.

At 13 Oct 1976 there were 30 Progressive-Conservatives, 17 Liberals, 3 Liberal Reform and 1 Independent.

The province is represented by 6 members in the Senate and by 7 members in the House of Commons of Canada.

Lieut.-Governor: G. A. Winter (assumed office 4 July 1974).
Flag: The British Union flag.

The Progressive-Conservative Executive Council was, in Feb. 1978, composed as follows:

Premier: Frank D. Moores.
Justice and Finance: T. A. Hickman, QC. *President of Executive Council, Transportation and Communications, Intergovernmental Affairs:* C. W. Doody. *Rural Development, Public Works and Services:* J. H. Lundrigan. *Forestry and Agriculture, President of Treasury Board:* E. M. Maynard. *Health:* H. A. Collins. *Industrial Development:* Dr T. C. Farrell. *Tourism:* J. C. Morgan. *Rehabilitation and Recreation:* T. V. Hickey. *Municipal Affairs and Housing:* J. W. Dinn. *Fisheries:* W. C. Carter. *Manpower and Labour:* J. G. Rousseau, Jr. *Mines and Energy:* B. Peckford. *Education:* H. W. House. *Social Services:* R. C. Brett. *Consumer Affairs and Environment:* A. J. Murphy.

Agent-General in London: H. Watson Jamer (60 Trafalgar Sq., WC2).

FINANCE. Budget[1] in Canadian $1,000 for fiscal years ended 31 March:

	1972–73	*1973–74*	*1974–75*	*1975–76*[2]	*1976–77*[2]	*1977–78*[3]
Gross revenue	390,767	484,754	592,284	708,955	825,639	955,978
Gross expenditure	399,698	457,919	586,648	708,104	824,423	947,396

[1] Current amount only. [2] Revised estimates. [3] Estimates.

Public debenture debt as at 31 March 1977 (preliminary) was $1,512·3m.; sinking fund, $179·7m.

ENERGY AND NATURAL RESOURCES

Electricity. The electrical energy requirements of the province are met mainly by hydro-electric power, with petroleum fuels being utilized to provide the balance. The total amount of energy generated in the province in 1976 was 39,190m. kwh., of which approximately 99% was derived from hydro-electric facilities. The greater part of the energy produced in 1976 came from Churchill Falls, of which 32,104m. kwh. was sold to Hydro-Quebec under the terms of a long-term contract. Energy consumed in the province during 1976 totalled 7,086m. kwh., with approximately 5,800m. kwh., or 95%, coming from hydro-electric facilities.

At 31 Dec. 1975 total electrical generating capacity in the province was 6·7m. kw., with hydro-electric plants accounting for 6·2m. kw., or 93%. A 75 mw hydro project will shortly be started at Hind's Lake in central Newfoundland and should be completed in 1981. It is estimated that potential additional hydro-electric generating capacity of up to 4·5m. kw. can be developed at various sites in the Labrador part of the province.

Oil. The province consumes refined petroleum at the rate of 43,000 bbls a day with 25% of this being refined in the province. While the refining capacity of the province is 114,000 bbls per day, there is presently only one refinery being operated, a 14,000 bbls-per-day refinery at Holyrood. Offshore exploration expenditures for oil and gas have increased substantially in recent years. The province has issued exploration permits to exploration companies, which operate for their own account or represent joint ventures, covering 168,993 sq. miles offshore on the continental shelf. In Oct 1974, two natural-gas finds off Labrador were announced. Tests of these two wells resulted in rates of flow of 13m. and 20m. cu. ft per day respectively, with some condensate and no water present. An additional natural gas find with a flow of 9·8m. cu. ft per day and significant condensates was announced in 1976. Additional drilling is required to delineate the reserves before the significance of the finds will be known.

Minerals. The mineral resources are vast but only partially documented. Large deposits of iron ore, with an ore reserve of over 5,000m. tons at Labrador City, Wabush City and in the Knob Lake area are supplying approximately half of Canada's production. Other large deposits of iron ore are known to exist in the Julienne Lake area. There are a variety of other minerals being produced in the province in more limited amounts.

Uranium deposits in the Kaipokak Bay area near Makkovik in Labrador are presently being studied by Brinex. The Central Mineral Belt, which extends from the Smallwood Reservoir to the Atlantic coast near Makkovik, holds uranium, copper, beryllium and molybdenite potential.

Production in 1976: Iron ore, 30·8m. tons ($643·5m.); copper, 7,456 tons ($10·2m.); zinc, 50,283 tons ($37·8m.); asbestos, 95,000 tons ($33·4m.); fluorspar ($2·2m.); lead, 10,199 tons ($4·6m.); silver, 512,000 troy oz. ($2·2m.); gold, 13,000 troy oz. ($1·6m.); cadmium, 10,000 lb. ($26,000); gypsum, 615,000 tons ($2·4m.); pyrophyllite ($416,000); silica ($218,000); cement ($5m.); clay products ($475,000); sand and gravel, 5·6m. tons ($9·2m.); stone, 900,000 tons ($2·7m.).

Agriculture. The estimated value of agricultural products sold, including livestock, 1976, was $20·6m.

Forestry. The forestry economy in the province is mainly dependent on the operation of 2 newsprint mills and a linerboard mill. In 1976 the 2 newsprint mills exported 513,485 tons of newsprint at a value of $151·3m., and the linerboard mill exported 109,955 tons of paper at a value of \$27·5m. Lumber mills, saw-log operations and miscellaneous cuttings in the province produced 37m. f.b.m.

Fisheries. The principal fish landings are cod, flounder, redfish, Queen crabs (in shell), lobster, salmon and herring. In 1975 some 4,700 persons were employed by the fish-processing industry and there were 15,313 full-, part-time and casual fishermen engaged in harvesting operations. 44 freezing plants and 57 saltfish plants were in operation. The production of fresh and frozen fish products was valued at \$191·3m. in 1976.

The total catch in 1976 was 317,199 tonnes valued at \$64·7m., of which the main items were: Cod, 99,241 tonnes (\$24·5m.); flounder, 82,607 (\$14·8m.); redfish, 40,075 (\$4·8m.); lobster, 2,254 (\$5·3m.); salmon, 2,012 (\$3·6m.). In addition, there were 48,922 tonnes (\$3·8m.) of herring landed.

The seal fishery in 1976 had 4 large licensed and 179 small licensed vessels with 881 men who landed 64,667 pelts. The number of pelts landed by 4,047 landsmen totalled 29,926.

INDUSTRY. The total value of manufacturing shipments in 1976 was \$585·9m. This consists largely of first-stage processing of primary resource products with two of the largest components being paper and fish products.

TRADE UNIONS. There were (1974) 344 unions representing 51,417 members of international and national unions, government employee associations as well as 5 local independent unions.

COMMUNICATIONS

Roads. In 1976 there were 5,564 miles, of which 2,825 were paved.

Railways. In 1976 there were 944 miles of railway, of which the Canadian National Railways operated 712 (3 ft 6 in.), the Quebec North Shore and Labrador Railway 357 (4 ft 8½ in.) and there were 25 miles of private line. Car and passenger ferries operate from Port aux Basques and Argentia to North Sydney, Nova Scotia. On the island of Newfoundland, the Canadian National Railways operates a trans-island bus and rail freight service in addition to a coastal service for both passengers and freight. In the months that the Labrador coast is ice-free, usually from June to Nov., the Canadian National Railways operates a scheduled coastal steamer service every week.

Aviation. The province is linked to the rest of Canada by regular air services provided by Air Canada, Eastern Provincial Airways, Quebecair and a number of smaller air carriers.

Shipping. At 31 Dec. 1976 there were 1,281 ships registered in Newfoundland.

Post. There were 486 post offices open in 1976, and 22 telegraph offices in the Newfoundland and Labrador postal district. Telephone connexions in the province numbered 211,581 in 1976.

EDUCATION. The number of schools in 1975–76 was 723. The enrolment was 157,682; teachers numbered 7,671. The Memorial University, offering courses in arts, science, engineering, education, nursing and medicine, had approximately 9,900 full- and part-time students. Total expenditure for education by the Government in 1976–77 was \$269m.

Books of Reference

Blackburn, R. H. (ed.), *Encyclopaedia of Canada: Newfoundland Supplement*. Toronto, 1949

Bruet, E., *Le Labrador et le Nouveau-Québec*. Paris, 1949

Horwood, H., *Newfoundland*. Toronto, 1969

Loture, R. de, *Histoire de la grande pêche de Terre-Neuve*. Paris, 1949

Mercer, G. A., *The Province of Newfoundland and Labrador: Geographical Aspects*. Ottawa, 1970

Perlin, A. B., *The Story of Newfoundland, 1497–1959*. St John's, 1959

Tanner, V., *Outlines of Geography. Life and Customs of Newfoundland–Labrador.* 2 vols. Helsinki, 1944, and Toronto, 1947
Taylor, T. G., *Newfoundland: A Study of Settlement.* Toronto, 1946

NOVA SCOTIA

HISTORY. The first permanent settlement was made by the French early in the 17th century, and the province was called Acadia until finally ceded to the British by the Treaty of Utrecht in 1713.

AREA AND POPULATION. The area of the province is 21,425 sq. miles (55,000 sq. km), of which 20,401 sq. miles are land area, 1,024 sq. miles water area. The population (census 1976) was 828,571; estimate (1977) 835,400.

Population of the principal cities and towns (census 1976): Halifax, 117,882; Dartmouth, 65,341; Sydney, 30,645; Glace Bay, 21,836; Truro, 12,840; New Glasgow, 10,672; Amherst, 10,263; Sydney Mines, 8,965; Yarmouth, 7,801.

Vital statistics, *see* pp. 259–60.
Religion, *see* p. 279.

CONSTITUTION AND GOVERNMENT. Under the British North America Act of 1867 the legislature of Nova Scotia may exclusively make laws in relation to local matters, including direct taxation within the province, education and the administration of justice. The legislature of Nova Scotia consists of a Lieut.-Governor, appointed and paid by the federal government, and holding office for 5 years, and a House of Assembly of 46 members, chosen by popular vote not more than every 5 years. The province is represented in the Canadian Senate by 10 members, and in the House of Commons by 11.

The franchise and eligibility to the legislature are granted to every person, male or female, if of age (19 years), a British subject or Canadian citizen, and a resident in the province for 1 year and 2 months before the date of the writ of election in the county or electoral district of which the polling district forms part, and if not by law otherwise disqualified. State of parties in Sept. 1977: 31 Liberals, 12 Progressive Conservatives, 3 New Democrats.

Lieut.-Governor: Dr Clarence L. Gosse.

Flag: A banner of the Arms, *i.e.*, white with a blue diagonal cross, bearing in the centre the royal shield of Scotland.

The members of the Liberal Ministry are as follows:

Premier and President of Executive Council: Gerald A. Regan, QC.

Minister of Finance, Deputy Premier: Peter Nicholson, QC. *Attorney-General, Minister in charge of Administration of the Human Rights Act:* Leonard L. Pace, QC. *Social Services, Minister responsible for Status of Women:* W. M. MacEachern. *Development, Minister in charge of Administration of the Civil Service Act, Minister in charge of Administration of the Research Foundation Corporation Act:* A. M. Sandy Cameron. *Education:* George M. Mitchell, QC. *Labour, Minister in charge of the Housing Development Act:* Walter R. Fitzgerald. *Recreation:* A. Garnet Brown. *Fisheries:* Daniel S. Reid. *Public Works, Minister in charge of Administration of the Liquor Control Act:* Benoit Comeau. *Municipal Affairs:* Glen M. Bagnell. *Tourism:* Maurice E. DeLory. *Mines, Minister in charge of the Nova Scotia Energy Council:* J. William Gillis. *Highways:* J. Fraser Mooney. *Agriculture, Marketing and Chairman of the Treasury Board:* John Hawkins. *Health, Minister in charge of Administration of the Drug Dependency Act, Registrar-General:* Maynard C. MacAskill. *Lands and Forests, Minister of the Environment, Minister in charge of Administration of the EMO (NS) Act and Regulations:* Vincent J. MacLean. *Consumer Affairs, Minister in charge of the Residential Tenancies Act:* Guy A. C. Brown. *Provincial Secretary, Minister in charge of Administration of the Communications and Information Act:* Harold M. Huskilson.

Agent-General in London: Adm. D. W. Piers (14 Pall Mall, SW1Y 5LU).

Local Government. The main divisions of the province for governmental purposes are the 3 cities, the 38 towns and the 24 rural municipalities, each governed by a council and a mayor or warden. The cities have independent charters, and the various towns take their powers from and are limited by The Towns Act, and the various municipalities take their powers from and are limited by The Municipal Act as revised in 1967. The majority of municipalities comprise 1 county, but 6 counties are divided into 2 municipalities each. In no case do the boundaries of any municipality overlap county lines. The 18 counties as such have no administrative functions.

Any city (of which there are 3) or incorporated town (of which there are 38) that lies within the boundaries of a municipality is excluded from any jurisdiction by the municipal council and has its own government.

FINANCE. Revenue is derived from provincial sources, payments from the federal government under the Federal-Provincial Fiscal Arrangements and Established Programs Financing Act (the '1977 Act'), and under various federal cost-shared programmes. Main sources of provincial revenues include income and sales taxes. Under the 1977 Act the Government of Canada makes payments designed to equalize tax revenues *per capita* available to the provinces. The 1977 Act also provides for the replacement of former cost-sharing arrangements for health and medical services and for post-secondary education with the transfer of additional personal income tax points to the provinces, plus an approximately equivalent amount in supplementary cash payments.

Ordinary expenditures include annual requirements for debt charges and provisions for the retirement of long-term debt (sinking fund instalments and serial retirements), thus funding capital requirements from current revenues.

Revenue, expenditure and debt (in Canadian $1m.) for fiscal years ending 31 March:

	1974	*1975*	*1976*	*1977*	*1978*[1]
Ordinary Revenue	726·5	855·2	985·9	1,120·1	1,248·9
Ordinary Expenditures	716·1	825·9	983·1	1,102·0	1,248·8
Net Revenue Surplus	10·4	29·3	2·8	18·1	0·1
Net Capital Expenditures	48·2	75·9	101·3	97·6	120·8
Direct Debt	1,233·0	1,359·7	1,485·8	1,558·3	—
Net Direct Debt	298·7	319·1	374·0	445·2	—

[1] Estimate.

NATURAL RESOURCES

Minerals. Principal minerals in 1976 were: Coal, 2·2m. tons, valued at $54·5m.; gypsum, 4·3m. tons, valued at $13·8m.; salt, 994,000 tons, valued at $17·6m.; sand and gravel, 9·5m. tons, valued at $14·4m. Total value of mineral production in 1976 was about $125,124,000.

Agriculture. Dairying, poultry and egg production, livestock and fruit growing are the most important branches. Farm cash receipts for 1976 were estimated at $124m., with an additional $9m. going to persons on farms as income in kind.

Cash receipts from sale of dairy products was $36·7m., with total milk production of 354m. lb.

The production of poultry meat in 1976 was 30·7m. lb., of which 23·7m. lb. were broilers and 3·1m. lb. were turkeys. Egg production was 16·1m. dozen.

The main 1976 fruit crops were apples, 2·3m. bu.; blueberries, 7m. lb.; and strawberries, 2·4m. quarts.

Forestry. The estimated forest area of Nova Scotia is 15,555 sq. miles, of which about 25% is owned by the province. The principal trees are spruce, balsam fir, hemlock, pine, larch, birch, oak, maple, poplar and ash. 106,982,173 cu. ft of round and sawn forest products were produced in 1976.

Fisheries. The fisheries of the province in 1976 had a landed value of $106·3m. of sea fish including scallop fishery, $37m., and lobster fishery, $22m. In 1975 there were about 4,354 employees in the fish processing industry; the value of shipment of goods was $149·7m.

INDUSTRY. The number of manufacturing establishments was 689 in 1975; the number of employees was 37,262; wage and salaries, $639·6m.; value of shipments in 1976 was $1,978·8m. The leading industries, according to value of shipments in 1976, were petroleum and coal products, food and beverages, transportation equipment and paper and allied industries.

TRADE UNIONS. The majority of unions are affiliated with the Canadian Labour Congress. Independent organizations with the largest union memberships are the Nova Scotia Government Employees Association, District 26, of the United Mine Workers of America and the Teamsters Union. In 1977 there were 554 local unions in Nova Scotia with a membership of 98,667.

COMMUNICATIONS

Roads. In March 1977 there were 15,660 miles of highways; 1,618 miles of paved arterial highways; 2,769 miles of collector highways (of which 2,467 miles are paved); 11,273 miles of local highways (of which 1,767 miles are paved). The figures are exclusive of highways within cities and towns.

Railways. The province is covered with a network of railways, 1,214 miles in extent.

Aviation. There is a direct air service to major Canadian and USA cities, London and Bermuda.

Shipping. Ferry services connect Nova Scotia with Newfoundland, Prince Edward Island, New Brunswick and Maine.

JUSTICE. There is a Supreme Court which is a Court of common law and equity possessing original and appellate jurisdiction in civil and in criminal cases. The Supreme Court consists of an appeal division of 4 judges and a trial division of 8 judges. There are also county courts, family courts, probate courts, magistrates' courts, municipal and justices' courts. Bodies, sometimes referred to as courts, are established for the revision of assessment rolls, voters' lists and like purposes. Juvenile courts under the auspices of the family courts throughout the province have power to try boys and girls under the age of 16 years.

For the year ending 31 Dec. 1976 there were 5,266 admissions to provincial jails, of these, 3,922 were sentenced. The Adult Probation Service handled 4,954 cases during 1976.

EDUCATION. Public education in Nova Scotia is free, compulsory and undenominational through elementary and high school. Attendance is compulsory to the age of 16. In addition to over 600 public schools there are the Intergovernmental Resource Centres for the Hearing Impaired and for the Visually Impaired; the Nova Scotia School for Boys; the Nova Scotia School for Girls, and the Nova Scotia Youth Training Centre for mentally deficient children. The province has 14 universities and colleges (including 3 junior colleges), of which the largest is Dalhousie University in Halifax. The Nova Scotia Agricultural College and the Nova Scotia Teachers College are located at Truro. The Nova Scotia Technical College at Halifax grants degrees in engineering and architecture.

The Adult Education programme of the Nova Scotia Department of Education operates through its applied arts and technology activity 2 institutes of technology, a nautical institute, and coalmining classes. It also provides in-school training for the Department of Labour Apprenticeship programme.

All training arrangements for adults including those financed by the federal Department of Manpower and Immigration are the responsibility of the Adult Vocational Activity of the Department of Education. Short courses for fishermen and farmers are conducted by the Departments of Fisheries and Agriculture respectively.

The Continuing Education Activity of the Department of Education offers financial support and organizational assistance to local school boards for provision of weekend and evening courses in academic and avocational subjects, and citizenship for new Canadians. It also provides local authorities with specialist support services to assist them in providing community workshops and short courses in fine arts and handicrafts; and it operates a correspondence study service for children and adults.

Occupational courses at the high school level are provided by 13 regional vocational schools under the jurisdiction (except in 3 amalgamated school areas) of the vocational education activity of the Department of Education Youth Education programme.

Total expenditure on public education for the year 1975–76 was $285,488,265, of which 72% was borne by the provincial government. In 1975–76, classrooms operated in 623 school houses, with 11,658 teachers and 206,783 pupils, of whom 109,782 were in elementary school grades and 97,001 in junior and senior high school grades.

Books of Reference

Atlantic Provinces Economic Council. *Atlantic Canada Today*. Halifax, 1969
Nova Scotia Economic Profile. Nova Scotia Dept. of Development. Halifax, 1972
Nova Scotia, Today's Economy. Nova Scotia Dept. of Development. Halifax, 1976
Proceedings and Transactions of the Nova Scotia Historical Society and Nova Scotian Institute of Science
Public Archives of Nova Scotia. *Place Names and Places of Nova Scotia*. Halifax, 1967
Beck, Murray, *The Government of Nova Scotia*. Toronto, 1957.—*Joseph Howe. The Voice of Nova Scotia*. 1964.—*The Evolution of Municipal Government in Nova Scotia, 1749–1973*. 1973
Bird, W. R., *This is Nova Scotia*. Toronto, 1955
Fergusson, C. B., *Nova Scotia* in *Encyclopedia Canadiana*, Vol. VII. Toronto, 1968
Raddall, T. H., *Halifax, Warden of the North*. Toronto, 1972

ONTARIO

AREA AND POPULATION. The total area is 412,582 sq. miles (1·55 sq. km), of which 344,092 sq. miles is land area and 68,490 sq. miles fresh water. The province extends 1,000 miles from east to west and 1,050 miles from south to north. About 82% of this area lies south of the isotherm of 60° F. (16° C.) mean July temperature, which is generally considered the northern limit for the economic production of cereals.

The province is bordered by Quebec on the east and Manitoba on the west. The southern boundary has a fresh-water shoreline of 2,362 miles on the Great Lakes; its northern limits have a salt-water shoreline of 680 miles.

The population of the province (census, 1 June 1976) was 8,264,465. Census population of the principal cities (1976): Toronto (provincial capital), 633,318 (city), 2,124,291 (metropolitan area), 2,803,101 (census metropolitan area); Hamilton, 312,003 (city), 529,371 (census metropolitan area); Ottawa (federal capital), 304,462 (city), 521,341 (census metropolitan area); London, 240,392 (city); Windsor, 196,526 (city), Kitchener, 131,870 (city), 272,158 (census metropolitan area); Sudbury, 97,604 (city), 167,705 (regional municipality).

Vital statistics, *see* pp. 259–60.

Religion, *see* p. 279.

CONSTITUTION AND GOVERNMENT. The provincial government is administered by a Lieut.-Governor, a cabinet and one chamber elected by a general franchise for a period of 5 years. Women have the vote and can be elected to the chamber. The minimum voting age is 18 years.

In June 1977 the provincial legislature was composed as follows: Progressive Conservatives, 58; Liberals, 34; New Democrats, 33; total 125.

Lieut.-Governor: Hon. Pauline M. McGibbon, QC, BA, LLD (appointed 10 April 1974).

Flag: The British Red Ensign with the shield of Ontario in the fly.

The members of the Executive Council in Feb. 1978 were as follows (all Progressive Conservatives):

Premier and President of the Council: William G. Davis, QC.

Culture and Recreation and Deputy Premier: Robert Welch, QC. *Chairman, Management Board of Cabinet:* James Auld. *Provincial Secretary for Resources Development:* Rene Brunelle. *Education:* Thomas L. Wells. *Environment:* George McCague. *Northern Affairs:* Leo Bernier. *Transportation and Communications:* James Snow. *Provincial Secretary for Social Development:* Margaret Birch. *Industry and Tourism:* John Rhodes. *Treasury, Economics and Intergovernmental Affairs:* W. Darcy McKeough. *Agriculture and Food:* William Newman. *Natural Resources:* Frank Miller. *Housing:* Claude Bennett. *Health:* Dennis Timbrell. *Provincial Secretary for Justice and Solicitor-General:* George Kerr, QC. *Revenue:* Lorne Maeck. *Colleges and Universities:* Harry Parrott. *Energy:* Reuben Baetz. *Labour:* Dr Bette Stephenson. *Attorney-General:* Roy McMurtry, QC. *Government Service and Chairman of Cabinet:* Lorne Henderson. *Community and Social Services:* Keith Norton. *Correctional Services:* Frank Drea. *Consumer and Commercial Relations:* Larry Grossman. *Without Portfolio:* Douglas Wiseman.

Local Government. Local government in Ontario is divided into two branches, one covering municipal institutions and the other education.

The present municipal system dates from The Municipal Corporations Act enacted by The Province of Canada in 1849. It has been considerably modified in recent years with the creation of the Municipality of Metropolitan Toronto in 1954 and the launching of the Government of Ontario's local government restructuring programme in 1968. Generally, there are two levels of municipal government in Ontario. The upper level consists of 27 counties plus 12 restructured regional municipalities. The local level comprises more than 800 cities, towns and townships. Cities in the traditional county system function independently of the county in which they lie, as do 5 towns which have been separated for municipal purposes. There are no separated municipal units in regional governments.

Ontario's local municipalities are governed by councils elected by popular vote.

A city council usually consists of a mayor, aldermen and, sometimes, an executive committee known as a board of control.

Councils of towns, villages and townships usually consist of a mayor, reeve, deputy reeve, councillors and, in the case of the newer regional municipalities, one or more regional councillors who represent the area municipalities on the regional council.

County and regional government councils are federated assemblies.

A county council consists of the reeves and deputy reeves of the towns, villages and townships. The head of the county council is the warden, who is elected by the council from among its own members.

A regional council consists of the heads of council of the local municipalities, as well as a varying number of regional councillors, who are elected on the basis of representation, either directly or indirectly. The head of the regional council is the chairman who is elected by council but who, unlike a county warden, need not have been a council member.

No municipality in Ontario may incur long-term debts without the sanction of the tribunal created by the Provincial Legislature and known as the Ontario Municipal Board. Debenture obligations incurred by municipalities for utility undertakings (water-works and electric light and power systems) are discharged ordinarily out of revenues derived from the sale of utility services and do not fall upon the ratepayers.

Municipal councils have no jurisdiction for education beyond the collection of taxes for school purposes. Responsibility for providing, operating and maintaining school facilities, and for the supply of teachers, rests with local education authorities known as boards of education or school boards. These boards are now generally organized on a county or regional basis. Apart from some of the larger cities, local municipal school boards no longer exist.

Municipal institutions come under the jurisdiction of the Provincial Ministry of Treasury, Economics and Intergovernmental Affairs. One of the principal functions of the Ministry is to advise and assist municipalities on such matters as accounting, reporting, auditing, budgeting and planning. Educational support and guidance at the provincial level is the responsibility of the Ministry of Education, which deals with the training of teachers and the formulation of curriculum. (At the university and community college level, education support services are provided by the Ministry of Colleges and Universities.)

There are considerable areas in the northernmost parts of Ontario where as yet there is little or no settlement of population. In such areas no municipal organization exists, and control for all purposes over such areas remains in the hands of the Provincial Government.

FINANCE. The gross revenue and expenditure and the net capital debt (in Canadian $1,000) for years ending 31 March were as follows:

	1972–73	*1973–74*	*1974–75*	*1975–76*	*1976–77*
Gross revenue	6,115,000	6,922,000	8,275,000	9,152,000	10,692,000
Gross expenditure	6,481,000	7,302,000	8,821,000	10,632,000	11,921,000
Net capital debt	2,522,000	2,902,000	3,448,000	4,928,000	6,157,000

Gross revenue includes capital receipts from sale of physical assets. Gross expenditure includes expenditure on physical assets.

ENERGY AND NATURAL RESOURCES

Electricity (1976). The Hydro-Electric Power Commission of Ontario recorded for the calendar year a dependable peak capacity of 19,677 mw and a net energy output generated and purchased of 97·5m. kwh.

Minerals (1975). The value of mineral production (in $1m.) of major metals was: Nickel, 811·3; copper, 361·4; iron ore, 291; gold, 123·7. The total value of mineral production was estimated at $2,350m. (1974, $2,422m.). The mining industry employed 47,190 people in 1975.

Agriculture. In 1976, 3·4m. hectares were under field crops with a farm value of $1,520m. This represented 12·2% of Canada's 28m. crop hectares.

Forestry. According to the most recent inventory (1963) the total area of productive forested land is 46,644,872 hectares, comprising: Softwoods, 23,591,147; hardwoods, 5,537,313; mixed woods, 14,270,428; reproducing forests, 3,245,983. The growing stock equals 4,266,868m. cu. ft. The estimated value of shipments by the forest products industry was (1974 census) $2,305m.

INDUSTRY AND TRADE

Industry (1976). Ontario is Canada's most highly industrialized province. In 1974, 69% of value added in commodity-producing industries was accounted for by manufacturing. Construction was next with 16%.

In 1976, the labour force was 3,931,000. Total salaries and wages paid, $39,447m. The Gross Provincial Product (GPP) was estimated at $77,300m.

The leading manufacturing industries are motor vehicles, iron and steel, motor vehicle parts and accessories, slaughtering and meat packing, pulp and paper, chemical, industrial petroleum refining and miscellaneous machinery and equipment.

Trade. In 1976 Ontario exported 41% ($15·7m.) of Canada's total foreign trade.

COMMUNICATIONS

Roads. There were, in 1975, 97,780·1 miles of roads. Motor licences numbered approximately 5·05m., of which 3·6m. were passenger cars, 583,000 trucks, 14,800 buses, 587,400 trailers, 77,300 motor cycles and 170,000 snow vehicles.

Railways. In 1976 the Ontario Northland Railway had 754 miles of track and the Algoma Central Railway had 325 miles and were provincially owned. The Canadian National and Canadian Pacific Railways operate a total of about 9,500 miles in Ontario.

Post (1976). Telephone service is provided by a small number of independent systems (258,000 telephones) and the Bell Telephone Co. (5·08m. telephones).

EDUCATION. There is a complete provincial system of elementary and secondary schools as well as private schools. In 1975 publicly financed elementary and secondary schools had a total enrolment of 1,994,638 pupils.

In 1965 Ontario established Colleges of Applied Arts and Technology (CAATS). There are now 22 of these publicly owned colleges with full-time enrolment of 58,000 in academic courses.

The University of Toronto, founded in 1827 (enrolment, 1976, 26,187), and 14 other major universities, all receive provincial grants. The net general expenditure of the provincial ministries of education and colleges and universities for the fiscal year ending 31 March 1976 was $3,042m.

Books of Reference

Statistical Information: Publications of the Ontario Ministry of Treasury, Economics and Intergovernmental Affairs include: *Ontario Statistics* (annual); *Ontario Budget*; *Public Accounts*; *Municipal Financial Information*; *Provincial Financial Assistance to Municipalities, Boards and Commissions*; County Restructuring Program *Status Reports*; *Municipal Directory*; *Ontario's Future: Trends and Options* (9 reports); *Design for Development, Northwestern Ontario:*

PRINCE EDWARD ISLAND

HISTORY. The earliest discovery of the island is not satisfactorily known, but the first recorded visit was by Jacques Cartier in 1534, who named it Isle St Jean; it was first settled by the French, but was taken from them in 1758. It was annexed to Nova Scotia in 1763, and constituted a separate colony in 1769. Prince Edward Island entered the Confederation on 1 July 1873.

AREA AND POPULATION. The province, which is the smallest in Canada, lies in the Gulf of St Lawrence, and is separated from the mainland of New Brunswick and Nova Scotia by Northumberland Strait. The area of the island is 2,184 sq. miles (5,656 sq. km). Total population (census, 1971), 111,641. Estimate (1976) 118,229. Population of the principal cities (1976): Charlottetown (capital), 17,063; Summerside, 8,592.

Vital statistics, *see* pp. 259–60.
Religion, *see* p. 279.

CONSTITUTION AND GOVERNMENT. The provincial government is administered by a Lieut.-Governor-in-Council (Cabinet) and a Legislative Assembly of 32 members who are elected for up to 5 years. At 15 Sept. 1977 parties in the Legislative Assembly were: Liberals, 24; Progressive Conservatives, 8. Two women sit in the Legislative Assembly and one is also a member of the Executive Council.

Lieut.-Governor: Gordon L. Bennett (sworn in 24 Oct. 1974).

Flag: A banner of the arms, *i.e.*, a white field bearing 3 small trees and a larger tree on a compartment, all green, and at the top a red band with a golden lion; on 3 sides a border of red and white rectangles.

Premier, President of the Executive Council, Minister of Justice: Alexander B. Campbell.

Development, Industry and Commerce: J. H. Maloney. *Public Works and Highways:* B. L. Stewart. *Education and Finance:* Bennett Campbell. *Municipal Affairs, Environment and Tourism, Parks and Conservation:* Gilbert Clements. *Health and Social Services:* Miss Catherine Callbeck. *Fisheries and Labour:* George

Henderson. *Agriculture and Forestry:* A. E. Ings. *Housing Authority:* George Proud. *Provincial Secretary:* Arthur J. MacDonald.

Local Government. The Village Service Act, 1954, provides for the incorporation of villages. The city of Charlottetown and the town of Summerside have been incorporated under Special Acts. The Town Act, 1951, provides for the incorporation of all towns. The Community Improvement Act, 1968, provides for the establishment of Community Improvement Committees in the unincorporated areas of the province.

FINANCE. Revenue and expenditure (in Canadian $) for 6 financial years ending 31 March:

	1971–72	*1972–73*	*1973–74*	*1974–75*	*1975–76*	*1976–77*
Revenue	91,962,083	102,226,137	130,289,697	150,861,505	176,856,206	193,668,328
Expenditure	96,577,541	107,263,198	130,007,139	148,583,657	180,399,067	193,790,131

Total sinking funds on 31 March 1977 amounted to $42,639,127.

NATURAL RESOURCES

Electricity. Electric power is supplied to 98% of the population. The province's consumption of electricity rose during 1976 by 5·9% to 445m. kwh.

Agriculture. Improved farm land occupies about 687,076 acres out of a total of 1,399,040 acres. Potatoes provided about 48% of total farm cash receipts in 1976, with dairy products, cattle, calves and hogs following in importance. Gross returns to producers in 1976 were $103m. The land in natural forest covers 920 sq. miles. For particulars of agricultural production and livestock, *see under* CANADA.

Fisheries. The fisheries of the province in 1976 amounted to 62·2m. lb. and had a landed value of $12·61m. The total processed value of all fishing products, including Irish moss, was $30m. Lobster accounted for $8·5m. or 67·5% of the total value of all fishery products, the highest return ever. The famous 'Malpeque' oyster industry had a landed value of $391,700 in 1976. Irish moss landings were 29m. lb. valued at $807,472; bluefin tuna, $528,734; scallop, $679,801.

INDUSTRY AND TRADE

Industry. Industrial establishments produced goods to a shipment value of $94·1m. in 1974.

Commerce. Average personal income rose from $3,400 in 1975 to $4,008 in 1976. The average wage rose from $147.50 per week to $168.40. The labour force grew by 2·1%. Total employment rose by almost 2·3% to 44,000 in 1976.

Farm cash receipts in 1976 were $102·6m. (1975, $67·4m.). Fisheries receipts in 1976, $12·4m. Value added in manufacturing (1975) was $33m. and the value added in the construction industry was $43m.

Continued growth in trade, commerce, finance and transport and other services is reflected by an increase of 10% in the value of retail trade.

Tourism. The value of the tourist industry was estimated at $26·5m. in 1976 with 213,013 tourist parties.

COMMUNICATIONS

Roads. The province has a total of 3,379 miles of road, including 1,896 miles of paved highway.

Railways. Rail service is provided over 283 miles of track within the province and connects with the national railways system *via* New Brunswick.

Aviation. Air service for passengers, mail and cargo is scheduled to provide 8 flights daily in each direction between the province and various points in eastern Canada. A daily bus service operates between various centres in the province as well as to Nova Scotia.

Shipping. A ferry service provides rail and highway communication with New Brunswick by means of 4 large ferries, 2 of which are powerful ice-breakers.

Another ferry service employing 2 ferries plus an additional 2 for summertime operates between the province and Nova Scotia throughout the season of open navigation. A third ferry service employing 1 ferry operates between the province and Magdalen Islands, Quebec, during the open navigation season.

Post. In 1976 there were approximately 52,500 telephones.

EDUCATION (1976–77). Under the regional school boards there are 69 schools, 1,475 teachers, 27,582 students. Two provincial vocational high schools have 777 students enrolled. There is one undergraduate university (1,500 full-time students), and a college of applied arts and technology (800 full-time students), both in Charlottetown. Total expenditure in education in the year ending 31 March 1977 is forecast to be $53,438,300.

Books of Reference

Clark, A. H., *Three Centuries and the Island.* Toronto, 1959
MacKinnon, F., *The Government of Prince Edward Island.* Toronto, 1951

QUEBEC—QUÉBEC

HISTORY. Quebec was formerly known as New France or Canada from 1534 to 1763; as the province of Quebec from 1763 to 1790; as Lower Canada from 1791 to 1846; as Canada East from 1846 to 1867, and when, by the union of the four original provinces, the Confederation of the Dominion of Canada was formed, it again became known as the province of Quebec (Québec).

The Quebec Act, passed by the British Parliament in 1774, guaranteed to the people of the newly conquered French territory in North America security in their religion and language, their customs and tenures, under their own civil laws.

AREA AND POPULATION. The area of Quebec (as amended by the Labrador Boundary Award) is 594,860 sq. miles (1,540,668 sq. km), of which 523,860 sq. miles is land area and 71,000 sq. miles water. Of this extent, 351,780 sq. miles represent the Territory of Ungava, annexed in 1912 under the Quebec Boundaries Extension Act. The population (census 1971) was 6,027,764. Estimate (1976) 6,234,445.

Principal cities (1976): Quebec (capital), 187,833; Montreal, 1,060,033; Laval, 228,010; Sherbrooke, 75,137; Verdun, 67,458; Hull, 61,039; Trois-Rivières, 51,772.

Vital statistics, *see* pp. 259–60.

CONSTITUTION AND GOVERNMENT. There is a Legislative Assembly consisting of 110 members, elected in 110 electoral districts for 4 years. There were, 15 Nov. 1976, 70 *Parti Québecois*, 1 *Ralliement Créditiste*, 1 *Parti National Populaire*, 27 Liberals and 11 Union National.

Lieut.-Governor: The Hon. Hughes Lapointe, QC, PC (sworn in 22 Feb. 1966).

Flag: The Fleurdelysé flag, blue with a white cross, and in each quarter a white fleur-de-lis.

The members of the Executive Council as on 26 Nov. 1976, are as follows:

Prime Minister: René Lévesque.

Vice-Prime Minister and Minister of Education: Jacques Yvan Morin. *House Leader and Minister of State for Parliamentary Reform:* Robert Burns. *Intergovernmental Affairs:* Claude Morin. *Finance and Revenue:* Jacques Parizeau. *Cultural Development:* Camille Laurin. *Social Development:* Pierre Marois. *Economic Development:* Bernard Landry. *Planning:* Jacques Léonard. *Justice:* Marc-André Bédard. *Transport and Public Works and Supply:* Lucien Lessard. *Environment:* Marcel Léger. *Youth Recreation and Sport:* Claude Charron. *Energy:*

Guy Joron. *Financial Institutions, Companies and Co-operatives:* Lise Payette. *Agriculture:* Jean Garon. *Social Affairs:* Denis Lazure. *Municipal Affairs:* Guy Tardif. *Labour and Manpower:* Pierre-Marc Johnson. *Immigration:* Jacques Couture. *Cultural Affairs and Communications:* Louis O'Neil. *Natural Resources and Lands and Forests:* Yves Bérubé. *Industry and Commerce:* Rodrigue Tremblay. *Tourism, Fish and Game:* Yves Duhaime. *Civil Service and Vice-President of the Treasury Board:* Denis de Belleval.

General-delegate in London: Gilles Loiselle (12 Upper Grosvenor St., W1X 9PA).

General-delegate in New York: Marcel Bergeron (17 West 50th St., Rockefeller Centre, New York 10020).

General-delegate in Paris: Jean Deschamps (66 Pergolèse, 75116 Paris).

ECONOMY

Budget. Ordinary revenue and expenditure (in Canadian $1,000) for fiscal years ending 31 March:

	1971–72	*1972–73*	*1973–74*	*1974–75*	*1975–76*
Revenue	3,908,238	4,376,775	5,032,850	6,474,367	7,917,716
Expenditure	4,257,223	4,690,396	5,290,578	6,761,470	8,791,122

The total net debt at 31 March 1976 was $4,023·7m.

ENERGY AND NATURAL RESOURCES

Electricity. Water power is one of the most important natural resources of the province of Quebec. Its turbine installation represents about 40% of the aggregate of Canada. At the end of 1976 the installed generating capacity was 12,409m. kwh. Production, 1976, was 60,822m. kwh.; energy sold to final consumer, 66,400m. kwh.

Minerals (1976). The value of the mineral production (metal mines only) was $740,181,000. Chief minerals: Iron ore, $318,744,000; copper, $166·8m.; zinc, $105,471,000; gold, $56·94m.

The second major iron-ore development in northern Quebec is, like the one at Knob Lake which gave birth to Schefferville, based on the Quebec–Labrador Trough which extends from Lac Jeannine to the northern tip of Ungava peninsula. The port of Sept-Iles and the railway connecting it with Schefferville allow easy shipment to the furnaces and steel mills of Canada, the USA and Europe. The setting-up of a steel industry is being explored.

Non-metallic minerals produced include: Asbestos ($373,963,000; about 80% of Canadian production), titane-dioxide ($73,121,000), industrial lime, dolomite and brucite, quartz and pyrite. Among the building materials produced were: Cement, $92,676,000; sand and gravel, $76m.; lime, $10,929,000; stone, $110·4m.

Agriculture. In 1976 the total area of the principal field crops was 5·61m. acres. The yield of the principal crops was (in 1,000):

Crops	*Yield*	*Crops*	*Yield*
Tame hay	5,211 tons	Fodder corn	2,840 tons
Oats for grain	24,304 bu.	Maize for grain	10,179 bu.
Potatoes	8,622 cwt	Barley	2,268 bu.
Mixed grains	5,425 bu.	Buckwheat	236 bu.

The farm cash receipts from farming operations in 1976 amounted to $1,331m. The principal items being: Livestock and products, $1,099·2m.; crops, $122·7m.; forest and maple products, $17·8m.; dairy supplements payments, $127·3m.

Forestry. Forests cover an area of 684,480 sq. km. About 490,693 sq. km are classified as productive forests, of which 611,625 sq. km are Provincial crown land and 70,912 sq. km are privately owned. Quebec leads the Canadian provinces in pulpwood production, having nearly half of the Canadian estimated total.

In 1974 production of saw lumber was 2,130·8m. f.b.m.; in 1976: Woodpulp, 6,404,645 tons; paper and paperboard, 6,055,861 tons.

Fishery. The principal fish are cod, herring, red fish, lobster and salmon. Total catch of sea fish, 1976, 83·6m. lb., valued at $14,956,329.

INDUSTRY AND TRADE

Industry. In 1975 there were 9,375 industrial establishments in the province; employees, 394,333; salaries and wages, $3,520·8m.; cost of materials, $13,662,494,000; value of shipments, $23,966·5m. Among the leading industries are pulp and paper, non-ferrous metal smelting and refining, chemical products, cotton yarn and cloth, men's and women's clothing, railway rolling stock, shipbuilding, brass and copper products, electrical apparatus, butter and cheese, slaughtering and meat packing, cigars and cigarettes, machinery, boots and shoes.

Commerce. In 1976 the value of Canadian exports through Quebec custom ports was $6,364·8m.; value of imports, $8,773·6m.

COMMUNICATIONS

Roads. In 1976 there were 49,072 miles of roads and 3,706,330 registered motor vehicles.

Railways. There were (1975) 5,398 miles of railway.

Aviation. In 1977 Quebec has 2 international airports (Dorval, Montreal) with landing runway of 27,600 ft and Mirabel, Montreal with 24,000 ft.

Post and Broadcasting. Telephones numbered 3·4m. in 1976 and there were 20 television and 83 radio stations.

Newspapers (1977). There are 10 French- and 3 English-language daily newspapers.

RELIGION AND EDUCATION

Religion. *See* p. 279.

Education. The province has 7 universities: 3 English universities, McGill (Montreal) founded in 1821, Bishop (Lennoxville) founded in 1845 and the Concordia University (Montreal) granted a charter in 1975; 4 French universities: Laval (Quebec) founded in 1852, Montreal University, opened in 1876 as a branch of Laval and became independent in 1920, Sherbrooke University founded in 1954 and University of Quebec founded in 1968. In 1975–76 there were 75,035 full-time university students and 5,562 teachers. There were also 66,037 part-time students.

In 1975–76, in kindergartens, there were 93,491 pupils and 2,418 teachers; in primary schools, 613,654 (24,824); in secondary schools, 643,924 (34,985).

Expenditure of the Department of Education for 1975–76 (Canadian $1,000), 2,417,721 net. This included 460,923 for universities, 598,653 for public elementary schools, 764,414 for public secondary schools, 68,555 for private elementary an secondary schools and 351,843 for colleges.

Books of Reference

Statistical Information: The Quebec Bureau of Statistics (Department of Industry and Commerce, Parliament Buildings, Quebec) was established in 1912. Its most important publication is the *Quebec Yearbook* (formerly *Quebec Statistical Year Book*; annually since 1914). Other annual publications include a *Directory of Manufactures* (occasional), a *Municipal Guide* (since 1914) and *Répertoire des publications gouvernementales du Québec. Revue Statistique du Québec* (a quarterly since 1963). *Quebec Economic Situation* (since 1962). *Statistiques agricoles* (since 1968).

Atlas du Québec: L'Agriculture. Ministère de l'Industrie et du Commerce, Quebec, 1966
Baudoin, L., *Le Droit civil de la province de Québec.* Montreal, 1953
Blanchard, R., *Le Canada-français.* Paris, 1959
Cook, R., *Canada and the French-Canadian Question.* Toronto, 1966
Ouellet, F., *Histoire de la Chambre de Commerce de Québec, 1809–1959.* Québec, 1959.
Raynauld, A., *Croissance et structure économiques de la province de Québec.* Québec, 1961
Trofimenkoff, S. M., *Action Française.* Univ. of Toronto Press, 1975
Wade, F. M., *The French Canadians, 1760–1967.* Toronto, 1968.—*Canadian Dualism: Studies of French–English Relations.* Quebec–Toronto, 1960

SASKATCHEWAN

HISTORY. Saskatchewan derives its name from its major river system, which the Cree Indians called 'Kis-is-ska-tche-wan', meaning 'swift flowing'. It officially became a province when it joined the Confederation on 1 Sept. 1905.

In 1670 King Charles II granted to Prince Rupert and his friends a charter covering exclusive trading rights in 'all the land drained by streams finding their outlet in the Hudson Bay'. This included what is now Saskatchewan. The trading company was first known as The Governor and Company of Adventurers of England; later as the Hudson's Bay Company. In 1869 the Northwest Territories was formed, and this included Saskatchewan. In 1882 the District of Saskatchewan was formed. By 1885 the North-West Mounted Police had been inaugurated, with headquarters in Regina (now the capital), and the Canadian Pacific Railway's transcontinental line had been completed, bringing a stream of immigrants to southern Saskatchewan. The Hudson's Bay Company surrendered its claim to territory in return for cash and land around the existing trading posts. Legislative government was introduced.

AREA AND POPULATION. Saskatchewan is bounded on the west by Alberta, on the east by Manitoba, to the north by the Northwest Territories; to the south it is bordered by the US states of Montana and North Dakota. The area of the province is 251,700 sq. miles (652,000 sq. km), of which 220,182 sq. miles is land area and 31,518 sq. miles is water. The population (1977 estimate) was 945,000. Population of principal cities (1976 estimate): Regina (capital), 157,059; Saskatoon, 138,376; Moose Jaw, 34,917; Prince Albert, 31,534; Yorkton, 15,315; Swift Current, 15,182; North Battleford, 13,890; Weyburn, 9,602; Estevan, 9,529; Melville, 5,463; Lloydminster, 4,935.

Vital statistics, *see* pp. 259–60.

Religion, *see* p. 279.

CONSTITUTION AND GOVERNMENT. The provincial government is vested in a Lieut.-Governor, an Executive Council and a Legislative Assembly, elected for 5 years. Women were given the franchise in 1916 and are also eligible for election to the legislature. State of parties in Sept. 1977: New Democratic Party, 39; Liberals, 11; Progressive Conservative, 11.

Lieut.-Governor: George Porteous, MBE, CM.

Flag: Green over gold, with the shield of the province in the canton, and a green and red prairie lily in the fly.

The NDP Ministry in Sept. 1977 was composed as follows:

Premier and President of the Executive Council: A. E. Blakeney, QC.

Attorney-General: R. J. Romanow, QC. *Mineral Resources:* J. R. Messer. *Finance:* W. E. Smishek. *Labour:* G. T. Snyder. *Northern Saskatchewan:* G. R. Bowerman. *Environment and Telephones:* N. E. Byers. *Municipal Affairs:* G. MacMurchy. *Highways and Transportation:* E. Kramer. *Provincial Secretary:* E. Cowley. *Health:* E. Tchorzewski. *Revenue and Co-operation and Co-operative Development:* W. A. Robbins. *Consumer Affairs:* E. C. Whelan. *Agriculture:* E. E. Kaeding. *Tourism and Renewable Resources:* A. Matsalla. *Social Services:* H. H. Rolfes. *Culture and Youth and Government Services:* E. B. Shillington. *Education and Continuing Education:* D. L. Faris. *Industry and Commerce:* N. Vickar.

Agent-General in London: M. Johnson, 14–16 Cockspur St., SW1.

Local Government. The organization of a city requires a minimum population of 5,000 persons; that of a town, 500; that of a village, 100 people. No requirements as to population exist for the rural municipality and the local improvement district.

Cities, towns, villages and rural municipalities are governed by elected councils, which consist of a mayor and 6–20 aldermen in a city; a mayor and 6 councillors in a town; a mayor and 2 other members in a village; a reeve and a councillor for each division in a rural municipality (usually 6). Local improvement districts are administered by the Department of Municipal Affairs.

FINANCE. Budget and net assets (years ending 31 March) in Canadian $1,000:

	1973–74	*1974–75*	*1975–76*	*1976–77*	*1977–78*[1]
Budgetary revenue	821,861	989,063	1,193,745	1,340,468	1,473,583
Budgetary expenditure	787,389	965,494	1,169,753	1,362,654	1,513,345
Net assets	63,502	63,707	64,081	64,607	...

[1] Estimate.

NATURAL RESOURCES. Agriculture used to dominate the history and economics of Saskatchewan, but the 'prairie province' is now a rapidly developing mining and manufacturing area. It is a major supplier of oil; has the world's largest deposits of potash; is the only source of helium in the 'free world' outside the USA, which limits production to internal use; and net value of non-agricultural production account for 76·2% of the provincial economy.

Electricity. The Saskatchewan Power Corporation generated 7m. kwh. in 1976.

Minerals. The 1976 mineral production was valued at $929·5m., including (in $1m.): Petroleum 443·7; natural gas, 10·6; coal, 15·2; gold, 2·1; silver, 1·4; copper, 14·5; zinc, 6·4; potash, 358·5; salt, 3·5; uranium, 44·8.

Agriculture. Saskatchewan produces normally about two-thirds of Canada's wheat. Wheat production in 1976, was 548m. bu. from 17·4m. acres; oats, 103m. bu. from 1·85m. acres; barley, 135m. bu. from 3m. acres; rye, 9·3m. bu. from 350,000 acres; rape seed, 19·4m. bu. from 850,000 acres; flax, 3·8m. bu. from 225,000 acres. Livestock (July 1977): Cattle, 2·94m.; swine, 500,000; sheep, 77,000. Poultry in 1977 (estimated): Chickens, 8m.; turkeys, 700,000. Cash income from the sale of farm products in 1975 was estimated at $2,469m. In all, there are 70,000 commercial farms in the province, each being a holding having agricultural sales of $2,500 or more.

The South Saskatchewan River irrigation project, whose main feature is the Gardiner Dam, was completed in 1967. It will ultimately provide for an area of 200,000 acres of irrigated cultivation in Central Saskatchewan. Currently, 40,000 acres are under development.

Forestry. Half of Saskatchewan's area is forested, but only 42,000 sq. miles are of commercial value at present. Forest products valued at $122·5m. were produced in 1976–77. The province's first pulp-mill, at Prince Albert, went into production in 1968; its daily capacity is 1,000 tons of high-grade kraft pulp.

Fur Production. In 1976–77 wild fur production was estimated at $6,763,000. Ranch-raised fur production amounted to $280,000.

Fisheries. The market value of the 1976–77 commercial fish catch of 10·8m. lb. was $2·7m.

INDUSTRY. In 1976 Saskatchewan had 678 manufacturing establishments. Total labour force (1976), 403,000. The net value of non-agricultural production was $2,021m. Manufacturing accounted for $455m., construction for $675m.

TOURISM. An estimated 1·2m. tourists spent $89m. in 1976.

COMMUNICATIONS

Roads. In 1976 there were 11,682 miles of provincial highways, 112,419 miles of municipal, local and rural roads; 2,815 miles of resources development roads. Motor vehicles registered totalled 654,002. Bus services are provided by 2 major lines.

Railways. There were (1976) approximately 8,690 miles of main railway track in operation.

Aviation. Saskatchewan had 2 major airports, 176 airports and landing strips in 1976.

Post and Broadcasting. There were (1976) 995 post offices, 20 sound broadcasting stations and 8 television stations. 501,000 telephones were connected to the Saskatchewan Telecommunications system.

EDUCATION. The University of Saskatchewan was established at Saskatoon on 3 April 1907. In 1977–78 it had about 11,500 (day-time) degree students and 1,350 full-time and part-time teaching staff at Saskatoon and 6,550 students and 330 full-time and 90 part-time faculty members at the University of Regina which was established 1 July 1974. The Saskatchewan public education system in 1976–77 consisted of 120 school units and districts serving 154,502 elementary pupils, 66,444 high-school students and 1,931 students enrolled in special classes. In addition, 3 provincial technical and vocational schools provided training for approximately 15,778 technical and 4,600 trade students (June 1976). There are also 17 Roman Catholic separate school districts and 2 separate high-school districts.

Books of Reference

Tourist and industrial publications, descriptive of the Government's programme, are obtainable from the Department of Industry and Commerce; other government publications from Government Information Services (Legislative Building, Regina).

Saskatchewan Economic Review. Executive Council, Regina. Annual.
Archer and Derby, *The Story of a Province.* Toronto, 1955
McCourt, E. A., *Saskatchewan.* Toronto, 1968
Morton, A. S., *Saskatchewan, the Making of a University.* Toronto, 1959
Richards, J. S., and Fung, K. I. (eds.), *Atlas of Saskatchewan.* Univ. of Saskatchewan, 1969
Wright, J. F. C., *Saskatchewan, the History of a Province.* Toronto, 1955

THE NORTHWEST TERRITORIES

AREA AND POPULATION. The total area of the Territories is 1,304,903 sq. miles (3,379,700 sq. km), divided into 3 districts, namely, Mackenzie (527,490 sq. miles), Keewatin (228,160 sq. miles) and Franklin (549,253 sq. miles). The population on 1 Jan. 1978 was 46,386, about two-thirds of whom were Indians or Eskimos. Main centres (census 1978): Inuvik (3,065), Fort Smith (2,410), Hay River (3,483), Frobisher Bay (2,626), Fort Simpson (1,083). Because of a transfer in governmental responsibility from Ottawa to the Territorial capital at Yellowknife, the population of Yellowknife was increased by the influx of civil servants from 3,741 in 1966 to 9,969 in 1978.

CONSTITUTION AND GOVERNMENT. The Northwest Territories comprises all that portion of Canada lying north of the 60th parallel of N. lat. except those portions within the Yukon Territory and the Provinces of Quebec and Newfoundland: it also includes the islands in Hudson Bay, James Bay and Ungava Bay except those within the Provinces of Manitoba, Ontario and Quebec.

The Northwest Territories is governed by a Commissioner and a Council. The Council is composed of 15 members elected for a 4-year term of office. The seat of government was transferred from Ottawa to Yellowknife when it was named territorial capital on 18 Jan. 1967.

Commissioner: S. M. Hodgson. *Deputy Commissioner:* J. H. Parker.

Flag: Vertically, blue, white, blue, with the white of double width and bearing the shield of the Territory.

Legislative powers are exercised by the Commissioner-in-Council on such matters as taxation within the Territories in order to raise revenue, maintenance of justice, licences, solemnization of marriages, education, public health, property, civil rights and generally all matters of a local nature.

The Territorial Government has now assumed responsibility for the administration of the entire Northwest Territories.

ENERGY AND NATURAL RESOURCES

Oil and Gas. As of 1 Dec. 1976, 5,837 permits for oil and gas exploration were held for 271,519,977 acres, of which 59,035,802 acres are on the mainland, 173,597,956 acres in the arctic islands and 39,886,219 acres in the arctic coast.

Crude oil, discovered in 1920, is produced and refined at Norman Wells on the Mackenzie River; value of crude oil produced was $8·4m. in 1976.

Minerals. Mineral production for the year 1976 was valued at $185·2m., of which zinc accounted for $119·6m.; lead, $26·8m.; gold, $23·12m.; silver, $14·9m.; copper, $660,000.

Yellowknife continues to be the centre of goldmining activity.

Trapping and Game. Fur produced during the 1976–77 season was valued at $3·7m. A herd of some 6,500 buffalo is protected in Wood Buffalo National Park. Barren ground caribou are increasing, due to more effective management techniques.

Forestry. The principal trees are white spruce, jack-pine, balsam, poplar and birch. In 1976, 1·52m. cu. ft measure of lumber, 153,000 cu. ft of round timber and 270,000 cu. ft of fuelwood were cut.

Fisheries. Commercial fishing, principally on Great Slave Lake, in 1977 produced fish valued at $3m., principally whitefish and lake trout.

CO-OPERATIVES. There are 43 co-operatives and 4 credit unions in the Northwest Territories. They are active in handicrafts, furs, fisheries, retail stores, print shops, provision of housing, contracting for services, etc. Total revenue in 1976 was $12,034,015.

COMMUNICATIONS

Roads. The Mackenzie Route connects Grimshaw, Alberta, with Hay River, Pine Point, Fort Smith, Fort Providence, Rae-Edzo and Yellowknife. The Mackenzie Highway extension to Fort Simpson and a road between Pine Point and Fort Resolution have both been opened. Clearing began in 1972 for extending the Mackenzie Highway north of Fort Simpson to the arctic coast.

Railways. The Great Slave Lake Railway runs from Pine Point and Hay River, on the south shore of Great Slave Lake, 435 miles south to Grimshaw, Alberta, where it connects with the CP Rail's main system.

Aviation (1977). Twelve licensed and 4 unlicensed airports are operated by the Ministry of Transport and there are 39 unlicensed private aerodromes. Regular mail, passenger and express services are maintained throughout the Territories. A seaplane base is operated by the Ministry of Transport and there are 27 licensed private seaplane bases. Scheduled services join major points with centres in southern Canada.

Shipping. A direct inland-water transportation route for about 1,700 miles is provided by the Mackenzie River and its tributaries, the Athabasca and Slave rivers. Subsidiary routes on Lake Athabasca, Great Slave and Great Bear River and Lake total more than 800 miles.

Post and Broadcasting (1978). There were 56 post offices. The CBC northern service operated radio stations at Yellowknife, Inuvik and Frobisher Bay. Virtually all communities of 500 or over were receiving television in 1978 *via* satellite. Telephone communication has been established between southern Canada and all areas in the Mackenzie district. Several arctic communities now receive telephone service *via* satellite. High-frequency telephone service is also available throughout the eastern Northwest Territories.

EDUCATION AND WELFARE

Education. In 1977–78 the Government of the Northwest Territories operated 64 schools with 580 teachers. In addition, one public school district operated at Yellowknife, one Roman Catholic separate school district at Yellowknife, and one school society operated a school at Rae-Edzo. The total enrolment was 12,718, of whom about 65% were Eskimos and Indians. Four large and 4 small residences accommodate 439 pupils. Free correspondence courses are available to any pupil in a settlement where appropriate instruction is not available. There is a full range of courses available in the school system: academic, industrial arts, home economics, commercial, technical and occupational training. The continuing and special education programme provides courses and financial assistance to residents who have left the school system or are taking post high school training.

Health. In 1978 there were 7 hospitals in the Territories, 3 operated by locally elected boards (Yellowknife, Hay River and Fort Smith) and 4 operated by the federal government. Forty nursing stations, 6 health stations and 8 health centres were in operation.

Welfare. Welfare services are provided by professional social workers. Facilities included (1978) 5 children's receiving homes, 1 home for the aged and 1 transit centre.

Books of Reference

Annual Report of the Department of Indian Affairs and Northern Development, 1974–75
Annual Report of the Government of the Northwest Territories, 1976
Boyle, E., and Sprudz, A., *Arctic Cooperatives, Canada 1965–68*
Dawson, C. A., *The New North-West.* Toronto, 1947
MacKay, D., *The Honorable Company.* Toronto, 1949
Wilson, C., *North of 55°.* Toronto, 1954

YUKON TERRITORY

AREA AND POPULATION. The exact area of Yukon is under study. It was commonly stated at 333,063 sq. km (207,076 sq. miles) but a federal review in 1976 placed the area at 299,600 sq. km (186,000 sq. miles). This new figure is also being reviewed for accuracy. The population reached its peak in 1901 with 27,219. The census population in 1971 was 18,388; 1976, 22,392. Principal centres are Whitehorse (capital), 14,606; Faro, 1,471; Watson Lake, 1,073; Dawson City, 827; Mayo, 470.

Vital statistics, *see* pp. 259–60.
Religion, *see* p. 279.

CONSTITUTION AND GOVERNMENT. The Yukon Territory was constituted a separate territory in June 1898. It is governed by a Commissioner (appointed) and a Legislative Assembly of 12 members who are elected for a 4-year term of office. The seat of government is at Whitehorse.

Commissioner: Dr Arthur M. Pearson (appointed 1 July 1976).

Flag: Vertically green, white, blue, in the proportions 2 : 3 : 2, charged in the centre with the arms of the Territory.

The legislative authority of the Assembly includes direct taxation, education, property and civil rights, territorial civil service, municipalities and generally all matters of local or private nature. All other major administration including Crown land, income tax and particularly that which requires the spending of large sums of money, is federally controlled.

ECONOMY

Planning. Proposed economic development of the Yukon Territory into the 1980s envisages a total expenditure of about $5,000m. Confirmed development projects include the construction of a natural gas pipeline through the territory to deliver Alaskan natural gas from Prudhoe Bay to the continental 48 states. Another confirmed project is the reconstruction and paving of 482 km of highways through south-western Yukon. Roads subject to this are the Haines Road and the Alaska Highway. Being considered is the possible opening of 5 new mines in eastern Yukon, extension of railways from southern Canada and Alaska and a proposed aluminium smelter. The federal government and Yukon Indians are currently negotiating a land claims settlement. It is anticipated these economic projects will result in a doubling of the current Yukon population by 1985.

Finance. The territorial revenue and expenditure (in Canadian $) for fiscal years ended 31 March was:

	1973–74	*1974–75*	*1975–76*	*1976–77*
Revenue	41,260,234	60,193,400	67,595,429	71,899,000
Expenditure	44,486,469	61,883,511	71,718,216	68,363,950

ENERGY AND NATURAL RESOURCES

Minerals. Mining remains the main industry. Silver, gold, lead, zinc, cadmium and copper are the chief minerals. Production figures (preliminary) for year ending March 1977 were: Gold, 17,272 oz. ($2,199,000); silver, 3,111,542 oz. ($13,846,000); lead, 87,173,664 lb. ($22,668,000); zinc, 160,602,595 lb. ($59,432,000); copper, 21,705,740 lb. ($15,411,000); cadmium, 6,107 lb. ($17,000); coal, 8,031 tons ($160,000); asbestos, 113,354 tons ($41·3m.). A series of labour strikes and changing world metal markets accounted for the decrease from previous years.

Land use permits issued during the 1976–77 fiscal year included: 3 oil and gas (drilling), 1 mining (drilling), 12 roads (private construction); letters of authorization in the non-land management zone, 3 mining (drilling), 11 roads (private construction), 3 mining (geophysical).

Forestry. The forests are part of the great Boreal forest region of Canada which stretches from the east coast of Canada into Alaska and north well above the Arctic Circle. Vast areas are covered by coniferous stands in the southern portion of Yukon with white spruce and lodgepole pine forming pure stands on wet sites and in northern aspects. Deciduous species form pure stands or occur mixed with conifers throughout forest areas.

Forest management is rudimentary, comprised largely of cut regulations and fire protection. The forest industry is small with approximately 14 active sawmills and timber operations. Most are portable 'bush' mills although a few semi-permanent mills have been established. Production in 1976–77 was over 73,787 cu. metres, including 41,137 cu. metres of sawlogs, 24,325 cu. metres of fuelwood and 2,325 cu. metres of round timber.

Game and Furs. The country abounds with big game, such as moose, goat, caribou, mountain sheep and bear (grizzly and black). The fur yield for 1976–77 was down 9% from the 1975–76 harvest for a total of 363,072 pelts. The lynx pelt harvest made up 44·8% of the total yield reflecting higher prices for furs.

TOURISM. In 1976, 305,373 tourists visited the Yukon and spent $25m.

COMMUNICATIONS

Roads. The Alaska Highway and its side roads connect Yukon's main communities with Alaska and the provinces and with adjacent mining centres. Interior roads connect the mining communities of Clinton Creek (asbestos), Elsa (silver–lead–zinc–cadmium), Faro (lead–zinc), Cantung (tungsten) and mineral exploration properties (lead–zinc–iron ore–tungsten) north of Ross River. The Dempster Highway north of Dawson City is under construction to Inuvik, on the Arctic coast. This road crossed the Arctic Circle during the 1977 summer and has been completed for 255 miles. The Carcross–Skagway road is under construction from Carcross, Yukon, and set for completion in Aug. 1978. There are 4,230 km of roads in the territory, of which less than 160 km are paved. The rest are all-weather gravel.

Railways. The 110-mile White Pass and Yukon Railway connects Whitehorse with year-round ocean shipping at Skagway, Alaska. A study is being undertaken to extend it from Whitehorse to join the British Columbia railway system to Yukon border near Watson Lake.

Aviation. Commercial airlines provide services every day between Whitehorse, Watson Lake, Vancouver and Edmonton, where they connect with transcontinental and international lines. Other services extend from Whitehorse to Mayo and Dawson, Clinton Creek, Old Crow, Inuvik, Yellowknife, Faro and Fairbanks, Juneau, and Anchorage, Alaska. Four commercial airlines operate schedule flights. There are also numerous commercial bush plane operations.

Shipping. Some goods are shipped into the Territory by air or *via* the Alaska Highway, but most are containerized in Vancouver and brought up the coast by ship to Skagway, Alaska. The containers are then taken by train from Skagway to Whitehorse, and then hauled by truck to the outlying communities. Many of these trucks then return to Whitehorse hauling ore to be shipped out. Some goods are transported within the Territory by air. Although navigable, the rivers are no longer used for shipping.

Post and Broadcasting. There are 2 radio stations in Whitehorse and 14 low-power relay radio transmitters in the Territory. There are also 5 cable-TV channels in Whitehorse. All telephone and telecommunications in the Territory are operated by Canadian National Telecommunications *via* pole lines and microwave. The communications satellite 'Anik' went into operation during 1973 providing live colour CBC national television. Communities served are Whitehorse, Clinton Creek, Dawson City, Elsa, Faro, Haines Junction, Keno, Mayo, Ross River, Teslin, Watson Lake, Old Crow, Destruction Bay, Burwash, Stewart Crossing, Beaver Creek, Carmacks and Carcross.

Newspapers. In 1978 there were 3 newspapers in Whitehorse.

EDUCATION (1976–77). The Territory had 23 schools with 5,297 pupils. In addition to the courses given in the Yukon Vocational and Technical Centre, the Yukon offers a limited number of post-secondary courses through the University of Alberta. A Yukon Teacher Education Programme started in 1977 to train local residents to obtain Bachelor of Education degrees in Education and a Teaching Certificate. The course is conducted by the University of British Columbia. The government provides financial assistance to students requiring further education elsewhere.

HEALTH. The health care system provides all residents with the care demanded by illness or accident. The federal government operates 1 general hospital at Whitehorse, 3 cottage hospitals, 2 nursing stations and 6 health centres. Negotiations are underway for the territorial government to take over the facilities and services administered by the federal government.

Books of Reference

Publications of the Department of Northern Affairs and National Resources, Ottawa: *The Yukon Act, Chapter 53, Statutes of Canada, 1953*, as amended.—*Mining in the North*. 1962.—*The Yukon Today*. 1968.

Annual Report of the Commissioner. 1972–73
Yukon Territorial Government, *Statistical Review*. 1970–74
Berton, P., *Klondike*. Toronto, 1963
McCourt, E., *The Yukon and Northwest Territories*. Toronto, 1969

CAPE VERDE

Capital: Praia
Population: 360,000 (1976)

República de Cabo Verde

HISTORY. The Cape Verde Islands were discovered in 1460 by Diogo Gomes, the first settlers arriving in 1462. In 1587 its administration was unified under a Portuguese governor.

On 30 Dec. 1974 Portugal transferred power to a transitional government headed by the Portuguese High Commissioner. Full independence was granted on 5 July 1975.

AREA AND POPULATION. Cape Verde is situated in the Atlantic ocean 350 miles WNW of Senegal and consists of 10 islands and 5 islets. Praia is the capital. The islands are divided into 2 groups, named Barlavento (windward) and Sotavento (leeward), the prevailing wind being north-east. The former is constituted by the islands of São Vicente, Santo Antão, São Nicolau, Santa Luzia, Sal and Boa Vista, and the small islands named Branco and Raso. The latter is constituted by the islands of Santiago, Maio, Fogo and Brava, and the small islands named Rei and Rombo. São Vicente is an oiling station which supplies all navigation to South America. The total area is 4,033 sq. km (1,557 sq. miles). The population (census, 1970) was 272,071.

Because of large-scale immigration from Angola the population was estimated at 360,000 in mid-1976.

GOVERNMENT. The National Assembly consists of 56 members all belonging to the African Party for the Independence of Guinea-Bissau and Cape Verde. The aim of the party is eventual union with Guinea-Bissau.

President: Aristides Pereira.
Prime Minister: Maj. Pedro Pires.
Foreign Minister: Abilio Duarte.

National flag: Horizontally yellow over green, with a vertical red strip in the hoist charged slightly above the centre with a black star surrounded by a wreath of maize, and beneath this a yellow clam shell.

INTERNATIONAL RELATIONS

Membership. Cape Verde is a member of UN and OAU.

ECONOMY

Budget. The revenue in 1972 was 631,918 contos and expenditure was 579,014 contos. Public debt, 1,117,863 contos.

AGRICULTURE. The chief products are bananas, salt, tunny, coffee, nuts and pozzolana. The coffee is of excellent quality; exports in 1973 were 20 tonnes. In 1976 there were 20,000 goats, 15,000 cattle, 18,000 pigs and 6,000 asses.

COMMERCE. Imports in 1973, 833,052 contos; exports, 477,802 contos. Trade of Cape Verde with UK (British Department of Trade returns, in £1,000 sterling):

	1974	*1975*	*1976*	*1977*
Imports to UK	721	175	139	158
Exports and re-exports from UK	761	2,097	2,218	1,564

COMMUNICATIONS

Roads. There were 1,946 km of roads in 1972.

Aviation. There is an airport at Ilha do Sal.

Shipping. In 1973, 4,053 vessels of 8m. NRT entered the ports.

Broadcasting. The private broadcasting stations are operating on short-waves. There were (1974) 21,000 radio receivers.

EDUCATION. There were, in 1971–72, 420 primary schools (55,062 pupils), 4 secondary schools (1,175 pupils), 5 secondary preparatory schools (2,238 pupils), 2 technical schools (336 pupils) and a church school (60 pupils).

DIPLOMATIC REPRESENTATIVES

OF CAPE VERDE TO THE UNITED NATIONS

Ambassador: Dr Amaro Alexandre da Luz.

Books of Reference

Annuário Estatistico de Cabo Verde. Praia. Annual
Cabo Verde. Agência-Geral do Ultramar. Lisbon, 1961

CAYMAN ISLANDS

Capital: George Town
Population: 13,000 (1975)

HISTORY. The Caymans were a dependency of Jamaica until 1959 when they became a separate dependent territory of UK.

AREA AND POPULATION. Cayman Islands consist of Grand Cayman, Little Cayman and Cayman Brac. Situated in the Caribbean Sea, about 200 miles NW of Jamaica, the islands were discovered by Columbus on 10 May 1503. Area, 100 sq. miles (260 sq. km). Census population of 1970, 10,249. Grand Cayman (population 8,932), 22 miles long, 4–8 miles broad; capital: George Town (population 3,975). Little Cayman, 10 miles long, 1 mile broad. Cayman Brac, 12 miles long and $1\frac{1}{4}$ miles wide. Total population of the lesser islands, 1,317. Vital statistics (1976): Births, 282; marriages, 76; deaths, 81.

CONSTITUTION AND GOVERNMENT. A new Constitution came into force in Aug. 1972. The Legislative Assembly consists of the Governor, not less than 2 nor more than 3 official members, and 12 elected members.

The Executive Council consists of 3 official members appointed from among the official members of the Legislative Assembly, and 4 elected members elected by the elected members of the Assembly from among the elected members of the Assembly with the Governor as Chairman.

Governor: Thomas Russell, CBE.

Flag: British Blue Ensign with the arms of the Colony on a white disc in the fly.

ECONOMY

Budget. Revenue 1976, CI$11,653,531; expenditure, CI$10,420,103. Public debt (1 Jan. 1977), CI$7,162,492; reserve fund, CI$633,601.

Banking. Fourteen commercial banks and trust companies have branches in George Town, including Barclays Bank International which also has branches at West Bay and Stake Bay, Cayman Brac.

INDUSTRY AND TRADE

Industry. Seafaring, banking and tourism are the main industries.

Commerce. Exports, 1976, totalled CI$550,476 (estimate) and included turtle shell, tropical fish and dried turtle meat. Imports, CI$29,779,506; principally foodstuffs, textiles, building materials, automobiles and petroleum products.

Tourism. Tourism is now the chief industry of the islands and in recent years 16 hotels have been completed. There were 54,145 visitors in 1975.

COMMUNICATIONS

Roads. There were (1977) about 110 miles of road and over 4,500 motor vehicles.

Aviation. *Lineas Aereas Constarricensus* operates regular services between Costa Rica, Grand Cayman and Miami. Cayman Airways provide regular services between Grand Cayman, Cayman Brac, Kingston and Miami. Southern Airways provide a daily service between Miami and Grand Cayman.

Shipping. Motor vessels ply regularly between the Cayman Islands, Jamaica and Florida. Shipping registered at George Town, 210 vessels of 55,134 net tons (1975).

Post and Broadcasting. There were 4,719 telephones in 1977 and there are 2 broadcasting stations in the islands.

EDUCATION AND WELFARE

Education. In 1977 there were 9 government primary schools with 1,402 pupils, a government comprehensive school with 1,384 pupils, 5 private elementary schools with 728 pupils and 2 private secondary schools with 161 pupils. There was also a private institution for further education and a school for the deaf with 7 pupils.

Health. In 1977 there was a general hospital, a dental clinic and 6 district clinics.

Book of Reference

Annual Report, 1976. Cayman Islands Government, 1977

CENTRAL AFRICAN EMPIRE

Capital: Bangui
Population: 1·64m (1971)
GNP per capita: US$230 (1976)

HISTORY. The Central African Empire became independent as the Central African Republic on 13 Aug. 1960, after having been one of the 4 territories of French Equatorial Africa (under the name of Ubangi Shari) and from 1 Dec. 1958 a member state of the French Community. In Jan. 1959 the 4 republics formed an 'economic, technical and customs union'.

AREA AND POPULATION. The Central African Empire is bounded north by Chad, east by Sudan, south by Zaïre and west by Cameroon. The area covers 625,000 sq. km; its population in 1971 was 1,637,000 (including refugees). The capital is Bangui (301,793 inhabitants).

CONSTITUTION AND GOVERNMENT. A new Constitution was adopted by a special congress of the *Mouvement pour l'évolution sociale de l'Afrique noire* on 4 Dec. 1976. It provided for the country to be a parliamentary democracy and to be known as the Central African Empire. President Bokassa became Emperor Bokassa I.

The Emperor: Jean Bedel Bokassa. Appointed President for life Feb. 1972, the coronation of the Emperor took place on 4 Dec. 1977.

Prime Minister: Ange Patassé.

Foreign Affairs: Jean-Paul Mokodopo.

National flag: Four horizontal stripes of blue, white, green, yellow; over all in the centre a vertical red strip, and in the canton a yellow star.

DEFENCE

Army. The Army consists of an infantry battalion of about 1,100 men.

Air Force. The Air Force has a few Douglas A-1D Skyraider attack aircraft, a number of Noratlas tactical transports, 1 DC-4 and 3 C-47 transports, 10 Aermacchi AL.60 and 6 Broussard liaison aircraft, 1 Alouette and 10 H-34 helicopters. It also maintains and operates the Dassault Falcon twin-jet presidential aircraft.

INTERNATIONAL RELATIONS

Membership. The Central African Empire is a member of UN, OAU and an ACP state of EEC.

FINANCE. The ordinary budget in 1974 envisaged expenditure at 17,200m. francs CFA and revenue at 15,706m.

PRODUCTION (in tonnes), 1971: Sorghum, 4,700; maize, 48,000; groundnuts, 7,400; coffee, 12,359; cotton, 54,000; diamonds (1974), 350,000 carats. Cotton and coffee are the main export crops. A record of 58,700 tonnes of cotton was produced in 1969–70. Livestock (1976): Cattle, 3·7m.; goats, 2·4m.

TRADE (in 1m. francs CFA):

	1971	*1972*	*1973*	*1974*
Imports	9,053	8,547	11,496	11,090
Exports	8,939	9,929	8,328	11,622

The main imports in 1971 were machinery, motor vehicles and cotton textiles. Exports were diamonds, coffee, cotton and wood.

Trade of the Central African Empire with UK (British Department of Trade returns, in £1,000 sterling):

	1972	*1973*	*1974*	*1975*	*1976*	*1977*
Imports to UK	575	728	515	287	1,635	278
Exports and re-exports from UK	95	317	409	342	312	868

EDUCATION. The University of Bangui was founded in 1970. In addition over 600 students attend higher education courses abroad. In 1971 there were 778 primary schools (178,550 pupils), 21 secondary schools (9,540), 15 technical schools (1,420).

DIPLOMATIC REPRESENTATIVES

OF CENTRAL AFRICAN EMPIRE IN GREAT BRITAIN

Ambassador: Gen. Sylvestre Bangui (resides in Paris).

OF GREAT BRITAIN IN CENTRAL AFRICAN EMPIRE

Ambassador: (Vacant).

OF CENTRAL AFRICAN EMPIRE IN THE USA
(1618 22nd St., NW, Washington, D.C. 20008)

Ambassador: Christophe Maidou.

OF THE USA IN CENTRAL AFRICAN EMPIRE
(Place de la République, Bangui)

Ambassador: Anthony C. E. Quainton.

OF THE CENTRAL AFRICAN EMPIRE TO THE UNITED NATIONS

Ambassador: Jean-Arthur Bandio.

CHAD

Capital: N'djamena
Population: 3·87m. (1973)
GNP per capita: US$120 (1976)

République du Tchad

HISTORY. The Republic of Chad became independent on 11 Aug. 1960, after having been one of the 4 territories of French Equatorial Africa and, from 28 Nov. 1958, a member state of the French Community. In Jan. 1959 it formed an 'economic and technical union' with the 3 other territories of the former government-general of French Equatorial Africa.

AREA AND POPULATION. Chad is bounded north by Libya, east by Sudan and south by the Central African Empire. Area, 1,284,000 sq. km; its population in 1973 was estimated at 3,869,000. The capital is N'djamena, formerly Fort Lamy (192,962 inhabitants).

CONSTITUTION AND GOVERNMENT. On 13 April 1975 President Nagarta Tombalbaye, was assassinated following an Army *coup d'état*. On 16 April 1975 a Military Higher Council of 9 members assumed power under the presidency of Gen. Félix Malloum and a new Constitution was adopted in Aug. 1975.

National flag: Three vertical strips of blue, yellow, red.

DEFENCE

Army. The Army consists of 3 infantry battalions, totalling 5,000 officers and men. The last French troops left on 27 Oct. 1975.

Air Force. The Air Force has 6 Douglas A-1D Skyraider attack aircraft, 1 Caravelle, 3 C-54 and 6 C-47 transports, 5 Reims-Cessna F337 light aircraft, 2 Turbo-Porter, 3 Broussard communication aircraft and several Puma and Alouette III helicopters.

INTERNATIONAL RELATIONS

Membership. Chad is a member of UN, OAU and is an ACP state of EEC.

AGRICULTURE. Cotton and animal husbandry are the most important industries. The cotton crop in 1972–73 was 104,215 tonnes of unginned cotton.

Livestock (1976): Cattle, 3·66m.; sheep, 2·4m.; goats, 2·4m.; poultry, 2·8m.

FISHERIES. Fish production was estimated at 110,000 tonnes in 1970.

TRADE (in 1m. francs CFA):

	1972	*1973*	*1974*	*1975*
Imports	15,476	18,213	17,363	25,800
Exports	9,028	8,483	10,222	9,280

Main imports, petroleum products, textile yarn, sugar and machinery. Exports were raw cotton and meat.

Trade with UK (British Department of Trade returns, in £1,000 sterling):

	1972	*1973*	*1974*	*1975*	*1976*	*1977*
Imports to UK	183	476	1,378	15	911	150
Exports and re-exports from UK	234	170	209	823	410	724

COMMUNICATIONS

Roads. In 1973 there were 30,725 km of roads.

Post and Broadcasting. In 1972 there were 5,096 telephones and (1972) 70,000 radios in use.

DIPLOMATIC REPRESENTATIVES

OF CHAD IN GREAT BRITAIN

Ambassador: Paul Ilamoko-Djel (resides in Brussels).

OF GREAT BRITAIN IN CHAD

Ambassador: J. R. Johnson (resides in London).

OF CHAD IN THE USA (2600 Virginia Ave., NW, Washington, D.C., 20037)

Ambassador: Abdoul Ousman.

OF THE USA IN CHAD (Rue du Lt. Col. Colonna D'Oranano, N'djamena)

Ambassador: William G. Bradford.

OF CHAD TO THE UNITED NATIONS

Ambassador: Beadengar Dessande.

Books of Reference

Aperçu sur le Tchad. Publication of the President. 2nd ed. N'djamena, 1973
L'essentiel sur le Tchad. Publication of the President. 2nd ed. N'djamena, 1972
Westebbe, R., *Chad: Development Potential and Constraints.* Washington, D.C., 1974

CHILE

República de Chile

Capital: Santiago
Population: 10·4m. (1974)
GNP per capita: US$1,050 (1976)

HISTORY. The Republic of Chile threw off allegiance to the crown of Spain, constituting a national government on 18 Sept. 1810, finally freeing itself from Spanish rule in 1818.

AREA AND POPULATION. Chile is bounded north by Peru, east by Bolivia and Argentina, and west by the Pacific ocean. All regions except 3 extend from the Pacific to the international boundary, while the inter-provincial boundaries in most cases now follow watersheds instead of rivers, thus confining within one province the waters of a single system and avoiding jurisdictional disputes.

Many islands to the north, west and south belong to Chile, including Easter Island (Isla de Pascua; 63·9 sq. miles), discovered in 1722. The coastline is about 2,650 miles in length; the average width of the country, 120 miles. Area, 741,767 sq. km or 286,397 sq. miles.

In 1940 Chile declared, and in each subsequent year has reaffirmed, its ownership of the sector of the Antarctic lying between 53° and 90° W. long.; and asserted that the British claim to the sector between the meridians 20° and 90° W. long. overlapped the Chilean by 27°. Five Chilean bases were established in Antarctica in 1947, 1948, 1951 and 1962. A law promulgated 21 July 1955 put the Intendente of the Province of Magallanes in charge of the 'Chilean Antarctic Territory'.

Three thinly-settled southern provinces of Magallanes, Chiloé and Aysén and the northern provinces of Arica and Iquique are known as 'free zones', for the severe restrictions on imports prevailing elsewhere are modified in respect of those areas.

The total population at the census of 30 June 1972 was 10,044,940. Estimate (1974) 10,405,123. Density per sq. km, 1972, was 13·54.

The areas of the provinces and their census populations at 30 June 1972 were as follows:

Provinces	*Area: sq. km*	*Population*	*Provinces*	*Area: sq. km*	*Population*
Aconcagua	10,204	181,660	Llanquihue	18,407	225,821
Antofagasta	123,063	283,029	Magallanes	135,418	101,368
Arauco	5,756	110,401	Malleco	14,277	200,894
Atacama	79,883	174,634	Maule	5,626	92,336
Aysén	88,984	55,201	Ñuble	14,211	351,277
Bío-Bío	11,248	216,789	O'Higgins	7,112	346,258
Cautín	17,370	465,695	Osorno	9,083	179,652
Chiloé	23,446	124,442	Santiago	17,422	3,724,540
Colchagua	8,431	184,837	Talca	9,640	257,937
Concepción	5,701	723,630	Tarapacá	55,287	204,745
Coquimbo	39,889	377,372	Valdivia	20,934	304,106
Curicó	5,737	126,565	Valparaíso	4,818	820,985
Linares	9,820	210,766			

Vital statistics (1971): Revised birth rate 27·6 per 1,000 population; death rate, 8·4; marriage rate, 8·6; infantile mortality rate, 70·9 per 1,000 live births.

The great majority of the population is mixed or *mestizo*, due to the free intermarriage between the early Spaniards and women of indigenous tribes; language and culture remain of European origin. The indigenous inhabitants are of three branches: The *Fuegians*, mostly nomadic, living in or near Tierra del Fuego; the *Araucanions* in the valleys or on the western slopes of the Andes; the *Changos*, who inhabit the northern coast region and work as labourers and fishermen.

The 3 leading cities, with the estimated population at 30 June 1975, are: Santiago, 3,186,000 (Greater Santiago, 3·3m.); Valparaíso, 248,972; Concepción, 169,570. Other towns, Viña del Mar, 229,000; Talcahuano, 183,591; Antofagasta, 149,720; Temuco, 138,430; Talca, 115,130; Chillán, 102,210; Valdivia, 89,500; Osorno, 71,000; Iquique, 63,600. Punta Arenas, on the Strait of Magellan, with a population of 67,600, is the southernmost city in the world. The Antarctic Territory proper is now stated to be 484,800 sq. miles.

There are 4 geographical zones in Chile—the arid 'desert' zone in the north, which for many years furnished the world's entire supply of natural nitrate of soda, 90% of its iodine and 18% of copper consumed; the agricultural 'Mediterranean' zone in the centre; the 'forest' zone to the south; and the 'Atlantic' zone in the extreme south, barren on the Pacific side, but with rich sheltered pampa on the Atlantic side.

CONSTITUTION AND GOVERNMENT. The Marxist coalition government of President Salvador Allende Gossens was ousted on 11 Sept. 1973 by the 3 Armed Services and the *Carabineros* (para-military police). These forces formed a government headed by a Junta of the 4 Commanders-in-Chief. Gen. Augusto Pinochet Ugarte, Commander-in-Chief of the Army, took over the presidency. President Allende committed suicide on the day of the *coup*.

While the Constitution of 1925 is still nominally in force, the National Congress has been dissolved. Marxist parties outlawed and all political activities banned. The new Government assumed wide-ranging powers but the 'state of siege' ended in March 1978. For details of the 1925 Constitution and earlier political history *see* THE STATESMAN'S YEAR-BOOK, 1975–76, p. 808.

In Jan. 1978 President Pinochet announced that there would be no elections for the next 10 years.

The capital is Santiago, founded on 12 Feb. 1541.

National flag: Two horizontal bands, white, red, with a white star on blue square in top sixth next to staff.

National anthem: Dulce patria, recibe los votos (words by E. Lillo, 1847; tune by Ramón Carnicer, 1828).

The following is a list of the presidents since 1927:

Gen. Carlos Ibáñez (Acting, then elected), 6 May 1927–26 July 1931 (resigned).
Pedro Opazo (Acting), 26–27 July 1931 (resigned).
Juan Esteban Montero (Acting), 27 July–18 Aug. 1931 (resigned).
Manuel Trucco (Acting), 18 Aug.–15 Nov. 1931.
Juan Esteban Montero, 15 Nov. 1931–4 June 1932 (deposed).
Socialist Junta (Carlos Dávila, Col. Marmaduke Grove, Gen. Arturo Puga), 4 June–8 July 1932.
Carlos Dávila (Acting), 8 July–13 Sept. 1932 (deposed).
Gen. Bartolomé Blanche (Acting), 13 Sept.–1 Oct. 1932 (resigned).
Abraham Oyanedel (Acting), 1 Oct.–24 Dec. 1932.
Arturo Alessandri, 24 Dec. 1932–24 Dec. 1938.
Pedro Aguirre Cerda, 24 Dec. 1938–25 Nov. 1941 (died).
Geronimo Méndez (succeeded as Vice-President), 25 Nov. 1941–1 April 1942.
Juan Antonio Rios, 1 April 1942–27 June 1946 (died).
Alfredo Duhalde (Acting), 27 June–3 Aug. 1946 (resigned).
Vice-Admiral Vicente Merino Bielech (Acting), 3 Aug.–3 Nov. 1946.
Gabriel González Videla, 3 Nov. 1946–3 Nov. 1952.
Carlos Ibáñez del Campo, 3 Nov. 1952–3 Nov. 1958.
Jorge Alessandri Rodriguez, 3 Nov. 1958–3 Nov. 1964.
Eduardo Frei Montalva, 3 Nov. 1964–3 Nov. 1970.
Salvador Allende Gossens, 3 Nov. 1970–11 Sept. 1973 (deposed).

President of the Republic: Gen. Augusto Pinochet
Minister of Foreign Affairs: Hernán Cubillos Sallato.

Local Government. For the purposes of local government the Military Junta in pursuance of its policy of administrative decentralization, has divided the republic into 13 regions (12 and Greater Santiago). Each Region is presided over by a *Gobernador*, while the Provinces (25 in all) included in it are in charge of an *Intendente* who represents the central government. The Provinces are divided into Municipalities under an *alcalde* (mayor). All these officials are appointed by the President.

DEFENCE. Chile on 9 April 1952 signed the Military Assistance pact with the US, promising access to raw materials and armed support in defence of the Western Hemisphere.

Army. The Chilean Army is a national militia in which all able-bodied citizens are obliged to serve. Liability extends from the 20th to the 45th year, inclusive. In many cases exemption can easily be obtained, as the supply exceeds the number that can adequately be trained. The annual intake has varied up to 20,000. Recruits are called up in their 20th year, and are trained for 24 months. After this training they pass into the reserve, which is estimated at 200,000.

The Army is organized in 22 infantry, 6 engineer, 6 cavalry (2 armoured, 1 helborne and 3 horsed), 10 transport, and 6 artillery regiments. Total strength, about 50,000 men.

Navy. The principal ships of the Chilean Navy are as follows:

Completed	*Name*	*Standard displacement Tons*	*Armour Belt In.*	*Armour Guns In.*	*Principal armament*	*Torpedo tubes*	*Shaft horse-power*	*Speed Knots*
				Cruisers				
1943	Latorre[2]	8,200	3–4	3–5	7·6-in.	—	100,000	33·0
1938	Prat[1]	10,000	4	3–5	15·6in.; 8 5-in.	—	100,000	32·5

[1] Ex-*Nashville*, purchased from USA in 1951 with sister ship *O'Higgins* (ex-*Brooklyn*) used as an alongside accommodation ship since she was damaged by grounding in Aug. 1974.
[2] Ex-*Göta Lejou*, purchased from Sweden in 1971.

There are also 2 new diesel powered patrol submarines (British 'Oberon' class), 1 old *ex*-US submarine, 6 destroyers, 5 frigates (2 new British 'Leander' class, *Cordell* and *Lynch*, and 3 old *ex*-US destroyer escort transports), 4 torpedo boats, 6 patrol vessels, 3 coastal patrol craft, 2 landing ships, 2 repair ships (*ex*-landing ships), 3 landing craft, 1 survey ship, 4 transports, 1 training ship, 1 antarctic patrol ship, 3 oilers, 2 floating docks and 7 tugs.

Naval personnel in 1977 totalled 23,000 (1,300 officers, 19,000 ratings, 2,700 marines).

Air Force. Approximate current strength is 10,000 personnel, with 70 first-line and 150 second-line aircraft, divided among 11 groups, each comprising one wing with supporting units. Group 1 has 16 twin-jet A-37Bs for light strike/reconnaissance duties. Group 2 has 8 HU-16B Albatross amphibians and some helicopters for coastal patrol, ASW, and search and rescue. Group 3 is equipped for general duties with 25 Lama, UH-1H Iroquois, Hiller UH-12E and S-55T helicopters. Groups 5 and 6 have 11 Twin Otters, 5 Twin Bonanzas and a King Air for light transport duties. Groups 7 and 9 are fighter-bomber units, each with a nominal strength of about 15 Hunter F.71s and T.77s. Group 8 received 15 F-5E Tiger II fighter-bombers and 3 F-5F trainers. Group 10 is a transport wing, with 2 C-130H Hercules, 4 C-118s, 4 DC-6Bs and about 12 C-47s. Group 11 has 8 twin-turboprop Beech 99A instrument/navigation trainers. Group 12 is a second A-37B strike/reconnaissance unit. Training aircraft include piston-engined T-34, T-41D and Brazilian-built T-25 Universal primary trainers; C-45 twin-engine trainers, and T-37B, Vampire and T-33 jets.

INTERNATIONAL RELATIONS

Membership. Chile is a member of the UN, OAS, the Andean Group and LAFTA.

External Debt. Total foreign debt at 31 Dec. 1976 amounted to the equivalent of US$5,195m.

ECONOMY

Budget. Revenue and expenditure were as follows (1,000 escudos):

	1971	*1972*	*1973*	*1974*	*1975*	*1976*[1,2]
Revenue	30,930,100	43,273,000	165,168,400	1,793,555,000	4,548,919,500	34,590,300,000
Expenditure	37,468,300	40,689,477	286,132,300	2,379,222,000	5,298,836,002	34,182,900,000

[1] Figures shown in new currency. [2] Estimate.

Since 1957 the estimates have consisted of a local currency budget (as above) plus a foreign-exchange budget (in US$1m.). The 1975 expenditures envisaged US$3,169m. for defence, US$3,687m. for education, US$883m. for agriculture, US$1,114m. for public works, US$1,395m. for housing and US$3,293m. for public health.

Currency. The old monetary unit was the gold *peso*, containing 0·183057 gramme of fine gold with, originally, a par value of £0·25 gold or 12·7 cents US$ gold (or 20·6 cents new US). From Dec. 1959 onwards the rate (used to value the gold stock) has been 1·049 *escudos* (1,049 *pesos*) to the dollar.

In Jan. 1960 a system came into force based on the *escudo* (equivalent of 1,000 *pesos*), the *centésimo* (10 *pesos*) and the *milésimo* (1 *peso*). On 29 Sept. 1975 the currency reverted to *pesos* with a value of 1,000 escudos to the new peso.

Banking. On 31 Dec. 1975 the Central Bank had gold and foreign exchange reserves as a deficit of US$1,081·8m. A foreign debt extending over an 8-year period, amounts to US$4,082m. Notes in circulation and deposits in currency were 23,985m. pesos at 30 July 1976; total deposits in the commercial banks stood at 5,725m. pesos, in the state bank at 4,525m. pesos and in the central bank a deficit of E.7,134m. on 31 Dec. 1974.

Commercial banks, since Sept. 1977, must maintain cash reserves of 63% of all sight deposits and 32% of time deposits over 30 days.

Inflation is severe but is decreasing. Approximately 70% in 1977.

Weights and Measures. The metric system has been legally established in Chile since 1865, but the old Spanish weights and measures are still in use to some extent.

ENERGY AND NATURAL RESOURCES

Electricity. In 1974 production of electricity was 9,297·3m. kwh.

Oil. Petroleum was discovered in 1945 in the southern area of Magallanes with an output of 19,500 bbls per day in 1977. Production of liquefied gas amounted to 6,718m. cu. metres in 1977.

Minerals. The wealth of the country consists chiefly in its minerals, especially in the northern provinces of Atacama and Tarapacá.

Copper is the most important source of foreign exchange (about 80% of exports) and Government revenues (over 30%). The copper industry, which is state-owned since July 1971, manages 5 large mines which in 1975 had proceeds returned to Chile amounting to US$1,054·3m. On the same basis the medium and small-sized companies recorded US$192·2m. Copper production for 1976 in the large mining sector was 846,800 tonnes fine plus 158,400 tonnes fine achieved by the medium and small miners. Exports during 1976 were valued at US$1,246·5m.

Chilean copper represents 40% of the world total.

Nitrate of soda is found in the Atacama deserts. Exports have gradually increased in recent years to approximately US$75m. in 1975. Production was 618,728 tonnes in 1976. Iodine is a by-product: 1976 production totalled 1,259 tonnes. The use of solar evaporation as a means of reducing costs has developed the production of potassium salts as an additional by-product.

Iron ore, of which high-grade deposits estimated at over 1,000m. tons exist in the provinces of Atacama and Coquimbo, has overtaken nitrate as Chile's second mineral. Production in 1976 was 9,978,649 tonnes.

Coal reserves exceed 2,000m. tons, partially low in thermal unit. Net 1976 production was 1,189,538 tonnes.

In 1976 other minerals include molybdenum (10,898 tonnes, pure), zinc (2,982 tonnes), manganese (24,399 tonnes), lead (102 tonnes).

Agriculture. Agriculture and forestry contribute one-twelfth of the national product, although one-third of the population take part in it. Total area of land being exploited (census of 1968) was 52·4m. hectares; 14·9% for agriculture, 26·7% for pasture, 28·8% for forest; 29·6% is desert or unproductive.

Chile used to import annually about two-thirds of the foodstuffs needed, a quarter of the total imports, but this has now been reduced by stimulating local production to about 12% of total imports.

Some principal crops were as follows:

Crop	*Area sown, 1,000 hectares 1975–76*	*Production, 1,000 tonnes 1975–76*	*Crop*	*Area sown, 1,000 hectares 1975–76*	*Production, 1,000 tonnes 1975–76*
Wheat	698	702	Potatoes	68	726
Oats	80	77	Beans	82	71
Barley	58	78	Lentils	12	16
Maize	96	273	Peas	64	11
Rice	29	73	Sugar-beet	23	2,067

There were in 1955 over 300 large farms, each with more than 12,250 acres, while 500,000 peasents live on less than 4 acres per family. As a result of the Agrarian Reform Bill the CORA (*Corporación de la Reforma Agraria*) had by March 1972 expropriated 3,601 farms totalling 7,068,780 hectares and settlements had been formed for 43,245 families. The military government has opted in most cases to increase the number of settlements with access to individual property. During 1974 some 5,000 property titles were issued, covering 138,500 hectares; most properties are operating in co-operative schemes.

Production of animal products in 1974 was (in 1,000 tonnes): Cattle, 147; sheep, 25; pork, 47; poultry, 53. Eggs, 1,339m.; milk, 906m. litres; new wool, 27,000 tonnes.

Livestock (1976): Cattle, 3·34m.; horses, 450,000; asses, 35,000; sheep, 5·61m.; goats, 800,000; pigs, 892,000; poultry, 19·8m.

Forestry. According to the Forestry Institute (census 1966) there were 277,944 hectares of artificial forests from Maule to Cautin, the most important species being the pine (*pinus radiata*) which covers 260,685 hectares. Eucalyptus covers 12,943 hectares, poplars 956 hectares. The volume of all species reaches 62m. cu. metres, of which 60m. correspond to pine. Native species of importance amounted to 5·9m. hectares in 1976.

Production during 1975 amounted to about 36·6m. in. of sawn timber. Exports in 1975 were valued at US$125·5m.

Paper production in 1974 was 300,000 tonnes and exports were valued at US$115·1m.

Fisheries. Chile's catch of fish in 1974 was 664,000 tonnes, including shell fish, 73,450 tonnes. Exports of seafood in 1975 were US$47·1m., of which fishmeal accounted for US$24·2m.

INDUSTRY AND TRADE

Industry. A nationally-owned steel plant has been established at Huachipato, near Concepción. Output, 1976, 447,700 tonnes of steel ingot. Cellulose and wood-pulp are two industries which are rapidly developing; in 1976, 1,310·4 tonnes of cellulose were produced and exports (1975) were valued at US$97·1m.

The textile industry consumes 70% of the wool clip of the country, or about 14,000 tonnes. In 1975 Chile produced 1,620 tonnes of rayon fibre and thread.

Labour. In March 1977 the 'economically active' numbered 3·62m. in the Santiago area. Professional and 'white-collar' workers numbered 687,500; agriculture employed 16,200; manufacturing, 327,800; mining, 10,700; construction, 62,200, and transport, 90,000.

Trade unions began in the middle 1880s.

Commerce. Imports and exports in US$1m.:

	1972	1973	1974	1975	1976	1977
Imports	941	1,608	2,239	1,776	1,594	2,221
Exports	855	1,323	2,043	1,498	2,069	2,171

In 1975 imports (in US$1m.) from USA, were valued at 390; Iran, 107; Federal Republic of Germany, 95; Brazil, 77; Ecuador, 52; Japan, 49; Argentina, 47; UK, 37. In 1975 exports to Federal Republic of Germany were valued at 239; Japan, 187; Argentina, 166; UK, 137; Brazil, 98; Netherlands, 91; Italy, 80; France, 70; Spain, 68; Belgium, 56.

In 1975 the principal imports were (in US$1m.): Industrial equipment, 382; live animals and foodstuffs, 314; fuels, 257; transport equipment, 165; chemicals, 119; and spares, 108. The principal exports in 1975 were (in US$1m.): Copper, 967; paper and pulp, 97; iron ore, 89; nitrate, 44.

Total trade between Chile and UK for 5 years (British Department of Trade returns, in £1,000 sterling):

	1973	1974	1975	1976	1977
Imports to UK	57,293	86,516	62,091	80,673	76,890
Exports and re-exports from UK	16,805	36,878	36,195	36,295	39,432

Tourism. There were 177,928 foreign visitors in 1972.

COMMUNICATIONS

Roads. In 1966 there were in Chile 66,000 km of highways, of which 8,847 first-class paved, 23,290 second class and 33,863 earth. There were in 1974, 235,335 automobiles, 149,642 goods vehicles, 15,682 buses and 28,833 motor cycles and scooters.

Railways. The total length of railway lines is 8,291 km, including 1,700 km electrified, of broad- and metre-gauge. Further electrification is in progress between Concepción and Puerto Montt (600 km). The initial line of an underground railway in Santiago was opened in Sept. 1975.

Aviation. There were, 1972, 5 customs airports, 11 military airports, 16 civilian airports and 287 landing grounds. Chile is served by 16 commercial air companies (2 Chilean). There are 5 international airports. In 1975, 235,300 passengers were carried into and out of Chile on international services; 228,800 passengers were carried on internal routes.

Shipping. The mercantile marine had, in 1976, 66 ships of over 100 tons (678,556 DWT) and owned by 17 companies. Valparaíso is the chief port. The free ports of Magallanes, Chiloé and Aysén serve the southern provinces. Chilean ports handled 21·9m. tons in 1974.

There are 2,185 km of navigable rivers.

Post and Broadcasting. There are 1,486 post offices and agencies. The length of telegraph lines in 1971 was 12,870 km. In 1977 there were 473,435 (Santiago, 300,651) telephones in use.

A chain of wireless stations along the coast for shore-to-ship transmission is operated by the Navy. At the end of 1974 there were some 150 commercial broadcasting stations. Three television stations are operated by the Universities and there is a national television station. On 9 Aug. 1968 the satellite station at Longovilo, 50 miles south-west of Santiago, was inaugurated to cover transmissions (including colour) from the USA and Europe.

Cinemas (1975). Cinemas numbered 196; 61 of them are in Santiago.

Newspapers (1975). There were 80 daily newspapers.

JUSTICE, RELIGION, EDUCATION AND WELFARE

Justice. There are a High Court of Justice in the capital, 12 courts of appeal distributed over the republic, tribunals of first instance in the departmental capitals and second-class judges in the sub-delegations. The police force had (1975) about 27,000 officers and men; it is organized and regulated by the Ministry of Defence.

Religion. The Roman Catholic religion was disestablished in 1925; it remains, however, a national Church in a state wherein 89·5% of the population are Catholics. There are 1 cardinal-archbishop, 5 archbishops, 22 bishops and 2 vicars apostolic. Latest estimates show 6·7m. Roman Catholics, 880,500 Protestants and 25,000 Jews.

Education. Education is in 3 stages: Basic (6–14 years), Middle (15–18) and University (19–23). Enrolment (1970): Pre-school (a new programme initiated in 1970), 60,360 children; primary school, 2,043,032; secondary school, 302,064.

University education is provided in the state university (founded in 1842), the Catholic University at Santiago (1888), the University of Concepción (1919), the Catholic University at Valparaíso (1928), the Universidad Técnica Federico Santa María at Valparaíso (1930), the Universidad Técnica del Estado (1952), Universidad Austral, Valdivia (1954) and Universidad del Norte, Antofagasta (1957) with a total student population of 96,000 in 1970.

Health. A national health service covered some 1·5m. employees (1977) and there are plans for an extension of the service to a further 1·5m.

DIPLOMATIC REPRESENTATIVES

OF CHILE IN GREAT BRITAIN (12 Devonshire St., London, W1N 2DS)

Ambassador: (Vacant).

OF GREAT BRITAIN IN CHILE (La Concepción 177, Casilla 72-D, Santiago)

Ambassador: (Vacant).

OF CHILE IN THE USA (1732 Massachusetts Ave., NW, Washington, D.C., 20036)

Ambassador: Jorge Cauas.

OF THE USA IN CHILE

Ambassador: George W. Landau.

OF CHILE TO THE UNITED NATIONS

Ambassador: Sergio Diez Urzua.

Books of Reference

Statistical Information: The Instituto Nacional de Estadística (Santiago), was founded 17 Sept. 1847. *Director General:* Sergio Chaparro Ruíz. Principal publications: *Anuario Estadística* and the bi-monthly *Estadística Chilena.*

Other sources are: *Geografía Económica,* by the Corporación de Fomento de la Production, and *Boletín Mensual,* by the Banco Central de Chile.

Allende, S., *Chile's Road to Socialism.* Harmondsworth, 1973
Butland, G. J., *Chile: An Outline of its Georgraphy, Economics and Politics.* 3rd ed. R. Inst. of Int. Affairs, 1956.—*The Human Geography of Southern Chile.* London, 1957
De Vylder, S., *Allende's Chile.* CUP, 1976
Empresa Periodística, *Diccionario biográfico de Chile.* 8th ed. Santiago, 1952
Horne, A., *Small Earthquake in Chile. A Visit to Allende's South America.* London, 1972
MacEoin, G., *No Peaceful Way: Chile's Struggle for Dignity.* New York, 1974
Petras, J., and Merino, H. Z., *Peasants in Revolt: A Chilean Case Study.* Univ. of Texas Press, 1972
Pinochet de la Barra, O., *La Antárctica Chilena.* Santiago de Chile, 1948

PEOPLE'S REPUBLIC OF CHINA

Capital: Peking
Population: 850m. (1977)
GNP per capita: US$410 (1976)

Chung-Hua Jen-Min Kung-Ho Kuo

HISTORY. In the course of 1949 the Communists obtained full control of the mainland of China, and in 1950 also over most islands off the coast, including Hainan.

On 1 Oct. 1949 Mao Tse-tung proclaimed the establishment of the People's Republic of China.

AREA AND POPULATION. China is bounded north by the USSR and Mongolia, east by Korea, the Yellow Sea and the East China Sea, with Hong Kong and Macao as enclaves on the south-east coast; south by Vietnam, Laos, Burma, India, Bhután and Nepál; west by India, Pakistan, Afghánistán and the USSR. China is composed of 22 provinces (this figure includes unliberated Taiwan), 5 autonomous regions originally entirely or largely inhabited by national minorities (owing to the immigration of Han Chinese the original nationality is sometimes outnumbered, *e.g.*, by 10 to 1 in Inner Mongolia), namely Inner Mongolia, Sinkiang–Uighur, Kwangsi–Chuang, Ninghsia–Hui, Tibet (and Chamdo area) and 3 centrally controlled municipalities (Peking, Shanghai, Tientsin).

The capital is Peking (Beijing).

See map in THE STATESMAN'S YEAR-BOOK, 1968–69.

The total area is estimated at 9,597,000 sq. km (3,704,400 sq. miles).

Population at the last census (1953): 601,938,035. This figure was arrived at as follows: Direct census, 574,205,940; Taiwan, 7,591,298; Chinese resident or studying abroad, 11,743,000; Chinese 'in remote border regions', 8,397,477. Urban population, 77·3m. (13·3%); rural population, 505·3m. According to Chinese sources in 1976 the population had reached over 800m., and the rate of increase was about 2% per year. In 1977 the Population Reference Bureau in Washington estimated the population to be at least 850m. Some 15% of the population is urban. Family planning is encouraged. The legal age for marriage is 18 for women and 20 for men but couples are encouraged to postpone marriage until 25 and 27 respectively and to confine their families to 2 children. The term 'Han' is used to distinguish racial Chinese from other Chinese citizens. Some 6% of the population are non-Han.

Population densities vary from 10 per sq. km in the West to over 100 per sq. km in the East.

Estimates of persons of Chinese race outside China, Taiwan and Hong Kong in 1974; Thailand 4m., Malaysia 4m., Indonesia 3·6m., Vietnam 1·8m., Singapore 1·5m., America 850,000, Burma 500,000, Philippine Islands 500,000, Democratic Kampuchea 250,000, Europe 150,000. China permits the emigration of a limited number of persons to Hong Kong annually. There were 20,735 in 1976.

A number of widely divergent varieties of Chinese are spoken. The official 'Common Speech' (*Putonghua*) is based on the dialect of North China, and the Government is promoting its use generally. The ideographic writing system is uniform throughout the country. Characters have been simplified, and in 1958 a 26-letter Roman alphabet (*pinyin*) was adopted as a means of transcribing *Putonghua* as a language-learning aid, for indexing etc.

From 1949 to 1955 the country was divided into 6 large administrative regions.

This system was terminated in 1955, but in 1961 was revived for Party purposes. These Party Regional Bureaux ceased to function during the Cultural Revolution but the 6 regions were reinstated in 1977 as part of the economic administration. The table below shows the Provinces, Autonomous Regions and Government-controlled Municipalities grouped regionally. The cities shown in brackets are the seats of the former Party Regional Bureaux.

	Area (in 1,000 sq. km)	Population: Census 1953 (in 1,000)	Population: Figures published in China 1976–77 (in 1m.)	Capital
North-Eastern Region (Shenyang)				
Heilungkiang	710·0	11,897	32·00	Harbin
Kirin	290·0	11,290	23·00	Changchun
Liaoning	230·0	18,545	36·00	Shenyang[1]
Northern Region (Peking)				
Hopei	202·7	35,985	47·00	Shihchiachuang
Inner Mongolia (Aut. Region)	450·0	6,100	8·50	Huhehot[2]
Peking (municipality)	17·8	2,768	8·00	—
Shansi	157·1	14,314	23·00	Taiyuan
Tientsin (municipality)	4·0	2,694	7·00	
Eastern Region (Shanghai)				
Shantung	153·3	48,877	70·00	Tsinan
Kiangsi	164·8	16,773	28·00	Nanchang
Kiangsu	102·2	41,252	55·00	Nanking
Shanghai (municipality)	5·8	6,204	10·00	—
Anhwei	139·9	30,344	45·00	Hofei
Chekiang	101·8	22,866	36·00	Hangchow
Fukien	123·1	13,143	24·00	Foochow
Taiwan[3]	36·0	7,591	16·50	Taipei
Central-Southern Region (Wuhan)				
Honan	167·0	44,215	60·00	Chengchow
Hupei	187·5	27,790	42·00	Wuhan
Hunan	210·5	33,227	50·00	Changsha
Kwangtung	231·4	34,770	53·50	Canton[4]
Kwangsi–Chuang (Aut. Region)	220·4	19,561	31·00	Nanning
South-Western Region (Chungking)				
Szechwan	569·0	62,304[5]	90·00	Chengtu
Kweichow	174·0	15,037	25·00	Kweiyang
Yunnan	436·2	17,473	28·00	Kunming
Tibet (Aut. Region)	1,221·6	1,273	1·60	Lhasa
North-Western Region (Sian)				
Shensi	195·8	15,881	27·00	Sian
Kansu	530·0	12,928	18·00	Lanchow
Ninghsia–Hui (Aut. Region)	170·0		3·00	Yinchuan[6]
Chinghai	721·0	1,677	3·00	Sining
Sinkiang–Uighur (Aut. Region)	1,646·8	4,874	11·00	Urumchi[7]

[1] Formerly Mukden. [2] Formerly Kweisui.
[3] Regarded by the People's Republic as part of China. *See* also p. 346.
[4] Now called Kwangchow.
[5] Plus most of the then 3·4m. population of the former province Sikang, incorporated Aug. 1955 in Szechwan province, except the area to the west of Yangtse River (Chamdo) which was united with Tibet.
[6] Formerly Ninghsia. [7] Formerly Tihwa.

Other large towns, with population in 1977: Chungking, 6m.; Canton, 5m.; Shenyang, 4·4m.; Lü-ta (formerly Port Arthur–Dairen, afterwards Lushun-Talien), 4·2m.; Wuhan (the former 3 towns: Hankow, Wuchang and Hanyang), 3·5m.; Nanking, 3 m; Harbin, 2·1m.

Manchuria, a term not used by the Chinese, is roughly identical with the 3 provinces of the N.E. Region.

Tibet. For events before the revolt of 1959 *see* THE STATESMAN'S YEAR-BOOK, 1964–65, under TIBET. After the revolt was suppressed the Preparatory Committee for the Autonomous Region of Tibet (set up 1955) took over the functions of local government, led by its Vice-Chairman, the Panchen Lama, in the absence of its Chairman, the Dalai Lama, who had fled to India in 1959. In Dec. 1964 both the Dalai and Panchen Lamas were removed from their posts. In March 1978 the Panchen Lama was elected to the Standing Committee of the Political Consultative Conference. On 9 Sept. 1965 Tibet became an Autonomous Region. 301 delegates were elected to the first People's Congress, of whom 226 were Tibetans. In 1976 the population was reported to be 1·6m. (120,000 in the capital, Lhasa) and the number of Chinese then in Tibet to be about 320,000. 90,000 Tibetans live in exile (mainly in India). Chinese efforts to modernize Tibet include irrigation, road-building and the establishment of light industry: more than 250 small and medium-sized factories have been set up making textiles, cement, matches, paper, chemicals and agricultural machinery. A coalmine was opened in 1970.

Agricultural communes were first introduced in 1965; by 1975 it was announced that 99% of villages had formed them. In 1975 Tibet became self-sufficient in grain for the first time.

Buddhist monasteries were suppressed during the Cultural Revolution, but 3 were reported functioning in 1976. Education has been secularized and made free and compulsory. In 1973 there were 10 secondary schools and, in 1975, 4,300 primary schools (1,600 in 1965). In 1975 it was claimed that some 200,000 persons were receiving education at all levels. In 1965 there were 15 hospitals and 149 clinics. In 1975 there were 6,000 'barefoot doctors'.

The Dalai Lama, *My Land and My People* (ed. D. Howarth). London, 1962
Dawa Norbu, *Red Star Over Tibet*. London, 1974
Jäschke, H. A., *A Tibetan–English Dictionary*. London, 1934
Mele, F., *Tibet*. Paris, 1975
Richardson, H. E., *Tibet and its History*. OUP, 1962
Shakabpa, T. W. D., *Tibet: A Political History*. Yale U.P. 1967
Thubten, J. N., and Turnbull, C., *Tibet: Its History, Religion and People*. Harmondsworth, 1972

CONSTITUTION AND GOVERNMENT. On 21 Sept. 1949 the 'Chinese People's Political Consultative Conference' met in Peking, convened by the Chinese Communist Party. The Conference adopted a 'Common Programme' of 60 articles and the 'Organic Law of the Central People's Government' (31 articles). Both became the basis of the Constitution adopted on 20 Sept. 1954 by the 1st National People's Congress, the supreme legislative body. The Consultative Conference never ceased to exist after 1954 as an advisory body but it had not met since 1964 when it was reactivated in March 1978 and Teng Hsiao-p'ing was elected as its head.

The 1954 Constitution was both a political and an organizational document. It indicated the steps to be taken to build a 'socialist' society, defined the structure and functions of government organs and the rights and duties of citizens appropriate in the period of transition to 'socialism'.

In Jan. 1975 the 4th National People's Congress approved a constitution, under which China was defined as a 'socialist state of the dictatorship of the proletariat'. The 1975 Constitution was a simpler document than its predecessor, emphasizing the role of politics in society, especially the thought of Mao, but giving fewer organizational details. In March 1978 the 5th National People's Congress adopted a new constitution of 60 articles which revives several of the provisions of the 1954 constitution dropped in the 1975 document and eliminates much of the latter's innovatory radicalism. More administrative detail is given. The people's right to strike and to criticize their leaders is reaffirmed.

The National People's Congress is the highest organ of state power which since 1978 has no longer been constitutionally under the direction of the Communist Party. It can amend the Constitution, elects and has power to remove from office the highest State dignitaries, decides on the national economic plan, etc. The Congress elects a *Standing Committee* of about 140 members which supervises the Commission for State Affairs and whose chairman is head of state. The present chairman (elected March 1978) is Yeh Chien-ying.

The Constitution provides that the Congress be elected for a 5-year term and should meet once a year. It is composed of deputies who are elected by local People's Congresses. When necessary a certain number of 'patriotic personages' may be specially invited to take part as deputies. 3,497 deputies were elected to the 5th Congress in March 1978.

The *Commission for State Affairs* is the executive organ of the Congress, that is, the Government. In May 1978 it consisted of the Prime Minister, Hua Kuo-Peng, 13 Deputy Prime-Ministers: Teng Hsiao-p'ing, Li Hsien-nien, Hsu Hsiang-chien (Minister of Defence), Chi Teng-k'uei, Yü Chiu-li (*Head of the State Planning Commission*), Ch'en Hsi-lien, Keng Piao, Ch'en Yung-kuei, Fang Yi (*Head of the State Science and Technology Commission*), Wang Chen, Ku Mu (*Head of the State Capital Construction Commission*), Kang Shih-en (*Head of the State Economic Commission*), Mme Chen Mu-hua (*Minister of Foreign Economic Relations*) and 30 other ministers including: Huang Hua (*Foreign Affairs*), Chao Tsang-pi (*Public Security*), Li Ch'iang (*Foreign Trade*), Yang Li-kung (*Agriculture*), Chang-Ching-fu (*Finance*), Liu Hsi-yao (*Education*), Chiang Yi-chen (*Health*).

Since 1970 when China began to emerge from the isolation of the Cultural Revolution, her diplomatic relations have expanded considerably. On 25 Oct. 1971 the United Nations voted for the People's Republic to take over the China seat from the Nationalists by 76 votes to 35 with 17 abstentions. Diplomatic relations have not been established with the United States, but President Nixon visited China in Feb. 1972 and in 1973 'liaison offices' were opened in the capitals of the two countries.

State emblem: 5 stars above Peking's Gate of Heavenly Peace, surrounded by a border of ears of grain entwined with drapings, which form a knot in the centre of a cogwheel at the base; the colours are red and gold.

National flag: Red with a large star and 4 smaller stars all in yellow in the canton.

National anthem: 'March on, brave people of our nation' (words composed 'collectively', 1978; tune by Nieh Erh).

De facto power is in the hands of the Communist Party of China, which was stated in 1977 to have over 35m. members. There are 8 other parties, all members of the United Front headed by Teng Hsiao-p'ing. Communist Party officials hold key positions in government organs and most social, economic and cultural organizations. In mid-1966 the Party Chairman, Mao Tse-tung, launched the 'Great Proletarian Cultural Revolution' to eradicate 'revisionism' and numerous Party and State officials were dismissed. The Cultural Revolution can be taken to have terminated by April 1969 when the long-delayed 9th Party Congress was convened, although it was not officially declared to have been brought to a 'victorious conclusion' until Aug. 1977. The 9th Congress adopted a new Party Constitution which proclaimed the leading rôle of the Party in the State and designated Lin Piao as Chairman Mao's successor. A factional dispute developed, however, centred on Lin Piao (killed in an air crash in Mongolia in Sept. 1971) and in Aug. 1973 the 10th Party Congress adopted amendments to the Party Constitution, removing references to Lin Piao and the succession to Chairman Mao, and electing a new Central Committee which appointed a new Politburo and Standing Committee. In Jan. 1975 the Central Committee appointed as a vice-chairman of the Politburo Teng Hsiao-p'ing, former Party Secretary-General dismissed during the Cultural Revolution. In April 1976 a 'radical' faction in the Politburo engineered a second dismissal of Teng from all his posts, and Hua Kuo-feng was appointed First Party Vice-Chairman as well as Premier. On the death of Mao Tse-tung on 9 Sept. 1976 Hua became Party Chairman. In Oct. 1976 the 'radical' faction (now identified and excoriated as the 'Gang of Four': Mao's widow, Chiang Ch'ing, Chang Ch'un-ch'iao, Wang Hung-wen and Yao Wen-yüan) were stripped of their offices and placed under arrest. At the 11th Party Congress in Aug. 1977 there was more emphasis on the need for realistic and efficient administration than on ideological fervour. A new Party Constitution was adopted which lays heavy stress on discipline, and a new Central Committee was elected. Changes in the leadership saw the elimination of the 'radical' faction and a second reinstatement of Teng to his Party and government posts. The full members of the Politburo in May 1978 were: *Chairman and Chief of the Military Affairs Commission:* Hua Kuo-feng. *Vice-Chairmen:* Yeh Chien-ying, Teng Hsiao-p'ing, Li Hsien-nien, Wang Tung-hsing (these five constituting the

Politburo's Standing Committee); Wei Kuo-ch'ing, Ulanfu, Fang Yi, Liu Po-ch'eng, Hsu Shih-yu, Chi Teng-k'uei, Su Chen-hua, Li Teh-sheng, Wu Teh, Yü Ch'iu-li, Chang T'ing-fa, Ch'en Yung-kuei, Ch-en Hsi-lien, Keng Piao, Nieh Jung-chen, Ni Chih-fu, Hsu Hsiang-chien, P'eng Chung; (candidate members) Mme Chen Mu-hua, Chao Tzu-yang, Saifudin.

Local Government. There are 4 administrative levels: (1) Provinces, Autonomous Regions and the municipalities directly administered by the Government; (2) prefectures; (3) *chou,* counties, autonomous counties and municipalities; (4) towns and rural communes. Local government is carried out by People's Congresses at level (1) and Revolutionary Committees at levels (2–4).

DEFENCE. The Party Chairman is *ex officio* supreme commander of the armed forces. China is divided into 11 military regions. The military commander also commands the air, naval and civilian militia forces assigned to each region.

Conscription is compulsory but for organizational reasons selective: only some 10% of potential recruits are called up. Service is 3 years with the Army, 4 years with the Air Force and 5 years with the Navy.

Military ranks were abolished in 1965 but restored, 1978; ranks are designated by function. Naval uniforms issued in 1974 distinguished officers from ratings.

The Chinese exploded their first nuclear device in May 1964, and their twenty-third in March 1978 and have tested guided missiles with nuclear warheads. Their first earth satellite was launched in April 1970, a seventh in Dec. 1976.

Army. The Army (PLA: 'People's Liberation Army') is divided into main and local forces. Main forces, administered by the military regions in which they are stationed but commanded by the Ministry of Defence, are available for operation anywhere and are better equipped. Local forces concentrate on the defence of their own regions. The Army consists of 261 divisions including 40 artillery, 12 armoured, 121 infantry, 3 airborne and 70 local force divisions. Total strength in 1977 was 3·25m.

The security forces, including the armed police, number some 300,000.

The People's Militia has a strength of over 5m.

Navy. There was a steadily accelerating new construction programme from 1960 to 1972 in modernized yards, but recently building schedules have been retarded, although it is questionable whether this was due to political decisions or production difficulties. Chinese naval strength, however, is an important element in the present and future balance of power east of Suez.

Present strength comprises 67 submarines, 9 destroyers, 12 frigates, 16 old escorts, 40 small corvettes and PC type patrol vessels, 120 missile boats, 438 fast gunboats, 18 fleet minesweepers, 240 fast torpedo boats, 40 coastal and river defence vessels, 33 landing ships, 480 landing craft, 1 submarine support ship, 1 repair ship, 4 range instrumentation ships, 11 survey and research ships, 6 boom defence vessels, 26 supply ships, 10 oilers, 1 training ship and 375 miscellaneous vessels and service craft.

Under construction are 1 nuclear powered ballistic missile submarine, 2 nuclear powered fleet submarines, 6 diesel powered patrol submarines, 2 guided missile destroyers, 2 frigates, 4 corvettes, 20 fast missile craft, 10 fast attack gunboats, 10 fast torpedo boats and 12 coastal patrol craft.

Active personnel (1978): 172,000 officers and men, including 38,000 marines and 20,000 naval airmen.

Main naval bases: Tsingtao, Lushun (North Sea Fleet); Shanghai, Chou Shan (East Sea Fleet); Whampao, Tsamkong (South Sea Fleet).

The naval air force of over 450 aircraft includes MiG-17, MiG-19 and MiG-21 fighters, some 100 Il-28 torpedo bombers, Madge flying boats, Hound M14 helicopters and communications and transport aircraft.

Air Force. In 1977 the Air Force was estimated at 5,000 front-line aircraft, organized in about 40 regiments of jet-fighters and several regiments of tactical bombers, plus reconnaissance, transport and helicopter units. Each regiment is made up of 3 or 4 squadrons (each 12 aircraft), and 3 regiments form a division.

Equipment is predominantly Russian in design and includes about 75 F-8 (MiG-21), 2,000 F-6 (MiG-19) and 1,900 F-4 (MiG-17) fighters, with about 400 Il-28 jet-bombers and 60 Chinese-built copies of the Soviet Tu-16 twin-jet strategic bomber, plus obsolete MiG-15s and a growing number of new F-9 twin-jet fighters evolved from the MiG-19. Transport aircraft include about 250 An-2, 100 Li-2, 30 Il-14 and 10 Il-18 fixed-wing types, plus 300 Mi-4 helicopters and 13 French-built Super Frelon heavy transport helicopters. The MiG fighters have been manufactured in China, initially under licence, and other types have been assembled there, including several hundred F-2 (MiG-15UTI) trainers.

Total strength (1977) about 400,000, including 100,000 in air defence organization.

INTERNATIONAL RELATIONS

Membership. The People's Republic of China is a member of UN.

ECONOMY

Planning. For planning history since 1953 *see* THE STATESMAN'S YEAR-BOOK, 1973–74, p. 817.

The current plan (it was disclosed in 1978) is running from 1976 to 1985. Priority is given to the development of agriculture. Steel production is scheduled to increase to 60m. tonnes, grain to 400m. tonnes. In 1977 new principles stressing discipline and technical competence were introduced into the administration of the economy, following the 'semi-anarchy' of the 'Gang of Four' period. A number of economic personnel were replaced.

Budget. The latest budget published was that for 1960 which balanced at 70,020m. yuan. A modest budgetary surplus was officially announced for 1973.

Communes pay an agricultural tax, and this accounts for almost 10% of budgetary revenue. 90% derives from industry and commerce. There is no personal taxation. Defence spending was estimated at 7·5–10% of GNP in 1976.

It is claimed that all national bonds have been redeemed and China has no internal or external debts. US claims in China are about US$196m., and Chinese claims in USA about US$78m.

China's gold and foreign exchange reserves were estimated at US$2,000m. in 1973.

Currency. The currency is called Renminbi (RMB, *i.e.*, People's Currency). The unit of currency is the *yuan* which is divided into 10 *chiao*, the *chiao*, into 10 *fen*. The official rate of exchange is £1 = 3·21 *yuan*; US$1 = 1·85 *yuan*; Hong Kong $1 = 0·983 *yuan*; 1 rouble = 2·222 *yuan* (non-commercial, 1 rouble = 1·29 *yuan*).

From 1 Dec. 1957 the People's Bank has issued small aluminium coins of 1, 2 and 5 *fen* (= 0·01, 0·02, 0·05 *yuan*) and also a new 10-*yuan* note.

Banking. Banking is controlled by the People's Bank which has 30,000 branches. It is both the bank of issue and the principal commercial and domestic bank. It is also the major instrument of economic policy through which enterprises are controlled or supervised by the Government. Its president has ministerial rank.

There are 2 specialized banks: the Construction Bank and the Bank of Communications, The Bank of China, which has branches abroad (including 1 in London) is an agency of the People's Bank.

Weights and Measures. The metric system is in general use. For older units of measurement, *see* THE STATESMAN'S YEAR-BOOK, 1975–76, p. 826 and 1954, pp. 877–88.

ENERGY AND NATURAL RESOURCES

Electricity. In 1976 coal provided over 80% of China's energy, although there is a large hydro-electric potential in the centre and sou. Generating is not centralized; local units range between 30 and 60 mw of output. Estimated output for 1975: 121,000m. kwh.

Oil. China has made rapid progress in oil extraction and refining. There are probably about 100 oilfields, of which the largest are at Taching, Shengli, Takang and Karamai. Offshore resources in Po Hai Bay are also being explored. Refining capacity is estimated at 45m. tons per annum. Oil reserves are thought to be at least 2,700m. tons and may be very much more. Crude oil production was 86m. tonnes in 1976.

Gas Natural gas is available from fields near Canton and Shanghai and in Szechwan province. Production is small (estimated 1,000m. cu. metres for 1967).

Minerals. *Coal.* Most provinces contain coal, and there are 70 major production centres, of which the largest are in Hopei, Shansi, Shantung and Kirin. Coal reserves are estimated at up to 100,000m. tonnes. Coal and lignite production was estimated at 450m. tonnes in 1976.

Iron. Iron ores are abundant in the anthracite field of Shansi, in Hopei, in Shantung and other provinces, and iron (found in conjunction with coal) is worked in Manchuria. 300m. tons of ore are estimated to be in Shansi; the principal iron-ore reserves total about 19,840m. tons. The Tayeh iron deposits, near Wuhan, are among the richest in the world. Estimated output of iron ore in 1972, 75m. tonnes. The biggest steel bases are at Anshan (in Manchuria) with a capacity of 6m. tons, Wuhan and Paotow (Inner Mongolia) (capacity 1·5m. tons).

Tin. Tin ore is plentiful in Yunnan, where the tin-mining industry has long existed. Tin production was estimated at 20,000 tonnes in 1967.

Tungsten. China is the world's principal producer of wolfram (tungsten ore), producing an estimated 10,000 tonnes in 1972. Mining of wolfram is carried on in Hunan, Kwangtung and Yunnan.

Estimated production of other minerals in 1973 (in tonnes): Phosphate rock, 1·2m.; salt, 18,000; aluminium, 150,000; copper, 100,000; lead, 800,000; zinc, 600,000; (1972) antimony, 14,000; (1969) asbestos, 160,000; manganese, 1m.; sulphur, 130,000; (1967) bauxite, 350,000. Other minerals produced: barite, bismuth, gold, graphite, gypsum, mercury, molybdenum, silver.

Agriculture. China remains essentially an agricultural country. Some 11% of the total land area is under cultivation. Intensive agriculture and horticulture have been practised for millennia. Present-day policy aims to avert the traditional threats from floods and droughts by soil conservancy, afforestation, irrigation and drainage projects, and to increase the 'high stable yields' areas by introducing fertilizers, pesticides and improved crops. Crop priorities: food grains; raw materials for industry (especially cotton); crops for export (especially oil seeds). Among livestock, priority is given to pig production.

In 1950 the land belonging to the fuedal nobility and to monasteries and other institutions was confiscated by the State. By the end of 1952 land reform and by the end of 1958 the socialization of agriculture was declared to be complete.

By the end of 1958 the peasant population had been organized into roughly 24,000 'communes', each consisting of a number of villages and 5,000–10,000 families. The commune took over the local government function at the village (*hsiang*) level. Centralized authority was discharged down through the production 'brigade' to the production 'team' of 10–50 families. Since 1958 some modifications have been made in the commune system, including reductions in their size. There were approximately 50,000 in 1977. Small private plots account for 20% or more of the average peasant's income.

In 1974 there were estimated to be 127m. hectares of arable land. In 1977 there were 43m. tractors (15 h.p. units).

Agricultural production (in 1m. tonnes) has been as follows (with the sown area (in 1m. hectares) in parentheses): Total grain, 1959, 167·6 (109·1); 1976, 285; rice, 1959, 80·2 (29·7); 1976, 125·5; wheat, 1959, 24·3 (24·3); 1963, 21·8 (24·2); potatoes, 1959, 21·6 (12·7); 1963, 24·3 (13·3).

Livestock. Official claim for 1959: Cattle, 65·43m.; horses, 7·6m.; sheep and goats, 112·53m.; pigs, 180m. Estimates based on official claims (1972): Sheep and goats, 148·23m.; large draught animals, 95·43m.; pigs, 259·88m. FAO estimates for milk production (1970), 3·2m. tonnes; meat, 11·3m. tonnes.

Forestry. Forests cover some 12m. hectares. The chief forested areas are in Heilungkiang, Szechwan and Yunnan. The most important tree is the tung (*Jatropha Curcas* L.), from which oil is produced: it grows chiefly in Szechwan. Tung-oil production amounted to 115,000 tonnes in 1948–49. Timber output in 1957 was 27·87m.; 1958, 35m.; 1959, 41·2m.

The most important timber product is teak. It is estimated that some 1·3m. hectares are afforested each year.

INDUSTRY AND TRADE

Industry. 'Cottage' industry is very old in the economy and persists into the 20th century. Modern industrial development began with the manufacture of cotton textiles, and the establishment of some silk filatures, steel plants, flour-mills and match factories. The first 5-year plan gave priority to the development of heavy industry, but since the withdrawal of Soviet aid and the failure of the 'Great Leap Forward' a more modest emphasis has been placed on it. Expanding sectors of manufacture are: steel, chemicals, cement, agricultural implements, plastics and lorries.

In 1970 a policy of establishing small-scale local industries was introduced.

Industrial production claimed for 1959, in 1m. tonnes: Coal, 347·8; pig-iron, 20·5; cement, 12·27; paper, 1·7; timber, 41·2m. cu. metres; electricity (1960), 55,000m. kwh.; cotton yarn, 8·2m. bales; textile fabrics (in 1m. metres): cotton, 7,500; woollen, 23·59; silk, over 190.

21m. tonnes of steel were produced in 1976, 25m. in 1975. 32m. tonnes of chemical fertilizer were produced in 1976.

Western estimates (in tonnes): Pig-iron (1974), 31·4m.; cement (1975), 40m.; aluminium (1971), 110,000.

Labour. In 1971 the industrial labour force was 30m. Factory wages in 1976 averaged 60 yuan a month. Wage increases affecting 40% of the non-agricultural workforce were introduced in Oct. 1977.

Commerce. Foreign trade is conducted through 8 national corporations under the Ministry of Foreign Trade. The China Council for the Promotion of International Trade is a non-governmental body in which the corporations are represented. It was officially announced in 1974 that China does not intend to allow foreign investment or the establishment of joint ventures with foreign firms and will not accept aid. China also does not accept credit (except short-term supplier credits which it terms 'deferred payments').

During the period of influence of the radical Politburo faction ('Gang of Four') China adopted a policy of reducing imports of foreign technology, but this policy is being reversed.

Imports include grain, cotton, rubber, fertilizers and advanced equipment, particularly civil aircraft; exports: farm produce (35% of all exports in 1976), processed agricultural products, textiles, wolfram, antimony and crude oil.

Estimated trade for 1976: Imports, US$6,200m.; exports, US$7,000m. In 1976 China's trade surplus with non-Communist countries was estimated at about US$700m.

Some 80% of China's trade is with non-Communist countries. Japan is China's biggest trading partner, and a long-term trade agreement was signed in 1977. Other major trading partners are Hong Kong, Federal Republic of Germany, France and Australia. Trade with USA amounted to US$934m. in 1974, but has declined since. In April 1978 a most-favoured-nation agreement was signed with EEC.

Total trade between UK and China (British Department of Trade returns, in £1,000 sterling):

	1973	*1974*	*1975*	*1976*	*1977*
Imports to UK	47,834	66,681	59,423	86,995	104,388
Exports and re-exports from UK	84,802	71,738	80,368	68,216	62,316

More than 95% of UK imports from China are free of quota restrictions.

COMMUNICATIONS

Roads. In 1976, 35,000 km of motor roads were built in rural areas. There were probably about 800,000 km of motor roads in 1976. 83% of communes could be reached by road in 1976. Highways are well graded but mostly unmetalled. In 1969 there were some 409,000 lorries, 60,000 cars and 30,000 buses.

In 1959 road haulage carried 155m. tons of freight.

Railways. Chinese railway history begins in 1876, when the Woosung–Shanghai line was opened. In 1976 there were some 48,000 km of railway.

The principal railways are:

(1) The great north–south trunk lines: (*a*) Peking–Canton Railway (over 2,300 km), *via* Chengchow–Wuhan–Chuchow–Hengyang.

(*b*) Tientsin–Shanghai Railway (1,500 km), *via* Pukow and Nanking (double-tracked in July 1976).

(*c*) Paochi–Chungking Railway, *via* Chengtu (1,174 km). Chungking with the east–west route from Hengyang to the Vietnam border, and to Kunming, connecting there with the Yünnan Railway to the Vietnam border. Two further lines connect Paochi (and ultimately Hanoi).

(2) Great east–west trunk lines: (*a*) Lung-Hai Railway; Lienyun–Hsuchow–Chengchow (on the Peking–Canton line)–Sian–Paochi–Tienshui–Lanchow (1,500 km). (*b*) Lanchow–Sinkiang Railway: Lanchow–Yumen–Hami–Turfan–Urumchi (1,800 km); (*c*) Shanghai–Yuyikuan (Vietnam border) *via* Hangchow, Nanchang, Hengyang (on the Peking–Canton line), Kweilin, Liuchow and Nanning. (*d*) Peking–Lanchow *via* Tsining (from which a branch connects with the lines through Mongolia to the Trans-Siberian Railway), Tatung (from which a branch serves the province of Shansi), Paotow and Yinchuan (Ninghsia). (*e*) Chuchow–Kweiyang (632 km).

Branches link coastal areas (*e.g.*, Fukien province) and smaller inland centres with the main parts of the system. Surveys have been made for a new 500-km railway, linking the trunk line with the oilfield of Karamai in Sinkiang.

(3) The Manchurian system: (*a*) Chinese Eastern (Changchun) Railway (2,370 km), from Manchouli on the Soviet border through northern Inner Mongolia and Manchuria *via* Tsitsihar, Harbin and Mutankiang to the Soviet border near Vladivostok. (*b*) South Manchuria Railway (705 km, 1120 km with branches), Changchun–Shenyang (formerly Mukden)–Talien. (*c*) Peking–Shenyang Railway, with branches in Manchuria (854 km, 1,350 km with branches).

Branches give connexions with outlying parts of Manchuria and Inner Mongolia as well as international links with Korean railways. Chinese railways are all constructed to the standard gauge except for some 600 km of metre gauge in Yünnan. The trans-Mongolian line, which was constructed to the Russian gauge, was converted to standard in 1965. Trunk routes are being converted from single to double track. The route between Paochi and Chengtu (676 km) was electrified in 1975 and that between Yangpingkuan (on the Paochi–Chengtu route) and Ankang in 1977.

Capacity is being expanded under the 1976–80 development plan. Lines are planned to link Tibet with the Chinese network and to bridge gaps in the system such as Liuchow–Canton and Kantang–Taiyuan.

In 1975 it is estimated the railways carried some 800m. tons of freight.

Aviation. The Civil Aviation Administration of China (CAAC) runs services from Peking to Tōkyō (*via* Osaka and Shanghai), Pyongyang (*via* Shenyang), Irkutsk, Rangoon, Paris (*via* Karachi), Tirana (*via* Tehran and Bucharest) and Moscow, and from Canton to Hanoi. Its inventory includes 10 Boeing 707s, 16 Tridents and 5 Il–62s. Japan Airlines have a route from Tōkyō to Peking (*via* Osaka and Shanghai), Air France Paris to Peking (*via* Athens and Karachi), Pakistan Airlines Karachi to Peking, Aeroflot Moscow to Peking, Ethiopian Airlines Addis Ababa to Shanghai, Tarom (Romania) Bucharest to Peking and Swissair Geneva to Peking and Shanghai.

In 1977 there were some 120 internal routes with 328 weekly flights.

Air services agreements were signed with Canada, Italy, Greece and Sweden in 1973, Japan and Laos in 1974 and Federal Republic of Germany in 1975.

Shipping. At the beginning of 1977 the ocean-going merchant fleet consisted of 400–450 vessels with a total DWT of 6·8m.

The major ports are at Tientsin, Shanghai, Tsingtao, Talien and Canton. New ports are under construction at Changchiang and Whampao. Ports cannot accommodate vessels over 100,000 GRT and most harbours have a draught limitation of 35 ft.

Inland waterways total about 150,000 km, of which 40,000 are navigable for steamers.

Pipeline. A pipeline links the Taching oilfield to the port of Talien and to refineries in Peking.

Post and Broadcasting. Number of post offices of all kinds in 1958 was 67,000. The use of *pinyin* transcription of place names has been requested for mail to addresses in China (*e.g.*, 'Beijing' *not* 'Peking'; 'Tianjin' *not* 'Tientsin'; 'Guangzhou' *not* 'Canton', etc.).

In 1975 there were 150 radio broadcasting stations. In 1964 there were some 7m. radio receivers. In 1977 there were 37 television stations and in 1974 331,000 TV receivers. Most are communally owned.

Cinemas. Cinemas numbered 1,386 in 1958.

Newspapers. The Party newspaper is *Jen Min Jih Pao* (or *Renmin Ribao*, People's Daily). In 1977 it had a daily circulation of 5m.

JUSTICE, RELIGION, EDUCATION AND WELFARE

Justice. Justice is administered by 'people's courts' which are divided into some 30 higher, 200 intermediate and 2,000 fundamental courts, and headed by the Supreme People's Court. The latter is accountable to the Standing Committee of the National People's Congress and tries cases, hears appeals, supervises the people's courts; it has been responsible for judicial administration since the abolition of the Ministry of Justice in 1959.

People's courts are composed of a president, vice-presidents and judges. Elected 'people's assessors' take part in trials alongside judges. Fundamental courts may establish 'people's tribunals' to try civil and minor criminal cases, and 'people's conciliation committees' are charged with settling disputes.

There are also special military courts.

The courts are responsible to the organs of government, and procuratorial powers and functions are exercised by the organs of public security (police) at various levels.

Religion. Confucianism, Buddhism and Taoism have long been practised. Confucianism has no ecclesiastical organization and appears rather as a philosophy of ethics and government. Taoism—of Chinese origin—copied Buddhist ceremonial soon after the arrival of Buddhism two millennia ago. Buddhism in return adopted many Taoist beliefs and practices. It is no longer possible to estimate the number of adherents to these faiths. A campaign against Confucianism was launched in 1973.

Ceremonies of reverence to ancestors have been observed by the whole population regardless of philosophical or religious beliefs.

Moslems are found in every province of China, being most numerous in the Ninghsia–Hui Autonomous Region, Yunnan, Shensi, Kansu, Hopei, Honan, Shantung, Szechwan, Sinkiang and Shansi. The total is estimated at 2–5% of the population.

Roman Catholicism has had a footing in China for more than 3 centuries. According to a Vatican estimate in 1977 it had about 2·5m. adherents who are members of the Patriotic Catholic Association, which declared its independence of Rome in 1958, and about 1,000 priests. In 1977 there were 78 bishops and 4 apostolic administrators, not all of whom were permitted to undertake religious activity. This figure included 46 'democratically elected' bishops not recognized by the Vatican.

Protestants are members of the All-China Conference of Protestant Churches.

Education. During the Cultural Revolution and the 'Gang of Four' period the educational system was in a turmoil of radical reformation. Reforms included an apparent reduction in the number of years in primary schools from 6 to 5, in middle schools from 6 to 4, the selection of students for higher institutes from among workers, soldiers, peasants and school graduates who had had 2–3 years experience in industry or agriculture, the application of a policy of part-work part-study, and more emphasis upon political education. Courses in higher institutes were from 2–3 years duration (3–4 years in medical schools). 1977 marked the beginning of a return to a more conventional system. Although some university entrants continue to be selected from workers, soldiers and peasants, entry now normally follows from secondary schooling and is dependent upon entrance examinations in which political reliability tests are accompanied by tests in academic subjects. The number of students at institutes of higher education was about 500,000 in 1975. A record number of university entrants was claimed for 1977, and primary and middle school pupils numbered some 100m.

The Academy of Sciences had in 1964 some 20 provincial branches.

Institutes of higher learning included in 1961: 61 universities, 271 engineering colleges, 113 colleges of agriculture and forestry, 174 teacher-training colleges and 142 medical schools.

Among the universities are the following: People's University of China, Peking (founded 1912 by Dr Sun Yat-sen; reorganized 1950; about 3,000 students); Peking University, Peking (1898, enlarged 1945; about 10,000 students); Amoy University, Fukien (1921 and 1937); Futan University, Shanghai (1905); Inner Mongolia University, Huhehot; Lanchow University, Lanchow (Kansu Prov.); Nankai University, Tientsin (1919); Nanking University, Nanking (1888 and 1928); People's University of North-East China, Changchun (Kirin Prov.); North-West University, Sian (Shensi Prov.); Shantung University, Tsingtao (1926); Sun Yat-sen University, Canton (founded 1924 by Dr Sun Yat-sen); Szechwan University, Chengtu (1931); Tsinghua University, Peking; Wuhan University, Wuhan (Hupeh Prov.; 1905 and 1928); Yunnan University, Kunming. In 1958 a university of science and technology was set up by the Academy of Sciences.

Health. Medical treatment is not free, but costs are partly borne by the patient's employing organization. Figures for doctors generally are not available, but it was reported in 1973 that there were 8,000 general practitioners in Inner Mongolia (*i.e.*, about 1 per 1,000 inhabitants). All doctors are trained in both Western and Chinese traditional methods.

In 1977 there were 1·8m. 'bare-foot doctors', who receive 3 months' training and remain in the community treating simple ailments and implementing public health directives.

Hospital care is organized in a hierarchy of clinics (per 1,000 population), commune hospitals (per 25,000), district hospitals (per 200,000) and the large teaching hospitals.

DIPLOMATIC REPRESENTATIVES

China and the USA established liaison offices in Washington and Peking in 1973. The head of the US office is Leonard Woodcock; of the Chinese, Chai Tse-Ming.

A Chinese ambassador is accredited to the EEC.

OF CHINA IN GREAT BRITAIN (31 Portland Place, London, W1N 3AG)

Ambassador: (Vacant).

OF GREAT BRITAIN IN CHINA
(11 Kuang Hua Lu, Chien Kuo Men Wai, Peking)

Ambassador: Sir Edward Youde, KCMG, MBE.

OF CHINA TO THE UNITED NATIONS

Ambassador: Chen Chu.

Books of Reference

The China Quarterly. London, from 1960
China's Foreign Trade. Bimonthly. Peking, from 1966
Bartke, W., *The Diplomatic Service of the People's Republic of China*. Hamburg, 1973
Berton, P., and Wu, E., *Contemporary China: A Research Guide*. Stanford U.P., 1967
Boardman, R., *Britain and the People's Republic of China, 1949–1974*. London, 1976
Boarman, P. M. (ed.), *Trade with China*. New York, 1974
Boorman, H. L., and Howard, R. C. (eds.), *Biographical Dictionary of Republican China*. 5 vols. Columbia U.P. 1967 ff.
Bouc, A., *La Chine à la Mort de Mao*. Paris, 1977
Brugger, W. C., *Contemporary China*. London, 1977
Clubb, O. E., *20th Century China*. 2nd ed. Columbia U.P., 1972
Deleyne, J., *The Chinese Economy*. London, 1973
Eckstein, A., *China's Economic Development*. Univ. of Michigan Press, 1975.
Etienne, G., *La Voie chinoise: la longue marche de l'économie, 1949–1974*. Paris, 1974
Fitzgerald, C. P., *Mao Tsetung and China*. London, 1976
Garth, B. G., and others. (eds.), *China's Changing Role in the World Economy*. New York, 1975
Gittings, J., *The World and China, 1922–1972*. London, 1974
Harrison, J. P., *The Long March to Power*. New York, 1972; London, 1973
Hermann, A., *An Historical Atlas of China*. Chicago, 1966
Hinton, H. C., *An Introduction to Chinese Politics*. Newton Abbot, 1973
Houn, F. W., *A Short History of Chinese Communism*. 2nd ed. Englewood Cliffs, N.J., 1973
How to Approach the China Market. Japan External Trade Organization, New York, 1972
Hsieh, C. M., *Atlas of China*. New York, 1973
Hsü, I. C. Y., *The Rise of Modern China*. 2nd ed. New York, 1975
Hsüeh, C.-T. (ed.), *Revolutionary Leaders of Modern China*. New York, 1971.—*Dimensions of China's Foreign Relations*. New York, 1977
Kaplan, F. M. (ed.), *Encyclopedia of China Today*. London, 1978
Karol, K. S., *La Deuxième révolution chinoise*. Paris, 1973
Klein, D. W., and Clark, A. B., *Biographic Dictionary of Chinese Communism, 1921–1965*. Harvard U.P., 1971
Latourette, K. S., *The Chinese, Their History and Culture*. 4th ed. New York, 1965
Lawrance, A. (ed.), *China's Foreign Relations Since 1949*. London, 1975
MacFarquahar, R., *The Origins of the Cultural Revolution*. London, 1974 ff.
MacInnis, D. E., *Religious Policy and Practice in Communist China*. New York and London, 1972
Mah, F.-H., *The Foreign Trade of Mainland China*. Chicago, 1971; Edinburgh, 1972
Mao Tse-tung, Selected works. 4 vols. London, 1954–56.—Vol. 2 of 2nd ed., Peking, 1965.—*Quotations from Chairman Mao Tse-tung*. Peking, 1966.—*On Revolution and War*. New York, 1969
Mathews, R. H., *Chinese–English Dictionary*. Cambridge, Mass., 1943–47.
Needham, J., *Science and Civilization*. CUP, 1954 ff.—*Within the Four Seas*. London, 1969
Neilan, E., and Smith, C. R., *The Future of the China Market*. Stanford U.P., 1974
Orleans, L. A., *Every Fifth Child: The Population of China*. London, 1972
Schram, S., *Mao Tse-tung*. Harmondsworth, 1966.—*The Political Thought of Mao Tse-tung*. New York, 1969.—*Mao Tse-tung Unrehearsed*. Harmondsworth, 1974.—*Authority, Participation and Cultural Change in China: Essays by a European Study Group*. CUP, 1973
Scott, G. L., *Chinese Treaties: The Post-revolutionary Restoration of International Law and Order*, New York, 1975
Shabad, T., *China's Changing Map: National and Regional Development, 1949–71*. Rev. ed. London, 1972
Skinner, G. W. (ed.), *Modern Chinese Society: An Analytical Bibliography*. 3 vols. Stanford U.P., 1974
Snow, E., *The Other Side of the River: Red China Today*. London, 1963.—*Red Star Over China*. Rev. ed. London, 1968.—*The Long Revolution*. London, 1973
Staiger, B. (ed.), *China in the Seventies*. Wiesbaden, 1975
Thornton, R. C., *China, the Struggle for Power 1917–1972*. Bloomington, 1973
The Times Atlas of China. London, 1974
Tregear, T. R., *An Economic Geography of China*. London, 1970
US Congress Joint Economic Committee. *China: A Reassessment of the Economy*. Washington, 1975
US Department of the Army, *Communist China: A Bibliographic Survey*. Washington, 1971
Wang, G.-W., *China and the World Since 1949*. London, 1977
Whitson, W. W. (ed.), *Doing Business with China: American Trade Opportunities in the 1970's*. New York and London, 1974
Whitson, W. W., and Huang, C.-H., *The Chinese High Command*. London, 1973.
Who's Who in Communist China. 2nd ed. Hong Kong, 1969
Wilson, I. (ed.), *China and the World Community*. Sydney, 1973
Worsley, P. M., *Inside China*. London, 1975
Wü, Y.-L. (ed.), *China: A Handbook*. Newton Abbot, 1973

REPUBLIC OF CHINA

Capital: Taipei
Population: 16·29m. (1977)
GNP per capita: US$1,070 (1976)

Taiwan

HISTORY. The island of Taiwan (Formosa) was ceded to Japan by China by the Treaty of Shimonoseki on 8 May 1895. After the Second World War the island surrendered to Gen. Chiang Kai-shek in Sept. 1945 and was placed under Chinese administration on 25 Oct. 1945.

AREA AND POPULATION. Taiwan lies between the East and South China Seas off the coast of Fukien province. The total area of Taiwan Island and the Penghu Archipelago is 13,892 sq. miles (35,981 sq km). Population (June 1977), 16·29m. (8·53m. males, 7·58m. females), of whom some 2m. are mainland Chinese who came with the Nationalist Government. There are also some 200,000 aboriginals. Population density: 458·8 per sq. km.

In 1976, birth rate was 2·6%; death rate, 0·47%; rate of growth, 2·12% per annum.

Taiwan is divided into a special municipality (Taipei, the capital, population 2m. in 1975), 4 municipalities (Kaohsiung, Keelung, Taichung, Tainan) and 16 counties (*hsien*): Changhua, Chiayi, Hsinchu, Hualien, Ilan, Kaohsiung, Miaoli, Nantou, Penghu, Pingtung, Taichung, Tainan, Taipei, Taitung, Taoyuan, Yunlin.

CONSTITUTION AND GOVERNMENT. Taiwan is controlled by the remnants of the Nationalist Government. On 1 March 1950, Chiang Kai-shek resumed the presidency of the 'Republic of China', and was re-elected for his fifth 6-year presidential term in March 1972. He died 5 April 1975 and was succeeded by Dr Yen Chia-kan. There are 3 political parties: the ruling Kuomintang (1·5m. members in 1976), which has a youth movement (China Youth Corps) of over 1m. members, the Young China Party and the China Democratic Socialist Party.

The National Assembly of the Republic of China was elected in 1947. It has 1,349 members. The highest legislative body is the Legislative Yuan (Council) elected in 1948 and now with 476 members. Terms of office in both bodies have been extended indefinitely. New regulations promulgated on 29 June 1972 provide for the augmentation of these bodies by the election of 53 and 51 new members respectively. Elections for the new National Assembly members were held in Dec. 1975. The Kuomintang gained 37 seats. The highest administrative organ is the Executive Yuan. There is also a Provincial Assembly of 73 members elected on 23 Dec. 1972 (the Kuomintang has 59 seats).

State emblem: A 12-pointed white sun in a blue sky.

National flag: Red with a blue first quarter bearing the state emblem in white.

National anthem: 'San Min Chu I', words by Dr Sun Yat-sen; tune by Cheng Mao-yun.

Prime Minister: Chiang Ching-kuo (eldest son of the late Chiang Kai-shek).

Vice-Premier: Hsu Ching-chung. *Foreign Minister:* Shen Ch'ang-huan. *Minister of National Defence:* Gen. Kao K'uel-yuan. *Minister of the Interior:* Chang Feng-shu. *Minister of Finance:* Walter H. Fei. *Governor of Taiwan:* Hsien Tung-ming.

DEFENCE. Army. The Army, which embodies the remnants of the forces which escaped to Taiwan with Chiang Kai-shek at the end of the civil war in 1949, numbered about 320,000 in 1977. It has been reorganized, re-equipped and trained by the USA and now consists of 2 armoured, 12 infantry and 6 light divisions. There is a conscription system for 2 years and reserve liability. Strong garrisons (about 80,000 men) are maintained on the Pescadores and the offshore islands of Quemoy and Matsu. US forces on Taiwan were reduced to about 1,400 in April 1977. US military aid worth US$65m. was granted in 1973.

Navy. The Nationalists have 2 old *ex*-US 'Tench' class diesel powered patrol submarines, 20 destroyers, 11 frigates, 3 escort vessels, 1 fast missile craft, 14 coastal minesweepers, 1 coastal minelayer, 8 minesweeping boats, 8 torpedo boats, 1 dock landing ship, 1 amphibious flagship, 28 landing ships, 22 landing craft, 2 repair ships, 3 surveying ships, 12 support ships, 2 transports, 9 oilers, 1 supply ship, 9 tugs, 5 floating docks and 25 service craft.

Under construction are 14 fast missile attack craft and 5 coastguard cutters (customs). Active personnel (1978): 7,000 naval officers and 28,000 ratings; 3,000 marine officers and 26,000 men.

Air Force. The Nationalist Air Force is equipped mainly with aircraft of US design, which continue to be supplied under military aid programmes. F-5E fighters are also built in Taiwan. It has 15 squadrons of F-104G Starfighters, F-5A/B/E supersonic fighter-bombers, and F-100 Super Sabre fighter-bombers, and 1 tactical reconnaissance squadron of RF-104G Starfighters. The transport squadrons are equipped with about 100 C-119Gs, C-123 Providers and C-47s. There is a naval cooperation squadron with S-2A Trackers. Search and rescue units operate Albatross amphibians and Iroquois helicopters, and there are other helicopter and large training elements. Total strength in 1977: 70,000 personnel and 296 combat aircraft.

INTERNATIONAL RELATIONS. By a treaty of 1 Dec. 1954 the USA is pledged to protect Taiwan.

The People's Republic took over the China seat in the United Nations from the Nationalists on 25 Oct. 1971.

ECONOMY

Planning. Taiwan is predominantly agricultural. Government policy is to 'develop industry through agriculture and expand agriculture through industry'. Regional planning was carried out through a series of 4-year plans, of which the sixth (1973–76) was terminated in 1975 because of difficulties arising from the international economic situation. The current 6-year programme (1976–81) envisages a GNP annual growth rate of 5·8% (previous target 9·5%). Emphasis is on heavy industry; there is some restriction of private spending.

Budget. The financial year ends 30 June. There are 2 budgets, the national together with a special defence budget (partly secret) and the provincial (*i.e.*, for Taiwan proper). For 1975–76 revenue was NT$155,719m. (including NT$106,983 from taxation) and expenditure, NT$142,107m. (including NT$54,810 on administration and defence, NT$24,836 on education and research and NT$16,947 on social affairs relief).

Currency. In 1945 the existing currency was converted into notes of the Bank of Taiwan. Taiwan dollars were linked to Chinese national currency at a fixed rate of exchange. When the Gold Yuan entered upon its last phase in early 1949, the Taiwan currency was detached and linked to the US$. Exchange rates: £1 = NT$73·81; US$1 = NT$38.

Banking. The Central Bank of China (reactivated in 1961) regulates the money market, manages foreign exchange and issues currency. The former Bank of China, a foreign exchange bank with branches in New York, Tōkyō, Sydney, Saigon and Bangkok, was reorganized in 1972 as a private bank for export financing and renamed the China International Commercial Bank (capital NT$1,000m.).

The Bank of Taiwan is the largest commercial bank and the fiscal agent of the Government.

Other banking institutions include the China Development Corporation.

ENERGY AND NATURAL RESOURCES

Electricity. Output of electricity in 1976 was 26,877m. kwh.; total generating capacity was 5·3m. kw. Two nuclear power-stations are under construction and a third is planned. All 3 should be fully operational by 1984.

Minerals. There are reserves of coal (220m. tonnes), gold (7·1m. tonnes), copper (12·6m. tonnes), sulphur (2·4m. tonnes), oil (3·1m. kl.) and natural gas (32,430 cu. metres). In 1976 an offshore gas-field south-west of Taiwan was discovered with an annual capacity of 500m. cu. metres. Coal production was 3·2m. tonnes in 1976.

Agriculture. The cultivated area was 919,700 hectares in 1976, of which 520,800 hectares were paddy fields. Production in 1,000 tonnes, in 1976 (and 1975): Rice, 2,713 (2,494); tea, 24·8 (26); bananas, 213·4 (196·6); pineapples, 278·8 (319); sugar-cane, 8,728 (7,687); sweet potatoes, 1,851 (2,403); wheat, 1·2 (3); soybeans, 53 (61·9); peanuts, 88·8 (91·5); cotton, 0·2 (0·2); jute, 0·2 (0·4).

Livestock (1976): Cattle, 253,297; pigs, 3·7m.; goats, 210,581.

Forestry. The total area of forests is 2·3m. hectares. Timber production in 1976 was 823,732 cu. metres.

Fisheries. The fleet comprised 27,043 vessels in 1976 (of which 11,849 were powered); the catch was 810,600 tonnes.

INDUSTRY AND TRADE

Industry. Output (in tonnes) in 1976 (and 1975): Steel, 1,309,136 (956,418); pig-iron, 104,829 (66,840); aluminium, 25,512 (28,111); shipbuilding, 171,573 (294,619); sugar, 779 (716); cement, 8·7m. (6·8m.); fertilizers, 1·6m. (1·5m.); paper, 500,495 (421,702); cotton fabrics, 811m. metres (761m.).

In 1976, 13,788m. litres of crude oil were refined; the main refinery at Kaohsiung has an annual capacity of 1m. tons.

Labour. In 1976 the non-agricultural labour force was 5,748,000, of whom 1·6m. worked in manufacturing, 0·4m. in building and 1·1m. in transport and communications. 85,000 were unemployed.

Commerce. Foreign trade affairs are handled by the China External Trade Development Council (founded 1970), which operates branches in 33 countries under the name of Far East Trade Service. Principal exports: textiles, bananas, chemicals, metals, machinery, sugar. Total trade, in US$m.:

	1969	*1970*	*1971*	*1972*	*1973*	*1974*	*1975*	*1976*
Imports	1,205	1,528	1,990	2,514	3,792	5,845	5,952	7,599
Exports	1,111	1,562	2,136	2,988	4,483	4,734	5,309	8,166

The USA and Japan are Taiwan's major trade partners followed by Federal Republic of Germany and the UK.

Total trade between UK and Taiwan (British Department of Trade returns, in £1,000 sterling):

	1972	*1973*	*1974*	*1975*	*1976*	*1977*
Imports to UK	27,712	51,996	66,663	73,045	97,027	138,730
Exports and re-exports from UK	10,975	25,465	39,152	33,829	52,605	61,607

The Anglo-Taiwan Trade Committee, a private business organization, helps British businessmen engaged in trade with Taiwan.

COMMUNICATIONS

Roads. In 1976 there were 17,172 km of roads (10,687 km surfaced). 2,341,298 motor vehicles were registered in 1976 including 170,984 passenger cars, 13,724 buses, 129,853 trucks and 2,009,698 motor cycles. 1,022m. passengers and 94m. tons of freight were transported (excluding urban buses).

Railways. Total route length in 1976 was 4,200 km, of which a large proportion is owned by the Taiwan Sugar Corporation and other concerns. Taiwan railways have various gauges, ranging from 3 ft 6 in. to 2 ft. Electrification of the west trunk line of the state network was started in 1973 and the first section between Keelung and

Chunan was energized in 1977. Freight traffic in 1976 amounted to 35·1m. tons and passenger traffic to 143m.

Aviation. There are 2 international airports: Taipei and Kaohsiung, and a third is being built at Taoyuan. There are 6 domestic airlines, including China Airlines (CAL), which also operates international services to Bangkok, Hong Kong, Kuala Lumpur, Manila, Seoul and Singapore.

Shipping. The merchant marine in 1976 comprised 7,255 vessels over 20 GRT, totalling 2,096,446 GRT; it included 28 passenger ships and 369 freighters. Ocean-going freight-traffic was 17·9m. tonnes.

The 3 international ports, Kaohsiung, Chilung and T'aichung, are being extensively redeveloped. The first two are container centres. The lesser ports of Hualien, Suao and Wuchi are also being built up.

Post and Broadcasting. In 1976 there were 9,727 postal establishments. Number of telephones in 1977, 1,396,022. In 1975 there were 3·5m. radio receivers and 2·3m. TV receivers. There are 3 TV networks, one state-owned.

Cinemas (1976). Cinemas numbered 489.

Newspapers (1976). There were 31 daily papers and 1,459 periodicals.

RELIGION, EDUCATION AND WELFARE

Religion. The predominant faith is Confucianism, and there were 5,000 temples in 1976. There are some 600,000 Christians, mainly in Hualien, of whom there were some 200,000 Presbyterians in 1978.

Education. Since 1968 there has been free compulsory education for 9 years (6–15). In that year the curriculum was modernized to give more emphasis to science while retaining the traditional basis of Confucian ethics. There were, in 1976–77, 2,353 primary schools with 64,468 teachers and 2,326,866 pupils; 975 secondary schools with 61,969 teachers and 1,530,745 pupils; 101 institutes of higher learning, including 8 universities, with 14,548 teachers and 299,414 students.

Health. In 1976 there were 66,781 registered medical personnel, including 16,982 doctors, 3,137 dentists and 3,469 'herb doctors', and 1,110 public medical institutions, including 31 general hospitals, 608 health centres and 413 mobile medical units.

DIPLOMATIC REPRESENTATIVES

OF TAIWAN CHINA IN THE USA (2311 Massachusetts Ave., NW, Washington, D.C., 20008)

Ambassador: James C. H. Shen.

OF THE USA IN TAIWAN

Ambassador: Leonard Unger.

Books of Reference

Statistical Yearbook of the Republic of China. Taipei, annual
China Yearbook. Taipei, annual
Taiwan Statistical Data Book. Taipei, annual
Chiu, H. (ed.), *China and the Question of Taiwan: Documents and Analysis.* New York, 1973
Goddard, W. G., *Formosa: A Study in Chinese History.* London, 1966
Li, V. H., *De-Recognizing Taiwan.* New York, 1977
Lin, C.-Y., *Industrialization in Taiwan, 1946–72.* New York, 1973
Lumley, F. A., *The Republic of China under Chiang Kai-shek: Taiwan Today.* London, 1976
Mendel, D., *The Politics of Formosan Nationalism.* California U.P., 1970
Sih, P. (ed.), *Taiwan in Modern Times.* New York, 1973

COLOMBIA

República de Colombia

Capital: Bogotá
Population: 25·2m. (1977)
GNP per capita: US$630 (1976)

HISTORY. The Vice-royalty of New Granada gained its independence of Spain in 1819, and was officially constituted 17 Dec. 1819, together with the present territories of Panama, Venezuela and Ecuador, as the state of 'Greater Colombia', which continued for about 12 years. It then split up into Venezuela, Ecuador and the republic of New Granada in 1830. The constitution of 22 May 1858 changed New Granada into a confederation of 8 states, under the name of Confederación Granadina. Under the constitution of 8 May 1863 the country was renamed 'Estados Unidos de Colombia', which were 9 in number. The revolution of 1885 led the National Council of Bogotá, composed of 2 delegates from each state, to promulgate the constitution of 5 Aug. 1886, forming the Republic of Colombia, which abolished the sovereignty of the states, converting them into departments, with governors appointed by the President of the Republic, though they retained some of their old rights, such as the management of their own finances. A decree of May 1928 abolished their right to borrow abroad without the sanction of the central government.

AREA AND POPULATION. Colombia is bounded north by the Caribbean sea, north-west by Panama, west by the Pacific ocean, south-west by Ecuador and Peru, north-east by Venezuela and south-east by Brazil. The estimated area of the Republic as given to the United Nations is 1,138,914 sq. km (456,535 sq. miles). It lies between lat. 12° 30′ N. and 4° 30′ S., and between long. 67° and 79° W. of Greenwich. It has a coastline of about 2,900 km, of which 1,600 km are on the Caribbean sea and 1,300 km on the Pacific Ocean. The area 1,138,914 sq. km (as estimated by the census bureau) and population 25,167,498 according to the estimate of 24 Oct. 1977, were as follows (the capitals in brackets):

	Area (sq. km)	*Population, 1977 Total*	*Per sq. km*
Departments			
Antioquia (Medellín)	62,870	3,542,902	56·35
Atlántico (Barranquilla)	3,270	1,166,860	356·84
Bolívar (Cartagena)	26,392	1,090,459	41·32
Boyacá (Tunja M.E.)	67,750	1,126,454	16·63
Caldas (Manizales)	7,283	748,980	102·84
Cauca (Popayán)	30,495	799,134	26·21
Cesar	23,792	615,934	25·89
Córdoba (Monteria)	25,175	789,995	31·38
Bogotá, D.E.	1,587	3,618,750	2,280·25
Cundinamarca[3]	23,960	1,169,876	52·59
Chocó (Quibdó)	47,205	224,310	4·75
Huila (Neiva)	19,990	534,742	26·87
La Guajira (Riohacha)	20,180	240,227	11·90
Magdalena (Santa Marta)	22,903	838,794	36·62
Meta (Villavicencio)	85,770	325,673	3·80
Nariño (Pasto)	31,045	917,510	29·55
Norte de Santander (Cúcuta)	20,815	843,297	40·51
Quindío[1] (Armenia)	1,825	368,993	202·19
Risaralda (Pereira)	3,962	515,132	130·02
Santander (Bucaramanga)	30,950	1,278,881	41·32
Sucre[2] (Sincelejo)	10,523	475,509	45·19
Tolima (Ibagué)	23,325	993,915	42·61
Valle del Cauca (Cali)	21,245	2,717,724	127·92
Intendencies			
San Andrés y Providencia (San Andrés)	44	22,719	516·34
Casanore[4]	44,532	...	...

[1] Formerly part of Caldas.
[2] Formerly part of Bolívar.
[3] Not including Bogotá, D.E.
[4] Formerly part of Boyacá.

Of the total population in 1964, 52% were urban. The bulk of the population lives at altitudes of from 4,000 to 9,000 ft above sea-level. It is divided broadly into: 68% mestizo, 20% white, 7% Indio and 5% Negro.

In 1971 births were 36·58 per 1,000; deaths, 9·49; marriages, 2·42.

The capital, Bogotá (population of Special District, 1972, 2,978,300), lies 8,661 ft above the sea. The chief commercial towns, with their population in 1973, are: Medellín, an industrial coffee and mining centre (1,269,900); Cali, an industrial and sugar centre (1,077,000); Barranquilla, international airport and river- and sea-port (721,900); Cartagena, an industrial port with the oil-pipe terminal (362,600); Manizales (318,600); Bucaramanga, tobacco and coffee centre (364,200); Cúcuta, coffee and industrial centre (259,400); Santa Marta, on the Caribbean, and terminus of the Ferrocarril del Atlántico (174,200); Pasto (140,700); Ibagué (226,500).

The language spoken is Spanish.

CONSTITUTION AND GOVERNMENT. The legislative power rests with a Congress of 2 houses, the Senate, of 112 members, and the House of Representatives, of 199 members, both elected for 4 years. In 1968 a congressional committee unanimously approved a constitutional amendment providing for progressive reductions in the membership of Congress to 90 senators and 162 representatives by 1974. Congress meets annually at Bogotá on 20 July. Women were given the vote, which is now open to citizens of either sex, over 18 years of age, on 25 Aug. 1954.

In the elections on 21 April 1974 the Liberal–Conservative alliance obtained 179 seats and the National Popular Alliance 20 seats in the lower house.

The President is elected by direct vote of the people for a term of 4 years, and is not eligible for re-election until 4 years afterwards. Congress elects, for a term of 2 years, one substitute to occupy the presidency in the event of a vacancy during a presidential term. There are 13 Ministries. The Governors of Departments and the Mayor of Bogotá are nominated by the national government.

A National Economic Council, functioning since May 1935, went through several transformations, becoming in 1954 a Directorate of Planning.

National flag: Three horizontal stripes of yellow, blue, red with the yellow of double width.

National anthem: Oh! Gloria inmarcesible (words by R. Núñez; tune by O. Síndici).

The following is a list of presidents since 1945:

Dr Alberto Lleras Camargo, 7 Aug. 1945–7 Aug. 1946.
Dr Mariano Ospina Pérez, 7 Aug. 1946–7 Aug. 1950.
Dr Laureano Gómez, 7 Aug. 1950–13 June 1953.
Gen. Gustavo Rojas Pinilla, 13 June 1953–10 May 1957.
Military Junta, Maj.-Gen. Gabriel París and 4 others, 10 May 1957–7 Aug. 1958.
Dr Alberto Lleras Camargo (Lib.), 7 Aug. 1958–7 Aug. 1962.
Dr Guillermo León Valencia (Cons.), 7 Aug. 1962–7 Aug. 1966.
Dr Carlos Lleras Restrepo (Lib.), 7 Aug. 1966–7 Aug. 1970.
Dr Misael Pastrana Borrero (Cons.), 7 Aug 1970–7 Aug. 1974.

President: Dr Alfonso López Michelsen, heading a dual administration composed of Conservatives and Liberals. He obtained 2,653,018 of the 4·8m. votes cast in the election on 21 April 1974 and took office on 7 Aug. 1974.

Minister of Foreign Affairs: Dr Indalecio Lievano Aguirre (L.).

Gibson, W. M., *The Constitutions of Colombia.* Durham, N.C. 1948, and London, 1949

DEFENCE. On 17 April 1952 Colombia signed the Military Assistance pact with the USA.

Army. Military service is compulsory between the years of 18 and 30. Service with the colours is for 1 year. From 30 to 45 years of age the citizens are on the reserved lists, classified in 1st, 2nd and 3rd classes, with the obligation of presenting themselves on being called up. The permanent Army consists of 10 infantry brigades and artillery, cavalry, engineers, motorized troops and the usual services. The peace effective is 42,000 men; reserves about 250,000. Number of national police, about 5,000.

Colombia was the only Latin American country participating in the Korean war, with a regiment of 1,000 men (three times relieved).

Navy. Colombia has 2 new Federal German-built 1,000-ton diesel-electric powered patrol submarines, 4 Italian-built midget submarines; 2 destroyers built in Sweden in 1958; 2 old former US destroyers; 3 old *ex*-US frigates (small DE and APD types); 4 river gunboats; 3 surveying vessels; 7 coastguard patrol vessels; 11 patrol motor launches; 1 oiler; 4 small transports, 1 training ship, 4 service craft, and 12 tugs. Personnel (1978), 700 officers and 6,500 men. The Navy has also a battalion of marines with 1,500 officers and men. There are American and British Naval Missions.

Air Force. Formed in 1922, the Air Force has been independent of the Army and Navy since 1943, when its reorganization began with US assistance. In 1977 it had about 200 aircraft, including a squadron of Mirage 5-COA fighter-bombers, 5-COR reconnaissance aircraft and 5-COD two-seat operational trainers; a squadron of 8 B-26 piston-engined bombers; a transport group equipped with 2 C-130s, 3 HS 748s, 4 Twin Otters, C-47s, C-54s and a small number of Otter, Beaver and Porter light transports; a presidential F-28 Fellowship jet transport; and a maritime reconnaissance and rescue unit with helicopters. Many of the transports are flown by the Air Force operated airline SATENA. Thirty Cessna T-41D primary trainer/light transports were delivered in 1968 and were followed by 10 T-37C jet advanced trainers to supplement piston-engined T-34s and T-33A armed jet trainers already in service. Total strength is about 6,500 personnel.

INTERNATIONAL RELATIONS

Membership. Colombia is a member of the UN, OAS, the Andean Group and LAFTA.

ECONOMY

Budget. Ordinary revenue and expenditure for calendar years in 1m. paper pesos:

	1973	*1974*	*1976*	*1977*	*1978*
Revenue	25,433	28,983	38,442	62,700	86,581
Expenditure	25,433	30,303	26,295	62,700	86,581

Reserves totalled US$1,800m. in Dec. 1977.

Currency. Coins include 50, 20 and 10 *centavos* (90% steel and 10% nickel) and 5, 2 and 1 *centavos* of various combinations of copper–nickel–bronze–steel. There are also notes representing 1, 5, 10, 20, 50, 100 and 500 *gold pesos*. Exchange rate Jan. 1977, 66·75 *pesos* = £1 sterling.

Banking. On 23 July 1923 the Banco de la República was inaugurated as a semi-official central bank, with the exclusive privilege of issuing bank-notes in Colombia; its charter, in 1951, was extended to 1973. Its note issues must be covered by a reserve in gold of foreign exchange of 25% of their value.

There are 26 domestic commercial banks of importance and 5 foreign banks (English, Canadian, American, French and Franco-Italian); but a high percentage of all commercial bank deposits are with the 4 largest domestic banks, which have branches throughout the country. In Nov. 1950 they were permitted to accept savings deposits, hitherto a government monopoly.

Weights and Measures. The metric system was introduced in 1857, but in ordinary commerce Spanish weights and measures are generally used; according to new definitions by the Ministry of Development, *e.g.*, *botella* (750 grammes), *galón* (5 *botellas*), *vara* (70 cm), *arroba* (25 lb., of 500 grammes; 4 *arrobas* = 1 quintal).

ENERGY AND NATURAL RESOURCES

Electricity. Capacity of electric power (1973) is 2,795,000 kw. Electric power produced in 1976, 13,695,000 kwh. There is increasing utilization of natural gas.

In Oct. 1954 the Department of Valle del Cauca established a local power corporation closely modelled on the Tennessee Valley Authority.

Oil. Petroleum production in 1977 was 49·8m. bbls (of 42 gallons) and 1976, 50·6m. bbls.

Minerals. Colombia is rich in minerals; gold is found chiefly in Antioquia and moderately in Cauca, Caldas, Tolima, Nariño and Chocó; output in 1976, 298,174 fine oz., highest in South America.

Other minerals are silver (105,720 troy oz. in 1976), copper, lead, mercury, manganese, emeralds and platinum (first discovered in Colombia in 1735 and the largest deposit in the world); export of platinum, 1967, 16,804 troy oz. The working of the government-controlled emerald mines has been resumed. The chief mines are those of Muzo and Chivor.

The Government holds the monopoly, which is leased to the Banco de la República, for extracting salts from the outstanding Zipaquirá mines (several hundred feet in depth and several hundred square miles in area) and for evaporating many sea salt pans; salt production in 1976 was 185,239 tonnes of land salt from the Zipaquirá mines and 500,786 tons of sea salt from Manaure and Galerazamba on the Caribe coast. Colombia's coal reserves are estimated at 13,200m. tonnes; production (1968) 3·3m. short tons.

Agriculture. Very little of the country is under cultivation, but much of the soil is fertile and is coming into use as roads improve. The range of climate and crops is extraordinary; the agricultural colleges have different courses for 'cold-climate farming' and 'warm-climate farming'. Some 6m. acres are described as arable, 96m. pasture and 148m. forest.

Colombia is the second largest producer of coffee and ranks first in the output of mild coffee, demand for which is unaffected by over-production in Brazil. Crops are grown by smallholders, and are picked all the year round. Production (1974, in tonnes): Sesame, 25,000; cotton, 330,000; rice, 648,000; barley, 62,000; maize, 500,000; potatoes, 500,000; soybean, 38,000; wheat, 76,000; bananas, 410,000; cacao, 23,900; sugar-cane, 820,000.

The rubber tree grows wild, and its cultivation has begun; output is a few hundred tons. Fibres are being exploited, notably the 'fique' fibre, which furnishes all the country's requirements for sacks and cordage; output about 12,000 tons. Tolú balsam is cultivated, and copaiba trees are tapped but are not cultivated. Tanning is an important industry, 12m. sq. ft of hides being exported in 1965.

Livestock (1976): 23·86m. cattle, 1·9m. pigs, 2·04m. sheep, 4·7m. poultry.

Fishery. In Sept. 1963 a *Sección de Caza y Pesca* was set up in the Ministry of Agriculture. It extended territorial waters to 200 nautical miles. The principal finance companies founded a development company with over 20m. pesos in Aug. 1966 (*Consorcio Pesquero Colombiano*).

INDUSTRY AND TRADE

Industry. Value of industrial output (located mainly in the Departments of Antioquia, Cundinamarca and Valle) by 456,188 production workers in 6,348 establishments in 1975 was 202,177m. pesos. There are 69 reassembly plants, apart from the motor industry. At the end of 1965 the 101 firms with more than 50% US control equalled an investment of US$510m.; they employed over 29,000 Colombians.

GDP *per capita* (1975) 16,952 pesos.

Trade Unions. The Colombian Federation of Labour (CTC) had, in 1947, 109,000 members out of a total of 165,000 organized workers. In 1946 there was established an association of trade unions, *Unión de Trabajadores Colombianos*. In May 1963, 8·6% of the 449,000 workmen in Bogotá were unemployed.

Commerce. For the 'Charter of Quito' trading agreement in 1948 between Colombia, Ecuador, Panama and Venezuela, *see* THE STATESMAN'S YEAR-BOOK, 1956, p. 882. Colombia's entry into the Latin American Free Trade Area (ALALC) was ratified on 29 Sept. 1961. A fresh impulse to this effort was given by the Bases for an Immediate Action Programme under the 'Charter of Bogotá' signed by Colombia, Chile, Ecuador, Peru and Venezuela on 16 Aug. 1966.

Imports (c.i.f. values) and exports (f.o.b. values) (excluding export tax) for calendar years (in US$1m.):

	1969	*1970*[1]	*1971*	*1972*	*1973*	*1974*	*1975*
Imports	685·3	843·0	929·4	859·0	1,061·5	1,597·2	1,416·9
Exports[1]	607·5	735·7	690·0	866·0	1,177·3	1,494·8	1,465·2

[1] Excluding export tax.

Trade by principal countries, in US$1m.:

	Imports (c.i.f.)[1]		*Exports (f.o.b.)*[1]	
	1974	*1975*[2]	*1974*	*1975*[2]
Belgium–Luxembourg	13·5	12·5	17·1	25·0
Canada	42·6	43·0	19·5	13·9
France	67·0	67·2	27·0	32·0
Germany (Fed. Republic of)	144·6	131·3	170·0	217·9
Italy	31·5	37·8	31·6	38·7
Japan	135·5	128·9	20·7	27·1
Netherlands	36·9	23·7	64·4	93·5
Spain	49·5	50·3	37·9	38·6
Sweden	27·5	26·1	32·7	46·4
Switzerland	59·0	40·3	8·0	7·1
UK	59·1	53·0	22·2	41·3
USA	639·0	640·4	514·5	441·9

[1] Excluding bullion and specie. [2] Provisional.

Important articles of export in 1973 (in US$1m.) were coffee (596·9), cotton (79·3), emeralds (79·6), petroleum (26·8), sugar (31·1), meat, fresh and frozen (40·1), fuel oil (22·5), skins and hides (20·2). The chief imports are machinery, vehicles, tractors, metals and manufactures, rubber, chemical products, wheat, fertilizers and wool.

Total trade between UK and Colombia (British Department of Trade returns, in £1,000 sterling).

	1972	*1973*	*1974*	*1975*	*1976*	*1977*
Imports to UK	9,771	9,705	12,458	24,095	25,818	31,641
Exports and re-exports from UK	17,121	15,477	24,213	28,692	28,854	41,685

Tourism. Foreign visitors totalled 362,900 in 1974.

COMMUNICATIONS

Roads. Owing to the mountainous character of the country, the construction of arterial roads and railways is costly and difficult. Total length of highways, 51,253 km in 1972. Of the 2,300-mile Simón Bolívar highway, which runs from Caracas in Venezuela to Guayaquil in Ecuador, the Colombian portion is complete. Buenaventura and Cali are linked by a highway (Carreterra al Mar). Motor vehicles numbered 433,845, of which 326,853 were passenger cars and 106,992 lorries in 1973.

Railways. There are 5 divisions of the State Railway, with a total length of 3,403 km in 1976 and a gauge of 3 ft. The Pacific Railway connects Bogotá with the port of Buenaventura. The Atlantic line from Bogotá to Sta. Marta was opened in July 1961. Three connecting links are planned to improve the operating efficiency of the network. Total railway traffic, 1976, was 4m. passengers and 2,411,372 tonnes of freight.

Aviation. In civil aviation Colombia ranks perhaps second, after Brazil, among South American countries. There are 675 landing grounds of all kinds. In 1976 the national airlines carried 4,356,738 passengers and 104,633 tonnes of cargo.

Shipping. Vessels entering Colombian ports in 1976 had a net registered tonnage of 10,731,046. The Colombian merchant fleet in 1966 owned 23 vessels of 187,906 net tons, and leased 20 of 164,360 net tons; in 1965 it carried 1·9m. tonnes. At present a cargo ship of 11,685 tons is being built in Spain.

The Magdelena River is subject to drought, and navigation is always impeded during the dry season, but it is an important artery of passenger and goods traffic. The river is navigable for 900 miles; steamers ascend to La Dorada, 592 miles from Barranquilla. In 1976 they carried 16,533 passengers and 3,268,977 tonnes of cargo.

Post and Broadcasting. The length of telephone lines in service is 705,852 km (Bogotá only); instruments in use, 1 Jan. 1977, 1,295,860, of which 437,000 in Bogotá. The cable company is government-owned. There are 223 broadcasting stations. Television was established in 1954. Bogotá is now the centre of a wide repeater network.

Cinemas (1973). There were 352 cinemas.

Newspapers (1973). There were 36 daily newspapers, with daily circulation totalling 1,448,467. There were 388 periodical publications.

JUSTICE, RELIGION, EDUCATION AND WELFARE

Justice. The Supreme Court, at Bogotá, of 20 members, is divided into 3 chambers—civil cassation (6), criminal cassation (8), labour cassation (6). Each of the 61 judicial districts has a superior court with various sub-dependent tribunals of lower juridical grade.

Communism was outlawed by government decree on 5 March 1956.

Religion. The religion is Roman Catholic, with the Cardinal Archbishop of Bogotá as Primate of Colombia and 7 other archbishops in Cartagena, Manizales, Medellín, Pamplona, Popayán, Cali and Tunja, 26 bishops, 1,546 parishes and 4,020 priests. Other forms of religion are permitted so long as their exercise is 'not contrary to Christian morals or to the law'; but since 1953 the 90,000 Protestants have complained of police prosecutions and religious disorders.

Education. Primary education is free but not compulsory, and facilities are limited. Schools are both state and privately controlled. In 1974 there were 30,558 primary schools with 3,844,257 pupils and 123,139 teachers. In 4,200 secondary schools there were 1,159,996 pupils with 62,000 teachers. In the 176 industrial schools, there were 27,808 pupils with 2,855 teachers. 178 night schools had 11,504 pupils with 1,668 teachers. 81 agricultural schools catered for 7,930 pupils with 815 teachers. There were 638 commercial schools catering for 69,233 pupils with 7,844 teachers. 110 art schools had 8,681 pupils and 709 teachers. Theological institutes (all private) numbered 22 with 674 students and 180 tutors. In *normalista* schools, of which there were 239, 54,198 pupils had 5,407 teachers.

The National University in Bogotá was founded in 1867 and there are 97 other universities with 171,002 students and 17,963 lecturers.

Of the population over 7 years of age in July 1964, the National Department of Statistics estimated that 27·1% were illiterate; intensive efforts to build new schools and to reduce illiteracy are being made.

Health. In 1976 there were 670 hospitals and clinics. There were also 1,499 health centres.

DIPLOMATIC REPRESENTATIVES

OF COLOMBIA IN GREAT BRITAIN (3 Hans Crescent, London, SW1X 0LR)

Ambassador: Dr Jaime Garcia-Parra (accredited 10 Feb. 1977).

OF GREAT BRITAIN IN COLOMBIA (Calle 38 13 35, Piso 9–11, Bogotá)

Ambassador: G. A. Crossley, CMG.

OF COLOMBIA IN THE USA (2118 Leroy Pl., NW, Washington, D.C., 20008)

Ambassador: Virgilio Barco.

OF THE USA IN COLOMBIA (Calle 37 8 40, Bogotá)

Ambassador: Diego C. Asencio.

OF COLOMBIA TO THE UNITED NATIONS

Ambassador: Dr Germán Zea.

Books of Reference

Anuario General de Estadistica de Colombia. Bogotá. Annual
Anuario de Comercio Exterior de Colombia. Annual
Anuario Estadístico Bogatá D.E. Annual
Boletín Mensual de Estadística. Monthly
Economía y Estadística. Occasional
Informe Financiero del Contralor General. Annual
Informe del Gerente de la Caja de Crédito Agrario, Industrial y Minero. Annual
Memorias (13) de los Ministros al Congreso Nacional. Annual
Charry Lara, Alberto, *Desarrollo histórico de la Estadística nacional en Colombia.* Nat. Dept of Statistics, Bogotá, 1954.—*El país en cifras.* 1964
Lebret, R. P. L. J., *Estudio sobre las condiciones dei desarrollo de Colombia. Informe de una Misión.* Bogotá, 1960
McGreevey, W. P., *An Economic History of Colombia, 1845–1930*, CUP, 1970
Wurfel S. W., *Foreign Enterprise in Colombia: Laws and Policies.* Univ. of N. Carolina Press, 1965

COMOROS

Etat Comorien

Capital: Moroni
Population: 344,000 (1976)
GNP per capita: US$180 (1976)

HISTORY. In the referendum held separately on each of the 4 islands on 22 Dec. 1974, 95·56% of the Comorans voted for independence, but the vote on Mayotte was 65% against independence. To avoid the expected separation of Mayotte, the Comoran Chamber of Deputies voted for an immediate unilateral declaration of independence on 6 July 1975. The next day it converted itself into the National Assembly and elected Ahmed Abdallah, President of the Executive Council since 26 Dec. 1972, as President of the new state. France retained responsibility for Mayotte, while the other 3 islands achieved *de facto* independence.

On 3 Aug. a *coup* mounted by the principal opposition parties, led by Ali Soilih, deposed President Abdallah. The following day a National Revolutionary Council, led by Prince Said Mohammad Jaffar, took office and abolished the National Assembly. On 10 Aug. the Revolutionary Council established a National Executive Council with Prince Said as its President. The four parties formed a coalition, the Front National Uni, which attempted unsuccessfully to persuade the Mayotte administration (the *Mouvement populaire mahouais*, led by Marcel Henry) to reunite with the other islands.

France recognized the independence of the three islands on 1 Jan. 1976. The next day the Executive Council and the Revolutionary Council elected Ali Soilih President. The Revolutionary Council was superseded by a National Institutional Council to oversee the actions of the Government.

A new referendum was held on 8 Feb. 1976 on Mayotte, which resulted in a 99·4% vote for retaining the island's links with France. In another referendum on 11 April Mayotte voted against remaining an Overseas Territory of France, preferring to become an Overseas Department. France has promised to implement the electorate's wishes accordingly. The UN recognized the State of Comoro as representative of the whole group. (For history prior to independence *see* THE STATESMAN'S YEAR-BOOK, 1976–77, p. 849.) All statistics prior to 1977 include Mayotte.

AREA AND POPULATION. The majority of the population throughout the islands speak Kiswahili, but a small proportion speak French or Arabic. On the three islands of the Comoro State, the majority of the population are Moslem, with about 2,000 Christians.

	Area sq. km	*Population census 1966*	*Population estimate 1972*	*Chief town*
Grande Comore	1,148	126,205	135,000	Moroni
Mohéli	290	10,300	12,000	Fomboni
Anjouan	424	80,082	105,000	Mutsamudu
	1,862	216,587	252,000	
Mayotte	374	31,930	38,000	Dzaoudzi

CONSTITUTION AND GOVERNMENT. The President appointed a Council of Ministers headed by a Prime Minister.

President: Ali Soilih (confirmed in office on 23 April 1977 after a referendum).

On 13 May 1978 a *coup* took place and the President was deposed (*see* Addenda).

National flag: Horizontally red over green with the red of double width and charged in the canton with a crescent and 4 white stars, all pointing to the lower fly.

DEFENCE

Air Arm. Initial equipment, acquired in 1977, comprises 3 SIAI-Marchetti SF-260W Warrior armed light trainers built in Italy.

INTERNATIONAL RELATIONS

Membership. Comoros is a member of UN.

ECONOMY

Budget. The ordinary budget for 1975 balanced at 2,949m. francs CFA.

Currency. The unit of currency is the franc CFA.

Banking. The Institut d'émission des Comores was established as the new bank of issue in 1975. The chief commercial bank is the Banque des Comores, established in 1974 by the separation of the former Comoran section of the Banque de Madagascar et des Comores.

Weights and Measures. The metric system is in force.

NATURAL RESOURCES

Agriculture. The chief product was formerly sugar-cane, but now vanilla, copra, cacao, sisal, coffee, cloves and essential oils (citronella, ylang, lemon-grass) are the most important products.

Livestock (1976): Cattle, 74,000; sheep, 8,000; goats, 81,000; asses, 3,000.

COMMERCE. Imports in 1971 amounted to 54,299 tonnes (2,834m. francs CFA), exports to 12,756 tonnes (1,572m. francs CFA). Vanilla exports were 206 tonnes (606m. francs CFA); sisal, 373 tonnes (268m. francs CFA); copra, 3,988 tons (206·5m. francs CFA); ylang, 67·4 tons (452m. francs CFA); basil, 6·5 tons (48·7m. francs CFA); coffee, 73 tons (15·4m. francs CFA). Grande Comore has a fine forest and produces timber for building.

Trade with UK (British Department of Trade returns, in £1,000 sterling):

	1974	*1975*	*1976*	*1977*
Imports to UK	11	—	78	3
Exports and re-exports from UK	25	13	19	69

COMMUNICATIONS

Roads. In 1973 there were 750 km of classified roads, of which 262 km were tarmac. There were 3,600 registered vehicles.

Aviation. The new international airport at Hahaya (on Grande Comore) came into service in 1975. Air Comores have twice-weekly flights to Antanarivo, Dar es Salaam and Mombasa. Air France and Air Madagascar also have twice-weekly flights to Antanarivo. Air Comores has daily internal flights between Moroni and Anjouan, and 5 per week between Moroni and Mohéli.

In 1973 nearly 16,000 passengers landed and 900 tonnes of freight was carried.

Shipping. In 1973, 279 vessels entered Comoran ports (excluding internal traffic) to discharge 54,391 tonnes and load 8,700 tonnes.

Post and Broadcasting. There were 1,035 telephones in 1977. *Comores-Inter* broadcasts in French and Comorian on short-wave and FM for approximately 8 hours a day. Number of radios (1975): 36,000.

Cinemas. In 1973 there were 2 cinemas with a seating capacity of 800.

EDUCATION AND WELFARE

Education. In 1974, 130 primary classes had 570 teachers and 21,557 pupils, 5 secondary schools had 121 teachers and 2,920 pupils.

Health. In 1975 there were 3 hospitals and a number of clinics.

CONGO

République Populaire du Congo

Capital: Brazzaville
Population: 1·32m. (1975)
GNP per capita: US$520 (1976)

HISTORY. The Republic of the Congo became independent on 15 Aug. 1960, after having been one of the 4 territories of French Equatorial Africa (under the name of Middle Congo) and from 28 Nov. 1958 a member state of the French Community. In Jan. 1959 it formed an 'economic, technical and customs union' with the other 3 territories of the former government-general of French Equatorial Africa.

AREA AND POPULATION. The area of the Congo Republic covers 342,000 sq. km; census population (1974), 1,300,020. Estimate (1975) 1·32m. The capital is Brazzaville (289,700), and other towns include Pointe-Noire, 141,700; Jacob, 30,600; Loubomo (Dolisie), 29,600.

CONSTITUTION AND GOVERNMENT. After the assassination of President Marien Ngouabi on 18 March 1977, the Constitution of 24 June 1973 was replaced by an *Acte Fondamental*. The Party Military Committee is the supreme organ of government.

President of the Republic: Col. Joachim Yhombi Opango.
Prime Minister: Maj. Louis Sylvain Goma.

National flag: Red, in the canton the national emblem of a crossed hoe and mattock, a green wreath and a gold star.

DEFENCE

Army. The Army consists of an armoured regiment, an infantry and a paracommando battalion. Total personnel (1977) 6,500.

Navy. The Navy has 3 gunboats, 4 river patrol craft and 12 small river patrol boats. Personnel (1977) 200.

Air Force. The Air Force has about 300 personnel, 8 MiG-15/17 jet fighters, 1 twin-turbofan F28 Fellowship transport, 1 Frégate and 4 Antonov An-24 turboprop transports, 3 C-47 and 5 Il-14 piston-engined transports, 2 Broussard communications aircraft and 4 Alouette II and Alouette III light helicopters.

INTERNATIONAL RELATIONS

Membership. Congo is a member of UN, OAU and is an ACP state of EEC.

ECONOMY

Budget. The ordinary budget in 1976 balanced at 52,042m. francs CFA. Investment budget (1972) 1,900m. francs CFA.

Currency. The unit of currency is the franc CFA.

ENERGY AND NATURAL RESOURCES

Oil. Oil reserves are estimated at 500–1,000m. tonnes, but production is low. Output 2·5m. tonnes in 1974 (1·8m. tonnes 1976).

Minerals. Lead, zinc and gold (82·8 kg in 1970) are the main minerals. The potash mine at Holle closed in Sept. 1977.

TRADE. Trade with UK (British Department of Trade returns, in £1,000 sterling):

	1972	*1973*	*1974*	*1975*	*1976*	*1977*
Imports to UK	1,698	3,231	5,206	6,765	1,683	1,822
Exports and re-exports from UK	1,074	1,448	1,324	1,460	1,784	3,478

COMMUNICATIONS

Roads. There are 8,270 km of roads, of which 4,500 km are good and 350 are tarred.

Railways. A railway (517 km, 3 ft 6 in. gauge) and a telegraph line connect Brazzaville with Pointe-Noire and a 200 km branch railway links Mont-Belo with Mbinda on the Gabon border.

Aviation. The principal airports are at Maya Maya and Pointe-Noire. In addition there are 22 airfields served by the local airline, Lina-Congo.

Shipping. Pointe-Noire handled (1975) 3·5m. tonnes of goods including manganese from Gabon.

Post. Telephones (1974) numbered 10,181, of which 6,119 were in Brazzaville.

Cinemas. In 1973 there were 7 cinemas with a seating caapicity of 5,100.

DIPLOMATIC REPRESENTATIVES

OF THE CONGO IN GREAT BRITAIN

Ambassador: Alexandre Denguet (resides in Paris).

OF GREAT BRITAIN IN THE CONGO

Ambassador: A. E. Donald (resides in Kinshasa).

OF CONGO TO THE UNITED NATIONS

Ambassador: Nicholas Mondjo.

Diplomatic relations with USA were broken off on 13 Aug. 1965 and re-established 30 Oct 1977.

Chargé d'Affairs: Jay Katzen.

COSTA RICA

República de Costa Rica

Capital: San José
Population: 2m. (1977)
GNP per capita: US$1,040 (1976)

HISTORY. The republic of Costa Rica (the 'Rich Coast') has been independent since 1821, although it formed, from 1824 to 1838, part of the Confederation of Central America.

AREA AND POPULATION. The area is estimated at 50,900 sq. km (19,653 sq. miles). The population at the census of 14 May 1973 was 1,871,780, compared with 800,875 shown in the 1950 census.

The area and official estimate of population for 1 Jan 1977 (2m.) was as follows:

Province	*Population*	*Area (sq. km)*	*Capital*	*Population*
San José	756,583	4,911	San José	233,691
Alajuela	353,837	9,503	Alajuela	35,715
Cartago	223,085	2,600	Cartago	23,675
Heredia	145,169	2,901	Heredia	24,965
Guanacaste	196,169	10,399	Liberia	18,601
Puntarenas	241,684	11,287	Puntarenas	29,851
Limón	127,710	9,301	Limón	27,349

Vital statistics for calendar years:

	Marriages	*Births*	*Deaths*	*Immigration*	*Emigration*
1973	13,047	53,455	9,702	339,888	330,359
1974	14,257	56,769	9,512	...	...
1975	14,683	58,140	9,685	...	...

Crude birth rate, 1974, was 29·5 per 1,000 population; crude death rate, 5; infantile death rate, 37·6 per 1,000 live births; crude marriage rate, 7·4 per 1,000 population. Males exceeded females by 15,088.

The population of European descent, many of them of pure Spanish blood, dwell mostly around the capital of the republic, San José, and in the principal towns of the provinces. Limón, on the Caribbean coast, and Puntarenas, on the Pacific coast, are the chief commercial ports. The United Fruit Company, who in 1941 abandoned their banana plantations on the Atlantic coast in favour of large new plantations on the Pacific coast, have constructed ports at Quepos and Golfito. The Standard Fruit Co. and others have cleared land since 1958 in the Atlantic coast area and now have 2,325 acres producing some 4·2m. stems a year. There are some 15,000 West Indians, mostly in Limón province. The indigenous Indian population is dwindling and is now estimated at 1,200.

Spanish is the language of the country.

CONSTITUTION AND GOVERNMENT. The constitution, promulgated on 7 Dec. 1871, has been modified very frequently, last in 1949. The constitution forbids the establishment or maintenance of an army. The legislative power is normally vested in a single chamber called the Legislative Assembly, which since 1962 consists of 57 deputies, 1 for every 25,214 inhabitants, elected for 4 years. The President is elected for 4 years; the candidate receiving the largest vote, provided it is over 40% of the total, is declared elected, but a second ballot is required if no candidate gets 40% of the total. By the election law of 18 Jan. 1946 all citizens who are 20 years of age are entitled to vote; married men and teachers, from the age of 18. Women over 21 were enfranchised in 1949. Elections are normally held on the first Sunday in February. Voting for President, Deputies and Municipal Councillors is secret and compulsory for all men under 70 years of age. Independent non-party candidates are barred from the ballot.

President: Rodrigo Carazo Odio, elected 5 Feb. 1978 and assumed office 8 May 1978.

Elections for the Legislative Assembly took place on 5 Feb. 1978; Opposition Party, 27; National Liberation Party, 25; People United, 3; Popular Front, 1; Cartago Agricultural Union, 1.

The administration is carried on by 13 ministers, appointed by the President. The powers of the President are limited by the constitution, which leaves him the power to appoint and remove at will members of his cabinet. All other public appointments are made jointly in the names of the President and of the minister in charge of the department concerned.

National flag: Five unequal stripes of blue, white, red, white, blue, with the national arms on a white disc near the hoist.

National anthem: Noble patria, tu hermosa bandera (words by J. M. Zeledón, 1903; tune by M. M. Gutiérrez, 1851).

DEFENCE.

Army. The Army was abolished in 1948, and replaced by a Civil Guard reputed to be 5,000 strong. There has never been compulsory military service or training.

Navy. The republic has 1 motor launch and 1 armed tug on the Atlantic coast and 3 small coastal patrol craft on the Pacific coast for revenue purposes, a tug and smaller craft. Personnel (1977) 50.

INTERNATIONAL RELATIONS

Membership. Costa Rica is a member of UN and OAS.

ECONOMY

Budget. The revenue and expenditure (in 1,000 colones) have been as follows (US$1 = 8·60 colones) for calendar years:

	1972	*1973*	*1974*	*1975*	*1976*	*1977*
Revenue	1,390,523	2,029,000	2,366,000	...	4,160,000	4,683,000
Expenditure	1,414,312	1,865,400	2,270,400	...	4,160,000	4,683,000

The income-tax law of 10 March 1972 raised the maximum rate to 50% for personal incomes of 350,000 colones and over, and to 40% for corporate incomes of 1m. colones and over.

Central government debt on 31 Dec. 1972 was 2,628m. colones. Debt service required 214·5m. colones in 1973.

Currency. A dual exchange rate was introduced June 1971. The official rate in April 1974 was ₡8·54 (buying) and ₡8·60 (selling) = US$1. The free market rate is ₡8·54 (buying) and ₡8·60 (selling) = US$1. The official rate is used for all imports on an essential list and by the Government and autonomous institutions. The free rate is for all other transactions.

The currency is chiefly notes. The Banco Central in 1951 printed and placed in circulation new notes for 5, 10, 20, 50, 100, 500 and 1,000 colones, replacing old notes previously issued by the Banco Nacional. Silver coins of 1 colone, 50 centimos and 25 centimos were in 1935 replaced by coins (2 and 1 colones and 50 and 25 centimos) made up of 3 parts copper and 1 part nickel, and given the same value as the subsidiary silver currency. There are copper coins (and chromium stainless steel coins) of 10 and 5 centimos.

Banking. By a law passed on 28 Jan. 1950 a Central Bank was established for the organization and direction of the national monetary system and of dealings in foreign exchange, the promotion of facilities for credit and the supervision of all banking operations in the country. The bank has a board of 7 directors appointed by the Government, including *ex officio* the Minister of Finance and the Planning

Office Director. On 31 Dec. 1974 it had foreign exchange of US$43·3m., compared with US$61·2m. in Dec. 1973; circulating media on 31 Dec. 1969 totalled 992·7m. colones.

In June 1948 the 3 small commercial banks were compulsorily nationalized; they held deposits of 1,005·3m. colones at 31 Aug. 1970 (962·1m. at 31 Dec. 1970).

The National Insurance Institute (*Instituto Nacional de Seguros*) is a Government organization, created in 1924, which has a monopoly of new insurance business.

Weights and Measures. The metric system is legally established; but in the country districts the following old Spanish weights and measures are found: *libra* = 1·014 lb. avoirdupois; *arroba* = 25·35 lb. avoirdupois; *quintal* = 101·40 lb. avoirdupois, and *fanega* = 11 Imperial bushels.

ENERGY AND NATURAL RESOURCES

Electricity. Electricity, derived from water power in the highlands, is increasingly used as motive power. Output, 1972, was 1,207m. kwh.

Minerals. Gold output is about 3,000 troy oz. per year. Salt production from sea water is about 10,000 tonnes annually. Haematite ore was discovered on the Nicoya Peninsula late in 1960 and sulphur near San Carlos in 1966. The United Nations have offered US$1m. towards a 3-year mining survey.

Agriculture. Agriculture is the principal industry. The cultivated area is about 1m. acres; grass lands cover 1·8m. acres; forests and woodlands, 9,855,000 acres. There are thousands of square miles of public lands that have never been cleared, on which can be found quantities of rosewood, cedar, mahogany and other cabinet woods. The principal agricultural products are coffee, bananas, sugar and cattle. Coffee normally accounts for about half the country's foreign-exchange earnings. Cocoa, maize, sugar, tobacco, rice and potatoes are commonly cultivated. The distillation of spirits is a government monopoly.

Coffee production in 1973–74 was 2·08m. quintals. Sugar production (1974–75) 3·5m. quintals.

Dairy-farming and cattle-raising are substantial pursuits. In 1973 cattle numbered 1·7m. and pigs 215,792.

Costa Rica is the seat of the Inter-American Institute of Agricultural Sciences, with headquarters at Turrialba.

INDUSTRY AND TRADE

Industry. A Ministry of Industry was formed in 1961, but industry is still on a small scale, though the Industrial Development and Protection Law of 1959 affords several facilities and advantages. Main manufactured goods are foodstuffs, textiles, fertilizers, pharmaceuticals, furniture, cement, tyres, canning, clothing, plastic goods, plywood and electrical equipment.

Industrial production was valued at 1·499m. colones in 1972, compared with 1·271m. in 1964.

Labour. As Costa Rica is still essentially an agricultural country, the organization of labour has made progress only in the larger centres of population, and even there it is not a strong movement. There are two main trade unions, *Rerum Novarum* (anti-Communist) and *Confederación General de Trabajadores Costarricenses* (Communist). It is estimated that they have under 10,000 members each. In addition there were (1963) 284 other trade unions and 34 employers' organizations.

Commerce. The value of imports into and exports from Costa Rica in 5 years was as follows in US$ (8·60 colones = US$1):

	1972	*1973*	*1974*	*1975*	*1976*
Imports	372,774,993	455,325,527	719,622,852	693,969,367	770,412,000
Exports	280,876,602	344,464,409	440,344,113	455,960,193	555,405,000

The value (in US$1m.) of the principal imports in 1976 were: Manufactures, 245·7; machinery, including transport equipment, 234·3; chemicals, 129·5; fuel and mineral oils, 73·8; foodstuffs, 55·6.

Chief exports (in US$1m.) in 1976 were: Manufactured goods and other products, 198·8; coffee, 164·9 (mostly to Federal Republic of Germany and USA); bananas, 131·1 (virtually all to USA); sugar, 22·7; cocoa, 6·9.

Total trade between UK and Costa Rica (British Department of Trade returns, in £1,000 sterling):

	1973	*1974*	*1975*	*1976*	*1977*
Imports to UK	771	1,085	8,946	496	1,378
Exports and re-exports from UK	7,257	7,025	9,144	8,614	10,647

Tourism. There was a total of 281,548 visitors in 1974.

COMMUNICATIONS

Roads. About 3,250 km of all-weather motor roads are open. On the Costa Rica section of the Inter-American Highway it is possible to motor to Panama during the dry season. The Pan-American Highway into Nicaragua is metalled for most of the way and there is now a good highway open almost to Puntarenas. Motor vehicles, 1973, numbered 86,460.

Railways. The nationalized railway system (*Ferrocarriles de Costa Rica*), totalling 602 km (3 ft 6 in. gauge), connect San José with Limón, the Atlantic port, and San José with Puntarenas, the Pacific port.

Aviation. Passenger movement in and out of Costa Rica is almost entirely by air *via* the local company, LACSA, PANAM and TACA. LACSA links San José by daily services with all the more important towns. The international airport at Juan Santamaría was opened in June 1955.

Shipping. In 1973, 1,606 ships entered and cleared the ports of the republic (Puerto Limón, Puntarenas and Golfito); combined cargo, 2,840,239 tonnes.

Post and Broadcasting. A telephone service covering (1976) 111,812 subscribers operates in and between San José and 6 other provincial centres; it has been transferred to a government Instituto Costarricense de Electricidad, which is installing a nationwide automatic system, and will eventually control all telecommunications.

The commercial wireless telegraph stations are operated by Cia Radiográfica Internacional de Costa Rica. The stations are located at Cartago, Limón, Puntarenas, Quepos and Golfito. The Government has 19 wireless telegraph stations in its local network. The principal or central station at San José also maintains international radio-telegraph circuits to Nicaragua, Honduras, San Salvador and Mexico. The Government has 202 telegraph offices and 88 official telephone stations. The official list of broadcasting stations shows 28 long-wave stations and 7 short-wave stations. Television was inaugurated in May 1960; there are 4 stations.

Cinemas (1975). Cinemas numbered 143, with seating capacity of 98,000.

Newspapers (1976). There were 6 daily newspapers all published in San José.

JUSTICE, RELIGION, EDUCATION AND WELFARE

Justice. Justice is administered by the Supreme Court, 4 appeal courts and the Court of Cassation. There are also subordinate courts in the separate provinces and local justices throughout the republic. Capital punishment may not be inflicted.

Religion. Roman Catholicism is the religion of the State, which contributes to its maintenance but controls the Church Patronage and insists on lay instruction in history, economics and similar subjects; there is entire religious liberty under the constitution, but religious appeals are forbidden in current political discussions. The Archbishop of Costa Rica has 4 bishops at Alajuela, Limón, San Isidro el General and Tilarán.

Protestants number about 40,000.

Education. Costa Rica has a very low illiteracy rate. Elementary instruction is compulsory and free; secondary education (since 1949) is also free. Elementary schools are provided and maintained by local school councils, while the national government pays the teachers, besides making subventions in aid of local funds. In 1976 there were 2,936 public primary schools with 13,226 teachers and administrative staff and 375,108 enrolled pupils; there were 225 public and private secondary schools with 143,390 pupils. The University of Costa Rica, founded in San José in 1843, has 1,195 professors in 13 faculties and 24,256 students. A medical school was opened in 1961. The budget for 1971 provides C250m. for public education. Since 1944 English has been taught in all secondary schools.

Social Welfare. The labour code of 1943 provides considerable protection for the workers, while a system of social insurance against sickness covering 130,024 workers in 1965, old age and death covering 68,949, is gradually being extended throughout the country.

DIPLOMATIC REPRESENTATIVES

OF COSTA RICA IN GREAT BRITAIN
(34 Chelwood Gdns., Richmond, Surrey)

Ambassador: (Vacant).

OF GREAT BRITAIN IN COSTA RICA
(3202 Paseo Colon, Apartado 10056, San José)

Ambassador and Consul-General: K. Hamylton Jones.

OF COSTA RICA IN THE USA
(2112 S St., NW, Washington D.C., 20008)

Ambassador: Ing. Rodolfo Silva.

OF THE USA IN COSTA RICA
(Avenida 3, Calle 1, San José)

Ambassador: Marvin Weissman.

OF COSTA RICA TO THE UNITED NATIONS

Ambassador: Fernando Salazar.

Books of Reference

Statistical Information: Official statistics are issued by the Director General de Estadística (Ministerio de Industria y Comercio, San José) as they become available. The compilation of statistics was started in 1861.

Bell, J. P., *Crisis in Costa Rica.* London and Austin, USA, 1971
Biesanz, J. and M., *Costa Rican Life.* 3rd printing. New York, 1946
Fernández Guardia, L., *Historia de Costa Rica.* 2nd ed., 2 vols. San José, 1941
Sandner, G., *Agrarkolonisation in Costa Rica.* Kiel, 1961
Trejos, Juan, *Geografía ilustrada de Costa Rica.* San José, 1948
uardia, L., *Historica de Costa Rica.* 2nd ed., 2 vols. San José, 1941
Sandner, G., *Agrarkolonisation in Costa Rica.* Kiel, 1961
Trejos, Juan, *Geografía ilustrada de Costa Rica.* San José, 1948

CUBA

República de Cuba

Capital: Havana
Population: 9·47m. (1976)
GNP per capita: US$860 (1976)

HISTORY. Cuba, except for the brief British occupancy in 1762–63, remained a Spanish possession from its discovery by Columbus in 1492 until 10 Dec. 1898, when the sovereignty was relinquished under the terms of the Treaty of Paris, which ended the struggle of the Cubans against Spanish rule. Cuba thus became an independent republic, but the United States stipulated under the 'Platt Amendment' (abrogated by Roosevelt in 1934) that Cuba must enter into no treaty relations with a foreign power, which might endanger its independence. A convention which assembled on 5 Nov. 1900 adopted the first constitution of the republic on 21 Feb. 1901.

The revolutionary movement against the Batista dictatorship, led by Dr Fidel Castro, started on 26 July 1953 (now a national holiday). It achieved power on 1 Jan. 1959 when Batista fled the country.

An invasion force of émigrés and adventurers landed in Cuba on 17 April 1961; the main body was defeated at the Bay of Pigs (Las Villas province) and mopped up by 20 April.

The US Navy blockaded Cuba from 22 Oct. to 22 Nov. 1962.

AREA AND POPULATION. The island of Cuba forms the largest and most westerly of the Greater Antilles group and lies 135 miles south of the tip of Florida, USA. It has an area of 44,206 sq. miles (114,524 sq. km); the Isle of Pines has 1,180 sq. miles, and other islands about 1,350 sq. miles. Estimated population in 1977 was 9·47m.

The area, population and density of population of the 6 provinces were as follows (1970 census):

	Area (sq. miles)	*Population*
Pinar del Rio	5,211	542,423
Havana[1]	3,173	2,335,344
Matanzas	3,259	501,273
Las Villas	8,264	1,362,179
Camagüey	10,169	813,204
Oriente	14,128	2,998,972
Total	44,206	8,553,395

[1] Isle of Pines, 30,103.

The country was divided in 14 politico administrative areas replacing the existing 6 provinces in 1976.

The chief towns (with population, census 1970) are: Havana, the capital, 1,735,360; Holguín, 422,329; Santa Clara, 331,655; Santiago de Cuba, 275,970; Cienfuegos, 225,615; Camagüey, 196,854; Matanzas, 160,097; Guantánamo, 131,466.

CONSTITUTION AND GOVERNMENT. The constitution has been suspended since Jan. 1959. The first socialist Constitution came into force on 24 Feb. 1976.

Since the last representative in Cuba of the King of Spain, Gen. Don Adolfo Jiménez Castellanos, handed over the island on 1 Jan. 1899 the following have been at the head of the administration:

	Took office
US Military Governors	
Maj.-Gen. John R. Brooke	1 Jan. 1899
Maj.-Gen. Leonard Wood	23 Dec. 1899
President of the Republic	
Tomas Estrada Palma	20 May 1902
	res. 28 Sept. 1906
US Provisional Governors	
William Howard Taft	29 Sept. 1906
Charles Edward Magoon	13 Oct. 1906
Presidents of the Republic	
Gen. José Miguel Gómez	28 Jan. 1909
Gen. Mario Garcia Menocal	20 May 1913
Dr Alfredo Zayas y Alfonso	20 May 1921
Gen. Gerardo Machado y Morales	20 May 1925
	dep. 12 Aug. 1933

	Took office
Dr Carlos Manuel de Céspedes	12 Aug. 1933
	dep. 5 Sept. 1933
Dr Ramón Grau San Martín	10 Sept. 1933
	res. 15 Jan. 1934
Col. Carlos Mendieta	Jan. 1934
	res. 12 Dec. 1935
Dr José A. Barnet	12 Dec. 1935
Dr Miguel Mariano Gómez y Arias	20 May 1936
	impeached 23 Dec. 1936
Dr Federico Laredo Bru	24 Dec. 1936
Gen. Fulgencio Batista y Zaldivar	10 Oct. 1940
Dr Ramón Grau San Martín	10 Oct. 1944
Dr Carlos Prío Socarrás	10 Oct. 1948
	dep. 10 March 1952
Gen. Fulgencio Batista y Zaldívar	10 March 1952
	abdicated 1 Jan. 1959

President: Dr Fidel Castro Ruz became President of the Council of State on 3 Dec. 1976. He is also President of the Council of Ministers and First Secretary of the Cuban Communist Party.

Minister for Foreign Affairs: Isidoro Malmierca Peoli.

Dr Castro on 2 Dec. 1961 proclaimed 'a Marxist–Leninist programme adapted to the precise objective conditions existing in our country'. The provisional *Organizaciones Revolucionarias Integradas* (ORI) were established as an intermediate stage towards a single (communist) party, and gave way to the *Partido Unido de la Revolución Socialista* (PURS). This brought together the *Partido Socialista Popular*, *Movimiento de 26 Julio* and (Students') *Directorio Revolucionario*. The PURS in turn became (3 Oct. 1965) the *Partido Comunista de Cuba*. The Communist Party had been outlawed by Batista in 1954, but legally reinstated after the revolution.

National flag: 3 blue, 2 white stripes (horizontal); a white 5-pointed star in a red triangle at the hoist.

National anthem: Al combate corred bayameses (words and tune by P. Figueredo, 1868).

Local Government. The country is divided into 14 provinces and 169 municipalities. Local Government is the responsibility of the organizations of Peoples' Power. Elections were held in 1976 for delegates to the provincial municipal assemblies and to the national assembly.

DEFENCE. The chief of the armed forces is *Comandante en Jefe* Fidel Castro, and his brother *Gen. de Ejercito* Raúl Castro Ruz, First Vice-President of the Council of State and Minister of Defence.

On 13 Nov. 1963 conscription was introduced for all men between the ages of 17 and 45 (3 years); women of the 17–35 age groups may volunteer (for 2 years).

Army. The strength was 160,000 officers and men in 1977. Reserves are estimated at 90,000.

The Army is organized in 15 infantry brigades, 3 armoured brigades, 8 independent battalions. It has over 600 Russian-built tanks. Para-military forces total 13,000 and the People's Militia, 100,000.

Navy. The Navy consists of 26 missile boats, 18 patrol vessels, 24 torpedo boats, 12 motor launches, 18 coastguard vessels, 6 survey vessels, 7 landing craft and 9 service craft. Personnel in 1977 totalled 6,000 officers and ratings. A very small and ancient cruiser, 3 old patrol frigates, 1 patrol escort (PCER) and 2 auxiliary coastguard cutters were operationally discarded in 1973 although one of the frigates still exists as a harbour ship. The USA is still in possession of the Guantánamo naval base, but the revolutionary government refuses to accept the nominal rent of US$5,000 per annum.

Air Force. The Air Force has been extensively re-equipped with aircraft supplied by USSR and in 1977 had a strength of some 20,000 officers and men and 200 combat aircraft. About 7 interceptor and 4 ground-attack squadrons fly MiG-21, MiG-19 and MiG-17 jet fighters, supplemented by Su-7B jet attack aircraft. There is a squadron of Il-14 twin-engined transports; some An-24 twin-turboprop transports, and Mi-4 helicopters, Zlin 326 piston-engined trainers and MiG-15UTI jet trainers. Many An-2M biplanes are operated by the Air Force, mainly on agricultural duties. Soviet-built surface-to-air ('Guideline' and 'Goa') and coastal defence ('Samlet') missiles are in service.

INTERNATIONAL RELATIONS

Membership. Cuba is a member of the UN and COMECON.

ECONOMY

Planning. The Cuban economy is now centrally planned. Since July 1972 Cuba has been a member of the Council for Mutual Economic Assistance (COMECON) and, since Jan. 1974, of the two COMECON international banks. Cuba has very large reserves of nickel and a guaranteed market in the USSR; output is currently some 36,000 tons per annum but it is to be increased to 60,000 tons after 1980. Sugar remains the mainstay of the economy. Investment in this and other agricultural sectors (rice, coffee, and dairy products) has recently been relatively high but output generally has failed to respond. Some items of food and clothing are rationed.

Budget. Revenue and expenditure (in 1m. pesos) for calendar years balanced as follows: 1963, 2,903·6; 1964, 2,399; 1965, 2,536.

The 1965 expenditure included (in 1m. pesos): Agriculture, forestry and fishery, 367·9; industry, 194·4; commerce, 14·2; communications, 12·9; transport, 41·6; basic community services, 128·7; education, 219; central, provincial and local administration, 143·8; labour, 173·8; industries, 194·4.

During 1960 long-term loans at low interest were negotiated with the following countries (expressed in US$1m.): USSR, 100; China, 60; Czechoslovakia, 40; Romania, 15; Hungary, 15; Poland, 12; German Democratic Republic, 10; Bulgaria, 5. The USSR is now subsidizing Cuba by permitting the accumulation in Soviet–Cuban trade of deficits which by 1965 exceeded US$600m.

Currency. The Cuban *peso* has been tied to the French franc since early 1972. In Sept. 1977, the sterling–peso rate was £1 = 1·38 *pesos*. The gold content is 0·888671 gramme of fine gold, thus 1 troy oz. of fine gold = 35 *pesos*. The law of 7 Nov. 1914, established that the monetary unit was a gold *peso* (equal to the US gold dollar) of 1·6718 grammes (1·5046 grammes fine) divided into 100 *centavos*. The old gold *pesos* and all US currency are no longer legal tender.

Copper–nickle coins of 40, 20, 5 and 1 *cent* are issued. Notes are for 100, 50, 20, 10, 5 and 1 *peso*.

Banking. On 23 Dec. 1948 the president signed the law creating a central bank (with capital of US$10m.) and which began operating on 27 April 1950.

On 14 Oct. 1960 all banks were nationalized, except the Royal Bank of Canada and the Bank of Nova Scotia, which were bought out later. All banking is now carried out by the National Bank of Cuba, through its 250 agencies. In 1964, 1·6m. small savings accounts totalled US$738m.

All insurance business was nationalized in Jan. 1964.

Weights and Measures. The metric system of weights and measures is legally compulsory, but the American and old Spanish systems are much used. The sugar industry uses the Spanish long ton (1·03 tonnes) and short ton (0·92 tonne). Cuba sugar sack = 329·59 lb. or 149·49 kg. Land is measured in *caballerías* (of 13·4 hectares or 33 acres).

ENERGY AND NATURAL RESOURCES

Electricity. Installed capacity 1974 was 1,673·6 mw. Production in 1963 was 2,529m. kwh.

Minerals. Iron ore abounds, with deposits estimated at 3,500m. tons, of which 90% were held as reserves by American steel interests but are now controlled by the Cuban Mining Institute; output (tonnes), wrought iron (1971), 111,107; steel (1971), 110,803.

Output of copper (1974) was 290 tonnes; refractory chrome (1974), 37,700 tonnes. Other minerals are nickel (1974: 33,900 tons nickel content), cobalt, silica and barytes. Gold and silver are also worked. Cuba has a small output of petroleum (1971: 4·3m. tonnes). Salt output from the solar evaporation of sea water was 138,300 tonnes in 1974.

All mineral resources were nationalized in 1960.

Agriculture. In May 1959 all land over 30 *caballerías* was nationalized and has since been turned into state farms. In Oct. 1963 private holdings were reduced to a maximum of 5 *caballerías* (approximately 67 hectares). By 1960, 764 co-operative farms had been formed, and by late 1966 almost 65% of farm land was state-owned; the balance being in private hands.

In 1963 the total cultivated land included 432,461 hectares under the Credit and Services Co-operative, and 509 people's farms (3,820,112 hectares).

The staple products are tobacco and sugar, of which latter Cuba is the world's second largest producer; with its by-products it furnishes nearly 80% by value of the national exports. The 1973–74 crop was 5·9m. tons. There are 152 mills, including 40 of the largest, which were taken over from US interests, and which represent 39% of total capacity. Coffee, cotton, maize, rice and potatoes are grown.

In 1974 production of other important crops was (in tonnes): Tobacco, 44,700; rice, 436,000; maize, 24,900; coffee 33,000.

Tobacco is grown mainly in the Vuelta–Abajo district, near Pinar del Río. Coffee is grown chiefly in the province of Oriente.

Output of henequén fibre in 1964 was 233,919 tons. A fast-growing fibre, *kenaf*, originally from India, soft in texture, is replacing jute for sacking; the tobacco industry uses *majagua*, another local fibre, while a third fibre, *yarey*, from palms is also used. 88,000 tonnes of potatoes were produced in 1974. A nitrate plant has been built at Nuevitas and a large British-built urea plant at Cienfuegos. The principal fruits exported are pineapples, citrus fruit, tomatoes and pimentos. Pángola is an increasingly important forage crop (15,000 *caballerías* in 1960). A rice cultivation plan began in 1967 in the south of Havana province. Cultivation is highly mechanized and the area so far sown produces two crops a year.

Despite the devastation caused by hurricane Flora in Oct. 1963, citrus fruit production, 112,000 tons in 1964, was some 11·4% above 1963. In 1974 production was 176,000 tonnes.

In 1962, 2,105 *caballerías* were allocated to cotton; cotton produced, 1964, was 2,653 tons against 13,000 tons in 1962.

In 1976 the livestock included 1·5m. hogs; 800,000 horses; 300,000 sheep, 92,000 goats; 5·5m. head of cattle.

Forestry. Cuba has extensive forest lands. These forests contain valuable cabinet woods, such as mahogany and cedar, besides dye-woods, fibres, gums, resins and oils. Cedar is used locally for cigar-boxes, and mahogany is exported. During the re-forestation campaign of 1959–60, 34,000 eucalyptus saplings were planted over 1,120 *caballerías*. Cedars, mahogany, *majagua*, teca, etc., are also being raised and planted out. Between 1960 and 1963 plantings included (in hectares): Pine, 9,947·81; eucalyptus, 52,699·43; *majagua preciosa*, 34,432·06; casuarina, 9,615·61.

INDUSTRY AND TRADE

Industry. Production in 1974 was: Cotton, 133·3m. sq. metres; rayon yarn, 5·7m. sq. metres; wheat flour, 184,300 tonnes; gasoline, 868,100 tonnes; 391,000 tyres; 246,000 tubes; shoes, 13·5m. pairs; paint, 201,000 hectolitres; soft drinks (1973), 1,795,600 hectolitres; cigarettes, 14·5m.; fertilizers, 728,000 tonnes.

Trade Unions. All trade unions are government-controlled. These are autonomous and are a counterweight to administration; they are not directly controlled by the Government but participate actively in social, political and mass organizations.

Commerce. Official Cuban statistics of imports and exports (including bullion and specie) for calendar years (in 1m. pesos):

	1971	*1972*	*1973*	*1974*	*1975*
Imports (c.i.f.)	1,387·5	1,189·8	1,467·0	2,225·9	3,113·1
Exports (f.o.b.)	861·2	770·9	1,153·8	2,236·5	2,946·6

Cuba's principal exports are sugar, minerals, tobacco and fish, which in 1974 were planned to furnish 86%, 6·4%, 2·7% and 2·3% respectively by value. The main imports from non-Communist countries are chemicals and engineering and electrical machinery and transport equipment.

Sugar accounts for approximately 80% of the exports. In 1973 over 2m. tons were sold in free world markets, the balance going mainly to Eastern Europe under long-term guaranteed price contracts. Tobacco, fish and nickel are the other major exports. Most trade is with Eastern Europe, particularly with the USSR which supplies approximately 50% of total Cuban imports.

Total trade between Cuba and UK (British Department of Trade returns, in £1,000 sterling):

	1972	*1973*	*1974*	*1975*	*1976*	*1977*
Imports to UK	5,039	13,250	19,952	6,318	25,602	9,732
Exports and re-exports from UK	16,732	17,538	23,926	36,977	42,925	27,455

COMMUNICATIONS

Roads. There are 27,013 km of highways open to traffic, including the Central Highway, traversing the island for 760 miles from Pinar del Río to Santiago. On 31 Dec. 1958 passenger automobiles numbered 143,828; hire cars, 29,710; coaches and buses, 4,306; lorries, 42,480; others, 12,987.

Railways. There are 5,053 km of public railway (mainly 4 ft 8½ in. gauge) owned by the National Railways (*Ferrocarriles Nacionales de Cuba*) formed on nationalization in 1960. In addition, the large sugar estates have 9,441 km of lines connecting them with the main lines.

Aviation. The state airline CUBANA operates all internal services, and from Havana to Mexico City, Madrid, Berlin, Montreal and Prague, and also to Lima, Panama, Kingston, Bridgetown, Port of Spain, Georgetown. The other regular foreign services are Mexican, Spanish, Soviet, Czech, German, Canadian and Belgian. In Dec. 1977 the first regular flights since 1960 started operating between USA and Cuba.

Shipping. The coastline is over 3,500 miles long and has many fine harbours. The merchant marine, in 1974, consisted of 51 sea-going vessels of over 550,000 DWT.

Post and Broadcasting. There are 3,545 miles of public and 8,902 miles of private telegraph wires. Cuba has 103 broadcasting stations and 2 television stations. Radio receiving sets, 1974, numbered 909,000; television sets, 300,000. The national telephone system (1972) had 274,949 instruments.

Cinemas (1972). There are 439 cinemas with seating capacity of 294,300.

Newspapers (1976). The government-controlled press includes 1 morning and 1 evening newspaper in Havana.

JUSTICE, RELIGION, EDUCATION AND WELFARE

Justice. There is a Supreme Court in Havana and 7 courts of appeal (one in each provincial capital and one in Holguín). The provinces are divided into judicial districts, with courts for civil and criminal actions, with municipal courts for minor offences. The civil code guaranteed aliens the same property and personal rights as are enjoyed by nationals.

The 1959 Agrarian Reform Law and the Urban Reform Law passed on 14 Oct. 1960 have placed certain restrictions on both. Revolutionary Summary Tribunals will have wide powers.

Religion. There is no state Church, though Roman Catholics predominate. There is a bishop of the American Episcopal Church in Havana; there are large congregations of Methodists in Havana and in the provinces. Protestants numbered 265,000 in 1962; they have been organized as the Cuban Council of Evangelical Churches. Dr Castro has promised that the State will not interfere with the freedom of religion.

Education. Education is compulsory (between the ages of 6 and 14) and free, and now available everywhere. The 1953 census showed that 22·8% of all those over 10 years of age were illiterate. It is claimed that the Year of Education (1961), in which higher-education students went out to all parts of the country, reduced this to 3·9%. In 1964 illiteracy was officially declared to have been completely eliminated.

In 1969–70 the 3 universities had 30,708 students. Primary schools had 1,560,193 pupils; general secondary schools, 700,000 pupils (1976); technical schools, 42,507 pupils; teachers' colleges, 35,000 students (1976); other schools (*e.g.*, for fishermen), 17,862 pupils; adult education classes, 404,149 pupils. In 1962–63 a system of 'popular teachers' was introduced, who teach in primary schools while in training; they numbered 11,985 in March 1964.

The Camilo Cienfuegos school city in the Sierra Maestra was designed for 12,000 boys and 8,000 girls by 1970 (1965: 4,000, total). In 1974 the V. I. Lenin vocational school opened as a forerunner of 6 such schools.

Health (1964). There were 4,855 posts for doctors, 154 hospitals with 47,861 beds. The 1965 health budget was $140·5m.

Free medical services are provided by the state polyclinics, though some doctors still have private practices. All serious tropical diseases are effectively kept under control, and virtually all children under the age of 15 have been vaccinated against poliomyelitis.

DIPLOMATIC REPRESENTATIVES

OF CUBA IN GREAT BRITAIN (57 Kensington Ct., London, W8 5DQ)

Ambassador: Jorge A. Bolaños.

OF GREAT BRITAIN IN CUBA
(Edificio Bolivar, Capdevilla 101–103, Havana)

Ambassador: J. E. Jackson, CMG.

OF CUBA TO THE UNITED NATIONS

Ambassador: Dr Ricardo Alaron de Quesanda.

The USA broke off diplomatic relations with Cuba on 3 Jan. 1961 but the first steps towards normal relations were taken in Sept. 1977 when missions were opened in both capitals.

Books of Reference

Anuario Estadístico de a República de Cuba. Havana, 1914, 1953, 1957, 1972, 1973 (these only)
Boletín Oficial, Ministerio de Comercio. Monthly
Estadística General: Commercio Exterior. Quarterly and Annual.—*Movimiento de Población.* Monthly and Annual. Havana
Anuario azucarero de Cuba. Havana, from 1937
Aguilar, L. E., *Cuba 1933.* Cornell Univ. Press, 1972
Canet, G., and Raisz, E., *Atlas de Cuba.* Cambridge, Mass., 1949
Carpentier, A., *Reasons of State.* London, 1976
Caute, D., *¿Cuba, yes?* London, 1974
Chaderick, L., *A Cuban Journey.* London, 1975
Draper, T., *Castro's Revolution: Myths and Realities.* New York, 1962.—*Castroism: Theory and Practice.* New York, 1965
Goldenberg, B., *The Cuban Revolution and Latin America.* New York, 1965
Guerra y Sánchez, R., and others, *Historia de la Nación Cubana.* 10 vols. Havana, 1952

Gonzalez, E., *Cuba under Castro: The Limits of Charisma*. Boston, 1974
International Commission of Jurists, *Cuba and the Rule of Law*. Geneva, 1962
Meyer, K. E., and Szulc, T., *The Cuban Invasion*. New York, 1962
Miller, W., *The Lost Plantation*. London, 1961
Montaner, C. A., *Informe secreto sobre la revolución cubana*. Madrid, 1975
Nelson, L., *Cuba: The Measure of the Revolution*. Univ. of Minnesota Press, 1972
Nûñez Jiménez, A., *Geografia de Cuba*. Havana, 1961
O'Connor, J., *The Origins of Socialism in Cuba*. London, Cornell Univ. Press, 1970
Ritter, A. R. M., *The Economic Development of Revolutionary Cuba: Strategy and Performance*. New York, 1974
Suchlicki, J. (ed.), *Cuba, Castro, and Revolution*. Univ. of Miami Press, 1972.—*Cuba: From Columbus to Castro*. New York, 1974
Thomas, H., *Cuba: Or the Pursuit of Freedom*. London, 1971

CYPRUS

Capital: Nicosia
Population: 639,000 (1975)
GNP per capita: US$1,480 (1976)

Kypriaki Dimokratia—Kıbrıs Cumhuriyeti

HISTORY. About the middle of the 2nd millennium B.C. Greek colonies were established in Cyprus and later it formed part of the Persian, Roman and Byzantine empires. In 1193 it became a Frankish kingdom, in 1489 a Venetian dependency and in 1571 was conquered by the Turks. They retained possession of it until its cession to England for administrative purposes under a convention concluded with the Sultan at Constantinople, 4 June 1878. On 5 Nov. 1914 the island was annexed by Great Britain and on 1 May 1925 given the status of a Crown Colony.

For the history of Cyprus from 1931 to 1958 *see* THE STATESMAN'S YEAR-BOOK, 1958, pp. 237–38, and 1959, p. 236.

On 1 April 1955 the Greek Cypriots embarked on a guerrilla struggle against the British. On 19 Feb. 1959, following discussions in Zürich between the Greek and Turkish Foreign Ministers, an agreement was signed in London by the Prime Ministers of Great Britain, Greece and Turkey, and by the representatives of the Greek Cypriots and Turkish Cypriots. This agreement was implemented on 16 Aug. 1960, when Cyprus became an independent republic. By treaties between the Republic of Cyprus, Great Britain, Greece and Turkey both Enosis and partition are precluded; and Britain retains sovereignty over the areas containing her military bases in the island.

When President Makarios proposed some incisive modifications of the Zürich–London agreements, violent clashes between Greek and Turkish Cypriots broke out on 22 Dec. 1963. First, a joint force of British, Greek and Turkish troops and later a UN peace force were sent to Cyprus. A UN mediator on 26 March 1965 submitted proposals for a settlement of the Cyprus problem. These were accepted by Greece and the Greek Cypriots, but rejected by Turkey; thereupon the mediator, Dr Galo Plaza (Ecuador), resigned. The UN General Assembly on 17 Dec. 1965 called upon all states to respect the sovereignty, unity, independence and territorial integrity of Cyprus and to refrain from any intervention.

In June 1968 representatives of the Greek and Turkish Cypriots started talks in Cyprus aiming at finding a solution to the Cyprus problem but without success.

On 15 July 1974 a *coup* was staged in Cyprus by the men of the Greek ruling junta, for the overthrow of President Makarios. The President left the island and the *coup* was short-lived. On 23 July power was handed over to the President of the House of Representatives, Glafcos Clerides, in accordance with the Constitution. He acted as President until the return of President Makarios on Dec. 7.

Turkey invaded the island on 20 July, eventually landing 40,000 troops supported with heavy armament and tanks. In two military operations 20–30 July and 14–16 August the Turkish troops managed to occupy 40% of the northern part of Cyprus. As a result 200,000 Greek Cypriots fled to live as refugees in the south. The Cyprus crisis was raised in the UN and the General Assembly unanimously adopted resolutions calling for the withdrawal of all foreign troops from Cyprus and the return of refugees to their homes, but without result.

On 13 Feb. 1975 at a special joint meeting of the executive council and legislative assembly of the Autonomous Turkish Cypriot Administration a Turkish Cypriot Federated State was proclaimed. Rauf Denktash was appointed President and he declared that the state would not seek international recognition. The proclamation was denounced by President Makarios and the Greek Prime Minister but welcomed by the Turkish Prime Minister.

AREA AND POPULATION. The island lies in the eastern Mediteranean, about 50 miles off the south coast of Turkey and (at the nearest points) 65 miles off the coast of Syria. Area 3,572 sq. miles (9,251 sq. km); about 140 miles is greatest length from east to west, and about 60 miles is greatest breadth from north to south. Populations by religions:

Religion	*1931*	*1946*	*1956*	*1960*	*1973*
Greek Orthodox	276,573	361,199	416,986	441,656	498,511
Turkish Moslem	64,238	80,548	92,642	104,942	116,000
Others	7,148	8,367	19,251	26,968	17,267
Total	347,959	450,114	528,879	573,566	631,778

Population estimate (1975) 639,000, of which 82% are Greek Cypriot (Armenian, Maronite and Latin minorities included) and 18% Turkish Cypriot. Principal towns with populations (1975 estimate): Nicosia (the capital), 147,100; Limassol, 80,600; Famagusta, 39,400; Larnaca, 19,800.

As a result of the Turkish invasion 207,500 Greek Cypriots were made homeless and of these 163,000 are still fully supported.

As a result of the Turkish invasion and the occupation of part of Cyprus, 200,000 Greek Cypriots were displaced and forced to find refuge in the south of the island. The urban centres of Famagusta, Kyrenia and Morphou were completely evacuated.

Vital statistics. The birth rate in 1975 was 16·9%; the death rate, 0·65% (1972); infantile mortality, 2·9%; marriage rate, 10·2%.

CONSTITUTION AND GOVERNMENT. The legislative power is exercised by the House of Representatives of 50 members, of whom 35 were elected by the Greek community and 15 by the Turkish community. As from Dec. 1963 the Turkish members have ceased to attend.

On 13 Dec. 1959 Archbishop Makarios was elected President of the Republic, having received 144,501 votes (against 71,753 cast for the candidate sponsored by the Left). Dr Fazil Kuchuk was elected Vice-President unopposed; he resigned on 4 Jan. 1964. On 13 Feb. 1975, Rauf Denktash the Turkish-Cypriot leader announced the formation of a Turkish-Cypriot state within a federal republic.

In the presidential elections of 25 Feb. 1968 Archbishop Makarios was re-elected President of the Republic, having received 220,911 votes (against 8,577 cast for the opposition candidate and 16,215 abstentions). When he died in July 1977 Spyros Kyprianou became acting President and was proclaimed President on 31 Aug. 1977 and was elected for a 5-year term on 26 Jan. 1978.

Flag: White with a copper-coloured outline of the island with 2 green olive-branches beneath.

The elections held on 5 Sept. 1976 returned 19 Democratic Front, 9 Akel Party (Communists), 4 EDEK (Socialist Party), 3 Independent. The Turks have not participated in the proceedings of the House since Dec. 1963.

On 16 Feb. 1961 the House of Representatives decided by 41 to 9 votes to apply for membership of the Commonwealth. Cyprus was admitted on 13 March.

The President reshuffled the Council of Ministers in March 1978:

External Affairs: Nicos Rolandis. *Finance:* Andreas Patsalides. *Interior and Defence:* Christodoulos Veniamin. *Education:* Chrysostomos Sofianos. *Agriculture and Natural Resources:* George Tombazos. *Commerce and Industry:* Andreas Papageorghiou. *Justice:* Petros Michaelides. *Labour and Social Insurance:* Emilos Theodoulou. *Communications and Works:* Marios Eliades. *Health:* Dr Andreas Mikellides.

DEFENCE. In 1964 compulsory conscription of 6 months was introduced and extended to 24 months in 1967. The National Guard, which was set up in 1964, is a modern and well-equipped force entrusted with the island's defence. The Cyprus Police Force is mainly employed for the maintenance of law and order, the preservation of peace and the prevention and detection of crime.

INTERNATIONAL RELATIONS

Membership. Cyprus is a member of UN, the Commonwealth and the Council of Europe.

ECONOMY

Planning. Under the Emergency Action Plan of 1975–76 the Government invested about £C34m. in restoring and building up manufacturing, agriculture, housing, transport and communications. The resulting budget deficit was met mainly from cash balances and domestic borrowing. Private sector investment at £C68m. met 90% of its required achievement. The Plan aimed at turning output towards foreign markets.

A second plan was launched in 1977 for 2 years; expenditure, 1977, £C26·9m. Agriculture and irrigation have been emphasized (expenditure, 1975–76, £C15·9m.; 1977 (planned) £C10·9m.).

Budget. Revenue and expenditure for calendar years (in £C):

Ordinary	*1972*	*1973*	*1974*	*1975*	*1976*
Revenue	50,816,887	59,603,112	55,207,730	56,02[illegible],900	76,957,000
Expenditure	...	55,239,283	60,840,032	67,745,048	69,727,000
Development					
Expenditure	13,197,714	14,862,832	10,612,936	11,894,869	18,433,000

Main sources of ordinary revenue in 1976 (in £C) were: Import duties, 12,637,915; excise duties, 9,838,424; income tax, 7,444,487; other duties, taxes and licences, 5,317,715; rents, royalties and interest, 5,660,114; fees and charges, 7,319,118; post office, 1,263,036.

Main divisions of ordinary expenditure in 1976 (in £C): Personal emoluments, 29,457,457; pensions and gratuities, 2,542,399; public works, 494,186; commodity subsidies, 5m.; subventions and contributions, 8,189,934; public debt charges, 6,044,327.

Development expenditure for 1976 (in £C) included 1,657,963 for water development, 2,027,834 for agriculture, forests and fisheries, 312,416 for rural development, 1,584,896 for roads, 513,267 for ports and 330,000 for tourism.

The outstanding public debt as at 31 Dec. 1976 was £C25,687,199 and accumulated sinking funds totalled £C3,694,213. Outstanding loans as at 31 Dec. 1976 totalled £C26,017,971; including £C7,883,926 to the Electricity Authority of Cyprus and £C2·98m. to the Cyprus Telecommunications Authority.

Currency. The Cyprus £ is divided into 1,000 *mils*. Notes of the following denominations are in circulation: £5, £1, 500 *mils*, 250 *mils*. Coins in circulation: Cupro-nickel: 100, 50, 25 *mils*; bronze: 5 and 3 *mils*; aluminium: 1 *mil*. Rate of exchange, Sept. 1977: £C = £1.40.

Banking. There is a Central and Issuing Bank exercising monetary functions, and the Cyprus Development Corporation created by the Government as a major source of loan funds for industrial development. Commercial banks carrying on business in Cyprus are: Bank of Cyprus Ltd, Turkish Bank of Nicosia, Banque Populaire de Chypre, Barclays Bank International, The Chartered Bank, National Bank of Greece, Turkiye Ish Bankasi, The Co-operative Central Bank, National & Grindlays Bank and Lombard Banking (Cyprus) Ltd.

The Central Bank of Cyprus, established in 1963, is responsible for the issue of currency, the regulation of money supply and credit, administration of the exchange control law and the foreign-exchange reserves of the Republic. The Bank also acts as a banker of the banks operating in Cyprus and of the Government.

At the end of March 1977 total deposits in banks were £C250m. The country's foreign exchange reserves at the end of Dec. 1976 were £C170m.

Weights and Measures. Cyprus weights and measures follow the standard weights and measures of Great Britain. The metric system may also be lawfully used. In internal trade the following special Cyprus weights and measures are in use: 1 *pic* = $\frac{2}{3}$ yd; 1 *oke* = 2·8 lb.; 1 *kilé* = 8 Imperial gallons. The Cyprus *donum is* approximately $\frac{1}{3}$ acre.

ENERGY AND NATURAL RESOURCES

Minerals. The principal minerals exported during 1976 were (in long tons): Iron pyrites, 145,000; cupreous concentrates, 41,000; asbestos, 33,000; chromium ores and concentrates, 12,000. Mining provided about 29·3% of all exports in 1976. Total value of minerals exported in 1976 was £C7·9m. No figures for copper cement at the Xeros mines as this is the Turkish occupied area.

Agriculture.[1] Chief agricultural products in 1976 (tonnes): Wheat, 34,000; barley, 55,000; olives, 10,000; carobs, 32,000; potatoes, 180,000; grapes, 165,000; wines including commandaria, 10·4m. gallons; oranges, 35,500; lemons, 9,500; grapefruit, 33,000; melons, 3,800; water melons, 21,000; carrots, 9,800; milk, 48,200; meat, 26,530.

Of the island's 2·3m. acres, approximately 1m. are cultivated. About 22·8% of the economically active population are engaged in agriculture.

Livestock in 1976 (in 1,000): Cattle, 17; sheep, 255; goats, 230; pigs, 141.

Forestry. During 1974 the Forest Department continued preserving and developing existing forests and salvaging timber burnt during the Turkish invasion. Estimated forest lost, 22,000 hectares. Total forest area, 670 sq. miles.

In 1974 the chief forest products were lumber, valued at £C199,000; of firewood, £C3,872.

[1] Production statistics for 1974, 1975 and 1976 refer to area of Cyprus not occupied by Turkey.

INDUSTRY AND TRADE

Industry. Cyprus has no heavy industry, but a wide variety of light manufacturing industries. The establishment of a Development Bank in 1963 has given further impetus to industrial activity. Manufacturing industry in 1976 contributed about 15·8% to the gross domestic product and gave employment to 14·5% of the economically active population. The GDP of manufacturing industries in 1976 was estimated at £C47·4m.

Since 1960, £C21m. has been spent on water dams, water supplies, hydrological research and geophysical surveys. Existing dams have (1976) a capacity of 12,825m. gallons as against 1,362m. gallons before independence.

Trade Unions and Associations. Cyprus has trade-union legislation on the lines of the British Trade Union Acts. Registration is compulsory and freedom of association is constitutionally and statutorily guaranteed. At the end of 1974 the trade unions were distributed as follows: Pancyprian Federation of Labour ('old' trade unions), 48,500 members in 16 unions; Cyprus Workers Confederation ('free' labour syndicates), 31,714 members in 47 unions; Pancyprian Federation of Independent Trade Unions, 941 members in 7 unions; Cyprus Turkish Trade Unions Federation, 5,662 members in 13 unions; Cyprus Democratic Labour Federation, 3,500 members in 4 unions; Civil Service and other trade unions, 13,617 members in 22 unions.

The 'old' trade unions are affiliated to the World Federation of Trade Unions, the 'free' labour syndicates and the Turkish Federation are affiliated to the International Confederation of Free Trade Unions.

In Dec. 1974 the total number of employers' associations was 23 with a total membership of 2,680. Most of the employers' associations are members of the Cyprus Employers' Federation, an organization with 11 trade associations consisting of 569 members.

Commerce. The commerce and the shipping, exclusive of coasting trade, for calendar years were (in £ sterling):

	1972	*1973*	*1974*	*1975*	*1976*
Imports[1]	121,480,403	157,442,382	148,027,511	159,192,811	248,868,170
Exports[2]	51,304,770	60,473,595	55,286,670	78,417,357	148,865,397
Bullion imports	518,760	563,942	213,081	957,769	1,252,578

[1] Excluding Naafi imports of about £1·3m. in 1976.
[2] Including re-exports and ships stores of about £28·8m. in 1976.

Chief civil imports, 1976 (in £1,000 sterling):

Meat and preparations	3,436	Textile yarn and fabrics made up	24,067
Sugar	2,744	Cereals and cereal preparations	18,013
Medicines	3,920	Petroleum and petroleum products	35,989
Egg and dairy products	3,656	Gas, natural and manufactured	1,531

Chief domestic exports, 1976 (in £1,000 sterling):

Grapes	3,607	Distilled alcoholic beverages	3,243
Grapefruit	2,963	Asbestos	4,642
Lemons	1,180	Copper cement	—
Oranges	2,889	Cupreous concentrates	4,675
Raisins (including sultanas)	427	Cupreous pyrites	—
Potatoes	24,789	Iron pyrites	897
Carobs: seed and kibbled	1,330	Cement	12,835
Carrots	713	Clothing	11,697
Wine	6,378	Footwear	6,379

In 1976 UK supplied 19·7% of the imports; other parts of the Commonwealth, 3·7%; the European countries, 51·1%; of the exports, 27·7% went to the UK, 2% to other parts of the Commonwealth, 22·1% to the European countries. In 1976 potatoes totalled 17% of all exports; industrial raw materials totalled 33% of all imports.

Total trade between Cyprus and UK (British Department of Trade returns, in £1,000 sterling):

	1972	*1973*	*1974*	*1975*	*1976*	*1977*
Imports to UK	21,690	28,010	30,599	30,365	63,315	79,749
Exports and re-exports from UK	32,709	40,406	38,605	27,155	51,009	82,906

Tourism. Foreign tourists (1976), 214,695.

COMMUNICATIONS

Roads. In 1975 the total length of roads was 9,686 km, of which 4,462 km were paved and 5,224 km were earth or gravel roads. The main paved roads which are maintained by the Ministry of Communications and Works (Public Works Department) totalled 2,365 km, of which 2,268 km were paved. The total of urban streets was 1,508 km, of which 1,001 were paved. Village roads and streets totalled 4,053 km, of which 1,192 km were paved, the rest being of earth or gravel surface. There were also 1,761 km of unpaved forest roads.

The area controlled by the Government of the Republic and that occupied by Turkey are now served by separate transport systems, and there are no services linking the two areas.

Aviation. Nicosia airport is the only civil airport of the country and has been closed since Aug. 1974. During 1976, 398,036 persons travelled and 13·9m. kg of commercial air-freight was handled through the airport.

Shipping. In 1976, 4,162 ships of 4,235,620 net tons entered and 4,134 of 4,212,950 cleared Cyprus ports. Ships under Cyprus registry (1976) numbered 1,006 of 2,967,946 tons. Famagusta has been closed to international traffic since Aug. 1974.

Post and Broadcasting (1976). There were 37 post offices and 599 postal agencies. There are 17 post offices and 368 postal agencies in the Turkish occupied area. Telephones (1977) 77,163. Wireless licences issued (1974) were 176,143, including television licences.

Cyprus Broadcasting Corporation broadcasts mainly in Greek, but also in Turkish, English, and Armenian on medium-waves. The corporation also broadcasts one TV programme.

Cinemas (1976). In the Greek part of Cyprus there were 66 winter cinemas (38,500 seats) and 17 open-air cinemas (9,700 seats).

Newspapers (1976). There are 1 English, 3 Turkish and 8 Greek daily newspapers and 11 Greek and 1 Turkish weeklies.

JUSTICE, RELIGION, EDUCATION AND WELFARE

Justice. Under the Constitution and other legislation in force the following judicial institutions are established: The Supreme Court of the Republic, the Assize Courts, District Courts and Communal and Ecclesiastical Courts.

The Supreme Court is composed of 5–7 judges (at present 6), one of whom is the President. The Supreme Court adjudicates exclusively and finally: on all constitutional and administrative law matters, including any recourse that any law or decision of the House of Representatives or the budget is discriminatory against either of the two Communities; on any conflict of competence between state organs, questions of unconstitutionality of any law or decisions on any question of interpretation of the Constitution in case of ambiguity, as well as recourses for annulment of administrative acts, decisions or omissions. The Supreme Court is the highest appellate court in the Republic and has jurisdiction to hear and determine all appeals from any court. It has exclusive jurisdiction to issue orders in the nature of *habeas corpus*, *mandamus*, prohibition, *quo warranto* and *certiorari* and in admiralty and matrimonial matters.

There are 6 Assize Courts and 6 District Courts, one for each district. The Assize Courts have unlimited criminal jurisdiction and power to order compensation up to £C800. The District Courts exercise original civil and criminal jurisdiction, the extent of which varies with the composition of the Bench. In civil matters (other than those within the original jurisdiction of Supreme Court) a District Court composed of not less than 2 and not more than 3 judges has unlimited jurisdiction. A President or a District Judge sitting alone has jurisdiction up to £C500, and is also empowered to deal with any action for the recovery of possession of any immovable property, and certain other specified matters. In criminal matters the jurisdiction of a District Court is exercised by its members sitting singly and is of a summary character. A President or a District Judge sitting alone has power to try any offence punishable with imprisonment up to 3 years, or with a fine up to £C500 or with both, and may order compensation up to £C500.

Civil disputes relating to personal status of members of the Turkish Community, including matrimonial cases and maintenance, are dealt with by 2 Turkish Communal Courts. There is a communal appellate court to which appeals may be made from the decision of the Courts of first instance.

There is a Greek Orthodox Church tribunal with exclusive jurisdiction in matrimonial causes between members of the Greek Orthodox Church. There is an appellate tribunal of that Church.

Education. Until 31 March 1965 each community in Cyprus managed its own schooling through its respective Communal Chamber. Intercommunal education had been placed under the Minister of the Interior, assisted by a Board of Education for Intercommunal Schools, of which the Minister was the Chairman. In 1965 the Greek Communal Chamber was dissolved and a Ministry of Education was established to take its place. Intercommunal education has been placed under this Ministry.

Greek-Cypriot Education. Elementary education is compulsory and is provided free in six grades to children between 6 and 14 years of age. In some towns and large villages there are separate junior schools consisting of the first three grades. In some large rural centres there are schools where children can take a 2-year post-elementary course if they are not proceeding to a secondary school. Apart from schools for the deaf and blind, and the Lambousa School for juvenile offenders, there are also 7 schools for handicapped children. The Ministry runs 9 kindergartens for children from low-income families; most pre-primary education is privately run.

Secondary education became free as from 1972–73 for the three grades of the lower cycle, the gymnasium, and is fee-paying for the rest, although senior pupils can be wholly or partially exempt from payment. The secondary school is 6 years, 3 years at the gymnasium followed by 3 years at the lykeion. There are 4 types of lykeia: classical, science, economic, agricultural. There are 5-year vocational (trade) schools and 6-year technical schools. There were also (1976) 9 foreign-language schools and 29 private schools.

Post-secondary education is provided at the Pedagogical Academy, which organizes 3-year courses for the training of elementary school teachers, and at the Higher Technical Institute, which provides 3-year courses for technicians in civil, electrical and mechanical engineering. There is also a 2-year Forestry College (administered by the Ministry of Agriculture) and a 3-year Nurses' School and 1-year School for Health Inspectors (Ministry of Health). Adult education is conducted through youth centres in rural areas, foreign language institutes in the towns and an apprenticeship scheme for young workers (in co-operation with the Ministry of Labour and Social Insurance).

Turkish-Cypriot Education. The Office of Education of the Turkish Community of Cyprus caters for some 18% of the island's population and (1976) administered 10 kindergartens, 167 elementary schools (16,014 pupils), 18 secondary schools (7,190 pupils), 6 technical schools (735 pupils) and 1 teacher-training college (13 students). There were 43 evening institutes for adult education.

Greek is the language of 80% of the population and Turkish of 18%. English is widely spoken. English and French are compulsory subjects in secondary schools. Illiteracy is largely confined to older people.

Social Security. The administration of the social-security services in Cyprus is in the hands of the Ministry of Labour and Social Insurance, with the Ministry of Health providing medical services through public clinics and hospitals on a means test, except medical treatment for employment accidents, which is given free to all insured employees and financed by the Social Insurance Scheme.

Social Insurance. The island's Social Insurance Scheme, which covers compulsorily both employees and self-employed persons, provides, in the case of employees, cash benefits for sickness, unemployment, maternity, marriage (females only), old-age, widowhood and death and cash benefits with free medical treatment for employment accidents and occupational diseases. Since the Turkish invasion many schemes have been suspended. Pensions have, however, been maintained.

Annual Holiday Scheme. An Annual Holidays with Pay Law, introduced in 1967, provides for a minimum of 9 days paid leave to all workers in the island. The law is implemented by means of regular contributions by employers into a fund administered by Government. Employers offering more than 9 days' paid leave by collective agreement or otherwise may be exempted from paying contributions into the fund.

Termination of Employment Scheme. A Termination of Employment law also enacted in 1967 provides for the establishment of a Redundancy Fund to which all employers contribute 0·5% of their pay-roll, for a maximum period of notice of 1 month in case of dismissal, and for compensation up to 1 year's wages payable direct by employers in case of arbitrary dismissal. Claims under both laws are adjudicated by a Labour Disputes Tribunal.

DIPLOMATIC REPRESENTATIVES

OF CYPRUS IN GREAT BRITAIN (93 Park St., London, W1Y 4ET)

High Commissioner: Costas Ashiotis, MBE.

OF GREAT BRITAIN IN CYPRUS (Alexander Pallis St., Nicosia)

High Commissioner: D. McD. Gordon, CMG.

OF CYPRUS IN THE USA (2211 R. St., NW, Washington, D.C., 20008)

Ambassador: Nicos G. Dimitriou.

OF THE USA IN CYPRUS (Therissos St., Nicosia)

Ambassador: William R. Crawford, Jr.

OF CYPRUS TO THE UNITED NATIONS

Ambassador: Zenon Rossides.

Books of Reference

Statistical Information: Statistics and Research Department, Nicosia.

Alastos, D., *Cyprus in History*. London, 1955.—*Cyprus Guerilla*. London, 1960
Bitsios, D. S., *Cyprus: The Vulnerable Republic*. Thessaloniki, 1975
Christodoulou, D., *The Evolution of the Rural Land use Pattern in Cyprus*. Bude, 1960
Crouzet, F., *Le Conflit de Chypre 1946–1959*. Brussels, 1973
Emilianides, A., *Histoire de Chypre*. Paris, 1962.—*The Zurich and London Agreements and the Cyprus Republic*. Athens, 1962
Hill, Sir George F., *A History of Cyprus*. 4 vols. Cambridge, 1940–52
Kosut, H., *Cyprus 1946–68*. New York, 1970
Luke, Sir Harry, *Cyprus*. Rev. ed. London, 1965
Markides, K. C., *The Rise and Fall of the Cyprus Republic*. Yale Univ Press, 1977
Politis, J. N., *Chypre*. Paris, 1959
Polyviou, P. G., *Cyprus: The Tragedy and the Challenge*. London, 1975.—*Cyprus in Search of a Constitution*. Nicosia, 1976
Spyridakis, C., *An Outline of the History of Cyprus*. Nicosia, 1957
Stavrinides, Z., *The Cyprus Conflict*. Nicosia, 1976
The Directory of the Republic of Cyprus [with Trade Index and Who's Who]. London, 1962
Vanezis, P. N., *Makarios: Faith and Power*. New York, 1972

CZECHOSLOVAKIA

Capital: Prague
Population: 14·86m. (1976)
GNP per capita: US$3,840 (1976)

Československá Socialistická Republika

HISTORY. The Czechoslovak State came into existence on 28 Oct. 1918, when the Czech *Národní Výbor* (National Committee) took over the government of the Czech lands upon the dissolution of Austria–Hungary. Two days later the Slovak National Council manifested its desire to unite politically with the Czechs. On 14 Nov. 1918 the first Czechoslovak National Assembly declared the Czechoslovak State to be a republic with T. G. Masaryk as President (1918–35).

The Treaty of St Germain-en-Laye (1919) recognized the Czechoslovak Republic, consisting of the Czech lands (Bohemia, Moravia, part of Silesia) and Slovakia. To these lands were added as a trust the autonomous province of Subcarpathian Ruthenia.

This territory was broken up for the benefit of Germany, Poland and Hungary by the Munich agreement (29 Sept. 1938) between UK, France, Germany and Italy.

In March 1939 the German-sponsored Slovak government proclaimed Slovakia independent, and Germany incorporated the Czech lands into the Reich as the 'Protectorate of Bohemia and Moravia'. A government-in-exile, headed by Dr Beneš, was set up in London in July 1940.

Liberation by the Soviet Army and US Forces was completed by May 1945.

Territories taken by Germans, Poles and Hungarians were restored to Czechoslovak sovereignty. Subcarpathian Ruthenia was transferred to the USSR.

Elections were held in May 1946, at which the Communist Party obtained about 38% of the votes.

A coalition government under a Communist Prime Minister, Klement Gottwald, remained in power until 20 Feb. 1948, when 12 of the non-Communist ministers resigned in protest against infiltration of Communists into the police.

In Feb. a predominantly Communist government was formed by Gottwald. In May elections resulted in an 89% majority for the government and President Beneš resigned.

In the first months of 1968 mounting pressure for liberalization culminated in the overthrow of the Stalinist President and Party Secretary, Antonín Novotný, and his associates. Under a new leadership the Communist Party introduced in April 1968 an 'Action Programme' of far-reaching political and economic reforms.

Soviet pressure to abandon this programme was exerted between May and Aug. 1968, and finally, Warsaw Pact forces occupied Czechoslovakia on 21 Aug. The enforced Moscow agreement of 26 Aug. bound the Czechoslovak government to a policy of 'normalization' (*i.e.*, abandonment of most reforms) and to the stationing of Soviet forces on Czechoslovak soil. This situation was confirmed by the Czechoslovak–Soviet 'Status of Forces Agreement' of 16 Oct. In 1969 and 1970 Soviet pressure led to extensive changes in the Party and in the federal and republican governments. In Oct. 1969 Czechoslovakia repudiated its condemnation of the Warsaw Pact invasion.

A Czechoslovak–Soviet 20-year Treaty of Friendship, Co-operation and Mutual Assistance was signed in May 1970.

On 11 Dec. 1973 the German Federal Republic and Czechoslovakia signed a treaty normalizing relations and annulling the Munich agreement of 1938. This was ratified by both countries' parliaments in July 1974.

AREA AND POPULATION. At the census of 1 Dec. 1970 the population was 14,344,987 (4,537,290 in Slovakia; 7·4m. females; 62% urban). Population in

1976 was 14,857,145 (4,763,609 in Slovakia; 7·6m. females). There are 12 administrative regions, one of which is the capital, Prague (Praha) and one the capital of Slovakia, Bratislava.

Region	Chief city	Area in sq. km	Population on 1 Jan. 1976
Czech			
Prague	—	496	1,169,567
Středočeský	Prague (Praha)	11,003	1,136,113
Jihočeský	České Budějovice	11,348	670,442
Západočeský	Plzeň (Pilsen)	10,872	875,351
Severočeský	Ústí nad Labem	7,810	1,139,806
Východočeský	Hradec Králové	11,240	1,227,110
Jihomoravský	Brno	15,027	1,971,982
Severomoravský	Ostrava	11,067	1,883,165
Slovak			
Bratislava	—	368	340,902
Západoslovenský	Bratislava	14,491	1,636,247
Středoslovenský	Banská Bystrica	17,976	1,462,050
Východoslovenský	Košice	16,179	1,324,410

The area of Czechoslovakia is 127,877 sq. km (49,365 sq. miles) (Slovakia, 49,014 sq. km). Population density in 1976: 116 per sq. km. Growth rate in 1975, 8 per 1,000. Expectation of life in 1973 was 66·3 (males); 73·3 (females).

Ethnic minorities have equal political and cultural rights. In 1975 there were (in 1,000): Czechs, 9,546; Slovaks, 4,458; Hungarians, 589; Germans, 79; Poles, 76; Ukrainians and Russians, 59. Gipsies are not recognized as a national minority. There were 293,000 in 1977.

The population of the principal towns in 1976 was as follows (in 1,000):

Prague (Praha)	1,169	Hradec Králové	89	Kladno	62
Brno	360	Pardubice	88	Most	60
Bratislava	341	České Budějovice	85	Žilina	58
Ostrava	301	Liberec	83	Nitra	57
Košice	174	Karviná	81	Banska Bystrica	56
Plzeň	156	Ústí nad Labem	76	Opava	55
Olomouc	96	Gottwaldov	...	Teplice	53
Havířov	92	Prešov	...	Trnava	51

Vital statistics for calendar years:

	Live births	Marriages	Divorces	Deaths
1973	274,461	141,108	29,458	167,818
1974	291,367	140,411	30,415	171,325
1975	289,342	141,045	32,308	169,566

CONSTITUTION AND GOVERNMENT. For details of previous constitutions, *see* THE STATESMAN'S YEAR-BOOK, 1968–69, pp. 927–28.

Since 1 Jan. 1969 Czechoslovakia has been a federal socialist republic consisting of two nations of equal rights: the Czech Socialist Republic (the Czech lands, previously Bohemia, Moravia and part of Silesia), and the Slovak Socialist Republic (Slovakia). Each Republic is governed by a National Council (the Czech with 200 deputies, the Slovak with 150), which delegates to an overall Federal Assembly responsibility for constitutional and foreign affairs, defence and important economic decisions. Centralized federal responsibility was increased by a constitutional amendment of Dec. 1970 to include several further spheres of administration, mainly economic. The Federal Assembly consists of the Chamber of Nations, which has 75 Czech and 75 Slovak delegates elected by their respective National Councils, and the Chamber of the People, which has 200 deputies elected by national suffrage.

The previous constitution (1960) remains in force where not specifically superseded, but since 1971 deputies are elected for a 5-year term so as to coincide with Communist Party congresses. Minimum age of voters is 18, of deputies, 21 years. The last elections to the superseded National Assembly were held in 1964; elections to the new Federal Assembly were postponed to 1971. By a law of 1968 more than one candidate was to be allowed to stand in each constituency, but this was repealed in 1971 and at the elections of Nov. 1971 the number of candidates was the same as the number of seats. At the elections of 22–23 Oct. 1976 a single list of National Front candidates was presented. Turnout was 10,617,152 from an electorate of 10,649,621 (99·7%). 99·97% of the votes were cast for the official candidates.

President of the Republic: Gustáv Husák (born 1913), succeeded Gen. Ludvík Svoboda, who was relieved of his duties on 27 May 1975 for reasons of ill-health. *President of the Federal Assembly:* Alois Indra.

The *de facto* primary source of power is the Communist Party of Czechoslovakia, of which the Communist Party of Slovakia (*First Secretary:* Josef Lenárt) is a constituent part. Communists head the National Front, which incorporates the remaining political parties (Czechoslovak Socialist Party, People's Party) and the trade unions and youth organizations. The Communist Party had 1,382,860 members in 1976. The day after the Warsaw Pact occupation (21 Aug. 1968) the Communist Party met in a secret Congress and elected a new Central Committee and Presidium. This Congress was subsequently annulled. In March 1978 the Presidium consisted of Gustáv Husák (*General Secretary*); Vasil Bil'ak; Peter Colotka (*Deputy Prime Minister*); Václav Hůla (*Deputy Prime Minister and Chairman, State Planning Committee*); Alois Indra; Antonín Kapek; Josef Kempný; Josef Korčák (*Deputy Prime Minister*); Josef Lenárt; Karel Hoffman (*Chairman, Central Council of Trade Unions*); Lubomír Štrougal (*Prime Minister*).

In May 1978 members of the government not mentioned above included: (*Deputy Prime Ministers*) Karol Laco; Matej Lúčan; Rudolf Rohlíček; Josef Šimon; Jindřich Zahradník; (other ministers) Andrej Barčák (*Foreign Trade*); Martin Dzúr (*Defence*); František Ondřich (*Chairman, Czechoslovak Control Committee*); Bohuslav Chňoupek (*Foreign*); Leopold Lér (*Finance*); Michal Štancel' (*Labour*); Jaromír Obzina (*Interior*); Vlastimir Ehrenberger (*Minister of Fuel and Power*).

The Czech Prime Minister is Josef Korcák; the Slovak, Peter Colotka.

National flag: White and red (horizontal), with a blue triangle of full depth at the hoist, point to the fly.

National anthem: Kde domov můj (words by J. K. Tyl; tune by F. J. Škroup, 1834); combined with, Nad Tatru sa blyska (words by J. Matuška, 1844).

DEFENCE. Defence is the responsibility of the Defence Council set up in Feb. 1969 and headed by the First Secretary of the Party. Army service lasts 2 years. There are 3 military districts. The security forces and frontier guards are organized in regiments and brigades repectively; total strength, 36,000.

The Warsaw Pact invasion of Aug. 1968 brought an estimated 500,000 occupation troops into the country. By early 1970 this number had been reduced to 80,000 Soviet troops, the presence of which is legalized by the Czech–Soviet 'Status of Forces' Agreement of Oct. 1968.

In Feb. 1969 the government announced an increase in defence capacity, and Czechoslovakia resumed participation in Warsaw Pact meetings.

Army. The Army is organized in 10 divisions (5 tank and 5 motorized divisions and 1 airborne brigade). The regular army had, in 1976, a total strength of about 135,000 men and 3,400 tanks, mainly T-55s, with some T-54s.

Air Force. The Air Force is organized as a tactical force, under overall army command, and has a strength of some 46,000 personnel and 550 combat aircraft. Service lasts 3 years. Six fighter regiments (each 3 squadrons of 14 aircraft) are equipped with MiG-21 jets, and there are 4 regiments of Su-7, MiG-21 and MiG-17 ground attack aircraft. MiG-21s and adapted L-29 Delfin jet trainers are used for tactical reconnaissance. Il-28s replaced in attack units have been converted for ECM duties. Transport units have An-24, Il-14 and Il-18 aircraft and Mil Mi-4 and Mi-8 helicopters. Training units are equipped with 2-seat MiG-21s and Czech-built aircraft, including L-29 Delfin and L-39 jet advanced trainers, totalling 300 in all. Surface-to-air ('Guideline' and 'Goa') missile units are operational.

INTERNATIONAL RELATIONS

Membership. Czechoslovakia is a member of UN, COMECON and the Warsaw Pact.

ECONOMY

Planning. For details of the first three 5-year plans *see* THE STATESMAN'S YEAR-BOOK, 1964–65, p. 922. The fourth 5-year plan ran from 1966 to 1970, the fifth from 1971 to 1975. It was officially announced that the social product and national income targets were fulfilled. Economic innovations introduced in the period 1965–68 have been substantially vitiated since the Soviet intervention of 1968, and the economy has reverted to a model closer to the traditional communist centrally planned type.

The sixth 5-year plan for 1976–80 envisages an increase of 32–34% in industrial (principally chemical, engineering and power) and of 14–15% in agricultural, production.

Budget. Budgets for calendar years (in Kčs. 1m.):

	1969	*1970*	*1971*	*1972*	*1973*	*1974*	*1975*
Revenue	184,429	205,860	219,021	223,503	242,258	263,755	278,113
Expenditure	176,942	194,313	212,632	216,569	237,200	259,185	273,774

Main items of the 1975 budget were (in Kčs. 1,000m.): Revenue: from the economy, 233; direct taxes, 31. Expenditure: national economy, 139; culture, health and social services,115; defence, 20; administration, 5.

Currency. The monetary unit in the Czechoslovak Republic is the *koruna* (Kčs.) or crown of 100 *haler*. Notes in circulation: Kčs. 10, 20, 50, 100, 500. Coin: 5, 10, 20, 50 *halers*, and Kčs. 1, 2, 5. The *koruna* is based on a gold content of 0·123426 gramme of pure gold and pegged on the rouble at Kčs. 1·80 = R.1. The International Monetary Fund did not approve this change of the par value, and Czechoslovak membership was terminated in 1954, and ceased to be a member of the International Bank. The official rates of exchange are £1 = Kčs. 9·80; US$1 = Kčs. 5·64; 1 Soviet rouble = Kčs. 8. Tourist rate: £1 = Kčs. 17·06.

In Sept. 1973 talks opened with USA with a view to settling mutual claims. It was announced in July 1974 that these had reached a satisfactory conclusion. USA was to return gold seized by Germany (18·4 tonnes), and Czechoslovakia was to pay compensation for nationalized US property. However on 15 Jan. 1975 the Czechoslovak Federal Assembly refused to ratify this agreement, on the grounds that USA was imposing unacceptable political conditions in its commercial treaties.

Banking. For previous banking history *see* THE STATESMAN'S YEAR-BOOK, 1971–72, pp. 858–59. The central bank and bank of issue is the State Bank (Statní Banka), which controls foreign exchange reserves, and is a savings bank and a commercial credit bank to enterprises, except foreign trade enterprises. These are financed by the Commercial Bank (Obchodní Banka) which carries out all foreign trade transactions. The Trade Bank (Živnostenská Banka) provides banking services for private foreign clients, and maintains branches abroad. There is also an Investment Bank (Investiční Banka), one of whose functions is to manage foreign securities. 'Foreign exchange points' (*e.g.*, hotels) have partial foreign exchange authorization.

Weights and Measures. The metric system is in force.

ENERGY AND NATURAL RESOURCES

Oil. There are 2 oil pipelines from the USSR, one to Bratislava and one to Zaluzi (near Most). A natural gas pipeline from USSR which supplies the German Federal and Democratic Republics, Austria and Italy as well as Czechoslovakia came into use in 1973, and a second is under construction.

Minerals. Czechoslovakia is not rich in minerals. Hard and soft coal reserves are ample (chief coalfields: Most, Chomutov, Kladno, Ostrava and Sokolov), and there is also iron ore, graphite, copper, lead, uranium, glass sand and salt. Production in 1975 (in tonnes): Iron ore, 1·8m; coal, 28m.; lignite and brown coal, 83·5m.

Agriculture. In 1975 there were 7m. hectares of agricultural land (5m. hectares arable, 0·9m. meadow, 0·8m. pasture). The area occupied by private plots (maximum size 1 hectare) was 219,000 hectares in 1974 and 171,000 hectares in 1975.

In 1975 there were 2,736 collective farms (6,270 in 1970) with 4,406,805 hectares of land, and 250 state farms with 1,421,000 hectares. Crop production in 1975 (in 1,000 tonnes): Wheat, 4,202; rye, 530; barley, 3,114; oats, 591; maize, 843; potatoes, 3,565; sugar-beet, 7,734.

Livestock. In 1975 the number of livestock was: Cattle, 4·55m. (including 1·9m. milch cows); horses, 62,000; pigs, 6·6m.; sheep, 805,000; poultry, 40·1m. In 1975 production of meat was 1,538,520 tonnes (live weight); milk, 5,298m. litres; 4,499m. eggs. In 1975 there were 241,088 tractors (in 15-h.p. units).

Forestry. Czechoslovakia is a richly wooded country, and the timber industry is important. Forest area in 1975 was 4,477,525 hectares (50% spruce, 16% beech and pine, 7% oak). The area reafforested in 1975 was 61,275 hectares. The timber yield was 16·7m. cu. metres in 1975.

INDUSTRY AND TRADE

Industry. Industrialization is well developed and antedates the Communist régime. All industry is nationalized.

Output in 1975 (in 1,000 tonnes): Pig-iron, 9,281; crude steel, 14,323; coke, 10,910; crude oil, 142; rolled-steel products, 10,027; cement, 9,305; paper, 761; sulphuric acid, 1,245; nitrogenous fertilizers, 446; phosphate fertilizers, 398; sugar, 840; beer, 22·6m. hectolitres; cars, 175,411 (no.).

Textile production (in 1m. metres) in 1975: Cotton, 556; linen, 77·7; woollen, 67·9. Leather shoes, 60·2m. pairs.

Production of electricity in 1975: 59,277m. kwh.

Labour. The total labour force in 1975 was 7,435,000 (48% female), of which 2·8m. worked in industry, 1·1m. in agriculture and forestry, 0·7m. in building and 0·7m. in commerce.

A 5-day 42-hour week with 4 weeks annual holiday is standard. Average monthly wage in 1977: Kčs. 2,427. In 1977 the trade union movement had 6·5m. members.

Commerce. Total trade (in Kčs. 1m.) for calendar years:

	1970	*1971*	*1972*	*1973*	*1974*	*1975*
Imports	26,605	28,870	30,912	35,805	43,974	50,716
Exports	27,305	30,095	32,588	33,322	41,213	46,651

In 1975, 66·5% of Czechslovakia's trade was with Communist countries (a half of this with the USSR). A Soviet–Czech trade agreement for 1976–80 envisages a certain degree of co-ordination of the two countries' 5-year plans. Trade exchanges are expected to rise by 40% in this period, to Kčs. 1,000m. in 1980. In 1975 Czechoslovakia imported from the USSR goods valued at Kčs. 16,276m. and exported to the USSR goods valued at Kčs. 15,387m.; followed by East Germany (imports, 6,188m.; exports, 5,725m.) and Poland (imports, 4,847m.; exports, 4,127m.). UK is Czechoslovakia's third biggest non-Communist trade partner after the Federal German Republic and Austria.

Major exports in 1975 (percentage of total): Machinery, 48; industrial consumer goods, 17·4; raw materials and fuel, 19·6. Imports: Machinery, 36·9; raw materials and fuel, 28·8.

There are 11 foreign trade agencies (independent legal entities with their own capital run by state-appointed managers). Western firms are permitted to set up their own offices on Czechoslovak soil. Enterprises must obtain agreement from the Ministry of Foreign Trade before trading with foreign firms. The 5-year plans envisage a certain degree of integration with the economies of other Comecon countries.

In 1972 an Anglo-Czech Agreement on Co-operation was signed. Under this an Anglo-Czech Joint Commission was established to further the development of trade and industrial and scientific co-operation.

UK–Czechoslovak trade has been conducted since 1 Jan. 1975 under terms negotiated by the EEC with Comecon.

Total trade between UK and Czechoslovakia for calendar years (British Department of Trade returns, in £1,000 sterling):

	1972	*1973*	*1974*	*1975*	*1976*	*1977*
Imports to UK	32,287	39,100	55,396	59,231	70,286	86,179
Exports and re-exports from UK	23,728	27,245	44,768	51,211	60,080	65,183

Tourism. In 1975 12,958,433 tourists visited Czechoslovakia (904,862 from the West) and 7,394,777 Czechoslovak citizens made visits abroad (293,909 to the West).

COMMUNICATIONS

Roads. In 1975 there were 73,712 km of motorways and first-class roads and 1,505,050 passenger cars. In 1975 state road transport carried 1,957m. passengers and 203m. tonnes of freight.

Railways. In 1975 the length of railway track was 13,215 km. Of this, 2,807 km was double-tracked and 2,707 km electrified. In 1975, 486m. passengers and 235·6m. tonnes of freight were carried.

Aviation. Air transport is run by ČSA (Czechoslovak Airlines). The main airports are: Prague (Ruzyně), Brno (Cernovice), Bratislava (Vajnory), Olomouc (Holice), Košice (Barca). In 1975, 1·9m. passengers and 28,502 tonnes of freight were flown. There are direct flights from Prague to some 50 cities, including most European capitals, Havana, Jakarta, Conakry, New York and Montreal. British Airways operates air traffic London–Prague, Air France Paris–Prague–Bucharest.

Shipping. In 1975 the Czechoslovak International Maritime Co. (founded 1959) had 12 ocean-going vessels of together 221,646 DWT, based on Szczecin. In 1975, 1,202m. tonnes of cargo were carried. River freight transport within Czechoslovakia totalled 5·65m. tonnes. There is an important Danube fleet.

A port under construction at Bratislava is scheduled to open in 1979.

Post and Broadcasting. Number of telephones in service on 1 Jan. 1976 was 2,614,761. *Çeskoslovenský Rozhlas*, the governmental broadcasting station, broadcasts on 2 networks; one from Prague with 3 programmes in Czech and Slovak and one from Bratislava with 2 programmes in Slovak and additional broadcasts in Hungarian and Ukrainian. *Československá Televise* broadcast 2 television programmes nationwide, including colour broadcasts. In 1975, 3·24m. people held wireless and 3·7m. TV licences.

Cinemas and Theatres (1975). There were 3,404 cinemas and 63 theatres. 62 full-length films were made in 1975.

Newspapers (1976). There were 28 daily newspapers, including 12 in Slovak. The party daily *Rudé Právo* has a circulation of about 1m.

JUSTICE, RELIGION, EDUCATION AND WELFARE

Justice. The criminal and criminal procedure codes date from 1 Jan. 1962. Amendments of April 1973 raised the maximum penalty for 'capital' (mainly political) offences from 15 to 25 years and tightened measures for dealing with prisoners and released prisoners. The death penalty is retained for exceptionally serious crimes.

Police powers were strengthened in July 1974.

There is a Federal Supreme Court and federal military courts, with judges elected by the Federal Assembly. Both republics have Supreme Courts and a network of regional and district courts whose professional judges are elected by the republican National Councils. Lay judges are elected by regional or district local authorities. Local authorities and social organizations may participate in the decision-making of the courts.

Religion. Churches are under the control of the state Secretariat for Church Affairs, and clergymen's salaries are paid by the state. In 1977 there were 18 different faiths with 4,860 clergy and 8,228 churches. The largest single church is the Roman Catholic (11m. members, 1973): its main support is in Slovakia. Cardinal František Tomašek was installed as archbishop of Prague in 1978. The archbishoprics of Olomonc and Trnava were vacant in 1978. In 1977 there were 5 bishops (the remaining 8 dioceses are directed by Government-appointed capitulary vicars). In 1970 there were 3,532 Roman Catholic priests (7,040 in 1948) and, in 1967, 3,200 churches (10,473 in 1948).

The Protestant (Hussite) Community was estimated (1962) at 1·2m., including 530,000 Reformed (360,000 Czech Brethren, 150,000 Reformed Church of Slovakia), 485,000 Lutherans (435,000 in Slovakia, 50,000 in Silesia), 10,000 Methodists, 10,000 Moravians, 10,000 Unity of Czech Brethren, 5,000 Baptists. In 1966 there were 15,000 Jews (mainly in Prague, where there is a synagogue). The Uniate Church was suppressed in 1950, when it had 305,645 adherents, 280 priests, 17 monasteries and 5 nunneries. It was permitted to revive in 1968.

Education. In 1975–76 there were 9,226 kindergartens for children from 3 to 6 years of age, with 34,755 teachers and 475,004 pupils. All children receive free education from the ages of 6 to 15, where possible remaining at a single school for the whole 9 years. In 1975–76 there were 9,285 schools with 1,881,414 pupils and 95,634 teachers.

Subsequent education is of 3 types. First, 3 final years of secondary school (in 1975–76, 340 schools with 8,236 teachers and 128,545 pupils). Secondly, technical, teachers' training and other vocational schools (1975–76, 599 schools with 293,718 students). Thirdly, university level (1975–96, 119,264 full-time students, and 32,018 part-time and correspondence students); academic staff numbered 17,009 in 1975–76. There are 36 institutions of higher education, with 103 faculties. These include 6 universities—the Charles University in Prague (founded 1348); the Purkyně (formerly Masaryk) University in Brno (1919); the Comenius University in Bratislava (1919); the Palacký University in Olomouc (1573); the Šafárik University in Košice (1959); the 17th of November University in Prague—and 12 technical universities or institutes.

In 1973 one-year residential adult education courses were introduced.

Welfare. Medical care is free. In 1975 Kčs. 2,538m. were spent on medicines and 20,540m. on health insurance benefits. There were, in 1975, 237 hospitals with a total of 115,674 beds, and 40,609 doctors and dentists. Family allowances (Kčs. per month): 1 child, 500; 2 children, 800; 3, 1,200. Old age pensions of 60% of salary are paid at the age of 60.

DIPLOMATIC REPRESENTATIVES

OF CZECHOSLOVAKIA IN GREAT BRITAIN (25 Kensington Palace Gdns, London, W8 4QY)

Ambassador: Dr Zdeněk Černík (accredited on 16 Nov. 1977).

OF GREAT BRITAIN IN CZECHOSLOVAKIA (Thunovská 14, Prague 1)

Ambassador: Peter J. E. Male, CMG, MC.

OF CZECHOSLOVAKIA IN THE USA (3900 Linnean Ave., NW, Washington, D.C., 20008)

Ambassador: Dr Jaromir Johanes.

OF THE USA IN CZECHOSLOVAKIA (Tržiste 15–12548 Praha, Prague)

Ambassador: Thomas Ryan Byrne.

OF CZECHOSLOVAKIA TO THE UNITED NATIONS

Ambassador: Ilja Hulinský.

Books of Reference

The Constitution of the Czechoslovak Socialist Republic [English ed.]. Prague, 1960
Statistical Survey of Czechoslovakia. Prague, annual since 1973
Statistická ročenka ČSSR [Statistical Yearbook]. Prague, annual since 1958
Czechoslovak Foreign Trade. Prague, monthly
Statistika. Prague, Statistical Office, monthly since 1964
Socialist Czechoslovakia. Prague, 1976
Demek, J., and others, *Geography of Czechoslovakia*. Prague, 1971
Hermann, A. H., *A History of the Czechs*. London, 1975
Hejzlar, Z., and Kusin, V. V., *Czechoslovakia, 1968–1969*. New York, 1975
Jancar, B. W., *Czechoslovakia and the Absolute Monopoly of Power*. New York and London, 1971
Korbel, J., *Twentieth-Century Czechoslovakia: The Meanings of its History*. Columbia Univ. Press, 1977
Krejčí, J., *Social Change and Stratification in Postwar Czechoslovakia*. London, 1972
Kusin, V. V. (ed.), *The Czechoslovak Reform Movement, 1968*. London, 1973
Littell, R. (ed.), *The Czech Black Book; prepared by the Institute of History of the Czechoslovak Academy of Sciences*. London, 1969
Mamatey, V. S., and Luža, R. (eds.), *A History of the Czechoslovak Republic 1918–1948*. Princeton Univ. Press, 1973
Oxley, A., Pravda, A., Richie, A., *Czechoslovakia: The Party and the People*. New York, 1973
Procházka, J., *English–Czech and Czech–English Dictionary*. 16th ed. London, 1959
Šik, O., *Czechoslovakia: The Bureaucratic Economy*. New York, 1972.
Teplý, J., *Économie Nationale de la Tchecoslovaquie Contemporaine*. Paris, 1977
Ulč, O., *Politics in Czechoslovakia*. San Francisco, 1974
Wallace, W. V., *Czechoslovakia*. London, 1977
Wheeler, G. S., *The Human Face of Socialism: The Political Economy of Change in Czechoslovakia*. New York, 1973

DENMARK

Kongeriget Danmark

Capital: Copenhagen
Population: 5·08m. (1977)
GNP per capita: US$7,599 (1976)

AREA AND POPULATION. According to the census held on 9 Nov. 1970 the area of Denmark proper was 43,074 sq. km (16,631 sq. miles) and the population 4,937,579. Population, Jan. 1977: 5,079,879.

Administrative divisions		*Area (sq. km) 1977*	*Population 1970*	*Population 1977*	*Population 1977 per sq. km*
København (Copenhagen)(city)		86	622,773	529,154	6,128
Frederiksberg	(borough)	9	101,874	91,278	10,408
Københavns	(county)	521	615,343	630,794	1,212
Frederiksborg	,,	1,347	259,442	313,693	233
Roskilde	,,	890	153,199	193,136	217
Vestsjællands	,,	2,984	259,057	271,005	91
Storstrøms	,,	3,398	252,363	257,364	76
Bornholms	,,	588	47,239	47,207	80
Fyns	,,	3,486	432,699	448,142	129
Sønderjyllands	,,	3,929	238,062	246,045	63
Ribe	,,	3,132	197,843	207,825	66
Vejle	,,	2,997	306,263	319,180	107
Ringkøbing	,,	4,853	241,327	256,739	53
Aarhus	,,	4,561	533,190	565,966	124
Viborg	,,	4,122	220,734	227,966	55
Nordjyllands	,,	6,172	456,171	474,385	77
Total		43,075	4,937,579	5,079,879	118

The population is almost entirely Scandinavian; in 1960, of the inhabitants of Denmark proper, 97·8% were born in Denmark.

On 9 Nov, 1970 the population of the capital, Copenhagen (comprising Copenhagen, Frederiksberg and Gentofte municipalities), was 802,391 (including suburbs, 1,380,204); Aarhus, 198,981; Odense, 137,276; Aalborg, 100,262; Esbjerg, 68,097; Randers, 58,409; Horsens, 44,120.

Vital Statistics for calendar years:

	Living births	*Stillbirths*	*Marriages*	*Divorces*	*Deaths*	*Emigration*	*Immigration*
1972	75,505	577	31,073	13,134	50,445	25,762	31,200
1973	71,895	523	30,813	12,637	50,526	29,703	41,948
1974	71,327	441	33,182	13,132	51,637	39,751	33,146
1975	72,071	483	31,782	13,264	50,895	40,659	31,946
1976	65,267	431	31,192	13,064	54,001	30,000	33,320

Illegitimate births: 1973, 17·1%; 1974, 18·8%; 1975, 21·8%; 1976, 27%.

REIGNING QUEEN. Margrethe II, born 16 April 1940; married 10 June 1967 to Prince Henrik, born Count de Monpezat; *offspring:* Crown Prince Frederik, born 26 May 1968; Prince Joachim, born 7 June 1969. She succeeded to the throne on the death of her father, King Frederik IX, on 14 Jan. 1972.

Mother of the Queen: Queen Ingrid, born Princess of Sweden, 28 March 1910.

Sisters of the Queen: Princess Benedikte, born 29 April 1944 (married 3 Feb. 1968 to Prince Richard of Sayn-Wittgenstein-Berleburg); Princess Anne-Marie, born 30 Aug. 1946 (married 18 Sept. 1964 to King Constantine of Greece).

The crown of Denmark was elective from the earliest times. In 1448 after the death of the last male descendant of Swein Estridsen the Danish Diet elected to the throne Christian I, Count of Oldenburg, in whose family the royal dignity remained for more than 4 centuries, although the crown was not rendered hereditary by right till 1660. The direct male line of the house of Oldenburg became extinct with King Frederik VII on 15 Nov. 1863. In view of the death of the king, without direct heirs, the Great Powers signed a treaty at London on 8 May 1852, by the terms of which the succession to the crown of Denmark was made over to Prince Christian of Schleswig-Holstein-Sonderburg-Glücksburg, and to the direct male descendants of his union with the Princess Louise of Hesse-Cassel, niece of King Christian VIII of Denmark. In accordance with this treaty, a law concerning the succession to the Danish crown was adopted by the Diet, and obtained the royal sanction 31 July 1853. Linked to the constitution of 5 June 1953, a new law of succession, dated 27 March 1953, has come into force, which restricts the right of succession to the descendants of King Christian X and Queen Alexandrine, and admits the sovereign's daughters to the line of succession, ranking after the sovereign's sons.

Queen Margrethe II has a civil list of 13·3m. kroner. Annuities to other members of the royal house amount to 3·35m. kroner.

Subjoined is a list of the kings of Denmark, with the dates of their accession, from the time of election of Christian I of Oldenburg:

House of Oldenburg

Christian I	1448	Christian IV	1588	Frederik V	1746
Hans	1481	Frederik III	1648	Christian VII	1766
Christian II	1513	Christian V	1670	Frederik VI	1808
Frederik I	1523	Frederik IV	1699	Christian VIII	1839
Christian III	1534	Christian VI	1730	Frederik VII	1848
Frederik II	1559				

House of Schleswig-Holstein-Sonderburg-Glücksburg

Christiana IX	1863	Christian X	1912	Margrethe II	1972
Frederik VIII	1906	Frederik IX	1947		

CONSTITUTION AND GOVERNMENT. The present constitution of Denmark is founded upon the 'Grundlov' (charter) of 5 June 1953.

The legislative power lies with the Queen and the *Folketing* (Diet) jointly. The executive power is vested in the Queen, who exercises her authority through the ministers. The judicial power is with the courts. The Queen must be a member of the Evangelical-Lutheran Church, the official Church of the State. The Queen cannot assume major international obligations without the consent of the *Folketing*. The *Folketing* consists of one chamber. All men and women of Danish nationality of more than 20 years of age and permanently resident in Denmark possess the franchise and are eligible for election to the *Folketing*, which is at present composed of 179 members; 135 members are elected by the method of proportional representation in 17 districts. In order to attain an equal representation of the different parties, 40 *tillægsmandater* (additional seats) are divided among such parties which have not obtained sufficient returns at the district elections. Two members are elected for the Faroe Islands and 2 for Greenland. The term of the legislature is 4 years, but a general election may be called at any time.

The *Folketing* must meet every year on the first Tuesday in October. Besides its legislative functions, it appoints every 6 years judges who, together with the ordinary members of the Supreme Court (*Højesteret*), form the *Rigsret*, a tribunal which can alone try parliamentary impeachments. The ministers have free access to the house, but can vote only if they are members.

Folketing, elected 15 Feb. 1977: 65 Social Democrats, 6 Radical Liberals, 15 Conservatives, 7 Socialist People's Party, 7 Communists, 11 Centre Democrats, 6 Christian People's Party, 21 Liberals, 5 Left Socialists, 26 Progress Party, 6 Single-Tax Party, 2 Faroe Islands and 2 Greenland representatives.

The executive (called the State Council (*Statsraadet*) when acting with the Queen presiding) is a minority Social Democratic government, was in Oct. 1977 as follows:

Prime Minister: Anker Jørgensen.

Minister for Foreign Affairs: K. B. Andersen. *Finance:* Knud Heinesen. *Economic Affairs:* Per Hækkerup. *Agriculture:* Poul Dalsager. *Justice:* Erling Jensen. *Defence:* Poul Søgaard. *Education:* Ritt Bjerregaard. *Interior:* Egon Jensen. *Ecclesiastical Affairs and Greenland:* Jørgen Peder Hansen. *Housing:* Ove Hove. *Inland Revenue:* Jens Kampmann. *Environment and Culture:* Niels Mattiasen. *Social Affairs:* Eva Gredal. *Labour:* Svend Auken. *Fisheries:* Svend Jacobsen. *Transport and Communications:* Kjeld Olesen. *Commerce:* Ivar Nørgaard. *Without Portfolio:* Lise Østergaard.

The ministers are individually and collectively responsible for their acts, and if impeached and found guilty, cannot be pardoned without the consent of the *Folketing*. In 1948 a separate legislature (*Lagting*) and executive (*Landsstyre*) were established for the Faroe Islands, to deal with specified local matters.

National flag: Red with white Scandinavian cross (Dannebrog).

National anthems: Kong Kristian stod ved højen Mast (words by J. Ewald, 1778; tune by J. E. Hartmann, 1780) and Der er et yndigt land.

Local Government. For administrative purposes Denmark is divided into 275 municipalities (*kommuner*); each of them has a district council of between 5 and 25 members, headed by an elected mayor. The city of Copenhagen forms a district by itself and is governed by a city council of 55 members, elected every 4 years, and an executive (*magistraten*), consisting of the chief burgomaster (*overborgmesteren*) and 6 burgomasters, appointed by the city council for 4 years. There are 14 counties (*amtskommuner*), each of which is administered by a county council (*amtsråd*) of between 13 and 31 members, headed by an elected mayor. All councils are elected directly by universal suffrage and proportional representation for 4-year terms. A third council, the Metropolitan Council, with a constitution similar to the counties was established 1 April 1974. The Metropolitan Council is responsible for overall development within Metropolitan Copenhagen.

The counties and Copenhagen are superintended by ministry of interior affairs. The municipalities are superintended by 14 local supervision committees, headed by a County Prefect (*amtmand*) who is a civil servant appointed by the Queen.

DEFENCE. The Danish military defence is organized in accordance with the Defence Act of 1969 (amended April 1973) and the overall organization of the Danish Armed Forces comprises the Defence Command, the Army, the Navy, the Air Force and inter-service authorities and institutions. To this should be added the Home Guard, which is an indispensable part of Danish military defence. The Home Guard is based on the Home Guard Act of 1961 (at the latest amended May 1973).

In accordance with the Defence Act the Chief of Defence has full command of the three services: the Army, the Navy and the Air Force. The Chief of Defence, the Chief of Defence Staff and the Chiefs of the Army, the Navy and the Air Force and their staffs, are integrated in the Defence Command.

The Minister of Defence is assisted by a Defence Council consisting of the Chief of Defence, the Chief of Defence Staff, the Chief of Danish Operational Forces, and the Chiefs of the Army, the Navy and the Air Force.

The Constitution of 1849 declared it the duty of every fit man to contribute to the national defence, and this provision is still in force. According to the Personnel Act, 1969 (amended April 1973), the military personnel comprises officers, n.c.o.s and privates. Private personnel are provided by enlistment and by recruiting of volunteers. Selection of conscripts takes place at the age of 19 years, and the conscripts are normally called up for 9 months service ½–1½ years later. Afterwards conscripts may be recalled for refresher training or musters.

Army. The Army comprises field army formations and the local defence forces. The field army formations are organized in an operationally balanced covering force and in reserve units. The covering force numbers about 13,000 men and comprises a standing force, and a supplementary force consisting of men newly released from service. The standing force number about 8,500 men organized in standing brigade units, headquarters units and support units. The brigade units are organized in 5 armoured infantry brigades. The field army is equipped with 200 medium battle tanks and about 650 armoured personnel carriers as well as artillery including 72 self-propelled howitzers. The local defence units consist of about 24,000 men organized in 21 infantry battalions and 7 artillery battalions. The men of the latest annual service groups form the troops of the line, while those of the previous years form the local defence, the reserve and the reserve for the Home Guard. The mobilization units of the field army and the local defence force will total about 65,000 men.

Navy. The Navy comprises the fleet and coast-defence. The fleet includes 52 warships, 19 special-purpose ships and a number of helicopters. The naval units are planned to constitute a balanced force consisting of 5 frigates/corvettes, 18 torpedo boats, 6 submarines, 4 minelayers, 3 small minelayers, 8 minesweepers, 8 seaward defence craft supported by 8 helicopters.

The special-purpose ships include 5 ocean escorts and cutters.

The coast-defence includes several permanent fortifications. Naval personnel in 1977 totalled 5,800 officers and men, with a reserve of 3,100 in the Naval Home Guard.

Air Force. The operational units of the Air Force comprise 2 surface-to-air missile battalions and 6 flying squadrons with a total of 116 aircraft.

The air defence force consists of the 2 surface-to-air missile battalions and 2 all-weather air-defence squadrons with a unit establishment of 20.

The fighter bomber force comprises 3 squadrons with a unit establishment of 20, and 1 reconnaissance squadron with a unit establishment of 16.

In addition the Air Force has a number of supplementary units, including 1 transport squadron, 1 helicopter rescue squadron, the control and warning system.

Total strength of the Air Force (1977) about 7,100. The Air Force Home Guard consists of about 12,000 volunteers.

Home Guard. The overall Home Guard organization comprises the Home Guard Command, the Army Home Guard, the Navy Home Guard and the Air Force Home Guard.

The personnel of the Home Guard is recruited on a voluntary basis. The personnel establishment of the Home Guard is at present 72,450 persons (55,625 in the Army Home Guard, 4,850 in the Navy Home Guard and 11,975 in the Air Force Home Guard).

INTERNATIONAL RELATIONS

Membership. Denmark is a member of UN and EEC.

ECONOMY

Budget. The budget (*Finanslovforslag*) must be laid before the Parliament (*Folketing*) not later than 4 months before the beginning of a new fiscal year.

The following shows the actual revenue and expenditure for 4 fiscal years ending 31 March and the budget for 1 year (in 1,000 kroner):

	1972–73	*1973–74*	*1974–75*	*1975–76*	*1976–77*
Revenue	45,793,038	53,479,514	59,630,815	62,004,533	66,920,975
Expenditure	43,449,276	48,006,593	60,011,977	71,697,864	79,194,460

Receipts and expenditures of special government funds and expenditures on public works are included.

The 1976–77 budget envisages revenue of 31,738m. kroner from income and property taxes and 32,076m. from consumer taxes.

The central government debt on 31 March 1975 amounted to 3,296m. kroner.

Currency. The monetary unit is the *krone* of 100 *øre*. In 1931 Denmark went off the gold standard, as established in 1873.

Small change: 5-kroner pieces of copper–nickel, 1-krone pieces of copper–nickel; 25-øre and 10-øre pieces of copper–nickel, and 5-øre pieces of copper–steel–copper clad.

Banking. On 31 Dec. 1976 the accounts of the National Bank balanced at 34,965m. kroner. The assets included 501m. kroner in gold bullion. The liabilities included 8,939m. kroner note issue, 50m. kroner general capital fund and 230m. kroner reserve fund.

On 31 Dec. 1976 there were 173 savings banks, with 6·3m. accounts and deposits of 33,592m. kroner. Their advances amounted to 26,762m. kroner.

On 31 Dec. 1976 there were 80 other banks for commercial, agricultural and industrial purposes; their deposits amounted to 77,904m. kroner; advances were 53,572m. kroner.

Weights and Measures. The use of the metric system of weights and measures has been obligatory in Denmark since 1 April 1912.

ENERGY AND NATURAL RESOURCES

Electricity. Owing to the concentration of power production, the number of generating power stations has declined from 371 in 1949–50 to 23 in 1974–75, while the net power production (in 1m. kwh.) has risen from 1,689 in 1949–50 to 17,423 in 1974–75.

Agriculture. The soil of Denmark is greatly subdivided. In 1976 the total number of farms was 124,231. There were 36,945 small holdings (0·5–10 hectares), 80,568 medium sized holdings (10–60 hectares) and 6,718 holdings with more than 60 hectares.

The number of agricultural workers has declined from 120,442 in July 1961 to 28,156 in June 1975, while the index of production was 100 in 1960 and 100 in 1972 (1963–64 = 100).

In June 1976 the cultivated area was utilized as follows (in 1,000 hectares): Grain, 1,787; peas and beans, 6; root crops, 295; other crops, 95; green fodder and grass, 726; fallow, 3; total cultivated area, 2,912.

	Area (1,000 hectares)			*Production (in 1,000 tonnes)*		
Chief crops	*1974*	*1975*	*1976*	*1974*	*1975*	*1976*
Wheat	110	102	127	592	520	592
Rye	46	49	72	168	163	213
Barley	1,437	1,443	1,478	5,967	5,156	4,801
Oats	122	111	98	472	367	263
Mixed grain	18	15	12	62	46	33
Potatoes	33	31	35	898	666	575
Root crops	248	267	260	12,129	11,733	10,120

Livestock, 4 June 1976: Horses, 60,000; cattle, 3·09m.; pigs, 7,701,000; sheep, 59,000; poultry, 15,759,000.

Production (in 1,000 tonnes) in 1976: Milk, 5,045; butter, 139; cheese, 157; beef, 264; pork and bacon, 759; eggs, 71.

In June 1976 farm tractors numbered 189,009 and harvester-threshers, 42,342.

Fisheries. The total value of the fish caught was (in 1m. kroner): 1950, 156; 1955, 252; 1960, 376; 1965, 650; 1970, 854; 1975, 1,442; 1976, 1,920. The fishing fleet in 1976 consisted of 7,430 motor boats, 101 sailing boats and 3,018 rowing boats.

INDUSTRY AND TRADE

Industry. The following table sets forth the gross factor income (in 1m. kroner) by industrial origin in 3 calendar years:

	1974		*1975*		*1976*	
	Current prices	*1955 prices*	*Current prices*	*1955 prices*	*Current prices*	*1955 prices*
Agriculture	12,244	5,837	12,285	5,177	13,199	4,760
Forestry	164	88	177	87	176	87
Gardening, fur-farming, etc.	934	660	1,057	610	1,211	620
Fishing	1,265	487	957	440	1,323	484
Peat and lignite production	44	25	46	23	59	28
Total	14,641	7,097	14,522	6,337	15,968	5,979

	1974		1975		1976	
	Current prices	*1955 prices*	*Current prices*	*1955 prices*	*Current prices*	*1955 prices*
Manufacturing industries	32,500	16,025	34,919	14,925	40,600	16,140
Handicrafts	15,035	4,290	16,710	4,265	18,975	4,475
Construction	16,195	4,475	16,919	4,055	20,213	4,480
Gas, electricity and water	3,066	2,219	3,793	2,263	3,939	2,497
Total	66,796	27,009	72,341	25,508	83,727	27,592
Wholesale and retail trade, etc	22,910	9,550	26,485	10,150	30,600	10,850
Banking and insurance	6,789	2,148	7,800	2,187	8,188	2,118
Catering establishments	2,085	619	2,384	649	2,775	691
Cinemas, theatres, etc.	335	62	376	61	387	57
Total	32,119	12,379	37,045	13,047	41,950	13,716
Foreign shipping	4,388	2,005	3,896	1,950	4,354	2,090
Other transportation	13,450	4,636	15,974	4,688	17,589	4,894
Total	17,838	6,641	19,870	6,638	21,943	6,984
Use of dwellings	10,040	2,925	11,485	3,026	13,263	3,107
Professions	3,228	662	3,624	687	4,138	711
Domestic services	408	54	519	60	637	65
Government services	37,270	6,785	43,585	6,941	48,445	7,119
Gross factor income	182,340	63,552	202,991	62,244	230,071	65,273
Plus indirect taxes	26,485	—	28,740	—	35,755	—
Less subsidies	5,285	—	4,686	—	6,483	—
Gross domestic product at market prices	203,540	69,002	227,045	68,019	259,343	71,373

Although only very few industrial raw materials are produced within the country, considerable industries have been developed.

According to the census of manufacturing, 2 June 1958, there were 65,700 establishments employing altogether 616,100 persons. The following are some data for the most important industries in 1975. The table covers establishments with 6 employees and more.

Branch of industry	*Number of wage-earners*	*Value of production (1,000 kroner)*	*Value added (1,000 kroner)*
Mining and quarrying	1,110	303,524	246,470
Food industry	39,118	25,976,882	6,630,010
Beverage industry	9,341	2,936,293	1,824,747
Tobacco industry	2,819	731,760	361,055
Textile industry	12,698	3,502,960	1,779,551
Footwear and clothing industry	13,974	2,081,933	1,044,832
Wood industry (except furniture)	7,253	1,628,846	644,339
Manufacturing of furniture	9,167	1,866,899	970,514
Paper industry	6,902	2,578,190	1,056,257
Graphic industry	16,123	4,593,888	3,073,033
Leather products (except footwear)	1,400	293,899	136,595
Rubber industry	2,220	521,202	275,957
Chemical industry	16,919	8,310,077	4,039,724
Oil and coal products	1,010	5,939,017	583,928
Stone, clay and glass industry	17,227	4,903,158	2,887,274
Iron and metal works	6,400	1,878,530	757,586
Iron and metalware industry	20,215	5,280,103	2,627,384
Engineering industry	36,807	10,164,114	5,605,365
Manufac. of electrical machines, etc.	16,647	4,360,823	2,370,020
Transportation equipment	27,449	6,058,084	3,140,937
Other manufacturing industries	9,012	2,480,867	1,463,787
Total	273,811	96,391,049	41,519,365

Labour. In 1970, 11% of the working population lived on agriculture, forestry and fishery, 29% on industries and handicrafts, 9% on construction, 15% on commerce, etc., 7% on transportation and communication, and 29% on administration, professional services, etc.

Commerce. The following table shows the value, in 1,000 kroner, of general imports and exports (excluding precious metal) for calendar years:

	1971[1]	*1972*[1]	*1973*[1]	*1974*[1]	*1975*[1]	*1976*[1]
Imports	34,177,369	35,326,397	46,968,945	60,479,570	59,707,627	75,010,879
Exports	27,366,029	30,833,419	37,548,669	46,921,919	50,031,127	55,034,147

[1] Including the Faroe Islands and Greenland.

Imports and exports (in 1,000 kroner) for calendar years:

	1975		*1976*	
Leading commodities	*Imports*	*Exports*	*Imports*	*Exports*
Live animals, meat, etc.	58,780	8,107,861	135,435	7,996,134
Dairy products, eggs	127,090	2,822,484	148,720	3,159,840
Fish and fish preparations	628,778	1,829,131	776,868	2,308,444
Cereals and cereal preparation	522,164	1,279,721	822,190	1,034,828
Sugar and sugar preparations	209,543	643,579	329,844	581,663
Coffee, tea, cocoa, etc.	771,244	82,023	1,308,673	126,184
Feeding stuff for animals	1,167,789	793,455	1,727,565	1,036,706
Wood, lumber and cork	895,112	188,721	1,403,990	200,647
Textiles, fibres, yarns, fabrics, etc.	2,710,525	1,433,705	3,553,068	1,578,580
Fuels, lubricants, etc.	10,936,671	1,587,820	12,100,083	1,858,228
Pharmaceutical products	546,949	914,819	678,498	1,040,732
Fertilizers, etc.	1,109,838	203,089	990,474	208,609
Metals, manufactures of metals	5,436,743	2,036,332	6,872,983	2,396,239
Machinery, electric. equipment, etc.	10,227,926	10,382,872	12,754,031	11,639,345
Transport equipment	6,209,056	3,823,385	8,476,155	3,420,071

Distribution of Danish foreign trade (in 1,000 kroner) according to countries of origin and destination, for calendar years:

	Imports			*Exports*		
Countries	*1974*	*1975*	*1976*	*1974*	*1975*	*1976*
Belgium	2,157,443	2,110,949	2,880,170	748,165	778,659	925,621
Finland	1,710,999	1,564,388	2,140,969	1,202,367	1,121,682	1,104,640
France	2,274,624	2,246,863	2,848,524	1,601,432	1,589,339	2,299,764
Germany (Fed. Rep.	11,196,653	11,774,711	15,635,146	6,002,665	6,647,532	7,900,421
Norway	2,680,094	2,891,542	3,513,106	2,927,333	3,285,168	3,702,203
Sweden	8,295,201	8,488,902	10,622,929	7,560,451	7,482,759	8,685,041
Switzerland	1,050,050	1,131,645	1,337,994	992,314	828,546	910,446
UK	6,605,368	6,117,491	7,665,358	8,024,228	9,413,646	9,417,899
USA	3,660,864	3,614,541	3,853,264	2,679,327	2,579,350	3,144,237
Allied forces in Fed. Rep. Germany	—	—	—	135,618	123,348	135,309

Total trade between Denmark (without the Faroe Islands) and UK (British Department of Trade returns, in £1,000 sterling):

	1973	*1974*	*1975*	*1976*	*1977*
Imports to UK	477,946	577,115	621,704	705,390	811,657
Exports and re-exports from UK	329,174	427,074	443,122	654,856	797,325

Tourism. In 1976, 16·2m. foreigners visited Denmark, spending some 4,860m. kroner.

Industrial Statistics. Danmarks Statistik. Copenhagen (annually)
Quarterly Statistics for the Industry: Commodity Statistics. Danmarks Statistik, Copenhagen
Statistics on Agriculture, Horticulture and Forestry. Danmarks Statistik. Copenhagen (annually)
Agriculture in Denmark. Agricultural Council of Denmark. Copenhagen, 1972
Agricultural Statistics 1900–1965. Vol. I: *Agricultural Area and Harvest and Utilization of Fertilizers.*—Vol. II: *Livestock and Livestock Products, and Consumption of Feeding Stuffs.* Danmarks Statistik. Copenhagen, 1968–69

Danish Industry in Facts and Figures. Federation of Danish Industries. Copenhagen (annually)
Energy Supply of Denmark, 1900–58 and *1948–65*. Danmarks Statistik. Copenhagen, 1959, 1967. Annual Supplements 1966–75 have been published in Statistical News
Report on Fisheries. Ministry of Fisheries, Copenhagen (annually)
Eckup, C., *The Danish Chemical Industry*. Lyngby, 1971
Nash, E. F., and Attwood, E. A., *The Agricultural Policies of Britain and Denmark*. London, 1961
The 1,000 Largest Companies in Denmark. 8th ed. Copenhagen, 1975

COMMUNICATIONS

Roads. Denmark proper had (1 Jan. 1977), 376 km of motorways, 4,272 km of other state roads, 6,822 km of provincial roads and 55,045 km of commercial roads. Motor vehicles registered at 31 Dec. 1976 comprised 1,327,421 passenger cars, 249,174 lorries, 10,958 taxicabs (including 3,431 for private hire), 6,302 buses and 36,544 cycles.

Railways. There were in 1977 railways of a total length of 2,479 km open for traffic. Of this total, 1,999 km belong to the State. The revenue for 1975–76 amounted to 790m. kroner from passenger transport (including bus traffic) and 900m. kroner from freight.

Aviation. On 1 Oct. 1950 the 3 Scandinavian airlines, Det Danske Luftfartsselskab, ABA and DNL, combined in Scandinavian Airlines System. In 1975 SAS flew 115·6m. km and carried 7,175,300 passengers.

SAS inaugurated its transpolar routes Copenhagen–Los Angeles on 15 Nov. 1954 and Copenhagen–Tōkyō on 25 Feb. 1957, and its trans-Asian express route Copenhagen–Bangkok–Singapore *via* Tashkent on 4 Nov. 1967.

Shipping. On 31 Dec. 1975 the Danish merchant fleet consisted of 3,337 vessels (above 20 GRT) of 4,725,693 GRT.

In 1974, 45,300 vessels of 28m. NRT entered the Danish ports, unloading 39m. tonnes and loading 15m. tonnes of cargo; traffic by passenger ships and ferries is not included.

Post and Broadcasting. There were, in 1976, 1,361 post offices. On 31 Dec. 1976 the length of telephone circuits of private companies was 8,924,127 km. On 1 Jan. 1977 there were 1,756,399 telephone subscribers. Postal revenues, 1975–76, 2,619m. kroner; expenditure, 2,726m. kroner.

Danmarks Radio is the government broadcasting station and is financed by licence fees. Television is broadcast by *Danmarks Radio* with colour programmes by PAL system. Number of receivers: Radio, 1·7m.; television, 1,634,000, including 511,000 colour sets.

Cinemas. In 1976 there were 391 cinemas with a seating capacity of 125,435.

Newspapers. In 1976 there were 49 daily newspapers with a combined circulation of 1·76m. on weekdays; 9 of them (866,000) appeared in Copenhagen.

JUSTICE, RELIGION, EDUCATION AND WELFARE

Justice. The lowest courts of justice are organized in 84 tribunals (*underretter*), where cases are dealt with by a single judge. The tribunals at Copenhagen have 30 judges, Aarhus 12, Odense 9, Aalborg 8, and the other tribunals have 1 to 4. Cases of greater consequence are dealt with by the superior courts (*Landsretterne*); these courts are also courts of appeal for the above-named cases. Of superior courts there are two: *Østre Landsret* in Copenhagen with 36 judges, *Vestre Landret* in Viborg with 20 judges. From these an appeal lies to the Supreme Court (*Højesteret*) in Copenhagen, composed of 15 judges. Judges under 70 years of age can be removed only by judicial sentence.

In 1976, 9,516 men and 801 women were convicted of crimes and delicts, fines not included. On 31 Dec. 1976, 1,294 men and 24 women were in the state prisons.

Religion. At the Reformation in 1536 the Danish Church ceased to exist as a legally independent unit, a part of the Roman Catholic Church, and became instead a

Lutheran Church under the direction of the State. Since that time the State has, in one form or another, continued to exercise supreme authority in the affairs of the Church, and has regulated these by the passing of laws, by royal decree, or other appropriate means. The great majority of Danish citizens (about 90%) belongs to the National Church. Administratively, Denmark is divided into 10 dioceses each with a Bishop who, within the framework of the law, is the supreme diocesan authority in ecclesiastical affairs. The Bishop together with the Chief Administrative Officer of the county make up the diocesan governing body, responsible for all matters of ecclesiastical local finance and general administration. Bishops are appointed by the Crown after an election at which the clergy and parish council members of the diocese have had the opportunity of voting for the candidates nominated. Each diocese is divided into a number of deaneries (about 100 in the whole country) each with its Dean and Deanery Committee, who have certain financial powers. Local government at parish level (there are about 2,100 parishes in all) is in the hands of Parish Councils, who are elected for a 4-year period of office.

Since the Constitution of 1849 complete religious toleration is extended to every sect, and no civil disabilities attach to Dissenters.

Kjær, J. C., *History of the Church of Denmark*. Blair, Nebr., 1945
Roesen, August, *Religion in Denmark*. Copenhagen, 1963

Education. Education has been compulsory since 1814. The primary and lower secondary education comprises a 1-year voluntary pre-school class (*børnehaveklassen*), a 9-year compulsory basic school and 1-year voluntary tenth form. Compulsory education may be fulfilled either through attending the public *folkeskole* or private schools or through home-instruction, the only requirement being that the instruction given should be comparable to that offered in the *folkeskole*. *Folkeskolen* are mainly municipal and no fees are paid. In the year 1976–77, 2,206 primary and lower secondary schools had 561,132 pupils in grades 1–7, and 193,657 pupils in grades 8–10, and employed 56,710 teachers. 13% of the total number of schools were private schools and they were attended by 6% of the total number of pupils in the primary and lower secondary schools. The 9-year compulsory basic school is in practice not streamed. However, a certain differentiation may take place in the eighth and ninth form.

Examination after finishing the primary and lower secondary school is voluntary. After the termination of the eighth and ninth form the pupils may sit for the leaving examination of the *folkeskole* (*folkeskolens afgangsprøve*). After the termination of the tenth form the pupils may sit for either the leaving examination of the *folkeskole* (*folkeskolens afgangsprøve*) or the extended leaving examination of the *folkeskole*.

Under certain conditions the pupils may continue their education either in a 3-year gymnasium ending with *studentereksamen* or in the 2-year higher preparatory school ending with the *højere forberedelseseksamen*. There were (1976–77) 125 of these upper secondary schools with 58,121 pupils and 5,717 teachers.

Youth and leisure-time education: 227 schools (continuation schools, youth residential schools, domestic science schools, folk high schools, youth high schools and agricultural schools) with 24,313 pupils.

Vocational training, technical and commercial education: 51 vocational and technical schools with 46,480 pupils, receiving vocational training as apprentices. 58 vocational and commercial schools with 17,243 pupils receiving vocational training as apprentices, and 15,072 other pupils.

Teacher-training institutions: 29 teacher-training colleges with 15,042 students. 26 colleges for training of teachers for kindergartens and leisure-time activities with 6,433 students.

Degree-courses in Engineering (1976): The Technical University of Denmark had 3,284 students. The Engineering Academy of Denmark had 1,209 students and 8 engineering colleges with 2,160 students.

Universities and University Centres (1976): The University of Copenhagen (founded 1479) 30,077 students. The University of Aarhus (founded in 1928) 15,364 students. The University of Odense (founded in 1964) 4,236 students. Roskilde

University Centre (founded in 1972) 1,508 students. Aalborg University Centre (founded in 1974) 2,324 students.

Other types of post-secondary education (1976): The Royal Veterinary and Agricultural College had 1,700 students. Two Colleges of Dentistry had 1,174 students. The Danish College of Pharmacy had 627 students. Eleven Colleges of Economics and Business Administration had 13,873 students. Two Schools of Architecture had 2,524 students. Five Academies of Music had 833 students. The Danish Library College had 1,314 students. The Royal Danish College of Educational Studies had 1,332 students. The Danish State Institute of Physical Education had 247 students. Four Colleges for Social Welfare Officers had 1,308 students. The Danish College of Journalism had 335 students. Six Therapeutists Colleges had 834 students. One State Midwife School had 121 students.

Schools and Education in Denmark. Copenhagen, 1972
Kirkegaard, P., *The Public Libraries in Denmark*. Copenhagen, 1950; French ed., 1960
Nellermann, A., *Schools and Education in Denmark*. Copenhagen, 1964
Rørdam, T., *The Danish Folk Schools*. Copenhagen, 1965
Skrubbeltrang, F., *The Danish Folk High Schools*. Copenhagen, 1947
Thomsen, O. B., *Some Aspects of Education in Denmark*. Toronto, 1976
Trane, E., *Education and Culture in Denmark*. Copenhagen, 1958

Security. The main body of Danish social welfare legislation is consolidated in 9 acts concerning (1) health insurance, (2) daily cash benefits, (3) disablement pensions, (4) old age pensions, (5) widows pensions, (6) employment injuries insurance, (7) employment services and unemployment insurance, (8) social assistance including assistance to handicapped, rehabilitation, child and juvenile guidance, care of the aged and sick, and (9) family allowances.

Health insurance, covering the entire population, provides free medical care, substantial subsidies for certain essential medicines together with some dental care and a funeral allowance. Hospitals are primarily municipal and the hospital treatment is normally free. Wage-earners are granted daily sickness allowances, others can have limited daily sickness allowances. Daily cash benefits are granted in the case of temporary incapacity for work because of illness, injury or childbirth to all persons who earn an income derived from personal work. The benefit is paid at the rate of 90% of the average weekly earnings. There is a maximum rate of 1,291 kroner a week.

Disablement and old-age pensions cover the entire population. Entitlement to benefits at the full rates is subject to the condition that the beneficiary has been ordinarily resident in Denmark for a number of years (40). For a shorter period of residence, the benefits are reduced proportionally. The basic amount of the old-age pension in 1977 was 30,816 kroner to married couples and 18,276 to single persons. Various supplementary allowances, depending on age and income, may be payable with the basic amount. Persons over 67 years of age are entitled to the basic amount. The pensions to a married couple are calculated and paid to the husband and the wife separately. Invalidity pension is payable, having regard to the degree of disability, at a rate of up to 39,648 kroner to a single person. The rate of the widow's pension corresponds more or less to that of the old-age pension. Invalidity and widow's pensions may be subject to income regulation.

Employment injuries insurance provides for disablement or survivors' pensions and funeral allowances. The scheme covers practically all employees.

Employment services are provided by regional public employment agencies. The insurance against unemployment provides daily allowances. The unemployment insurance funds had at 1 June 1977 a membership of about 1,146,000 full-time workers.

The *Social Assistance Act* applies to the field of social legislation which rules the individually granted benefits in contrast to the other fields of social legislation which apply to fixed benefits.

Total social expenditure, including hospital and health services, amounted in the financial year 1974–75 to 42,445m. kroner.

Bibliography of Foreign Language Literature on Industrial Relations and Social Services in Denmark. Ministries of Labour and Social Affairs, Copenhagen, 1975
Social Conditions in Denmark. Vols. 1–8. Ministries of Labour and Social Affairs, Copenhagen
Jensen, O., *Social Welfare in Denmark.* 3rd ed. Copenhagen, 1972
Kuhlman, S., *Danish Labour Market Conditions, 1974.* Ministry of Labour, Copenhagen, 1974

THE FAROE ISLANDS

Færøerne

AREA AND POPULATION. Area, 1,399 sq. km (540 sq. miles); population (1 Jan. 1977), 41,575.

GOVERNMENT. The parliament (*Lagting*), elected on 7 Nov. 1974, consists of 26 members: 7 Social Democrats, 5 Samband Party, 5 Folkeflok, 1 Progressive Party, 2 Home Rule Party, 6 Republicans.

Flag: White with a red blue-edged Scandinavian cross.

From 1 Jan. 1972 the Faroe Islands were no longer members of EFTA.

BUDGET.

COMMERCE. The main industries are fisheries and crafts. Exports, mainly fresh, frozen, filleted and salted fish, amounted to 631·4m. kroner in 1976; imports to 730m. kroner.

Total trade with UK (British Department of Trade returns, in £1,000 sterling):

	1972	*1973*	*1974*	*1975*	*1976*	*1977*
Imports to UK	1,331	3,411	3,571	4,180	7,637	9,791
Exports and re-exports from UK	1,097	1,134	2,834	1,845	2,061	3,277

BROADCASTING. *Utvarp Føroya* is the broadcasting station and the number of receivers 11,000.

Faroes in Figures. Thorshavn, annual, from 1956
West, J. F., *Faroe.* London, 1973
Williamson, K., *The Atlantic Islands: A Study of the Faroe Life and Scene.* London, 1970

GREENLAND

Grønland

AREA AND POPULATION. Area 2,175,600 sq. km (840,000 sq. miles), made up of 1,833,900 sq. km of ice cap and 341,700 sq. km of ice-free land. The population, 1 Jan. 1976, numbered 49,666; West Greenland, 44,440; East Greenland, 3,029; North Greenland (Thule), 749, and 1,448 not belonging to any specific municipality. Of the total, 9,276 were born outside Greenland.

CONSTITUTION. On 5 June 1953 Greenland became an integral part of the Danish Realm with the same rights as other counties in Denmark and with a democratically elected council (*landsråd*). A Danish–American agreement for the common defence of Greenland was signed on 27 April 1951.

INDUSTRY. Until the beginning of this century, the hunting of land and sea mammals, especially seals, was the main occupation of the population; now fishing is most important. Fish-processing industries, construction and trade are also important occupations.

Coal production ceased in 1972. A deposit of the valuable mineral cryolite has been mined at Ivigtut. The interest of oil and mining companies in obtaining licences and concessions in and offshore Greenland has grown considerably during the last years and in Jan. 1971 the Danish company Greenex A/S was granted a concession for lead and zinc near Umanak and a mine has been constructed. In April 1975, 19 international oil companies and 1 Danish company were granted 13 oil concessions off the west coast. Production of lead and zinc started in 1973.

COMMERCE. Imports (c.i.f. Greenland) (in 1,000 kroner): 1972, 502,661; 1973, 565,711; 1974, 633,691; 1975, 741,910. Exports (f.o.b. Greenland) (in 1,000 kroner): 1972, 152,620; 1973, 191,084; 1974, 551,094; 1975, 509,271. Trade is mainly with Denmark.

Total trade with UK (British Department of Trade returns, in £1,000 sterling):

	1972	*1973*	*1974*	*1975*	*1976*	*1977*
Imports to UK	313	114	41	52	61	2,211
Exports and re-exports from UK	1,384	269	1,550	4,857	5,856	5,329

BROADCASTING. *Grønlands Radio* broadcasts in Greenlandic and Danish. The short wave transmitters are located at Godthoab. Number of receivers, 7,300.

Greenland. R. Danish Ministry of Greenland. Copenhagen. Annual from 1968
Meddelelser om Grønland. Ed. Kommissionen for videnskabelige undersøgelser i Grønland. Copenhagen, 1897 ff.
Birket-Smith, K. (ed.), *Grønlandsbogen.* 2 vols. Copenhagen, 1950
Gad, F., *A History of Greenland.* Vol. 1. London, 1970.—Vol. 2. London, 1973
Hertling, K. (ed.), *Greenland Past and Present.* Copenhagen, 1972

DIPLOMATIC REPRESENTATIVES

OF DENMARK IN GREAT BRITAIN (55 Sloane St., London, SW1X 9SR)

Ambassador: Jens Christensen (accredited 30 Nov. 1977).

OF GREAT BRITAIN IN DENMARK (36–40 Kastelsvej, DK-2100, Copenhagen Ø)

Ambassador: Anne Marion Warburton, CMG, CVO.

OF DENMARK IN THE USA (3200 Whitehaven St., NW, Washington, D.C., 20008)

Ambassador: Otto R. Borch.

OF THE USA IN DENMARK (Dag Hammarskjolds Alle 24, Copenhagen)

Ambassador: John Gunther Dean.

OF DENMARK TO THE UNITED NATIONS

Ambassador: Henning Hjorth-Nielsen.

Books of Reference

Statistical Information: Danmarks Statistik (Sejrøgade 11, 2100 Copenhagen Ø.) was founded in 1849 and reorganized in 1966 as an independent institution; it is administratively placed under the Minister of Economic Affairs. *Chief:* N. V. Skak-Nielsen. Its main publications are: *Statistik Årbog* (Statistical Yearbook). From 1896; *Statistiske Efterretninger* (Statistical News). From 1909; *Statistiske Meddelelser* (Statistical Reports). From 1852; *Handelsstatistiske Meddelelser* (Reports on Foreign Trade). From 1910; *Statistiske Tabelværker* (Statistical Tables). From 1850; *Statistiske Undersøgelser* (Statistical Inquiries). From 1958.

Ministry of Foreign Affairs, *Danish Foreign Office Journal. Commercial and General Review.—Denmark.* 1961.—*Economic Survey of Denmark* (annual).—*Facts About Denmark.* 1959.—Hæstrup, J., *From Occupied to Ally: the Danish Resistance Movement.* 1963
Atlas over Danmark. R. Danish Geog. Society. Copenhagen, 1963
Bibliografi over Danmarks Offentlige Publikationer. Institut for International Udveksling, Copenhagen. Annual
Dania polyglotta. Annual Bibliography of Books ... in Foreign Languages Printed in Denmark. State Library, Copenhagen. Annual

Kongelig Dansk Hof og Statskalender. København. Annual
Brynildsen, F., *A Dictionary of the English and Dano-Norwegian Languages*. 2 vols. Copenhagen, 1902–07
Danstrup, J., *History of Denmark*. 2nd ed. Copenhagen, 1949
Frils, H. (ed.), *Scandinavia Between East and West*. Cornell Univ. Press, Ithaca, 1950
Gedde, K., *This is Denmark*. Copenhagen, 1948
Krabbe, L., *Histoire de Danemark*. Copenhagen and Paris, 1950
Lauring, P., *A History of Denmark*. Copenhagen, 1960
Nielsen, B. K., *Engelsk–Dansk Ordbog*. Copenhagen, 1964
Outze, B. (ed.), *Denmark During the German Occupation*. Copenhagen, 1946
Trap, J. P., *Kongeriget Danmark*. 5th ed. 11 vols. Copenhagen, 1953 ff.
Vinterberg H., and Bodelsen, C. A., *Dansk-engelsk ordbog*. Copenhagen, 1966

National Library: Det Kongelige Bibliotek, Copenhagen. *Librarian:* P. Birkelund.

REPUBLIC OF DJIBOUTI

Capital: Djibouti
Population: 125,000 (1974)

HISTORY. At a referendum held on 19 March 1967, 60% of the electorate voted for continued association with France rather than independence and the new statute for the territory came into being on 5 July 1967. In Jan. 1976, following discussions between Ali Aref and President Giscard d'Estaing, it was announced that the French Government affirmed that the Territory of the Afars and the Issas was destined for independence but no date was fixed. Legislative elections were held on 8 May and independence as the Republic of Djibouti was achieved on 27 June 1977.

AREA AND POPULATION. Djibouti is situated in the Gulf of Aden between the Somali Republic and Ethiopia. The frontier starts from Loyada, on the coast, 20 km south-east of Djibouti, passes by Djalelo, the Degoueiné Mountains, crosses the Addis Ababa railway at Kilometre 110, 6 km to the north of Daouenlé, encloses the Gobaad Plain and Lake Abbé, passes Mount Moussa Ali near Daddato, and terminates at Cape Doumeirah, opposite Perim, on the Straits of Bab el Mandeb.

Djibouti has an area of 23,000 sq. km (8,500 sq. miles). The population was estimated in 1974 at 125,000, including: Somalis, 58,240; Arabs, 8,285; Afars, 42,270; Europeans, 10,255; foreigners, 37,850. Djibouti, the seat of government, had 62,000 inhabitants.

CONSTITUTION AND GOVERNMENT. On 8 May 1977 a 65-seat Chamber of Deputies was elected comprising 33 Issa (Somali), 30 Afar and 2 Arab members.

The cabinet at 5 Feb. 1978 was composed as follows:

President: Hassan Gouled Aptidon.

Prime Minister, Foreign Affairs and Defence: Abdallah Mohamed Kamil.

Justice and Penal Affairs: Ismael Ali Youssef. *Interior:* Moumin Bahdon Farah. *Finance and Economy:* Abdulkader Waheri Askar. *Commerce, Transport, Civil Aviation, Tourism and Industry:* Mohamed Djaba Elabe. *Education:* Hassan Hussein Banabila. *Agriculture and Animal Production:* Idriss Farah Abane. *Posts:* Ahmed Youssef Houmed. *Labour and Social Welfare:* Djama Djilal Djama. *Public Health and Social Affairs:* Mohammed Ahmed Issa. *Public Service:* Ahmed Hassan Liban. *Public Works:* Omar Kamil Warsama. *Administration of Industry:* Ali Mohammed Houmed. *Youth and Sports:* Hamad Abdallah Hamad.

National flag: Horizontally blue over green, with a white triangle based on the hoist charged with a red star.

INTERNATIONAL RELATIONS

Membership. Djibouti is a member of UN, OAU and the Arab League.

ECONOMY

Budget. The ordinary budget for 1977–78 envisaged an expenditure of 10,000m. Djibouti francs.

Currency. The Djibouti franc was introduced on 17 March 1949. The currency is covered 100% by a US dollar fund.

MINERALS. Minerals supposed to exist are gypsum, mica, amethyst and sulphur.

AGRICULTURE. Mainly market gardening at the oasis of Ambouli and near urban areas. Livestock (1976): 18,000 cattle, 98,000 sheep, 580,000 goats, 3,000 donkeys, 25,000 camels.

COMMERCE. The chief imports are cotton goods, sugar, cement, flour and benzene; the chief exports are hides, cattle and coffee (transit from Ethiopia). Special trade in 1,000 tonnes and 1m. Djibouti francs:

	1967		*1968*		*1972*	
	Quantity	*Value*	*Quantity*	*Value*	*Quantity*	*Value*
Imports	105·5	6,713	97·9	8,195	19·1	10,733
Exports	1·9	604	2·2	817	4·5	1,627

Trade with UK (British Department of Trade returns, in £1,000 sterling):

	1973	*1974*	*1975*	*1976*	*1977*
Imports to UK	69	608	124	82	99
Exports and re-exports from UK	2,008	2,711	3,957	5,046	7,432

COMMUNICATIONS

Roads. In 1970 there were operating 7,200 passenger cars, 1,062 lorries, 481 motor cycles and 852 motorized bicycles.

Railway. For the line Djibouti–Addis Ababa *see* p. 437. In 1969–70 the railway carried goods traffic of 411,460 tons and 457,000 passengers.

Shipping. In 1970 there entered at Djibouti 1,217 vessels, unloading 232,866 tons and loading 88,092 tons of merchandise.

Post and Broadcasting. Number of telephones (1975), 3,399. *Office de Radiodiffusion-Télévision Française* broadcasts on medium- and short-waves in French, Somali, Afar and Arabic. There is a low-power television transmitter in Djibouti, broadcasting for 19 hours a week. Number of receivers (1973): radio, 10,000; TV, 2,500.

Cinemas. In 1975 there were 4 cinemas with a seating capacity of 5,800.

EDUCATION. In 1970–71 there were 137 public classes with 4,973 pupils and 37 private classes with 1,449 pupils for primary education. There were 1,475 pupils receiving a secondary education in high school, technical school and private secondary schools.

HEALTH. The medical services in 1971 included a hospital (671 beds), a military hospital (120 beds), 7 dispensaries in Djibouti, 4 dispensaries (140 beds) and 5 infirmaries in other localities outside Djibouti.

DIPLOMATIC REPRESENTATIVES

OF GREAT BRITAIN IN DJIBOUTI

Ambassador: B. L. Strachan (resides in Sana'a).

OF DJIBOUTI IN THE USA

Chargé d'Affaires: Walter S. Clarke.

Books of Reference

Poinsot, J.-P., *Djibouti et la Côte française des Somalis.* Paris, 1965
Thompson, V., and Adloff, R., *Djibouti and the Horn of Africa.* Stanford Univ. Press, 1967
La Côte des Somalis. Paris, 1961

DOMINICAN REPUBLIC

Capital: Santo Domingo
Population: 4·7m. (1978)
GNP per capita: US$780 (1976)

República Dominicana

HISTORY. On 5 Dec. 1492 Columbus discovered the island of Santo Domingo, which he called La Española; for a time it was called Hispaniola. The city of Santo Domingo, founded by his brother, Bartholomew, in 1496, is the oldest city in the Americas. The western third of the island—now the Republic of Haiti—was later occupied and colonized by the French, to whom the Spanish colony of Santo Domingo was also ceded in 1795. In 1808 the Dominican population, under the command of Gen. Juan Sánchez Ramirez, routed an important French military force commanded by Gen. Ferrand, at the famous battle of Palo Hincado. This battle was the beginning of the end for French rule in Santo Domingo and culminated in the successful siege of the capital. Eventually, with the aid of a British naval squadron, the French were forced to capitulate and the colony returned again to Spanish rule, from which it declared its independence in 1821. It was invaded and held by the Haitians from 1822 to 1844, when they were expelled, and the Dominican Republic was founded and a constitution adopted. Great Britain, in 1850, was the first country to recognize the Dominican Republic. The country was occupied by American Marines from 1916 until 1924. In 1936 the name of the capital city was changed from Santo Domingo to Ciudad Trujillo; and back again in 1961.

AREA AND POPULATION. The Dominican Republic occupies the eastern portion (about two-thirds) of the island of Hispaniola, Quisqueya or Santo Domingo, the western division forming the Republic of Haiti. It consists of the National District (containing the capital, Santo Domingo; population, census 1970, 817,067), and 26 provinces. Area is 48,442 sq. km (18,700 sq. miles) with 870 miles of coastline, 193 miles of frontier line with Haiti (marked out in 1936).

The populations of the 26 provinces at the 1970 census were:

La Altagracia	87,180	Puerto Plata	185,800
Azua	91,511	La Romana	56,995
Bahoruco	66,572	Salcedo	89,773
Barahona	112,914	Samaná	53,893
Dajabón	50,780	Sánchez Ramírez	106,177
Duarte	200,813	San Cristóbal	324,395
Espaillat	139,579	San Juan	191,065
La Estrelleta	53,228	San Pedro de Macorís	105,490
Independencia	32,580	Santiago	386,269
María Trinidad Sánchez	97,043	Santiago Rodríguez	49,958
Montecristi	69,276	El Seibo	132,795
Pedernales	12,547	Valverde	76,608
Peravia	127,587	La Vega	293,694

Census population of 1970 was 4,006,005 (1,998,990 males and 2,007,015 females) with 48% of population under 15 years and only 2% over 65.

Population of the principal municipalities (1969): National District (including Santo Domingo) 822,862; Santiago de los Caballeros, 351,656; San Cristóbal, 360,247; La Vega, 295,273; La Romana, 80,873; Azua, 102,407; Bahoruco, 66,223; Barahona, 102,481; Dajabón, 61,590; Duarte, 213,920; Espaillat, 141,356; Independencia, 35,208; María Trinidad Sánchez, 135,081; Montecristi, 74,966; Peravia, 134,860; Puerto Plata, 192,170; Salcedo, 93,669; Sánchez Ramírez, 145,276; Santiago Rodríguez, 48,367; El Seibo, 144,517; Valverde, 99,424.

The population is partly of Spanish descent, but is mainly composed of a mixed race of European and African blood.

CONSTITUTION AND GOVERNMENT. A new constitution was promulgated on 28 Nov. 1966.

The President is elected for 4 years, by direct vote. In case of death, resignation or disability, he is succeeded by the Vice-president. There are 12 secretaries of state, a judicial adviser with secretary-of-state rank and 2 ministers without portfolio in charge of departments. Citizens are entitled to vote at the age of 18, or less when married.

Recent Presidents have been: Gen. Rafael Leonidas Trujillo Molina, 1930–38, 1942–52 (assassinated 30 May 1961); Héctor Bienvenido Trujillo Molina, 1952–60; Dr Joaquín Balaguer, 4 Aug. 1960–62; Lic. Rafael Bonnelly, 18 Jan. 1962; Professor Juan Bosch, 27 Feb.–25 Sept. 1963 (deposed); Dr Héctor Gracía Godoy, 3 Sept. 1965–1 July 1966; Joaquin Balaguer, 1 July 1966–15 Aug. 1978.

President: Antonio Guzman (elected May 1978).

The country's first free elections for nearly 40 years were held in Dec. 1962 when Juan Bosch was elected President with a clear majority, after which a new Constitution was approved on 29 April 1963. Bosch was overthrown by a military *coup d'état* in Sept. 1963 and the declared aim of the Constitutionalist side in the Civil War of April–Sept. 1965 was the restoration of Bosch as President and a return to the 1963 Constitution.

On 30 April 1965 USA landed a force of 23,000 Marine and Army, later assisted by Organization of American States contributions. The capital remained divided between these forces and various rival factions of nationals. A provisional government was eventually installed on 3 Sept. 1965.

Until elections on 1 June 1966 there was government by decree. The voting on 16 May 1974 was 924,779 votes for Dr Joaguín Balaguer (Reformist Party). The general election of May 1978, *see* Addenda.

National flag: Blue, red; quartered by a white cross.

National anthem: Quisqueyanos valientes, alzemos (words by E. Prud'homme; tune by J. Reyes, 1883).

DEFENCE. The armed forces are under the command of the President of the Republic, acting through the Secretary of State for the Armed Forces.

Army. The Army has a strength of about 11,000 all ranks. It is organized in 3 infantry brigades, 1 artillery regiment and 1 anti-aircraft regiment, and has some light tanks and armoured cars.

Navy. The Navy consists of 3 frigates, including the presidential yacht (*ex*-frigate) used for training midshipmen, 2 ocean corvettes, 2 escort (*ex*-fleet) minesweepers, 3 patrol vessels, 1 landing ship (LSM), 2 landing craft (LDM), 6 coastguard vessels, 8 motor launches, 2 oilers, 4 survey craft and 8 tugs. Personnel, 1978: 3,800 officers and men.

Air Force. The Air Force, with HQ at San Isidoro, has 2 operational squadrons, each with 10 to 20 first-line aircraft. One is equipped with F-51D Mustang piston-engined interceptors; the other with jet-powered Vampire Mk. 1 and Mk. 50 fighter-bombers and 3 B-26 piston-engined light bombers. There are also transport (C-47, etc.), helicopter and training units. Total strength (1978) was about 3,500 personnel and 100 aircraft.

INTERNATIONAL RELATIONS

Membership. The Dominican Republic is a member of UN and OAS.

ECONOMY

Budget. The receipts and disbursements for calendar years, in 1m. Dominican gold pesos (RD$), equal to the US$, were:

	1973	*1974*	*1975*	*1976*	*1977*[1]	*1978*[1]
Revenue	325·3	383·4	657·4	...	547·7	620·3
Expenditure	325·3	383·4	665·0	...	547·7	620·3

[1] Estimated.

Income tax, established in 1949, was replaced in 1950 by an identity-card tax, known as the 'cédula tax', but re-introduced in 1962.

Currency. In Oct. 1947 the *peso oro*, equal to the US$, was formally made the unit of currency, replacing the USA gold dollar, which had been the standard since 1 July 1897. On 31 Dec. 1972 the Banco Central had gold and foreign exchange worth 213·2m. pesos. Money supply was 234·7m. pesos.

There are silver coins for 50, 25 and 10 centavos, a copper–nickel 5-centavo piece and a copper 1-centavo piece.

Banking. On 24 Oct. 1941 a law was passed for the creation of a Dominican commercial bank (government controlled) to be known as the Banco de Reservas de la República Dominicana, with a capital of RD$1m., now increased to RD$20m. This bank, starting with branches purchased from the National City Bank of New York, opened for business on 27 Oct. 1941 and now has 11 branches covering the country. It is authorized to perform all customary banking transactions. On 31 Oct. 1966 its assets and liabilities totalled RD$142,126,322. There are 4 foreign banks—the Royal Bank of Canada with 5 branches, the Bank of Nova Scotia, the Citibank and the Chase Manhattan Bank. An agricultural and mortgage bank, with paid-up capital of RD$500,000, was established in 1945; in 1950 its capital was increased to RD$5m.; in 1952 steps were begun to raise it to cover a 5-year programme of agricultural expansion; it stood at RD$100m. in Nov. 1962.

In 1947 the Central Bank of the Dominican Republic was launched. Chief liability was note circulation, chiefly bank-notes of 1, 5 and 10 pesos (RD$104·5m. in 1966); total assets and liabilities were RD$215·8m. The net reserve of foreign exchange was US$32m. at 31 Aug. 1966.

A new Banco Popular Dominicano, with an authorized capital of RD$5m., opened in Jan. 1964.

Weights and Measures. The metric system was nominally adopted on 1 Aug. 1913, but English and Spanish units have remained in common use in ordinary commercial transactions; on 17 Sept. 1954 a more drastic law requiring the decimal metric system was passed.

ENERGY AND NATURAL RESOURCES

Electricity. The electricity production capacity in 1971 was 257,000 kw. and 1,201m. kwh. was generated in 1972.

Minerals. The Aluminium Company of America sent its first shipment of bauxite for smelting, to Texas, on 13 Jan. 1959. Output in 1972 was 1,087,000 tonnes. Silver and platinum have been found, and near Neiba there are several hills of rock salt (production 1972, 31,000 tonnes). Copper production (1969) 1,200 tonnes.

Agriculture. Agriculture is the chief source of wealth, sugar cultivation being the principal industry. Of the total area, 9,900 sq. miles are cultivable, and about 3,700 are under cultivation. 50% is under subsistence farming—small-holdings each of 15 *tareas* ($2\frac{1}{2}$ acres) or less.

Livestock in 1976: 2m. cattle, 800,000 pigs, 51,000 sheep.

The largest sugar estates are in the south-eastern part of the republic. Sugar production, 1974, was 1,505,000 tonnes. Two companies (one American-owned, the other expropriated after the downfall of the Trujillo family) produce four-fifths of the total, but in all there are 16 sugar 'centrals'.

Coffee is exported mainly to USA. Output, 1972, 42,000 tonnes. Production of rice for home consumption and export is fostered; output, 1974, 344,000 tonnes. Cocoa is the second principal crop and covers 2m. *tareas* (340,000 acres); output in 1974, 41,000 tonnes. Other principal exports are leaf tobacco and molasses (22,000 tonnes in 1970). There are useful crops of yuca (1973: 195,000 tonnes) and beans

(1973: 34,000 tonnes) for local consumption. Scientific growing of bananas (1970: 275,000 tonnes) and of tobacco (1973: 44,000 tonnes) is progressing.

INDUSTRY AND TRADE

Commerce. Total imports and exports in RD$1m. (equal to US$1m.):

	1971	*1972*	*1973*	*1974*	*1975*	*1976*
Imports	311·1	337·7	421·9	673·0	773·1	763·6
Exports	246·6	347·6	442·1	636·8	893·8	716·4

The principal exports in 1974 were (in RD$1m.): Sugar and by-products, 340; coffee, 45; cocoa and by-products, 47·9; tobacco, 39·2; meat, 9·3; fruit and vegetables, 8·8; ferronickel, 93·1; bauxite, 17·8.

Total trade between the Dominican Republic and UK (British Department of Trade returns, in £1,000 sterling):

	1973	*1974*	*1975*	*1976*	*1977*
Imports to UK	4,716	10,553	6,123	4,063	2,025
Exports and re-exports from UK	4,666	6,396	7,522	9,537	10,501

Industry. In 1967, 1,230 industrial establishments employed 107,595 men and women, who earned RD$79·6m. Output was valued at RD$423·5m. There were 1,036 establishments in 1970. Important manufactures are sugar (1,173,000 tonnes in 1972), textiles (7m. metres of cotton fabric in 1972), cement (678,000 tonnes in 1972), glass bottles, paper and matches. Oil refining capacity was 1·5m. tonnes in 1972, and chemical plants produced 57,000 hectolitres of ethyl alcohol.

Tourism. 232,902 tourists visited the Dominican Republic in 1975 spending US$79,631,499.

COMMUNICATIONS

Roads. Three main trunk highways, with branches, extend from Santo Domingo eastward to Higuey (106 miles), northward to Santiago and Montecristi and Dajabón (204 miles) and westward to San Juan (128 miles) and Elías Piña on the Haitian border (161 miles). At Elías Piña the road joins the Haitian road to Port-au-Prince. Total highway system in 1963 was 4,250 km first- and 2,000 km second-class roads; there were 647 bridges. Road transport is the chief means of travel. There were 54,657 cars, 26,981 commercial vehicles and 29,332 motor cycles in 1975.

Railways. Some 100 km of the Dominican Government Railway remains in use between La Vega and the port of Sánchez. Other lines, including the Central Romana Railway, exist to serve the sugar industry.

Aviation. The country is reached from the American continent and the Caribbean islands by 8 international airlines. Two local aviation companies provide interior services and connect Santo Domingo with San Juan in Puerto Rico, Curaçao, Aruba and Miami.

Shipping. Santo Domingo is the leading port; Puerto Plata ranks next. In 1971, vessels of 9,833,000 tons entered the ports to discharge 3,009,000 tonnes of cargo, and vessels of 5,276,000 tons cleared the ports having loaded 1,986,000 tonnes.

Post and Broadcasting. Number of telephone instruments (1977), 127,332, of which 96,680 in Santo Domingo. The telephone system is mainly operated by an American company. The telegraph has a total length of about 500 km, privately owned; they have been leased to All-America Cables, Inc., which also controls submarine cables connecting, in the north, Puerto Plata with Puerto Rico and New York, and in the south, Santo Domingo with Puerto Rico, Cuba and Curaçao.

There are 95 broadcasting stations in Santo Domingo and other towns; this includes the 2 government stations. There are 4 television stations. In 1972 there were 170,000 radio receivers and 150,000 television receivers.

Cinemas (1971). Cinemas numbered 82, with seating capacity of 40,600.

Newspapers (1972). There were 7 daily newspapers with a circulation of 155,000.

JUSTICE, RELIGION, EDUCATION AND WELFARE

Justice. The judicial power resides in the Supreme Court of Justice, the courts of appeal, the courts of first instance, the communal courts and other tribunals created by special laws, such as the land courts. The Supreme Court consists of a president and 8 judges chosen by the Senate, and the procurator-general, appointed by the executive; it supervises the lower courts. Each province forms a judicial district, as does the *Distrito Nacional*, and each has its own procurator fiscal and court of first instance; these districts are subdivided, in all, into 72 municipalities and 18 municipal districts, each with one or more local justices. The death penalty was abolished in 1924.

Religion. The religion of the state is Roman Catholic; other forms of religion are permitted. There is a papal nuncio as well as an archbishop, known as the Primate of the Indies.

Education. Primary instruction (5,245 schools) is free and obligatory for children between 7 and 14 years of age; there are also secondary, normal, vocational and special schools, all of which are either wholly maintained by the state or state-aided; in 1975, primary schools had 15,216 teachers and 833,439 pupils; 997 intermediate and secondary schools had 4,950 teachers and 142,501 pupils. The campaign against adult illiteracy dates from 1941, but in 1964 about 65% of the population were still illiterate.

The University of Santo Domingo (founded 1538) had (1975) 27,675 students; 5 other universities had 14,573 students.

Health. In 1964, 78 towns had complete waterworks. There were, in 1975, 1,310 doctors, 121 hospitals, health centres and polyclinics with 8,389 beds.

DIPLOMATIC REPRESENTATIVES

OF THE DOMINICAN REPUBLIC IN GREAT BRITAIN
(4 Braemar Mansions, London, SW7 4AG)

Ambassador: Alfredo A. Ricart.

OF GREAT BRITAIN IN THE DOMINICAN REPUBLIC
(Ave. Independencia No. 84, Santo Domingo)

Ambassador and Consul-General: C. Spearman.

OF THE DOMINICAN REPUBLIC IN THE USA
(1715–22nd St., NW, Washington, D.C., 20008)

Ambassador: Dr Horacio Vicioso-Soto.

OF THE USA IN THE DOMINICAN REPUBLIC
(Calle Cesar Nicolas Pensen, Santo Domingo)

Ambassador: (Vacant).

OF THE DOMINICAN REPUBLIC TO THE UNITED NATIONS

Ambassador: Dr Alfonso Moseno Martinez.

Books of Reference

Anuario estadístico de la República Dominicana, 1944–45. Ciudad Trujillo. 1949. This has been succeeded by separate annual reports covering foreign trade, vital statistics, banking, insurance, housing and communications.

Dirección General de Estadística. *21 años de estadísticas dominicanas 1936–1956.* Ciudad Trujillo, 1957

The Dominican Republic: Rebellion and Depression. London and New York, 1973

ECUADOR

República del Ecuador

Capital: Quito
Population: 6·5m. (1974)
GNP per capita: US$640 (1976)

HISTORY. The Spaniards under Francisco Pizarro founded a colony after their victory at Cajamarca (16 Nov. 1532). Their rule was first challenged by the rising of 10 Aug. 1809. Marshal Sucre defeated the Spaniards at Pichincha in 1821, and in 1822 Bolívar persuaded the new republic to join the federation of Gran Colombia. The Presidency of Quito became the Republic of Ecuador by amicable secession 13 May 1830.

AREA AND POPULATION. Ecuador is bounded on the north by Colombia, on the east and south by Peru, on the west by the Pacific Ocean. The frontier with Peru has long been a source of dispute between the two countries. The latest delimitation of it was in the treaty of Rio, 29 Jan. 1942, when, after being invaded by Peru, Ecuador ceded the latter over half her Amazonian territories. Ecuador unilaterally denounced this treaty in Sept. 1961. *See* map in THE STATESMAN'S YEAR-BOOK, 1942.

No definite figure of the area of the country can yet be given, as a portion of the frontier has not been delimited. One estimate of the area of Ecuador is 268,178 sq. km, excluding the litigation zone between Peru and Ecuador, which is 190,807 sq. km.

Ecuador has 3 distinct zones: the *Sierra* or uplands of the Andes, consisting of high mountain ridges with valleys, with 2·57m. of the population and high-priced farming land; the *Costa*, the coastal plain between the Andes and the Pacific, with 2·02m., whose permanent plantations furnish bananas, cacao, coffee, sugar-cane and many other crops; the *Oriente*, the upper Amazon basin on the east, consisting of tropical jungles threaded by large rivers.

The population is predominantly of Amerindians, with small proportions of people of European or African descent.

The official language is Spanish. The Amerindians of the highlands speak mainly the Quechua language; in the Oriental Region various tribes have languages of their own.

Ecuador's first census of population was taken on 29 Nov. 1950; it showed a total of 3,202,757 (1,594,803 males and 1,607,954 females). The census was hampered by strong opposition from the Indian villages. The working population was given as 1,940,628, of which two-thirds were agricultural. Census population in 1974, 6,521,710.

The population (census at 8 April 1974) was distributed by provinces (capitals in brackets):

Provinces	*Area (sq. km)*	*Population 1974*
Azuay (Cuenca)	7,799	367,324
Bolívar (Guaranda)	3,216	144,593
Cañar (Azogues)	2,677	146,570
Carchi (Tulcán)	3,582	120,857
Chimborazo (Riobamba)	6,161	304,316
Cotopaxi (Latacunga)	4,614	236,313
El Oro (Machala)	7,451	262,564
Esmeraldas (Esmeraldas)	15,866	203,151
Guayas (Guayaquil)	21,259	1,512,333
Imbabura (Ibarra)	4,903	216,027
Loja (Loja)	28,900	342,339

Provinces	Area (sq. km)	Population 1974
Los Rios (Babahoyo)	5,937	383,432
Manabí (Portoviejo)	18,963	817,966
Pichincha (Quito)	16,438	988,306
Tungurahua (Ambato)	3,204	279,920
Napo (Tena)	296,390	62,186
Pastaza (Puyo)		23,465
Morona-Santiago (Macas)		53,325
Zamora-Chinchipe (Zamora)		34,493
Colon (Galápagos)	7,844	4,037
Totals	455,454	6,521,710

There are 115 cantons, 212 urban parishes and 715 rural parishes. The chief towns (population census, 1974) are the capital, Quito (559,828), Guayaquil (823,219), Cuenca (104,470), Ambato (77,955), Machala (69,170), Esmeraldas (60,364), Portoviejo (59,550), Riobamba (58,087).

Vital statistics for calendar years: Births, (1964) 219,137, (1965) 226,436, (1966) 220,930; deaths, (1964) 58,989, (1965) 60,202, (1966) 59,618.

CONSTITUTION AND GOVERNMENT. On 22 June 1970 President José Maria Velasco Ibarra assumed dictatorial powers, following months of strife between student and security forces. For details of governments 1963–70, *see* THE STATESMAN'S YEAR-BOOK, 1974–75, pp. 875–76. On 15 Feb. 1972 President Ibarra was deposed. A National Military Government under Brig.-Gen. Guillermo Rodriguez Lara was formed and the 1945 Constitution reintroduced. President Velasco resigned in Jan. 1976 and a military junta assumed power in Jan. 1976. A referendum on the future Constitution took place in Jan. 1978 and Presidential elections are to be held on 16 July.

National flag: Three horizontal stripes of yellow, blue, red, with the yellow of double width, and in the centre over all the national arms.

National anthem: Salve, on patria! (words by J. L. Mera; tune by A. Neumann, 1866).

The following is a list of the presidents and provisional executives since 1940:

Carlos Alberto Arroyo del Rio, elected 12 Jan. 1940; resigned 30 May 1944.
Dr José María Velasco Ibarra, elected by Constituent Assembly, Aug. 1944; re-elected 11 Aug. 1946, but deposed 24 Aug. 1947.
Col. Carlos Mancheno, seized power 24 Aug. 1947; deposed 3 Sept. 1947.
Mariano Suárez Veintimilla (Vice-President), 3–15 Sept. 1947.
Carlos Julio Arosemena Tola (provisional), 15 Sept. 1947–31 Aug. 1948.
Galo Plaza Lasso, 1 Sept. 1948–31 Aug. 1952
Dr José María Velasco Ibarra, 1 Sept. 1952–31 Aug. 1956.
Dr Camilo Ponce Enríquez, 1 Sept. 1956–31 Aug. 1960.
Dr José María Velasco Ibarra, 1 Sept. 1960–8 Nov. 1961 (withdrew).
Dr Carlos Julio Arosemena Monroy, 8 Nov. 1961–11 July 1963 (deposed).
Military Junta, 11 July 1963–31 March 1966.
Clemente Yerovi Indaburu, 31 March–16 Nov. 1966 (interim).
Dr Otto Arosemena Gómez, 17 Nov. 1966–1 Sept. 1968.
Dr José María Velasco Ibarra, 1 Sept. 1968–15 Feb. 1972 (deposed).
Gen. Guillermo Rodriguez Lara, 16 Feb. 1972–11 Jan. 1976 (resigned).

President: Vice-Adm. Alfredo Povedo Burbano.

Minister of Foreign Affairs: Lic. José Ayala Lasso.

Local Government. The country is divided politically into 20 provinces; 4 of them comprise the 'Región Oriental' and one the Archipelago of Galápagos, officially called 'Colón', situated in the Pacific Ocean about 600 miles to the west of Ecuador and comprising 15 islands. The provinces are administered by governors, appointed by the Government; their sub-divisions, or cantons, by political chiefs and elected cantonal councillors; and the parishes by political lieutenants. The Galápagos Archipelago is administered by the Ministry of National Defence.

DEFENCE. Military service is selective, with a 2-year period of conscription. The country is divided into 4 military zones, with headquarters at Quito, Guayaquil, Cuenca and Pastaza.

Army. The Army consists of 11 infantry battalions, 3 artillery groups, 3 reconnaissance squadrons, 2 engineer battalions, 1 anti-aircraft battalion and 10 independent infantry companies. A military academy for cadets and a war academy for officers are maintained at Quito. Total strength (1977) 17,500.

Navy. The Navy consists of 2 new Federal Republic of Germany-built diesel-electric powered patrol submarines; 3 frigates (comprising 2 British 'Hunt' class escort destroyers acquired in 1955 and a US destroyer escort transport acquired in 1967), 2 escort vessels, 3 missile boats, 3 torpedo boats, 2 gunboats, 5 patrol boats, 2 medium landing ships, 1 supply ship, 1 water carrier, 2 survey vessels, 2 coastguard service craft, 1 training ship, 1 floating dock and 3 tugs. Two more submarines are reportedly ordered from the Federal Republic of Germany. Naval personnel in 1978 totalled 3,800.

Air Force. The Air Force, formed with Italian assistance in 1920, was reorganized and re-equipped with US aircraft after Ecuador signed the Rio Pact of Mutual Defence in 1947 but latest equipment acquired from Europe. Current strength of about 3,000 personnel and 48 combat aircraft includes a strike squadron equipped with 10 single-seat and 2 two-seat Jaguars; a bomber squadron with 5 Canberra B.6s; a squadron of 7 Meteor FR.9 day reconnaissance-fighters; 2 counter-insurgency units equipped with 12 Cessna A-37B and 14 Strikemaster light jet attack and training aircraft, 1 squadron of DC-6B and C-47 piston-engined transports, 4 Electra, 2 Buffalo, 4 HS 748, 3 Twin Otter and 6 Arava turboprop transports, Alouette III, SA 330 Puma and SA 315B Lama helicopters, and Cessna 150, T-28, T-33, T-34C and T-41A/D trainers. On order are 16 single-seat and 2 two-seat Mirage F.1 fighters from France.

INTERNATIONAL RELATIONS

Membership. Ecuador is a member of UN and OAS.

ECONOMY

Budget. Estimated revenue and expenditure for 1976 was US$17·4m.

The division of the budget under main heads was, for 1976 (in 1m. sucres): Education and social development, 4,487; defence, 2,592; public works, 1,834; economic development including agriculture, 2,050. The budget deficit for 1976 was estimated at 1,250m. sucres.

Net international reserves at 30 Sept. 1975 were US$204·7m. (1974, US$330·3m.).

Currency. The monetary unit is the *sucre*, divided into 100 *centavos*. In circulation are a pure nickel 1-sucre and copper–nickel and copper–zinc 50-, 20-, 10- and 5-centavo pieces. The currency consists mainly of the notes of the Central Bank in denominations of 5, 10, 20, 50, 100, 500 and 1,000 sucres. In Aug. 1970 the US$1 stood at 25 sucres and (Jan. 1973) the £ at 57·75 sucres in the official exchange.

Banking. The Central Bank of Ecuador, at Quito, with a capital of 20m. sucres, is modelled after the Federal Reserve Banks of US: through branches opened in 12 towns it now deals in mortgage bonds. On 31 July 1970 the Central Bank had gold and foreign-exchange reserves worth US$62m. Banks must hold cash equal to 21% of sight, short-term and savings deposits.

All commercial banks must be affiliated to the Central Bank; the commercial banks, 31 Oct. 1967, had capital and reserves of 463m. sucres and total assets of 4,536m. sucres. In circulation, Dec. 1972, 7,321m. sucres.

The Bank of London and Montreal, Ltd, had branches in Quito and Guayaquil.

Weights and Measures. By a law of 6 Dec. 1856 the metric system was made the legal standard but the Spanish measures are in general use. The quintal is equivalent to 101·4 lb.

The meridian of Quito has been adopted as the official time.

ENERGY AND NATURAL RESOURCES

Electricity. In 1972, total capacity of hydraulic and thermal plants was 357,000 kw. Estimated output was 1,117m. kwh.

Oil. Exports of crude petroleum in 1976 were 47·6m. US bbls. New drilling along the coast has had some success, but Ecuador has to import some crude oil. Drilling near the river Putumayo started in 1967, and oil is reported to have been found in commercial quantities. Of 53 wells drilled in 1973 only 6 were dry.

Minerals. A few firms are engaged in stoping mineralized vein material for copper, gold, silver, lead and zinc. Production is small: that of silver was 2 tonnes in 1972.

The country has some copper, iron and lead. There are coal deposits in the Biblián area, but their exploitation has so far proved uneconomic. Output of sea salt in 1970 was 40,000 tonnes.

Agriculture. Ecuador is divided into two agricultural zones: the coast and lower river valleys, where tropical farming is carried on in an average temperature of from 18° to 25° C.; and the Andean highlands with a temperate climate, adapted to grazing, dairying and the production of cereals, potatoes, pyrethrum and vegetables suitable to temperate climes. Some wheat has to be imported.

124,000 acres of rich virgin land in the Santo Domingo de los Colorados area has been set aside for settlement of smallholders.

Excepting the two agricultural zones and a few arid spots on the Pacific coast, Ecuador is a vast forest. Roughly estimated, 10,000 sq. miles on the Pacific slope extending from the sea to an altitude of 5,000 ft on the Andes, and the Amazon Basin below the same level containing 80,000 sq. miles, nearly all virgin forest, are rich in valuable timber, but much of it is still not commercially accessible.

The staple export products are bananas, cacao and coffee. These make up over 82% of her exports; the value of the bananas being some 46%. The production of wheat is increasing. Sugar is becoming important; some tea is being produced, mostly for export. Main crops, in 1,000 tonnes, in 1972: Rice, 242; wheat, 51; potatoes, 473; maize, 271; coffee, 58·4; barley, 73; cocoa, 64·9; bananas (1969), 118m. stems.

Livestock (1976): Cattle, 2·7m.; sheep, 2·2m.; pigs, 2·7m.

Fisheries. Fisheries and fish product exports were valued at US$9·6m. in 1970; of these, shrimps comprised about half.

INDUSTRY AND TRADE

Industry. The Industrial Development Law of 1965 has stimulated the establishment of new industries, including textiles, refrigerators, pharmaceuticals, tinned food, batteries etc. In 1971 there were 1,053 manufacturing units employing 50,000 people who earned 1·1m. sucres. Value of gross output, 11,172m. sucres. Cement output, 1972, from the country's 3 plants was 482,000 tonnes. Production (in tonnes) of sawn wood was 792,000; fuel oils, 691; motor spirit, 407; sugar, 275.

GNP *per capita* (1975) US$635.

Commerce. Imports and exports for calendar years, in US$1m.:

	1973	*1974*	*1975*	*1976*	*1977*
Imports (c.i.f.)	397·3	678·2	987·0	860·7	1,288·7
Exports (f.o.b.)	532·0	1,123·5	973·9	1,127·3	1,189·4

Of the total exports in 1969 (and 1970) the largest items were: Bananas, $107·1m. ($122·8m.); coffee, $26·6m. ($50·5m.); cocoa, $24·5m. ($22·3m.). Other exports include sugar, castor-oil seed, pharmaceuticals, toquilla straw ('Panama') hats, balsa wood, rice, pyrethrum and fish products.

USA furnished 35% of imports in 1970 and took 43% of the exports.

Total trade between Ecuador and UK (British Department of Trade returns, in £1,000 sterling):

	1973	*1974*	*1975*	*1976*	*1977*
Imports to UK	2,250	2,170	2,065	2,540	4,978
Exports and re-exports from UK	11,822	13,600	17,307	23,260	59,522

COMMUNICATIONS

Roads. There are 17,195 km of roads of all types in this mountainous country, but most are narrow and subject to landslides. A trunk highway through the coastal plain is under construction which will link Machala in the extreme south-west with Esmeraldas in the north-west and with Quito and the northern section of the Pan-American Highway.

In 1971 there were 30,000 passenger cars and 44,300 commercial vehicles.

Railways. A railway is open from Durán (opposite Guayaquil) to Quito (463 km). The Quito–San Lorenzo extension was officially opened in Aug. 1957. The total length of the Ecuadorean State Railways in operation is 965 km. Modernization of the Durán–Quito section was in progress in 1971.

Aviation. The following international lines operate: Air France, Avianca, Braniff, Ecuatoriana de Aviación, KLM, Lufthansa, Iberia, LAN Chile, and Aerovías Peruanas. They connect Quito with Panama, Bogotá (Colombia), Guayaquil, New York and Europe. All the leading towns are connected by an almost daily service, but landing fields are small.

Shipping. Ecuador has 7 seaports, of which Guayaquil is the chief. The merchant navy comprises 39,964 tons of seagoing and 21,232 tons of river craft. In 1970 ships totalling 8·88m. GRT entered Ecuadorean ports, unloading 1·52m. tons, and loading 1·77m. tons.

There is river communication, improved by dredging, throughout the principal agricultural districts on the low ground to the west of the Cordillera by the rivers Guayas, Daule and Vinces (navigable for 200 miles by river steamers in the rainy season).

Post and Broadcasting. Quito is connected by telegraph with Colombia and Peru, and by cable with the rest of the world. The main towns in the country are connected by radio-telephone. There are over 300 radio stations.

In 1977 there were 174,046 telephones in use, 74,240 in Quito and 64,200 in Guayaquil; most were operated by the Government; 90% were automatic. Television was inaugurated in 1960 in Guayaquil, in 1961 in Quito and in 1967 in Cuenca. In 1971 there were 1·7m. radio receivers and 280,000 television receivers.

Cinemas (1974). Cinemas numbered about 185 with total seating capacity of 114,600.

Newspapers (1971). There were 22 daily newspapers with an aggregate daily circulation of 283,000; 7 papers in Quito and Guayaquil have the bulk of the circulation.

JUSTICE, RELIGION, EDUCATION AND WELFARE

Justice. The Supreme Court in Quito is the highest tribunal and consists of 5 justices and the Minister Fiscal. Of the 15 superior courts, 4 are composed of 6 judges and 11 of 3 judges each. There are numerous lower courts. The popular jury was abolished in 1928, and criminal cases are heard before a 'special jury' consisting of 1 judge and 3 members of the Ecuadorean bar, appointed annually by the superior courts. Capital punishment and all forms of torture are prohibited under the constitution, as are imprisonment for debt and contracts involving personal servitude or slavery. Substantial amendments expediting judicial procedure were introduced in 1936, and salaries for all judicial officials replaced remuneration by fees.

Religion. The state recognizes no religion and grants freedom of worship to all. Civil registration of births, deaths and marriages is obligatory. Divorce is permitted. Illegitimate children have the same rights as legitimate ones with respect to education and inheritance.

The Catholic Church has 1 cardinal, 3 archbishops and 18 bishops. A *modus vivendi* was concluded with the Holy See on 24 July 1937, governing the relations between the Catholic Church and the state. Protestants numbered 19,200 in 1966.

Education. Primary education is free and in principle obligatory. Private schools, both primary and secondary, are under some state supervision. There were (1976–

77) primary schools with 1,318,475 pupils; secondary schools with 431,226 pupils and universities with 170,173 students.

Social Welfare. From 1 May 1964 social benefits are extended to professional men, artisans and domestic workers; and to agricultural workers from 1 May 1965. The Ministry of Social Welfare and Labour was in 1967 divided into the Ministries of Social Welfare and of Public Health. In 1970 there were 199 hospitals with 14,024 beds.

DIPLOMATIC REPRESENTATIVES

OF ECUADOR IN GREAT BRITAIN (3 Hans Crescent, London, SW1X 0LS)

Ambassador: Dr Agustin Carlos Arroyo (accredited 13 Oct. 1977).

OF GREAT BRITAIN IN ECUADOR (Calle Gonzalez Suarez 111, Quito)

Ambassador: J. K. Hickman, CMG.

OF ECUADOR IN THE USA (2535–15th St., NW, Washington, D.C., 20009)

Ambassador: Gustavo Ycaza Borja.

OF THE USA IN ECUADOR (120 Avenida Patria, Quito)

Ambassador: Richard J. Bloomfield.

OF ECUADOR TO THE UNITED NATIONS

Ambassador: Dr Miguel A. Albornoz.

Books of Reference

Anurio de Legislación Ecuatoriana. Quito. Annual
Boletin del Banco Central. Quito
Boletin General de Estadistica. Tri-monthly
Boletín Mensual del Ministerio de Obras Públicas. Monthly
Informes Ministeriales. Quito. Annual
Bibliografia Nacional, 1756–1941. Quito, 1942
Blanksten, G. I., *Ecuador: Constitutions and Caudillos.* Univ. of California Press, 1951
Bromley, R. J., *Development Planning in Ecuador.* London, 1977
Buitrón, Aníbal, and Collier, Jr., J., *The Awakening Valley: Study of the Otavalo Indians.* New York, 1950
Hagen, V. W. von, *Ecuador and the Galápagos Islands.* Norman, Okla., 1949
Holdridge, L. R., and others, *The Forests of Western and Central Ecuador.* Washington, 1947
Linke, L., *Ecuador, Country of Contrasts.* R. Inst. of Int. Affairs, 3rd ed., 1959
Luna Yepes, J., *Síntesis histórica y geográfica del Ecuador.* Madrid, 1951

ARAB REPUBLIC OF EGYPT

Capital: Cairo
Population: 39m. (1976)
GNP per capita: US$280 (1976)

HISTORY. On 1 Feb. 1958 President Nasser of Egypt and President Kuwatly of Syria proclaimed in Cairo the union of their countries, under one head of state, with a common legislature, a unified army and one flag.

On 8 March the Kingdom of Yemen federated with the United Arab Republic under the name of the United Arab States.

On 26–28 Sept. 1961 Syria broke away and resumed its independence. President Nasser accepted the situation on 29 Sept.

On 26 Dec. 1961 Egypt also declared the union with Yemen terminated; but in Nov. 1962 concluded a defence pact with the republican regime.

On 13 Aug. 1964 the UAR, Iraq, Kuwait, Jordan and Syria signed a document forming an Arab Common Market, which aims at the free movement of the currency and products of the member countries. The market was to come into being on 1 Jan. 1965, but this has not taken place.

A decision to bring about full political union between Egypt and Libya by 1 Sept. 1973 was announced on 2 Aug. 1972.

In Aug. 1973 it was agreed by Egypt and Libya that the merger should nominally come into force but that each country should remain independent. Total union should take place over a period of time.

EVENTS. In Nov. 1977 President Sadat travelled to Israel for talks with Prime Minister Begin about peace in the Middle East.

AREA AND POPULATION. The total area of Egypt is about 386,198 sq. miles (1m. sq. km), but the cultivated and settled area, that is, the Nile valley, delta and oases, covers only about 13,500 sq. miles (35,500 sq. km). Canals, roads, date plantations, etc., cover 1,900 sq. miles; 2,850 sq. miles constitute the surface of the Nile, marshes and lakes.

Egypt is divided into two districts—'Wagh-el-Bahari', Lower Egypt and 'El-Saïd', Upper Egypt.

The following table gives the area of the settled land surface, and the results of the census taken in 1966:

Governorates[1]	*Area in sq. km*	*1966 census (in 1,000)* *Males*	*Females*	*Total*
Cairo	214·2	2,158	2,062	4,220
Alexandria	289·5	921	881	1,801
Suez	306·9	137	127	264
Port Said	828·8	144	139	283
Ismailia	397·4	175	170	348
Damietta	599·2	220	211	432
Behera (Damanhûr)	4,592·5	980	999	1,979
Gharbîya (Tanta)	1,994·5	949	952	1,901
Daqahlîya (Mansûra)	3,462·1	1,147	1,138	2,285
Sharqîya (Zagazig)	4,701·5	1,059	1,049	2,108
Menûfîya (Shibin-el-Kôm)	1,514·2	734	724	1,458
Qalyûbîya (Benha)	943·6	619	592	1,212
Kafr el Sheikh	3,492·4	553	565	1,118
Gîza	1,078·5	839	812	1,650
Beni Suef	1,312·8	458	470	928
Faiyûm	1,792·1	467	468	935
Minya	2,273·9	858	847	1,706
Asyût	1,553·0	723	695	1,418

[1] Capitals in brackets, where different from the name of the governorate.

Governorates	Area in sq. km	1966 census (in 1,000) Males	Females	Total
Sohag	1,540·2	850	840	1,689
Qena	1,810·7	738	733	1,471
Aswân	882·2	264	256	521
Red Sea	—	22	16	38
New Valley	—	31	29	59
Matruh	—	63	61	124
Sinai	—	67	64	131
Total (excluding deserts)	35,500	...	...	30,076

The density of population was 732 per sq. km. The nomadic population of about 78,000 is not included in the above table.

The principal towns, with their estimated 1974 populations (in 1,000), are: Cairo (city only) 5,715; Alexandria, 2,259; Gîza, 854; Suez, 368; Subra-El Khema, 346; Port Said, 342; Mahalla el Kûbra, 288; Tanta, 278; Aswân, 246; Mansûra, 232; Asyût, 197; Zagazig, 195; Ismailia, 190; Damanhûr, 176; Faiyûm, 167; Minya, 131.

Estimated population in 1976 was 39m. (census, 1966, 30,075,858) and Greater Cairo, 8·3m.

Vital statistics for 1971: Births, 1,479,000; deaths, 445,000.

Crude birth rate (1971), 34·6 per 1,000 population; crude death rate, 13·1; marriage rate, 10; divorce rate, 2·1.

CONSTITUTION AND GOVERNMENT. The constitution was proclaimed by President Nasser on 25 March 1964.

The constitution defines the UAR as 'a democratic socialist state' and the Egyptian people as 'part of the Arab nation'; with Islam as a state religion and Arabic as the official language. The national economy is directed by the state; the 3 sectors of state, co-operative and private ownership are supervised and controlled by the people. 'Freedom of belief is absolute; freedom of the press, printing and publication is guaranteed within the limits of the law'. Public education is free at all stages.

The People's Assembly is elected by universal suffrage and has 360 members; the President of the Republic may appoint up to 10 additional members. The President of the Republic is nominated by the People's Assembly and confirmed by plebiscite for a 6-year term. He is the supreme commander of the armed forces and presides over the defence council.

On 26 March 1973 President Sadat assumed the post of Prime Minister and announced a new cabinet of 12 members.

The constitution is supplemented by the Charter of 21 May 1962, which sketches the principles and aims of the regime since the overthrow of the monarchy on 23 July 1952; and by the Statute of the Arab Socialist Union of 7 Dec. 1962; and by the October paper, presented by President Sadat in April 1974, which envisages development from now until 2000. This organization has been created as 'the socialist vanguard' for safeguarding and furthering the 'socialist revolution' on all levels of local, district and national administration.

General elections took place on 28 Oct. and 4 Nov. 1976 for 342 of the 350 elective seats in the People's Assembly. There were about 9·5m. registered voters and voting was compulsory for men. The 'centrists' won 280 of the 360 seats. On 11 Nov. President Sadat announced the creation of 3 political parties (the first since 1953). They were the Free Socialists, the Arab Socialists and National Progressive Unionists.

President of the Republic: Mohammed Anwar El Sadat (sworn in on 17 Oct. 1970 and re-elected 16 Sept. 1976).

The Cabinet, reshuffled in May 1978, was composed as follows:

Prime Minister: Mamduh Salem.
Deputy Prime Ministers: (Vacant) (*Economic Affairs*); Dr Hafez Ghanem (*Social Development*); Mohammad Ibrahim (*Foreign Affairs*); Gen. Mohammed Abdel-Ghani al-Gamassi (*War Production*); Ahmad Sultan (*Production and Energy*).

Manpower: Abdel-Latif Baltiya. *Social Affairs:* Dr Aisha Rateb. *Education:* Dr Mustafa Kamal Hilmi. *Interior:* Maj.-Gen. al-Sayyid Hussain Fahmi. *Petroleum:* Ahmad Izzeddin Hilal. *Agriculture:* Abdel-Azim Abu al-Ata. *Industry:* Isa Abdel-Hamid Shaheen. *Tourism and Aviation:* Ibrahim Naguib. *Trade and Supply:* Zakariya Tawfiq Abdel-Fattah. *Finance:* Dr Mahmoud Sataheddin Hamid. *Planning:* Dr Mohammed Mahmoud al-Imam. *People's Assembly Affairs:* Dr Ahmed Fuad Mohieddin. *Health:* Dr Ibrahim Mustafa Badran. *Housing:* Hasan Mohammad Hasan. *Justice:* Ahmad Samih Talaat. *Waafs and Azhar Affairs:* Mohammed Mutawalli Abdel-Hafez al-Sharaawi. *Transport:* Abdel-Fattah Abdullah Mahmoud. *Information and Culture:* Dr Gamal al-Otaifi. *Economy and Economic Co-operation:* Dr Hamid Abdel-Latif al Sayih.

There are 7 Ministers of State.

National flag: Three horizontal stripes of red, white, black, with the federal emblem in the centre in gold.

DEFENCE. At the outbreak of the 4th Arab-Israeli war the total strength of the defence forces was about 298,000. There was also a national guard of about 100,000.

Army. Service in the Army is compulsory for all male citizens at the age of 18. The Army comprised (Jan. 1976) 2 armoured divisions, 3 mechanized infantry divisions, 5 infantry divisions, 3 independent armoured and 7 independent infantry brigades, a parachute brigade, 2 airborne brigades, 6 artillery brigades and 26 commando battalions. Its tank strength (Jan. 1976) was about 2,000, mainly USSR. Total strength is about 300,000 men; reserves totalled, 500,000.

Navy. There are 12 submarines, 5 destroyers, 3 old frigates, 10 fleet minesweepers, 4 inshore minesweepers, 30 torpedo boats, 16 missile boats, 12 submarine chasers, 25 coastal patrol boats, 2 training ships, 3 medium landing ships, 14 landing craft, 6 auxiliary vessels, 10 service craft and 4 tugs. Naval personnel in 1978: 17,500 officers and men, including the Coastguard, but not reserves of about 12,000.

Air Force. The Air Force is equipped largely with aircraft of USSR design, but re-equipment will include aircraft bought in the West. Current strength is about 30,000 personnel and 500 combat aircraft, of which the interceptors are operated by an independent Air Defence Command, in conjunction with many 'Guideline', 'Goa' and 'Gainful' missile batteries. There are about 25 Tu-16 twin-jet strategic bombers, some equipped to carry 'Kelt' air-to-surface missiles. The main strike force consists of about 60 Su-7B, 25 Su-20 and 24 MiG-23 supersonic fighter-bombers. Other interceptor/ground attack fighter divisions are equipped with 32 Mirage IIIEs, 14 Mirage 5s, 24 MiG-23s, about 200 MiG-21s and 100 MiG-17s. Transport units have an estimated 20 An-12 and 4 C-130E Hercules turboprop heavy freighters, 30 Il-14 twin-engined transports, a few An-24s and up to 150 Gazelle, Mi-4, Mi-8 and Sea King/Commando helicopters; 2 EC-130E Hercules are equipped for ECM duties. Training units are equipped with Gomhouria and Yak-18 piston-engined trainers, Czech-built L-29 Delfin jet trainers, single-seat and two-seat versions of the MiG-15, and two-seat MiG-21Us and Su-7Us.

INTERNATIONAL RELATIONS

Membership. Egypt is a member of UN, OAU, the Arab League and OAPEC.

ECONOMY

Planning. A 'permanent council of national production' was established in 1952.

The 10-year development plan 1973–83 envisages an initial investment by the public and private secors of £E8,400m.

In 1961–62 a number of sweeping socialist measures were carried out, which contributed largely to the Syrian defection in Sept. 1961. In addition to the nationalization of banks, insurance companies, etc. (*see* below under BANKING), about 1,000 private businessmen had their property confiscated by Jan. 1962. In 1963 complete nationalization was enforced of all cotton exporting and ginning firms, pharmaceutical factories and some 400 other companies in which the state had previously held a half-share. Share owners were compensated by government bonds redeemable over 15 years at 4% interest.

Budget. Ordinary revenue and expenditure for fiscal years ending 30 June, in £E1,000:

	1974	*1975*	*1976*[1]
Revenue	2,641·9	3,961·5	5,976
Expenditures	2,909·3	4,345·5	5,976

[1] Estimates.

Currency. By decree of 18 Oct. 1916 (20 Zi-El-Higga 1934), the monetary unit of Egypt is the gold Egyptian pound of 100 *piastres* of 1,000 *millièmes*. Coins in circulation are 20, 10, 5, 2 piastres (silver); 2, 1 piastre, 5 millièmes, 1 millième (bronze). Gold coins are no longer in circulation. Silver coin is legal tender only up to £E2, and bronze coins up to 10 piastres. The Treasury issues 5- and 10-piastre currency notes. Bank-notes are issued by the National Bank in denominations of 5, 10, 25 and 50 piastres, £E1, 5 and 10.

Banking. On 18 Aug. 1960 a Central Bank of Egypt was established by decree. It manages the note issue, the Government's banking operations and the control of commercial banks. At the same date the National Bank founded in 1898 ceased to be the central bank and became a purely commercial bank. The position of the bank in June 1967 was (in £E1m.): Foreign assets and gold, 37·6; government securities and treasury bills, 40·5; notes issued, 441; advances and bills discounted, 270·6; clearing and other accounts, 35·4. Liabilities, government deposits, 4·5; bankers' deposits, 124·5; other deposits, 153·1; clearing and other accounts, 118·7.

In 1901 a post office savings bank was opened; on 31 Dec. 1959 the total deposits amounted to £E38·6m.

Commercial banks in Egypt numbered 27 in Dec. 1959, including 16 Egyptian joint-stock companies (of which by far the most important are Bank Misr and Bank of Alexandria), the rest being branches of foreign banks. On 15 Jan. 1957 all English and French banks and insurance companies were nationalized. All banks and insurance companies must now be limited-liability companies with a paid-up capital of not less than £E500,000 for banks and £E100,000 for insurance companies; all shareholders, directors and managers must be Egyptian nationals.

The Bank el Goumhouria subsequently took over the Ottoman Bank and the Ionian Bank; the Bank of Cairo took control of the Crédit Lyonnais and the Comptoir National d'Escompte de Paris; the Bank of Alexandria was established to take over the 40 branches of Barclays Bank International, and the Banque de l'Union Commerciale took over the Crédit d'Orient.

Other banks in Egypt include the Crédit Foncier Egyptien (founded in 1880) and the Land Bank of Egypt (1905), both for mortgage lending, the Crédit Agricole et Coopératif (1931), the Crédit Hypothécaire d'Egypte (1932) and the Industrial Bank (1949). The National Bank and the Bank Misr were nationalized on 11 Feb. 1960.

Weights and Measures. In 1951 the metric system was made official with the exception of the feddân and its subdivisions.

Capacity. Kadah = 1/96th ardeb = 3·36 pints. *Rob* = 4 kadahs = 1·815 gallons. *Keila* = 8 kadahs = 3·63 gallons. *Ardeb* = 96 kadahs = 43,555 gallons, or 5·44439 bu., or 198 cu. decimetres.

Weights. Rotl = 144 dirhems = 0·9905 lb. *Oke* = 400 dirhems = 2·75137 lb. *Qantâr* or 100 rotls or 36 okes = 99·0493 lb. 1 *Qantâr* of unginned cotton = 315 lb. 1 *Qantâr* of ginned cotton = 99·05 lb. The approximate weight of the ardeb is as follows: Wheat, 150 kg; beans, 155 kg; barley, 120 kg; maize, 140 kg; cotton seed, 121 kg.

Surface. Feddân, the unit of measure for land = 4,200·8 sq. metres = 7,468·148 sq. pics = 1·03805 acres. 1 sq. pic = 6·0547 sq. ft = 0·5625 sq. metre.

ENERGY AND NATURAL RESOURCES

Electricity. Electricity generated in 1969 was 7,316m. kw.

Oil. The first commercial discovery of oil in the Middle East outside Iran was made in Egypt in 1909, but production long remained low and often insufficient to meet Egypt's domestic requirements. By the end of 1975, however, production was rising again and with the newly-regained Sinai oilfields was of the order of 300,000 bbls per day. In 1976 a major exploration effort was being mounted and the Egyptian Government hoped that, as a result, production will reach 1m. bbls a day by 1980.

Policy is controlled by the Egyptian General Petroleum Corporation (EGPC) a wholly state-owned corporation answerable to the Minister of Petroleum, EGPC is whole or part-owner of the various production and refining companies and controls supplies to the domestic marketing companies.

EGPC has absolute control of the foreign exchange derived from the signature bonuses paid by international companies for exploration concessions, some US$70m. to date, and also has an annual foreign exchange budget of its own from the Government.

Amoco and, to a much lesser extent, Phillips have been exploring and producing successfully in Egypt since 1963, under joint venture concessions. In 1973 a new 80/20 production sharing concession agreement was introduced and some 28 concessions have been taken out by international companies. Under these agreements these companies are committed to spend some US$600m. on exploration in Egypt over the next 7 or 8 years. About 80% of this expenditure will probably be in foreign exchange.

The Italian SAIPEM consortium is currently constructing an 80m. tonne per annum crude pipeline between the Gulf of Suez and the Mediterranean for the SUMED Company (EGPC 50%, Kuwait 15%, Saudi Arabia 15%, Abu Dhabi 15% and Qatar 5%). The consultants are the Bechtel Corporation, and the work is due to be finished in late 1976 at a cost of over US$400m.

Minerals. Production (in tonnes):

	1970	*1971*	*1972*	*1973*
Phosphate rock	584,000	657,000	562,000	553,000
Iron ore	453,000	473,000	427,000	656,000
Salt, marine	376,000	385,000	388,000	454,000

Agriculture. Rain seldom falls in Upper Egypt, and only at irregular intervals in Cairo, where the average for the year is no more than 1·2 in. At Alexandria the average is 8 in.

The cultivated area of Egypt proper was estimated in 1971 at 10·74m. feddâns (1 feddân = 1·038 acres) and of this 4,869,000 feddâns were under winter crops, 5,012,000 under summer crops and 613,000 under Nile crops.

The Agricultural Reform Decree of Sept. 1952 limits agricultural ownership to 200 feddâns, reduced to 100 feddâns in July 1961. Foreigners were debarred in 1963 from owing any land. Holdings in excess of this limit will be redistributed; compensation, equivalent to 10 times the rental value of the land, will take the form of 3% (from 1958: 1½%) bonds redeemable within 30 years (from 1958: 40 years). All national *waqfs* are to be dissolved.

Irrigation occupies a predominant place in the economic development of the country. The Aswân reservoir can now hold up to 5,500m. cu. metres of water, and the Gebel Aulia reservoir, completed in 1937, holds 2,000m. cu. metres. Barrages have been erected at Esna, Nag' Hammâdi, Asyût and Zifta, and at the bifurcation of the Nile below Cairo. Nag' Hammâdi barrage, completed in 1930, ensures full basin supplies even in low flood to Girga province, and will facilitate perennial irrigation when basin lands are converted. Asyût barrage, having been remodelled, will meet the greater demands of the area it now commands. The Esna barrage now secures basin irrigation to lands in Qena province. New barrages (Mohamed Ali barrages) have been completed at the bifurcation of the Nile below Cairo to rcplace the existing structures which, built in 1861, are now unable to meet the conditions following the increase in summer supplies, the reclamation of large areas of waste lands and the earlier watering of food crops.

On 8 Nov. 1959 the United Arab Republic and Sudan concluded agreements on the sharing of the Nile waters (after construction of the Aswân High Dam), and trade, payments and Customs dues. The agreement provides that from the time the High Dam starts to store water (15 May 1964) Sudan will be entitled to 18,500m. cu. metres of the total annual flow, instead of 4,000m., and Egypt to 55,500m. compared with the present 48,000m. Egypt is to pay £E15m. to meet the cost of providing new homes and lands for between 60,000 and 70,000 Sudanese living in Wadi Halfa and other areas which will be inundated by the waters.

The area and production of raw cotton for crop years ending 31 Aug. were:

	Area in 1,000 feddâns	*Crop in 1,000 qantârs*		*Area in 1,000 feddâns*	*Crop in 1,000 qantârs*
1961	1,986	6,344	1970	1,627	8,914
1962	1,657	8,479	1971	1,525	9,002
1963	1,627	8,334	1972[1]	1,552	9,028
1964	1,611	9,117	1973[1]	1,600	9,790

[1] Provisional.

In 1971 the area and yield (both in 1,000) of wheat were, 1,349 feddâns and 11,529 ardebs; barley, 70 feddâns and 634 ardebs; beans, 288 feddâns and 1,653 ardebs; lentils, 65 feddâns and 311 ardebs; onions, 36 feddâns and 12,685 qantârs; maize, 1,171 feddâns and 16,727 ardebs; millet, 462 feddâns and 6,097 ardebs; sugar-cane, 193 feddâns and 166,612 qantârs.

The rice crop was 1·48 tonnes in 1974–1975.

Livestock (1976): 2·4m. cows, 2·4m. buffaloes, 2m. sheep, 1·4m. goats, 100,000 camels and 16,000 pigs.

Fisheries. The catch of the Egyptian sea, Nile and lake fisheries in 1957 amounted to 102,600 tonnes. In 1952 there were 48,947 men and 16,347 boys engaged in fishing and 11,739 boats used for fishing.

INDUSTRY AND TRADE

Industry. The census of industrial production (1966) showed 875,000 persons engaged in 4,000 industrial establishments employing 10 or more persons. Total value of industrial production in 1963 was £E952·6m.

Production in 1962 of pig-iron was 99,770 tonnes; of steel ingots and castings, 149,655 tonnes.

Electricity generated in 1969 was 7,316m. kw.

Labour. A comprehensive labour code was issued in April 1959. It applies to all categories of workers, including agricultural workers, encourages the formation of trade unions, organizes conciliation and arbitration procedures (strikes and lock-outs being forbidden) and provides for an 8-hour working day and paid holidays.

In 1959 a Labour Stability and Social Insurance Code revised the legislation of 1955 and set up a Social Insurance Institution with regional and local branch offices. It covers employment injuries, old age, invalidity benefits.

Trade unions were first recognized in 1942. In 1952 the acts concerning trade unions, individual contracts, and conciliation and arbitration were recast. Employment exchanges and unemployment statistics were introduced in 1953. Social insurance was enacted in 1955.

Commerce. Imports and exports for 6 years (in £E1,000):

	1969	*1970*	*1971*	*1972*	*1973*	*1974*
Imports	277,300	341,100	400,000	381,400	357,500	919,200
Exports	323,400	331,200	342,200	258,800	444,200	593,300

Raw cotton and cotton products represent over 60% of total exports.

Total trade between Egypt and UK for calendar years (British Department of Trade returns, in £1,000 sterling):

	1973	*1974*	*1975*	*1976*	*1977*
Imports to UK	23,734	37,317	40,943	65,254	88,065
Exports and re-exports from UK	27,116	52,360	107,735	171,851	190,516

Tourism. In 1974, 680,900 foreigners visited Egypt.

COMMUNICATIONS

Roads. Egypt had 12,087 km of highways and 13,889 km of desert roads in 1971–72. Motor vehicles, as at 31 Dec. 1959: 57,296 private cars, 10,143 taxis, 16,225 trucks, 3,894 buses.

Railways. In 1976 there were 4,856 km of state railways. The state railways have a gauge of 4 ft 8½ in., except that to the Western Oases, which is 2 ft 5½ in.

In 1974 the railways ran 8,500m. passenger-km and 2,561m. ton-km.

Aviation. There is an international aerodrome at Cairo. A new airport at Cairo began operations in 1977. The national airline Egyptair has a fleet of 20 aircraft, Egyptair operates scheduled flights connecting Cairo with Athens, Rome, Frankfurt, Geneva, Zürich, London, Khartoum, Tōkyō, Bangkok, Hong Kong, Bombay, Asmara, Aden, Jeddah, Doha, Dharan, Kuwait, Beirut, Jerusalem, Baghdad and Tripoli. In addition, Egyptair operates scheduled flights on a wide-spread domestic network connecting Cairo with Port Said, Mersa Matruh, Assiout, Luxor, Aswân.

Shipping. The Egyptian merchant navy in 1966 consisted of 37 steamers of 291,000 tons and 2 sailing ships of 930 tons each.

In 1971, excluding warships and vessels requisitioned by the military authorities, 2,751 steamers of 7,006 NRT entered at, and 2,596 steamers of 6,459 NRT departed from, all the Egyptian ports.

Suez Canal. The Suez Canal was opened for navigation on 17 Nov. 1869. By the convention of Constantinople of 29 Oct. 1888 the canal is open to vessels of all nations and is free from blockade, except in time of war, but the UAR Government does not allow Israeli ships to use the canal. It is 101 miles long (excluding 7 miles of approach channels to the harbours), connecting the Mediterranean with the Red Sea. Its minimum width is 197 ft at a depth of 33 ft, and its depth permits the passage of vessels up to 38ft draught; this was to have been widened and deepened with the help of a Kuwait loan, so as to enable the Canal to take tankers of 110,000 tons by 1972.

On 26 July 1956 President Nasser proclaimed the nationalization of the Suez Canal Company, the concession of which was to expire on 17 Nov. 1968. The shareholders of the Suez Canal Company received £28m. compensation; the final instalment was paid in Jan. 1963. The Company, now the Suez Financial Company, continues as an investment trust.

On 22 Dec. 1959 the World Bank granted Egypt a loan of US$56·5m. for the deepening, widening and general improvement of the Canal and Port Said harbour. The interest of the loan is 6%; amortization will extend over 15 years.

The number and net tonnage of vessels that have passed through the Suez Canal (including warships), and the transit receipts (in £E1m.), have been as follows:

	No. of transits	*Suez net tonnage*	*Receipts*		*No. of transits*	*Suez net tonnage*	*Receipts*
1961	18,148	187,059,000	52	1964	19,943	227,991,000	78
1962	18,518	197,837,000	54	1965	20,289	246,817,000	86
1963	19,146	210,498,000	71	1966	21,250	274,466,000	...

Vessels passing through Suez Canal, 1966, included 3,601 British, 2,721 Liberian, 2,271 Norwegian, 1,493 Greek, 1,236 Italian, 1,469 USSR, 1,108 French, 947 German, 864 Dutch, 801 USA, 659 Panamanian, 484 Swedish, 465 Danish, 94 UAR.

The number of passengers who went through the canal was, in 1952, 571,416; 1955, 520,774; 1956 (Jan.–Oct.), 319,798; 1957 (April–Dec.), 188,361; 1958, 342,404; 1961, 323,000; 1962, 270,000; 1963, 298,000; 1964, 270,000; 1965, 291,000; 1966, 300,000.

The total rates payable by all ships were raised as from 29 June 1964 so as to provide an extra $3·45m. revenue.

During the war with Israel in June 1967 Egypt blocked the Canal. The canal was cleared and re-opened to shipping on 5 June 1975. This is part of a programme to develop and rebuild the whole area of Suez to make it one of the largest tax-free industrial zones. Canal toll fees reached £E230m. in 1976 and over 12,000 vessels went through the canal.

Baxter, R. R., *The Law of International Waterways.* Harvard Univ. Press, 1964
Lauterpacht, E. (ed.), *The Suez Canal Settlement, 1956–59.* London, 1960
Marlow, J., *The Making of the Suez Canal.* London, 1964

Post and Broadcasting. The telephone service was taken over by the Egyptian Government in April 1918. In 1958–59 the state telegraphs had a length of 15,381 km of wire, and telephones, 1,076,159 km. There were, in 1971–72 (provisional figures), 1,448 postal agencies, 1,763 mobile offices, 1,489 government and 2,576 private post offices. Number of telephones in 1975, 503,200. Number of wireless licences in 1964, 864,000.

The internal telecommunications system is owned and operated by the Telecommunications Organization. Government landlines connect with those of the Gaza sector and the Sudan.

Cinemas (1971). There were 152 cinemas with a seating capacity of 140,900.

Newspapers. On 23 May 1960 all newspapers were nationalized.

JUSTICE, RELIGION, EDUCATION AND WELFARE

Justice. The national courts, established in 1883, consist of 165 summary tribunals and of 14 judicial delegations, each presided over by a single judge, with civil jurisdiction in matters up to £E250 in value, and criminal jurisdiction in offences punishable by fine or by imprisonment up to 3 years (*i.e.*, police offences and misdemeanours), except in cases relating to the trafficking in narcotics, where the period rises up to perpetual hard labour and a fine not exceeding £E10,000. There are also 19 central tribunals, each of the chambers of which is also (since 1959) presided over by a single judge; and 5 courts of appeal each consisting of 3 judges. Civil cases not within the competence of the summary tribunals are heard in first instance by the central tribunals, with an appeal to one of the courts of appeal. The central tribunals also hear civil and criminal appeals from the summary tribunals. Serious crimes, trafficking in narcotics and Press offences are tried at the central tribunals by 3 judges of the court of appeal sitting as an assize court, assizes being held monthly.

In 1931 a court of cassation above the courts of appeal was set up. It is composed of a president, 4 deputy presidents and 36 judges and divided into 3 chambers, one for criminal, one for civil and commercial and one for personal law.

There is also an administrative court, created in 1946 at the Conseil d'Etat; it is composed of 3 judges, or of 5 in cases when the validity of administrative regulations is contested.

All religious courts, Moslem as well as non-Moslem, were abolished by decree of 21 Sept. 1955, effective from Jan. 1956.

Religion. In 1947 the population (excluding Nomads) consisted of 17,397,946 Moslems (91·46%); 1,186,353 Orthodox Copts; 86,918 Protestant Copts; 72,764 Roman Catholic Copts; 89,062 other Orthodox; 50,200 other Roman Catholics; 16,338 other Protestants; 1,547 Jews, other and unknown.

There are in Egypt large numbers of native Christians connected with the various Oriental Churches; of these, the largest and most influential are the Copts, who adopted Christianity in the 1st century. Their head is the Coptic Patriarch. There are 25 metropolitans and bishops in Egypt; 4 metropolitans for Ethiopia, Jerusalem, Khartoum and Omdurman, and 12 bishops in Ethiopia. Priests must be married before ordination, but celibacy is imposed on monks and high dignitaries. The Copts use the Diocletian (or Martyrs') calendar, which begins in A.D. 284.

Education. Education was made compulsory for all children between the ages of 6 and 12 in 1933; primary education (6 years) was made free in 1944, secondary and technical education in 1950. Compulsory education is provided in primary schools (6 years). In the 5 years 1965–66/1970–71, the number of pupils in all stages of education increased by 120%.

Statistics for state and private schools in the school year 1970–71; Primary schools, 8,415 with 3,740,551 pupils; preparatory schools, 1,362 with 851,936 pupils; secondary schools, 604 with 569,456 pupils.

Teachers' training colleges in 1970–71 numbered 56 with 25,526 students.

There are 4 universities in Egypt. Cairo University, founded in 1908 as a private institution and taken over by the Government in 1925, had, in 1970–71, 50,320 students; Alexandria University, founded by the Government in 1942, had 41,177 students; the Ein Shams University, founded by the Government in Cairo in 1950, had 46,636 students; Asyût University, opened in 1957, had 14,149 students. There are various other faculties in Mansûra, Zagazig and Tanta, as well as High Institutes.

The principal seat of Koranic learning is the Mosque and University of Al-Azhar at Cairo, founded in the year 361 of the Hegira (A.D. 972). The University had, in 1970–71, 25,673 students, including 2,810 women, first admitted in Oct. 1962.

Health. In 1966 there were about 6,000 doctors and (1970–71) 72,976 hospital beds.

DIPLOMATIC REPRESENTATIVES

OF EGYPT IN GREAT BRITAIN (26 South St., London, W1Y 8EL)

Ambassador: Mohamed Samih Anwar (accredited 31 Oct. 1975).

OF GREAT BRITAIN IN EGYPT (Ahmed Raghab St., Garden City, Cairo)

Ambassador: Sir Willie Morris, KCMG.

OF EGYPT IN THE USA (2310 Decatur Pl, NW, Washington, D.C., 20008)

Ambassador: Ashraf A. Ghorbal.

OF THE USA IN EGYPT (5 Sharia Latin America, Cairo)

Ambassador: Hermann F. Eilts.

OF EGYPT TO THE UNITED NATIONS

Ambassador: Dr Ahmed Esmat Abdel Meguid.

Books of Reference

Statistical Information: The Department of Statistics and Census (15, Sharia Mansour, Cairo) was formed in 1905. *Chief:* Under-Secretary of State for Statistical Affairs, Dr Hasan M. Husein. Previously, various government departments had their own statistical sections. Estimates of population were made in 1800, 1821 and 1846; the first census took place in 1873. Among the publications of the Department are the following: *Annuaire Statistique* (Arabic and French). *Annual Return of Shipping* (Arabic and English). *Monthly Summary, and Annual Statement of Foreign Trade* (Arabic and English). *Monthly Bulletin of Agriculture and Economic Statistics* (Arabic and English). *Vital Statistics* (Arabic and English). *Statistical Pocket Year-Book* (Arabic and English).

The Egyptian Almanac. Annual
Le Mondain Egyptien (*Who's Who*). Cairo. Annual
Aatikiotos, P. J., *The Modern History of Egypt.* London, 1969
Barbour, K. M., *The Growth, Location and Structure of Industry in Egypt.* London and New York, 1972
Dawisha, A. I., *Egypt in the Arab World.* London, 1976
Elias, E. A., *Modern Dictionary English–Arabic.* 5th ed. Cairo, 1946
Fedden, R., *Egypt: Land of the Valley.* London, 1977
O'Brien, P., *The Revolution in Egypt's Economic System, 1952–65.* OUP, 1966
Mabro, R., and Radwan, S., *The Industrialization of Egypt 1939–1973.* Oxford, 1976
Nelson, N., *Egypt.* London, 1976
Richmond, J. C. B., *Egypt 1798–1952.* London, 1977
Rubinstein, A. Z., *Red Star on the Nile: The Soviet–Egyptian Relationship Since the June War.* Princeton Univ. Press, 1977
Saab, G. S., *The Egyptian Agrarian Reform, 1952–62.* OUP, 1967

EL SALVADOR

República de El Salvador

Capital: San Salvador
Population: 4m. (1976)
GNP per capita: US$490 (1976)

HISTORY. In 1839 the Central American Federation, which had comprised the states of Guatemala, El Salvador, Honduras, Nicaragua and Costa Rica, was dissolved, and El Salvador declared itself formally an independent republic in 1841. There have since been a number of attempts to restore some looser form of Central American unity, the latest being the founding in 1951 of the Organization of Central American States (with Secretariat in San Salvador) and the Central American Common Market.

AREA AND POPULATION. El Salvador is the smallest and most densely populated of the Central American states. Its area (including 247 sq. km of inland lakes) is estimated at 21,393 sq. km (8,236 sq. miles) with population (census 1971) of 3,712,622. Estimate (1976) 4m. The capital is San Salvador (500,000 inhabitants in 1976).

The republic is divided into 14 departments, each under an appointed governor. Their areas (in sq. km) and populations at census 1971 were:

Department	*Area*	*Population*	*Department*	*Area*	*Population*
Ahuachapán	1,281	183,682	La Paz	1,155	194,196
Santa Ana	1,829	375,186	Cabañas	1,075	139,312
Sonsonate	1,133	239,688	San Vicente	1,175	160,534
Chalatenango	2,507	186,003	Usulután	1,780	304,369
La Libertad	1,650	293,076	San Miguel	2,532	337,325
San Salvador	892	681,656	Marazán	1,364	170,706
Cuscatlán	766	158,458	La Unión	1,738	230,103

Important towns (with population census 1971) are: Santa Ana, 96,306; Zacatecoluca, 57,001; San Miguel, 59,304; Mejicanos, 54,916; Ahuachapán, 53,386; Sonsonate, 33,562.

There has been considerable emigration into nearby states. There are no tribal Indians. The language of the country is Spanish.

CONSTITUTION AND GOVERNMENT. The latest Constitution was enacted in Jan. 1962, slightly amending that of 1950. The Executive Power is vested in a President elected for a non-renewable term of 5 years, with Ministers and Under-Secretaries appointed by him. The Legislative power is an Assembly of 52 members elected by universal suffrage and proportional representation for a term of 2 years. The judicial power is vested in a Supreme Court, of a President and 9 magistrates elected by the Legislative Assembly for renewable terms of 3 years; and subordinate courts.

A new Partido de Conciliación Nacional won all the seats of a new Assembly elected on 17 Dec. 1961. Its president, Dr Eusebio Cordón, was elected Provisional President of the Republic when it promulgated the new Constitution on 25 Jan. 1962. In Presidential elections on 29 April, Col. J. A. Rivera was returned without opposition and held office 1962–67. The elections of 13 March 1966 resulted in 31 Partido de Conciliación Nacional being elected against the opposition Partido Demócrata Cristiano (15) and various minor parties (6).

At the elections held 20 Feb. 1977 Col. Carlos Humberto Romera, of the ruling *Partido de Conciliación Nacional*, was elected President.

President: Col. Carlos Humberto Romero, assumed office 1 July 1977 for 5 years.

Vice-President and Minister of the Presidency: Dr Julio Ernesto Astacio. *Interior:* Gen. Armando Léonidas Rojas. *Foreign Affairs:* Alvaro Ernesto Martínez. *Finance:* René López Beltrán. *Economy:* Roberto Ortiz Avalos. *Development and Public Works:* Léon Rivas Durbán. *Agriculture and Livestock:* Rutilio Aguilera. *Education:* Carlos Herrera Rebollo. *Justice:* Dr Rafael Flores y Flores. *Health and Social Welfare:* Dr César Augusto Escalante. *Labour and Social Security:* Lieut.-Col. Roberto Escobar García. *Defence:* Gen. Federico Castillo Yanes. *Planning and Co-ordination for Economic and Social Development:* Dr Eduardo Reyes.

National flag: Blue, white, blue (horizontal): the white stripe charged with the arms of the republic.

National anthem: Saludemos la patria orgullosos (words by J. J. Cañas; tune by J. Aberle).

DEFENCE

Army. The Army is organized in 3 territorial divisions of 4 infantry battalions, 2 artillery battalions, 1 air defence battalion, and 1 cavalry squadron. Total strength, 6,000 men. There are also the National Guard, the National Police and the Treasury Police.

Navy. The Navy includes 2 patrol boats and 2 other small coastguard craft. Personnel in 1978 totalled 130 officers and men.

Air Force. The Air Force underwent a major re-equipment programme in 1974–75, with most aircraft coming from Israel and US aid for transport units. Combat squadron now has 18 Ouragan jet fighter-bombers. Transports include 6 C-47s, 2 C-54s and 4 Israeli-built light twin-engined Aravas, plus an FH-1100 light helicopter. Training types include 6 Israeli-built Magister jets, and about 8 piston-engined T-6s and T-34s. A few Cessna liaison aircraft are also in service. Strength totalled about 1,000 personnel and 50 aircraft in 1978.

INTERNATIONAL RELATIONS

Membership. El Salvador is a member of UN and OAS.

ECONOMY

Budget. Revenue and expenditure for fiscal years ending 31 Dec., in 1,000 colones (2·5 colones = US$1):

	1971	*1973*	*1974*	*1975*	*1976*	*1977*
Revenue	299,751	421,500	557,900	729,700	1,069,000	1,252,000
Expenditure	256,677	421,500	557,900	729,700	1,069,000	1,252,000

External debt amounted to US$175·4m. on 30 June 1975.

Currency. The monetary unit is the *colón* of 100 *centavos.* Its exchange value since July 1934 had been kept at 40 cents US, and on 30 June 1942 the bank's gold stock was revalued, making it exactly equal to the exchange value of 40 cents. The country left the gold standard on 9 Oct. 1931. On 20 April 1961 exchange control was introduced to prevent the transfer of capital abroad. This control has since been extended to limit the length of credit on the import of consumer goods. The buying/selling rate for the £ is 6 and 6·06 colones respectively.

The colón is issued in denominations of 1, 2, 5, 10, 25 and 100 colones; 25 and 50 centavos (silver); 1, 2, 3, 5 and 10 centavos (copper–nickel and copper–zinc).

Money in circulation (including sight deposits) was 351·6m. colones on 31 March 1972.

Banking. There are 6 native commercial banks, including the Banco Salvadoreño (paid-up capital, 6m. colones). The Bank of London and Montreal and the Citibank are the only foreign institutions. The Central Reserve Bank of El Salvador, constructed in 1934 out of the Banco Agricola Comercial, was nationalized on 20 April 1961. Bank deposits, both term and sight, were 567m. colones in 1972. Total gold and dollar reserves of the Banco Central on 30 June 1966 were 136·5m. colones compared with 166·99m. in March 1972. A stock exchange was officially inaugurated in Oct. 1962 with the declared intention of promoting investments in Central America; it began operations on 17 Aug. 1964 with a capital of 100,000 colones subscribed by 360 shareholders. Its activities have been limited.

Weights and Measures. On 1 Jan. 1886 the metric system was made obligatory. But other units are still commonly in use, of which the principal are as follows: *Libra* = 1·014 lb. av.; *quintal* = 101·4 lb. av.; *arroba* = 25·35 lb. av.; *fanega* = 1·5745 bushels.

ENERGY AND NATURAL RESOURCES

Electricity. El Salvador's biggest national enterprise, begun in 1950, is the construction of a 200-ft high dam across the (unnavigable) Lempa River, 35 miles north-east of San Salvador, designed to double the country's electric-power resources, from 31,000 to 78,000 kw. Production in 1975, 935·3m. kwh.; consumption, 831·9m. kwh.

Oil. Production of petrol lubricants and other petroleum derivatives during 1970 totalled ₡15·8m.

Minerals. The mineral output of the republic is now negligible, but the Ministry of Public Works has recently started to investigate 2 new silver mines in the department of Morazán.

Agriculture. El Salvador is predominantly agricultural; 32·5% of its total area is used for crops and 30·2% for pasture. Area devoted to coffee is about 308,000 acres, almost entirely owned by nationals.

Rice is important for home consumption; other agricultural products are maize (359,000 tonnes in 1974), cacao, tobacco, indigo, henequén and sugar (2·4m. tonnes in 1973). A little rubber is exported.

Livestock (1976: 1·1m. cattle, 4,000 pigs, 400,000 sheep, 11,000 goats.

Forestry. In the national forests are found dye woods and such woods as mahogany, cedar and walnut. Balsam trees also abound: El Salvador is the world's principal source of this medicinal gum.

INDUSTRY AND TRADE

Industry. Total production was valued at C550·2m. in 1972, which included: Footwear and clothing, C61·3m.; textiles, C70·2m.; food, ₡157·7m.; chemicals, C42.

GDP *per capita* (1972) US$307.

Labour. A decree of Aug. 1950 permits the formation of trade unions except among agricultural workers and those engaged in seasonal work such as coffee-milling and sugar-refining; trade-union posts must be filled by natives, not foreigners.

Commerce. The imports (including parcels post) and exports have been as follows in calendar years in 1,000 colones:

	1970	*1971*	*1972*	*1973*	*1974*	*1975*
Imports	533,900	619,500	691,400	934,423	1,408,548	1,495,734
Exports	571,000	569,500	694,000	895,745	1,156,188	1,281,387

Of total exports, coffee furnishes about 20% by weight and 51% by value. The coffee is of the 'mild' variety; it is sold in bags of 60 kg, but trade statistics use a bag of 69 kg. Exports in 1966 were 97,000 tonnes (valued at 227m. colones), of which 45% went to the Federal Republic of Germany and 43% to USA.

In 1970 US took 122·3m. colones of exports and furnished 157·5m. colones of the imports. The chief imports are normally wheat, flour, fuel-oil, fertilizers, machinery, vehicles and iron and steel manufactures. The other Central American Republics, the Federal Republic of Germany, Japan, the Netherlands and the UK are also important trading partners.

Total trade between El Salvador and UK for 5 years (British Department of Trade returns, in £1,000 sterling):

	1973	*1974*	*1975*	*1976*	*1977*
Imports to UK	297	897	6,413	1,603	3,138
Exports and re-exports from UK	3,393	3,857	8,333	12,478	11,770

Tourism. There were 285,415 visitors in 1974 (236,137 in 1973).

COMMUNICATIONS

Roads. In 1974 there were 10,972 km of national roads in the republic, including 1,373 km of paved road; 4,868 km are usable all the year round and 4,622 only in the dry season. Motor vehicles registered, 1969, 63,949.

Railways. A railway connects the port of Acajutla with Santa Ana, Sonsonate and San Salvador, the capital. It links San Salvador with the American-owned International Railways of Central America, which runs from the eastern to the western boundary of El Salvador, and extends into Guatemala City and Puerto Barrios on the north coast and on the Mexican border. Total length of railway open, about 1,031 km, all of 3 ft gauge.

Aviation. International air traffic is expanding and in 1972 there were 80 flights a week. There is a modern airport at Ilopango, 5 miles from San Salvador, equipped to handle jet aeroplanes.

Shipping. The principal ports are La Unión, La Libertad and Acajutla, all on the Pacific. Passengers (and some freight) use the Guatemalan port of Puerto Barrios on the Atlantic, reaching El Salvador by rail or road.

Post and Broadcasting. The telephone and telegraph systems are government-owned; the radio-telephone systems are partly private, partly government-owned. Telephone instruments, 1977, 54,156. Two radio transmitting and receiving stations at San Salvador maintain communications with Latin America. El Salvador has, 1965, over 500,000 wireless receiving sets. In 1973, there were 3 commercial television channels and 2 educational channels sponsored by the Ministry of Education.

Cinemas (1976). Cinemas numbered 65.

Newspapers (1970). There are 4 daily newspapers in San Salvador and 1 each in Santa Ana and San Miguel.

JUSTICE, RELIGION, EDUCATION AND WELFARE

Justice. Justice is administered by the Supreme Court of Justice, courts of first and second instance, besides minor tribunals. Magistrates of the Supreme Court and courts of second instance are elected by the Legislative Assembly for a renewable 3-year term.

An anti-Communist law, effective 29 Sept. 1962, has made the propagation of totalitarian or Communist doctrines an offence punishable by imprisonment; supplementary offences, contrary to democratic principles, are punished by prison terms of from 3 to 7 years.

Religion. The dominant religion is Roman Catholicism. Under the 1962 constitution churches are exempted from the property tax; the Catholic Church is recognized as a legal person, and other churches are entitled to secure similar recognition. There is an archbishop in San Salvador and bishops at Santa Ana, San Miguel, San Vicente, Santiago de María and Usulután.

Education. Education is free and obligatory. In 1929 the State took over control of all schools, public and private, but the provision that the teaching in government schools must be wholly secular was removed in 1945.

In Dec. 1970 there were 2,892 (2,937 in 1972) primary schools (state, municipal and private), with 531,309 (869,065 in 1974) pupils and 14,193 teachers. Secondary education was given at 860 schools (86,853 pupils). The national university and the Catholic University had 186,500 students in 1974.

Social Welfare. The Social Security Institute now administers the sickness, old age and death insurance, covering industrial workers and employees earning up to ₡700 a month. Employees in other private institutions with salaries over this amount are included but are excluded from the medical and hospital benefits.

DIPLOMATIC REPRESENTATIVES

OF EL SALVADOR IN GREAT BRITAIN (9B Portland Place, London, W1N 3AA)

Ambassador: Dr Manuel Arturo Calderón.

OF GREAT BRITAIN IN EL SALVADOR (11a Ave. Norte, 611 Colnia Dueñas, San Salvador)

Ambassador and Consul-General: A. S. Papadopoulos, MVO, MBE.

OF EL SALVADOR IN THE USA (2308 California St., NW, Washington, DC., 20008)

Ambassador: Roberto Quinonez Meza.

OF THE USA IN EL SALVADOR (25 Ave. Norte, Colnia Dueñas, San Salvador)

Ambassador: Frank J. Devine.

OF EL SALVADOR TO THE UNITED NATIONS

Ambassador: Dr Miguel Rafael Urquia.

Books of Reference

Statistical Information: The Dirección General de Estadistica y Censos (Villa Fermina, Calle Arce, San Salvador) dates from 1937. *Director General:* Lieut.-Col. José Castro Meléndez. Its publications include *Anuario Estadistico*. Annual from 1911.—*Boletin Estadístico*. Quarterly.—*El Salvador en Gráficas*. Annual.—*Atlas Censal de El Salvador*. 1955 only.

Angel Gallardo, M., *Cuatro Constituciones Federales de Centro América y Las Constituciones Políticas de El Salvador*. San Salvador, 1945
Browning, D., *El Salvador: Landscape and Society*. OUP, 1971
Vogt, W., *The Population of El Salvador and Its Natural Resources*. Washington, D.C., 1946
Wallich, H. C. (ed.), *Public Finance in a Developing Country: El Salvador*. Harvard Univ. Press, 1951
White, A., *El Salvador*. New York, 1973

EQUATORIAL GUINEA

Capital: Malabo
Population: 290,000 (1970)
GNP per capita: US$330 (1976)

República de Guinea Ecuatorial

HISTORY. The Republic of Equatorial Guinea became independent on 12 Oct. 1968 after having been a Spanish colony (Territorios Españoles del Golfo de Guinea) until 1959. From 1959 to 1963 the territory was made into two Spanish provinces with a status comparable to the metropolitan provinces. From 1964 to 1968 this Equatorial Region became an autonomous entity still retaining the status of two Spanish provinces, but with a certain amount of internal self-government. Serious political disturbances in Rio Muni occurred in March–April 1969. This led to the partial withdrawal of the Spanish community. Agreements for co-operation in education and economic development were signed with Spain in 1971 and 1972. The Republic still depends heavily on Spanish economic aid but has, in recent years, tended to rely increasingly on the Soviet bloc including Cuba and the People's Republic of China.

AREA AND POPULATION. The total area is 28,051 sq. km (10,831 sq. miles). Total population, 245,989 (1960 census); 1976 estimate, 250,000.

The republic consists of 2 provinces: (1) the continental Mbini (formerly Rio Muni) (26,017 sq. km including the adjacent islets of Corisco, Elobey Grande and Elobey Chico which cover 17 sq. km). The administrative and economic capital is Bata (3,548 inhabitants in 1960). Total population was 183,377, including 2,864 Europeans at the census of 1960; 1970 estimate, 290,000; (2) the island of Macías Nguema, formerly Fernando Poo (2,034 sq. km including Pigalu, formerly Annobón, 17 sq. km). The capital is Malabo, formerly Santa Isabel, which is also the capital of the Republic (19,869 inhabitants in 1960). Total population at the census of 1960 was 62,612 (including 1,415 for Pigalu), including 4,220 Europeans: 1968 estimate about 70,000—80,000 with a significant increase of Nigerian plantation workers, but there has been considerable withdrawal of Nigerian workers because of the deterioration of economic conditions since independence. In 1976 the colony of Nigerian citizens was expelled.

The majority of the Mbini population is Fang (Pámues in Spanish). Along the coast and in the islets are the Combes, the Bengas, the Bujebas, etc.

In Macías Nguema the aborigines are called Bubis. These are now a minority (perhaps 15,000). Other ethnic groups are the Fernandinos (descendants of English-speaking Creoles), the Fangs, coast people from Mbini and formerly naturalized migrant workers from Nigeria, Cameroon and São Tomé. A fluctuating mass of plantation workers were about twice as numerous as the Equatorial Guineans. Pigalu is peopled by descendants of slaves brought by the Portuguese; they still speak a Portuguese patois. Pidgin English was the lingua franca in Macías Nguema in spite of the official Spanish. Because of political and economic difficulties about 100,000 citizens are reported to live in neighbouring countries and Spain.

CONSTITUTION AND GOVERNMENT. Following the referendum of 11 Aug. and the elections of 22 and 29 Sept. 1968, Equatorial Guinea has become a sovereign state consisting of two provinces. The Republic is administered by a President who is chief of the armed forces and head of government.

The first Assembly elected in 1968 was dissolved in 1971. The first President was appointed for life on 14 July 1972. There is a cabinet of 10 ministers. A new

Constitution was adopted in July 1973. All power rests with the Life President and the nominal autọmony of the provinces does not exist.

Life President and Minister of Defence and Foreign Affairs: Francisco Macias Nguema.

National flag: Three horizontal stripes of green, white, red; a blue triangle based on the hoist; in the centre the national arms.

DEFENCE. The *Guardia Nacional* consisted mainly of Fang soldiers with Spanish officers of the *Guardia Civil* seconded to it. Total strength about 1,000. Since 1969 all Spanish troops have been repatriated. There is a militia of young partisans.

INTERNATIONAL RELATIONS

Membership. Equatorial Guinea is a member of UN, OAU and is an ACP state of EEC.

ECONOMY

Budget. The budget for 1969–70 envisaged revenue of 712·5m. pesetas and expenditure of 1,139m. Spanish subsidies normally balance the budget.

Currency. In July 1973 the Guinean *peseta* was redesignated the *Ekpwele.*

Banking. The Banco Central de Guinea Ecuatorial in Malabo was established in 1969 with Spanish technical and financial assistance.

NATURAL RESOURCES

Agriculture. The chief products are cocoa (56,400 hectares in 1966), coffee (12,000 hectares) and wood; in 1976 production was 14,000 tonnes of cocoa, most of it high-grade exported to Spain and the US. Production declined by 56%, 1965–76. Coffee, of mediocre quality, is chiefly a Fang product. Production (1975) 7,200 tonnes and is gradually decreasing. With the departure of Nigerian workers, Fang labourers from Mbini have been recruited forcibly in 1976.

Livestock (1976): Cattle, 4,000; sheep, 31,000; goats, 7,000; poultry, 82,000.

Forestry. Wood was almost entirely exported from Mbini to Spain and the Federal Republic of Germany (337,438 tonnes to Spain in 1967). Production ceased in 1969 but is slowly recovering (920,000 tonnes in 1973). Plantations in the hinterland have been abandoned by their Spanish owners and except for cocoa, commercial agriculture is under serious difficulties.

INDUSTRY AND TRADE

Industry. Macías Nguema has very few industries. Electricity production in 1967: Fernando Poo, 9·47m. kwh.; Mbini, 5·7m. kwh. Mbini has no industry except lumbering. In Macías Nguema a fish-processing industry is developing. Hopes based on the 4-year development plan (1964–68) have not materialized. Post-independence political conditions have not been conducive to private investment.

Trade. In 1965 Equatorial Guinea exported 330,100 tonnes (value, 1,635·6m. pesetas; 1966, 1,817m.), of which 326,000 tonnes to Spain (value, 1,581·6m. pesetas). In 1970 total exports were 1,741m. EG pesetas, of which 91% went to Spain. Imports were 1,472m. EG pesetas, of which 80% came from Spain. In 1975 cocoa exports were US$13·4m. and coffee, US$7m.

Total trade between UK and Equatorial Guinea (British Department of Trade returns, in £1,000 sterling):

	1976	*1977*
Imports to UK	214	—
Exports and re-exports from UK	5	37

COMMUNICATIONS

Roads. Macías Nguema had a good tarmac road network, but Mbini had few surfaced roads; the main artery is Rio Benito–Bata–Micomeseng–Ebebiyin. Road reconstruction is envisaged.

Aviation. An international airfield exists in Malabo (28,029 passengers in 1967). Bata has more modest facilities (15,031 passengers in 1967). The line Madrid–Malabo–Bata is subsidized by Spain. Links with Douala (from Santa Isabel) and Libreville (Gabon) exist.

Shipping. Malabo is the main port. The other ports are Luba, formerly San Carlos (bananas, cocoa) in Macías Nguema and Bata, Puerto Iradier and Rio Benito (wood) in Mbini. A new harbour in Bata has been completed. In 1966 in the 5 ports 141,600 tonnes were unloaded and 429,000 loaded.

Post. Estimated number of telephones (1969), 1,451.

JUSTICE, RELIGION, EDUCATION AND WELFARE

Justice. The Constitution guarantees an independent judiciary. The Supreme Tribunal is the highest court of appeal and is located at Malabo.

Religion. The population of Equatorial Guinea is nominally Roman Catholic (227,517 in 1966) with influential Protestant groups in Santa Isabel and Mbini. By order of the President most churches were closed in 1975.

Education. Elementary schools provided compulsory education up to 12 years and primary schools continued it to 14 years. There were in 1966, 147 elementary and 32 primary schools with 21,421 and 1,565 pupils respectively. There were 271 teachers (17 Europeans). Malabo and Bata had a secondary school each, with together 31 teachers and 936 pupils. Malabo had also an 'Escuela Superior provincial' with 100 students and a teacher-training school. Bata had a normal school and a technical secondary school. In 1967 there were only about a dozen university graduates. Schooling has deteriorated consistently since independence and a significant number of teachers live in exile.

Health. Equatorial Guinea has a fairly adequate health service with 2 large hospitals in Malabo and Bata. With the exception of 3 African doctors in 1967, doctors come from Spain and other countries. A leper hospital exists in Micomeseng (200 beds with about 300 patients). About 10 European doctors remained in 1975.

DIPLOMATIC REPRESENTATIVES

OF GREAT BRITAIN IN EQUATORIAL GUINEA

Ambassador: A. E. Saunders, CMG, OBE (resident in Yaoundé).

OF EQUATORIAL GUINEA TO THE UNITED NATIONS

Ambassador: Evuna Owono Asangono.

The US Embassy was closed on 14 March 1976.

Books of Reference

Atlas Histórico y Geográfico de Africa Española. Madrid, 1955

Plan de Desarrollo Económico de la Guinea Ecuatorial. Presidencia del Gobierno. Madrid, 1963

Resumén estadistico del Africa española, 1965–66. Madrid, 1967

Berman, S., *Spanish Guinea: An Annotated Bibliography.* Microfilm Service, Catholic University. Washington, D.C. 1961

Pélissier, R., *Les Territoires espagnols d'Afrique.* Paris, 1963.—*Los territorios españoles de Africa.* Madrid, 1964.—*Etudes Hispano-Guinéennes.* Paris, 1969

ETHIOPIA

Capital: Addis Ababa
Population: 29·4m. (1977)
GNP per capita: US$100 (1976)

HISTORY. The ancient empire of Ethiopia has its legendary origin in the meeting of King Solomon and the Queen of Sheba. Historically, the empire developed in the centuries before and after the birth of Christ, at Aksum in the north, as a result of Semetic immigration from South Arabia. The immigrants imposed their language and culture on a basic Hamitic stock. Ethiopia's subsequent history is one of sporadic expansion southwards and eastwards, checked from the 16th to early 19th centuries by devastating wars with Moslems and Gallas. Modern Ethiopia dates from the reign of the Emperor Theodore (1855–68).

Menelik II (1889–1913) defeated the Italians in 1896 and thereby safeguarded the empire's independence in the scramble for Africa. By successful campaigns in neighbouring kingdoms within Ethiopia (Jimma, Kaffa, Harar, etc.) he united the country under his rule and created the Empire as it is today.

In 1936 Ethiopia was conquered by the Italians, who were in turn defeated by the Allied forces in 1941 when the Emperor returned.

The former Italian colony of Eritrea, from 1941 under British military administration, was in accordance with a resolution of the General Assembly of the United Nations, dated 2 Dec. 1950, handed over to Ethiopia on 15 Sept. 1952. Eritrea thereby became an autonomous unit within the federation of Ethiopia and Eritrea, under the Ethiopian Crown.

This federation became a unitary state on 14 Nov. 1962 when Eritrea was fully integrated with Ethiopia.

A provisional military government assumed power on 12 Sept. 1974 and deposed the Emperor. The deposed Emperor Hailé Selassié I, was born 23 July 1892; crowned King (Negus), on 7 Oct. 1928, proclaimed Emperor, after the death of the Empress Zauditu, on 2 April 1930, and crowned on 2 Nov. 1930. He married in 1911 Menen, who died on 15 Feb. 1962. The Emperor died on 27 Aug. 1975. There are a son and a daughter surviving. On 25 Jan. 1931 the eldest son, Asfa Wossen, was proclaimed Crown Prince and heir to the throne. On 14 April 1974 the Emperor named his grandson, Prince Zare Yacob as Crown Prince, but following the military takeover Asfa Wossen was invited to be crowned King, but this offer was later rescinded.

EVENTS. In early 1978 a reversal of the position in the armed struggle in the Ogaden area of Ethiopia with Somali forces took place. After an offensive mounted with strong USSR and Cuban support the area was recaptured and in March Somalia withdrew all troops from the area.

AREA AND POPULATION. The total area of the Empire is approximately 395,000 sq. miles or 1m. sq. km (Ethiopia 350,000, Eritrea, 45,000).

The official estimate of the population in 1977 was 29,416,000.

The dominant race of Ethiopia, the Amhara, inhabit the central Ethiopian highlands. To the north of them are the Tigréans, akin to the Amhara and belonging to the same Christian church, but speaking a different, though related, language. Both these races are of mixed Hamitic and Semitic origin, and further mixed by intermarriage with Galla and other races. The Gallas, some of whom are Christian, some Moslem and some pagan, comprise about 40% of the entire population, and are a pastoral and agricultural people of Hamitic origin. Somalis, another Hamitic race, inhabit the south-east of Ethiopia, in particular the Ogaden desert region. These like the closely related Afar people, are Moslem. The Afar stretch northwards from Wollo region into Eritrea.

The country is divided into 14 administrative regions, each under a Chief Administrator, and under the administrative control of the Minister of the Interior. Each province is divided into about 7 districts under a district administrator. All revenues collected in the provinces are under the control of the Minister of Finance.

Province	Area (sq. km)	Population 1974	Chief town	Population 1974
Arussi	23,500	892,700	Assela	22,100
Bale	124,600	739,600	Goba	15,650
Begemdir	74,200	1,418,700	Gondar	43,040
Eritrea	117,600	2,070,100	Asmara	296,044
Gemu Goffa	39,500	730,700	Arba Minch	8,790
Gojjam	61,600	1,829,600	Debre Markos	33,730
Hararge	259,700	3,510,000	Harar	53,560
Illubabor	47,400	719,400	Mattu	7,820
Kefa	54,600	1,768,700	Jimma	52,420
Shoa	85,400	5,712,100	Addis Ababa (capital)	1,083,420
Sidamo	117,300	2,595,600	Awassa	19,550
Tigre	65,900	1,916,600	Mekele	34,290
Wollega	71,200	1,326,800	Lekemti	21,260
Wollo	79,400	2,570,200	Dessie	54,910

Other large towns (population, 1974): Dire Dawa, in Harar, 72,860; Nazret, in Shoa, 50,550.

CONSTITUTION AND GOVERNMENT. On 24 Nov. 1974 the Provisional Military Government announced that on 23 Nov. it had executed 60 former military and civilian leaders including Gen. Aman Andom who was then Head of State and Chairman of the Provincial Military Administrative Council.

On 3 Feb. 1977 it was announced that Brig.-Gen. Teferi Bante, the Head of State and Chairman of PMAC and 6 other members of the ruling military council were executed.

Chairman of the Provisional Military Administration Council: Lieut.-Col. Mengistu Haile Mariam.

National flag: Three horizontal stripes of green, yellow, red; over all in the centre the Lion of Judah in brown.

National anthem: Ityopya, Ityopia Kidemi (tune by Daniel Yohannes, 1975).

DEFENCE

Army. The Army, trained by British officers from 1947 to 1951 and by Swedish officers until 1964, comprises 5 divisions, including 3 made up of 3 infantry brigades, 1 division composed of 1 mechanized, 1 motorized and 1 infantry brigade, and 1 counter-insurgency division. It is recruited by voluntary enlistment. Five artillery battalions, 5 anti-aircraft batteries, 2 combat engineer battalions, an airborne infantry battalion and ancillary service, make up the ground forces to a total of 70,000.

In addition, a people's militia of around 100,000 has been set up. This force was still being expanded in Oct. 1977.

A US military advisory and administrative group, established since 1954, working down to divisional level, was asked by the Ethiopian government to disband in April 1977. Ethiopia's military rulers have moved away from US military assistance since they came to power and now rely on USSR for most of their military aid. Large amounts of USSR military equipment have been sent to help her in her conflict with Somalia over the Ogaden desert region. Ethiopian officers are trained at the National Military Academy, Harar, and at the National Military Training Centre, Holletta, near Addis Ababa.

Navy. The Navy, with headquarters at Addis Ababa, consists of a training ship (1,768 tons; *ex*-US seaplane tender), 1 *ex*-Netherlands coastal minesweeper, 5 patrol craft (*ex*-US coastguard motor gunboats), 1 *ex*-Yugoslav submarine chaser, 4 harbour defence craft and 4 small landing craft. The Naval Base and College is at Massawa.

Personnel, 1978, totalled 1,500 officers and men.

Air Force. The Air Force, trained originally by Swedish and American personnel, has its headquarters at Debre Zeit, near Addis Ababa. It includes a training school and a central workshop. Before fighting with Somalia began, there were 1 bomber, 1 ground-attack, 2 day-fighter/ground-attack and 1 fighter/reconnaissance combat squadrons, equipped with Canberras, F-5s, F-86s and T-28Ds, and 1 transport squadron equipped with jet-augmented C-119Ks, C-54s, C-47s and Doves. USSR equipment since supplied is reported to include 48 MiG-21 fighters. Training aircraft include two-seat F-5Bs, T-33 jet advanced trainers and piston-engined Cessna 310s, T-28s and Saab-91s. A few Agusta-Bell 204, Alouette III, Mi-6 and Mi-8 helicopters are in service. Personnel, 330 officers and 1,790 men.

The frontier guard patrols the Somalia border, and commando police units are being employed to assist the Army and police in border patrols and anti-terrorist operations in Eritrea. Total paramilitary force, 20,000.

INTERNATIONAL RELATIONS

Membership. Ethiopia is a member of UN, OAU and is an ACP state of EEC.

ECONOMY

Planning. The second 5-year plan (1962–67) which envisaged a total expenditure of E$1,451m., including E$376m. for industrial development, was claimed to have been fulfilled to 95%. The third 5-year plan (1969–73, which was extended to 1974) involved a total expenditure of E$2,865m. (of which E$565m. for industry and E$624m. for transport and communications) and hoped to achieve a growth rate of 6% per annum. Actual growth rate was below 4% and the fourth 5-year plan was replaced in 1975 by a policy statement embodying a package approach to rural development.

Budget. Revenue and expenditure estimates for financial years (ended 7 July) were as follows (in E$1m.):

	1971–72	*1972–73*	*1973–74*	*1974–75*	*1975–76*
Revenue	714·9	732	832·2	881·9	1,174·9
Expenditure	732·9	757	857·2	918·8	1,331·0

Of the estimated revenue in 1975–76, E$252m. is expected to come from customs duties and taxes, E$190·9m. from indirect taxes, E$182·2m. from direct taxes and E$100·5m. from external assistance. Of the expenditure, E$174·4m. is to be allocated to defence, E$178·4m. to education and culture and E$267·8m. to social services. The deficit is to be covered by external loans and credits E$214m. and internal borrowing E$156m.

Currency. The Ethiopian *birr*, divided into 100 cents, is the unit of currency; it is based on 5·52 grains of fine gold. It consists of notes of $1, 5, 10, 50 and 100 denominations, and bronze 1-, 5-, 10- and 25-cent coins. The former dollar notes were replaced by the new *birr* in Oct. 1976. Currency is issued by the National Bank, and, as at 30 Sept. 1975, was notes, E$673·7m.; coins, E$169·7m. The note issue, under the Banking Proclamation of 1963, must be backed by gold and foreign securities in the international reserve fund to at least 25% of its value. At 30 Sept. 1975, the fund stood at E$491·6m. The Ethiopian dollar = 48 cents US; E$4.31 = £1 sterling (on 14 Oct. 1975).

Banking. The State Bank was renamed the National Bank of Ethiopia in Oct. 1963, when its commercial activities were transferred to the newly established Commercial Bank of Ethiopia. At the same time another new bank, the Investment Bank of Ethiopia, was set up with a capital of E$10m., of which the Government held the majority of shares. In Sept. 1965 it became the Ethiopian Investment Corporation, which is a substantial shareholder in a number of industrial and other ventures.

The Investment Corporation has now been merged with the Development Bank of Ethiopia and the two are now known as the Agricultural and Industrial Development Bank, SC.

Two Italian banks have subsidiaries in Asmara, and one has a subsidiary in Addis Ababa. The Addis Ababa Bank Share Co. is connected with National & Grindlays Bank Ltd.

On 1 Jan. 1975 the Government nationalized all banks, mortgage and insurance companies.

Weights and Measures. The metric system of weights and measures is officially in use. Traditional weights and measures vary considerably in the various provinces: the principal ones are: *Frasilla* = approximately $37\frac{1}{2}$ lb.; *gasha*, the principal unit of land measure, which is normally about 100 acres but can vary between 80 and 300 acres, depending on the quality of the land.

ENERGY AND NATURAL RESOURCES

Electricity. Installed electricity generating power of the Ethiopian Electric Light and Power Authority was 185 mw in 1972 and production in 1972 totalled 431m. kwh.

Oil. A Russian built state-owned oil refinery at Assab came on stream in 1967 with a capacity of 600,000 tonnes of crude.

Minerals. Ethiopia has little proved mineral wealth. Salt (122,000 tonnes in 1974) is produced mainly in Eritrea, while a placer goldmine is worked by the Government of Adola in the south. Gold production, in 1974, was 15,754 troy oz. Small quantities of other minerals are produced including platinum. The potash deposits in the Dankali salt plains in the north-east part of the country were investigated by 2 US companies in 1966–70 but no exploitation has taken place. Japanese interests were engaged in the exploitation of significant copper deposits near Asmara, but the mine was closed down in March 1974 as a result of damage caused by ELF dissidents. A natural gas-strike was made offshore near Massawa in Decc. 1969, but it was not exploited. Encouraging traces of gas and oil have been found in south-east Ethiopia and exploration has been intensified by US concerns.

Agriculture. Coffee is by far the most important source of rural income. Harari coffee (long berry Mocha) is cultivated in the east; Abyssinian coffee is produced in Kaffa and the surrounding provinces, much of it growing wild.

Teff (*Eragrastis abyssinica*) is the principal food grain, followed by barley, wheat, maize and durra. Pulses and oilseeds are imported for local consumption and export. Cane sugar is an important crop.

Livestock: 23·1m. sheep, 26m. cattle, 17·1m. goats; smaller numbers of donkeys, horses, mules and camels. Hides and skins and butter (ghee) are important for home consumption and export. Sheep, cattle and chickens (51·3m.) are the main providers of meat. All agricultural land was nationalized in March 1975, and a radical land reform was carried out. Tenants were given possessory rights to the land they tilled, absentee landlords were abolished, and a ceiling on landholding was instituted.

INDUSTRY AND TRADE

Industry. The most important products of the small but growing industries are cotton yarn and fabrics, cement, sugar, salt, cigarettes, canned foodstuffs, building materials, footwear, pharmaceuticals, tyres and paint. Most industry is centred around Addis Ababa and Asmara. Industry around Asmara has been severely hit by actions of Eritrean guerrillas.

Foreign investment is encouraged by 5-year tax holiday for new investment greater than E$200,000; expansion of existing plant and investments of less than E$200,000 are given a 3-year tax holiday. Imports for processing are duty free.

Commerce. Coffee is by far the most important export, followed by pulses, oilseeds, hides and skins. Imports are textiles, foodstuffs, vehicles, machinery, manufactured goods and petroleum products. Coffee exports, 1973, were 76,082 tonnes.

Imports and exports (in E$1m.) for 6 years (ending 9 Dec.):

	1969	*1970*	*1971*	*1972*	*1973*	*1974*
Imports	388·2	429·0	469·6	435·6	448·2	569·2
Exports	292·6	294·6	309·9	376·9	494·9	556·2

In 1973 the main supplying countries were: Italy (E$66·6m.), Japan (E$60·4m.), Federal Republic of Germany (E$52·1m.), UK (E$41·9m.), USA (E$38·1m.), Iran

(E$30m.), France (E$19·9m.). The principal purchasing countries were: (USA E$149·6m.), Federal Republic of Germany (E$43·4m.), Italy (E$38·6m.), French Terr. of Afars and Issas (E$36·6m.), Saudi Arabia (E$31·2m.), Japan (E$22·7m.).

The chief items of import in 1973 were: Machinery and transport equipment (E$146·1m.), manufactured goods (E$102·4m.). The main items of export were: Coffee (E$189·8m.), pulses (E$75m.), hides and skins (E$68·6m.).

Total trade between Ethiopia and UK (British Department of Trade returns, in £1,000 sterling):

	1972	*1973*	*1974*	*1975*	*1976*	*1977*
Imports to UK	2,248	3,559	4,804	3,762	14,913	4,689
Exports and re-exports from UK	5,620	6,980	9,815	8,709	12,584	19,111

COMMUNICATIONS

Roads. Loans totalling E$83·75m. have been made between 1951 and 1968 by the International Bank and the International Development Agency for 3 programmes for improving and extending the road system. A fourth programme began in 1968 and is being financed by E$190m. in foreign loans and was completed in 1972. A fifth programme is near completion with a projected cost of E$60m. A sixth programme, estimated to cost E$133m., is underway which will include about 400 km of gravel-surfaced feeder roads. The Highway Authority now maintains some 7,600 km of roads and is engaged in constructing another 850 km of all-weather roads. Chief motor roads: Massawa–Asmara–Sudan; Asmara–Dessie–Addis Ababa; Asmara–Gondar–Addis Ababa; Addis Ababa–Jimma; Addis Ababa–Lekemti; Addis Ababa–Nazareth; Dire-Dawa–Hargeisa; Dessie–Assab; Addis Ababa–Adola.

Estimated number of motor vehicles (1973): Cars, 55,000; lorries and trucks, 7,000; buses, 3,500; tractors, 3,000.

Railways. The Franco-Ethiopian Railway Co., owned by the 2 governments, operates the line from Djibouti to Addis Ababa. The line is of 1 metre gauge, with a total length of 782 km. Trains run three times weekly in each direction, covering the distance in one night and one day. The railway carried 397,852 tons of freight and 361,120 passengers in 1971–72. The line has been out of action since June 1977 when Somali guerrillas destroyed several bridges. The Northern Railway of Ethiopia from Massawa to Asmara and Agordat (306 km, 950 mm gauge) is owned and operated by the Ethiopian Government. It carried 146,600 tons of freight and 1,000 passengers in 1971–72, but services have ceased because of terrorist activity.

Aviation. Ethiopian Air Lines, formed in 1946, provides services to Cairo, Athens, Frankfurt, London, Khartoum, Lagos, Accra, Rome, Nairobi, Entebbe, Kinshasa, Kigali, Dar es Salaam, Djibouti, Aden, Paris, Duala, Taiz, Jedda, Peking and Delhi, in addition to internal services. The following airlines operate through Asmara and Addis Ababa: Alitalia, Kenya Airways, Air India, Lufthansa, Egyptair, Yemen Airlines and Saudi Arabia Airlines. Air-France, British Airways and Air Djibouti operate through Addis Ababa only.

Shipping. A state shipping line was established in 1964. In May 1973 it owned 4 cargo vessels and 2 tankers.

Post and Broadcasting. The postal system serves 301 offices in the Empire, mainly by air-mail. All the main centres are connected with Addis Ababa by telephone or radio telegraph. International telephone services are available at certain hours to most countries in Europe, North America and India. Number of telephones (1977), 73,486 and 194 telex subscribers (1972).

The Ethiopian Broadcasting Service makes sound broadcasts on the medium and short waves in English, Amharic and in the vernacular languages spoken within the country. Radio Voice of the Gospel, owned by the Lutheran World Federation, was nationalized in March 1977 and renamed Radio Voice of Revolutionary Ethiopia. It broadcasts from Addis Abba in English, French, Amharic, Arabic, Somali and Afar. Television was introduced in 1964 and programmes broadcast from Addis Ababa for a radius of about 100 miles to the south and south-east of the capital and in Asmara from June 1977.

Cinemas (1974). There were 31 cinemas, with seating capacity of about 25,600.

Newspapers. In Addis Ababa there is 1 English, 1 French and 1 Amharic dailies, and in Asmara 2 Italian dailies, 1 part-Tigrinya, part-Arabic, and 1 Amharic weekly. All the papers are government-controlled and have small circulations, varying between 2,000 and 20,000.

JUSTICE, RELIGION, EDUCATION AND WELFARE

Justice. The legal system is said to be based on the Justinian Code. A new penal code came into force in 1958 and Special Penal Law in 1974. Codes of criminal procedure, civil, commercial and maritime codes have since been promulgated.

The extra-territorial rights formerly enjoyed by foreigners have been abolished, but any person accused in an Ethiopian court has the right to have his case transferred to the High Court, provided he asks for this before any evidence has been taken in the court of first instance.

Provincial and district courts have been established, and High Court judges visit the provincial courts on circuit. The Supreme Imperial Court at Addis Ababa is presided over by the Chief Justice.

Police. In 1948 the regular police force of the capital and some provincial cities was amalgamated with the irregular territorial forces under the provincial governors-general. The total force now numbers about 32,000 officers and other ranks.

Religion. Since the conversion of the Amharas to Christianity in the 4th century they have retained their connexion with the Alexandrian Church through the Abuna, or Metropolitan who was always an Egyptian Copt, and who was appointed and consecrated by the Coptic Patriarch of Alexandria. Both the Egyptian and Ethiopian Coptic Churches are monophysite, rejecting the decrees of the Council of Chalcedon (A.D. 451). After the restoration of the Emperor relations between the Ethiopian and Egyptian churches were strained until the summer of 1948, when an agreement was reached which envisaged the appointment of an Ethiopian Archbishop, and in Jan. 1951 Abuna Basilios (who died in 1970) was elected Archbishop of Ethiopia. A further agreement in 1959 made the Ethiopian Church autocephalous, and Basilios assumed the rank of Patriarch, with seniority immediately after the Patriarch of Alexandria. Abuna Theophilos was elected to the Patriarchate by an electoral college representing clergy, laity and Government and consecrated by the Ethiopian Archbishops in May 1971. In Aug. 1976 the third Patriarch, Abuna Tekle Haimanot, was invested. The clergy is very numerous and the Church holds a considerable proportion of the land. Christianity is predominant in the following provinces in the north: Tigré, Gondar, Gojjam, Shoa. Wollo province in the north-east is half Christian, half Moslem. In the southern half of the country the provinces of Hararge and Arssi have Moslem majorities, while all the other southern provinces have considerable Moslem minorities. In addition, the province of Gamu Gofa on the Kenya border and parts of Sidamo and Arssi have considerable pagan elements. Eritrea is half Moslem and half Christian. Each province now forms a diocese.

Islam is widely practised in the south and east of the Empire. Moslem minorities are found in Addis Ababa and in other commercial centres. The rite is mainly shafeitic. Harar is the most important Moslem centre. There are mosques and government schools for Moslems in most towns.

Education. In the academic year 1971–72 there were more than 2,600 primary, secondary and church schools providing education for 872,000 pupils. Higher education is co-ordinated under the National University, chartered in 1961. The University College, the Engineering, Building and Theological Colleges are in Addis Ababa, the Agricultural College in Harar and the Public Health College in Gondar. It is intended to develop these provincial colleges into universities in their own right. In 1971–72 the University of Asmara had 1,500 students. Altogether they provided tuition for about 5,884 students.

Since the military takeover in 1974 education has been in a state of flux. A campaign, known as *zemetcha*, lasting from Dec. 1974 to July 1976, was launched, in which all higher academic institutions were closed and the students sent into the countryside to preach the revolution. Academic institutions are now in operation again, although it is not clear if numbers have recovered to a pre-1974 level.

The main language of instruction from the secondary level upwards is English.

Health. In 1972 there were 350 doctors and 8,415 hospital beds.

DIPLOMATIC REPRESENTATIVES

OF ETHIOPIA IN GREAT BRITAIN (17 Prince's Gate, London, SW7 1PZ)

Ambassador: Ato Ayalew Wolde-Giorgis.

OF GREAT BRITAIN IN ETHIOPIA (Fikre Mariam, Abatecham St., Addis Ababa)

Ambassador: D. M. Day, CMG.

OF ETHIOPIA IN THE USA (2134 Kalorama Rd, NW, Washington, D.C., 20008)

Chargé d'Affaires: Tibabu Bekele.

OF THE USA IN ETHIOPIA (Entoto St., Addis Ababa)

Chargé d'Affaires: Arthur T. Tienkin.

OF ETHIOPIA TO THE UNITED NATIONS

Ambassador: Mohamed Hamid Ibrahim.

Books of Reference

Area Handbook for Ethiopia. US Govt. Printing Office, Washington, 1971
Trade Directory and Guide Book of Ethiopia. Addis Ababa, 1971
Clapham, C., *Haile Selassie's Government.* London, 1969
Greenfield, R., *Ethiopia: A New Political History.* London, 1967
Hess, R. L., *Ethiopia: The Modernization of Autocracy.* Cornell Univ. Press, 1970
Mosley, L., *Haile Selassie.* London, 1964
Rasmussen. *Welcome to Ethiopia.* Addis Ababa, 1967
Thompson, B., *Ethiopia: The Country That Cut Off Its Head.* London, 1975
Trevaskis, G. K. N., *Eritrea.* London, 1960
Wolde-Mariam, M., *An Atlas of Ethiopia.* Rev. ed. Addis Ababa, 1970

FALKLAND ISLANDS AND DEPENDENCIES

Capital: Stanley
Population: 1,903 (1976)

AREA AND POPULATION. The Crown Colony is situated in the South Atlantic Ocean about 480 miles north-east of Cape Horn. The numerous islands cover 4,700 sq. miles. The main East Falkland Island, 2,610 sq. miles; the West Falkland, 2,090 sq. miles, including the adjacent small islands. The Dependency of South Georgia lies 800 miles south-east of the Falklands, has an area of 1,450 sq. miles; the South Sandwich group, 470 miles south-east of South Georgia, has an area of 130 sq. miles.

The population of the Falkland Islands on 31 Dec. 1976 was 1,903. The only town is Stanley, in East Falkland, with a population of just over 1,000. The population of South Georgia varies with the season, but the resident population in 1976 was 22 (males).

The South Shetlands are uninhabited.

South Georgia, once a base for whaling and sealing operations, is now occupied by members of the British Antarctic Survey at the base at King Edward Point.

The population of the Falkland Islands and Dependencies is white and almost exclusively of British birth or descent.

CONSTITUTION AND GOVERNMENT. The Colony is administered by a Governor, assisted by an Executive Council consisting of the Chief Secretary and Financial Secretary, both *ex-officio*; 2 members elected by the Legislature and 2 appointed members; and a Legislative Council composed of the Chief Secretary and Financial Secretary, both *ex-officio*; 2 elected members representing Stanley, 1 elected member from the East Falkland and 1 from the West Falkland and 1 representing the Camp as a whole.

Governor and Commander-in-Chief: J. R. W. Parker, OBE.
Chief Secretary: John D. Mossingham.
Flag: British Blue Ensign with arms of Colony on a white disc in the fly.

ECONOMY

Budget. Revenue and expenditure (in £ sterling) for fiscal years ending 30 June:

	1972–73	*1973–74*	*1974–75*	*1975–76*	*1976–77*	*1977–78*[1]
Revenue	465,525	716,684	939,553	1,294,447	1,185,359	1,405,441
Expenditure	525,120	600,856	908,360	1,013,235	1,206,065	1,351,865

[1] Estimates.

Chief source of revenue (1976–77): Customs, £110,000; internal revenue, £347,329; investment, £215,628; posts and telecommunications, £124,815.

Currency. The Falkland £ is at parity with the £ sterling.

Banking. On 30 June 1977 the government savings bank held a balance of £1,685,303 belonging to 1,907 depositors. Some banking facilities are also offered by Lloyds Bank and Hambros Bank.

SHEEP FARMING. The whole acreage of the Colony is divided into large sheep runs. Wool is the principal product, but hides are exported. In 1976–77 there were 638,116 sheep, 9,111 cattle and 2,621 horses in the islands.

DEVELOPMENT. In recent years development aid has provided extra concrete roads in Stanley, improved education facilities throughout the Colony, radio-telephone services to many countries, including the UK, New Zealand and Australia, and telex and telecommunication facilities. In 1974 Cable and Wireless Ltd assumed control of the external communications of the colony. Studies are at present in hand with a view to developing the tourist potential of the islands. Recent and current development projects, for which Britain has granted Development Aid, include: a grant of £66,400 and a loan of £100,000 for the extension of the power station and electricity supply system, and grants of £4·2m. for the construction of an international airfield near Stanley, as well as £50,000 for a fencing subsidy scheme. A comprehensive Development Plan for the 5-year period 1973–78 has recently been approved, and capital expenditure in excess of £600,000 is allocated to various communication projects, assistance to the sheep-farming industry and to educational developments.

TRADE. Total imports, 1976, amounted to £1,063,116 and exports to £2,373,976.

COMMUNICATIONS

Roads. There are no made-up roads in the islands beyond the immediate vicinity of Stanley.

Aviation. There is a small internal air service. Communication between Stanley and the outside world is effected by a weekly air service by F27 aircraft to Comodoro Rivadavia, Argentina.

Shipping. A charter vessel calls 4 or 5 times a year to/from the UK. Communication with the Colony, the Dependencies and the British Antarctic Territory is kept up by the Royal research ships *John Biscoe* and *Bransfield* and by the ice-patrol vessel HMS *Endurance*.

In 1976 the total tonnage of shipping entered and cleared was 126,741.

Post and Broadcasting. There is a government-operated broadcasting station at Stanley and the Government also operates a wired broadcasting service to subscribers.

EDUCATION AND WELFARE

Education. Education is compulsory between the ages of 5 and 15 years. In 1976 there were 331 children receiving education in the colony. This includes Stanley schools, Darwin Boarding School and settlement schools, as well as pupils taught by itinerant teachers in rural areas. 31 children were being educated abroad.

Health. The Falkland Islands Medical Department, under the supervision of the senior medical officer, is responsible for the public health and sanitation of the colony. The government medical department employs the following: 3 registered medical practitioners; 4 registered nurse/midwives; 6 partially trained nurses; 1 laboratory and X-ray technician and 1 dental surgeon. There is 1 general hospital situated in Stanley with 27 beds. There is also a routine/emergency flying doctor service operated to the outlying farm settlements.

WILD LIFE. The Falkland Islands and South Georgia are noted for their outstanding wild life, including penguin and seal. Four Nature Reserves have been declared and 18 Wild Animal and Bird Sanctuaries gazetted. The brown trout introduced between 1947 and 1952 can now be found in nearly all the rivers.

Books of Reference

Falkland Islands and Dependencies. Biennial Report: 1970–71. HMSO, 1973
Falkland Islands Journal. Stanley, from 1967
Strange, I. J., *The Falkland Islands.* Newton Abbot, 1972

FIJI

Capital: Suva
Population: 588,068 (1976)
GNP per capita: US$1,150 (1976)

HISTORY. The Fiji Islands were discovered by Tasman in 1643 and visited by Capt. Cook in 1774, but first recorded in detail by Capt. Bligh after the mutiny of the *Bounty* (1789). In the 19th century the search for sandalwood, in which enormous profits were made, brought many ships. Deserters and shipwrecked men stayed on; fire-arms salvaged from wrecks were used in native wars, new diseases swept the islands, and rum and muskets became regular articles of trade. Tribal wars became bloody and general until Fiji was ceded to Britain on 10 Oct. 1874, after a previous offer of cession had been refused. British administrators produced order out of chaos, and since then there has been steady political, social and economic progress. Fiji gained independent status on 10 Oct. 1970.

AREA AND POPULATION. Fiji comprises about 844 islands and islets (about 106 inhabited) lying between 15° and 22° S. lat. and 174° E. and 177° W. long. The largest is Viti Levu, area 4,010 sq. miles; next is Vanua Levu, area 2,137 sq. miles. The island of Rotuma (18 sq. miles), about 12° 30′ S. lat., 178° E. long., was added to the colony in 1881. Total area, 7,055 sq. miles (18,272 sq. km).

A population census is taken every 10 years. Total population (census, 15 Sept. 1976), 588,068. In Sept. 1966 it was 476,727. The 1976 total population consisted of the following: 259,932 Fijians; 292,896 Indians; 10,276 Part Europeans; 4,929 Europeans; 6,822 Rotumans; 4,652 Chinese; 7,291 other Pacific Islanders; 1,270 others.

Suva, the capital, is on the south coast of Viti Levu; population (census 1976), 63,622. Suva was proclaimed a city on 2 Oct. 1953.

Vital statistics, 1975:

	Fijians	*Indians*	*Others*[1]	*Total*
Births	7,202	8,281	1,019	16,502
Deaths	1,505	2,208	234	3,947

[1] Includes Europeans, Part-Europeans, Rotumans, Other Pacific Islanders and Chinese.

CONSTITUTION AND GOVERNMENT. Fiji became an independent nation with Dominion status within the Commonwealth on 10 Oct. 1970. This had been agreed at a constitutional conference held in London in April 1970. There is also an Upper House, the Senate, of 22 members (8 nominations by the Council of Chiefs, 7 by the Prime Minister, 6 by the Leader of the Opposition and 1 by the Rotuma Council).

At elections held in Sept. 1977 for the 52 seats in the House of Representatives the Alliance Party won 36 seats, two factions of the National Federation Party won 15 seats and there was 1 independent.

Local Government. The Fijian Administration, established in 1876, had jurisdiction over all Fijians.

Fiji is divided into 14 provinces, each with its own council. Elections to these councils in 90 constituencies were conducted for the first time in 1967 on a full adult franchise amongst Fijians.

The councils have wide powers to make by-laws and draw up their own budget subject to confirmation by the Fijian Affairs Board. Each council has its own treasury and levies rates to raise its revenue. These provincial rates vary from $F6 to $F9 per annum for every male adult, but those maintaining 5 or more children pay lower rates until their children become taxpayers. A start has been made, however, to change over to a system of land rating based upon the unimproved value of Fijian-owned land. This is considered to be more equitable and related to ability to pay.

These newly elected councils held their inaugural and 1968 budget meetings towards the end of 1967, when the chairman for each of these 14 councils was also elected from among its members. Members were elected for 2 years and new elections were held in 1969.

At the apex of the Fijian Administration is the Great Council of Chiefs presided over by the Minister for Fijian Affairs and Rural Development. The Council of Chiefs consists of 22 Fijian members elected to the House of Representatives, 30 representatives, elected by the Provincial Councils and 15 representatives nominated by the Minister for Fijian Affairs and Rural Development.

The Council of Chiefs advises the Government generally on Fijian affairs.

Governor-General: Ratu Sir George Cakobau, GCMG, GCVO, OBE.

Prime Minister: Ratu Sir Kamisese Mara, KBE.

Flag: Light blue with the Union Flag in the canton and the shield of Fiji in the fly.

DEFENCE. The Fiji Military Forces Ordinance, 1949, provides for the maintenance of a small regular force, with territorial units and trained reserves.

Navy. A naval squadron has been raised to perform fishery protection, surveillance, hydrographic surveying and coastguard duties. Present strength is 3 coastal minesweepers (*ex*-US MSC) and 1 survey craft. Naval personnel in 1978 numbered 160.

INTERNATIONAL RELATIONS

Membership. Fiji is a member of the UN, the Commonwealth, the Colombo Plan and is an ACP state of the EEC.

ECONOMY

Budget. The financial year corresponds with the calendar year. All figures are in $ Fijian.

	1971	*1972*	*1973*	*1974*	*1975*	*1976*
Revenue	53,008,798	59,100,000	72,500,000	80,900,000	110,900,000	128,785,048
Expenditure	46,806,723	56,700,000	70,400,000	79,000,000	109,100,000	129,667,658

For budget purposes, revenue and expenditure are divided into two parts: Operating and Capital Operating. Revenue comes mainly from taxation, customs and excise duty, licences and fees. In 1976, of the total revenue collected over $F46m. was derived from customs and excise duty and over $F59m. from income tax collections. The total capital expenditure in 1976 was $F40,717,783.

GDP at factor cost in 1976 was $F531·3m. (1975, $F476m.), and GDP *per capita* at factor cost was $F919m. (1975, $F837m.). The annual real growth between 1971 and 1976 was 4·7% and the real growth in GDP *per capita* was 2·9%.

Currency. Fiji changed to decimal currency on 13 Jan. 1969, with the major unit being $1.

Banking. The Bank of New South Wales has 6 branches and 9 agencies; the Bank of New Zealand has 6 branches, 1 sub-branch and 17 agencies; the Australia and New Zealand Bank has 3 branches, 1 sub-branch and 1 agency and the Bank of Baroda has 5 branches, 2 sub-branches and 5 agencies in Fiji.

The National Bank of Fiji had, at the end of 1976, deposits amounting to $F10,396,000 due to 170,086 accounts. The headquarters are at the General Post Office, Suva, and there are 58 branches throughout Fiji.

NATURAL RESOURCES

Agriculture. Some 600,000 acres of land are in agricultural use. Sugar-cane is the principal cash crop, accounting for more than two-thirds of Fiji's export earnings; one quarter of the population depend on it directly for their livelihood. Copra, Fiji's second major cash crop, provides coconut oil and other products for export and employs nearly as many workers as the sugar industry. Ginger is the third major export crop replacing bananas which has declined through disease and hurricane. Other agricultural products include rice, cocoa, maize, tobacco and a variety of fruits and vegetables.

Fiji has a small but fast developing livestock industry.

Livestock (1976): Cattle, 156,000; horses, 35,000; goats, 55,000; pigs, 31,000; poultry, 785,000.

Forestry. Fiji supplies the bulk of its own timber requirements. A comprehensive pine scheme has been implemented with the aim of planting 186,000 acres by 1988. So far some 59,954 acres have been planted with a further 13,000 acres being developed a year. The Government provides extension and research services, agricultural subsidies, training and marketing services.

INDUSTRY AND TRADE

Industry. Major industries include 4 large sugar-mills, the goldmines (66,000 fine oz. in 1976) and 3 mills which process copra into coconut oil and coconut meal. There is a great variety of light industries.

Trade Unions. In July 1977 there were 43 trade unions registered with the Registrar-General's office.

Commerce. Exports in 1976: Sugar, 246,000 tons ($F67,704,000); coconut oil, 14,000 tons ($F4,564,000); gold, 66,000 fine oz. ($F7·25m.); oil seed, cake and meal, 4,000 tonnes ($F271,000); cement, 190,000 cwt ($F305,000).

Total trade (in $F) in calendar years:

	1972	*1973*	*1974*	*1975*	*1976*
Imports	131,549,479	174,644,907	219,331,159	220,967,274	238,040,052
Exports	65,582,377	74,425,887	123,740,332	142,292,948	122,523,214

Imports in 1976 (in $F1,000) from Australia were 68,189; Japan, 42,792; New Zealand, 32,507; UK, 25,645; Singapore, 21,794.

Exports in 1976 (in $F1,000) to UK were 50,547; New Zealand, 12,860; Australia, 12,596; Singapore, 6,207.

Total trade between Fiji and UK (British Department of Trade returns, in $1,000 sterling):

	1972	*1973*	*1974*	*1975*	*1976*	*1977*
Imports to UK	10,830	11,301	21,474	51,094	25,145	45,948
Exports and re-exports from UK	9,785	9,689	9,744	11,810	13,482	12,584

COMMUNICATIONS

Roads. There is a principal highway round Viti Levu, the distance from Suva to Lautoka *via* Ra, Tavua and Ba (King's Road) being 166 miles and *via* Navua and Sigatoka and Nadi (Queen's Road) being 156 miles. Branch roads run 34 miles along the Sigatoka Valley, 18 miles to Nadarivatu and Navai, 5½ miles to Vatukoula Goldfields, 35 miles to Serea and 7 miles to Vunidawa.

On Vanua Levu highways are in the neighbourhood of Labasa (Nasea) and Nasavusavu (Valeci). There are highways, 92 miles south and 36 miles west of Labasa. A highway extends to Buca Bay, 45 miles east of Nasavusavu. Coastal roads connect villages and plantations on parts of the islands of Taveuni and Ovalau. Work was proceeding (1976) on the reconstruction of the new bitumen surfaced highway between Suva and Nadi. The construction of a new gravel surfaced highway on Vanua Levu to link the towns of Vanua Levu and Labasa is almost complete.

Total road mileage is 2,019, of which 218 are sealed (paved), 1,663 are gravelled and 138 are unimproved.

Railway. There is a private 2-ft-gauge railway (South Pacific Sugar Mills Railway) of 400 miles from Tavua to Sigatoka serving most of the sugar-cane producing area.

Aviation. Fiji provides an essential staging point for long-haul trunk-route aircraft operating between North America, Australia and New Zealand. Under the South Pacific Air Transport Council, which comprises the UK, Australia, New Zealand and Fiji, the international airport at Nadi has been developed and administered. Four other airports are in use for domestic services.

Long-haul services touching Nadi airport are operated by PANAM (USA, Honolulu, Sydney), Air New Zealand (Auckland, Pago Pago, Honolulu, Los

Angeles), Qantas (Sydney, Honolulu, San Francisco; Sydney, Tahiti, Mexico), Union de Transports Aériens (Sydney, Nouméa, Tahiti, Los Angeles), Canadian Pacific Airlines (Vancouver, Honolulu, Auckland, Sydney).

Domestic and regional services are operated by Air Pacific (Tonga, also including Australia (Brisbane) and New Zealand (Auckland), New Hebrides, Solomon Islands, Gilbert Island, Tuvalu, Western Samoa); Polynesian Airlines (Western Samoa) and Air Nauru.

Shipping. In 1976, 20 vessels of 918 net tons were registered with the Fiji Marine Board. Suva has 4 slipways of 100, 200, 500 and 1,500 tons, and there are 3 shipbuilding and repair firms.

Post. There are 35 post offices and 156 agencies. Overseas postal communications are excellent. There is a daily air service to the major countries of the world and frequent dispatches by sea to UK, Australia, New Zealand and North America. Overseas telephone and telegram services are available through the Commonwealth cable to most countries except those in the South Pacific, which are served by direct radio circuits. The automatic telex network operates through New Zealand into the international telex system. There are ship-to-shore radio facilities. There were 30,759 telephones in 1977.

Cinemas. In 1977 there were 30 cinemas with a seating capacity of 15,000.

JUSTICE, RELIGION AND EDUCATION

Justice. Fijian courts have been abolished and merged into the magistrates' court.

Religion. The 1976 census showed: Christians, 299,960; Hindus, 234,520; Muslims, 45,247; Confucians, 731.

Education (1975). School attendance is not compulsory in Fiji. There were 780 schools scattered over 55 islands, staffed by 5,694 teachers, of whom about 75% were trained. There were also 117 pre-schools. The primary schools had 133,529 pupils and secondary 30,712. The technical and vocational schools had 1,586 students and the teachers' colleges 506. There were 3 teacher-training colleges, 1 medical and 1 agricultural school.

The University of the South Pacific opened in Feb. 1968 at Laucala Bay in Suva. It had 1,031 full-time students in 1975. The University has 3 schools, social and economic development, natural resources and education.

The main libraries are at Suva and Lautoka and there are also public libraries at Nadi, Ba, Sigatoka and Labasa. There is a national archives library, confined mainly to Fijiana and Oceania.

The Fiji museum in Suva contains a fine historical and ethnological collection relating to Fiji and Western Pacific territories.

Total government expenditure on education in 1975 was over $F25m.

DIPLOMATIC REPRESENTATIVES

OF FIJI IN GREAT BRITAIN (34 Hyde Park Gate, London, SW7 5DN)

High Commissioner: J. D. Gibson.

OF GREAT BRITAIN IN FIJI (Civic Centre, Stinson Parade, Suva)

High Commissioner: Lord Dunrossil.

OF FIJI IN THE USA (Suite 520, 1629 K. St., NW, Washington, DC., 20006)

Ambassador: Berenado Vunibobo.

OF THE USA IN FIJI (Ratu Sukuna Hse., Suva)

Chargé d'Affaires: Robert L. Flanegin.

OF FIJI TO THE UNITED NATIONS

Ambassador: Berenado Vunibobo.

Books of Reference

Statistical Information: A Government Statistical Office was set up in 1950 (Government Buildings, Suva). *Government Statistician:* M. A. Sahib.

Annual Report, 1973. HMSO, 1973
Trade Report. Annual (from 1887 [covering 1883–86]). Suva
Journal of the Fiji Legislative Council. Annual (from 1914 [under different title from 1885]). Suva
Fiji Today. Annually. Suva
Report of Commission of Inquiry Into Natural Resources and Population Trends in Fiji. Suva, Government Press, 1960
Ashford, J. E., *Social Security in Fiji*. Suva Government Press, 1964
Burns, Sir Alan, *Fiji*. HMSO, 1963
Capell, A., *New Fijian Dictionary*. 2nd ed. Glasgow, 1957
France, P., *The Charter of the Land*. OUP, 1969
Nayacakalom, R. R., *Leadership in Fiji*. OUP, 1976
Roth, G. K., *The Fijian Way of Life*. 2nd ed. OUP, 1973
Sahlins, M. D., *Moala: Culture and Nature on a Fijian Island*. Univ. of Michigan Press, 1962
Spate, O. H. K., *The Fijian People: Economic Problems and Prospects*. Suva, Government Press, 1959
Ward, R. G., *Land Use and Population in Fiji*. HMSO, 1965
Watters, R. F., *Koro: Economic Development and Social Change in Fiji*. OUP, 1969

FINLAND

Suomen Tasavalta—Republiken·Finland

Capital: Helsinki
Population: 4·73m. (1977)
GNP per capita: US$5,620 (1976)

HISTORY. Since the Middle Ages Finland was a part of the realm of Sweden. In the 18th century parts of south-eastern Finland were conquered by Russia, and the rest of the country was ceded to Russia by the peace treaty of Hamina in 1809. Finland became an autonomous grand-duchy which retained its previous laws and institutions under its Grand Duke, the Emperor of Russia. After the Russian revolution Finland declared itself independent on 6 Dec. 1917. The country was freed from Russian troops in a war from Jan. to May 1918, in which, simultaneously, domestic groups advocating a socialist system of government were defeated.

On 30 Nov. 1939 Soviet troops invaded Finland, after Finland had rejected territorial concessions demanded by the USSR. These, however, had to be made in the peace treaty of 12 March 1940, amounting to 32,806 sq. km and including the Carelian Isthmus, Viipuri and the shores of Lake Ladoga.

When the German attack on the USSR was launched in June 1941 Finland again became involved in the war against the USSR. On 19 Sept. 1944 an armistice was signed in Moscow. Finland agreed to cede to Russia the Petsamo area in addition to cessions made in 1940 (total 42,934 sq. km) and to lease to Russia for 50 years the Porkkala headland to be used as a military base. Further, Finland undertook to pay 300m. gold dollars in reparations within 6 years (later extended to 8 years). The peace treaty was signed in Paris on 10 Feb. 1947. The payment of reparations was completed on 19 Sept. 1952. The military base of Porkkala was returned to Finland on 26 Jan. 1956.

AREA AND POPULATION. The area and the population of Finland on 31 Dec. 1977 (Swedish names in brackets):

Province	*Area (sq. km)*	*Population*[2]	*Population per sq. km*[2]
Uusimaa (Nyland)	9,859	1,104,780	112·1
Turku-Pori (Åbo-Björneborg)	21,924	700,004	31·9
Ahvenanmaa (Åland)	1,481	22,455	15·2
Häme (Tavastehus)	17,156	660,072	38·5
Kymi (Kymmene)	10,736	346,215	32·2
Mikkeli (St Michel)	16,425	209,253	12·7
Pohjois-Karjala (Norra Karelen)	17,986	176,507	9·8
Kuopio	16,719	251,290	15·0
Keski-Suomi (Mellersta Finland)	16,430	240,560	14·6
Vaasa (Vasa)	26,119	425,841	16·3
Oulu (Uleåborg)	56,707	410,048	7·2
Lappi (Lappland)	93,932	195,269	2·1
Total	305,475	4,742,294	15·5

[1] Excluding inland water area which totals 31,577 sq. km. [2] Resident population.

The growth of the population, which was 421,500 in 1750, has been:

End of year	*Urban*	*Rural*	*Total*	*Percentage urban*
1800	46,600	786,100	832,700	5·6
1900	333,300	2,322,600	2,655,900	12·5
1950	1,302,400	2,727,400	4,029,800	32·3
1960	1,707,000	2,739,200	4,446,200	38·4
1970	2,340,308	2,258,028	4,598,336	50·9

The population on 31 Dec. 1976 by language primarily spoken: Finnish, 4,415,572 (93·3%); Swedish, 300,704 (6·4%); other languages, 8,553; unknown 6,007.

The principal towns with resident census population, 31 Dec. 1976, are (Swedish names in brackets):

Helsinki (Helsingfors)—capital	491,516	Kotka	34,247
(metropolitan area)	825,407	Savonlinna (Nyslott)	28,191
Tampere (Tammerfors)	165,769	Rauma (Raumo)	30,395
(metropolitan area)	271,207	Kouvola	30,363
Turku (Åbo)	164,380	Rovaniemi	28,968
(metropolitan area)	239,672	Kemi	28,080
Espoo (Esbo)	124,629	Mikkeli (St Michel)	27,704
Vantaa (Vanda)	123,088	Varkaus	24,424
Lahti	94,919	Riihimäki	23,933
Oulu (Uleåborg)	92,463	Seinäjoki	22,768
Pori (Björneborg)	80,356	Valkeakoski	22,686
Kuopio	72,438	Karhula	22,679
Jyväskylä	62,228	Kuusankoski	22,668
Vaasa (Vasa)	53,963	Kokkola (Gamlakarleby)	21,952
Lappeenranta (Villmanstrand)	53,345	Iisalmi	21,768
Joensuu	42,902	Kajaani	21,667
Hämeenlinna (Tavastehus)	41,102	Kerava	21,575
Hyvinkää (Hyvinge)	36,535	Anjalankoski	20,771
Imatra	35,737	Tornio	20,626

Vital statistics in calendar years:

	Living births	*Of which illegitimate*	*Still-born*	*Marriages*	*Deaths (exclusive of still-born)*	*Emigration*
1973	56,787	4,501	423	34,883	43,418	10,309
1974	62,472	5,648	464	34,533	44,674	12,027
1975	65,719	6,670	378	31,547	43,828	12,237
1976	66,846	...	377	32,004	44,786	17,346
1977	65,681	...	...	31,554	44,391	16,657

In 1977 the rate per 1,000 was: Births, 13·9; infantile deaths (per 1,000 births), 11·7; marriages, 6·7; deaths, 9·4.

General Census of Population 1970. 16 vols. Helsinki, 1973
Vital Statistics. Annual, Helsinki

CONSTITUTION AND GOVERNMENT. Finland is a republic according to the Constitution of 17 July 1919.

Parliament consists of one chamber of 200 members chosen by direct and proportional election, in which all Finnish citizens (men or women) who are 18 years have the vote (since 1969). The country is divided into 15 electoral districts with a representation proportional to their population. Every citizen over the age of 20 is eligible for Parliament, which is elected for 4 years, but can be dissolved sooner by the President.

The President is elected for 6 years by a college of 300 electors, elected by the votes of the citizens in the same way as the members of Parliament.

President of Finland: Dr Urho Kekkonen (elected 15 Feb. 1956, re-elected 15 Feb. 1962, 15 Feb. 1968, mandate extended by special law to March 1978 on 17–18 Jan. 1973 and re-elected 15 Feb 1978 for a further 6-year term).

State of Parties (March 1978) for Parliament elected on 28–29 Sept. 1975: Conservative 34; Liberals, 8; Swedish Party, 10 (including 1 for Coalition of Åland); Centre, 41; Rural, 2; Social Democratic Party, 54; Democratic League, 40; Christian League 9; Constitutional People's, 2.

The Council of State (Cabinet), appointed by the President in May 1977 and reshuffled March 1978, was composed as follows:

Prime Minister: Kalevi Sorsa.

Deputy Prime Minister and Minister of Agriculture and Forestry: Johannes

Virolainen. *Foreign Minister:* Paavo Väyrynen. *Justice:* Paavo Nikula. *Interior:* Eino Uusitalo. *Defence:* Taisto Tähkämaa. *Finance:* Paul Paavela. *Economics and Finance:* Esko Rekola. *Education:* Jaakko Itälä. *Education (Deputy):* Kalevi Kivistö. *Communications:* Veikko Saarto. *Trade and Industry:* Eero Rantala. *Social Affairs and Health:* Pirkko Työläjärvi. *Social Affairs and Health (Deputy):* Olavi Martikainen. *Labour:* Arvo Aalto.

National flag: White with a blue Scandinavian cross.

National anthem: Maamme; Swedish: Vårt land (words by J. L. Runeberg, 1843; tune by F. Pacius, 1948).

Finnish and Swedish are the official languages of Finland.

Local Government. For administrative purposes Finland is divided into 12 provinces (*lääni,* Sw.: *län*). The administration of each province is entrusted to a governor (*maaherra,* Sw.: *landshövding*) appointed by the President. He directs the activities of the provincial office (*lääninhallitus,* Sw.: *länsstyrelse*) and of local sheriffs (*nimismies,* Sw.: *länsman*). In 1976 the number of sheriff districts was 228.

The unit of local government is the commune. Main fields of communal activities are local planning, roads and harbours, sanitary services, education, health services and social aid. The communes raise taxes independent from state taxation. Two different kinds of communes are distinguished: Urban communes (*kaupunki* Sw.: *stad*) and rural communes. In 1977 there were altogether 464 communes, of which 84 were urban and 380 rural. In all communes communal councils are elected for terms of 4 years; all inhabitants (men and women) of the commune who have reached their 18th year are entitled to vote and eligible. The executive power is in each commune vested in a board which consists of members elected by the council and one or a few chief officials of the commune. Several communes often form an association for the administration of some common institution, *e.g.*, a hospital or a vocational school.

The autonomous county (*landskap*) of Åland has a county council (*landsting*) of one chamber, elected according to rule corresponding to those for parliamentary elections. In addition to its provincial governor it has a county board with executive power in matters within the field of the autonomy of the county.

Constitution Act and Parliament Act of Finland. Helsinki, 1967
The Finnish Parliament. Porvoo, 1969
Local Self-Government in Finland and the Finnish Municipal Law. Helsinki, 1960
Democracy in Finland. Studies in Politics and Government. Political Science Association. Helsinki, 1960

DEFENCE. The period of military training is 240 to 330 days. Total strength of trained and equipped reserves is about 700,000.

Army. The country is divided into 7 military districts. The Army consists of 1 armoured brigade, 6 infantry brigades, 8 independent infantry battalions, 3 field-artillery regiments, 5 independent field-artillery battalions, 2 coastal artillery regiments, 3 independent coastal artillery battalions, 1 anti-aircraft regiment and 3 independent anti-aircraft battalions, 2 independent engineer battalions, 1 signal regiment and 1 independent signal battalion, making a total strength in 1978, about 34,000.

Navy. The Fleet comprises 2 frigates (*ex*-Soviet), 2 corvettes, 1 coastal minelayer, 5 missile craft, 15 fast patrol boats, 6 inshore minesweepers, 5 patrol boats (*ex*-inshore minesweepers), 13 patrol boats, 4 coastguard patrol vessels, 3 support ships, 2 headquarters ships, 11 transport craft, 44 small transport boats, 5 coastguard cutters, 100 small coastguard craft, 1 training ship, 6 tugs, 10 icebreakers, 1 supply ship and a cable ship. There is a naval academy. Personnel in 1978 totalled 2,500 (200 officers and 2,300 ratings).

Air Force. The Air Force has 3 fighter squadrons, a military school of aviation and air force technical school, a depot, a transport squadron and a signal school. The fighter squadrons have MiG-21bis ('Fishbed-N') and Saab J35 Draken aircraft. Other equipment includes Saab-91D Safir piston-engined primary trainers (to be replaced by Valmet Vjinka trainers of Finnish design), Magister jet basic trainers (to be replaced by Hawks), MiG-15UTI and MiG-21UTI jet advanced trainers, C-47 transport aircraft, Il-28 target tugs and Mi-8, Mi-4, Hughes 500 and Agusta-Bell 206 helicopters. Personnel total 3,000 officers and men.

INTERNATIONAL RELATIONS

Membership. Finland is a member of UN, the Nordic Council, OECD and EFTA.

Treaties. A Treaty of friendship, co-operation and mutual assistance between Finland and the USSR was concluded in Moscow on 6 April 1948 for 10 years, extended on 19 Sept. 1955 to cover a period of 20 years and extended on 19 July 1970 for a further period of 20 years.

Treaty of Peace with Finland (10 Feb. 1947). Cmd. 7484

ECONOMY

Budget. Actual revenue and expenditure for the calendar years 1971–76, the ordinary budget for 1977 and the proposed budget for 1978 in 1m. marks:

	1971	*1972*	*1973*	*1974*	*1975*	*1976*	*1977*	*1978*
Revenue	12,166	14,304	16,896	20,931	25,108	32,132	33,125	35,721
Expenditure	11,944	13,970	16,961	21,307	27,546	31,094	33,122	37,601

Of the total revenue, 1976, 36% derived from direct taxes, 46% from indirect taxes, 4% from social-security contributions. Of the total expenditure, 1976, 18% went to education, 11% to social security, 9% to health, 12% to agriculture and forestry, 13% to transport and communications, 5% to defence and 2% to the public debt.

At the end of Dec. 1976 the foreign loans totalled 2,248m. marks, of which 2,201m. were long-term loans, 46m. promissory notes to international organizations. The internal loans amounted to 2,375m. marks, of which, 2,175m. were consolidated debt and 200m. short-term loans. The cash deficit was 882m. marks. The total public debt was 4,623m. marks.

Currency. The unit of currency, starting 1 Jan. 1963, is the new *mark* of 100 *pennis*, equalling 100 old *marks*. The gold standard was suspended on 12 Oct. 1931. Aluminium bronze coins are 50, 20 and 10 *pennis*; copper coins, 5 and 1 *pennis*; aluminium coins, 1 *pennis*; silver, 1 *mark* pieces. Exchange rate from 28 Feb. 1978: 8·105 = £1; 4·182 = US$1.

Banking. The Bank of Finland (founded in 1811) is owned by the State and under the guarantee and supervision of Parliament. It is the only bank of issue, and the limit of its right to issue notes is fixed equal to the value of its assets of gold and foreign holdings plus 500m. marks. Notes of 500, 100, 50, 10, 5 and 1 marks are in circulation, and their total value at the end of 1976 was 2,635m. marks.

At the end of 1976 the deposits in banking institutions totalled 44,025m. marks and the loans granted by them 50,749m. marks. The most important groups of banking institutions were:

	Number of institutions	*Number of offices*	*Deposits (1m. marks)*	*Loans (1m. marks)*
Commercial banks	7	1,097	15,819	19,090
Savings banks	280	1,307	11,751	10,616
Post office savings bank	1	22[1]	5,910	6,012
Co-operative banks	380	1,225	9,290	9,247

[1] In addition: 3,093 post offices.

Bank of Finland Monthly Bulletin. Helsinki, from 1926
Unitas. Quarterly Review, issued by Union Bank of Finland. Helsinki, from 1929
Economic Review (issued quarterly by Kansallis–Osake–Pankki). Helsinki, from 1948

Weights and Measures. The metric system of weights and measures was introduced in 1887 and is officially and universally employed.

Economic Survey of Finland. Annual

ENERGY AND NATURAL RESOURCES

Electricity. Electricity production was (in 1m. kwh.) 8,605 in 1960; 26,524 in 1974; 25,134 in 1975; 27,804 in 1976 and 31,556 in 1977, of which 39% was hydro-electric.

Minerals. The most important mines are Outokumpu (copper, discovered in 1910) and Otanmäki (iron, discovered in 1953). In 1977 the metal content (in tonnes) of the output of copper concentrates was 46,776, of zinc concentrates 61,317, of nickel concentrates 5,810, of iron concentrates and pellets 753,060 and of lead concentrates 627.

Agriculture. Agriculture is one of the chief occupations of the people, although the cultivated area covers only 9% of the land. The arable area was divided in 1974 into 248,736 farms, and the distribution of this area by the size of the farms was: Less than 5 hectares cultivated, 80,967 farms; 5–20 hectares, 142,027 farms; 20–50 hectares, 23,305 farms; 50–100 hectares, 2,085 farms; over 100 hectares, 321 farms.

The principal crops (area in 1,000 hectares, yield in tonnes) were in 1975:

Crop	*Area*	*Yield*	*Crop*	*Area*	*Yield*
Rye	47	180,000	Oats	465	1,216,000
Barley	583	1,447,400	Potatoes	46	736,500
Wheat	131	294,900	Hay	616	1,879,200

The total area under cultivation in 1975 was 2,641,300 hectares. Creamery butter products in 1977 was 73,420 tonnes, and production of cheese was 60,245 tonnes.

Livestock (1977): Horses, 29,300; milch cows, 751,600; other cattle, 1,010,700; sheep excluding lambs, 54,800; pigs, 1·19m.; poultry, 8·6m.; reindeer, 193,000.

Forestry. The total forest land amounts to 30–31m. hectares. The productive forest land covers 19·73m. hectares. The growing stock was valued at 1,488m. cu. metres in 1971–76 and the annual growth at 57·4m. cu. metres.

In 1977 there were exported: Round timber, 1,101,783 cu. metres; sawn wood, 4,354,899 cu. metres; plywood and veneers, 605,405 cu. metres.

Census of Agriculture 1969. Helsinki, 1969
Westermarck, N., *Finnish Agriculture*. Helsinki, 1963

INDUSTRY AND TRADE

Industry. The following data cover establishments with a total personnel of 5 or more in 1975:

Industry	*Establishments*	*Personnel*[1]	*Value of production* Gross (1m. marks)	Value (1m. marks)
Mining and quarrying	100	7,092	655	388
Metal ore mining	13	4,675	399	229
Other mining	87	2,397	256	139
Manufacturing	6,106	521,427	75,951	27,055
Manufacture of food, beverages and tobacco	1,185	62,151	14,518	3,565
Textile, wearing apparel and leather industries	896	73,309	5,367	2,379
Manufacture of textiles	298	28,585	2,563	1,054
Manufacture of wearing apparel, except footwear	438	35,532	2,099	1,024
Manufacture of wood and wood products, incl. furniture	553	49,555	4,737	1,547
Manufacture of paper and paper prod., printing, publishing	752	82,692	16,816	5,548
Manufacture of paper and paper products	173	51,685	13,577	3,739
Printing, publishing, etc.	579	31,007	3,240	1,809
Manufacture of chemicals and chemical, petroleum, coal, rubber and plastic products	379	37,835	9,920	2,955
Manufacture of industrial chemicals	128	14,334	4,059	1,378
Manufacture of other chemical products	111	9,275	1,179	580
Petroleum refineries	3	2,353	3,422	357
Manufacture of non-metallic mineral products	379	22,615	2,398	1,173
Basic metal industries	74	20,489	4,901	1,333
Iron and steel basic industries	61	15,041	3,419	1,081
Non-ferrous metal basic industries	33	5,448	1,482	252

[1] Working proprietors, salaried employees and wage earners.

Industry	Establishments	Personnel[1]	Value of production: Gross (1m. marks)	Value of production: Value (1m. marks)
Manufacture of fabricated metal products, machinery, etc.	1,452	167,761	16,965	8,366
Manufacture of fabricated metal prod., excl., machinery	453	29,818	2,871	1,504
Manufacture of machinery, except electrical	572	63,984	6,138	3,186
Manufacture of electrical machinery apparatus, etc.	165	31,773	2,947	1,482
Manufacture of transport equipment	213	38,030	4,721	2,020
Other manufacturing industries	116	5,020	329	189
Electricity, gas and water	487	23,906	7,765	3,009
All industry	6,693	552,425	84,371	30,452

[1] Working proprietors, salaried employees and wage earners.

GDP *per capita* (1977) 24,915 marks.

Industrial Statistics of Finland. Annual
Knoellinger, C. E., *Labor in Finland.* Harvard Univ. Press, 1960

Commerce. Imports and exports for calendar years, in 1m. marks:

	1973	1974	1975	1976	1977
Imports	16,599	25,666	28,002	28,555	30,712
Exports	14,605	20,686	20,247	24,505	30,945

The trade with some principal import and export countries was (in 1,000 marks):

Country	Imports 1976	Imports 1977	Exports 1976	Exports 1977
Argentina	14,025	15,670	49,321	71,711
Australia	10,405	10,045	229,851	220,145
Austria	420,084	368,049	170,223	265,524
Belgium–Luxembourg	507,959	531,494	418,068	639,397
Brazil	177,466	54,495	120,950	141,713
Canada	116,619	131,019	144,182	168,279
China	43,231	46,509	100,572	86,081
Colombia	162,572	273,481	21,233	24,556
Czechoslovakia	135,798	134,237	133,632	114,968
Denmark	860,878	880,670	937,735	1,112,557
France	784,888	847,248	867,294	1,063,383
Germany (Dem. Rep.)	136,947	176,456	204,797	249,950
Germany (Fed. Rep.)	4,570,544	468,588	2,407,802	3,251,248
Greece	8,246	9,991	111,921	272,744
Hungary	122,888	118,843	132,482	174,372
Iran	247,624	349,122	277,168	348,538
Ireland	30,884	34,385	127,844	162,023
Israel	77,487	84,675	89,901	111,953
Italy	527,205	548,242	385,720	360,923
Japan	445,366	559,665	165,149	257,777
Netherlands	863,021	1,023,809	741,014	1,068,655
Norway	866,583	1,121,634	831,942	1,605,326
Poland	478,212	678,514	268,956	215,359
Portugal	85,599	99,595	71,046	81,374
Romania	39,568	51,363	16,203	43,561
Spain	363,834	363,172	242,152	261,687
Sweden	5,200,667	4,900,186	4,350,034	5,104,272
Switzerland	...	994,861	...	590,354
USSR	5,732,232	5,922,833	4,903,460	5,886,756
UK	2,277,189	2,778,092	3,492,854	3,741,285
USA	2,154,421	1,939,888	659,478	1,275,266

Principal imports 1977 (in 1m. marks): Food and live animals, 2,323; crude materials, inedible, except fuels, 1,813; mineral fuels, lubricants, etc., 7,250; chemicals, 2,715; textile yarn, fabrics, etc., 1,403; iron and steel, 1,051; machinery apparatus and appliances, 9,282; road vehicles, 1,942.

Principal exports in 1977 (in 1m. marks): Food and live animals, 1,163; wood shaped or simply worked, 2,375; wood pulp, 1,568; veneers, plywood, etc., and other wood manufactures, 799; paper and paper-board, 7,049; clothing, 1,518; machinery and transport equipment, 8,057; road vehicles, 552.

Total trade between UK and Finland (British Department of Trade returns, in £1,000 sterling):

	1973	*1974*	*1975*	*1976*	*1977*
Imports to UK	331,574	493,384	400,402	562,462	593,675
Exports and re-exports from UK	167,757	228,485	264,466	288,960	345,957

Finnish Foreign Trade Directory, 1971. Helsinki, 1971

COMMUNICATIONS

Roads. In Jan. 1977 there were 40,075 km of highways and 36,688 km of other public roads. At the end of 1977 there were 1,075,399 registered cars, 50,291 lorries, 85,920 vans and 8,771 buses.

Railways. On 31 Dec. 1976 the total length of the railways was 6,042 km, of which all except 6 km was owned by the State. The gauge is 5 ft. In 1977 the number of passengers carried was 37m. and the amount of goods carried was 22·1m. tonnes. The total revenue in 1977 was 1,297m. marks and the total expenditure 1,877m. marks.

Aviation. The scheduled traffic of Finnish airlines covered 30m. km in 1977. The number of passengers was 1,836,292 and the number of passenger-km 1,395m. The air transport of freight and mail amounted to 38·69m. tonne-km.

Shipping. The total registered mercantile marine on 31 Dec. 1977 was 446 vessels of 2·27m. gross tons. In 1977 the total number of vessels arriving in Finland from abroad was 16,124 and the goods discharged amounted to 25·6m. tonnes. The goods loaded for export from Finland ports amounted to 14m. tonnes.

The lakes, rivers and canals are navigable for about 6,600 km. Timber floating is important, and there are about 41,500 km of floatable inland waterways. In 1976, timber floated by vessels, 186,778 tonnes (rafts, 6·58m.).

On 27 Aug. 1963 the USSR leased to Finland the Russian part of the canal connecting Lake Saimaa with the Gulf of Finland. After extensive rebuilding the canal was opened for traffic in 1968. The Saimaa Canal and deepwater channels on Lake Saimaa (520 km) can be used by vessels with dimensions not larger than as follows: length 82 metres, width 11·8 metres, draught 4·4 metres and height of mast 24·5 metres.

Post and Broadcasting. In 1976 there were 4,178 post offices and 906 telegraph offices. The total length of telegraph wires was 483,840 km and that of telephone wires (1975) 10,057,072 km. The number of telephones (1977) was 1,935,683. All post and telegraph systems are administered by the State jointly with a large part of the telephone services. The total revenues from postal services were 949m. marks and from (wire and radio) telegraph services 1,274m. marks.

On 31 Dec. 1976 the number of combined wireless and television licences, 1,454,454; licences for colour television, 431,147. *Oy Yleisradio AB* broadcasts 2 programmes in Finnish and 1 in Swedish on long-, medium- and short-waves, and on FM. Two TV programmes (1 commercial) are broadcast.

Cinemas. In Dec. 1976 there were 314 cinemas with a seating capacity of 94,213.

Newspapers. In 1976 the number of newspapers published more often than once a week was 121, of which 107 in Finnish, 13 in Swedish and 1 bilingual.

JUSTICE, RELIGION, EDUCATION AND WELFARE

Justice. The lowest courts of justice are the municipal courts in towns and district courts in the country. Municipal courts are held by the burgomaster and at least 2 members of court, district court by judge and 5 jurors, the judge alone deciding, unless the jurors unanimously differ from him, when their decision prevails. From these courts an appeal lies to the courts of appeal (*Hovioikeus*) in Turku, Vaasa,

Kuopio and Helsinki. The Supreme Court (*Korkein oikeus*) sits in Helsinki. Judges can be removed only by judicial sentence.

Two functionaries, the *Oikeuskansleri* or Chancellor of Justice, and the *Oikeusasiamies*, or Solicitor-General, exercise control over the administration of justice. The former acts also as counsel and public prosecutor for the Government; while the latter, who is appointed by the Parliament, exerts a general control over all courts of law and public administration.

At the end of 1976 the prison population numbered 5,575 men and 131 women; the number of convictions in 1976 was 298,050, of which 268,891 were for minor offences with maximum penalty of fines and 29,154 with penalty of imprisonment.

Merikoski, V., *Précis du droit public de la Finlande*. Helsinki, 1954

Religion. Liberty of conscience is guaranteed to members of all religions. National churches are the Lutheran National Church and the Greek Orthodox Church of Finland. The Lutheran Church is divided into 8 bishoprics (Turku being the archiepiscopal see), 72 provostships and 593 parishes. The Greek Orthodox Church is divided into 2 bishoprics (Kuopio being the archiepiscopal see) and 25 parishes, in addition to which there are a monastery and a convent.

Percentage of the total population at the end of 1974: Lutherans, 91·5; Greek Orthodox, 1·2; others, 1·1; not members of any religion, 6·2.

Education (1975–76). *Primary and secondary education:*

	Number of institutions	*Teachers*	*Students*
First-level Education	*4,351*	*24,490*	*453,700*
(Lower sections of the comprehensive schools, grades I–VI, regular primary schools and junior secondary schools, grades I–II)			
Second-level Education	*1,533*	*32,890*	*419,800*
General education	1,013	23,130	337,600
(Upper sections of the comprehensive schools, grades VII–IX, primary continuation schools, junior secondary schools, grades III–VI and senior secondary schools)			
Vocational education	520	9,760	82,200

Higher Education. Education at the third level (including universities) was provided at 30 institutions with 4,600 teachers and 114,300 students. General adult education (at civic institutes, folk high schools and study centres) had 656,100 students.

University Education. The institutions of academic education and the number of teachers and students are:

	Founded	*Teachers*	*Students Total*	*Students Women*
Universities				
Helsinki	1640[1]	1,526	22,961	12,113
Turku (Swedish)	1919	220	3,247	1,608
Turku (Finnish)	1922	676	8,590	4,643
Jyväskylä	1958[2]	442	6,161	3,691
Oulu	1958	657	6,568	3,066
Tampere	1966[3]	373	8,356	4,902
Joensuu	1969	157	1,934	1,279
Kuopio	1972	129	711	356
Polytechnic, Lappeenranta	1969	71	489	53
Polytechnic, Helsinki	1849	411	6,132	905
Polytechnic, Tampere	1972	144	1,674	172
College of Veterinary Medicine, Helsinki	1946	46	226	98
Schools for Economics				
Helsinki (Finnish)	1911	144	4,167	1,951
Helsinki (Swedish)	1927	77	1,557	683
Turku (Swedish)	1927	35	630	285
Turku (Finnish)	1950	54	1,185	527
Vaasa	1968	50	854	584

[1] In Turku, moved to Helsinki in 1828.
[2] Previously teachers' training college since 1934.
[3] Previously College for Social Services in Helsinki since 1925.

	Founded	Teachers	Students Total	Students Women
Swedish school of social sciences and local administration	1964[1]	16	323	235
Teachers' training colleges[2]				

[1] Previously Swedish Civic College since 1943.
[2] Included in data for the universities above.

Higher Education and Research in Finland. Ministry of Education. Helsinki, 1968
Niini, A., *Vocational Education.* National Board for Vocational Education. Helsinki, 1968

Health. In 1976 there were 7,068 physicians, 3,366 dentists and 72,366 hospital beds.

Social Security. The Social Insurance Institution administers general systems of old age pensions (to all persons over 65 years of age and disabled younger persons) and of health insurance. An additional system of compulsory old age pensions paid for by the employers is in force and works through the Central Pension Security Institute. Systems for child welfare, care of vagrants, alcoholics and drug addicts and other public aid are administered by the communes and supervised by the National Social Board and the Ministry of Social Affairs and Health.

The total cost of social security amounted to 18,205·4m. marks in 1975. Out of this 4,914m. (27%) was spent for health, 522m. (2·9%) for industrial accidents, 809m. (4·4%) for unemployment, 7,880m. (43·3%) for old age and disability, 2,604m. (4·4%) for family allowances and child welfare, 231m. (1·3%) for general welfare purposes, 615m. (3·4%) for war-disabled, etc., and 334m. (1·8%) as tax reductions for children. Out of the total expenditure 26% was financed by the State, 15% by local authorities, 48% by employers and 11% by the beneficiaries.

Labour Protection and Legislation. Helsinki, 1977
Social Welfare and Social Allowances. Helsinki, 1976
Social Security in the Nordic Countries 1972. Statistical Reports of the Nordic Countries, vol. 29. Copenhagen, 1976
Ellala, Esa, Suominen, Risto, and Kotiranta, Maija-Liisa, *The Development of Social Security in Finland from 1950–1974.* Official statistics of Finland, special social studies XXXII:48. Helsinki, 1976
Ellala, Esa, and Kortiranta, Maija-Liisa, *Social Expenditure in 1975 and Preliminary Data for 1976.* Official statistics of Finland, special social studies XXXII:53. Helsinki, 1978

DIPLOMATIC REPRESENTATIVES

OF FINLAND IN GREAT BRITAIN (38 Chesham Place, London SW1X 8HW)

Ambassador: Dr Richard Tötterman, GCVO, OBE (accredited 20 March 1975).

OF GREAT BRITAIN IN FINLAND (16–20 Uudenmaankatu, Helsinki, 12)

Ambassador: Sir James Cable, KCVO, CMG.

OF FINLAND IN THE USA (1900–24th St., NW, Washington, D.C., 20008)

Ambassador: Jaakko Iloniemi (accredited 10 Sept. 1977).

OF THE USA IN FINLAND (Itäinen Pulstotie 14A, Helsinki)

Ambassador: Rozanne L. Ridgway.

OF FINLAND TO THE UNITED NATIONS

Ambassador: Jaako Pekka Blomberg.

Statistical Information: The Central Statistical Office (Tilastokeskus, Swedish: Statistikcentralen; address: P.O. Box 504, 00101 Helsinki 10) was founded in 1865 to replace earlier official statistical services dating from 1749 (in united Sweden–Finland). Statistics on foreign trade, agriculture, forestry, navigation, health and social welfare are produced by other state authorities. Its publications include: *Statistical Yearbook of Finland* (from 1879) and

Bulletin of Statistics (monthly, from 1924). A bibliography of all official statistics of Finland is published in Finnish, Swedish and English in each *Statistical Yearbook*.

Books of Reference

Constitution Act and Parliament Act of Finland. Helsinki, 1978
Suomen valtiokalenteri (*State Calendar of Finland*; a Swedish version ***Finlands statskalender*** is published separately). Helsinki. Annual
Facts about Finland. Helsinki. Annual (Union Bank of Finland)
Finland: Creation and Construction. London, 1968
Finland in Figures. Helsinki, 1978
Finland Press Laws. Helsinki, 1978
Statistical Yearbook of Finland. Helsinki, Annual
Yearbook of Finnish Foreign Policy. Helsinki, Annual
Finnish Foreign Policy: Studies in Foreign Politics. Political Science Association, Helsinki, 1963
Hall, W., *The Finns and their Country.* London, 1967
Hurme-Pesonen, *Finnish–English General Dictionary.* Helsinki, 1973
Jakobson, M., *Finnish Neutrality.* London, 1968
Jutikkala, E., and Pirinen, K., *A History of Finland.* 2nd ed. New York, 1974
Kekkonen, U., *Neutrality: The Finnish Position.* 2nd ed. London, 1973
Nousiainen, J., *The Finnish Political System.* Harvard Univ. Press, 1971
Platt, R. R. (ed.): *Finland and its Geography.* New York, 1955
Puntila, L. A., *The Political History of Finland, 1809–1966.* Helsinki, 1974
Suomen Kartasto/Atlas of Finland/Atlas over Finland (ed. L. Aario). Finnish Geogr. Society, Helsinki, 1960
Suomi: Handbook of Finnish Geography. Finnish Geogr. Society, Helsinki, 1962
Törnudd, K., *The Electoral System of Finland.* London, 1968
Tuomikoski, A., and Sloor, A., *English–Finnish Dictionary.* Helsinki, 1973
Uotila, J., *The Finnish Legal System.* Helsinki, 1966
Wuorinen, J. H., *A History of Finland.* Columbia Univ. Press, 1965

FRANCE

République Française

Capital: Paris
Population: 53·09m. (1977)
GNP per capita: US$6,550 (1976)

AREA AND POPULATION.

Departments	*Area (sq. km)*	*Census population March 1946*	*March 1968*	*April 1975*
Ain[1]	5,756	298,556	339,262	376,477
Aisne	7,378	453,411	526,346	533,862
Allier	7,327	373,481	386,533	378,406
Alpes-de-Haute-Provence	6,944	83,354	104,813	112,178
Alpes (Hautes-)	5,520	84,932	91,790	97,358
Alpes-Maritimes	4,294	453,073	722,070	816,681
Ardèche	5,523	254,598	256,927	257,065
Ardennes	5,219	245,335	309,380	309,306
Ariège	4,890	145,956	138,478	137,857
Aube	6,002	235,237	270,325	284,823
Aude	6,232	268,889	278,323	272,366
Aveyron	8,735	307,717	281,568	278,306
Belfort (Territoire de)	610	86,648	118,450	128,125
Bouches-du-Rhône	5,112	971,935	1,470,271	1,632,974
Calvados	5,536	400,026	519,695	560,967
Cantal	5,741	186,843	169,330	166,549
Charente	5,953	311,137	331,016	337,064
Charente-Maritime	6,848	416,187	483,622	497,859
Cher	7,228	286,070	304,601	316,350
Corrèze	5,860	254,574	237,858	240,363
Corse-du-Sud (Ajaccio) } Haute-Corse (Bastia) }	8,681	267,873	269,831	289,842
Côte-d'Or	8,765	335,602	421,192	456,070
Côtes-du-Nord	6,878	526,955	506,102	525,556
Creuse	5,559	188,669	156,876	146,214
Dordogne	9,184	387,643	374,073	373,179
Doubs	5,228	298,255	426,363	471,082
Drôme	6,525	268,233	342,891	361,847
Essonne[1]	1,811	294,482	674,157	923,061
Eure	6,004	315,902	383,385	422,952
Eure-et-Loir	5,876	258,110	302,207	335,151
Finistère	6,785	724,735	768,929	804,088
Gard	5,848	380,837	478,544	494,575
Garonne (Haute-)	6,301	512,260	690,712	777,431
Gers	6,254	190,431	181,577	175,366
Gironde	10,000	858,381	1,009,390	1,061,474
Hauts-de-Seine[1]	175	992,859	1,461,619	1,438,930
Hérault	6,113	461,100	591,397	648,202
Ille-et-Vilaine	6,758	578,246	652,722	702,199
Indre	6,778	252,075	247,178	248,523
Indre-et-Loire	6,124	349,685	437,870	478,601
Isère[1]	7,474	542,573	768,450	860,378
Jura	5,008	216,386	233,547	238,856
Landes	9,237	248,397	277,381	288,323
Loir-et-Cher	6,314	242,419	267,896	283,686
Loire	4,774	631,591	722,383	742,396
Loire (Haute-)	4,965	228,076	208,337	205,491
Loire-Atlantique	6,893	665,064	861,452	934,499
Loiret	6,742	346,918	430,629	490,189
Lot	5,228	154,897	151,198	150,725
Lot-et-Garonne	5,358	265,449	290,592	292,616

[1] Population in 1946 adjusted to area at 1 March 1968.

Departments	Area (sq. km)	Census population March 1946	March 1968	April 1975
Lozère	5,168	90,523	77,258	74,825
Maine-et-Loire	7,132	496,068	584,709	629,849
Manche	5,947	435,468	451,939	451,662
Marne	8,163	386,926	485,388	530,399
Marne (Haute-)	6,216	181,840	214,336	212,304
Mayenne	5,171	256,317	252,762	261,789
Meurthe-et-Moselle	5,235	528,805	705,413	722,587
Meuse	6,220	188,786	209,513	203,904
Morbihan	6,763	506,884	540,474	563,588
Moselle	6,214	622,145	971,314	1,006,373
Nièvre	6,837	248,559	247,702	245,212
Nord	5,738	1,917,452	2,417,899	2,510,738
Oise	5,857	396,724	540,988	606,320
Orne	6,100	273,181	288,524	293,523
Paris (Ville de)[1]	105	2,725,374	2,590,771	2,299,830
Pas-de-Calais	6,639	1,168,545	1,397,159	1,403,035
Puy-de-Dôme	7,955	478,903	547,743	580,033
Pyrénées (Atlantiques)	7,629	415,795	508,734	534,748
Pyrénées (Hautes-)	4,507	201,954	225,730	227,222
Pyrénées-Orientales	4,086	228,776	281,976	299,506
Rhin (Bas-)	4,787	673,281	827,367	882,121
Rhin (Haut-)	3,523	471,705	585,018	635,209
Rhône[1]	3,215	958,534	1,325,611	1,429,647
Saône (Haute-)	5,343	202,573	214,176	222,254
Saône-et-Loire	8,565	506,749	550,362	569,810
Sarthe	6,210	412,214	461,839	490,385
Savoie	6,036	235,965	288,921	305,118
Savoie (Haute-)	4,391	270,565	378,550	447,795
Seine	...	4,775,711	—	—
Seine-Maritime	6,254	846,131	1,113,977	1,172,743
Seine-et-Marne	5,917	407,137	604,340	755,762
Seine-et-Oise	...	1,414,910	—	—
Seine-Saint-Denis[1]	236	730,361	1,251,792	1,322,127
Sèvres (Deux-)	6,004	312,756	326,462	335,829
Somme	6,175	441,368	512,113	538,462
Tarn	5,751	298,117	332,011	338,024
Tarn-et-Garonne	3,716	167,664	183,572	183,314
Val-de-Marne[1]	244	672,037	1,121,340	1,215,674
Val-d'Oise[1]	1,249	344,744	693,269	840,885
Var	5,999	370,688	555,926	626,093
Vaucluse	3,566	249,838	353,966	390,446
Vendée	6,721	393,787	421,250	450,641
Vienne	6,985	313,932	340,256	357,366
Vienne (Haute-)	5,512	336,313	341,589	352,149
Vosges	5,871	342,315	388,201	397,957
Yonne	7,425	266,014	283,376	299,851
Yvelines[1]	2,271	430,764	853,386	1,082,255
Total	543,998[2]	40,506,639[3]	49,778,540	52,655,802

[1] Population in 1946 adjusted to area at 1 March 1968.
[2] 212,919 sq. miles.
[3] Not including military, air and naval forces, crews of the commercial navy abroad and the personnel of the military government in Germany and Austria, numbering 312,105.

The figures include 2,664,060 foreigners in 1968.

The following table gives the area and census population of metropolitan France:

	Area (sq. km)	Domiciled population	Inhabitants per sq. km	Annual increase per 10,000
1801	537,699	27,349,003	51	—
1821	—	30,461,875	57	54
1841	—	34,230,178	64	58
1861	550,986	37,386,313	69	44
1866	—	38,067,064	69	36
1872	536,464	36,102,921	67	−88[1]

[1] Decrease.

	Area (sq. km)	Domiciled population	Inhabitants per sq. km	Annual increase per 10,000
1881	—	37,672,048	70	47
1891	—	38,342,948	71	18
1901	—	38,961,945	73	16
1911	—	39,604,992	74	16
1921	550,986	39,209,518	71	−10[1]
1931	—	41,834,923	76	65
1946	—	40,506,639	74	−22[1]
1954	—	42,777,174	78	67
1962	551,601	46,519,997	84	100
1968	543,998	49,778,540	92	101
1975	543,814	52,655,802	97	82

[1] Decrease.

Live birth rate in 1976 was 13·6 per 1,000 inhabitants; death rate, 10·5; marriage rate, 7·1; divorce rate, 1; infantile mortality, 12·6 per 1,000 live births.

Vital statistics for calendar years:

	Marriages	Divorces	Living births	Still-born	Deaths
1971	406,416	47,000	878,647	14,030	551,514
1972	416,521	48,400	875,093	13,400	547,487
1973	400,700	50,000	854,900	12,800	556,500
1974	394,755	50,000	799,217	11,400	550,550
1975	386,900	...	742,200	...	558,100
1976	374,400	...	717,800	...	555,200

Principal conurbations and towns (*agglomérations*) (census 1975, provisional):

	Con-urbation	Town		Con-urbation	Town
Paris	8,424,092	2,290,252	Metz	181,189	111,757
Lyon	1,152,863	456,674	Angers	180,512	137,347
Marseille	1,004,536	907,854	Dunkerque	164,819	83,091
Lille	928,569	175,477	Limoges	164,729	143,689
Bordeaux	591,447	223,131	Avignon	153,961	90,901
Toulouse	495,203	373,670	Amiens	152,503	131,013
Nice	...	...	Béthune	145,198	—
Nantes	437,566	344,451	Thionville	141,902	—
Rouen	389,462	114,415	Briey	132,612	—
Grenoble	389,076	166,733	Montbeliard	130,170	—
Toulon	378,609	181,841	Nîmes	129,924	187,635
Strasbourg	355,262	252,959	Troyes	128,050	74,814
St Etienne	334,596	219,722	Denain	126,411	—
Lens	313,081	—	Pau	125,703	83,143
Nancy	278,617	107,682	Besançon	124,011	120,387
Rennes	273,293	197,399	Bayonne	120,374	—
Le Havre	263,978	219,073	Saint-Nazaire	119,293	69,189
Cannes	255,089	70,527	Bruay-en-Artois	116,310	—
Tours	235,059	140,617	Perpignan	114,220	106,366
Clermont-Ferrand	224,700	156,800	Lorient	105,745	69,737
Valenciennes	223,752	—	Valence	104,296	68,560
Mulhouse	218,524	116,685	Calais	100,443	78,820
Montpellier	204,953	191,034	Angoulême	98,054	—
Orléans	204,536	106,226	Boulogne-sur-Mer	95,482	—
Douai	203,497	—	La Rochelle	95,295	75,367
Dijon	203,139	151,614	Béziers	92,530	88,131
Reims	196,331	177,639	Poitiers	...	81,312
Brest	186,426	167,519	Chambéry	88,123	54,368
Le Mans	184,812	152,031	Bourges	83,720	77,146
Caen	182,687	119,781	Roanne	83,527	55,166

Occupational structure (1975 census). Out of an economically active population of 21,061,215 persons, there are 2·01m. engaged in agriculture; 1,841,083 in building and public works; 6,327,818 in other manufacturing industries; 829,289 in transport; 3,632,478 in business, banking and insurance; 3,543,881 in services; 2,522,544 in commerce.

Recensement de la population de 1975. Paris, Institut National de la Statistique et des Etudes Economiques, 1975
Demangeon, A., *La France économique et humaine*. Paris, 1946
Ormsby, H., *France, a Regional and Economic Geography*. 2nd ed. London, 1950

CONSTITUTION AND GOVERNMENT. The constitution of the Fifth Republic, superseding that of 1946, came into force on 4 Oct. 1958. A referendum held in the French Republic and the oversea departments and territories on 28 Sept. 1958 approved the constitution drawn up by a committee which General de Gaulle had appointed in June. Apart from French Guinea, which voted over 90% against the constitution and for independence, the final result for metropolitan France, Algeria, the oversea departments and territories, and from French citizens living abroad or in trusteeship territories was as follows: Electorate, 45,840,642; voters, 36,893,979; valid votes, 36,486,251; Yes, 31,066,502; No, 5,419,749.

The Constitution consists of a preamble, dealing with the Rights of Man, and 92 articles. Emphasis is placed on the rôle of the President of the Republic. 'He sees that the Constitution is respected; he ensures, through his arbitration, the regular functioning of public powers as well as the continuity of the state. He is the guarantor of national independence' (Art. 5). He nominates and dismisses the Prime Minister and the other members of the government (Art. 8). He can dissolve the National Assembly after consultation with the Prime Minister and the presidents of the assemblies (Art. 12). He appoints to all military and civil offices of the Republic (Art. 13). 'When the institutions of the Republic, the independence of the nation, the integrity of its territory or the fulfilment of its international commitments are threatened with immediate and grave danger, and when the regular functioning of constitutional public powers is interrupted, the President of the Republic takes the measures demanded by the circumstances, after official consultation with the Prime Minister, the presidents of the assemblies and the Constitutional Council' (Art. 16).

Under the revised article 6 of the constitution (6 Nov. 1962) the President of the Republic is now elected by direct universal suffrage. His term of office is 7 years.

'The government determines and conducts the policy of the nation' (Art. 20); 'the government may ask parliament for authority to take, by decrees and within a limited period, such measures as are normally within the province of the law' (Art. 38). Ministers must not be members of parliament (Art. 23). Votes of censure can only be carried by a majority of the members constituting the Assembly (Art. 49). The 2 ordinary sessions in autumn and spring are curtailed to a total of 5 months (Art. 28).

The 'Constitutional Council' has to uphold the fairness of the elections and act as a guardian of the constitution. It is composed of 9 members, 3 of whom are nominated by the President of the Republic, 3 by the President of the National Assembly and 3 by the President of the Senate. In addition, past Presidents of the Republic are, by right, members of the Constitutional Council (Art. 56).

The Senate is composed of 295 members representing Metropolitan Departments, 9 Overseas Departments, 3 Oversea Territories, 6 Frenchmen residing outside France.

The elections for the National Assembly took place in March 1978. The National Assembly was composed of 491 members: 153 RPR (Gaullists); 137 UDF (Giscardians and centrist allies); 10 *Radicaux de gauche*; 104 *Parti socialiste*; 86 *Parti communiste*; 1 far left.

President of the Republic: Valéry Giscard d'Estaing; elected 19 May 1974. Assumed office 27 May 1974.

The Cabinet, as at June 1978:

Prime Minister: Raymond Barre.
Justice: Alain Peyrefitte.
Defence: Yvon Bourges.
Foreign Affairs: Louis de Guiringaud.
Economic Affairs: René Monory.
Education: Christian Beullac.
Co-operation: Robert Galley.
Interior: Christian Bonnet.
Labour: Robert Boulin.

Health: Simone Veil.
Industry: André Giraud.
Environment: Michael D'Ornano.
Agriculture: Pierre Mehaignerie.
External Trade: Jean François Deniau.
Budget: Robert Paon.
Universities: Alice Saunier-Séïté.
Transport: Joël le Theule.
Commerce: Jacques Barrot.
Youth and Sport: Jean-Pierre Soisson.
Culture and Communications: Jean-Philippe Lecat.

There are also 25 Secretaries of State.

National flag: The Tricolour of three vertical stripes of blue, white, red.
National anthem: La Marseillaise (words and tune by C. Rouget de Lisle, 1792).

Local Government. For administrative purposes metropolitan France is divided into 96 departments, since 1960, the departments have been re-grouped into 22 programme regions (or regional constituencies for operation to serve in effect as background for national development work, for planning and for budgetary policy).

The unit of local government is the *commune*, the size and population of which vary very much. There were, in 1975, in the 95 metropolitan departments, 36,034 communes. Most of them (31,259) had less than 1,500 inhabitants, and 16,372 had less than 300, while 199 communes had more than 30,000 inhabitants. A law of 16 July 1971 causes the smallest administrative area roughly equivalent to parish (*communes*), either to merge or to re-group themselves into combined administrative units of 'communes' or into urban communities. The local affairs of the commune are under a Municipal Council, composed of from 10 to 36 members, elected by universal suffrage, and by the *scrutin de liste* for 6 years by French citizens of 21 years or over after 6 months' residence.

Each Municipal Council elects a mayor, who is both the representative of the commune and the agent of the central government. He is the head of the local police and, with his assistants, acts under the orders of the prefect.

In Paris the Municipal Council is composed of 90 members. The 20 *arrondissements* into which the city is subdivided have been grouped in 9 sectors, each of which has its own mayor.

The next unit is the *canton* (3,209 in 1968), which is composed of an average of 12 communes, although some of the largest communes are, on the contrary, divided into several cantons.

The district, or *arrondissement* (322 in 1968), has an elected *conseil d'arrondissement*, with as many members as there were cantons, its chief function being to allot among the communes their respective parts of the direct taxes assigned to each *arrondissement* by the Council General.

Avril, P., *Le Régime politique de la Ve république*. Paris, 1964
d'Estaing, V. G., *French Democracy*. New York, 1977
Hayward, J., *The One and Indivisible French Republic*. New York, 1973
Suleiman, E. N., *Politics, Power, and Bureaucracy in France: The Administrative Elite*. Princeton Univ. Press, 1974

DEFENCE. The President of the Republic exercises command over the Armed Forces. He is assisted by the research organization of the High Council of Defence (*Conseil Supérieur de la Défense Nationale*) and two Committees (*Comité de Défense* and *Comité de Défense restreint*) which formulate directives. The Prime Minister is responsible for the national defence; he exercises his military responsibilites through the General Secretariat of National Defence (SGDN). Under the Prime Minister's authority, the *Comité d'Action Scientifique de Défence* co-ordinates research.

On 5 July 1969 the Army Ministry was replaced by the Ministry of State for National Defence which is responsible for the Army, Air Force and Navy. In addition to the powers of the Army Ministry, the Ministry of State prepares general directives for negotiations relating to defence. It has SGDN at its disposal for exercising these powers. It is assisted by the Departmental Assistant for Weapons, the

Secretary-General for Administration, the Chief of Staff of the Armed Forces and the Chiefs of Staff of the 3 Armed Forces—Army, Navy and Air.

In 1962 the Armed Forces were reorganized in 3 groups: (1) nuclear strategic force; (2) operational forces; (3) home defence forces.

(1) The Nuclear Strategic Force (FNS), which is directly under the President's authority, will comprise three generations: at present, the Mirage IV and the 'A' bomb operated by the Air Force; as from 1971, ground-to-ground strategic ballistic missiles (SSBS); as from 1971, the nuclear submarine missile launcher (SNLE). Each of these weapons systems is intended to exist alongside the preceding one and to supplement it. The strategic nuclear weapons will be supplemented as from 1972 by a tactical nuclear weapons system.

(2) The Land, Sea and Air Forces consist of: (*a*) 5 mechanized divisions forming the land forces which comprise the First Army. Since 1 Aug. 1969 these have been placed under a single command (3 divisions in metropolitan France—2 in the Federal Republic of Germany); 1 division specializing in overseas operations; national reserves in metropolitan France; troops, chiefly marines, stationed overseas and organized in 3 commands in the departments and French overseas territories and 3 inter-service commands in the African states and Madagascar; (*b*) a naval force of 2 squadrons, comprising aircraft carriers, escorts and amphibious craft; (*c*) tactical aircraft (Mirage III), helicopters (Frelon), transports (Transall), etc.

(3) Organized in 7 defence zones, 7 military regions and 21 territorial divisions, with co-ordination of civil and military authorities; also comprising all 3 services. The majority consists of 20 army home defence regiments, manned by conscripts.

French forces are not formally committed to NATO.

Army. The Army consists of regular officers and n.c.o.s, long-term n.c.o.s and soldiers, and conscripts serving 12 months.

The peace-time units comprise infantry, armoured troops and cavalry, artillery, engineering, signals, transport, matériel, naval infantry and artillery. In addition, there are the Foreign Legion, mountain and airborne troops and other specialized units.

In 1977 the effective strength of the Army was 330,000 all ranks.

Higher military instruction is provided in 3 stages: the staff school (*École d'État-major*) for officers of formation staffs; the *École Supérieure de Guerre* for officers earmarked for the higher command; the *Institut des Hautes Études de Défense Nationale* where high-ranking officers and civilians study together the problems of national defence.

Light Army Aircraft. Formed in 1952, the *Aviation Légère de l'Armée de Terre* (ALAT) is a well-equipped force, with 150 light aeroplanes and nearly 400 helicopters for observation, reconnaissance, combat area transport, liaison and supply duties. Effective strength, 1977, 5,500.

The *Gendarmerie* is an integral part of the Army but also co-operates with the civil administration in maintaining public order. Effective strength, 1977, 76,200.

Navy. The Navy is under the supreme direction of the Minister of Defence, being administered by the Chief and Deputy Chiefs of Naval Staff.

All naval aircraft and coastal defences are under the control of the Navy, and have been reorganized in 3 coast 'naval frontier' districts (with headquarters in Cherbourg, Brest and Toulon), in relation to the aircraft attached to the active fleet.

The French Navy is manned partly by conscription but mainly by voluntary enlistment. In 1978 the active personnel was 69,000 officers and men.

The following is a summary of the strength of the fleet at the periods shown:

	Completed at end of								
	1969	*1970*	*1971*	*1972*	*1973*	*1974*	*1975*	*1976*	*1977*
Aircraft carriers	4[1]	4[1]	4[1]	4[1]	4[1]	3[3]	3[3]	3[3]	3[3]
Submarines	21	20	21	22[2]	23[2]	23[2]	24[4]	24[4]	26[4]
Cruisers	2	2	2	2	1	1	1	1	1
Destroyers	17	17	16	16	20	22	21	20	21
Frigates	30	29	30	30	31	28	28	27	29

[1] Including 2 helicopter-carriers. [2] Including 3 nuclear-powered ballistic missile submarines.
[3] Including 1 helicopter-carrier. [4] Including 4 nuclear-powered ballistic missile submarines.

The principal surface ships of the French Navy are as follows:

Completed	Name	Standard displacement Tons	Armour Belt In.	Armour Guns In.	Principal armament	Shaft horse-power	Speed Knots
			Aircraft Carriers				
1963	Foch	22,000	—	—	8 3·9 in. (40 aircraft)	126,000	32·0
1961	Clemenceau						

The battleship *Richelieu* was relegated to an accommodation ship in 1960 and sold for scrap in 1968; and the battleship *Jean Bart* was similarly reduced in 1961 and condemned in 1968.

Completed	Name	Standard displacement Tons	Armour Belt In.	Armour Guns In.	Principal armament	Shaft horse-power	Speed Knots
			Helicopter Carriers				
1964	Jeanne d'Arc[1]	10,000	—	—	4 3·9-in. (8 helicopters)	40,000	26·5

[1] Cruiser type forward, flat-topped midships to aft.

The helicopter carrier *Arromanches* (former British fixed-wing aircraft carrier *Colossus*) was listed for disposal in 1974.

Completed	Name	Standard displacement Tons	Armour Belt In.	Armour Guns In.	Principal armament	Shaft horse-power	Speed Knots
			Cruisers				
1959	Colbert	8,500	—	—	1 twin 'Masurca' guided missile launcher; 2 3·9 in. AA	86,000	32·0

The command cruiser *De Grasse* was condemned in 1973.

There are also 4 nuclear-powered ballistic missile submarines of 7,500 tons, 22 diesel-powered submarines, 2 guided-missile destroyer leaders of 5,100 tons, 3 guided-missile leaders of 4,580 tons, 1 missile leader of 3,500 tons, 15 destroyers of 2,750 tons, 29 escorts (frigates), of 1,170 to 1,750 tons, 2 assault landing ships, 5 missile boats, 13 ocean minesweepers (6 converted for hunting), 5 coastal mine-hunters, 40 coastal minesweepers (14 used as patrol vessels), 5 inshore minesweepers (used as patrol craft), 10 surveying vessels, 11 patrol vessels, 7 coastal patrol craft, 5 landing ships, 13 landing craft, 9 maintenance, repair and depot ships, 10 oilers, 14 boom defence vessels, 5 support ships, 13 transports, 4 sail training vessels and 140 auxiliary ships and service craft.

Two more nuclear-powered ballistic-missile submarines, 1 diesel-electric submarine, 3 guided-missile leaders and 4 *avisos* (escorts) are under construction. A prototype nuclear-powered helicopter carrier, 1 prototype nuclear-powered fleet (hunter-killer) submarine and 10 escorts are projected.

The naval air arm, known usually as *Aéronavale*, has 2 squadrons of nationally designed Etendard IV-M transonic fighter-bombers, 1 squadron of Etendard IV-P reconnaissance fighters, 2 squadrons of US-built Crusader all-weather fighters, 3 squadrons of Alizé turboprop anti-submarine aircraft, 5 maritime reconnaissance squadrons with Atlantic and Neptune aircraft and 3 anti-submarine and assault squadrons with Super Frelon and Sikorsky HSS-1 helicopters. Strength is approximately 12,000 personnel and 350 aircraft, of which 200 are combat types.

Air Force. Formed as the *Service Aéronautique* in April 1910, the *Armeé de l'Air* is organized in 7 major commands. Its bases and installations were regrouped and modernized in 1967. The *Commandement des Forces Aériennes Stratégiques* (CFAS) commands the nuclear deterrent force. The *Commandement de la Force Aérienne Tactique* (FATAC) directs the tactical air forces, commands the air force reserve and is responsible for support of the ground forces. Under FATAC the 1st *Commandement Aérien Tactique* (1° CATAC) controls tactical air units based in eastern France; the 2nd *Commandement Aérien Tactique* (2° CATAC) controls the reserve forces and the air component of the *Force d'Intervention*. The *Commandement du Transport Aérien Militaire* (COTAM) is responsible for air transport operations and for the training and transport of airborne forces. The *Commandement Air des Forces de Défense Aérienne* (CAFDA) controls air defence forces. The *Commandement des Écoles de l'Armée de l'Air* (CEAA) is responsible for training the personnel for all branches of the Air Force. The *Commandement des Transmissions* has responsibility for communications and electronic warfare. Finally, the *Commandement du Génie de l'Air*, made up mainly of Army personnel, undertakes airbase construction and maintenance under Air Force control.

The home-based French Air Force is divided territorially among 4 metropolitan air regions (Metz, Villacoublay, Bordeaux, Aix-en-Provence); overseas, small air units are integrated into the local joint-service commands. There are about 37 combat squadrons plus transport, helicopter and support squadrons, and the Air Force uses a total of 66 bases.

The strategic, tactical and air defence forces are equipped entirely with jet aircraft. The CFAS has 32 first-line Mirage IV supersonic nuclear bombers, and reserves, deployed in 2 wings (each 3 squadrons) supported by 11 C-135F refuelling tanker transports. Some of these Mirage IVs are equipped also for reconnaissance missions. The 1° CATAC deploys 7 wings (20 squadrons), consisting of about 200 Mirage III-E and 5F ground-attack and III-R reconnaissance fighters, 120 Jaguar strike aircraft and a training squadron of Mirage III-Bs. The air defence forces have 4 wings, with 6 squadrons of Mirage F.1 multi-mission fighters and 2 squadrons of Mirage III-Cs. The COTAM is equipped with 3 wings of turboprop Transall C.160 and Noratlas piston-engined transports, supplemented by 2 groups of DC-8, Caravelle, Nord 262, Mystère 20 and M.S. 760 Paris aircraft. Other units are equipped with Broussard observation and general-purpose monoplanes, and about 100 Alouette III and Puma helicopters. Training aircraft include Magister jet basic trainers, Mystère IV, T-33 and Mirage III-B advanced trainers, and two-seat Jaguars. Replacement of the Magisters with Alpha Jets has begun.

Total aircraft in service on 1 Jan. 1976, 1,637, plus 390 supporting types, of which 700 were combat aircraft, including reserves. Total personnel, 100,990.

INTERNATIONAL RELATIONS

Membership. France is a member of UN, the Council of Europe, NATO and EEC.

ECONOMY

Planning. The post-war reconstruction and expansion of the French economy began under the guidance of the first 'Monnet plan' (1947–50), named after the then director of the planning office, Jean Monnet. This was followed by the second and third plans (1954–57, 1958–61), an intermediate plan for 1960 and 1961, the fourth plan, 1962–65, fifth plan, 1966–70, sixth plan, 1971–75, and seventh plan, 1976–80.

Bauchet, P., *La Planification Française. Vingt Ans d'Expérience*. Paris, 1966
Caire, G., *La Planification, Techniques et Problèmes*. Paris, 1967
Carré, J.-J., Dubois, P., and Malinvaud, E., *French Economic Growth*. Stanford Univ. Press, 1975
Treize, A., *La Planification en Pratique*. Paris, 1971

Budget. Budgets (in 1m. francs) for calendar years:

	1972	*1973*	*1974*	*1975*
Total revenue	198,208	225,278	272,898	270,800
Total expenditure[1]	193,073	220,018	254,148	270,800
of which Civil	160,244	183,675	213,114	218,600
Military	33,716	36,273	41,004	43,800

[1] Some expenditure has not been divided between civil and military expenditures.

The accounts of revenue and expenditure (in 1m. francs) are examined by a special administrative tribunal (*Cour des Comptes*), instituted in 1807.

Revenue	*1971*	*1972*	*1973*	*1974*
Taxes and monopolies	173,959	196,004	220,323	267,644
State industries	1,537	1,937	2,335	4,671
State domains	181	267	269	313
Total (including all others)	175,677	198,208	225,278	272,898

Civil expenditure	*1971*	*1972*	*1973*	*1974*
Public debt	13,631	15,427	18,993	23,079
Supply services	60,179	67,148	...	...
President and Parliament	379	447	553	611
Economic state intervention	48,359	53,331	62,859	70,864
Total	122,548	136,353	158,657	185,335
Civil equipment and reconstruction	21,613	23,984	25,018	27,778
Total civil expenditure	144,161	160,337	183,675	213,114

The French public debt was as follows on 31 Dec. (in 1m. francs):

National Debt:	*1971*	*1972*	*1973*	*1974*
A. Funded debt—				
(*a*) *Interior:* Perpetual	554	554	554	554
Long term	12,569	11,926	...	...
Treasury bonds	57,414	52,100	...	...
Liability towards issuing houses	9,835	10,039	...	...
(*a*) Total	80,372	74,616	...	...
(*b*) Foreign debt	2,447	2,100	1,570	1,278
B. Floating debt—				
(*a*) Interior	7,407	3,787	...	...
(*b*) Foreign	6,299	6,231	...	...
Posts and telecommunications	4,890	6,102	6,801	9,270
Total debt	101,415	92,836	93,122	105,022

Bloch-Laine, F., *La Zone Franc.* Paris, 1956
Lattre, A. de, *Les Finances extérieures de la France, 1945–58.* Paris, 1959
Mérigot, J. G., and Coulbois, P., *Le Franc, 1938–50.* Paris, 1950

Currency. A new currency, the 'heavy franc' or '*nouveau franc*' (NF) worth 100 'light francs', was introduced on 1 Jan. 1960.

Franc coins are issued for 1, 5, 10 and 20 centimes, ½, 1, 5 and 10 francs; and bank-notes for 5, 10, 50, 100 and 500 francs.

Banking. The Bank of France, founded in 1800, and placed under state control in 1806, has the monopoly (since 1848) of issuing bank-notes. Note circulation on 31 Dec. 1976 was 16,090m. francs.

On 2 Dec. 1945 a law was passed to nationalize the Banque de France and the 4 principal deposit banks. It also established a new body, the National Credit Council, formed to regulate banking activity and consulted in all political decisions on money. This new body comprises 45 members nominated by the Government; its president is the Minister for the Economy and Finance, its vice-president is the Governor of the Bank of France.

The following are the principal banks: those nationalized in 1945 are Crédit Lyonnais (founded 1863), Banque Nationale de Paris (an amalgamation on 1 July 1966 of the Banque Nationale pour le Commerce et l'Industrie and the Comptoir National d'Escompte de Paris), and the Société Générale (founded 1864); other banks are Crédit Industriel et Commercial, Crédit Commercial de France, the Banque de Paris et des Pays Bas and the Banque de l'Union Parisienne–Crédit du Nord. Total deposits and short- and medium-term bonds held by the banks on 31 Dec. 1975 was 612,000m. francs.

The ordinary savings banks number about 600. In addition, the state savings organization (*Caisse nationale d'épargne*) is administered by the post office on a giro system. On 31 Dec. 1975 ordinary savings banks had 154,000m. francs in deposits; the state savings banks had 85,000m. francs in deposits. Deposited funds are centralized by a non-banking body, the Caisse de Dépôts et Consignations, which finances a large number of local co-operatives and state-aided housing projects, and carries an important portfolio of transferable securities.

Weights and Measures. The metric system is in general use.

ENERGY AND NATURAL RESOURCES

Electricity. Production of electrical (and percentage of hydro-electric) power (in 1m. kwh.): 1967, 111,637 (40%); 1968, 117,925 (43%); 1969, 131,516 (40%); 1970, 140,708 (40%); 1971, 148,998 (33%); 1972, 163,652 (30%); 1973, 174,480 (28%); 1974, 180,022 (30%); 1975, 177,500; 1976, 194,900.

Oil. Output of petroleum in 1969, 2·5m.; 1970, 2·31m.; 1971, 1·86m.; 1972, 1·48m.; 1973, 1·25m.; 1974, 1·1m. tonnes. The greater part came from the Parentis oilfield in the Landes. France has an important oil-refining industry, utilizing imported crude oil. Total yearly capacity at the end of 1975 was about 169·5m. tonnes. The principal plants are situated in Basse Seine (production in tonnes, 1972), 31·2m.; Mediterranean, 24·6m.; Atlantic, 15·4m.; Alsace, 12·6m., and Nord, 9m.

There has been considerable development of the production of natural gas and sulphur in the region of Lacq in the foothills of the Pyrenees. Production of natural gas was 10,284m. cu. metres in 1970; 10,789m. in 1971; 10,925m. in 1972; 10,948m. in 1973.

In 1m. tonnes of oil equivalent, 1975 production of fuels was: Coal and lignite, 17·9; natural gas, 6·7.

Minerals. Principal minerals produced, in 1,000 tonnes:

	1970	*1971*	*1972*	*1973*	*1974*
Coal	37,254	33,014	29,763	26,400	24,000
Lignite	2,785	2,752	2,962	2,764	2,790
Iron ore	56,805	55,852	54,246	54,282	54,260
Bauxite	3,051	3,184	2,358	3,299	2,938
Potash salts	1,904	2,000	1,760	2,263	2,275
Pig-iron	19,221	18,345	19,001	20,304	22,519
Crude steel	23,773	22,859	24,054	25,264	27,023
Aluminium	381	384	392	358	393

Agriculture. Of the total area of France (54·9m. hectares in 1972) 16·7m. are under cultivation, 13·9m. are pasture, 1·3m. are under vines, 13·9m. are forests and 7·7m. are uncultivated land.

The following table shows the area under the leading crops and the production for 5 years:

	Area (1,000 hectares)					*Produce (1,000 quintals)*				
Crop	*1970*	*1971*	*1972*	*1973*	*1974*	*1970*	*1971*	*1972*	*1973*	*1974*
Wheat	3,746	3,978	3,949	3,960	4,143	129,216	154,818	180,461	178,502	191,405
Rye	135	129	126	122	113	2,871	2,937	3,284	3,272	3,106
Barley	2,953	2,671	2,676	2,799	2,659	81,264	89,095	104,664	109,485	98,137
Oats	805	831	761	693	659	21,025	25,405	24,784	22,079	20,466
Potatoes	401	362	301	309	305	86,942	88,292	72,446	72,093	73,560
Industrial beet	403	425	448	512	534	175,215	199,511	192,757	226,884	215,561
Maize	1,483	1,642	1,895	1,942	1,906	75,809	89,535	82,516	106,918	86,915

Other crops in 1974 (figures for 1973 in brackets) include (in 1,000 quintals): Rice, 492 (693); tobacco, 523 (504); hops, 20 (21); flax, 2,744 (2,588).

The annual production of wine and cider (in 1,000 hectolitres) appears as follows:

	Vineyards (1,000 hectares)	*Wine produced*	*Wine import*	*Wine export*	*Cider produced*
1938	1,513	60,332	16,257	1,032	34,601
1948	1,433	47,437	9,894	620	13,092
1958	1,315	47,735	19,862	1,266	27,440
1971	1,293	62,287	4,941	4,483	...
1972	1,295	59,469	8,324	5,425	...
1973	1,303	58,998	9,508	6,691	...

The production of fruits (other than for cider making) and nuts for 1974 (figures for 1973 in brackets) is given in 1,000 quintals, as follows: Apples, 16,103 (20,596); pears, 4,262 (4,905); plums, 1,514 (812); peaches, 4,339 (5,986); apricots, 582 (1,540); cherries, 1,050 (1,128); nuts, 278 (414); grapes, 2,975 (3,122); strawberries, 737 (782).

In 1976 the numbers of farm animals (in 1,000) were (figures for 1975 in brackets): Horses, 402 (413); cattle, 24,247 (24,119); sheep, 10,707 (10,568); goats, 988 (959); pigs, 12,028 (12,031).

Fisheries (1976). There were 30,321 fishermen, and 12,756 sailing-boats, steamers and motor-boats. Catch (in 1,000 tonnes): Fresh fish, 381; frozen fish, 51·5; crustaceans, 31·4; shell fish, 89·4; oysters, 90·6.

INDUSTRY AND TRADE

Industry (1974) (1973 in brackets). *Engineering:* 3,075,109 (3,217,899) vehicles (excluding small vehicles), 1,694,000 (1,695,000) television sets, 3,374,000 (3,017,000) radio sets, 45·4m. (45·7m.) tyres.

Chemicals (in 1,000 tonnes): Sulphuric acid, 4,689 (4,383); caustic soda, 1,427 (1,392); sulphur, 1,852 (1,753); polystyrene, 189 (191); polyvinyl, 622 (656); polyethylene, 900 (785); ammonia, 2,114 (1,923); nitric acid, 834 (758).

Textiles (in 1,000 tonnes): Woollen, 67·5 (71·6); cotton, 208·9 (211·8); linen, 13·3 (13·5); silk, 52 (51); man-made fibres, yarns, 128·5 (138·5); jute, 26 (30).

Food (in 1,000 tonnes): Cheese, 860 (828); chocolate, 101 (104); biscuits, 317 (302); sugar 2,709 (2,916); fish preparations, 101·2 (90·7); jams and jellies, 107 (113).

Construction: Cement, 32·3 (30·6) tonnes.

See map in THE STATESMAN'S YEAR-BOOK, 1968–69, Industrial Redeployment.

Trade Unions. The main unions considered as nationally representative are the CGT (Confédération Générale du Travail), which was founded in 1895 and has about 2·4m. members; the CGT–FO (Confédération Générale du Travail–Force Ouvrière) which broke away from the CGT in 1948 as a protest against Communist influence therein and has about 850,000 members; the CFTC (Confédération Française des Travailleurs Chrétiens), which was founded in 1919 and has about 200,000 members following its break-away in 1964 from the main body of the union which continues under the new name of CFDT (Confédération Française Démocratique du Travail) and has about 770,000 members; the CGC (Confédération Générale des Cadres) formed in 1944 which only represents managerial and supervisory staff and has about 250,000 members.

Membership is estimated because unions are not required to publish figures; some publish none, others define 'membership' in different terms.

Except for the CGC unions operate within the framework of industries and not of trades. Their main fields of influence are: CGT—steel, metallurgy, building, chemicals, mining, printing, ports and dockyards, electricity and gas, railways; CGT–FO—Civil service, Paris transport, agricultural and food trades, banking, insurance, electrical engineering, building and civil engineering, clothing, leather and hides; CFDT—metallurgy, rubber, oil, textiles, electrical engineering, banking, insurance; CFTC—mining, banking, insurance, air traffic control, oil, glass, pottery.

An Outline of French Trade Unionism. French Embassy, London, 1975
Chardonnet, J., *L'Économie Française.* 2 vols. Paris, 1958–59
Ehrmann, H. W., *Organized Business in France.* Princeton Univ. Press, 1957
Jeanneney, J.-M., *Forces et faiblesses de l'économie française, 1945–59.* 2nd ed. Paris, 1959
Lorwin, V. R., *The French Labor Movement.* Harvard Univ. Press, 1955
Pilliet, G., *Inventaire économique de la France.* Annual from 1945. Paris

Commerce. Imports (calculated c.i.f. since 1972) and exports (f.o.b. figures) in 1m. francs for 6 calendar years were (including gold):

	1972	*1973*	*1974*	*1975*	*1976*	*1977*
Imports	135,998	166,298	254,891	231,766	308,000	346,364
Exports	133,387	162,462	222,741	227,198	266,200	312,072

The chief imports for home use and exports of home goods are to and from the following countries, in 1m. francs (including gold):

Countries	*Imports (c.i.f.)*		*Exports (f.o.b.)*	
	1974	*1975*	*1974*	*1975*
Franc area	8,804	7,578	9,749	11,014
UK	11,311	10,986	14,380	14,604
Germany (Fed. Rep.)	48,915	43,571	37,882	36,986
Belgium–Luxembourg	25,746	22,016	24,900	22,770
Switzerland	6,366	6,590	13,062	10,623
Italy	19,009	20,342	25,636	21,594
USA	19,661	17,497	10,770	8,794

Countries	Imports (c.i.f.) 1974	Imports (c.i.f.) 1975	Exports (f.o.b.) 1974	Exports (f.o.b.) 1975
Brazil	1,805	1,419	1,659	1,519
Argentina	686	458	684	606
Australia and New Zealand	2,402	1,784	960	764
Canada	2,493	1,987	1,965	2,002
Sweden	4,570	4,036	2,929	3,127
Netherlands	14,444	14,653	11,823	11,719

Total trade between France and UK (British Department of Trade returns, in £1,000 sterling):

	1973	1974	1975	1976	1977
Imports to UK	979,552	1,349,153	1,627,770	2,091,308	2,660,123
Exports and re-exports from UK	678,336	914,639	1,164,441	1,710,262	2,147,613

I.N.S.E.E., *Statistiques et indices du commerce extérieur*. Paris, 1964

Tourism. In 1971 foreign visitors contributed about 8,060m. francs to the French economy; 9,006m. in 1972; 10,022m. in 1973; 12,018m. in 1974.

COMMUNICATIONS

Roads. At the end of 1974 the French road system consisted of 1,520,805 km, namely 31,199 km of national roads (excluding 2,629 km of motorway), 328,429 km of departmental roads and about 424,953 km of local roads.

Railways. As from 1 Jan. 1938 all the independent railway companies were merged with the existing state railway system in a Société Nationale des Chemins de Fer Français, in which the State holds 51% of the shares.

The length of lines in 1976 (and 1975) was 34,717 km (34,787 km), of which 9,374 km were electrified. The railways, in 1976, carried 675m. passengers and 227m. tonnes of goods. Railway receipts, 1975, 22,959m. francs; 1976, 26,530m.; expenses, 1975, 24,142m.; 1976, 27,646m. In 1977 construction work began on the high-speed (260 km/h) line between Paris and Lyon.

The Paris transport network consisted in 1976 of 258 km of underground railway (métro) and 2,214 km of bus routes. In 1976 it carried 1,181m. passengers on the métro and 686m. by bus. In Dec. 1977 the central section of the RER (*Réseau Express Régional*) was opened to form the first 92 km of an integrated network.

Lartilleux, H., *Géographie des chemins de fer français*. 2 vols. Paris, 1946–48.
Peyret, H., *Histoire des chemins de fer en France*. Paris, 1949

Aviation. Air France, UTA and Air Inter, the national airlines, had (31 Dec. 1973) a fleet of 180 aircraft, servicing Europe, North America, Central and South America, West and East Africa, Madagascar, the Near, Middle and Far East. There are local networks in the West Indies and Central America.

In 1975 Air France, UTA and Air Inter flew 1,014m. tonne-km and 23·7m. passenger-km (13,247,000 passengers).

Shipping. French merchant ships of more than 100 tons, with gross tonnage, on 1 Jan.: 1972, 550 (6·98m.); 1973, 531 (7·44m.); 1974, 498 (8·18m.).

Shipping (excluding fishing vessels) in foreign trade in 1973: Entered, 84,243 vessels and disembarked 239,124,000 tonnes of imports; cleared, 84,196 vessels and loaded 56,126,000 tonnes of exports. Total cargo traffic (1975) 266m. tonnes.

In 1974 there were 8,623 km of navigable rivers, waterways and canals, with a total traffic (1975) of 94,543,000 gross tons.

Post and Broadcasting. In 1970 the receipts on account of posts, telegraphs and telephones amounted to 15,852·3m. francs; 1971, 19,302·9m.; 1973, 25,061·9m.

On 1 Jan. 1977 the telephone system (government-owned) had 15,553,798 subscribers; the Paris region (including the Paris and Seine-et-Marne, Yvelines, Essonne, Hauts-de-Seine, Seine-Saint-Denis, Val-de-Marne and Val-d'Oise departments) accounted for 3,713,830 in 1976.

Radio and television broadcasting was reorganized under the Act of 7 Aug. 1974 which replaced the Office de Radiodiffusion Télévision Française with 4 broadcasting companies, a production company and an audio-visual institute. Organization, development, operation and the maintenance of networks and installations became the responsibility of the Public Broadcasting Establishment. Radio programmes are broadcast from 247 transmitters (including 196 VHF) by 3 stations: *France Inter, France Musique* and *France Culture*. Television programmes are broadcast from 135 transmitters and 3,000 relay stations on 3 channels. There were about 14m. sets in 1975.

Cinemas (1975). There were 4,328 cinemas with a seating capacity (1974) of 1,844,200.

Newspapers (1975). There were 85 daily papers published in the provinces with a circulation of 7·5m. copies, and 9 published in Paris with a national circulation of 3·8m. Among Paris dailies *Le Parisien Libéré* sells 786,000; *France-Soir* 727,000; *Le Monde* 432,000 and *Le Figaro* 402,000. Among provincial dailies *Ouest-France* (Rennes) sells 636,000; *Le Progrès* (Lyon) 436,000; *La Voix du Nord* (Lille) 389,000; *Sud-Ouest* (Bordeaux) 383,000; *La Dauphine Libérée* (Grenoble) 362,000 and *Le Provençal* (Marseilles) 312,000.

There are 33 main weekly periodicals, their circulation varying in 1974 between 419,000 and 4·7m. (excluding television weeklies), and about 24 main monthlies, circulation varying between 695,000 and 7·36m.

JUSTICE, RELIGION, EDUCATION AND WELFARE

Justice. The French judicial system has been reorganized by a number of ordinances and decrees dated 22 Dec. 1958.

Before this reform, the lowest courts were those of the Justices of Peace (*juges de paix*), 1 in each *canton*, who tried less important civil cases. The Tribunals of First Instance (*Tribunaux de Première Instance* or *Tribunaux Civils*), 1 in each *arrondissement*, dealt with more important civil cases and served as Tribunals of Appeal for the Justices of Peace, when their decisions were susceptible of appeal.

Since 1976, 468 *tribunaux d'instance* (10 in overseas departments), under a single judge each and with increased material and territorial jurisdiction, have replaced the cantonal justices of the peace; and 181 *tribunaux de grande instance* (6 in overseas departments) have taken the place of the 357 *tribunaux de première instance*.

The *tribunaux de grande instance* usually have a collegiate composition, however a law dated 10 July 1970 has allowed them to administer justice under a single judge in some civil cases.

All petty offences (*contraventions*) are disposed of in the Police Courts (*Tribunaux de Police*) presided over by a Judge on duty in the *tribunal d'instance*. The Correctional Courts pronounce upon all graver offences (*délits*), including cases involving imprisonment up to 5 years. They have no jury, and consist of 3 judges who administer both criminal and civil justice. An Act of 29 Dec. 1972 established that there is only 1 judge; in some cases, the correctional courts may consist of a single judge each. In all cases of a *délit* or a *crime* the preliminary inquiry is made in secrecy by an examining magistrate (*juge d'instruction*), who either dismisses the case or sends it for trial before a court where a public prosecutor (*Procureur*) endeavours to prove the charge.

The Conciliation Boards (*Conseils des Prud'hommes*) composed of an equal number of employers and employees deal with small trade and industrial disputes. Commercial litigation goes to the Commercial Courts (*Tribunaux de Commerce*) composed of tradesmen and manufacturers elected for 2 years. The judges hold office for 2 years and they can be re-elected; 3 years for the President.

When the decisions of any of these Tribunals are susceptible of appeal, the cases go to the Courts of Appeal (*Cours d'Appel*). There are 34 Courts of Appeal (3 in overseas departments and 1 in an overseas territory), composed each of a president and a variable number of members.

The Courts of Assizes (*Cours d'Assises*), composed each of a president, assisted by 2 other magistrates who are members of the Courts of Appeal, and by a jury of 9 people, sit in every *département*, when called upon to try very important criminal cases. The decisions of the Courts of Appeal and the Courts of Assizes are final; however, the Court of Cassation (*Cour de Cassation*) has discretion to verify if the law has been correctly interpreted and if the rules of procedure have been followed exactly. The Court of Cassation may annul any judgment, and the cases have to be tried again by a Court of Appeal or a Court of Assizes.

A State Security Court has been established by 2 laws dated 15 Jan. 1963. It is usually composed of 3 civilian judges, including the president, and 2 judges of general or field officer rank, and has jurisdiction to deal with subversion in peace-time.

The French penal institutions have been reorganized by the procedural code which came into force on 2 March 1959 and was modified by a law dated 17 July 1970 and by a *décret* of 25 May 1975. They consist of: (1) *maisons d'arrêt* and *de correction*, where persons awaiting trial as well as those condemned to short periods of imprisonment are kept; (2) central prisons (*maisons centrales*) for those sentenced to long imprisonment; (3) special establishments, namely (*a*) schools for young adults, (*b*) hostels for old and disabled offenders, (*c*) hospitals for the sick and psychopaths, (*d*) institutions for recidivists. Special attention is being paid to classified treatment and the rehabilitation and vocational re-education of prisoners including work in open-air and semi-free establishments.

Juvenile delinquents go before special judges and courts; they are sent to public or private institutions of supervision and re-education.

On 24 Jan. 1973 the first Ombudsman (*médiateur*) was appointed for a 6-year period.

The population at 1 Jan. 1977 of all penal establishments was 31,442 men and 945 women.

Religion. No religion is officially recognized by the State. Under the law promulgated on 9 Dec. 1905, which separated Church and State, the adherents of all creeds are authorized to form associations for public worship (*associations culturelles*). The law of 2 Jan. 1907 provided that, failing *associations culturelles*, the buildings for public worship, together with their furniture, would continue at the disposition of the ministers of religion and the worshippers for the exercise of their religion; but in each case there was required an administrative act drawn up by the *préfet* as regards buildings belonging to the State or the departments, and by the *maire* as regards buildings belonging to the communes.

There are 18 archbishops and 92 bishops of the Roman Catholic Church, with (1974) 43,557 clergy of various grades and 45·3m. church members. The Protestants of the Augsburg confession are, in their religious affairs, governed by a General Consistory, while the Reformed Church is under a Council of Administration, the seat of which is in Paris. In 1975 communicant Protestants numbered 750,000. There were (1978) about 2m. Moslems.

Education. The primary, secondary and higher state schools constitute the 'Université de France'. The Supreme Council of 84 members has deliberative, administrative and judiciary functions, and a Consultative Committee advise respecting the working of the school system, but the inspectors-general are in direct communication with the Minister. For local education administration France is divided into 25 academic areas, each of which has an Academic Council whose members include a certain number elected by the professors or teachers. The Academic Council deals with all grades of education. Each is under a Rector, and each is provided with academy inspectors, 1 for each department.

By decree of 6 Jan. 1959 the whole system of public instruction was reorganized and the structure of the Ministry of National Education has consequently been modified. A further Education Act was passed on 11 July 1975. Compulsory education is now provided for children of 6–16. The educational stages are as follows:

1. Non-compulsory pre-school instruction for children aged 2–5, to be given in infant schools or infant classes attached to primary schools.

2. Compulsory elementary instruction for children aged 6–11, to be given in primary schools and certain classes of the *lycées*. It consists of 3 courses: preparatory (1 year), elementary (2 years), intermediary (2 years). Physically or mentally handicapped children are cared for in special institutions or special classes of primary schools.

3. *Enseignement du Second Degré*, for pupils aged 11–18:

(*a*) *Enseignement du 1er cycle du Second Degré;* 4 years of study in the *Lycées, Collèges d'Enseignement Secondaire* or *Collèges d'Enseignement Général.*

(*b*) *Enseignement du Second Cycle:*

Long, général or *professionel* provided by the *lycées* and leading to the *baccalauréat* or to the *baccalauréat de technicien* after 3 years.

Court, professional courses of 3, 2 and 1 year are taught in the *Collèges d'enseignement technique*, or the specialized sections of the *lycées*, CES or CEG.

In addition students are also prepared for the *Sections de Techniciens Supérieurs* and the preparatory classes of the *Grandes Écoles.*

The following table shows the various types of schools in 1974–75 and the numbers of enrolled pupils:

Description	*Pupils* *State*	*Private*	*Total*	*Schools*
Pre-primary	2,194,347	346,122	2,540,469	59,838
Primary	4,005,651	656,267	4,661,918	200,281
Secondary:				
First cycle	2,561,291	564,447	3,125,738	27,975
Second cycle				
'short'	546,184	167,018	713,202 }	69,170
'long'	724,888	221,419	946,307 }	
Total	3,832,363	952,884	4,785,247	357,264
Preparation for *Grandes Écoles* and the *Brevets de technicien supérieur*	56,927	15,308	72,235	

The state schools in 1974 had 50,986 nursery, 182,657 primary, 16,064 special school, 24,133 'first cycle' secondary and 89,631 'second cycle' secondary school teachers.

Higher Instruction is supplied by the State in the universities and in special schools, and by private individuals in the free faculties and schools. The law of 12 July 1875 provided for higher education free of charge. This law was modified by that of 18 March 1880, which granted the state faculties the exclusive right to confer degrees. A decree of 28 Dec. 1885 created a general council of the faculties, and the creation of universities, each consisting of several faculties, was accomplished in 1897, in virtue of the law of 10 July 1896.

The law of 12 Nov. 1968 laying down future guidelines for higher education redefined the activities and working of universities. Bringing several disciplines together, 780 units for teaching and research (U.E.R.—Unités d'Enseignement et de Récherche) were formed which decided their own teaching activities, research programmes and procedures for checking the level of knowledge gained. They and the other parts of each university must respect the rules designed to maintain the national standard of qualifications.

The following table shows the year of foundation and the total number of students of the universities in 1973–74 (1972–73 in brackets):

Universities	*Students*		*Universities*	*Students*	
Aix-Marseille (1409)	41,966	(42,816)	Nancy (1572)	27,538	(26,781)
Amiens (1964)	8,931	(8,824)	Nantes (1961)	22,348	(21,940)
Besançon (1485)	10,478	(11,010)	Nice (1965)	16,722	(17,601)
Bordeaux (1441)	39,858	(40,134)	Orleans (1961)	16,979	(17,004)
Caen (1432)	11,830	(11,234)	Paris (1150)	248,297	(236,894)
Clermont-Ferrand (1808)	13,809	(14,690)	Poitiers (1431)	12,546	(12,813)
Dijon (1722)	12,460	(12,599)	Reims (1961)	10,305	(10,315)
Grenoble (1339)	27,622	(27,399)	Rennes (1735)	28,112	(28,102)
Lille (1530)	34,680	(36,341)	Rouen (1964)	11,158	(11,873)
Limoges	6,852	(7,076)	Strasbourg (1567)	24,325	(23,491)
Lyon (1808)	39,775	(41,647)	Toulouse (1230)	41,649	(41,071)
Montpellier (1289)	33,834	(33,580)			

The following table shows the number of students in state institutions, by faculties or schools, for 5 years:

Students of	*1970–71*[1]	*1971–72*	*1972–73*	*1973–74*	*1974–75*
Law and economics	147,700	153,681	160,041	169,170	178,215
Medicine	113,900	119,201	133,011	130,012	146,912
Science	117,400	120,808	117,324	118,153	117,389
Letters	225,700	246,885	253,975	236,703	233,954
Pharmacy	22,200	23,519	25,462	28,032	31,599
Technology	24,400	33,697	35,422	38,943	41,949
Multi-discipline courses	—	—	—	—	4,843
Total	651,400	697,791	735,235	742,074	754,861

[1] Provisional.

The other higher institutions under the Ministry of Public Instruction are the Collège de France (founded by Francis I in 1530), which has courses of study bearing on various subjects (literature and language, archaeology, mathematical, natural science, psychology and social science, political economy, etc.); the Museum of Natural History, giving instruction in science and natural history; the École Pratique des Hautes Études (history and philology, mathematical and physico-chemical sciences, natural science, theology, economics and social science), having its seat at the Sorbonne; the École Normale Supérieure, which prepares teachers for secondary education and, since 1904, follows the curricula of the Sorbonne without special teachers of its own; the École des Chartes, which train archivists and palaeographers; the École des Langues Orientales vivantes; the École du Louvre, devoted to art and archaeology; the Bureau des Longitudes, the central meteorological bureau; the Observatoire de Paris; and the French Schools at Athens, Rome, Cairo and South-East Asia.

Outside Paris there are 12 observatories (Meudon, Besançon, Bordeaux, etc.). The observatory at Nice belongs to the University of Paris.

There are free faculties in Paris (the Catholic Institute of Paris comprising theology and literary studies) and in some other major towns.

Professional and Technical Instruction. The principal institutions of higher or technical instruction are: The *Grandes Écoles* with 98,443 students in 1974–75, the Conservatoire des Arts et Métiers at Paris (with 20 evening courses on the applied sciences and social economy), the École Central des Arts et Manufactures (953 students in 1971–72), the École des Hautes Études Commerciales (803 students in 1972–73), 17 higher schools of commerce (4,461 pupils in 1969–70), under the Ministry of Public Instruction; the National Agronomic Institute at Paris, the veterinary school at Maisons-Alfort, Lyon and Toulouse, a school of forestry at Nancy, Écoles Nationales Supérieures Agronomiques at Grignon, Rennes, Montpellier, Nancy and Toulouse, 98 schools of agriculture, etc., under the Ministry of Agriculture; the École Supérieure de Guerre, the École Polytechnique, the military school at Coëtquidan (formerly St Cyr), the École d'Artillerie at Fontainebleau, the École de Cavalerie at Saumur and other schools under the Ministry of War; the Naval School at Brest under the Ministry of Marine; the School of Mines at Paris, the School of Civil Engineering at Paris, the School of Mines at St Etienne and the Schools of Miners at Alès and Douai with other schools under the Ministry of Public Works; the École Nationale Supérieure des Beaux Arts, the École Nationale Supérieure des Arts Décoratifs and the Conservatoire de Musique et de Déclamation under the Department of Fine Arts, which is attached to the Ministry of Cultural Affairs. In the provinces there are national schools of fine arts, and schools of music, and several municipal schools, as well as free subventional schools, etc.

Health. At the end of 1973 there were 69,810 physicians, 27,835 pharmacists and 24,379 dentists practising. There were 1,870 public hospitals (492,041 beds), 135 public mental hospitals (120,000 beds), 1,935 private hospitals (100,232 beds) and 158 private mental homes (10,236 beds) at the end of 1971.

Social Welfare. An order of 4 Oct. 1945 laid down the framework of a comprehensive plan of Social Security and created a single organization which superseded the various laws relating to social insurance, workmen's compensation, health insurance, family allowances, etc. All previous matters relating to Social Security are dealt with in the Social Security Code, 1956; this has been revised several times, and finally by orders laid down on 21 Aug. 1967, which were ratified on 31 July 1968. The Social Security general scheme covers all wage-earning workers in industry and commerce that are not covered by a special scheme of their own.

Contributions. All wage-earning workers or those of equivalent status are insured regardless of the amount or the nature of the salary or earnings. The funds for the general scheme are raised mainly from professional contributions, these being fixed within the limits of a ceiling (assessed at 37,920 francs per annum on 1 Jan. 1976) and calculated as a percentage of the salaries. The calculation of the contributions payable for family allowances, old age and industrial injuries relates only to this amount; on the other hand, the amount payable for sickness, maternity expenses, disability and death is calculated partly within the limit of the 'ceiling' and partly on the whole salary. These contributions are the responsibility of both employer and employee, except in the case of family allowances or industrial injuries, where they are the sole responsibility of the employer.

Self-employed Workers. From 17 Jan. 1948 allowances and old-age pensions were paid to self-employed workers by independent insurance funds set up within their own profession, trade or business. Schemes of compulsory insurance for sickness were instituted in 1961 for farmers and in 1966, with modifications in 1970, for other non-wage-earning workers.

Social Insurance. The orders laid down in Aug. 1967 ensure that the whole population can benefit from the Social Security Scheme; at present all elderly persons who have been engaged in the professions, as well as the surviving spouse, are entitled to claim an old-age benefit; 98% of the population, both working and retired, are covered by a compulsory scheme of insurance for sickness, the remaining 2% who are not covered by a compulsory insurance scheme have been able to participate in a voluntary scheme since 1967; the whole population benefit from the legislation regarding family allowances.

Sickness Insurance refunds the costs of treatment required by the insured, of the needs of his wife, of children under 16 and a half who are in his care and not earning, under 18 who are apprenticed, under 20 who are still studying or who cannot work on account of some chronic illness or infirmity, as well as relations, older or younger or of similar age living under the same roof who are engaged exclusively in domestic duties and in the education of at least 2 children under 14. A decree of 12 Oct. 1976 laid down conditions on which students of 20 or over at public or private educational institutions, who do not benefit from a social security scheme in their own right, are guaranteed insurance benefits for sickness or maternity, holding their parents entitlement until the end of the academic year in which they attain their 21st birthday, provided they have proof that their studies have been interrupted by illness. The general principles relating to medical care consist of: a free choice by the patient of his doctor, his pharmaceutical chemist, his place of treatment, etc.; the medical practitioner is granted freedom of prescription. Reimbursement is not as a rule made in full; the insured person usually pays between 10% and 30% of the legal rate except in cases of exemption. The insured who is recognized as medically unfit for work receives daily allowances equal to half of the wage which has been used to calculate the contributions, or to two-thirds of this if the person has 3 or more children. These allowances may be paid for 3 years, plus one additional year if the insured undergoes re-adaptation treatment or takes up fresh vocational training.

Maternity Insurance covers the costs of medical treatment relating to the pregnancy, confinement and lying-in period; the beneficiaries being the insured person or the spouse. The daily allowances are equal to 90% of the salary on which contributions were calculated.

Insurance for Invalids is divided into 3 categories: (1) those who are capable of working; (2) those who cannot work; (3) those who, in addition, are in need of the help of another person. According to the category, the pension rate varies from 30 to 50% of the average salary for the last 10 years, with a minimum additional allowance for home help of 20,078·32 francs per year for the third category.

Old-age Pensions for workers were introduced in 1910 and revised in 1930, 1935, 1941 and 1945 and are now fixed by the Social Security Code of 28 Jan. 1972. After 1975 people who have paid insurance for at least 37½ years (150 quarters) will receive at 60 a pension equal to 25% of basic annual salary, to be increased by 1·25% of the basic salary for every quarter that realization is deferred; thus at 65 the pension will be equal to 50% of basic salary. People who have paid insurance for less than 37½ years but not less than 15 years can expect a pension equal to as many 1/150ths of the full pension as their quarterly payments justify. In 1976 the maximum retainable number of years insurance was 37½, and a pension at 65, after a maximum period of insurance, would be equal to 50% of basic annual salary. In the event of death of the insured person, the husband or wife of the deceased person receives half the pension received by the latter. Compulsory supplementary schemes ensure for those to whom they apply benefits additional to the old-age pensions.

Family Allowances. The system comprises: (*a*) Family allowances proper, equivalent to 22% of the basic monthly salary (694·50 francs) for 2 dependent children, 37% for the third and fourth child, and 33% for the fifth and each subsequent child; a supplement equivalent to 9% of the basic monthly salary for the second and each subsequent dependent child more than 10 years old and 16% for each dependent child over 15 years. (*b*) Single wage-earner allowance (when the wife does not work), according to the number of dependent children. (*c*) Housewife allowance (when an employer's or self-employed person's wife does not work), according to the number of dependent children and the amount of net annual taxable income. (*d*) Maintenance grant for children under 3 years for families who do not receive either of the above grants, and to individual recipients whose resources are less than a maximum which varies according to the number of dependent children. (*e*) Antenatal grants. (*f*) Maternity grant equal to 260% of basic salary. (*g*) Allowance for supervision. (*h*) Allowance for specialized education of crippled minors. (*i*) Allowance for orphans. (*j*) Allowance for handicapped minors. (*k*) Allowance for opening of school term. (*l*) Allowance for accommodation, under certain circumstances (since July 1972 older persons and young workers enjoy equal benefit from the accommodation allowance). The allowance for single wage (*b*) allowance for the mother in the home (*c*) and the allowance for expenses respecting supervision have been subjected to an annual ceiling of resources. The regional abatements have been abolished since 1 Jan. 1973 and the amount is from now on identical over the whole territory.

Workmen's Compensation. The law passed by the National Assembly on 30 Oct. 1946 supersedes the Act of 9 April 1898 and forms part of the Social Security Code. It is administered by the Social Security Organization. Employers are invited to take preventive measures. The application of these measures is supervised by consulting engineers (assessors) of the local funds dealing with sickness insurance, who may compel employers who do not respect these measures to make additional contributions; they may, in like manner, grant rebates to employers who have in operation suitable preventive measures. The injured person receives free treatment, the insurance fund reimburses the practitioners, hospitals and suppliers chosen freely by the injured. In cases of temporary disablement the daily payments are equal to half the total daily wage received by the injured. In case of permanent disablement the injured person receives a pension, the amount of which varies according to the degree of disablement and the salary received during the past 12 months.

A law promulgated on 11 Oct. 1946 has created a medical labour service of doctors who hold a diploma of 'industrial health specialists'. These doctors are entrusted with the control of hygiene and health matters in all industrial undertakings or groups of undertakings. In addition, it is the duty of this medical service to examine wage-earners when they are engaged, to carry out periodical medical examinations and to ensure the application of the existing rules relating to safety in work.

Unemployment Benefits vary according to circumstances (full or partial unemployment) and means test. Since 1926 unemployment benefits have been paid from public funds. Full unemployment benefit amounts to 13·50 francs per day for the head of the family and 5·40 francs for the spouse or a dependent person. After 3 months the payment is reduced to 12·40 francs.

A collective agreement signed on 31 Dec. 1958 between the national council of employers and certain trade unions has established a system of special allowances for unemployed workers in industry and trade. The costs are shared by employers (1·92%) and employees (0·48%) and the benefits amount to 35% of the wages for 12 months, to be extended for workers of old age and long employment. The system is administered by commissions composed of representatives of employers and employees in equal proportion. A similar agreement of 22 Feb. 1968 extends the system to partial unemployment.

Social Security in France. I.N.S.E.E., 1970
Questions de Sécurité Sociale. Paris, 1970

DIPLOMATIC REPRESENTATIVES

OF FRANCE IN GREAT BRITAIN (58 Knightsbridge, London, SW1X 7JT)

Ambassador: Jean Sauvagnargues. (accredited 10 Nov. 1977)

OF GREAT BRITAIN IN FRANCE (35 rue du Faubourg St. Honoré, Paris)

Ambassador: Sir Nicholas Henderson, GCMG.

OF FRANCE IN THE USA (2535 Belmont Rd., NW, Washington, D.C., 20008)

Ambassador: François de Laboulaye.

OF THE USA IN FRANCE (2 Ave. Gabriel, Paris)

Ambassador: Arthur A. Hartman.

OF FRANCE TO THE UNITED NATIONS

Ambassador: Jacques Leprette.

Books of Reference

Statistical Information: The Institut national de la Statistique et des Études économiques (29, Quai Branly, Paris 7e) is the central office of statistics. It was established by a law of 27 April 1946, which amalgamated the Service National des Statistiques (created in 1941 by merging the Direction de la Statistique générale de la France and the Service de la Démographie) with the Institut de Conjoncture (set up in 1938) and some statistical services of the Ministry of National Economy. The Institut comprises the following departments: Metropolitan statistics, Overseas statistics, Market research and economic studies, Documentation, Research statistics and economics, Informatics, Foreign Economic Studies.

The main publications of the Institute include:

Annuaire statistique de la France (from 1878)
Annuaire statistique des Territoires d'Outre-Mer (from 1959)
Bulletin mensuel de statistique (monthly)
Documentation économique (bi-monthly)
Données statistiques africaines et Malgaches (quarterly)
Economie et Statistique (monthly)
Tableaux de l'Economie Française (biennially, from 1956)
Tendances de la Conjoncture (monthly)

Bonnefous, E., Duroselle, J. B., and Gerbet, P., *L'année politique, économique, sociale et diplomatique en France*. Paris, 1970
Coffey, P., *The Social Economy of France*. London, 1973
Hoffman, S., *Decline or Renewal? France Since the 1930's*. New York, 1973
Ouston, P. A., *France in the Twentieth Century*. London, 1972
Pinchemel, P., *La France*. 2 vols. Paris, 1969
Tint, H., *French Foreign Policy Since the Second World War*. New York, 1972

OVERSEAS DEPARTMENTS

GUADELOUPE AND DEPENDENCIES

HISTORY. Guadeloupe has been a French possession since 1635; it was occupied by the British in 1759–63, 1794, 1810–16.

AREA AND POPULATION. Guadeloupe, situated in the Lesser Antilles, consists of 2 islands separated by a narrow channel, called Rivière Salée. That on the west is called Guadeloupe proper, the principal town of which is Basse-Terre, and that to the east Grande Terre; the chief town of Grande Terre is Pointe-à-Pitre. The 2 islands have a combined area of 1,434 sq. km (583 sq. miles). There are 5 dependencies, consisting of the smaller islands, Marie Galante (population, 15,867), Les Saintes (population, 3,269), Désirade (population, 1,559), St Barthélemy, a Swedish possession from 1784 to 1877 (population, 2,351) and St Martin (population, 5,061); the total area with these is 1,702 sq. km (657 sq. miles), and the total population in 1974 was 334,900. Les Saintes and St Barthélemy are still inhabited by the white descendants of the Normans and Bretons who came there 300 years ago. St Martin was occupied simultaneously by the French and the Dutch in 1648; by virtue of an agreement dated 23 March 1648, the island was divided, France receiving about two-thirds of the island, the capital of which is Marigot, a free port.

The seat of government is Basse-Terre (15,690 inhabitants). Pointe-à-Pitre (29,538 inhabitants) has a fine harbour.

GOVERNMENT. On 19 March 1946 the status of Guadeloupe was changed to that of an overseas department. The department is under a prefect and an elected general council of 36 members; it is represented in the National Assembly by 3 deputies, in the Senate by 2 senators and on the Economic and Social Council by 1 councillor.

Prefect: M. Aurousseau.

ECONOMY

Budget. The budget for 1969 balanced at 362,849,695 francs.

Banking. The Bank of Guadeloupe (founded 1851), with a capital of 2·4m. francs and reserve funds amounting to 1·44m. francs, advances loans chiefly for agricultural purposes. The Crédit Guadeloupéen has a capital of 5m. francs. The Banque Nationale de Paris has 3 and the Banque Antillaise has 2 branches in the department. The Royal Bank of Canada has a branch at Pointe-à-Pitre. The Caisse Centrale de Coopération économique is the official banking institution of the department, enjoying the privilege of issuing bank-notes. Silver coin has disappeared from circulation.

AGRICULTURE. Chief products (1974) are bananas (162,000 tonnes), sugar (97,000 tonnes), rum (114,871 hectolitres in 1971), coffee (230 tonnes), cocoa (80 tonnes) and pineapples (2,000 tonnes).

Livestock (1976): Cattle, 86,000; goats, 17,000; pigs, 26,000; poultry, 103,000.

COMMERCE. Trade for 1974 (in 1m. francs) was imports 1,104 and exports 278. The majority of the trade was with France and the balance with USA.

There are Chambers of Commerce and Industry at Basse-Terre and Pointe-à-Pitre. There is a British consular agent at Pointe-à-Pitre.

COMMUNICATIONS

Roads. In 1970 there were 323 km of national roads, 507 km of departmental roads and 866 km of local roads.

Aviation. Air France, British West Indian Airways, PANAM, Caribair and Air Antilles call at Guadeloupe.

Shipping. Guadeloupe is in direct communication with France by means of 4 steam navigation companies. In 1967, 1,157 vessels of 2·41m. tons entered the department.

Post and Broadcasting. In 1966 there were 42 post offices, 2,300 km of telephone circuits and (1977) 26,798 telephones. ORTF broadcasts for 16 hours a day in French and television broadcasts for 25 hours a week on 3 transmitters. Wireless licences total 25,000 and TV 10,000.

EDUCATION. In 1974 there were 2 *lycées* with 3,128 pupils, 4 *Collèges d'Enseignement Secondaire* (CES) with 4,343 pupils and 36 *Collèges d'Enseignement Général* (CEG) and 5 *Collèges d'Enseignement Technique* (CET) with 3,206 pupils. Primary education was given in 312 public schools (68,964 pupils) and 25 private schools (5,152 pupils).

HEALTH. The medical services in 1971 included 11 public hospitals (2,860 beds), 17 private clinics (1,285 beds) and 39 dispensaries. There were 174 doctors and 45 dentists.

Books of Reference

Information: Office du Tourisme du département, Pointe-à-Pitre. *Director:* R. Fortuné.
Lasserre, G., *La Guadeloupe, étude géographique.* 2 vols. Bordeaux, 1961

GUIANA

Guyane Française

HISTORY. From 1854 to 1938. Cayenne had a penal settlement for habitual criminals. The last convicts were, after 1945, sent back to France.

AREA AND POPULATION. Area about 91,000 sq. km (34,740 sq. miles), is situated on the north-east coast of South America, and population 49,200 (estimate 31 Dec. 1971), of whom 3,000 are tribal Indians. Cayenne, the chief town, has a population of 24,581. These figures are exclusive of the floating population of miners, officials and troops.

GOVERNMENT. On 19 March 1946 the status of Guiana was changed to that of an overseas department. It is administered by a prefect, has an elected council-general of 16 members and is represented in the National Assembly and the Senate by 1 deputy each. On 17 March 1969 the administration of Guiana was modified by dividing the territory into 2 *arrondissements* (Cayenne and Saint-Laurent-du-Maroni) sub-divided into 19 communes.

Prefect: Hervé Bourseiller.

ECONOMY

Budget. The budget for 1976 balanced at 190,577,559 francs.

Banking. The Bank of Guiana had a capital of 5m. francs and reserve fund of 1·3m. francs in 1972. Loans totalled 52·4m. francs in Dec. 1976.

AGRICULTURE. The country has immense forests (about 80,000 sq. km) rich in many kinds of timber. Only about 3,000 hectares are under cultivation. The crops consist of rice (100 tons in 1973), maize (500 tons), manioc (15,000 tons), bananas

(2,000 tons) and sugar-cane (5,000 tons). The fishing of shrimps has been taken up by American companies.

Livestock, 1973: 1,430 cattle, 3,200 swine, 400 sheep and 60,000 poultry.

COMMERCE. Trade in 1,000 tonnes and 1m. francs:

	1973		*1974*		*1975*	
	Quantity	*Value*	*Quantity*	*Value*	*Quantity*	*Value*
Imports	116·57	250·71	101·45	271·11	103·94	307·16
Exports	11·83	23·15	9·56	20·22	5·31	10·63

In 1975 imports (in 1m. francs) came from: France, 217; USA, 13; Surinam, 5; Brazil, 4; and exports went to Surinam, 39,000; USA, 5; France, 2·64.

Total trade between Guiana and UK (British Department of Trade returns, in £1,000 sterling):

	1973	*1974*	*1975*	*1976*	*1977*
Imports to UK	48	42	63	187	10
Exports and re-exports from UK	3,011	497	422	405	849

COMMUNICATIONS

Roads. Three chief and some secondary roads connect the capital with most of the coastal area by motor-car services. There are 259 km of national and 244 km of departmental roads. Connexions with the interior are made by waterways which, despite rapids, are navigable by local craft.

Aviation. Air France calls at Cayenne 4 times a week, and Cruseiro do Sul twice a week; GAT airline services interior connexions. The airport at Cayenne-Rochambeau registered 4,050 arrivals and departures of aircraft in 1975, transporting 70,627 passengers and 1,865 tonnes of freight. In 1977 a new route, Paris–Cayenne–Linta opened.

Shipping. There are 5 ports: Cayenne, Larivot, St-Laurent-du-Maroni, Dégrad des Cannes and Kourou. Cayenne is visited regularly by ships of the Compagnie Générale Transatlantique and the Société Générale de Transports Maritimes. There is also steamboat communication between the capital and the other towns of the department. In 1975, 134 arrivals and departures of vessels were registered (4 passengers and 117,780 tonnes of freight arrived and 4 passengers and 3,318 tonnes of freight departed).

Post and Broadcasting. A telegraph system connects Cayenne with Macouria, Kourou, Sinnamary, Iracoubo and St-Laurent-du-Maroni. Number of telephones (1977), 8,885. There are wireless stations at Cayenne, Oyapoc, Régina, St-Laurent, Maripassoula, Saül, Camopi.

Office de Radiodiffusion-Télévision Française broadcasts on medium- and short-waves and FM in French and television is broadcast for 116 hours each week. Wireless licences (1973), 2,558; TV, 3,017.

JUSTICE. At Cayenne there are a court of first instance, and a superior court of appeal, with jurisdiction in other localities.

EDUCATION. Primary education has been free since 1889 in lay schools for the two sexes in the communes and many villages. In 1976 public primary schools had 480 teachers and 10,472 pupils, the *lycées* and *collèges d'enseignement supérieur*, 315 teachers and 1,356 pupils.

Private schools had 95 teachers and 2,144 pupils.

Books of Reference

Abonnec, A., Hurrault, J., Saban, R., *Bibliographie de la Guyane Française*. 2 vols. Paris, 1957

Henry, *Guyane Française, son histoire 1604–1946*. Cayenne

Hurault, J., *Guide du voyageur en Guyane*. Paris, 1949

MARTINIQUE

HISTORY. Martinique has been in French possession since 1635, except during the Seven Years' War (1762–63) and the French Revolution and Empire (1794–1802, 1809–15) when it was under British occupation.

AREA AND POPULATION. Area, 1,100 sq. km (420 sq. miles), divided into 34 communes; population (census, 1974), 324,832.

Vital statistics (1971): Births, 9,214; deaths, 2,230.

The capital and chief commercial town is Fort-de-France (census, 1974, 98,807), with a landlocked harbour nearly 40 sq. km in extent.

GOVERNMENT. On 19 March 1946 the status of Martinique was changed to that of an overseas department. The department is under a prefect. An elected general council of 36 members votes the budget, and elective municipal councils administer the 34 communes. Martinique is represented in the National Assembly by 3 deputies, in the Senate by 2 senators and in the Economic and Social Countil by 1 councillor.

Prefect: Paul Noirot-Cosson.

ECONOMY

Budget. The budget, 1977, balanced at 891·69m. francs.

Banking. The Institut d'Émission des Départements d'Outre-mer is the official bank of the department. The Caisse Centrale de Coopération économique is used by the Government in assisting the economic development of the department.

La Banque des Antilles françaises with a capital of 5m. francs and a reserve fund of 2m. francs, the Crédit Martiniquais and a capital of 2·1m. francs, branches of the Banque Nationale de Paris, The Chase Manhattan Bank and the Royal Bank of Canada are operating at Fort-de-France. There is also a post office savings bank.

AGRICULTURE. Bananas, sugar and rum are the chief productions, followed by pineapples, food and vegetables. In 1970 there were 7,992 hectares under sugar-cane, 9,409 hectares under bananas, 1,050 hectares under pineapples and 1,100 hectares food-producing crops. In 1976 livestock numbered 47,000 cattle, 35,000 sheep, 40,000 pigs, 13,000 goats and 4,000 horses. There are 3 sugar works with distilleries attached, 20 agricultural distilleries producing rum and 3 factories for canning pineapples. In 1972–73 production of sugar was 25,311 tonnes; rum, 117,700 hectolitres.

COMMERCE. Trade in 1,000 tonnes and 1m. francs:

	1974		*1975*		*1976*	
	Quantity	*Value*	*Quantity*	*Value*	*Quantity*	*Value*
Imports	898·53	1,405·11	859·74	1,453·19	897·57	1,965·14
Exports	474·01	380·62	411·68	419·16	498·77	594·04

In 1969 the main items of import were foodstuffs; main items of export were sugar (20·76m. francs), bananas (98·6m. francs) and rum (24·8m. francs).

Total trade of the French West Indian Islands with UK (British Department of Trade returns, in £1,000 sterling):

	1973	*1974*	*1975*	*1976*	*1977*
Imports to UK	72	...	257	1,421	1,031
Exports and re-exports from UK	1,872	602	1,102	1,664	1,717

The Chamber of Commerce and Industry administers the port, airport and industrial zones.

COMMUNICATIONS

Roads. There are 238 km of national roads, 560 km of district roads and 713 km of local roads.

Aviation. In 1972, 323,672 passengers arrived and departed by air.

Shipping. The island is visited regularly by French and American steamers. In 1972, 1,011 vessels called at Martinique.

Post and Broadcasting. There were, in 1972, 43 post offices and, 1977, 34,714 telephones. Radio-telephone service to Europe is available. Wireless licences in 1974 totalled 33,000 and TV 13,000.

JUSTICE. Justice is administered by 5 tribunals of the first instance, a superior court, a regional court of appeal, a commercial court, a court of assizes and an administrative court.

EDUCATION. Education is compulsory between the ages of 6 and 16 years. In 1974, 110,560 children received primary and secondary education. The *Institut Henri Vizioz* had (1975) 1,200 students of law, politics and economics.

Books of Reference

Annuaire statistique de la Martinique. Paris. (Latest issue, 1959–60)
Monographie de la Martinique. Préfecture, Martinique, 1964
Hannau, H. W., *Martinique*. Munich, 1966
Nicolas, M., *Guide Touristique de la Martinique*. 2nd ed. Martinique, 1969

MAYOTTE

HISTORY. Mayotte was a French colony from 1843 until 1914, when it was attached to Madagascar. For subsequent history prior to 1976 see under 'Comores'. Following the accession to independence of the other 3 islands of the Comores group, a referendum was held on 8 Feb 1976, resulting in a 99·4% vote for retaining the island's links with France. In another referendum on 11 April, Mayotte voted against remaining an Overseas Territory of France and became an Overseas Department in 1977.

AREA AND POPULATION. Mayotte, east of the Comoro Islands, has an area of 374 sq. km (144 sq. miles) and a 1966 Census population of 31,930; estimate (1972) 38,000. The chief town is Dzaoudzi. The main languages are Swahili and French, and a majority of the population are Christian, with a substantial Moslem minority.

GOVERNMENT. The department is under a Prefect and an elected general council of 17 members. Mayotte is represented by 1 deputy in the National Assembly and by 1 member in the Senate.

Prefect: Jean-Marie Coussirou.

AGRICULTURE. The main products are vanilla, ylang-ylang and copra.

FISHERIES. A lobster and shrimp industry has recently been created. Annual catch is about 2,000 tonnes.

COMMERCE. Total trade between Mayotte and UK (1977): Imports to UK, £42,000 and exports and re-exports from UK, £33,000.

LA RÉUNION

AREA AND POPULATION. Réunion (or Bourbon), about 569 miles east of Madagascar, has belonged to France since 1642. It has an area of 2,511·6 sq. km (968·5 sq. miles) and a population of 476,700 (Oct. 1974). The chief towns are: St-Denis, the capital, with 90,000 inhabitants; St-Paul, 50,000; St-Pierre, 45,000; Le

Tampon, 35,000; St-Louis, 30,000. Elected municipal councils administer the 24 communes.

GOVERNMENT. On 19 March 1946 the status of Réunion was changed to that of an overseas department. Since 1974 Réunion has been part of a région. The région is under a prefect, an elected general council of 36 members and an elected regional council of 46 members. Réunion is represented in the National Assembly by 3 deputies, in the Senate by 2 senators, and in the Economic and Social Council by 1 councillor.

Prefect: Bernard Landouzy.

ECONOMY

Budget. The budget for 1976 balanced at 2,000m. French francs.

Banking. The Institut d'émission des Départements d'Outre-mer has the right to issue bank-notes. Banks operating in Réunion are the Banque de la Réunion (Crédit Lyonnais), the Banque Nationale pour le Commerce et l'Industrie, the Caisse Régionale de Crédit Agricole Mutuel de la Réunion and the Banque française Commerciale (B.F.C.).

AGRICULTURE. The chief productions are sugar (33,600 hectares), rum, maize, vanilla, essences and tobacco. The forests occupy about 98,000 hectares. The production of spirit (expressed as 100% alcohol) in 1976 amounted to 88,920 hectolitres of rum. The sugar production in 1976 was 249,949 tonnes.

Livestock (1976): 23,500 cattle, 123,560 swine, 35,000 sheep and goats.

FISHERIES. In 1976 the catch was 1,808 tonnes.

INDUSTRY (1976). Total number of workers (in 403 firms employing 10 or more) 17,334. The sugar industry employed 6,350.

COMMERCE. Trade in 1,000 tonnes and 1,000 French francs:

	1973		*1974*		*1975*		*1976*	
	Quantity	*Value*	*Quantity*	*Value*	*Quantity*	*Value*	*Quantity*	*Value*
Imports	1,270	63·5	710	1,593	641	1,757	809	2,152
Exports	366	18·3	218	327	156	257	251	450

The chief imports in 1976 were (in tonnes): Rice, 54,952; cement, 31,102. Chief exports (1976): Sugar, 208,495 tons; molasses, 24,185 tons; rum, 5,082 tons.

Total trade between Réunion and UK (British Department of Trade returns, in £1,000 sterling):

	1973	*1974*	*1975*	*1976*	*1977*
Imports to UK	261	159	51	4,469	19,585
Exports and re-exports from UK	500	693	1,138	1,742	1,807

COMMUNICATIONS

Roads. There were, in 1976, 2,172 km of roads, 1,764 km of which are bitumenized.

Aviation. Air France maintains an air service 7 times a week.

Shipping. Four shipping lines serve the island. In 1976, 402 vessels (97 of them French) visited the island.

Post and Broadcasting. There is telephone and telegraph connexion with Mauritius, Madagascar and metropolitan France. There are 50 post offices and a central telephone office; number of telephones (1977), 31,709.

France Regions 3 broadcasts in French on medium- and short-waves for more than 18 hours a day. There is 1 television programme *via* 14 transmitters for 21 hours a week. Number of receivers (1973): radio, 67,000; TV, 24,000.

JUSTICE. There is 1 *tribunal d'Instance*, 2 *tribuneaux de grande instance* and 1 *Cour d'Appel.*

EDUCATION. Réunion had (1977) 5 *lycées*, 49 *collèges*, 9 *lycées d'enseignement technique* with 52,198 pupils and 4 private secondary schools with 1,195 pupils. Primary education is given in 441 public and 30 private schools. Teachers number 3,956 in the public and 441 in the private schools. The public schools were attended by 118,141 pupils; the private schools by 9,630 pupils. University courses are given in 6 high schools to 2,201 students by 58 teachers.

Books of Reference

Bulletin de l'Académie de la Réunion. Biennial
Bulletin de la Chambre d'Agriculture de la Réunion
Statistiques et Indicateurs Economiques, 1976. Département de la Réunion, 1977

ST PIERRE AND MIQUELON

Departement de Saint-Pierre et Miquelon

AREA AND POPULATION. The department consists of a group of 8 small islands off the south coast of Newfoundland. Area of St Pierre group, 26 sq. km (10 sq. miles); population (census 18 Feb. 1974), 5,232; area of Miquelon-Langlade group, 216 sq. km (83·5 sq. miles); population, census, 1974, 608; total area, 242 sq. km (93·5 sq. miles). Population (estimate Dec. 1976), 6,100. Vital statistics (1976): Births, 100; marriages, 42; deaths, 45.

GOVERNMENT. The department changed its status from that of a territory in July 1976 and is represented in the National Assembly and the Senate by 1 deputy each.

Prefect: Pierre Eydoux.

A general council of 14 elected members was set up by decree of 25 Oct. 1946. Chief town, St Pierre, is also the seat of the court of appeal and the see of the Apostolic Vicariate.

BUDGET. The ordinary budget for 1976 balanced at 28·57m. francs CFA, the extraordinary budget at 2·7m. francs CFA.

INDUSTRY. The islands, being mostly barren rock, are unsuited for agriculture. The chief industry is fishing. The imports comprise textiles, salt, wines, coal, petrol, foodstuffs, meat; and the exports (in 1976), dried and salted fish (12 tons; 97,000 francs CFA); frozen and smoked fish (569 tons; 928,000 francs CFA); cattle, from quarantine station (355 tons; 18·46m. francs CFA).

COMMERCE. Trade in tonnes and 1m. francs CFA:

	1974		*1975*		*1976*	
	Quantity	*Value*	*Quantity*	*Value*	*Quantity*	*Value*
Imports	83,330	123,553	75,354	102,396	89,470	129,437
Exports	1,724	25,241	2,229	26,669		38,491

Total trade between St Pierre and Miquelon and UK (British Department of Trade returns, in £1,000 sterling):

	1973	*1974*	*1975*	*1976*	*1977*
Imports to UK	51	16	1	16	7
Exports and re-exports from UK	84	217	188	209	356

COMMUNICATIONS

Aviation. Air Saint-Pierre connects the department with Sydney (Nova Scotia), and there are occasional flights to and from St John's (Newfoundland), Gander and New York.

Shipping. St Pierre is in regular motor-vessel communication with North Sydney, Fortune (Newfoundland) and Halifax, and is connected by radio-telecommunication with most countries of the world.

Post and Broadcasting. There were 1,430 telephones in 1975. *France Regions 3* broadcasts in French on medium-waves.

Cinemas. There were (1973) 2 cinemas with a seating capacity of 800.

EDUCATION. Primary instruction is free. There were, in 1978, 7 nursery and primary schools with 50 teachers and 1,158 pupils; 3 secondary schools (including 1 technical school) with 74 teachers and 633 pupils.

Books of Reference

De Curton, E., *Saint-Pierre et Miquelon.* Paris, 1944
De La Rüe, E. A., *Saint-Pierre et Miquelon.* Paris, 1963
Ribault, J. Y., *Histoire de Saint-Pierre et Miquelon: Des Origines à 1814.* St Pierre, 1962

OVERSEAS TERRITORIES

SOUTHERN AND ANTARCTIC TERRITORIES

Terres Australes et Antarctiques Françaises

The Territory of the TAAF was created on 6 Aug. 1955. It comprises the islands of Saint Paul and Amsterdam, formerly Nouvelle Amsterdam, the Kerguelen and Crozet islands, and Terre Adélie.

The Administrator is assisted by a consultative council which meets twice yearly in Paris; its members are nominated by the Government for 5 years. Members of the Scientific Council are appointed by the Senior Administrator after approval by the Minister in charge of scientific research. The administration has its seat in Paris.

Administrator: Roger Barberot.

There are 4 postal agencies; the TAAF has its own postage stamps.

The scientific stations of the TAAF which took an important part in the International Geophysical Year, 1956–58, have been made permanent; the staff of the French bases is renewed annually.

Kerguelen islands, situated 48–50° S. lat., 68–70° E. long., consists of 1 large and 300 small islands with a total area of 7,215 sq. km (2,786 sq. miles). It was discovered in 1772 by Yves de Kerguelen, but was effectively occupied by France only in 1949. Port-aux-Français has several scientific research stations (92 members). Reindeer, trout and sheep have been acclimatized.

Crozet islands, situated 46° S. lat., 50–52° E. long., consists of 5 larger and 15 tiny islands, with a total area of 300 sq. km (116 sq. miles); the western group includes Apostles, Pigs and Penguins islands; the eastern group, Possession and Eastern islands. The archipelago was discovered in 1772 by Marion Dufresne, whose mate, Crozet, annexed it for Louis XV. A meteorological and scientific station on Possession Island (28 members) was built in 1964.

Saint Paul island, situated 38° S. Lat., 77° E. long., has an area of 7 sq. km (2·7 sq. miles). It is uninhabited. It was perhaps discovered in 1559 by Portuguese sailors.

Amsterdam island, situated 37° S. lat., 70° E. long., with an area of 60 sq. km (25 sq. miles). It was discovered in 1522 by Magellan's companions, but first visited (together with Saint Paul) by a Dutch skipper. In 1950 an administrative office, research stations (37 members) and a hospital were established.

Terre Adélie comprises the antarctic continent between 136° and 142° E. long., south of 60° S. lat. It was discovered in 1840 by Dumont d'Urville. A research station (34 members) is situated at Base Dumont d'Urville, which is kept by the French Polar Expeditions.

Books of Reference

T.A.A.F. Revue trimestrielle. Paris, 1957 ff.
Expéditions Polaires Françaises. Etudes et Rapports. Paris, 1948–59

FRENCH POLYNESIA

Polynésie Française

GOVERNMENT. These islands, formerly called 'French Settlements in Oceania', scattered over a wide area in the eastern Pacific, opted in Nov. 1958 for the status of an Overseas Territory within the French Community. They are administered by a governor, a government council (over which the governor presides), consisting of 5 members elected by the assembly and a territorial assembly of 30 members elected every 5 years on the basis of universal suffrage. French Polynesia is represented in the National Assembly by 1 deputy, in the Senate by 1 senator and in the Economic and Social Council by 1 councillor.

Governor: Charles Schmitt.

French Polynesia is administratively divided into the following *circonscriptions*:

1. The **Windward Islands** (Iles du Vent), comprising Tahiti with an area of about 1,042 sq. km and (census 1970) 84,552 inhabitants; Moorea with an area of 132 sq. km and 4,842 inhabitants; Maio, 216 inhabitants. The most important island is **Tahiti** with 79,494 inhabitants; its chief town is Papeete.

2. The **Leeward Islands** (Iles sous le Vent) (15,718 inhabitants), comprising Huahine, Raiatéa, Tahaa, Bora-Bora and Maupiti. The chief town is Uturoa (2,681 inhabitants) on Raiatéa.

The Windward and Leeward Islands together are called the Society Archipelago (Archipel de la Société).

3. The **Tuamotu group,** consisting of two parallel ranges of islands between 135° and 143° W. long. and 14° and 23° S. lat., east of the Society Archipelago, with a population of 6,664; chief centres, Rangiroa and Anaa. The **Gambier group** (of which Mangareva is the principal) have 30 sq. km of area; chief centre, Rikitea. The whole circonscription had 8,226 inhabitants in 1971.

4. The **Austral Islands,** of which Rurutu is the largest, Tubuai, Raivavae, Rimatara and, far to the south, Rapa, have together an area of 174 sq. km and 5,079 inhabitants.

5. The **Marquezas Islands,** with a total area of 1,274 sq. km and 5,593 inhabitants, the two largest islands being Nuku-Hiva and Hiva-Oa.

The total area is estimated at 3,941 sq. km (1,522 sq. miles); their population (census, 1977) was 137,382. The uninhabited island of Clipperton is under the authority of the Governor as Delegate of the French Government.

FINANCE. The ordinary budget for 1977 balanced at 9,343·9m. francs CFP.

COMMERCE. Trade in 1,000 tonnes and 1m. francs du Pacifique (= 0·055 metropolitan francs):

	1970		*1971*		*1972*	
	Quantity	*Value*	*Quantity*	*Value*	*Quantity*	*Value*
Imports	334	13,642	342	14,073	324	14,270
Exports	19	1,840	14	1,749	18	1,341

Total trade between the French possessions in the Pacific and UK (British Department of Trade returns, in £1,000 sterling):

	1973	*1974*	*1975*	*1976*	*1977*
Imports to UK	3	16	5	—	11
Exports and re-exports from UK	2,713	1,060	1,214	1,647	1,768

An important product is copra (coconut trees covering the coastal plains of the mountainous islands and the greater part of the low-lying islands), production (1973) 14,000 tonnes. Other produce for export are coffee, vanilla and mother-of-pearl, whereas tropical fruits, such as bananas, pineapples, oranges, etc., are grown only for local consumption.

Chief imports (by value) include metalwork, textiles, petrol, sugar and flour. Chief exports were copra, vanilla, coffee, citrus fruit, mother-of-pearl (1972: 75 tonnes). Tourism is very important, earning almost half as much as the visible exports. There were 91,993 tourists in 1976.

COMMUNICATIONS

Aviation. Six international airlines connect Tahiti with Paris, Honolulu, USA, Mexico and New Zealand. There is also a regular air service between Tahiti and the Leeward Isles with occasional connexions to the other groups. In 1974, 331,216 passengers arrived by air.

Shipping. Several shipping companies connect France, San Francisco, New Zealand and Australia with Papeete.

Post and Broadcasting. Number of telephones (1977), 14,679. Radio Tahiti belongs to *Office de Radiodiffusion-Télévision Française* and broadcasts in French, Tahitian and English on medium- and short-waves and also broadcasts 1 television programme *via* 5 transmitters. Number of receivers (1973): radio, 62,000; TV, 12,000.

RELIGION. In 1971 it was estimated that 70,000 inhabitants were Protestants and 35,000 Roman Catholics.

EDUCATION. Education at primary level was re-organized in 1974 and secondary education in 1975. There were, in 1972, 160 primary schools (33,166 pupils), 14 secondary schools (6,294 pupils) and 3 technical schools (853 pupils).

Books of Reference

Journal Officiel des Etablissements Françaises de l'Océanie, and *Supplement Containing Statistics of Commerce and Navigation*. Papeete

Andrews, E., *Comparative Dictionary of the Tahitian Language*. Chicago, 1944

Luke, Sir Harry, *The Islands of the South Pacific*. London, 1961

O'Reilly, P., and Reitman, E., *Bibliographie de Tahiti et de la Polynésie française*. Paris, 1967

O'Reilly, P., and Teissier, R., *Tahitiens. Répertoire bio-bibliographique de la Polynésie française*. Paris, 1963

NEW CALEDONIA AND DEPENDENCIES

Nouvelle Calédonie

AREA AND POPULATION. New Caledonia is situated between 20° 8′ and 22° 25′ S. lat., and 164° 15′ and 162° 15′ E. long. It has a total length exceeding

397 km and an average breadth of 50 km. Area, including dependencies, 19,103 sq. km (7,374 sq. miles). In 1974 the population was 131,665, including 51,582 Europeans (majority French), 53,725 Melanesians, 4,213 Vietnamese and Indonesians, 10,518 Polynesians and Wallisians. Nouméa had 59,869 inhabitants.

GOVERNMENT. From Jan. 1976 State affairs are administrated by the High Commissioner and Territorial affairs by a Council of Government of 7 elected members (until 1976 the Council was advisory). A Territorial Assembly of 35 elected members decides the more important territorial affairs including local revenue.

The Territory is divided into 31 communes which are administered by locally elected councils and mayors.

High Commissioner for the Pacific Ocean and the New Hebrides and Governor of New Caledonia and Dependencies: Jean-Gabriel Eriau.

The territory is represented in the National Assembly and the Senate by 2 deputies and 1 senator.

ECONOMY

Budget. Expenditure for 1975 was 9,699m. francs CFP and revenue 9,990m. francs CFP. Revenues included special grants by France totalling 4,341m. francs CFP.

Banking. There are branches of the Banque de l'Indochine, the Banque Nationale de Paris, the Banque de Paris et Pays-Bas, and the Société Générale, in addition to the Banque de la Nouvelle Calédonie.

MINERALS. The mineral resources are very great; nickel, chrome and iron abound; silver, gold, cobalt, lead, manganese, iron and copper have been mined at different times. The nickel deposits are of special value, being without arsenic. Production of nickel ore in 1974, 6·96m. tonnes. About 467,000 hectares of mining land are owned, and 97,000 hectares have been granted for exploitation. In 1973 the furnaces produced 18,837 tonnes matte of nickel and 48,533 tonnes of ferro-nickel. Local industries are developing; there are a chlorine and oxygen plant, barking mills for coffee and an important construction industry.

AGRICULTURE. Of the total area only about 6% is cultivable; about 416,000 hectares are pasture land; about 6,000 hectares are commercially cultivated and about 250,000 hectares contain forest; forest produce, 1974, 17,714 cu. metres. There are 4 forms of landownership: native reserves belonging to the local tribes, private estates, public land belonging to the New Caledonian territory and public land belonging to the metropolitan government. The chief agricultural products are coffee, copra, maize, fruits and vegetables. Some meat is produced locally but insufficient to satisfy domestic consumption.

Livestock (1976): Cattle, 92,000; pigs, 30,000; goats, 10,000; poultry, 166,000.

COMMERCE. Trade in 1m. CFP francs[1]:

	1970	*1973*	*1974*	*1975*
Imports	23,271	17,748	24,635	27,049
Exports	19,362	15,675	23,333	22,380

[1] 18·18 CFP francs = 1 French franc.

In 1974, 40·8% of the imports came from, and 43·2% of the exports went to France.

Chief imports in 1974 were (in CFP1m.): Food, 5,141; machines, electrical products, 2,747. Chief exports: Nickel metal, 17,787; nickel ore, 5,729; other, 33.

COMMUNICATIONS

Roads. There were, in 1974, 5,214 km of roads.

Aviation. New Caledonia is connected by air routes with France (by UTA), Australia (UTA, Air Pacific and Qantas), New Zealand (UTA and Air New

Zealand), Fiji (by Air Pacific), the New Hebrides, Wallis archipelago and Tahiti (by UTA).

Shipping. In 1975, 508 vessels entered Nouméa and unloaded 1·1m. tonnes of goods and loaded 2·6m. tonnes. A new harbour for deep-water alongside discharge was completed in 1974.

Post and Broadcasting. There were 52 post offices and telex, telephone, radio and television services. There were (1977) 20,612 telephones. Radio Nouméa belongs to *Societé Mahande des Programmes* and broadcasts in French on medium- and short-waves and also broadcasts 1 television programme 28 hours a week. Number of receivers (1975): radio, 60,000; TV, 20,000.

EDUCATION. In 1974, 37,508 persons received instruction: 30,278 in 240 primary schools, 5,012 in 8 secondary schools and 2,095 in technical and vocational schools.

Dependencies of New Caledonia:

1. The Isle of Pines, 30 miles to the south-east, with an area of 153 sq. km and a population of 1,175 (census 1974).
2. The Loyalty Islands, 60 miles east of New Caledonia, consisting of 3 large islands, Maré, Lifou and Uvéa, and many small islands with a total area of about 2,072 sq. km and a population of 13,392, nearly all Melanesians (census, 1974). The chief culture in the islands is that of coconuts: the chief export, copra.
3. The Huon Islands, 170 miles north-west of New Caledonia, a most barren group.
4. The Bélep Archipelago, about 7 miles north-east of New Caledonia.
5. Chesterfield Islands are on the 20° S. parallel, about 342 miles west of the northern headland of New Caledonia.
6. Walpole lies south-east of Maré (Loyalty Islands) and east of the Isle of Pines, about 93 miles from each of these islands.

Books of Reference

Journal Officiel de la Nouvelle Calédonie et Dépendances
Annuaire Statistique de la Nouvelle Calédonie et Dependances

WALLIS AND FUTUNA

On 22 Dec. 1959 the inhabitants of these islands voted with an overwhelming majority in favour of exchanging their status from a protectorate to an oversea territory, which was granted by the French Parliament on 29 July 1961. The Senior Administrator of the Wallis and Futuna Isles carries out the duties of the Head of the Territory. He is assisted by a Territorial Council.

The Wallis Archipelago, north-east of Fiji, has an area of 96 sq. km and 7,000 inhabitants. The archipelago is in regular communication with Nouméa *via* Port Vila. Futuna and Alofi, south of the Wallis Islands have an area of 159 sq. km and 2,900 inhabitants.

ANGLO-FRENCH CONDOMINIUM

NEW HEBRIDES. *See* p. 889

GABON

République Gabonaise

Capital: Libreville
Population: 950,000 (1974)
GNP per capita: US$2,590 (1976)

AREA AND POPULATION. The Gabon Republic is bounded west by the Atlantic ocean and north by Equatorial Guinea and Cameroon and east and south by Congo. The area covers 267,667 sq. km; its population in 1974 (estimate) was about 950,000, including about 12,000 Europeans. The capital is Libreville (251,400 inhabitants), Port Gentil (77,111).

CONSTITUTION AND GOVERNMENT. The Gabonese Republic became independent on 17 Aug. 1960 after having been one of the 4 territories of French Equatorial Africa and, from 28 Nov. 1958, a member state of the French Community. In Jan. 1959 it formed an 'economic, technical and customs union' with the other 3 territories of the former government-general of French Equatorial Africa.

President of the Republic: Albert-Bernard Bongo (re-elected for 7-year term on 25 Feb. 1973).

Prime Minister: Léon Mebiame.

Foreign Minister: Okoumba D'Okwatseque.

Flag: Three horizontal stripes of green, yellow, blue.

DEFENCE

Army. The Army consists of 1 infantry battalion and 2 commando battalion companies, totalling 950 men.

Air Force. The Air Force has ordered 3 of single-seat and 2 two-seat Mirage 5 ground-attack aircraft. It has 2 Hercules turboprop transports, 2 twin-jet Gulfstream IIs and 1 twin-jet Falcon 20, 2 Cessna Skymaster communications aircraft, and 3 Puma and 4 Alouette III helicopters. Other transport aircraft are operated on a joint military/civilian basis. Personnel number between 100 and 150.

INTERNATIONAL RELATIONS

Membership. Gabon is a member of UN, OAU and is an ACP state of EEC.

FINANCE. The ordinary budget for 1975–76 provided for expenditure of 193,114m. francs CFA, and the development expenditure, 134,926m. GDP *per capita* (1972) US$828.

NATURAL RESOURCES

Oil. The petroleum refinery at Port Gentil, a joint venture of the governments of the five members of the Central African Customs and Economic Union (UDEAC) and foreign petroleum companies, began trial operations in Oct. 1967. The refinery produced 10·8m. tons of crude oil in 1976. *La Société Gabonaise de raffinerie* produced 191,000 tonnes in 1974.

Minerals. Production 1974: Manganese dioxide, 2,129 tonnes; uranium concentrates, 1,713 tonnes; natural gas, 45·6m. cu. metres; gold, 227 kg; timber (okoumé), 1·04m. tonnes.

A large deposit of iron ore estimated at 1,000m. tonnes was discovered in 1971 at Mékambo near Belinga.

TRADE. In 1975 imports totalled 100,560m. francs CFA and exports 201,920m. francs CFA. France, UK, USA, the Netherlands and the Federal Republic of Germany are Gabon's principal trading partners. Petroleum makes up 80% of exports.

Trade with the UK (British Department of Trade returns, in £1,000 sterling):

	1972	*1973*	*1974*	*1975*	*1976*	*1977*
Imports to UK	2,506	10,258	28,397	3,759	9,160	3,216
Exports and re-exports from UK	1,808	2,833	3,565	2,828	4,041	5,626

COMMUNICATIONS

Roads. There were (1977) 6,848 km of roads.

Railways. A 1,435-mm gauge railway is under construction from Libreville and Owendo to Booué and Franceville. The first section was due to open in late 1978.

Aviation. There are 3 airports at Port Gentil, Franceville and Libreville.

Shipping. Libreville and Port Gentil are the main ports. Together with Pointe-Noire (Congo), they received 1,531 vessels in 1963; merchandise unloaded was 176,400 tonnes; loaded, 1,319,000 tonnes.

Post. Telephones (1969), 4,300.

Cinemas. In 1971 there were 2 cinemas with a seating capacity of 1,700.

EDUCATION. In 1977 there were nearly 700 primary and secondary schools with 100,000 pupils. There were 900 students receiving higher education.

DIPLOMATIC REPRESENTATIVES

OF GABON IN GREAT BRITAIN
(48 Kensington Ct., London, W8)

Ambassador: Edouard Teale (accredited 18 Feb. 1977).

OF GREAT BRITAIN IN GABON

Ambassador; A. C. D. S. MacRae.

OF GABON IN THE USA
(2034 20th St., NW, Washington, D.C., 20008)

Ambassador: Jean-Daniel Mambouka.

OF THE USA IN GABON
(Blvd de la Mer, Libreville)

Ambassador: Andrew L. Steigman.

OF GABON TO THE UNITED NATIONS

Ambassador: Léon N'Dong

Books of Reference

Lasserre, G., *Libreville, la ville et sa région.* Paris, 1958
Thiery, Y., and Delarozière, R., *Carte ethnique du Gabon.* Paris, 1945

THE GAMBIA

Capital: Banjul
Population: 493,197 (1973)
GNP per capita: US$180 (1976)

HISTORY. The Gambia was discovered by the early Portuguese navigators, but they made no settlement. During the 17th century various companies of merchants obtained trading charters and established a settlement on the river, which, from 1807, was controlled from Sierra Leone; in 1843 it was made an independent Crown Colony; in 1866 it formed part of the West African Settlements, but in Dec. 1888 it again became a separate Crown Colony. The boundaries were delimited only after 1890. The Gambia achieved full internal self-government on 4 Oct. 1963 and became an independent member of the Commonwealth on 18 Feb. 1965.

A referendum was held in Nov. 1965 to decide whether The Gambia was to become a republic. The referendum failed, as any alteration of the constitution requires a two-thirds majority. A further referendum was held in April 1970 and 84,968 were cast in favour of a republic and 35,683 against. The Gambia became a republic within the Commonwealth on 24 April 1970.

AREA AND POPULATION. The Gambia is bounded west by the Atlantic ocean and on all other sides by Senegal. Area of Banjul (formerly Bathurst) and environs, 87·8 sq. km; population (1973) 39,476. In the Provinces (area, 10,601·5 sq. km) the settled population (1971) was 275,469, not including temporary immigrants. Total population (census, April 1973), 493,197. The largest tribe is the Mandingo (186,241), followed by the Fulas (79,994), Woloffs (69,291), Jolas (41,988) and Sarahulis (38,478). The capital is Banjul (39,476), and the other chief town is Kombo St Mary (38,934). There are 1,159 non-Africans.

CONSTITUTION AND GOVERNMENT. Parliament consists of the House of Representatives which consists of a Speaker and 32 elected members; in addition, 4 Chiefs are elected by the Chiefs in Assembly; 3 nominated members are without votes and the Attorney-General is nominated and has a vote.

At the general election of 4–5 April 1977, the People's Progressive Party obtained 27, the National Convention Party 5, and the United Party 2 seats.

The Cabinet comprises the President and 11 Ministers from the Legislature.

The Government was in June 1977 composed as follows:

President: Sir Dawda Kairaba Jawara.

Vice-President and Minister for Local Government and Lands: Assan Musa Camara. *Agriculture and Natural Resources:* Alhaji Yaya Ceesay. *Minister of External Affairs:* Alhaji Alieu Badara N'Jie. *Health, Social Welfare and Labour:* Alhaji Kalilou Singhateh. *Attorney-General:* Mohamadu Lamin Saho. *Works and Communications:* Alhaji Sir Alieu Sulayman Jack. *Information and Tourism:* B. L. K. Sanyang. *Education, Youth, Sport and Culture:* Alhaji Momodu C. Cham. *Finance and Trade:* Dembo Jatta. *Minister of State, President's Office:* K. N. Leigh. *Economic Planning and Industrial Development:* L. B. M'Boge.

National flag: Three horizontal stripes of red, blue, green, with blue edged in white.

Local Administration. The Gambia is divided into 35 districts, each traditionally under a Chief, assisted by Village Heads and advisers. These districts are grouped into 6 Area Councils containing a majority of elected members, with the Chiefs of the district as *ex-officio* members. The city of Banjul is administered by a City Council.

INTERNATIONAL RELATIONS

Membership. The Gambia is a member of UN, OAU, the Commonwealth and is an ACP state of EEC.

ECONOMY

Budget. Revenue and expenditure for years ending 30 June are (in 1,000 *dalasi*):

	1971–72	*1972–73*	*1973–74*	*1974–75*	*1975–76*[1]
Revenue	22,698	23,881	27,716	29,702	37,139
Expenditure	22,754	20,970	24,936	32,731	39,964

[1] Estimates.

Currency. In July 1971 a new currency unit (*dalasi*) was introduced. It is divided into 100 *butut*. 4 *dalasi* = £ sterling; 1 *dalasi* = US$0.50 (March 1976).

Banking. There are 4 banks in the Gambia, the Standard Bank of West Africa Ltd, Central Bank of the Gambia, Commercial and Development Bank and la Banque Internationale pour le Commerce et l'Industrie (BICI). On 30 June 1974 the government savings bank had over 35,000 depositors holding 664,748 *dalasi*.

NATURAL RESOURCES

Minerals. Deposits of ilmenite exist on old storm beaches along the Atlantic coast. No other workable mineral deposits are known.

Agriculture. Almost all commercial activity centres upon the marketing of groundnuts, which is the only export crop of financial significance. Rice is of increasing importance for local consumption.

Livestock (1976). 300,000 cattle, 90,000 goats, 9,500 sheep, 8,000 pigs and 300,000 poultry.

LABOUR. There are 4 large and 10 small trade unions.

TRADE. Chief items of imports are textiles and clothing, vehicles and machinery, metal goods and petroleum products.

Imports and exports, in 1,000 *dalasi*:

	1970–71	*1971–72*	*1972–73*	*1973–74*	*1974–75*
Imports	42,587	46,216	54,419	63,495	90,834
Exports	30,911	35,491	33,690	67,607	84,840

Chief items of exports are groundnuts, palm kernels, dried and smoked fish, hides and skins and groundnut oil.

Trade between the Gambia and UK (British Department of Trade returns, in £1,000 sterling):

	1972	*1973*	*1974*	*1975*	*1976*	*1977*
Imports to UK	4,598	4,204	8,438	8,240	6,761	8,503
Exports and re-exports from UK	3,197	3,225	4,437	7,554	10,865	12,362

TOURISM. In 1975–76, 25,372 tourists visited the Gambia.

COMMUNICATIONS

Roads. There are 733 miles of motorable roads, of which 470 miles rank as all-season. Number of licensed motor vehicles (1974–75): 11,765 private cars, 5,777 commercial vehicles, 240 buses and coaches, 410 tractors and 143 trailers.

Aviation. Air movements at Yundum Airport in 1975 numbered 2,756, including scheduled services.

Shipping. The chief port, Banjul, handled 303 ships of 686,300 DWT in 1975–76. The first phase of development of the port was completed in 1974; a new 400 ft berth will take one large vessel of up to 36 ft draught. Internal communication is maintained by steamers and launches.

Post and Broadcasting. There are several post offices and agencies; postal facilities are also afforded to all river towns by means of a travelling post office on the government river mail-steamers. Banjul is connected with St Vincent (Cape Verde islands) and with Sierra Leone by cable. Banjul is in wireless communication with London and the main centres up river. A trans-Gambia telephone system provides direct communications with Dakar and Ziguinchor. Telephones numbered 2,752 in Jan. 1977. A telex service was introduced in 1968.

Radio Gambia, a government station, broadcasts for about 12 hours a day.

Newspapers. There is an official (three times weekly) and several duplicated news-sheets.

Cinemas. In 1971 there were 8 cinemas.

RELIGION, EDUCATION AND WELFARE

Religion. The population is mainly Moslem. Banjul is the seat of an Anglican and a Roman Catholic bishop. There are some Methodist missions.

Education (1975–76). There were 96 primary schools (797 teachers, 24,629 pupils), 17 secondary technical schools (180 teachers, 4,282 pupils), 7 senior secondary schools (103 teachers, 1,897 pupils) and 5 post-secondary schools (40 teachers, 461 pupils).

Health. In 1972 there were 19 doctors and about 500 hospital beds.

DIPLOMATIC REPRESENTATIVES

OF THE GAMBIA IN GREAT BRITAIN (60 Ennismore Gdns., London, SW7)

High Commissioner: Bocar Ousman Semega-Janneh, MBE.

OF GREAT BRITAIN IN THE GAMBIA (78B Wellington St., Banjul)

High Commissioner: M. H. G. Rogers.

OF THE USA IN THE GAMBIA (16 Buckle St., Banjul)

Ambassador: Herman J. Cohen (resides in Dakar).

Books of Reference

The Gambia Independence Act, 1964
The Gambia Independence Order, 1965
Gailey, Jr, H. A., *A History of the Gambia.* London, 1964
Rice, B., *Enter Gambia.* Sydney, 1968

GERMANY

POST-WAR HISTORY. Since the unconditional surrender of the German armed forces on 8 May 1945 there has been no central authority whose writ runs in the whole of Germany. Consequently no peace treaty has been signed with a government representing the whole of Germany, and the country is virtually partitioned between the Federal Republic of Germany and the German Democratic Republic.

By the Berlin Declaration of 5 June 1945 the governments of the USA, the UK, the USSR and France assumed supreme authority over Germany. Each of the 4 signatories was given a zone of occupation, in which the supreme power was to be exercised by the C.-in-C. in that zone (*see* map in THE STATESMAN'S YEAR-BOOK, 1947). Jointly these 4 Cs.-in-C. constituted the Allied Control Council in Berlin, which was to be competent in all 'matters affecting Germany as a whole'. The territory of Greater Berlin, divided into 4 sectors, was to be governed as an entity by the 4 occupying powers.

At the Potsdam Conference (17 July–2 Aug. 1945) the northern part of the Province of East Prussia, including its capital Königsberg (renamed Kaliningrad), was transferred to the Soviet Union, pending final ratification by a peace treaty; and it was agreed that, pending the final peace settlement, Poland should administer those parts of Germany lying east of a line running from the Baltic Sea immediately west of Swinemünde along the river Oder to its confluence with the Western Neisse and thence along the Western Neisse to the Czechoslovak frontier.

The agreements between the war-time allies concerning the occupation zones (12 Sept. 1944) and control of Germany (1 May 1945) were repudiated by the USSR on 27 Nov. 1958.

A Treaty was signed in East Berlin between the German Democratic Republic and the Federal Republic of Germany on 21 Dec. 1972 agreeing the basis of relations between the two countries.

GERMAN DEMOCRATIC REPUBLIC

Capital: Berlin (East)
Population: 16.8m. (1976)
GNP per capita: US$4,220 (1976)

Deutsche Demokratische Republik

HISTORY. For the immediate post-war history *see* p. 493.

AREA AND POPULATION. Area and population (31 Dec. 1976):

Districts	*Area in sq. km.*	*Population Male*	*Female*	*Total*	*Per sq. km.*
Berlin (East)	403	503,378	602,889	1,106,267	2,745
Cottbus	8,262	413,916	460,091	874,007	106
Dresden	6,738	835,209	990,607	1,825,816	271
Erfurt	7,349	580,297	657,934	1,238,231	168
Frankfurt	7,186	328,033	362,197	690,230	96
Gera	4,004	343,393	393,835	737,228	184
Halle	8,771	872,734	990,766	1,863,500	212
Karl-Marx-Stadt	6,009	898,184	1,064,049	1,962,233	327
Leipzig	4,966	657,187	778,237	1,435,424	289
Magdeburg	11,525	599,917	683,442	1,283,359	111
Neubrandenburg	10,792	299,120	325,938	625,058	58
Potsdam	12,572	523,119	593,985	1,117,104	89
Rostock	7,074	414,577	456,649	871,226	123
Schwerin	8,672	278,291	310,812	589,103	68
Suhl	3,856	258,534	289,710	548,244	142
German Democratic Republic	*108,179*	*7,805,889*	*8,961,141*	*16,767,030*	*155*

An agreement proclaiming the Oder–Neisse line the permanent frontier between Germany and Poland was concluded between the German Democratic Republic and Poland on 6 July 1950. A protocol on the delimitation of the frontier was signed on 27 Jan. 1951.

Resident population of the principal towns as at 31 Dec. 1976:

Berlin (East), capital	1,106,267	Halle	234,261	Gera	117,394
Leipzig	564,596	Rostock	217,022	Cottbus	110,051
Dresden	510,408	Erfurt	205,483	Schwerin	101,265
Karl-Marx-Stadt	307,554	Zwickau	122,168	Jena	100,810
Magdeburg	279,430	Potsdam	121,923	Dessau	100,726

Vital statistics:

	Live births	*Marriages*	*Divorces*	*Deaths*
1974	179,127	138,816	41,615	229,062
1975	181,798	142,130	41,632	240,389
1976[1]	195,483	144,592	44,805	234,811

[1] Preliminary.

Crude birth rate per 1,000 population was 18·8 in 1971; 11·8 in 1972; 10·6 in 1973; 10·6 in 1974; 10·8 in 1975; 11·6 in 1976; marriage rate, 7·6 in 1971; 7·8 in 1972; 8·1 in 1973; 8·2 in 1974; 8·4 in 1975; 8·6 in 1976; death rate, 13·8 in 1971 and 1972; 13·7 in 1973; 13·5 in 1974; 14·3 in 1975; 14 in 1976; infantile mortality per 100 live births, 1·8 in 1971 and 1972; 1·6 in 1973, 1974 and 1975; 1·4 in 1976 (Preliminary).

CONSTITUTION AND GOVERNMENT. Upon the establishment of the

Federal Republic of Germany, the People's Council of the Soviet-occupied zone, appointed in 1948, was converted into a provisional People's Chamber.

On 7 Oct. 1949 the provisional People's Chamber enacted a constitution of the 'German Democratic Republic'.

In July 1952 the 5 Länder of Mecklenburg, Saxony-Anhalt, Brandenburg, Saxony and Thuringia were replaced by 14 districts (*Bezirke*).

A new 'socialist constitution' was approved by a referendum on 6 April 1968, when 94·54% of the electorate voted for the constitution; it came into force on 8 April, 1968. The People's Chamber, of 500 deputies, is 'the supreme organ of state power'; it elects the Council of State, the Council of Ministers, the National Defence Council and the judges of the Supreme Court.

Council of State. After the death of President Wilhelm Pieck (7 Sept. 1960), the People's Chamber on 12 Sept. 1960 abolished the office of president and elected instead a council of state. This consists of a chairman, 6 deputy chairmen, 18 members and a secretary. The Council is authorized to issue decrees and decisions with the force of law and to interpret existing laws. The Chairman of the Council of State represents the GDR in international law. *Chairman:* Erich Honecker.

On 20 Sept. 1961 the People's Chamber passed a 'law for the defence of the GDR'; the People's Chamber is authorized to declare a 'state of defence'.

At the elections held on 16 Oct. 1976, the list of the National Front received 99·86% of the valid votes.

The cabinet was, in Jan. 1977, composed as follows:

Chairman: Willi Stoph.

First Deputy Chairmen: Alfred Neumann, Werner Krolikowski.

Deputy Chairmen: Günther Kleiber, Wolfgang Rauchfuss, Gerhard Schürer, Dr Gerhard Weiss, Dr Herbert Weiz, Manfred Flegel, Hans-Joachin Heusinger, Hans Reichelt, Rudolph Schulze.

Members of the Presidium of the Council of Ministers: All members of the cabinet and Siegfried Böhm, Heinz Kuhrig, Walter Halbritter.

Considerable political power is exercised by the Politburo of the SUP.

National flag: Black, red, golden (horizontal); in the centre, on both sides, the coat of arms showing a hammer and compass with a wreath of grain entwined with a black, red and golden ribbon.

National hymn: Auferstanden aus Ruinen (words by Johannes R. Becher, tune by Hanns Eisler).

East Berlin ('Democratic Berlin') is the capital of the German Democratic Republic. *Head of the Administration* (*Magistrat*): Erhard Krack.

DEFENCE. On 18 Jan. 1956 the Diet passed laws for the establishment of a 'national people's army' and a defence ministry. A 12-member defence council, under the chairmanship of E. Honecker, General Secretary of the Central Committee, was set up on 10 Feb. 1960.

The 'law for the defence of the GDR', of 20 Sept. 1960, makes military service (in case of emergency) and civil defence compulsory for all citizens.

Conscription for men between 18 and 25 years was introduced on 24 Jan. 1962 (18 months' service in the army, 2 years in the navy and air force).

Twenty Soviet divisions of about 258,000 men with about 1,000 heavy tanks and 6,000 armoured vehicles are stationed in the German Democratic Republic, chiefly along the Polish border.

Army. The Army, set up on 1 March 1956, is organized in 2 army corps, including 2 armoured divisions and 4 motorized infantry divisions. Operationally these divisions are subordinate to the Soviet formations of the Warsaw Pact forces. They are armed with about 2,000 tanks (mostly Soviet T-54, T-55 and T-62), 300 self-propelled guns and ground-to-air 'Guideline' missiles. The Border Police was incorporated in the Army in Sept. 1961. Total army strength was (1977) 105,000 all ranks.

Police. The Police force (*Volkspolizei*) numbered 25,000 security and 48,000 border troops. There are also 500,000 militiamen organized in combat groups. The militia receive military instruction by the People's Police.

Navy. The 'People's Navy' includes 2 small frigates, 15 missile boats, 63 torpedo boats, 18 patrol vessels, 52 coastal minesweepers, 3 intelligence ships, 4 patrol boats, 18 coastguard boats, 2 tank landing ships, 18 landing craft, 4 oilers, 4 training ships (including 3 fleet minesweepers), 4 supply ships, 4 survey vessels, 17 buoy tenders, 4 diving vessels, 1 cable layer, 2 torpedo recovery craft, 3 icebreakers, 10 auxiliary ships and 13 tugs. Personnel (1978) 1,800 officers and 15,200 men.

Air Force. The *ex*-'air-police', set up in Nov. 1950, had in 1977 a strength of about 36,000 officers and men and 425 combat aircraft. Two fighter divisions consist respectively of 2 and 4 wings (each with at least 3 squadrons of 16 aircraft), plus a fighter training division. Operational units are equipped mainly with MiG-21 supersonic day and all-weather interceptors and about 90 Su-7 supersonic ground attack fighters. MiG-17 fighters remain in service, mainly for training. Other units include a wing of Mi-2, Mi-4 and Mi-8 helicopters, a wing of Il-14, An-24, Tu-124 and Tu-134 transports and a Flight Training Division with Yak-18, Trener, L-29 Delfin, MiG-15UTI and MiG-21UTI training aircraft. 'Guideline' and 'Goa' surface-to-air missile units are operational.

INTERNATIONAL RELATIONS

Membership. The German Democratic Republic is a member of UN and Comecon.

ECONOMY

Budget. The budget of the German Democratic Republic was as follows (in M 1m.) for calendar years:

	1971	*1972*	*1973*	*1974*	*1975*	*1976*
Revenue	80,206	86,935	94,946	104,645	114,662	117,588
Expenditure	79,125	85,748	93,277	103,292	114,160	117,128

Of the 1976 expenditures, 41,443m. was earmarked for health and social services, education and *Kultur*.

Currency. The circulating Reichsmark notes were in June 1948 exchanged for 'Deutsche Mark' (East), renamed 'Mark of the German Bank of Issue' (MDN) from 1 Aug. 1964 and further renamed 'the Mark of the GDR' M from 1967. The circulation of notes and coins at 31 Dec. 1976 was 10,488m. M. Since 1 Nov. 1953 the M currency has been based on gold, the gold content of the M being fixed at 0·399902 gramme. The Federal German *Deutschmark* also became legal tender in 1978.

Banking. The most important banking institutions of the GDR are the Staatsbank der DDR Berlin, which is the bank of issue, and the Industrie- und Handelsbank der DDR. Savings, as at 31 Dec. 1975, totalled 75,315m. M.

Weights and Measures. The metric system is in force.

ENERGY AND NATURAL RESOURCES

Electricity. Generation of electric power (in 1m. kwh.): 1950, 19,466; 1960, 40,305; 1969, 65,463; 1970, 67,650; 1971, 69,420; 1972, 72,828; 1973, 76,908; 1974, 80,286; 1975, 84,505; 1976, 89,150.

Minerals. In the production of lignite, the German Democratic Republic takes first place in world output. Rare metals, such as uranium, cobalt, bismuth, arsenic and antimony, are being exploited in the western Erzgebirge and eastern Thuringia.

The principal minerals raised are as follows (in 1,000 tonnes):

	1973	*1974*	*1975*	*1976*		*1973*	*1974*	*1975*	*1976*
Coal	753	594	539	...	Iron ore	52	53	59	...
Lignite	246,245	243,468	246,706	246,897	Potash	2,556	2,864	3,019	3,161

Agriculture. In 1976 the arable land was 4,751,762 hectares; meadows and pastures, 1,295,091 hectares; forests, 2,950,994 hectares. Since 1945, the estates of Junkers, war criminals and leading Nazis have been sequestrated; 3·1m. hectares have been distributed among farmers. In 1976 there were 3,582 collective farms of 5·3m. hectares, 424 state farms of 119,961 hectares.

The yield of the main crops in 1976 was as follows (in 1,000 tonnes): Wheat, 2,715; rye, 1,455; barley, 3,456; oats, 506; potatoes, 6,816; sugar-beet, 5,106.

Livestock (in 1,000) in 1976: Cattle, 5,471 (including 2,146 milch cows); pigs, 11,291; sheep, 1,870; goats, 42; horses, 68; poultry, 48,445.

Fisheries. Total catch (1976) 279,353 tonnes. Inland catch was 13,187 tonnes, of which 9,167 tonnes was carp.

INDUSTRY AND TRADE

Industry. Industry produced about 59·1% of the national income in 1976; the nationally owned and co-operative undertakings were responsible for 96·8% of the net product. The percentage of privately owned enterprises was 31·8 in 1950 and 3·2 in 1976.

There were, at 31 Dec. 1976, 7,254 industrial establishments with 3,092,125 employees.

Production of iron and steel (in 1,000 tonnes):

	1971	*1972*	*1973*	*1974*	*1975*	*1976*
Crude steel	5,350·1	5,670·2	5,891·7	6,165·2	6,472·4	6,732·0
Pig-iron	2,027·4	2,150·6	2,201·6	2,280·1	2,455·5	2,527·9
Rolled steel	3,550·5	3,708·2	3,876·0	4,098·7	4,280·6	4,593·4

Leading chemical products in 1976 were (in 1,000 tonnes): Nitrogen fertilizers, 776; synthetic rubber, 145; sulphuric acid, 957; calcined soda, 829; caustic soda, 441; ammonia, 1,361; other industrial products: cement, 11,344; cotton fabrics, 274m. sq. metres; leather shoes, 42·8m. pairs; plastics and synthetic resins, 679.

The 340-km pipeline from Schwedt on the Oder to Leuna near Halle was completed in Jan. 1967; it carried Soviet oil direct to the industrial centre of the GDR. Total pipeline length within GDR (1976) 952 km.

Commerce. Total trade was as follows (in 1m. Valuta-Mark):

	Total Import	*Total Export*		*Total Import*	*Total Export*
1970	20,357·2	19,240·2	1973	27,330·3	26,171·4
1971	20,920·1	21,320·5	1974	33,569·5	30,443·2
1972	22,851·3	23,931·1	1975	39,289·0	35,104·6

In 1973 goods valued at 8,638m. Valuta-Mark came from, and 9,888·5m. went to, the USSR.

Total trade between the German Democratic Republic and UK (British Department of Trade returns, in £1,000 sterling):

	1972	*1973*	*1974*	*1975*	*1976*	*1977*
Imports to UK	21,644	26,318	44,552	38,826	60,299	95,446
Exports and re-exports from UK	14,974	13,656	39,100	32,495	44,811	54,440

COMMUNICATIONS

Roads. There were, in 1976, 47,530 km of classified roads. Road traffic amounted to 18,655m. ton-km of goods and 21,870m. passenger-km (by buses). Motor vehicles included, 2,052,240 passenger cars, 312,941 lorries, 3·54m. motor cycles and mopeds.

Railways. There were, in 1976, 14,306 km of railway line, of which 1,508 km were electrified. Traffic amounted to 51,792m. ton-km of goods and 21,955m. passenger-km.

Aviation. Interflug operates services between Berlin and Prague, Warsaw, Budapest, Bucharest, Moscow, Sofia, Belgrade, Tirana, Cairo, Baghdad, Beirut and other capitals. Passengers carried (1976), 1,087,800; freight, 25,054 tonnes.

Shipping. The port of Rostock is being reconstructed and enlarged so as to absorb the sea-going traffic of the German Democratic Republic and the Czechoslovak hinterland. Sea-going traffic in 1976 was 5,100 vessels of 15m. BRT. In 1976 navigable inland waterways had a length of 2,538 km; they handled 1,947m. ton-km of goods. The state-owned merchant fleet had, in 1976, 198 vessels of 1,211,898 BRT.

Post and Broadcasting. In 1976 there were 12,035 post offices and agencies and (1977) 2,750,597 telephone subscribers. *Staatliches Kommittee für Rundfunk*, the governmental broadcasting station, broadcasts 4 programmes on long-, medium- and short-waves, and on FM. The foreign service is broadcast in 11 languages on medium- and short-waves, using the name Radio Berlin International. The transmitters are located at Königswusterhausen, Leipzig and Nauen. Radio Volga transmits on long-waves from Burg and broadcasts in Russian for the Soviet Armed Forces in Germany. More than 80% of the programmes are relays from Radio Moscow. Radio Moscow is using relay transmitters on medium-waves at Leipzig for programmes in German. *Deutsche Freiheitssender 904* and *Deutsche Soldatensender* are clandestine stations claiming to be operating from the Federal Republic although they are located not far from Burg. *Fernsehen der DDR* broadcasts 2 TV programmes, of which the second broadcasts in colour, using SECAM-system. Number of wireless licences, 6·21m.; television licences, 5·35m.

Cinemas (1976). There were 833 cinemas with a seating capacity of 283,018.

Newspapers (1976). There were 39 daily newspapers with a combined circulation of 6·8m.

RELIGION, EDUCATION AND WELFARE

Religion. According to the census of 1950, 80·5% of the population were Protestants and 11% were Roman Catholics.

Education. There are 2 types of schools: (*a*) the General polytechnical secondary schools, with 10 grades (the former elementary and middle schools), numbering (1976) 5,037 with 2,532,924 pupils; (*b*) the Extended polytechnical secondary schools, with the 11th and 12th grades, numbering (1976) 284 with 47,562 pupils.

In addition there were (1976), 977 vocational schools (*Berufsschulen*) with 15,213 teachers and 433,600 pupils and 233 technical schools with 159,955 pupils. There were also 54 universities and other high schools with (1976 preliminary) 130,201 students, including 62,134 women.

Health. In 1976, 571 hospitals had 180,466 beds. There were 534 polyclinics each with at least 6 special branches. There were 32,097 physicians and 8,108 dentists.

Social Welfare. Expenditure for social welfare in state budget, M 3,066m., and social insurance, M 22,195m. in 1976.

DIPLOMATIC REPRESENTATIVES

OF THE GERMAN DEMOCRATIC REPUBLIC IN GREAT BRITAIN
(34 Belgrave Sq., London, SW1X 8QB)

Ambassador: Karl-Heinz Kern.

OF GREAT BRITAIN IN THE GERMAN DEMOCRATIC REPUBLIC
(108 Berlin, Unter den Linden 32/34)

Ambassador: P. M. Forster.

OF THE GERMAN DEMOCRATIC REPUBLIC IN THE USA
(1717 Massachusetts Ave., NW, Washington, D.C. 20036)

Ambassador: Dr Rolf Sieber.

OF THE USA IN THE GERMAN DEMOCRATIC REPUBLIC
(108 Berlin, Neustadtische Kirchstrasse 4-5)

Ambassador: David B. Bolen.

OF THE GERMAN DEMOCRATIC REPUBLIC TO THE UNITED NATIONS

Ambassador: Peter Florin.

Books of Reference

Statistical Information: The central statistical agency is the Staatliche Zentralverwaltung für Statistik (Hans-Beimler-Str. 70–72, 102, Berlin).

The Zentralverwaltung publishes: *Statistisches Jahrbuch der Deutschen Demokratischen Republik* (from 1956).—*Statistisches Taschenbuch der DDR* (annual, from 1959; also Arabic, English, French, Russian, Spanish editions).—*Statistische Praxis* (bi-monthly, from 1946).

Jahrbuch der Deutschen Demokratischen Republik, ed. Institut für Zeitgeschichte (latest issue, 1961).

Childs, D., *East Germany.* London, 1969

Krisch, H., *German Politics under Soviet Occupation.* New York and London, 1974

National Library: Deutsch Bücherei, Leipzig C.1. *Director:* Helmut Rötzsch.—Deutsche Staatsbibliothek, Berlin. *Director:* Professor H. Kunze.

FEDERAL REPUBLIC OF GERMANY

Bundesrepublik Deutschland

Capital: Bonn
Population: 61·44m. (1976)
GNP per capita: US$7,380 (1976)

HISTORY. The Federal Republic of Germany became a sovereign independent country on 5 May 1955 and is a member of EEC, the Council of Europe, Western European Union, NATO, the European Coal and Steel Community, Euratom, the European Monetary Agreement and the Agencies of the UN.

In June 1948 USA, UK and France agreed on a central government for the 3 western zones. An Occupation Statute, which came into force on 31 Sept. 1949, reduced the responsibilities of the occupation authorities. Formally, the Federal Republic of Germany came into existence on 21 Sept. 1949. The Petersberg Agreement of 22 Nov. 1949 freed the Federal Republic of numerous restrictions of the Occupation Statute. In 1951 USA, UK and France as well as other states terminated the state of war with Germany; the Soviet Union followed on 25 Jan. 1955. On 5 May 1955 the High Commissioners of USA, UK and France signed a proclamation revoking the Occupation Statute. On the same day, the Paris and London treaties, signed in Oct. 1954, came into force and established the sovereignty of the Federal Republic of Germany.

AREA AND POPULATION. On April 1949 some minor frontier rectifications were carried out in favour of the Netherlands (68 sq. km), Belgium (18 sq. km), Luxembourg (6 sq. km) and France (7 sq. km), subject to a final peace settlement. Belgium (1956) and the Netherlands (1963) returned most of this territory to Germany.

Area and estimated population as at 31 Dec. 1976:

Länder	*Area in sq. km.*	*Population Male*	*Female*	*Total*	*Per sq. km*
Schleswig-Holstein	15,696	1,239,200	1,343,500	2,582,700	165
Hamburg	747	788,000	910,600	1,698,600	2,273
Lower Saxony	47,423	3,456,400	3,770,500	7,226,900	152
Bremen	404	333,400	376,600	710,000	1,757
North Rhine-Westphalia	34,056	8,146,900	8,926,300	17,073,200	501
Hessen	21,112	2,657,100	2,881,300	5,538,400	262
Rhineland-Palatinate	19,838	1,740,500	1,908,500	3,649,000	184
Baden-Württemberg	35,751	4,374,100	4,745,200	9,119,300	255
Bavaria	70,547	5,147,300	5,656,900	10,804,200	153
Saarland	2,570	516,600	572,400	1,089,000	424
Berlin (West)	480	863,300	1,087,400	1,950,700	4,064
Federal Republic	*248,624* [1]	*29,262,800*	*32,179,200*	*61,442,000*	*247*

[1] 95,995 sq. miles.

Vital statistics for calendar years:

	Marriages	*Live births*	*Of these illegitimate*	*Deaths*	*Divorces*
1974	377,265	626,373	39,277	727,511	98,584
1975	386,681	600,512	36,774	749,260	106,829
1976 [1]	365,620	602,851	38,251	733,140	—

[1] Preliminary.

The annual rate of the population increase or decrease (including migration) was 0·8% in 1971; 0·5% in 1972; 0·5% in 1973; −0·2% in 1974; −0·6% in 1975; −0·3% in 1976.

Crude birth rate was 10·3 per 1,000 population; marriage rate, 6·4; death rate, 11·8; infantile mortality, 2·3 per 100 live births.

Migrants from Eastern Germany to the Federal Republic, including West Berlin, totalled about 2,022,000 between 1955 and 1961. The East German Government tried to stop the outflow by erecting a concrete wall which later became a heavily fortified barrier along the border in Berlin on 13 Aug. 1961; despite the Berlin wall, the figures registered for persons moving from Eastern Germany and East Berlin into the Federal Republic were 20,700 in 1967, 18,600 in 1968, 20,600 in 1969, 20,700 in 1970, 19,900 in 1971, 19,700 in 1972, 17,300 in 1973, 16,200 in 1974, 20,300 in 1975 and 17,100 in 1976; most of them are older people with permission to emigrate. Migrants from the Federal Republic to Eastern Germany totalled about 279,000 between 1955 and 1961, 4,300 in 1966, 3,600 in 1967, 2,900 in 1968, 2,500 in 1969, 2,100 in 1970, 1,900 in 1971, 1,800 in 1972, 1,700 in 1973, 1,500 in 1974, 1,400 in 1975 and 1,300 in 1976.

The resident population of the principal towns was estimated as follows on 31 Dec. 1976:

Town	*Land*	*Population*
Berlin (West)	Berlin (West)	1,950,706
Hamburg	Hamburg	1,698,615
München	Bavaria	1,314,572
Köln	N. Rhine-Westph.	981,021
Essen	N. Rhine-Westph.	670,221
Frankfurt (Main)	Hessen	626,251
Dortmund	N. Rhine-Westph.	623,677
Düsseldorf	N. Rhine-Westph.	615,494
Stuttgart	Baden-Württ.	590,135
Duisburg	N. Rhine-Westph.	581,971
Bremen	Bremen	568,217
Hannover	Lower Saxony	547,077
Nürnberg	Bavaria	492,447
Bochum	N. Rhine-Westph.	412,889
Wuppertal	N. Rhine-Westph.	401,609
Gelsenkirchen	N. Rhine-Westph.	317,980
Bielefeld	N. Rhine-Westph.	314,258
Mannheim	Baden-Württ.	309,059
Bonn	N. Rhine-Westph.	284,957
Karlsruhe	Baden-Württ.	276,620
Braunschweig	Lower Saxony	267,124
Münster (Westf.)	N. Rhine-Westph.	266,083
Mönchengladbach	N. Rhine-Westph.	260,076
Kiel	Schleswig-H.	259,403
Wiesbaden	Hessen	249,199
Augsburg	Bavaria	246,193
Aachen	N. Rhine-Westph.	242,701
Oberhausen	N. Rhine-Westph.	234,580
Lübeck	Schleswig-H.	230,407
Hagen	N. Rhine-Westph.	226,301
Krefeld	N. Rhine-Westph.	226,042
Saarbrücken	Saarland	203,429
Kassel	Hessen	201,705
Herne	N. Rhine-Westph.	188,357
Mülheim a.d. Ruhr	N. Rhine-Westph.	187,677
Mainz	Rhinel.-Pal.	183,911
Freiburg im Breisgau	Baden-Württ.	175,044
Hamm	N. Rhine-Westph.	171,765
Solingen	N. Rhine-Westph.	169,584
Ludwigshafen am Rhein	Rhinel.-Pal.	166,083
Leverkusen	N. Rhine-Westph.	164,754
Osnabrück	Lower Saxony	160,242
Neuss	N. Rhine-Westph.	148,790
Bremerhaven	Bremen	141,755
Darmstadt	Hessen	135,823
Oldenburg	Lower Saxony	134,611
Remscheid	N. Rhine-Westph.	131,528
Regensburg	Bavaria	130,346
Heidelberg	Baden-Württ.	129,361
Wolfsburg	Lower Saxony	126,511
Göttingen	Lower Saxony	123,932
Recklinghausen	N. Rhine-Westph.	121,583
Koblenz	Rhinel.-Pal.	116,960
Siegen	N. Rhine-Westph.	116,060
Würzburg	Bavaria	115,946
Salzgitter	Lower Saxony	115,925
Bottrop	N. Rhine-Westph.	115,724
Offenbach (Main)	Hessen	113,141
Heilbronn	Baden-Württ.	112,411
Pforzheim	Baden-Württ.	107,877
Witten	N. Rhine-Westph.	107,722
Paderborn	N. Rhine-Westph.	105,809
Hildesheim	Lower Saxony	104,278
Wilhelmshaven	Lower Saxony	102,539
Erlangen	Bavaria	101,057
Moers	N. Rhine-Westph.	100,893
Kaiserslautern	Rhinel.-Pal.	100,383

CONSTITUTION. The Constituent Assembly (known as the 'Parliamentary Council') met in Bonn on 1 Sept. 1948, and worked out a Basic Law which was approved by a two-thirds majority of the parliaments of the participating Länder and came into force on 23 May 1949.

The Basic Law (*Grundgesetz*) consists of a preamble and 146 articles. The first section deals with the basic rights which are legally binding for legislation, administration and jurisdiction.

The Federal Republic of Germany is a democratic and social federal state. For the time being the Basic Law applies to the Länder Baden-Württemberg, Bavaria, Bremen, Greater Berlin (temporarily suspended), Hamburg, Hessen, Lower Saxony, North Rhine-Westphalia, Rhineland-Palatinate, Saarland and Schleswig-Holstein. The Basic Law decrees that the general rules of international law form part of the federal law. The constitutions of the Länder must conform to the principles of a republican, democratic and social state based on the rule of law. Executive power is vested in the Länder, unless the Basic Law prescribes or permits otherwise. Federal law supersedes Land law.

The organs of the Federal Republic are:

The Federal Diet (*Bundestag*), elected in universal, direct, free, equal and secret elections, for a term of 4 years.

The Federal Council (*Bundesrat*), consisting of members of the governments of the Länder. Each Land has at least 3 votes. Länder with more than 2m. inhabitants have 4, Länder with more than 6m. inhabitants have 5 votes.

The Federal President (*Bundespräsident*) is elected by the Federal Assembly for a term of 5 years and represents the Federal Republic in international relations. Re-election is admissible only once. The Federal Assembly (which meets only for the election of the Federal President) consists of the members of the Federal Diet and an equal number of members elected by the popular representative bodies of the Länder according to a particular system of semi-proportional representation.

The Federal Government consists of the Federal Chancellor, elected by the Federal Diet on the proposal of the Federal President, and the Federal Ministers, who are appointed and dismissed by the Federal President upon the proposal of the Federal Chancellor.

The Federal Republic has exclusive legislation on: (1) foreign affairs; (2) federal citizenship; (3) freedom of movement, passports, immigration and emigration, and extradition; (4) currency, money and coinage, weights and measures, and regulation of time and calendar; (5) customs, commercial and navigation agreements, traffic in goods and payments with foreign countries, including customs and frontier protection; (6) federal railways and air traffic; (7) post and telecommunications; (8) the legal status of persons in the employment of the Federation and of public law corporations under direct supervision of the Federal Government; (9) trade marks, copyright and publishing rights; (10) co-operation of the Federal Republic and the Länder in the criminal police and in matters concerning the protection of the constitution, the establishment of a Federal Office of Criminal Police, as well as the combating of international crime; (11) federal statistics.

For concurrent legislation in which the Länder have legislative rights if and as far as the Federal Republic does not exercise its legislative powers, *see* THE STATESMAN'S YEAR-BOOK, 1956, p. 1038.

Federal laws are passed by the Federal Diet and after their adoption submitted to the Federal Council, which has a limited veto. The Basic Law may be amended only upon the approval of two-thirds of the members of the Federal Diet and two-thirds of the votes of the Federal Council.

The foreign service, federal finance, railways, postal services, waterways and shipping are under direct federal administration.

In the field of finance the Federal Republic has exclusive legislation on customs and financial monopolies and concurrent legislation on: (1) excise taxes and taxes on transactions, in particular, taxes on real-estate acquisition, incremented value and on fire protection; (2) taxes on income, property, inheritance and donations; (3) real estate, industrial and trade taxes, with the exception of the determining of the tax rates.

Customs, the yield of monopolies, excise taxes with the exception of the beer tax, the transportation tax, the turnover tax and property dues serving non-recurrent purposes accrue to the Federal Republic. The Federal Republic can, by federal law, claim part of the income and corporation taxes to cover its expenditures not covered by other revenues. Financial jurisdiction is uniformly regulated by federal legislation.

National flag: Three horizontal stripes of black, red, gold.

National anthem: Einigkeit und Recht und Freiheit (words by H. Hoffmann, 1841; tune by J. Haydn, 1797).

Hiscocks, R., *Democracy in Western Germany*. OUP, 1957
Mangoldt, H., *Das Bonner Grundgesetz* (*Kommentar*). 2nd ed. Berlin, 1960
Maunz, Th., *Deutsches Staatsrecht*. 12th ed. Munich, 1963
Schäfer, H., *Der Bundesrat*. Cologne, 1955

GOVERNMENT. The *Federal Diet*, elected on 3 Oct. 1976, is composed of 496 members. In addition, there are 22 members for Berlin (11 CDU, 10 SPD, 1 FDP), who, however, have no vote.

State of the parties: Social Democrats (SPD), 214 (1972: 230); Christian Democrats (CDU; CSU), 243 (225); Free Democrats (FDP), 39 (41); other parties failed to obtain 5% of the votes or to elect a representative in a constituency, and therefore returned no members.

Bonn on the Rhine is the capital of the Federal Republic.

Federal President: Walter Scheel (elected 15 May 1974).

The cabinet, a coalition of Social Democrats and Free Democrats, on 3 Feb. 1978, was as follows:

Chancellor: Helmut Schmidt (SPD).
Deputy Chancellor, Minister of Foreign Affairs: Hans-Dietrich Genscher (FDP).
Interior: Werner Maihofer (FDP).
Justice: Hans-Jochen Vogel (SPD).
Finance: Hans Matthöfer (SPD).
Economics: Dr Otto Graf Lambsdorff (FDP).
Food, Agriculture and Forests: Josef Ertl (FDP).
Labour and Social Affairs: Herbert Ehrenberg (SPD).
Defence: Hans Apel (SPD).
Family Affairs: Antje Huber (SPD).
Transport, Posts and Telecommunications: Kurt Gscheidle (SPD).
State and Town Planning, and Housing: Dieter Haack (SPD).
Internal German Relations: Egon Franke (SPD).
Research and Technology: Volker Hauff (SPD).
Education and Science: Jürgen Schmude (SPD).
Economic Co-operation: Rainer Offergeld (SPD).

DEFENCE. The Paris Treaties, which entered into force in May 1955, stipulated a contribution of the Federal Republic to western defence within the framework of NATO and the Western European Union. In 1977 the Federal Armed Forces (*Bundeswehr*) had a total strength of 489,000 all ranks (235,000 conscripts).

Army. In 1978 the Army consisted of 16 armoured brigades, 12 armoured infantry brigades, 3 Jager brigades, 2 mountain brigades, 3 airborne brigades; total strength 341,000.

The principal combat unit is still the Brigade, however, under the 'Brigade 80' concept the number of battalions per brigade goes up, although the number of men per battalion comes down. The armoured brigade has 3,026 men and the armoured infantry 3,730. The main emphasis of the concept is to improve the anti-armour capability and the brigades will have to look to the divisional troops for reconnaissance, artillery and air-defence support in points of main effort. The Army is at present converting to the 'Brigade 80' concept. There are 3 corps and 12 divisions, each of 3 brigades. The Army has 1,400 M-48A2 Patton and 2,400 Leopard I medium tanks with a further 1,000 Leopard II tanks on order; 7,700 armoured personnel carriers; 1,400 artillery pieces; 70 *Honest John*, 20 *Sergeant* and 26 *Lance* surface-to-surface missiles.

Territorial Army. The Territorial Army lies outside the Authority of Supreme Commander NATO, but is tasked with securing the freedom of manoeuvre of NATO forces under national command as well as protecting points of military relevance. There are 3 Territorial Commands and 6 Home Defence Groups. Peacetime strength, 63,000.

Navy. At the end of 1977 the Navy had 24 diesel-powered coastal submarines, 1 old experimental oceangoing submarine, 3 guided missile armed destroyers, 8 other destroyers, 6 frigates, 6 corvettes, 30 fast missile boats (Exocet armed) of 234–295 tons, 10 fast torpedo boats, a light cruiser type training ship, 13 escort and support ships, 18 coastal minesweepers and minehunters, 22 fast minesweepers, 18 inshore minesweepers, 41 landing craft, 13 supply ships, 11 replenishment ships and oilers, 7 coast patrol ships, 8 coastguard cutters, 3 repair ships and 92 auxiliaries and service craft.

The new construction programme includes 10 large hydrofoil patrol (missile) vessels (202 tons). The project to build 4 guided missile frigates was cancelled, but 4 (initially, to replace old *ex*-US destroyers) and eventually 12 (to replace 'Hamburg' class destroyers and 'Köln' class frigates) of 2,500 tons are projected under a future development programme.

The Naval Air Arm has 2 wings (each 2 squadrons of 18 aircraft) of F-104G Starfighters and 1 wing of Breguet Atlantic maritime patrol bombers, supplemented by an anti-submarine helicopter wing. Albatross amphibians and Do 27 aircraft from an air-sea rescue wing.

Navy personnel in 1978 totalled 38,300 officers and men, including 6,000 of the Naval Air Arm.

Air Force. Since Oct. 1970, the *Luftwaffe* has comprised the following commands: German Air Force Tactical Command, German Air Force Support Command (including two German Air Force Regional Support Commands—North and South) and General Air Force Office. Its strength in mid-1977 was approximately 110,000 officers and other ranks and about 500 first-line combat aircraft. Combat units, including 12 heavy fighter-bomber squadrons, 5 light ground attack/reconnaissance squadrons, 4 reconnaissance squadrons, 8 missile squadrons, and an air defence force of 4 interceptor squadrons, 24 batteries of *Nike-Hercules* and 34 batteries of *Hawk* surface-to-air missiles, are assigned to NATO. There are 4 F-4F Phantom interceptor squadrons, 8 F-104G fighter-bomber squadrons, 4 attack squadrons of F-4Fs, 4 RF-4E Phantom reconnaissance squadrons and 4 light attack/reconnaissance squadrons of Fiat G 91s (to be replaced with Alpha Jets). Five transport squadrons (each 15 aircraft) with turboprop Transall C-160 aircraft and 1 wing of 4 helicopter squadrons with UH-1D Iroquois add to the air mobility of the *Bundeswehr*. There are also VIP, support and light transport aircraft, and Piaggio P.149D initial training aircraft. Guided weapons in service include 2 wings of *Pershing* surface-to-surface missiles and 6 battalions of *Nike-Hercules* and 9 battalions of *Hawk* surface-to-air missiles.

All F-104 and Phantom pilots undergo basic and advanced training in USA.

INTERNATIONAL RELATIONS

Membership. The Federal Republic of Germany is a member of UN, OECD, EEC, NATO and the Council of Europe.

External Debt. On 27 Feb. 1953 several agreements were signed in London settling Germany's external pre-war and post-war debts. These agreements entered into force on 16 Sept. 1953.

The claims arising from the post-war economic assistance given to Germany by the UK (£201·8m.), France (US$15·79m.) and the USA (US$3,014m.) were fixed at £150m., US$11·84m. and US$1,000m. respectively, of which only the claims of the USA bear interest at $2\frac{1}{2}$%. Up to March 1961 the claims were paid off by regular and premature redemption as follows: Great Britain except for £67·5m., France except for US$5,328,000 and the USA except for US$787·37m. In April/May 1961 the Deutsche Bundesbank repaid on behalf of the Federal Republic the total claims of Great Britain and France and the amount of US$587m. to the USA. The debt still outstanding on 30 Dec. 1966 (US$195·94m.) was also repaid by the Deutsche Bundesbank on behalf of the Federal Republic.

On 31 Dec. 1968 the London Debts Agreement of 27 Feb. 1953 was in force in a total of 56 foreign countries. 90% of all debts were claims of the USA, Great Britain, France and Switzerland.

Of the approximately DM 4,000m. of public pre-war debts, the sum of DM

1,705m. and of the approximately DM 2,200m. of private pre-war debts the amount of DM 253m. had still to be paid back on 31 Dec. 1968.

ECONOMY

Budget. The budget of the Federal Government shows the following figures (in DM 1m.) for calendar years:

	1974	*1975*	*1976*	*1977*[1]
Revenues				
Federal taxes and customs duties	34,551	33,611	35,647	37,295
Share of Federal Government in joint taxes and trade tax levy	84,112	85,600	95,253	108,105
Tax-like charges	11	2	—	—
Others	4,113	3,945	4,884	4,763
Total revenue	122,787	123,157	135,784	150,163
Expenditures				
Defence	30,674	32,101	33,300	34,638
Social security	38,056	57,051[2]	59,188	62,340
Agriculture and food	2,183	2,255	1,919	2,019
Transport and communications	11,005	11,468	11,491	12,037
Electricity, gas, water supply, industries and services	3,205	3,257	2,567	3,739
Education and science	7,500	8,476	8,450	8,907
Housing and settlements	1,696	1,714	2,046	2,080
All other expenditure	38,935	39,942	42,711	45,546
Total expenditure	133,251	156,262	161,672	171,306
Balance of transitory means	+ 126	+ 23	+ 31	—
Net financing balance	−10,337	−33,083	−25,856	−21,143
Financed from:				
Loans	−15,329	−36,754	−46,316	−35,401
Coinage	− 252	− 805	− 74	− 450
Less:				
Redemption payments	+ 5,854	+ 6,829	+20,533	+14,708
Withdrawals from reserves	− 610	− 2,354	—	—

[1] Provisional.
[2] Not completely comparable with previous years.

The total debt of the Federal Republic, the Equalization of Burdens Fund, ERP-Special Fund and the Länder was DM 82,971m., as at 31 Dec. 1969.

Currency. Pursuant to the laws issued on the monetary reform by the military governors of the British, American, and French Zones, from 18 to 26 June 1948, the 'Reichmark' was replaced by the 'Deutsche Mark'. The RM notes circulated by the former Reichsbank were exchanged for DMs at the rate of 1 to 1 up to the amount of RM 60, and all amounts exceeding RM 600 as well as all bank and saving deposits at the ratio of RM 100 to DM 6·5. All RM liabilities, including securities, were depreciated at the ratio of 10 to 1.

On 31 Aug. 1977 the circulation of coins in the Federal Republic amounted to DM 5,958m.; that of notes and coins to DM 68,597m.

The rate of exchange for DM (West) was fixed at 3·66 to the US$ from 26 Oct. 1969, and at 8·78 to the £ after the revaluation of DM in Oct. 1969.

Banking. On 14 Feb. 1948 the Bank of German Länder (Bank deutscher Länder) was established in Frankfurt as the central bank of issue for the Federal Republic and designated the exclusive agency for issuing notes and coins.

The Land Central Banks and the Berlin Central Bank were merged with the Bank deutscher Länder as from 1 Aug. 1957. The Bank deutscher Länder became the Deutsche Bundesbank.

The most important items of the balance sheets of the Deutsche Bundesbank in Frankfurt on 31 Aug. 1977 were as follows (in DM 1m.):

Assets	
Gold	14,034·4
Balances at foreign banks and money market investments abroad	52,711·9
Foreign notes, coins, bills and cheques	1,686·0
Loans to international institutions and consolidation loans	11,760·2
Domestic bills of exchange and advances against securities	18,149·6
Equalization claims [1]	8,136·3
Liabilities	
Bank-notes in circulation	62,639·3
Deposits	64,804·0

[1] From the monetary reform.

Weights and Measures. The metric system is in force.

ENERGY AND NATURAL RESOURCES

Electricity. In 1976, 336,651m. kwh. were produced.

Oil. In 1976, 17,573 tonnes of petroleum and 9,768 tonnes of diesel oil were produced.

Minerals. The great bulk of the minerals in Germany is produced in North Rhine-Westphalia (for coal, iron and metal smelting-works), Central Germany (for brown coal), Lower Saxony (Salzgitter for iron ore; the Harz for metal ore). The chief oilfields are in Lower Saxony (Emsland).

The quantities of the principal minerals raised in the Federal Republic were as follows (in 1,000 tonnes):

Minerals	*1971*	*1972*	*1973*	*1974*	*1975*	*1976*
Coal	110,795	102,470	97,339	94,876	92,393	89,269
Lignite	104,478	110,415	118,658	126,044	123,377	134,535
Iron ore	6,391	6,117	6,429	5,671	4,273	3,034
Metal ore	1,448	1,507	1,385	995	1,032	1,034
Potash	22,306	23,023	24,950	26,202	22,006	20,815
Crude oil	7,420	7,098	6,638	6,191	5,741	5,524

The production of iron and steel in the Federal Republic was (in 1,000 tonnes):

	1971	*1972*	*1973*	*1974*	*1975*	*1976*
Pig-iron	29,990	32,002	36,828	40,221	30,074	31,849
Steel ingots and castings	40,313	43,705	49,521	53,232	40,415	42,415
Rolled products finished	28,717	31,192	36,706	39,615	29,487	30,398

Agriculture. The agricultural area of Germany within the boundaries of 1937 comprised 28·5m. hectares, of which 13·5m. are now situated in the Federal Republic. In 1976 the arable land within the Federal Republic was 7,532,000 hectares; meadows and pastures, 5,219,000 hectares; gardens, vineyards, orchards, nurseries, 518,000.

The total number of agricultural holdings (with an agricultural area of 0·5 hectare or more) in the Federal Republic, and their classification by size, according to the agricultural area, were as follows (spring 1976):

	Total	*0·5–5 hectares*	*5–20 hectares*	*20–100 hectares*	*Over 100 hectares*
Schleswig-Holstein	38,645	9,789	7,586	20,315	955
Hamburg	2,146	1,518	360	259	9
Lower Saxony	153,586	56,804	44,049	51,346	1,387
Bremen	701	338	119	242	2
North Rhine-Westphalia	130,933	56,284	42,583	31,552	514
Hessen	84,337	42,426	28,888	12,810	213
Rhineland-Palatinate	82,974	41,864	29,262	11,751	97
Baden-Württemberg	195,746	107,005	67,901	20,595	245
Bavaria	321,713	113,919	157,354	49,900	540
Saarland	9,573	6,289	1,902	1,352	30
Berlin (West)	252	181	42	29	—
Federal Republic	*1,020,606*	*436,417*	*380,046*	*200,151*	*3,992*

There were a further 8m. households with a total area of less than 0·5 hectare used for horticultural, agricultural or forestry purposes (1% microcensus April 1970).

Area (in 1,000 hectares) and yield (in 1,000 tonnes) of the main crops in the Federal Republic, were as follows:

	Area				Yield			
	1974	*1975*	*1976*	*1977*[1]	*1974*	*1975*	*1976*	*1977*[1]
Wheat	1,631	1,569	1,632	1,589	7,761	7,014	6,702	7,126
Rye	708	624	663	701	2,559	2,125	2,100	2,549
Barley	1,665	1,756	1,735	1,791	7,048	6,971	6,487	7,548
Oats	851	920	855	795	3,482	3,445	2,497	2,740
Potatoes	467	415	415	396	14,548	10,853	9,808	11,347
Sugar-beet	369	426	440	427	16,499	18,203	18,011	19,385

[1] Preliminary results.

Wine must production (in 1m. hectolitres): 7·4 in 1960; 6·1 in 1967; 6 in 1968; 5·9 in 1969; 9·9 in 1970; 6 in 1971; 7·5 in 1972; 10·7 in 1973; 6·8 in 1974; 9·2 in 1975; 8·7 in 1976.

Livestock on 3 Dec. 1976 were as follows: Cattle, 14,496,400 (including 5,387,400 milch cows); horses, 355,000; sheep, 1,091,300; pigs, 20,589,200; goats, 38,000 (1973); poultry, 90,461,200.

Forestry. Forestry is an industry of great importance, conducted under the care of the State on scientific methods. The forest area of Germany within the boundaries of 1937 was 12·9m. hectares, of which 7·2m. are now in the Federal Republic. In 1976 cuttings amounted to 29m. cu. metres in the Federal Republic.

Fisheries. In 1976 the yield of sea and coastal fishing in the Federal Republic was 426,000 tonnes live weight, valued at DM 437m.

At the end of 1976 the number of vessels of the fishing fleet was 66 trawlers (114,011 gross tons), 5 luggers and 720 cutters.

INDUSTRY AND TRADE

Industry. In 1976, 51,071 establishments (with 10 and more employees) in the Federal Republic employed 7,428,331 persons; of these 1,002,288 were employed in machine construction; 341,707 in textile industry; 964,543 in electrical engineering; 246,584 in mining; 571,367 in chemical industry.

The production of important industrial products in the Federal Republic was as follows:

Products	*1973*	*1974*	*1975*	*1976*
Aluminium (1,000 tonnes)	533	689	678	697
Potassium fertilizers, K_2O (1,000 tonnes)	2,548	2,620	2,222	1,925
Sulphuric acid, SO_3 (1,000 tonnes)[1]	4,138	4,188	3,394	3,811
Soda, Na_2CO_3 (1,000 tonnes)[1]	1,422	1,456	1,249	1,364
Cement (1,000 tonnes)[1]	41,011	35,977	36,500	34,155
Rayon:				
Staple fibre (1,000 tonnes)	98	99	63	75
Continuous rayon filament (1,000 tonnes)[1]	71	74	53	71
Cotton yarn (1,000 tonnes)[1]	215	214	192	208
Woollen yarn (1,000 tonnes)[1]	65	55	51	60
Passenger cars (1,000)[2]	3,643	2,840	2,905	3,548
Commercial cars and buses (1,000)	292	246	267	310
Bicycles (1,000)	2,604	2,444	2,466	2,845

[1] Including the quantities processed in the same factories.
[2] Including dual-purpose vehicles.

Fachserie 4 Produzierendes Gewerbe. Ed. Statistisches Bundesamt, Wiesbaden
Gutmann, G., and others. *Die Wirtschaftsverfassung der Bundesrepublik*. Stuttgart, 1964

Labour. The economically active persons (excluding the armed forces) totalled 25,752,000 at the 1%-sample survey of the microcensus of May 1976. Of the total, 2·33m. were self-employed, 1,188,000 unpaid family workers and 22,234,000 dependently employed persons. 1,612,000 were engaged in agriculture and forestry; 11,741,000 in power supply, mining, manufacturing and building; 4·62m. in commerce and transport; 7·78m. in other industries and services; 944,000 were unemployed.

In June 1976 foreign workers numbered 1,937,000, including 527,000 Turks, 390,000 Yugoslavs, 276,000 Italians, 179,000 Greeks, 111,000 Spaniards.

Commerce. The distribution of the imports and exports of the Federal Republic according to principal countries was as follows (in DM 1m.):

	Imports			*Exports*		
Country	*1974*	*1975*	*1976*	*1974*	*1975*	*1976*
Argentina	721·1	633·2	892·1	1,044·7	795·5	873·4
Australia	1,055·1	2,280·0	1,537·9	1,965·3	1,482·4	1,781·9
Austria	3,516·2	3,788·3	5,149·7	10,152·1	9,824·3	12,543·8
Belgium–Luxembourg	15,917·2	15,742·6	19,102·1	17,583·6	16,866·4	20,266·3
Brazil	2,016·1	2,211·4	2,414·6	3,862·3	2,946·5	2,736·9
Canada	1,998·4	1,754·2	2,321·6	1,893·3	1,915·3	2,018·0
Denmark	2,455·0	2,786·2	3,321·6	4,638·3	4,635·2	6,647·9
Finland	1,212·2	1,174·9	1,557·2	2,539·0	2,413·3	2,494·3
France	20,898·2	22,147·3	25,830·6	27,344·8	25,962·3	33,665·6
Greece	1,368·0	1,691·4	1,931·1	2,204·4	2,682·5	2,695·2
India	418·4	482·9	750·1	894·7	862·6	922·1
Iran	3,198·2	3,634·9	4,982·5	2,933·5	5,192·0	5,758·1
Italy	14,975·6	17,227·7	18,900·2	18,730·8	16,190·4	18,998·1
Japan	3,477·9	4,294·9	5,437·4	3,243·6	2,350·5	2,796·2
Libya	4,247·9	3,446·7	5,272·3	1,035·2	1,321·0	1,314·9
Netherlands	25,219·0	25,730·6	30,585·0	23,470·3	22,192·3	24,845·4
Norway	1,816·4	1,870·3	2,358·2	2,980·0	3,488·5	3,955·1
South Africa	1,944·5	2,178·7	2,254·4	3,640·8	3,389·6	3,149·0
Spain	2,142·7	2,169·6	2,753·2	4,339·8	3,764·7	4,338·0
Sweden	4,280·4	4,252·7	4,705·9	7,873·3	8,097·7	9,027·1
Switzerland	4,878·8	5,471·4	6,964·5	11,535·6	9,567·7	11,576·9
USSR	3,269·2	3,240·2	4,357·1	4,773·7	6,948·2	6,755·0
UK	6,266·8	6,939·3	8,539·1	11,011·0	10,094·8	12,184·1
USA	13,971·5	14,226·4	17,555·6	17,342·7	13,146·4	14,412·6

The main items of imports in 1976 were finished manufactures (US$32,269m.) and raw materials (US$14,369m.); exports, finished manufactures (US$69,193m.) and semi-finished manufactures (US$18,157m.).

Fachserie 7 Aussenhandel. Ed. Statistisches Bundesamt, Wiesbaden

Total trade between the Federal Republic of Germany and UK (British Department of Trade returns, in £1,000 sterling):

	1973	*1974*	*1975*	*1976*	*1977*
Imports to UK	1,351,236	1,892,651	1,996,903	2,757,025	3,574,241
Exports and re-exports from UK	785,167	1,011,271	1,272,446	1,834,438	2,501,120

Tourism. In 1976 there were 7·9m. tourists spending DM 8,083m.

COMMUNICATIONS

Roads. On 1 Jan. 1976 the total length of classified roads in the Federal Republic was 169,146 km, including 6,213 km *autobahn*, 32,490 km federal highways, 65,484 km first-class and 64,959 km second-class country roads. Motor vehicles licensed in the Federal Republic on 1 July 1976 numbered 22,108,084 (including 291,858 motor cycles, 18,919,738 passenger cars, 1,122,372 trucks, 62,118 buses and 1,582,519 tractors; not including 220,253 motor cycles and motor vehicles up to 50 cm³ cylinder capacity and 1,848,548 mopeds).

Road casualties in 1976 totalled 480,581 injured and 14,820 killed.

Railways. The total operative length of railway line in the Federal Republic was 31,817 km (28,576 Federal Railway, 3,241 private railways) on 31 Dec. 1976; of these, 10,349 km were electrified. In 1976 the railways (including ships owned by the Federal Railways) carried 971m. passengers and 326m. tonnes of freight.

Aviation. The Deutsche Lufthansa AG (set up on 6 Jan. 1953, as AG für Luftverkehrsbedarf and renamed on 6 Aug. 1954), with headquarters at Cologne, has capital of DM 600m. The Federal Republic owns 74·3%, Land North Rhine-Westphalia 2·2%, the Federal Railways, 0·9%, Federal Post 1·8%, Kreditanstalt für Wiederaufbau 3% and private industry 17·8%.

Lufthansa operate internal, European, African, North and South Atlantic, Near and Far East routes. In 1976 the Lufthansa carried 11·2m. passengers, 304,927 tonnes of cargo and 43,104 tonnes of mail.

Shipping. On 31 Dec. 1976 the Federal German mercantile marine comprised 1,757 ocean-going vessels of 9,036,209 BRT.

The inland-waterways fleet in the Federal Republic on 31 Dec. 1976 comprised 4·21m. tons. The length of the navigable rivers and canals in use was 4,283 km.

Sea-going ships (foreign trade only) in 1976 loaded 29m. tonnes clearing and unloaded 110·9m. tonnes entering in the ports of the Federal Republic. Inland waterways carried 230m. tonnes in 1976.

Post and Broadcasting. The Federal Republic had, on 31 Dec. 1975, 21,320 post and telecommunications offices. Number of telephones (1977), 21,161,787.

The postal bus services covered, in 1975, 225m. km and carried 428m. passengers.

The post office savings banks had, on 31 Dec. 1975, 17,526,000 depositors with DM 19,405m. to their credit.

In the financial year 1975 the postal revenues amounted to DM 28,825m. and the expenditure to DM 26,738m.

Arbeitsgemeinschaft der öffentlich-rechtlichen Rundfunkanstalten der Bundesrepublik Deutschland (ARD) is an organization for co-operation between the German broadcasting stations. ARD also broadcast a common TV programme under the name *Deutsches Fernsehen* throughout the Federal Republic. In addition regional programmes are broadcast. Number of wireless licences, 19,558,000; of television licences, 17,796,000.

Cinemas (31 Dec. 1976). There were 3,016 cinemas with a seating capacity of 1·05m. and 19 drive-in cinemas for 18,382 cars.

Newspapers (1976). There were 413 daily newspapers with a combined circulation of 25m.

JUSTICE, RELIGION, EDUCATION AND WELFARE

Justice. Justice is administered by the federal courts and by the courts of the Länder. In criminal procedures, civil cases and procedures of non-contentious jurisdiction the courts on the Land level are the local courts (*Amtsgerichte*), the regional courts (*Landgerichte*) and the courts of appeal (*Oberlandesgerichte*). On the federal level decisions regarding these matters are taken by the Federal Court (*Bundesgerichtshof*) at Karlsruhe. In labour law disputes the courts of the first and second instance are the labour courts and the Land labour courts and in the third instance, the Federal Labour Court (*Bundesarbeitsgericht*) at Kassel. Disputes about public law in matters of social security, unemployment insurance, maintenance of war victims and similar cases are dealt with in the first and second instances by the social courts and the Land social courts and in the third instance by the Federal Social Court (*Bundessozialgericht*) at Kassel. In most tax matters the finance courts of the Länder are competent and in the second instance, the Federal Finance Court (*Bundesfinanzhof*) at Munich. Other controversies of public law in non-constitutional matters are decided in the first and second instance by the administrative and the higher administrative courts (*Observerwaltungsgerichte*) of the Länder, and in the third instance by the Federal Administrative Court (*Bundesverwaltungsgericht*) at Berlin.

For the inquiry into maritime accidents the admiralty courts (*Seeämter*) are competent on the Land level and in the second instance the Federal Admiralty Court (*Bundesoberseeamt*) at Hamburg.

The constitutional courts of the Länder decide on constitutional questions. The Federal Constitutional Court (*Bundesverfassungsgericht*) as the supreme German court decides such questions as loss of basic rights, unconstitutional character of political parties, validity of laws, charges against judges and complaints regarding violations of basic rights by the public force.

The death sentence is abolished.

Religion. Of the population 49% are Protestants, 44·6% Roman Catholics and 0·1% Jews (census, 1970).

The Evangelical Church in Germany consists of 17 member-churches in the Federal Republic of Germany and West Berlin (10 Lutheran Churches, 5 United-Lutheran-Reformed-Churches, 2 Reformed Churches and 1 Confederation of United member Churches: 'Church of the Union'). Its organs are the Synod, the Church Conference and the Council under the chairmanship of Bishop D. Helmut Class (elected 2 June 1973). The Protestants numbered about 27·2m. in 1976. There are also some 12 Evangelical Free Churches. The 8 territorial churches in German Democratic Republic established the Federation of Evangelical Churches in 1969.

There are 5 Roman Catholic archbishops and 17 bishoprics. Chairman of the Bishops' Conference is Cardinal Höffner, Archbishop of Cologne. A concordat between Germany and the Holy See was signed on 20 July and ratified on 10 Sept. 1933.

The 'Old Catholics', who are in full communion with the Anglican Churches, numbered about 30,000 in 1977; they have a bishop at Bonn.

Kirchliches Jahrbuch für die Evangelische Kirche in Deutschland. Gütersloh, 1884 ff.
Taschenbuch der evangelischen Kirche in Deutschland. Stuttgart,1974
Kirchliches Handbuch. Amtliches statistisches Jahrbuch der Katholischen Kirche Deutschlands. Vol. 28. Cologne, 1976
Alt-Katholisches Jahrbuch. Bonn, 1978
Luckey, G., *Free Churches in Germany.* Bad Nauheim, 1956
Katholiken und ihre Kirche, Protestanten und ihre Kirche. Munich, 1977

Education. Schools providing general education are primary and post-primary schools (*Grund- und Hauptschulen*), special schools (*Sonderschulen*), secondary modern schools (*Realschulen*), grammar schools (*Gymnasien*) and comprehensive schools. Primary schools: Attendance is compulsory for all children having completed their 6th year of age. Compulsory education extends 9 years. After the first 4 (or 6) years at primary school children may attend post-primary schools, secondary modern schools, grammar schools and other schools of general secondary education. The secondary modern school comprises 6, the grammar school 9 years. The final Grammar School Certificate (Arbitur-Higher School Certificate) entitles the holder to enter any institution of higher education. There are also special schools for retarded, physically or mentally handicapped and socially maladjusted children.

In 1976 there were in the Federal Republic 18,255 primary and post-primary schools with 6,287,642 pupils; 2,696 special schools with 398,190 pupils, 2,450 secondary modern schools with 1,218,653 pupils; 2,407 grammar schools with 1,910,617 pupils; 232 comprehensive schools (primary and secondary stage) with 201,889 pupils.

Vocational education is provided in part-time, full-time and advanced vocational schools (*Berufs-*, *Berufsaufbau-*, *Berufsfach-* and *Fachschulen*, including *Fachschulen für Technik* and *Schulen des Gesundheitswesens*). Running parallel to the occupation, part-time vocational schools offer 6 to 12 hours per week of additional compulsory schooling. All young people who are apprentices, in some other employment or even unemployed have to attend them in general up to the age of 18 years or until the completion of the practical vocational training. Full-time vocational schools comprise courses of at least one year. They prepare for commercial and domestic occupations as well as specialized occupations in the field of handicrafts. Advanced full-time vocational schools are attended by pupils having completed their 18th year of age; courses vary from 6 months to 3 or more years.

In Nov. 1975 there were 5,802 full- and part-time vocational schools with 24,337 teachers (9,622 female) and 2,082,843 pupils (898,670 female); 4,318 full-time vocational schools with 461,692 pupils (251,215 female); 3,068 advanced vocational schools with 7,190 teachers (3,324 female) and 205,663 pupils (119,280 female).

Higher Education. Universities and equivalent institutions; teacher-training colleges and equivalent institutions which train teachers for primary schools, special schools, intermediate schools and schools providing vocational education; colleges of music, fine arts and the college for physical education in Cologne.

Higher technical colleges offer highly qualified full-time vocational instruction.

There were, in the winter term 1976–77, 149 higher technical colleges with 157,093 students (36,363 female).

During the winter term 1976–77 there were 278 academic institutions of higher education with 877,328 students (294,208 female; 49,977 foreigners); they comprise 49 universities with 581,142 students (188,945 female); 7 Roman Catholic theological colleges and 4 Protestant theological colleges with together 1,994 students (463 female).

In the winter term 1976–77 there were 33 teacher-training colleges and equivalent institutions with 72,833 students (47,447 female).

In the winter term 1976–77 there were 15 colleges of music, 10 colleges of fine arts and the college of film and television with together 15,272 students (6,508 female).

Health. There were in 1975, 3,481 hospitals with 729,791 beds in the Federal Republic. In 1975 public assistance (including aid to tuberculars) and aid to war victims amounted to DM 9,382m. or DM 151.73 per head of population.[1]

[1] All subsequent statistics relate to the end of 1975 or the calendar year 1975.

Social Welfare. *Social Health Insurance* (originally introduced in 1883). Compulsory insurants are in particular wage-earners and apprentices, salaried employees with an income below the limit of compulsory insurance and the social-insurance pensioners. Voluntary insurance is possible; insurants may voluntarily continue to insure when no longer liable to do so.

Benefits: Medical treatment, medicaments, hospital and nursing care, maternity benefits, death benefits for the insured and their families, sickness payments and out-patients' allowances.

Number of insurants, 33·5m., including compulsory insurants (19·1m.) and pensioners (9·6m.). Number of the cases of incapacity for work 20·4m. Total expenditure, DM 61,631m.

Accident Insurance (originally introduced in 1884). Insured are all persons in employment or service, apprentices and the greater part of the self-employed and the unpaid family workers.

Benefits in the case of industrial injuries and occupational diseases: Medical treatment and nursing care, sickness payments, pensions and other payments in cash and in kind, surviving dependants' pensions.

Number of insurants, 27·3m.; number of current pensions, 1m.; total expenditure, DM 7,180m.

Workers' and Employees' Old-age Insurance Funds (originally introduced in 1889). Compulsory insurants are all wage-earners and salaried employees, the members of certain liberal professions and—subject to certain conditions—self-employed craftsmen. Insurants may voluntarily continue to insure when no longer liable to do so or increase the insurance.

Benefits: Measures designed to maintain, improve and restore the earning capacity; pensions paid to persons incapable for work, old age and surviving dependants' pensions.

Number of pensions paid, 11·1m., of which pensions to insurants, 7·2m.; pensions to widows and widowers, 3·4m.; pensions to orphans, 0·5m. Total expenditure, DM 104,903m.

Miners' Pension Insurance Funds. Compulsory insurants are all persons employed in mining, excluding salaried employees functioning as employers. Insurants may voluntarily continue to insure when no longer liable to do so or increase the insurance.

Benefits: Measures designed to maintain, improve and restore the earning capacity; pensions paid to underground workers because of partial disability to work in mines, miners' pensions in the case of complete disability, miners' retirement benefits, surviving dependants' pensions.

Number of pensions paid, 0·7m., of which pensions to insurants, 0·4m.; pensions to widows and widowers, 0·3m.; pensions to orphans, 0·03m. Total expenditure, DM 9,768m.

Farmers' Old-age Pension Funds: Unemployment Insurance and *Unemployment Relief* granted to unemployed persons who are not entitled to unemployment pay.

Number of insured, 0·7m.; number of current pensions, 0·3m. Total expenditure, DM 1,883,000.

Assistance for War Victims (war-disabled and surviving dependants of war victims).

Benefits: Medical treatment and nursing care, aid to war victims, disablement pensions, basic and equalization pensions paid to widows and orphans, parents' pensions, allowances for nursing care, compensation for occupational detriment, funeral allowances, lump-sum indemnification and idemnification paid upon marriage.

Persons (including those with permanent residence abroad) qualifying for pensions, 2·2m., of which disabled persons, 1·1m.; widows and widowers, 1m.; orphans, 0·03m.; parents, 0·1m. Total expenditure, DM 11,135m.

Equalization of Burdens (public relief and compensation payments). Eligible are expellees and persons who suffered damage because of the war or in connexion with the currency reform.

Benefits: Basic compensation, war-damage pensions, compensation for household equipment, accommodation assistance, currency-conversion compensation, compensation for holders of 'old savings', training grants, loans and other promotive measures.

Number of recipients of war damage pensions, 0·4m.; payments made (1 Sept. 1952–31 Dec. 1975), DM 89,783m., including basic compensation, DM 20,515m.; war damage pension, DM 33,916m.; accommodation assistance, DM 5,611m.; compensation for household equipment, DM 9,005m.

Family Assistance. From 1 Jan. 1975, children's allowances are being paid, beginning with the first child, to all persons living in the area of application of the law, the income limit being abolished. The monthly allowance is for the first child DM 50, for the second child DM 70 and for the third and any further child DM 120 each. Before, the Federal Law on Children's Allowances (*Bundeskindergeldgesetz*) had provided that all persons living in the area of application of the law were to be paid children's allowances for the third and any further child, unless the beneficiaries were public service employees or recipients of social benefits and as such already entitled to children's allowances. For the second child allowances were paid only to persons who together with their husband/wife had a yearly income not exceeding DM 15,000 (as of 1 Jan. 1973 = DM 16,800, as of 1 Jan. 1974 = DM 18,360); this limitation did not apply in the case of persons with 3 or more children.

Accommodation Allowances for tenants, owners of a homestead, a freehold flat or a small-holder's cottage.

Public Welfare. Public assistance or welfare (the latter from 1 June 1962) for needy persons, namely livelihood aid and aid in special situations (including aid to tuberculars) provided outside and inside institutions, homes and similar establishments.

Aid provided outside institutions, DM 3,682m.; aid provided inside institutions, DM 4,723m.

Aid to War Victims. Benefits for disabled persons and members of their families as well as for surviving dependants, namely vocational assistance, education allowances, supplementary livelihood aid; recovery, accommodation and special assistance. Total expenditure, DM 974m.

Public Youth Welfare. In particular, supervision of foster children, official guardianship, assistance with adoptions and affiliations, social assistance in juvenile courts, educational assistance and correctional education under a court order. Total expenditure, DM 3,369m.

Übersicht über die soziale Sicherung in Deutschland. Bundesministerium für Arbeit und Sozialordnung. 9th ed. Bonn, 1974

Tietz, G., *Zahlenwerk zur Sozialversicherung in der Bundesrepublik Deutschland* (and supplements). Berlin, 1963

Arbeits- und Sozialstatistik. Bundesminister für Arbeit und Sozialordnung, Bonn (from 1950)

Fachserie 13 Sozialleistungen. Statistisches Bundesamt (from 1951)

Fachserie 12 Gesundheitswesen. Statistisches Bundesamt (from 1946)

DIPLOMATIC REPRESENTATIVES

OF THE FEDERAL REPUBLIC OF GERMANY IN GREAT BRITAIN
(21–23 Belgrave Sq., London, SW1X 8PZ)

Ambassador: Hans Hellmuth Ruete.

OF GREAT BRITAIN IN THE FEDERAL REPUBLIC OF GERMANY
(53 Bonn, Friedrich-Ebert-Alle 77)

Ambassador: Sir Oliver Wright, KCMG, DSC.

OF THE FEDERAL REPUBLIC OF GERMANY IN THE USA
(4645 Reservoir Rd, NW, Washington, D.C. 20007)

Ambassador: Berndt von Staden.

OF THE USA IN THE FEDERAL REPUBLIC OF GERMANY
(Mahlemer Ave., 5300, Bonn)

Ambassador: William J. Stoessel, Jr.

FEDERAL REPUBLIC OF GERMANY TO THE UNITED NATIONS

Ambassador: Rüdiger von Wechmar.

Books of Reference

Statistical Information: The central statistical agency is the Statistisches Bundesamt, 62 Wiesbaden, Gustav Stresemann Ring 11. *President:* Dr Hildegard Bartels. Its publications include:

Statistisches Jahrbuch für die Bundesrepublik Deutschland (latest issue, 1977); *Wirtschaft und Statistik* (monthly, from 1949); *Das Arbeitsgebiet der Bundesstatistik* (latest issue 1976; also in English: *Survey of German Federal Statistics*).

Documents on Germany under Occupation, 1945–54. Ed. B. Ruhm von Oppen. R. Inst. of Int. Affairs, 1955
Bluhm, G., *Die Oder-Neisse-Linie in der Deutschen Aussenpolitik*. Freiburg, 1963
Dickinson, R. E., *The Regions of Germany*. London, 1945
Grosser, A., *Germany in our Time: A Political History of the Postwar Years*. New York, 1971
Pounds, N. J. G., *The Economic Pattern of Modern Germany*. 2nd ed. London, 1966
Roberts, G. K., *West German Politics*. London, 1972
Ryder, A. J., *Twentieth-Century Germany: From Bismarck to Brandt*. London, 1973
Trene, W., *Germany Since 1884*. Bad Godesberg, 1969
Wiskemann, E., *Germany's Eastern Neighbours*. R. Inst. of Int. Affairs, 1956

National Library: Deutsche Bibliothek, Zeppelinallee 4–8; Frankfurt (Main). *Director:* Professor Dr Kurt Köster.

THE LÄNDER

BADEN-WÜRTTEMBERG

AREA AND POPULATION. Baden-Württemberg comprises 35,751 sq. km, with a population (at 30 June 1977) of 9,120,678 (4,375,923 males, 4,744,755 females).

The Land is administratively divided into 4 areas, 9 urban and 35 rural districts, and numbers 1,111 communes. The capital is Stuttgart.

Vital statistics for calendar years:

	Live births	*Marriages*	*Divorces*	*Deaths*
1974	102,206	53,647	13,268	93,127
1975	97,019	53,637	13,921	95,646
1976	95,492	51,129	14,795	94,426

CONSTITUTION. The Land Baden-Württemberg is a merger of the 3 Länder, Baden, Württemberg-Baden and Württemberg-Hohenzollern, which were formed in 1945. The merger was approved by a plebiscite held on 9 Dec. 1951, when 70% of the population of the 3 Länder voted in its favour.

The Diet, elected on 4 April 1976, consists of 71 Christian Democrats, 41 Social Democrats, 9 Free Democrats.

The government is formed by Christian Democrats, with Dr Hans Filbinger (CDU) as Prime Minister.

AGRICULTURE. Area and yield of the most important crops:

	Area (in 1,000 hectares)			*Yield (in 1,000 tonnes)*		
	1974	*1975*	*1976*	*1974*	*1975*	*1976*
Rye	16·8	15·7	18·8	56·3	51·0	54·9
Wheat	254·5	241·0	248·7	1,140·9	940·2	997·5
Barley	165·7	177·4	168·0	637·6	609·6	611·4
Oats	91·8	100·0	97·6	400·9	375·9	300·7
Potatoes	55·4	50·6	49·6	1,751·5	1,215·6	1,425·8
Sugar-beet	22·0	25·1	25·3	1,096·3	1,240·1	1,169·0

Livestock (3 Dec. 1976): Cattle, 1,827,751 (including 688,619 milch cows); horses, 38,141; pigs, 2,109,747; sheep, 167,399; poultry, 9,021,514.

INDUSTRY. In June 1977, 8,124 establishments (with 20 and more employees) employed 1,386,142 persons; of these, 242,708 were employed in machine construction (excluding office machines, data processing equipment and facilities); 105,782 in textile industry; 233,527 in electrical engineering; 178,182 in car building.

LABOUR. The economically active persons totalled 4,017,500 at the 1%-sample survey of the microcensus of May 1976. Of the total 355,900 were self-employed, 199,200 unpaid family workers, 3,462,400 employees; 265,900 were engaged in agriculture and forestry; 2,072,500 in power supply, mining, manufacturing and building, 590,900 in commerce and transport, 1,088,200 in other industries and services.

ROADS. On 1 Jan. 1977 there were 27,440 km of 'classified' roads, including 774 km of autobahn, 4,765 km of federal roads, 12,705 km of first-class and 9,196 km of second-class highways. Motor vehicles, at 1 July 1977, numbered 3,627,868, including 3,088,330 passenger cars, 7,439 buses, 155,390 lorries, 282,858 tractors and 63,209 motor cycles.

JUSTICE. There are a constitutional court (*Staatsgerichtshof*), 2 courts of appeal, 17 regional courts, 108 local courts, a Land labour court, 20 labour courts, a Land social court, 8 social courts, a finance court, a higher administrative court (*Verwaltungsgerichtshof*), 4 administrative courts.

RELIGION. At the census of 1 Jan. 1976, 44·8% of the population were Protestants and 47·1% Roman Catholics.

EDUCATION. In 1976 there were 2,650 primary schools with 30,657 teachers and 912,637 pupils; 531 special schools with 6,073 teachers and 66,553 pupils; 412 intermediate schools with 9,030 teachers and 228,847 pupils; 407 high schools with 13,808 teachers and 305,538 pupils; 14 *Freie Waldorf* schools with 416 teachers and 7,451 pupils; 19 *Integrierte Gesamtschulen* (comprehensive schools) including stage of orientation, with 702 teachers and 12,446 pupils; 153 *Berufliche Gymnasien* (technical secondary schools) with 21,682 pupils; 375 part-time vocational schools with 217,215 pupils; 841 full-time vocational schools with 66,419 pupils; 177 advanced vocational schools with 8,066 pupils; 245 schools for public health occupations with 11,735 pupils; there were also 86 (full- and part-time) institutions for the training of technicians with 4,548 participants and 30 *Fachhochschulen* (colleges of engineering and others) with 23,419 students; in all vocational schools there were 11,190 teachers.

In the winter term 1976–77 there were 9 universities (Freiburg, 16,869 students;

Heidelberg, 18,498; Konstanz, 2,921; Tübingen, 18,076; Karlsruhe, 11,593; Stuttgart, 11,373; Hohenheim, 2,763; Mannheim, 6,738; Ulm, 1,804); 10 teacher-training colleges with 19,861 students; 5 colleges of music and 2 colleges of fine arts, comprising together 2,855 students.

Statistical Information: Statistisches Landesamt Baden-Württemberg (P.O.B. 898, D7000 Stuttgart 1) (*President:* Prof. Klaus Szameitat), publishes: *Statistische Monatshefte Baden-Württemberg; Jahrbücher für Statistik und Landeskunde von Baden-Württemberg; Statistik von Baden-Württemberg* (series); *Statistisches Handbuch Baden-Württemberg* (1955 and 1958); *Statistisches Taschenbuch* (latest issue 1977). *Die Stadt- und Landkreise Baden-Württembergs in Wort und Zahl.*

Spreng, R., and others, *Die Verfassung des Landes Baden-Württemberg.* Stuttgart, 1954

BAVARIA

Bayern

AREA AND POPULATION. Bavaria has an area of 70,547 sq. km. The capital is Munich. There are 7 areas, 96 urban and rural districts and 3,918 communes. The population (31 March 1977) numbered 10,806,804 (5,149,257 males, 5,657,547 females).

Vital statistics for calendar years:

	Live births	*Marriages*	*Divorces*	*Deaths*
1974	114,060	64,081	15,550	123,980
1975	108,544	64,355	16,527	127,931
1976	108,995	62,425	16,504	124,580

CONSTITUTION. The Constituent Assembly, elected on 30 June 1946, passed a constitution on the lines of the democratic constitution of 1919, but with greater emphasis on state rights; this was agreed upon by the Christian Social Union and the Social Democrats.

The elections for the Diet, held on 27 Oct. 1974, had the following results: 132 Christian Social Union, 64 Social Democrats, 8 Free Democrats. The cabinet of the Christian Social Union is headed by Minister President Dr Alfons Goppel (CSU).

AGRICULTURE. Area and yield of the most important products:

	Area (1,000 hectares)			*Yield (1,000 tonnes)*		
	1975	*1976*	*1977*[1]	*1975*	*1976*	1977[1]
Wheat	486·2	499·8	493·2	2,029·3	1,982·0	2,213·9
Rye	71·5	79·1	87·7	215·0	219·0	286·5
Barley	456·1	439·4	445·4	1,664·6	1,499·3	1,707·4
Oats	170·8	169·7	155·7	609·9	474·8	564·7
Potatoes	160·1	159·3	148·0	4,375·7	4,053·3	4,520·1
Sugar-beet	92·0	92·0	91·5	4,817·7	4,077·0	...

[1] Preliminary results.

Livestock (3 Dec. 1976): 4,575,300 cattle (including 1,921,100 milch cows); 50,300 horses; 271,100 sheep; 3,970,800 pigs; 15,775,600 poultry.

INDUSTRY. In July 1977, 8,598 establishments (with 20 and more employees) employed 1,232,208 persons; of these, 239,913 were employed in electrical engineering; 159,750 in mechanical engineering; 85,228 in clothing industry.

LABOUR. The economically active persons totalled 4,910,800 at the 1% sample survey of the microcensus of May 1976. Of the total, 550,600 were self-employed, 386,500 unpaid family workers, 3,973,700 employees; 2,170,100 in power supply, mining, manufacturing and building; 801,300 in commerce and transport; 1,370,600 in other industries and services.

ROADS. There were, on 1 Jan 1977, 38,489 km of 'classified' roads, including 1,299 km of autobahn, 7,265 km of federal roads, 13,515 km of first-class and 16,410 km of second-class highways. Number of motor vehicles, at 1 Jan. 1977, was 4,160,865, including 3,341,797 passenger cars, 190,907 lorries, 10,725 buses, 507,844 tractors, 109,592 motor cycles.

JUSTICE. There are a constitutional court (*Verfassungsgerichtshof*), a supreme Land court (*Oberstes Landesgericht*), 3 courts of appeal, 21 regional courts, 72 local courts, 2 Land labour courts, 11 labour courts, a Land social court, 7 social courts, 2 finance courts, a higher administrative court (*Verwaltungsgerichtshof*), 6 administrative courts.

RELIGION. At the census of 27 May 1970 there were 69·9% Roman Catholics and 25·7% Protestants.

EDUCATION. In 1976–77 there were 2,914 primary schools with 44,672 teachers and 1,183,337 pupils; 384 special schools with 3,701 teachers and 55,031 pupils; 321 intermediate schools with 7,546 teachers and 163,632 pupils; 387 high schools with 16,280 teachers and 303,404 pupils; 227 part-time vocational schools with 5,274 teachers and 339,311 pupils; 493 full-time vocational schools with 2,828 teachers and 63,310 pupils including 204 schools for public health occupations with 508 teachers and 13,473 pupils; 257 advanced full-time vocational schools with 1,532 teachers and 21,695 pupils; 79 vocational high schools (*Berufsoberschulen, Fachoberschulen*) with 1,127 teachers and 21,432 pupils.

In the winter term 1976–77 there were 7 universities with 92,372 students (Augsburg, 3,655 students; Bayreuth, 687 students; Erlangen–Nürnberg, 16,126 students; München, 36,314; Regensburg, 9,486; Würzburg, 12,795; the Technical University of München, 13,309); 4 *Gesamthochschulen* with 5,655 students; the college of philosophy, München (247) and the Roman Catholic theological college, Passau (89). There were also 2 colleges of music, 2 colleges of fine arts and 1 college of television and film, with together 1,854 students; 11 vocational colleges (*Fachhochschulen*) with 26,444 students.

Statistical Information: Bayerisches Statistisches Landesamt, 51 Neuhauser St. 8000 Munich, was founded in 1833. *President:* Dr Günther Scheingraber. It publishes: *Statistisches Jahrbuch für Bayern.—Bayern* in *Zahlen.* Monthly (from Jan. 1947).—*Zeitschrift des Bayerischen Statistischen Landesamts.* July 1869–1943; 1948 ff.—*Beiträge zur Statistik Bayerns.* 1850 ff.—*Statistische Berichte.* 1951 ff.—*Schaubilderhefte.* 1951 ff.—*Kreisdaten.* 1976.—*Gemeindedaten* (Stand: 1 Jan. 1976).

Nawiasky, H., and Luesser, C., *Die Verfassung des Freistaates Bayen vom 2. Dez. 1946.* Munich, 1948; supplement, by H. Nawiasky and H. Lechner, Munich, 1953

State Library: Bayerische Staatsbibliothek, Munich 22. *Director-General:* Dr Hans Striedl.

BERLIN

GOVERNMENT. Greater Berlin was under quadripartite Allied government (Kommandatura) until 1 July 1948, when the Soviet element withdrew. On 30 Nov. 1948, a separate Municipal Government was set up in the Soviet Sector (*see* p. 493).

AREA. The total area of Berlin is 883 sq. km, of which Western Berlin covers 480 sq. km and the Soviet Sector 403 sq. km. The *British Sector* includes the administrative districts of Tiergarten, Charlottenburg, Wilmersdorf and Spandau; the *American Sector* those of Kreuzberg, Neukölln, Tempelhof, Schöneberg, Zehlendorf and Steglitz; the *French Sector* covers the administrative districts of Wedding and Reinickendorf, and the *Soviet Sector*, those of Mitte, Friedrichshain, Prenzlauer Berg, Pankow, Weissensee, Lichtenberg, Treptow and Köpenick. The British, American and French sectors form an administrative unit, called Berlin (West).

On 13 Aug. 1961 the East German government completely severed all communications between West and East Berlin.

BERLIN (WEST)

POPULATION. Population, 31 Dec. 1976, 1,950,706 (863,309 males, 1,087,397 females). According to the census of 27 May 1970, 70·2% were Protestants and 12·5% Roman Catholics.

Vital statistics for calendar years:

	Live births	*Marriages*	*Divorces*	*Deaths*
1974	18,254	13,699	6,650	38,492
1975	17,716	14,505	7,100	39,181
1976	17,677	12,691	7,005	37,670

CONSTITUTION AND GOVERNMENT. According to the constitution of 1 Sept. 1950, Berlin is simultaneously a *Land* of the Federal Republic (though not yet formally incorporated) and a city. It is governed by a House of Representatives (at least 200 members); the executive power is vested in a Senate, consisting of the Ruling Burgomaster, the deputy Burgomaster and not more than 16 senators.

In the municipal elections, held on 2 March 1975, the Social Democrats obtained 67 seats; the Christian Democrats, 69 seats; the Free Democrats, 11 seats. The government is a coalition of Social Democrats and Free Democrats.

Governing Mayor: Dietrich Stobbe (Social Democrat).

ECONOMY

Currency. The legal tender of Berlin is the German Mark (DM), viz., the DM (East) in the Soviet Sector and the DM (West) in the Western Sectors.

Banking. On 20 March 1949 when the DM (West) became the only legal tender of the Western Sectors, the Zentralbank of Berlin was established. Its functions were similar to those of the Zentralbanks of the Länder of the Federal Republic. The Berlin Central Bank was merged with the Bank deutscher Länder as from 1 Aug. 1957, when the latter became the Deutsche Bundesbank. The legal tender for the Western Sectors of Berlin is being issued by the Deutsche Bundesbank (formerly Bank deutscher Länder).

AGRICULTURE. Agricultural area (May 1977), 1,650 hectares, including 1,307 hectares arable land and 161 hectares gardens, orchards, nurseries.

Livestock (3 Dec. 1976): Cattle, 1,008; pigs, 6,835; horses, 2,490; sheep, 246.

INDUSTRY. In 1976 (monthly averages), 1,567 establishments (with 10 or more employees) employed 192,140 persons; of these, 69,591 were employed in electrical engineering, 21,180 in machine construction, 4,409 in cloth manufacture, 8,162 in steel construction.

LABOUR. The economically active persons totalled 827,700 at the 1%-sample survey of the microcensus of May 1976. Of the total, 68,600 were self-employed including unpaid family workers, 759,100 employees; 8,000 were engaged in agriculture and forestry; 306,700 in power supply, manufacturing and building; 163,800 in commerce and transport; 349,200 in other industries and services.

ROADS. There were, on 1 Jan. 1976, 117 km of 'classified' roads, including 25 km of autobahn and 92 km of federal roads. On 1 Jan. 1977, 557,900 motor vehicles were registered, including 508,501 passenger cars, 33,891 lorries, 10,683 motor cycles, 2,225 buses and 2,600 tractors.

JUSTICE. There are a court of appeal (*Oberlandesgericht*), a regional court, 7 local courts, a Land labour court, a labour court, a Land social court, a social court, a higher administrative court, an administrative court and a finance court.

EDUCATION. In 1976 (preliminary figures) there were 457 schools providing general education (excluding special schools) with 13,626 teachers and 244,490 pupils; 63 special schools with 1,324 teachers and 11,719 pupils. There were further 39 vocational schools with 786 teachers and 32,462 pupils; 21 full-time vocational schools with 363 teachers and 3,815 pupils; 11 *Fachoberschulen* (full-time vocational schools leading up to vocational colleges) with 122 teachers and 1,574 pupils; 35 advanced full-time vocational schools with 272 teachers and 4,621 pupils; 87 schools for public-health occupations with 313 teachers and 4,944 pupils. Moreover, there were 3 schools for technicians with 49 teachers and 683 participants.

In the winter term 1976–77 there was 1 university (32,240 students); 1 technical university (21,712); 1 theological (evangelical) college (282); 1 teacher-training college with 5,601 students; 1 college of fine arts with 2,031 students; 1 vocational college (for economics) (1,275); 2 colleges for social work (1,097); 1 technical college (3,146), 1 college of the Federal postal administration (441) and 1 college for public administration (1,409).

Statistical Information: The Statistisches Landesamt Berlin, formerly Statistisches Amt der Stadt Berlin, was founded in 1862 (Fehrbelliner Platz 1, 1000 Berlin 31). *Director:* Prof. Dr Hanisch. It publishes: *Statistisches Jahrbuch* (from 1867): *Berliner Statistik* (monthly, from 1947).—*100 Jahre Berliner Statistik* (1962).

BREMEN

Freie Hansestadt Bremen

AREA AND POPULATION. The area of the Land, consisting of the towns and ports of Bremen and Bremerhaven, is 404 sq. km. Estimated population, 31 Dec. 1975, 716,805 (337,034 males, 379,771 females).

Vital statistics for calendar years:

	Live births	*Marriages*	*Divorces*	*Deaths*
1974	6,594	4,329	2,130	9,251
1975	6,429	4,775	2,364	9,347
1976	6,392	4,461	2,184	9,115

CONSTITUTION. Political power is vested in the House of Burgesses (*Bürgerschaft*), which appoints the executive, called the Senate.

The elections of 28 Sept. 1975 had the following result: 52 Social Democratic Party, 35 Christian Democratic Union, 13 Free Democratic Party. The Senate is only formed by Social Democrats; its president is Hans Koschnick (Social Democrat).

AGRICULTURE. Agricultural area comprised (1976), 16,753 hectares: yield of grain crops, 6,012 tonnes; potatoes, 687 tonnes.

Livestock (3 Dec. 1976): 17,037 cattle (including 4,605 milch cows); 8,977 pigs; 402 sheep; 1,530 horses; 47,283 poultry.

FISHERIES. In 1976 the yield of sea and coastal fishing was 98,696 tonnes valued at DM 175·8m.

INDUSTRY. In June 1977, 295 establishments (20 and more employees) employed 86,893 persons; of these, 18,464 were employed in shipbuilding (except naval engineering); 7,885 in machine construction; 11,224 in electrical engineering; 5,904 in coffee processing.

LABOUR. The economically active persons totalled 299,500 at the 1%-sample survey of the microcensus of April 1976. Of the total, 18,600 were self-employed, 3,700 unpaid family workers, 277,200 employees; 1,500 were engaged in agriculture and forestry, 104,300 in power supply, mining, manufacturing and building, 87,600 in commerce and transport, 106,100 in other industries and services.

ROADS. On 1 Jan. 1976 there were 139 km of 'classified' roads, including 45 km of autobahn, 82 km of federal roads, 7 km of first-class and 5 km of second-class highways. Registered motor vehicles on 1 Jan. 1977 numbered 232,000, including 211,000 passenger cars, 15,000 trucks, 2,000 tractors, 640 buses and 2,500 motor cycles.

SHIPPING. Vessels entered in 1976, 11,415 of 39,401,171 net tons; cleared, 11,027 of 39,160,951 net tons. Sea traffic, 1976, incoming 15,070,026 tonnes; outgoings, 8,122,472 tonnes.

JUSTICE. There are a constitutional court (*Staatsgerichtshof*), a court of appeal, a regional court, 3 local courts, a Land labour court, 2 labour courts, a Land social court, a social court, a finance court, a higher administrative court, an administrative court.

RELIGION. On 27 May 1970 (census) there were 82·4% Protestants and 10·2% Roman Catholics.

EDUCATION. In 1976 there were 269 new system schools with 5,105 teachers and 110,735 pupils; 25 special schools with 482 teachers and 4,506 pupils; 22 part-time vocational schools with 21,766 pupils; 16 full-time vocational schools with 3,317 pupils; 14 advanced vocational schools (including institutions for the training of technicians) with 2,204 pupils; 10 schools for public health occupations with 1,008 pupils.

In the winter term 1976–77 about 4,850 students were enrolled at the university. In addition to the university there were 6 other colleges in 1976 with about 3,600 students.

Statistical Information: The Statistisches Landesamt Bremen (An der Weide 14–16 (P.B. 101309), D2800 Bremen 1) was founded in 1850. *Director:* Ltd Reg.-Dir. Dr Matti. Its current publications include: *Statistische Mitteilungen Freie Hansestadt Bremen* (from 1948).—*Monatliche Zwischenberichte* (1949–53); *Statistische Monatsberichte* (from 1954).—*Statistische Berichte* (from 1956).—*Statistisches Handbuch für das Land Freie Hansestadt Bremen* (*1950–60*, 1961; *1960–64*, 1967; *1965–69*, 1971; *1970–74*, 1975).

Beutin, L., *Bremen und Amerika*. Bremen, 1953

University Library: Klagenfurter Str., D2800 Bremen 33. *Director:* Dr Kluth.

HAMBURG

Freie und Hansestadt Hamburg

AREA AND POPULATION. In 1938 the territory of the Free Hanse Town was reorganized by the amalgamation of the city and its 18 rural districts with 3 urban and 27 rural districts ceded by Prussia. Total area, 753 sq. km, including the islands Neuwerk and Scharhörn (5·8 sq. km) joined to the territory of Hamburg on 1 Oct. 1969. Population (31 Dec. 1976), 1,698,615 (788,035 males, 910,580 females).

Vital statistics for calendar years:

	Live births	*Marriages*	*Divorces*	*Deaths*
1974	13,535	10,406	5,694	25,291
1975	13,192	10,494	6,110	26,099
1976	13,601	9,724	5,864	25,300

CONSTITUTION. The constitution of 1 July 1952 vests the supreme power in the House of Burgesses (*Bürgerschaft*) of 120 members. The executive is in the hands of the Senate, whose 11 members are elected by the Bürgerschaft.

The elections of 3 March 1974 had the following results: Social Democrats, 56; Christian Democrats, 51; Free Democrats, 13. The First Burgomaster is Hans-Ulrich Klose (Social Democrat).

By a law of 21 Sept. 1949 the territory has been divided into 7 administrative districts, each with a mayor and council.

AGRICULTURE. The agricultural area comprised 30,900 hectares in 1974. Yield, in tonnes, of cereals, 20,300; potatoes, 1,800.

Livestock (3 Dec. 1975): Cattle, 14,500 (including 3,700 milch cows); pigs, 10,800; horses, 3,200; sheep, 1,500; poultry, 114,500.

FISHERIES. In 1975 the yield of sea and coastal fishing was 28,600 tonnes valued at DM 29·2m.

INDUSTRY. In June 1977, 784 establishments (with 20 and more employees) employed 160,168 persons; of these, 22,109 were employed in electrical engineering; 18,696 in machine construction; 15,165 in shipbuilding (except naval engineering); 14,812 in chemical industry.

LABOUR. The economically active persons totalled 732,000 at the 1%-sample survey of the microcensus of May 1976. Of the total, 65,100 were self-employed, 11,800 unpaid family workers, 655,100 employees; 9,300 were engaged in agriculture and forestry, 235,000 in power supply, mining, manufacturing and building, 230,100 in commerce and transport, 257,200 in other industries and services.

ROADS. On 1 Jan. 1976 there were 218 km of 'classified' roads, including 60 km of autobahn, 157 km of federal roads. Number of motor vehicles (1 July 1977), 571,728, including 520,911 passenger cars, 38,393 lorries, 1,703 buses, 4,401 tractors, 6,320 motor cycles.

SHIPPING. Hamburg is the largest port in the Federal Republic.

Vessels		*1938*	*1958*	*1968*	*1975*	*1976*
Entered:	Number	18,149	19,033	18,802	17,763	17,926
	Tonnage	20,567,311	27,454,640	37,073,215	49,416,283	52,614,410
Cleared:	Number	19,316	20,363	19,320	18,717	18,823
	Tonnage	20,547,148	27,579,914	36,820,828	49,853,412	52,704,474

JUSTICE. There is a constitutional court (*Verfassungsgericht*), a court of appeal, a regional court, 6 local courts, a Land labour court, a labour court, a Land social court, a social court, a finance court, a higher administrative court, an administrative court.

RELIGION. On 25 May 1970 (census) Evangelical Church and Free Churches 73·6%; Roman Catholic Church 8·1%.

EDUCATION. In 1976 there were 413 new system schools (not including *Internationale Schule*) with 11,954 teachers and 235,160 pupils; 63 special schools with 1,061 teachers and 10,486 pupils; 42 part-time vocational schools with 39,587 pupils; 17 schools with 693 pupils in their vocational preparatory year; 15 schools with 1,323 pupils in manual instruction classes; 55 full-time vocational schools with 8,609 pupils; 8 economic high schools with 1,652 pupils; 24 advanced vocational schools with 4,177 pupils; 44 schools for public health occupations with 2,483 pupils; 13 vocational introducing schools with 520 pupils and 21 technical superior schools with 2,168 pupils; all these vocational and technical schools have a total number of 3,936 teachers.

In the winter term 1976–77 there was 1 university with 27,569 students; 1 college of music and 1 college of fine arts with together 1,413 students; 1 high school of the *Bundeswehr* with 1,671 students; 1 professional high school (*Fachhochschule*) with 6,131 students, 1 college for economics and politics with 896 students, as well as 1 private professional high school with 154 students.

Statistical Information: The Statistisches Landesamt Hamburg (Steckelhörn 12, D2000 Hamburg 11) was founded in 1866. Among its older publications, the *Statistik des Hamburgischen Staates* (from 1867) is the most important. Current publications include: *Statistisches Jahrbuch für die Freie und Hansestadt Hamburg*, formerly 'Statistisches Handbuch für den Hamburgischen Staat' (from 1874).—'Hamburger Statistische Monatsberichte' (1924–26).—'Aus Hamburgs Verwaltung und Wirtschaft' (1927–39).—*Hamburg in Zahlen* (from 1947).—*Statistische Berichte*, formerly *Hamburger Statistische Informationen* (from Jan. 1954).—*Handel und Schiffahrt des Hafens Hamburg*, formerly '*Tabellarische* Übersichten des Hamburgischen Handels' and 'Hamburgs Handel und Schiffahrt' (annual, from 1845), since 1959 included the series 'Statistik des Hamburgischen Staates', H. 54.

Studt-Olsen, B., *Hamburg, die Geschichte einer Stadt*. Hamburg, 1951

HESSEN

AREA AND POPULATION. The state of Hessen comprehends the areas of the former Prussian provinces Kurhessen and Nassau (excluding the exclaves belonging to Hesse and the rural counties of Oberwesterwald, Unterwesterwald, Unterlahn and St Goarshausen) and of the former Volksstaat Hessen, the provinces Starkenburg (including the parts of Rheinhessen east of the river Rhine) and Oberhessen. Hessen has an area of 21,112 sq. km. Its capital is Wiesbaden. There are 2 areas, 26 urban and rural districts and 423 communes. Population, 31 March 1977, was 5,538,042 (2,656,363 males, 2,881,679 females).

Vital statistics for calendar years:

	Live births	*Marriages*	*Divorces*	*Deaths*
1974	55,077	33,179	9,117	63,267
1975	53,176	33,070	10,350	64,760
1976	53,126	31,529	10,393	64,624

CONSTITUTION. The constitution was put into force by popular referendum on 1 Dec. 1946. The Diet, elected on 27 Oct. 1974, consists of 53 Christian Democrats, 49 Social Democrats, 8 Free Democrats.

The Social Democrat and Free Democrat cabinet is headed by Minister President Holger Börner (SPD).

AGRICULTURE. Area and yield of the most important crops:

	Area (in 1,000 hectares)			*Yield (in 1,000 tonnes)*		
	1974	*1975*	*1976*	*1974*	*1975*	*1976*
Wheat	141·6	141·4	144·1	695·6	694·6	561·9
Rye	52·9	43·6	46·5	203·6	141·4	156·3
Barley	119·1	127·6	125·0	504·5	514·0	448·9
Oats	84·3	88·2	87·5	323·5	322·0	240·1
Potatoes	38·6	33·8	33·7	1,096·7	844·2	673·2
Sugar-beet	21·8	24·9	24·8	942·4	1,062·8	976·9

Livestock, 3 Dec. 1976: Cattle, 862,000 (including 307,200 milch cows); horses, 30,800; pigs, 1,384,500; sheep, 125,000; poultry, 5,113,500.

INDUSTRY. In Sept. 1976, 4,464 establishments (with 10 and more employees) employed 653,704 persons; of these, 89,852 were employed in chemical industry; 86,158 in electrical engineering; 84,981 in machine construction; 66,636 in car building.

LABOUR. The economically active persons totalled 2·31m. at the 1%-sample survey of the microcensus of May 1976. Of the total, 188,000 were self-employed, 91,000 unpaid family workers, 2·08m. employees; 118,000 were engaged in agriculture and forestry, 1,056,000 in power supply, mining, manufacturing and building, 438,000 in commerce and transport, 698,000 in other industries and services.

ROADS. On 1 Jan. 1977 the Land Hessen had 16,296 km of 'classified' roads, including 828 km of autobahn, 3,426 km of federal highways, 7,111 km of first-class highways and 4,932 km of second-class highways. Motor vehicles licensed on 1 July 1977 totalled 2,205,529, including 1,913,824 passenger cars, 5,028 buses, 104,911 trucks, 134,107 tractors and 34,339 motor cycles.

JUSTICE. There are a constitutional court (*Staatsgerichtshof*), a court of appeal, 9 regional courts, 58 local courts, a Land labour court, 12 labour courts, a Land social court, 7 social courts, a finance court, a higher administrative court (*Verwaltungsgerichtshof*), 4 administrative courts.

RELIGION. On 27 May 1970 (census) there were 60·5% Protestants and 32·8% Roman Catholics.

EDUCATION. In 1976 there were 1,702 primary schools with 14,998 teachers and 434,654 pupils; 241 special schools with 2,569 teachers and 30,667 pupils; 172 intermediate schools with 2,772 teachers and 70,101 pupils; 153 high schools with 6,969 teachers and 142,438 pupils; 150 *Gesamtschulen* (comprehensive schools) with 8,860 teachers and 185,307 pupils; 111 part-time vocational schools with 2,696 teachers and 135,477 pupils; 218 full-time vocational schools with 1,895 teachers and 32,546 pupils; 65 advanced vocational schools with 331 teachers and 5,471 pupils; 162 schools for public health occupations with 7,789 pupils; there were a further 36 full- and part-time institutions for the training of technicians with 2,747 participants.

In the winter term 1976–77 there were 3 universities (Frankfurt/Main, 22,473 students; Giessen, 14,218; Marburg, 13,260); 1 technical university in Darmstadt (10,660); 1 *Gesamthochschule* (5,647); 10 *Fachhochschulen* (15,877); 3 Roman Catholic theological colleges and 1 Protestant theological college with together 323 students; 1 college of music and 2 colleges of fine arts with together 913 students.

Statistical Information: The Hessisches Statistisches Landesamt (Rheinstr. 35–37, D6200 Wiesbaden), was established in Dec. 1945. *President:* Dr Heinrich Benz. Main publications: *Statistisches Handbuch für das Land Hessen* (1972).—*Statistisches Taschenbuch für das Land Hessen* (1977).—*Staat und Wirtschaft in Hessen* (monthly).—*Hessische Bevölkerungs- und Wirtschaftskunde* (2nd ed., 1969).—*Die hessischen Landkriese und kreisfreien Städte* (3rd ed., 1967).—*Hessen im Wandel der letzten 100 Jahre* (2nd ed., 1969).—*Hessen unter den Ländern der Bundesrepublik* (2nd ed., 1970).—*Die hessischen Gemeinden* (1966).—*Beiträge zur Statistik Hessens.*—*Statistische Berichte.*—*Hessische Gemeindestatistik 1960–61* (5 vols., 1963 ff.).—*Hessische Gemeindestatistik 1970* (5 vols., 1972 ff.).

LOWER SAXONY

Niedersachsen

AREA AND POPULATION. Lower Saxony (excluding the town of Bremerhaven, and the districts on the right bank of the Elbe in the Soviet Zone) comprises 47,430 sq. km, and is divided into 4 administrative districts, 37 rural districts, 9 towns and 1,026 communes; capital, Hanover.

Estimated population, on 31 Dec. 1976, was 7,226,897 (3,456,414 males, 3,770,483 females).

Vital statistics for calendar years:

	Live births	*Marriages*	*Divorces*	*Deaths*
1974	76,318	43,418	10,532	87,385
1975	71,970	44,160	11,081	90,030
1976	72,434	42,185	11,261	87,034

GOVERNMENT. The Land Niedersachsen was formed on 1 Nov. 1946 by merging the former Prussian province of Hanover and the *Länder* Brunswick, Oldenburg and Schaumburg-Lippe. The Diet, elected on 9 June 1974, consists of 77 Christian Democratic Union, 67 Social Democrats and 1 Free Democrats.

The cabinet of the Christian Democratic Union is headed by Minister President Dr Ernst Albrecht (CDU).

AGRICULTURE. Area and yield of the most important crops:

	Area (in 1,000 hectares)			*Yield (in 1,000 tonnes)*		
	1974	*1975*	*1976*	*1974*	*1975*	*1976*
Wheat	243·9	243·8	257·0	1,231·0	1,157·0	1,160·0
Rye	294·5	266·4	270·0	1,048·6	919·2	849·0
Barley	387·5	407·2	408·0	1,693·8	1,641·3	1,614·0
Oats	206·5	218·8	209·0	887·7	860·4	671·0
Potatoes	96·3	85·7	87·0	3,184·0	2,231·9	1,974·0
Sugar-beet	126·7	147·6	157·0	5,095·0	5,525·4	5,911·0

Livestock, 3 Dec. 1976: Cattle, 3,007,501 (including 1,029,519 milch cows); horses, 81,681; pigs, 6,066,935; sheep, 147,429; poultry, 38,307,528.

FISHERIES. In 1975 the yield of sea and coastal fishing was 175,287 tonnes valued at DM 165m.

INDUSTRY. In Sept. 1976, 4,626 establishments (with 10 and more employees) employed 689,172 persons; of these 64,548 were employed in machine construction; 111,260 in car building; 72,322 in electrical engineering; 24,963 in textile industry.

LABOUR. The economically active persons totalled 2,943,000 at the 1%-sample survey of the microcensus of May 1976. Of the total 280,000 were self-employed, 172,000 unpaid family workers, 2,491,000 employees; 245,000 were engaged in agriculture and forestry, 1,207,000 in power supply, mining, manufacturing and building, 556,000 in commerce and transport, 936,000 in other industries and services.

ROADS. At 1 Jan. 1977 there were in Lower Saxony 27,486 km of 'classified' roads, including 884 km of autobahn, 5,261 km of federal roads, 8,639 km of first-class and 12,702 km of second-class highways.

Number of motor vehicles, 1 July 1977, was 2,780,774, including 2,355,202 passenger cars, 170,910 lorries, 7,473 buses, 236,035 tractors, 53,086 motor cycles.

JUSTICE. There are a constitutional court (*Staatsgerichtshof*), 3 courts of appeal, 11 regional courts, 79 local courts, a Land labour court, 15 labour courts, a Land social court, 8 social courts, a finance court, a higher administrative court (together with Schleswig-Holstein), 3 administrative courts.

RELIGION. On 27 May 1970 (census) there were 74·6% Protestant and 19·6% Roman Catholics.

EDUCATION. In 1976 there were 2,457 primary schools with 30,451 teachers and 676,779 pupils; 279 special schools with 4,519 teachers and 47,910 pupils; 333 stages of orientation with 3,731 teachers and 137,548 pupils; 269 intermediate schools with 6,988 teachers and 147,230 pupils; 242 grammar schools with 10,435 teachers and 194,522 pupils; 5 evening high schools with 112 teachers and 634 pupils; 13 integrated comprehensive schools with 1,286 teachers and 15,214 pupils; 16 co-operative comprehensive schools with 771 teachers and 7,897 pupils; 142 part-time vocational schools with 187,742 pupils; 67 year of basic vocational training with 3,569 pupils; 590 full-time vocational schools with 36,768 pupils; 75 *Fachgymnasien* with 6,924 pupils; 123 *Fachoberschulen* with 6,934 pupils (full-time vocational schools leading up to vocational colleges); 68 vocational extension schools with 1,821 pupils; 172 advanced full-time vocational schools (including schools for technicians) with 10,890 pupils; 235 public health schools with 10,747 pupils.

In the winter term 1976–77 there were the University of Göttingen (19,587 students); 3 technical universities (Braunschweig, 8,484; Clausthal, 2,778; Hanover, 13,402); the medical college of Hanover (1,530) and the veterinary college in Hanover (1,079). There were also 5 teacher-training colleges with 10,804 students; 1 college of music and 1 college of fine arts with together 1,367 students.

Statistical Information: The Niedersächsisches Landesverwaltungsam.—Statistik' (Geibelstr. 65, D3000 Hanover 1) fulfils the function of the 'Statistisches Landesamt für Niedersachsen'. *Head of Division:* Abteilungsdirektor Dr Hans Kraus. Main publications are: *Statistisches Jahrbuch für Niedersachsen* (from 1950).—*Statistische Monatshefte für Niedersachsen* (from 1947).—*Statstik von Niedersachsen.*

State Library: Niedersächsische Staats- und Universitätsbibliothek. Prinzenstr. 1, 3400, Göttingen. *Director:* Prof. W. Grunwald.

NORTH RHINE-WESTPHALIA

Nordrhein-Westfalen

AREA AND POPULATION. The Land comprises 34,057 sq. km. It is divided into 5 areas, 23 urban and 31 rural districts. Capital Düsseldorf. Population, 31 Dec. 1976, 17,073,192 (8,146,896 males, 8,146,896 females).

Vital statistics for calendar years:

	Live births	*Marriages*	*Divorces*	*Deaths*
1974	169,031	107,294	24,266	197,905
1975	164,228	112,685	26,361	205,057
1976	166,128	105,283	27,604	199,930

GOVERNMENT. The Land Nordrhein-Westfalen is governed by a coalition of Social Democrats and Free Democrats; Minister President, Heinz Kühn (SPD). The Diet, elected on 4 May 1975, consists of 95 Christian Democrats, 91 Social Democrats, 14 Free Democrats.

AGRICULTURE. Area and yield of the most important crops:

	Area (in 1,000 hectares)			*Yield (in 1,000 tonnes)*		
	1974	*1975*	*1976*	*1974*	*1975*	*1976*
Wheat	213·7	212·3	219·6	1,089·4	1,005·2	931·5
Rye	137·5	113·4	114·0	532·7	436·1	412·6
Barley	307·6	314·1	326·4	1,486·6	1,425·2	1,371·9
Oats	132·6	151·2	134·1	558·8	593·6	438·1
Potatoes	44·3	38·3	38·6	1,497·2	1,095·4	877·5
Sugar-beet	77·9	88·2	89·9	3,537·7	3,471·2	3,873·6

Livestock, 3 Dec. 1976: Cattle, 1,911,138 (including 654,735 milch cows); pigs, 4,587,272; sheep, 161,945; horses, 85,990; poultry, 16,860,870.

INDUSTRY. In June 1977, 10,629 establishments (with 20 and more employees) employed 2,194,760 persons; of these, 187,170 were employed in mining; 300,746 in machine construction; 214,250 in iron and steel production; 210,875 in chemical industry; 178,194 in electrical engineering; 93,749 in textile industry.

Output and/or production in 1,000 tonnes, 1976: Hard coal, 79,974; lignite, 119,103; pig-iron, 20,671; raw steel ingots, 26,852; rolled steel, 18,178; castings (iron, steel and malleable castings), 1,866; cement, 12,655; fireproof products, 1,492; sulphuric acid (including production of cokeries), 2,134; staple fibres and rayon, 16; metalworking machines, 145; equipment for smelting works and rolling mills, 168; machines for mining industry, 240; cranes and hoisting machinery, 70; installation implements, 60; cables and electric lines, 246; springs of all kinds, 201; chains of all kinds, 138; locks and fittings, 241; spun yarns, 210; electric power, 165,693m. kwh.; gas (including cokery-gas of industry), 6,096m. cu. metres. Of the total population, 13·4% were engaged in industry.

LABOUR. The economically active persons totalled 6,729,000 at the 1%-sample survey of the microcensus of May 1976. Of the total, 527,600 were self-employed, 178,000 unpaid family workers, 6,023,400 employees; 189,900 were engaged in agriculture and forestry, 3,375,700 in power supply, mining, manufacturing and building, 1,193,400 in commerce and transport, 1·97m. in other industries and services.

ROADS. There were (1 Jan. 1977) 29,139 km of 'classified' roads, including 1,425 km of autobahn, 5,714 km of federal roads, 12,259 km of first-class and 9,741 km of second-class highways. Number of motor vehicles, 1 July 1977, 6,133,845, including 5,092,848 passenger cars, 366,848 lorries, 291,249 motor lorries/trucks, 15,498 buses, 201,714 tractors and 132,480 motor cycles.

JUSTICE. There are a constitutional court (*Verfassungsgerichtshof*), 3 courts of appeal, 19 regional courts, 143 local courts, 2 Land labour courts, 29 labour courts, a Land social court, 8 social courts, 2 finance courts, a higher administrative court, 7 administrative courts.

RELIGION. On 27 May 1970 (census) there were 41·9% Protestants and 52·5% Roman Catholics.

EDUCATION. In 1976 there were 4,898 primary schools with 65,493 teachers and 1,735,526 pupils; 708 special schools with 10,542 teachers and 122,386 pupils; 544 intermediate schools with 12,897 teachers and 330,318 pupils; 36 *Gesamtschulen* (comprehensive schools) with 2,242 teachers and 35,709 pupils; 642 high schools with 26,706 teachers and 577,368 pupils; in 1976 there were 303 part-time vocational schools with 433,057 pupils; vocational preparatory year 234 with 17,440 pupils; 345 full-time vocational schools with 89,175 pupils; 255 full-time vocational schools leading up to vocational colleges with 35,129 pupils; 157 advanced full-time vocational schools with 14,240 pupils; 626 schools for public health occupations with 9,138 teachers and 30,126 pupils.

In the winter term 1976–77 there were 7 universities (Bielefeld, 5,341 students; Bochum, 22,628; Bonn, 25,490; Dortmund, 4,647; Düsseldorf, 6,774; Cologne, 25,349; Münster, 28,646); the Technical University of Aachen (21,971); 1 Roman Catholic and 2 Protestant theological colleges with together 731 students. There were also 3 teacher-training colleges with 28,810 students; 3 colleges of music, 1 college of fine arts and the college for physical education in Cologne with together 6,626 students; 17 *Fachhochschulen* (vocational colleges) with 48,297 students, and 6 *Gesamthochschulen* with together 37,696 students.

Statistical Information: The *Landesamt für Datenverarbeitung und Statistik Nordrhein-Westfalen* (Mauerstr. 51, D4000 Düsseldorf 1) was founded in 1946, by amalgamating the provincial statistical offices of Rhineland and Westphalia. *President:* A. Benker. The Landesamt publishes: *Statistisches Jahrbuch Nordrhein-Westfalen.* From 1949.—*Statistisches Taschenbuch Nordrhein-Westfalen.* From 1955 to 1971.—More than 550 other publications yearly.

Land Library: Universitätsbibliothek, Grabbeplatz 7, Dusseldorf. *Director:* Dr G. Gattermann.

RHINELAND-PALATINATE

Rheinland-Pfalz

AREA AND POPULATION. Rhineland-Pfalz comprises 19,838 sq. km. Capital Mainz. Population (at 31 Dec. 1976), 3,649,001 (1,740,467 males, 1,908,534 females).

Vital statistics for calendar years:

	Live births	*Marriages*	*Divorces*	*Deaths*
1974	35,885	24,444	5,427	43,487
1975	34,377	25,674	6,357	44,943
1976	34,544	24,199	6,120	44,706

CONSTITUTION. The constitution of the Land Rheinland-Pfalz was approved by the Consultative Assembly on 25 April 1947 and by referendum on 18 May 1947, when 579,002 voted for and 514,338 against its acceptance.

The elections of 9 March 1975 returned 55 Christian Democrats, 40 Social Democrats, 5 Free Democrats.

The cabinet is headed by Bernhard Vogel (Christian Democrat).

AGRICULTURE. Area and yield of the most important products:

	Area (1,000 hectares)			*Yield (1,000 tonnes)*		
	1974	*1975*	*1976*	*1974*	*1975*	*1976*
Wheat	127·7	118·8	122·1	585·2	505·8	385·5
Rye	33·3	30·2	37·1	126·2	100·6	104·3
Barley	123·3	131·5	129·6	487·1	499·0	341·0
Oats	66·1	69·2	62·8	249·1	240·2	101·5
Potatoes	38·9	32·4	32·6	1,074·6	781·6	603·3
Sugar-beet	24·0	27·1	27·3	1,175·4	1,351·3	1,189·2
Wine (1,000 hectolitres)	57·0	57·7	58·6	5,467·1	6,642·4	6,028·2
Tobacco	1·3	1·4	1·4	...	...	...

Livestock (3 Dec. 1976): Cattle, 654,000 (including 232,800 milch cows); horses, 21,000; sheep, 83,000; pigs, 683,100; poultry 4,341,600.

INDUSTRY. In June 1976, 2,647 establishments (with 10 and more employees) employed 362,637 persons; of these 72,451 were employed in chemical industry; 24,378 in production of leather goods and footwear; 41,256 in machine construction; 17,560 in processing stones and earthenware.

LABOUR. The economically active persons totalled 1·51m. at the census of May 1976. Of the total, 146,000 were self-employed, 87,000 unpaid family workers, 1,276,000 employees; 120,000 were engaged in agriculture and forestry, 643,000 in power supply, mining, manufacturing and building, 266,000 in commerce and transport, 481,000 in other industries and services.

ROADS. There were (1 Jan. 1977) 18,552 km of 'classified' roads, including 591 km of autobahn, 3,296 km of federal roads, 6,870 km of first-class and 7,795 km of second-class highways. Number of motor vehicles, 1 July 1977, was 1,476,222, including 1,124,655 passenger cars, 68,497 lorries, 4,242 buses, 137,730 tractors and 37,617 motor cycles.

JUSTICE. There are a constitutional court (*Verfassungsgerichtshof*), 2 courts of appeal, 8 regional courts, 47 local courts, a Land labour court, 4 labour courts, a Land social court, 3 social courts, a finance court, a higher administrative court, 2 administrative courts.

RELIGION. On 27 May 1970 (census) there were 40·7% Protestants and 55·7% Roman Catholics.

EDUCATION. In 1976 there were 1,238 primary schools with 16,141 teachers and 404,584 pupils; 161 special schools with 2,125 teachers and 19,783 pupils; 102 intermediate schools with 2,643 teachers and 63,556 pupils; 136 high schools with 5,780 teachers and 117,888 pupils; 90 vocational schools with 97,079 pupils; 97 advanced vocational schools and institutions for the training of technicians (full- and part-time) with 5,364 pupils; 115 schools for public health occupations with 1,908 teachers and 6,111 pupils.

In the summer term 1977 there were the University of Mainz (18,345 students), the University of Kaiserslautern (1,957 students), the University of Trier (2,694 students) and the Roman Catholic Theological College in Trier (292 students). There were also the Teacher-Training College of the Land Rheinland-Pfalz (*Erziehungswissenschaftliche Hochschule*) with 3,180 students and the *Fachhochschule des*

Landes Rheinland-Pfalz (college of engineering) with 6,964 students; also 2 private colleges for social-pedagogy (769 students).

Statistical Information: The Statistisches Landesamt Rheinland-Pfalz (Mainzer St., 15–16, D5427 Bad Ems) was established in 1948. *President:* Dr Nellessen. Its publications include: *Statistisches Jahrbuch für Rheinland-Pfalz* (from 1948); *Statistische Monatshefte Rheinland-Pfalz* (from 1958); *Statistik von Rheinland-Pfalz* (from 1949) 281 vols. to date; *Rheinland-Pfalz im Spiegel der Statistik* (1968); *Die Kreisfreien Städte und Landkreise in Rheinland-Pfalz* (1977); *Rheinland-Pfalz heute* (from 1973); *Benutzerhandbuch des Landesinformationssystems* (1976); *Rheinland-Pfalz heute und morgen* (Mainz, 1974); *Raumordnungsbericht 1975 den Landesregierung Rheinland-Pfalz* (Mainz, 1976).

Klöpper, R., and Korber, J., *Rheinland-Pfalz in seiner Gliederung nach zentralörtlichen Bereichen.* Remagen, 1957
Süsterhenn, A., and Schäfer, H., *Verfassung von Rheinland-Pfalz: Kommentar.* Koblenz, 1950

SAARLAND

HISTORY. In 1919 the Saar territory was placed under the control of the League of Nations. Following a plebiscite, the territory reverted to Germany in 1935. In 1945 the territory became part of the French Zone of occupation, and was in 1947 accorded an international status inside an economic union with France. In pursuance of the German–French agreement signed in Luxembourg on 27 Oct. 1956 the territory returned to Germany on 1 Jan. 1957. Its re-integration with Germany was completed by 5 July 1959.

AREA AND POPULATION. Saarland has an area of 2,569 sq. km. Estimated population, 31 Dec. 1976, 1,089,000 (516,600 males, 572,400 females). The capital is Saarbrücken.

Vital statistics for calendar years:

	Live births	*Marriages*	*Divorces*	*Deaths*
1974	9,868	7,789	872	13,241
1975	9,585	8,355	1,200	13,269
1976	9,601	7,635	1,178	13,570

CONSTITUTION. Saarland now ranks as a *Land* of the Federal German Republic and is represented in the Federal Diet by 8 members. The constitution passed on 15 Dec. 1947 is being revised.

The Saar Diet, elected on 4 May 1975, is composed as follows: 25 Christian Democrats, 22 Social Democrats, 3 Free Democrats.

Saarland is governed by Christian Democrats and Free Democrats in spite of deadlock in Parliament. Minister President: Dr Franz Josef Röder (Christian Democrat).

AGRICULTURE AND FORESTRY. The cultivated area occupies 129,800 hectares or slightly more than half the total area; the forest area comprises nearly 32% of the total.

Area and yield of the most important crops:

	Area (1,000 hectares)			*Yield (1,000 tonnes)*		
	1974	*1975*	*1976*	*1974*	*1975*	*1976*
Wheat	12·0	10·2	12·0	49·1	37·1	36·8
Rye	7·3	5·7	7·5	25·7	19·3	21·2
Barley	12·4	13·8	12·8	48·8	51·1	33·6
Oats	8·9	9·7	9·0	33·7	34·8	16·7
Potatoes	6·9	6·5	6·7	200·6	147·1	89·9
Sugar-beet	...	...	...	1·0	1·0	0·7

Livestock, 3 Dec. 1975: Cattle, 72,700 (including 26,000 milch cows); pigs, 52,600; sheep, 10,300; horses, 4,100; poultry, 656,800.

INDUSTRY. In June 1976, 566 establishments (with 10 and more employees) employed 152,119 persons; of these 22,306 were engaged in coalmining, 36,373 in iron and steel production, 11,183 in machine construction, 9,840 in steel construction. In 1976 the coalmines produced 9·3m. tonnes of coal. Four iron foundries had 12 blast furnaces working and produced 4·4m. tonnes of pig-iron and 5m. tonnes of crude steel.

LABOUR. The economically active persons totalled 400,000 at the 1%-sample survey of the microcensus of April 1975. Of the total, 28,000 were self-employed, 19,000 unpaid family workers, 361,000 employees; 9,000 were engaged in agriculture and forestry, 196,000 in power supply, mining, manufacturing and building, 90,000 in commerce and transport, 105,000 in other industries and services.

ROADS. At 1 Jan. 1976 there were 2,045 km of 'classified' roads, including 128 km of autobahn, 435 km of federal roads, 750 km of first-class and 733 km of second-class highways. Number of motor vehicles, 1 July 1976, 369,630, including 330,989 passenger cars, 20,019 lorries, 1,377 buses, 11,289 tractors and 5,956 motor cycles.

JUSTICE. There are a constitutional court (*Verfassungsgerichtshof*), a court of appeal, a regional court, 11 local courts, a Land labour court, 3 labour courts, a Land social court, a social court, a finance court, a higher administrative court, an administrative court.

RELIGION. On 27 May 1970 (census) 73·8% of the population were Roman Catholics and 24·1% were Protestants.

EDUCATION. In 1976–77 there were 334 primary schools with 4,325 teachers and 112,223 pupils; 55 special schools with 579 teachers and 7,012 pupils; 33 intermediate schools with 919 teachers and 20,788 pupils; 38 high schools with 1,808 teachers and 36,229 pupils; 1 *Gesamtschule* (comprehensive school) with 66 teachers and 1,327 pupils; 1 *Freie Waldorfschule* with 5 teachers and 125 pupils; 43 part-time vocational schools with 28,959 pupils; year of commercial basic training: 63 institutions with 159 classes and 3,126 pupils; 24 advanced full-time vocational schools and schools for technicians with 1,710 pupils; 88 full-time vocational schools with 7,298 students; 26 vocational extension schools with 2,509 pupils; 18 *Fachoberschulen* (full-time vocational schools leading up to vocational colleges) with 1,845 students; 40 schools for public health occupations with 2,379 pupils; 1 school for mining engineers with 158 students; 2 evening high schools and 1 *Saarland-Kolleg* with together 408 pupils; 1 vocational special school with 208 pupils. Teachers of all vocational schools 1,469 including *Referendare*.

In the winter term 1975–76 there was the University of the Saar with 11,451 students; 1 academic institution of higher education (teacher-training institution) with 726 students; 1 conservatory with 204 students; 1 *Studienkolleg* (special institution leading up to university qualification) with 47 students; 1 vocational college (economics, engineering and design) with 1,609 students; 1 *Fachhochschule* (vocational college) for social affairs with 99 students.

Statistical Information: The Statistical Office of the Saar (Saarbrücken 1, Hardenbergstrasse 3) was established on 1 April 1938. As from 1 June 1935, it was an independent agency; its predecessor, 1920–35, was the Statistical Office of the Government Commission of the Saar. *Chief:* Direktor Dr Kunkel. The most important publications are: *Statistisches Handbuch für das Saarland*, from 1950.—*Statistisches Taschenbuch für das Saarland*, from 1959.—*Saarländische Bevölkerungsund Wirtschaftszahlen*. Quarterly, from 1949.—*Saarland in Zahlen* (special issues).—*Einzelschriften zur Statistik des Saarlandes*, from 1950.

Fischer, P., *Die Saar zwischen Deutschland und Frankreich*. Frankfurt, 1959
Freymond, J., *Le Conflit sarrois, 1945–55*. Brussels, 1959. [*The Saar Conflict*. New York, 1960]
Schmidt, R. H., *Saarpolitik 1945–57*. 3 vols. Berlin, 1959–62

SCHLESWIG-HOLSTEIN

AREA AND POPULATION. The area of Schleswig-Holstein is 15,696 km; it is divided into 4 urban and 11 rural districts and 1,159 communes. The capital is Kiel. The population (estimate, 31 Dec. 1976) numbered 2,582,718 (1,239,187 males, 1,343,531 females).

Vital statistics for calendar years:

	Live births	*Marriages*	*Divorces*	*Deaths*
1974	25,545	14,979	4,610	32,084
1975	24,282	14,970	5,487	32,993
1976	24,861	14,495	...	32,185

GOVERNMENT. The elections of 13 April 1975 gave the Christian Democratic Union 37, the Social Democratic Party 30, the Free Democratic Party 5 and the South Schleswig Association 1 seat. Minister President, Dr Gerhard Stoltenberg (Christian Democrat).

AGRICULTURE. Area and yield of the most important crops:

	Area (1,000 hectares)			*Yield (1,000 tonnes)*		
	1974	*1975*	*1976*	*1974*	*1975*	*1976*
Wheat	109·1	113·8	126·5	591·4	636·8	638·3
Rye	85·3	75·9	88·2	299·3	236·9	277·3
Barley	121·8	126·5	124·0	573·4	558·0	559·0
Oats	95·9	110·6	84·7	434·7	402·4	250·7
Potatoes	9·9	7·7	7·7	298·0	159·1	109·1
Sugar-beet	16·7	20·7	24·1	637·0	734·9	813·1

Livestock, 3 Dec 1976: 32,100 horses, 1,559,800 cattle (including 513,300 milch cows), 1,695,600 pigs, 124,200 sheep, 4,626,000 poultry.

FISHERIES. In 1976 the yield of small-scale deep-sea and inshore fisheries was 62,100 tonnes valued at DM 53m.

INDUSTRY. In 1976 (average), 1,503 establishments (with 10 and more employees) employed 171,400 persons; of these, 20,600 were employed in shipbuilding (except naval engineering); 26,400 in machine construction; 23,100 in food and kindred industry; 18,000 in electrical engineering.

LABOUR. The economically active persons totalled 1·05m. at the 1%-sample survey of the microcensus of April 1976. Of the total, 103,000 were self-employed, 44,000 unpaid family workers, 913,000 employees; 76,000 were engaged in agriculture and forestry, 364,000 in power supply, mining, manufacturing and building, 222,000 in commerce and transport, 396,000 in other industries and services.

ROADS. There were (1 Jan 1977) 9,509 km of 'classified' roads, including 275 km of autobahn, 1,989 km of federal roads, 3,612 km of first-class and 3,634 km of second-class highways. Number of motor vehicles, 1 July 1977, was 979,098, including 837,931 passenger cars, 45,433 lorries, 2,424 buses, 71,841 tractors, 11,402 motor cycles.

SHIPPING. The Kiel Canal, 98·7 km (51 miles) long, is on Schleswig-Holstein territory. In 1938, 53,530 vessels of 22·6m. net tons passed through it; in 1974, 68,456 vessels of 50·5m. net tons; in 1975, 60,281 vessels of 43·5m. net tons; in 1976, 60,323 vessels of 45·7m. net tons.

JUSTICE. There are a court of appeal, 4 regional courts, 43 local courts, a Land labour court, 6 labour courts, a Land social court, 4 social courts, a finance court, an administrative court.

RELIGION. On 27 May 1970 (census) there were 86·5% Protestants and 6% Roman Catholics.

EDUCATION. In 1976–77 there were 737 primary schools with 7,361 teachers and 251,940 pupils; 158 special schools with 1,486 teachers and 21,874 pupils; 146 intermediate schools with 3,063 teachers and 83,609 pupils; 93 high schools with 3,491 teachers and 76,253 pupils; 5 *Integrierte Gesamtschulen* (comprehensive schools) with 171 teachers and 3,138 pupils; 55 part-time vocational schools with 1,043 teachers and 65,496 pupils; 145 full-time vocational schools with 369 teachers and 8,628 pupils; 66 advanced vocational schools with 316 teachers and 5,045 pupils; 59 schools for public health occupations with 2,859 pupils; 29 vocational grammar schools with 341 teachers and 4,387 pupils; 4 *Fachhochschulen* (vocational colleges) with 3,835 pupils in the winter term 1976–77.

In the winter term 1976–77 the University of Kiel had 12,010 students, 2 teacher-training colleges had 3,658 students, 1 music college had 243 students and 1 *Medizinische Hochschule* in Lübeck had 318 students.

Statistical Information: Statistisches Landesamt Schleswig-Holstein (Mühlenweg 166, 2300 Kiel 1). *Director:* Dr Mohr. Publications: *Statistisches Taschenbuch Schleswig-Holstein*, from 1954.—*Statistisches Jahrbuch Schleswig-Holstein*, from 1951.—*Statistische Monatshefte Schleswig-Holstein*, from 1949.—*Statistische Berichte*, from 1947.—*Beitrage zur historischen Statistik Schleswig-Holstein*, from 1967.

Baxter, R. R., *The Law of International Waterways.* Harvard University Press, 1964
Brandt, O., *Grundriss der Geschichte Schleswig-Holsteins.* 5th ed. Kiel, 1957
Handbuch für Schleswig-Holstein. 16th ed. Kiel, 1972

State Library: Schleswig-Holsteinische Landesbibliothek, Kiel, Schloss. *Director:* Prof. Dr Klaus Friedland.

GHANA

Capital: Accra
Population: 9·6m. (1976)
GNP per capita: US$580 (1976)

HISTORY. The State of Ghana came into existence on 6 March 1957 when the former Colony of the Gold Coast and the Trusteeship Territory of Togoland attained Dominion status. The name of the country recalls a powerful monarchy which from the 4th to the 13th century A.D. ruled the region of the middle Niger.

The Ghana Independence Act received the royal assent on 7 Feb. 1957. The General Assembly of the United Nations in Dec. 1956 approved the termination of British administration in Togoland and the union of Togoland with the Gold Coast on the latter's attainment of independence.

The country was declared a Republic within the Commonwealth on 1 July 1960 with Dr Kwame Nkrumah as the first President. On 24 Feb. 1966 the Nkrumah regime was overthrown in a military *coup* and ruled by the National Liberation Council until 1 Oct. 1969 when the military regime handed over power to a civilian regime under a new constitution. Dr K. A. Busia was the Prime Minister of the Second Republic. In Aug. 1975 the Government announced that they would commemorate the late Dr Nkrumah as 'a great Ghanaian responsible for taking the country to independence'.

On 13 Jan. 1972 the armed forces and police took over power again from the civilian regime in a *coup*.

In Oct. 1975 the National Redemption Council was subordinated to a Supreme Military Council (SMC).

AREA AND POPULATION. The area of Ghana is 92,010 sq. miles (238,305 sq. km); census population 1970 (preliminary), 8,545,561. Estimate (1976) 9·6m.

The capital is Accra (population, 1970, 636,067).

Ghana is divided into 9 regions:

Regions	*Area (sq. km)*	*Population census 1970*	*Capital*	*Population census 1970*
Eastern	19,833	1,262,882	Koforidua	69,804
Western	24,214	770,089	Sekondi-Takoradi	254,543
Central	9,469	890,135	Cape Coast	71,594
Ashanti	25,123	1,505,049	Kumasi	351,629
Brong-Ahafo	39,709	766,509	Sunyani	61,772
Northern	70,338	728,572	Tamale	120,000
Volta	20,651	947,012	Ho	46,348
Upper	16,877	862,723	Bolgatanga	18,896
Greater Accra	2,023	903,445	Accra	636,067

Other chief towns (population, census, 1970); Asamankese, 101,144; Nsawam, 57,350; Oda, 40,740; Obuasi, 40,001; Winneba, 36,104; Keta, 27,461; Swedru (Agona), 23,843.

Estimated birth rate, between 47 and 52 per 1,000; death rate, about 23 per 1,000.

CONSTITUTION AND GOVERNMENT. Following a bloodless *coup* on 13 Jan. 1972 the armed forces of Ghana took over the government from Dr K. A. Busia. A National Redemption Council (NRC) was established to administer the affairs of the country.

The Constitution of the Second Republic of Ghana which came into force on 22 Aug. 1969 was suspended. The office of President was abolished and the National Assembly dissolved.

On 9 Oct. 1975 the National Redemption Council was replaced by the Supreme Military Council as the highest legislative and administrative authority in the country. The Supreme Military Council is headed by the Head of State Gen. I. K. Acheampong as Chairman. Other members are Chief of Defence Staff, the Army

Commander, the Navy Commander, the Air Force Commander, the Border Guards Commander and the Inspector-General of Police. All members other than the Chairman hold office by virtue of their service appointments.

The reconstituted National Redemption Council is a subordinate body also headed by the Head of State and composed of members appointed by virtue of their service appointments in the Government and armed forces.

For earlier political history of Ghana *see* THE STATESMAN'S YEAR-BOOK, 1971–72.

Head of State, Chairman of the National Redemption Council: Gen. I. K. Acheampong.

For administrative purposes Commissioners have been appointed to head the various ministries and include:

Defence: Gen. I. K. Acheampong. *Internal Affairs* (*Inspector-General of Police*): Ernest Ako. *Agriculture:* Col. S. M. Akwagyiram. *Education and Culture:* E. Owusu-Fordwouh. *Economic Planning:* Dr Robert Gardiner. *Foreign Affairs:* Col. R. J. A. Felli. *Health:* A. Karbo. *Justice and Attorney-General:* Dr Koranteng Addow. *Industries:* Col. B. K. Ahlijah. *Information:* Col. P. H. S. Yarney. *Labour, Social Welfare and Co-operatives:* Nii Anyetei Kwakwranyai. *Lands and Mineral Resources:* Brig. O. I. Boateng. *Local Government:* C. K. Tedam. *Trade and Tourism:* Col. K. A. Quarshie. *Transport and Communications:* E. R. K. Dwemoh. *Works and Housing:* Maj. E. Yirimambo. *Cocoa Affairs:* Cdr Parker H. S. Yarmey, *Finance:* Dr A. K. Appiah.

Regional Organization. Ghana is divided into 9 regions: Eastern, Western, Ashanti, Northern, Volta, Central, Upper, Brong-Ahafo; and the Greater Accra Area. Each region is administered by a Regional Commissioner, who is an army officer.

National flag: Red, gold, green (horizontal); a black star in the centre.

National anthem: Hail the name of Ghana.

DEFENCE. The Ministry of Defence is responsible for the armed services, the military academy and the border guards. The Military Academy provides a 2-year course for army officers, a 1-year course for later entrants in the flying-training school and a preliminary 6-month course for navy cadets.

Army. The Ghana Army consists of 6 infantry battalions, 1 reconnaissance battalion, 1 field engineer battalion, 5 with armoured cars, and ancillary units. Total strength, about 15,000. There are also 3 border battalions and a paramilitary militia of 3,000.

Navy. The Ghana Navy was formed in 1959. It comprises 2 British-built 500-ton corvettes, 2 new patrol craft, a coastal minesweeper, 2 inshore minesweepers, 2 seaward defence boats and a maintenance repair craft. A frigate (to have been named *The Black Star*) was built in Britain to the order of Ghana, but the contract was rescinded in 1966; she was completed in 1968 and taken over by Britain in 1972, and was commissioned in the Royal Navy in 1973 as HMS *Mermaid* but was transferred to Malaysia in 1977. Naval personnel in 1978 numbered 2,000 officers and ratings.

Air Force. The Ghana Air Force was formed in 1959, when an Air Force Training School was established at Accra. Its first combat unit has 6 Italian-built Aermacchi M.B.326K light ground attack jets ordered in 1976. It has, for training, transport, search and rescue, and air survey operations, 5 Fokker Friendship twin-turboprop transports, and a twin-turbofan Fokker Fellowship for Presidential use, all built in the Netherlands; 6 Short Skyvan and 8 Britten-Norman Islander twin-engined STOL transports and 12 Bulldog primary trainers, all built in the UK; 2 Bell 212 helicopters built in the US; 4 French-built Alouette III helicopters, and 7 Aermacchi M.B.326F armed jet trainers. There are air bases at Takoradi and Tamale. Personnel strength about 1,250.

INTERNATIONAL RELATIONS

Membership. Ghana is a member of UN, Commonwealth, OAU and is an ACP state of EEC.

ECONOMY

Planning. The 1975–80 Development Plan was launched in 1977.

Budget. Revenue and expenditure for fiscal years ending 30 June (excluding Ghana Railway and Takoradi Harbour accounts), in ₵1,000:

	1972–73	*1973–74*	*1974–75*
Revenue[1]	391,654	583,574	804,800
Expenditure[2]	545,114	738,521	1,161,400

[1] Excludes redemption of loans.
[2] Excludes contribution to sinking funds, repayment of loans, loans and refunds of revenue.

The main items of expenditure envisaged for 1969–70 were (in ₵1,000): Social services, 132,944; general services, 144,841; economic services, 70,534; community services, 41,687.

The development budget for 1975–76 was ₵322m.

Currency. The monetary unit is the *cedi* (₵), divided into 100 *pesewas* (P) and equivalent to £0·51 or US$0·87. Notes are issued of 1, 2, 5 and copper coins of ½ and 1 P, and cupro-nickel coins of 2½, 5, 10 and 20 P.

The internal debt was ₵2,436m. in 1976.

Banking. The Bank of Ghana was established in Feb. 1957 as the central bank of the country. The Ghana Commercial Bank, also established in Feb. 1957, is the former Bank of the Gold Coast. It is a purely commercial institution and has 120 branches in the country, 1 in London and 1 in Lomé (Togo). Barclays Bank (Ghana) Ltd has 54 branches and agencies and the Standard Bank (Ghana) Ltd has 27 branches.

The Ghana National Investment Bank, opened in June 1963, is a finance-cum-development agency. The former post office savings bank has been transformed into the Ghana Savings Bank. The Bank for Housing and Construction opened in 1973.

ENERGY AND NATURAL RESOURCES

Oil. The Government announced in Jan. 1978 that oil had been found in commercial quantities.

Minerals. In 1975 gold production was 513,830 fine oz.; diamonds, 2,258,014 carats; manganese, 328,294 tons; bauxite, 292,464 long tons. Old mines are being re-opened and exploration of mineral oil deposits, bauxite, limestone and iron ore is now extensive.

Agriculture. Cocoa is by far the most important crop and covers about 2m. acres. There has been a considerable increase in cocoa yields as a result of the Capsid control and the introduction of improved varieties. A Cocoa Affairs Ministry has been established to formulate policy and provide technical supervision for developing cocoa, coffee, shea-nuts, copra and bananas. Coffee, improved types of oil-palm and coconut are being planted on an increased scale and production from these crops is increasing. Progress has been made in the planting of Clonal rubber in south-west Ghana. In the south-east coastal belt irrigation works have been constructed and black-clay farming is being successfully undertaken in the Accra plains.

Of the main foodstuffs in south and central Ghana, maize, rice, cassava, plantain, groundnuts, yam and cocoyam predominate. Tobacco is proving an attractive and very important cash crop in food-crop producing areas.

In northern Ghana the chief food crops are groundnuts, rice, maize, guinea corn, millet and yams, with tobacco and cotton as important cash crops.

The State Farms Corporation has been reorganized and is now to concentrate on the development of large-scale tree-crop plantations such as palm-oil, rubber, coconut, kola and cashew. All its available food farms have been transferred to the newly formed Food Production Corporation. The Corporation undertakes the growing of maize, guinea corn, rice, vegetables, cassava, plaintain, yams, etc.

An agricultural crash programme, 'Operation Feed Yourself', and 'Operation

Feed Your Industries' are under way, designed to produce the country's food requirements and industrial crops to supply the existing factories and for export. Large areas of land hitherto lying fallow are now thriving with a variety of staple crops. The country is now self-sufficient in maize and rice. Guaranteed prices have been fixed for maize, yam, plantain and cassava to encourage production on a large scale. Agricultural cash crops, *e.g.*, pepper, ginger, pineapple, avocado and citrus, etc., are being extensively cultivated for export. Active steps have also been taken to provide within the next few years industrial raw materials, *e.g.*, kenaf, cotton, tobacco, palm-oil, mango, pineapple, sugar-cane, etc., to feed the local factories. The trend is towards diversification of agriculture.

About ₵37m. was allocated for the development of agriculture for 1975–76. Development is being concentrated on increased production of selected industrial and cash crops such as rubber, sugar-cane, cotton, oil-palm, bast fibre, groundnut, cashew, etc. Infrastructural facilities necessary for commercial livestock development is being provided and small-scale fishermen are getting assistance.

A Food Production Corporation has been established to see to the production and efficient and equitable distribution of foodstuffs throughout the country. The state farms have been transferred to the Corporation.

In the 1975–76 budget ₵10m. was allocated for irrigation works including ₵5·7m. for projects at Tono, ₵775,000 at Dawhenya and ₵245,000 at Kyereko.

Production of main food crops (1975) was: Cassava, 2,360m. tons; coco yam, 1,082m. tons; plantain, 1,226m. tons; yam, 698,000 tons.

Livestock, 1976: Cattle, 1·1m.; sheep, 1·8m.; goats, 2m.; horses, 4,000; pigs, 400,000; poultry, 11m. The Central Veterinary Laboratory is located at Pong-Tamale under the Veterinary Research Officer. The efficient control of rinderpest and bovine pleuro-pneumonia, the two main killing diseases of cattle, has made it possible to quadruple the cattle in the past 20 years. The control of imported livestock is effected by 8 quarantine stations along the frontier, and newly established veterinary centres are being established.

Forestry. The total area of closed forest is 82,576 sq. km, of which 16,852·2 sq. km are reserved. Exports (1975) of logs, was 1,524m. cu. metres.

The destruction of unreserved forests by farming is threatening the timber supply for exports. Reafforestation is going ahead to counteract this and the Upper and Northern Regions included to arrest the Sahelian threat.

Fisheries. ₵ 3·3m. is to be spent on the development of the fisheries sector of the economy, including fishing harbours and landing stages, workshops for repair and maintenance of outboard motors; development of fish culture and expansion of fish farms, establishment of fishing complexes, purchase of refrigerated vans for fish distribution and the establishment of more cold-stores.

COMMERCE. Total trade, in ₵1,000, for calendar years:

	1972	*1973*	*1974*	*1975*
Imports	393,293	525,950	943,706	909,300
Exports	564,412	730,440	840,933	928,260

Principal exports in ₵1,000	*1971*	*1972*	*1973*	*1974*
Cocoa	195,066	289,058	344,833	466,427
Timber (logs)	32,753	42,292	88,551	63,955
Gold	28,454	510,089	71,016	94,843
Diamonds	11,752	18,544	13,063	14,570
Manganese	6,641	8,170	7,315	10,519
Bauxite	2,290	3,683	2,574	3,465

In 1974 the most important items of imports were food, mineral fuels, chemicals, manufactured goods, machinery and transport equipment.

Total trade between Ghana and UK (British Department of Trade returns, in £1,000 sterling):

	1973	*1974*	*1975*	*1976*	*1977*
Imports to UK	48,702	70,755	57,954	82,230	126,632
Exports and re-exports from UK	30,383	51,013	50,458	79,563	100,072

West African Common Market. On 4 May 1967, 12 West African countries (Benin, Ghana, Ivory Coast, Liberia, Mali, Mauritania, Niger, Nigeria, Senegal, Sierra Leone, Togo and Upper Volta) signed articles of association in Accra, setting up a common market for goods and services among them and eliminating customs and trade barriers.

COMMUNICATIONS

Roads. The total mileage of roads maintained by the Public Works Department in 1974 was 21,762, of which 2,746 miles were bitumen surfaced and 5,016 miles gravel surfaced.

The number of vehicles with valid licences at 31 Dec. 1969 was 53,717. The principal categories were: Cars, 34,222 (including taxis); goods vehicles, 13,137; motor cycles, 3,550; special-purpose vehicles, 2,808.

Railways. The total railway mileage open in 1976 was 592, including a link of 51 miles between the Central Province line at Achiasi and the Accra–Kumasi line at Kotoku opened in Feb. 1956. The main line runs from Takoradi to Kumasi, thence to Accra (355 miles); with branches: Takoradi Junction–Sekondi (3 miles), Tarkwa–Prestea (19 miles), Hunni Valley–Kade (99 miles, Central line), Dunkwa–Awaso (46 miles), Achimota–Tema (16 miles), Achiasi–Kotoku (51 miles) and Accra–Accra Beach (2 miles). All are 3 ft 6 in. gauge. During 1973–74 capital expenditure was ₵2·9m., revenue was ₵11·7m. and expenditure (including renewals) ₵21m.

Aviation. There are 4 major airports in Ghana, situated at Accra, Takoradi, Kumasi and Tamale; and 3 airstrips for domestic services. Accra airport is an international airport. The following airlines operate scheduled services: Ghana Airways, Air France, Nigerian Airways, Air Mali, United Arab Airlines, KLM, Swissair, PANAM, British Caledonian and several other companies. Total aircraft movement in 1970 was 31,611.

Shipping. The chief ports are Takoradi and Tema; the 'surf' ports at Accra, Winneba, Cape Coast and Keta ceased to operate when Tema harbour was opened in 1962, 18 miles east of Accra. In 1970, 4,164,329 tons of cargo were imported and 2,154,759 tons were exported by 3,116 ships.

Post and Broadcasting. There were (31 Dec. 1974) 2,190 miles of telegraph land wire, 20,948 miles of telephone trunks, 237 post offices and 710 postal agencies. There were 431 telephone exchanges and 742 call offices with (1977) 66,287 telephones in use and 29,227 miles of underground and overhead land wires in the exchange areas. There are internal wireless stations at Accra, Kumasi, Bawku, Lawra, Kete-Krachi, Tamale, Yendi, Kpandu, Tumu and Sekondi-Takoradi.

Newspapers. There are 5 daily and 7 weekly papers, 8 fortnightly and 5 monthly magazines.

JUSTICE, EDUCATION AND WELFARE

Justice. The judicial power of Ghana is vested in the Judiciary with the Chief Justice as the Head. It has jurisdiction in all civil and criminal matters.

The Courts of Ghana are constituted as follows: *Superior Courts of Ghana*, the Court of Appeal and the High Court of Justice. The Supreme Court of Ghana, created by the suspended Constitution in 1969, has been abolished and its functions taken over by the Court of Appeal.

The Court of Appeal. The Court of Appeal replaces the former Supreme Court of Ghana as the highest and final Court of Appeal in and for Ghana. It has all the power, authority and jurisdiction vested in any Court established in the country. The Court of Appeal consists of the Chief Justice, together with not less than 6 other Justices of the Appeal Court and such other Justices of Superior Courts as the Chief Justice may nominate. The Court is duly constituted by 3 justices. A full Bench of the Court of 5 Judges has jurisdiction to review and determine, among other things, a decision of the Court of Appeal or any justice or division thereof upon a question of law, including matters relating to aspects of the Chieftaincy Act

1971. Divisions of the Appeal Court may be created, subject to the discretion of the Chief Justice.

The High Court of Justice. This Court has jurisdiction in civil and criminal matters as well as those relating to industrial and labour disputes, including administrative complaints. It has supervisory jurisdiction over all interior and traditional courts, but has no power in a trial for offences involving treason, to convict any person for any offence other than treason. The High Court consists of the Chief Justice and not less than 12 other Judges as may be appointed by the Chief Justice. A High Court Judge can sit alone or with a jury.

The country has been divided into circuits, and there are Circuit Judges sitting in these courts with original jurisdiction in all criminal cases, except offences where the maximum punishment is death. The original jurisdiction in civil matters is restricted to cases where the subject-matter of the suit is not more than ₵8,000 or, in respect of liquidated sums, ₵15,000 involving ownership or occupation of land. *District District Courts* (Grade I and II), sitting throughout the country in the magisterial districts. *Juvenile Courts,* dealing with persons under the age of 17, have been established in Accra, Cape Coast, Sekondi, Kumasi and Koforidua.

Police. The force was established in Oct. 1874. It is headed by an Inspector-General and consists of 7 divisions with a (1975) strength of 15,817.

Education. A complete re-organization of the system took place in 1974. There are kindergartens for the age-groups 4–6 years. Primary schools are free and attendance is compulsory. In 1973–74 there were 6,843 primary schools with 1,014,964 pupils. The 4,000 secondary schools had about 500,000 pupils. In 1974–75 there were 6,006 students at the 3 universities (University of Ghana, the University of Science and Technology and the University of the Cape Coast).

Health. Medical facilities include 50 government hospitals, 116 health centres and posts, 4 university hospitals, 3 mental hospitals, 4 leprosaria, 7 military hospitals, 1 prison hospital, 40 mission hospitals and 16 private hospitals. In addition, there are 30 nurses and midwives training schools.

There were 1,224 doctors, 7,608 nurses and 4,168 midwives at work in 1976.

DIPLOMATIC REPRESENTATIVES

OF GHANA IN GREAT BRITAIN (13 Belgrave Sq., London, SW1X 8PR)

High Commissioner: Col. Samuel McGal Asante (accredited 6 Nov. 1975).

OF GREAT BRITAIN IN GHANA (Barclays Bank Bldg., High St., Accra)

High Commissioner: J. Mellon.

OF GHANA IN THE USA (2460 16th St., NW, Washington, D.C. 20009)

Chargé d'Affaires: Moses Kwasi Agyeman.

OF THE USA IN GHANA (Liberia and Kinbu Rds., Accra)

Ambassador: Robert B. Smith.

OF GHANA TO THE UNITED NATIONS

Ambassador: Frank Edmund Boaten.

Books of Reference

Digest of Statistics. Accra. Quarterly (from May 1953)
Ghana. Official Handbook. Annual
Trade Directory of the Republic of Ghana. 5th ed. London, 1967
The Volta River Project. 3 vols. HMSO, 1956
Acquah, L., *Accra Survey.* Univ. of London Press, 1958
Afrifa, A. A., *The Ghana Coup 24th February 1966.* London, 1966

Austin, D., *Politics in Ghana, 1946–60*. OUP, 1964
Boateng, E. A., *A Geography of Ghana*. 2nd ed. CUP, 1966
Davidson, B., *Black Star*. London, 1973
James, C. L. R., *Nkrumah and the Ghana Revolution*. London, 1977
Jones, T., *Ghana's First Republic 1960–1966*. London, 1975
Lystad, R. A., *The Ashanti*. Rutgers Univ. Press, 1966
Manshard, W., *Die geographischen der Wirtschaft Ghanas*. Wiesbaden, 1961
Timothy, B., *Kwame Nkrumah: His Rise to Power*. London, 1964
Wills, J. B. (ed.), *Agriculture and Land Use in Ghana*. OUP, 1962

GIBRALTAR

Population: 29,278 (1977)

HISTORY. The Rock of Gibraltar was settled by Moors in 711; they named it after their chief Jabal Tariq, 'the Mountain of Tarik'. In 1462 it was taken by the Spaniards, from Granada. It was captured by Admiral Sir George Rooke on 24 July 1704, and ceded to Great Britain by the Treaty of Utrecht, 1713. The cession was confirmed by the treaties of Paris (1763) and Versailles (1783).

On 10 Sept. 1967, in pursuance of a United Nations resolution on the decolonization of Gibraltar, a referendum was held in Gibraltar in order to ascertain whether the people of Gibraltar believed that their interests lay in retaining their link with Britain or in passing under Spanish sovereignty. Out of a total electorate of 12,762, 12,138 voted to retain the British connexion, while 44 voted for Spain.

AREA AND POPULATION. Area, $2\frac{1}{2}$ sq. miles (6·5 sq. km). Total population, including port and harbour (census, 6 Oct. 1970), 26,833 (13,501 males; 13,322 females). Estimate (1977) 29,278 (15,041 males; 14,237 females). The population are mostly of Genoese, Portuguese and Maltese as well as Spanish descent.

Vital statistics (1977): Births, 506; marriages, 461; deaths, 248.

GOVERNMENT. Following a Constitutional Conference held in July 1968, a new Constitution was introduced in 1969. The Legislative and City Councils were merged to produce an enlarged legislature known as the Gibraltar House of Assembly. Executive authority is exercised by the Governor, who is also Commander-in-Chief. The Governor, while retaining certain reserved powers, is normally required to act in accordance with the advice of the Gibraltar Council, which consists of 4 *ex-officio* members (the Deputy Governor, the Deputy Fortress Commander, the Attorney-General and the Financial and Development Secretary) together with 5 elected members of the House of Assembly appointed by the Governor after consultation with the Chief Minister. Matters of primarily domestic concern are devolved to elected Ministers, with Britain responsible for other matters, including external affairs, defence and internal security. There is a Council of Ministers presided over by the Chief Minister.

The House of Assembly consists of a Speaker appointed by the Governor, 15 elected and 2 *ex-officio* members (the Attorney-General and the Financial and Development Secretary).

A Mayor of Gibraltar is elected from among the members of the Assembly by the elected members of the Assembly.

Governor and C.-in-C.: Gen. Sir William Jackson, GBE, KCB, MC.

Chief Minister: Sir Joshua Hassan, CBE, MVO, QC.

Flag: White with a red strip along the bottom, a red triple-towered castle with a gold key depending from the gateway.

DEFENCE. The Gibraltar Regiment is a part-time infantry battalion with a small regular cadre.

ECONOMY

Budget. Revenue and expenditure (in £ sterling):

	1972–73	*1973–74*	*1974–75*	*1975–76*	*1976–77*
Revenue	5,614,920	6,710,196	8,790,210	11,807,045	18,207,859
Expenditure	5,674,270	6,906,250	8,653,078	10,322,937	17,709,855

Currency. The legal currency consists of Gibraltar Government notes and UK coins. The amount of local currency notes in circulation at 31 March 1977 was £3,951,346.

Banking. There are 6 banks, including a branch of Barclays Bank International. Government savings banks, with 13,582 depositors, had £1,481,021 deposits at 31 March 1976.

INDUSTRY AND TRADE

Industry. There are a number of relatively small industrial concerns engaged in the bottling of beer and mineral waters, etc., mainly for local consumption. There is a small but important commercial ship-repair yard. Tourism is of increasing importance.

Labour. The full-time labour force in Dec. 1976 was (estimate) 12,123. The labour supply from the local population is insufficient to meet the demand and since the withdrawal of the Spanish frontier workers in June 1969, a substantial part of the labour has had to come from other places. A quota system is in existence which takes into account the demand from the various industries and seasonal variations and the issue of employment permits is based on this. More than one-half of the local labour force is employed by the UK departments or the Gibraltar government.

A considerable proportion of the workers are organized in one or other of the 14 registered employees' trade unions, of which the Transport and General Workers Union has the largest membership; 7 of these are local branches of parent associations in the UK.

Commerce. Imports and exports (in £ sterling):

	1972–73	*1973–74*	*1974–75*	*1975–76*	*1976–77*
Imports	12,777,294	15,511,005	25,088,714	27,027,401	32,415,906
Exports	3,025,501	4,663,540	10,484,352	10,753,448	13,727,865

Britain and the Commonwealth provide the bulk of the imports, but fresh vegetables, fruit and fish come mainly from Morocco, Portugal and the Netherlands. Exports of local produce are negligible. Gibraltar depends largely on tourism, the entrepôt trade and the provision of supplies to visiting ships.

COMMUNICATIONS

Roads. There are 30 miles of roads including 4 miles of pedestrian way.

Aviation. There are 5 weekly flights between London and Gibraltar (3 operated by Gibraltar Airways and 2 by British Airways) during the winter; these are increased to daily flights during the summer.

The unilateral closure by Spain of their land frontier with Gibraltar makes overland travel from or to Spain impossible. However, there is a regular car ferry service and air services to Tangier and Morocco from where it is possible to cross over to the Spanish mainland.

Shipping. Gibraltar is a naval and air base of strategic importance. There is a deep Admiralty harbour of 440 acres. A total of 2,553 merchant ships, 19,113,544 NRT, entered the port during 1976. An additional 2,758 calls were made by yachts, 35,965 NRT.

Post. An automatic telephone system exists in the town, and there is world-wide communication *via* the cable and/or wireless circuits of Cable & Wireless Ltd. Airmails arrive by British Airways daily. A direct air-mail service between Gibraltar and Tangier is run by Gibraltar Airways, Ltd. Surface mails arrive direct and through France, Spain and Tangier.

Cinemas. In 1978 there were 3 cinemas with a seating capacity of 2,400.

JUSTICE, RELIGION, AND EDUCATION

Justice. The judicial system is based on the English system. There is a Court of Appeal, a Supreme Court, presided over by the Chief Justice, a court of first instance and a magistrates' court.

Religion. Religion of civil population mostly Roman Catholic; 1 Anglican and 1 Roman Catholic cathedral and 2 Anglican and 6 Roman Catholic churches; 1

Presbyterian and 1 Methodist churches and 4 synagogues; annual subsidy to each communion, £500.

Education. Free compulsory education is provided for children between ages 5 and 15 years. Scholarships are made available for universities, teacher-training and other higher education in Britain. The comprehensive system was introduced in Sept. 1972. There are 12 government primary schools and 2 comprehensive schools, 1 for boys and 1 for girls. There is also 1 private primary school, 1 Hebrew primary school, 2 Services primary schools and 1 school for handicapped children. Total number of pupils was 5,514, including 59 in technical and vocational schools.

Books of Reference

Annual Report on Gibraltar, 1972. London, 1974
Gibraltar Directory and Guide Book. Gibraltar, 1961
Dennis, P., *Gibraltar*. Newton Abbot, 1977
Ellicott, D., *Our Gibraltar*. Gibraltar, 1975
Garcia, J., *Gibraltar Who's Who and Year-Book, 1974–75*. Gibraltar, 1974
Garcia, S., *Gibraltar: An Analysis of How the Economy was Affected by the Spanish Restrictions 1963–72* (unpublished). Garrison Library, 1974
Hills, G., *Rock of Contention: A History of Gibraltar*. London, 1974
Howes, H. W., *The Story of Gibraltar*. London, 1946

GILBERT ISLANDS

Capital: Tarawa
Population: 57,816 (1973)

HISTORY. The Gilbert and Ellice Islands were proclaimed a protectorate in 1892 and annexed (at the request of the native governments) as the Gilbert and Ellice Islands Colony on 10 Nov. 1915 (effective on 12 Jan. 1916). On 1 Oct 1975 the former Ellice Islands severed its constitutional links with the Gilbert Islands and took a new name Tuvalu.

Internal self-government was obtained on 1 Nov. 1976 and independence is expected in 1978 although Ocean Island is aiming at separation from the Gilberts.

AREA AND POPULATION. The Colony comprises 3 groups of atolls together with the adjacent Ocean Island (Banaba). Total population at 8 Dec. 1973 was 57,816. Tarawa (capital) 17,188.

Ocean Island (Banaba) is situated at 0° 52′ S. lat., 169° 35′ E. long., and is approximately 2 sq. miles in area. Population (Dec. 1973) 2,314, including 160 Europeans and 26 Chinese. This island was annexed and included in the Colony (at that time a protectorate) by a proclamation of 28 Nov. 1900.

The **Gilbert Islands** between 4° N. and 3° S. lat. and 172° and 177° E. long. comprise Makin, Butaritari, Marakei, Abaiang, Tarawa (headquarters of the colony and Gilbert Islands district), Maiana, Abemama, Kuria, Aranuka, Nonouti, Tabiteuea, Beru, Nikunau, Onotoa, Tamana and Arorae. Population (Dec. 1973) 47,714, including about 300 Europeans; area approximately 102 sq. miles (264 sq. km). The Gilbertese are classed as Micronesians; their language is known as Gilbertese.

The **Phœnix Islands** between 3° and 5° S. lat. and 170° and 175° W. long. comprise the islands of Canton, Enderbury, Birnie, McKean, Phœnix, Hull, Sydney and Gardner. Area approximately 11 sq. miles (28 sq. km).

The Phœnix Islands were included in the Colony by an Order in Council of 18 March 1937. In March 1938 the USA claimed sovereignty over Canton and Enderbury. On 6 April 1939 the UK and US Governments agreed, without prejudice to their respective claims, to exercise joint control over the 2 islands for a period of 50 years. Canton used to be an international airport on the trans-Pacific route between Fiji and Honolulu, but, with the use of long-range jet aircraft, is no longer serviced by scheduled flights and is now uninhabited.

The southern Phœnix Islands of Hull, Sydney and Gardner were colonized by Gilbertese between 1938 and 1940, but due to long droughts permanent settlement on them ceased between 1955 and 1964. Enderbury, Phœnix, Birnie and McKean Islands are also uninhabited. The Phoenix Islands are now administered by the secretary to the Chief Minister.

The **Line Islands** between 4° 40′ and 2° N. lat. and 160° 20′ and 157° W. long. comprise Fanning, Washington and Christmas Islands. Fanning Island: population (Dec. 1973) 340, including 2 Europeans; area approximately 13 sq. miles (33 sq. km). Washington Island: population (Dec. 1973) 458; area approximately 5 sq. miles (13 sq. km). Christmas Island (headquarters of the Line Islands district): population (Dec. 1973) 674; area approximately 139 sq. miles (359 sq. km). Fanning and Washington Islands were annexed in 1889 and a repeating station for the Pacific cable was established on Fanning; they were included in the Colony in 1916. Both islands are worked as copra plantations by Fanning Island Plantations, Ltd, using Gilbertese labour. The Cable & Wireless Station at Fanning Island closed early in 1964, after operating for 62 years. Christmas Island was discovered by Capt. Cook in 1777, annexed by Great Britain in 1888 and included in the Colony in 1919. It is reputed to be the largest atoll in the world. The island is worked as a copra plantation by the Government.

The following 5 Line Islands became part of the Gilbert Islands by Order in Council from 1 Jan. 1972. **Starbuck Island,** 5° 35′ S. lat., 155° 52′ W. long.; area 1 sq. mile, uninhabited. **Maiden Island,** 4° S. lat., 155° W. long.; area 35 sq. miles (90 sq. km), containing deposits of guano of doubtful value, uninhabited. **Flint Island,** 11° 26′ S. lat., 151° 48′ W. long., and **Caroline Island,** 10° S. lat., 150° 14′ W. long., were, in 1951, leased to commercial interests in Tahiti. **Vostock Island,** 10° 06′ S. lat., 152° 23′ W. long., uninhabited.

GOVERNMENT. The Colony formerly came under the jurisdiction of the High Commissioner for the Western Pacific, but from 1 Jan. 1972 is headed by a Governor with direct access to London.

The Gilbert and Ellice Islands Order 1974, established a Council of Ministers which is presided over by the Governor and a House of Assembly which is presided over by a Speaker appointed by the Governor. The Council of Ministers comprises the Chief Minister, who is elected to the Council by the elected members of the House of Assembly, 7 ministers appointed by the Chief Minister and 1 *ex-officio* member.

The House of Assembly consists of the official members of the Council of Ministers plus a further 13 elected members. It has a life of 4 years and its main function is to legislate.

The Gilbert Islands are divided into 21 electoral districts. A General Election under the new Constitution was held at the beginning of 1974.

A form of local government was to be found on each of the islands as early as 1915, but it is only recently that a unified form of island administration has been created by the Local Government Ordinance of 1966. Under its provision Island Councils have been set up each being elected by the adult population of the island. They are empowered to enact by-laws and are responsible for providing social services on the islands. They also prepare yearly estimates of revenue and expenditure.

The Gilbert Islands have there own High Court, with right of appeal to the Fiji Court of Appeal. Island Courts are now capable of jurisdiction over all the races, both in civil and criminal fields, subject to review by the Senior Magistrate.

Governor: R. J. Wallace.

Chief Minister: Jeremiah Tabai.

Flag: British Blue Ensign with the shield of the Colony in the fly.

ECONOMY

Budget. Revenue for the calendar year 1976 amounted to $A26,355,717; principal items: customs duties, 5A1,761,130; direct taxation, 5A472,755; taxation on phosphate, 5A22,783,367. Expenditure in 1975 amounted to 5A30,405,012.

Currency. The currency in use is the Australian dollar.

AGRICULTURE. The land is basically coral reefs upon which coral sand has built up, and then been enriched by humus from rotting vegetation and flotsam which has drifted ashore. The principal tree is the coconut, which grows prolifically on all the islands except some of the Phœnix Islands. Other food-bearing trees are the pandanus palm and the breadfruit. As the amount of soil is negligible, the only vegetable which grows in any quantity is a coarse calladium (alocasia) with the local name 'babai', which is cultivated most laboriously in deep pits. There is also a little taro cultivated in the Ellice group. Pigs and fowls are kept throughout the Colony, and there is an abundance of fish.

Copra production is mainly in the hands of the individual landowner, who collects the coconut products from the trees on his own land.

Livestock (1976): Pigs, 10,000; poultry, 154,000.

TRADE. The principal imports are rice, flour, cotton piece-goods, tobacco and manufactured articles such as bicycles. The value of imports for 1975 amounted to $A9,280,546. Exports are almost exclusively phosphate and copra. The British Phosphate Commissioners exported 521,400 tons in 1975, valued at $A26,745,026 and 15,575 tons of copra valued at $951,367.

COMMUNICATIONS

Aviation. Air Pacific operates a weekly service, Fiji–Funafuti–Tarawa and Fiji–Funafuti–Tarawa–Nauru on alternate 2 weeks, using a HS748 aircraft. The BAC1-11 because of costly operations is used only at peak periods. Air Nauru operates a weekly service between Nauru and Tarawa using a F-28 aircraft. Air Pacific also runs the internal air service and there are air links between Tarawa and 6 outer islands which have airfields—Abemama, Butaritari, Tabiteuea, Marakei, Nonouti and Beru—the last 3 were recently completed under Government's plans to expand the air service internally. The type of aircraft used for the domestic service is the Trislander.

Cinemas. In 1974 there were 5 cinemas with a seating capacity of 2,000.

JUSTICE, EDUCATION AND WELFARE

Justice. In 1976 the Colony had a police force of 168 under the command of a Commissioner of Police. The force is deployed throughout the Colony covering all inhabited islands in the Gilbert Islands, Ellice Islands, Line Islands and Ocean Island. The Commissioner of Police is also responsible for prisons, immigration, fire service (both domestic and airport) and firearms licensing.

Education (1977). The Government maintains a co-educational boarding school, the King George V and Elaine Bernacchi School at Tarawa, with 211 boys and 178 girls, 5 primary schools, with a total of 13,350 pupils, and 4 community high schools with 168 pupils attending the first year of a new rurally oriented 3-year post-primary course. The Government also maintains a teachers' training college with 79 students and a marine training school with 149 full-time students. The Tarawa Technical Institute at Betio offers a variety of part-time and evening technical and commercial courses to about 500 students each year in addition to providing full-time courses for 34 students.

In 1975, 150 islanders were in overseas countries for secondary and further education or training expenses being met by the Gilbert Islands, UK, Australian and New Zealand Governments and other aid sources.

Welfare. Government maintains free medical and other services. There are few towns, and the people are almost without exception landed proprietors, thus eliminating child vagrancy and housing problems to a large extent, except in the Tarawa urban area. Destitution is almost unknown.

Books of Reference

Report on the Gilbert and Ellice Islands, 1970. HMSO, 1971

Grimble, Sir Arthur, *A Pattern of Islands*. London, 1953.—*Return to the Islands*. London, 1957

Kennedy, D. G., *Handbook of the Languages of the Ellice Islands*. Suva, 1945

Maude, H. E., *Of Islands and Men*. London, 1968

GREECE

Elliniki Dimokratia

Capital: Athens
Population: 9·2m. (1977)
GNP per capita: US$2,590 (1976)

HISTORY. Greece gained her independence from Turkey in 1821–29, and by the Protocol of London, of 3 Feb. 1830, was declared a kingdom, under the guarantee of Great Britain, France and Russia. For details of the subsequent history to 1947 *see* THE STATESMAN'S YEAR-BOOK, 1957, pp. 1069–70 and for details of the monarchy *see* THE STATESMAN'S YEAR-BOOK, 1973–74, p. 1000.

AREA AND POPULATION. Greece is bounded north by Albania, Yugoslavia and Bulgaria, east by Turkey and the Aegean Sea, south by the Mediterranean and west by the Ionian Sea. The total area is 131,986 sq. km (50,960 sq. miles), of which the islands account for 24,761 sq. km (9,560 sq. miles).

The population was 8,768,641 according to the census of 14 March 1971. Estimate (1977), 9·2m.

Athens is the capital; population of Greater Athens, in 1971, 2,540,241.

The following table shows the prefectures (*Nomoi*) and their population:

Nomoi	*Area in sq. km*	*Population 1971*	*Capital*	*Population 1971*
Greater Athens[1]	*433*	*2,540,241*		
Central Greece and Euboea[2]	*24,475*	*992,077*		
Aetolia and Acarnania	5,447	228,989	Missolonghi	11,614
Attica[2]	2,496	201,948	Athens	867,023
Boeotia	3,211	114,675	Levadeia	15,445
Euboea	3,908	165,369	Chalcis	36,300
Evrytania	2,045	29,533	Karpenissi	4,414
Phthiotis	4,368	154,542	Lamia	37,872
Phokis	2,121	41,361	Amphissa	6,605
Piraeus[2]	879	55,660	Piraeus	187,458
Peloponnessos	*21,439*	*986,912*		
Argolis	2,214	88,698	Nauplion	9,281
Arcadia	4,419	111,263	Tripolis	20,209
Akhaïa	3,209	239,859	Patras	111,607
Elia	2,681	165,056	Pyrgos	20,599
Korinthia	2,289	113,115	Korinthos	20,773
Lakonia	3,636	95,844	Sparte	10,549
Messenia	2,991	173,077	Calamata	39,133
Ionian Islands	*2,307*	*184,443*		
Zakynthos	406	30,187	Zante	9,339
Kerkyra	641	92,933	Kerkyra	28,630
Kefallenia	935	36,742	Argostolion	7,060
Lefkas	325	24,581	Levkas	6,818
Epirus	*9,203*	*310,344*		
Arta	1,612	78,376	Arta	19,498
Thesprotia	1,515	40,684	Hegoumenitsa	4,109
Yannina	4,990	134,688	Yannina	40,130
Preveza	1,086	56,586	Preveza	11,439
Thessaly	*13,904*	*659,913*		
Karditsa	2,576	133,776	Karditsa	25,685
Larissa	5,354	232,226	Larisa	72,336
Magnessia	2,636	161,392	Volos	51,290
Trikkala	3,338	132,519	Trikkala	34,794

[1] Comprising parts of Attica and Piraeus prefectures.

[2] Excluding figures for the parts of Attica and Piraeus prefectures within Greater Athens.

Nomoi	Area in sq. km	Population 1971	Capital	Population 1971
Macedonia	*34,203*	*1,890,684*		
Grevena	2,338	35,275	Grevena	8,016
Drama	3,468	91,009	Drama	29,692
Imathia	1,699	118,103	Verria	29,528
Thessaloniki	3,560	710,352	Thessaloniki	345,799
Kavala	2,109	121,593	Kavala	46,234
Kastoria	1,685	45,711	Kastoria	15,407
Kilkis	2,597	84,375	Kilkis	10,538
Kozani	3,562	135,709	Kozani	23,240
Pella	2,506	126,085	Edessa	13,967
Pieria	1,548	91,728	Katerini	28,808
Serres	3,987	202,898	Serres	39,897
Florina	1,863	52,264	Florina	11,164
Khalkidiki	2,945	73,850	Polyghyros	3,707
Mount Athos	336	1,732	Karyai	301
Thrace	*8,578*	*329,582*		
Evros	4,242	138,988	Alexandroupolis	22,995
Xanthi	1,793	82,917	Xanthi	24,867
Rodopi	2,543	107,677	Komotini	28,896
Aegean Islands	*9,071*	*417,813*		
Cyclades	2,572	86,337	Hermoupolis	13,502
Lesvos	2,154	114,802	Mitylini	23,426
Samos	778	41,709	Limin Vatheos	5,146
Khios	904	53,948	Khios	24,084
Dodecanese	2,663	121,017	Rhodes	32,092
Crete	*8,331*	*456,642*		
Iraklion	2,641	209,670	Heraklion	77,506
Lassithi	1,818	66,226	Aghios Nikolaos	6,176
Rethymnon	1,496	60,949	Rethymnon	14,969
Canea	2,376	119,797	Canea	40,564

In 1971 cities (*i.e.*, communes of more than 10,000 inhabitants, including Greater Athens) had 4,667,489 inhabitants (53·2%), towns (*i.e.*, communes with between 2,000 and 9,999 inhabitants), 1,028,769 (11·7%), villages and rural communities (under 2,000 inhabitants), 3,072,383 (35·1%).

Mount Athos, the easternmost of the three prongs of the peninsula of Chalcidice, is a self-governing community composed of 20 monasteries. (*See* THE STATESMAN'S YEAR-BOOK, 1945, p. 983.) For centuries the peninsula has been administered by a Council of 4 members and an Assembly of 20 members, 1 deputy from each monastery. The Greek Government on 10 Sept. 1926 recognized this autonomous form of government; Articles 109–112 of the Constitution of 1927 gave legal sanction to the Charter of Mount Athos, drawn up by representatives of the 20 monasteries on 20 May 1924. Article 103 of the 1952 Constitution confirms the special status of Mount Athos.

Vital statistics (1971): 141,126 live births; 1,920 still births; 1,732 illegitimate births; 73,350 marriages; 73,819 deaths; 61,745 emigrants; 24,709 immigrants.

GOVERNMENT AND CONSTITUTION. A *coup d'état* took place on 21 April 1967, 'to avert the danger of a communist threat against the nation'. A National Government was formed, which suspended certain articles of the 1952 Constitution. Following the unsuccessful counter-*coup* in 1967, King Constantine went abroad. Voting took place on 29 July 1973 in the referendum to change Greece from a Monarchy to a Republic and to elect a President. 77·2% of the valid votes were cast for a republican regime.

On 25 Nov. 1973, in a bloodless *coup*, President Papadopoulos was overthrown and Lieut.-Gen. Phaedon Ghizikis was sworn in. The military dictatorship collapsed on 23 July 1974 and the 1952 Constitution was reintroduced in a modified form. A new Constitution was introduced in June 1975.

A further referendum on the Monarchy took place on 8 Dec. 1974 and 69·2% of the valid votes were cast for an 'uncrowned democracy'.

General elections were held on 20 Nov. 1977 for 300 seats. The results were: New Democracy, 173; Pan-Hellenic Socialist Movement, 92; Union of Democratic

Centre, 15; Communists, 11; National Camp, 5; Alliance of Progressive and Left-Wing Forces, 2; Neo-Liberal Party, 2.

President: Konstantinos Tsatsos (elected President on 19 June 1975, by 210 votes to 65 against).

The cabinet in May 1978:

Prime Minister: Konstantinos Karamanlis.

Deputy Prime Minister: C. Papakonstantinou. *Co-ordination and Planning:* C. Mitsotakis. *Presidency of the Government:* C. Stephanopoulos. *Foreign Affairs:* G. Rallis. *National Defence:* E. Averof. *Interior:* Ch. Stratos. *Justice:* G. Stamatis. *Public Order:* A. Balkos. *Culture and Sciences:* G. Plytas. *Education:* I. Varvitsiotis. *Finance:* A. Kanellopoulo. *Agriculture:* I. Boutos. *Industry:* M. Evert. *Commerce:* G. Panayatopoulos. *Labour:* C. Laskaris. *Social Services:* S. Doxiadis. *Public Works:* N. Zardinidis. *Communications:* A. Papadongonas. *Merchant Marine:* E. Kephaloyannis. *Northern Greece:* N. Martis. *Without Portfolio (with special responsibility for the EEC):* G. Kontogeorgis.

National flag: (land) Blue with white cross; (sea) Nine horizontal stripes of blue and white, with a canton of blue with a white cross.

National anthem: Se gnorizo apo tin kopsi (words by Dionysios Solomos, 1824; tune by N. Mantzaros, 1828).

DEFENCE. In Aug. 1950 the Ministries of War, Marine and Military Aviation were fused into a single Ministry of National Defence. The General Staff of National Defence is directly responsible to the Minister on general defence questions, besides the special staffs for Army, Navy and Air Force. Defence expenditure in 1976 was 41,481m. drachmai.

Army. Military service is compulsory and universal. Liability begins in the 21st year and lasts up to the 50th. The normal term of service in the active Army is for 24–32 months for all arms, followed by 19 years in the first reserve of the active Army and 10 years in the second. The normal annual contingent of recruits in peace-time is about 50,000. Every 3 months a quarter of the current year's contingent is called up for service.

Since 1945, the organization and establishment of the Army units have been adapted to British models. In Feb. 1952 an American Mission took over from a British Military Mission the training of the Army.

The Army consists of 11 infantry and 1 armoured division, 13 infantry brigades and 1 commando brigade, with a total strength of 160,000 men.

Navy. The Hellenic Navy includes 7 submarines, 12 fleet destroyers, 4 frigates, 5 escort minesweepers (corvettes), 2 coastal minelayers, 10 fast missile boats, 5 patrol vessels, 15 coastal minesweepers, 19 fast torpedo boats, 1 repair ship, 1 dock landing ship, 15 landing ships, 8 landing craft, 1 salvage vessel, 8 oilers, 2 transports, 1 repair ship, 1 depot ship, 5 surveying craft, 2 lighthouse tenders, 8 water carriers, 1 netlayer and 12 fleet tugs. Personnel (1978): 1,900 officers and 15,700 ratings (called up for 24 months, or enlisted).

On 1 Nov. 1975 an agreement was signed to build 3 submarines of improved type in the Federal Republic of Germany, with a contract for a fourth in Sept. 1976.

Air Force. The Hellenic Air Force has a strength of about 23,000 officers and men and some 250 combat aircraft, consisting of 2 squadrons of F-4E Phantom air-superiority fighters, 1 squadron of F-104G Starfighters, 2 squadrons of Mirage F.1 fighters, 3 squadrons of A-7H Corsair II attack aircraft, 3 squadrons of F-5 fighters, 3 squadrons of RF-4E and RF-5A reconnaissance fighters and 1 squadron of HU-16B Albatross ASW amphibians. There are also transport squadrons equipped with C-130H Hercules (8), Noratlas and C-47 aircraft, 6 Canadair CL-215 twin-engined amphibians, training and helicopter units, and anti-aircraft units equipped with Nike-Hercules and Hawk surface-to-air missiles. Latest deliveries include 40 T-2E Buckeye training/attack aircraft.

The HAF is organized into Tactical, Training and Materiel Commands.

INTERNATIONAL RELATIONS

Membership. Greece is a member of UN, Associate of EEC and has applied for full membership, the Council of Europe and the political wing of NATO.

ECONOMY

Budget. The revenue and expenditure for calendar years were as follows (in 1m. drachmai):

	1970	*1971*[1]	*1972*[1]	*1973*[1]	*1974*[1]	*1975*	*1976*[1]
Revenue	65,130	73,277	86,230	105,240	129,380	138,320	174,362
Expenditure	65,126	59,277	86,229	105,234	129,380	170,496	210,231

[1] Estimates.

Currency. On 11 Nov. 1944 the Green currency was stabilized at 1 new *drachma* equalling 50,000m. old *drachmai.* Further readjustments took place in 1946, 1949 and 1953. A 'new issue' of notes and coins was put into circulation on 1 May 1954, 1 new drachma equalling 1,000 old drachmai (72 drachmai = £1; 30 drachmai = US$1). The 'new issue' comprises notes of 50, 100, 500 and 1,000 drachmai and metal coins of 1, 2, 5, 10 and 20 drachmai and 10, 20 and 50 *lepta.* Rate of exchange, 1977, £1 = 62·5 drachmai.

Banking. The Bank of Greece (*Trapeza Tis Ellados*) is the bank of issue. On 31 Dec. 1975 bank-notes in circulation amounted to 93,996m. drachmai.

In 1953 the National Bank of Greece and the Bank of Athens were amalgamated; in 1957 its name was changed to National Bank of Greece (*Ethniki Trapeza tis Ellados*).

The National Investment Bank for industrial development was set up in Dec. 1963; of its capital of 180m. drachmai, the National Bank provided 60%.

Other important banks are the Ionian and Popular Bank of Greece, the Commercial Bank of Greece, the National Mortgage Bank, the Hellenic Industrial Development Bank, the Investment Bank, the Commercial Credit Bank and the General Bank of Greece.

On 31 Dec. 1976, total private bank deposits were 347,252m. drachmai (107,941m. in 1970); total money supply was 160,062m. drachmai.

Post office savings bank deposits amounted to 39,449m. drachmai in Aug. 1974.

Weights and Measures. The metric system was made obligatory in 1959; the use of other systems is prohibited. The Gregorian calendar was adopted in Feb. 1923.

ENERGY AND NATURAL RESOURCES

Electricity. Total installed capacity of the Public Power Corporation was 3·99m. kw as at 31 Dec. 1974. Total net production in 1974 was 13,724m. kwh. (11,384m. thermal, 2,340m. hydraulic). Total production (1976) 16,321m. kwh.

Minerals. Greece produces a variety of ores and minerals, including iron-pyrites (180,000 tonnes in 1976), bauxite (2·75m. tonnes), nickel (2,205,000 tonnes), magnesite (1·5m. tonnes), dead burnt magnesite (342,000 tonnes), mixed sulphur ores (752,000 tonnes), barytes, chromite, marble (white and coloured) and various other earths, chiefly from the Laurium district, Thessaly, Euboea and the Aegean islands. There is little coal, and lignite of indifferent quality (22·2m. tonnes). Oil was struck in 1963 by British Petroleum at Kleisoura in west central Greece. Salt production (1970) 68,471 tons.

Agriculture. Of the total area only 33% is cultivable, but it supports about 45% of the whole population. The total area under cultivation in 1971 was 3,586,232 hectares, forest area (1965) was 2,512,418 hectares (445,715 of which were privately owned). The average holding was 3·42 hectares in 1975.

Yield (1,000 tonnes) of the chief crops (1976):

Wheat	2,450	Table grapes	220
Tobacco	139	Wine	452
Cotton	323	Citrus fruit	801
Sugar-beet	2,860	Other fruit	850
Currants and raisins	149	Milk	1,693
Olive oil	258	Meat	509

About 496,260 hectares of olives are under cultivation.

Rice is cultivated in Macedonia, the Peloponnese, Epirus and Central Greece. Successful experiments have been made in growing rice on alkaline land previously regarded as unfit for cultivation. The main kinds of cheese produced are sliced cheese in brine (commercially known as Fetta) and hard cheese, such as Kefalotyri.

Livestock (1976): 1·3m. cattle, 7,000 buffaloes, 800,000 pigs, 8·9m. sheep, 4·7m. goats, 200,000 horses, 100,000 mules, 300,000 asses, 30·9m. poultry.

Fisheries. In 1968, 16,435 fishermen were active. 55,000 kg of sponges were produced in 1970.

INDUSTRY AND TRADE

Industry. The main products are canned vegetables and fruit, fruit juice, beer, wine, alcoholic beverages, cigarettes, textiles, yarn, leather, shoes, synthetic timber, paper, plastics, rubber products, chemical acids, pigments, pharmaceutical products, cosmetics, soap, disinfectants, fertilizers, glassware, porcelain sanitary items, wire and power coils and household instruments.

Production, 1976 (1,000 tonnes): Textile yarns, 137; cement, 8,714; fertilizers, 1,554; ammonia, 287; iron (concrete-reinforcing bars), 589; iron–nickel, 16; alumina, 450; aluminium, 133; electrical domestic goods (1,000 pieces), 325.

Labour. Of the economically active population in 1971, 1·96m. were engaged in agriculture, 677,451 in industry and 1,000,684 in other employment.

Pepelasis, A. A., and Yotopoulos, P. A., *Surplus Labor in Greek Agriculture, 1953–60.* Athens, 1962

Trade Unions. The status of trade unions in Greece is regulated by the Associations Act 1914. Trade-union liberties are guaranteed under the Constitution, and the right to strike is subject to the Settlement of Collective Labour Disputes Act of 21 Nov. 1935, which, while not making strikes illegal, introduced the principle of compulsory arbitration.

The national body of trade unions in Greece is the Greek General Confederation of Labour.

Commerce. Foreign trade (in 1m. drachmai) for 6 calendar years was:

	1971[1]	*1972*	*1973*	*1974*	*1975*	*1976*
Imports	62,078	70,374	102,979	132,181	175,536	200,016
Exports	24,638	26,126	42,812	60,891	70,360	80,208

[1] Estimate.

Leading exports (1970, in 1,000 drachmai): Food and live animals, 19,518,588; beverages and tobacco, 5,820,228; chemicals, 2,344,680; manufactured goods, 39,454,200; crude materials, 7,558,652.

Textiles were the highest-valued exports in 1976. Percentage distribution of foreign trade by area (1976):

	Imports	*Exports*
EEC	43·8	50·0
Arab states	19·5	19·5
USA	8·4	5·7
Eastern Europe	7·9	11·3
Western Europe (non-EEC)	7·7	6·7
Rest	12·7	6·8

Total trade between Greece and UK (British Department of Trade returns, in £1,000 sterling):

	1972	*1973*	*1974*	*1975*	*1976*	*1977*
Imports to UK	17,338	46,757	68,180	65,237	64,606	95,563
Exports and re-exports from UK	67,580	99,241	105,079	117,207	149,207	220,393

Tourism. Tourists visiting Greece in 1976 numbered 4,257,000, coming mainly from USA, UK, Federal Republic of Germany, Yugoslavia, Italy, Sweden and Switzerland. They spent the equivalent of US$824m. At 31 Dec. 1976 there were 213,000 hotel beds.

COMMUNICATIONS

Roads. There were, in 1970, 35,257 km of roads, of which 8,004 were national and 27,253 provincial roads. Number of motor vehicles in Dec. 1970: 226,499 passenger cars, 106,729 goods vehicles, 10,503 buses.

Railways. Total length of the Greek railway system was 2,572 km in 1975, and all lines are state-owned except Hellenic Electric Railways Co. Ltd (27 km). In 1976 the state system moved 844m. tonnes-km of freight and 1,582m. passenger-km.

Aviation. Olympic Airways connects Athens with all important cities of the country, Europe, the Middle East and USA. Thirty-four foreign companies connect Athens with the principal cities of the world. The principal airport is at Athens. In 1974, 59,120 aircraft arrived, carrying 3·26m. passengers.

Shipping. In 1976 the merchant navy comprised 3,321 vessels of 26,623,376 GRT. Greek-owned ships under foreign flags totalled more than 23·09m. GRT.

There is a canal (opened 9 Nov. 1893) across the Isthmus of Corinth (about 4 miles).

There is (since 1925) in the town and port of Thessaloniki a free zone, covering today a land area of 536 sq. km. In the same port there was established in 1923 and operating since 1929 a Yugoslav free zone with 94 sq. km total area of land and seaway. In 1923 there was created a free zone in the town of Piraeus, covering a land area of 181·5 sq. km.

Post and Broadcasting. In 1973 there were 3,200 telephone exchanges, 1·8m. installed capacity of telephone exchanges, handling 8,000m. calls. There were (1977) 2,180,243 telephones.

Elliniki Radiophonia Tileorasis (ERT), the Hellenic National Radio and Television Institute, is the government broadcasting station. *Ypiressia Enimerosseos Enoplon Dhynameon Helladhos* (YENED), the Greek Armed Forces Information Service, broadcasts from a central station in Athens *via* medium- and short-waves and has regional stations in 11 towns. ERT and YENED each broadcasts 1 TV programme. AFRTS broadcasts 1 TV programme in Iraklion (Crete). Number of receivers: radio, 2·8m.; television, 850,000.

Cinemas (1965). There were 1,400 cinemas.

Newspapers (1974). There were 12 daily newspapers published in Athens.

JUSTICE, RELIGION, EDUCATION AND WELFARE

Justice. There are administrative, civil and criminal courts and they are organized by special laws.

Religion. The Christian Eastern Orthodox faith is the established religion to which 98% of the population belong.

The Greek Orthodox Church is under an archbishop and 67 metropolitans, 1 archbishop and 7 metropolitans in Crete, and 4 metropolitans in the Dodecanese. The Roman Catholics have 3 archbishops (in Naxos and Corfu and, not recognized by the State, in Athens) and 1 bishop (for Syra and Santorin). The Exarchs of the Greek Catholics and the Armenians are not recognized by the State.

Complete religious freedom is recognized by the Constitution of 1968, but proselytizing from, and interference with, the Greek Orthodox Church is forbidden.

Education. Public education is provided in nursery, primary and secondary schools, starting at 6 years of age and since 1963 free at all levels.

In Dec. 1976 there were 3,275 nursery schools with 3,645 staff and 105,042 pupils; 9,705 public day primary schools with 29,804 staff and 926,628 pupils. There were 1,105 secondary schools with 19,279 staff and 521,141 pupils. There were 406 public and 706 private technical and vocational schools with 117,006 students.

In 1976 there were 4 universities at Athens. Thessaloniki, Patras and Ioannina with 84,600 students and 5,038 lecturers. New universities are planned at Rethymnon (Crete) and Komotini (Thrace).

Illiteracy in the age groups of 10 years and over was 18% in 1961 (8% among men). 1972 estimate 12%.

The Greek langugage consists of 2 branches, *katharevousa*, a conscious revival of classical Greek, used for official purposes and in newspapers, and *demotiki*, the spoken language.

Health (1974). There were 725 hospitals and sanatoria with a total of 56,885 beds. There were 17,942 doctors and 5,283 dentists.

DIPLOMATIC REPRESENTATIVES

OF GREECE IN GREAT BRITAIN
(1A Holland Park, London, W11 3TP)

Ambassador: Stavros G. Roussos.

OF GREAT BRITAIN IN GREECE
(1 Ploutarchou St., Athens 139)

Ambassador: I. J. M. Sutherland, CMG.

OF GREECE IN THE USA (2221 Massachusetts Ave., NW, Washington, D.C. 20008)

Ambassador: Menelas D. Alexandrakis.

OF THE USA IN GREECE
(91 Vasilissis Sophias Blvd, Athens)

Ambassador: William E. Schaufele, Jr.

OF GREECE TO THE UNITED NATIONS

Ambassador: George Papoulias.

Books of Reference

Campbell, J., and Sherrard, P., *Modern Greece*. London, 1968
Forster, E. S., *A Short History of Modern Greece*. 3rd ed. London, 1958
Holden, D., *Greece Without Columns: The Making of the Modern Greeks*. London, 1972
Katris, J. A., *Eyewitness in Greece: The Colonels Come to Power*. St Louis, 1971
Kayser, B., *Géographie humaine de la Grèce*. Paris, Presses Universitaires, 1964
Kolodny, E. Y., *La Population des Îles de la Grèce*. Aix-en-Provence, 1973
Kousoulas, D. G., *Revolution and Defeat: The Story of the Greek Communist Party*. OUP, 1965
Kykkotis, I., *English–Modern Greek and Modern Greek–English Dictionary*. 3rd ed. London, 1957
Munkman, C. A., *American Aid to Greece*. New York, 1958
Phillipson, A., *Die griechischen Landschaften: eine Landeskunde*. 4 vols. Frankfurt, 1951–59
Spring, J. T., *The Oxford Dictionary of Modern Greek*. 2 vols. OUP, 1966–67
Woodhouse, C. M., *The Struggle for Greece, 1941–1949*. London, 1976
Xydis, S. G., *Greece and the Great Powers, 1944–47*. Thessaloniki, 1963
Young, K., *The Greek Passion*. London, 1967

GRENADA

Capital: St. George's
Population: 107,779 (1975)
GNP per capita: US$420 (1976)

HISTORY. Grenada became an independent nation within the Commonwealth on 7 Feb. 1974. Grenada was formerly an Associated State under the West Indies Act, 1967. Independence followed a Constitutional conference held in London in May 1973.

AREA AND POPULATION. Grenada is the most southerly island of the Windward Islands with an area of 133 sq. miles (344 sq. km); population, census 1970, 92,775, of which 29,860 are in the parish of St George; estimated population 1975, 107,779. The largest of the Grenadines attached to Grenada is Carriacou, area 6,500 acres; population 1970, 5,950.

Vital statistics (1975): Births, 2,890; deaths, 619; infant deaths, 68; marriages, 293.

CONSTITUTION AND GOVERNMENT

Governor-General: Sir Leo de Gale, GCMG, CBE.

Prime Minister: Rt. Hon. Eric M. Gairy, PC.

National flag: Divided into 4 triangles of yellow, top and bottom, and green, hoist and fly; in the centre a red disc bearing a gold star; along the top and bottom edged red stripes each bearing 3 gold stars; on the green triangle near the hoist a pod of nutmeg.

INTERNATIONAL RELATIONS

Membership. Grenada is a member of the UN, OAS, Caricom, the Commonwealth and is an ACP state of EEC.

ECONOMY

Budget. The 1976 estimates balanced at $27,559,541. Public debt at 31 Dec. 1970 was $15,168,705.

Banking. In 1976 there were 6 commercial banks in Grenada; Barclays Bank International, Royal Bank of Canada, Bank of Nova Scotia, Canadian Imperial Bank of Commerce, Grenada National Bank and the Grenada Co-operative Bank. The Grenada Agricultural Bank was established in 1965 to encourage agricultural development.

AGRICULTURE (1976). The principal crops grown are: Cocoa (15,000 acres), nutmegs (6,500 acres), bananas (4,000 acres), coconuts (3,000 acres), citrus (1,200 acres) and sugar-cane (800 acres), in addition to small scattered cultivations of cotton, cloves, cinnamon and coffee.

Livestock (1976): Cattle, 5,000; sheep, 7,000; goats, 5,000; pigs, 10,000; poultry, 256,000.

COMMERCE (1976). Total value of imports, $66,215,392; exports, $34,121,010. Chief exports: Cocoa (6·9m. lb.) $10·4m.; nutmegs (6·1m. lb.) $12m.; mace (1m. lb.) $3m.; bananas (3·4m. lb.) $8m.

Value of imports (1974): From UK, $9,799,063; Canada, $3,331,099; USA, $2,978,139. Value of exports (1974): To UK, $7,504,198; USA, $427,436; Canada, $346,184.

Total trade between UK and Grenada (British Department of Trade returns, in £1,000 sterling):

	1976	*1977*
Imports to UK	3,782	4,493
Exports and re-exports from UK	2,603	4,294

TOURISM. In 1976, 24,551 visitors (excluding cruise passengers), spending an estimated $15m.

COMMUNICATIONS

Roads. The scheduled road mileage is 577, of which 377 have an oiled surface and 210 are graded as third-and fourth-class roads.

Aviation. International Aeradio Ltd control by radio all plane movements within this area, and keep Pearls Airport in contact with St George's, on official airways business.

Shipping. Total shipping for 1976 was 895 motor and steamships and 249 sailing and auxiliary vessels, with a total net tonnage of 3,831,659 and 9,856 respectively.

Post and Broadcasting. The telephone system is owned and operated by the Grenada Telephone Co. Ltd. The Government of Grenada is a shareholder. The system is completely automatic, and in 1977 served 5,072 subscribers. Cable & Wireless (W.I.) Ltd operates a VHF radio system (telephone and telegraph) to Trinidad and Barbados, from where connexion is made to all principal West Indian islands and all other parts of the world.

Radio Grenada is government owned and operated.

DIPLOMATIC REPRESENTATIVES

OF GRENADA IN GREAT BRITAIN (King's Hse, 10 Haymarket, London, SW1Y 4DA)

High Commissioner: Oswald M. Gibbs.

OF GREAT BRITAIN IN GRENADA

High Commissioner: H. S. H. Stanley, CMG (resides in Port-of-Spain).

OF GRENADA IN THE USA (927 15th St., NW, Washington, DC., 20005)

Ambassador: Franklin O'Brien Dolland.

OF THE USA IN GRENADA

Ambassador: Theodore R. Britten (resides in Bridgetown).

OF GRENADA TO THE UNITED NATIONS

Ambassador: Franklin O'Brien Dolland.

GUATEMALA

República de Guatemala

Capital: Guatemala City
Population: 6·3m. (1976)
GNP per capita: US$630 (1976)

HISTORY. From 1524 to 1821 Guatemala was a Spanish captaincy-general, comprising the whole of Central America. It became independent in 1821 and formed part of the Confederation of Central America from 1823 to 1839, when Rafael Carrera dissolved the Confederation.

AREA AND POPULATION. Guatemala is bounded on the north and west by Mexico, south by the Pacific ocean and east by El Salvador, Honduras and Belize, and the area is 108,889 sq. km (42,042 sq. miles). In March 1936 Guatemala, El Salvador and Honduras agreed to accept the peak of Mount Montecristo as the common boundary point.

The population was 6·3m. in 1976. About 45% are pure Indians, of 21 different groups descended from the Maya-Quiché tribe; most of the remainder are mixed Indian and Spanish (*ladinos*); and these supply the ruling classes. Density of population, 1973, 48 per sq. km.

Vital statistics, 1974: Births, 253,055; deaths, 69,820; marriages, 25,155; infant deaths, 19,089.

Guatemala is administratively divided into 22 departments, each with a governor appointed by the Head of Government. Population, 1976:

Departments	*Area (sq. km)*	*Population*	*Departments*	*Area (sq. km)*	*Population*
Alta Verapaz	8,686	372,572	Petén	35,854	71,463
Baja Verapaz	3,124	136,747	Quezaltenango	1,951	383,470
Chimaltenango	1,979	233,287	Quiché	8,378	363,579
Chiquimula	2,376	212,869	Retalhuleu	1,858	159,085
El Progreso	1,922	92,453	Sacatepéquez	465	116,259
Escuintla	4,384	353,302	San Marcos	3,791	473,341
Guatemala	2,126	1,239,749	Santa Rosa	2,955	225,597
Huehuetenango	7,403	422,717	Sololá	1,061	156,548
Izabal	9,038	205,305	Suchitepéquez	2,510	257,439
Jalapa	2,063	145,091	Totonicapán	1,061	207,954
Jutiapa	3,219	290,511	Zacapa	2,690	138,292

The capital is Guatemala City with 717,322 inhabitants (1973), almost all *ladinos*. Other towns are Quezaltenango (65,733), Puerto Barrios (38,956), Mazatenango (38,319), Antigua (26,631), Zacapa (35,769) and Cobán (43,538). An earthquake in central Guatemala in Feb. 1976 killed 24,103 people and destroyed 200,000 dwellings.

CONSTITUTION AND GOVERNMENT. Following the revolution of June 1954 the Constitution of 1945 was replaced in Aug. 1954 by a 'Political Statute'. A new Constitution was promulgated in 1965 with effect from 6 May 1966.

President of the Republic and C.-in-C.: Gen. Romeo Lucas García, elected by Congress for a 4-year term beginning 1 July 1978.

Minister of Foreign Affairs: Dr Adolfo Molina Orantes.

The administration is carried on, under the President, by the Cabinet; the Council of State of 14 members from the 3 branches of Government; the municipalities; the University of San Carlos; agriculture; commerce; industry; banking; labour. Mayors of municipalities, with their councils, are elected.

National flag: Three vertical strips of blue, white, blue, with the national arms in the centre.

National anthem: ¡Guatemala! feliz (words by J. J. Palma; tune by R. Alvarez).

DEFENCE

Army. Military service (2 years) is compulsory, but not universal, between the ages of 18 and 50 (from 18 to 30 in the special reserves), and conscripts may be called upon for work in communications, reforestation and agriculture. The Army numbers 13,500, organized in 10 infantry, 1 parachute and 1 engineer battalions and some motorized units with some tanks. The Policía Nacional has 3,000 personnel.

Navy. A Naval force was formed in 1959. In 1978 it comprised 11 small patrol craft, 7 landing craft, 8 service craft, 6 motor launches and 2 yachts. Personnel: 400 officers and men (including 210 marines).

Air Force. There is a small Air Force with 8 A-37B light attack aircraft, 1 C-54, 6 C-47 and 10 Israeli-built Arava transports, T-33 and T-37 jet and T-6 piston-engined trainers, and a number of light aircraft and helicopters, including 6 UH-1 Iroquois. Total strength is about 1,000 personnel and 50 aircraft.

INTERNATIONAL RELATIONS

Membership. Guatemala is a member of UN, OAS and CACM.

External Debt. In 1976 the external debt was Q.170m.

ECONOMY

Planning. A 5-year development plan (1971–75) aimed at increasing the value of exports, improving the collection of revenues from taxation and making the best use of foreign credits (Q.453m. in the period) to bring about a cumulative annual growth rate of 7·8% in the GDP by 1975. A new 3-year plan is now being prepared.

Budget. The estimates of ordinary revenue and expenditure balanced as follows, in quetzales (1 quetzal = US$): 1975, 422·6m.; 1976, 553·7m.; 1977, 797·7m.; 1978, 942·6m. Income tax was introduced for the first time in 1963.

Currency. The gold *quetzal* was established 7 May 1925 equal to 60 old Guatemala paper pesos, with a gold content equal to that of the US$. The exchange rate has remained at $1 since 1926. Gold coins have been withdrawn from circulation. New coins of 25, 10, 5 and 1 *centavos* were issued by the Banco de Guatemala on 16 Sept. 1965; they are of a lower content value than the previous ones. There are also paper notes of 100, 50, 20, 10, 5, 1 and ½ *quetzales* (50 *centavos*).

Banking. By an Act effective 4 Feb. 1946 the Central Bank of Guatemala (founded in 1926 as a mixed central and commercial bank) was superseded by a new institution, the Banco de Guatemala, to operate solely as a central bank. Savings and term deposits at commercial banks were Q.495m. at the end of 1975. Total currency circulation (backed by a gold reserve fixed by law at a minimum of 40%) on 31 Dec. 1975 was Q.429·1m.; total net international reserves amounted to Q.280·2m. on 31 Dec. 1975. In July 1965 the country's quota with the IMF was increased from US$15m. to 25m.

There are 11 banks, including the Banco de Guatemala, Banco Nacional de Desarollo, set up in 1971 to promote agricultural development, its counterpart for small industries (Banco de los Trabajadores) set up in Jan. 1966 with initial capital of US$1·3m., a branch of the Bank of London and Montreal Ltd and a branch of the Bank of America.

Weights and Measures. The metric system has been officially adopted, but is little used in local commerce.

Libra of 16 oz.	= 1·014 lb.	*League*	= 3 miles
Arroba of 25 libras	= 25·35 lb.	*Vara*	= 32 in.
Quintal of 4 arrobas	= 101·40 lb.	*Manzana*	= 100 varas sq.
Tonelada of 20 quintals	= 18·10 cwt	*Caballeria* of 64 manzanas	= 110 acres
Fanega	= 1½ Imp. bushels		

ENERGY AND NATURAL RESOURCES

Electricity. 666m. kwh. of electricity were generated in 1973. A new thermo-electric plant of 14,000 kw. capacity was inaugurated at Escuintla in Sept. 1965 and another of 13,000 kw. at Los Esclavos on 24 Sept. 1966. A large-scale hydro-electric development costing US$350m. is now underway.

Minerals. Mineral production includes zinc and lead concentrates, some antimony and tungsten, a small amount of cadmium and silver; some copper is also being mined. Exports (1975) Q.8·4m. In 1965 a subsidiary of International Nickel Co. of Canada was granted a 40-year concession to extract and process nickel ore in northern Guatemala. Production and export started in 1977.

Agriculture. The Cordilleras divide Guatemala into two unequal drainage areas, of which the Atlantic is much the greater. The Pacific slope, though comparatively narrow, is exceptionally well watered and fertile between the altitudes of 1,000 and 5,000 ft, and is the most densely settled part of the republic. The Atlantic slope is sparsely populated, and has little of commercial importance beyond the chicle and timber-cutting of the Petén, coffee cultivation of Cobán region and banana-raising of the Motagua Valley and Lake Izabal district. Soil erosion is serious and a single week of heavy rains suffices to cause flooding of fields and much crop destruction.

On 17 June 1952 an 'Agrarian Reform Law' was enacted providing for the expropriation (with eventual compensation) of those parts of landed estates which were not under cultivation. The US Government in 1953 protested against the expropriation of 234,000 acres belonging to the United Fruit Company. Under the new government the expropriation was halted and the 'Agrarian Reform Law' was superseded by a 'Statute' early in 1956, which provided small holdings to several thousand peasant farmers. This distribution of land continues, now under the provisions of the 'Agrarian Transformation Law' of 1962. In 1966, 24 state farms and 17 farms owned by banks were transformed into co-operatives.

The principal crop is coffee; there are about 12,000 coffee plantations with 138m. coffee trees on about 338,000 acres, but 80% of the crop comes from 1,500 large coffee farms employing 426,000 workers. Coffee exports in 1975 were valued at Q.164·1m. mainly to USA and Federal Republic of Germany.

Bananas are still an important export crop, but exports have at times been seriously reduced, partly by labour troubles and by hurricanes. Exports 1975 were worth Q.17m.

Cotton has become an important export and in 1975 was valued at Q.75·9m. Other important exports (1975) were sugar, Q.115·5m.; beef, Q.16·9m. Guatemala is, after Mexico, the largest producer of chicle gum (used for chewing-gum manufacture in USA). Rubber development schemes are under way, assisted by US funds. Guatemala is one of the largest sources of essential oils (citronella and lemon grass); exports in 1974 were valued at Q.4·8m. Cattle-grounds (*potreros*) occupy about 758,000 acres. There were (1974) some 1·5m. head of cattle (mostly beef) in the country.

Forestry. The forest area has an extent of 17,784,000 acres. The department of Petén is rich in mahogany and other woods.

Fisheries. Exports were about Q.4·1m. in 1975.

INDUSTRY AND TRADE

Industry. The principal industries are food and beverages, tobacco, chemicals, hides and skins, textiles, garments and non-metallic minerals. New industries include electrical goods, plastic sheet and metal furniture.

Trade Unions. Trade unions are small. In 1954 the trade unions were ordered to reorganize and there are now two main federations.

Commerce. Values in Q.1,000 (1 quetzal = US$1) were:

	1971	*1972*	*1973*	*1974*	*1975*	*1976*
Imports (c.i.f.)	303,283	323,984	431,002	700,473	732,679	981,600
Exports (f.o.b.)	283,231	327,484	436,151	572,133	623,503	782,400

Value (in Q.1,000) of principal imports, 1972: Chemicals, 65,046; foodstuffs, 24,361; petroleum products, 21,305. Chief exports are coffee, cotton, bananas, beef, essential oils, timber, chicle and shrimps. The main trading partners are USA and Federal Republic of Germany, and the partners of the Central American Common Market.

Total trade between Guatemala and UK for 6 years (British Department of Trade returns, in £1,000 sterling):

	1972	*1973*	*1974*	*1975*	*1976*	*1977*
Imports to UK	1,884	4,667	7,410	31,918	2,133	3,600
Exports and re-exports from UK	4,724	5,145	6,948	9,838	14,022	16,676

Tourism. There were 412,342 foreign visitors in 1974 spending approximately US$50m.

COMMUNICATIONS

Roads. In 1977 there were 13,632 km of roads, of which 2,638 are paved. There is a trunk highway from coast to coast *via* Guatemala City. There are 2 trunk highways from the Mexican to the Salvadorean frontier: the Pacific Highway serving the fertile coastal plain and the Pan-American Highway running through the highlands and Guatemala City. Motor vehicles number about 90,000.

Railways. The principal railway system is the government-owned (since 1968) International Railways of Central America. All railways are of 3 ft gauge. Total length of all lines is 819 km. Passengers carried, 1974, numbered 1,663,282, and freight carried (1976), 918,600 short tons. The bridge across the Suchiate River between Mexico and Guatemala in 1942 linked the railways of North and Central America, though differences in gauge make it necessary to change trains at Ayutla.

Aviation. The government-owned airline, Aviateca, furnishes both domestic and international services; 6 other airlines handle international traffic. In 1974 air cargo amounted to 16·6m. kg; number of passengers, 293,000.

Shipping. The chief ports on the Atlantic coast are Puerto Barrios and Santo Tomás de Castilla: on the Pacific coast, San José and Champerico. Total tonnage handled was, 1974, 3m. tons.

Post and Broadcasting. The Government own and operate the telegraph and telephone services; there are (1973) 45,137 telephone instruments. There are some 70 broadcasting stations. Radio receiving sets in use, 1974, numbered about 590,000. There are 3 commercial television stations.

Cinemas (1976). Cinemas numbered approximately 100.

Newspapers (1976). There are 8 daily newspapers.

JUSTICE, RELIGION, EDUCATION AND WELFARE

Justice. Justice is administered in a Supreme Court, 6 appeal courts and 28 courts of first instance. Supreme Court and appeal court judges are appointed by the Head of Government. Judges of first instance are appointed by the Supreme Court.

All holders of public office have to show on entering office, and again on leaving, a full account of their private property and income.

Religion. Roman Catholicism is the prevailing faith; but all other creeds have complete liberty of worship. Guatemala has an archbishopric.

Education. In 1974 there were 6,010 primary schools with 25,297 teachers and an attendance of 753,932 pupils; these figures include private schools. There are 357 secondary and other schools having 7,051 teachers and an attendance of 104,800 pupils; the autonomous University of San Carlos de Borromeo, founded in 1678, was reopened in 1910 with 7 faculties and schools and there are 4 new universities. Total university enrolment (1972) approximately 18,488. All education is in theory free, but owing to a grave shortage of state schools private schools flourish. The 1964 census showed that 63% of those 10 years of age and older were illiterate.

Social Welfare. A comprehensive system of social security was outlined in a law of 30 Oct. 1946. Medical personnel include about 1,250 doctors and 275 dentists for the whole republic. There are about 60 public hospitals and about 100 dispensaries.

DIPLOMATIC REPRESENTATIVES

OF GUATEMALA IN THE USA (2200 R St., NW, Washington, D.C. 20008)

Ambassador: Jorge Lamport-Rodil.

OF THE USA IN GUATEMALA (7–01 Avenida de la Reforma, Zone 10, Guatemala)

Ambassador: David E. Boster.

OF GUATEMALA TO THE UNITED NATIONS

Ambassador: Julio Ascensio-Wunderlich.

Guatemala broke off diplomatic relations with UK on 31 July 1963.

Books of Reference

The official gazette is called *Diario de Centro America.*

Adler, J. H., and others, *Public Finance and Economic Development in Guatemala.* Stanford Univ. Press, 1952
Banco de Guatemala, *Memoria annual y Estudio económico*
Bianchi, W. J., *Belize.* New York, 1959
Bloomfield, L. M., *The British Honduras–Guatemala Dispute.* Toronto, 1953
Holleran, M. P., *Church and State in Guatemala.* New York, 1949
Humphreys, R. A., *The Diplomatic History of British Honduras 1638–1901.* London, 1961
Male, P. J. E., *Economic and Commercial Conditions in Guatemala.* HMSO, 1956
Mendoza, J. L., *Britain and Her Treaties on Belize.* Guatemala, 1946
Morton, F., *Xeláhuh.* London, 1959
Rosenthal, M., *Guatemala.* New York, 1961
Whetton, N. L., *Guatemala: The Land and the People.* Yale Univ. Press, 1961

National Library: Biblioteca Nacional, 5a Avenida y 8a Calle, Zona 1, Guatemala City.

GUINEA

Capital: Conakry
Population: 5·14m. (1972)
GNP per capita: US$150 (1976)

République de Guinée

HISTORY. The independent republic of Guinea was proclaimed on 2 Oct. 1958, after the territory of French Guinea had decided at the referendum of 28 Sept. to leave the French Community. The constitution provides for the limitation or renunciation of sovereignty in favour of African unity.

Co-operation with France in economic and cultural matters was established by a convention signed on 22 May 1963.

AREA AND POPULATION. Guinea is bounded north-west by Guinea-Bissau and south by Liberia and Sierra Leone.

The area is 245,857 sq. km (95,000 sq. miles), and the estimated population in 1972 was 5,143,284 and Conakry, the capital, had 525,671 inhabitants. In 1964 Kankan had 29,100 inhabitants; Kindia, 25,000; Siguiri, 12,700; Labé, 12,500, and N'Zérékoré, 8,600.

The most important ethnic groups are the Peuls (1·02m.), Malinké (600,000), Soussou (325,000) and Kissi (160,000).

CONSTITUTION AND GOVERNMENT. The constitution of 12 Nov. 1958 declared Guinea 'a democratic, secular and social republic'. The President of the republic is elected for a 7-year term and can be re-elected.

President and Prime Minister: Sékou Touré (elected Jan. 1961, re-elected Jan. 1968 and Dec. 1974).

Foreign Affairs: El Hadj Diallo Saifoulaye.

Elections for the National Assembly, held on 1 Jan. 1968, returned the 75 members (including 16 women) from the single official list of the Parti Démocratique de Guinée.

National flag: Three vertical strips of red, gold, green.

The official language is French.

DEFENCE

Army. The Army of 5,000 men has been equipped with Soviet, Czech and Chinese weapons, armoured cars and artillery.

Air Force. An Air Force has been formed with Soviet assistance; it is reported to be equipped with 8 MiG-17 jet-fighters and 2 MiG-15UTI trainers, 2 Il-18 turboprop transports, 4 An-14 and 4 Il-14 piston-engined transports, all Russian built, plus a few helicopters, piston-engined Yak-18 and L-29 jet trainers. Personnel about 800. An operational base for Soviet maritime reconnaissance aircraft has been established at Conakry.

INTERNATIONAL RELATIONS

Membership. Guinea is a member of UN, OAU and is an ACP state of EEC.

ECONOMY

Budget. The budget for 1972–73 balanced at 4,500m. sylis.

Currency. The monetary unit is the *syli*, divided into 100 *cauris*, introduced in 1972. The issue consists of notes of 100, 50, 25 and 10 *sylis*, and coins of 50 *cauris* 5, 2 and 1 *sylis*.

Banking. The Banque de la République de Guinée, with a capital of 500m. francs, is controlled by a governor with ministerial rank. It is the sole bank of issue. In Jan. 1962 all insurance companies and the Banque de l'Afrique Occidentale, the only private bank in Conakry, were nationalized.

ENERGY AND NATURAL RESOURCES

Electricity. Production of electrical energy was 450m. kwh. in 1971.

Minerals. Diamonds are found in the Macenta district (80,000 carats in 1973). Bauxite exists in the Los islands, the Boké district and the Kindia–Telimélé district; output, 1973, 3·7m. tonnes. Production of iron ore in the Kaloum peninsular was 1·04m. tonnes in 1970.

Agriculture. The chief products are rice, palm-nuts, bananas, coffee, pineapples, orange juice, groundnuts, millet. Coffee is grown in forest districts. There are experimental fruit gardens at Camayenne near Conakry, Kindia and Dalaba, 2 stations for rice selection (Kankan, Koba) and an experimental quinine station at Sérédou. Fouta Djallon contains cattle in abundance. In 1976 there were 1·55m. cattle and 805,000 sheep and goats.

Agricultural production, 1973 (in 1,000 tonnes): Bananas, 90; cassava, 420; maize, 260.

COMMERCE. In 1972 imports totalled US$90m.; exports, US$60m. Alumina forms about 60% of the exports.

Total trade between Guinea and the UK (British Department of Trade returns, in £1,000 sterling):

	1973	*1974*	*1975*	*1976*	*1977*
Imports to UK	416	409	22	54	205
Exports and re-exports from UK	772	1,692	3,644	4,508	5,399

COMMUNICATIONS

Roads. There are 3,500 km of all-weather roads and 7,000 km of dry-season roads.

Railways. A railway connects Conakry with Kankan (662 km) and may be extended to Bamako in Mali, by Chinese engineers. A line 134 km long linking bauxite deposits at Sangaredi with Port Kamsar was opened in 1973.

Aviation. There are airports at Conakry and Kankan; in 1973, 55,000 passengers disembarked and embarked.

Shipping. Conakry port facilities are being expanded 1976–80.

Post. The territory is connected by cable with France and Pernambuco; also with Freetown, Monrovia and other places. There is a wireless station at Conakry affording communication with all territories of West Africa. Telephones, 1972, numbered about 7,488.

EDUCATION AND WELFARE

Education. There were, in 1970, 191,287 pupils in primary schools, 59,918 in secondary schools and 2,013 in technical schools. There were 1,478 students at teacher-training colleges.

Health. The medical service maintains 6 hospitals and 32 dispensaries.

DIPLOMATIC REPRESENTATIVES

OF GUINEA IN GREAT BRITAIN

Ambassador: Seydou Keita (resides in Rome).

OF GREAT BRITAIN IN GUINEA

Ambassador: J. E. Powell-Jones, CMG (resides in Dakar).

OF GUINEA IN THE USA (2112 Leroy Pl., NW, Washington, D.C., 20008)

Ambassador: Ibrahima Camara.

OF THE USA IN GUINEA (2nd Blvd. and 9th Ave., Conakry)

Ambassador: Oliver S. Crosby.

OF GUINEA TO THE UNITED NATIONS

Ambassador: Sekou Mouke Yansane.

Books of Reference

Bulletin Statistique et Economique de la Guinée. Monthly. Conakry
Adamolekun, L., *Sékou Touré's Guinea*. London, 1976
Camara, S. S., *La Guinée sans la France*. Paris, 1976
Rivière, C., *Guinea: The Mobilization of a People*. Cornell Univ. Press, 1977
Taylor, F. W., *A Fulani–English Dictionary*. Oxford, 1932

GUINEA-BISSAU

Capital: Bissau
Population: 800,000 (1978)
GNP per capita: US$140 (1978)

HISTORY. Guinea-Bissau, formerly Portuguese Guinea, on the coast of Guinea, was discovered in 1446 by Nuno Tristão. It became a separate colony in 1879. It is bounded by the limits fixed by the convention of 12 May 1886 with France. In 1951 Guinea-Bissau became an overseas province of Portugal. The armed struggle against colonial rule began in 1963. On 10 Sept. 1974 Portugal formally recognized the independence of Guinea-Bissau.

AREA AND POPULATION. Guinea-Bissau is bounded by Senegal in the north and by Guinea in the east and south. It includes the adjacent archipelago of Bijagoz, with the island of Bolama. The capital and chief port is Bissau, estimated population (1971), 65,000. Other ports are Bolama and Cacheu. Area is 36,125 sq. km (13,948 sq. miles); population (census, 1970), 487,448; estimate (1978), 800,000.

CONSTITUTION AND GOVERNMENT. The Constitution, as established by the National People's Assembly, designates the *Partido Africano da Independencia da Guiné e Cabo Verde* (PAIGC) as the only permitted Party, and provides for eventual union between Guinea-Bissau and Cape Verde. Executive powers are vested in the Council of State of 15 members, elected for 3 years by the Assembly from its own members, while administrative functions are exercised by the Council of State Commissioners, appointed by the President.

President of the Council of State: Luis Cabral.

Commissioners of State: Victor Maria Saude (*Foreign Affairs*); Vasco Cabral (*Planning and Development*); Mario Cabral (*Education*); Fidelis Almada (*Justice*); João da Costa (*Health*); Carlos Correia (*Finance*); Samba Lamine (*Agriculture*).

National flag: Horizontally yellow over green with red vertical strip in the hoist bearing a black star.

INTERNATIONAL RELATIONS

Membership. Guinea-Bissau is a member of UN, OAU and is an ACP state of EEC.

ECONOMY

Budget. The revenue in 1972 was 577,216 contos; the expenditure, 552,127 contos, and the public debt, 809,785 contos.

Currency. The monetary unit is the *escudo.*

NATURAL RESOURCES

Minerals. Mining is very little developed although bauxite (200m. tonnes) has been located in the Boké area. Exploration for oil is taking place but no reports of finds have been reported.

Agriculture. Chief products are rice, palm-oil, groundnuts, coconuts, timber, hides, seeds, wax. Rice production had fallen by 1975 to 40,000 tonnes and caused large rice imports.

Livestock (1976): Cattle, 258,000; pigs, 176,000; goats, 180,000.

COMMERCE. Imports in 1973, 1,076,528 contos; exports, 78,957 contos (special commerce).

Total trade between Guinea-Bissau and UK (British Department of Trade returns, in £1,000 sterling):

	1974	*1975*	*1976*	*1977*
Imports to UK	146	89	15	2
Exports and re-exports from UK	1,208	279	327	516

COMMUNICATIONS

Roads. There were (1972) 3,570 km of roads.

Shipping. In 1972, 112 vessels of 232,912 net tons entered the ports.

Post. In 1972 there were 2,764 telephones.

Cinemas. There were 7 cinemas (1972) with a seating capacity of 3,000.

EDUCATION. There were, in 1976, 343 primary schools with 80,000 pupils and 1,000 teachers; 2 secondary preparatory schools with 4,000 pupils; 4 technical schools with 694 pupils and a secondary school with 692 pupils.

HEALTH. In 1970 there were about 30 doctors and 900 hospital beds.

DIPLOMATIC REPRESENTATIVES

OF GREAT BRITAIN IN GUINEA-BISSAU

Ambassador: J. E. Powell-Jones, CMG (resides in Dakar).

OF GUINEA-BISSAU IN THE USA

Ambassador: Gil Vicente Vaz Fernandes.

OF THE USA IN GUINEA-BISSAU
(Ave. Domingos Ramos, Bissau)

Ambassador: Edward Marks.

OF GUINEA-BISSAU TO THE UNITED NATIONS

Ambassador: Gil Vicente Vaz Fernandes.

Books of Reference

Anuário da Guiné Portuguesa. Bissau (latest issue, 1956–58)
Relatório e Mapas do Movimento Comercial e Maritimo da Guiné. Bolama. Annual
Guine. Agencia-Geral do Ultramar. Lisbon, 1961
Davidson, B., *Growing from the Grass Roots.* London, 1974
Mota, T. de, *Guiné Portuguesa.* Lisbon, 1954
Rudebeck, L., *Guinea-Bissau: A Study of Political Mobilization.* Uppsala, 1974

GUYANA

Capital: Georgetown
Population: 800,000 (1977)
GNP per capita: US$540 (1976)

HISTORY. The territory, including the counties of Demerara, Essequibo and Berbice, named from the 3 rivers, was first partially settled by the Dutch West Indian Company about 1620. The Dutch retained their hold until 1796, when it was captured by the English. It was finally ceded to Great Britain in 1814 and named British Guiana. On 26 May 1966 British Guiana became an independent member of the Commonwealth under the name of Guyana and the world's first Co-operative Republic on 23 Feb. 1970.

AREA AND POPULATION. Guyana is situated on the north-east coast of South America on the Atlantic Ocean, with Surinam on the east, Venezuela on the west and Brazil on the south and west. Area, 83,000 sq. miles (210,000 sq. km). Estimated population (Dec. 1977), 800,000. Births (1972), 25,065; deaths (1974), 3,418. The Greater Georgetown area had in 1975 an estimated population of 182,000.

In Nov. 1940 sites on the bank of the Demerara River, about 25 miles from the sea, and at Makouria, about 40 miles up the Essequibo River, were leased to the USA as military bases. The site on the Demerara River is being operated by the Guyana Government as a civil airport. The US Government relinquished its claims to Atkinson on Guyana's attainment of independence. On 1 May 1969 the airport and surrounding area (formerly Atkinson) were renamed Timehri.

CONSTITUTION AND GOVERNMENT. The constitution is based on the agreement reached at the independence conference in London in Nov. 1965. It provides for a unicameral national assembly of 53 elected members. Elections are held under the single-list system of proportional representation, with the whole of the country forming one electoral area and each voter casting his vote for a party list of candidates. The legislature is elected for 5 years unless earlier dissolved.

The elections held on 16 July 1973 gave the People's National Congress 37 seats, the People's Progressive Party 14 seats, the Liberator Party 2 seats. The PNC with an overall majority formed a 25-member cabinet. Thirteen of these are non-elected members.

President: Arthur Chung.

National flag: Green with a yellow triangle based on the hoist, edged in white, charged with a red triangle edged in black.

The cabinet was in May 1978 composed as follows:

Prime Minister: L. F. S. Burnham.

Deputy Prime Minister and Minister of National Development: Dr P. A. Reid. *Economic Development and Co-operatives:* H. D. Hoyte. *Health, Housing and Labour:* H. Green. *Energy and Natural Resources:* H. O. Jack. *Finance:* F. E. Hope. *Works and Transport:* S. S. Naraine. *Trade and Consumer Protection:* G. A. King. *Agriculture:* G. B. Kennard. *Foreign Affairs and International Trade:* R. E. Jackson. *Justice:* M. Shahabuddeen. *Information:* S. M. Field-Ridley. *Parliamentary Affairs and Leader of the House:* B. Ramsaroop. *Home Affairs:* C. V. Mingo. *Education, Social Development and Culture:* V. R. Teekah. *Ministers of State:* C. A. Nascimento (*Office of the Prime Minister*), P. Duncan (*Economic Development and Co-operatives*), J. R. Thomas (*Health, Housing and Labour*), R. H. O. Corbin (*National Development*), O. E. Clarke, K. B. Bancroft, J. P. Chowritmootoo, A. Salim, F. U. A. Carmichael (*Regional*).

DEFENCE

Army. The Guyana army has a strength of 2,500, including a women's army corps.

Air Force. The Air Wing was equipped initially with 2 Helio H-295 Courier STOL liaison aircraft and has since received 3 Islander twin-engined STOL transports and 2 Hughes 269 light helicopters.

INTERNATIONAL RELATIONS

Membership. Guyana is a member of UN, the Commonwealth, Caricom and is an ACP state of EEC.

ECONOMY

Budget. Revenue and expenditure for calendar years (in G$1,000):

	1971	*1972*[1]	*1973*	*1974*	*1975*[1]	*1976*[2]
Revenue	162,693	189,257	257,931	395,317	585,491	449,762
Expenditure	180,856	209,503	294,736	358,553	602,518	663,944

[1] Revised estimates. [2] Provisional.

These figures are exclusive of special receipts from the Colonial Development Fund, US grant and the related expenditure.

Chief items of revenue 1975 (in G$1,000): Customs and excise, 330,746; internal revenue, 124,071; fees, fines, etc., 4,082; rents, royalties, etc., 1,197; posts, 3,841; miscellaneous, 16,201. Expenditure: Health, 29,248; education, 59,433; public works, 91,522; post and telecommunications, 19,716; agriculture, 60,443.

Public debt, 31 Dec. 1975, was G$676·8m.

Currency. Accounts are kept in dollars and cents (G$ = £0·21). The Bank of Guyana, established in 1965, issued Guyana dollar notes of $1, 5, 10 and 20 and coins of 1-, 5-, 10-, 25- and 50-cent pieces. The face value of Guyana notes in circulation at 31 Dec. 1975 was G$97·9m.

Banking. Barclays Bank International and the Royal Bank of Canada maintain branches in Berbice, Demerara and Essequibo while the Bank of Baroda (India) has branches in Demerara and Berbice. The Chase Manhattan Bank (USA) and the Bank of Nova Scotia each have a branch in Georgetown. The Guyana National Co-operative Bank opened in Feb. 1970 with headquarters at Georgetown and branches in Berbice, Linden and Essequibo. In 1973 the Guyana Agricultural Co-operative Bank and the Guyana Mortgage Finance Bank were established.

As at 31 Dec. 1975 the Bank of Guyana had external assets totalling $254·2m.

NATURAL RESOURCES

Minerals. Placer gold mining commenced in 1884, and was followed by diamond mining in 1887. From 1884 to 1973 the output of gold was 431,413 bullion oz. (15,600 oz. in 1976). From 1901 to 1973 the production of diamonds was 4,008,211 metric carats (14,000 in 1976). There are large deposits of bauxite; 4,851,000 tons and 247,000 tons of alumina were produced in 1976. Full-scale production of manganese began in 1960 and 114,988 wet tons were produced in 1968. The North West Guyana Mining Co. Ltd, operating through the Manganese Mines Ltd, closed operation in Guyana by the end of 1968.

Agriculture. Production, 1976: Sugar-cane, 332,000 tons; rice, 110,000 tons. Other important products are coconuts, coffee, cocoa, ground provisions and citrus fruit. Other tropical fruits and vegetables are grown mostly in scattered plantings; they include mangoes, papaws, avocado pears, melons, bananas and gooseberries. Other important crops are tomatoes, cabbages, black-eye peas, peanuts, carrots, onions, turmeric, ginger, red kidney beans, soybeans, eschallot and tobacco. Large areas of unimproved land in the coastal region, which vary in width up to about 30 miles from the sea, are still available for agricultural and cattle-grazing projects.

Livestock estimate (1974): Cattle, 265,000; pigs, 90,000; sheep, 100,000; goats, 30,000; poultry, 4·2m.

Forestry. Guyana can be divided roughly into 3 regions: (1) A low coastal region varying in width up to about 30 miles and constituting the agricultural area; (2) an intermediate area about 100 miles wide, of slightly higher undulating land containing the chief mineral and forest resources of the country; and (3) a hinterland of several mountain ranges and extensive savannahs. Approximately 87% of the land area is forested, and about 60,000 sq. miles of this is still available for timber exploitation. Only about 20% of the forest area is at present regarded as being reasonably accessible for timber extraction on an economic basis, however. In 1972 this area accounted for the production of 8,233,743 cu. ft of wood and wood products.

COMMERCE. Imports and exports (in G$) for calendar years:

	1972	*1973*	*1974*	*1975*	*1976*
Imports	297,880,887	372,502,862	567,054,570	810,641,316	927,299,000
Exports	299,877,830	286,978,072	596,200,403	849,478,101	668,723,000

Chief imports (1976): Wheat flour, 4,136,000 lb., $1,514,000; unmilled wheat, 90,617,000 lb., $24,921,000; milk, 26·49m. lb., $21,724,000; textile fabrics, 42·52m. sq. yd, $38,639,000; footwear, 89,000 doz. pairs, $8,587,000; motor vehicles and parts, 51,571,000, $203,439,000.

Chief domestic exports (1976): Sugar, 297,000 tons, $233,471,000; rum, 2,585,000 proof gallons, $12,901,000; rice, 72,000 tons, $73,593,000; timber, 1,112,000 cu. ft, $9·7m.; diamonds, 12,000 carats, $802,000; bauxite, 1·65m. tons, $229,003,000; alumina, 247,000 tons, $61,157,000; molasses, 1,227,000 cwt, $6·02m.

Imports (exclusive of transhipments), 1975, from USA, 29·3%; from UK, 21·4%; from CARICOM Territories, 21·3%; from Canada, 4·3%; exports (exclusive of transhipments) to UK, 28·4%; to USA, 21·9%; to CARICOM Territories, 12·2%; to Canada, 3·1%.

Total trade between UK and Guyana (British Department of Trade returns, in £1,000 sterling):

	1974	*1975*	*1976*	*1977*
Imports to UK	30,509	48,112	46,414	46,447
Exports and re-exports from UK	19,275	29,620	37,977	33,441

COMMUNICATIONS

Roads. Roads and vehicular trails in the national, provincial and urban systems amount to 1,810 miles, of which 595 miles are maintained by government, 836 miles by local authorities and 269 miles by 5 municipalities. There are 422 miles of road on the coastal and lower riverain areas of which 308 miles are paved; and 651 miles of road and vehicular trail in the upper riverain and interior areas of which only 16 miles are paved. A new road, which will eventually link up with the Pan American Highway, is now under construction in the Guyana interior. The road extends from Mahdia on the Potaro River to Annai in the Rupununi. Work on the road is being undertaken on a self-help basis. Motor vehicles, as of 31 Dec. 1976, totalled 64,272, including 26,599 passenger cars, 6,979 lorries and vans, 9,072 tractors and trailers, and 19,109 motor cycles.

Railways. The 19-mile government-owned West Coast Railway ceased operation in June 1974. Passenger and cargo services between Vreed-en-Hoop on the West Bank of the Demerara River and Parika at the mouth of the Essequibo River are carried out by buses owned by the Guyana Transport Services.

In addition, there is a short, government-owned railway in the North West District, while the Guyana Bauxite Co. operates a standard-gauge railway of 80 miles from Linden on the Demerara River to Ituni. In March 1967 a bridge (740 ft) across the Demerara River was opened to enable the company to resume mining operations on the west bank of the river.

Aviation. Guyana Airways Corporation operates scheduled services within the state. Other services in operation: British Airways 4 times weekly to the Caribbean, Europe and North America: PANAM 3 times weekly to North, Central and South America: Air France, to and from Guadeloupe, Paramaribo and Cayenne 4 times a week; British West Indian Airways, Ltd, to and from Trinidad 3 times a week, providing direct connexion with New York and London; Cubana Airlines once weekly. All-cargo services are provided by Guyana Airways out of Guyana through the major Caribbean countries to the USA (Miami) and also to Brazil.

Shipping. In 1975, 1,273 vessels of 2,823,912 NRT entered and 1,225 of 2,266,220 NRT cleared the port of Georgetown.

Guyana is in direct sea-communication with the UK, France, Canada, USA, the West Indies, and Netherlands and French Guiana. There are 217 nautical miles of river navigation. There are ferry services across the mouths of the Demerara, Berbice and Essequibo rivers, the last providing a link between the West Coast Railway and the islands of Leguan and Wakenaam and the mainland at Adventure, and a number of coastal and river-boat services carrying both passengers and cargo. A number of launch services are operated in the more remote areas by private concerns.

Georgetown harbour, about ½ mile wide and 2½ miles long, has a minimum depth of 24 ft. New Amsterdam harbour is situated at the mouth of the Berbice River; there are wharves for coastal vessels only. Bauxite is loaded on ocean-going freighters at Mackenzie, 67 miles up the Demerara River, and at Everton on the Berbice River, about 10 miles from the mouth of the waterway. The Essequibo River has several timber-loading berths ranging from 20 to 40 ft. Springlands on the Corentyne River is the point of entry and departure of passengers travelling by launch services to and from Surinam. It is also a shipping point for rice and other produce from the Corentyne to Georgetown.

Post and Broadcasting. The inland public telegraph and radio communication services are operated and maintained by the Telecommunication Corporation, established on 1 March 1967. On 31 Dec. 1976 there were 57 post offices and 94 agencies (including travelling post offices and agencies).

The telephone exchanges had at the end of 1975 a total of 17,311 direct exchange lines with 21,074 telephone instruments. The number of route miles in the coastal and inland areas was 2,982 km. 39 land-line stations were maintained at post offices in the coastal area, and 8 telegraph stations in the interior provide communication with the coastal area through a central telegraph office in Georgetown.

Overseas radio-telephone and telegraphic communication were provided by Cable & Wireless (W.I.) Ltd, but were nationalized in 1977 and the service is now provided by the Guyana International Telecommunications Corporation Ltd (Guyintel). In Georgetown a central radio station provides facilities for radio communication with 5 branch offices operated in combination with the wireless telegraph stations mentioned above. 92 stations operated by other government departments, 31 stations operated by private concerns (including mining, ranching, timber and other commercial interests) and 12 coastal ships and launches. This system is linked with the telephone system and is available to the general public.

A Tropospheric Scatter System, operated by Guyintel, was opened on 26 March 1969. It provides for a maximum of 32 channels linking Guyana with the rest of the world *via* Trinidad, the nearest point for connexion in the company's broad band system. The Guyana United Broadcasting Co. Ltd, operates 1 station on a commercial basis. The Government established a national broadcasting service on 1 Oct. 1968 which is also operating on a commercial basis.

Cinemas (1975). There are 51 cinemas with seating capacity of 38,375.

Newspapers (1977). There are 2 daily newspapers with a combined circulation of 64,000 and 5 weekly papers with a combined circulation of 138,000.

JUSTICE, EDUCATION AND WELFARE

Justice. The law, both civil and criminal, is based on the common and statute law of England, save that the principles of the Roman–Dutch law have been retained in respect of the registration, conveyance and mortgaging of land.

The Supreme Court of Judicature consists of a Court of Appeal and a High Court.

Education. In Sept 1976 the government assumed total responsibility for education from nursery school to university. Private education was abolished. In Sept. 1977, the total number of schools was 916: Nursery, 400; primary, 445; secondary, 71.

There are now 5 technical and vocational schools and 2 schools for the teaching of home economics and domestic crafts. Training in co-operatives is provided by the Kuru-Kuru Co-operative College and agriculture by the Guyana School of Agriculture and the Burnham Agricultural Institute. The training of primary and secondary school teachers is undertaken by 3 institutions. Higher education is also provided by the University of Guyana which was established in 1963 with faculties of natural science, social science, art, technology and education as well as first year students in law. There were 2,250 students in Oct. 1976.

Health. In 1977 there were 23 hospitals, 132 health centres and stations, 29 dispensaries and 13 medical outposts. There were 114 doctors and 11 dentists.

DIPLOMATIC REPRESENTATIVES

OF GUYANA IN GREAT BRITAIN (3 Palace Court, London, W2)

High Commissioner: Dr Cedric Hilburn Grant (accredited 12 Oct. 1977).

OF GREAT BRITAIN IN GUYANA (44 Main St., Georgetown)

High Commissioner: P. Gautrey, CMG, CVO.

OF GUYANA IN THE USA (2490 Tracey Place, NW, Washington, D.C., 20008)

Ambassador: Laurence E. Mann.

OF THE USA IN GUYANA (31 Main St., Georgetown)

Ambassador: John R. Burke.

OF GUYANA TO THE UNITED NATIONS

Ambassador: (Vacant).

Books of Reference

Daly, P. H., *From Revolution to Republic.* Georgetown, 1970
Daly, Vere T., *A Short History of the Guyanese People.* Rev. ed. London, 1975
Newman, P., *British Guiana—Problem of Cohesion in an Immigrant Society.* OUP, 1964
Report of the British Guiana Commission of Inquiry of the International Commission of Jurists on Racial Problems in the Public Service. Geneva, 1965
Smith, R. T., *British Guiana.* OUP, 1962
Swan, M., *British Guiana.* HMSO, 1957

HAITI

République d'Haiti

Capital: Port-au-Prince
Population: 4·58m. (1975)
GNP per capita: US$200 (1976)

HISTORY. Haiti occupies the western third of the large island of Hispaniola which was discovered by Christopher Columbus in 1492. The Spanish colony was ceded to France in 1697 and became her most prosperous colony. After the extirpation of the Indians by the Spaniards (by 1533) large numbers of African slaves were imported whose descendants now populate the country. The slaves obtained their liberation following the French Revolution, but subsequently Napoleon sent his brother-in-law, Gen. Leclerc, to restore French authority and re-impose slavery. Toussaint Louverture, the leader of the slaves who had been appointed a French general and governor, was kidnapped and sent to France, where he died in gaol. However, the reckless courage of the Negro troops and the ravages of yellow fever forced the French to evacuate the island and surrender to the blockading British squadron.

The country declared its independence on 1 Jan. 1804, and its successful leader, Gen. Jean-Jacques Dessalines, proclaimed himself Emperor of the newly-named Haiti. After the assassination of Dessalines (1806) a separate regime was set up in the north under Henri Christophe, a Negro general who in 1811 had himself proclaimed King Henry. In the south and west a republic was constituted, with the mulatto Alexander Pétion as its first President. Pétion died in 1818 and was succeeded by Jean-Pierre Boyer, under whom the country became re-united after Henry had committed suicide in 1820. From 1822 to 1844 Haiti and the eastern part of the island (later the Dominican Republic) were united. After one more monarchical interlude, under the Emperor Faustin (1847–59), Haiti has been a republic. From 1915 to 1934 Haiti was under United States occupation.

AREA AND POPULATION. The area is 27,750 sq. km (10,700 sq. miles), of which about three-quarters is mountainous. The population at the census in 1975 was 4,583,785m. (highest density in Latin America), of which 85% are living in rural areas. The capital, Port-au-Prince (Ouest) census (1975) population 458,675. Other estimates (1970): Cap Haitien (Nord), 30,000; Les Cayes (Sud), 14,000; Gonaives (Artibonite), 14,000, and Jérémie (Sud), 12,000; Port de Paix (Nord-Ouest), 6,500. Infant deaths per 1,000 live births in 1970 were estimated at 147.

The country is divided into 9 *Départements*: the original Nord-Ouest, Artibonite, Nord, Ouest, Sud; plus (1962) Nord Est, Centre, Sud Est and Grande Anse. The Ile de la Gonave, some 40 miles long, lies in the gulf of the same name. Among other islands is La Tortue, off the north peninsula. The majority of the population are Negroes, with an important minority of mulattoes and only about 5,000 white residents, almost all foreign.

Haiti is the only French-speaking republic in the Americas. The standard French of government, parliament and the press is spoken by the small literate minority, but the great majority of the people habitually speak the dialect known as Créole.

CONSTITUTION AND GOVERNMENT. The 1950 constitution, under which Dr François Duvalier was elected president on 22 Oct. 1957, provided that no president was immediately re-eligible. The new constitution later in 1957 did not forbid re-election.

A single-chamber legislature of 58 deputies elected for a 6-year term was established in April 1961, and new chambers were elected in 1967 and 1973.

In 1964 the constitution was again rewritten and Dr Duvalier named Life President (22 June); the deputies were made capable of indefinite re-election.

President of the Republic: In April 1961 elections were held for the Legislative Chamber, and afterwards it was announced that Dr Duvalier had been re-elected President for a further 6 years (on 22 June 1964 extended to 'life'), although the next presidential election was not due until 1963 and there had been neither nominations nor campaign. (For the series of *coups d'état* in 1956–57, *see* THE STATESMAN'S YEAR-BOOK, 1960, p. 1085.). Dr Duvalier died 21 April 1971. He was succeeded, as President for Life, by his son, Jean-Claude Duvalier whom he nominated as his successor under Article 102 of the 1964 Constitution as amended 14 Jan. 1971.

National flag: Vertically black and red, with a small white panel in the centre bearing the national arms.

National anthem: 'La Dessalinienne': Pour le pays, pour les ancêtres (words by J. Lhérisson; tune by N. Geffrard, 1903).

DEFENCE. The Haitian Defence Force (*Forces Armées d'Haiti*) totalling about 6,550 men, is divided into Army, Navy, and Air Force. The President is Commander-in-Chief and appoints the officers.

Army. Total strength about 6,000 organized into 9 Military Departments and the 'Leopards'. Three of the Departments are in Port-au-Prince and consist of the Presidential Guard (4 Companies); the Dessalines Barracks (7 Companies including the Dessalines Battalion and Headquarters troops); and the Port-au-Prince Police (6 Companies in blue uniforms.) The other 6 Military Departments are located outside Port-au-Prince; their troops (21 Companies) operate as District Police. The Fire Brigade and the Prison Guard Company are also part of the Armed Forces. Only the Presidential Guard, the Dessalines Battalion and the Leopards (two companies of 'Commandos' or Special Forces) with a third company of about 200 recruits, now in training, have any potential for tactical military operations. They are armed mainly with light infantry weapons but have a few elderly pieces of light artillery, 9 light tanks and 6 V150 commando vehicles.

Navy. The Navy/coastguard of 40 officers and approximately 260 men has 11 patrol vessels, of which 5 are operational, a landing craft transport in reserve and a yacht.

Air Force. Personnel strength is about 250, with about 45 aircraft of some 12 varieties, of which only about 30 are operational. They include 3 C-45 transports, 2 T-28s, 5 S-58 helicopters, 1 S-58T helicopter, 4 Hughes helicopters and 12 Cessna Skymaster search and rescue aircraft.

Militia. There is in addition a volunteer civilian force, the *Volontaires de la Sécurité Nationale*, whose total strength is now estimated at about 5,000–7,000, about half of whom have access to antiquated rifles. This force, formerly of some importance as Dr François Duvalier's 'private army' of tough, devoted followers (sometimes called Tontons Macoute or Bogeymen) is much less prominent since his death, having been reduced in strength and reorganized under Defence Force Headquarters on lines roughly parallel to the regional Military Departments.

INTERNATIONAL RELATIONS

Membership. Haiti is a member of UN and OAS.

ECONOMY

Budget. Revenue and expenditure (fiscal year ending 30 Sept.) in US$1m. (5 gourdes = US$1), balanced as follows: 1971–72, 29·6; 1972–73, 31·3; 1973–74, 33·2; 1974–75, 38·9; 1975–76, 43·3.

Proposed expenditures for the year 1974–75 (in US$1m.) are: Interior and defence, 9·9; health, 5; education, 4·6; debt service, 3·4; the chief sources of revenue are customs duties, 15·2; export taxes, 3·9, and internal taxes, 18·6. A revised income tax, on individuals and companies, became effective in April 1973. These figures do not give a full picture of Haiti's financial situation, since the State also draws substantial revenue from other sources, mainly the tobacco monopoly, which deals in various fields besides tobacco; these revenues are 'unfiscalized' and neither the amount realized nor the purposes for which the money is spent are made public.

The development budget (1975–76) balanced at US$103·9m. and includes US$66·4m. in foreign aid.

The total public debt at Dec. 1974 was approximately US$102m., of which about $54·2m. is owed abroad.

Currency. The unit of currency is the *gourde* and its value fixed at 5 *gourdes* = US$1. The total currency in circulation on 1 Oct. 1974 was 158·8m. gourdes. There are copper–nickel coins for 50, 20, 10 and 5 centimes and copper–zinc–nickel coins of 10 and 5 centimes. The amount of US currency in circulation is not known, due to the fact that it is used freely with the local currency, and is legal tender.

Banking. The Banque Nationale de la République d'Haiti, owned by the State, was established 21 Oct. 1910 with a capital of US$5m., and has a monopoly of the note issue. US dollars may be included in the minimum required reserves. The Royal Bank of Canada, the Citibank, the Bank of Nova Scotia, the Bank of Boston, the Banque de l'Union Haitienne (mainly local capital with participation from American, Canadian and Dominican Republic Banks), Banque Nationale de Paris and First National Bank of Chicago all have branches in Port-au-Prince.

Weights and Measures. The metric system is officially accepted.

ENERGY AND NATURAL RESOURCES

Electricity. The hydro-electric plant at Péligre, which was inaugurated in July 1971, provides some 45m. kw. to the capital. The thermal plant in Port-au-Prince, formerly US and now state owned, is now on standby for emergencies. Generating capacity at Cap Haitien is 3·1m. kw.

Minerals. A US company is engaged in mining bauxite (792,600 tonnes in 1973–74). A Canadian firm mining copper (144,430 tonnes in 1970) had to suspend operations at the end of 1971, as uneconomical because of the world price of copper, but indications are that copper mining may start again. Haiti may possess undeveloped mineral resources of oil, gold, silver, antimony, sulphur, coal and lignite, nickel, gypsum and porphyry.

Agriculture. Only one-third of the country is arable and most people own the tiny plots they farm; the resulting pressure of population is the main cause of rural poverty. Number of farms is estimated at over 500,000.

The occupations of Haiti are nine-tenths agricultural, carried on in 7 large plains, from 200,000 to 25,000 acres, and in 15 smaller plains down to 2,000 acres. Irrigation is used in some areas. Haiti's most important product is coffee of good quality, classified as 'mild', and grown by peasants. Production in 1973–74 totalled about 600,000 bags (of 60 kg). In 1974–75, 300,000 bags were exported. Second most important crop is sugar. Sisal is grown extensively. Much of the fibre is exported as or for cordage. New types of cotton are being tried with success. New varieties of rice should significantly boost future production, especially in the Artibonite Valley. Output of main crops in 1972–73 (short tons) was: Sugar, 72,500; sisal, 18,000; (tonnes) cocoa, 3,000; tobacco, 2,000; maize, 257,000; rice, 83,000.

Rum and other spirits are distilled. Essential oils from lime, vetiver, neroli and amyris are important. Cattle and horse breeding are encouraged.

Livestock (1976): Cattle, 747,000; sheep, 81,000; pigs, 1·8m.; goats, 1·4m.; horses, 387,000; poultry, 3·4m.

INDUSTRY AND TRADE

Industry. Light manufacturing industries assembling or finishing goods for re-export constitute the fastest growing sector. Their foreign exchange earnings are second only to those of coffee. There are 2 textile mills producing cheap denim with a total of 550 looms and 14,000 spindles. Soap factories produce laundry soap, toilet soap and detergent. A cement factory located near the capital produced 140,000 tons in 1973–74 and is extending to 300,000 tons per year. A steel plant making rods, beams and angles was opened in 1974. There are also a pharmaceutical plant, a tannery, a plastics plant, 2 paint works, 2 shoe factories, a large factory producing enamel cookingware, 2 pasta-making factories, a tomato cannery and a flourmill, all located in or near Port-au-Prince.

Labour. Trade unions were recognized in Feb. 1946. Strong government influence is exercised over the insignificant portion of the labour force that is unionized and organized labour has virtually no strength in Haiti.

Commerce. Imports and exports for fiscal years ending 30 Sept. (in US$1m.):

	1969–70	*1970–71*	*1971–72*	*1972–73*	*1973–74*[1]
Imports	51·7	59·2	65·8	76·7	119·9
Exports	40·5	48·2	42·3	51·3	100·8

[1] Provisional.

Chief exports from Haiti during the period 1 Oct. 1973–30 Sept. 1974 were (in US$1m.) as follows: Coffee, 23·9; light industrial products assembled for re-export, 18·6; bauxite, 12·1; sugar, 0·9; essential oils, 6·5; handicrafts, sisal and sisal products are also normally significant.

Of total imports in 1971–72 (US$65·8m.), USA supplied US$28·1m., Japan US$5·8m., Canada US$4·9m. (mostly wheat), France US$3·6m., Federal Republic of Germany US$3·4m., UK US$3m., Curaçao US$2·8m. (petroleum products); of exports (US$48·2m.) the main destinations were: USA US$26·7m., Belgium US$3·2m., France US$3·2m., Italy US$2·3m., Netherlands US$1·9m. Coffee was the main export to Europe.

The leading imports are foodstuffs, textiles, machinery, mineral oils, raw materials for transformation industries and vehicles.

Total trade between Haiti and UK (British Department of Trade returns, in £1,000 sterling):

	1972	*1973*	*1974*	*1975*	*1976*	*1977*
Imports to UK	74	154	199	139	882	1,063
Exports and re-exports from UK	1,280	1,470	2,000	2,143	2,697	3,394

Tourism. In 1974, 209,000 tourists visited Haiti.

COMMUNICATIONS

Roads. Total length of roads is some 4,000 km, little of which is practicable in ordinary motors in the rainy season. Four-wheel drive vehicles are widely used as well as lorries. A major road-building programme is in progress (1976) financed by the World Bank, the Inter-American Development Bank and France. There are about 21,500 vehicles in Haiti.

Railways. The only railway is owned by the Haitian American Sugar Company.

Aviation. An airport capable of handling jets was opened at Port-au-Prince in 1965. US and French carriers provide daily direct services to New York, Miami, Jamaica, Puerto Rico and the French Antilles. There are also services to the Dominican Republic, the Bahamas and the Netherlands Antilles. A Haitian company provides a cargo service to the US and Puerto Rico. Air services connecting Port-au-Prince with other Haitian towns are operated by Haiti Air Inter, under a management contract, with Turks and Caicos Airways who provide aircraft and personnel.

Shipping. US, French, Federal Republic of Germany, Dutch, British, Canadian and Japanese lines connect Haiti with the US, Latin America (except Cuba), Canada, Jamaica, Europe and the Far East.

Post. Most principal towns are connected by the government telegraph system, telephones and wireless.

Cables run from Port-au-Prince to Puerto Plata (Dominican Republic) and to New York and South America.

The telephone company, of which the Haitian Government is now the majority stockholder, is in process of being modernized. Telephone subscribers totalled 17,800 in 1977.

Cinemas (1975). There were 19 cinemas and 4 drive-in cinemas in Port-au-Prince.

Newspapers (1975). There were 6 daily newspapers in Port-au-Prince, also a monthly in English and 1 weekly newspaper in Cap Haitien.

JUSTICE, RELIGION, EDUCATION AND WELFARE

Justice. Judges, both of the lower courts and the court of appeal, are appointed by the President. The legal system is basically French. The divorce law has recently been amended to permit parties to obtain 'quick and painless' divorces at a moderate cost, in the hope of attracting the US trade, now that the Mexican 'divorce mills' have closed down. This has developed a useful flow of dollar revenue.

Police. The Police number about 600 in Port-au-Prince and are part of the armed forces.

Religion. Since the Concordat of 1860, the official religion is Roman Catholicism, under an archbishop with 5 suffragan bishops. There are still quite a number of foreigners, French and French Canadians mainly, among the clergy but the first Haitian archbishop took office in 1966. The Episcopal Church now has its first Haitian bishop who was consecrated in 1971. Other Christian churches number perhaps 10% of the population. The folk religion is Voodoo.

Education. Education is divided into primary (first 6 years), secondary (the next 7 years) and finally superior or university. The school system is modelled on that of France. The law calls for free and compulsory elementary education in the French language.

For the 1973–74 academic year, urban primary schools numbered 360 (221 lay and 139 religious) attended by 127,330 pupils with 3,532 teachers. There were, for the same period, at the secondary level, 21 public secondary *lycées* with 15,760 students (4,163 of them girls), 563 teachers (39 of them women). In the private secondary sector, 129 schools were reported with 35,414 students (16,398 girls), 1,172 teachers (107 women). Professional education is divided into 3 categories: (*a*) 41 pre-vocational schools; (*b*) 18 vocational schools which prepare trained workers, and (*c*) 5 vocational schools preparing technicians. There were also 10 licensed private commercial schools. The total number of students was 13,000, 2,000 of whom were in the private sector.

Adult education decreed by a law enacted in 1958 is under the responsibility of an autonomous organization related to the Ministry of Education called *Office National d'Alphabétisation et d'Action Communautaire* (ONAAC). According to statistics available on ONAAC, the number of illiterate adults, on 10 May 1971, was 1,916,685. During the 1972–73 academic year, 53,000 of them learned how to read and write Creole, thus becoming apt for the passage to French.

The country is divided into *centres*. The action of ONAAC extends, so far, to four-fifths of the Republic with 3,724 *centres*. The average annual attendance is 590,000. Each *centre* has 1 teacher.

Rural education falls into the attributions of the Ministry of Agriculture. It is estimated that rural school population is about 1·3m. but only about 14% regularly attended classes in 1973–74.

Higher education is offered at the following faculties of the University of Haiti: medicine and pharmacy, odontology (dentistry), science (engineering, architecture, natural sciences, physics, chemistry, biology) with a school of surveying, law and economic sciences, agronomy and veterinary medicine, ethnology, and the Institute of Administration and Management. A new Faculty of Arts (Sciences and Humanities) was opened in Nov. 1974. The École Normal Superièure has replaced the faculty of Letters and Pedagogy.

Health. There were, in 1972, 332 doctors and 104 dentists in practice, 44 hospitals, and 196 health centres and rural clinics. The hospitals had 3,329 beds, of which 776 were in private and charitable establishments.

DIPLOMATIC REPRESENTATIVES

OF HAITI IN GREAT BRITAIN
(17 Queen's Gate, London, SW7 5JE)

Ambassador: (Vacant).

OF GREAT BRITAIN IN HAITI
(residence at Kingston, Jamaica)

Ambassador: J. K. Drinkall, CMG.

OF HAITI IN THE USA (4400–17th St., NW, Washington, D.C., 20011)

Ambassador: Georges Salomon.

OF THE USA IN HAITI (Harry Truman Blvd., Port-au-Prince)

Ambassador: William B. Jones.

OF HAITI TO THE UNITED NATIONS

Ambassador: Serge Elie Charles.

Books of Reference

The official gazette is *Le Moniteur*.
Revue Agricole d'Haïti. From 1946. Quarterly
Bellegarde, D., *Histoire du Peuple Haïtien*. Port-au-Prince, 1953
De Young, M., *Man and Land in the Haitian Economy*. Univ. of Florida Press, 1958
Diedrich, B., and Burt, D., *Papa Doc*. London, 1969
Institut Haïtien de Statistique, *Guide Économique de la République d'Haïti*
James, C. L. R., *The Black Jacobins*. New York, 1963
Layburn, J. G., *The Haitian People*. Yale Press, 1966
Rodman, S., *Haiti, the Black Republic*. New York, 1973
Talleyrand and Talleyrand. *Digest of the Laws of Haiti*. Port-au-Prince, 1964
Turnier, A., *Les Etats-Unis et le Marché Haïtien*. Washington, D.C., 1955

National Library: Bibliothèque Nationale, Rue du Centre, Port-au-Prince.

HONDURAS

República de Honduras

Capital: Tegucigalpa
Population: 3·04m. (1976)
GNP per capita: US$390 (1976)

HISTORY. On 5 Nov. 1838 Honduras declared itself an independent sovereign state, free from the Federation of Central America, of which it had formed a part.

AREA AND POPULATION. Honduras is bounded north by the Caribbean, east and north-east by Nicaragua, west by Guatemala, south-west by El Salvador and south by the Pacific. Area is 112,088 sq. km (43,227 sq. miles), with a population, census (1974) of 2,752,000. Estimate (1976) 3,036,004.

The capital of Honduras is Tegucigalpa with (1974) a population of 270,645. The next most important town is San Pedro Sula, 133,730. The main ports are Amapala (6,900) on the Pacific, and, on the Atlantic, La Ceiba (44,057), Puerto Cortés (29,981) and Tela (19,658). The port of entry for the Bay Islands is Roatán.

The republic is divided into 18 departments with their populations: Francisco Morazán (483,200); Atlántida (139,700); Colón (64,700); Comayagua (143,999); Copán (176,899); Cortés (311,599); Choluteca (227,601); El Paraíso (149,599); Gracias a Dios (17,801); Intibucá (95,301); Islas de La Bahía (10,100); La Paz (70,200); Lempira (144,899); Ocotepeque (63,300); Olancho (151,800); Santa Barbara (240,399); Valle (106,800); and Yoro (179,501).

Aboriginal tribes number over 35,000, principally Miskito, Payas and Xicaques Indians and Sambos (the latter a mixture of Miskito and Negro), each speaking a different dialect. The Spanish-speaking inhabitants are chiefly *mestizos*, Indians with an admixture of Spanish blood. Gracias a Dios is still practically unexplored and is inhabited by pure native races who speak little or no Spanish.

In 1971 there were 117,430 live births and 20,405 deaths. Crude birth rate was 45·2 per 1,000 population; crude death rate, 7·9; marriage rate, 33; infant mortality rate, 39·5 per 1,000 live births.

CONSTITUTION AND GOVERNMENT. Until a change of Government on 4 Dec. 1972, legislative power had been vested in a single chamber, the Congress of Deputies consisting of 64 members, chosen for 6 years by popular vote, in the ratio of 1 per 30,000 inhabitants. It used to meet for 180 days beginning 26 May and ending 26 Oct. A permanent commission of 5 members used to sit while Congress was not in session for the transaction of routine or emergency business. All men and women over 18 are entitled to vote.

In March 1971, Dr Ramón Ernesto Cruz (National Party) was elected President, defeating Dr Jorge Bueso Arias (Liberal Party). The former President, Gen. López, who was debarred from standing for re-election in 1971, seized power in a bloodless *coup* on 4 Dec. 1972. Since that date Congress has been suspended and Government is by decree. Gen Oswaldo López Arellano was deposed in a military *coup* in April 1975. It is the military government's declared policy to return to constitutional rule in 1979.

President: Col. Juan Melgar Castro.

National flag: Three horizontal stripes of blue, white, blue, with 5 blue stars in the centre.

National anthem: Tu bandera es un lampo de cielo (words by A. C. Coello; tune by C. Hartling).

DEFENCE

Army. Every male citizen is liable to serve in the Army from the age of 18 to 50.

Service in the active Army is for approximately 1 year. Although there is no actual reserves programme, those men who have served on active duty for 1 year or more, are eligible for recall. The size of the regular Army is approximately 13,000 men; this does not include the National Police Force, which numbers 3,000. The Army is organized into 5 battalions and minor units.

Air Force. Equipment, mostly of US origin, includes 12 J52-engined Supere Mystère fighters acquired from Israel, 6 A-37B jet light attack aircraft, 9 F4U-5 Corsair piston-engined fighter-bombers, 1 or 2 F-86K jet fighters, 3 RT-33A reconnaissance aircraft, 4 T-28E armed piston-engined trainers, 1 C-54, 7 C-47 and 3 Israeli-built Arava and 1 Westwind transports, T-33A, T-41A and T-6 trainers. Total strength is about 1,200 personnel, of whom 400 are civilian maintenance staff.

INTERNATIONAL RELATIONS

Membership. Honduras is a member of UN and OAS.

ECONOMY

Budget. The fiscal and calendar years have coincided since 1 Jan. 1957. Recent budgets (in 1m. lempiras) balance as follows: 1974, 329·1; 1975, 325; 1976, 493·1; 1977, 625·7; 1978, 831·9.

The largest sources of income (1972) were (in 1m. lempiras): Import duties, 51·7; income tax, 39·6; production taxes, 68·8.

Total external debt stood at US$111m. on 31 Dec. 1975 and net reserves of foreign currency in 1974 at US$30·5m.

Currency. The unit of the monetary system is the *lempira* also known as a *peso*, comprising 100 *centavos*. Notes are issued by the Banco Central de Honduras which has the sole right to issue, in denominations of 100, 50, 20, 10, 5 and 1 *lempiras*. Coins in circulation are 50 and 20 *centavos* in silver, 10 and 5 *centavos* in cupro-nickel and 2 and 1 *centavos* in copper.

Rate of exchange, 9 Feb. 1978: 2 *lempiras* = US$1, 4·67 *lempiras* = £1.

Banking. The central bank of issue is the Banco Central de Honduras. The Banco Atlántida (controlled by Chase Manhattan) has branches in Tegucigalpa, San Pedro Sula, Comayaguela, Puerto Cortés, La Ceiba, Tela, El Progreso, Choluteca and other towns. The Banco de Honduras which operates in many parts of the country is controlled by the Citibank. The Bank of America has branches in Tegucigalpa and San Pedro Sula. The Bank of London and Montreal has branches in Tegucigalpa, San Pedro Sula, Comayaguela and La Ceiba. The Central American Bank for Economic Integration has its head office in Tegucigalpa.

Weights and Measures. The metric system has been legal since 1 April 1897, but English pounds and yards and the old Spanish system are still in use: 1 *vara* = 32 in.; 1 *manzana* (10,000 sq. *varas*) = 700 sq. metres; 1 *arroba* = 25 lb.; 1 *quintal* = 100 lb.; 1 *tonelada* = 2,000 lb.

NATURAL RESOURCES

Minerals. Mineral resources include gold, silver, lead, tin, zinc and mercury, which are exported. There are probably reserves of other minerals which have not yet been exploited. The Rosario Resources Company, which owned and operated the famous Rosario mines near Tegucigalpa from 1882 to 1954, developed and now operates a mine at El Mochito (Department of Santa Barbara) while the Compañia Minera Los Angeles SA has a mine currently extracting lead, zinc and silver at Valle de Angeles (Department of Francisco Morazán).

Agriculture. Although Honduras is essentially an agricultural country, less than a quarter of the total land area is cultivated and by far the larger portion of this is on the Caribbean and Pacific coastal plains. Agriculture employs 65% of the working population and provides 80% of the exports. The chief products exported during 1972 were (in 1m. lempiras): Bananas, 176·9; coffee, 54·5; cotton, 1·4; maize, 1·3; beans, 4; tobacco, 4·4; sugar, 4·1; tinned fruit, 4·6.

Livestock (1976): Cattle, 1·8m.; sheep, 5,000; pigs, 520,000; goats, 58,000; horses, 280,000; poultry, 7·8m.

Forestry. Forests cover nearly 45% of the total land area. Honduras has an abundance of hard- and softwoods. Large stands of mahogany and other hardwoods—granadino, guayacán, walnut and rosewood—grow in the north-eastern part of the country, in the interior valleys, and near the southern coast. Stands of pine occur almost everywhere in the interior, but are severely damaged by bark beetle and fires. In 1972, total wood exports amounted to 54·2m. lempiras. The Olancho Forest Development Programme involving the construction of saw- and pulp-mills was in progress in 1978.

Fisheries. Commercial fishing in territorial waters is restricted to Honduran nationals and Honduran companies in which the controlling share of the capital is owned by a Honduran national. 2,206,043 kg (6·58m. lempiras) of shrimp, fish and other sea foods were exported in 1971.

INDUSTRY AND TRADE

Industry. Small-scale local industries include beer and mineral waters, cement, flour, vegetable lard, coconut oil, sweets, cigarettes, cigars, textiles and clothing, panama hats, plastics, nails, matches, plywood, furniture, paper bags, soap, candles, fruit juices and household chemicals. An important hydro-electric scheme has been built at Rio Lindo to serve the Central and North Coast regions. A small integrated steel-mill may be erected in Agalteca (Department of Francisco Morazán). The manufacturing industry employed 9% of the working population in 1975.

GDP *per capita* (1972) US$301.

Labour. The organization of trade unions was begun in 1954 with the assistance of ORIT (Inter-American Regional Organization) sponsored by the USA trade unions. In 1972 there were 166 trade unions, of which only 119 were active, with about 67,956 members. A 'Charter of Labour' was granted in Feb. 1955 and an advanced Labour Code and Social Security Bill passed into law in May 1959. A Ministry of 'Labour, Social Assistance and the Middle Class' was created in 1955; the last four words of its title were expunged in 1957.

Commerce. Imports and exports (including re-exports) for fiscal years (in 1m. lempiras):

	1969	*1970*	*1971*	*1972*
Imports	368·5	441·3	387·8	484·4
Exports	333·7	347·7	364·4	463·6

Imports (1972) in 1m. lempiras: Food products, 34·9; beverages and tobacco, 1·5; crude material inedible, 6·6; mineral fuel and lubricants, 38·4; animal and vegetable oils and fats, 3·6; chemicals, 62·1; manufactured goods, 112; machinery and transport equipment, 101·1.

Exports (1972) in 1m. lempiras: Bananas, 176·9; coffee, 54·5; timber, 54·2; silver, 8·2; lead and zinc, 13·7; refrigerated meats, 32·1; beans, 4; cotton, 1·4; tobacco, 4·4; livestock, 1·8.

Trade with main countries in £1m. sterling (1972) was: USA, 31·6; UK, 10·5; Japan, 4·8; Federal Republic of Germany, 3; Nicaragua, 1·1; Guatemala, 0·6.

Total trade between Honduras and UK (British Department of Trade returns, in £1,000 sterling):

	1973	*1974*	*1975*	*1976*	*1977*
Imports to UK	398	447	714	483	1,107
Exports and re-exports from UK	1,522	3,321	4,187	4,580	6,965

COMMUNICATIONS

Roads. Honduras is connected with Guatemala, El Salvador and Nicaragua by the Pan-American Highway. Out of a total of 3,500 miles of road, 730 are paved. There are good asphalted highways between Puerto Cortés in the north and Choluteca in the south passing through San Pedro Sula and Tegucigalpa with branches to Guatemala and El Salvador.

Railways. Only 3 railways exist; they are confined to the north coastal region and are used mainly for transportation of bananas. Tegucigalpa, the capital, is not served by any railway, and there are no international railway connexions. The total railways operating at Dec. 1975 were 991 km of 1,065 mm and 914 mm gauge.

Aviation. Over a large part of the country the aeroplane is the normal means of transport for both passengers and freight. There are international airports at Tegucigalpa, San Pedro Sula, La Ceiba and over 30 smaller airstrips in various parts of the country.

Shipping. Sailings to the Atlantic coast port of Puerto Cortés from Europe are frequent, mainly operated by Cia Generale Transatlantique, the Royal Netherlands Steamships Co., Hapag Lloyd and vessels owned or chartered by the United Fruit Co. and the Standard Fruit Co.

Post and Broadcasting. The Government at April 1972 operated 18,845 km of telephone lines and 12,526 km of telegraph lines. Number of government telephones in use, 1975, 14,984; telephone exchanges, 52; number of telegraph offices, 210; combined telephone and telegraph offices, 179. There are 421 post offices and agencies, 100 commercial broadcasting stations. Commercial television began with a station in Tegucigalpa in Sept. 1959. There were 5 commercial channels and about 27,000 receivers in use. Transmission in colour commenced mid-1973.

Cinemas (1972). Cinemas numbered about 46 with seating capacity of some 40,000.

Newspapers (1973). The 5 most important daily papers are *El Día*, *El Cronista* and *La Noticia* in Tegucigalpa, *La Prensa* and *El Tiempo* in San Pedro Sula. Several others exist but their circulation is low and their influence is very limited.

JUSTICE, RELIGION, EDUCATION AND WELFARE

Justice. The judicial power resides in the Supreme Court, with 7 judges elected by the National Congress for 6 years; it appoints the judges of the courts of appeal, labour tribunals and the district attorneys who, in turn, name the justices of the peace.

Religion. Roman Catholicism is the prevailing religion, but the constitution guarantees freedom to all creeds, and the State does not contribute to the support of any.

Education. Instruction is free, compulsory (from 7 to 15 years of age) and secular. In 1973 the 4,151 primary schools had 420,000 children (12,000 teachers); the 154 secondary, normal and technical schools had 45,000 pupils (2,983 teachers); the teachers' college had 1,025 students (59 teachers); 6 university faculties (1973) had 8,070 students (427 teachers) at Tegucigalpa offering economics, engineering, law, medicine, dentistry, chemistry and pharmacy. Other courses offered are: Public administration, journalism, business administration, auditing and accounting, nursing, psychology, mechanical engineering, social service, agronomy (La Ceiba) and economics (San Pedro Sula).

The illiteracy rate was 50% of those 10 years of age and older in 1970.

Health. In 1972 there were 780 doctors and 4,500 hospital beds.

DIPLOMATIC REPRESENTATIVES

OF HONDURAS IN GREAT BRITAIN (48 George St., London, W1H 5RF)

Ambassador: Ricardo Pineda-Milla.

OF GREAT BRITAIN IN HONDURAS

Ambassador and Consul-General: J. B. Weymes (resides in San José).

OF HONDURAS IN THE USA (4715–16th St., NW, Washington, D.C., 20011)

Ambassador: Dr Roberto Lazarus.

OF THE USA IN HONDURAS (Ave. La Paz, Tegucigalpa)

Ambassador: Mari-Luci Jaramillo.

OF HONDURAS TO THE UNITED NATIONS

Ambassador: Dr Mario Carías.

Books of Reference

The *Anuario Estadístico* (latest issue, *Comercio Exterior de Honduras*, 1967) is published by the Dirección de Estadíaricas y Censos, Tegucigalpa. *Director:* Carlos Raudeles.

Banco Central de Honduras: *Monthly Bulletin*

Checchi, V. (and others), *Honduras, a Problem in Economic Development*. New York, 1959

Rubio Melhado, A., *Geografía General de la Republica de Honduras*. Tegucigalpa, 1953

Stokes, W. S., *Honduras: An Area Study in Government*. Madison, Wisc., 1950

HONG KONG

Population: 4·5m. (1977)
GNP per capita: US$2,110 (1976)

HISTORY. The Crown Colony of Hong Kong was ceded by China to Great Britain in Jan. 1841; the cession was confirmed by the treaty of Nanking in Aug. 1842, and the charter bears date 5 April 1843. Since then Hong Kong has been under British administration, with the exception of the period from 25 Dec. 1941 to 30 Aug. 1945, when it was occupied by the Japanese.

AREA AND POPULATION. Hong Kong island is 20 miles east of the mouth of the Pearl River and 91 miles south-east of Canton. The area of the island is 29 sq. miles. It is separated from the mainland by a fine natural harbour. On the opposite side is the peninsula of Kowloon (3½ sq. miles), which, with Stonecutters Island (¼ sq. mile), was added to the colony by the Convention of Peking, 1860. By a further convention, signed at Peking on 9 June 1898, 365½ sq. miles, consisting of all the immediately adjacent mainland and numerous islands in the vicinity, were leased to Great Britain by China for 99 years. This area is known as the New Territories. Total area of the territory, 404 sq. miles (including recent reclamations), a large part of it being steep and unproductive hillside. Shortage of land suitable for development for housing and industry, is a serious problem. Since 1945, the government has reclaimed about 1,080 hectares from the sea, principally from the sea fronts of Hong Kong and Kowloon, fronting the harbour. In the New Territories, the new town of Tsuen Wan, incorporating Tsuen Wan, Kwai Chung and Tsing Yi, is well advanced and already houses over half of its planned ultimate population of 900,000. The construction of two further new towns at Sha Tin and Tuen Mun is now well underway and the development programmes envisage them being complete in about 10 years' time with population capacities of 530,000 and 486,000 respectively. Extensive development and re-development of Crown land for all purposes is proceeding.

The climate is sub-tropical, the winter being cool and dry and the summer hot and humid. The average rainfall is 2,168·8 mm. (85·39 in.), May to Sept. being the wettest months.

The population was 3,948,179 at 1971 census. Estimate (1977) 4·5m. During the war years the population of Hong Kong fluctuated sharply. In Sept. 1945, at the end of the Japanese occupation, it was about 600,000. In mid-1950 it was estimated at 2·24m. Since 1963 the net annual increase has been between 32,000 and 95,100. Of the present population about 41% are under 20 years of age. About 59% of the population was born in Hong Kong.

CONSTITUTION AND GOVERNMENT. The administration is in the hands of a Governor, aided by an Executive Council, composed of the Commander, British Forces, the Colonial Secretary, the Attorney-General, the Secretary for Home Affairs, the Financial Secretary (who are members *ex officio*) and such other members, both official and unofficial, as may be appointed by the Queen upon the Governor's nomination. In 1977 there were, in addition to the 5 *ex-officio* members, 1 nominated official and 8 nominated unofficial members. There is also a Legislative Council, presided over by the Governor. On 1 Sept. 1976, the Legislative Council was enlarged. It consists of 5 *ex-officio* members, namely the Chief Secretary, the Attorney-General, the Secretary for Home Affairs and the Financial Secretary, 8 new nominated unofficial members and 5 official members, bringing the total number of members to 22 unofficial and 19 official. Chinese and English are the official languages.

Governor and C.-in-C.: Sir Murray MacLehose, KCMG, KBE.
Commander British Forces: Lieut.-Gen. Sir John Archer, KCB, OBE.
Chief Secretary: Sir Denys Roberts, KBE, QC.
Flag: British Blue Ensign with the arms of the Colony on a white disc in the fly.

DEFENCE. The British Armed Forces, comprising 4 infantry battalions, 3 of them Gurkha, 5 Royal Navy patrol craft and a RAF helicopter squadron, are stationed in Hong Kong to assist the Hong Kong Government in maintaining security and stability in the territory.

Army. The local Auxiliary Defence Units, consisting of the Royal Hong Kong Regiment and the Royal Hong Kong Auxiliary Air Force, are administered by the Hong Kong Government, but, in a crisis, would come under the command of the Commander British Forces. The Royal Hong Kong Regiment (The Volunteers) has a strength of almost 700. It is fully mobile and its role is to operate in support of regular army battalions stationed in Hong Kong.

Navy. The indigenous maritime force comprises 2 command vessels, 29 patrol craft, 2 logistic boats and 11 motor launches. Personnel in 1978 numbered 1,300 (70 officers, 330 n.c.o.s and 90 constables).

The 6th Patrol Squadron of the Royal Navy is based in Hong Kong, being maintained on HMS *Tamar* the shore establishment on the site of the former dockyard. It comprises 5 coastal patrol vessels (modified coastal minesweepers).

Air Force. Formed on 1 May 1949, the Royal Hong Kong Auxiliary Air Force is intended mainly for internal security and air-sea rescue duties. It has a strength of about 90 volunteer members, including 15 pilots, and operates 3 Alouette III helicopters, 2 Bulldog primary trainers, 1 Musketeer light aircraft and 1 twin-engined Islander transport, training, rescue and survey aircraft.

ECONOMY

Budget. The public revenue and expenditure for the financial year ending 31 March were as follows (in HK$):

	1973–74	*1974–75*	*1975–76*	*1976–77*
Revenue	5,240,805,405	5,875,309,787	6,519,539,700	6,898,462,881
Expenditure	5,169,157,030	6,255,150,534	6,032,190,492	5,995,850,489

The revenue is derived chiefly from rates, licences, duties on liquor, tobacco and hydrocarbon oils, a tax on earnings and profits, land sales and stamp duties.

Currency. The unit of currency is the Hong Kong dollar. Bank-notes (of denominations of $5 upwards) are issued by the Hongkong and Shanghai Banking Corporation, the Chartered Bank and the Mercantile Bank Ltd. Their combined note issue was, at the end of Aug. 1975, HK$3,737·28m. Subsidiary currency consisting of HK$1, 50-cent, 20-cent, 10-cent, 5-cent copper-nickel-alloy coins and 1-cent notes is issued by the Hong Kong Government and at the end of Aug. 1975 totalled HK$334,692,765.

Banking. There are 74 licensed banks and 100 banks maintaining representative offices in Hong Kong. Deposits in 1977 totalled HK$53,019m.

Weights and Measures. The *Tael* (*leung*) = $1\frac{1}{3}$ oz. avoirdupois; the *Picul* (*taam*) = $133\frac{1}{3}$ lb. (often taken as $\frac{1}{17}$ of a ton); the *Catty* (*kan*) = $1\frac{1}{3}$ lb. avoirdupois; the *Chek* (Chinese foot) = $14\frac{5}{8}$ in. (but varying from $11\frac{1}{2}$ to $14\frac{5}{8}$ in. according to the custom of various trades, the commonest equivalent being 14·14 in.); the *Tsuen* (Chinese inch) = $\frac{1}{10}$ of a *Chek*; the *Cheung* = 10 *Chek*; the *Lei* (Chinese mile) = 707–744 yd.

Besides the above weights and measures of China, those of Great Britain are in general use.

AGRICULTURE. Livestock (1976): Cattle, 11,000; pigs, 440,000; poultry, 4m.

WATER. A serious problem is the provision of storage of the summer rainfall to meet the water requirements, particularly during the dry winter months. The raising of the Plover Cove dams was completed in 1973, giving the reservoir a capacity of 230m. cu. metres. Storage capacity now stands at 306m. cu. metres distributed in 17 reservoirs, supplemented by 109m. cu. metres annually purchased from China. By 1979, it is hoped to complete the High Island scheme, involving the conversion of another sea inlet (as was the case with Plover Cove), which will almost double the total available storage. A desalting plant (capacity 180,000 cu. metres) at Lok On Pai, near Tuen Mun, was completed in 1975.

INDUSTRY AND TRADE

Industry. An economic policy based on free enterprise and free trade; an industrious work force; an efficient and aggressive commercial infrastructure; modern and efficient sea-port (including container shipping terminals) and airport facilities: its geographical position relative to markets in North America and its traditional trading links with Britain have all contributed to Hong Kong's success as a modern industrial complex.

In 1977, there were 23,507 factories employing 670,325 people out of a total population of approximately 4·4m. The type of factory involved ranges from the small cottage type to large highly complex modern establishments. Given the scarcity of land it is most common for light industry to operate in multi-storey buildings specially designed for this purpose. The main industry is textiles and clothing, which employs 46% of the labour force and accounts for 47% of total domestic exports. Other major light manufacturing industries include electronic products, clocks and watches, toys, plastic products, metalware, footwear, cameras and travel goods. Heavy industry includes ship-building, ship-repairing, aircraft engineering and iron and steel rolling. Agriculture, fishing and some mining are the main primary industries.

Commerce. Hong Kong's industries are mainly export oriented. The total value of domestic exports in 1977 was HK$35,004m. The major markets were USA (39%), Federal Republic of Germany (10%), UK (9%), Australia (4%), Japan (4%), and Canada (3%). There is also a sizeable and flourishing entrepôt trade which accounted for another HK$9,829m. in 1977.

The total value of imports in 1977 was HK$48,701m., mainly from Japan (24%), China (17%), USA (13%), Taiwan (7%), Singapore (6%) and UK (5%).

The chief import items were machinery (19%), textiles (17%), foodstuffs (15%), chemicals (7%), petroleum products (6%) and crude raw materials (2%).

Imports from the Commonwealth countries (HK$7,827m. in 1977) amounted to 16% of total imports and exports to the Commonwealth countries (HK$7,832m.) accounted for 22% of Hong Kong's domestic exports.

Duties are levied only on tobacco, hydrocarbon oils and alcoholic liquors (including proprietary medicines and toilet preparations containing more than 2% of proof spirit), whether imported into or manufactured in Hong Kong for local consumption.

All imports (apart from foodstuffs, which are subject to a flat charge of HK$2 per shipment) and exports are subject to an 0·05% *ad valorem* charge.

The adverse balance on visible trade is offset by a favourable balance from exchange, shipping and insurance transactions, an inflow of capital, ship-repairing, a flourishing tourist industry, remittances from overseas Chinese, etc.

Hong Kong has a free exchange market. Foreign merchants may remit profits or repatriate capital. Import and export controls are kept to the minimum, consistent with strategic requirements.

The trade of Hong Kong and UK (British Department of Trade returns, in £1,000 sterling) is given as follows:

	1972	*1973*	*1974*	*1975*	*1976*	*1977*
Imports to UK	184,700	263,442	292,268	306,967	439,605	454,056
Exports and re-exports from UK	100,945	126,915	158,429	157,376	204,430	271,194

Tourism. Tourists spent an estimated HK$4,000m. in Hong Kong in 1977. During the year tourists totalled nearly 1·75m.

COMMUNICATIONS

Roads. In Dec. 1977 there were 1,092 km of roads, distributed as follows: Hong Kong Island, 342; Kowloon and New Kowloon, 316, and New Territories, 415·7. A mile-long cross-harbour tunnel, opened to traffic in Aug. 1972, now links Hong Kong Island with the Kowloon peninsula.

Railways. There is an electric tramway of 19½ miles, and a cable tramway connecting the Peak district with the lower levels in Victoria. A railway, now being modified to include two tracks, 21 miles in length 4 ft 8½ in. gauge, owned by the Government, runs between Kowloon and the Chinese frontier. Passengers travelling to China disembark at the Chinese frontier and walk across to board a Chinese train. Goods trains go right through. A 17-mile underground railway is under construction between Hong Kong Island and Kwun Tong on Kowloon with a branch to Tsuen Wan.

Aviation. Hong Kong International Airport is situated on the north shore of Kowloon Bay. It is regularly used by 30 airlines and many charter airlines which provide frequent services throughout the Far East to Europe, North America, Africa, Australia and New Zealand. British Airways operates 20 services per week, to UK, Australia, Africa and Japan. Cathay Pacific Airways, the Hong Kong-based airline, operates 88 passenger services to the Far East and Australia. Over 900 scheduled services are operated weekly to and from Hong Kong by scheduled airlines. In 1977, 50,050 aircraft arrived and departed on international flights, carrying 5m. passengers, 1,097 tonnes of mail and 184,000 tonnes of freight. Flights to Canton resumed in 1978.

Shipping. The total vessels entering and clearing Hong Kong and engaged in foreign trade during the year ending 31 Dec. 1977 amounted to 17,884 ocean-going vessels of 85,727,242 net tons. Launches and junks engaging in local trade, totalled, 32,499 vessels of 4,721,655 net tons. 477 vessels (834,587 gross tons) were registered in Hong Kong as British ships.

Post and Broadcasting. There were 73 post offices in 1977; postal revenue totalled HK$290·7m.; expenditure, HK$152·3m. Telephone services are provided by the Hong Kong Telephone Co. Ltd. It operates through a network of 62 fully automatic main exchanges and served (1977) 1,132,435 subscribers. Cable & Wireless Ltd is responsible for all external telecommunications and also provides for marine, meteorological and aeronautical communications. Telecommunication systems employed in Hong Kong include satellite, tropospheric scatter, HF, VHF, UHF, submarine and land coaxial cables. Services provided to the community include international telephone, telegram, telex, leased circuits, data transmission, facsimile and ship-shore communications.

There is a government broadcasting station, Radio Television Hong Kong, with daily transmissions in English and Chinese. Wireless licences were abolished as from 1 March 1967. A commercial station, the Commercial Broadcasting Co. Ltd transmits daily in English and Cantonese.

Television Broadcasts Ltd and Rediffusion Television Ltd transmit commercial television in English and Chinese on four channels, mainly in colour. A further licence, Commercial Television Ltd, began single-channel station broadcasting only in Chinese in 1975.

Cinemas. In 1977 there were 75 cinemas with a seating capacity of 94,092. Attendance 60m. in 1977.

Newspapers. In 1977 there were 118 daily or weekly newspapers, registered and in circulation, including 4 English-language papers; the remainder in Chinese.

JUSTICE, EDUCATION AND WELFARE

Justice. There is a Supreme Court, having original, bankruptcy and companies winding-up, criminal, probate, divorce, admiralty and prize jurisdiction, and a court of appeal. There are also 3 district courts and 9 magistracies, most containing several courts. The district courts, apart from hearing civil cases where the claim does not amount to more than HK$10,000, also have jurisdiction over certain criminal matters. A tenancy tribunal hears cases covering disputes between landlord and tenant, etc.

Police. The police force numbered, in 1977, 22,164, composed of 1,808 gazetted and inspectorate officers, 15,554 rank and file, who are predominantly Chinese. These figures include 1,738 women police officers, who are being completely integrated throughout the force.

Education. The majority of schools have to be registered with the Education Department under the Education Ordinance. They are required to comply with regulations as to staff, building, fire and health requirements. From Sept. 1971, free primary education was introduced in government and the majority of government-aided schools. At the same time the Director of Education was given powers to order parents to send their children to school in cases where it appears to him that the parents are withholding their children between the ages of 6 and 11 from attending primary school without good reason. Parents may appeal to a specially constituted board of review if they so wish.

In 1977 there were 171,879 pupils in kindergartens (all private), another 591,267 in primary schools and 488,044 in secondary schools. 495,846 primary pupils were in government or fully aided schools while 138,996 pupils in secondary schools were receiving education financed wholly or partly financed by the government.

There are 3 colleges of education maintained by the Government. Northcote College of Education had 249 students (including 173 women); Grantham College of Education, 301 (including 167 women), and Sir Robert Black College of Education, 250 (including 167 women). The Hong Kong Technical Teachers' College, which is also run by the Government, had an enrolment of 438 (including 29 women).

The University of Hong Kong had 4,693 students. The Chinese University of Hong Kong, inaugurated in Oct. 1963, had 4,715 students. The Hong Kong Polytechnic had a total of 5,931 full-time and 18,593 part-time students.

Health. In 1972 there were 2,533 doctors and about 17,000 hospital beds.

Books of Reference

Statistical Information: The Census and Statistics Department is responsible for the preparation and collation of Government statistics. These statistics are published mainly in the Special Supplement No. 4 to the *Hong Kong Government Gazette* at the end of each month; the Special Supplements are also available in a collected annual edition. The Department publish monthly trade statistics and economic indicators. The Commerce and Industry Department issues an annual review of overseas trade. Statistical information is also published in the annual reports of Government departments. Full details of all Government publications are obtainable from the Information Services Department, Beaconsfield House, Hong Kong. The Trade Development Council issues a monthly *Hong Kong Enterprise*.

Hong Kong 1978. Hong Kong Government Press, 1978
Hong Kong Bibliography. Hong Kong Government Press, 1965
Endacott, G. B., *A History of Hong Kong*. 2nd ed. OUP, 1973.—*Government and People in Hong Kong, 1841–1962. A Constitutional History*. OUP, 1965
Hopkins, K., *Hong Kong: The Industrial Colony*. OUP, 1971
Miners, N., *The Government and Politics of Hong Kong*. OUP, 1976
Rabushka, A., *The Changing Face of Hong Kong: New Departures in Public Policy*. Washington, 1973
Szcepanik, T. F., *The Economic Growth of Hong Kong*. OUP, 1958
Tregear, E. R., *Land Use in Hong Kong*. Hong Kong Univ. Press, 1958.—*Hong Kong Gazetteer*. Hong Kong Univ. Press, 1958.—*The Development of Hong Kong as Told in Maps*. Hong Kong Univ. Press, 1959

HUNGARY

Magyar Népköztársaság

Capital: Budapest
Population: 10·67m. (1976)
GNP per capita: US$2,280 (1976)

HISTORY. Hungary first became an independent kingdom in 1001. For events in Hungary since 1918 *see* THE STATESMAN'S YEAR-BOOK, 1945, pp. 1006–7, and 1957, p. 1096.

On 23 Oct. 1956 an anti-Stalinist revolution broke out, and the newly formed coalition government of Imre Nagy on 1 Nov. withdrew from the Warsaw Pact and asked the UN for protection. János Kádár formed a counter-government on 3 Nov. and asked the USSR for support.

Russian troops suppressed the revolution and abducted Nagy and his Ministers, who were later secretly executed.

On 7 Sept. 1967 the Soviet–Hungarian treaty of friendship was renewed for 20 years.

In 1978 the crown of St Stephen, the symbol of Hungarian nationhood, which had been in US hands since 1945, was returned to Hungary.

AREA AND POPULATION. Hungary is bounded north by Czechoslovakia, north-east by the USSR, east by Romania, south by Yugoslavia and west by Austria. The peace treaty of 10 Feb. 1947 restored the frontiers as of 1 Jan. 1938. The area of Hungary is 93,032 sq. km (35,911 sq. miles).

The official language is Hungarian (Magyar), which is a member of the Finno-Ugrian group.

At the census of 1 Jan. 1970 the population was 10,314,152 (4,991,000 males and 5,323,000 females). Population in 1976: 10,672,000.

48% of the population is urban (20% in Budapest). Population density, 114 per sq. km. Birth rate, 1975, 18 per 1,000; growth rate, 6‰; expectation of life: males, 67; females, 73. In 1970 there were some 1·25m. Hungarian émigrés. There are Hungarian minorities in Romania, Yugoslavia and Czechoslovakia.

Vital statistics, 1975: Births, 195,740; marriages, 103,636; divorces, 26,200; deaths 130,954; infant mortality, 32·6 per 1,000 live births.

Area (in sq. km) and population (in 1,000) of counties, county boroughs and county towns:

Counties (1975)	*Area*	*Population*	*Chief town (1975)*	*Population*
Baranya	4,388	433	Pécs	163
Bács-Kiskun	8,362	568	Kecskemét	90
Békés	5,669	433	Békéscsaba	62
Borsod-Abaúj-Zemplén	7,024	588	Miskolc	199
Csongrád	4,149	455	Hódmezővásárhely	55
Fejér	4,374	407	Székesfehérvár	95
Győr-Sopron	3,837	419	Győr	119
Hajdú-Bihar	5,766	539	Debrecen	187
Heves	3,638	342	Eger	56
Komárom	2,249	313	Tatabánya	71
Nógrád	2,544	234	Salgótarján	44
Pest	6,394	935	Budapest	2,065
Somogy	6,082	632	Kaposvár	69
Szabolcs-Szatmár	5,936	571	Nyíregyháza	91
Szolnok	5,571	442	Szolnok	72
Tolna	3,609	253	Szekszárd	30
Vas	3,340	279	Szombathely	76
Veszprém	5,187	423	Veszprém	49
Zala	3,285	262	Zalaegerszeg	49

County boroughs (1 Jan. 1975)	*Area*	*Population*	*County boroughs (1 Jan. 1975)*	*Area*	*Population*
Budapest (capital)	525	2,047	Szeged	145	165
Miskolc	224	193	Pécs	113	159
Debrecen	446	177	Győr	175	113

Ethnic minorities in 1974 (in 1,000): Germans, 200; Slovaks, 110; Croats and Serbs, 80; Romanians, 25.

CONSTITUTION AND GOVERNMENT. On 1 Feb. 1946 the National Assembly proclaimed a republic.

The present People's Republic was established by a constitution adopted on 18 Aug. 1949. Supreme power is vested in Parliament. Parliament elects a Presidential Council, which exercises the functions of Parliament between sessions. It can dissolve government bodies and annul legislation. The 1949 Constitution was amended in 1972. The distinction between 'working people' and 'citizens' disappears. Citizens are stated to have both indirect (through elected representatives) and direct (through local and enterprise councils) democratic rights. State and co-operative property are recognized as co-existing with equal status. Personal property is 'recognized and protected' up to the limit set by law (this includes for private artisans, places of business and machinery).

Ethnic minorities have equal rights and education in their own tongue.

National flag: Three horizontal stripes of red, white, green.

National anthem: God bless the Hungarians—Isten áldd meg a magyart (words by Ferenc Kölcsey, tune by Ferenc Erkel).

Chairman of the Presidential Council (*Head of State*): Pál Losonczi, appointed on 14 April 1967. *Deputy Chairmen:* Sándor Gáspár and Rezső Trautmann.

In 1949 the Hungarian Working People's Party (Communists), the Smallholders' Party, the National Peasant Party, the Trade Union Federation, the Association of Working Peasants, the Democratic Women's Association and the Federation of Working Youth were merged in the Hungarian People's Independence Front. In 1954 a new comprehensive organization was formed, the People's Patriotic Front. The Communist Youth Association (KISZ) had 800,000 members in 1975.

The Communist Party was reorganized after the 1956 revolution and changed its name to 'Hungarian Socialist Workers' Party'. It had 754,353 members in 1975 (32% women; 46% manual workers and peasants). Supreme *de facto* power is in the hands of the Party's Politburo, composed in March 1978 of: János Kádár, *First Secretary of the Central Committee*: György Aczél; Antal Apró; Valéria Benke; Béla Bisku; Jenő Fock; Sándor Gáspár; István Huszár; György Lázár; Pál Losonczi; Lásló Márothy; Dezső Nemes; Károly Nemeth; Miklos Ovári; István Sárlos.

The Government was in May 1978 composed as follows:

Prime Minister: György Lázár.

Deputy Prime Ministers: György Aczél, János Borbándi, Ferenc Havasi, István Huszár (*Chairman, State Planning Committee*), Jozsef Marjai Gyula Szekér. *Finance:* Lájos Faluvégi. *Foreign Affairs:* Frigyes Puja. *Speaker, National Assembly:* Antal Apró. *Interior:* András Benkei. *Education:* Károly Polinszky. *Defence:* Gen. Lájos Czinege. *Foreign Trade:* József Biró. *Justice:* Imre Markoja.

Parliament consists of 352 deputies, elected for a 5-year term by all citizens over 18 years. At the elections held on 15 June 1975, 7,527,169 votes were cast (*i.e.*, 97·6% of the electorate). 101 women deputies were elected.

The right to select candidates is vested solely in pre-election nomination meetings open to all voters. More than one candidate is permitted to stand in each constituency. Such 'alternative' candidates must receive 30% of the votes at nomination meetings. All candidates must support the Patriotic Front. To be elected candidates must gain at least 50% of the votes cast. In 1975 alternative candidates stood in 34 constituencies.

Local Government. Hungary is divided into the capital, Budapest, 19 counties (*megyek*) and 5 county boroughs (large towns with county status), which are subdivided into districts, towns and boroughs. All of these are administered by a hierarchy of local councils which in turn elect Executive Committees to carry on day-to-day administration. Members of county councils are elected by the lower councils. The last local elections were held in April 1973. The term of office of the councils then elected has been prolonged to 1980 to coincide with the 5-year plan period. Elections thereafter will be held every 5 years.

DEFENCE. The 1947 Treaty authorized Hungary to have an army up to a strength of 65,000 personnel, and an air force of 90 aircraft, of which not more than 70 may be combat types with a personnel strength of 5,000.

By a law of 1976 the Presidential Council may establish a National Defence Council which in times of war would exercise supreme control over defence.

Men between the ages of 18 and 23 are liable for 24 months' conscription. Compulsory military service age-limits are 18 to 55 (18 to 45 women).

The security police (BKH) is controlled by the Ministry of the Interior.

The Workers' Militia is a para-military organization armed with automatic weapons. Its strength in 1966 was about 35,000.

Four Soviet divisions are stationed in Hungary.

Army. Hungary is divided into 4 army districts: Budapest, Debrecen, Kiskunfélegyháza, Pécs. The strength of the Army is 83,000 men. It is organized in 1 tank and 5 motorized divisions not all up to full strength, with about 1,500 T-54, T55 and T62 tanks.

Navy. There is a military marine service of about 500 officers and men operating 10 patrol craft of 100 tons, 5 utility landing craft and a number of river mine-warfare vessels, troop transports, river monitors and watch pickets, constituting the River Guard, and Army vessels are active along the Danube.

Air Force. The Air Force is an integral part of the Army, with a strength of about 20,000 officers and men and 140 combat aircraft, in 2 fighter divisions. The interceptor division has 3 regiments of MiG-21 and MiG-19 fighters. Su-7 fighter-bombers equip the other division. Transport units are equipped with An-2, An-26, Il-14 and Li-2 (DC-3) aircraft. Other types in service include Ka-26, Mi-4 and Mi-8 helicopters and L-29 Delfin and MiG-15UTI trainers. 'Guideline' surface-to-air missiles are also operational.

INTERNATIONAL RELATIONS

Membership. Hungary is a member of UN and Comecon.

External Debt. Hungary settled its debt to the UK in 1967. By an agreement of 6 March 1973 Hungary is to meet claims of US$18·9m. arising from war damage and nationalization in 20 yearly instalments.

ECONOMY

Planning. For details of past plans *see* THE STATESMAN'S YEAR-BOOK, 1975–76. A 'New Economic Mechanism' (NEM) came into effect on 1 Jan. 1968. It restricts central direction to overall policies, replaces direct by financial control and gives local managers more initiative. Although the NEM was initially successful, the detrimental effect of the rise in world prices (including Soviet) has reinforced tendencies hostile to it. Its chief architect. Resző Nyers, was dismissed in 1974. Since Jan. 1976, enterprises have been required to repay state investment credits in full (instead of up to 80%), usually over 10 years, and to cover unscheduled increases in costs themselves. Under the sixth 5-year plan (1976–80) industrial production is scheduled to rise by 34%, agricultural production by 17%, national income by 30%. Priority is given to the aluminium, petrochemical, computer and natural gas industries. 1976 production was below plan, especially in agriculture.

Budget. The budget for calendar years was as follows (in 1,000m. forints):

	1971	*1972*	*1973*	*1974*	*1975*	*1976*	*1977*[1]
Revenue	193·061	209·400	229·500	280,807	313,264	320,400	359,000
Expenditure	195·226	212·000	232·200	284,297	316,224	322,900	362,000

[1] Estimates.

1974 revenue included 216,461m. forints from enterprises and 15,385m. from personal taxation. Expenditures: Economy, 153,398m.; welfare, 48,367m.; defence, 10,564m.; interest on domestic and international loans, 22,220m.

Currency. A decree of 26 July 1946 instituted a new monetary unit, the *forint* subdivided into 100 *fillér*. The official rate of exchange is 34·92 forints to the £ sterling, 20·30 forints = US$1, 13 forints = 1 rouble. Tourist rate: 69·64 forints = £1 sterling, 40·60 forints = US$1.

Banking. All banking activities are controlled by the National Bank, including the National Savings Bank, which handles local government, as well as personal, accounts. (Deposits in 1975: 81,255m. forints.) The National Bank finances investment to individual enterprises and is the main authority over foreign-exchange transactions. There is also a Foreign Trade Bank for Hungarian enterprises trading abroad. The State Development Bank (formerly Investment Bank) finances large-scale investment projects and oversees national investment trends.

The National Credit Institute of Co-operatives handles all credit transactions for farmers, artisans and co-operatives. The Hungarian International Trade Bank opened in London in 1973.

Weights and Measures. The metric system of weights and measures is in use. For land measure a cadastral yoke (1 acre = 0·7033 cadastral yoke) is used.

ENERGY AND NATURAL RESOURCES

Electricity. An 880-mw nuclear power station is being built with Soviet help at Paks to begin producing in 1980. A 750 kv power line linking Albertirsa in Hungary with the Soviet grid at Vinnitsa come into operation in 1978.

Oil. Oil and natural gas have been found in the Szeged basin and in Zala county. There are pipelines for crude oil ('Friendship' I and II from USSR) and natural gas totalling 3,650 km in 1975. The 2,700-km Orenburg–Hungary natural gas pipeline is due to come on stream in 1980. Imports in 1975 (1,000 tonnes): oil, 7,800; gas, 500. The Hungarian section of the Adria oil pipeline (from Rijeka to Czechoslovakia) came on stream in 1978.

Minerals. Coal and bauxite are mined, and there is some iron ore.

Agriculture. The large private holdings which characterized pre-war agriculture were broken up by the Communist government and distributed as individual smallholdings. After 1950 this policy was superseded by collectivization. A land law of 1968 permits collectives to own land, and guarantees individuals' rights to private plots. Collectives meet in a National Council of Agricultural Co-operatives.

In 1975 the agricultural area was (in 1,000 hectares) 6,770, of which 4,976 were arable, 1,257 meadows and pastures, 206 vineyards and 313 gardens.

In 1975 there were 1,599 collective farms with 5·9m. hectares of land (including 589,000 hectares of household plots) and 151 state farms with 984,000 hectares of land. The irrigated area was 155,000 hectares; 62,000 tractors were in use.

Production statistics (in 1,000 tonnes):

Crops	*1973*	*1974*	*1975*	*Crops*	*1973*	*1974*	*1975*
Wheat	4,498	4,968	4,005	Maize	5,911	6,211	7,088
Rye	175	175	147	Potatoes	1,163	1,364	1,268
Barley	871	894	669	Sugar-beet	2,752	3,662	4,089
Oats	67	78	87	Sunflowers	560	575	154

Livestock in 1976 was (in 1,000 head) as follows: Cattle, 1,900; pigs, 6,950; poultry, 53,400; sheep, 2,000; horses, 135,000.

Livestock products (1975): Eggs, 4,000m.; milk, 1,920m. litres; wool, 8,393 tonnes; animals for slaughter, 1·86m. tonnes.

The north shore of Lake Balaton and the Tokai area are important wine-producing districts. Tokaj viticulture was neglected before the 1970s, but now a Reconstruction Committee is reimposing rigorous standards. Wine production in 1975 was 506m. litres.

Forestry. The area under forest in 1975 was 1·55m. hectares. 30,000 hectares were afforested and 5·25m. cu. metres of timber were cut.

Fisheries. Hungary retains important fishery preserves in the Danube and Tisza rivers and in Lake Balaton. Catch in 1975: 23,000 tonnes.

INDUSTRY AND TRADE

Industry. For a summary of the successive stages of nationalization from 1946 to 1952, *see* THE STATESMAN'S YEAR-BOOK, 1954, p. 1115.

Production statistics (in 1,000 tonnes):

	1971	*1972*	*1973*	*1974*	*1975*
Coal[1]	27,424	25,841	26,800	25,800	24,900
Iron ore	687	695	681	545	642
Pig-iron	1,970	2,044	2,087	2,290	2,219
Crude steel	3,111	3,273	3,332	3,466	3,671
Rolled steel	2,064	2,410	2,280	2,391	2,675
Bauxite	2,090	2,358	2,600	2,751	2,800
Aluminium	67	68	68	69	70
Alumina	467	520	655	693	756
Crude oil	5,502	6,332	6,921	8,406	2,006[2]
Natural gas (1m. cu. metres)	3,713	4,086	4,813	5,094	5,175
Electricity (1m. kwh.)	14,990	16,318	17,641	18,946	20,457
Cement	2,712	2,969	3,405	3,437	3,759
Nitrogenous fertilizers	1,841	1,824	1,969	1,908	...
Superphosphates	922	951	1,002	1,076	...
Sulphuric acid	468	566	648	657	630
Sugar	241	298	300	267	308
Cotton cloth (1m. sq. metres)	306	312	346	355	351
Woollen (1m. sq. metres)	41	38	38	40	39
Silk and rayon (1m. sq. metres)	56	57	53	52	55
Flax and hemp (1m. sq. metres)	27	27	25	24	24
Leather footwear (1m. pairs)	38	37	41	41	43

[1] Including lignite and brown coal. [2] Figures for previous years include products.

Labour. In 1975 there were 5·08m. wage-earners (2·2m. female) including: Industry, 1·8m.; agriculture, 1·16m.; commerce, 0·46m.; building, 0·4m.; transport and communications, 0·39m. The labour code contains regulations in line with the 'New Economic Mechanism', abolishing many of the restrictions on the termination of employment and the obligation of the State to fix wages. Trade unions play an increased role. A 44-hour week has been introduced progressively in most branches of industry since 1970. Average monthly wages in 1975: state sector, 2,865 forints; socialist sector, 2,829 forints. Wages were raised in 1977. Trade union membership was 3,957,120 in 1975.

Commerce. Hungary is heavily dependent on foreign trade, which even under the 'New Economic Mechanism' remains basically under state control. Trade for calendar years (in 1m. forints):

	1970	*1971*	*1972*	*1973*	*1974*	*1975*
Imports	29,410	35,098	34,093	37,299	51,010	61,500
Exports	27,196	29,355	35,583	42,038	46,927	52,200

In 1974, 62% of Hungary's trade was with communist countries (33% with USSR). Major exports to communist countries: Machinery, industrial consumer goods, raw materials; elsewhere, raw materials and industrial consumer goods.

All exports and imports require licensing by the Ministry of Foreign Trade, and may be handled by 29 specialized foreign-trade agencies. Under a law of Oct. 1974 enterprises may handle their own foreign trade relations, set up companies abroad and participate in foreign companies. Hard currency is available through the National Bank for enterprises permitted to trade directly with foreign customers. The Marketexpo branch of the Hungarian National Market Research Institute will conduct research for foreign firms. The agency Interag acts for Western firms in Hungary. Main imports from the West are machinery, fuel and consumer goods.

Joint ventures with Western firms holding up to 49% of the capital have been permitted since 1972 on Hungarian soil. Foreign companies may set up offices in

Hungary. In March 1978 the US and Hungary initialled a most-favoured-nation trade agreement.

Total trade between Hungary and UK (British Department of Trade returns, in £1,000 sterling):

	1972	*1973*	*1974*	*1975*	*1976*	*1977*
Imports to UK	11,760	16,830	25,007	26,137	30,771	43,203
Exports and re-exports from UK	22,901	21,467	44,050	44,449	49,515	61,894

COMMUNICATIONS

Roads. In 1975 there were 30,000 km of roads. In 1975 passenger cars numbered 580,000 (551,000 private). 191m. tonnes of freight and 640m. passengers were transported by road in 1975 (excluding urban traffic).

Railways. Route length of public lines in 1975, 8,392 km, of which 1,303 km are electrified. 132m. tonnes of freight and 463m. passengers were carried. In 1972, 80% of trains were hauled by electricity or diesel.

Aviation. Hungarian Air Lines (Malév) operate from Ferihegy airport, 16 km from Budapest. In 1975, 464,945 passengers were carried. Malév operates flights to Austria, Belgium, France, Federal Republic of Germany, Greece, Italy, Scandinavia, Egypt, UK and European communist capitals. Western airlines, with flights to Budapest: British Airways, PANAM, Air France, SABENA, Swissair, OS, Lufthansa and KLM.

Shipping. Navigable waterways have a length of 1,688 km; 3·4m. tons of cargo and 4·6m. passengers were carried in 1975.

Post and Broadcasting. Number of post offices (1975), 2,496; number of telephones, 1,076,064 (1977). Wireless licences (1975), 2,538,000; television licences, 2·39m. *Magyar Rádio és Televízió* broadcasts 3 programmes on medium-waves and FM and also regional programmes, including transmissions in German and Serbo-Croat. One TV programme is broadcast. Colour broadcasts are only transmitted in Budapest, using the SECAM system.

Cinemas (1975). There were 3,595 cinemas; attendance totalled 74m. 37 full-length feature films were made.

Newspapers. In 1975 there were 29 dailies and 479 other periodicals. The Party daily is *Népszabadság* ('People's Freedom') (average daily circulation, 800,000).

JUSTICE, RELIGION, EDUCATION AND WELFARE

Justice. The administration of justice is the responsibility of the Procurator-General, who is elected by Parliament for a term of 6 years. Civil and criminal cases fall under the jurisdiction of the district courts, county courts and the Supreme Court in Budapest. Criminal proceedings are dealt with by district courts through 3-member councils and by county courts and the Supreme Court in 5-member councils. A new Civil Code was adopted in 1978.

District Courts act only as courts of first instance; county courts as either courts of first instance or of appeal. The Supreme Court acts normally as an appeal court, but may act as a court of first instance in cases submitted to it by the Public Prosecutor. All courts, when acting as courts of first instance, consist of 1 professional judge and 2 lay assessors, and, as courts of appeal, of 3 professional judges. Local government Executive Committees may try petty offences.

District or county judges and assessors are elected by the district or county councils, all members of the Supreme Court by Parliament.

There are also military courts of the first instance. Military cases of the second instance go before the Supreme Court.

Judges are elected by the Presidential Council.

Religion. There are 20 authorized religious denominations which share proportionally an annual state subsidy of 70m. forints. 8·5m. of the population professed a religious faith in 1976; the number of active church members was put between 1m. and 1·5m.

Senior church appointments require the consent of the Presidential Council. Lower ones are ratified by the State Office for Church Affairs. Certain appointments become valid if the Office makes no comment within 15 days, and for the most minor church appointments neither state consent nor prior notification is required. Ecclesiastics are required to take an oath of allegiance to the state.

In 1976 there were 5·25m. Roman Catholics with 11 dioceses, 4,000 priests and 4,400 churches. There were 7 theological colleges with 60 teachers and 8 secondary schools.

The Primate of Hungary is the Archbishop of Esztergom, Laszló Lekai, appointed Feb. 1976. There is also an archbishop of the diocese of Eger, a diocesan bishop of Székesfehérvár and bishops of the dioceses of Csanad, Hajdudorog, Szombathely, Vác and Veszprém. The Vatican has lifted its excommunication of priests who work with the Government.

In 1976 there were 2m. Calvinists with 4 dioceses, 1,300 ministers and 1,500 churches. There were 2 theological colleges with 16 teachers, and one secondary school. There were 500,000 Lutherans with 16 dioceses, 374 ministers and 673 churches. There is a theological college with 6 teachers. The 10 denominations in the Association of Free Churches had 37,000 members, 230 ministers and 675 churches. There are 4 Orthodox denominations. The Unitarian Church has 10,000 members, 11 ministers and 6 churches. There were 130 synagogues, 26 rabbis, a rabbinical college with 6 teachers and a Jewish secondary school.

Education. Education is free and compulsory from 6 to 16. 'General' schooling ends at 14; secondary schooling is available at general, technical, or vocational schools.

In 1975–76 there were 4,077 kindergartens with 20,512 teachers and 329,000 pupils; 4,468 general schools with 66,861 teachers and 1·05m. pupils; 528 secondary schools with 14,078 teachers and 382,000 pupils.

There are 4 universities proper (Budapest, Pécs, Szeged, Debrecen), and 14 specialized universities (6 technical, 4 medical, 3 arts, 1 economics). At these and at 38 other institutions of higher education there were, in 1975–76, 108,000 students and 12,135 teachers.

Libraries. In 1975 there were 5,111 public and 3,185 trade union libraries. Major national libraries (1975): National Széchenyi, 4·9m. volumes; Academy of Sciences, 1·4m.; Budapest University, 1·3m.

Health. In 1975 there were 27,057 doctors and dentists and 88,992 hospital beds.

Social Security. Medical treatment is free. Patients bear 15% of the cost of medicines. Sickness benefit is 75% of wages, old age pensions (at 60 for men, 55 for women) 60–70%. in 1976, 50m. forints were paid out in social insurance benefits.

Family allowances were raised by 17% in 1977.

DIPLOMATIC REPRESENTATIVES

OF HUNGARY IN GREAT BRITAIN (35 Eaton Place, London, SW1X 8BY)

Ambassador: János Lörincz-Nagy (accredited 10 Nov. 1976).

OF GREAT BRITAIN IN HUNGARY (Harmincad Utca 6, Budapest V)

Ambassador: R. E. C. F. Parsons, CMG.

OF HUNGARY IN THE USA (3910 Shoemaker St., NW, Washington, D.C., 20008)

Ambassador: Ferenc Esztergalyos

OF THE USA IN HUNGARY (Szabadság Tér 12, Budapest V)

Ambassador: Philip N. Kaiser.

OF HUNGARY TO THE UNITED NATIONS

Ambassador: Imre Hollai.

Books of Reference

Report of the Hungarian Statistical Office on the Economic Development and Plan Fulfilment. Budapest, annual from 1973
Statisztikai Évkönyv. Budapest, annual; occasional editions in English (latest, 1972)
Statistical Pocket Book of Hungary (in English). Budapest, annual from 1962
Hungarian Review. Budapest, monthly
Hungary 66 (*67* etc.). Budapest, annual from 1966
Marketing in Hungary. Budapest, quarterly
Bako, E., *Guide to Hungarian Studies.* 2 vols. Stanford Univ. Press, 1973
Berend, I. T., and Ranki, G., *Hungary: A Century of Economic Development.* New York and Newton Abbot, 1974
Bonis, J. de, *En Direct avec un Dirigeant Hongrois: György Aczél.* Paris, 1975
Enyedi, G., *Hungary: An Economic Geography.* Boulder, Colorado, 1976
Ignotus, P., *Hungary.* London, 1972
Kádár, J., *For a Socialist Hungary.* Budapest, 1974
Lauter, G. P., *The Manager and Economic Reform in Hungary.* New York, 1972
Macartney, C. A., *Hungary: A Short History.* London, 1962
Országh, L., *Magyar-Angol Szótár.* Budapest, 1968.—*Angol-Magyar Szótár.* Budapest, 1968
Pamlényi E. (ed.), *A History of Hungary.* Budapest, 1975
Pécsi, J., and Sárfalvi, B. *The Geography of Hungary.* Budapest, 1964
Robinson, R. F., *The Pattern of Reform in Hungary.* London, 1973
Shawcross, W., *Crime and Compromise: Janos Kadar and the Politics of Hungary Since the Revolution.* London, 1974
Toma, P. A., and Volgyes, I., *Politics in Hungary.* San Francisco, 1977

ICELAND

Lýðveldið Ísland

Capital: Reykjavík
Population: 220,918 (1976)
GNP per capita: US$6,100 (1976)

HISTORY. The first settlers came to Iceland in 874. Between 930 and 1264 Iceland was an independent republic, but by the 'Old Treaty' of 1263 the country recognized the rule of the King of Norway. In 1381 Iceland, together with Norway, came under the rule of the Danish kings, but when Norway was separated from Denmark in 1814, Iceland remained under the rule of Denmark. Since 1 Dec. 1918 it has been acknowledged as a sovereign state. It was united with Denmark only through the common sovereign until it was proclaimed an independent republic on 17 June 1944.

AREA AND POPULATION. Iceland is a large island in the North Atlantic, close to the Arctic Circle, and comprises an area of about 103,000 sq. km (39,758 sq. miles), with its extreme northern point (the Rifstangi) lying in 66° 32′ N. lat., and its most southerly point (Dyrhólaey, Portland) in 63° 24′ N. lat., not including the islands north and south of the land; if these are included, the country extends from 67° 10′ N. (the Kolbeinsey) to 63° 19′ N. (Geirfuglasker, one of the Westman Islands). It stretches from 13° 30′ (the Gerpir) to 24° 32′ W. long. (Látrabjarg). The skerry *Hvalbakur* (The Whaleback) lies 13° 16′ W. long.

The 25 constituencies of the country are now grouped in 7 districts.

District	*Inhabited land (sq. km)*	*Mountain pasture (sq. km)*	*Waste-land (sq. km)*	*Total area (sq. km)*	*Population (1 Dec. 1976)*
Reykjanes area	1,266	716	—	1,982	130,918
West	5,011	3,415	275	8,711	14,047
Western Peninsula	4,130	3,698	1,652	9,470	10,080
Northland West	4,867	5,278	2,948	13,093	10,203
Northland East	9,890	6,727	5,751	22,,368	24,322
East } South }	16,921	17,929	12,555	21,991 / 25,214	12,260 / 19,088
Iceland	42,085	37,553	23,181	102,819	220,918

In 1976, 28,344 were domiciled in rural districts and 192,574 in towns and villages (of over 200 inhabitants.) The population is almost entirely Icelandic.

In 1976 foreigners numbered 3,005; of these 987 were Danish, 599 US, 285 British, 251 Norwegian and 248 German (Fed. Rep.) nationals.

The capital, Reykjavík, had on 1 Dec. 1976, a population of 84,493; other towns are Akranes, 4,654; Akureyrí, 12,299; Bolungarvik, 1,134; Dalvik, 1,207; Eskifjörður, 1,033; Grindavik, 1,723; Hafnarfjörður, 11,739; Húsavik, 2,282; Ísafjörður, 3,136; Keflavík, 6,313; Kópavogur, 12,848; Neskaupstaður, 1,684; Ólafsfjörður, 1,143; Sauðarkrökur, 1,898; Seltjarnarnes, 2,630; Seyðisfjörður, 959; Siglufjörður, 2,067; Vestmannaeyjar, 4,568.

Vital statistics for calendar years:

	Living births	*Still-born*	*Marriages*	*Divorces*	*Deaths*	*Infant deaths*
1972	4,676[1]	50	1,692	319	1,447	53
1973	4,598[1]	43	1,753	334	1,475	44
1974	4,276[1]	34	1,891	364	1,495	50
1975	4,384	33	1,689	397	1,412	55
1976	4,261	27	1,645	383	1,343	33

[1] Revised.

CONSTITUTION AND GOVERNMENT. On 24 May 1944 the people of Iceland decided in a referendum to sever all ties with the Danish Crown. The voters were asked whether they were in favour of the abrogation of the Union Act, and whether they approved of the bill for a republican constitution: 70,725 voters were for severance of all political ties with Denmark and only 370 against it; 69,048 were in favour of the republican constitution, 1,042 against it and 2,505 votes were invalid. On 17 June 1944 the republic was formally proclaimed, and as the republic's first president the Alþingi elected Sveinn Björnsson for a 1-year term (re-elected 1945 and 1949; died 25 Jan. 1952). The President is now elected for a 4-year term.

President of the Republic of Iceland: Kristján Eldjárn (elected 30 June 1968, with 67,544 out of 102,972 valid votes, inaugurated 1 Aug. 1968; re-elected unopposed in 1972 and 1976).

National flag: Blue with a red white-bordered Scandinavian cross.

National anthem: Ó Guð vors lands (words by M. Jochumsson, 1874; tune by S. Sveinbjørnsson).

The official language is Icelandic (*íslenzka*).

The *Alþingi* (Parliament) is divided into two Houses, the Upper House and the Lower House. The former is composed of one-third of the members elected by the whole Alþingi in common sitting. The remaining two-thirds of the members form the Lower House. The members of the Alþingi receive payment for their services.

The budget bills must be laid before the two Houses in joint session, but all other bills can be introduced in either of the Houses. If the Houses do not agree, they assemble in a common sitting and the final decision is given by a majority of two-thirds of the voters, with the exception of budget bills, where a simple majority is sufficient. The ministers have free access to both Houses, but can vote only in the House of which they are members.

The electoral law enacted in 1959 provides for an Alþingi of 60 members. Of these, 49 are elected in 8 constituencies by proportional representation; the remaining 11 are apportioned to the parties according to their total vote.

At the elections held on 30 June 1974 the following parties were returned: Independence Party, 25; Progressives, 17; People's Alliance, 11; Social Democrats, 5; Union of Liberals and Leftists, 2.

The executive power is exercised under the President by the Cabinet. The coalition Cabinet, constituted on 4 Aug. 1974, is now composed as follows:

Prime Minister: Geir Hallgrímsson (Ind.).

Foreign Minister: Einar Ágústsson (Progress). *Justice and Church, Commerce:* Ólafur Jóhannesson (Progress). *Manufacturing Industries, Social Affairs:* Gunnar Thoroddsen (Ind.). *Agriculture and Communications:* Halldór E. Sigurðsson (Progress). *Finance:* Matthías Á. Mathiesen (Ind.). *Education:* Vilhjalmur Hjálmarsson (Progress). *Fisheries, Health and Social Welfare:* Matthías Bjarnason (Ind.).

The ministers are responsible for their acts. They can be impeached by the Alþingi, and in that case their cause will be decided by the *Landsdómur*, a special tribunal for parliamentary impeachments.

Local Administration. For administrative purposes Iceland is divided into 17 provinces (*syslur*), each under a chief executive (*syslumaður*). Each province forms one or two municipal districts with a council superintending the 203 rural municipalities. There are also 21 urban municipalities with a town council, independent of the provinces, and forming by themselves administrative districts co-ordinate with the provinces. The municipal councils are elected direct by universal suffrage (men and women over 20 years of age), in urban municipalities by proportional representation, but in rural municipalities by simple majority.

DEFENCE. Iceland possesses neither an army nor a navy. Under the North Atlantic Treaty, US forces are stationed in Iceland as the Iceland Defence Force. Six armed fishery protection vessels are maintained by the Coastguard, with 2 patrol aircraft and 1 helicopter. Coastguard Service personnel in 1977 totalled about 160 officers and men.

INTERNATIONAL RELATIONS

Membership. Iceland is a member of UN, ETFA, OECD, the Council of Europe, NATO and the Nordic Council.

ECONOMY

Budget. Current revenue and expenditure for calendar years (in 1,000 kr.):

	1972	*1973*	*1974*	*1975*	*1976*	*1977*
Revenue	16,898,872	21,970,325	29,179,784	47,625,680	60,342,390	89,956,581
Expenditure	16,549,552	21,457,234	29,402,110	47,225,533	58,857,251	89,153,247

Main items of the Treasury accounts for 1976 in (1,000 kr.):

Revenue		*Expenditure*	
Direct taxes	11,498,529	Presidency	25,931
Indirect taxes	58,666,297	Alþingi	443,280
Profit from government enterprises	245,509	Cabinet	55,509
		Justice and ecclesiastical affairs	4,535,108
		Culture and education	11,392,165
		Social affairs	3,227,321
		Commerce	5,241,558
		Foreign affairs	917,106
		Fisheries and agriculture	5,782,402
		Finance	2,901,382
		Communications	7,945,139

The public debt of Iceland was on 31 Dec. 1976, 30,339m. kr., of which the foreign debt amounted to 5,643m. kr. and the internal debt to 24,696m. kr.

Currency. The Icelandic monetary unit is the *króna*, pl. *krónur*. Devaluations took place in 1960, 1961, 1967, 1968 and 1972. In April 1973 the *króna* was revalued by 6% and during the following summer some minor revaluations took place. Since the beginning of 1974 the *króna* has been floating downwards, and on 2 Sept. 1974 a 17% devaluation was carried out. In Feb. 1975 the *króna* was further devalued by 20·01%. The selling rate 30 Sept. 1977 of the US$1 = kr. 208·60; £1 = 364·35. Note circulation, 31 Dec. 1976, was 5,740m. kr.

Banking. By Act of 29 March 1961 the Central Bank of Iceland was established, which took over the central bank function up to that date exercised by the *Landsbanki Íslands* (The National Bank of Iceland, owned entirely by the State). Other banks are: *Búnaðarbanki Íslands* (the Agricultural Bank of Iceland), a state bank, founded in 1930; *Útvegsbanki Íslands* (the Fisheries Bank of Iceland), founded in 1930 as a joint-stock bank, which in 1957 became a state bank; *Ísnaðarbanki Íslands* (Industrial Bank of Iceland Ltd), a joint-stock bank, established 1953, part of the shares being owned by the Government; *Verzlunarbanki Íslands* (Iceland Bank of Commerce Ltd), established in 1961; *Samvinnubanki Íslands* (The Icelandic Co-operative Bank), established in 1963; *Alþýðubankinn* (The People's Bank Ltd) established 1971. On 30 June 1977 the accounts of the Central Bank balanced at 74,934m. kr.

At the end of 1976 there were 43 savings banks with deposits amounting to 10,630m. kr.

Weights and Measures. The metric system of weights and measures is obligatory.

ENERGY AND NATURAL RESOURCES

Electricity. The installed capacity of public power plants at the end of 1976 totalled 503,000 kw, of which 392,000 kw. comprised hydro-electric plants. Total energy production in public-owned plants in 1976 amounted to 2,421m. kwh.; in privately-owned plants, 5m. kwh.

Agriculture. Of the total area of Iceland, about six-sevenths is unproductive, but only about 0·5% is under cultivation, which is confined to hay, potatoes and turnips. In 1977 the total hay crop from cultivated and uncultivated land was 389,727 tonnes; the crop of potatoes, 7,641 tonnes, and of turnips 653 tonnes. At the end of

1977 the livestock was as follows: Horses, 49,528; cattle, 62,677 (including 36,859 milch cows); sheep, 896,192; pigs, 8,387; poultry, 277,726.

Fisheries. Fishing vessels in Dec. 1976 numbered 882 with a gross tonnage of 97,156. Total catch in 1976, 975,145 tonnes; 1977, 1,373,954.

The Icelandic Government announced that the fishery limits off Iceland were extended from 12 to 50 nautical miles from Sept. 1972. An interim agreement for 2 years signed by the UK and Iceland in Nov. 1973 expired in Nov. 1975.

On 15 July 1975 the Icelandic Government issued a decree that from 15 Oct. 1975 the fishery limits of Iceland were extended from 50 to 200 nautical miles. The Icelandic Government maintain that this extension is necessary to protect the fish stocks in Icelandic waters because the fishing industry is of vital importance to the national economy.

COMMERCE. Total value of imports and exports in 1,000 kr.:

	1973	*1974*	*1975*	*1976*	*1977*
Imports	31,856,300	52,568,600	75,062,400	85,659,600	120,969,100
Exports	26,019,200	32,876,900	47,436,600	73,499,700	101,889,300

Leading exports (in 1,000 kg and 1,000 kr.):

	1975		*1976*	
	Quantity	*Value*	*Quantity*	*Value*
Fish and whale products	368,758·8	37,339,100	329,305·4	53,367,600
Agricultural products	7,770·6	1,373,300	8,157·8	1,872,200

Leading imports (in 1,000 tonnes and 1,000 kr.):

	1975		*1976*	
	Quantity	*Value*	*Quantity*	*Value*
Ships (number)	32	5,723,400	21	2,249,700
Fuel oil	454,132·6	6,859,900	406,142·4	7,451,600
Cereals	13,507·1	723,400	15,067·6	989,800
Animal feed	55,367·2	1,677,200	67,045·9	2,342,000
Gasoline	78,246·6	1,656,600	79,825·3	2,058,300
Motor vehicles (number)	3,835	2,001,800	4,806	3,187,300
Fishing nets and other gear	1,549·7	1,162,200	1,682·9	1,136,400

Value of trade with principal countries for 3 years (in 1,000 kr.):

	1974		*1975*		*1976*	
	Imports (c.i.f.)	*Exports (f.o.b.)*	*Imports (c.i.f.)*	*Exports (f.o.b.)*	*Imports (c.i.f.)*	*Exports (f.o.b.)*
Austria	303,500	65,000	414,400	26,700	515,900	43,000
Belgium	1,083,200	295,600	1,902,200	366,400	2,659,300	588,400
Brazil	308,000	199,300	614,700	243,600	918,900	479,800
Canada	249,400	43,300	151,100	72,700	208,000	155,600
Czechoslovakia	515,200	178,500	624,200	640,800	688,700	751,900
Denmark	4,966,100	1,903,100	7,535,700	1,840,500	8,156,700	2,301,900
Faroe Islands	30,200	230,900	45,900	245,900	29,900	397,300
Finland	1,448,900	386,500	1,741,700	690,900	1,736,400	1,257,700
France	1,094,100	304,400	1,967,600	391,400	1,718,200	410,100
German Dem. Rep.	129,400	308,700	141,700	44,800	185,300	167,600
Germany, Fed. Rep. of	6,353,200	2,884,800	8,044,100	3,013,800	9,307,900	7,723,600
Greece	2,800	424,300	6,800	570,500	7,300	904,000
Hungary	15,500	39,700	35,300	7,500	54,600	321,000
India	44,300	—	105,300	—	88,200	—
Irish Republic	29,000	4,400	66,200	300	144,000	5,200
Israel	43,900	1,200	70,100	—	81,400	—
Italy	754,000	972,700	1,045,300	1,121,200	1,320,400	2,361,500
Japan	1,397,300	1,369,300	1,733,600	434,900	3,481,300	1,110,100
Netherlands	3,526,400	288,300	5,101,100	233,600	5,206,400	603,300
Nigeria	3,500	58,200	3,000	631,800	1,300	802,500
Norway	4,436,800	1,064,400	7,957,100	884,400	7,160,700	1,917,600
Poland	1,372,500	1,094,400	705,400	584,100	857,900	2,186,600
Portugal	215,600	3,388,900	343,300	5,583,800	268,500	7,671,800

	1974		*1975*		*1976*	
	Imports (c.i.f.)	*Exports (f.o.b.)*	*Imports (c.i.f.)*	*Exports (f.o.b.)*	*Imports (c.i.f.)*	*Exports (f.o.b.)*
Spain	1,296,200	1,480,300	702,200	2,053,000	707,500	1,872,800
Sweden	3,692,800	683,600	4,513,400	1,044,400	5,477,600	1,997,300
Switzerland	524,200	1,880,000	673,500	800,700	801,000	2,376,900
USSR	4,999,700	2,500,700	7,781,400	5,050,700	10,024,300	4,028,800
UK	5,716,200	2,804,900	8,006,700	4,718,400	8,645,100	8,833,500
USA	4,169,400	7,264,000	6,952,100	13,884,900	9,002,900	21,183,400

Total trade between Iceland and UK (British Department of Trade returns, in £1,000 sterling):

	1973	*1974*	*1975*	*1976*	*1977*
Imports to UK	13,903	12,826	16,240	31,659	44,880
Exports and re-exports from UK	15,419	20,839	24,936	26,215	39,276

TOURISM. There were 72,690 visitors to Iceland in 1977.

COMMUNICATIONS

Roads. There are no railways in Iceland. Iceland possesses between 11,000–12,000 km of high roads and country roads. Motor vehicles registered at the end of 1976 numbered 73,410, of which 66,699 were passenger cars and 6,711 trucks; there were also 465 motor cycles. On 26 May 1968 Iceland changed from left-hand to right-hand traffic.

Aviation. One large and some small companies maintain regular services between Reykjavík and various places in Iceland (the large one 1976: 205,756 passengers; 678 tonnes of mail; 4,387 tonnes of freight). The two chief companies maintain regular services between Iceland and the UK and Europe. Another Icelandic company provides regular air service between the Scandinavian countries, Luxembourg and the UK on the one hand and USA on the other hand. In 1976 the two companies carried in scheduled foreign flights 381,993 passengers, 952 tonnes of mail and 5,182 tonnes of freight.

Shipping. The mercantile marine of Iceland consisted in Dec. 1976 of 6 steam vessels (2,971 gross tons) and 987 motor vessels (178,066 gross tons).

Post and Broadcasting. At the end of 1976 the number of post offices was 195 and telephone and telegraph offices 158, number of telephones 91,406. The government station, *Rikisutvarpid*, broadcasts 1 programme on long- and medium-waves and on FM. *Rikisutvarpid-Sjonvarp* uses 81 transmitters and broadcasts 1 TV programme. Number of licenced receivers: radio, 63,000; television, 55,000.

Cinemas (1976). There were 29 cinemas with a seating capacity of 9,727.

Newspapers (1976). There are 6 daily newspapers, all in Reykjavík, with a combined circulation of about 121,000.

JUSTICE, RELIGION, EDUCATION AND WELFARE

Justice. The lower courts of justice are those of the provincial magistrates (*syslumenn*) and town judges (*bæjarfógetar*). From these there is an appeal to the Supreme Court (*hæstiréttur*) in Reykjavík, which has 5 judges.

Religion. The national church, and the only one endowed by the State, is Evangelical Lutheran. But there is complete religious liberty, and no civil disabilities are attached to those not of the national religion. The affairs of the national church are under the superintendence of a bishop. In 1976, 3,494 persons (1·6%) were Dissenters and 2,537 persons (1·1%) did not belong to any religious community.

Education. There is a university in Reykjavík, inaugurated on 17 June 1911, with an enrolment of about 2,800 students. In 1975–6 there were 7 grammar schools (3,500 pupils), 124 general secondary schools (16,800 pupils), 6 vocational schools of home economics for women (178 pupils), 1 training college for primary and secondary school teachers (181 pupils) and 3 other teachers' training colleges (143 pupils); 2 agricultural and 1 horticultural school (146 pupils), 3 schools of navigation (192 pupils), 1 school of nautical engineering (398 students), 2 commercial high schools (551 pupils), 18 part-time vocational training schools for apprentices in trade (about 3,000 pupils), 1 technological college (210 pupils), 7 schools for training of nurses, midwives, etc. (435 pupils), 1 college of music (57 students), 1 arts college (139 students) and 1 drama school (42 students). There are also many part-time schools of cultural activities, such as 26 schools of music, 3 schools of art and crafts, 3 schools of dance and drama and 1 school of athletics. There are also some courses on various subjects for adults and continuation schools for young people. Elementary instruction is compulsory for children from 7 to 15 years.

Social Welfare. The main body of the Icelandic social welfare legislation is consolidated in six main acts:

(*i*) *The social security legislation* (*a*) health insurance, including sickness benefits; (*b*) social security pensions, mainly consisting of old age pension, disablement pension and widows' pension, and also children's pension; (*c*) employment injuries insurance.

(*ii*) *The unemployment insurance legislation*, where daily allowances are paid to those who have met certain conditions.

(*iii*) *The subsistence legislation.* This is controlled by municipal government, and social assistance is granted under special circumstances, when payments from other sources are not sufficient.

(*iv*) *The tax legislation.* In 1975 family allowances were abolished and children's support included in the tax legislation, according to which a certain amount is subtracted from levied taxes for each child in a family.

(*v*) *The rehabilitation legislation.*

(*vi*) *Child and juvenile guidance.*

Health insurance covers the entire population. Citizenship is not demanded and there is no waiting period. Most hospitals are both municipally and state run, a few solely state run and all offer free medical help. Medical treatment out of hospitals is partly paid by the patient, the same applies to medicines, except medicines of life-long necessary use, which are paid in full by the health insurance. Dental care is free for the age groups 6–15, but is paid 50% for old age and disablement pensioners, pregnant women and children at the age of 3–5. Sickness benefits are paid to those who lose income because of periodical illness. The daily amount is fixed and paid from the 11th day of illness. In 1976 it was 944 kr. a day.

Entitlement to old age and disablement pensions at the full rates is subject to the condition that the beneficiary has been resident in Iceland for 40 years at the age period of 16–67. For a shorter period of residence, the benefits are reduced proportionally. Entitled to old age pension are all those who are 67 years old, and have been residents in Iceland for 3 years of the age period of 16–67. Entitled to disablement pension are those who have lost 75% of their working capacity and have been residents in Iceland for 3 years before application or have had full working capacity at the time when they became residents. Old age and disablement pension are of equally high amount, in the year 1976 the total sum was Kr. 230,649 for an individual. Married pensioners are paid 90% of two individuals pensions. In addition to the basic amount, supplementary allowances are paid according to social circumstances and income possibilities. Widows' pensions are the same amount as old age and disablement pension, provided the applicant is over 60 when she becomes widowed. Women at the age 50–60 get reduced pension. Women under 50 are not entitled to widows' pension.

The employment injuries insurance covers medical care, daily allowances, disablement pension and survivors' pension and is applicable to practically all employees.

All benefits within the above-mentioned laws shall go up in step with general wages within 6 months from their increase.

Social assistance is primarily municipal and granted in cases outside the social security legislation. Domestic assistance to old people and disabled is granted within this legislation, besides other services.

Child and juvenile guidance is performed by chosen committees according to special laws, such as home guidance and family assistance. In cases of parents' disablement the committees take over the guidance of the children involved.

Total social expenditure in 1974 including tax relief in respect of children is Kr. 15,151m.

DIPLOMATIC REPRESENTATIVES

OF ICELAND IN GREAT BRITAIN (1 Eaton Terrace, London, SW1N 8EY)

Ambassador: Siguorður Bjarnason.

OF GREAT BRITAIN IN ICELAND (Laufasvegur 49, Reykjavík)

Ambassador and Consul-General: K. A. East, CMG.

OF ICELAND IN THE USA (2022 Conneticut Ave., NW, Washington, D.C., 20008)

Ambassador: Hans G. Andersen.

OF THE USA IN ICELAND (Laufasvegur 21, Reykjavík)

Ambassador: James J. Blake.

OF ICELAND TO THE UNITED NATIONS

Ambassador: Thomas Tomasson.

Books of Reference

Statistical Information: The Icelandic Statistical Office, Hagstofa Islands (Reykjavík) was founded in 1914. *Director:* Klemens Tryggvason. Its main publications are:

Hagskýrslur Islands. Statistics of Iceland (from 1912)
Hagtíðindi (Statistical Journal) (from 1916)
Statistical Bulletin. Issued quarterly by the Statistical Bureau of Iceland and the Central Bank of Iceland (from 1931 to 1962, monthly)
Heilbriðoisskýrslur. Public Health in Iceland (latest issue for 1956; published 1959)
Briem, Helgi P., *Iceland and the Icelanders.* Maplewood, 1945
Cleasby, R., *An Icelandic–English Dictionary.* 2nd ed. Oxford, 1957
Foss, H. (ed.), *Directory of Iceland.* Annual. Reykjavík, 1907–40, 1948 ff.
Hansson, Ólafur, *Facts about Iceland.* Reykjavík, 1951
Hermannsson, Halldór, *Islandica.* An annual relating to Iceland and the Fiske Icelandic Collection in Cornell University Library. Ithaca (from 1908)
Hood, J. C. F., *Icelandic Church Saga.* London, 1946
Leaf, H., *Iceland Yesterday and Today.* London, 1949
Magnússon, S. A., *Northern Sphinx: Iceland and the Icelanders from the Settlement to the Present.* London, 1977
Nordal, J., and Kristinsson, V. (eds), *Iceland 874–1974.* Central Board of Iceland, Reykjavík, 1975
Þorðarson, Björn, *Iceland: Past and Present.* 2nd ed. Oxford, 1945
Þorðarson, Matthias, *The Althing, Iceland's Thousand-Year-Old Parliament, 930–1930.* Reykjavík, 1930
Þorsteinsson, Þorsteinn, *Iceland, 1946: A Handbook Published on the 60th Anniversay of the National Bank of Iceland.* 4th ed. Reykjavik, 1946
Trial, G. T., *History of Education in Iceland.* Cambridge, 1945
Zoëga, G. T., *Íslensk-ensk (and Ensk-íslensk) orðabók.* 3rd ed. 2 vols. Reykjavík, 1932–51

National Library: Landsbókasafnið, Reykjavík, *Librarian:* Dr Finnbogi Gudmundsson.

INDIA

Capital: New Delhi
Population: 605m. (1976)
GNP: US$150 (1976)

Bharat

HISTORY. The Indus civilization was fully developed by *c.* 2500 B.C., and collapsed *c.* 1750 B.C. An Aryan civilization spread from the west as far as the Ganges valley by 500 B.C.; separate kingdoms were established and many of these were united under the Mauryan dynasty established by Chandragupta in *c.* 320 B.C. The Mauryan Empire was succeeded by numerous small kingdoms. The Gupta dynasty (A.D. 320–600) was followed by the first Arabic invasions of the north-west. Moslem, Hindu and Buddhist states developed together with frequent conflict until the establishment of the Mogul dynasty in 1526. The first settlements by the East India Company were made after 1600 and the company established a formal system of government for Bengal in 1700. During the decline of the Moguls frequent wars between the Company, the French and the native princes led to the Company's being brought under British Government control in 1784; the first Governor-General of India was appointed in 1786. The powers of the Company were abolished by the India Act, 1858, and its functions and forces transferred to the British Crown. Representative government was introduced in 1909, and the first parliament in 1919. The separate dominions of India and Pakistan became independent within the Commonwealth in 1947 and India became a republic in 1950.

EVENTS. *See* Andhra Pradesh, p. 624.

AREA AND POPULATION. India is bounded north-west by Pakistan, north by China, Tibet, Nepál and Bhután, east by Burma, south-east, south and south-west by the Indian ocean. The far eastern states and territories are almost separated from the rest by Bangladesh as it extends northwards from the Bay of Bengal. The area of the Indian Union (excluding the Pakistan and China-occupied parts of Jammu and Kashmir) is 3,166,828 sq. km). Its population according to the 1971 census was 547,949,809 (excluding Sikkim and the occupied area of Jammu and Kashmir); this represents an increase of 24·8% since 1961. Sex ratio was 929 females per 1,000 males (941 in 1961); density of population, 178 per sq. km. Estimated population (1976) 605m.

Many births and deaths go unregistered. Data from certain areas of better registration and field studies suggest that the 1973 birth rate was about 34 per 1,000 population, the death rate 15 per 1,000. In 1971 the age-group 0–14 years represented 42% of the population and only 5·2% were over 60. In 1971–75 expectation of life for men was 50·7 years, for women 49·3.

Marriages and divorces are not registered. The minimum age for a civil marriage is 18 for women and 21 for men; for a sacramental marriage, 14 for girls and 18 for youths.

The main details of the census of 1 March 1961 and of 1 March 1971 are:

Name of State	Land area in sq. km (1971)	Population 1961	Population 1971
States			
Andhra Pradesh	276,814	35,983,447	43,502,708
Assam [1]	78,523	11,872,772	14,625,152
Bihar	173,876	46,455,610	56,353,369
Gujarat	195,984	20,633,350	26,697,475
Haryana	44,222	—	10,036,808
Himachal Pradesh	55,673	1,351,144	3,460,434

[1] In 1961 population included areas now separate (Meghalaya and Mizoram).

Name of State	Land area in sq. km (1971)	Population 1961	Population 1971
States			
Jammu and Kashmir[1]	101,283	3,560,976	4,617,000
Karnataka	191,773	23,586,772	29,299,014
Kerala	38,864	16,903,715	21,347,375
Madhya Pradesh	442,841	32,372,408	41,654,119
Maharashtra	307,762	39,553,718	50,412,235
Manipur	22,356	780,037	1,072,753
Meghalaya	22,489	—	1,011,699
Nagaland	16,527	369,200	516,449
Orissa	155,782	17,548,846	21,944,615
Punjab[4]	50,362	20,306,812	13,551,060
Rajasthan	342,214	20,155,602	25,765,806
Tamil Nadu	130,069	33,686,953	41,199,168
Tripura	10,477	1,142,055	1,556,342
Uttar Pradesh	294,413	73,746,401	88,341,144
West Bengal	87,853	34,926,279	44,312,011
Union Territories			
Andaman and Nicobar Islands	8,293	63,548	115,133
Arunachal Pradesh	83,578	336,558	467,511
Chandigarh	114	—	257,251
Dadra and Nagar Haveli	491	57,963[2]	74,170
Delhi	1,485	2,658,612	4,065,698
Goa, Daman and Diu	3,813	626,667[3]	857,771
Lakshadweep	32	24,108	31,810
Mizoram	21,087	—	332,390
Pondicherry	480	369,079	471,707
Grand total	3,159,530	439,072,582	547,949,809

[1] Excludes the Pakistan-occupied area.
[2] 1962 census.
[3] 1960 Portuguese census.
[4] By the creation of Haryana (1966) Punjab has lost *c.* 7m. people to the new state, 89,000 to the new Union territory of Chandigarh and a further 1·5m. to Himachal Pradesh.

Sikkim was added to the Union as a state in 1975; area, 7,298 sq. km, population (1977 estimate), 250,000.

Greatest density occurs in Delhi (2,738 per sq. km), Chandigarh (2,257), Lakshadweep (994) and Pondicherry (983). The lowest occurs in Arunachal Pradesh (6).

There were (1971) 283,936,000 males and 264,013,200 females.

In 1971, 43·89 crores were rural (*c.* 80%) and 10·91 crores were urban. There were 575,721 villages: 318,611 of these had less than 500 inhabitants.

Cities and Urban Agglomerations (with states in brackets) having more than 100,000 population at the 1971 census were:

Agra (U.P.)	637,785
Ahmedabad (Guj.)	1,741,522
Ahmednagar (Mah.)	117,275
Ajmer (Raj.)	262,480
Akola (Mah.)	168,454
Aligarh (U.P.)	254,008
Allahabad (U.P.)	513,997
Alleppey (Ker.)	160,064
Alwar (Raj.)/Har.	100,791
Ambala (Har.)	102,519
Amravati (Mah.)	193,636
Amritsar (Pun.)	432,663
Asansol (W.B.)	157,388
Aurangabad (Mah.)	150,514
Bangalore (Kar.)	1,653,779
Bareilly (U.P.)	326,127
Behrampur (Ori.)	117,635
Belgaum (Kar.)	213,830
Bellary (Kar.)	125,127
Bhadravati (Kar.)	101,315
Bhagalpur (Bih.)	172,700
Bhavnagar (Guj.)	226,072
Bhopal (M.P.)	392,077
Bhubaneswar	105,514
Bihar (Bih.)	100,052
Bijapur (Kar.)	103,308
Bikaner (Raj.)	188,598
Bilaspur (M.P.)	130,804
Bokaro Steel City (Bih.)	108,012
Bombay (Mah.)	5,970,575
Burdwan (W.B.)	144,970
Burhanpur (M.P.)	105,349
Calcutta (W.B.)	7,031,382
Chandigarh (Ch.)	233,004
Cochin (Ker.)	438,420
Cuddalore (T.N.)	101,345
Cuttack (Ori.)	194,036
Darbhanga (Bih.)	132,129
Dehra Dun (U.P.)	199,443
Delhi	3,647,023
Devanagere (Kar.)	121,018
Dhanbad (Bih.)	433,085
Dhulia (Mah.)	137,089
Dindigul (T.N.)	127,406
Durgapur (W.B.)	207,232
Durg-Bhilainagar (M.P.)	245,333
Eluru (A.P.)	127,047
Erode (T.N.)	103,704
Faizabad (U.P.)	109,765
Farrukhabad-Fatehgar (U.P.)	111,373
Firozabad (U.P.)	133,945
Gauhati (Ass.)	122,981

Gaya (Bih.)	179,826	Machilipatnam (A.P.)	112,636	Rohtak (Har.)	124,783
Ghaziabad (U.P.)	128,036	Madras (T.N.)	3,169,930	Rourkela (Ori.)	172,536
Gorakhpur (U.P.)	230,701	Madurai (T.N.)	548,298	Sagar (M.P.)	154,811
Gulbarga (Kar.)	145,630	Malegaon (Mah.)	191,784	Saharanpur (U.P.)	225,698
Guntur (A.P.)	269,941	Mangalore (Kar.)	214,093	Salem (T.N.)	308,303
Gwalior (M.P.)	406,755	Mathura (U.P.)	140,468	Sangli (Mah.)	115,052
Hubli-Dharwar (Kar.)	379,555	Meerut (U.P.)	367,821	Shahjahanpur (U.P.)	144,058
Hyderabad (A.P.)	1,796,339	Mirzapur (U.P.)	105,920	Shimoga (Kar.)	102,703
Imphal (Man.)	100,605	Monghyr (Bih.)	102,462	Sholapur (Mah.)	398,122
Indore (M.P.)	572,622	Moradabad (U.P.)	272,355	Singanallur (T.N.)	113,397
Jabalpur (M.P.)	533,751	Muzaffar Nagar (U.P.)	114,859	Srinagar (J. & K.)	403,612
Jaipur (Raj.)	613,144	Muzaffarpur (Bih.)	127,045	Surat (Guj.)	471,815
Jalgaon (Mah.)	106,739	Mysore (Kar.)	355,636	Tenali (A.P.)	102,943
Jammu (J. & K.)	155,249	Nadiad (Guj.)	108,268	Thana (Mah.)	170,167
Jamnagar (Guj.)	214,853	Nagercoil (T.N.)	141,207	Thanjavur (T.N.)	140,470
Jamshedpur (Bih.)	465,200	Nagpur (Mah.)	866,144	Tiruchirapalli (T.N.)	306,247
Jhansi (U.P.)	198,101	Nanded (Mah.)	126,400	Tirunelveli (T.N.)	108,509
Jodhpur (Raj.)	318,894	Nasik (Mah.)	176,187	Tiruppur (T.N.)	113,171
Jullundur (Pun.)	296,103	Nellore (A.P.)	133,607	Trivandrum (Ker.)	409,761
Kakinada (A.P.)	164,172	Nizamabad (A.P.)	114,868	Tuticorin (T.N.)	154,804
Kanchipuram (T.N.)	110,505	Patiala (Pun.)	151,903	Udaipur (Raj.)	162,934
Kanpur (U.P.)	1,275,242	Patna (Bih.)	490,265	Ujjain (M.P.)	209,118
Kharagpur (W.B.)	161,911	Pune (Mah.)	1,135,034	Ulhasnagar (Mah.)	168,128
Kolhapur (Mah.)	259,068	Quilon (Ker.)	124,072	Vadodara (Guj.)	467,422
Kotah (Raj.)	213,005	Raipur (M.P.)	205,909	Varanasi (U.P.)	582,915
Kozikhode (Ker.)	333,980	Rajahmundry (A.P.)	188,841	Vellore (T.N.)	138,220
Kumbakonam (T.N.)	112,971	Rajkot (Guj.)	300,152	Vijayawada (A.P.)	343,664
Kurnool (A.P.)	136,682	Rampur (U.P.)	161,802	Visakhapatnam (A.P.)	362,270
Lucknow (U.P.)	826,246	Ranchi (Bih.)	256,011	Warangal (A.P.)	207,130
Ludhiana (Pun.)	401,124	Ratlam (M.P.)	118,625		

Report of the Officials of the Government of India and the People's Republic of China on the Boundary Question. New Delhi, Ministry of External Affairs, 1961
1961 Census: Final General Totals. 1962
Census of India, 1951 and 1961: Reports and Papers, Decennial Series. (All published by Government of India.)
Annual Report on the Working of Indian Migration. Government of India, from 1956
Report of the Commissioner for Scheduled Castes and Scheduled Tribes. Government of India. Annual
Public Health. Report of the Public Health Commission with the Government of India. Annual
Agarwala, S. N., *India's Population.* London, 1960
Hutton, J. H., *Caste in India.* 3rd ed. Bombay, 1961
Mamoria, C. B., *India's Population Problem.* Allahabad, 1961
Mayer, A. C., *Caste and Kinship in Central India.* London, 1960
Misra, B. B., *The Indian Middle Classes.* R. Inst. of Int. Affairs, 1961
Sovani, N. V., *Urbanization and Urban India.* London, 1966
Turner, R. (ed.), *India's Urban Future.* Univ. of California Press and CUP, 1962

CONSTITUTION AND GOVERNMENT. On 26 Jan. 1950 India became a sovereign democratic republic. India's relations with the British Commonwealth of Nations were defined at the London conference of Prime Ministers on 27 April 1949. Unanimous agreement was reached to the effect that the Republic of India remains a full member of the Commonwealth and accepts the Queen as 'the symbol of the free association of its independent member nations and, as such, the head of the Commonwealth'. This agreement was ratified by the Constituent Assembly of India on 17 May 1949.

The constitution was passed by the Constituent Assembly on 26 Nov. 1949 and came into force on 26 Jan. 1950. It has since been amended 44 times.

India is a Union of States and comprises 22 States and 9 Union territories. Each State is administered by a Governor appointed by the President for a term of 5 years while each Union territory is administered by the President through an administrator appointed by him.

The capital is New Delhi.

Presidency. The head of the Union is the President in whom all executive power is vested, to be exercised on the advice of ministers responsible to Parliament. He is elected by an electoral college consisting of all the elected members of Parliament and of the various state legislative assemblies. He holds office for 5 years and is eligible for re-election. He can be removed from office by impeachment for violation of the constitution.

There is also a Vice-President who is *ex-officio* chairman of the Upper House of Parliament.

Central Legislature. The Parliament for the Union consists of the President, the Council of States (*Rajya Sabha*) and the House of the People (*Lok Sabha*). The Council of States, or the Upper House, consists of not more than 250 members; in 1977 there were 232 elected members and 12 members nominated by the President. The election to this house is indirect; the representatives of each State are elected by the elected members of the Legislative Assembly of that State. The Council of States is a permanent body not liable to dissolution, but one-third of the members retire every second year. The House of the People, or the Lower House, consists of 544 members, 525 directly elected on the basis of adult suffrage from territorial constituencies in the States, and 17 members to represent the Union territories, chosen in such manner as the Parliament may by law provide; in May 1977 there were 542 elected members and 2 members nominated by the President. The House of the People unless sooner dissolved continues for a period of 6 years from the date appointed for its first meeting.

State Legislatures. For every State there is a legislature which consists of the Governor, and (*a*) 2 Houses, a Legislative Assembly and a Legislative Council, in the States of Andhra Pradesh, Jammu and Kashmir, Karnataka, Madhya Pradesh, Maharashtra, Tamil Nadu and Uttar Pradesh, and (*b*) 1 House, a Legislative Assembly, in the other States. Every Legislative Assembly, unless sooner dissolved, continues for 6 years from the date appointed for its first meeting. Every State Legislative Council is a permanent body and is not subject to dissolution, but one-third of the members retire every year. Parliament can, however, abolish an existing Legislative Council or create a new one, if the proposal is supported by a resolution of the Legislative Assembly concerned.

Legislative Councils have one-third of the total membership of the Assemblies but not less than 40 members, of whom one-third are elected by local authorities, one-third by members of the Assembly, one-twelfth by state university graduates and one-twelfth by teachers of secondary school upwards; the rest are named by the Governor. Legislative Assemblies have between 60 and 500 directly elected members.

Legislation. The various subjects of legislation are enumerated in three lists in the seventh schedule to the constitution. List I, the Union List, consists of 97 subjects (including defence, foreign affairs, communications, currency and coinage, banking and customs) with respect to which the Union Parliament has exclusive power to make laws; the State legislature has exclusive power to make laws with respect to the 66 subjects in list II, the State List—these include police and public order, agriculture and irrigation, education, public health and local government; the powers to make laws with respect to the 47 subjects (including economic and social planning, legal questions and labour and price control) in list III, the Concurrent List, are held by both Union and State governments, though the former prevails. But Parliament may legislate with respect to any subject in the State List in circumstances when the subject assumes national importance or during emergencies.

Other provisions deal with the administrative relations between the Union and the States, interstate trade and commerce, distribution of revenues between the States and the Union, official language, etc.

Fundamental Rights. Two chapters of the constitution deal with fundamental rights and 'Directive Principles of State Policy'. 'Untouchability' is abolished, and its practice in any form is punishable. The fundamental rights can be enforced through the ordinary courts of law and through the Supreme Court of the Union. The directive principles cannot be enforced through the courts of law; they are nevertheless fundamental in the governance of the country.

Citizenship. Under the Constitution, every person who was on the 26 Jan. 1950, domiciled in India and (*a*) was born in India or (*b*) either of whose parents was born in India or (*c*) who has been ordinarily resident in the territory of India for not less than 5 years immediately preceding that date became a citizen of India. Special provision is made for migrants from Pakistan and for Indians resident abroad. Under the Citizenship Act, 1955, which supplemented the provisions of the Constitution, Indian citizenship is acquired by birth, by descent, by registration and by naturalization. The Act also provides for loss of citizenship by renunciation, termination and deprivation. The right to vote is granted to every person who is a citizen of India and who is not less than 21 years of age on a fixed date and is not otherwise disqualified.

Parliament. Parliament and the state legislatures are organized according to the following schedule (figures show distribution of seats in May 1977):

	Parliament		*State Legislatures*	
	House of the People (Lok Sabha)	*Council of States (Rajya Sabba)*	*Legislative Assemblies (Vidhan Sabhas)*	*Legislative Councils (Vidhan Parishads)*
States:				
Andhra Pradesh	42	18	294	90
Assam	14	7	126	—
Bihar	54	22	324	—
Gujarat	26	11	182	—
Haryana	10	5	90	—
Himachal Pradesh	4	3	68	—
Karnataka	28	12	224	63
Kerala	20	9	140	—
Madhya Pradesh	40	16	320	90
Maharashtra	48	19	288	78
Manipur	2	1	60	—
Meghalaya	2	1	60	—
Nagaland	1	1	60	—
Orissa	21	10	147	—
Punjab	13	7	117	—
Rajasthan	25	10	200	—
Sikkim	1	1	32	—
Tamil Nadu	39	18	234	63
Tripura	2	1	60	—
Uttar Pradesh	85	34	425	108
West Bengal	42	16	294	—
Jammu and Kashmir	6	4	76[2]	36[4]
Union Territories:				
Andaman and Nicobar Islands	1	—	—	—
Arunachal Pradesh	2	1[3]	30	—
Chandigarh	1	—	—	—
Dadra and Nagar Haveli	1	—	—	—
Delhi	7	3	61	—
Goa, Daman and Diu	2	—	30	—
Lakshadweep	1	—	—	—
Mizoram	1	1	30	—
Pondicherry	1	1	30	—
Nominated by the President under Article 80 (1) (a) of the Constitution	—	12	—	—
Total	544[1]	244	4,034	528

[1] Includes 2 nominated members to represent Anglo-Indians.
[2] Excludes 25 seats for Pakistan-occupied areas of the State which are in abeyance.
[3] Nominated by the President.
[4] Excludes seats for the Pakistan-occupied areas.

The number of seats allotted to scheduled castes and scheduled tribes in the House of the People is 77 and 42 respectively. Out of the 3,864 seats allotted to the

Legislative Assemblies, 521 are reserved for scheduled castes and 329 for scheduled tribes.

Following the general election of March 1977 the composition of the House of the People was: Janata Alliance 346 (Janata 271, Congress for Democracy 28, Communist Party (Marxist) 22, Akali Dal 9, Others 20); Congress 150; Anna Dravida Munnetra Kazhagam 19; Communist Party of India 7; others 16.

National flag: Three horizontal stripes of saffron (orange), white and green, with the wheel of Asoka in the centre in blue.

National anthem: Jana-gana-mana (words by Rabindranath Tagore).

Indian Independence Act, 1947. (Ch. 30.) London, 1947
The Constitution of India (*Modified up to 15 April 1967*). Delhi, 1967
Appadorai, A., *Documents on Political Thought in Modern India.* OUP, 1974
Austin, G., *The Indian Constitution.* OUP, 1966
Basu, D. D., *Commentary on the Constitution of India.* 3rd ed. 2 vols. Calcutta, 1956
Gandhi, I., *The Speeches and Reminiscences of Indira Gandhi.* London, 1975
Mansergh, N., ed. *The Transfer of Power 1942–47.* 5 vols. HMSO, 1970–75
Menon, V. P., *Transfer of Power in India.* Bombay, 1957
More, S. S., *Practice and Procedure of Indian Parliament.* Bombay, 1960
Morris-Jones, W. H., *Parliament in India.* London, 1957.—*The Government and Politics of India.* London, 1964
Pylee, M. V., *Constitutional Government in India.* 2nd ed. Bombay, 1965
Rao, K. V., *Parliamentary Democracy of India.* 2nd ed. Calcutta, 1965
Seervali, H. M., *Constitutional Law of India.* Bombay, 1967
Sinha, S., *Indian Independence in Perspective.* London, 1965

Language. The constitution provides that the official language of the Union shall be Hindi in the Devanagari script. It was originally provided that English should continue to be used for all official purposes until 1965. But the Official Languages Act 1963 provides that, after the expiry of this period of 15 years from the coming into force of the constitution, English might continue to be used, in addition to Hindi, for all official purposes of the Union for which it was being used immediately before that day, and for the transaction of business in Parliament. The Official Languages Amendment Act, 1967, provides that bilingualism shall continue; central government officers will choose their medium for official business. Translations will be provided for them until they attain a working knowledge of Hindi.

The following 15 languages are included in the Eighth Schedule to the Constitution: Assamese, Bengali, Gujarati, Hindi, Kannada, Kashmiri, Malayalam, Marathi, Oriya, Punjabi, Sanskrit, Sindhi, Tamil, Telugu, Urdu.

The number of mother tongues (including 103 non-Indian languages) returned in 1961 Census was 1,652. Hindi or Urdu languages (including mother tongues grouped under each) are spoken by 30·4% and 5·31% of the population respectively.

Ferozsons English–Urdu, Urdu–English Dictionary. 2 vols. 4th ed. Lahore, 1961
Fallon, S. W., *A New English–Hindustani Dictionary.* Lahore, 1941
Grierson, Sir G. A., *Linguistic Survey of India.* 11 vols. (in 19 parts). Delhi, 1903–28
Mehta, B. N. and B. B., *Modern Gujarati–English Dictionary.* 2 vols. Baroda, 1925
Mitra, S. C., *Student's Bengali–English Dictionary.* 2nd ed. Calcutta, 1923
Scholberg, H. C., *Concise Grammar of the Hindi Language.* 3rd ed. London, 1955
University of Madras, *Tamil Lexicon.* 7 vols. Madras, 1924–39
Vyas, V. G., and Patel, S. G., *Standard English–Gujarati Dictionary.* 2 vols. Bombay, 1923

Government. *President of the Republic:* Neelam Sanjiva Reddy (sworn in Aug. 1977).

Vice-President: B. D. Jatti.

There is a Council of Ministers to aid and advise the President of the Republic in the exercise of his functions; this comprises Ministers who are members of the Cabinet, Ministers of State who are not members of the Cabinet and Deputy Ministers. A Minister who for any period of 6 consecutive months is not a member of either House of Parliament ceases to be a Minister at the expiration of that period. The Prime Minister is appointed by the President; other Ministers are appointed by the President on the Prime Minister's advice.

The salary of each Minister is Rs 27,000 per annum, and that of each Deputy Minister is Rs 21,000 per annum. Each Minister is entitled to the free use of a furnished residence throughout his term of office. At the administrative head of each Ministry is a Secretary of the Government.

Following is the composition of the Cabinet following elections March 1977:

Prime Minister: Morarji R. Desai.
Home Affairs: Charan Singh.
Finance, Revenue and Banking: H. M. Patel.
Irrigation and Agriculture: S. S. Barnala.
Law, Justice and Company Affairs: Shanti Bhushan.
Industry: George Fernandes.
Education and Social Welfare, and Department of Culture: Pratap C. Chunder.
Railways: Madhu Dandavate.
External Affairs: Atal Behari Vajpayee.
Tourism and Civil Aviation: Purushottam Kaushik.
Defence: Jagjivan Ram.
Health and Family Welfare: Raj Narain.
Chemicals, Fertilizers and Petroleum: H. Nandan Bahuguna.
Parliamentary Affairs and Labour: Ravindra Varma.
Energy: P. Ramachandran.
Communications: B. Lal Verma.
Information and Broadcasting: L. Advani.
Commerce, Civil Supplies and Co-operatives: Mohan Dharia.
Works, Housing, Supply and Rehabilitation: Sikander Bakht.
Steel and Mines: Biju Patnaik.

Local Government. There were in 1971, 32 municipal corporations, 1,493 municipalities, 249 town area committees, 202 notified area committees and 62 cantonment boards. The municipal bodies have the care of the roads, water supply, drainage, sanitation, medical relief, vaccination and education. Their main sources of revenue are taxes on the annual rental value of land and buildings, octroi and terminal, vehicle and other taxes. The municipal councils enact their own bye-laws and frame their budgets, which in the case of municipal bodies other than corporations generally require the sanction of the State government. All municipal councils are elected on the principle of adult franchise.

For rural areas there is a 3-tier system of *panchayati raj* at village, block and district level, although the 3-tier structure may undergo some changes in State legislation to suit local conditions. All *panchayati raj* bodies are organically linked, and representation is given to special interests. Elected directly by and from among villagers, the *panchayats* are responsible for agricultural production, rural industries, medical relief, maternity and child welfare, common grazing grounds, village roads, tanks and wells, and maintenance of sanitation. In some places they also look after primary education, maintenance of village records and collection of land revenue. They have their own powers of taxation. There are some judicial *panchayats* or village courts.

Panchayati raj now cover all the States with the exception of Nagaland and Meghalaya, although Nagaland has area, range and tribal councils. They exist in all the Union Territories except Mizoram and Lakshadweep. In Pondicherry they have been created by declaring existing Municipal Communes to be Commune Panchayat Councils; this is a transition arrangement. In Arunachal Pradesh and Chandigarh the 3-tier system of *panchayati raj* has been introduced. In Jan. 1977 there were 221,727 village *panchayats* covering a population of 441·6m. In addition, there are 4,017 *panchayat samitis* (block level) and 262 *zila parishads* (district level). With most of the country covered by *panchayati raj*, the emphasis now is on consolidation and clarifying their role in rural development.

The powers and responsibilities of *panchayati raj* institutions are derived not only from State Legislatures, but also from the procedures—administrative and financial—laid down by the State governments to give effect to statutory provisions.

NAGARLOK (Municipal Affairs Quarterly). Quarterly. Institute of Public Administration. Delhi

Proceedings of the 13th Meeting of the Central Council of Local Self Government. Delhi, 1970

Report of the Committee on Budgetary Reforms in Municipal Administration. Delhi, 1974

State Machinery for Municipal Supervision. Institute of Public Administration. Delhi, 1970
Statistical Abstract of India. Annual. Delhi.
Khera, S. S., *District Administration in India.* London, 1964
Roy, N. C., *The Civil Service in India.* 2nd ed. Calcutta, 1960

DEFENCE. The Supreme Command of the Armed Forces vests in the President of the Indian Republic. Policy is decided at different levels by a number of committees, including the Political Affairs Committee presided over by the Prime Minister and the Defence Minister's Committee. Administrative and operational control rests in the respective Service Headquarters, under the control of the Ministry of Defence.

The Ministry of Defence is the central agency for formulating defence policy and for co-ordinating the work of the three services. Among the organizations directly administered by the Ministry are the Research and Development Organization, the Production Organization, the National Defence College, the National Cadet Corps and the Directorate-General of Armed Forces Medical Services.

The Research and Development Organization (headed by the Scientific Adviser to the Minister) has under it about 30 research establishments. The Production Organization controls 8 public-sector undertakings and 28 ordnance and 2 departmental factories; the total value of production in 1971–72 was estimated at Rs 352 crores.

The National Defence College, New Delhi, was established in 1960 on the pattern of the Imperial Defence College (UK): the 1-year course is for officers of the rank of brigadier or equivalent and for senior civil servants. The Defence Services Staff College, Wellington, trains officers of the three Services for higher command for staff appointments. There is an Armed Forces Medical College at Pune.

The National Defence Academy, Khadakvasla, gives a 3-year basic training course to officer cadets of the three Services prior to advanced training at the respective Service establishments.

Army. The Army Headquarters functioning directly under the Chief of the Army Staff is divided into the following main branches: General Staff Branch; Adjutant-General's Branch; Quartermaster-General's Branch; Master-General of Ordnance Branch; Engineer-in-Chief's Branch; Military Secretary's Branch.

The Army is organized into 4 commands—eastern, central, western and southern—each divided into areas, which in turn are subdivided into sub-areas.

Recruitment of permanent commissioned officers is through the Indian Military Academy, Dehra Dun. It conducts courses for ex-National Defence Academy, National Cadet Corps and direct-entry cadets, and for serving personnel and technical graduates.

The Territorial Army came into being in Sept. 1949, its role being to: (1) relieve the regular Army of static duties and, if required, support civil power; (2) provide anti-aircraft units, and (3) if and when called upon, provide units for the regular Army. The Territorial Army is composed of practically all arms of the Services.

The authorized strength of the Army is 826,000, that of the Territorial Army, 50,000. There are 2 armoured, 14 infantry and 10 mountain divisions, 5 independent armoured brigades, 7 independent infantry and 1 parachute brigade.

Mason, P., *A Matter of Honour.* London, 1974

Navy. Since 26 Jan. 1950 the former Royal Indian Navy, which traced its history in an unbroken line from the foundation in 1613 of the East India Company's Marine, has been known as 'Indian Navy', and the ships referred to as 'INS' instead of 'HMIS'. There are 3 commands: Eastern, Western and Southern.

Principal ships of the Indian Navy:

Completed	*Name*	*Standard displacement Tons*	*Armour Belts in.*	*Armour Turrets in.*	*Principal armament*	*Shaft horse-power*	*Speed Knots*
		Aircraft Carrier					
1961	Vikrant (*ex*-Hercules)	16,000	—	—	15 40 mm. AA	40,000	24·5

Com-pleted	Name	Standard displace-ment Tons	Armour Belts in.	Armour Turrets in.	Principal armament	Shaft horse-power	Speed Knots
		Cruisers					
1940	Mysore (*ex*-Nigeria)	8,700	3–4½	2	9 6-in.; 8 4-in.	72,500	31·5
1933	Delhi (*ex*-Achilles)	7,114	2–4	1	6 6-in.; 8 4-in.	72,000	32·0

The fleet also includes 8 ex-Soviet submarines, 4 new broad beam 'Leander' class general purpose frigates (built in India), 2 anti-submarine frigates, 2 smaller anti-submarine frigates, 3 anti-aircraft frigates (all 7 built in Great Britain, 1958–60), 4 frigates (including 1 'Hunt' class small escort destroyer acquired from Great Britain, 1953), 10 Soviet-built escorts, 4 coastal minesweepers acquired from Great Britain in 1956, 4 inshore minesweepers (2 acquired from Great Britain in 1955), 16 missile boats, 8 patrol craft, 7 landing ships, 3 surveying vessels, a repair ship, a submarine parent ship, a submarine rescue ship, 5 oilers, 4 harbour defence motor launches, 5 yard service craft and an ocean tug.

Two more general-purpose frigates of the British 'Leander' class are being built in India. INS *Nilgiri* was commissioned in 1972; *Himgiri* in 1974; *Udaygiri* in 1975, and *Dunagiri* in 1976. 'Nanuchka' class guided missile corvettes are being acquired from the USSR.

The major training establishments of the Navy include INS *Venduruthy* at Cochin (Basic and Divisional, Gunnery, Torpedo and Anti-Submarine, Navigation and Direction, Communication), INS *Vaisura* at Jamnagar (Electrical), INS *Shivaji* at Lonavla (Engineering), INS *Hansa* at Goa (Aviation), INS *Hamla* at Bombay (Supply and Secretariat) and INS *Circars* at Vishakhapatnam (Boys' Training).

At the naval base at Cochin, the Fleet Requirement Unit of the Naval Aviation Station, INAS *Garuda*, has been developed. This unit was equipped with Firefly target tugs and Vampire aircraft which work with the ships and naval training schools. Sea Hawk fighters, Alizé anti-submarine aircraft and Sea King anti-submarine helicopters were acquired for the aircraft carrier.

Naval personnel in 1978 comprised 46,000 officers and ratings, including the Naval Air Arm.

Air Force. The Indian Air Force Act was passed in 1932, and the first flight was formed in 1933.

The Air Headquarters, under the Chief of Air Staff, consists of 4 main branches, viz., Air Staff, Administration, Policy and Plans, and Maintenance. Units of the IAF are organized into 3 operational commands—Western at Delhi, Central at Allahabad, Eastern at Shillong—plus an operational group at Jodhpur administered directly by Air HQ. Training Command HQ is at Bangalore, Maintenance Command at Nagpur. Nominal strength in 1977 was about 100,000 personnel and 670 combat aircraft in 35 squadrons, supported by 11 transport squadrons, 12 helicopter squadrons, training units and 20 sites equipped with surface-to-air missiles.

Air defence units include 7 squadrons of Gnat Mk 1 fighters (being replaced by a Mk 2 version known as the Ajeet), 11 squadrons of MiG-21s and batteries of 'Guideline' and Tigercat surface-to-air missiles. Initial delivery of MiG-21s from the Soviet Union has been followed by large-scale licence production in India, with new MiG-21MF version in current production. There are 4 squadrons of Sukhoi Su-7s, 4 of Canberra (3 bomber, 1 reconnaissance), 5 of Hunter F56s and 4 of Hindustan HF-24 Marut supersonic fighter-bombers.

The large transport force includes An-12s, jet-boosted C-119Gs, C-47s, HS 748s, Caribou, Il-14s, Otters, Tu-124s and smaller aircraft and helicopters for VIP and other duties. Helicopter units have Mi-8s, Mi-4s, Chetaks (Aérospatiale Alouette IIIs) and licence-built Cheetahs (Aérospatiale Lamas); main training types are the Hindustan HT-2 and Kiran, Polish-built Ts-11 Iskra, Hunter T.66 and MiG-21UT1.

Primary flying training is provided at the Elementary Flying School, Bidar, and advanced flying training at the Air Force Academy, Dundigal, Hyderabad. The IAF Technical College, Jalahalli, imparts technical training, while the IAF Administrative College, Coimbatore, trains officers of the ground duty branch. There are also land–air warfare, flying instructors' and medical schools.

INTERNATIONAL RELATIONS

Membership. India is a member of the UN, the Commonwealth and the Colombo Plan.

External Debt. On 31 March 1976 India's external public debt was Rs. 7,031·95 crores.

Treaties. India pursues a general policy of non-alignment; the exception is a Treaty of Peace, Friendship and Co-operation with the USSR, 1971; the parties agreed to mutual support short of force in the event of either being attacked by a third party.

ECONOMY

Planning. The third five-year plan ended in March 1966 and 3 annual plans, as periods of stabilization, led up to the beginning of the fourth plan in April 1969. The formal fifth plan document was placed before Parliament on 19 Dec. 1973. The fifth plan stresses agriculture, mining and manufacturing industries and aims at a 4½% growth rate.

Outlay is set at Rs 53,411 crores, of which Rs 37,250 are for the public sector. Goals are an increase of 4·67% in agricultural production, 8·2% in mining and manufacturing, and 7·6% in exports. States now have more initiative in forming their development programmes.

Priority is given to increasing the income of the worst-off 30% of the population.

For power, the objective is a net installed capacity of 23m. kw., which will allow for obsolete plant to be taken out of service. Outlay is Rs 210 crores for continuing generating schemes, including Rs 120 crores for nuclear generation.

In Nov. 1977 the Government defined a new long-term economic policy under which agriculture would receive at least 40% of public sector resources. In industry no new capital-intensive enterprises in the field of consumer goods would be permitted if those goods could be made by cottage or small industry. This would stimulate employment in rural areas.

Estimated net national product, 1975–76, Rs 602,930m. Annual plan expenditure, budget estimates 1977–78, Rs 99,600m.

Ministry of Agriculture. *Serving the Small Farmer: Policy Choices in Indian Agricultural Development.* 1975
Dutt, A. K. (ed.), *India: Resources, Potentialities and Planning.* Rev. ed. Dubuque, India, 1973
Singh, T., *India's Development Experience.* London, 1975

Budget. Revenue and expenditure (on revenue account) of the central government[1] for years ending 31 March, in crores of rupees:

	1972–73[2]	*1973–74*[2]	*1974–75*[2]	*1975–76*[2]	*1976–77*[2]
Revenue	4,464·7	5,733·65	6,484·68	8,023	8,401
Expenditure	4,124·3	5,585·45	5,860·00	7,117	9,647

Under the Constitution (Part XII and 7th Schedule), the power to raise funds has been divided between the central government and the states. Generally, the sources of revenue are mutually exclusive. Certain taxes are levied by the Union for the sake of uniformity and distributed to the states. The Finance Commission (Art. 280 of the Constitution) advises the President on the distribution of the taxes which are distributable between the centre and the states, and on the principles on which grants should be made out of Union revenues to the states. The main sources of central revenue are: customs duties; those excise duties levied by the central government; corporation, income and wealth taxes; estate and succession duties on non-agricultural assets and property, and revenues from the railways and posts and telegraphs. The main heads of revenue in the states are: taxes and duties levied by the state governments (including land revenues and agricultural income tax); civil administration and civil works; state undertakings; taxes shared with the centre; and grants received from the centre.

[1] Excluding states' share of excise duties and other taxes.
[2] Revised.

Important items of revenue and expenditure charged to revenue of the central government for 1976–77 (revised), in Rs 1m.:

Revenue		*Expenditure*	
Taxes on personal income	6,856	Education	17,805
Land tax	1,997	Agriculture and industry	26,284
Estate duty	84	Health	6,912
Excise duties	14,085	River and irrigation schemes	6,663
Turnover tax	21,509		

Debt. On 31 March 1976 the interest-bearing obligations of the Government of India were estimated to amount to Rs 19,829·56 crores, of which total obligations in India were Rs 12,797·61 crores.

Bhargava, R. N., *Indian Public Finance.* London, 1962
Cheliah, R. J., *Fiscal Policy in Underdeveloped Countries, with Special Reference to India.* London, 1960
Misra, B. R., *Indian Federal Finance.* Rev. ed. Bombay, 1960
National Council of Applied Economic Research, *Management of Public Debt in India.* New Delhi, 1965
Premchand, A., *Control of Public Expenditure in India.* New Delhi, 1963

Currency. A decimal system of coinage was introduced in 1957. The Indian *rupee* is divided into 100 *paise* (until 1964 officially described as *naye paise*), the decimal coins being 1, 2, 5, 10, 25 and 50 *paise* (or *naye paise*) and rupee.

On the devaluation of the £ in Nov. 1967, the £ became equivalent to Rs 18. Value (1977): £1 = Rs 15·2. The rupee is valued in relation to a package of main currencies.

The paper currency consists of: (1) Reserve Bank notes in denominations of Rs 2, 5, 10, 100, 1,000, 5,000 and 10,000; and (2) Government of India currency notes of denominations of Re 1 (issued in 1917), Rs 2½, 5, 10, 20, 50 and 100. Re 1 notes of a different type, issued since 1940, are deemed to be included in the expression 'rupee coin' for the purposes of the Reserve Bank of India Act, 1934. Bank and Government notes bearing the king's effigy and other earlier issues have ceased to be legal tender, 28 Oct. 1957, except at the issue department of the Reserve Bank, government treasuries and sub-treasuries, and agency branches of the State Bank of India and its subsidiaries.

According to the Reserve Bank of India, the total value of currency with the public in 1975 was Rs 122,300m.

100,000 rupees are called 1 lakh and are written thus: Rs 1,00,000; 100 lakhs are called 1 crore and are written thus: Rs 100,00,000. A lakh of rupees at the exchange rate of Rs 15·2 = £1 is equivalent to £6,500.

Sadeque, A., *Indian and Pakistan Currency.* Dacca, 1965

Banking. The Reserve Bank, the central bank for India, was established in 1934 and started functioning on 1 April 1935 as a shareholder's bank; it became a nationalized institution on 1 Jan. 1949. It has the sole right of issuing currency-notes. The Bank acts as adviser to the government on financial problems and is the banker for central and state governments, commercial banks and some other financial institutions. The Bank manages the rupee public debt of central and state governments. It is the custodian of the country's exchange reserve and supervises repatriation of export proceeds and payments for imports. The Bank gives short-term loans to state governments and scheduled banks and short- and medium-term loans to state co-operative banks and industrial finance institutions. The Bank has extensive powers of regulation of the banking system, directly under the Banking Regulation Act, 1949, and indirectly by the use of variations in bank rate, variation in reserve ratios, selective credit controls and open market operations. Bank rate was raised to 9% in the financial year 1974–75. The statutory cash reserves were raised to the level of 6% from Nov. 1976 and as much as 10% of the incremental demand and time liabilities were impounded from 14 Jan. 1977. With a view to restricting to a minimum the commercial banks' use of Reserve Bank's credit facilities, the system of Net Liquidity Ratio, which regulated the cost of refinance from the Reserve Bank, was given up in Nov. 1975. Automatic recourse to borrowings from the Reserve Bank was severely cut, being limited to a basic quota equivalent to 1% of a bank's demand and time liabilities, and to a proportion of a bank's incremental lendings for public food procurement operations and for exports. All other recourse to Reserve Bank facilities, including rediscount of bills, was placed on a discretionary basis. The Bank provides short-term credit (for financing seasonal agricultural operations) to state co-operative banks at 2% below the Bank rate. The Bank also provides financial accommodation to State Co-operative Banks at the Bank rate for financing and industrial co-operative societies and industrial societies and units outside the co-operative sector. The net profit of the Reserve Bank of India for the year ended 30 June 1977 amounted to Rs 200 crores.

The commercial banking system consisted of 113 scheduled banks (*i.e.*, banks which are included in the 2nd schedule to the Reserve Bank Act) and 6 non-scheduled banks on 31 Dec. 1976; scheduled banks included 40 Regional Rural Banks. Total number of offices was 23,655. Total deposits in commercial banks, 31 Dec. 1976, stood at Rs 17,132 crores; in post office savings banks 31 March 1975 deposits were Rs 1,266 crores. The business of non-scheduled banks forms less than 1% of commercial bank business. Of the 113 scheduled banks, 14 are foreign banks which specialize in financing foreign trade but also compete for domestic business. The largest scheduled bank is the State Bank of India, constituted by nationalizing the Imperial Bank of India in 1955. The State Bank acts as the agent of the Reserve Bank and the subsidiaries of the State Bank act as the agents of the State Bank for transacting government business as well as undertaking commercial functions. Fourteen banks with aggregate deposits of not less than Rs 50 crores were nationalized on 19 July 1969. Public sector banks accounted for 85% of deposits and 86% of credit on 31 Dec. 1976.

Reserve Bank of India: Report on Currency and Finance.—Report on the Trend and Progress of Banking in India.—Report of the Central Board of Directors. Annual. Bombay
Reserve Bank of India—Functions and Working. Reserve Bank of India, 1970

Weights and Measures. A complete change to the metric system was envisaged by the Standards of Weights and Measures Act, 1956, which provided for a transition period of 10 years. So far the system has been fully adopted in trade transactions but there are a few fields such as engineering, survey and land records and the building and construction industry where it has not; efforts are being made to complete the change as early as possible.

An expert committee (Weights and Measures (Law Revision) Committee) was set up by the Central Government to suggest a revised Bill which was passed by Parliament in April 1976. The new Standards of Weights and Measures Act, 1976, has recognized the International System of Units and other units recommended by the General Conference on Weights and Measures and is in line with the recommendations of the International Organisation of Legal Metrology (OIML). The new Act also covers the system of numeration, the approval of models of weights and measures, regulation and control of inter-state trade in relation to weights and measures, commodities sold by weight, measure or number and indication of net weight, measure or number on packaged commodities, etc. A (model) State Weights and Measures Bill has also been prepared by the committee for adoption by states on a uniform basis throughout the country and, in some states, has already been adopted.

While the Standards of Weights and Measures are laid down in the Central Act, enforcement of weights and measures laws is the responsibility of the state governments; the central Directorate of Weights and Measures is responsible for co-ordinating activities so as to ensure national uniformity.

To give immediate effect to the main features of the new Central Act relating to packaged commodities, a Packaged Commodities Order, 1975, was promulgated under the Defence and Internal Security of India Rules. It enjoined that all packaged commodities, with certain exceptions, should bear on the container the name of the manufacturer or packer, the identity of the commodity, its net weight, measure or number and the date of its packing. This was intended to protect the interest of consumers and to entail discipline among manufacturers, packers and retailers in the sale of packaged commodities. Six months after the ending of the State of Emergency DISIR Orders ceased to be operative and the relevant provisions of the 1976 Act took their place on 26 Sept. 1977.

An Indian Institute of Legal Metrology trains officials of the Weights and Measures departments of India and different developing countries. The Institute is being modernized with technical assistance from the Federal Republic of Germany.

There are 2 Regional Reference Standards laboratories in the country which (besides calibrating secondary standards of physical measurements) also provide testing facilities in metrological and industrial measurements. These laboratories are equipped with Standards next in line to the National Standards of physical measurements which are maintained at the National Physical Laboratory in New Delhi.

For weights previously in legal use under the Standards of Weight Act, 1956, *see* THE STATESMAN'S YEAR-BOOK, 1961, p. 171.

Calendar. The dates of the Saka era (named after the north Indian dynasty of the first century A.D.) are being used alongside Gregorian dates in issues of the *Gazette of India*, news broadcasts by All-India Radio and government-issued calendars, from 22 March 1957, a date which corresponds with the first day of the year 1879 in the Saka era.

ENERGY AND NATURAL RESOURCES

Electricity. In 1969, 2,618 towns and 67,710 villages had electric power in the States, and 59 towns and 3,700 villages in the Union Territories. Total villages with electricity, 1974, was 154,786 (27·3%). Total installed capacity (1975) was 22m. kw., of which 8·4m. was hydro-electricity. In 1975 production of electricity was 85,613m. kwh., of which 33,247m. kwh. was hydro-electricity.

Oil. The Oil and Natural Gas Commission began commercial production from the Bombay High offshore fields in 1975: production, 1977, 2m. tonnes.

Water. The net area of 44·7m. hectares (1974) under irrigation exceeds that of any other country except China, and equals about 28% of the total area under cultivation. Irrigation projects have formed an important part of all three Five-Year Plans. The possibilities of diverting rivers into canals being nearly exhausted, the emphasis is now on damming the monsoon surplus flow and diverting that. Usable surface and groundwater resources were assessed (1972) at 870,000m. cu. metres. Utilization (1974) 337,000m. cu. metres. In 1977 India and Bangladesh reached an agreement to share the water of the Ganges at the Farakka barrage: India needs this supply to supplement the Hooghly River in flushing silt from Calcutta port.

Minerals. Bihar, West Bengal and Madhya Pradesh produce 42%, 25% and 19% of all coal, respectively. The coal industry was nationalized in 1973; planned state investment 1976–86, Rs 4·0 crores. Production, 1975, 92m. tonnes. Production of other minerals, 1975 (1,000 tonnes): Iron ore, 26,002; bauxite, 1,273; chromium ore, 242; copper ore, 23·8; lead ore, 12·3; magnesite, 314; manganese ore, 575·4; zinc ore, 22; salt, 5,918; phosphate rock, 459; asbestos, 20; diamonds 20,000 metric carats (of which 16,000 were gem diamonds); gold, 1,611 kg; silver, 3 tonnes.

Agriculture. The chief industry of India has always been agriculture. About 70% of the people are dependent on the land for their living. In 1971 agriculture employed about 126m. people; in 1977 it provided 43% of national income.

Agricultural commodities account for about 20% by value of Indian exports, while agricultural commodities, machinery and fertilizers account for about 25–30% of imports. Tea accounts for about 40% of agricultural exports.

An increase in food production of at least 2% per annum is necessary to keep pace with the rising population. There was no increase in foodgrain production in the first 3 years of the third Plan: 82·7m. tons in 1961–62, 78·4m. tons in 1962–63, 80·2m. tons in 1963–64; a rise to 89m. tons in 1964–65 and a severe setback because of the unprecedented drought in 1965–66, with a harvest of only 72·3m. tons.

The harvest by 1970–71 had risen to 108·4m. tons. By 1972–73 it was down to 97m. tons but rose again to 118m. tons in 1975–76.

The Indian Council of Agricultural Research, established in 1929 by the Government of India and registered as a Society under the Societies Registration

Act, 1960 (21 of 1860), became a fully autonomous organization with effect from 1 April 1974. It is a National Apex Body to plan, undertake, promote and co-ordinate education and research in agriculture and animal husbandry and their application in practice.

The Council at present works through 22 Research Institutes, 2 Technological Research Laboratories and a Directorate of All India Soil and Land Use Survey, Universities (including Agricultural Universities) and other public and quasi-public research and educational bodies. It supports the establishment of at least one agricultural university in each of the States; it also supports research in agriculture, animal husbandry, fisheries and allied subjects through a national grid of All-India Co-ordinated Research Projects and a number of *ad-hoc* research schemes.

Land Tenure. There are three main systems of land tenure: *ryotwari* tenure, where the individual holders, usually peasant proprietors, are responsible for the payment of land revenues; *zamindari* tenure, where one or more persons own large estates and are responsible for payment (in this system there may be a number of intermediary holders); and *mahalwari* tenure, where village communities jointly hold an estate and are jointly and severally responsible for payment.

Agrarian reform, initiated in the first Five-Year Plan, being undertaken by the state governments includes: (1) The abolition of intermediaries under *zamindari* tenure. Formerly the *zamindari* system prevailed in about 43% of the country, but by 1958 it had been abolished, usually in favour of *ryotwari* tenure, in all except about 5%. The total amount payable in compensation had been estimated at Rs 570 crores, payable in cash in some states and in transferable bonds in others. (2) Tenancy legislation designed to scale down rents to $\frac{1}{4}$-$\frac{1}{5}$ of the value of the produce, to give permanent rights to tenants (subject to the landlord's right to resume a minimum holding for his personal cultivation), and to enable tenants to acquire ownership of their holdings (subject to the landlord's right of resumption for personal cultivation) on payment of compensation over a number of years. (3) Fixing of ceilings on existing holdings and on future acquisition following a census of land holdings. Based on the recommendations of the Central Land Reforms Committee made in July 1972, the Government of India decided to keep the holding of a family between 4·05 and 7·28 hectares if it has assured irrigation to produce two crops a year; a ceiling of 10·93 hectares for land with irrigation facilities for only one crop a year; and a ceiling of 21·85 hectares for all other categories of land.

A family unit for the ceiling consists of husband, wife and 3 minor children. Additional land can be retained by large families subject to a maximum of twice the ceiling. Tea, coffee, cocoa and cardamom plantations have been exempted from the ceiling. Until Aug. 1973, 13 States had passed legislation to implement the ceiling law. (4) The consolidation of holdings in community project areas (45·3m. acres had been consolidated by 31 March 1965, mainly in the Punjab, Madhya Pradesh and Uttar Pradesh) and the prevention of fragmentation of holdings by reform of inheritance laws. (5) Promotion of farming by co-operative village management (*see* p. 615).

The average size of holding for the whole of India is 2·63 hectares. Andhra Pradesh, 2·87; Assam, 1·46; Bihar, 1·53; Gujarat, 4·49; Jammu and Kashmir, 1·43; Kerala, 0·75; Madhya Pradesh, 3·99; Tamil Nadu, 1·49; Maharashtra, 4·65; Karnataka, 4·11; Orissa, 1·98; Punjab, 3·85; Rajasthan, 5·5; Uttar Pradesh, 1·78; West Bengal, 1·56.

Of the total 71m. rural households possessing operational holdings, 34% hold on the average less than 0·20 hectare of land each.

The table opposite shows, in 1,000 hectares, according to state and territories, the net area and the classification of areas of India that were in 1974 cultivated, and uncultivated, and the areas under forests and irrigation.

Agricultural production, 1975 (1,000 tonnes): Rice, 74,186; barley, 3,135; maize, 7,036; wheat, 24,104; potatoes, 6,225; groundnuts, 6,991; coffee, 92·5; tobacco, 363; cotton, 1,193; wool, 35; sugar, 5,048.

The tea industry is important, with production concentrated in Assam, West Bengal, Tamil Nadu, Kerala and Karnataka. Total crop in 1975, about 500,000 tonnes from 361,000 hectares.

State or Territory	Geo-graphical area	Reporting area	Permanent pasture and other grazing land	Area irrigated (net)	Area sown	Area cropped	Forests	Fallow land	Other un-cultivated land
Andhra Pradesh	27,676	27,440	1,028	2,998	11,269	12,652	6,240	855	2,313
Assam	7,853	7,807	234	572	2,235	2,834	2,080	166	1,787
Bihar	17,388	17,330	173	2,384	8,276	10,683	2,797	903	1,080
Gujarat	19,598	18,562	1,019	1,209	9,322	9,933	1,634	392	4,200
Haryana	4,422	4,402	47	1,565	3,567	5,048	110	—	186
Himachal Pradesh	5,567	5,082	1,186	91	548	901	2,783	2	116
Jammu and Kashmir	22,224	4,523	133	264	706	861	2,776	11	244
Karnataka	19,177	18,943	1,592	1,373	10,331	10,988	2,895	644	861
Kerala	3,886	3,859	28	439	2,187	2,958	1,055	23	69
Madhya Pradesh	44,284	44,238	3,141	1,643	18,461	20,892	14,405	865	2,315
Maharashtra	30,776	30,747	1,666	1,344	16,575	17,481	5,417	1,473	1,802
Manipur	2,236	2,211	—	65	140	147	602	—	1,419
Meghalaya	2,248	2,248	—	37	162	193	187	—	1,900
Nagaland	1,653	1,351	—	12	62	63	266	—	1,023
Orissa	15,584	15,540	725	1,149	6,119	7,042	4,973	95	802
Punjab	5,036	5,031	5	2,955	4,076	5,724	127	—	198
Rajasthan	34,222	34,109	1,805	2,173	15,263	16,773	1,401	1,884	4,705
Tamil Nadu	13,007	13,004	229	2,710	6,348	7,642	2,007	540	805
Tripura	1,048	1,048	34	22	240	355	630	2	6
Uttar Pradesh	29,441	29,806	78	6,989	17,317	23,025	4,952	554	1,418
West Bengal	8,785	8,852	—	1,489	5,712	7,271	1,101	160	1,272
Andaman and Nicobar Islands	829	790	3	—	19	19	740	3	1
Arunachal Pradesh	8,358	6,353	—	23	115	130	5,154	118	37
Dadra and Nagar Haveli	49	49	4	—	23	24	21	—	—
Delhi	149	148	1	46	76	118	1	8	16
Goa, Daman and Diu	381	370	1	8	133	139	105	—	16
Lakshadweep	3	3	—	—	3	3	—	—	—
Mizoram	2,109	2,092	—	2	47	40	1,298	—	747
Pondicherry	48	47	—	26	32	55	—	—	—
	328,048	305,985	13,132	31,593	139,365	164,002	65,757	8,696	29,338

Figures are for 1973 with the following exceptions:

Assam, 1969–70. Gujarat, 1969–70. Jammu and Kashmir, 1970–71. Excludes Pakistan-occupied area. Manipur, estimates. Meghalaya (equivalent area) 1969–70. Nagaland (equivalent area) 1968–69. West Bengal, 1967–68, area cropped, estimate. Arunachal Pradesh (equivalent area) 1970–71. Mizorum (equivalent area) 1969–70. Goa, Daman and Diu, estimates.

Production of natural rubber (1975) was 136,000 tonnes. Kerala produced about 93% of this.

Livestock (1975). Cattle, 180·2m.; sheep, 40m.; pigs, 7·1m.; horses, 900,000; asses, 100,000.

There were 215,000 tractors in use in 1975.

Opium. By international agreement the poppy is cultivated under licence, and all raw opium is sold to the central government. Opium, other than for wholly medical use, is available only to registered addicts.

Fisheries. Total catch (1975) was 2·32m. tonnes, of which Kerala produced 510,000; Tamil Nadu, 314,000, and Maharashtra, 267,000.

Forestry. The lands under the control of the state forest departments are classified as 'reserved forests' (forests intended to be permanently maintained for the supply of timber, etc., or for the protection of water supply, etc.), 'protected forests' and 'unclassed' forest land.

In 1974 the total forest area was 74·6m. hectares, or 23% of the land area. Forest revenue was Rs 1,508m., or 2·2% of national income. Production is low at 0·28 cu. metres per hectare per year (France, 3·9 cu. metres; Japan, 2·8 cu. metres; USA, 1·25 cu. metres). About 16% of the area is inaccessible, of which about 45% is potentially productive. Production of roundwood, 1975, 120·4m. cu. metres. Outlay on forests for the Fifth Plan period is envisaged at about Rs 2,205m. as against Rs 930m. for the Fourth Plan. Distribution of plantations (1973–74):

Plantations of quick growing species (1,000 hectares)	510
Economic plantations of industrial and commercial uses (1,000 hectares)	850
Farm forestry (1,000 hectares)	80
Mixed plantations including fuel wood (1,000 hectares)	140
Communications (1,000 km)	45

INDUSTRY AND TRADE

Industries. The most important traditional industry, after agriculture, is the weaving of cotton cloth. Others are silk-rearing and weaving, shawl and carpet weaving, wood-carving and metal-working. Silk production, 1974, was 2,400 tonnes of mulberry silk and 675 tonnes of wild silk. In 1973 there were about 20m. people engaged in village industries, of whom about 5m. were in handloom industries.

Indian Government industrial policy aims to further a socialist pattern of society. Railways, air transport, armaments and atomic energy are government monopolies. In a number of industries (including the manufacture of iron and steel and mineral oils, shipbuilding and the mining of coal, iron and manganese ores, gypsum, gold and diamonds) new units are set up only by the state. In a further group of industries (road transport, manufacture of chemicals such as drugs, dyestuffs, plastics and fertilizers) the state established new undertakings, but private enterprise may develop either on its own or with state backing, which may take the form of loans or purchase of equity capital. Under the Industries (Development and Regulation) Act, 1951, as amended, industrial undertakings are required to be licensed; 162 industries are within the scope of the Act. The Government are authorized to examine the working of any undertaking, to issue directions to it and to take over its control if this be deemed necessary. A Central Advisory Council has been set up consisting of representatives of industry, labour, consumers and primary producers. There are 16 Development Councils for individual industries.

Foreign investment is encouraged by a tax holiday on income up to 6% of capital employed for 5 years. There are special depreciation allowances, and customs and excise concessions for export industries.

In the cotton industry production of yarn in 1975 was 989,300 tonnes and of cloth, 8,034m. metres (mill cloth accounts for about 58% of total production, the balance being produced by handloom and small industries). In 1974 there were about 900,000 workers in the mills and 10m. handloom weavers.

Oil refinery installed capaicity, 1975, was 27·82m. tonnes. The Indian Oil Corporation was established in 1964 and had (1973–74) 61·2% of the market.

Industrial production, 1975 (1,000 tonnes): Pig-iron and ferro-alloys, 8,558; crude steel, 7,884; aluminium, 167; smelted copper, 16; petroleum products, 19,283 (distillate fuel oils, 7,130; residual fuel oils, 5,073; kerosene, 2,323; naphtha, 1,915; motor spirit, 1,222; bitumen, 708; jet fuel, 912); coke, 8,846; cement, 16,235; wool yarn, 13·3 (1974); rayon and acetate yarn, 119; wood pulp, 20; newsprint, 52; other paper products, 830; synthetic rubber, 23; sulphuric acid, 1,333; hydrochloric acid, 165·9; benzine, 56·8; fertilizers, 1,828; woollen fabrics, 38m. metres; rayon and acetate fabric, 846m. metres; sawnwood, 2·2m. cu. metres; motor vehicles (no.), 70,000 (including 38,000 commercial vehicles).

Labour. At the 1971 census there were 180·3m. workers, of whom 78m. were cultivators, 37·4m. agricultural labourers, 17m. in manufacturing, processing and servicing, 2·2m. in construction, 10m. in trade and commerce and 4·4m. in transport, communications and storage. There were 847 central unions registered and 19,865 state unions. In 1974, 62,833 manufacturing units (employing 10 or more persons with power, or 20 or more without power) employed 5·2m. people earning Rs 22,600m.; value added by manufacture, Rs 47,913m. Bond labour system was abolished in 1975. In the autumn of 1977 the number of unemployed was estimated at 40m.

Companies. The total number of companies limited by shares at work in India, 31 March 1976, was 44,489; aggregate paid-up capital was Rs 8,836·9 crores. There were 7,869 public limited companies with an aggregate paid-up capital of Rs 2,535·3 crores, and 36,620 private limited companies (Rs 6,301·6 crores). There were also 15 companies with unlimited liability.

During 1975–76, 2,988 new limited companies were registered in the Indian Union under the Companies Act 1956 with a total authorized capital of Rs 1,094·4 crores; 280 were public limited companies (Rs 183 crores) and 2,708 were private limited companies (Rs 911·4 crores). There were also 11 private companies with unlimited liability, authorized capital Rs 0·5 crores. Of the new companies, 113 had an authorized capital of Rs 1 crore and above, and 69 of between Rs 50 lakhs and Rs 1 crore; 75 were government companies (*i.e.*, companies in which Government owns at least 51% of share capital). During 1975–76, 165 companies with an aggregate paid-up capital of Rs 638 lakhs went into liquidation and 137 companies (Rs 36 lakhs) were struck off the register.

On 31 March 1976 there were 651 government companies at work with a total paid-up capital of Rs 6,122·2 crores; 243 were public limited companies and 408 were private limited companies.

On 31 March 1976, 481 companies incorporated elsewhere were reported to have a place of business in India; of these 277 were of UK and 80 of USA origin.

On 13 May 1971 the General Insurance (Emergency Provisions) Ordinance vested the management of all insurance companies operating in India in the Government. This covered 106 companies, 42 of them foreign-owned, with total assets of Rs 2,400m. A bill to nationalize all these, as the General Insurance Corporation of India, passed the Rajya Sabha in Sept. 1972.

Department of Company Affairs, Govt. of India. *Joint Stock Companies in India*. New Delhi.

Co-operative Movement. in 1971–72 there were 322,868 co-operative societies of all types with a membership of 56·8m., and working capital of Rs 2,071·88 crores. In 1974 there were 26 state co-operative banks with outstanding loans of Rs 706 crores. The central co-operative banks (including banking unions) numbered 341, total advances were Rs 12,88 crores, funds and deposits Rs 10,00 crores. Agricultural primary credit societies (which constitute the base of the co-operative credit structure of the country) 153,808, with a membership of 35m. and deposits of Rs 89 crores. There were 19 central land development banks and 869 primary land development banks. Total credit made available by all co-operatives to members was Rs 920 crores.

Following the recommendations (1954) of a committee appointed by the Reserve Bank of India, the co-operation movement was extended from its chief function of providing credit to include marketing, processing, warehousing, etc. In 1971–72 there were 142,597 non-credit societies including 3,654 primary marketing societies,

144 sugar factories, 1,341 agricultural processing societies, 9,605 farming societies, 12,273 primary weavers' societies, 33,736 other industrial societies; there were 13,278 primary consumers' stores.

In 1974 non-credit societies marketed agricultural produce worth Rs 809 crores, agricultural requisites worth Rs 614 crores and consumer goods worth Rs 536 crores. Co-operative sugar factories accounted for 40% of national output.

Indian Labour Guide. Monthly. Delhi
Co-operative Movement in India, Statistical Statements Relating to. Annual. Reserve Bank of India, Bombay
Das, N., *Industrial Enterprise in India.* 3rd ed. Bombay, 1961
Dube, R. N., *The Economic Geography of the Indian Republic.* Allahabad, 1954
Ghose, B. C., *Industrial Organization.* 2nd ed. OUP, 1959
Ghosh, A., *Indian Economy, its Nature and Problems.* 7th ed. Calcutta, 1963
Hough, E. M., *Co-operative Movement in India.* 4th ed. OUP, 1959
Karnik, V. B., *Indian Trade Unions.* 2nd ed. Bombay, 1966
Kust, M. J., *Foreign Enterprise in India.* Bombay, 1964
Neale, W. C., *Economic Change in Rural India.* Yale Univ. Press, 1962
Pant, S. C., *Indian Labour Problems.* Allahabad, 1965
Rangnekar, D. K., *Poverty and Capital Development in India.* OUP, 1958
Rao, R., *Surveys of Indian Industries.* 2 vols. OUP, 1957–58
Sharma, T. R., and Singh Chauhan, S. D., *Indian Industries.* 2nd ed. Agra, 1965
Sharma, V. S., *Sahayoga, or Indian Co-operation.* Hoshiarpur, 1964
Thorner, D., *Agricultural Co-operatives in India.* Bombay, 1964
Turner, R. (ed.), *India's Urban Future.* California Univer. Press, 1961
Venkatasubbiah H., *Indian Economy Since Independence.* 2nd ed. London, 1961

Commerce. The external trade of India (excluding land-borne trade with Tibet and Bhután) was as follows (in 1,000 rupees):

	Imports		*Exports and Re-exports*	
	Merchandise[1]	*Treasure*	*Merchandise*	*Treasure*
1971–72	1,824,54,24	26,93,11	1,608,22,37[3]	48
1972–73	1,867,43,80	80,72	1,970,83,19	2,77
1973–74	2,955,36,92	69,12	2,523,39,98	1,39
1974–75	4,468,10,37	7,65	3,304,14,11	3,72
1975–76	5,264,77,87	7,40	4,036,25,87	4,32
1976–77	5,015,14,94	8,84[2]	4,981,01,37	3,88[2]

[1] Excludes certain consignments of foodgrains and stores awaiting adjustment.
[2] Provisional.
[3] Allows for incomplete recording of exports to Bangladesh during early transactions.

The distribution of commerce by countries and areas was as follows in the year ended 31 March 1977 (in 1,000 rupees):

Countries	*Exports to*	*Imports from*
Afghánistán	21,60,40	26,84,36
Argentina	2,28,79	1,07,83
Australia	64,68,98	249,56,63
Belgium	98,05,24	57,10,12
Burma	9,04,08	55,16
Canada	48,58,40	129,40,13
Czechoslovakia	43,05,36	34,12,77
Denmark	23,89,59	5,26,92
Federal Rep. of Germany	223,96,29	305,64,30
France	160,82,10	140,21,27
German Dem. Republic	42,46,23	30,13,66
Hungary	21,14,36	14,77,33
Iran	144,58,09	507,87,48
Italy	116,65,12	57,44,28
Japan	538,87,45	297,05,48
Kenya	17,50,91	6,99,65
Malaysia	29,41,31	33,93,23
Nepál	50,64,53	33,48,86
Netherlands	185,61,30	65,21,99
New Zealand	12,98,78	69,31
Poland	112,34,93	37,99,20
Saudi Arabia	74,36,80	331,98,35
Singapore	57,62,05	8,78,98
Sri Lanka	38,92,72	1,14,74
Sudan	51,14,92	19,03,68
Sweden	25,41,75	35,74,94
Switzerland	69,15,93	49,04,29
USSR	440,36,95	307,23,78
UAR	90,75,33	21,14,54
UK	508,84,60	321,29,30
USA	547,23,17	1055,53,36
Yemen	44,49,12	1,26,06
Yugoslavia	49,21,61	23,86,63

The value (in 1,000 rupees) of the leading articles of merchandise was as follows in the year ended 31 March 1977:

Exports	*Value*
Fish	178,22,97
Edible nuts and fresh fruits	115,15,06
Coffee	114,04,98
Tea and mate	292,86,99
Spices	72,92,33
Oilseed, oilnuts and oil kernels	71,16,26
Tobacco	96,61,81
Hides and skins, undressed	22,73
Wood (unworked)	16,55,43
Wool and other animal hair	8,04,71
Cotton, raw	38,74,06
Cottonwaste; shoddy	39,15
Stone, sand and gravel	8,22,77
Iron ore and concentrates	238,48,87
Iron and steel scrap	9,75,47
Ore and concentrates, non-ferrous base metals	49,40,18
Coal, coke and briquettes	14,33,92
Fixed vegetable oils	48,57,71
Leather	246,29,53
Textile yarn and thread	54,46,63
Textile fabrics (woven) except cotton and jute	39,32,83
Cotton manufactures except yarn, thread and clothing	331,24,33
Jute manufactures except twist and yarn	197,46,46
Floor coverings, tapestries, except cotton and jute	76,66,13
Manufactures of leather or artificial leather	8,68,51
Imports	
Milk and cream	30,99,25
Wheat, spelt and meslin	807,10,33
Rice	45,98,07
Edible nuts and fresh fruit	28,49,36
Pulp and waste paper	6,07,76
Wool and other animal hair	27,97,86
Cotton, raw	129,48,72
Jute	6,76,33
Vegetable fibres except cotton and jute	3,02,45
Crude fertilizers	25,02,78
Sulphur and unroasted iron pyrites	38,47,76
Petroleum, crude and partly refined	1,151,61,64
Petroleum products	260,44,60
Animal oils and fats	16,16,50
Fixed vegetable oils	100,61,19
Organic chemicals	88,72,97
Medical and pharmaceutical products	42,14,47
Manufactured fertilizers	197,71,99
Plastic materials	27,34,78
Chemical materials and products	26,33,41
Paper, paperboard and manufactures	62,17,58
Pearls, precious and semi-precious stones	180,63,82
Iron and steel bars, angles, shapes, sections	26,94,58
Iron and steel universals, plates and sheets	87,66,81
Iron and steel tubes, pipes, fittings	78,75,10
Copper	46,15,55
Zinc	35,59,80
Tin	20,47,37
Machinery other than electrical	658,73,37
Electrical machinery	173,00,74
Transport equipment	147,40,37

The trade between India and UK (British Department of Trade returns, in £1,000 sterling):

	1972	*1973*	*1974*	*1975*	*1976*	*1977*
Imports to UK	112,205	148,609	203,330	237,136	855,074	383,462
Exports and re-exports from UK	141,203	132,911	127,133	164,535	206,918	278,098

Annual Statement of the Foreign Trade of India. 2 vols. Calcutta

Review of the Trade of India. Annual. Delhi
India—Handbook of Commercial Information. 3 vols. Calcutta
Guide to Official Statistics of Trade, Shipping, Customs and Excise Revenue of India. Rev. ed. Calcutta

Tourism. There were 465,275 visitors to India in 1975. They spent the equivalent of US$124m.

COMMUNICATIONS

Roads. In 1973 there were about 1,337,000 km of roads, of which 485,000 km were metalled. Roads are divided into 5 main administrative classes, namely, national highways, state highways, major district roads, district roads and village roads. The national highways (28,819 km in 1973) connect capitals of states, major ports and foreign highways. The national highway system is linked with the ECAFE (Economic Co-operation Administration Far East) international highway system. The state highways are the main trunk roads of the states, while the major district roads connect subsidiary areas of production and markets with distribution centres, and form the main link between headquarters and neighbouring districts.

There were (31 March 1974) 2,243,249 motor vehicles in India, comprising 693,697 private cars and jeeps, 784,178 motor cycles and auto-rickshaws, 185,128 public service vehicles, 393,070 goods vehicles.

Railways. The Indian railway system is government-owned and (under the control of the Railway Board) is divided into 9 zones, with route km as follows at 31 March 1975:

Zone	*Headquarters*	*Broad gauge*	*Metre gauge*	*Narrow gauge*	*Total*
Central	Bombay	4,840	382	839	6,016
Eastern	Calcutta	4,100	—	130	4,230
Northern	Delhi	6,998	3,430	260	10,687
North Eastern	Gorakhpur	52	4,947	—	4,999
North East Frontier	Gauhati	639	2,901	87	3,628
Southern	Madras	2,341	4,958	153	7,452
South Central	Secunderabad	2,918	2,873	369	6,160
South Eastern	Calcutta	5,514	—	1,479	6,993
Western	Bombay	2,878	6,112	1,202	10,192

Passengers carried in 1973–74 were approximately 2,654m. (1963–64, 1,892·6m.); freight, 184·9m. (192·3m.) tonnes; this includes freight carried for railway purposes. Railway staff on 31 March 1973 numbered 1·43m. Total route, 31 March 1975: 60,357 km.

Indian Railways pay to the central government a fixed dividend of 4½% on capital-at-charge.

Financial years	*Gross traffic receipts (Rs crores)*	*Working expenses (Rs crores)*	*Net revenues (Rs crores)*	*Net surplus or deficit (Rs crores)*
1971–72[1]	1,078·00	734·32	161·23	+ 9·08
1972–73	1,162·42	982·62	164·43	+ 2·92
1973–74[1]	1,170·00	1,084·02	68·85	− 99·75
1974–75[2]	1,427·15	1,279·37	128·88	− 52·79

[1] Revised estimate. [2] Budget.

Prasad, A., *Indian Railways*. Bombay and London, 1960
Saxena, K. K., *Indian Railways*. Bombay, 1962

Aviation. The air transport industry in India was nationalized in 1953 with the formation of two Air Corporations: Air India for operating long-distance international air services, and Indian Airlines for operating air services within India and to adjacent countries. Air India has 5 Boeing 747s and 9 707s; it operates daily to New York *via* London with halts in the Middle East and Europe, 6 flights a week to London with halts in the Middle East and 2 flights per week to London *via* Moscow and Tehrán. Other scheduled flights are made to Perth and Sydney, Kuala Lumpur, Singapore, Tōkyō, Osaka, Bangkok and Hong Kong, Nairobi, Aden and Addis Ababa, Lagos and Accra, Kuwait, Cairo, Baghdad, Mauritius, Seychelles, Dhahran, Jeddah, Bahrain, Doha, Abu Dhabi, Dubai and Muscat. A fleet of 46 aircraft consisting of Airbus A-300, Caravelle, Viscount, Boeing 737, F-27 and HS-748 aircraft are flown by India Airlines on 192 daily flights covering 43,632 route km.

In 1976 Indian aircraft flew 76·9m. km, carrying about 4·5m. passengers and 81,805 tonnes of cargo and mail. At Dec. 1976, there were 661 aircraft with certificates of registration and 250 with certificates of airworthiness.

The Civil Aviation Department maintains and operates 85 aerodromes. The management of the 4 international airports at Bombay (Santa Cruz), Calcutta (Dum Dum), Delhi (Palam) and Madras is vested in the International Airports Authority of India.

Shipping. In June 1977, 368 ships totalling 5,257,968 GRT were on the Indian Register; of these, 77 ships of 432,162 GRT were engaged in coastal trade, and 291 ships of 4,825,807 GRT in overseas trade. Traffic of major ports, 1976–77, was as follows:

Port	*Ships entered*	*Imports (1m. tonnes)*	*Exports (1m. tonnes)*
Calcutta	990	4·86	3·16
Bombay	2,503	12·25	5·04
Madras	843	4·77	3·06
Cochin	976	3·56	1·19
Marmagoa	542	0·61	12·85
Vishakhapatnam	529	2·54	6·16
Kandla	306	3·13	0·34
Paradip	177	0·28	3·03
New Mangalore	157	0·30	0·13
New Tuticorin	78	0·32	0·31
	7,101	32·62	35·27

The shipyard at Vishakhapatnam is capable of building vessels of a maximum of 21,500 DWT. Present capacity is 3 ships of 21,500 DWT each per year. The Cochin Shipyard is building Panamax type bulk carriers of 75,000 DWT each. On full development the capacity of the shipyard will be 2 such ships a year. Garden Reach Shipbuilders and Engineers are building bulk carriers of 26,000 DWT each while the Mazagoan Dock at Bombay has developed capacity to build ships up to 27,000 DWT each. There are about 14,150 km navigable inland waterways, one fifth-navigable by steamers.

Post and Broadcasting. On 31 March 1976 there were 118,481 post offices and 19,844 telegraph offices (including 3,285 licensed offices, 16,253 combined offices and 306 DTOs). Of the post offices, 106,424 were rural and 12,057 urban.

The telephone system is in the hands of the Indian Posts and Telegraphs Department. On 31 March 1976 there were 5,240 departmental exchanges with 1,913,824 telephones. There were 69 telex exchanges and 11,823 subscribers.

There were (1974) 70 radio stations of All India Radio, 2 commercial stations and 4 auxiliary centres; on 31 Dec. 1974, 14,848,097 receiver licences were in force and programmes were sent out from 141 transmitters, of which 109 were medium-wave. 'Home Service' broadcasts were 42·2% music. The television service was started at Delhi, 15 Sept. 1959. There were (1974) 275,424 television receiver licences. There were 7 television centres and a relay station at Pune. Entertainment films occupy 29·3% of broadcasting time, news and current affairs, 21·3%.

Cinemas. In 1975 there were 8,734 cinemas, including about 3,260 touring cinemas, with 5m. seats: 435 feature films were produced.

Newspapers. In Dec. 1974 the total number of newspapers and periodicals was 12,185. Maharashtra published 1,750; 30·9% of all papers were published in Delhi, Bombay, Calcutta and Madras. Papers in 6 principal languages included 2,453 English papers with a circulation of 7,764,000; 3,200 Hindi, 7,408,000. Highest daily circulation, *Ananda Bazar Patrika* (Bengali), 3m. Total circulation, 33m.

Annual Report of the Register of Newspapers for India. New Delhi
Natarajan, S., *History of the Press in India.* London, 1962

JUSTICE, RELIGION, EDUCATION AND WELFARE

Justice. All courts form a single hierarchy, with the Supreme Court at the head, which constitutes the highest court of appeal. Immediately below it are the high courts and subordinate courts in each state. Every court in this chain, subject to the usual pecuniary and local limits, administers the whole law of the country, whether made by Parliament or by the state legislatures.

The states of Andhra Pradesh, Assam (in common with Nagaland, Meghalaya, Manipur and Tripura and the Union territories of Arunachal Pradesh and Mizoram), Bihar, Gujarat, Himachal Pradesh, Jammu and Kashmir, Karnataka, Kerala, Madhya Pradesh, Maharashtra, Orissa, Punjab (in common with the state of Haryana and the Union Territory of Chandigarh), Rajasthan, Tamil Nadu, Uttar Pradesh, West Bengal and Sikkim have each a High Court. There is a Court of Judicial Commissioners, which is in status equivalent to a High Court, in the Union Territory of Goa. There is a separate High Court for Delhi. For the Andaman and Nicobar Islands the Calcutta High Court, for Pondicherry the High Court of Madras, and for Lakshadweep the High Court of Kerala are the highest judicial authorities; in Dadra and Nagar Haveli the High Court of Bombay is the highest judicial authority. The Allahabad High Court has a Bench at Lucknow, the Bombay High Court has a Bench at Nagpur, the Madhya Pradesh High Court has Benches at Gwalior and Indore, the Patna High Court has a Bench at Ranchi and the Rajasthan High Court has a Bench at Jaipur. Judges and Division Courts of the Gauhati High Court also sit in Meghalaya, Manipur, Nagaland and Tripura. Below the High Court each state is divided into a number of districts under the jurisdiction of district judges who preside over civil courts and courts of sessions. There are a number of judicial authorities subordinate to the district civil courts. On the criminal side magistrates of various classes act under the overall supervision of the High Court.

The Code of Criminal Procedure, 1898, has been replaced by the Code of Criminal Procedure, 1973 (2 of 1974), which came into force with effect from 1 April 1974. The new Code provides for complete separation of the Judiciary from the Executive throughout India.

Police. The states control their own police force through the state Home Ministers. The Home Minister of the central government co-ordinates the work of the states and controls the Central Detective Training School, the Central Forensic Laboratory, the Central Fingerprint Laboratory as well as the National Police Academy at Mount Abu (Rajasthan) where the Indian Police Service is trained. This service is recruited by competitive examination of university graduates and provides all senior officers for the state police forces. The Central Bureau of Investigation functions under the control of the Cabinet Secretariat.

The cities of Pune, Ahmedabad, Nagpur, Bangalore, Calcutta, Madras, Bombay and Hyderabad have separate police commissionerates.

Total sanctioned strength of police was 706,895 in 1971.

Sarkar, P. C., *Civil Laws of India and Pakistan*. 2 vols. Calcutta, 1953.—*Criminal Laws of India and Pakistan*. 2nd ed. 2 vols. Calcutta, 1956
Setalvad, M. C., *The Common Law of India*. London, 1960
Sharma, S. R., *Supreme Court in the Indian Constitution*. Delhi, 1959

Religion. The principal religions in 1971 (census) were: Hindus, 453·2m. (82·7%); Sikhs, 10·3m. (1·89%); Jains, 2·6m. (0·47%); Buddhists, 3·8m. (0·7%); Moslems, 61·4m. (11·21%); Christians, 14·2m. (2·6%).

In 1971 the Christian population consisted of 8·2m. Roman Catholics, 2·69m. Anglicans of the Church of South India, 1·37m. Anglicans of the Church of North India and about 2m. nonconformists

Sundkler, B., *Church of South India*. London, 1954

Education. *Literacy*. According to the 1971 census the literacy percentage in the country (excluding age-group, 0–4) was 34·45 (28·3 in 1961): 45·95% among males, 21·97% among females. Of the states and territories, Chandigarh (70·43%) and Kerala (69·75%) respectively have the highest rates.

Educational Organization. In the states the general control over education rests with the state government. In the union territories it is the responsibility of the union governments under the control of the central government. The Union Government is directly responsible for the central universities and all institutions declared by parliament to be of national importance; the promotion of Hindi as the federal language; co-ordinating and maintaining standards in higher education, research, science and technology. Professional education rests with the Ministry or Department concerned, *e.g.*, medical education, the Ministry or Department of Health. The Union Minister of Education is in overall charge of the separate Departments of Education, Culture and Social Welfare, assisted by 2 Ministers of State. There are several autonomous organizations attached to the Department of Education. The Central Advisory Board of Education meets periodically (in average intervals of 1 year) to recommend directions for educational policy. The University Grants Commission is a statutory body and is responsible for the funding of the central universities, besides providing developmental assistance to the state universities as well. The Commission also influences the policies and the course curricula of the universities. The National Council of Educational Research and Training provides advisory and consultancy services in respect of school education, and also produces standard school textbooks which can be used all over the country. The Union Ministry of Education is also concerned with non-formal education, youth activities, promotion of regional languages, sports, the institution of scholarships, the award of foreign scholarships, liaison with Unesco and its organizations and promoting book production.

School Education. The school system in India can be divided into four states: pre-primary, primary, middle and high or higher secondary.

There are as yet not many pre-primary schools in India.

Primary education is imparted either at independent primary (or junior basic) schools or primary classes attached to middle or high schools. The period of instruction in this stage varies from 4 to 5 years and the medium of instruction is the mother tongue of the child or the regional language. Legislation for compulsory and free primary education has been passed by almost all state governments but it is not practicable to enforce compulsion and attendance is more often ensured by incentive.

The period for the middle stage varies from 2 to 4 years and instruction is given in middle classes of high schools or middle schools, the latter having, generally, primary classes attached to them. At this stage English is usually taught as a compulsory subject.

The high-school extends from 2 to 4 years. Education is given in higher classes of high schools, which have middle or primary (or both) departments attached. English is generally taught as a compulsory subject. The medium of instruction is mostly the mother tongue or the regional language.

The eventual pattern is to be 10 years general school education and 2 years high secondary education with diversified courses.

There are, in addition, schools for professional subjects such as agriculture, commerce, fine arts, forestry, medicine, veterinary science, physical education, social service, teachers' training, technical, industrial and crafts subjects. There are also special schools for the physically and mentally handicapped and reformatory pupils. There are schools of oriental studies and adult education centres.

Higher Education. Higher education is given in arts, science or professional colleges, universities and all-India educational or research institutions. In 1977 there were 105 universities, 9 institutions of national importance and 10 institutions deemed as universities. Of the 105 universities, 7 are central: Aligarh Muslim University; Banaras Hindu University; University of Delhi; University of Hyderabad; Jawaharlal Nehru University; North Eastern Hill University; Visva Bharati. The rest are state universities.

Grants are paid through the University Grants Commission to the central universities for their maintenance and development and to state universities and institutions deemed to be universities for their development projects only. Their maintenance is the concern of State governments or of the institutions themselves. During 1975–76 the University Grants Commission sanctioned grants of Rs 58·30 crores.

Technical Education. The number of institutions awarding degrees in engineering and technology in 1976–77 was 143 (in 1947: 38), and those awarding diplomas in engineering and technology numbered 299 (in 1947: 53); the former admitted about 22,000, the latter about 46,000 students; enrolment has been less than capacity, following a period of unemployment in engineering. There were also 8 rural institutes and 28 Girls' Polytechnics with about 700 and 3,470 students respectively. For training high-level engineers and technologists 5 Institutes of Technology, the Indian Institute of Science, Bangalore, and 65 other institutions conduct post-graduate and research courses.

Adult Education. In spite of the improvement in the literacy rate, the number of adult illiterates over 14 was 210m. in 1971. Adult education is, therefore, being accorded a high priority. Existing programmes include the Farmers' Functional Literacy Project, adult education programmes for urban workers, the Non-Formal Education Programme for the age-group 15–25, assistance to voluntary organizations working in the field of adult education and the production of literature. The Government are also planning to launch (with effect from 2 Oct. 1978) a massive programme of adult education to produce another 100m. literate adults in the age-group 15–35 within a period of 10 years.

Educational Statistics for the year 1976–77:

Type of recognized institution	*No. of institutions*	*No. of students on rolls*	*No. of teachers*
Primary/junior basic schools	466,332	67,529,903	1,339,865
Middle/senior basic schools	94,214	17,007,599	715,663
High/higher secondary schools	43,880	8,773,362	736,053
Training schools and colleges	1,462	165,065	—
Arts, Science and Commerce colleges	3,166	2,972,085	—

Primary pupils represent 80·9% of the age-group 6–11; middle school pupils, 37% of 11s–14s; high school pupils, 20·9% of 14s–17s.

Expenditure (on recognized institutions) during the Fifth Plan (1974–79) is estimated at Rs 1,285 crores.

University Development in India: A Statistical Report, 1961–62. New Delhi, 1962
Mudal ar, A. L., *Education in India.* London, 1960
Rawat, P. L., *History of Indian Education.* 4th ed. Agra, 1965
Vakil, K. S., and Natarajan, S., *Education in India.* 3rd ed. Bombay, 1966

Health. Health programmes are primarily the responsibility of the state governments. The Union Government has sponsored and supported major schemes for disease prevention and control which are implemented nationally. These include the prevention and control of malaria, filaria, tuberculosis, leprosy, venereal diseases, smallpox, trachoma and cancer. There are also Union Government schemes in connexion with water supply and sanitation, and with nutrition. The Nutrition Advisory Committee of the Indian Council of Medical Research sponsors schemes for research and advises the Government. The National Nutrition Advisory Committee is to formulate a national nutrition policy and recommend measures for improving national standards.

Medical relief and service is primarily the responsibility of the states. By 1974 there were 303,000 hospital beds. There were 5,288 primary health centres, 138,000 active doctors, 88,000 nurses. Medical education is also a state responsibility, but there is a co-ordinating Central Health Educational Bureau. In 1974 there were 105 medical colleges and 74 colleges for homeopathic medicine. There were 601 nursing schools. In 1977 there were 38 mental hospitals and 51 institutions for the mentally handicapped and retarded; there were 600 TB clinics.

Family planning is centrally sponsored and locally implemented. The goal is to reduce the birth-rate by means of education in family planning methods.

DIPLOMATIC REPRESENTATIVES

OF INDIA IN GREAT BRITAIN (India House, Aldwych, London, WC2B 4NA)

High Commissioner: N. G. Goray.

OF GREAT BRITAIN IN INDIA (Chanakyapuri, New Delhi 21, 1100–21)
High Commissioner: John Thomson, CMG.

OF INDIA IN THE USA (2107 Massachussetts Ave., NW, Washington, D.C., 20008)

Ambassador: N. A. Palkhivala.

OF THE USA IN INDIA (Shanti Path, Chanakyapuri, New Delhi 21)

Ambassador: Robert F. Goheen.

OF INDIA TO THE UNITED NATIONS

Ambassador: Rikhi Jaipal

Books of Reference

Special works relating to States are shown under their separate headings.

The Gazetteer of India. Central Gazetteers Unit. Delhi, 1965
India: A Reference Annual. Delhi Govt. Printer. Annual
Cambridge History of India. 6 vols. CUP, 1922–47. Supp., 1953
The Times of India Directory and Yearbook. Bombay and London. Annual
Handbook for Travellers in India, Pakistan, Burma and Ceylon. 19th ed. by L. F. Rushbrook Williams. London, 1962
Bhatia, K., *Indira: A Biography of Prime Minister Gandhi.* New York, 1974
Chatterjee, S. P., *Indian Climatology.* Calcutta, 1956.—(ed.), *National Atlas of India (Preliminary* [Hindi] *edition).* Calcutta, 1957
Desai, A. R., *The Social Background of Indian Nationalism.* Bombay, 1954
Griffiths, P. J., *The British Impact on India.* London, 1952
Hanson, A. H., and Douglas, J., *India's Democracy.* London, 1972
Kesavan, B. S., and Kulkarni, V. Y. (eds), *The National Bibliography of Indian Literature, 1901–53*, New Delhi, 1963 ff.
Kundra, J. C., *Indian Foreign Policy, 1947–54.* Bombay, 1955
Lipton, M., and Firn, J., *The Erosion of a Relationship: India and Britain Since 1960.* OUP, 1975
Majumdar, R. C., Raychandhuri, H. C., and Datta, K., *An Advanced History of India.* 2nd ed. London, 1950
Mitra, H. N., *The Indian Annual Register.* Calcutta, from 1953
Nanda, B. R. (ed.), *Socialism in India.* Delhi, Bombay, Bangalore, Kanpur, London, 1972
Philips, C. H. (ed.), *The Evolution of India and Pakistan: Select Documents.* OUP, 1962 ff.—*Politics and Society in India.* London, 1963
Platt, R. (ed.), *India: A Compendium.* New York, 1962
Poplai, S. L. (ed.), *India, 1947–50* [select documents]. 2 vols. Bombay and London, 1959
Smith, V. E., *Oxford History of India.* 3rd ed. OUP, 1958
Spear, P., *India: A Modern History.* 2nd ed. Univ. of Michigan Press, 1972
Sukhwal, B. L., *India: A Political Geography.* Bombay and New Delhi, 1971
Sutton, S. C., *Guide to the India Office Library [founded in 1801].* HMSO, 1952
Yasdani, C. (ed.), *Early History of the Deccan.* 2 vols. London, 1960

STATES AND TERRITORIES

The Republic of India is composed of the following 22 States and 9 centrally administered Union Territories:

States	*Capital*	*States*	*Capital*
Andhra Pradesh	Hyderabad	Manipur	Imphal
Assam	Dispur	Meghalaya	Shillong
Bihar	Patna	Nagaland	Kohima
Gujarat	Ahmedabad	Orissa	Bhubaneswar
Haryana	Chandigarh	Punjab	Chandigarh
Himachal Pradesh	Simla	Rajasthan	Jaipur
Jammu and Kashmir	Srinagar	Sikkim	Gangtok
Karnataka	Bangalore	Tamil Nadu	Madras
Kerala	Trivandrum	Tripura	Agartala
Madhya Pradesh	Bhopal	Uttar Pradesh	Lucknow
Maharashtra	Bombay	West Bengal	Calcutta

Union Territories

Andaman and Nicobar Islands; Arunachal Pradesh; Chandigarh, Dadra and Nagar Haveli; Delhi; Goa, Daman and Diu; Lakshadweep; Mizoram; Pondicherry.

States Reorganization. The Constitution, which came into force on 26 Jan. 1950, provided for 9 Part A States (Assam, Bihar, Bombay, Madhya Pradesh, Madras, Orissa, Punjab, Uttar Pradesh and West Bengal) which corresponded to the previous governors' provinces; 8 Part B States (Hyderabad, Jammu and Kashmir, Madhya Bharat, Mysore, Patalia–East Punjab (PEPSU), Rajasthan, Saurashtra and Travancore–Cochin) which corresponded to Indian states or unions of states; 10 Part C States (Ajmer, Bhopal, Bilaspur, Coorg, Delhi, Himachal Pradesh, Kutch, Manipur, Tripura and Vindhya Pradesh) which corresponded to the chief commissioners' provinces; and Part D Territories and other areas (*e.g.*, Andaman and Nicobar Islands). Part A States (under governors) and Part B States (under rajpramukhs) had provincial autonomy with a ministry and elected assembly. Part C States (under chief commissioners) were the direct responsibility of the Union government, although Kutch, Manipur and Tripura had legislatures with limited powers. Andhra was formed as a Part A State on its separation from Madras in 1953. Bilaspur was merged with Himachal Pradesh in 1954.

The States Reorganization Act, 1956, abolished the distinction between Parts A, B and C States and established two categories for the units of the Indian union to be called States and Territories. The following were the main territorial changes: the Telugu districts of Hyderabad were merged with Andhra; Mysore absorbed the whole Kannada-speaking area (including Coorg, the greater part of 4 districts of Bombay, 3 districts of Hyderabad and 1 district of Madras); Bhopal, Vindhya Pradesh and Madhya Bharat were merged with Madhya Pradesh, which ceded 8 Marathi-speaking districts to Bombay; the new state of Kerala, comprising the majority of Malayalam-speaking peoples, was formed from Travancore–Cochin with a small area from Madras; Patalia–East Punjab was included in Punjab; Kutch and Saurashtra in Bombay; and Ajmer in Rajasthan; Hyderabad ceased to exist.

On 1 May 1960 Bombay State was divided into two parts: 17 districts (including Saurashtra and Kutch) in the north and west became the new state of Gujarat; the remainder was renamed the state of Maharashtra.

In Aug. 1961 the former Portuguese territories of Dadra and Nagar Haveli became a Union territory. The Portuguese territory of Goa and the smaller territories of Daman and Diu, occupied by India in Dec. 1961, were constituted a Union territory in March 1962. In Aug. 1962 the former French territories of Pondicherry, Karikal, Mahé and Yanaon were formally transferred to India and became a Union territory. In Sept. 1962 the Naga Hills Tuensang Area was constituted a separate state under the name of Nagaland. On 1 Nov. 1966, under the Punjab Reorganization Act 1966, a new state of Haryana and a new Union Territory of Chandigarh were created from parts of Punjab (India); for details, *see* pp. 631 and 661. On 26 Jan. 1971 Himachal Pradesh became a state. In 1972 the North East Frontier Agency and Mizo hill district were made Union territories (as Arunachal Pradesh and Mizoram) and Manipur, Meghalaya and Tripura full states. Sikkim became a state in 1975.

Report of the States Reorganization Commission. Government of India. Delhi, 1956
Menon, V. P., *The Story of the Integration of the Indian [Princely] States.* London, 1956
Santhanam, K., *Union–State Relations in India.* London, 1961

ANDHRA PRADESH

HISTORY. Andhra was constituted a separate state on 1 Oct. 1953, on its partition from Madras, and consisted of the undisputed Telugu-speaking area of that state. To this region was added, on 1 Nov. 1956, the Telangana area of the former Hyderabad State, comprising the districts of Hyderabad, Medak, Nizamabad,

Karimnaga, Warangal, Khammam, Nalgonda and Mahbubnaga, parts of the Adilabad district and some taluks of the Raichur, Gulbarga and Bidar districts, and some revenue circles of the Nanded district. On 1 April 1960, 221·4 sq. miles in the Chingleput and Salem districts of Madras were transferred to Andhra Pradesh in exchange for 410 sq. miles from Chittoor district. The district of Ongole was formed by an Ordinance of 2 Feb. 1970.

EVENTS. About 250 sq. miles of the state was devastated by cyclones in Nov. 1977. Coastal settlements and fertile inland farms were equally affected and crops of cotton, tobacco and rice destroyed. The number of dead was placed at over 50,000 and about 2m. have lost their homes or livelihood. The tidal wave which accompanied the cyclone moved inland for 18 miles and carried villages, people and livestock back as it retreated. It has left farmland which is useless until it can be cleaned of salt.

AREA AND POPULATION. Andhra Pradesh is in south India and is bounded south by Tamil Nadu, west by Mysore, north and northwest by Maharashtra, northeast by Madhya Pradesh and Orissa, east by the Indian Ocean. The state has an area of 275,281 sq. km and a population (1971) of 43·39m. Density, 157 per sq. km. The principal language is Telugu. Cities with over 100,000 population (1971 census), *see* pp. 600–601.

CONSTITUTION AND GOVERNMENT. Andhra Pradesh has a bicameral legislature. A regional committee composed of the elected members of Telangana Region is consulted by the Government on matters pertaining to that region.

For administrative purposes there are 21 districts in the state. The capital is Hyderabad.

There are 294 seats in the Legislative Assembly and 90 in the Legislative Council. Following the elections of Feb. 1978 the state of the parties in the Legislative Assembly was: Indira Congress, 175; Janata, 60; Congress, 30; others, 29.

Governor: S. Mukherjee.
Chief Minister: Chenni Reddi.

BUDGET. The budget estimates for 1968–69 showed total revenue receipts of Rs. 199 crores, and expenditure of Rs 204·67 crores.

ENERGY AND NATURAL RESOURCES

Electricity. There are hydro-electric plants at Machkund, Upper Sileru, Nizam Sagar, Nellore, Ramagundam and Kothagudam. Installed capacity, 1974, 888 mw. In 1972 there were 9,252 electrified villages.

Water. The Tungabhadra dam, inaugurated in 1953, has been completed, thus irrigating about 492,800 hectares in Andhra Pradesh and Karnataka. The Nagarjunsaga project, which incorporates canals and a dam (the tallest masonry dam in the world) on the Krishna River 160 km from Hyderabad, will irrigate over 1,305,000 hectares on completion of the final phase. The Pochambad dam on the Godavari River will irrigate 230,000 hectares.

Minerals (1970). Production of principal minerals (in 1,000 tonnes): Manganese, 139; mica, 8; iron ore, 92; limestone, 1,435; coal, 3,700; barytes, 35; clay, 54; steatite, 12.

Agriculture. There are about 14·3m. hectares of cultivable land, of which 31% is irrigated. Production of principal crops (in tonnes), 1972–73: Foodgrains, 6·7m.; sugar-cane, 1·1m.; oilseeds, 1·1m.; cotton, 1·12m. bales (of 180 kg).

Livestock (1966 census): Cattle, 12·34m.; buffaloes, 6·79m.; goats, 3·76m.; sheep, 8m.

Forests. In 1975 it was estimated that forests occupy about 22·5% of the total area of the state; main forest products are timber, bamboo and casuarina.

INDUSTRY. The main industries are textile manufacture, sugar-milling and paper-making. Other industries include cement, tanning and glass. There is an oil refinery at Vishakhapatnam, where India's only major shipbuilding yards are situated.

Cottage industry includes the manufacture of carpets, wooden and lacquer toys, brocades, bidriware, filigree and lace-work. The wooden toys of Nirmal and Kondapalli are particularly well known.

COMMUNICATIONS

Roads. In 1972 there were 72,702 km of roads, including 41,820 km of surfaced roads. Number of vehicles, 1972: 136,882.

Railways. In 1971 there were approximately 4,510 route km of railway, of which 2,888 km were broad gauge, 1,599 km metre gauge and 32 km narrow gauge.

Aviation. There are airports at Hyderabad, Tirupati, Vijayawada and Vishakapatnam, with regular scheduled services to Bombay, Calcutta, Delhi and Madras.

Shipping. The chief port is Vishakhapatnam. There are minor ports at Kakinada, Machilipatnam, Bheemunipatnam, Narsapur, Krishnapatnam, Vadarevu and Calingapatnam.

JUSTICE, RELIGION AND EDUCATION

Justice. The High Court of Judicature at Hyderabad has a Chief Justice and 17 puisne judges.

Religion. At the 1961 census Hindus numbered 31,813,944; Moslems, 2,715,021; Christians, 1,428,819; Jains, 9,012; Sikhs, 8,563; Buddhists, 6,753.

Education. In 1971, 24·56% of the population were literate. There were, in 1970, 42,664 recognized educational institutions, with 4,982,798 pupils, namely, 53 pre-primary, 36,757 primary, 2,919 upper primary, 2,925 secondary schools. Education is free for children up to 14.

Osmania University, Hyderabad (founded in 1918), had (1969–70) 38 day colleges for men, 9 for women, 15 evening colleges for men, 1 for women and 84 junior colleges; Andhra University, Waltair (1926), had 46 day colleges for men, 11 for women, 8 evening colleges for men, 48 junior colleges; Sri Venkateswara University, Tirupati (1954), had 23 day colleges for men, 4 for women, 7 evening colleges for men, 38 junior colleges. The AP Agricultural University, inaugurated in Rajendra Nagar, Hyderabad, in 1964, had 3 agricultural colleges for men, 2 veterinary science colleges for men, I home science college for women and 1 college of basic courses for men.

ASSAM

HISTORY. Assam first became a British Protectorate at the close of the first Burmese War in 1826. In 1832 Cachar was annexed; in 1835 the Jaintia Hills were included in the East India Company's dominions, and in 1839 Assam was annexed to Bengal. In 1874 Assam was detached from Bengal and made a separate chief commissionership. On the partition of Bengal in 1905, it was united to the Eastern Districts of Bengal under a Lieut.-Governor. From 1912 the chief commissionership of Assam was revived, and in 1921 a governorship was created. On the partition of India almost the whole of the predominantly Muslim district of Sylhet was merged with East Bengal (Pakistan). Dewangiri in North Kamrup was ceded to Bhután in 1951. The Naga Hill district, administered by the Union government since 1957, became part of Nagaland in 1962. The autonomous state of Meghalaya within Assam, comprising the districts of Garo Hills and Khasi and Jaintia Hills, came into existence on 2 April 1970, and achieved full independent statehood in Jan. 1972, when it was also decided to form a Union Territory, Mizoram, from the Mizo Hills district.

AREA AND POPULATION. Assam is in eastern India, almost separated from central India by Bangladesh. It is bounded west by West Bengal, north by Bhután and the Territory of Arunachal Pradesh, east by Nagaland, Manipur and Burma, south by Meghalaya, Bangladesh and Tripura. The area of the state is now approximately 78,523 sq. km. Its population (1971 census) 14·6m. Principal towns with population (1971) are; Gauhati, 122,981; Dibrugarh, 80,344; Tinsukia, 55,392; Nowgong, 52,892; Silchar, 52,612. The principal language is Assamese.

CONSTITUTION AND GOVERNMENT. Assam has a unicameral legislature of 126 members. The state of the parties in the Legislative Assembly in March 1978 was: Janata, 53; Congress, 26; CPI(M), 11; Indira Congress, 8; others, 28.

There are 10 districts. The capital is Dispur, near Gauhati.

Governor: L. P. Singh.
Chief Minister: S. C. Sinha.

BUDGET. The budget estimates for 1977–78 showed total revenue receipts of Rs 232·36 crores and expenditure of Rs 211·35 crores. Capital receipts are estimated at Rs 77·81 crores and expenditure at Rs 105·24 crores.

ENERGY AND NATURAL RESOURCES

Electricity. In 1973–74 there was an installed capacity of 121 mw and 1,241 villages (out of 21,995) with electricity. A further 42·5 mw capacity has since been installed and another 30 mw planned for 1978. New power stations also were under construction in 1977 at Bongaigaon and Lakwa; 1,810 villages had electricity by 1978.

Oil. Assam contains important oilfields and produces about 50% of India's crude oil.

Water. Twelve irrigation projects are due to be completed during the Fifth Plan period, affecting 70,000 hectares.

Minerals. Coal production (1973), 436,000 tonnes. The state also has limestone, refractory clay, dolomite, corundum and natural gas.

Agriculture. There are about 750 tea plantations, and growing tea is the principal industry. Assam produces over 50% of Indian tea. Over 72% of the cultivated area is under food crops, of which the most important is rice. Total foodgrains, 1976–77, 21.47m. tonnes. Main cash crops: jute, tea, cotton, oilseeds, sugarcane, fruit and potatoes. Wheat has been introduced recently and yielded 71,045 tonnes in 1976–77.

Forestry. There are 1·62m. hectares of reserved forests under the administration of the Forest Department and 1,229,000 hectares of unclassed forests, altogether about 35% of the total area of the state.

INDUSTRY. Sericulture and hand-loom weaving, both silk and cotton, are important home industries together with the manufacture of brass, cane and bamboo articles. The main heavy industry is petro-chemicals; there are 3 oil refineries. Other industries include manufacturing paper, fertilizers, sugar, jute and plywood products, rice and oil milling.

COMMUNICATIONS

Roads. In 1972 there were 17,839 km of road maintained by the Public Works Department in Assam, including national highway. There were 43,869 motor vehicles in the state.

Railways. The open length of railways in 1974 was 2,193·65 km, of which 105·22 km are broad gauge.

Aviation. Daily scheduled flights connect the principal towns with the rest of India. There are airports at Gauhati, Tezpur, Jorhat, Dimapur, Silchar and Dibrugarh.

Shipping. Water transport is important in Lower Assam; the main waterway is the Brahmaputra river.

JUSTICE, RELIGION AND EDUCATION

Justice. The seat of the High Court is Gauhati. It has a Chief Justice and 6 puisne judges.

Religion. At the 1971 census Hindus numbered 10,604,618; Moslems, 3,592,124; Christians, 381,010; Buddhists, 22,565; Jains, 12,914; Sikhs, 11,920.

Education. The 1971 census showed 28·74% of the population to be literate.

In 1976 there were 26,000 primary schools; 2,504 middle schools; 1,657 high schools; 70 higher secondary schools; 133 general colleges; 5 vocational colleges; 1 Ayurvedic college and 3 universities.

Goswami, P. C., *Economic Development of Assam.* London, 1963
Reid, Sir Robert, *History of the Frontier Areas Bordering on Assam.* Shillong, 1942

BIHAR

The state contains the 2 ethnic areas of Bihar and Chota Nagpur. In 1956 certain areas of Purnea and Manbhum districts were transferred to West Bengal.

AREA AND POPULATION. Bihar is in north India and is bounded north by Nepal, east by West Bengal, south by Orissa, southwest by Madhya Pradesh and west by Uttar Pradesh. The area of Bihar is 173,876 sq. km and its population (1971 census), 56,353,369, a density of 324 per sq. km. Population of principal towns, *see* pp. 600–601.

The official language is Hindi.

CONSTITUTION AND GOVERNMENT. Bihar has a unicameral legislature. The Legislative Assembly consists of 324 elected members. After the elections of June 1977 Janata held 214 seats; Congress, 57; Communist Party of India, 21; independents, 22; others, 9; vacant, 1.

For the purposes of administration it is divided into 5 divisions covering 23 districts. The capital is Patna; the hot-weather seat is Ranchi.

Governor: R. D. Bhandare.
Chief Minister: K. Thakur.

BUDGET. The budget estimates for 1972–73 show total revenue receipts of Rs 3,11,10·00 lakhs and expenditure of Rs 3,16,38·00 lakhs.

ENERGY AND NATURAL RESOURCES

Electricity. Installed capacity (1974) 1,314 mw. There were 9,687 villages with electricity.

Minerals. Bihar is the foremost state for mineral deposits. Coal is the principal mineral, but copper, of which Bihar is the only Indian producer, iron ore, ruby mica, kyanite and bauxite are important. The recently discovered large deposits of pyrites in the Shahabad district are being exploited.

Agriculture. About 26% of the cultivable area is irrigated. Main crops are rice, wheat, jowar, bajra and maize; total foodgrains (1974), 7·73m. tonnes.

Livestock (1961 census): Buffaloes, 3,698,000; other cattle, 16,104,000; sheep, 1,156,000; goats, 8,671,000; horses and ponies, 133,000.

INDUSTRY. Main plants are the Tata Iron and Steel Co., the Tata Engineering and Locomotive Co., the steel plant at Bokaro, oil refinery at Barauni and aluminium plant at Muri. Other important industries are machine tools, fertilizers, sugar-milling, paper-milling, manufacturing explosives and cement.

COMMUNICATIONS

Roads. In 1972 the state had 116,575 km of highway (including 88,040 km of unmetalled roads). Passenger transport has been nationalized in 7 districts.

Railways. The North Eastern and Eastern railways traverse the province.

Aviation. There are airports at Patna and Ranchi with regular scheduled services to Calcutta and Delhi.

Shipping. The length of waterways open for navigation is 900 miles.

JUSTICE, RELIGION AND EDUCATION

Justice. There is a High Court (constituted in 1916) at Patna with a Chief Justice, 17 puisne judges and 6 additional judges.

Police. The police force is under an inspector-general; there is 1 policeman to 1,211 of the population.

Religion. At the 1961 census Hindus numbered 39,347,050; Moslems, 5,785,631; Christians, 502,195; Sikhs, 44,413; Jains, 17,598; Buddhists, 2,885.

Education. At the census of 1971 the proportion of literates was 19·97%.

There were, 1971, 2,581 high and higher secondary schools with 601,000 pupils, 8,025 middle schools with 965,000 pupils, 46,582 primary schools with 5,009,000 pupils. Primary schools had 144,559 teachers, higher secondary and high schools 25,740. Education is free for children aged 6–11.

There were 7 universities in academic year 1972–73; Patna University (founded 1917) with 12,577 full-time students (1970); Bihar University, Muzaffarpur (1952) with 4 constituent colleges, 35 affiliated colleges and 41,640 students (1970); Bhagalpur University (1960) with 40,746 students (1970); Ranchi University (1960) with 36,892 students (1968–69); Darbhanga Sanskrit University (1961); Magadha University, Gaya (1962) and Mithila University (1972), Darbhanga.

GUJARAT

HISTORY. On 1 May 1960, as a result of the Bombay Reorganization Act, 1960, the state of Gujarat was formed from the north and west (predominantly Gujarati-speaking) portion of Bombay State, the remainder being renamed the state of Maharashtra. Gujarat consists of the following districts of the former state of Bombay: Banas Kantha, Mehsana, Sabar Kantha, Ahmedabad, Kaira, Panch Mahals, Vadodara, Bharuch, Surat, Dangs, Amreli, Surendranagar, Rajkot, Jamnagar, Junagadh, Bhavnagar, Kutch, Gandhinagar and Bulsar.

AREA AND POPULATION. Gujarat is in western India and is bounded north by Pakistan and Rajasthan, east by Madhya Pradesh, southeast by Maharashtra, south and west by the Indian Ocean and Arabian Sea. The area of the state is 195,984 sq. km and the population at the 1971 census was 26,697,475; a density of 136 per sq. km. The chief cities, *see* pp. 600–601. Gujarati and Hindi in the Devanagari script are the official languages.

CONSTITUTION AND GOVERNMENT. Gujarat has a unicameral legislature, the Legislative Assembly, which has 182 elected members.

The capital is Gandhinagar. There are 19 districts.

Governor: K. K. Viswanathan.
Chief Minister: B. Patel.

BUDGET. Budget estimates, 1977–78, showed total revenue of Rs 5,74,39·22 lakhs, and expenditure of Rs 4,82,12·03 lakhs. Receipts included: Taxes on income except corporation tax, Rs 38,20·0 lakhs; state excise, Rs 2,00·0 lakhs; estate duty, Rs 48·0 lakhs; registration fees, Rs 1,29·55 lakhs; stamps, Rs 15,57·45 lakhs; sales tax, Rs 2,00,00·0 lakhs; vehicle taxes, Rs 14,09·0 lakhs; land revenue, Rs 8,29·0 lakhs. Expenditure included: Education, Rs 1,18,47·75 lakhs; public works and improvements, Rs 12,88·39 lakhs; irrigation, embankment, etc., Rs 34,98·29 lakhs; medical, and public health, Rs 38,65·56 lakhs; police, Rs 30,16·88 lakhs; agriculture, Rs 20,52·14 lakhs; general administration, Rs 10,17·28 lakhs; extraordinary, including community projects and local development, Rs 27,96·26 lakhs; industries, Rs 3,94·31 lakhs. Annual Plan expenditure for 1977–78 (estimate), Rs 2,80·78 crores, including Rs 23·5 crores for the Tribal Area Sub-plan.

ENERGY AND NATURAL RESOURCES

Electricity. In 1977 the total generating capacity was 1,802 mw of electricity, serving 6,971 towns and villages and 133,848 wells and tube-wells.

Oil and Gas. There were crude oil and gas reserves in 20 fields in 1975. Production: Crude oil, 4·1m. tonnes; gas, 632 cu. metres. Crude oil and natural gas was produced from 23 fields in 1976; production, 4,127,861 tonnes of oil and 567,054,672 cu. metres of gas.

Minerals. Chief minerals produced in 1976 (tonnes) included chalk (65,102), limestone (2·5m), agate stone (3,732), calcite (4,402), quartz (41,784), bauxite (1·56m.), china clay (45,208), other clays (252,618), dolomite (165,620), crude fluorite (37,160), silica-glass sand (84,202) and lignite (10,382).

Agriculture. Cropped area, 1972–73, was 10·3m. hectares. Area and production of principal crops, 1976–77 (1,000 hectares and 1,000 tonnes): Rice, 466, 567; groundnuts, 1,886, 1,898; cotton, 1,726, 1,630,400 bales of 170 kg.

Livestock (1972): Buffaloes, 3·46m.; other cattle, 6,457,284; sheep, 1,722,057; goats, 3,209,502; horses and ponies, 63,018.

Fisheries. There were (1977) about 49,227 active fishermen and 140 fishing co-operatives. There were 7,050 fishing vessels (4,667 motor vessels). The catch for 1976–77 (estimate) was 241,000 tonnes.

INDUSTRY. Gujarat is one of the 4 most industrialized states. In 1975 there were over 9,000 registered factories employing an estimated 527,225 workers. This figure includes over 1,900 textile factories. There were about 82 industrial estates. Principal industries are textiles, general and electrical engineering, vegetable oils, chemicals, soda ash and cement. Large fertilizer plants have been set up at Jawaharnagar, Kandla and Kalol. There is an oil refinery at Koyali near Vadodara, with a developing petro-chemical complex. Industrial production (1976) in tonnes: Cement, 5·3m; hydrogenerated oil, 46,763; soda ash, 530,000; caustic soda, 40,426; sugar, 119,961; sulphuric acid, 216,813; cotton yarn, 198,744; superphosphate, 62,361; paper and paper-board, 41,353; ceramics, 15,130; cotton cloth, 1,306,655,000 metres; powered pumps, 46,000 (no.); diesel engines, 11,543 (no.); clocks, 95,000 (no.).

COMMUNICATIONS

Roads. In 1975–76 there were 39,885 km of roads. Gujarat State Transport Corporation operated 7,588 routes over 37·86 crore route km.

Railways. In 1973 the state had 3,381 km metre-gauge railway, 1,141 km narrow gauge and 1,134 km broad gauge.

Aviation. Ahmedabad is the main airport. There are 6 services daily between Bombay, Ahmedabad and Delhi. There are 8 other airports.

Shipping. The largest port is Kandla. There are 45 other ports, including Okha, Bedi, Bhavnagar, Verawal, Sikka and Porbandar.

Post. There were (1977) 7,304 post offices, 735 telegraph offices. Ahmedabad has direct dialling telephone connexion with Delhi, Bombay, Pune, Rajkot, Vadodara, Nadiad, Gaudhinagar and Surat, and telex connexions with other cities.

JUSTICE, RELIGION, EDUCATION AND WELFARE

Justice. The High Court of Judicature at Ahmedabad has a Chief Justice and 10 puisne judges.

Religion. At the 1971 census Hindus numbered 23,835,471; Moslems, 2,249,055; Jains, 451,578; Christians, 109,341; Sikhs, 18,233; Buddhists, 5,469.

Education. Literacy is 35·8% of the population. Primary and secondary education are free. In 1972–73 there were an estimated 21,831 primary schools; nearly all villages with more than 500 people have one. In 1972–73 there were 2,468 secondary schools with 855,000 pupils.

There are 5 universities in the state. Gujarat University, Ahmedabad, founded in 1949, is teaching and affiliating; it has 147 affiliated colleges. The Maharaja Sayajirao University of Vadodara (1949) is residential and teaching. The Sardar Vallabhnhai Vidyapeeth, Anand (1955) has 18 constituent and affiliated colleges. The 2 newer universities (1967) are Saurashtra University at Rajkot with 53 affiliated colleges, and South Gujarat at Surat with 34. Gujarat Vidyapeeth at Ahmedabad is of university status. In 1976–77 the total number of students was 219,078. There were also 1 agricultural and 1 Ayurvedic university.

Health. In 1977 there were 251 primary health centres and 19,369 hospital beds. The annual intake at medical colleges was 675.

Rushbrook Williams, L. F., *The Black Hills: Kutch in History and Legend.* London. 1958
Desai, I. F., *Untouchability in Rural Gujarat.* Bombay, 1977

HARYANA

HISTORY. The state of Haryana, created on 1 Nov. 1966 under the Punjab Reorganization Act, 1966, was formed from the Hindi-speaking parts of the state of Punjab (India). It comprises the districts of Hissar, Mohindergarh, Gurgaon, Rohtak and Karnal; parts of Sangrur and Ambala districts; and part of Kharar tehsil.

AREA AND POPULATION. Haryana is in north India and is bounded north by Himachal Pradesh, east by Uttar Pradesh, south and west by Rajasthan and northwest by Punjab. Delhi forms an enclave on its eastern boundary. The state has an area of 44,222 sq. km and a population (1971) of 10,036,808; density, 226 per sq. km. The principal language is Hindi.

CONSTITUTION AND GOVERNMENT. The state has a unicameral legislature with 90 members. After the elections of March 1977 Janata held 75 seats, Congress, 3; Vishal Haryana, 5; independents, 7. The state shares with Punjab (India) a High Court, a university and certain public services. The capital (shared with Punjab) is Chandigarh (*see* p. 661). There are 7 districts.

Governor: B. N. Chakravati.
Chief Minister: B. D. Gupta.

BUDGET. Budget estimates for 1968–69 showed a total revenue of Rs 67,98·72 lakhs, and expenditure of Rs 66,35·37 lakhs.

ENERGY AND NATURAL RESOURCES

Electricity. Approximately 1,000 mw are supplied to Haryana, mainly from the Bhakra Nangar system. In 1975 installed capacity was 552 mw and all the 3,302 villages had electric power.

Agriculture. Haryana has sandy soil and erratic rainfall. Total irrigated area, 1973, was 43·7% of the cultivable area of 3,738,000 hectares. Agriculture employs over 82% of the working population. During 1972–73 foodgrain production was 4·07m. tonnes; sugar (gur), 560,000 tonnes; oilseeds, 99,000 tonnes, and cotton, 423,000 bales (of 180 kg).

INDUSTRY. Number of registered working factories (1970), 1,260, employing 83,178 workers. The main industries are cotton textiles, agricultural machinery, woollen textiles, scientific instruments, glass, cement, paper and sugar milling.

COMMUNICATIONS

Roads. There were (1971) about 13,259 km of metalled roads and 262 km unsurfaced. Road transport was nationalized by 1971; Haryana Roadways has a fleet of 725 vehicles running on 335 routes and daily carrying 125,255 passengers over 149,630 km.

Railways. The state is crossed by lines from Delhi to Agra, Ajmer, Ferozpur and Chandigarh. The main stations are at Ambala and Kurukshetra.

Aviation. There is no airport within the state but Delhi is on its eastern boundary.

JUSTICE AND EDUCATION

Justice. Haryana shares the High Court of Punjab and Haryana at Chandigarh which had (1968) a Chief Justice and 16 puisne judges.

Education. In 1969–70 there were 5,967 schools and colleges with 1,250,590 attending. This includes 4,362 primary schools, 776 high and higher secondary schools, 777 middle schools and 47 colleges.

HIMACHAL PRADESH

HISTORY. The territory came into being on 15 April 1948 and comprised 30 former Hill States. The state of Bilaspur was merged with Himachal Pradesh in 1954. The 6 original districts were: Mahasu, Sirmur, Mandi, Chamba, Bilaspur and Kinnaur. On 1 Nov. 1966, under the Punjab Reorganization Act, 1966, certain parts of the state of Punjab (India) were transferred to Himachal Pradesh. These comprise the districts of Simla, Kulu, Kangra, and Lahaul and Spiti; and parts of Hoshiarpur and Ambala districts, with an estimated population (1967) of 1·5m.

AREA AND POPULATION. Himachal Pradesh is in north India and is bounded north by Kashmir, east by Tibet, southeast by Uttar Pradesh, south by Haryana, southwest and west by Punjab. The area of the state is 55,673 sq. km and it had a population at the 1971 census of 3,460,434. Density, 62 per sq. km. Principal language is Pahari.

CONSTITUTION AND GOVERNMENT. Full statehood was attained, as the 18th state of the Union, on 25 Jan. 1971.

On 1 Sept. 1972 districts were reorganized and 2 new districts created, Hamirpur and Una, making a total of 12. The capital is Simla.

There is a unicameral legislature. The Legislative Assembly has 68 seats of which Janata holds 53 and Congress 9.

Governor: S. Chakravarti.
Chief Minister: S. Kumar.

BUDGET. Total revenue for 1974–75 was (on budget estimates) Rs 82,88·26 lakhs. Expenditure was Rs 82,37·00 lakhs. Receipts included: Contribution and adjustments between central and state governments, Rs 48,26·29 lakhs; forests, Rs 8,20 lakhs. Expenditure included: Education, Rs 19,08·38 lakhs; public works and improvements, Rs 1,29·00 lakhs; agriculture, Rs 5,04·18 lakhs.

ENERGY AND NATURAL RESOURCES

Electricity. Power generated (1973) 162m. kwh.

Agriculture. Main crops are seed potatoes and fruits such as apples, peaches, apricots, nuts, pomegranates.

Production of foodgrains (1974) 990,000 tonnes.

Livestock (1966 census): Buffaloes, 415,356; other cattle, 1,048,917; goats, 813,041.

Salt is another important item. Handicrafts, which include Pashmina shawls, wool of quality, resin, herbs, musk and skins, are other sources of income.

Forestry. Himachal Pradesh forests supply the largest quantities of coniferous timber in northern India. They are the main source of revenue of Pradesh. The forests also ensure the safety of the catchment areas of the Jumna, Sutlej, Beas, Ravi and Chenab rivers.

INDUSTRY. The main sources of employment are the forests and their related industries, salt production and handicrafts, including weaving.

COMMUNICATIONS

Roads. The national highway from Chandigarh runs through Simla; other main highways from Simla serve Kulu, Manali, Kangra, Chemba and Pathankot. The rest are minor roads. Pathankot is also on national highways from Punjab to Kashmir.

Railways. There is a line from Chandigarh to Simla, and the Jammu–Delhi line runs through Pathankot.

Aviation. The state has no airport, but Chandigarh is on its southern boundary.

JUSTICE. The state has its own High Court at Simla.

JAMMU AND KASHMIR

HISTORY. The state of Jammu and Kashmir, which had earlier been under Hindu rulers and Moslem sultans, became part of the Mogul Empire under Akbar from 1586. After a period of Afghan rule from 1756, it was annexed to the Sikh kingdom of the Punjab in 1819. In 1820 Ranjit Singh made over the territory of Jammu to Gulab Singh. After the decisive battle of Sobraon in 1846 Kashmir also was made over to Gulab Singh under the Treaty of Amritsar. British supremacy was recognized until the Indian Independence Act, 1947, when all states decided on accession to India or Pakistan. Kashmir asked for standstill agreements with both. Pakistan agreed, but India desired further discussion with the Government of Jammu and Kashmir State. In the meantime the state became subject to armed attack from the territory of Pakistan and the Maharajah acceded to India on 26 Oct. 1947, by signing the Instrument of Accession. India approached the UN in Jan. 1948; India–Pakistan conflict ended by ceasefire in Jan. 1949. Further conflict in 1965 was followed by the Tashkent Declaration on Jan. 1966. Following further hostilities between India and Pakistan a ceasefire came into effect on 17 Dec. 1971, followed by the Simla Agreement in July 1972, whereby a new line of control was delineated bilaterally through negotiations between India and Pakistan and came into force on 17 Dec. 1972.

AREA AND POPULATION. The state is in the extreme north and is bounded north by China, east by Tibet, south by Himachal Pradesh and Punjab and west by Pakistan. The area is 222,236 sq. km, of which about 78,932 sq. km is occupied by Pakistan and 42,735 sq. km by China; the population of the territory on the Indian side of the line, 1971 census, was 4,617,000. For the population of Srinagar and Jammu, *see* pp. 600–601. The official language is Urdu; other commonly spoken languages are Kashmiri, Dogri, Balti, Ladakhi, Pahari and Punjabi, of which 18·59% was urban.

CONSTITUTION AND GOVERNMENT. The Maharajah's son, Yuvraj Karan Singh, took over as Regent in 1950 and, on the ending of hereditary rule (17 Oct. 1952), was sworn in as Sadar-i-Riyasat. On his father's death (26 April 1961) Yuvraj Karan Singh was recognized as Maharajah by the Indian Government; he decided not to use the title while he was elected head of state.

The permanent Constitution of the state came into force in part on 17 Nov. 1956 and fully on 26 Jan. 1957. It is unique in Indian states in that the Governor is bound by the advice of the Chief Minister. There is a bicameral legislature; the Legislative Council has 36 members and the Legislative Assembly has 76, of which 24 are reserved for the Pakistan-occupied areas. The state of the parties in the Legislative Assembly in 1978 was: Congress, 10; National Conference, 48; Janata, 13; others, 5. Since the 1967 elections the 6 representatives of Jammu and Kashmir in the central House of the People are directly elected; there are 4 representatives in the Council of States. The Council of Ministers consists of 4 Ministers, 11 Ministers of State and 1 Chief Parliamentary Secretary with the status of Minister of State.

In Nov. 1977 measures were passed allowing detention for up to two years without stated reason, banning entry to certain areas and censoring the press.

Kashmir Province has 4 districts and Jammu Province has 6 districts; the frontier district of Ladakh is in the former. Srinagar is the summer and Jammu the winter capital.

Governor: L. K. Jha.

Chief Minister: Shaikh Mohammed Abdullah.

BUDGET. Budget estimates for 1976–77 show total revenue of Rs 1,01,92 lakhs, and expenditure of Rs 1,42,22 lakhs.

Total planning expenditure for 1976–77 was Rs 87,93 lakhs, of which Rs 11,16 lakhs were allocated to agriculture and allied programmes, Rs 37,63 lakhs to irrigation and power, Rs 550 lakhs to industry and mining, Rs 13,79 lakhs to transport and communication, Rs 15,14 lakhs to social and community services and Rs 4,35 lakhs to the development of backward areas.

Per capita annual income, 1973–74, was Rs 309,53.

ENERGY AND NATURAL RESOURCES

Electricity. Installed capacity (1974) 83 mw.

Agriculture. About 77% of the population are supported by agriculture. Rice, wheat, maize, barley, bajra and jawar are the major cereals. The total area under crops (1976) was estimated at 2,256,000 acres. Total foodgrains produced, 1975–76, 1m. quintals. The size of units has been limited to 12 standard acres—the standard acre being determined by soil fertility, availability of irrigation, etc. Fruit is important; exports (1975–76), 230,000 tonnes.

Livestock (1972 census): Cattle, 1,791,000; buffaloes, 493,000; sheep, 1,072,000; goats, 569,000; horses, 60,000, and poultry, 1,654,000.

Forestry. Forests cover about one-eighth of the area of the state, forming an important source of revenue, besides providing employment to a large section of the population. About 7,480 sq. km of forests yield valuable timber; output in 1974–75 was 362,320 cu. metres. Most forests yield medicinal drugs.

INDUSTRY. The chief industry is tourism, and after that sericulture, which dates back to the 16th century. It employs about 45,000 people. There are 25 main industrial units, 19 in the public sector. Of these, 18 are run by Jammu and Kashmir Minerals Ltd and Jammu and Kashmir Industries Ltd.

COMMUNICATIONS

Roads. Kashmir is linked with the rest of India by the motorable Jammu–Pathankot road. The Jawahar Tunnel, through the Banihal mountain, connects Srinagar and Jammu, and maintains road communication with the Kashmir Valley during the winter months. In 1976 there were 7,874 km of roads.

Railways. Kashmir was linked with the Indian railway system on 3 Dec. 1972 when the line between Jammu and Pathankot was opened.

Aviation. Major airports, with daily service from Delhi, are at Srinagar and Jammu. Srinagar airport accommodates jet aircraft and is linked with international routes *via* Delhi and Kábul.

Post. There were 890 post offices in 1967. In 1975 there were 51 telephone exchanges and approximately 10,000 private telephones. There is direct dialling between Srinagar, Jammu and Delhi.

JUSTICE, RELIGION, EDUCATION AND WELFARE

Justice. The High Court, at Srinagar and Jammu, has a Chief Justice and 4 puisne judges.

Religion. The majority of the population, except in Jammu, are Moslems. At the 1971 census Moslems numbered 3,040,129; Hindus, 1,404,292; Sikhs, 105,873; Buddhists, 57,956; Christians, 7,182; Jains, 1,150.

Education. The proportion of literates was 18·63% in 1972. Education is free. There are 8,246 schools and about 600,000 children attend. Jammu and Srinagar Universities (founded 1948) have 31 teaching departments and 40 affiliated colleges (1972). There are 2 medical colleges, an engineering college, 1 agricultural college, 2 polytechnics, 2 fine art colleges, 1 commercial college and an Ayurvedic college.

Health. In 1975 there were 35 hospitals, 273 primary health units and centres, about 620 clinics and dispensaries, and 307 mobile medical units. There were 1,334 doctors. Expenditure on health *per capita* was Rs 14·75 in 1973.

Bamzai, P. N. K., *A History of Kashmir*. Delhi, 1962
Birdwood, Lord, *Two Nations and Kasmir*. London, 1956
Gupta, S., *Kashmir: A Study in India–Pakistan Relations*. London, 1967
Khan, S. M. I., *The Kashmir Saga*. Lahore, 1965
Korbel, J., *Danger in Kasmir*. Rev. ed. Princeton Univ. Press, 1966

KARNATAKA

HISTORY. The state of Karnataka, constituted as Mysore under the States Reorganization Act, 1956, brought together the Kannada-speaking people distributed in 5 states, and consisted of the territories of the old states of Mysore and Coorg, the Bijapur, Kanara and Dharwar districts and the Belgaum district (except one taluk) in former Bombay, the major portions of the Gulbarga, Raichur and Bidar districts in former Hyderabad, and South Kanara district (apart from the Kasaragod taluk) and the Kollegal taluk of the Coimbatore district in Madras. The state was renamed Karnataka in 1973.

AREA AND POPULATION. The state is in south India and is bounded north by Maharashtra, east by Andhra Pradesh, south by Tamil Nadu and Kerala, west by the Indian Ocean and northeast by Goa. The area of the state is 191,773 sq. km, and its population (1971 census), 29,299,014, an increase of 24·07% since 1961. Kannada is the language of administration and is spoken by about 60% of the people. Other languages include Telugu (8·7%), Urdu (8·6%), Marathi (4·5%), Tamil (3·6%), Tulu and Konkani. Principal cities, *see* pp. 600–601.

CONSTITUTION AND GOVERNMENT. Karnataka has a bicameral legislature. The Legislative Council has 63 members. The Legislative Assembly consists of 223 elected members and 1 nominated member. Seats in spring 1978: Indira Congress, 149; Janata, 59; Congress, 3; Communist Party of India, 3; independents and others, 10.

The state has 19 districts (of which Coorg is one) in 4 divisions: Bangalore, Mysore, Belgaum and Gulbarga. The capital is Bangalore.

Governor: Govind Narain.
Chief Minister: D. D. Urs.

BUDGET. Budget estimates for 1976–77 showed total revenue of Rs 513·94 crores; expenditure 499·78 crores.

ENERGY AND NATURAL RESOURCES

Electricity. In 1975–76 the state's power stations generated 966·6m. kwh. of electricity.

Water. About 1·26m. hectares were irrigated in 1976.

Minerals. Karnataka has India's only sources of gold; production, 1975, 2,824 kg, about 65% of which came from the Kolar Gold Fields and the remainder from those at Hutti; about 30,000 men are employed in the goldfields. Production of other minerals in 1975 included iron ore, 3,825,493 tonnes; manganese ore, 464,806 tonnes, and silver, 224 kg.

Agriculture. Agriculture forms the main occupation of more than three-quarters of the population. Physically, Karnataka divides itself into four regions—the coastal region, the southern and northern 'maidan' or plain country, comprising roughly the districts of Bangalore, Tumkur, Chitaldrug, Kolar, Bellary, Mandya and Mysore, and the 'malnad' or hill country, comprising the districts of Chickmagalur, Hassan and Shimoga. Rainfall is heavy in the 'malnad' tracts, and in this area there is dense forest. The greater part of the 'maidan' country is cultivated. Coorg district is essentially agricultural.

In 1975–76, 7·48m. hectares were under foodgrains (production, 5·53m. tonnes); other crops included oilseeds (950,000 tonnes), cotton (700,000 bales of 180 kg), chillies, tobacco, sugar-cane and rubber. Yield of raw rubber from 1,120 hectares, 2 tonnes per day. There were, in 1977, 956,040 hectares under cotton, 957,855 under groundnuts, 1·2m. under rice, 2m. under jowar, 9·78m. under ragi and 529,528 under maize.

Livestock (1977): Buffaloes, 3,215,873; other cattle, 10,018,714; sheep, 662,420; goats, 726,016.

Forestry. Total forest area in the state (1976) is 2,875,623 hectares, producing sandalwood, bamboo and other timbers, and ivory.

INDUSTRY. The Visvesvaraya Iron and Steel Works is situated at Bhadravarti, while at Bangalore are national undertakings for the manufacture of aircraft, machine tools, light engineering and electronics goods. Other industries include textiles, cement, chemicals, sugar, paper, porcelain and soap. In addition, much of the world's sandalwood is processed, the oil being one of the most valuable productions of the state. Sericulture is a more important cottage industry giving employment, directly or indirectly, to perhaps 1m. persons; production in 1974 was about 2m. kg of silk, nearly half the Indian total. Industrial production, 1972 (tonnes): Iron, 180,637; steel, 290,307; paper, 71,618; cement, 1·2m. and sugar, 254,000.

COMMUNICATIONS

Roads. In 1977 the state had 89,496 km of roads.

Railways. In 1976 there were 2,803 km of railway (including 154 km of narrow gauge) in the state.

Aviation. There are airports at Bangalore, Mangalore and Belgaum, with regular scheduled services to Bombay, Calcutta, Delhi and Madras.

Shipping. Mangalore is a deep-water port for the export of mineral ores. Karwar is being developed as an intermediate port.

JUSTICE, RELIGION AND EDUCATION

Justice. The seat of the High Court is at Bangalore. It has a Chief Justice and 11 puisne judges.

Religion. At the 1971 census Hindus numbered 25,332,388; Moslems, 3,113,298; Christians, 613,026; Jains, 218,862; Buddhists, 114,139; Sikhs, 6,830.

Education. The proportion of literates to the total population, according to the 1971 census, was 31·52% (males, 41·62%; females, 20·97%). In 1977 the state had 33,137 primary schools, 2,326 high schools, 314 schools for professional and technical education and 30 polytechnic and engineering schools. Education is free up to pre-university level.

The University of Mysore (founded in 1916) at Mysore has 3 university colleges at Mysore and 134 affiliated colleges. Karnatak University (1950) at Dharwar has 4 constituent colleges and 95 affiliated colleges. Bangalore University (1964) has 46 constituent colleges, the University of Agricultural Sciences, Hebbal, Bangalore, (1964) has 3 constituent colleges. The Indian Institute of Science, Bangalore, is unaffiliated; it conducts diploma courses in engineering, metallurgy and technology. There are 415 other colleges, including medical, law and commercial.

Learmouth, A. T. A., and Bhat, L. T., *Mysore State.* 2 vols. London, 1961–62
Prakasa, Rao, V. L. S., *Towns of Mysore State.* London, 1964

KERALA

HISTORY. The state of Kerala, created under the States Reorganization Act, 1956, consists of the previous state of Travancore–Cochin, except for 4 taluks of the Trivandrum district and a part of the Shencottah taluk of Quilon district. It took over the Malabar district (apart from the Laccadive and Minicoy Islands) and the Kasaragod taluk of South Kanara (apart from the Amindivi Islands) from Madras State.

AREA AND POPULATION. Kerala is in south Indian and is bounded north by Karnataka, east and southeast by Tamil Nadu, southwest and west by the Indian Ocean. The state has an area of 38,855 sq. km. The 1971 census showed a population of 21,347,375; density of population was 549 per sq. km (highest of any state). Population of principal cities, *see* pp. 600–601.

Languages spoken in the state are Malayalam, Tamil and Kannada.

The physical features of the land fall into three well-marked divisions: (1) the hilly tracts undulating from the Western Ghats in the east and marked by long spurs, extensive ravines and dense forests; (2) the cultivated plains intersected by numerous rivers and streams; and (3) the coastal belt with dense coconut plantations and rice fields.

CONSTITUTION AND GOVERNMENT. The state has a unicameral legislature of 140 members including the Speaker. The state of the parties in Oct. 1977 was: United Front, 111 (of which, Congress, 38) and opposition alliance, 29 (of which, Communist Party of India (Marxist), 17).

The state has 11 districts. The capital is Trivandrum.

Governor: N. N. Wanchoo.
Chief Minister: A. K. Antony.

BUDGET. Budget estimates for 1975–76 showed total revenue of Rs 2,95,29·09 lakhs, and expenditure of Rs 3,16,26·35 lakhs. Receipts included: Taxes on income except corporation tax, Rs 21,56·43 lakhs; state excise, Rs 15,20 lakhs; stamps and registration fees, Rs 12,25·57 lakhs; sales tax, Rs 76,81 lakhs; vehicles taxes, Rs 873·50 lakhs; land revenue, Rs 2,86·78 lakhs; tax on electricity, Rs 3,20 lakhs; tax on goods and passengers, Rs 4,40 lakhs. Expenditure included: Education, Rs 1,17,77·97 lakhs; medical, Rs 21,80 lakhs; police, Rs 14,10·97 lakhs; industries, Rs 2,05·92 lakhs. Annual Plan expenditure, 1974–75, Rs 73·68 crores.

ENERGY AND NATURAL RESOURCES

Electricity. Installed capacity (1974), 621,500 kw.; energy generated in 1973–74 was 2,510·5m. kw., mainly by the Sabaragiri, the Sengulam, the Neriamaugalam, the Poringalkuthu and the Pallivasal hydro-electric schemes. A hydro-electric scheme at Idukki has been built at a cost of Rs 110 crores for commissioning in Jan. 1976.

Minerals. Next to Bihar, Kerala possesses the widest variety of economic mineral resources among the Indian States. The beach sands of Kerala contain monazite, ilmenite, rutile, zircon, sillimanite, etc. There are extensive white-clay deposits; other minerals of commercial importance include mica, graphite, limestone, quartz sand and lignite.

Agriculture. The chief agricultural products of the state are rice, tapioca, coconut, arecanut, oilseeds, pepper, sugar-cane, rubber, tea, coffee and cardamom. About 98% of Indian black pepper and about 95% of Indian rubber is produced in Kerala. Area and production of principal crops, 1973–74 (1,000 hectares and 1,000 tonnes): Rice, 874·7, 1,257; black pepper, 118, 27; ginger (dry), 12, 26; arecanut, 90·7, 13,459 (million nuts); bananas and other plantains, 46·7, 354; cashewnuts, 103·3, 116; coconuts, 744·3, 3,703 (million nuts); tea, 37·7, 48; coffee, 35·8, 15·5; rubber, 199·6, 118; tapioca, 306·4, 5,660; cardamom, 47·5, 1·5.

Livestock (1972, provisional); Buffaloes, 469,515; other cattle, 2,855,856; sheep, 10,390; goats, 1,450,587.

Forestry. About a third of the area is comprised of forests, including teak, sandalwood, ebony and black-wood and varieties of softwood. Forest revenue, 1973–74, Rs 11·26 crores, from timber, bamboos, reeds and ivory.

Fisheries. Fishing is a flourishing industry; the annual catch is about 470,000 tonnes.

INDUSTRIES. Most of the major industrial concerns are either owned or sponsored by the Government. The Government owns 11 industrial concerns and has substantial shares in more than 40. Among the privately owned factories are the numerous cashew and coir factories. Other important factory industries are rubber, tea, tiles, oil, textiles, ceramics, fertilizers and chemicals, sugar, cement, rayon, glass, matches, pencils, monazite, ilmenite, titanium oxide, rare earths, aluminium, electrical goods, paper, shark-liver oil, etc.

The number of factories registered under the Factories Act 1948 on 31 Dec. 1972 was 3,487, with daily average employment of 226,088.

Among the cottage industries, coir-spinning and handloom-weaving are the most important, forming the means of livelihood of a large section of the people. Other industries are the village oil industry, ivory carving, furniture-making, bell metal, brass and copper ware, leather goods, screw-pines, mat-making, rattan work, bee-keeping, pottery, etc. These have been organized on a co-operative basis.

COMMUNICATIONS

Roads. In 1970 there were 14,735 km of roads in the state; national highways, 448 km; state highways, 2,144 km; major district roads, 5,143 km. Total for 1973, 18,432 km, of which 15,123 was surfaced.

Railways. There is a coastal line from Mangalore (Karnataka) which serves Mahe, Kozhikode, Ernakulam (for Cochin) and Quilon, and connects them with main towns in Tamil Nadu.

Aviation. There are airports at Cochin and Trivandrum with regular scheduled services to Bombay and Madras.

Shipping. Port Cochin, administered by the central government, is one of India's 6 major ports. There are 10 other ports and harbours.

JUSTICE, RELIGION AND EDUCATION

Justice. The High Court at Ernakulam has a Chief Justice and 11 puisne judges and 4 additional judges.

Religion. At the 1971 census Hindus numbered 12,683,277; Christians, 4,494,089; Moslems, 4,162,718; Jains, 3,336.

Education. Kerala is the most literate Indian State—60·42% at the 1971 census. Education is free up to the age of 14.

In 1974–75 there was a total school enrolment of 5·35m. students. There were 44 primary schools, 7 high schools per lakh of population.

Kerala University (established 1937) at Trivandrum, is affiliating and teaching; in 1974 it had 57 affiliated arts and science colleges, 20 junior colleges and 25 affiliated professional colleges. The University of Cochin is federal, and for post-graduate studies only. The University of Calicut (established 1968) is teaching and affiliating and has 65 affiliated colleges. Kerala Agricultural University (established 1971) has 3 constituent colleges.

Mankekar, D. R., *The Red Riddle of Kerala*. Bombay, 1966
Pillai, V. R., and Panikar, P. G. K., *Land Reclamation in Kerala*. London, 1965
Woodcock, G., *Kerala*. London, 1968

MADHYA PRADESH

HISTORY. Under the provisions of the States Reorganization Act, 1956, the State of Madhya Pradesh was formed on 1 Nov. 1956. It consists of the 17 Hindi districts of the previous state of that name, the former state of Madhya Bharat (except the Sunel enclave of Mandsaur district), the former state of Bhopal and Vindhya Pradesh and the Sironj subdivision of Kotah district, which was an enclave of Rajasthan in Madhya Pradesh.

For information on the former states, *see* THE STATESMAN'S YEAR-BOOK, 1958, pp. 180–84.

AREA AND POPULATION. The state is in central India and is bounded north by Rajasthan and Uttar Pradesh, east by Bihar and Orissa, south by Andhra Pradesh and Maharashtra, west by Gujarat. Madhya Pradesh is the largest Indian state in size, with an area of 442,841 sq. km. In respect of population it ranks seventh. Population (1971 census), 41,654,119, an increase of 28·04% since 1961.

Cities with over 100,000 population, *see* pp. 600–601.

The number of persons speaking each of the more prevalent languages (1971 census) were: Hindi, 32,873,079; Urdu, 988,275; Marathi, 1,385,952; Gujarati, 155,723.

CONSTITUTION AND GOVERNMENT. Madhya Pradesh is one of the 9 states for which the Constitution provides a bicameral legislature, but the Vidhan Parishad or Upper House (to consist of 90 members) has yet to be formed. The Vidhan Sabha or Lower House has 320 elected members. The state of the parties after the elections of June 1977 was: Janata, 230; Congress, 84; independents, 6.

For administrative purposes the state has been split into 11 divisions with a Commissioner at the head of each; the headquarters of these are located at Bhopal, Bilaspur, Gwalior (2), Hoshangabad, Indore, Jabalpur, Raipur, Rewa, Sagar and Ujjain. There are 45 districts, each under a Collector, 190 tehsils, 6 municipal corporations and 181 municipalities.

The seat of government is at Bhopal.

Governor: N. N. Wanchoo.
Chief Minister: Kailash Joshi.

BUDGET. Budget estimates for 1977–78 showed total revenue of Rs 6,91,59·22 lakhs, and expenditure of Rs 6,10,66·43 lakhs. Receipts included: Contributions and adjustments between central and state governments, Rs 1,65,87·84 lakhs; taxes on income, Rs 55,00 lakhs; state excise, Rs 40,50 lakhs; stamps and registration, Rs 13,57 lakhs; forests, Rs 99,06 lakhs; sales tax, Rs 1,50·41 lakhs; vehicles taxes, Rs 39,01 lakhs; debt services, Rs 34,00·36 lakhs; civil administration, Rs 14,92·49 lakhs; land revenue, Rs 12,69·81 lakhs. Expenditure included: Education, Rs 1,23,48·54 lakhs; public works and improvements, Rs 32,84·93 lakhs; irrigation, embankment, etc., Rs 12,97·60 lakhs; medical, and public health, Rs 66,64·82 lakhs; police, Rs 37,05·21 lakhs; agriculture, Rs 25,28·16 lakhs; general administration, Rs 12,92·09 lakhs; debt services, Rs 56,37·78 lakhs; community projects and local development, Rs 13,63·64 lakhs; industries, Rs 5,34·57 lakhs; forests, Rs 52,29·03 lakhs; social security and welfare, Rs 35,81·32 lakhs.

ENERGY AND NATURAL RESOURCES

Electricity. Madhya Pradesh is rich in low-grade coal suitable for power generation, and also has immense potential hydro-electric energy. The present installed capacity is 1,012·5 mw; of this 819·50 mw is from thermal and 193 mw from hydro-electric power stations. The thermal power stations are at Korba in Bilaspur district, Amarkantak in Shahdol district and Satpura in Betul district; new stations are being built. The only hydro-electric power station is at Gandhi Sagar lake in Mandsaur district; this, with a maximum water surface of 165 sq. miles, is the biggest man-made lake in Asia.

Water. Major irrigation projects include the Chambal Valley scheme (started in 1952 with Rajasthan) which irrigates some 700,000 acres, the Tawa project in Hoshangabad district (750,000 acres), the Barna and Hasdeo schemes, the Mahanadi canal system (140,000) and schemes under construction (Bargi, Narmadasagar, and Bansagar). Up to the end of the Fourth Plan period works by the State had an irrigation potential of 12·46 lakh hectares. Target for the Fifth Plan, a further 8·77.

Minerals. The state has extensive mineral deposits including coal, iron ore and manganese, bauxite, ochre, sillimanite, limestone, dolomite, rock phosphate, copper, lead, tin, fluorite, barytes, china clay and fireclay, corundum, gold, diamonds, pyrophyllite and diaspore, lepidolite, asbestos, vermiculite, mica, glass sand, quartz, felspars, bentonite and building stone.

In 1972 the output of major minerals was (in tonnes): coal, 13,988m.; china clay, 14,565; limestone, 4,698; ochre, 22,585; dolomite, 512,871; fireclay, 1,277; quartz corundum, 201; diamonds, 20,009 carats; bauxite, 238,479m.; iron ore, 2,001m.; manganese ore, 237,844.

Agriculture. Agriculture is the mainstay of the state's economy and 83% of the people depend on it. Over 42% of the land area is cultivable, of which 9·6% is irrigated. The Malwa region abounds in rich black cotton soil, the low-lying areas of Gwalior, Bundelkhand and Baghelkhand and the Chhatisgarh plains have a lighter sandy soil, while the Narmada valley is formed of deep rich alluvial deposits. Production of principal crops, 1975–76 (tonnes): Foodgrains, 12m.; sugar-cane, 247,000; oilseeds, 846,000, and cotton, 272,000 bales (of 180 kg).

Livestock (1977 census): Buffaloes, 5,852,549; other cattle, 34,256,725; sheep, 968,595; goats, 6,573,467; horses and ponies, 121,908.

Forestry. Nearly 35% of the state's area is covered by forests. The forests are chiefly of sal, babul, salai, dhavra, tendu, mahua, bamboo, teak, anjan and harra. They are the chief source in India of best-quality teak.

INDUSTRY. The major industries are the steel plant at Bhilai, Bharat Heavy Electricals at Bhopal, the aluminium plant at Korba, the security paper mills at Hoshangabad, the Bank Note Press at Dewas, the newsprint mill at Nepanagar and alkaloid factory at Neemuch, cement factory at Mandhar, vehicle factory, ordnance factory, and gun carriage factory. There are also 20 textile mills, 7 of them nationalized.

The Bhilai steel plant near Durg is one of the 6 major steel mills. A power station at Korba (Bilaspur) with a capacity of 420 mw serves Bhilai, the aluminium plant and the Korba coalfield.

The heavy electricals factory was set up by the Government of India at Bhopal during the second-plan period. This is India's first heavy electrical equipment factory and also one of the largest of its type in Asia. It makes a variety of highly complicated equipment required for generation, transmission, distribution and utilization of electric power.

Other industries include cement, sugar, straw board paper, vegetable oil, refractories, potteries, textile machinery, steel casting and rerolling, industrial gases, synthetic fibres, drugs, biscuit manufacturing, engineering, tools, rayon and art silk. The number of heavy and medium industries in the State is 168 and the number of small-scale industries in production is 18,636. Thirty-six out of forty-five districts in the state are categorized as industrially backward districts.

The main industrial development agencies are Madhya Pradesh Financial Corporation, Madhya Pradesh Audyogik Vikas Nigam Ltd, Madhya Pradesh State

Industries Corporation, Madhya Pradesh Laghu Udyog Nigam, Madhya Pradesh State Textile Corporation, Madhya Pradesh Handicrafts Board, Khadi and Village Industries Board and Madhya Pradesh State Mining Corporation.

The state is known for its traditional village and home crafts such as handloom weaving, best developed at Chanderi and Maheshwar, toys, pottery, lace work, woodwork and metal utensils. The ancillary industries of dyeing, calico printing and bleaching are centred in areas of textile production.

COMMUNICATIONS

Roads. Total length of roads in 1977 was 50,748·76 km, of which 38,101·5 km were surfaced.

Railways. Bhopal, Bilaspur, Katni, Khandwar and Ratlam are important junctions for the central and northern networks.

Aviation. There are airports at Bhopal, Indore, Jabalpur, Khajuraho and Raipur with regular scheduled services to Bombay, Calcutta and Delhi.

JUSTICE, RELIGION AND EDUCATION

Justice. The High Court of Judicature at Jabalpur has a Chief Justice and 17 puisne judges.

Religion. At the 1961 census Hindus numbered 30,425,798; Sikhs, 65,715; Moslems, 1,317,617; Jains, 247,927; Buddhists, 113,365; Christians, 188,314.

Education. The 1971 census showed 22·3% of the population to be literate. Education is free for children aged up to 14.

In 1975–76 there were 355 higher educational institutions. Primary schools (1974–75) had 3·5m. pupils and higher secondary schools, 620,897 pupils.

There are 10 universities in Madhya Pradesh: the University of Sagar (established 1946), at Sagar, had 53 affiliated colleges and 26,516 students in 1975; Jabalpur University (1957) had 30 affiliated colleges and 12,962 students; Vikram University (1957), at Ujjain, had 46 affiliated colleges and 38,011 students; Indira Kala Sangeet Vishwavidyalaya (1956), at Khairagarh, had 9 affiliated colleges and 1,164 students on roll (this university teaches music and fine arts); Indore University (1964) had 21 affiliated colleges and 22,915 students; Jivagi University (1963), at Gwalior, had 43 affiliated colleges and 31,462 students; Jawaharlal Nehru Krishi University (1964), at Jabalpur, had 9 affiliated colleges and 2,274 students in 1964; Ravishankar University (1964), at Raipur, had 63 affiliated colleges and 41,607 students. In 1975–76 there were 256 degree-granting colleges, 19 teacher-training colleges, and 71 professional colleges including polytechnics.

MAHARASHTRA

HISTORY. Under the States Reorganization Act, 1956, Bombay State was formed by merging the states of Kutch and Saurashtra and the Marathi-speaking areas of Hyderabad (commonly known as Marathwada) and Madhya Pradesh (also called Vidarbha) in the old state of Bombay, after the transfer from that state of the Kannada-speaking areas of the Belgaum, Bijapur, Kanara and Dharwar districts which were added to the state of Mysore, and the Abu Road taluka of Banaskantha district, which went to the state of Rajasthan.

By the Bombay Reorganization Act, 1960, which came into force 1 May 1960, 17 districts (predominantly Gujarati-speaking) in the north and west of Bombay State became the new state of Gujarat, and the remainder was renamed Maharashtra.

The state of Maharashtra consists of the following districts of the former Bombay State: Ahmednagar, Akola, Amravati, Aurangabad, Bhandara, Bhir, Buldana, Chanda, Dhulia (West Khandesh), Greater Bombay, Jalgaon (East Khandesh), Kolaba, Kolhapur, Nagpur, Nanded, Nasik, Osmanabad, Parbhani, Pune, Ratnagiri, Sangli, Satara, Sholapur, Thana, Wardha, Yeotmal; certain portions of Thana and Dhulia districts have become part of Gujarat.

AREA AND POPULATION. Maharashtra is in central India and is bounded north and east by Madhya Pradesh, south by Andhra Pradesh, Karnataka and Goa, west by the Indian Ocean and northwest by Daman and Gujarat. The state has an area of 307,762 sq. km. The population at the 1971 census was 50,412,235 (an increase of 27·45% since 1961), of whom about 30m. were Marathi-speaking. The area of Greater Bombay was 603 sq. km. and its population 5,970,575. For other principal cities, *see* pp. 600–601.

CONSTITUTION AND GOVERNMENT. Maharashtra has a bicameral legislature. The Legislative Council has 78 members. The Legislative Assembly has 287 elected members and 1 member nominated by the Governor to represent the Anglo-Indian community.

The Council of Ministers consists of the Chief Minister, 13 other Ministers, 12 Ministers of State and 5 Deputy Ministers.

Following the elections of Feb. 1978 the state of the parties in the Legislative Assembly was: Janata, 99; Congress, 69; Indira Congress, 62; others, 58.

The capital is Bombay.

Governor: Sadiq Ali.
Chief Minister: V. B. Patil.

BUDGET. Budget estimates, 1976–77, showed total revenue of Rs 11,21,74 lakhs; expenditure, Rs 10,53,59 lakhs. Receipts included: taxes, Rs 78,299 lakhs; non-tax revenue, Rs 33,875 lakhs. Expenditure included: Education, Rs 204,17 lakhs; housing and urban development, Rs 27,54 lakhs; medical and public health, Rs 82,73 lakhs; agriculture and community development, Rs 1,91,35 lakhs; general administration, Rs 1,37,02 lakhs; debt services, Rs 1,19,90 lakhs; industries and minerals, Rs 468 lakhs.

Capital expenditure on development, 1976–77: Agriculture and allied services, Rs 228 lakhs; industries and minerals, Rs 578 lakhs; water and power development, Rs 86,51 lakhs; schemes for transport and communications, Rs 10,79 lakhs; public health, Rs 809 lakhs.

AGRICULTURE. Area (in 1,000 hectares) and production (in 1,000 tonnes) of principal crops in 1973–74: Rice, 1,351, 1,637; wheat, 965, 547; jowar, 6,088, 2,819; bajri, 2,215, 850; total cereals, 11,091, 6,177; total pulses, 2,762, 868; total foodgrains, 13,853, 7,045; sugar-cane, 215 (of gur, 1,544); groundnuts, 758, 566; cotton, 2,348 (1,058 bales of 180 kg).

Livestock (1972 census): Buffaloes, 3,300,746; other cattle, 14,705,147; sheep, 2,128,036; goats, 5,910,554; horses and ponies, 58,287; poultry, 12,216,567.

INDUSTRY. The number of factories on 31 Dec. 1974 was 10,975 employing (daily average) 1,038,868 workers.

The textile industry is dominant in production. On 31 Dec. 1974 there were 123 cotton textile (spinning and composite) mills with an average daily employment of about 158,703 workers. There are 26 woollen mills employing about 6,158. There are 74 sugar mills employing about 27,364 workers daily, 775 chemical factories employing about 82,967, and in engineering there are 1,079 factories employing about 86,341 workers.

COMMUNICATIONS

Roads. On 31 March 1975 there were 89,007 km of roads, of which 41,484 km were surfaced. Passenger and freight transport has been nationalized.

Railways. The total length of railway is about 5,162 km. The main junctions and termini are Bombay, Manmad, Akola, Nagpur, Pune and Sholapur.

Aviation. The main airport is Bombay, which has national and international flights. Nagpur airport is on the route from Bombay to Calcutta and there are also airports at Pune and Aurangabad.

Shipping. Maharashtra has a coastline of 720 km. Bombay is the major port, and there are 42 minor ports.

JUSTICE, RELIGION AND EDUCATION

Justice. The High Court has a Chief Justice and 27 judges. There are 8 additional judges. The seat of the High Court is Bombay, but it has a bench at Nagpur.

Religion. At the 1961 census Hindus numbered 32,530,901; Moslems, 3,034,332; Buddhists, 2,789,501; Christians, 560,594; Jains, 485,672; Sikhs, 57,617.

Education. The proportion of literates to the total population, according to the 1971 census, was 39·08% (males, 51·3%; females, 25·9%).

The total number of recognized institutions in 1975 was 56,656, with 10,528,258 students. Higher and secondary schools numbered 6,579 with 2,986,636 pupils; primary schools, 48,018, with 7,367,045 pupils; pre-primary schools, 827 with 62,781.

Bombay University, founded in 1857, is mainly an affiliating university. It has 99 constituent colleges and 21 post-graduate departments in Bombay with a total (1975–76) of 137,922 students. Colleges in Goa can affiliate to Bombay University. Nagpur University (1923) is both teaching and affiliating. In addition to the 26 post-graduate departments there were (1975–76) 140 affiliated colleges and constituent colleges with 87,153 students. Pune University, founded in 1948, is teaching and affiliating; in 1975–76 it had 103 affiliated colleges and constituent colleges, 26 post-graduate departments and a total of 88,232 students. The SNDT Women's University had, in 1975–76, 16 constituent colleges and affiliated colleges with a total of 9,911 students. Marathwada University, Aurangabad, was founded in 1958 as a teaching and affiliating body to control colleges in the Marathwada or Marathi-speaking area, previously under Osmania University; in 1975–76 there were 82 affiliated and constituent colleges and 6 post-graduate departments and 71,419 students. Shiwaji University, Kolhapur, was established in 1963 to control affiliated colleges previously under Pune University. In 1975–76 it had 84 affiliated and constituent colleges and 14 post-graduate departments and 65,526 students. There are 4 agricultural universities with 16 affiliated colleges and 6,114 students in 1975–76.

There were altogether 682 institutions for higher education in 1975–76, with 474,067 students.

Statistical Information: The Director of Publicity, Sachivalaya, Bombay.

Annual Statistical Abstract (from 1951)

State Library: Central Library, Town Hall, Bombay.

MANIPUR

HISTORY. Formerly a state under the political control of the Government of India, Manipur, on 15 Aug. 1947, entered into interim arrangements with the Indian Union and the political agency was abolished. The administration was taken over by the Government of India on 15 Oct. 1949 under a merger agreement, and it is centrally administered by the Government of India through a Chief Commissioner. In 1950–51 an Advisory form of Government was introduced. In 1957 this was replaced by a Territorial Council of 33 elected and 2 nominated members. Later in 1963 a Legislative Assembly of 30 elected and 3 nominated members was established under the Government of Union Territories Act 1963. Because of the unstable party position in the Assembly, it had to be dissolved on 16 Oct. 1969 and President's Rule introduced. The status of the administrator was raised from Chief Commissioner to Lieut.-Governor with effect from 19 Dec. 1969. On the 21 Jan. 1972 Manipur became a state and the status of the administrator was changed from Lieut.-Governor to Governor.

AREA AND POPULATION. The state is in northeast India and is bounded north by Nagaland, east by Burma, south by Burma and Mizoram, and west by Assam. Manipur has an area of 22,356 sq. km and a population (1971) of 1,072,753. Density, 48 per sq. km. The valley, which is about 1,813 sq. km, is 2,600 ft above sea-level. The hills rise in places to nearly 10,000 ft, but are mostly about 5,000–6,000 ft. The average annual rainfall is 65 in. The hill areas are inhabited by various hill tribes who constitute about one-third of the total population of the state. There are about 40 tribes and sub-tribes falling into two main groups of Nagas and Kukis. A large number of dialects are spoken, while Hindi is gradually becoming prevalent.

CONSTITUTION AND GOVERNMENT. With the attainment of statehood, Manipur has a Legislative Assembly of 60 members, of which 19 are from reserved tribal constituencies. The leading party in the Assembly is the Janata party. There are 5 districts. Capital, Imphal (population, 1971, 100,366).

Governor: L. P. Singh.
Chief Minister: Y. Shaiza.

BUDGET. Revised estimates for 1969–70 show revenue of Rs 1,89·06 lakhs and expenditure on revenue account of Rs 14,41·73 lakhs.

ENERGY AND NATURAL RESOURCES

Electricity. Installed capacity, 1973–74, 7·6 mw. There were 214 villages with electricity.

Agriculture. Rice is the principal crop; production, 1972–73, 169,800 tonnes from 238,600 hectares. Total foodgrains, 1973–74, 198,000 tonnes.

INDUSTRY. Handloom weaving is a popular industry. Many development schemes are in progress under the 5-year plans.

COMMUNICATIONS. A national highway from Kazirangar (Assam) runs through Imphal to the Burmese frontier. There are no railways. There is an airport at Imphal with regular scheduled services to Gauhati and Calcutta.

EDUCATION AND HEALTH

Education. In 1973–74 there were 1,199 primary schools, 455 middle schools, 123 high schools and 13 colleges. The number enrolled at the schools (1970) was 230,000.

Health. In 1973–74 there were 25 hospitals (including primary health centres) and 105 dispensaries (including primary health centres).

MEGHALAYA

HISTORY. The state was created under the Assam Reorganization (Meghalaya) Act 1969 and inaugurated on 2 April 1970. Its status was that of a state within the State of Assam until 21 Jan. 1972 when it became a fully independent State of the Union. It consists of the former Garo Hills district and United Khasi and Jaintia Hills district of Assam.

AREA AND POPULATION. Meghalaya is bounded north and east by Assam, south and west by Bangladesh. In 1971 (census figure) the area was 22,489 sq. km and the population 1,011,699. Density 45 per sq. km. The people are mainly of the Khasi, Jaintia and Garo tribes.

CONSTITUTION AND GOVERNMENT. Meghalaya has a unicameral legislature. The Legislative Assembly has 60 seats. State of the parties following elections in Feb. 1978: All-Party Hill Leaders' Conference, 16; Congress, 20; HSPDP, 14; independents, 10.

There are 2 districts. The capital is Shillong, shared at present with Assam.

Governor: L. P. Singh.
Chief Minister: Capt. W. Sangma.

BUDGET. The outlay on the 1971–72 annual plan was Rs 7·95 crores, with Rs 7·44 crores provided by central assistance. Allocations were: Agriculture, Rs 131 lakhs; transport and communications, Rs 337 lakhs; social services, Rs 161·5 lakhs; irrigation and power, Rs 43 lakhs; industry and mining, Rs 42·5 lakhs; co-operation and community development, Rs 40 lakhs.

ENERGY AND NATURAL RESOURCES

Electricity. The United Khasi and Jaintia Hills district produces coal, sillimanite (95% of India's total output), limestone, white clay and corundum. The state also has deposits of coal (estimated reserves 1,200m. tonnes), limestone (2,100m.), fire-clay (100,000) and sandstone which are virtually untapped because of transport difficulties.

Agriculture. About 80% of the people depend on agriculture, and 27% of the cultivable area is irrigated. Principal crops are potatoes, fresh fruit and cotton. Production 1971–72 (1,000 tonnes): Foodgrains, 137; potatoes, 71; tapioca, 5; tobacco (1971), 0·23; areca nuts (1971), 3; jute, 50,000 bales (of 180 kg); mesta (1971), 2,130 bales (of 180 kg). Annual production (1,000 tonnes, estimated) of pineapples, 70; oranges, 80; bananas, 35.

Forest products are the state's chief resources.

INDUSTRY. Apart from agriculture the main source of employment is the extraction and processing of minerals.

COMMUNICATIONS. A national highway from Gauhati (Assam) runs through Dispur and Shillong. The state has no railways. There is no airport but Gauhati airport is on the northern boundary.

JUSTICE. There is a High Court at Shillong which is common to Assam, Meghalaya, Nagaland, Manipur, Tripura and the Union Territories of Mizoram and Arunachal Pradesh.

NAGALAND

HISTORY. The territory was constituted by the Union Government in Sept. 1962. It comprises the former Naga Hills district of Assam and the former Tuensang Frontier division of the North-East Frontier Agency; these had been made a Centrally Administered Area in 1957, administered by the President through the Governor of Assam. In Jan. 1961 the area was renamed and given the status of a state of the Indian Union, which was officially inaugurated on 1 Dec. 1963.

For some years a section of the Naga leaders sought independence. Military operations from 1960 and the prospect of self-government within the Indian Union led to a general reconciliation, but rebel activity continued. A 2-month amnesty in mid-1963 had little effect. A 'ceasefire' in Sept. 1964 was followed by talks between a Government of India delegation and rebel leaders. The peace period was extended and the 'Revolutionary Government of Nagaland' (a breakaway group from the Naga Federal Government) was dissolved in 1973. Further talks with the Naga underground movement resulted in the Shillong Peace Agreement of Nov. 1975.

AREA AND POPULATION. The state is in the extreme north-east and is bounded west and north by Assam, east by Burma and south by Manipur. Nagaland has an area of 16,527 sq. km and a population (1971 census) of 516,449. Density 31 per sq. km. Towns include Kohima, Mokokchung, Tuensang and Dimapur. The chief tribes in numerical order are: Angami, Ao, Sema, Konyak, Chakhesang, Lotha, Phom, Khiamngan, Chang, Yimchunger, Zeliang-Kuki, Rengma and Sangtam.

CONSTITUTION AND GOVERNMENT. An Interim Body (Legislative Assembly) of 42 members elected by the Naga people and an Executive Council (Council of Ministers) of 5 members were formed in 1961, and continued until the State Assembly was elected in Jan. 1964. The initial strength of this Assembly was 46, with 8 cabinet ministers. Since 1974 there have been 60 members. The Cabinet comprises the Chief Minister, 5 Cabinet Ministers and 2 Deputy Ministers. The Governor has extraordinary powers, which include special responsibility for law and order. The state of the parties following elections in Nov. 1977: United Democratic Front, 35; Congress, 15; National Convention of Nagaland, 1; independent, 9.

The state has 7 districts (Kohima, Mon, Zunheboto, Wokha, Phek, Mokokchung and Tuensang). The capital is Kohima.

Governor: L. P. Singh.
Chief Minister: M. Vizol.

BUDGET. Budget estimates for 1974–75 show total revenue of Rs 47,43·32 lakhs and expenditure of Rs 47,53·19 lakhs. Receipts included: Statutory grant under the Finance Commission award, Rs 23,77 lakhs; share of central taxes and duties, Rs 117·18 lakhs; grants-in-aid for plan expenditure, Rs 640·80 lakhs; loans from the Government of India, Rs 71·20 lakhs; grant for roads, Rs 3,64·94 lakhs.

AGRICULTURE. More than 80% of the people derive their livelihood from agriculture. The Angamis, in Kohima district, practise a fixed agriculture in the shape of terraced slopes, and wet paddy cultivation in the lowlands. In the other two districts there is a traditional form of shifting cultivation (*jhumming*). About 1,223,000 hectares were under cultivation in 1977. Production of rice (1977) was 94,530 tonnes.

COMMUNICATIONS. There is a national highway from Kaziranga (Assam) to Kohima and on to Manipur. There are no railways, and no airports.

RELIGION. At the 1971 census Christians numbered 344,798; Hindus, 59,031; Islam, 2,966; others, 108. The Naga Baptist Christian Convention had, 1969, 632 churches and a total church membership of 73,500.

EDUCATION. The 1971 census records 27·4% literacy. In 1976 there were 2 government and 5 private colleges, 45 government and 41 private high schools, 171 government and 88 private middle schools and 916 lower primary schools, 1 polytechnic, 3 teacher-training schools and 151 adult literary centres.

Aram, M., *Peace in Nagaland*, New Delhi, 1974
Elwin, V., *Nagaland.* Shillong, 1961
Fürer-Haimendorf, C. von, *The Naked Nagas.* 2nd ed. Calcutta, 1962
Mankekar, D. R., *Slippery Slope of Nagaland.* New Delhi, 1965
Rattan, H. R., *Nagaland is Born.* Calcutta, 1964

ORISSA

HISTORY. Orissa, ceded to the Mahrattas by Alivardi Khan in 1751, was conquered by the British in 1803. In 1804 a board of 2 commissioners was appointed to administer the province, but in the following year it was designated the district of Cuttack and was placed in charge of a collector, judge and magistrate. In 1823 it was split up into 3 regulation districts of Cuttack, Balasore and Puri, and the non-regulation tributary states which were administered by their own chiefs under the ægis of the British Government. Angul, one of these tributary states, was annexed in 1847, and with the Khondmals, ceded in 1835 by the tributary chief of the Boudh state, constituted a separate non-regulation district. Sambalpur was transferred from the Central Provinces to Orissa in 1905. These districts formed an outlying tract of the Bengal Presidency till 1912, when they were transferred to Bihar, constituting one of its divisions under a commissioner. Orissa was constituted a separate province on 1 April 1936, some portions of the Central Provinces and Madras being transferred to the old Orissa division.

The rulers of 25 Orissa states surrendered all jurisdiction and authority to the Government of India on 1 Jan. 1948, on which date the Provincial Government took over the administration. The administration of 2 states, viz., Saraikella and Kharswan, was transferred to the Government of Bihar in May 1948. By an agreement with the Dominion Government, Mayurbhanj State was finally merged with the province on 1 Jan. 1949. By the States Merger (Governors' Provinces) Order, 1949, the states were completely merged with the state of Orissa on 19 Aug. 1949.

AREA AND POPULATION. Orissa is in eastern India and is bounded north by Bihar, north-east by West Bengal, east by the Bay of Bengal, south by Andhra Pradesh and west by Madhya Pradesh. The area of the state is 155,782 sq. km, and its population (1971 census), 21,944,615, density 141 per sq. km. The second-largest city next to Cuttack (*see* pp. 600–601) is Rourkela, with 90,287 inhabitants. The principal language is Oriya.

CONSTITUTION AND GOVERNMENT. The Legislative Assembly has 147 members. State of the parties after the elections of June 1977: Janata, 110; Congress, 26; independents, 9; others, 2.

The state consists of 17 districts, of which 4 are linked with other districts for administrative purposes.

The capital is Bhubaneswar (18 miles south of Cuttack).

Governor: A. A. Khan.
Chief Minister: N. Routray.

BUDGET. Budget estimates, 1968–69 showed total revenue of Rs 1,23,07·84 lakhs and expenditure of Rs 1,22,18·90 lakhs.

ENERGY AND NATURAL RESOURCES

Electricity. The Hirakud Dam Project on the river Mahanadi (started 1949) irrigates 1·8m. acres and has a scheduled capacity of 270,000 kw. The dam (the largest earth dam in the world) was completed in 1957. Hydro-electric power totalling 85,000 kw. is now serving Cuttack, Puri and Dhenkanal districts. The installed capacity of the Machkund hydro-electric project (financed jointly with Andhra Pradesh) is 114,750 kw. Total installed capacity, 1975, 914 mw. There were 11,868 electrified villages.

Minerals. The chief minerals are iron ore, manganese ore (about 20% of India's total), coal, limestone and dolomite. About 36,000 workers are employed in the mines. Mineral production, 1973, 11·5m. tonnes.

Agriculture. The cultivation of rice is the principal occupation of nearly 80% of the population. The area under paddy, 1969–70, was 4·5m. hectares and production amounted to 4·31m. tonnes; only a very small amount of other cereals is grown. Production of foodgrains (1973–74) totalled 5·5m. tonnes from 5·6m. hectares. Jute (500,000 bales (of 180 kg)), wheat (100,000 tonnes), oilseeds (200,000 tonnes) and sugar-cane (200,000 tonnes) are also grown. Turmeric is cultivated in the uplands of the districts of Ganjam, Phulbani and Koraput, and is exported.

Livestock (1961 census): Buffaloes, 1,075,000; other cattle, 9·81m.; sheep, 994,000; goats, 2,382,000; horses and ponies, 58,000.

Forests. Forests occupy about 43% of the area of the state, the most important species being sal.

Fisheries. There were, in 1974, 156 fishery co-operative societies.

INDUSTRY. Thirty-eight large industries have been set up, mostly based on minerals, including the steel plant of Hindustan Steel Ltd at Rourkela, a pig-iron plant at Barbil, a ferro-chrome plant, 2 ferro-manganese plants at Joda and Jeypore, 1 ferrosilicon plant at Theruvelli and an aluminium smelter plant at

Hirakud, 3 refractory plants at Belpahar, Rajgangpur and Laitkata and 2 cement plants at Bargarh and Rajgangpur. There are 3 large paper mills at Rayagada, Chowdwar and Brajrajnagar, a fertilizer plant at Rourkela, a caustic soda plant, a salt manufacturing unit and an industrial explosives plant.

Other industries of importance are sugar, glass, aluminium, heavy machine tools, a re-rolling mill and textile mills, and fertilizer plants.

There are cottage and small-scale industries in the state, *e.g.*, handloom weaving and the manufacture of baskets, wooden articles, hats and nets; silver filigree work and hand-woven fabrics are specially well known.

COMMUNICATIONS

Roads. On 31 March 1974 length of roads was: State highway, 2,175 km; major district roads, 5,213 km; other district roads, 2,320 km; village roads, about 6,118 km. An 80-km expressway connects the Daitari mining area with Paradip Port.

Railways. The total length of railway in 1971 was 1,875·8 km, of which 1,382 km was single line.

Aviation. There is an airport at Bhubaneswar with regular scheduled services to Calcutta and Hyderabad.

Shipping. Paradip was declared a 'major' port in 1966 and has been developed to handle 2m. tons of traffic. Other minor ports at Chandbali and Gopalpur.

JUSTICE, RELIGION AND EDUCATION

Justice. The High Court of Judicature at Cuttack has a Chief Justice and 6 puisne judges.

Religion. There were in 1961: Hindus (including scheduled castes and scheduled tribes), 17,123,194; Moslems, 215,319; Christians, 201,017; Buddhists, 454; Sikhs, 5,030; Jains, 2,295.

Education. The percentage of literates in the population is 21·7% (males, 34·7%, females, 8·6%).

In 1970 there were 24,000 primary and 900 secondary schools.

Utkal University was established in 1943 at Cuttack and moved to Bhubaneswar in 1962; it is both teaching and affiliating. It has 2 university colleges (engineering and law) and 43 affiliated colleges. Berhampur University has 15 affiliated colleges and Orissa University of Agriculture 4 constituent colleges.

PUNJAB (INDIA)

HISTORY. The Punjab was constituted an autonomous province of India in 1937. In 1947, the province was partitioned between India and Pakistan into East and West Punjab respectively, under the Indian Independence Act, 1947, the boundaries being determined under the Radcliffe Award. The name of East Punjab was changed to Punjab (India) under the Constitution of India. On 1 Nov. 1956 the erstwhile states of Punjab and Patiala and East Punjab States Union (PEPSU) were integrated to form the state of Punjab. On 1 Nov. 1966, under the Punjab Reorganization Act, 1966, the state was reconstituted as a Punjabi-speaking state comprising the districts of Gurdaspur (excluding Dalhousie), Amritsar, Kapurthala, Jullundur, Ferozepore, Bhatinda, Patiala and Ludhiana; parts of Sangrur, Hoshiarpur and Ambala districts; and part of Kharar tehsil. The remaining area comprising an area of 18,000 sq. miles and an estimated (1967) population of 8·5m. was shared between the new state of Haryana and the Union Territory of Himachal Pradesh. The existing capital of Chandigarh was made the joint capital of Punjab and Haryana.

AREA AND POPULATION. The Punjab is in north India and is bounded at its northernmost point by Kashmir, north-east by Himachal Pradesh, south-east by Haryana, south by Rajasthan, west and north-west by Pakistan. The area of the state is 50,376 sq. km, with census (1971) population of 13,551,060. Density 270 per sq. km. The largest cities, *see* pp. 600–601. The official language is Punjabi.

CONSTITUTION AND GOVERNMENT. Punjab (India) has a unicameral legislature of 117 members. The Legislative Council was abolished in Jan. 1970. The state of parties in the Legislative Assembly after the elections of June 1977, was: Akali Dal, 58; Janata, 24; Congress, 17; Communist Party of India, 7; Communist Party of India (Marxist), 8; independents, 2; vacant, 1.

There are 12 districts. The capital is Chandigarh (*see* p. 661). There are 104 municipalities, 116 community development blocks and 9,331 elected village *panchayats*.

Governor: M. M. Chaudhury.
Chief Minister: P. S. Badal.

BUDGET. Budget estimates for 1974–75 show total revenue of Rs 234·93 crores and expenditure, Rs 213·61 crores. Receipts included: Grants-in-aid, Rs 24,58 lakhs; share from central taxes, Rs 28,13 lakhs; other tax revenue, Rs 38,14 lakhs; state excise, Rs 35,41 lakhs; non-tax receipts, Rs 47,45 lakhs; sales tax, Rs 60,06 lakhs; land revenue, Rs 1,16 lakhs. Expenditure included: Scientific and education departments, Rs 54,21 lakhs; multi-purpose irrigation schemes and public works and improvements, Rs 15,28 lakhs; medical, and public health, Rs 20,62 lakhs; agriculture, Rs 19,83 lakhs; community development, Rs 13,98 lakhs; debt services, Rs 59,50 lakhs; communications, Rs 18,81 lakhs.

Expenditure under the fourth Five-Year Plan was Rs 293·56 crores.

ENERGY AND NATURAL RESOURCES

Electricity. Installed capacity, 1974, was 576 mw; over 7,000 villages had electricity.

Agriculture. About 70% of the population depends on agriculture. Agricultural prosperity is mainly due to irrigation. The irrigated area rose from 2·21m. hectares in 1950–51 to 2·95m. hectares in 1972–73: total production of foodgrains rose from 1·99m. tonnes to 7·7m. tonnes in 1972–73. Production in 1,000 tonnes (area in 1,000 hectares) in 1972–73: Wheat, 5,361 (2,386); maize, 738 (549); rice, 1,163 (508); oilseeds, 287 (347); sugar-cane (gur), 597 (112); cotton, 961,000 bales (of 180 kg) from 499,000 hectares.

Livestock (1972 census): Buffaloes, 3,839,200; other cattle, 3·41m.; sheep and goats, 1,205,400; horses and ponies, 54,700; poultry, 3m.

Forestry. In 1974 there were 215,665 hectares of forest land, of which 99,849 hectares belonged to the Forest Department.

INDUSTRY. In Jan. 1974 the number of registered factories in the Punjab (India) was 5,136; 4,933 operational factories employed about 127,451 people. The chief manufactures are textiles, sewing machines, sports goods, sugar, starch, fertilizers, bicycles, scientific instruments, electrical goods, machine tools and pine oil. There were 32,646 industrial units employing about 177,000 workers.

COMMUNICATIONS

Roads. The total length of metalled roads on 31 March 1973 was 18,207 km. State transport services cover 249,350 route km daily with a fleet of 1,405 buses carrying a daily average of 350,000 passengers. Coverage by private operators is estimated as 40%.

Railways. The Punjab possesses an extensive system of railway communications, served by the Northern Railway. Total length, 3,371 km.

Aviation. There is an airport at Amritsar, and Chandigarh airport is on the north-eastern boundary; both have regular scheduled services to Delhi.

JUSTICE, RELIGION, EDUCATION AND WELFARE

Justice. The Punjab and Haryana High Court exercises jurisdiction over the states of Punjab and Haryana and the territory of Chandigarh. It is located in Chandigarh. It consists (1973) of a Chief Justice and 17 puisne judges.

Religion. At the 1971 census Hindus numbered 5,037,235; Sikhs, 8,159,172; Moslems, 114,447; Christians, 162,202; Jains, 21,383; Buddhists, 1,374.

Education. Compulsory education was introduced in April 1961; at the same time free education was introduced up to 8th class for boys and 9th class for girls as well as fee concessions. The aim is education for all children of 6–11.

In 1974–75 there were 8,969 primary schools, 1,220 middle schools and 1,478 higher secondary schools.

Punjab University was established in 1947 at Chandigarh as an examining, teaching and affiliating body. It is shared with Haryana and Himachal Pradesh. In 1962 Punjabi University was established at Patiala and an agricultural university at Ludhiana. Guru Nanak University has been established at Amritsar to mark the 500th anniversary celebrations for Guru Nanak Dev, first Guru of the Sikhs. Altogether there are 179 affiliated colleges, 151 for arts and science, 14 for teacher training, 5 medical, 1 dental, 2 engineering and 6 for other studies.

Health. Punjab claims the longest life expectancy (58·6 years for women, 63·5 for men) and lowest death rate (7·48 per 1,000). There were (1974) 888 medical institutions, including 126 hospitals, 296 Ayurvedic dispensaries, 128 primary health centres and 338 dispensaries.

Darling, M. L., *The Punjab Peasant in Prosperity and Debt.* 4th ed. London, 1949
Mangat Rai, E. N., *Civil Administration in the Punjab.* Cambridge, Mass., 1963
Singh, Khushwant, *A History of the Sikhs.* 2 vols. Princeton and OUP, 1964–67

RAJASTHAN

HISTORY. As a result of the implementation of the States Reorganization Act, 1956, the erstwhile state of Ajmer, Abu Taluka of Bombay State and the Sunel Tappa enclave of the former state of Madhya Bharat were transferred to the state of Rajasthan on 1 Nov. 1956, whereas the Sironj subdivision of Rajasthan was transferred to the state of Madhya Pradesh.

AREA AND POPULATION. Rajasthan is in north-west India and is bounded north by Punjab, north-east by Haryana and Uttar Pradesh, east by Madhya Pradesh, south by Gujarat and west by Pakistan. The area of the state is 342,214 sq. km and its population (1971) census, 25,765,806, density 75 per sq. km. The chief cities, *see* pp. 600–601.

CONSTITUTION AND GOVERNMENT. There is a unicameral legislature, the Legislative Assembly, having 200 members. The state of the parties in the Assembly after the election of June 1977, was: Janata, 150; Congress, 41; Communist Party of India, 1; CPI (Marxist), 1; independents, 6 (including the Speaker); vacant, 1.

The capital is Jaipur. There are 26 districts.

Governor: Raghukul Tilak.
Chief Minister: B. Singh Shekhawat.

BUDGET. Budget estimates for 1977–78 show total revenue of Rs 448·26 crores, and expenditure of Rs 456·93 crores. Receipts included: Contributions and adjustments between central and state governments, Rs 83·69 crores; taxes on income, Rs 30,97·35 lakhs; state excise, Rs 25,00 lakhs; sales tax, Rs 90,00 lakhs; vehicles taxes, Rs 7,50 lakhs; land revenue, Rs 18,34 lakhs. Expenditure included: Education, Rs 102,80 lakhs; irrigation, embankment, etc., Rs 130,80 lakhs; medical and public health, Rs 62,00 lakhs; agriculture, Rs 68,78 lakhs.

ENERGY AND NATURAL RESOURCES

Electricity. Installed capacity in 1975–76, 802·12 mw. By March 1977 8,518 villages and 108,080 wells had electric power, and 106 rural electrification schemes were in progress.

Minerals. The state is rich in minerals. In 1976 7m. tonnes of gypsum and 581,000 tonnes of rock phosphate were produced. Other minerals include silver, asbestos, felspar, copper, limestone and salt. Total value of principal mineral production in 1976 was Rs 42 crores.

Agriculture. The sown area is (1976–77) about 16·7m. hectares, of which 2·9m. is irrigated. Production of principal crops (1,000 tonnes), 1976–77: Jowar, 358; bajra, 1,321; maize, 580; wheat, (1975–76) 2,290; barley, 1,005; pulses (Kharif), 602; sugar-cane (gur), 1,990; total oilseeds, 343; cotton, 404,000 bales (of 180 kg). Total food-grains, 1977, 74,80. Tractors numbers 31,658 in 1975.

Livestock (1972): Buffaloes, 4,592,489; other cattle, 12,469,509; sheep, 8,557,295; goats, 12,162,441; horses and ponies, 48,089; poultry, 1,235,036.

INDUSTRY. In 1976 there were 3,812 (1,949 in 1965) factories subject to the Factories Act, 1948. Chief manufactures are cotton textiles, cement, glass and sugar. Production, 1976 estimate: Cloth, 68·9m. metres; yarn, 38m. kg; cement, 1·64m. tonnes; sugar, 32,000 tonnes.

COMMUNICATIONS

Roads. In 1976–77 there were 38,883 km of roads including 11,151 km of un-surfaced roads in Rajasthan; there were 2,089 km of national highway. Motor vehicles numbered 171,011 in 1976.

Railways. Jodhpur, Marwar, Udaipur, Ajmer, Jaipur and Sawai Madhopur are important junctions of the north-western network.

Aviation. There are airports at Jaipur, Jodhpur and Udaipur with regular scheduled services to Bombay and Delhi.

JUSTICE, RELIGION, EDUCATION AND WELFARE

Justice. The seat of the High Court is at Jodhpur. There is a Chief Justice and 11 puisne judges. There is also a bench of 5 judges at Jaipur.

Religion. At the 1971 census Hindus numbered 23,093,895; Moslems, 1,778,275; Jains, 513,548; Sikhs, 341,182; Christians, 30,202.

Education. The proportion of literates to the total population was 19·07% at the 1971 census.

In 1976–77 enrolment in 26,563 schools was 3,452,000; 19,943 primary schools (including nursery and junior basic schools) had 2·55m. students, 5,066 middle schools had 604,000 students and 1,554 secondary and higher schools had 298,000. Elementary education is free but not compulsory. The percentage in 1976–77 of children attending schools in the age-group 6–11 was 61·6 (40·9 in 1961), in the 11–14 age-group 26·9 (14·4).

In 1977 there were 88 government or aided colleges and 18 unaided. Enrolment at these and at the universities of Rajasthan, Jodhpur and Udaipur was 97,354. Rajasthan University, established at Jaipur in 1947, is teaching and affiliating; Jodhpur University was founded in 1962; Udaipur University and Rajasthan Agricultural University are both at Udaipur. There are also 4 agricultural colleges, 1 veterinary and animal science college, 4 engineering colleges, 5 government or aided Ayurvedic colleges and 6 polytechnics.

Health. In 1975–76 there were 1,102 hospitals and dispensaries. Rajasthan had 1,981 doctors and 8,077 nurses and assistants. There are 5 medical colleges.

In 1976–77 there were 2,294 Ayurvedic hospitals and dispensaries, 62 Unani, 32 homoeopathic and 3 naturopathy hospitals.

SIKKIM

HISTORY. Sikkim became the twenty-second state of the Indian Union in May 1975. It is inhabited chiefly by the Lepchas, who are a tribe indigenous to Sikkim with their own dress and language, the Bhutias, who originally came from Tibet, and the Gorkhalis (Nepalis), who entered from Nepál in large numbers in the late 19th and early 20th century. The main languages spoken are Sikkimese, Bhutia, Lepcha and Khaskura (Nepali). Being a small country Sikkim had frequently been involved in struggles over her territory, and as a result her boundaries have been very much reduced over the centuries. In particular the Darjeeling district was acquired from Sikkim by the British East India Company in 1839. The Namgyal dynasty had been ruling Sikkim since the 14th century; the first consecrated ruler was Phuntsog Namgya who was consecrated in 1642 and given the title of 'Chogyal', meaning 'Divinely appointed King', derived from Cho—religion and Gyalpo—king.

Sikkim is a land of wide variation in altitude, climate and vegetation, and is known for the great number and variety of birds, butterflies, wild flowers and orchids to be found in the different regions. It is a fertile land and to the Sikkimese is known as Denjong, The Valley of Rice.

AREA AND POPULATION. Sikkim is in the Eastern Himalayas and is bounded north by Tibet, east by Tibet and Bhután, south by West Bengal and west by Nepál. Area, 7,298 sq. km. Census population (1971), 208,609, of whom 15,000 lived in the capital, Gangtok. Population estimate, 1977, 250,000.

CONSTITUTION AND GOVERNMENT. Sikkim was joined to the British Empire by a treaty in 1886 until 1947, but that relationship ceased when Britain withdrew from India in 1947. Thereafter there was a standstill agreement between India and Sikkim until a treaty was signed on 5 Dec. 1950 between India and Sikkim by which Sikkim became a protectorate of India and India undertook to be responsible for Sikkim's defence, external relations and strategic communications.

The Chogyal had governed Sikkim with the help of the Sikkim Council, consisting of 18 elected members and 6 members nominated by the Chogyal. Sikkim parties represented were: National Party, Sikkim National Congress and, later, Sikkim Janta Congress.

Political reforms were demanded by the National Congress and the Janta Congress in March–April 1973 and Indian police took over control of law and order at the request of the Chogyal. On 13 April it was announced that the Chogyal had agreed to meet most of the political demands. Elections were held in April 1974 to a popularly-elected assembly. By the Government of Sikkim Act, June 1974, the Chogyal became a constitutional monarch with power of assent to the Assembly's legislation. By the Constitution (Thirty-Sixth Amendment) Act 1974 Sikkim became a state associated with the Indian Union. The office of Chogyal was abolished in April 1975. By the Constitution (Thirty-Eighth Amendment) Act 1975 Sikkim became the twenty-second state of the Indian Union. The Assembly has 32 members with a cabinet of 8 ministers including the Chief Minister. The Janata party holds 25 seats.

Governor: B. B. Lal.
Chief Minister: K. L. Dhorji.

The official language of the Government is English. Lepcha, Bhutia and Nepali have also been declared official languages.

Sikkim is divided into 4 districts for administration purposes, Gangtok, Mangan, Namchi and Gyalshing being the headquarters for the Eastern, Northern, Southern and Western districts respectively. Each district is administered by a District Collector. Within this framework are the *Panchayats* or Village Councils, representing the villages.

ECONOMY

Planning. The fifth Five-Year Plan began in April 1976.

Budget. The annual revenue exceeded Rs 33·8m. in 1976.

ENERGY AND NATURAL RESOURCES

Electricity. There are 5 hydro-electric power stations including the Lagyap project which has been implemented by the Government of India as aid to meet the growing demand for electrical power for new industries.

Agriculture. The economy is mainly agricultural; main crops are cardamom (a spice), mandarin oranges, apples, potatoes, rice, maize, millett, ginger and soybean. A tea plantation has recently been started. Forests occupy about 1,000 sq. km. of the land area (excluding hill pastures) and the potential for a timber and wood pulp industry is being explored. Some medicinal herbs are exported.

INDUSTRY AND TRADE

Industry. There is a distillery at Rangpo and a fruit preservation factory at Singtam. Copper, zinc and lead are mined by the Sikkim Mining Corporation. A recent survey by the Geological Survey of India and the Indian Bureau of Mines has confirmed further deposits of copper, zinc, silver and gold in Dikchu, North Sikkim. There is a jewel-bearing factory for the production of industrial jewels and transistor radios are also made. A watch factory has been set up in collaboration with Hindustan Machine Tools (India). A number of small manufacturing units for leather, wire nails, storage cells batteries, candles, safety matches and carpets, are already producing in the private sector. Local crafts include carpet weaving, making handmade paper, wood carving and silver work. To encourage trading in indigenous products, particularly agricultural produce, the State Trading Corporation of Sikkim has been established.

Tourism. There is great potential for the tourist industry; a 72-bed hotel at Gangtok was built in 1977–78 and a tourist lodge in West Sikkim was commissioned.

COMMUNICATIONS

Roads. There are 531 miles of motorable roads, all on mountainous terrain, and 27 major bridges under the Public Works Department. Public transport and road haulage is nationalized.

Railways. The nearest railhead is at Siliguri, (72 miles from Gangtok).

Aviation. The nearest airport is at Bagdogra, (80 miles from Gangtok).

Post and Broadcasting. There are 790 telephones (1977) and (1972) 32 wireless stations.

RELIGION, EDUCATION AND WELFARE

Religion. The state religion is Mahayana Buddhism, but a large proportion of the population is Hindu. There are some Christians, Moslems and members of other religions.

Education. Sikkim has 260 primary schools and 49 secondary schools (1,670 teachers), providing education for over 37,039 children. Education is free up to class X for girls and class VIII for boys. There is also a training institute for primary teachers and degree college with day and evening courses.

Health. There are 5 hospitals, serving the 4 districts, at Gangtok, Singtam, Gyalshing, Namchi and Mangan, with a total of 292 beds, besides 26 dispensaries, 4 sub-dispensaries and mobile dispensaries, a maternity ward, chest clinic and two blocks for tuberculosis patients. There are 7 primary health centres with 10 beds each and 21 primary sub-centres. There are 52 doctors. Medical and hospital treatment is free; there is a hospital or dispensary within 10 miles of every homestead. Malaria and Kala-azar have been completely eliminated and many schemes for the provision of safe drinking water to villages and bazaars have been implemented.

Coelho, V. H., *Sikkim and Bhutan*. New Delhi, 1970
Olschak, B. C., *Sikkim*. Zürich, 1965
Mele, F., *Sikkim*. Paris, 1974

TAMIL NADU

HISTORY. The first trading establishment made by the British in the Madras State was at Peddapali (now Nizampatnam) in 1611 and then at Masulipatnam. In 1639 the English were permitted to make a settlement at the place which is now Madras, and Fort St George was founded. By 1801 the whole of the country from the Northern Circars to Cape Comorin (with the exception of certain French and Danish settlements) had been brought under British rule.

Under the provisions of the States Reorganization Act, 1956, the Malabar district (excluding the islands of Laccadive and Minicoy) and the Kasaragod district taluk of South Kanara were transferred to the new state of Kerala; the South Kanara district (excluding Kasaragod taluk and the Amindivi Islands) and the Kollegal taluk of the Coimbatore district were transferred to the new state of Mysore; and the Laccadive, Amindivi and Minicoy Islands were constituted a separate Territory. Four taluks of the Trivandrum district and the Shencottah taluk of Quilon district were transferred from Travancore–Cochin to the new Madras State. On 1 April 1960, 405 sq. miles from the Chittoor district of Andhra Pradesh were transferred to Madras in exchange for 326 sq. miles from the Chingleput and Salem districts. In Aug. 1968 the state was renamed Tamil Nadu.

AREA AND POPULATION. Tamil Nadu is in south India and is bounded north by Karnataka and Andhra Pradesh, east and south by the Indian ocean and west by Kerala. Area, 130,357 sq. km. Population (1971 census), 41,103,125, density of 313 per sq. km. Tamil is the principal language and has been adopted as the state language with effect from 14 Jan. 1958. The principal towns, *see* pp. 600–601.

CONSTITUTION AND GOVERNMENT. The Governor is aided by a Council of 16 ministers. There is a bicameral legislature; the Legislative Council has 63 members and the Legislative Assembly has 234 members. State of the parties following the elections of June 1977: Auna-DMK, 130; DMK, 48; Congress, 27; CPI (Marxist), 12; Janata, 10; CPI, 5; others, 2.

There are 14 districts. The capital is Madras.

Governor: P. B. Patwari.
Chief Minister: M. G. Ramachandran.

BUDGET. Budget estimates for 1974–75, receipts, Rs 4,68·00 crores; disbursements, Rs 4,72·84 crores.

ENERGY AND NATURAL RESOURCES

Electricity. Production 1973–74 amounted to 7,105m. units; 61,171 towns, hamlets and villages were supplied with electricity.

Agriculture. Agriculture engages 29% of the population. The land is a fertile plain watered by rivers flowing east from the Western Ghats, particularly the Cauvery and the Tambaraparani. Temperature ranges between 18° C. and 43° C., rainfall between 25 in. and 75 in. Of the total land area (13·01m. hectares), 76·98 lakh hectares were cultivable and 27·10 lakh hectares were irrigated in 1972. The staple food crops grown are paddy, maize, jawar, bajra, pulses and millets. Important commercial crops are sugar-cane, oilseeds, cotton, tobacco, coffee, tea, rubber and pepper. The production of foodgrains was 72·84 lakh tonnes; sugar-cane and oilseeds, 13·73, and 12·97 lakh tonnes respectively.

Livestock (1966 census): Buffaloes, 2,753,049; other cattle, 11,009,368; sheep, 6,641,843; goats, 3,796,736; swine, 874,880; horses, ponies, mules, camels, etc., 185,336; poultry, 10,898,862.

Forestry. The revenue from forests in 1973–74 was Rs 735·40 lakhs: sandalwood, Rs 282·19 lakhs; timber, Rs 108·24 lakhs; firewood, Rs 107·91 lakhs. Area of forest land, 1973, 20,925 sq. km.

INDUSTRY AND TRADE

Industry. The contribution of the industrial sector to the state income was Rs 373 crores in 1972–73. The number of registered factories was 6,713 in 1973. The consumption of power in the industrial sector was 49·5% of total state consumption in 1974. The biggest central sector project is Salem steel plant.

Cotton textiles is one of the major industries. There are nearly 180 cotton textile mills and most of the spinning mills supplying yarn to the decentralized handloom industry. Other important industries are tanning, manufacture of textile machinery, power-driven pumps, bicycles, electrical machinery, tractors, rubber tyres and tubes, bricks and tiles and silk. Tamil Nadu is the second largest producer of cement, while its sugar industry has been expanding rapidly.

Public sector undertakings include the Neyveli lignite complex, integral coach factory, high-pressure boiler plant, photographic film factory, surgical instruments factory, teleprinter factory, oil refinery, continuous casting plant and defence vehicles manufacture. The state produces limestone, manganese, mica, quartz, feldspar, salt, bauxite and gypsum. Main exports: tanned hides and skins, leather and cotton goods, tea, coffee, spices, engineering goods, motor-car ancillaries.

Tourism. In 1973, 50,074 tourists visited the state, 35,929 of whom came by air and 14,145 by sea.

COMMUNICATIONS

Roads. At the end of 1973 the state had approximately 78,463 km of roads (about 50,000 km metalled). In 1973 there were 162,413 registered motor vehicles.

Railways. In 1970 there were 6,038 km of railway. Madras and Madurai are the main centres.

Aviation. There are airports at Madras, Tiruchirapalli and Madurai, with regular scheduled services to Bombay, Calcutta and Delhi. Madras is the main centre of airline routes in South India.

Shipping. Madras is the chief port. Important minor ports are Cuddalore and Nagapattinam. There are 9 intermediate ports. A harbour is under construction at Tuticorin.

JUSTICE, RELIGION AND EDUCATION

Justice. There is a High Court at Madras with a Chief Justice and 18 judges.

Police. Strength of armed police battalions, 1973, 4,420; strength of the armed reserve (1972) in the state and in Madras, 356,461.

Religion. At the 1971 census Hindus numbered 36,674,150 (89·2%), Christians, 5·75%; Moslems, 5·11%.

Education. At the 1971 census 39·39% of the total population was literate.

Education is free up to pre-university level. In 1973–74 there were 2,823 high schools with a total enrolment of 1,627,030 students. The number of primary schools was 26,726, and their enrolment, 3,759,140; 5,773 upper primary schools had 2,113,981 pupils. Allotment of expenditure for education for 1974–75, Rs 1,08·52 crores.

There are 3 universities. Madras University (founded in 1857) is affiliating and teaching. It had (1968) 119 colleges for arts and sciences with 106,571 students. Annamalai University, Annamalainagar (founded 1928) is residential; Madurai University (founded 1966) is an affiliating and teaching university.

Statistical Information: The Department of Statistics (Fort St George, Madras) was established in 1948 and reorganized in 1953. *Director:* D. S. Rajabushanam, MA. Main publications: *Annual Statistical Abstract; Decennial Statistical Atlas; Season and Crop Report; Quinquennial Wages Census; Quarterly Abstract of Statistics.*

National Council of Applied Economic Research, *Economic Atlas of Madras State*. New Delhi, 1962.

TRIPURA

HISTORY. A Hindu state of great antiquity having been ruled by the Maharajahs for 1,300 years before its accession to the Indian Union on 15 Oct. 1949. With the reorganization of states on 1 Sept. 1956 Tripura became a Union Territory. The Territory was made a State on 21 Jan. 1972.

AREA AND POPULATION. Tripura is bounded on the north, west and south by Bangladesh, and on the east by Mizoram. The major portion of the state is hilly and mainly jungle. It has an area of 10,477 sq. km and a population of 1,556,342 (1971 census).

GOVERNMENT. There is a Legislative Assembly of 60 members. The election of Jan. 1978 was won by the Communist Party of India (Marxist). The territory has 1 district, divided into 10 administrative sub-divisions, namely, Sadar, Khowai, Kailasahar, Dharmanagar, Sonamura, Udaipur, Belonia, Kamalpur, Sabroom and Amarpur.

The capital is Agartala (population, 1961, 54,878).

Governor: L. P. Singh.
Chief Minister: P. K. Das.

BUDGET. Budget estimates 1976–77 show revenue receipts of Rs 37,78·94 lakhs, of which grants from the central government amounted to Rs 29,15·73 lakhs, and expenditure on revenue account of Rs 39,43·45 lakhs, of which education cost Rs 9,81·35 lakhs and public works, Rs 8,38·02 lakhs.

ENERGY AND NATURAL RESOURCES

Electricity. Installed capacity (1976), 9·7 mw; there were 245 electrified villages.

Agriculture. About 8% of the cultivated area is irrigated. The tribes practise shifting cultivation, but this is being slowly replaced by modern methods. The main crops are rice, jute, mesta, potatoes, cotton, oilseeds and sugar-cane. Rice production (1976 estimate), 366,000 tonnes.

Forestry. Forests cover about 60% of the land area.

COMMUNICATIONS

Roads. Total length of motorable roads (1974) 3,692 km, of which 1,123 km were surfaced. Vehicles registered, 31 March 1975, 5,526.

Railways. There is a railway between Dharmanagar and Kalkalighat (Assam).

Aviation. There is 1 airport and 3 airstrips. The airport (Agartala) has regular scheduled services to Calcutta.

UTTAR PRADESH

HISTORY. In 1833 the then Bengal Presidency was divided into two parts, one of which became the Presidency of Agra. In 1836 the Agra area was styled the North-West Province and placed under a Lieut.-Governor. The two provinces of Agra and Oudh were placed, in 1877, under one administrator, styled Lieut.-Governor of the North-West Province and Chief Commissioner of Oudh. In 1902 the name was changed to 'United Provinces of Agra and Oudh', under a Lieut.-Governor, and the Lieut.-Governorship was altered to a Governorship in 1921. In 1935 the name was shortened to 'United Provinces'. On Independence, the states of Rampur, Banaras and Tehri-Garwhal were merged with United Provinces. In 1950 the name of the United Provinces was changed to Uttar Pradesh.

AREA AND POPULATION. Uttar Pradesh is in north India and is bounded north by Himachal Pradesh, Tibet and Nepál, east by Bihar, south by Madhya

Pradesh and west by Rajasthan, Haryana and Delhi. The area of the state is 294,413 sq. km. Population (1971 census), 88,341,144, a density of 300 per sq. km. Cities with more than 100,000 population, *see* pp. 600–601. The official language is Hindi.

CONSTITUTION AND GOVERNMENT. Uttar Pradesh has had an autonomous system of government since 1937. There is a bicameral legislature. The Legislative Council has 108 members; the Legislative Assembly has 425. State of the parties following the elections of June 1977: Janata, 351; Congress, 46; CPI, 9; independents, 16; CPI (Marxist), 1; vacant, 2.

There are 11 administrative divisions, each under a Commissioner, and 54 districts. The number of municipalities (1968) is 142, that of *Zila Parishads* 51 and that of *Antarim Zila Parishads* 3. On 23 March 1970 all *Zila Parishads* were dissolved for 2 years or until their reconstitution.

The capital is Lucknow.

Governor: M. Channa Reddy.
Chief Minister: R. N. Yadav.

BUDGET. Budget estimates, 1968–69, show total revenue of Rs 3,55,63·69 lakhs and expenditure of Rs 3,54,86·53 lakhs.

ENERGY AND NATURAL RESOURCES

Electricity. The State Electricity Board had, 31 March 1975, an installed capacity of 1,886 mw. There were 30,465 villages with electricity.

Agriculture. Agriculture occupies 75% of the population. Production of foodgrains (1974), 15·56m. tonnes; sugar-cane, 60·8m.; oilseeds, 1·55m. The state is one of India's main producers of sugar.

INDUSTRY. Sugar and cotton processing are the leading industries.

COMMUNICATIONS

Roads. There were, 31 March 1973, 112,243 km of roads, of which 36,437 km were metalled. (This excludes forest roads.)

Railways. Lucknow is the main junction of the northern network; other important junctions are Agra, Kanpur, Allahabad and Varanasi.

Aviation. There are airports at Lucknow, Kanpur, Varanasi and Gorakhpur.

JUSTICE, RELIGION AND EDUCATION

Justice. The High Court of Judicature at Allahabad (with a bench at Lucknow) has a Chief Justice, 40 puisne judges including additional judges. There are 45 sessions divisions in the state.

Religion. At the 1961 census Hindus numbered 62,437,313; Moslems, 10,788,089; Sikhs, 283,737; Jains, 122,108; Christians, 101,641; Buddhists, 12,893.

Education. For secondary education there were, in 1973–74, an estimated 3,793 schools, with 1,193,000 scholars, and for primary education, 62,486 schools, with 11,912,000 scholars. Compulsory education for boys was in force in 95 municipalities and for girls in 10 municipalities in 1967.

Uttar Pradesh has 11 universities: Allahabad University (founded 1887) with 3 university colleges, 6 associated colleges and 8,992 students in 1973; Agra University (1927) with 68 affiliated colleges and 74,156 full-time students; the Banaras Hindu University, Varanasi (1916) with 2 constituent colleges, 4 affiliated colleges and 12,999 students; Lucknow University (1921) with 3 university colleges and 26,186 students; Aligarh Muslim University (1920) with 8,000 students in 1963; Rookee University (1948), formerly Thomason College of Civil Engineering (established in 1847) with 1,396 students; Gorakhpur University (1957), with 63 affiliated colleges and 42,524 students; Varanasaya Sanskrit Vishwavidyalaya, Varanasi (1958) with about 1,000 students, and Uttar Pradesh Agriculture University, Phoolbagh (1960) with about 1,870 students. Kanpur University and Meerut University were founded in 1966. The Indian Institute of Technology, Kanpur (1960), has university status; in 1962–63 there were 288 post-graduate students. In 1966–67 an estimated 39,775 students were studying in the universities and 65,084 in the affiliated colleges.

Brass, P. R., *Factional Politics in an Indian State: The Congress Party in Uttar Pradesh*. Univ. of California Press, 1965.

WEST BENGAL

HISTORY. For the history of Bengal under British rule, from 1633 to 1947, *see* THE STATESMAN'S YEAR-BOOK, 1952, p. 183.

Under the terms of the Indian Independence Act, 1947, the Province of Bengal ceased to exist. The Moslem majority districts of East Bengal, consisting of the Chittagong and Dacca Divisions and portions of the Presidency and Rajshahi Divisions, became what was then East Pakistan.

AREA AND POPULATION. West Bengal is in north-east India and is bounded north by Sikkim and Bhután, east by Assam and Bangladesh, south by the Bay of Bengal and Orissa, west by Bihar and north-west by Nepál. The total area of West Bengal is 87,853 sq. km. At the 1971 census its population was 44,312,011, an increase of 27% since 1961, the density of population 507 per sq. km. Population of chief cities, *see* pp. 600–601. The principal language is Bengali.

CONSTITUTION AND GOVERNMENT. The state of West Bengal came into existence as a result of the Indian Independence Act, 1947. The territory of Cooch-Behar State was merged with West Bengal on 1 Jan. 1950, and the former French possession of Chandernagore became part of the state on 2 Oct. 1954. Under the States Reorganization Act, 1956, certain portions of Bihar State (an area of 3,157 sq. miles with a population of 1,446,385) were transferred to West Bengal.

The Legislative Assembly has 294 seats. Distribution March 1978: Communist Party of India (Marxist), 178; Forward Bloc, 26; Revolutionary Socialist Party, 20; others of the 'Left Front', 7; Janata, 29; Congress, 20; others of the opposition bloc, 14.

The capital is Calcutta.

For administrative purposes there are 2 divisions (Burdwan and Presidency), under which there are 15 districts, excluding Calcutta. The Calcutta Metropolitan Development Authority has been set up to co-ordinate development in the metropolitan area (1,000 sq. km). For the purposes of local self-government there are 15 district boards, 325 *anchalik parishads* (regional boards), 2,926 *anchal* (regional) *panchayats* and 19,662 *gram* (village) *panchayats*. There is no district board in Cooch-Behar district. There are 90 municipalities. The Calcutta Corporation was reconstituted in 1969 with a mayor and deputy mayor, a commissioner, aldermen and standing committees.

Governor: A. L. Dias.
Chief Minister: J. Basu.

BUDGET. The revised estimates for 1975–76 show total revenue of Rs 5,57,44·21 lakhs and expenditure of Rs 5,41,94·17 lakhs. Receipts included: Contributions and adjustments between central and state governments, Rs 1,48,97·64 lakhs; taxes on income, Rs 63,75 lakhs; state excise, Rs 26,50 lakhs; stamps, Rs 21,52 lakhs; sales tax, Rs 1,54,54 lakhs; vehicles taxes, Rs 100 lakhs; debt services, Rs 13,33·36 lakhs; civil administration, Rs 35,35·38 lakhs; land revenue, Rs 9,80·12 lakhs. Expenditure included: Education, Rs 1,18,59·65 lakhs; public works and improvements, Rs 17,68·67 lakhs; medical, and family planning, Rs 55,18 lakhs; police, Rs 47,04·25 lakhs; agriculture, Rs 37,31 lakhs; general administration, Rs 4,54·05 lakhs; debt services, Rs 64,13·75 lakhs; extraordinary, including community projects and local developments, Rs 11,61·49 lakhs; industries, Rs 8,21·10 lakhs.

ENERGY AND NATURAL RESOURCES

Electricity. Installed capacity, 1975, 1,367 mw. In 1975–76, 10,448 villages had electricity.

Water. Important major irrigation and power schemes at present under construction are the Damodar Valley scheme; the Kansabati project; and the Mayurakshi River project. The Canada Dam on the Mayurakshi was opened on 1 Nov. 1955 and the reservoir irrigates 560,000 acres.

Agriculture. About 70% of the cultivated area is rice-paddy, one-third of it irrigated. Total foodgrain production, 1975–76, 8·6m. tonnes; oilseeds, 85,000.

Livestock (1971 census): 11,878,083 cattle, 824,161 buffaloes, 793,369 sheep, 5,211,445 goats, 14,548 horses and 15,491,905 poultry; tractors numbered 692.

INDUSTRY. The jute textile industry in 1975 employed 243,799 workers. The total number of registered factories, 1975, was 5,977. The coalmining industry had 101 units employing 170,000 workers. There are about 300 tea estates which employ about 214,000 workers.

There is a large automobile factory at Uttarpara, and there are aluminium rolling-mills at Belur and Asansol. At Durgapur a major steel plant was completed in 1962. Durgapur has other industries under the state sector—a thermal power plant, coke oven plant, fertilizer factory, alloy steel plant and ophthalmic glass plant. There are a locomotive factory and cable factory at Chittaranjan and Rupnarayanpur. A refinery and fertilizer factory are under construction at Haldia.

COMMUNICATIONS

Roads. In April 1972 the length of national highway was 1,481 km and of other motorable roads 75,081 km. On 31 March 1972 the state had 190,279 motor vehicles.

Railways. The length of railways within the state is 2,908 km. The main centres are Calcutta and Durgapur.

Aviation. The main airport is Calcutta which has national and international flights. The second airport is at Bagdogra in the extreme north, which has regular scheduled services to Calcutta.

Shipping. Calcutta is the chief port: a barrage is being built at Farakka to control the flow of water and to provide a rail and road link between North and South Bengal. A second port is being developed at Haldia, halfway between the present port and the sea, which is intended mainly for bulk cargoes. West Bengal possesses 779 km of navigable canals.

JUSTICE, RELIGION AND EDUCATION

Justice. The High Court of Judicature at Calcutta has a Chief Justice and 38 puisne judges. The Andaman and Nicobar Islands (*see* p. 660) come under its jurisdiction.

Police. In 1975–76 the police force numbered 48,421, under an inspector-general. Calcutta has a separate force under a commissioner directly responsible to the Government; its strength was 19,737.

Religion. At the 1971 census Hindus numbered 34,611,864; Moslems, 9,064,338; Christians, 251,752; Buddhists, 121,504; Sikhs, 35,084; Jains, 32,203.

Education. At the 1971 census literacy was 33·05%. In 1972 recognized educational institutions numbered 42,786, with about 5m. pupils. There were 35,484 primary and junior basic schools, with about 3·5m. pupils and 4,133 secondary schools with about 1m. pupils. Primary education is free.

The University of Calcutta (founded 1857) is affiliating and teaching; in 1972–73 it had 24 constituent colleges and 283 affiliated institutions. Visva Bharati, Santiniketan, was originally established by Tagore and is residential and teaching. The University of Jadavpur, Calcutta (1955), had 5,192 students in 1970. Burdwan

University was established 15 June 1960 with 31 affiliated colleges previously under the supervision of the University of Calcutta; in 1972–73 there were 196,257 students. Kalyani University was established in 1961. The University of North Bengal had 26,191 students in 1972–73. Rabindra Bharati University had 30 affiliated colleges in 1972.

Chatterjee, S. P., *Bengal in Maps*. Bombay, 1950

UNION TERRITORIES

ANDAMAN AND NICOBAR ISLANDS. The Andaman and Nicobar Islands are administered by the President of the Republic of India acting through a Chief Commissioner. There is an Advisory Committee of 20 members associated with the Chief Commissioner and another 12 members associated with the Union Home Minister. The seat of administration is at Port Blair, which is connected with Calcutta (1,255 km away) and Madras (1,190 km) by steamer service which calls about every 10 days; there is a bi-weekly air service from Calcutta. There are 2 districts, each with a Deputy Commissioner.

The population (1971 census) was 115,133.

Revised estimates for 1976–77 show total revenue receipts of Rs 390·94 lakhs, and total expenditure on revenue account of Rs 23,08·69 lakhs, and total capital expenditure of Rs 9,81·74 lakhs.

Chief Commissioner: S. M. Krishnatry.

The **Andaman Islands** lie in the Bay of Bengal, 193 km from Cape Negrais in Burma, 1,255 from Calcutta and 1,190 from Madras. Five large islands grouped together are called the Great Andamans, and to the south is the island of Little Andaman. There are some 204 islets, the two principal groups being the Ritchie Archipelago and the Labyrinth Islands. The total area is about 6,475 sq. km. The Great Andaman group is about 467 km long and, at the widest, 51 km broad.

The original inhabitants live in the forests by hunting and fishing; they are of a small Negrito type and their civilization is about that of the Stone Age. Their exact numbers are not known, as they avoid all contact with civilization. The total population of the Andaman Islands (excluding the aboriginals) was in 1951, 18,962 (12,734 males and 6,228 females). Under a central government scheme started in 1953, some 4,000 displaced families, mostly from East Pakistan, had been settled in the islands by May 1967.

Japanese forces occupied the Andaman Islands on 23 March 1942. Civil administration of the islands was resumed on 8 Oct. 1945.

From 1857 to March 1942 the islands were used by the Government of India as a penal settlement for life and long-term convicts, but the penal settlement was abolished on re-occupation in Oct. 1945.

The Great Andaman group, densely wooded, contains many valuable trees, both hardwood and softwood. The best known of the hardwoods is the *padauk* or Andaman redwood; *gurjan* is in great demand for the manufacture of plywood. Large quantities of softwood are supplied to match factories. Annually the Forest Department export about 25,000 tons of timber to the mainland. Coconut, coffee and rubber are cultivated. The islands are slowly being made self-sufficient in paddy and rice, and now grow approximately half their annual requirements. The average yield of rice in 1966–67 was 1·24 tonnes per hectare. Total livestock (1961 census) was 38,617. There is a saw-mill at Port Blair and a coconut-oil mill at Dunbar Point. There are about 338 km of black top road in the entire territory.

The islands possess a number of harbours and safe anchorages, notably Port Blair in the south, Port Cornwallis in the north and Elphinstone and Mayabandar in the middle.

The **Nicobar Islands** are situated to the south of the Andamans, 121 km from Little Andaman. The British formally took possession in 1869. There are 19 islands, 7 uninhabited; total area, 1,645 sq. km. The islands are usually divided into 3 subgroups (southern, central and northern), the chief islands in each being respectively,

Great Nicobar, Camotra with Nancowrie and Car Nicobar. There is a fine land-locked harbour between the islands of Camotra and Nancowrie, known as Nancowrie Harbour.

The population numbered, in 1961, 14,563. The coconut and arecanut are the main items of trade, and coconuts are a major item in the people's diet.

The Nicobar Islands were occupied by the Japanese in July 1942; and Car Nicobar was developed as a big supply base. The Japanese built some roads in Car Nicobar and small jetties at Malacca in Car Nicobar, and in the harbour at Nancowrie. The Allies reoccupied the islands on 9 Oct. 1945.

Sen. P. K., *The Land and People of the Andamans*. Calcutta, 1962

ARUNACHAL PRADESH. On 21 Jan. 1972 the former North East Frontier Agency of Assam was created a Union Territory. The territory includes the Kameng, Tirap, Subansiri, Siang and Lohit frontier divisions and has an area of 81,426 sq. km and a population (1971 census) of 444,744.

There is a Legislative Assembly of 30 members and a Council of Ministers. The election of 1978 was won by the Janata party.

There are 5 districts. The centre of administration is at Shillong.

Administrator: B. K. Nehru.
Chief Minister: Prem Khandu Thungon.

About 60% of the land area is forest. In 1970 there were 200,000 acres under cultivation, 32,600 acres of it irrigated. Food production was 70,500 tons. There were about 100 co-operatives.

CHANDIGARH. On 1 Nov. 1966 the city of Chandigarh and the area surrounding it was constituted a Union Territory. Population (1971), 257,251. Area, 114 sq. km. It serves as the joint capital of both Punjab (India) and the new state of Haryana, and is the seat of a High Court and of a university serving both states. The city will ultimately be the capital of just the Punjab; joint status is to last while a new capital is built for Haryana.

Evenson, N., *Chandigarh*. Berkeley, Cal., 1966

DADRA AND NAGAR HAVELI. By the 10th amendment to the constitution the Portuguese territories of Dadra and Nagar Haveli (area, 491 sq. km; population (1971), 74,170; density, 152 per sq. km) became a centrally administered Union Territory with effect from 11 Aug. 1961, forming an enclave at the southernmost point of the border between Gujarat and Maharashtra. Formerly for administrative purposes a part of Damão (on the south Gujarat coast), they were separated from it by a 26-km strip of Indian territory. In July 1954 'nationalist volunteers' occupied Dadra and Nagar Haveli and a pro-India administration was formed; this body made a request for incorporation into the Union, 1 June 1961, and has been recognized by the Indian Government as able to exercise an advisory role on the pattern of territorial councils. The Indian Government appointed an Administrator in Oct. 1960. Headquarters are at Silvassa. Dadra has 3 villages, Nagar Haveli 69. Languages used are Gujarat, Varli, Marathi, Dhodia, Konkani and Hindi.

Administrator: S. K. Banerji.

Budget. Revised estimates for 1972–73 show provsion of Rs 168·63 lakhs.

Electricity. Electricity is supplied by Gujarat. A Silvassa sub-station is being built, and 44 villages had been electrified by 1977.

Agriculture. Farming is the chief occupation, and 18,000 hectares were under crops in 1976–77. Much of the land is terraced and there is a 75% subsidy for soil conservation. The major food crops are rice and ragi; 9,600 hectares were under paddy cultivation and 11,285 under ragi and pulses in 1976–77. There is little irrigation (502 hectares). There are veterinary centres, an agricultural research centre and 2 breeding centres to improve strains of cattle and poultry.

Forests. About 41·5% of the total area is forest, mainly of teak and khair.

Industry. An industrial estate has been set up at Piparia which had 48 operating factories in 1977 for chemical products, engineering, textiles, plastics, fertilizers and other manufactures. There were 31 units operating outside the estate. Concessions are available for small industries. Estimated employment (total) in 1977, 1,800.

Communications. There are (1977) 158 km of motorable road. The railway line from Bombay to Ahmedabad runs through Silvassa. The nearest airport is Bombay.

Justice. The territory is under the jurisdiction of the Bombay (Maharashtra) High Court. There is a District and Sessions Court and one junior Division Civil Court at Silvassa.

Education. Literacy was 14·86% of the population at the 1971 census. In 1978 there were 4 pre-primary schools, 144 government primary schools, 13 mission schools, 1 higher secondary school and 4 high schools. Total primary enrolment was 11,066; high-school, 900.

Health. The territory has 1 hospital (25 beds), 2 primary health centres and 3 dispensaries.

DELHI. Delhi became a Union Territory on 1 Nov. 1956.

Area and Population. The territory forms an enclave inside the eastern frontier of Haryana in north India. Delhi has an area of 1,485 sq. km. At the 1971 census its population was 4,065,698 (density per sq. km, 2,738). In the rural area of Delhi there are 258 villages in 5 community development blocks.

Government. Delhi is administered by an elected Metropolitan Council consisting of 61 members including 5 nominated by the President of India. State of the parties after elections of June 1977: Janata, 51; Congress, 10. The Lieut-Governor is the Administrator, assisted by 4 Executive Councillors (1 Chief Executive Councillor and 3 Executive Councillors) appointed by the President of India on the recommendation of the Union Home Ministry. The Territory is covered by 3 local bodies: Delhi Municipal Corporation, New Delhi Municipal Committee and Delhi Cantonment Board.

Lieut.-Governor: Dalip Rai Kohli.
Chief Executive Councillor: Kidar Nath Sahani.

Budget. Budget estimates 1976–77 show total revenue of Rs 1,36,12·79 lakhs and expenditure of Rs 2,14,84·09 lakhs. Biggest items of expenditure were social and community services, Rs 73,01·59 lakhs; general schemes, Rs 31,06·18 lakhs.

Agriculture. About 120,000 hectares are cultivated. Animal husbandry is increasing and mixed farms are common. Chief crops in 1975–76, production in 1,000 tonnes (area in 1,000 hectares), were: Wheat, 98 (47); jowar and bajra, 11 (27); gram, 5 (5); sugar-cane (gur), 1 (1); fruit, vegetables and flowers.

Industry. The modern city of Delhi and New Delhi is not only the largest commercial centre in northern India but is also an important industrial centre. Since 1947 a large number of industrial concerns have been established; these include factories for the manufacture of razor blades, sports goods and parts for radios, bicycles and station wagons. The number of industrial units functioning was 38,000 in 1976; average number of workers employed was 266,000. Production was worth Rs 428 crores and investment was Rs 295 crores.

Some traditional handicrafts, for which Delhi was formerly famous, still flourish; among them are ivory carving, miniature painting, gold and silver jewellery and papier mâché work. The handwoven textiles of Delhi were particularly fine; this craft is being successfully revived.

Roads. Three national highways pass through the city. There were (1976) 378,918 registered motor vehicles in Delhi including 4,996 taxis. The city transport service had 2,245 buses in 1976–77.

Railways. Delhi is an important rail junction.

Aviation. Delhi is served by 2 airports.

Religion. At the 1971 census Hindus numbered 3,407,835; Sikhs, 291,123; Moslems, 263,019; Jains, 50,513; Christians, 43,720; Buddhists, 8,720.

Education. The proportion of literates to the total population was 56·61% at the 1971 census.

The total number of educational institutions in 1976–77 was 2,746, with an enrolment of 1,212,059 students.

The University of Delhi was founded in 1922; it has 64 constituent colleges and institutions with, 1977, a total of 82,057 students.

GOA, DAMAN AND DIU. The coast was captured for Portugal by Afonso de Albuquerque in 1510 and the inland area was added in the 18th century. Daman (Damão) on the Gujarat coast, 70 miles north of Bombay, was seized by the Portuguese in 1531 and ceded to them (1539) by the Shar of Gujarat. The island of Diu, captured in 1534, lies off the south-east coast of Kathiawar (Gujarat); there is a small coastal area. In Dec. 1961 the territories were occupied by India and incorporated into the Indian Union.

Area and Population. Goa, bounded on the north by Maharashtra and on the east and south by Karnataka, has a coastline of 105 km. The area of the territory is 3,813 sq. km, that of Goa itself being about 3,701 sq. km. Daman, 72 sq. km; Diu, 40 sq. km. Population (1971) 857,771: Goa, 795,120; Daman, 38,739; Diu, 23,912. Density, 225 per sq. km. Panaji is the largest town, population (urban agglomeration, 1971) 59,258. The languages spoken are Gujarati and Konkani.

Government. The Indian Parliament passed legislation in March 1962 by which Goa, Daman and Diu became a Union Territory with retrospective effect from 20 Dec. 1961. Goa is represented by 2 elected members in the Indian House of the People. For judicial purposes the territory comes under the High Court of Bombay. The capital is Panaji. There are 194 village *panchayats*.

There is a Legislative Assembly of 30 members. Following the elections of June 1977 the Maharashtrawadi Gomantak party held 15 seats; Congress, 10; Janata, 3; independents, 2.

Lieut-Governor: S. K. Banerji.
Chief Minister: Mrs S. Kakodkar.

Budget. Budget estimates, 1968–69, show total revenue of Rs 10,56·77 lakhs, expenditure of Rs 10,56·77 lakhs. Contributions and adjustments between central and state governments brought receipts of Rs 5,20·76 lakhs, sales tax brought Rs 1,20 lakhs. Expenditure was highest on education, Rs 2,09·01 lakhs. An estimated Rs 8·62 crores was spent on development during 1967–68. Annual Plan expenditure, 1971–72, Rs 81·5m. Expected outlay, 1972–73, Rs 86·8m.: Agriculture, Rs 17·63m.; irrigation and power, Rs 20·80m.; social services, Rs 30·09m.

Electricity. Units sold, 140·99m. kwh. in 1975–76. Thirteen towns and 331 villages were supplied with electric power by March 1976. Power is generated in neighbouring states.

Minerals. Resources include manganese ore and iron ore, both of which are exported. There are also reserves of bauxite, limestone and clay.

Agriculture. Agriculture is the main occupation; important crops are rice, wheat, ragi, pulses, groundnuts, fruit and coconuts. The net area sown is 128,429 hectares in Goa, 4,353 in Daman and 793 in Diu. Area irrigated, 11,277 hectares. Rice is the main crop in Goa; production of paddy 1975–76, 128,796 tonnes, with 23,077 hectares under high yielding varieties. Government poultry and dairy farming schemes yielded 766,667 eggs and 1·46m. litres of milk in 1975–76, with 3,679 kg of butter and ghee.

Fisheries. The fishing industry is important; fish is the territory's staple food. In 1975 the catch of seafish was 46,235 tonnes (value Rs 5,85·4 lakhs). The whole territory has a coastline of about 140 km. There are about 4,950 active fishing vessels.

Industry. At 19 Jan. 1977 there were 8 large industrial projects and 1,711 small units registered, the largest being a fertilizer factory (investment, Rs 500m.). There were 5 government industrial estates. Small units were mainly occupied in rice- and flour-milling, boat repairs and forest products.

Employment. In 1975 there were 77 unions with 26,880 members.

Roads. In 1975 there were 2,642 km of motorable road (national highway, 223 km). A road bridge on national highway 17 is being built at Zuari. In 1976 there were 31,939 registered vehicles.

Railways. There is a metre gauge line from the Pune–Bangalore line into Goa. There are no railways on Diu or in Daman.

Aviation. There are regular services to Bombay and Bangalore.

Shipping. The main port is Marmagoa. There is a daily steamer service between Panaji and Bombay, and weekly service between Bombay and Cochin, calling at Marmagoa.

Post and Telegraphs. There are (1977) 171 post offices and 21 telephone exchanges with 5,520 lines. There are 2 telex exchanges.

Justice. The territory comes under the High Court of Bombay.

Religion. About 62% of the population is Hindu, 36% Christian, 2% Muslim and other communities.

Education. The 1971 census recorded 44·53% literacy. Education is free up to grade VIII. In 1976–77 primary schools numbered 1,116 with 117,727 pupils, middle schools 355 with 56,393 pupils and secondary schools 233 with 32,316 pupils. There were 9 arts, commercial and science colleges with 6,092 students. There were also 6 professional colleges, a polytechnic, 3 elementary teachers' training colleges and 5 industrial training institutes.

Health. There are (1976–77) 32 government hospitals (2,362 beds) including 3 tuberculosis hospitals; also mobile and specialist clinics. There were also 37 private hospitals and nursing homes. Two health centres were opened in 1972; there are 786 doctors and 678 nurses. There is 1 medical college.

National Council of Applied Economic Research, *Techno-economic Survey of Goa, Daman and Diu.* New Delhi, 1964

LAKSHADWEEP. The territory consists of a group of 27 islands (10 inhabited), about 300 km off the west coat of Kerala. It was constituted a Union Territory in 1956 as the Laccadive, Minicoy and Amindivi Islands, and renamed in Nov. 1973. The total area of the islands is 32 sq. km. The northern portion is called the Amindivis. The remaining islands are called the Laccadives (including Minicoy Island). Minicoy is the largest island, 4·8 sq. km, and is considerably to the south of the other islands. An Advisory Committee associated with the Union Home Minister and an Advisory Council to the Administrator assist in the administration of the islands; these are constituted annually. Population (1971 census, provisional), 31,810, nearly all Moslems. The language is Malayalam, but the language in Minicoy is Mahl. There were, in 1976, 1 higher secondary school, 6 high schools and 26 nursery/junior basic schools, 7 senior basic schools and 1 junior college. There are 2 hospitals and 7 primary health centres. The staple products are coconut-husk fibre (coir), coconuts and fish. Headquarters of administration, Kavaratti Island.

Administrator: M. C. Verma.

MIZORAM. On 21 Jan. 1972 the former Mizo Hills District of Assam was created a Union Territory. The area is approximately 21,230 sq. km and the population approximately 400,000, of whom 44% are literate and 80% are Christian.

There is a Council of Ministers responsible to a Legislative Assembly with 30 seats. Presidential rule was imposed in 1977. The main town is Aizawl, which is connected by a main road (not a national highway) to Silchar, Assam; Silchar is also the nearest airport. There are no railways.

Lieut.-Governor: S. K. Chibber.

PONDICHERRY. Formerly the chief French settlement in India, was founded by the French in 1674, taken by the Dutch in 1693 and restored to the French in 1699. The English took it in 1761, restored it in 1765, re-took it in 1778, restored it a second time in 1785, retook it a third time in 1793 and finally restored it to the French in 1814. Administration was transferred to India on 1 Nov. 1954. A Treaty of Cession (together with Karikal, Mahé and Yanaon) was signed on 28 May 1956; instruments of ratification were signed on 16 Aug. 1962 from which date (by the 14th amendment to the Indian Constitution) Pondicherry, comprising the 4 territories, became a Union Territory.

Area and Population. The territory forms an enclave on the Coromandel Coast of Tamil Nadu, with Karikal forming a separate enclave further south. The total area of Pondicherry (with Karikal, Mahé and Yanaon) is 480 sq. km, divided into 16 Communes. Population (1971), 471,707; Pondicherry city had 90,637 inhabitants. The principal languages spoken are French, English, Tamil, Telegu and Malayalam.

Government. By the Government of Union Territories Act 1963 Pondicherry is governed by a Lieut.-Governor, appointed by the President, and a Council of Ministers (4) responsible to a Legislative Assembly of 30 members. Distribution of seats following the elections of June 1977; Anna-DMK, 14; Janata, 7; DMK, 3; others, 6.

Lieut.-Governor: B. T. Kulkarni.
Chief Minister: S. Ramaswany.

Budget. Budget estimates for 1976–77 show revenue receipts of Rs 10,43·84 lakhs and expenditure on revenue account of Rs 19,32·18 lakhs. Main sources of revenue were grants in aid from central government, Rs 7,88·46 lakhs; income from power schemes, Rs 249 lakhs; state excise, Rs 3,28·61 lakhs; sales tax, Rs 221 lakhs. Main items of expenditure were: Education, Rs 3,88·73 lakhs; electricity schemes, Rs 2,30·37 lakhs; medical, and public health, Rs 2,56·09 lakhs; interest payments, Rs 85·47 lakhs; police, Rs 87·82 lakhs; social security and welfare, Rs 87·81 lakhs. The fifth plan provdes for an outlay of Rs 32·00 crores; plan outlay for 1976–77, Rs 697 lakhs.

Agriculture. The main food crop is rice. Estimated foodgrain production, 1·3m. tonnes in 1975–76; cash crops include groundnuts, cotton and sugar-cane. Sugar-cane production (1975–76) was 99,840 tonnes.

Industry. The main industry is cotton textiles (2,681 looms and 127,848 spindles on monthly average producing cloth worth Rs 2·5 crores in 1973).

Railways. Pondicherry is on a branch from the main Madurai–Madras line.

Aviation. The nearst airport is Madras.

Education. There are 9 university colleges in the territory, 4 of them affiliated to the University of Madras, as are the medical and law colleges; 2 are affiliated to the University of Andhra, 1 to Rennes, France, and 1 is non-affiliated.

REPUBLIC OF INDONESIA

Capital: Jakarta
Population: 133m. (1978)

Republik Indonesia

HISTORY. In the 16th century Portuguese traders in quest of spices settled in some of the islands, but were ejected by the British, who in turn were ousted by the Dutch (1595). From 1602 the Netherlands East India Company conquered the Netherlands East Indies, and ruled them until the dissolution of the company in 1798. Thereafter the Netherlands Government ruled the colony from 1816 to 1941, when it was occupied by the Japanese until 1945. An independent republic was proclaimed by Dr Sukarno and Dr Hatta on 17 Aug. 1945.

Complete and unconditional sovereignty was transferred to the Republic of the United States of Indonesia on 27 Dec. 1949, except for the western part of New Guinea, the status of which was to be determined through negotiations between Indonesia and the Netherlands within one year after the transfer of sovereignty. A union was created to regulate the relationship between the two countries. A settlement of the New Guinea (Irian Jaya) question was, however, delayed until 15 Aug. 1962, when, through the good offices of the United Nations, an agreement was concluded for the transfer of the territory to Indonesia on 1 May 1963. In Feb. 1956 Indonesia abrogated the union and in Aug. 1956 repudiated Indonesia's debt to the Netherlands.

During 1950 the federal system which had sprung up in 1946–48 (*see* THE STATESMAN'S YEAR-BOOK, 1950, p. 1233) was abolished, and Indonesia was again made a unitary state. The provisional constitution was passed by the Provisional House of Representatives on 14 and came into force on 17 Aug. 1950. On 5 July 1959 by Presidential decree, the Constitution of 1945 was reinstated and the Constituent Assembly dissolved.

On 12 Jan. 1960 President Sukarno issued a decree enabling him to control the political parties, with the power (on the recommendation of the Supreme Court) to dissolve them. He also set up a mass organization, the National Front, and a supreme State body called the Provisional People's Consultative Assembly.

On 6 March 1960 the President prorogued Parliament to be reorganized on the basis of the 1945 constitution. Local administrations nominated 130 members representing political parties and 153 members representing functional groups, who formed the new 'Mutual Co-operation House of Representatives'.

A communist second attempt to overthrow the government in Sept./Oct. 1965 was suppressed by the army. Some 80,000 communists are said to have been killed, and the communists killed 6 generals and several officials of the armed forces. The Communist Party was banned on 12 March 1967.

The 3-year 'confrontation' with Malaysia ended on 11 Aug. 1966, when an agreement was signed in Jakarta, terminating hostilities and re-establishing diplomatic relations.

AREA AND POPULATION. Indonesia, covering a total land area of 735,000 sq. miles (1,903,650 sq. km), consists of the islands of Sumatra, Java and Madura, Sulawesi (Celebes), Kalimantan (Borneo), Nusa Tenggara (Lesser Sundas), Maluku (Moluccas), Irian Jaya (the western half of New Guinea) and some 3,000 smaller islands and islets. It extends about 3,200 miles east to west through three time-zones (East, Central and West Standard time) of 1 hour's difference. Indonesia has a tropical climate with two monsoons; the dry (June–Sept.) and the wet (Oct.–April).

The total population in 1971 (census) was 119,232,499, distributed as follows:

Java and Madura, 76·1m.; Sumatra, 20·8m.; Sulawesi, 8·5m.; other islands (including Loro Sae, formerly East Timor), 9·2m.; Kalimantan, 5·2m. Main cities (1971 census): Jakarta Raya (capital), 4·6m.; Surabaya, 1·6m.; Bandung, 1·2m.; Semarang, 646,500; Malang, 422,400; Surakarta, 414,200; Yogyakarta, 342,200.

Estimated population, 1978, was 133m.

Indonesia is divided into the following provinces (capitals in brackets): Aceh (Banda Aceh, formerly Kutaraja), North Sumatra (Medan), West Sumatra (Padang), Riau (Pakan Baru), Jambi (Telanaipura, formerly Jambi), South Sumatra (Palembang), West Java (Bandung), Central Java (Semarang), East Java (Surabaya), West Kalimantan (Pontianak), South Kalimantan (Banjarmasin), East Kalimantan (Samarinda), Central Kalimantan (Palangka Raja, formerly Pahandut), North Sulawesi (Menado), South Sulawesi (Makassar), Bali (Den Pasar), West Nusa Tenggara (Mataram), East Nuse Tenggara (Kupang), Maluku (Ambon), Irian Jaya (Jayapura, formerly Sukarnapura).

East Timor, the former Portuguese colony, became the 27th province on 17 July 1976.

The principal ethnic groups are the Acinese, Bataks and Minangkabaus in Sumatra, the Javanese and Sundanese in Java, the Madurese in Madura, the Balinese in Bali, the Sasaks in Lombok, the Menadonese and Buginese in Sulawesi, the Dayaks in Kalimantan, Irianese in Irian Jaya and the Ambonese in the Moluccas.

Bahasa Indonesia is the official language of the Republic.

GOVERNMENT AND CONSTITUTION. Indonesia is a sovereign, independent republic.

On 11–12 March 1966 the military commanders under the leadership of Lieut.-Gen. Suharto took over the executive power while leaving President Sukarno as the head of State. The Communist Party was at once outlawed and the National Front was dissolved in Oct. 1966. On 22 Feb. 1967 Sukarno handed over all his powers to Gen. Suharto.

The People's Consultative Assembly is the supreme power. It has 920 members and it sits at least once every 5 years. The House of People's Representatives has 460 members, 360 of them elected, and sits for a 5-year term. Functional Group members have 236 seats; Muslim parties, 94; Nationalists, 20.

General elections to the 360 elected seats in the House of Representatives were held on 2 May 1977. The results were *Sekber Golker*, 232 seats (39,750,096 votes); *Partai Persatuan Pembangunan*, 99 (18,743,491); *Partai Demokrasi Indonesia*, 29 (5,504,757).

President, Prime Minister and Minister of Defence: Gen. Suharto, elected by the People's Consultative Assembly in March 1968 and re-elected in 1973 and 1978.

National flag: Horizontally red over white.

National anthem: Indonesia Raya (tune by Wage Rudolf Supratman, 1928).

Feith, H., *The Decline of Constitutional Democracy in Indonesia.* Cornell Univ. Press, 1962
Palmier, L. H., *Indonesia and the Dutch.* OUP, 1961
Schiller, A. A., *The Formation of Federal Indonesia, 1945–49.* The Hague, 1955

DEFENCE. The Indonesian Armed Forces were formally set up on 5 Oct. 1945. On 11 Oct. 1967 the Army, Navy, Air Force and Police were unified under the Ministry of Defence and Security. Their commanders no longer hold cabinet rank. There is selective military service.

Army. There are 1 cavalry brigade, 15 infantry brigades, 2 airborne infantry brigades, 1 para-commando regiment, 6 artillery regiments, 4 air defence regiments and 8 armoured battalions. Total strength in 1977 was 180,000.

Navy. The Navy, in 1978, included 3 diesel powered patrol submarines, 11 small frigates, 13 missile boats, 5 fleet minesweepers, 5 torpedo boats, 16 coastal gunboats, 11 patrol vessels, 2 coastal minesweepers, 18 small patrol craft and motor launches, 9 landing ships, 2 landing craft, 1 training ship, 4 surveying vessels, 8 oilers, 2 command and support ships, 1 destroyer depot ship, 1 repair ship, 1 cable ship and 4 tugs. Not all the warships are effective. The (*ex*-Soviet) cruiser was on the disposal list in 1972; and no more than 3 of the 10 (originally 14) old submarines or any of the 8 old destroyers acquired from the USSR remain. Three small frigates of 1,400 tons are being built in the Netherlands. The naval air arm has 15 helicopters.

Naval personnel total 39,000 officers and men, including 1,000 naval air arm and 5,000 marine commando corps.

Air Force. Operational combat units comprise 1 squadron with 16 Avon-Sabre jet fighters provided by Australia, 1 squadron of 7 P-51D Mustang piston-engined fighter-bombers, 1 squadron with a few B-26 Invader piston-engined bombers and 1 squadron with 16 OV-10F Bronco twin-turboprop counter-insurgency aircraft. Large numbers of combat aircraft supplied by the Soviet Union, including MiG-21, MiG-19 and MiG-17 fighters, and Tu-16 and Il-28 twin-engined bombers, are currently inactive, as are Soviet-built 'Guideline' surface-to-air missiles at several sites. There are 2 transport squadrons, equipped with turboprop C-130B Hercules, CASA Aviocar and F-27 Friendship, and piston-engined C-47 aircraft; 1 maritime patrol squadron with Albatross amphibians; and an assortment of other aircraft in transport, helicopter and training units. Personnel (1978) approximately 28,000.

INTERNATIONAL RELATIONS

Membership. Indonesia is a member of UN and ASEAN.

ECONOMY

Planning. On 15 Aug. 1960 the National Planning Council produced the draft of the First National Overall Development Plan, which the Consultative Assembly subsequently ratified. The second Five-Year Development Plan (1974–79) provides funds from central government for food production and other programmes implemented by village, region, province and municipal authority. Village projects include building and credits to farmers; regions and municipalities implement schemes to create employment, often in road-making; provinces receive sums for specific projects. Aid is also provided for school building, health centres, irrigation and fertilizer plant. The largest single programme is that for increased production of paddy, secondary and horticultural crops (7·6% of plan budget). Other important programmes are those for stimulating fisheries and stock-farming, and for generally lessening dependence on rice by encouraging other food crops.

Budget. The ordinary budget, excluding the development budget, was as follows in 1973–74 (in Rp. 1m.): gross revenue, 967,700; gross expenditure, 713,000. Revenue from direct taxes, 505,000, including 344,600 oil corporation tax; from indirect taxes, 412,900, including 128,200 import duties. Expenditure included 268,900 on employment, 108,600 on regional subsidies. Development expenditure was 336,800, including 79,500 on agriculture, 69,800 on regional development. Development budget for 1975–76 was 1,268,000. In March 1974 foreign investment was US$459·9m. in 29 projects.

Currency. The monetary unit is the *rupiah* (abbreviated Rp.), divided into 100 *sen*. There are bank-notes of 1, 2½, 5, 10, 25, 50 and 100 rupiahs and aluminium coins of 1, 5, 10, 25 and cupro-nickel coins of 50 sen.

On 24 Aug. 1959 the currency denominations were reduced to a tenth of their nominal value. Further devaluations took effect on 14 Dec. 1965, when a new *rupiah* worth 1,000 old rupiahs was introduced, and on 22 Dec. 1965, when the *rupiah* for imports and exports was revalued at Rp. 10,000 = US$1.

Special bank-notes—called 'Irian jaya rupiah'—were issued on 1 May 1963 for the province of Irian Jaya. Money in circulation in March 1974 (provisional), Rp. 785,200m.

In May 1976 foreign exchange reserves stood at US$2,000m.

Banking. The Bank Indonesia, formerly the Java Bank, established in 1828, was made the central bank of Indonesia on 1 July 1953. It had an original capital of Rp. 25m.; a reserve fund of Rp. 18m. and a special reserve of Rp. 84m.

Bank Negara Indonesia is a state bank and is designed to act as a source of credit for reconstruction purposes. The Bank Pembangunan Indonesia accords long-term credits for agricultural, industrial and mining projects. The Bank Koperasi Tani & Nelayan extends credits to co-operative societies and smaller business men.

There are 7 major commerical banks and 10 foreign banks; the latter include the Chartered Bank, the Hongkong and Shanghai Banking Corporation, the Bank of America, the Citibank and the Bank of Tōkyō.

In Aug. 1973, 18,377 co-operative societies, including 17,589 primary co-operatives with 2·8m. members and savings of Rp. 4,530m. (provisional), had a combined membership of 6·8m.

Weights and Measures. The metric system of weights and measures was officially introduced in Feb. 1923, and came into full operation on 1 Jan. 1938.

The following are the old weights and measures: *Pikol* = 136·16 lb. avoirdupois; *Katti* = 1·36 lb. avoirdupois; *Bau* = 1·7536 acres; *Square Pal* = 227 hectares = 561·16 acres; *Jengkal* = 4 yd; *Pal* (Java) = 1,506 metres; *Pal* (Sumatra) = 1,852 metres.

ENERGY AND NATURAL RESOURCES

Electricity. All gas and electricity undertakings were nationalized by presidential decree of 3 Oct. 1953, retroactive from 23 Dec. 1952. Three large-scale hydro-electric plants are operating on the Jatiluhur and Brantas rivers in Java and on the Asahan River in Sumatra. Electricity generated, 1973–74, 2,932,480 mwh.

Oil. Oil plays an important part in Indonesian economy, being a major source of revenue and providing employment for some 50,000. Indonesia is the principal producer of petroleum in the Far East, production coming from Sumatra, Kalimantan (Indonesian Borneo) and Java, where Anglo-Dutch and US interests operate. Indonesia is the tenth largest OPEC producer. The 1973 output of crude oil was 508·4m. bbls. Oil refined in 1973: 118·3m. bbls. Production rate, 1977, 1·72m.–1·74m. bbls per day. On 1 Nov. 1960 the Government announced a new regulation providing that all mineral oil and gas exploitation must be exclusively in the hands of Indonesian Government mining companies. Mining rights held by oil and gas companies issued before the new regulation continued.

Minerals. The high cost of extraction means that little of the large mineral resources outside Java is exploited; however, there is copper mining in Irian Jaya, nickel mining and processing on Sulawesi, aluminium smelting in northern Sumatra. The tin mines of Bangka, Billiton and Riouw are worked by the Government. In 1973–74 their total yield was 22,600 tonnes. Output (in tonnes) of bauxite was 1,204,706; coal, 145,900; nickel, 989,900; iron sand, 321,700; copper, 146,600; gold, 345 kg.

Agriculture. Indonesian agriculture is divided between estate and smallholders cultivation.

Rice production (1974), 15·2m. tons. Other main crops are maize, rubber, cassava, sweet potatoes, copra, coffee, palms. In 1973 production on estates was (1,000 tons): Rubber, 137; palm oil, 207; sugar 693; tea, 43; palm kernel, 46.

Livestock (1976): Cattle, 6·8m.; buffaloes, 2·8m.; horses, 704,000; sheep, 3·2m.; goats, 7·5m.; pigs, 4·4m.

Salt is a government monopoly; production in 1973, 30,000 tons.

Forestry. The forest area is 902,808 sq. km. Production, 1973 (provisional): All timber, 24,800 cu. metres, of which 676 was teak.

Fisheries. In 1971 (provisional) the catch of sea fisheries was 824,000 tonnes; inland fisheries, 402,000 tonnes.

INDUSTRY AND TRADE

Industry. At the beginning of Dec. 1957 the trade unions expropriated all Dutch-owned banks, trading firms, hotels, etc., which were then placed under government control. On 3 Dec. 1958 parliament passed a bill for the nationalization of all Dutch-owned businesses.

In Nov. 1963 all business enterprises owned 'wholly or partly by Malaysian nationals or Indonesian nationals domiciled in Malaysia' were sequestrated by presidential decree.

There are shipyards at Jakarta Raya, Surabaya, Semarang and Amboina. There are many textile factories (total production in 1973–74, 920m. metres), large paper factories (47,000 tonnes, 1973–74), match factories, automobile and bicycle assembly works, large construction works, tyre factories, glass factories, a caustic soda and other chemical factories. Production (1973–74): Cement, 818,000 tons; fertilizers, 241,000 tons; glass, 59,000 tons; 2,200,324 cycle tyres; 1,351,400 motor vehicles; 4,635,100 cu. metres of oxygen; 99,100 cu. metres of acetylene.

There were (1975) 8 oil refineries with a combined capacity of over 400,000 bbls per day. Domestic consumption takes about 12% and the remainder is exported mainly to Japan and USA.

Trade Unions. The largest group of trade unions in Indonesia is the Serekat Organasasi Karyawan Seluruh Indonesia (SOKSI), the Central Council of All Indonesia Trade Unions, with a membership of 2·6m., to which 28 national unions and 832 local unions are affiliated. The second largest is the Kongres Buruh Seluruh Indonesia (KBSI), the All Indonesia Trades Union Congress, with a membership of nearly 400,000. To the KBSI 25 national unions and 54 local unions are affiliated. There are also the HISSBI (Federation of Indonesian Trade Unions) with a membership of 180,203, and the KBKI (Indonesian Democratic Labour Organization), with a membership of 94,477. In addition, there are also trade-union centres which are closely connected with the Islamic Parties, viz., Serikat Buruh Islam Indonesia, with a membership of 275,000; the Sarekat Buruh Muslimin Indonesia, with a membership of 11,950, and the Gerakan Organisasi Buruh Sjarekat Islam Indonesia, with a membership of 1,347.

Commerce. Imports and exports (including oil) in US$1m. for year April–March:

	1974	*1975*	*1976*	*1977*	*1978*
Imports	3,367	5,160	5,745	6,395	7,120
Exports	7,449	4,810	5,200	5,850	6,750

The main export items (in US$1m.) in 1973 were: Rubber, 483·7; oil, 3,613; copra, 18·6; tin ore, 97; tobacco, 37·8; palm-oil and kernels, 95·1; tea, 31·5; coffee, 78·6. In 1976 oil exports were worth US$6,081m.; timber, US$781m.; rubber, US$535m.; coffee, US$250m.; tin, US$154m.

The main import items are non-crude oil, rice, consumer goods, fertilizer, chemicals, weaving yarn, iron and steel, industrial and business machinery.

Total trade between UK and Indonesia (British Department of Trade returns, in £1,000 sterling):

	1972	*1973*	*1974*	*1975*	*1976*	*1977*
Imports to UK	9,309	14,947	14,419	15,100	22,321	28,740
Exports and re-exports from UK	19,872	32,834	46,693	59,533	80,616	86,683

Tourism. In 1973 about 273,300 tourists visited Indonesia, spending US$41m.

COMMUNICATIONS

Roads. The projected Trans-Sumatra trunk road will connect Aceh (north) and Lampung (south). The feeder-road between West Sumatra and Riau provinces was completed with the building of the bridge over the Kampar River at Pekanbaru in 1974. Motor vehicles, at 1 Jan. 1973, totalled 307,740 passenger cars, 144,060 vans and trucks, 30,368 buses and about 400,000 motor cycles.

Railways. In 1973 the state-controlled railway company (PJKA) carried 29·3m. passengers and 4·9m. tons of goods over 7,891 km. During the second plan period up to 1979, PJKA is upgrading track on all main lines, installing modern signalling and telecommunications systems, and acquiring 60 diesel-electric locomotives.

Aviation. The Government and KLM in 1949 set up 'Garuda Indonesian Airways' as a mixed enterprise on a 50–50 capital basis under KLM management. The agreement was to last until 1960. In 1954, however, the Government bought up the shares held by KLM for 15m. guilders and nationalized GIA; and in Jan. 1958, the Government unilaterally terminated the contracts with the technical assistants provided by KLM. GIA maintains a direct service between Jakarta and Manila, Bangkok, Hong Kong, Tōkyō and Amsterdam. In 1973 the company flew 33,000 km and carried 1·6m. passengers and 13,790 tons of goods on domestic flights, and on international flights flew 10·3m. flying hours, carried 97m. passengers and 3,125 tons of goods.

Shipping. The national shipping company Pelajaran Nasional Indonesia (PELNI) had in 1973 a fleet of 312 vessels, maintains interinsular communications. The Jakarta Lloyd maintains regular services between Jakarta, Amsterdam, Hamburg and London.

Post and Broadcasting. In 1974 the postal and telegraph services of Indonesia included 950 post offices. There were 660 telegraph offices which handled 3·9m. domestic and 488,000 international cables. Post offices handled 176m. letters and Rp. 250,000m. in money orders, Giro and postal cheques. Deposits with post office savings accounts, Rp. 31,210m. Number of telephones (1977), 314,445.

Radio Republik Indonesia, under the Department of Information, operates 26 stations. Television broadcasting covers 40m. people in an area of 72,100 sq. km. There were, in 1973, 6 studios broadcasting from 22 stations.

Newspapers (1973). There were 117 daily newspaper publishers with estimated circulation of 1·6m. There were 374 publishers of weekly papers with a circulation of 3·3m.

JUSTICE, RELIGION, EDUCATION AND WELFARE

Justice. The judicial organization is under the direction of the Minister of Justice. There are courts of first instance, high courts of appeal in the larger towns and a Supreme Court of Justice for the whole of Indonesia in the capital.

In civil law the population is divided into three main groups: Indonesians, Europeans and foreign Orientals, to whom different law systems are applicable. When, however, people from different groups are involved, a system of so-called 'inter-gentile' law is applied.

The present criminal law, which has been in force since 1918, is codified and is based on European penal law. This law is equally applicable to all groups of the population. For private and commercial law, however, there are various systems applicable for the various groups of the population. For the Indonesians, a system of private and agrarian law is applicable; this is called Adat Law, and is mainly uncodified. For the other groups the prevailing private and commercial law system is codified in the Private Law Act (1847) and the Commercial Law Act (1847). These Acts have their origins in the French *Code Civile* and *Code du Commerce* through the similar Dutch codifications. These Acts are entirely applicable to Indonesian citizens and to Europeans, whereas to foreign Orientals they are applicable with some exceptions, mainly in the fields of family law and inheritance.

Religion. Religious liberty is granted to all denominations. The majority of the Indonesians are Moslems. There are nearly 6m. Christians; their main strength is in Central and East Java, North Sulawesi, East Nusa Tenggara, the Moluccas and Irian Jaya. There are also about 1m. Buddhists, probably for the greater part Chinese. Hinduism has 6m. members, of whom 2·5m. are on Bali.

In 1973 there were 387,720 Islamic houses of worship, 17,565 Christian (3,409 of them Catholic), 4,105 Hindu and 605 Buddhist.

Education. The following table shows the number of school and college students in 1978 (1,000):

Total population aged 7–13	23,000
Pupils in public and private elementary schools	13,612[1]
Pupils in Islamic schools	3,032[1]
Total population aged 13–18	16,196[1]
Junior high school pupils	2,056
Senior high school pupils	886
Academy and university students	401

[1] 1973.

English is the first foreign language taught in schools.

There are 51 universities (23 are private).

Higher education is given at the University of Indonesia (at Jakarta and Bogor), the University of Gajah Mada (at Yogyakarta), Airlangga University (at Surabaya, Malang and Bali), Andalas University (1956) (at Bukittinggi, Payakumbuh, Padang and Batusangkar), Hasanuddin University (1956) (at Ujung Pandang and Tondano), Pajajaran University (1958) (at Bandung), the University of North Sumatra (at Medan), and the Institute of Technology (at Bandung), the State Institute of Islam (1960) (at Yogyakarta), the Sriwijaja University (1960) (at Palembang and Tanjungkarang), the Lambung Mangkurat University (1960) (at Banjarmasin), the University of Sjah Kuala (at Banda Aceh), the University of Diponegoro (at Semarang), the University of North and Central Sulawesi (at Menado), the Institute of Technology (at Surabaya) and the new universities of Riau (at Pakanbaru), Maluku (at Ambon), East Nusa Tenggara (at Kupang), West Nusa Tenggara (at Mataram), and Cendrawasih (at Jayapura), Mulawarman (at Samarinda), Brawijaja (at Malang), Pancasila (at Jakarta) and Bung Karno (at Surakarta) universities. In 1961 a separate Department of Higher Education and Science was set up. Five training centres for technical education were opened in May 1975.

Health. In 1973 there were 2,343 public health centres, 6,800 mother-and-child clinics, 1,147 dispensaries, 1,848 doctors and 4,601 nurses and midwives.

DIPLOMATIC REPRESENTATIVES

OF INDONESIA IN GREAT BRITAIN
(38 Grosvenor Sq., London, W1X 9AD)

Ambassador: Saleh Basarah (accredited 31 May 1978)

OF GREAT BRITAIN IN INDONESIA
(Jalan, MH, Thamrin, 25, Jakarta)

Ambassador: T. J. O'Brien.

OF INDONESIA IN THE USA (2020 Massachusetts Ave., NW, Washington, D.C., 20036)

Ambassador: D. Ashari.

OF THE USA IN INDONESIA (Medan Merdeka Selatan 5, Jakarta)

Ambassador: Edward E. Masters.

OF INDONESIA TO THE UNITED NATIONS

Ambassador: Dr Anwar Sani.

Books of Reference

Indonesian Handbook 1975. Dept. of Information, Jakarta, 1976

Bemmelen, R. W. van, *Geology of Indonesia*. 2 vols. The Hague, 1949

Echols, J. M., and Shadily, H., *An Indonesian–English Dictionary*. 3rd ed. Cornell Univ. Press, 1975

Grant, B., *Indonesia*. Melbourne Univ. Press, 1964

Helsdingen, W. H. van, and Hoogenberk, H. (ed.), *Mission Interrupted; The Dutch in the East Indies . . . in the 20th century*. Amsterdam, 1946

Hindley, D., *The Communist Party of Indonesia, 1951–63*. California Univ. Press and CUP, 1965

Kroef, J. M. van der, *Indonesian Social Evolution*. Amsterdam, 1958.—*The Communist Party of Indonesia*. Univ. of Br. Columbia Press, 1965

Legge, J. D., *Sukarno: A Political Biography*. London, 1972

Neill, W. T., *Twentieth-Century Indonesia*. Columbia Univ. Press, 1973

Paauw, D. S., *Financing Economic Development: The Indonesian Case*. Glencoe, Ill., 1960
Palmier, L. H., *Social Status and Power in Java*. Athlone Press, London, 1960
Polomka, P., *Indonesia Since Sukarno*. London, 1971
Schrieke, B., *Indonesian Sociological Studies*. The Hague, 1955
Taylor, A. M., *Indonesian Independence and the United Nations*. Cornell Univ. Press, 1960
Weinstein, F. B., *Indonesian Foreign Policy and the Dilemma of Dependence*. Cornell Univ. Press, 1977

IRAN

Capital: Tehrán
Population: 34m. (1977)
GNP cer capita: US$2,220 (1977)

Keshvaré Shahanshahiyé Irân

AREA AND POPULATION. Iran is bounded north by the USSR and the Caspian Sea, east by Afghánistán and Pakistan, south by the Persian Gulf and the Gulf of Oman, west by Iraq and Turkey. Iran has an area of about 1,648,000 sq. km (634,000 sq. miles), but a vast portion is desert, and the average density is only 15 inhabitants to the sq. km.

According to the results of the census taken in Nov. 1976, the population of Iran was 33,591,875. Estimate (1977) 34m. Population of Tehrán, the capital (1976) 4,496,159.

The principal cities and their population are: Esfahán, 671,825; Meshed, 670,180; Tabriz, 598,576; Shiráz, 414,408; Rezáyeh, 163,991; Abadan, 296,081; Ahwaz, 329,006; Qum, 246,831; Rasht, 187,203; Hamadán, 155,848.

The 14 *ustáns* are as follows:

The central province; capital Tehrán; population, 4,950,394. Khorásán; capital Meshed; population, 2,494,283. Esfáhán; capital Esfáhán; population, 1·7m. Eastern Azerbáiján; capital Tabriz; population, 2·6m. Western Azerbáiján; capital Rezáyeh; population, 1m. Khuzistán; capital Ahwáz; population, 1·6m. Mázándárán; capital Sári; population, 1·8m. Fárs; capital Shiráz; population, 1·5m. Gilán; capital Rasht; population, 1·7m. Kermán; capital Kermán; population, 773,669. Kermánsháhán; capital Kermánsháh; population, 776,409. Ports and Islands of the Sea of Oman; capital Bándár Abbás; population, 605,387. Báluchestán and Sistán; capital Záhedán; population, 454,996. Kurdestán; capital Sánándáj; population, 624,256.

REIGNING KING (SHAH). Mohammad Reza Pahlavi (born 26 Oct. 1919) was sworn before the Majles on 16 Sept. 1941 on the abdication of his father Reza Shah Pahlavi (died 25 July 1944), who after the overthrow of the Qajar dynasty had been elected Shah on 12 Dec. 1925. After the dissolution of two former marriages, the Shah on 20 Dec. 1959 married Farah Diba, daughter of an army officer. *Offspring:* Prince Reza Pahlavi, born 31 Oct. 1960 (*Heir apparent*); Princess Farahnaz, born 12 March 1963; Prince Ali Reza Pahlavi, born 28 April 1966; Princess Leila, born 27 March 1970.

The Shah crowned himself and the Queen on 26 Oct. 1967.

Minister of the Court: Amir Asadullah Alam.

CONSTITUTION AND GOVERNMENT. In Jan. 1906 the Shah, up to then an absolute ruler, gave his consent to the establishment of a National Assembly, or *Majles*, which drew up a Constitution, which received the Shah's approval on 30 Dec. 1906. The Constitution also provided for the establishment of a Senate, but this body was constituted only in Feb. 1950; 30 of its 60 members are nominated by the Shah, while the other 30 are elected. As the result of constitutional amendments approved since 1949 the number of *Majles* deputies has been increased from the original 136 to 268 and the term of each *Majles* has been extended from 2 to 4 years; the Shah has the right to dissolve either or both Houses of Parliament and to return to the *Majles* finance bills for further consideration. All other legislation approved by Parliament the Shah is obliged to sign and promulgate as law.

On 2 March 1975 the Shah announced the formation of the National Political

Resurrection Movement and the dissolution of the two-party system. The first general election under the single party system was held in June 1975.

In Aug. 1977 the Cabinet was composed as follows:

Prime Minister: Jamshid Amouzegar.

Foreign Affairs: Abbas Ali Khalatbari. *War:* Gen. Reza Azimi. *Interior:* Assadollah Nasr Esfahani. *Finance and Economic Affairs:* Houshang Ansari. *Information and Tourism:* Daryush Homayoun. *Education:* Manuchehr Ganji. *Industry and Mines:* Mohammad Reza Amir. *Agriculture and Rural Development:* Dr Ahmed Ali Ahmedi. *Posts and Telecommunications:* Karim Motamedi. *Commerce:* Kazem Kosrowshahi. *Housing and Urban Development:* Firuz Towfiq. *Roads and Transport:* Morteza Salehi. *Arts and Culture:* Mehrdad Pahlbod. *Justice:* Gholamreza Kiyanpour. *Labour and Social Affairs:* Amir Qassem Moini. *Health and Welfare:* Dr Sheykhole Eslamzadeh. *Energy:* Taki Tavakoli. *Minister of State in charge of Economic Affairs:* Safi Asfia. *Minister of State and Director of the Plan and Budget Organization:* Mohammad Yeganeh. *Minister of State in charge of the Prime Minister's Relations with Parliament:* Mahmud Kashefi. *Minister of State for Executive Affairs:* Manuchehr Agah. *Minister of State for Women's Affairs:* Mahnaz Afkhami.

The country is divided into 21 *ustán* (administrative provinces), 2 governor-generalships, 153 governorships and 461 districts. The provinces are divided into *shahrestán* (counties), each under a *farmándár* (governor). the *shahrestáns* are subdivided into *bakhsh* (districts) under a *bakhshdár* and *dehistán* (group of villages) under a *dehdár*. Each village has a *kadkhodá* (headman). All these officials, with the exception of the village headmen, are appointed, directly or indirectly, by the central government.

On 3 Nov. 1955 Iran joined the Baghdad pact between Turkey, Iraq, Pakistan and Great Britain; now, without Iraq, known as CENTO.

National flag: Three horizontal stripes of green, white, red, with the national emblem in gold in the centre.

National anthem: Shahanshah é ma zendeh bad (words by Prince Afsar, tune by Da'ud Najmi Moghaddam).

DEFENCE

Army. The Army consists of about 220,000 men organized in 4 infantry divisions, 4 independent infantry brigades, 3 armoured divisions, and auxiliary units. Two years' military service is compulsory. *Gendarmerie* strength is about 70,000. Its function is internal security in rural areas.

A US Military Mission is attached in an advisory capacity to the Army and another to the *Gendarmerie*.

Navy. The Navy comprises 3 destroyers, 4 fast frigates, 4 corvettes, 3 coastal minesweepers, 2 inshore minesweepers, 17 patrol boats, 14 hovercraft, 2 landing ships, 1 landing craft, 2 fleet supply ships, 1 repair ship, 2 Imperial yachts, 2 oilers, 3 survey vessels, 1 water carrier and 3 tugs. There are also 30 coastguard cutters and 2 custom craft.

A British 'Battle' class destroyer (*ex*-HMS *Sluys*) was sold to Iran in 1966 and modernized in 1969, and 4 Vosper Mark 5 frigates were built in Britain in 1967–72.

The order for 6 large destroyers to be built in USA was reduced to 4. There is tentative agreement for the transfer of 3 old diesel-powered patrol submarines from the US Navy in 1978, 1979 and 1980. Twelve fast missile craft of 250 tons under construction in France are to be completed by mid-1979. Two new landing ships are projected.

The naval air arm comprises 12 patrol, transport and command aircraft and 36 helicopters.

In 1978 naval personnel totalled 22,000 officers and ratings including cadets and apprentices under training, and a marine battalion being formed.

Air Force. In Aug. 1955 the Air Force became a separate and independent arm, and is being built up to a strength of about 22 first-line squadrons (each 15 aircraft, plus reserves), with 100,000 personnel. When current deliveries have been completed, there will be 4 squadrons of F-14 Tomcat interceptors, with Phoenix missiles, 8 squadrons of F-5E Tiger II fighter-bombers, 10 squadrons of F-4D and F-4E Phantom interceptor/fighter bombers, 7 Boeing E-3A warning and control aircraft and 1 reconnaissance squadron of RF-4Es (160 F-16s have been ordered for delivery from 1980). Six P-3F Orions have been acquired for long-range anti-submarine duties. A transport wing is equipped with 57 C-130E/H Hercules and 25 F-27 Friendship turboprop transports and smaller types. Eleven Boeing 707-320C tanker-transports support the tactical fighter and anti-submarine squadrons. The Air Force also operates some of the many hundreds of new turbine-powered helicopters acquired for the Iranian services, including twin-engined CH-47C Chinooks, and Model 214 utility helicopters. Training aircraft include Bonanza basic trainers, T-33 advanced trainers and two-seat F-5B/Fs. Missiles in service include Rapier and Tigercat surface-to-air weapons.

INTERNATIONAL RELATIONS

Membership. Iran is a member of UN, OPEC, CENTO and the Colombo Plan.

ECONOMY

Planning. The fifth development plan 1973–78 originally envisaged an expenditure of US$36,000m. In Aug. 1974 it was decided to increase this to US$69,000m. Of this amount $23,000m. is allotted to the private sector.

GDP *per capita* (1972) US$571.

Budget. Budget estimate for year commencing 21 March 1976 totalled 3,105,000 rials, of which 27% was allocated to defence.

The main items of the budget for 1972–73 are (in 1m. rials): Receipts, 256,500; income tax, 270,000; customs duties, 29,100; treasury share of oil revenues, 150,300. Expenditure, 302,800; education, 23,200; defence, 92,000; capital expenses, 118,700; agriculture, 6,100; health, 6,500.

The estimated budget for the fourth 5-year development plan which began in 1968 was more than $11,000m., the major portion of which was covered by oil revenue.

Currency. The Iranian unit of currency is the *rial* sub-divided into 100 *dinars*.

Notes in circulation are of denominations of 50–10,000 *rials*. Coins in circulation are bronze–aluminium and copper, 50 *dinar*; silver alloy, 1, 2, 5, 10 and 20 *rials*. There are also gold *pahlavi* and ½ *pahlavi* pieces containing 7·322382 and 3·661191 grammes of gold respectively which do not constitute part of monetary circulation, but have a market value as any other commodity.

Government control of foreign exchange was introduced on 1 March 1936. Up to Feb. 1975 the official parity of the rial was 75·75 rials = US$1. This parity was used only in calculating the value of the gold and foreign exchange held as reserve for the note cover. In Feb. 1975 the rial was linked to the IMF Special Drawing Rights (SDR) and divorced from the US$1. Median exchange rate: SDR = 82·2425 rials. The effective rates for all authorized foreign-exchange payments are: Buying, £1 sterling = 124·50 rials, US$1 = 70·50 rials; selling, £1 = 124·30 rials, US$1 = 70·75 rials.

Banking. The following banks are established in Iran: Bank Markazi (Central Bank), which was officially established in 1961 under the Monetary and Banking Law of May 1960 to implement the monetary and credit policy of the country. The Central Bank took over from the Bank Melli many of its functions, including the issue of bank-notes.

The liabilities and assets of the Bank Markazi on 20 March 1972 were as follows (in rials): Liabilities: notes in circulation, 61,500m.; assets, 324,734m.; bank deposits, 48,770m.; capital, 3,600m.

Bank Melli Iran, founded in 1927, continues to be the leading commercial bank with branches all over the country. The National Savings Bank, founded in 1939, is a branch of the Bank Melli. Bank Keshavarzi Iran (Agricultural Bank), formerly a section of the Bank Melli Iran, was made a separate establishment in 1933. It has a nominal capital of 1,500m. rials and has branches at the principal agricultural centres in Iran. The bank gives assistance for the agricultural development of the country. The Bank Sepah, founded in 1926, deals principally in inland exchange and manages army accounts; paid-up capital, 400m. rials. Bank Rahni Iran (Mortgage Bank), founded in 1939, has an authorized capital of 720m. rials and fulfils the functions of a building society. Bank Tows'eh Sanati va Madani (Industrial and Mining Development Bank) was founded in 1959 under the 7-year plan with a paid-up capital of 400m. rials with the object of assisting the modernization and development of Iran's industries. The Foreign Trade Bank of Iran, with a capital of 275m. rials, of which 51% belong to the Bank Melli, 24% to American and 12½% each to German and Italian banks. Bank Sakhtemani (Building Bank) was formed with an authorized capital of 150m. rials with the object of building and selling houses to the poorer classes. Bank Omran (Development Bank) was founded in 1953 with a nominal capital of 15m. rials to finance farmers and peasants who come into possession of land by virtue of the distribution of Crown lands. Sherkat Sahami Bimeh Iran (The Iran Insurance Co.), in 1954 inaugurated a banking department. In addition, there are 19 privately owned banks.

The Russo-Iran Bank is the oldest foreign bank operating in Iran; it finances Soviet–Iranian trade. An Irano-French bank (Bank Etabarate) opened in 1958. The Irano-British Bank, the Bank of Iran and the Middle East, the Mercantile Bank of Iran and Holland, and the Bank of Iran and Japan opened in 1959.

Most banks are now authorized to deal in foreign exchange.

Weights and Measures. By a law passed on 8 Jan. 1933, the official weights and measures are those of the metric system.

The Iranian year is a solar year running from 21 March to 20 March; the Hejra year 1357 corresponds to the Christian year 21 March 1977–20 March 1978.

ENERGY AND NATURAL RESOURCES

Electricity. Energy produced in 1972 was 351·88m. tonnes of coal equivalent. Electric energy installed capacity, 1971, was 2,807,000 kw., and 9,100m. kwh. was generated in 1972.

Oil. The exploitation of Iran's large oil resources was undertaken by the Anglo-Persian (later Anglo-Iranian) Oil Company, which held a concession for a considerable area of southern Iran, built a large refinery and produced the following quantities of crude oil (in long tons): 1946, 19,189,551; 1948, 24,871,058; 1950, 31,750,147; 1951 (Jan.–Oct.), 16,176,000.

This concession was terminated as a result of the nationalization of the Iranian oil industry in 1951. The ensuing dispute (*see* THE STATESMAN'S YEAR-BOOK, 1954, p. 1294) led to the cessation of oil exports in June 1951, and of the company's operations in Iran in Oct. 1951. The dispute was finally settled on 5 Aug. 1954, and on 29 Oct. 1954, the date when the Shah signed it, an agreement came into force between the Iranian Government and the National Iranian Oil Company, on the one hand, and 17 international oil companies, on the other; of these, the British Petroleum Co. Ltd. holds 40% of the shares. These companies came to be known collectively as the Consortium.

The agreement is for 25 years with provisions for three 5-year extensions, at the option of the Consortium under specific terms and conditions. Two operating companies—Iraanse Aardolie Exploratie en Producte Maatschappij (Iranian Oil Exploration and Producing Company) NV and Iraanse Aardolie Raffinage Maatschappij (Iranian Oil Refining Company) NV—were formed by Consortium member companies and they received the necessary rights and powers from Iran to be solely responsible respectively for exploration and production in a defined area in South Iran and for the operation of the Refinery of Abadan. While the National Iranian Oil Company, the shares of which are held by the Iranian Government, is the owner of the fixed assets of the oil industry in South Iran, the Operating Companies have the unrestricted use of them. The two Operating Companies do not sell the oil; their function is solely to produce and refine it. So-called Trading Companies, subsidiaries representing Consortium members, deal individually and independently of each other with the buying and selling in Iran of oil for export.

The National Iranian Oil Company was united in Jan. 1955 with the Iran Oil Company, whose object is the exploration and production of oil throughout Iran except in regions subject to special agreements. The National Iranian Oil Company operates the Naft-i-Shah oilfield and the Kermánsháh refinery in West Iran and is solely responsible for the distribution and marketing of oil in Iran. The net effect of the financial aspects of the sale of oil by the National Iranian Oil Company to the Trading Companies for export is to bring about an equal sharing between Iran and each Trading Company of the profits arising in Iran from the Trading Companies operations.

The Shah signed a new 20-year agreement with a western Consortium on 31 July 1973 bringing the oil industry totally under the control of the National Iranian Oil Company.

Crude oil production figures since the Consortium began operations in Oct. 1954 have been (in tonnes): 1961, 56·3m.; 1962, 64·5m.; 1963, 66m.; 1964, 84m.; 1965, 92m.; 1966, 106m.; 1967, 121m.; 1968, 133m.; 1969, 153m.; 1970, 222m.; 1971, 227m.; 1972, 258m.; 1973, 293m.

Refining capacity in 1972 was 31m. tonnes.

Production of residual fuel oils was 11·3m. tonnes; distillate fuel oils, 4·8m.; motor spirit, 3·5m., and kerosene, 2·7m.

Minerals. Iran has substantial mineral deposits relatively underdeveloped. Production figures for 1973 (in 1,000 tonnes): Iron ore, 900; lead and zinc, 1,140; chromite, 200; salt, 500; natural gas, 17·2m. cu. metres.

Land Reform. Before the enactment of the 1962 land reform law most of the more than 50,000 villages in Iran were owned by absentee landlords. Several earlier land reform laws presented to the Majlis by the government had remained ineffective, and the only large-scale distribution of land to smallholders was that of the Crown property, which the Shah began in 1951. However, as a result of the implementation of the 1962 land reform law, all the large estates coming under the land reform law have been purchased from the landlords by the Government and distributed among the farmers. Up to 1968 more than 3m. farm families comprising some 14m. farmers have become the owners of the land they till.

Agriculture. Reliable statistics of production are not available. It is estimated, however, that out of 164·8m. hectares of land area only 16,857,000 are crop land (including 10,300 hectares fallow), 27·8m. hectares are forests and ranges and 32·7m. hectares are potentially cultivable waste.

Crop returns for 1975 (in 1,000 tonnes): Wheat, 5,507; oats, 1,438; rice, 954; sugar-beet, 4,585; tobacco, 14.

Wool comes principally from Khorásán, Kermánsháh, Mázandarán and Azerbáiján. Production, 1972, 20,000 tonnes.

Rice is grown largely on the Caspian shores.

Tobacco is grown along the shores of the Caspian. It is purchased by the Tobacco Monopoly and manufactured in the government factory at Tehrán.

Opium, until 1955, was an important export commodity in Iran. On 7 Oct. 1955 an Act was approved by Parliament to prohibit the cultivation and usage of opium. The Government has been contemplating reintroducing poppy cultivation on a limited scale and under rigid state control in an effort to fight narcotic trafficking and addiction.

Livestock (1976): 35·3m. sheep, 14·3m. goats, 6·7m. cattle, 350,000 horses, 60,000 camels, 68,000 pigs and 1·8m. donkeys.

Fisheries. The Caspian Fisheries Co. (Shilát) is a government monopoly. Exports of caviar (1975) were valued at US$72m.

INDUSTRY AND TRADE

Industry. Iran's chief natural products are oil, wool, cotton, silk, fruit, nuts, cereals, vegetables, gum, timber, oil seeds, copper and other metalliferous ores, coal, cattle, sheep and goats. Its principal manufactured or processed products are textiles, carpets, skins, casings, vegetable oil, soap, metal products, plastic products, furniture, beet sugar, tea, tobacco and cigarettes, wine, vodka, soft drinks, caviar, footwear, petroleum products, glass products, tiles, bricks, cement, leather and leather goods, dairy products and manufactured foodstuffs, and printed matter.

In 1975 there were 215,087 manufacturing units employing about 2m. people.

Apart from the oil industry, the industries employing most workers are textiles, sugar refining, flour-milling, fruit processing, tea, furniture, printing, leather, matches, glass, building materials and light metal goods. The most popular carpets are manufactured in the environs of Tabriz, Kermán, Arák, Káshán, Esfahán, Shiráz and Hamadán. Esfahán is the traditional textile manufacturing centre, but in recent years important textile mills, particularly cotton, have been built in other towns, including Tehrán. A number of automobile assembly plants have been set up in recent years employing several thousand workers. A steel-mill, a machine-tool factory, a tractor plant and a huge petrochemical complex are also going into production.

In March 1975 it was decreed that 99% of shares in all state-owned factories were to be sold to their workers and the public. This did not apply to the key industries—oil, steel, copper and transport. Production, 1972, in 1,000 tonnes: Cement, 3,600 (1975, 5,145); nitrogenous fertilizers, 108; hydrochloric acid, 15·6; sugar, 598 (1975, 558); wheat flour, 3,800; cotton yarn, 42; wool yarn, 29·2; ethyl alcohol, 33,000 hectolitres; woven silks, 7m. metres; cotton fabrics, 482m. metres, and woollen fabrics, 13m. metres.

Labour. Legislation regulating conditions of employment in certain industrial undertakings was first introduced in 1949. The subsequent adoption of certain international minimum standards led to the enactment of the Labour Act of 1959, which establishes basic provisions dealing with hours of work; holidays with pay; the payment of wages, salaries and overtime; the formation, registration and activities of employers' and workers' organizations; employment contracts and collective agreements; the settlement of disputes; industrial safety, health and welfare; and labour inspection. Regulations concerning safety, health and welfare in industrial premises, conciliation procedure and the settlement of disputes, the formation, registration and activities of trade unions, the duties and powers of labour inspectors have since been promulgated. The employment of foreigners is controlled by regulations promulgated in 1960. Responsibility for the enforcement of the Labour Act, 1959, and supporting legislation is entrusted to provincial and district departments of labour.

According to a survey of manpower undertaken in 1958, the country's non-agricultural work force numbered about 1·37m., of whom nearly 70,000 were women and about 33,000 were under 13 years of age. Just over half (718,000) were engaged in crafts, production process and related occupations, while 18% were employed in sales and related occupations.

Commerce. Imports and exports were as follows for years ending 20 March (1m. rials):

	1975	*1976*
Imports	400,600	694,100
Exports	1,435,800	1,370,100

Total trade between Iran and UK (British Department of Trade returns, in £1,000 sterling):

	1973	*1974*	*1975*	*1976*	*1977*
Imports to UK	237,381	513,270	700,933	1,049,263	789,819
Exports and re-exports from UK	169,412	278,580	494,621	510,901	654,661

COMMUNICATIONS

Roads. In 1970 there were 10,749 km of completely surfaced roads and 1,537 km of roads in the process of surfacing. First- and second-class (graded, all weather) roads total (1975) 16,000 km and third-class roads 30,000 km.

In 1974 passenger cars and taxis numbered 119,851; commercial vehicles, 13,193; buses, 2,611, and motor cycles, 19,785.

Railways. The Iranian State Railways have a total length of 4,944 km, distributed as follows: Tehrán–Bandar Sháh, 464; Tehrán–Bandar Sháhpoor, 928; Ahwáz–Khorramshahr, 121; Tehrán–Tabriz, 734; Garmsar–Meshed, 813; Qum–Káshán, 98; Tabriz–Julfa, 145; Soofian–Sharaf Kháneh, 52; Zâhedán–Mirjáveh, 92; oil company railways, 165; Tehrán–Shahr Rey, 8; Bandar Sháh–Gorgán, 36. Extensive plans exist

(1977) for construction of new routes and upgrading existing lines, and an underground railway in Tehrán began in 1977.

Aviation. The principal airlines which link Tehrán with Europe and the Middle East are Air France, British Airways, Ariana, Iraqi Airways, Alitalia, PANAM, Swissair, LIA, KLM, PIA, SAS, Qantas, SABENA, El Al, Lufthansa, Aeroflot and Middle East Air Lines. British Airways, Qantas, Lufthansa, PANAM and Air France also connect Tehrán with the Far East. Aryana (Afghánistán) Airline connects Tehrán with Lebanon, Syria and Afghánistán. British Airways, KLM and SAS operate services to Abadán and Iran National Airlines Corporation, registered on 29 March 1962, has monopoly rights on all internal flights and also operates in the Persian Gulf; in 1965 it inaugurated European services. The Iranian Government owns 51% of its shares.

Shipping. During the year ended 21 March 1970, 1,790 vessels of 19,369,000 tons entered at ports of the Persian Gulf, and 619 vessels totalling 195,095 tons entered ports on the Caspian Sea. In 1973, 211,005,000 tonnes of goods were loaded at Iranian ports and 3,766,000 tonnes were unloaded.

Navigation on the Lake of Rezáyeh, from Sharaf-Khaneh to Kolmankháneh, is served by some 5 tugs and 9 barges for the transport of goods and passengers. The service runs twice a week. On the river Karun likewise, from Khorramshahr to Ahwáz, an irregular service for cargo only both ways is run by the Iran Transport Co. and the Karun Navigation Co., and some local firms run daily trips by motor boat, for passengers and merchandise. By changing into lighter-draught boats at Ahwáz both can be taken up to Shallili near Shushtar.

Post and Broadcasting. Postal, telegraph and telephone services are administered by the Iranian Ministry of Posts, Telegraphs and Telephones.

The Indo-European Telegraph Company relinquished its lines in Iran in 1931, while the telephone system was nationalized in 1952. There is wireless-telegraph communication between Tehrán and Tabriz, Meshed, Kermánsháh, Kermán, Khorramshahr, Bushehr, Yazd, Shiráz and Lingeh and a wireless-telephone link between Tehrán and Tabriz. Tehrán is also in wireless communication with Europe and is linked by wireless telephone with Baghdad, London, Berne and New York. In 1977 the number of telephones was 781,537, of which some 369,500 were in Tehrán. Wireless sets numbered 7m. in 1972, and television sets 1m.

Cinemas (1975). There were 430 cinemas with 299,191 seats.

Newspapers. There were in 1972, 39 daily papers in Tehrán and other cities. Their circulation is relatively small, *Ettela'át* and *Kayhán* leading with about 100,000 each. Total circulation was 750,000. Two English-language and a French-language daily appear in Tehrán.

JUSTICE, RELIGION, EDUCATION AND WELFARE

Justice. The judicial system is modelled on that of France. There are justices of the peace in villages and small towns, higher courts in the large towns, police magistrates in all important places, courts of appeal in Tehrán, Tabriz, Shiráz, Kermánsháh, Esfahán, Meshed, Kermán and Ahwáz, and a court of cassation, or supreme court, in Tehrán. The courts are supervised by the Ministry of Justice. New civil, criminal and commercial codes based on French and Swiss codes were introduced in the early 1930s.

Religion. The official religion is the Shia branch of Islam, known as the *Ithna-Ashariyya*, which recognizes 12 Imáms or spiritual successors of the Prophet Mohammad. Of the total population, 850,000 are of the Sunnî sect, 19,816 are Parsîs (Zartushti), 60,682 Jews, 108,421 Armenians, 20,000 Nestorians and 8,500 Protestants.

The Shia Moslems reject the *Sunna* or tradition, as distinct from the actual text of the Koran, both of which are recognized by the Sunnî Moslems. The power of the clergy has diminished, as the result of the increased power of the central government. The highest authority is the leading *ayatullah*, at present *ayatullah* Hakim.

All mosques and shrines have some endowments (*ouqáf*, sing, *vaqf*), now devoted to charitable and educational institutions and administered by the Ministry of Education. The shrines of some favourite saints are richly endowed and own extensive property.

The Gregorian National Armenians form 3 dioceses. There are also a few thousand Roman Catholic Armenians, who have a bishop of their own rite at Esfahán, the bishop of the Latin rite residing at Rezayeh (Urmia). There is an Anglican bishop residing at Esfahán.

Education. A law providing for the gradual establishment of compulsory primary education was passed in July 1943. In 1972 schooling was available for 80% of the children of school age. The literate population is estimated at 36·9%.

The influence of the French educational system has been prominent. As in France, education is highly centralized.

The curricula for primary and secondary schools are drawn up by the Ministry of Education.

The great majority of primary and secondary schools are state schools. Grants are made to private schools. Elementary education in state schools and university education are free; small fees are charged for state-run secondary schools. Textbooks are issued free of charge to pupils in the first 4 grades of elementary schools.

In 1975–76 there were 6·63m. pupils attending 44,242 schools. Approximately 4·46m. of these were at primary schools.

Higher education is provided by universities and technical colleges. In 1975–76, 705,009 students were attending institutes of higher education. Tehrán University (with 11 constituent faculties) is the largest in Iran; it maintains a secondary teachers' training college and a midwifery school. There are also universities at Shiráz (letters, agriculture, science, medicine), Tabriz (letters, agriculture, science, medicine, pharmacy), Rezayeh (agriculture), Esfahán (letters, pharmacy, medicine), Meshed (medicine, letters, theology) and Ahwáz (agriculture, science, medicine). There are in Tehrán an Institute of Technology for the training of teachers of vocational subjects at secondary-school level; a Polytechnic with institutes of mechanical, textile and electrical engineering and building construction; and the National University, a private institution for fee-paying students. The National Iranian Oil Company maintains an institute of technology at Abadán. The Central Treaty Organization in 1959 set up an institute of nuclear science in Tehrán (which has now been handed over to Iran), and in 1961 opened an agricultural machinery and soil conservation training centre at Karaj near Tehrán, and in 1960 a vocational training centre south of Tehrán.

Health. The Ministry of Health controls the health of the country through the Department of Public Health, which has achieved some remarkable results in the fight against malaria; large areas along the Caspian and the Persian Gulf and in Azerbáiján are now free from malaria. Opium addiction has been greatly reduced, and the cultivation of the poppy has been practically eradicated. Programmes to combat tuberculosis, smallpox, trachoma, venereal diseases, etc., have been introduced.

In 1975 about 45,604 hospital beds (half of them in Tehrán) were available in 498 hospitals. Medical personnel included 10,054 physicians and surgeons and 1,462 dentists.

Numerous health centres, dispensaries and maternal and child health clinics and 14 schools of nursing have been set up.

Social Security. A system of social security benefits covering accident, sickness, retirement, death, marriage, maternity and childbirth and free medical attention and hospitalization for insured contributors and their families is embodied in the Workers' Social Insurance Law, 1960. This law provides for the insurance under the scheme of all workers in receipt of wages or salaries, but is at present being applied to some 683,496 workers employed mainly in industrial and mining establishments employing 10 or more workers. It also provides for the compulsory payment by employers of family allowances to workers with 2 or more children.

DIPLOMATIC REPRESENTATIVES

OF IRAN IN GREAT BRITAIN (16 Prince's Gate, London, SW7 1PX)

Ambassador: Parviz C. Radji.

OF GREAT BRITAIN IN IRAN (Ave. Ferdowsi, Tehrán)

Ambassador: Sir Anthony Parsons, KCMG, MVO, MC.

OF IRAN IN THE USA (3005 Massachusetts Ave., NW, Washington, D.C., 20008)

Ambassador: Ardeshir Zahedi.

OF THE USA IN IRAN (260 Takhte Jamshid Ave., Tehrán)

Ambassador: William H. Sullivan.

OF IRAN TO THE UNITED NATIONS

Ambassador: Fereydoun Hoveyda.

Books of Reference

Statistical Information: The principal statistical agencies of the Government are: (1) Department of Census, Civil Registration, and Statistics (Ministry of the Interior). *Director-General:* Sayyed Mehdi Hesabi; Publications on demographical statistics, in Persian. (2) Publicity and Information Department of the Seven-year Plan Organization. *Director:* Dr Mohammed Ali Rashti; Publications on industry, labour, agriculture, in English and Persian. (3) Statistical and Economic Research Department of the Bank Melli Iran; Publishes *Monthly Bulletin*, in English and Persian. (4) Customs Department (Ministry of Finance), publishes monthly and annual reports, in French and Persian. (5) and (6) Ministry of Labour and Ministry of Industry and Mines, publish statistical year-books.

H.M. The Shah, *Mission for My Country*. 1961.—*The White Revolution*. 1967 (both in Persian)

Adli, Abolfazi, *Aussenhandel und Aussenwirtschaftspolitik des Iran*. Berlin, 1960

Arberry, A. J. (ed.), *The Cambridge History of Iran*. 8 vols. CUP, 1968 ff.

Benedick, R. E., *Industrial Finance in Iran*. Harvard Univ. Press, 1964

Bharier, J., *Economic Development in Iran, 1900–1970*. OUP, 1971

Farahmand, S., *Der Wirtschaftsaufbau des Iran*. Basel, 1965

Haim, S., *Shorter Persian–English Dictionary*. Tehran, 1958

Handley-Taylor, G., *Bibliography of Iran*. London, 1964; latest ed., 1968

Lambton, A. K. S., *Landlord and Peasant in Persia*. OUP, 1953.—*Persian Vocabulary*. CUP, 1954

Lenczowski, George, *Russia and the West in Iran*. Cornell Univ., 1948; supplement, 1954

Looney, R. E., *The Economic Development of Iran: A Recent Survey with Projections to 1981*. New York, 1973

Malek-Mahdavi, Ahmed, *Le Parlement Iranien*. Univ. of Neuchâtel, 1954

Ramazani, R. K., *The Persian Gulf: Iran's Role*. Univ. Press of Virginia, 1972.—*Iran's Foreign Policy 1941–1973*. Univ. Press of Virginia, 1975

Steinglass, F. J., *A Comprehensive Persian–English Dictionary*. 2nd ed. London, 1930

Ward, P., *Touring Iran*. London, 1971

Wilber, D. N., *Iran Past and Present*. 6th ed. Princeton Univ. Press, 1967

Zakhoder, B. N. (ed.), *Sovremennyi Iran*. Moscow, 1957

IRAQ

al Jumhouriya al 'Iraqia

Capital: Baghdad
Population: 11·5m. (1976)
GNP per capita: US$1,390 (1976)

HISTORY. On 14 July 1958 the Republic of Iraq was declared by a group of Army officers, after an armed *coup d'état* in which the reigning King Faisal II and his uncle, the ex-Regent the Emir Abdul Ilah, and the Prime Minister, Nuri al Said, lost their lives. For the next 4 years the country was under the control of Gen. Qasim, who was executed on 9 Feb. 1963, following a *coup d'état* by the Army and Air Force on the previous day.

The republican regime terminated the adherence of Iraq to the Arab Federation (*see* THE STATESMAN'S YEAR-BOOK, 1958, p. 806).

The provisional constitution on 4 May 1964 declared Iraq to be an 'Arab, Islamic, independent and sovereign republic' based on democracy and socialism; complete Arab unity was the aim. The National Council for the Revolutionary Command, which took office on 8 Feb. 1963, following the overthrow of Gen. Qasim, affirmed its adherence to the spirit of the 14 July Revolution. It abolished the Sovereignty Council, which had exercised the functions of the Presidency since 1958, and appointed a new President and Cabinet. It reached agreement with Kuwait on the question of Kuwaiti sovereignty, which Gen. Qasim had disputed, but failed to find a peaceful solution to the 2-year-old Kurdish revolt. Increasing domination of the government by Ba'ath Party members and consequent estrangement from Egypt led to a military *coup d'état* on 18 Nov. 1963. In April 1966 Field Marshal Abdul Salam Muhammad Arif, who came to power in Feb. 1963, and survived the revolution of Nov. 1963, was killed in a helicopter crash. His brother, Abdul Rahman Muhammad Arif, was elected President by the National Defence Council.

A cease-fire in Kurdistan was proclaimed on 10 Feb. 1964, but fighting was resumed in April 1965. In June 1966 the Government announced a peace plan which the Kurds accepted in principle. In March 1970 the Revolutionary Command Council announced a complete and constitutional settlement of the Kurdish issue.

AREA AND POPULATION. Iraq is bounded north by Turkey, east by Iran, south-east by the Persian Gulf, south by Saudi Arabia, west by Jordan and Syria. The country has an area of 438,446 sq. km (171,267 sq. miles) and a population (census 14 Oct. 1965) of 8,097,230. Estimated population (1976) 11,505,234. The capital is Baghdad (2,969,000).

Each Governorate is administered by a Governor, and is subdivided into *qadhas* (under Qaimaqams) and *nahiyahs* (under Mudirs). The following are the area (in sq. km) and population (in 1,000, estimated, 1975) for each Governorate:

Maysan	17,945	362	Thi-Qar	13,900	549
Arbil	15,315	491	Al-Anbar	137,969	387
Baghdad	22,973	3,523	Sulaimaniya	11,993	555
Basrah	18,022	947	Al-Muthanna	74,536	152
Diyala	15,742	496	Ta'min[1]	19,543	600
Al-Qadisiya	9,359	416	Kerbela	7,170	588
Babylon	6,889	594	Neutral Zone, water territories	4,446	...
Wasit	14,814	386			
Nineveh	38,670	909			
D'hok	9,754	168			

[1] Formerly Kirkuk governorate.

Two new governorates were announced in Feb. 1976: Salah ad-Din and Najaf.

Vital statistics, registered in 1973: Births, 166,387; deaths, 40,750, infant mortality, 4,559.

The largest towns are Baghdad, Basra, Mosul, Kirkuk and Najaf.

On 25 Nov. 1933 the Council of the League of Nations fixed the boundary between Iraq and Syria, including the whole of the Jebel Sinjar in Iraq.

CONSTITUTION AND GOVERNMENT. Under the 1970 Constitution supreme power is vested in the Revolutionary Command Council, which elects the President and Vice-President pending the establishment of an elected National Assembly. The only legal political movement is the National Progressive Front, a coalition between the Ba'ath Party and the Iraq Communist Party. Two amendments to the Constitution were introduced in 1973 and 1974. The second granted autonomy to the area whose population was predominantly Kurdish.

President, Chairman of the Revolutionary Command Council, Minister of Defence: Maj.-Gen. Ahmed Hassan Bakr.

Deputy Chairman of the Revolutionary Command Council: Saddam Hussein al Takriti.

Vice-President: Taha Moheddin Marouf.

National flag: Three horizontal stripes of red, white, black, with 3 green stars on the white stripe.

DEFENCE. Military training is compulsory for all men when they reach the age of 18. This consists of 2 years' service with the colours and 18 years on the reserve. However, a man may volunteer for service in the army or change his conscript service into voluntary service. In such circumstances voluntary service is for 2 years, and he may extend it by periods of 2 years until he reaches the age of 45. The 2-year compulsory service can be extended in a national emergency. Many technicians and technically qualified officers serve up to 4 or 5 years.

Army. The strength of the Iraqi Army in 1977 was 160,000, organized into 4 infantry divisions, 4 armoured divisions, 3 independent brigades and Ministry of Defence troops.

Navy. The Navy comprises 12 *ex*-Soviet missile boats, 12 *ex*-Soviet torpedo boats, 3 *ex*-Soviet submarine chasers, 2 fleet minesweepers, 3 inshore minesweepers, 30 gunboats, 5 coastal craft and harbour patrol boats, 1 harbour authority craft (former presidential yacht) and a tug.

In 1978 naval personnel totalled 3,000 officers and ratings, recently increased on the acquisition of further fast craft from the USSR.

Air Force. Except for 2 squadrons of Hunter jet fighter-bombers bought from Britain and about 40 Alouette III, 10 Super Frelon and Gazelle helicopters acquired from France, the combat and transport squadrons are equipped primarily with aircraft of Soviet design, including 4 Tu-16 medium bombers, 50 Su-7 fighter-bombers, 90 MiG-23 and 120 MiG-21 interceptors, 30 MiG-17d night fighters and MiG-17c day interceptor and ground attack fighters, Mi-4, Mi-6 and Mi-8 helicopters, and An-12 and An-24 transports. A few Il-14s and smaller types are used in a transport-communications role, while Hunter, Jet Provost and L-29 Delfin aircraft are employed with Soviet-MiG-15UTI trainers and other types in the Air Force College and operational conversion unit. Total strength is about 25,000 personnel and 300 combat aircraft. Soviet 'Guideline', 'Goa' and 'Gainful' surface-to-air missiles are operational. Orders placed in 1977 are reported to include 36 Mirage F1 fighters from France, with an option on 36 more.

INTERNATIONAL RELATIONS

Membership. Iraq is a member of UN and the Arab League.

ECONOMY

Planning. Investment in the second 5-year economic plan 1965–70 totalled I.D.446·7m. and the third 5-year plan 1970–74 envisages total investment of I.D.1,169,000 including I.D.336·5m. for agricultural projects.

Budget. Revenue and expenditure (in 1,000 Iraqi dinars) for fiscal years ending 31 March:

	1968–69	*1969–70*	*1970–71*	*1971–72*	*1972–73*
Revenue	220,419	250,591	292,562	344,805	270,530
Expenditure	241,933	289,249	303,425	341,412	345,359

The above figures relate to the ordinary state budget; development expenditure is financed through a separate budget. Until the 1959–60 budget, 70% of the Iraqi government's share of oil revenues was allocated to development, the remainder going to the ordinary state budget. In 1959, however, the proportions were altered and the amount assigned to development was to be not less than 50% (1967–68: 158m. dinars).

Oil revenues account for nearly 50%, customs and excise for about 26% of the total revenue. The 1970–74 National Development Plan takes about 1,169,000 dinars, and education about 20% of the expenditure.

The public debt was 260m. dinars on 31 Dec. 1972.

Currency. The monetary unit is the *Iraqi dinar* (I.D.) = 1,000 *fils* = 10 *riyals* = 20 *dirhams*. Silver alloy coins for 100 and 50 fils (*dirham*) and 25 fils are in circulation, and other coins for 10, 5 and 1 fils. Notes are for $\frac{1}{4}$, $\frac{1}{2}$ and 1 dinar, and for 5 and 10 dinars. The total currency in circulation in Dec. 1972 amounted to 207m. dinars. The currency was formerly controlled by an Iraqi Currency Board sitting in London, but was taken over by the National Bank of Iraq on 1 July 1949, which in 1956 was re-named the Central Bank of Iraq.

Banking. The British Bank of the Middle East and the Eastern Bank and all other banks were nationalized on 14 July 1964.

In 1941 the Rafidain Bank, financed by the Iraqi Government, was instituted to carry out normal banking transactions with head office in Baghdad and branches in the chief towns and abroad, including London. In addition, there are 4 government banks which are authorized to issue loans to companies and individuals: the Industrial Bank, the Agricultural Bank, the Estate Bank, and the Mortgage Bank.

In March 1972 post office savings amounted to 8,437,000 dinars held by 201,455 depositors.

Weights and Measures. The metric system is in general use.

ENERGY AND NATURAL RESOURCES

Oil. The greater part of Iraq's oil production comes from the Iraq Petroleum Company's field at Kirkuk (found in 1927). This company, an international group, has constructed pipelines to the Mediterranean, including one to Banias on the Syrian coast, with a throughput of about 35m. tons in 1960. The Mosul Petroleum Co. Ltd holds a concession for oil covering Iraqi territory west of the Tigris and north of the 33rd parallel of latitude. Oil was found at Ain Zalah, north-west of Mosul, and the company has laid a pipeline from there to Baiji. The Basra Petroleum Company have been granted a concession for oil covering the southernmost part of Iraq (the old Basra vilayet). High-grade quality oil has been found here, and production started in Dec. 1951. Production at the oilfield of Rumaila started in Dec. 1954; its pipeline is linked to the Zubair–Fao system. An oilfield near Khanaqin, in the area known as the Transferred Territories near the Iranian frontier, was, until Nov. 1958, operated by the Khanaqin Oil Company, a subsidiary of the British Petroleum Company, and is now being operated by the Iraqi Government. There is a pipeline to a refinery near Khanaqin. Oil for consumption in Iraq is refined by the government oil refineries administration (GORA) and is distributed and marketed in Iraq at cheap prices by the Ministry of Oil and Minerals.

Under an agreement dated 3 Feb. 1952 between the Government and the Iraq, Basra and Mosul Petroleum Companies, the Government receives 50% of the profits before the deduction of foreign taxes, and in any case not less than I.D.25m. in

1955 and thereafter, from which date onward the minimum rate of oil-production will be 30m. tons annually. On 11 Dec. 1961, on the severance of the negotiations with the oil companies, the Iraqi Government enacted a law defining the areas in which the Iraq Petroleum Company and its associates may carry out operations. The defined areas total less than ½% of the concessions.

The total crude petroleum production was 89·6m. tonnes in 1974. Revenue received by the Iraqi Government from oil amounted to I.D.140·8m. in 1966; I.D.131·7m. in 1967; I.D.174m. in 1968; I.D.170m. in 1969.

An oil refinery (annual output, 1m. tons) at Daura near Baghdad, and a bitumen refinery (annual output 60,000 tons) at Gayyarah in the Mosul district both started production in 1955 under the direction of the GORA. The Daura refinery has a capacity of 70,000 bbls per annum. A lubricating oil plant (annual output, 36,000 tons) had been added to the Daura refinery and started production in May 1957.

On 1 June 1972 President Bakr announced the nationalization of the Iraq Petroleum Company's concessions and the formation of a State company to manage the funds, assets and rights of IPC. IPC would be paid compensation although the company's alleged debts would be deducted from the amount. On 1 March 1973 the Mosul Petroleum Company was amalgamated with the Iraq Petroleum Company.

On 7 Oct. 1973 the Government nationalized the 23·75% share in the Basra Petroleum Company which was held by the American Near East Development Corporation.

Water. Iraq is a land of great potentialities. The soil of the country is rich, but there are vast areas which can be cultivated only if irrigated by canals or pumps. The Irrigation Ministry operates several canal systems, new dams have been completed and other irrigation works are under construction.

Agriculture. An Agrarian Reform Law, issued in Sept. 1958, limits land ownership to 1,000 *dunums* for flow-irrigated land and to 2,000 *dunums* for rain-irrigated land.

In 1957–58, 16m. *mesharas* were planted, 13m. lay fallow, 2m. were uncultivable, 595,000 were orchards and vineyards, 18,000 were pasture and 45,000 woodland. About 13m. *mesharas* were irrigated.

The chief winter crops (1974) are wheat, 1,339,000 tonnes and barley, 533,000 tonnes. The chief summer crop is rice, 68,000 tonnes. The date crop is important (1974 production, 385,000 tons), the country furnishing about 80% of the world's trade in dates (exports, 1972, 314,395 tonnes); the chief producing area is the totally irrigated riverain belt of the Shatt-el-Arab. Wool is also an important export (1972: 3,854 tonnes). In 1972, 3,071 tonnes of cotton were exported.

Livestock (1976): Cattle, 2·1m.; buffaloes, 175,000; sheep, 8·4m.; goats, 2·6m.; horses, 83,000; camels, 330,000; chickens, 17·5m.

Forestry. Up to 1969, 614,953 *dunums* have been demarcated and surveyed in Arbil, Mosul and Sulaimaniya Governorates.

INDUSTRY AND TRADE

Industry. Industrial and constructional establishments in 1974 numbered 26,332. Constructional establishments employed the largest number of workers. Other large employers were the brick industry, water and electricity services, date packing, the textile industry, cigarette factories, oil refining and the cement industry. Iraq is still relatively under-developed industrially but work has begun on 13 new industrial plants which are being established with Soviet equipment and technical assistance. A light-industries company was formed in 1960 to foster smaller industries.

On 14 July 1964 all banks, insurance companies and 32 of the largest industrial and commercial companies were nationalized. The nationalized industries comprise cement, asbestos, cigarettes, spinning and weaving, steel, paper, leather tanning, flour-mills and trading companies. Small firms in these fields were left in the private sector, except for cement, asbestos and cigarettes, which will be entirely in the public sector. The owners of the nationalized companies are to compensated for the value of their shares with state bonds maturing in 15 years and bearing 3% interest.

From the 1970–74 National Development Plan for industrialization, the sum of 208m. Iraqi dinars has been set aside to improve the country's industries.

Commerce. Imports and exports for 5 calendar years were as follows (in 1,000 Iraqi dinars):

	1971	*1972*	*1973*	*1974*	*1975*
Imports	247,870	234,680	270,317	700,087	1,044,664
Local exports	22,782	28,614	32,523	28,130	35,595
Transit	33,801	65,485	56,095	...	118,141

Movements of gold bullion and currency are excluded from the above table. Import values are c.i.f. plus landing charges, and include all goods cleared for home consumption whether subsequently re-exported or not. Exports do not include shipments of oil or re-exports, and are valued f.o.b.

The total trade between Iraq and UK for 5 years (British Department of Trade returns, in £1,000 sterling):

	1973	*1974*	*1975*	*1976*	*1977*
Imports to UK	30,678	106,577	102,525	279,530	331,714
Exports and re-exports from UK	27,057	59,838	136,472	149,853	166,940

COMMUNICATIONS

Roads. About 5,824 miles of roads and tracks have been developed for vehicular traffic. The main surfaced roads are: (1) the road north from Baghdad *via* Kirkuk, Arbil and Nineveh to a point near the Turkish frontier at Zakho, with branches from Kirkuk to the northern province of Sulaimaniya, from Arbil to the Iranian frontier, and from Nineveh to Sinjar; (2) about 350 miles of the main road west from Baghdad to the Jordan frontier; (3) the road east of Baghdad, which connects the road system of Iran near Khanaqin; and (4) the road south from Baghdad to Hilla and the holy city of Kerbela.

Vehicles registered in 1973 totalled 142,826, including 83,263 passenger cars, 28,353 lorries, 14,318 buses.

Railways. The Iraqi state railway system consists of a metre-gauge line from Basra, at the head of the Arabian Gulf, to Baghdad, 669·2 km. From Baghdad the line extends through Juloula (Qaraghan), which is 147·8 km from Baghdad on to Kirkuk 321·8 km, thence to the terminal station of Arbil 104·9 km. Khanaqin on the Iraqi–Iranian frontier is served by a branch line from Juloula (27·9 km). There is also a standard gauge (4 ft 8½ in.) line from Basra to Tel-Kotchek on the Syrian frontier; following the right bank of the Tigris *via* Nineveh, it links with the Syrian railway system at Tel-Kotchek, thus establishing a through service from the Gulf to Turkey, Egypt and Europe. The total length of track open in 1972 was 2,203 km. Proposals are being studied for a 404 km. standard-gauge line from Baghdad to Husaiba on the Syrian frontier, which would form part of a route to the Mediterranean port of Latakia and would serve phosphates deposits at Akashat by a 155 km branch line.

Aviation. Baghdad and Basra airports are served by British Airways, Lufthansa, Alitalia, Swissair, KLM, Middle East Air Lines, PIA, Iraqi Airways, Iranian Airways, Air Liban, United Arab Airlines and Aeroflot. In 1975 there arrived by air 390,440 passengers; 402,903 passengers left Iraqi airports on 7,979 flights.

Shipping. In 1975, 828 vessels of 8,343,000 NRT entered the ports of Basra and Um Kaser.

Post and Broadcasting. In 1973 there were 352 post and telegraph offices. Wireless telegraph services exist with UK, USA, UAR, Lebanon and Saudi Arabia, and wireless telephone services with UK, USA, Italy, UAR and USSR. Telephones, 1977, 319,591.

Cinemas (1976). There were 24 cinemas in Baghdad.

Newspapers (1976). In Baghdad there are 5 daily newspapers (one of which is in English).

JUSTICE, RELIGION, EDUCATION AND WELFARE

Justice. The courts are established throughout the country as follows: For civil matters: the court of cassation in Baghdad; 6 courts of appeal at Baghdad (2), Basra, Babylon, Mosul and Kirkuk; 16 courts of first instance with unlimited powers and 150 courts of first instance with limited powers, all being courts of single judges. In addition, 6 peace courts have peace court jurisdiction only. Tribal law was abolished in Aug. 1958.

For *Shara*' (religious) matters: the Shara' courts at all places where there are civil courts, constituted in some places of specially appointed Qadhis (religious judges) and in other places of the judges of the civil courts. For criminal matters: the court of cassation; 6 sessions courts (2 being presided over by the judge of the local court of first instance and 4 being identical with the courts of appeal). Magistrates' courts at all places where there are civil courts, constituted of civil judges exercising magisterial powers of the first and second class. There are also a number of third-class magistrates courts, powers for this purpose being granted to municipal councils and a number of administrative officials. Some administrative officials are granted the powers of a peace judge to deal with cases of debts due from cultivators.

Special religious courts for non-Catholic Christians at Baghdad, Basra and Nineveh which dealt with matters of personal status, such as divorce, separation and maintenance between husband and wife, have now been abolished, cases being dealt with by the civil courts.

The prison population at the end of 1973 was 6.025 men and 83 women, including persons on remand and in the reformatory school.

Religion. In 1965 there were 7,711,712 Moslems, 232,406 Christians, 3,187 Jews, 69,653 Yazidis and 14,262 Sabians.

Education. Primary and secondary education is free and primary education became compulsory in Sept. 1976. Primary school age is 6–12. Secondary education is for 6 years, of which the first 3 are termed intermediate. The medium of instruction is Arabic; Kurdish is used in primary schools in northern districts.

There were, in 1974–75, 202 kindergartens with 35,551 pupils and 1,397 teachers; 6,170 primary schools with 1,521,604 pupils and 57,490 teachers, and 1,099 secondary schools with 452,911 pupils and 16,644 teachers. Seventy-one vocational schools had 18,025 students.

There are 5 universities in Iraq: in 1974–75 Baghdad University had 26,961 students; Basrah, 7,835; Mosul, 7,325; Sulaimaniya, 2,289; Al-Mustransiriya, 18,903.

Health. In 1974 there were 4,734 doctors (including dentists); 162 hospitals with 21,582 beds.

DIPLOMATIC REPRESENTATIVES

OF IRAQ IN GREAT BRITAIN (21–22 Queen's Gate, London, SW7 5JG)

Ambassador: Taha Ahmed Al-Dawood.

OF GREAT BRITAIN IN IRAQ (Sharia Salah, Ud-Din, Karkh, Baghdad)

Ambassador: A. J. D. Stirling, CMG.

OF IRAQ TO THE UNITED NATIONS

Ambassador: Mohammed Said Al-Sahhaf.

Iraq broke off diplomatic relations with USA on 7 June 1967.

Books of Reference

Statistical Information: The Central Statistical Organization, Ministry of Planning, Baghdad (*President:* Dr Salah Al-Shaikhly) publishes an annual *Statistical Abstract* (latest issue 1973). Foreign Trade statistics are published annually by the Ministry of Planning.

Arfa, H., *The Kurds.* OUP, 1966

Langley, K. M., *The Industrialization of Iraq.* Harvard Univ. Press, 1961

IRISH REPUBLIC

Capital: Dublin
Population: 3·19m. (1977)
GNP per capita: US$2,560 (1976)

Éire

HISTORY. In April 1916 an insurrection against British rule took place and a republic was proclaimed. The armed struggle was renewed in 1919 and continued until 1921. The independence of Ireland was reaffirmed in Jan. 1919 by the National Parliament (*Dáil Éireann*), elected in Dec. 1918.

In 1920 an Act was passed by the British Parliament, under which separate Parliaments were set up for 'Southern Ireland' (26 counties) and 'Northern Ireland' (6 counties). The Unionists of the 6 counties accepted this scheme, and a Northern Parliament was duly elected on 24 May 1921. The rest of Ireland, however, ignored the Act.

On 6 Dec. 1921 a treaty was signed between Great Britain and Ireland by which Ireland accepted dominion status subject to the right of Northern Ireland to opt out. This right was exercised, and the border between *Saorstát Éireann* (26 counties) and Northern Ireland (6 counties) was fixed in Dec. 1925 as the outcome of an agreement between Great Britain, the Irish Free State and Northern Ireland. The agreement was ratified by the three parliaments.

Subsequently the constitutional links between *Saorstát Éireann* and the UK were gradually removed by the *Dáil*. The remaining formal association with the British Commonwealth by virtue of the External Relations Act, 1936, was severed when the Republic of Ireland Act, 1948, came into operation on 18 April 1949.

AREA AND POPULATION. The Republic lies in the Atlantic Ocean, separated from Great Britain by the Irish Sea to the east, and bounded north-east by Northern Ireland.

Counties and county boroughs	*Area in sq. miles*[1]	*Census population, 1971*		
		Males	*Females*	*Total*
Province of Leinster				
Carlow	346	17,502	16,735	34,237
Dublin County Borough	45	267,801	300,065	567,866
Dublin[2]	305	114,144	117,038	231,182
Dun Laoghaire Borough	7	24,063	29,108	53,171
Kildare	654	37,279	34,698	71,977
Kilkenny	796	31,828	29,645	61,473
Laoighis	664	23,805	21,454	45,259
Longford	403	14,891	13,359	28,250
Louth	317	37,511	37,440	74,951
Meath	903	36,977	34,752	71,729
Offaly	771	27,029	24,800	51,829
Westmeath	681	27,544	26,026	53,570
Wexford	908	43,768	42,583	86,351
Wicklow	782	33,318	32,977	66,295
Total of Leinster	7,580	737,460	760,680	1,498,140
Province of Munster				
Clare	1,231	39,002	36,006	75,008
Cork County Borough	14	61,731	66,914	128,645
Cork	2,866	115,055	109,183	224,238
Kerry	1,815	58,404	54,368	112,772
Limerick County Borough	7	27,626	29,535	57,161
Limerick	1,030	43,160	40,138	83,298

[1] Exclusive of certain rivers, lakes and tideways.
[2] Excludes Dun Laoghaire borough.

Counties and county boroughs	Area in sq. miles[1]	Census population, 1971 Males	Females	Total
Province of Munster—contd.				
Tipperary, N.R.	771	28,190	26,147	54,337
Tipperary, S.R.	872	35,333	33,895	69,228
Waterford County Borough	4	15,421	16,547	31,968
Waterford	706	23,349	21,998	45,347
Total of Munster	9,315	447,271	434,731	882,002
Province of Connacht				
Galway	2,293	77,842	71,381	149,223
Leitrim	589	15,269	13,091	28,360
Mayo	2,084	56,402	53,123	109,525
Roscommon	951	28,294	25,225	53,519
Sligo	693	25,887	24,388	50,275
Total of Connacht	6,611	203,694	187,208	390,902
Province of Ulster (part of)				
Cavan	730	27,819	24,799	52,618
Donegal	1,865	55,424	52,920	108,344
Monaghan	498	24,092	22,150	46,242
Total of Ulster (part of)	3,093	107,335	99,869	207,204
Total	26,599[2]	1,495,760	1,482,488	2,978,248

[1] Exclusive of certain rivers, lakes and tideways.
[2] 68,893 sq. km.

The population has declined since 1841, when the 26 counties had 6,528,799 inhabitants; there were 3,221,823 in 1901; 3,139,688 in 1911; 2,971,992 in 1926; 2,968,420 in 1936; 2,955,107 in 1946; 2,898,264 in 1956; 2,818,341 in 1961; 2,884,002 in 1966, and 2,978,248 in 1971.

Vital statistics for 4 calendar years:

	Births	Marriages	Deaths		Births	Marriages	Deaths
1973	68,713	22,816	34,192	1975	67,178	21,280	33,173
1974	68,907	22,883	34,921	1976[1]	68,167	20,431	33,284

[1] Provisional.

Passenger movements by sea were in 1976, outward, 847,155; inward, 865,706.

CONSTITUTION AND GOVERNMENT. The Irish Republic is a sovereign independent, democratic republic. Its parliament exercises jurisdiction in 26 of the 32 counties of Ireland.

The first constitution of the Irish Free State came into operation on 6 Dec. 1922. Certain provisions which were regarded as contrary to the national sentiments were gradually removed by successive amendments, with the result that at the end of 1936 the text differed considerably from the original document. On 14 June 1937 a new constitution was approved by Parliament (*Dáil Éireann*) and enacted by a plebiscite on 1 July 1937. This constitution came into operation on 29 Dec. 1937. Under it the name Ireland (Éire) was restored.

The constitution provides that, pending the reintegration of the national territory, the laws enacted by the Parliament established by the constitution shall have the same area and extent of application as those of the Irish Free State.

The *Oireachtas* or National Parliament consists of the President and two Houses, viz., a House of Representatives, called *Dáil Éireann*, and a Senate, called *Seanad Éireann*, consisting of 60 members. The *Dáil*, consisting of 148 members, is elected by adult suffrage. Of the 60 members of the Senate, 11 are nominated by the *Taoiseach* (Prime Minister), 6 are elected by the universities and the remaining 43 are elected from 5 panels of candidates established on a vocational basis, representing the following public services and interests: (1) national language and culture, literature, art, education and such professional interests as may be defined by law for the purpose of this panel; (2) agricultural and allied interests, and fisheries; (3) labour, whether organized or unorganized; (4) industry and commerce, including banking, finance, accountancy, engineering and architecture; (5) public administration and social services, including voluntary social activities. The electing body is a college of about 900 members, comprising members of the *Dáil*, Senate, county boroughs and county councils.

A maximum period of 90 days is afforded to the Senate for the consideration or amendment of Bills sent to that House by the *Dáil*, but the Senate has no power to veto legislative proposals.

No amendment of the constitution can be effected except with the approval of the people given at a referendum.

Agreement on the establishment of a Council of Ireland was reached at a meeting held at Sunningdale on 6–9 Dec. 1973. Members of the Irish and UK governments attended together with the Northern Ireland Executive-designate.

Irish is the first official language; English is recognized as a second official language.

For further details of the Constitution *see* THE STATESMAN'S YEAR-BOOK, 1952, pp. 1123–34.

President: Pádraig Óhlrighile (Patrick Hillery), installed on 3 Dec. 1976. The President holds office for 7 years.

Former Presidents: Dr Douglas Hyde (1938–45; Seán T. O. Ceallaigh (1945–59; 2 terms); Éamon de Valéra (1959–73; 2 terms); Erskine Childers (1973–74; died in office); Cearbhall Ó Dálaigh (1974–76; resigned).

A general election was held on 16 June 1977: Fianna Fáil, 84 (1973 election, 69); Fine Gael, 43 (54); Labour Party, 17 (19); Independents, 4 (2).

There are no formal party divisions in the Senate.

The Fianna Fáil Government consisted of the following members in Feb. 1978:

Taoiseach (*Prime Minister*): Sean Ó Loinsigh (John Lynch).

Tánaiste (*Deputy Prime Minister*), *Minister for Finance and Minister for the Public Service:* Seoirse Ó Colla (George Colley). *Fisheries:* Brian Ó Luineacháin (Brian J. Lenihan). *Environment:* Salbhastar Baireád (Sylvester Barrett). *Agriculture:* Séamus MacGiobúin (James Gibbons). *Labour:* Eoghan MacGearailt (Gene FitzGerald). *The Gaeltacht:* Donncha Ó Gallchobhair (Denis Gallagher). *Tourism and Transport and Posts and Telegraphs:* Pádraig Ó Fachtna (Patrick Faulkner). *Foreign Affairs:* Micheál Ó Cinneíde (Michael O'Kennedy). *Education:* Sean P. Mac Uilliam (John Patrick Wilson). *Industry, Commerce and Energy:* Deasún Ó Máille (Desmond J. O'Malley). *Justice:* Gearóid Ó Coileáin (Gerard Collins). *Defence:* Roibéard Ó Maoildhia (Robert Molloy). *Economic Planning and Development:* Mháirtín Ó Donnchadha (Martin O'Donoghue). *Health and Social Welfare:* Cathal Ó hEochaidh (Charles J. Haughey). *Attorney-General:* Antoine Ó hEadramáin (Anthony J. Hederman).

There were 10 Ministers of State.

National flag: Three vertical strips of green, white, orange.

National anthem: The Soldier's Song (words by P. Kearney; music by P. Heaney).

Local Government. The elected local authorities comprise 27 county councils, 4 county borough corporations, 7 borough corporations, 49 urban district councils and 28 town commissions. All the members of these authorities are elected under a system of proportional representation, normally every 5 years. All residents of an area who have reached the age of 18 are entitled to vote in the local election for their area. Women are eligible for election as members of local authorities in the same manner and on the same conditions as men. Elected members are not paid, but provision is made for the payment of travelling expenses and subsistence allowances.

The range of services for which local authorities are responsible are broken down into 8 main programme groups as follows: Housing and Building; Road Transportation and Safety; Water Supply and Sewerage; Development Incentives and Controls; Environmental Protection; Recreation and Amenity; Agriculture, Education, Health and Welfare and Miscellaneous Services. Because of the small size of their administrative areas the functions which are actually carried out by town commissioners and many of the urban district councils have tended to become increasingly limited, and the more important tasks of local government have become the responsibility of the county councils.

The local authorities have a system of government which combined an elected council and a whole-time manager. The elected members have specific functions reserved to them which include the making of rates (local tax), the borrowing of money, the adoption of development plans, the making, amending or revoking of bye-laws and the nomination of persons to other bodies. The managers, who are paid officers of their authorities, are responsible for the performance of all functions which are not reserved to the elected members, including the employment of staff, making of contracts, management of local authority property, collection of rates (tax) and rents and the day-to-day administration of local authority affairs. The manager for a county council is manager also for every borough corporation, urban district council and board of town commissioners whose functional area is wholly within the county. A central body called the Local Appointments Commission is charged with the duty of selecting suitable persons to be appointed by local authorities to chief executive offices, professional offices and other prescribed offices. Where a prescribed office becomes vacant, the local authority must request the Commissioners to recommend to them a suitable persn. The Commissioners normally select persons for appointment by the machinery of selection boards.

The revenue expenditure of local authorities is financed by a local tax, called rates, on the occupation of non-domestic property, grants and subsidies from the central government and payments for certain services which they provide. Capital expenditure is financed mainly by means of borrowing from the Local Loans Fund, which is operated by the central government, and from banking and insurance institutions.

Local authorities use a scheme of combined purchasing to obtain commodities of standard quality at the lowest possible price. Official supply contractors are appointed annually by the Minister for Local Government on the recommendation of an advisory committee.

DEFENCE. Under the direction of the President, and subject to the provisions of the Defence Act, 1954, the military command of the Defence Forces is exercisable by the Government through the Minister for Defence. To aid and counsel the Minister for Defence on all matters in relation to the business of the Department of Defence on which he may consult it, there is a Council of Defence consisting of the Parliamentary Secretary to the Minister, the Secretary of the Department of Defence, the Chief of Staff, the Adjutant-General and the Quartermaster-General. Establishments provide at present for a Permanent Defence Force of approximately 15,000 all ranks including the Air Corps and the Naval Service. The Defence Estimates for the year ending 31 Dec. 1977 provide for approximately 18,665 all ranks of the Reserve Defence Force. Recruitment is on a voluntary basis. Minimum term of enlistment is 4 years in the Permanent Defence Force.

The Defence Estimates for the year ending 31 Dec. 1977 provide for an expenditure of £85,223,000.

From July 1960 to June 1964, Irish troops formed part of the UN Force in the Congo, which from Jan. 1961 to March 1962, was under an Irish Commander.

An Irish contingent formed part of the UN Force in Cyprus from April 1964 to Oct. 1973, when the contingent was transferred to the UN Emergency Force in the Middle East. The contingent continued to serve with the latter force until May 1974. Irish officers have served also with the UN in the Lebanon and in Papua New Guinea. Twelve officers served with the UN Observation Mission from Sept. 1965 to March 1966. Irish officers are at present serving with the UN Truce Supervision Organization and the UN Disengagement Observer Force in the Middle East.

Army. There are at present 6 brigades in the Army. Each comprises 3 infantry battalions and a squadron or company from each Corps (except Ordnance and Air).

Navy. The Naval Service comprises 2 new all-weather fishery protection vessels or corvettes completed in the Irish Republic in 1972 and 1977, 3 coastal minesweepers acquired from Britain in 1971 for fishery protection, 1 training ship and 1 tender. Naval personnel (1978) totalled 650 officers and ratings.

Air Force. The Air Corps has a personnel strength of approximately 700 all ranks and 40 aircraft. There are 8 Cessna FR-172H aircraft for border patrol, 6 Magister armed jet trainers and 10 SIAI-Marchetti SF.260W armed piston-engined trainers with dual combat responsibility; 8 Alouette III helicopters; a twin-turboprop Super King Air for coastal fishery patrol; a Dove light transport and some Provost trainers.

INTERNATIONAL RELATIONS

Membership. The Irish Republic is a member of UN, OECD, the Council of Europe and EEC.

ECONOMY

Budget. Receipts and expenditures (in £1m.):

	1974[1]	*1975*[2]
Receipts		
Customs duties	108·6	175·4
Excise duties	89·3	157·4
Income tax and surtax	170·5	331·7
Corporation profits tax, etc.	19·0	26·5
Value-added tax	112·3	175·1
Stamp duties	9·4	13·3
Estate, etc., duties	11·5	13·5
Motor vehicle duties	19·1	27·9
Post Office	42·5	69·0
Capital taxes	—	3·7
Agricultural levies	2·6	2·1
Total (including other items)	651·4	1,091·2
Current expenditure		
Debt service	141·0	241·1
Agriculture, etc.	54·9	95·7
Education	48·6	183·1
Transport	34·5	56·7
Post Office	37·0	66·5
Defence	31·2	59·2
Justice (including Police)	29·4	56·4
Social Welfare	119·0	212·9
Health	102·4	207·5
Superannuation	22·0	37·7
Industry	17·1	40·0
Total (including other items)	743·7	1,350·0

[1] From 1 April to 31 Dec. [2] From 1 Jan. to 31 Dec.

Capital expenditure amounted to £334·6m. in 1975, and the estimate for 1976 is £419·9m.

On 31 Dec. 1975 the liabilities totalled £2,651m. The assets were: Electricity scheme, £50·1m.: local loans fund, £607·5m.; national transport organization, £17·4m.; industrial credit, £26·7m.; turf development, £17·7m.; reconstruction finance, £22m.; shares in companies established under state auspices, £99m.; exchequer balance, £605,500; other assets, £235m.; total, £1,076m.

Currency. The unit of currency is the Irish *pound,* which since June 1972 has been floating in line with the pound sterling against other currencies, the one-for-one relationship between the two currencies being maintained. The dollar rate of the

Irish pound at end-Oct. 1976 was £1 = $1.60. The Central Bank has the sole right of issuing legal tender notes; token coinage is issued by the Minister for Finance through the Bank. Decimal currency was adopted in 1971.

The volume of legal-tender notes outstanding at 2 Dec. 1975 was £294,429,000. Total notes and coins in circulation in Dec. 1975 amounted to £314,557,000.

Banking. The Central Bank, which was established as from 1 Feb. 1943, in accordance with the Central Bank Act, 1942, replaced the Currency Commission, which was set up under the Currency Act, 1927, and had been responsible *inter alia* for the regulation of the note issue. In addition to the powers and functions of the Currency Commission the Central Bank has the power of receiving deposits from banks and public authorities, of rediscounting Exchequer bills and bills of exchange, of making advances to banks against such bills or against Government securities, of fixing and publishing rates of interest for rediscounting bills, or buying and selling certain Government securities and securities of any international bank or financial institution formed wholly or mainly by governments. The Bank also collects and publishes information relating to monetary and credit matters. The Central Bank Act, 1971, gives further powers to the Central Bank in the regulation of banking including licensing of banks, the supervision of their operations and control of liquidity and reserve ratios. The capital of the Bank is £40,000, of which £24,000 has been paid up and is held by the Minister for Finance.

The Board of Directors of the Central Bank consists of a Governor, appointed by the President of the Republic on the advice of the Government, and 8 directors, all appointed by the Minister for Finance, 6 direct and 2 from among directors of the Associated Banks (the term applied to the 4 shareholding banks associated with the former Currency Commission).

There are 4 commercial banks associated with the Central Bank: The Bank of Ireland, Allied Irish Banks Ltd, the Ulster Bank and the Northern Bank.

At 31 Dec. 1975 the Associated Banks had total liabilities and assets balancing at £3,257·7m., including £1,761·2m. current deposit and other accounts, £838·3m. loans and advances, £524·2m. government bills and investments and £222·3m. balance (inclusive of statutory deposits) with the Central Bank. The commercial banking system also includes 39 licensed banks not 'associated' with the Central Bank. At 31 Dec. 1976 these non-associated banks had total liabilities and assets balancing at £1,417·4m.

The post office savings bank has approximately 2,142,000 (including 1·07m. dormant) accounts and the amount due at 31 Dec. 1975 was £180·5m. The trustee savings banks had deposits of £85·3m. at 31 Dec. 1975.

Weights and Measures. The Imperial system is in use but conversion to metric is in progress.

ENERGY AND NATURAL RESOURCES

Electricity. The generating and supplying of electricity and the construction and maintenance of the nationwide electricity distribution system is the function of the Electricity Supply Board, a State-sponsored body established in 1927. The total generating capacity is 2,290 mw. In the year ending 31 March 1977 the total sales of electricity amounted to 6,783m. units supplied to 959,428 consumers. Nuclear energy is not yet produced or used in the Irish energy sector. In late 1973, however, a Nuclear Energy Board was established to advise the Government on proposals for construction of nuclear power stations and on all aspects of the installation, operation and supervision of such stations.

Agriculture. General distribution of surface (in acres) in 1976: Crops and pasture, 11,977,900; other land, including grazed mountain, 5,045,800; total, 17,023,700.

Estimated area (statute acres) under principal crops, and estimated yield (in 1,000 tons), calculated from sample returns:

	Area		*Produce*	
Crops	*1974*	*1975*	*1974*	*1975*
Wheat	140,900	110,147	250	192
Oats	116,900	121,045	167	162
Barley	608,500	605,704	1,024	1,003

Crops	Area 1974	Area 1975	Produce 1974	Produce 1975
Rye	1,000	714	...	...
Potatoes	104,000	100,275	1,154	1,002
Turnips	62,600	54,748	1,280	1,020
Mangels	13,200	10,592	322	253
Sugar-beet	63,400	82,173	911	1,407
Hay	1,706,300	1,830,700	3,754	3,661
Grass for silage	848,600	...	8,130	...

Gross agricultural output (excluding value changes in livestock) for the year 1975 was valued at £908,976,000.

Livestock (1976): Cattle, 6·7m.; sheep, 3·9m.; pigs, 1m.; horses, 98,000; poultry, 10m.

Forestry. The total area of state forests at 31 Dec. 1976 was 268,595 hectares.

Fisheries. The number of vessels and men engaged in fishing in 1976 were 1,237 motor, 1,225 boats propelled by outboard engines, sails and oars; men 7,393. The quantities and values of fish landed during 1976 were: Demersal fish, 22,796,691 kg, value £4,579,915; pelagic fish, 39,257,669 kg, value £3,945,934; shellfish, 11,813,216 kg, value £3,909,858. Total value, £12,435,713.

INDUSTRY AND TRADE.

Industry. The census of industrial production for 1973 gives the following details of the values (in £1,000) of gross and net output for the principal manufacturing industries. The figures for net output are those of gross output minus cost of materials, including fuel, light and power.

	Gross output	Net output
Tobacco	85,867	12,871
Creamery butter, cheese, condensed milk, chocolate crumb, ice-cream and other edible milk products	232,822	33,874
Grain milling and animal feeding stuffs	93,150	19,691
Bacon factories	84,605	16,189
Assembly, construction and repair of mechanically propelled road and land vehicles	77,200	22,650
Manufacture and refining of sugar and manufacture of cocoa, chocolate and sugar confectionary	51,761	19,336
Bread, biscuit and flour confectionery	48,845	23,550
Slaughtering, preparation and preserving of meat other than by bacon factories	149,066	19,373
Brewing[1]	51,390	40,504
Metal trades (excluding machinery and transport equipment)	99,707	44,983
Woollen and worsted (excluding clothing)	44,859	17,673
Printing, publishing and allied trades	50,288	33,949
Manufacture of paper and paper products	45,081	20,650
Manufacture of electrical machinery, apparatus and appliances	81,513	35,075
Hosiery	38,898	18,862
Boot and shoe (wholesale factories)	20,564	10,940
Clothing (wholesale factories), women's and girls' readymade clothing (other than hosiery)	27,441	13,779
Structural clay products, asbestos goods, plaster, gypsum and concrete products, slate, dressed stone and cement	61,504	33,129
Linen and cotton spinning, weaving and manufactures	15,896	5,856
Fertilizers	37,492	15,781
Jute, canvas, rayon, nylon, cordage and miscellaneous textiles	41,181	17,654
Oils, paints, inks and polishes	20,274	6,005
Fellmongery, tanning and dressing of leather	19,606	5,151
Clothing (wholesale factories), men's and boys' readymade suits, overcoats, hats and caps	17,767	8,723
Manufacture and assembly of machinery except electrical	29,380	13,605
Manufactures of wood and cork except furniture	28,715	12,275
Canning of fruit and vegetables and manufacture of preserves, jams, jellies, etc.	22,587	9,030
Manufacture of furniture and fixtures: brushes and brooms	19,163	9,012
Chemicals and drugs	56,488	34,521
Glass and glassware, pottery, china and earthenware	18,021	12,640

[1] Excluding excise duty £39,174,598.

	Gross output	*Net output*
Aerated and mineral waters	17,918	11,627
Clothing (wholesale factories) shirtmaking	9,955	5,111
Margarine, compound cooking fats and butter blending	6,275	2,305
Manufacture of railroad equipment	5,527	3,818
Malting	7,715	2,298
Ship- and boatbuilding and repairing	15,655	5,324
Soaps, detergents and candles	5,180	2,652
Manufacture of made-up textile goods except apparel	8,311	3,030
Miscellaneous food preparations including canning and preserving of fish	13,741	4,513
Distilling	4,493	2,094
Assembly, construction and repair of vehicles other than mechanically propelled road and land vehicles	8,024	5,014
Clothing (wholesale factories) miscellaneous articles of apparel	2,531	1,184
Manufacture of leather and leather substitutes, except footwear and other wearing apparel	2,427	1,294
Total (including all other manufacturing industries)	1,924,832	696,084

Labour. The Department of Labour is responsible for the administration of legislation concerning: (i) the safety, health and welfare mainly of industrial workers, and those employed in mining and quarrying; (ii) conditions of employment and holidays with pay in the non-agricultural sectors; (iii) National Manpower Service; (iv) industrial training (through *An Chomhairle Oiliúna*—the Industrial Training Authority); (v) redundancy payments and resettlement allowances; (vi) industrial relations; and (vii) trade unions.

An Industrial Training Authority (ANCO) was established by the Minister for Labour under the Industrial Training Act, 1967, to assist in the improvement of industrial training: ANCO's programme covers apprentice recruitment and training, the training and retraining of adult workers in industrial training centres and the designation and levying of industries for training purposes under the Act. Levy-grant schemes, the purpose of which is to stimulate training by industry itself, are in operation for 7 designated industries.

The Redundancy Payments Acts provide for financial compensation to workers who lose their employment as a result of redundancy. Workers with a minimum of 2 years' service with their employers are entitled to benefit under the Act.

The Resettlement Assistance Scheme, administered by the Department of Labour, provides financial assistance for workers who have to move to new areas to take up employment arranged through the manpower service. Grants and allowances are payable towards the costs involved for the workers in transferring dependants and household effects to the new employment areas.

The National Manpower Service is responsible for the development of job placement and post-school guidance work throughout the country and for the collection and dissemination of information on manpower.

The Labour Court was established by the Industrial Relations Act, 1946. Provisions of that Act relating to the Court's constitution and operation were amended by the Industrial Relations Act, 1969. The Court consists of a neutral chairman and 2 deputy chairmen with employers' representatives nominated by the Federated Union of Employers and workers' representatives nominated by the Irish Congress of Trade Unions. The Court can investigate and/or conciliate in a trades dispute; assist in the formation of joint industrial councils and decide on the validity of registered agreements between employers and trade unions. When a dispute is referred to the Court by either the trade unions or the employers or both the Act requires that the Court normally appoint an Industrial Relations Officer to mediate in the dispute and try to secure agreement through the medium of conciliation conferences. Should conciliation fail to find a settlement, both parties may request an investigation and recommendation by the Court. An investigation is normally held in private and neither party is under any legal obligation to accept the recommendation.

The Rights Commission Service was established under the Industrial Relations Act, 1969. The Rights Commission Service is free. A Commissioner may investigate a trade dispute referred to him by a party to a dispute. However he may not investigate a dispute without the consent of both parties, nor can he investigate disputes connected with rates of pay, hours of work of a body of workers. The Rights Commissioner's recommendation in trade disputes may be referred to the Labour Court on appeal.

The Department is responsible for dealing with EEC labour policy and legislation and for the promotion of standards contained in the Conventions and Recommendations of the International Labour Organization. It also services the Manpower and Social Affairs Committee of the OECD.

Labour and Employment. The total labour force at mid-April 1974 was 1·12m., of which 64,000 persons were out of work.

The number of trade unions holding negotiation licences in March 1974 was 86, 66 of which were workers' trade unions and the remainder employers' trade unions. The total membership of these unions was estimated at an earlier date at 364,000, 7,000 of whom were in the employers' trade unions. Of the 357,000 workers in trade unions approximately 230,000 were organized in 6 general unions catering for both white collar and manual workers. Trade unions representing the majority of workers in the Public Service and their membership are not included in these figures as, generally, they are not obliged to hold negotiation licences.

European Social Fund. The Department of Labour has been designated by the Irish Government as the national agency responsible for formulating and transmitting to the EEC Commission Irish applications for assistance from the European Social Fund. Assistance is available from the Fund towards expenditure on certain schemes of training, retraining and resettlement of workers and of vocational rehabilitation of the handicapped, provided that those schemes receive financial assistance from public funds.

Commerce. Value of imports and exports of merchandise (excluding bullion and specie and goods transhipped under bond) for calendar years (in £):

	1972	*1973*	*1974*	*1975*	*1976*
Imports	838,053,271	1,137,236,398	1,626,311,286	1,740,115,620	2,335,792,979
Exports	635,533,904	869,186,046	1,134,279,721	1,441,156,566	1,857,880,544
Re-exports	12,014,599				

The values of the chief imports and total exports are shown in the following table (in £):

	Imports		*Exports*	
	1975	*1976*	*1975*	*1976*
Live animals and food	191,317,486	251,902,919	642,674,810	735,089,335
Raw materials	70,440,255	110,580,149	67,078,985	78,002,087
Mineral fuels and lubricants	243,706,014	312,968,305	19,092,857	12,303,481
Chemicals	191,914,901	256,788,502	108,194,524	167,196,598
Manufactured goods	332,991,806	463,017,371	200,688,911	279,479,284
Machinery and transport equipment	419,201,498	594,499,370	161,227,216	253,836,806
Manufactured articles[1]	157,742,505	222,991,057	140,751,754	189,572,867

[1] Not elsewhere specified.

Distribution of trade, by principal countries of origin in the case of imports and destination in the case of exports (in £):

	Imports		*Total exports*	
Country	*1974*	*1975*	*1974*	*1975*
Argentina	5,220,449	2,950,285	697,054	778,606
Australia	3,593,071	2,436,494	11,575,221	9,900,069
Belgium and Luxembourg	35,029,045	30,677,106	36,801,145	53,700,003
Brazil	6,534,852	4,107,335	1,638,410	1,005,548
Canada	24,499,187	17,620,234	16,431,509	16,742,327
Denmark	14,985,037	13,290,482	4,109,048	5,157,592
Finland	25,686,683	18,888,850	2,506,740	4,493,245
France	87,500,532	85,954,326	35,865,521	63,776,579
Germany, Fed. Rep. of	125,947,565	119,587,404	66,875,364	114,656,960
Ghana	8,172,085	5,904,282	353,214	658,817

Country	Imports 1974	Imports 1975	Total exports 1974	Total exports 1975
Hong Kong	5,783,519	4,539,748	1,338,464	1,445,369
India	6,435,850	9,087,676	2,194,268	391,096
Iran	21,952,301	28,132,156	1,413,753	5,559,044
Iraq	9,617	5,055,697	780,445	981,231
Israel	3,384,402	3,820,915	2,570,867	5,164,424
Italy	33,801,702	42,721,583	17,559,623	39,779,077
Japan	21,674,890	29,866,981	9,484,806	9,109,605
Kuwait	22,920,802	32,539,517	486,720	984,411
Malaysia	4,584,246	2,431,289	1,432,615	1,375,818
Morocco	9,987,221	4,271,768	13,019	449,833
Netherlands	55,785,795	54,816,322	46,330,581	86,037,288
New Zealand	4,955,487	4,045,447	1,536,701	1,547,150
Nigeria	2,574,435	2,392,934	3,859,957	11,450,313
Northern Ireland	51,862,173	64,358,672	104,715,622	153,534,521
Norway	9,451,725	8,441,424	3,992,327	3,598,666
Poland	15,019,002	13,700,592	2,386,261	3,157,785
Portugal	6,151,583	6,040,278	3,286,131	1,030,789
Saudi Arabia	41,189,959	26,744,626	1,033,099	1,291,962
South Africa, Rep. of	4,698,461	6,141,715	5,989,839	7,027,655
Spain	10,220,710	10,983,393	13,365,398	11,102,972
Sri Lanka	1,187,440	1,076,042	864,884	198,075
Sweden	40,215,106	36,191,601	12,133,740	15,172,425
Switzerland	11,227,989	12,193,297	5,897,846	6,931,104
USSR	14,907,435	18,040,767	8,257,248	10,050,242
UK	706,603,923	763,799,367	529,939,196	627,748,448
USA	105,728,791	122,454,623	109,292,515	27,856,187
Venezuela	11,491	2,503	1,698,246	2,787,948

An Anglo-Irish free-trade agreement to remove progressively all duties between July 1966 and July 1975 was signed in London on 14 Dec. 1965.

Trade with UK (British Department of Trade returns, in £1,000 sterling):

	1973	1974	1975	1976	1977
Imports to UK	526,603	809,704	920,925	1,008,434	1,282,560
Exports and re-exports from UK	625,713	820,463	906,564	1,246,575	1,640,311

Tourism. Estimated number of visits by foreigners (including cross-border movement) in 1976 was 9·5m.; they spent an estimated £137·2m.

COMMUNICATIONS

Roads. At 31 March 1975 there were 55,306 miles of public roads, consisting of 3,226 miles of national roads, 6,678 miles of main (trunk and link) roads other than national roads, 44,023 miles of county roads and 1,379 miles of county borough and urban roads; of the total mileage 49,775 (90%) was paved.

Number of licensed motor vehicles at 30 Sept. 1976: Private cars, 551,117; public-service vehicles, 6,716; goods vehicles, 53,532; agricultural tractors, 64,463; motor cycles, 36,025; other vehicles, 12,963.

The total number of miles run by road motor passenger vehicles of the omnibus type during 1976 was 53,119,790. Passengers carried numbered 277,097,612 and the gross receipts from passengers were £31,315,503.

Railways. The total length of railway open for traffic at 31 Dec. 1976 was 1,248 route miles, all 5 ft 3 in. gauge, Córas Iompair Éireann, the national transport undertaking, operates all rail services in the State.

Railway statistics for years ending 31 Dec.	1975	1976
Passengers (no.)	13,891,000	13,608,000
Miles run by coaching trains	4,677,000	4,279,000
Merchandise and mineral traffic conveyed (tons)	3,385,266	3,477,899
Livestock conveyed (no.)	14,367	—[1]
Miles run by freight trains	2,515,000	2,523,000
Receipts (£)	20,270,940	23,262,004
Expenditure (£)	38,412,539	44,960,231

[1] The carriage of livestock was discontinued in 1975.

Aviation. During the year ended 31 March 1977 Aer Lingus–Irish International Airlines carried 1,684,250 passengers, 44,590 short tons of cargo and 2,320 short tons of mail on its European services and 214,330 passengers, 13,760 short tons of cargo and 454 short tons of mail on its trans-Atlantic services.

Shipping. The total number of vessels with cargo and in ballast in the foreign trade which arrived at ports in the country during 1976 was 11,780 of 18,960,765 NRT; of these, 1,358 of 2,299,072 NRT, were Irish registered vessels. The Irish merchant fleet, of vessels of 100 gross tons or over, consisted of 55 vessels totalling 177,223 GRT at 31 Oct. 1976.

Inland Waterways. The principal inland waterways open to navigation are the Shannon Navigation (130 miles) and the Grand Canal and Barrow Navigation (156 miles). Merchandise traffic is not now transported on them and navigation is confined to pleasure craft operated either privately or commercially.

Post and Broadcasting (30 June 1976). Number of post offices, 2,191; telegraph offices, 1,345; telephones, 458,000; public telephones, 3,900; telephone exchanges, 1,030.

Radio and television broadcasting is operated by Radio Telefis Éireann, a statutory public body appointed by the Minister for Posts and Telegraphs under the Broadcasting Authority Acts. In July 1976 there were 450,559 holders of current monochrome television licences and 97,334 holders of current colour television licences.

Cinemas. There were (1976) 203 cinemas.

Newspapers (1976). There are 7 daily newspapers (all in English) with a combined circulation of 699,182; 5 of them are published in Dublin (circulation, 598,927).

JUSTICE. RELIGION, EDUCATION AND WELFARE

Justice. The Constitution provides that justice shall be administered in public in Courts established by law by Judges appointed by the President on the advice of the Government. The jurisdiction and organization of the Courts are dealt with in the Courts (Establishment and Constitution Act, 1961), the Courts (Supplemental Provisions) Acts, 1961–77. These Courts consist of Courts of First Instance and a Court of Final Appeal, called the Supreme Court. The Courts of First Instance are the High Court with full original jurisdiction and the Circuit and the District Courts with local and limited jurisdiction. A judge may not be removed from office except for stated misbehaviour or incapacity and then only on resolutions passed by both Houses of the *Oireachtas*. Judges of the Supreme, High and Circuit Courts are appointed from among practising barristers. Judges of the District Court (called District Justices) may be appointed from among practising barristers or practising solicitors.

The Supreme Court, which consists of the Chief Justice (who is *ex officio* an additional judge of the High Court) and 5 ordinary judges, has appellate jurisdiction from all decisions of the High Court. The President may, after consultation with the Council of State, refer a Bill, which has been passed by both Houses of the *Oireachtas* (other than a money bill and certain other bills), to the Supreme Court for a decision on the question as to whether such Bill or any provision thereof is or are repugnant to the Constitution.

The High Court, which consists of a President (who is *ex officio* an additional Judge of the Supreme Court) and 9 ordinary judges, has full original jurisdiction in and power to determine all matters and questions, whether of law or fact, civil or criminal. In all cases in which questions arise touching the validity of any law having regard to the provisions of the Constitution, the High Court alone exercises original jurisdiction. The High Court on Circuit acts as an appeal court from the Circuit Court.

The Court of Criminal Appeal consists of the Chief Justice or an ordinary Judge of the Supreme Court, together with either 2 ordinary judges of the High Court or the President and one ordinary judge of the High Court. It deals with appeals by persons convicted on indictment where the appellant obtains a certificate from the trial judge that the case is a fit one for appeal, or, in case such certificate is refused, where the court itself, on appeal from such refusal, grants leave to appeal. The decision of the Court of Criminal Appeal is final, unless that court or the Director of Public Prosecutions certifies that the decision involves a point of law of exceptional public importance, so that an appeal should be taken to the Supreme Court.

The High Court exercising criminal jurisdiction is known as the Central Criminal Court. It consists of a judge or judges of the High Court, nominated by the President of the High Court. The Court sits in Dublin and tries criminal cases which are outside the jurisdiction of the Circuit Court or which may be sent forward to it for trial from the Circuit Court on the application of the Director of Public Prosecution or the accused person.

The country is divided into a number of circuits for the purposes of the Circuit Court. The President of the Circuit Court is *ex officio* an additional judge of the High Court. The jurisdiction of the court in civil proceedings is limited to £2,000 in contract and tort, £2,000 in actions founded on hire-purchase and credit-sale agreements, £5,000 in equity and £5,000 in probate and administration, save by consent of the parties, in which event the jurisdiction is unlimited. In criminal matters it has jurisdiction in all cases except murder, treason, piracy and allied offences. The Circuit Court acts as an appeal court from the District Court.

The District Court has a summary jurisdiction in a large number of criminal cases where the offence is not of a serious nature. In civil matters the Court has jurisdiction in contract and tort (except slander, libel, criminal conversation, seduction, slander or title, malicious prosecution and false imprisonment) where the claim does not exceed £250; in proceedings founded on hire-purchase and credit-sale agreements, the jurisdiction is £250.

All criminal cases, except those of a minor nature, are tried by a judge and a jury of 12. Juries are also used in many civil cases in the High Court. In a criminal case the jury must be unanimous in reaching a verdict, but in a civil case the agreement of 9 members is sufficient.

Religion. According to the census of population taken in 1971 the principal religious professions were as follows:

	Leinster	*Munster*	*Connacht*	*Ulster (part of)*	*Total*
Roman Catholics	1,387,644	849,382	378,613	180,027	2,795,666
Church of Ireland	60,115	17,807	6,084	13,733	97,739
Presbyterians	5,172	627	347	9,906	16,052
Methodists	3,187	1,321	248	890	5,646
Other religious denominations	6,914	1,269	272	426	8,881
Not stated or no religion	35,108	11,596	5,338	2,222	54,264

Education. *Elementary.* Elementary education is free and was given in 3,429 ordinary national schools (with 100 attached special classes) and 92 special schools in 1975–76. The total enrolment of pupils in 1975–76 was 528,398; the number of teachers of all classes 17,389. There are 5 state-aided training colleges with a 3-year training course as from 1974. The estimated state expenditure on elementary education for 1976 (1 Jan.–31 Dec.) is £104,631,000, excluding the cost of administration.

Satisfactory progress is being made in the provision of up-to-date facilities and accommodation for primary school children including disadvantaged children.

The state is pursuing a policy of grouping children in larger educational units, involving the closing of small schools and the conveyance of pupils to larger schools by state-aided transport services. Over 1,300 small schools have been closed since this policy was initiated in 1964.

Special provision is made for handicapped and deprived children in special schools which are recognized on the same basis as primary schools, in special classes attached to ordinary schools and in certain voluntary centres where educational services appropriate to the needs of the children are provided.

A new child-centred curriculum was formally introduced into the primary schools in 1971. In-service training of teachers is proceeding to familiarize them with the philosophy and methods of the new programme.

Secondary. The secondary schools are under private control and are conducted in many cases by religious orders; all schools receiving grants from the state are open to inspection by inspectors of the Department of Education. The number of recognized secondary schools during the school year 1975–76 was 539, and the number of pupils in attendance was 183,225. Total estimated state expenditure for 1976 (1 Jan.–31 Dec.) is £68,649,000 (including the cost of community and comprehensive schools).

Grants for the provision of a wide range of audio visual teaching aids are available to secondary schools. The schools television service, *Telefís Scoile*, provides programmes in Irish, English, history, geography, mathematics and science subjects for senior and junior pupils. The vast majority of secondary schools now have at least one television receiving set which was purchased with the aid of a state grant.

Continuation and Technical. Vocational centres provide courses of continuation and technical education, apprentice training, courses of technician training and courses leading to professional qualifications (*e.g.*, architecture, engineering, accountancy). These centres are controlled by the local Vocational Education Committees, and are maintained partly from the rates and partly by state grants. The estimated state expenditure for 1976 (1 Jan.–31 Dec.) is £43,436,000, excluding the cost of administration, and the estimated expenditure from the local rates, £1,896,315.

Comprehensive Schools which are established and financed by the State combine academic and technical subjects in one broad curriculum so that each pupil may be offered an education structured to his needs, abilities and interests. Pupils are prepared for the State examinations and for entrance to universities and institutes of further education. To date, 14 comprehensive schools have been built.

Community Schools continue to be established through the amalgamation of existing voluntary secondary and Vocational Education Committee schools; in new areas a single larger school is considered preferable to 2 smaller schools under separate managements. These schools cater for all aspects of second-level education and will provide adult education facilities in the areas in which they are situated. They will also make facilities available to voluntary organizations and to the adult community generally. The estimated cost for 1976 (1 Jan.–31 Dec.) is £10,392,900 for community and comprehensive schools.

Regional Technical Colleges have been set up in 8 provincial centres, Athlone, Carlow, Cork, Dundalk, Galway, Letterkenny, Sligo and Waterford. The colleges provide senior-cycle post-primary, apprentice, technician, professional and other courses. The estimated state expenditure on the colleges for 1975, including capital costs and student aid, is £8,861,000. This expenditure is included in state expenditure on continuation and technical education.

University Education is provided by the National University of Ireland, founded in Dublin in 1908, and by the University of Dublin (Trinity College), founded in 1592. The National University comprises 3 constituent colleges—University College, Dublin, University College, Cork, and University College, Galway—and a recognized college, St Patrick's College, Maynooth, Co. Kildare. St Patrick's College is a national seminary for Catholic priests and a pontifical university with the power to confer degrees up to doctoral level in philosophy, theology and canon law. It now admits lay students (men and women) to the courses in arts, celtic studies, science and education which it provides as a recognized college of the National University. Other recognized colleges are the National Institute for Higher Education, Limerick, and the teacher-training colleges, St Patrick's College of Education, Dublin, Our Lady of Mercy College of Education, Dublin, and Mary Immaculate College of Education, Limerick.

Statistics for the academic year 1975–76:

Universities	*Academic staff*	*Full-time students*
University College, Dublin	648	8,955
University College, Cork	547	3,984
University College, Galway	362	3,125
Trinity College, Dublin	455	4,256
St Patrick's College, Maynooth	114	997

The National Institute for Higher Education, Limerick, was opened in Sept. 1972 and in 1976 became a recognized college of the National University of Ireland. The Institute provides courses primarily of a technological character, with a significant element of the humanities, leading to the award of degrees and diplomas.

Agricultural. Full-time instruction in agriculture is provided for all sections of the farming community. There are 4 state agricultural colleges for young men, administered by the Department of Agriculture and Fisheries, and 7 private state-aided agricultural colleges, at each of which a 1-year course in agriculture is given. Second-year courses in general agriculture, farm machinery, dairying and beef cattle and sheep production are provided at a number of the colleges. Advanced courses in pig and poultry husbandry and management are also provided. Scholarships tenable at these colleges, all of which are residential, are awarded by the County Committees of Agriculture. These Committees provide a comprehensive agricultural advisory service and also conduct winter classes in agriculture and horticulture at local centres. A more comprehensive course is provided in winter farm schools, which are intended, in general, for persons of not less than 17 years of age who are engaged in farming.

Horticultural. A 2-year course in commercial horticulture is provided at 3 residential colleges. There is also a 2-year course in amenity horticulture at the National Botanic Gardens in Dublin.

Poultry-keeping and Farm Home Management. An advanced 3-year residential course is provided at the Munster Institute, Cork, for young women who wish to qualify for teaching and advisory posts in farm home management. The farm home management course includes instruction in poultry-keeping, butter- and cheese-making, general farming and home management. A 1-year non-residential course of instruction for the training of young men and women as technicians in poultry husbandry is also provided at the Munster Institute (which is administered by the Department of Agriculture and Fisheries). In addition, a 15-month non-residential course in poultry husbandry and management is provided for young men at the Munster Institute.

Rural Home Economics and Rural Science. A 1-year course for young women in poultry-keeping, dairying and rural home economics is given at 5 private residential colleges of rural home economics and 1 private residential school of home economics. The County Committees of Agriculture award scholarships tenable at these institutions. Classes in poultry-keeping and farm home management are also conducted by the County Committees at local centres.

A scheme of farm apprenticeship and a trainee farmer scheme are operated by the Farm Apprenticeship Board, which represents various agricultural interests. The scheme provides for practical training on well-managed commercial farms.

Higher Education in Agriculture, Horticulture, Dairy Science and Veterinary Science. Higher education in general agriculture and horticulture, leading to University degrees, is provided by University College, Dublin, and in dairy science by University College, Cork. Training in veterinary medicine and surgery, leading to University degrees, is provided at the Veterinary College, Ballsbridge, Dublin, by University College, Dublin, and Trinity College.

Health Services. Persons in the lower income group (those who are unable to provide medical services from their own resources, and their dependants) are entitled to free general medical practitioner attention, including any medicines or appliances that may be necessary, free hospital and specialist treatment, free maternity care and infant-welfare services, free dental, ophthalmic and aural services. Persons in the middle-income groups—insured manual workers irrespective of their incomes, insured non-manual workers up to a limit of £3,000, uninsured persons up to an income limit of £3,000 and farmers whose valuation does not exceed £60 and their dependants are entitled to in-patient and out-patient hospital services (including mental hospital) and specialist services, free maternity care and infant-welfare services and help towards the cost of drugs and medicines. Such persons must pay a contribution of £15 a year, or £0·33 a week, towards the cost of these services. All insured persons, irrespective of income, qualify for the benefit of assistance towards the cost of prescriptions, which limits the total outlay of a family to £6·50 per month. Hospital treatment for tuberculosis and certain other infectious diseases as well as for children suffering from certain long-term diseases and disabilities is provided free of charge to all classes of the community. Persons suffering from diabetes and other specified long-term conditions are eligible for a free supply of drugs and other necessary medicines, etc.

Pupils of national (elementary) schools are provided with a free school health-examination service and are also eligible for free hospital and specialist treatment and free dental, ophthalmic and aural services for defects discovered at school health examinations.

A free child-welfare clinic service for children under 6 years of age is available in many urban areas. A disabled persons maintenance allowance is payable in cases of need to chronically disabled persons over 16 who are not living in institutions. There are also schemes which provide for the education of the blind, and for the training and placement in suitable employment of the blind and the disabled. All these services are provided by regional health boards under the direction and control of the Minister for Health.

Social Security. Social-welfare services concerned primarily with income maintenance are under the general control of the Minister for Social Welfare. The services administered by the Department of Social Welfare are divided into Insurance and Assistance schemes.

Insurance Services. All employees irrespective of their level of earnings are compulsorily insured from age 16 to 67 years and pay weekly flat-rate contributions. Pay-related contributions are also payable by persons paying certain flat rate contributions. (The insured population is approximately 1m.) Subject to appropriate statutory conditions (but without regard to the recipients' means) the following flat-rate insurance benefits are available: Disability benefit, invalidity pension, unemployment benefit, maternity benefit, widow's pension, deserted wife's benefit, orphan's allowance, treatment benefit, retirement pension payable at 65, old-age pension payable at the age of 67 and a death grant. Pay-related benefit is payable with disability benefit, unemployment benefit, maternity allowance and injury benefit to persons liable for pay-related contributions. The cost of the flat-rate benefits is met by flat-rate contributions from employers and employees and by a state grant; the cost of pay-related benefits is met by pay-related contributions from employers and employees alone.

The insurance services also provide for payment of benefits in respect of injury, disablement or death, as well as medical care resulting from an occupational accident or disease. These benefits are available to employees, irrespective of age, and are paid from an Occupational Injuries Fund which is financed by employers' contributions and income from investments.

Assistance Services. Children's allowances are payable without a means test in respect of each child under 16 years of age and children between 16 and 18 who are at school, in apprenticeship or incapacitated for a prolonged period. The following Assistance services are subject to means and, sometimes, residence tests: Non-contributory widows and orphans' pensions to the survivors of persons whose lack of insurance (or inadequate insurance record) precludes payment of contributory pensions; deserted wife's allowance to women under 67 years of age who have been deserted by their husbands and for whom the deserted wife's benefit is similarly precluded; allowances for unmarried mothers, prisoners' wives and single women between the ages of 58 and 67 years; old age pensions payable at age 67 to persons not entitled to insurance pensions; blind pensions (under the same general conditions as apply to old age pensions) payable at age 21; unemployment assistance payable during unemployment to persons not entitled to receive unemployment benefit.

A person unable to provide the necessaries of life for herself is eligible for public assistance; failing assistance in an institution, such a person must be given home assistance, generally in the form of a cash payment on a weekly basis, but, in particular cases, in kind.

DIPLOMATIC REPRESENTATIVES

OF THE IRISH REPUBLIC IN GREAT BRITAIN
(17 Grosvenor Place, London, SW1X 7HR)

Ambassador: Paul John Geoffrey Keating (accredited 22 March 1977).

OF GREAT BRITAIN IN THE IRISH REPUBLIC
(33 Merrion Rd., Dublin, 4)

Ambassador: W. R. Haydon, CMG.

OF THE IRISH REPUBLIC IN THE USA (2234 Massachusetts Ave, NW, Washington, D.C. 20008)

Ambassador: John G. Molloy.

OF THE USA IN THE IRISH REPUBLIC
(42 Elgin Rd., Ballsbridge, Dublin)

Ambassador: William V. Shannon.

OF THE IRISH REPUBLIC TO THE UNITED NATIONS

Ambassador: Dr Eamonn L. Kennedy.

Books of Reference

Statistical Information: The Central Statistics Office (Earlsfort Terrace, Dublin, 2) was established in June 1949, and is attached to the Department of the Taoiseach. *Director:* T. P. Linehan, B.E., B.Sc.

The Central Statistics Office took over the work carried out since 1922 by the Statistics Branch, Department of Industry and Commerce, which in turn had continued the statistical work carried out by the Department of Agriculture and Technical Instruction (since 1900) and by the Irish Department of the Ministry of Labour, London (since 1919). Vital statistics from 1864, annual agricultural statistics prior to 1900 and decennial census of population were compiled by the Registrar-General for Ireland. The population censuses were carried out in 1926, 1936 and 1946 by the Statistics Branch of the Department of Industry and Commerce and are now the responsibility of the Central Statistics Office, which has also, as from July 1950, taken over from the Registrar-General the compilation of Vital Statistics. The Statistics Act 1926 confers wide powers for the collection, compilation and publication of statistics. Other Acts under which statistics are collected are Workmen's Compensation Act, Merchant Shipping Act, Customs Consolidation Act and Road Transport Act.

Principal publications of the Central Statistics Office are *National Income and Expenditure* (annually), *Statistical Abstract* (annually), *Census of Population Reports*, *Census of Industrial Production Reports*, *Trade and Shipping Statistics* (annually and monthly), *Trend of Employment and Unemployment* (annually), *Reports on Vital Statistics* (annually), *Irish Statistical Bulletin* (quarterly).

Facts About Ireland. Dublin Department of Foreign Affairs, 1973
The Gill History of Ireland. 11 vols. Dublin
Bartholomew, P. C., *The Irish Judiciary.* Dublin, Institute of Public Administration, 1974
Chubb, B., *The Government and Politics of Ireland.* OUP
Delaney, V. T. H., *The Administration of Justice in Ireland.* Dublin, Institute of Public Administration, 1962
Eager, A. R., *Guide to Irish Bibliographical Materials.* London, 1964
Encyclopaedia of Ireland. Dublin, 1968
Freeman, T. W., *Ireland: A General and Regional Geography.* 2nd ed. London, 1965
Harbison, P., *Guide to the National Monuments of Ireland.* Dublin, 1975
Johnston, T. J., and others, *A History of the Church of Ireland.* Dublin, 1953
Keatinge, P., *Formulation of Irish Foreign Policy.* Dublin, Institute of Public Administration, 1973
Kee, R., *The Green Flag.* London, 1972
Kelly, J. M., *Fundamental Rights in the Irish Law and Constitution.* Dublin, 1966
Lehane, B., *The Companion Guide to Ireland.* London, 1973
Lyons, F. S. L., *Ireland Since the Famine.* London, 1971
McDunphy, Michael, *The President of Ireland: His Powers, Functions and Duties.* Dublin, 1945
MacLiammoir, Micheál, and Smith, Edwin, *Ireland.* London, 1966
MacManus, F. (ed.), *The Years of the Great Test, 1926–1939.* Cork, 1967

Meenan, J., *The Irish Economy Since 1922.* Liverpool, 1970
Nevill, W. E., *Geology and Ireland.* Dublin, 1963
O'Donnell, J. P., *How Ireland is Governed.* 5th ed. Dublin, Institute of Public Administration
O'Mahony, David, *The Irish Economy.* Cork University Press, 1966
O'Mahony, D., *The Irish Economy.* Cork Univ. Press
O'Neill's Commercial Who's Who and Industrial Directory of Ireland. 18th ed. Dublin, 1963
Thom's Directory of Ireland. 3 vols. (Dublin, Professional, Commercial). Dublin, 1960–67

ISRAEL

Medinat Israel—State of Israel

Capital: Jerusalem
Population: 3·8m. (1978)
GNP per capita: US$3,920 (1976)

HISTORY. In 1967, following some years of uneasy peace, local clashes on the Israeli-Syrian border were followed by Egyptian mass concentration of forces on the borders of Israel. The UN emergency force was expelled and a blockade of shipping to and from Israel was imposed by Egypt in the Red Sea. Israel struck out at Egypt on land and in the air on 5–9 June 1967. Jordan joined in the conflict which spread to the Syrian borders. By 11 June the Israelis had occupied the Gaza Strip and the Sinai peninsula as far as the Suez Canal in Egypt, West Jordan as far as the Jordan valley and the heights east of the Sea of Galilee, including the town of Quneitra in Syria.

A further war broke out on 6 Oct. 1973 when an Egyptian offensive was launched across the Suez Canal and Syrian forces struck on the Golan Heights. Following UN Security Council resolutions a ceasefire finally came into being on 24 Oct. In Dec. agreement was reached by Egypt and Israel on disengagement and a disengagement agreement was signed with Syria on 31 May 1974. A further disengagement agreement was signed between Israel and Egypt in Sept. 1975.

Developments in 1977 included President Sadat of Egypt's visit to Israel and peace initiative and in March 1978 Israeli troops entered southern Lebanon but later withdrew after the arrival of a UN peace-keeping force.

AREA AND POPULATION. The area of Israel, within the boundaries defined by the 1949 armistice agreements with Egypt, Jordan, the Lebanon and Syria, is 20,700 sq. km (7,993 sq. miles), with a population (May 1972 census) of 3·2m. (estimated, Jan. 1978, 3·6m.). The area within the ceasefire lines is 89,359 sq. km (34,493 sq. miles). Population of areas which came under Israeli administration as a result of the 6-day war was approximately 1m.; Judaea and Samaria (West Bank), 674,500, Gaza Strip and Northern Sinai, 418,800 and a few thousand on the Golan Heights.

Crude birth rate per 1,000 population of Jewish population (1974), 24·7; non-Jewish, 44·6; crude death rate, Jewish, 7·5; non-Jewish, 5·4; infant mortality rate per 1,000 live births, Jewish, 19·2; non-Jewish, 37.

Israel is administratively divided into 6 districts:

District	*Area (sq. km)*	*Population*[1]	*Chief town*
Northern	3,489	473,700	Nazareth
Haifa	855	480,800	Haifa
Central	1,243	572,300	Ramla
Tel Aviv	171	905,100	Tel Aviv
Jerusalem[2]	557	338,600	Jerusalem
Southern	14,387	351,300	Beersheba
	20,702	3,124,000	

[1] Census 1972. [2] Includes East Jerusalem, annexed from Jordan after 1967 War.

On 23 Jan. 1950 the Knesset proclaimed Jerusalem the capital of the State. Population of the main towns (31 Dec. 1974): Tel-Aviv/Jaffa, 357,600; Jerusalem, 344,200; Haifa, 225,000; Ramat Gan, 120,200; Bat-Yam, 114,000; Holon, 110,300; Petach Tikva, 103,000; Beersheba, 93,400; Netanya, 79,500.

The official languages are Hebrew and Arabic.

Immigration. The following table shows the numbers of Jewish immigrants entering Palestine (Israel), including persons entering as travellers who subsequently registered as immigrants. For a year-by-year breakdown, *see* THE STATESMAN'S YEAR-BOOK, 1951, p. 1167.

1919–32	84,093	1940–47	92,563	1969–74	259,237
1933–39	218,099	1948–68	1,290,610		

During the period 1948–68, 45·5% of the immigrants came from Europe and America and 54·5% from Asia and Africa; during the period 1969–74, 78% came from Europe and America and 22% from Asia and Africa.

The Jewish Agency, which, in accordance with Article IV of the Palestine Mandate, played a leading role in laying the political, economic and social foundations on which the State of Israel was established, continues to be instrumental in organizing immigration.

CONSTITUTION AND GOVERNMENT. Israel is an independent sovereign republic, established by proclamation on 14 May 1948. For the history of the British Mandate, *see* THE STATESMAN'S YEAR-BOOK, 1920–49, under PALESTINE.

In 1950 the Knesset (*Parliament*), which in 1949 had passed the Transition Law dealing in general terms with the powers of the Knesset, President and Cabinet, resolved to enact from time to time fundamental laws, which eventually, taken together, would form the Constitution. The first of these fundamental laws, dealing with the Knesset, Israel Lands and the President, were passed in 1958, 1960 and 1964 respectively.

National flag: White with 2 horizontal blue stripes, the blue Shield of David in the centre.

National anthem: Hatikvah (The Hope). Words by N. N. Imber (1878); adopted as the Jewish National Anthem by the first Zionist Congress (1897).

The Knesset, a one-chamber Parliament, consists of 120 members. It is elected for a 4-year term by secret ballot and universal direct suffrage. The system of election is by proportional representation. In Jan. 1976 the Knesset was composed as follows: 'Labour Alignment', consisting of the Labour Party (a merger of Mapai, Abduth Ha'avoda and Rafi) and left wing Mapam, 51; Arab and Druse lists, 3; Moked-Maki, 1; Citizens Rights, 3; National Religious Party, 11; Independent Liberals, 4; New Communist list, 4; Torah Front (formed by Agudat Israel and Poalei Agudat Israel), 5; Likud (formed by Herut Liberals, National List and Free Centre), 39. The President is elected by the Knesset by secret ballot by a simple majority; his term of office is 5 years. He may be re-elected once.

Former Presidents of the State: Chaim Weizmann (1949–52); Izhak Ben-Zvi (1952–63); Zalman Shazar (1963–68); Ephraim Katzir (1963–1978).

President: Yitzhak Navon, elected 19 April 1978 by 86 votes to none with 23 abstentions.

The Cabinet in Feb. 1978 was composed as follows:

Prime Minister: Menachem Begin (L-H).

Deputy Prime Minister: Yigal Yadin (DMC). *Foreign Affairs:* Moshe Dayan (I). *Religious Affairs:* Abaron Abou Hassira (NR). *Finance:* Simha Ehrlich (L-Lib). *Interior:* Dr Yosef Burg (NR). *Industry, Commerce and Tourism:* Yigal Hurvitz (L-L). *Education and Culture:* Zevulun Hammer (NR). *Defence:* Ezer Weizman (L-H). *Absorption:* David Levi (L-H). *Energy and Infrastructure:* Yitzhak Moday (L-Lib). *Construction and Housing:* Gideon Patt (L-Lib). *Health:* Eliezer Shostak (L-L). *Agriculture:* Ariel Sharon (L). *Justice:* Shmuel Tamir (DMC). *Social Betterment:* Dr Israel Katz (DMC). *Transport and Communications:* Meir Amit (DMC). *Without Portfolio:* Haim Landau (L-H), Moshe Nissim (L-Lib).

Local Government. Local authorities are of three kinds, namely, municipal corporations, local councils and regional councils. Their status, powers and duties are prescribed by statute. Regional councils are local authorities set up in agricultural areas and include all the agricultural settlements in the area under their jurisdiction. All local authorities exercise their authority mainly by means of bye-laws approved by the Minister of the Interior. Their revenue is derived from rates and a surcharge on income tax. Local authorities are elected for a 4-year term of office concurrently with general elections.

There are 31 municipalities (2 Arab), 115 local councils (46 Arab and 6 Druze) and 49 regional councils (1 Arab) comprising 700 villages.

DEFENCE. The Defence Service Law of 8 Sept. 1949, as amended, provides a compulsory 30-month conscription (extended to 36 months in 1968) for men between the ages of 18 and 26 and a 2-year conscription for men in the age-group of 27–29 years. Unmarried women aged 18–26 serve 20 months. After their term of military service, men and childless women are on the reserves until the ages of 55 and 34 years respectively. Until they are 40, men usually report for 31 days training annually and from then until they are 55, for 14 days. Commissioned and n.c.o.s usually serve 7 extra days a year.

The Israel Defence Force is a unified force, in which army, navy and air force are subordinate to a single chief-of-staff. The Minister of Defence is *de facto* commander-in-chief but from Oct. 1973 the cabinet formed a defence committee with authority to make decisions on military operations.

Army. The regular army had a strength in 1977 of 138,000 (18,000 regulars) including 12,000 women, organized in 10 armoured, 9 mechanized, 9 infantry, 3 artillery and 5 parachute brigades. There is a reserve army of about 375,000 on mobilization.

The highest army rank is that of Lieut.-General (*Rav Alouf*), and the Chief-of-Staff, who is the C.-in-C., holds that rank. A divisional commander is a Brigadier (*Tat Alouf*), and a brigade commander a Colonel (*Alouf Mishne*).

Navy. The Navy includes 2 diesel-powered patrol submarines (acquired from Britain), 20 missile boats, 63 patrol craft, 2 transports, 3 medium landing ships, 6 landing craft, 1 support ship, 1 training ship, 4 coastguard cutters and 3 minor landing craft.

New construction includes 2 diesel-electric patrol submarines being built in Britain and 4 steel-hulled guided-missile boats of 415 tons displacement being built in Israel.

The former Nautical School in Haifa has been reorganized as a Naval Officers' School in Acre. Naval personnel in 1977 totalled 350 officers and 4,150 men, of whom 1,000 are conscripts, including a Naval Commander. There are also 5,000 naval reserves.

Air Force. The Air Force has a personnel strength of about 21,000, with more than 500 first-line aircraft, all jets, of Israeli, US and French manufacture. They include about 25 surviving Mirage III supersonic multi-mission fighters, at least 100 Israeli-built Kfirs based on the Mirage airframe, nearly 200 F-4E Phantom fighter-bombers, 12 RF-4E reconnaissance fighters and about 225 A-4E/H/N Skyhawk light attack aircraft. Deliveries of the F-4E are continuing. One interceptor squadron is re-equipping with F-15 Eagles. There are also transport squadrons of turbo-prop C-130/KC-130 Hercules, C-47, Arava, and locally modified Boeing 707 and 'swing-tail' Stratocruiser aircraft (used also for ECM and flight refuelling duties), helicopter squadrons of CH-53, S-61R, CH-47C Chinook, Super Frelon, Agusta-Bell 205 and Alouette aircraft, and training units with locally-built Magister jet trainers, which can be used also in a light ground attack role. On order are 4E-2C Hawkeye airborne early warning aircraft. Missiles in service include surface-to-air Hawks and surface-to-surface Lances.

INTERNATIONAL RELATIONS

Membership. Israel is a member of UN.

ECONOMY

Budget. The budget year runs from 1 April to 31 March (in I£1m.):

	1974–75	*1975–76*
Revenue	31,915·5	85,200·0[1]
Revenue for development budget	8,734·5	17,900·0
Business enterprises	6,009·3	11,604·6
Expenditure	46,659·3	85,200·0

[1] Estimate.

New economic measures were introduced in Sept. 1975; purchase tax was increased by 10% on luxury goods, and 5% on many basic consumer items. On 5 Jan. 1976, the Israeli pound was devalued from I£7.10 to the US$ to I£7.24.

In 1973–74 the main items of expenditure (in I£1m.) were: Defence, 15,340; education, 1,603·3; commerce and industry, 170·5; health, 587·5; social welfare, 202·3; housing, 38·8.

Income tax is levied progressively up to a maximum of 71·9%. A Defence Levy of 10% on income tax paid was introduced during the 6-day war.

Currency. The unit of currency is the Israeli £ (I£), divided into 100 *agorot* (up to 31 Dec. 1959; 1,000 *prutah*). There are coins of I£½ and I£1 as well as of 1 *agora*, 5, 10 and 25 *agorot* and bank-notes of I£1, 5, 10, 50 and 100. Currency in circulation on 31 Dec. 1975 was I£4,172·2m. (bank-notes and coins).

Banking. The Bank of Israel was established by law in 1954 as Israel's central bank. Its Governor is appointed by the President on the recommendation of the Cabinet for a 5-year term. He acts as economic adviser to the Government and has ministerial status. The assets of the Bank of Israel on 31 Dec. 1974 totalled I£20,551m., of which I£7,762m. was in foreign currencies and I£235m. in gold.

There are 21 commercial banks headed by Bank Leumi Le Israel, Bank Hapoalim and Israel Discount Bank.

Weights and Measures. The metric system is in general use. The (metrical) *dunam* = 1,000 sq. metres (about 0·25 acre).

Jewish Year. The Jewish year 5736 corresponds to 6 Sept. 1975–24 Sept. 1976; 5737 to 25 Sept. 1976–12 Sept. 1977; 5738 to 13 Sept. 1977–1 Oct. 1978.

ENERGY AND NATURAL RESOURCES

Electricity. Electric-power consumption amounted during 1974–75 to 7,915m. kwh.

Oil and Gas. Oil was first discovered in Sept. 1955 at Heletz in the Negev. Crude oil production in 1974 was 45m. litres and natural gas 66m. metres.

Minerals. The most valuable natural resources of the country are the potash, bromine and other salt deposits of the Dead Sea, which are exploited by the Dead Sea Works, Ltd. Geological research and exploration of the natural resources in the Negev are undertaken by the Israel Mining Corporation. Copper is being worked at Timna near Eilat; production in 1974 was 9,500 tons. Potash production in 1974 was 950,000 tons.

A plant for the production of 46,000 tons of magnesium and 80,000 tons of hydrochloric acid per annum is being erected in the Arad area.

Agriculture. In the coastal plain (Sharon, Emek Hefer and the Shephelah) mixed farming, poultry raising, citriculture and vineyards are the main agricultural activities. The Emek (the Valley of Jezreel) is the main agricultural centre of Israel. Mixed farming is to be found throughout the valleys; the sub-tropical Beisan and Jordan plainlands are also centres of banana plantations and fish breeding. In Galilee mixed farming, olive and tobacco plantations prevail. The Hills of Ephraim are a vineyard centre; many parts of the hill country are under afforestation. In the northern Negev farming has been aided by the Yarkon–Negev water pipeline. This has become part of the overall project of the 'National Water Carrier', which is to take water from the Sea of Galilee (Lake Kinnereth) to the south. The plan includes a number of regional projects such as the Lake Kinnereth–Negev pipeline which came into operation in 1964; it has an annual capacity of 320m. cu. metres.

A land-utilization survey has graded the country as follows: 3,392,000 dunams under dry farming and 3,938,000 dunams under irrigation suitable for all types of cultivation, 697,000 dunams under dry farming and 1,339,000 dunams under irrigation suitable for plantations, 8·49m. dunams suitable for pasture, 882,000 dunams suitable for afforestation, 470,000 dunams unfit for any type of cultivation.

The area under cultivation (in 1,000 dunams) in 1974–75 was 4,350, of which 1,825 were under irrigation. Of the total cultivated area 2,800 dunams were under field crops, 390 under vegetables, potatoes, pumpkins and melons, 875 under citrus and orchards, 56 under fish ponds and 189 under miscellaneous crops, including auxiliary farms, nurseries, flowers etc.

Industrial crops, such as cotton and sugar-beet, have successfully been introduced. In 1973–74 the area under cotton totalled 333,700 dunams and under sugar-beet 18,800.

Livestock (1976) included 323,000 cattle, 342,000 sheep and goats, 11·5m. laying hens.

Characteristic types of rural settlement are, among others, the following: (1) The *Kibbutz* and *Kvutza* (communal collective settlement), where all property and earnings are collectively owned and work is collectively organized. (2) The *Moshav Ovdim* (workers' co-operative smallholders' settlement) which is founded on the principles of mutual aid and equality of opportunity between the members, all farms being equal in size; hired labour is prohibited. (3) The *Moshav Shitufi* (co-operative settlement), which is based on collective ownership and economy as in the *Kibbutz*, but with each family having its own house and being responsible for its own domestic services. (4) The *Moshav* (smallholders' settlement), which resembles the *moshav ovdim* but lacks the latter's rigid ideological basis; hired labour, for instance, is permitted. (5) The *Moshava* (village), in which land and property are privately owned and every resident is responsible for his own well-being. In 1974, of the 785 rural settlements in Israel, 227 were kibbutzim (population, 94,200), 350 were moshavim (129,300), 27 moshavim shitufiim (6,100), 98 were small villages (70,200), 88 Arab villages (165,100, not including 49,300 Bedouin); the rest were temporary settlements and educational institutions.

INDUSTRY AND TRADE

Industry. A wide range of products is manufactured, processed or finished in the country, including chemicals, metal products, textiles, tyres, diamonds, paper, plastics, leather goods, glass and ceramics, building materials, precision instruments, tobacco, foodstuffs, electric goods, including refrigerators and radios.

A law for the encouragement of capital investment, passed on 29 March 1950, grants substantial privileges to foreign investors; the law was amended in 1955, 1957, 1959 and 1967 to extend the scope of the benefits. An Investment Centre was established in May 1950, and had by early-1971 approved investments totalling I£1,000m.

GDP *per capita* (1972) US$2,279.

Labour. The General Federation of Labour (Histadrut) founded in 1920, had, in 1973, 1,259,200 members (including 89,000 Arab and Druse members); including workers' families, this membership represents 56·1% of the population covering 85% of all wage-earners. Several trades unions of lesser importance also exist.

Histadrut participates in over 70% of Israeli agriculture and 23% of industrial production; it runs the Kuput Holim (workers' health service) and has large interests in banking, insurance, retail business, construction and building.

In 1974 the average daily number of registered unemployed was 844.

Commerce. External trade, in US$1,000, for calendar years:

	1969	*1970*	*1971*	*1972*	*1973*	*1974*	*1975*
Imports	1,332,000	1,433,497	1,811,605	1,961,362	2,968,579	4,197,856	4,151,119
Exports	723,983	778,735	957,609	1,146,972	1,458,990	1,824,859	1,941,202

In 1974, of the imports 56·1% came from Europe (EEC, EFTA and COMECON countries), 18·6% from the US and Canada, 6·1% from Asia and Africa; of the exports 53·3% went to European countries, 18% to US and Canada, 21·8% to Africa and Asia.

The main exportable commodities are citrus fruit and by-products, fruit-juices, wines and liquor, sweets, polished diamonds, chemicals, motor cars, tyres, textiles, electrical goods, flowers. The main exports were, in 1975 ($1m.): Diamonds, 641; chemical and oil products, 185·7; citrus fruit, 176·8, and food, beverages and tobacco, 125·7.

Total trade with UK (British Department of Trade returns, in £1,000 sterling):

	1973	*1974*	*1975*	*1976*	*1977*
Imports to UK	69,942	78,701	91,253	127,796	159,025
Exports and re-exports from UK	187,248	219,206	237,243	249,398	273,925

COMMUNICATIONS

Roads. There were 10,657 km of paved roads in 1976. Registered motor vehicles in 1974 totalled 408,280, including 5,615 buses, 94,758 trucks and 267,425 private cars.

Railways. Internal communications (1977) are provided by 902 km of standard gauge line. Surveys are being made (1977) of 215 km of new line linking Eilat on the Gulf of Aqaba with Sedom and the existing rail network by means of the 34 km line opened between Oron and Nahal Zin in Nov. 1977. In 1974–75, 3·6m. passengers and 3·6m. tonnes of freight were carried by rail.

Aviation. Air communications are centred in the airport of Lod, near Tel-Aviv. In 1974, 9,182 planes landed at Israeli airports on international flights; 870,600 passengers arrived, 876,000 departed; 28,191 tonnes of freight were loaded and 20,860 tonnes unloaded. The Israeli airline El Al maintains regular flights to London, Paris, Rome, Amsterdam, Brussels, Athens, Vienna, New York, Zürich, Munich, Nicosia, Istanbul, Tehrán, Johannesburg, Mexico, Nairobi, Frankfurt and Copenhagen. In 1975–76 El Al carried 819,890 passengers.

Shipping. Israel has 3 commercial ports, Haifa, Ashdod and Eilat. The deep-water port at Ashdod came into use at the end of 1965, when the ports of Tel-Aviv and Jaffa were closed for freight services. An Israel Ports Authority began to operate in 1962. In 1974, 2,991 ships anchored in Israeli ports; 9·97m. tons of freight (not including oil in bulk tankers) were handled. The Israeli merchant fleet consisted in 1974 of 106 vessels, totalling 2,304,253 GRT.

Post and Broadcasting. The Ministry of Posts controls the postal, telegraph and telephone service. In 1974–75 there were 591 post offices and postal agencies, 43 mobile post offices and (1977) 869,042 telephones.

The broadcasting station in Jerusalem, *Kol Israel*, is controlled by the Broadcasting Authority, established in 1965. Wireless licences in 1974 numbered approximately 460,000 and television licences 385,000.

Cinemas (1974). There were 242 cinemas with a seating capacity of approximately 165,400.

Newspapers (1974). There were 27 daily newspapers, including 13 in Hebrew, 4 in Arabic, 1 each in German, English, French, Hungarian, Yiddish, Russian, Romanian, Bulgarian, Spanish and Polish, with a total circulation of over 500,000.

JUSTICE, RELIGION, EDUCATION AND WELFARE

Justice. *Law.* Under the Law and Administration Ordinance, 5708/1948, the first law passed by the Provisional Council of State, the law of Israel is the law which was obtaining in Palestine on 14 May 1948 in so far as it is not in conflict with that Ordinance or any other law passed by the Israel legislature and with such modifications as result from the establishment of the State and its authorities.

Capital punishment was abolished in 1954, except for support given to the Nazis and for high treason.

The law of Palestine was derived from three main sources, namely, Ottoman law, English law (Common Law and Equity) and the law enacted by the Palestine legislature, which to a great extent was modelled on English law. The Ottoman law in its turn was derived from three main sources, namely, Moslem law which had survived in the Ottoman Empire, French law adapted by the Ottomans and the personal law of the non-Moslem communities.

Civil Courts. Municipal courts, established in certain municipal areas, have criminal jurisdiction over offences against municipal regulations and bye-laws and certain specified offences committed within a municipal area.

Magistrates courts, established in each district and sub-district, have limited jurisdiction in both civil and criminal matters.

District courts, sitting at Jerusalem, Tel-Aviv and Haifa, have jurisdiction, as courts of first instance, in all civil matters not within the jurisdiction of magistrates courts, and in all criminal matters, and as appellate courts from magistrates courts and municipal courts.

The Supreme Court has jurisdiction as a court of first instance (sitting as a High Court of Justice dealing mainly with administrative matters) and as an appellate court from the district courts (sitting as a Court of Civil or of Criminal Appeal).

In addition, there are various tribunals for special classes of cases, such as the Rents Tribunals and the Tribunals for the Prevention of Profiteering and Speculation. Settlement Officers deal with disputes with regard to the ownership or possession of land in settlement areas constituted under the Land (Settlement of Title) Ordinance.

Religious Courts. The rabbinical courts of the Jewish community have exclusive jurisdiction in matters of marriage and divorce, alimony and confirmation of wills of members of their community other than foreigners, concurrent jurisdiction with the civil courts in such matters of members of their community who are foreigners if they consent to the jurisdiction, and concurrent jurisdiction with the civil courts in all other matters of personal status of all members of their community, whether foreigners or not, with the consent of all parties to the action, save that such courts may not grant a decree of dissolution of marriage to a foreign subject.

The courts of the several recognized Christian communities have a similar jurisdiction over members of their respective communities.

The Moslem religious courts have exclusive jurisdiction in all matters of personal status over Moslems who are not foreigners, and over Moslems who are foreigners, if under the law of their nationality they are subject in such matters to the jurisdiction of Moslem religious courts.

Where any action of personal status involves persons of different religious communities, the President of the Supreme Court will decide which court shall have jurisdiction, and whenever a question arises as to whether or not a case is one of personal status within the exclusive jurisdiction of a religious court, the matter must be referred to a special tribunal composed of 2 judges of the Supreme Court and the president of the highest court of the religious community concerned in Israel.

Religion. Religious affairs are under the supervision of a special Ministry, with departments for the Christian and Moslem communities. The religious affairs of each community remain under the full control of the ecclesiastical authorities concerned: in the case of the Jews, the Sephardi and Ashkenazi Chief Rabbis, in the case of the Christians, the heads of the various communities, and in the case of the Moslems, the Qadis. The Druze were officially recognized in 1957 as an autonomous religious community.

In 1974 (estimate) there were: Moslems, 392,500; Christians, 84,500; Druze and others, 41,600.

The Jewish Sabbath and Holy Days are observed as days of rest in the public services. Full provision is, however, made for the free exercise of other faiths, and for the observance by their adherents of their respective days of rest and Holy Days.

The General Assembly of the United Nations proposed, in its resolution of 29 Nov. 1947, the establishment of an international regime for the Jerusalem area. Following the war of June 1967 and the unification of Jerusalem, Israel has maintained freedom of access and worship for all faiths in their holy places. Moslem holy places are administered by their own administration, the Wakf and Christian holy places are still administered in accordance with the *status quo* defined in Ottoman days.

Education. The school system is under the direction of the Ministry of Education and Culture, and comprises kindergarten, primary, secondary and technical schools.

A law passed by the Knesset on 12 Sept. 1949 provides for free and compulsory primary education from 5 to 15 years of age. Youths in the age groups 14–18, who have not completed their primary schooling, must attend special classes.

The State Education Law of 12 Aug. 1953 established a unified state-controlled elementary school system with a provision for special religious schools. The standard curriculum for all elementary schools is issued by the Ministry with a possibility of adding supplementary subjects comprising not more than 25% of the total syllabus. Many schools in towns are private, a number are maintained by municipalities and some are administered by teachers' co-operatives or trustees.

Statistics relating to schools under government supervision, 1974–75:

Type of School	*Schools*	*Teachers*	*Pupils*
Hebrew Education—Total	*6,265*	*52,824*	*868,037*
Kindergartens	4,279	4,637	186,625
Primary schools	1,213	24,670	374,443
Schools for handicapped children	164	1,780	11,594
Schools for working youth	80	235	2,992
Schools of intermediate division	176	6,512	50,882
Secondary schools	206		54,878
Vocational schools	306	15,384	64,505
Agricultural schools	27		5,877
Teachers' training colleges	49	2,214	10,356
Arab Education—Total	*355*	*6,371*	*146,377*
Kindergartens	254	507	15,934
Primary schools	287	4,525	105,373
Schools for handicapped children	4	21	117
Schools for working youth	5	18	182
Schools of intermediate division	33	660	8,929
Secondary schools	77		12,860
Vocational schools	24	1,145	1,572
Agricultural schools	2		687
Teachers' training colleges	2	88	723

There are also a number of private schools maintained by religious foundations—Jewish, Christian and Moslem—and also by private societies.

The Hebrew University of Jerusalem, founded in 1925, comprises faculties of the humanities, social sciences, law, science, medicine and agriculture. In 1974–75 it had a teaching staff of 2,000 and 16,000 students.

The Technion in Haifa had, in 1974–75, 21 faculties and departments with 1,500 teachers and 9,500 students. The Weizmann Institute of Science in Rehovoth is engaged in research in chemistry, mathematics, physics and biology; founded in 1949, it had a staff of 400 in 1974–75.

In 1974–75 the Tel Aviv University had 16 faculties, some 1,150 teachers and 15,400 students. The religious Bar-Ilan University at Ramat Gan, opened in 1965 had, in 1974–75, 5 faculties (Jewish studies, humanities, natural sciences, social sciences, philology), 850 teachers and 7,000 students. The Haifa University had, in 1974–75, 29 faculties with 700 teachers and 6,000 students. The Ben Gurion University had, in 1974–75, 28 departments with 900 teachers and 3,600 students.

Social Welfare. In 1974 Israel had 126 hospitals with 23,077 beds. The 'Malben' organization cares for the aged. The Women's International Zionist Organization has a number of children's homes, crèches and kindergartens as well as vocational schools and training institutions for nurses. In addition, there are several other voluntary bodies providing specific services to the community.

The National Insurance Law, which took effect in April 1954, provides for old-age pensions, survivors' insurance, work-injury insurance, maternity insurance, family allowances and unemployment benefits.

DIPLOMATIC REPRESENTATIVES

OF ISRAEL IN GREAT BRITAIN (2 Palace Green, London, W8 4QB)
Ambassador: Abraham Kidron.

OF GREAT BRITAIN IN ISRAEL (192 Rehov Hayarkon, Tel Aviv 63405)
Ambassador: J. C. M. Mason, CMG.

OF ISRAEL IN THE USA (1621–22nd St., NW, Washington, D.C., 20008)
Ambassador: Simcha Dinitz.

OF THE USA IN ISRAEL (71 Hayarkon St., Tel Aviv)

Ambassador: Samuel W. Lewis.

OF ISRAEL TO THE UNITED NATIONS

Ambassador: Chaim Herzog.

Books of Reference

Statistical Information: There is a Central Bureau of Statistics and Economic Research at the Prime Minister's Office, Jerusalem. It publishes monthly bulletins of economic statistics, social statistics, foreign trade statistics and an English summary.

Government Yearbook. Government Printer, Jerusalem. 1951 ff. (latest issue, 1971/72)
Facts about Israel 1972. Government Printer, Jerusalem, 1972
Statistical Abstract of Israel. Government Printer, Jerusalem (from 1949/50)
Israel Yearbook. Tel-Aviv, 1948–49 ff.
Statistical Bulletin of Israel. 1949 ff.
Reshumoth (Official Gazette)
Middle East Record, ed. Y. Oron. London, 1960 ff.
Laws of the State of Israel. Authorized translation. Government Printer, Jerusalem, 1958 ff.
Alkalay, R., *The Complete English–Hebrew Dictionary.* 4 vols. Tel-Aviv, 1959–61
Atlas of Israel. Amsterdam, Jerusalem and London, 1970
Badi, J., *The Government of the State of Israel.* New York, 1963
Ben-Gurion, D., *Ben-Gurion Looks Back.* London, 1965.—*The Jews in Their Land.* London, 1966.—*Israel: A Personal History.* New York, 1971
Bentwich, J. S., *Education in Israel.* London, 1965
Bentwich, N., *The New–Old Land of Israel.* London, 1960
Comay, J., *Israel.* London and New York, 1969
Churchill, R. S. and W. S., *The Six-Day War.* London, 1967
Crossman, R., *Nation Reborn.* London, 1960
Drabkin-Darin, H., *The Other Society.* London, 1962
Eigenstadt, S. N., *Israel Society.* London, 1969
Elizur, Y., and Salpeter, E., *Who Rules Israel?* New York, 1973
Horowitz, D., *The Economics of Israel.* New York and Oxford, 1967.—*The Enigma of Economic Growth: A Case Study of Israel.* New York, 1972
Hyamson, A. M., *Palestine under Mandate, 1920–48.* London, 1951
Jiryis, S., *The Arabs in Israel.* New York, 1976
Karmon, Y., *Israel: A Regional Geography.* London, 1971
Laquer, W. (ed.), *The Israel–Arab Reader.* London 1970.—*A History of Zionism.* New York, 1972
Likhovski, E. S., *Israel's Parliament: The Law of the Knesset.* Oxford, 1971
Luttwak, E., and Horowitz, D., *The Israeli Army.* London, 1975
Meir, G., *My Life.* New York, 1975
Orni, E., and Efrat, E., *Geography of Israel.* Jerusalem and London, 1966
Pryce-Jones, D., *The Face of Defeat: Palestinian Refugees and Guerrillas.* New York, 1973
Safran, N., *Israel: The Embattled Ally.* Harvard Univ. Press, 1978
Segal, R., *Whose Jerusalem? The Conflicts of Israel.* London, 1973
Sykes, C., *Crossroads to Israel.* London, 1965
Weizmann, C., *Trial and Error.* London, 1949
Who's Who in Israel. Tel-Aviv, 1965

National Library: The Jewish National and University Library, Jerusalem. *Director:* Dr C. Worman.

ITALY

Repubblica Italiana

Capital: Rome
Population: 56·3m. (1976)
GNP per capita: US$3,050 (1976)

HISTORY. On 10 June 1946 Italy became a republic on the announcement by the Court of Cassation that a majority of the voters at the referendum held on 2 June had voted for a republic. The final figures, announced on 18 June, showed: For a republic, 12,718,641 (54·3% of the valid votes cast, which numbered 23,437,143); for the retention of the monarchy, 10,718,502 (45·7%); invalid and contested, 1,509,735. Total 24,946,878, or 89·1% of the registered electors, who numbered 28,005,449. For the results of the polling in the 13 leading cities, *see* THE STATESMAN'S YEAR-BOOK, 1951, p. 1175. Voting was compulsory, open to both men and women 21 years of age or older, including members of the Civil Service and the Armed Forces; former active Fascists and a few other categories were excluded.

On 18 June the then Provisional Government without specifically proclaiming the republic, issued an 'Order of the Day' decreeing that all court verdicts should in future be handed down 'in the name of the Italian people', that the *Gazzetta Ufficiale del Regno d'Italia* should be re-named *Gazzetta Ufficiale della Repubblica Italiana*, that all references to the monarchy should be deleted from legal and government statements and that the shield of the House of Savoy should be removed from the Italian flag.

Thus ended the reign of the House of Savoy, whose kings had ruled over Piedmont for 9 centuries and as Kings of Italy since 18 Feb. 1861. (For fuller account of the House of Savoy, *see* THE STATESMAN'S YEAR-BOOK, 1946, p. 1021.) The Crown Prince Umberto, son of King Victor Emmanuel III, became Lieut.-Gen. (*i.e.*, Regent) of the kingdom on 5 June 1944. Following the abdication and retirement to Egypt of his father on 9 May 1946, Umberto was declared King Umberto II; his reign lasted to 13 June, when he left the country. King Victor Emmanuel III died in Alexandria on 28 Dec. 1947.

AREA AND POPULATION. The population (present in actual boundaries) at successive censuses were as follows:

31 Dec. 1871	27,577,640	21 April 1931	40,582,043
31 Dec. 1881	29,277,927	21 April 1936	42,302,680
10 Feb. 1901	33,370,138	4 Nov. 1951	47,158,738
10 June 1911	35,694,582	15 Oct. 1961	49,903,878
1 Dec. 1921	37,403,956	24 Oct. 1971	53,744,737

The following table gives area and population of the Regions (census of 24 Oct. 1971 and estimate 1976):

Regions	*Area in sq. km (1971)*	*Resident pop. census, 1971*	*Resident pop. estimate, 1976*	*Density per sq. km (1971)*
Piemonte	25,399	4,432,313	4,542,787	175
Valle d'Aosta	3,262	109,150	114,112	33
Lombardia	23,834	8,543,387	8,865,759	358
Trentino-Alto Adige	13,613	841,886	869,458	62
Bolzano-Bozen	*7,400*	*414,041*	*429,079*	56
Trento	*6,213*	*427,845*	*440,379*	69
Veneto	18,368	4,123,411	4,300,674	224
Friuli-Venezia Giulia	7,846	1,213,532	1,244,114	155
Liguria	5,413	1,853,578	1,864,762	342
Emilia Romagna	22,123	3,846,755	3,946,832	174
Toscana	22,992	3,473,097	3,578,581	151
Umbria	8,456	775,783	799,196	92

Regions	Area in sq. km (1971)	Resident pop. census, 1971	Resident pop. estiimate 1976	Density per sq. km (1971)
Marche	9,692	1,359,907	1,396,950	140
Lazio	17,203	4,689,482	4,958,554	273
Abruzzi	10,794	1,166,694	1,220,574	108
Molise	4,438	319,807	330,604	72
Campania	13,595	5,059,348	5,334,796	372
Puglia	19,347	3,582,787	3,818,708	185
Basilicata	9,992	603,064	617,257	60
Calabria	15,080	1,988,051	2,048,508	132
Sicilia	25,708	4,680,715	4,902,302	182
Sardegna	24,090	1,473,800	1,568,077	61
Total	301,245	54,136,547	56,322,605	180

Vital statistics for calendar years:

	Marriages	Living births: Legitimate	Illegitimate	Total	Deaths: Still-born	excl. of still-born
1971	404,464	885,192	20,990	906,182	13,407	522,654
1972	418,944	866,255	21,948	888,203	12,453	523,828
1973	418,334	852,427	22,119	874,456	11,668	547,487
1974	403,215	846,558	22,324	868,882	10,691	532,043
1975[1]	374,354	803,564	23,956	827,520	9,168	550,552
1976[1]	355,273	758,785	22,785	781,570	8,088	546,912

[1] Provisional.

Emigrants to non-European countries, by sea and air: 1972, 29,944; 1973, 24,832; 1974, 24,960; 1975, 20,641; 1976, 24,216. Since 1960 nearly nine-tenths of these emigrants have gone to Canada, USA and Australia.

Communes of more than 100,000 inhabitants, with population resident on 31 Dec. 1976:

Roma (Rome)	2,883,996	Cagliari	240,256	La Spezia	121,075
Milano (Milan)	1,705,086	Brescia	215,156	Monza	120,574
Napoli (Naples)	1,223,927	Modena	178,530	Siracusa (Syracuse)	120,569
Torino (Turin)	1,190,621	Parma	177,894	Vicenza	119,132
Genova (Genoa)	800,532	Reggio di C.	177,883	Sassari	115,990
Palermo	673,163	Livorno (Leghorn)	177,687	Terni	112,523
Bologna	485,648	Salerno	161,645	Forlì	109,618
Firenze (Florence)	464,792	Ferrara	155,172	Piacenza	109,250
Catania	399,773	Prato	154,362	Ancona	107,829
Bari	384,374	Foggia	153,334	Bolzano	106,913
Venezia (Venice)	362,494	Ravenna	138,172	Udine	103,627
Verona	271,392	Perugia	136,799	Pisa	103,479
Trieste	267,857	Pescara	135,167	Alessandria	102,910
Messina	265,318	Reggio nell'E.	129,674	Cosenza	102,375
Taranto	243,750	Bergamo	127,816	Novara	102,132
Padova (Padua)	242,186	Rimini	125,816		

CONSTITUTION AND GOVERNMENT. The new constitution was passed by the constituent assembly by 453 votes to 62 on 22 Dec. 1947; it came into force on 1 Jan. 1948. The constitution consists of 139 articles and 18 transitional clauses. Its main dispositions are as follows:

Italy is described as 'a democratic republic founded on work'. Parliament consists of the Chamber of Deputies and the Senate. The Chamber is elected for 5 years by universal and direct suffrage and it consists of 630 deputies. The Senate is elected for 5 years on a regional basis; each Region having at least 6 senators, consisting of 315 elected senators; the Valle d'Aosta is represented by 1 senator only. The President of the Republic can nominate 5 senators for life from eminent men in the social, scientific, artistic and literary spheres. On the expiry of his term of office, the President of the Republic becomes a senator by right and for life, unless he declines.

The President of the Republic is elected in a joint session of Chamber and Senate, to which are added 3 delegates from each Regional Council (1 from the Valle d'Aosta). A two-thirds majority is required for the election, but after a third indecisive scrutiny the absolute majority of votes is sufficient. The President must be 50 years or over; his term lasts for 7 years. The President of the Senate acts as his deputy. The President can dissolve the chambers of parliament, except during the last 6 months of his term of office.

The Cabinet can be forced to resign only on a motivated motion of censure; the defeat of a government bill does not involve the resignation of the Government.

A Constitutional Court, consisting of 15 judges who are appointed, 5 each, by the President of the Republic, Parliament (in joint session) and the highest law and administrative courts, has rights similar to those of the Supreme Court of the USA. It can decide on the constitutionality of laws and decrees, define the powers of the State and Regions, judge conflicts between the State and Regions and between the Regions, and try the President of the Republic and the Ministers. The court was set up in Dec. 1955.

The reorganization of the Fascist Party is forbidden. Direct male descendants of King Victor Emmanuel are excluded from all public offices, have no right to vote or to be elected, and are banned from Italian territory; their estates are forfeit to the State. Titles of nobility are no longer recognized, but those existing before 28 Oct. 1922 are retained as part of the name.

National flag: Three vertical strips of green, white, red.

National anthem: Fratelli d'Italia (words by G. Mameli; tune by M. Novaro, 1847).

The peace treaty was signed in Paris on 10 Feb. 1947, and ratified on 15 Sept. 1947. Italy ceded to France 4 frontier districts on the Little St Bernard Pass, the Mont-Cenis Plateau, the Mont-Thabor and Chaberton areas, and the upper valleys of the Tinée, Vésubie and Roya (*see* map in THE STATESMAN'S YEAR-BOOK, 1948); to Yugoslavia, nearly the whole of the provinces of Venezia Giulia, the commune of Zara and the island of Pelagosa; to Greece, the Dodecanese; to Albania, the island of Saseno; to China the Italian concession at Tientsin. Italy also gave up her former colonies.

Under the peace treaty Italy was to pay reparations to the following states: Greece, US$105m.; Yugoslavia, US$125m.; USSR, US$100m.; Ethiopia, US$25m.; Albania, US$5m. By Nov. 1967 the whole debt had been paid.

Head of State: On 24 Dec. 1971 Chamber and Senate in joint session elected by an absolute majority (518 votes out of 1,008 votes cast) Giovanni Leone (Christian Democrat; born 1908), President of the Republic.

Former Presidents of the Republic: Luigi Einaudi (1948–55); Giovanni Gronchi (1955–62); Antonio Segni (1962–64); Giuseppe Saragat (1964–71).

General elections for the Senate and Chamber of Deputies took place on 20 June 1976.

Senate. Christian Democrats, 135; Communists, 116; Socialists, 29; Italian Social Movement, 15; Social Democrats, 6; Republicans, 6; other groups, 8. Total: 315.

Chamber. Christian Democrats, 262; Communists, 228; Socialists, 57; Italian Social Movement, 35; Republicans, 14; Social Democrats, 15; other groups, 19. Total: 630.

A coalition government was formed on 13 March 1978 and it included, for the first time, members of the Communist Party.

Prime Minister: Giulio Andreotti.

Foreign Affairs: Arnaldo Forlani. *Interior:* Francesco Paolo Cossiga. *Justice:* Francesco Bonifacio. *Defence:* Attilio Ruffini. *Budget and Economic Planning:* Tommaso Morlino. *Finance:* Franco M. Malfatti. *Treasury:* Filippo M. Pandolfi. *Education:* Mario Pedini. *Public Works:* Gaetano Stammati. *Agriculture and Forestry:* Giovanni Marcora. *Transport and Merchant Navy:* Vittorino Colombo. *Industry and Commerce:* Carlo Donat Cattin. *Post and Telecommunications:* Antonino Gullotti. *Civil Service:* Antonio Bisagalia. *Employment and State Insurance:* Vincenzo Scotti. *Foreign Trade:* Dr Rinaldo Ossola. *Health:* Tina Anselmi. *Tourism and Entertainment:* Carlo Pastorino. *Culture:* Dario Antoniozzi. *Without portfolio dealing with Mezzogiorno:* Ciriaco De Mita.

Adams, J. C. and Barile, P., *The Government of Republican Italy.* Boston, Mass., 1961
Allum, P. A., *Italy: Republic Without Government.* New York, 1974

Cross, E. (ed.), *La Constitution Italienne de 1948.* Paris, 1950
Lucarini, S., *Democrazia in Crisi.* Milan, 1970
Ruini, M., and others, *La Nuova Costituzione Italiana.* Rome, 1947
Spriano, P., *Stori a del Partito Comunistà Italiano.* Milan, 1967
Vedovato, G., *Il Trattato di Pace con l'Italia.* Rome, 1947

Regional Administration. Italy is administratively divided into regions (*regioni*), provinces (*province*) and municipalities (*comuni*).

Art. 116 of the 1948 constitution provided for the establishment of 5 autonomous regions with special statute (*regioni autonome con statuto speciale*) and 15 autonomous regions with ordinary statute (*regioni autonome con statuto normale*). The regions have their own parliaments (*consiglio regionale*) and governments (*giunta regionale e presidente*) with certain legislative and administrative functions adapted to the circumstances of each region. A government commissioner is in charge of co-ordination between regional and national activities.

The division into 20 autonomous regions has been completed. The results of the last regional elections were as follows:

Regions	*Election date*	*Christian Democrats*	*Communists*	*Socialists*	*Social Movement*	*Social Democrats*	*Republicans*	*Liberals*	*Others*	*Total*
Piemonte	15 June 1975	20	22	8	2	4	2	2	—	60
Valle d'Aosta[1]	10 June 1973	7	7	3	1	1	—	—	16[2]	35
Lombardia	15 June 1975	32	25	11	3	3	2	2	2	80
Trentino-Alto Adige[1]	18 Nov. 1973	26	5	6	2	3	1	1	26[3]	70
Veneto	15 June 1975	31	14	8	2	3	1	1	—	60
Friuli-Venezia Giulia[1]	17 June 1973	26	13	8	4	4	1	2	3[4]	61
Liguria	15 June 1975	13	16	5	2	2	1	1	—	40
Emilia-Romagna	15 June 1975	13	26	4	1	2	2	1	1	50
Toscana	15 June 1975	15	25	4	2	2	1	—	1	50
Umbria	15 June 1975	9	14	4	1	1	1	—	—	30
Marche	15 June 1975	16	15	4	1	2	1	—	1	40
Lazio	15 June 1975	20	21	6	6	3	2	1	1	60
Abruzzi	15 June 1975	18	13	4	2	2	1	—	—	40
Molise	15 June 1975	16	6	3	1	2	1	1	—	30
Campania	15 June 1975	23	16	6	7	4	2	1	1	60
Puglia	15 June 1975	21	15	5	5	2	1	1	—	50
Basilicata	15 June 1975	13	9	4	2	2	—	—	—	30
Calabria	15 June 1975	17	10	6	3	2	1	—	1	40
Sicilia[1]	20 June 1976	39	24	10	9	2	4	2	—	90
Sardegna[1]	16 June 1974	32	22	9	6	3	1	1	1[5]	75

[1] Autonomous regions with special statute.
[2] Including 8 Democrates Populaires, 4 Union Valdôtaine, 2 Union Valdôtaine Progressiste and 1 Rassemblement Valdôtain.
[3] Including 20 Südtiroler Volkspartie.
[4] Including 1 Slovenian Union.
[5] Sardinian Action Party.

DEFENCE. Most of the restrictions imposed upon Italy in Part IV of the peace treaty signed on 10 Feb. 1947 were repudiated by the signatories on 21 Dec. 1951, only the USSR objecting.

Head of the armed forces is the Defence Chief of Staff. In 1947 the ministries of war, navy and air were merged into the ministry of defence. The technical and scientific council for defence directs all research activities.

National service lasts 12 months in the Army and Air Force, and 18 months in the Navy.

Army. The Army is divided into the expeditionary force and the national defence force. It is composed of 5 infantry divisions, 2 armoured divisions (with M-47, M-60 and Leopard tanks), 5 Alpini brigades, 4 infantry brigades, 1 parachute brigade, 1 cavalry brigade (with M-47 tanks), 1 rocket brigade, 4 surface-to-air missile battalions and various special and support units. Total strength, 218,000.

Navy. Particulars of the principal surface ships in the Italian Navy:

Completed	*Name*	*Standard displacement Tons*	*Armour Belt in.*	*Armour Big guns in.*	*Principal armament*	*Torpedo tubes*	*Shaft horse-power*	*Speed Knots*
				Cruisers				
1969	Vittorio Veneto	7,500	—	—	8 3-in.; twin 'Terrier'; 9 helicopters	6	73,000	32
1964	Andrea Doria [1]	6,000	—	—	8 3-in.; twin 'Terrier'; 4 helicopters	6	60,000	31
1964	Caio Duilio [1]							

[1] Rated as guided-missile escort cruisers.

There are also 9 diesel-powered submarines, 4 guided-missile destroyers, 1 large destroyer (*ex*-light cruiser converted), 4 destroyers, 11 frigates, 12 corvettes, 1 vedette, 4 ocean minesweepers, 30 coastal minesweepers, 10 inshore minesweepers, 1 hydrofoil missile boat, 6 fast torpedo-boats, 4 fast gunboats, 2 landing ships, 3 surveying vessels, 1 salvage ship, 1 transport, 1 support ship, 4 training ships, 1 oiler, 15 water carriers, 2 netlayers, 7 repair craft, 18 auxiliaries, 10 coastal transports (landing craft), 59 motor transports (minor landing craft), and 60 tugs. The guided-missile cruiser *Giuseppe Garibaldi* was deleted from the list in 1972. The construction of 5 missile boats and the projection of a nuclear-powered fast fleet replenishment ship were rescinded.

Two diesel-powered submarines, 4 frigates, and 6 missile hydrofoils are under construction.

The coastline of the peninsula is divided into zones, with headquarters at Spezia, Naples, Taranto and Ancona; all are under the jurisdiction of flag officers with the status of C.-in-C. The admirals commanding on the coasts of Sardinia and Sicily do not rank as C.-in-C.

Other localities of strategic importance under naval administration are Brindisi, where there is an admiral commanding, and Genoa, Leghorn, Augusta and Venice, each of which is under a senior naval officer.

The personnel of the Navy in 1978 numbered 42,700 officers and ratings, including the naval air arm and the marine force.

Air Force. Control is exercised through 2 regional HQ near Taranto and Milan. All units except single squadrons of G91 fighter-bombers and C-119 transports are assigned to NATO. They comprise the 1st air brigade of Nike surface-to-air missiles, 6 fighter-bomber, 2 light attack, 6 interceptor and 3 tactical reconnaissance squadrons, with supporting transport, search and rescue, and training units. One of the fighter-bomber squadrons has F-104G Starfighters, 3 have F-104S Starfighters, and 2 have Aeritalia G91Ys. The light attack squadrons operate G91Rs. F-104S Starfighters have been standardized throughout the interceptor squadrons. The reconnaissance force operates RF-104G Starfighters.

One transport squadron has turboprop C-130H Hercules aircraft; 2 more are replacing their present C-119Gs with turboprop Aeritalia G222s. There is a VIP and personnel transport squadron, equipped with DC-9, DC-6B, C-47, PD-808 and P.166M aircraft.

ECM duties are performed by specially equipped EC-119s, EC-47s, F.27 Friendships, PD-808s and a C-130. Two land-based anti-submarine squadrons operate Breguet Atlantics and S-2F Trackers. ASW helicopters, including Italian-built SH-3D Sea Kings, operate from ships of the Italian Navy. There are also strong support and training elements. Air Force strength in mid-1975 was about 70,000 officers and men, about 300 combat aircraft, 500 fixed-wing second-line aircraft and over 100 helicopters.

INTERNATIONAL RELATIONS

Membership. Italy is a member of UN, NATO and EEC.

ECONOMY

Budget. Total revenue and expenditure for fiscal years, in 1m. lire:

	Revenue	*Expenditure*		*Revenue*	*Expenditure*
1969	12,563,386	13,932,700	1973	18,640,892	23,807,890
1970	12,709,776	14,313,803	1974	22,930,800	29,557,700
1971	14,380,400	16,929,800	1975	32,312,962	40,201,458
1972	15,563,400	19,102,600	1976	37,882,716	50,036,796

In the revenue for 1976 turnover and other business taxes accounted for 4,434,740m. lire, customs duties and indirect taxes for 11,288,285m. lire.

The public debt at 31 Dec. 1976 totalled 52,492,900m. lire, including consolidated debt of 42,200m. lire and the floating debt 38,379,300m. lire.

Currency. The standard coin is the *lira*. From 30 March 1960 the gold standard was formally established as equal to 0·00142187 gramme of gold per lira.

State metal coins are of 1, 2, 5, 10, 20, 50, 100, 200, 500 and 1,000 lire. There are also in circulation State notes of 500 and bank-notes of 1,000, 2,000, 5,000, 10,000, 20,000, 50,000 and 100,000 lire; they are neither convertible into gold as foreign moneys nor exportable abroad, nor importable from abroad into Italy (except for certain specified small amounts).

Circulation of money at 28 Feb. 1977: State coins and notes, 355,600m. lire; bank-notes, 13,578,000m. lire.

In Aug. 1977 the rate of exchange was 882·25 lire per US$1 and 1,535·35 lire per £1 sterling.

Banking. According to the law of 6 May 1926 there is only one bank of issue, the Banca d'Italia. Its gold reserve amounted to 8,176,600m. lire in Feb. 1977; the foreign credit reserves of the Exchange Bureau (*Ufficio Italiano Cambi*) amounted to 2,555,400m. lire at the same date.

Since 1936, all credit institutions have been under the control of a state organ, named 'Inspectorate of Credit'; the Bank of Italy has been converted into a 'public institution', whose capital is held exclusively by corporate bodies of a public nature. Other credit institutions, totalling 1,073, are classified as: (1) 6 chartered banks (Banco di Napoli, Banco di Sicilia, Banca Nazionale del Lavoro, Monte dei Paschi di Siena, Istituto di S. Paolo di Torino, Banca di Sardegna); (2) 3 banks of national interest (Banca Commerciale Italiana in Milan, Credito Italiano in Genoa and Banco di Roma); (3) banks and credit concerns in general, including 155 joint-stock banks and 171 co-operative banks; (4) 89 savings banks and Monti di pegno (institutions granting loans against personal chattels as security), and (5) 644 *Casse rurali e agrarie* (agricultural banks, established as co-operative institutions with unlimited liability of associates).

At the end of 1976 there were 322 credit institutes handling 97% of all deposits and current accounts, with capital and reserves of 5,095,271m. lire.

On 31 May 1977 the post office savings banks had deposits and current accounts of 17,822,000m. lire; ordinary credit institutions, 130,928,000 lire.

Insurance. By a decree of 29 April 1923 life-assurance business is carried on only by the National Insurance Institute and by other institutions, national and foreign, authorized by the Government. At 31 Dec. 1976 the insurances vested in the *Istituto Nazionale delle Assicurazioni* amounted to 4,288,000m. lire, including the decuple of life annuities.

Weights and Measures. The metric system is in general use.

ENERGY AND NATURAL RESOURCES

Electricity. Italy has greatly developed her water-power resources. In 1976 the total power generated was 155,833m. kwh., of which 40,757m. kwh. were generated by hydro-electric plants.

Oil. The Sicilian district of Ragusa, Gela and Fontanarossa is rapidly developing into one of the largest European oilfields. Production in 1976 amounted to 1,108,546 tonnes, of which 820,745 came from Sicily.

Minerals. The Italian mining industry is most developed in Sicily (Caltanissetta), in Tuscany (Arezzo, Florence and Grosseto), in Sardinia (Cagliari, Sassari and Iglesias), in Lombardy (particularly near Bergamo and Brescia) and in Piedmont.

Italy's fuel and mineral resources are wholly inadequate. Only sulphur and mercury outputs yield a substantial surplus for exports. In 1976 outputs, in tonnes, of coal and similar fuels was 2,027,991, cast-iron ingots, 11,630,592; raw steel, 23,446,624; rolled iron, 18,832,352.

Production of metals and minerals (in tonnes) was as follows:

	1971	*1972*	*1973*	*1974*	*1975*	*1976*
Iron pyrites	1,503,650	1,382,236	1,169,425	1,168,388	808,731	854,477
Iron ore	683,097	615,605	522,019	659,417	631,542	514,172
Manganese	30,604	25,637	25,529	14,008	...	4,461
Zinc	229,164	283,468	256,263	262,024	234,052	274,725
Crude sulphur	573,823	830,279	777,846	473,301	499,246	349,132
Bauxite	193,887	96,528	49,951	31,640	32,265	24,200
Mercury	1,471	1,441	1,155	896	1,094	757
Lead	48,486	50,138	35,127	43,460	33,197	42,601
Aluminium	136,413	149,459	184,179	212,225	190,070	205,723

Agriculture. The area of Italy on 30 June 1976 comprised 301,260 sq. km, of which 270,310 sq. km was agricultural and forest land and 30,950 sq. km was unproductive; the former was mainly distributed as follows (in 1,000 hectares): Cereals, 5,156; leguminous plants, 406; garden produce, 436; vines, 1,320; olive trees, 1,054; woods, 6,308; forage and pasture, 9,417; vines grown among other crops, 569; olive trees grown among other crops, 1,111.

At the second general census of agriculture (25 Oct. 1970) agricultural holdings numbered 3,620,799 and covered 25,091,267 hectares. 3,142,608 owners (86·8%) farmed directly 14,706,204 hectares (58·6); 278,157 owners (7·7%) worked with hired labour on 8,523,107 hectares (34%); 130,648 share-croppers (3·6%) tilled 1,271,485 hectares (5·1%); the remaining 69,408 holdings (1·9%) of 590,471 hectares (2·3%) were operated in other ways.

According to the labour force survey in April 1972 persons engaged in agriculture numbered 3·37m. (2·35m. males and 1·02m. females).

In 1976, 865,715 farm tractors were being used.

The production of the principal crops (in 1,000 quintals) in 1976: Wheat, 95,280; barley, 7,603; oats, 4,397; rye, 351; maize, 53,374; sugar-beet, 154,422; potatoes, 29,885; tomatoes, 29,853; rice, 9,068; olive oil, 2,957; hemp, 1; oranges, 19,057; tangerines, 3,588; lemons, 7,921; other citrus fruit, 431.

Production of wine, 1976, 65·85m. hectolitres; of tobacco, 10,631 tonnes.

In 1975 consumption of chemical fertilizers in Italy was as follows (in 1,000 tons): Perphosphate, 632·6; deposed slags, 51·7; sulphate of ammonium, 440·8; nitrate of ammonia, 558·3; nitrate of calcium $\frac{15}{16}$, 136·3; potash salts, 149·7.

Livestock estimated in 1976: Cattle, 8·8m.; pigs, 9·1m.; sheep and goats, 9,393,400; horses, 263,800; donkeys, 163,100; mules, 113,700.

Facca, V., and Martella, T., *Esami operativi della produttivita in agricoltura.* Bologna, 1959
Problemi d'agricoltura meridionale. Naples, Cassa per il Mezzogiorno, 1953
Merlini, G., *Le regioni agrarie in Italia.* Bologna, 1948

Fisheries. The Italian fishing fleet comprised in 1975, 19,691 motor boats (257,460 gross tons) and 22,850 sailing vessels (31,035 gross tons). The catch in 1976 was 366,580 tonnes.

INDUSTRY AND TRADE

Industry. The textile industry is the largest and most important. Silk culture, while flourishing most extensively in Lombardy, Piedmont and Venezia, is carried on all over Italy. Output of raw silk in 1975 amounted to 55 tonnes. The production of artificial and synthetic fibre (including staple fibre and waste) in 1973 was 546,661 tonnes in 30 factories. Output, 1974 (in tonnes): Pure cotton yarns, 140,040; jute yarns, 11,845; pure wool yarns, 50,347.

The chemical industry produced, in 1976 (in tonnes): Sulphuric acid (at 50 Be), 4,633,364; mineral phosphate, 814,233; sugar, 16,129,357.

Production of motor vehicles was 1,590,677 in 1976.

Labour. The census of industry and commerce, of 25 Oct. 1971, recorded 2,425,204 establishments employing 11,077,533 workers. Mining employed 71,460 workers; food and tobacco manufacture, 400,699; textile industries, 541,030; clothing, shoes, skins and leather industries, 645,310; engineering, 1,905,316; metallurgy, 245,648; chemical, rubber and paper industries, 427,586; building, 997,534; transport and communications, 894,567; commerce, 2,796,897; banking and insurance, 293,005; electricity, gas and water works, 155,156.

As at July 1977, 20·2m. persons were employed, 1·7m. unemployed (figures from a new series of statistics on the labour force, 1977, which is not comparable with previous series).

Trade Unions. Membership of the 4 main groups: Confederazione Generale Italiana del Lavoro (Communist-dominated), 4,485,930 (1977); Confederazione Italiana Sindacati Lavoratori (Catholic), 2,823,735 (1976); Unione Italiana del Lavoro, 1,151,370 (1977); Confederazione Italiana Sindacati Nazionali Lavoratori, 1,015,988 (1961).

Commerce. The territory covered by foreign trade statistics includes Italy, the Republic of San Marino, but excludes the municipalities of Livigno and Campione.

The following table shows the value of Italy's foreign trade (in 1m. lire):

	1970	*1971*	*1972*	*1973*	*1974*	*1975*	*1976*
Imports	9,355,946	9,901,308	11,264,615	16,343,378	26,714,957	25,199,599	36,305,883
Exports	8,253,889	9,361,694	10,849,428	12,989,282	19,826,059	22,866,426	30,904,160

The following table shows trade by countries in 1m. lire:

	Imports into Italy from			*Exports from Italy to*		
Countries	*1974*	*1975*	*1976*	*1974*	*1975*	*1976*
Argentina	376,470	216,962	342,312	123,855	115,066	113,249
Australia	156,908	172,931	326,171	168,733	136,121	216,041
Austria	450,682	392,993	639,906	399,160	482,512	726,997
Belgium–Luxembourg	890,839	799,761	1,334,688	733,557	766,203	1,194,324
France	3,509,453	3,354,770	4,928,258	2,497,842	3,025,299	4,650,521
Germany, Fed. Rep. of	4,733,703	4,316,247	6,167,224	3,662,115	4,293,155	5,854,854
Japan	288,024	299,045	490,271	211,252	195,270	266,045
Netherlands	1,150,321	1,189,153	1,711,324	888,248	971,014	1,264,753
Switzerland	549,215	583,440	867,283	825,233	862,035	1,147,910
USSR	522,634	587,357	1,140,379	403,571	667,031	821,015
UK	808,910	839,545	1,268,628	1,024,727	1,045,512	1,484,208
USA	2,037,464	2,193,760	2,854,319	1,503,632	1,489,646	1,998,867
Yugoslavia	300,734	223,698	380,755	561,186	505,780	450,963

In 1976 the main imports were maize, wood, greasy wool, metal scrap, pit-coal, petroleum, raw oils, meat, paper, rolled iron and steel, copper and alloys, mechanical and electric equipment, motor vehicles. The main exports were fruit and vegetables, fabrics, footwear and other clothing articles, rolled iron and steel, machinery, motor vehicles, plastic materials and petroleum by-products.

Italy's balance of trade (in 1,000m. lire) has been estimated as follows:

	Goods and services			*Income from investments and work, balance*	*Net balance*
	Export	*Import*	*Balance*		
1972	13,965	13,411	+ 554	+374	+ 928
1973	16,681	18,727	−2,046	+331	−1,715
1974	24,350	29,479	−5,129	− 61	−5,190
1975	28,177	28,368	− 188	−353	− 541
1976	37,505	39,713	−2,203	−470	−2,678

Remittances from Italians abroad (in US$1m. until 1969 and then 1,000m. lire): 1950, 72; 1955, 80; 1960, 214; 1969, 426; 1970, 289; 1971, 336; 1972, 340; 1973, 360; 1974, 351; 1975, 338; 1976, 385.

Total trade between Italy and UK (British Department of Trade returns, in £1,000 sterling):

	1973	*1974*	*1975*	*1976*	*1977*
Imports to UK	504,384	723,541	809,641	1,106,165	1,532,155
Exports and re-exports from UK	386,059	510,039	563,258	826,403	978,368

Tourism. In 1976, 37·7m. foreigners visited Italy; they included 7·5m. German, 6·2m. Swiss, 6m. French, 3·7m. Austrian, 3·1m. Yugoslav, 1·7m. British, 1·7m. USA and 1·5m. Dutch citizens. They spent about 2,101,200m. lire.

COMMUNICATIONS

Roads. Italy's roads totalled (31 Dec. 1976) 292,343 km, of which 44,761 km were state roads, 100,351 km provincial roads, 141,702 km communal roads. Motor vehicles, Dec. 1976: Cars, 15,925,267; buses, 47,099; lorries, 1,179,698; motor cycles, light vans, etc., 4,700,414.

The Mont Blanc tunnel road (11·6 km) from Entreves to Les Pelerins (France) was opened on 16 July 1965.

Railways. Railway history in Italy begins in 1839, with a line between Naples and Portici (8 km). Length of railways (31 Dec. 1976), 20,088 km, including 16,143 km of state railways, of which 8,006 had not yet been electrified. The first section of a new high-speed direct railway linking Rome and Florence opened in Feb. 1977. In 1976 the state railways carried 374,397,000 passengers and 48·43 tonnes of goods.

Aviation. The Italian airline Alitalia (with a capital of 100,000m. lire, of which 98·7% is owned by the State) operates flights to every part of the world. Airports include 21 international, 32 national and 75 club airports. Domestic and international traffic in 1976 registered 11,116,408 passengers arrived and 11,133,289 departed, while freight and mail (excluding luggage) amounted to 153,707 tonnes unloaded and 198,334 tonnes loaded.

Shipping. The mercantile marine at 31 Dec. 1976 consisted of 3,253 vessels of 11,241,185 gross tons, not including pleasure boats (yachts, etc.), sailing and motor vessels. There were 1,461 motor vessels of 100 gross tons and over.

In 1976, 269·5m. tonnes of cargo were unloaded, and 84,484,000 tonnes of cargo were loaded in Italian ports.

In 1972 navigable waterways had a length of 2,237 km (849 km of which were canals).

Post and Broadcasting. On 31 Dec. 1976 there were 13,872 post offices and 12,941 telegraph offices. The maritime radio-telegraph service had 22 coast stations. On 1 Jan. 1977 the telephone service had 15,246,223 apparatus. *Radiotelevisione Italiana* broadcasts 3 programmes and additional regional programmes, including transmissions in English, French, German and Slovenian on medium- and short-waves and on FM. It also broadcasts 2 TV programmes. Radio licences numbered 647,389; television and radio licences, 13,024,001.

Cinemas. There were 8,558 cinemas with a seating capacity of about 5m. in 1976.

Newspapers. There were 78 daily newspapers with a combined circulation of 2·02m. copies; of the papers 17 are published in Rome and 9 in Milan. One daily each is published in German and Slovene, and 2 in English.

JUSTICE, RELIGION, EDUCATION AND WELFARE

Justice. Italy has 1 court of cassation, in Rome, and is divided for the administration of justice into 23 appeal court districts (and 3 detached sections), subdivided into 159 tribunal districts, and these again into *mandamenti* each with its own magistracy (*Pretura*), 899 in all. There are also 89 first degree assize courts and 26 assize courts of appeal. For civil business, besides the magistracy above mentioned, *Conciliatori* have jurisdiction in petty plaints.

On 31 Dec. 1976 there were 388 establishments for preventive custody (with 21,297 male and 916 female prisoners), 72 penal establishments (with 6,238 male and 126 female prisoners) and 33 establishments for preventive measures of safety (with 1,313 male and 78 female prisoners).

Religion. The treaty between the Holy See and Italy, of 11 Feb. 1929, confirmed by article 7 of the constitution of the Republic, lays down that the Catholic Apostolic Roman Religion is the only religion of the State. Other creeds are permitted, provided they do not profess principles, or follow rites, contrary to public order or moral behaviour.

The appointment of archbishops and of bishops is made by the Holy See; but the Holy See submits to the Italian Government the name of the person to be appointed in order to obtain an assurance that the latter will not raise objections of a political nature.

Catholic religious teaching is given in elementary and intermediate schools. Marriages celebrated before a Catholic priest are automatically transferred to the civil register. Marriages celebrated by clergy of other denominations must be made valid before a registrar. In 1972 there were 279 dioceses with 28,154 parishes and 43,714 priests. There were 187,153 members (154,796 women) of about 20,000 religious houses.

In 1962 there were about 100,000 Protestants and about 50,000 Jews.

Annuario Cattolico d'Italia, a cura del CNEC. 14th ed. 1969–70, Rome, 1970
Annuario di Pastorale. Rome, 1970
Burgalassi, S., *La Sociologia della Religione in Italia dalle originial 1967.* Rome, 1967

Education. Education is compulsory from 6 to 14 years of age. An optional pre-school education is given to the children between 3 and 5 years in the preparatory schools (kindergarten schools). Illiteracy of males over 6 years was 4% in 1971, of females 6·3%.

Compulsory education can be classified as primary education (5-year course) and junior secondary education (3-year course).

Senior secondary education is subdivided in classical (*ginnasio* and classical *liceo*), scientific (scientific *liceo*) and technical education: agricultural, industrial, commercial, technical, nautical institutes, institutes for surveyors, institutes for girls (5-year course) and teacher-training institutes (4-year course).

University education is given in Universities and in University Higher Institutes (4, 5, 6 years, according to degree course).

Statistics for the academic year 1975–76:

Elementary schools	*No.*	*Teachers*	*Pupils*
Kindergarten	29,397	72,571	1,822,527
Public elementary schools	30,811	242,866	4,504,630
Private elementary schools	1,405	6,839	181,424
Private elementary recognized schools (*partificate*)	1,017	5,562	147,361

Government secondary schools	*No.*	*Students* *Males*	*Females*	*Total*
Junior secondary schools	9,827	1,457,150	1,321,447	2,778,597
Classical lyceum	772	86,076	104,798	190,874
Lyceum for science	987	211,894	161,720	373,614
Teachers' schools	192	—	27,330	27,330
Teachers' institutes	643	15,265	155,831	171,096
Technical and professional institutes	1,748	190,390	157,203	347,593
Industrial institutes	610	303,146	11,524	314,670
Commercial institutes	905	174,351	217,546	391,897
Surveyors' institutes	450	121,158	6,689	127,847
Agricultural institutes	76	21,591	2,019	23,610
Nautical institutes	44	16,118	521	16,639
Technical institutes for tourism	15	1,687	7,072	8,759
Managerial institutes	79	3,591	22,823	26,414
Girls technical schools	85	—	22,167	22,167
Artistic studies	219	21,502	32,570	54,072

Universities and higher institutes	*Date of foundation*	*Students*	*Teachers*	*Universities and higher institutes*	*Date of foundation*	*Students*	*Teachers*
Ancona	1965	5,308	106	Bergamo	1970	1,390	71
Arezzo	1971	1,009	...	Bologna	1200	57,142	1,966
Bari	1924	40,701	1,259	Brescia	1970	2,291	44

Universities and higher institutes	Date of foundation	Students	Teachers
Cagliari	1626	18,240	1,001
Camerino	1727	2,351	188
Cassino	1968	2,202	28
Catania	1434	33,056	900
Chieti	1965	4,072	81
Cosenza	1972	2,644	341
Feltre (Belluno)	1969	390	10
Ferrara	1391	6,888	379
Firenze	1924	41,256	1,472
Genova	1243	31,285	1,259
L'Aquila	1956	5,587	268
Lecce	1959	7,043	202
Macerata	1290	3,729	141
Messina	1549	23,998	900
Milano	1924	95,699	2,439
Modena	1678	7,479	446
Napoli	1224	94,346	2,200
Padova	1222	47,063	1,774
Palermo	1805	40,860	1,272
Parma	1502	16,904	714
Pavia	1390	16,322	819
Perugia	1276	17,744	755
Pescara	1965	5,624	51
Piacenza	1924	506	43
Pisa	1338	26,983	1,296
Reggio di C.	1968	6,108	58
Roma	1303	137,862	3,793
Salerno	1944	19,728	300
Sassari	1677	6,220	350
Siena	1300	7,758	461
Teramo	1965	3,539	41
Torino	1404	51,133	1,867
Trento	1965	2,952	91
Trieste	1924	10,546	693
Udine	1969	1,020	44
Urbino	1564	10,163	303
Venezia	1868	11,768	459
Verona	1969	6,886	...

Health. In 1976 there were 130,846 doctors and 588,103 hospital beds.

Social Security. Social expenditure is made up of transfers which the central public departments, local departments and social security departments, make to families. Payment is principally for pensions, family allowances and health services. Expenditure on subsidies, public assistance to various classes of people and people injured by political events or national disasters are also included.

In 1975 government expenditure on social welfare amounted to 27,291,000m. lire.

DIPLOMATIC REPRESENTATIVES

OF ITALY IN GREAT BRITAIN (14 Three Kings Yard, London, W1Y 2EH)

Ambassador: Roberto Ducci.

OF GREAT BRITAIN IN ITALY
(Via XX Settembre 80A, I-00187, Rome)

Ambassador: Sir Alan Campbell, KCMG.

OF ITALY IN THE USA (4400 Broad Branch Rd., Washington, D.C., 20009)

Ambassador: Roberto Gaja.

OF THE USA IN ITALY (Via Veneto 119/A, Rome)

Ambassador: Richard N. Gardner.

OF ITALY TO THE UNITED NATIONS

Ambassador: Piero Vinci.

Books of Reference

Statistical Information: The Istituto Centrale di Statistica (16 Via Cesare Balbo 00100 Rome) was set up by law of 9 July 1926 as the central institute in charge of census and all statistical information. *President:* Prof. Giuseppe de Meo. *Directors-General:* Dr Carlo Viterbo and Dr Luigo Pinto. Its publications include:

Annuario statistico italiano. 1977
Compendio statistico italiano. 1977
Bollettino mensile di statistica. Monthly, from 1950
Annuario di statistiche industriali. 1977
Annuario di statistiche demografiche. 1973
Popolazione e movimento anagrafico dei Comuni. Vol. XX, 1976. Vol. XXI, 1977

Annuario di statistica agraria. 1976
Statistica della navigazione marittima. 1976
Annuario statistico del commercio interno. 1976
Statistica annuale del commercio con l'estero. 1975
Statistica mensile del commercio con l'estero. Monthly
Annuario di statistiche del lavoro. 1976
Censimento generale dell'agricoltura, 1970. 7 vols.
Censimento generale della popolazione, 1971. 11 vols.
Censimento generale dell'industria e del commercio, 1971. 9 vols.
Sintesi Statistica di un Ventennio di Vita Economica Italiana, 1952–71

Italy. Documents and Notes. Servizi delle Informazioni, Rome. 1952 ff.
Italian Books and Periodicals. Bimonthly from 1958
A Quick Glimpse at Italy. Rome, 1970
Banco di Roma, *Review of the Economic Condition in Italy* (in English). Bimonthly, 1947 ff.
Credito Italiano, *The Italian Economic Situation*. Bimonthly. Milan, from June 1961 (in Italian), from June 1962 (in English)
Compendio Economico Italiano. Rome, Unione Italiana delle Camere di Commercio. Annually from 1954
Twentyfive Years of the Italian Republic, 1946–1971. Rome 1971
Allum, P. A., *Italy; Republic Without Government*. London, 1973
Almagià, R., *L'Italia*. 2 vols. Turin, 1959
Carone, G., *Il Turismo nell'economia internazionale*. Milan, 1959
Clough, S. B., *The Economic History of Modern Italy*. Columbia Univ. Press, 1964
Danielli, G., *Atlante Fisico Economico d'Italia*. Milan, 1950
Di Vittorio, G. (ed.), *I sindacati in Italia*. Bari, 1955
Grindrod, M., *The Rebuilding of Italy, 1945–55*. R. Inst. of Int. Affairs, 1955
Hildebrand, G. H., *Growth and Structure in the Economy of Modern Italy*. Harvard Univ. Press, 1965
Kogan, N., *A Political History of Postwar Italy*. London, 1966
Lutz, V., *Italy: A Study in Economic Development*. R. Inst. of Int. Affairs, 1962
Nichols, P., *Italia, Italia*. London, 1974
Wiskemann, E., *Italy Since 1945*. London, 1971
Woolfe, S. J. (ed.), *The Rebirth of Italy, 1943–50*. New York, 1972
Zanetti, G., and Filippi, E., *Finanze e sviluppo della grande industria in Italia*. 2 vols. Milan, 1967

National Library: Biblioteca Nazionale Centrale Vittorio Emanuele II Viale Castro Pretorio, Rome. *Director:* Dr L. M. Crisari.

IVORY COAST

République de Côte d'Ivoire

Capital: Abidjan
Population: 6,673,013 (1975)
GNP per capita: US$610 (1976)

HISTORY. France obtained rights on the coast in 1842, but did not actively and continuously occupy the territory till 1882. On 1 Jan. 1933 a portion of Upper Volta was added to the Ivory Coast, but on 1 Jan. 1948 the districts of Bobo-Dioulasso, Gaoua, Kondougou, Ougadougou, Kaya, Tenkodogo and Dédougou were transferred to the reconstituted Upper Volta.

AREA AND POPULATION. The Republic is situated between Liberia and Ghana and has common frontiers with the Republics of Guinea, Mali and Upper Volta. Area, 322,463 sq. km; total population (census, 1975), 6,673,013. The seat of administration and of the court of appeal is at Abidjan (population estimate (1976) 850,000); the office of agriculture, at Bingerville. Other important towns (population estimate, 1974): Bouaké, 200,000; Daloa, 100,000; Man, 100,000.

The principal ethnical groups are the Agnis-Ashantis, Kroumen, Mandé, Baoulé, Dan-Gouro and Koua.

Of the total population, 23·5% are Moslems, 12·5% Christians and 65% animists.

CONSTITUTION AND GOVERNMENT. The Republic of Ivory Coast became independent on 7 Aug. 1960, after having been a territory of French West Africa from 1904. The Republic was admitted to the UN on 20 Sept. 1960.

The legislative assembly has 120 members; all of them, elected on 27 Nov. 1970, belong to the *Parti Démocratique de la Côte d'Ivoire*. The Republic is administratively divided into 24 departments.

The Government was in July 1977 composed as follows:

President: Félix Houphouët-Boigny. (Re-elected for a fourth 5-year term in 1975. He was the sole candidate and received 99% of the votes cast.)

Minister of State: Auguste Denise. *Minister of State responsible for Reform of State-owned Companies:* Mathieu Ekra. *Public Health, Population and Social Affairs:* Jean-Baptiste Mockey. *Minister of State:* Nanlo Bamba. *Justice:* Camille Alliali. *Defence and Civic Service:* Kouadio M'Bahia Blé. *Interior:* Alexis Thierry-Lebbe. *Foreign Affairs:* Siméon Ake. *Economy, Finance and Planning:* Abdoulaye Koné. *Agriculture:* Denis Bra Kanon. *Scientific Research:* Jean Lorougnon Guédé. *Technical Education and Vocational Training:* Ange Barry-Battesti. *National Education:* Paul Akoto Yao. *Cultural Affairs:* Bernard Dadié. *Commerce:* Maurice Seri Gnoleba. *Construction and Town Planning:* Désiré Boni. *Animal Production:* Dicoh Garba. *Labour and 'Ivorization' of Personnel:* Albert Vanié Bi Tra. *Youth, Popular Education and Sport:* Etienne Ahin. *Information:* Laurent Dona Fologo. *Mining:* Paul Gui Dibo. *Water Resources and Forests:* Théodore Koffi Attobra. *Primary Education and Educational Television:* Pascal N'Gouessan Dikébié. *Internal Security:* Gaston Ouassenan Koné. *Posts and Telecommunications:* Bangali Koné. *Navy:* Lamine Fadiga. *Public Service:* Emile Kei Boguinard. *Women's Affairs:* Jeanne Gervais. *Tourism:* Ibrahima Koné. *Relations with the National Assembly:* Emile Brou.

National flag: Three vertical strips of orange, white, green.

DEFENCE

Army. The Army consisted of 3 infantry battalions and support units in 1978; total strength, 4,500.

Air Force. The Air Force, formed in 1962, has 2 turbofan F-28 Fellowship, 1 turboprop Gulfstream I, 2 turboprop F-27 Friendship and 1 C-47 transports, 1 Gulfstream II and 1 Falcon light jet transport, 7 Broussard and 1 Aero Commander 500 communications aircraft, 3 Reims-Cessna 150s and 3 Reims-Cessna 337s for liaison and training, and 3 SA330 Puma and 5 Alouette II/III helicopters. On order are 6 Alpha Jet advanced trainers, with combat potential. Personnel total 300.

INTERNATIONAL RELATIONS

Membership. Ivory Coast is a member of UN and OAU.

ECONOMY

Budget. The budget for 1976 balanced at 140,200m. francs CFA. Reserves (Nov. 1974) US$47·7m.

Currency. The currency is the franc CFA divided into 100 centimes. £ sterling = 425 francs CFA (Feb. 1978).

NATURAL RESOURCES

Minerals. Diamond fields are being exploited; 299,708 carats in 1973. Manganese deposits yielded 123,060 tonnes in 1970.

Agriculture. Coffee is the largest export commodity (1974), 3·1m. bags (of 60 kg). Production (1974–75) cocoa, 215,000 tonnes; palm oil, 135,000 tonnes. Other crops include maize, yams, sweet potatoes, cassava and plantains. The cultivation of cotton has been developed. Production (1973) 53,800 tonnes. Output, 1970–71, 94,000 tonnes. Coconuts and a small quantity of rubber are collected. The mahogany forests inland are worked.

Several factories produce palm-oil, fruit preserves and fruit juice.

Livestock, 1976: 600,000 cattle, 1m. sheep, 1m. goats, 210,000 pigs, 1,000 horses and 1,000 donkeys.

TRADE. Trade for calendar years in 1,000 francs CFA:

	1973	*1974*	*1975*	*1976*
Exports	190·8	291·7	254·6	392·5
Imports	157·5	232·3	241·4	311·6

In 1973 exports of timber furnished 66,092m.; coffee, 44,136m., and cocoa, 29,600m. Of the exports, 26% went to France, 41% to EEC and 11% to the USA. Of the imports, 44% came from France, 19% from EEC and 9% from the USA. Chief imports were metalwork, cement, wine, motor fuel and oils.

Total trade between the Ivory Coast and UK (British Department of Trade returns, in £1,000 sterling):

	1973	*1974*	*1975*	*1976*	*1977*
Imports to UK	15,249	19,928	18,836	45,105	79,541
Exports and re-exports from UK	3,937	6,528	12,288	17,848	25,173

COMMUNICATIONS

Roads. In 1973 roads totalled 1,400 km bitumenized, 18,000 km all-weather, 16,600 km secondary. In 1964 there were 28,074 cars and 24,700 lorries and tractors.

Railways. From Abidjan a railway runs to Léraba (652 km) and thence through Upper Volta to Ouagadougou in Upper Volta. An extension to Tambao is proposed and a new network for the export of iron ore from the port of San Pedro is under study. In 1973 the railways carried 883m. passenger-km and 550m. ton-km of freight.

Aviation. The main airport is at Abidjan-Port-Buet. In 1967 it handled 153,381 passengers and 5,597 tons of freight and 660 tons of mail.

Shipping. The main ports are Abidjan, Sassandra and Tabou. In 1972 Abidjan port handled 5,925,000 tonnes. The 4 main rivers, Comoé, Bandama, Sassandra and Cavally, are practically not navigable because of rapids and cataracts.

Post. There were 58,796 telephones in 1977.

Cinemas. There were 80 cinemas in 1972 with a seating capacity of 80,000.

JUSTICE, EDUCATION AND WELFARE

Justice. There are a court of first instance, 2 courts of second instance and a court of appeal.

Education. There were, in 1969–70, 464,817 pupils in primary schools, 54,838 in secondary schools, and 4,895 in technical and vocational schools. The university of Abidjan had 3,400 students in 1970.

Health. In 1969 there were 8,683 hospital beds. There were 252 doctors, 15 dentists, 217 midwives, 2,656 nurses and 31 pharmacists.

DIPLOMATIC REPRESENTATIVES

OF THE IVORY COAST IN GREAT BRITAIN (2 Upper Belgrave St., London, SW1X 8BJ)

Ambassador: Louis Antoine Aduko (accredited 1 Feb. 1974).

OF GREAT BRITAIN IN THE IVORY COAST (Immeuble Shell, Ave. Lamblin, Abidjan)

Ambassador: J. B. Wright.

OF THE IVORY COAST IN THE USA (2424 Massachusetts Ave., NW, Washington, D.C., 20008)

Ambassador: Timothée N'Guetta Ahoua.

OF THE USA IN THE IVORY COAST (5 Rue Jesse Owens, Abidjan)

Ambassador: Monteagle Stearns.

OF THE IVORY COAST TO THE UNITED NATIONS

Ambassador: Louis Antoine Aduko.

Books of Reference

Statistical Information: Service de la Statistique, Abidjan. It publishes *Bulletin Statistique Mensuel* and (1958) *Inventoire Économique de la Côte d'Ivoire, 1947–56*

Panorama de la Côte d'Ivoire, 1960, ed. Direction de l'Information, Abidjan

Rapport sur l'évolution économique et sociale de la Côte d'Ivoire, 1960–64. Abidjan, 1965

Holas, B., *Industries et cultures en Côte d'Ivoire*. Abidjan, 1965

JAMAICA

Capital: Kingston
Population: 2·08m. (1976)
GNP per capita: US$1,070 (1976)

HISTORY. Jamaica was discovered by Columbus in 1494, and was occupied by the Spaniards between 1509 and 1655, when the island was captured by the English; their possession was confirmed by the Treaty of Madrid, 1670. Self-government was introduced in 1944 and gradually extended until Jamaica achieved complete independence within the Commonwealth on 6 Aug. 1962.

AREA AND POPULATION. The area of Jamaica is 4,243·6 sq. miles (10,991 sq. km). The population at the census of 7 April 1970 was 1,861,300, distributed on the basis of the 14 parishes of the island as follows: Kingston, 117,400; St Andrew, 432,700; St Thomas, 71,400; Portland, 68,500; St Mary, 100,000; St Ann, 121,300; Trelawny, 61,300; St James, 103,700; Hanover, 59,000; Westmoreland, 113,200; St Elizabeth, 126,000; Manchester, 123,500; St Catherine, 186,000; Clarendon, 176,600.

Estimated population, 31 Dec. 1976 was 2,084,500.

Vital statistics (1975): Births, 61,400; deaths, 14,000; infant deaths, 1,440; emigrants to USA, 11,076; to Canada, 8,500, and to UK, 1,394.

CONSTITUTION AND GOVERNMENT. A new Constitution was enacted with independence in Aug. 1962. The Crown is represented by a Governor-General appointed by the Crown on the advice of the Prime Minister. The Governor-General is assisted by a Privy Council.

The Legislature comprises two chambers, an elected House and a nominated Senate. The executive is chosen from both chambers.

The Executive comprises the Prime Minister, who is the leader of the majority party, and Ministers appointed by the Prime Minister. Together they form the Cabinet, which is the highest executive power. An Attorney-General is a member of the House and is legal adviser to the Cabinet.

The Senate consists of 21 senators appointed by the Governor-General, 13 on the advice of the Prime Minister, 8 on the advice of the Leader of the Opposition. The House of Representatives (60 members, Dec. 1976) is elected by universal adult suffrage for a 5-year period. Electors and elected must be Jamaican or Commonwealth citizens resident in Jamaica for at least 12 months before registration. The powers and procedure of Parliament correspond to those of the British Parliament.

The Privy Council consists of 6 members appointed by the Governor-General in consultation with the Prime Minister.

Governor-General: Florizel Augustus Glasspole.

National flag: A yellow diagonal cross dividing triangles of green, top and bottom, and black, hoist and fly.

The elections to the House of Representatives, held on 15 Dec. 1976 returned 47 members of the People's National Party and 13 members of the Jamaica Labour Party.

Prime Minister: Michael Manley.
Deputy Prime Minister: David Coore, QC.

DEFENCE

Army. The Jamaica Defence Force consists of a Regular and a Reserve Force. The Regular Force is comprised of the 1st battalion, Jamacia Regiment and Support Services which include the Air Wing and Coast Guard. The Reserve Force consists of the 3rd battalion, Jamaica Regiment.

Air Force. The Air Wing of the Jamaica Defence Force was formed in July 1963 and has since been expanded and trained successively by the British Army Air Corps and Canadian air force personnel. Equipment for army liaison, search and rescue, police co-operation, survey and transport duties includes a Twin Otter; 2 Defender armed STOL transports; 1 Beech King Air and 3 Duke light transports; 3 JetRanger, 2 Bell 47 and 3 Bell 212 light helicopters; and 2 Cessna 185 Skywagons.

INTERNATIONAL RELATIONS

Membership. Jamaica is a member of UN, the Commonwealth, OAS and is an ACP state of EEC.

ECONOMY

Budget. Revenue and expenditure for fiscal years ending 31 March (in J$):

	1970–71	*1971–72*	*1972–73*	*1973–74*	*1974–75*	*1975–76*
Revenue	249,857,477	248,982,757	369,292,577	419,124,673	517,100,000	859,650,000
Expenditure	168,845,062	302,528,084	373,262,525	432,032,208	709,700,000	923,000,000

The chief heads of recurrent revenue are customs and excise duties, income tax, motor vehicle licences and post office receipts. Capital revenue is derived mainly from royalties.

Public debt at 31 Dec. 1975, J$837·6m.

Remittances from overseas amounted to approximately J$49·5m. in 1975.

Currency. On 8 Sept 1969 Jamaica adopted decimal currency, the dollar, divided into 100 cents. The Jamaican dollar was devalued in Jan. 1973. J$ = £0·47 and US$1.10. Currency circulation in July 1976 was J$137,498,000, comprising notes of J$126,885,000 and J$10,613,000 coin.

Banking. On 1 May 1961 the Bank of Jamaica opened for business as Jamaica's Central Bank. It has the sole right to issue notes and coins in Jamaica, acts as Banker to the Government and to the commercial banks, and administers the island's external reserves and exchange control.

There are 9 commercial banks in operation, with main offices in Kingston. They are the Bank of Nova Scotia (Jamaica) Ltd, the Royal Bank Ja. Ltd, the Bank of Commerce Ja. Ltd, National Commercial Bank of Jamaica Ltd, the Citibank N.A., the First National Bank of Chicago (Ja) Ltd, Jamaica Citizens' Bank, and the Workers Savings and Loan Bank.

ENERGY AND NATURAL RESOURCES

Electricity. The Jamaica Public Service Company is the public supplier of electricity. The bauxite companies, sugar estates and the Caribbean Cement Co. generate their own electricity.

Minerals. Bauxite, ceramic clays, marble, silica and gypsum are commercially valuable. Jamaica has become the world's second largest producer of bauxite and alumina. The deposits are worked by a Canadian and 5 American companies. Four companies process bauxite into alumina. In 1975, 11,388,000 tons of bauxite ore and 2,999,000 tons of alumina were mined. Gypsum production in 1975 was 235,795 tons.

Agriculture (1975). Production: Sugar, 354,882 long tons (1973, 337,087); rum and other spirits, 7·7m. proof gallons; molasses, 119,716 long tons; copra, 7,000 short tons. Exportable commodities: Bananas, 68,099 tons (exported); cocoa, 1,771 tons; coffee, 380,000 boxes; citrus fruit, 1,028,000 boxes; pimento, 3,873,000 lb. (exported); ginger, 630,000 lb. (exported). Agricultural exports (1974–75), J$177m.

Livestock (1976): Cattle, 280,000; goats, 330,000; pigs, 235,000; poultry, 3·77m.

INDUSTRY AND TRADE

Industry. At the end of 1975 there were 191 firms operating under the Industrial Incentive Laws, implemented by the Industrial Development Corporation. From processing only a few agricultural products—sugar, rum, condensed milk, oils and fats, cigars and cigarettes—the island is now producing a wide range of manufactures using both local and imported raw materials. Among the manufactured goods are clothing, footwear, textiles, paints, building materials, including cement, agricultural machinery and toilet articles. An oil refinery in Kingston meets local fuel demand. In 1975 manufacturing and processing contributed J$426·7m. to the total GNP.

Commerce. Value of imports and domestic exports for calendar years (in J$m.):

	1972	*1973*[1]	*1974*[1]	*1975*	*1976*
Imports	493·2	604·5	850·8	1,021·4	829·8
Domestic exports	292·6	347·7	653·1	699·4	561·6

[1] Provisional.

Principal imports in 1975 (in J$1,000): Raw materials, 494·3; consumer goods, 212·6; capital goods, 314·5.

Principal exports, 1975 (in J$m.): Bauxite and alumina, 453·8; sugar, 140.

In 1975 total trade with USA, UK and Canada amounted to J$1,746·6m.

Total trade with UK (British Department of Trade returns, in £1,000 sterling):

	1972	*1973*	*1974*	*1975*	*1976*	*1977*
Imports to UK	38,684	44,714	46,704	80,244	63,193	78,229
Exports and re-exports from UK	41,508	43,478	50,122	61,002	50,605	39,650

Tourism. In 1975, 553,258 tourists stayed in Jamaica, spending about J$116·8m.

COMMUNICATIONS

Roads (1975). The island has 2,784 miles of main roads, maintained by the Ministry of Public Utilities, Communication and Transport or the councils, and in Kingston and St Andrew by the corporation.

Railways. There are 229 miles of railway open of 4 ft 8½ in. gauge, operated by the Jamaica Railway Corporation, which also operates 19½ miles (Alcoa Mineral Railway) on behalf of one of the bauxite companies. In 1975 operating receipts were J$6·2m. and working expenditure (including interest) J$7·6m.

Aviation. In 1975, 13 scheduled commercial international airlines served Jamaica, operating through the Norman Manley and Donald Sangster international airports at Palisadoes and Montego Bay. Trans-Jamaica Airlines Ltd operates internal flights. Air Jamaica, originally set up in conjunction with BOAC and BWIA in 1966, became a new company, Air Jamaica (1968) Ltd, and is affiliated to Air Canada. In 1969 it began operations as Jamaica's national airline. In 1975 Air Jamaica had a revenue of J$61,484,000 and operating expenses of J$62,258,000.

Shipping. Jamaica has 19 specified ports. In 1975 the port of Kingston unloaded 1·27m. tons of cargo.

Post and Broadcasting. Post and telecommunications are the responsibility of the Ministry of Works and Communications. At 31 Dec. 1975 there were 311 post offices, 475 postal agencies and 33 sub-agencies.

The Jamaica Telephone Company operates the telephone system. In Dec. 1977 there were 108,500 telephones in use. All telephone exchanges are automatic. Jamaica is linked to USA by a submarine telephone cable. Jamaica International Telecommunications Ltd (JAMINTEL) established in 1971, provides a wide range of international telecommunications services for Jamaica.

There are 1 commercial and 1 publicly owned broadcasting stations; the latter also operates a television service.

Cinemas. In 1974 there were 24 cinemas and 1 drive-in cinema for 400 cars.

JUSTICE, RELIGION, EDUCATION AND WELFARE

Justice. The Judicature comprises a Supreme Court, a court of appeal, a revenue court, resident magistrates' courts, petty sessional courts, coroners' courts, a traffic court and a family court (for Kingston and St Andrew) which was instituted in 1975. The Chief Justice is head of the judiciary. All prosecutions are initiated by the Director of Public Prosecutions.

Police. The Constabulary Force in 1975 stood at 4,390 officers, sub-officers and constables (men and women). There are, in addition, district constables and special constables.

Religion. There is no established Church. Adherents of the various religious communities at the census of 1960 numbered: Anglican, 318,643; Baptist, 306,037; Church of God, 191,231; Roman Catholic, 115,291; Methodist, 107,858; Presbyterian, 82,698; Seventh Day Adventist, 78,360; Moravian, 52,467; Congregationalist, 22,440; Pentecostal, 14,739; Plymouth Brethren, 14,555; Salvation Army, 10,416; Society of Friends, 3,977; Pocomania, 811; Christian Science, 341; Hindu, 1,181; Jews, 600; others, 14,876; no religion, 183,738; not specified, 89,555.

Education. In Sept. 1973 education became free for all government grant-aided schools (the majority of all schools) and for all Jamaicans entering the University of the West Indies, the College of Arts Science and Technology and the Jamaica School of Agriculture. In Sept. 1975 there were 804 primary and all-age schools with 440,525 enrolled, and 114 schools offering secondary education with 113,532 enrolled. There are 4 comprehensive schools, 3 vocational schools, 25 industrial training centres, 6 technical high schools, the Jamaica School of Agriculture, and a College of Arts, Science and Technology. There are 8 training colleges, providing 2- and 3-year courses for primary-school teachers.

Degrees in Arts, Natural and Social Sciences, Education, Medicine and General Studies are offered at the Mona Campus of the University of the West Indies. The faculties of Engineering and Agriculture are at the St Augustine Campus in Trinidad, and the Law Faculty is at Cave Hill in Barbados.

Health. In 1976 there were about 390 doctors and 30 hospitals with 7,000 beds.

DIPLOMATIC REPRESENTATIVES

OF JAMAICA IN GREAT BRITAIN
(48 Grosvenor St., London, W1X 0BJ)

High Commissioner: (Vacant).

OF GREAT BRITAIN IN JAMAICA (Trafalgar Rd., Kingston 10)

High Commissioner: J. K. Drinkall, CMG.

OF JAMAICA IN THE USA (1666 Connecticut Ave., NW, Washington, D.C., 20009)

Ambassador: Alfred A. Rattray.

OF THE USA IN JAMAICA (2 Oxford Rd., Kingston)

Ambassador: Frederick Irving.

OF JAMAICA TO THE UNITED NATIONS

Ambassador: Donald O. Mills.

Books of Reference

Statistical Information: The Department of Statistics (93 Hanover St., Kingston) was set up in 1945—the nucleus being the Census Office, which undertook the operations of the 1943 Census of Jamaica and its Dependencies. *Director:* Dexter Rose. Publications of the Bureau include the *Bulletin of Statistics on External Trade* and the *Annual Abstract of Statistics.*

Economic and Social Survey, Jamaica 1976. National Planning Agency. Yearly
Social and Economic Studies. Institute of Social and Economic Research, Univ. of the West Indies. Quarterly
Black, C. V., *History of Jamaica.* London, 1965.
Cassidy, F. G., and Le Page, R. B., *Dictionary of Jamaican English.* CUP, 1966
Clarke, C. G., *Jamaica in Maps.* London, 1974
Delattre, R., *A Guide to Jamaica Reference Material.* Kingston, 1965

Hurwitz, S. J., and Hurwitz, E. F., *Jamaica: A Historical Portrait*. New York, 1971 and London, 1972
Jefferson, O., *The Post-War Economic Development of Jamaica*. Kingston, 1972
Kuper, A., *Changing Jamaica*. London and Boston, 1976
Manley, M., *A Voice at the Work Place*. London, 1975.—*The Politics of Change*
Nettleford, R., *Mirror Mirror*
Stone, C., *Class, Race and Political Behaviour in Urban Jamaica*. Kingston, 1973
Bibliography of Jamaica, 1900–1963. Jamaica Library Service, 1963

Libraries: Institute of Jamaica, Kingston. Jamaica Library Service, Kingston.

JAPAN

Nippon (*or* Nihon)

Capital: Tōkyō
Population: 113·1m. (1976)
GNP per capita: US$4,910 (1976)

HISTORY. The house of Yamato, from about 500 B.C. the rulers of one of several kingdoms, in about A.D. 200 united the nation; the present imperial family are their direct descendants. From 1186 until 1867 successive families of Shoguns exercised the temporal power. In 1867 the Emperor Meiji recovered the imperial power after the abdication on 14 Oct. 1867 of the fifteenth and last Tokugawa Shogun Keiki (in different pronunciation: Yoshinobu). In 1871 the feudal system (Hōken Seido) was abolished; this was the beginning of the rapid westernization.

At San Francisco on 8 Sept. 1951 a Treaty of Peace was signed by Japan and representatives of 48 countries. For details *see* THE SATESMAN'S YEAR-BOOK, 1953, p. 1169. On 26 Oct. 1951 the Japanese Diet ratified the Treaty by 307 votes to 47 votes with 112 abstentions. On the same day the Diet ratified a Security Treaty with the US by 289 votes to 71 votes with 106 abstentions. The treaty provided for the stationing of American troops in Japan until she was able to undertake her own defence. The peace treaty came into force on 28 April 1952, when Japan regained her sovereignty. In 1960 Japan signed the Japan–US Mutual Security Treaty, valid for 10 years, which was renewed in 1970. In June 1971 the Okinawa Reversion Agreement providing for the return from the US to Japan of Okinawa on 15 May 1972 was signed.

AREA AND POPULATION. Census population, 1 Oct. 1976, was 113,086,000 (including Okinawa) with density of 300·6 per sq. km (55m. males, 56m. females). Foreigners registered, June 1977, were 757,866, of whom 653,913 were Koreans, 47,337 Chinese, 20,998 Americans, 4,182 British, 3,174 Philippine, 2,703 Germans, 1,715 Indians, 1,550 Canadians.

Japanese overseas, Oct. 1976, 409,398; of these 145,838 lived in Brazil, 114,345 in USA, 15,794 in Argentina, 11,602 in Peru, 9,705 in Canada.

The leading cities, with census population, 1 Oct. 1975 (in 1,000), are:

Akita	261	Kawasaki	1,015	Sakai	751
Amagasaki	546	Kitakyushu	1,058	Sapporo	1,241
Aomori	264	Kōbe	1,361	Sasebo	251
Asahikawa	321	Kochi	281	Sendai	615
Chiba	659	Koriyama	265	Shimonoseki	267
Fujisawa	266	Kumamoto	488	Shizuoka	447
Fukushima	247	Kurashiki	393	Suita	301
Fukuoka	1,002	Kure	243	Takamatsu	299
Fukuyama	330	Kyōto	1,461	Takatsuki	331
Funabashi	423	Maebashi	250	Tokushima	239
Gifu	409	Matsudo	345	Tōkyō	8,643
Hachioji	323	Matsuyama	367	Toyama	290
Hakodate	307	Nagano	307	Toyohashi	285
Hamamatsu	469	Nagasaki	450	Toyonaka	398
Higashiosaka	525	Nagoya	2,080	Urawa	331
Himeji	436	Niigata	423	Utsunomiya	344
Hiroshima	853	Nishinomiya	401	Wakayama	390
Ichinomiya	238	Oita	320	Yao	262
Ishikawa	319	Okayama	513	Yokkaichi	247
Iwaki	330	Omiya	328	Yokohama	2,622
Kagoshima	457	Osaka	2,779	Yokosuka	390
Kanazawa	395	Otaru	184		
Kawaguchi	346	Sagamihara	377		

Vital statistics (in 1,000) for calendar years:

	1968	*1969*	*1970*	*1971*	*1972*	*1973*	*1974*	*1975*	*1976*
Births	1,870	1,890	1,934	2,001	2,039	2,101	2,030	1,901	1,833
Deaths	686	697	713	685	684	706	710	702	703

Crude birth rate of Japanese nationals in present area, 1976, was 16·3 per 1,000 population (1947: 3·43); crude death rate, 6·3; crude marriage rate, 7·8; infant mortality rate per 1,000 live births, 9·3.

EMPEROR. The Emperor bears the title of Nihon-koku Tennō ('Emperor of Japan'). **Hirohito,** born in Tōkyō, 29 April 1901; succeeded his father, Yoshihito, 25 Dec. 1926; married 26 Jan. 1924, to Princess Nagako, born 6 March 1903. Living sons: (1) Prince Akihito (Tsugunomiya), born 23 Dec. 1933; formally installed as Crown Prince on 10 Nov. 1952; married to Miss Michiko Shoda (born 20 Oct. 1934), 10 April 1959. *Offspring:* Prince Naruhito (Hironomiya), born 23 Feb. 1960; Prince Fumihito (Ayanomiya), born 30 Nov. 1965; Princess Sayako (Norinomiya), born 18 April 1969. (2) Prince Masahito (Hitachinomiya), born 28 Nov. 1935; married to Miss Hanako Tsugaru, 30 Sept. 1964.

By the Imperial House Law of 11 Feb. 1889, revised on 16 Jan. 1947, the succession to the throne was fixed upon the male descendants.

CONSTITUTION AND GOVERNMENT. Japan's Government is based upon the Constitution of 1947 which superseded the Meiji Constitution of 1889. In it the Japanese people pledge themselves to uphold the ideas of democracy and peace. The Emperor is the symbol of the States and of the unity of the people. Sovereign power rests with the people. The Emperor has no powers related to government. Japan renounces war as a sovereign right and the threat or the use of force as a means of settling disputes with other nations. Fundamental human rights are guaranteed.

National flag: White, with a red disc.

National anthem: Kimi ga yo wa (words 9th century, tune by Hiromori Hayashi, 1881).

Legislative power rests with the Diet, which consists of the House of Representatives (of 491 members), elected by men and women over 20 years of age for a 4-year term, and the House of Councillors of 252 members (100 elected at large and 152 from prefectural districts), one-half of its members being elected every 3 years. The Lower House controls the budget and approves treaties with foreign powers.

The former House of Peers is replaced by the House of Councillors, whose members, like those of the House of Representatives, are elected as representatives of all the people. The House of Representatives has pre-eminence over the House of Councillors.

In Oct. 1977 the House of Representatives consisted of 258 Liberal-Democrats, 122 Socialists, 56 Komeito, 28 Democratic Socialists, 19 Communists, 18 New Liberal Club, 8 Independents.

The Cabinet, as constituted in Nov. 1978, was as follows:

Prime Minister: Takeo Fukuda.

Justice: Mitsuo Setoyama. *Foreign Affairs:* Sunao Sonoda. *Finance:* Tatsuo Murayama. *Education:* Shigetami Sunada. *Health and Welfare:* Tatsuo Ozawa. *Agriculture and Forestry:* Ichito Nakagawa. *Interantional Trade and Industry:* Toshio Komoto. *Transport:* Kenji Fukunaga. *Postal Services:* Yasushi Hattori. *Labour:* Katsushi Fujii. *Construction:* Yoshio Sakurauchi. *Home Affairs:* Takenori Kato.

Local Government. The country is divided into 47 prefectures (*Yodōfuken*), including Tōkyō-to (the capital), Ōsaka-fu and Kyōto-fu, Hokkai-dō, and 42 *Ken*. Each *Todōfuken* has its governor (*Chiji*) elected by the voters in the area. The prefectural government of Tōkyō-to is also responsible for the urban part (formerly Tōkyō-shi) of the prefecture. Each prefecture, city, town and village has a representative assembly elected by the same franchise as in parliamentary elections.

New legislation, which came into effect on 1 July 1954, has given the central government complete control of the police throughout the country.

DEFENCE

Army. The 'Ground Self-Defence Force' had in 1977 an authorized strength of 154,800 uniformed personnel, plus a reserve of 39,000 men. The Army is organized in 12 infantry divisions, 1 mechanized division, 1 airborne brigade, 1 artillery, 5 engineer, 1 signal, 1 mixed and 1 helicopter brigades in addition to 8 Anti-aircraft Artillery groups. Equipment includes 790 tanks.

The Northern Army, stationed in Hokkaido, consists of 4 divisions (1 of which is mechanized), an artillery brigade, an Anti-aircraft Artillery Brigade, a tank brigade and an engineering brigade. The Western Army, stationed in Kyushu, consists of 2 divisions. The North-Eastern Army (2 divisions), the Eastern Army (2 divisions) and 1 Airborne Brigade, the Middle Army (3 divisions). The infantry division establishment is approximately 9,000 with 4 infantry regiments or 7,000 (lower establishment) with 3 infantry regiments. Each infantry division has an artillery unit, an anti-tank unit, a tank battalion and an engineering battalion in addition to administrative units.

Navy. The 'Maritime Self-Defence Force' comprises 16 submarines, 2 destroyers of 4,700 tons each carrying 3 helicopters, 2 guided-missile destroyers, 27 destroyers, 16 frigates, 2 minelayer/support ships, 16 large patrol vessels, 2 modern purpose-built training ships (destroyer and frigate types, with helicopters), 30 coastal minesweepers, 2 minesweeper support ships, 4 auxiliary minesweepers, 2 submarine rescue vessels, 6 minesweeping boats, 5 fast torpedo-boats, 10 patrol boats, 6 landing ships, 6 surveying vessels, 1 icebreaker (antarctic support ship), 1 cable (*ex*-mine) layer, 1 oiler, 31 tugs, 12 tenders, 18 auxiliaries and 60 minor craft.

Two helicopter carrying destroyers, 2 guided-missile destroyers, 5 submarines, 3 fleet destroyers, 3 frigates, 5 landing ships, 3 fast torpedo-boats and 3 missile boats are under construction, only part of the schedule of over 70 ships projected under the fourth 5-year defence programme (1973–77) and fifth (1977–81) new construction plan.

Personnel in 1978 numbered 42,200 officers and ratings including the Naval Air Arm.

The Navy has a strong air arm, including 28 S2F and 94 P2 anti-submarine patrol, 66 trainers, 91 helicopters and 11 other aircraft.

Coastguard. The 'Maritime Safety Agency' (Coastguard) consists of 11 regional MS headquarters, 65 MS offices, 5 MS bases, 12 air bases, 3 hydrographic observatories and 145 navigation aids offices (with 4,614 navigation aids facilities) and controls 10 large patrol vessels, 57 medium patrol vessels, 20 small patrol vessels, 210 patrol craft, 27 hydrographic service vessels, 11 firefighting vessels, 50 miscellaneous craft and 100 navigation aids service supply vessels. Personnel in 1978 numbered 11,200 officers and men.

The Coastguard aviation service includes 15 aircraft and 20 helicopters.

Air Force. An 'Air Self-Defence Force' was inauguarated on 1 July 1954. In 1977 its equipment included 6 interceptor squadrons of F-104J Starfighters, and 4 of F-4EJ Phantoms (1 more squadron to be equipped); 3 squadrons of F-86F Sabres; 1 squadron of Mitsubishi F-1 close-support fighters (2 more to be formed to replace F-86Fs); 1 squadron of RF-4E reconnaissance fighters; 2 squadrons of turbofan Kawasaki C-1 and 1 squadron of NAMC YS-11 turboprop transports. About 25 helicopters, including S-62s and KV107s, and MU-2S twin-turboprop aircraft perform search, rescue and general duties. Training units use piston-engined T-34 Mentor basic trainers (being replaced with Fuji KM-2Bs), Fuji T-1 jet intermediate trainers, T-33 jet advanced trainers and supersonic Mitsubishi T-2s. Five surface-to-air missile battalions are in service. Total strength is about 365 combat aircraft and 43,000 officers and men.

INTERNATIONAL RELATIONS

Membership. Japan is a member of UN, the Colombo Plan and OECD.

ECONOMY

Planning. The National Income Doubling Plan 1961–70 was replaced by the Economic and Social Development Programme, 1967–72, which was then replaced by the Plan for Social and Economic Development 1973–78. This has been superseded by the 1976–80 Plan. The Plan envisages an annual growth rate of slightly over 13·1% in nominal terms but 6·7% in real terms.

Budget. Ordinary revenue and expenditure for fiscal year ending 31 March 1978 balanced at 28,514,300m. yen.

Of the proposed revenue in 1977 (in 1m. yen), 18·24m. was to come from taxes and stamps, 8·48m. from public bonds. Main items of expenditure: Local government, 4,932,600; public works, 4,281,000; social security, 5,691,900; education, 3,430,100; defence, 1,690,600.

The outstanding national debt incurred by public bonds was estimated in March 1977 to be 22,965,447m. yen, including 29,729m. yen of Japan's foreign currency bonds. *Local.* The estimated 1977–78 budgets of the prefectures and other local authorities forecast a total revenue of 28,836,500m. yen, to be made up partly by local taxes and partly by government grants and local loans.

Currency. Coins of 1, 5, 10, 50 and 100 *yen* are in circulation as well as notes of the Bank of Japan, of 100, 500, 1,000, 5,000 and 10,000 *yen*. Bank-notes for 100 *yen* are still in circulation in country districts but are gradually being replaced by coins.

In Dec. 1976 the currency in circulation consisted of 14,020,074m. yen Bank of Japan notes and 754,599m. yen subsidiary coins.

Banking. The modern banking system dates from 1872. The Nippon Ginko (Bank of Japan) was founded in 1882. The Bank of Japan has undertaken to finance the Government and the banks; its function is similar to that of a Central Bank in other countries. The Bank undertakes the actual management of Treasury funds and foreign exchange control.

Gold bullion and cash holdings of the Bank of Japan at 31 Dec. 1976 stood at 116,428m. yen.

The Yokohama Specie Bank (specializing in foreign exchange) became the Bank of Tōkyō in Aug. 1954. Total assets of all banks at the end of 1976 was 162,101,200m. yen.

The post office savings bank is modelled upon the British; deposits amounted to 29,218,645m. yen in 1976.

Many foreign banks operate branches in Japan including: Bank of Indo-China, Hongkong & Shanghai Banking Corporation, Chartered Bank of India, Australia and China, Bank of India, Mercantile Bank of India, Bank of Korea, Bank of China, Algemene Bank Nederland NV, National Handelsbank NV, Bank of America, National City Bank of New York, Chase Manhattan Bank, Bangkok Bank and American Express Co.

Weights and Measures. The metric system was made obligatory by a law passed in March 1921, and the period of grace for its compulsory use ended on 1 April 1966.

ENERGY AND NATURAL RESOURCES

Electricity. In 1974 generating facilities were capable of an output of 112m. kw.; electricity produced was 475·794m. kwh.

Oil and Gas. Output of crude petroleum, 1975, was 705,000 kl, almost entirely from oilfields on the island of Honshu, but 262,806m. kl crude oil had to be imported. Output of natural gas, 1975, was 2,436m. cu. metres.

Minerals. Ore production in tonnes, 1975, of copper, 84,980; lead, 50,566; manganese, 157,931; iron, 602; zinc, 254,423; tungsten, 1,330; coal, 18,999; chromite, 23,149,000; molybdenum, 263,000; gold, 4,463 kg; silver, 271,640 kg.

Agriculture. Agricultural workers in full-time employment in 1976 were 7·48m.; 12·6% of the labour force as opposed to 24·7% in 1962. The arable land area in 1976 was 5,536,000 hectares (5,796,000 in 1970). Division of ordinary fields to non-agricultural use accounted largely for this decrease. Rice cultivation accounted for 2·76m. hectares in 1977. The area planted with industrial crops such as rapeseed, tobacco, tea, rush, etc., was 241,800 hectares in 1976.

In 1976 there were 3·92m. power cultivators and tractors in use together with 1·3m. power sprayers and 1·59m. power dusters.

Output of rice was 14m. tonnes in 1973, 12·3m. in 1974, 13·17m. in 1975 and 11.77m. in 1976.

Production in 1976 (in 1,000 tonnes) of barley was 170; wheat, 220. Production of soybeans in 1975 was 126. Sweet potatoes, which in the past mitigated the effects of rice famines, have, in view of rice over-production, decreased from 4·6m. tons in 1965 to 1·42m. tons in 1975. Domestic sugar-beet and sugar-cane production accounted for only 16% of requirement in 1975. In 1975, 2·47m. tonnes were imported, 24·1% of this being imported from Philippines, 17·4% from Cuba, 15·6% from Brazil, 14·3% from South Africa, 12·5% from Thailand, 9·3% from Australia.

Fruit production, 1975 (in 1,000 tonnes): Peaches, 270; pears, 460; apples, 898; grapes, 284; persimmons, 275; and mandarins, 3,665.

Livestock (1976): 3·72m. cattle (including 1·81m. milch cows), 36,000 horses, 7·46m. pigs, 10,000 sheep, 94,000 goats, 249m. chickens. Milk output is increasing—in 1975, 5m. tonnes.

Forestry. Forests and grasslands cover about 25m. hectares (nearly 70% of the whole land area), with an estimated timber stand of 2,073·7m. cu. metres in 1974. In 1974, 47·5m. cu. metres were felled.

Fisheries. Before the War, Japanese catch represented one-half to two-thirds of the world's total fishing, in 1974 it was 15·4%. The catch in 1975 was 10·5m. tonnes, excluding whaling. Japan is the leading whaling nation, occupying 80% of the world's total catch. Output of whale oil, 1975, 39,000 tonnes from 9,450 whales caught.

INDUSTRY AND TRADE

Industry. Japan's industrial equipment, 1974, numbered 696,795 plants of all sizes, employing 11,487 production workers.

Since 1920 there has been a shift from light to heavy industries. The production of electrical appliances and electronic machinery has made great strides: television sets (1976: 15m.), radio sets (1975: 12·77m.), cameras (1976: 8m.), computing machines and automation equipment are produced in increasing quantities. The chemical industry ranks third in production value after machinery and metals (1974). Production, 1975, included (in tonnes): Ammonium sulphate, 1·9m.; calcium superphosphate, 494,000; sulphuric acid, 6m.; caustic soda 2·9m.

Output (1974), in 1,000 tonnes, of pig iron was 86,877; crude steel, 102,313; ordinary rolled steel, 76,514.

In 1975 paper production was 7·7m. tonnes; paperboard, 5·9m. tonnes.

Japan's textile industry before the War had 13m. cotton-yarn spindles. After the War she resumed with 2·78m. spindles; in 1964, 8·42m. spindles were operating. Output of cotton yarn, 1975, 460,483 tonnes, and of cotton cloth, 2,124 sq. metres.

In wool, Japan aims at wool exports sufficient to pay for the imports of raw wool. Output, 1975, 142,244 tonnes of woollen yarns and 357 sq. metres of woollen fabrics.

Output, 1974, of rayon woven fabrics, 839m. sq. metres; synthetic woven fabrics, 2·4m. sq. metres; silk fabrics, 160m. sq. metres.

Since 1955 Japan has led the world in shipbuilding, and in 1975 accounted for about 50% of the world's launchings. In 1975, 17·99m. gross tons were launched, of which 12·6m. were exported. In Aug. 1977, the world's largest oil tanker, the *Esso-Atlantic* (508,731 DWT) was launched from a Japanese shipyard.

Labour. Total labour force, Aug. 1976, was 53·45m., of which 6·63m. were in agriculture and forestry, 430,000 in fishing, 190,000 in mining, 4·98m. in construction, 13·31m. in manufacturing, 9·02m. in commerce and finance, 3·31m. in transport and other public utilities, 9m. in services (including the professions) and 1·9m. in government work.

In 1976 there were 12,509,000 workers organized in 70,039 unions. The largest federation is the 'General Council of Japanese Trade Unions' (Sōhyō) with 4·58m. members. The 'Japanese Confederation of Labour' (Dōmei Kaigi) had 2·2m. members. The 'Federation of Independent Unions' (Chūritsu Rōren) founded in 1956 had 1·35m. members.

In Oct. 1976, 1m. (1·8%) were unemployed. In 1976, 3·25m. working days were lost in industrial stoppages.

Harari, E., *The Politics of Labor Legislation in Japan.* Univ. of California Press, 1973
Okochi, K., Karsch, B. and Levine, S. B. (eds.), *Workers and Employers in Japan.* Univ. of Tokyo Press, 1974

Commerce. Trade, excluding bullion and specie (in US$1m.; US$1 = 360 yen, 1,000 yen = US$2.77; from 1 Jan. 1972, US$1 = 308 yen, 1,000 yen = US$3.24):

	1970	*1971*	*1972*	*1973*	*1974*	*1975*	*1976*
Imports	18,881	19,712	23,471	38,314	62,110	57,863	64,799
Exports	19,318	24,019	28,591	28,930	55,536	55,753	67,225

Distribution of trade by countries (customs clearance basis) (in US$1m.):

	Exports		*Imports*	
	1975	*1976*	*1975*	*1976*
South-east Asia	12,543	14,047	10,586	13,411
Hong Kong	1,378	1,840	245	342
Thailand	959	1,070	724	848
Philippines	1,026	1,114	1,121	793
Latin America	2,368	2,340	1,701	1,797
Africa	5,556	5,889	2,320	2,076
USA	11,149	15,690	11,608	11,809
Canada	1,150	1,552	2,499	2,715
Australia	1,739	2,309	4,156	5,360
Fed. Rep. of Germany	1,661	2,243	1,139	1,228
UK	1,473	1,400	810	843
USSR	1,626	2,252	1,169	1,167
China	2,259	1,663	1,531	1,371

Principal items in 1976, with value in US$1m. were:

Imports, c.i.f.		*Exports, f.o.b.*	
Mineral fuels	28,287	Machinery and transport equipment	39,627
Foodstuffs	9,376	Metals and metal products	13,170
Metal ores and scrap	4,579	Textile products	4,216
Machinery and transport equipment	4,608	Chemicals	3,747
Textile fibres	1,796		

Total trade between Japan and UK for calendar years (British Department of Trade returns, in £1,000 sterling):

	1973	*1974*	*1975*	*1976*	*1977*
Imports to UK	443,394	570,099	671,745	796,259	1,065,355
Exports and re-exports from UK	272,598	319,047	308,470	359,126	469,308

Tourism. In 1975, 811,700 foreigners visited Japan, 276,300 of whom came from USA, 46,600 from UK. Japanese travelling abroad totalled 1,323,700. Japanese tourist payment showed a deficit of US$1,115m.

COMMUNICATIONS

Roads. The total length of roads (including urban and other local roads) was 1,059,101 km at 31 March 1974; the 'national' roads extended 32,782 km, of which 30,372 km were paved. Motor vehicles, at 31 Dec. 1975, numbered 27·5m., including 17·24m. passenger cars and 10·27m. commercial vehicles.

Railways. The first railway was completed in 1872, between Tōkyō and Yokohama (29 km). Total length of railways, in 1974, was 28,024 km, of which the national railways had 22,230 km (8,444 km electrified) and private railways, 5,794 km (5,058 km electrified). In 1974 the national railways carried 7,113m. passengers (private, 10,476m.) and 158m. tons of freight (private, 48m.).

Aviation. The principal airlines are Japan Airlines and All Nippon Airways. Japan Airlines, founded in 1953, operate international services from Tōkyō to the USA, Europe, the Middle East and Southeast Asia, including flights to London over the North Pole and to Moscow by way of Siberia. In 1975 Japanese companies carried 25m. passengers in domestic services and 2·6m. passengers in international services.

Shipping. On 1 July 1975 the merchant fleet consisted of 8,832 vessels (over 100 gross tons) of 38·19m. gross tons; there were 716 ships for passenger transport (1,032,000 gross tons), 5,503 cargo ships (19·58m. gross tons) and 1,893 oil tankers (17·41m. gross tons).

Post and Broadcasting. The telephone services, operated by a public corporation, at 31 March 1976 had 43,232,000 instruments.

In 1975, 98% of all households owned television sets and 99% had radio sets.

Cinemas (1976). Cinemas numbered 2,480 with an annual attendance of 171m. (1960: 1,014m.).

Newspapers (1976). Daily newspapers numbered 123 with aggregate circulation of 60·78m., including 4 major English-language newspapers.

JUSTICE, RELIGION, EDUCATION AND WELFARE

Justice. The Supreme Court is composed of the Chief Justice and 14 other judges. The Chief Justice is appointed by the Emperor, the other judges by the Cabinet. Every 10 years a justice must submit himself to the electorate. All justices and judges of the lower courts serve until they are 70 years of age.

Below the Supreme Court are 8 regional higher courts, district courts (*Chihō-saibansho*) in each prefecture (4 in Hokkaidō) and the local courts.

The Supreme Court is authorized to declare unconstitutional any act of the Legislature or the Executive which violates the constitution.

Religion. There has normally been religious freedom, but Shintō (literally, The Way of the Gods) was given the status of *quasi*-state-religion in the 1930s; in 1945 the Allied Supreme Command ordered the Government to discontinue state support of Shintō. State subsidies have ceased for all religions, and all religious teachings are forbidden in public schools.

In Dec. 1975 Shintoism claimed 89,062,866 adherents, Buddhism 86,607,272; these figures obviously overlap. Christians numbered 866,662, of whom 457,421 are Protestants and 349,241 Catholics.

Education. Education is compulsory and free between the ages of 6 and 15. All institutions are co-educational. On 1 May 1976 there were 13,489 kindergartens with 89,600 teachers and 2,370,400 pupils; 24,716 elementary schools with 424,000 teachers and 10,610 pupils; 10,719 junior high schools with 237,600 teachers and 4,386,100 pupils; 4,978 senior high schools with 226,800 teachers; 511 junior colleges with 15,800 teachers and 364,900 pupils.

There were also 603 special schools for handicapped children (21,200 teachers, 65,700 pupils).

Japan has 7 main state universities, formerly known as the Imperial Universities: Tōkyō University (1877); Kyōto University (1897); Tōhoku University, Sendai (1907); Kyūshū University, Fukuoka (1910); Hokkaidō University, Sapporo (1918); Osaka University (1931), and Nagoya University (1939). In addition, there are various other state and municipal as well as private universities of high standing, such as Keio (founded in 1859), Waseda, Rikkyo, Hosei, Meiji universities, and several women's universities, among which Tōkyō and Ochanomizu are most notable. There are 423 colleges and universities with (1 May 1976) 1,734,100 students and 92,900 teachers.

Social Welfare. Hospitals at the end of 1975 numbered 8,294 with 1,164,098 beds. Physicians at the end of 1975 numbered 132,479; dentists, 43,586.

There are in force various types of social security schemes, such as health insurance, unemployment insurance and old-age pensions. The total population come under one or more of these schemes.

In 1977 some 160,000 welfare commissioners were employed. In April 1977 some 1·37m. persons received some form of regular public assistance.

DIPLOMATIC REPRESENTATIVES

OF JAPAN IN GREAT BRITAIN (43 Grosvenor St., London, W1X OBA)

Ambassador: Tadao Kato.

OF GREAT BRITAIN IN JAPAN (1 Ichiban-cho, Chiyoda-ku, Tōkyō 102)

Ambassador: Sir Michael Wilford, KCMG.

OF JAPAN IN THE USA (2520 Massachusetts Ave., NW, Washington, D.C. 20008)

Ambassador: Fumihiko Togo.

OF THE USA IN JAPAN (10–5, Akasaka 1-chrome, Minato-Ku, Tōkyō)

Ambassador: Michael J. Mansfield.

OF JAPAN TO THE UNITED NATIONS

Ambassador: Isao Abe.

Books of Reference

Statistics Bureau of the Prime Minister's Office: *Statistical Year-Book* (from 1949).—*Statistical Abstract* (from 1950).—*Statistical Handbook of Japan 1977.*—*Monthly Bulletin* (from April 1950)

Economic Planning Agency: *Economic Survey* (annual), *Economic Statistics* (monthly), *Economic Indicators* (monthly)

Ministry of International Trade: *Foreign Trade of Japan* (annual)

The Bank of Japan Research Department. *Money and Banking in Japan.* London, 1973

Japan Times Year Book. (*I. Year Book of Japan. II. Who's Who in Japan. III. Business Directory of Japan.*) Tokyo, first issue 1933

Treaty of Peace with Japan. (Cmd. 8392.) HMSO, 1951; (Cmd. 8601). HMSO, 1952

Ackerman, E. A., *Japan's Natural Resources.* Univ. of Chicago Press, 1953

Allen, G. C., *Short Economic History of Modern Japan.* London, 1946.—*Japan's Economic Recovery.* R. Inst. of Int. Affairs, 1957.—*Japan's Economic Expansion.* CUP, 1965

Asahi Newsprinting Co., *This is Japan.* Tokyo, annual from 1954

Baerwald, H. H., *Japan's Parliament.* CUP, 1974

Boltho, A., *Japan: An Economic Survey, 1953–1973.* OUP, 1976

Brown, D. M., *Nationalism in Japan.* Univ. of California Press, 1955

Fistié, P., *La Rentrée en Scène du Japon.* Paris, 1972

Hirschmeier, J., and Tsunehiko, Y., *The Development of Japanese Business, 1600–1973.* London, 1976

Jones, F. C., *Japan's New Order in East Asia, 1937–45.* OUP, 1954

Kenkyusha's *New Japanese–English* [*and English–Japanese*] *Dictionary.* 2 vols. New ed. Cambridge, Mass., and Berkeley, Cal., 1960

Kennedy, M. D., *A History of Japan.* London, 1963

Kitamura, H., *Choices for the Japanese Economy.* London, 1976

Langdon, F. C., *Japan's Foreign Policy.* Univ. of British Columbia Press, 1973

McNelly, T., *Politics and Government in Japan.* 2nd ed. London, 1972

Miyazaki, S., *The Japanese Dictionary Explained in English.* Tokyo, 1950

New Japan. Mainichi Newspapers, Tokyo, annual, from 1948

Nihon Keizai Shimbun, *Industrial Review of Japan.* Tokyo, annual, from 1956

Nippon: A Chartered Survey of Japan. Tsuneta Yano Memorial Society. Tokyo, annual

Norbury, P., and Bownes, G. (ed.), *Business in Japan.* London, 1974

Ohkawa, K., and Rosovsky, H., *Japanese Economic Growth: Trend Acceleration in the Twentieth Century.* Stanford Univ. Press, 1973

Richardson, B. M., *The Political Culture of Japan.* Univ. of California Press, 1974

Sansom, G. B., *The Western World and Japan.* New York, 1950.—*A History of Japan.* 3 vols. London, 1958–64

Schwind, M., *Das Japanische Inselreich.* 3 vols. Berlin, 1967 ff.

Simonis, H. and U. E. (ed.), *Japan: Economic and Social Studies in Development.* Wiesbaden, 1974

Takekazu Ogura (ed.), *Agricultural Development in Modern Japan*. Tokyo, 1963

Tanaka, K., *Building a New Japan: A Plan for Remodelling the Japanese Archipelago*. Tokyo, 1973

Trewartha, G. T., *Japan: A Physical, Cultural and Regional Geography*. Madison, Wisconsin, and London, 1945

Yabuki, K. (ed.), *Japan Bibliographic Annual*. 2 vols. Tokyo, annual

THE HASHEMITE KINGDOM OF JORDAN

Capital: Amman
Population: 2·75m. (1976) E. Bank
0·8m. (1976) W. Bank
GNP per capita: US$610 (1976)

Al Mamlaka al Urduniya al Hashemiyah

HISTORY. By a Treaty, signed in London on 22 March 1946, Britain recognized Transjordan as a sovereign independent state. A new Anglo-Transjordan treaty was signed in Amman on 15 March 1948. The treaty was to remain in force for 20 years, but by mutual consent was terminated on 13 March 1957.

The Arab Federation between the Kingdoms of Iraq and Jordan, which was concluded on 14 Feb. 1958, lapsed after the revolution in Iraq of 14 July 1958, and was officially terminated by royal decree on 1 Aug. 1958.

On 25 May 1946 the Amir Abdullah assumed the title of King, and when the treaty was ratified on 17 June 1946 the name of the territory was changed to that of 'The Hashemite Kingdom of Jordan'. The legislature consists of a lower house of 60 members elected by universal suffrage (30 from East Jordan and 30 from West Jordan), and a senate of 30 members nominated by the King. Elections took place on 16 April 1967.

AREA AND POPULATION. The part of Palestine remaining to the Arabs under the armistice with Israel 3 April 1949, with the exception of the Gaza strip, was in Dec. 1949 placed under Jordan rule and formally incorporated in Jordan on 24 April 1950; for the frontier lines *see* map in THE STATESMAN'S YEAR-BOOK, 1951. On 10 Aug. 1965 a treaty with Saudi Arabia provided for an exchange of about 6,000–7,000 sq. km in order to facilitate the development of the port of Aqaba.

Total East Bank area, 91,000 sq. km. West Bank enclaves 5,000 sq. km: census population (18 Nov. 1961), 1,706,226; estimate, 1976, 2,751,968 (1,951,968 in East Bank, 800,000 in West Bank). In 1961, 805,450 lived in West Jordan and 834,589 in East Jordan, including some 550,000 refugees from Palestine but excluding some 53,000 nomads. About 63,000 Jordanians live abroad. Density of population per sq. km, 51 in East Jordan, 143 in West Jordan.

The country is divided into 8 districts (*muhafaza*), viz., Amman, Irbid, Balqa, Karak, Ma'an, Jerusalem, Hebron and Nablus. The last 3 named districts are known collectively as the West Bank, which, since the hostilities of June 1967, has been occupied by Israel.

The largest towns, with estimated population, Dec. 1976: Amman, the capital, 700,000; Zarka, 258,000; Irbid, 134,000.

In 1975 registered births numbered 81,659; deaths, 6,788; marriages, 14,137; divorces, 2,345.

KING. The Kingdom is a constitutional monarchy headed by His Majesty King **Hussein**, GCVO, eldest son of King Talal, who, being incapacitated by mental illness, was deposed by Parliament on 11 Aug. 1952 and died 8 July 1972. The King was born 14 Nov. 1935, and married Princess Dina Abdul Hamid on 19 April 1955 (divorced 1957), Toni Avril Gardiner (Muna al Hussein) on 25 May 1961 (divorced 1972) and Alia Toukan on 26 Dec. 1972 (died in air crash 1977). *Offspring:* Princess Alia, born 13 Feb. 1956; Prince Abdulla, born 30 Jan. 1962; Prince Faisal, born 11 Oct. 1963; Princesses Zein and Aisha, born 23 April 1968; Princess Haya, born 3

May 1974; Prince Ali, born 23 Dec. 1975. *Crown Prince* (appointed 1 April 1965): Prince Hassan, younger brother of the King.

CONSTITUTION AND GOVERNMENT. The Constitution passed on 7 Nov. 1951 provides that the Cabinet is responsible to Parliament.

On 9 Nov. 1974 both Houses of Parliament approved amendments to the Constitution by which the King was empowered to dissolve Parliament and delay calling elections for 12 months.

On 5 Feb. 1976 both Houses of Parliament approved amendments to the Constitution by which the King was empowered to postpone calling elections until further notice. The lower house was dissolved. This step was taken because no elections could be held in the West Bank which has been under Israeli occupation since June 1967.

On 12 Aug. 1975 Jordan and Syria concluded an agreement by which a high political command of both countries would co-ordinate their policy and work for closer relations in political, military and economic fields.

The cabinet, on 28 Nov 1976, was composed as follows:

Prime Minister and Minister of Defence and Foreign Affairs: Muhar Badran.

Education: Dr Abdul Salam Al-Majaly. *Information:* Adnan Abu Oudeh. *Tourism and Antiquities:* Ghaleb Barakat. *Finance:* Salem Massa'deh. *Public Works:* Ahmad Al-Shoubaki. *Interior, Municipal and Rural Affairs:* Marwan Humoud. *Health:* Dr Mohammed al Beshir. *Transport:* Mahmoud E. Hawamdeh. *Justice:* Ahmad Tarawneh. *Industry and Trade:* Dr Rajai Al-Mousher. *Supply and Agriculture:* Salah Jum'ah. *Minister of State for Foreign Affairs, and Reconstruction and Development:* Hassan Ibrahim. *Labour:* Isam Al-Ajlouni. *Interior:* Suleiman Arar. *Minister of State for Prime Ministerial Affairs:* Marwan Kassem. *Communications:* Abd Al-Ra'ouf Rawabdeh. *Wakf and Islamic Affairs, and Shrines:* Kamel Al-Sharif.

National flag: Three horizontal stripes of black, white, green, with a red triangle based on the hoist, bearing a white 7-pointed star.

The official language of the country is Arabic.

DEFENCE

Army. The Army is organized in 2 armoured, 2 mechanized and 2 infantry divisions. In addition there is an independent infantry brigade group which includes 1 armoured car regiment. Total strength (1977) 61,000 men.

Navy. The Coastal Guard or Jordan Sea Force consists of 10 motor launches based at Aqaba. Personnel (1978) totalled 300 officers and ratings.

Air Force. The Air Force has 2 squadrons of F-5A supersonic fighter-bombers, 1 squadron of F-5E Tiger II interceptors (second squadron equipping) and 1 squadron of F-104A Starfighter interceptors. There are a few C-130B Hercules and 4 CASA Aviocar turboprop transports, piston-engined Dove transports, Alouette III helicopters, and T-37B jet trainers. Basic training on piston-engined Bulldogs is centred at the civil Royal Academy of Aeronautics. Hawk surface-to-air missiles are being delivered to equip 14 batteries. Strength is about 6,600 officers and men.

INTERNATIONAL RELATIONS

Membership. Jordan is a member of the UN and the Arab League.

ECONOMY

Planning. A 5-year plan (1976–80) aims at achieving a growth rate of 12% per annum but in 1975 the increase was only 6%.

Budget. The budget estimates for the year 1976–77 provide for revenue of JD.332·6m.

Currency. On 1 July 1950 Jordan began to issue its own currency, the Jordan *dinar*, divided into 1,000 *fils*. The Jordan dinar equals £1·5. Jordan is a member of the sterling area. The following bank-notes and coins are in circulation: 10, 5 dinars, 1 dinar, 500 fils (notes), 250, 100, 50, 25, 20 fils (cupro-nickel), 10, 5, 1 fils (bronze). Circulation on 31 Dec. 1976 was JD.164·93m.

Banking. The Central Bank of Jordan started operations on 1 Oct. 1964, taking over the sterling assets and the commitments of the Jordan Currency Board.

NATURAL RESOURCES

Minerals. Phosphate rock production in 1976 was 1,767,933 tons. Potash is found in the Dead Sea. Oil prospecting in the southern area is being undertaken by the Government in association with INA of Yugoslavia. Cement production (1976), 533,000 tons.

Agriculture. The country east of the Hejaz Railway line is largely desert; north-western Jordan is potentially of agricultural value but entirely dependent on the rainfall. The resources are agricultural and pastoral products; hillsides are being terraced, fruit-trees planted, irrigation has started. Most of the 93,000 farms are owner-operated and are less than 25 acres.

Production in 1975 included (in tonnes): Wheat, 500,165; barley, 117,671; tomatoes, 145,059; citrus fruits, 122,752; water melons, 503,787. Olive production was very poor.

Livestock (1976): 818,000 sheep; 474,000 goats; 35,000 cattle; 18,000 camels. 2,923 tractors and 189 cultivators were in use in 1975.

COMMERCE. Imports in 1976 were valued at JD.349·5m. and exports and re-exports at JD.49·5m.

Total trade with UK (British Department of Trade returns, in £1,000 sterling):

	1973	*1974*	*1975*	*1976*	*1977*
Imports to UK	465	1,631	733	892	1,996
Exports and re-exports from UK	13,408	20,648	36,847	55,737	48,974

TOURISM. In 1976, 1,063,262 foreigners visited Jordan.

COMMUNICATIONS

Roads. Asphalt roads connect Amman with all the chief towns in the country. Unmetalled roads have been constructed, making motor traffic possible from Amman to most other areas. The road from Amman to Ma'an and Aqaba (394 km) has branches to Karak, Tafileh, Shobak and Wadi Musa (Petra). The town of Jerash is joined by a good road to Amman. The normal asphalted route from Amman to Deraa (in Syria) and thence to Damascus is through Jerash. The oasis of Azraq may be reached by motor car from Mafraq, Zarka or Amman. Total length of public highways, 4,095 km. Motor vehicles in 1975 included 33,132 private passenger cars and taxis, 8,378 goods vehicles, 1,887 motor cycles, 729 buses.

Railways. The 1,050 mm Hejaz Railway runs from the Syrian border at Nassib to Ma'an and Naqb Ishtar and Aqaba Port. The railway linking Damascus with Ma'an passes through Amman. The line linking Ma'an with Aqaba Port was opened for phosphates traffic in Oct. 1975.

Aviation (1975). The Royal Jordanian Airlines (ALIA) maintains services from Amman to Amsterdam, Athens, Abu Dhabi, Aleppo, Aqaba, Baghdad, Bahrain, Bangkok, Beirut, Brussels, Cairo, Casablanca, Colombo, Copenhagen, Damascus, Deir ez Zor, Dubai, Dhahran, Doha, Frankfurt, Geneva, Istanbul, Jidda, Kuala Lumpur, Kuwait, London, Madrid, Oman, Paris, Rome, Singapore, Tehrán and Vienna. Alitalia, KLM, Middle East Airways, Egyptian Airlines, Saudi Arabian, Iraqi, Kuwaiti, British Airways, Swissair, Syrian Arab Airlines, and Aeroflot also operate in Jordan.

Shipping (1976). 1,064 vessels called at the port of Aqaba, handling 3,000,503 tons.

Post. There were 43,720 telephones in 1977 (13,854 in Amman).

Cinemas (1975). Cinemas numbered 40 with a total attendance of 4,341,900.

Newspapers (1976). There were 6 daily (including 1 in English) and 5 weekly papers.

EDUCATION (1975–76, East Bank only). Government schools, 1,861; private schools, 303; UNRWA schools, 191. Number of pupils, 577,469 (including 256,751 girls); number of teachers, 19,826. Budget provision for education in 1975 was JD.18,610,500. The University of Jordan, inaugurated on 15 Dec. 1962 had 5,307 students (including 1,694 girls) and 302 teachers. The Yarmouk University (Irbid) was inaugurated in 1976 with 640 students.

Seven teacher-training colleges had 5,104 students (including 1,870 girls) and 229 teachers. Three agricultural schools had 40 teachers and 591 students; 10 industrial schools had 157 teachers and 1,911 pupils, and 3 nursing, midwifery and childcare schools had 25 teachers and 323 students. One social service institute had 6 teachers and 52 students. Six vocational centres had 32 teachers and 424 pupils.

HEALTH (1975). There were 796 physicians, 145 dentists and 31 hospitals with 3,274 beds.

DIPLOMATIC REPRESENTATIVES

OF JORDAN IN GREAT BRITAIN (6 Upper Phillimore Gdns, London, W8 7HB)

Ambassador: Salah Abuzeid.

OF GREAT BRITAIN IN JORDAN (Third Circle, Jebel Amman)

Ambassador: J. C. Moberly, CMG.

OF JORDAN IN THE USA (2319 Wyoming Ave., NW, Washington, D.C., 20008)

Ambassador: Abdullah Salah.

OF THE USA IN JORDAN (Jebel Amman, Amman)

Ambassador: Thomas R. Pickering.

OF JORDAN TO THE UNITED NATIONS

Ambassador: Dr Hazem Nuseibeh.

Books of Reference

The Department of Statistics, Ministry of National Economy, publishes a *Statistical Yearbook* (in Arabic and English), latest issue 1968, and a *Statistical Guide*, latest issue 1965.—*External Trade Statistics*, 1968.—*National Accounts and Input–Output Analysis, 1959–65*, 1967

The Constitution of the Hashemite Kingdom of Jordan. Amman, 1952

Aruri, N. H., *Jordan: A Study in Political Development (1921–1965)*. The Hague, 1972

Glubb, J. B., *The Story of the Arab Legion*. London, 1948.—*A Soldier with the Arabs*. London, 1957

Haas, J., *Husseins Königreich: Jordaniens Stellung in Nahen Osten*. Munich, 1975

Morris, J., *The Hashemite Kings*. London, 1959

Seton, C. R. W., *Legislation of Transjordan, 1918–30*. London, 1931. [Continued by the Government of Jordan as an annual publication: *Jordan Legislation*. Amman, 1932 ff.]

Toni, Y. T., and Mousa, S., *Jordan: Land and People*. Amman, 1973

DEMOCRATIC KAMPUCHEA

Capital: Phnom Penh
Population: 8m. (1977)
GNP per capita: No accurate estimate available (1978)

Cambodia

HISTORY. The recorded history of Cambodia, starts at the beginning of the Christian era with the Kingdom of Fou-Nan, whose territories at one time included parts of Thailand, Malaya, Cochin-China and Laos. The religious, cultural and administrative inspirations of this state came from India. The Kingdom was absorbed at the end of the 6th century by the Khmers, under whose monarchs was built, between the 9th and 13th centuries, the splendid complex of shrines and temples at Angkor. Attacked on either side by the Vietnamese and the Thai from the 15th century on, Cambodia was saved from annihilation by the establishment of a French protectorate in 1863. Thailand eventually recognized the protectorate and renounced all claims to suzerainty in exchange for Cambodia's north-western provinces of Battambang and Siem Reap, which were, however, returned under a Franco-Thai convention of 1907, confirmed in the Franco-Thai treaty of 1937. In 1904 the province of Stung Treng, formerly administered as part of Laos, was attached to Cambodia. For history to 1949 *see* THE STATESMAN'S YEAR-BOOK, 1973–74, p. 1112.

In 1949 Cambodia was granted independence as an Associate State of the French Union. The transfer of the French military powers to the Cambodian government of 9 Nov. 1953 is considered in Cambodia as the attainment of sovereign independence. In Jan. 1955 Cambodia became financially and economically independent, both of France and the other two former Associate States of French Indo-China, Vietnam and Laos.

Anti-French guerrilla bands had operated in the jungle from 1945, the most important being a nationalist group known as the Khmer Issarak led by Son Ngoc Thanh, who had, briefly, been Prime Minister during the Japanese occupation. By 1953 Communist bands drawn from the Vietnamese minority and controlled by the Vietminh were active, and in 1954 regular Vietminh forces invaded Cambodia. Fighting came to an end with the conclusion on 21 July 1954, at the Geneva Conference, of the agreement on Cambodia, which ensured the withdrawal of French and Vietminh troops, and most of the Khmer Issarak bands then surrendered.

The International Control Commission was withdrawn in Dec. 1969 at the request of Prince Sihanouk.

Following a period of increasing economic difficulties and growing indirect involvement in the Vietnamese war Prince Sihanouk was deposed in March 1970 and on 9 Oct. 1970 the Kingdom of Cambodia became the Khmer Republic. From 1970 hostilities extended throughout most of the country involving North and South Vietnamese and US forces as well as Republican and anti-Republican Khmer troops. During 1973 direct American and North Vietnamese participation in the fighting came to an end, leaving a civil war situation which continued during 1974 with large-scale fighting between forces of the Khmer Republic supported by American arms and economic aid and the forces of the United National Cambodian Front including 'Khmer Rouge' communists supported by North Vietnam and China.

After unsuccessful attempts to capture Phnom Penh in 1973 and 1974, the Khmer Rouge ended the 5-year war in April 1974, when the remnants of the republican forces surrendered the city.

AREA AND POPULATION. Kampuchea is bounded north by Laos and Thailand, in the west by Thailand, east by Vietnam and south by Kerala and the Gulf of Thailand. It has an area about 181,000 sq. km (71,000 sq. miles), divided into 17 provinces: Kompong Thom (population, 322,000), Kompong Cham (820,000), Battambang (551,860), Kampot (337,879), Siem Reap (313,000), Kompong Chhang (273,000), Kompong Speu (307,000), Takeo (467,000), Kratié (136,000), Stung Treng (136,000), Svay Rieng (287,000), Prey Veng (492,000), Pursat (180,000), Kandal (population, excluding Phnom Penh, 706,000), Ratanakiri (49,400), Mondolkiri (14,300), Koh Kong (38,700).

The total population of 8m. (1977) included Vietnamese, Chinese, Chams and Europeans. No estimates were possible in 1978. In the uplands and in the north-east live various groups of hillmen, known as Khmer-Loeu.

The chief towns are Phnom Penh, the capital located at the junction of the Mekong and Tonle Sap rivers, and Battambang. Populations of major towns have fluctuated greatly since 1970 by flows of refugees from rural areas and from one town to another. Phnom Penh formerly had a population of at least 2·5m. but a 1977 estimate puts it at 50,000. Khmer is the official language.

GOVERNMENT. The Royal Government of National Union for Cambodia (GRUNC) was set up by Prince Sihanouk in exile in Peking in 1970. Many of its members led the fighting in Cambodia against Marshal Lou Nol's Republican Forces.

For period 1972–75 *see* STATESMAN'S YEAR-BOOK, 1975–76, p. 1100.

A new Constitution was approved on 15 Dec. 1975 and on 22 March 1976 a legislature was elected consisting of 204 men and 46 women. On 5 April Prince Sihanouk resigned and Khieu Samphan became Head of State on 14 April.

Prime Minister: Pol Pot. *Vice Premier for Foreign Affairs:* Son Sen.

National flag: Red with a silhouette of the temple of Angkor Wat in the centre in yellow.

DEFENCE. Since the end of the war in April 1975 there has been no accurate data on defence and the three sections below should be treated with reserve.

Army. The Army has 1 armoured brigade, 1 engineer brigade, 1 parachute brigade, 1 artillery brigade and 30 infantry brigades (about 220 battalions), and the normal communications, logistic and training elements. Strength (1977) about 200,000.

Navy. The Marine Royale Khmer was established on 1 March 1954 and became Marine Nationale Khmer on 9 Oct. 1970. It includes 7 landing craft, 23 seaward patrol craft and coastal boats, 1 tug, 65 river patrol craft and 100 small craft, converted junks, etc. Two patrol vessels and 2 support (landing) gunboats escaped from Khmer Rouge, and 2 torpedo boats are believed to have sunk. Personnel in 1976 numbered about 11,000 officers and men, including 4,000 of marine infantry but the 1978 figure is obscure.

Air Force. In 1974 the Air Force had a strength of about 7,000 officers and men, including 120 pilots, with about 200 aircraft, none of them jets. Combat squadrons operated approximately 60 T-28 piston-engined light attack aircraft. The remaining equipment comprised C-123 and C-47 transports, UH-1H helicopters, and U-1A, O-1A/D and AU-24A light aircraft. It is not known how many of these aircraft remain serviceable.

ECONOMY

Currency. Under the Paris agreements of 29 Dec. 1954, between the Associate States and France, the parity of the Cambodian *piastre* (henceforth to be known as a *riel*) was to be maintained for the time being at 10 francs = 1 *riel.* On 31 Dec. 1954 the quadripartite Institut d'Emission ceased operations and a new Cambodian National Bank became responsible for the issue of currency. In Nov. 1955 Vietnamese and Laotian bank-notes ceased to be legal tender in Kampuchea. During 1973–74 the *riel* declined in value with repeated devaluations. By 1978 money had been officially abolished. No wages or salaries are paid.

Banking. In 1964 all bank functions were taken over by government banks. In 1972 legislation permitted the re-opening of foreign banks but by the end of Dec. 1973 only a few representational offices had opened.

NATURAL RESOURCES

Minerals. A phosphate factory, jointly controlled by the state and private interests, was set up in 1966 near a deposit of an estimated 350,000 tons. Another deposit of about the same size is earmarked for exploitation. High-grade iron-ore deposits (possibly as much as 2·5m. tons) exist in Northern Khmer, but are not exploited commercially because of transportation difficulties. Some small-scale gold panning (6,687 troy oz. in 1963) and gem (mainly zircon) mining is carried out at Pailin where there is potential for considerable expansion. In Sept. 1972 a French company began drilling for oil in offshore waters.

Agriculture. The overwhelming majority of the population is normally engaged in agriculture, fishing and forestry. Of the country's total area of 44m. acres, about 20m. are cultivable and over 20m. are forest land. Some 4m. acres are cultivated, well over half being devoted to rice production. Before the spread of war the high productivity provided for a low, but well-fed standard of living for the peasant farmers, the majority of whom owned the land they worked. A relatively small proportion of the food production entered the cash economy. The war and unwise pricing policies have led to a disastrous reduction in production to a stage in which the country had become a net importer of rice in 1972 and 1973 and continued to be so in 1974. Since April 1975 a vigorous agricultural programme has been implemented to meet food shortages.

A crop of about 635 tonnes of paddy were produced in 1974. Rubber production in 1968 amounted to 49,000 tonnes but less than 10,000 tonnes in 1972.

Other products are maize, and, in usual order of value, livestock, timber, pepper, haricot beans, soybeans and fish.

Livestock (1976) FAO estimate: Cattle, 1·9m.; buflaloes, 869,000; sheep, 2,000; horses, 12,000; poultry, 4·3m.

Forestry. Much of Kampuchea's surface is covered by potentially valuable forests, 3·8m. hectares of which are reserved by the Government to be awarded to concessionaires, and are not at present worked to an appreciable extent. The remainder is available for exploitation by the local residents, and as a result some areas are over-exploited and conservation is not practised. There are substantial reserves of pitch pine.

Fisheries. Kampuchea has the greatest fresh-water fish resources in South-East Asia but production in 1970 (30,000 tons) was about a third of that for 1966.

INDUSTRY AND TRADE

Industry. Some development of industry had taken place before the spread of open warfare in 1970. Industry established and in operation in Jan. 1970 included a motor-vehicle assembly plant, 3 cigarette manufacturing concerns, a modern factory, several metal fabricating concerns, a distillery, a saw-mill, textile, fish canning, plywood, paper, cement, sugar sack, tyre, pottery and glassware factories and a cotton-ginnery. In the private sector there are about 3,200 manufacturing enterprises, producing a wide range of goods; most of them are small family concerns. An oil refinery at Kompong Som came into production in 1969 but was put out of action by an attack in early 1971. Since April 1975 a programme for repairing factories has been started and some 70 are back in production.

Commerce. Principal imports by order of value (1972) were petroleum products, metals and machinery (including vehicles), general foodstuffs and chemicals.

The only recorded export in 1972 was 7,328 tonnes of rubber. Much of the country's trade is with Hong Kong and Singapore.

Total trade with UK (British Department of trade returns, in £1,000 sterling):

	1972	*1973*	*1974*	*1975*	*1976*	*1977*
Imports to UK	23	4	269	147	228	86
Exports and re-exports from UK	592	204	872	456	61	92

COMMUNICATIONS

Roads. There were, in 1970, 2,574 km of asphalt roads (including the 'Khmer–American Friendship Highway' from outside Phnom Penh to close to Kompong Som, built under the United States aid programme and opened in July 1959), 359 km of macadamized roads, and about 1,213 km of improved dirt roads. Since 1970 many road bridges have been destroyed and long stretches of highway closed to traffic or open only to escorted convoys.

Railways. A line of 385 km (metre gauge) links Phnom Penh to Poipet (Thai frontier). In 1969 traffic amounted to 170m. passenger-km and 76m. ton-km. Work was completed during 1969 on a line Phnom Penh–Kompong Som *via* Takeo and Kampot. Total length, 649 km but by 1973 only a short stretch between Battambang and the Thai border remained in operation, the remainder having been closed by military action. Restoration of some lines is now in progress.

Aviation. The Pochentong airport is 10 km from Phnom Penh. The airport at Siemreap has been closed to international traffic since 1971. Minor airports have been expanded since 1970 and there are regular services between Phnom Penh and provincial capitals using DC-3 aircraft.

Shipping. The port of Phnom Penh can be reached by the Mekong (through Vietnam) by ships of between 3,000 and 4,000 tons. In 1970, 97 ocean-going vessels imported 51,300 tons of cargo at Phnom Penh and exported 86,400 tons.

A new ocean port has been built under the French aid programme at Kompong Som (formerly Sihanoukville) on the Gulf of Siam and is being increasingly used by long-distance shipping. In 1970, 339,288 tons were imported and 257,659 tons were exported in 175 vessels (279 in 1969).

Post. There were 58 post offices functioning in 1968 but in 1978 it was doubtful if any offices operate. There are telephone exchanges in all the main towns; number of telephones in 1968, 6,325. Phnom Penh has a direct telephone link with Hong Kong, Paris and Tōkyō; and is linked by teletype with Hong Kong, Osaka, Paris and Saigon. Hong Kong is by far the most important link for both systems. There is an International Telex network in Phnom Penh and direct telephone and telegraphic links with Singapore.

RELIGION. The majority of the population practise Theravada Buddhism. The Constitution 1976 ended Buddhism as the State religion. There are small Roman Catholic and Mohammedan minorities.

EDUCATION (1970–71). There were 1,490 primary schools (337,290 pupils) compared with 5,699 and 989,464 in 1969–70, 95 secondary schools (81,611 pupils) and 12,453 students in higher education. These figures show the disruption caused by the spread of war in 1970 which lead to the concentration of all university education in Phnom Penh and closed many schools in rural areas and provincial towns. The situation continued to deteriorate during 1973 and 1974.

DIPLOMATIC REPRESENTATIVES

OF DEMOCRATIC KAMPUCHEA IN GREAT BRITAIN
(26 Townsend Road, London, NW8 6LE)

Embassy closed.

OF GREAT BRITAIN IN DEMOCRATIC KAMPUCHEA
(96 Moha Vithei, Phnom Penh)

All staff temporarily withdrawn from post.

OF DEMOCRATIC KAMPUCHEA IN USA (4500–16th St., NW, Washington, DC., 20011)

Embassy closed.

OF THE USA IN DEMOCRATIC KAMPUCHEA

Embassy closed on 12 April 1975.

Books of Reference

Annuaire Statistique Retrospectif du Cambodge. Vol. I, 1937–57; vol. II, 1958–60. Ministry of Planning, Phnom-Penh
Indo-China: Geographical Appreciation. Department of Mines and Technical Surveys. Ottawa, 1953
Barron, J., and Paul, Z., *Murder of a Gentle Land*, New York, 1977.—*Peace With Horror*. London, 1977
Debré, F., *La Révolution de la Forêt*. Paris, 1976
Herz, M. F., *A Short History of Cambodia*. New York and London, 1958
Kirk, D., *Wider War*. London, 1971
McDonald, M., *Angkor*. London, 1958
Migozzi, J., *Cambodge*. Paris, 1973
Ponchaud, F., *Cambodia, Year Zero*. London, 1978

KENYA

Djumhuri ya Kenya

Capital: Nairobi
Population: 13·8m. (1976)
GNP per capita: US$240 (1976)

HISTORY. Until Kenya became independent on 12 Dec. 1963, it consisted of the colony and the protectorate. The protectorate comprised the mainland dominions of the Sultan of Zanzibar, viz., a coastal strip of territory 10 miles wide, to the northern branch of the Tana River; also Mau, Kipini and the Island of Lamu, and all adjacent islands between the rivers Umba and Tana. The Sultan on 8 Oct. 1963 ceded the coastal strip to Kenya with effect from 12 Dec. 1963.

The colony and protectorate, formerly known as the East African Protectorate were, on 1 April 1905, transferred from the Foreign Office to the Colonial Office and in Nov. 1906 the protectorate was placed under the control of a governor and C.-in-C. and (except the Sultan of Zanzibar's dominions) was annexed to the Crown as from 23 July 1920 under the name of the Colony of Kenya, thus becoming a Crown Colony. The territories on the coast became the Kenya Protectorate.

A treaty was signed (15 July 1924) with Italy under which Great Britain ceded to Italy the Juba River and a strip from 50 to 100 miles wide on the British side of the river. Cession took place on 29 June 1925. The northern boundary is defined by an agreement with Ethiopia in 1947.

AREA AND POPULATION. Kenya is bounded by Ethiopia in the north, Uganda in the west, Tanzania in the south and the Somali Republic and the Indian ocean in the east. The total area is 224,960 sq. miles (582,600 sq. km), of which 219,790 sq miles is land area. In the 1969 census, the population was 10,942,708, of which 10,735,192 were Africans, 139,037 Asians, 40,593 Europeans, 27,886 Arabs. Estimate (1976) 13·8m.

On the coast the Arabs and Swahili predominate, farther inland the races speaking Bantu languages, and non-Bantu tribes, such as the Luo, the Nandi and Kipsigis, the Masai, the Somali and the Gallas.

Population of the Provinces (1975): Nyanza, 2·65m.; Central, 2·03m.; Rift Valley, 2·67m.; North Eastern, 0·3m.; Eastern, 2·28m.; Western, 1·67m.; Nairobi district, 0·7m.; Coast, 1·16m.

Nairobi, the capital, was given a Royal charter on 30 March 1950; the 1969 census showed a population of 509,286, including 19,195 Europeans and 67,189 Asians. Estimate (1975) 700,000.

Population of the largest towns: Mombasa, 340,000; Kisumu, 149,000; Nakuru, 66,000; Eldoret, 30,000.

GOVERNMENT. A constitution conferring internal self-government was brought into force on 1 June 1963, and full independence was achieved on 12 Dec. 1963. On 12 Dec. 1964 Kenya became a republic.

National flag: Three horizontal stripes of black, red, green, with the red edged in white; bearing in the centre an African shield in black and white with 2 crossed spears behind.

President of the Republic: Mzee Jomo Kenyatta. *Vice-President and Minister of Home Affairs:* Daniel Arap Moi.

The House of Representatives and the Senate were in Dec. 1966 amalgamated into one National Assembly. Elections took place in 1974.

On 10 Nov. 1964 Kenya became a one-party state of the Kenya African National Union (KANU) when the voluntary dissolution of the Kenya African Democratic

Union (KADU) was declared. Later a second party, the Kenya People's Union (KPU) was formed but on 30 Oct. 1969 was proscribed.

The Cabinet was composed in March 1978 as follows:

Finance and Planning: Mwai Kibaki. *Defence:* J. S. Gichuru. *Agriculture:* J. J. Nyagah. *Health:* James C. N. Osogo. *Local Government:* Robert S. Matano. *Works:* Nathan Munoko. *Labour:* James Nyamweya. *Power and Communications:* Daniel Mutinda. *Tourism and Wild Life:* Matthew J. Ogutu. *Lands and Settlement:* J. H. Angaine. *Housing and Social Services:* Z. Onyonka. *Education:* Taaitta Toweett. *Attorney-General:* C. Njonjo. *Information and Broadcasting:* I. O. Okero. *Natural Resources:* S. S. Oloitiptip. *Co-operatives:* Paul Ngei. *Commerce and Industry:* Eliud Mwamunga. *Minister of State:* Mbiyu Koinange. *Foreign Affairs:* Munyua Waiyaki. *Water Development:* J. G. Kiano.

Administration. The country is divided into the Nairobi Area and 7 provinces over which there are local councils with administrative functions. The provinces are: Coast, Central, Eastern, Rift Valley, Western, Nyanza and North Eastern.

Swahili became the official language in 1974 but English is in general use.

DEFENCE

Army. The Army consists of 4 infantry battalions and a support battalion which includes a paratroop company; total strength, 6,500.

Navy. The Navy consists of 7 large patrol craft and personnel (1977) 400.

Air Force. An air force, formed 1 June 1964, has been built up with RAF assistance. Current equipment includes 12 F-5E/F-5F supersonic combat aircraft/trainers, 3 Hunter single-seat jet fighter-bombers and 1 Hunter two-seat trainer, 5 BAC 167 Strikemaster light jet attack/trainers, 4 twin-turboprop Buffalos, 4 twin-engined Caribou and 11 single-engined Beavers for transport, air ambulance, anti-locust spraying and security duties, 2 Navajo light twins, 14 Bulldog piston-engined primary trainers and a few Alouette II and Bell 47 light helicopters. Personnel total about 700.

INTERNATIONAL RELATIONS

Membership. Kenya is a member of UN, the Commonwealth, OAU and is an ACP state of EEC.

ECONOMY

Budget. Revenue and expenditure (in Kenya £1,000) for fiscal years 1 July–30 June:

	1972–73	*1973–74*	*1974–75*	*1975–76*[1]	*1976–77*[1]
Net revenue	140,259	172,492	224,420	295,255	277,170
Net expenditure	122,544	147,493	194,005	228,436	248,288
Development revenue	42,677	34,012	40,316	89,270	69,418
Development expenditure	58,906	64,595	88,852	123,880	118,060

[1] Estimates.

Funded public debt at 31 March 1977 was Sh.3,569·76m.

Currency. The monetary unit is the Kenya shilling divided into 100 cents.

Banking. Banks operating in Kenya: the National & Grindlays Bank International, Ltd; the Standard Bank, Ltd; Barclays Bank International; Algemene Bank Nederland NV; Bank of India, Ltd; Bank of Baroda, Ltd; Habib Bank (Overseas), Ltd; African Banking Corporation (E.A.), Ltd; Commercial Bank of Africa, Ltd; The Co-operative Bank of Kenya, Ltd; National Bank of Kenya, Ltd; The Kenya Commercial Bank; Citibank.

NATURAL RESOURCES

Minerals. By mid-1970 over 75% of the area of Kenya had been geologically mapped. A special and 2 ordinary oil-prospecting licences were extant at the end of 1969, together covering 22,250 sq. miles. A joint UN–Kenya Government project is investigating the mineral resources in western Kenya and the exploration and development of mineral deposits is proceeding.

Mineral production during 1973, excluding much building material and manufactured cement, was valued at K£3,445,687. The main products in 1975 (provisional) were: Soda ash, 91,733 tons; gold (refined), 3,062 grammes; limestone and products, 197,414 tons; diatomite, 1,799 tons; salt, 5,553 tons. Other minerals comprised barytes, magnesite, felspar, sapphires, guano, fluospar ore, garnets, sand and raw soda.

Agriculture. As agriculture is possible from sea-level to altitudes of over 9,000 ft, tropical, sub-tropical and temperate crops can be grown and mixed farming can be advocated. Four-fifths of the country is range-land which produces mainly livestock products and wild game which constitutes the major attraction of the country's tourist industry.

The main areas of crop production are the Central, Rift Valley, Western and Nyanza Provinces and parts of Eastern and Coastal Provinces. Coffee, tea, sisal, pyrethrum, maize and wheat are crops of major importance in the Highlands, while coconuts, cashew nuts, cotton, sugar, sisal and maize are the principal crops grown at the lower altitudes. Principal crops with production for sale (in 1,000 tonnes, 1975): Wheat, 159·1; maize (estimate), 493·5; rice paddy, 31·6; pyrethrum extract, 0·2; sugar-cane, 1,735·4; seed cotton, 19·6; clean coffee, 63·8; sisal, 48·4; tea, 54.

Livestock (1976): Cattle, 7·5m.; sheep, 3·6m.; goats, 4·1m.; pigs, 67,000; poultry, 15·43m.

Forestry. The total area of gazetted forest reserves in Kenya amounts to 16,800 sq. km, of which the greater part is situated between 6,000 and 11,000 ft above sea-level, mostly on Mount Kenya, the Aberdares, Mount Elgon, Tinderet, Londiani, Mau watershed, Elgeyo and Charangani ranges. These forests may be divided into coniferous, broad-leaved or hardwood and bamboo forests. The upper parts of these forests are mainly bamboo, which occurs mostly between altitudes of 8,000 and 10,000 ft and occupies some 10% of the high-altitude forests. Plantations established by 31 Dec. 1975 (provisional) total 142,500 hectares, of which 121,600 are exotic softwood. In addition 3,100 hectares of pines have been planted for pulp-wood. The Forest Department employs about 11,000 men and primary forest industries about 8,000. Water catchment is no longer considered to be the primary role of forests. Revenue from timber royalties, fuel royalties and from exports of forest-based products continues to increase. Exports of forest-based products earned K£6,101,240 in 1969. The revenue to the Forest Department from timber royalties and miscellaneous produce amounted to K£437,000. In 1975 (provisional), 230,000 cu. metres of softwood logs and 69,000 cu. metres of hardwood were sold as timber.

COMMERCE. Total domestic exports (1976), K£268·8m.; imports, K£393·8m.

The chief areas of origin in 1976 were: Western Europe, K£182·6m.; Middle East, K£97·4m. Chief areas of destination: Western Europe, K£138·5m.; Africa, K£34·2m.

Total trade between Kenya and UK (British Department of Trade returns, in £1,000 sterling):

	1972	*1973*	*1974*	*1975*	*1976*	*1977*
Imports to UK	29,070	38,747	44,043	38,792	61,473	155,067
Exports and re-exports from UK	55,552	60,887	78,681	85,615	97,713	118,464

TOURISM. In 1976, 424,200 overseas visitors travelled to Kenya.

COMMUNICATIONS

Roads. In 1976 there were 4,045 km of bitumen surfaced roads and 46,046 km of gravel-surfaced roads.

Railways. On 11 Feb. 1977 the independent Kenya Railways Corporation was formed following break-up of the East African Railways administration. The network totals 2,051 km of metre-gauge.

Aviation. Total number of passengers handled at the 4 airports (1976) was 2,188,000.

Shipping. The port of Lamu was being expanded in 1978.

Post and Broadcasting. The Voice of Kenya operates 2 national services (Swahili–English) from Nairobi and regional services in Kisumu, Nairobi and Mombasa. The television service provides programmes mainly in English and Swahili. A new television station opened in Mombasa in 1970. Telephones (1977) 131,843.

Cinemas (1971). Cinemas numbered 32, with seating capacity of 18,800.

JUSTICE, RELIGION, EDUCATION AND WELFARE

Justice. The courts of justice comprise the High Court, established in 1921, with full jurisdiction both civil and criminal over all persons and all matters in Kenya, including Admiralty jurisdiction arising on the high seas and elsewhere, and Subordinate Courts. The High Court has its headquarters at Nairobi and consists of the Chief Justice and 11 puisne judges; it sits continuously at Nairobi, Mombasa, Nakuru and Kisumu; civil and criminal sessions are held regularly at Eldoret, Nyeri, Meru, Kitale, Kisii and Kericho.

The Subordinate Courts are presided over by Senior Resident, Resident or District Magistrates and are established in the main centres of all districts. They sit throughout the year. There are also Moslem Subordinate Courts established in areas where the local population is predominantly Mohammedan; they are presided over by Kadhis and exercise limited jurisdiction in matters governed by Mohammedan law.

Religion. The indigenous African background is largely influenced by belief in God in Judaic forms, but Christianity is making an important contribution to the life of the whole territory, not only through the educational and medical services of Christian missions, but by the growth of churches under African leadership, and by its impact on the thought and policy of the country. The Roman Catholic Church (about 1·5m. adherents) has been developed mainly by Irish, British, Dutch and Italian missionary bodies and is now organized in 12 dioceses under the archbishop of Nairobi.

The Protestant Churches (about 950,000 adherents) were started mainly by British and American mission societies; most of them are now linked together by the National Christian Council of Kenya. The Church of the Province of Kenya, formerly the Anglican Church Province of East Africa, was inaugurated on 3 Aug. 1970; at the same time the first Archbishop of Kenya was enthroned. The East African Yearly Meeting of Friends (Religious Society of Friends) has 90,000 adherents.

The Arabs on the coast are Moslems, and Islam has spread among some of the African coastal tribes and the cities. The Asians are Hindus and Moslems, with the exception of the Goans, who are Roman Catholics.

Education. *Primary* (1975). 8,161 primary schools (7,989 maintained, 142 assisted and 30 unaided), with together 2,881,155 children, of whom 1,319,654 were girls and 1,561,501 boys.

Secondary (1975). There were 1,160 secondary schools (379 maintained, 43 assisted and 738 unaided), with a total enrolment of 226,835, of whom 81,529 are girls and 145,306 are boys.

Technical (1976). The Kenya Polytechnic in Nairobi, with an enrolment of 1,860 students, and Mombasa Technical Institute, with an enrolment of 805 students, are the most advanced institutions.

Teacher training (1975). 8,630 students were training as primary teachers, 488 as secondary teachers (recruitment from university graduates only) and 36 teachers for the deaf.

Higher Education. The University of East Africa, which had 3 constituent Colleges, Makerere University College in Kampala, Uganda, the University College in Nairobi, Kenya, and University College in Dar es Salaam, Tanzania, was disbanded in 1970. The University of Nairobi was inaugurated on 10 Dec. 1970. The University of Nairobi is now wholly supported by Kenya Government, and provides courses in arts, science, education, agriculture, medicine, art, architecture, engineering, veterinary, law and domestic science. In 1975–76 there were some 5,950 Kenya students at college in East Africa, 4,060 of them at University of Nairobi. In 1976, 5,813 Kenya students were enrolled in diploma and degree courses in education at the universities.

Health. In 1974 beds in hospitals (including mission hospitals) totalled 16,934. 603 health centres, including sub-centres and dispensaries, were in operation. Total expenditure of the Ministry of Health in 1974–75 was £16,902,965 on health services. Development expenditure on health services totalled £4,471,000 in 1975–76 (provisional). Free medical service for all children and adult out-patients was launched in 1965.

DIPLOMATIC REPRESENTATIVES

OF KENYA IN GREAT BRITAIN (45 Portland Pl., London, W1N 4AS)
High Commissioner: Dr. F. Ng'ethe Njoroge.

OF GREAT BRITAIN IN KENYA (Bruce Hse, Standard St., Nairobi)
High Commissioner: S. J. G. Fingland, CMG.

OF KENYA IN THE USA (2249 R. St., NW, Washington, D.C., 20008)
Ambassador: John P. Mbogua.

OF THE USA IN KENYA (Cotts Hse., Wabera St., Nairobi)
Ambassador: William J. Le Melle.

OF KENYA TO THE UNITED NATIONS
Ambassador: Charles Gatere Maina.

Books of Reference

Statistical Abstract. Government Printer, Nairobi, 1969
Standard English–Swahili Dictionary. Ed. Inter-territorial Language Committee of East Africa. 2 vols. London, 1939
Arnold, G., *Kenyatta and the Politics of Kenya.* London, 1974
Bienen, H., *Kenya: The Politics of Participation and Control.* Princeton Univ. Press, 1974
Bolton, K., *Haramble Country: A Guide to Kenya.* London, 1970
Harbeson, J. W., *Nation-Building in Kenya: The Role of Land Reform.* Northwestern Univ. Press, 1973
Hill, M. F., *Permanent Way, the Story of the Kenya and Uganda Railway.* E.A. Railways and Harbours, Nairobi, 1950
Huxley, E., and Perham, M. *Race and Politics in Kenya.* Rev. ed. London, 1956
Leys, C., *Underdevelopment in Kenya.* London, 1975
Mboya, T. J., *Freedom and After.* London, 1963
Murray-Brown, J., *Kenyatta.* London, 1972
Rothchild, D., *Racial Bargaining in Independent Kenya.* OUP, 1973
Werlin, H. W., *Governing an African City: A Study in Nairobi.* New York, 1974

KOREA

Han Kook

Capital: Seoul
Population: 35·9m. (1976)
GNP per capita: US$670 (1976)

HISTORY. Korea was united in a single kingdom under the Silla dynasty from 668. China, which claimed a vague suzerainty over Korea, recognized Korea's independence in 1895. Korea concluded trade agreements with the USA (1882), Great Britain, Germany (1883). After the Russo-Japanese war of 1904–5 Korea was virtually a Japanese protectorate until it was formally annexed by Japan on 22 Aug. 1910 thus ending the rule of the Yi dynasty which had begun in 1392.

Following the collapse of Japan in 1945, American and Russian forces entered Korea to enforce the surrender of the Japanese troops there, dividing the country for mutual military convenience into two portions separated by the 38th parallel of latitude. Negotiations between the American and Russians regarding the future of Korea broke down in May 1946.

On 25 June 1950 the North Korean forces crossed the 38th parallel and invaded South Korea. The same day, the Security Council of the United Nations asked all member states to render assistance to the Republic of Korea. When the UN forces had reached the Manchurian border Chinese troops entered the war on the side of the North Koreans on 26 Nov. 1950 and penetrated deep into the south. By the beginning of April 1951, however, the UN forces had regained the 38th parallel.

On 23 June 1951 Y. A. Malik, President of the Security Council, suggested a cease-fire, and on 10 July representatives of Gen. Ridgway met representatives of the North Koreans and of the Chinese Volunteer Army. An agreement was signed on 27 July 1953.

For the contributions of member-nations of the United Nations to the war, *see* THE STATESMAN'S YEAR-BOOK, 1954, p. 1195, and 1956, p. 1180.

On 16 Aug. 1953 the USA and Korea signed a mutual defence pact and on 28 Nov. 1956 a treaty of friendship, commerce and navigation.

On 4 July 1972 it was announced in Seoul and Pyongyang (North Korea) that talks had taken place aimed at 'the peaceful unification of the fatherland as early as possible'. By late 1975 no progress had been made.

On 18 Aug. 1976 North Korean soldiers killed 2 US officers of a UN command pruning a tree at Panmunjon in the demilitarized zone. This led to a North Korean–UN agreement on 6 Sept. 1976 establishing a joint security area 850 metres in diameter and divided into 2 equal parts to ensure the separation of the two sides.

AREA AND POPULATION. After a transfer of some frontier districts by the United Nations command on 12 Aug. 1954 the area of South Korea is now 38,002 sq. miles (98,447 sq. km). The population (census 1975) was 34,708,542 (male, 17,451,946). The population of the largest cities was as follows: Seoul, the capital, 6,889,470; Pusan, 2,454,051; Taegu, 1,311,078; Inchŏn, 799,982; Kwangchu, 607,058; Taejŏn, 506,703; Masan, 371,937; Chonchu, 311,432, Seongnam, 272,329; Ulsan, 252,639; Suweon, 224,177.

South Korea includes 9 provinces and the cities of Seoul and Pusan, which have provincial status.

CONSTITUTION AND GOVERNMENT. The first general election was held, under United Nations observation, on 10 May 1948. The National Assembly adopted a constitution on 17 July, elected Dr Syngman Rhee President of the Republic on 20 July and proclaimed the Republic of Korea on 15 Aug., when US military government ended.

President Syngman Rhee was re-elected on 5 Aug. 1952, 15 May 1956 and 15 March 1960, but was forced to resign and leave the country at the end of April 1960. The National Assembly on 15 June 1960 amended the constitution, changing the presidential-government system to a cabinet system, with the president as the symbolic head of state. A joint session of both Houses of Parliament on 12 Aug. 1960 elected the Democratic leader, Posun Yun, president.

The elections held on 29 July 1960 gave the Democratic Party 31 out of 58 seats in the House of Councillors and 181 out of 233 seats in the National Assembly.

The democratically elected government of Dr Myun Chang was overthrown by a military revolution on 16 May 1961. The National Assembly was dissolved and political parties were banned. The rule of the 'Supreme Council for National Reconstruction' under Gen. Chung Hee Park ended on 15 Oct. 1963 with his election as President of the Republic.

A new constitution was approved by a referendum on 17 Dec. 1962. On 14 Sept. 1969, the National Assembly passed a constitutional amendment bill, and the revision of the constitution was approved by a referendum on 17 Oct. 1970. The principal contents of the constitutional revision bill were that the number of members of the National Assembly shall be determined by law and shall not be more than 250 persons and the President may be elected for a maximum of 3 consecutive terms. The elections held on 26 Nov. 1963 and on 8 June 1967 gave Gen. Park's Democratic Republican Party a large majority.

Martial law was lifted on 13 Dec. 1972 and a new National Assembly was formed on 7 March 1973. The constitution was suspended for a time in 1974, but reinstated in Aug. 1974.

President of the Republic: Chung Hee Park (re-elected 27 April 1971).
Premier: Choi Kyu Hah. *Foreign Minister:* Park Tong Jin.
National flag: White with a blue and red moon in the centre, flanked by 4 black trigrams.

DEFENCE

Army. The Army, in 1977, had 560,000 men in 19 infantry divisions, 2 armoured brigades equipped with 840 M-47, M-48 and M-60 tanks, 30 artillery battalions, SS and SA missile batteries. Reserves, 1m. and Popular Militia, 1m.

Navy. The Navy comprises 9 destroyers, 9 frigates (3 of destroyer-escort type and 6 former fast transports, *ex*-destroyer escorts), 8 fast missile patrol craft, 10 corvettes, 8 fast attack craft, 30 patrol boats, 10 coastal minesweepers, 1 minesweeping boat, 1 dock landing ship, 20 landing ships, 2 landing craft, 1 repair ship, 3 surveying vessels, 6 supply ships, 4 oilers, 13 auxiliary ships, 35 service craft, 25 auxiliary cutters and 2 tugs. Personnel in 1978: 20,000 (2,400 officers and 17,600 ratings) in Navy; 20,000 (2,300 officers and 17,700 men) in Marine Corps.

New construction includes 4 frigates reportedly to be built in South Korean yards where 3 high-speed interdiction craft are being built.

The Korean Coastguard operates 25 vessels including rescue craft and tugs.

Air Force. With a 1977 strength of about 30,000 men, the Air Force is undergoing rapid expansion with US assistance. Its combat aircraft include about 70 F-4D/E Phantoms, 70 F-5A/B tactical fighters, 120 F-5E Tiger II tactical fighters, 24 OV-10G Bronco light attack/reconnaissance aircraft, 10 RF-5A reconnaissance fighters and some Tracker anti-submarine aircraft. There are also C-54 and C-46 piston-engined transports, 2 VIP HS 748s, a few UH-19, UH-1D and Bell 212 helicopters, and T-28 and T-33 trainers. Aircraft entering service include 100 Hughes 500M-D Defender light anti-tank/observation helicopters.

ECONOMY

Planning. The 5-year plan 1962–66 aimed at achieving a self-sufficient agricultural economy on which two-thirds of the population is dependent. The second 5-year plan (1967–71) envisaged an annual growth rate of 10%; emphasis is placed on industrial development. The third 5-year plan for 1972–75 has been turned into a long-range development programme, aimed at self-sufficiency by 1980.

Budget. The 1975 budget envisaged expenditure of 1,697,414m. won and revenue at 1,382,331m. won.

Currency. On 14 June 1949 a presidential decree established a dual rate of exchange for the *won*, one of 450 *won* = US$1 for government transactions and another of 900 *won* = $1 for all other transactions. Severe inflation followed until on 17 Feb. 1953 President Rhee abolished the *won*, substituting a new unit, the *hwan*, equal to 100 *won*. The *hwan* depreciated from 60 in Feb. 1953 to 1,300 to US$1 in April 1961. On 10 June 1962 the *hwan* was revalued at the rate of 10 *hwan* = 1 *won*. The exchange rate is determined daily by the Foreign Exchange Bank of Korea; it was (1975) about 500 *won* = US$1. Total money supply in Sept. 1977, was 2,000,000m. *won*, of which 1,208,009m. was in deposits and 791,700m. in circulation.

Banking. State-run banks include the Bank of Korea, the Korean Construction Bank, the Medium Industry Bank, the Citizen's National Bank, the Foreign Exchange Bank, the National Agricultural Co-operatives Federation, Federation of Fisheries Co-operatives serving as banking and credit institutions for farmers and fishermen, Trust Bank of Korea, the Korea Housing Bank, Korea Development Finance Corporation.

There are 5 commercial banks: the Bank of Seoul Ltd, the Cho Heung Bank Ltd, the Commercial Bank of Korea, the First City Bank of Korea, the Hanil Bank, Ltd, the Taegu Bank Ltd. The Bank of Korea is the central bank and the only note-issuing bank, the authorized purchaser of domestically produced gold. All foreign exchange is held by the Foreign Exchange Bank.

In addition, there are non-bank financial institutions consisting of 19 insurance companies, the Land Bank of Korea, the Credit Guarantee Fund, 10 short-term financial companies, 211 mutual credit companies, and the Merchant Banking Corporation. Institutions operating in the securities market include the Korea Stock Exchange and 27 member firms of the Exchange. The Securities Exchange Commission and the Securities Regulatory Board, the Korea Securities Finance Corporation and 2 Investment Trust Companies play important roles in the issuing and trading market.

ENERGY AND NATURAL RESOURCES

Electricity. Electricity generated (1974) was 16,835m. kwh.

Minerals. In 1976, 985 mining companies employed 65,800 people. Mineral deposits are mostly small, with the exception of tungsten; the Sangdong mine is one of the world's largest deposits of tungsten. Korea's output, 1976, included (in 1,000 tonnes): Anthracite coal, 16,427; iron ore, 755; tungsten concentrate, 4,660 short tons; kaolin, 470; copper ore, 15; lead ore, 29; gold refined, 583 kg; silver refined, 57,800 kg.

Agriculture. The arable land in South Korea comprises 24·4m. acres, of which over 5·5m. acres are cultivated.

The chief crops are rice (1976: 5·21m. tonnes), barley, wheat, beans, grain of all kinds and tobacco.

Output of tobacco manufactures, a government monopoly, was 138,500 tonnes in 1977.

Raising of livestock has recently become a flourishing industry. In 1976 cattle numbered 1·56m.; hogs, 1·95m.; poultry, 26·28m.

Fisheries. Deep-sea fishing fleets increased from 5 ships (600 gross tons) in 1962 to 455 ships (160,000 gross tons) in 1972 and 833 ships (316,000 gross tons) in 1975. In 1976, 849 Korean deep-sea fishing vessels were engaged based on 25 overseas fishing bases, 345 in the Atlantic, 143 in the Indian and 361 in the Pacific oceans.

The Government plans a US$404,266,000 inshore development programme up to 1981, increasing the annual incomes of fishing households by 165% in that year compared with 1975.

INDUSTRY AND TRADE

Industry. Manufacturing industry, which (Dec. 1972) employed 5m. persons, was concentrated primarily in the production of light consumer goods for domestic consumption and export. This is now shifting towards heavy and petro-chemical industries rapidly.

Output of principal products in 1976 (in tonnes): Cotton yarn, 244,276; Portland cement, 14·1m.; fertilizers, 1·88m.

GNP, 1974, US$17,300m.

Trade Unions. Membership of trade unions at 31 Aug. 1971 was 493,711.

Commerce. In 1976 the total exports were equal to US$7,715m., while imports (including 'aid goods') were US$8,773m.

Total trade between Korea and UK (British Department of Trade returns, in £1,000 sterling):

	1973	*1974*	*1975*	*1976*	*1977*
Imports to UK	27,017	50,985	74,543	135,723	178,693
Exports and re-exports from UK	21,439	36,045	52,577	63,125	75,855

COMMUNICATIONS

Roads. In 1976 there were 45,514 km of roads. Motor vehicles (1976) totalled 226,320 including 93,885 trucks, 23,643 buses, 96,009 passenger cars.

Railways. In 1976, 5,678 km of railways existed, including 424 km electrified between Seoul and Bukpyong.

Shipping. In 1976, there were registered 2,226 vessels of 3,127,206 tons.

Post. Post offices total 1,980; telephones (all government-owned) were 1,515,910 in Aug. 1977; a direct distance dialling telephone system was completed in 1976.

Cinemas. In 1974 there were 689 with a seating capacity of 429,200.

Newspapers (1974). There were 30 daily papers, including 7 national dailies and 2 in English appearing in Seoul.

RELIGION, EDUCATION AND WELFARE

Religion. Basically the religions of Korea have been Animism, Buddhism (introduced A.D. 372) and Confucianism, which was the official faith from 1392 to 1910. Catholic converts from China introduced Christianity in the 18th century, but the ban on Roman Catholics was not lifted until 1882. Estimated Christian population in 1976 was 5·71m. (1,052,691 Catholics, 4,658,700 Protestants).

Education. In April 1977 Korea had 5,515,397 pupils enrolled in 6,419 elementary schools, 2,258,713 pupils in 2,266 middle schools and 1,426,566 pupils in 1,339 high schools (including 623 vocational schools).

For higher education, 347,887 students who attended 215 universities, colleges and junior colleges. There are 87 graduate schools granting master's degrees in 2 years and doctor's degrees in 4 years, where 17,220 pupils attend.

The Korean language belongs to the Ural–Altaic group, is polysyllabic, agglutinative and highly developed syntactically. The modern Korean alphabet of 10 vowels and 14 consonants forms a script known as Hangul.

Health. In Dec. 1976 there were 17,848 physicians, 2,744 dentists, 2,855 herb doctors, 4,028 midwives, 26,949 nurses, 37,953 assistant nurses, 4,712 technicians and 20,718 pharmacists. There were 11,181 hospitals and clinics.

DIPLOMATIC REPRESENTATIVES

OF KOREA IN GREAT BRITAIN (4 Palace Gate, London, W8 5NF)
Ambassador: Dr Pyo Wook Han.

OF GREAT BRITAIN IN KOREA (4 Chung-Dong, Sudaemoon-Ku, Seoul)
Ambassador and Consul-General: W. S. Bates, CMG.

OF KOREA IN THE USA (2370 Massachusetts Ave., NW, Washington, D.C., 20008)
Ambassador: Yong Shik Kim.

OF THE USA IN KOREA (Sejong-Ro, Seoul)

Ambassador: Richard L. Sneider.

Books of Reference

Economic Planning Board. *Guide to Investment in Korea*. Seoul, 1973.—*Korean Economy: Present and Future*. Seoul, 1973
Korea Annual 1974. 11th ed. Seoul, 1973
Korea: Its Land, People and Culture of All Ages. Seoul, 1960
Korea: Past and Present. Seoul, 1972
Korea Statistical Year Book. Seoul, 1974
UNESCO Korean Survey. Seoul, 1960
Guide to Geographical Names in Korea (Chosen). United States Board of Geographical Names. Washington, 1945
Major Economic Indicators, 1958–69. Seoul, 1970
Monthly Statistics of Korea. Seoul, 1975
Bartz, P. M., *South Korea*. OUP, 1972
Lew, H. J., *New Life Korean–English, English–Korean Dictionary*. 2 vols. Seoul, 1947–50
Martin, S. F. (ed.), *A Korean–English Dictionary*. Yale Univ. Press, 1968
Wright, E. R., *Korean Politics in Transition*. Univ. of Washington Press, 1976

NORTH KOREA

Capital: Pyongyang
Population: 16m. (1975)
GNP per capita: US$470 (1976)

Chosun Minchu-chui Inmin Konghwa-guk

HISTORY. In northern Korea the Russians, arriving on 8 Aug. 1945, one month ahead of the Americans, established a Communist-led 'Provisional Government'. The newly created Korean Communist Party merged in 1946 with the New National Party into the Korean Workers' Party. In July 1946 the KWP, with the remaining pro-Communist groups and non-party people, formed the United Democratic Patriotic Front. On 25 Aug. 1948 the Communists organized elections for a Supreme People's Assembly, both in Soviet-occupied North Korea (212 deputies) and in US-occupied South Korea (360 deputies, of whom a certain number went to the North and took their seats). A People's Democratic Republic was proclaimed on 9 Sept. 1948. On 17 May 1973 North Korea was admitted to the World Health Organization by 66 votes to 41 with 22 abstentions, and in June 1973 was granted observer status at the UN.

AREA AND POPULATION. The area of North Korea is 47,225 sq. miles (122,370 sq. km). Population in 1975, 16m. Rate of population increase, 2·8% per annum. Marriage is discouraged before the age of 32 for men and 29 for women. Expectation of life (1977): Men, 70; women, 76. The capital is Pyongyang, with 1·5m. inhabitants.

The country is divided into 11 administrative units: 2 cities (Pyongyang and Kaesong) and 9 provinces (capitals in brackets): South Pyongan (Nampo), North Pyongan (Sinuiji), Jagang (Kanggye), South Hwanghai (Haeju), North Hwanghai (Sariwon), North Kangwon (Wonsan), South Hamgyong (Hamheung), North Hamgyong (Chongjin), Yanggang (Hyesan).

CONSTITUTION AND GOVERNMENT. The political structure is based upon the Constitution of 27 Dec. 1972, which supersedes that of 1948 as amended in 1954 and 1955. The Constitution provides for a Supreme People's Assembly elected every 4 years by universal suffrage. Citizens of 17 years and over can vote and be elected. Elections were held in 1948, 1957, 1962, 1972 and 11 Nov. 1977. At the latter it was claimed that 100% of the electorate voted for the candidates presented. There are 579 deputies.

In practice the country is ruled by the Korean Workers' (*i.e.*, Communist) Party which elects a Central Committee which in turn appoints a Politburo. In April 1978 this was composed of: Marshal Kim Il Sung, *General Secretary of the Party, President of the Republic, Supreme Commander of the Armed Forces*; Kim Il (*Vice-President of the Republic*); Li Jong Ok, *Prime Minister*; Gen. Choe Hyon; Kim Yong Ju; O Jin Yu (*Defence Minister*); Kim Dong Gyu; So Chol; Kim Jung Rin; Han Ik Su. There are also 4 'alternate members'.

Ministers not in the Politburo include Ho Dam (*Deputy Prime Minister, Foreign Minister*); Kye Ung Tae (*Deputy Prime Minister, Foreign Trade*); Kim Gyong Ryon (*Finance*); Kim Il Dae (*Education*); Hong Song Ryong (*Chairman, State Planning Commission*); Choe Won Ik (*Public Security*).

In 1972 the Party had some 1·5m. members.

There are also the puppet religious Chongu and North Korean Democratic Parties, and various organizations combined in a Fatherland Front.

National flag: Blue, red and blue horizontal stripes separated by narrow white bands. The red stripe bears a white circle within which is a red 5-pointed star.

National anthem: The Song of General Kim Il Sung.

Local government is administered by People's Assemblies at city (or province), county (or district) and *ri* (town, workers' or rural commune) level. The latest elections were on 4 March 1977.

DEFENCE. Military service is compulsory at the age of 17 and lasts 3–4 years.

Army. In 1977 the Army was believed to number about 430,000 men, organized in 2 armoured and 23 infantry divisions, with 800 Soviet tanks; it has about 300 Guideline surface-to-air missiles, and Soviet Sam-2 rockets, Frog-5 and Frog-7 missiles.

Navy. The Navy comprises 13 diesel-powered patrol submarines (9 *ex*-Chinese and 4 *ex*-Soviet), 2 small frigates, 18 missile boats, 160 fast torpedo boats, 44 fast gunboats, 20 patrol vessels, 30 coastal patrol craft, 90 minor landing craft, 20 light gunboats and minesweeping boats, 30 auxiliaries and 100 service craft and armed junks. Personnel in 1978: 18,000 officers and men, plus 40,000 reservists.

Air Force. With Chinese and Soviet assistance, the Air Force has been increased to a total of about 600 aircraft and 40,000 personnel. Equipment is believed to include about 150 supersonic MiG-21 interceptors, 325 MiG-17s for ground attack and reconnaissance, at least 30 Su-7 fighter-bombers, 60 Il-28 twin-jet light bombers, and a variety of transport and training aircraft and helicopters.

ECONOMY

Planning. Past plans: 3-year plan, 1954–56, rehabilitated the country after the Korean War (1950–53); 5-year plan, 1957–61; 7-year plan, extended in 1966 to 1970; 6-year plan, 1971–76, during which an average annual industrial growth rate of 16·3% was claimed. 1977 was a year of planning hiatus ('readjustment'), but it was finally announced in that year that all the 1971–76 plan targets had been reached, and a 7-year plan for 1978–84 was adopted which gives priority to the fuel and mining industries (particularly coal) and expects an annual industrial growth rate of 12·1%.

Budget (in 1m. won) for calendar years:

	1972	*1973*	*1974*	*1975*	*1976*	*1977*	*1978*[1]
Revenue	7,430	8,599	10,015	11,586	12,626	13,789	15,923
Expenditure	7,387	8,313	9,672	11,367	12,326	13,349	15,923

[1] Estimate.

In 1977, 15·7% of budget expenditure was on defence. Average monthly income was 70 won in 1970. Personal taxation was abolished in 1974.

Currency. The monetary unit is the *won*, divided into 100 *jun*. Official rate of exchange: US$1 = 0·996 *won*.

Weights and Measures. While the metric system is in force traditional measures are in frequent use. The *jungbo* = 1 hectare; the *ri* = 3,927 metres.

ENERGY AND NATURAL RESOURCES

Electricity. There are thermal power stations at Pyongyang, Unggi and Chongchongang. There are hydro-electric plants at Kanggye, Unbong and Sodusu, and another is under construction at Taedonggang. Output in 1975, was 28,000m. kwh. Hydro-electric potential exceeds 8m. kw. In 1972 thermal power generation accounted for 38% of total output. An oil pipeline from China was opened in Jan. 1976.

Minerals. North Korea is rich in minerals (coal, iron, lead, zinc, copper, tungsten, nickel, manganese and graphite) and has important metallurgical works. Oilwells went into production in 1957. Coalmines are being enlarged and modernized. There are large open-cast workings at Yonghung. 50m. tonnes of coal were mined in 1975. 7·4m. tonnes of iron ore and 12,000 tonnes of copper ore were extracted in 1969.

Agriculture. Only 2m. hectares of the land area are cultivable. Intensive water and soil conservancy is practised and land reclamation from the sea has a high priority.

In 1946 all Japanese-owned and landowners' property above 5 *jungbo* was distributed among some 724,500 landless peasants and smallholders.

Collectivization took place between 1954 and 1958, when there were 13,309 'co-operatives' averaging 130 *jungbo*. In 1958 these were merged into 3,843 larger units (*ri*), averaging 500 *jungbo*, modelled on the Chinese communes. 90% of the cultivated land is farmed by co-operatives. A law of 1977 proclaims that there is no private property in land; land belongs either to the State or to co-operatives, and it is intended gradually to transform the latter into the former. Livestock farming is mainly carried on by large state farms.

Some 3m. *jungbo* are under cultivation, of which 1m. *jungbo* have regular irrigation. There were 37,600 km of irrigation canals in 1976. The 6-year plan (1971–76) extended irrigation so as to make possible 2 rice harvests a year. In 1974 the number of tractors (15 h.p. units) was between 70,000 and 80,000. The technical revolution in agriculture (nearly 95% of ploughing, etc., is mechanized) considerably increased the yield of grain (sown on 2·3m. *jungbo* of land); this was 8·5m. tonnes in 1977 (mainly rice). Maize is being fostered to replace millet as the major dry-field crop.

Livestock (FAO estimates for 1976): 816,000 cattle, 1·6m. pigs.

Forestry. Between 1961 and 1970, 800,000 hectares were afforested, 500,000 hectares of oil-bearing trees are scheduled for planting.

Fishery. The annual catch is about 1·6m. tonnes. There is a fishing fleet of about 3,400 modern motor and sailing fishing craft, equipped with factory and refrigerator ships.

INDUSTRY AND TRADE

Industry. Industries were intensively developed by the Japanese, notably cotton spinning, hydro-electric power, cotton, silk and rayon weaving, and chemical fertilizers. Production (in tonnes) in 1975: Chemical fertilizers, 3m.; cement, 8m.; steel, 4m.; textiles, 600m. sq. metres. Industrial workers make up some 40% of the total work force. There is a steel complex at Kangson with an annual productive capacity of 4m. tonnes. Average wage 1977: Workers, 70 won per month; managers, 200 won per month. Workers have 2 weeks, managers 4 weeks, annual holiday.

Commerce. Foreign trade is almost exclusively with Communist countries. In 1977 North Korea's indebtedness was estimated at US$700m. to Communist countries and US$430m. to Japan and the West. Trade with Japan amounted to some US$200m. in 1974. The chief exports are metal ores and products, the chief imports machinery and petroleum products.

Exports to the USSR in 1976 (and 1975) were worth 118·7m. (151·4m.) roubles; imports from the USSR, 181·8m. (186·8m.) roubles.

Total trade between North Korea and UK (British Department of Trade returns, in £1,000 sterling):

	1972	*1973*	*1974*	*1975*	*1976*	*1977*
Imports to UK	188	379	2,026	1,425	1,408	3,262
Exports and re-exports from UK	409	826	12,911	600	930	1,288

COMMUNICATIONS

Roads. Motor transport is very important, as about one-third of the inhabited places are without railway communications. Roads are bad and mostly unpaved; statistics about their length, etc., are lacking. In 1961 lorries and coaches transported 17·7m. tons of freight.

Railways. Extensive railway construction was carried out under the Japanese occupation. Because these lines served strategic purposes, however, and because of the separation of North and South Korea, not all of them were suitable for inclusion in the present railway network. The two trunk-lines Pyongyang–Sinuiji and Pyongyang–Myongchon are both electrified, and the Pyongyang–Sariwon trunk is in course of electrification. The 'Wonra' line runs from Wonsan to Rajin and is electrified from Myongchon to Rajin. The Sepo–Inchon line was opened in 1972 and the Sinchon–Unryul line in 1973. Lines are under construction from Pukchong to Toksong, from

Palwon to Kujang and Kanggye *via* Hyesan to Musan. The Hyesan–Samsok section of the latter opened to traffic in 1971. In 1971 there were some 15,000 km of track, about 35% electrified. In 1977, 66% of trains were hauled by electricity and 30·6m. tonnes were transported in 1969. Further electrification was in progress including 100 km Chongjin–Puryong–Musan line.

Aviation. There are weekly flights to Moscow and Peking. Domestic lines: Pyongyang–Hamheung–Chongjin.

Shipping. The leading ports are Chongjin and Heungnam (near Hamheung). Nampo, the port of Pyongyang, has been dredged and expanded. Pyongyang is connected to Nampo by railway and river.

The biggest navigable river is the Yalu, 698 km up to the Hyesan district.

Broadcasting. In 1961 there were 600,000 radio receivers. The Pyongyang central broadcasting station was rebuilt about 1955.

Newspapers. The party newspaper is *Nodong* (or *Rodong*) *Sinmun* (Labour Party News).

JUSTICE, EDUCATION AND WELFARE

Justice. The judiciary consists of the Supreme Court, whose judges are elected by the Assembly for 3 years; provincial courts; and city or county people's courts. The procurator-general, appointed by the Assembly, has supervisory powers over the judiciary and the administration; the Supreme Court controls the judicial administration.

Education. In 1975–76 the 10-year system of free compulsory universal technical education was extended to 11 years (1 pre-school year, 4 years primary education starting at the age of 6, followed by 6 years secondary).

In 1970–71, 9,260 schools of all grades were attended by 3·2m. pupils, including 214,000 students in 569 institutes of higher education, two-thirds of whom were studying technical and engineering subjects. There were some 100,000 teachers. In 1975–76 there were 5–6m. children in the 11-year system and nearly 1m. students in higher education.

There are 3 universities—Kim Il Sung University (founded 1946), Kim Chaek Technical University, Pyongyang Medical School—and an Academy of Sciences (founded 1952).

In 1977–78 Kim Il Sung University had some 17,000 students.

Health. Medical treatment is free and in 1977 there was 1 doctor for every 600 inhabitants.

Books of Reference

Baik Bong, *Kim Il Sung: Biography*. 3 vols. New York, 1969–70

Brun, E., and Hersh, J., *Socialist Korea: A Case Study in the Strategy of Economic Development*. New York, 1976

Chung, J. S.-H., *The North Korean Economy: Structure and Development*. Stanford, 1974

Kim, I. J., *Communist Policies in North Korea*. New York, 1975

Kim Il Sung, *Selected Works*. Pyongyang, 1965 in progress

Kiyosaki, W. S., *North Korea's Foreign Relations*. New York, 1976

Koreiskaya Narodno-Demokraticheskaya Respublika. Moscow, 1975

Paige, G. D., *The Korean People's Democratic Republic*. Stanford, Cal., Hoover Institution, 1966

Rees, D., *North Korea: Undermining the Truce*. London, 1976

Scalapino, R. A., and Lee, C.-S., *Communism in Korea. Part I: The Movement. Part II: The Society*. Univ. of Calif. Press, 1972

United States Department of the Army. *Communist North Korea: A Bibliographic Survey*. Washington, 1971

KUWAIT

Dowlat al Kuwait

Capital: Kuwait
Population: 1·07m. (1976)
GNP per capita: US$15,480 (1976)

HISTORY. The independent and sovereign State of Kuwait is situated on the north-western coast of the Arabian Gulf. The ruling dynasty was founded by Shaikh Sabah al-Owel, who ruled from 1756 to 1772. In 1899 the then ruler Shaikh Mubarak concluded a treaty with Great Britain wherein, in return for the assurance of British protection, he undertook not to alienate any of his territory without the agreement of Her Majesty's Government. In 1914 the British Government recognized Kuwait as an independent government under British protection. On 19 June 1961 an agreement reaffirmed the independence and sovereignty of Kuwait and recognized the government of Kuwait's responsibility for the conduct of internal and external affairs; the agreement of 1899 was terminated and Her Majesty's Government expressed their readiness to assist the government of Kuwait should they request such assistance.

AREA AND POPULATION. Area, about 9,375 sq. miles (24,280 sq. km); the total population at the census of 1976 was 1,066,400, of which about 53% were non-Kuwaitis.

The country is divided into 3 governates, Kuwait (the capital, 80,405 population 1970; metropolitan area, 217,749), Ahmadi and Hawali (106,542).

The Neutral Zone (3,560 sq. miles, 5,700 sq. km), jointly owned and administered by Kuwait and Saudi Arabia from 1922 to 1966, was partitioned between the two countries in May 1966, but the exploitation of the oil and other natural resources will continue to be shared.

RULER. HH Shaikh Jabir al-Ahmad al-Jabir al-Sabah the 13th Amir of Kuwait, succeeded on 31 Dec. 1977.

CONSTITUTION AND GOVERNMENT. Elections for a National Assembly of 50 members were held on 27 Jan. 1975 but in Aug. 1976 the Amir dissolved the Assembly because it had 'exploited democracy for private gain'. At the same time parts of the Constitution were suspended.

The official language is Arabic; English is used as the second language.

Prime Minister: Shaikh Saad al Abdallah al-Sabah (appointed 8 Feb. 1978).

Deputy Prime Minister and Information: Jabir al Ali as Salim al-Sabah. *Deputy Prime Minister and Foreign Affairs:* Shaikh Sabah al-Ahmad al-Jabir al-Sabah. *Oil:* Ali al-Khalifah al-Adhibi. *Planning:* Mohammed Youssef al-Adasani.

Flag: Three horizontal stripes of green, white, red, with a black trapezium based on the hoist.

DEFENCE

Army. Kuwait maintains a small (8,500 men), well-equipped and mobile army of 3 brigades.

Air Force. From a small initial combat force of 4 Hunter ground-attack fighters and 2 (now 5) Hunter 2-seat fighter trainers the Air Force has grown rapidly. It has 1 squadron of 10 Lightning F.53 supersonic fighters and 2 Lightning T.55 2-seat trainers; 1 squadron with 18 Mirage F.1C fighters and 2 Mirage F.1B 2-seat trainers; and 2 squadrons with 36 A-4KU/TA-4KU Skyhawk attack aircraft. Other equipment includes 2 DC-9 jet transports, 2 C-130 Hercules turboprop transports, 2

Caribou twin-engined STOL transports, 12 BAC 167 Strikemaster armed jet trainers, 6 Agusta-Bell 204B/205, 10 Puma and 20 Gazelle helicopters. Hawk surface-to-air missiles are in service. Personnel strength about 1,000.

INTERNATIONAL RELATIONS

Membership. Kuwait is a member of UN, the Arab League and OPEC.

ECONOMY

Budget. The financial year runs 1 April–31 March. In 1975–76 revenue, KD 2,004·5m.; expenditure, KD 908·6m.

Currency. The Kuwait *dinar* of 1,000 *fils* replaced the Indian external rupee on 1 April 1961; £1 sterling = 0·524 KD (May 1976). Coins in circulation are, 1, 5, 10, 20, 50 and 100 *fils*. The amount of currency in circulation in 1974 was KD 81·7m.

Banking. Five banks operate in Kuwait: the British Bank of the Middle East, the Kuwait National Bank, the Commercial Bank of Kuwait Ltd, the Gulf Bank of Kuwait and the Ahlly Bank.

Weights and Measures. The metric system was adopted in 1962.

ENERGY AND NATURAL RESOURCES

Oil. Kuwait oil comes mainly from the Burgan oilfields, the residential and administrative centre for oil operations being at Ahmadi. Oil reserves in Kuwait and its share of the neutral zone was estimated at 77,000m. bbls in 1975. The Kuwait Petroleum Gas and Energy Company (KPGEC) formed in 1974 as a result of the Government's take-over of 60% of oil production, is controlling all oil exploration and the processing and marketing of oil and gas. Production of crude oil production (in 1m. bbls): 1970, 1,091; 1971, 1,166; 1972, 1,202; 1973, 1,011; 1974, 929 (estimate).

Agriculture. Livestock (1976): Cattle, 9,000; sheep, 111,000; goats, 86,000; poultry, 5·8m.

Fisheries. Shrimp fishing is becoming one of the important non-oil industries.

INDUSTRY AND TRADE

Industry. Industries include boat building, fishing, food production and construction. A second cement plant was being built in 1975 and a steel works is planned. The manufacture or import of alcoholic drinks is prohibited.

Labour. Of the working population 75% are foreigners.

Commerce. The port of Kuwait formerly served mainly as an entrepôt for goods for the interior, for the export of skins and wool, and for pearl fishing. Entrepôt trade continues but, with the development of the oil industry, is declining in importance. Pearl fishing is now on a small scale. Dhows and launches of traditional construction are still built.

Trade in calendar years, in Kuwaiti dinars:

	1968	*1969*	*1970*	*1971*	*1972*	*1973*
Imports	218,300,000	230,800,000	223,300,000	232,300,000	236,800,000	266,100,000
Exports[1]	20,858,169	23,100,000	26,400,000	34,400,000	40,500,000	52,600,000

[1] Excluding oil.

In 1973 the main imports were (in. 1m. Kuwaiti dinars): Machinery and transport equipment, 10·93; fabrics and yarns, 7·65; wheat and flour, 7·04; transport equipment, 6·27. The main suppliers were: USA, 11%; UK, 9%; Federal Republic of Germany, 9%; Syria, 8%; Lebanon, 6%; Japan, 5%.

Total trade with UK (British Department of Trade returns, in £1,000 sterling):

	1973	*1974*	*1975*	*1976*	*1977*
Imports to UK[1]	235,305	549,501	419,291	587,067	541,262
Exports and re-exports from UK	36,101	59,573	99,227	144,343	243,341

[1] Including oil.

COMMUNICATIONS

Aviation. British Airways, Kuwait Airways, Iraqi Airways, Iranian Airways, United Arab Airlines, Middle East Airlines, Saudi Arabian Airways, Lebanese International Airways, Air Liban, Air India, Lufthansa, Japanese Airlines, TWA, PIA, KLM and Gulf Aviation operate scheduled air services.

Shipping. Ships of 27 lines make regular calls at Kuwait, but in 1977 there was severe congestion at the port.

Post and Broadcasting. Wireless communication was taken over by the Kuwait Government in 1956, internal postal services in Feb. 1958 and external postal services in 1959. There were (1977), 139,880 telephones in Kuwait. There are a broadcasting and a television station.

Cinemas. In 1973 there were 8 cinemas with a seating capacity of 11,000.

EDUCATION AND WELFARE

Education. In 1976 there were 201,907 pupils at 326 government schools. In 1969–70 there were 2,200 students at teacher-training institutes (354 teachers) and teacher-training colleges had 100 students (28 teachers). A technical college was opened in 1954 and in 1970 had 931 students (212 teachers). The University of Kuwait had 6,500 students in 1976.

Health. Medical services are free to all residents. There are altogether 12 hospitals with over 3,381 beds in the State, including 3 tuberculosis sanatoria, 2 mental hospitals and over 150 clinics. The Ministry of Health employs 575 physicians and 63 dentists.

DIPLOMATIC REPRESENTATIVES

OF KUWAIT IN GREAT BRITAIN (45 Queen's Gate, London, SW7)

Ambassador: Shaikh Saud Nazir al-Sabah.

OF GREAT BRITAIN IN KUWAIT (Arabian Gulf St., Kuwait)

Ambassador: S. J. G. Cambridge.

OF KUWAIT IN THE USA (2940 Tilden St., NW, Washington, D.C., 20008)

Ambassador: Khalid M. Jaffar.

OF THE USA IN KUWAIT (P.O. Box 77, Kuwait)

Ambassador: Frank E. Maestrone.

OF KUWAIT TO THE UNITED NATIONS

Ambassador: Abdalla Yaccoub Bishara.

Books of Reference

Education in Kuwait, 1969–70. Kuwait Government Press, 1971
Kuwait Economy 1968–69. Kuwait Government Press, 1970
The Oil of Kuwait: Facts and Figures. 3rd ed. Kuwait Government Press, 1970
Dickson, H. R. P., *Kuwait and Her Neighbours.* London, 1956
Shiber, S. G., *The Kuwait Urbanization.* Kuwait Government Press, 1964
Winstone, H. V. F., and Freeth, Z., *Kuwait: Prospect and Reality.* London, 1972

LAOS

Capital: Vientiane
Population: 2·9m. (1976)
GNP per capita: US$90 (1976)

HISTORY. The Lao People's Democratic Republic was founded on 2 Dec. 1975. Until that date Laos was a Kingdom, once called Lanxang (the land of a million elephants).

In 1893 Laos became a French protectorate and in 1907 acquired its present frontiers. In 1941 French authority was suppressed by the Japanese. When the Japanese withdrew in 1945 an independence movement known as Lao Issara (Free Laos) set up a government under Prince Phetsarath, the Viceroy of Luang Prabang. This government collapsed with the return of the French in 1946 and the leaders of the movement fled to Thailand.

Under a new Constitution of 1947 Laos became a constitutional monarchy under the Luang Prabang dynasty, and in 1949 became an independent sovereign state within the French Union. Most of the Lao Issara leaders returned to Laos but a few remained in dissidence under Prince Souphanouvong, who allied himself with the Vietminh and subsequently formed the 'Pathet Lao' (Lao State) rebel movement.

The war in Laos from 1953 to 1973 between the Royal Lao Government (supported by American bombing and Thai mercenaries) and the dissident communist-led *Pathet Lao* (supported by large numbers of North Vietnamese troops) ended in 1973 when an agreement and a protocol were signed. A provisional coalition government was formed by the two sides in 1974. However, after the communist victories in neighbouring Vietnam and Cambodia in April 1975, the *Pathet Lao* took over the running of the whole country, although maintaining the façade of a coalition. On 29 Nov. 1975 HM King Savang Vatthana signed a letter of abdication and the People's Congress proclaimed a People's Democratic Republic of Laos. For the history of *Pathet Lao* and the military intervention of the Vietminh, *see* THE STATESMAN'S YEAR-BOOK, 1971–72, pp. 1126–28 and 1975–76 ed., pp. 1115–16.

AREA AND POPULATION. Laos is a land-locked country of about 91,000 sq. miles (235,700 sq. km) bordered on the north by China, the east by Vietnam, the south by Democratic Kampuchea (Cambodia) and the west by Thailand and Burma. Apart from the Mekong River plains along the border of Thailand, the country is mountainous, particularly in the north, and in places densely forested. The climate is of a tropical monsoon type with a wet season from May to Oct. and a dry one from Nov. to April. Most of northern Laos receives about 40–80 in. of rainfall annually, while parts of the Bolovens Plateau in southern Laos have over 150 in.

There has been no complete census in Laos, but estimates place the population at about 2·9m. The most heavily populated areas are the Mekong River plains by the Thailand border. Otherwise, the population is sparse and scattered, particularly in the northern provinces, and the eastern part of the country has been depopulated by war. The majority of the population is officially divided into 4 groups: about 40% Lao-Lum (Valley-Lao), 16% Lao-Tai (tribal Tai); 34% Lao-Theung (Lao of the mountain sides); and 9% Lao-Soung (Lao of the mountain tops), who comprise the Meo and Yao. Other minorities include Vietnamese, Chinese, Europeans, Indians and Pakistanis.

The Lao-Lum and Lao-Tai belong to the Lao branch of the Tai peoples, who migrated into South-East Asia at the time of the Mongol invasion of South China. The valley Lao are Buddhists, following the Hinayana (Theravada) form. The Lao-Tai, who live mainly in northern Laos, are mostly patrilineal, believing in ancestral deities. The majority of the Lao-Theung—a diverse group consisting of many tribes—are animists.

The Meo and Yao live in northern Laos. Far greater numbers live in both North Vietnam and China, having migrated over the last century. Their religions have strong Confucian and animistic features but some are Christians.

There are 24 provinces. Compared with other parts of Asia, Laos has few towns.

The administrative capital and largest town is Vientiane, with a population of (census, 1973) 176,637. Other important towns are Luang Prabang, the royal capital, 44,244; Pakse, 44,860, in the extreme south, and Savannakhet, 50,690.

Language: Lao is the official language of the country, but French is also widely used in the various administrative departments and English is becoming more widely spoken, particularly by the young. The liturgical language of Theravada Buddhism is Pali.

GOVERNMENT. On 1–2 Dec. 1975 a national congress of 264 people's representatives met and declared Laos a People's Democratic Republic. A People's Supreme Council was appointed to draw up a new Constitution.

President: Prince Souphanouvong.

Prime Minister: Kaysone Phomvihane.

There are 3 deputy prime ministers.

National flag: Three horizontal stripes of red, blue, red, with blue of double width with in the centre a large white disc.

National anthem: Peng Sat Lao (Hymn of the Lao People).

Provincial Administration: All provincial administration is in the hands of the *Pathet Lao*. Orders come from the Central Committee through a series of 'People's Revolutionary Committees' at the province, town and village level.

DEFENCE

Army. Since the Communist victory in 1975 the Royal Lao Army has partly been integrated with the *Pathet Lao*, the rest being disbanded. The 'Lao People's Liberation Army', as the *Pathet Lao* is more correctly known, is about 46,000 strong. There are about 10,000 active North Vietnamese troops in Laos.

Navy. In 1978 there were 4 river squadrons comprising 42 craft of 6 different types, of which 14 were in commission and 28 in reserve. Naval personnel totalled 550 officers and ratings.

Air Force. In spring 1975, the Air Force had about 139 aircraft, including 70 T-28D piston-engined light strike aircraft, some AC-47 ground-attack aircraft, 10 C-123 and 10 C-47 transports, about 28 UH-34 and Alouette III helicopters, observation and light communications aircraft. Personnel strength, about 2,250. Since then it has begun to re-equip with aircraft supplied by the USSR, including 10 MiG-21 fighters, 6 An-24 turboprop transports and some Mi-8 helicopters.

INTERNATIONAL RELATIONS

Membership. Laos is a member of UN.

ECONOMY

Planning. A development plan for the period 1975–78 was drawn up in Sept. 1974. The large projects include extending the Nam Ngum Dam and development of the infrastructure. The other projects, particularly the project for the integrated agricultural development of the Vientiane Plain, emphasize development of the productive sector, particularly agriculture, to attain self-sufficiency in food.

Budget. The budget for the Laotian fiscal year 1974–75 (ended 30 June) was estimated as follows: Revenue K.19,600m.; expenditure K.37,046m., of which the military budget appropriated K.13,000m. Much of the deficit was made up by foreign aid in the form of donations to a Foreign Exchange Operations Fund (Stabilization Fund). The fund was administered by agreement between the Laotian Government and the donor countries who were the USA, UK, Australia, France and Japan, and assisted in supporting the convertibility for foreign trade transactions. It has now been wound up.

Currency. The National Bank issues the currency, the *kip*, whose value is normally expressed in US$. The official rate of exchange was (1976) K.200 = US$1, but the black market rate in 1977 was estimated at up to ten times this.

ENERGY AND NATURAL RESOURCES

Electricity. Only a few towns in Laos have an electricity service. A power plant with a capacity of 8,000 kw. is installed at Vientiane, but there are only small thermo-electric plants in other towns. The Nam Ngum Dam situated about 45 miles north of Vientiane was inaugurated in Dec. 1971 with an initial installed capacity of 30,000 kw. and a planned ultimate capacity of 135,000 kw. Transmission lines to Vientiane and to Thailand have been constructed. Other sources of electric power are the dams on the Sedone River about 20 miles north of Pakse and on the Nam Dong about 5 miles south of Luang Prabang, with installed capacities of 2,400 and 1,200 kw. respectively.

Minerals. Various minerals are found, but only tin is mined to any significant extent at present, and only at 2 mines (1974 production, 1,423 tonnes of 50% concentrate). There are extremely rich deposits of high-quality iron in Xieng Khouang province and potash near Vientiane.

Agriculture. The chief products are rice (production in 1974 about 540,000 tonnes), maize (production 27,200 tonnes), tobacco (4,200 tonnes), cotton (2,100 tonnes), citrus fruits, sticklack, benjohn tea and in the Boloven plateau coffee (2,070 tonnes), potatoes, cardamom and cinchara. Opium is produced but is the subject of legislation designed to control its manufacture and trafficking.

Forestry. The forests in the north produce valuable woods, teak in particular; the logs are floated southwards on the Mekong. Elephants are trained in forest work.

INDUSTRY AND TRADE

Industry. Industry is limited to beer, rubber sandals, cigarettes, matches, soft drinks, plastic bags, saw-mills, rice-mills, weaving, pottery, distilleries, ice, plywood, bricks, etc. Many of these industries are not in full operation since Dec. 1975. Plans for increased production are limited by lack of funds and skilled machine operators.

Commerce. In 1973 imports amounted to K.34,298m. and exports to K.3,055m. The main imports were agricultural products, petroleum products and agricultural and other machinery. The chief supplying countries were Thailand, Japan, USA and Indonesia. The main exports were tin, timber and raw cotton.

Total trade with UK (British Department of Trade returns, in £1,000 sterling):

	1972	*1973*	*1974*	*1975*	*1976*	*1977*
Imports to UK	2	16	10	15	2	4
Exports and re-exports from UK	283	557	852	504	178	340

COMMUNICATIONS

Roads. In 1974 there were 3,412 km of all-weather, asphalted or permanent roads and 4,000 km of non-all-weather roads.

Railways. There is no railway in Laos, but the Thai railway system extends to Nongkhai, on the Thai bank of the Mekong, which is connected by ferry with Thadeua about 12 miles east of Vientiane.

Aviation. Lao Aviation provides scheduled domestic air services linking major towns in Laos and international services to Bangkok and Hanoi. Thai Airways, Aeroflot and Air Vietnam provide direct flights from Bangkok, Hanoi, Rangoon and Moscow.

Shipping. The river Mekong and its tributaries are an important means of transport, but rapids, waterfalls and narrow channels often impede navigation and make transhipments necessary.

Telecommunications. The British Government has provided a radio network for Laos (with contributions of equipment from the USA, Australia and the Federal Republic of Germany). A team of technical experts to advise on and assist in the running of the system were asked to leave in May 1976. The main station in Vientiane became operational on 6 Aug. 1968.

In 1974 there were 5,506 telephones in Laos. A telephone link with Bangkok was opened in 1967, and telephonic communication was established with most parts of the world in 1968.

RELIGION, EDUCATION AND WELFARE

Religion. The majority of the population is Buddhist (Hinayana).

Education. At the end of the 1972–73 school year there were 2,018 elementary schools and 145 private schools (estimated 281,000 pupils); 22 colleges, 4 *lycées* and 3 technical schools provided secondary education for an estimated 9,000 pupils.

There is 1 teachers' training college, 1 college of education, 1 school of medicine, 1 agricultural college and an advanced school of Pali.

Health. In 1973 there were 250 doctors and 2,500 hospital beds.

DIPLOMATIC REPRESENTATIVES

OF LAOS IN GREAT BRITAIN (5 Palace Green, London, W8 4QA)

Ambassador: Platthana Choulamany.

OF GREAT BRITAIN IN LAOS (Rue Pandit J. Nehru, Vientiane)

Ambassador and Consul-General: J. A. B. Stewart.

OF LAOS IN USA (2222 S St., NW, Washington, D.C., 20008)

Ambassador: (Vacant).

OF USA IN LAOS (Rue Bartholonie, Vientiane)

Ambassador: (Vacant).

OF LAOS TO THE UNITED NATIONS

Ambassador: (Vacant).

Books of Reference

La Constitution du Laos. Notes et Etudes. 1957

International Conference on the Settlement of the Laotian Question. Geneva, 12th May 1961–23rd July 1962 (Cmnd. 1828). HMSO, 1962

Declaration and Protocol on the Neutrality of Laos. Geneva, 23rd July 1962 (Cmnd. 2025). HMSO, 1963

White Book on the Violations of the Geneva Accords of 1962 by the Government of North Vietnam. Ministry of Foreign Affairs, Vientiane, 1968

Berval, Rene De and others, *Kingdom of Laos.* Saigon, 1959

Halpern, Joel M., *Economy and Society of Laos: Brief Survey.* Yale University Press, 1964.—*Government, Politics and Social Structure in Laos.* Yale University Press, 1964

Zasloff, J. J., *The Pathet Lao: Leadership and Organization.* Lexington, Toronto and London, 1973

LEBANON

al-Jumhouriya al-Lubnaniya

Capital: Beirut
Population: 2·78m. (1974)
GNP per capita: US$1,070 (1974)

HISTORY. After 20 years' French mandatory regime, the Lebanon was proclaimed independent at Beirut on 26 Nov. 1941. On 27 Dec. 1943 an agreement was signed between representatives of the French National Committee of Liberation and of Lebanon, by which most of the powers and capacities exercised hitherto by France were transferred as from 1 Jan. 1944 to the Lebanese Government. The evacuation of foreign troops was completed in Dec. 1946.

In early May 1958 the opposition to President Chamoun, consisting principally (though not entirely) of Moslem pro-Nasserist elements, rose in insurrection; and for 5 months the Moslem quarters of Beirut, Tripoli, Sidon and the northern Bekaa were in insurgent hands. On 15 July the USA Government acceded to President Chamoun's request and landed a considerable force of army and marines who re-established the authority of the government.

In the subsequent presidential elections, Gen. Fouad Chehab replaced President Chamoun and a return to normality enabled US forces to be withdrawn.

In 1970 Suleiman Frangié succeeded President Helou. His term of office ended in 1976.

Israeli attacks on Lebanon and some internal problems resulted from the presence and activities of armed Palestinian resistance units on Lebanese territory. But a secret Cairo agreement in 1969 and new agreements in 1972 and 1973 have regulated these activities. From March 1975, Lebanon was beset by civil disorder causing considerable loss of life and economic life was brought to a virtual standstill.

By Nov. 1976 it was estimated that 40,000 people had been killed and up to 100,000 injured. During this period there were over 50 ceasefire agreements but, by the end of 1976, the intervention of the Syrian dominated Arab Deterrent Force had ensured sufficient security to permit Lebanon to establish normal conditions under the guidance of President Sarkis. Only the south of Lebanon remained unsettled in late 1977. However in early 1978 there was a full-scale Israeli invasion of Lebanon with the aim of destroying Palestinian resistance units. Israeli troops withdrew from the majority of the area in March on the arrival of UN peace-keeping forces.

AREA AND POPULATION. The Lebanon is a mountainous country about 135 miles long and varying between 20 and 35 miles wide, bounded on the north and east by Syria, on the west by the Mediterranean and on the south by Israel. Between the two parallel mountain ranges of Lebanon and Anti-Lebanon lies the fertile Bekaa Valley. About one-half of the country lies at an altitude of over 3,000 ft.

The area of Lebanon is estimated at 10,400 sq. km (3,400 sq. miles) and the population at 2·78m. (1974). The principal towns, with estimated population, are: Beirut (the capital), 702,000; Tripoli, 175,000; Zahlé, 46,800; Saida (Sidon), 24,740; Tyre, 14,000.

Vital statistics, 1971: Births, 76,099; deaths, 12,799; marriages, 16,516; divorces, 1,382.

The official language is Arabic. French and, increasingly, English are widely spoken in official and commercial circles.

CONSTITUTION AND GOVERNMENT. Lebanon is an independent republic and a member of the United Nations and the Arab League. The first constitution was established under the French Mandate on 23 May 1926. It has since been amended in 1927, 1929, 1943 (twice) and 1947. It is a written constitution based on the classical separation of powers, with a President, a single chamber elected by universal adult suffrage, and an independent judiciary. The Executive consists of the President and a Prime Minister and Cabinet appointed by him. The system is, however, adapted to the peculiar communal balance on which Lebanese political life depends. This is done by the electoral law which allocates deputies according to the confessional distribution of the population, and by a series of constitutional conventions whereby, *e.g.*, the President is always a Maronite Christian, the Prime Minister a Sunni Moslem and the Speaker of the Chamber a Shia Moslem. There is no highly developed party system other than on religious confessional lines.

At a special meeting of Parliament on 11 April 1976, 89 deputies voted unanimously in favour of an amendment to the Constitution to allow a new President to be elected up to 6 months before the end of the incumbent's term. President Frangié delayed signing the amendment until 22 April.

President of the Republic: Elias Sarkis (elected on 8 May and took office on 23 Sept. 1976).

The government, formed 9 Dec. 1976, was composed as follows:

Prime Minister, Economy, Trade, Industry, Petroleum, Information: Dr Selim Hoss (Sunni Moslem).

Deputy Prime Minister, Foreign Affairs, Defence: Fuad Boutos (Greek Orthodox). *Interior, Housing and Co-operatives:* Dr Salah Salman (Druse). *Health, Hydraulic and Electricity Resources:* Dr Ibrahim Cheito (Shia Moslem). *Public Works and Transport, Tourism:* Amin Bizri (Sunni Moslem). *Industry and Petroleum, Agriculture:* Michel Doumet (Maronite Christian). *Labour and Social Affairs, National Education and Art:* Assaed Rizk (Greek Catholic). *Justice, Finance, Posts and Telegraphs:* Farid Raphael (Maronite).

National flag: Three horizontal stripes of red, white, red, with the white of double width and bearing in the centre a green cedar of Lebanon.

National anthem: Kulluna lil watan lil 'ula lil' alam (words by Rashid Nachleh, tune by Mitri El-Murr).

DEFENCE

Army. The Army strength was about 17,000, the *gendarmerie* about 5,000, the police force about 600 and the security force about 350 men. Army and *gendarmerie* use mainly British, American and French equipment.

Navy. The Navy consisted in 1978 of 4 patrol boats and 1 landing craft. The new patrol craft ordered from the Federal Republic of Germany in 1976 were not delivered. Personnel totalled 250 officers and men.

Air Force. The Air Force has about 1,000 men and 50 aircraft. In addition to a single combat squadron of Hunter jet fighter-bombers, it has (partly in storage) 10 Mirage III supersonic fighters. Other aircraft include 1 Dove light transport, 17 Alouette II and III and 4 Agusta-Bell 212 helicopters, and Fouga Magister jet and piston-engined Bulldog trainers.

INTERNATIONAL RELATIONS

Membership. Lebanon is a member of UN.

ECONOMY

Planning. Since the civil war a Development and Reconstruction Council has been responsible for co-ordinating all efforts.

Budget. The general budget for 1977 provides for a total expenditure of £Leb.1,661m. (1,608m. in 1975).

Currency. The Lebanese pound, divided into 100 *piastres*, is issued by the Banque du Liban, which commenced operations on 1 April 1964. There is a fluctuating official rate of exchange, fixed monthly (March 1976: £Leb.4·92 = £1 sterling, £Leb.24·42 = US$1), but this in practice is used only for the calculation of *ad-valorem* customs duties on Lebanese imports and for import statistics. For other purposes the free market is used; the rate of the £ sterling on 31 Aug. 1974 was £Leb.5·15 = £1; the US$ rate was £Leb.3·08 = $1.

On 28 Oct. 1977 the note circulation was £Leb.1,353m.

Banking. Beirut is an important international financial centre, and there were 75 banks registered with the central bank at 31 Dec. 1973, including 2 British banks, the British Bank of the Middle East and the Chartered Bank.

Weights and Measures. The use of the metric system is legal and obligatory throughout the whole of the country. In outlying districts the former weights and measures may still be in use. They are: 1 *okiya* = 0·47 lb.; 6 *okiyas* = 1 *oke* = 2·82 lb.; 2 *okes* = 1 *rottol* = 5·64 lb.; 200 *okes* = 1 *kantar*.

ENERGY AND NATURAL RESOURCES

Oil. There are 2 oil refineries in Lebanon, one at Tripoli, which refines oil brought by ship from Iraq, and the other at Sidon, which refines oil brought from Saudi Arabia by a pipeline owned by the Trans-Arabian Pipeline Company. These refineries received 2·3m. tonnes of crude oil in 1973 and their production is sufficient to meet the country's requirements of refined fuel.

Minerals. Iron ore exists but is difficult to work. Other minerals known to exist are iron pyrites, copper, bituminous shales, asphalt, phosphates, ceramic clays and glass sand; but the available information is of doubtful value.

Agriculture. Lebanon is essentially an agricultural country, although owing to its physical character only about 38% of the total area of the country is at present cultivated. The forests of the past have been denuded by exploitation and the unrestricted grazing of goats, and only about 80,000 hectares of indifferent timber remain, and soil erosion is considerable.

The estimated yield (in 1,000 tonnes) of the main crops in 1972 was as follows: Citrus fruits, 296: apples, 220; grapes, 109; potatoes, 117; sugar-beet, 190; wheat, 64; olives, 40; bananas, 39.

Livestock (estimated, 1976): Goats, 330,000; sheep, 234,000; cattle, 84,000; camels, 1,000; hogs, 23,000; horses, 4,000; donkeys, 26,000; mules, 4,000.

INDUSTRY AND TRADE

Industry. Industry suffered badly during the civil war. The manufacturing industry was small but had doubled in size in the 10 years before the war.

Commerce. Foreign as well as local wholesale and retail trade is the principal source of income in Lebanon and provides about 31% of the total. Because of the protectionist policies followed in some neighbouring countries, this sector has been declining, the sectors to gain being those of banking, real estate, government and services (especially tourism, £Leb.573m., 1973).

In 1972 imports were valued at £Leb.2,819·9m.; exports were valued at £Leb.1,168·2m. Imports came mainly from USA, Federal Republic of Germany, France, Italy and UK. Exports went mainly to Saudi Arabia, Kuwait, Syria, Libya and Iraq.

Total trade with UK (British Department of Trade returns, in £1,000 sterling):

	1973	*1974*	*1975*	*1976*	*1977*
Imports to UK	8,012	28,603	8,025	6,065	8,365
Exports and re-exports from UK	41,959	60,750	69,528	10,052	48,591

Customs duties are usually imposed on an *ad valorem* basis: the receipts are the Lebanese Government's main source of income; actual yield in 1973, £Leb.361m. The considerable adverse balance of trade is offset by invisible receipts, including foreign capital investment in Lebanese real estate, remittances from émigrés and receipts from tourism and international arbitrage operations.

Tourism. Receipts from tourism were £Leb.573m. in 1973.

COMMUNICATIONS

Roads. The main roads in Lebanon are good. The surface is normally of asphalt and they are normally well maintained. In Dec. 1971 there were 570 km of international roads, 1,420 km of main roads and 4,310 km of secondary and local roads, all asphalted. The main arterial routes are the north–south coastal road and the west–east trunk road (Beirut to Damascus).

Passenger transport outside the town of Beirut is provided by a great number of small private companies running cheap and regular bus services and long-distance taxi services. Most goods traffic is hauled by road.

At 31 Dec. 1973 there were 185,935 cars and taxis, 2,258 buses and 19,151 commercial vehicles.

Railways. There are 3 railway lines in Lebanon, all operated by the Office des Chemins de Fer de l'Etat Libanais (CFL): (1) Nakoura–Beirut–Tripoli (standard gauge); the Nakoura–Sidon section has been idle since the establishment of Israel: (2) a narrow-gauge line running from Beirut to Riyak in the Bekaa Valley and thence to Damascus, Syria; (3) a standard-gauge line from Tripoli to Homs and Aleppo in Syria, providing access to Ankara and Istanbul. From Homs a branch of the CFL line extends south and re-enters Lebanon, terminating at Riyak. Total length 417 km.

The railway system is operated at a considerable annual loss, attributable largely to unrestricted competition from road transport. 36,000 passengers and 512,000 tons of goods were carried in 1973. No passengers were being carried in 1977, and certain routes are still not operating at all.

Aviation. Beirut International Airport is used by many international airlines which connect Lebanon with most countries in the world. Extensive local services cover the Middle East, Persian Gulf and Europe. There are 2 national airlines, Middle East Airlines/Air Liban and Trans-Mediterranean Airways. In 1974, 44,406 flights passed through Beirut international airport, carrying a total of 2,806,632 passengers 1973: 2,258,475) and 145,897 tonnes of freight (1973: 109,927).

Shipping. Beirut is by far the largest and busiest port. In 1973, 3,415 vessels (total tonnage 5,150,254) were handled. Activity in the port of Tripoli is growing due to increased movements in goods and petroleum. The small port of Sidon in the south, near to the closed Lebanese–Israeli frontier, is at present of little importance. General activity since the civil war has been reduced to about 60%, but was increasing in late 1977.

Post and Broadcasting. There is an automatic telephone system in Beirut, Tripoli, Sidon, Zahlé and several other towns and villages, which is being extended to all parts of the country. There are no telegraph, postal or telephone communications with Israel. Number of telephones (1971), 192,000.

The state radio transmits in Arabic, French, English and Armenian. There are 2 commercial television stations, transmitting in Arabic, French and English. There were 325,000 sets in 1975.

Cinemas (1970). There were 170 cinemas with a seating capacity of about 86,600.

Newspapers (1977). There were about 30 daily newspapers in Arabic, 2 in French, 1 in English and 4 in Armenian, with a total circulation of 215,000.

RELIGION, EDUCATION AND WELFARE

Religion. About half the population are Christians, who have been indigenous since the earliest time of Christianity. There were in 1958, 792,000 Christians, of whom 424,000 were Maronites, 150,000 Greek Orthodox, 69,000 Armenians, 91,000 Greek and Roman Catholics, 14,500 Armenian Catholics, 14,000 Prostestants. Moslems numbered 536,000, of whom 286,000 were Sunnis and 250,000 Shiites. There were also 88,000 Druzes and 6,600 Jews.

Education. Government schools in 1970 comprised 1,290 primary and secondary schools. There were also 1,484 private primary and secondary schools. There are also 5 teachers' training colleges and 5 universities, namely the Lebanese (State) University, the American University of Beirut, the French University of St Joseph (founded in 1875), the Arab University, a branch of Alexandria University and Beirut University College. The French Government runs the École Supérieure de Lettres and the Centre d'Études Mathématiques.

The Lebanese Academy of Fine Arts includes schools of architecture, art, music, political and social science.

Health. In 1973 there were 2,300 physicians and 8,000 hospital beds.

DIPLOMATIC REPRESENTATIVES

OF THE LEBANON IN GREAT BRITAIN (21 Kensington Palace Gdns, London, W8 4QM)

Ambassador: Nadim Dimechkié (accredited 18 July 1966).

OF GREAT BRITAIN IN THE LEBANON (Ave. de Paris, Ras Beirut)

Ambassador: Sir Peter Wakefield, KBE, CMG.

OF THE LEBANON IN THE USA (2560-28th St., Washington, D.C., 20008)

Ambassador: Najati Kabbani.

OF THE USA IN THE LEBANON (Corniche at Rue Ain Mreisseh, Beirut)

Ambassador: Richard B. Parker.

OF THE LEBANON TO THE UNITED NATIONS

Ambassador: Ghassan Tueni.

Books of Reference

Statistical Information: Import and export figures are produced by the Conseil Supérieur des Douanes. The Service de Statistique Générale (M. A. G. Ayad, *Chef du Service*) publishes a quarterly bulletin (in French and Arabic) covering a wide range of subjects, including foreign trade, production statistics and estimates of the national income.

Binder, L. (ed.), *Politics in Lebanon.* New York, 1966
Cowan, J. M., *Dictionary of Modern Arabic.* Wiesbaden, 1961
Hitti, P. K., *A Short History of Lebanon.* London, 1965
Murray, G., *Lebanon: The New Future.* London, 1974
Naccache, G., *Les Partis libanais en 1959.* Beirut, 1959
Rizk, C., *Le Régime politique libanais.* Paris, 1966
Salem, E. A., *Modernization Without Revolution: Lebanon's Experience.* Indiana Univ. Press, 1973
Salibi, K. S., *Modern History of Lebanon.* London, 1965
Ward, P., *Touring Lebanon.* London, 1971

National Library: Dar el Kutub, Parliament Sq., Beirut.

LESOTHO

Capital: Maseru
Population: 1·18m. (1975)
GNP per capita: US$170 (1976)

HISTORY. Basutoland first received the protection of Britain in 1868 at the request of Moshesh, the first paramount chief. In 1871 the territory was annexed to the Cape Colony, but in 1884 it was restored to the direct control of the British Government through the High Commissioner for South Africa.

On 4 Oct. 1966 Basutoland became an independent and sovereign member of the Commonwealth under the name of the Kingdom of Lesotho.

AREA AND POPULATION. Lesotho is bounded on the west by the Orange Free State, on the north by the Orange Free State and Natal, on the east by Natal and East Griqualand, and on the south by the Cape Province. The altitude varies from 5,000 to 11,000 ft. The climate is dry and rigorous, with extremes of heat and cold both seasonal and diurnal. The temperature varies between 93° F. (34° C.) and 3° F. (−16° C.). The rainfall is variable, the average being about 29 in. per annum.

The area is 11,716 sq. miles (30,340 sq. km). Lesotho is a purely African territory, and the few European residents are government officials, traders, missionaries and artisans. The capital is Maseru (population, 1975, 30,000).

The census taken on 14 April 1966 showed a total population of 969,634 persons (465,784 males, 503,850 females), of whom 97,529 males and 19,744 females were absent. Estimate (1975), 1·18m.

CONSTITUTION AND GOVERNMENT. On 4 Oct. 1966 the country became the Kingdom of Lesotho, with the Paramount Chief as King.

Parliament consists of the National Assembly (60 members elected by adult suffrage) and a Senate (22 principal chiefs and 11 members nominated by the King). The general election held on 30 April 1965 returned 31 members of the National Party, 25 members of the Congress Party and 4 members of the Marematlou Freedom Party. The elections of 27 Jan. 1970 were declared invalid on 31 Jan. Parliamentary rule, with a National Assembly of nominated members, was re-introduced in April 1973. A Constitution is being drafted.

National flag: Blue with a white Basuto hat; in the hoist 2 vertical strips of green and red.

King of Lesotho: Moshoeshoe II.

Prime Minister: Chief Leabua Jonathan. *Deputy Prime Minister and Public Works:* Chief Sekhonyana 'Maseribane.

The College of Chiefs settles the recognition and succession of Chiefs and adjudicates cases of inefficiency, criminality and absenteeism among them.

Local Government. The country is divided into 9 districts as follows: Maseru, Qacha's Nek, Mokhotlong, Leribe, Butha-Buthe, Teyateyaneng, Mafeteng, Mohale's Hoek, Quthing. Each district is subdivided into wards, most of which are presided over by hereditary chiefs allied to the Moshoeshoe family.

District councils, established in 1944, were abolished on 17 Jan. 1966; their functions are now exercised by officials appointed by the Ministry of Local Government.

INTERNATIONAL RELATIONS

Membership. Lesotho is a member of UN, OAU, the Commonwealth and is an ACP state of the EEC.

ECONOMY

Budget. The financial year ends on 31 March.

	1969–70[1]	*1970–71*[1]	*1971–72*	*1972–73*	*1973–74*	*1974–75*
Revenue	11,322,650	11,704,510	12,409,839	16,052,000	26,516,000	33,320,000
Expenditure	10,497,380	11,041,480	12,440,471	17,187,000	20,900,800	24,203,000

[1] Estimates.

The major items of expenditure in 1974–75 were education (R4·7m.), health (R1·7m.), police (R1·8m.) and agriculture (R1·7m.). The revenue situation was greatly improved by the re-negotiation of the Republic of South Africa's customs agreement in 1970. Of the 1974–75 revenue R30m. was generated from domestic sources including the Customs Union.

Currency. The currency is the South African Rand (R1·63 = £1).

Banking. The Standard Bank of South Africa and Barclays Bank International have branches at Maseru, Mohale's Hoek and Leribe.

AGRICULTURE. The chief crops are wheat, maize and sorghum; barley, oats, beans, peas and other vegetables are also grown. The land is held in trust for the nation by the King and may not be alienated.

Soil conservation and the improvement of crops and pasture are matters of vital importance. A total area of 1,006,817 acres has been protected against soil erosion by means of terracing, training banks, tree planting and grass strips. Efforts are being made to secure the general introduction of rotational grazing in the mountain area.

Livestock (1976): Cattle, 600,000; horses, 60,000; donkeys, 4,000; sheep, 1·6m.; goats, 900,000; mules, 2,000.

INDUSTRY AND TRADE

Industry. Industrial development is progressing under the National Development Corporation. Diamond exports, 1974, were valued at R752,000.

Commerce. Lesotho, Botswana and Swaziland are members of the South African customs union, by agreement dated 29 June 1910.

Total values of imports and exports into and from Lesotho (in R1,000):

	1971	*1972*	*1973*	*1974*
Imports	28,000	43,000	60,500	79,120
Exports	3,000	6,100	8,770	9,809

Principal imports in 1974 were food, livestock, drink and tobacco (R16m.), mineral fuels and lubricants (R5m.), manufactured goods (R41m.), machinery and transport equipment (R8m.); principal exports were cattle (R1m.), wool and mohair (R5m.).

The majority of international trade is with the Republic of South Africa.

Total trade of Lesotho with UK (British Department of Trade returns, in £1,000 sterling):

	1974	*1975*	*1976*	*1977*
Imports to UK	71	69	331	188
Exports and re-exports from UK	335	376	755	807

Tourism. In 1974 there were 75,000 visitors. The Lesotho National Development Corporation is helping the development of tourism and more hotels and resorts are planned.

COMMUNICATIONS

Roads. There were (1975) 125 miles of tarred roads and 529 miles of gravel-surfaced roads along the western border of Lesotho, with outlets to the border ports of exit. Regular motor services of the South African Railways operate between Zastron (OFS) and Quthing, Zastron (OFS) and Mohale's Hoek, and between Fouriesburg (OFS) and Butha Buthe. In addition to the main roads there were (1975) 1,029 miles of tracks leading to trading stations and missions. Communications into the mountainous interior are by means of bridlepaths suitable only for riding and pack animals, but a mountain road of 80 miles has been constructed, and some parts are accessible by air transport, which is being used increasingly.

Railways. A railway built by the South African Railways, 1 mile long, connects Maseru with the Bloemfontein–Natal line at Marseilles.

Aviation. There is a scheduled passenger service between Maseru and Jan Smuts Airport, Johannesburg operated jointly by Lesotho National Airways and SAA. There are also 30 airstrips for light aircraft.

Post. There were 3,726 telephones on 1 Jan. 1975.

Cinemas. In 1971 there were 2 cinemas with a seating capacity of 800.

JUSTICE, RELIGION, EDUCATION AND WELFARE

Justice. An appeal court for Lesotho was established at Maseru on 4 Oct. 1966.

The police force on 31 Dec. 1972 had an establishment of 111 officers and subordinate officers and 1,194 other ranks.

Religion. About 70% of the population are Christians, 40% being Roman Catholics.

Education. Education is largely in the hands of the 3 main missions (Paris Evangelical, Roman Catholic and English Church), under the direction of the Ministry of Education. In 1974 the total enrolment in 1,087 primary schools was 218,038; in 84 secondary schools, 14,908; in 7 teacher-training schools enrolment was 510 in 1972. University education was provided at the University of Botswana, Lesotho, Swaziland, which now has a campus in each of the 3 countries. Total enrolment in 1974–75 was 538, of which 322 were Basotho students. In 1975 a National University was established. Recurrent government expenditure on education was estimated at R3,948,700 in 1973–74. Bursaries are provided at all stages for secondary, teacher-training and university work. In 1972, 106 Basotho were studying at universities and places of higher education, outside Lesotho.

Health. The government medical staff of the territory consists of 1 Permanent Secretary for Health and chief medical officer, 1 medical superintendent, 26 medical officers, 1 medical officer of health and 6 specialist physicians and surgeons.

There are 10 government hospitals staffed by 333 matrons, sisters and nurses. There is accommodation for 2,106 patients in government hospitals. The 316-bed Queen Elizabeth II hospital in Maseru was completed in 1957. There are 9 mission hospitals subsidized by the Government with 729 beds. Health centres and mountain dispensaries provide outpatient medical facilities and maternity services to people living in remote areas. The leper settlement 5 miles out of Maseru had 189 patients at the end of 172.

Typhus and plague occur.

DIPLOMATIC REPRESENTATIVES

OF LESOTHO IN GREAT BRITAIN (16A St James's St., London, SW1A 1EU)

High Commissioner: Marion Likhapha Sehlabo (accredited 24 Feb. 1977).

OF GREAT BRITAIN IN LESOTHO

High Commissioner: O. G. Griffith.

OF LESOTHO IN THE USA (1601 Connecticut Ave., NW, Washington, D.C., 20009)

Ambassador: Thabo R. Makeka.

OF THE USA IN LESOTHO

Ambassador: Donald R. Norland (resides in Gaborone).

OF LESOTHO TO THE UNITED NATIONS

Ambassador: Mooki V. Malopo.

Books of Reference

Statistical Information: Bureau of Statistics, P.O.B.455, Maseru, Lesotho.

Lesotho: Report for 1968. Maseru, 1969
Ashton, H., *The Basuto*. 2nd ed. OUP, 1967
Hailey, Lord, *The Republic of South Africa and the High Commission Territories*. OUP, 1963
Khaketla, B. M., *Lesotho 1970*. London, 1971
Spence, J. E., *Lesotho*. OUP, 1968

LIBERIA

Capital: Monrovia
Population: 1·5m. (1974)
GNP per capita: US$450 (1976)

HISTORY. The Republic of Liberia had its origin in the efforts of several American philanthropic societies to establish freed American slaves in a colony on the West African coast. In 1822 a settlement was formed near the spot where Monrovia now stands. On 26 July 1847 the state was constituted as the Free and Independent Republic of Liberia. The new state was first recognized by Great Britain and France, and ultimately by other powers.

AREA AND POPULATION. Liberia has about 350 miles of coastline, extending from Sierra Leone, on the west, to the Ivory Coast, on the east, and it stretches inland to a distance, in some places, of about 250 miles. The boundaries were determined by the Anglo-Liberian agreement of 1885 and the Franco-Liberian agreements of 1882 and 1907–10. In 1911 the territory of Kailahun was transferred to Sierra Leone in exchange for a strip on the south side of Mano River, which now is the boundary.

The total area is about 43,000 sq. miles (112,600 sq. km). A census taken in 1973–74 gave the total population as 1,523,050. The indigenous natives belong in the main to 4 principal stocks: Mendetan, West Atlantic, Mande-fu, and Kru. These are in turn subdivided into 16 major tribes, namely: Bassa, Belle, Gbandi, Mende, Gio, Dey, Mano, Gola, Kpelle, Kissi, Krahn, Kru, Loma, Mandingo, Vai and Grebo.

Monrovia, the capital, had (1974) a population of 171,680 and is administered as a district by a mayor to be elected by popular vote. It is one of the 4 ports of entry along the 350 miles of coast, the others being Buchanan (Grand Bassa), River Cess, Greenville (Sinoe), Harper (Maryland). Other towns are Kolahun, Voinjama, Tubmanburg, Bentol, Zorzor, Kakata, Suakoko, Gbarnga, Ganta, Sanniquellie, Saclape, Tappita, Robertsport and Yekepa.

The country is divided into 9 counties and 6 territories.

CONSTITUTION AND GOVERNMENT. The constitution of the Republic is modelled on that of the US. The executive power is vested in a President and the legislative power in a legislature of 2 Houses, the Senate (18 members) and the House of Representatives (71 members). The President is elected for 8 years in the first instance, the House of Representatives for 4 and the Senate for 6 years. A Legislative Act was approved on 22 July 1974, setting up a National Commission to give consideration to possible changes in the Motto, Flag, Anthem and the Constitution of Liberia.

President: Dr William Richard Tolbert, Jr.

Foreign Affairs: C. Cecil Dennis, Jr. *Finance:* James T. Phillips, Jr. *Justice:* Oliver Bright. *Postal Affairs:* J. Jenkins Peal. *National Defence:* Burlergh Holder. *Local Government, Rural Development and Urban Reconstruction:* Samuel D. Hill. *Education:* Dr Advertus Hoff. *Public Works:* Gabriel Tucker. *Agriculture:* Florence Chenoweth. *Health and Social Welfare:* Abeodu Jones. *Commerce, Industry and Transportation:* William E. Dennis. *Information, Cultural Affairs and Tourism:* Dr Edward B. Kesselly. *Planning and Economic Affairs:* D. Franklin Neal. *Action for Development and Progress:* Levee K. Moulton. *Minister of State for Presidential Affairs:* E. Reginald Townsend. *Land and Mines:* Aaron Holmes. *Labour, Youth and Sports:* Estrada Bernard.

The President may be elected once for an 8-year term, whereas before 1972 he could be re-elected for any number of subsequent 4-year terms. He must be a citizen of over 25 years' residence and have unencumbered real estate to the value of US$2,500. Electors must be citizens and owners of land. By the end of 1945, legislation was passed granting manhood suffrage to the tribes in the hinterland who are now represented in the legislature. In 1947 the franchise was extended to women. In 1973 the voting age was changed from 21 to 18 years.

The official language is English.

National flag: Six red and 5 white horizontal stripes alternating. In the upper corner, nearest the staff, is a square of blue covering a depth of 5 stripes. In the centre of this blue field is a 5-pointed white star.

National anthem: All hail, Liberia, hail! (words by President Warner; tune by O. Luca, 1860).

On 22 Dec. 1950 an agreement of assistance and co-operation was signed in Washington whereby a development programme is implemented under control of a joint American–Liberian Commission.

In 1963 the US Agency for International Development announced loans for the construction of a hydro-electric project (US$24·3m.), schools (US$1·7m.) and hospitals (US$4·7m.); Federal Republic of Germany made a loan for road construction (US$8·2m.).

DEFENCE. For defence every citizen from 16 to 45 years of age capable of bearing arms is liable to serve. On 31 March 1942 an agreement was signed between the USA and Liberia by which the US were given the right to construct, control, operate and defend airports in Liberia for the duration of the war. On 8 June 1943 a further mutual aid agreement was concluded with the US, which extended lend-lease aid to Liberia for the purpose of defence and enabled it to increase its Armed Forces.

Army. The establishment organized on a militia basis numbers 5,020, divided into 5 infantry regiments. There is in addition an enlisted frontier force, the Liberian National Guard, of 93 officers and 2,200 men.

Navy. The small naval service or coastguard comprises 1 motor gunboat, 2 small patrol boats, the Presidential yacht and a few landing craft for transport and general utility. Personnel in 1978 totalled 200 officers and men.

Air Force. The nucleus of an Air Force has been formed, as the Air Reconnaissance Unit, to support the Liberian Army. Equipment includes 2 C-47 transports and about 10 Cessna 172, 185 and 207 light aircraft.

INTERNATIONAL RELATIONS

Membership. Liberia is a member of UN, OAU and is an ACP state of EEC.

ECONOMY

Budget. The budgets for calendar years were as follows (in US$1,000):

	1972	*1973*	*1974*	*1975*	*1976*
Revenue	80,900	91,093	108,600	125,343	149,800
Expenditure	78,000	87,941	198,400	118,859	136,000

Currency. The legal currency of Liberia is the dollar which is equivalent to US$1 which itself has been in circulation since 3 Nov. 1942, but there is a Liberian coinage in silver and copper. Official accounts are kept in dollars and cents. The Liberian coins are as follows: Silver, US$1, 50-, 25-, 10- and 5-cent pieces; alloy, 2- and 1-cent pieces. The Government has not yet issued paper money.

British currency ceased to be legal tender after the end of 1943, and on 1 Jan. 1944 the Liberian dollar was raised to parity with the US$.

Banking. The Bank of Liberia, Inc., was founded on 28 July 1955. An Italian bank, Tradevco, started business in 1955. The International Trust Co. of Liberia opened a commercial banking department at the end of 1960. The Commercial Bank of Liberia and a branch of the Chase Manhattan Bank opened in 1961. The Union National Bank (Liberia) Inc., opened in 1962. The National Bank of Liberia opened on 22 July 1974, to act as a central bank. The National Housing and Savings Bank opened on 20 Jan. 1976.

Weights and Measures. Weights and measures are the same as in UK and USA.

NATURAL RESOURCES

Minerals. Mineral resources have not been completely surveyed. However, the Liberia Mining Co. at Bomi Hills, the National Iron Ore Co. near the Mano River, the Liberian Swedish Mineral Co. in the Nimba Mountains and the Bong Mining Co. (DELIMCO) at Bong Mountain Range are exploiting their iron-ore concession areas. Iron ore exports amounted to 20·05m. long tons in 1976. Gold and diamonds are found on a small scale.

A pelletizing and washing plant was inaugurated in 1968 for the American–Swedish Minerals Co. near the port of Buchanan. Another pelletizing and washing plant was inaugurated in 1971 for the Bong Mining Co.

Agriculture. The soil is productive, but due to excessive rainfall (from 160 to 180 in. per year), there are large swamp areas. Rice, cassava, coffee, citrus and sugar-cane are cultivated. Rice production is inadequate for local needs, but strenuous efforts are being made to increase production by the substitution of swamp rice for hill rice cultivation. Total rice production increased from 472,000 acres 1975 to 495,000 acres in 1976. The Government is negotiating the financing of large-scale investment in rice production on over 50,000 acres, aimed at transforming the country from a rice-importing to a rice-exporting nation. Sugar-cane is grown for manufacture of locally consumed rum. In 1973, Liberia signed an agreement with China for the development of a sugar industry in Liberia. The project is to be carried out in two phases, the first involving an investment of US$15m. on 10,000 acres of land, for the production of 10,000–12,000 tons of sugar and 3,000 tons of molasses per year, and the second entailing an investment of US$25·6m. for the production of 73,000–80,000 tons yearly. The sugar will be under the management of LIBSUCO, in Maryland County. Coffee, cocoa and palm-kernels are produced mainly by the traditional agricultural sector. In 1976, the total volume of coffee and cocoa exports alone were 9·3m. lb. (US$6·6m.), and 5·5m. lb. (US$4·1m.), respectively.

The Liberia Produce Marketing Corporation (LPMC) operates an oil-mill in Monrovia, processing most of the palm-kernels. There were 2 large commercial oil-palm plantations in the country. The Liberia Industrial Co-operative (LBINC) has 6,000 acres of oil-palm (of which 5,000 acres are in production) in Grand Bassa County, and West Africa Agricultural Co. (WAAC) has 4,020 acres in production in Grand Cape Mount County.

Forestry. The Firestone Plantation Co. have large rubber plantations, employing over 40,000 men. Their concession comprises about 1m. acres and expires in the year 2025. About 100,000 acres have been planted. Independent producers have a further 65,000 acres planted. In 1976 the total area under rubber cultivation was 294,400 acres, of which 195,800 acres were under actual production.

The B. F. Goodrich Co. was, on 9 July 1954, granted an 80-year concession to produce rubber; part of the 12,300 acres planted came into production in 1963. Other rubber-producing companies include Allen L. Grant, L. A. C. and Salala Rubber Co. Together, the foreign concessions produced 128m. lb. in 1975 while independent Liberian farmers produced 53·4m. lb. amounting to a total rubber production in 1975 of 181·4m. lb.

Logs and lumber are now the country's fourth most important export.

INDUSTRY AND TRADE

Industry. There are a number of small factories (brick and tile, soap, nails, mattresses, shoes, plastics, paint, oxygen, acetylene, tyre retreading, a brewery, soft drinks, cement, matches, candy and biscuits).

Commerce. Foreign trade for 6 calendar years was as follows (in US$1m.):

	1971	*1972*	*1973*	*1974*	*1975*	*1976*
Imports	162·4	178·7	188·0	289·4	331·0	399·2
Exports	224·0	244·4	289·5	400·3	394·0	457·0

The principal exports in 1976 were: Iron ore, and concentrates, US$331·6m.; rubber, US$53·3m.; logs and lumber, US$32·4m. The principal imports in 1976 were machinery and transport equipment (US$152·1m.) and manufactured goods (US$795·4m.). Main suppliers in 1976 were: EEC (US$142·3m.), USA (US$119·1m.), Asia (US$98·8m.), other West European countries (US$24·1m.).

According to British Department of Trade returns, the value of the trade between UK and Liberia was as follows (in £1,000 sterling):

	1973	*1974*	*1975*	*1976*	*1977*
Imports to UK	7,381	6,494	6,085	10,035	14,052
Exports and re-exports from UK	17,625	13,990	23,752	23,893	21,539

The figures for exports from the UK include the value of shipping transferred to the Liberian flag; the genuine exports are considerably lower.

Liberia was placed in the American account area in 1952.

COMMUNICATIONS

Roads. There are over 4,500 miles of state roads, suitable for motor traffic, as well as roads on private plantations. The principal highway connects Monrovia with the road system of Guinea, with branches leading into the Eastern and Western areas of Liberia. The latter branch reaches the Sierra Leone border and joins the Sierra Leone road system. A bridge over the St Paul River carries road and rail traffic to the iron-ore mines at Bomi Hills.

In the interior, communication is maintained by tracks, all goods being carried by native porters, but secondary roads are being constructed by local communities with state assistance, and transportation by vehicle is becoming increasingly common. A 5-year road improvement plan was in operation until 1977.

Railway. A railway (for freight only) was built in 1951, connecting Monrovia with the Bomi Hills iron-ore mines about 43 miles distant; this has been extended to the National Iron Ore Co. area by 49 miles. A line from Nimba to Lower Buchanan (165 miles) was completed in 1963 and another line from Bong to Monrovia (47 miles) was completed in 1965.

Aviation. The airport for Liberia is Roberts Airport (30 miles from Monrovia). The James Spriggs Payne Airfield, 5 miles from Monrovia, can be used by light aircraft and mini jumbo jets. Air services are maintained by PANAM, Ghana Airways, Nigeria Airways, UTA, Middle East Airlines, Air Mali, Air Afrique, SAS, KLM, Swissair, Liberian National Airlines, British Caledonian, Air Guinée, SABENA, Iberia Airlines and Romanian Airline.

Shipping. In 1976, 2,229 main-line ships entered Monrovia.

The Liberian merchant navy, in 1976, consisted of 2,666 ships of 76,412,842 GRT. The Liberian Government requires only a modest registration fee and an almost nominal annual charge and maintains no control over the operation of ships flying the Liberian flag.

Constructed under the auspices of the USA Government under lend-lease terms, the port of Monrovia, a free port, was opened on 26 July 1948.

A modern port for the shipment of iron-ore from the mines at Nimba has been built at Lower Buchanan, capable of accommodating vessels up to 75,000 tons.

The river St Paul is navigable for a distance of 8 miles from its mouth for small craft of shallow draught. The Cavalla River is navigable for 8 miles.

Post and Broadcasting. There is cable communication (French) with Europe and America *via* Dakar, and a wireless station is maintained by the Government at Monrovia. There is a telephone service (3,400 telephones, 1974), in Monrovia, which is gradually being extended over the whole country. An earth station constructed by Itacable in 1976 is equipped for 24 telephone type channels and its traffic can be increased to 60 telephone type channels. With the aid of the satellite the average traffic each day now stands at 900.

There are wireless stations at Monrovia, Bassa, Harper, Kolahun, Cape Mount and Sinoe. The wireless stations at Harbel, Montserrado county, Maryland county, and Gedetarbo, have since 1928 been operated as a public utility by the US–Liberia Radio Corporation, a subsidiary of Firestone Plantation Co.

A commercial broadcasting station, ELBC, opened in Dec. 1959 and a television service on 1 Jan. 1964. Other broadcasting stations around Monrovia include ELWA, operated by the Sudan Interior Mission and the Voice of America.

JUSTICE, RELIGION, EDUCATION AND WELFARE

Justice. Justice is administered by a Supreme Court of 5 judges, circuit courts and lower courts. A new Liberian code of laws has been published (5 vols. to 1956).

Religion. The main denominations represented in Liberia are Methodist, Baptist, Episcopalian, African Methodist, Pentecostal, Seventh Day Adventist, Lutheran and Roman Catholic, working through missionaries and mission schools. There is also a fairly large Muslim community.

Education. Schools are classified as: (1) Public schools, maintained and run by the Government; (2) Mission schools, supported by foreign Missions and subsidized by the Government, and operated by qualified Missionaries and Liberian teachers; (3) Private schools, maintained by endowments and sometimes subsidized by the Government.

By the end of 1976 there were estimated to be 1,281 schools with 6,108 teachers and 209,909 pupils. In 1975, 800 US Peace Corps Volunteers were teaching in schools throughout the country.

Health. There were 132 doctors in 1973 and about 2,500 hospital beds.

DIPLOMATIC REPRESENTATIVES

OF LIBERIA IN GREAT BRITAIN (21 Prince's Gate, London, SW7 1QB)

Ambassador: H. R. Wright Brewer (accredited 7 Feb. 1975).

OF GREAT BRITAIN IN LIBERIA (Mamba Point, Monrovia)

Ambassador and Consul General: John H. Reiss, OBE.

OF LIBERIA IN THE USA (5201–16th St., NW, Washington, D.C., 20011)

Ambassador: Francis Dennis.

OF THE USA IN LIBERIA

Ambassador: W. Beverly Carter.

OF LIBERIA TO THE UNITED NATIONS

Ambassador: David M. Thomas.

Books of Reference

Presidential Papers, July 1971–July 1972. Monrovia, 1973

Economic Survey of Liberia, 1975. Ministry of Planning and Economic Affairs.

Clower, R. W. (ed.), *Growth Without Development: An Economic Survey of Liberia.* Evanston, North-western Univ. Press, 1966

Cole, H. B. (ed.), *The Liberian Year Book.* Monrovia, 1962

Fraenkel, M., *Tribe and Class in Monrovia.* OUP, 1964

McLaughlin, R. U., *Foreign Investment and Development in Liberia.* New York, 1966

Richardson, N. R., *Liberia's Past and Present.* London, 1959

Welch, G., *The Jet Lighthouse.* London, 1960

Wilson, C. M., *Liberia: Black Africa in Microcosm.* New York, 1971

SOCIALIST PEOPLE'S LIBYAN ARAB JAMAHIRIYAH

Capital: Tripoli
Population: 2·63m. (1977)
GNP per capita: US$6,310 (1976)

Al-Jamahiriyah Al-Arabiya Al-Libya Al-Shabiya Al-Ishtirakiya

HISTORY. Tripoli fell under Turkish domination in the 16th century, and though in 1711 the Arab population secured some measure of independence, the country was in 1835 proclaimed a Turkish vilayet. In Sept. 1911 Italy occupied Tripoli and on 19 Oct. 1912, by the Treaty of Ouchy, Turkey recognized the sovereignty of Italy in Tripoli.

After the expulsion of the Germans and Italians in 1942 and 1943, Tripolitania and Cyrenaica were placed under British, and the Fezzan under French, military administration. Britain recognized the Amir Mohammed Idris Al-Senussi as Amir of Cyrenaica in June 1949.

Liby became an independent, sovereign, federal kingdom under the Amir of Cyrenaica, Mohammed Idris Al-Senussi, as King of the United Kingdom of Libya, on 24 Dec. 1951, when the British Residents in Tripolitania and Cyrenaica and the French Resident in the Fezzan transferred their remaining powers to the federal government of Libya, in pursuance of decisions passed by the United Nations in 1949 and 1950. The King is married to his cousin Fatima and to Aliyah Lamlun. In Nov. 1956 the King announced the appointment of HRH Prince Al Hassan Rida as Crown Prince unless he himself should have an heir.

On 1 Sept. 1969 King Idris was deposed by a group of army officers, and now lives in exile in Egypt. Twelve of the group of officers formed the Revolutionary Command Council which rules the country with the assistance of a, mainly, civilian cabinet. One member died in Aug. 1972 and has not been replaced and another member, Maj. Muhaishi, was dismissed in 1976.

The Confederation of Arab Republics, comprising Libya, Egypt and Syria was created in 1971. Libya and Egypt announced in Aug. 1972 their intention of complete union of their two countries by 1 Sept. 1973.

A decision to bring about political union between Libya and Egypt by 1 Sept. 1973 was announced on 2 Aug. 1972. A proposed merger between Tunisia and Libya was announced on 12 Jan. 1974. Neither of these proposals had been implemented by April 1978.

AREA AND POPULATION. The area is estimated at 1,759,540 sq. km (679,358 sq. miles). The population, according to the census of 1973, was 2·26m. Estimate (1977) 2·63m.

According to an arrangement with France (12 Sept. 1919) the western frontier extends in a curve from west of Ghadames to south of Tummo, including Ghat. According to the agreement with France of 7 Jan. 1935, the southern frontier runs along a line between Tummo and a cross-point indicated by 24° E. long. from Greenwich and 18° 45′ N. lat. Further frontier agreements with France were signed on 10 Aug. 1955 and 26 Dec. 1956. In 1926 Egypt ceded the oasis of Jarabub to Italy, in exchange for a rectification of the frontier near Sollum. The eastern boundary follows in general the 25° parallel E. long. (*See* map in THE STATESMAN'S YEAR-BOOK, 1952.)

The country is administratively divided into the following 10 divisions (with population, 1973, census): Tripoli (735,083), Benghazi (337,423), Sebha (113,006), Zawia (247,628), Kalig (106,647), Khoms (162,126), Misurata (177,939), Derna (122,984), Jebel Akhdar (131,940), Gharian (155,958).

The 3 most important towns are Tripoli (551,477 inhabitants), Misurata (103,302), Benghazi (282,192).

CONSTITUTION AND GOVERNMENT. Until 1963 Libya was a federal state, each of the 3 provinces, Tripolitania, Cyrenaica and Fezzan, being administered by a governor assisted by an executive and legislative council. In April 1963, however, comprehensive unity was proclaimed and the federal system (together with the governors and the executive and legislative councils) abolished. The country is divided into 10 divisions, each administered by a commissioner (*muhafidh*).

Arabic is the official language. Tripoli is the capital.

Secretary-General of the General Secretariat of the SPLAJ: Col. Muammar al-Qadhifi.

Foreign Affairs: Dr Ali Abdul Salam Treiki.

National flag: Plain green.

DEFENCE

Army. The Army, of 22,000 men, is organized in 1 armoured, 1 National Guard, and 2 mechanized brigades, 1 commando and 5 artillery battalions.

Navy. The Libyan Government stated in Nov. 1975 that submarines (6?) of the Soviet 'F' class would be provided by the USSR. The training of Libyans in the Soviet Union offered confirmation of this. First delivery was early 1977, named *Babr*. Four submarines of the French 'Daphne' class were ordered (under licence from Paris) from Spain in 1976 and delivery could be in 1980–81.

A fast frigate was completed by Vosper-Thornycroft in 1973. Three fast missile patrol boats of the gas-turbine MTB type and a logistic support ship (dock type) were completed in Britain by Vosper-Thornycroft in 1968–69. Four patrol boats were completed in Britain by Brooke Marine in 1969–70. A corvette was built in Britain by Vosper in 1965–66. There are also a maintenance repairs craft purchased from Britain in 1966 and 7 coastguard patrol boats (Vosper-Thornycroft). Personnel in 1978 totalled 2,200 officers and ratings, including coastguard.

Four missile corvettes were ordered from Italy for completion by 1978, and 10 missile fast attack craft and 2 tank landing ships from France; and some 24 fast missile boats were transferred from the USSR from 1977 onwards. Libya is thus apparently procuring naval equipment and weapons from both the East and the West; and the eventual considerable-sized and up-to-date fleet will constitute a force of critical importance in the Mediterranean.

Air Force. The creation of an Air Force began in 1959. In 1974, delivery was completed of a total of 110 Mirage III/5 combat aircraft and trainers, some of which are believed to be in store. They have been followed by 12 Tu-22 supersonic reconnaissance bombers and 30 MiG-23 variable-geometry fighter-bombers from the USSR, and 38 Mirage F-1 aircraft are reported to have been ordered from France. Other equipment includes 8 C-130H Hercules and 9 C-47 transports, 9 Super Frelon and 8 Agusta-built CH-47C Chinook heavy-lift helicopters, and a total of about 24 Bell 47, Alouette II/III and Mi-8 helicopters. Training is performed on Yugoslav-built Galeb and Magister jet aircraft; 2 Dassault Falcons equipped with Mirage avionics and controls are used for operational training of combat pilots. Personnel total about 5,000.

INTERNATIONAL RELATIONS

Membership. Libya is a member of UN, OAU and the Arab League.

ECONOMY

Planning. A plan of economic and social transformation was published in 1976 covering the period 1976–78.

Budget. The administrative budget for the fiscal year ending 31 Dec. 1974 showed expenditure of LD310m.

Currency. The Libyan *dinar* is divided into 1,000 *millemes*.

Banking. A National Bank of Libya was established in 1955; it was renamed the Central Bank of Libya in 1972. On 31 Dec. 1972, its assets amounted to LD953·1m. and currency in circulation to LD151,586. All foreign banks were nationalized by Dec. 1970. In 1972 the Libyan Government set up the Libyan Arab Foreign Bank whose function is overseas investment and to participate in multinational banking corporations. The National Agricultural Bank, which has been set up to give loans and subsidies to farmers to develop their land and to assist them in marketing their crops, has offices in Tripoli, Benghazi, Sebha and other agricultural centres. The National Industrial and Real Estate Bank, which has been established to give loans to house buyers and to give short and medium loans to private sector industrial ventures, also has offices in Tripoli and Benghazi.

Weights and Measures. Although the metric system has been officially adopted and is obligatory for all contracts, the following weights and measures are still used: *oke* = 1·282 kg; *kantar* = 51·28 kg; *draa* = 46 cm; *handaza* = 68 cm.

ENERGY AND NATURAL RESOURCES

Electricity. Electricity output capacity in 1972 was 190 mw and was increased to 581 mw by the end of 1975.

Oil. In 1968, 41 companies were working concession areas; the most important discoveries so far made are: (i) Zelten, about 200 miles south from Benghazi and 100 miles from the nearest point on the coast; discovered by Esso (the local subsidiary of the Standard Oil Company of New Jersey) in April 1959. Exports from this field began at the end of 1961, the oil being piped to the port of Marsa Bregha. (ii) Dahra, roughly midway between Tripoli and Benghazi and about 90 miles from the coast, discovered in 1958–59; a pipeline to Ras El Sidr was completed in 1962. (iii) Beida, about 140 miles from the coast and just east of the Tripolitanian/Cyrenaican border, discovered by Caltex in 1959. (iv) Other discoveries, either non-commercial or not yet evaluated, have been made by Mobiloil of Canada, Shell, Gulf, CPTL. British Petroleum has also discovered oil in commercial quantities in southern Cyrenaica some 400 miles from the coast, connected to the Tobruk terminal by pipeline. Occidental Oil Company have made 2 high-yield strikes and are planning the construction of a pipeline and terminal at Zueitina.

In 1974 production averaged 1·4m. bbls per day. On 7 Dec. 1971 the British Petroleum Exploration (Libya) Company was nationalized and on 11 June 1973 its partner Nelson Bunker Hunt. The rights and concessions were listed in the Arabian Gulf Exploration Company. The Oasis and Occidental companies agreed in Aug. 1973 to 51% participation by the Libyan National Oil Company in their rights and operations. A decree of 1 Sept. 1973 nationalized 51% of the rights and assets of the following companies: Mobil, Exxon, Amoco, Amoseas and Shell. On 11 Feb. 1974 Amoco and Amoseas were totally nationalized. Compensation has been paid to Shell, BP and Bunker Hunt.

Minerals. The production of cement was 726,000 tonnes in 1975, though the existing 2 cement plants are being expanded to give a future combined production of 850,000 tonnes per annum. Studies are now being carried out to build a third cement factory in eastern Libya. A limestone factory is also to be built shortly in Benghazi. Gypsum output (1975) 15,000 tonnes.

Agriculture. Tripolitania has 3 zones from the coast inland—the Mediterranean, the sub-desert and the desert. The first, which covers an area of about 17,231 sq. miles, is the only one properly suited for agriculture, and may be further subdivided into: (1) the oases along the coast, the richest in North Africa, in which thrive the date palm, the olive, the orange, the peanut and the potato; (2) the steppe district, suitable for cereals (barley and wheat) and pasture; it has olive, almond, vine, orange and mulberry trees and ricinus plants; (3) the dunes, which are being gradually afforested with acacia, robinia, poplar and pine; (4) the Jebel (the mountain district,

Tarhuna, Garian, Nalut-Yefren), in which thrive the olive, the fig, the vine and other fruit trees, and which on the east slopes down to the sea with the fertile hills of Msellata. Of some 25m. acres of productive land in Tripolitania, nearly 20m. are used for grazing and about 1m. for static farming. The sub-desert zone produces the alfa plant. The desert zone and the Fezzan contain some fertile oases, such as those of Ghadames, Ghat, Socna, Sebha, Brak.

Cyrenaica has about 10m. acres of potentially productive land, most of which, however, is suitable only for grazing. Certain areas, chief of which is the plateau known as the Barce Plain (about 1,000 ft above sea-level), are suitable for dry farming; in addition, grapes, olives and dates are grown. With improved irrigation, production, particularly of vegetables, could be increased, but stock raising and dry farming will remain of primary importance. About 143,000 acres are used for settled farming; about 272,000 acres are covered by natural forests. The Agricultural Development Authority plans to reclaim 6,000 hectares each year for agriculture.

In the Fezzan there are about 6,700 acres of irrigated gardens and about 297,000 acres are planted with date palms.

A 10-year agricultural plan totalling over LD700m. was announced in May 1973. The plan aims to reclaim and develop land in the Gefara plain, the Jebel Akhdar, the Fezzan and the Kufra/Sarir areas. Future agricultural activity will concentrate on building up local production of cereals, dairy farming, sheep rearing, poultry farming and the cultivation of fruits and vegetables.

Production (1975, in tonnes): Wheat, 107,000; barley, 216,000; vegetables, 620,000; milk, 85,000; meat, 46,000. Olive trees number about 3·4m. and productive date-palm trees about 3m.

Livestock (1976): 3·4m. sheep, 1·13m. goats, 123,000 cattle, 1·5m. poultry.

INDUSTRY AND TRADE

Industry. Among the traditional industries of Tripolitania and Cyrenaica are sponge fishing, tunny fishing, tobacco growing and processing, dyeing and weaving of local wool and imported cotton yarn, and olive oil. Tripolitania also produces bricks, salt, leather and esparto grass for paper-making. Home industries of both territories include the making of matting, carpets, leather articles and fabrics embroidered with gold and silver. The government has embarked on an ambitious programme of industrial development aimed at the local manufacture of building materials (steel and aluminium pipes and fittings, electric cables, cement, bricks, glass, etc.), foodstuffs (dairy products, flour, tinned fruits and vegetables, dates, fish processing and canning, etc.), textiles and footwear (ready-made clothing, woollen and cotton cloth, blankets, leather footwear, etc.) and development of mineral deposits (iron ore, phosphates, mineral salts). Private sector industrialization is encouraged by government loans and subsidies.

Production (1975): Footwear, 680,000 pairs; hides, 70,000 sq. ft. On 21 Sept. 1969 a decree laid down that all business concerns should be 100% Libyan-owned, but oil companies and banks were excluded.

Commerce. Total imports into Libya in 1973 were valued at LD516·43m. (c.i.f.) and exports of LD1,224·13m. (f.o.b.), mostly crude oil.

Total trade between Libya and UK (British Department of Trade returns, in £1,000 sterling):

	1973	*1974*	*1975*	*1976*	*1977*
Imports to UK	164,515	390,132	127,800	166,608	141,472
Exports and re-exports from UK	61,057	62,538	107,041	134,647	173,333

COMMUNICATIONS

Roads. Good motor roads connect Tripoli through Zuara with Tunis, and through Homs and Misurata with Benghazi and thence with Tobruk and Alexandria. Other roads go south and south-west from Tripoli to Tiagura, Garian, Yefren, Nalut and Ghadames. A road connects Sebha in the south with the main coastal road. An ambitious road building programme is being implemented and a road will eventually link Libya with Chad and Niger through Sebha. A further main road is being built to link Kufra, a major agricultural centre in the south-eastern part of Libya with the coastal road.

Surface communication between Benghazi and Tripoli is by frequent bus service, and there are also bus services between Benghazi and Alexandria, and between Tripoli, Tunis and Algiers.

Aviation. Benghazi and Tripoli are both served by international airlines, linking them with each other and Athens, Cairo, Rome, Malta, Tunis, Frankfurt, Paris, Amsterdam, Algiers, Khartoum, Lagos and London. British Caledonian has 3 flights weekly between Tripoli and London.

A national airline, the Libyan Arab Airlines (LAA), was inaugurated on 30 Sept. 1965. Apart from internal flights LAA operate to Athens, London, Rome, Beirut, Cairo, Paris, Malta, Algiers, Khartoum and Tunis.

Post and Broadcasting. Tripoli is connected by telegraph cable with Malta and by microwave link with Bengardane (Tunis). There are overseas wireless-telegraph stations at Benghazi and Tripoli, and radio-telephone services connect Libya with the UK and most countries of western Europe. In 1971 some 41,495 telephones were in use and in 1975 there were 77,000 radio sets.

JUSTICE, RELIGION, EDUCATION AND WELFARE

Justice. The Civil, Commercial and Criminal codes are based mainly on the Egyptian model. Matters of personal status of family or succession matters affecting Moslems are dealt with in special courts according to the Moslem law. All other matters, civil, commercial and criminal, are tried in the ordinary courts, which have jurisdiction over everyone. In 1971 the Revolutionary Command Council set up a Commission with the task of revising Libyan laws.

There are civil and penal courts in Tripoli and Benghazi, with subsidiary courts at Misurata and Derna; courts of assize in Tripoli and Benghazi, and courts of appeal in Tripoli and Benghazi.

Religion. Islam is declared the State religion, but the right of others to practise their religions is provided for.

Education. Pupils spend 6 years in elementary schools, 3 in primary and 3 in secondary. In 1975 there were 554,000 pupils in government and private schools. The Libyan University had, in 1961, 8,220 undergraduates studying arts and teaching, commerce and economics, engineering and science. In 1960 Libyan university students abroad numbered 279 (135 in Egypt, 54 in the UK, 26 in USA, 24 in Italy, 17 in Turkey, the remainder in western Europe).

There are several schools, mainly in Tripoli, providing British, French, Italian, American and Dutch curricula, mainly on elementary and intermediate levels and chiefly for the non-Libyan communities.

Social Welfare. In 1975 there were 12,241 hospital beds and 42 hospitals with surgical facilities.

DIPLOMATIC REPRESENTATIVES

OF LIBYA IN GREAT BRITAIN (5 St James's Sq., London, SW1)

Ambassador: Muhammad Yunis Al-Mismari.

OF GREAT BRITAIN IN LIBYA (30 Trig al Fatah, Tripoli)

Ambassador: A. J. Williams, CMG.

OF LIBYA IN THE USA (1118 22nd St., NW, Washington, D.C., 20037)

Ambassador: (Vacant).

OF THE USA IN LIBYA (Shari Mohammad Thabit, Tripoli)

Ambassador: (Vacant).

OF LIBYA TO THE UNITED NATIONS

Ambassador: Mansur Rashid Kikhia.

Books of Reference

The Economic Development of Libya. International Bank, 1960
Ansell, M. O., and al-Arif, I. M., *The Libyan Revolution.* London, 1972
Bianco, M., *Gadafi: Voice from the Desert.* London, 1975
Khadduri, M., *Modern Libya.* Johns Hopkins Press, 1963
Ward, P., *Touring Libya.* 3 vols. London, 1967–69
Wright, J., *Modern Libya.* London, 1969

LIECHTENSTEIN

Capital: Vaduz
Population: 24,169 (1976)
GNP per capita: US$8,000 (1974)

HISTORY. The Principality of Liechtenstein, situated between the Austrian province of Vorarlberg and the Swiss cantons of St Gallen and Graubünden, is a sovereign state whose history dates back to 3 May 1342, when Count Hartmann III became ruler of the county of Vaduz. Additions were later made to the count's domains, and by 1434 the territory reached its present boundaries. It consists of the two former counties of Schellenberg and Vaduz (until 1806 immediate fiefs of the Roman Empire). The former in 1699 and the latter in 1712 came into the possession of the house of Liechtenstein and, by diploma of 23 Jan. 1719, granted by the Emperor Charles VI, the two counties were constituted as the Principality of Liechtenstein.

AREA AND POPULATION. Liechtenstein is bounded on the east by Austria and the west by Switzerland. Area, 160 sq. km (61·8 sq. miles); population, of Alemannic race (census 1976), 24,169. In 1976 there were 350 births and 180 deaths. Population of Vaduz (census 1976) 4,620.

REIGNING PRINCE. Francis Joseph II, born 16 Aug. 1906; succeeded his great uncle, 26 July 1938; married on 7 March 1943 to Countess Gina von Wilczek; there are 4 sons, Princes Hans Adam (*heir apparent*, born 14 Feb. 1945; married on 30 July 1967 to Countess Marie Kinsky), Philip Erasmus (married on 11 Sept. 1971 to Isabelle de l'Arbre de Malander), Nikolaus Ferdinand and Franz Josef Wenzel, and one daughter, Princess Nora Elisabeth. The monarchy is hereditary in the male line.

National flag: Horizontally blue over red, with a gold coronet in the first quarter.

National anthem: Oben am jungen Rhein (words by H. H. Jauch, 1850; tune, 'God save the Queen').

CONSTITUTION AND GOVERNMENT. Liechtenstein is a constitutional monarchy ruled by the hereditary princes of the House of Liechtenstein. The present constitution of 5 Oct. 1921 provides for a unicameral parliament (Diet) of 15 members elected for 4 years. Election is by universal adult male suffrage and is on the basis of proportional representation. The prince can call and dismiss the parliament. On parliamentary recommendation, he appoints the prime minister and the 4 councillors for a 4-year term. Any group of 600 persons or any 3 communes may propose legislation (initiative). Bills passed by the parliament may be submitted to popular referendum. A law is valid when it receives a majority approval by the parliament and the prince's signed concurrence. The capital and seat of government is Vaduz and there are 10 more communes all connected by modern roads. The 11 communes are fully independent administrative bodies within the laws of the principality. They levy additional taxes to the state taxes. Since Feb. 1921 Liechtenstein has had the Swiss currency, and since 29 March 1923 has been united with Switzerland in a customs union. Switzerland has also since 1919 represented the Principality diplomatically.

At the elections for the Diet, on 3 Feb. 1978, the Fatherland Union obtained 8 seats, the opposition Progressive Citizen's Party, 7 seats.

Head of Government: Hans Brunhart.

INTERNATIONAL RELATIONS

Membership. Liechtenstein is a member of EFTA and the International Court of Justice.

ECONOMY

Budget. Budget estimates for 1977: Revenue, 189,670,600 Swiss francs; expenditure, 189,322,600 Swiss francs. There is no public debt.

Currency. The Swiss franc.

Banking. There were (1978) 3 banks: Liechtensteinische Landesbank, Bank in Liechtenstein Ltd, Verwaltungs- und Privatbank Ltd.

Weights and Measures. The metric system is in force.

ENERGY AND NATURAL RESOURCES

Electricity. Electricity produced in 1976 was 48,255,500 kwh.

Agriculture. The rearing of cattle, for which the fine alpine pastures are well suited, is highly developed. In 1976 there were 5,897 cattle (including 2,368 milch cows), 20 horses (agriculture only), 1,860 sheep, 52 goats, 3,905 pigs. Total production of dairy produce, 1976, 6·67m. kg.

INDUSTRY AND TRADE

Industry. The country has a great variety of light industries (textiles, ceramics, steel screws, precision instruments, canned food, pharmaceutical products, heating appliances, etc.).

Liechtenstein has during the past 30 years changed from a predominantly agricultural country to a highly industrialized country. The farming population has gone down from 70% in 1930 to only 3% in 1976. The rapid change-over has led to the immigration of foreign workers (Austrians, Germans, Italians, Spaniards). Industrial undertakings in 1976 employed 5,096 workers earning 159·2m. Swiss francs.

Commerce. Exports of home produce in 1976 amounted to 597,766,576 Swiss francs. 47·9% went to EFTA countries and 30·4% to EEC countries. The biggest customer is Switzerland (236·8m., 39·6%).

Total trade with UK is included with Switzerland from 1968.

Tourism. In 1976, 77,462 foreign visitors stayed in Liechtenstein.

COMMUNICATIONS

Roads. There are 250 km of roads. Postal buses are the chief means of public transportation within the country and to Austria and Switzerland.

Railways. The 18·5 km of main railway passing through the country is operated by Austrian Federal Railways.

Post and Broadcasting. In 1976 there were 8,246 telephones, 256 telex, 5,415 wireless sets and 4,566 television sets. The post and telegraphs are administered by Switzerland.

Cinemas. There were 3 cinemas in 1978.

Newspapers. In 1978 there was 2 daily newspapers with a total circulation of 11,800.

JUSTICE, RELIGION, EDUCATION AND WELFARE

Justice. The principality has its own civil and penal codes. The lowest court is the county court, *Landgericht*, presided over by one judge, which decides minor civil cases and summary criminal offences. The criminal court, *Kriminalgericht*, with a bench of 5 judges is for major crimes. Another court of mixed jurisdiction is the court of assizes (with 3 judges) for misdemeanours. The superior court, *Obergericht*, and Supreme Court, *Oberster Gerichtshof*, are courts of appeal for civil and criminal cases (both with benches of 5 judges). An administrative court of appeal from government actions and the State Court determines the constitutionality of laws.

Police. The principality has no army. Police force, 37; auxiliary police, 29.

Religion. In 1970, 90% of the population was Roman Catholic.

Education (1976). In 14 primary, 2 upper, 4 secondary and 1 grammar school there were 3,738 pupils and 244 teachers. There is also an evening technical school, a music school, 3 schools for backward children and a children's pedagogic-welfare day school.

Health. In 1978 there was 1 hospital, but Liechtenstein has an agreement with the Swiss cantons of St Gallen and Graübunded that her citizens may use certain hospitals.

DIPLOMATIC REPRESENTATIVES

British Consul-General: J. E. Reeve (resident in Zürich).
USA Consul-General: Clarke N. Ellis (resident in Zürich).

Books of Reference

Statistical Information: Press and Information Service, Vaduz. *Chief:* Walter Kranz.

Rechenschaftsbericht der fürstlichen liechtensteinischen Regierung. Vaduz. Annual, from 1922
Jahrbücher der Historischen Vereins. Vaduz. Annual since 1900
Batliner, E. H., *Das Geld- und Kreditwesen des Fürstentums Liechtenstein.* Winterthur, 1959
d'Havrincourt, H., *Liechtenstein.* Lausanne, 1964
Greene, B., *Liechtenstein, Valley of Peace.* Vaduz, 1967
Kranz, W., *Principality of Liechtenstein—Documentary Handbook.* Vaduz, 1973
Steger, G., *Fürst und Landtag nach Liechtensteinischen Recht.* Vaduz, 1950

LUXEMBOURG

Grand-Duché de Luxembourg

Capital: Luxembourg
Population: 356,400 (1976)
GNP per capita: US$6,460 (1976)

AREA AND POPULATION. Luxembourg has an area of 2,586 sq. km (998 sq. miles) and is bounded on the west by Belgium, south by France, east by the Federal Republic of Germany. The population (31 Dec. 1976) was 356,400. The capital, Luxembourg, had 78,400 inhabitants; Esch-Alzette, the centre of the mining district, 27,800; Differdange, 18,300; Dudelange, 14,700, and Petange, 12,100. In 1977 the foreign population was about 86,000.

Vital statistics (1976): 3,915 births, 4,507 deaths, 2,249 marriages.

REIGNING GRAND DUKE. Jean, born 5 Jan. 1921, son of Grand Duchess Charlotte and the late Prince Felix of Bourbon-Parma; succeeded 12 Nov. 1964 on the abdication of his mother; married to Princess Joséphine-Charlotte of Belgium, 9 April 1953. *Offspring:* Princess Marie Astrid, born 17 Feb. 1954; Prince Henri, *heir apparent*, born 16 April 1955; Prince Jean and Princess Margareta, born 15 May 1957; Prince Guillaume, born 1 May 1963.

The civil list is fixed at 300,000 gold francs per annum, to be reconsidered at the beginning of each reign.

On 28 Sept. 1919 a referendum was taken in Luxembourg to decide on the political and economic future of the country. The voting resulted as follows: For the reigning Grand Duchess, 66,811; for the continuance of the Nassau-Braganza dynasty under another Grand Duchess, 1,286; for another dynasty, 889; for a republic, 16,885; for an economic union with France, 60,133; for an economic union with Belgium, 22,242. But France refused in favour of Belgium, and on 22 Dec. 1921 the Chamber of the Grand Duchy passed a Bill for the economic union between Belgium and Luxembourg. The agreement, which is for 60 years, provides for the disappearance of the customs barrier between the two countries and the use of Belgian, in addition to Luxembourg, currency as legal tender in the Grand Duchy. It came into force on 1 May 1922.

The Grand Duchy was under German occupation from 10 May 1940 to 10 Sept. 1944. The Grand Duchess Charlotte and the Government carried on an independent administration in London. Civil government was restored in Oct. 1944.

National flag: Three horizontal stripes of red, white, blue.

National anthem: Ons Hemecht (words by M. Lentz, 1859; tune by J. A. Zinnen).

CONSTITUTION AND GOVERNMENT. The Grand Duchy of Luxembourg is a constitutional monarchy, the hereditary sovereignty being in the Nassau family. The constitution of 17 Oct. 1868 was revised in 1919, 1948 and 1956. The revision of 1948 has abolished the 'perpetually neutral' status of the country and introduced the concepts of right to work, social security, health services, freedom of trade and industry, and recognition of trade unions. The revision of 1956 provides for the devolution of executive, legislative and judicial powers to international institutions.

The national language is Luxemburgish; French, German and English are widely used.

The country forms 4 electoral districts. An elector must be a citizen (male or female) of Luxembourg and have completed 18 years of age; to be eligible for election the citizen must have completed 21 years of age.

The Chamber of Deputies consists of 18 Christian Social, 17 Socialists, 14 Democrats, 5 Social Democrats and 5 Communists (elections of 26 May 1974). Members are elected for 5 years; they receive a salary and a travelling allowance.

The head of the state takes part in the legislative power, exercises the executive power and has a certain part in the judicial power. The constitution leaves to the sovereign the right to organize the Government, which consists of a Minister of State, who is President of the Government, and of at least 3 Ministers.

The Cabinet was, in Oct. 1977, composed as follows:

Minister of State, President of the Government, Foreign Affairs, National Economy, Middle Classes: Gaston Thorn (Lib.).

Vice-President, Labour and Social Security, Family, Social Living and Social Solidarity: Bernard Berg (Soc.). *Treasury:* Jacques F. Poos (Soc.). *Tourism, Transport and Energy:* Joseph Barthel (Lib.). *Public Health and Environment, Civil Service, Public Forces, Sport;* Emile Krieps (Lib.). *Interior:* Joseph Wohlfart (Soc.). *National Education, Justice:* Robert Krieps (Soc.). *Agriculture and Viticulture, Public Works, Deputy Foreign Affairs:* Jean Hamilius (Lib.). *Secretaries of State: Agriculture and Viticulture:* Albert Berchem (Lib.); *National Education:* Guy Linster (Soc.); *Labour and Social Security:* Maurice Thoss (Soc.).

Besides the Cabinet there is a Council of State. It deliberates on proposed laws and Bills, on amendments that might be proposed; it also gives administrative decisions and expresses its opinion regarding any other question referred to it by the Grand Duke or the Government. The Council of State is composed of 21 members chosen for life by the sovereign, who also chooses a president from among them each year.

DEFENCE. A law passed by Parliament on 29 June 1967 abolished compulsory service and instituted a battalion-size army of volunteers enlisted for 3 years. Strength (1977) 630. The defence estimates for 1977 amounted to 1,000m. francs. Luxembourg is an original member of NATO and the battalion is committed to NATO ACE mobile force.

INTERNATIONAL RELATIONS

Membership. Luxembourg is a member of the UN, Benelux, the EEC, OECD, the Council of Europe, NATO and WEU.

ECONOMY

Budget. Revenue and expenditure (including extraordinary) for years ending 30 April (in 1m. francs):

	1973	*1974*	*1975*	*1976*[1]	*1977*[2]	*1978*[2]
Revenue	20,959·5	25,692·1	28,370·3	33,112·4	35,924·7	39,110·9
Expenditure	19,724·6	23,542·8	27,956·2	32,796·2	36,637·0	39,363·0

[1] Provisional. [2] Budget.

Consolidated debt at 31 Dec. 1976 amounted to 16,522m. francs (long-term) and 2,341m. francs (short-term).

Currency. On 14 Oct 1944 the Luxembourg franc was fixed at par value with the Belgian franc. Notes of the Belgian National Bank are legal tender in Luxembourg.

Banking. On 31 Dec. 1976 there were 288,816 depositors in the State Savings Bank with a total of 21,460m. francs to their credit.

Weights and Measures. The metric system is in force.

ENERGY AND NATURAL RESOURCES

Electricity. Power production was 1,543m. kwh. in 1976.

Minerals. The mining and metallurgical industries are the most important. In 1976 production (in tonnes) of iron ore was 2,078,655; of pig-iron, 3,756,113; of steel, 4,565,773.

Agriculture. Agriculture is carried on by about 8,900 of the population; 131,393 hectares were under cultivation in 1976. The principal crops are potatoes, barley, beet, oats and wheat.

Livestock (May 1976): 1,751 horses, 213,745 cattle, 82,943 pigs, 3,837 sheep.

COMMERCE. By treaty of 5 Sept. 1944, signed in London, and the treaty of 14 March 1947, signed in The Hague, the Grand Duchy, together with Belgium and the Netherlands, became a party to the Benelux Customs Union, which came into force on 1 Jan. 1948. For further particulars *see* p. 202 and 881.

Total trade between Luxembourg and UK (British Department of Trade returns, in £1,000 sterling) from 1974 included with Belgium:

	1970	*1971*	*1972*	*1973*
Imports to UK	4,306	4,616	6,363	7,847
Exports and re-exports from UK	5,653	7,601	8,030	8,580

TOURISM. In 1976 there were approximately 500,000 tourists.

COMMUNICATIONS

Roads. In 1976 the network had a total of 5,051 km. Motor vehicles registered in Luxembourg on 1 Jan. 1977 included 130,719 passenger cars, 9,687 trucks, 651 buses, 15,296 tractors and special vehicles.

Railways. In 1976 there were 274 km of railway (standard gauge).

Aviation. Findel is the airport for Luxembourg.

Post and Broadcasting. In 1976 the telephone system had 2,224 km of telegraph and telephone line (1977), 157,829 telephones, 95 post offices and 459 telegraph offices. *Compagnie Luxembourgeoise de Télédiffusion* broadcasts 1 programme in Luxembourgian on FM. Powerful transmitters on long-, medium- and short-waves are used for commercial and religious programmes in French, Dutch, German, English and Italian. Five TV programmes are broadcast. Colour transmission by SECAM system. Number of receivers (estimate): radio, 200,000; television, 115,000.

Cinemas (1977). There were 20 cinemas.

Newspapers (1976). There were 6 daily newspapers with an aggregate circulation of 130,000.

RELIGION, EDUCATION AND WELFARE

Religion. The population is Catholic, save (31 Dec. 1970) 3,900 Protestants, 700 Jews, 2,100 belonging to other denominations and 3,700 without religion (or having given no indication on this subject). The Protestant Church is organized on an inter-denominational basis.

Education (1976–77). Education is compulsory for all children between the ages of 6 and 15. The primary schools had 34,500 pupils; state grammar schools had 8,400 pupils.

Middle, technical and vocational schools had 14,700 pupils. One teachers' training college had 140 students.

Health. In 1973 there were 375 doctors and about 4,000 hospital beds.

DIPLOMATIC REPRESENTATIVES

OF LUXEMBOURG IN GREAT BRITAIN
(27 Wilton Crescent, London, SWIX 8SD)

Ambassador: André Philippe, GCVO (accredited as ambassador, 9 March 1972).

OF GREAT BRITAIN IN LUXEMBOURG (28 Boulevard Royal, Luxembourg)

Ambassador and Consul-General: P. R. H. Wright.

OF LUXEMBOURG IN THE USA (2200 Massachusetts Ave. NW, Washington, D.C., 20008)

Ambassador: Adrien Meisch.

OF THE USA IN LUXEMBOURG (22 Blvd. Emmanuel Servais, Luxembourg)

Ambassador: James G. Lowenstein.

OF LUXEMBOURG TO THE UNITED NATIONS

Ambassador: Paul Peters.

Books of Reference

Statistical Information: The Service Central de la Statistique et des Études Économiques was founded in 1900 and reorganized in 1962 (48, rue Charles Arendt, C.P. 304 (Luxembourg-City). *Director:* Georges Als. Main publications: *Bulletin du Statec.—Annuaire statistique.—Cahiers économiques.*

Bulletin de Documentation. Government Information Service. From 1945 (monthly)
Luxembourg 963–1963. Le livre du millénaire. Luxembourg, 1963
Tausend Jahre Luxemburg. Luxembourg, 1963
Cooper-Pritchard, A. H., *History of the Grand-Duchy of Luxembourg.* Luxembourg, 1950
Majerus, P., *Le Luxembourg indépendant.* Luxembourg, 1948.—*L'État Luxembourgeois.* Luxembourg, 1948
Petit, J., *Luxemburg, plateforme internationale.* Luxembourg, 1960
Weber, P., *Histoire du Grand-Duché de Luxembourg.* Brussels, 1949.—*Histoire de l'économie luxembourgeoise.* Luxembourg, 1950

Archives of the State: Luxembourg-City. *Director:* Paul Spang.
National Library: Luxembourg-City, 14a Boulevard Royal. *Director:* Gilbert Trausch.

MADAGASCAR

Capital: Antananarivo
Population: 8m. (1977)
GNP per capita: US$200 (1976)

The Democratic Republic of Madagascar

HISTORY. Madagascar was discovered by the Portuguese, Diego Diaz, in 1500. On the return of Diaz to Portugal the King concluded that the island must be Madagascar, about which he had read in Marco Polo's 'Voyages'. Polo, however, had not been there, but believing his Arab informants, ascribed to an island what was really the kingdom of Mogadisho, on the east coast of Africa. Mispronouncing and mis-spelling the name, he coined the word Madagascar.

The last native sovereign in Madagascar, Queen Ranavalona III (born 1845, died 1917), succeeded in 1883. The French claimed a portion of the north-west coast as having been transferred to them by local chiefs, and hostilities were carried on in 1883–85 against the Merina, who refused to recognize the cession. In 1885 peace was made, Diégo-Suarez having been surrendered to France. A French expedition was dispatched in May 1895 to enforce the claims of France and on 1 Oct. the Queen accepted the protectorate.

By a law promulgated 6 Aug. 1896 the island and its dependencies were declared a French colony.

On 14 Oct. 1958 Madagascar was proclaimed a republic. The republic was admitted to the UN on 21 Sept. 1960.

AREA AND POPULATION. Madagascar is situated off the south-east coast of Africa, from which it is separated by the Mozambique Channel, the least distance between island and continent being 250 miles; its length is 980 miles; greatest breadth, 360 miles.

The area is 594,180 sq. km (229,233 sq. miles). In 1973 the population was 7,185,000 (48% under 18 years). Estimate (1977) 8m.

In 1978 there were 30,000 Europeans, mainly French, resident on the island. Indians, 16,000, and Chinese, 9,000, carry on small retail trade.

Population (and area in sq. km) of the provinces (1 Jan. 1971): Diégo-Suarez, 621,549 (43,900); Fianarantsoa, 1,861,492 (103,270); Majunga, 918,263 (152,860); Toamasina, 1,223,377 (72,080); Tananarive, 1·86m. (59,090); Toliary, 1,168,872 (166,590).

The populations of the chief towns were in 1978, the capital Antananarivo, formerly Tananarive, 400,000; Toamasina, 59,100; Majunga 57,500; Fianarantsoa, 55,500; Diégo-Suarez, 48,000; Toliary, 34,000.

Vital statistics, 1971: Births, 279,583; deaths, 85,129.

CONSTITUTION AND GOVERNMENT. The constitution of the republic was promulgated on 29 April 1959 and amended in June 1960. It provided for a national assembly of 107 and a senate of 52 members. The government consisted of a president and 38 ministers. On 18 May 1972 the government was dissolved. A decree issued later gave Gen. Gabriel Ramanantsoa supreme power for up to 5 years. A provisional Constitutional law was issued on 8 Oct. 1972.

On 5 Feb. 1975 Col. Richard Ratsimandrava became Head of State and also held the portfolios of Defence and Planning. Col. Ratsimandrava was assassinated on 11 Feb. 1975 and the Minister of State without Portfolio, Brig.-Gen. Gilles Andriamahazo immediately declared martial law and on 12 Feb. established a National Military Directorate. Capt. Ratsiraka was sworn in as President on 21 Dec. 1975 when a new Constitution was approved.

The republic is divided into the 6 provinces and each is under the supervision of a field officer. The provinces are subdivided into prefectures, sub-prefectures, arrondissements and cantons. Each canton comprises a number of *fokontany*.

President: Didier Ratsiraka.

The Cabinet was in Aug. 1977 composed as follows:

Prime Minister: Lieut.-Col. Désiré Rakotoarijaona.

Foreign Affairs: Richard Christian Rémi. *National Defence:* Capt. Guy Sibon. *Primary and Secondary Education:* Théophile Andrianoelisoi. *Scientific Research and Higher Education:* Ignace Rakoto. *Information and Ideological Guidance:* Georges Ruffin. *Revolutionary Art and Culture:* Giselle Rabesahala.

National flag: Horizontally red over green, in the hoist a vertical white strip.

National anthem: Ry tanindrazanay malala ô!

Malagasy, which is a language of Malayo-Polynesian origin, is the official language. French and English is understood and taught in Malagasy schools.

DEFENCE

Army. The Army in 1977 had a strength of 9,550 organized in 2 infantry battalions, 1 engineer battalion and 1 service battalion.

Air Force. Created in 1961 and maintained with French Air Force assistance, the Malagasy Air Force is equipped for transport and communications duties, with 1 Britten-Norman Defender armed transport, 10 C-47s, 5 Flamants, 4 Broussards, 1 Aztec, 3 Cessna Skymasters, 4 Cessna 172Ms and 4 helicopters, comprising 1 Bell 47, 1 Alouette II and 2 Alouette IIIs.

INTERNATIONAL RELATIONS

Membership. Madagascar is a member of UN, OAU and is an ACP state of EEC.

ECONOMY

Planning. A development plan, 1974–77, provided for a total expenditure of 169,239m. francs. The main aim is to increase agricultural production through the rural reform plan based on the *fokonolama* communes and distributive co-operatives.

Budget. The local revenue is derived chiefly from income tax, from customs and other indirect taxes, from territorial lands, from posts and telegraphs, markets and miscellaneous sources. The chief branches of expenditure are general administration, public works, health services, education, the post office and the public debt. The general budget for 1977 provided for an expenditure of 137,400m. FMG.

Currency. The Malagasy franc (FMG) = 0·02 French francs.

Banking. The Banque Nationale Malagasy de Développement (BNM) created in 1963 to replace the Société Malgache d'Investissement et de Crédit is the national investment bank. The Banque de Madagascar et des Comores was formerly the bank of issue, but this privilege was, on 8 March 1962, transferred to a new national institute, the Institut d'Emission Malgache and later, in July 1973, this institute was replaced by the Central Bank. The other commercial banks are: Banque Malagasy d'Escompte et de Crédit (BAMES) (the Comptoir National d'Escompte de Paris holds 65% of its capital, the rest being owned by the Malagasy Government) with 9 offices throughout the island and 2 sub-offices in Antananarivo; the Banque Nationale pour le Commerce et l'Industrie (BNCI) with 9 offices and 2 sub-offices (in Antananarivo); the Banque Française pour le Commerce which has 1 office and 2 sub-offices in Antananarivo and 1 office in Toamasina.

The savings bank had, at 30 Sept. 1972, 90,071 depositors.

Weights and Measures. The metric system is in use.

ENERGY AND NATURAL RESOURCES

Electricity. The consumption of electric power in 1971 amounted to 210m. kwh.

Minerals. Mining production (in tonnes) included: Mica (1975), 1,914; graphite

(1976), 17,402; chrome (1975), 194,127; ilmenite, 1,857; zircon, 209; beryl, 1971 (industrial), 52; gold (1971), 17 kg; garnet, 1971 (industrial), 40.

Agriculture. The principal agricultural products in 1975 were (in 1,000 tonnes): Rice, 1,813; cloves, 4·5; vanilla, 1·43; coffee, 65; groundnuts, 38·6; sugar, 1,092; tobacco, 3·3; pepper, 2·6; cotton, 30·7; cape peas, 15·8.

Cattle breeding and agriculture are the chief occupations. There were, in 1976, 9·84m. cattle, 680,000 pigs, 700,000 sheep, 1·3m. goats and 13m. poultry.

Forestry. The forests contain many valuable woods, while gum, resins and plants for tanning, dyeing and medicinal purposes abound.

Fisheries. The fish catch in 1974 was 50,000 tonnes

INDUSTRY AND TRADE

Industry. Industry, hitherto confined mainly to the processing of agricultural products, is now extending to cover other fields. Thus in addition to rice milling, sugar making, distilling, oil-seed crushing, meat, fruit and vegetable canning, cigarette and chewing-tobacco production, soap and rope manufactures, cotton spinning and weaving, brewing, processing of cashew nuts, fruit juices and jams and meat canning, it now includes an oil refinery, a paper-mill, 2 vehicle assembly plants, plants for the assembly of batteries, transistor radio and television sets and bicycles, a plastics factory, 2 paint factories, metal furniture and window making, tyre-retreading and foam-rubber plants, an animal-feed factory, an iron-sheeting and nail-making plant, a metal packing plant, 2 undertakings producing aluminium ware, a chemical works and 2 biscuit and confectionery factories. The oil refinery at Toamasina, which came on stream in 1966, has a capacity of 12,500 bbls a day. A second cotton-mill started production in 1970. A second cement factory is projected; the existing one produced 71,000 tonnes in 1972.

Commerce. Trade in 1m. FMG:

	1974	*1975*	*1976*
Imports	70,028	80,701	64,577
Exports	57,733	70,791	65,370

In 1972 the chief imports (in 1m. FMG) were: Metalware, 5,509; chemicals, 5,453; mineral products, 5,061; wines, 553; food, 17,136. The chief exports in 1972 were: Foodstuffs, 75,802; textiles, 24,962; animal products, 1,479.

Total trade between Malagasy Republic and UK (British Department of Trade returns, in £1,000 sterling):

	1973	*1974*	*1975*	*1976*	*1977*
Imports to UK	1,922	3,183	5,629	4,032	3,826
Exports and re-exports from UK	763	1,870	1,764	2,698	2,786

COMMUNICATIONS

Roads. At the end of 1968 there were 40,000 km of roads suitable for motor traffic, of which 8,364 km are practicable all the year round. There is a motor-car service with a network of routes covering about 2,797 km. Motor vehicles registered at 1 Jan. 1971 included 45,992 passenger cars, 3,149 buses, 2,882 commercial vehicles, 31,147 lorries, 2,660 tractors and 4,724 motor cycles.

Railways. Four railways are operating, namely: between Antananarivo and Toamasina (376 km); between Antananarivo and Antsirabe (noted for its thermal springs), 158 km: the branch line of the Toamasina railway, from Moramanga to Lake Alaotra (168 km) and the line from Fianarantsoa Manakara on to the east coast (165 km). All metre-gauge. In 1972, 2·2m. passengers and 623,000 tonnes of cargo were transported.

Aviation. Air France and Air Madagascar connect Antananarivo with Paris, Alitalia connects with Rome. Several weekly services operated by Air Madagascar connect the capital with the ports and the chief inland towns. The main airfields are at Ivato, Toamasina, Tuléar and Majunga. In 1968, 67,365 passengers, 2,446 tonnes of cargo and 82 tonnes of mail departed on international flights.

Shipping. Toamasina, Majunga, Diégo-Suarez, Tuléar, Nossi-Bé and Manakara are the principal ports. In 1968, 5,237 vessels of 1,090,846 tons entered these ports.

Post and Broadcasting. There were in 1971, 547 post offices and agencies and 55 wireless telegraph stations. The telegraph line has a length of 17,400 km. There were 66,000 km of telephone line and 29,324 telephone subscribers. Direct telephone communications exist between Antananarivo, Paris, Mauritius and Réunion. Wireless telegraph was established between Antananarivo and Fianarantsoa in Oct. 1962 and between Antananarivo and Paris in April 1972.

Cinemas. There were, in 1974, 31 cinemas with a seating capacity of 12,500.

RELIGION, EDUCATION AND WELFARE

Religion. Since 1818 a large portion of the Merina and other ethnic groups in the central districts have been Christianized. Many of the missionary societies which worked in Madagascar have now established churches. The 2 largest religious bodies are Roman Catholics with 1·4m. members (5,000 churches) and Fiangonan'i Jesosy Kristy eto Madagascar (FJKM) with 1·03m. members and 5,161 churches. There are also other smaller Christian churches and 75 mosques.

Education. Education is compulsory from 6 to 14 years of age in the primary schools. In 1972 there were 938,015 pupils in public primary schools and 260,726 in private schools. The total number of primary schools was 6,054. There were 508 colleges of general education and 18 *lycées* with a total of 105,320 students. There is a co-educational university at Antananarivo with faculties of Law, Science and Letters. The total student body in 1972 was 5,648.

There are also 4 agricultural schools at Nanisana, Ambatondrazaka, Marovoay and Ivoloina.

Health. In 1973 there were 700 doctors.

DIPLOMATIC REPRESENTATIVES

OF THE MALAGASY REPUBLIC IN GREAT BRITAIN
(33 Thurloe Sq., London, SW7 2SB)

Ambassador: (Vacant).

OF GREAT BRITAIN IN THE MALAGASY REPUBLIC
(41 Lalana Razanakombana, Antananarivo)

Ambassador: M. Brown, CMG, OBE (resides at Dar es Salaam).

OF THE MALAGASY REPUBLIC IN THE USA
(2374 Massachusetts Ave., NW, Washington, D.C., 20008)

Chargé d'Affaires: Norbert Rakotomalala.

OF THE USA IN THE MALAGASY REPUBLIC
(14 rue Rainitovo, Antsohavola, Antananarivo)

Chargé d'Affaires: Robert S. Barett.

OF THE MALAGASY REPUBLIC TO THE
UNITED NATIONS

Ambassador: Blaise Rabetafika.

Books of Reference

Statistical Information: The Service de Statistique Générale in Antananarivo published the *Bulletin mensuel de Madagascar* (from 1971); continuation of the trimestrial *Bulletin de statistique générale* (1949–71), the *Revue de Madagascar*, the *Madagascar à travers ses provinces* (latest issue, 1953), the *Annuaire Statistique de Madagascar* (vol. 1, 1938–51, published 1953, the *Situation Economique au Janvier 1968, Population de Madagascar au 1er* Jan. 1971, and the *Statistiques du Commerce Extérieur de Madagascar*).

Bulletin de l'Académie Malgache (from 1902)
Deschamps, H., *Histoire de Madagascar*. Paris, 1960
Heseltine, N., *Madagascar*. London and New York, 1971
Saron, G., *Madagascar et les Comores*. Paris, 1953
Thompson, V., and Adloff, R., *The Malagasy Republic*. Stanford Univ. Press, 1965

MALAWI

Capital: Lilongwe
Population: 5·31m. (1977)
GNP per capita: US$140 (1976)

HISTORY. Malawi was formerly the Nyasaland (until 1907 British Central Africa) Protectorate, constituted on 15 May 1891.

Nyasaland became a self-governing country on 1 Feb. 1963, and on 6 July 1964 an independent member of the Commonwealth under the name of Malawi. It became a Republic on 6 July 1966.

AREA AND POPULATION. Malawi lies along the southern and western shores of Lake Malawi (the third largest lake in Africa), and is otherwise bounded north by Tanzania, south by Mozambique and west by Zambia. Land area (excluding inland water of Lakes Palombe, Chilwa and Chiuta) 36,325 sq. miles, divided into 3 regions and 24 districts, each administered by a District Commissioner.

Lake Malawi waters belonging to Malawi are 9,250 sq. miles and the whole Lake Malawi (including the waters under Mozambique by an agreement made between the two countries in 1950) is 11,650 sq. miles.

The results of the census held in Aug. 1966: 4,020,724 Africans, 11,299 Asians, 7,395 Europeans, 165 undetermined; total 4,039,583 (1,913,262 males, 2,126,321 females). Estimate (1977), 5·31m. Over 90% of the population live in rural areas.

Population of main towns (census 1977) was as follows: Blantyre, 228,520; Lilongwe, 102,924; Zomba, 15,705; Mzuzu, 16,119. The capital was Zomba, and on 1 Jan. 1975 Lilongwe, in the Central Region, was officially declared the capital. All ministries were to be located there by 1977–78.

Population of the regions, 1966 (and census 1977): Northern, 497,491 (643,485); Central, 1,474,952 (2,122,010); Southern, 2,067,140 (2,806,072).

CONSTITUTION AND GOVERNMENT. The President of the Republic is also head of Government and of the Malawi Congress Party.

Malawi is a one-party state. Parliament is composed of 87 elected members and up to 15 nominated members.

The Cabinet was in Oct. 1977 composed as follows:

Life President, External Affairs, Agriculture and Natural Resources, Justice, Works and Supplies: Ngwazi Dr H. Kamuzu Banda.

Youth and Culture: Gwanda Chakuamba Phiri. *Without Portfolio:* E. B. Muluzi. *Finance:* D. T. Matenje. *Education:* W. A. H. Lweya. *Trade, Industry and Tourism:* Edward Bwanali. *Health:* S. H. M. Chinsamba Kwenda. *Transport and Communications:* Robson Chirwa. *Local Government:* T. T. Phaiya. *Community Development and Social Welfare:* R. Kapichila Banda. *Labour:* W. B. Deleza. *Minister at Large:* R. B. Chidzanja Nkhoma. *Regional Ministers:* M. Malani Lungu (North), Joseph R. Mlelemba (South), Aaron Gadama (Centre).

National flag: Three equal horizontal stripes of black, red, green, with a red rising sun on the centre of the black stripe.

DEFENCE

Army. The army consists of a headquarters—a large infantry battalion complete with its own supporting arms and services—and a depot back-up of an engineering workshop and an ordnance depot in Zomba, Lilongwe and at Mzuzu. The total strength is 54 officers and 1,050 other ranks.

Navy. There are 3 small lake patrol boats.

INTERNATIONAL RELATIONS

Membership. Malawi is a member of UN, the Commonwealth, OAU and is an ACP state of EEC.

ECONOMY

Planning. The Government of Malawi operates a 3-year 'rolling' public-sector investment programme, revised annually to take into account changing needs and the expected level of resources available. The greatest part of the development programme is annually financed from external aid, and priority in the use of resources has always been given to providing the counterpart contributions to funds received from external sources. The balance of these local resources is used for financing projects commanding high national priority for which no external funds can be secured.

The two tables below give a summary of the Government's Development Programme for the 3 years 1977–78–1979–80 and the sources of finance (in K.1m.):

Government Development Expenditure	*1977–78*	*1978–79*	*1979–80*	*Total 3 Years*	%
Agriculture and natural resources	22·1	19·1	18·7	59·9	17·2
Transportation	50·3	58·9	51·8	161·0	46·4
Posts and telecommunications	4·2	4·4	1·4	10·0	2·9
Power	10·5	14·8	15·0	40·3	11·6
Education	5·9	6·4	5·2	17·5	5·0
Health	1·9	2·8	2·2	6·9	2·0
Water supplies and sanitation	6·4	5·5	3·1	15·0	4·3
New capital—Lilongwe	2·7	1·2	0·8	4·7	1·4
Housing	3·0	2·5	1·7	7·2	2·1
Other	8·5	11·3	4·9	24·7	7·1
Total	115·5	126·9	104·8	347·2	100·0

Finance					
British government loan	11·5	10·6	11·2	33·3	9·5
Other externally financed	2·8	1·5	—	4·3	1·2
External Financed	88·1	101·2	80·4	269·7	77·7
Counterpart to external aid	8·9	9·0	8·3	26·2	7·6
Wholly locally financed projects	4·2	4·6	4·9	13·7	3·9
Total	115·5	126·9	104·8	347·2	100·0

Budget. Revenue Account receipts and expenditure (in K.1,000) for years ending 31 March:

	1972–73	*1973–74*	*1974–75*	*1975–76*	*1976–77*[1]
Revenue	56,945	63,097	78,687	89,701	89,860
Expenditure	57,031	61,733	73,831	84,422	90,827

[1] Provisional.

Main revenue items (in K.1,000) in 1976–77 are: Direct taxes, 34,902; indirect taxes, 34,805.

Main expenditure items (in K.1,000) in 1975–76 were: Public debt charges, 12,714; education, 11,867; general administration, 9,152.

Currency. In 1971 a new decimalized currency was introduced. the *kwacha* (dawn), which is subdivided into 100 *tambala* (cockerels). From 9 June 1975 the kwacha has been pegged to Special Drawing Rights. Official exchange rate 5 Sept. 1977: £1 sterling = K1·5768, US$1 = K0·9070.

Banking. In July 1964 the Reserve Bank of Malawi was set up with a capital of K1m. to be responsible for the issue of currency and the holding of external reserves and to issue treasury bills and local registered stock on behalf of the Government. Since then, the Reserve Bank has fully assumed the responsibilities of a Central Bank.

The National Bank of Malawi has a total of 10 branches in major urban areas and 19 static and 35 mobile agencies in rural areas. The Commercial Bank of Malawi Ltd opened in 1970 and has branches at Limbe and Lilongwe and an agency in Dedza and headquarters at Blantyre.

In 1972 The Investment Development Bank of Malawi was established in

Blantyre. Its resources are derived from domestic and foreign official sources and its objective is to provide medium and long-term credits to private entities considered of importance to the economy.

The post office savings bank has 223 offices conducting savings business throughout the country, and the New Building Society has agencies in Limbe, Zomba and Lilongwe with its head office in Blantyre. Two finance houses now operate in Malawi, providing longer-term industrial and consumer finance.

Total money in the country, 1976, K.58·4m.; total domestic credit, K.141·5m.

Weights and Measures. British measures are in use; the metric system is being introduced gradually.

ENERGY AND NATURAL RESOURCES

Electricity. The first stage of the Tedzani Project, two 8 mw. sets, was commissioned in July 1973 which, together with the 24 mw. Nkula hydro-electric station, will meet the power demands of the interconnected systems of the Southern Region and Lilongwe. With the completion of a barrage at Tedzani these machines will be uprated to 10 mw. each and, with the addition of thermal plant to the system, sufficient power will be available to meet forecast demands prior to the commissioning in 1977 of the second stage of the Tedzani Project, a further two 10 mw. sets. The Electricity Supply Commission also operates stations at Mangochi, Mzuzu, Kasungu, Liwonde, Chikwawa and Salima. A total of 252·96m. kwh. were sold by the Electricity Supply Commission in 1976.

Minerals. The main product in 1976 was marble (149,254 tonnes) for the manufacture of cement.

Agriculture. Malawi is predominantly an agricultural country. Up to March 1977 519,300 of the rural population had been reached by self-help piped water projects, of which 427,700 were in the Southern region. In 1976 agriculture contributed 46·1% to the GDP, and agricultural produce accounted for over 79% of total exports. Of the total area of 23·3m. acres, 13·1m. could be cultivated and, in 1969, 3·36m. were being cultivated, of which 2·64m. were under maize. Maize is the main subsistence crop and is grown by over 95% of all smallholders. Almost all the surplus crops produced by smallholders are sold to the Agricultural Development and Marketing Corporation. In 1976 the corporation purchased: Groundnuts, K.5·38m.; tobacco, K.6·03m.; cotton, K.3·02m.; maize, K.3·54m.; rice, K.2·42m.; pulses, K.1·9m.

Livestock in 1976: Cattle, 728,500; sheep and goats, 850,000; pigs, 190,000.

Forestry. In 1976 (estimate) 535,510 cu. ft of sawn timber were produced, valued at K.1·3m. The value of other forest products was K.536,986.

Fisheries. Landings in 1976 (provisional) were 80,800 short tons valued at K.8m.

INDUSTRY AND TRADE

Industry. Index of manufacturing output (1970 = 100): manufacturing for domestic consumption, 177·7 (186·5 in 1975); of this consumer goods were at 191·9 (194·8) and intermediate goods mainly for building and construction were at 128·6 (157·6). Manufacturing for export, 172·3 (154).

Labour:

	1976		
	Private	*Government*	*Total*
Agriculture, forestry, fishing	70,934	6,947	79,227
Mining and Quarrying	707	3	710
Manufacturing	32,319	1,116	33,435
Electricity and Water	2,196	878	3,074
Building and Construction	15,735	5,389	21,124
Trade, Hotels, Restaurants	21,558	—	21,558
Transport, Storage, Communications	9,476	2,926	12,402
Financial Services	3,231	68	3,299
Community, Social, Personal Services	10,354	51,819	62,173
Total	166,510	70,492	237,002

Commerce. The main items of export in 1976 were (in K.): Tobacco, 65·2m.; tea, 26·2m.; sugar, 17·4m.; groundnuts, 11·3m. Malawi's imports in the same year included consumer goods, 25·2m.; capital equipment, 58·8m.; building materials, 19·5m.; means of transport, 26·4m.

Trade statistics for calendar years are (in K.):

	1973	*1974*	*1975*	*1976*
Imports	114,651,000	157,726,000	218,663,000	188,074,000
Exports	79,919,000	101,306,000	122,122,000	146,363,000

Total trade between UK and Malawi (British Department of Trade returns, in £1,000 sterling):

	1974	*1975*	*1976*	*1977*
Imports to UK	16,088	28,282	35,496	51,040
Exports and re-exports from UK	10,552	17,575	16,594	18,359

Tourism. There were 57,702 visitors to Malawi in 1975. They spent about K.70·36 per person.

COMMUNICATIONS

Roads. In 1976 there were 1,877 miles of main road, of which 772 were bitumen-surfaced and 206 gravel; 1,520 miles of secondary roads, of which 215 were surfaced; 3,426 miles of district and other roads, of which 148 were surfaced. Motor vehicles licensed, 29,085, of which 10,222 were cars and 10,642 goods vehicles.

Railways. Malawi Railways (541 km—1,067 mm gauge) operates a main line from Salima to the Mozambique border near Nsanje, from which running powers over the Trans-Zambesia Railway allow access to the port of Beira; a branch opened in 1970 runs eastwards from a point 10 miles south of Balaka to the Mozambique border to give a direct route to the deep-water port of Nacala. The 16-mile section from Nsanje to the border is operated by the Central Africa Railway Co. Ltd. The construction of another railway line (102 km) from Salima through Lilongwe to the Zambian border was opened in May 1978. In 1976 (provisional) 1m. passengers were carried; freight (1m. net ton-miles), 135·8.

Aviation. In 1976 Chileka airport handled 173,468 passengers and 11,451·8 tonnes of freight. Lilongwe airport handled 28,752 and 324·6 tonnes.

Shipping. In 1976 lake ships carried 131,000 passengers and 33,000 short tons of freight.

Newspapers (1977). *The Daily Times* (English, Monday to Friday); 5,700–6,300 copies daily. *Malawi News* (English and Chichewa, Saturdays); 6,700 copies weekly. *The African* (English and Chichewa, Fortnightly).

JUSTICE, RELIGION, EDUCATION AND WELFARE

Justice. Justice is administered in the High Court, the magistrates' courts and traditional courts. There are 23 magistrates' courts, 176 traditional courts and 23 local appeal courts.

Appeals from traditional courts are dealt with in the traditional appeal courts and in the national traditional appeal court. Appeals from magistrates' courts lie to the High Court, and appeals from the High Court to Malawi's Supreme Court of Appeal.

Religion. In 1972 the Roman Catholic Church claimed 1,073,000 members; the Presbyterian Church of Central Africa, 846,000; the Diocese of Malawi (part of the Province of Central Africa of the Anglican Communion), 79,000; Seventh Day Adventist Church, 93,000; Zambezi Evangelical Church (formerly Nayas Mission), 36,000; Assemblies of God, 7,000; Seventh-Day Baptists (Central Africa conference), 11,000; Churches of Christ, 21,000; African Evangelical Church, 7,000; Evangelical Church of Malawi, 18,000. Moslems are estimated to number between 500,000 and 1m.

Education (1975–76). The Ministry of Education controls all aspects of education.

The number of pupils in the 2,091 primary schools was 641,709; in the 61 secondary schools, 14,489. There were 10,588 teachers in primary schools and 748 in secondary schools. The primary school course is of 8 years duration, followed by a 4-year secondary course. English is taught from the 1st year and becomes the general medium of instruction from the 4th year.

Teacher-training is undertaken in 8 residential colleges, 2 of which are directly controlled by the Ministry; the others receive grants in aid as assisted institutions. Courses last 3 years. Enrolment 1,100. Technical and trade courses are offered in commerce, building, woodwork and mechanical engineering, as well as home craft for girls; 1,904 trainees undertook courses at government and voluntary schools in 1966.

The University of Malawi was inaugurated on 6 Oct. 1965. In 1975–76 there were 1,148 students taking degree and diploma courses.

Health. In 1975 there were 482 medical institutions and 8,991 hospital beds.

DIPLOMATIC REPRESENTATIVES

OF MALAWI IN GREAT BRITAIN
(33 Grosvenor St., London, W1)

High Commissioner: Victor Timothy Likaku (accredited 8 Feb. 1977).

OF GREAT BRITAIN IN MALAWI (Lingadzi Hse, Lilongwe, 3)

High Commissioner: M. Scott, CMG, MVO.

OF MALAWI IN THE USA (1400 20th St., NW, Washington, D.C., 20036)

Ambassador: Jacob T. X. Muwamba.

OF THE USA IN MALAWI (P.O. Box 30016, Lilongwe)

Ambassador: Robert A. Stevenson.

OF MALAWI TO THE UNITED NATIONS

Ambassador: T. J. X. Muwamba.

Books of Reference

General Information: The Chief Information Officer, P.O. Box 494, Blantyre.
Clutton-Brock, G., *Dawn in Nyasaland.* London, 1964
Debenham, F., *Nyasaland.* HMSO, 1964
Gelfand, M., *Lakeside Pioneers. Socio-medical Study of Nyasaland, 1875–1920.* Oxford, 1964
Jones, G., *Britain and Nyasaland.* London, 1964
McMaster, C., *Malawi: Foreign Policy and Development.* London, 1974
Pike, J. G., *Malawi, A Political History.* London, 1967
Pike and Rimmington, *Malawi, a Geographical Study.* Oxford, 1965
Read, F. E., *Malawi, Land of Promise.* Govt. Dept. of Information, 1967.—*Malawi, Land of Progress.* Govt. Dept. of Information, 1969

MALAYSIA

Capital: Kuala Lumpur
Population: 12·63m. (1976)
GNP per capita: US$860 (1976)

HISTORY. On 16 Sept. 1963 Malaysia came into being, consisting of the Federation of Malaya, the State of Singapore and the colonies of North Borneo (renamed Sabah) and Sarawak. The agreement between the UK and the 4 territories was signed on 9 July (Cmnd. 2094); by it, the UK relinquished sovereignty over Singapore, North Borneo and Sarawak from independence day and extended the 1957 defence agreement with Malaya to apply to Malaysia. Malaysia became automatically a member of the Commonwealth of Nations. *See* map in THE STATESMAN'S YEAR-BOOK, 1964–65.

On 9 Aug. 1965, by a mutual agreement dated 7 Aug. 1965 between Malaysia and Singapore, Singapore seceded from Malaysia to become an independent Sovereign nation.

POPULATION. The 1970 census gave a total of 8,809,557. Estimates, 1976, 12,629,381; 10,713,187 for Peninsular Malaysia; 765,915 in Sabah, and 1,150,279 in Sarawak.

CONSTITUTION AND GOVERNMENT. The Constitution of Malaysia is based on the Constitution of the former Federation of Malaya, but includes safeguards for the special interests of Sabah and Sarawak.

The federal capital is Kuala Lumpur, established on 1 Feb. 1974 with an area of approximately 94 sq. miles. The official language is Malay.

The Constitution provides for one of the 9 Rulers of the Malay States to be elected from among themselves to be the Yang di-Pertuan Agong (Supreme Head of the Federation). He holds office for a period of 5 years. The Rulers also elect from among themselves a Deputy Supreme Head of State, also for a period of 5 years.

Supreme Head of State (*Yang di-Pertuan Agong*): HM Al-Sultan Yahya Petra Ibrahim ibni Al-Marhum Sultan, DK, DMN, SMN, SPMK, SJMK, SPSK, Ruler of Kelantan (elected 21 Sept. 1975).

Raja of Perlis: HRH Tuanku Syed Putra ibni Al-Marhum Syed Hassan Jamalullail, DK, DKM, DMN, SMN, SPMP, acceded 12 March 1949.

Sultan of Kedah: HRH Tuanku Haji Abdul Halim Mu'adzam Shah ibni Al-Marhum Sultan Badlishah, DK, DKH, DKM, DMN, DJK, SPMK, SSDK, acceded 20 Feb. 1959.

Sultan of Pahang: HRH Sultan Haji Ahmad Shah Al-Musta'in Billah ibni Al-Marhum Sultan Abu Bakar Ri'ayatuddin Al-Mu' Adzam Shah, DK, DMN, SIMP, acceded 7 May 1974 (Deputy Head of State, elected 8 May 1975).

Sultan of Johore: HRH Sultan Ismail ibni Al-Marhum Sultan Ibrahim, DK, DMN, SMN, SPMJ, acceded 10 Feb. 1960.

Regent of Kelantan: HRH Tengku Ismail Petra ibni Al-Sultan Yahya Petra, DK, SPMK, appointed 21 Sept. 1975.

Sultan of Selangor: HRH Sultan Salahuddin Abdul Aziz Shah ibni Al-Marhum Sultan Hisamuddin 'Alam Shah Al-Haj, DK, DMN, SPMS, acceded 28 June 1961.

Sultan of Perak: HRH Sultan Idris Al-Mutawakkil Alallahi Shah ibni Al-Marhum Sultan Iskandar Shah Kadasallah, DK, DMN, SPMP, acceded 26 Oct. 1963.

Yang di-Pertuan Besar of Negri Sembilan: HRH Tuanku Ja'afar ibni Al-Marhum Tuanku Abdul Rahman, DMN, DK, acceded 8 April, 1968.

Sultan of Trengganu: HRH Sultan Ismail Nasiruddin Shah ibni Al-Marhum Sultan Zainal Abidin, DK, DKM, DMN, SPMT (acceded 6 June 1949).

Governor of Malacca: HE Tan Sri Syed Zahiruddin bin Syed Hassan, PSM, SPMP, JMN, PJK, appointed 23 May 1975.

Governor of Sarawak: HE Datuk Pattinggi Abang Muhammed Salahuddin, DP, appointed 2 April 1977.

Yang di-Pertua Negara Sabah: HE Datuk Ahmad Koroh, SPDK, appointed 11 Oct. 1977.

Governor of Penang: HE Tan Sri Datuk Sardon bin Haji Jubir, PMN, DUPN, SPMJ, appointed 5 Feb. 1975.

Parliament consists of the *Yang di-Pertuan Agong* and two *Majlis* (Houses of Parliament) known as the *Dewan Negara* (Senate) of 58 members and *Dewan Rakyat* (House of Representatives) of 154 members. There are 149 members from the states in Malaysia and 5 from the Federal Territory. Appointment to the Senate is for 6 years. The maximum life of the House of Representatives is 5 years, subject to its dissolution at any time by the *Yang di-Pertuan Agong* on the advice of his Ministers.

National flag: Fourteen horizontal stripes of red and white, with a blue quarter bearing a crescent and a star of 14 points, all in gold.

The elections to the House of Representatives held on 24 Aug. 1974, returned the following members: National Front, 135; Democratic Action Party, 9; Sarawak National Party, 9; PEKEMAS, 1.

The Cabinet was in Nov. 1977 composed as follows:

Prime Minister and Minister of Defence: Datuk Hussein bin Onn, DK.

Deputy Prime Minister, Finance and Education: Dr Mahathir bin Mohamad. *Agriculture and Rural Development:* (Vacant). *Labour and Manpower:* Datuk Lee San Choon, SPMJ, KMN. *Communications:* Tan Sri V. Manickavasagam, PMN, SPMS. *Lands, Mines and Special Functions:* Datuk Haji Mohd. Asri bin Haji Muda, SPMK, SPDK. *Trade and Industry:* Datuk Haji Hamzah bin Datuk Abu Samah, SMK, SIMP. *Local Government and Environment:* Tan Sri Ong Kee Hui, PMN, PNBS. *Home Affairs:* Tan Sri Haji Muhammad Ghazali bin Shafie, PMN, SIMP, DPK. *Transport and Works:* Datuk Haji Abdul Ghani Gilong, SPDK, JP. *Health:* Tan Sri Lee Siok Yew, PMN, PJK. *Law and Attorney-General:* Tan Sri Datuk Haji Abdul Kadir bin Yusof, PMN, SPDK, SPMJ. *Welfare Services:* Puan Hajjah Aishah binti Haji Abdul Ghani, JMN. *Information and Special Functions:* Datuk Amar Haji Abdul Taib bin Mahmud, PDK, PGDK. *Culture, Youth and Sports:* Datuk Ali bin Haji Ahmad, SPMJ. *Foreign Affairs:* Y. M. Tengku Ahmad Rithauddeen Al-Haj bin Tengku Ismail, PMK. *Power, Technology and Research:* Datuk Haji Mohamed bin Yaacob, PGDK, PMK, SMT. *Housing and New Villages:* Encik Michael Chen Wing Sum. *Primary Industry:* Datuk Musa bin Hitam, SPMJ. *Co-ordination of Public Corporations:* Datuk Mohamed Yacob.

DEFENCE. The Malaysian Armed Forces is made up of the Malaysian Army, the Royal Malaysian Navy and the Royal Malaysian Air Force. Each Service has its own component of reserves.

The Malaysian Constitution provides for the *Yang di-Pertuan Agong* (Supreme Head of State) to be the Supreme Commander of the Armed Forces who exercises his powers and authority in accordance with the advice of the Cabinet. Under the general authority of the Yang di-Pertuan Agong and the cabinet, there is the Armed Forces Council which is responsible for the command, discipline and administration of all other matters relating to the Armed Forces, other than those relating to its operational use.

The Armed Forces Council is chaired by the Minister of Defence and its membership consists of the chief of the Armed Forces Staff, the 3 Service Chiefs and 2 other senior military officers, the Secretary-General of the Ministry of Defence, a representative of State Rulers and an appointed member.

The chief of the Armed Forces Staff is the professional head of the Armed Forces and the senior military member in the Armed Forces Council. He is the principal adviser to the Minister of Defence on the military aspects of all defence matters.

The chief of the Armed Forces Staff's committee, established under the authority of the Armed Forces Council, is the highest level at which joint planning and co-ordination with the Armed Forces are carried out. The Committee is chaired by the chief of the Armed Forces Staff and its membership consists of the chief of the Army, Navy and Air Force, the chief of Personnel Staff, the chief of Logistic Staff and the chief of Staff of the Ministry of Defence.

Army. The active army is an all regular force consisting of 8 brigade groups in 2 infantry divisions and 1 semi-independent regional security command. Each brigade consists of infantry, reconnaissance, artillery, signals, engineers and is supported by adequate logistic units. The Army is still at its phase of expansion. The total strength is approximately 52,500.

The Royal Military College, founded in 1953, is now accommodated at Sungei Besi near Kuala Lumpur. It has a Boys' Wing which prepares young Malaysians 'to take their places as officers in the Armed Forces, in the higher divisions of the public service and as leaders in the professional, commercial and industrial life of the country'. The Cadet Wing trains officers for both regular and short service commissions.

Navy. The Royal Malaysian Navy is commanded by the Chief of the Naval Staff from the integrated Ministry of Defence in Kuala Lumpur. The main naval bases are KD Malaya situated on Singapore Island and KD Sri Labuan on Labuan Island. These establishments are responsible for the operation and administration of the ships, and KD Malaya for the training of personnel.

The ships include 3 frigates, 6 coastal minesweepers, 8 fast missile craft, 6 fast gunboats, 24 patrol craft, 3 landing ships, 1 diving tender and 1 survey vessel. The peace-time tasks include fishery protection and anti-piracy patrols. There are also 27 armed patrol launches, 25 operated by the Royal Malaysian Police and 2 by the Government of Sabah (North Borneo) which also operates 4 patrol boats and a yacht. Naval personnel, 1978: 6,000 officers and ratings, plus 1,000 reservists.

The British frigate *Mermaid* was transferred to Malaysia in April 1977. Four 'Spica' class large torpedo boats (fast attack craft) were ordered from Sweden in 1976 for delivery in 1979. A new survey ship is being completed.

Air Force. Formed on 1 June 1958, the Royal Malaysian Air Force is equipped primarily to provide air defence and air support for the Army, Navy and Police. Its secondary rôle is to render assistance to Government departments and civilian organizations, especially during periods of national disasters. There are 11 squadrons, of which 8 operate transport aircraft and helicopters. Equipment includes 14 F-5E Tiger II jet fighter-bombers and 2 F-5B trainers, 20 Canadair CL-41G Tebuan dual-purpose light jet strike and training aircraft, 6 C-130H Hercules four-turboprop heavy transports, 2 F.28 Fellowship VIP transports, 16 Caribou twin-engined STOL transports, 2 Heron and 2 Dove light liaison/communications aircraft, 35 Sikorsky S-61A-4 Nuri heavy troop and cargo transport helicopters, 23 Alouette III, 20 Gazelle, 3 Agusta-Bell 212, 9 Bell 47 and 5 Bell 206B Jet-Ranger helicopters, 12 Cessna 402Bs for twin-engine training and liaison, 14 piston-engined Bulldog basic trainers and 2 H.S. 125 Merpati twin-jet executive transports.

Volunteer Forces. The Army Volunteer Force (Territorial Army) consists of first-line infantry, signals, engineer and logistics units able to take the field with the active army, and a second-line organization to provide local defence. There is also a small Naval Volunteer Reserve with Headquarters in Penang and Kuala Lumpur. The Royal Malaysian Air Force Volunteer Reserve has both air and ground elements.

INTERNATIONAL RELATIONS

Membership. Malaysia is a member of UN, the Commonwealth and the Colombo Plan.

ECONOMY

Planning. The first 5-year plan, 1966–70, envisaged an outlay of M$14,742m. The second 5-year plan, 1971–75, envisaged an expenditure of M$16,150m. and aimed at the eradication of poverty and the restructuring of society.

Budget. Revenue and expenditure for calendar years, in M$1m.:

	1975	*1976*	*1977*[1]	*1978*[2]
Revenue	5,117	6,157	7,515	8,320
Operating expenditure[3]	4,900	5,828	7,160	8,058
Development expenditure	2,151	2,335	3,000	3,400

[1] Latest estimate.
[2] Budget estimate.
[3] Including contribution to sinking fund from 1975.

Currency. Bank Negara Malaysia (Central Bank of Malaysia) assumed sole currency issuing authority in Malaysia on 12 June 1967. The unit of currency issued by Bank Negara Malaysia is the Malaysian dollar, which is divided into 100 *sen.* Currency notes are of denominations of $1, 5, 10, 50, 100 and $1,000. Coins are of denominations of 1 *sen,* 5, 10, 20, 50 *sen* and $1, $5 and $100. The circulation of currency on 31 Dec. 1976 was M$2,789·5m.

Banking. Thirty-six banks were operating in Dec. 1976; of these 19 were domestic banks with a total of 282 banking offices. Five were banks incorporated in Singapore with 63 banking offices and the remaining 12 banks were foreign incorporated with 85 banking offices. Total deposits amounted to M$10,531m. on 31 Dec. 1976 and loans and advances amounted to M$8,061·4m.

The post office savings bank held M$522m. due to 2,595,149 depositors at 31 Dec. 1974.

TRADE. Total trade of Malaysia with UK (British Department of Trade returns, in £1,000 sterling):

	1974	*1975*	*1976*	*1977*
Imports to UK	128,582	116,094	157,150	223,558
Exports and re-exports from UK	113,410	114,535	118,175	147,450

COMMUNICATIONS

Post. The Postal Services in Malaysia are under the Ministry of Communications and are headed by the Director-General of Post, Malaysia.

Cinemas. In 1974 there were 500 cinemas with a seating capacity of 345,400.

JUSTICE. The judicial power of the Federation is vested in the High Court in Peninsular Malaysia and the High Court in East Malaysia and also in subordinate courts. Legally the 2 High Courts are known as High Court and High Court Borneo. Above the High Courts there also exists a Federal Court with its main registry in Kuala Lumpur, with exclusive jurisdiction to determine appeals from decisions of any High Court.

The Supreme Head of the Judiciary is the Lord President of the Federal Court, consisting of himself and 2 Chief Justices of the High Courts and Judges of the Federal Court. Every proceeding in the Federal Court is heard and disposed of by 3 judges or such greater uneven number of judges as the Lord President in any particular case may order. In his absence, the senior member of the court presides.

On 17 Dec. 1977 the Malaysian Parliament abolished the right of appeal to the British Privy Council.

DIPLOMATIC REPRESENTATIVES

OF MALAYSIA IN GREAT BRITAIN
(45 Belgrave Sq., London, SW1X 8QT)

High Commissioner: Datuk Abdullah bin Ali.

OF GREAT BRITAIN IN MALAYSIA (Wisma Damansara, Jalan Semantan, Kuala Lumpur)

High Commissioner: D. F. Hawley, CMG, MBE.

OF MALAYSIA IN THE USA (2401 Massachusetts Ave., NW, Washington, D.C., 20008)

Ambassador: Azraai Zain.

OF THE USA IN MALAYSIA
(A.I.A. Bldg., Jalan Ampang, Kuala Lumpur)

Ambassador: Robert H. Miller.

OF MALAYSIA TO THE UNITED NATIONS

Ambassador: Tan Sri Zaiton Ibrahim.

Books of Reference

Statistical Information: The Department of Statistics, Malaysia, Kuala Lumpur, was set up in 1963, taking over from the Department of Statistics, States of Malaya. *Chief Statistician:* R. Chandler. Main publications: *Peninsular Malaysia Monthly* and *Annual Statistics of External Trade*; *Malaysia External Trade* (quarterly); *Peninsular Malaysia Statistical Bulletin* (monthly); *Rubber Statistics* (monthly); *Rubber Statistics Handbook* (annual); *Oil Palm Statistics* (monthly); *Oil Palm, Coconut and Tea Statistics* (annual); *Survey of Manufacturing Industries, 1972*; *National Accounts of Peninsular Malaysia, 1960–1971*; *Malaysia Industrial Classification, 1972*; *Monthly Industrial Statistics, Malaysia*; *Census of Selected Service Trades, 1973.*

Books About Malaysia. Singapore, National Library, 1965
The Economic Aspects of Malaysia. Report by the International Bank. Singapore, 1963
Harrison, B., *South-east Asia, A Short History*, 3rd ed. London, 1966
Means, G. P., *Malaysian Politics.* 2nd ed. London, 1976

PENINSULAR MALAYSIA

AREA AND POPULATION. The total area of Peninsular Malaysia is about 50,806 sq. miles (131,587 sq. km). The federal capital is Kuala Lumpur.

State	*Area (sq. miles)*	*Population (1970 Census)*	*Capital*	*Population (1970 Census)*
Johore	7,330	1,277,180	Johore Bharu	136,229
Kedah	3,639	954,947	Alor Star	66,260
Kelantan	5,765	684,738	Kota Bharu	55,124
Malacca	637	404,125	Malacca	87,160
Negri Sembilan	2,565	481,563	Seremban	80,921
Pahang	13,886	504,945	Kuantan	43,358
Penang	399	776,124	Georgetown	269,247
Perak	8,110	1,569,139	Ipoh	247,969
Perlis	307	121,062	Kangar	8,758
Selangor	3,166	1,630,366	Shah Alam	451,810
Trengganu	5,002	405,368	Kuala Trengganu	53,320
Peninsular Malaysia	50,806	8,809,557		

Population by races (1970 Census): 4,671,874 Malays; 3,131,320 Chinese; 936,341 Indians and Pakistani; 70,022 others. In 1974 Kuala Lumpur became a Federal District. Shah Alam became capital of Selangor. Vital statistics (1974): Births, 312,749; deaths, 63,000.

CONSTITUTION AND GOVERNMENT. The States of the Federation of Malaya, now known as Peninsular Malaysia, comprises the 11 States of Johore, Pahang, Negri Sembilan, Selangor, Perak, Kedah, Perlis, Kelantan, Trengganu, Penang and Malacca. On 31 Aug. 1957 the Federation became the 11th sovereign member-state of the Commonwealth of Nations. For earlier history of the States and Settlements *see* THE STATESMAN'S YEAR-BOOK, 1957, pp. 241 f.

The Constitution is based on the agreements reached at the London conference of Jan.–Feb. 1956, between HM Government in the UK, the Rulers of the Malay States and the Alliance Party (which at the first federal elections on 27 July 1955 obtained 51 of the 52 elected members), and subsequently worked out by the Constitutional Commission appointed after that conference.

ECONOMY

Budget. Revenue and expenditure for calendar years, in M$1m.:

	1973	*1974*[2]	*1975*[2]
Revenue	525·6	663·6	664·1
Current expenditure[1]	572·1	730·6	761·2
Development expenditure	165·7	254·9	490·6
Less Federal reimbursement	22·6	28·8	47·1

[1] Excluding contribution to development and water supply funds but including recurrent expenditure from water supply fund, loan repayments and interest.
[2] Estimates.

Weights and Measures. The standard measures are the imperial yard, pound and gallon.

ENERGY AND NATURAL RESOURCES

Electricity. In 1976, 6,024·7m. kwh. were generated; commerce and industry are the main consumers.

Minerals. Production: Tin-in-concentrates (in 1,000 long tons): 1975, 63·3; 1976, 62·4. Iron ore (in 1,000 tons): 1975, 343; 1976, 303. Bauxite: 1975, 692·5; 1976, 649·8. Ilmenite (exports) (in 1,000 tons): 1975, 110·5; 1976, 177·2. Gold: 1975, 2,484; 1976, 3,574 troy oz.

Agriculture. Total area under agricultural crops, 1974, 8m. acres. This included 536,300 acres of second season rice crops.

Rice: Production in 1976, 1,117,900 tons from 1,433,400 acres, which includes second crop acreage.

Rubber: Production in 1976, 1,539,000 tons. Oil-palms: Production in 1976, 1,233,000 tons of palm oil; 250,541 tons of kernels; 71,483 tons of coconut oil.

Tea: Production in 1976, 6,719,000 lb.

Livestock (1975); Oxen, 386,000; buffaloes, 213,000; sheep, 45,000; swine, 1,168,000; goats, 329,000.

Forestry (1976). Reserved forests, 12·8m. acres; productive, 5·43m. acres. Production of round timber, 236·6m. cu. ft and outturn of sawn timber, 122m. cu. ft. Production of plywood, 734·5m. sq. ft. Exports of veneer, 321·6m. sq. ft.

Fisheries. Landings in 1975, 375,235 tons; 1976, 410,968 tons. Number of vessels in 1976, 16,516 motor, 4,100 sailing.

INDUSTRY AND TRADE

Commerce. Imports and exports for calendar years in M$1m.:

	1971	*1972*	*1973*	*1974*	*1975*	*1976*
Imports	3,414·2	3,877·1	5,143·6	8,550·0	7,483·1	8,521·6
Exports	3,917·0	4,024·7	6,026·7	8,437·5	7,695·8	10,043·6

Chief imports (1976): Machinery and transport equipment, M$2,657·4m.; food and live animals, $1,232·6m.; manufactured goods, $1,407·6,.

Chief exports (1976): Rubber, 1,519,555 long tons (M$2,990·5 m.); tin metal and tin-in-concentrates, 80,240 long tons ($1,526·5m.); palm-oil, crude, 737,256 long tons ($674·5m.); sawn timber, 1,864,970 tons of 50 cu. ft ($733·7m.); saw logs, 260,310 tons of 50 cu. ft ($36·1m.); bauxite, 515,545 long tons ($10·2m.).

In 1976 imports came chiefly from Japan (M$1,740·4m.), USA ($1,030·4m.), Australia ($667·5m.), UK ($634·9m.), Singapore ($608·5m.), Federal Republic of Germany ($489·9m.) Thailand ($360·2m.), China ($248·4m.). Saudi Arabia ($217·9m.), Indonesia ($87·5m.). Exports went mainly to Singapore (M$1,825·9m.), USA ($1,686·4m.), Netherlands ($836·5m.), Japan ($780·2m.), UK ($581·9m.), Federal Republic of Germany ($521·5m.), Sabah ($360·9m.), Sarawak ($347·4m.), USSR ($302m.), Italy ($245·2m.), France ($233·1m.).

Trade Unions. There were, on 31 Dec. 1976, 366 registered trade unions with 515,078 members in Malaysia.

Tourism. In 1976, 2,617,514 foreigners visited Peninsular Malaysia.

COMMUNICATIONS

Roads. In 1973 the Public Works Department maintained 11,419 miles of public road, of which 8,146 miles was of bituminous metalled surface, 1,380 bitumen surface waterbound, 525 earth surface.

At June 1975, 1·18m. motor vehicles were registered, including 378,622 private cars, 8,198 buses, 86,907 lorries and vans, 666,489 motor cycles.

Railways. The Malayan Railway main line runs from Singapore to Butterworth opposite Penang Island. From Bukit Mertajam 8 miles south of Butterworth a branch line connects Peninsular Malaysia with the State Railways of Thailand at the frontier station of Padang Besar. Other branch lines connect the main line with Port of Klang, Teluk Anson, Port Dickson and Port Weld. The east-coast line, branching off the main line at Gemas, runs for over 300 miles to Tumpat, Kelantan's northernmost coastal town; a short branch line linking Pasir Mas with Sungei Golok makes a second connexion with Thailand. The route mileage in 1975 is 1,337 (metre gauge) and the annual budget is about M$100m.

Aviation (1974). There are 8 aerodromes used by scheduled air services in Peninsular Malaysia. International air services are operated into Kuala Lumpur and Penang airports. The national carrier, Malaysian Airlines System (MAS), began operation on 1 Oct. 1972 to provide both domestic and international services. The Malaysian Airlines System (MAS) operate international services to Bandar Seri Bengawan, Bangkok, Haadyai, Hong Kong, Jakarta, Kuwait, London, Madras, Manila, Medan, Singapore, Sydney, Taipei and Tōkyō. The number of domestic points served by the airline is 35. Charter services are provided within Peninsular Malaysia by Malaysia Air Charter Company and Kris Udara Malaysia. The following airlines operate scheduled services through Kuala Lumpur besides MAS, Air Ceylon, Aeroflot Soviet Airlines, Air India, Air Vietnam, British Airways, Cathay Pacific Airways, China Airlines, Czechoslovakia Airlines, Garuda Indonesian Airways, Japan Airlines, Royal Dutch Airlines (KLM), PANAM, Qantas Airways, Royal Air Laos, SAS, SABENA, Singapore Airlines. Thai International Airways and Trans Mediterranean Airways. The airlines operating scheduled services through Penang besides MAS are Merpati Nusantara Airlines, Thai Airways Co. and Thai Airways International.

Civil aviation statistics for airports in Peninsular Malaysia (1974): Aircraft movements, 61,956; terminal passengers, 2,071,986; freight, 13,996 tons; mail, 2,662 tons.

Shipping. The major ports of Peninsular Malaysia are Penang, Malacca, Port Klang, Tumpat, Dungun, Port Dickson, Teluk Anson and Kuantan. The volume of shipping (vessels of over 75 NRT only) handled at these ports, exclusive of coasting trade, was as follows (in 1,000 NRT):

		Arrivals		*Departures*	
Ports		*Number*	*Tonnage*	*Number*	*Tonnage*
Penang	1975	1,753	7,072	1,758	7,093
	1976	1,916	7,601	1,896	7,568
Port Klang	1975	2,749	13,567	2,733	13,469
	1976	2,794	14,807	2,796	14,821
Total (all ports)	1975	5,198	23,971	5,185	23,913
	1976	5,417	26,295	5,396	26,205

The total cargo handled in all ports during 1975 was 15·04m. tons; 1976, 17·01m. tons.

Post and Broadcasting. As at 31 Dec. 1976, 400 post offices, 1,204 postal agencies, 145 mobile post offices and 2 riverine postal agencies were operating in Malaysia, and the cash turnover for the year amounted to M$3,153,695,746.

There were 278,548 telephones on 31 Dec. 1976 serviced by 299 exchanges with 14 satellite exchanges. In 1976, 368,282 wireless licences were issued and 548,790 television licences were issued.

JUSTICE, RELIGION, EDUCATION AND WELFARE

Justice. The Courts Ordinance, 1948, established sessions court, magistrates' courts and Penghulu's courts. There are also juvenile courts for offenders under the age of 17.

There are 17 penal institutions, including 4 Borstal establishments and 1 open prison camp. The average prison population (1977) was 7,351.

Religion. More than half the population are Muslims, and Islam is the official religion. In 1970 there were 4,673,670 Muslims, 765,250 Hindus, 220,897 Christians and 2,495,739 Buddhists.

Education (1976). The number of schools (fully assisted, partially assisted and private) of all types, of teachers and pupils of both sexes were (as at 31 Jan.) as follows:

	Malay	*Malay and English*	*English*	*Chinese*	*Tamil*	*Total*
Schools	2,620	123	835	1,045	611	5,234
Teachers	31,444	5,188	24,597	15,088	3,539	79,856
Pupils	957,193	141,837	741,833	514,633	80,237	2,435,733

Upper secondary vocational training is given in 18 assisted secondary vocational schools (8,205 pupils), and upper secondary technical education in 9 assisted secondary technical schools (4,774 pupils). Vocational training is also given in 36 private vocational institutes.

Post-secondary professional education (1974–76) is given at the University of Technology (formerly the National Institute of Technology), Kuala Lumpur (218 lecturers and tutors, 2,249 students), the University of Agriculture (5 professors, 249 lecturers and tutors, 2,542 students), Ungku Omar Polytechnic, Ipoh (80 lecturers and instructors, 1,145 students), Mara Institute of Technology, Shah Alam (12 professors, 544 lecturers and instructors, 6,900 students), Tunku Abdul Rahman College (121 lecturers and instructors, 4,036 students), University of Science (formerly University of Penang), Penang (18 professors, 331 lecturers, tutors, researchers and language teachers, 2,184 full-time students), University Kebangsaan, Kuala Lumpur (12 professors, 448 lecturers, readers and tutors, 2,572 students) and the University of Malaya, Kuala Lumpur (38 professors, 864 lecturers, readers, tutors and language teachers, 8,056 students).

Primary teachers are trained at the Sultan Idris Teachers' College in Perak (700 students), the Malay Women's Teachers' College in Malacca (440 students), the Kota Bharu Teachers' College, Kelantan (339 students), Seri Kota Teachers' College, Kuala Lumpur (391 students), Sri Pinang Teachers' College, Penang (396 students), Mohd. Khalid Teachers' College, Johore (412 students), Raja Melewar Teachers' College, Negri Sembilan (395 students), and the Day Training Teachers' College, Perak (372 students).

Secondary teachers are trained at the Malayan Teachers' College in Penang (419 students), Temenggong Ibrahim Teachers' College, Johore (674 students), the Language Institute, Kuala Lumpur (275 students), the Specialist Teachers' Training College, Kuala Lumpur (496 students), and the Technical Teachers' Training College, Kuala Lumpur (673 students).

In 1974 further education classes were provided by the Government throughout the country (119 centres, 710 classes, 2,012 teachers and 20,368 students).

Health. In 1976 Government maintained 58 general, district hospitals with 19,094 beds, 2 institutions with 2,688 beds for the treatment of Hensens' disease, 2 mental institutions with 6,577 beds and 1 institution (293 beds) for tuberculosis treatment. For the care of the rural population there were 2,975 medical and health facilities comprising 62 main health centres, 248 health sub-centres, 1,310 midwives' clinics, 363 static, 269 travelling dispensaries, 682 dental clinics, 41 maternal and child health clinics. The Government also maintains an Institute for Medical Research with 2 branch laboratories at Ipoh and Penang.

Books of Reference

Gullick, J. M., *Malaya.* 2nd ed. London, 1965
Jin-Bee, Ooi, *Land, People and Economy in Malaya.* London, 1963
Kennedy, J., *A History of Malaya.* London, 1962
O'Ballance, E., *Malaya: The Communist Insurgent War, 1948–60.* London, 1966
Ratnam, K. J., *Communalism and the Political Process in Malaya.* OUP, 1965

Wilkinson, R. J., *Malay–English Dictionary*. 2 vols. New ed. London, 1956
Winstedt, Sir R., *Malaya and Its History*. 3rd ed. London, 1953.—*An English–Malay Dictionary*. 3rd ed. Singapore, 1949.—*The Malays: A Cultural History*. London, 1959

SABAH

HISTORY. The territory now named Sabah, but until Sept. 1963 known as North Borneo, was in 1877–78 ceded by the Sultans of Brunei and Sulu and various other rulers to a British syndicate, which in 1881 was chartered as the British North Borneo (Chartered) Company. The Company's sovereign rights and assets were transferred to the Crown with effect from 15 July 1946. On that date, the island of Labuan (ceded to Britain in 1846 by the Sultan of Brunei) became part of the new Colony of North Borneo. On 16 Sept. 1963 North Borneo joined the new Federation of Malaysia and became the State of Sabah.

AREA AND POPULATION. Area, about 29,388 sq. miles (80,520 sq. km), with a coastline of about 900 miles. The interior is mountainous, Mount Kinabalu being 13,455 ft (4,175 metres) high. Population (1970 census), 655,295, of whom 421,962 were natives, 140,969 Chinese, 2,489 Europeans and 97,717 others. The native population comprises Kadazans (largest and mainly agricultural), Bajaus and Bruneis (agriculture and fishing), Muruts (hill tribes), Suluks (mainly seafaring) and several smaller tribes.

The island of Labuan, 35 sq. miles (75 sq. km) in area, lying 6 miles off the north-west coast of Borneo is a free port. It has a fine port, Victoria Harbour.

The principal towns are situated on or near the coast. They include Kota Kinabalu, the capital (formerly Jesselton), 1970 census population, 40,939, Sandakan (41,413), Tawau (24,247), Kudat (5,089); and Keningau in the hinterland (2,037).

CONSTITUTION AND GOVERNMENT. The Constitution of the State of Sabah provides for a Head of State, called the *Yang Dipertua Negeri Sabah*. Executive authority is vested in the State Cabinet headed by the Chief Minister.

Head of State: Datuk Ahmad Koroh, SPDK.

Flag: Four horizontal stripes of red, white, yellow and blue, with a green quarter bearing an outline of Mount Kinabalu in brown.

The Cabinet was composed as follows in Oct. 1977:

Chief Minister and Minister of Natural Resources: Datuk Harris bin Mohd. Salleh, SPDK.

Deputy Chief Minister/Industrial and Rural Development: Datuk James Peter Ongkili, DIMP. *Finance:* Tuan Hj. Mohd. Noor Mansoor. *Agriculture and Fisheries:* Datuk Suffian Koroh, PGDK. *Communications and Works:* Datuk Lim Guan Sing, DK. *Social Welfare and National Unity:* Toh Puan Hajjah Rahimah Stephens, PGDK. *Local Government and Housing:* Encik Joseph Pairin Kitingan. *Manpower and Environmental Development:* Datuk Yap Pak Leong, PGDK. *Culture, Youth and Sports:* Pengiran Awang Othman bin Pengiran Haji Rauf.

The Legislative Assembly consists of the Speaker, 48 elected members and not more than 6 nominated members.

The official language was English for a period of 10 years from Sept. 1963 but in Aug. 1973 Bahasa Malaysia was introduced and in 1974 was declared the official language.

ECONOMY

Budget. Budgets for calendar years, in M$:

Ordinary Budget	*1972*	*1973*	*1974*	*1975*	*1976*
Revenue	168,522,766	299,239,434	380,349,513	265,757,626	427,683,597
Expenditure[1]	234,833,994	213,361,906	345,645,805	414,619,046	299,707,169

[1] Includes contributions to Development Budget: 1972, $80m.; 1973, $65m.; 1974, Nil; 1975, $85m.; 1976, $95m.

Development Budget	*1972*	*1973*	*1974*	*1975*	*1976*
Revenue[1]	119,695,040	94,319,970	135,836,231	133,855,491	137,946,010
Expenditure[1]	93,384,695	93,084,147	124,263,362	160,517,426	140,033,443

[1]Excluding federal accounts on federal subjects in the State.

Banking. There are branches of The Chartered Bank at Kota Kinabalu, Sandakan, Tawau, Labuan, Kudat, Tenom and Lahad Datu. The Hongkong and Shanghai Bank has branches at Kota Kinabalu, Sandakan, Labuan, Beaufort, Papar and Tawau. The Hock Hua Bank (S) has branches at Kota Kinabalu, Sandakan and Tawau. The Chung Khiaw Bank has branches at Kota Kinabalu, Tuaran and Sandakan. Malayan Banking Ltd has branches at Kota Kinabalu, Tawau, Semporna and Sandakan. United Overseas Bank and the Overseas Chinese Banking Corporation have each a branch at Kota Kinabalu. Bank Bumiputra Malaysia has branches at Kota Kinabalu, Lahad Datu, Sandakan and Keningau. Overseas Union Bank and the Development and Commercial Bank have each a branch at Sandakan.

The National Savings Bank has taken over the functions of the post office savings bank as from 1 Dec. 1974 and had (1976) $12·9m. due to 47,348 depositors. It also provides additional services to depositors including the granting of loans for housing.

COMMERCE. The main imports are machinery, tobacco, provisions, petroleum products, metals, rice, textiles and apparel, vehicles, sugar, building material. Statistics for calendar years, in M$:

	1971	*1972*	*1973*	*1974*	*1975*
Imports	585,446,404	589,511,666	704,913,606	1,192,314,365	1,011,576,867
Exports	577,465,595	590,463,830	1,011,791,294	1,193,509,274	1,011,229,092

The main imports and exports were (in M$1m.):

Imports	*1955*	*1960*	*1970*	*1974*	*1975*
Rice	6·4	8·4	15·4	48·0	42·0
Provisions	13·0	22·3	45·7	89·9	93·6
Textiles and apparel	5·9	9·2	20·5	39·4	50·2
Tobacco, cigars and cigarettes	4·2	12·8	32·9	43·2	47·4
Sugar	2·5	3·5	6·7	28·2	31·6
Vehicles	2·2	8·1	47·6	117·3	70·0
Machinery	6·9	30·0	109·0	244·4	129·8
Petroleum products	5·0	16·1	28·6	85·5	95·2
Metals	7·5	12·1	36·8	169·8	134·6
Building materials	2·1	2·8	11·6	30·8	14·2
Exports					
Rubber	45·9	49·5	36·5	50·5	40·0
Timber	21·6	90·7	396·8	871·4	568·6
Hemp	2·2	5·2	0·3	—	—
Fish, fresh, dried and salted	0·4	0·9	8·0	13·3	13·6
Copra (including re-exports)	14·2	40·2	6·8	10·7	14·4
Cocoa beans	—	15·8	4·4	16·0	17·0
Veneer sheets	—	0·5	2·5	8·5	3·0
Palm oil	—	—	18·1	105·5	131·0
Copper concentrates	—	—	—	—	11·3

TOURISM. In 1976 some 71,262 tourists visited Sabah.

COMMUNICATIONS

Roads (1975). There were 2,381 miles of roads, of which 664 miles were bitumen surfaced, 1,428 miles gravel surfaced and 289 miles of earth road. Work is in progress on a network of roads, notably the Kota Kinabalu–Sandakan and Sandakan–Lahad Datu road links.

Railways. A metre-gauge railway, 87 miles, runs from Kota Kinabalu on Gaya Bay to Tenom in the interior.

Aviation. External communications are provided from the international airport at Kota Kinabalu by Cathay Pacific Airways Ltd to Hong Kong; Malaysian Airways to Hong Kong, Manila, Brunei, Kuching, Singapore and Kuala Lumpur and Brunei Airways to Brunei and Kuching.

The total air traffic handled at Sabah aerodromes during 1976 was 1,249,499 passengers, 11,673,568 kg freight and 2,351,013 kg mail.

Shipping (1976). Merchant shipping totalling 14,952,441 gross tons, used the ports, handling 8,021,950 tons of cargo.

Post. As at 31 Dec. 1976 there were 32 post offices, 13 mobile post offices and 84 postal agencies. There were 23,068 telephones on 1 Jan. 1977.

JUSTICE, EDUCATION AND WELFARE

Justice. When Sabah attained independence on 16 Sept. 1963 the Supreme Court of Sarawak, North Borneo and Brunei was replaced by the High Court in Borneo with 2 registries for Sarawak (at Kuching) and Sabah (at Kota Kinabalu).

There are native courts with jurisdiction in cases concerning local native customs. Appeals from native courts go to administrative officers, with a final appeal to the Native Court of Appeal.

In 1975, 1,341 convictions were obtained in 2,258 cases taken to court.

Education. In 1976, there were 127,271 primary and 52,152 secondary pupils. There are 803 primary schools (613 government, 181 grant-aided and 9 private), and 94 general secondary schools (44 government, 37 grant-aided and 13 private) throughout the State. There are 3 teacher-training colleges, Gaya College (298 students), Kent College (327 students) and Sandakan Teacher Training College (152 students).

The Government also runs 2 vocational schools in Kota Kinabalu and Sandakan offering carpentry, motor mechanics, electrical installation, fitting/turning, radio and television and heavy plant fitting.

The Department of Education also runs further education classes in most towns and districts. The main medium of instruction in primary schools is Bahasa Malaysia although there are some Chinese medium primary schools. Secondary education is principally English but this is progressively being replaced by Bahasa Malaysia.

Health. The principal diseases are malaria, pulmonary tuberculosis and intestinal infestations. Specific control programmes for malaria and tuberculosis have drastically reduced the incidence of these two diseases.

There are 3 general hospitals (893 beds) with specialist facilities and 11 district hospitals (739 beds). Forty-three dispensaries in outlying districts providing in-patient and out-patient care are staffed by hospital assistants under the supervision of district medical officers. There is a mental hospital at Sandakan (330 beds). A new mental hospital at Kota Kinabalu with 300 beds was opened in 1972. There are 15 district health centres and 163 village group sub-centres throughout the State providing maternal and child health care.

Book of Reference

Statistical Information: Director, Federal Department of Information, Kota Kinabalu.

Tregonning, K. G., *North Borneo.* HMSO, 1960

SARAWAK

HISTORY. The Government of part of the present territory was obtained on 24 Sept. 1841 by Sir James Brooke from the Sultan of Brunei. Various accessions were made between 1861 and 1905. In 1888 Sarawak was placed under British protection. On 16 Dec. 1941 Sarawak was occupied by the Japanese. After the liberation the Rajah took over his administration from the British military authorities on 15 April

1946. The Council Negri, on 17 May 1946, authorized the Act of Cession to the British Crown by 19 to 16 votes, and the Rajah ceded Sarawak to the British Crown on 1 July 1946.

On 16 Sept. 1963 Sarawak joined the Federation of Malaysia.

AREA AND POPULATION. The area is about 48,250 sq. miles (121,400 sq. km), with a coastline of 450 miles and many navigable rivers.

The population at 1970 census was 975,918, including 386,260 Dayaks; 182,700 Malays; 103,194 other natives; 294,020 Chinese; 9,735 others. The annual rate of increase is 2·8% (estimate). Working population (1970), 361,171.

The chief towns are the capital, Kuching, about 21 miles inland, on the Sarawak River (1970 population: 63,535), Sibu, 80 miles up the Rejang River, which is navigable by large steamers (1970 population: 50,635), and Miri, the headquarters of the Sarawak Shell Ltd (1970 population: 35,702).

CONSTITUTION AND GOVERNMENT. On 24 Sept. 1941 the Rajah began to rule through a constitution. Since 1855 two bodies, known as the Supreme Council and the Dewan Undangan Negri (State Legislature), had been in existence. By the constitution of 1941 they were given, by the Rajah, powers roughly corresponding to those of a colonial executive council and legislative council respectively. Sarawak has retained a considerable measure of local autonomy in state affairs. The State or Legislature consists of 48 elected members and sits for 5 years unless sooner dissolved.

A ministerial system of government was introduced in 1963. The Chief Minister presides over the Supreme Council, which contains no more than 8 other Council Negri members, all of whom are Ministers.

Elections to the State Legislature on 14 Sept. 1974 returned 30 members of the Sarawak Barisan Nasional comprising the Party Pesaka Bumiputra Bersatu and the Sarawak United Peoples' Party, and 18 of Sarawak National Party. Since the 1974 elections, Sarawak United Peoples' Party has joined again with the Party Pesaka Bumiputra Bersatu forming Sarawak Barisan Government. The Sarawak National Party has joined the Sarawak Barisan Government since Aug. 1976.

Sarawak has 24 seats in the Malaysia Parliament.

Head of State: Datuk Patinggi Abang Muhammad Salahuddin.

Chief Minister: Datuk Patinggi Tan Sni Haji Abdul Rahman Ya'kub, DP, PMN, SPMJ, SPMK, SIMP, SPDK, PNBS.

Deputy Chief Ministers: Datuk Sim Kheng Hong, PNBS (*Finance and Development*), Datuk Dunstan Endaurie Anak Enchana, PNBS (*Communications and Works*), Datuk Alfred Jabu Anak Numpang, PNBS (*Lands and Mineral Resources*). *Welfare Services:* Nyipa Bato, JBS. *Housing:* Ahmad Zaidi. *Agriculture and Community Development:* Dr Wong Soon Kai, PBS. *Culture, Youth and Sports:* Celestine Ujang Anak Jilan. *Local Government:* Leo Moggie Anak Irak.

State Secretary: Tan Sri Gerusin Lembat, PSM, PNBS. *Deputy State Secretary:* Datuk Abang Haji Yusuf Puteh, PNBS, JSM. *State Attorney-General:* Jemuri Serjan, PBS, JBS. *State Financial Secretary:* Haji Bujang bin Nor, JBS, JSM.

The official languages are Malay and English. The continuing use of English as official language in Sarawak will be reviewed in 1979.

Flag: Horizontally red over white with a blue triangle based on the hoist.

ECONOMY

Budget. In 1977 estimated State revenue was $177·1m. (of which the statutory Federal grants were $28·5m.); estimated expenditure, $182·7m. The revenue is mainly derived from royalties on oil and timber.

The third Malaysian 5-year development plan (1976–80) provides for Sarawak an expenditure of $1,600m.; of this sum $629·9m. is to be spent on roads and bridges, land development, port development, education, electricity and water supply and agriculture.

Currency. The Malaysian dollar is based on gold, 0·290299 gramme to a dollar, which is on a par of £0·24 or US$0.40.

Banking. The post office savings bank had 40,810 depositors at the end of 1976; the amount to their credit was $16,201,000. There is a branch of Bank Negara Malaysia in Kuching, and branches of the Chartered Bank, the Hong-kong & Shanghai Bank, the Overseas Chinese Banking Corporation, the Malayan Bank and 8 other banks.

PRODUCTION. The State produces rubber (exports, 1976, 39,767 net tons, $64·3m.; 1975, 28,579 net tons, $35·8m.), timber logs (exports, 1976, 1·6m. tons, $242m.; 1975, 0·7m. tons, $63·7m.), sawn timber (exports, 1976, 203m. tons, $116·9m.; 1975, 170m. tons, $62m.), sago (exports, 1976, 27,593 tons, $6·7m.; 1975, 22,506 tons, $5·3m.), pepper (exports, 1976, 34,851 tons, $124·4m.; 1975, 29,873 tons, $100·8m.), and other jungle produce. There are also gold (1976, 965 troy oz.; 1975, 1,192 troy oz.) and antimony ore (1976, 592 tons; 1975, 577 tons).

COMMERCE. Export of crude oil and petroleum in 1976 was 5·6m. tons ($1,533m.), about 69% of total exports. The bulk of crude production was exported to Japan, Singapore, Philippines and Thailand.

Total import value, 1976, $1,068m.; 1975, $850·9m. Export, 1976, $2·22m.; 1975, $1,387m.

COMMUNICATIONS

Roads. There are no railways. In 1976 there were 2,561 miles of roads, consisting of 557 miles of bitumen surfaced, 1,310 miles of gravel or stone surfaced and 694 miles of earth roads.

Aviation. There are daily Malaysian Airline System (MAS) flights between Kuching and Kuala Lumpur *via* Singapore. Scheduled flights between Kuching, Brunei and Hong Kong started in Oct. 1974. Major towns in Sarawak are linked up by internal air routes.

Shipping. In 1976 Sarawak ports loaded 7·92m. tons (1975: 4·91m. tons) and discharged 1·27m. tons (1975: 1·13m. tons). New Kuching wharf, operational since Dec. 1974, can accommodate vessels up to 15,000 tons.

Post and Broadcasting. There are 46 post offices (including 3 mobile offices) and wireless-telegraph stations and 53 agencies. A telephone system with 57 exchanges (28,028 telephones) covers the country. There is communication by wireless with Singapore and other Commonwealth countries. The government radio and television service had, at the end of 1976, 38,733 registered receivers.

Newspapers (1977). There are 2 English and 7 Chinese daily; 1 Malay weekly; 1 Malay and 1 Iban (Sea Dayak) monthly newspapers as well as a weekly news review in Malay and Iban published by government.

JUSTICE, RELIGION, EDUCATION AND WELFARE

Justice (1976). There are 6 prisons including 2 centres of protective custody. There were 2,002 admissions, of whom 872 were sentenced to penal imprisonment and 504 committed on remand or awaiting trial, and 47 paid fines. Daily average prison population was 364.

Police. There is a Royal Malaysia Police, Sarawak Component, with a total establishment of about 7,600 regular officers and men.

Religion. There are Church of England, Roman Catholic, American Methodist, Seventh Day Adventist and Borneo Evangelical missions. There is a large Moslem population and many Buddhists. Islam is the state religion.

Education (1976). All schools (government, missions, local authorities) numbered 1,366 with 251,916 pupils, of whom 69,980 were in secondary classes. There are 3 teacher-training centres and an agricultural university campus conducting pre-university courses.

Health. At the end of 1976 there were 14 government and private hospitals (2,424 beds), 61 static and 49 travelling dispensaries, 1 urban health centre, 82 public dental and school dental clinics and 183 maternal and child health centres. There were 135 registered doctors.

Books of Reference

Population and Housing Census of Malaysia, 1970. Dept. of Statistics, Kuala Lumpur
Sarawak Annual of Statistics. Dept. of Statistics, Kuching, 1976
Sarawak Annual External Trade Statistics. Dept. of Statistics, Kuching, 1976
1976 Sarawak Budget. Information Dept., Sarawak
Dickson, M. G., *Sarawak and its People.* New ed. Kuching, 1962
MacDonald, M., *Borneo People.* London, 1956
Milne, R. S., and Ratnam, K. J., *Malaysia, New States in a New Nation: Political Development of Sarawak and Sabah in Malaysia.* London, 1974
Runciman, S., *The White Rajahs.* CUP, 1960
Scott, N. C., *Sea Dyak Dictionary.* Govt. Printing Office, Kuching, 1956

National Library: The Sarawak Central Library, Kuching.

REPUBLIC OF MALDIVES

Capital: Malé
Population: 140,000 (1976)

HISTORY. The islands were under British protection from 1887 to mid-1965. They now enjoy complete independence under the agreement signed in Colombo on 26 July 1965. Maldives became a republic on 11 Nov. 1968.

AREA AND POPULATION. The Republic of Maldives, 400 miles to the south-west of Sri Lanka, consists of some 2,000 low-lying coral islands (only 220 inhabited), grouped into 12 clearly defined clusters of atolls but divided into 19 for administrative purposes. Area 115 sq. miles (298 sq. km). Population (census 1971), 118,818. Estimate (1976) 140,000. Capital Malé (17,000 inhabitants).

CONSTITUTION AND GOVERNMENT. The President is elected every 5 years by universal adult suffrage. He is assisted by the Ministers' *Majlis*, a cabinet of ministers of his own choice whom he may dismiss at will. There is also a Citizens' *Majlis* (House of Representatives) which consists of 48 members, 8 nominated by the President, 2 elected from Malé and 2 elected from each of the 19 atolls. The life of the Citizens' *Majlis* is 5 years.

President and Prime Minister: Amir Ibrahim Nasir.

The people are Moslems, and Islam is reflected in the constitution and judicial system.

The official language is Divehi, which is akin to Elu or old Sinhalese.

National flag: Red with a green panel bearing a white crescent.

ECONOMY. The islands are covered with coconut palms and yield millet and fruit as well as coconut produce.

The Maldivian economy is based on the fishing industry. Bonito ('Maldive fish') is the main export commodity and Japan the main buyer. Tourism, introduced in 1972, is expanding and there were 15,000 visitors in 1976. There is no direct taxation. Exports to UK (1977), £40,000; imports, £168,000.

COMMUNICATIONS

Aviation. The 1965 agreement which allowed the British Government staging and communications facilities on Gan island and part of Hittadu island in Addu atoll, the southernmost of the group, was terminated in 1976, when the RAF staging post on Gan closed down. There is another civil airstrip at Hulule in the Malé atoll, some 300 miles from Gan, which is being extended.

Shipping. The merchant fleet consists of about 50 vessels of 200,000 GRT.

Post and Broadcasting. In Jan. 1977 there were 480 telephones.

DIPLOMATIC REPRESENTATIVES

OF GREAT BRITAIN IN THE REPUBLIC OF MALDIVES

Ambassador: D. P. Aiers, CMG (resides in Colombo).

OF THE REPUBLIC OF MALDIVES TO THE UNITED NATIONS

Ambassador: Fathulla Jameel.

Book of Reference

Bell, H. C. P., *History, Archaeology and Epigraphy of the Maldive Islands.* Ceylon Govt. Press, Colombo, 1940

MALI

Capital: Bamako
Population: 6·3m. (1976)
GNP per capita: US$100 (1976)

République du Mali

HISTORY. Annexed by France, it formed from 1895 the territory of French Sudan as a part of French West Africa. It became an autonomous state within the French Community on 24 Nov. 1958, and on 4 April 1959 joined with Senegal to form the Federation of Mali. The Federation of Mali achieved independence on 20 June 1960, but Senegal seceded from the Federation on 22 Aug. and Mali proclaimed itself an independent republic on 22 Sept. The National Assembly was dissolved on 17 Jan. 1968 by President Modibo Keita, whose government was then overthrown by an Army *coup* on 19 Nov. 1968.

AREA AND POPULATION. The frontiers of the former territory were re-adjusted in 1904, 1933, 1948 and 1954 (*see* THE STATESMAN'S YEAR-BOOK. 1959, p. 1011). The Republic is bounded north-west by Mauritania, north-east by Algeria and east by Niger and covers an area of 1,204,021 sq. km with a census population of 6,308,000 in 1976. The most densely populated and richest of the 19 districts are those of San, Mopti, Sikasso, Koutiala, Bamako and Ségou. Bamako, the capital (population, 400,022), Ségou (36,400), Kayes (34,100), Mopti (32,400), Sikasso (26,600), Gao (15,600), San (14,900) and Tombouctou (9,000) are important towns.

CONSTITUTION AND GOVERNMENT. The Republic of Mali became independent on 22 Sept. 1960, after having been the territory of French Sudan and, from Jan. 1959 to 22 Sept. 1960, a partner (together with Senegal) of the Federation of Mali. The Republic was admitted to the UN on 29 Sept. 1960.

A National Liberation Committee assumed all political and administrative functions on 19 Nov. 1968 and rules by decree. A new constitution was approved by a national referendum on 21 June 1974; it provides for a single permitted political party, and an elected President and National Assembly. Elections will take place in 1979, until which time the CMLN will retain all powers.

Chief of State, President of the Government: Col. Moussa Traoré.
National flag: Three vertical stripes of green, yellow, red.

DEFENCE

Army. The Army consists of 5 infantry battalions; strength, 4,200.

Air Force. The Air Force has received at least 5 MiG-17 jet fighters, 1 MiG-15UTI jet trainer, some Yak-18 piston-engined trainers, 2 Il-14 and 3 An-2 transports and 2 Mi-4 helicopters from USSR, Yak-12M liaison aircraft from Poland and 2 C-47 transports from USA. Personnel total about 400.

INTERNATIONAL RELATIONS

Membership. Mali is a member of UN, OAU and is an ACP state of EEC.

ECONOMY

Planning. The 1974–78 development plan envisages expenditure of 386,000m. Mali francs and a 7·1% annual increase in GDP (estimated to be 166,000m. Mali francs in 1971).

Budget. The ordinary budget for 1974 balanced at 31,823m. Mali francs.

Currency. On 5 May 1967 the Mali franc was devalued from MF 246·853 to MF 493·706 per US$. In Feb. 1967 Mali signed a monetary agreement with France whereby Mali re-entered the French franc zone which it had abandoned in 1962, and in March 1968 the Mali franc became convertible at the rate of MF 100 to 1 French franc.

AGRICULTURE. Production of cotton increased from 22,000 tons (1961–65) to 42,000 tons (1973) with an area under cultivation of 70,000 hectares in 1973.

Production in 1973 included (in 1,000 tonnes) millet (600), rice (100), maize (60), groundnuts (147). In 1976 there were 4·08m. head of cattle, 150,000 horses, 400,000 asses, 4·22m. sheep, 3·9m. goats and 178,000 camels.

Important irrigation schemes have been carried out in the Ségou and Mopti districts on the Niger River, of which the Sansanding Barrage is the centre; 50,000 hectares of cotton and rice lands are being irrigated.

TRADE. Imports in 1974 totalled 42,900m. Mali francs, exports, 16,990m. Chief imports are foodstuffs, automobiles, petrol, building material, sugar, salt, beer. Chief exports are groundnuts, karité, gum, dried fish and skins.

Trade with UK (British Department of Trade returns, in £1,000 sterling):

	1973	*1974*	*1975*	*1976*	*1977*
Imports to UK	782	2,505	576	1,797	2,124
Exports and re-exports from UK	431	1,436	1,697	1,453	1,554

COMMUNICATIONS

Roads. There are 12,080 km of roads, of which 7,500 km are usable in all seasons; they include 669 km of the metalled road Dakar–Niger (1,250 km). There were 2,002 road vehicles in 1971.

Railways. Mali has a railway from Kayes to Koulikoro by way of Bamako, a continuation of the Dakar–Kayes line in Senegal. An agreement was signed in May 1968 between Mali, Guinea and China to extend the railway from Kourousa–Kankan in Guinea to Bamako, though no work had been done in 1976. Total length 645 km.

Aviation. Air services connect the Republic with Paris, Dakar and Abidjan. The chief airport is at Bamako. In 1973 aircraft disembarked and embarked 63,000 passengers and 3,945 tonnes of freight and mail.

Shipping. For about 7 months in the year small steamboats perform the service from Koulikoro to Tombouctou and Gao, and from Bamako to Kouroussa.

Post and Broadcasting. There were, in 1969, 7,800 telephones and (1975) 81,000 radio receivers.

EDUCATION AND WELFARE

Education. There were in 1969–70, 218,400 pupils in primary schools, 4,300 in secondary schools and 2,900 in technical schools

Health. In 1971 there were 124 doctors.

DIPLOMATIC REPRESENTATIVES

OF MALI IN GREAT BRITAIN

Ambassador: Mamadou Traoré (resides in Brussels).

OF GREAT BRITAIN IN MALI

Ambassador: J. E. Powell-Jones, CMG (resides in Dakar).

OF MALI IN THE USA (2130 R. St., NW, Washington, D.C., 20008)

Ambassador: Ibrahima Sima.

OF THE USA IN MALI (Rue Testard and Rue Mohamed V, Bamako)
Ambassador: Patricia M. Byrne.

OF MALI TO THE UNITED NATIONS
Ambassador: Mamadou Boubacar Kante.

Book of Reference

Hopkins, N. S., *Popular Government in an African Town.* Univ. of Chicago Press, 1972

MALTA

Capital: Valletta
Population: 304,997 (1976)

Repubblika Ta Malta

HISTORY. Malta was held in turn by Phoenicians, Carthaginians and Romans, and was conquered by Arabs in 870. From 1090 it was joined to Sicily until 1530, when it was handed over to the Knights of St John, who ruled until dispersed by Napoleon in 1798. The Maltese rose in rebellion against the French and the island was subsequently blockaded by the British aided by the Maltese from 1798 to 1800. The Maltese people freely requested the protection of the British Crown in 1802 on condition that their rights and privileges be preserved. The islands were finally annexed to the British Crown by the Treaty of Paris in 1814.

On 17 April 1942, in recognition of the steadfastness and fortitude of the people of Malta during the Second World War, King George VI awarded the George Cross to the island.

AREA AND POPULATION. The area of Malta is 246 sq. km (94·9 sq. miles); Gozo, 67 sq. km (25·9 sq. miles); Comino, 3 sq. km (1·1 sq. miles); total area, 316 sq. km (121·9 sq. miles). Population, census 27 Nov. 1967, 314,216; estimate (31 Dec. 1976) 304,997. (Malta, 282,628; Gozo and Comino, 22,369.) Chief town and port, Valletta, population 14,071 (1976).

Vital statistics, 1976: Births, 5,696; deaths, 2,967; marriages, 2,938; net emigration, 1,365; gross emigration (including emigrants who later returned), 1,107.

CONSTITUTION AND GOVERNMENT. Malta was granted a measure of self-government (subject to the reservation of certain powers to the Governor) under a constitution introduced by letters patent dated 5 Sept. 1947. On the resignation of the Government led by D. Mintoff on 24 April 1958 and the disturbances that followed, a state of emergency was declared on 30 April 1958, and the direct administration of the island was assumed by the Governor. On 15 April 1959 the state of emergency was brought to an end and the 1947 constitution was replaced by an interim constitution. A new Constitution was introduced by the Malta (Constitution) Order in Council, 1961, under which the island became known as 'the State of Malta'. The UK Government retained responsibility for defence and external affairs.

On 20 Aug. 1962 the Prime Minister made a formal request for independence within the Commonwealth. Following a constitutional conference in July 1963 and further talks in London, a referendum was held in the island in May 1964 to decide on the form of the Independence Constitution. A Malta Independence Bill was passed by the House of Commons and by the Malta Legislative Assembly. The Maltese Parliament also agreed to Malta's applying for Commonwealth membership. Malta became independent on 21 Sept. 1964.

Malta became a republic within the Commonwealth on 13 Dec. 1974.

Malta is a democratic republic and the Constitution, which was amended in 1965, 1966, 1970, 1972 and 1974, provides for a parliament consisting of a House of Representatives of elected members and a Cabinet consisting of the Prime Minister and such number of Ministers as may be appointed. The Constitution makes provision for the protection of fundamental rights and freedom of the individual, and ensures that all persons in Malta shall have full freedom of conscience and religious worship.

Maltese and English, and such other language as may be prescribed by Parliament, are the official languages.

National flag: Vertically white and red, with a representation of the George Cross medal in the canton.

Elections were held on 17 and 18 Sept. 1976. State of parties in Sept. 1976: Malta Labour Party, 34; Nationalist Party, 31.

The Cabinet (Malta Labour Party) was as at Feb. 1978:

President: Dr Anton Buttigieg.

Prime Minister, Minister of Commonwealth and Foreign Affairs and Minister of the Interior: Dom Mintoff.

Justice, Lands, Housing and Parliamentary Affairs: Dr Joseph Cassar. *Labour, Welfare and Culture:* Agatha Barbara. *Finance, Customs and People's Financial Investments:* Dr Joseph Abela. *Tourism:* Dr Daniel Piscopo. *Works and Sport:* Lorry Sant. *Development, Energy, Ports and Telecommunications:* Wistin Abela. *Parastatal and People's Industries:* Freddie Micallef. *Trade:* Dr Patrick Holland. *Health and Environment:* Dr Vincent Moran. *Industry, Fisheries and Agriculture:* Danny Cremona. *Education:* Dr Philip Muscat.

DEFENCE. The Maltese armed forces are reported to have received a few Dornier Do 27 communications aircraft from Federal Republic of Germany, to supplement 4 Bell 47G–2 and 1 JetRanger light helicopters received in 1971–73. Personnel consisted (1978) of one regular unit and 2 para-military corps.

INTERNATIONAL RELATIONS

Membership. Malta is a member of UN, the Commonwealth and the Council of Europe.

ECONOMY

Planning. The basic economic objective of the 1973–80 development plan is to lead the Maltese Islands to a situation of economic viability whereby the earnings derived from the British military base, on which Malta's economy was traditionally dependent, will be phased out completely by March 1979 when the base closes. The manufacturing industry has been expanded and is largely oriented towards the export market, agriculture, tourism, commerce and other services. Other objectives include the development of Malta as a leading ship-repair and shipbuilding centre in the Mediterranean by the construction of the Red China Dock, which will be capable of taking vessels of up to 300,000 DWT and by the new Marsa shipbuilding yard for the building of vessels of up to 120,000 tons. In its programme of economic restructuring, Malta is also seeking to exploit its strategic position in the centre of the Mediterranean, and intensive efforts are now under way to turn the island into a major transhipment centre by the development of a new harbour at Marsaxlokk Bay.

Budget. Revenue and expenditure (in £M) for financial years ending 31 March:

	1973–74	*1974–75*	*1975–76*	*1976–77*	*1977–78*
Revenue	55,850,380	74,453,497	88,358,156	100,820,470	94,595,000
Expenditure	55,731,672	63,789,284	94,043,698	96,097,392	103,015,000

The most important sources of revenue are customs duties, income tax, licences, stamp duties, fees of office and reimbursements, receipts from the Central Bank of Malta and rent for defence facilities.

Currency. Central Bank of Malta notes of £M1, £M5 and £M10 denominations are in circulation. On 16 May 1972 a new decimal system was introduced and UK coinage previously in circulation ceased to be legal tender in Malta after 4 Oct. 1972. Malta coins are issued in the following denominations: 50, 25, 10, 5, 2 and 1 cents; 5, 3 and 2 *mils*. Total notes in circulation on 31 Dec. 1976 was £M120m.; coins, £M2·8m.

Banking. The Central Bank of Malta was founded in 1968. Commercial banking facilities are provided by Bank of Valletta Ltd, Lombard Bank Malta Ltd and Mid Med Bank Ltd. The other domestic banking institutions are the government savings bank and the Investment Finance Bank.

ENERGY AND NATURAL RESOURCES

Electricity. All towns and villages in Malta and Gozo are provided with electric current. The islands obtain their electricity power supplies from 2 interconnected power stations located at Marsa (Malta) having a total installed capacity of 115 mw. The bigger power station with a generating capacity of 85 mw is also equipped with distillation plant capable of also producing fresh water for public consumption at the rate of 4·5m. gallons per day.

The gross electricity generated in 1976 was 387m. kwh.

Agriculture. In 1976 agriculture contributed £M10·3m. to the Gross Domestic Product as against £M8·4m. in 1975. (The 1976 figure represents a share of 5·45% in the GDP.) In 1976 there was a slight increase in the area cultivated, which totalled 12,857 hectares as against 12,618 hectares in 1975. In 1976 agriculture employed 6,019 full-time farmers, 546 full-time wage earners and 10,778 part-time farmers against 5,916, 470 and 9,224 respectively in 1975. (The 1976 figure for full-time farmers and full-time wage earners represents 5·95% of the gainfully occupied population.)

In 1976 the value of Malta's main agricultural exports reached £M2·5m. as against £M1·1m. in 1975. The 1976 exports consisted of: potatoes, £M1,532,046; onions, £M173,256; wine, £M189,808; live animals, £M69,823; meat and meat products, £M164,469; seeds, cut-flowers and plants, £M328,951; hides and skins, £M63,614.

Fisheries. In 1976 the fishing industry occupied 895 motor and 139 other fishing boats, engaging 440 full-time and 567 part-time fishermen. The catch in 1976 was, 1,552 tonnes valued at £M775,137 at first sale of which 200 tonnes valued at £M58,649 were landed by the government trawlers.

INDUSTRY AND TRADE

Industry. Investors in industry in Malta are offered the following advantages: political stability, excellent industrial relations, a strategic geographic location, favourable customs tariffs with the EEC, a fully developed and highly functional infrastructure, free repatriation of profits and capital, easily trainable and highly adaptable labour force, financing facilities at favourable rates of interest, ready-built factories at very low rents. About 200 aided projects are in operation in various industrial sectors, of which the majority are foreign-owned or have foreign interests. The Malta Development Corporation is the Government agency responsible for promoting and implementing new industrial projects, including joint ventures. The Corporation may also participate by way of equity capital, up to a maximum of 20%, in certain projects jointly with Maltese or foreign industrialists.

Labour. The total work force at 15 Nov. 1976 was 115,311; males, 85,458; females, 29,853, distributed as follows: Agriculture and fisheries, 7,209; manufacturing, 27,959; building, construction and quarrying, 4,705; services, 32,332; electricity, gas and drydocks, 6,066; government, 20,303; armed forces, 634; Malta Pioneer Corps, Dirghajn il-Maltin and auxiliary workers, 7,876; military base department and British Services, 3,329. The number of registered unemployed as at 31 Dec. 1976 was 4,898.

There were 60 trade unions registered as at 31 Dec. 1976, with a total membership of 42,622.

Commerce. Imports and exports including bullion and specie (in £M1,000);

	1970	*1971*	*1972*	*1973*	*1974*	*1975*	*1976*
Imports	67,121	65,377	67,210	88,100	138,969	144,448	179,900
Exports	16,065	18,815	25,722	35,961	51,582	63,899	97,400

In 1976 the principal items of imports were: Semi-manufactures, £M56·2m.; food, £M36·2m.; machinery and transport, £M34·3m.; fuels, £M15·8m.; manufactures, £M14·4m.; beverages and tobacco, £M5·8m.; others, £M17·2m. Of domestic exports: Manufactures, £M54·4m.; semi-manufactures, £M8·3m.; machinery and transport, £M8·2m.; food, £M5·2m.; beverages and tobacco, £M2·6m.; others, £M1·4m.

In 1976, £M43·8m. of the imports came from UK, £M31·4m. from Italy, £M21·7m. from USA, £M18·6m. from Federal Republic of Germany, £M14·8m. from Asia, £M10·9m. from other European countries, £M6·8m. from the EFTA, £M4·8m. from Oceania, £M2·6m. from Africa; of domestic exports, £M23·4m. to Federal Republic of Germany, £M15·9m. to UK, £M10·3m. to Africa, £M6·8m. to Asia, £M5·1m. to EFTA, £M4m. to Italy, £M1·6m. to USA and £M0·6m. to other European countries.

Total trade of Malta with UK (British Department of Trade returns, in £1,000 sterling):

	1974	*1975*	*1976*	*1977*
Imports to UK	15,322	17,091	25,528	34,041
Exports and re-exports from UK	34,269	40,822	49,187	64,339

Tourism. In 1976, 339,537 tourists visited Malta, 214,076 from UK, 23,052 from Italy, 10,303 from Scandinavia, 18,003 from Federal Republic of Germany, 12,446 from Libya, 9,450 from USA annd 9,656 from France.

COMMUNICATIONS

Roads. Every town and village is served by motor omnibuses. There are ferry services running between Malta and Gozo; cars can be transported on the ferries. Motor vehicles registered during 1976 totalled 75,244 of which 53,360 were private cars, 3,025 hire cars, 12,609 commercial vehicles, 622 buses, 4,665 motor cycles and 963 other motor vehicles.

Aviation. In 1976 the principal airlines, British Airways, Air Malta, Alitalia, Libyan Arab Airlines, Union de Transports Aeriens, Yugoslav Air Transport and Zambia Airways, operated scheduled services between Malta and UK, Italy, France, Libya, Yugoslavia and Zambia. In 1976 there were 9,828 civil aircraft movements at Luqa Airport. 745,537 passengers and 6,690 tonnes of freight (excluding mail) were handled.

Shipping. The number of ships registered in Malta on 31 Dec. 1976 was 183, 83,626 GRT. Ships entering harbour during 1976, 3,497 of 5·7m. tons.

Post. There is a government system of telephones with exchanges at Malta and Gozo. On 1 Jan. 1977 there were 62,234 telephones.

Cinemas (1976). There were 37 cinemas with a seating capacity of 30,000.

Newspapers. There are 2 English, 3 Maltese daily newspapers and 4 Sunday papers.

JUSTICE, RELIGION, EDUCATION AND WELFARE

Justice. The number of persons convicted in 1976 of crimes was 1,473; those convicted for contraventions against various laws and regulations numbered 3,368. 101 were committed to prison and 6,259 were awarded fines. 6 male juveniles were committed to St Philip Neri School.

Police. On 31 Dec. 1976 police numbered 40 officers and 1,377 other ranks, including 16 women police.

Religion. The majority of the population belong to the Roman Catholic Church.

Education. Education in Malta is compulsory between the ages of 6 and 16 and free in government schools. As a result of the launching of a kindergarten scheme for the 4-year olds by the Government, 218 kindergarten groups with over 3,000 children were opened in 59 centres throughout Malta and Gozo in 1976–77. The primary level enrols children between 5 and 11 years in a 6-year course. There were 23,447 children (12,158 boys and 11,289 girls) in 100 government schools. There were 41 government secondary schools with a total of 19,484 (8,662 boys, 10,822 girls). Secondary schools run 5-year courses leading to GCE 'O' level; upper secondary schools offer 2-year courses leading to 3 GCE 'A' levels. Enrolment in craft and technician courses in 3 technical institutes amounted to 1,296, while 3,251 (2,623 boys and 628 girls) were enrolled in the 9 trade schools for boys and 5 trade schools for girls. Trade schools offer 2- to 4-year courses in specialized trades and are open to students who finish their third year of secondary education. Another 84 students were enrolled in the Nautical School and the Training Centre in Industrial Electronics. The number of children in special education amounted to 594.

There were 81 private schools with a population of 3,868 at the nursery level, 7,534 at the primary level and 7,325 at the secondary level. Government subsidises recognized private secondary schools on a *per capita* basis.

5,860 students (2,887 males and 2,973 females) attended evening courses in academic, commercial, technical and practical subjects established in 82 centres. The School of Art had an enrolment of 249 students while another 717 students enrolled in courses organized by the School of Music. 370 members of a para-military labour corps were given intensive trade training by the Education Department.

The 2 institutes of higher education are the Malta College of Arts, Science and Technology and the University of Malta. The former had an enrolment of 1,313 students in 1976 which included 273 teachers in training. Enrolment at the university was 971.

Welfare. The National Insurance Act, 1956, provides cash benefits for marriage (women only), sickness, unemployment, widowhood, orphanhood, invalidity, old age, children's allowances and industrial injury. An agreement, signed on 26 Oct. 1956, established reciprocity in matters of social insurance between Malta and the UK.

The total number of persons in receipt of benefits on 31 March 1976 was 67,984, viz., 1,236 in receipt of sickness benefit, 1,081 unemployment benefit, 198 injury benefit, 159 disablement benefit, 88 death benefit, 18,166 retirement pensions, 5,383 widows' pensions, 14 guardian's allowance, 1,659 invalidity pensions and 40,000 children's allowances.

The National Assistance Act, 1956, provides for the payment of social assistance and medical assistance, while the Old Age Pensions Act of 1948 provides for the payment of non-contributory old-age pensions to persons over 60 years of age and to blind persons over the age of 14 years.

The number of households in receipt of social assistance and of medical assistance on 31 March 1976 was 3,895 and 4,800 respectively, and the number of old-age pensioners under the Old Age Pensions Act, 1948, was 8,523.

DIPLOMATIC REPRESENTATIVES

OF MALTA IN GREAT BRITAIN (24 Haymarket, London, SW1Y 4DJ)

High Commissioner: Arthur J. Scerri.

OF GREAT BRITAIN IN MALTA (7 St Anne St., Floriana, Valletta)

High Commissioners: N. Aspin, CMG.

OF MALTA IN THE USA (2017 Connecticut Ave., NW, Washington, D.C., 20008)

Chargé d'Affaires: Victor Gauci.

OF THE USA IN MALTA (Development Hse., St Anne St., Floriana, Valletta)

Ambassador: L. Bruce Laingen.

OF MALTA TO THE UNITED NATIONS

Ambassador: (Vacant).

Books of Reference

Statistical Information: The Central Office of Statistics (1 Windmill Street, Valletta) was set up in 1947. It publishes *Statistical Abstracts of the Maltese Islands*, a quarterly digest of statistics, monthly vital statistics and annual publications on foreign trade, shipping and aviation, education, taxation, agriculture and industry.

Government publications: The Department of Information (Auberge de Castille, Valletta), set up in 1955, publishes *The Malta Government Gazette* (twice weekly), *Il Gzejjer* (monthly), *Malta*

Today (quarterly), *Malta Handbook, Economic Survey, Development Plan for Malta 1973–80, Paper Currency in Malta, Heritage of an Island.*

Malta Independence Constitution (Cmnd 2406). HMSO, 1964
Constitution of the Republic of Malta. Department of Information, 1975
Malta Who's Who. Malta, 1969–70
Economic Survey 1976. Malta, 1976
The Malta Year Book. Malta from 1952
Malta Handbook 1977. Department of Information, 1977
Blouet, Brian, *The Story of Malta.* London, 1967
Busuttil, E. D., *Kalepin Dizzjunarju Malti-Ingliz.* Valletta, 1941
Cassar, P., *Medical History of Malta.* London, 1966
Cremona, J. J., *The Malta Constitution of 1835 and its Historical Background.* Malta, 1959.—*The Constitutional Developments of Malta under British Rule.* Malta University Press, 1963.—*Human Rights Documentation in Malta.* Malta University Press, 1966
Dobie, E., *Malta's Road to Independence.* University of Oklahoma, Norman, USA, 1967
Luke, Sir Harry, *Malta.* 2nd ed. London, 1962
Price, G. A., *Malta and the Maltese: A Study in 19th-century Migration.* Melbourne, 1954
Smith, Harrison, *Britain in Malta.* 2 vols. Malta, 1954

MAURITANIA

Capital: Nouakchott
Population: 1·48m. (1977)
GNP per capita: US$340 (1976)

République Islamique de Mauritanie

HISTORY. The Islamic Republic of Mauritania became independent on 28 Nov. 1960, after having been a French protectorate (1903) and colony (1920).

AREA AND POPULATION. The Republic is divided into 10 administrative areas, and the district of Nouakchott, with a total area of 1,030,700 sq. km. Two additional regions (88,667 sq. km) have been formed from the portion of Western Sahara occupied by Mauritania.

The population is estimated (1977) at 1,481,000. Nouadhibou (135,000 inhabitants), F'Derik (18,000), Kaédi (13,000), Atar (13,000) and Rosso (13,000) are the principal towns, Nouakchott (70,000) is the capital.

The official languages are French and Arabic. The population is 80% Arabic and 20% Bantu.

The Republic is administered by a government council of 16 ministers. The national assembly consists of 70 members, elected by universal suffrage. The President appoints a Council of Ministers (16 members) to assist him. Since 1964 the only legal political party has been the Parti du peuple mauritanien (PPM), who nominate the candidates for President and for the National Assembly. Seven additional members were nominated on 8 Aug. 1976 to represent the newly-acquired territory of the former Western Sahara.

President of the Republic, Prime Minister: Moktar ould Daddah (re-elected for a fourth 5-year term in 1976).

Foreign Affairs: Hamdi ould Mouknass.

National flag: Green, with a crescent beneath a star in yellow in the centre.

DEFENCE

Army. The Army consists of 5 infantry battalions, 1 paracommando company and 3 motorized reconnaissance squadrons; total strength, 7,000.

Air Force. The Air Force has 6 Britten-Norman Defender armed light transports, 1 C-54, 3 C-47, 1 Caravelle, 2 Buffalo and 2 Skyvan transports and 2 Broussard, 3 Reims-Cessna 337 Milirole Skymaster and 1 Aermacchi AL.60 light aircraft. Personnel (1978) 150.

INTERNATIONAL RELATIONS

Membership. Mauritania is a member of UN, OAU, the Arab League and is an ACP state of EEC.

ECONOMY

Budget. The ordinary budget for 1972 balanced at 10,004m. francs CFA, the capital budget at 1,413m.

Currency. The monetary unit is *ougiya* which is divided into 5 *khoums*. Bank-notes of 1,000, 200 and 100 *ougiyas* and coins of 20, 10, 5 and 1 *ougiya* and 1 *khoum* are in circulation. The *ougiya* is equal to 5 francs CFA.

NATURAL RESOURCES

Minerals. Huge deposits of iron ore (Fort Gouraud) and copper (Akjoujt) are being exploited. Iron ore exports in 1972, 8·6m. tonnes; copper 5·3m. tonnes.

Agriculture. Chief products are cattle, millet, gum, salt, niébé (a kind of haricot), béref (*citrullus vulgaris*), and dried and salted fish.

In 1976 there were 748,000 camels, 2m. cattle, 264,000 asses, 29,000 horses, 5·6m. sheep and goats. Production (tonnes) (1970) of millet, 40,000; dates, 15,000; niébé, 4,000; maize, 3,000; sweet potatoes, 2,000; rice, 1,000. The 1970 harvest was exceptionally poor because of drought conditions. Rubber production (1970–71) 5,464 tonnes.

Fisheries. Export of salted and dried fish in 1971, 4,958 tonnes.

TRADE. There is a chamber of commerce for Western Mauritania in Nouakchott. In 1974 imports totalled 5,543m. ougiyas and exports 8,199m.

Total trade between Mauritania and UK (British Department of Trade returns, in £1,000 sterling):

	1973	*1974*	*1975*	*1976*	*1977*
Imports to UK	14,463	13,303	15,238	14,948	11,825
Exports and re-exports from UK	857	4,554	3,959	6,176	4,364

COMMUNICATIONS

Roads. There were 6,904 km of roads in 1975.

Railways. A mineral railway was opened between the port of Nouadhibou and Tazadit (650 km) in 1963. Passenger trains also run.

Aviation. In 1973 aircraft disembarked and embarked 55,000 passengers and 1,495 tonnes of freight and mail.

Post and Broadcasting. There were, in 1977, over 2,000 telephones and 82,000 radio receivers.

Cinemas. In 1971 there were 10 cinemas with a seating capacity of 1,000.

EDUCATION AND WELFARE

Education. There were, in 1970–71, 31,945 pupils in primary schools and (1971–72) 3,745 in secondary schools.

Health. There were 68 doctors in 1970.

DIPLOMATIC REPRESENTATIVES

OF MAURITANIA IN GREAT BRITAIN

Ambassador: Ahmed Ould Ghanahalla (resides in Paris).

OF GREAT BRITAIN IN MAURITANIA

Ambassador: J. E. Powell-Jones, CMG (resides in Dakar).

OF MAURITANIA IN THE USA (2129 Leroy Pl., NW, Washington, D.C., 20008)

Ambassador: Mohammed Nassim Kochman.

OF THE USA IN MAURITANIA (P.O. Box 222, Nouakchott)

Ambassador: E. Gregory Kryza.

OF MAURITANIA TO THE UNITED NATIONS

Ambassador: Moulaye El Hassan.

MAURITIUS

Capital: Port Louis
Population: 880,781 (1976)
GNP per capita: US$680 (1976)

HISTORY. Mauritius was known to Arab navigators probably not later than the 10th century. It was probably visited by Malays in the 15th century, and was discovered by the Portuguese between 1507 and 1512, but the Dutch were the first settlers (1598). In 1710 they abandoned the island, which was occupied by the French under the name of Ile de France (1715). The British occupied the island in 1810, and it was formally ceded to Great Britain by the Treaty of Paris, 1814. Mauritius attained independence on 12 March 1968.

AREA AND POPULATION. The island situated 20% S. lat., 57½° E. long., is of volcanic origin. The climate is free from extremes of weather, except for tropical cyclones at times. Yearly rainfall varies from 30 in. on the north-west coast to 200 in. in the uplands.

Mauritius has an area of about 720 sq. miles (1,865 sq. km). According to the census of 30 June 1972, the population of the island was 826,199 (413,648 males, 412,551 females); that of the dependencies was 25,135 (30 June 1972). The estimated population of the island at the end of 1976 was 880,781, and the population of Port Louis, the capital with its suburbs, numbered 141,343. Port Louis was granted city status on 25 Aug. 1966.

Rodrigues (formerly a dependency but now a part of Mauritius) is about 350 miles east of Mauritius, 9½ miles long, 4½ miles broad. Area, 40 sq. miles (103·6 sq. km). Population (census 1972), 24,769; estimated population on 31 Dec. 1976, 27,049 (13,251 males; 13,798 females). Imports, 1974, Rs 16,804,280; 1975, Rs 19,161,796. Exports, 1974, Rs 3,441,089; 1975, Rs 3,329,680. There are 2 government, 5 aided primary and 1 private secondary school.

Vital statistics, June 1976: Births, 22,250 (25·6 per 1,000); marriages, 8,262 (19 per 1,000); deaths, 6,815 (7·8 per 1,000).

The official language is English.

Dependencies. Agalega and St Brandon Group. St Brandon is 250 miles from Mauritius. Area, 71 sq. km. Total population of the lesser dependencies, census 1972, 366; estimated population on 31 Dec. 1976, 350. The main exports (to Mauritius) in 1974 were 227 tonnes of salted fish.

In 1965 the Chagos Archipelago was transferred to the newly created colony of British Indian Ocean Territory (*see* SEYCHELLES, p. 1043).

CONSTITUTION AND GOVERNMENT. Mauritius became an independent state and a monarchial member of the British Commonwealth on 12 March 1968 after 7 months of internal self-government. The Governor-General is the local representative of HM the Queen, who remains the Head of the State.

In accordance with the Mauritius Independence Order 1968 the Cabinet is presided over by the Prime Minister. Each of the other 19 members of the Cabinet is responsible for the administration of specified departments or subjects and is bound by the rule of collective responsibility. There are also 9 Parliamentary Secretaries appointed by the Governor-General on the advice of the Prime Minister.

The Legislative Assembly consists of a Speaker and 62 elected members (3 each for the 20 constituencies of Mauritius and 2 for Rodrigues) and 8 additional seats in order to ensure a fair and adequate representation of each community within the Assembly. General Elections are held every 5 years on the basis of universal adult suffrage.

The Constitution also provides for the Public Service Commission and the Judicial and Legal Service Commission, which have both assumed executive powers for appointments to the Public Service. An Ombudsman assumed office on 2 March

1970. Adequate provision is also made for the protection of fundamental rights and freedoms of the individual.

Acting-Governor-General: William Henry Garrioch.
Prime Minister: Dr The Rt. Hon. Sir Seewoosagur Ramgoolam, Kt.
National flag: Horizontally 4 stripes of red, blue, yellow and green.

DEFENCE. The Mauritius Police, which is responsible for defence, is equipped with arms; its strength at 1 July 1977 was 3,922 officers and men.

INTERNATIONAL RELATIONS

Membership. Mauritius is a member of UN, the Commonwealth, OAU and is an ACP state of EEC.

ECONOMY

Budget. Revenue and expenditure (in Rs) for years ending 30 June:

	1972–73	*1973–74*	*1974–75*	*1975–76*	*1976–77*
Revenue	376,729,269	515,442,360	744,940,161	1,075,657,316	1,210,676,709
Expenditure	326,428,453	534,775,320	734,310,871	1,071,038,550	1,260,978,369

Principal sources of revenue, June 1977: Direct taxes, Rs 437,278,066; indirect taxes, Rs 643,902,599; receipts from public utilities, Rs 47,096,123; receipts from public services Rs 24,177,215; interest and royalties, Rs 44,441,355; reimbursement, Rs 10,266,492. Capital expenditure, 1977, was Rs 485,377,265. Capital revenue, Rs 285,736,213.

On 30 June 1977 the public debt of Mauritius was Rs 1,250,289,392 after deducting the value of accumulated sinking funds.

Currency. The unit of currency is the Mauritius Rupee, divided into 100 cents.

The currency consists of: (i) Bank of Mauritius notes of Rs 50, 25, 10 and 5; (ii) Cupro-nickel coins of 1 rupee, rupee, rupee and 10 cents; (iii) Bronze coins of 5 cents, 2 cents and 1 cent.

Notes and coins in circulation as at 31 Dec. 1977 amounted to Rs 779·4m. and Rs 21·7m. respectively.

Banking. The Bank of Mauritius was established in 1966, with an authorized capital of Rs 10m., to exercise the function of a central bank. There are 10 commercial banks, the Mauritius Commercial Bank Ltd (established 1838), Barclays Bank International, the Bank of Baroda Ltd, The Mercantile Bank Ltd, the Mauritius Co-operative Central Bank Ltd, Banque Nationale de Commerce et d'Industrie (Ocean Indien), the Habib Bank (Overseas) Ltd, Citibank, the State Commercial Bank and the Bank of Credit and Commerce International SA. Other financial institutions include the Mauritius Housing Corporation, the Development Bank of Mauritius and the post office savings bank.

On 30 June 1976 the post office savings bank held deposits amounting to Rs 72·4m., belonging to 121,917 depositors.

NATURAL RESOURCES

Agriculture (1976). The area planted with sugar-cane is 214,954 acres. There were 21 factories in operation and the amount of sugar produced was 52,745 tonnes of white sugar and 637,187 tonnes of raw sugar. 199,421 tonnes of molasses were also produced.

The main secondary crops are tea (13,691 acres, yielding 4,335 tonnes of black tea), tobacco (1,389 acres, yielding 700 tonnes of tobacco), aloe (1,713 arpents, yielding 676 tonnes of fibre), potatoes (1,868 arpents, yielding 11,945 tonnes) and onions (391 arpents, yielding 1,264 tonnes of green onions).

Livestock (1976): Cattle, 53,000; goats, 67,000; poultry, 1·1m.

Forestry. The total forest area is estimated at 20,200 hectares including some 9,700 hectares of plantations; if scrub and grazing lands are included the total area is approximately 57,400 hectares.

In 1976 sales of forest produce from Crown land totalled 23,110 cu. metres, worth Rs 1,562,000. Free collections of firewood could not be accurately estimated, nor could the production from private lands.

INDUSTRY AND TRADE

Labour. There were on 31 Dec. 1976, 177 registered trade unions with a total membership of 69,695 (on roll).

Commerce. Total trade in rupees for calendar years:

	1972	*1973*	*1974*	*1975*	*1976*
Imports[1]	635,800,000	915,800,000	1,759,800,000	1,995,300,000	2,398,700,000
Exports[2]	573,800,000	748,300,000	1,786,400,000	1,838,900,000	1,769,800,000

[1] Excluding bullion and specie.
[2] Including value of sugar quota certificates.

In 1976, Rs 390·2m. of the imports came from UK, Rs 237·9m. from South Africa and Rs 116·3m. from Australia; Rs 1,226·7m. of the exports went to UK, Rs 103·5m. to USA and Rs 67m. to Canada.

Sugar exports in 1975, 497,500 tonnes (Rs 1,548·8m.); 1976, 544,500 tonnes (Rs 1,321·5m.).

Total trade between Mauritius and UK (British Department of Trade returns, in £1,000 sterling):

	1972	*1973*	*1974*	*1975*	*1976*	*1977*
Imports to UK	27,091	28,328	47,012	103,080	99,995	102,906
Exports and re-exports from UK	8,122	10,538	19,479	23,934	27,766	34,403

Tourism. In 1976, 92,561 tourists visited Mauritius, spending about Rs 184m.

COMMUNICATIONS

Roads. There are 9·5 miles of motorway, 351 miles of main roads, 369 miles of urban roads and 380 miles of rural roads. All the main urban and rural roads have a bitumen surface. At 31 Dec. 1976 there were 20,656 cars, including 2,288 for public hire, 1,186 buses, 6,455 motor cycles and 9,447 auto cycles. Commercial vehicles comprised 8,804 lorries and vans.

Aviation. Mauritius is linked by air with Europe, Africa, India and Australia by the following airlines: Air France, Air India, Air Malawi, Air Mauritius, Alitalia, British Airways, Kenya Airways, Lufthansa, South African Airways and Zambia Airways. In addition to passenger services a weekly cargo flight is operated by Air France on the Mauritius–Paris route. The Government is presently planning for the construction of a new airport at Plaine des Roches.

Air Mauritius operates a Boeing 707 service to London *via* Nairobi and to Bombay *via* the Seychelles, and Twin Otter services to Réunion and Rodrigues. The Company has commercial arrangements with Air France, Lufthansa, Alitalia, Zambia Airways and Air Malawi for the operation of services to Paris, Frankfurt, Rome, Lusaka and Blantyre.

Shipping. The registered shipping, as at 31 Dec. 1976, consisted of 16 motor vessels (23,687 NRT). In 1976, 920 vessels of 2,368,860 NRT entered and 916 vessels of 2,372,773 NRT cleared Mauritius.

Post and Broadcasting. In Dec. 1976 there were 26 telephone exchanges and 26,505 individual telephone installations. Communication with other parts of the world is established *via* radio links. A radio-telephone service operates with countries all over the world.

Television was introduced in Feb. 1965. At 31 Dec. 1976 there were 45,826 television sets and 87,380 radio sets.

Cinemas (1974). There were 50 cinemas, with a seating capacity of 48,000.

Newspapers. There are 8 French daily papers (with occasional articles in English) with a combined circulation of 67,000 and 2 Chinese daily papers with a combined circulation of 5,000.

RELIGION, EDUCATION AND WELFARE

Religion. At the 1972 census there were 245,556 Roman Catholics, 7,047 Protestants (Church of England and Church of Scotland). The Hindus numbered 421,705 and the Moslems, 136,996. State aid is granted to the churches and amounted to Rs 1,924,770 in 1976–77.

Education. Primary education is free but not compulsory, though under the Education Ordinance of 1957 compulsion may be introduced as circumstances permit. In Jan. 1978 there were 186 government and 50 state-aided schools. Average attendance at government schools was 100,612 and at state-aided primary schools 30,688. There were 3 junior technical schools for boys and girls providing a free 3-year post-primary pre-vocational course with emphasis on handicraft and homecraft, 107 unaided primary schools with an enrolment of 1,943, 6 grant-aided and 32 unaided secondary schools with primary sections with an enrolment of 3,255.

For secondary education there were in Jan. 1978, 5 government boys' schools (one of which has technical and commercial streams) and 2 government girls' schools with 3,809 pupils, and 22 aided (including Mahatma Gandhi Institute with 10,431 pupils) and 86 unaided secondary schools for boys and girls, with a roll of 26,566 and 24,751 respectively.

There is also a teachers' training college, 589 on roll (including 252 working under supervision in primary schools) and 10 vocational and technical training centres (1,032 on roll and 308 students following part-time courses).

Government expenditure on education in 1977–78 was Rs 222·5m.

Health. In 1972 there were 160 doctors and 3,200 hospital beds.

DIPLOMATIC REPRESENTATIVES

OF MAURITIUS IN GREAT BRITAIN (32–33 Elvaston Pl., London, SW7)

High Commissioner: Sir Leckraz Teelock, CBE.

OF GREAT BRITAIN IN MAURITIUS (Cerne Hse, Chausee, Port Louis)

High Commissioner: William Alec Ward.

OF MAURITIUS IN THE USA (4301 Connecticut Ave., NW, Washington, D.C., 20008)

Ambassador: Pierre G. G. Balancy, CBE.

OF THE USA IN MAURITIUS (Anglo-Mauritiuse Hse., Port Louis)

Ambassador: Robert V. Keeley.

OF MAURITIUS TO THE UNITED NATIONS

Ambassador: Radha Krishna Ramphul.

Books of Reference

Statistical Information: The Central Statistical Information Office (Rose Hill, Mauritius) was founded in July 1945. Its main publication is the *Bi-annual Digest of Statistics.*

Barnwell, P. J., and Toussaint, A., *A Short History of Mauritius.* London, 1949
Brouard, N. R., *A History of Woods and Forests in Mauritius.* Government Printer, 1964
Buckory, S., *Our Constitution.* Port Louis, 1971.—*An Outline of Local Government.* Port Louis, 1970
Central Statistical Office, *Population Census of Mauritius and its Dependencies.* 2 vols. 1962
Chelin, A., *Une île et son passé (1507–1947).* Mauritius Printing, 1973
Fougere, H., *A Survey of the Fisheries of Mauritius.* Government Printer, 1964
Jessop, A., *A History of the Mauritius Government Railways 1864–1964.* Government Printer, 1964

Leys, Colin, *The Development of a University College of Mauritius*. Government Printer, 1964
Lockwood, J. F., *An Examination of the Possibility of Setting up a University College in Mauritius*. London, 1962
Meade, J. E., *The Economic and Social Structure of Mauritius*. Government Printer, 1960
Ministry of Industry. *Handbook of Commerce and Industry*. Port Louis, 1970
Ministry of Information and Broadcasting, *Mauritius at a Glance*. Mauritius Printing, 1972
Napal, D. *Les constitutions de l'île Maurice*. Port Louis, 1962
Société de l'Histoire de l'Ile Maurice. *Dictionnaire de biographie mauricienne*. Port Louis, 1967
Titmuss, R., and Abel-Smith. B., *Social Politics and Population Growth in Mauritius*. London, 1961
Toussaint, A., *History of Mauritius*. London, 1978.
Toussaint, A., and Adolphe, H., *Bibliography of Mauritius (1502–1954)*. Port Louis, 1956
The Census of Industrial Production, 1964. Government Printer, 1965
10 années de réalisations. Ministry of Information and Broadcasting, 1967
Bi-annual Survey of Employment and Earnings in Large Establishments, 30 March 1972. Government Printer, 1972
Development Strategy (1971–1980), Ministry of Economic Planning and Development, Port Louis, 1970
4-Year Plan for Social and Economic Development 1971–75. Government Printer, 1971
5-Year Plan for Social and Economic Development 1975–80. Government Printer, 1975

Library: The Mauritius Institute Public Library, Port Louis.

MEXICO

Capital: Mexico City
Population: 62·33m. (1976)
GNP per capita: US$1,090 (1976)

Estados Unidos Mexicanos

HISTORY. Mexico's history falls into four epochs: the era of the Indian empires (before 1521), the Spanish colonial phase (1521–1810), the period of national formation (1810–1910), which includes the war of independence (1810–21) and the long presidency of Porfirio Díaz (1876–80, 1884–1911), and the present period which began with the social revolution of 1910–21 and is regarded by Mexicans as the period of social and national consolidation.

AREA AND POPULATION. Mexico is at the southern extremity of North America and is bounded in the north by USA, west and south west by the Pacific, south by Guatemala and Belize and east by the Gulf of Mexico and comprises 1,967,183 sq. km (761,530 sq. miles), excluding inland waters and uninhabited islands (5,363 sq. km) offshore. The language is Spanish.

Census results for 1970 and estimates for 1976 are shown in the following table (capital of states in brackets):

States	*Area (sq. km)*	*Census 1970*	*Estimate 1976*	*Approx. density per sq. km in 1970*
Aguascalientes (Aguascalientes)	5,589	338,142	430,000	60·50
Baja California (Mexicali)	70,113	870,421	1,253,000	12·41
Baja California, T.S. (La Paz)	73,677	128,019	181,000	1·74
Campeche (Campeche)	51,833	251,556	337,000	4·85
Coahuila (Saltillo)	151,571	1,114,956	1,334,000	7·36
Colima (Colima)	5,455	241,153	317,000	44·21
Chiapas (Tuxtla Guitiérrez)	73,887	1,569,053	1,933,000	21·24
Chihuahua (Chihuahua)	247,087	1,612,525	2,000,000	6·53
Distrito Federal (México City)	1,499	6,874,165	8,906,000	4,585·83
Durango (Durango)	119,648	939,208	1,122,000	7·85
Guanajuato (Guanajuato)	30,589	2,270,370	2,811,000	74·22
Guerrero (Chilpancingo)	63,794	1,597,360	2,013,000	25·04
Hidalgo (Pachuca)	20,987	1,193,845	1,409,000	56·88
Jalisco (Guadalajara)	80,137	3,296,586	4,157,000	41·14
México (Toluca)	21,461	3,833,185	6,245,000	178·61
Michoacán (Morelia)	59,864	2,324,226	2,805,000	38·83
Morelos (Cuernavaca)	4,941	616,119	866,000	124·70
Nayarit (Tepic)	27,621	544,031	699,000	19·70
Nuevo León (Monterrey)	64,555	1,694,689	2,344,000	26·25
Oaxaca (Oaxaca)	95,364	2,015,424	2,337,000	21·13
Puebla (Puebla)	33,919	2,508,226	3,055,000	73·95
Querétaro (Querétaro)	11,769	485,523	618,000	41·25
Quintana Roo (Chetumal)	50,350	88,150	131,000	1·75
San Luis Potosi (San Luis Potosi)	62,848	1,281,996	1,527,000	20·40
Sinaloa (Culiacán)	58,092	1,266,528	1,714,000	21·80
Sonora (Hermosillo)	184,934	1,098,720	1,414,000	5·94
Tabasco (Villa Hermosa)	24,661	768,387	1,054,000	31·16
Tamaulipas (Ciudad Victoria)	79,829	1,456,858	1,901,000	18·25
Tlaxcala (Tlaxcala)	3,914	420,638	498,000	107·47
Veracruz (Jalapa)	72,815	3,815,422	4,917,000	52·40
Yucatán (Mérida)	39,340	758,355	904,000	19·28
Zacatecas (Zacatecas)	75,040	951,462	1,097,000	12·68
Total	1,967,183[1]	48,225,238	62,329,000	24·51

[1] Excludes islands (5,363 sq. km).

At the census of 28 Jan. 1970, 24,065,614 were males and 24,159,624 females (1976, estimate, 31,466,000 males and 30,863,000 females). Urban population, 1974, was 26m. and rural population was 33m. There are five basic language groups (Náhuatl, Maya, Zapotec, Otomi and Mixtec) from which are derived a total of 59 dialects spoken by 3,111,415 inhabitants (1970 census).

Estimates (1975) of the largest cities (proper) were:

México[1]	8,591,750	Cuernavaca	273,986	Nuevo Laredo	193,145
Guadalajara[2]	1,560,805	Veracruz Llave	266,255	Durango	191,034
Monterrey[3]	1,049,957	Torreón	251,294	Matamoros	172,195
Ciudad Juárez	520,539	Hermosillo	247,887	Jalapa	171,937
Léon de los Aldamas	496,598	Culiacán	244,645	Poza Rica de Hidalgo	160,682
Puebla de Zaragoza	482,155	Mérida	239,222	Mazatlán	154,140
Tijuana	386,852	Tampico	222,188	Ciudad Obregón	152,834
Acapulco de Juárez	352,673	Aguascalientes	221,538	Querétaro	150,226
Chihuahua	346,003	Saltillo	211,129	Villahermosa	142,384
Mexicali	331,059	Morelia	209,014	Toluca de Lerdo	141,726
San Luis Potosí	281,534	Reynosa	193,653	Irapuato	140,342

[1] Greater Mexico City, 13m. [2] Greater Guadalajara, 1,856,879.
[3] Greater Monterrey, 1,543,399.

Movement of population for 3 years:

	Marriages	*Births*	*Deaths*	*Immigration*	*Emigration*
1971	378,222	2,231,999	458,323	3,035,115	2,400,617
1972	612,057[1]	2,346,002	476,206	3,530,918	2,797,048
1973	452,640	2,572,287	458,915	3,986,574	3,118,598

[1] This figure is composed of 423,776 registered marriages plus 198,281 marriages registered in 1972 during the government 'Mexican Family' campaign among indigenous classes.

Crude birth rate has been maintained at approximately 45 per 1,000 population for several years; crude death rate (1976), 9 (26·1 in 1932); infant mortality rate, 77 per 1,000 live births (375 in 1933); crude marriage rate (1973), 8·1 per 1,000 population; divorces (1973), 13,517, or 3·2% of marriages.

For the regulations governing immigration, *see* THE STATESMAN'S YEAR-BOOK, 1951, p. 1234. An Immigration Tax law came into effect 1 Jan. 1951. The net immigration in 1975 included: 693 US subjects; 611 Spaniards; 182 Germans (GDR); 86 Argentinians; 85 Cubans; 82 Italians; 69 French; 63 Canadians; 38 Colombians; 37 British; 33 Japanese; 28 Swedish; 26 Swiss; 22 Germans (FRG).

CONSTITUTION AND GOVERNMENT. A new constitution, amending the constitution of 1857, was promulgated on 5 Feb. 1917, and has been amended from time to time. Mexico is a federal republic, divided into 31 states and 1 federal district, each of which has the right to manage its own local affairs. Citizenship, including the right of suffrage, is vested in all nationals who are 18 years old and have 'an honourable means of livelihood'; women were given equal citizenship and suffrage with men in 1952–53. Thumbprints are taken of registered voters.

Congress consists of a Chamber of Deputies elected for 3 years by universal suffrage, and a Senate of 64 members, 2 for each state and the federal district, elected for 6 years. In the elections of July 1976, 63 seats were won by the Partido Revolucionario Institucional and 1 seat by the Partido Popular Socialista. Since 1964 additional 'party deputies' have also been elected to the Chamber according to a system of partial proportional representation. There are (1978) 250 seats, of which the 3 small opposition parties hold 40. Senators and deputies are ineligible for re-election until another term has elapsed. Congress sits from 1 Sept. to 31 Dec. During the recess there is a permanent committee consisting of 14 senators and 15 representatives appointed by the respective Houses.

The President is elected by direct popular vote in a general election, and holds office for 6 years. He can never be re-elected. If the office falls vacant during the first 2 years a general election must be held; if after the first 2 years, then Congress elects a successor who completes the term. The administration is carried on under the direction of the President and a cabinet formed by the secretaries of 15 ministries, the Attorney-General and the heads of 3 departments.

The names of the presidents from 1920 are as follows:

Gen. Alvaro Obregón, 1 Dec. 1920–30 Nov. 1924
Gen. Plutarco Elias Calles, 1 Dec. 1924–30 Nov. 1928.
Emilio Portes Gil (Provisional).[1] 1 Dec. 1928–4 Feb. 1930.
Pascual Oritz Rubio, 5 Feb 1930–3 Sept. 1932.[2]
Gen. Abelardo L. Rodriguez, 4 Sept. 1932–30 Nov. 1934.
Gen. Lázaro Cárdenas, 1 Dec. 1934–30 Nov. 1940.
Gen. Manuel Avila Camacho, 1 Dec. 1940–30 Nov. 1946.
Miguel Alemán Valdés, 1 Dec. 1946–30 Nov. 1952.
Adolfo Ruiz Cortines, 1 Dec 1952–30 Nov. 1958.
Adolfo Lopez Mateos, 1 Dec. 1958–30 Nov. 1964.
Gustavo Diaz Ordaz, 1 Dec. 1964–30 Nov. 1970.
Luis Echeverría Alvarez, 1 Dec 1970–30 Nov. 1976.

[1] Took office after the assassination on 17 July 1928, of Gen. Obregón, the President-elect.
[2] Resigned.

President: José Lopez Portillo (born in 1916), formerly Minister of Finance, elected 4 July 1976 to serve for 6 years. He polled 17,695,043 votes out of the total of 25,913,215 (assumed office on 1 Dec. 1976).

Minister of the Interior: Jesús Reyes Heroles. *Foreign Affairs:* Santiago Roel García. *National Defence:* Félix Galvan López. *Navy:* Adm. Ricardo Cházaro Lara. *Finance:* David Ibarra Munõz. *National Property:* José Andrés Oteyza. *Industry and Commerce:* Jorge de la Vega Domínguez. *Agriculture and Livestock:* Francisco Merino Rábago. *Communications and Transport:* Emilio Mujica Montoya. *Public Works:* Pedro Ramírez Vásquez. *Public Education:* Fernando Solando Morales. *Labour and Social Affairs:* Pedro Ojeda Paullada. *Secretariat of Programming and Budget:* Ricardo García Sainz. *Agrarian Reform:* Jorg Rojo Lugo. *Health and Public Welfare:* Emilio Martinez Manautou. *Tourism:* Guillermo Rossel de la Lama. *Hydraulic Resources:* Jesús Robles Linares. *Attorney-General of the Republic:* Oscar Flores Sánchez. *Regent of the Federal District:* Carlos Hank González. *Attorney-General of the Federal District:* Augustín Alanís Fuentes. *Director of the Federal Electricity Commission:* Hugo Cervantes del Río.

National flag: Three vertical strips of green, white, red, with the national arms in the centre.

National anthem: Mexicanos, al grito de guerra (words by F. González Bocanegra; tune by Jaime Nunó, 1954).

Local Government. Mexico is divided into 31 states. 1 federal district (comprising México City and 10 surrounding towns). Each state has its own constitution, government taxes and laws, and its governor, legislature and judicial officers popularly elected. Inter-state customs duties are not permitted. The President appoints the chief of the federal district.

DEFENCE. Supreme command is vested in the President, exercised through the Ministries of Defence (for Army and Air Force) and Marine.

Army. The country is divided into 35 zones in which both the regular army and volunteer corps are trained. The Army, in 1976, had 1 mechanized, 1 infantry and 1 parachute brigade, 64 garrison battalions and 23 cavalry regiments. Peace-time strength is 69,000. Military education is provided for officers, at the National Military School, the Application Centre for Army Officers and the Staff College, as well as in other specialized schools. To combat illiteracy in the Army, schools have been established in every regular and volunteer group.

Navy. The Navy consists of 2 (former US) destroyers, 6 frigates (including 4 former US destroyer escort transports), 18 fleet minesweepers, 17 escort minesweepers, 21 new fishery protection cutters of 130 tons built in Britain in 1974–76 and 10 built in Mexico. 14 patrol boats, 1 survey ship, 1 transport, 3 landing ships (2 used for rescue and 1 repair), 2 oilers, 1 training ship and 6 tugs. There are 4 naval districts on the Atlantic and 4 on the Pacific coast. Naval personnel in 1978 totalled 11,000 officers and men including naval air force, coastguard and marines. There were

7 companies of marines on active duty, with 1 regiment (3 companies) in reserve, formed by military service conscripts.

Air Force. The Air Force has a strength of about 6,000 officers and men, and 200 aircraft. These include 15 T-33A dual purpose jet-trainer/fighter-bombers, C-118A, C-54, C-47, Israeli-built Arava and LASA-60 transports, 30 T-28A and 45 T-6 armed piston-engined trainers and 3 Puma, 10 Bell 205 Iroquois, 5 JetRanger II and other light helicopters. One HS 125, a JetStar and 13 Islanders are employed on general and VIP transport duties. Primary trainers comprise 20 Beech Musketeers and 20 Bonanzas.

INTERNATIONAL RELATIONS

Membership. Mexico is a member of UN and OAS.

External Debt (Dec. 1976). US$19,600m. (public sector); US$7,000m. (private sector).

ECONOMY

Budget. Ordinary receipts and expenditure in 1m. pesos for calendar years:

	1973	*1974*	*1975*	*1976*
Revenue	52,217	71,996	102,592	134,082
Expenditure	48,022	68,228	92,560	125,532

In 1976, 40,000m. pesos was spent on education.

The proposed budget expenditure for 1976 was 392,389m. pesos, 209,510m. from the federal government and 182,879m. from the decentralized agencies. 29·7% to be allotted to the industrial sector, 22·9% to social welfare programmes, 20% to agricultural development, 16·8% to general administrative expenses, 10·2% to transportation and communication projects and 0·4% to tourism.

Currency. The monetary unit is the *peso* divided into 100 *centavos.*

There are coins for 1, 5 and 10 pesos and 50, 20, 10 and 5 centavos; notes for 10,000, 5,000, 500, 100, 50, 20, 10 and 5 pesos.

Rate of exchange, Feb. 1978: 22·60 pesos = US$1.

Banking. The Bank of Mexico, established 1 Sept 1925, is the central bank of issue; it is modelled on the Federal Reserve system, with large powers to 'manage' the currency. The Government holds 51% of the capital stock.

In 1976 metallic monetary reserves, gold, silver and foreign exchange were US$1,540m.

Weights and Measures. The metric system was introduced in 1896, and its sole use is enjoined by law of 14 Dec. 1928.

ENERGY AND NATURAL RESOURCES

Electricity. In 1974 the 2,770 electric generating plants had installed capacity of 9·6m. kw.; consumption, including imports, was 41·15m. kwh.

Oil. The chief Mexican oilfields, with proven reserves, in 1975, of 3,086·89m. bbls of crude oil, 2,239m. bbls of natural gas and 449·55m. bbls of condensed gas, are located in 3 widely separated regions. These were originally discovered and developed by international companies which were expropriated by government decree, 18 March 1938. The only foreign concession left, Mexican Gulf Oil was purchased by the Government in Dec. 1950. In 1969, the contracts with foreign companies were rescinded. The importance of the oil industry can be seen in the following indicators: in 1973 it generated 4·2% of the gross national product; employed 75,000 persons; and supplied about 92% of the energy consumed in the country. Since the nationalization of the industry in 1938, Petróleos, Mexicanos, a government-owned enterprise, has exclusive rights to the exploitation, refining and sale of oil and its by-products. PEMEX is exploiting mainly the rich Poza Rica and Faja de Oro fields in the state of Veracruz (discovered in 1938), which extend into the Gulf of Mexico shelf and the nearby fields in Escolín and Mecatepec. New discoveries in Reforma, state of Chiapas, and Samaria, state of Tabasco, however, increased oil production in 1974 over the previous year by 25%. 43% of the current national yield is obtained from these two states. Exploration has been intensified in various states throughout Mexico leading to important discoveries in Cotaxtla, state of Veracruz, and Chac, state of Campeche. Crude petroleum output was 39,403,000 cu. metres in 1975. Natural gas production came to 22,273m. cu. metres. Mexico exports crude oil but still imports petrol, gasoil (diesel), fuel oil and some petroleum gas.

Minerals. Mining is an important industry and, of the 48 principal non-metallic minerals in the world. Mexico produces at least 23. However, in view of the international price of mineral-metallurgical products, mining production, lacking incentives, has been both sluggish and fluctuating. Mining policy is aimed at the rational exploitation and increased industrialization of its mineral resources, procuring, at the same time, to completely Mexicanize the firms dedicated to this activity. This policy is implemented by the law regulating Article 27 of the Constitution regarding the exploitation and use of mineral resources. Based on this legislation, 769 mining companies had been Mexicanized by the end of Aug. 1972. The contribution, in monetary terms, of the Mexican mining companies to total national mining output soared from 26% in 1964 to 98% in Aug. 1972. In addition to the uranium deposits discovered in the states of Chihuahua, Durango, Sonora and Querétaro announced in 1959, rich deposits have been located at General Bravo, state of Nuevo León, with up to 450 tonnes of uranium oxide. Total reserves (estimate 1976) 2,860 tonnes of uranium 308.

Silver output (in tonnes) was 1,179 in 1975; 1,168 in 1974. About half the production is minted, including a 'token' coin (1949) weighing 1 troy oz. Gold output: 1975, 4,452 kg; 1974, 4,182 kg.

Mexico has large coal resources, calculated at 675m. tonnes, including high-grade coking coal at Sabinas in Coahuila; output of coke alone reached 2,066,025 tonnes in 1975. 744,673m. cu. metres of natural gas were produced in 1975. There are large underdeveloped reserves of iron ore with known reserves of 300m. tonnes; the new Peña Colorado field in Colima State seems to be promising. Output, 1975 (in tonnes): Iron ore, 3,388,272; billet steel, 5,077,000.

Quantities of mineral products (in tonnes) for 6 calendar years:

Metals	*1970*	*1971*	*1972*	*1973*	*1974*	*1975*
Copper	61,012	63,150	78,720	80,501	82,670	78,196
Lead	176,597	156,852	161,358	179,296	218,021	178,615
Zinc	266,400	264,972	271,844	271,373	262,716	228,851
Antimony	4,468	3,361	2,976	2,388	2,407	3,137
Graphite	55,648	50,916	55,110	65,392	62,551	60,804
Quicksilver	1,043	1,220	776	197	894	490
Arsenic	6,922	8,717	4,482	3,852	7,199	4,636
Bismuth	571	570	629	585	718	445
Cadmium	1,967	1,662	1,757	1,477	1,960	1,581
Tin	533	479	362	292	400	378
Tungsten	288	408	354	348	309	277
Manganese	98,609	96,081	106,424	131,049	145,128	154,245
Barytes	319,092	279,742	261,403	255,257	271,710	299,985
Sulphur	1,380,812	1,178,454	944,190	1,608,245	2,322,288	2,164,348
Cement	7,266,744	7,521,000	8,753,000	9,918,000	10,504	11,463
Fluorite	978,485	1,180,955	1,042,392	1,085,894	1,112,247	1,088,816

Agriculture. About 80% of Mexico's territory is made up of arid and semi-arid lands. Irrigation is needed, 43% of the land having less than 500 mm of rain a year. The 1970 census indicated Mexico had 24m. hectares of arable land, of which 13·9m. hectares were cultivated and 10·6m. harvested. In 1975, land under cultivation came to 17·77m. hectares and the total area covered by irrigation was almost 900,000 hectares. Grains occupy 68% of the cultivated land, with about 53% given to maize and about 9% to wheat. In the 1970 census there were 91,354 tractors. It is estimated that Mexico should be self-supporting with at least 17m. hectares of land under irrigation and 20·3m. hectares under cultivation. Government agricultural programmes are being carried out by the National Basic Commodities Company (CONUSUPO) and the National Deposit Warehouses (ANDSA) which regulate the market, intervening in the marketing process and protecting the low-income producers as well as the low-income consumer by assuring him access to basic commodities. ANDSA has undertaken the construction of silos, warehouses, storage, machinery and equipment.

The volume of credit channelled towards agriculture is dealt with by the National Ejidal Credit Bank. In addition, the Fund for Technical Assistance and Agricultural Credit Guarantees was set up in recent years to assist government and private banks in projects to finance and provide technical assistance, organizational counselling, primary industrialization and marketing to small farm producers.

Livestock (1975): Cattle, 28·2m.; sheep, 5·7m.; hogs, 11·7m.; horses, 4·3m.; goats, 10·1m.; mules, 2·7m.; donkeys, 2·9m.

Production of hides reached 3·69m. in 1973; production of meat, 664,980 tonnes.

Mexico's basic food crop is maize, and a rapid expansion of this crop is one of the chief aims of Mexican agricultural policy, balanced by the demand for 'cash crops' for export, such as cotton, sugar, garbanzos (chick peas), bananas, winter vegetables and coffee. Local production of nitrogen fertilizers in 1973 was 1,161,000 tonnes, and of phosphatic, 485,100 tonnes.

Principal products in tonnes for 1975 were: Maize, 9,001,000; rice, 623,000; sugarcane, 32,368,000; wheat, 2,735,000; coffee, 3·75m.; beans, 1,202,000; tomatoes, 1,127,000; oranges, 2,477,000; mangoes, 360,000; bananas, 1,241,000; cotton, 231,000; sorghum, 3,419,000; safflower, 531,000; soybeans, 545,000.

More than 50% of coffee output goes to world markets, and as a result of the policy adopted by the Mexican Coffee Institute to expand markets, exports have tended to increase.

Sugar-cane is also linked closely with the export markets, although not to the same degree as coffee, in view of the fact that despite the large crop, the national consumption of sugar, at approximately 35 kg a year per person, is one of the highest in the world. Exports have however remained more or less stable; 1972 exports represented 25% of total output.

The Yucatán peninsula produces about 50% of the world's supply of sisal (known locally as henequén).

Forestry. Timber lands represent 22% of the Mexican territory and are estimated to extend over 43m. hectares (about 43% of commercial importance), containing pine, spruce, cedar, mahogany, logwood and rosewood. Despite the existence of forests that would support a higher production, output for 20 years up to 1973, averaged an annual growth of only 1·1%. In 1973 only 15·7% of the productive capacity of the country's forests was being exploited. Reckless lumbering had destroyed the timber stands on many watersheds, resulting in spring floods and lowered water supplies in summer. In 1951 federal edicts had halted all timber-cutting in 22 states, regardless of concessions; but they have been resumed under strict supervision. There are 14 forest reserves (nearly 800,000 hectares) and 47 national park forests of 750,000 hectares. In 1973 wood products amounted to 4,026,000 cu. metres; others in tonnes: chicle, 1,312; pitch, 10,640; resins, 54,338; turpentine, 2,250; ixtle, 4,120; other fibres, 3,261; vegetable waxes, 1,428; tree barks, 896.

Fisheries. Fishing is important because of Mexico's 9,903 km of coastline. Catch (1975, tonnes): Sardine, 76,196; shrimp, 43,786; oysters, 26,988; tuna, 17,607; sea bass, 13,015; sea perch, 11,033; mackerel, 9,011; bonito, 6,394; shark, 6,192. Total catch in 1975 was 451,330 tonnes for human consumption and 157,795 tonnes for industrial use.

INDUSTRY AND TRADE

Industry. In 1975 the economically active population was 16,597,000, 40% of which were engaged in agriculture. GDP contribution by agriculture, 9·7%; industry and construction, 29·9%; mining, 4·2%; electricity, gas, water, transport, communications and other services, 56·2%.

Commerce. Trade for calendar years in 1m. pesos:

	1972	*1973*	*1974*	*1975*
Imports	33,981	47,668	75,709	82,252
Exports	20,926	25,880	35,625	35,733

Export figures for metals and for certain foreign-owned agricultural products are heavily undervalued to reduce export taxes.

Of total imports (1m. pesos) in 1975, 51,406 came from USA, 6,005 from Federal Republic of Germany, 3,730 from Japan, 2,410 from UK, 2,303 from France and 1,823 from Canada. Leading imports were cereals, machine tools, iron and steel products, electrical machinery and parts, car parts and components.

Of total exports (1m. pesos) in 1975, 22,146 went to USA, 1,612 to Japan, 1,119 to Federal Republic of Germany, 378 to Switzerland, 349 to UK and 272 to France. The main visible exports were manufactured products, petroleum, coffee, sugar and cotton.

Total trade between UK and Mexico (British Department of Trade returns, in £1,000 sterling):

	1973	*1974*	*1975*	*1976*	*1977*
Imports to UK	10,268	17,868	10,889	25,432	40,312
Exports and re-exports from UK	39,650	60,012	111,734	119,889	79,006

Tourism. Tourism is the largest single source of dollar income and in 1974 3,362,000 tourists visited Mexico. Tourist income in 1975, including border visitors, amounted to US$2,240m.

COMMUNICATIONS

Roads. Total length, 31 Dec. 1974, 175,540 km, of which 122,040 km are hard-surfaced highroads and 53,500 km gravelled.

Motor vehicles registered at 31 Dec 1975 included 2,669,213 passenger cars, 49,264 buses, 874,758 trucks and 238,472 motor cycles.

Railways. In 1937 the main railway lines were nationalized. The two principal groups are now the National Railways and the Pacific Railroad. In 1977 the Pacific Railroad, with 3 other large independent railways, were merged into the National Railways, creating a network of 19,665 km. In 1976 the National Railways alone carried 51·3m tonnes of freight.

Aviation. Mexico has an excellent air service. Each of the larger states has a local airline which links them with main airports, which, in turn, furnish services to US. Central and South America and Europe. Thirty companies in 1976 maintained international services, of these 2 were Mexican. Domestic flights are handled by 77 companies. In 1975 commercial aircraft carried 9·63m. national and international passengers with 127,025 tonnes of baggage and some 97,923 tonnes of mail and freight.

Shipping. Mexico has 49 ocean ports, of which, on the Gulf coast, the most important include Tampico, Veracruz, Coatzacoalcos, Progreso and Yucalpetón. On the Pacific are Ensenada, La Paz, Santa Rosalía, Guaymas, Mazatlán, Manzanillo. Acapulco and Salina Cruz.

Merchant shipping loaded 33·9m. tonnes and unloaded 29·2m. tonnes in 1975. Passengers (1973), embarked, 342,887; landed, 346,183.

Post and Broadcasting. On 31 Dec. 1975 the federal, state and private telegraph and telephone system had 5,938 offices and 220,442 km of telegraph lines and 16·2m. km of telephone line. *Teléfonos de México*, a state-controlled company, controls about 98% of all the telephone service. Telephones in use, Dec. 1976, 3·23m.; 96·3% were automatic.

In 1976 there were 674 commercial broadcasting stations and 22 cultural government radio stations which reached about 7·7m. homes. Commercial television stations numbered 85 and cultural government stations 4; there were about 4·5m. homes with receiving sets.

Cinemas (1975). Cinemas numbered 1,783 with annual attendance of 257m.

Newspapers (1974). There were 178 dailies and 21 weeklies, with an aggregate circulation in excess of 5m.; 23 in México City have about half of the total circulation.

JUSTICE, RELIGION, EDUCATION AND WELFARE

Justice. Magistrates of the Supreme Court are appointed for 6 years by the President and confirmed by the Senate; but the judges of the Supreme Court can be removed only on impeachment. The courts include the Supreme Court with 21 magistrates, 6 circuit courts with 3 judges each, 6 unitary and 47 district courts with 1 judge each.

The penal code of 1 Jan. 1930 abolished the death penalty, except for the Army, and set up a commission of alienists and other specialists, in place of courts, to deal with criminal cases (for federal offences); each state appoints its own local magistrates also.

The Mexican Constitution provides a guarantee of individual rights by means of a judicial procedure known as *amparo*, which gives any injured person whose constitutional rights have, in his opinion, been infringed, right to immediate access to the courts and full remedy, combining the swiftness of the Anglo-Saxon writ of *habeas corpus* and the breadth of remedy available through the injunction.

Religion. The prevailing religion is the Roman Catholic (46·38m. members at the census of 1970); with (1976) 2 cardinals, 9 archbishops and 84 bishops, but by the constitution of 1857, the Church was separated from the State, and the constitution of 1917 provided strict regulation of this and all other religions. No ecclesiastical body may acquire landed property, and since 1917 the property of the Church has been held to belong to the State. In the 1920s the Government suppressed the political influence of the priesthood and temporarily (1929–31) closed the churches. An understanding between State and Church was, however, reached, and all churches eschewing public affairs flourish freely. At the 1970 census 876,879 Protestants, 49,181 Jews and 150,329 members of other religions were also numbered.

Education. Primary and secondary education is free and compulsory, and secular. Clergy are forbidden to establish primary schools. All private schools must conform to government standards. Military drill is compulsory for boys of 18 years. In the Federal District education is controlled by the national government; elsewhere by the state authorities.

In 1975 there were:

	Schools	*Pupils*
Kindergarten	3,647	490,462
Primary	53,469	12,700,000
Secondary	5,894	2,024,042
Preparatory/Vocational	1,325	590,089
Professional and special	279	89,865
University level	507	451,947

There are 507 institutes of higher education, of which 48 are for post-graduate studies only.

The most important university is the Universidad Nacional Autónoma de México (UNAM) in México City which, with its associated universities and schools, had, in 1974–75, 238,375 pupils and 10,800 teachers. UNAM was founded in 1551, reorganized in 1910, and granted full autonomy in 1920. Other universities of particular importance in México City are El Colegio de México, a small, independent university concentrating on research in the humanities and social sciences, the Instituto Politecnico Nacional, specializing in applied science. Universidad Autónoma Metropolitana, recently opened by the federal government in order to meet the demand for higher education institutions in the federal district, and the Universidad Iberoamericana, a private university. Outside México City the more notable universities are, in Monterrey, the Universidad de Nuevo León and the Instituto Tecnólogico de Estudios Superiores de Monterrey; in Guadalajara, the Universidad de Guadalajara and the Universidad Autónoma de Guadalajara; and in Xalapa, the Universidad Veracruzana.

Health. In 1974 Mexico had 45,322 physicians; there were 5,469 state and private hospitals and clinics with 76,413 beds.

DIPLOMATIC REPRESENTATIVES

OF MEXICO IN GREAT BRITAIN (8 Halkin St., London, SW1X 7DW)

Ambassador: Manuel Tello Macias, CMG (accredited 16 March 1977).

OF GREAT BRITAIN IN MEXICO (Lerma 71, Col. Cuauhtémoc, Mexico City 5, D.F.)

Ambassador: N. E. Cox, CMG.

OF MEXICO IN THE USA (2829–16th St., NW, Washington, D.C., 20009)

Ambassador: Hugo B. Margáin, GCVO.

OF THE USA IN MEXICO (Paseo de la Reforma 305, Mexico City 5, D.F.)

Ambassador: Patrick J. Lucey.

OF MEXICO TO THE UNITED NATIONS

Ambassador: Lic. Roberto Rosenzweig-Díaz Azmitia

Books of Reference

Anuario Estadístico de los Estados Unidos Mexicanos. Annual (latest issue 1965)
México A Vuelo de Pajaro. Secretaria de la Presidencia, 1976
Mexico Statistical Data. Banco Nacional de México, 1975
Petroleos Mexicanos: Anuario Estadístico, 1975. Mexico City
Revista de Estadística (Monthly); *Revista de Economia* (Monthly)
Alba, V., *A Concise History of México.* London, 1973
Banco de México S.A., Annual report (latest, 42nd, 1964)
Banco Nacional de Comercio Exterior. *Comercio Exterior*, monthly.—*Mexico 1973.* Annual (in Spanish or English)
Bazant, J., *A Concise History of Mexico.* CUP, 1977
Bulletin of the International Commission of Jurists, No. 24, Dec. 1965: *Mexico, Constitutional Changes in the Electoral System*
Calvert, P., *Mexico.* London, 1973
Cheetham, N., *New Spain, the Birth of Modern Mexico.* London, 1974
Davies, N., *The Aztecs.* London, 1973
Ker, A. M., *Mexican Government Publications: A Guide, 1821–1936.* Washington, 1940
López-Portillo, J., *Mexico in Facts and Figures.* Mexico City, 1976
Parkes, H. B., *A History of Mexico.* Rev. ed. Boston, 1950
Peña, M. T. de la, *El Pueblo y su Tierra.* Mexico City, 1964
Ross, J. B., *The Economic System of Mexico.* Stanford, 1971
Smith, B., *Mexico: A History in Art.* London, 1975

MONACO

Capital: Monaco
Population: 25,029 (1976)

HISTORY. Monaco is a small Principality on the Mediterranean, surrounded by the French Department of Alpes Maritimes except on the side towards the sea. From 1297 it belonged to the house of Grimaldi. In 1731 it passed into the female line, Louise Hippolyte, daughter of Antoine I, heiress of Monaco, marrying Jacques de Goyon Matignon, Count of Torigni, who took the name and arms of Grimaldi. The Principality was placed under the protection of the Kingdom of Sardinia by the Treaty of Vienna, 1815, and under that of France in 1861. Prince Albert I (reigned 1889–1922) acquired fame as an oceanographer; and his son Louis II (1922–49) was instrumental in establishing the International Hydrographic Bureau.

AREA AND POPULATION. The area is 189 hectares or 467 acres. The Principality is divided into 4 districts: Monaco-Ville, la Condamine, Monte-Carlo and Fontvieille. Population (1976), 25,029. The official language is French.

REIGNING PRINCE. Rainier III, born 31 May 1923, son of Princess Charlotte, Duchess of Valentinois, daughter of Prince Louis II, 1898–1977 (married 19 March 1920 to Prince Pierre, Comte de Polignac, who had taken the name Grimaldi, from whom she was divorced 18 Feb. 1933). Prince Rainier succeeded his grandfather Louis II, who died on 9 May 1949. He married on 19 April 1956 Miss Grace Kelly, a citizen of the USA. *Issue:* Princess Caroline Louise Marguerite, born 23 Jan. 1957; Prince Albert Alexandre Louis Pierre, born 14 March 1958 (*heir apparent*); Princess Stephanie Marie Elisabeth, born 1 Feb. 1965.

CONSTITUTION AND GOVERNMENT. Prince Rainier III on 28 Jan. 1959 suspended the Constitution of 5 Jan. 1911, thereby dissolving the National Council and the Communal Council. On 28 March 1962 the National Council (18 members) and the Communal Council (16 members) were re-established as elected bodies. Elections took place on 16 Jan. 1978.

On 17 Dec. 1962 a new constitution was promulgated. It maintains the hereditary monarchy, though Prince Rainier renounces the principle of divine right. The supreme tribunal becomes the custodian of fundamental liberties, and guarantees are given for the right of association, trade union freedom and the right to strike. It provides for votes for women and the abolition of the death penalty.

The constitution can be modified only with the approval of the elected National Council. Women were given the vote in 1945.

Monegasque relations with France were based on a convention of neighbourhood and administrative assistance of 1951. This was terminated by France on 11 Oct. 1962, but has been replaced by several new conventions signed on 18 May 1963.

National flag: Horizontally red over white.

ECONOMY

Planning. A 54-acre site has been reclaimed from the sea at Fontvieille. This land has been earmarked for office and residential development. The present industrial zone is to be reorganized and developed with a view to attracting new light industry to the Principality.

Budget. The budget (in 1,000 francs) was as follows:

	1972	*1973*	*1974*	*1975*[1]	*1976*[1]
Revenue	259,021	281,102	339,165	330,249	528,246
Expenditure	180,339	433,420	512,467	387,402	464,421

[1] Estimate.

Currency. The monetary unit is the French *franc* divided into 100 *centimes.*

Weights and Measures. The metric system is in use.

INDUSTRY AND TRADE

Tourism. There were 137,000 tourists in 1974.

Trade Unions. Membership of trade unions is estimated at 4,500 out of a work force of 17,000.

Commerce. International trade is included with France.

COMMUNICATIONS

Roads. There were 46 km of roads in 1976.

Railways. The 1·6m. km of main line passing through the country is operated by the French National Railways (SNCF).

Aviation. The nearest airport is at Nice, France.

Shipping. The harbour has an area of 47 acres, depth at the entrance 90 ft, and alongside the quay 24 ft at least. In 1975 there were 2 registered ships with a total of 14,588 GRT.

Post and Broadcasting. Telephones numbered 23,740 in 1977. Monaco issues its own postage-stamps.

Radio Monte Carlo broadcasts 2 commercial programmes in French and Italian on long-, medium- and short-waves. Radio Monte Carlo owns 55% of Radio Monte Carlo Relay Station on Cyprus and 80% of Radio Monte Carlo is owned by France. The foreign service is dedicated exclusively to religious broadcasts and is maintained by free-will contributions. It operates in 36 languages under the name 'Trans World Radio' and has relay facilities on Bonaire, West Indies, and is planning to build relay facilities in the southern parts of Africa. *Télé Monte-Carlo* broadcasts 1 TV programme. Number of receivers: radio, 6,700; TV, 16,000.

Cinemas. In 1974 there were 2 cinemas with seating capacity of 800.

JUSTICE, RELIGION, EDUCATION AND WELFARE

Justice. The Code Louis, adopted in 1919, is based upon the French codes. There is a Court of First Instance as well as a Juge de Paix's Court. A semi-military police force has taken the place of the 'guard of honour' and troops formerly maintained.

Religion. There has been since 1887 a Roman Catholic bishop, directly dependent on the Holy See.

Education. In 1975 there were 4,937 pupils with over 300 teachers.

Health. In 1972 there were 290 hospital beds and 53 physicians.

DIPLOMATIC REPRESENTATIVES

British Consul-General (resident in Marseille): E. A. W. Bullock.
Consul-General for Monaco in London: I. S. Ivanovic.
USA Consul (resident in Nice): Jon G. Edensword.

Books of Reference

Journal de Monaco. Bulletin Officiel. 1858 ff.
Handley-Taylor, G., *Bibliography of Monaco.* London, 1968
La Gorce, P. M. de., *Monaco.* Lausanne, 1969

MONGOLIAN PEOPLE'S REPUBLIC

Capital: Ulan Bator.
Population: 1·5m. (1977)
GNP per capita: US$860 (1976)

Bügd Nayramdakh Mongol Ard Uls

HISTORY. Outer Mongolia was a Chinese province from 1691 to 1911, an autonomous state under Russian protection from 1912 to 1919 and again a Chinese province from 1919 to 1921. On 13 March 1921 a Provisional People's Government was established which declared the independence of Mongolia and on 5 Nov. 1921 signed a treaty with Soviet Russia annulling all prevous unequal treaties and establishing friendly relations. On 26 Nov. 1924 the Government proclaimed the country the Mongolian People's Republic.

On 5 Jan. 1946 China recognized the independence of Outer Mongolia after a plebiscite in Mongolia (20 Oct. 1945) had resulted in an overwhelming vote for independence. A Sino-Soviet treaty of 14 Feb. 1950 guaranteed this independence.

AREA AND POPULATION. Mongolia is bounded north by the USSR, east and south and west by China. Area, 1,565,000 sq. km (610,350 sq. miles); population (1977), 1·5m. (640,700 urban; 50% male in 1974). Density, 0·96 per sq. km. Birth rate (1968), 42 per 1,000; death rate, 9 per 1,000. Rate of increase, 1971–75, 3%. The population is predominantly made up of Mongolian peoples (75% Khalkha). There is a Turkic Kazakh minority (5·2% of the population) and 8 Mongol minorities. The official language is Mongol.

The Republic is administratively divided into 3 cities (Ulan Bator, the capital, population, 400,000 in 1977; Darkhan, 55,000, and Erdenet, 10,000), and 18 provinces (*aimag*). Local government is administered by People's Deputies' Khurals. The provinces are subdivided into districts (*somon*).

CONSTITUTION AND GOVERNMENT. According to the fourth constitution (1960) power is vested in the *People's Great Khural* of deputies elected for 4 years by universal suffrage of voters over 18 years of age on a basis of 1 deputy per 2,500 inhabitants. It elects from its number 9 members of the Presidium, which carries on current state affairs. *De facto* power is in the hands of the only political party, the Mongolian People's Revolutionary (*i.e.*, Communist) Party, which had 67,000 members and candidates in 1976. The youth organization had over 140,000 members in 1975.

The last general election took place on 19 June 1977; 99% of an electorate of 694,855 were said to have voted for the 354 deputies (152 professional, 104 agricultural and 98 industrial workers; 82 women).

National flag: Red–sky-blue–red (vertical), with a golden 5-pointed star and under it the golden *soyombo* emblem on the red stripe nearest to the flag-pole.

The *Chairman of the Presidium of the Khural* and head of state is Yumjagiin Tsedenbal, who is also *First Secretary of the People's Revolutionary Party*. The *Prime Minister* is Dr. Jambyn Batmunkh. The other members of the Politburo of the Party are: D. Maydar, *First Deputy Prime Minister and Chairman, State Committee for Science and Technology*; T. Ragchaa, *First Deputy Prime Minister*; N. Luvsanravdan, D. Molomjamts, S. Jalanaajav, N. Jagvaral, D. Gombojav, B.-O. Altangerel. Ministers not in the Politburo include: *Chairman, State Planning*

Commission: D. Sodnom; *Minister of Defence:* Gen. B. Dorj; *Minister of Public Security:* Bugyn Dezhid; *Foreign Minister:* Mangalyn Dügesüren; *Minister of Foreign Trade:* Yë Ochir. *Minister of Agriculture:* L. Rinchin.

DEFENCE. Military service is 2 years. The Army was estimated to number some 28,000 in 1976. It is equipped with Soviet weapons and includes mechanized units. The Air Force is engaged primarily in running civil air services. It has non-combat aircraft, helicopters, plus a few MiG-15 fighter-bombers. There is a para-military security force of about 18,000 men. A civil defence force was set up in 1970. There are some 25,000 Soviet service personnel in the country.

INTERNATIONAL RELATIONS

Membership. Mongolia is a member of UN and Comecon.

Aid. Mongolia receives economic aid from the USSR and other communist countries. There is also a UN development aid programme running at US$1m. per annum.

Treaties. Relations with the USSR were based on treaties of friendship and mutual aid (27 Feb. 1946), trade (17 Dec. 1957), economic and technical assistance (9 Sept. 1960), now replaced by a 20-year treaty of friendship, co-operation and mutual assistance (15 Jan. 1966).

Relations with China were based on treaties of economic and cultural co-operation (4 Oct. 1952), economic and technical aid (29 Aug. 1956), friendship and mutual aid (31 May 1960), commerce (26 April 1961 and 18 March 1963) and a border agreement (26 Dec. 1962). Sino-Mongolian relations have deteriorated since the estrangement between China and USSR.

On 28 Oct. 1961 Mongolia was admitted to the United Nations.

ECONOMY

Planning. Mongolia has had for centuries a traditional nomadic pastoral economy, which the government aims to transform into an 'agricultural–industrial economy'. For earlier plans *see* THE STATESMAN'S YEAR-BOOK, 1976–77, p. 1156. The current 5-year plan (1976–80) aims to increase national income by 42%, industrial production by 63%, agricultural production by 30% and livestock by 7–9%. Capital investment is expected to increase by 80% (37% to industry). Emphasis is placed on the development of state farms, the extension of the arable area, mining and house building. Electricity output of 1,440m. kwh. is scheduled for 1980.

Budget (in 1m. tugriks):

	1972	*1973*	*1974*	*1975*	*1976*	*1977*
Revenue	2,246	2,678	2,716	2,696	2,988	3,312
Expenditure	2,165	2,530	2,670	2,686	2,973	3,300

In the 1971–75 planning period 5,500m. *tugriks* were invested in the national economy and social and cultural measures. 800m. *tugriks* were allocated for health purposes in the 1976–80 planning period.

Currency. 100 *möngö* = 1 *tugrik*. Official exchange rates: £1 = 5·60 *tugriks*; 1 rouble = 4·44 *tugriks*.

Weights and Measures. The metric system is in use.

ENERGY AND NATURAL RESOURCES

Electricity. There are power stations at Ulan Bator, Choybalsan, Tolgoyt, Sükh Bator and Darkhan. Production of electricity, 1973, 669m. kwh.

Minerals. Large deposits of copper, molybdenum, phosphorites, tin, fluorite and other minerals are claimed. Joint Soviet–Mongol enterprises are constructing a copper–molybdenum complex at Erdenet and a phosphorite mine at Hobsgol. Wolfram and fluorspar are exported. There are major coalmines near Ulan Bator and Darkhan. Coal production in 1976 was 2·9m. tonnes. Oil was produced in the eastern Gobi desert at Dzüünbayan (production was 45,000 tonnes in 1969), but is no longer being extracted. There are reports of uranium and gold deposits.

Agriculture. The economy remains predominantly agricultural (mainly stock-raising). In 1975 there were 2·25m. horses, 617,000 camels, 2·42m. cattle, 14·5m. sheep and 4·59m. goats. The total herd of all animals numbered 24·5m. in 1976. Pastures occupy 84% of the total area, forests 10·5%. In 1976 there were 259 collective farms and 45 state farms. All cultivated land and 80% of livestock belong to collective or state farms. Farms cover vast areas. In 1976 collective farms averaged 69,000 head of cattle and state farms 36,000.

Collectivization was carried through at the end of the 1950s. In the 1960s a virgin lands campaign to grow grain was instituted.

The sown area in 1977 was some 600,000 hectares, 500,000 hectares of which were sown to grain. The 1976 crop was 340,000 tonnes of grain. Production of hay fodder was 800,000 tonnes in 1976. In 1976 each state farm had an average of 240 tractors (15 h.p. units), 45 grain harvesters and 33 lorries.

Forestry. Forests, chiefly larch, cedar, fir and birch, occupy 150,000 sq. km. Production, 1973: 814,500 cu. metres of timber.

INDUSTRY AND TRADE

Industry. Industry though still small in scale and local in character, is being vigorously developed and now accounts for a greater share of GNP than agriculture. The main industrial centre is Ulan Bator; others are being built at Darkhan, Erdenet and Choybalsan. Production figures (1975): Fluorspar, 209,000 tonnes; washed wool, 11,200 tonnes; leather footwear, 1·9m. pairs; processed leather, 2·9m. pieces; woollen textiles, 848,000 sq. metres; processed meat, 41,600 tonnes.

Employment. The non-agricultural labour force was 222,900 in 1973.

There is a serious labour shortage necessitating the employment of military personnel, and workers from the USSR and Eastern Europe.

Commerce. Foreign trade is a state monopoly. Trade figures for 1975 (in 1m. tugriks): exports, 828; imports, 1,847, Mongolia has been a member of Comecon since 1962. The main exports are live cattle and horses, wool and hair, meat, grain, hides, furs, ores, and butter. 95% of foreign trade is with communist countries (80% with USSR). There is a chronic trade deficit. Just over half the imports are consumer goods and just under half are machinery and industrial raw materials. In 1976 trade with China was 28m. tugriks. Trade with Japan, previously valued at US$1m. per annum, increased slightly after the establishment of diplomatic relations in 1972.

Mongolia exported goods to the UK valued at £1,128,000 in 1977 (1970: £2,000) and imported from the UK goods valued at £55,000 (1970: nil) (British Department of Trade and Industry returns). In 1972 contracts were placed for UK agricultural and textile machinery and exports of furs to UK increased. Exports to USSR in 1976 (and 1975): 139·8m. (125·3m.) roubles; imports: 474·7m. (355·1) roubles.

COMMUNICATIONS

Roads. There are surfaced roads in and around Ulan Bator, from Ulan Bator to Darkhan and at points on the frontier with USSR. Truck services run throughout the country where there are no surfaced roads. 70m. passengers and 10·1m. tons of freight were carried in 1973.

Railways. The Trans-Mongolian Railway (1,425 km in 1973) connects Ulan Bator with the Soviet Union and China. The Moscow–Ulan Bator–Peking express runs each way once a week. There are spur lines to the coalmines at Nalaykha and Sharin Gol. A separate line connects Choybalsan in the east with Borzya on the Trans-Siberian railway. 1·1m. passengers and 6·9m. tons of freight were carried in 1975.

Aviation. Mongolair operates internal services and a flight to Irkutsk which links with the Moscow service. 5,000 tons of freight were carried in 1975 and 300,000 passengers. Soviet airlines (Aeroflot) and Mongolair jointly operate an approximately twice-weekly service to Moscow.

Shipping. There is a steamer service on the Selenge River and a tug and barge service on Khövsgöl Lake. 40,000 tonnes of freight were carried in 1973.

Post and Broadcasting. There were, in 1975, 391 post offices, 211 telephone exchanges and 31,000 telephones. Number of telephones (1977), 37,792.

There are wireless stations at Ulan Bator and Olgiy. In 1975 there were 116,500 radio and 31,400 television receivers. Television services began in 1967. A Mongolian television station opened in 1970.

Cinemas. In 1975 there were 21 cinemas, 446 mobile cinemas and 12 theatres.

Newspapers. The Party daily paper *Ünen* ('Truth') had a circulation of 110,000 in 1975. There were 37 other newspapers.

JUSTICE, RELIGION, EDUCATION AND WELFARE

Justice. The Procurator-General is appointed, and the Supreme Court elected, by the *Khural* for 4 years. There are also courts at province, town and district level. Lay assessors sit with professional judges.

Religion. Tibetan Buddhist Lamaism was the prevalent form of religion. The church was suppressed in the 1930s, and only one functioning monastery exists today, at Ulan Bator.

Education. Schooling begins at the age of 8. There are 8- and 10-year schools. In 1976 there were 30,000 children in kindergartens, 302,000 pupils in 559 'general' schools and 17,000 teachers and scientists engaged in public education. There is a state university (founded 1942) at Ulan Bator (40 professors, 240 lecturers and 2,500 students in 1967), and other institutes of higher learning (teacher training, medicine, agriculture, economics, etc.) under the supervision of an Academy of Sciences (founded 1953; reorganized, 1961). In 1977 there were 23,550 students in institutes of higher learning, and some 6,000 students a year are sent to study abroad, principally in the USSR.

In 1946 the Mongolian alphabet was replaced by one based on Russian, but now enjoys a limited revival.

Health. In 1976 it was estimated that there were 2 doctors and 10 hospital beds per 1,000 of the population.

DIPLOMATIC REPRESENTATIVES

OF MONGOLIA IN GREAT BRITAIN (7 Kensington Ct., London, W8 5DL)

Ambassador: Denzengiin Tserendondov.

OF GREAT BRITAIN IN MONGOLIA (30 Enkh Taivny Gudamzh, Ulan Bator)

Ambassador: J. D. N. Hartland-Swann.

OF MONGOLIA TO THE UNITED NATIONS

Ambassador: Tsevegzhavyn Puntsagnorov.

Books of Reference

The Central Statistical Office: *Economic Statistics of the MPR for 40 Years.* 1961.—*40 Years of the MPR Revolution.* 1961.—*National Economy MPR 1973.* 1974

Bavrin, E. P., *Mongol'skaya Narodnaya Respublika: Spravochnik.* Moscow, 1976

Bawden, C. R., *The Modern History of Mongolia.* London, 1968

Boberg, F., *Mongolian–English, English–Mongolian Dictionary.* 3 vols. Stockholm, 1954–55

Haltod, M. (ed.), *Mongolian–English Dictionary.* Berkeley, Cal., 1961

Lattimore, O., *Nationalism and Revolution in Mongolia.* Leiden, 1955.—*Nomads and Commissars.* OUP, 1963

Petrov. V. P., *Mongolia: A Profile.* London, 1971

Rupen, R. A., *Mongols of the Twentieth Century.* Indiana Univ. Press, 1964

Sandag, S., *The Mongolian People's Struggle for National Independence*. Ulan Bator, 1966
Sanders, A. J. K., *The People's Republic of Mongolia: A General Reference Guide*. OUP, 1968
Shirendev, B., and Sanjdorj, M. (eds.), *History of the Mongolian People's Republic*. Vol. 3 (vols. 1 and 2 not translated). Harvard Univ. Press, 1975
Zhukov, E. M., and others (eds.). *History of the Mongolian People's Republic*. Moscow, 1973

MONTSERRAT

Capital: Plymouth
Population: 12,162 (1976)
GNP per capita: US$500 (1976)

HISTORY. Montserrat was discovered by Colombus in 1493 and colonized by Irish settlers in 1632.

AREA AND POPULATION. Montserrat is situated in the Caribbean sea 25 miles south-west of Antigua. The area is 39·5 sq. miles (106 sq. km). Population, 1976, 12,162. Chief town, Plymouth, 3,000 inhabitants.

CONSTITUTION AND GOVERNMENT. Montserrat is a crown colony. The Executive Council is composed of 4 unofficial members (the Chief Minister and 3 other Ministers) and 2 official members (Attorney-General and Financial Secretary). The Legislative Council consists of 7 elected, 1 nominated and 2 official members (the Attorney-General and Financial Secretary). The Executive Council is presided over by the Governor and the Legislative Council by the Speaker.

Governor: G. W. Jones, CBE.
Chief Minister: P. A. Bramble.
Flag: The British Blue Ensign with the shield of Montserrat in the fly.

FINANCE. In 1976 the budget estimates balanced at EC$10,175,020 (including grant-in-aid).

TRADE. Imports in 1975 totalled EC$16,543,866; domestic exports, EC$489,838. Chief imports were manufactured goods, food and beverages. Chief exports in 1975 were cotton, cattle and Irish potatoes.

TOURISM. In 1976, 11,211 tourists arrived in Montserrat.

COMMUNICATIONS

Aviation. At the modernized Blackburne airport 2,200 aircraft landed in 1976, disembarking 14,941 passengers and 452 tons of cargo.

Shipping. In 1976, 462 vessels arrived, landing 22,100 and loading 1,105 tons of cargo.

Post. A modern automatic telephone system, catering for 2,000 subscribers was installed by Cable & Wireless (West Indies) Ltd in 1967, under a 20-year agreement. By the end of 1976 the number of registered stations was 1,930.

JUSTICE, EDUCATION AND WELFARE

Justice. There are 2 magistrates' courts, at Plymouth and Cudjoe Head. Strength of the police force (1976), 2 graduate officers, 1 chief inspector, 3 inspectors and 88 other ranks.

Education. There are 12 government elementary, 1 government secondary, 2 grant-aided denominational elementary schools, 2 junior secondary schools, 2 preparatory private schools for children between the ages of 5 and 12 and 10 nursery schools. In 1976, 2,635 children were enrolled in the primary schools, with 110 teachers; 483 in the secondary schools, with 32 teachers. There was 1 technical college with 65 students and 7 teachers.

Health. In 1977 there were 7 doctors and 65 hospital beds.

Books of Reference

Overseas Trade 1975. Montserrat Government
Statistical Digest 1976. Montserrat Government

Library: Public Library, Plymouth. *Librarian:* Mrs J. Grell.

MOROCCO

al-Mamlaka al-Maghrebia

Capital: Rabat
Population: 17·8m. (1976)
GNP per capita: US$540 (1976)

HISTORY. From 1912 to 1956 Morocco was divided into a French protectorate (established by the treaty of Fez concluded between France and the Sultan on 30 March 1912), a Spanish protectorate (established by the Franco-Spanish convention of 27 Nov. 1912) and the international zone of Tangier (set up by France, Spain and Great Britain on 18 Dec. 1923).

On 2 March 1956 France and the Sultan terminated the treaty of Fez; on 7 April 1956 Spain relinquished her protectorate, and on 29 Oct. 1956 France, Spain, Great Britain, Italy, USA, Belgium, the Netherlands, Sweden and Portugal abolished the international status of the Tangier Zone.

A tripartite agreement was announced on 14 Nov. 1975 providing for the transfer of power from Spanish Sahara (Western Sahara) to the Moroccan and Mauritanean governments on 28 Feb. 1976. Spanish troops left El Aaiún on 20 Dec. 1975. On 14 April 1976 a Convention was signed by Mauritania and Morocco in which the 2 countries agreed on their borders in Western Sahara.

AREA AND POPULATION. As the south-eastern boundaries of Morocco have not been delimited, no exact figure can be given, but the total area is officially given as 659,970 sq. km. On 30 June 1969 the former Spanish province of Ifni was returned to Morocco, *see* THE STATESMAN'S YEAR-BOOK, 1969–70, p. 1322.

The population (census) June 1971 totalled 16,309,000, of whom 5·4m. were urban and 9·97m. rural; foreigners numbered 145,675. Estimate (1976) 17,825,700.

The population of the largest municipalities (census) June 1971: Casablanca, 1,506,373: Rabat (capital), 367,620; Marrakesh, 332,741; Fez, 325,327; Meknès, 248,369; Tangier, 187,894; Oujda, 175,532; Salè, 155,557; Kénitra, 139,206; Tétuan, 139,105; Safi, 129,113; Khouribga, 73,667; Mohammedia, 70,392; Agadir, 61,192; El Jadida, 55,501.

The prefectures and provinces (and their Moslem population 1975, Rabat-Sale and Casablanca being urban prefectures) are Casablanca (2,010,800), Fez (1·13m.). Marrakesh (1,109,300), Kenitra (1,043,500), Agadir (847,900), Rabat-Sale (745,800), Settat (744,100), Meknès (687,000), Oujda (669,700), El Jadida (655,900), Tetuan (607,400), Safi (595,300), Taza (588,400), Ouarzazate (581,400), Nador (531,300), El Kelaa-Sraghna (515,700), Beni-Mellal (489,700), Essaouira (404,900), Tiznit (389,400), Khémisset (387,600), Khouribga (372,000), Ksar-es-Souk (366,900), Azilal (365,100), Tangier (330,700), Chaouen (278,600), Khénifra (275,100), Al Hoceima (273,000), Boulemane (129,800), Figuig (98,600), Tarfaya (79,700).

With the incorporation of the northern portion of the former Spanish Sahara, administrative changes have resulted in the creation of 3 new provinces.

The official language is Arabic; French and Spanish are considered subsidiary languages.

REIGNING KING. Hassan II, born on 9 July 1929, succeeded on 3 March 1961, on the death of his father Mohammed V, who reigned 1927–61. The royal style was changed from 'His Sherifian Majesty the Sultan' to 'His Majesty the King' on 18 Aug. 1957. *Heir apparent:* Crown Prince Sidi Mohammed, born 21 Aug. 1963.

The King holds supreme civil and religious authority; the latter in his capacity of Emir-el-Muminin or Commander of the Faithful. He resides usually at Rabat, but occasionally in one of the other traditional capitals, Fez (founded in 808), Marrakesh (founded in 1062), Meknès and Tangier.

CONSTITUTION AND GOVERNMENT. The constitution was approved by referendum on 7 Dec. 1962 (3,919,737 for, 113,199 against, 72,722 void) and was promulgated on 14 Dec. 1962. In July 1970 a modification of the 1962 constitution was approved by referendum. A new constitution was approved by referendum on 15 March 1972. The Kingdom of Morocco is a constitutional monarchy with a legislature of a single chamber composed of 264 deputies. Deputies for 88 seats are elected by indirect vote through an electoral college representing the town councils, the regional assemblies, the chambers of commerce, industry and agriculture, and the trade unions. Deputies for the remaining 176 seats are by general election. The King, as sovereign head of State, appoints the Prime Minister and other Ministers, has the right to dissolve Parliament and approves legislation.

National flag: Red, with a green pentacle star in the centre.

Municipal elections were held on 12 Nov. 1976, general elections on 3 June 1977 and indirect elections on 21 June 1977. Cabinet on 10 Oct. 1977:

Prime Minister: Ahmed Osman.

Foreign Affairs and Co-operation: Mohamed Boucetta. *Interior:* Mohamed Benhima. *Posts and Telecommunications:* Mahjoubi Ahardane. *Cultural Affairs:* Mohamed Bahnini. *Parliamentary Relations:* Haddou Chiguer. *Finance:* Abdellatif Ghissassi. *Agriculture and Agrarian Reform:* Mustapha Faris. *Commerce and Industry:* Kamal Reghaye. *Mines and Energy:* Moussa Saadi. *Supply Equipment and National Promotion:* Mohamed Douiri. *Transport:* Mohamed Nasser. *Justice:* Maati Bouabid. *Education and Executive Training:* Azedine Laaraki. *Information:* Laarbi Khattabi. *Public Health:* Rahal Rahali. *Labour and Professional Training:* Mohamed Bouamoud. *Urban Affairs and Housing:* Abbes Fassi. *Tourism:* Mausouri Benali. *Administrative Affairs:* Mohamed Benyakheef. *Youth and Sports:* Abdelhafid Kadiri. *Handicrafts and Social Affairs:* Abdallah Gharnit. *Waqfs and Islamic Affairs:* Ahmed Ramzi. *Secretary-General of the Government:* Abbas el Kaissi. *Secretaries of State:* Othman Slimani (*Economic Affairs*); Tayeb Bencheikh (*Planning and Regional Development*); Abdeslam Zmined (*General Affairs*); Abderrahman Baddou (*Foreign Affairs*); Said Belbachir (*Higher Education and Scientific Research*); Driss Basri (*Interior*); Abdelhaq Tazi (*Executive Training*).

The country is administratively divided into 34 provinces and 2 urban prefectures. The provinces are: Agadir, Alhouceima, Azilal, Beni Mellal, Benslimane, Bonjdour, Boulmane, Chaouen, El Jadida, El Kalâat Srarhna, Errachidia, Essaouira, Fez, Figuif, Kenitra, Khemisset, Khenifra, Khouribga, Marrakesh, Meknes, Nador, Ouar Zazate, Oujda, Safi, Setlat, Smara, Ta-Ta, Tangier, Tantan, Tarfaya, Taza, Tetouan, Tiznit. The prefectures are: Casablanca and Rabat-Salé.

DEFENCE

Army. The Army numbers 90,000 officers and men, organized in 9 motorized infantry brigades, 5 armoured battalions, 1 light security brigade, 2 engineer battalions, 1 paratroop brigade, 22 infantry battalions and desert troops.

Navy. The Navy includes 2 new large patrol vessels or small corvettes, 1 coastal minesweeper, 1 patrol vessel, 1 gunboat, 1 seaward patrol craft, 6 new patrol boats and 4 landing craft acquired from France, 1 yacht and 1 training vessel. Personnel in 1978 totalled 2,000 officers and ratings including 500 marines. There are also 12 small customs cutters and a coastguard picket. Another 9 coastal patrol boats are under construction.

Air Force. The Air Force, formed in Nov. 1956, received from the Soviet Union about 20 jet combat aircraft and trainers, of which 12 were MiG-15UTIs and MiG-17s, now in storage. Equipment in current use is mainly of US and West European origin. It includes 17 F-5A supersonic fighter-bombers, 2 RF-5A reconnaissance-fighters and 3 two-seat F-5Bs, a total of about 45 T-28 and T-6 armed piston-engined trainers, 22 Magister armed jet basic trainers, 10 Swiss-built Bravo primary trainers, Agusta-Bell 205 and 212, Puma and JetRanger helicopters, 6 C-130H and some C-47 transport aircraft and 6 turboprop King Air light transports. Personnel strength is about 5,500. On order are 50 Mirage F-1 fighters, 9 C-130H transports and 12 T-34C turboprop armed basic trainers.

INTERNATIONAL RELATIONS

Membership. Morocco is a member of UN, OAU and the Arab League.

ECONOMY

Planning. A 5-year plan (1973–77) envisaged a total investment of 11,751,874m. dirhams. A new 5-year plan (1978–82) is under preparation.

GDP *per capita* (1977) 1,839 DH.

Budget. The ordinary budget for 1977 envisaged revenue of 17,405m. DH. The main items of revenue in 1977 were (in 1m. DH): Direct taxation, 2,482; customs, 2,001; indirect taxes, 3,160; registration and stamp duties, 660.

Currency. In Oct. 1959, a national currency was introduced. Its unit is the *dirham* (abbreviated DH), equalling 100 *centimes* (1 French franc = 1·025 DH; US$1 = 5·01 DH; £1 = 10·135 DH. Notes: 5, 10, 50, 100 DH; coins: 0·02, 0·05, 0·10; 0·20, 0·50, 1 DH. The exchange rate in Oct. 1977 was: £1 sterling = 7·88 DH.

Banking. The bank of issue is the Banque du Maroc in Rabat. Other important institutions are the Banque Marocaine du Commerce Extérieur (Casablanca), the Banque Nationale pour le Développement Economique (Rabat) and the Caisse de prêts immobiliers (Casablanca). There are 23 other banks in Casablanca, 3 in Tangier and 1 each in Tetouan, Fez, Kenitra, Meknès, Oujda and Rabat.

Weights and Measures. The metric system of weights and measures is the sole legal system.

ENERGY AND NATURAL RESOURCES

Electricity. Electric power-plants produced 3,340m. kwh. in 1976.

Oil. Crude oil production 25,300 tonnes in 1975.

Minerals. The principal mineral exploited is phosphate, the output of which (under a state monopoly) was 17·79m. tonnes in 1975. Other important minerals (in 1,000 tonnes) are: Iron ore (53·3), lead (151), cobalt (12·5), zinc (27), manganese (178), silver (1969, 773,000 troy oz.). Production of minerals (1974) 4,760m. dirhams.

Agriculture. Agriculture is by far the most important industry, on which 70% of the population exists. The principal crops are cereals, especially wheat and barley; beans, chickpeas, fenugreek and other legumens; canary seed; cumin and coriander; linseed; olives; almonds and other fruits, especially citrus. The almost universal wild palmetto is put to various uses, including the manufacture of *crin végétal*. The trees include, cork, cedar, arar, argon, oak and various conifers. Wine production, 1975, 830,000 hectolitres. Tizra wood is exported for tanning purposes. Stock-raising is an important industry.

Production (in 1,000 tonnes) in 1974: Wheat, 3,048; barley, 2,062; citrus fruit, 987.

Livestock (1975, in 1,000 heads): Camels, 115 (1973); horses, 380 (1973); cattle, 2,445; pigs, 10 (1973); sheep, 12,295; goats, 5,527; poultry, 15,000 (1973).

Fishing. The coasts abound in fish. The chief fishing centres are Agadir, Safi, Essaouira and Casablanca. There were 500 fishing vessels of different tonnage along the coastal areas of Morocco. Total catch in 1976 was 292,867 tonnes.

COMMERCE. Imports and exports were (in 1m. dirhams):

	1972	*1973*	*1974*	*1975*	*1976*
Imports	3,577	4,684	8,292	10,394	11,555
Exports	2,953	3,746	7,937	6,238	5,580

Main imports, 1974, consumer goods and industrial products. Main exports, 1974, citrus fruit (338m. dirhams), phosphates (4,075m. dirhams) and minerals.

Main trading partners (1974): Exports, France (23%), Federal Republic of Germany (7%), Italy (7%). Imports, France (28%), Federal Republic of Germany (10%), USA (9%).

A royal proclamation of 30 Aug. 1959 abrogated the former economic status of Tangier and integrated the zone in the kingdom. However, Tangier was declared a free port from 1 Jan. 1962; and commercial transactions within the free zone were further liberalized by decree of 8 Nov. 1965.

Total trade between Morocco and UK (British Department of Trade returns, in £1,000 sterling):

	1972	*1973*	*1974*	*1975*	*1976*	*1977*
Imports to UK	16,127	23,123	52,506	51,910	56,784	46,268
Exports and re-exports from UK	13,290	14,192	28,127	35,474	60,498	67,971

TOURISM. In 1976, 1,212,742 foreign visitors came to Morocco.

COMMUNICATIONS

Roads. In 1975 there were 52,205 km of classified roads, of which 21,639 km were surfaced. At the end of 1975 there were in use 107,000 lorries, 14,200 tractors, 320,000 private cars and 16,045 motor cycles.

Railways. In 1975 there were 2,071 km of railways, of which 819 km were electrified. The principal standard-gauge lines are from Casablanca eastward to the Algerian border, forming part of the continuous rail line to Tunis; Casablanca to Marrakesh with 2 important branches, one eastward to Oued Zem tapping the Khouribga phosphate mines, the other westward to the port of Safi. Another branch serves the manganese mines at Bou Arfa. Two new double-track electrified lines are to serve a new deep-water port at Jorf Lasfar, and a 650 km south-east extension from Marrakesh to Laayoun in the south Sahara is planned.

In 1976–77 Moroccan railways carried 832m. passenger-km and 3,191m. tonne-km of goods.

Aviation. There are 19 airfields, of which Casablanca–Arfa and Casablanca–Nouaceur are the most important. Total international air services in 1976 comprised 1,878,558 passengers arrived and departed; 20,585 tonnes of freight and (1975) 1,407 tons of mail handled.

Shipping. In 1976, 19,259 vessels of 30·5m. net tons entered and cleared the ports of Morocco. In 1976 Casablanca handled 40·5m. tonnes of maritime traffic.

Post and Broadcasting. Communication with Europe is maintained by cables between Casablanca and Brest, Tangier–Casablanca–Le Havre, Tangier–Gilbraltar, Tangier–Cádiz, Larache–Cádiz *via* Algeciras.

Telephone subscribers totalled 204,500 at the end of 1977; of these, 52,544 were in Casablanca and 33,449 in Rabat.

Broadcasting is done in Arabic, Berber, French, Spanish and English from Rabat and Tangier; television in Arabic and French began in 1962.

Cinemas. There were about 235 cinemas in 1971.

JUSTICE, RELIGION, EDUCATION AND WELFARE

Justice. A uniform legal system is being organized, based mainly on French and Islamic law codes and French legal procedure. The judiciary consists of a Supreme Court, courts of appeal, regional tribunals and magistrates' courts.

Religion. Islam is the established state religion. The majority of the Moroccans are Sunni Moslems of the Malekite school. The French and Spanish settlers are Roman Catholics under the Archbishop of Rabat. The once large Jewish population is diminishing (180,000 in 1961).

Education. In 1959 a standardization of the various school systems (French, Spanish, Israeli, Moslem, etc.) was begun. Education has been made compulsory from the age of 7 to 13.

In 1977–78, 1·75m. children were enrolled in state primary schools, 550,000 in state secondary schools, 500,000 in coranic schools and 500,000 in private primary schools.

The language of instruction in primary schools is Arabic during the first 2 years, and half-Arabic and half-French during the following 3 years; in secondary schools lessons are in French and Arabic. A third language of the choice of the student is learnt during the last 3 years of secondary education.

There are four universities, Mohamed V at Rabat, Hassan II at Casablanca, Mohamed Ben Abdallah at Fez and Quaraouyine at Fez, with a total enrolment of 35,037 in 1975.

Health. In 1976 there were 1,474 doctors and 23,146 hospital beds.

DIPLOMATIC REPRESENTATIVES

OF MOROCCO IN GREAT BRITAIN (49 Queen's Gate Gdns, London, SW7 5NE)

Ambassador: Badreddine Senoussi.

OF GREAT BRITAIN IN MOROCCO (28 bis, Ave. Allal ben Abdallah, Rabat)

Ambassador: J. S. R. Duncan, CMG, MBE.

OF MOROCCO IN THE USA (1601 21st St., NW, Washington, D.C., 20009)

Ambassador: Ali Benjelloun.

OF THE USA IN MOROCCO
(2 Ave. de Marrakech, Rabat)

Ambassador: Robert Anderson.

OF MOROCCO TO THE UNITED NATIONS

Ambassador: (Vacant).

Books of Reference

Statistical Information: The Service Central des Statistiques (BP 178, Rabat) was set up in 1942. Its publications include: *Annuaire de Statistique Générale* (latest issue, 1952).—*La Conjoncture Économique Marocaine* (monthly; with annual synthesis).—*Résultats du Recensement général de la population de 1971.*—*Bulletin économique et social du Maroc* (trimestral).—*La situation Economique du Maroc, 1975*

Bulletin Official (in Arabic and French). Rabat. Weekly
La situation Economique du Maroc en 1970. Rabat, 1971
Ashford, D. E., *Political Change in Morocco.* Princeton University Press, 1961
Barber, N., *Survey of North Africa,* 2nd ed. OUP, 1962.—*Morocco.* London, 1965
Decroux, P., *Les sociétés au Maroc.* Paris, 1950
D'Étienne, J., and others, *L'évolution sociale du Maroc.* Paris, 1950
Drague, G., *Esquisse d'histoire religieuse du Maroc.* Paris, 1951
Joly, F., and others, *Géographie du Maroc.* Paris, 1949
Kinross, Lord, and Hales-Gary, D., *Morocco.* London, 1971
Mercier, H., *Dictionnaire arabe–français.* Rabat, 1951
Miège, J.-L., *Morocco.* New York, 1953
Rivière, P. L., *Précis de Législation marocaine.* New ed. in collaboration with G. Catteriz. 2 vols. Caen, 1942–46
Sonnier, E., *Code des eaux du Maroc.* Rabat, 1954
National Library: Bibliothèque Générale et Archives, Rabat.

MOZAMBIQUE

The People's Republic of Mozambique

Capital: Maputo
Population: 10m. (1977)
GNP per capita: US$170 (1976)

HISTORY. Mozambique was discovered by Vasco da Gama's fleet on 1 March 1498, and was first colonized in 1505. The frontier with British Central and South Africa was fixed between Great Britain and Portugal in June 1891. The border with Tanzania, according to agreements of 1886 and 1890, runs from Cape Delgado at 10° 40′ S. lat. till it meets the courses of the Rovuma, which it follows to the point of its confluence with the 'Msinje, the boundary thence to Lake Nyasa being the parallel of latitude of this point. The Treaty of Versailles, 1919, allotted to Portugal the original Portuguese territory south of the Rovuma, known as the 'Kionga Triangle' (formerly part of German East Africa).

After ten years of conflict preceding the coup in Portugal talks took place June–Sept. 1974 between *Frente de Libertação de Moçambique*, FRELIMO and Portugal and a transitional government was sworn in on 20 Sept. 1974 comprising FRELIMO and Portuguese elements. Complete independence was achieved on 25 June 1975.

AREA AND POPULATION. Mozambique is bounded east by the Indian Ocean, south by South Africa, southwest by Swaziland, west by South Africa and Rhodesia and north by Zambia, Malawi and Tanzania. It has an area of 784,961 sq. km (303,070 sq. miles) and a population, according to the census of 1970, of 8,233,834. Estimate (1977) 10m. The country is divided into 11 provinces. The capital is Maputo. The official language is Portuguese. The climate is mainly tropical.

CONSTITUTION AND GOVERNMENT. A Constitution was published on 25 June 1975. The legislative organ is the People's Assembly of 210 members. The Council of Ministers sworn in on 1 July 1975 consisted of:

President: Samora Moïses Machel (assumed office 25 June 1975).

Development and Economic Planning: Marcelino dos Santos. *Foreign Affairs:* Joaquim Alberto Chissano. *Defence:* Alberto Joaquim Chipande. *Information:* Jorge Rebelo. *Labour:* Mariano de Arnajo Matsinha. *Minister of State in the President's Office:* José Oscar Monteiro. *Agriculture:* Joaquim Ribeiro de Carvalho. *Education and Culture:* Graça Simbine. *Health:* Helder Fernandes Brigido Martins. *Commerce and Industry:* Mário Fernandes da Graça Machungo. *Transport and Communications:* José Luis Cabaco. *Justice:* Dr Rui Baltasar dos Santos Alves. *Works and Housing:* Julio Zamith Carrilho. *Finance:* Salomão Munguambe.

Flag: Four rays coloured green, red, black and yellow, with white fimbriations, radiating from the upper hoist corner, in which is placed over all the national emblem in colour.

DEFENCE. The FPLM (Mozambique People's Liberation Forces) consist of an Army of about 20,000 men, armed with Chinese and Soviet light weapons, medium armour and some SAM missiles, and a fledgling Air Force and Navy. The former has several primary trainers and *ex*-Portuguese Air Force transport aircraft, the latter some gunboats. Substantial Soviet arms deliveries have taken place in 1977.

INTERNATIONAL RELATIONS

Membership. Mozambique is a member of UN and OAU.

Aid. After UN appeals in 1976 assistance was received from countries including

Sweden, UK and USA. There are also technical co-operation agreements with China, Cuba, the German Democratic Republic, the USSR and Portugal.

ECONOMY

Budget. In 1977 the revenue was 6,527,000 contos; expenditure, 10,030,910 contos (deficit 3,503,910 contos).

Currency. The Mozambique *escudo* is divided into 100 *centavos*. 1 *conto* = 1,000 *escudos*.

Banking. Barclays Bank is represented through the Banco Comercial de Angola, with branches in Maputo and Beira, and the Standard Bank through Banco Standard Totta.

Weights and Measures. The metric system is in force.

AGRICULTURE. Production in tonnes: (1974) cereals, 901,000; tea, 18,795; tobacco, 7,000; cotton fibre (1973), 35,308; rice (1972), 100,000; maize (1972), 430,000; bananas (1972), 66,000; sisal (1972), 24,000.

Livestock 1972: 1,355,613 cattle, 568,330 goats, 129,604 sheep, 178,558 pigs, 18,981 asses (1969).

INDUSTRY AND TRADE

Industry. There is very little industry and government plans are for the development of the agricultural and mineral wealth.

Commerce. The chief agricultural exports in 1973 were (in tonnes): Sugar, 178,864; cotton, 48,858; copra, 48,243; sisal, 19,826; cashew nuts, 33,195; tea, 17,545. Mining products in 1973: Gold, 0·1 kg (1972); beryl, 31 tonnes; bauxite, 5,594 tonnes; coal, 394,195 tonnes.

Imports, 1973, amounted to 11,415,260 contos; exports, 5,540,628 contos.

Total trade between Mozambique and UK (British Department of Trade returns, in £1,000 sterling):

	1974	*1975*	*1976*	*1977*
Imports to UK	16,893	10,271	23,160	41,650
Exports and re-exports from UK	16,881	17,242	17,020	18,163

COMMUNICATIONS

Roads. There were, in 1973, 38,560 km of road, of which 11,423 km are main roads. Motor vehicles, in 1971, included 83,841 passenger cars, 20,215 lorries and buses and 4,081 motor cycles. These numbers have been reduced by the exodus of Portuguese settlers. The Government is devoting effort to constructing a new North/South road link, and to improving provincial rural feeder road systems.

Railways. The Mozambique State Railways consist of 5 independent networks known as the Maputo, Mozambique, Sofala (Beira), Inhambane and Gaza, and Quelimane systems. The Maputo system has links with the Republic of South Africa, Swaziland and Rhodesia railways; the Sofala system links with Rhodesia at Machipanda and by way of the Trans-Zambesia Railway with Malawi at Dona Ana; and the Mozambique system links with Malawi at Entre Lagos. The Inhambane and Quelimane systems have no international connections. Total route-km (1975), 3,696 km (1,067 mm gauge), and 147 km (762 mm gauge). Trans-Zambesia Railway, 318 km (1,067 mm gauge). Since the closure of Mozambique's border with Rhodesia in March 1976 the rail links with Rhodesia do not operate.

Aviation. Regular air services exist between Maputo and Johannesburg, Mbabane, Lusaka, Dar es Salaam and Lisbon; and between Beira and Blantyre.

Shipping. The principal ports are: Maputo (1,880 vessels of 9,522,105 net tons handled in 1972), Beira (1,043 vessels of 4,254,728 net tons), Mozambique (71 vessels of 263,841 net tons) and Nacala (345 vessels of 1,261,379 net tons). Planning studies have begun on the expansion of Maputo and Beira port capacity.

Post and Broadcasting. Maputo is connected by telegraph with the Transvaal system. Quelimane has telegraphic communication with Chiromo. In 1971 there were 103,533 km of telegraph line, 37 wireless stations, 125 telephone stations and 217 telegraph stations; length of telephone lines, 103,533 km, including 86,018 km of conductor wires in cable; number of telephones (1977), 52,270. North–south telecommunications have been severely disrupted by fighting with Rhodesia during 1976–77.

Radio Moçambique broadcasts 5 programmes in Portuguese, English, Afrikaans, Ronga and Shangane as well as 4 regional programmes in 8 languages. Number of receivers (1974): radio, 110,000; TV, 1,000.

Cinemas. There were, in 1971, 31 cinemas with a seating capacity of 20,195.

Newspapers. There are two daily newspapers in Mozambique: *Noticias,* published in Maputo, and *Noticias de Beira*. There is also a weekly magazine, *Tempo*. The Mozambique News Agency (*AIM*) was established in 1976.

EDUCATION AND WELFARE

Education. Efforts are being made to expand primary and secondary schooling, and institute an adult literacy programme, despite a lack of trained teachers. There are also a number of professional and technical schools, and one university, *Universidade Eduardo Mondlane*, in Maputo.

Health. There were (1972) about 500 doctors and 12,500 hospital beds.

DIPLOMATIC REPRESENTATIVES

OF GREAT BRITAIN IN MOZAMBIQUE (Ave. Vladimir 1 Lenine, 310, Maputo)

Ambassador: J. H. Lewen, CMG.

OF USA IN MOZAMBIQUE (35 Rua Da Mesquita, Maputo)

Ambassador: Willard A. De Pree.

OF MOZAMBIQUE TO THE UNITED NATIONS

Ambassador: José Carlos Lobo.

Books of Reference

Boletim da Republica (Government Gazette). Maputo, 1975
Boletim Mensal de Estatistica. Maputo, 1976

NAURU

Population: 8,007 (1976)

HISTORY. The island was discovered by Capt. Fearn in 1798, annexed by Germany in Oct. 1888, and surrendered to the Australian forces in 1914. It was administered under a mandate, effective from 17 Dec. 1920, conferred on the British Empire and approved by the League of Nations until 1 Nov. 1947, when the United Nations General Assembly approved a trusteeship agreement with the governments of Australia, New Zealand and UK as joint administering authority.

AREA AND POPULATION. The island is situated 0° 32′ S. lat. and 166° 55′ E. long. Area, 5,263 acres (2,130 hectares). It is an oval-shaped upheaval coral island of approximately 12 miles in circumference, surrounded by a reef which is exposed at low tide. There is no anchorage. On the seaward side the reef dips abruptly into the deep waters of the Pacific at an angle of 45°. On the landward side of the reef there is a sandy beach interspersed with coral pinnacles. From the sandy beach the ground rises gradually, forming a fertile section ranging in width from 150 to 300 yd and completely encircling the island. On the inner side of the fertile section there is a coral cliff which rises to a height of 200 ft. Above the cliff there is an extensive plateau bearing phosphate of a high grade, the mining rights of which were vested in the British Phosphate Commissioners until 1 July 1970, subject to the rights of the Nauruan landowners. In July 1970 the Nauru Phosphate Corporation assumed control and management of the enterprise. It is chiefly on the fertile section of land between the sandy beach and the plateau that the Nauruans have established themselves. With the exception of a small fringe round a shallow lagoon, about 1 mile inland, the plateau, which contains the phosphate deposits, has few food-bearing trees and is not settled by the Nauruans.

At 31 July 1976 the population totalled 8,007, of whom 4,032 were Nauruans. A census was held in 1977.

Vital statistics, 1975: Births, 333; deaths, 54.

CONSTITUTION AND GOVERNMENT. A Legislative Council was established by the Nauru Act, passed by the Australian Parliament in Dec. 1965 and was inaugurated on 31 Jan. 1966. The trusteeship agreement terminated on 31 Jan. 1968, on which day Nauru became an independent republic but having special relationship with the Commonwealth. An 18-member Parliament is elected on a 3-yearly basis.

President and Minister for Foreign Affairs: Hammer DeRoburt, OBE.

National flag: Blue with a narrow horizontal gold stripe across the centre, beneath this near the hoist a white star of 12 points.

FINANCE. Revenue and expenditure (in $A) for financial year ending 30 June 1977: revenue, 22,643,375; expenditure, 28,052,000 (health, 715,110; education, 1,179,581).

The interests in the phosphate deposits were purchased in 1919 from the Pacific Phosphate Company by the governments of the UK, the Commonwealth of Australia and New Zealand, at a cost of £Stg3·5m., and a Board of Commissioners representing the 3 governments was appointed to manage and control the working of the deposits. In May 1967, in Canberra, the British Phosphate Corporation agreed to hand over the phosphate industry to Nauru and on 15 June 1967 agreement was reached that the Nauruans could buy the assets of the B.P.C. for approximately $A20m. over 3 years. Final payment was made on 23 April 1969 and control was handed over on 1 July 1970.

It is estimated that the deposits will be exhausted by the end of the century.

COMMERCE. The export trade consists almost entirely of phosphate shipped to Australia, New Zealand and Japan. Phosphate exported, 1971–72, 750,000 tons. The imports consist almost entirely of food supplies, building construction materials and machinery for the phosphate industry. Value of imports, 1970–71, $A4·5m.

Trade with the UK (British Department of Trade returns, in £1,000 sterling):

	1973	*1974*	*1975*	*1976*	*1977*
Imports to UK	—	249	31	2	4
Exports from UK	15	458	336	367	484

COMMUNICATIONS

Aviation. There is an airfield on the island capable of accepting medium size jet aircraft. Air Nauru, a wholly owned government subsidiary, operates services with Boeing 727 and 737 aircraft to Melbourne, Hong Kong, Apia, Honiara, Guam, Tarawa, Majuro, Wallis, Kagoshima, Noumea, Port Vila, Fiji, Ponape, Manila and Taipei.

Shipping. The Nauru Local Government Council, through its agency the Nauru Pacific Shipping Line, owns 5 ships and has 3 on charter. These ships ply between Australia, Pacific Islands and Japan. Other shipping coming to the island consists of those under charter to the phosphate industry.

Telecommunications. Direct daily schedules are maintained with Sydney (N.S.W.), Suva and Nandi (Fiji), Tarawa, Ocean Island and Port Moresby, and with merchant shipping—both long- and short-wave transmission. A radio-telephone circuit is maintained Mondays to Sundays with Sydney. A separate tele-radio service exists between Nauru and Ocean Island. An earth satellite radio station is installed and became operational in 1976.

Cinemas. In 1973 there were 2 cinemas with a seating capacity of 800.

EDUCATION. Attendance at school is compulsory for all children between the ages of 6 and 15 (if European) and 6 and 16 (if Nauruan). In Dec. 1977 there were 8 infant and primary schools and 2 secondary schools. There were 111 teachers and 1,165 pupils in infant, primary and secondary schools. Scholarships are available for Nauruan children to receive secondary and higher education and vocational training in Australia and New Zealand. In Dec. 1977, 65 Nauruans were receiving secondary education abroad in Australia and New Zealand and 12 were enrolled in university and vocational training courses in Australia, New Zealand and Fiji.

DIPLOMATIC REPRESENTATIVE

OF GREAT BRITAIN IN NAURU

Ambassador: Lord Dunrossil (resides in Suva).

Books of Reference

Report to the General Assembly of the United Nations on the Administration of the Territory of Nauru. 1949 to date
Text of Trusteeship Agreement. (Cmd. 7290; Treaty Series No. 89, 1947)
Territory of Nauru—Annual Report. Dept. of Territories. Canberra, 1920–40 and from 1947–48
Packett, C. N., *Guide to the Republic of Nauru.* Bradford, 1970
Pittman, G. A., *Nauru, the Phosphate Island.* London, 1959
Viviani, N., *Phosphate and Political Progress.* Canberra, 1970

NEPÁL

Capital: Káthmándu
Population: 11·7m. (1973)
GNP per capita: US$120 (1976)

HISTORY. From 1846 to 1951 Nepál was virtually ruled by the Ráná family, a member of which always held the office of prime minister, the succession being determined by special rules. The last Ráná prime minister (and, until 18 Feb. 1951, Supreme C.-in-C.) was HH Máháràja Mohan Shumsher Jung Bahádur Ráná, who resigned in Nov. 1951.

AREA AND POPULATION. Nepál, situated between 26° 20′ and 30° 10′ N. lat. and between 80° 15′ and 88° 15′ E. long., is bounded on the north by Tibet, on the east by Sikkim and West Bengal, on the south and west by Bihar and Uttar Pradesh. On 5 Oct. 1961 a treaty was signed in Peking, according to which the Chinese–Nepalese boundary line 'runs generally south-eastwards along the mountain ridge, passing through Cho Oyu mountain, Pumoli mountain, Mount Chomo Lungma (the Chinese name for Everest) and Lhotse Too Makalu mountain'. Nepál gained about 300 sq. miles of territory. Area about 54,600 sq. miles (141,400 sq. km); population (estimate, 1973), 11·7m.

In 1966 about 7,000 refugees from Tibet were living in Nepál.

Capital, Káthmándu, 75 miles from the Indian frontier; population about 195,260, and of the surrounding valley 415,000 including Pátan with a population of 135,230, and Bhádgáon with 84,240.

The aboriginal stock is Mongolian with a considerable admixture of Hindu blood from India. They were originally divided into numerous hill clans and petty principalities, one of which, Gorkha or Gurkha, became predominant in 1559 and has since given its name to men from all parts of Nepál. The 15 feudal chieftainships were integrated into the kingdom on 10 April 1961.

The country is administratively divided into 14 zones and 75 development districts.

RULING KING. The sovereign is HM Mahárájádhirája **Birendra Bir Bikram Sháh Dev**, who succeeded his father Mahendra Bir Bikram Sháh Dev on 31 Jan. 1972.

CONSTITUTION AND GOVERNMENT. On 18 Feb. 1951 the King proclaimed a constitutional monarchy, and on 16 Dec. 1962 a new constitution of the 'Constitutional Monarchical Hindu State'. The village and town *panchayat*, recognized as the basic units of democracy, elect the district *panchayat*, these elect the zonal *panchayat*, and these finally the 112 members of the national *panchayat*. The Constitution was amended in 1975. In addition, 23 representatives of professional organizations and royal nominees not exceeding 15% of the elected members, will be included in the national *panchayat*. The executive power is vested in the King, who appoints a council of ministers from the national *panchayat*. A state council will advise the King and proclaim the successor or, if the heir is a minor, a regency council. Art. 81 empowers the King to declare a state of emergency and to suspend the constitution.

On 25 Aug. 1963 the King formed a National Guidance Council and in Jan. 1973 appointed a new cabinet which was reshuffled Nov. 1974.

Relations with the UK are regulated by the treaty of peace and friendship signed on 29 Oct. 1950, which supersedes the treaties of 1792, 1815 and 1923. Diplomatic relations with the USA were established in 1947.

The Cabinet appointed on 12 Sept. 1977 was as follows:

Prime Minister, Palace Affairs and Defence: Kirti Nidhi Bista.

Home Affairs and Panchayat: Khadga Bahadur Singh. *Food, Agriculture and Irrigation:* Rabindra Nath Sharma. *Communications:* Hari Bahadur Basnyat. *Law and Justice:* Hom Bahadur Shrestha. *Foreign Affairs:* Krishna Raj Aryal. *Without Portfolio:* Damodar Shumshere Jung Bahadur Rana. *Finance:* Dr Bekh Bahadur Thapa. *Industry and Commerce:* Pitamber Dhoj Khati.

There are also 8 Ministers of State.

National flag: Two triangular parts of red, with a blue border all round, bearing symbols of the moon and the sun in white.

National anthem: 'May glory crown our illustrious sovereign' (1952).

DEFENCE

Army. The Army consists of about 20,000 men, mainly infantry, all of whom are regulars. It is being modernized with the aid of Britain and USA. Equipment delivered to date includes at least 1 C-47 and 2 Skyvan transport aircraft, a Puma helicopter and 3 Alouette III helicopters. Another Skyvan Executive, an H.S. 748 turboprop transport and a Puma helicopter are operated by the Royal Flight.

INTERNATIONAL RELATIONS

Membership. Nepál is a member of UN and the Colombo Plan.

ECONOMY

Planning. The fifth plan runs from 1975 to 1980. Its cost is estimated at NRs 10,110m. Priority was given to transport, communications, power, agriculture, irrigation, training of technicians and schools.

Budget. The general budget for the fiscal year 1974–75 envisages total expenditure of NRs 1,740·8m., of which development expenditure amounts to NRs 1,153·3m. Current revenues are estimated at NRs 959·7m. The deficit is to be financed by foreign aid and loans. The main sources of foreign aid are India, USA, Mainland China, UK and Federal Republic of Germany.

Currency. The Nepalese *rupee* is 171 grains in weight, as compared with the Indian rupee, which weighs 180 grains. The rate of exchange is 135 Nepalese rupees for 100 Indian rupees. 100 Nepalese *pice* = 1 Nepalese rupee. Coins of all denominations are minted. The Rástra Bank also issues notes of 1, 5, 10, 100 and 1,000 rupees.

AGRICULTURE. Nepál has valuable forests in the southern part of the country. In the northern part, on the slopes of the Himálayas, there grow large quantities of medicinal herbs which find a world-wide market. Of the total area, nearly one-third (11·2m. acres) is under forest; 5·4m. acres is covered by perpetual snow; 9·6m. acres is under paddy, 2·9m. maize and millet, 0·8m. wheat.

Livestock (1976): Cattle, 6·65m., including 3·2m. cows, 3·1m. oxen and 3·7m. buffaloes; sheep and goats, 2·68m.; hogs, 338,000; poultry, 20·53m.

INDUSTRY AND TRADE

Industry. New industries, such as jute- and sugar-mills, match, leather, cigarette, and shoe factories, and chemical works have been established, including two industrial estates at Patan and Balaju. The third economic plan envisages a 60,000-kw. capacity from hydro-electric plants.

Commerce. The principal articles of export are food grains, jute, timber, oilseeds, ghee (clarified butter), potatoes, medicinal herbs, hides and skins, cattle. The chief imports are textiles, cigarettes, salt, petrol and kerosene, sugar, machinery, medicines, boots and shoes, paper, cement, iron and steel, tea. The trade is mostly financed by the Nepál Bank, Ltd (established in 1937) and the Rástra Bank of Nepál (established in 1956). A large proportion of international trade is with India.

Imports and exports in NRs 1,000:

	1969–70	*1970–71*	*1971–72*	*1972–73*
Imports	122,049	84,311	79,609	111,826
Exports	114,730	84,964	185,973	135,051

Total trade between Nepál and UK (British Department of Trade returns, in £1,000 sterling):

	1972	*1973*	*1974*	*1975*	*1976*	*1977*
Imports to UK	201	221	452	473	539	680
Exports and re-exports from UK	551	532	1,485	2,253	1,532	2,747

Tourism. There were 90,000 (estimate) tourists in 1974.

COMMUNICATIONS

Roads. With the co-operation of India and the USA 900 miles of motorable roads are being constructed, including the East–West Highway through southern Nepál. A road from the Tibetan border to Káthmándu was recently completed with Chinese aid.

There are about 1,300 miles of motorable roads. A ropeway for the carriage of goods covers the 14 miles from Dhursing above Bhimphedi into the Káthmándu valley.

A road connects Káthmándu with Birgung.

Railways. Railways (2 ft 6 in. gauge) connect Jayanagar on the North Eastern Indian Railway with Janakpur and thence with Bijulpura (33 miles).

Aviation. The Royal Nepal Airline Corporation has linked Káthmándu, the capital, with 11 districts of Nepál; and 23 more airfields are under construction. The Royal Nepalese Airline Corporation has services between Káthmándu and Calcutta, Patna, New Delhi, Bangkok, Rangoon and Dacca, employing Boeing 727 jet aircraft.

Post and Broadcasting. Káthmándu is connected by telephone with Birganj and Raxaul (North Eastern Indian Railway) on the southern frontier with Bihar; and with the eastern part of the Terai foothills; an extension to the western districts is being completed. Number of telephones (1974) 9,162, of which 7,793 in Káthmándu. Under an agreement with India and the USA, a network of 91 wireless stations exists in Nepál, with further stations in Calcutta and New Delhi. Radio Nepál at Káthmándu broadcasts in Nepáli and English. Wireless telecommunication was inaugurated on 1 Oct. 1964.

All post, telephone and telegraph services have been taken over from India. The Indian, originally English, post office, established in 1816, closed on 13 April 1965.

JUSTICE, RELIGION, EDUCATION AND WELFARE

Justice. The Supreme Court Act, 1956, established a uniform judicial system, culminating in a supreme court of a Chief Justice and no more than 6 judges. Special courts to deal with minor offences may be established at the discretion of the Government.

Religion. Sánáton of Pauranic, *i.e.*, traditional or ancient Hinduism, and Buddhism are the religions of the bulk of the people. Christian missions are admitted, but conversion is forbidden.

The royal family is Hindu.

Education. In 1970 there were 7,256 primary schools, 1,036 secondary schools, 49 colleges and the Tribhuvan University (founded 1960).

About 16% of the population are literate. The national language is Nepáli.

Health. There were 130 doctors and 2,000 hospital beds in 1972.

DIPLOMATIC REPRESENTATIVES

OF NEPÁL IN GREAT BRITAIN (12a Kensington Palace Gdns, London, W8 4QU)

Ambassador: Jharenda Narayan Singha, CVO (accredited 9 Feb. 1978).

OF GREAT BRITAIN IN NEPÁL (Láincháur Káthmándu)

Ambassador: J. B. Denson, CMG, OBE.

OF NEPÁL IN THE USA (2131 Leroy Pl. NW. Washington, D.C., 20008)

Ambassador: Padma Badahur Khatri.

OF THE USA IN NEPÁL (Pani Pokhari, Káthmándu)

Ambassador: L. Douglas Heck.

OF NEPÁL TO THE UNITED NATIONS

Ambassador: Shailendra Kumar Upadhyay.

Books of Reference

Statistical Information: A Department of Statistics was set up in Káthmándu in 1950.

Karan, P. P., and Jenkins, W. M., *Nepal: A Cultural and Physical Geography.* Univ. of Kentucky Press, 1960
Mihaly, E. B., *Foreign Aid and Politics in Nepal.* OUP, 1965
Muni, S. D., *Foreign Policy of Nepal.* New Delhi, 1973
Regmi, D. R., *Modern Nepal.* Calcutta, 1961
Shaha, R., *Nepali Politics: Retrospect and Prospect.* OUP, 1975

THE NETHERLANDS

Capital: The Hague
Population: 13·81m. (1976)
GNP per capita: US$6,200 (1976)

Koninkrijk der Nederlanden

HISTORY. William of Orange (1533–84), as the German count of Nassau, inherited vast possessions in the Netherlands and the Princedom of Orange in France. He was the initiator of the struggle for independence from Spain (1568–1648); in the Republic of the United Netherlands he and his successors became the 'first servants of the Republic' with the title of 'Stadhouder' (governor). In 1689 William III acceded to the throne of England, becoming joint sovereign with Mary II, his wife. William III died in 1702 without issue, and after a stadhouderless period a member of the Frisian branch of Orange-Nassau was nominated hereditary stadhouder in 1747; but his successor, Willem V, had to take refuge in England, in 1795, at the invasion of the French Army. In Nov. 1813 the United Provinces were freed from French domination. The Congress of Vienna joined the Belgian provinces, the 'Austrian Netherlands' before the French Revolution, to the Northern Netherlands. The son of the former stadhouder Willem V was proclaimed King of the Netherlands at The Hague on 16 March 1815 as Willem I. The union was dissolved by the Belgian revolution of 1830, and the treaty of London, 19 April 1839, constituted Belgium an independent kingdom.

Netherlands Sovereigns

Willem I	1815–40 (died 1843)	Wilhelmina	1890–1948 (died 1962)
Willem II	1840–1849	Juliana	1948–
Willem III	1849–1890		

AREA AND POPULATION. The Netherlands is bounded north and west by the North Sea, south by Belgium and east by the Federal Republic of Germany. Growth of census population:

1829	2,613,298	1889	4,511,415	1930	7,935,565
1849	3,056,879	1909	5,858,175	1947	9,625,499
1869	3,579,529	1920	6,865,314	1960	11,461,964

Area, density and estimated population on 31 Dec. 1966 and 1976:

Province	*Land area (in sq. km) 1975*	*Population 1966*	*Population 1976*	*Density per sq. km 1976*
Groningen	2,329·83	508,173	544,264	234
Friesland	3,340·13	506,311	566,042	169
Drenthe	2,645·09	348,001	409,874	155
Overjissel	3,804·08	887,261	992,953	261
Gelderland	5,010·29	1,434,439	1,653,516	330
Utrecht	1,328·32	758,007	873,753	658
Noord-Holland	2,655·63	2,200,602	2,299,410	866
Zuid-Holland	2,869·06	2,902,572	3,049,570	1,063
Zeeland	1,789·95	295,374	335,624	188
Noord-Brabant	4,911·13	1,700,866	1,991,176	405
Limburg	2,166·49	980,276	1,055,619	487
Dronten[1]	296·82	—	17,232	58

[1] Dronten is a municipality and has not yet been incorporated into any province.

Province	Land area (in sq. km) 1975	Population 1966	Population 1976	Density per sq. km 1976
Zuidelijke IJsselmeerpolders[1]	664·41	8,765	23,443	35
Central Register of population[2]	—	4,660	2,019	—
Total	33,811·23	12,535,307	13,814,495	409

[1] The Zuidelijke IJsselmeerpolders (drained in 1957) are part of the former Zuiderzee, now called IJsselmeer; they have not yet been incorporated into any province.

[2] The Central Register of population includes persons who are residents of the Netherlands but who have no fixed residence in any particular municipality (living in caravans and house-boats, population on inland vessels, etc.).

Of the total population on 31 Dec. 1976, 6,871,547 were males, 6,942,948 females.

The total area of the Netherlands up to the low water line (*i.e.* sea-level at low tide) is 41,160 sq. km (15,892 sq. miles), of which 33,811·23 sq. km (13,054·54 sq. miles) is land area.

On 14 June 1918 a law was passed concerning the reclamation of the Zuiderzee. The work was begun in 1920; the following sections have been completed: 1. The Noordholland–Wieringen Barrage (2·5 km), 1924; 2. The Wieringermeer Polder (210 sq. km), 1930 (inundated by the Germans in 1945, but drained again in the same year); 3. The Wieringen–Friesland Barrage (30 km), 1932; 4. The Noordoost Polder (501 sq. km), 1942; 5. Oost Flevoland (651 sq. km), 1957; 6. Zuidelijk Flevoland (428 sq. km), 1967.

The polder Markerwaard (400 sq. km) is being reclaimed. A portion of what used to be the Zuiderzee behind the barrage will remain a fresh-water lake: IJsselmeer (1,250 sq. km). The 'Delta-project', scheduled to be completed in about 1980, comprises the building of enclosure dams in the estuaries between the islands in the south-western part of the country, excluding the sea-entrances to the ports of Rotterdam and Antwerp; it will also create fresh-water reservoirs. *See* map in The Statesman's Year-Book, 1959.

Vital statistics for calendar years:

	Live births Total	Live births Illegitimate	Still births	Marriages	Divorces	Deaths	Net migration
1974	185,982	3,686	1,651	109,607	19,167	109,250	+33,141
1975	177,876	3,820	1,373	100,081	20,093	113,737	+72,055
1976	177,090	4,297	1,434	97,056	20,889	114,454	+21,423

Population of principal municipalities on 1 Jan. 1977:

Alkmaar	67,554	Dordrecht	102,688	Heerlen	70,933
Almelo	62,501	Ede (Gld.)	80,142	Den Helder	60,828
Alphen a/d Rijn	47,110	Eindhoven	192,566	Hellendoorn	32,266
Amersfoort	87,222	Emmen	87,355	Helmond	58,930
Amstelveen	70,924	Enschede	141,423	Hengelo (O.)	73,084
Amsterdam	738,441	Epe	32,384	's-Hertogenbosch	86,809
Apeldoorn	135,251	Etten-Leur	26,613	Hilversum	93,951
Arnhem	125,576	Geldrop	26,202	Hoogeveen	42,836
Assen	44,490	Geleen	36,110	Hoogezand-	
Baarn	25,036	Goes	28,870	Sappemeer	34,979
Barneveld	35,074	Gorinchem	28,539	Hoorn	27,464
Bergen op Zoom	42,133	Gouda	57,773	Huizen	27,602
Beverwijk	36,942	's-Gravenhage	471,137	Kampen	29,584
De Bilt	33,028	Groningen	161,825	Katwijk	37,674
Breda	118,845	Haarlem	162,774	Kerkrade	46,732
Brunssum	26,126	Haarlemmermeer	74,271	Krimpen a/d IJssel	26,927
Bussum	37,056	Hardenberg	29,102	Leeuwarden	85.435
Capelle a/d IJssel	37,528	Harderwijk	28,707	Leiden	101,524
Delft	85,144	Heemskerk	31,702	Leidschendam	29,859
Deurne	27,016	Heemstede	27,292	Maassluis	29,364
Deventer	65,140	Heerenveen	35,256	Maastricht	110,191
Doetinchem	35,332	Heerhugowaard	27,376	Middelburg	37,327

Nieuwegein	25,212	Sneek	28,044	Vlaardingen	79,068
Noordoostpolder	35,361	Soest	40,728	Vlissingen	43,415
Nijmegen	148,094	Spijkenisse	32,519	Voorburg	45,456
Oldenzaal	27,284	Stadskanaal	33,959	Waalwijk	27,277
Oosterhout	41,368	Terneuzen	34,205	Wageningen	28,818
Oss	45,582	Tiel	25,778	Wassenaar	27,884
Purmerend	33,212	Tietjerksteradeel	28,547	Weert	37,374
Renkum	34,401	Tilburg	150,738	Winterswijk	27,618
Rheden	49,361	Uden	30,421	Zaanstad	125,409
Ridderkerk	44,976	Utrecht	245,290	Zeist	58,910
Rijswijk (Z.-H.)	53,532	Valkenswaard	26,980	Zevenaar	27,231
Roermond	36,533	Veendam	26,718	Zoetermeer	49,638
Roosendaal	52,652	Veenendaal	36,829	Zutphen	29,727
Rotterdam	601,012	Veldhoven	30,870	Zwijndrecht	39,192
Schiedam	76,865	Velsen	63,023	Zwolle	78,585
Sittard	34,162	Venlo	61,636		
Smallingerland	45,692	Venray	32,509		

Urban agglomerations as at 1 Jan. 1977: Rotterdam, 1,022,711; Amsterdam, 975,506; The Hague, 677,506; Utrecht, 467,902; Eindhoven, 360,722; Arnhem, 282,495; Heerlen-Kerkrade, 265,374; Enschede-Hengelo, 240,097; Haarlem, 230,394; Nijmegen, 214,977; Tilburg, 212,814; Groningen, 200,768; Dordrecht-Zwijndrecht, 188,868; Geleen-Sittard, 180,203; 's-Hertogenbosch, 180,499; Leiden, 169,125; Breda, 151,594; Maastricht, 145,203; Zaanstad, 137,940; Velsen-Beverwijk, 131,667; Hilversum, 111,024.

REIGNING QUEEN. Juliana Louise Emma Marie Wilhelmina, born 30 April 1909, daughter of Queen Wilhelmina (born 31 Aug. 1880, died 28 Nov. 1962) and Prince Henry of Mecklenburg-Schwerin (born April 1876, died 3 July 1934); succeeded to the throne on the abdication of her mother, 4 Sept. 1948, and was enthroned on 6 Sept.; married to Prince Bernhard Leopold Frederick Everhard Julius Coert Karel Godfried Pieter of Lippe-Biesterfeld (born 29 June 1911) on 7 Jan. 1937. *Offspring:* Princess Beatrix Wilhelmina Armgard, born 31 Jan. 1938 (*heir presumptive*), married to Claus von Amsberg on 10 March 1966 (*sons:* Prince Willem-Alexander, born 27 April 1967; Prince Johan Friso, born 25 Sept. 1968; Prince Constantijn, born 11 Oct. 1969); Princess Irene Emma Elisabeth, born 5 Aug. 1939, married to Prince Charles Hugues de Bourbon-Parma on 29 April 1964 (*sons:* Prince Carlos Javier Bernardo, born 27 Jan. 1970; Prince Jaime Bernardo, born 13 Oct. 1972; *daughter:* Princess Margarita Maria Beatrix, born 13 Oct. 1972); Princess Margriet Francisca, born in Ottawa, 19 Jan. 1943, married to Pieter van Vollenhoven on 10 Jan. 1967 (*son:* Prince Maurits, born 17 April 1968; Prince Bernhard, born 25 Dec. 1969; Prince Pieter, born 22 March 1972; Prince Floris, born 10 April 1975); Princess Maria Christina, born 18 Feb. 1947, married to Jorge Guillermo on 28 June 1975 (*son:* Prince Bernardo, born 17 June 1977).

The Queen's civil list was in Nov. 1968 fixed at 4·75m. guilders.

CONSTITUTION AND GOVERNMENT. According to the Constitution of the Kingdom of the Netherlands, the Kingdom consists of the Netherlands and the Netherlands Antilles. Their relations are regulated by the 'Statute' for the Kingdom, which came into force on 29 Dec. 1954. Each part enjoys full autonomy; they are united, on a footing of equality, for mutual assistance and the protection of their common interests.

The first Constitution of the Netherlands after its restoration as a Sovereign State was promulgated in 1814. It was revised in 1815 (after the addition of the Belgian provinces and the assumption by the Sovereign of the title of King), 1840 (after the secession of the Belgian provinces), 1848, 1884, 1887, 1917, 1922, 1938, 1946, 1948, 1953, 1956, 1963 and 1972.

The Netherlands is a constitutional and hereditary monarchy. The royal succession is in the direct male line in the order of primogeniture; in default of male heirs, the female line ascends the throne. The Sovereign comes of age on reaching his 18th year. During his minority the royal power is vested in a Regent—designated by law—and in some cases in the Council of State.

The central executive power of the State rests with the Crown, while the central legislative power is vested in the Crown and Parliament (the *Staten-Generaal*), consisting of 2 Chambers. After the 1956 revision of the Constitution the Upper or First Chamber is composed of 75 members, elected by the members of the Provincial States, and the Second Chamber consists of 150 deputies, who are elected directly. Members of the States-General must be Netherlanders or recognized as Netherlands subjects and 25 years of age or over; they may be men or women. They receive an allowance.

First Chamber (as constituted in 1977): Labour Party, 25; Christian Democrats, 24; Party for Freedom and Democracy, 15; Radicals, 5; Communists, 2; Political Calvinist Party, 1; Farmers' Party, 1; Calvinist Political Association, 1; Pacifist Socialists, 1.

Second Chamber (elected on 25 May 1977): Labour Party, 43; Christian Democrats, 49; Party for Freedom and Democracy, 28; Democrats 1966, 8; Radicals, 3; Farmers' Party, 1; Democratic Socialists, 1970, 1; Pacifist Socialist Party, 1; Political Calvinist Party, 3; Communists, 2; Calvinist Political Association, 1.

The revised Constitution of 1917 has introduced an electoral system based on universal suffrage and proportional representation. Under its provisions, members of the Second Chamber are directly elected by citizens of both sexes who are Netherlands subjects not under 18 years (since 1972). Criminals, lunatics and certain others are disqualified; for certain crimes and misdemeanours there may be temporary disqualification.

The members of the Second Chamber are elected for 4 years, and retire in a body, whereas the First Chamber is elected for 6 years, and every 3 years one-half retires by rotation. The Sovereign has the power to dissolve both Chambers of Parliament, or one of them, subject to the condition that new elections take place within 40 days, and the new House or Houses be convoked within 3 months.

The Sovereign and the Second Chamber may propose Bills; the First Chamber can only approve or reject them without inserting amendments. The meetings of both Chambers are public, though each of them may by a majority vote decide on a secret session. It is a fixed custom, that Ministers and Secretaries of State, on their own initiative or upon invitation of the Parliament, attend the sessions to defend their policy, their budget, their proposals of Bills, etc., when these are in discussion. A Minister or Secretary of State, however, cannot be a member of Parliament at the same time.

The Constitution can be revised only by a Bill declaring that there is reason for introducing such revision and containing the proposed alterations. The passing of this Bill is followed by a dissolution of both Chambers and a second confirmation by the new States-General by two-thirds of the votes. Unless it is expressly stated, all laws concern only the realm in Europe, and not the overseas parts of the kingdom.

Every act of the Sovereign has to be covered by a responsible Minister.

The Ministry was composed as follows in May 1978:

Prime Minister, Minister of General Affairs: Andreas van Agt (CDA).

Deputy Prime Minister, Minister of the Interior: Hans Wiegel (VVD). *Foreign Affairs:* Christoph van der Klaauw (VVD). *Justice:* Job de Ruiter (CDA). *Education and Science:* Arie Pais (VVD). *Finance:* Frans Andriessen (CDA). *Economic Affairs:* Gijsbert van Aardenne (VVD). *Social Affairs:* Willem Albeda (CDA). *Housing and Planning:* Pieter Beelaerts van Blokland (CDA). *Defence:* Willem Sholten. *Agriculture and Fisheries, Antilles Affairs:* Alfons van der Stee (CDA). *Culture, Recreation and Social Work:* Mathilda Gardeniers-Berendsen (CDA). *Public Health and Environment:* Leendert Ginjaar (VVD). *Transport and Public Works:* Daniel Tuynman (VVD). *Minister without Portfolio for Development Aid:* Jan de Koning (CDA). *Minister without Portfolio for Science Policy:* Rinus Peijnenburg (CDA).

There are also 16 state secretaries (10 from CDA and 6 from VVD).

The Council of State (*Raad van State*), appointed and presided over by the Sovereign, is composed of a vice-president and not more than 16 members. It can be consulted on all legislative matters. Decisions of the Crown in administrative disputes are prepared by a special committee of the Council.

The Hague is the seat of the Court, Government and Parliament.

National flag: Three horizontal stripes of red, white, blue.

National anthem: Wilhelmus van Nassouen (words by Philip Marnix van St Aldegonde, *c.* 1570).

Local Government: The kingdom is divided in 11 provinces and about 840 municipalities. Each province has its own representative body, the Provincial States. The members are elected for 4 years, directly from the Netherlands inhabitants of the province who are 21 years of age. The electoral register is the same as for the Second Chamber. The members retire in a body and are subject to re-election. The number of members varies according to the population of the province, from 83 for South Holland to 43 for Zeeland. The Provincial States are entitled to issue ordinances concerning the welfare of the province, and to raise taxes pursuant to legal provisions. The provincial budgets and the provincial ordinances and resolutions relating to provincial property; loans, taxes, etc., must be approved by the Crown. The members of the Provincial States elect the First Chamber of the States-General. They meet twice a year, as a rule in public. A permanent commission composed of 6 of their members, called the 'Deputy States', is charged with the executive power and, if required, with the enforcement of the law in the province. Deputy as well as Provincial States are presided over by a Commissioner of the Sovereign, who in the former assembly has a deciding vote, but attends the latter in only a deliberative capacity. He is the chief magistrate in the province. The Commissioner and the members of the Deputy States receive an allowance.

Each municipality forms a Corporation with its own interests and rights, subject to the general law, and is governed by a Municipal Council, directly elected for 4 years, by the electorate registered for the Provincial States, provided they are residents of the municipality. All Netherlands inhabitants 21 years of age are eligible, the number of members varying from 7 to 45, according to the population. The Municipal Council has the right to issue bye-laws concerning the communal welfare. The Council may levy taxes pursuant to legal provisions; these ordinances must be approved by the Crown. All bye-laws may be vetoed by the Crown. The Municipal Budget and resolutions to alienate municipal property require the approbation of the Deputy States of the province. The Council meets in public as often as may be necessary, and is presided over by a Burgomaster, appointed by the Sovereign. The day-to-day administration is carried out by the Burgomaster and 2–7 Aldermen (*wethouders*), elected by and from the Council; this body is also charged with the enforcement of the law. The Burgomaster may suspend the execution of a resolution of the council for 30 days, but is bound to notify the Deputy States of the province. In maintaining public order, the Burgomaster acts as the chief of police. The Burgomaster and Aldermen receive allowances.

DEFENCE. The Netherlands are bordered on the south by Belgium, on the east by the Federal Republic of Germany. On both sides the country is quite level and has no natural defences, except the barriers of some large rivers, running east to west and south to north. The country has an excellent roadnet and a vast railway system, enabling rapid movement. The west part of the country is densely populated.

Army. Service is partly voluntary and partly compulsory; the voluntary enlistments bear a small proportion to the compulsory. The total peacetime strength amounts to 75,000, including Military Police. The number of regulars is 23,800 (officers, n.c.o.s and technical specialists). The technical specialists serve for a period of 4–6 years and receive military and vocational training. On completing the latter training they will be given an official civilian certificate. The Army also employs 13,500 civilians. The legal period of active service for national servicemen is 22–24 months; the actual service period is 14 months for enlisted personnel and 16 months for reserve-officers and n.c.o.s. The balance may be spent at will as 'short-term leave'. After their period of actual service the conscript personnel are granted long-term leave. However, they will be liable to being called up for refresher training or in case of mobilization until they have reached the age of 35 (n.c.o.s 40, reserve officers 45).

The Netherlands have the 1st Netherlands Army Corps assigned to NATO. It consists of active and mobilizable units.

The active part of the Corps comprises 2 armoured brigades, 4 armoured infantry brigades and 40% of the Corps troops (headquarters, combat-support and service-support units); the brigades and the division-type headquarters may be grouped into 2 mechanized divisions. Part of this force is stationed in the Federal Republic of Germany. The peacetime strength of the active brigades is 80% of the war-authorized strength.

The mobilizable part of the Corps comprises 1 motorized infantry division, 1 independent infantry brigade and the remaining Corps troops.

The mechanized units comprise tank battalions (Leopard and Centurion), armoured infantry battalions, heavy (175 mm) and medium (155 mm and 105 mm) artillery battalions (mainly self-propelled), armoured engineer units, armoured reconnaissance units and armoured tank-destroyer units. Helicopter squadrons are also available.

The National Territorial Command forces consist of territorial units, security forces, some logistical units and staffs. The major part of the national logistic units is placed under the National Logistic Command. In event of mobilization, territorial brigades with support and logistical units are called up. Some units in the Netherlands are earmarked for assignment to the United Nations as peace-keeping forces. A group of officers is permanently attached to the UN Truce Supervision Organization force in the Middle East. For civil defence purposes there are a number of military (mobilizable) fire-fighting, rescue and medical battalions. In time of war these units turn to the command of the National Commander of the Civil Defence.

Navy. The Royal Netherlands Navy has its main base in the Netherlands at Den Helder and minor bases at Flushing and Curaçao (Netherlands Antilles).

Principal surface ships of the Royal Netherlands Navy:

Completed	*Name*	*Standard displacement (tons)*	*Principal armament*	*Shaft horse-power*	*Max. speed (knots)*
1976 1975	De Ruyter Tromp	4,300	2–4·7 in.; 1 Tartar launcher; Seasparrow PDMS; 2 × 4 Harpoon; 1 Lynx helicopter	50,000	30

The *De Zeven Provincien*, converted to guided missile cruiser in 1962–64, was placed on the disposal list at the end of 1976. Her unconverted sister ship *Ruyter* was sold to Peru in 1973 and re-named *Almirante Grau*.

There are also 6 diesel-powered patrol submarines, 10 destroyers, 6 frigates, 6 corvettes, 3 mine countermeasures support ships (*ex*-ocean minesweepers), 1 torpedo trials ship (*ex*-ocean minesweeper), 5 patrol vessels, 3 survey ships, 11 coastal minesweepers, 4 coastal minehunters and 3 diving vessels (converted coastal minesweepers), 16 inshore minesweepers, 2 fast combat support ships, 11 minor landing craft, 2 training ships, 16 auxiliary ships and 5 service craft.

Two more guided-missile armed destroyer leaders (large frigates) were planned by 1983; and 8 missile armed general purpose frigates are under construction with 4 more projected. The future construction programme includes 15 minehunters.

On 1 Jan. 1978 naval personnel totalled 18,000 officers and other ranks, including the Naval Air Service, the Royal Netherlands Marine Corps and the Women's Royal Netherlands Naval Service.

The naval air service maintains 15 Lockheed Neptunes (SP-2H), 8 Breguet Atlantics, and 19 helicopters. 16 Lynx helicopters are ordered to replace the ageing helicopters.

Naval estimates (in 1m. guilders): 1970, 936; 1971, 998; 1972, 1,135; 1973, 1,254; 1974, 1,362; 1975, 1,618; 1976, 1,683; 1977, 1,885.

Air Force. The Royal Netherlands Air Force was established 1 July 1913. Its current strength is approximately 17,700 personnel and it has a first-line combat force of 9 squadrons of aircraft and 15 squadrons of surface-to-air missiles. Two F-104G Starfighter interceptor squadrons are operated by Tactical Air Command, which also controls a USAF squadron of F-4E Phantom II tactical fighter-bombers based in the Netherlands; also 2 squadrons of F-104G Starfighter and 4 of NF-5 fighter-bombers, and 1 reconnaissance squadron of RF-104G aircraft. The single-seat NF-5A and two-seat NF-5B aircraft were built in Canada.

There are 4 Nike-Hercules surface-to-air missile (high-altitude) squadrons and 11 Hawk surface-to-air missile (low-altitude) squadrons.

In addition the RNIAP comprises 1 transport squadron (Fokker Friendship), 1 squadron of Lynx helicopters for search and rescue, casualty evacuation and pilot training, and 3 observation and communication squadrons of MBB BO 105 and Alouette III helicopters. The observation and communication squadrons are under the operational command of the Army.

Training of RNIAF pilots is undertaken in Canada.

INTERNATIONAL RELATIONS

Membership. The Netherlands is a member of UN, EEC, OECD, the Council of Europe and NATO.

ECONOMY

Budget. The revenue and expenditure of the central government (ordinary and extraordinary) were, in 1m. guilders, for calendar years:

	1971[2]	*1972*[2]	*1973*[2]	*1974*[3]	*1975*[3]	*1976*[4]	*1977*[5]
Revenue[1]	35,067	40,373	49,637	53,446	62,041	69,671	77,623
Expenditure[2]	37,556	41,393	49,316	57,635	70,394	83,264	92,191

[1] Without the revenue of loans. [2] Accounts. [3] Preliminary accounts. [4] Revised budget figures. [5] Budget estimates.

The revenue and expenditure of the Agriculture Equalization Fund, the Fund for Central Government roads, the Property Acquisition Fund (established in 1971) and of the Fund for the Development of a Fast Breeder Reactor (established in 1972) have been incorporated in the general budget.

The national debt, in 1m. guilders, was on 31 Dec.:

	1970	*1971*	*1972*	*1973*	*1974*	*1975*
Internal funded debt	23,462	24,599	26,651	27,489	29,880	34,725
,, floating ,,	9,410	10,467	9,856	11,264	11,411	12,000
External funded ,,	98	74	59	39	23	12
Total	32,970	35,140	36,566	38,792	41,314	46,777

Currency. The monetary unit is the *gulden* (guilder, florin) of 100 cents. The official rate of exchange is US$1 = 2·78 guilders since 17 Sept. 1973 (guilders per troy oz. fine gold: 117·427).

Legal tender are bank-notes, currency notes of 2½ and 1 guilders, silver 10-guilder pieces, nickel 2½- and 1-guilder pieces, 25-cent, 10-cent pieces, bronze 5-cent and 1-cent pieces. Note circulation, 1 Sept. 1975, 14,017m. guilders and 1 Sept. 1976, 15,563m.

Banking. The Netherlands Bank, founded as a private institution, was nationalized on 1 Aug. 1948, the shareholders receiving, for a share of 1,000 guilders, a security of 2,000 guilders on the 2½% National Debt. Since 1863 the bank has the sole right of issuing bank-notes. The bank does the same business as other banks, but with more guarantees. The capital amounts to 20m. guilders.

In the year 1975 the state post office savings bank had deposits of 3,671m. guilders and withdrawals of 2,771m. guilders. Private savings banks: Deposits, 7,946m. guilders; withdrawals, 7,715m. guilders.

Weights and Measures. The metric system of weights and measures was adopted in the Netherlands in 1820.

ENERGY AND NATURAL RESOURCES

Electricity. The total production of electrical energy (in 1m. kwh.) amounted in 1938 to 3,688; 1958, 13,854; 1970, 40,859; 1973, 52,628; 1974, 55,350; 1975, 54,259; 1976, 58,138. Production of manufactured gas (milliard kcal): 1973, 52,717; 1974, 52,263; 1975, 52,565; 1976, 43,293. Production of natural gas in 1950, 8m. cu.

metres; 1955, 139; 1960, 384; 1970, 31,688; 1973, 70,834; 1974, 83,725; 1975, 90,853; 1976, 97,302.

Minerals. On 1 Jan. 1975 all coalmines were closed.

The production of crude petroleum (in 1,000 tonnes) amounted in 1943 (first year) to 0·2; 1953, 820; 1969, 2,020; 1970, 1,919; 1972, 1,597; 1973, 1,492; 1974, 1,461; 1975, 1,419; 1976, 1,371.

There are saltmines at Hengelo and Delfzijl; production (in 1,000 tonnes), 1950, 412·6; 1960, 1,096; 1970, 2,871; 1971, 3,169; 1972, 2,803; 1973, 3,044; 1974, 3,387; 1975, 2,690; 1976, 3,026.

Agriculture. The net area of all holdings was divided as follows (in hectares):

	1972[1]	*1973*[1]	*1974*[1]	*1975*[1]	*1976*[1]
Field crops	685,548	674,876	675,270	674,756	683,315
Grass	1,317,056	1,310,810	1,298,476	1,286,195	1,270,103
Market gardening	87,332	89,404	92,160	92,435	91,894
Land for flower bulbs	12,503	13,271	13,416	13,010	12,743
Flower cultivation	3,093	3,449	3,804	4,119	4,248
Nurseries	4,130	4,602	4,987	5,129	5,360
Fallow land	6,648	5,848	5,371	6,320	5,442
Total	2,116,310	2,102,260	2,093,484	2,081,964	2,073,105
Plantations with undercropping	*2,508*	*2,102*	*1,899*	...	...
Total agricultural area	2,133,802	2,100,158	2,091,585	2,081,964	2,073,105

[1] Excluding holdings of less than 10 SFU (SFU = standard farm unit). 10 SFU is equal to a computed net value added at factor cost of about 2,000 guilders, in 1968.

The net areas[1] under special crops were as follows (in hectares):

Products	*1975*	*1976*	*Products*	*1975*	*1976*
Autumn wheat	64,864	109,045	Colza	14,110	12,339
Spring wheat	42,068	21,149	Flax	5,126	5,306
Rye	18,196	21,226	Agricultural seeds	20,756	15,253
Autumn barley	6,065	9,526	Potatoes, edible[2]	78,145	89,037
Spring barley	77,069	51,833	Potatoes, industrial[3]	73,024	71,536
Oats	34,346	25,360	Sugar-beet	136,515	139,089
Peas	6,026	4,499	Fodder-beet	3,482	3,079

[1] Excluding non-agrarian holdings of less than 10 SFU.
[2] Including early and seed potatoes. [3] Including seed potatoes.

The yield of the more important products, in tonnes, was as follows:

Crop	*Average 1940–49*	*Average 1950–58*	*1974*[1]	*1975*[1]	*1976*[1]
Wheat	322,003	348,464	745,883	527,793	709,585
Rye	439,055	454,992	77,837	62,815	65,231
Barley	145,892	258,049	314,991	335,924	263,397
Oats	315,642	464,041	163,297	158,127	103,390
Field beans	15,799	5,693	...	...	...
Peas	65,460	93,664	23,286	21,917	15,903
Colza	24,763	18,358	44,907	36,600	34,207
Flax, fibre	82,906	138,165	43,136	23,138	22,338
Potatoes, edible[2]	2,861,793	2,745,505	3,211,299	2,574,283	2,776,314
Potatoes, industrial	1,242,326	1,003,994	2,883,528	2,428 847	2,006,561
Sugar-beet	1,667,711	2,935,881	4,910,771	5,926,777	6,484,355
Fodder-beet	...	...	306,166	249,604	206,320

[1] Excluding holdings of less than 10 SFU. [2] Including early potatoes.

Livestock, May 1976: 4,964,100 cattle, 7,507,100 pigs; 18,700 horses (3 years old and over, for agricultural purposes), 780,000 sheep, 68·6m. poultry.

In 1974 the production of butter, under state control, amounted to 202,843 tonnes; that of cheese, under state control, to 377,932 tonnes. Export value of arable crops amounted to 9,755m. guilders; animal produce, 10,024m. guilders and horticultural produce, 4,821m. guilders.

Fisheries. The total produce of fish landed from the sea and inshore fisheries in 1976 was valued at 447m. guilders; the total weight amounted to 252,692 tonnes. In

1976 the herring fishery had a value of 76m. guilders and a weight of 48,108 tonnes. The quantity of oysters produced in 1975 amounted to 1,302 tonnes (15m. guilders).

INDUSTRY AND TRADE

Industry. Numbers employed (in 1,000) and turnover (in 1m. guilders) in manufacturing enterprises with 10 employees and more, excluding building:

Class in industry	*Numbers employed* 1975	1976	*Turnover* 1975	1976
Mining and quarrying	7·0	6·8	9,410	12,410
Manufacturing industry	935·0	933·1	137,280	154,880
Foodstuffs and tobacco products	148·3	145·2	38,810	42,820
Textile industry	48·6	46·1	4,170	4,480
Clothing	27·1	24·9	2,090	2,040
Leather and footwear	9·7	9·3	640	700
Wood and furniture industry	36·4	36·8	2,990	3,420
Paper industry	29·2	28·9	3,470	3,960
Graphic industry, publishers	60·0	59·4	6,040	6,640
Petroleum industry	10·5	10·2	12,990	15,940
Chemical industry, artificial yarns and fibre industry	90·3	88·8	17,070	20,510
Rubber and synthetic materials processing industry	24·8	24·7	2,550	3,020
Building materials, earthenware and glass	38·5	37·2	3,800	4,200
Basic metal industry	38·5	39·3	5,410	6,540
Metals products (excl. machinery and means of transport)	89·6	88·3	7,270	8,230
Machinery	88·4	86·9	8,200	8,890
Electrical industry	116·6	112·3	10,990	12,340
Means of transport	82·2	80·1	9,380	9,490
Instrument making and optical industry	9·3	9·6	1,050	1,210
Other industries	5·0	5·0	350	440
Public utilities	44·6	44·6	7,680	9,930

Commerce. On 5 Sept. 1944 and 14 March 1947 the Netherlands signed agreements with Belgium and Luxembourg for the establishment of a customs union. On 1 Jan. 1948 this union came into force and the existing customs tariffs of the Belgium–Luxembourg Economic Union and of the Netherlands were superseded by the joint Benelux Customs Union Tariff. It applies to imports into the 3 countries from outside sources, and exempts from customs duties all imports into each of the 3 countries from the other two. The Benelux tariff has 991 items and 2,400 separate specifications.

Returns of special imports and special exports (including parcel post and diamond trade, excluding unrefined and partly-worked gold, gold coins and coins in current circulation made of other metal) for calendar years (in 1,000 guilders):

	Imports	*Exports*		*Imports*	*Exports*
1949	5,331,569	3,851,126	1973[1]	66,560,222	66,879,265
1959	14,968,454	13,702,927	1974[1]	87,820,513	87,992,705
1969	39,796,506	36,073,810	1975[1]	88,010,009	88,655,462
1972[1]	54,720,893	53,898,886	1976[1]	104.249,868	106,016,987

[1] Including unrefined and partly worked gold and gold coins.

Value of the trade (including parcel post and diamond trade, excluding unrefined and partly-worked gold, gold coins and coins in current circulation made of other metal) with leading countries (in 1,000 guilders):

Country	*Imports* 1974	1975	1976	*Exports* 1974	1975	1976
Belgium–Luxembourg	11,665,106	11,509,912	13,165,170	12,362,395	12,279,756	15,655,724
France	6,369,225	6,773,918	7,336,289	8,693,637	9,127,287	11,273,951
Germany (Fed. Rep.)	23,235,148	22,354,051	25,177,822	26,515,314	26,940,651	32,762,340
Indonesia	274,651	314,323	364,189	317,409	408,570	566,051
Italy	2,977,634	3,093,340	3,517,587	4,661,124	4,481,615	5,475,517
Kuwait	306,261	1,226,748	1,632,688	99,274	113,543	140,030

Country	Imports 1974	Imports 1975	Imports 1976	Exports 1974	Exports 1975	Exports 1976
Sweden	1,792,842	1,716,288	1,993,151	2,047,994	1,895,534	2,196,577
UK	4,790,466	5,096,679	6,473,076	8,018,472	8,120,900	8,800,232
USA	7,943,876	8,771,327	9,585,322	3,508,656	2,439,898	3,010,616
Venezuela	115,178	171,453	168,744	164,858	229,941	189,957

Total trade between the Netherlands and UK for calendar years (British Department of Trade returns, in £1,000 sterling):

	1973	1974	1975	1976	1977
Imports to UK	911,732	1,637,020	1,872,819	2,427,921	2,491,986
Exports and re-exports from UK	603,568	982,318	1,113,460	1,500,350	2,138,789

Tourism. There were 2·68m. visitors in 1974 spending US$1,030m.

COMMUNICATIONS

Roads. In 1975 the length of the Netherlands network of surfaced inter-urban roads was 51,544 km, of which 1,430 km were motor highways. Buses and trams transported in 1976, 963m. passengers, 645m. of them in local traffic. Number of private cars (1976), 3·8m.

Railways. All railways are run by the mixed company 'N.V. Nederlandsche Spoorwegen'. Length of line in 1977 was 2,825 km, of which 1,719 km were electrified. Passengers carried (1976), 172m.; goods transported, 17·7m. tonnes.

Aviation. The Royal Dutch Airlines (KLM) was founded on 7 Oct. 1919. The company has a paid-up capital of 711m. guilders (31 March 1977). Revenue traffic, 1976: Passengers, 3·7m.; freight, 165m. kg; mail, 6·9m. kg.

Sea-going Shipping. Survey of the Netherlands mercantile marine as at 1 Jan. (capacity in 1,000 GRT):

Ships under Netherlands flag (including Netherlands Antilles)	*1976 Number*	*1976 Capacity*	*1977 Number*	*1977 Capacity*
Passenger ships[1]	10	129	9	126
Freighters (500 GRT and over)	387	2,400	408	2,401
Freighters (under 500 GRT)	219	98	175	78
Tankers	98	2,533	98	2,472
	714	5,160	690	5,077

[1] With accommodation for 13 or more cabin passengers.

In 1976, 46,032 sea-going ships of 320·1m. gross tons entered Netherlands ports (1975, 45,314 ships of 306·9m. gross tons).

Total goods traffic by sea-going ships in 1976 (with 1975 figures in brackets), in 1m. tonnes, amounted to 255·8 (242·6) unloaded, of which 146 (136·9) tankershipping, and 82·5 (80·1) loaded, of which 47 (46·8) tankshipping. The total seaborne freight traffic at Rotterdam was 283·1m (269·3m.) and at Amsterdam 18·9m. (19m.) tonnes.

The number of containers at Rotterdam in 1976 was: unloaded from ships, 409,919, of which 156,051 from North America, and 406,262 loaded into ships, of which 117,338 to North America.

Inland Shipping. The total length of navigable rivers and canals is 4,360 km, of which about 1,950 km is for ships with a capacity of 1,000 and more tonnes. On 1 Jan. 1977 the Netherlands inland fleet actually used for transport (with carrying capacity in 1,000 tonnes) was composed as follows:

	Number	*Capacity*
Self-propelled barges	6,416	3,739
Dumb barges	721	770
Pushed barges	378	595
	7,515	5,104

In 1976, 260m. (1975: 236m.) tonnes of goods were transported on rivers and canals, of which 166m. (156m.) was international traffic. Goods transport on the

Rhine (Lobith) amounted to 41·5m. (44·4m.) tonnes downstream and 77 (74·7m.) upstream.

Post and Broadcasting. On 1 Jan. 1977 there were 3·6m. telephone connexions (26 per 100 inhabitants). Number of telex lines, 24,854; teleprinters, 26,799. *Nederlandse Omroep Stitching* (NOS) provides 4 programmes on medium-waves and FM in co-operation with broadcasting organizations. Regional programmes are also broadcast.

Advertisements are transmitted. NOS broadcasts 2 TV programmes. Advertisements are restricted to 180 minutes weekly. Television sets totalled 3·8m.: holders of television licences may, in addition, have wireless receiving sets.

Cinemas (end 1975). There were 419 cinemas with a seating capacity of 171,920.

Newspapers (1975). There were 72 daily newspapers with a total circulation of over 4·6m.

JUSTICE, RELIGION, EDUCATION AND WELFARE

Justice. Justice is administered by the High Court of the Netherlands (Court of Cassation), by 5 courts of justice (Courts of Appeal), by 19 district courts and by 62 cantonal courts; trial by jury is unknown. The Cantonal Court, which deals with minor offences, is formed by a single judge; the more serious cases are tried by the district courts, formed as a rule by 3 judges (in some cases one judge is sufficient); the courts of appeal are constituted of 3 and the High Court of 5 judges. All judges are appointed for life by the Sovereign (the judges of the High Court from a list prepared by the Second Chamber of the States-General). They can be removed only by a decision of the High Court.

At the district court the juvenile judge is specially appointed to try children's civil cases and at the same time charged with the administration of justice for criminal actions committed by young persons who are between 12 and 18 years old, unless imprisonment of 6 months or more ought to be inflicted; such cases are tried by 3 judges.

Number of persons convicted (tax offenders excluded):

Major offences	*1973*	*1974*	*1975*	*Minor offences*	*1974*	*1975*	*1976*
Males	40,576	42,364	46,183	Males	1,286,207	1,326,557	1,446,624
Females	3,409	3,305	3,573	Females	161,267	170,972	211,969

In addition, prosecution was evaded by paying a fine to the police in 813,570 cases in 1973, 794,460 in 1974, 829,707 in 1975 and 926,415 in 1976.

Police. There are both State and Municipal Police. The State Police, about 5,900 men strong, serves 720, and the Municipal Police, about 16,000 men strong, serves 140 municipalities. The State Police includes ordinary as well as water, mounted and motor police. The State Police Corps is under the jurisdiction of the Police Department of the Ministry of Justice, which also includes the National Criminal Investigation Office, which deals with serious crimes throughout the country, and the International Criminal Investigation Office, which informs foreign countries of international crimes.

Religion. Entire liberty of conscience is granted to the members of all denominations. The royal family belong to the Dutch Reformed Church.

The number of adherents of the Churches according to the census of 1971 was: Dutch Reformed Church, 3,075,565; Reformed Churches (excluding other reformed denominations), 937,840; Roman Catholics, 5,273,665; other creeds (including other reformed denominations), 694,405; no religion, 3,078,640; total, 13,060,115.

The government of the Reformed Church is Presbyterian. On 1 July 1972 the Dutch Reformed Church had 1 synod, 11 provincial districts, 54 classes, 147 districts and 1,905 parishes.

Their clergy numbered 2,000. The Roman Catholic Church had, Jan. 1973, 1 archbishop (of Utrecht), 6 bishops and 1,815 parishes and rectorships. The Old Catholics had (1 July 1972) 1 archbishop (Utrecht), 2 bishops and 29 parishes. The Jews had, in 1970, 46 communities.

Education. Statistics for the scholastic year 1975–76:

	Full-time Schools	*Pupils* Total	*Pupils* Female	*Part-time*[1] Schools	*Pupils* Total	*Pupils* Female
Nursery schools	7,568	518,890	252,806	—	—	—
Primary schools	8,568	1,453,467	714,053	—	—	—
Special schools	885	83,364	26,948	—	—	—
Secondary general schools	1,514	766,391	380,114	69	32,649	15,010
Secondary vocational schools:						
Junior—						
Technical, nautical	526	192,793	5,984	...[1]	113,386[1]	31,321[1]
Agricultural	134	20,089	2,815	209	3,948	641
Domestic science	597	143,638	141,920	48	3,021	3,015
Other	184	46,387	22,585	...	539	—
Senior—						
Technical, nautical	118	46,198	2,012	86	7,657	206
Agricultural	50	7,911	885	33	563	3
Domestic science	231	26,033	25,534	20	3,150	3,063
Teachers' training (nursery schools)	48	10,830	10,789	45	4,267	4,262
Other	115	23,315	7,685	80	12,161	6,234
Third level non-university training:						
Technical, nautical	62	28,038	2,931	45	5,252	492
Agricultural	23	3,009	340	—	—	—
Arts	37	8,552	3,758	19	2,978	1,279
Teachers' training:						
Primary schools	91	25,225	12,908	—	—	—
Secondary general schools	26	15,680	6,288	194	28,886	12,480
Secondary vocational schools	57	3,789	3,395	49	7,391	572
Other	87	26,956	13,955	48	12,136	5,628

[1] Including apprenticeship schemes, young workers' educational institutes.

Full-time: 1976–77[1]

	Schools	*Pupils* Total	*Pupils* Female
University education:			
Humanities	14	29,475	12,808
Social sciences		45,837	12,133
Natural sciences		12,904	2,100
Technical sciences		16,728	658
Medical sciences		17,356	4,448
Agricultural sciences		5,344	1,338

[1] Provisional figures.

Health. In 1972 there were 6,000 doctors and 53,000 hospital beds.

DIPLOMATIC REPRESENTATIVES

OF THE NETHERLANDS IN GREAT BRITAIN
(38 Hyde Park Gate, London, SW7 5DP)

Ambassador: Robbert Fack.

OF GREAT BRITAIN IN THE NETHERLANDS
(Lange Voorhout, 10, The Hague)

Ambassador: Sir Richard Sykes, KCMG.

OF THE NETHERLANDS IN THE USA (4200 Linnean Ave, NW, Washington, D.C., 20008)

Ambassador: A. R. Tammenoms Bakker.

OF THE USA IN THE NETHERLANDS (Lange Voorhout, 102, The Hague)
Ambassador: Robert James McCloskey.

OF THE NETHERLANDS TO THE UNITED NATIONS
Ambassador: Dr Johan Kaufmann.

Books of Reference

Statistical Information: The 'Centraal Bureau voor de Statistiek' at Voorburg, near The Hague, is the official Netherlands statistical service. *Director-General of Statistics:* Prof. Dr W. Begeer.

The Bureau was founded in 1899. Prior to that year, statistical publications were compiled by the 'Centrale commissie voor de statistiek', the 'Vereniging voor staathuishoudkunde en statistiek' and various government departments. These activities have gradually been taken over and co-ordinated by the Central Bureau, which now compiles practically all government statistics.

Its current publications include:

Statistical Yearbook of the Netherlands. From 1923/24 (preceded by *Jaarciifers voor het Koninkrijk der Nederlanden, 1898–1922*); latest issue, 1976
Statistisch zakboek (*Pocket Year Book*). From 1899/1924 (1 vol.); latest issue, 1976
Maandstatistiek van de buitenlandse handel (*monthly statistical bulletin of foreign trade*). From 1917
Nationale Rekeningen (*National Accounts*), from 1948–50; latest issue, 1976
Uitkomsten van de 14e Algenene volkstelling, 28 Feb 1971 (*Results of the Fourteenth Census. Population and Housing, 28 Feb. 1971*)
Statistische onderaoekingen (*Statistical Studies*). From 1977

Benelux Information. *See* p. 201.

Other Official Publications

Central Economic Plan. Centraal Plan-bureau, The Hague (Dutch text), annually, from 1946
Netherlands. Organization for Economic Co-operation and Development. Paris, annual from 1964
Staatsalmanak voor het Koninkrijk der Nederlanden. Annual. The Hague, from 1814
Staatsblad van het Koninkrijk der Nederlanden. The Hague, from 1814
Staatscourant (*State Gazette*). The Hague, from 1813
Atlas van Nederland. Government Printing Office, The Hague, 1970 and supplements up to and including 1973
De Nederlandse Economie in 1980. Centraal Planbureau, The Hague, 1976
Memoranda on the Condition of the Netherlands State Finances. Ministry of Finance, The Hague, from 1906
Basic Guide to the Establishing of Industrial Operations in the Netherlands 1976. Ministry of Economic Affairs, The Hague, 1976
The Kingdom of the Netherlands. Ministry of Foreign Affairs, The Hague, 1974–75
Huggett, F. E., *The Dutch Today.* Ministry of Foreign Affairs, The Hague, 1973

Non-Official Publications

Huggett, F. E., *The Modern Netherlands.* London, 1971
Jansonius, H., *Groot Nederlands–Engels Woordenboek Voor Studie en Praktijk.* 3 vols. Leiden, 1972 (Vols. 1 and 2)
Newton, G., *The Netherlands: An Historical and Cultural Survey, 1795–1977.* Boulder, 1978
Veldman, J., *Agriculture in the Netherlands.* Utrecht, 1974
Pyttersen's Nederlandse Almanak. Zaltbommel, annual, from 1899
Commerce and Industry in the Netherlands. Amsterdam–Rotterdam Bank. Amsterdam, 1974
Foreign Investment in the Netherlands. The Hague, 1975
The Information You Need When Planning a Business in the Netherlands. Algemene Bank Nederland. Amsterdam, 1975
A Compact Geography of the Netherlands. Utrecht, 1974
De Economische Geschiedenis van Nederland. Groningen, 1977

National Library: De Koninklijke Bibliotheek, Lange Voorhout, 34, The Hague, *Director:* Dr C. Reedijk.

THE NETHERLANDS ANTILLES

De Nederlandse Antillen

AREA AND POPULATION. The Netherlands Antilles are an integral part of the Netherlands and comprises two groups of islands, viz. the Leeward Islands, Curaçao, Aruba and Bonaire, and the Windward Islands, St. Maarten, St Eustatius and Saba. The Leeward Islands are situated 40–70 miles north of the Venezuelan coast between 12° and 13° N. lat. and 68° and 71° W. long. The Windward group lies east of Puerto Rico. For the constitutional position of the Netherlands Antilles *see* p. 875. The total area is 993 sq. km (383 sq. miles) and the population was 234,374 on 31 Dec. 1974.

Leeward group	*Sq. km*	*Population*	*Windward group*	*Sq. km*	*Population*
Curaçao	444	154,928	St Maarten (St Martin)[1]	34	10,310
Aruba	193	61,788	St Eustatius	21	1,421[2]
Bonaire	288	8,400	Saba	13	951

[1] The southern part belongs to the Netherlands Antilles, the northern to France. [2] 1973.

In 1972, 4,941 births, 1,138 deaths, 1,471 marriages and 350 divorces were registered.

GOVERNMENT. Since Dec. 1954, the Netherlands Antilles have been fully autonomous in internal affairs, and constitutionally equal with the Netherlands and Surinam. The Sovereign of the Kingdom of the Netherlands is Head of the Government of the Netherlands Antilles and is represented by a Governor.

The executive power in internal affairs rests with the Governor and the Council of Ministers, who together form the government. The Ministers are responsible to the unicameral legislature (*Staten*). This consists of 22 members (12 from Curaçao, 8 from Aruba, 1 from Bonaire, 1 from the Windward Islands) and is elected by general suffrage. It was agreed in 1977 that the 2 smallest islands, Saba and St Eustatius would each have a representative (non-voting) in the *Staten*.

The executive power in external affairs is vested in the Council of Ministers of the Kingdom, in which the Antilles is represented by a Minister Plenipotentiary with full voting powers.

In 1951 the Netherlands Antilles Islands Regulation provided for self-government of each of the 4 insular communities Aruba, Bonaire, Curaçao and the Windward Islands. The autonomous powers of the insular communities are divided between the Island Council (elected by general suffrage), the Executive Council and the Lieut.-Governor (*Gezaghebber*), who is responsible for maintaining public peace and order.

Governor: Dr B. M. Leito.

Prime Minister: S. G. M. Rozendal.
Deputy Prime Minister: L. A. I. Chance.

Flag: White, with a red vertical strip crossed by a blue horizontal strip bearing 6 white stars.

Dutch is the official language. Spanish and English are also spoken. In addition a 'lingua franca', *Papiamento*, has evolved out of Spanish, Dutch and some other languages.

FINANCE. The central budget for 1972 envisaged 121,796,700 guilders revenue and 121,231,500 guilders expenditure.

The public debt was 252m. guilders as at 31 Dec. 1971.

The official rate of exchange is £1 = 4·33 (buying) and 4·27 (selling) Netherlands Antilles guilders.

ENERGY AND NATURAL RESOURCES

Oil. The economy of the Netherlands Antilles is almost entirely based on the refining of oil imported from Venezuela to Curaçao and Aruba. About 25% (Curaçao) and 30% (Aruba) of the gainfully occupied are working at the refineries or their shipping establishments. On account of the activities of the oil companies (affiliated to the Royal Dutch/Shell and the Standard Oil of New Jersey), the prosperity on Curaçao and Aruba is good in comparison with the other islands.

Minerals. About 100,000 tons of calcium phosphate are annually mined in Curaçao.

Agriculture. Livestock (1976): Cattle, 8,000; goats, 21,000; poultry, 100,000.

INDUSTRY AND TRADE

Industry. In Aruba there are some petrochemical factories; Curaçao has a paint factory, 2 cigarette factories, a textile factory, a brewery and some smaller industries. The Texas Instruments Co. and Electronic Fabriek have established electronic factories. Almost all products needed for consumption and production are imported, as the rocky soil permits little agriculture and local fishing is insufficient for home consumption. Bonaire has a textile factory and a modern-equipped salt plant. St Maarten has a rum factory and fishing is important. St Eustatius and Saba are of less economic importance.

Trade (1971). Total imports amounted to 1,493m. guilders; total exports to 1,274m. guilders, of which oil and oil products accounted for 1,196m. guilders.

Total trade between the Netherlands Antilles and UK (British Department of Trade returns, in £1,000 sterling):

	1973	*1974*	*1975*	*1976*	*1977*
Imports to UK	14,222	37,760	31,219	49,675	26,075
Exports and re-exports from UK	10,236	8,684	12,044	14,945	71,096

The Free-Zones Ordinance of 1956 has established free zones in the ports of Curaçao and Aruba.

Tourism. In 1972, 552,776 foreign tourists visited the Netherlands Antilles including 269,850 cruise tourists.

COMMUNICATIONS

Roads. In 1972 the Netherlands Antilles had 1,150 km of surfaced highway distributed as follows: Curaçao, 929; Aruba, 389; Bonaire, 125; St Maarten, 60. Number of motor vehicles (31 Dec. 1972): 32,355 in Curaçao, 12,743 in Aruba.

Shipping (1971). There entered the port of Curaçao, 5,333 vessels of 42m. gross tons; Aruba, 2,394 vessels of 34·8m. gross tons. Curaçao has a dry dock of 120,000 tons.

Post and Broadcasting. Number of telephones, 1 Jan. 1977, 48,000. Eight radio stations are operating on medium-waves from Curaçao, Aruba, Bonaire, and Saint Maarten. These stations broadcast in Papiamento, Dutch, English and Spanish and are mainly financed by income from advertisements. In addition, Radio Nederland and Trans World Radio have powerful relay stations operating on medium- and short-waves from Bonaire.

Cinemas (1973). Curaçao and Aruba had 13 cinemas with a seating capacity of 11,000. There is a drive-in for 500 cars in Curaçao, for 200 cars in St Maarten and for 350 cars at Aruba.

RELIGION, EDUCATION AND WELFARE

Religion. In 1960, 82% of the population were Roman Catholics, 8% were Protestants.

Education (1972). Schools numbered 280, with 66,409 pupils and 2,516 teachers.

Health. In June 1973 there were 155 physicians, 55 specialists, 33 dentists and 18 pharmacists. In 1973, 11 hospitals had 2,037 beds.

DIPLOMATIC REPRESENTATIVE

USA Consul-General: Grover W. Penberthy.

The British consulate closed on 1 Sept. 1976.

Books of Reference

Statistical Information: Statistical publications (on population, trade, cost of living, etc., are obtainable on request from the Statistical Office, Willemstad, Curaçao. *Statistical Jaarboek 1970* (text in Dutch, English and Spanish).

De West Indische Gids. The Hague. Monthly from 1919
Braam, H. L., *Hoe ons land geregeerd wordt*. Willemstad, 4th ed. 1972
Hartog, J., *Aruba*. Oranjestad, 1953.—*Bonaire*. Oranjestad, 1958.—*Curaçao*. Oranjestad, 1961
Nordlohne, E., *De Economisch-geographische Structuur der Benedenwindse Eilanden*. Rotterdam, 1951
Poll, W. van de, *De Nederlandse Antillen*. The Hague, 1950
Walle, J. van de, *De Nederlandse Antillen*. Willemstad, 1954
Westerman, J. H., *Overzicht van de geologische en mijnbouwkundige kennis der Nederlandse Antillen*. Amsterdam, 1949

NEW HEBRIDES CONDOMINIUM

Capital: Vila
Population: 97,468 (1976)

Nouvelles Hébrides

HISTORY. The group is administered for some purposes jointly, for others unilaterally, as provided for by Anglo-French Convention of 27 Feb. 1906, ratified 20 Oct. 1906, and a protocol signed at London on 6 Aug. 1911 and ratified on 18 March 1922.

AREA AND POPULATION. The New Hebrides group lies roughly 500 miles west of Fiji and 250 miles north-east of New Caledonia. The estimated land area is 5,700 sq. miles (14,760 sq. km). The larger islands of the group are: Espiritu Santo, Malekula, Epi, Pentecost, Aoba, Maewa, Paama, Ambrym, Efate, Erromanga, Tanna and Aneityum.

There are 3 active volcanoes, on Tanna, Ambrym and Lopevi, respectively. Earth tremors are of common occurrence. Rainfall at Vila (the capital, population (1972) 12,536) averages 90 in. per annum.

The first complete census was taken in 1967. The total population was found to be 77,988, of whom 72,243 were New Hebrideans. Estimate, June 1976, 97,468.

CONSTITUTION AND GOVERNMENT. The interests of British, French and New Hebrideans, respectively, are protected; the conditions of land-holding in the islands fixed, and the regulation of the recruitment of native labour provided for. Britain and France are represented by High Commissioners who delegate their powers to Resident Commissioners stationed in the group.

General elections took place in Nov. 1975 to elect a 42-member Representative Assembly, replacing the former advisory council. A committee system was instituted and the Assembly chose its own President from its own members in 1977. The President replaced the Co-presidents, who were the Resident Commissioners. Complete independence is envisaged in 1980.

Flag: On land, the British Union flag is flown side by side with the French tricolour; at sea, the British Blue Ensign with the badge of the New Hebrides in the fly.

British Resident Commissioner: J. S. Champion, OBE.
French Resident Commissioner: R. Langlois.

ECONOMY

Planning. A Joint Office of Development planning was established in 1976. There are planners from Britain and France, and it is charged with the preparation of recommendations to the Resident Commissioners concerning development strategies for the group. The draft plan should be drafted by 1977, and should run from 1978 to 1980. Finance for the Development Plan will be sought mainly from Britain and France. Assistance will also be available from the usual multilateral agencies. The Condominium itself usually appropriates an annual amount towards the financing of development projects.

In 1970 a joint development plan was prepared for the 5-year period 1971–75. The plan provided for a balanced and co-ordinated programme of development in those sectors of the economy for which the joint administration is responsible. It is financed from Condominium funds, grants from the British and French Governments, and loans. The plan envisages a total expenditure of $A8,884,500 on public works, communications, urban development and national resources. The new Vila deep-water quay was completed in 1972.

Budget. The Condominium budget for 1975: Revenue, 737m. NH francs; expenditure, 1,028m. NH francs. The main sources of revenue were (1975) import duties (388m. NH francs) and export duties (30m. NH francs).

Currency. In Dec. 1976 100 NH francs = $A1.20. Australian decimal currency was introduced in 1966. It and the New Hebrides franc are the currencies in use.

Banking. Because of the absence of direct taxation, with the exception of an added value tax on sales of sub-divided land, there has been growing interest in the New Hebrides as a finance centre. There were 10 banks in Vila in 1976 and there has been a corresponding growth in other professions associated with the finance industry. There are branches of the Bank of Indo-China at Vila and Santo and savings bank agencies of the Commonwealth Bank of Australia at Vila, Santo, Tanna and Aoba. The Bank of Australia and New Zealand and Barclays Bank International have branches in Vila.

PRODUCTION. The main commercial crops are copra, cocoa and coffee. Yams, taro, manioc and bananas are grown for local consumption. A large number of cattle are reared on plantations, and an up-grading programme using pure-bred Charolais, Limousins and Illawarras has begun. A beef industry is developing.

Livestock (1976): Cattle, 110,000; goats, 7,000; pigs, 64,000; poultry, 131,000.

The manganese mine, established at Forari on Efate by the Compagnie Française de Phosphates de l'Océanie, closed in 1968 but was reopened in 1970 by Southland Mining of Australia. Manganese exports, 1975, 65·7m. NH francs. Timber exports fell sharply in 1974 with the closing of the mill on Erromanga. Frozen fish exports by a British/Japanese company have declined from 888m. NH francs in 1973 to 258m. NH francs in 1975. There is no heavy industry but there is increasing activity in light industry. Industries include a brick and pipe works, a ready-mixed cement works, a sawmill, a stone-crushing company, a soft drinks factory, meat canneries and a modern abattoir, and a fish-freezing plant. A few indigenous crafts, such as basketry, canoe-building and pottery, are practised. Subsistence fishing is done by the New Hebrideans, and a plant for freezing of tuna and bonito commenced operation in 1957. This plant, which is sited on Santo, freezes and packages for export to Japan and elsewhere, fish caught by Taiwanese and other vessels under contract to the British company running the plant. There is a shipyard at Santo.

COMMERCE. In 1975 imports totalled 1,498m. NA francs and exports 2,489m. NA francs.

Australia and France were the major sources of imports and principal imports were machinery and transport equipment, foodstuffs, manufactured goods and mineral fuels.

COMMUNICATIONS

Roads. The Public Works Department maintains limited roads on Efate, Santo, Tanna, Pentecost and Malekula. There are, in addition, tracks usable by motor vehicles on some of the other islands.

Aviation. External air services are provided by Air Pacific, UTA (Unions de Transports Aériens) and Air Nauru. Air Pacific has two services a week Nandi–Vila–Honiara–Brisbane, and one Nandi–Vila–Noumea–Brisbane. UTA has daily flights from Noumea, and a weekly flight to Wallis. Air Nauru gives a weekly service Vila–Nauru. Inter-island flights are provided by Air Melanesiae. The principal airports are Bauer Field (for Vila) and Pekoa (for Santo). Twelve smaller airfields provide an internal network. In 1975 there were 737 overseas aircraft arrivals in Vila, carrying 21,264 passengers.

Shipping. Several international shipping lines serve the New Hebrides, linking the Condominium with Australia, New Zealand, other Pacific territories notably Hong Kong and Japan, and Europe. A deep-water wharf built with financial aid from Britain and France was opened in 1973. Small vessels provide a frequent but mostly unscheduled inter-island service. Ports of entry are Vila and Santo. In 1975, 393 vessels totalling 898,862 net tons entered, loaded 91,815 tons of cargo and discharged 84,293 tons.

Telecommunications. Telegraphic communication is by direct wireless contact with Suva, Honiara, Noumea and Sydney, and there is an internal network of teleradio stations. There is also a radio-telephone service with Honiara, Noumea, Suva and Sydney, from where the service can be extended to USA, Europe, etc. Air radio facilities are provided. Marine coast station facilities are available at Vila and Santo. Telex became available in Vila in 1973.

Radio Vila operates a broadcasting service on 6 days a week for limited periods.

JUSTICE, EDUCATION AND WELFARE

Justice. There are Condominium and English and French national courts. A study is being made which could lead to unification of the judicial system. Condominium regulations apply to all courts.

Education. Education is the responsibility of the British and French National Services, which organize parallel and separate systems. The Condominium Government makes an annual subsidy to each administration ($A278,813 in 1976). The British National Service finances 1 secondary school and a primary teacher-training college. Grant-aid is given to 3 voluntary agency junior secondary schools each with forms 1 to 3. Grant-aid is also given to 4 district education committees with 110 primary schools and to the Diocese of the New Hebrides with 21 primary schools. In 1976, 118 students, sponsored by the British National Service were studying overseas.

Health. Medical care is provided through a network of 106 hospitals, health centres, clinics and dispensaries administered by the French and British medical departments with the help of WHO, and a number of voluntary agencies. Public health measures and the control of communicable diseases are the responsibility of the joint Condominium public health administration. Local training schemes are devoted to basic community nurse training at both British and French hospitals in Vila, to rural health training and refresher courses at a special training health centre in North Efate, or by attachment to other suitable clinics and health centres, and to training of village sanitarians or health orderlies.

Malaria is still the most serious of the major endemic diseases which also include tuberculosis, leprosy, filariasis and venereal disease. During 1975–76 yaws recurred on some islands and there were epidemic outbreaks of dengue, influenza and gastro-enteritis.

For professional and technical education in medicine, nursing, X-ray, dentistry, laboratory work, health inspection, selected students or suitable in-service staff are awarded scholarships and fellowships for overseas training in Solomon Islands, Papua New Guinea, Fiji, New Zealand, Australia, New Caledonia and other countries.

Book of Reference

Annual Report 1968–69. HMSO

NEW ZEALAND

Capital: Wellington
Population: 3·15m. (1976)
GNP per capita: US$4,250 (1976)

HISTORY. The first European to discover New Zealand was Tasman in 1642. The coast was explored by Capt. Cook in 1769. From about 1800 onwards, New Zealand became a resort for whalers and traders, chiefly from Australia. By the Treaty of Waitangi, in 1840, between Governor William Hobson and the representatives of the Maori race, the Maori chiefs ceded the sovereignty to the British Crown and the islands became a British colony. Then followed a steady stream of British settlers.

The Maoris are a branch of the Polynesian race, having emigrated from the eastern Pacific before and during the 14th century. Between 1845 and 1848, and between 1860 and 1870, misunderstandings over land led to war, but peace was permanently established in 1871, and the development of New Zealand has been marked by racial harmony and integration.

AREA AND POPULATION. New Zealand lies south-east of Australia in the south Pacific, Wellington being 1,233 miles from Sydney by sea. There are two principal islands, the North and South Islands, besides Stewart Island, Chatham Islands and small outlying islands, as well as the territories overseas (*see* p. 907).

New Zealand (*i.e.*, North, South and Stewart Islands) extends over 1,750 km from north to south. Area, excluding territories overseas, 268,704 sq. km.; North Island, 11,469,000 hectares; South Island, 15,046,000 hectares; Stewart Island, 174,000 hectares; Chatham Islands, 96,000 hectares; minor islands, 82,900 hectares. Census population, exclusive of territories overseas:

	Total population	*Average annual increase %*		*Total population*	*Average annual increase %*
1858	115,462	—	1921	1,271,644	2·27
1874	344,984	—	1926	1,408,139	2·06
1878	458,007	7·33	1936	1,573,810	1·13
1881	534,030	5·10	1945[1]	1,702,298	0·83
1886	620,451	3·05	1951[1]	1,939,472	2·37
1891	668,632	1·50	1956[1]	2,174,062	2·31
1896	743,207	2·13	1961[1]	2,414,984	2·12
1901[1]	815,853	1·89	1966[1]	2,676,919	2·10
1906	936,304	2·75	1971[1]	2,862,631	1·34
1911	1,058,308	2·52	1976[1]	3,129,383	1·71
1916[1]	1,149,225	1·50			

The census of New Zealand is quinquennial, but the census falling in 1931 was abandoned as an act of national economy, and owing to war conditions the census due in 1941 was not taken until 25 Sept. 1945.

[1] Excluding members of the Armed Forces overseas.

The areas and populations of statistical areas (with principal centres) at 23 March 1976 were as follows[1]:

Statistical area[2]	*Sq. km*	*Total population*
Northland (Whangarei)	12,639	107,013
Central Auckland (Auckland)	5,569	797,406
South Auckland—Bay of Plenty (Hamilton)	36,744	472,083
East Coast (Gisborne)	10,878	48,147
Hawke's Bay (Napier, Hastings)	11,033	145,061
Taranaki (New Plymouth)	9,713	107,071
Wellington (Wellington)	28,153	591,612
Total, North Island	*114,729*	*2,268,393*

[1] For statistical purposes, the 9 provincial districts have now been replaced by 13 statistical areas.
[2] Listed from north to south.

Statistical area[1]	*Sq. km*	*Total population*
Marlborough (Blenheim)	10,930	35,030
Nelson (Nelson)	17,897	75,562
Westland (Greymouth)	15,566	24,049
Canterbury (Christchurch)	43,431	428,586
Otago (Dunedin)	36,441	188,903
Southland (Invercargill)	29,681	108,860
Total, South Island	*153,946*	*860,990*
Total, New Zealand	268,675	3,129,383

[1] Listed from north to south.

New Zealand-born residents made up 83·25% of the population at the 1976 census. Foreign-born: UK, 291,490; Australia, 61,810; Netherlands, 21,990; Western Samoa, 19,430; Cook Islands, 11,000; USA, 8,440; Republic of Ireland, 5,930; others, 105,220.

Maori population: 1896, 42,113; 1936, 82,326; 1945, 98,744; 1951, 115,676; 1961, 171,553; 1966, 201,159; 1971, 227,414; 1976 (estimated), 257,770.

Populations of statistical divisions and urban areas at 23 March 1976 were as follows:

Auckland	797,406	Invercargill	53,762
Christchurch	325,710	Masterton	21,001
Dunedin	120,426	Nelson	42,433
Hamilton	154,606	New Plymouth	43,914
Napier–Hastings	109,010	Rotorua	46,650
Palmerston North	88,724	Tauranga	48,153
Wellington	349,628	Timaru	29,958
Urban areas:		Wanganui	39,679
Gisborne	31,790	Whangarei	39,069

Vital statistics for calendar years:

	Total live births	*Ex-nuptial births*	*Deaths*	*Marriages*	*Divorces (decrees absolute)*
1974	59,336	9,370	25,261	25,412	4,457
1975	56,639	9,407	25,114	24,535	4,761
1976	55,105	9,597	25,457	24,154	5,401

Birth rate, 1976, 17·68 per 1,000; death rate, 8·17 per 1,000; marriage rate, 7·75 per 1,000; infant mortality, 13·9 per 1,000 live births.

External migration (exclusive of crews and through passengers) for years ended 31 March:

	Arrivals	*Departures*
1972	408,281	397,430
1973	469,382	443,907
1974	598,099	564,932
1975	678,655	649,514
1976	678,664	673,472
1977	667,224	683,494

Population and Migration: Part B—External Migration. Dept. of Statistics, Wellington, Annually

CONSTITUTION AND GOVERNMENT. Definition was given the status of New Zealand by the (Imperial) Statute of Westminster of Dec. 1931, which had received the antecedent approval of the New Zealand Parliament in July 1931. The Governor-General's assent was given to the Statute of Westminster Adoption Bill on 25 Nov. 1947.

The powers, duties and responsibilities of the Governor-General and the Executive Council under the present system of responsible government are set out in Royal Letters Patent and Instructions thereunder of 11 May 1917, published in the *New Zealand Gazette* of 24 April 1919. In the execution of the powers vested in him the Governor-General must be guided by the advice of the Executive Council.

The following is a list of Governors-General, the title prior to June 1917 being Governor:

Earl of Liverpool	1917–20	Lord Norrie	1952–57
Viscount Jellicoe	1920–24	Viscount Cobham	1957–62
Sir Charles Fergusson, Bt	1924–30	Sir Bernard Fergusson	1962–67
Lord Bledisloe	1930–35	Sir Arthur Porrit, Bt	1967–72
Viscount Galway	1935–41	Sir Denis Blundell	1972–77
Sir Cyril Newall	1941–46	Sir Keith Holyoake	1977–
Lord Freyberg, VC	1946–52		

National flag: The British Blue Ensign with 4 stars of the Southern Cross in red, edged in white, in the fly.

National anthem: God Save the Queen.

National song: God Defend New Zealand (words by Thomas Bracken, music by John J. Woods).

Parliament consists of the House of Representatives, the former Legislative Council having been abolished since 1 Jan. 1951.

The statute law on elections and the life of Parliament is contained in the Electoral Act, 1956. In 1974 the voting age was reduced from 20 to 18 years.

The House of Representatives consists of 87 members, including 4 Maoris, elected by the people for 3 years. The 4 Maori electoral districts cover the whole country and adult Maoris of half or more Maori descent are the electors. From 1976 a descendant of a Maori is entitled to register either for a general or a Maori electoral district. Women's suffrage was instituted in 1893: women became eligible as members of the House of Representatives in 1919. The House in 1976 included 4 women members.

During Parliamentary sittings the proceedings of the House are broadcast regularly on sound radio.

House of Representatives as composed following the General Election in Nov. 1975: National Party, 55; Labour, 32; total 87.

The Executive Council was composed as follows in May 1978:

Governor-General and C.-in-C.: Sir Keith Holyoake, GCMG, CH.

Prime Minister, Minister of Finance, Minister in charge of the Legislative Department, Minister in charge of Audit Department, Minister in charge of the New Zealand Security Intelligence Service: R. D. Muldoon.

Deputy Prime Minister, Minister of Foreign Affairs, Minister of Overseas Trade: B. E. Talboys.

Minister of Labour, Minister of State Services: J. B. Gordon.

Minister of Agriculture, Minister of Maori Affairs, Minister in charge of the Rural Banking and Finance Corporation: D. MacIntyre.

Minister of Trade and Industry: L. R. Adams-Schneider.

Minister of Justice: D. S. Thomson.

Minister of Energy Resources, Minister of Electricity, Minister of Mines, Minister of National Development, Minister of Regional Development: G. F. Gair.

Minister of Defence, Minister of Police, Minister in charge of War Pensions, Minister in charge of Rehabilitation: A. McCready.

Minister of Education, Minister of Science and Technology: L. W. Gandar.

Minister of Health, Minister of Immigration: T. F. Gill.

Minister of Transport, Minister of Civil Aviation and Meteorological Services, Minister of Railways: C. C. A. McLachlan.

Minister of Works and Development: W. L. Young.

Minister of Housing, Minister in charge of Public Trust Office: E. S. F. Holland.

Minister of Social Welfare, Minister in charge of the Government Life Insurance Office, Minister in charge of the Earthquake and War Damage Commission: H. J. Walker.

Minister of Internal Affairs, Minister of Local Government, Minister of Recreation and Sport, Minister of Civil Defence, Minister for the Arts: D. A. Highet.

Attorney-General, Minister of Customs, Postmaster-General: P. I. Wilkinson.

Minister of Lands, Minister of Forests, Minister for the Environment, Minister in charge of the Valuation Department: V. S. Young.

Minister of Tourism, Minister in charge of Publicity, Minister in charge of the Government Printing Office: H. R. Lapwood.

Minister of Statistics, Minister of Broadcasting, Associate Minister of Finance, Minister in charge of the Inland Revenue Department, Minister in charge of Friendly Societies: H. C. Templeton.

Minister of Fisheries, Associate Minister of Agriculture: J. B. Bolger.

The Prime Minister (provided with residence) had at Dec. 1976 a salary of NZ$29,667 plus a tax-free expense allowance of $7,000 per annum; Ministers with portfolio, $19,564 plus a tax-free expense allowance of $2,800 (Minister of Foreign Affairs $4,800) per annum; Ministers without portfolio, $16,906 plus a tax-free expense allowance of $2,600 per annum; Parliamentary Under-Secretaries, $14,779 plus an expense allowance of $2,240 per annum. In addition, Ministers and Parliamentary Under-Secretaries not provided with residence at the seat of Government receive $600 per annum house allowance. An allowance of $30 per day while travelling within New Zealand on public service is payable to Ministers.

The Speaker of the House of Representatives received $17,969 plus an expense allowance of $4,650 per annum in addition to his electorate allowance, and residential quarters in Parliament House, and the Leader of the Opposition $19,564 plus expense allowance of $2,800 per annum, and allowances for travelling and housing amounting to $1,875.

Members were paid $12,486 per annum, plus an expense allowance varying from $3,400 to $5,220 according to the area of electorate represented.

There is a compulsory contributory superannuation scheme for members; retiring allowances are payable to a member after 9 years' service and the attainment of 50 years of age.

Dollimore, H. N., *The Parliament of New Zealand and Parliament House.* 2nd ed. Wellington, 1964
Milne, R. S., *Political Parties in New Zealand.* OUP, 1966
Scott, K. J., *The New Zealand Constitution.* OUP, 1962

Local Government. For purposes of local government New Zealand is divided into counties, district councils, boroughs and town districts. Some counties are subdivided into ridings. There are also numerous other local authorities created for specific functions, such as electric-power districts, river (*i.e.*, river protection) districts, gas districts, pest destruction districts, etc.

DEFENCE. The control and co-ordination of defence activities is obtained through the Ministry of Defence. This is a unitary department combining not only all joint-Service functions but also the former Departments of Army, Navy and Air.

Army. The Army is organized into a Home Command and a Field Force Command, each of which is responsible to Defence Headquarters. A regular force battalion is stationed in Malaysia.

Regular personnel, in 1977, totalled 5,441 all ranks; territorial personnel totalled 7,932; the cadet corps totalled 4,700 cadets.

Navy. The Royal New Zealand Navy is administered by the Chief of Naval Staff and the Deputy Chief of Naval Staff at Defence Headquarters.

The RNZN ships include 4 frigates, 1 surveying vessel, 4 new patrol craft, 7 old harbour defence motor launches, 1 oceanographic research ship and 2 tenders.

Personnel, in 1977, totalled 2,726 officers and ratings and 3,206 in the naval reserve. There were 1,170 sea cadets.

Air Force. The Chief of Air Staff and Air Officer Commanding the RNZAF exercises command and administration of the RNZAF. Operational squadrons are No. 1 Squadron, No. 3 (Sioux, UH-1H Iroquois and Wasp helicopters) Squadron, No. 5 (Orion) Squadron, No. 14 (Skyhawk/Strikemaster) Squadron, No. 40 (Hercules) Squadron, No. 41 (Iroquois) Squadron stationed at Singapore, No. 42 (Andover) Squadron and No. 75 (Skyhawk) Squadron. Training aircraft comprise Airtrainers, Harvards, the dual-role Strikemasters and two-seat TA-4K Skyhawks.

The strength on 31 March 1977 was 4,289 regular personnel, 1,260 non-regular personnel and 2,610 ATC cadets. About one-quarter of the 105 aircraft are combat types.

INTERNATIONAL RELATIONS

Membership. New Zealand is a member of UN, the Commonwealth, OECD and the Colombo Plan.

ECONOMY

Budget. The following tables of revenue and expenditure relate to the Consolidated Revenue Account, which covers the ordinary revenue and expenditure of the general government—*i.e.*, apart from capital items, commercial and special undertakings, advances, etc. Revenue in the Account (in NZ$1m.) was as follows:

Year ended 31 March	*Customs and excise*	*Sales tax*	*Income tax*	*Other taxes*	*Trading profits and departmental receipts*	*Interest*	*Total*
1974	245·8	206·4	1,697·9	141·5	90·5	127·5	2,509·6
1975	275·3	234·7	2,136·0	114·5	115·6	145·6	3,020·7
1976	265·4	311·4	2,295·8	211·4	116·7	184·9	3,385·6
1977	299·3	353·3	2,828·5	256·7	149·4	227·9	4,164·9

Expenditure from Consolidated Revenue Account was as follows (in NZ$1m.):

Year ended Debt 31 March	*Debt services*	*Social services*[1]	*Industrial development*	*Defence*	*Total (including other)*
1974	251·9	1,476·6	141·9	140·5	2,509·8
1975	271·8	1,750·2	183·5	166·9	3,034·9
1976	322·8	2,131·1	311·5	193·5	3,684·6
1977	431·3	2,411·1	304·0	214·8	4,225·1

[1] Includes education, health and social welfare.

Taxation receipts in 1976–77 for all purposes amounted to $3,844,935,000, giving an average of $1,023 per head of mean population. Included in the total taxation is $107·4m. National Roads Fund taxation. The estimate for 1977–78 is $4,756m., the total being inclusive of an estimated $126m. of National Roads Fund taxation.

The gross public debt at 31 March 1977 was $6,289m., of which $4,462m. was held in New Zealand, $1,158m. in London and Europe, $246m. in USA and $59m. with the World Bank. The gross annual interest charge on the public debt at 31 March 1977 was $367,037,000.

National Income. Some of the more important national income aggregates for 4 years are given in the following tables (in NZ$1m.):

Year ended 31 March	*Private income*	*National income at factor cost (national income)*	*National income at market prices*	*Gross national product*
1973	6,938	6,481	6,983	7,498
1974	8,057	7,494	8,046	8,636
1975	8,934	8,184	8,777	9,452
1976	10,504	9,522	10,164	10,928

The source of private income for 4 years ended 31 March was as follows (in NZ$1m.):

	1973	*1974*	*1975*	*1976*
Salary and wage payments	3,993	4,768	5,678	6,476
Pay and allowances, Armed Forces	70	79	84	95
Social security benefits and pensions	488	594	675	846
Rental value, owner occupied houses	201	217	225	304
Other personal income	1,307	1,363	1,262	1,628
Company income	891	1,021	989	1,174
Producer Board surpluses	−3	−10	−25	−19

Currency. The monetary unit is the New Zealand dollar, divided into 100 cents. As from July 1973 it has been set in a constant average relationship with the currencies of New Zealand's main trading partners.

Banking. The Reserve Bank is the sole note-issuing authority. Six denominations of Reserve Bank notes are issued: NZ$1, 2, 5, 10, 20, 100.

The New Zealand banking system comprises a central bank—the Reserve Bank of New Zealand—5 commercial or trading banks and 18 savings banks (including the post office savings bank). The trading banks have operated savings-bank facilities from 1 Oct. 1964.

The primary functions of the Bank are to act as the central bank, to advise the Government on matters relating to monetary policy, banking and overseas exchange, and to give effect to the monetary policy of the Government.

Of the 5 trading banks 3 are primarily Australian concerns, 1 has its head office in London and the Bank of New Zealand has been state owned since 1 Nov 1945.

At the end of March 1976 the amount on deposit at trading banks was $2,902·1m., while advances amounted to $2,283·7m. The weekly average of bank debits for 1976 was $1,791·8m.

The number of accounts with the post office savings bank at 31 March 1977 was 3·15m.; amount deposited during year, $1,328m.; withdrawn, $1,282m., total amount to credit of depositors at end of year, $1,336m. At 31 March 1977, $959·2m. was on deposit in 12 Trustee Savings Banks to the credit of 1,963,000 depositors. The amount to the credit of depositors with savings accounts in the trading banks was $621·9m. at 31 March 1977.

Weights and Measures. Conversion to the metric system of weights and measures has been completed.

ENERGY AND NATURAL RESOURCES

Electricity. The general policy of the Government in regard to electric power is to supply power in bulk, leaving the reticulation and retail supply in the hands of local authorities; some of these are cities and boroughs but most are electric power boards. Hydro energy provides over 80% of the national electricity supply, the balance coming from coal, oil, natural gas and geothermal energy. The last is obtained from Wairakei in the thermal region; natural steam is used to drive the turbines.

The transmission systems of the North and South Islands are linked by a high-voltage direct-current transmission and 40 km of submarine cable in Cook Strait.

Principal statistics for 4 years ended 31 March are:

	1974	*1975*	*1976*	*1977*
Number of establishments	77	77	79	79
Generators (capacity) AC (1,000 kw.)	4,543	4,784	5,038	5,366
Units generated (1m. kwh.)	18,114	18,352	20,071	20,914
Revenue ($1,000)	302,108	328,935	377,520	542,164
Expenditure:				
Operating ($1,000)	168,294	188,649	202,520	320,215
Management, etc. ($1,000)	29,439	35,260	57,643	63,642
Capital charges ($1,000)	99,019	111,434	127,666	168,623
Capital outlay:				
During year ($1,000)	127,962	188,727	265,047	285,083
To date ($1,000)	1,724,383	1,913,187	2,178,634	2,463,995

Natural Gas. Resources discovered in the Taranaki area of the North Island in 1961 are now supplying gas for household use to North Island cities including Auckland and Wellington. The much larger Maui offshore gas field was discovered in 1969 and is at present being developed.

Minerals. New Zealand's production of minerals in 1975 included 85·4 kg of gold, 3,055 tonnes of diatomite earth, 5,246 tonnes of bentonite, 211,423 tonnes of clay for bricks, tiles, etc., 26,997 tonnes of potters' clays, 2,297,056 tonnes of iron sand, 1,502,496 tonnes of limestone for agriculture and 125,314 tonnes of limestone for industry, 1,838,299 tonnes of limestone, marl, etc., for cement, 37,857 tonnes of pumice, 60,069 tonnes of serpentine, 147,738 tonnes of silicasand. Mineral fuel production amounted to 2,412,393 tonnes of coal, 226,299 cu. metres of petroleum condensate and 524·9m. cu. metres of natural gas. Salt produced by the solar evaporation of sea water amounted to 40,000 tonnes. Mineral production for the year was valued at $84,345,000.

Agriculture. Two-thirds of the surface of New Zealand is suitable for agriculture and grazing. The total area under cultivation at 30 June 1974 was 9,917,000 hectares (including residential area and domestic orchards). There were 8,894,600 hectares of sown pasture, including areas sown with crops, and 624,900 hectares of timber plantations. The area of Crown lands (other than reserves) leased under various tenures at 31 March 1976 was 5,817,114 hectares.

The largest freehold estates are held in the South Island. The extent of occupied holdings as at 30 June 1974 (exclusive of holdings within borough boundaries) was as follows:

Size of holdings (hectares)	*Number*	*Aggregate area (hectares)*	*Size of holdings (hectares)*	*Number*	*Aggregate area (hectares)*
Under 5	3,903	11,300	400–799	4,326	2,370,700
5–19	7,138	74,900	800–999	805	712,500
20–39	6,127	180,400	1,000–1,199	465	511,400
40–79	12,950	742,500	1,200–1,999	932	1,422,200
80–99	4,486	396,800	2,000–3,999	582	1,602,900
100–149	6,994	857,400	4,000 and over	607	8,429,200
150–199	4,928	854,100			
200–299	6,147	1,500,100	Total	63,455	20,722,000
300–399	3,065	1,055,600			

The area and yield for each of the principal crops are given as follows (area and yield for threshing only, not including that grown for chaff, hay, silage, etc.):

	Wheat		*Maize*		*Barley*	
Crop years	*Area (1,000 hectares)*	*Yield (1,000 tonnes)*	*Area (1,000 hectares)*	*Yield (1,000 tonnes)*	*Area (1,000 hectares)*	*Yield (1,000 tonnes)*
1975	57·7	179·9	20·6	157·6	104·5	157·6
1976	103·7	388·2	25·9	183·9	84·7	183·8

Private air companies are carrying out such aerial work as top-dressing, spraying and crop-dusting, seed-sowing, rabbit poisoning, aerial photography and surveying, and dropping supplies to deer cullers and dropping fencing materials in remote areas. The main aerial activity was top-dressing, statistics for the year ended Dec. 1975 being: Hours flown, 141,098; fertilizer distributed, 0·9m. tonnes.

Livestock in 1977: 9,472,000 cattle (including 2·07m. milch cows), 56·4m. sheep and 536,000 pigs. Total meat produced in the year ended 30 Sept. 1976 was estimated at 1,243,000 tonnes (including 599,000 tonnes of beef and 357,000 tonnes of lamb). Total liquid milk produced in the year ended 31 May 1977 was 6,442m. litres; of this, 5,775m. were used for butter and cheese products.

Production of wool for the 12 months ended 30 June 1976, 312,000 tonnes (greasy basis).

Agricultural Statistics. Dept. of Statistics, Wellington. Annual
National Resources Survey. West Coast Region: Bay of Plenty Region: Northland Region: Nelson Region. Ministry of Works, Wellington, 1959, 1962
New Zealand Agriculture. Ministry of Agriculture and Fisheries, Wellington, 1974
Evans, B. L., *A History of Agricultural Production and Marketing.* Palmerston North, 1969
Poole, A. L., *Forestry in New Zealand: The Shaping of Policy.* London, 1969
Smallfield, P. W., *The Grasslands Revolution in New Zealand.* London, 1970

Forestry. Of the 6·2m. hectares of indigenous forest only about 1m. hectares are merchantable; they are being depleted at the rate of 5,000 hectares a year (although the rate of cutting is diminishing) and mainly for sawn timber. There are about 730,000 hectares of productive exotic forest, and this produces far more timber than the indigenous forests. Introduced conifer pines form the bulk of the large exotic forest estate and among these radiata pine is the best multi-purpose tree, reaching saw-log size in 25–30 years. Other major species are Douglas fir, Corsican pine and ponderosa pine. The table below shows the quantities of timber produced in 1,000 cu. metres for years ending 31 March:

	Softwoods		*Hardwoods*		
	Indigenous	*Exotic*	*Indigenous*	*Exotic*	*Total*
1973	340	1,402	40	5	1,787
1974	341	1,668	40	5	2,054
1975	328	1,716	39	3	2,086
1976	326	1,618	48	11	2,003

Forest industries consist of 420 saw-mills, 9 plywood and veneer plants, 3 particle board mills, 6 pulp and paper mills and 2 fibreboard mills.

The basic products of the pulp and paper mills are mechanical and chemical pulp which are converted into newsprint, kraft and other papers, paperboard and fibreboard. Production of woodpulp for the calendar year 1976 amounted to 1,038,000 tonnes and of paper (including newsprint paper and paperboard) to 608,000 tonnes.

Fisheries. At the peak of the 1976 season about 400 foreign vessels were within New Zealand's 200 miles fisheries management zone. The annual catch of all species was about 300,000 tonnes, mainly tuna and squid; New Zealand catch, about 60,000 tonnes.

Exports of fisheries products for the year ended 30 June 1977 had a value of $48·4m., of which the value of rock lobster exports of 1,785 tonnes was $21·5m. Live eel exports of 565 tonnes were worth $700,000 and paua (abalone) exports of 459 tonnes, $2·8m.

INDUSTRY AND TRADE

Industry. Major industrial developments in recent years have included the establishment of an oil refinery, an iron and steel industry using New Zealand iron sands and an aluminium smelter using hydro-electric power.

Statistics of manufacturing industries for 3 years:

Production year	*Persons engaged*	*Salaries and wages paid (NZ$1,000)*	*Cost of materials (NZ$1,000)*	*Value of production (NZ$1,000)*	*Net output (net value added) (NZ$1,000)*
1972–73	235,648	875,420	2,787,201	4,611,256	1,301,701
1973–74	244,528	1,042,214	3,112,806	5,250,878	1,502,387
1974–75	300,945	1,391,000	4,665,000	6,499,000	2,210,000

The following is a statement of the value of the products (including repairs) of the principal industries for the year 1973–74 (in NZ$1,000):

Industry group	*Value of production*	*Industry group*	*Value of production*
Food	1,441,483	Chemicals and chemical products	253,019
Beverages	100,664	Petroleum and coal products	110,232
Tobacco manufactures	34,094	Non-metallic mineral products, n.e.i.	158,653
Textiles	408,874	Basic metal manufactures	192,305
Footwear, other wearing apparel, and made-up textile goods	250,055	Metal products (except machinery and transport equipment)	367,989
Wood and cork products (except furniture)	287,172	Machinery (except electrical)	272,189
Furniture and fixtures	90,612	Electrical machinery and appliances	175,283
Paper and paper products	276,074	Transport equipment	358,597
Printing, publishing, etc.	178,746	Miscellaneous	186,184
Leather and leather products (except footwear and apparel)	45,084		
Rubber products	63,571	Total	5,250,878

Industrial Production. Dept. of Statistics, Wellington. Annual

Labour. In Dec. 1976 there were 294 industrial unions of workers with a total of 464,453 members.

The industrial distribution of the labour force as estimated in Oct. 1976 was: Primary industries, 148,500; manufacturing, 289,200; construction, 90,600; commerce, 190,100; transport and communication, 110,700; services, 269,100; armed forces, 11,200; unemployed, 4,800; total labour force, 1,206,800.

By the Accident Compensation Act 1972 immediate compensation without proof of fault is provided for every injured person and wherever the accident occurred. Compensation is paid both for permanent physical disability and also—in the case of earners—for income losses on an income related basis. Regular adjustment in the level of payment is provided for in accordance with variations in the value of money. Non-earners such as tourists, housewives, children, students, and retired people do not normally qualify for earnings related compensation but are eligible for all other benefits. These are not taxable. Housewives—including visiting women from overseas—who are non-earners are eligible for the benefits available to non-earners and home help can be paid for or the husband compensated for loss of earnings while he is looking after the home until the injured wife can resume her duties.

After the first week's incapacity and for the ensuing 4 weeks the earner can be paid 80% of his average earnings for the 28 days preceding the accident; after that the 80% is related to average earnings over the 12 preceding months. In addition—for earners—lump sums are payable for impairment, pain and disfigurement and for funeral expenses and weekly sums and lump payments to their widows and dependent children.

All employees are covered by the Accident Compensation Act 1972.

Commerce. Trade (excluding specie and bullion) in NZ$1,000 for 12 months ended 30 June:

	Total merchandise imported (c.d.v.)[2]	*Exports of domestic produce*	*Re-exports*	*Total merchandise exported (f.o.b.)*
1973–74	1,842,263	1,744,741	42,822	1,787,563
1974–75	2,470,434	1,548,715	63,892	1,612,607
1975–76	2,693,728	2,246,828	124,777	2,371,605
1976–77[1]	3,168,288	3,057,649	89,847	3,147,497

[1] Provisional figures. [2] Current domestic value in country of export.

The principal imports for the 12 months ended 30 June 1977:

Commodity	*Value (NZ$1,000) (c.d.v.)*
Cereals and cereal preparations	3,791
Fruit and vegetables	35,546
Sugar and sugar preparations	45,676
Coffee, tea, cocoa, spices, etc.	41,651
Beverages	15,832
Tobacco and manufactures	12,801
Crude rubber	22,068
Textile fibres	14,518
Crude fertilizers and minerals other than coal	56,116
Petroleum and petroleum products	468,430
Chemical elements and compounds	146,020
Dyeing, tanning, etc. materials	21,513
Medicinal and pharmaceutical products	72,477
Fertilizers, manufactured	24,736
Plastic materials, etc.	105,454
Miscellaneous chemical materials and products	35,134
Rubber manufactures (n.e.s.)	24,945
Paper and paperboard manufactures	36,655
Textile yarn and fabrics, etc.	226,702
Non-metallic mineral manufactures (n.e.s.)	37,197
Iron and steel	228,472
Nonferrous metals	69,975
Manufactures of metals	86,350
Machinery, other than electric	456,560
Electric machinery	201,788
Transport equipment	357,718
Scientific instruments, watches, etc.	83,772
Miscellaneous manufactured articles (n.e.s.)	102,815
Commodities not classified (mainly arms of war)	19,654

The principal exports of New Zealand produce for the 12 months ended 30 June 1977 were:

Commodity	*Quantity (in tonnes)*	*Value (NZ$1,000)*	*Commodity*	*Quantity (in tonnes)*	*Value (NZ$1,000)*
Meat			Hides and skins	...	127,854
Beef	249,809	294,328	Wood and cork	...	31,221
Veal	8,544	14,562	Pulp and waste paper	427,607	70,010
Lamb	294,329	316,251	Wool	253,388	645,308
Mutton	100,736	64,018	Sausage casings	6,487,642h.	25,700
Edible offals	49,155	41,927	Tallow	...	32,921
Dairy products			Casein	95,314	28,832
Milk and cream	...	106,399	Newsprint	61,623	50,424
Butter	212,264	253,118	Other machine paper	172,769	25,509
Cheese	77,887	83,385	Textile yarn, etc.	76,829	56,260
Fish	...	48,379	Nonferrous metals	...	117,013
Cereals	...	20,088	Metal manufactures	...	25,620
Apples	56,954	15,512	Machinery, other than electric	...	36,689
Animal feeding stuff	276,833	50,896	Electric machinery, etc	...	34,970

The following table shows the trade with different countries (in NZ$1,000):

Countries	*Imports c.d.v. from*		*Exports and re-exports f.o.b. to*		
	1976[1]	*1977*[1]	*1975*[1]	*1976*[1]	*1977*[1]
Australia	514,464	653,583	188,288	288,360	383,502
Bahrain	34,112	33,156	1,199	1,306	3,441
Belgium and Luxembourg	16,797	22,992	16,341	25,371	39,256
Canada	53,454	80,607	45,081	60,040	65,884
China	10,808	17,228	10,183	25,399	25,075
Fiji	13,465	17,204	23,393	30,846	39,954
France and Monaco	25,468	32,089	43,398	65,376	78,191
Germany (Fed. Rep. of)	96,148	131,330	41,900	61,578	96,069
Greece	242	812	29,953	42,519	42,299
Hong Kong	40,766	56,368	17,219	24,222	44,479
India	22,447	19,383	796	927	2,218
Iran	99,404	138,715	16,911	33,664	43,157
Italy and San Marino	33,372	35,842	20,969	38,028	61,455
Japan	401,897	472,978	186,756	323,377	403,691
Kuwait	60,027	39,144	2,181	2,547	3,734
Malaysia	19,121	18,393	20,973	26,130	31,486
Netherlands and Antilles	32,919	64,084	36,090	55,101	84,126
Philippines	5,969	3,180	29,247	34,749	38,264
Saudi Arabia	33,771	76,326	1,689	2,203	4,231
Singapore	85,211	54,194	20,621	51,980	61,287
Sweden	49,764	24,818	4,401	3,666	7,999
UK	457,345	530,565	344,078	449,415	642,012
USSR	1,414	5,084	45,410	62,130	144,073
USA	394,779	427,215	189,817	277,029	353,666

[1] Provisional.

The total trade between UK and New Zealand was as follows (British Department of Trade returns, in £1,000 sterling):

	1974	*1975*	*1976*	*1977*
Imports to UK	247,603	267,522	320,824	383,163
Exports and re-exports from UK	255,596	252,828	251,199	286,891

Tourism. The country has a growing tourist industry. In the year ended 31 March 1977, 380,222 travellers visited New Zealand (including 306,378 tourists), compared with 384,586 (including 312,824 tourists) in 1975–76.

COMMUNICATIONS

Roads. Total length of formed roads and streets in New Zealand at 31 March 1975 was 95,026 km. There were 13,383 bridges of over 3 metres in length with a total length of 313,296 metres at 31 March 1975. The network of state highways comprised, at 31 March 1975, 11,225 km, including the principal arterial traffic routes.

Total expenditure on roads, streets and bridges by the central government and local authorities combined for the financial year 1975–76 amounted to $178,833,000.

In the main, roads are financed from the National Roads Fund which is administered by the National Roads Board. This fund which is derived largely from petrol tax is used for the maintenance and improvement of existing roads. The board's income is currently of the order of $120m. per annum, and is apportioned according to fixed percentages, with 50% allocated to state highways, 23% to counties and 16% to municipalities. These sector percentages have been varied twice in the last 10 years in the light of changing needs.

At 31 March 1977 motor vehicles licensed numbered 2,023,621, of which 1,213,460 were cars, 4,518 omnibuses and contract vehicles, 232,202 goods service vehicles. Included in the remaining number were 104,359 motor cycles, 2,879 power cycles and 111,979 farm tractors, road graders, etc. Licensed road goods services for the year ended 31 March 1975 recorded total vehicle journeys of 700m. km. Total revenue amounted to $362m. The road passenger services journeys amounted to 145·3m. km.

Railways. On 31 March 1977 there were 4,658 km of 3 ft 6 in. gauge railway open for traffic. Operating earnings from government railways, 1976–77, $202,419,337; operating expenses, $214,795,654. In 1976–77 the tonnage of goods (including livestock) carried was 13,576,749 tonnes, and passengers numbered 18,478,134. In addition, the railways road motor services carried 21m. passengers. Four rail/road ferries maintain a regular service between the North and South Islands.

The total revenue (including road motor and other subsidiary services) amounted to $248,069,785, and total expenditure $260,072,954 in 1976–77.

Aviation. Domestic scheduled passenger services are mainly operated by the New Zealand National Airways Corporation. International services are operated to and from New Zealand by a state-owned company, Air New Zealand Ltd, and by a number of overseas companies. Non-scheduled services are run by the main companies and also by a number of small operators and aero clubs.

Domestic scheduled services during the 12 months ended Dec. 1975: Passengers carried, 2,312,000; mail, 1,617,000 tonne-km; freight, 24,539,000 tonne-km. International services: Passengers carried 1,179,000; mail, 2,270 tonnes; freight, 30,877 tonnes.

Shipping. Container ships operate from Auckland and Wellington to the UK and North America. The government-owned New Zealand Shipping Corporation has begun to increase its activity into New Zealand–UK and Pacific trades.

Entrances and clearances of vessels from overseas:

	Entrances		*Clearances*	
	No.	*Tons*	*No.*	*Tons*
1974	3,831	20,536,000	3,817	20,397,000
1975	3,692	20,098,000	3,688	19,976,000
1976	3,762	20,886,000	3,754	20,780,000

Post and Broadcasting. Receipts of the Post Office for year ended 31 March 1977 were $367·5m.; total expenditure was $346·3m. Personnel numbered 38,230.

The telegraph and telephone systems are operated by the Post Office. At 31 March 1977 there were 1,078,034 telephone subscribers and 1,674,132 telephones. The telecommunications receipts for the year 1975–76 were $279,387,000.

An earth satellite station has been built north of Auckland to link with the Pacific satellite Intelsat III to augment the Compac and Seacon telecommunications systems which link New Zealand with overseas countries.

There are 2 TV channels both operated by the state-owned New Zealand Broadcasting Corporation, which also operates most of the broadcasting stations. Over 85% of New Zealand households have TV sets. There are 52 medium-wave broadcasting stations and 2 short-wave transmitters. Some commercial material is broadcast by both sound and TV services. Number of TV receiving licences at 31 March 1977 was 815,000.

Cinemas. There were in 1975, 203 cinemas with a seating capacity of 119,000.

Newspapers. There were (1975), 35 daily newspapers (8 morning and 27 evening) with a combined circulation of 972,000. Eight of these newspapers (2 each in Auckland, Wellington, Christchurch and Dunedin) had a circulation of 718,000.

JUSTICE, RELIGION, EDUCATION AND WELFARE

Justice. The judiciary consists of the Chief Justice, 3 judges of the Court of Appeal and 20 Supreme Court judges, 1 judge of the Industrial Court and 1 judge each for the Courts of Compensation and Land Valuation. At the end of March 1977 the gaols and Borstal institutions contained 2,893 prisoners, 2,786 males and 107 females. In 1976, 5,504 persons were received into all penal institutions. The death penalty for murder was replaced by life imprisonment in 1961.

The Criminal Injuries Act, 1963, which came into force on 1 Jan. 1964, provided for compensation of persons injured by certain criminal acts and the dependants of persons killed by such acts. Since 1970 legal aid in civil proceedings (except divorce) has been available for persons of small means. For the year ended 31 March 1977 expenditure amounted to $1,360,100 and 11,035 applications for aid were granted.

Police. The police in New Zealand are a national body maintained wholly by the central government. The total strength at 31 March 1977 was 4,466, the proportion of police to population being 1 to 703. The total cost of police services for the year 1976–77 was NZ$54·7m., equivalent to $17 per head of population. In New Zealand the police do not control traffic.

Ombudsmen. The office of Ombudsman was created in 1962. From 1975 additional Ombudsmen have been authorized. There are currently three. Ombudsmen's functions are to investigate complaints from members of the public relating to administrative decisions of government departments, local authorities and statutory organizations. The Chief Ombudsman is also the Privacy Commissioner for the Government Computer Centre.

From 1 Oct. 1962 to 31 March 1977, 14,184 complaints were received, 1,569 of which were held to be justified and were acted upon by the department or organization concerned. No complaint of actual malpractice has been found justified.

Religion. No direct state aid is given to any form of religion. For the Church of England the country is divided into 7 dioceses, with a separate bishopric (Aotearoa) for the Maoris. The Presbyterian Church is divided into 23 presbyteries and the Maori Synod. The Moderator is elected annually. The Methodist Church is divided into 10 districts; the President is elected annually. The Roman Catholic Church is divided into 4 dioceses, with the Archbishop of Wellington as Metropolitan Archbishop.

Religious denomination	*Number of clergy (Feb. 1975)*	*Number of adherents 1966 census*	*1971 census*
Church of England	736	901,701	895,839
Presbyterian	664	582,976	583,701
Roman Catholic (including 'Catholic' undefined)	883	425,280	449,974
Methodist	336	186,260	182,727
Baptist	223	46,748	47,350
Brethren	135	23,139	25,768
Ratana	133	27,570	30,156
Protestant (undefined)	—	46,090	37,475
Salvation Army	244	17,737	19,371
Church of Christ	63	10,301	8,930
Latter-Day Saints (Mormon)	118	25,564	29,785
Congregationalist	11	12,101	7,704
Seventh-Day Adventist	42	9,551	10,477
Ringatu	66	5,605	5,635
Christian (undefined)	—	21,548	33,187
Christian Scientist	—	1,161	816
Jehovah's Witnesses	76	7,455	10,318
Hebrew	6	4,104	3,803
Lutheran	16	5,730	5,930
Other bodies[1]	418	47,893	65,648
Unspecified	—	19,300	103,533
Object to state	—	216,325	247,019
No religion (so returned)	—	32,780	57,485
Total	4,170	2,676,919	2,862,631

[1] Including the Society of Friends with 887 members in 1966 and 966 in 1971.

Education. New Zealand has 6 universities, the University of Auckland, University of Waikato (at Hamilton), Victoria University of Wellington, Massey University (at Palmerston North), the University of Canterbury (at Christchurch) and the University of Otago (at Dunedin). There is, in addition, Lincoln College near Christchurch, a university college of agriculture, which is a constituent college of the University of Canterbury. The number of students in 1976 was 45,032. There were 9 teachers' training colleges with 7,521 students in 1976.

At 1 July 1976 there were 248 state secondary schools with 11,014 full-time teachers and 193,894 pupils. There were also 39 district high schools with 2,856 scholars in the secondary division. At 1 July 1976, 97,648 part-time pupils attended technical classes, and 21,712 received part-time instruction from the technical correspondence institute. At 1 July 1976, 762 pupils received tuition from the secondary department of the correspondence school. There were 108 registered private secondary schools with 1,353 teachers and 32,379 pupils.

At 1 July 1976, there were 2,507 state primary schools (including intermediate schools and departments), with 475,113 pupils; the number of teachers was 19,500. A correspondence school for children in remote areas and those otherwise unable to attend school had 1,021 primary pupils. There were 327 registered private primary schools with 1,839 teachers and 49,899 pupils.

Education is compulsory between the ages of 6 and 15. Children aged 3 and 4 years may enrol at the 424 free kindergartens maintained by Free Kindergarten Associations, which receive government assistance. There are also 697 play centres which also receive government subsidy. In July 1976 there were 34,075 and 24,065 children on the rolls respectively.

Total expenditure out of government funds in 1976–77 upon education was NZ$699·4m.

The universities and the affiliated agricultural colleges are autonomous bodies. Most secondary schools are controlled by their own boards. Virtually all state primary schools are controlled by the district education board: there are 10 education districts. The Department of Education exercises certain defined functions in connexion with the general supervision of the education provided in state primary and secondary schools and disburses the government grants payable to controlling authorities for the running of those schools. Education in state schools is free for children under 19 years of age. Private schools are regularly visited by state school inspectors.

Report of the Minister of Education ('E.1. Report'). Annually. Wellington, Government Printer
NZ Committee on Secondary Education. *Towards Partnership.* Dept. of Education, 1976
Bates, R. J. (ed.), *Prospects in New Zealand Education.* Auckland, 1970
Ewing, J. L. *Compulsory Education in New Zealand.* Paris, UNESCO, 1969
Watson, J. E., *Intermediate Schooling in New Zealand.* Wellington, 1964

Social Welfare. New Zealand's record for progressive legislation reaches back to 1898, when it was second only to Denmark in introducing non-contributory old-age pensions.

The present system came into operation from 1 April 1972. It provides for retirement, unemployment, widowhood, invalidity and sickness, as well as hospital and other medical care. Since 1 April 1969 the scheme has been financed from general taxation. Previously there was a special social security tax on virtually all income of individuals and companies in excess of $4 a week which met approximately three-quarters of the cost of the scheme, the balance being met from general taxation.

At 31 March 1977 the current weekly rates of widows', invalids', sickness, domestic purposes, unemployment and miners' benefits were $64 for a married couple and $38.40 for an unmarried person.

There are additional payments for dependent children.

All benefits except superannuation and family allowances are subject to an income test.

Family Benefit. A family benefit of $3 a week is payable for each dependent child.

Unemployment Benefit. The payment is subject to the condition that the applicant is capable and willing to undertake suitable employment.

Sickness Benefit. Payment is subject to medical evidence of incapacity of a person who has suffered a loss of weekly earnings as a result.

Other benefits include emergency benefits and additional benefits for those in need but who either do not qualify for one of the standard benefits or who have special needs or commitments for which a benefit at the standard rate is insufficient.

Medical, Hospital and Related Benefits. Medical, hospital and other related benefits are also provided under the Social Welfare scheme. These consist mainly of the payment of certain fees for medical attention by private practitioners, free treatment in public and mental hospitals, certain fees for treatment in private hospitals, maternity benefits (including ante-natal and post-natal treatment and services of doctors and nurses at confinements), pharmaceutical benefits (medicines, drugs, etc., prescribed by medical practitioners), etc. There are also benefits in connexion with dental services up to the age of 16, X-ray diagnosis, massage, home-nursing, artificial aids, etc.

Pensions. Provision is made for the payment of pensions and allowances to members or dependants of disabled, deceased or missing members, of the New Zealand Forces who served in the South African War, the two World Wars, the Korean War and the Vietnam War, to members of the New Zealand Mercantile Marine during the Second World War, or in connexion with any emergency whether arising out of the obligations undertaken by New Zealand in the Charter of the United Nations or otherwise. Principal rates are: War pensions are payable to widows at a rate of $16.30 a week, together with a mother's allowance of $19.12 a week, increased by $3 a week for the second child and $1.25 for each additional child, in addition to the normal child allowances of $3 per week for each child. The rate for total disablement is $22.10. These rates may be increased by an amount not exceeding $13.30 per week if the pensioner is suffering from total blindness, two or more serious disabilities or one extremely severe disability.

An 'economic pension' is defined as a supplementary pension granted on economic grounds and is additional to any pension payable as of right in respect of death or disablement. The maximum weekly rates are $32 to a married person (if unmarried, $38.40); to the widow or dependent widowed mother of a member, $38.40.

War veterans' allowances are $32 weekly plus an equal amount to a wife, increased by $1.50 a week each at age 65, subject to income qualifications.

Domestic Purposes Benefit. A domestic purposes benefit is payable to unsupported male and female solo parents including divorced, separated and unmarried persons, prisoners' spouses and also to those who are required to give full-time care to a person (other than their spouse) who would otherwise have to be admitted to hospital.

Death Benefit. A death benefit of $1,000 is payable to a widow or widower if totally dependent on the deceased plus $500 for each dependent child but not exceeding $1,500.

Social Welfare Benefits and War Pensions:

Benefits	*Number in force at 31 March 1977*	*Total payments 1976–77 (NZ$1,000)*
SOCIAL WELFARE:		
Monetary—		
Superannuation	371,697	274,411
Age	...	326,879
Widows	16,211	39,045
Orphans	420	516
Family	464,156	156,614
Invalids	10,707	23,130
Miners	37	96
Unemployment	3,651	13,428
Sickness	8,367	24,414
Supplementary Assistance	...	...
Family (capitalization)	...	...
Domestic Purposes	28,401	80,774
Total	903,647	939,309

Benefits	Number in force at 31 March 1977	Total payments 1976/77 (NZ$1,000)
Health, etc—		
Medical		33,697
Hospital		17,398
Maternity		5,022
Pharmaceutical		84,851
Supplementary		20,368
Total		161,336
WAR PENSION, ETC.:		
First World War	4,847	8,605
Second World War	22,169	35,922
South African War	...	...
Korean War	1	4
Vietnam War	247	154
War veterans' allowances	186	90
Mercantile Marine	6,642	21,140
K Force	19	28
Other	7,687	619
Total	41,798	66,562

Reciprocity with Other Countries. There are reciprocal arrangements between New Zealand and Australia in respect of age, invalids', widows', family, unemployment and sickness benefits, and between New Zealand and the UK in respect of family, age, superannuation, widows', orphans', invalids', sickness and unemployment benefits.

Superannuation. Following the change of Government in Dec. 1975 the earnings-related superannuation scheme described in THE STATESMAN'S YEAR-BOOK, 1977–78, was abolished. Under the new system (operative from Feb. 1977) superannuation is payable to all New Zealanders on reaching the age of 60. It is taxable but not subject to an income test. The rates are based on the national average wage, of which initially married couples received 70·1% and single persons 60% of the married rate.

Health. In 1975 there were 3,867 doctors in general and specialist practice. At 31 March 1976 there were 31,735 hospital beds, of which 3,051 were for maternity cases.

MINOR ISLANDS

The minor islands (total area, 320 sq. miles, 775 sq. km) included within the geographical boundaries of New Zealand are the following: Kermadec Islands, Three Kings Islands, Auckland Islands, Campbell Island, Antipodes Islands, Bounty Islands, Snares Islands, Solander Island. With the exception of Raoul Island in the Kermadec Group (population, 9) and Campbell Island (population, 11) none of these islands is inhabited.

The **Kermadec Islands**, which were annexed to New Zealand in 1887, have no separate administration and all New Zealand laws apply to them. Situation, 29° 10′ to 131° 30′ S. lat., 177° 45′ to 179° W. long., 600 miles N.N.E. of New Zealand. Area, 13 sq. miles (33·5 sq. km). The largest of the group is Raoul or Sunday Island, 20 miles in circuit, while Macaulay Island is 3 miles in circuit.

A meteorological station and an aeradio station have been established on Raoul Island, the official staff of 9 being the only inhabitants.

TERRITORIES OVERSEAS

Territories Overseas coming within the jurisdiction of New Zealand consist of Tokelau and the Ross Dependency.

Tokelau. Situated some 480 km to the north of Western Samoa between 8° and 10° S. lat., and between 171° and 173° W. long., are the 3 atoll islands of Atafu, Nukunonu and Fakaofo of the Tokelau (Union) group. Formerly part of the Gilbert and Ellice Islands Colony, the group was transferred to the jurisdiction of New Zealand on 11 Feb. 1926. By legislation enacted in 1948, the Tokelau Islands were declared part of New Zealand as from 1 Jan. 1949. The area of the group is 1,011 hectares; the population at 25 Oct. 1976 was 1,575.

By the Tokelau Islands Act 1948 the Tokelau Group was included within the territorial boundaries of New Zealand; legislative powers are now invested in the Governor-General in Council. The inhabitants are British subjects and New Zealand citizens. In Dec. 1976 the territory was officially renamed 'Tokelau', the name by which it has customarily been known to its inhabitants.

From 8 Nov. 1974 the office of Administrator was invested in the Secretary of Foreign Affairs. Certain powers are delegated to the district officer in Apia, Western Samoa.

Because of the very restricted economic and social future in the atolls, the islanders agreed to a proposal put to them by the Minister of Island Territories in 1965 that over a period of years most of the population be resettled in New Zealand. Up to March 1975, 528 migrants entered New Zealand as permanent residents under Government sponsorship. At the request of the people the scheme has now been suspended.

New Zealand Government aid to Tokelau totalled $551,000 for 1976–77.

Ross Dependency. By Imperial Order in Council, dated 30 July 1923, the territories between 160° E. long. and 150° W. long. and south of 60° S. lat. were brought within the jurisdiction of the New Zealand Government. The region was named the Ross Dependency. From time to time laws for the Dependency have been made by regulations promulgated by the Governor-General of New Zealand.

The mainland area is estimated at 400,000–450,000 sq km and is completely ice-covered. In Jan. 1957 a New Zealand expedition under Sir Edmund Hillary established a base in the Dependency. In Jan. 1958 Sir Edmund Hillary and 4 other New Zealanders reached the South Pole.

The main base—Scott Base—at Pram Point, Ross Island—is manned throughout the year, about 12 people being present during winter. Vanda Station in the dry ice-free Wright Valley is manned every summer.

Quartermain, L. B., *New Zealand and the Antarctic.* Wellington, 1971

SELF-GOVERNING TERRITORY OVERSEAS

THE COOK ISLANDS

HISTORY. The Cook Islands, which lie betwen 8° and 23° S. lat., and 156° and 167° W. long., were proclaimed a British protectorate in 1888, and on 11 June 1901 were annexed and proclaimed part of New Zealand. The islands within the territory fall roughly into two groups—the scattered islands towards the north (Northern group) and the islands towards the south known as the Lower group.

AREA AND POPULATION. The names of the islands with their populations as at the Census of 1 Dec. 1976 were as follows:

Lower Group—	*Population*	*Northern Group—*	*Population*
Rarotonga	9,811	Nassau	113
Mangaia	1,530	Palmerston (Avarau)	53
Atiu	1,312	Penrhyn (Tongareva)	531

Lower Group (contd.)—	*Population*	*Northern Group* (contd.)—	*Population*
Aitutaki	2,414	Manihiki (Humphrey)	263
Mauke (Parry Is.)	710	Rakahanga (Reirson)	283
Mitiaro	305	Pukapuka (Danger)	786
Manuae and Te au-o-tu	—	Suwarrow (Anchorage)	1
		Total	18,112

Total area of the Cook Islands, excluding Niue, is about 93 sq. miles (241 sq. km). Rarotonga is 20 miles in circumference; Atiu, 20 miles; Aitutaki, 14·5 miles.

In 1975, 516 live births and 120 deaths were registered.

CONSTITUTION AND GOVERNMENT. The Cook Islands Constitution Act 1964, which provides for the establishment of internal self-government in the Cook Islands, came into force on 4 Aug. 1965.

The Act establishes the Cook Islands as fully self-governing but linked to New Zealand by a common Head of State, the Queen, and a common citizenship, that of New Zealand. It provides for a ministerial system of government with a Cabinet consisting of a Premier and 6 other Ministers. The Resident Commissioner became the High Commissioner of the Cook Islands, who exercises the dual functions of representative of the Queen and of the New Zealand Government. New Zealand continues to be responsible for the external affairs and defence of the Cook Islands, subject to consultation between the New Zealand Prime Minister and the Premier. The changed status of the Islands does not affect the consideration of subsidies or the right of free entry into New Zealand for exports from the group.

ECONOMY AND TRADE

Budget. Revenue is derived chiefly from customs duties which follow the New Zealand customs tariff, income tax and stamp sales. Tax receipts (not including customs duties), in 1971 included income tax, $566,238; customs duties, $403,530; sales tax, $103,700, and stamp sales, $70,970.

Grants from New Zealand, mainly for medical, educational and general administrative purposes totalled $7,002,000 in 1975–76.

Commerce. Exports, mainly to New Zealand, were valued at $2·39m. in 1975. Main items of export were fruit juice, citrus fruit, copra and clothing. Imports in 1973 totalled $4,947,000. The main items were foodstuffs, drapery and piece-goods, motor vehicles, petrol and oil.

COMMUNICATIONS

Aviation. New Zealand has financed the construction of an international airport at Rarotonga which became operational for jet services in Sept. 1973.

Shipping. A monthly passenger-cargo shipping service is provided between New Zealand and Rarotonga.

Telecommunications. Wireless stations are maintained at all the permanently inhabited islands.

EDUCATION AND HEALTH

Education. Twenty-four primary schools are established in the various islands. There are also 6 Roman Catholic missionary schools and a Seventh Day Adventist mission school. Post-primary education is provided for by 4 government and 2 mission schools on Rarotonga. The instruction given in government schools is similar to that of the New Zealand state schools, but with a special syllabus suited to the requirements of the people. Regular instruction is given in the Maori language in all classes, while during the first 2 years all instruction is in the vernacular, English being taught only as a subject. Numbers of pupils on the rolls (31 March 1976): 6,572. At the same date 88 students were receiving education or vocational training in New Zealand.

Health. All Cook Islanders receive free medical and surgical treatment in their villages, the hospital and the tuberculosis sanatorium. Cook Island Maori patients in the hospital and the sanatorium and all schoolchildren receive free dental treatment.

NIUE ISLAND

History. Niue Island achieved internal self-government in Oct. 1974.

Area and Population. Distance from Auckland, New Zealand, 1,343 miles; from Rarotonga, 580 miles. Area, 100 sq. miles; circumference, 40 miles; height above sea-level, 220 ft. Population at 31 Dec. 1976 was 3,954. During 1973 live births registered numbered 105, deaths 26. Migration to New Zealand is the main factor in population change.

Government. There is an Island Assembly, and legislative measures apply as in the case of the Cook Islands.

Budget. Financial aid from New Zealand, 1975–76, totalled $2·6m.

Agriculture. The most important products of the island are copra, passion fruit, honey and limes.

Trade. Exports, 1973, $137,000; imports, $858,000.

Communications. There is a wireless station at Alofi, the port of the island. A weekly commercial air service links Niue with Tonga and Western Samoa.

Education. There were 10 government schools with 1,503 pupils in 1973.

Quarterly Statistical Bulletin. Statistics Office, Rarotonga

Buck, P. H., *Vikings of the Sunrise.* New York, 1938.—*The Coming of the Maori.* Wellington, 1950

Ross, A. (ed.), *New Zealand's Record in the Pacific Islands in the Twentieth Century.* Auckland, 1969

DIPLOMATIC REPRESENTATIVES

OF NEW ZEALAND IN GREAT BRITAIN (New Zealand House, Haymarket, London, SW1Y 4TQ)

High Commissioner: Sir Douglas J. Carter, KCMG.

OF GREAT BRITAIN IN NEW ZEALAND (Reserve Bank of New Zealand Bldg, 2 The Terrace, Wellington,1)

High Commissioner: H. Smedley, CMG, MBE.

OF NEW ZEALAND IN THE USA (19 Observatory Cir., NW, Washington, D.C., 20008)

Ambassador: G. D. L. White, MVO.

OF THE USA IN NEW ZEALAND (IBM Centre, 29 Fitzherbert Terrace, Wellington)

Ambassador: Armistead I. Selden.

OF NEW ZEALAND TO THE UNITED NATIONS

Ambassador: M. J. C. Templeton.

Books of Reference

Statistical Information: The central statistical office for New Zealand is the Department of Statistics (Wellington, 1).

The beginning of a statistical service may be seen in the early 'Blue books' prepared annually from 1840 onwards under the direction of the Colonial Secretary, and designed primarily for the information of the Colonial Office in England. A permanent statistical authority was created in 1858. The Department of Statistics functions under the Statistics Act 1975 and reports to

Parliament through the Minister of Statistics. A comprehensive statistical service has been developed to meet national requirements, and close control is maintained with the United Nations Statistical Office and other international statistical organizations; through the Conference of Asian Statisticians assistance is being given with the development of statistics in the region.

The oldest publications consist of (*a*) census results from 1858 onwards and (*b*) annual volumes of statistics (first published 1858 but covering years back to 1853). Main current publications:

New Zealand Official Yearbook. Annual, from 1893
Catalogue of New Zealand Statistics. 1972
Statistical Reports of New Zealand. Annual
Monthly Abstract of Statistics. From 1914
Pocket Digest of Statistics. Annual, 1927–31, 1938 ff.

Parliamentary Reports of Government Departments. Annual
Pacific Islands Yearbook. Sydney, 1977
Dictionary of New Zealand Biography. 2 vols. Wellington, 1940
Encyclopaedia of New Zealand. 3 vols. Wellington, 1966
National Bibliography. Wellington, 1968
New Zealand Financial System. Wellington, 1966
Oxford New Zealand Encyclopaedia. London, 1965
Best, Elsdon, *The Maori As He Was*. Wellington, 1974
Bright, T. N., *Banking Law and Practice in New Zealand*. 2nd ed. Wellington, 1969
Firth, R., *Economics of the New Zealand Maori*. Wellington, Government Printer, 1959
Hall, D. O. W., *Portrait of New Zealand*. 3rd ed. Wellington, 1961
Holcroft, M. H., *New Zealand*. Wellington, 1968
Holmes, F. W., *Money, Finance and the Economy*. Auckland, 1972
Institute of Public Administration. *Administration in New Zealand's Multi-racial Society*. Wellington, 1968
Kennaway, R., *New Zealand Foreign Policy, 1951–71*. Wellington and London, 1973
Metge, J., *The Maoris of New Zealand*. London, 1976
Morrell, W. P., and Hall, D. O. W., *A History of New Zealand Life*. Christchurch and London, 1957
Oliver, W. H., *The Story of New Zealand*. London, 1963
Polaschek, R. J. (ed.), *Local Government in New Zealand*. Wellington, 1956.—*Government Administration in New Zealand*. Wellington, 1958
Robson, J. L. (ed.), *New Zealand: the Development of its Laws and Constitution*. 2nd ed. London, 1967
Rowe, J. W. and M. A., *New Zealand*. London, 1967
Shadbolt, M. F. R., *The Shell Guide to New Zealand*. Christchurch, 1976
Sinclair, K., *A History of New Zealand*. Penguin, 1969
Traue, J. E., *Who's Who in New Zealand*. 11th ed. Wellington, 1977
Wards, I., *A Descriptive Atlas of New Zealand*. Wellington, Government Printer, 1976
Watters, R. F. (ed.), *Land and Society in New Zealand*. Wellington, 1965
Wise's New Zealand Guide. 6th ed. Dunedin, 1974

NICARAGUA

República de Nicaragua

Capital: Managua
Population: 2·25m. (1976)
GNP per capita: US$750 (1976)

HISTORY. Active colonization of the Pacific coast was undertaken by Spaniards from Panama, beginning in 1523. After links with other Central American territories, and Mexico, Nicaragua became completely independent in 1838, but subject to a prolonged feud between the 'Liberals' of León and the 'Conservatives' of Granada. Mosquitia remained an autonomous kingdom on the Atlantic coast, under British protection until 1860.

On 5 Aug. 1914 the Bryan–Chamarro treaty between Nicaragua and the US was signed, under which the US in return for $3m. acquired a permanent option for a canal route through Nicaragua and a 99-year option for a naval base in the Bay of Fonseca on the Pacific coast and Corn Island on the Atlantic coast. It was ratified by Nicaragua on 7 April 1916 and by the US on 22 June 1916. US Marines finally left in 1933.

The Bryan–Chamarro treaty was abrogated on 14 July 1970.

AREA AND POPULATION. Area estimated at 148,000 sq. km (57,143 sq. miles) or 139,000 sq. km (54,296 sq. miles) if the lakes are excluded. The coastline runs 336 miles on the Atlantic and 219 miles on the Pacific. Population at the census of April 1971 was 1,911,543 (922,433 males, 989,110 females). Estimate (1976) 2,253,095.

Nicaragua is the largest in area and most thinly populated of the Central American republics. Crude birth rate, 1975, 42·59 per 1,000 population; crude death rate, 6·72; infantile mortality rate (1974), 41·19 per 1,000 live births; crude marriage rate (1974), 5·64 per 1,000 population.

In 1974 about 48% of the inhabitants lived in urban areas and 52% in rural areas.

The people of the western half of the republic are principally of mixed Spanish and Indian extraction, some of pure Spanish descent and many Indians. The population of the eastern half is composed mainly of Mosquito and other Indians and Zambos, and Negroes from Jamaica and other islands of the Caribbean. The main ethnic groups in 1974 were: Mestizo, 69%; white, 19%; Negro, 9%; Indio, 5%.

Nicaragua is administratively divided into the following 16 departments and 1 territory, with population as on 31 Dec. 1975:

Boaco	76,104	Jinotega	104,942	Nueva Segovia	79,249
Carazo	90,406	Leon	205,265	Río San Juan	23,581
Chinandega	184,062	Madriz	60,679	Rivas	88,916
Chontales	81,768	Managua	556,470	Zelaya	166,282
Esteli	90,585	Masaya	114,060		
Granada	91,421	Matagalpa	187,521	Cabo Gracias a Dios	4,249

Of the 134 *municipios*, 98 have from 2,000 to 50,000 inhabitants. The capital is Managua, situated on the lake of the same name, 180 ft above sea level, with (1974) 499,568 inhabitants. On 23 Dec. 1972 Managua was almost totally destroyed. Other cities: León, 61,649; Matagalpa, 61,383; Granada, 40,200; Chinandega, 36,885; Masaya, 34,127; Estelí, 26,764; Diriamba, 24,177; Boaco, 20,428; Juigalpa, 18,259; Bluefields, 17,706; Jinotepe, 15,957.

CONSTITUTION AND GOVERNMENT. On 31 Aug. 1971 the Congress voted in favour of dissolution and the abrogation of the Constitution. A 100-member Constituent Assembly started its discussions on a new Constitution in May 1972.

On 14 March 1974 the new Constitution came into force and provides for a national congress consisting of a Chamber of Deputies of 70 members and a Senate of 30 members.

President: Gen. Anastasio Somoza Debayle, elected for a 6-year term beginning 1 Dec. 1974 (Gen. Somoza was President 1967–72).

Minister for Foreign Affairs: Dr Julio César Quintana.

Ministers, who are heads of departments, are chosen by the President and cannot be members of Congress.

The republic is divided into 16 departments and 1 territory, each of which is under a political head (appointed by the President), who has supervision of finance, education and other matters. The departments have 134 *municipios*, headed by a mayor (*alcalde*). The Mosquito Reserve now forms part of the departments of Zelaya and Río San Juan.

National flag: Three horizontal stripes of blue, white, blue, with the national arms in the centre.

National anthem: Salve a ti Nicaragua (words by S. Ibarra Mayorga, 1937).

DEFENCE

Army. The National Guard (which functions as police force and army) numbered (1977) 5,400 officers and other ranks, besides 4,000 in the trained reserve. Period of enlistment, 3 years, but military service may be made compulsory at any time. There is a military academy.

Navy. Ten small coastguard boats operated by the marine section of the National Guard patrol the east and west coasts. An ancient patrol boat is used for training. Personnel in 1978 totalled 200 officers and men.

Air Force. Formed in June 1938 as the Nicaraguan Army Air Force, the Air Force has been semi-independent since 1947. Its combat units have about 6 T-33 armed jet trainers, 4 B-26 light piston-engined bombers and 4 T-28 armed piston-engined trainers. Other equipment includes 5 Spanish-built Aviocar and 2 Israeli-built Arava STOL transports, T-6 piston-engined trainers and smaller communications aircraft and helicopters. Approximate strength is 1,000 personnel and 40 aircraft.

INTERNATIONAL RELATIONS

Membership. Nicaragua is a member of the UN, OAS and the Central American Common Market.

ECONOMY

Planning. The objects of the National Reconstruction Plan 1975–79 include the reconstruction of Managua which will take one-third of the US$6,000m. envisaged for the plan.

Budget. Revenue and expenditure for fiscal years, ending 30 June, in 1m. córdobas:

	1973	*1974*	*1975*	*1976*	*1977*	*1978*
Revenue	1,203·0	2,093·2	2,020·7	2,200	2,652	3,577
Expenditure	1,203·6	2,030·9	2,093·8	2,200	2,652	3,577

The 1976 budget included 85·1m. córdobas for the Ministry of Finance and Public Credit, 244·6m. for education, 49·1m. for commerce and public works, 159m. for defence and 60·5m. for health.

The external debt at the end of 1976 was 164·4m. córdobas; the internal debt was 17·6m. córdobas.

Currency. The monetary unit is the *córdoba* (C$), divided into 100 *centavos*. Its exchange parity with gold is managed by the Central Bank of Nicaragua and the Government. On 31 Dec. 1976 total money supply was 1,675·4m. córdobas. Gold and silver coins provided by law (Oct. 1974) were struck in denominations of 200, 500, 1,000 and 2,000 córdobas. National bank-notes form the greater part of the currency, in denominations from 1,000 córdobas to 1 córdoba. Silver coins struck, but now out of circulation, are 50, 25 and 10 centavos; copper–nickel and copper–zinc coins, 1 córdoba, 50, 25, 10 and 5 centavos; copper coin, 1 centavo.

Rate of exchange, Dec. 1975: 7 córdobas = US$1.

Banking. The National Bank of Nicaragua at Managua, founded in 1912, owned by the Government since 1924 was completely reorganized in May 1940. On 31 Dec. 1975 its capital was increased to C$175m. and a new law gave it increased responsibilities as a development bank. The Central Bank of Nicaragua came into operation on 1 Jan. 1961 as an autonomous bank of issue, absorbing the issue department of the National Bank. The total gold and foreign-exchange reserve of the Central Bank was, as of 31 Dec. 1975, equivalent to C$849·2m. Money supply was C$1,313·7m.

In May 1974 a private investment company, Inter Financiera SA, opened in Managua with a capital of C$3m. The next year a saving and loan company, *Nicaraguense de ahorro y préstamo*, opened in Managua and a private investment company, Financiera de Occidente SA, opened in León with a capital of C$10m. A new private bank, Banco de Centroamerica, opened in Managua in Dec. 1972 with a capital of C$3m. The legal minimum cash holding for commercial private banks with the Central Bank is 35% on demand deposits and 10% on savings and time deposits. For the National Bank the minimum cash holding is 26% on demand deposits and 10% on saving and time deposits.

Weights and Measures. Since 1893 the metric system of weights and measures has been recommended.

ENERGY AND NATURAL RESOURCES

Electricity. Installed capacity for electric energy was 205,552 kw. in 1973 and 1,298m. kwh. was produced.

Minerals. Production of gold in 1972 was 2,550 kg.; of silver, 9 tonnes; of copper, 4,000 tonnes. There is no iron or coalmining. Large deposits of tungsten in Nueva Segovia were announced in 1961. Exploration for petroleum began off the Pacific and Atlantic coasts in 1965. A petroleum refinery of 650,000 tonnes capacity is functioning at Managua.

Agriculture. Agriculture is the principal source of national wealth, finding work for 65% of the labour force, and furnishing, 1975, 22% of the gross national product.

Production. Of the total land area (about 36·5m. acres), about 17·5m. acres are under timber, 0·9m. acres are used for grazing and 2·1m. acres are arable. The unit of area used locally is the *manzana* (= 1·73 acres). Of the arable only 1·2m. acres are actively cultivated, 780,000 in annual crops such as cotton and rice and the remainder in perennial crops such as coffee and sugar-cane, or in two harvests a year in the cases of maize, sorghum and beans. 65% of the working population is in agriculture.

There are plans to increase its efficiency by means of irrigation schemes depending on the Tipitapa and Tuma rivers. The principal production of the eastern part of the republic was formerly bananas, but the exports in 1975 were only 6·63m. boxes. An American company, in 1961, laid out banana plantations on the west coast on new soil which should be free of the Panama disease. The Chinandega crop was valued at C$20m. in 1963–64; it suffered heavy storm damage in Feb. 1965, which destroyed 50% of the trees. Cotton production in 1975 was 118,000 tonnes. Plantains, oranges, pine apples, sweet potatoes and yucca are raised for home consumption.

The products of the western half are much more varied, the most important being cotton, coffee, now under the aegis of the new *Instituto del Café*, sugar-cane, cocoa, maize, sesame and beans. A firm has been organized to produce soluble banana, cocoa and coffee powder, principally for export. Sugar-cane output, 1975–76, was 2·5m. tonnes. The first shipments of a Havana-type tobacco were made in 1964 from a farm controlled by the *Instituto de Fomento Nacional*. A US company bought the entire crop, valued at C$1·2m.

Rice is grown (estimated at 58,000 tonnes in 1975) and wheat in León and the hilly Jinotega district, while tobacco is cultivated round Masaya, Somoto, Estelí and Nueva Segovia. Sesame seed is the country's only oilseed of importance, but it is ninth after coffee, gold, cotton, meat, sugar, powdered coffee, cotton seed and copper as an export. An experimental planting of castor seed was made in May 1957. The coffee crop was 48,000 tonnes in 1975. There are 67 processing plants. Maize production, 1975, was 190,000 tonnes. With the exception of plantains and yucca or cassava, the greater part of the food supply of the eastern section is imported from the US.

The western half of the country produces much of its own food, but is seriously dependent upon weather conditions. There were about 2·6m. head of cattle in 1975. There are now 4 modern meat-packing plants; slaughterings were 324,600 heads in 1975. There were 1·3m. pigs. Beef exports in 1975 were valued at US$26·9m., fourth only to coffee, cotton and sugar-cane. A big programme for the improving of the quality of the cattle was jointly introduced in 1965 by the National Development Institute and the National Bank of Nicaragua.

Forestry. Timber production has been declining, though the forests, which cover 10m. acres and 4 distinct zones, contain mahogany and cedar, which were formerly largely exported, three varieties of rosewoods, guayacán (*lignum vitae*) and dyewoods. In 1968–69 exploitation of these vast areas of timber with a potential production of 300,000 tonnes per annum was begun. Production of sawn wood in 1972, 270,000 tonnes.

Fishery. On the Atlantic coast fisheries are an important subsistence activity. Over 6·6m. lb. of shrimps were exported in 1975 and were processed in 3 plants at Schooner Cay, El Bluff and Corn Island. The fishing limit off the coast has been defined as 200 nautical miles. Within that limit, fishing is subject to the provisions of the National Resources Exploration Law.

INDUSTRY AND TRADE

Industry. Chief local industries are matches, cigarettes, beer, soap, leather, plastics, metal products, flour, cement (99,000 tonnes in 1972), cotton and silk, strong and soft drinks, soluble coffee, dairy products, meat, plywood, cosmetics, detergents and paints. Production of oil products, in 1975, was valued at 476·2m. córdobas; food products, 2,539m.; beverages, 387·7m.; textiles, 284·8m.; chemical substances and products, 704·5m. In 1964 almost 100 new enterprises received tax incentive authorization under the law. Revenue from the tourist industry, 1972, $15m.

GDP *per capita* (1972) US$496.

Labour. In 1975 there were some 654,683 persons gainfully employed; of these: agriculture, 47·9%; manufacturing, construction, mining and power, 15·4%; services, transport and commerce, 35%.

Commerce. The foreign trade of Nicaragua, in US$1m., was as follows in calendar years:

	1974	*1975*	*1976*	*1977*
Imports	561·7	516·9	504·5	701·8
Exports	380·9	375·2	526·5	655·5

The main imports in 1975 (in US$1m.) were: Crude oil, 63·4; machinery and vehicles, 143·6; chemicals, 105·8; foodstuffs, 22·1. These were supplied mainly by USA, Venezuela. Federal Republic of Germany, Japan, Costa Rica and Guatemala. Imports from the Central American Common Market (CACM) countries were almost double those of 1972.

In 1975 the main exports (in US$1m.) were: Cotton, 95·6; coffee, 48·1; sugar, 42·6; meat, 27; timber, 5·6; bananas, 4·9; soluble coffee, 0·9.

Total trade between Nicaragua and UK (British Department of Trade returns, in £1,000 sterling):

	1972	*1973*	*1974*	*1975*	*1976*	*1977*
Imports to UK	353	459	1,360	9,890	1,174	1,393
Exports and re-exports from UK	2,687	2,692	7,710	5,247	8,335	8,841

COMMUNICATIONS

Roads. In 1975, 1,600 km were paved, out of a total of 12,500 km. The whole 368·5 km of the Nicaraguan section of the Pan-American Highway is now paved. The all-weather Roosevelt Highway linking Managua with the river port Rama was completed in 1968, to provide the first overland link with the Atlantic coast. There are paved roads to San Juan del Sur, Puerto Somoza and Corinto. In 1973 there were 32,123 passenger cars and vans in use.

Railways. The Pacific Railroad of Nicaragua, owned and operated by the Government, has a total length of 373 km, all single-track, and connects Corinto, Chinandega, León, Managua, Masaya and Granada. Passengers carried (1975) 441,154; freight, 65,320 tonnes.

Aviation. LANICA, the Nicaraguan airline, 77% national and 23% Pan-American owned, has 3 flights a week to Miami and to Bluefields, Puerto Cabezas and the mining towns of Siuna and Bonanza. PANAM and TACA (Transportes Aéreos Centroamericanos), a US-owned line registered in El Salvador, have daily services to Panama, Mexico, the other central American countries and USA. Craft Airlines, a new airline, has begun daily service between Managua, Nicaragua, and San José, Costa Rica. In 1972, 105,000 passengers were carried and 2m. km flown.

Shipping. The Pacific ports are Corinto (the largest), San Juan del Sur and Puerto Somoza through which pass most of the external trade. The chief eastern ports are El Bluff (for Bluefields) and Puerto Cabezas. The merchant marine consists solely of the Mamenic Line with 4 vessels owned and 5 chartered. In 1975, 971,000 short tons of goods were loaded and 1·34m. tonnes unloaded at Nicaraguan ports.

Post and Broadcasting. There are (1976) 16,000 km of (government-owned) telegraph wire and 326 offices; also 31,300 lines and 45,000 instruments. There are 233 post offices, and good service between the chief towns of the western section; service into the interior is carried by air-mail. All American Cable Co. connects with New York and has a powerful station at San Juan del Sur.

The Tropical Radio Telegraph Company maintains a powerful station at Managua, and branch stations at Bluefields and Puerto Cabezas. The Government operates the National Radio with 47 broadcasting stations: there are 31 commercial stations and some 70 others. Number of wireless sets in 1972 was 115,000 and television sets 60,000. There is a television station at Managua.

Cinemas. Cinemas numbered over 100 in 1965 and seated over 60,000.

Newspapers. There are 7 daily newspapers (5 in Managua and 2 in León), with a total circulation of about 75,000.

JUSTICE, RELIGION, EDUCATION AND WELFARE

Justice. The judicial power is vested in a Supreme Court of Justice at Managua, 5 chambers of second instance (León, Masaya, Granada, Matagalpa and Bluefields) and 153 judges of inferior tribunals.

Religion. The prevailing form of religion is Roman Catholic, but religious liberty is guaranteed by the Constitution. The republic constitutes 1 archbishopric (seat at Managua) and 7 bishoprics (Léon, Granada, Estelí, Matagalpa, Juigalpa, Masaya and Puerto Cabezas). Protestants, established principally on the Atlantic coast, numbered 54,100 in 1966.

Education. There were, in 1974, 2,186 elementary schools, of which 1,913 were state and 223 private, with a total of 333,406 pupils; and 246 secondary schools, 161 of which were private, with 27,401 pupils. Illiterate persons, of all ages, number 63·7% of the population. The National University at León has faculties of medicine, law, pharmacy, dentistry, engineering (at Managua) and economics. It had 14,000 students in León, Managua and Carazo in 1975–76.

The Roman Catholic university, founded in Managua in 1961, with faculties of engineering, public administration, law, zootechnics, veterinary science and humanities, had 6,200 students in 1975–76.

Social Welfare. From 26 May 1963 a minimum daily wage of 6 córdobas was introduced nationally to be increased every 2 years thereafter. In 1975–76 it ranged from 6·33 to 18 córdobas daily according to different zones and workers' classifications. In 1974 there were 62 hospitals with 4,841 beds.

DIPLOMATIC REPRESENTATIVES

OF NICARAGUA IN GREAT BRITAIN (8 Gloucester Road, London, SW7 4PP)

Chargé d'Affaires: Dr José Rigo Castellón.

OF GREAT BRITAIN IN NICARAGUA

Ambassador and Consul-General: K. Hamylton Jones (resides in San José).

OF NICARAGUA IN THE USA (1627 New Hampshire Ave., NW, Washington, D.C., 20009)

Ambassador: Dr Guillermo Sevilla-Sacasa.

OF THE USA IN NICARAGUA (Km. 4½ Carretera Sur., Managua)

Ambassador: Mauricio Solaun.

OF NICARAGUA TO THE UNITED NATIONS

Ambassador: Dr Guillermo Sevilla-Sacasa.

Books of Reference

Dirección General Estadística y Censos, *Boletín de Estadística* (irregular intervals); and *Indicadores Economicos.*
Memoria de la Recaudaciòn General de Aduanas (Customs statistics). Annual
Boletín de la Superintendencia de Bancos. Banco Central, Managua
National Library: Biblioteca Nacional, Managua, D.N.

NIGER

République du Niger

Capital: Niamey
Population: 4·24m. (1974)
GNP per capita: US$160 (1976)

HISTORY. The Republic of the Niger became independent on 3 Aug. 1960, after having been a territory of French West Africa from 1904.

AREA AND POPULATION. Niger is bounded north by Algeria and Libya, east by Chad, south by Nigeria, south-west by Dahomey and Upper Volta and west by Mali. Area 1,187,000 sq. km. The territory is divided into 7 *départements* with 33 *arrondissements*. Population (1974), 4,239,000. Niamey is the capital (102,000 inhabitants), Zinder (39,000), Maradi (37,000), Tahoua (31,000). The population is composed chiefly of Hausa (2·3m.), Jerma and Sanghai (1m.), Peulh (450,000), Beriberi-Manga (386,600) and Tuareg (127,000). Precipitation determines the geographical division into a southern zone of agriculture, a central zone of pasturage and a desert-like northern zone. The country lacks water, with the exception of the western districts, which are watered by the Niger and its tributaries, and the southern zone, were there are a number of wells.

The official language is French.

CONSTITUTION AND GOVERNMENT. On 15 April 1974 President Hamani was overthrown in a military *coup*. Lieut.-Col. Seyni Kountche suspended the Constitution, dissolved the National Assembly and banned political groups.

President: Seyni Kountche.

DEFENCE

Army. The Army consists of 4 motorized infantry companies and an armoured-car squadron; total strength, 2,000.

Air Force. The Air Force has 100 officers and men, 3 ex-*Luftwaffe* Noratlas transports, 2 DC-6B and 4 C-47 transports, 1 Flamant light transport, 2 Cessna Skymasters, 4 Broussards and 1 Aero Commander 500 for communications duties.

INTERNATIONAL RELATIONS

Membership. Niger is a member of UN, OAU and is an ACP state of the EEC.

ECONOMY

Planning. An economic development plan, covering the period 1965–68 was followed by a 3-year preparatory plan and was part of a 10-year economic programme (1965–74).

Compared with an initial estimate of 23,000m. francs CFA for the preparatory plan, investments under the 1965–68 plan totalled 43,000m. francs CFA. Some 4,000m. francs CFA was used for the development of water resources and 5,000m. francs CFA for the general improvement of agricultural production.

Budget. The ordinary budget for 1976 balanced at 24,200m. francs CFA.

NATURAL RESOURCES

Minerals. Large uranium deposits have been discovered about 200 miles north of Agadez. A mining company has been formed with the Government of Niger and the French Atomic Energy Commission. The construction of a uranium-ore concentrate plant was begun in 1968, with production starting in 1970. Production (1973) 949 tonnes. Salt and natron are produced at Manga and Agadez, tin ore in Aïr.

Agriculture. The chief agricultural produce are millet, groundnuts (258,000 tonnes, 1972), and beans, manioc and, in the river districts, cotton and rice. Gum arabic at Gouré, nearly all of which is exported to Nigeria. In 1976 there were 200,000 horses, 2·7m. cattle, 7·4m. sheep and goats, 350,000 asses, 260,000 camels.

TRADE. Imports in 1974 were valued at 23,144m. francs CFA and exports at 12,621m. francs CFA.

Trade with the UK (British Department of Trade returns, in £1,000 sterling):

	1973	*1974*	*1975*	*1976*	*1977*
Imports to UK	123	1,381	1,485	820	450
Exports and re-exports from UK	577	3,380	2,667	1,101	3,549

COMMUNICATIONS

Roads. There are 7,000 km of roads. Niamey and Zinder are the termini of two trans-Sahara motor routes; the Hoggar–Aïr–Zinder road extends to Kano and Fort Lamy. There were (1973), 2,274 motor vehicles.

Aviation. At Niamey airport 56,900 passengers and 6,770 tonnes of freight and mail were dealt with in 1973.

Post and Broadcasting. There were, in 1966, 35 post offices and (1977) 8,147 telephones. In 1975 there were 100,000 radio receivers.

Cinemas. In 1970 there were 4 cinemas with a seating capacity of 3,800.

RELIGION, EDUCATION AND WELFARE

Religion. 85% of the population is Moslem.

schools and 179 in a technical school.

Health. In 1972 there were 97 doctors.

DIPLOMATIC REPRESENTATIVES

OF NIGER IN GREAT BRITAIN

Ambassador: Amadou Seydou (accredited 5 Nov. 1975, resides in Paris).

OF GREAT BRITAIN IN NIGER

Ambassador: J. B. Wright (resides in Abidjan).

OF NIGER IN THE USA (2204 R. St., NW, Washington, D.C., 20008)

Ambassador: André Wright.

OF THE USA IN NIGER (P.O. Box 201, Niamey)

Ambassador: Charles A. James.

OF NIGER TO THE UNITED NATIONS

Ambassador: Jean Poisson.

Books of Reference

Bonardi, P., *La République du Niger*. Paris, 1960
Séré de Rivières, E., *Histoire du Niger*. Paris, 1965

NIGERIA

Federal Republic of Nigeria

Capital: Lagos
Population: 73m. (1974)
GNP per capita: U$380 (1976)

HISTORY. The Federal Republic comprises a number of areas formerly under separate administrations. Lagos, ceded in Aug. 1861 by King Docemo, was placed under the Governor of Sierra Leone in 1866. In 1874 it was detached, together with Gold Coast Colony, and formed part of the latter until Jan. 1886, when a separate 'colony and protectorate of Lagos' was constituted. Meanwhile the National African Company had established British interests in the Niger valley, and in July 1886 the company obtained a charter under the name of the Royal Niger Company. This company surrendered its charter to the Crown on 31 Dec. 1899, and on 1 Jan. 1900 the greater part of its territories was formed into the protectorate of Northern Nigeria. Along the coast the Oil Rivers protectorate had been declared in June 1885. This was enlarged and renamed the Niger Coast protectorate in 1893; and on 1 Jan. 1900, on its absorbing the remainder of the territories of the Royal Niger Company, it became the protectorate of Southern Nigeria. In Feb. 1906 Lagos and Southern Nigeria were united into the 'colony and protectorate of Southern Nigeria', and on 1 Jan. 1914 the latter was amalgamated with the protectorate of Northern Nigeria to form the 'colony and protectorate of Nigeria', under a Governor. On 1 Oct. 1954 Nigeria became a federation under a Governor-General.

On 1 Oct. 1960 Nigeria became sovereign and independent and a member of the Commonwealth and on 1 Oct. 1963 Nigeria became a republic.

At the plebiscite held on 11 Feb. 1961 the northern portion of the trusteeship territory of the Cameroons voted to join Nigeria while the southern Cameroons opted for unification with the Republic of Cameroon.

On 15 Jan. 1966 a group of 25 officers staged a military *coup d'état* and killed the Federal Prime Minister, Sir Abubakar Tafawa Balewa, the Federal Minister of Finance, Chief Festus Okotie-Eboh, the Premier of Northern Nigeria, Sir Ahmadu Bello, the Premier of Western Nigeria, Chief S. L. Akintola, the Adjutant-General of the Army, Lieut.-Col. Jack Pam, and other officers. By 17 Jan. Maj.-Gen. Johnson Aguiyi-Ironsi, head of the army, had suppressed the revolt and assumed supreme power.

AREA AND POPULATION. Area approximately 356,669 sq. miles (923,773 sq. km). Census population, Nov. 1963, 55,670,052. In Feb. 1976 there were 19 states:

States	*Area (in sq. km)*	*Population (in 1m.)*	*States*	*Area (in sq. km)*	*Population (in 1m.)*
Anambra	21,189	3·6	Kwara	73,400	1·7
Bauchi	17,926	2·4	Lagos	14,712	1·4
Bendel	39,737	2·5	Niger	17,344	1·2
Benue	19,200	2·4	Ogun	13,600	1·6
Borno	116,589	3·0	Ondo	14,400	2·7
Cross River	35,149	3·5	Oyo	17,600	5·2
Gongola	13,664	2·6	Plateau	31,350	2·0
Imo	8,720	3·7	Rivers	17,941	1·7
Kaduna	68,989	4·1	Sokoto	149,066	4·5
Kano	42,593	5·8			

The results of the 1973 census were abandoned in Aug. 1975 because they 'will not command general acceptance throughout the country'. There is considerable uncertainty over the total population, but one estimate is 73m. in 1974 (1973 census, preliminary) 79·8m.

The populations of the largest towns were (1975 estimate) as follows: Lagos, 1,060,848; and (in 1,000) Ibadan, 847; Ogbomosho, 432; Kano, 399; Oshogbo, 282; Ilorin, 282; Abeokuta, 253; Port Harcourt, 242; Zaria, 224; Ilesha, 224; Onitsha, 220; Iwo, 214; Ado-Ekiti, 213; Kaduna, 202; Mushin, 197; Maiduguri, 189; Enugu, 187; Ede, 182; Aba, 177; Ife, 176; Ila, 155; Oyo, 152; Ikere-Ekiti, 145; Benin, 136; Iseyin, 129.

It was announced in Feb. 1976 that the federal capital would be moved inland from Lagos to Abuja area north of river Niger.

Topography and Climate. A belt of mangrove swamp forest lies along the entire coastline. North of this there is a zone of tropical rain forest and oil-palm bush some 50–100 miles wide. Farther inland the country rises and the vegetation changes to open woodland and savannah. In the extreme north the country is almost desert. There are few mountains except along the eastern boundary and on the northern plateau, where peaks of over 5,000 ft occur. The Niger, Benue and Cross are the main rivers.

The climate varies with the types of country, but Nigeria lies wholly within the tropics, and temperatures are high. Temperatures of over 100° are common in the north; coast temperatures are seldom over 90°, but the humidity at the coast is much higher than in the north. Most of the rain falls between April and Sept. in the north and between March and Nov. in the south; rainfall varies from under 25 in. a year to 150 in. During the dry-season the 'harmattan' wind, laden with fine particles of dust, blows from the north-east.

CONSTITUTION. Gen. Ironsi suspended the constitution in 1966 and set up a supreme military council. All political parties and tribal associations were abolished. On 24 May the 'regions' were replaced by 'provinces' and the name of the Federation was changed to 'Republic of Nigeria'.

On 29 July 1966 the regime of Gen. Ironsi was overthrown by a military *coup*, leaders of which accepted Lieut.-Col. Yakubu Gowon as a compromise leader. By decree of 31 Aug. he restored, as from 1 Sept., the federal system of government. The National Military Government was renamed the Federal Military Government, the provinces became again regions and the capital territory of Lagos again the federal territory of Lagos.

On 30 May 1967 Lieut.-Col. Ojukwu, the Military Governor of the Eastern States, announced secession from the Federal Republic of Nigeria and renamed the region as the Republic of Biafra. In Aug. the Mid-West State was taken by Col. Ojukwu's forces but recaptured by the federal army later that year. By April 1968 the federal army had reconquered the greater part of the breakaway states. In Jan. 1970 the rebellion had collapsed and Col. Ojukwu fled the country leaving Col. Philip Effiong to surrender to federal forces.

On 29 July 1975 Gen. Gowon was overthrown and Brig. (later Gen.) Murtala Ramat Mohammed became Head of State and on 13 Feb. 1976 there was an attempted *coup* and Gen. Mohammed was killed.

A Constituent Assembly of 203 members was drafting a new Constitution in 1977–78, and free elections have been promised for 1979.

The official language is English.

Head of State: Lieut.-Gen. Olusegun Obasanjo.

National flag: Three vertical strips of green, white, green.

Local Government. Important in the Federal Military Government's political programme for the return to democratic civilian rule by 1979 is the reform of the local government system. The federal government have given a suggested framework for a national system of local government and as an interim measure a sum of ₦100m. was allocated for local governments in 1976–77. In Dec. 1976, the local government elections were held in all the states of the Republic.

DEFENCE

Army. The Army consists of 4 infantry divisions, 4 reconnaissance, 4 artillery and 4 engineer regiments. Total strength (1977) 221,000.

Navy. The Nigerian Navy was established in 1956. Administered by a rear-admiral as Chief of Naval Staff and a captain as Chief of Staff. The Navy includes the frigate *Nigeria* (built in the Netherlands in 1964–65), the corvettes *Dorina* and *Otobo* built in Britain in 1970–72 (2 more are being completed), 8 patrol craft, 1 landing craft, 1 supply ship, 2 survey craft, 1 training ship and 1 tug. There are also 8 small patrol launches operated by the Nigerian Police. Naval personnel (1978), 260 officers and 2,700 ratings, plus 2,000 reservists.

Air Force. The Nigerian Air Force was established in Jan. 1964. Pilots were trained initially in Canada, India and Ethiopia. The Air Force was built up subsequently with the aid of a Federal Republic of Germany mission; much first-line equipment has since been received from the Soviet Union. It includes 20 MiG-21 supersonic jet-fighters, about 10 MiG-17 fighter-bombers, a few MiG-15UTI fighter-trainers and a small number of Il-28 twin-jet bombers, and L-29 Delfin armed jet trainers from Czechoslovakia. Four BO 105 twin-turbine helicopters have been acquired from the Federal Republic of Germany for search and rescue. Transport units operate 6 C-130H Hercules 4-turboprop heavy transports, a Fokker F.28 Fellowship twin-turbofan airliner for Presidential use, 9 turboprop Friendships, 6 twin-engined Noratlas, about 7 DC-3s, 2 Navajos and a Navajo Chieftain. Training types include 32 Scottish Aviation Bulldog primary trainers, a few Do 27s and Do 28s, and 4 twin-engined Dornier Sky-servants for instrument training, transport and ambulance duties. Two medium-lift Aérospatiale Pumas and a few light helicopters are also in service. Personnel total about 6,000.

INTERNATIONAL RELATIONS

Membership. Nigeria is a member of UN, the Commonwealth, OAU and is an ACP state of EEC.

Treaties. Under a convention concluded in May 1964, Nigeria, Niger, Chad and Cameroon agreed to develop the basin of Lake Chad as a single economic region.

ECONOMY

Planning. The first national development plan ran from 1962 to 1968; the second plan (1970–74) was launched in 1970 and provided for a total expenditure of £1,596m. The third national development plan will run from 1975 to 1980 and provides for an expenditure of ₦40,000m.

Budget. Revenue for 1977–78 was ₦7,650m. Expenditure, ₦3,097m. for recurrent items; defence taking 26%. Capital expenditure, ₦5,503m.

In March 1976 reserves were ₦3,521m.

Currency. Since 1 Jan. 1973 a decimal currency has been issued by the Central Bank of Nigeria, consisting of *Naira* (₦) and divided into 100 *kobe* (k). Notes in circulation ₦20, ₦10, ₦5, ₦1, 50k. Coins, 25k, 10k, 5k, 1k, ½k.

Banking. In Aug. 1967 the statutory foreign-exchange cover of the Central Bank was reduced from 40 to 25%, and the percentage of government securities the Bank is permitted to hold was raised from 33½ to 50% of its total liabilities.

The Central Bank of Nigeria, the Standard Bank of Nigeria, Ltd, Barclays Bank of Nigeria, Ltd, the National Bank of Nigeria, the African Continental Bank, the Merchants' Bank, Ltd, the United Bank for Africa, the Bank of America, the Chase Manhattan Bank, the Bank of the North and the Co-operative Bank are the principal banks operating in Nigeria. All banks are required to be registered as Nigerian companies from 1969. In 1976 the Government took a 60% shareholding in all foreign banks.

In Aug. 1974 the post office savings bank had 400,000 depositors holding ₦4,664,468.

Weights and Measures. The metric system is in force and the transitional period from the imperial system ended in 1977.

ENERGY AND NATURAL RESOURCES

Electricity. The National Electric Power Authority generated 2,664m. kwh. in 1973–74. The Niger dams at Kainji were completed in early 1969 (investment of £87m.) and provide cheap hydro-electricity for rapid industrialization.

Oil. There is a refinery at Port Harcourt and 2 more are being built at Warri and Kaduna. Oil represents 93% of exports. Production, 1975, 89,099,000 tonnes.

Gas. Natural gas is being used at electric power stations at Afam and Ughelli to generate power. Production, 1972, 601,237,000 cu. ft.

Minerals. Production (1975): Tin, 7,300 tonnes; columbite (the world's largest producer), 1,000 tonnes; coal, 274,000 tonnes. There are large deposits of iron ore, coal (reserves estimate 245m. tonnes), lead and zinc. There are small quantities of gold and uranium.

Agriculture. Groundnuts, cotton and soybean come mainly or wholly from the north, palm produce, cocoa, timber and rubber from the south. Tobacco is grown in commercial quantities in parts of the Northern and Western States. Production (estimates) 1975–76 were (in tonnes): Groundnuts, 5,000; palm kernels, 400,000; cocoa, 220,000; cotton, 300,000 bales.

Livestock. In 1976 there were 11·3m. cattle, 7·9m. sheep, 23m. goats, 900,000 pigs and 91m. poultry.

Forestries. There are plywood factories at Epe, Sapele and Calabar, and numerous saw-mills. The most important timber species include mahogany, iroko, obeche, abwa, ebony and camwood, the main sources of which are the high forest zones in the south.

INDUSTRY AND TRADE

Industry. Timber and hides and skins are other major export commodities. Industrial products include soap, cigarettes, beer, margarine, groundnut oil, meat and cake, concentrated fruit juices, soft drinks, canned food, metal containers, plywood, textiles, ceramic products and cement. Of growing importance is the local assembly of motor vehicles, bicycles, radio equipment, electrical goods and sewing machines.

Under a decree on indigenization Nigerians must have a minimum of 40% shareholding in all foreign enterprises.

Trade Unions. The trade union decrees of 1973 and 1974 make provision for the formation, registration and organization of trade unions.

Commerce. There is a great deal of internal commerce in local foodstuffs and imported goods moving by rail, lorry and pack animals overland, and by launches, rafts and canoes along an extensive and complex network of inland waterways. Kano is still, as it has been for centuries, the focus of caravan routes linking a territory which stretches from the Sudan in the east to Senegal in the west, with branches northwards across the Sahara.

Total trade in ₦m. for 4 years:

	1972	*1973*	*1974*	*1975*
Imports (c.i.f.)	990·1	1,224·8	1,721·3	3,721·5
Exports and re-exports (f.o.b.)	1,444·2	2,277·4	5,794·8	4,924·7

The steep rise in oil prices is reflected in the 1974 export figures.

Total trade between UK and Nigeria (according to British Department of Trade returns, in £1,000 sterling):

	1973	*1974*	*1975*	*1976*	*1977*
Imports to UK	206,836	368,280	310,155	316,697	219,286
Exports and re-exports from UK	172,654	222,386	512,302	774,179	1,068,707

COMMUNICATIONS

Roads (1972). There are about 55,000 miles of maintained roads, of which 9,500 miles are tarred.

In 1969, 133,577 vehicles were registered. Bus services, by private owners, operate in the larger towns and between the main towns in Eastern and Western Nigerian, but the bulk of passenger and goods traffic by road is carried in lorries (mammy wagons). Taxis are available in the large towns.

Railways. There are 2,680 route miles of line 3 ft 6 in. gauge.

Aviation. There is an extensive system of internal and international air routes, serving Europe, South and West Africa. Regular services are operated by Nigerian Airways (WAAC), British Caledonian, UTA, KLM, Sabena, Swissair, PANAM and other lines. Aircraft arrivals from outside Nigeria in 1961 totalled 3,804, carrying 726 tons of freight. In 1962, 60,036 passengers and 924 tons of mail and freight were carried on internal services. In 1972, 112,000 passengers arrived at Nigerian airports and 119,000 passengers departed.

Shipping. The principal ports are Lagos, Port Harcourt, Warri and Calabar.

Post and Broadcasting. Postal facilities are provided at 1,667 offices and agencies; telegraph, money order and savings bank services are provided at 280 of these. Most internal letter mail is carried by air at normal postage rates. External telegraph services are owned and operated by Nigerian External Telecommunications, Ltd, at Lagos, from which telegraphic communication is maintained with all parts of the world. There were 121,032 telephones in use in 1977, of which 42,626 were in Lagos and 9,919 in Ibadan. There is also a telex service.

Federal and some state governments have established commercial corporations for sound and television broadcasting, which are widely used in schools.

Cinemas (1974). There were 120 cinemas, with a seating capacity of 60,000. Mobile cinemas are used by the Federal and States Information Services.

Newspapers. There are 49 newspapers and magazines; the highest circulation of a daily is about 125,000. Most of the papers are published in English.

JUSTICE, RELIGION, EDUCATION AND WELFARE

Justice. The highest court is the Federal Supreme Court, which consists of the Chief Justice of the Republic, not less than 2 Federal Judges and the Chief Justice of each State. It has original jurisdiction in any dispute between the Federal Republic and any State or between States; and to hear and determine appeals from any of the High Courts and from any court or tribunal established by Parliament. It may be given powers of advisory jurisdiction by Parliament in respect of the exercise of the prerogative of mercy by the Heads of State of the Republic or the States.

High Courts, presided over by a Chief Justice, are established in most of the states. Magistrates' courts are established throughout the Republic, and customary law courts in Western, Eastern, South Eastern, East Central and Lagos States of Nigeria. In Northern States of Nigeria there are the Sharia Court of Appeal and the Court of Resolution. Moslem Law has been codified in a Penal Code and is applied through Alkali courts.

The Advisory Judicial committee has powers of appointment and discipline.

Religion. The 1963 census figures were: Moslems, 26·2m.; Christians, 19·2m.; others, 10·1m. Northern Nigeria is mainly Moslem; Southern Nigeria is predominantly Christian. The Protestant and Roman Catholic Churches have 2·5m. each.

Education. On 1 Oct. 1954 education became the responsibility of the Regional Governments, the Federal Government retaining responsibility for education in Lagos and for those institutions of higher learning which have Nigerian significance, such as the University of Ibadan, King's College and the Man o' War Bay Training Centre. Free education for all primary school children within the 6–12 year age group was implemented in the Western State in Jan. 1955 and in Lagos and the Eastern State in Jan. 1957 and in Sept. 1976 primary education became free throughout the country.

In 1973 there were 14,525 primary schools with 4·7m. pupils and (1971) 116,640 teachers. The demand for secondary education continues to exceed the number of places available, particularly in Eastern and Western States and in Lagos. In 1973 there were 1,499 secondary schools, including some secondary modern schools, with 448,904 pupils and (1971) 18,351 teachers. All external examinations of the Universities of London and Cambridge have been taken over by the West African Examination Council.

Teacher-training institutions totalled 157 in 1973. There were also 67 trade centres and vocational training institutes for sub-professional technicians and tradesmen.

There are 13 universties in Nigeria, providing 3–5-year courses leading to the award of a first degree in various disciplines. There are also opportunities for taking higher degrees. Free tuition was provided from 1977.

The University of Ibadan was founded in 1948, and was an autonomous University College in special relationship with the University of London. Its graduates were prepared for degrees of the University of London. In 1962 the College was transformed into a full University, awarding its own degrees. In 1976 there were 6,961 full-time students. A 500-bed teaching hospital was opened in 1957. The University of Nigeria, opened Oct. 1960, had 6,005 students in 1976. The Ahmadu Bello University was opened in Oct. 1962 at Zaria in Northern Nigeria. It had 7,455 students in 1976. The University of Benin opened in 1970 and had 1,054 students in 1976.

The University of Ife, in the Western State, founded in Oct. 1961 and formally opened in 1962, includes the Ibadan branch of the former Nigerian College of Arts, Science and Technology. It had 1,781 students in 1971.

The University of Lagos, concentrating initially on law, medicine and business administration, was opened in Oct. 1962. It had 4,382 students in 1976. Total enrolment at Nigerian universities in 1974 was about 20,000.

Health. Most tropical diseases are endemic to Nigeria. Blindness, yaws, leprosy, sleeping sickness, worm infections, malaria are major health problems which, however, are yielding to remedial and preventative measures. In co-operation with the World Health Organization river blindness and malaria are being tackled on a large scale, while annual campaigns are undertaken against the danger of smallpox epidemics. Over 33m. people were vaccinated against smallpox in 1968. Dispensaries and travelling dispensaries are found in most parts of the country.

The teaching hospital at Lagos University has 350 beds; there is also a nursing school and a teaching hospital at Ibadan University. There are medical courses at Ahmadu Bello University, University of Ife, Benin University and at Nsukka.

DIPLOMATIC REPRESENTATIVES

OF NIGERIA IN GREAT BRITAIN
(9 Northumberland Ave., London, WC2N 5BX)

High Commissioner: H. O. I. Monu.

OF GREAT BRITAIN IN NIGERIA
(Kajola Hse, 62–64 Campbell St., Lagos)

High Commissioner: Sir Sam Felle, KCVO, CMG, DSC.

OF NIGERIA IN THE USA (2201 M. St., NW, Washington, D.C., 20037)

Ambassador: O. Jolaoso.

OF THE USA IN NIGERIA (1 King's College Rd, Lagos)

Ambassador: Donald B. Easum.

OF NIGERIA TO THE UNITED NATIONS

Ambassador: Leslie O. Harriman.

Books of Reference

National Development Plan, 1962–68. Ministry of Economic Development, 1962
Economic Survey of Nigeria, 1959. Federal Government Printer, Lagos, 1959
Nigeria Digest of Statistics. Lagos, 1951 ff. (quarterly)
Annual Abstract of Statistics. Federal Office of Statistics. Lagos, 1960 ff.
Nigeria Trade Journal. Federal Ministry of Commerce and Industries (quarterly)
Nigeria Handbook 1975–76. Ministry of Information, Lagos, 1975

Afolabi Ojo, G. J., *Yoruba Culture*. Univ. of London Press, 1967
Arnold, G., *Modern Nigeria*. London, 1977
Blitz, F. (ed.), *The Politics and Administration of Nigerian Government*. Lagos and London, 1965
Buchanan, K. H., and Pugh, J. C., *Land and People in Nigeria*. Univ. of London Press, 1955
Burns, Sir Alan, *History of Nigeria*. 8th ed. London, 1972
Crowder, M., *The Story of Nigeria*. 3rd ed. London, 1973
Damachi, U. G., *Nigerian Modernization: The Colonial Legacy*. New York, 1972
Isichei, E., *History of the Igbo People*. London, 1976
Luckham, R., *The Nigerian Military: A Sociological Analysis of Authority and Revolt, 1960–67*. CUP, 1971
Nwabueze, B. O., *The Machinery of Justice in Nigeria*. London, 1964
Panter-Brick, S. K., *Nigerian Politics and Military Rule: Prelude to Civil War*. London, 1970
Peil, M., *Nigerian Politics: The People's View*. London, 1976
Williams, G., *Nigeria: Economy and Society*. London, 1977

NORWAY

Kongeriket Norge

Capital: Oslo
Population: 4m. (1977)
GNP per capita: US$7,420 (1976)

HISTORY. By the Treaty of 14 Jan. 1814 Norway was ceded to the King of Sweden by the King of Denmark, but the Norwegian people declared themselves independent and elected Prince Christian Frederik of Denmark as their king. The foreign Powers refused to recognize this election, and on 14 Aug. a convention proclaimed the independence of Norway in a personal union with Sweden. This was followed on 4 Nov. by the election of Karl XIII (II) as King of Norway. Norway declared this union dissolved, 7 June 1905, and Sweden agreed to the repeal of the union on 26 Oct. 1905. The throne was offered to a prince of the reigning house of Sweden, who declined. After a plebiscite, Prince Carl of Denmark was formally elected King on 18 Nov. 1905, and took the name of Haakon VII.

Norwegian Sovereigns

Inge Baardssøn	1204	Erik of Pomerania	1389
Haakon Haakonssøn	1217	Kristofer af Bavaria	1442
Magnus Lagabøter	1263	Karl Knutssøn	1449
Eirik Magnussøn	1280	Same Sovereigns as in Denmark	1450–1814
Haakon V Magnussøn	1299	Christian Frederik	1814
Magnus Erikssøn	1319	Same Sovereigns as in Sweden	1814–1905
Haakon VI Magnussøn	1355	Haakon VII	1905
Olav Haakonssøn	1381	Olav V	1957
Margreta	1388		

AREA AND POPULATION. Norway is bounded north by the Arctic Ocean, east by the USSR, Finland and Sweden, south by the Skagerrak Straits and west by the North Sea.

Fylker (*counties*)	*Area* (*sq. km*)	*Census population 1 Nov. 1970*	*Population 1 Jan. 1977*	*Pop. per sq. km* (*total area*) *1977*
Oslo (City)	453·28	477,898	462,497	1,020·3
Akershus	4,908·56	322,321	357,866	72·9
Østfold	4,183·43	220,892	229,444	54·6
Hedmark	27,343·96	178,923	184,206	6·7
Oppland	25,312·71	172,163	178,549	7·1
Buskerud	14,933·22	198,225	211,343	14·2
Vestfold	2,215·77	174,640	183,365	82·8
Telemark	15,315·32	156,405	160,096	10·5
Aust-Agder	9,211·71	80,575	87,076	9·5
Vest-Agder	7,280·33	124,013	132,877	18·3
Rogaland	9,140·57	268,171	291,065	31·8
Hordaland	15,633·73	372,172	388,048	24·8
Sogn og Fjordane	18,565·99	100,761	103,682	5·6
Møre og Romsdal	15,075·81	223,360	233,049	15·5
Sør-Trøndelag	18,918·76	233,420	242,416	12·8
Nord-Trøndelag	22,463·25	117,718	123,317	5·5
Nordland	38,327·01	240,461	242,723	6·3
Troms	25,953·88	136,224	144,276	5·6
Finnmark	48,648·96	75,791	79,307	1·6
Total	323,886·16[1]	3,874,133	4,035,202	12·5

[1] 125,053 sq. miles.

In 1977, 2,242,372 persons lived in rural municipalities and 1,792,830 in towns.

Conjugal condition of the domiciled population over 15 years of age, 1977: Unmarried: 461,032 males, 365,646 females; married: 954,558 males, 952,592 females; separated, widowed or divorced: 103,366 males, 253,289 females.

Population of the principal towns at 1 Jan. 1977:

Oslo	462,497	Ålesund	40,941	Halden	27,056
Bergen	212,755	Sandnes	34,558	Gjøvik	26,030
Trondheim	135,558	Sandefjord	33,533	Moss	25,720
Stavanger	87,360	Porsgrunn	31,710	Lillehammer	21,496
Kristiansand	60,037	Bodø	31,471	Harstad	21,225
Drammen	50,821	Ringerike	30,335	Molde	20,624
Skien	47,345	Fredrikstad	28,893	Steinkjer	20,491
Tromsø	44,409	Haugesund	27,214	Kongsberg	20,189

Vital statistics for calendar years:

	Marriages	*Divorces*	*Births*	*Still-born*	*Illegitimate*[2]	*Deaths*
1974	27,344	5,156	59,603	524	5,543	39,464
1975	25,898	5,577	56,345	458	5,790	40,061
1976	25,389	5,825	53,474	400	5,824	40,155[1]

[1] Provisional figures. [2] Excluding still-born.

REIGNING KING. Olav V, born 2 July 1903, married on 21 March 1929 to Princess Märtha of Sweden (born 28 March 1901, died 5 April 1954), daughter of the late Prince Carl (son of King Oscar II). He succeeded on the death of his father, King Haakon VII, on 21 Sept. 1957. *Offspring:* Princess Ragnhild Alexandra, born 9 June 1930 (married, 1953, Hr. Erling Lorentzen); Princess Astrid Maud Ingeborg, born 12 Feb. 1932 (married, 12 Jan. 1961, Hr. Johan Martin Ferner); Crown Prince Harald, born 21 Feb. 1937, married, 29 Aug. 1968, Sonja Haraldsen. *Offspring:* Princess Märtha Louise, born 22 Sept. 1971; Prince Haakon Magnus, born 20 July 1973.

CONSTITUTION AND GOVERNMENT. Norway is a constitutional and hereditary monarchy. The royal succession is in direct male line in the order of primogeniture. In default of male heirs the King may propose a successor to the Storting, but this assembly has the right to nominate another, if it does not agree with the proposal.

The constitution, voted by the constituent assembly at Eidsvoll on 17 May 1814 and modified at various times, vests the legislative power of the realm in the Storting (Parliament). The royal veto may be exercised twice; but if the same Bill passes three Stortings formed by separate and subsequent elections it becomes the law of the land without the assent of the sovereign. The King has the command of the land, sea and air forces, and makes all appointments.

Since June 1938 all branches of the Government service, including the state church, are open to women.

National flag: Red with a blue white-bordered Scandinavian cross.

National anthem: Ja, vi elsker dette landet (words by B. Bjørnson, 1865; tune by R. Nordraak, 1865).

The Storting assembles every year. The meetings take place *suo jure*, and not by any writ from the King or the executive. They begin on the first weekday in October each year, until June the following year. Every Norwegian subject of 20 years of age is entitled to vote, unless he is disqualified for a special cause. Women are, since 1913, entitled to vote under the same conditions as men. The mode of election is direct and the method of election is proportional. The country is divided into 19 districts, each electing from 4 to 15 representatives.

At the elections for the Storting held on 11–12 Sept. 1977 the following parties were elected: Labour, 76; Conservative, 41; Centre Party, 12; Christian Popular, 22; Socialist Left Party, 2 and Liberal, 2.

The Storting, when assembled, divides itself by election into the *Lagting* and the *Odelsting*. The former is composed of one-fourth of the members of the Storting, and the other of the remaining three-fourths. Each Ting (the Storting, the Odelsting and the Lagting) nominates its own president. Most questions are decided by the

Storting, but questions relating to legislation must be considered and decided by the Odelsting and the Lagting separately. Only when the Odelsting and the Lagting disagree, the Bill has to be considered by the Storting in plenary sitting, and a new law can then only be decided by a majority of two-thirds of the voters. The same majority is required for alterations of the Constitution, which can only be decided by the Storting in plenary sitting. The Storting elects 5 delegates, whose duty it is to revise the public accounts. The Lagting and the ordinary members of the Supreme Court of Justice (the *Høyesterett*) form a High Court of the Realm (the *Riksrett*) for the trial of ninisters, members of the *Høyesterett* and members of the Storting. The impeachment before the *Riksrett* can only be decided by the Odelsting.

The executive is represented by the King, who exercises his authority through the Cabinet or Council of State (*Statsråd*), composed of a Prime Minister (*Statsminister*) and 14 ministers (*Statsråder*). The ministers are entitled to be present in the Storting and to take part in the discussions, but without a vote.

A Labour Government was formed and took office on 15 Jan. 1976:

Prime Minister: Odvar Nordli.

Foreign Affairs: Knut Frydenlund. *Agriculture:* Oskar Øksnes. *Commerce and Shipping:* Hallvard Bakke. *Justice:* Inger Louise Valle. *Ecclesiastical Affairs and Education:* Kjølv Egeland. *Local Government and Labour:* Leif Aune. *Industry:* Bjartmar Gjerde. *Communications:* Ragnar Christiansen. *Environment:* Gro Harlem Brundtland. *Social Affairs:* Ruth Ryste. *Consumer Affairs and Government Administration:* Annemarie Lorentzen. *Fisheries:* Eivind Bolle. *Finance:* Per Kleppe. *Defence:* Rolf Hansen. *Maritime Law:* Jens Evensen.

The official languages are Bokmål (or Riksmål) and Nynorsk (or Landsmål).

Local Government. For the purposes of administration the country is divided into 19 counties (*fylker*), in each of which the central government is represented by a county governor (*fylkesmannen*). In addition, there are 47 urban districts (*bykommuner*) and 407 rural districts (*herredskommuner*), each of which usually corresponds in size to a parish (*prestegjeld*). The districts are administered by district councils (*kommunestyrer*), whose membership may vary between 13 and 85 councillors, and by a committee (*formannskap*) which is elected by and from the members of the council. The council is four times the size of the committee. The council elects a chairman and a vice-chairman from among its members. Councillors are elected in accordance with rules which are in most cases identical with the rules governing election to Parliament.

Each of the 18 counties forms a county district (*fylkeskommune*), while the remaining one, Oslo, comprises an urban district. The supreme authority in a county district is the county council (*fylkesting*). Every district council has until now elected its district representatives in the proportion of one to every 6,000 inhabitants, though no one district may elect more than one-third of the total number of representatives in the county council. From 1 Jan. 1976, members of the county council will be elected directly by the electors of the county and the number of representatives varies between 25 and 85. In a county district the county committee (*fylkesutvalg*) occupies a position corresponding to that of the committee (*formannskap*) in the primary districts. The county committee is elected by and from among the members of the county council. The number of county committee members is one-fourth of the membership of the county council, but must be not more than 15. The county council elects from among the members of the county committee a county sheriff (*fylkesordfører*) and a deputy sheriff.

DEFENCE. Service is universal and compulsory, liability in peace-time commencing at the age of 19 and continuing till the age of 44. The training period in the Army is 12 months, in the Navy and Air Force, 15 months. The Norwegian Defence forces are organized into 2 integrated regional commands.

Army. Major units are organized mainly in Regimental Combat Teams. Peace establishment includes 1 RCT, a number of independent units and supporting elements as well as training units. Tanks include 78 Leopard and 38 M-48. Total strength, 20,000 officers and men.

Navy. The Navy consists of the coastal batteries and the following naval units: 15 coastal submarines, 5 frigates, 2 minelayers, 2 corvettes, 10 coastal minesweepers, 26 fast missile boats, 20 fast torpedo-boats, 1 coastal (controlled) minelayer, 7 landing craft, 1 depot ship, the royal yacht *Norge* and 1 defence research vessel.

Personnel in 1978 totalled 8,000 officers and ratings including 1,600 in the Coast Artillery.

The new construction programme includes 14 fast missile boats.

Projected ships include a new class of patrol submarines of 750 tons to be built in the Federal Republic of Germany.

Coastguard. The Coastguard was set up in 1976 for the dual roles of Fishery Protection and Oil Rig Patrol, at present comprising the 6 corvette-type fishery protection ships formerly under separate administration from the Navy, it will be expanded by a new class of 7 frigate-size patrol vessels under construction with helicopter, decompression chamber and fire-fighting and anti-oil pollution equipment, and a new type of support ship designed to operate deep-diving vehicles.

Air Force. The Royal Norwegian Air Force consists of 3 squadrons of F-5 supersonic fighter-bombers, 1 squadron equipped with RF-5A reconnaissance fighters, 2 squadrons of F-104G and CF-104 Starfighters, 1 maritime patrol squadron of P-3B Orions, 1 squadron of C-130H Hercules transports, and a number of UH-1B Iroquois helicopter, communications and training units, as well as 4 Nike surface-to-air missile batteries and several light anti-aircraft artillery units. Ten Westland Sea King helicopters are used for search and rescue duties.

Total strength is approximately 9,500 officers and men.

Home Guard. The Home Guard is organized in small units equipped and trained for special tasks in their home area. Compulsory service after basic training is 50 hours a year. The total strength is approximately 85,000.

INTERNATIONAL RELATIONS

Membership. Norway is a member of UN, NATO, EFTA, OECD, the Council of Europe and the Nordic Council.

ECONOMY

Budget. Current revenue and expenditure for years ending 31 Dec. (in 1,000 kroner):

	1972	*1973*	*1974*	*1975*	*1976*	*1977*[1]
Revenue	24,447,032	27,042,507	30,459,009	34,667,531	41,663,412	46,807,000
Expenditure	27,886,738	30,848,984	35,226,986	44,024,575	52,655,159	63,696,000

[1] Voted budget.

National debt[1] for years ending 31 Dec. (in 1,000 kroner):

1969	15,824,100	1972	25,671,200	1975	41,082,800
1970	18,878,700	1973	29,521,000	1976	50,290,300
1971	21,636,900	1974	33,943,000	1977	54,022,000

[1] At the rate of par on foreign loans: including treasury bills (in 1m. kroner) which amounted to nil in 1969; 1,345 in 1971; 1,942 in 1972; 2,773 in 1973; 2,229 in 1974, and 499 in 1975.

Currency. By a treaty signed 16 Oct. 1875 Norway adopted the same monetary system as Sweden and Denmark. The Norwegian *krone*, of 100 *øre*, is of the value of about 10 *kroner* to £1 sterling. National bank-notes of 10, 50, 100, 500 and 1,000 *kroner* are legal means of payment.

On 31 Aug. 1976 the nominal value of the coin in circulation was 508m. kroner; notes in circulation, 12,161m. kroner.

Banking. The Norges Bank is a joint-stock bank; in 1949 the state acquired all the shares hitherto privately owned. The bank is governed by laws enacted by the State, and its directors are elected by the Storting, except the president and vice-president of the head office, who are nominated by the King. It is the only bank of issue.

At the end of 1976 there were 27 private joint-stock banks. Their total amount of capital and funds was 3,055m. kroner (capital 1,644m., funds 1,411m.). Deposits amounted to 38,015m. kroner, of which 9,964m. kroner were at call and notice, and 28,051m. kroner on time.

The number of savings banks at the end of 1976 was 368. The total amount of funds of the savings banks amounted to 1,205m. kroner, and total deposits 35,379m. kroner, of which 6,960m. kroner were at call and notice and 28,419m. kroner on time.

Weights and Measures. The metric system of weights and measures has been obligatory since 1875.

ENERGY AND NATURAL RESOURCES

Electricity. Norway is a large producer of hydro-electric energy. The potential total hydro-electric power, for a whole year at regulated minimum water flow and by 82% efficiency, is estimated at 15m. kw. or about 131,000m. kwh. annually. About 60% of the water power suitable for development consists of waterfalls with a height of at least 900 ft.

By the end of 1975 the capacity of the installations for production of thermo-electric energy amounted to only 159,657 kw. On 31 Dec. 1975, the total capacity of generators (of hydro-electric plants) was 19·22m. kva.

In 1975 the total production of electricity amounted to 77,486m. kwh., of which 99·9% was produced by hydro-electric plants.

Most of the electricity is used for industrial purposes, especially by the chemical and basic metal industries for production of nitrate of calcium and other nitrogen products, carbide, ferrosilicon and other ferro-alloys, aluminium and zinc. The paper and pulp industries are also big consumers of electricity.

Bjerve. P. J., *Planning in Norway 1947–1956*. Amsterdam, 1959
Bourneuf, A., *Norway, the Planned Revival*. Cambridge, Mass., 1958
Galenson, W., *Labor in Norway*. Cambridge, Mass., and London, 1949
Leiserson, M. W., *Wages and Economic Control in Norway, 1945–57*. Harvard Univ. Press, 1959

Minerals. Production and value of the chief concentrates, metals and alloys were:

	1974		1975	
Concentrates and minerals	*Tonnes*	*1,000 kroner*	*Tonnes*	*1,000 kroner*
Copper concentrates	77,562	156,836	105,965	124,341
Pyrites	658,626	38,086	475,112	32,717
Iron ore and titaniferous concentrates	4,751,983	...	4,635,955	...
Zinc and lead concentrates	48,675	68,617	52,646	56,449
Molybdenum concentrates	—	—	—	—
Metals and alloys				
Copper	31,737	...	26,349	...
Nickel	43,224	...	37,056	...
Aluminium	648,213	729,054	594,828	2,464,550
Ferro-alloys	874,384	1,646,922	560,309	1,269,852
Semi-finished steel	816,842[2]	1,185,543	609,067[2]	1,004,875
Pig-iron	647,980	...	637,885	...
Zinc	72,434[1]	...	60,891[1]	...
Lead and tin	485[3]	...	326[3]	...

[1] Primary for sale and own use. [2] For sale and own use. [3] Secondary.

Agriculture. Norway, including Svalbard and Jan Mayen, is a barren and mountainous country. The arable soil is found in comparatively narrow strips, gathered in deep and narrow valleys and around fiords and lakes. Large, continuous tracts fit for cultivation do not exist. Of the total area, 80% is unproductive, 18% productive forest and 2% under cultivation.

	Area (hectares)			Produce (tonnes)		
Principal crops	*1974*	*1975*	*1976*	*1974*	*1975*	*1976*
Wheat	14,175	15,644	20,138	62,095	48,065	65,268
Rye	2,849	1,410	2,149	11,047	4,226	6,500
Barley	170,243	179,632	172,830	649,109	444,648	486,186
Oats	103,185	102,601	102,454	404,035	258,649	286,886
Mixed corn	535	386	496	1,870	806	1,353
Potatoes	29,726	24,854	27,908	847,238	435,386	483,941
Hay	366,508	362,202	364,667	2,407,048	2,132,307	2,264,147

Livestock, 20 June 1976: 21,750 horses, 921,231 cattle (385,669 milch cows), 1,667,488 sheep, 67,758 goats, 697,822 pigs, 3,798,369 hens.

Fur production in 1976–77 was as follows (1975–76 in brackets): Silver fox, 2,500 (2,100); blue fox, 267,000 (249,500); mink, 950,000 (1·05m.).

Forestry. The forests are one of the chief natural sources of wealth. The total area covered with forests is estimated at 83,300 sq. km, of which 64,800 sq. km is productive forest. 81% of the productive forest area consisted of conifers and 19% of broadleaves. Forests in public ownership cover 8,970 sq. km of productive forests and 5,820 sq. km of unproductive forests. Besides the home consumption of timber and fuel wood, the essential part of the cut is consumed as raw material in sawmills and the pulp and paper industry. The annual natural increase is about 13·2m. cu. metres. In 1975–76, 8·1m. cu. metres were cut for production of pulp, sawn timber and other industrial wood products.

Fisheries. The total number of persons engaged in fisheries in 1976 was 33,262, of whom 8,492 had another chief occupation. The number of fishing vessels with motor was 28,818 in 1976, and of these, 20,917 were open boats.

The value of sea fisheries in 1m. kroner in 1976 was: Cod, 876: mackerel, 163; coal-fish (saithe), 180; deep-water prawn, 155; haddock, 93; herring, 53; dogfish, 28. The catch totalled in 1976, 3·1m. tonnes, valued at 2,600m. kroner.

From 1 Jan. 1977 Norway established an economic zone of 200 nautical miles, and from 3 June 1977 a fishery protection zone of 200 nautical miles around Svalbard.

INDUSTRY AND TRADE

Industry. Industry is chiefly based on raw materials produced within the country (wood, fish, etc.) and on water power, of which the country possesses a large amount. The pulp and paper industry, the canning industry and the chemical and basic metal industries are the most important export manufactures. In the following table are given figures for industrial establishments in 1975, excluding one-man shops. Electrical plants, construction and building industry are not included. The values are given in 1m. kroner.

Industries	*Establish-ments*	*Number of Salaried staff*	*Number of Wage earners*	*Gross value of production*	*Value added by manufacture*
Coalmining	1	145	557	101	45
Crude petroleum and natural gas	1	623	392	4,296	3,815
Metal-mining	18	978	3,983	1,067	452
Other-mining	596	482	2,923	733	434
Food manufacturing	2,820	8,736	38,785	17,212	2,085
Beverages	75	1,157	3,556	1,556	980
Tobacco	6	423	808	771	616
Textiles	467	2,390	9,967	1,877	720
Clothing, etc.	452	1,598	8,304	1,053	483
Footwear	68	224	1,566	197	91
Leather	94	211	1,123	200	82
Wood	1,801	4,109	19,272	5,803	2,030
Furniture and fixtures	654	1,527	8,370	1,711	706
Pulp and paper	213	4,245	16,199	7,092	1,835
Printing and publishing	1,445	9,910	22,685	4,320	2,084
Chemical, industrial	63	3,035	5,510	3,290	1,194
Chemical, other	191	3,313	4,505	3,219	776
Petroleum, refined	7	300	385	4,167	449
Petroleum and coal	49	348	1,220	723	231
Rubber	92	619	2,223	423	189
Plastics	331	2,147	5,257	1,351	553
Ceramics	37	321	1,303	182	112
Glass	57	573	1,603	350	154
Other mineral products	522	2,065	6,656	2,417	975
Metal products, except machinery	1,509	5,742	21,746	4,942	2,195
Machinery and equipment	971	7,789	22,168	9,898	2,928
Transport equipment	956	9,616	42,414	11,927	4,118
Total (all included)	14,357	86,363	286,728	106,023	36,444

The following table sets forth the estimated value of net production, at factor cost by industries, in 1m. kroner:

	1971[1]	*1972*[1]	*1973*[1]	*1974*[1]	*1975*[1]	*1976*[1]
Agriculture	2,661	2,789	2,852	3,297	3,744	5,473
Forestry	870	767	835	1,164	1,536	1,588
Fishing	945	803	1,215	1,172	813	1,279
Mining and quarrying	506	571	635	726	742	832
Manufacturing	16,459	18,744	21,722	26,432	29,841	33,554
Crude petroleum and gas production and pipelines for crude oil transport	−389	−152	−317	−692	2,378	3,631
Electricity, gas and water	1,330	1,504	1,804	2,360	2,577	2,968
Construction[2]	6,070	6,558	6,997	8,469	9,414	10,142
Wholesale and retail trade	7,633	8,173	9,407	11,426	12,929	14,611
Restaurants and hotels	887	1,034	1,121	1,284	1,587	1,873
Water transport	4,500	4,526	5,705	6,234	3,805	3,070
Other transport	3,920	4,518	4,937	5,678	6,646	7,714
Financial institutions	2,253	2,571	3,084	3,930	4,242	5,235
Real estate	2,919	3,204	3,598	4,029	4,443	4,888
Business services	1,517	1,739	1,886	2,198	2,669	3,101
Government services, social and personal services	14,748	16,828	19,387	22,029	26,744	31,299
Imputed bank service charge	−2,015	−2,316	−2,758	−3,635	−4,061	−4,850
Net production at factor cost	64,814	71,861	82,110	96,101	110,049	126,408
+ Indirect taxes	16,597	18,193	20,331	22,745	26,471	31,165
− Subsidies	4,715	5,233	5,975	7,514	9,339	11,378
Net production (market price)	76,696	84,821	96,466	111,332	127,181	146,195

[1] Provisional figures.
[2] Including drilling of crude oil and natural gas wells.

Labour. The distribution of the population according to professions in 1970, showed 296,667 (7·7%) dependent on agriculture, forestry and gardening; 1,300,490 (33·6%) on mining, manufacturing, building, etc.; 447,248 (11·5%) on commerce; 353,207 (9·1%) on transport; 68,627 (1·8%) on fishery, sealing and whaling; 653,450 (16·9%) on public administration, liberal professions and services.

Commerce. Total imports and exports in calendar years (in 1,000 kroner):

	1971	*1972*	*1973*	*1974*	*1975*	*1976*
Imports	28,715,001	28,808,488	36,040,510	46,555,707	50,544,836	60,532,915
Exports	18,003,138	21,624,522	27,085,334	34,731,723	37,922,338	43,330,277

Trading according to countries was as follows (in 1,000 kroner):

	1975		*1976*	
Countries	*Imports*	*Exports*	*Imports*	*Exports*
Argentina	57,635	37,369	80,330	22,747
Australia and New Zealand	278,853	167,276	463,231	145,080
Belgium and Luxembourg	1,309,036	734,931	1,518,529	650,227
Brazil	544,153	327,637	558,516	328,753
Canada	975,889	303,624	1,105,775	529,657
Czechoslovakia	196,141	121,651	162,354	116,213
Denmark	2,934,085	2,745,227	3,341,356	3,057,156
Fed. Republic of Germany	7,920,009	3,727,208	9,381,313	4,122,121
Finland	1,461,190	1,037,904	1,368,261	932,618
France	1,897,796	1,371,495	2,218,758	1,098,754
India	38,427	45,776	72,919	75,619
Italy	784,924	589,251	1,024,253	755,210
Netherlands	2,279,765	1,266,062	3,319,422	1,563,835
Poland	365,075	330,804	896,011	594,954
Portugal	286,978	191,582	301,698	247,798
Spain	299,784	308,916	336,913	269,665
Sweden	9,725,138	6,010,574	11,110,582	6,137,209
Switzerland	909,412	291,622	1,075,773	374,444
UK	4,897,960	9,184,412	5,925,611	12,890,910
USA	3,609,447	2,191,151	5,646,989	2,031,250
USSR	449,464	496,814	470,289	417,823

Principal items of import in 1976 (in 1,000 kroner): Machinery, transport equipment, etc., 25,220,278; base metals and manufactures thereof, 5,855,210; fuel oil, etc., 6,781,527; textiles, 3,775,027; chemicals and related products, 3,451,904.

Principal items of export in 1976 (in 1,000 kroner): Machinery and transport equipment, 11,255,350; base metals and manufactures thereof, 8,573,928; crude oil, 6·7m.; pulp and paper, 3,217,847; edible animal products, 2,778,440.

Total trade between Norway and UK (British Department of Trade returns, in £1,000 sterling):

	1973	*1974*	*1975*	*1976*	*1977*
Imports to UK	325,217	408,394	593,227	622,816	846,669
Exports and re-exports from UK	240,897	333,611	390,768	473,539	761,851

COMMUNICATIONS

Roads. On 31 Dec. 1976 the length of the public roads (including roads in towns) was 78,116 km. Of these, 55,833 km were main roads; 36,976 km had some kind of paving, mostly bituminous and oil-gravel treatment, the rest being gravel-surfaced.

Number of registered motor vehicles (31 Dec. 1976) was 1,414,527, including 1,022,918 passenger cars (including taxis), 138,709 lorries and vans, 9,215 buses, 135,122 motor cycles and mopeds. The scheduled bus and lorry services in 1974 drove 4,058m. passenger-km and 307m. net ton-km.

Railways. The length of state railways on 31 Dec. 1976 was 4,241 km; of private companies, 16 km. On 2,440 km of state and 16 km of private railways electric power is installed. Total receipts of the state railways and road traffic in 1976 were 1,443m. kroner; total expenses (excluding interest on capital), 1,896m. kroner. The state railways carried 29·2m. tonnes of freight (of which, 17·9m. was iron ore on the Ofoten railway) and 32·7m. passengers.

Aviation. Det Norske Luftfartselskap (DNL) started its post-war activities on 1 April 1946. On 1 Aug. 1946 DNL, together with DDL (Danish Airlines) and ABA/SILA (Swedish Airlines), formed the 'Scandinavian Airlines System'—SAS. The 3 companies remained independent units, but all services were co-ordinated. In 1951 a new agreement was signed (retroactive from 1 Oct. 1950) according to which the 3 national companies became holding partners in a new organization which took over the entire operational system. Denmark and Norway hold each two-sevenths and Sweden three-sevenths of the capital, but they have joint responsibility towards third parties.

In the autumn of 1977 SAS had a fleet of 72 jet planes. Length of route network, about 262,000 km. Scheduled air services are run by SAS, Braathens South-American and Far East Air transport service (SAFE) and Wideroes Flyveselskap service. The Norwegian share of the scheduled air service run by SAS is two-sevenths of the SAS service on international routes and the total service in Norway.

	1,000 km flown	*Passengers carried*	*1,000 passenger-km*	*Post, luggage, freight and passengers (1,000 ton-km) Total*	*Of which post*
1974	48,372	3,367,534	2,738,000	348,000	12,000
1975	49,450	3,530,463	2,880,000	354,000	12,000
1976	52,266	3,853,483	3,180,000	397,000	13,000

Shipping. The total registered mercantile marine on 1 Jan. 1977 was 2,042 vessels, 27m. gross tons (steam and motor vessels above 100 gross tons). These figures do not include fishing and catching boats, tugs, salvage vessels, ice-breakers and similar special types of vessels, totalling 810 vessels of 346,000 gross tons.

Vessels in foreign trade 1972	*With cargoes*		*In ballast*		*Total*	
	No.	*Net tons*	*No.*	*Net tons*	*No.*	*Net tons*
Entered:						
Norwegian	6,450	7,238,172	2,583	2,397,882	9,033	9,636,054
Foreign	6,029	10,849,845	4,174	10,479,550	10,203	21,329,395
Total entered	12,479	18,088,017	6,757	12,877,432	19,236	30,965,449

Vessels in foreign trade 1972	With cargoes No.	Net tons	In ballast No.	Net tons	Total No.	Net tons
Cleared:						
Norwegian	7,723	7,744,639	1,325	1,881,453	9,048	9,626,092
Foreign	7,663	14,419,118	2,530	6,946,180	10,193	21,365,298
Total cleared	15,386	22,163,757	3,855	8,827,633	19,241	30,991,390

Goods (in 1,000 tonnes) in 1976 discharged, 21,966; loaded, 34,218, of which 17,513 was Swedish iron ore shipped from Narvik.

Post and Broadcasting. Number of telephones on 31 Dec. 1976 was 1,476,091 (37 per 100 of population). Receipts, 2,476·7m. kroner; expenses, 2,308·4m. kroner (interest on capital included). *Norsk Rikskringkasting* is a non-commercial enterprise operated by an independent state organization and broadcasts 1 programme on long-, medium, and short-waves and on FM. Local programmes are also broadcast. It broadcasts 1 TV programme from 817 transmitters. Colour programmes are broadcast by PAL system. Number of licences: radio, 1·3m.; television, 1,086,671.

Cinemas. There were 451 cinemas with a seating capacity of 143,256 in 1975.

Newspapers. There were 72 daily newspapers with a combined circulation of 1,619,000 in 1976.

JUSTICE, RELIGION, EDUCATION AND WELFARE

Justice. The judicature in Norway is common to both civil and criminal cases. The same judges, who are state officials, preside over both kinds of cases. The participation of lay assessors and jurors, summoned for each case, varies according to the civil or criminal nature of the case.

The ordinary Court of First Instance (*Herreds- og byrett*) is presided over by a judge who in criminal cases is, and in civil cases may be, assisted by 2 lay assessors, chosen by ballot from a panel elected by the district council. In criminal matters the Court of First Instance is generally competent in cases where the maximum penalty incurred is 5 years imprisonment. Altogether there are 100 Courts of First Instance. There is a Conciliation Council (*Forliksråd*) for each community, consisting of 3 men or women, elected by the district council, before which, as a general rule, civil cases must first be brought for mediation.

The Court of Second Instance (*Lagmannsrett*) is presided over by a judge, together with 2 other judges. In civil matters they may be assisted by lay assessors, ordinarily 4 but in some cases 2, chosen and elected in the same way as mentioned above. In criminal cases the lay element is a jury composed of 10 jurors. This court is a court of appeal in both civil and criminal cases. In addition, as a court of first instance, it takes cognizance of all criminal cases (other than those coming under the *Riksrett*—the court for impeachments) which do not come under the competence of the Court of First Instance. The kingdom is divided into 5 districts (*Lagdømmer*) for the purpose of the Courts of Second Instance.

The Supreme Court (*Høyesterett*) is the ultimate court of appeal. In criminal cases competence of the court, however, is limited to complaints against the application of laws, measuring out of the penalty and trial of the case of the subordinate courts. The Supreme Court consists of a president and 19 judges. In each single case the court consists of 5 judges. Criminal procedure is at present under revision.

All serious offences are prosecuted by the State. The public prosecution is led by a general prosecutor (*riksadvokat*) and there are 15 district prosecutors (*statsadvokater*). Counsel for the defence is, generally, paid by the State.

There are 3 central penal and correctional institutions for delinquents: inmates (17 Sept. 1977), 260 males and 26 females. There are also 35 local prisons in which were detained (17 Sept. 1977) 1,341 persons.

Religion. There is complete freedom of religion, the Evangelical Lutheran Church, however, being the national church, endowed by the State. Its clergy are nominated by the King. Ecclesiastically Norway is divided into 10 *Bispedømmer* (bishoprics), 90 *Prostier* (provostships or archdeaconries) and 604 *Prestegjeld* (clerical districts). There were 119,974 members of registered religious communities outside the

Evangelical Lutheran Church, subsidized by central government and local authorities in 1973. The Roman Catholics are under a Bishop at Oslo, a Vicar Apostolic at Trondheim and a Vicar Apostolic at Tromsø.

Education. In Norway the children normally start their school attendance the year they complete 7 and finish compulsory school the year they complete 16.

On 1 Oct. 1974 the number of primary schools and pupils were as follows: 3,423 primary schools, 584,978 pupils; 1 continuation school, 89 pupils; 88 special schools for the handicapped, 3,396 pupils.

On 1 Oct. 1974 the number of upper secondary schools, *i.e.*, folk high schools, secondary general schools and vocational schools, was 972 with 151,994 pupils.

There are in Norway 4 universities and 8 institutions equivalent to universities. In autumn 1976 the total number of students was 40,883. The University of Oslo, founded in 1811, had in 1976, 19,964 students. The University of Bergen, founded in 1948, had in 1976, 7,898 students. The University of Trondheim consists, for the time being, of the Norwegian Institute of Technology, founded in 1910, and the College of Arts and Science, founded in 1925. At each of them the number of students was in autumn 1976, 4,088 and 3,339 respectively. The University of Tromsø was established in 1968; 1,371 students were registered in autumn 1976. The Norwegian School of Economics and Business Administration had in 1976, 1,050 students, the Agricultural University of Norway, 1,030 students, the Free Faculty of Theology (Church of Norway), Oslo, 942 students, the State Veterinary College, 246 students, the Norwegian College of Physical Education and Sports, 361 students, the Oslo School of Architecture, 200 students, the State Academy of Music, 255 students and the National Academy of Liberal Arts, 114 students.

In 1976 there were 3,775 Norwegian students and pupils attending foreign universities and schools.

Health. In 1975 there were 7,302 doctors and 65,294 hospital beds.

Social Security. In 1976, 24,128m. kroner were paid under different social insurance schemes, amounting to 19·6% of the net national income.

The National Insurance Act of 17 June 1966, which came into force on 1 Jan. 1967, replaced the schemes relating to old age pensions, disability benefits, widows' and mothers' pensions, benefits to unmarried women 'survivors' benefit for children and rehabilitation aid. Schemes relating to health insurance, unemployment insurance and occupational injury insurance were revised and incorporated in National Insurance Scheme on 1 Jan. 1971.

The following conspectus gives a survey of schemes established by law. Many municipalities grant additional benefits to old-age, disablement and survivor's pensions.

Type of scheme	*Introduced*[1]	*Scope*	*Principal benefits as from 1 May 1977*[6]
National insurance	1967 (1977)		
Sickness benefits[2]	1911	All residents	Medical benefits: hospital expenses; about ¾ of doctors' fees, daily sickness allowances as from 1 May 1977: kr. 8 to 129 per day cash
Unemployment benefits[2]	1939	Nearly all wage-earners	Daily allowance during unemployment kr. 26 to 153 per day, contributions to training and retraining, removal expenses, wage subsidies in the case of relief work
Rehabilitation benefits[3]	1961	Persons unfit for work because of disablement and persons whohaveasubstantially limited general functional capacity.	Training; treatment; rehabilitation allowance grants and loans

For notes *see* bottom of table on p. 937.

Type of scheme	*Introduced*[1]	*Scope*	*Principal benefits as from 1 May 1977*[6]
Disability benefits[3]	1961	All residents disabled before the age of 67	*A basic grant* (15, 23 or 30% of the basic amount) and *an assistance grant* (25% of the basic amount) to persons with special needs. *Disability pension* to persons between 16 and 67 years of age, disabled by at least 50%, unfit for rehabilitation Full disability pension equals old age pension
Occupational injury benefits[2] (industrial workers 1895; fishermen 1909; seamen 1913; military personnel 1953, combined in the act of occupational injury insurance *1960*)	1960	All employed persons, school children and students; self-employed on a voluntary basis	The ordinary benefits of the National Insurance, *e.g.*, sickness and rehabilitation benefits, basic grants, assistance grants, disability pensions, and benefits to survivors granted according to special rules which in almost all cases are more favourable for the insured person—or his survivors than the ordinary rules *An occupational injury compensation*, alone or in addition to a disability pension
Old age pensions[3]	1937	All persons above 67 years of age	Basic pensions: Single, kr. 13,400; couples, kr. 20,100 per annum; supplementary pensions based on previous contributions; various allowances
Death grants	1967	All residents	20% of basic amount (kr. 13,400); 25% of basic amount in addition if deceased left a spouse or children
Survivors' benefits[3]	1965	All residents	Full pension = kr. 13,400 per annum + 55% of the supplementary pension due to the deceased, *transitional benefits*, assistance grant and educational allowances
Children's pension[3]	1958	Under 18 years, after loss of one or both parents	40% of basic amount (kr. 13,400) for first child, 25% for each additional child. If both parents are dead, full survivors' pension for first, 40% of basic amount for second, 25% third, etc., child
Benefits for unmarried mothers[3]	1965	Unmarried mothers	Maternity grant kr. 4,958, transitional benefit, full amount kr. 13,400 per annum, assistance grant and educational allowances
Benefits to unmarried persons forced to live at home[3]	1965	Unmarried persons under 67 years having stayed at home for at least 5 years to give necessary care and attention to parents or other near relatives	A transitional benefit, an educational allowance or a pension that equals the basic amount
Special supplement to National Insurance pensions or transitional benefits	1969 (1977)	Pensioners and persons with transitional allowance on basic rates	Full special supplement as from 1 May 1977 to married pensioner 30% of basic amount, others 31% of basic amount

For notes *see* bottom of table on p. 937.

Type of scheme	*Introduced*[1]	*Scope*	*Principal benefits as from 1 May 1977*[6]
Compensation supplement to National Insurance pensions or transitional benefits	1970	Pensioners, persons with transitional benefits (except unmarried mothers) or rehabilitation allowances	Full compensation supplement kr. 500 for single persons and kr. 750 for married couples
Family allowances	1946 (1976)	All families with children under 16 years	Kr. 708, for the first child, kr. 1,932 for the second, kr. 2,952 for the third, kr. 3,228 for the fourth and kr. 3,516 for the fifth and each additional child
War pensions	1946 (1977)	War victims, 1939–45	Pensions up to kr. 67,440 per annum; widows' and children's pensions
Special pension schemes:		Persons with at least:[4]	Maximum old-age pension for couples:
Seamen	1948 (1977)	150 months service (360 ,, ,,)	Kr. 43,848[5] per annum (officers) Kr. 31,320[5] ,, ,, (others)
Forestry workers	1952 (1976)	750 premium weeks (1,500 ,, ,,)	Kr. 12,000 per annum
Fishermen	1958 (1976)	750 premium weeks (1,500 ,, ,,)	Kr. 18,000 ,, ,,

[1] Date of latest revision in brackets.
[2] Transferred to national insurance scheme and revised in 1971.
[3] Transferred to national insurance scheme and revised in 1967.
[4] Requirements for maximum pensions in brackets.
[5] Supplements for service during war not included.
[6] Rates valid from 1 May.

Provisions have been laid down for the integration of more than one benefit, pension, etc., so as to limit the total amount.

SVALBARD

An archipelago situated between 10° and 35° E. long. and between 74° and 81° N. lat. Total area, 62,000 sq. km (24,000 sq. miles).

The main islands of the archipelago are Spitsbergen (formerly called Vestspitsbergen), Nordaustlandet, Edgeøya, Barentsøya, Prins Karls Forland, Bjørnøya, Hopen, Kong Karls Land, Kvitøya, and many small islands. The arctic climate is tempered by mild winds from the Atlantic.

The archipelago was probably discovered by Norsemen in 1194 and rediscovered by the Dutch navigator Barents in 1596. In the 17th century the very lucrative whale-hunting caused rival Dutch, British and Danish–Norwegian claims to sovereignty and quarrels about the hunting-places. But when in the 18th century the whale-hunting ended, the question of the sovereignty of Svalbard lost its significance; it was again raised in the 20th century, owing to the discovery and exploitation of coalfields. By a treaty, signed on 9 Feb. 1920 in Paris, Norway's sovereignty over the archipelago was recognized. On 14 Aug. 1925 the archipelago was officially incorporated in Norway.

Coal is the principal product. Of the 3 Norwegian and 3 Soviet mining camps, only 1 Norwegian and 2 Soviet camps are operating. A second Norwegian mining camp, Sveagruva, is being prepared for re-opening. Total population on 31 Dec. 1976 was 3,495, of which 1,171 in Norwegian communities, and 2,324 in Soviet communities. In 1976, 454,261 tonnes of coal were exported from the Norwegian and 454,942 tonnes from the Soviet mines.

Norwegian and foreign companies have been prospecting for oil. So far 3 deep drillings have been made, but oil and gas finds have not been reported.

There are Norwegian meteorological and radio stations at the following places: Bjørnøya, Hopen, Isfjord, Longyearbyen and Ny-Ålesund (for research). An airport near Longyearbyen opened in 1975.

Norsk Polarinstitutt, Skrifter. Oslo, from 1948 (under different titles from 1922)
Svalbard-Spitsbergen. Bergen, 1961
Greve, T., *Svalbard: Norway in the Arctic*. Oslo, 1975
Orvin, A. K., 'Twenty-five Years of Norwegian Sovereignty in Svalbard 1925–1950' (in *The Polar Record, 1951*)

JAN MAYEN

This bleak, desolate and mountainous island of volcanic origin and partly covered by a glacier, is situated 71° N. lat. and 8° 30′ W. long., 300 miles NNE of Iceland. The total area is 380 sq. km (147 sq. miles). Beerenberg, its highest peak, reaches a height of 2,277 metres. Volcanic activity, which had been dormant, was reactivated in Sept. 1970.

The island was possibly discovered by Henry Hudson in 1608, and it was first named Hudson's Tutches (Touches). It was again and again rediscovered and renamed. Its present name derives from the Dutch whaling captain Jan Jacobsz May, who indisputably discovered the island in 1614. It was uninhabited, but occasionally visited by seal hunters and trappers, until 1921 when Norway established a radio and meteorological station. On 8 May 1929 Jan Mayen was officially proclaimed as incorporated in the Kingdom of Norway. Its relation to Norway was finally settled by law of 27 Feb. 1930. A LORAN station (1959), a landing strip for aircraft (1963); and a CONSOL station (1968) have been built.

BOUVET ISLAND
Bouvetøya

This uninhabited volcanic island, mostly covered by glaciers and situated 54° 26′ S. lat. and 3° 24′ E. long., was discovered in 1739 by a French naval officer, Jean Baptiste Lozier Bouvet, but no flag was hoisted till, in 1825, Capt. Norris raised the Union Jack. In 1928 Great Britain waived its claim to the island in favour of Norway, which in Dec. 1927 had occupied it. A law of 27 Feb. 1930 declared Bouvetøya a Norwegian dependency. The area is 48 sq. km (19 sq. miles).

PETER I ISLAND
Peter I Øy

This uninhabited island, situated 68° 48′ S. lat. and 90° 35′ W. long., was sighted in 1821 by the Russian explorer, Admiral von Bellingshausen. The first landing was made in 1929 by a Norwegian expedition which hoisted the Norwegian flag. On 1 May 1931 Peter I Island was placed under Norwegian sovereignty, and on 24 March 1933 it was incorporated in Norway as a dependency. The area is 180 sq. km (69 sq. miles).

QUEEN MAUD LAND
Dronning Maud Land

On 14 Jan. 1939 the Norwegian Cabinet placed that part of the Antarctic Continent from the border of Falkland Islands dependencies in the west to the border of the Australian Antarctic Dependency in the east (between 20° W. and 45° E.) under

Norwegian sovereignty. The territory had been explored only by Norwegians and hitherto been ownerless. Since 1949 expeditions from various countries have explored the area. In 1957 Dronning Maud Land was given the status of a Norwegian dependency.

DIPLOMATIC REPRESENTATIVES

OF NORWAY IN GREAT BRITAIN (25 Belgrave Sq., London, SW1X 8QD)

Ambassador: Frithjof Jacobsen.

OF GREAT BRITAIN IN NORWAY (Thomas Heftyesgate 8, Oslo, 2)

Ambassador: A. T. Lamb.

OF NORWAY IN THE USA (3401 Massachusetts Ave., NW, Washington, D.C., 20007)

Ambassador: S. Chr. Sommerfelt (accredited 9 Nov. 1973).

OF THE USA IN NORWAY (Drammensveien 18, Oslo, 1)

Ambassador: Louis A. Lerner.

OF NORWAY TO THE UNITED NATIONS

Ambassador: Ole Ågård.

Books of Reference

Statistical Information: The Central Bureau of Statistics, Statistisk Sentralbyrå (Dronningensgate 16, Oslo 1), was founded in 1876 as an independent state institution. *Director:* Peter Jakob Bjerve. The earliest census of population was taken in 1769. The Sentralbyrå publishes the series *Norges Offisielle Statistikk*, Norway's official statistics (from 1828), and *Social Economic Studies* (from 1954). The main publications are:

Statistisk Årbok for Norge (annual, from 1880; from 1952 with English explanations)
Økonomisk Utsyn (annual, from 1935; with English summary from 1952)
Historisk Statistikk 1968 (historical statistics; bilingual Norwegian–English)
Statistisk Månedshefte (monthly, from 1880; with English index)

Norges Statskalender. From 1816; annual from 1877
Facts about Norway. Ed. by Aftenposten. 15th ed. Oslo, 1975
Andenaes, T., *The Constitution of Norway.* Oslo, 1951
Angerman, H., *The Fishing Industry in Norway.* Oslo, 1971
Bjorge, J. H. B., *Engelsk–amerikansk–norsk ordbok.* Oslo, 1959
Derry, T. K., *A History of Modern Norway, 1814–1972.* OUP, 1973
Ekeland, S., *Norway in the Modern World.* Oslo, 1976
Gleditsch, Th., *Engelsk–norsk ordbok.* 2nd ed. Oslo, 1948
Grønland, E., *Norway in English. Books on Norway . . . 1742–1959.* Oslo, 1961
Haugen, E., *Norwegian–English Dictionary.* Oslo, 1965
Helvig, M., *Norway: Land, People, Industries, a Brief Geography.* 3rd ed. Oslo, 1970
Holtedahl, O. (ed.), *Geology of Norway.* Oslo, 1960
Hove, O., *The System of Education.* Oslo, 1968
Knudsen, O., *Norway at Work.* Oslo, 1972
Larsen, K., *A History of Norway.* New York, 1948
Midgaard, J., *A Brief History of Norway.* Oslo, 1969
Nielsen, K., and Nesheim, A., *Lapp Dictionary: Lapp–English–Norwegian.* 5 vols. Oslo, 1963
Orvik, N. (ed.), *Fears and Expectations: Norwegian Attitudes Toward European Integration.* Oslo, 1972
Paine, R., *Coast Lapp Society.* 2 vols. Tromsø, 1957–65
Popperwell, R. G., *Norway.* London, 1972
Udgaard, N. M., *Great Power Politics and Norwegian Foreign Policy.* Oslo, 1973
Vorren, Ø. (ed.) *Norway North of 65,* Oslo, 1960

National Library: The University Library, Drammensvein 42b, Oslo. *Director:* John Brandrud.

OMAN

Capital: Muscat
Population: 750,000 (1977)
GNP per capita: US$2,680 (1976)

Saltanat Oman

AREA AND POPULATION. The Sultanate of Oman, known as the Sultanate of Muscat and Oman until 1970, is an independent sovereign state, situated in south-east Arabia. Its coastline is over 1,000 miles long and extends from the Ras al Khaimah Shaikdom near Bukha on the west side of the Musandum Peninsula to Ras Dharbat Ali, which marks the boundary between Oman and the territory of the People's Democratic Republic of Yemen. The Sultanate extends inland to the borders of the Rub' al Khali ('Empty Quarter') across three geographical divisions—a coastal plain, a range of hills and a plateau. The coastal plain varies in width from 10 miles near Suwaiq to practically nothing in the vicinity of Mutrah and Muscat towns, where the hills descend abruptly into the sea. These hills are for the most part barren except at the highest part of the mountainous region of the Jebel Akhdar (summit 9,998 ft) where there is some cultivation. The plateau has an average height of 1,000 ft. With the exception of oases there is little or no cultivation. North-west of Muscat the coastal plain, known as the Batinah, is fertile and prosperous. The date gardens extend for over 150 miles. Whereas the coastline between the capital, Muscat, and the southern province of Dhofar is barren, Dhofar itself is highly fertile. Its principal town is Salalah on the coast which is served by the port of Raysut.

In the valleys of the interior, as well as on the Batinah, date cultivation has reached a high level, and there are possibilities of agricultural development subject to present water resources and soil surveys. The average annual crop of dates is estimated at 50,000 tons, most of which is exported to India. Camels are bred in large numbers by the inland tribes. There are no industries of any importance, although copper will be an established industry by 1980, but fishing, water resources, soil and agricultural surveys are being undertaken.

The area has been estimated at about 105,000 sq. miles and the population at 750,000, chiefly Arabs; of these, some 40,000 live in Dhofar. The town of Muscat is the capital which, while formerly of some commercial importance, has now lost most of its trade to the adjacent port of Mutrah (combined populations, 25,000), the starting point for the trade routes into the interior. The population of both towns consists of pure Arabs, Indians, Pakistanis and Negroes; numerous merchants are Khojas (from Sind and Kutch) and Hindus (mostly from Gujarat and Bombay). Other ports are Sohar, Khaburah and Sur, Rasut in the south; none, however, affords shelter from bad weather.

The port of Gwadur and a small tract of country on the Balúchistán coast of the Gulf of Oman were handed over to Pakistan on 8 Sept. 1958.

The **Kuria Muria** islands were ceded to the United Kingdom in 1854 by the Sultan of Muscat and Oman for the purpose of a cable station. On 30 Nov. 1967 the islands were retroceded to the Sultan of Muscat and Oman, in accordance with the wishes of the population.

RULER. The present Sultan is Qaboos bin Said (born Nov. 1940). He took over from his father Said bin Taimur, on 23 July 1970 in a Palace *coup.*

National flag: Red, with a white panel in the upper fly and a green one in the lower fly, and in the canton the national emblem in white.

The Treaty of Friendship, Commerce and Navigation between Britain and the Sultan, signed on 20 Dec. 1951, reaffirmed the close ties which have existed between the British Government and the Sultanate of Oman for over a century and a half.

DEFENCE

Army. The Army is of 8 battalions with personnel of 11,800 with an artillery regiment, signals regiment, sapper company and armoured-car squadron.

Navy. The Navy comprises 7 fast missile armed patrol boats, an armed royal yacht, 2 patrol vessels (*ex*-Netherlands coastal minesweepers), a training ship, a support ship, 3 landing craft and 7 coastal patrol craft. Naval personnel in 1978 totalled 450 officers and ratings.

Air Force. The Air Force, formed in 1959, is being built up rapidly. It had in 1977 a ground attack squadron of Hunters, a counter-insurgency squadron of Strikemaster light jet attack aircraft, 3 BAC One-Eleven twin-turbofan transports, 2 Caribou, 7 Defender, 15 Skyvan and 2 Turbo-Porter light transports, and up to 35 Agusta-Bell 205, 214A and JetRanger helicopters for security duties. Delivery of 12 Jaguar supersonic attack aircraft was under way. Air defence force has more than 2 batteries of Rapier low-level surface-to-air missiles. Personnel about 750.

INTERNATIONAL RELATIONS

Membership. Oman is a member of UN and the Arab League.

ECONOMY

Budget. Revenue (1976) R.O. 577·3m. (454·7m. from oil); expenditure, 581·1m. (defence, 288·3m.).

Currency. The *Rial Omani* was introduced in Nov. 1972 replacing the *Rial Saidi*. It is divided into 1,000 *baiza*. There are notes of 100, 250 and 500 *baiza* and 1, 5 and 10 *Rial Omani* and coins of 2, 5, 10, 20, 50 and 100 *baiza*. The exchange rate in July 1975 was £1 = 748 *baiza*; US$1 = 340 *baiza*.

Weights and Measures. The metric system of measurement is being gradually introduced. The weights in use are 1 *kiyas* = the weight of 6 dollars of 5·9375 oz.; 24 kiyas = 1 Muscat *maund*; 10 maunds = 1 *farásala*; 200 maunds = 1 *bahár*. Rice is sold by the bag; other cereals by the following measures: 40 *palis* = 1 *ferrah*; 20 ferrah = 1 *khandi*.

OIL. The economy of Oman is dominated by the oil industry, which provides all Government revenue. Known reserves (1974) 6,000m. bbls. In 1937 Petroleum Concessions (Oman) Ltd, a subsidiary of the Iraq Petroleum Co., was granted a 75-year oil concession extending over the whole area except the district of Dhofar. A concession covering Dhofar was granted in 1953 to Dhofar Cities Service Petroleum Corporation; it expires in 25 years from the date of commercial production, with option to renew for another 25 years.

In 1964 Petroleum Development (Oman) Ltd, re-formed in 1967 as a subsidiary of Royal Dutch Shell (with an 85% interest), Compagnie Française des Pétroles (with 10%) and Gulbenkian interests with their traditional 5% announced that drilling had proved sufficient reserves for the company to go into commercial production. The production of oil began in 1967 at a rate of 200,000 bbls per day and expanded to 360,000 bbls per day by the end of 1969. However, during late 1970 and early 1971 technical difficulties affected production and the 1971 production of 105·56m. bbls was 15m. down on 1970. Production (1976) averaged 365,000 bbls per day; total production for 1976 was 133·8m. bbls. Total oil exports in 1972 were 103·2m. bbls and in 1973, 106·9m. bbls.

In 1973 the 4 connected oilfields at Fahud, Natih, Yibal and Al-Huwaisah together produced at an average rate of 292,947 bbls per day. The average rose to about 375,000 bbls per day from Jan. 1975, when the 3 Ghaba fields started producing. The Saih Rawl field, when fully operational, should increase daily production to around 400,000 bbls per day.

Petroleum Development (Oman) Ltd is also drilling in the north of Dhofar, where quantities of relatively heavy oil are known to exist. It is not yet clear whether this will be a commercial proposition.

The German company Wintershall A.G. heads a consortium exploring an off-shore concession in the Gulf of Oman. Other off-shore concessions are held by Sun

Oil (south-west of Masirah Island) and ELF–ERAP (off the Musandam coast). None of these companies has yet announced finds.

Early in 1974 the Oman Government purchased a 25% share in Petroleum Development (Oman) Ltd, increasing this in July to 60%. Shell interest is now only 34%. Oman is not a member of the Organization of Petroleum Exporting Companies (OPEC) nor of the Organization of Arab Petroleum Exporting Countries (OAPEC), but under the terms of the concessions granted to the companies the Government of the Sultanate is assured of treatment equal to that received by members of OPEC.

COMMERCE. Trade is mainly with UK, India, Australia, Japan and the neighbouring Gulf States. In the calendar year 1975 imports amounted to R.O. 231·4m., excluding duty-free imports for government use. Chief imports were rice, wheat, flour, milk and milk products, machinery, cement, vehicles and accessories, electrical goods, petroleum products and building materials. The main countries exporting to Oman in 1973 were UK, UAE, Japan, India, Australia, Netherlands and the Federal Republic of Germany.

Exports, which, excluding oil, consisted of dates, limes, dried fish, tobacco leaf, fruits and vegetables, were valued at R.O. 347m. in 1975 (non-oil, R.O. 1·1m.).

Trade with UK (British Department of Trade returns, in £1,000 sterling):

	1972	*1973*	*1974*	*1975*	*1976*	*1977*
Imports to UK	2,895	15,930	32,814	113,997	73,234	15,147
Exports and re-exports from UK	17,210	22,199	42,927	97,994	102,288	172,856

COMMUNICATIONS

Roads. A network of adequate graded roads links all the main sectors of population, and only a few mountain villages are not accessible by Land-Rover. A rapid road construction programme began in 1976, and by the end of the year there were 1,272 km of paved roads and 8,500 km of graded roads. The road from Sohar to Buraimi is complete. In Dhofar tarmac roads have been completed from Raysut through Salalah to Taqa and also Bid Bid to Sur. Proposed future contracts for tarmac roads include: Al Qabil to Ibri, 140 miles; Ibri to Nizwa, 80 miles.

Aviation. Gulf Air run regional services in and out of Seeb international airport (20 miles from Muscat) to Bahrain, Doha, Abu Dhabi, Dubai, Karachi and Bombay. They and British Airways each operate daily flights to and from London. Other airlines serving Muscat are MEA, Kuwait Airlines, PIA, Air India, Iran Air, TMA (cargo) and Trade Winds (cargo).

Shipping. In Mutrah the new deep-water port (named Mina Qaboos) was completed in 1974 at a cost of R.O. 18·2m. It provides 12 berths, 9 of which are deep-water berths, warehousing facilities and a harbour for dhows and coastal vessels. The annual handling capacity has been raised to 1·5m. tons.

Post and Broadcasting. There are Sultanate post offices in Muscat and Mutrah, relying solely upon a Post Office Box system for delivery. Omantel maintain a telegraph office at Muscat and an automatic telephone exchange (7,307 lines, 1977) which includes Mutrah, Bait-al-Falaj and Mina al-Fahal, the oil company terminal. A high-frequency radio link with Bahrain was opened in Aug. 1972 providing communications with other parts of the world. Internally, there are radio telephone, telex and telegraph services direct between Salalah and Muscat, and a VHF radio link between Seeb international airport and Muscat. The airport is also served by a SITA telex system.

A colour television service covering Muscat and the surrounding area started transmission in Nov. 1974. A television service for Dhofar opened in 1975.

EDUCATION AND WELFARE

Education. Until 1970 there were only 3 schools in Oman, and it has been estimated that as many as 80% of Omanis are still illiterate. In Sept. 1976 there were 216 schools (64,975 pupils), and over 30% of children of primary school age were receiving education. Secondary education is still extremely limited, and all Omanis with secondary or further education have obtained it abroad, but plans are being implemented for the development of technical and agricultural training and craft training at intermediate and secondary level. There are also programmes to combat adult illiteracy.

Health. Health services in 1976 were widely spread with 13 hospitals in use and 1 more planned, 11 health centres and 40 dispensaries. There are also Save the Children Fund Welfare Clinics at Sohar and Sur.

DIPLOMATIC REPRESENTATIVES

OF OMAN IN GREAT BRITAIN (64 Ennismore Gdns, London, SW7 5DN)

Ambassador: Nasir bin Seif El Bualy.

OF GREAT BRITAIN IN OMAN (PO Box 300, Muscat)

Ambassador: C. J. Treadwell, CMG.

OF OMAN IN THE USA (2342 Massachusetts Ave., NW, Washington, DC., 20008)

Ambassador: Farid Mubarak Al-Henai.

OF THE USA IN OMAN (PO Box 966, Muscat)

Ambassador: William D. Wolle.

OF OMAN TO THE UNITED NATIONS

Ambassador: Mahoud Aboul-Nasr.

Books of Reference

Achievements. Ministry of Health. Oman, 1975
Phillips, W., *Unknown Oman*. London, 1967.—*Oman: A History*. London, 1968
Skeet, I., *Muscat and Oman: The End of an Era*. London, 1974
Thesiger, W., *Arabian Sands*. London, 1959

PAKISTAN

Capital: Islamabad
Population: 74·9m. (1977)
GNP per capita: US$170 (1976)

Islamic Republic of Pakistan

HISTORY. Pakistan was constituted as a Dominion on 14 Aug. 1947, under the provisions of the Indian Independence Act, 1947, which received the royal assent on 18 July 1947. The Dominion consisted of the following former territories of British India: Balúchistán, East Bengal (including almost the whole of Sylhet, a former district of Assam), North-West Frontier, West Punjab and Sind; and those States which had acceded to Pakistan.

On 23 March 1956 an Islamic republic was proclaimed after the Constituent Assembly had adopted the draft constitution on 29 Feb.

On 7 Oct. 1958 President Mirza declared martial law in Pakistan, dismissed the central and provincial Governments, abolished all political parties and abrogated the constitution of 23 March 1956. Field Marshal Mohammad Ayub Khan, the Army Commander-in-Chief, was appointed as chief martial law administrator and assumed office on 28 Oct. 1958, after Maj.-Gen. Iskander Mirza had handed all powers to him. His authority was confirmed by a ballot in Feb. 1960. He proclaimed a new constitution on 1 March 1962.

On 25 March 1969 President Ayub Khan resigned and handed over power to the army under the leadership of Maj.-Gen. Agha Muhammad Yahya Khan who immediately proclaimed martial law throughout the country, appointing himself chief martial law administrator on the same day. On 29 March 1970 the Legal Framework Order was published, defining a new constitution: Pakistan to be a federal republic with a Moslem Head of State; the National Assembly and Provincial Assemblies to be elected in free and periodical elections, the first of which was held on 7 Dec. 1970.

At the general election the Awami League based in East Pakistan and led by Sheikh Mujibur Rahman gained 167 seats and the Peoples' Party 90. Martial law continued pending the settlement of differences between East and West, which developed into civil war in March 1971. The war ended in Dec. 1971 and the Eastern province declared itself an independent state, Bangladesh. On 20 Dec. 1971 President Yahya Khan resigned and Mr Z. A. Bhutto became President and chief martial law administrator. On 30 Jan. 1972, Pakistan withdrew from the Commonwealth.

A new Constitution was adopted by the National Assembly on 10 April 1973 and enforced on 14 Aug. 1973. It provided for a federal parliamentary system with the President as constitutional head and the Prime Minister as chief executive. President Bhutto stepped down to become Prime Minister and Fazal Elahi Chaudhry was elected President.

Governors-General of Pakistan: Quaid-I-Azam Mohammed Ali Jinnah (14 Aug. 1947–11 Sept. 1948); Khawaja Nazimuddin (14 Sept. 1948–18 Oct. 1951; took over the premiership after the assassination of Liaquat Ali Khan); Ghulam Mohammad (19 Oct. 1951–6 Oct. 1955); Maj.-Gen. Iskander Mirza (assumed office of President on 6 Oct. 1955, elected President on 5 March 1956).

EVENTS. As a result of a deadlock between the Government and various political parties in discussing issues concerning the general elections held in March 1977 and the possibility of new elections, the maintenance of law and order deteriorated. With the aim of avoiding chaotic conditions, the Chief of the Army Staff, Gen. M. Zia-ul-Haq, proclaimed martial law throughout the country on 5 July 1977, and the armed forces took control of the administration. The General also assumed the office of chief martial law administrator.

He announced that the elections due to be held on 18 Oct. 1977 would have to be postponed because of the volatile political situation and the fact that many cases (ranging from alleged murder to corruption) involving leaders of the previous regime were pending in the superior courts. A fresh date for elections would be announced as soon as the courts had given their verdict in these cases.

AREA AND POPULATION. Pakistan is bounded north-west by Afghánistán, north by the USSR and China, east by India and south by the Arabian Sea. The total area of Pakistan is 307,374 sq. miles (796,095 sq. km); population (1972 census), 64·89m.; males, 34,417,000; females, 30,475,000. Density, 212 per sq. mile. Estimate (1977) 74,955,000. This excludes Jammu and Kashmir, Gilgit and Baltistan, Junagadh, Manavadar and Pakistan enclaves in India. In 1976 the birthrate was 40·5 per 1,000 population.

The population of the principal cities (census of 1972) is:

Bahawalpur	133,956	Jhang	135,722	Multan	542,195	Sargoda	201,407
Gujranwala	360,419	Karachi	3,498,634	Peshawar	268,366	Shah Faisa-labad	820,000
Gujrat	100,581	Kasur	102,531	Quetta	156,000		
Hyderabad	628,310	Lahore	2,165,372	Rawalpindi	615,392	Sialkot	203,779
Islamabad	77,318	Mardan	115,218	Sahiwal	106,213	Sukkur	158,876

Population of the provinces (census of 1972) was:

	Area (sq. miles)	*Total population (1,000)*	*Male (1,000)*	*Female (1,000)*	*Density per sq. mile*
North-West Frontier Province	28,773	8,402	4,376	4,026	296
Federally Administered Tribal Areas	10,510	2,507	1,291	1,216	237
Federal Capital Territory, Islamabad	350	235	130	105	671
Punjab	79,284	37,374	19,871	17,503	475
Sind	54,407	13,965	7,474	6,491	260
Balúchistán	134,050	2,409	1,275	1,134	18

Language. The commonest languages are Urdu and Punjabi. English is used in business and in central government.

CONSTITUTION AND GOVERNMENT. Under the Constitution of 1973 Parliament is bi-cameral, comprising the National Assembly and the Senate. The strength of the National Assembly is 210 including 10 women. The Senate consists of 63 members, 14 from each Province, 5 from Federally-Administered Tribal areas and 2 from the federal capital area, elected by the members of the Provincial Assemblies. A constitutional amendment of 29 March 1976 provided 6 National Assembly seats reserved for non-Moslem minority representatives.

With the proclamation of martial law the Constitution has been kept in abeyance, but not abrogated: it is subject to the laws (Continuance in Force) Order, 1977, and any Order made by the President and any Regulation issued by the Chief Martial Law Administrator. All existing laws, other than the Constitution (subject to any Order of the President or Regulation made by the Chief Martial Law Administrator and until altered, amended or repealed by the competent authority) will continue in force.

President: Fazal Elahi Chaudhry.

Chief Martial Law Administrator responsible for law administrator's secretariat, defence, defence production, information and broadcasting, atomic energy commission, health, population planning and social welfare, science and technological research, aviation, culture and sports, tourism: Gen. M. Zia-ul-Haq, assumed office 5 July 1977.

Council of advisers:

Secretary-general in chief, planning and co-ordination of inter-departmental and inter-provincial affairs: G. Ishaq Khan. *Law and parliamentary affairs, religious and minority affairs:* A. N. Brohi. *Establishment:* Lieut.-Gen. F. A. Chisti. *Shipping, ports and export promotion:* M. Gokal. *Industries and production:* Lieut.-Gen. H. Khan. *Security, labour, local government, rural development:* Lieut.-Gen. G. H.

Khan. *Interior:* Air Marshal Iham ul-Haq. *Secretary-general, finance and economic co-ordination, economic affairs, statistics, water and power, agrarian management:* A. G. N. Kazi. *Railways:* N. A. Aureshi. *Chairman of the National Council of social welfare, environment and urban affairs, housing and works:* M. Ali. *Political affairs and commerce:* S. M. B. Somroo. *Education:* M. A. Hoti. *Food, agriculture, co-operatives and livestock:* A. Mohammad. *Attorney-General:* S. Pirzada. *Secretary-general, foreign affairs:* A. Shahi. *Petroleum and natural resources:* Rear-Adm. R. M. Sheikh.

National flag: Green, charged at the centre, with a white crescent and white 5-pointed star, a white vertical stripe at the mast to one-quarter of the flag.

Local Government. Pakistan comprises the provinces of the Punjab, the North-West Frontier, Sind and Balúchistán, the states of Bahawalpur and Khairpur, the Balúchistán States Union, the frontier states and the tribal areas of Balúchistán and the north-west. These were merged into a single unit on 14 Oct. 1955. In July 1970 the single unit was dissolved into the original 4 provinces. The provincial capitals are Peshawar (NW Frontier Province), Lahore (Punjab), Karachi (Sind) and Quetta (Balúchistán). Provincial governments are elected and are led by a Chief Minister and his cabinet. Provincial governors are appointed by the President.

Within the provinces there are divisions (15 in 1977) administered by Commissioners appointed by the President; the divisions are divided into districts and agencies (51 in 1977) administered by Deputy Commissioners or Collectors who are responsible to the Provincial Governments.

Kashmir. Between one-third and one-half of Kashmir is controlled by Pakistan. This area is known as Azad (Free) Kashmir, and is the northern and western portion of the country. The people of Azad Kashmir have their own Constitution known as 'The Azad Jammu and Kashmir Interim Constitution Act 1974', which is in accordance with the concept of the local Government in the State, having its own Assembly (42 members including 2 women), their own Council (of 14 members), High Court and Supreme Court. The Act envisages a Parliamentary form of Government with a Prime Minister as the executive head and the President as the Constitutional head.

Interim Government at 1 March 1978:

President: Sardar Mohammad Ibrahim.

Chief Executive: Brig. Mohammad Hayat Khan.

Elections to the Legislative's 40 general seats are to be held within 10 days of the general elections in Pakistan, according to a presidential proclamation of 8 Oct. 1977. The seat of government is Muzaffarabad.

(For the area on the Indian side of the cease-fire line in Kashmir, *see* p. 633.)

DEFENCE

Army. The Pakistan Army consists of 14 infantry divisions and 2 armoured divisions, 2 independent armoured brigades and 1 air defence brigade. Total strength, 400,000. General headquarters is at Rawalpindi. The entire officers cadre receives its precommission training in the Military Academy at Kakul.

Navy. The fleet comprises 4 diesel-powered patrol submarines (built in France in 1967–71), 6 midget submarines, 1 light cruiser (cadet training ship), 6 destroyers, 2 fast anti-submarine frigates, 14 fast gunboats, 6 fast (hydrofoil) torpedo boats, 1 survey ship (*ex*-frigate), 7 coastal minesweepers, 3 patrol craft, 2 oilers, 1 rescue ship, 1 water carrier and 3 tugs.

Two 'Whitby' class frigates to have been acquired from Britain were not taken up; instead 2 destroyers were purchased from USA in 1977.

The principal naval base and dockyard are at Karachi. Naval personnel in 1978 totalled 950 officers and 10,050 ratings.

The submarine *Ghazi* (*ex*-USS *Diablo*), transferred from the US Navy in 1964, was sunk during the India–Pakistan war in Dec. 1971. The destroyer *Khaibar* (*ex*-HMS *Cadiz*), purchased from Britain in 1956, was also sunk in Dec. 1971, as were 3 patrol craft built in Britain in 1965 and a coastal minesweeper acquired from USA in 1955.

Air Force. The Pakistan Air Force came into being on 14 Aug. 1947. It has its headquarters at Peshawar and is organized within 3 air defence sectors, in the northern, central and southern areas of the country. Tactical units include 1 squadron of B-57B (Canberra) bombers, 4 squadrons of Mirage III-EP/5 supersonic fighters, 7 squadrons of MiG-19 (F-6) supersonic fighter-bombers acquired from China, Mirage III-RP and RT-33 jet reconnaissance aircraft, C-130 Hercules turboprop transports and CH-47 Chinook troop-carrying helicopters. Flying training schools are equipped with Saab Supporter armed piston-engined primary trainers, T-37B/C jet trainers supplied by the USA, Mirage III-DPs, MiG-15Us, F-86Fs and other types. Three Breguet Atlantics, Albatros amphibians and Sea King and HH-43 helicopters, plus a small number of Alouette III helicopters, perform maritime reconnaissance, search and rescue duties. There is a flying college at Risalpur and an apprentices' college at Korangi Creek. Total strength in 1977 was about 300 combat aircraft and 18,000 all ranks.

INTERNATIONAL RELATIONS

Membership. Pakistan is a member of UN and the Colombo Plan.

Treaties. A mutual defence assistance agreement between Pakistan and the USA was signed in Karachi on 19 May 1954.

ECONOMY

Planning. All government plans and policies aim primarily at economic self-reliance. The fourth 5-year plan (1970–75) target was a 6·5% annual growth rate and an expenditure of Rs 75,000m. (49,000m. for the public sector). The fourth plan aimed at an increasingly self-reliant economy, with less disparity in *per capita* income and a workable synthesis between economic growth and social justice. Main concerns were power, water supply, preventing water-logging and salinity, improving transport and communication systems, especially in backward areas, and increasing industrial investment. The GNP increased by 5% during 1975–76, when fixed capital investment stood at Rs. 22,500m.

Agriculture had been subsidized at Rs 300m. to Rs 400m. a year, excluding indirect subsidies through price maintenance. During the fourth plan the subsidies policy was reviewed and agricultural policy reconsidered with particular reference to the need for expansion in processing and exporting food surplus. More funds were allocated to housing, slum clearance, sewerage and domestic water supply. The People's Works Programme, the Integrated Rural Development Programme and the Agrovilles were set up to develop rural areas and generate employment.

A draft fifth plan (1977–83) provides for a total investment of Rs 215,000m.

Budget. The following table shows the budget for the years 1976–77 and 1977–78 in Rs 1m.:

	1976–77	*1977–78*
Gross revenue receipts	20,012·2	23,956·6
Less provincial share in federal taxes	2,913·0	3,273·4
Net federal revenue	17,099·2	20,683·2
Non-development revenue expenditure	16,147·1	20,282·4
Capital:		
Internal resources	2,593·7	3,525·2
External resources	12,713·7	11,983·6
Total resources	15,307·4	15,508·8
Development outlay	17,000·0	17,000·0

Currency. The monetary unit is the Pakistan *rupee*. The official rate is Rs = £0·06. Decimal coinage was introduced on 1 Jan. 1961. The rupee, which previously consisted of 64 *pice*, now consists of 100 *paisas*. The notes are of Rs 100, 50, 10 and 5 denominations issued by the State Bank in the name of the Government, and Re 1 issued by the State Bank incurring no liability; the coinage in the decimal series is 0·5, 0·25, 0·05 and 0·01 rupee.

Currency in circulation in May 1977 amounted to Rs 16,471·5m.

Banking. The State Bank of Pakistan is the central bank; it came into operation as the Central Bank on 1 July 1948 with an authorized capital of Rs 30m. and was nationalized in Jan. 1974. As on 30 June 1976 total assets or liabilities of the issue department amounted to Rs 13,395·2m. and those of the banking department Rs 14,665·4m.; reserve fund, Rs 100m. and total deposits, Rs 10,120·8m. It is the sole bank of issue for Pakistan, custodian of foreign exchange reserves and banker for the federal and provincial governments and for scheduled banks. It also manages the rupee public debt of federal and provincial governments. It provides short-term loans to the Government and commercial banks and short- and medium-term loans to Provincial Co-operative banks and specialized banks. The State Bank raised the bank rate from 9 to 10% with effect from 7 June 1977, but it provides finance for export sales of locally manufactured machinery at 3% per annum below bank rate and for local sales at 2% per annum below the rate charged by the financing institutions.

There were 24 scheduled banks (banks with capital and reserves of an aggregate value of not less than Rs 0·5m.) in Pakistan on 30 Dec. 1976. Of these 9 were Pakistani including 5 commercial banks (National Bank of Pakistan, Habib Bank Ltd, United Bank Ltd, Muslim Commercial Bank Ltd and Allied Bank Ltd), 2 specialized banks (Agricultural Development Bank of Pakistan and Industrial Development Bank of Pakistan) and 2 co-operative banks (Punjab Provincial Co-operative Bank and Federal Bank for Co-operatives). Pakistani scheduled banks were nationalized in Jan. 1974. In addition, there were 15 foreign banks operating in Pakistan on 30 Dec. 1976. The total number of offices of scheduled banks was 6,103. Total deposits of all the scheduled banks stood at Rs 33,513·7m. and total assets at Rs 66,881·3m. on 30 June 1976. The National Bank of Pakistan acts as an agent of the State Bank for transacting Government business and managing currency chests at places where the State Bank has no offices of its own.

Weights and Measures. The principal units in all the scales of weights are the maund, seer and tola, and the standard weights for each of these are 82·29 lb., 2·057 lb. and 11·664 grammes respectively.

The decimal system already used in coinage is to be introduced in weights and measures in some Government agencies.

ENERGY AND NATURAL RESOURCES

Electricity. Installed capacity (1970) by type of generation: Steam and gas turbine, 1,028,700 kw.; hydro-electric, 667,800 kw.; diesel, 46,900 kw.; captive industrial capacity, 180,000 kw. Total available electrical energy at the end of 1970, 6,700m. kwh.; total installed capacity, 1·92m. kw.

Oil. Oil comes mainly from the Potowar Plain, from fields at Meyal, Tut, Balkassar, Joya Mair and Dhullian. Production in 1977, 453,000 tonnes. Oil reserves were also found at Dhodak in Dec. 1976.

Gas. Gas pipelines from Sui to Karachi (345 miles) and Multan (200) supply natural gas to industry and domestic consumers. Gas currently provides about 38% of all energy. Reserves are estimated at 17,000,000m. cu. ft; additional pipelines completed or under construction will enable production to increase. Production, 1977 (provisional), 192,000m. cu. ft.

Water. The Indus water treaty of 1960, concluded between India and Pakistan, has created the basis for a large-scale development programme. The Indus Basin Development Fund Agreement has been subscribed by Australia, Canada, Federal Republic of Germany, New Zealand, UK and USA and is administered by the International Bank; the works to be constructed call for expenditure of US$1,000m. The main purpose of the treaty is the division of the water power of the Indus and its 5 tributaries between India and Pakistan. After the construction of some 460 miles of canals, the Indus and the 2 western tributaries will serve Pakistan and the entire flow of the 3 eastern tributaries will be released for use in India.

The largest project is the construction of the Tarbela Dam, an earth-and-rock-filled dam on the river Indus, 485 ft high, which is designed to irrigate 1m. acres and to provide power.

The Lloyd Barrage and Canal Construction Scheme, which consists of a barrage across the river Indus at Sukkur and 7 canals—4 on the left and 3 on the right bank—is designed to provide an assured supply of water to an area of about 1·83m. acres in territory which used to be dependent upon inundation canals. It also brings under irrigation a further area of 3·62m. acres in Sind, the Khairpur state and the Nasirabad tehsil in Balúchistán.

Another barrage across the Indus, 4½ miles north of Kotri, called the Ghulam Muhammad Barrage, was completed in 1955; the fourth and last of the main canals taking off it was opened in 1958. The irrigable area to be served by this scheme is about 2·75m. acres in the Lower Sind area.

The Tausa barrage on the Indus, 80 miles downstream of Kalabagh, was completed in 1958. It will eventually irrigate 1·4m. acres in the Muzaffargah and Dera Ghazi Khan districts.

The Gudu barrage, 10 miles from Kashmore, serves 2·6m. acres of the rice-growing tracts north of Sukkur; it was completed in 1962.

The province of the Punjab set up in 1949 the Thal Development Authority to colonize the Thal desert between the Indus and Jhelum rivers. The project envisages the irrigation of some 2m. acres and the establishment of a balanced economy of agriculture, trade and industry.

The Chashma canal, to be completed by 1982, will carry water 172 miles across Dera Ismail Khan from the Chashma barrage on the Indus, irrigating 350,000 acres of virgin land. The canal will extend into Punjab and there irrigate 220,000 acres.

The Mangla Dam on the Jhelum was inaugurated in Nov. 1967; it generates 400,000 kw. of hydro-electric power.

Minerals. Coal is mined at Sharigh and Harnai on the Sind–Pishin railway and in the Bolan pass, also in Sor Range in the Quetta–Pishin district; total recoverable reserves, about 450m. tonnes, mainly low-grade. Chromite is extracted in the Zhob district near Hindubagh. Limestone is quarried in small quantities. Gypsum is mined in the Sibi district near Spintangi railway station. Iron ore is being worked in Kalabagh. Uranium has been found in Dera Ghazi Khan and copper at Saindak (about 524m. tonnes of ore). The quantity (in 1,000 tonnes) of the chief minerals produced in 1975–76 was as follows: Chromite, 10; gypsum, 429; limestone, 2,743; rock salt, 419; coal, 1,212.

Agriculture. The entire area in the north and west is covered by great mountain ranges. The rest of the country consists of a fertile plain watered by 5 big rivers and their tributaries. Agriculture is the occupation of a vast majority of the population, and is dependent almost entirely on the irrigation system based on these rivers. The main crops are wheat, cotton, maize, sugar-cane and rice, while the Quetta and Kalat divisions (Balúchistán) are known for their fruits and dates.

By 31 March 1977, 3·34m. acres of land had been taken away from landlords, and 1·48m. acres had been distributed to 137,005 tenants. An ordinance of Jan. 1977 reduced the upper limit of land holding to 100 irrigated or 200 non-irrigated acres; it also replaced the former land revenue system with a new agricultural income tax, from which holders of up to 25 irrigated or 50 unirrigated acres are exempt. Land resumed by the Government, unless required for public purposes, is granted free to tenants who were in possession and cultivating during certain seasons of 1975 and 1976. About 9·5m. of the 10m. landowners held less than 25 acres; about 35,000 landowners would have had to surrender land. Of the surveyed area of 156m. acres, cultivated land accounts for 63m. acres, of which 11m. acres consist of fallow land, so that the net area sown is 52m. acres. The Mangla Dam scheme has begun the reclamation of 3m. acres of salt-affected land; this and other schemes had reclaimed between 7m. and 8m. acres by 1976. The main problem in agriculture is pest control; pesticide imports for 1976–77 are estimated at 6,045 tonnes valued at Rs 293·8m., increasing the acreage sprayed from 8·56m. to 11·92m.

Production, 1976–77 (in 1,000 tons): Rice (cleaned), 2,589; wheat, 9,000; sugar-cane (gur), 27,709; cotton (lint, 1,000 bales), 2,416.

Livestock (FAO estimate, 1976): Cattle, 13·6m.; buffaloes, 10·8m.; sheep, 19·19m.; goats, 14·1m.; poultry, 34·6m.

Forestry. There were (1976) 7·3m. acres of reserved and protected forests and 10·6m. acres managed as pasture ranges by the Forest Department. Of the forests 1·5m. acres are in Punjab, 1·66m. in Balúchistán, 1·46m. in Sind and 2·65m. in the North-

West Frontier Province. Forests produce an annual average of over 20m. cu. ft of timber and 16m. cu. ft of fuel. Annual value of this and other produce, about Rs. 60m. Forest lands are also used as national parks, wildlife and game reserves.

Fisheries. Landings (1975) in inland waters, 37,600 tonnes; of sea fish, 161,500 tonnes.

INDUSTRY AND TRADE

Industry. Industry employs about 10% of the population. Woollen and other cottage industries, especially cotton weaving (with 220,000 workers) and carpet weaving, have made great strides. The population engaged in the fishing industry is about 39,000. In 1972 public sector companies were re-organized under a Board of Industrial Management. In 1976 all cotton-ginning, rice-husking and flour-milling plants, were nationalized (except small flour-mills of less than 6 rollers outside Balúchistán). Pakistan is self-sufficient in cotton cloth and sugar. Capacity of chemical fertilizer plants in 1976–77 was 335,000 tons; cement plants, 3·4m. tons; both are being expanded (to 1·29m. tons and 5·8m. tons respectively). A public sector steel-mill is being built at Karachi, capacity 1·1m. tons and begins trial production in 1978–79. Also recently completed are a heavy mechanical complex and a heavy forge and foundry plant at Taxila.

Production 1975–76: Cotton cloth, 622m. yd; cotton yarn, 770·8m. lb., cement, 3·15m. tons; refined sugar, 630,000 tons; fertilizers, 832,124 tonnes.

Labour. The Labour Force Survey of 1974–75 gave the total work force as 20·42m., of whom 54·8% (11·22m.) were engaged in agriculture, forestry and fishing, 13·6% (2·8m.) in manufacturing; the textile industry was the largest single manufacturing employer.

Commerce. Total value of exports during 1975–76 amounted to Rs 11,212m., and the total value of imports to Rs 20,007m. The value of the chief articles imported into and exported from Pakistan in 1975–76 was (in Rs 1m.):

Imports		*Exports*	
Machinery and transports equipment	4,149	Cotton, raw	980
Chemicals and fertilizers	1,798	Cotton manufactures	3,585
Vegetable oils	1,020	Rice	2,476
Iron and steel	1,514	Leather	556
Electrical goods	1,188	Fish	279
Paper	223	Carpets and rugs	719

Total trade with UK (British Department of Trade returns, in £1,000 sterling):

	1972[1]	*1973*	*1974*	*1975*	*1976*	*1977*
Imports to UK	34,802	31,044	39,779	38,012	40,421	48,790
Exports and re-exports from UK	35,506	34,305	45,808	77,203	92,723	121,051

[1] Including Bangladesh.

Mutual trade relations with India were re-established in Jan. 1975.

Tourism. About 152,000 tourists visited the country in 1974.

COMMUNICATIONS

Roads. At the end of financial year 1975–76 Pakistan had 31,029 miles of roads, of which 16,875 miles were all-weather roads. The fourth plan allocated Rs 100m. to building and improving 3,500 miles.

Railways. Pakistan Railways had (1977) a route kilometrage of 8,808 mainly on 1,600 mm. gauge, with some metre gauge and narrow gauge line. During 1975–76, 146·2m. passengers and 15m. tonnes of freight were carried. A spur line is being built to link the capital, Islamabad, to the national network.

Aviation. Karachi is served by British Airways, KLM, PANAM, Lufthansa, Swissair, SAS, Iran National Airlines, Air France, Garuda, Gulf Air and by Philippine, Japanese, Chinese, East African, Syrian, Iraqui, Kuwait, Jordanian, Saudi Arabian, Romanian, Egyptian and Russian airlines.

Pakistan International Airlines (founded 1955; the majority of shares is held by the Government) had 4 DC-10s, 7 Boeing 707Cs, 5 720Bs, 2 747Bs and 8 Fokker F-27s in 1977; 2 other Boeing 720Bs were on lease to Air Malta. Services operate to 20 home airports, New York, Paris, Amsterdam, Copenhagen, İstanbul, Athens, Rome, Cairo, Tripoli, Nairobi, Dhahran, Damascus, Amman, Baghdad, Persian Gulf points, Tōkyō, Peking, Zahedan, Singapore, Manila, Kuala Lumpur, Bangkok, Colombo, London, Frankfurt, Bombay, Delhi, Dacca, Kabul, Tehrán and Jeddah.

Shipping. There is a seaport at Karachi. A second port is being built at Phitti Creek on the Makram coast, 26 miles east of Karachi, to be called Port Muhammad Bin Qasim. The merchant fleet consists of 41 dry cargo, 3 passenger ships, 4 passenger and cargo vessels, 1 oil tanker; total carrying capacity 590,992 tons and 4,709 passengers. National flag carriers now operate between Pakistan and UK, Continental USA–Canada; Adriatic–Turkey–Black Sea; Persian Gulf, Red Sea; Sri Lanka–Bangladesh; China–Far East and Indonesia–Australia. There is a shipyard at Karachi with capacity for shipbuilding, ship-repairs and engineering.

Post and Broadcasting. The telegraph and telephone system is government-owned. Telephones, on 30 June 1977, numbered 269,281; a nationwide dialling system is in course of installation between 50 cities. In 1977 there were 9,043 post offices and 2,585 telegraph offices; in 1976–77 emphasis was laid on improving rural communications and 197 public call offices, 43 small exchanges and 37 telegraph offices were opened. Pakistan has international telephone connections by 48 satellite, 10 HF, 4 microwave and 8 carrier circuits. Television stations operate in Lahore, Karachi, Peshawar, Quetta and Rawalpindi–Islamabad.

Cinemas (1972). There are 578 cinemas seating 300,000.

Newspapers. Dailies and periodicals numbered 1,200 in 1973: 19 were English language dailies, 83 were vernacular dailies and the rest were periodicals in English and regional languages.

JUSTICE, RELIGION, EDUCATION AND WELFARE

Justice. The Central Judiciary consists of the Supreme Court of Pakistan, which is a court of record and has three-fold jurisdiction, namely, original, appellate and advisory. There are 4 High Courts in Lahore, Peshawar, Quetta and Karachi. Under the Constitution, each has power to issue directions of writs of *Habeas Corpus*, *Mandamus*, *Certiorari* and others. Under them are district and sessions courts of first instance in each division; they have also some appellate jurisdiction. Criminal cases not being sessions cases are tried by district magistrates and subordinate magistrates. There are subordinate civil courts also.

Jurisdiction of the Judicial Committee of the Privy Council ceased on 30 April 1950.

The Constitution provides for an independent judiciary, as the greatest safeguard of citizens' rights. There is an Attorney-General, appointed by the President, who has right of audience in all courts.

Religion. Religious groups (1972 census): Moslems, 63·28m.; Christians, 907,861; Scheduled Castes, 603,369; Caste Hindus, 296,837; Parsees, 9,589; Buddhists, 4,318; others, 205,250. There is a Ministry to safeguard the constitutional rights of religious minorities.

Education. At the census of 1972, there were about 9·3m. people in Pakistan who were able to read and write, representing 21·7% of the population over 10 years old.

The principle of free and compulsory primary education has been accepted as the responsibility of the state. The duration of primary education has been fixed provisionally at 5 years. It is hoped that universal primary education for boys will be achieved by 1983 and for girls by 1987. Adult literacy programmes have been established. Present policy stresses vocational and technical education, disseminating a common culture based on the precepts of Islamiat.

	1974–75	*1976–77*
Number of primary schools	51,568	56,357
Enrolment	5,080,000	5,709,920
Number of secondary schools	7,652	8,698
Enrolment	1,599,000	2,000,000

	1974–75	1976–77
Primary school teachers	122,600	—
Secondary school teachers	92,700	—
Colleges and Universities:		
Colleges (general education)	400	400
Enrolment	203,200	209,800
Engineering colleges	5	—
Enrolment	4,615	—
Number of universities	12	12
Enrolment	21,391	25,970
Polytechnics, monotechnics and technical institutions	333	333
Enrolment	43,700	—

Health. In 1974 there were 4,234 hospitals (36,417 beds) and 17,194 doctors.

DIPLOMATIC REPRESENTATIVES

OF PAKISTAN IN GREAT BRITAIN (35–36 Lowndes Sq., London, SW1X 9JN)

Ambassador: Maj.-Gen. Mohammed Akbar Khan (accredited 17 May 1978)

OF GREAT BRITAIN IN PAKISTAN (Diplomatic Enclave, Ramna 5, Islamabad)

Ambassador: J. C. W. Bushell, CMG.

OF PAKISTAN ON THE USA 2315 Massachusetts Ave., NW, Washington, D.C., 20008)

Ambassador: Sahabzada Yaqub-Khan.

OF THE USA IN PAKISTAN (Diplomatic Enclave, Ramna 4, Islamabad)

Ambassador: Arthur W. Hummel, Jr.

OF PAKISTAN TO THE UNITED NATIONS

Ambassador: Iqbal A. Akhund

Books of Reference

Pakistan Year-Book 1973
Ahmad, K. S., *A Geography of Pakistan.* OUP, 1964
Anwar, M. R., *Presidential Government in Pakistan.* 2nd ed. Lahore, 1964
Burke, S. M., *Pakistan's Foreign Policy.* OUP, 1973
Feldman, H., *Pakistan—An Introduction.* OUP, 1968.—*Revolution in Pakistan: A Study of the Martial-law Administration.* OUP, 1957
Griffin, K., and Khan, A. R. (ed.), *Growth and Inequality in Pakistan.* London and New York, 1972
Jennings, Sir Ivor, *Constitutional Problems in Pakistan.* CUP, 1957
Khalid bin Sayeed, *Pakistan, the Formative Phase.* Karachi, 1961
Office of the Economic Adviser, *Pakistan—Basic Facts.* Rawalpindi, 1973–74
Papnek, G. F., *Pakistan's Development—Social Goods and Private Incentives.* OUP, 1968
Siddiqui, K., *Conflict, Crisis and War in Pakistan.* London, 1972
Stephens, I., *Pakistan.* New York, 1963
Suleri, Zia-ud-din Ahmad, *Politicians and Ayub: A Survey of Pakistani Politics from 1948 to 1964.* Lahore, 1965
Tayyeb, A., *Pakistan: A Political Geography.* OUP, 1966
Williams, L. F. R., *The State of Pakistan.* 2nd ed. CUP, 1966

PANAMA

República de Panamá

Capital: Panama City
Population: 1·7m. (1976)
GNP per capita: US$1,310 (1976)

HISTORY. A revolution, inspired by the USA, led to the separation of Panama from the United States of Colombia and the declaration of its independence on 3 Nov. 1903. The *de facto* Government was on 13 Nov. recognized by the USA, and soon afterwards by the other Powers. In 1914 Colombia agreed to recognize the independence of Panama. This treaty was ratified by the USA and Colombia in 1921, and on 8 May 1924 diplomatic relations between Colombia and Panama were established.

For the treaties regulating the relations between Panama and the USA *see* p. 957 and map in this edition.

AREA AND POPULATION. Panama is bounded north by the Caribbean, east by Colombia, south by the Pacific and west by Costa Rica. Extreme length is about 480 miles; breadth between 37 and 110 miles; coastline, 426 miles on the Atlantic and 767 on the Pacific; total area (excluding the Canal Zone) is 29,201 sq. miles (75,650 sq. km); population according to the census of 10 May 1970 was 1,428,082 (estimated population in Dec. 1976 was 1·7m.). No recent figures are available of the racial composition of the population; the 1940 census gave 12% white, 14·5% Negro, 72% mixed and 1·5% other races.

There are approximately 8,000 British Commonwealth citizens from the Caribbean area.

The capital is Panama City, on the Pacific coast; estimated population, 1976, 460,000. There are 9 provinces (with populations, 1970) as follows (the capitals in brackets): Bocas del Toro (Bocas del Toro), 50,300; Chiriquí (David), 265,000, includes 40,367 in Comarca de Barú; Coclé (Penonomé), 133,000; Colón (Colón), 152,000, including 24,681 in Comarca de San Blas; Los Santos (Las Tablas), 75,000; Herrera (Chitré), 79,000; Darién (La Palma), 24,000; Panama (Panama City), 737,000; Veraguas (Santiago), 162,900. The port of Colón on the Atlantic coast had 95,300. Smaller ports on the Pacific are Aguadulce, Pedregal, Montijo, Puerto Mutis and Puerto Armuelles; in the Atlantic, Bocas del Toro, Almirante, Portobello, Mandinga and Permé. A fishing port is being built at Vacamonte.

Birth rate, 1975, was 32 per 1,000 population; death rate, 4·9; marriage rate, 19·7; infantile death rate, 33 per 1,000 live births; divorce rate, 64·6 per 10,000 couples. The figures exclude the tribal Indians.

CONSTITUTION AND GOVERNMENT. The constitution of 1946 contained provisions for a National Assembly of 42 members with a mandate for 4 years. The term of the President of the Republic, elected by direct vote, was 4 years, he was not eligible for the two succeeding terms. Women had equal rights with men.

There were normally 2 vice-presidents, elected every 4 years by direct popular vote, and a cabinet of 7 ministers nominated by the President, who might attend and address the legislature but could not vote. The Comptroller-General was elected by the National Assembly for 4 years.

On 11 Oct. 1968, however, the newly elected President, Dr Arnulfo Arias, was deposed after only 11 days in office, in a *coup* conducted by the National Guard. The National Assembly was suspended and a provisional government set up consisting of a two-man military Junta and a civilian cabinet. In Dec. 1969 the military members of the Junta resigned and were replaced by civilians after an abortive attempt to depose the Commander of the National Guard, Brig.-Gen. Omar Torrijos.

In 1972 a 505-member Assembly was directly elected to approve a new constitution. Under this constitution there is an indirectly elected President, Vice-President and Legislative Council but full executive powers were given to Gen. Torrijos for a period of 6 years as a 'transitory provision' of the constitution.

President of the Republic: Demetrio Lakas.
Vice-President of the Republic: Gerardo Gonzalez V.
Minister for Foreign Affairs: Nicolás González Revilla.
Commander-in-Chief of the National Guard: Brig.-Gen. Omar Torrijos.

The official language is Spanish.

National flag: Rectangle of 4 quarters: white with blue star, blue, white with red star, red.

National anthem: Alcanzamos por fin la victoria (words by J. de la Ossa; tune by Santos Jorge, 1903).

DEFENCE

Army. The *Guardia Nacional* is the only military type force with police as well as military and para-military functions. It has a strength of about 11,000 and includes a coastguard section.

Air Force. The air wing has 1 DC-6, 4 C-47s, 2 Islanders, 1 Israeli-built Westwind jet and 1 Twin Otter transport, 11 Cessna and 5 DHC-3 Otter liaison aircraft and 12 UH-1H Iroquois, twin-engined UH-1N and FH-1100 helicopters.

INTERNATIONAL RELATIONS

Membership. Panama is a member of UN and OAS.

ECONOMY

Budget. Total public sector expenditure (in balboas): 1972, 359m.; 1973, 408m.; 1974, 529m.; 1975, 684m.

Net receipts from transactions with the Panama Canal Zone were estimated at 222m. balboas in 1975.

Consolidated public sector debt was 1,186m. balboas in Dec. 1975.

Currency. The monetary unit is the *balboa*, which is of the same size and fineness as the US silver dollar but is maintained equivalent to the gold dollar. Other coins whose metallic content is required by law to correspond exactly to that of similar US coins are the half-balboa (equal to 50 cents US); the quarter and tenth of a balboa piece; a cupro-nickel coin of 5 cents, and a copper coin of 1 cent. US coinage is also legal tender. Volume of the currency has not been disclosed since 31 Dec. 1950, when it stood at 1·5m.; 5·1m. balboas of Panamanian coin had been minted up to 31 Dec. 1963. The only paper currency used is that of the USA.

Banking. There is no statutory central bank. The Government accounts are handled through the *Banco Nacional de Panama.* The number of commercial banks rose from 9 in 1964 to 72 by Sept. 1977. Leading banks are the Citibank, The Bank of London and South America, and the Chase Manhattan Bank of New York. Other foreign-owned banks include the Bank of America, as well as Canadian, Colombian, Swiss, Federal German, French, Spanish, Dutch, Taiwan, Japanese and Brazilian banks.

Weights and Measures. English weights and measures are in general use; those of the metric system are also used.

ENERGY AND NATURAL RESOURCES

Electricity. Production of electric energy, 1975, amounted to 1,382·1m. kwh. (Panama City and Colón).

Minerals. It is reported that Panama has 3 valuable copper deposits. There are known to be copper deposits in the provinces of Chiriqui, Colón and Darien. The most important is Cerro Colorado (Chiriqui) on which a feasibility study by Texasgulf is nearing completion. The Petaquilla (Colón) exploration concession contract was awarded to a Japanese group.

Agriculture. Of the whole area (1975) 18·5% is cultivated, 57·1% is natural or artificial pasture land and 9·5% is fallow. Of the remainder only a small part is cultivated, though the land is rich in resources. About 60% of the country's food requirements are imported. The Ministry of Agricultural Development (MIDA) buys leading crops at field prices. Of the land under cultivation, 26·4% is owned and 44·7% is usufructuary. The most important export products are bananas, grown by an affiliate of the United Brands Company and sugar from 4 state-owned and 2 private mills. Value of exports of these commodities in 1976 was 64m. balboas and 30m. balboas respectively. Most important food crop, for home consumption, is rice, grown on 80% of the farms; Panama's *per capita* consumption is very high. Output of rough rice from 105,200 hectares, was 4·5m. quintals in 1975–76. Other products are maize (65,700 hectares, yielding 1·5m. quintals in 1975–76), cocoa, coffee and coconuts. Beer, whisky, rum, 'seco', anise and gin are produced. Coffee is grown in the province of Chiriqui, near the Costa Rican frontier; total production in 1975–76 was 105,850 quintals, and small amounts were exported to Federal Republic of Germany and USA. The country has great timber resources, notably mahogany. According to the livestock estimate of July 1975 there were 1,347,900 cattle, 166,100 pigs and 3,704,300 poultry. Hides are among minor articles of export.

INDUSTRY AND TRADE

Industry. Local industries include cigarettes, clothing, food processing, shoes, soap, cement factories; foreign firms are being encouraged to establish industries, and a petrol refinery is operating in Colón.

GDP *per capita* (1976) 1,200 balboas.

Commerce. The imports and exports (including re-exports) for the Republic of Panama, for 6 calendar years are as follows (in 1,000 balboas; 1 balboa = US$1):

	Imports	*Exports*		*Imports*	*Exports*
1971	358,974	116,539	1974	730,900	200,500
1972	399,461	122,841	1975	789,700	262,000
1973	448,881	135,655	1976	783,500	378,200

The USA have the right to import into the Canal Zone supplies of all descriptions required for canal construction, maintenance and protection and for the use of their employees, free of all taxes.

The huge adverse visible trade balance is mainly with the USA and is due to the heavy import of consumer goods, most of it covered by a large invisible surplus, for sale to the Canal Zone employees and to the big transient population. In 1974 the USA furnished 30·8% of Panama's imports and took 49·7% of her exports. The UK was the eighth largest supplier.

A Free Zone exists at Colón for the storage, processing, repacking and re-exporting or sale of goods in transit. The imports and exports (including re-exports) for the Colón Free Zone, for 6 calendar years are as follows (in 1,000 balboas):

	Imports	*Exports*		*Imports*	*Exports*
1971	216,456	255,177	1974	475,900	510,800
1972	247,091	313,960	1975	415,700	543,100
1973	311,101	378,881	1976	558,033	651,020

Chief exports (virtually all to the USA) in 1976 (in 1m. balboas) were: Petroleum products, 178·9; bananas, 64; sugar, 30.

Chief imports, 1976, were valued (in 1m. balboas f.o.b.): Machinery and transport material, 176; manufactured goods, 201·2; fuel, minerals and similar, 250; chemicals, 78·8; food, 57·9.

Total trade between Panama (including Colón Free Zone) and UK (British Department of Trade returns, in £1,000 sterling):

	1973	*1974*	*1975*	*1976*	*1977*
Imports to UK	2,323	773	2,334	1,068	732
Exports and re-exports from UK[1]	9,540	13,654	15,827	18,995	16,928

[1] Including new ships built for foreign owners and registered in Panama.

Tourism. In 1976, 307,601 foreigners visited Panama earning 119·4m. balboas.

COMMUNICATIONS

Roads. Panama had on 31 Dec. 1975, 7,323 km of roads. The road from Panama City westward to the cities of David and Concepción and to the Costa Rican frontier, with several branches, is part of the Pan-American Highway. In 1972 work was started on the Pan-American Highway link with Colombia and has reached a point about 70 miles east of Panama City. The Darien gap prevents through transit. A concrete highway, maintained by the USA until 1975, connects Panama City and Colón.

On 31 Dec. 1975 registered motor vehicles, private and commercial, numbered 87,875; this excludes vehicles owned by government departments. Vehicles registered in the Canal Zone numbered 21,944 (1973–74).

Railways. The Panama Railroad (1,524 mm gauge) (owned by the Panama Canal Company), which connects Ancón on the Pacific with Cristóbal on the Atlantic, is the principal railway. It is 76 km long and lies entirely within the Canal Zone territory. As most vessels unload their cargo at Cristóbal (Colón), on the Atlantic side, the greater portion of the merchandise destined for Panama City is brought overland by the Panama Railroad. The United Brands owned railway runs from Almirante to Guabito on the Costa Rica border and on to Fields in Costa Rica (51 miles).

The Chiriquí National Railroad (914 mm gauge) operates 169 km between David and Puerto Armuelles (United Brands).

Aviation. Commercial aviation has developed rapidly. PANAM, Braniff Airways, British Airways, KLM and other international companies operate at Tocumen Airport, 17 miles from Panama City. Air Panama provides services between Panama City and New York, Los Angeles, Miami, Central America and some countries in South America. The Compañía Panameña de Aviación (COPA) and Aerolineas Las Perlas provide a local service between Panama City and the provincial towns. COPA also provides an international service to Central America. In 1975 a total of 328,281 passengers arrived by air, excluding direct transits.

Shipping. Ships under Panamanian registry on 31 Dec. 1974 numbered 8,843 of 17,319,007 gross tons; most of these ships elect Panamanian registry because fees are low and labour laws lenient. All the international maritime traffic for Colón and Panama runs through the Canal Zone ports of Cristóbal, Balboa together with Bahia Las Minas (Colón); Almirante is used for both the provincial and international trade.

Post and Broadcasting. There are telegraph cables from Panama to North America and Central and South American ports, and from Colón to the USA and Europe. There is also inter-continental communication by satellite. There are 93 licensed commercial broadcasting stations, nearly all operated by private companies, one of which functions in the Canal Zone. There are 3 television stations, one of them run by the US Army in the Canal Zone. At the end of 1976 there were 154,598 telephones installed including those in the Canal Zone.

Cinemas. In 1976 there were 47 cinemas in the district of Panama. All films must have Spanish subtitles.

Newspapers. There are 1 English language and 3 Spanish language daily morning newspapers and 1 English/Spanish evening newspaper.

JUSTICE, RELIGION AND EDUCATION

Justice. The Supreme Court consists of 9 justices appointed by the executive. There is no death penalty.

Religion. The 1950 census showed that 95% of the population was Roman Catholic and 5% Protestant. There is freedom of religious worship and separation of Church and State. Clergymen may teach in the schools but may not hold public office.

Education. Elementary education is compulsory for all children from 7 to 15 years of age, with an estimated 512,000 students in schools throughout the Republic in 1975. The University of Panama at Panama City, inaugurated on 7 Oct. 1935, had a total enrolment (1975) of 25,046 students in the schools of law, science and other professional subjects; the university was granted autonomy on 28 Sept. 1946. Up to the academic year 1956–57 the university was a centre of evening studies (except for the faculty of medicine); since 1956–57 all faculties hold day classes as well. A new site, called University City, was inaugurated in June 1950. The Catholic university Sta. Maria La Antigua, inaugurated on 27 May 1965, had 1,243 students in Sept. 1975.

The 1970 census showed that 17·8% of the population over 10 years old were illiterate, excluding the tribal Indians (compared with 28·3% in 1950).

DIPLOMATIC REPRESENTATIVES

OF PANAMA IN GREAT BRITAIN (116 Knightsbridge, London, SW1X 7PJ)

Ambassador: Roger Decerega Smith (accredited 18 March 1976).

OF GREAT BRITAIN IN PANAMA (Via España 120, Panama City)

Ambassador: Robert M. John.

OF PANAMA IN THE USA (2862 McGill Terr., NW, Washington, D.C., 20008)

Ambassador: Gabriel Lewis.

OF THE USA IN PANAMA
(Ave. Balbao y Calle 38, Panama City)

Ambassador: William J. Jorden.

OF PANAMA TO THE UNITED NATIONS

Ambassador: Dr Jorge Enrique Illucca.

Books of Reference

Statistical Information: The Comptroller-General of the Republic (Contraloria General de la República, Calle 35 y Avenida 6, Panama City) publishes an annual report and other statistical publications.

Fiscal Survey of Panamá. Johns Hopkins Press, 1964
Biesanz, J. M., *The People of Panama.* Columbia Univ. Press, 1955
Castillero, Ernesto J., *Historia de Panamá.* 5th ed. Panama City, 1965
Howarth, D., *The Golden Isthmus.* London, 1966
Larsen, H. and M., *The Forests of Panama.* London, 1964
Susto, J. A., *An Introduction to Panamanian Bibliography* (Publications of the National Library, No. 4). Panama, 1946

National Library: Biblioteca Nacional, Departamento de Información. Calle 22, Panama.

THE PANAMA CANAL AND THE CANAL ZONE

On 18 Nov. 1903 a treaty between the USA and the Republic of Panama was signed making it possible for the US to build and operate a canal connecting the Atlantic and Pacific oceans through the Isthmus of Panama. The treaty granted the US in perpetuity the use, occupation and control of a Canal Zone, approximately 10 miles wide, in which the US would possess full sovereign rights 'to the entire exclusion of the exercise by the Republic of Panama of any such sovereign rights, power or authority'. In return the US guaranteed the independence of the Republic and agreed to pay the Republic $10m. and an annuity of $250,000. The US purchased the French rights and properties—the French had been labouring from 1879 to 1899 in an effort to build the Canal—for $40m. and in addition, paid private landholders within what would be the Canal Zone a mutually agreeable price for their properties.

In Aug. 1977, 2 new Treaties were agreed in principle. The first gave Panama full control of the canal and the Canal Zone by the year 2000 and the second guaranteed the neutrality of the area. Details of the ratification by Panama after a referendum and its approval by the US Congress are given on the map of the area in rhis edition.

The Treaties were finally signed in Panama in June 1978.

The treaty of 1936 increased the annuity to $430,000 and, as desired by Panama, withdrew the guarantee of independence. In 1955 the annuity was increased to $1·93m., and the Panama Canal Company turned over to the Republic the Panama City railroad yards and other properties valued at $22m. At the end of 1962 the US completed the construction of a high-level bridge over the Pacific entrance of the Canal, and the flags of Panama and the US were flown jointly over areas of the Canal Zone under civilian authority. Following the devaluation of the dollar in 1972 and 1973, the annuity was adjusted proportionally to $2·1m. and $2·33m., respectively.

The Canal Zone Government is responsible for such functions as police and fire protection, postal service, and schools and hospital services (such as the Gorgas hospital, greatly enlarged in 1964). The Panama Canal Company is concerned primarily with the actual operation of the Canal. On 8 July 1974 and 17 Nov. 1976 tolls were increased. These were the first increases of toll rates in the history of the Canal.

The changes were designed to continue the approximately break-even financial operating results after paying its own expenses for reimbursing the US Treasury for the net cost of the Canal Zone Government and paying interest on the net direct investment of the US in the Canal.

Governor of the Canal Zone and President of the Panama Canal Company: Maj.-Gen. H. R. Parfitt, US Army.

Lieut.-Governor and Vice-President: Col. Richard L. Hunt, US Army.

The area of the Canal Zone, including land and water, is 647·29 sq. miles (1,676·3 sq. km). The water area of the zone, including the water area within the 3-mile limit from the Atlantic and Pacific ends, is 274·97 sq. miles (712·17 sq. km).

The total civilian and military population of the Canal Zone is 41,800, of whom about 37,400 are US citizens. The total full-time permanent force employed by the Panama Canal Company and the Canal Zone Government on 30 June 1976 numbered 3,540 US citizens and 9,438 others, mostly Panamanian citizens.

There are 144·4 miles of improved streets and highways in the zone, exclusive of those within Armed Forces reservations. Motor vehicles number over 25,000.

The Canal was opened to commerce on 15 Aug. 1914. It is 85 ft above sea-level. It is 51·2 statute miles in length from deep water in the Caribbean Sea to deep water in the Pacific ocean, and 36 statute miles from shore to shore. The channel ranges in bottom-width from 500 to 1,000 ft; the widening of Gaillard Cut to a minimum width of 500 ft was completed in 1969. Normally, the average time of a vessel in Canal waters is 18·5 hours, 8 of which are in transit through the Canal proper. A map showing the Panama, Suez and Kiel canals on the same scale will be found in THE STATESMAN'S YEAR-BOOK, 1959 and a new map in this edition.

Particulars of the ocean-going commercial traffic through the canal are given as follows (vessels of 300 tons Panama Canal net and 500 displacement tons and over; cargo in long tons):

Fiscal year ending 30 June	*North-bound (Pacific to Atlantic)*		*South-bound (Atlantic to Pacific)*		*Total*		*Tolls levied (in $)*
	Vessels	*Cargo*	*Vessels*	*Cargo*	*Vessels*	*Cargo*	
1973	6,759	52,709,535	7,082	73,394,494	13,841	126,104,029	111,032,543
1974	6,866	56,575,399	7,167	91,331,515	14,033	147,906,914	119,419,878
1975	6,859	56,009,293	6,750	84,092,166	13,609	140,101,459	141,898,218
1976	5,988	51,216,598	6,169	65,995,668	12,157	117,212,266	134,204,402

In the fiscal year ending 30 June 1976, of the 12,157 toll-paying ships which passed through the Canal 1,777 were Liberian; 1,285 British; 1,064 US; 1,008 Japanese; 930 Panamanian; 885 Greek; 685 Norwegian; 626 Federal German; 332 Swedish; 300 Netherlands.

Books of Reference

Statistical Information: The Panama Canal Information Office, Balboa Heights, Canal Zone. *Information Officer:* Frank A. Baldwin.

Annual Reports on the Panama Canal, by the Governor of the Canal Zone.

Rules and Regulations Governing Navigation of the Panama Canal. Balbao Heights, CZ *or* Washington, DC

Baxter, R. R., *The Law of International Waterways.* Harvard Univ. Press, 1964

Cameron, I., *The Impossible Dream.* London, 1972

Du Val, M. P., *Cadiz to Cathay: The Diplomatic Struggle for the Panama Canal.* 2nd ed. Stanford Univ. Press, 1947.—*And the Mountains will Move: The Building of the Panama Canal.* Stanford Univ. Press, 1947

Le Feber, W., *The Panama Canal: The Crisis in Historical Perspective.* OUP, 1978

McCullough, D., *The Path Between the Seas.* New York and London, 1978

PAPUA NEW GUINEA

Capital: Port Moresby
Population: 2·6m. (1978)
GNP per capita: US$490 (1976)

HISTORY. To prevent that portion of the island of New Guinea not claimed by the Netherlands from passing into the hands of a foreign power, the Government of Queensland annexed Papua in 1883. This step was not sanctioned by the Imperial Government, but on 6 Nov. 1884 a British Protectorate was proclaimed over the southern portion of the eastern half of New Guinea, and in 1887 Queensland, New South Wales and Victoria undertook to defray the cost of administration, and the territory was annexed to the Crown the following year. The Federal Government took over the control in 1901; the political transfer was completed by the Papua Act of the Federal Parliament in Nov. 1905, and on 1 Sept. 1906 a proclamation was issued by the Governor-General of Australia declaring that British New Guinea was to be known henceforth as the Territory of Papua. The northern portion of New Guinea was a German colony until the First World War. It became a League of Nations mandated territory in 1921, administered by Australia, and later a UN Trust Territory (of New Guinea).

The Papua New Guinea Act 1949–1972 provides for the administration of the UN Australian Trust Territory of New Guinea in an administrative union with the Territory of Papua, in accordance with Art. 5 of the New Guinea Trusteeship Agreement, under the title of Papua New Guinea.

Australia granted Papua New Guinea self-government on 1 Dec. 1973 and, on 16 Sept. 1975, Papua New Guinea became a fully independent state.

AREA AND POPULATION. Papua New Guinea extends from the equator to Cape Baganowa in the Louisiade Archipelago to 11° 40′ S. lat. and from the border of West Irian to 160° E. long. with a total area of 462,840 sq. km. According to the census the 1971 population was 2,489,935 (1978, estimated, 2·6m.), 1,797,803 resided in New Guinea and 692,132 in Papua. Port Moresby, census population (1971) 76,507; Lae, 38,707; Rabaul, 26,619; Madang, 16,865; Wewak, 15,015; Goroka, 12,065; Mount Hagen, 10,261. Area and population of the provinces at the 1971 census:

Provinces	*Sq. km*	*Population*	*Capital*
Milne Bay	20,200	109,460	Samarai
Northern	23,300	66,514	Popondetta
Central	31,100	193,837	Port Moresby
Gulf	38,900	58,564	Kikori
Western	103,600	70,898	Daru
Southern Highlands	16,100	192,854	Mendi
Western Highlands	23,800	346,032	Mount Hagen
Chimbu	7,300	160,245	Kundiawa
Eastern Highlands	12,900	239,640	Goroka
Morobe	32,900	249,032	Lae
Madang	28,000	170,953	Madang
East Sepik	27,200	181,893	Wewak
West Sepik	51,000	93,978	Aitape
Manus	2,100	24,866	Lorengau
West New Britain	18,400	61,515	Hoskins
East New Britain	18,100	113,750	Rabaul
New Ireland	9,800	59,543	Kavieng
Bougainville	10,600	96,363	Sohano
Total	475,300	2,489,935	

A 19th province, Enga, has subsequently been created.

ISLAND DISTRICTS

New Guinea Islands. The archipelago comprises 4 main islands and some 100 smaller islands. There are 5 administrative districts: East New Britain, West New Britain, New Ireland, Manus and Bougainville. The estimated indigenous population as at 30 June 1974 was 383,500. The main towns (census, 1971) are Rabaul, 22,393; Lorengau, 3,915; Kavieng, 2,797.

New Britain, the largest island of this group, has a mean breadth of 50 miles and a length of 300 miles. The estimated indigenous population (including adjacent small islands) was 189,000 at 30 June 1974. A mountain chain traverses the entire length of the island, and in the centre consists of several irregular ranges. There are several active volcanoes. The highest known peak is the Father, about 7,500 ft high, which is an active volcano. The island has very fine harbours; the principal town is Rabaul.

The chief export products are copra, cocoa and timber. An oil palm industry is being established on the north coast. Non-indigenous census population in July 1971 was 6,244.

New Ireland, the second in size and importance, is situated north of New Britain, from which it is separated by St George's Channel. The chief town is Kavieng, at the north-west extremity of the island. The only other town is Namatanai on the south-east coast. The island has a long range of mountains running through it. It is of older formation than New Britain, and does not show any signs of recent volcanic activity.

The principal harbour is Nusa Bay on the north coast, on which Kavieng, the seat of the local administration, is situated. The estimated indigenous population at 30 June 1974 was 64,500, including adjacent islands; non-indigenous 1971 census population was 1,036.

The soil is reasonably fertile. The chief industry is coconut growing. There are numerous plantations around the coast near Kavieng. Smaller islands include Tabar, Lihir, Tanga, Feni, Nissan (Green Island), Nuguria, Mussau and Emirau groups.

The Solomon Islands. The portion of the Solomon Islands group within the area of Papua New Guinea consists of Bougainville, Buka and adjacent islands, including Kilinailau (Carteret Island), Taku (Mortlock) and Nukumanu (Tasman) Islands. Bougainville has an area of 4,100 sq. miles, and the estimated indigenous population at 30 June 1974 was 102,400, including Buka, which has an area of 190 sq. miles; non-indigenous 1971 census population was 5,981. Smaller islands have a total area of 30 sq. miles. The islands are very mountainous. Of the several volcanic cones Bagana (in the Crown Prince range) and Balbi are the only active volcanoes.

The principal harbours are Kieta, situated on the east coast of Bougainville and Raua and Tinputz on the north-east coast of Bougainville. There is a good harbour on the west side of Buka, named Carola Hafen.

Copper is the most important resource of Bougainville. Bananas, coconuts, taro, sweet potatoes and cocoa are grown by the indigenous population.

The Admiralty Islands are the most important of the small groups. The chief island is Manus; the chief town is Lorengau on its north-east coast. The estimated indigenous population of the group at 30 June 1974 was 27,600; non-indigenous census population in July 1971 was 510. Coconuts are the chief cultivated crop and marine shell is taken for commercial purposes.

CONSTITUTION AND GOVERNMENT. At present Papua New Guinea has a Westminster type of government. A single legislative house, known as the National Parliament, is made up of 109 members from all parts of the country. The members are elected under universal suffrage and general elections are held every 5 years. All persons over the age of 18 who are Papua New Guinea citizens are eligible to vote and stand for election. Voting is by secret ballot and follows the preferential system.

The First Legislative Council was established in 1951. It was abolished in 1964 and replaced with the House of Assembly. In 1950 the first village council was formed which established the basis of the now extensive local government system. A system of provincial government was introduced in 1976.

The elections in 1972 saw the formation of the first indigenous controlled central government in the history of the country. It also saw the emergence of four major political parties—the Pangu Pati, United Party, People's Progress Party and the New Guinea National Party. A number of other parties had also been formed before these elections. A coalition group was formed and the group was able to place its members in the ministerial postions, and with its combined majority in the House of Assembly, also formed a working government.

Also in 1972, the coalition government appointed a constitutional planning committee to make recommendations for a Constitution specifically suited to conditions in the country. The committee's final report was presented to the House of Assembly in 1974 and provided the basis for the Constitution of the Independent State of Papua New Guinea introduced in 1975. In 1977, following the first general election since independence, the Pangu Pati, the People's Progress Party and independent members formed a coalition with support from 69 members of Parliament.

Governor-General: Sir Tore Lokoloko, GCMG, OBE.

The cabinet at Aug. 1977 was as follows:

Prime Minister, responsible for National Planning and the Public Services Commission: Michael T. Somare.

Deputy Prime Minister and Minister for Primary Industry: Julius Chan. *Foreign Affairs and Trade:* Ebia Niwia Olewale. *Labour and Industry:* Jacob Lemeki. *Finance:* Barry Holloway. *Decentralization:* John Momis. *Transport and Civil Aviation:* Bruce Jephcott. *Natural Resources:* Boyamo Sali. *Education, Science and Culture:* Oscar Tammur. *Defence:* Louis Mona. *Justice:* Delba Biri. *Public Utilities:* Gabriel Bakani. *Commerce:* Pita Lus. *Environment, Conservation and Human Settlements:* Stephen Tago. *Health:* Wiwa Korowi. *Youth, Recreation, Social Development and Women's Affairs:* Pato Kakarya. *Media:* Tom Koraea. *Corrective Institutions and Liquor Licensing:* Nahau Rooney. *Works and Supply:* Yano Belo. *Housing:* Thomas Kavali. *Minerals and Energy:* Karl Kitchens.

The seat of the government is at Port Moresby.

National flag: Diagonally ochre-red over black, on the red a bird of paradise in gold, and on the black 5 stars of the Southern Cross in white.

DEFENCE. The Papua New Guinea Defence Force has a total strength of 3,500 (1977) consisting of land, maritime and air elements. The nucleus of an Air Force was formed by 4 C-47 piston-engined transports delivered from Australia in 1975. They have been followed by 3 Australian-built Mission Master twin-turboprop support transports.

INTERNATIONAL RELATIONS

Membership. Papua New Guinea is a member of UN, the Commonwealth and the Colombo Plan.

ECONOMY

Budget. Receipts (in $A1,000) for years ended 30 June were:

Source	*1975*	*1976*	*1977*[1]
Civil aviation	336	902	2,130
Customs	51,595	57,864	66,388
Licences	1,724	2,096	2,683
Stamp duties	755	1,086	1,472
Land revenue	1,768	1,693	2,008
Mining receipts	3,212	2,358	2,979
Fees and fines	1,227	1,449	1,382

[1] Estimates.

Source	*1975*	*1976*	*1977*[1]
Health revenue	550	554	594
Forestry	1,643	1,538	1,614
Agriculture	2,772	2,878	2,290
Direct taxation	81,016	81,149	82,100
Public utilities	736	799	761
Miscellaneous	25,236	63,305	50,928
Recoveries, A.S.A.G. expenditure[2]	5,013	3,521	...
Total local revenue	177,585	221,191	217,329
Loans	50,330	43,857	28,630
Grants from the Australian Government	156,282	119,391	190,000
Other	10,000	47,566	...
Total receipts	394,196	432,004	435,959

[1] Estimates. [2] Australian Staffing Assistance Group.

Currency. The unit of currency is the *kina* divided into 100 *toea* and is the sole legal tender. 1 kina = US$1.30 (Nov. 1977).

Banking. The Bank of Papua New Guinea assumed the central banking functions formerly undertaken by the Reserve Bank of Australia on 1 Nov. 1973.

A national banking institution, which has been named the Papua New Guinea Banking Corporation, has been established. This bank has assumed the Papua New Guinea business of the Commonwealth Trading Bank of Australia except where certain accounts give rise to special financial or contractual problems.

The subsidiaries of 3 Australian commercial banks also operate in Papua New Guinea. These are the Australia and New Zealand Banking Group (PNG) Ltd, the Bank of New South Wales (PNG) Ltd, and the Bank of South Pacific Ltd, all of which offer trading and savings facilities. As from 1 Nov. 1973 these banks operated under Papua New Guinea banking legislation.

In addition to the subsidiaries of Australian banks operating in Papua New Guinea, the Papua New Guinea Development Bank has provided long-term development finance with particular attention to the needs of small-scale enterprises since 1967 and includes 14,422 loans totalling K59·8m. by 30 June 1976.

Weights and Measures. The metric system is in force.

ENERGY AND NATURAL RESOURCES

Minerals. Copper is the main mineral product. Oil companies have been searching for oil, but no commercial deposits have yet been found. Several wells of natural gas have been discovered in commercial quantities. In Papua New Guinea gold, copper and silver are the only minerals produced in quantity. Major copper deposits in the Kieta district of Bougainville have proven reserves of about 900m. tonnes. Copper deposits have been found in the Star mountains of the Western Province and exploration is continuing. Production of copper concentrates for export began in 1972 (1973–74, K311,909,036). The total value of mineral production in 1973–74 was K260m. (including K52,214,000 gold and K2,843,000 silver mined in the copper concentrate found by Bougainville Copper Ply Ltd). The total value of production in 1974–75 was estimated at about K200m.

Agriculture. Agricultural activity in Papua New Guinea is carried out by non-indigenous and indigenous occupiers on plantations and by indigenous smallholders. At 30 June 1975, 406,360 hectares of land had been leased to non-indigenous occupiers, of which 151,144 hectares were for agricultural purposes, the principal crops being coconuts, cocoa, coffee and rubber. Indigenous sago is plentiful in the Western Province. Oil palm, pyrethrum, tea, rice, sweet potatoes, yams, taro, sago and bananas are grown on a smaller scale. Tropical fruits grow abundantly. There is extensive grassland and a beef-cattle industry is being developed. Number of cattle (beef and dairy), 155,000.

Forestry. Timber production is of growing importance for both local consumption and export. In 1974–75, about 938,000 cu. metres of logs were harvested; logs exported, 383,000 cu. metres. Production of plywood, 1974–75, 16,000 cu. metres; exports of veneer, 3,796 cu. metres.

Fisheries. Prawn fishing is one of the main sources of income from marine fisheries. Exports of prawns and other fish, 1974–75: Prawns, K998,120; crayfish, K257,596; pearls, K1,500,507; tuna, K8,835,839; barramundi, K81,854; marine shell (mother-of-pearl, trochus and turtle shell), K177,376; Katsuobushi, K197,340.

INDUSTRY AND TRADE

Industry. Secondary and service industries are expanding for the local market. Industries include the manufacture of paint, gases, concrete, twist tobacco, matches, brewing, boat-building, furniture and the assembly of electrical appliances. In 1975 there were 706 factories employing 17,255 persons. Value of output K217m.

Labour. In 1976 about 352,000 indigenous wage-earners were in regular employment.

Trade. Imports (in K1,000) during the years ended 30 June:

	1972	*1973*	*1974*	*1975*
Food and live animals	45,412	47,734	57,404	71,364
Beverages and tobacco	5,973	5,025	4,289	5,597
Crude materials, inedible, except fuels	1,007	749	769	1,246
Minerals fuels, lubricants and related materials	12,843	11,102	19,642	38,292
Oils and fats (animal and vegetable)	296	357	471	805
Chemicals	12,694	12,435	13,624	22,939
Manufactured goods, chiefly by material	41,383	39,214	38,964	61,631
Machinery and transport equipment	93,066	73,533	61,666	112,151
Miscellaneous manufactured articles	23,959	21,791	22,202	30,117
Commodities and transactions of merchandise trade, not elsewhere specified	16,149	13,556	6,950	9,278
Total, excluding outside packages	252,782	225,495	225,982	353,421
Outside packages	3,034	3,604	2,893	3,974
Total imports	256,386	228,815	228,875	357,395

Exports (in K1,000) during the years ended 30 June:

	1972	*1973*	*1974*	*1975*
Coconut and copra products—				
Whole coconut	7	4	3	2
Desiccated coconut	1,065	1,192	498	...
Copra	9,392	8,083	23,672	28,841
Copra (coconut) oil	5,880	4,982	13,761	14,284
Copra oil pellets	588	950	1,012	1,211
Total	16,932	15,212	38,948	44,338
Coffee beans	20,454	23,395	28,847	33,554
Cocoa beans	11,021	11,175	23,338	40,067
Crude rubber	1,995	1,998	3,563	2,585
Tea	1,500	2,048	2,602	3,866
Peanuts	616	305	324	47
Pyrethrum extract	227	192	215	190
Passionfruit juice and pulp	288	226	83	250
Forest and timber products—				
Logs	4,997	5,646	11,588	7,671
Sawn timber	1,991	2,688	5,163	3,285
Veneers	213	287	470	345
Plywood	1,998	2,368	3,569	2,663
Other	21	9	249	1,589
Total	45,321	50,334	79,588	96,112

	1972	*1973*	*1974*	*1975*
Crocodile skins	198	650	585	403
Fresh fish	2,979	3,191	10,536	8,921
Crayfish and prawns	2,051	1,355	3,432	1,256
Gold	792	953	1,622	3,411
Other domestic produce	24,766	128,848[1]	318,298[1]	248,119[2]
Total domestic produce	93,039	200,542	453,009	402,560
Re-exports	34,142	29,072	30,723	20,945
Total exports	127,181	229,614	483,731	423,505

[1] Includes K311,903 for copper ore concentrate.
[2] Includes K236,660 for copper ore concentrate..

Trade between Papua New Guinea and UK (British Department of Trade returns, in £1,000 sterling):

	1972	*1973*	*1974*	*1975*	*1976*	*1977*
Imports to UK	6,737	8,772	19,279	13,693	16,453	30,577
Exports and re-exports from UK	2,578	2,104	3,124	5,834	7,079	10,038

COMMUNICATIONS

Roads. In June 1975 there were approximately 18,188 km of roads including approximately 1,016 km of urban roads. Motor vehicles numbered (1976) 42,575 including 13,480 cars.

Aviation. Frequent air services operate to and from Australia, and there is a weekly flight from Sydney through Port Moresby to Manila, Hong Kong and Japan. A weekly service is maintained to Honiara in the Solomon Islands (UK) and a weekly flight to Port Moresby from Fiji *via* Vila (New Hebrides) and Honiara.

An air service is maintained between Madang and Djajapura in West Irian once a fortnight. On 1 Nov. 1973 a government-owned airline Air Niugini, was established.

Shipping. There are regular shipping services between Australia and PNG ports, and also services to New Zealand, Europe and Asia. Small coastal vessels run between the various ports. There is also a connecting service to Nauru, North America, through the New Hebrides and New Caledonia. Overseas and inter-island vessels cleared from PNG ports in 1974–75 totalled 4·26m. net tons. In 1972–73 cargo discharged from overseas was 1·2m. tons; cargo loaded for overseas was 1·3m. tons.

Post and Broadcasting. Telephones numbered 37,531 on 1 Jan 1977. The National Broadcasting Commission broadcasts on short-wave and medium-wave from Port Moresby, Rabaul, Wewak, Goroka, Lae and Madang. There are 10 other stations broadcasting on short-wave only, at a number of centres, broadcasting programmes in several local languages.

Cinemas (1972): 28 with a total seating capacity of 18,800.

EDUCATION. At 30 June 1976 about 255,500 children attended 1,861 primary schools and 41,100 enrolled in 184 secondary, technical and vocational schools. The University of Papua New Guinea and the Papua New Guinea University of Technology had 2,869 students in 1976.

DIPLOMATIC REPRESENTATIVES

OF PAPUA NEW GUINEA IN GREAT BRITAIN
(14 Waterloo Pl., London, SW1R 4AR)

High Commissioner: Frederick B. C. Reiher (accredited 4 May 1977).

OF GREAT BRITAIN IN PAPUA NEW GUINEA
(Douglas St., Port Moresby)

High Commissioner: D. K. Middleton.

OF PAPUA NEW GUINEA IN THE USA (1776 Massachusetts Ave., NW, Washington D.C., 20036)

Ambassador: Paulias Nguna Matane, OBE.

OF THE USA IN PAPUA NEW GUINEA (Armit St., Port Moresby)

Ambassador: Mary S. Olmsted.

OF PAPUA NEW GUINEA TO THE UNITED NATIONS

Ambassador: Paulius N. Matane, OBE.

Books of Reference

The Territory of Papua. Annual Report. Commonwealth of Australia. 1906–1940–41 and from 1945–46

The Territory of New Guinea. Annual Report. Commonwealth of Australia. 1914–1940–41 and from 1946–47

Papua New Guinea, Annual Report. From 1970–71

Report on New Guinea. UN visiting missions to . . . Nauru and New Guinea. New York, 1962

Bettison, D. G., and others, *Independence of Papua–New Guinea*, Sydney, 1962.—*The Papua–New Guinea Elections 1964.* Canberra, 1966

Essal, B., *Papua and New Guinea.* Melbourne, 1961

Hasluck, P., *A Time for Building.* Melbourne Univ. Press, 1976

Hastings, P. (ed.), *Papua New Guinea: Prospero's Other Island.* London, 1971

Ross, A. C., and Langmore, J., *Alternative Strategies for Papua New Guinea.* OUP, 1974

Ryan, J., *The Hot Land.* London, 1970

Ryan, P. (ed.), *Encyclopaedia of Papua and New Guinea.* Melbourne Univ. Press, 1972

Simpson, C., *Plumes and Arrows Inside New Guinea.* Sydney, 1962

Wilkes, J. (ed.), *New Guinea and Australia.* Austral. Inst. of Political Science, 1959

PARAGUAY

Capital: Asunción
Population: 2·75m. (1976)
GNP per capita: US$640 (1976)

República del Paraguay

HISTORY. The Republic of Paraguay gained its independence from Spain on 14 May 1811. In 1814 Dr José Gaspar Rodríguez de Francia was elected dictator, and in 1816 perpetual dictator by the National Assembly. He died 20 Sept. 1840. In 1844 a new constitution was adopted, under which Carlos Antonio López (first elected in 1842, died 10 Sept. 1862) and his son, Francisco López, ruled until 1870. During the devastating war against Brazil, Argentina and Uruguay (1865–70) Paraguay's population was reduced from about 600,000 to 232,000. Argentina, in Aug. 1942, and Brazil, in May 1943, voided the reparations which Paraguay had never paid. Further severe losses were incurred during the war with Bolivia (1932–35) over territorial claims in the Chaco. A peace treaty by which Paraguay obtained most of the area her troops had conquered was signed in July 1938.

AREA AND POPULATION. The area of the Oriental section is officially estimated at 159,827 sq. km (61,705 sq. miles) and the Occidental section at 246,925 sq. km (95,337 sq. miles), making the total area of the republic 406,752 sq. km (157,042 sq. miles).

The population according to official estimates in 1976 was 2·75m. The capital, Asunción, had 500,000 inhabitants.

The 16 provinces had the following populations in 1972:

Central	310,101	Caazapá	103,002
Caaguazú	213,356	Alto Paraná	78,037
Paraguari	211,704	Neembucu	72,978
Itapua	201,776	Misiones	69,315
Cordillera	194,365	Amambay	65,527
San Pedro	138,091	Presidente Hayes	38,515
Guairá	124,843	Boquerón	26,142
Concepción	108,198	Olimpo	5,368

Number of births, 1976, was 88,371; deaths, 13,754.

The population is overwhelmingly *mestizo* (mixed Spanish and Guaraní Indian) forming a homogeneous stock. There are some 46,700 unassimilated Indians of other tribal origin, in the Chaco and the forests of eastern Paraguay. There are some small traces of Negro descent. About half the population speak only Guaraní; some 4% speak only Spanish; the rest are bilingual.

Mennonites who arrived in 3 groups (1927, 1930 and 1947) are settled in the Chaco and Oriental Paraguay and were estimated in 1969 to number 13,000, of whom 2,000 came from Canada and 11,000 from Germany. The Japanese colonists in the Oriental section, who first came in 1935, were reckoned to number 7,000 in 1969. Under an agreement signed with Japan in 1959 up to 85,000 Japanese were to be admitted over 30 years. An agreement with Korea was signed in 1966 and there are now (1978) about 3,000 Korean families living in Paraguay.

CONSTITUTION AND GOVERNMENT. A new constitution replacing that of 1940 was drawn up by a Constituent Convention in which all legally recognized political parties were represented and was signed into law on 25 Aug. 1967. It provides for a two-chamber parliament consisting of a 30-seat Senate and a 60-seat Chamber of Deputies. Two-thirds of the seats in each Chamber are allocated to the majority party and the remaining one-third shared among the minority parties in proportion to the votes cast. Voting is compulsory for all citizens over 18.

The President appoints the Cabinet and during parliamentary recess can govern by decree through the Council of State, the members of which are representatives of the Government, the armed forces and other bodies.

On 6 Feb. 1977 elections were held for a 60-member Constitutional Assembly to revise the 1967 Constitution.

President: Gen. Alfredo Stroessner, Commander-in-Chief, elected 11 July 1954 to complete the presidential period of his predecessor. He was re-elected as 'Colorado' candidate in 1958, 1963, 1968, 1973 and 1978.

The following is a list of past presidents since 1940, with the date on which each took office:

Gen. Higinio Morinigo, 7 Sept. 1940 (resigned)
Dr Juan Manuel Frutos, 3 June 1948.[1]
Dr J. Natalicio González, 15 Aug. 1948 (deposed).
Gen. Raimundo Rolón, 30 Jan. 1949.
Dr Felipe Molas López, 26 Feb. 1949[1] (resigned).
Dr Federico Chávez, 16 July 1950 (resigned)
Tomás Romero Pereira, 4 May 1954.

[1] Provisional, *i.e.*, following a *coup d'état.*

The President has a cabinet of 11 ministers.

Interior: Dr Sabino A. Montanaro. *Foreign Affairs:* Dr Alberto Nogués. *Finance:* César Barrientos. *Education and Worship:* Dr Raúl Peña. *Public Works and Communications:* Gral. Juan A. Cáceres. *Agriculture and Livestock:* Ing. Hernando Bertoni. *National Defence:* Gral. Marcial Samaniego. *Public Health and Social Welfare:* Dr Adan Godoy Giménez. *Justice and Labour:* Dr Saúl González. *Industry and Commerce:* Dr Delfín Ugarte Centurion. *Without Portfolio:* Tomás Romero Pereira.

National flag: Red, white, blue (horizontal); the white stripe charged with the arms of the republic on the obverse, and, on the reverse, with a lion and the inscription *Paz y Justicia*—the only flag in the world with different obverse and reverse.

National anthem: ¡Paraguayos, repúplica o muerte! (words by F. Acuña de Figueroa; tune by F. Dupey).

The country is divided into 2 sections: the 'Oriental', east of Paraguay River, and the 'Occidental', west of the same river. The Oriental section is divided into 15 departments. The more important departments are supervised by a *Delegado* appointed by and directly responsible to the central government. The Occidental section, or Chaco, is under military government and divided into 4 departments.

DEFENCE. The army, navy and air forces are separate services under a single command. The President of the Republic is the active Commander-in-Chief. The armed forces total about 17,000 officers and men. Of these, the Army account for about 12,500 (75% conscripts) the Navy about 1,900 (25% conscripts) and the Air Force about 2,500 (25% conscripts). There are also about 4,000 armed police (75% conscripts). Military service is compulsory between the ages of 18 and 20 but there are many exemptions.

Army. The main units of the Army are: a Presidential escort regiment, 6 infantry regiments, a cavalry brigade with 4 regiments, 3 artillery batteries and an engineer command with 5 battalions. Strength (1977), 12,500.

Navy. The Navy consists of 5 armoured river defence gunboats (2 monitors of 636 tons built in Italy and 3 *ex*-Argentinian minesweepers of 620 tons), 1 helicopter lighter, 1 river patrol boat, 2 patrol launches, 6 coastal patrol craft, 2 landing craft, 5 service craft and 3 tugs. Personnel (1978) totalled 1,900 officers and men including coastguard and 500 marines.

Air Force. The Air Force came into being in the early thirties as a combat service, but now has only transport and training formations, although some trainers have COIN capability. It is equipped with a number of DC-6B and C-54 four-engined and C-47 twin-engined transports, 1 Convair 240, a Twin Otter, an Otter, 12 T-6 Texan armed basic trainers and light helicopters. Latest equipment comprises 8 Brazilian-built Uirapuru primary trainers. HQ and flying school are at Campo Grande, Asunción. Personnel total about 2,500.

INTERNATIONAL RELATIONS

Membership. Paraguay is a member of UN, OAS and LAFTA.

ECONOMY

Budget. Revenue and expenditure, in Gs.1m. for calendar years:

	1971[1]	*1972*	*1973*	*1974*	*1975*	*1976*
Revenue	10,255	12,186	12,696	37,198	49,260	61,656
Expenditure	10,522	13,019	13,335	37,052	50,482	59,175

[1] Estimate.

The 1977 budget provided Gs.32,494m. for current and 39,750m. for capital expenditure. The budget revenue includes 7,565m. foreign loans and 17·5m. grants. Total external debt outstanding at the end of Dec. 1976 was US$222m.

Currency. The *guarani* was established on 5 Oct. 1943 equal to 100 old paper pesos. Total monetary circulation was Gs.31,882m. in Aug. 1977; of this, notes were Gs.8,093m. and the remainder money at sight.

Rate of exchange, Aug. 1977: 132 *guaranies* = US$1; 220 *guaranies* = £1.

Banking. The Banco Central del Paraguay opened 1 July 1952 to take over the central banking functions previously assigned to the National Bank of Paraguay, which had opened in March 1943 and been reorganized as the Banco del Paraguay in Sept. 1944 with a monetary, a banking and a mortgage department. The Banco del Paraguay closed in Nov. 1961 and has been replaced, with the aid of a US loan of US$3m., by the Banco Nacional de Fomento; the latter's authorized capital was increased on 13 June 1966 by Gs.600m. to 2,100m.

The Banco Central on 30 Aug. 1973 had gold amounting to US$89m. and foreign exchange equal to US$30m. exclusive of IMF drawing rights.

The Banco Nacional de Fomento, Bank of London and South America, Ltd, Banco Exterior do Brasil, Citibank, Banco de Asunción, Banco Exterior SA, Banco Paraguayo de Comercio, Banco Real del Paraguay SA, Banco Aleman Transatlantico, Banco Holandés Unido, Banco Nacional del Estado de São Paulo. Bank of America all have agencies in Asunción and branches in some main towns.

Weights and Measures. The metric system was officially adopted on 1 Jan. 1901.

ENERGY AND NATURAL RESOURCES

Electricity. Electricity from a 90,000 kw. hydro-electric plant at Acaray, which is to be increased to 180,000 kw. and supplies Asunción, reached 80 population centres in 1972. Electricity is exported to Argentina and Brazil. Paraguay has signed agreements with Brazil to build jointly a 10m. kw. scheme on the river Paraná and with Argentina another which will yield approximately 3m. kw.

Oil. The oil refinery at Villa Elisa, which has been in operation since 1966, has a production of about 3,500 bbls a day. Exploration for petroleum in the Chaco yielded negative results and was abandoned in 1978.

Minerals. Iron, manganese and other minerals have been reported but have not been shown to be commercially exploitable. There are large deposits of limestone, and also salt, kaolin and apatite. *Pennzoil Paraguay* and other national and international firms have acquired licences to prospect for oil and natural gas in the Chaco.

Agriculture. In 1976 it was estimated that agriculture absorbs some 1·5m. hectares.

Area (in hectares) and yield (in tonnes per hectare) of the main agricultural products in 1974:

	Area	*Yield*		*Area*	*Yield*
Cotton	93,200	962	Wheat	30,300	1,163
Maize	206,100	1,366	Soybeans	127,300	1,424
Tobacco	24,200	1,341	Mandioca	90,100	15,484

Wheat, soybean, cotton, sugar, tobacco, coffee are increasing in importance, as are also essential oils and oilseeds. *Yerba maté*, or strongly flavoured Paraguayan tea, continues to be produced but is declining in importance.

The principal sources of finance for agricultural development are USAID and Interamerican Development Bank loans and, for the wheat programme, suppliers' or other credits administered by the National Development Bank.

Livestock. In 1977 Paraguay had about 5·4m. cattle, 315,000 horses, 800,000 pigs, 355,000 sheep. Exports of meat products in 1976 were 12,647 tonnes (US$20·9m.). In 1976 production of fresh meat was 74,000 tonnes; of processed meat, 16,000 tonnes.

Forestry. In the Oriental section there are huge reserves of hardwoods and cedars that have scarcely been exploited. Palms, tung and other trees are exploited for their oils. The Japanese are experimenting with mulberries for silk growing. Pines and firs have been introduced under a United Nations project. In the Chaco the accessible Quebracho forests have nearly been worked out but plans are being made to open up new areas.

INDUSTRY AND TRADE

Industry. There are 3 main meat-packing plants and other factories producing vegetable oils. A textile industry in Pilar and Asunción meets a large part of local needs. As a result of government restrictions on the export of logs the sawmilling and woodworking industry has recently been expanding. A cement works at Valle-mi, with a capacity of 7,000 bags a day, was inaugurated in Jan. 1970. In 1972 the GDP was estimated at about Gs.79,824m., of which 51% originated in agriculture, livestock and forestry, hunting and fishing, mining, industry, building, 5·1% in electricity, water and sanitary services, transport and communications and 48·1% in trade and finance, government, housing and other services. Foreign investment is encouraged by industries being exempted from 30–50% of their tax bill for 5 years. In development areas this may be increased up to 100% for 10 years. Various degrees of duty exemption are permitted on capital equipment and raw materials.

Labour. Trade unionists number about 30,000 (*Confederación Paraguaya de Trabajadores and Confederación Cristiana de Trabajadores*).

Commerce. Imports and exports (in US$1m.):

	1971	*1972*	*1973*	*1974*	*1975*	*1976*	*1977*
Imports	76·2	82·6	83·2	198·3	212·7	180·2	250·4
Exports	64·1	86·2	65·0	169·8	176·2	181·8	278·9

Chief exports in 1976 included (in US$1m.): Cotton, 34·6; meat products, 21; tobacco, 14·7; timber, 12·1; essential oils, 11·6.

Of the imports in 1976 (principally foodstuffs and beverages, vehicles and machinery, chemicals, fuels and lubricants; in US$m.) 37·8 came from Argentina, 31·2 from Brazil, 18·4 from USA, 15·3 from Federal Republic of Germany and 13·7 from the UK.

The trade between Paraguay and UK (British Department of Trade returns, in £1,000 sterling):

	1972	*1973*	*1974*	*1975*	*1976*	*1977*
Imports to UK	4,935	3,897	2,466	6,837	7,897	8,183
Exports and re-exports from UK	2,342	2,786	4,452	6,484	5,478	8,318

Tourism. Visitors numbered 93,023 in 1972; 95,086 in 1973.

COMMUNICATIONS

Roads. In 1976 there were 8,477 km of roads, of which 905 were paved, 582 of gravel and 6,990 of earth. The principal paved roads are Route No. 2/7 running from Asunción to the bridge over the Paraná at Puerto Presidente Stroessner, and thence down to the ocean at Paranaguá; and Route No. 1 to Encarnación in the south. The other main arteries (unpaved) are the road from Coronel Oviedo, on the Asunción–Puerto Presidente Stroessner road, to Pedro Juan Caballero in the north, and the trans-Chaco road which starts from the ferry across the Paraguay River north of Asunción and ends near Nueva Asunción on the Bolivian border. Work has begun to pave this road from Asunción up to Mcal. Estigarribia, about 500 km.

Unpaved roads are closed when it rains. In the Argentine, a paved road starts from Pilcomayo, opposite Asunción, and provides good communication with Buenos Aires, Motor cars, 1976, numbered 17,600; commercial vehicles, 15,200, and passenger vehicles, 7,580.

Railways. The President Carlos Antonio López (formerly Paraguay Central) Railway runs from Asunción to Encarnación, on the Rio Alto Paraná, with a length of 441 km (1,435 mm gauge). Traffic fell sharply in 1976 to 16m. passenger-km and 16·1m. tonne-km.

Aviation. International services are operated by 9 airlines (domestic and foreign) and internal routes by military airlines and some small private lines.

Shipping. In flood the Paraguay River, which divides the country into two distinct parts, is navigable for 12-ft-draught vessels as far as Concepción, 180 miles north of Asunción, and for smaller vessels for a further distance of 600 miles northward. Drought conditions often restrict navigation to lighter traffic. The Paraná River is navigable by large boats from Corrientes up to Puerto Aguirre, at the mouth of the Yguazú River. Boats of a few hundred tons capacity navigate the tributary rivers.

Asunción, the chief port, is 950 miles from the sea. In June 1945 the Government formed—after a break of 80 years—a national merchant marine which operates in the river Plate basin, connecting with Argentine, Uruguayan and Brazilian ports. The cargo fleet includes 25 vessels of 300–1,000 tons, 3 tankers of 1,100–1,700 tons, 2 passenger river boats and 1 ocean-going freighter of 713 tons.

Post and Broadcasting. The national telegraph (137 offices) connects Asunción with Corrientes and Posadas in the Argentine Republic, and thus with the outside world; new direct links have been opened with the Federal Republic of Germany, USA, Bolivia and Chile. In addition, 34 stations are operated by the President Carlos Antonio López Railway; total, 2,070 miles. Three companies (12 stations) offer radio-telegraph and telex services to several countries. The telephone system has been under government control since 5 Oct. 1945; a new government agency, the National Telephone Administration, took over the telecommunication services in July 1947. Telephone lines, 1949, 5,225 miles; instruments, 1977, 41,644, of which 33,501 were in Asunción and were automatic. There are 1 state and 7 commercial radio stations in Asunción, 20 in provincial towns, and a commercial television station in Asunción.

Cinemas (1974). Cinemas numbered 65 in Asunción. The larger country towns usually have an outdoor cinema.

Newspapers (1977). There are 5 daily newspapers in Asunción with an aggregate circulation of about 180,000.

JUSTICE, RELIGION AND EDUCATION

Justice. The highest court is the Supreme Court with 5 members. There are special Chambers of Appeal for civil and commercial cases, and criminal cases. Judges of first instance deal with civil, commercial and criminal cases in 6 departments. Minor cases are dealt with by Justices of the Peace.

The Attorney-General represents the State in all jurisdictions, with representatives in each judicial department and in every jurisdiction. In matters of revenue, taxes, etc., the State is represented by the Abogado del Tesoro.

Religion. Religious liberty is guaranteed by the 1967 constitution. Article 6 thereof recognizes Roman Catholicism as the official religion of the country. The same article disposes that relations between Paraguay and the Holy See shall be regulated by concordats or other bilateral agreements, but no such agreements have yet been negotiated.

The Roman Catholic Church is organized into the Archdiocese of Asunción, 3 other dioceses (San Juan Bautista de las Misiones, Concepción and Villarrica); 4 Prelatures (Coronel Oviedo, Encarnación, Alto Paraná and Caacupé); and 2 Vicariates Apostolic (Chaco and Pilcomayo). The bishops meet in a Conference of Paraguayan Bishops. Only civil marriages are legally valid. There are numerous non-catholic communities, the largest of whom are the Mennonites. There is a small

Anglican church in Asunción, with missions in the Chaco, which comes under the jurisdiction of an Anglican Bishop resident in Asunción.

Education. Education is free and nominally compulsory, but schools are not everywhere available, and the system has been extensively revised to provide, *inter alia*, primary education for adults. Illiteracy is estimated at 22% (urban) and 30% (rural). In 1973 there were 2,288 government primary schools and 421 private schools, with 459,393 pupils and 15,871 teachers; 652 secondary schools had 66,746 students and 6,729 teachers. In 1978 there was an intensive school building programme in progress. The National University in Asunción had, in 1973, 7,919 students and 1,209 professors. In 1973 the Catholic University and associated colleges had 4,546 students and 355 professors.

DIPLOMATIC REPRESENTATIVES

OF PARAGUAY IN GREAT BRITAIN
(51 Cornwall Gdns, London, SW7 4AQ)

Ambassador: Lic. Numa A. Mallorquin (accredited 5 Dec. 1969).

OF GREAT BRITAIN IN PARAGUAY (25 de Mayo, 171, Asunción)

Ambassador and Consul-General: C. W. Wallace, CVO.

OF PARAGUAY IN THE USA (2400 Massachusetts Ave., NW, Washington, D.C., 20008)

Ambassador: Mario López Escobar.

OF THE USA IN PARAGUAY (1776 Mariscal López Ave., Asunción)

Ambassador: Robert E. White.

OF PARAGUAY TO THE UNITED NATIONS

Ambassador: Dr Francisco Barreiro.

Books of Reference

Gaceta Oficial, published by Imprenta Nacional, Estrella y Estero Bellaco, Asunción
Anuario Daumas. Asunción
Anuario Estadístico de la República del Paraguay. Asunción. Annual
Report of the Council of the Corporation of Foreign Bondholders. Annual. London
Pendle, G., *Paraguay, A Riverside Nation*. R. Inst. of Int. Affairs, 3rd ed., 1967
Raine, P., *Paraguay*. New Brunswick, N.J., 1956

National Library: Biblioteca Nacional, De la Rosidenta, Asunción.

PERU

Capital: Lima
Population: 15·5m. (1977)
GNP per capita: US$800 (1976)

República del Perú

HISTORY. The Republic of Peru, formerly the most important of the Spanish vice-royalties in South America, declared its independence on 28 July 1821; but it was not till after a war, protracted till 1824, that the country gained its actual freedom.

AREA AND POPULATION. The total area of Peru is estimated to be 1,285,215 sq. km (496,093 sq. miles).

The long-standing dispute with Chile over the provinces of Tacna and Arica (*see* THE STATESMAN'S YEAR-BOOK, 1928, p. 1198) reached an amicable settlement on 3 June 1929 at Lima, Tacna going to Peru and Arica to Chile. In response to demands by Bolivia for permanent access to the Pacific Coast, proposals for a Bolivian corridor to the sea and a new Bolivian port to be built in the disputed area have been put forward by Chile and Peru. To date, little progress has been made. One result has been increased tension along the Chilean–Peruvian border, with reports of an arms build-up by both countries. For an account of the settlement of other boundary disputes, *see* THE STATESMAN'S YEAR-BOOK, 1948, p. 1173.

A map of the boundary with Ecuador is to be found in THE STATESMAN'S YEAR-BOOK, 1942.

The census taken on 4 June 1972 gave the population as 13,572,052. Estimate (1977) 15·5m. Children under 15 years, 7·2m. (45% of total population). Birthrate, 4·2%; death, 1·3%. Lima, the capital, had 3,158,417 population. Other major cities (with census population 1972), are Callao (296,220), Arequipa (304,653), Trujillo (241,882), Chiclayo (189,685), Chimbote (159,045), Piura (126,702), Cuzco (120,881), Huancayo (115,693), Iquitos (111,327). The language is Spanish, but the Indian population speak either Quechua (the second official language) or Aymará.

The area of the 23 departments and the constitutional province of Callao are given below with the population, according to the official census of 1961 and 1972. The area of the department of Puno includes the Peruvian zone of Lake Titicaca, 4,996·28 sq. km. The chief towns are shown in brackets:

Departments	*Area (sq. km) 1959*	*Population* 2 July 1961 (census)	2 June 1972 census (provisional)	*Pop. per sq. km 1961*
Amazonas (Chachapoyas)	41,297·1	129,003	196,469	2·85
Ancash (Huaraz)	36,308·3	605,548	726,665	16·20
Apurímac (Abancay)	20,654·6	303,648	307,805	16·36
Arequipa (Arequipa)	63,527·6	407,163	530,528	6·47
Ayacucho (Ayacucho)	45,503·1	430,289	459,747	9·85
Cajamarca (Cajamarca)	35,417·8	786,599	916,331	21·15
Callao (Callao)[1]	73·8	219,420	315,605	2,901·46
Cuzco (Cuzco)	84,140·9	648,168	708,719	7·30
Huancavelica (Huancavelica)	22,870·9	315,730	331,155	13·07
Huánuco (Huánuco)	35,314·6	355,003	420,764	10·24
Ica (Ica)	21,251·4	261,126	357,973	11·48
Junín (Huancayo)	32,354·4	548,662	691,216	15·64
La Libertad (Trujillo)	23,241·3	609,105	806,368	25·29
Lambayeque (Chiclayo)	16,585·9	353,657	515,363	20·93
Lima (Lima)	33,894·9	2,093,435	3,485,411	68·42
Loreto (Iquitos)	478,336·2	411,340	494,895	0·69

[1] With Province.

Departments	Area (sq. km.) 1959	Population 2 July 1961 (census)	2 June 1972 census (provisional)	Pop. per sq. km. 1961
Madre de Dios (Maldonado)	78,402·7	25,269	21,968	0·19
Moquegua (Moquegua)	16,174·7	53,260	74,573	3·60
Pasco (Cerro de Pasco)	21,854·1	150,575	176,750	5·79
Piura (Piura)	33,067·1	692,414	854,668	21·68
Puno (Puno)	72,382·4	727,309	779,594	10·20
San Martín (Moyobamba)	53,063·6	170,456	224,310	3·06
Tacna (Tacna)	14,766·6	67,800	95,623	4·68
Tumbes (Tumbes)	4,731·5	57,378	75,399	21·10
Total	1,285,215·6	10,420,357	13,567,939	8·06

CONSTITUTION AND GOVERNMENT. On 3 Oct. 1968 a military junta overthrew the government of President Fernando Belaúnde Terry and installed Gen. Juan Velasco Alvarado as President of a 'Revolutionary Government' with a cabinet composed entirely of officers of the armed services. Gen. Velasco was ousted in a bloodless *coup* in Aug. 1975 and was replaced by Gen. Francisco Morales Bermudez. Congress has been suspended and rule is by Decree Law.

The Government have stated that the existing Constitution will be revised by 1979 before fresh elections are held. Return to civilian rule by 1980 is envisaged.

At present the Constitution provides for a Legislature consisting of a Senate (45 members) and a Chamber of Deputies (140 members) and an Executive formed of the President of the Republic and a Council of Ministers appointed by him. Elections are to be held every 6 years with the President and Congress elected, at the same time, by separate ballots. All literate Peruvians (native-born or naturalized) over the age of 21 are eligible to vote; in Dec. 1970 the number of registered voters was 2,829,728, including 1m. in Lima province. Voting is compulsory; women were fully enfranchised in 1955.

Augusto Bernardino Leguia, 4 July 1919–24 Aug. 1930.[1]
Gen. Manuel Ponce (Acting), 24 Aug. 1930–28 Aug. 1930.[2]
Col. Louis M. Sánchez Cerro (Acting), 28 Aug. 1930–1 March 1931.[2]
Richardo Leoncio Elias (Acting), 1 March 1931–5 March 1931.[2]
Col. Gustavo A. Jiménez (Acting), 5 March 1931–10 March 1931.[2]
David Samanez Ocampo (Acting), 10 March 1931–8 Dec. 1931.
Gen. Luis M. Sánchez Cerro (Constitutional), 8 Dec. 1931–30 April 1933.[3]
Gen. Oscar Raimundo Benavides, 30 April 1933–8 Dec. 1939.
Dr Manuel Pradoy Ugarteche, 8 Dec. 1939–28 July 1945.
Dr José Luis Bustamante y Rivero, 28 July 1945–27 Oct. 1948.[1]
Gen. Manuel A. Odría (Acting), 27 Oct. 1948–1 June 1950.[2]
Gen. Zenón Noriega, 1 June 1950–28 July 1950.
Gen. Manuel A. Odría, 28 July 1950–28 July 1956.
Dr Manuel Prado y Ugarteche, 28 July 1956–July 1962.
Gen. Ricardo Pérez Godoy, 18 July 1962–3 March 1963.[1]
Gen. Nicolás Lindley López, 3 March–28 July 1963.
Fernando Belaúnde Terry, 28 July 1963–3 Oct. 1968.[1]
Gen. Juan Velasco Alvarado, 3 Oct. 1968–29 Aug. 1975.[1]

[1] Deposed. [2] Resigned. [3] Assassinated.

President: Gen. Francisco Morales Bermúdez.

Prime Minister and Minister of War: Gen. Oscar Molina Pallochia.

Interior: Gen. Fernando Velit Sabattini. *Foreign Affairs:* Dr José de la Puente Radbill. *Labour and Indian Affairs:* José Garcia Calderón Koechlin. *Health:* Oscar Davila Zumaeta. *Navy:* Jorge Parodi Galliani. *Air Force:* Jorge Tamayo de la Flor. *Energy and Mines:* Juan Sánchez González. *Transport and Communications:* Elivio Vaninni Chumpitazi. *Industry, Tourism, Integration and Commerce:* Gabriel Lanatta. *Agrarian Reform and Food:* Luis Arbulú Ibáñez. *Economy and Finance:* Javier Silva Rueke. *Education:* Otto Eléspuru Revoredo. *Housing and Construction:* Gerónimo Cafferata Marazzi. *Fisheries:* Francisco Mariátegui Angulo.

As of 30 June 1965 the 23 departments are divided into 148 provinces (plus the constitutional province of Callao) and 1,662 districts; the province of Callao has some of the functions of a department.

National flag: Three vertical strips of red, white, red, with the national arms in the centre.

National anthem: Somos Libres, seámoslo siempre (words by J. de la Torre Ugarte; tune by J. B. Alcedo, 1821).

DEFENCE. The national budget for 1977 included a defence estimate of S/.30,000m.

Army. While military service is compulsory youths are only conscripted to fill the annual quota. The term of service is 2 years and all males of 20–25 years of age are liable. The country is divided into 5 military regions.

The Army comprises approximately 46,000 all ranks, of which some 6,000 are regular officers. There are 8 infantry, 1 commando and 1 armoured brigade, and mountain, parachute, artillery and engineer battalions. There is an air element of 4 Helio Courier 395 communications aircraft. Equipment consists of approximately 360 tanks (T-55, AMX13 and Sherman) over 100 light armoured fighting vehicles and 105-mm./155-mm. field artillery.

The section of the national police force with a para-military role is known as the *Guardia Civil* and comprises approximately 20,000 personnel.

Navy. The Peruvian Navy consists of 8 submarines comprising 2 West German-built completed in 1975–76, 4 completed in USA in 1954–57 and 2 older *ex*-USN; 3 cruisers, *Almirante Grau* (ex-*De Ruyter*) acquired from the Netherlands in 1973, *Capitan Quinones*[1] (ex-*Almirante Grau*, ex-*Newfoundland*) and *Coronel Bolognesi* (ex-*Ceylon*), acquired from Great Britain in 1959–60; 2 'Daring' class destroyers delivered from Britain during 1973; 2 destroyers acquired from USA during 1960–61; 2 frigates (former US destroyer escorts); 2 landing ships; 2 medium landing ships; 3 river patrol launches; 5 river gunboats; 8 small patrol craft; 2 transports; 2 hospital craft; 1 research craft; 1 training ship (attack cargo ship); 7 oilers; 2 survey vessels; 3 floating docks; 1 water carrier, and 2 tugs.

[1] When the Dutch cruiser *De Ruyter* was purchased in 1973 she was re-named *Almirante Grau* after Peru's principal naval hero. In consequence the cruiser whose name had been changed from *Newfoundland* to *Almirante Grau* when she was purchased from Britain in 1959 was again re-named *Capitan Quinones*, after an air force hero.

All naval training takes place in the Callao area at various schools. The main naval base and dockyard are also in Callao. Smaller bases are at Iquitos on the Amazon, and at San Lorenzo. Naval personnel in 1978 totalled 1,200 officers and 12,800 men including the Naval Air Arm and 1,000 marines.

The new construction programme includes 4 frigates (2 being built in Italy and 2 sister ships to be built in Peru), 2 patrol submarines to be built in the Federal Republic of Germany, 1 oceanographic survey ship, and 1 oiler.

The Coast Guard includes 2 corvettes (*ex*-fleet minesweepers acquired from the US Navy in 1960–61), 6 fast patrol vessels built in Britain in 1964–65, 2 former US gunboats, and 6 new large patrol craft.

Air Force. The Air Force is under the direction of the Air Minister, who is also C.-in-C.

The operational force consists of 3 combat groups. No. 13 Group has 2 squadrons of Mirage 5 jet fighters; No. 21 Group has 2 squadrons of Canberra light jet bombers and 1 squadron of A-37B light jet attack aircraft; No. 12 Group has 1 squadron of F-86F and 1 of Hunter F.4/52 jet day fighters, supplemented by AT-33 armed jet trainers. Other aircraft in service include medium transports (DC-9, F.28 Fellowship, An-26, C-54, C-130 and C-118), 40 light transports (C-47, Twin Otter, Buffalo and Turbo-Porter), 30 helicopters (including Mi-8, Bell 212, Alouette II/III and Bell JetRanger and 47G), 100 training aircraft (including T-33, T-37, Beech T-42A and Cessna T-41D) and a small number of miscellaneous types for photographic and communications duties. The 2 DC-9s and some of the C-47, C-54 and C-130 aircraft are used by the Air Force to run a commercial airline network (SATCO). There are military airfields at Talara, Chiclayo, Piura, Pisco, Lima (2),

Iquitos and La Joya, and a seaplane base at Iquitos. All officers and pilots are trained at the Air Academy at Lima (Las Palmas). The approximate strength of the Peruvian Air Force is 10,000 personnel and 135 combat aircraft. An order for 36 Soviet-built Su-22 variable-geometry fighter-bombers was placed in 1976, and 12 MiG-21s were obtained from Cuba for conversion training.

INTERNATIONAL RELATIONS

Membership. Peru is a member of UN, OAS and LAFTA.

ECONOMY

Planning. Peru has had a National Planning Institute since 1963. The plans it has published are of an indicative nature. The Institute accounced in May 1975 a comprehensive plan for economic and social development in the years 1975–78. The plan provides for an annual growth rate of 6·5%.

Budget. On a cash-flow basis (*i.e.*, development loans considered as receipts and debt service included in payments) the revenue and expenditure for calendar years were as follows (in 1m. soles):

	1967[1]	*1968*[2]	*1969*[3]	*1970*	*1971–72*[3]
Revenue	28,222	30,745	32,300	42,715	114,760
Expenditure	33,183	30,745	32,300	44,877	115,605

[1] Budget year 15 months ending 31 March 1968. [2] Estimates. [3] Biennial basis.

In the 1971–72 budget proposed expenditure included (in 1m. soles): Defence, 18,780; economy and finance, 25,515 (including 13,757 for debt refinancing); interior, 11,230; education, 23,009; health, 6,487; transport and communications, 6,545; agriculture, 7,491; energy and mines, 3,926; housing, 1,940.

The external debt rose from US$311m. in 1964 to 3,013m. in 1975.

Currency. The monetary unit is the *sol.* On 28 June 1976 the *sol* was devalued to the rate of 65 = US$1, and on 20 Sept. 1976 there was introduced a policy of frequent mini-devaluations which brought the exchange rate to 67·21 = US$1 in Nov. 1976. In May 1970 exchange control was imposed on the small free exchange market. Foreign residents were exempted from a number of the regulations but Peruvian citizens were required to repatriate overseas bank deposits and declare all foreign assets. The official exchange rate is S/.106 = £1 for normal transactions.

Coins include the 10- and 5-sol pieces (copper 75%; nickel 25%), the sol and half sol (copper 30%; zinc 70%), the 20, 10 and 5 centavos (copper–zinc); the 2- and 1-centavo pieces (zinc) have been discontinued. Peru has a paper currency issued by the Banco Central de la Reserva in denominations of 1,000, 500, 200, 100, 50, 10 and 5 soles. Money in circulation at 30 June 1972 was S/.22,318·2m.

Banking. The Government bank of issue is the Banco Central de la Reserva del Perú, which was established in 1922. A new charter for the bank was promulgated in Aug. 1968; this, *inter alia,* extended the bank's authority with regard to the organization of the commercial banking system. This bank also regulates the certificate exchange market through which import, export and foreign currency loan operations are channelled. As at March 1971 its paid-up capital and reserves stood at 311m. soles and its net foreign currency reserves at US$219m.

The Government's fiscal agent is the Banco de la Nación which, since May 1970, has control of the 'giro' market through which most non-trade foreign currency transactions are channelled. As at March 1971 it had a paid-up capital and reserves of 563m. soles.

Banks, domestic and foreign, are supervised by the Superintendent of Banks and Insurance. There were in March 1971, 7 state banks, 11 commercial banks (of which 3 were controlled by the Banco de la Nación), 6 regional banks (with head office outside Lima or Callao) and 4 foreign banks (1 British, 2 American and 1 Japanese). In March 1971 Peruvian currency deposits of the banking system (excluding state banks) amounted to 36,935,000 soles and advances to 25,398,000 soles.

Weights and Measures. The metric system of weights and measures was established by law in 1869, and since 1916 has come into general use.

ENERGY AND NATURAL RESOURCES

Electricity. In 1972 control of electricity production and distribution passed to ELECTROPERU, a state company. In 1970 the production of electric energy was 5,003m. kw. The installed capacity in 1970 was 1,684 kw.

Oil. Proven oil reserves in the jungle region amount to about 105m. tonnes. A further 75m. tonnes have been found in the north-west, some of it offshore. The new 850 km pipeline, linking the new jungle oilfields to coastal terminals, was opened in 1977. Throughput will amount to about 100,000 bbls per day by 1978. Peru is expected to become self-sufficient in oil by 1978. The total value of exports in 1975 of petroleum and derivatives was US$13m.

Minerals. Mineral exports accounted for about 50% of value of exports in 1976. Lead, copper, iron, silver, zinc and petroleum are the chief minerals exploited. Mineral exports in 1975: Copper, US$165m.; silver, US$83m.; lead, US$73m.; zinc, US$173m.; iron ore, US$55m. Crude petroleum output in 1970 was 26·3m. bbls. Mine production (in tonnes, 1970) of copper, 215,000; lead, 170,000; zinc, 320,000; antimony, 780, tungsten, 1,591; bismuth, 765; molybdenum, 810; cadmium, 285; mercury, 121; tin, 71; manganese (37·8%), 12; silver, 38m. troy oz.; gold, 90,000 grammes. Diamonds were discovered during 1966 in the department of Cuzco (Canchis). Iron deposits are large; production (62% Fe), 1970, 10·1m. long tons. Excellent coal deposits, with an ash content of from 5–7%, lie near by; output, 1969, 161,769 tonnes. Nepheline was discovered in Puno department in 1962. Titanium was discovered off the northern coast in 1972.

In Sept. 1969 a law was introduced to force the major mining companies to work their hitherto unexploited concessions or lose them. In June 1971 a Mining Law was published which introduced a new tax structure for the industry and stated that as a matter of policy the State would undertake the marketing and refining of minerals.

The government-controlled guano deposits on Huanillos, Punta Lobos and other islands are important; the 1966 production was 55,505 tonnes.

Production of domestic and industrial salt in 1970 was 103,400 tonnes.

Agriculture. There are 4 natural zones: the coast strip, with an average width of 80 km; the Sierra or Uplands, formed by the coast range of mountains and the Andes proper; the Montaña or high wooded region which lies on the eastern slopes of the Andes, and the jungle in the Amazon Basin, known as the Selva. Land under cultivation, 1967, was about 2·75m. hectares. There are 4 fertilizer factories, near Callao and in Cuzco.

Peru is a substantial importer of foodstuffs, chiefly cereals (1975, US$150m.), but also fats and oil, meat and dairy products. In 1971 imports and primary agricultural products were valued at 510·5m. soles and capital goods at 553·4m. soles.

Nearly half of the population is dependent on agriculture, which accounted for 15% of the GDP in 1970. Peru's third land reform law, that of June 1969, is the most comprehensive. It provides for the large sugar estates in the north of Peru to be turned into co-operatives. Maximum permitted sizes for other types of land holding are stipulated for the various regions of the country. These range from 150 hectares for irrigated land on the coast to an area capable of supporting 5,000 sheep for pasture land in the Sierra. These sizes may be increased if certain efficiency criteria are met. Holdings too small to be economically viable are to be consolidated into co-operative units. The chief agricultural productions of Peru are, in the order named: Sugar, cotton, coffee and wool. The cotton industry was nationalized on 1 Oct. 1974.

Production in 1971 (in 1,000 tonnes): Sugar-cane, 823; cotton, 250; coffee, 69; wool, 8. Sugar (1975), 543m. tonnes.

Output of cattle hides (in tonnes), 1970, 1,200; sheepskins, 1,110; goatskins, 953. Output of sheep wool in 1970 was 13,121 tonnes. Alpaca and llama wool and vicuña hair, 4,458 tonnes; exports, 1970, were sheep wool, unwashed, 606 tonnes; llama, alpaca and vicuña wool, 1,537 tonnes.

Livestock (1972): 1·19m. llamas, alpacas, etc., 1·54m. horses, 3·82m. cattle, 1·87m. goats, 12·83m. sheep, 1·7m. swine, 21·33m. poultry.

Fisheries. Peru is the world's foremost fishing nation in terms of value of catch, most of which is anchoveta which is reduced into fishmeal for export as animal feed. Peru produces around 45% of the world's total fishmeal supplies or nearly 2m. tons a year. There were in Dec. 1971, 109 fishmeal plants employing about 3,000 workers spread among the 22 ports of the 1,400-mile Peruvian coastline. Over 30% of the capacity is in Chimbote. There are approximately 1,300 fishing boats employing 20,000 full-time fishermen. In 1971 exports of fishmeal amounted to 1·75m. tonnes valued at US$327·7m., production (1975) was 706,370 tonnes and the anchovy catch was 10·27m. tonnes (1975, 6m.). Abnormal marine conditions prevailed in 1976 with a catch of 3·9m. tonnes. Other fish caught include tuna (exports in 1969 of canned tuna were 2,753 tonnes and of frozen tuna (1970) 2,753 tonnes); bonito (1969 exports were 1,600 tons for canned and 1,207 tons for frozen); barrilete; merluza; swordfish. Increasing importance is being placed on the development of the table fish industry. Exports of fishmeal in 1972 declined sharply owing to the departure of anchovy for other waters, driven by temporarily abnormal ocean currents.

INDUSTRY AND TRADE

Industry. The Industrial Promotion Law, 1959, succeeded in encouraging local enterprises. The manufacturing industry has been the fastest growing sector of the economy in recent years. The average compounded annual growth rate for the period 1968–72 was 9·2% per annum. In 1970 it was estimated that the manufacturing industries accounted for 20% of the GNP. In July 1970 a new Law of Industry was promulgated. This classifies industries according to national priorities and defines certain basic industries which it will be in the interests of the economy for the State to control. It also provides for worker participation in industrial companies to the extent that they will share both in the profits and ultimately, through the creation of an industrial community, own 50% of all companies. In future foreign owned companies must either become Peruvianized or operate under a special contract with the Government, which will enable them to recover their investment and reasonable profits, but eventually for the enterprise to pass to the hands of the Peruvian Government. Cars and station wagons assembled in 1971 were 11,059 and commercial vehicles 5,580. The Government in an attempt to rationalize the industry, has stipulated that as from 1 Jan. 1971 there will only be 5 plants assembling automobiles. The aim of the Government is progressively to increase the proportion of nationally produced vehicle parts and components. About 70% of Peru's manufacturing industries are located in or around the Lima/Callao metropolitan area.

Peru's first iron and steel mill came into production at Chimbote in April 1958. Products include pig-iron, blooms, billets, largets, round and round-deformed bars, wire rod, black and galvanized sheets and galvanized roofing sheets. Refractories are manufactured at Lima.

The Government has a monopoly of the import and/or local manufacture and sale of guano, salt, alcohol and explosives. The monopoly of matches was abandoned in 1954 and that of tobacco in June 1955.

Output of Peru's manufacturing industry grew 10·5% in 1970 and annual production in the following industries was (in tonnes):

Refined copper	35,900	Vehicle assembly, cars (units)	10,300
Refined zinc	69,000	Lorries and buses (units)	4,200
Refined lead	72,200	Tyres (units)	456,000
Sulphuric acid	45,000	Radio receivers (units)[3]	27,000
Caustic soda[1]	26	TV receivers (units)[3]	32,000
Cement	1,138,000	Non-cellulose fibres (lb.)	3,000,000
Cast iron[2]	176,000	Rayon and acetate filament threads (lb.)	3,700,000
Crude steel[2]	153,000		

[1] 1968. [2] 1969. [3] 1967.

In 1972 the Andean Group allocated 24 different metal manufacturing industries to Peru for meeting the Group's needs in those industries by 1980.

Labour. In 1976 the total labour force was considered to number 5m. persons, of which 40% either under-employed or unemployed. This was 52% of the urban population of the country or about 30% of the country's population. The population was distributed roughly as follows in 1972: Agriculture, stock-raising and fishing, 2m.; manufacturing industry, 611,000; construction, 183,000; mining, 98,000; government, 317,000; commerce, 475,000; services, 477,000.

Trade Unions. Trade unions have about 2m. members (approximately 1·5m. in peasant organizations and 0·5m. in industrial). The major trade union organization is the *Confederación de Trabajadores del Perú*, which was reconstituted in 1959 after being in abeyance for some years. The other labour organizations recognized by the Government are the *Confederación General de Trabajadores del Perú*, the *Confederación Nacional de Trabajadores* and the *Central de Trabajadores de la Revolución Peruana*.

Commerce. The value of trade has been as follows (in US$1m.):

	1972	*1973*	*1974*	*1975*	*1976*	*1977*
Imports	660	886	1,276	1,380	1,359	1,726
Exports	943	1,047	1,511	2,480	2,100	2,095

On 2 May 1961 Peru ratified the Montevideo treaty and thereby became one of the members of the Latin American Free Trade Area (LAFTA).

On 26 May 1969 Peru signed the Cartagena Agreement between Bolivia, Colombia, Chile and Ecuador establishing the Andean Group but withdrew in Jan. 1977, the aim of which is to accelerate the process of economic integration and development on a sub-regional basis within the ambit of LAFTA.

In 1970 the principal imports were: Machinery and appliances (25%); foodstuffs, beverages and tobacco (20%); metals and manufactures (11%); chemicals and allied products (12%); vehicles and transport equipment (10%); wood, pulp and paper (6%); textiles (4%); fuel, lubricants and other non-metallic minerals (3%); rubber, plastics, etc. (5%); miscellaneous (5%).

The principal exports were: Minerals and metals (48%); marine products (32%); cotton (5%); sugar (6%); coffee (4%); wool (1%); petroleum (1%); miscellaneous (3%).

The major suppliers were (in S/.1m.):

	Imports from		*Exports to*	
	1969	*1970*	*1969*	*1970*
USA	7,196	7,697	11,560	13,334
Germany (Fed. Rep.)	2,642	2,917	4,051	6,084
Japan	1,673	1,893	5,413	5,490
Argentine	2,404	1,547	592	539
UK	1,020	1,037	1,047	1,019
Italy	636	699	877	973
Belgium/Netherlands	...	1,078	...	5,756

Principal exports have been (in S/.1m.):

	1969	*1970*
Copper	10,038	10,418
Iron (ore)	2,549	2,544
Lead (metal content)	1,336	1,362
Petroleum	240	288
Silver (metal content)	2,224	2,391
Zinc (metal content)	1,504	1,816
Cotton	2,522	2,056
Fish and fish products	8,552	13,107
Sugar	1,522	2,563
Coffee	1,166	1,730

Total trade between Peru and UK (British Department of Trade returns, in £1,000 sterling):

	1973	*1974*	*1975*	*1976*	*1977*
Imports to UK	19,126	35,788	28,794	41,873	34,634
Exports and re-exports from UK	14,154	21,884	51,034	35,761	34,585

COMMUNICATIONS

Roads. There were at 30 June 1966, 45,549 km, of which 17,114 km were made up and 4,547 km asphalted. Work on the Carretera Marginal de la Selva (South American Marginal Forest Highway) started in 1965; the 5,600 km road between the Colombian–Venezuelan border and Sta. Cruz, Bolivia, of which the Peruvian portion consists of 394 km already existing, 503 km now under construction and 1,565 km outstanding, to make a sectional total of some 2,460 km.

In 1974 there were 266,910 private cars and 139,950 commercial vehicles.

Railways. Since 1972 all public railways are nationalized and run by Peruvian National Railways (ENAFER). Total length (1975), 1,628 km on 1,435- and 914-mm gauges.

Aviation. Air services connect Lima and the capitals of every South American republic.

Shipping. In 1966, 6,900 vessels of 26,602,270 tons entered, and 6,871 of 26,610,772 tons cleared the ports. Since 1928 the coasting trade has been largely reserved for Peruvian-owned vessels with Peruvian crews; in 1960 it handled 2,246,000 tonnes, valued at 1,665m. soles.

Post and Broadcasting. An earth satellite ground communication station at Lurin connects Peru through Intelsat. III to the US and Europe. In 1975 there were 333,346 telephones, 245,701 in Lima. Length of telegraph lines was 26,121 km. In 1970 the Lima Telephone Co. was nationalized and the Government have announced their intention to nationalize progressively the entire telephone and communications network. Radio-telephone circuits connect Lima with distant towns. Three submarine telegraph cables connect Peru and Chile, and one connects Peru and the republics to the north. There are 153 broadcasting stations, of which 29 are in Lima. Wireless receiving sets, about 2m. There are 7 television stations in Lima, 16 in the provinces and 45 relay stations. All radio and television stations are controlled by the Government.

Cinemas. In 1972 there were 276 cinemas.

Newspapers. The main Lima newspapers, all controlled by the government, are *La Prensa, El Comercio, Expreso, Correo* and *La Nueva Crónica.*

JUSTICE, RELIGION, EDUCATION AND WELFARE

Justice. The Peruvian judicial system is a pyramid at the base of which are the justices of the peace who decide minor criminal cases and civil cases involving small sums of money. The apex is the Supreme Court with 17 members; in between are the judges of first instance, who usually sit in the provincial capitals, and the superior courts of which there are 18.

The Revolutionary Government decreed in Dec. 1969 that all judges, except justices of the peace, will in future be elected by the National Council of Justice, composed of representatives of the Executive, the Legislature, the Judiciary, the National Federation of the College of Lawyers and 2 of the university law faculties. Justices of the peace will be appointed, as before, by the superior courts.

Religion. Religious liberty exists, but the Roman Catholic religion is protected by the state, and since 1929 only Roman Catholic religious instruction is permitted in schools, state or private. In 1972 there were 1 Roman Catholic cardinal, 7 archbishops, 14 bishops, 3 vicars-general, 8 vicars apostolic, 2,672 priests, 506 cloistered monks and 4,558 members of religious orders.

Protestants numbered 128,000 in 1966.

All marriages must be civil, regardless of religion and preceded by medical examination; there are liberal divorce regulations, including divorce for 'absence without just cause for more than 2 years', and by mutual consent. Divorcees may remarry immediately. A law of 1936 emphasizes that the religious obligations of marriage are fully recognized.

Education. A new law for education was promulgated in March 1972. Elementary education is compulsory and free for both sexes between the ages of 7 and 16; secondary education is also free. But schools, despite substantial increases, are still too few. The system is highly centralized; all teaching appointments are made by the Minister of Education for the public schools; for the private schools he supervises plant and equipment and limits fees but does not appoint teachers.

In 1970 there were 20,034 public, private and primary schools with 64,004 teachers and 2·75m. pupils; 1,452 secondary schools, with 21,863 teachers and 674,000 students. Training in 414 public technical schools is also free; in 1970 they had 6,333 teachers and 223,300 pupils. The 90 teacher-training schools had 1,075 teachers and 18,000 pupils. Total literacy (1975) was 68% of total population.

Because of the increase in the number of pupils state schools have divided their teaching timetable into three divisions, morning, afternoon and evening. Those pupils in the last shift have to spend an extra year at school to make up for the difference in the length of the daily timetable.

In 1970 the total number of university students was 105,600.

Social Welfare. Contributory social security schemes exist for employees and workers. These are administered by the Ministry of Labour. There were in 1975, 182 hospitals (33,350 beds). In addition in 1969 there were 63 health centres, 307 medical posts and 842 sanitary posts, all administered by the authorities. In 1975 there were 9,445 doctors, 2,119 obstetricians, 115 chemists and 8,920 trained nurses.

DIPLOMATIC REPRESENTATIVES

OF PERU IN GREAT BRITAIN (52 Sloane St., London, SW1X 9SP)

Ambassador: Dr Don Gonzalo Fernandez-Puyo (accredited 1 June 1978).

OF GREAT BRITAIN IN PERU
(Edificio El Pacifico, Washington Ave., Arequipa, Lima)

Ambassador: G. W. Harding, CMG, CVO.

OF PERU IN THE USA (1700 Massachusetts Ave., NW, Washington, D.C., 20036)

Ambassador: Carlos Garcia-Bedoya.

OF THE USA IN PERU (PO Box 1995, Lima)

Ambassador: Harry W. Shlandeman.

OF PERU TO THE UNITED NATIONS

Ambassador: Dr Carlos Alzamora.

Books of Reference

The official gazette is *El Peruano*, Lima.

Anario Estadistico del Perú. Annual.—*Boletin de Estadistica Peruana.* Quarterly.—*Demarcarción Política del Perú.* (Dirección Nacional de Estadística), Lima

Censo Nacional Población, 4 June 1972. Lima, 1972

Estadística del Comercio Exterior (*Superintendencia de Aduanas*). Lima

Banco Central de Reserva. Monthly Bulletin.—*Renta Nacional del Perú.* Annual, Lima

Ministerio de Fomento Lima publishes separate annual statistics on the mining and petroleum industries and on general industry; the wool textile and cotton textile industries, the Peruvian Chamber of Commerce furnish annual studies.

Alba, V., *Peru.* Boulder, 1977

Bourricaud, F., *Pouvoir et Société dans le Pérou contemporain.* Paris, 1965

Fitzgerald, E. V. K., *The State and Economic Development: Peru since 1968.* CUP, 1976

Hemming, J., *The Conquest of the Incas.* London, 1970

Lowenthal, A. F., *The Peruvian Experiment.* Princeton Univ. Press, 1975

Marrett, Sir R., *Peru.* London, 1969

Mejia Baca, J., and Tauro, A., *Diccionário Enciclopédico del Perú.* 3 vols. 1966

Owens, R. J., *Peru.* OUP, 1964

Pike, *A Modern History of Peru.* London, 1967

Sharp, D. A. (ed.), *US Foreign Policy and Peru.* Univ. of Texas Press, 1972

Vargas, Padre, *Historia General del Perú.* Lima, 1967

Webb, R. C., *Government Policy and the Distribution of Income in Peru, 1963–1973.* Harvard Univ. Press, 1977

National Library: Avenida Abancay, Lima. *Director:* Dr Estuardo Náñez.

REPUBLIC OF THE PHILIPPINES

Capital: Manila
Population: 43·94m. (1976)
GNP per capita: US$410 (1976)

República de Filipinas—
Republika ñg Pilipinas

HISTORY. Before the Spanish discovery of the Philippines, the native Filipinos came in contact with India, China and Arabia. According to the early records of China, 'some Filipinos from the country of Ma-i arrived in Canton and sold their merchandise' as early as 982. The Philippines was discovered by Magellan in 1521 and conquered by Spain in 1565. Following the Spanish–American war, the islands were ceded to the USA on 10 Dec. 1898, after the Filipinos had tried in vain to establish an independent republic in 1896.

The Republic of the Philippines came into existence on 4 July 1946, by agreement with the US Government embodied in an Act of Congress signed by President Roosevelt on 24 March 1934, accepted the the Philippine Legislature on 1 May 1934 and ratified at a plebiscite on 14 May 1935. This Act established a 10-year transitional period, designated as that of the Philippine Commonwealth, at the end of which complete independence was automatically effective.

AREA AND POPULATION. The Philippines is situated between 21° 25′ and 4° 23′ N. lat. and between 116° and 127° E. long. It is composed of 7,100 islands and islets, 2,773 of which are named. Approximate land area, 115,830 sq. miles (300,000 sq. km). The 16 most important islands with their areas (in sq. miles) are: Luzon, 40,420; Mindanao, 36,537; Samar, 5,050; Negros, 4,906; Palawan, 4,550; Panay, 4,446; Mindoro, 3,759; Leyte, 2,786; Cebu, 1,707; Bohol, 1,492; Masbate, 1,262; Sulu group, 379; Tawi-tawi, 229; Romblon, 32; Marinduque, 347, and Siquijor, 129.

Census population 1975 was 42,070,660. Estimate (1976) 43·94m.

The population of Manila, the present capital, in 1975 was 1,454,352 (metropolitan Manila, 4·5m.). The old capital, Quezon City, just north-east of Manila, had a population of 960,341. Other cities, with their population in May 1975 are: Iloilo on Panay, 227,374; Cebu on Cebu, 408,173; Zamboanga on Mindanao, 261,978; Davao on Mindanao, 482,233; Basilan on Basilan Island (abolished in Dec. 1975), 22,536; Bacolod on Negros, 222,735; San Carlos on Negros Occidental, 91,042; San Carlos on Pangasinan, 90,358; Pasay on Rizal, 186,920.

On 7 June 1946 the President of the Philippines approved a law, effective 4 July 1946, making a new language (Pilipino) based on Tagalog (a Malayan dialect) the official national language of the republic. In 1970 about 16,409,133 people spoke English and about 1,335,945 Spanish; for government and commercial purposes these two languages are commonly used. Some 77 native languages are spoken in the Philippines, of which 9 are of major importance; they belong to the Malayo-Polynesian family.

CONSTITUTION AND GOVERNMENT. The republic was governed by a constitution adopted on 14 May 1935 and amended in 1940 and 1946. On 17 Jan. 1973 a new constitution was ratified naming President Marcos President and Prime Minister without a fixed term of office. The President is assisted by 20 departmental secretaries and several officials with cabinet rank in charge of Foreign Affairs, Finance, Justice, Agriculture, Public Works, Transportation and Communications, Education and Culture, Labour, National Defence, Energy, Trade, Health, Social Services and Development, Agrarian Reforms, Public Information, Local

Government and Community Development, Tourism, Industry, Public Highways, Natural Resources, Youth and Sports Development, Energy, Presidential Executive Assistance Office, Central Bank of the Philippines, Budget Commission, Commission of National Integration, Solicitor-General, Commission on Elections, Commission on Audit, Civil Service Commission and Presidential Assistance on National Minorities.

President and Prime Minister: Ferdinand E. Marcos.

Martial law was introduced on 21 Sept. 1972. A referendum held in Dec. 1977 decreed that President Marcos should remain in power. On 12 June 1978 a limited experiment in parliamentary democracy began and the President also became Prime Minister. Limited power to legislate was given to the new Assembly but the right to legislate by decree was retained by the President and no date was given for lifting the martial law.

The 1973 Constitution provides that all male and female citizens 15 years of age or older who can read or write Spanish, English or a native dialect and who meet certain residential qualifications are entitled to vote.

The constitution vests in the republic all ownership of the country's natural resources, which, apart from public agricultural land, may not be alienated. An agreement with the USA signed on 4 July 1946, ratified by plebiscite on 11 March 1948 and expired in 1974, granted American interests or companies the exploitation of any resources and public-utility business open to Filipinos. Concessions and leases are limited to 25 years; maximum area of agricultural public land which any corporation may acquire or lease is 1,024 hectares (2,529 acres) and not more than 2,000 hectares (4,940 acres) are used for grazing purposes.

National flag: Horizontally blue over red, with a white triangle based on the hoist bearing a gold sun of 8 rays and 3 gold stars.

National hymn: 'Tierra adorado', 'Land of the morning', lyric in English by M. A. Sane and C. Osias, in Spanish by José Palma (1899), tune by Julian Felipe (1898); 'Pambansang Awit ñg Pilipinas', Tagalog lyric by the Institute of National Language, music by Julian Felipe.

Local Government. The country is administratively divided into 12 regions, 72 provinces, 60 cities, 1,445 municipalities, 42,000 *barangays* with 252,000 councilmen. On 14 Nov. 1975 the name of provincial boards and city or municipal boards or councils was changed into *Sangguniang Bayan.* The latter assumes all the powers and responsibilities on matters of legislation of the defunct provincial, city or municipal boards.

The *Sangguniang Pambayan* is the direct successor of the old municipal council; *Sangguniang Panglunsod* for the old city council; *Sangguniang Panlalawigan* for the province and *Batasang Pambansa* for the defunct Congress.

DEFENCE. On 14 March 1947 the Philippine and US Governments signed a 99-year military-base arrangement since reduced to 25 years and will end in 1991. The USA was granted the use of a series of army, navy and air bases, with the right to use a number of others on mutual agreement. On 21 March a second agreement provided for a US Military Advisory Group as well as military assistance. A treaty of mutual assistance was signed in Washington on 30 Aug. 1951; the instruments of ratification were exchanged in Manila on 27 Aug. 1952. The Philippines is also a signatory of the S.E. Asia Collective Defence Treaty.

The Chief of Staff of the Armed Forces has overall command over the Army, Air Force, Navy and Constabulary.

Army. The Army consists of 63,000 officers and men in the active force. It is organized in 4 light infantry divisions, 1 independent brigade, 1 artillery group and 10 engineer construction battalions, equipped with M-41 tanks.

Navy. The Navy includes 10 old frigates (4 former US destroyer escorts and 6 *ex*-USCG cutters, *ex*-USN seaplane tenders); 12 escort vessels (4 *ex*-US fleet minesweepers and 8 *ex*-US escorts), 2 coastal minesweepers, 5 patrol vessels, 5 gunboats, 36 patrol boats, 4 hydrofoil patrol craft, 27 landing ships, 4 medium landing ships, 8 landing craft (4 LSSL and 4 LSIL), 2 repair ships, 7 oilers, 4 water carriers, 1 supply ship, 4 survey ships, 5 tenders, 70 minor landing craft, 1 geodetic service vessel, 8 tugs and 33 coastguard utility cutters, all *ex*-USA. Naval personnel in 1977 totalled 2,000 officers and 15,000 men, including coastguard and trainee conscripts. There are also 500 officers and 5,000 enlisted men in the marine corps.

The Philippine Navy was considerably increased in 1976 by taking over many vessels (nearly all former US warships) from the South Vietnamese Navy which escaped from Indo-China when the Saigon government collapsed in 1975. They included 3 destroyer escorts, 6 frigate-size coastguard cutters, 2 fleet minesweepers, 3 escorts, 1 patrol vessel, 1 gunboat, 13 landing ships, 3 medium landing ships, 6 landing craft, 2 repair ships, 5 oilers, 3 water carriers and several auxiliary ships.

Air Force. The Air Force has a strength of some 15,000 officers and men, with 140 aircraft, and was built up with US assistance. Its fighter-bomber wing is equipped with 2 squadrons of supersonic F-5A/Bs and 1 squadron of F-86F Sabre jets; but the Sabres are used mainly for tactical training and are being replaced by 25 F-8H Crusaders. There are transport, observation, air/sea rescue, helicopter and training units, for which recently acquired equipment has included 12 Australian-built Nomad twin-turboprop STOL light transports and a total of 48 Italian-built SF.260WP (armed) and SF.260MP piston-engined trainers. Many of the Air Force's other trainers are armed for counter-insurgency duties. No. 16 squadron of the 15th Strike Wing operates 16 T-28Ds. No. 17 has 16 SF.260WPs. No. 19 has 11 AC-47A gunships and No. 18 has 18 UH-1H Iroquois helicopters.

Police. Public order is maintained partly through the Philippine constabulary and partly through the local police forces. The constabulary now forms part of the Armed Forces and has 27,000 personnel.

INTERNATIONAL RELATIONS

Membership. The Republic of the Philippines is a member of UN and the Colombo Plan.

External Debt. At 31 Dec. 1975 the external debt amounted to US$2,233·7m.

ECONOMY

Budget. The revenues and expenditures of the central government for fiscal years (ending 30 June) were, in 1m. Philippine pesos, as follows:

	1971–72	*1972–73*	*1973–74*	*1974–75*
Revenue	5,100	7,157	11,088	15,072
Expenditure	5,562	7,909	12,897	16,684

Taxation furnished P.1,560m. of the revenue for 1964–65, P.6,239m. for 1972–73, P.10,094m. for 1973–74, P.12,278m. for 1974–75.

Expenditure (1974) included (in 1m. pesos): National defence and police, 1,564, education, health and welfare, 2,260; general administration, 771; economic development, 3,701; public debt, 606.

At 31 Dec. 1975 the total internal public debt outstanding of the national and local governments, including those of the government corporations, stood at P.20,838·5m.

Currency. The republic is on a free foreign-exchange market with the *peso* equivalent to about 13 cents US (Nov. 1975). Total money supply, Dec. 1976, was P.12,074·9m., of which P.5,651·8m. was currency in circulation and P.6,423·1m. were demand deposits. The coins used are: 5 *peso*, 1 *peso*, one-half *peso*, quarter *peso*, media *peseta* (10 *centavos*), all contain 70 grammes copper, 18 grammes zinc and 12 grammes nickel; 5 *centavo* in copper and zinc, and 1 *centavo* in aluminium and magnesium zinc. Central Bank notes are issued in 2, 5, 10, 20, 50, 100 *pesos* denominations.

Banking. On 30 June 1977 there were 1,145 branches of commercial banks operating under 31 head offices, with 4 overseas, 1 each in New York, Hong Kong, Taipei and London. Agencies exist in Honolulu, San Francisco and Los Angeles. Total deposits of the commercial banks in 1976 were P.29,468·7m.

Under the law passed 15 June 1948 the Central Bank of the Philippines was created to have sole control of the credit and monetary supply, independent of the Treasury. It has a capital of P.10m. furnished solely by the Government. Its total assets, at 31 Dec. 1976 were P.28,972·2m.

Weights and Measures. The metric system of weights and measures was established by law in 1869, and since 1916 has come into general use.

ENERGY AND NATURAL RESOURCES

Electricity. Government and private electric systems furnish the Philippines with electric power, with a total installed capacity of 3,123,655 kw. Private electric systems include the Manila Electric Co., with a total generating capacity of 1,521,000 kw. and the government's National Power Corporation produces 666,550 kw. (June 1975).

Minerals. Mineral production in 1976 (in tonnes): Lead, 5,493; zinc, 22,544; copper concentrates, 857,085; copper direct shipping ore, 21,503; manganese, 857; chromite, 520,038; iron, 570,999; coal, 157,861; salt, 70,625; gypsum (natural), 6,867, (synthetic), 111,116; quicksilver, 8·4; gold, 15,607·53 kg; silver, 50,373 kg. Other minerals include cement, rock asphalt, sand and gravel.

Agriculture. Of the total area of 30m. hectares, 7,573,000 hectares are commercial forests; 5,699,000 hectares non-commercial forests; 2·11m. hectares open grassland; 129,000 hectares mangrove and marshes; 14,489,000 hectares cultivated.

About 98·4% of the total cultivated area is owned by Filipinos; the average size of the farm is 3·21 hectares. The principal products are unhusked rice (palay), Manila hemp (abaca), copra, sugar-cane, maize and tobacco. In Aug. 1976, 8·1m. persons were employed in agriculture (52·7% of the working population).

The products (in tonnes) are (1976): Rough rice, 6·16m.; copra, 5·33m.; coconut, 3·42m.; sugar (muscovado and centrifugal), 3·58m.; shelled corn, 2·77m.; tobacco, 59,857; abaca fibre, 133,600.

Minor crops are fruits, nuts, root crops, vegetables, onions, beans, coffee, cacao, peanuts, ramie, rubber, maguey and kapok.

Livestock, estimated in 1974: 5,233,000 carabaos (water buffaloes), 2,237,000 cattle, 11,653,000 hogs, 1,526,000 goats and 60·83m. poultry.

Forestry. The forests covered some 13,272,136 hectares at 30 June 1976. Log production, 8,645,835 cu. metres, of which 2,331,297 cu. metres were exported in 1976.

Fisheries. Fish production from all sources was 1,336,800 tonnes and was valued at P.5,919,100 in 1975.

INDUSTRY AND TRADE

Industry. Manufacturing is largely carried on in homes (chiefly embroidery, buntal hats, woven cloths, mats and pottery). In 1974 there were 20 coconut-oil mills, 25 cigar and cigarette factories, 31 rice-mills, 74 shoe factories, 35 sugar-mills, 18 cement plants and 12 hydro-electric plants. The non-agricultural labour force in Aug. 1976 was 7,301,000 out of a total of 15,427,000 employed.

Commerce. The values of imports and exports (f.o.b.) for calendar years are stated as follows in US$1m.:

	1974	*1975*	*1976*	*1977*
Imports	3,143	3,459	3,633	3,210
Exports	2,725	2,294	2,574	2,550

The principal exports in 1976 were (in US$1m.): Centrifugal sugar, 429·2; coconut oil (crude), 298·7; copper concentrates, 265·9; logs and lumber, 203·4; copra, 149·7; bananas and plantains, 75·6; gold from copper, ores and concentrates, 65·3; pineapples (in syrup), 46·7; nickel, 59·5; copra, oilcake or meal, 54·5.

Main imports in 1976 (in US$1m.): Machinery, 625·3; mineral fuels, lubricants and related products, 890·7; transport equipment, 276·1; base metals, 245·2; cereals and cereal preparations, 157·7; electric machinery, apparatus and appliances, 187·2; explosives and miscellaneous chemical materials and products, 115·3; textile fibres (unmanufactured) and waste silk, 80·3; chemical elements and compounds, 141·8, and manufacture of metals, 80·9.

For over a half-century the foreign trade has been chiefly with the USA. The trade relationship of the two countries is governed by the Philippine Trade Act of 1946 as amended.

Philippine products entering the USA paid 10% of the US tariff in 1959–61, 20% in 1962–64, 40% in 1965–67, 60% in 1968–70, 80% in 1971–73 and 100% from 1 Jan. 1974.

Total trade between the Philippines and UK (British Department of Trade returns, in £1,000 sterling):

	1972	*1973*	*1974*	*1975*	*1976*	*1977*
Imports to UK	5,231	9,754	16,791	40,574	33,485	44,696
Exports and re-exports from UK	20,262	29,111	49,276	54,606	86,180	92,721

COMMUNICATIONS

Roads. In 1976 highways extended 112,881 km. In 1975 there were registered 885,366 motor vehicles of all types.

Railways. Railway tracks (1976), 1,057 km in Luzon. In 1975–76, 8,467,367 passengers and 243,062 tonnes of freight were carried by rail.

Aviation. The Philippine Air Lines, Inc., with a capital of P.898m., in 1975 carried 2,780,974 passengers, 54,655,005 kg of cargo and 830,493 kg of mail.

Shipping. In 1976, 79,490 vessels of 22,523,374 net tons entered and 79,145 vessels of 22,418,335 net tons cleared all ports.

Post and Broadcasting. In 1976 there were in operation 1,682 post offices and 1,354 telecommunication stations. The Philippine Long Distance Telephone Company has 441,037 telephones in service while the Government Telephone System which operates 13 automatic exchanges within the Greater Manila Area has 17,863 subscribers. The Republic Telephone Company, Inc. (Retelco) had 29,918 telephone units in service in 1976.

Licensed radio stations in 1975 numbered 12,244, including 1,681 ship stations and 820 aircraft stations.

Newspapers (1975). There were 1,401 (800 published in Manila) newspapers and magazines, 12 of which were dailies, with a combined circulation of 9m.

JUSTICE, RELIGION, EDUCATION AND WELFARE

Justice. There is a Supreme Court which is composed of a chief justice and 14 associate justices; it can declare a law or treaty unconstitutional by the concurrent votes of the majority sitting. There is a court of appeal; headed by a presiding justice, with 35 associate justices. There are 16 judicial districts sub-divided into 357 branches, each with a presiding judge of first instance. Every city has a city court and every municipality has 1 municipal judge. In addition, the juvenile and domestic relations court in Manila has exclusive jurisdiction to try all cases involving minors and matrimonial disputes.

Religion. In 1970 there were 31,169,488 Roman Catholics; 1,434,688 Aglipayans, 1,584,963 Moslems, 1,122,999 Protestants, 475,407 members of the Iglesia ni Kristo, 33,639 Buddhists and 863,302 others.

The Roman Catholics are organized in 12 archbishoprics, 30 bishoprics, 12 prelatures nullius, 4 apostolic vicariates, 4 apostolic prefectures and some 1,633 parishes. The Philippine Independent Church, founded in 1902, and comprising about 3·9% of the population, denies the spiritual authority of the Roman Pontiff. It is divided into two groups, one of which has accepted ordinations by the Episcopalian Church.

Education. Bilingual education as the medium of instruction in the elementary and secondary schools was implemented in 1974. Bilingual education is defined as the separate use of Pilipino and English as the media of instruction in definite subject areas, though Arabic can be used in areas where it is necessary. Pilipino is used as the medium of instruction in the following subjects: social studies/social sciences, character education, work education, health and physical education for both elementary and secondary schools. In Grades I and II the vernacular used in the locality or place where the school is located is the auxiliary medium of instruction. Tertiary institutions (collegiate and graduate levels) are given discretion to develop their own schedule of implementation provided that by school-year 1984, all college graduates should be able to pass examinations in English/Pilipino for the practice of their profession. In 1975, of the persons 10 years old and over, 86·5% were literate.

In 1974–75, 8,364,406 attended elementary, 2,158,983 secondary and 916,190 collegiate schools. There were 418,161 private elementary school pupils, 1,186,532 secondary and 800,618 collegiate. The University of the Philippines (founded in 1908) had about 24,000 students in 1976–77.

Health. In 1970 there were 14,000 doctors and 45,000 hospital beds.

Social Welfare. The government programme includes the purchase and subdivision of big landed estates for resale on easy instalment plans to tenants, the opening of virgin lands and settlement of landless families, the granting of bank loans to such families for seeds and the building of homes, the opening of rural roads and rural schools, the setting up of travelling medical clinics and the distribution of relief goods, including food, clothing and medicine, to families who have been displaced due to the depredations of the communist outlaws.

DIPLOMATIC REPRESENTATIVES

OF THE PHILIPPINES IN GREAT BRITAIN (9A Palace Green, London, W8 4QE)

Ambassador: José Manuel Stillianopoulos.

OF GREAT BRITAIN IN THE PHILIPPINES (115 Esteban St., Manila)

Ambassador: W. Bentley.

OF THE PHILIPPINES IN THE USA (1617 Massachusetts Ave., NW, Washington, D.C., 20036)

Ambassador: Eduardo Z. Romualdez.

OF THE USA IN THE PHILIPPINES (1201 Roxas Blvd., Manila)

Ambassador: David D. Newsom.

OF THE PHILIPPINES TO THE UNITED NATIONS

Ambassador: Alejandro D. Yango.

Books of Reference

Republic of the Philippine Government Manual, 1950. Manila, 1950
Gazetteer of the Philippine Islands. United States Department of Commerce. Washington, 1945
Averch, H. A., *The Matrix of Policy in the Philippines.* Princeton Univ. Press, 1971
Burley, T. M., *The Philippines. An Economic and Social Geography.* London, 1973
Chapman, A., *Philippine Nationalism.* New York, 1950
Forbes, W. C., *The Philippine Islands.* 3 vols. Rev. Cambridge, Mass., 1945
Golay, F. H., *The Philippines: Public Policy and National Economic Development.* Cornell Univ. Press, 1961
Hainsworth, R. G., and Moyser, R. T., *Agricultural Geography of the Philippine Islands.* Washington, 1945
Kurihara, K. K., *Labor in the Philippine Economy.* Stanford University Press, 1945
Lightfort, K., *The Philippines.* London, 1973
Meyer, M. W., *A Diplomatic History of the Philippine Republic.* Univ. of Hawaii Press, 1965
Mills, L. A., *The New World of Southeast Asia.* University of Minnesota Press, 1949
Zafra, U. A., *Philippine Economic Handbook.* Silver Spring, Md., 1960

PITCAIRN ISLAND

HISTORY. It was discovered by Carteret in 1767, but remained uninhabited until 1790, when it was occupied by 9 mutineers of HMS *Bounty*, with 12 women and 6 men from Tahiti. Nothing was known of their existence until the island was visited in 1808. In 1856 the population having become too large for the island's resources, the inhabitants (194 in number) were, at their own request, removed to Norfolk Island; but 43 of them returned in 1859–64.

AREA AND POPULATION. Pitcairn Island (1·75 sq. miles; 4·6 sq. km) is situated in the Pacific ocean, nearly equidistant from New Zealand and Panama (25° 04′ S. lat., 130° 06′ W. long). The population has been declining and on 30 June 1977 it was 65.

The uninhabited islands of Henderson (12 sq. miles), Dulcie ($1\frac{1}{2}$ sq. miles) and Oeno (2 sq. miles) were annexed in 1902 and are included in the Pitcairn group.

CONSTITUTION. Pitcairn was brought within the jurisdiction of the High Commissioner for the Western Pacific in 1898 and transferred to the Governor of Fiji in 1952. When Fiji became independent in Oct. 1970, the British High Commissioner in New Zealand was appointed Governor.

The Local Government Ordinance of 1964 constitutes a Council of 10 members, of whom 4 are elected, 5 are nominated (3 by the 4 elected members and 2 by the Governor) and the Island Secretary is an *ex officio* member. The Island Magistrate, who is elected triennially, presides over the Council; other members hold office for only 1 year. Liaison between Governor and Council is through a Commissioner in the Auckland, New Zealand, office of the British Consulate-General.

TRADE. Fruit, vegetables and curios are sold to passing ships; flour, sugar and other foodstuffs are imported.

Governor: Harold Smedley, CMG, MBE.
Island Magistrate: Ivan Christian (elected Dec. 1975).

Books of Reference

A Guide to Pitcairn. British South Pacific Office, Suva, Fiji, 1963, revised ed. 1976
Ross, A. S. C., and Moverly, A. W., *The Pitcairnese Language.* London, 1964

POLAND

Polska Rzeczpospolita Ludowa

Capital: Warsaw
Population: 34·5m. (1977)
GNP per capita: US$2,860 (1976)

HISTORY. In 1966 Poland celebrated its millennium, but modern Polish history begins with the partitions of the once-powerful kingdom between Russia, Austria and Prussia in 1772, 1793 and 1795. After the creation by Napoleon I of a semi-independent Grand Duchy of Warsaw, the country was again partitioned at the Congress of Vienna in 1815 between Russia (Congress Poland), Austria (Galicia) and Prussia (Grand Duchy of Posen), and the free city of Cracow.

The Polish revolution of 1830–31 caused the suppression of the 1815 constitution and made 'Congress Poland' virtually a Russian province. The revolution of 1846–48 led to the incorporation of Cracow in Austria, the abolition of the Grand Duchy of Posen and further repression in 'Congress Poland', which was intensified after the revolution of 1863–64.

During the First World War Russian Poland was occupied by the Austro-German forces. On 10 Nov. 1918 independence was proclaimed by Józef Piłsudski, the founder of the Polish Legions during the war. On 28 June 1919 the Treaty of Versailles recognized the independence of Poland.

On 1 Sept. 1939 Germany invaded Poland, on 17 Sept. 1939 Russian troops entered eastern Poland, and on 29 Sept. 1939 the fourth partition of Poland took place. After the German attack on Russia, the Germans occupied the whole of Poland. War casualties and victims of German terror amounted to 6–7m. people. By March 1945 the country had been liberated by the Russians.

In July 1944 the USSR recognized the Polish Committee of National Liberation (*Polski Komitet Wyzwolenia Narodowego*) established in Lublin as an executive organ of the National Council of the Homeland (*Krajowa Rada Narodowa*). The Committee was transformed into the Provisional Government in Dec. 1944, and on 28 June 1945, supplemented by members of the Polish Government in London (which had been recognized by the UK and USA), it was re-established—in Moscow—as the Polish Provisional Government of National Unity and on 6 July recognized as such by the UK and USA.

Elections were held on 19 Jan. 1947. Of the 12·7m. votes cast, 11·24m. were recognized as valid and 9m. were given for the Communist-dominated 'Democratic Bloc'.

After riots in Poznań in June 1956 nationalist anti-Stalinist elements gained control of the Communist Party, under the leadership of Władysław Gomułka.

In 1970 West Germany recognized Poland's western boundary as laid down by the Potsdam Conference of 1945 (the 'Oder–Neisse line').

In Dec. 1970 strikes and riots in Gdańsk, Szczecin and Gdynia led to the resignation of a number of leaders including Gomułka. He was replaced by Edward Gierek (born 1913).

The introduction of price rises in June 1976 was again followed by strikes and riots. The rises were withdrawn 'for further study' and demonstrators were given severe sentences. In the campaign of protest which followed a Committee for the Defence of the Workers was formed and some sentences were reduced. Following a recommendation from Gierek, all prisoners were released by July 1977. Subsequently several other oppositional movements made an appearance.

AREA AND POPULATION. Poland is bounded north by the Baltic and the R.S.F.S.R., east by Lithuania, White Russia and the Ukraine, south by Czechoslovakia and west by the German Democratic Republic. Poland comprises an area of 312,677 sq. km (120,624 sq. miles). In 1975 the administrative structure was reorganized. (For previous administrative divisions see THE STATESMAN'S YEAR-BOOK, 1975–76.) The country is divided into 49 voivodships (*wojewodztwo*) (including 3 urban: Warsaw, Kraków and Łódź) and these in turn are divided into 808 towns and 2,128 wards (*gmina*). The capital is Warsaw (Warszawa).

Area (in sq. km) and population (in 1,000, with percentage urban in brackets) in 1977:

Voivodship	*Area*	*Population*	*Voivodship*	*Area*	*Population*
Biała Podlaska	5,348	618 (49)	Opole	8,535	971 (47)
Białystok	10,053	280 (26)	Ostrołęka	6,472	362 (25)
Bielsko	3,703	779 (43)	Piła	8,205	417 (48)
Bydgoszcz	10,352	995 (60)	Piotrków	6,261	583 (37)
Chełm	3,867	221 (33)	Płock	5,114	481 (38)
Ciechanów	6,362	399 (27)	Poznań	8,152	1,171 (68)
Częstochowa	6,189	727 (45)	Przemyśl	4,430	374 (32)
Elbląg	6,103	423 (54)	Radom	7,294	678 (39)
Gdańsk	7,389	1,249 (75)	Rzeszów	4,399	610 (31)
Gorzów	8,484	434 (55)	Siedlce	8,499	601 (24)
Jelenia Góra	4,379	487 (62)	Sieradz	4,870	387 (27)
Kalisz	6,512	644 (40)	Skierniewice	3,957	389 (36)
Katowice	6,649	3,488 (86)	Słupsk	7,453	356 (49)
Kielce	9,211	1,037 (38)	Suwałki	10,489	415 (41)
Konin	5,139	426 (31)	Szczecin	9,980	854 (72)
Koszalin	8,471	435 (57)	Tarnobrzeg	6,282	535 (27)
Kraków (Cracow)	3,254	1,120 (68)	Tarnów	4,152	578 (31)
Krosno	5,701	422 (28)	Toruń	5,345	587 (55)
Legnica	4,036	414 (58)	Wałbrzych	4,167	714 (71)
Leszno	4,153	343 (41)	Warsaw	3,794	2,155 (88)
Łódź	1,520	1,079 (91)	Włocławek	4,404	403 (39)
Łomża	6,709	320 (27)	Wrocław	6,289	1,026 (71)
Lublin	6,792	885 (50)	Zamość	6,986	472 (20)
Nowy Sącz	5,576	599 (32)	Zielona Góra	8,867	580 (56)
Olsztyn	12,329	663 (49)			

Population (in 1,000) of the largest towns (1977):

Warsaw	1,316	Bydgoszcz	330	Sosnowiec	198
Łódź	810	Lublin	282	Radom	180
Kraków (Cracow)	701	Bytom	236	Toruń	158
Wrocław (Breslau)	585	Gdynia	225	Kielce	157
Poznań	527	Zabrze	204	Chorzów	157
Gdańsk (Danzig)	434	Częstochowa	203	Ruda Śląska	152
Szczecin (Stettin)	376	Białystok	201	Tychy	140
Katowice	349	Gliwice	200	Wałbrzych	129

At the census of 30 March 1974 the population was 33,636,000 (16·2m. males; 18·2m. urban). Population on 1 Jan. 1977, 34,528,000 (16·8m. males; 19·5m. urban; density, 109 per sq. km). Vital statistics, 1976 (per 1,000): Marriages, 9·5; divorces, 1·1; live births, 19·5; deaths, 8·8, infant mortality (per 1,000 live births), 24.

The rate of natural growth declined from 19·5 in 1955 to 8·2 in 1969, since when it has been rising again (9·7 in 1976). Expectation of life in 1974 was 67·8 years for males, 74·6 years for females. In 1976, 37·3% of the population was under 19.

Ethnic minorities in 1963: 180,000 Ukrainians, 165,000 Byelorussians, 21,000 Slovaks, 10,000 Lithuanians. There were 10,000 Jews in 1977. By a treaty of March 1976, Poland agreed to repatriate 125,000 ethnic Germans by 1980 and thereafter to issue exit permits to the remaining 155,000.

In 1969, 10·33m. Poles lived abroad (6·5m. in USA, 1·4m. in USSR, 150,000 (1976) in UK). In 1972 there were 1,800 immigrants and 19,100 emigrants.

CONSTITUTION AND GOVERNMENT. The present Constitution was adopted on 22 July 1952. Constitutional amendments were adopted in Feb. 1976. Two amendments referring to the leading role of the Communist Party and the special relationship with the USSR provoked a wave of protest when circulated in draft form and were adopted in a modified form.

The titular head of state is the Chairman of the Council of State, Henryk Jabłoński.

Supreme *de facto* power is in the hands of the Politburo of the Polish United Worker's (*i.e.*, Communist) Party, in June 1978 composed as follows: Edward Gierek, *First Secretary of the Central Committee*; Edward Babiuch; Piotr Jaroszewicz, *Chairman of the Council of Ministers* (*Prime Minister*); Władysław Kruczek, *Chairman, Central Council of Trade Unions*; Emil Wojtaszek, *Foreign Minister*; Jan Szydlak, *Deputy Prime Minister*; Józef Tejchma; Gen. Wojciech Jaruzelski, *Minister of Defence*; Mieczysław Jagielski; Zdzisław Grudzień; Stanisław Kania; Józef Kepa, *Deputy Prime Minister*; Stanisław Kowalczyk, *Minister of the Interior*. Candidate members: Kazimierz Barcikowski; Tadeusz Wrzaszczyk, *Deputy Prime Minister and President of the Planning Commission*; Jerzy Łukaszewicz. Ministers not in the Politburo include: Jerzy Olszewski (*Foreign Trade*); Henryk Kisiel (*Finance*); Jerzy Bafia (*Justice*); Leon Klonica (*Agriculture*).

In 1977 the Polish United Workers' Party had 2,568,400 members, the Democratic Party, 94,100, and the United Peasants' Party, 420,400 members.

The authority of the Republic is vested in the Sejm, elected for 4 years by all citizens over 18. The Sejm elects a Council of State, composed of a Chairman, the Secretary and 14 members, including 4 vice-chairmen; and a Council of Ministers. Local government is carried out by People's Councils elected every 4 years at voivodship and community level. Alongside these are the offices of state administration. The chairman of the People's Council is the Secretary of the regional Party organization for the area.

The last local elections were held on 5 Feb. 1978.

The last elections for the Sejm were held on 21 March 1976. 631 candidates stood on the single list of the National Unity Front for the 460 constituencies. 98·27% of the electorate voted; 14,923 votes were spoiled. The 460 seats are distributed as follows: 261 United Worker's Party, 113 United Peasant's Party, 37 Democratic Party, 49 independents, including 5 Catholic representatives nominated by the Government but repudiated by the Church. There are 95 women deputies.

National flag: Horizontally white over red.

National anthem: Jeszcze Polska nie zginęła (words by J. Wybicki, 1797; tune by M. Ogiński, 1796).

DEFENCE. Poland is divided into 3 military districts: Warsaw (the eastern part of Poland); Pomerania (Baltic coast, part of central Poland; headquarters at Bydgoszcz); Silesia (Silesia and southern Poland; headquarters at Wrocław).

The armed forces are on Soviet lines and divided into army and air force (2 years' service), navy (3 years), anti-aircraft, rocket and radio-technological units (3 years) and internal security forces (2 years). In 1965 the security forces were taken away from the Ministry of Internal Affairs and placed under the Defence Ministry. The military age extends from the 19th to the 50th year. The strength of the armed forces is estimated at 307,000, plus 97,000 security and frontier forces. Security forces include armoured brigades.

Army. The Army consists of 5 armoured, 8 motorized, 1 airborne and 1 amphibious assault divisions (not all at full strength). Total strength, 220,000. Tanks (mostly T-54) number 3,400.

Navy. The Navy comprises 4 submarines, 3 destroyers (including 2 inactive), 24 fleet minesweepers, 12 missile craft, 29 patrol boats, 21 torpedo boats, 23 medium landing ships, 7 training ships, 15 minor landing craft, 20 minesweeping boats, 2 surveying vessels, 6 oilers, 20 tugs and 12 auxiliaries. The Fleet Air Arm has 50 naval aircraft (mostly MiG-17 and IL-28) and helicopters. Personnel in 1978 totalled 2,800 officers and 22,000 men.

Air Force. The Air Force has a strength of some 62,000 officers and men and 750 first-line jet aircraft of Soviet design. There are 3 divisions (more than 30 16-aircraft squadrons) of MiG-21 supersonic interceptors, and 4 regiments (at least 12 squadrons) operating variable-geometry Su-20, Su-7B and some MiG-17 close-support fighters. Another fighter division supports the Navy. There are also reconnaissance, transport, helicopter and training units. Soviet 'Guide-line' and 'Goa' surface-to-air missiles are operational.

Two Soviet armoured divisions are stationed on Polish territory.

INTERNATIONAL RELATIONS

Membership. Poland is a member of UN, Comecon and the Warsaw Pact.

ECONOMY

Planning. Before 1940 Poland was a predominantly agricultural country, but by 1975 only 27% of the population made a living by agriculture. In the mid-1960s some steps were taken towards decentralizing the economy. In 1973 the former three-tier hierarchy of industry (ministries–industrial associations–enterprises) began to be modified to include specializing combines and large enterprises ('big economic organizations') containing 'inner units'. By 1975 these proposals had been extended to firms producing two-thirds of the country's output, but the system was then suspended on the grounds that it was causing economic disequilibrium by its excessive demands on labour and investment resources and a tendency to generate imports. To restore the balance between supply and demand the system was modified on 18 March 1977 to increase the authority of the various economic ministries as intermediaries between the 'big economic organizations' and the central planning body. The modified system was put into effect first in the machine, chemical and light industries.

The current plan is running from 1976 to 1980. Under it, national income is scheduled to rise by 7% per annum, and industrial and agricultural production are expected to rise by 48–50% and 16–19% by 1980 respectively.

Budget. Budget in 1m. złotys, for calendar years:

	1971	*1972*	*1973*	*1974*	*1975*	*1976*
Revenue	403,500	438,300	483,800	604,100	720,000	884,100
Expenditure	392,500	433,300	482,200	602,300	713,800	740,100

Main items of 1976 revenue (in 1m. złotys): Sales tax and profits tax from state enterprises, 660,500; finance and insurance, 143,500; payroll tax, 9,300.

Main items of 1976 revenue (in 1m. złotys): State enterprises, 384,700; welfare, 57,800; education, 56,100; defence, 51,200; administration, 36,100.

In 1975 a 'wealth tax' of 10–50% on assets over 700,000 złotys was instituted.

Polish debts to UK have been fully repaid. Poland does not accept liability for the £495,000 debts of Danzig (Gdańsk). Gold seized by the Nazis from Danzig was returned to Poland by the USA in 1976.

Currency. The currency unit is the *złoty*, divided into 100 *groszy*. The currency consists of notes of 50, 100, 1,000 and 2,000 złotys; and of coins of 10, 20 and 50 groszy and 1, 2, 5, 10 and 20 złotys. The official rate of exchange is £1 sterling = 34 złotys, US$ = 19·98 złotys, 1 rouble = 4·44 złotys. Tourist rates: £1 = 58 złotys, US$ = 33·30 złotys.

Banking. The National Bank of Poland (established 1945) is the central bank, has exclusive authority to issue currency, is charged with control of money and credit, and has responsibility for financial implementation of the national economic plan. Since its merger with the former Investment Bank on 1 Jan. 1970 it exercises centralized control over investment financing.

The Agricultural Bank (Bank Rolny) has exclusive responsibility for direct financing of rural areas through both short-term and investment loans. It operates banks. The General Savings Bank (Powszechna Kasa Oszczędności) exercises central control over savings activities, transfers and checking transactions, including activities of workers' co-operative banks.

In addition to the National Bank of Poland, other authorized foreign-exchange banks are: Bank for the National Economy, the Polish Welfare Bank (Bank Polska Kasa Opieki SA) and the Commercial Bank of Warsaw (Bank Handlowy w Warszawie SA).

Deposits in savings institutions amounted to 276,200m. złotys on 31 Dec. 1976.

Weights and Measures. The metric system is in general use.

ENERGY AND NATURAL RESOURCES

Oil. In 1975 there were 1,851 km of oil pipeline delivering 30·52m. tonnes of oil.

Minerals. Poland is a major producer of coal (reserves of some 71,000m. tonnes) and sulphur. Copper reserves are estimated at 10m. tonnes. There is also iron ore, lead and zinc. Production in 1976 (in 1,000 tonnes): Coal, 179,000; brown coal, 39,300; copper ore, 16,963; iron ore, 1,192; zinc-lead ores, 4,598.

Agriculture. In 1976 there were 19·2m. hectares of agricultural land, of which 15·2m. were in private hands, 0·3m. in co-operatives, 3·3m. in state farms. Private holdings average 5·3 hectares, and may not exceed 50 hectares. 14·8m. hectares were arable, 0·3m. orchards, 2·6m. meadows, 1·6m. pasture lands.

Collectivization has been largely abandoned (there were only 1,492 co-operatives in 1976) but remains a long-term aim of the Government which makes use of economic incentives to foster the formation of new collective farms. Existing co-operatives are encouraged to specialize and merge with others. From 1980 retirement pensions will be given to farmers (men at 65, women at 60) who leave their farms to the state or to an heir, who must have an agricultural qualification. A new approach is being tried with 'agricultural circles' (35,600 with 2·8m. members in 1975). In 1976 there were 2,895 state farms.

	Area (1,000 hectares)			*Yield (1,000 tonnes)*		
Crops	*1974*	*1975*	*1976*	*1974*	*1975*	*1976*
Wheat	2,022	1,842	1,832	6,414	5,211	5,741
Rye	3,138	2,792	2,934	7,877	6,271	6,914
Barley	1,230	1,335	1,210	3,914	3,652	3,609
Oats	1,182	1,291	1,115	3,242	2,932	2,696
Potatoes	2,684	2,581	2,466	48,635	46,456	50,012
Sugar-beet	440	496	555	12,971	15,339	15,170

Livestock (1976): 12·8m. cattle (6m. cows), 18·8m. pigs, 3·4m. sheep, 2·1m. horses, 93·3m. poultry. Milk production in 1976 was 16,000m. litres.

Tractors in use in 1975: 520,700 (in 15-h.p. units).

Forestry. In 1976 8·6m. hectares were forests (predominantly coniferous). 97,000 hectares were afforested in 1976, and 24·2m. cu. metres of timber gained.

Fisheries. In 1975 the fishing fleet had 130 deep-sea vessels totalling 196,100 GRT. The catch was 648,000 tonnes.

In 1966 Poland joined the Fisheries Convention of 1964, extending the fishing limits from 3 to 12 miles.

INDUSTRY AND TRADE

Industry. Production in 1975 (and 1976) (in 1,000 tonnes): Coke, 18,300 (18,100); pig-iron, 8,206 (8,213); crude steel, 15,007 (15,641); rolled steel, 11,085 (11,502); cement, 15,500 (19,800); sulphuric acid (100%), 3,410 (3,289); fertilizers, 2,362 (2,593); aluminium, 103 (103); electrolytic copper, 249 (270); lead, 76·2 (80·6); zinc, 243 (237); crude oil, 553 (455); salt, 3,513 (3,818); sugar, 1,699 (1,467); electricity, 97,200m. kwh. (104,000m.); natural gas, 5,963m. cu. metres (6,699m.). In 1975, 83 ships over 100 DWT were built (1,023,000 DWT), 164,000 cars and 64,900 lorries.

Output of light industry in 1975 (and 1976): Cotton fabrics, 948m. metres (885); woollen fabrics, 125m. metres (126); silk and synthetic fibres, 180m. metres (191); shoes, 162m. pairs (163); household glass, 44,800 tonnes (45,900); paper, 981,000 tonnes (1,046,000).

Labour. In 1976 the total number in employment was 17m., of whom 12·3m. worked in the state-controlled sector and 4·7m. in the private sector, and including in agriculture 5·2m., industry 5·2m., building 1·4m., trade 1·2m. and transport and communications 1·1m. 5m. women were employed in the state-controlled sector. Trade union membership (1976), 12m. (4·7m. women). Monthly industrial wage: legal minimum, 1,000 złotys; average earnings (1976), 3,969 złotys (not including private earnings). Saturday work is being progressively abolished.

Commerce. Trade statistics for calendar years (in 1m. złotys):

	1971	*1972*	*1973*	*1974*	*1975*	*1976*
Imports	16,151	19,612	26,103	34,823	41,645	46,100
Exports	15,489	18,133	21,355	27,625	34,161	36,600

Main imports in 1976 (in tonnes): Iron ore, 15·8m.; petroleum and products, 18·3m.; fertilizers, 6m.; wheat, 2·3m.; coal, 1·1m.; passenger cars, 32,100 units.

Main exports in 1976 (in tonnes): Coal, 40m.; lignite, 3·1m.; coke, 3·1m.; fertilizers, 981,300; ships, 71,700 DWT.

53% of Poland's trade is with Communist countries. UK is Poland's seventh largest trade partner after USSR, the German Democratic Republic and the Federal Republic of Germany, Czechoslovakia, France and USA.

Foreign trade deals should be made directly with the appropriate foreign trade enterprise. Information may be obtained from the Polish Chamber of Foreign Trade, Trebacka 4, 00–950 Warsaw. Joint ventures with Western firms are encouraged both at home and abroad. The Western partner may own up to 49% of the shares of ventures on Polish soil, and is guaranteed a share of profits and interest.

In 1972 a 5-year trade agreement was signed with the USA, and the US Export-Import Bank granted Poland a credit of US$150m. Six co-operation agreements were signed with the USA in 1974. Under these, a Polish–American Economic Council has been set up. In Dec. 1975 a Soviet–Polish trade and payments agreement for 1976–80 was signed. Under it trade is to amount to 28,000m. roubles. In Nov. 1976 the USSR granted Poland a credit of 1,000m. roubles repayable in 5–10 years at 2%. Soviet exports include plant and equipment and raw materials; Polish exports, machinery, ships, coal, chemicals and consumer goods.

Total trade between Poland and UK for 5 years (British Department of Trade returns, in £1,000 sterling):

	1973	*1974*	*1975*	*1976*	*1977*
Imports to UK	95,124	110,330	114,320	154,150	174,265
Exports and re-exports from UK	111,192	138,676	182,172	189,473	200,409

An Anglo-Polish 10-year agreement on the development of economic, industrial, scientific and technical co-operation was signed on 20 March 1973, and a 10-year programme implementing this was signed on 4 Sept. 1975. A UK–Polish 5-year economic agreement was signed in Dec. 1976. Some Polish imports are subject to quota restrictions.

By treaties of March 1976 the Federal Republic of Germany will make available to Poland credits of DM 1,000m. at 2·5% interest, and pay DM 1,300m. in settlement of Polish pension claims.

COMMUNICATIONS

Roads. In 1976 Poland had 143,349 km. of hard-surfaced roads. A road-improvement programme is bringing 75% of all roads up to suitability for heavy traffic. Number of motor vehicles: Passenger cars, 1,290,100 (of which, 1,250,500 private); lorries, 467,100 (56,000 private); motor cycles, 1,896,900 (1,888,000 private).

In 1976 road transport carried 2,315m. passengers and 1,901m. tonnes of freight.

Railways. The length of the standard gauge railway system was (1976) 23,885 km (5,988 km electrified); of narrow gauge, 2,879 km. In 1977 the second section of a new central trunk railway was opened bringing the line to Warsaw. Branches from this are being built to Bydgoszcz and Wrocław. In 1975 the railways carried 464·2m. tons of freight and 1,108m. passengers.

Aviation. In 1976 the state airline 'Lot' had 35 aircraft including Il-62s, operated 11 internal routes and flew services to 30 countries. 1,596,000 passengers were flown and 20,316 tonnes of freight. There are British Airways, SABENA, KLM, PANAM, Alitalia, Swissair, Air France, Austrian Airlines and Lufthansa services to Okęcie (Warsaw) airport.

Shipping. The principal ports are Gdynia, Gdańsk (Danzig) and Szczecin (Stettin). A new port (Port Pólnocny) to take ships of 100,000 DWT is under construction near Gdańsk. The merchant marine is grouped into Polish Ocean Lines (179 vessels totalling 1·04m. DWT in 1975), based on Gdynia and operating regular liner services, and the Polish Shipping Company based on Szczecin and operating cargo services. Poland also has a share in the Gdynia America Line. There are 4,572 km of inland navigable waterways. 16·6m. tonnes of freight were carried in 1976.

In 1976 the merchant marine had 320 vessels totalling 2,718,900 GRT (including 37 vessels over 20,000 tons). There are regular lines to London, Hull, China, Indonesia, Australia, Vietnam and some African and Latin-American countries.

Total shipping entering Polish ports in 1976 was 12,174 vessels of 27·7m. NRT. Freight traffic in 1976 was 35·5m. tonnes.

Post and Broadcasting. In 1976 there were 8,088 post offices and 1·7m. telephone subscribers, including 945,800 private persons.

Polskie Radio i Telewizja broadcasts 3 programmes in Polish on long-, medium- and short-waves and on FM. There are 2 TV programmes. Colour programmes are transmitted by SECAM system. Wireless licences in 1975 numbered 8·1m.; television licences, 6·5m.

Cinemas and Theatres. In 1976 there were 2,524 cinemas, 98 theatre and 38 concert halls. Cinema attendance was 144·2m.; theatre, 9·9m.

Newspapers (1976). There were 87 papers with an overall circulation of 2,694m. 2,580 periodicals were published. The Party newspaper is *Trybuna Ludu* (People's Tribune), weekend circulation 1·1m.

JUSTICE, RELIGION, EDUCATION AND WELFARE

Justice. A new penal code was adopted in 1969. Espionage and treason carry the severest penalties and severer punishment is provided for 'serious crimes'. For minor crimes there is more provision for probation sentences and fines. Previous jurisprudence was based on a penal code of 1932 supplemented by the Concise Penal Code of 1946.

There exist the following courts: The Supreme Court; voivodship, district and special courts. Judges and lay assessors are elected. The State Council elects the judges of the Supreme Court for a term of 5 years, and appoints the Prosecutor-General. The office of the Prosecutor-General is separate from the judiciary.

340,400 crimes were reported in 1975 (339,500 in 1974).

Religion. The population is predominantly Roman Catholic, and the proportion of active believers is perhaps as high as 80%. Church–State relations are regulated by agreements of 1950, 1956 and 1972. On 28 Nov. 1976 a pastoral letter was read in all churches in which the Polish bishops deplored the 'constant threat to the Catholic faith' in Poland. The Church has a university (Lublin), an Academy of Catholic Theology and a seminary in every diocese. Religious education of children is conducted in 'catechism centres', of which there were 18,254 in 1973–74.

The archbishop of Warsaw and Gniezno is the primate of Poland (since 1948, Stefan, Cardinal Wyszyński). The Vatican considers the archbishops of Lwów and Vilnius (incorporated in the USSR in 1940) as still being under Polish jurisdiction. In 1976 there were 5 archbishoprics, 27 dioceses and 6,716 parishes, 75 bishops, some 19,500 priests, 30,162 monks and nuns and over 13,000 churches and chapels. In 1975 some 4,000 students were studying for the priesthood. In 1973, 557 priests were ordained.

On 28 June 1972 the Vatican adjusted the Church boundaries, to coincide with the State's western frontier ('Oder–Neisse line') and the 4 apostolic administrators in the former German territories became bishops.

Figures for other churches in 1976: Polish Autocephalous Orthodox, 4 dioceses, 233 parishes, 300 churches, 216 priests, 2 monsteries (460,000 adherents in 1975). Lutheran, 6 dioceses, 122 parishes, 356 churches, 100 parsons (100,000 adherents in 1975). Uniate, 3 dioceses, 84 parishes, 89 churches, 103 priests (200,000 adherents in 1975). Old-Catholic Mariavite, 3 dioceses, 41 parishes, 56 churches, 33 priests (30,000 adherents in 1975). Methodist, 5 districts, 66 parishes, 66 chapels, 38 parsons (4,133 adherents in 1975). United Evangelical, 207 congregations, 65 chapels, 207 parsons. Seventh Day Adventist, 3 communities, 124 churches, 58 parsons. Baptist, 127 congregations, 60 parsons, 53 chapels (2,300 adherents in 1975). Moslems, 6 communities, 2 mosques, 6 imams. Jews, 16 congregations, 24 synagogues.

Education. Basic education from 7 to 15 is free and compulsory. Free secondary education is then optional in general or vocational schools. Primary schools are organized in complexes based on wards under one director ('gmina collective schools'). In 1976–77 there were: Kindergartens, 10,300 with 709,000 pupils and 37,300 teachers; primary schools, 14,738 (of which 1,512 gmina collective schools) with 4,309,800 pupils and 191,200 teachers; secondary schools, 895 with 472,000 pupils and 25,600 teachers; primary schools for adults, 2,111 with 137,700 pupils; secondary schools for adults, 373 with 150,000 pupils; vocational schools, 10,095 with 2,060,500 pupils and 74,700 teachers, and 89 institutions of higher education (including 10 universities, 18 polytechnics, 7 agricultural schools, 6 schools of economics, 12 teachers' training colleges and 10 medical schools) with 464,900 students (282,900 full-time) and 48,821 teaching staff.

Health. In 1976 there were 673 hospitals (including 36 mental hospitals) with 229,500 beds, 5,828 dispensaries and 3,130 health centres. There were 60,000 doctors and 16,400 dentists.

DIPLOMATIC REPRESENTATIVES

OF POLAND IN GREAT BRITAIN (47 Portland Place, London, W1N 3AG)

Ambassador: Artur Starewicz (accredited 16 Dec. 1971).

OF GREAT BRITAIN IN POLAND (Aleje Roz No. 1, Warsaw)

Ambassador: K. R. C. Pridham.

OF POLAND IN THE USA (2640–16th St., NW, Washington, D.C., 20009)

Ambassador: Dr Witold Trampczyński.

OF THE USA IN POLAND (Aleje Ujazdowskie 29/31, Warsaw)

Ambassador: Richard T. Davies.

OF POLAND TO THE UNITED NATIONS

Ambassador: Henryk Jaroszek.

Books of Reference

Statistical Information: The Central Statistical Office, Warsaw (Wawelska 1–3), publishes *Statistical News* (Aug. 1945–49; restarted Sept. 1956, bimonthly); *Statistical Studies and Works* (from 1950); *Statistics of Poland* (20 vols. 1946–51; restarted 1957 as *Biuletyn statystyczny*, monthly); *Rocznik statystyczny* (annual); *Concise Statistical Year Book of Poland.*

Constitution of the Polish People's Republic. Warsaw, 1964
Beneš, V. L., and Pounds, N. G. J., *Poland.* London, 1970
Bromke, A., and Strong, J. W. (eds.) *Gierek's Poland.* New York, 1973
Bulas, K., and others, *English–Polish and Polish–English Dictionary.* 2 vols. The Hague, 1959–61
Davies, N., *Poland, Past and Present: A Select Bibliography of Works in English.* Newtonville, 1977
Dziewanowski, M. K., *Poland in the Twentieth Century.* Columbia Univ. Press, 1977
Feiwel, G. R., *Poland's Industrialization Policy: A Current Analysis.* New York, 1971.—*Problems in Polish Economic Planning.* New York, 1971
Gieysztor, A., and others, *History of Poland.* Warsaw, 1969
Halecki, O., *A History of Poland.* 3rd ed. London, 1978.—(ed)., *Poland.* New York, 1957
Kieniewicz, S. (ed.) *History of Poland.* Warsaw, 1977
Lane, D., and Kolankiewicz, G. (ed.) *Social Groups in Polish Society.* London, 1973
Poland: The Country and its People. Warsaw, 1971
Poland: A Handbook. Warsaw, 1974
Poland Among the European Countries, 1950–1970. Warsaw, 1971
Roos, H., *A History of Modern Poland.* London, 1966

Szczepański, J., *Polish Society*. New York, 1970
Wielka Encyklopedia Powszechna. 13 vols. Warsaw, 1962–70
Woiciechowski, B., *Foreign Trade of Poland: Its Growth, Structure and Economic System*. Warsaw, 1974
Zielinski, J. G., *Economic Reforms in Polish Industry*. OUP, 1973

National Library: Biblioteka Narodowa, Rakowiecka 6, Warsaw.

PORTUGAL

República Portuguesa

Capital: Lisbon
Population: 8·75m. (1975)
GNP per capita: US$1,690 (1976)

AREA AND POPULATION.

	Area (sq. km)	*Population 1960 (census)*	*Population 1970 (census)*[2]
Continent	88,500	8,292,975	8,074,960
Islands	3,131	596,417	536,150
Portugal (total)	91,631[1]	8,889,392	8,611,110
Districts:			
Aveiro	2,708	524,592	545,230
Beja	10,240	276,895	204,440
Braga	2,730	596,768	609,405
Bragança	6,545	233,441	180,395
Castelo Branco	6,704	316,536	254,355
Coimbra	3,956	433,656	399,380
Évora	7,393	219,916	178,475
Faro	5,072	314,841	268,035
Guarda	5,496	282,606	210,720
Leiria	3,516	404,500	376,940
Lisboa	2,762	1,382,959	1,568,020
Portalegre	5,882	188,482	145,545
Porto	2,282	1,193,368	1,309,560
Santarém	6,689	461,707	427,995
Setúbal	5,152	377,186	469,555
Viana do Castelo	2,108	277,748	250,510
Vila Real	4,239	325,358	265,605
Viseu	5,019	482,416	410,795
Islands:			
Angra do Heroismo	703	96,174	85,650
Funchal	796	268,937	251,135
Horta	780	49,382	40,600
Ponta Delgada	852	181,924	158,765

[1] 34,861 sq. miles. [2] Provisional.

In 1970 the population consisted of 4,089,165 males and 4,521,960 females, or 109 females to every 100 males.

The Azores islands are divided into 3 widely separated groups, with clear channels between, São Miguel together with Santa Maria being in the most easterly. About 100 miles north-west of them lies the central cluster of Terceira, Graciosa, São Jorge, Pico and Faial. Still another 150 miles to the north-west are Flores and Corvo, the latter being the most isolated and primitive of the islands. São Miguel, Terceira and Pico are the largest, the first measuring 41 miles in length and 9 in breadth, and containing over half the total population of the archipelago. For political and administrative purposes they are divided into 3 districts, each sending its representatives to the Chamber at Lisbon. The capitals of the 3 districts are the chief seaports, Ponta Delgada on São Miguel Island, Horta on Faial Island and Angra do Heroísmo on Terceira Island.

Vital statistics for calendar years:

	Births	*Still-births*	*Marriages*	*Divorces*	*Deaths*	*Emigrants*
1974	171,979	2,963	81,724	777	96,928	43,397
1975	179,648	2,781	203,125	2,552	97,936	24,811
1976	186,712	2,735	101,599	...	...	...

In 1975 the births included 93,099 (1976: 96,582) boys and 86,549 (1976: 90,130) girls; deaths, 51,261 (1974: 49,477) males and 46,675 (1974: 47,451) females.

At the census of 15 Dec. 1970 the population of Lisbon (capital) was 760,150 (metropolitan area, 1,034,141); Porto, 300,925 (metropolitan area, 693,170). According to 1970 census (provisional figures): Vila Nova de Gaia, 50,805; Coimbra, 55,985; Setubal, 49,670; Braga, 48,735; Amadora, 65,870; Matosinhos, 22,505; Almada, 38,990; Barreiro, 53,690; Evora, 23,665; Guimarães, 24,280; Covilhã, 26,530; Moscavide, 21,765; Faro, 20,470.

In 1975, 2,553 emigrants went to Brazil and 8,975 to USA.

CONSTITUTION AND GOVERNMENT. Portugal has been an independent state since the 12th century; until 1910 it was a monarchy. The last King was Manuel II of the house of Braganza-Coburg, born 15 Nov. 1889, died 2 July 1932. On 5 Oct. 1910 the republic was proclaimed with Dr Teófilo Braga as the provisional president (5 Oct. 1910 to 24 Aug. 1911). Thereafter there were duly elected presidents, as follows:

Dr Manuel de Arriaga, 24 Aug. 1911–29 May 1915.[1]
Dr Joaquim Teófilo Braga, 29 May 1915–5 Oct. 1915.
Dr Bernardino Luis Machado Guimarães, 5 Oct. 1915–11 Dec. 1917.[2]
Dr Sidonio Bernardino Cardoso da Silva Pais, 11 Dec. 1917–14 Dec. 1918.[3]
Adm. João de Canto e Castro Silva Antunes, 16 Dec. 1918–5 Oct. 1919.
Dr António José de Almeida, 5 Oct. 1919–5 Oct. 1923.
Manuel Teixeira Gomes, 5 Oct. 1923–11 Dec. 1925.[1]
Dr Bernardino Luís Machado Guimarães, 11 Dec. 1925–1 June 1926.[1]
Provisional government, 1 June–29 Nov. 1926.
Marshal António Oscar Fragoso Carmona, 29 Nov. 1926–18 April 1951.
Marshal Francisco Higino Craveiro Lopes, 22 July 1951–9 Aug. 1958.
Rear-Adm. Américo de Deus Rodrigues Tomás, 9 Aug. 1958–25 April 1974.[2]
Gen. Antonio de Spinola, 25 April 1974–30 Sept. 1974.[4]
Gen. Francisco da Costa Gomes, 30 Sept. 1974–27 June 1976.

[1] Resigned. [2] Deposed. [3] Assassinated. [4] Not elected.

National flag: Vertical green and red, with the red of double width, and over all on the dividing line the national arms.

National anthem: A Portuguesa (words by Lopes de Mendonça, 1890; tune by Alfredo Keil).

In 1933 a constitution declared that the Portuguese state was a unitary and corporative republic, and the Constitution was adopted by plebiscite. The president was to be elected for 7 years by an electoral college, constituted of members of the National Assembly and the Corporative Chamber, with representatives of municipalities and oversea legislative councils.

On 25 April 1974 a military *coup* led by Gen. Antonio de Spinola overthrew the government of Dr Caetano. Gen. Spinola announced on 26 April that there would be elections within 12 months, that political prisoners would be released and that there would be freedom of expression and the Press. The deposed President, Rear-Adm. Tomás and deposed Prime Minister, Dr Caetano, were taken to Madeira.

General Spinola resigned as President on 30 Sept. 1974.

Several military officers attempted to overthrow the Portuguese Government on 11 March 1975. Gen. Spinola went into exile but denied taking part in the *coup*.

Following the failure of the *coup* a new Supreme Revolutionary Council, of 28 members, was sworn in on 17 March.

At the legislative elections held on 25 April 1976 the Socialists gained 34·97% of the votes cast, 107 seats in the Assembly; Popular Democrats, 24·03%, 73 seats; Centre Democratic Social Party, 15·91%, 42 seats; Communist Party, 14·56%, 40 seats; Democratic Popular Union, 1·69%, 1 seat.

At the presidential elections held on 27 June 1976 Gen. Ramalho Eanes gained 61·59% of the votes cast; Adm. José Baptista Pinheiro de Azevedo, 14·37%; Octávio Pato, 7·59%; Otelo Nuno Romão Saraiva de Carvalho, 16·4%.

President: Gen. António dos Santos Ramalho Eanes.
Prime Minister: Dr Mario Soares.
Foreign Minister: Vitor Sá Machado.

DEFENCE. Continental Portugal is divided into 4 military regions with headquarters at Coimbra, Oporto, Évora, Lisbon and insular Portugal territorial military command of Madeira and the Azores.

Every Portuguese citizen in good physical condition is subject to compulsory military service from the age of 20 to 45 years for a period of 2 years.

Pre-military training is entrusted to the *Colégio Militar* and the *Instituto Técnico e Profissional dos Pupilos do Exército*, with particular emphasis on physical and moral training of youths aged from 9 to 19 years.

Army. The Army consisted of 1 tank, 2 cavalry and 15 infantry regiments, 5 artillery regiments, 2 engineer and 1 signal battalions. Effective strength (1978), 36,000 all ranks.

In 1978 the Republican Guard (*Guarda Nacional Republicana*) consisted of 11,800 all ranks, the Police (*Policia de Legurança Pública*) of 11,000 all ranks and the Fiscal Guard (*Guarda Fiscal*) of 6,504 all ranks.

Navy. The Navy comprises 3 diesel-powered patrol submarines, 17 frigates, 10 patrol vessels, 4 coastal minesweepers, 8 patrol launches, 1 sail training ship, 5 surveying vessels, 1 fleet oiler, 1 depot ship, 1 fishery protection vessel, 1 landing craft, 13 minor landing craft, 3 tugs and 1 harbour tanker. The navy personnel in 1978 totalled approximately (running down) 12,000 officers and men including marines.

Following the withdrawal from Africa there is a considerable disposal list of some 80 warships and the Navy is now comparatively small.

Air Force. Formed in 1912, the Air Force has been independent since 1952, when it was combined with the naval air service and given equal status with the Army and Navy.

In 1977, it had a strength of about 10,000 officers and men, with 50 first-line aircraft. It contributes 1 maritime reconnaissance squadron to NATO.

Equipment comprises 1 interceptor squadron of F-86F Sabre jets, a light strike unit of G-91Rs; 1 squadron of P2V-5 Neptune ASW reconnaissance aircraft; air transport units with 5 C-130H Hercules and 24 Spanish-built CASA 212 Aviocars, of which 4 are equipped for photographic duties; 32 Cessna 337 Skymasters for counter-insurgency and liaison duties; and a strong force of Puma and Alouette III helicopters. Other aircraft in service include Chipmunk piston-engined trainers, T-37C jet basic trainers, T-33 and G-91T jet advanced trainers.

There is a parachute regiment of 2,000, which comes under Air Force command.

INTERNATIONAL RELATIONS

Membership. Portugal is a member of UN, EFTA, OECD and NATO.

ECONOMY

Planning. For 1977 investment included (in 1m. escudos): Education, 2·8m.; housing and urbanization, 15·2m.; agriculture, forestry and livestock, 5·1m.; transport and communications, 7·7m.

Budget. Revenue and expenditure for calendar years (in 1,000 contos):

	1971	*1972*	*1973*	*1974*	*1975*	*1976*	*1977*[1]
Revenue	36,930	42,103	50,034	61,274	79,683	125,373	159,173
Expenditure	36,648	40,868	48,894	63,415	86,620	124,688	159,173

[1] Estimates.

Main items of estimated revenue and expenditure (in 1,000 escudos):

	1976	*Expenditure*	*1976*
Current revenue	71,430,758	Defence	13,889,978
Direct taxes	21,029,795	Co-operation	75,590
Indirect taxes	44,681,064	Domestic administration	5,992,147
Taxes, fines and other penalties	541,644	Justice	794,370
Property incomes	3,564,529	Finance[1]	14,794,336
Transferences	425,764	Social and environment	10,316,855

[1] Includes 7,650m. escudos for servicing the public debt.

	1976
Permanent properties sale	6,025
Services and other non-permanent properties sale	1,170,637
Other current revenues	11,300
Capital revenues	349,405
Investment properties sale	1,388
Transferences	33,909
Financial assets	314,108
Repositions non-deducted in payment	749,450
Bank accounts	3,936,078
Total of ordinary revenue	76,465,691
Extraordinary revenue	48,907,661
Total	125,373,352

Expenditure	*1976*
Education and scientific research	17,052,202
Labour	305,328
Social affairs	8,354,332
Social communications	660,666
Agriculture and fisheries	1,178,864
Industry and technology	442,648
Foreign trade	1,298,915
Domestic trade	184,907
Transport and communications	3,848,613
Total ordinary	80,811,852
Extraordinary	43,876,386
Total	124,688,238

On 31 Dec. 1976 the public debt was as follows: Consolidated debt: 4% (1940) (centenarios), 1,114,199 contos; 3½% (1941), 376,870 contos; 3% (1942), 2,542,453 contos; 2¾% (1943), 903,986 contos; public debt certificates (4%), 6·48m. contos; public debt certificates (5%), 6,143,500 contos. The internal redeemable debt was as follows: Titles, 98,222,741 contos; Caixa Geralde Depósitos, 274,317 contos. Public debt certificate: 4·58m. contos. External redeemable debt: 10,728,133 contos.

Currency. The unit of currency is the *escudo* of 100 *centavos*, which contains 0·66567 gramme of fine gold. It was stabilized on 9 June 1931, and the paper currency re-linked to gold when the notes of the Bank of Portugal became payable in gold or its equivalent in foreign currency. 1,000 escudos is called a *conto*.

At present there are silver coins of 50, 20, 10 and 5 escudos; 10, 5 and 2½ escudos (nickel and copper); alpaca coins of 1 and ½ escudo (50 centavos); bronze coins of 1 and ½ escudo and 20 and 10 centavos, and aluminium coins of 10 centavos.

The 20- and 10-centavo coins, issued in 1943, were made of an alloy of 95% copper, 3% zinc and 2% tin.

Banking. The one bank of issue for the mainland of the country and adjacent islands is the Bank of Portugal, founded 19 Nov. 1846. By decree of 29 June 1962, its constitution was modified and its privileges were prolonged until 30 June 1991. The capital of the bank was fixed at 200m. escudos. The bank is the treasury of the State, and its reserve must be not less than 50% of the total amount of its notes in circulation and other sight liabilities. Not less than 25% of the amount of the notes in circulation and other sight liabilities must be represented by gold (coin or bullion). The bank issues notes of 1,000, 500, 100, 50 and 20 escudos. All Portuguese banks and insurance companies were nationalized in March 1975.

The National Development Bank began operations on 4 Jan. 1960. Of its total capital of 1,500m. escudos, 650m. have been subscribed by the Government and 75m. by the Bank of Angola.

There are 16 banks registered on the mainland and 1 in the islands, with cash in hand on 31 Dec. 1976, 4,303m. escudos; bills, 168,076m. escudos; deposits, 118,640m. escudos. The deposits in the savings banks and general deposit bank (state) amounted to 275,923m. escudos.

Weights and Measures. The metric system of weights and measures is the legal standard.

ENERGY AND NATURAL RESOURCES

Electricity. Total production of electrical power in 1975 was 10,728m. kwh. (1976: 10,145m.) ; the installed capacity totalled 3,936,704 kva. (1976: 4,288,068), of which 2,437,587 kva. (1976: 2,523,604) were hydro-electric. New power plants were inaugurated in 1951 (Castelo do Bode, Venda Nova, Belver), 1953 (Salamonde), 1954 (Cabrill), 1955 (Caniçada and Bouçã), 1958 (Picote), 1960 (Miranda), 1964 (Bemposta), 1965 (Tàvora), 1970 (Drives and Bugalheira), 1971 (Carrapatelo) and 1975 (France, Fratel, Valeira).

Minerals. Portugal possesses considerable mineral wealth. Production in tonnes:

	1974	*1975*	*1976*		*1974*	*1975*	*1976*
Coal	230,209	221,621	193,443	Beryl	17	21	...
Cupriferous pyrites	510,573	461,923	416,205	Wolframite	2,488	2,411	2,146
Tin ores	606	529	474	Hematite	24,498	33,850	29,081
Kaolin	60,724	59,355	63,895	Magnetite	...	1,818	2,353
Gold (refined)	0·357	0·356	0·312	Manganese	71	...	...

Agriculture. The following figures show the area (in hectares) and yield (in tonnes) of the chief crops:

	1974		*1975*		*1976*	
Crop	*Area*	*Yield*	*Area*	*Yield*	*Area*	*Yield*
Wheat	461,646	533,603	462,259	601,204	531,805	685,744
Maize	359,794	485,545	371,531	451,272	348,542	378,529
Oats	170,596	99,141	206,630	120,675	215,241	126,714
Barley	93,540	74,524	100,502	86,457	143,137	116,774
Rye	209,831	142,834	210,828	145,909	218,709	164,842
Rice	32,969	129,457	30,225	39,305	22,284	97,235
Dried beans	297,418	39,580	301,066	1,012,686	269,956	31,742
Potatoes	111,764	1,111,519	107,219	1,052,686	116,124	918,103

Wine production (in hectolitres), 1975, 8,773,335; 1974, 13,872,572; olive oil, 1975, 538,943; 1974, 525,596. In 1955, 228,996 hectolitres of port wine were exported; 1968, 337,986; 1969, 327,207; 1970, 352,090; 1971, 372,802; 1972, 445,741; 1973 (tonnes), 48,244; 1974, 43,063; 1975, 37,712.

Livestock. In 1976 Portugal (continental only) possessed 27,000 horses, 88,000 mules, 180,000 asses, 1m. cattle, 653,000 goats and 1·68m. pigs.

Forestry. Forest area covers 3·2m. hectares, of which 1·41m. are pine, 758,000 cork oak, 704,000 other oak, 75,000 chestnut, 155,000 eucalyptus and 135,000 other species.

Portugal surpasses the rest of the world in the production of cork, 1973 (in tonnes), 188,405; 1974, 149,579; 1975, 115,073; 1976, 95,929. Most of it is exported crude; exports of cork and cork products totalled (in tonnes) 162,227 in 1972; 153,702 in 1973; 138,421 in 1974; 103,967 in 1975. Production of resin (in tonnes) was 120,660 in 1972; 137,662 in 1973; 146,968 in 1974; 137,774 in 1975; 100,319 in 1976, more than two-thirds are exported. Exports of turpentine (in tonnes) were 14,229 in 1972; 12,953 in 1973; 14,012 in 1974; 6,816 in 1975.

Fisheries. The fishing industry for the continent and adjacent isles is of importance. At 31 July 1976 there were 31,611 men and boys employed, with 8,767 boats. The sardine catch, 1975, was 95,486 tonnes valued at 409,778 contos; 1976, 79,246 tonnes valued at 625,131 contos. Exports of tinned sardines (in tonnes) amounted to 22,001 in 1974, 23,293 in 1975 and 28,577 in 1976. The most important centres of the sardine industry are at Matosinhos, Setubal, Portimão and Olhão.

TRADE

Commerce. Imports for consumption and exports (exclusive of coin and bullion and re-exports) for calendar years, in 1,000 escudos:

	1971	*1972*	*1973*	*1974*	*1975*	*1976*
Imports	52,416,220	60,683,574	74,775,538	118,094,938	99,474,040	130,858,582
Exports	30,248,315	35,255,334	45,410,493	58,014,289	49,328,112	55,088,512

The principal articles of imports and exports (in 1,000 escudos):

Imports	*1974*	*1975*	*1976*	*Exports*	*1974*	*1975*	*1976*
Dried cod	850,061	584,105	799,642	Sardines	754,638	897,545	1,129,270
Wheat	2,099,536	1,784,131	1,225,604	Cork	3,797,679	2,971,193	3,741,299
Tobacco, un-manuf'd	331,976	366,902	431,032	Wine	3,804,669	3,329,774	3,551,895
				Olive oil	219,481	182,408	131,231
Oil seeds	1,725,124	2,437,131	3,047,811	Resin	1,510,665	734,570	950,176
Coffee	444,720	396,612	913,859	Turpentine	153,439	67,459	125,714
Sugar	3,255,555	5,186,517	3,456,580	Pyrites	27,981	19,693	7,988
Hides	514,844	371,142	591,686	Wolfram	461,019	333,956	452,158

Imports	*1974*	*1975*	*1976*
Ammonium sulphate	288	644	177
Iron and steel:			
Ingots	6,354,416	4,604,516	5,224,413
Manuf'd	1,616,700	1,691,830	2,236,582
Coal etc.	525,766	773,418	968,083
Cotton, raw	3,154,705	3,107,330	4,497,460
Dyes	285,884	160,217	376,628
Motor vehicles	5,145,834	4,266,957	6,014,718
Petroleum and shale oil, crude	11,475,712	12,843,224	17,384,258
Fuel and gas oil	863,962	922,768	1,053,406

Exports	*1974*	*1975*	*1976*
Pit-props	40,027	33,551	34,494
Pulpwood	2,517,324	2,392,390	3,554,420
Fuel and gas oils	1,026,728	423,975	424,861
Rubber tyres and tubes	236,586	216,856	154,313

The distribution of the imports and exports (in 1,000 escudos):

From or to	*Imports from* 1974	1975	1976	*Exports to* 1974	1975	1976
Angola	9,223,994	3,055,668	1,261,883	3,510,856	1,741,667	880,068
Belgium	3,952,056	2,815,760	3,576,676	1,616,348	1,581,911	1,912,272
France	9,159,648	7,416,246	10,918,171	3,448,986	3,264,060	4,601,833
Germany, Fed. Rep. of	15,863,223	11,107,397	12,216,793	4,646,931	5,027,741	10,162,926
Great Britain	10,929,961	8,498,691	6,123,596	13,234,472	10,468,060	2,062,189
Italy	6,289,619	4,876,881	1,472,973	1,884,483	1,617,364	819,727
Mozambique	2,600,787	1,475,590	4,883,978	1,814,132	1,261,069	1,872,096
Netherlands	4,171,734	3,476,038	6,101,106	1,475,999	1,407,406	1,156,179
Spain	5,365,090	4,163,692	13,856,295	1,200,065	1,328,135	3,702,677
USA	11,087,598	12,146,329	15,205,333	5,760,555	3,559,322	5,907,922

Total trade between Portugal (excluding the Azores and Madeira) and UK (British Department of Trade returns, in £1,000 sterling):

	1972	*1973*	*1974*[1]	*1975*	*1976*	*1977*
Imports to UK	125,667	188,564	236,176	201,081	199,124	229,889
Exports and re-exports from UK	111,635	147,452	185,637	157,606	223,317	299,321

[1] Including Azores and Madeira.

Trade Unions. 331 unions had in 1977 a membership of 1,436,142. A single confederation for trade unions was established by law in Jan. 1975.

Tourism. Tourism is of increasing importance for the invisible balance of payments. In 1976, 2m. visitors (1975: 2m.) spent about 9,980m. escudos (1975: 6,502m.); they included, in 1976, 244,552 British and 82,105 US citizens.

COMMUNICATIONS

Roads (1976). There were 32,137 km of road. There were registered in continental Portugal in 1976, 1,254,406 motor vehicles, including 86,376 motor cycles and 67,836 tractors; not counting vehicles used by the armed forces.

Railways. A decree of 9 May 1951, based on the law of 7 Sept. 1945, merged all leases and concessions in a single concession for all Portuguese railways, granted to the *Companhia dos Campinhos de Ferro Portugueses*, except the Estoril railway (Lisbon–Cascais), of 26 km length. In 1976 total railway length was 3,519 km (1,676 mm and metre gauges), of which 406 km of broad-gauge was electrified. In 1976, 191,676,000 passengers were carried and 3·42m. tons of merchandise transported.

Aviation. Regular services connect Lisbon with Brussels, Johannesburg, New York, Madrid, Paris, London, Frankfurt, Rio de Janeiro, Zürich, Copenhagen, Dusseldorf, Amsterdam, Buenos Aires, Boston, Montreal, Las Palmas, Salisbury, Geneva, Recife, Sal Island, Beira, Luanda, Maputo and Bissau. These lines in 1976 carried 1·65m. passengers and 29,858 tonnes of freight.

Shipping. In 1976, 13,927 vessels of 61,453,907 tons entered the ports (continental and islands). Of those entering 6,050 (14,659,694 tons) were Portuguese, 610 (5,663,093 tons) British and 666 (2,095,074 tons) Spanish. On 31 Dec. 1976 the merchant marine consisted of 118 transport vessels of 1,122,646 tons.

Post and Broadcasting (1976). The length of telegraph lines was 500,217 km; number of offices, 1,708. The state owned 2,448,023 km of telephone line and the *Telefones de Lisboa e Porto* owned 2,223,489 km of lines. Number of telephones was 1,118,970, of which 363,664 were government-owned.

Cable and Wireless, Ltd, operate in Portugal (Carcavelos), the Azores, Madeira and Cape Verde Islands, connecting Portugal with Great Britain, North and South America, and West and South Africa.

Emissora Nacional de Radiodifusão broadcasts 2 programmes on medium- and short-waves and on FM as well as 3 regional services. *Radiotelevisão Portuguesa SARL* broadcasts 2 commercial TV programmes. *Radio Clube Português* is a commercial, nationwide network. In addition there are 6 local, commercial stations, operating on medium-waves. Radio Trans Europe is a high-powered short-wave station, retransmitting programmes of different broadcasting organizations, *e.g.*, IBRA, Radio Canada and Deutsche Welle. Radio Free Europe also has relay facilities on short-waves in Portugal. Number of receivers (1975): Radio, 1,510,703; TV, 722,315.

Cinemas (1976). There were 475 cinemas with a seating capacity of 263,849.

Newspapers (1976). There were 36 daily newspapers with a combined circulation of 226,263; 17 of these, with a combined circulation of 147,238, appeared in Lisbon.

JUSTICE, RELIGION AND EDUCATION

Justice. Portuguese law distinguishes civil (including commercial) and penal, labour, administrative and fiscal law, each branch having its lower courts, courts of appeal and the Supreme Court.

The republic is divided for civil and penal cases into 196 *comarcas*; in every comarca there is a lower court. In the comarca of Lisbon there are 46 lower courts (22 for criminal procedure and 24 for civil or commercial cases); in the comarca of Oporto there are 25 lower courts (13 for criminal and 12 for civil or commercial cases); at Barcelos, Vila Nova de Famalicáo, Braga, Setúbal, Guimarães, Santarém, Leiria, Aveiro, Viseu, Almada, Feira, Anadia, Cascais, Loures, Oeiras, Sintra, Vila Franca de Xira and Vila Nova Degaja there are 2 courts; at Coimbra and Funchal there are 3 courts. There are 4 courts of appeal (Tribunal de Relação) at Lisbon, Coimbra, Evora and Oporto, and a Supreme Court in Lisbon (Supremo Tribunal de Justiça). There are also 16 municipal courts, which are lower courts, similar to those of the comarcas; their jurisdiction is, however, limited.

Capital punishment was abolished completely after the new constitution of 1976.

The prison population as at 31 Dec. 1975 was 6,112.

Religion. The predominant faith is the Roman Catholic, but there is freedom of worship, both in public and private, with the exception of creeds incompatible with morals and the life and physical integrity of the people.

Education. According to the latest statistics, 70% of the population over 7 years could read and write. Compulsory education has been in force since 1911. In 1975–76 there were 10,979 public primary schools with 882,910 pupils and 36,593 teachers. Private elementary schools numbered 605 with 39,294 pupils and 2,113 teachers. Basic preparatory schools numbered 1,527 with 288,948 pupils. Secondary instruction is supplied in two types of schools: in the *liceus* and other grammar schools, and in schools of technical instruction. In 1975–76 there were 449 *liceus* and 318 institutions of *liceu* standard, with 216,323 pupils, and 183 professional and technical secondary schools, with 123,044 pupils. There were also 14 schools which taught art activities (cinema, music and theatre) with 4,273 students. For higher education there are 6 universities; at Aveiro (founded in 1973), Lisbon (founded in 1911), Coimbra (founded 1290), Porto (founded 1911), Minho (founded 1974) and a new university at Lisbon (founded 1974). In 1975–76 the number of students at the universities was 38,375; and the Technical University at Lisbon (founded in 1930) had 13,039 students. There are also a military and a naval school, art schools in Lisbon and Porto (2,372 students) and 1 college of music (127 students). At upper level there are other colleges, public and private, which were attended by 13,868 and 3,151 students respectively.

DIPLOMATIC REPRESENTATIVES

OF PORTUGAL IN GREAT BRITAIN
(11 Belgrave Sq., London, SW1X 8PP)

Ambassador: Armando Martins.

OF GREAT BRITAIN IN PORTUGAL (35–39 Rua S. Domingos à Lapa, Lisbon)

Ambassador: Lord Moran, CMG.

OF PORTUGAL IN THE USA (2125 Kalorama Rd., NW, Washington, D.C., 20008)

Ambassador: João Manuel Hall Themido.

OF THE USA IN PORTUGAL (Ave. Duque de Loule 39, Lisbon)

Ambassador: Frank C. Carlucci.

OF PORTUGAL TO THE UNITED NATIONS

Ambassador: Vasco Futscher Pereira.

Books of Reference

Statistical Information: The Instituto Nacional de Estatistica (Avenida Dr António José de Almeida, Lisbon) was set up in 1935 in succession to the Direcção-Geral de Estatistica. The Centro de Estudos Económicos and the Centro de Estudos Demográficos were affiliated to the Instituto in 1944. The main publications are:

Anuário Estatistico. Annuaire statistique. Annual, from 1875
Estatísticas do Comércio Externo. 2 vols. Annual from 1967 (replacing *Comércio Externo*, 1936–66, and *Estatística Comercial*, 1865–1935)
Censo da População de Portugal. 1864 ff. Decennial (latest ed. 1972)
Estatistica da Organização Corporativa, 1938–49; Estatisticas da Organização Corporativa e Previdência Social. 1950 ff.
Estatisticas das Finanças, Publicas and *Estatísticas Nometárias.* 1969 ff. (replacing *Estatísticas Financeiras.* 1947–68 and *Situação Bancária*, 1919–46)
Estatísticas Agricolas. Statistique Agricole. 1943–64; replaced by *Estatísticas Agrícolas e Alimentares.* From 1965. Annual
Estatísticas Industrials. 1967 ff. (replacing *Estatística Industrial. Statistique Industrielle.* 1943–66)
Estatísticas Demográficas. From 1967 (replacing *Anuário Demográfico*, 1929–66)
Boletim Mensal do Instituto Nacional de Estatística. Monthly since 1929
Centro de Estudos Económicos. Revista. 1945 ff.
Centro de Estudos Demográficos. Revista. 1945 ff.
Estatísticas das Contribuições e Impostos. Annual from 1967 (replacing *Anuário Estatístico das Contribuições e Impostos*, 1936–66)
Estatisticas da Educação. 1940 ff.
Estatísticas da Justica. 1968 ff. (replacing *Estatísticas Judiciária.* 1936–66)
Estatísticas das Sociedades. 1939 ff.
Estatísticas do Turismo. 1969 ff.
Estatísticas do Energia. 1969 ff.

Azevedo, Gonzaga de, *Historia de Portugal.* 6 vols. Lisbon, 1935–44
Bradford, S., *Portugal.* London, 1973
Brazão, E., *The Anglo-Portuguese Alliance.* London, 1957
Bruce, N., *Portugal: The Last Empire.* Newton Abbot, 1975
Ferreira, J. A., *Dictionário inglês-portugês.* 2 vols. Porto, 1948
Figueiredo, A. de, *Fifty Years of Dictatorship.* Harmondsworth, 1975
Guerreiro, A. D. (ed.), *Bibliografia sobre a economia portuguesa, 1948–69.* 21 vols. Lisbon, 1958–72
Livermore, H. V., *Portugal: A Short History.* Edinburgh, 1973
Marques, A. H. de O., *History of Portugal.* 2 vols. Columbia Univ. Press, 1973
Mota, J. G., *A Resistência.* Lisbon, 1976
Nowell, C. E., *Portugal.* New Jersey, 1973
Pereira, A. M., *Organização politica e administrativa de Portugal.* Oporto, 1949
Rodrigues, A., Borga, C. and Cardosa, M., *Portugal depois de Abril.* Lisbon, 1976
Salazar, A. de O., *Doctrine and Action: Integral and Foreign Policy of the New Portugal, 1928–39.* London, 1939.—*Discursos, 1928–58.* 5 vols. 5th ed. Coimbra, 1958.—*Politica Portuguesa.* Santiago de Chile, 1952

Soares, M., *Le Portugal Bâillonné: Une Témoignage*. Paris, 1972
Sobel, L. A. (ed.), *Portuguese Revolution 1974–76*. New York, 1976
Spinola, A. de, *Portugal e o Futoro*. Lisbon, 1974
Stanislawski, D., *The Individuality of Portugal: A Study in Historical-Political Geography*. Univ. of Texas Press, 1959
Taylor, J. L., *Portuguese–English Dictionary*. London, 1959

National Library: Biblioteca Nacional, Campo Grande, Lisbon. *Director:* A. H. C. Marques.

OVERSEAS TERRITORIES

On 11 June 1951 the status of the Portuguese overseas possessions was changed from 'colonies' to 'overseas territories'. In 1972 greater autonomy was granted to the overseas territories. Angola and Mozambique became States instead of overseas provinces and had their own legislative assemblies. A Governor-General from each State would continue to be appointed by Lisbon but he would have the rank of Minister of State. On 6 Sept. 1961 all Africans were given full Portugese citizenship, thereby achieving the same status as the inhabitants of Portugese India and the other provinces. On 27 July 1974 Gen. Spinola announced that Portugal was prepared to offer independence to her African overseas territories of Angola, Mozambique and Portuguese Guinea (Guinea-Bissau) and to 'recognize the right of the populations of our overseas territories to take their destinies into their own hands'. A new constitutional law on decolonization, published on 24 July, formally repealed the section of 1933 Constitution which forbade the surrender of Portugal's overseas territories.

During 1974–76 independence was achieved by Angola (11 Nov. 1975); Cape Verde (5 July 1975); Guinea-Bissau (10 Sept. 1974); Mozambique (25 July 1975); São Tomé e Principe (12 July 1975)

East Timor was invaded by Indonesian forces on 7 Dec. 1975 after civil war had raged since August. On 17 July 1976 East Timor became a province of Indonesia and was renamed Loro Sae.

Approval has also been given for greater autonomy in Madeira and the Azores.

Books of Reference

Atlas de Portugal Ultramarino. Lisbon: Ministério das Colónais. 1948
Anuàrio Estatìstico, II: Ultramar. Annuaire statistique, II: Outre-mer. Lisbon, 1961 ff (1950–60 under the title *Anuário Estatístico do Ultramar*)
Boletin da Agência Geral do Ultramar. Lisbon. Monthly
Documentacão ultramarina portuguesa. Centro de Estudos Históricos Ultramarinos. Lisbon, 1960
Andrade, A. A., *O Tradicional Anti-Racismo da Acção Civilizadora Portuguesa* (in Portuguese and English). Lisbon, 1953
Bahia dos Santos, F., *Unidade e cooperação entre a metrópole e o ultramar*. Lisbon, 1953
Boxer, C. R., *Race Relations in the Portuguese Empire*. OUP, 1963
Caetano, M., *Tradições, Princípios e Métodos da Colonização Portuguesa* (in Portuguese, French and English). Lisbon, 1951
Cunha, S., *O Sistema Português de Politica Indigena*. Lisbon, 1953
Duffy, J., *Portuguese Africa*. Harvard Univ. Press, 1959.—*Portugal in Africa*. Harmondsworth, 1962
Freyer, G., *The Portuguese and the Tropics*. Lisbon, 1961
Galvão, H., and Selvagem, C., *Império Ultramarino Português*. 4 vols. Lisbon, 1950–53
Nogueira, F., *The United Nations and Portugal*. London, 1963
Oliveira, J. da Costa. *Aplicação de capitais nas províncias ultramarinas*. Lisbon, 1961
Pattee, R., *Portugal na Africa contemporânea*. Coimbra, 1959

MACAO

AREA AND POPULATION. Macao, in China, situated on a peninsula of the same name at the mouth of the Canton River, which came into possession of the

Portugese in 1557, forms with the 2 small adjacent islands of Taipa and Colôane a province divided into 2 wards, each having its own administrator. The boundaries have not yet been definitely agreed upon; at present Portugal holds the territory in virtue of the treaty with China of 1 Dec. 1887. Talks took place in Macao in Oct. 1974, but no firm plans emerged for granting independence or decolonization. An 'organic statute' was published on 17 Feb. 1976. It defined the territory as a collective entity, *pessoa colectiva*, with internal legislative authority which, while remaining subject to Portuguese constitutional laws, would otherwise enjoy administrative, economic and financial autonomy. The area of the province is 16 sq. km (6 sq. miles). The population, according to the census of 1970, is 248,636. Estimate (1975) 260,227.

BUDGET. Revenue in 1972 was 464,510 contos; expenditure, 432,002 contos, and public debt, 258,244 contos. The currency is the *pataca*.

COMMERCE. The trade, mostly transit, is handled by Chinese merchants. Imports, in 1973, 3,713,976 contos; exports, 2,460,471 contos.

COMMUNICATIONS. The province is served by a Portuguese and various British and Dutch steamship lines. In 1973, 22,673 vessels of 6,844,619 gross tons entered the port.

The province has 860 km of telephone line (8,468 instruments in 1973). There were 11,765 telephones in 1977. One government and 1 private commercial radio station are in operation on medium-waves broadcasting in Portuguese and Chinese. Number of receivers (1974), 65,000.

EDUCATION. Education (1972–73) is provided at 33 secondary schools (7,389 pupils), 85 elementary schools (22,699 pupils), 3 secondary preparatory schools (396 pupils), 21 technical schools (2,717 pupils), 1 church school (2 pupils) and an art school (110 pupils).

Governor: José Garcia Leandre.

Books of Reference

Anuário Estatístico de Macau. Macao
Brazáo, E., *Macau.* Lisbon, 1957

STATE OF QATAR

Capital: Doha
Population: 202,000 (1975)
GNP per capita: US$11,400 (1976)

HISTORY. The State of Qatar declared its independence from Britain on 1 Sept. 1971, ending the Treaty of 3 Nov. 1916 which was replaced by a Treaty of friendship between the 2 countries.

AREA AND POPULATION. The State of Qatar, which includes the whole of the Qatar peninsula, extends on the landward side from Khor al Odeid to the boundaries of the Saudi Arabian province of Hasa. Area, about 4,247 sq. miles (11,000 sq. km); population estimate in 1975 about 202,000, including a number of migrant labourers from neighbouring states. In 1976, 70% of employed population (44,000) where foreigners.

The capital is Doha (population, 130,000), which is the main port. Other towns are Dukhan, the centre of oil production, and Umm Said, oil-terminal of Qatar.

RULER. *The Amir:* HH Shaikh Khalifa bin Hamad Al-Thani, assumed power on 22 Feb. 1972. On 31 May 1977, HH Shaikh Hamed bin Khalifa Al-Thani, was appointed Heir Apparent of the State of Qatar, the portfolio of Minister of Defence was added to his existing responsibility of Commander-in-Chief of the Armed Forces.

Foreign Minister: Shaikh Suhaim bin Hamad Al-Thani.

Flag: Maroon, with white serrated border on hoist.

DEFENCE. The Qatar Public Security Forces have 3 Hunter jet fighter-bombers, 1 Hunter 2-seat trainer, 4 Commando and 3 Lynx helicopters, 1 Islander twin-engined light transport and Tigercat surface-to-air missile systems.

INTERNATIONAL RELATIONS

Membership. Qatar is a member of UN and the Arab League.

ECONOMY

Budget. Revenue (1977) 8,948m. riyals, of which oil, 8,138m. The Development budget 1977–78 envisaged expenditure of 6,301m. riyals.

Currency. On 13 May 1973 the Qatar *Riyal* was introduced. £1 = 7·08 *riyals*, US$1 = 3·93 *riyals*.

Banking. Banks operating in Qatar include: Qatar National Bank, the Commercial Bank of Qatar (also Qatari-owned), the Arab Bank, Bank Al Mashrek, Bank Saderat Iran, Banque de Paris et des Pays Bas, British Bank of the Middle East, the Chartered Bank, the First National City Bank, Grindlays Bank, the Bank of Oman and United Bank.

OIL. On 9 Feb 1977 Qatar gained national control over its 2 natural resources, oil and gas, with the signing of an agreement with Shell Qatar over the procedure for the transfer to the State of the company's remaining 40% share. A similar agreement had been reached with the Qatar Petroleum Company on 16 Sept. 1976.

The Qatar General Petroleum Corporation (QGPC) had been established by decree in July 1974 to assume overall responsibility for the State's domestic and foreign oil interests and operations. On 16 Oct. 1976 the Qatar Petroleum Producing Authority (QPPA) was established to serve as the executive arm of the QGPC. A subsidiary of the QGPC, the QPPA, oversees onshore and offshore oil operations.

The terminal of Halul Island was completed in March 1966; from it about 11m. tons of oil were exported in 1972. Production, 1975, 160m. bbls; 1976, 178m. bbls. Reserves (1974) 6,000m. bbls.

TRADE. In 1976 oil exports totalled US$2,065m. (1975, US$1,753m.), imports (1975) totalled 1,610m. riyals.

Total trade between Qatar and UK (British Department of Trade returns, in £1,000 sterling):

	1973	*1974*	*1975*	*1976*	*1977*
Imports to UK	47,293	166,005	156,670	248,813	100,761
Exports and re-exports from UK	19,410	22,081	55,741	86,696	116,611

COMMUNICATIONS

Roads. There are 600 miles of road.

Aviation. The Gulf Aviation Co., Ltd (owned equally by Qatar, Bahrain, Oman and the UAE), operates daily services from Bahrain; British Airways, Middle East and about 15 other airlines operate regular international flights from Doha airport.

Shipping. Ships of several lines used to call at Umm Said; with the completion in 1969 of the new Doha port, it has become the main port of Qatar.

Post. Telephone and radio-telephone services connect Qatar with Europe and America; there were 24,403 telephones in Jan. 1977. An earth satellite station was inaugurated in March 1976.

Cinemas. In 1973 there were 8 cinemas with a seating capacity of 7,000.

EDUCATION. There were, in 1975–76, 17,479 boys at 63 elementary schools with 1,056 teachers; 59 girls' schools had 13,680 pupils and 896 teachers. Total number of pupils in schools (1976–77) 32,400. In addition, 1,915 boys and 895 girls were attending 4 secondary schools. Students in higher institutions and universities numbered 1,800, of whom 767 attended the 2 colleges of education in Doha, the nucleus of the University of the Lower Gulf. 231 university students graduated, including 117 from the colleges of education. Post-graduate students abroad numbered 53.

HEALTH. There are 5 hospitals (including 1 for women and 1 for gynaecology and obstetrics) with a total of 682 beds. The 660-bed hospital at Doha is nearing completion and clinics are being built throughout the State.

DIPLOMATIC REPRESENTATIVES

OF QATAR IN GREAT BRITAIN (10 Reeves Mews, London, W1Y 3PB)

Ambassador: Rashid Mohammed Al-Khater (accredited on 21 Dec. 1977).

OF GREAT BRITAIN IN QATAR (Doha, Qatar)

Ambassador: D. G. Crawford.

OF QATAR IN THE USA (600 New Hampshire Ave., NW, Washington, D.C., 20037)

Ambassador: Abdullah Saleh Al-Mana.

OF THE USA IN QATAR (Doha, Qatar)

Ambassador: Andrew I. Killgore.

OF QATAR TO THE UNITED NATIONS

Ambassador: Jasim Yousif Jamal.

Book of Reference

Qatar into the Seventies. Information Ministry, Doha, 1973

RHODESIA

Capital: Salisbury
Population: 6·5m. (1976)
GNP per capita: US$550 (1976)

HISTORY. Prior to Oct. 1923 Southern Rhodesia, like Northern Rhodesia, was under the administration of the British South Africa Company. In Oct. 1922 Southern Rhodesia voted in favour of responsible government. On 12 Sept. 1923 the country was formally annexed to His Majesty's Dominions, and on 1 Oct. 1923 government was established under a governor, assisted by an executive council, and a legislature, with the status of a self-governing colony.

AREA AND POPULATION. Rhodesia is situated between the northern border of the Transvaal and the Zambezi River and is bordered on the east by Mozambique and on the west by the republic of Botswana. The area is 150,820 sq. miles (390,622 sq. km). The capital is Salisbury. The growth of the population is given in the following table:

	European (census)			*Asiatic and Coloured*	*African total (estimated)*	*Total population (estimated)*
	Males	*Females*	*Total*			
1911	15,580	8,026	23,606	2,912	745,000	772,000
1931	27,280	27,630	49,910	4,102	1,076,000	1,130,000
1941	36,615	32,339	68,954	6,521	1,404,000	1,479,000
1951	71,307	64,289	135,596	10,283	2,170,000	2,320,000
1961	111,720	109,784	221,504	17,812	3,618,150[1]	3,857,466
1974	—	—	273,000	29,300	5,800,000	6,100,000
1975	—	—	274,000	29,800	5,900,000	6,310,000
1976	—	—	277,000	31,500	6,220,000	6,530,000

[1] Actual Census, April–May 1962.

Estimated (1976) population of main urban areas:

	Europeans	*Africans*	*Asiatic*	*Coloured*	*Total*
Salisbury	124,000	430,000	4,600	7,400	566,000
Bulawayo	59,000	270,000	2,800	8,200	340,000
Umtali	9,600	49,000	600	600	60,000
Que Que	4,200	47,000	300	300	52,000
Gwelo	9,100	56,000	400	1,000	67,000
Gatooma	2,700	29,000	200	300	32,000
Fort Victoria	2,800	17,000	200	300	20,000
Shabani	1,900	15,000	—	100	17,049
Wankie	2,900	26,000	—	100	29,000

Vital statistics (European):

	1970	*1971*	*1972*	*1973*	*1974*	*1975*	*1976*
Births	4,370	4,495	4,713	4,401	4,528	4,347	4,079
Deaths	1,645	1,757	2,047	2,042	2,122	2,016	2,085
Immigrants	12,227	14,743	13,966	9,433	9,649	12,425	7,782

In 1973 the birth rate was 16 per 1,000; the crude death rate, 7·5 per 1,000, and infant mortality, 20 per 1,000 for Europeans. Figures for Africans were estimated as follows (1969): Births, 52 per 1,000; deaths, 16 per 1,000.

In 1973, 7,750 Europeans left the country and 9,649 Europeans immigrated in 1974.

CONSTITUTION AND GOVERNMENT. The government proposals for a new constitution were endorsed by 41,949 votes against 21,846 at a referendum on 26 July 1961.

By an Order in Council dated 6 Dec. 1961, Southern Rhodesia was granted the new constitution. Under this the Legislative Assembly consists of 65 members—50 on the upper roll and 15 on the lower roll, thus ensuring African representation.

Most of the reserved rights of the UK were replaced by a Declaration of Rights, a Constitutional Council and other safeguards.

After the dissolution of the Federation of Rhodesia and Nyasaland on 31 Dec. 1963 Southern Rhodesia reverted to the status of a self-governing colony within the Commonwealth, but, at the same time, became responsible for those powers which had been surrendered to the federal government on its formation and which, once again, became its responsibility. These included agriculture (European), defence, education (non-African), external affairs, health services, taxation and other fiscal responsibilities, posts, trade, transport and power.

The Legislative Assembly, elected on 7 May 1965, consisted in Oct. 1968 of 50 Rhodesian Front, 10 United People's Party, 3 independents and 2 Democratic Party.

Ian Smith, Prime Minister from 14 April 1964, had discussions about independence in London with the Prime Ministers, Sir Alec Douglas-Home (7–8 Sept. 1964) and Harold Wilson (4–11 Oct. 1965); and in Salisbury with the Prime Minister, the Commonwealth Secretary and the Attorney-General (25–30 Oct. 1965).

On 5 Nov. 1965 Prime Minister Smith declared a state of emergency, overriding normal constitutional safeguards. After abortive appeals by Prime Minister Wilson (10–11 Nov.) the Smith government issued a unilateral declaration of independence on 11 Nov. Thereupon the Governor dismissed Smith and his cabinet. The British Government reasserted its own formal responsibility for Rhodesia, excluded Rhodesia from Commonwealth preference in trade and from the sterling area; and had an enabling bill passed by Parliament on 15 Nov., which gave the Government power to deal with the situation by Orders-in-Council. Effective internal government was nevertheless carried on by the Smith cabinet.

The United Nations Security Council on 20 Nov. called upon all member states to break off economic relations with Rhodesia. Only Portugal and the Republic of South Africa did not impose an embargo, which from 17 Dec. also included oil.

In Sept. 1966 the conference of the Commonwealth Prime Ministers urged the British Government to approach the United Nations with a view to imposing mandatory selective sanctions, unless Rhodesia returned to legality by the end of 1966. From 1 to 3 Dec. Prime Minister Wilson, the Commonwealth Secretary, the Attorney-General, the Governor and the Chief Justice of Rhodesia met Mr Smith and a colleague of his on board HMS *Tiger*. They drafted a 'Working Document' on the procedure for progress towards legal independence on the basis of the 1961 Constitution and the so-called 'six principles'. This statement was approved by the British cabinet on 4 Dec., but rejected by the Smith government on 5 Dec. As a result the British Government approached the United Nations and on 16 Dec. 1966 the Security Council voted for mandatory sanctions including oil; France and USSR abstained.

Further talks based on the *Tiger* proposals were held between the British and Rhodesian Prime Ministers aboard HMS *Fearless* at Gibraltar on 10–13 Oct. 1968. On 2 March 1970 the Smith government declared Rhodesia a republic and adopted a new constitution. A general election was held on 10 April 1970. The Rhodesian Front Party won 50 of the 66 seats. On 28 May the first Republican Parliament was opened by the President.

The British Government stated on 3 March 1970 that 'The purported assumption of a republican status by the régime in Southern Rhodesia is, like the 1965 declaration of independence itself, illegal.'

On 24 Nov. 1971 an agreement was signed between Britain and Rhodesia following an announcement made on 8 Oct. 1970 that Britain would attempt further negotiations. The terms of the agreement of British recognition of the independence of Rhodesia included the principle that the British Government would need to be satisfied that any basis proposed for independence was acceptable to the people of Rhodesia as a whole. In 1972 a Commission arrived in Rhodesia to carry out a test of acceptability and found that the proposals were not acceptable to the people of Rhodesia as a whole. A new move towards a constitutional conference was begun in Nov. 1974 between the Rhodesian Government and leaders of the Rhodesian African Council in Lusaka, but the agreement which was reached, broke down when violations of the ceasefire clause were caused by increased terrorist activities in

Rhodesia. A further constitutional conference was arranged between the two parties to take place on the Victoria Falls railway bridge in Aug. 1975, but again broke down resulting in a split of the Rhodesian African National Council.

In Feb.–March 1976 there was a further attempt at reaching agreement but without success. In Sept. 1976, after discussions between Dr Kissinger, Ian Smith, and B. J. Vorster, an agreement for establishing an interim government leading to a new Constitution was accepted. A conference, held in Geneva, to discuss and implement this agreement, reached deadlock in Dec. 1976 and the conference was adjourned until an unspecified date.

The UK UN representative, Ivor Richard, visited Rhodesia in early 1977 with fresh proposals for a settlement but these were rejected although negotiations continued. In April Dr David Owen met Ian Smith in Cape Town and Salisbury about a constitutional settlement and in Sept. David Owen and Andrew Young of the US presented the Rhodesian Government with a fresh set of proposals.

A general election was held on 31 Aug. 1977 and the Rhodesian Front again held all 50 European seats.

On 3 March 1978 Ian Smith signed a constitutional agreement with the internally-based black nationalist leaders. It decrees independence, as Zimbabwe, on 31 Dec. 1978. Ian Smith retains his constitutional position as elected Prime Minister but acts as a co-equal with Abel Muzorewa, Ndabaningi Sithole and Jeremiah Chirau, who compose the executive council of the transitional administration. The agreement was rejected by the Patriotic Front and opposed by OAU and the UN Security Council.

Flag: Three vertical strips of green, white, green, with the arms of Rhodesia in the centre.

Internal Affairs. In 1962 the Ministry of Internal Affairs took over all functions performed by the then Department of Native Affairs, except in the field of agriculture which was taken over by the Ministry of Agriculture and the administration of Native Purchase Areas which was taken over by the Ministry of Mines and Lands. The Ministry of Internal Affairs is responsible for district and general government administration and the development of the Tribal Trust Land. The land areas previously known as Native Reserves and Special Native Areas have been reclassified as Tribal Trust Land and are set aside entirely for African occupation. In 1969 the Ministry of Internal Affairs took control of development of African agriculture. On 2 March 1970 the Land Tenure Act came into effect and distribution of land was (in 1m. acres): European area, 44·95; African area, 44·95; National area reserved for wild life conservation and national parks, 6·60.

All judicial functions (excluding Native Customary Law civil cases) previously performed by the Department of Native Affairs have been transferred to the Ministry of Justice. The Ministry of Internal Affairs is responsible for the supervision of the Government's policy of community development.

African Councils, formed for communities wanting to become responsible for local government, may be authorized to provide services, facilities and amenities and establish and maintain any undertaking for the benefit of the area. Councils have powers to impose rates on adults in the area in regard to stock or buildings and on the value of any land and grazing right.

There were (1976) 240 established African Councils which, in general, meet at monthly intervals.

Under the Quinet Commission which was set up by the government to enquire into racial discrimination, it was recommended that the Tribal Trust Lands should remain as they are, and abandonment of the two main land classifications in favour of free land for all, namely state land and private land. This has been accepted by government only in part, that is, all rural agricultural land and urban land zoned for industrial purposes, and commercial land in the main business centres to be open to all races. European and African residential Areas continue to be reserved.

DEFENCE

Army. The Rhodesia Army consists of (*a*) the Regular Force, (*b*) the territorial force, (*c*) the Class A and B reserves, together with the appropriate ancillary units.

Control is effected through the Army Headquarters (established in Salisbury and Bulawayo). Organized into 3 brigades, each of 1 regular battalion and several battalions of the territorial force. In addition, there are 8 each of reserve battalions and an artillery regiment of the territorial force and the various supporting units necessary for an independent command. The Regular Army consists of approximately 8,250 (including 3,250 conscripts) officers and other ranks. The Territorial Force (including the Reserve) totals approximately 55,000.

Air Force. The Rhodesia Air Force (regular) has a strength of about 1,300 personnel and 130 aircraft in 7 squadrons, of which 1 is intended primarily for a training role. Headquarters RhAF and New Sarum RhAF station are in Salisbury; the second main base is at Thornhill, Gwelo, with many secondary airfields throughout the country. Equipment includes 1 squadron of Canberra bombers with added under fuselage rocket racks; 1 squadron of Hunter FGA.9 fighter-bombers; 1 squadron of Vampire FB.9 fighter-bombers; a dual-role reconnaissance and training squadron with T.52 (armed) Provosts and two-seat Vampires; a light transport and scouting squadron with 14 twin-engined Islanders, a Cessna 310 and about 10 Italian-built AL.60F5 Trojan utility lightplanes; a transport squadron with C-47s; and a helicopter squadron with up to 50 Alouette IIs and IIIs. Latest acquisitions are reported to be 20 French-built Cessna 337 Milirole counter-insurgency light twins, known as Lynx in Rhodesia.

ECONOMY

Budget. Revenue and expenditure (in R$1,000) for years ending 30 June:

	1972–73	*1973–74*	*1974–75*[1]	*1975–76*	1976–77	1977–78[1]
Revenue	267,374	313,684	397,322	...	...	646,120
Ordinary expenditure:						
From revenue and loan funds	282,609	326,996	414,920	...	...	727,446

[1] Estimate.

Receipts during the year ended 30 June 1977 were (in R$1,000): Income and profits tax, 312,800; sales tax, 224,500; miscellaneous, 5,420.

Principal items of expenditure from revenue funds were (in R$1,000): Goods and services, 368,462; transfers (including pensions) 294,295.

The gross amount of the public debt outstanding in June 1977 was R$806,172,000.

Currency. On 17 Feb. 1970 decimal currency was adopted. The unit of currency is the Rhodesian dollar divided into 100 cents.

Banking. The Reserve Bank of Rhodesia is the country's central bank; it became operative when the Bank of Rhodesia and Nyasaland ceased operations on 1 June 1965. It acts as banker to the Government and to the commercial banks and as agent of the Government for important financial operations. It is also the central note-issuing authority and co-ordinates the application of the Government's monetary policy. The British Government dismissed the governor and directors on 3 Dec. 1965 and appointed a new board in London.

The post office savings bank had R29m. fixed deposits at 30 June 1975.

The leading banks are Barclays Bank International, National & Grindlays Bank, RHO Bank of Rhodesia, Standard Bank Ltd.

Weights and Measures. The British imperial system is in use but the US short ton is also used.

NATURAL RESOURCES

Natural Resources. The Natural Resources Board, set up in 1941, is the trustee of the natural resources of Rhodesia. The resources are defined as the soil, water and minerals, the animals, bird and fish life; the trees, grasses and other vegetation; the springs, marshes, swamps and public streams; other features the President may proclaim as natural resources such as landscapes and scenery. The principal executive bodies are the Conservation Area Committees of which there were 99 in

1977, covering the whole of the European farming area and about 77% of the African Purchase Areas. In the Tribal Trust Areas the Board had established 96 Tribal Trust Land Committees by 1977.

Minerals. The total value of all minerals produced in 1974 was £165·2m. Output (in 1,000 tons) and value (in £1,000):

	Output			*Value*		
	1963	*1964*	*1965*	*1963*	*1964*	*1965*
Asbestos	142·3	153·4	176·1	5,996·8	6,849	8,525
Gold (1,000 oz.)	566·3	574·4	549·6	7,101·2	7,228	6,895
Chrome ore	412·4	493·3	645·5	1,895·0	2,219	2,624
Coal	3,021·0	3,047·0	3,868·3	3,077·6	3,431	3,872
Copper	18·5	18·3	19·8	3,233·6	4,156	6,283

Production figures 1966–77 have not been published.

Agriculture. The most important single food crop in Rhodesia is maize, the stable food of a large proportion of the population; production in 1971 was 18m. bags (of 200 lb.). The livestock industry is second to tobacco as regards its export potential. Dairying forms the foundation of many mixed farms. The annual production of milk is approximately 10m. gallons.

Since U.D.I. agricultural production figures have not been published.

Fish farming is being developed and large catches are taken from Lake Kariba, where a fish freezing plant was completed in 1964.

Sugar is being produced in the Triangle and Hippo Valley estates (2·9m. tons of cane from 59,200 acres in 1966).

The citrus estates of the British South Africa Company, the state-owned deciduous orchards at Inyanga and a scheme for large-scale citrus growing at Hippo Valley form the basis of the citrus fruit industry in Rhodesia. However, many parts of the country between 2,500 and 4,000 ft above sea-level are suitable for citrus culture, and large numbers of deciduous fruit trees planted in the Melsetter and Inyanga areas are coming into production.

In 1973 cotton production was 1,557m. kg and irrigated wheat production (1973) amounted to 3,932m. kg.

Rhodesia has 7 large tea plantations, 2 of which are in the Inyanga district and 5 in Chipinga; production in 1966 was 2,500 short tons. Other crops grown in substantial quantities include small grains (sorghums and millet), rice, groundnuts, cassava. These crops form the basis of much subsistence farming undertaken by the African population.

Tobacco is the most important single product, amounting to about half the total agricultural output (by value). In 1965 tobacco accounted for £32·6m. out of a total agricultural output of £66·5m. In 1970 tobacco yields were 140·5m. lb.

Livestock (1973): European, 2·57m. cattle; African, 3m. cattle.

INDUSTRY AND TRADE

Industry. Manufacturing industries are becoming increasingly important and have been stimulated by the abrogation of the Customs Convention with the Union in 1955 and the substitution of a trade agreement. In 1973 agriculture formed 10·4% and manufacturing 23·4% of the total economy.

Labour. In 1972 the monthly average of Non-Africans in employment was 112,000 and of Africans, 890,000. Largest employers of African labour were agriculture (349,000), manufacturing (120,000), construction (58,000), mining (54,000), hotels and restaurants (63,000) and domestic service (125,000).

The conditions of service for all workers in all industries other than agriculture and private domestic service are negotiated through the 27 Industrial Councils and the 54 Industrial Boards established under the Industrial Conciliation Act. The training, including full-time technical training, and conditions of employment for apprentices are determined by Apprenticeship Committees established in terms of the Apprenticeship Act. There is a system of national employment exchanges including youth employment and careers advisory services.

Workmen's compensation is by compulsory insurance through a Government established fund. Health and safety in industry is safeguarded through the Factories and Works Act.

Commerce. The leading commodities exported from Rhodesia are tobacco, asbestos, copper, clothing, meat, chrome ore, sugar, pig-iron and coal. Statistics in £ sterling until 1968 and then Rhodesian dollars:

	1968	*1969*	*1970*	*1971*	*1972*
Imports	103,524,000	199,426,000	234,881,000	282,379,000	274,245,000
Exports	91,734,000	218,979,000	253,558,000	277,238,000	328,474,000

Total imports of merchandise in 1965 from UK amounted to £36·36m.; from the Republic of South Africa, £27·46m.; from USA, £8·2m. Domestic exports to UK were £31·15m.; to the Republic of South Africa, £12·8m.

Principal exports in 1965: Copper, £6,056,240; tobacco, £46,968,149; asbestos, £10,761,271; chrome ore, £3,809,799; coal, £2,222,679; ferrochrome, £1,690,620; pig-iron, £2,472,537; sugar, £3,482,485; meat, £4,227,722; meat preparations, £2,523,107; clothing, £5,417,452.

Total trade between Rhodesia and UK (British Department of Trade returns, in £1,000 sterling):

	1973	*1974*	*1975*	*1976*	*1977*
Imports to UK	60	105	151	211	208
Exports and re-exports from UK	794	831	1,219	1,205	1,057

Tourism. In 1976, 157,000 tourists visited Rhodesia.

COMMUNICATIONS. The Minister of Transport and Power is responsible for the Government's relations with the Rhodesia Railways and with the Air Rhodesia Corporation.

Roads. Main roads connect all the main centres of the country with one another and with adjacent territories, and secondary roads serve rural areas. The total of surfaced roads maintained by the central government was 8,568 km and a further 69,394 km of secondary roads were maintained by local councils in 1971.

Number of motor vehicles excluding military (Oct. 1966) in Rhodesia: Private cars, 109,408; commercial vehicles (excluding farm tractors), 32,515.

Railways. Rhodesia is served by the Rhodesia Railways, which connect with the South African Railways to give access to the South African ports; with the Mozambique Railways to give access to the ports of Beira and Maputo; and with the Zambia railway system. The Mozambique and Zambia links were still closed at June 1978. In Sept. 1974 another branch of Rhodesia Railways was opened, which connects with South African Railways at Beitbridge. There were 3,250 km in 1975. In 1976 Rhodesia Railways carried 11·3m. tons of freight and (1974) 3.25m. passengers.

Aviation. The Air Rhodesian Corporation, in association with Central African Airways, South Africa Airways, Air Malawi and DETA, operates regular scheduled services to Malawi, Mauritius, Mozambique and the Republic of South Africa. In 1972–73 the Corporation flew 202,146 passenger-miles.

Shipping. Rhodesia outlets to the sea are through the South African ports.

Post and Broadcasting. At 1 Jan. 1977 there were 190,303 telephones in Rhodesia. Rhodesia Broadcasting Corporation is an independent statutory body broadcasting general service in English and African service in English, Shona, N'debele and Nyanja and 3 regional commercial services in English on medium- and short-waves. Rhodesia Television Ltd broadcasts one programme 42 hours a week *via* 3 transmitters. In June 1973 there were 177,541 radio licences and 61,716 combined radio and television licences.

JUSTICE, RELIGION, EDUCATION AND WELFARE

Justice. The High Court consists of an appellate division and a general division. The appellate division consists of the Chief Justice, the Judge President and at least one other judge of appeal. The general division consists of the Chief Justice and 5 puisne judges. The appellate division considers appeals from the general division and the lower courts; the general division has full jurisdiction, civil and criminal, over all persons and matters within Rhodesia. The Chief Justice is the head of the judiciary of Rhodesia. The Judge President presides over the appellate division in the absence of the Chief Justice. The Courts sit at Salisbury and Bulawayo, and sittings of the general division are held at 3 other principal towns three times a year.

Regional Courts, established in Salisbury and Bulawayo, are intermediate in jurisdiction between the magistrates courts and the High Court, but have no civil jurisdiction. There are 19 principal courts of magistrates and 64 periodical courts presided over by magistrates.

African Courts have jurisdiction over African persons in civil matters which are decided in accordance with African law and custom.

Religion. The largest religious groups are the Anglicans with 86,000 members (36% of the non-African populations), the Presbyterians with 29,000 members (12%) and the Roman Catholics with 35,500 (15%). There are no accurate figures for Africans.

Education. On 1 Jan. 1964 Rhodesia assumed responsibility for all education services which were under the control of the Federal Government. For administrative reasons the educational system of the country was divided between Africans and Non-Africans, and separate ministries were charged with the responsibility for the educational needs of these two groups. At present all educational services are under one ministry.

Total Government expenditure on education for the financial year 1973–74 was over R$52·47m.

African Education. There were (1977) 3,526 primary schools with 855,025 pupils, 156 secondary schools (47,333 pupils), 9 special schools for the physically handicapped (783), 19 homecraft schools (1,175 pupils) and 4,664 pupils enrolled in part-time classes and study groups.

Non-African Education. The total enrolment of Non-African pupils for 1974 was 60,107 in 236 schools.

Higher Education. The University of Rhodesia provides facilities for higher education. In 1977 the total enrolment of students was 1,423, including 796 Africans.

Health. In 1977 there were 114 hospitals, clinics and health centres operated by the Ministry of Health; 63 hospitals and clinics were operated by medical missions with government grants-in-aid and 46 without government grants. There was one medical practitioner for every 7,174 inhabitants in Rhodesia and there was 1 hospital bed for every 347 inhabitants.

Social Welfare. The Children's Protection and Adoption Act provides for the establishment of juvenile courts, the protection, welfare and supervision of children and juveniles; the establishment of corrective institutions and the treatment therein; the recognition, registration and inspection of certified institutions for the reception and custody of juveniles; for the adoption of minors and other matters. Administrative procedures make provision for public assistance and certain grants-in-aid.

Books of Reference

Statistical Information: The Central Statistical Office, PO Box 8063, Causeway, Salisbury, Rhodesia, originated in 1927 as the Southern Rhodesian Government Statistical Bureau. Ten years later its name was changed to Department of Statistics, and in 1948 it assumed its present title when it took over responsibility for certain Northern Rhodesian and Nyasaland statistics (which it relinquished in Dec. 1963 on the dissolution of the Federation). It publishes *Monthly Digest of Statistics.*

Rhodesia: Documents Relating to Proposals for a Settlement, 1966. (Cmd. 171) HMSO, 1966
Akers, M., *Encyclopaedia Rhodesia.* Salisbury, 1973
Blake, R., *A History of Rhodesia.* London, 1977
Bowman, L. W., *Politics in Rhodesia: White Power in an African State.* OUP, 1974
Cann, L. H., *A History of Southern Rhodesia to 1934.* London, 1965
Davies, D. K., *Race Relations in Rhodesia.* London, 1975
Good, R. C., *U.D.I.: The International Politics of the Rhodesian Rebellion.* London, 1973

Gray, R., and Gelfand, L. H., *Huggins of Rhodesia*. London, 1964
Hanna, A. I., *The Story of the Rhodesias and Nyasaland*. 2nd ed. London, 1965
Howarth, D., *The Shadow of the Dam: The Story of Lake Kariba*. London, 1961
Lardner-Burke, D., *Rhodesia: The Story of the Crisis*. London, 1966
Murphee, M. W. (ed.), *Education, Race and Employment*. Lichfield, 1975
O'Meara, P., *Rhodesia: Racial Conflict or Co-Existence*. Cornell Univ. Press, 1975
Palley, C., *The Constitutional History and Law of Southern Rhodesia, 1888–1965*. OUP, 1966
Palmer, R., *Land and Racial Domination in Rhodesia*. London, 1977
Rayner W., *The Tribe and its Successors: An Account of Traditional Life and European Settlement in Southern Rhodesia*. London, 1962
Sithole, N., *Roots of a Revolution*. OUP, 1977
Vambe, L., *From Rhodesia to Zimbabwe*, London, 1976.
Wills, A. J., *An Introduction to the History of Central Africa*. 2nd ed. OUP, 1967
Windrich, E., *The Rhodesian Problem: A Documentary Record 1923–73*. London, 1975
Young, K., *Rhodesia and Independence*. London, 1969

Reference Library: National Archives of Rhodesia. PO Box 8043, Causeway, Salisbury.

ROMANIA

Capital: Bucharest
Population: 21·25m. (1975)
GNP per capita: US$1,450 (1976)

Republica Socialistă România

HISTORY. For the history and constitution of Romania from 1859 to 1947, *see* THE STATESMAN'S YEAR-BOOK, 1947, pp. 1187–89. On 30 Dec. 1947 King Michael abdicated under Communist pressure and parliament proclaimed the 'People's Republic'.

AREA AND POPULATION. The area of Romania is 237,500 sq. km (91,699 sq. miles). Pre-war Romania had an area of 113,918 sq. miles. Population at censuses: 1930, 18,057,208 (14,280,729 within present-day Romania); 1948, 15,872,624 (48·3% male); 1966, 19,103,163 (49% male, 38·2% urban).

On 1 July 1975 the population was 21·25m. (49% male, 43% urban), density per sq. km, 89·5. Vital statistics, 1975 (per 1,000 population): Live births, 19·7; deaths, 9·3; marriages, 8·9; divorces, 1·6; stillborn (per 1,000 live births), 10; infant mortality (per 1,000 live births), 34·7; population growth rate, 10·4 per 1,000.

Administratively, Romania is divided into 40 districts (*judeţ*), 236 towns (*oraş*) (of which 47 are municipalities) and 2,706 local authorities (*comune*). The capital is Bucharest (Bucureşti) a municipality with district status.

District	*Area in sq. km*	*Population 1975*	*Capital*	*Population 1975*
Alba	6,231	403,622	Alba Iulia	34,676
Arad	7,654	497,143	Arad	147,145
Argeş	6,801	607,255	Piteşti	98,316
Bacău	6,603	685,670	Bacău	111,296
Bihor	7,535	628,421	Oradea	159,096
Bistriţa-Năsăud	5,305	294,023	Bistriţa	35,689
Botoşani	4,965	492,037	Botoşani	50,396
Braşov	5,351	504,644	Braşov	202,761
Brăila	4,724	378,165	Brăila	169,578
Buzău	6,072	523,563	Buzău	84,432
Caraş-Severin	8,514	373,935	Reşita	76,835
Cluj	6,650	695,304	Cluj-Napoca	222,429
Constanţa	7,055	554,446	Constanţa	198,429
Covasna	3,705	194,948	Sf. Gheorghe	32,015
Dîmboviţa	3,738	468,625	Tîrgovişte	45,313
Dolj	7,413	750,131	Craiova	197,820
Galaţi	4,425	565,909	Galaţi	201,607
Gorj	5,641	333,739	TBrgu Jiu	51,333
Harghita	6,610	314,874	Miercurea Ciuc	23,958
Hunedoara	7,016	518,811	Deva	52,858
Ialomiţa	6,211	395,863	Slobozia	23,359
Iaşi	5,469	736,065	Iaşi	216,206
Ilfov	8,225	811,295	Bucharest (*see below*)	
Maramureş	6,215	492,054	Baia Mare	93,393
Mehedinţi	4,900	329,543	Drobeta-Turnu Severin	71,107
Mureş	6,696	616,531	Tîrgu Mureş	114,326
Neamţ	5,890	543,226	Piatra Neamţ	69,893
Olt	5,507	521,159	Slatina	35,147
Prahova	4,694	793,904	Ploieşti	178,256
Satu Mare	4,405	391,602	Satu Mare	91,675
Sălaj	3,850	272,942	Zalău	25,595
Sibiu	5,422	460,090	Sibiu	131,361
Suceava	8,555	652,441	Suceava	54,012

District	Area in sq. km	Population 1975	Capital	Population 1975
Teleorman	5,872	543,192	Alexandria	29,002
Timiş	8,678	650,386	Timişoara	213,054
Tulcea	8,430	263,072	Tulcea	51,503
Vaslui	5,300	483,508	Vaslui	34,970
Vîlcea	5,705	408,155	Rîmnicu Vîlcea	47,094
Vrancea	4,863	387,992	Focşani	49,34347
Bucharest[1]	605	1,706,818	Bucharest[2]	1,588,592

[1] Total conurbation. [2] Central area.

The 1966 census listed the following ethnic groups (in 1,000): Romanians, 16,747; Hungarians, 1,620; Germans, 383.

The official language is Romanian.

CONSTITUTION AND GOVERNMENT. The present Constitution was adopted on 21 Aug. 1965 and supersedes those of 13 April 1948 and 24 Sept. 1952. Under it Romania becomes a 'Socialist' (as opposed to 'People's') Republic. The leading role of the Communist Party is reaffirmed. The Grand National Assembly of 349 is elected for 5 years (before 1972 for 4 years). It holds short sessions twice a year, and between sessions delegates its legislative rights to the State Council (the President, head of state; 4 Vice-presidents, 1 secretary and 20 members). By a law of Nov. 1969 the policy of ministries is shaped by deliberative collegiate bodies of which the minister is the chairman. All citizens of 18 and over have the right to vote and electoral law provides for the nomination of 'one or more' candidates in each constituency.

The National Council of the Socialist Unity Front functions as a consultative body on home and foreign affairs. It has a central and local councils in which workers, peasants, professional bodies, ethnic minorities and the Communist Party are represented. It replaces the Popular Democratic Front which was a coalition formed in 1948 of the Romanian Workers Party (a merger of the Communist and Social Democratic Parties), the Ploughmen's Front (a pro-Communist Peasant Party), the National Popular Party and the Hungarian Popular Union.

Elections were held on 30 Nov. 1952, 3 Feb 1957, 5 March 1961, 7 March 1965, 2 March 1969 and 9 March 1975 (postponed from 1974 so that subsequent elections may be synchronized with Party Congresses).

At the 1975 elections 99·96% of the 14·9m. electorate voted. In 139 constituencies 2 candidates stood.

In 1965 the Romanian Workers' Party was renamed the Romanian Communist Party. The Party Congress elects the General Secretary, and its Central Committee elects the Executive Committee (26 full and 20 candidate members), the Permanent Bureau (*see below*) and the Secretariat (General Secretary and 6 secretaries). The Party had 2·48m. members in 1974.

President of the Republic and Chairman of the State Council: Nicolae Ceauşescu, succeeded Chivu Stoica in Dec. 1967. *Vice-Chairmen:* Emil Bodnaraş, Stefan Voitec, Vasîle Vilcu.

In June 1978 the Permanent Bureau of the Party consisted of: Nicolae Ceauşescu (*General Secretary*); Ştefan Andrei; Elena Ceaşescu; Manea Mănescu; Gheorghe Oprea; Ion Păţan; Gheorghe Rădulescu.

Council of Ministers (June 1978). *Chairman* (*Prime Minister*): Manea Mănescu. *First Vice-Chairman:* Gheorge Oprea; Ilie Verdeţ (*Chairman, Economic Council, Chairman, State Planning Committee*). *Vice-Chairman:* Virgil Cazacu; Gheorghe Cioara; Janos Fazekaş; Col-Gen. Ion Ionaţă. Cornel Burtica (*Minister of Foreign Trade*); Gheorghe Rădulescu; Trajan Dudas (*Minister of Transport*); Paul Niculescu-Mizil (*Minister of Finance*); *Interior:* Teodor Coman; *Foreign Affairs:* Ştefan Andrei; *Armed Forces:* Gen. Ion Coman; *Justice:* Gheorghe Statescu; *Chairman, Supreme Council of Economic and Social Development:* Nicolae Ceauşescu.

Since the mid-1960s Romania has been taking an increasingly independent stand in foreign affairs. In July 1970 Romania signed a treaty of friendship, co-operation and mutual assistance with the USSR. A previous such treaty had expired in 1968.

National flag: Three vertical strips of blue, yellow, red, with the national arms in the centre.

National anthem: Tre culori (Three colours). Introduced, 1977.

DEFENCE. Defence is the responsibility of the Defence Council, which is controlled by the Council of State and headed by President Ceauşescu.

Army. Service is 16 months. Strength in 1977 was 140,000 men plus 37,000 in para-military forces (frontier troops, internal-security troops, militia, military firemen).

Units of the Ministry of the Armed Forces are under one of the 3 military regions of Iaşi, Bucharest and Cluj. There are 2 tank and 8 infantry divisions (not all at full strength), 2 mountain brigades and 1 airborne regiment. The AA artillery consists of 14 regiments. There are 1,700 T-34, T-54 and T-55 tanks. A Territorial Defence Force was set up in 1970.

Navy. The fleet comprises 3 coastal escorts, 5 missile boats, 22 torpedo boats, 18 fast gunboats, 3 old patrol vessels, 4 old minesweepers, 12 inshore minesweepers, 1 training ship, 8 minesweeping boats, 9 river patrol craft, 19 coastal patrol boats, 12 landing craft, 2 survey vessels, 10 transports, 3 oilers and 2 tugs. Headquarters of the Danube flotilla and main river port is Brăila. The naval school is in Constanţa. Personnel in 1978 totalled 10,000 officers and ratings including 2,000 Coastal Defence. National service is 2 years.

Air Force. Service is 2 years. The Air Force numbers some 30,000 men, with 320 combat aircraft. These are organized into 5 fighter regiments with MiG-21 fighters and 2 ground-attack regiments and other close-support squadrons with Su-7 and MiG-17 fighters. There are also 200 training aircraft, transports and helicopters. 'Guideline' surface-to-air missiles are operational, and short-range surface-to-surface missiles have been displayed.

INTERNATIONAL RELATIONS

Membership. Romania is a member of UN, Comecon and the Warsaw Pact.

ECONOMY

Planning. Economic policy is implemented by the State Planning Committee. Annual growth targets of the firth 5-year plan (1976–80): GNP, 9%; national income, 10·5%; industrial production, 11·2%; agricultural production, 6–7·2%; foreign trade, 12·3%. Industries scheduled for particular development: machine-building, iron and steel, non-ferrous metals, chemicals and electric power. An earthquake in March 1977 caused damage estimated at £300m. (For previous plans *see* The Statesman's Year-Book, 1976–77.)

Economic reforms were introduced in 1967 to give enterprises 'functional autonomy', but there is no move towards any fundamental decentralization of planning authority. In 1971 economic units were set up intermediate between ministries and enterprises. The number of these was reduced from 207 to 102 in 1974.

Budget. Revenue and expenditure (in 1m. lei) for calendar years:

	1970	*1971*	*1972*	*1973*	*1974*	*1975*
Revenue	133,342	138,630	153,382	175,972	210,111	238,553
Expenditure	130,900	134,237	145,432	168,091	207,322	236,169

In 1974 a Court of Preventive Financial Control was set up to oversee most official transactions and combat waste and corruption.

155m. on the economy, 51m. social and cultural, 12m. on administration and defence.

The revenues of local councils yielded 42m. lei in 1975.

In 1974 a Court of Preventive Financial Control was set up to oversee most official transactions and combat waste and corruption.

By an agreement signed 12 Jan. 1976 Romania is to pay £3·5m. as 'full and final settlement' of defaulted Romanian bonds held by UK citizens in 4 annual instalments of £875,000 starting at the end of 1976. Payments of £1·25m. in settlement of UK claims arising out of the peace treaty were completed by 31 Jan. 1967.

Currency. The monetary unit is the *leu*, pl. *lei* (of 100 *bani*). On 1 Feb. 1954 the gold content of the leu was changed to 0·148112 gramme of fine gold. Exchange rates: £1 = 14·4 lei; US$1 = 6 lei; 1 rouble = 6·67 lei. Tourist rates: £1 = 25 lei; US$1 = 18 lei; 1 rouble = 8·30 lei.

Bank-notes of 1, 3, 5, 10, 25 and 100 *lei* are issued by the National Bank, and there are coins of 5, 10, 15 and 25 *bani* and 1 and 3 *lei*.

Banking. The National Bank of Romania (founded 1880, nationalized 1946) is the State Bank under the Minister of Finance. Half its profits are allotted to the State budget. There are also a Bank of Investments, a Foreign Trade Bank, an Agriculture and Food Industry Bank and a Savings Bank. In 1972 Romania joined IMF. The US Export-Import Bank has granted Romania borrowing rights. In 1974 the American bank Manufactures Hanover Trust Co. opened a branch in Bucharest, the first Western bank to do so in a Communist country.

Weights and Measures. The Gregorian calendar was adopted in 1919. The metric system is in use. Tubes and pipes are measured in *tol* (= 1 inch).

ENERGY AND NATURAL RESOURCES

Electricity. The second 10-year power plan (1966–75) envisaged an output of electric power of 55,000–60,000m. kwh. by 1975. Installed electric power in 1975: 11,578,000 kw; output, 53,721m. kwh. A joint Romanian–Yugoslav hydro-electric power plant on the Danube at the 'Iron Gates' was opened in 1972; yearly output is 11,000m. kwh. Atomic power stations are being built.

Oil. The oilfields are in the Prahova, Băcau, Gorj, Crişana and Argeş districts. Refining capacity (13m. tons per annum) exceeds production of crude oil and efforts are being made to expand it; some crude is imported.

Minerals. The principal minerals are oil and natural gas, salt, brown coal, lignite, iron and copper ores, bauxite, chromium, manganese and uranium. Salt is mined in the lower Carpathians and in Transylvania; production in 1973 was 3·3m. tonnes.

Output, 1975 (and 1974) (in 1,000 tonnes): Iron ore, 3,065 (3,265); crude oil, 14,590 (14,486); coal, 29,385 (29,207); methane gas (cu. metres), 27,001m. (24,217m.).

Agriculture. Utilization of the land in 1975 (in 1,000 hectares): Arable, 9,741; meadows and pasture, 4,446; vineyards and fruit trees, 759.

Production in 1975 (in 1,000 tonnes): Wheat, 4,912; barley, 952; maize, 9,241; potatoes, 2,716; sunflower seed, 728; sugar-beet, 4,905.

Livestock (1976): 5·9m. cattle, 8·8m. pigs, 13·9m. sheep and 78·6m. poultry.

In 1975 there were 4,649 collective farms, with 9m. hectares of land (7·2m. arable; 973,000 in private plots). State farms numbered 391 (200 in 1971), with 2·1m. hectares of land, of which 1·66m. hectares were arable. A further 2·5m. hectares of land were in the hands of other state agricultural organizations. There were 743 agriculture mechanization stations with 88,461 tractors. Total national tractor strength (in 15-h.p. units), 213,652. Individual holdings totalled 1·41m. hectares. The National Union of Agricultural Co-operatives promotes self-management in collective farms, and gives guidance on planning and marketing. In 1973 a minimum income was guaranteed to peasants (960 lei per month in 1973). In 1975 there were 1,424,200 hectares of irrigated land.

Forestry. Total forest area was 6·32m. hectares in 1975. In 1973 the output of sawn timber was 5·3m. cu. metres. In 1973, 73,023 hectares were afforested.

INDUSTRY AND TRADE

Industry. Output of main products in 1975 (and 1974) (in 1,000 tonnes); Pig-iron, 6,602 (6,081); steel, 9,549 (8,848); steel tubes, 1,151 (973); metallurgical coke, 2,277 (1,832); rolled steel, 6,810 (6,253); chemical fertilizers, 1,729 (1,200); washing soda, 693 (807); caustic soda, 566 (444); paper, 518 (514); cement, 11,520 (11,195); sugar, 516 (516); edible oils, 321 (332); butter, 33 (30). Fabrics (in 1m. sq. metres): Cotton, 591 (612); woollens, 96 (94); silk, 89 (78). Light industry (in 1,000 units): Radio sets, 712 (602); TV sets, 512 (451); bicycles, 239 (244); footwear, 87m. pairs (91); washing machines, 178 (162); refrigerators, 332 (279).

Labour. The employed population in 1975 was 10·15m., of whom 3·84m. worked in agriculture and 3·93m. industry and building. A law of 1974 provides for wage differentials in accordance with the 'social evaluation' of the work and a range of incentives for productivity. The average monthly non-agricultural wage was 975 lei in 1976. Real wages rose 22% in the 1971–75 planning period, and are scheduled to rise 18–20% by 1980. A 5-day week is to be introduced in 1978. Men retire at 62, women at 57. Since 1977 the chairman of the trade union organization has exercised the functions of Minister of Labour.

Commerce. Some 60% of external trade is with Communist countries (15% with the USSR).

In 1975 exports totalled 26,547m. lei and imports 26,548m. lei.

Principal exports in 1975 were (in 1,000 tonnes): Petroleum products, 6,176; cement, 2,835; cereals, 1,164; tractors, 35,714 units; oilfield equipment, 713m. lei; equipment for cement mills, 43m. lei; equipment for chemical factories, 196m lei; shipbuilding, 495m. lei. Principal imports (in 1,000 tonnes): Iron ore, 10,879; industrial coke, 2,537; rolled ferrous metals, 1,570; electrical equipment, 937m. lei; motor cars, 3,898 units, and industrial and agricultural equipment.

In 1975 Romania's main trading partners (trade in 1m. lei) were: USSR (9,858), Federal Republic of Germany (5,039), German Democratic Republic (2,909), Czechoslovakia (2,447), Italy (2,273), China (2,164), Poland (2,073), Switzerland (2,069), Iran (1,702), France (1,689), Hungary (1,603), UK (1,503), and Austria (1,493).

Total trade between Romania and UK for calendar years (British Department of Trade returns, in £1,000 sterling):

	1973	*1974*	*1975*	*1976*	*1977*
Imports to UK	31,788	34,252	36,081	49,514	52,448
Exports and re-exports from UK	34,161	33,485	39,802	49,173	80,477

On 18 Sept. 1975 Romania and the UK signed a 10-year economic co-operation agreement. In Nov. 1976 Romania and the USA signed a 10-year commercial agreement. Both the UK and the USA have joint economic commissions with Romania.

As a reaction to international economic difficulties it became offical policy in 1975 to restrict imports and co-operation with foreign firms to strict necessities and the honouring of agreements already made.

In 1974 the 'industrial centrals' lost many of their powers to engage directly in foreign trade to the Ministry of Foreign Trade and International Co-operation. Joint companies with Western firms have been set up; at least 51% of the capital must be in Romanian hands. The 'Romconsult' and 'Publicom' agencies will carry out respectively market research and publicity campaigns on behalf of foreign firms.

Romania has a trade link with EEC under the generalized preference system.

On 1 Jan. 1975 a 2-tier tariff system was introduced, graded according to the grant of most favoured nation status to Romania.

COMMUNICATIONS

Roads. There were in 1975, 12,918 km of national roads, of which 10,193 km were modernized. Freight carried, 419m. tons; passengers, 814m.

Railways. Length of track (1,435 mm gauge) in 1975 was 10,403 km and (narrow-gauge), 591 km. A total of 1,296 km is electrified. Freight carried, 228m. tons; passengers, 366m.

Aviation. TAROM (*Transporturi Aeriene Române*), the state airline, operates all internal services, and also services to Amsterdam, Athens, Beirut, Belgrade, Berlin, Brussels, Budapest, Cairo, Cologne, Copenhagen, Düsseldorf, Frankfurt, Istanbul, London, Moscow, Paris, Prague, Rome, Sofia, Tel-Aviv. Vienna, Warsaw and Zürich. Bucharest is also served by British Airways, PANAM, SABENA, Aeroflot, Air France, Interflug, ČSA, MALEV, Austrian Air Lines, SAS, Lot, TABSO, El Al, Alitalia, Lufthansa and Swissair. An air agreement with China was signed in 1973.

Bucharest's airports are at Băneasa (internal flights) and Otopeni (international flights; 12 miles from Bucharest). Air transport in 1975 carried 1,397,000 passengers and 24,000 tons of freight.

Shipping. The main ports are Constanţa on the Black Sea and Galaţi and Brăila on the Danube. A new port is under construction at Mangalia on the Black Sea. The largest shipyard is at Galaţi.

In 1975 the mercantile marine (NAVROM) had 94 ships totalling 1,365,000 DWT. In 1975 sea-going transport carried 6·46m. tons of freight; river transport, 6·1m. tons.

Post and Broadcasting. *Radio-televiziunea Româna* broadcasts 3 programmes on medium-waves and FM. There are also 6 regional programmes, including transmission in Hungarian, German and Serbo-Croat. Two TV programmes are broadcast. Number of telephone subscribers, in 1975, 1,076,566. Radio receiving sets, in 1975, 3·1m.; television sets, 2·7m.

Cinemas and Theatres. There were, in 1975, 6,099 cinemas and 145 theatres and concert halls. 23 full-length feature films were made in 1975.

Newspapers. There were, in 1975, 59 newspapers and 394 periodicals. These figures include 35 in minority languages. The party newspaper is *Scînteia* ('The Spark').

JUSTICE, RELIGION, EDUCATION AND WELFARE

Justice. Justice is administered by the Supreme Court, the 40 district courts, and lower courts. Lay assessors (elected for 4 years) participate in most court trials, collaborating with the judges. The Procurator-General exercises 'supreme supervisory power to ensure the observance of the law' by all authorities, central and local, and all citizens. The Procurator's Office and its organs are independent of any organs of justice or administration, and only responsible to the Grand National Assembly (which appoints the Procurator-General for 4 years) and between its sessions, to the State Council. The Ministry of the Interior is responsible for ordinary police work. State security is the responsibility of the State Security Council. A new penal code came into force on 1 Jan. 1969. It is based on 'the rule of law' and is aimed at preventing illegal trials. The death penalty is retained for 'specially serious offences' (treason, some classes of murder, theft of state property having serious consequences).

Religion. Churches are organized and function in accordance with art. 30 of the Constitution. Churches administer their own affairs and run seminaries for the training of priests. Expenses and salaries are paid by the State. There are 15 Churches, all under the control of the 'Department of Cults'. The largest is the Romanian Orthodox Church, which claimed 13·67m. members in 1950. It is autocephalous, but retains dogmatic unity with the Eastern Orthodox Church. It is administered by the consultative Holy Synod and National Ecclesiastical Assembly and the executive National Ecclesiastical Council and Patriarchal Administration. It is organized into 12 dioceses grouped into 5 metropolitan bishoprics (Hungaro-Wallachia; Moldavia-Suceava; Transylvania; Olt; Banat), and headed by Patriarch Justinian Marina (since May 1948). There are some 11,800 churches, 2 theological colleges and 6 'schools of cantors', as well as seminaries.

The Uniate (Greek Catholic) Church severed its connexion with the Vatican (formed 1698) to rejoin the Romanian Orthodox in 1948. It had 1·6m. adherents and 1,818 priests. Estimates for 1973: 700,000 adherents and 600 priests.

Other churches: Serbs have a Serbian Orthodox Vicariate at Timişoara. There is a Roman Catholic archbishopric of Bucharest and a bishopric of Alba Iulia. There were 820 priests and 254 monks in 1958. The Church has not secured approval for a Statute and has no hierarchical ties with the Vatican.

Calvinists (780,000; mainly Hungarian) have bishoprics at Cluj and Oradea; Lutherans (250,000, mainly Germans) a bishopric at Sibiu and Unitarians bishoprics at Cluj and Timişoara. These sects share a seminary at Cluj.

In 1973 there were 70 Jewish communities comprising some 90,000 persons under a Chief Rabbi (Moses Rosen). There were 130 synagogues.

Moslems have a Muftiate at Constanţa.

Education. Education is free and compulsory for 10 years (6 to 16), consisting of 8 years of primary school and 2 years of secondary (gymnasium). Further secondary education is available at *lycées*, professional schools or advanced technical schools.

In 1975–76[1] there were 13,537 kindergartens with 33,789 teachers and 812,420 children; 14,695 primary and secondary schools with 144,978 teachers and 3,019,776 pupils; 1,064 *lycées* with 41,617 teachers and 901,977 pupils; 426 professional schools with 5,391 teachers and 122,630 pupils; and 280 advanced technical schools with 1,647 teachers and 35,191 pupils. There are general and secondary schools for minorities, with over 250,000 pupils.

There are universities at Iaşi (founded 1860), Bucharest (1864), Cluj (1919), Timişoara (1962), Craiova (1965) and Braşov (1971). In 1975–76 there were in all 137 faculties of higher education, with a student population of 164,567.

The Academy, with seat at Bucharest, has 2 branches at Iaşi and Cluj. The National Council for Scientific Research co-ordinates research.

[1] Figures include evening classes.

Health. In 1975 there were 196,236 hospital beds and 34,005 doctors.

DIPLOMATIC REPRESENTATIVES

OF ROMANIA IN GREAT BRITAIN (4 Palace Green, London, W8 4QD)

Ambassador: Pretor Popa (accredited 9 Feb. 1973).

OF GREAT BRITAIN IN ROMANIA (24 Strada Jules Michelet, Bucharest)

Ambassador: R. L. Secondé, CMG, CVO.

OF ROMANIA IN THE USA (1607–23rd St., NW, Washington, D.C., 20008)

Ambassador: Rudolph Aggrey.

OF THE USA IN ROMANIA (7–9 Strada Tudor Arghezi, Bucharest)

Ambassador: Harry G. Barnes, Jr.

OF ROMANIA TO THE UNITED NATIONS

Ambassador: Ion Datcu

Books of Reference

Academia Republicii Socialiste România. *Dicţionar Englez-Român.* Bucharest, 1974
Atlas Geografic Republica Socialistă România. Bucharest, 1965
Anuarul Statistic al R.S.R. Statistical Pocket Book of the Socialist Republic of Romania. Bucharest, both annual
Buletin Statistic Trimestrial (with Russian and French translations). Bucharest
Mic Dicţionar Enciclopedic. Bucharest, 1973
Catchlove, D., *Romania's Ceausescu.* Tunbridge Wells, 1972
Ceauşescu, N., *Romania: Achievements and Prospects.* Bucharest, 1969.—*Romania on the Way of Completing Socialist Construction.* 3 vols. Bucharest, 1968–69.—*Romania on the Way of Completing the Many-sided Developed Socialist Society.* Bucharest, 1970
Confederation of British Industry, *Romania: An Opportunity for Joint Investment.* London, 1974
Dicţionar Enciclopedic Român. Bucharest, 1962–66
Revista de Statistică. Bucharest, monthly
Economic and Commercial Guide to Romania. Bucharest, annual since 1969
Fischer-Galati, S. A., *Rumania: A Bibliographical Guide.* Library of Congress, 1963.—*The New Rumania.* Mass. Inst. of Technology, 1968.—*The Socialist Republic of Rumania.* Baltimore, 1969.—*Twentieth Century Rumania.* New York, 1970
Gilberg, T., *Modernization in Romania Since World War II.* New York, 1975
Giurescu, C. C. (ed.), *Chronological History of Romania.* 2nd ed. Bucharest, 1974

Ionescu, A. (ed.), *The Grand National Assembly of the Socialist Republic of Romania: A Brief Outline*. Bucharest, 1974
Morariu, T., and others, *The Geography of Rumania*. 2nd ed. Bucharest, 1969
Leviţchi, L., *Dictionar Român-Englez*. 2nd ed. Bucharest, 1965
Ratiu, I., *Contemporary Romania: Her Place in World Affairs*. Richmond (UK), 1975
Spigler, I., *Economic Reform in Rumanian Industry*. OUP, 1973
Turnock. D., *An Economic Geography of Romania*. London, 1974

RWANDA

Capital: Kigali
Population: 5·5m. (1969)
GNP per capita: US$110 (1976)

HISTORY. From the 16th century to 1959 the Tutsi kingdom of Rwanda shared the history of Burundi (*see* p. 252). In 1959 an uprising of the Hutu destroyed the Tutsi feudal hierarchy and led to the departure of the Mwami Kigeri V. Elections and a referendum under the auspices of the United Nations in Sept. 1961 resulted in an overwhelming majority for the republican party, the Parmehutu (Parti du Mouvement de l'Emancipation du Bahutu), and the rejection of the institution of the Mwami. The republic proclaimed by the Parmehutu on 28 Jan. 1961 was recognized by the Belgian administration (but not by the United Nations) in Oct. 1961. Internal self-government was granted on 1 Jan. 1962, and by decision of the General Assembly of the UN the Republic of Rwanda became independent on 1 July 1962. An agreement, signed with Burundi under United Nations auspices at Addis Ababa in April 1962, provided for a monetary and customs union. These and other common organizations came to an end by 1 Oct. 1964.

AREA AND POPULATION. Rwanda lies between lat. 1° and 3° S. and long. 29° and 31° E., with an area of 26,330 sq. km (10,166 sq. miles). The Nile–Congo mountain divide (about 9,000 ft) and the Kirunga volcanoes (Mt. Karisimbi, 14,825 ft), rising steeply from Lake Kivu in the west, slope down first to a hilly central plateau (7,000–5,000 ft) and farther eastwards to a complex of marshy lakes in the upper reaches of the Kagera River. Rwanda is bounded in the south by Burundi, in the west by Lake Kivu and the Congo, in the north by Uganda and in the east by Tanzania.

The population, the densest in Africa outside the Nile delta, was estimated (1969) at 5·5m. There are 3 ethnic groups, the Tutsi (Nilotic), the Hutu (Bantu) and a few Twa (pygmoid). The Tutsi, traditionally the ruling caste and about 15% of the population have greatly diminished in number since the troubles of 1959–61, as a result of which over 140,000 took refuge in neighbouring territories. In Jan. 1964 several thousand Tutsi were massacred by the Hutu, and an exodus of 12,000 more Tutsi followed. The Tutsi now form only 9% of the population. There are some 1,200 Europeans and 750 Asians.

Kigali, the capital, had an estimated population of 54,403 in Dec. 1970. Nyanza (between Kigali and Butare) is the seat of the High Court. Other centres are Gisenyi and Cyangugu on Lake Kivu, and Gitarama.

GOVERNMENT. Rwanda is a republic with an executive President as Head of State, assisted by a Council of 12 Ministers. The National Assembly consists of 47 members elected by universal suffrage for 4 years. The administrative divisions are 10 prefectures (Kigali, Kibungo, Byumba, Ruhengeri, Gisenyi, Kibuye, Gitarama, Gikongoro, Butare, Cyangugu) and 144 communes.

On 5 July 1973 President Gégoire Kayibanda who had been in office since 1961 was deposed in a bloodless *coup*.

President: Maj.-Gen Juvénal Habyarimana. *Foreign Affairs:* Lieut.-Col. Aloys Nsekolije.

Flag: Three equal vertical panels of red, yellow and green (left to right), the letter 'R' in black superimposed on the centre panel.

DEFENCE

Army. The national army has a strength of 3,750 all ranks, including a Belgian cadre.

Air Force. Initial equipment ordered for the Air Force in 1972 comprised 3 Italian-built Aeritalia/Aermacchi AM.3C liaison aircraft, since joined by 3 armed Magister jet trainers, 2 C-47 transports, 1 Islander light transport and 2 Alouette III helicopters. Personnel, about 150.

INTERNATIONAL RELATIONS

Membership. Rwanda is a member of UN, OAU and is an ACP state of EEC.

ECONOMY

Budget. The budget for 1970 showed an overall surplus, the first time since independence, of 187m. Rwanda francs.

Currency. On 12 April 1966 the Rwanda franc was devalued. The previous official rate of Rwanda francs 140 = £1 and the free rate of about Rwanda francs 330 = £1 were abolished and a single official rate of Rwanda francs 235 = £1 substituted; since Nov. 1967 the rate is 240 francs to the £.

Banking. On 5 April 1967 a Development Bank was created with a capital of 50m. Rwanda francs, of which 27·5m. can be held only by the government or public bodies. There are 4 other banks in Rwanda.

AGRICULTURE. Subsistence agriculture accounts for most of the gross national product. Staple food crops are beans, cassava, maize, sweet potatoes, peas, groundnuts and sorghum. The annual rainfall varies from under 40 in. in the north-east to 60 in. in the west and over 70 in. in the extreme north-west.

The main cash crop is *aravica* coffee as in Burundi; the 1970 crop was about 16,000 tons. Tea and pyrethrum are also produced on a limited scale. There is a pilot rice-growing project.

On 30 July 1964 the Rwanda Industrial Produce Bureau was established, which is responsible for organizing and controlling the quality of Rwandese agricultural exports, notably coffee. Coffee exports (1970) 14,700 tons earning 1,423m. Rwanda francs.

Tea plantations are being developed and projects are being financed by the World Bank and the African Development Bank. Fresh vegetables are produced for export (600 tonnes, 1975).

Long-horned Ankole cattle, 717,000 head in 1976, play an important traditional role. Efforts are being made to improve their present negligible economic value. There were (1976) 570,000 goats and some 252,000 sheep.

INDUSTRY. There is no general industrial development apart from mining. About 3,500 tons of cassiterite were produced in 1970. There are 4 hydro-electric installations and a large modern brewery. Methane gas is abundant under Lake Kivu.

COMMERCE. Trade between Rwanda and UK (British Department of Trade returns, in £1,000 sterling):

	1973	*1974*	*1975*	*1976*	*1977*
Imports to UK	522	640	2,516	3,924	6,115
Exports and re-exports from UK	284	435	559	844	1,085

COMMUNICATIONS

Roads. There are about (1968) 1,500 miles of main and 2,200 miles of secondary roads. There are road links with Burundi, Uganda, Tanzania and Zaïre. There were in 1967 2,122 cars and 1,243 trucks. Because of the strained political relations with Burundi nearly all goods traffic passes through Kampala and Mombasa.

Shipping. Shipping on Lake Kivu in 1967 amounted to 70,000 tonnes. Kigali has an international airport, with services to Bujumbura, Bukavu *via* Kamembe, Entebbe, Goma, Lubumbashi, Athens and Brussels.

Post. Telephones (1976) 3,378.

Cinemas. In 1975 there were 3 cinemas with a seating capacity of 1,000.

RELIGION. The population is predominantly Roman Catholic; there is an archbishop (Kabgayi) and 3 bishops. The Ruanda Mission of the Church Missionary Society have 4 stations.

EDUCATION. In 1965 there were 352,406 children attending primary schools. There were 25 secondary schools of various types with a total of 7,800 pupils; but only 135 completed the full 6-year course. The National University, opened at Butare in 1963, had over 300 students in 1969.

The local language is Kinyarwanda, a Bantu language. French is also an official language, and Kiswahili is spoken in the commercial centres.

DIPLOMATIC REPRESENTATIVES

OF RWANDA IN GREAT BRITAIN

Ambassador: (Vacant).

OF GREAT BRITAIN IN RWANDA
(PO Box 320, Kigali)

Ambassador: A. E. Donald.

OF RWANDA IN THE USA
(1714 New Hampshire Ave, NW, Washington, D.C., 20009)

Ambassador: Bonaventure Ubalijoro

OF THE USA IN RWANDA (Blvd. Central, Kigali)

Ambassador: T. Frank Crigler.

OF RWANDA TO THE UNITED NATIONS

Ambassador: Ignace Karuhije.

Books of Reference

Hance, W. A., *African Economic Development*. London, 1967
Lacroix, B., *Le Rwanda*. Montreal, 1966
Northumb, D., *Un Humanisme Africain*. Brussels, 1965

ST HELENA

Capital: Jamestown
Population: 5,147 (1976)

AREA AND POPULATION. St Helena, of volcanic origin, is 1,200 miles from the west coast of Africa. Area, 47 sq. miles (121·7 sq. km), with a cultivable area of about 600 acres (243 hectares). The port of the island is Jamestown.

Population (1976), 5,147. Births (1976), 102; deaths, 55; marriages, 52.

GOVERNMENT. The Government of St Helena is administered by a Governor, with the aid of a Legislative Council consisting of the Governor, 2 *ex-officio* members (the Government Secretary and the Treasurer) and 12 elected members. Committees of the Legislative Council are responsible for the general oversight of the activities of government departments and have, in addition, statutory and administrative functions.

The Governor is also assisted by an Executive Council consisting of the 2 *ex-officio* members and the chairmen of the Council committees.

Governor and C.-in-C.: G. C. Guy, CMG, CVO, OBE.

Government Secretary: C. B. Kendall.

Flag: The British Blue Ensign with the shield of the colony in the fly.

FINANCE AND TRADE, for years from 1 April–31 March, in £ sterling:

	1971–72	*1972–73*	*1973–74*	*1974–75*	*1975–76*	*1976–77*
Revenue[1]	954,709	826,956	997,777	1,356,049	1,481,539	2,014,981
Expenditure[1]	853,255	804,868	963,795	1,520,101	1,544,027	1,952,642
Imports[2]	403,832	499,146	654,571	1,115,341	1,192,418	1,430,168

[1] Including imperial grants (1971–72, £479,993; 1972–73, £460,100; 1973–74, £588,201; 1974–75, £937,888; 1975–76, £1,060,342; 1976–77, £1,461,739).

[2] Excluding government stores.

The revenue from customs was, in 1971–72, £66,677; 1972–73, £84,745; 1973–74, £76,605; 1974–75, £91,998; 1975–76, £93,039; 1976–77, £122,029.

The colony's assets at 31 March 1977 exceeded the liabilities by £47,056.

Total trade between Ascension and St Helena and UK (British Department of Trade returns, in £1,000 sterling):

	1971	*1972*	*1973*	*1974*	*1975*	*1976*	*1977*
Imports to UK	32	33	49	194	120	109	156
Exports and re-exports from UK	1,006	1,070	1,000	1,288	1,675	1,632	2,387

BANKING. Savings-bank deposits on 31 March 1977, £726,660, belonging to 2,753 depositors.

COMMUNICATIONS

Shipping. The number of merchant vessels that called in 1977 was 40; total tonnage entered and cleared was 168,000. There were 48·6 miles of all-weather motor roads.

Post and Broadcasting. The Cable & Wireless Ltd cable connects St Helena with Cape Town and Ascension Island. There is a telephone service with 85 miles of wire and 267 telephones.

St Helena Government Broadcasting Station broadcasts in English on medium-waves. Number of radio receivers, 775.

JUSTICE, RELIGION, EDUCATION AND WELFARE

Justice. Police force, 32; cases dealt with by police magistrate, 159 in 1976.

Religion. There are 10 Anglican churches and 4 Baptist chapels.

Education. Three pre-school playgroups, 8 primary, 3 senior and 1 secondary schools controlled by the Government had 1,368 pupils in Sept. 1976.

Health. There were 3 doctors and 55 hospital beds in 1972.

Ascension is a small island of volcanic origin, of 34 sq. miles (88 sq. km), 700 miles north-west of St Helena. In Nov. 1922 the administration was transferred from the Admiralty to the Colonial Office and annexed to the colony of St Helena. There are 10 acres under cultivation providing vegetables and fruit. Population, 31 Dec. 1946, was 292; 1973, St. Helenians 691, others 460.

The island is the resort of sea turtles, which come to lay their eggs in the sand annually between Jan. and May. Rabbits, wild goats and partridges are more or less numerous on the island, which is, besides, the breeding ground of the sooty tern or 'wideawake', these birds coming in vast numbers to lay their eggs every eighth month.

Cable & Wireless Ltd own and operate a cable station, connecting the island with St Helena, Sierra Leone, St Vincent, Rio de Janeiro and Buenos Aires. There is an airstrip (Miracle Mile) near the settlement of Georgetown.

Administrator: Brig. Gordon McDonald, CBE.

Tristan da Cunha, a small group of islands in the Atlantic, half-way between the Cape and South America, in 37° 6′ S. lat., 12° 1′ W. long. Besides Tristan da Cunha and Gough Island, there are Inaccessible and Nightingale Islands, the former 2 and the latter 1 mile long, and a number of rocks. As from 12 Jan. 1938 the 4 islands have become dependencies of St Helena.

Tristan consists of a volcano rising to a height of 6,760 ft, with a circumference at its base of 21 miles. The volcano, believed to be extinct, erupted unexpectedly early in Oct. 1961. The whole population was evacuated without loss and settled temporarily in the United Kingdom. In 1963 they returned to Tristan.

Before the disaster occurred the habitable area was a small plateau on the north-west side of about 12 sq. miles, 100 ft above sea-level. Only about 30 acres was under cultivation, three-quarters of it for potatoes. There were apple and peach trees; bullocks, sheep and geese were reared, and fish are plentiful.

The island is extremely lonely, but the community is growing. In 1880 it numbered 109, in 1973, 292. The original inhabitants were shipwrecked sailors and soldiers who remained behind when the garrison from St Helena was withdrawn in 1817.

At the end of April 1942 Tristan da Cunha was commissioned as HMS *Atlantic Isle*, and became an important meteorological and radio station. In Jan. 1949 a South African company commenced crawfishing operations. An Administrator was appointed at the end of 1948 and a body of basic law brought into operation. The Island Council, which was set up in 1932, consists of 3 nominated and 8 elected members under the chairmanship of the Administrator, with the Society for the Propagation of the Gospel in Foreign Parts' missionary and the company manager as *ex-officio* members. Women's affairs are discussed by the Island Women's Council, which presents them for consideration to the general council.

Administrator: Stanley Graham Trees, MVO, OBE.

Books of Reference

Annual Report, 1970–73. HMSO
Blakeston, O., *Isle of St Helena.* London, 1957
Booy, D. M., *Rock of Exile: A Narrative of Tristan da Cunha.* London, 1957
Holdgate, M., *Mountains in the Sea.* London, 1958
Munch, P. A., *Sociology of Tristan da Cunha.* Oslo, 1945
Stonehouse, B., *Wideawake Island* [Ascension]. London, 1960

SAN MARINO

Capital: San Marino
Population: 19,168 (1974)

Repubblica di San Marino

HISTORY. On 22 March 1862 San Marino concluded a treaty of friendship and good co-operation, including a *de facto* customs union with the kingdom of Italy, preserving the independence of the ancient republic, although completely surrounded by Italian territory. The treaty was renewed on 27 March 1872, 28 June 1897 and 31 March 1939, with 7 amendments in 1943–71.

The republic has extradition treaties with UK, Belgium, France, the Netherlands and USA.

AREA AND POPULATION. San Marino is a land-locked state in central Italy, 20 km from the Adriatic. The frontier line is 38·6 km in length, area is 61·19 sq. km (24·1 sq. miles) and the population (30 June 1974), 19,168; some 20,000 citizens live abroad.

CONSTITUTION AND GOVERNMENT. The legislative power is vested in the Great and General Council of 60 members elected every 5 years by popular vote, 2 of whom are appointed every 6 months to act as regents (*Capitani reggenti*).

The elections held on 28 May 1978 gave 26 seats to the Christian Democrats, 8 to the Left-wing Socialists (the government coalition), 16 to the Communists, 15 to Socialist parties, 3 to others. (Full details not available at the time of going to press.)

The regents exercise executive power together with the Congress of State (*Congresso di Stato*), which comprises 10 departments, and through Commissions on social welfare, public works, etc.

National flag: Horizontally white over light blue, with the national arms over all in the centre.

DEFENCE. The militia consists, in case of necessity, of all able-bodied citizens between the ages of 16 and 55, with certain exceptions (teachers and students, etc.).

ECONOMY. The budget (ordinary and extraordinary) for the financial year ending 31 Dec. 1973 balanced at 14,912,266,209 lire.

The chief exports are wine, textiles, tiles, varnishes, ceramics and the building stone quarried on Mount Titano.

Italian and Vatican City currency is in general use, but the republic issues its own postage stamps.

In 1973, 2·58m. tourists visited San Marino.

COMMUNICATIONS

Roads. A bus service connects San Marino with Rimini.

Aviation. There is a helicopter service to Rimini in summer.

Post. In 1976 there were 5,216 telephones.

Cinemas. In 1974 there were 8 cinemas with a seating capacity of 2,300.

JUSTICE. Law is administered by a Commissioner for civil and commercial cases and a Commissioner for criminal cases (acting with a penal judge), from whom appeals can be made to a civil appeals judge and a criminal appeals judge respectively. The highest legal authority is, in certain cases, the *Consiglio dei XII.*

EDUCATION. There are 16 infant schools, 16 elementary schools, a secondary school and a grammar school, the diplomas of which are recognized by Italian universities. Civil marriage was instituted in Sept. 1953.

DIPLOMATIC REPRESENTATIVES

British Consul-General (resides at Florence): R. A. Vining, MBE.
USA Consul-General (resides at Florence): Robert C. F. Gordon.
Consul-General in London: Charles Forte.

Books of Reference

Information: Segreteria di Stato per gli Affari Esteri: Ente Governativo per il Turismo.

Garbeletto, A., *Evoluzione storica della costituzione di S. Marino.* Milan, 1956
Packett, C. N., *Guide to the Republic of San Marino.* Bradford, 1970
Rossi, G., *San Marino.* San Marino, 1954

SÀO TOMÉ E PRINCIPE

Capital: São Tomé
Population: 76,430 (1973)
GNP per capita: US$490 (1976)

HISTORY. The islands of São Tomé and Principe, which are about 125 miles off the coast of Africa, in the Gulf of Guinea, were discovered in 1471 by Pedro Escobar and João Gomes, and from 1522 until independence had constituted a province of Portugal.

On 26 Nov. 1974 the Government of Portugal and the liberation movement of São Tomé e Principe signed an agreement granting independence to the archipelago on 12 July 1975 to become the Democratic Republic of São Tomé e Principe.

AREA AND POPULATION. The country also includes the islands of Pedras Tinhosas and Rolas. The fort of St Jean Baptiste d'Ajudá on the coast was annexed by the Dahomey republic on 1 Aug. 1961. Area of the islands 964 sq. km (372 sq. miles). Total population (census, 1970) 73,631 (São Tomé, 60,032; Principe, 4,599). Estimate (1973) 76,430. Vital statistics (1972): Births, 3,392; deaths, 840; marriages, 141.

CONSTITUTION AND GOVERNMENT. The cabinet was composed as follows in July 1975:

President: Dr Manuel Pinta do Costa (*also Minister of Agriculture, Land Reform and Defence*).

Prime Minister, Economic Co-ordination and Tourism: Miguel Tronvoado.

Foreign Affairs: Leonel Mario d'Alva. *Interior:* José Fret Lau Chong. *Health and Social Affairs:* Manuel Q. dos Santos Costa. *Education and Culture:* Alda G. do Espirito Santo. *Domestic Administration:* Maj. Daniel Daio. *Social Equipment and Environment:* Xavier Daniel Dias.

Flag: Three horizontal stripes of green, yellow, green, with the yellow of double width and bearing 2 black stars; in the hoist a red triangle over all.

INTERNATIONAL RELATIONS

Membership. São Tomé e Principe is a member of UN and OAU.

DEFENCE. Armed forces strength (estimate, 1976) 160.

FINANCE. In 1974 the budget balanced at 150m. escudos.

AGRICULTURE. The chief commercial products are cacao, copra, coconut, coffee, palm-oil and cinchona. In 1976 there were 1,000 goats, 1,000 sheep, 3,000 pigs and 2,000 cattle.

COMMERCE. Imports (1974), 247·3m. escudos; exports, 322·6m. escudos. The main exports were copra, coffee, bananas, palm oil.

Total trade between São Tomé e Principe and UK (British Department of Trade returns, in £1,000 sterling):

	1974	*1975*	*1976*	*1977*
Imports to UK	81	7	75	9
Exports and re-exports from UK	285	118	373	701

COMMUNICATIONS

Roads. There were 288 km of roads in 1973.

Shipping. In 1973, 220 vessels of 435,971 net tons entered the ports.

Post. There were, in 1973, 3 wireless stations, 352 km of telephone lines and a telephone exchange (with 727 instruments in 1976).

Cinemas. In 1972 there was 1 cinema with a seating capacity of 1,000.

EDUCATION. There were, in 1971–72, 46 primary schools with 10,015 pupils, a secondary preparatory school with 1,621 pupils, 3 technical schools with 280 pupils and a secondary school with 493 pupils.

Book of Reference

S. Tomé e Principe. Agência-Geral do Ultramar, 1964

SAUDI ARABIA

Capital: Riyadh
Population: 9·16m. (1976)
GNP per capita: US$4,480 (1976)

al-Mamlaka al-'Arabiya as-Sa'udiya

HISTORY. Saudi Arabia was founded by Abdul-Aziz ibn Abdur-Rahman al-Faisal Al Sa'ud, GCB, GCIE (born about 1880; died 9 Nov. 1953), who had been proclaimed King of the Hejaz on 8 Jan. 1926 and had in 1927 changed his title of Sultan of Nejd and its dependencies to that of king, thus becoming 'King of the Hejaz and of Nejd and its Dependencies'. On 20 May 1927 a treaty was signed at Jidda between Great Britain and Ibn Sa'ud, by which the former recognized the complete independence of the dominions of the latter. The name of the State was changed to 'The Saudi Arabian Kingdom' by decree of 23 Sept. 1932.

In Nov. 1937 a general agreement between Saudi Arabia and the Yemen concerning the settlement of disputes was ratified, and an agreement regarding the delimitation of the frontiers was negotiated.

In March 1953 the treaty of Taif, first signed with the Yemen in May 1934, was extended for 20 lunar years.

In 1942 Saudi Arabia and the British Government, acting on behalf of the Shaikh of Kuwait, signed agreements for friendship and neighbourly relations, for the extradition of offenders and for the regulation of trade between Saudi Arabia and Kuwait.

In Aug. 1962 Saudi Arabia and Jordan agreed on measures of co-operation in the military, political and economic fields.

King Faisal ibn Abdul-Aziz was assassinated on 25 March 1975 by his nephew. There appeared to be no political motive.

AREA AND POPULATION. The total area of Saudi Arabia is estimated to be 927,000 sq. miles (2·4m. sq. km).

The principal cities of the Hejaz are: Mecca, 366,801; Jidda, 561,104; Medina, 198,186 and Taif, 204,857.

Taif, about 3,800 ft above sea-level and some 50 miles from Mecca, is a summer resort.

The principal cities of the Nejd are: Riyadh, the capital (666,840), Buraida (69,940), Anaiza, Hail, Jauf and Sakaka.

The total population was (1974 census) 7,012,642, of which 5,128,655 were categorized as settled and 1,883,987 as nomadic. Estimate (1976) 9,156,581.

Slavery was declared illegal in Nov. 1962.

KING. Khalid ibn Abdul-Aziz; succeeded on 25 March 1975, after King Faisal's assassination. *Crown Prince:* Prince Fahd ibn Abdul-Aziz, Deputy Prime Minster, younger brother of the King.

National flag: Green, with the text 'There is no God but Allah and Mohammed is his prophet' in white Arabic script, and beneath this a white sabre.

GOVERNMENT AND CONSTITUTION. The Kingdom has been welded together from Hejaz, Nejd, Asir and Al-Hassa. Riyadh is the political capital and Mecca the religious capital.

In May 1958 a 'Cabinet system' was instituted under which, from 1962, effective power devolved upon the President of the Council of Ministers.

The King has the post of Prime Minister.

Deputy Prime Minister: Crown Prince Fahd ibn Abdul Aziz.
Second Deputy Prime Minister: Prince Abdullah ibn Abdul Aziz.

Foreign Minister: Prince Saud al Faisal.
Interior: Prince Nayef ibn Abdul Aziz.
Petroleum and Natural Resources: Sheikh Ahmed Zaki Yamani.
Finance and Economy: Sheikh Muhammad Ali Aba al Khail.
Defence and Aviation: Prince Sultan ibn Abdul Aziz.

The religious law of Islam is the common law of the land, and is administered by religious courts, at the head of which is a chief judge, who is responsible for the Department of Sharia (legal) Affairs. The constitution also provides for the setting up of certain advisory councils, comprising a consultative Legislative Assembly in Mecca, municipal councils in each of the towns of Mecca, Medina and Jidda, and village and tribal councils throughout the provinces. The country is divided for administrative purposes into 6 major and 12 minor provinces.

DEFENCE. In 1937 a Ministry of Defence and a training school for officers were established. British Military and Civil Air Missions helped in training the Army and civil aviation from 1947 to 1951. The United States now maintains a Military Mission (with an Air Force element). Personnel are now trained in Saudi Arabia and the UK.

Army. The Army comprises 4 infantry brigades, and 1 parachute, 1 armoured, 2 reconnaissance, 1 Royal Guard and 3 artillery battalions, 6 AA battalions and 10 Hawk missile batteries. Service is voluntary and the strength (1977) 45,000; paramilitary, 41,500.

Air Force. Formed as a small army support unit in 1932, the Air Force has been built up considerably with British and US assistance since 1946. Complete re-equipment began in 1966 and main combat units now include 2 squadrons of Lightning F.53 supersonic interceptors, supported by a conversion unit with Lightning fighters and 2-seat fighter-trainers. There are 2 squadrons of F-5E Tiger II supersonic fighter-bombers, 2 squadrons of F-5B combat trainers. Two squadrons of Strikemaster light jet attack/trainers are based at the King Faisal Air Academy, Riyadh, together with Cessna T-41A piston-engined primary trainers. Other types in current service include 11 C-130E, 14 C-130H and 4 KC-130H Hercules transports and tankers, 2 Boeing 707s, 2 JetStar VIP jet transports, nearly 50 Agusta-Bell 205 and JetRanger helicopters, and communications aircraft. Personnel, about 5,500.

Navy. The Navy has about 1,500 personnel.

INTERNATIONAL RELATIONS

Membership. Saudi Arabia is a member of UN and the Arab League.

ECONOMY

Planning. A 5-year plan was adopted in May 1975; the GNP having risen by 150% in 1973–74 and by 37% in 1974–75, allocations were based on an average annual growth rate of 45%. To water resources, 34,000m. rials was allocated; to agriculture, 4,000m. rials; to education, 73,000m. rials, and to electrical projects, 6,000m. rials.

Budget. The fiscal year runs from 15 Oct. to 14 Oct. The budget for 1975–76 balanced at SR95,847m. and that for 1974–75 at SR98,247m. Receipts from the oil companies account for 80% of revenue.

The main items of expenditure in 1975–76 were (in SR1m.): Education, 6,615; defence and national guard, 4,169; health, 1,136; interior, 3,756; agriculture and irrigation, 460.

Currency. In 1960 the Saudi Arabian Monetary Agency announced the issue of a paper *rial* to replace the 'pilgrims' receipts'; the paper *rial* is divided into 100 *nilalas*.

Money supply at 9 July 1975 was 10,684·1m. *rials*.

Banking. Branches of the Algemene Bank, Nederland NV, the Banque de l'Indochine, the British Bank of the Middle East, the Arab Bank (of Jerusalem), the Banque de Caire, the National Bank of Pakistan and the Banque de Liban et d'Outremer conduct banking business in Jidda. The Banque de l'Indochine, the British Bank of the Middle East, the Algemene Bank Nederland, the Banque de Caire and the Arab Bank have branches in Al Khobar and Dammam; the last two banks have also branches in Riyadh. The locally-controlled National Commercial Bank has branches in Jidda, Mecca, Taif, Medina, Riyadh, Al Khobar and Dammam.

ENERGY AND NATURAL RESOURCES

Electricity. Energy produced in 1972 was 379m. tonnes of coal equivalent. Electric energy installed capacity was 268,000 kw. in 1971, and 1,000m. kwh. was generated in 1972.

Oil. The geologic–geographical mapping of Saudi Arabia was completed in 1961 under the joint sponsorship of the Saudi Arabian and US governments.

Oil operations are chiefly carried out by the Arabian American Oil Co. (Aramco). Since 1974 the Government has owned a 60% share in the producing assets of Aramco, although this excludes the Ras Tanura refinery complex. Other American interests have secured a concession of Saudi Arabia's oil rights in the Kuwait/Saudi Arabia Neutral Zone. Here first shipments began in 1954. In 1958 a Japanese concern obtained concessions for both the Saudi and Kuwait half-shares in the Neutral Zone offshore. Crude oil production was 146,000 bbls daily in 1946 and 3m. bbls daily in 1970. Production, 1975, was 350m. tonnes and oil revenues were 798,247m. rials.

The operating centre is at Dhahran, and the principal oilfield at Abqaiq; the next most important producers are in Ain Dar and the Dammam oilfield, where the original discovery of oil was made in 1938. Several other oilfields, notably the great Ghawar field south of Ain Dar and the offshore wells of Safaniya, are being developed.

Of the 1948 concession area, Aramco had by March 1963 retained only 105,000 sq. miles, *i.e.*, about 20%.

Some crude oil is refined in a large refinery at Ras Tanura (11m. tonnes in 1960), and some is transported by pipeline to Bahrain Island, for refining there. Crude oil is also shipped from the Persian Gulf. In addition, some 15m. long tons of crude oil is annually transported along the Trans-Arabian Pipeline system (TAPline). This 1,068-mile long pipeline connects the oilfields to a Mediterranean oil port at Saida; it came into operation at the end of 1950. Oil refining capacity, 1971, was 24·7m. tonnes.

The government-established General Petroleum and Mineral Organization (Petromin) works to set up new oil- and mineral-related industries, and to co-ordinate national interest in oil production. Petromin handles exploration and concession agreements and is active in drilling, distribution and marketing. It has 75% interest in a new refinery at Jidda and is building another at Riyadh. Production of residual fuel oils in 1972 was 16·9m. tonnes; distillate fuel oils, 3·3m.; motor spirit, 4·5m., and jet fuel, 2·1m.

Agriculture. The Saudi Arabian Agricultural Bank in Riyadh had (1970) capital of SR30m. Most of the loans granted were for agricultural equipment or for drilling or deepening wells. SR300m. has been allocated to major projects of desert reclamation, including irrigation schemes, land preparation and sowing, drainage and control of surface water, control of moving sands and distribution of undeveloped land to farmers. A full survey of water resources is in progress; there are 3 sea-water desalination plants working and 4 others proposed.

Medina produces excellent dates in abundance; Taif and other oases in the mountains and valleys produce honey and a fair variety of fruit, while Beduin products are hides, wool, charcoal and clarified butter. The products of Nejd are dates, wheat (150,000 tonnes estimated for 1972), barley (20,000 tonnes estimated for 1972), coffee, limes, henna, pearls, hides, wool, oil, clarified butter (*saman* or *ghi*) and abaas (Arab cloaks), besides camels, horses, donkeys and sheep.

Livestock estimates for 1976 include 180,000 cattle and 1·38m. sheep.

COMMERCE. Exports amounted to 4,708m. rials in 1973 and imports 31,866m. rials. In 1975 Japan was the main supplier, accounting for 30·3% of the total. Other major supplying countries were the USA (29·9%), Federal Republic of Germany (12·2%) and the UK (10%). Foodstuffs accounted for 30% and machinery, electrical appliances and transport items for another 30%.

Total trade with UK (British Department of Trade returns, in £1,000 sterling):

	1973	*1974*	*1975*	*1976*	*1977*
Imports to UK	322,183	1,178,149	856,618	978,472	1,095,116
Exports and re-exports from UK	58,466	119,698	199,773	400,399	576,904

COMMUNICATIONS

Roads. There are asphalted roads from Jidda to Mecca, to Medina, to Taif and to Riyadh. There is also a track from Mecca eastward through Riyadh to Uqair and Dhahran on the Gulf, a distance of 829 miles, which is used for motor transport. Motor cars can travel between Riyadh and Kuwait, Riyadh and Hail, Jauf and the northern frontier towns, Jidda and Hail, and between Jidda and Jizan and Sabya. In 1970 there were 64,900 cars in use and 50,400 commercial vehicles.

Railways. A railway from Riyadh to Damman on the Gulf (612 km, 1,435 mm gauge) *via* Dhahran and the oilfields Abqaiq, Ithmaniya (near Hofuf) and Haradh was completed in Oct. 1951. That section of the Hejaz Railway which is in Saudi Arabian territory is not now in working order.

Aviation. Saudi Arabian Air Lines, a government-owned company managed in conjunction with Trans-World Airlines, operates regular internal air services, and services to Cairo and other North African countries, to other Middle East centres, to Europe and to London, as well as special flights for pilgrims. The pilots are mainly Americans, with a growing number of Saudi-Arabian co-pilots. The main airports are at Jidda, Dhahran and Riyadh.

Shipping. The ports of Dammam on the Gulf and Jidda on the Red Sea have deep-water piers. In 1971, 185·82m. tonnes of goods were loaded and 2,955,000 tonnes unloaded.

Post and Broadcasting. Jidda, Mecca, Taif, Riyadh and Dammam are linked by telephone, Jidda and Cairo by radio-telephone. An international radio-telephone station at Riyadh was opened in 1956. Number of telephones (1977), 160,000. Number of post offices (1970) about 400. In 1971 there were 87,000 radio receivers and 18,000 television receivers.

Newspapers. In 1976 there were 6 daily newspapers in Arabic and 2 in English.

EDUCATION AND WELFARE

Education. Administration is in educational districts (23 in 1969). Schooling is in three stages, elementary, intermediate and secondary which is to prepare older pupils for college. Education is free in all these stages; monthly scholarships are paid to students in higher education. Girls' education is separate. In 1973–74 there were 1,472 elementary schools with 342,600 pupils. In 1970 the pre-primary schools had 185 teachers and 5,694 pupils; elementary schools had 17,435 teachers and 422,744 pupils; intermediate schools had 5,064 teachers and 89,226 pupils and secondary schools had 697 teachers and 8,492 pupils. There are also adult literacy schools, special schools, commercial, agricultural and industrial schools including the Royal Vocational Institute in Riyadh which can take 8,000 students on two daily shifts.

There were 34 teacher-training schools in 1968.

The University of Riyadh (founded 1957) has faculties of arts, science, pharmacy, commerce, agriculture, engineering, education and medicine. The Islamic University at Medina was founded in 1961. The King 'Abdal-Aziz' University in Jidda opened in 1967. Other universities are the Imam Muhammad bin Saud University in Riyadh (for training in Islamic law and theology), the King Faisal University in Dammam and the University of Petroleum and Minerals in Dhahran.

Welfare. The Ministry of Health is responsible for 10 administrative districts, serving both Saudi citizens and pilgrims. In 1970 there were 47 hospitals, 67,870 beds,

180 clinics and 270 health units. The Jidda Quarantine Centre, designed by WHO and primarily for pilgrims, can take 2,400 patients. In 1970 there were 3 nursing schools and 3 sanitation training institutes. There is a strict system of health controls for visiting pilgrims and strict supervision of sanitation and water supply.

DIPLOMATIC REPRESENTATIVES

OF SAUDI ARABIA IN GREAT BRITAIN
(30 Belgrave Sq., London, SW1X 8QB)

Ambassador: Shaikh Faisal Aziz Alhegelan (accredited 16 Dec. 1976).

OF GREAT BRITAIN IN SAUDI ARABIA (PO Box 393, Jidda)

Ambassador: A. J. Wilton, CMG, MC.

OF SAUDI ARABIA IN THE USA (1520–18th Street, NW, Washington, D.C., 20036)

Ambassador: Ali Abdallah Alireza.

OF THE USA IN SAUDI ARABIA (Palestine Rd., Ruwais, Jidda)

Ambassador: John C. West.

OF SAUDI ARABIA TO THE UNITED NATIONS

Ambassador: (Vacant).

Books of Reference

The Business Directory of Saudi Arabia. London, 1974
Doughty, C. M., *Travels in Arabia Deserta.* 2 vols. London, 1936
El Wassie, A., *Education in Saudi Arabia.* London, 1970
Ingrams, H., *Arabia and the Isles.* 2nd ed. London, 1952
Lewis, B., *Handbook of Diplomatic and Political Arabic.* London, 1947
Meulen, D. van der, *The Wells of Ibn Sa'ud.* London, 1957
Pesce, A., *Jiddah: Portrait of an Arabian City.* 3rd ed. Cambridge, 1978
Philby, H. St. J. B., *Arabian Jubilee.* London, 1952.—*Sa'udi Arabia.* London, 1955
Twitchell, K. S., and Jurji, E. J., *Saudi Arabia: With an Account of the Development of Its Natural Resources.* 2nd ed. Princeton, 1953

SENEGAL

Capital: Dakar
Population: 5·09m. (1976)
GNP per capita: US$390 (1976)

République du Sénégal

HISTORY. The Republic of Senegal became independent on 20 Aug. 1960, after having been a French territory (1659 foundation of Saint-Louis, 1854–65 occupation of the hinterland), a member state of the French Community (from 25 Nov. 1958) and, from Jan. 1959 to 20 Aug. 1960, a partner (together with Sudan) of the Federation of Mali.

AREA AND POPULATION. The Republic has a total area of 197,722 sq. km; the population (census, 1976) 5,085,388. The capital is Dakar (population, 581,000). Kaolack (96,238), Thiès (90,456), Saint-Louis (81,204), Rufisque (48,101), Ziguinchor (45,772) and Diourbel (40,230) are other important towns. The country is divided in 7 regions.

The principal autochthonous tribes are the Ouolofs (about 700,000, mostly Moslems), Bambaras, Mandingos, Peuls (Fulbés) and Toucouleurs. In 1971 some 71,473 refugees from Portuguese Guinea were living in Senegal.

CONSTITUTION AND GOVERNMENT. The Republic is administered by a government council of 7 ministers and 2 secretaries of state and 8 other ministers. The national assembly consists of 80 members, elected by universal suffrage for a 4-year term. There are 3 legal political parties.

President of the Republic: Léopold Sédar Senghor (re-elected for further 5-year term, Feb. 1978).

Prime Minister: Abdou Diouf.

National flag: Three vertical strips of green, yellow, red, with a green star in the centre.

DEFENCE

Army. The Army has a strength of 5,500, organized in 3 motorized infantry battalions and minor units.

Navy. The Navy has 3 large patrol boats, 14 small patrol craft and 1 landing craft. Personnel (1978) 250.

Air Force. The Senegal Air Force, formed with French assistance, has 4 C-47 transports, 2 F.27 twin-turboprop transports, 1 Cessna 337 and 1 Aztec light transport, 2 Broussard liaison aircraft, 2 Bell 47, 1 Gazelle and 2 Alouette II helicopters. Personnel total about 200.

INTERNATIONAL RELATIONS

Membership. Senegal is a member of UN, OAU and is an ACP state of EEC.

ECONOMY

Planning. A second development plan, covering 1965–69, was adopted on 1 July 1965, and a third plan, covering 1969–73, was adopted on 1 July 1969.

Budget. The ordinary budget for 1971–72 balanced at 57,040m. francs CFA.

Currency. The currency is the franc CFA.

Banking. Under an agreement with the Crédit Lyonnais a new commercial bank, the Union Sénégalaise de la Banque pour le Commerce et l'Industrie, was established in Sept. 1961; the Senegal government holds the larger part of its capital.

At 31 Dec. 1972 the savings banks had deposits of 664m. francs CFA.

AGRICULTURE. The soil is generally sandy. Production (1972) in 1,000 tonnes: Millet, 582·7; maize, 38·5; rice, 108·2; groundnuts, 988·5. Livestock (1976): 2·6m. sheep and goats, 2·4m. cattle, 160,000 pigs, 196,000 asses, 25,000 camels and 226,000 horses.

INDUSTRY. Dakar has numerous industrial works. In 1972 the production of phosphate rock was 1·3m. tonnes; cement, 334,900 tonnes. The discovery of iron-ore deposits at La Faleme has created the possibility that Senegal could become one of Africa's major producers. Reserves are estimated at 980m. tonnes.

TRADE. The chief imports (1972) (in tonnes): Rice (169,905), sugar (80,144), petroleum products (604,773), textiles and machinery. The chief exports were: Groundnuts (557,740), phosphates (1·43m.) and preserved fish (9,078).

Imports in 1975 totalled 119,472m. francs CFA; exports, 96,151m.

Total trade with UK (British Department of Trade returns, in £1,000 sterling):

	1973	*1974*	*1975*	*1976*	*1977*
Imports to UK	3,003	9,637	14,359	22,738	31,369
Exports and re-exports from UK	2,717	3,260	5,659	9,385	9,521

COMMUNICATIONS

Roads. The length of roads (1971) was 15,422 km.

Railways. There are 5 railway lines: Dakar–Kidira (continuing in Mali), Thiès–Saint-Louis (193 km), Guinguinéo–Kaolack (22 km), Louga–Linguère (129 km), and Diourbel–Touba (46 km). Total length, 1,034 km (metre gauge).

Aviation. In 1972 aircraft disembarked 116,756 and embarked 118,752 passengers and disembarked 2,345 tonnes and embarked 4,547 tonnes of freight at Yoff (Dakar). Extensions to the airport were completed in 1976.

Shipping. In 1971, 5,541 vessels entered the port of Dakar. There is a river service on the Senegal from Saint-Louis to Podor (140 miles) open throughout the year, and to Kayes (924 km) open from July to October. The Senegal River is closed to foreign flags. The Saloum River is navigable as far as Kaolack, the Casamance River as far as Ziguinchor.

Post and Broadcasting. There were, in 1972, 74 post offices. Telephones in 1977 numbered 39,029, of which 30,604 were in Dakar. In 1975 there were 287,000 radio receivers and 1,800 television sets.

Cinemas. In 1975 there were 77 with a seating capacity of 33,500.

EDUCATION. Education is provided at 11 *lycées*, 66 *collèges d'enseignement secondaire*, 2 *lycées techniques*, 2 *écoles normales* and 3 *cours normaux*. Total pupils in the elementary schools on 1 Jan. 1972 was 269,997, including 33,421 attending private schools; in the secondary schools, 57,720 (of whom 15,980 attend private colleges). The University in Dakar was established on 24 Feb. 1957, with faculties of law, science, the arts and a school of medicine and pharmacy; it had 5,561 students in 1972.

DIPLOMATIC REPRESENTATIVES

OF SENEGAL IN GREAT BRITAIN (11 Phillimore Gdns., London, W8 7QG)

Ambassador: Saliou Diodj Faye.

OF GREAT BRITAIN IN SENEGAL (20 Rue du Docteur Guillet, Dakar)

Ambassador: J. E. Powell-Jones, CMG.

OF SENEGAL IN THE USA (2112 Wyoming Ave., NW, Washington, D.C., 20008)

Ambassor: André Coulbary.

OF THE USA IN SENEGAL (PO Box 49, Dakar)

Ambassador: Herman J. Cohen.

OF SENEGAL TO THE UNITED NATIONS

Ambassador: Médoune Fall.

Books of Reference

Crowder, M., *Senegal: A Study in French Assimilation.* OUP, 1962
Samb, M. (ed.), *Spotlight on Senegal.* Dakar, 1972

SEYCHELLES

Capital: Victoria
Population: 59,000 (1976)

HISTORY. The islands were first colonized by the French in the middle of the 18th century, in order to establish plantations of spices to compete with the Dutch monopoly. They were captured by the English in 1794 and incorporated as a dependency of Mauritius in 1814. In 1888 the office of administrator was created, with an Executive Council and a Legislative Council. In 1897 the Administrator was given full powers as Governor, and in Nov. 1903 he was raised to the rank of Governor with the Seychelles archipelago becoming a separate colony. In June 1976, Seychelles attained independence and is now a republic within the Commonwealth.

British Indian Ocean Territory, a British colony created in 1965, consists of the Chagos Archipelago (formerly a dependency of Mauritius). Aldabra, Farquhar and Desroches. These latter 3 islands returned to Seychelles in June 1976.

AREA AND POPULATION. Seychelles and its Dependencies consist of 87 islands and islets with a total estimated area of about 156 sq. miles (404 sq. km). The principal island is Mahé 57 sq. miles (144 sq.km), smaller islands of the group being Praslin, Silhouette, La Digue, Curieuse and Félicité. Among the outer islands are the Amirantes, Assumption Island, Astove Island, Cosmoledo Island, Providence Island, Coetivy Island and Platte Island.

The capital is Victoria on Mahé, which has a good harbour and improved port facilities have recently (1975) become available. The population (census 1971) was 52,650. Population (1976, estimate) 59,000.

Vital statistics (1976): Births, 1,642; deaths, 466.

CONSTITUTION AND GOVERNMENT. A new Constitution was introduced in Nov. 1970. The Legislative Assembly consists of 15 elected members, 3 *ex-officio* members and a Speaker. In the election, the Seychelles Democratic Party obtained 10 seats and the Seychelles Peoples United Party 5 seats. In the 1974 elections the Seychelles Democratic Party obtained 13 seats and the Seychelles Peoples United Party 2 seats. A Constitutional Conference opened in London in March 1975. A coalition government was formed on 1 June 1975 with 8 ministers, including the Prime Minister, 1 from the Seychelles Democratic Party and 4 Ministers from the Seychelles Peoples United Party. On 5 June 1977 President Mancham was deposed in a *coup* and F. Albert René became president forming a government entirely from the Seychelles People's United Party. On 1 Oct. 1975 Seychelles became internally self-governing. Independence was granted in June 1976. The official languages are English and French.

President: Hon. F. Albert René.

National flag: Horizontally green over red, with the green of double width and divided from the red by a white wavy stripe.

INTERNATIONAL RELATIONS

Membership. Seychelles is a member of UN, OAU and is an ACP state of EEC.

ECONOMY

Budget, in rupees, for calendar years, excluding Overseas Aid Scheme:

	1972	*1973*	*1974*	*1975*	*1976*
Total revenue	79,921,000	83,895,000	97,804,000	109,300,000	120,176,114
of which overseas loans and grants	37,734,000	28,990,000	32,832,000	31,000,000	...
Total expenditure	81,233,000	87,839,000	98,829,000	107,500,000	...
of which capital expenditure	38,142,000	29,119,000	32,683,000	310,000	...

Chief items of revenue, 1976: Customs, Rs 35m.; direct taxes, Rs 24m.; fees and fines, Rs 7m.

Chief items of expenditure, 1974: Education, Rs 8,924,000; medical, Rs 6,463,000; agriculture, Rs 6,884,000; police, Rs 4,983,000; electricity, Rs 6,683,000.

Currency. The currency is the Seychelles rupee.

Banking. Barclays Bank International and Standard Bank have branches in Victoria, Mahé.

AGRICULTURE. Chief products are copra and cinnamon bark. Food crop production is being increased for home consumption and fishing is actively pursued mainly for home consumption but also for export as frozen fish.

Livestock (1976): Cattle, 5,000; pigs, 20,000; poultry, 87,000.

INDUSTRY AND TRADE

Industry. Local industry is expanding, the largest development in recent years being the brewery.

Commerce. Total trade, in rupees, for calendar years:

	1973	*1974*	*1975*	*1976*
Imports (less re-exports)	135,100,000	160,500,000	191,350,000	290,620,000
Domestic exports	12,969,000	18,721,000	12,903,000	17,408,000

Principal imports (1976): Food, Rs 58·12m., of which rice, Rs 13,725,000; fruit and vegetables, Rs 7,308,000; other major imports, mineral fuels, Rs 56·32m.; manufactured goods, Rs 48m.

Principal exports (1976): Copra, Rs 8,817,000; cinnamon bark, Rs 3,601,000; frozen fish, Rs 3,354,000; hides, Rs 287,000; guano, Rs 1·11m.; coconuts, Rs 445,000.

Imports (1976) from: UK, Rs 86,436,000; Kenya, Rs 46,408,000; Republic of South Africa, Rs 20,916,000; Australia, Rs 15,107,000; Singapore, Rs 15,363,000.

Exports (1976) to: Pakistan, Rs 8,473,000; Mauritius, Rs 1,798,000; USA, Rs 1,567,000.

Tourism. Tourism has now established itself as an important sector of the economy. The number of visitors has grown very rapidly since the opening of the international airport in 1971 and in 1976 there were 49,500. The number of hotel beds available has expanded under a strictly controlled hotel construction programme and there are now 4 hotels with over 200 beds each and the total number of hotel beds available in Seychelles is about 1,870 at Dec. 1976.

COMMUNICATIONS

Roads. There is a good system of tarmac (84 miles) and earth roads (21 miles) in Mahé; Praslin and La Digue have 28 miles (9 miles tarmac); extensive roadmaking is being undertaken.

Aviation. British Airways operates 3 services a week between London and Seychelles, twice weekly from Colombo, Hong Kong and Tōkyō, and once a week from Mauritius and Johannesburg. Air Malawi operate weekly services from Blantyre. Air France operate a weekly service from Paris *via* Djibouti, Réunion and Mauritius. South African Airways operate weekly services from Johannesburg and Hong Kong.

Shipping. Shipping (1975), goods unloaded, 102,800 tonnes, of which petroleum, 42,100, and cement, 13,400; goods loaded, 10,800 tonnes, of which guano, 3,900. There are regular cargo vessels from Australia and the Far East, South Africa and Europe. The vessel *Nordvaer* travels to and from Mombasa and occasionally visits the outlying islands.

Post and Broadcasting. Services operated by Cable & Wireless Ltd provide telegraphic communications with all parts of the world by satellite, the company's radio-telephone service also extends to all principal countries in the world, In 1969, a telex system was introduced. Telephones in Jan. 1977 numbered 3,874.

Cinemas. In 1974 there was one cinema with seating capacity of 500.

JUSTICE, EDUCATION AND WELFARE

Justice. In 1976, 4,729 criminal and other cases were recorded by the police. The police force numbered 450 all ranks and 87 special constabulary.

Education. In Jan. 1976 there were 35 primary schools, 13 junior secondary schools, 2 secondary grammar schools, 5 vocational and technical schools and 1 teacher-training college.

In Jan. 1976 there were 5,043 boys and 5,106 girls in primary schools, 1,208 boys and 1,615 girls in junior secondary and secondary grammar schools, 147 boys and 160 girls in vocational and technical schools and 141 in the teacher-training college. A total of 122 students were undergoing training overseas, mainly in the UK; 68 were in university, 35 were undergoing professional/technical training, 12 teacher-training and 7 nursing.

Health. In 1978 there was 1 hospital with 140 beds and 21 doctors in government service.

DIPLOMATIC REPRESENTATIVES

OF SEYCHELLES IN GREAT BRITAIN
(2 Mill St, London, W2R 9TE)

High Commissioner: Ralph Louis Joseph Adam (accredited 27 Oct. 1977).

OF GREAT BRITAIN IN SEYCHELLES (Victoria Hse., Victoria)

High Commissioner: J. A. Pugh, OBE.

OF THE USA IN SEYCHELLES

Ambassador: Wilbert J. Le Melle (resides in Nairobi).

Books of Reference

Statistical Information: Information Office, 52 Kingsgate House, Victoria, Mahé.
Report of Seychelles Constitutional Conference. HMSO, 1970
Population Census 1960.—Agricultural Census 1960. Government Printer, 1961
Seychelles Handbook. Government Printer, 1976
Benedict, B., *People of the Seychelles.* HMSO, 1966
Lionnet, G., *The Seychelles.* Newton Abbot, 1972
Webb, A. W. T., *Story of Seychelles.* Government Printer, 1965

SIERRA LEONE

Capital: Freetown
Population: 3m. (1974)
GNP per capita: US$200 (1976)

HISTORY. The Colony of Sierra Leone originated in the sale and cession, in 1787, by native chiefs to English settlers, of a piece of land intended as a home for natives of Africa who were waifs in London, and later it was used as a settlement for Africans rescued from slave-ships. The hinterland was declared a British protectorate on 21 Aug. 1896.

AREA AND POPULATION. Sierra Leone is bounded on the north-west, north and north-east by the Republic of Guinea, on the south-east by Liberia and on the south-west by the Atlantic Ocean. The coastline extends from the boundary of the Republic of Guinea to the north of the mouth of the Great Scarcies River to the boundary of Liberia at the mouth of the Mano River, a distance of about 212 miles.

The area of Sierra Leone is 27,925 sq. miles (73,326 sq. km). Population (census Dec. 1974, provisional), 3,002,426, of whom about 2,000 are Europeans, 3,000 Asiatics and 30,000 non-native Africans. The capital is Freetown, with 274,000 inhabitants.

Sierra Leone is divided into 3 provinces (Eastern, Southern, Northern) covering 12 districts, each administered by a Resident Minister. The principal peoples are the Temnes, Limbas, Lokos and Korankos in the north, the Temnes in the centre, the Mendis in the south, and the Kissis and Konos in the east.

CONSTITUTION AND GOVERNMENT. The Constitution embodied in the Sierra Leone (Constitution) Order in Council 1961, came into force at Independence on 27 April 1961 when Sierra Leone became a sovereign and independent member state of the Commonwealth of Nations. Sierra Leone was accordingly admitted to the United Nations as the 100th member.

Subject to the provisions of the 1971 Constitution, executive power is vested in the President who is Head of State and Commander of the Armed Forces.

The House of Parliament consists of 12 paramount chiefs representing the 12 districts in the provinces, 85 elected members and 3 members appointed by the President. There is a Speaker and Deputy Speaker.

After the elections held on 17 March 1967 the Governor-General Sir Henry Lightfoot-Boston, GCMG, JP, appointed Siaka Stevens, leader of the All People's Congress, Prime Minister on 21 March. On the same day, however, the Government was overthrown by a military coup under the Army Commander, Brig. David Lansana. On 23 March 1967 there was a counter-coup by senior army and police officers who proclaimed the National Reformation Council on 25 March with Brig. Andrew Juxon-Smith as Chairman, Commissioner of Police L. W. Leigh as Deputy Chairman and 6 others.

On the night of 17–18 April 1968 the National Reformation Council was overthrown by army and police non-commissioned officers, who announced the formation of the Anti-Corruption Revolutionary Movement. The ACRM appointed an Interim Council, but later decided, in concurrence with the elected parliamentarians, that there should be a national government comprising candidates drawn from both political parties, independent candidates and paramount chiefs.

On 26 April 1968 constitutional government and civilian rule was restored.

Elections were held in May 1977 but because of outbreaks of violence, 8 seats in the Bo district were not filled until October.

Composition of Parliament in March 1978: All People's Congress, 74; Sierre Leone People's Party, 11; nominated members, 15.

The Cabinet consists of 28 Ministers representing the ruling All People's Congress (APC), including 3 paramount chiefs; the Force Commander, Brig. J. S. Momoh and the Commissioner of Police, P. C. Kaetu Smith. The latter two and the paramount chiefs are Ministers of State. The President, Dr Siaka Stevens is head of the Cabinet.

Sierra Leone became a republic on 19 April 1971.

National flag: Three horizontal stripes of green, white, blue.

Local Government. The Provinces are administered through the Ministry of the Interior and divided into 167 Chiefdoms, each under the control of a Paramount Chief and Council of Elders known as the Tribal Authorities, who are responsible for the maintenance of law and order and for the administration of justice (except for serious crimes). 143 of these Chiefdoms have been organized into local government units, empowered to raise and disburse funds for the development of the Chiefdom concerned. There are 12 administrative districts each with a committee of management.

DEFENCE

Army. The Army consists of 1 infantry battalion with supporting services including a signals squadron. Strength, 2,000 officers and men.

Air Force. The nucleus of an air arm for the defence forces came into existence in 1973, with the delivery of 2 Saab/MFI-15 light training aircraft (since increased to 4) and 1 Hughes 300 light helicopter from Sweden. These have been supplemented by 2 Hughes 500 helicopters.

INTERNATIONAL RELATIONS

Membership. Sierra Leone is a member of UN, OAU, the Commonwealth and is an ACP state of EEC.

ECONOMY

Budget. Revenue and expenditure (in leone) for years ending 30 June.

	1970–71	*1971–72*	*1972–73*	*1973–74*	*1974–75*
Revenue	51,000,000	54,000,000	59,100,000	82,500,000	86,700,000
Expenditure	41,300,000	55,000,000	58,200,000	82,500,000	86,700,000

Currency. The Bank of Sierra Leone, which was established on 4 Aug. 1964, is responsible for providing the currency in the country. It introduced on 4 Aug. 1964 a decimal currency, the *leone* and the *cent.* The paper currency consists of 1, 2, 5 *leone* and 50-*cent* notes; the coinage of 1, 5, 10, 20 and 50 *cents.*

The currency is interchangeable with sterling at par. At 30 June 1976 total Sierra Leone notes and coins in circulation was Le. 39·19m.

Banking. The Standard Bank Sierre Leone, the National Commercial Bank and Barclays Bank Sierre Leone have their headquarters at Freetown; the Standard Bank has 13 and Barclays Bank 12 branches and agencies.

NATURAL RESOURCES

Minerals. The chief minerals mined are diamonds, bauxite and rutile. There minerals accounted for 70% of domestic exports in 1975. Molybdenite and gold are being prospected.

Agriculture. In the western area farming is largely confined to the production of cassava and garden crops, such as maize and vegetables, for local consumption. In the provincial areas the principal products include rice, which is the staple food of the country, and export crops such as palm kernels, cocoa beans, coffee and ginger. Cattle production is important in the northern part of the country, and most of the poultry, eggs and pork are produced in the western area.

The second agricultural statistical survey showed that in 1970–71 there were 286,137 small holdings cultivating 1,286,348 acres; large farmers cultivated 18,806 acres. Rice plantations covered 807,557 acres; groundnuts, 34,128 acres; coffee, 176,078 acres.

Livestock (rough estimate): Cattle, 170,000; goats, 1·35m.; sheep, 45,800; chickens, 928,700.

Fisheries. There has been a gradual expansion of the fishing industry due to the introduction of new fishing techniques and gear. The estimated tonnage of catch of all species of fish during 1973–74 was over 50,000 tonnes. The FAO has carried out a 5-year survey of pelagic fish resources along the coastline and continental shelf.

Total catch of fish is still below the demand of the country. In 1975, 94,601 cwt of fish were imported. Total catch for 1975 was 206,000 tons.

INDUSTRY AND TRADE

Industry. Four pioneer oil-mills for the expressing of palm-oil are operated by the Sierra Leone Produce Marketing Board. Government also operates 4 rice-mills, and there are a number of privately owned mills. At Kenema the Government Department of Forest Industries produces sawn timber, joinery products (including prefabricated buildings) and high-class furniture. In addition, there is a smaller privately owned sawmill at Panguma and several small furniture workshops throughout the country. All these products are used internally. Village industries include fishing, fish curing and smoking, weaving and hand methods of expressing palm-oil and cracking palm kernels.

Labour. A large proportion of the population was engaged in agriculture and about 125,000 workers were in wage-earning employment. The number of workers in establishments employing 6 or more persons was 72,314 in 1975, distributed as follows: Agriculture, forestry and fishing 5·1%; mining and quarrying, 15%; manufacturing, 8·1%; construction, 12·4%; electricity and water services, 2·6%; commerce, 8·7%; transport, storage and communications, 14·9%; services, 33·2%.

The wage negotiation machinery was recently reorganized and wages and conditions of employment are now regulated by a Joint National Negotiating Board and 14 Trade Group Councils as provided for in the Regulation of Wages and Industrial Relations Act, 18 of 1971.

There are 27 registered trade unions (22 workers and 5 employers). The number of persons registered for employment at the end of 1971 was 7,210, excluding maritime, articled and the dock workers who are registered in the Port Labour (Maritime, Articled and Harbour) Pools; registrations in these Pools numbered 8,471.

Commerce. Total trade (in leone) for calendar years:

	1970	*1971*	*1972*	*1973*	*1974*	*1975*
Imports	88,080,000	94,267,571	86,780,000	116,300,000	170,770,000	152,760,000
Exports	85,550,000	82,068,109	91,610,000	106,570,000	122,950,000	116,470,000

Of the imports (1971) 28·8% came from UK, 10·2% from Japan, 7·1% from Federal Republic of Germany. Of the exports (1971) 62·8% went to UK, 9·4% to Netherlands, 6·8% to Japan and 6·5% to the USA.

Total trade between Sierra Leone and UK (British Department of Trade returns, in £1,000 sterling):

	1972	*1973*	*1974*	*1975*	*1976*	*1977*
Imports to UK	29,078	40,116	41,897	32,608	35,531	40,053
Exports and re-exports from UK	10,348	12,716	18,733	21,104	17,935	19,669

Tourism. Tourism is being developed.

COMMUNICATIONS

Roads. There were (1977) about 4,406 miles of main roads, of which 665 miles are surfaced with bitumen.

Motor vehicles licensed in 1975 totalled 21,135: passenger cars, 14,267; buses and trucks, 3,384, and motor cycles, 3,484.

Railways (1977). The government railway closed in 1974, and an 84-km mineral line of 1,067-mm gauge connecting Marampa with the port of Pepel was closed in 1975.

Aviation. Freetown Airport (Lungi), situated north of Freetown in the Port Loko District, is the only international airport in Sierra Leone and all aircraft entering and leaving the territory must land at Lungi.

The airport is served by Sierra Leone Airways, Ghana/Nigeria Airways, British

Caledonian, Union de Transport Aériens, KLM, Air Afrique, United Arab Airlines and Czechoslovakia Airlines. A once weekly non-stop flight from London (Gatwick) to Freetown and vice versa is also provided.

Sierra Leone Airways provide domestic flights daily (except Sundays) from Hastings (14 miles from Freetown) to Gbangbatoke, Bo, Kenema, Yengema, twice weekly to Bonthe and occasional flights to Marampa and Port Loko on charter basis.

Shipping. During 1975 the total imports handled by the port of Freetown amounted to 361,454 freight tons and exports 110,316 freight tons; a total of 704 vessels called at Freetown; 699 were cargo vessels and 5 were tourist ships with a total of 793 passengers.

Bonthe-Sherbro, 80 miles south of Freetown, is used for the shipment of piassava, palm kernels, rutile and bauxite. Pepel, lies some 12 miles from Freetown but is no longer in use.

Post and Broadcasting. The Posts and Telecommunications Department maintains a trunk network of radio and overhead telephone and telegraph routes of approximately 3,000 miles linking the western area with the other provinces. Automatic telephone exchanges have been introduced at the provincial centres of Bo, Kenema and Makeni; microwave radio relay link now replaces overhead open wire on main trunk routes. An extension programme to link important mining areas at Koidu and Mokanji to the national network by microwave links is well on the way.

The wired broadcasting relay service was replaced in Jan. 1964 by a transistor radio service. Approximately 20,000 transistor radios purchased under this scheme are now in service.

Number of telephones (1977) 11,600. Telegraphic facilities are provided at 58 offices.

There are 137 post offices and postal agencies.

The number of private wireless-licence holders at 30 June 1972 was 23,958 and 732 television sets were in operation.

JUSTICE, RELIGION, EDUCATION AND WELFARE

Justice. The High Court has jurisdiction in civil and criminal matters. Subordinate courts are held by magistrates in the various districts. Native Courts, headed by court Chairmen, apply native law and custom under a criminal and civil jurisdiction. Appeals from the decisions of magistrates' courts are heard by the High Court. Appeals from the decisions of the High Court are heard by the Sierra Leone Court of Appeal. Appeal lies from the Sierra Leone Court of Appeal to the Supreme Court which is the highest court.

Police. The police force at 31 Dec. 1975 had an authorized strength of 82 superior police officers, 211 junior police officers and 3,833 other ranks including 382 women. In the provinces each Chiefdom keeps an additional force known as Chiefdom Police.

A non-pensionable force, known as the Auxiliary Force and consisting of 2 junior police officers and 272 other ranks, are helping the regular force in maintaining law and order in the diamond protected area in the Eastern Province.

Religion. The majority of the population follow traditional tribal religions. Islam was brought to the region by the nomadic cattle-rearing Fula people from the north around 1600. The Temne people in the north-west form the main part of the Moslem community who were estimated in 1977 to comprise about 20% of the population.

Christianity came to West Africa in the 16th century from Portugal and Spain. The Roman Catholics have 2 dioceses in Sierra Leone and number about 25,000 (1977).

The Evangelical group who led the anti-slavery movement in England founded the Sierra Leone Company in 1791 to setttle freed slaves in and around Freetown. In 1966 there were 16 Protestant denominations with a total community of 77,000. Members of the Sierra Leone Church (Anglican) were 25,000 in 1977.

Education (1975–76). There were over 1,974 registered primary schools with a total enrolment of over 205,910. Primary education is as yet neither free nor compulsory but parents and guardians are urged to send their children and wards to school.

School attendance varies considerably in different parts of the country. There were 132 secondary schools with a total enrolment of 48,609 pupils; 71 of these schools are fully assisted by the Government. Technical education was provided in 2 technical institutes, 2 trade centres and in the technical training establishments of the mining companies. There is also a rural institute.

Non graduate teacher-training is offered at two levels: the teachers certificate trains teachers for primary schools and the higher teachers certificate trains teachers for the lower forms of secondary schools.

Fourah Bay College (1,016 students) and Njala University College (586 students) are the 2 constituent colleges of the University of Sierra Leone. The Institute of Education, which is part of the University, is now responsible for teacher education, educational research and curriculum development in the country.

Health (1977). In the western area there are 12 government hospitals (1,108 beds and 217 cots), including a maternity hospital, a children's hospital and an infectious diseases hospital near Freetown. There are 6 government health centres in the Western Area. Three private hospitals are located in Freetown with 108 beds. A mental hospital at Kissy has accommodation for 224 patients. In the provinces there are 14 government hospitals, 4 hospitals associated with mining companies and 7 mission hospitals. There is a school of nursing in Freetown. There are 156 government dispensaries and health treatment centres and two military hospitals with 124 beds.

DIPLOMATIC REPRESENTATIVES

OF SIERRA LEONE IN GREAT BRITAIN
(33 Portland Pl., London, W1N 3AG)

High Commissioner: (Vacant).

OF GREAT BRITAIN IN SIERRA LEONE (Standard Bank, Sierra Leone, Ltd Bldg., Wallace Johnson St., Freetown)

High Commissioner: Michael Hugh Morgan.

OF SIERRA LEONE IN THE USA (1701 19th St., NW, Washington, D.C., 20009)

Ambassador: Philip J. Palmer.

OF THE USA IN SIERRA LEONE
(Corner Walpole and Siaka Stevens St., Freetown)

Ambassador: John Andrew Linehan.

OF SIERRA LEONE TO THE UNITED NATIONS

Ambassador: Shirley Yema Gbujama.

Books of Reference

Atlas of Sierra Leone. Ed. Survey and Lands Dept. Freetown, 1953
Sierra Leone Studies. Ed. J. D. Hargreaves. Freetown, 1953 ff.
Fyfe, C., *A History of Sierra Leone*. OUP, 1962.—Fyfe, C., and Jones, E. (ed.), *Freetown*. Sierra Leone Univ. Press and OUP, 1968
Kup, A. P., *Sierra Leone*. Newton Abbot, 1975
Lewis, R., *Sierra Leone*. HMSO, 1954
Porter, A. T., *Creoledom: A Study in the Development of Freetown Society*. OUP, 1963
Saylor, R. G., *The Economic System of Sierra Leone*. Duke Univ. Press, 1968

REPUBLIC OF SINGAPORE

Population: 2·28m. (1976)
GNP per capita: US$2,700 (1976)

HISTORY. For the early history of the settlement (1819) and colony (1867) *see* THE STATESMAN'S YEAR-BOOK, 1959, pp. 246 f.

By an agreement entered into between the Governments of Malaysia and of the State of Singapore on 7 Aug. 1965, effective on 9 Aug. 1965, Singapore ceased to be one of the 14 states of the Federation of Malaysia and became an independent sovereign state. The separation was ratified by the Constitution and Malaysia (Singapore Amendment) Act of the Malaysian Parliament on 9 Aug. The 2 governments agreed to enter into a treaty on external defence and mutual assistance. The Singapore Government retains its executive authority and legislative powers under its State Constitution and took over the powers of the Malaysian Government under the Malaysian Constitution in Singapore. The sovereignty and jurisdiction of the head of the Malaysian State was transferred to the Singapore Government. Civil servants working in Singapore for the Federal Departments became Singapore civil servants. Singapore citizens ceased to be Malaysian citizens.

Singapore accepted responsibility for international agreements entered into by the Malaysian Government on its behalf.

AREA AND POPULATION. The Republic of Singapore consists of Singapore Island itself, and some 54 islets.

Singapore Island is situated off the southern extremity of the Malay peninsula, to which it is joined by a causeway carrying a road, railway and water pipeline. The Straits of Johore between the island and the mainland are about three-quarters of a mile wide. The island is some 26 miles (41·8 km) in length and 14 miles (22·5 km) in breadth, and about 232·4 sq. miles (602 sq. km) in area, including the adjacent islets.

Census of population (1970): 1,579,866 Chinese, 311,379 Malays, 145,196 Indians and 38,093 others; total 2,074,507. Estimate (mid-1976), 2,278,200.

Report on the Census of Population 1970. Dept. of Statistics, Singapore, 1973

CONSTITUTION AND GOVERNMENT. By a constitutional amendment the name of the state was changed to 'Republic of Singapore', the head of state was named 'President of Singapore' and the legislative assembly was renamed 'Parliament'.

Malay, Chinese, Tamil and English are the official languages; English is the language of administration.

Parliament consists of 69 members, elected by secret ballot from single-member constituencies, and is presided over by a Speaker, chosen by Parliament from its own members or from outside the Assembly. In the latter case, the Speaker has no vote. With the customary exception of those serving criminal sentences, all citizens over 21 are eligible to vote irrespective of sex, race, education or property qualification. There is a common roll without communal electorates. Citizenship is automatic by birth; it can also be acquired by registration or by naturalization.

A Presidential Council was established under Part IVA of the Constitution enacted on 9 Jan. 1970. The general function of the Council is to consider and report on matters affecting persons of any racial or religious community in Singapore as referred to it by Parliament or the Government. The Council will draw attention to any bill or subsidiary legislation which in the opinion of the Council is a differentiating measure.

Parliament, elected on 23 Dec. 1976, is composed of 69 People's Action Party members.

The People's Action Party cabinet at Jan. 1978 was composed as follows:

President of Singapore: Dr Benjamin Henry Sheares (sworn in 2 Jan. 1971).

Prime Minister: Lee Kuan Yew.

Deputy Prime Minister and Minister of Defence: Dr Goh Keng Swee. *Culture:* Ong Teng Cheong. *Foreign Affairs:* S. Rajaratnam. *Labour:* Ong Pang Boon. *National Development and Communications:* Lim Kim San. *Law and Environment:* E. W. Barker. *Health:* Dr Toh Chin Chye. *Home Affairs and Education:* Chua Sian Chin. *Science and Technology:* E. W. Barker. *Social Affairs:* Dr Ahmad Mattar. *Finance:* Hon Sui Sen. There are also 10 Ministers of State.

National flag: Horizontally red over white, with a crescent and a circle of 5 stars, all in white in the canton.

DEFENCE. The Ministry of Defence exercises command and control over all armed forces in the Republic. It comprises 5 major divisions, *i.e.*, the general staff, manpower, logistic, security and intelligence and finance divisions. Compulsory military service in peace-time was introduced in 1967.

The governments of Australia, Britain, Malaysia, New Zealand and Singapore continue to co-operate closely in defence arrangements and have agreed on a new 5-nation defence set-up in South-east Asia designed to protect Malaysia and Singapore against outside attack. The new defence arrangement came into force on 1 Nov. 1971.

Army. Eight active infantry battalions have been raised and they are organized into 3 infantry brigades. The support arms of the artillery, the engineers and the signals have been expanded. There is an armoured unit of light tanks and armoured assault vehicles. In addition to the battalions which are performing full-time duties, reserve battalions have also been raised as full-time national servicemen are released into reserve service. The People's Defence Force consists of 6 infantry battalions, 2 volunteer battalions and a PDF women's company. Regular strength, 30,000, and reserves, 45,000.

Navy. Naval vessels comprise 6 missile boats of German design, 6 fast patrol craft built by Vosper Thornycroft (2 at Portsmouth, Britain, and 4 in Singapore), 2 *ex*-US coastal minesweepers, 1 seaward defence boat, 4 coastal patrol craft (marine police), 6 landing ships (*ex*-USN LST), 1 training ship and 6 small landing craft. Personnel in 1978: 3,000 officers and men.

Air Defence Command. The formation of an Air Defence Command began in 1968, with *ab initio* training on Cessna 172 light aircraft. The Republic of Singapore Air Force now has 2 fighter-bomber squadrons equipped with 40 A-4S Skyhawks, supported by 7 TA-4S two-seat trainers; 2 squadrons of Hunter jet fighters and reconnaissance-fighters, supported by Hunter 2-seat trainers, a radar unit and a Bloodhound surface-to-air missile squadron; a squadron of Strikemaster light jet attack/trainers; 6 Skyvan 3M STOL transports, some equipped for search and rescue; a primary training squadron of SIAI–Marchetti SF.260Ms and armed SF.260Ws; and a squadron of Alouette III helicopters, since supplemented by 20 Bell UH-1H Iroquois and 212s. On order are F-5E Tiger II supersonic fighter-bombers. With the withdrawal of British forces, Bukit Gombak Station, which has one of the most advanced radar shields in SE Asia, the Joint Air Traffic Control Centres at Paya Leba, Seletar, Tengah and Changi Air Bases were handed over to the Singapore Air Defence Command by the RAF. Personnel strength about 4,000.

INTERNATIONAL RELATIONS

Membership. Singapore is a member of UN, the Commonwealth and the Colombo Plan.

ECONOMY

Planning. The GDP in 1976, at current prices was estimated at $14,420m., an increase of 9% in 1975. Gross Domestic Fixed Capital formation advanced at constant prices by 12% to $2,926m., of which the public sector accounted for 37%.

Increasing efforts were made in the development of two-way foreign trade. The Commercial Secretaries' Service was expanded to provide local manufacturers and traders with better access to the latest information and contacts. In 1976, 6 trade missions visited over 10 countries, reciprocated by 20 which came to Singapore.

The Bureau of Joint Ventures established by the Economic Development Board provided valuable assistance to facilitate and speed up the establishment of joint projects between foreign and local parties. A small-industries finance scheme was established with the backing of the Economic Development Board and the Development Bank of Singapore to support the growth and development of local industries by providing tax incentives and training grants.

Budget. Public revenue and expenditure for financial years, in Singapore dollars (S$1 = £0·13):

	1973–74[1, 2]	*1974–75*[1, 2]	*1975–76*[1, 2]	*1976–77*[1, 2]	*1977–78*[1, 2]
Revenue	1,874,900,000	2,322,950,000	2,647,461,000	3,107,570,000	5,459,839,200
Expenditure	1,874,900,000	2,322,950,000	2,647,461,000	3,107,570,000	5,459,839,200

[1] Financial year from 1 April to 31 March of the following year. [2] Estimated figures.

Currency. The Singapore dollar (S$) is divided in 100 cents.

Banking. The functions of the Commissioner of Banking have been assumed by the Monetary Authority of Singapore from 1 Jan. 1971.

The Development Bank of Singapore was established in 1968, primarily to provide long-term financing of manufacturing and other industries. At 31 Dec. 1976, the net cumulative long-term financing was S$1,959m.

There were 72 commercial banks with 250 banking offices operating in Singapore on 31 Dec. 1976. Total deposits amounted to S$8,600m. on 31 Dec. 1976.

The amount deposited in the Singapore Post Office Savings Bank was S$1,004·4m.

Weights and Measures. The metric system or the International System of Units (SI) has been introduced in Singapore. The Metrication Board was set up on 11 Dec. 1970 to stimulate the conversion from the British to the metric system and to co-ordinate the changeover in the various sectors of Singapore's economy. During 1973 the Metrication Board concentrated on conversion in the textile trade, building and construction, and the standardization of packing. By the end of this decade metric measures will be used almost exclusively. All government departments and statutory bodies and 75% of industries with external trade dealings adopted the metric system by 1976 and the system is to be universal by 1980.

ENERGY AND NATURAL RESOURCES

Electricity. The Public Utilities Board is responsible for the production and distribution of electricity, gas and water. Electrical power is generated by 5 power stations, with a total generating capacity of 1,390 mw at the end of 1976.

Fisheries. As the prospect of increasing fish production from inshore waters is poor, in 1967 various projects were introduced, with the aim of making Singapore self-sufficient in fish as well as a major fishing base in the region.

The Jurong fishing port and fish market began operating 26 Feb. 1969. A Fishery Training Institute was established at Changi with the assistance of the United Nations Development Programme (Special Fund) to train youths and fishermen in modern fishing techniques. At Changi, too, a Marine Fisheries Research Department was set up under the sponsorship of the South-east Asian Fisheries Development Centre. Research on fish culture and ornamental fish was carried out at the Freshwater Fisheries Laboratory at Sembawang. Ornamental fish industry is fast becoming a valuable foreign exchange earner. Export of ornamental fish in 1976, S$11·8m. The total supply of fresh fish in 1976 was 60,751 tonnes.

INDUSTRY AND TRADE

Industry. The largest industrial area is the Jurong Industrial Estate with 675 factories in production and 102 factories under planning and construction.

Industries in Jurong include shipbuilding and those manufacturing steel rods, steel pipes, tyres, chemicals, pharmaceuticals, plywood and veneer, plastics, cement, bricks, cables, textiles and wiremesh. Smaller industrial estates have light industry factories producing food, paper and miscellaneous consumer goods.

Labour. The principal occupations in Singapore are in the manufacturing sector; community, social and personal services, commerce, warehousing and transport and communications.

In June 1976, 870,400 persons were employed, of whom 713,200 were employees, 36,100 were employers, 95,100 were self-employed and 26,000 were unpaid domestic workers. Persons engaged in manufacturing numbered 234,000, the highest among all industries.

There were 143 registered trade unions comprising 91 employee unions, 51 employer unions and 1 federation of trade unions as at Dec. 1976. The total membership of employee unions numbered 221,936; that of employer unions, 6,852.

The Employment Act and the Industrial Relations Act provide principal terms and conditions of employment such as hours of work, sick leave and other fringe benefits. A new labour legislation was introduced allowing youths of 14–16 years to work in industrial establishments, and also children from 12–14 years to be employed in approved apprenticeship schemes. A trade dispute may be referred to the Industrial Arbitration Court which was established in 1960.

The Ministry of Labour operates 3 employment exchanges to assist job seekers to obtain suitable employment and employers to recruit suitable workers. The Central Provident Fund was established in 1955 to make provision for employees in their old age. At Dec. 1976 the fund had 1,177,538 accounts with assets of S$4,066·1m.

Commerce. The imports during 1976 amounted to S$22,404m., the exports to S$16,266m. (inclusive of trade with West Malaysia).

The principal trading countries for 1976 were Malaysia (15% of total trade), USA (14%) and Japan (14%). In 1976, imports (S$22,404m.) rose by 16%, mainly due to more imports of raw materials and semi-manufactured goods. Exports (S$16,266m.) increased more rapidly, by 28%, mainly due to increases in petroleum products, crude rubber and machinery equipment.

In the following table (British Department of Trade returns, in £1,000 sterling) the imports include produce from Borneo, Sarawak and other eastern places, transhipped at Singapore, which is thus entered as the place of export:

	1973	*1974*	*1975*	*1976*	*1977*
Imports to UK	85,376	74,758	64,558	94,358	102,611
Exports and re-exports from UK	100,601	153,533	157,096	168,235	201,162

COMMUNICATIONS

Roads. Singapore has 2,218 km of public roads. In 1976 motor vehicles registered in Singapore included 136,574 private cars, 5,217 buses, 5,473 taxis and 84,016 motor cycles and scooters.

Railways. A 16-mile (25·8-km) main line runs through Singapore, connecting with the States of Malaysia and as far as Bangkok. Branch lines serve the port of Singapore and the industrial estate at Jurong.

Aviation. The new international airport at Changi was under construction in 1978 and is to be completed in 1980.

Shipping. A total of 77,040 vessels of 208·6m. NRT entered into and cleared from Singapore during 1976.

Post. In 1976, 60 post offices and 43 postal agencies were in operation. Telephones numbered 388,709 at 31 March 1977.

Cinemas (1976). There were 73 cinemas with a seating capacity of 62,682.

Newspapers (1976). There were 10 daily newspapers, in 5 languages, with a total daily circulation of 477,000.

JUSTICE, EDUCATION AND WELFARE

Justice. There is a Supreme Court in Singapore which consists of the High Court, the Court of Appeal and the Court of Criminal Appeal. The Supreme Court is composed of a Chief Justice and 6 Judges. An appeal from the High Court lies to the Court of Appeal in civil matters and to the Court of Criminal Appeal in criminal matters. Further appeal can in certain cases be made to the Judicial Committee of the Privy Council. The High Court has original civil and criminal jurisdiction as well as appellate civil and criminal jurisdiction in respect of appeals from the Subordinate Courts. There are 8 district courts, 13 magistrates' courts, 1 juvenile court and 2 coroners' courts.

Education. Statistics of registered institutions for 1976:

Classification	*Schools*	*Enrolment*	*Teachers*
Government schools	262	341,297	13,423
Government-aided schools	233	150,846	5,516
Private schools	60	7,129	339
Total	555	499,272	19,278

The University of Singapore has 7 faculties: arts and social sciences, law, science, medicine, dentistry, engineering, architecture and building; 3 schools: accountancy and business administration, post-graduate medical and dental studies; and 1 department: Department of Extramural Studies. It numbered 6,199 students (excluding 52 non-graduating) in 1976–77. The Nanyang University, established in 1953 and began functioning in 1956, has 4 Colleges of Arts, Science, Commerce and Graduate Studies in addition to a Computer Centre. There were 2,362 students in 1976–77. The Singapore Polytechnic had 8,440 students and the Ngee Ann Technical College had 2,094 students in 1976–77. The Institute of Education, established on 1 April 1973, is now the only institution responsible for teacher education in Singapore and for promoting research in education. There were 1,378 students in 1976–77. There were also 11 vocational institutes and a technical institute with an enrolment of 8,355 students in 1976. The Adult Education Board conducts secondary education classes as well as language, technical, commercial and recreational courses. Enrolment in 1976 totalled 56,235.

Health. There were 1,565 doctors and 8,000 hospital beds in 1972.

DIPLOMATIC REPRESENTATIVES

OF SINGAPORE IN GREAT BRITAIN
(2 Wilton Cres., London, SW1X 8RW)

High Commissioner: Jek Yeun Thong (accredited 1 Dec. 1977).

OF GREAT BRITAIN IN SINGAPORE
(Tanglin Circus, Singapore, 10)

High Commissioner: J. D. Hennings.

OF SINGAPORE IN THE USA (1824 R St, NW, Washington, D.C., 20009)

Ambassador: P. Coomaraswamy.

OF THE USA IN SINGAPORE
(30 Hill St., Singapore)

Ambassador: John H. Holdridge.

OF SINGAPORE TO THE UNITED NATIONS

Ambassador: T. T. B. Koh.

Books of Reference

Statistical Information: The Department of Statistics (PO Box 3010, Singapore) was established 1 Jan. 1922. Its publications include: *Singapore External Trade Statistics* (quarterly), *Monthly Digest of Statistics, Yearbook of Statistics, Population Estimates of Singapore* (bi-annual). *Census of Population 1970. Acting Chief Statistician:* Khoo Chian Kim.

National Library. *Books about Singapore*. Singapore. Biennial
National Trades Union Congress. *Singapore. Towards Tomorrow*. Singapore, 1973

Singapore. Constitution. The Constitution of Singapore. Singapore, 1966
Singapore. Singapore, Publicity Division, Ministry of Culture (formerly *Annual Report*)
Singapore. Government Gazette (published weekly with supplement)
Singapore Government Directory. Singapore, Publicity Division, Ministry of Culture
The Statutes of the Republic of Singapore. 8 vols., 1970 (with annual supplements)
Buchanan, I., *Singapore in South East Asia: An Economic and Political Appraisal*. London, 1972
Gamer, R. E., *The Politics of Urban Development in Singapore*. OUP, 1972
George, T. J. S., *Lee Kuan Yew's Singapore*. London, 1973
Goh, K. S., *The Economics of Modernisation*. Singapore, 1972
Hughes, H. (ed.), *Foreign Investment and Industrialisation in Singapore*. Canberra, 1969
Josey, A., *Lee Kuan Yew, The Struggle for Singapore*. Sydney, 1974
Ooi, J. B. (ed.), *Modern Singapore*. Singapore, 1969
Wilson, R., *The Future Role of Singapore*. OUP, 1972
You, P. S., and Lim, C. Y. (ed.), *The Singapore Economy*. Singapore, 1971

National Library: National Library, Stamford Rd, Singapore. *Director:* Mrs Hedwig Anuar.

SOLOMON ISLANDS

Capital: Honiara
Population: 196,823 (1976)

HISTORY. The Solomon Islands were discovered in 1568 by Alvaro de Mendana, on a voyage of discovery from Peru; 200 years passed before European contact was again made with the Solomons. The Solomon Islands lie within the area 5° to 12° 30′ S. lat. and 155° 30′ to 169° 45′ E. long. The group includes the main islands of Guadalcanal, Malaita, San Cristobal, New Georgia, Santa Isabel and Choiseul; the smaller Florida and Russell groups; the Shortland, Mono (or Treasury), Vella La Vella, Kolombangara, Ranongga, Gizo and Rendova Islands; to the east, Santa Cruz, Tikopia, the Reef and Duff groups; Rennell and Bellona in the south; Ontong Java or Lord Howe to the north; and innumerable smaller islands.

The 4 first-named were placed under British protection in 1893; the other islands were added in 1898 and 1899.

AREA AND POPULATION. The land area of the Solomons is estimated at 11,500 sq. miles (29,785 sq. km). The larger islands are mountainous and forest-clad, with flood-prone rivers of considerable energy potential. Guadalcanal has the largest land area and the greatest amount of flat coastal plain.

The population of Guadalcanal (including Honiara the main town) was 46,619 at census date (Feb. 1976); Malaita (58,721).

The total population of the Solomon Islands was 196,823, over 50% being under 20 years (183,665 Melanesians, 7,821 Polynesians, 452 Chinese, 1,359 Europeans, 2,753 Gilbertese and 773 others).

The islands are administratively divided into 4 districts with Central 70,615, Western 40,329, Malaita 60,043 and Eastern 25,836. However, while the administrative breakdown still exists more important now is the Council system. Eight Councils cover the local administration and are virtually in charge of the development of their areas. The population at census 1976 of each of these was as follows: Western 40,329, Isabel 10,420, Central Islands 13,576, Guadalcanal 31,677 Honiara 14,942, Malaita 60,043, Makira and Ulawa 14,891 and Eastern Islands 10,945.

The capital, Honiara, on Guadalcanal, is the largest urban area, with census population in 1976 of 14,942. Rainfall at Honiara (which lies in a rain shadow) is 90 in. per annum; elsewhere as high as 300 in.; the average is 120–140 in.

CONSTITUTION AND GOVERNMENT. In 1960, a Legislative Council was established with an Executive Council.

1969 saw a further change in the Constitution, making provision for an elected majority in a single Governing Council with an Executive Council. Elections were held in 1970 with the newly constituted council consisting of 3 *ex officio*, 6 public service and 17 elected members. By the end of 1971, the 6 public service members were withdrawn and a Solomon Islander appointed as chairman presiding over public meetings.

The transition to a ministerial form of government took place during 1974. The Governing Council became the Legislative Assembly, and in Aug. the elected members chose a Chief Minister.

A Council of Ministers was also appointed, and the High Commissioner redesignated Governor. He, in consultation with the elected members, appointed the first Solomon Islander Speaker of the Assembly.

Constitutional changes and developments are aimed at protecting the fundamental rights and freedoms of individual Solomon Islanders, to provide an independent Public Service Commission to oversee the Public Service in replacement of the Public Service Advisory Board established in 1968, and to see that its islands move smoothly and flexibly towards self-government.

The Solomon Islands achieved internal self-government on 2 Jan. 1976. In the same year a general election was held and 38 members were returned to the Legislative Assembly. These members elected a chief minister who appointed from them the 8 ministers who with the chief minister form the Council of Ministers (*i.e.*, Cabinet). The Constitution provides for 2 additional ministers if required.

The Governor retains control over security, defence and external affairs, but on all other matters his powers are exercised in accordance with the advice of the Council of Ministers.

A Constitutional Conference was held in London during Sept. 1977, where it was agreed that full independence for the Solomon Islands should be granted on 7 July 1978.

Considerable control over local affairs has been devolved on the 5 district councils whose members are elected under popular franchise.

Governor: Colin Hamilton Allan, CMG, OBE.

Chief Minister: Peter Kenilorea.

Flag: British Blue Ensign with the arms of the Colony on a white disc in the fly.

ECONOMY

Planning. The overall objective of the $A60m. first National Development Plan covering the years 1975–79 was to provide guidelines for the development of the country. A review of the first 2 years of operation of the plan has shown that many of the targets have been met, while the prospects for the rest of the Plan period appear cautiously optimistic, with increased production and export earnings, a likely favourable balance of trade and improved revenue from local taxation.

Budget. The budget for the calendar year 1975 had a deficit of $A1,657,540 covered by a British grant-in-aid. In 1976 total revenue, including UK aid, was $A17·76m. and total expenditure was $A17·74m.

Currency. The medium of exchange is Australian decimal currency introduced in Feb. 1966, but the Solomon Island dollar was introduced in 1977. The estimated amount of currency in circulation at the end of Dec. 1970 was $A4·3m.

NATURAL RESOURCES

Agriculture. Coconuts, cocoa, rice and other minor crops are grown. Oil-palm is being developed successfully with a total of about 6,800 acres having been planted. Production of copra (1976), 22,500 tonnes.

An oil-mill became operational in 1976 and 3,205 hectares of oil-palms have been planted. 3,500 tons of palm-oil out of 300 tons of palm-kernels were exported in 1976.

Rice-cropping in 1976 from 834 hectares yielded 1,850 tonnes of milled rice.

Timber extraction is an important development in the Solomons. Timber (logs, sawn timber and veneer sheets) exports for 1976 were 242,700 cu. metres ($A6,244,000), an increase of 12,300 cu. metres over 1975 exports.

Livestock (1976): Cattle, 23,000; pigs, 34,000; poultry, 133,000.

Fisheries. A total catch of 15,200 tonnes of skipjack was made in 1976, an increase of 8,000 tonnes over 1975. Exports of fish totalled $A9·11m. in 1976.

COMMERCE (1976). The main imports were food, fuels and capital goods and totalled $A21m. Exports comprised copra (23,015 tonnes), frozen fish (12,160 tonnes), rough timber (241,000 cu. metres), canned fish (672 tonnes), palm-oil (3,799 tonnes), marine shell, cocoa and manufactured tobacco. Australia supplied 38% of the imports; Japan, 13%; Singapore, 10%, and of the exports, 36% went to Japan, 13% to UK, 11% to Puerto Rico and 11% to American Samoa.

COMMUNICATIONS

Aviation. Regular flights from Fiji and Australia (*via* Papua New Guinea) provide the main communication link. Solair, the internal airline, and innumerable small ships, provide inter-island transport.

Shipping. Shipping services are maintained with Australia, New Zealand, UK and the Far East.

Post. Number of telephones (Aug. 1977), 1,888. A VHF radio telephone service operates internally as well as overseas.

Newspapers. There are 4 weekly newspapers, 1 with a circulation of 4,000 and the other 3 with 3,000.

EDUCATION AND WELFARE

Education. In 1974, a Ministry of Education and Cultural Affairs was created. Library, museum services, sociological researches, the national archives and church schools come under this ministry.

Primary education is still largely in the hands of the churches. Of the 323 registered schools in 1974, 5 were run by the Government, 35 by local councils, 6 by others and 277 by the churches. The enrolment at primary schools was 24,088. There are 6 secondary schools of which 5 are run by the churches. The enrolment was 1,566.

In 1974, the Government's recurrent expenditure on education totalled $A1·5m. $A700,000 of this went in grants to various kinds of schools controlled by churches, the local councils and other authorities. About $A543,500 was spent on various school capital projects under the Sixth Development Plan (1971–74), and a further $A357,000 provided scholarships to students overseas.

Health. In 1971 there were 1,413 hospital beds.

Books of Reference

B.S.I.P. Annual Report, 1969. Honiara, 1970
Pacific Islands Year Book and Who's Who. Sydney, 1968
Building the Nation. Honiara, 1975
Amhurst, Lord, and Thompson, B., *The Discovery of the Solomon Islands in 1568*. London, 1967
Fox, C. E., *The Threshold of the Pacific*. London, 1924
Kent, J., *The Solomon Islands*. Newton Abbot, 1972
Miller, J., *Guadalcanal: The First Offensive*. Washington, 1949

SOMALI DEMOCRATIC REPUBLIC

Capital: Mogadiscio
Population: 3·2m. (1976)
GNP per capita: US$110 (1976)

Al-Jumhouriya As-Somaliya Al-Domocradia

HISTORY. The Somali Republic came into being on 1 July 1960 as a result of the merger of the British Somaliland Protectorate, which became independent on 26 June 1960, and the Italian Trusteeship Territory of Somalia. For the previous history of these territories *see* THE STATESMAN'S YEAR-BOOK, 1960, pp. 337 and 1367.

AREA AND POPULATION. The Somali Republic has a total area of about 630,000 sq. km (246,000 sq. miles) with an estimated population (1976) of 3,221,050. Mogadiscio is the capital (population, 350,000). Other towns: Hargeisa (60,000), Kisimayu (60,000), Merca (56,000), Berbera (50,000). There has never been a census.

There are long-standing territorial disputes with Kenya and Ethiopia.

CONSTITUTION AND GOVERNMENT. The constitution of the Somali Republic was established under the Italian trusteeship during 1960. It was provisionally adopted on 1 July 1960 by the two regions by means of an Act of Union and approved by a national referendum in June 1961. The Somali armed forces took over supreme power in the country from the civilian Government on 21 Oct. 1969. The Parliament was dismissed, the constitution suspended and Supreme Court dissolved.

A Supreme Revolutionary Council was formed which took over the responsibility of Legislature, Executive and Judiciary. Fourteen civilian Secretaries of State responsible for Government Ministries were appointed by the Revolutionary Council. The Supreme Court was re-established with new Judges by the Revolutionary Council.

The Somali Democratic Republic is administratively divided into 11 regions, Migiurtinia, Hiran, Mudugh, Benadir, Upper Giuba, Lower Giuba, North Western Province (consisting of Hargeisa, Berbera and Borama districts) and North-Eastern Province (consisting of Burao, Erigavo and Las Anod).

The national language is Somali. Arabic, Italian and English are all official languages of the Government, and all 3 are extensively spoken.

President of the Supreme Revolutionary Council: Maj.-Gen. Mohammed Siyad Barre.

Vice-Presidents: Maj.-Gen. Hussein Kulmia Afrah, Gen. Ismail Ali Aboker (*Secretary-General for Party Affairs*) and Lieut.-Gen. Mohamed Ali Sameter (*Commander of the Army*).

The Central Committee of the Somali Socialist Revolutionary Party comprises the President, the Vice-President and the Head of the National Security Service.

National flag: Light blue with a white star in the centre.

DEFENCE

Army. The Army of 22,000 includes 6 tank battalions, 9 mechanized infantry battalions, 6 field artillery, 5 AA artillery and 2 commando battalions. Border guards number 500.

Navy. The Navy has 2 submarine chasers, 10 motor torpedo boats, 4 landing craft. Personnel (1978) 300.

Air Force. Formed with a nucleus of aircraft taken over from the former Italian Air Corps of Somalia, in 1960, the Air Corps was built up with Soviet aid. Current equipment includes 12 MiG-21 supersonic fighters, about 40 MiG-17 and MiG-15 jet-fighters and two-seat advanced trainers, a few Il-28 light jet bombers, and small transport, helicopter and training units. Personnel total about 1,000.

INTERNATIONAL RELATIONS

Membership. Somalia is a member of UN, OAU, the Arab League and is an ACP state of EEC.

ECONOMY

Planning. The 1974–78 development plan envisages expenditure of Som.Sh.3,863m., of which 40% is allocated to livestock, agriculture and mineral development, 11% to health, education and housing and 25% to transport and communications.

Budget. The budget for 1973 envisaged Som.Sh.418·6m. expenditure and Som.Sh.480·6m. revenue. Indirect taxation accounts for more than 80% of the revenue. The deficit is expected to be covered by foreign assistance.

Currency. The currency is the Somali shilling, divided into 100 cents (10·49 Somali shillings = £1 sterling). The money is issued in notes of 1, 5, 10, 20 and 100 shillings and coins of 1, 5, 10, 50 cents and 1 shilling. Currency in circulation (1974) Som.Sh.589·9m.

Banking. The Banco di Roma, Napoli, National & Grindlays Bank and Banco di Portsaid have all more than one branch each in the country. The Somali National Bank and the Somali Development Bank are both state-owned.

Weights and Measures. The metric system is used in 6 provinces and the Imperial system in 2; the latter is gradually disappearing.

NATURAL RESOURCES

Minerals. Deposits of iron ore in the south and gypsum in the north are known to exist. Beryl and columbite are also found in the north. None are commercially exploited. Several firms hold exploration and drilling licences for oil. Uranium is found in Juiba region.

Agriculture. Somalia is essentially a pastoral country, and about 80% of the inhabitants depend on livestock-rearing (cattle, sheep, goats and camels). In Southern Somalia, especially along the Shebeli and Giuba rivers, there are Somali and Italian plantations with a cultivated area of some 90,000 hectares. Estimated production, 1975 (in 1,000 tons): Sugar, 280; sugar from sugar-cane, 37; bananas, 140; maize, 168; cassava, 28. Fresh fruit and oil seeds are grown in increasing quantities.

Livestock (1976). 8m. goats; 7m. sheep; 2m. camels; 2·6m. cattle; 22,000 horses and mules.

INDUSTRY AND TRADE

Industry. In 1971, 195 industrial establishments employed 6,304 workers and produced a gross output of Som.Sh.219m., of which Som.Sh.166m. was in food manufacturing. Electricity production (1971) was 38·3m. kwh. A sugar refinery at Jowhar had 5,300 workers; a textile factory at Balad employed 750; and a meat canning plant at Kisimayu employed 500; there is also a fish processing plant at Las Korey, and a milk bottling plant at Mogadiscio.

Trade. In 1973 imports were Som.Sh.638m. and exports Som.Sh.340m. The chief exports are fresh fruit, livestock, hides and skins.

Total trade between the Somali Republic and UK (British Department of Trade returns, in £1,000 sterling):

	1972	*1973*	*1974*	*1975*	*1976*	*1977*
Imports to UK	70	126	1,704	239	766	257
Exports and re-exports from UK	1,833	2,050	2,918	3,829	5,628	14,198

COMMUNICATIONS

Roads. Somalia has no developed transport system. Internal freight and passenger transport is almost entirely by means of road haulage. There are 8,115 miles of roads (1,243 miles are paved). In 1973 there were 8,200 passenger cars and 5,200 commercial vehicles, including buses. The Chinese were providing aid (1976) to construct a 649-mile road from Beletwein to Buroa.

Aviation. There is a commercial national airline, Somali Airlines. Mogadiscio airport is used by Alitalia, Alyemda, Aeroflot and Kenya Airways. Through Nairobi to the south and Aden to north there are reasonable connexions for travelling to any part of the world.

Shipping. There are 2 deep-water harbours at Kisimayu and Berbera. A third is being built at Mogadiscio. Because of the shape of the country, coastal shipping is an important form of internal transport. The merchant fleet (1973) is 1,613,000 gross tons. In 1973, 900,000 tonnes of international seaborne goods were handled in the main ports.

Post and Broadcasting. There is a manual telephone system in several towns, but Mogadiscio has an automatic system; number of telephones (1971), about 4,740. The state radio stations transmit in Somali, Arabic, English and Italian from Mogadiscio, Hargeisa, Anhazic, Koti.

Cinemas. In 1970 there were 26 cinemas with a seating capacity of 23,000.

RELIGION, EDUCATION AND WELFARE

Religion. The population is almost entirely Sunni Moslems. There are very few Roman Catholics, mainly in the capital.

Education. The nomadic life of a large percentage of the population inhibits educational progress. In 1973–74 there were 69,000 primary pupils, 27,000 secondary pupils and 2,000 vocational students. In 1972 the Somali script was introduced and in 1975 a mass literacy campaign was launched. Teachers in training (1974) 900.

The National University of Somalia in Mogadiscio (founded 1959) had 2,809 students in 1975.

Health. In 1972 there were 153 doctors, 21 pharmacists, 280 medical assistants, 480 nurses, 193 midwives, 58 hospitals and 187 dispensaries. There was a total of 5,163 beds.

DIPLOMATIC REPRESENTATIVES

OF SOMALIA IN GREAT BRITAIN (60 Portland Place, London, W1N 3DG)

Ambassador: Ahmed Mohamed Adan.

OF GREAT BRITAIN IN SOMALIA (Waddada Xasan Geeddi Abtoow 7/8, Mogadiscio)

Ambassador: A. H. Brind, CMG.

OF SOMALIA IN USA (600 New Hampshire Ave., NW, Washington, D.C., 20037)

Ambassador: Dr Adbullahi Ahmed Addou.

OF USA IN SOMALIA (Corso Primo Luglio, Mogadiscio)

Ambassador: John L. Loughran.

OF SOMALIA TO THE UNITED NATIONS

Ambassador: Abdirizak Haji Hussen.

Books of Reference

The Agricultural Economy of Somalia. US Dept. of Agriculture, Washington, 1971
Drysdale, J., *The Somali Dispute.* London, 1964
Karp, M., *The Economics of Trusteeship in Somalia.* Boston Univ. Press, 1960
Lewis, I. M., *A Pastoral Democracy.* London, 1962.—*The Modern History of Somaliland.* London, 1965
Lytton, The Earl of, *The Stolen Desert.* London, 1966
Touval, S., *Somali Nationalism.* Harvard Univ. Press and OUP, 1963

REPUBLIC OF SOUTH AFRICA

Capital: Pretoria
Population: 26m. (1976)
GNP per capita: US$1,340 (1976)

Republiek van Suid-Afrika

HISTORY. The Union of South Africa was formed in 1909 and comprised the former self-governing British colonies of the Cape of Good Hope, Natal, the Transvaal and the Orange Free State. The Union remained a member of the British Commonwealth until it became a Republic on 31 May 1961.

AREA AND POPULATION. South Africa is bounded north by South West Africa, Botswana and Rhodesia, north-east by Mozambique and Swaziland, east by the Indian Ocean, south and west by the South Atlantic. Lesotho forms an enclave between the Orange Free State and Natal. The total area of the Republic is 455,694[1] sq. miles (1,177,854 sq. km), divided between the provinces as follows: Cape Province, 260,323 (674,016); Natal, 34,055 (90,767); Transvaal, 110,450 (283,918); Orange Free State, 49,866 (129,153).

On 25 Dec. 1947 the Union formally took possession of Prince Edward Island and, on 30 Dec., of Marion Island, about 1,200 miles south-east of Cape Town.

[1] Excludes Walvis Bay (434 sq. miles), which is an integral part of the Cape Province but is administered under Act No. 24 of 1922 by South West Africa, and Transkei (16,675 miles, 43,188 km).

The census taken in 1904 in each of the 4 colonies was the first simultaneous census taken in South Africa. In 1911 the first Union census was taken.

	All races			*Whites*		*Non-whites*	
	Total	*Whites*	*Non-Whites*	*Males*	*Females*	*Males*	*Females*
1904	5,174,827	1,117,234	4,057,593	635,317	481,917	2,046,370	2,011,223
1911	5,972,757	1,276,319	4,696,438	685,206	591,113	2,383,879	2,312,559
1921	6,927,403	1,521,343	5,406,060	783,006	738,337	2,753,188	2,652,872
1936	9,587,863	2,003,334	7,584,529	1,017,557	985,777	3,818,211	3,766,318
1946	11,415,925	2,372,044	9,043,881	1,194,201	1,177,843	4,610,862	4,433,019
1951	12,671,452	2,641,689	10,029,763	1,322,754	1,318,935	5,109,331	4,920,432
1960	15,994,181	3,080,159	12,914,022	1,534,923	1,545,236	6,504,317	6,409,705
1970[1]	21,402,470	3,726,540	17,675,930	1,856,180	1,870,360	8,689,920	8,986,010

[1] Census, May 1970.

Of the non-White population in 1970, 15,036,360 were Bantu, 618,140 Asiatic and 2,021,430 Coloured. The numerically leading Bantu nations are the Zulu (4·02m.), Xhosa (3·9m.), Tswana (1·7m.), Sepedi (North Sotho) (1·6m.), Seshoeshoe (South Sotho) (1·4m.).

In 1970 Afrikaans was the home language of 1,797,059 Whites, English of 1,119,826 Whites. Of the 15,036,360 Bantu about 50% can read and write, and 3·2m. (80%) of Bantu children of school-going age were attending school in 1972.

Vital statistics for calendar years:

	Whites					*Asians and Coloureds*		
	Births	*Deaths*	*Marriages*	*Immi-grants*	*Emigrants*	*Births*	*Deaths*	*Marriages*
1972	...	33,686	41,294	32,776	7,803	...	32,381	22,551
1973	90,501	33,757	40,602	24,016	6,290	97,150	13,160	23,876
1974	83,651	34,794	41,066	35,847	7,212	90,504	34,274	23,549
1975	80,026	35,035	41,333	50,464	10,255	87,835	32,449	24,632

The registration of Bantu essential data was introduced on a compulsory basis many years ago. However, despite serious efforts on the part of the registering authorities, the Bantu are still largely reluctant to have their essential data registered. Consequently no complete vital statistics are available for this population group.

Principal cities (excluding suburbs) according to the latest statistics (1970) are:

Town	*Whites*	*Africans*	*Coloureds*	*Asians*	*Total*
Alberton	26,802	2,567	793	160	30,322
Benoni	43,928	98,183	389	7,063	149,563
Bloemfontein	74,516	95,510	10,152	1	180,179
Boksburg	37,038	56,041	10,876	329	104,284
Brakpan	30,374	82,560	178	3	113,115
Cape Town	378,505	107,877	598,952	11,263	1,096,597
Carletonville	22,025	70,077	932	31	93,065
Durban	257,780	224,819	43,699	317,029	843,327
East London	56,809	51,244	13,249	1,994	123,294
Germiston	95,768	29,886	4,461	2,158	132,273
Johannesburg	501,061	809,595	82,639	39,348	1,432,643
Kempton Park	32,349	3,239	138	41	35,767
Kimberley	29,397	48,797	24,657	938	103,789
Krugersdorp	34,844	52,600	3,047	711	91,202
Pietermaritzburg	45,503	68,262	8,756	36,400	158,921
Port Elizabeth	149,569	201,574	112,154	5,280	468,577
Pretoria	304,618	234,695	11,343	11,047	561,703
Roodepoort Maraisburg	56,734	54,217	2,174	1,066	114,191
Springs	44,627	55,892	2,234	1,337	104,090
Vereeniging	34,568	122,052	1,951	1,982	169,553
Welkom	31,381	98,988	1,398	—	131,767

Bruwer, J. P., *Die Bantoe van Suid-Afrika.* Johannesburg, 1958
Millin, Sarah G., *The People of South Africa.* London, 1951
Patterson, Sheila, *Colour and Culture in South Africa.* London, 1953
Ritter, E. A., *Shaka Zulu.* London, 1955
Saron, G., and Hotz, L., *The Jews in South Africa.* London, 1955
Schapera, I., *The Bantu-speaking Tribes of South Africa.* Cape Town, 1953

CONSTITUTION AND GOVERNMENT. The Republic of South Africa Constitution Act 1961 established with effect from 31 May 1961, the Republic, consisting of the 4 provinces—the Cape of Good Hope, Natal, the Transvaal and the Orange Free State—which until then comprised the Union of South Africa.

On 5 Oct. 1960 a referendum was held among the white voters (1,800,426 on roll) to decide whether the Union should become a republic. Of the 1,634,240 votes polled, 850,458 were in favour of a republican constitution, 775,878 against it; 7,904 votes were invalid. The voting was as follows: Transvaal, 406,632 for, 325,041 against; Cape Province, 271,418 for, 269,784 against; Orange Free State, 110,171 for, 33,438 against; Natal, 42,299 for, 135,598 against; South West Africa, 19,938 for, 12,017 against.

The head of the Republic is the State President; he is elected for a 7-year term (at a meeting specially convened for the purpose) by an electoral college consisting of the members of the Senate and the House of Assembly and presided over by the Chief Justice or a judge of appeal designated by him.

Legislative power is vested in a Parliament consisting of the State President, a Senate and a House of Assembly. The State President has power to summon, prorogue and dissolve Parliament, either both Houses simultaneously or the House of Assembly alone. He may also dissolve the Senate at any time within 120 days of any dissolution of the House of Assembly or the expiry of the term of office of a provincial council.

A session of Parliament must be held once at least in every year.

The Senate consists of 54 members, 10 being nominated by the State President-in-Council (2 for each of the Provinces and 2 for South West Africa) and 44 being elected (15 in the Transvaal, 11 in the Cape Province, 8 in Natal, 8 in the Orange Free State, 2 in South West Africa). A senator must be a white South African citizen, at least 30 years of age, qualified as a voter in one of the provinces and resident for 5 years within the Republic. Senators hold their seats for 5 years, subject to a prior dissolution of the Senate.

At least one of the 2 senators nominated by the State President from each province should be thoroughly acquainted with the needs of the Coloured population. Similarly, one of the senators nominated from South West Africa should be selected mainly for his thorough acquaintance with the reasonable wants and wishes of the Coloured races of the Territory.

The House of Assembly consists of 164 members chosen in electoral divisions as follows: Cape of Good Hope, 55; Natal, 20; Transvaal, 75; Orange Free State, 14.

A member of the House of Assembly must be a white South African citizen, qualified as a voter and resident for 5 years within the Republic. Every House of Assembly continues for 5 years unless sooner dissolved.

Only the House of Assembly can originate money bills, but may not pass a bill for taxation or appropriation unless it has been recommended by the State President during the session. Restrictions are placed on the amendment of money bills by the Senate. Provision is made respecting disagreements between the Houses and the State President's assent to bills.

A member of one House cannot be elected to the other, but a minister and a deputy minister may sit and speak, but not vote, in the House of which he is not a member. To hold an office of profit under the State (with certain exceptions) is a disqualification for membership of either House, as are also insolvency, crime and insanity. Pretoria is the seat of government, and Cape Town is the seat of legislature.

The state of the parties in the House of Assembly after the general election of Nov. 1977 was as follows: National Party, 134; Progressive Federal Party, 17; New Republic Party, 10; South African Party, 3.

In the Senate the National Party had 42 members; the United Party, 10, and the Progressive Reformed Party, 2.

The Executive Council (National Party) was, on 25 Jan. 1978, composed as follows:

State President: Dr Nicolaas Diederichs (elected 21 Feb., installed 10 April, 1975).

Prime Minister: B. J. Vorster.

Transport: S. L. Muller. *Finance:* Senator O. P. F. Horwood. *Agriculture:* H. Schoeman. *Defence:* P. W. Botha. *Indian Affairs, Tourism and Community Development:* S. J. M. Steyn. *Foreign Affairs:* R. F. Botha. *Posts and Telecommunications, Social Welfare and Pensions:* F. W. de Klerk. *Plural Relations Administration and Development and Information:* Dr C. P. Mulder. *Justice, Police and Prisons:* J. T. Kruger. *National Education, Sport and Recreation:* Dr P. G. J. Koornhof. *Economic Affairs:* J. C. Heunis. *Water Affairs and Forestry:* A. J. Raubenheimer. *Immigration, Public Works and the Interior:* A. L. Schlebusch. *Health, Planning, Environment and Statistics:* Dr S. W. van der Merwe. *Coloured, Rehoboth and Nama Relations:* Hennie H. Smit. *Labour and Mines:* S. P. Botha. *Education and Training:* W. A. Cruywagen.

The following are Deputy Ministers, who do not have Cabinet rank and are not members of the Executive Council: *Agriculture:* J. J. Malan. *Plural Relations Administration and Education:* Dr Andries Treurnicht. *Bantu Development:* Dr F. Hartzenberg. *Social Welfare, Pensions, Planning and Environment and Statistics:* T. N. H. Janson. *Information and Interior:* Louis le Grange.

The Prime Minister receives an annual salary of R24,000; a member of the Cabinet an annual salary of R16,000 and a reimbursive allowance of R3,000; and a Deputy Minister an annual allowance of R12,000 and a reimbursive allowance of R4,500.

The English and Afrikaans languages are both official, subject to amendments carried by a two-thirds majority in joint session of both Houses of Parliament.

National flag: Orange, white, blue (horizontal), with the flags of the Orange Free State, the South African Republic and the Union Jack superimposed on the white stripe.

National anthem: The Call of South Africa/Die Stem van Suid-Afrika (words by C. J. Langenhoven, 1918; tune by M. L. de Villiers, 1921).

Provincial Administration. In each province there is an Administrator appointed by the State President-in-Council for 5 years, and a provincial council elected for 5 years, each council electing an executive committee of 4 (either members or not of the council), the Administrator acting as chairman. Members of the provincial council are elected on the same system as members of Parliament. The provincial committees and councils have authority to deal with local matters, of which provincial finance, education (primary and secondary, other than higher education and technical education), hospitals, roads and bridges, townships, horse and other racing, and game and fish preservation are the most important. In 1953 the administration and control of Bantu education was transferred from the provincial councils to the central government. All ordinances passed by a provincial council are subject to the veto of the State President-in-Council.

Bantu Administration. In 1951 the Bantu Authorities Act was enacted to provide a system of Bantu tribal, regional and territorial authorities. These were given limited administrative, executive and judicial functions and limited legislative powers. In 1959 the main ethnic groups received legislative recognition by the passing of the Promotion of Bantu Self-Government Act, which provided *inter alia* for the various ethnic groups to develop into self-governing national units, each with a Commissioner-General representing the Government of the Republic.

As the territorial authorities became experienced an executive body in the form of a government service was set up for each authority to increase their administrative power.

As the Act envisages eventual political autonomy for each of the various national units and as representation in the highest White governing bodies is regarded as a retarding factor, the representation of Bantu by Whites in Parliament and the Cape Provincial Administration was abolished with effect from 30 June 1960.

In 1968 the Ciskei (whose people are also Xhosa-speaking) and the Tswana Territorial Authorities were established, followed by the Lebowa (North Sotho), Machangana (Tsonga-Shangaan), Venda and South Sotho Territorial Authorities in 1969 and the Zulu Territorial Authority in 1970.

During 1971 these authorities, with the exception of the Zulu, were granted increased powers in terms of the Bantu Homelands Constitution Act 1971. In terms of the provisions of part I of this Act, 6 of the existing 7 territorial authorities in the Republic of South Africa (the Transkei became a self-governing territory in 1963 by virtue of the provisions of the Transkei Constitution Act of 1963) have been converted to Legislative Assemblies with extended legislative and administrative powers.

Part II of the Bantu Homelands Constitution Act makes provision for the areas of these legislative assemblies to be proclaimed self-governing territories with *inter alia* the power to repeal or amend, with minor exceptions, acts of the Republican Parliament. Executive power is vested in an Executive Council. These Councils, each headed by a Chief Councillor, consist of 6 members, except in the case of the South Sotho, where there are only 4. Each of these Councillors is responsible for the administration of a Department. A civil service has been established in each instance, staffed by citizens of the respective homelands. White officials will serve the homeland governments on secondment, until trained Bantu citizens are able to take over all duties.

In 1961 the ex-chief of the Umvoti Mission reserve, Albert Luthuli, was awarded the Nobel Peace Prize for his advocacy of peaceful means in the achievement of Bantu aspirations.

The Coloured Peoples Representative Council consists of 40 elected and 20 nominated members. Elections took place in Sept. 1969 and Tom Swartz, leader of the Federal Party, was appointed Chairman of the Council by the State President. On his death in 1975 he was succeeded by Dr W. Bergins. The Council has legislative powers and its Executive, consisting of 5 members, is responsible on behalf of the Coloured community for the management of finance, education, community welfare and pensions, local government and rural areas and settlements. The

Administration of Coloured Affairs has approximately 20,000 administrative and professional posts for Coloureds.

The South African Indian Council is a statutory body consisting of 25 nominated representatives of Indian communities in the Transvaal, Natal and the Cape Province. It advises the Government on the economic, social, cultural and political interests of the Indian population. The S.A. Indian Council Amendment Bill of 1972 enlarges the Council to 30 representatives, the additional 5 to be elected. Voters rolls are being compiled. The number of elected representatives can be amended in the future.

In 1971 the Zulus established a Legislative Assembly. Their seat of government is Ulundi.

The Transkei, territory of the Xhosa nation, became independent on 25 Oct. 1976 (*see* p. 1091) and Bophuthatswana on 6 Dec. 1977 (*see* p. 1089).

Rhoodie, N. J., and Venter, H. J., *Apartheid: A Socio-Historical Exposition of the Origin and Development of the Apartheid Idea*. Cape Town, 1959

DEFENCE. The South African Defence Force comprises a Permanent Force, a Citizen Force and a Commando organization. The Permanent Force consists of professional soldiers, airmen and seamen who are responsible for the administration and training of the whole Defence Force in peace-time, but who are gradually absorbed into the Citizen Force in time of war. The Permanent Force and the Citizen Force consist of Army, Air Force and Naval components; the Commando organization is an army and air organization.

Every citizen between the ages of 18 and 65 is liable to undergo training and to render personal service in time of war. Those between the ages of 16 and 25 are liable to undergo a compulsory course of peace training. Peace-time training in Commando organizations extends over a period of 16 years' intermittent training. Training in the Citizen Force takes the form of 2 years of continuous training, followed by 9 years during which training takes place at regular intervals.

Aliens have become liable for military service after 5 years' residence by Act of Parliament, 1967.

The S.A. Defence Force is administered by the Chief of the Defence Force, his advisers being the Chief of the Army, Chief of the Air Force and Chief of the Chief of Staff Operations, Chief of Staff Personnel, the Chief of Staff Management Services and the Surgeon-General.

Army. South Africa is divided into 9 territorial Commands: Western Province, Eastern Province, Natal, Orange Free State, North Western, Northern Transvaal, Witwatersrand, South West Africa and Southern Cape Commands. Within the various Commands are training units, of which members of the Permanent Force form the permanent staff. Courses of various types are held also at the S.A. Military College. Equipment includes 141 Centurion and 20 Comet tanks. Total strength, 41,000 and 138,000 Citizen Force.

Navy. The South African Navy has its headquarters at Simonstown where HM Dockyard was transferred to the Republic of South Africa on 2 April 1957. The Navy includes 3 French-built diesel-powered patrol submarines, 3 British-built anti-submarine frigates, 1 destroyer (*Jan van Riebeck*, *ex*-HMS *Wessex*), 10 coastal minesweepers, 5 seaward defence boats (1 used for surveying), 1 modern British-built survey ship (specifically designed), 6 fast missile armed patrol vessels of the 'Reshef' class (3 built in Durban and 3 in Israel), 1 fleet replenishment ship, 1 boom defence vessel, 1 small training vessel, 1 torpedo recovery vessel, 4 rescue launches and 2 tugs. Naval personnel in 1978 totalled 500 officers and 4,200 ratings, including 1,400 national service men.

New construction (programme amended) includes 2 or 4 small frigates similar to the French 'A 69' class armed with Exocet missiles, to be built in Lorient; 2 ocean-going diesel-electric patrol submarines of the 'Agosta' class to be built in France.

A newly constructed submarine base incorporating an operations centre alongside a Syncholift marine elevator capable of docking all South African warships except the large tanker, was opened at Simonstown in July 1972, known as SAS *Drommedaris*. A new maritime headquarters was opened at Silvermine in March 1973.

Air Force. Units of the South African Air Force are organized in Strike, Transport, Maritime, Light Aircraft, Training and Air Logistics Commands. There is 1 light bomber squadron with 6 Canberra B.12 and 3 Canberra T.4; 1 light bomber squadron with 9 Buccaneer Mk.50; 1 maritime reconnaissance squadron equipped with 7 Shackletons; 1 coastal patrol squadron with Piaggio P.166S; 2 fighter-bomber squadrons with 32 Mirage F1.AZ ground attack aircraft; 1 general-purpose fighter squadron with Mirage IIIEZ fighter-bombers, Mirage IIICZ interceptors and 20 Mirage IIIRZ reconnaissance fighters; and 1 squadron with Mirage F1.CZ interceptors. Transport squadrons have 9 Transall C-160s, 7 C-130B/E Hercules, 23 C-47s, 4 C-54s, 1 Viscount, 4 twin-jet HS.125s and 7 twin-turboprop Merlin IVA light transports. Four helicopter squadrons have 40 Alouette IIIs, 11 Wasps, 20 Pumas and 15 Super Frelons. T-6Gs are used for primary training, followed by advanced training on Impalas, weapons training on Impalas and Sabre 6s, and multi-engine/crew training on C-47s. Built under licence in the Republic of South Africa, about 150 two-seat Impala Mk. 1s are being followed by an initial batch of 50 single-seat Impala Mk. 2s, based on the Aermacchi MB.326M and 326K respectively. Various types of light aircraft are also in service.

The Citizen Force has 4 squadrons of Impalas and 2 of Harvards for counter-insurgency duties and 1 squadron of AM.3C liaison aircraft. CF personnel have additional functions in regular SAAF squadrons, notably those equipped with C-47 transports and P.166 light transport/coastal patrol aircraft. Total strength is about 5,800 regular officers and men and 3,000 Citizen Force in training at one time.

INTERNATIONAL RELATIONS

Membership. The Republic of South Africa is a member of UN.

ECONOMY

Budget. A new basis of subsidy has, with effect from the 1971–72 financial year, been brought into operation by the Government following the investigation of the commission of enquiry into the financial relations between the central government and the provinces. The formula on which this subsidy is based is mainly derived from the calculation of: (1) The needs of the various provinces in respect of the services which they have to provide in the fields of education, health, roads and miscellaneous services; (2) the capacity to pay of the various provinces in respect of the different sources from which their 'own' revenue has to be derived; (3) the deficit which arises when the available revenue of each province, as reflected in its capacity to pay, is subtracted from its expenditure, as adjusted in accordance with its needs.

Ordinary revenue and expenditure of the central government (excluding Railways and Harbours Administration) in R1m.:

	1972–73	*1973–74*	*1974–75*	*1975–76*	*1976–77*
Revenue	2,916·4	3,800·2	4,474·7	5,046·0	6,051·8
Expenditure[1]	2,867·7	3,466·7	5,622·8	6,787·8	7,932·9

[1] Excluding subsidies.

Details of ordinary revenue (1976) and expenditure (1975) of the central government for years ended 31 March (in R1,000):

Revenue	*1976*
Customs	318,500
Excise	604,065
Income tax	3,301,500
Licences, stamp duties and fees	91,000
Interest	211,109

Expenditure	*1975*
Bantu administration and development	320,161
Bantu education	59,177
Foreign affairs	13,871
Defence	699,049
Public debt	304,675
Provincial administration	1,109,069
Education	172,413
Social welfare and pensions	267,212
Public health	98,142
Police	156,692
Indian affairs	52,868
Coloured relations—Rehoboth affairs	144,252

Public debt on 31 Dec. 1976, R12,106m., of which R1,325m. was foreign debt; internal debt, R10,781m.

Currency. The Decimal Coinage Act, 1959, introduced the decimal system, the units being the *rand* (abbreviated as R) and the *cent* (abbreviated as c). The rand/cent coinage system came into operation on 14 Feb. 1961. The decimal coins are: *Gold coins.* 2 rand; 1 rand. *Silver coins.* 50 cents; 20 cents; 10 cents; 5 cents. *Bronze coins.* 2 cents; 1 cent.

Banking. Statistics of the South African Reserve Bank,[1] Dec. 1976, are as follows (in R1m.):

Liabilities		*Assets*	
Notes in circulation	1,179	Gold coin and bullion	374
Deposits:		Foreign assets	360
Bankers	279	Domestic discounts and advances	720
Government and others	368	Government Securities	458

[1] In Dec. 1920, under the South African Currency and Banking Act, 1920, a Central Reserve Bank was established at Pretoria. It commenced operations in June 1921, and began to issue notes in April 1922. The bank has branches in Pretoria (Head Office), Johannesburg, Cape Town, Durban, Port Elizabeth, East London, Bloemfontein, Pietermaritzburg and Windhoek.

Ratio of legal reserve to liabilities to the public was 22% on 30 April 1977.

The number of depositors in the post office savings bank at the end of March 1975 was 1,885,000, and the amount standing to their credit R162,258,000.

Weights and Measures. Prior to 1969 the imperial system of weights and measures was generally used in the country. However, during 1969 the Weights and Measures Act was amended to provide for the gradual change-over to the metric system of weights and measures.

ENERGY AND NATURAL RESOURCES

Electricity. The total capacity of the power plants controlled by the Electricity Supply Commission was 15,344 mw at the end of 1976; production, 63,356 Gwh.; average price per kw. sold, 1·036 cents. Total generation by all power stations, 70,287 Gwh. Power sold in 1976 was 63,356m. kwh.

Water. The government activities in respect of the control and utilization of water are governed by the Water Act, 1956 (as amended), which is administered by the Department of Water Affairs. The Department's expenditure for 1971–72 is: Revenue account, R17m.; Local account, R101·5m.; South West Africa account, R13·2m.

The Orange River Project, launched in 1966, will take about 30 years to complete. It is to embrace 3 major dams on the Orange River, 9 smaller dams or weirs, a 51½ mile tunnel, 20 hydro-electric power stations and a system of canals. The first of the major dams—the Hendrik Verwoerd Dam—was built 5 miles upstream from Norvalspont. A Water Research Commission was established in 1971 to co-ordinate and promote research; it is responsible for hydrological research, major water resource development, water pollution control.

Minerals. Value of the mineral production sales (in R1,000):

	1973	*1974*	*1975*	*1976*
Antimony	12,455	19,428	22,275	22,329
Asbestos	46,963	54,071	91,542	117,647
Chrome ore	16,942	19,694	40,834	60,841
Coal	152,106	199,852	316,100	517,776
Copper	171,176	204,859	146,308	171,794
Diamonds	162,367	131,519	174,221	215,073
Fluorspar	4,681	5,144	24,812	26,565
Gold	2,559,810	2,403,211	2,560,395	2,380,170
Granite	10,773	10,691	10,179	11,184
Iron ore	35,329	35,186	42,114	60,092
Iron pyrites	3,887	3,836	5,069	9,136
Lime and limestone	24,926	28,906	38,993	50,279
Manganese	52,990	72,752	102,054	131,309
Nickel	30,677	47,398	61,623	80,620

	1973	*1974*	*1975*	*1976*
Phosphate	14,343	17,265	24,812	26,565
Silver	7,331	9,309	10,012	10,618
Tin	7,264	11,905	12,714	14,579
Vanadium	23,848	27,142	38,001	49,742
Vermiculite	3,524	3,922	5,819	6,246
Zinc	2,925	8,236	14,886	22,344

Mineral production, 1976: Gold, 713,390 kg; silver, 87,736 kg; vanadium (pentoxide content), 17,628 tonnes; iron ore, 15,663,000 tonnes; copper, 196,880 tonnes; manganese ore, 5,503,000 tonnes; chromite, 2·4m. tonnes; coal, 76·45m. tonnes; asbestos, 369,840 tonnes; diamonds, 7,022,770 carats; phosphates (1975), 11,626,000 tonnes; nickel, 22,371 tonnes; vermiculite, 222,077 tonnes; zinc concentrates, 149,922 tonnes.

In 1976 the number of persons engaged in mining totalled 657,512. Of these, 401,907 were engaged in goldmining. Total salaries R1,178,135,068.

The Mineral Resources of the Union of South Africa, With a Summary of the Mineral Resources South West Africa. Geological Survey, Department of Mines. 5th ed. Pretoria, 1976

Minerals. A Quarterly Report of Production and Sales. Department of Mines. Pretoria, from 1936

Agriculture. The number of farms in white areas in 1973 was 81,935 with an area of 87·9m. hectares.

South African farmers produced mainly the following crops for the years indicated:

Product (1,000 tonnes)	*1972–73*	*1973–74*	*1974–75*	*1975–76*
Maize	4,160	11,105	9,131	7,395[1]
Sorghum	222	682	401	290[1]
Wheat	1,746	1,871	1,596	1,792
Barley	33	32	50	51
Oats	105	91	103	99
Rye	7	6	5	4
Groundnuts	138	373	179	106[1]
Sunflower seed	233	253	209	253[1]
Sugar-cane	16,805	15,454	16,895	16,159[1]
Deciduous fruit	1,599	1,550[1]	1,729[1]	1,762[1]
Citrus fruit	681	758	656	694[1]
Subtropical fruit	306	355	339	343[1]
Vegetables	1,726	1,855	1,889	1,968[1]

[1] Preliminary.

Livestock, in 1,000 (1975–76): 12,477 cattle; 28,929 sheep; 4,355 goats; 1,206 pigs. In 1975, 1·84m. cattle and 6,336,000 sheep and goats were slaughtered.

The 1975–76 production of butter was 26,883 tonnes; condensed milk, 53,740 tonnes; milk powder, 28,459 tonnes; cheese, 29,589 tonnes.

Wool produced in 1975–76 was 107,300 tonnes.

Cotton-growing is now undertaken by many farmers, the plant being found a better drought resistant than either tobacco or maize.

During 1974–75, 589·6m. litres of wine were produced, of which 292·7m. litres were distilled.

In 1975–76 the gross value of agricultural production was R2,767m. (field crops, R1,166·9m.; livestock products, R1,113·1m.; horticultural products, R487·1m.).

Forestry. The forested surface occupies about 1·25m. hectares, of which 0·25m. hectares are indigenous trees and 1m. hectares exotic trees (pine, gum, wattle). The annual output of forest products is about 85m. cu. metres. Production now meets about 90% of domestic need. Capital invested is about R600m., and the number of employees about 100,000.

Fisheries. The catch of offshore whaling in 1975 was 1,817 whales. Whaling is conducted off the Natal coast and from Donkergate whaling station, Saldanha Bay, but on a small scale owing to the danger of whales becoming extinct.

In 1975, 1·17m. tonnes of fish were landed, including 617,595 tonnes of pilchards and 447,883 of anchovies.

INDUSTRY AND TRADE

Industry. Net value of sales of the principal groups of industries (in R1,000) in 1976: Food, beverages and tobacco, 4,028,850; motor vehicles, 1,213,676; basic metals, 2,134,541; chemicals and products, 3,457,986; non-electrical machinery, 1,227,213; non-metallic mineral products, 677,713; electrical machinery, 1,119,722; clothing, 599,211; paper and products, 692,398; textiles, 1,086,866; total net value including other groups, 20,602,408. Manufacturing industry contributed 24·8% to gross domestic product in 1976.

Industrial employment (except mining) in 1976: Manufacturing employed 1,269,700 workers (earning R3,500,452,000); construction, 446,900 (R1,004m.); transport, communications, 324,800 (R1,175,644,000); motor trade, 110,800 (R83,632,000); wholesale trade, 207,200 (R626m.); retail trade, 359,800 (R655,675,000).

Of the above figures the following proportion of jobs and salaries were held by white South Africans: Total jobs in manufacturing, 275,500 (earning R1,887,493,000); construction, 60,500 (R401,651,000); transport, communications, 156,170 (R948,188,000); motor trade, 43,900 (R59,476,000); wholesale trade, 82,800 (R450,524,000); retail trade, 134,200 (R411,309,000).

In 1976 in private manufacturing 159,800 workers were employed in the food industry (earning R336,583,000); textiles employed 112,300 (R204m.); clothing, 98,300 (R147,302,000); transport equipment, 92,400 (R318,651,000); non-metallic mineral products, 85,200 (R180,771,000).

Motor trade excludes motor-cycle dealers. Communications comprises the Department of Posts and Telegraphs. Transport comprises South African Railways and Harbours.

Domestic Trade. The distributive trade in South Africa has developed to the stage where it ranks second only to manufacturing industry as the principal contributor to the gross domestic product of the country. In 1974 the contribution by the group of undertakings classified as wholesale, retail, catering and accommodation establishments to the gross domestic product was 13·5%.

Retail distributors include general dealers, departmental and chain stores, bazaars, supermarkets, discount houses, speciality shops and consumer co-operatives.

Trade Unions. At the end of 1970 there were 182 trade unions with a total membership of 405,032 Whites and 182,210 Coloureds and Asians.

The total revenue of trade unions in 1964–65 was R3,857,545; their total assets were valued at R10,624,661.

Although there is no legal provision for Bantu trade unions, there is no legal prohibition of trade unions by Bantu workers. However, the vast majority of Bantu workers have not shown much interest in trade unionism.

The Wage Board inquires into the wage levels of numerous categories of workers, particularly the Bantu, and it fixes minimum levels of pay and other conditions of employment. Special machinery exists under the Bantu Labour (Settlement of Disputes) Act to safeguard the interests of Bantu workers. This Act provides for the establishment by Bantu workers of local labour committees which are linked with regional committees.

The latter committees are in contact with the Central Bantu Labour Board, which, together with Bantu Labour Officers, attends the meetings of the Wage Board and the other industrial bodies. Bantu Labour Officers also maintain close contact with employers of Bantu.

Doxey, G. V., *The Industrial Colour Bar in South Africa.* OUP, 1961
Horrell, M., *South African Trade Unionism.* Johannesburg, 1961
Walker, I. D., and Weinbren, B. *2000 Casualties: A History of the Trade Unions and the Labour Movement in the Union of South Africa.* Johannesburg, 1961

Commerce. South Africa, Botswana, Lesotho, Swaziland and Transkei are members of a customs union and the foreign trade statistics shown below represent the combined imports and exports of these countries. The total value of the imports and exports, exclusive of specie and gold bullion, was as follows (in R1m.):

Imports		*Exports*	
1972	2,812·6	1972	2,040·8
1973	3,275·4	1973	2,421·3
1974	4,908·8	1974	3,350·1
1975	5,561·8	1975	3,989·6
1976	5,888·6	1976	4,471·7

Agricultural products to the value of R1,183·8m. were exported in 1975. Processed products accounted for roughly half of this figure. Maize, sugar, wool and fruit provide the bulk of agricultural exports, while rice, tea, raw rubber, coffee and cocoa are the major agricultural imports. Total agricultural imports for 1975 were R103·6m.

The principal commodity groups of imports and exports (in R1m.) in 1976 were:

Imports		*Exports*	
Food, beverages and tobacco	247·5	Manufactured goods	1,331·9
Chemicals	593·2	Machinery and transport equipment	213·9
Manufactured goods	896·3	Inedible raw materials (excl. fuels)	1,073·5
Metals and metal manufactures	347·5	Food, beverages and tobacco	1,003·5
Machinery and transport equipment	3,217·1		

The geographical origin of South Africa's imports and the direction of its export trade were mainly as follows (in R1m.) in 1976:

Imports				*Exports*			
Africa	309·8	America	1,400·8	Africa	453·1	America	700·2
Europe	3,206·1	USA	1,226·8	Europe	2,495·1	USA	456·5
UK	1,030·7	Asia	836·3	UK	997·0	Asia	764·0
Fed. Rep. of Germany	1,058·7	Japan	600·4	Fed. Rep. of Germany	472·8	Japan	514·8

Trade with UK (British Department of Trade returns, in £1,000 sterling):

	1973	*1974*	*1975*	*1976*	*1977*
Imports to UK	399,514	465,194	540,289	612,992	879,724
Exports and re-exports from UK	374,400	526,291	684,769	645,363	581,063

COMMUNICATIONS

Roads. The railway administration operated road motor services over 52,645 route km in 1976; during that year 19·1m. passengers were conveyed and 3·7m. tons of goods were carried.

There were at 31 March 1975, 185,900 km of roads, of which some 1,887 km of national roads and 39,184 km of provincial roads were tarred.

Motor vehicles in operation in 1976 included 2,151,904 passenger cars, 761,253 commercial vehicles, 73,322 buses and 131,064 motor cycles. Motor vehicles licensed in 1976, 3,356,889.

Railways. Railway history in South Africa begins in 1860 with the line Durban–Point. With the formation of the Union in 1910, the state-owned lines in the 4 provinces (12,194 km) were amalgamated into one state undertaking, which also took over the control of the harbours—the South African Railways and Harbours Administration.

Government-owned lines operated by the administration at 31 Dec. 1976 totalled 22,430 km, of which 4,800 km were electrified. Two important lines were completed during 1976: a privately owned railway linking Sishen with the port of Saldanha Bay (860 km) for the export of iron ore; and a 509 km link comprising new construction and upgraded lines between Broodsnyersplaas and the new deep-water port of Richards Bay, for the export of coal. Passenger journeys, 1976, 643m.; goods traffic, 1976, 119·9m. tonnes.

Aviation. Civil aviation in South Africa is controlled by the Department of Transport, which administers the following state-owned airports: Jan Smuts Airport, Johannesburg; D. F. Malan Airport, Cape Town; Louis Botha Airport, Durban; J. B. M. Hertzog Airport, Bloemfontein; J. G. Strydom Airport, Windhoek; Ben Schoeman Airport, East London; H. F. Verwoerd Airport, Port Elizabeth; B. J. Vorster Airport, Kimberley; J. G. H. van der Wath Airport,

Keetmanshoop; Upington Airport. At 13 other airports the Department provides air navigation services.

South African Airways, as the national air carrier, operate scheduled international air services within Africa and to Europe, South America, the USA and Australia. Twenty-three other lines also operate scheduled international air services; they include British Airways, PANAM, KLM, SAS, TAP, Swissair, Olympic Air, El-Al, Alitalia, SABENA, Lufthansa, DETA, Air Rhodesia, Iberia, DJA, UTA, LUXAIR, Lesotho Airways, Swazi Air, Air Malawi, Air Madagascar. Luxavia operate international non-scheduled flights.

South African Airways, Pacair, Avne, Margate Air Services, Protea Airways, National Airways, The John Andrew Co., Avex Air, Commercial Air Services Ltd, Suidwes Lugdiens and Namakwaland-lugdiens operate scheduled air services within South Africa.

During 1976 South African Airways carried 2,936,789 passengers and 53,876 kg of freight and mail.

Shipping. The 4 main ports are Durban, Cape Town, Port Elizabeth and East London. Smaller ports are Mossel Bay, Port Nolloth, Saldanha, Richards Bay, Walvis Bay and Lüderitz. During 1975 these ports handled 36m. tonnes of cargo, of which 11,841,000 tonnes were landed and 24,064,000 loaded. Durban handled 16,454,000 tonnes.

Post and Broadcasting. On 31 March 1975 there were in South Africa 2,937 post and telegraph offices. In 1975 post office income amounted to R454·8m.

In 1972 the international telex switchboard enabled telex subscribers in South Africa to communicate with telex subscribers in 123 countries. Some 7,071 teleprinters were in use in 1972. There were 231 automatic telephone exchanges, 27,559 trunk (long-distance) lines in operation in 1973. There were 1,745,540 telephone stations and 20,767 public call offices and (1976) 2,072,131 telephones.

The South African Broadcasting Corporation had, in Sept. 1974, 2·41m. listeners' licences.

On 5 Jan. 1976 the South African Television Service began official transmissions. A Bantu programme is planned for 1980.

Cinemas (1971). There were 686 with 498,000 seats.

Newspapers (1974). There are 7 Afrikaans and 15 English daily newspapers with a combined circulation of about 1,369,881, of which 1,109,784 are English.

JUSTICE, RELIGION, EDUCATION AND WELFARE

Justice. The common law of the Republic is the Roman–Dutch law—that is, the uncodified law of Holland as it was at the date of the cession of the Cape in 1806. The law of England as such is not recognized as authoritative, though by statute the principles of English law relating to evidence and to mercantile matters, *e.g.*, companies, patents, trademarks, insolvency and the like, have been introduced. In shipping and insurance, English law is followed in the Cape Province, and it has also largely influenced civil and criminal procedure throughout the Republic. In all other matters, family relations, property, succession, contract, etc., Roman–Dutch law rules, English decisions being valued only so far as they agree therewith.

The Supreme Court of South Africa is constituted as follows: (i) The Appellate Division, consisting of the Chief Justice and as many Judges of Appeal as the State President may stipulate, is the highest court and its decisions are binding on all courts. It has no original jurisdiction, but is purely a Court of Appeal. (ii) The Provincial Divisions: In each province there is a provincial division of the Supreme Court, while in the Cape there are three such divisions possessing both original and appellate jurisdiction. (iii) The Local Divisions: There is a local division each in the Transvaal and Natal exercising the same original jurisdiction within limited areas as the provincial divisions.

The judges hold office till they attain the age of 70 years. No judge can be removed from office except by the State President upon an address from both Houses of Parliament on the ground of misbehaviour or incapacity. The circuit system is fully developed.

The Bantu appeal courts and 3 Bantu divorce courts have jurisdiction to some extent concurrent with and in certain respects exclusive of that of the Supreme Court in cases in which the parties are Bantu.

Each province is further divided into districts with a magistrate's court having a prescribed civil and criminal jurisdiction. From this court there is an appeal to the provincial divisions of the Supreme Court, and thence to the appellate division. Magistrates' convictions carrying sentences above a prescribed limit are subject to automatic review by a judge. In addition, several regional divisions consisting of a number of districts have been constituted. Convictions of such courts are not subject to automatic review by a judge.

Courts of Bantu affairs commissioners have been constituted in defined areas to hear all civil cases and matters between Bantu and Bantu only. An appeal lies to the Bantu appeal court, whose decision is final, unless the court consents to an appeal to the appellate division of the Supreme Court on a point stated by the court itself. Bantu affairs commissioners have concurrent criminal jurisdiction with magistrates' courts in respect of certain offences committed by Bantu, while a limited civil and criminal jurisdiction is conferred upon the Bantu chief or headman over his own tribe.

Police. In 1971 the police force consisted of 1,703 White officers and 6,674 n.c.o.s, 7 Coloured officers and 250 n.c.o.s, 11 Bantu officers and 2,036 n.c.o.s, 3 Indian officers and 139 n.c.o.s. There were 8,397 White, 1,150 Coloured, 590 Indian and 11,148 Bantu constables.

Religion. A sample tabulation of the 1970 census results as regards religious denominations shows the following: *Whites:* Nederduits Gereformeerde Kerk, 1,487,080; Anglicans, 399,950; Methodists, 357,410; Roman Catholics, 304,840; Nederduits Hervormde Kerk, 224,400; Jews, 117,990; Presbyterians, 117,250; Gereformeerde Kerk, 113,620; Apostolics, 110,960; Congregationalists, 19,640; other Christians, 321,030; others, 111,200. *Non-Whites:* Bantu Churches, 2,761,120; Methodists, 1,794,430; Roman Catholics, 1,539,430; Afrikaans Churches, 1,504,610; Anglicans, 1,276,850; Lutherans, 843,500; Hindus, 423,180; Presbyterians, 337,210; Congregationalists, 330,150; Mohammedans, 254,780; Apostolics, 191,330; other Christians, 1,721,130; others and unspecified, 4,698,080.

Education. *Higher Education.* There are 16 universities in the Republic: (1) The University of Cape Town. (2) The University of Natal, Durban and Pietermaritzburg. (3) The University of the Orange Free State at Bloemfontein. (4) Potchefstroom University for Christian Higher Education, Potchefstroom. (5) The University of Pretoria. (6) Rhodes University, Grahamstown, C.P. (7) The University of Stellenbosch. (8) The University of the Witwatersrand, Johannesburg. (9) The University of South Africa, with its seat in Pretoria, which conducts a Division of External Studies by means of correspondence and vacation courses; it is also an examining body. (10) The University of Port Elizabeth. (11) Rand Afrikaans University, Johannesburg.

The University of Fort Hare (12), the University of the North (13) near Pietersburg and the University of Zululand (14) near Empangeni, Natal, are operated by the Department of Bantu Education and provide education at university level for the Bantu, the University of the Western Cape (15), Bellville (Cape), offers university facilities to the Coloured population and is administered by the Department of Coloured Affairs; while the University for Indians (16), the University of Durban-Westville, at Durban falls under the Department of Indian Affairs.

The following statistics refer to 1970:

		Lecturers		
University	*Professors*	*Full-time*	*Part-time*	*Students*
Cape Town	79	339	490	7,968
Fort Hare	29	56	—	613
Natal	84	396	166	6,258
North	22	72	—	810
Orange Free State	46	162	45	4,222
Port Elizabeth	34	96	24	1,142
Potchefstroom	77	182	53	4,212

University	Professors	Lecturers Full-time	Lecturers Part-time	Students
Pretoria	160	453	308	12,464
Rand Afrikaans	50	91	13	1,240
Rhodes	34	152	133	1,803
Salisbury Island (Durban)	16	145	—	1,654
South Africa	81	31	59	21,886
Stellenbosch	109	349	698	7,778
West Cape	11	56	23	936
Witwatersrand	116	454	174	9,368
Zululand	18	64	—	574

In 1975 there were 10 White universities with 73,463 students and 5 non-White with 8,561 students; Arts courses have the highest enrolment (22,885) followed by Commerce and Administration for White students, Medicine for non-White.

Technical and Vocational Education. Technical, vocational and special education for persons other than those for whom specific provisions is made (*e.g.*, Bantu): The Department of National Education is responsible for the maintenance, management and control of or the payment of subsidies to colleges for advanced technical education, technical colleges, technical institutes, special schools, schools of industries and reform schools. Colleges for advanced technical education provide education on an advanced level for a variety of technical, commercial and general courses of study as well as secondary education on a part-time basis. Technical colleges and technical institutes are mainly responsible for the training of apprentices and the education, on a part-time basis, of persons not subject to compulsory school attendance. Special schools for handicapped children cater for the educational needs of those who are blind, partially sighted, deaf, hard of hearing, epileptic, cerebral palsied and physically handicapped. Children found to be in need of care by a children's court, are admitted to schools of industries and reform schools.

The Department of Coloured Affairs has taken over all schools of this nature for Coloureds.

In 1973, 26 technical colleges for Whites had 19,571 students; 5 for Coloureds had 2,841 students; 1 for Asians had 6,978 students. In addition there are 16 teacher-training colleges for Coloureds and Asians. Provision is made for technical education for the Bantu at 2 institutions for advanced technical education and 42 industrial or trade schools; total enrolment at these institutions was about 4,600 in 1974. Forty-six schools for the physically handicapped had 6,729 pupils in 1975.

State and State-aided Education other than Higher Education. Primary and secondary public education, other than that specifically provided elsewhere, falls under the Provincial Administration. In terms of the National Education Policy Act, 1967, the Minister of Education, Arts and Science may, after consultation with the Provincial Administrators and the National Advisory Education Council, determine general educational policy within the framework of the Act. Bantu education is the responsibility of the Department of Bantu Education, while education for Coloureds and Indians is controlled by the Departments of Coloured Affairs and Indian Affairs respectively.

Public schools in 1975: 2,386 for Whites with 42,754 teachers and 871,407 pupils; 2,270 for Coloureds and Asians with 26,274 teachers and 820,368 pupils; 11,823 for Bantu (in the Republic) with 55,026 teachers and 3,698,921 pupils.

Private Schools. To a certain extent the activities of private schools are controlled by government regulations. Their pupils generally sit for the state schools' examinations. These schools make provision for kindergarten, elementary and preparatory, general primary, secondary and commercial education.

In 1975, 157 private or aided schools for Whites had 2,995 teachers and 44,076 students. In 1972, 1,310 schools for Coloureds had 6,912 teachers and 216,639 students; 173 for Asians had 1,845 teachers and 53,511 students; 416 for Bantu had 1,878 teachers and 80,904 students.

Teacher-training colleges in 1975: 23 for Whites had 1,194 teachers and 11,611 students; 16 for Coloureds and Asians had 409 teachers and 5,108 students; 38 for Bantu had 6,936 teachers and 14,686 students.

Health. In 1974 there were 12,654 medical practitioners, 3,105 specialists, 821 hospital interns, 1,899 dental specialists and dentists; in 1971 there were 109,892 hospital beds, excluding private and mission hospitals. More tuberculosis patients were treated as outpatients than in hospital.

Social Welfare. *Social Security.* Pensions paid in 1974–75:

	Beneficiaries	*Amount (R1,000)*
Old age	383,725	130,844
War veterans	21,837	14,673
Blind	7,375	1,615
Disability grants	121,954	35,339
Maintenance	59,112	35,714

Welfare Services. South Africa is not a welfare state, yet provides many services for the community. Welfare work on behalf of the Government is done by the Departments of Social Welfare and Pensions, Coloured Affairs, Indian Affairs, and Plural Relations and Development.

There are also a great number of voluntary welfare societies which undertake a variety of welfare services. Social assistance is not based on compulsory insurance but is financed from taxation.

The Department of Social Welfare and Pensions formulates the broad policy and takes care of the co-ordination of the various welfare services. The National Council for Welfare, a statutory body set up under the National Welfare Act of 1965, among others, is used by the Government for the execution of this policy. Four specialized commissions serve under the National Council. These are: the Social Work Commission, the Commission for Family Life, the Commission for Welfare Planning and the Commission for Welfare Organizations. The Department also provides such personal services as pensions and allowances, and practical assistance to individuals or families who may have social problems, neglected and uncared-for children, juvenile delinquents, adults needing special guidance and alcoholics. There is assistance for mental or physical disability, death or absence of the breadwinner. There are professional field services and institutions available as well as financial help.

Voluntary Welfare Societies. These organizations supply supplementary services to those provided by the Government. Voluntary welfare organizations must register at the Department of Social Welfare and Pensions under the National Welfare Act of 1965. There are more than 2,000 registered welfare organizations; they have organized themselves into national and provincial councils so as to co-ordinate their activities.

Funds for these voluntary services are raised from Government subsidies and by public subscription.

In the past the State, with the assistance of local authorities, voluntary welfare agencies and church organizations, provided welfare services for the Bantu, the voluntary agencies being controlled by White committees. However, this situation is gradually changing as more Bantu are taking an interest in welfare work. The various Bantu nations are being encouraged and assisted to form their own voluntary agencies and so to provide, as far as possible, welfare services for their own people. As far as is practicable, the institutions required for the care of the aged and the disabled and for needy children are sited in the homelands, and are staffed by Bantu.

Child and Family Welfare. Welfare or professional officers employed by the State are responsible for the implementation and administration of the Children's Act (amended and consolidated in 1960). This Act makes provision for the prevention and treatment of neglected and maladjusted children, with the full integration of the services of voluntary child and family welfare organizations. Children's institutions, mainly established and controlled by private organizations, are subsidized by the State, as are crèches, community centres and other projects in aid of child and family welfare.

DIPLOMATIC REPRESENTATIVES

OF SOUTH AFRICA IN GREAT BRITAIN (South Africa House, Trafalgar Sq., London, WC2N 5DP)

Ambassador: Mattys Izak Botha (accredited 15 March 1977).

OF GREAT BRITAIN IN SOUTH AFRICA (6 Hill St., Arcadia, Pretoria, 0002)

Ambassador: Sir David Scott, KCMG.

OF SOUTH AFRICA IN THE USA (3051 Massachusetts Ave., NW, Washington, D.C., 20008)

Ambassador: D. B. Sole.

OF THE USA IN SOUTH AFRICA (225 Pretorius St., Pretoria)

Ambassador: William G. Bowdler.

OF SOUTH AFRICA TO THE UNITED NATIONS

Ambassador: J. A. Eksteen.

Books of Reference

Statistical Information: The Bureau (formerly Office) of Census and Statistics (Schoeman St., Pretoria), established on 1 April 1917 as a division of the Department of the Interior and now directly under the Minister of Economic Affairs, is based mainly on the Consolidated Census Act, No. 76, of 1957, and the Consolidated Statistics Act, No. 73, of 1957. Main publications.

Official Year Book of the Union of South Africa and of Basutoland, Bechuanaland Protectorate and Swaziland. From 1918 (preceded by the *Statistical Year Book, 1913–17*)
Union Statistics for 50 Years: Jubilee Issue, 1910–1960 (1960)
Statistical Year Book. From 1964
Statistics of Production: Industrial. Annual, from 1915/16 (but suspended from 1929/30 to 1931/32 and from 1938 to 1942)
Statistics of Production: Agricultural. Annual, from 1917/18 (but suspended from 1920/30 to 1931/32 and from 1939 to 1946)
Monthly Bulletin of Statistics (from 1922)
Population Census, 1970. (Various special reports in course of publication)
South African Reserve Bank, *Quarterly Bulletin of Statistics*
South Africa Year Book 1976
Official South African Municipal Year Book 1977
Homelands: The Role of the Corporations in the Republic of South Africa. Johannesburg, 1976

The Customs and Excise Office, Pretoria, publishes *Monthly Abstract of Trade Statistics* (from 1946) and *Trade and Shipping of the Union of South Africa* (annually, 1910–55); *Foreign Trade Statistics* (annually, from 1956)

Barber, J., *South Africa's Foreign Policy*. OUP, 1973
Bate, H. M., *South Africa Without Prejudice*. London, 1956
Bosman, D. B., *Tweetalige Woordeboek*. 2 vols. Cape Town, 1946–49
Brotz, H., *The Politics of South Africa: Democracy and Racial Diversity*. OUP, 1977
Davenport, T. R. H., *South Africa: A Modern History*. London, 1977
de Villiers, L., *South Africa: A Skunk Among Nations*. London, 1975
Friedman, B., *Smuts: A Reappraisal*. London, 1975
Heard, K. A., *General Elections in South Africa, 1943–70*. OUP, 1974
Hepple, A., *Verwoerd*. Harmondsworth, 1967
Kruger, D. W., *The Making of a Nation*. Johannesburg, 1969
Lacour-Gayet, R., *A History of South Africa*. London, 1977
Metrowich, F. R., *Africa in the Sixties*. Pretoria, 1970
Muller, C. F. J., *500 Years of South African History*. Pretoria, 1969
Talbot, A. M. and W. J., *Atlas of South African History*. Pretoria, 1969
Troup, F., *South Africa: An Historical Introduction*. London, 1972
Walker, E. A., *History of Southern Africa*. London, 1957
The Oxford History of South Africa. OUP, Vol. 1, 1969; Vol. 2, 1971

PROVINCE OF THE CAPE OF GOOD HOPE

Kaapprovinsie

HISTORY. The colony of the Cape of Good Hope was founded by the Dutch in the year 1652. Britain took possession of it from 1795 to 1803 and again in 1806, and it was formally ceded to Great Britain by the Convention of London, 13 Aug. 1814. Letters patent issued in 1850 declared that in the colony there should be a Parliament which should consist of the Governor, a Legislative Council and a House of Assembly. On 31 May 1910 the colony was merged in the Union of South Africa, thereafter forming an original province of the Union.

AREA AND POPULATION. The following table gives the population of the Cape of Good Hope[1] (area (1970) 261,790 sq. miles) at the last census:

		All races		*Whites*		*Non-Whites*	
	Total	*Males*	*Females*	*Males*	*Females*	*Males*	*Females*
1921	2,781,542	1,347,791	1,433,751	329,367	321,268	1,018,424	1,112,483
1936	3,527,865	1,663,169	1,864,796	396,058	394,993	1,267,011	1,469,803
1946	4,051,424	1,924,334	2,127,090	433,849	436,300	1,490,485	1,690,790
1951	4,426,726	2,110,674	2,316,052	463,917	471,168	1,646,757	1,844,884
1960	5,360,234	2,553,245	2,806,989	493,370	507,398	2,059,875	2,299,591
1970	6,731,820	3,177,420	3,554,400	546,680	561,370	2,630,740	2,993,030

[1] Excluding Walvis Bay (434 sq. miles).

Present area (excluding Griqualand East, which has been transferred to Natal), 260,323 sq. miles.

Of the non-White population in 1970, 21,617 were Asians, 4,235,376 were Bantu and 1,751,546 Coloureds.

Vital statistics for calendar years:

		Whites			*Asians and Coloureds*	
	Births	*Deaths*	*Marriages*	*Births*	*Deaths*	*Marriages*
1961	23,448[1]	9,641	8,510	66,597[1]	21,649	9,175
1962	23,160[1]	10,088[1]	...	69,185[1]	21,616[1]	...
1966	...	10,290	10,055	...	24,110	9,758

[1] Preliminary.

ADMINISTRATION. At the provincial council election in 1977 the following parties were returned: National Party, 44; Progressive Federal Party, 6; South Africa Party, 3; New Republic Party, 2.

Cape Town is the seat of the provincial administration.

Administrator: L. A. P. A. Munnik.

The province is divided into 109 magisterial districts and 91 divisional council divisions. Each division has a council of at least 6 members (15 in the Cape Division) elected quinquennially by the owners or occupiers of immovable property. The duties devolving upon divisional councils include the construction and maintenance of roads and bridges, local rating, vehicle taxation (except motor vehicle taxation) and preservation of public health.

There are 173 municipalities, each governed by a mayor and councillors. Municipal elections are held biennially. There are also 73 village management boards and 9 local boards.

FINANCE. In 1974–75 revenue amounted to R435,655,000 and expenditure to R486,532,000.

MINING. For mineral production, *see* pp. 1070–71.

AGRICULTURE. Viticulture in the Republic is almost exclusively confined to the Cape Province, but practically all other forms of agricultural and pastoral activity are pursued.

INDUSTRY. The province has brick, tile and pottery works, saw-mills, engineering works, foundries, grain-mills, distilleries and wineries, clothing factories, furniture, boot and shoe factories, etc.

RELIGION. Sample tabulation, 1960 census. *Whites:* Nederduits Gereformeerde Kerk, 532,343; Gereformeerde Kerk, 12,153; Nederduits Hervormde Kerk, 8,033; Anglicans, 146,870; Presbyterians, 30,899; Congregationalists, 8,824; Methodists, 79,098; Lutherans, 11,244; Roman Catholics, 58,514; Apostolics, 21,979; other Christians, 46,141; Jews, 32,389; others, 14,720. *Non-Whites*[1]*:* Afrikaans Churches, 497,603; Anglicans, 503,650; Presbyterians, 105,125; Congregationalists, 218,296; Methodists, 748,100; Lutherans, 108,278; Roman Catholics, 229,862; Apostolics, 92,206; Bantu Churches, 478,594; other Christians, 196,795; Mohammedans, 89,082; Hindus, 4,852; others, 1,067,070.

[1] Excludes 20,133 Bantu omitted from sample.

EDUCATION. *Training.* Higher education is under the control of the Department of National Education, Pretoria. Primary and secondary education (including vocational education and the training of primary teachers) are controlled by the Provincial Administration in respect of White pupils, by the Department of Bantu Education in respect of Bantu pupils and by the Administration of Coloured Affairs in respect of Coloured pupils. Education is compulsory for all White children. Primary and secondary education is free to the end of the calendar year in which the age of 19 years is attained.

Whites (1973). There were 1,074 government and aided schools with 12,027 teachers and 234,665 pupils; 8 teacher-training colleges with 264 teachers and 2,652 pupils; 91 private schools with 1,106 teachers and 15,285 pupils.

Coloureds (1973). There were 1,656 government and aided schools with 16,296 teachers and about 500,000 pupils; 11 teacher-training schools with about 4,000 students (Coloured and Asian); 18 private schools with 97 teachers and 2,133 pupils; 3 vocational schools with about 1,500 pupils.

Bantu (1974). There were 1,034 public and private school sections with 4,088 teachers and 225,502 pupils.

Asians (1970). There is 1 private school with 3 teachers and 20 pupils.

Books of Reference

Official Guide. Cape Town, 1953
Du Toit, P.S., *Onderwuys in Kaapland, 1652–1939.* Pretoria, 1940
Kilpin, R., *The Parliament of the Cape.* London, 1939
Marais, J. S., *The Cape Coloured People, 1652–1937.* London, 1939

PROVINCE OF NATAL

HISTORY. Natal was annexed to Cape Colony in 1844, placed under separate government in 1845, and on 15 July 1856 established as a separate colony. By this charter partially representative institutions were established, and in 1893 the colony obtained responsible government. The province of Zululand was annexed to Natal on 30 Dec. 1897. The districts of Vryheid, Utrecht and part of Wakkerstroom, formerly belonging to the Transvaal, were annexed in Jan. 1903. On 31 May 1910 the colony was merged in the Union of South Africa as an original province of the Union.

AREA AND POPULATION. The province (including Zululand, 10,375 sq. miles) has an area of 34,055 sq. miles, with a seaboard of about 360 miles. The climate is sub-tropical on the coast and somewhat colder inland. It is well suited to White persons. The province is divided into 45 magisterial districts.

The returns of the total population at the census were:

		All races		*Whites*		*Non-Whites*	
	Total	*Males*	*Females*	*Males*	*Females*	*Males*	*Females*
1921	1,429,398	707,600	721,798	70,506	66,381	637,094	655,417
1936	1,946,468	944,220	1,002,248	95,157	95,392	849,063	906,856
1946	2,202,392	1,073,510	1,128,882	117,425	119,272	956,085	1,009,600
1951	2,415,318	1,182,931	1,232,387	136,300	137,940	1,046,631	1,094,447
1960	2,977,034	1,443,561	1,535,473	166,404	222,750	1,277,157	1,362,468
1970	4,236,770	2,009,410	2,227,360	171,005	214,960	1,794,430	2,004,610

Of the non-White population in 1967, 514,803 were Asians, 66,821 Coloureds and 1,114,184 Bantu.

Vital statistics for calendar years:

	Whites			*Asians and Coloureds*		
	Births	*Deaths*	*Marriages*	*Births*	*Deaths*	*Marriages*
1961	7,301[1]	3,412	2,803	19,234[1]	3,509	3,617
1962	7,622[1]	3,561[1]	...	18,575[1]	3,728	...
1966[1]	...	3,901	3,612	...	4,008	4,446

[1] Preliminary.

ADMINISTRATION. At the provincial council elections in 1977 there were returned: United Party, 12; National Party, 8.

The seat of provincial government in Natal is Pietermaritzburg.

Administrator: W. Havemann.

FINANCE. In 1974–75 revenue amounted to R188·8m. and expenditure to R182·6m.

MINING. The province is rich in mineral wealth, particularly coal. For figures of mineral production, *see* pp. 1070–71.

AGRICULTURE. Sugar and citrus growing are of major importance. On the coast and in Zululand there are vast plantations of sugar-cane (about 800,000 acres), producing, in 1967, 15,547,000 tons. Cereals of all kinds (especially maize), fruits, vegetables, the *Acacia molissima* (the bark of which is much used for tanning purposes) and other crops are produced. Large areas are being afforested.

INDUSTRY. Natal is highly industrialized. There are metallurgical, chemical, paper, rayon, and food-processing plants, iron and steel foundries, petrol refineries, pulp-mills, explosives and fertilizer plants, milk- and meat-canning factories.

RELIGION. Sample tabulation, 1960 census. *Whites:* Nederduits Gereformeerde Kerk, 64,052; Gereformeerde Kerk, 2,895; Nederduitse Hervormde Kerk, 5,319; Anglicans, 94,349; Presbyterians, 25,852; Congregationalists, 4,652; Methodists, 53,283; Lutherans, 7,226; Roman Catholics, 35,747; Apostolics, 9,827; other Christians, 18,973; Jews, 6,266; others, 11,794. *Non-Whites:* Afrikaans Churches, 25,411; Anglicans, 128,400; Presbyterians, 35,013; Congregationalists, 16,267; Methodists, 173,088; Lutherans, 122,052; Roman Catholics, 270,744; Apostolics, 25,229; Bantu Churches, 495,747; other Christians, 95,828; Mohammedans, 59,957; Hindus, 282,797; others, 909,152.

EDUCATION. The Natal Provincial Administration controls primary and secondary technical and vocational education for Whites. Higher technical and vocational education for all races is provided by the central government. *See also* p. 1075.

Whites (1973). There were 297 government and aided schools with 99,078 pupils; 3 teacher-training colleges with 1,110 students; 35 private schools with 1,875 pupils.

Coloureds (1973). There were 55 government and aided schools with 760 teachers and 22,432 pupils; 2 teacher-training colleges with 214 students; 1 private school with 2 teachers and 46 pupils.

Bantu (1974). There were 968 school sections with 3,844 teachers and 195,344 pupils.

Asians (1973). There were 302 government and aided schools with 5,536 teachers and 153,918 pupils; 18 private schools with 5,536 pupils; 1 teacher-training school with 35 teachers and 407 students.

Books of Reference

Town and Regional Planning Commission, Natal: *The Tugela Basin* (1952), *Towards a Plan for the Tugela Basin* (1960), *The Population and Labour Resources of Natal* (1960)

Cullingvorsh's *Natal Almanac*. Annual. Durban

Doke, C. M., and Vilakazi, B. W., *Zulu–English Dictionary*. Johannesburg, 1948

Fair, T. J. D., *Natal Regional Survey*. 3 vols. OUP, 1955

Kuper, H., *Indian People in Natal*. Natal Univ. Press, 1960

Tatlow, A. H., *Natal Province: Descriptive Guide and Official Handbook*. Durban and London. Annual

PROVINCE OF THE TRANSVAAL

HISTORY. The Transvaal was one of the territories colonized by the Boers who left the Cape Colony during the Great Trek in 1831 and following years. In 1852, by the Sand River Treaty, Great Britain recognized the independence of the Transvaal, which, in 1853, took the name of the South African Republic. In 1877 the Republic was annexed by Great Britain, but the Boers took up arms towards the end of 1880. In 1881 peace was made and self-government, subject to British suzerainty and certain stipulated restrictions, was restored to the Boers. The London Convention of 1884 removed the suzerainty and a number of these restrictions but reserved to Great Britain the right of approval of the Transvaal's foreign relations, excepting with regard to the Orange Free State. In 1886 gold was discovered on the Witwatersrand, and this discovery, together with the great influx of foreigners which it occasioned, gave rise to many grave problems. Eventually, in 1899, war broke out between Great Britain and the Transvaal. Peace was concluded on 31 May 1902, the Transvaal and the Orange Free State both losing their independence. The Transvaal was governed as a crown colony until 12 Jan. 1907, when responsible government came into force. On 31 May 1910 the Transvaal became one of the four provinces of the Union.

AREA AND POPULATION. The area of the province is 109,621 sq. miles, divided into 53 districts. The following table shows the population at each of the last censuses:

		All races		*Whites*		*Non-Whites*	
	Total	*Males*	*Females*	*Males*	*Females*	*Males*	*Females*
1921	2,087,636	1,159,430	928,206	285,185	259,788	874,245	668,418
1936	3,341,470	1,846,576	1,494,894	424,470	396,286	1,422,108	1,098,608
1946	4,283,038	2,374,323	1,908,715	541,053	522,068	1,833,270	1,386,647
1951	4,812,838	2,619,314	2,193,524	737,194	731,111	2,575,119	2,230,053
1960	6,270,711	3,310,948	2,959,763	735,845	729,730	2,575,103	2,230,034
1970	8,717,530	4,460,130	4,257,400	946,430	938,210	3,513,700	3,319,190

Of the non-White population in 1970, 4,264,775 were Bantu, 80,556 Asians and 150,831 Coloureds.

Important towns of the province are listed on p. 1065.

Vital statistics for calendar years:

		Whites			*Asians and Coloureds*	
	Births	*Deaths*	*Marriages*	*Births*	*Deaths*	*Marriages*
1951	39,725[1]	11,658	14,555	6,194[1]	1,900	941
1962	40,199[1]	12,600[1]	...	6,330[1]	2,242[1]	...
1966	...	13,440	...	...	2,322	1,290

[1] Preliminary.

ADMINISTRATION. At the provincial council election in 1977 there were returned: National Party, 65; Progressive Federal Party, 10; New Republic Party, 1.

The seat of provincial government is at Pretoria, which is also the administrative capital of the Republic of South Africa.

Administrator: S. G. J. van Niekerk.

FINANCE. In 1974–75 revenue amounted to R532,071,000 and expenditure to R536,864,000.

MINING. For mineral production, *see* pp. 1070–71. Gold output in 1967 was 19,591,000 oz. worth R492,978,000.

AGRICULTURE. The province is in the main a stock-raising country, though there are considerable areas well adapted for agriculture, including the growing of tropical crops.

INDUSTRY. The province has iron and brass foundries and engineering works, grain-mills, breweries, brick, tile and pottery works, tobacco, soap, and candle factories, coach and wagon works, clothing factories, etc.

RELIGION. Sample tabulation, 1960 census. *Whites:* Nederduits Gereformeerde Kerk, 539,491; Gereformeerde Kerk, 72,404; Nederduits Hervormde Kerk, 167,693; Anglicans, 137,207; Presbyterians, 50,196; Congregationalists, 3,071; Methodists, 123,218; Lutherans, 13,880; Roman Catholics, 91,235; Apostolics, 67,550; other Christians, 90,504; Jews, 74,221; others, 37,635. *Non-Whites:* Afrikaans Churches, 278,006; Anglicans, 309,047; Presbyterians, 50,924; Congregationalists, 29,839; Methodists, 318,424; Lutherans, 365,836; Roman Catholics, 270,493; Apostolics, 179,739; Bantu Churches, 1,030,853; other Christians, 310,162; Mohammedans, 42,707; Hindus, 23,190; others, 1,595,952.

EDUCATION. All education for Whites except that of universities is under the provincial authority. The province has been divided for the purposes of local control and management into 21 school districts. Instruction in government schools, both primary and secondary, is free. The medium of instruction is the home language of the pupil. The teaching of the other language begins at the earliest stage at which it is appropriate on educational grounds. Both languages are taught as examination subjects to every pupil.

Whites (1973). There were 909 public schools with 18,993 teachers and 446,083 pupils; 4 teacher-training colleges with 7,500 students; 109 private schools with 1,560 teachers and 27,595 pupils.

Coloureds (1973). There were 67 state and state-aided schools with 1,292 teachers and 39,675 pupils; 1 teacher-training college with 301 students; 4 private schools with 1,292 pupils; 1 vocational school with 412 pupils.

Asians (1973). There were 65 public schools with 927 teachers and 22,739 pupils; 1 teacher-training college with 25 teachers and 241 students.

Bantu (1974). There were 1,956 public and private school sections with 12,429 teachers and 645,355 pupils.

Books of Reference

Transvaal Official Guide. Cape Town, 1955
Eliovson, E., *Johannesburg, the Fabulous City*. Cape Town, 1956
Symonds, F. A., *The Johannesburg Story*. London, 1953

PROVINCE OF THE ORANGE FREE STATE

Oranje-Vrystaat

HISTORY. The Orange River was first crossed by Europeans in the middle of the 18th century. Between 1810 and 1820, settlements were made in the southern parts of the Orange Free State, and the Great Trek greatly increased the number of settlers during and after 1836. In 1848, Sir Harry Smith proclaimed the whole territory between the Orange and Vaal rivers as a British possession called the 'Orange River sovereignty'. However, in 1854, by the Convention of Bloemfontein, British sovereignty was withdrawn and the independence of the country was recognized.

During the first 5 years of its existence the Orange Free State was much harassed by incessant raids by the Basutos. These were at length conquered, but, owing to the intervention of the British Government, the treaty of Aliwal North incorporated only part of the territory of the Basutos in the Orange Free State.

On account of the treaty with the South African Republic, the Orange Free State took a prominent part in the South African War (1899–1902) and was annexed on 28 May 1900 as the Orange River Colony. Crown colony government continued until 1907, when responsible government was introduced. On 31 March 1910 the Orange River Colony was merged in the Union of South Africa as the province of the Orange Free State.

AREA AND POPULATION. The area of the province is 49,866 sq. miles; it is divided into 34 administrative and 57 magisterial districts. The census population has varied as follows:

		All races		*Whites*		*Non-Whites*	
	Total	*Males*	*Females*	*Males*	*Females*	*Males*	*Females*
1921	628,827	321,373	307,454	97,948	90,900	223,425	216,554
1936	772,060	381,903	390,157	101,872	99,106	280,031	291,051
1946	879,071	432,896	446,175	101,874	100,203	331,022	345,972
1951	1,016,570	519,166	497,404	115,637	112,015	403,529	385,389
1960	1,386,202	731,486	654,716	139,304	137,103	601,182	553,613
1970	1,716,350	899,140	817,210	148,110	148,030	751,030	669,180

Of the non-White population in 1970, 1,319,510 were Bantu, 36,192 Coloureds and 5 Asians.

Vital statistics for calendar years:

		Whites			*Asians and Coloured*	
	Births	*Deaths*	*Marriages*	*Births*	*Deaths*	*Marriages*
1961	7,136[1]	2,297	2,314	781[1]	467	126
1962	7,088[1]	2,441[1]	...	858[1]	527[1]	...
1966	...	2,450[1]	2,855[1]	...	...	...

[1] Preliminary.

ADMINISTRATION. At the provincial council election in 1977 there were returned 28 National Party.

The seat of provincial government is at Bloemfontein. There are 68 municipalities and 8 village management boards.

Administrator: A. C. van Wyk.

FINANCE. In 1974–75 revenue amounted to R123m. and expenditure to R118·8m.

MINING. For mineral statistics, *see* pp. 1070–71. The production of the goldfields in the province has increased tremendously since 1951, when the output was 18,545 oz. valued at R230,186. The output in 1961 was 7,235,647 oz. valued at R181,320,401.

AGRICULTURE. The province consists of undulating plains, affording excellent grazing and wide tracts for agricultural purposes. The rainfall is moderate. The country was mainly devoted to stock-farming, but now a rapidly increasing quantity of grain is being raised, especially in the eastern districts.

INDUSTRY. The more important manufacturing industries in the province are the oil-from-coal factory (as well as industries based on its by-products) at Sasolburg; fertilizer, agricultural implements, blanket and woollen products, clothing, hosiery, cement and pharmaceutical factories, grain-mills and brick, tile and pottery works.

RELIGION. Sample tabulation, 1960 census. *Whites:* Nederduits Gereformeerde Kerk, 190,458; Gereformeerde Kerk, 14,018; Nederduits Hervormde Kerk, 9,297; Anglicans, 11,433; Presbyterians, 3,926; Congregationalists, 109; Methodists, 14,226; Lutherans, 1,281; Roman Catholics, 7,303; Apostolics, 8,344; other Christians, 10,480; Jews, 3,190; others, 2,680. *Non-Whites:* Afrikaans Churches, 210,379; Anglicans, 80,554; Presbyterians, 21,414; Congregationalists, 8,309; Methodists, 193,439; Lutherans, 16,504; Roman Catholics, 119,629; Apostolics, 78,001; Bantu Churches, 183,109; other Christians, 52,083; others, 146,374.

EDUCATION. *Whites.* Primary, secondary and vocational education and the training of primary teachers are controlled and financed by the Provincial Administration. The province is divided into 11 school board areas.

Education is free in all public schools up to the university matriculation standard. Attendance is compulsory between the ages of 7 and 16, but exemption may be granted in special cases. The home language of the pupil is the medium of instruction.

There were in 1973, 280 government and aided schools with 5,031 teachers and 72,248 pupils, and 1 private school with 1 teacher and 13 pupils.

Coloureds (1973). There were 45 government and aided schools with 303 teachers and 9,040 pupils.

Bantu (1974). There were 1,648 school sections with 4,558 teachers and 246,072 pupils.

Books of Reference

Orange Free State Official Guide. Cape Town, 1956
Orange Free State Bulletin. 1961 ff.

SOUTH WEST AFRICA
Suidwes-Afrika—Namibia

HISTORY. The territory (excluding Walvis Bay and certain islands) was proclaimed a German protectorate in 1884, but was surrendered to the Forces of the Union of South Africa on 9 July 1915 at Khorab. The administration was vested in the Government of the Union of South Africa by mandate of the League of Nations dated 17 Dec. 1920. In 1921 the Governor-General delegated certain of his functions to the Administrator of the Territory, who was assisted by an Advisory Council and, from 1925, by an Executive Committee and the Legislative Assembly. On 18 July 1966 the International Court of Justice decided, by the President's casting vote, that Ethiopia and Liberia had no legal right in applying for a decision on the international status of South West Africa. In 1971 the International Court of Justice ruled in an advisory opinion that the Republic of South Africa's presence in South West Africa was illegal. In Dec. 1973 the UN appointed Sean McBride as UN Commissioner for Namibia. The Republic of South Africa was given until May 1975 to declare its intentions on the future of Namibia, by the UN.

On 25 April 1978 the Prime Minister of the Republic of South Africa announced his government's acceptance of the proposals to give South West Africa (Namibia) independence on 31 Dec. 1978.

AREA AND POPULATION. The total area of the Territory, including the Caprivi-Zipfel, is 318,261 sq. miles (824,269 sq. km); this figure includes that of Walvis Bay, administered by South West Africa, 434 sq. miles (1,124 sq. km).

The country is bounded on the north by Angola and Zambia, on the west by the Atlantic Ocean, on the south and southern portion of the easten boundary by the Cape Province, and on the remainder of the eastern boundary by Botswana and Zambia. There are 3 main regions: the Namib, an extremely arid and desolate region stretching along the entire coastline to a width of between 80 to 130 km. The major portion of the Namib receives an annual rainfall of less than 50 mm. per annum; the Central Plateau is the region lying to the east of the Namib. It varies in altitude between 1,000 and 2,000 metres and offers a diversified landscape of rugged mountains, rocky outcrops, sand-filled valleys and plains. It covers approximately 50% of the total area; the Kalahari covers the eastern, north-eastern and northern areas of South West Africa.

The dominant feature of this region is its thick cover of terrestrial sands and limestones and its near-total lack of surface water.

The rainfall increases steadily from less than 50 mm. in the west and south-west up to 600 mm. in the Caprivi Strip.

The Kunene River and the Okavango, which form portions of the northern border of the country, the Zambesi, which forms the eastern boundary of the Caprivi-Zipfel, the Kwando or Mashi, which flows through the Caprivi-Zipfel from the north between the Okavango and the Zambesi, and the Orange River in the south, are the only permanently running streams. But there is a system of great, sandy, dry river-beds throughout the country, in which water can generally be obtained by sinking shallow wells. In the Grootfontein area there are large supplies of underground water, but except for a few springs, mostly hot, there is no surface water in the country.

On 13 Oct. 1964 and 29 Jan. 1969 the Republic of South Africa and Portugal signed agreements on the common use of the Kunene River.

Owing to the difficulty of satisfactorily controlling that part of the Caprivi-Zipfel, east of the line running due south from Beacon 22, situated west of the Kwando (or Mashi) River, the control of this area was in Aug. 1939 transferred to the Union Department of Native Affairs.

The population at the census 1960 and 1970 and estimate 1977 was:

	1960	*1970*	*1977*
Ovambos	239,363	342,455	418,300
Whites	73,464	90,658	105,600
Damaras	44,353	64,973	80,500
Hereros	35,354	49,203	58,900
Namas	34,806	32,853	40,400
Kavangos	27,871	49,577	61,400
East Caprivians	15,840	25,009	31,200
Coloureds	12,708	28,275	34,000
Rehobothers	11,257	16,474	20,800
Bushmen	11,762	21,909	27,500
Tswana and others	9,992	18,400	22,500
Kaokovelders	9,234	6,467	7,200
	526,004	746,328	908,800

The population grew at a rate of 3·7% per annum between 1960 and 1970.

The Ovambos are a Bantu race and are both agriculturists and owners of stock. They still possess tribal organization to its full extent.

The Hereros are a pastoral people who formerly owned enormous herds of cattle. Wars with Namas and Germans destroyed their tribal organization. Under the Union and Republic administration, reserves have been set apart and they have considerably increased in numbers and in animal wealth.

The ethnic origin of the Bergdamaras or Damara is still not certain. They were alternatively the slaves of the Hereros and the Namas, whose language they now speak, in pre-European days.

The Namas consist of 2 distinct sections: one, the Hamitic, whose remnants are found in the central portions of the country, being of pure native extraction, is thought to have migrated from the region of the Central African lakes in prehistoric times; the other, the Khoisan, is composed of tribes whose members are descended from persons born in the Cape a couple of centuries ago with an admixture of European and Nama blood.

The Bushmen are among the oldest inhabitants of southern Africa.

In the centre of the country just south of the Windhoek district is the Rehoboth Gebiet, occupied by a race known as the Basters, who are of mixed Nama–European descent and whose ordinary language is Afrikaans.

ADMINISTRATION. The South West Africa Affairs Amendment Act, 1949, abolished the Advisory Council and the nominated members of the Legislative Assembly. All 18 members of the Assembly are now elected by the registered voters of the Territory. The election held on 24 April 1974 returned 18 Nationalists.

The Territory is represented in the South African House of Assembly by 6 members elected by the registered voters of the Territory, and in the Senate by 4 Senators, of which number 2 are elected by the members of the Legislative Assembly and the representatives of the Territory in the House of Assembly, and 2 nominated by the President of the Republic. One of the nominated Senators is selected mainly on the ground of his acquaintance with the conditions of the coloured races of South West Africa.

A commission of inquiry, appointed by the South African Government, in 1964 recommended the establishment of 'homeland areas' for the non-White groups. All these areas should be governed by legislative councils, headed by executive committees; franchise should be granted to males and females over 18 years who qualify for citizenship in their respective homelands.

On 17 Oct. 1968, 22 Oct. 1970 and 15 March 1973 respectively the first sessions of the Legislative Councils of Ovambo (77 members), Kavango (30 members) and Eastern Caprivi (28 members) were opened. On 1 May 1973 and 9 May 1973 respectively Ovambo and Kavango obtained self-government.

On 13 Oct. 1966 the security and apartheid laws of the Republic of South Africa were extended to South West Africa, retrospective to 1950. The Legislative Assembly adopted a resolution on 22 Nov. 1974 inviting the representatives of the various population groups to deliberate with the representatives of the Whites on the manner in which they should exercise their right of self-determination in view of the South African government's desire that the inhabitants of South West Africa should themselves decide upon their future.

The seat of the White administration is Windhoek. The country is divided into 19 districts controlled by magistrates and commissioners.

Administrator-General: M. T. Steyne.

ECONOMY

Budget. The revenue and expenditure (in R1,000) were:

	1971–72	*1972–73*	*1973–74*	*1974–75*	*1975–76*
Revenue	104,639	112,863	161,048	181,252	227,787
Expenditure	139,410	132,166	159,138	174,626	233,946

Banking. Barclays Bank International, Volkskas Bank, Standard Bank, French Bank, Netherlands Bank, Trust Bank, South African Reserve Bank and Boland Bank have branches in the Territory. The only indigenous bank, The Bank of South West Africa, was established in 1973.

NATURAL RESOURCES

Minerals. Mineral export/sales amounted to R142,979,648 in 1972. Diamonds, which constitute the principal production, are mainly recovered from alluvial terraces on a 60-mile stretch along the coastline from the Orange River mouth northward.

Agriculture. South West Africa is essentially a stock-raising country, the scarcity of water and poor rainfall rendering agriculture, except in the northern and north-eastern portions, almost impossible. Generally speaking, the southern half is suited for the raising of small stock, while the central and northern portions are better fitted for cattle.

Livestock (1974): 1,415,283 cattle, 4,177,507 sheep, 732,413 goats. In 1976, 260,864 head of cattle and 290,948 head of small stock were exported.

In 1971–72, 1·8m. lb. of butter and 137,800 lb. of factory cheese were manufactured.

The production of karakul pelts is of increasing importance. In 1973, 3,144,800 pelts, worth R28,963,000 were exported.

Fisheries. The total catch in 1976 was 585,000 tonnes. The sales value of fish products was R116m.

COMMERCE. The statistics concerning the external trade of South West Africa are included in those of the Republic of South Africa (*see* p. 1073).

The bulk of the direct imports into the country is landed at Walvis Bay.

Total trade between South West Africa and UK (British Department of Trade returns, in £1,000 sterling):

	1973	*1974*	*1975*	*1976*	*1977*
Imports to UK	32,637	21,857	24,257	33,323	26,122
Exports and re-exports from UK	535	1,735	2,979	2,914	1,348

COMMUNICATIONS

Roads. In 1977 there were 3,812 km of trunk roads, 8,953 km of main roads, 19,579 km of district roads, of which 3,070 km are bitumen surfaced. In 1974 there were 71,272 registered motor vehicles.

Railways. The South West Africa system connects with the main system of the South African Railways at De Aar. The total length of the line inside South West Africa is 2,340 km of 1,065 mm gauge.

Aviation. In 1976–77 the Territory's 4 major airports handled 143,622 passengers and 1,715,000 kg of freight.

Shipping. In 1976–77 Walvis Bay harbour handled 838,157 tons of cargo and Luderitz, 23,875.

Post and Broadcasting. At 31 March 1977 there were 99 post offices and postal agencies, and 826 private bag services distributed by rail or road transport.

There were 25,434 circuit km of trunk lines, 606,137 km of carrier circuits, 330,747 km of telegraph circuits and 472,650 km of farm telephone lines; 85 telegraph offices, 141 telephone exchanges, and 48,365 telephones. There are 1 post-office and 1,256 licensed radio stations in operation.

In 1977, 56,698 wireless licences were issued. There were 11,049 km of broadcast circuits.

A post office savings bank was established in 1916. The number of accounts open at 31 March 1974 was 38,364 with a credit of R4,249,889. Savings certificates of a value of R200 are also issued. The balance due to holders as at 31 March 1974 amounted to R429,000.

EDUCATION AND WELFARE

Education (1977). There were 862 schools for all races, 201,890 pupils and 6,263 teachers. This included 17 academic high schools, a centre for handicapped children and 2 agricultural colleges.

Health (1975–76). There were 176 hospitals and clinics. The ratio of beds per population was 5 per 1,000 and the ratio of doctors to population was 1 per 4,000 inhabitants (excluding the Eastern Caprivi). Nursing staff numbered 3,641.

Books of Reference

The Territory of South West Africa. (In *Official Year Book of the Republic of South Africa*)
Department of Foreign Affairs, *South West Africa Survey 1967*
Department of Mines: *Quarterly Information Circulars: Industrial Minerals*
Cockram, G.-M., *South West African Mandate.* Cape Town, 1976
Serfontein, J. H. P., *Namibia?* London, 1977
Wipplinger, O., *The Storage of Water in Sand.* Windhoek, 1959
Vigne, R., *A Dwelling Place of Our Own: The Story of the Namibian Nation.* London, 1973

BOPHUTHATSWANA

HISTORY. Bophuthatswana was first to obtain self-government under the Bantu Homelands Constitution Act of 1971 and is the second black homeland to ask the Republic of South Africa for full independence, which was granted on 6 Dec. 1977.

AREA AND POPULATION. The total area is 38,261 sq. km.

In 1976 Bophuthatswana had a *de jure* population of 2,103,000, of which 65% lived in the White areas. The remaining 35% (736,000) lived in the homeland. In addition, the homeland has a further population of about 300,000 non-Tswanas, giving the homeland a *de facto* population of about 1,036,000.

CONSTITUTION AND GOVERNMENT. The Bophuthatswana Government is a compromise between the traditional chief-in-council system and a democratic electoral system. There are 48 nominated and 48 elected members in the Legislative Assembly. Self-government was granted in 1972. Each regional authority (coinciding with the 12 districts of the homeland) nominates 4 members (usually chiefs or headmen), and each district elects the same number to the Legislative Assembly.

Executive power vests in the chief Minister, who is elected by the Assembly, and his cabinet.

The first general election was held in Oct. 1972, 4 political parties taking part. Chief Lucas Mangope's Bophuthatswana National Party (BNP) won 20 of the 24 contested seats, but in 1974 he formed the Bophuthatswana Democratic Party which in 1978 holds two-thirds of the seats in the Assembly.

Members of regional authorities are elected from among the tribal and community authorities in their area.

Chief Minister: Chief L. L. M. Mangope.

Minister of the Interior: Chief B. L. M. Motsatsi. *Justice:* Chief T. V. R. Makapan. *Education:* M. Setlogelo. *Agriculture:* Chief S. V. Suping. *Health and Social Welfare:* T. M. Molatihwa. *Works*: D. P. Kgotleng.

INTERNATIONAL RELATIONS

Aid. The Republic of South Africa granted aid of R51m. in 1977–78.

ECONOMY

Budget. The 1977–78 budget balanced at R72m.

Currency. The South African Rand.

NATURAL RESOURCES

Water. The Department of Agriculture inherited the following improvements from South Africa: 2,833 reservoirs; 6,845 boreholes, of which more than 4,000 have been equipped; 648 earth dams.

Minerals. The territory is particularly rich in minerals. In 1976 there were 34 mines employing 53,000 people. Minerals include platinum, asbestos, iron ore, manganese, chrome, vanadium, limestone, diamonds and fluorspar.

Exploration for more platinum, chrome and coal is currently being carried out both by the private sector and by the Bantu Mining Corporation. The platinum mines around Rustenburg produce about 66% of the free world's total production. The major chrome mines are near Rustenburg and Marico, while vanadium is mined in the Odi district near Brits.

The Rustenburg, Western and Impala Platinum mines which Bophuthatswana shares with the Republic of South Africa produce about 1·9m. oz. a year.

AGRICULTURE. Bophuthatswana is a semi-arid area of bushveld and grass veld suitable for stock farming. The annual rainfall is 300 mm in the west and 700 mm in the east and there are 3 river catchment areas—those of the Molopo, Limpopo and Vaal rivers.

Although the land tenure system militates against establishing large farms, some land which is unsuitable for building on is leased by the government to successful farmers.

Livestock (1977): Cattle, 380,000.

Only 6·6% of the territory is suited to dryland cropping, but crop yields have shown a steady improvement in recent years. Plant production in 1972 yielded R2·4m. In the Ditsobotla district, 3,500 hectares of fertile land has been developed by 3 primary co-operatives comprising 190 Tswana farmers.

INDUSTRY. The first industries were started on an agency basis at Babelegi; the fastest growing industrial area in the homeland, in 1977 it covered 183 hectares and by March 1976 more than R56m. had been invested in the project. Other industries include 2 breweries at Thlabane and Garankuwa. There is also a furniture factory near Heystekrand, and a tannery at Montshiwa. Border industries are also promoted by the central government, notably Rosslyn where 128 industries had been established by Dec. 1975.

COMMUNICATIONS

Roads. Total length (1977) 6,300 km, of which 63 km are tarred. 1976–77, 32 km were covered by bus, and 116m. passengers transported.

EDUCATION AND WELFARE

Education. In 1976 the territory's total school attendance was 383,000 at 921 educational institutions which include special schools and technical schools. Primary school attendance grew from 252,000 (1970) to 327,000 (1976) and secondary school enrolment increased from 15,000 (1970) to 56,000 (1976). The number of pupils to one teacher was 55 in 1976, but the situation should improve since 3,000 pupil teachers entered the 6 training colleges, and 6,967 qualified in that year.

Education is free apart from a nominal contribution to school funds, and hostel fees at post-primary schools.

Instruction from Grade I to Standard 4 is in Tswana, while the senior standards are taught in English. The education of the Black population is controlled by the Department of Bantu Education.

Health. In 1975 Bophuthatswana had 10 hospitals in the homelands, 116 clinics, 5,355 hospital beds, 127 doctors and 2,805 nurses. The health budget in 1975–76 was R17m.

Book of Reference

The Independence of Bophuthatswana. Dept. of Information, South African Embassy, London

TRANSKEI

HISTORY. Transkei is the homeland of the Xhosa nation and was granted self-government by the Republic of South Africa in 1963. Over 1·5m. Transkeians live permanently in the Republic of South Africa but were deprived of their South African citizenship on independence.

AREA AND POPULATION. The total area is 16,675 sq. miles (43,188 sq. km). Population (1976 estimate) 1·9m., of which coloured 7,650 and whites 10,000. The capital is Umtata (population (1976) 24,805; 20,196 blacks, 1,067 coloured and 3,542 whites). Other towns include Gcuwa, Kwabhaca and Umzimvubu.

CONSTITUTION AND GOVERNMENT. The Status of Transkei Bill passed its third reading in the South African House of Assembly on 11 June 1976 and received its second reading in the Senate on 17 June. The Bill gave Transkei a unicameral National Assembly instead of the then existing Legislative Assembly.

General elections were held on 29 Sept. 1976 and the Transkei National Independence Party gained 69 of the 75 elective seats in the National Assembly. Members were elected for a 5-year period. In addition there are 75 traditional (co-opted) members (70 chiefs and 5 paramount chiefs).

President: Chief Botha Sigcau.

Chief Minister: Paramount Chief K. D. Matanzima.

Foreign Affairs and Information: Digby S. Koyana. *Justice, Police and Prisons:* Chief George Matanzima. *Finance and Auditor-General:* Tsepo Letlaka. *Planning and Commerce:* Ramsay Madikizela. *Interior:* Stella N. Sigeau. *Local Government and Land Tenure:* Chief George S. Naabankulu. *Posts and Telecommunications, and Transport:* Armstrong N. Jonas. *Education:* W. Silas Mbanga. *Health and Welfare:* Hubert L. Mlonyeni. *Agriculture and Forestry:* Saul Ndzumo. *Works and Energy:* T. Vike.

FINANCE. The budget (1976–77) balanced at R136m.

AGRICULTURE. *Livestock* (1976): Cattle, 1·3m.; sheep, 2·5m.; goats, 1·25m.

COMMUNICATIONS

Roads. There are above 8,800 km of roads.

Railways. There is a 209 km railway line linking Umtata with the port of East London in the Republic of South Africa.

Aviation. An international airport exists at Umtata.

Shipping. A start was made in 1978 on a 'free port' at Mnganzana. It will be completed in 5–6 years at a cost of R125m. by a French consortium.

DIPLOMATIC REPRESENTATIVES

No country, other than the Republic of South Africa, recognized Transkei as an independent state and in April 1978 Transkei severed diplomatic relations with the Republic.

SPAIN

Capital: Madrid
Population: 35·7m. (1976)
GNP per capita: US$2,920 (1976)

Estado Español

HISTORY. The Spanish State was established by Gen. Franco on 1 Oct. 1936. For a short account of the Civil War in Spain, 17 July 1936 to 1 April 1939, *see* THE STATESMAN'S YEAR-BOOK, 1939, pp. 1325–26.

On 19 April 1937 the various political groups in the Nationalist Movement were united by Gen. Franco into one single political party, under the title *Falange Española Tradicionalista y de las Juntas de Ofensiva Nacional Sindicalistas* comprising the *falange española* created on 29 Oct. 1933 by José Antonio Primo de Rivera, eldest son of the general who was Dictator of Spain from 1923 to 1930, and the traditionalists. On 30 Jan. 1938 the first civil government was proclaimed, with Gen. Franco, possessing dictatorial powers, at its head.

On 31 March 1947 Gen. Franco announced that Spain would eventually become a monarchy, with a regency council and himself as the head of state.

On 6 July 1947 the 'Law of Succession' was approved by a referendum; out of a total of 17,178,812 electors, 14,145,163 voted for, and 722,656 against it; 351,744 votes were invalid.

In July 1969, Prince Don Juan Carlos de Borbón was sworn in as successor to the Head of State and he had the title of HRH Prince of Spain until he became King.

Prince Juan Carlos was appointed acting Head of State on 30 Oct. 1975 because of Gen. Franco's illness.

Gen. Francisco Franco y Bahamonde died on 20 Nov. 1975 and on 22 Nov. Prince Juan Carlos de Borbón y Borbón took the oath as Juan Carlos I, King of Spain.

AREA AND POPULATION. Spain is bounded north by the Bay of Biscay and the Pyrenees (which form the frontier with France), east and south by the Mediterranean and the Straits of Gibraltar, southwest by the Atlantic and west by Portugal and the Atlantic. Continental Spain has an area of 492,592 sq. km, and including the Balearic and Canary Islands 504,879 sq. km (194,883 sq. miles).

The growth of the population has been as follows:

Census year	*Population*	*Rate of annual increase*	*Census year*	*Population*	*Rate of annual increase*
1860	15,655,467	0·34	1940	25,877,971	0·98
1910	19,927,150	0·72	1950	27,976,755	0·81
1920	21,303,162	0·69	1960	30,903,137	0·88
1930	23,563,867	1·06	1970	33,823,918	. .

Area and registered population of the provinces, as at (census) 1970:

Area (sq. km)	*Population*	*Per sq. km*	*Province*	*Area (sq. km)*	*Population*	*Per sq. km*
3,047	204,323	67	Cádiz	7,385	885,433	120
14,858	335,026	23	Castellón	6,679	385,823	58
5,863	920,105	157	Ciudad-Real	19,749	507,650	26
8,774	375,004	43	Córdoba	13,718	724,116	53
8,048	203,798	25	Coruña (La)	7,876	1,004,188	127
21,657	687,599	32	Cuenca	17,061	247,158	14
5,014	558,287	111	Gerona	5,886	414,397	70
7,733	3,929,194	508	Granada	12,531	733,375	59
14,369	358,075	25	Guadalajara	12,190	147,732	12
19,945	457,777	23	Guipúzcoa	1,997	631,003	316

Province	Area (sq. km)	Population	Per sq. km	Province	Area (sq. km)	Population	Per sq. km
Huelva	10,085	397,683	39	Santa Cruz de Tenerife	3,208	590,514	184
Huesca	15,671	222,238	14	Santander	5,289	467,138	88
Jaén	13,498	661,146	49	Segovia	6,949	162,770	23
León	15,468	548,721	35	Sevilla	14,001	1,327,190	95
Lérida	12,028	347,015	29	Soria	10,287	114,956	11
Logroño	5,034	235,713	47	Tarragona	6,283	431,961	69
Lugo	9,803	415,052	42	Teruel	14,804	170,284	12
Madrid	7,995	3,792,561	474	Toledo	15,368	468,925	31
Málaga	7,276	867,330	119	Valencia	10,763	1,767,327	164
Murcia	11,317	832,313	74	Valladolid	8,202	412,572	50
Navarra	10,421	464,867	45	Vizcaya	2,217	1,043,310	471
Orense	7,278	413,733	57	Zamora	10,559	251,934	24
Oviedo	10,565	1,045,635	99	Zaragoza	17,194	760,186	44
Palencia	8,029	198,763	25				
Palmas (Las)	4,065	579,710	143				
Pontevedra	4,477	750,701	168				
Salamanca	12,336	371,607	30	Total	504,750	33,823,918	70

In 1970 there were 16,619,144 males and 17,413,657 females.

By decree of 21 Sept. 1927 the islands which form the Canary Archipelago were divided into 2 provinces, under the name of their respective capitals: Santa Cruz de Tenerife and Las Palmas de Gran Canaria. The province of Santa Cruz de Tenerife is constituted by the islands of Tenerife, Palma, Gomera and Hierro, and that of Las Palmas by Gran Canaria, Lanzarote and Fuerteventura, with the small barren islands of Alegranza, Roque del Este, Roque del Oeste, Graciosa, Montaña Clara and Lobos. The area of the islands is 7,273 sq. km; population (census 1970), 1,138,801. Places under Spanish sovereignty in Morocco are: Alhucemas, Ceuta, Chafarinas, Melilla and Peñón de Vélez.

The following were the registered populations of principal towns at census 1970:

Town	Population	Town	Population	Town	Population
Albacete	93,233	Hospitalet	241,978	Palma de Mallorca	234,098
Alcoy	61,371	Huelva	96,689	Pamplona	147,168
Algeciras	81,662	Jaén	78,156	Pontevedra	52,452
Alicante	184,716	Jérez de la Frontera	149,867	Puertollano	53,001
Almeria	114,510	La Coruña	189,654	Rens	59,095
Avilés	81,710	La Laguna	79,963	Sabadell	159,408
Badajoz	101,710	Langreo	58,864	Salamanca	125,220
Badalona	162,888	Las Palmas	287,038	San Fernando	60,187
Baracaldo	108,757	Leganés	57,537	San Sebastián	165,829
Barcelona	1,745,142	León	105,235	Sta Coloma de Grammanet	106,711
Bilbao	410,490	Lérida	90,884	Sta Cruz de Tenerife	151,361
Burgos	119,915	Linares	50,516	Santander	149,704
Cáceres	56,064	Logroño	84,456	Santiago de Compostela	70,893
Cádiz	135,743	Lorca	60,609	Sevilla	548,072
Cartagena	146,904	Lugo	63,830	Tarragona	78,238
Castellón	93,968	Madrid	3,146,071	Tarrasa	138,697
Córdoba	253,632	Málaga	374,452	Valencia	653,690
Cornellá	77,314	Manresa	57,846	Valladolid	236,341
Elche	122,663	Mataró	73,129	Vigo	197,144
El Ferrol	87,736	Mieres	64,552	Virotia	136,873
Gerona	50,338	Murcia	243,759	Zaragoza	479,845
Getafe	69,424	Orense	73,379		
Gijón	187,612	Oviedo	154,117		
Granada	190,429	Palencia	58,370		

Vital statistics for calendar years:

	Marriages	Births	Deaths	Immigrants[1]	Emigrants[1]
1971	253,475	664,770	301,670	11,594	8,785
1972	262,481	665,569	280,335	1,798	1,083
1973	268,981	666,336	296,524	1,731	482
1974	267,171	582,010	295,275	2,009	404
1975[2]	268,207	661,292	289,179	925	288
1976[2]	259,640	662,084	291,573	1,040	142

[1] Transoceanic movements by sea. [2] Provisional figures.

KING. Juan Carlos I, born 5 June 1938. The eldest son of Don Juan, Conde de Barcelona. Juan Carlos was given precedence over his father as pretender to the Spanish throne in an agreement in 1954 between Don Juan and Gen. Franco. King Juan Carlos married, in 1962, Princess Sophia of Greece, daughter of the late King Paul of the Hellenes and Queen Frederika.

GOVERNMENT AND CONSTITUTION. The constitutional regulations contained in the Law of the Cortes, the Succession Act, the Fuero of the Spaniards, the Fuero of Labour, etc. (*see* THE STATESMAN'S YEAR-BOOK, 1966–67, pp. 1425 f.) were consolidated and partly modified by the 'Organic Law of the Spanish State' (*La Ley Orgánica del Estado Español*), unanimously approved by the Cortes on 22 Nov. 1966 and ratified by a national referendum on 14 Dec. 1966.

It was announced in June 1978 that a referendum on the new Constitution would take place in Oct. 1978.

A general election took place on 15 June 1977 to choose members for a new bicameral Parliament to replace the, largely appointed, Cortes.

Congress of Deputies (350 members): Centre Democrats, 165; Socialist Workers, 118; Communists, 20; Popular Alliance, 16; Catalan Democrats, 11; Basque Nationalists, 8; Socialist Union, 6; others, 6.

Senate (248 members): Centre Democrats, 105; Socialist Workers, 35; Communists, 12; Democratic Senate, 12; others, 12. In addition there are 41 senators appointed by the King.

The Cabinet in Feb. 1978 was composed as follows:

Prime Minister (*Presidente del Gobierno*): Adolfo Suarez Gonzalez.

First Deputy Prime Minister and Minister of Defence: Manuel Gutierrez Mellado. *Second Deputy Prime Minister and Minister of Economics:* Fernando Abril Martorell. *Foreign Affairs*: Marcelino Oreja Aguirre. *Justice:* Landelino Lavilla Alsina. *Finance:* Francisco Fernandez Ordoñez. *Interior:* Rodolfo Martin Villa. *Education:* Iñigo Cavero Lataillade. *Industry and Energy:* Agustin Rodriguez Sahagun. *Transport and Communications:* Salvador Sanchez Teran. *Agriculture:* Jaime Lamo de Espinosa. *Tourism and Commerce:* Juan Antonio Garcia Diez. *Public Works and Urbanization:* Joaquin Garrigues Walker. *Labour:* Rafael Calvo Ortega. *Culture:* Pio Cabanillas Gallas. *Presidency of Government:* Jose Manuel Otero Novas. *Health and Social Security:* Enrique Sanchez de Leon. *Minister for the Regions:* Manuel Clavero Arevalo. *Minister for Relations with the EEC:* Leopoldo Calvo Sotelo y Bustelo.

National flag: Three horizontal stripes of red, yellow, red, with the yellow of double width, bearing the national arms in the centre.

National anthem: Marcha real.

Local Government. The provinces are constituted by the association of municipalities (8,655 in 1970). All municipalities are autonomous in their respective spheres, and at their heads stands the *Ayuntamiento*. The municipal councils are elected by the heads of family. The *Alcalde* or Mayor is appointed by the Minister of the Interior in municipalities of over 10,000 inhabitants, and elsewhere by the Civil Governors. The *Diputaciones Provinciales* have entire jurisdiction over their own province and are their sole administrators. Each island of the Canaries has a corporation known as *Cabildo Insular*, to rule their special interests; the Balearic Islands have the same provincial administration as the mainland. Each province of Spain has its own Assembly, the *Diputación Provincial.*

The reconstruction of devastated regions is under the care of the *Instituto de la Vivienda* and by the *Banco de Crédito a la Reconstrucción*, whose duty is to grant and administer loans approved for reconstructing buildings, and the *Banco de Crédito Agricola* and *Banco de Crédito Industrial* with regard to industries, agriculture, commerce and mining, and merchant vessels.

DEFENCE. On 26 Sept. 1953 the US and Spain signed three agreements covering the construction and use of military facilities in Spain by the US, economic assistance, and military end-item assistance. These agreements were renewed for another

5 years on 26 Sept. 1963. The American naval and air base at Rota (near Cádiz) is connected by pipelines with the American bomber bases at Morón de la Frontera (near Seville), Torrejón (near Madrid) and Zaragoza.

A further agreement was signed on 6 Aug. 1970 replacing the one signed in 1953 which was due to expire on 26 Sept. 1970 having been extended for 18 months in 1969. The agreement will expire in 1975 but could be extended for a further period of 5 years.

Length of service is 16 months in the army, 24 months in the navy and 18 months in the air force.

Army. The Army consists of 1 armoured division with AMX-30, M-47 and M-48 tanks, 2 mechanized infantry divisions, 2 mountain divisions, 10 independent infantry brigades, 1 armoured cavalry brigade, 1 high mountain brigade, 1 parachute brigade, 1 airportable brigade and 1 battalion with surface-to-air missiles.

Army personnel consisted (1977) of 220,000 officers and other ranks. Total strength in Africa, about 35,000 men, including 3 regiments of the Foreign Legion.

Navy. Particulars of the principal ships:

Completed	*Name*	*Standard displacement Tons*	*Principal armament*	*Aircraft*	*Shaft horse-power*	*Speed Knots*
			Helicopter Carrier			
1943	Dedalo[1]	13,000	26 40-mm. A.A.	Vertical lift aircraft and 20 helicopters	100,000	32

[1] The former US fixed-wing aircraft carrier *Cabot*, converted in 1966 and transferred to Spain on loan in 1967 and purchased in 1973.

The heavy cruiser *Canarias* was placed on the ineffective list at the end of 1976.

The anti-aircraft cruiser *Méndez Nunez* was stricken from the list in 1963 and the cruisers *Almirante Cervera*, *Galicia* and *Miguel de Cervantes* in 1964–66.

There are also 9 diesel-powered patrol submarines (4 new French-built and 5 old *ex*-US), 16 destroyers, 5 new large frigates (of US destroyer escort type), 2 old frigates, 5 corvettes, 6 new fast patrol craft, 3 old patrol vessels, 10 ocean minesweepers, 12 coastal minesweepers, 3 seaward defence launches, 8 motor launches, 6 coastguard patrol vessels, 1 dock landing ship, 6 survey ships, 3 landing ships, 8 landing craft, 79 minor landing craft, 14 oilers, 2 attack transports, 1 attack cargo ship, 2 tenders, 1 training ship, a boom defence vessel, 12 tugs, 14 harbour tugs, 1 royal yacht and 40 service craft.

The Spanish Navy is being renewed and modernized. Ships under construction include 4 more patrol submarines of French design, 7 small frigates, 6 patrol vessels and 6 fast patrol craft. Ships projected include 1 helicopter carrier, 3 patrol frigates, 2 corvettes and 2 survey ships, although a reduced new construction programme is being considered.

Shipbuilding is mainly carried on at the dockyards at El Ferrol and Cartagena, Cádiz having a smaller share in it.

There are naval wireless telegraphic stations at Cádiz, Barcelona, Mahón, Pontevedra, Cartagena and El Ferrol.

Barcelona, Bilbao, Seville and Cádiz are the chief naval yards.

In 1978 naval personnel totalled 55,400, comprising 4,700 officers, 32,700 ratings, 8,000 civil branch and 10,000 marine other ranks.

Air Force. The Air Force is organized as an independent service, dating from 1939. It comprises air regions (with HQ at Madrid, Seville and Zaragoza), an overseas air zone (Canary Islands) and a separate Air Defence Command which controls interceptor squadrons (including USAF elements) and the control and warning radar network, and Tactical and Transport Commands. Strength is about 40,000 and 200 combat aircraft.

The *Avacïon Tactica* has 2 fighter-bomber and tactical reconnaisance squadrons of Spanish-built Northrop SF-5s, 1 squadron of HA-200D S Saeta and HA-220 Super

Saeta light attack jet aircraft of Spanish design and manufacture, 1 aero-naval co-operation squadron with 3 P-3A Orion and about 11 HU-16B Albatross anti-submarine aircraft, 3 COIN and transport squadrons in the Canaries equipped with HA-200Ds, T-6s and CASA 212 Aviocars respectively, and a liaison flight at Tablada with CASA 127s and Bird Dogs. Air Defence Command has 2 squadrons of Mirage III-Es, 2 squadrons of F-4C Phantom IIs and a single squadron of Mirage F1-Cs, plus a group of T-33As for advanced training. Three KC-130H tankers support the F-4C squadrons. Three transport wings operate a total of more than 100 C-130 Hercules, Canadair CL-215 amphibians, C-54s, C-47s, Caribou and Spanish-built CASA Aviocars and Azors.

American-built Bonanza and T-6 piston-engined aircraft are used for basic training, together with HA-200 Saeta twin-jet training aircraft. T-33A jet aircraft and 2-seat versions of operational types are used as advanced trainers. There are also large air rescue and helicopter units.

INTERNATIONAL RELATIONS

Membership. Spain is a member of UN and OECD.

ECONOMY

Budget. Revenue and expenditure in 1m. pesetas:

	1971	*1972*	*1973*	*1974*	*1975*	*1976*
Revenue	370,169	419,290	474,283	551,698	656,000	785,000
Expenditure	370,169	419,290	474,283	551,698	656,000	785,000

The budget is made up as follows (in 1m. pesetas):

Revenue (1976)

Direct taxes	287,500
Indirect taxes	394,700
Levies and taxes	47,000
Current transactions	19,600
Investment income	33,600

Expenditure (1975)

Chief of State		56
Regency council		...
Cortes		...
National Council		...
Court of Accounts		...
Public Debt		13,485
National fund		22,071
Presidency of the Government		9,336
Ministry of Foreign Affairs		3,905
,,	Justice	11,797
,,	Defence	55,842
,,	Marine	20,390
,,	Interior	90,329
,,	Public Works	71,177
,,	Education	105,582
,,	Labour	27,631
,,	Industry	17,492
,,	Agriculture	36,449
,,	Air	26,832
,,	Commerce	17,006
,,	Information and Tourism	11,139
,,	Housing	17,976
,,	Finance	10,093
Other charges		60,161

Currency. The *peseta* of 100 *céntimos* had the nominal value of a pre-war franc, 25·22 *pesetas* to the £ sterling.

Bank-notes of 1,000, 500, 100, 50, 25, 5 and 1 *peseta* and coins of 5 and 10 *céntimos* (aluminium, tin and copper), 1 *peseta* (copper and aluminium), 5, 25, 50 *pesetas* (nickel and copper) and 100 *pesetas* (silver) are in circulation. In 1975 the circulation of bank-notes was 580,014m. *pesetas* and of coins, 18,515m. *pesetas*.

Banking. On 1 Jan. 1922 the Bank of Spain came under the Bank Ordinance Law, according to which the Government participate in its net profits.

In 1963 the Banco Central set up the Banco de Fomento (capital, 225m. pesetas) for long-term financing; the new bank is to absorb the Banco Central's investment company (Hispana de Inversiones), after which its capital is to be increased by 75m.

On 30 Dec. 1970 the gold and foreign currency holdings of the Bank of Spain amounted to 114,477m. pesetas (paper). A decree of 11 July 1941 established the voluntary nationalization of foreign banks in Spain, and the transference and amalgamation of the business of national banks.

Savings bank deposits (Popular Savings Banks) in Spain, 31 Dec. 1970, amounted to 325,661m. pesetas. Post office savings banks opened on 12 March 1916. Deposits, 31 Dec. 1967, amounted to 37,965m. pesetas; private banks saving deposits, 564,468m. pesetas.

By a decree of 20 Nov. 1941 the post office savings bank opens an account with an initial entry of 1 peseta for every Spanish child born.

Weights and Measures. On 1 Jan. 1859 the metric system of weights and measures was introduced.

ENERGY AND NATURAL RESOURCES

Electricity. Electric power-stations in 1971 had a total installed capacity of 19m. kw., of which 8m. was hydro-electric. The total output (1974) amounted to 80,855m. kwh. Gas production in 1975 was 797m. cu. metres.

Minerals. Spain is rich in minerals. The production of the more important minerals in 1976 (provisional) were as follows (in 1,000 tonnes):

Anthracite	3,570	Iron ore	7,980	Tin ore	1·0
Coal	6,970	Lead ore	92	Zinc ore	146·4
Lignite	4,140	Manganese ore	...	Wolfram ore	0·5

Agriculture. Spain is mainly an agricultural country. In 1973 the total value of agricultural produce was 299·4m. pesetas; of livestock, 195·5m.; of forestry, 18·3m. Land under cultivation in 1974 (in 1,000 hectares) included: Cereals, 7,519; vegetables, 749; potatoes, 832. In 1970, 261,844 tractors and 32,220 harvesters were in use.

Principal crops	*Area (in 1,000 hectares)*				*Yield (in 1,000 tonnes)*			
	1972[1]	*1973*[1]	*1974*[1]	*1975*[1]	*1972*[1]	*1973*[1]	*1974*[1]	*1975*[1]
Wheat	3,587	3,151	3,163	2,661	4,562	3,966	4,533	4,302
Barley	5,520	2,773	3,027	3,262	4,358	4,402	5,404	6,728
Oats	467	471	475	457	440	425	558	609
Rye	278	268	249	228	263	252	254	240
Rice	59	61	61	62	346	387	367	378
Maize	467	523	501	485	1,923	2,038	1,992	1,793
Potatoes	401	409	407	385	5,210	5,579	5,693	5,337
Sugar-beet	207	190	142	200	5,166	5,501	3,989	6,336
Tomatoes	74	73	82	81	1,953	2,029	2,399	2,488

[1] Provisional.

In 1975, 1,611,000 hectares were under vines; in 1974 production of wine was 36m. hectolitres. The area of onions in 1975 was 33,000 hectares, yielding 820,000 tons. Production of oranges and mandarines in 1974 was 2,478,000 tons. Other products are esparto (41,477 tons in 1964), flax, hemp and pulse. Spain has important industries connected with the preparation of wine and fruits. Silk culture is carried on in Murcia, Alicante and other provinces; 27 tons were produced in 1969. Spain produced in 1968, 8,951 tons of honey and 500 tons of beeswax. Alcoholic beverages produced totalled 232·8m. litres in 1975.

Tobacco crop in 1975 was 25,000 tons; sugar-cane, 273,000 tons.

Livestock. The number of farm animals in 1976 was as follows: Horses, 262,000; mules, 281,000; asses, 258,000; cows, 4·4m.; sheep, 14·7m.; goats, 2·2m.; pigs, 9·2m.

Forestry. Total forests (1975) 26m. hectares; production value, 31,389m. pesetas.

Fisheries. The most important catches are those of sardines, tunny fish and cod. The total catch amounted in 1975 to 1·22m. tons, representing a value of 56,721·1m. pesetas. In the tinned fish industry there were, in 1972, 495 factories, producing 106,944 tons. The Spanish fishing fleet in 1975 consisted of 16,853 vessels of 781,213 tons.

INDUSTRY AND TRADE

Industry. The manufacture of cotton and woollen goods is important, principally in Catalonia. In 1970 there were 3,626 textile factories in operation. Production, in 1,000 tonnes (1975): Wool yarn, 28; cotton (yarn, 68; fabrics, 57); rayon fabrics, 6. 275 paper-mills produced in 1975, 1·9m. tonnes of writing, printing, packing and other paper. The production of cork and cork products was 51,300 tonnes. The production of cement reached 23,968,090 tonnes in 1975.

Spanish shipyards launched 1,690,066 BRT in 1975. In 1975, 936,988 vehicles were built, including 696,682 passenger cars.

Labour. The daily minimum wage for workers is 500 pesetas (Jan. 1978).

The economically active population numbered 11,908,100 at the end of 1970. Of these, 2·95m. were occupied in agriculture and fishing, 3·02m. in manufactures, 1·81m. in trade, 1·87m. in public and personal services.

Commerce. Foreign trade of Spain (Peninsula, Baleares, Canaries, Ceuta, Melilla) (in 1m. pesetas):

	1971	*1972*	*1973*	*1974*	*1975*	*1976*
Imports	347,415	437,566	561,543	888,688	931,986	1,169,412
Exports	205,645	245,215	302,670	407,972	441,091	583,222

In 1975 the most important items of import were (in 1m. pesetas): Manufactures, 441,314; mineral fuels and lubricants, 240,081; food drink and tobacco, 117,210; animal and vegetable oils and fats, 114,583. The main items of exports were: Manufactured goods, 314,958; food, drink, tobacco, 95,753.

In 1975 the main supplying countries were (in 1m. pesetas); USA, 148,067; Federal Republic of Germany, 95,515; France, 77,670; UK, 49,841; Italy, 47,717. The main receiving countries were (in 1m. pesetas): France, 60,254; Federal Republic of Germany, 47,194; USA, 46,308; UK, 33,596; Italy, 15,063.

Of the 115·9m. litres of sherry exported in 1972, 57·9m. went to the UK. In 1972, 113·6 litres of wine were exported.

Total trade between Spain and UK (British Department of Trade returns, in £1,000 sterling):

	1972	*1973*	*1974*	*1975*	*1976*	*1977*
Imports to UK	138,952	203,864	261,826	277,830	360,354	435,176
Exports and re-exports from UK	170,613	199,286	260,292	294,796	368,483	464,829

Trade of the Spanish territories with UK (British Department of Trade returns, in £1,000 sterling):

	Imports to UK			*Exports from UK*		
	1975	*1976*	*1977*	1975	*1976*	*1977*
Canary Islands	36,047	54,200	52,601	38,635	39,504	45,367
North Africa	1	8	181	1,913	2,725	4,733

Tourism. In 1976, 30m. foreigners visited Spain.

COMMUNICATIONS

Roads. In 1974 the total length of highways and roads in Spain was 142,585 km, of which 56,106 km were macadamized. Number of motor cars was 7,600,532 in 1976.

Railways. The total length of the state railways in 1975 was 13,497 km, mostly 1,676-mm gauge. There are 3,143 km of lines electrified. On 1 Feb. 1941 the Spanish railways, of broad gauge only, passed into state ownership; they are under a board known as the *Red Nacional de Ferrocarriles Españoles* (RENFE). The gauge of the principal Spanish railways has, for strategic reasons, been kept different from that of France; passengers therefore must change trains at the frontier stations except by certain trains having variable gauge axles. Number of passengers carried in 1975 by government-owned lines was 199·6m.; freight carried was 37·6m. tonnes. A further 2,757 km of route is being electrified during 1974–77 development plan period and a high-speed 1,435-mm gauge line from the French frontier at Port Bou to Barcelona and Madrid is planned.

Aviation. The most important Spanish airline is 'Iberia': it maintains a regular service with Tangier, Morocco, the Balearic and Canary Islands, Lisbon, Switzerland,

London, Buenos Aires, Venezuela, Cuba, Canada and USA. There are 37 civilian and 7 military airports.

Aircraft movements in 1975 (provisional), 312,441 internal and 230,491 international, carrying 37·8m. passengers and 287,497 tonnes of merchandise.

Shipping. The merchant navy in 1973 contained 3,040 vessels of a gross tonnage of 4,840,665.

1972, 98,021 (1973: 97,704) ships entered Spanish ports, carrying 3,061,848 (1973: 3,355,665) passengers and discharging 107·8m. (1973: 104m.) tons of cargo; 98,590 (1973: 97,662) ships cleared, carrying 3,087,569 (1973: 3,174,557) passengers and loading 51m. (1973: 49m.) tons of cargo.

Post and Broadcasting. The receipts of the post office in 1970 were 6,280m. pesetas; expenses, 6,050m. pesetas. There were in 1974, 12,745 post offices and (1977) 8,597,781 telephones nearly all privately operated.

The length of telegraph lines in 1975 was 36,675 km; number of telegraph offices, 8,830. Total receipts (1975), 2,271m. pesetas; expenses, 4,391m. pesetas.

The 'Compañia Nacional de Telegrafia sin Hilos' holds the government concession for the public service with ships, and between the Peninsula and the Canary Islands, and the international service with England, Italy, France, Switzerland and America, as well as various special press services. The National Radio Service 'Redera' operates a broadcasting station at Arganda, 15 miles from Madrid.

The overseas radio-telegraph circuits are operated in Spain mainly by Trans-radio Española, SA. Under an agreement with Cable and Wireless, Ltd, London, Transradio Española lease and operate the Bilbao end of the Bilbao–Great Britain cable and the Barcelona end of the Barcelona–Marseilles cable.

Radio Nacional de España broadcasts 4 programmes on medium-waves and FM, as well as 4 regional programmes. *Television Española* broadcasts 2 programmes. Colour transmissions are carried by PAL system. Number of receivers: radio, 5·1m.; television, 4·4m. (including 3,000 colour sets).

Cinemas (1974). There were 8,586 cinemas with an estimated seating capacity of 5m.

Newspapers (1975). There appeared 247 daily newspapers with a total daily circulation of about 7·3m. copies. Thirteen of them were published in Madrid and 10 in Barcelona; all must be printed in Castilian.

JUSTICE, RELIGION, EDUCATION AND WELFARE

Justice. Justice is administered by *Tribunales* and *Juzgados* (Tribunals and Courts), which conjointly form the *Poder Judicial* (Judicial Power). Judges and magistrates cannot be removed, suspended or transferred except as set forth by law.

The Judicature is composed of the *Tribunal Supremo* (Supreme High Court); 15 *Audiencias Territoriales* (Division High Courts); 50 *Audiencias Provinciales* (Provincial High Courts); 579 *Juzgados de Primera Instancia* (Courts of First Instance), and 9,203 *Juzgados Municipales, Comarcales y de paz* (District Court, or Court of Lowest Jurisdiction held by Justices of the Peace).

The *Tribunal Supremo* consists of a President (appointed by the Government) and various judges distributed among 6 chambers: 1 for trying civil matters, 3 for administrative purposes, 1 for criminal trials and 1 for social matters. The *Tribunal Supremo* has disciplinary faculties; is court of cassation in civil criminal trials; for administrative purposes decides in first and second instance disputes arising between private individuals and the State, and in social matters resolves in the last instance all cases involving over 100,000 pesetas.

The *Audiencias Territoriales* have power to try in second instance sentences passed by judges in civil matters.

The *Audiencias Provinciales* try and pass sentence in first instance on all cases filed for delinquency. The jury system is in operation except for military trials.

The *Juzgados Municipales* try small civil cases and petty offences. The *Juzgados Comarcales* deal with the same charges, but their jurisdiction embraces larger districts.

Military cases are tried by the *Tribunal Supremo de Justicia Militar*.

The prison population was, on 31 Dec. 1976, 9,937.

Police. The Minister of the Interior (*Gobernación*) controls the armed police, the secret police and the para-military *Guardia Civil.*

Religion. Catholicism is again established as the religion of the State. Religious bodies have recovered their legal status; confiscated property has been returned; allowances to clergy are again paid by the State; divorce is suppressed; cemeteries are brought back to ecclesiastical jurisdiction. There are 10 metropolitan sees and 64 suffragan sees, the chief being Toledo, where the Primate resides.

A concordat was signed in Rome on 27 Aug. 1953 to replace the concordat of 1851, which the Republic had denounced in 1931.

There are about 26,000 Protestants, with 200 churches and chapels, outside which no public ceremonies are permitted. The British and Foreign Bible Society was, on 10 March 1963, allowed to resume its activities.

The first synagogue since the expulsion of the Jews in 1492 was opened in Madrid on 2 Oct. 1959. The number of Jews is estimated at about 1,000.

Education. Spain is divided into 12 educational districts, with the universities as centres. Primary education is compulsory and free. The *Frente de Juventudes* (Youth Front) was created by law of 6 Dec. 1940; it comprises 3 sections (educational, labour, rural). There is also the University Militia for army training under conscription.

In 1973–74 there were 138,114 primary schools attended by 4,945,774 pupils, with 169,977 teachers. Secondary education is conducted by 4,312 middle schools, with 56,379 teachers and 1,012,945 pupils. For higher education, there are 410 centres with 399,500 pupils and 26,800 teachers. There are 13 universities, attended (1965–66) by 125,771 students, with 3,078 teachers. The universities are at Barcelona, Granada, Madrid, Murcia, Oviedo, Salamanca, Santiago, Sevilla, Valencia, Valladolid, Zaragoza, Pamplona and La Laguna (Canaries). There is, besides, a medical and science faculty at Cádiz in connexion with the University of Seville.

In 1972 the government announced the creation of 4 new universities at Málaga, Córdoba, Santander and the first 'university of the air'. A further 2 universities are envisaged.

Social Security. Schemes of wide social range include the Labour Charter (*Fuero del Trabajo*) of 9 March 1938, for a better distribution and remuneration of the working classes, with uninterrupted Sunday and feast-day wages. The law of Family Subsidy (*Subsidio Familiar*), which came into force on 1 March 1939, makes all working people contribute 1% of their earnings, plus an additional 6% from the employers, in a system of social insurance which entitles all families with from 2 to 12 children under 14 years of age to a proportional monthly allowance ranging from 60 to 4,500 pesetas, with an additional 3,000 pesetas for each child in excess of 12 (2 Sept. 1955). Married workers receive an additional bonus. Since 1949, old age pensions and health and maternity insurances have been added; workers contribute 1% and employers 5%.

A decree of 22 Feb. 1941 established state loans on marriage to help large families, and the institution known as *Auxilio Social*, the funds of which are derived among other channels from a fortnightly public collection throughout the country, for supplying food and clothing to needy persons and the maintenance of nurseries and infirmaries. A national health insurance for all workers is now also in operation.

By a law dated 27 Feb. 1908 the *Instituto Nacional de Previsión* was founded for the purpose of granting old age pensions and administering a system of social insurance. The family-allowance and health-insurance schemes, described above, have been incorporated in the *Instituto*.

DIPLOMATIC REPRESENTATIVES

OF SPAIN IN GREAT BRITAIN (24 Belgrave Sq., London SW1X 8QA)

Ambassador: Don Luis Guillermo Perinat y Elio, Marquess de Perinat (accredited 24 March 1976).

OF GREAT BRITAIN IN SPAIN (Calle de Fernando el Santo, 16, Madrid, 4)
Ambassador: Sir Antony Acland, KCVO, CMG.

OF SPAIN IN THE USA (2700–15th St., NW, Washington, D.C., 20009)
Ambassador: Juan José Rovira.

OF THE USA IN SPAIN (Serrano 75, Madrid)
Ambassador: Wells Stabler.

OF SPAIN TO THE UNITED NATIONS
Ambassador: Jaime de Piníes.

Books of Reference

Statistical Information: The Instituto Nacional de Estadistica (Generalisimo 91, Madrid) combines the administrative work of a government department attached to the Presidency of the Government with a centre of statistical studies. *Director-General:* Benito Martinez-Echevarria. Its publications include: *Anuario Estadístico de España.* Annual (latest vol., 1966). *Edición manual* (latest vol., 1973).—*Reseñas estadísticos provinciales.*—*Nomenclator de las ciudades, villas lugares, aldeas, y demás entidades de población de España,* 6 vols. Madrid, 1963.—*Censo de Población de España,* Madrid, 1960.—*Diccionario Corográfico de España,* 4 vols. Madrid, 1948.—*Boletin de Estadística.* Madrid. (No. 1, Jan.–March 1939; monthly from 1948).—*Estadística española. Revista trimestral* (from 1959).

Spain at a Glance, 1972. Servicio Informativo Español, Madrid, 1972

Aguilar (ed.), *Nuevo Atlas de España.* Madrid, 1961
Altamira y Crevea, R., *A History of Spain.* New York and London, 1950
Anuario del Mercado Español. Madrid, 1965
Enciclopedia Universal Ilustrada. 70 vols., 10 appendices, 10 supplements. Madrid
Garcia Venero, M., *Historia del Nacionalismo Vasco, 1793–1936.* Madrid, 1945
Hermet, G., *L'Espagne de Franco.* Paris, 1974
Lafuente, M., and Valera, J., *Historia General de España.* New ed. 25 vols. Barcelona, 1925
López Oliván, J., *Repertorio Diplomático Español.* [*Collection of treaties, 1125–1935.*] Madrid, 1944
Roman M., *The Limits of Economic Growth in Spain.* New York, 1971 and London, 1972
Russell, P. E. (ed.), *Spain: A Companion to Spanish Studies.* 6th ed. London, 1973
Vicens Vives, J., *Historia Económica de España.* 5 vols. Barcelona, 1959
Wright, A., *The Spanish Economy 1959–1976.* London, 1977

National Library: Biblioteca Nacional, Madrid. *Director:* Guillermo Cuastavino Callent.

FORMER PROVINCE IN AFRICA (WESTERN SAHARA)

It was announced in Madrid on 14 Nov. 1975 that Spain, Morocco and Mauritania had reached agreement on the transfer of power over Western Sahara to Morocco and Mauritania on 28 Feb. 1976. Morocco occupied El Aiaún in late Nov. and on 12 Jan. 1976 the Spanish army withdrew from Western Sahara which had ceased to be a Spanish province on 31 Dec. 1975. The country was partitioned by Morocco and Mauritania with the new border passing north of Dakhla (Villa Cisneros), turning east and then turning south-east.

Algeria stated that the former province should be handed over to the people of the territory, objected to the partition and is (1977) backing the claims of *Frente Polisario* for an independent state. In spite of occupation of all centres by Moroccan and Mauritanian troops, Saharan guerrillas based in Algeria continue to attempt to liberate their country. They have renamed it the Democratic Saharan Arab Republic.

The area was 266,000 sq. km (102,680 sq. miles). The population at the census (1970) was 76,425; Saharans, 59,777 and 16,648 Europeans. The capital was El Aaiún (population, 24,048).

Rich phosphate deposits were discovered in 1963. Morocco holds 65% of the shares of the former Spanish state-controlled company. While production reached 5·6m. tonnes in 1975, exploitation has been severely reduced by guerrilla activity in 1976 and 1977.

Books of Reference

Atlas Histórico y Geográfico de Africa Española. Madrid, 1955
Resumén estadistico del Africa aspañola. 1965–66. Madrid, 1967
Caro Baroja, J., *Estudios saharianos.* Madrid, 1955
Hernández-Pacheco, E., and others, *El Sahara español.* Madrid, 1949
Mercer, J., *Spanish Sahara.* London, 1976
Pélissier, R., *Les Territoires Espagnols d'Afrique.* Paris, 1963.—*Los Territorios Españoles de Africa.* Madrid, 1964
Rumeu de Armas, A., *España en el Africa Atlántica.* 2 vols. Madrid, 1956–57

SRI LANKA

Ceylon

Capital: Colombo
Population: 14·27m. (1976)
GNP per capita: US$200 (1976)

HISTORY. According to the Mahawansa chronicle, an Indian prince from the valley of the Ganges, named Vijaya, arrived in the 6th century B.C. and became the first king of the Sinhalese. The monarchical form of government continued until the beginning of the 19th century when the British subjugated the Kandyan Kingdom in the central highlands.

In 1505 the Portuguese formed settlements on the west and south, which were taken from them about the middle of the next century by the Dutch. In 1796 the British Government annexed the foreign settlements to the presidency of Madras. In 1802 Ceylon was constituted a separate colony. Passing through various stages of increasing self-government, Ceylon reached fully responsible status within the British Commonwealth when the Ceylon Independence Act, 1947, came into force on 4 Feb. 1948. Sri Lanka became a republic in 1972.

EVENTS. In Aug. 1977 exceptionally serious rioting took place between the Sinhalese and Tamil communities. This has re-emphasized the Tamils' request for a separate state; government policy is to establish rights for the Tamils within the existing, unified, state.

AREA AND POPULATION. Sri Lanka lies off the south-east coast of the Indian State of Tamil Nadu, separated from it by the Indian ocean but almost joined to it by the chain of islands called Adam's Bridge. On 28 June 1974 the frontier between India and Sri Lanka in the Palk Strait was re-defined, giving to Sri Lanka the island of Kachchativu. Area (in sq. miles) and census population on 9 Oct. 1971:

Provinces	*Area*	*Population*	*Provinces*	*Area*	*Population*
Western	1,432	3,404,444	North-Central	4,140	553,065
Central	2,158	1,956,755	Uva	3,874	807,820
Southern	2,146	1,666,710	Sabaragamuwa	1,892	1,313,804
Northern	3,429	877,768			
Eastern	3,242	722,883	Total	25,332	12,711,143[1]
North-Western	3,016	1,407,894			

[1] 25,422,286 sq. km.

Population (1971 census), 12,711,143, an increase of 20·5% since 1963. Estimate (1976) 14·27m. Population (in 1,000) according to race and nationality at the 1971 census: 9,147 Sinhalese, 1,416 Ceylon Tamils, 824 Ceylon Moors, 44 Burghers, 42 Malays, 1,195 Indian Tamils, 29 Indian Moors. Non-nationals of Sri Lanka totalled 1,224,784. By agreement with the Government of India in 1964 and 1974, Indian nationals who have not been granted Sri Lanka citizenship were to be repatriated. The 1964 agreement covered 525,000 people; the 1974 agreement, 150,000.

Vital statistics, 1972 (provisional): Births, 383,070; marriages, 90,094; deaths, 103,104. 1973 (provisional): Births, 366,186; deaths, 100,850.

The urban population is 22·4% of the total population. The principal towns and their population according to the census of 1971 are: Colombo, 562,160; Dehiwela–Mt. Lavinia, 154,785; Jaffna, 107,663; Kotte, 92,042; Kandy, 93,602; Galle, 72,720; Moratuwa, 96,489; Negombo, 57,115; Kurunegala, 25,189; Nuwara Eliya, 16,347.

The official language is Sinhala. English is a major second language. The use of Tamil for some official purposes was approved by Parliament in 1966.

CONSTITUTION AND GOVERNMENT. Prior to independence the Ceylon and UK governments concluded agreements on defence, external affairs and public officers. The defence agreement provided that the UK and Ceylon would give to each other such military assistance as it may be in their mutual interest to provide. The UK may base such naval and air forces and maintain such land forces in Ceylon as may be required for these purposes, and as may be mutually agreed. The UK naval base at Trincomalee and the air base at Katunayake were taken over by Ceylon on 15 Oct. and 1 Nov. 1957 respectively.

The agreement on external affairs declared the readiness of Ceylon to adopt and follow the resolutions of past imperial conferences; provides that in external affairs generally the two governments will conform to the principles and practice observed by other members of the Commonwealth; provides that Ceylon will enjoy reciprocal rights and benefits enjoyed by the UK, and bear the obligations carried by the UK, which arise out of any valid international instrument which applies to Ceylon.

The public officers agreement protected the positions of specified classes of person holding office in the public service of Ceylon.

Parliament consists of one chamber, the National State Assembly, composed of 168 members elected by universal suffrage, and 6 are nominated. The Senate was abolished by constitutional amendment in Sept. 1971.

The House of Representatives as a Constituent Assembly framed a new republican constitution providing for a President and a Council of Ministers headed by the Prime Minister and responsible to a National Assembly.

This constitution came into force on 22 May 1972. Sovereignty is vested entirely in the National Assembly, which sits for 6 years and combines legislative and executive functions. The Public Service Commission and Judicial Commission were abolished.

In Oct. 1977 the constitution was amended to provide a presidential form of government. The office of President would be held by the then Prime Minister: Mr Jayawardene took office on 4 Feb. 1978 for a 6-year term with wide executive powers, including the right to preside over the cabinet and to assign any ministry to himself.

The electorate consists of all over 18 years of age.

National flag: A yellow field bearing 2 panels: in the hoist 2 vertical strips of green and orange; in the fly, dark red with a gold lion holding a sword and in each corner a gold 'bo' leaf.

The Cabinet in June 1978 was as follows:

President, Defence and Planning: J. R. Jayawardene.

Prime Minister: Ranasingle Premadasa.

Irrigation, Power and Highways: Gamini Dissanayake. *Foreign Affairs:* A. C. S. Hameed. *Trade:* Lalith Athulathmudali. *Shipping, Aviation and Tourism:* Wimala Kannangara. *Education:* N. P. Wijeyeratna. *Finance and Economic Affairs:* Ronnie de Mel. *Labour:* Capt. C. P. J. Seneviratne. *Industries and Scientific Affairs:* Cyril Mathew. *Local Government, Housing and Construction:* R. Premadasa. *Cultural Affairs:* E. L. B. Hurulle. *Fisheries:* F. Perera. *Health:* Gamini Jayasooriya. *Information and Broadcasting:* D. B. Wijetunge. *Parliamentary Affairs and Sports:* M. Vincent Perera. *Transport:* H. M. Mohamed. *Agriculture and Land:* E. L. Senanayake. *Posts and Telecommunications:* D. Shelton Jayasinghe. *Plantation Industries:* M. D. H. Jayawardene. *Textile Industry:* Wijepala Mendis. *Justice:* K. W. Dewanayagam. *Social Services:* Asoka Karunaratne. *Food and Co-operatives:* S. B. Herath.

For purposes of general administration, the island is divided into 22 districts, each presided over by a government agent with assistants. There are 12 municipalities, with 39 urban councils, 85 town councils and 542 village committees. People's Committees inaugurated on 1 Sept. 1971, consisting of 11 members drawn from co-operatives, trade unions, rural development societies and local government bodies, have been abandoned.

The capital is Colombo.

DEFENCE

Army. The Army was constituted on 10 Oct. 1949 and consists of the Regular Force, the Regular Reserve, the Volunteer Force and the Volunteer Reserve. Strength, 8,900, organized into 1 brigade of 3 battalions, 1 reconnaissance regiment and 1 artillery regiment. Reserves, 12,000.

Navy. The Navy was constituted on 9 Dec. 1950. It comprises a frigate, 6 (1 *ex*-Soviet and 5 *ex*-Chinese) fast gunboats, 22 small patrol boats, and 4 survey craft. *Gemunu* and *Rangalla* are commissioned as shore establishments. Personnel in 1978 numbered 200 officers and 2,100 ratings. Naval personnel are sent to the UK for training. There is also a Naval Reserve, a Volunteer Naval Force and a Voluntary Naval Reserve.

Air Force. The Air Force was formed on 10 Oct. 1950. Its flying bases are at Katunayake and China Bay, Trincomalee. In 1975 equipment included 5 MiG-17F jet fighter-bombers, 1 MiG-15UTI jet trainer, 4 Jet Provosts (armed), 7 Chipmunk and 5 Cessna 150 trainers, 4 Heron and 3 Dove light transports (also used for coastal reconnaissance), 1 Convair 440 and 4 Cessna Skymasters for transport duties, and 2 Kamov Ka-26, 7 JetRanger and 5 Bell 47G helicopters for internal security operations. Total strength is about 2,000 officers and airmen. There is also an Air Force Reserve.

INTERNATIONAL RELATIONS

Membership. Sri Lanka is a member of UN, the Commonwealth and the Colombo Plan.

External debt. External debt in 1976 was Rs 6,620m., of which Rs 4,968m. was long-term debt and Rs 916m. IMF drawings.

Agreement. In 1952 Sri Lanka and China signed the 'Rice–Rubber Agreement', whereby Sri Lanka agreed to supply rubber in return for rice. This established China as a major trading partner.

ECONOMY

Budget. Revenue and expenditure of central government in Rs 1m. for financial years ending 30 Sept.:

		Expenditure		
Year	*Revenue*	*Recurrent*	*Capital*	*Total*
1974–75	5,085·7	5,153·1	1,960·4	6,886·6
1975–76	4,493·6	4,593·2	1,968·4	6,651·6
1976–77	6,497·0	6,195·0	3,054·0	9,249·0
1977–78[1]	10,830·0	10,070·0	5,180·0	15,250·0

[1] Estimate.

The principal sources of revenue in 1975–76 were (in Rs 1m.): Income tax, 633·1; import duties, 252·3; export duties, 742·3; other indirect taxes, 2,453·9.

The principal items of expenditure in 1975–76 (in Rs 1m.): Defence, 146; food, subsidies, 1,092; education, 718·3; health, 406·8; agriculture, 484·2; communications, 445.

The net public debt on 30 Dec. 1975 was Rs 12,959·7m., consisting of domestic loans (9,254·8m.) and foreign loans (3,704·9m.).

Currency. The Monetary Law (Amendment) Act No. 16 of 1967 provides that the standard monetary unit is the Ceylon rupee having a par value equal to 0·149297 of a grain of fine gold. Following the devaluation of sterling in Nov. 1967, the Ceylon rupee was devalued by 20%.

The Central Bank is the sole authority for the issue of currency and all currency notes and coins issued by the Central Bank are legal tender for the payment of any amount. Currency notes are issued in the denominations of Re 1, Rs 2, 5, 10, 50 and 100. The following coins are legal tender: (1) nickel brass. 10 and 5 cents; (2) cupro-nickel, Re 1, 50 and 25 cents; (3) aluminium, 2 and 1 cent, and copper, ½ cent. The note circulation stood at Rs 1,090·4m. on 31 Dec. 1970. The official rate between Sri Lanka and the UK (1977) was Rs 29·94 to £1.

Banking. National reserves at 1 Sept. 1976 stood at Rs 651·2m.

The leading banks in Sri Lanka are: The Bank of Ceylon and the People's Bank (state-managed), the Mercantile Bank Ltd, the State Bank of India, National &

Grindlays Bank, the Hongkong and Shanghai Banking Corporation, the Chartered Bank, the Commercial Bank of Ceylon, the Hatton Bank, the Habib Bank (Overseas) Ltd and the Indian Overseas Bank Ltd. Nationalization of foreign banks (except Indian and Pakistani) was proposed in 1976.

The state-owned Ceylon Insurance Corporation has a monopoly of all insurance business.

The Sri Lanka Savings Bank had deposits amounting to Rs 180m. in March 1972. It has been amalgamated with the post office savings bank and Ceylon Savings Movement to form the Sri Lanka National Savings Bank. The post office savings bank on 31 March 1972 had a balance to depositors' credit of Rs 653·7m. The loans granted by the Sri Lanka State Mortgage Bank for the year ended 30 Sept. 1973 amounted to Rs 6·3m.

Weights and Measures. The Imperial weights and measures of the UK are established as the standard weights and measures of Sri Lanka. Local and customary weights and measures are still used in parts of the country.

ENERGY AND NATURAL RESOURCES

Electricity. Installed capacity of electric energy (1974), 281,000 kw., of which 195,000 kw. is hydro-electricity. Energy produced, 1,050m. kwh., of which 800m. kwh. is hydro-electricity.

Water. The Mahaweli Ganga power and irrigation scheme has been inaugurated. It is to be completed within 5 years and will benefit 896,000 acres. Two major diversions, at Polgolla near Kandy and at Bowatenna on the Amban Ganga River, will benefit 120,000 acres of land already cultivated and irrigate an extra 104,000 acres of new land.

Minerals. Graphite is the chief mineral mined and exported. There were 8 mines working at the end of 1968. The total quantity of graphite exported during 1975 was 5,886 tonnes.

The Sri Lanka Mineral Sands Corporation is running a plant at Pulmoddai on the NE coast for the recovery of ilmenite, production in 1974 was 10·26m. long tons. There are several gem pits from which sapphire, ruby, aquamarine, moonstone, topaz, chrysoberyl (cat's eye), zircon, spinel, tourmaline and other semi-precious stones are obtained. There are also deposits of kaolin, iron-ore and glass sand. The miocene limestone of the north is the basis of the cement industry.

Manufacture of salt is a government monopoly. Production (1974) 120,000 tonnes.

Agriculture. The area of the island is approximately 16,212,480 acres, of which about 4·9m. acres are under cultivation, and about 456,000 acres pasture land. The acreage and production of the main crops in 1976 were as follows: Paddy, 1·71m. (60m. bushels); rubber, 561,000 (152,000 tonnes); tea, 597,691 (196,000 tonnes); other crops were coffee and maize.

In March 1976 the Sri Lanka State Plantation Corporation took over management of all private tea and rubber estates. Compensation is paid on condition that it be re-invested in Sri Lanka. The Sri Lanka Tea Corporation was formed in March 1972.

Livestock in 1976: 1·7m. cattle, 850,000 buffaloes, 36,000 swine, 600,000 goats and 30,000 sheep.

Fisheries. The Government is implementing a programme for the development of fisheries in inland as well as deep-sea waters. Production for 1974 was 108,952 tons valued at Rs 313,458.

INDUSTRY AND TRADE

Industry. The Business Undertakings (Acquisition) Act was passed in May 1971 empowering the Government to acquire any business for the state. The British Ceylon Corporation Ltd and its subsidiaries were nationalized in Feb. 1972. The nationalization of the oil industry was completed in Dec. 1971. The first objective was the development of heavy industry through state investment in small companies and the setting up of public corporations. Three such corporations have been established for the mining and processing of graphite; the importing, manufacture and distribution of pharmaceuticals; the importing and distribution of materials for textile manufacture. Present government policy favours private investment. Other important manufactures are ceramics, vegetable oils, fertilizers, cement, wood and paper products, leather, rubber products and sugar. Foreign investment is encouraged by a 5-year tax holiday for approved industries. Export profits may have a 3-year tax holiday.

Trade Unions. The registration and control of trade unions are regulated by the Trade Unions Ordinance (Ch. 138 of the Legislative Enactments). As at 31 Dec. 1973 there were 1,644 unions; 590 employees' unions reported a membership of 1,216,252; and 16 employers' unions reported 1,488 members.

Commerce. State Trading Corporations handle all imports and the private sector handles most exports. The values of total imports and exports (both including bullion, specie and postal articles; exports, including re-exports and ship's stores) for calendar years (in Rs 1,000):

	1973	*1974*	*1975*	*1976*
Imports	2,714,688	4,554,000	5,251,300	4,406,000
Exports	2,617,100	3,471,900	3,933,400	4,805,000

Principal exports (domestic) in 1975 (in Rs 1m.): Tea, 1,931·6; cocoa, 3·6; copra, coconut oil and desiccated coconut, 387·5; cardamoms, 12·7; rubber, 653·6; coir fibre products, 79·1.

Principal imports in 1975 were food and drink, consumer goods, investment goods and intermediate goods.

In 1975 the principal sources of imports were (in Rs 1m.): China, 661·5; Saudi Arabia, 636·6; Japan, 447; Australia, 429·5; France, 429·1; Thailand, 355·6; USA, 336·6; Federal Republic of Germany, 252; UK, 223·5.

Of the 453·1m. lb. of black tea in 1973, the following countries received the largest amounts: UK, 72m.; Pakistan, 66·8m.; Iraq, 44·4m.; USA, 39m.; Australia, 24·4m. South Africa, 23·6m.; UAR, 20·6m.; Saudi Arabia, 16·6m.; Syria, 13·2m.; New Zealand, 12·5m.; Canada 12·3m.; Netherlands, 11·4m.

Trade with UK (British Department of Trade returns, in £1,000 sterling):

	1973	*1974*	*1975*	*1976*	*1977*
Imports to UK	22,957	30,436	27,178	35,518	50,793
Exports and re-exports from UK	10,189	10,042	15,882	17,913	27,872

Tourism. Over 85,000 tourists visited the country in 1974.

COMMUNICATIONS

Roads. There are about 16,333 miles of motorable roads, of which 12,039 are black-topped.

Number of motor vehicles, 31 Dec. 1973, 183,929, including 89,771 private cars and cabs, 34,633 lorries and vans, 12,192 buses and coaches, 16,726 tractors, 8,052 trailers, 22,134 motor cycles, 411 ambulances and hearses.

Railways. There are 1,395 km of railway open, 1,676 mm gauge apart from 139 km of 762 mm gauge line.

Aviation. Air Sri Lanka Ltd operates internal and international services.

Foreign airlines which operate scheduled services to Sri Lanka are British Airways, UTA, Qantas, India Airlines Corporation, Swissair, Aeroflot, TWA, Malaysian Airways, Singapore Airlines, Pakistan International Airlines; various others operate charter services. In 1974 aircraft flew 4m. km., carried a total of 90,000 passengers and 2·6m. tonnes of freight per km.

Shipping. In 1973, 1,966 ocean-going merchant vessels totalling 5,245,878 NRT entered and 1,971 vessels of 8,001,830 NRT cleared the ports of Sri Lanka. In 1974, 1·12m. tonnes of goods were loaded at ports and 3m. tonnes unloaded. Total income of Sri Lanka Shipping Corporation (1975) Rs 185m.

Post and Broadcasting. In 1973 there were 322 post offices, 2,265 sub-post offices, 11 receiving offices for postal business. There were 1,503 telegraph offices. There were (1976) 72,059 telephones, of which 22,318 were in Colombo. Throughout the Greater Colombo Area inter-dialling facilities are now available between 19 stations.

The Overseas Telecommunication Service operates telegraph and telephone services through submarine cables and/or VHF radio circuits to most parts of the world. There is a telex service to 66 countries. Broadcasting is provided by the Sri Lanka Broadcasting Corporation, which assumed the functions of Radio Ceylon on 5 Jan. 1967.

Cinemas. In 1975 there were 346 cinemas with a seating capacity of 181,675. The State Film Corporation established in 1972 has exclusive rights to import films and equipment and arranges distribution of foreign and local films.

Newspapers. In 1974 there were 26 daily newspapers and 149 others. In Jan. 1972 a Press Council was set up. Of the main newspaper groups two, Associated Newspapers (publishers of the *Ceylon Daily News*) and the *Times of Ceylon* group, are owned by the Government.

JUSTICE, RELIGION, EDUCATION AND WELFARE

Justice. The systems of law which obtain in Sri Lanka are the Roman-Dutch law, the English law, the Tesawalamai, the Moslem law and the Kandyan law.

The Kandyan law applies to the Kandyan Sinhalese in the Central, North-Central, Uva and Sabaragamuwa provinces in respect of all matters relating to inheritance, matrimonial rights and donations. The law of England is observed in most commercial matters. The law of Tesawalamai is applied to all Tamil inhabitants of Jaffna, in all matters relating to inheritance, marriages, gifts, donations, purchases and sales of land. The Moslem law is applied to all Moslems in respect of succession, donations not involving Fidei Commissa, marriage, divorce and maintenance. These customary and religious laws have been modified in many respects by local enactments.

The court of original jurisdiction are the High Courts, district courts and magistrates' courts. The High Courts try major crimes and also exercise election and admiralty jurisdiction in addition to their power to grant injunctions. The district court has unlimited civil jurisdiction and criminal jurisdiction carrying punitive power to impose sentences of imprisonment up to 5 years and fines up to Rs 5,000. The magistrates' courts exercise civil jurisdiction where the value of the subject-matter does not exceed Rs 1,500, and has criminal jurisdiction carrying the power to impose terms of imprisonment not exceeding 18 months and fines not exceeding Rs 1,500. The Supreme Court is the sole appellate tribunal to which a single appeal lies from decisions of any court. A system of mandatory conciliation also obtains since the establishment of conciliation boards in 1958. The Minister of Justice appoints panels of conciliators from which the conciliation boards are constituted. Wherever such a panel has been appointed all civil disputes and specified criminal offences must be submitted to these boards for conciliation before recourse can be had to the regular courts of law.

Police. The strength of the police service on 31 Dec. 1974 was 16,116.

Religion. Buddhism was introduced from India in the 3rd century B.C.. and is the religion of 67·4% of the inhabitants. There were (1971) 8,567,570 Buddhists, 2,239,310 Hindus, 986,687 Christians, 909,941 Moslems and 7,635 others.

Education. Education is free from the kindergarten to the university and is imparted in the medium of the mother tongue.

In 1974 there were 9,390 schools including 8,571 government schools, 45 private and 774 estate schools. The government schools had about 110,000 teachers and 2·6m. students from grades I to XII. Of current government expenditure, 13% is on education. Education is now administered in 25 education districts under 17 regional directors of education.

The overall control of the education districts is vested in the Ministry of Education.

About 55% of the teachers in these schools are trained. This training has been carried on in the university departments of education for graduates and in 27 training colleges for non-graduates. In 1974 there were 7,565 non-graduates and 131 graduates in training.

In 1972 the 4 universities and the College of Technology at Katubedde were amalgamated as the University of Ceylon, with a Vice-Chancellor, and a President for each of 5 campuses (the 4 universities and 1 college). A sixth campus was established at Jaffna in 1975. The first University of Ceylon was founded in 1942, superseding the Ceylon Medical College founded in 1870 and the Ceylon University College founded in 1921. In 1973 the University had faculties of oriental studies, arts, science, medicine, law, engineering, geology, agriculture and veterinary science with a total of 14,000 students.

Vidyalankara University, established in 1959, provides courses in languages (Pali, Sinhalese, Sanskrit, English, Hindi), humanities and fine arts. Vidyodaya, Colombo and Peradeniya provide courses in sciences, geography, economics, mathematics, business and public administration, in education and in estate management.

Health. In 1973 there were 456 hospitals with 39,732 beds and (1972) there were 3,251 doctors.

Social Security. The activities of the Department of Social Services fall into five main divisions:

Public assistance (monthly allowances); casual relief; relief to leprosy and tuberculosis patients and their dependants.

Relief of widespread distress due to failure of crops, floods, storms, etc., including relief to individual cases of distress among fishermen due to acts of God such as fire, storms and accidents; rehabilitation and resettlement of flood victims.

State homes for the aged; grants-in-aid to voluntary agencies and local authorities for the running of charitable and welfare institutions, homes for children, homes for the aged and crèches.

Services for orthopaedically handicapped persons; services for the deaf and blind; vagrancy and administration of the house of detention.

The payment of compensation to workmen meeting with accidents in the course of their work is provided for under the Workmen's Compensation Ordinance No. 19 of 1934, as amended in 1957, 1959 and 1966. It was brought into operation in 1935, and has been administered by the Director of Social Services, who is Commissioner for Workmen's Compensation, since 1948.

DIPLOMATIC REPRESENTATIVES

OF SRI LANKA IN GREAT BRITAIN (13 Hyde Park Gdns., London, W2 2LX)

High Commissioner: Nanediri Wimalasena (accredited 20 Dec. 1977)

OF GREAT BRITAIN IN SRI LANKA (Galle Rd., Kollupitiya, Colombo 3)

High Commissioner: D. P. Aiers, CMG.

OF SRI LANKA IN THE USA (2148 Wyoming Ave., NW, Washington, D.C., 20008)

Ambassador: W. S. Karunaratne.

OF THE USA IN SRI LANKA (44 Galle Rd., Kollupitiya, Colombo 3)

Ambassador: (Vacant).

OF SRI LANKA TO THE UNITED NATIONS

Ambassador: Hamilton Shirley Amerasinghe.

Books of Reference

The Sri Lanka Year Book
Census Publications from 1871

Collins, Sir C., *Public Administration in Ceylon*. London, 1951
de Silva, K. M. (ed.), *Sri Lanka: A Survey*. London, 1977
Farmer, B. H., *Pioneer Peasant Colonization in Ceylon*. R. Inst. of Int. Affairs, 1957
Ferguson's *Ceylon Directory*. Annual (from 1858)
Jennings, Sir I., *The Constitution of Ceylon*. 3rd ed. London, 1953
Kearney, R. N., *The Politics of Ceylon (Sri Lanka)*. Cornell Univ. Press, 1973
Ludowyk, E. F. G., *The Story of Ceylon*. London, 1962
Pickens, V. L., *Serendipity*. New York, 1964
Ratnasuriya, M. D., and Wijeratne, P. B. F., *Shorter Sinhalese–English Dictionary*. Colombo, 1949
Robinson, M. S., *Political Structure in a Changing Sinhalese Village*. CUP, 1975
Snodgrass, D. R., *Ceylon: An Export Economy in Transition*. Homewood, Ill., 1966
Williams, H., *Ceylon*. London, 1963
Wilson, A. J., *Politics in Sri Lanka 1947–73*. London, 1974
Wriggins, W. H., *Ceylon: Dilemma of a New Nation*. Princeton Univ. Press, 1960

THE DEMOCRATIC REPUBLIC OF THE SUDAN

Jamhuryat es-Sudan Al Democratia

Capital: Khartoum
Population: 17m. (1977)
GNP per capita: US$290 (1976)

HISTORY. Sudan was proclaimed a sovereign independent republic on 1 Jan. 1956. On 19 Dec. 1955 the Sudanese parliament passed unanimously a declaration that a fully independent state should be set up forthwith, and that a Council of State of 5 should temporarily assume the duties of Head of State. The Co-domini, the UK and Egypt, gave their assent on 31 Dec. 1955.

For the history of the Condominium and the steps leading to independence, *see* THE STATESMAN'S YEAR-BOOK, 1955, pp. 340–41.

On 8 July 1965 the Constituent Assembly elected Ismail El-Azhari as President of the Supreme Council. Following a crisis in the coalition Cabinet the Prime Minister, Mohammed Ahmed Mahgoub resigned on 23 April 1969. For political history *see* THE STATESMAN'S YEAR-BOOK, 1973–74, p. 1333. The Government was taken over by a 10-man Revolutionary Council on 25 May 1969 under the Chairmanship of Col. Jaafar M. al Nemery. This Council was dissolved in 1972.

AREA AND POPULATION. The Sudan is bounded north by Egypt, north-east by the Red Sea, east by Eritrea and Ethiopia, south by Kenya, Uganda and Zaïre, west by the Central African Empire and Chad, north-west by Libya. The Sudan covers an area of 967,500 sq. miles (2·5m. sq. km). The Eritrea–Sudan frontier and the frontier with Chad and the Central African Empire have been delimited and demarcated, as also has the greater part of the frontier with Ethiopia.

The population according to the 1973 census was 14,171,732 (estimate (1977) 17m.), and consists mainly (two-thirds to four-fifths) of Moslem Arabs, and Nubians in the north and Nilotic and Negro tribes in the south.

The capital is Khartoum (census 1973, 333,921). Other important cities are: Omdurman (299,401), Khartoum North (150,991), Port Sudan (132,631), Wadi Medani (106,776), Kassala (98,751), El Obeid (90,060), Al-Qadarif (66,465), Atbara (66,116), Kosti (65,257).

In 1973 there were 9 provinces.

CONSTITUTION AND GOVERNMENT. A new Constitution was introduced in 1973. Legislative power lies with a People's Assembly of 250 members. The President nominates 25 and 225 are elected for 4-year terms by universal adult suffrage. Executive power lies with the President.

A measure of autonomy has been given to southern Sudan and a People's Assembly of 60 was elected in Dec. 1973. The Assembly is situated at Juba.

President and Prime Minister: Jafaar M. al Nemery (re-elected for a second term in April 1977).

First Vice-President: Maj. Abou Kassem Mohammed Ibrahim.
Foreign Affairs: Rashid Al Tahir Bakr.

On 9 Dec. 1965 the Constituent Assembly proscribed the Communist Party.

National flag: Three horizontal stripes of red, white, black, with a green triangle based on the hoist.

DEFENCE. The Army is organized in 2 armoured, 1 parachute and 7 infantry brigades, with 6 artillery and 1 engineer regiment. There are about 150 Russian tanks. Total strength (1977), 50,000.

The Navy was established in 1962 with a nucleus of 4 patrol boats built in Yugoslavia and a 10-year training mission from the Yugoslav Navy. Since then 8 more patrol boats, 5 landing craft, an oiler, a water carrier and a survey ship have been acquired from Yugoslavia and 3 coastguard cutters from Iran. Personnel in 1978 totalled 600 officers and men.

The Air Force has been built up with Soviet and Chinese assistance. Two combat squadrons are equipped with about 10 MiG-21 supersonic fighters and 12 MiG-17 fighter-bombers. There is 1 transport squadron, with 6 C-130H Hercules, 4 DHC-50 Buffalo, 5 An-24 and 2 F.27 Friendship turboprop transports; 1 helicopter squadron with 10 Mi-8s and 4 Mi-4s; and 10 armed Jet Provost trainers which are reported to be in store. Fourteen Mirage 50 fighters have been ordered from France, with an option on 14 more, to replace the MiGs. Personnel total about 1,500.

INTERNATIONAL RELATIONS

Membership. Sudan is a member of UN, OAU, the Arab League and is an ACP state of EEC.

ECONOMY

Planning. The 10-year plan 1961/62–1970/71 envisaged a total expenditure on social and economic development of £S565·4m. A 5-year plan for 1971–75, extended to 1977, is now in operation with an estimated total investment of £S666·3m.

Budget. Revenue and expenditure in Sudanese pounds for financial years ending 30 June:

	1970–71	*1971–72*	*1972–73*	*1973–74*	*1974–75*[1]
Revenue	158,016,360	192,706,350	191,286,658	222,835,190	277,182,654
Expenditure	150,416,360	184,485,889	189,586,658	217,119,090	268,291,277

[1] Estimates.

Currency. The monetary unit is the Sudanese *pound* (£S) divided into 100 *piastres* and 1,000 *milliemes*. Sudanese bank-notes of £S10, £S5, £S1, 50 and 25 *piastres* and Sudanese coins of P. 10, 5, 2; m/ms 10, 5, 2, 1 are in circulation. Currency in circulation at 5 Feb. 1975 totalled £S233·75m.

Banking. The Bank of Sudan opened in Feb. 1960 with an authorized capital of £S1·5m. as the central bank of the country; it has the sole right to issue currency. Its foreign reserves stood at £S24·8m. as at 15 Sept. 1974. All foreign banks were nationalized in 1970.

The post office savings bank had 212,090 depositors each with an average balance of £S61 as at 31 May 1974.

Weights and Measures. The metric system is in use.

ENERGY AND NATURAL RESOURCES

Minerals. The following minerals are known to exist in the Sudan: gold, graphite, sulphur, chromite (20,500 tonnes in 1965), iron-ore, manganese-ore, copper-ore, zinc-ore, fluorspar, natron, gypsum and anhydrite, magnesite, asbestos, talc, halite, kaolin, white mica, coal, diatomite (kieselguhr), limestone and dolomite, pumice, lead-ore, wollastonite, black sands, vermiculite pyrites.

Gold is being exploited on a small scale at Gabeit and at Abirkateib (in Kassala Province); alluvial gold is occasionally exploited in Southern Fung and Equatoria. Total gold production in 1972, 95 troy oz. Iron-ore was discovered in Red Sea area in 1976 with estimated reserves of 250m. tonnes.

About 10m. tons of copper ore were proved at Hofrat-en-Nahas, an ancient copper working. Manganese mining activities started in the 1950s but this industry did not develop well and by 1967 only 2,500 tons had been exported. Processed and scrap white mica have been mined since the late fifties; it went out of production for almost a decade, but started again in 1970 when 170 tonnes were produced. A big deposit of vermiculite and a medium-sized deposit of pyrophyllite are known to occur in the Sinkat District. Reserves of metallurgical grade chromite occur in the Ingessana Hills, Southern Blue Nile Province, but only 47,060 tons of this mineral were exported in 1970. Huge reserves of chrysotile asbestos are proved in this vicinity and also in Qala El Nahal area, Kassala Province. Deposits of magnesite, with or without talc, are known to occur in the Ingessana Hills and Qala El Nahal areas in addition to other occurrences in the Halaib area, Northern Red Sea Hills Province, but only 400 tonnes of magnesite were shipped in 1970.

Reserves of high grade gypsum and anhydrite are known to occur in the Red Sea Hills Province 40 miles north of Port Sudan. Salt pans at Port Sudan supply the whole needs of the country and a surplus of about 70,000 tonnes was shipped in 1970. High grade quartz for the glass industry occurs in the Sinkat area and reserves of limestone occur in the Atbara and Rabak areas supplying the needs of cement factories in these areas. Wolfram and tin occur in the Halaib area and nickel, with or without platinum, occurs in the Halaib and Ingessana Hills areas.

Agriculture. In the Sudan, a predominantly agricultural country, cotton is by far the most important cash crop on which the Sudan depends for earning foreign currency. The two types of cotton grown in the Sudan are: (*a*) long staple sakellaridis and sakel types (derivatives of sakellaridis), grown in Gezira, White Nile, Abdel Magid and private pump schemes; (*b*) short staple, mainly American types, in Equatoria and Nuba Mountains, generally by rain cultivation.

Production (1975) in 1,000 tonnes: Sorghum, 1,875; millet, 470; wheat, 362; groundnuts, 991; sesame, 271; sugar-cane, 1,409; cotton, 670.

The Rural Water Supplies and Soil Conservation Board, set up in Oct. 1944, was in May 1956 replaced by the Land Use and Rural Water Development Board and an executive department.

Livestock (1976): Cattle, 15·4m.; sheep, 15·3m.; goats, 10m.

Forestry. The forests of the Sudan, their extent and dominant species are approximately as follows: (1) desert, 728,800 sq. km; (2) semi-desert, 491,000 sq. km (*Acacia Tortilis, Maerua crassifolia*); (3) woodland savannah: (*a*) low rain, 691,000 sq. km (*Acacia melifera, Acacia seyal, Acacia senegal, cambretum*), (*b*) high rain, 347,000 sq. km (*Anogeissus, Khaya, Isoberlinia*); (4) flood region, 246,000 sq. km (*Papyrus*); (5) montane vegetation, 6,000 sq. km (*Podocarpus, Olea*).

Gum arabic, mainly hashab gum from *Acacia senegal*, is the sole forest produce exported from the Sudan on a major scale. About 50,000 tons (95% of the total world supply) are exported annually, fetching about £S6m. It ranks as the second cash crop to cotton. The bulk of gum production originates from Kordofan, Darfur, Kassala and Blue Nile Provinces.

A forest research and education institute has been established by the Sudan Government in co-operation with the United Nations Special Fund.

COMMERCE. Total trade for calendar years, in £S:

	1972	*1973*	*1974*
Imports[1]	111,560,000	151,840,000	223,580,000
Exports	124,350,000	151,710,000	122,010,000

[1] Including government imports.

Principal items of imports and exports in 1974 (quantities in tonnes, value in £S1,000):

	Quantity	*Value*
Imports:		
Cotton fabrics (yards)	96·32m.	11,338
Sugar	120,964	29,821
Motor vehicles (number)	3,468	8,040
Tea (kg)	17·22m.	5,857
Wheat flour	16,815	859
Coffee (kg)	8·6m.	2,709
Cigarettes and tobacco (kg)	876,694	1,955
Machinery	...	62,888
Fertilizers	691,049	120,059

	Quantity	Value
Exports:		
Cotton, ginned	102,788	57,806
Gum arabic	19,805	14,374
Sesame	107,852	21,168
Groundnuts	130,044	24,502
Dura	98,992	4,817
Cottonseed	4,752	241
Animal feeding stuff	96,813	3,614
Vegetable oils (not processed)	6,980	1,457
Sheep (number)	290,823	4,015
Hides and skins	6,712	4,491

Principal sources of import into the Sudan in 1971: UK (14·2%), US (8·7%), India (4·2%). Principal countries of export from the Sudan: China (17·8%), Italy (11·6%), Germany (11·2%).

Trade with UK (British Department of Trade returns, in £1,000 sterling):

	1973	*1974*	*1975*	*1976*	*1977*
Imports to UK	8,377	8,357	8,559	14,209	13,164
Exports and re-exports from UK	26,879	35,974	63,937	91,975	86,234

COMMUNICATIONS

Roads. In the Northern Sudan there are about 550 km of asphalted roads, other than town roads. The remaining roads are only cleared tracks mostly impassable directly after rain. A network of 1,700 km asphalted, all-weather roads was under construction in 1975. In Upper Nile Province motor traffic is limited mostly to the months Jan.–May. In Equatoria and Bahr El Ghazal Provinces there are a number of good gravelled roads with permanent bridges which can be used all the year round, though minor roads become impassable after rain.

Railways. The main railway lines run from Khartoum to El Obeid *via* Wad Medani, Sennar Junction, Kosti and El Rahad (701 km); El Rahad to Nyala *via* Abu Zabad, Babanousa and Ed-Daein (698 km); Sennar Junction to Kassala *via* Gedaref (455 km) and to Roseires *via* Singa (220 km); Kassala to Port Sudan *via* Haiya Junction and Sinkat (550 km); Khartoum to Wadi Halfa *via* Shendi, El Dammer, Atbara, Berber and Abu Hamad Junction (924 km); Abu Hamad to Karima (248 km); Atbara to Haiya Junction (271 km); Babanousa to Wau (444 km). The main flow of exports and imports is to and from Port Sudan *via* Atbara and Kassala. The total length of line open for traffic (1976) was 4,556 km. The gauge is 3 ft 6 in. Several new lines are planned, including a link from Wadi Halfa across the Egyptian border.

Aviation. Sudan Airways is a government-owned airline, with its headquarters in Khartoum, operating domestic and international services. The latter include services to Asmara, Addis Ababa, Aden, Jiddah, Cairo, Athens, Rome, London, Beirut, Nairobi, N'djamena, Tripoli and Entebbe. In 1972 Sudan Airways carried 135,496 passengers and 1,273,000 kg of mail and freight.

Shipping. Supplementing the railways are regular river steamer services of the Sudan Railways, between Karima and Dongola, 319 km; from Khartoum to Kosti, 319 km; from Kosti to Juba, 1,436 km, and from Kosti to Gambeila, 1,069 km. Port Sudan is the country's only seaport; it is equipped with 13 berths.

Post and Broadcasting (1975). There are 213 permanent post and telegraph offices, 24 travelling post and telegraph offices and 372 agencies. There are 27 wireless telegraph and 99 radio-telephone stations, 36 automatic telephone exchanges and 340 telephone call boxes; number of telephones in 1977 was 43,288 (19,602 in Khartoum).

Cinemas. In 1973 there were 52, seating capacity 47,300.

JUSTICE, RELIGION, EDUCATION AND WELFARE

Justice. The judiciary is a separate and independent department of state directly and solely responsible to the President of the Republic. The general administrative supervision and control of the judiciary is vested in the High Judicial Council.

Civil Justice is administered by the courts constituted under the Civil Justice Ordinance, namely the High Court of Justice—consisting of the Court of Appeal and Judges of the High Court, sitting as courts of original jurisdiction—and Province Courts—consisting of the Courts of Province and District Judges. The law administered is 'justice, equity and good conscience' in all cases where there is no special enactment. Procedure is governed by the Civil Justice Ordinance.

Justice in personal matters for the Moslem population is administered by the Mohammedan law courts, which form the Sharia Divisions of the Court of Appeal, High Courts and Kadis Courts; President of the Sharia Division is the Grand Kadi. The religious law of Islam is administered by these courts in the matters of inheritance, marriage, divorce, family relationship and charitable trusts.

Criminal Justice is administered by the courts constituted under the Code of Criminal Procedure, namely Major Courts, Minor Courts and Magistrates' Courts. Serious crimes are tried by Major Courts, which are composed of a President and 2 members and have the power to pass the death sentence. Major Courts are, as a rule, presided over by a Judge of the High Court appointed to a Provincial Circuit or a Province Judge. There is a right of appeal to the Chief Justice against any decision or order of a Major Court, and all its findings and sentences are subject to confirmation by him.

The President of the Supreme Council of the Armed Forces has power to commute a capital sentence. The Chief Justice has power to remit any case subject to confirmation by him to the Court of Criminal Appeal composed of the Chief Justice and 2 Magistrates of the first class, one of whom has to be a Judge of the High Court.

Lesser crimes are tried by Minor Courts consisting of 3 Magistrates and presided over by a Second Class Magistrate, and by Magistrates' Courts consisting of a single Magistrate or a bench of lay magistrates. In Provinces in which circuits of the High Court exist the High Court Judge, in other cases the Province Judge, exercises an appellate jurisdiction and a general supervision over these courts. The greater part of the criminal law is codified in the Sudan Penal Code.

Religion. The population of the 6 northern provinces is almost entirely Moslem (Sunni), the majority of the 3 southern provinces is pagan. There are small Christian communities, with 2 Coptic Bishops, a Greek Orthodox metropolitan, an Anglican bishop and assistant bishop, 4 Roman Catholic bishops and Greek Evangelical, Evangelical and Maronite congregations. In 1962 Protestants numbered about 95,000. Some of the foreign missionaries were expelled from the southern provinces in March 1964.

Education (1975–76). Private kindergartens had 5,010 pupils; government elementary schools, 745,959 boys and 370,149 girls; private elementary schools, 7,543 boys and 7,081 girls; government intermediate schools, 34,304 boys and 6,777 girls; government senior secondary schools, 95,819 boys and 34,220 girls; private junior secondary schools, 10,989 boys and 4,999 girls. In 1975 Khartoum University with 10 faculties had 6,942 students. The Khartoum branch of Cairo University with 4 faculties had 12,671 students and the Islamic University of Omdurman with 3 faculties had 754 students. There were also 1,702 students at 16 higher specialized institutions and colleges.

Health. In 1974 the Ministry of Health maintained 122 hospitals, 1,500 dispensaries and dressing stations, 139 health centres and 620 clinics (with together 15,391 beds) and 1,413 doctors.

DIPLOMATIC REPRESENTATIVES

OF THE SUDAN IN GREAT BRITAIN (3 Cleveland Row, London, SW1A 1DD)

Ambassador: Sayed Amir El-Sawi.

OF GREAT BRITAIN IN THE SUDAN (New Aboulela Bldg, Barlaman Ave, Khartoum)

Ambassador: D. C. Carden, CMG.

OF THE SUDAN IN THE USA (600 New Hampshire Ave., NW, Washington, D.C., 20037)

Ambassador: Omer Salih Eissa.

OF THE USA IN THE SUDAN (Gamhouria Ave., Khartoum)

Ambassador: Donald C. Bergus.

OF THE SUDAN TO THE UNITED NATIONS

Ambassador: Mustafa Medani.

Books of Reference

Sudan Almanac. Khartoum (annual)
Trade Directory of the Republic of the Sudan; with Who's Who in the Sudan. 8th ed. London. 1966
Barbour, K. M., *The Republic of the Sudan.* London, 1967
Barnett, T., *The Gezira Scheme: An Illusion of Development.* London, 1977
Duncan, J. S. B., *The Sudan's Path to Independence.* London, 1957
Fabunni, L. A., *The Sudan in Anglo-Egyptian Relations.* London and New York, 1960
Fawzi, Saad Ed-Din, *The Labour Movement in the Sudan, 1946–55.* R. Inst. of Int. Affairs, 1957
Gaitskell, A., *Gezira: A Study of Development in the Sudan,* London, 1959
Henderson, K. D. D., *The Sudan Republic.* London, 1965
Hill, R., *Sudan Transport: A History of Railway, Marine and River Services.* OUP, 1965
Holt, P. M., *A Modern History of the Sudan.* New York, 1961
Jackson, H. C., *Behind the Modern Sudan.* London, 1956
Lebon, J. H. G., *Land Use in Sudan.* Bude, 1965
Macmichael, Sir H. A., *The Anglo-Egyptian Sudan.* London, 1954
Said, Beshir M., *The Sudan.* London, 1965
Trimingham, J. S., *Islam in the Sudan.* London, 1949
Wai, D. M., (ed.) *The Southern Sudan: The Problem of National Integration.* London, 1973
Wickens, G. E., *The Flora of Jebel Marra.* London, 1977

SURINAM

Capital: Paramaribo
Population: 414,000 (1976)

HISTORY. At the peace of Breda (1667) between Great Britain and the United Netherlands, Surinam was assigned to the Netherlands in exchange for the colony of New Netherland in North America, and this was confirmed by the treaty of Westminster of Feb. 1674. Since then Surinam has been twice in British possession, 1799–1802 (when it was restored to the Batavian Republic at the peace of Amiens) and 1804–16, when it was returned to the Kingdom of the Netherlands according to the convention of London of 13 Aug. 1814, confirmed at the peace of Paris of 20 Nov. 1815. On 25 Nov. 1975, Surinam gained full independence and was admitted to the UN on 4 Dec. 1975.

AREA AND POPULATION. Surinam is situated on the north coast of South America and bounded on the north by the Atlantic Ocean, on the east by the Marowijne River, which separates it from French Guiana, on the west by the Corantijn River, which separates it from Guyana, and on the south by forests and savannas, which separate it from Brazil.

Area, 163,265 sq. km. Census population (1971), 384,900 (estimate (1976) 414,000), including 39,500 Bush Negroes and 10,200 aboriginal Indians. The capital, Paramaribo, had (1971 census) 151,500 inhabitants. Annual rate of growth decreased from 4·34% during 1950–64 to 2·3% during 1964–71, mainly through severe migration primarily to the Netherlands. It is estimated that Surinam lost a total of 62,700 persons by migration.

Birth-rate 32·8 per 1,000, death-rate 6·4 per 1,000.

The official languages are Dutch and English. English is widely spoken next to Hindi, Javanese and Chinese as inter-group communication. A vernacular, called 'Sranan Tongo' or 'Surinamese', is used as a lingua franca. In 1976 the Government announced that Spanish would become the nation's principal working language.

CONSTITUTION AND GOVERNMENT. The Government consists of the President of the Republic of Surinam and the Council of Ministers. The Governor is the constitutional head of the Government. He is assisted by an Advisory Council of 6 members.

President: Dr J. H. E. Ferrier.

There is a council of 13 ministers who are responsible to the Legislative Council (*Staten van Suriname*). The Legislative Council (39 members) is elected for a 4-year period by universal adult suffrage. Seven political parties are represented in the Legislative Council. Elections were held on 31 Oct. 1977 and the National Party Alliance gained 22 seats and the United Democratic Party, 17.

Surinam is divided into 9 districts: Paramaribo (urban district), Commewijne, Coronie, Marowijne, Nickerie, Saramacca, Suriname, Brokopondo and Para.

Flag: Horizontally green, red, green with the red of double width with yellow 5-pointed star in centre of red bar.

INTERNATIONAL RELATIONS

Membership. Surinam is a member of UN and OAS.

DEFENCE. Armed forces of the Republic of Surinam consist of regular local officers and conscripted personnel with a strength of about 600 at the time of independence.

ECONOMY

Planning. A 10-year development plan was launched in 1955 and later extended for

2 years. The first 5-year plan was completed in 1972 and a second 5-year plan (1972–76) is being executed.

For 15 years from independence approximately 3,500m. guilders will be available from the Netherlands to carry out an extensive social and economic development programme devised by a joint Dutch and Surinamese team of experts. This programme envisages the extension of Surinam's economic strength, the creation of greater employment and the improvement of the living conditions of the people.

Budget. The expenditures and local revenues (derived from import, export and excise duties, taxes on houses and estates, personal imports and some indirect taxes) are as follows (in 1,000 Surinam guilders):

	1972	*1973*	*1974*[1]	*1975*	*1976*	*1977*
Revenues	183,200	185,000	204,579	234,600	354,600	541,100
Expenditures	222,500	219,000	249,700	363,900	404,900	581,500

[1] Provisional figures.

Outstanding loans in 1974: Local, 31·7m.; foreign, 184·9m. Surinam guilders. Public debt as at 30 March 1974, 216·6m. Surinam guilders.

Currency. Surinam florin notes ranging from 5 to 1,000 Surinam florins are legal tender. Currency notes of 1·00 and 2·50 guilders are issued by the Government. US$1 = 1·80 Surinam florins; £1 sterling = Sfl3·12 and 1 Netherlands florin = Sfl73·80.

Banking. The Central Bank of Surinam is a bankers' bank and also a bank of issue; the Surinaamsche Bank, the Algemene Bank Nederland and the O.R.G. Vervuurt's Banking Corporation Ltd, are commercial banks; the Surinam People's Credit Bank operates under the auspices of the Government; Surinaamse Postspaarbank (postal savings bank), Surinaamse Hypotheekbank NV (mortgage bank); Surinaamse Investerings Mij. NV (investment bank); Agentschap van de Maatschappij tot financiering van het Nationaal Herstel NV (long-term investments); National Development Bank; The Agrarian Bank.

Weights and Measures. The metric system is in force.

NATURAL RESOURCES

Minerals. Bauxite is the most important mineral; it is being mined in the Suriname and Marowijne districts. Fresh deposits have been found in the western areas. The ore is exported mainly to USA, but partly processed locally into alumina and aluminium. Production in 1975: Bauxite, 4·75m. tonnes; gold (1973, 14 kg; alumina, 1,148,602 tonnes; aluminium, 39,964 tonnes.

Agriculture. Agriculture is restricted to the alluvial coastal zone; cultivated area in 1973, 54,656 hectares. The staple food crop is rice; 46,471 hectares of paddy were planted in 1973, chiefly in the Nickerie, Commewijne, Saramacca and Coronie districts.

Principal products (in 1,000 units) in 1975:

Sugar-cane (kg)	159,543	Maize on cob (kg)	365	Oranges (pieces)	15,036
Cocoa (kg)	55	Bananas (kg)	43,095	Grapefruit (pieces)	5,530
Coffee (kg)	88	Rum 50% (litres)	2,422	Coconuts (pieces)	5,525
Paddy (kg)	174,845	Molasses (kg)	5,727		

Livestock, 1976: 28,000 head of cattle, 10,000 sheep and goats, 7,000 pigs, 908,000 poultry.

Forestry. Surinam has great timber resources. Production 1975 included 29 tonnes of balata, 12,775 cu. metres of sleepers, 1,397 cu. metres of fuel wood, 14,225 cu. metres of plywood and 9,054 cu. metres of particle board, chiefly from the Suriname and Marowijne districts.

Fishery. The catch in 1975 amounted to 2,634 tonnes.

INDUSTRY AND TRADE

Industry. There are 3 large bauxite plants, 1 alumina and 1 aluminium smelting plants, sugar- and rice-mills, 2 paint factories, a fruit-juice plant, 2 shrimp freezing plants, a plywood factory, timber-mills, a milk pasteurization plant, a butter and margarine factory and a considerable number of various medium and small industries.

Commerce. Imports and exports in calendar years (in 1,000 Surinam guilders):

	1969	*1970*	*1971*	*1972*	*1973*	*1974*[1]
Imports	207,700	217,700	237,800	258,200	281,000	390,000
Exports	250,200	235,000	294,500	305,700	319,800	420,000

[1] Estimate.

Principal exports in 1973 (value in 1,000 Surinam guilders): Rice, 20,600; citrus fruits, 12,500; bananas, 3,800; shrimp and other fisheries products, 1,300; bauxite, 85,000; alumina, 143,600; aluminium, 44,800; particle board, 2,157; plywood, 6,384.

Principal imports in 1973 (value in 1,000 Surinam guilders): Fuels and lubricants, 36,100; raw and auxiliary materials, 108,600; textile yarn and fabrics, 7,300; foodstuffs, cars and motor cycles, 6,300; investment goods, 48,500.

Total trade with UK (British Department of Trade returns, in £1,000 sterling):

	1973	*1974*	*1975*	*1976*	*1977*
Imports to UK	4,071	4,873	4,745	24,030	16,525
Exports and re-exports from UK	2,904	4,099	5,760	6,109	9,458

COMMUNICATIONS

Roads. There are 1,335 km of main roads. Two of them lead from Paramaribo to the bauxite centres of Smalkalden (29 km) and Paranam (30 km) and to the airport of Zanderij (49 km). Another main road runs across the districts of Saramacca (71 km) and Coronie (68 km), a fourth across the Commewijne district (41 km) and a fifth in the Marowijne district, from the bauxite centre Moengo to Albina (45 km).

The 'East–West connexion' is almost completed, linking the Corantijn and the Marowijne rivers (375 km).

In 1974 there were 23,227 passenger cars, 5,369 trucks, 1,898 buses, 34,799 powered bicycles and 4,354 motor cycles and scooters.

Railway. There is one single-track railway, running from Onverwacht to Bronsweg (86 km); part of the track, from Paramaribo to Onverwacht (34 km) has been removed.

Aviation. Regular air services are maintained by KLM, SLM, Air France and Cruzeiro do Sul. The international airfield at Zanderij is capable of handling all types of planes.

Surinam Airways Ltd provides daily services between all major districts and maintains also a charter service.

In 1975, 1,205 aircraft landed at Zanderij airport with 40,416 passengers and 1,225 tons of incoming mail and freight.

Shipping. The Royal Netherlands Steamship Co. plies between Amsterdam, Rotterdam, Antwerp, Hamburg and Paramaribo, and New York, Baltimore, New Orleans and Paramaribo. Regular sailings are made to Georgetown, Ciudad Bolivar and most Caribbean ports. The Surinam Navigation Co. maintains services from Paramaribo to Georgetown and Cayenne, and once a month to the Caribbean area. A French and an Italian company maintain passenger services to Europe. The Alcoa Steamship Co. has a fortnightly service to New York, Baltimore, Mobile and New Orleans; a Japanese line sails once a month from Hong Kong and Yokohama to Paramaribo; the Boomerang Line maintains a monthly freight and passenger service between Surinam and Australia. In 1974, 615 vessels totalling 3·58m. GRT entered and in 1975 1,172 of 6·5m. GRT cleared Paramaribo.

Post and Broadcasting. Automatic telephone service links most of the districts in the interior. In 1977 there were 18,566 telephones. Wireless telephone connects Surinam with the Netherlands, USA, Curaçao, Guyana, French Guiana and Trinidad. There are 6 broadcasting and 1 television stations. In 1974 there were 170,000 radios and 36,000 TV sets. Automatic telex was established in 1972.

Cinemas (1973). There are 31 cinemas with a seating capacity of 19,000, and one drive-in cinema.

Newspapers (1973). There are 5 daily newspapers and 5 weeklies with a combined circulation of over 30,000.

JUSTICE, RELIGION, EDUCATION AND WELFARE

Justice. There is a court of justice, whose members are nominated by the President. There are 3 cantonal courts.

Religion. There is entire religious liberty. At the end of 1971 the various religious bodies were: Reformed and Lutheran, 3,911; Moravian Brethren, 51,868; Roman Catholics, 70,175; Moslems, 74,078; Hindus, 112,047; Confucians, 80; others, 27,228.

Education. During school-year 1975–76 there were 413 schools with a total of 134,656 pupils and 4,813 teachers. There are also a University with faculties of medicine and law, social and economic studies, 3 technical schools and 5 teachers' training colleges.

Schooling is compulsory from 6 to 12 years of age. Primary education is free and is undertaken by the Government in public schools and by the Roman Catholic and Protestant Missions in denominational schools.

Social Security. The Government subsidizes orphanages and other religious or philanthropical institutions, and maintains an almshouse and institutions for delinquent boys and girls. There are 13 modern hospitals in the country, 4 of which are operated by missions, 2 by a private company, 1 by the military forces and 6 by the Government.

DIPLOMATIC REPRESENTATIVES

OF GREAT BRITAIN IN SURINAM

Ambassador: P. Gautrey, CMG, CVO.

OF SURINAM IN THE USA (2600 Virginia Ave., NW, Washington, D.C. 20037)

Ambassador: Roel F. Kamamat.

OF THE USA IN SURINAM

Ambassador: J. Owen Zurhellen, Jr (Dr Sophie Redmondstraat, Paramaribo)

OF SURINAM TO THE UNITED NATIONS

Ambassador: Henricus A. F. Heidweiller.

Books of Reference

Statistical Information: The General Bureau of Statistics in Paramaribo was established on 1 Jan. 1947. Its publications comprise trade statistics, *Surinam in Figures* (including, from 1953, the former *Handelsstatistiek*) and *Statistische Berichten.*

Economische Voorlichting Suriname. Ministry of Economic Affairs, Paramaribo
Annual Report of the Central Bank of Surinam

SWAZILAND

Capital: Mbabane
Population: 527,791 (1976)
GNP per capita: US$470 (1976)

HISTORY. The Swazi migrated into the country to which they have given their name, in the last half of the 18th century. They settled first in what is now southern Swaziland, but moved northwards under their chief, Sobhuza—known also to the Swazi as Somhlolo. Sobhuza died in 1838 and was succeeded by Mswati. The further order of succession has been Mbandzeni and Bhunu, whose son, Sobhuza II, was installed as King of the Swazi nation in 1921 after a long minority.

The independence of the Swazis was guaranteed in the conventions of 1881 and 1884 between the British Government and the Government of the South African Republic. In 1890, soon after the death of Mbandzeni, a provisional government was established representative of the Swazis, the British and the South African Republic Governments. In 1894 the South African Republic was given powers of protection and administration. In 1902, after the conclusion of the Boer War, a special commissioner took charge, and under an order-in-council in 1903 the Governor of the Transvaal administered the territory, through the Special Commissioner.

AREA AND POPULATION. Swaziland is bounded on the north, west and south by the Transvaal Province, and on the east by Portuguese territory and Zululand. The area is 6,705 sq. miles (17,400 sq. km).

The country is divided geographically into 4 longitudinal regions running from north to south; 3 of roughly equal width—Highveld (westernmost), Middleveld, Lowveld—and the Lubombo plateau in the east. The mountainous region on the west rises to an altitude of over 6,000 ft (1,800 metres). The Middleveld is mostly between 1,700 and 3,000 ft, while the Lowveld has an average height of not more than 1,000 ft (300 metres). The whole country is now virtually free from malaria. The Highveld and the Middleveld are well watered. Innumerable small streams unite with the large rivers, notably the Usutu and Komati, which traverse the country from west to east. Except for these the Lowveld is not very well watered. The climate is good except for a few months in summer, when the heat is somewhat excessive in low-lying parts.

Population (census 1976), 527,791. Mbabane, the administrative capital (22,262). The main urban areas with 1971 populations are: Manzini 16,000); Havelock Mine (4,500); Siteki (3,600); Big Bend (2,900); Mhlume (2,200); Nhlangano (1,700) and Pigg's Peak (1,400).

CONSTITUTION AND GOVERNMENT. Swaziland became independent on 6 Sept. 1968.

On 25 April 1967 the British Government gave the country internal self-government. It changed the country's status to that of a protected state with the Ngwenyama, Sobhuza II, recognized as King of Swaziland and head of state. Britain's protection ended at independence, when a constitution similar to the 1967 constitution was brought into force. The general elections (by universal adult franchise) in April 1967 gave the royalist and traditional Imbokodvo National Movement all 24 seats. The Parliament consists of a House of Assembly, with 24 elected and 6 nominated members and the Attorney-General, who has no vote, and a Senate comprising 12 members, 6 of whom are elected by the House of Assembly and 6 appointed by the King. The executive authority is vested in the King and exercised through a Cabinet presided over by the Prime Minister, and consisting of the Prime Minister, the Deputy Prime Minister and up to 8 other ministers. In April 1973 the King assumed supreme power and the Constitution was suspended and in 1976 it was abolished.

His Majesty the King: Sobhuza II, KBE.
Prime Minister: Prince Makhosini.

National flag. Horizontally 5 unequal stripes of blue, yellow, red, yellow, blue; in the centre of the red strip an African shield of black and white, behind which are 2 assegais and a staff, all laid horizontally.

Local Government. In Dec. 1963 the former 6 districts were replaced by the 4 districts of Shiselweni, Lubombo, Manzini and Hhohho. They are administered by District Commissioners.

INTERNATIONAL RELATIONS

Membership. Swaziland is a member of UN, OAU, the Commonwealth and is an ACP state of EEC.

ECONOMY

Budget. Revenue and expenditure (in 1,000 emalangeni) for financial years ending 31 March:

	1971–72	*1972–73*	*1973–74*	*1974–75*
Revenue	21,608	28,172	38,237	55,135
Expenditure	20,000	24,443	32,289	37,158

Chief items of estimated revenue, 1974–75: Customs and excise, E18·7m.; income tax, E9·8m.

The public debt expenditure was estimated at R935,060 in 1970–71.

Currency. The currency in circulation in Swaziland, from 1974, is the *emalangeni*, but remains in the rand monetary area.

Banking. Barclays Bank International and the Standard Bank Ltd maintain branches at Mbabane and Manzini; sub-branches and agencies are operated in 17 other places. Bank rates are those in force throughout South Africa and are prescribed by the main South African offices of the 2 banks. The Swaziland Credit and Savings Bank, a statutory body, was opened in 1965. It specializes in credit for agriculture and low-cost housing. Its head office is in Mbabane and it has branches or agencies at 3 other places.

ENERGY AND NATURAL RESOURCES

Minerals. Swaziland produces a large tonnage of iron ore from the Ngwenya mine near Mbabane (2·53m. short tons worth R12m. in 1969) and asbestos from the Havelock Mine (40,200 short tons worth R5m. in 1969). Coal is mined at Mpaka (121,600 short tons worth R260,000 in 1969). Small quantities of quarry stone, kaolin, barytes and pyrophyllite are also mined. Total mineral production was valued in 1968, R18,277,300.

A railway has been built from the Ngwenya hæmatite deposits to Goba, in Mozambique, chiefly for the transportation of iron ore. The Swaziland Iron Ore Development Company has entered into a contract to supply Japanese buyers with 14·5m. tons of ore over 10 years; first shipments began in Nov. 1964. The extensive deposits of low-volatile bituminous coal in the Lowveld are being worked to provide coal for the railway, sugar-mills and export.

Agriculture. Some 56% of the country, which covers 4,290,944 acres, is reserved for occupation by the Swazi. The main crops are sugar, citrus and rice, all of which are grown under irrigation, and cotton, maize (the staple product), sorghum, tobacco and pineapples. It is usually necessary to import maize from South Africa. Sugar, first produced in 1958, and wood-pulp and other forest products are the two main agricultural exports (worth E70·2m. and E12·5m respectively in 1975).

Livestock (1976): Cattle, 600,000; goats, 300,000; sheep, 35,000; poultry, 600,000.

COMMERCE. By agreement with the Republic of South Africa, Swaziland is united in a customs union with the Republic and receives a *pro rata* share of the customs dues collected.

Total exports in 1975 amounted to E132m. The chief items were: Iron ore, E11·9m.; wood-pulp and other forest products, E9·3m.; sugar, E70·2m.; asbestos,

E9·3m.; meat and meat products, E1·6m.; citrus fruit, E3·6m. Imports in 1975 were E57·5m.

Total trade of Swaziland with UK (British Department of Trade returns, in £1,000 sterling):

	1972	*1973*	*1974*	*1975*	*1976*	*1977*
Imports to UK	9,868	12,962	16,119	30,538	30,188	13,340
Exports and re-exports from UK	316	151	511	521	710	559

COMMUNICATIONS

Roads. There is daily (except Sundays) communication by railway motor-buses between Manzini, Mbabane and Breyten; Manzini, Mankayana and Piet Retief. There are 101 miles of tarred trunk roads, 930 miles of gravelled main road and 470 miles of branch roads.

Railways. Swaziland's railway, constructed in 1962–64, is 139 miles long, starting at Kadake, operated by Mozambique State Railways, and connecting at the Mozambique frontier with an extension to the Mozambique State Railways between Maputo and Goba.

Post. There were (1975) 32 post offices, 2 telephone–telegraph agencies and 6 telephone agencies. There were, in Jan. 1977, 8,207 telephones in the country.

Aviation. The country's chief airport is at Matsapa. It is served by Swazi Air and South African Airways, connecting with Johannesburg and Durban, and DETA connecting with Maputo.

Cinemas. There were 4 cinemas in 1975 with a total seating capacity of 1,300.

JUSTICE, RELIGION, EDUCATION AND WELFARE

Justice. The judiciary is headed by the Chief Justice. A High Court having full jurisdiction and subordinate courts presided over by Magistrates and District Officers are in existence. During 1969 there were 6,624 convictions in subordinate courts and 36 convictions in the High Court.

There is a Court of Appeal with a President and 3 Judges. It deals with appeals from the High Court. There are 16 Swazi courts of first instance, 2 Swazi courts of appeal and a Higher Swazi Court of Appeal. The channel of appeal lies from Swazi Court of first instance to Swazi Court of Appeal, to Higher Swazi Court of Appeal, to the Judicial Commissioner and thence to the High Court of Swaziland.

The police force in 1969 had a strength of 30 senior and 188 subordinate officers and 448 other ranks.

Religion. It is estimated that more than 60% of the population is Christian, but no accurate figures are available. The remainder hold traditional beliefs. A large number of churches and missionary societies are established throughout the country and, in addition to evangelism, are doing important work in the fields of education and medicine. In the larger centres there are churches of several denominations—Protestant, Roman Catholics and others.

Education. In 1974 there were 469 schools with 86,110 pupils in primary classes and 6,911 in secondary classes. The Swaziland Agricultural College and University Centre at Luyengo was opened in Oct. 1966. Technical and vocational training classes are run at the Government's Industrial Training Institute and its Staff Training Institute. The Government also operates a police college. There are 2 teacher-training colleges. In 1975 Botswana and Swaziland formed a joint university with campuses in each territory.

Health. In 1974 there were 64 doctors and about 1,750 hospital beds.

DIPLOMATIC REPRESENTATIVES

OF SWAZILAND IN GREAT BRITAIN (58 Pont St., London SW1X 0AE)

High Commissioner: George Mbikwakhe Mamba (accredited on 16 Feb. 1978).

OF GREAT BRITAIN IN SWAZILAND (Allister Miller St., Mbabane)

High Commissioner: J. E. A. Miles, OBE.

OF SWAZILAND IN THE USA (4301 Connecticut Ave., NW, Washington, D.C., 20008)

Ambassador: Simon M. Kunene.

OF THE USA IN SWAZILAND (PO Box 199, Mbabane)

Ambassador: Donald R. Norland (resides in Gaborone).

OF SWAZILAND TO THE UNITED NATIONS

Ambassador: N. M. Malinga.

Books of Reference

The Kingdom of Swaziland. Swaziland Government Information Services, 1968
Post Independence Development Plan. Mbabane, 1969
Barker, D., *Swaziland.* HMSO, 1965
Holleman, J. F. (ed.), *Experiment in Swaziland: Sample Survey 1960.* OUP, 1964
Kuper, H., *An African Aristocracy.* New ed. London, 1961.—*The Uniform of Colour.* Johannesburg, 1947.—*The Swazi: An Ethnographical Survey.* London, 1952
Potholm, C. P., *Swaziland: The Dynamics of Political Modernization.* Univ. of California Press, 1972

SWEDEN

Konungariket Sverige

Capital: Stockholm
Population: 8·2m. (1976)
GNP per capita: US$8,670 (1976)

AREA AND POPULATION. The first census took place in 1749, and it was repeated at first every third year, and, after 1775, every fifth year. Since 1860 a general census has been taken every 10 years and, in addition, in 1935, 1945, 1965 and 1975.

Latest census figures: 1940, 6,371,432 (annual increase since 1935: 0·38%); 1945, 6,673,749 (0·94% since 1940); 1950, 7,041,829 (1·1% since 1945); 1960, 7,495,316 (0·64% since 1950); 1965, 7,766,424 (1·04% since 1960); 1970, 8,076,903 (1·04% since 1965); 1975, 8,208,544 (1·02% since 1970).

Counties (Län)	*Land area: sq. km*	*Census population 1 Nov. 1975*	*Estimated population 31 Dec. 1976*	*Pop. per sq. km 1976*
Stockholm (city)[1] / Stockholm (county)[1]	6,494	1,493,052	1,500,868	230
Uppsala	6,987	229,879	233,115	33
Södermanland	6,060	252,030	251,996	42
Östergötland	10,566	387,104	389,431	37
Jönköping	9,943	301,905	302,142	30
Kronoberg	8,459	169,454	170,319	20
Kalmar	11,171	240,768	240,969	22
Gotland	3,140	54,447	54,621	17
Blekinge	2,909	155,391	154,962	53
Kristianstad	6,048	272,090	273,941	45
Malmöhus	4,909	740,137	739,682	151
Halland	5,448	219,767	222,985	40
Göteborg and Bohus	5,110	714,660	714,374	140
Älvsborg	11,394	418,150	420,192	37
Skaraborg	7,937	263,382	264,286	33
Värmland	17,584	284,442	284,529	16
Örebro	8,514	273,994	273,819	32
Västmanland	6,302	259,872	260,164	41
Kopparberg	28,350	281,082	283,350	10
Gävleborg	18,191	294,595	294,627	16
Västernorrland	21,771	268,202	268,237	12
Jämtland	49,857	133,559	133,752	3
Västerbotten	55,429	236,367	237,705	4
Norrbotten	98,906	264,215	266,113	3
Total	411,479	8,208,544	8,236,179	20

[1] From Jan. 1968 Stockholm city and Stockholm county have been united in Stockholm county.

On 31 Dec. 1976 there were 4,092,582 males and 4,143,597 females.

On 1 July 1976 aliens employed in Sweden numbered 266,677. Of these, 117,972 were Finns, 30,963 Yugoslavs, 21,997 Danes, 14,347 Greeks, 13,791 Norwegians, 12,718 Germans, 4,576 Italians and 3,092 Austrians.

Vital statistics for calendar years:

	Total living births	*Of which illegitimate*	*Still-born*	*Marriages*	*Divorces*	*Deaths exclusive of still-born*
1974	109,874	34,451	732	44,864	26,802	86,316
1975	103,632	33,543	603	44,103	25,383	88,208
1976	98,345	32,656	545	44,790	21,702	90,677

Immigration: 1974, 37,430; 1975, 44,133; 1976, 45,492. Emigration: 1974, 28,352; 1975, 27,249; 1976, 25,522.

In 1860 the town population numbered 435,000 (11% of the total population) and on 31 Dec. 1965, 4,177,212 (54%); including other densely populated areas, the urbanized population in 1965 was 77·4%.

On 1 Nov. 1975, population in densely populated areas was 6,789,432 (82·7%).

Population of largest communities, 31 Dec. 1976:

Stockholm	661,258	Karlstad	72,677	Falun	48,454
Göteborg	442,410	Botkyrka	71,242	Mölndal	46,937
Malmö	240,220	Kristianstad	67,598	Uddevalla	46,668
Uppsala	139,893	Luleå	67,190	Borlänge	46,059
Norrköping	119,967	Huddinge	64,065	Skövde	45,665
Västerås	118,055	Nyköping	62,932	Sollentuna	44,585
Örebro	117,383	Växjö	62,537	Sandviken	43,330
Linköping	110,053	Örnsköldsvik	60,740	Varberg	43,302
Jönköping	108,171	Karlskrona	60,232	Täby	42,513
Borås	104,415	Nacka	55,782	Västervik	41,681
Helsingborg	101,323	Östersund	54,792	Kungsbacka	39,792
Sundsvall	94,148	Gotland	54,621	Norrtälje	39,425
Eskilstuna	92,158	Solna	52,841	Landskrona	37,952
Gävle	87,408	Kalmar	52,583	Karlskoga	37,724
Södertälje	77,799	Järfälla	51,696	Lidingö	36,955
Lund	76,536	Trollhättan	50,791	Hudiksvall	36,702
Umeå	76,276	Haninge	50,717	Piteå	36,463
Halmstad	74,718	Motala	49,625	Lidköping	34,617
Skellefteå	72,929	Hässleholm	48,574	Trelleborg	34,488

Befolkningsförändringar (*Population Changes*). Annual. 3 vols. National Central Bureau of Statistics, Stockholm
Folkmängd 31 Dec. (*Population*). Annual. 3 vols. National Central Bureau of Statistics, Stockholm
Historisk statistik för Sverige. I: Befolkning (*Population*). *1720–1967*. 2nd ed. Stockholm, 1969

REIGNING KING. Carl XVI Gustaf, born 30 April 1946, succeeded on the death of his grandfather Gustaf VI Adolf, 15 Sept. 1973, married 19 June 1976 to *Silvia* Renate Sommerlath, born 23 Dec. 1943 (Queen of Sweden). *Daughter:* Princess Victoria Ingrid Alice Desirée, born 14 July 1977 (Princess of Sweden).

Sisters of the King. Princess Margaretha, born 31 Oct. 1934, married 30 June 1964 to Mr John Ambler; Princess Birgitta (Princess of Sweden), born 19 Jan. 1937, married 25 May 1961 (civil marriage) and 30 May 1961 (religious ceremony) to Johann Georg, Prince of Hohenzollern; Princess Désirée, born 2 June 1938, married 5 June 1964 to Baron Niclas Silfverschiöld; Princess Christina, born 3 Aug. 1943, married 15 June 1974 to Tord Magnuson.

Uncles of the King. Sigvard, Count of Wisborg, born on 7 June 1907; Prince Bertil, Duke of Halland, heir-presumptive, born on 28 Feb. 1912, married 7 Dec. 1976 to Lilian May Davies, born 30 Aug. 1915 (Princess of Sweden, Duchess of Halland); Carl Johan, Count of Wisborg, born on 31 Oct. 1916.

Aunt of the King. Princess Ingrid (Princess of Sweden), born 28 March 1910, married 24 May 1935 to Frederik, Crown Prince of Denmark (King Frederik IX), died 14 Jan. 1972.

The following is a list of the kings and queens of Sweden, with the dates of their accession from the accession of the House of Vasa:

House of Vasa

Gustaf I	1523
Eric XIV	1560
Johan III	1568
Sigismund	1592
Carl IX	1600
Gustaf II Adolf	1611
Christina	1632

House of Pfalz-Zweibrücken

Carl X Gustaf	1654
Carl XI	1660
Carl XII	1697
Ulrica Eleonora	1718

House of Hesse

Fredrik I	1720

House of Holstein-Gottorp

Adolf Fredrik	1751
Gustaf III	1771
Gustaf IV Adolf	1792
Carl XIII	1809

	House of Bernadotte		
Carl XIV Johan	1818	Gustaf V	1907
Oscar I	1844	Gustaf VI Adolf	1950
Carl XV	1859	Carl XVI Gustaf	1973
Oscar II	1872		

The royal family of Sweden have a civil list of 6·3m. kronor; this does not include the maintenance of the royal palaces.

CONSTITUTION AND GOVERNMENT. Sweden's present constitution came into force in 1975 and replaced the 1809 constitution. Under the present constitution Sweden is a representative and parliamentary democracy. Parliament (*Riksdag*) is declared to be the central organ of government. The executive power of the country is vested in the Government, which is responsible to Parliament. The King is Head of State, but he does not participate in the government of the country. Since 1971 Parliament has consisted of one chamber. It has 349 members, who are elected for a period of 3 years in direct, general elections.

Every man and woman who has reached the age of 18 years on election-day itself, and who is not under wardship has the right to vote and to stand for election.

The manner of election to the *Riksdag* is proportional. The country is divided into 28 constituencies. In these constituencies 310 members are elected. The remaining 39 seats constitute a nation-wide pool intended to give absolute proportionality to parties that receive at least 4% of the votes. A party receiving less than 4% of the votes in the country is, however, entitled to participate in the distribution of seats in a constituency, if it has obtained at least 12% of the votes cast there.

A state subsidy is given to all political parties which have obtained at least one seat in the *Riksdag* at the last election. The subvention (53·1m. kr. in 1977–78) is distributed in the ratio of 115,000 kr. per seat. Furthermore a municipal subsidy may be decided by the regional councils and the local councils. The subsidy is distributed in a fixed ratio per seat in the council. The counties subsidy is estimated at 30,136,700 kr. for 1977 and the municipalities at 38·5m. kr. for 1974.

The *Riksdag*, elected 19 Sept. 1976, has 152 Social Democrats, 86 Centre Party, 55 Conservatives, 39 Liberals and 17 Communists.

A New Cabinet with Centre Party, Conservatives and Liberals was appointed on 8 Oct. 1976, composed as follows in June 1978.

Prime Minister: Thorbjörn Fälldin (CP).

Deputy Prime Minister: Ola Ullsten (Lib.). *Foreign Affairs:* Karin Söder (CP). *Justice:* Sven Romanus (Non-Party). *Defence:* Erick Krönmark (Con.). *Health and Social Affairs:* Rune Gustavsson (CP). *Communications:* Bo Turesson (Con.). *Economy:* Gösta Bohman (Con.). *Finance:* Ingemar Mundebo (Lib.). *Education:* Jan-Erik Wikström (Lib.). *Agriculture:* Anders Dahlgren (CP). *Commerce:* Staffan Burenstam-Linder (Con.). *Industry:* Nils G. Åsling (CP). *Labour:* Rolf Wirtén (Lib.). *Housing:* Elvy Olsson (CP). *Local Government:* Johannes Antonsson (CP). *Without Portfolio:* Britt Mogård (Con.), Ingegärd Troedsson (Con.), Olof Johansson (CP), Birgit Friggebo (Lib.).

All the members of the Cabinet are responsible for the acts of the Government.

Public administration in Sweden is characterized by a unique degree of functional decentralization. The Ministries are not really administrative agencies. They prepare bills for the *Riksdag*, issue general directives and make higher appointments, but, as a rule, do not take individual administrative decisions. The routine administrative work is attended to by the central boards (*centrala ämbetsverk*). Each board's sphere of activity depends partly on its organization which is decided by the appropriations granted by the Riksdag. The Government often asks the boards' opinion on proposed measures.

National flag: Blue with a yellow Scandinavian cross.

National anthem: Du gamla, du fria, du fjällhöga nord (words by R. Dybeck, 1844; folk-tune).

The official language is Swedish. The capital is Stockholm.

Local Government. For administrative purposes Sweden is divided into 24 counties (*län*), in each of which the central government is represented by a county administrative board (*länsstyrelse*). The governor (*landshövding*), appointed by the government, is chairman of the board, which in addition to the governor has 14 members elected by the county council.

Local government and the levying of local taxes are based on the fundamental law and are regulated by the municipal law and special acts. According to the municipal law Sweden is divided into communes in which all men and women who have reached the age of 18 on election-day itself, and not under wardship, are entitled to elect the commune council. These councils are named *kommunfullmäktige*. The number of communes has, since 1951, been reduced from about 2,500 to 277. The communes deal with a great variety of different tasks such as social welfare, education and culture, public health, town planning, housing etc. Each county, except Gotland, which consists of only one commune, has a county council (*landsting*) elected by men and women who enjoy municipal suffrage. The county councils chiefly administer the health service. Ecclesiastical affairs in all parishes with more than 1,000 inhabitants are dealt with by church councils (*kyrkofullmäktige*); smaller parishes may make the same arrangement. All elections are conducted on a proportional basis.

Andrén, N., *Modern Swedish Government*. 2nd ed. Stockholm, 1968
Elder, N. C. M., *Government in Sweden: The Executive at Work*. Oxford, 1970
Lewin, L., Jansson, B., and Sörbom, D., *The Swedish Electorate 1887–1968*. Stockholm, 1972
Vinde, P., *Swedish Government Administration: An Introduction*. Stockholm, 1971

DEFENCE. A Supreme Commander is, under the Government, in command of the three services. He is assisted by the Defence Staff under a chief of staff.

The military forces are recruited on the principle of national service, supplemented by voluntarily enlisted personnel who form the permanent cadres for training purposes, staff duties, etc.

Liability to service commences at the age of 18, and lasts till the end of the 47th year. The period of training for the Army and Navy is 7½–15 months and for the Airforce 8–15 months.

The territorial organization consists of 6 military commands each one under a general officer commanding.

Army. The C.-in-C. of the Royal Swedish Army has at his disposal the Army Staff under a chief of staff.

The peace-time Army consists for training purposes of 16 infantry, 5 armour, 7 artillery, 6 AA, 3 engineer, 3 signal and 4 Army Service Corps units, most of which are called 'regiments' (*regementen*), each usually consisting of several battalions.

The Army is organized and equipped with regard to the varying geographical and climatic conditions of the country. The Home Guard (*Hemvärnet*) raised during the War continues to be in force.

Sweden's ground forces can be said to consist of a standing Army which for the most part is on indefinite leave, but which on short notice can be ready for action. One of the basic principles of the Swedish system of mobilization is the local recruitment of as many units as possible. Efforts are also made to decentralize as much as possible the storage of equipment and supplies.

The active personnel of the Army comprises about 45,000, including 36,500 conscripts.

Navy. The C.-in-C. of the Royal Swedish Navy has at his disposal the Chief of Naval Staff, the Chief of Naval Material Department and the C.-in-C. of the Fleet. The Navy is divided into two branches, the Royal Swedish Navy and the Royal Coast Artillery. There are 3 Naval Base Areas: those of the southern, eastern and western coast.

There are 18 submarines, 6 destroyers, 4 frigates, 1 guided missile armed fast patrol boat (prototype) and 16 building, 2 minelayers and submarine support ships, 1 minelayer and seagoing training ship, 18 coastal minesweepers, 20 inshore minesweepers, 29 large and 12 small torpedo boats, 27 patrol launches, 9 mining tenders, 2 mine transports, 37 minelaying boats, 7 tenders, 5 surveying vessels, 7 icebreakers, 1 oiler, 1 salvage vessel, 9 artillery landing craft, 79 utility craft, 54 minor landing craft, 2 sail training ships, 1 supply ship, 2 water carriers, 5 fleet tugs, 13 harbour tugs and 2 icebreaking tugs.

Ships under construction include 2 submarines, 1 minelayer, 9 minehunters and 5 landing craft.

Ships projected include 2 submarines, 3 corvettes of a new type (flotilla leaders for fast attack craft) and 1 survey ship.

The Naval Air Arm comprises 10 Boeing Vertol 107 helicopters, 10 JetRanger helicopters and 5 Alouette II helicopters.

The coast artillery defence areas are those of the Stockholm archipelago, Blekinge, Gothenburg, Gotland and Norrland. There are 5 coastal artillery regiments. The active personnel of the navy and coast artillery in 1978 totalled 15,000 officers and men, comprising 4,500 regular service, 3,000 reserve service and 7,500 national service (additionally 7,000 conscripts train annually).

Air Force. The C.-in-C. of the Royal Swedish Air Force has at his disposal the Air Staff under a chief of staff. Directly subordinate to the C.-in-C. of the Air Force are also the Inspectors of Air Base Control and Reporting Services, and of Flying Safety. Technical matters are managed by the Air Materiel Department (formerly Air Force Board) which is the Air Force section of the Materiel Administration of the Swedish Armed Forces.

The combat units consist of 8 fighter-interceptor and 4 ground-attack wings (*flottiljer*), each with 2–4 squadrons of 12–15 aircraft, including 5 reconnaissance squadrons (*divisioner*). Total peace-time strength of the combat units is about 25 squadrons with about 400 first-line aircraft.

Standard night- and all-weather-fighter is the Swedish-built Saab J35 Draken. The ground-attack wings have 5½ squadrons of Saab AJ37 Viggens, and there are 5 light ground-attack squadrons of twin-jet Saab-105s (Sk60s). The present 3 reconnaissance squadrons of Draken and Lansen (Saab S35 and S32) are re-equipping with SF37 (overland) and SH37 (maritime) Viggen reconnaissance aircraft; the fighter-interceptor force will have eventually 8 squadrons of JA37 Viggens; plus transport, helicopter and other support units, as at present. Bloodhound surface-to-air missile squadrons are operational. One reconnaissance squadron has also the Sk60B/C versions of the Saab-105 twin-jet light multi-purpose aircraft. The Sk60A version is the Air Force's standard advanced trainer, to which pupils progress after initial training on piston-engined Scottish Aviation Bulldogs. Other trainers in service include the Sk35C Draken and Sk37 Viggen.

Active strength consists of about 10,300 personnel, including 5,400 conscripts.

INTERNATIONAL RELATIONS

Membership. Sweden is a member of UN and EFTA.

ECONOMY

Budget. Revenue and expenditure of the ordinary budget for fiscal years ending 30 June (in 1,000 kr.):

	Revenue	*Expenditure*		*Revenue*	*Expenditure*
1972–73	52,646,738	54,699,216	1975–76	91,367,610	89,228,047
1973–74	59,327,787	64,003,776	1976–77	102,065,945	106,681,410
1974–75	70,022,245	74,922,769	1977–78	111,557,904	120,002,277

The actual revenue and expenditure (current accounts) for the financial year 1 July 1976 to 30 June 1977 was as follows (in 1,000 kr.):

Current revenue:		*Current expenditure:*	
Income and property taxes	45,020,315	Royal household	15,144
Death duty and other stamp-duties	1,315,760	Justice	4,171,350
Motor-car duty	5,718,746	Foreign affairs	3,294,558
Special employer's fee	6,997,238	Defence	10,692,362
Customs duties	1,170,057	Social welfare	32,310,461
Purchase tax	21,721,477	Communications	4,781,868
Excise on spirits, tobacco, etc.	11,190,894	Finance	6,823,128
Civil service fees, etc.	2,177,545	Religion and education	15,022,580
Miscellaneous	1,039,623	Agriculture	4,808,562
		Commerce	366,466

Net receipts from state capital funds:	
State enterprises:	
Posts, Telecommunications	146,172
Hydro-electric power	830,090
Forests	55,287
Railways	3,577
Defence factories	25,378
Civil aviation	42,240
Real estate funds	636,841
Interest on state-owned shares	81,842
Interest on outstanding loans	3,039,665
Other funds	303,197
Shares in the profits of Bank of Sweden	550,000
Current expenditure (contd.):	
Labour	7,170,972
Housing and physical planning	4,506,941
Industry	2,431,479
Local government	1,558,455
Expenses for the Diet, etc.	158,206
Unforeseen expenses	90,367
Expenditure on state funds:	
National debt (interest, etc.)	5,416,337
Depreciation of new capital investment	2,161,174
Appropriation for covering capital losses	901,000

Net capital investments (in 1,000 kr.): 1972–73, 4,628,994; 1973–74, 4,834,194; 1974–75, 5,523,917; 1975–76, 5,437,236; 1976–77, 5,647,438.

Revenue and expenditure of state business enterprises (in 1m. kr.):

	Revenue	*Expenditure*
Forest Service, 1975	934·8	789·8
Power Administration, 1975	2,404·7	1,731·6
Railways, 1974–75	3,657·0	3,456·1
Post Office, 1974–75[1]	2,853·2	2,852·1
Telecommunications, 1974–75	4,307·7	4,127·7

[1] Not comparable with previous years.

On 31 Dec. 1976 the national debt amounted to 80,411m. kr.

Riksgäldskontoret [National Debt Office], *årsbok*. Annual. Stockholm, from 1920
Riksskatteverket [National Tax Board], *årsbok*. Annual. Stockholm, from 1971
The Swedish Budget. Ministry of the Budget, from 1962/63

Currency. The Swedish *krona*, of 100 *öre*, averaged in 1975 of the value of approximately 7·89 kr. to the £ sterling and 4·36 kr. to the US$.

Gold coins do not exist as a currency. National bank-notes for 5, 10, 50, 100, 1,000 and 10,000 kr. are legal means of payment, and the bank is formally bound to exchange them for gold on presentation, but the obligation to redemption is suspended.

Banking. The Riksbank, or National Bank of Sweden, belongs entirely to the State and is managed by directors elected for 3 years by the Diet, except the chairman, who is designated by the King. The bank is under the guarantee of the Diet, its capital and reserve capital are fixed by its constitution. The note circulation is fixed at 13,000m. kr. Since 1904, only the Riksbank has the right to issue notes. On 31 Dec. 1976 its note circulation amounted to 22,113m. kr.; its combined gold and net foreign-exchange holdings (including surplus value of gold) totalled 10,657m. kr.

There are 14 commercial banks. On 31 Dec. 1976 their total deposits amounted to 100,653m. kr.; domestic bills and loans to 88,576m. kr.

The savings-banks statistics (exclusive of post office) are as follows, at the end of the year:

	1971	*1972*	*1973*	*1974*	*1975*	*1976*
Depositors' accounts, 1,000	10,217	9,228	9,380	9,574	9,711	9,944
Deposits, 1m. kr.[1]	35,628	38,781	42,682	46,907	52,224	56,554
Capital and reserve funds, 1m. kr.	1,091	1,127	1,173	1,219	1,252	1,294

[1] Including interest.

On 30 June 1974 the post office bank had 5·6m. depositors and 11,553m. kr. of deposits, including interest.

Sveriges Riksbank, årsbok. Annual. Stockholm, from 1908
Skandinaviska Enskilda Banken, Kvartalskift. Quarterly Review (in English). Stockholm, from 1920

Weights and Measures. The metric system is obligatory.

ENERGY AND NATURAL RESOURCES

Electricity. Sweden is rich in water power resources. The total electric energy production in 1976 was 86,416m. kwh. About 63% of this energy was produced in hydro-electric plants. The development of water power will in the future be insignificant and the new plants must be based on thermal power, mainly nuclear.

Minerals. Sweden is one of the leading exporters of iron ore. The largest deposits are found north of the polar circle in the area of Kiruna and Gällivare–Malmberget. The ore is exported *via* the Norwegian port of Narvik and the Swedish port of Luleå. There are also important resources of iron ore in southern Sweden (Bergslagen). The most important fields are Grängesberg and Stråssa and the ores are shipped *via* the port of Oxelösund. Some of the southern deposits have, in contrast to the fields in North Sweden, a low phosphorus content.

There are also some deposits of copper, lead and zinc ores especially in the Boliden area in the north of Sweden. These ores are often found together with pyrites. Non-ferrous ores, except zinc ores, are used in the Swedish metal industry and barely satisfy domestic needs.

The total production of iron ores amounted to 29·9m. tons in 1976 and exports to 22m. tons. The production of copper ore was 187,833 tons, of lead ore 114,234 tons, of zinc ore 225,793 tons.

There are also deposits of raw materials for aluminium not worked at present. In southern Sweden there are big resources of alum shale, containing oil and uranium.

Agriculture. According to the farm register which is revised annually the following data was provided for 1976. The number of farms in cultivation of more than 2 hectares of arable land, was 130,945; of these there were 86,513 of 2–20 hectares; 41,408 of 20–100 hectares; 3,033 of above 100 hectares. Of the total land area of Sweden (41,147,900 hectares), 3,003,057 hectares (except kitchen gardens and fruit gardens) were arable land, 249,177 hectares cultivated pastures and 22,598,565 hectares forests.

	Area (1,000 hectares)[1]			*Production (1,000 tonnes)*		
Chief crops	*1974*	*1975*	*1976*	*1974*	*1975*	*1976*
Wheat	340·1	302·8	397·5	1,793	1,455	1,765
Rye	108·0	96·1	124·0	433	326	427
Barley	638·0	648·6	595·0	2,356	1,903	1,826
Oats	468·1	497·5	483·2	1,656	1,321	1,251
Mixed grain	76·7	70·6	68·3	244	165	165
Peas and vetches	9·2	9·0	9·5	19	19	22
Potatoes	47·5	42·9	45·1	1,257	837	1,058
Sugar-beet	46·7	52·5	53·4	2,140	1,992	2,077
Tame hay	716·3	693·9	686·9	2,501[2]	2,772	2,966[2]
Oil seed	160·5	173·0	147·6	353	328	281

[1] Figures refer to holdings of more than 2 hectares of arable land.
[2] Figures refer only to the first harvest.

Area of rotation meadows for pasture was (in 1,000 hectares): 1974, 214; 1975, 212; 1976, 209.

Total production of milk (in 1,000 tonnes): 1974, 3,112; 1975, 3,168; 1976, 3,247. Butter production in the same years was (in 1,000 tonnes): 58, 56, 61; and cheese, 75, 81, 84.

Livestock, 1976: Cattle, 1,862,614; sheep, 389,478; pigs, 2,547,832.

Number of farm tractors in 1976, 209,186; combines in 1976, 50,040.

The number of pelts produced in 1975 was as follows: Fox, 31,606; mink, 1·2m.; others, 0·2m.

Forestry. Nearly 23·5m. hectares or 57% of the total land area are covered with forests. The total amount of standing timber is estimated at 2,448m. cu. metres with bark; 83% of this volume consists of coniferous wood (pine and spruce). Half of the forest area is privately owned, the other half is equally divided between public authorities (Crown, Church, communities, etc.) and joint-stock companies. The total cut in 1976 was 54m. cu. metres solid volume (without bark); of these, 23m. were coniferous timber, 29m. pulpwood, 1m. fuel wood and 1m. other wood. In 1975 the total cut was 56m. cu. metres.

In 1973 there were about 900 saw-mills with 5 or more workers, the total production of which—representing some 90% of the country's total production—amounted to 11·3m. cu. metres sawn and planed wood. The production of the 89 pulp-mills in Sweden in 1976 amounted to 8·3m. tonnes pulp (dry weight). There was an export of approximately 1·5m. cu. metres of roundwood; exports of sawn coniferous wood amounted to 6·6m. cu. metres, of plywood (including blockboards) to 21,800 tonnes, of pulp 3·3m. tonnes and of particle board 272,200 tonnes.

Fisheries. In 1976 the total value of the catches of the sea fisheries was 271m. kr.; of this sum, 165m. kr. came from Göteborg, Bohus and Halland.

INDUSTRY AND TRADE

Manufacturing. The most important sector of Swedish manufacturing is the production of metals, metal products, machinery and transport equipment, covering almost half of the total value added by manufacturing. Production of high-quality steel is an old Swedish speciality. A large part of this production is exported. The production of ordinary steel is slightly decreasing and is still short of domestic demand. The total production of steel amounted to 5·1m. tons in 1974, 28% of which was high-quality steel. There is also a large production of other metals (aluminium, lead and copper) and rolled semi-manufactured goods of these metals.

These basic metal industries are an important basis for the production of more developed metal products, machinery and equipment, which are to a large extent sold on the world market, *i.e.*, hand tools, mining drills, ball-bearings, turbines, pneumatic machinery, refrigerating equipment, machinery for pulp and paper industries, etc., sewing machines, machine tools, office machinery, high-voltage electric machinery, telephone equipment, cars and trucks, ships and aeroplanes.

Another important manufacturing sector is based on Sweden's forest resources. This sector includes saw-mills, plywood factories, joinery industries, pulp- and paper-mills, wallboard and particle board factories, accounting for about 15% of the total value of manufacturing. A fast increasing sector is the chemical industry, especially the petro-chemical branch. Minerals industries include production of building materials, decorative arts products of glass and china.

Industry groups	*No. of establishments*		*Average no. of wage-earners*		*Sales value of production (gross) in 1m. kr.*	
	1974	*1975*	*1974*	*1975*	*1974*	*1975*
Mining and quarrying	*169*	*167*	*11,240*	*11,485*	*3,001*	*3,310*
Metal-ore mining	58	56	9,813	10,406	2,748	2,996
Other mining	111	111	1,427	1,439	253	314
Manufacturing	*12,261*	*12,216*	*667,391*	*669,169*	*176,062*	*189,663*
Manufacture of food, beverages and tobacco	1,311	1,227	52,942	54,085	23,498	25,239
Textile, wearing apparel and leather industries	1,268	1,218	49,629	46,392	6,938	6,959
Manufacture of wood products including furniture	2,196	2,152	66,601	62,968	15,450	14,278
Manufacture of paper and paper products, printing and publishing	1,183	1,205	73,677	73,632	25,068	26,148
Manufacture of chemicals and chemical, petroleum, coal, rubber and plastic products	828	817	45,448	44,773[2]	18,856	19,682
Manufacture of non-metallic mineral products, except products of petroleum and coal	718	678	25,500	24,933	4,636	5,108
Basic metal industries	184	188	52,402	52,907	16,989	16,490
Manufacture of fabricated metal products, machinery and equipment	4,408	4,558	296,282	304,570	63,899	74,951
Other manufacturing industries	165	173	4,910	4,909	728	807
Electricity, gas and water	*1,111*	*1,060*	*11,750*	*11,662*	*12,773*	*14,442*
Electricity, gas and steam	951[1]	903[1]	10,458	10,429	12,121	13,671
Water works and supply	160	158	1,292	1,233	652	771

[1] Number of power stations. [2] Partly calculated.

Arbetsmarknadsstatistik (*Labour Market Statistics*). Monthly. National Labour Market Board, Stockholm, from 1963
Arbetsmarknadsstatistisk Årsbok (*Year Book of Labour Statistics*). National Central Bureau of Statistics, Stockholm, from 1973
Carlson, B., *Trade Unions in Sweden*. Stockholm, 1969
Historisk statistik för Sverige, II (Climate, land surveying, agriculture, forestry, fisheries). Stockholm, 1959
Johansson, Ö. *The Gross Domestic Product of Sweden and its Composition 1861–1955*. Stockholm, 1967
Jörberg, L., *A History of Prices in Sweden 1732–1914*. 2 vols. Stockholm, 1972
Jordbruksekonomiska meddelanden (Journal of Agricultural Economics, published monthly by the National Agricultural Market Board). Stockholm, from 1939
Jordbruksstatistisk årsbok (Yearbook of Agricultural Statistics). Stockholm, from 1965
The Swedish Economy. The Economic Department of the Ministry for Economic Affairs and National Institute of Economic Research. Stockholm, from 1960
The Swedish Economy, 1971–75, and the General Outlook up to 1990. Ministry of Finance. Stockholm, 1971
The 1,000 Largest Companies in Sweden. Stockholm, from 1972

Commerce. The imports and exports of Sweden, unwrought gold and coin not included, have been as follows (in 1m. kr.):

	1970	*1971*	*1972*	*1973*	*1974*[1]	*1975*[1]	*1976*[1]
Imports	36,251	36,192	38,618	46,336	72,800	74,000	84,000
Exports	35,150	38,224	41,749	53,153	70,514	72,012	80,195

Imports and exports by products (in 1m. kr.):

	Imports		*Exports*	
	1975[1]	*1976*[1]	*1975*	*1976*
Food and live animals chiefly for food	4,933	6,057	1,741	1,784
Cereals and cereal preparations	282	295	947	837
Vegetables and fruit	1,474	1,752	96	141
Coffee, tea, cocoa, spices and manufactures thereof	1,009	1,719	115	159
Feeding stuff for animals (not including unmilled cereals)	416	511	15	20
Beverages and tobacco	650	643	65	76
Crude materials, inedible, except fuels	3,526	3,559	11,182	12,450
Hides, skins and furskins, raw	158	243	162	238
Crude rubber (including synthetic and reclaimed)	225	229	39	48
Cork and wood	667	771	2,950	3,905
Pulp and waste paper	62	56	5,526	5,478
Textile fibres (other than wool tops) and their wastes (not manufactured into yarn or fabric)	182	169	101	113
Crude fertilizers and crude minerals (excluding coal, petroleum and precious stones)	641	546	114	130
Metalliferous ores and metal scrap	1,026	920	2,066	2,336
Mineral fuels, lubricants and related materials	12,907	14,707	1,134	1,351
Coal, coke and briquettes	864	925	18	27
Petroleum, petroleum products and related materials	11,797	13,449	903	994
Chemicals and related products, n.e.s.	5,925	6,559	3,236	3,768
Artificial resins and plastic materials, and cellulose esters and ethers	1,631	1,947	964	1,214
Manufactured goods classified chiefly by material	14,957	15,616	18,584	19,989
Paper, paperboard, and articles of paper pulp, of paper or of paperboard	697	845	6,130	6,892
Textile yarn, fabrics, made-up articles, n.e.s., and related products	2,773	3,154	1,023	1,135
Non-metallic mineral manufactures, n.e.s.	1,186	1,251	576	667
Iron and steel	4,593	4,357	5,581	5,442

[1] *See* note on p. 1134.

	Imports		Exports	
	1975[1]	1976[1]	1975	1976
Non-ferrous metals	2,036	2,093	1,045	1,290
Manufactures of metal, n.e.s.	2,122	2,222	2,847	2,957
Machinery and transport equipment	23,468	25,877	31,231	35,217
Power generating machinery and equipment	1,852	1,922	1,761	2,185
Machinery specialized for particular industries	2,494	2,972	3,741	4,086
Metalworking machinery	1,140	955	924	958
General industrial machinery and equipment, n.e.s. and machine parts, n.e.s	4,406	4,376	5,792	5,653
Office machines and automatic data processing equipment	1,342	1,534	1,344	1,347
Telecommunications and sound recording and reproducing apparatus and equipment	1,532	1,910	3,085	3,347
Electrical machinery apparatus and appliances, n.e.s., and electrical parts thereof (including non-electrical counterparts, n.e.s., of electrical household type equipment)	3,641	4,026	2,711	3,175
Road vehicles (including air cushion vehicles)	5,227	6,544	7,971	8,402
Other transport equipment	1,835	1,637	3,904	6,063
Miscellaneous manufactured articles	8,112	9,814	4,332	5,133

[1] *See* note below next table.

Principal import and export countries (in 1m. kr.):

	Imports from		Exports to	
	1975[1]	1976[1]	1975	1976
Belgium–Luxembourg	2,742	2,683	2,041	2,397
Denmark	5,285	5,861	6,213	7,827
Federal Republic of Germany	14,348	15,676	7,196	7,918
Finland	4,174	4,768	5,160	5,163
France	3,129	3,341	3,443	4,394
Italy	1,980	2,244	1,944	2,093
Netherlands	3,479	3,715	2,909	3,366
Norway	4,960	5,107	8,032	9,014
Switzerland	1,797	1,899	1,345	1,404
USSR	2,205	2,069	1,213	1,225
UK	8,183	8,760	7,851	9,034
USA	4,887	5,597	3,760	3,682

[1] On 1 Jan. 1974 a new Customs procedure for the imports was introduced. This means that a great part of the imports are now recorded in the statistics with an extra delay of up to 2 weeks as compared to the registration before 1974. The import values for the first months of 1974 and especially Jan. are, therefore, underestimated.

A series of monthly totals, for 1974 and 1975, preliminary adjusted for the effects of the time-lags, have been calculated in order to facilitate comparisons with earlier years and to show the development of the trade balance. For 1975 the adjusted import value is about 74,000m. kr. The registered import value is 74,865,378,000 kr. For 1976 the adjusted import value is about 84,000m. kr. The registered import value is 83,225,897,000 kr.

Adjustments have not been made by commodity and country. For this reason the adjusted import value is used in the summary table only, while the data in the other tables are unadjusted.

Total trade between Sweden and UK (British Department of Trade returns, in £1,000 sterling):

	1973	1974	1975	1976	1977
Imports to UK	739,996	929,112	885,752	1,187,887	1,259,859
Exports and re-exports from UK	514,300	723,340	825,642	1,045,046	1,196,773

Historisk Statistik för Sverige, III: Utrikeshandel (Foreign Trade), *1732–1970*. Stockholm, 1972

Utrikeshandel (Foreign Trade). National Central Bureau of Statistics, Stockholm. Annually, 2 vols, from 1911

Utrikeshandel, kvartalsstatistik (Foreign Trade, Quarterly Bulletin). National Central Bureau of Statistics, Stockholm, from 1961. From 1976 published in *Statistical Reports*, Series H

Utrikeshandel, månadsstatistik (Foreign Trade, Monthly Bulletin). National Central Bureau of Statistics, Stockholm, from 1913. From 1976 published in *Statistical Reports*, Series H

COMMUNICATIONS

Roads. On 1 Jan. 1977 there were 97,402 km of public roads, of which 51,899 km were surfaced. Motor vehicles on 31 Dec. 1976 included 2,888,131 passenger cars, 178,392 buses and lorries and 28,396 heavy motor cycles.

Railways. At the end of 1976 the total length of railways was 12,061 km, of which 11,361 km belonged to the State; 7,484 km were electrified. In 1976 the number of passengers on the railways was 79m.; weight of goods, including Lapland ore, 63m. tonnes.

Aviation. Commercial air traffic is maintained in (1) Sweden and other parts of the world by Scandinavian Airlines System (SAS), of which AB Aerotransport (ABA = Swedish Air Lines) is the Swedish partner (DDL = Danish Air Lines and DNL = Norwegian Air Lines being the other two); (2) only within Sweden by Linjeflyg AB. Scandinavian Airlines System have a joint paid-up capital of about Sw. kronor 858m. Capitalization of ABA, Sw. kronor 350m., of which 50% is owned by the Government and 50% by private enterprises. Capitalization of Linjeflyg, Sw. kronor 31m., of which 50% is owned by SAS and 50% by ABA.

In scheduled air traffic during 1976 the total number of km flown was 63·5m.; passenger-km, 4,040·8m.; goods, 154·5m. ton-km; mail, 18·1m. ton-km. These figures represent the Swedish share of the SAS traffic (Swedish domestic and three-sevenths of international traffic) and the Linjeflyg traffic.

Shipping. The Swedish mercantile marine consisted on 1 Jan. 1977 of 562 vessels of 7·01m. gross tons (only vessels of at least 100 gross tons, and excluding fishing vessels and tugs). Stockholm and Göteborg, with together 296 vessels of 5·35m. gross tons in Jan. 1977 are the two largest ports.

Vessels entered from and cleared for foreign countries, exclusive of passenger liners and ferries, with cargoes and in ballast, in 1976, are as follows (only vessels of at least 20 net tons included): With cargoes, 32,121 of 45·9m. net tons; in ballast, 17,744 of 30·2m. net tons.

Post and Broadcasting. The length of telegraph circuits in Dec. 1975 was 1,502,000 km. The circuits of the telephone had a length of 24·48m. km. On 1 Jan. 1977 there were 5,673,427 instruments employed in the telephone service.

Number of combined radio and television reception fees paid at the end of 1976 was 2,988,000, of which 1,737,000 included extra fees for colour television; radio reception fees paid, 215,000.

Sveriges Radio AB is a non-commercial semi-governmental corporation, transmitting 3 programmes on long-, medium-, and short-waves and on FM. There are also regional programmes. It also broadcasts 2 TV programmes. Colour programmes are broadcast by PAL system.

The overseas radio-telegraph and radio-telephone services are conducted by the Swedish Telecommunications Administration.

The number of post offices at the end of 1976 was 2,077. For receipts of the post and telecommunication services see the section on Economy.

Cinemas (1976). There were 1,192 cinemas.

Newspapers (1976). There were 144 daily newspapers with a total circulation of 4·7m.

JUSTICE, RELIGION, EDUCATION AND WELFARE

Justice. The administration of justice is entirely independent of the Government. The *Justitiekansler*, or Chancellor of Justice (a royal appointment) and the *Justitieombudsmän* (Judicial Commissioners appointed by the Diet), exercise a control over the administration. In 1968 a reform was carried through which meant that the offices of the former *Justitieombudsman* (Ombudsman for civil affairs) and the *Militieombudsman* (Ombudsman for military affairs) were turned into one sole institution with 3 Ombudsmen, each styled *Justitieombudsman*. They exert a general supervision over all courts of law, the civil service, military laws and the military services. In 1976 they received altogether 177 cases; of these, 78 were instituted on their own initiative and 1,622 on complaints. They dismissed 678 cases, investigated

742 without taking direct action, offered criticisms in 348 cases, instituted 3 prosecutions and made 4 proposals to government.

Bruzelius, A. and Ginsburg, R. B., *The Swedish Code of Judicial Procedure*. South Hackensack, 1968
Justitieombudsmännens ämbetsberättelse avgiven till Riksdagen. Annual. Stockholm
The Penal Code of Sweden: As Amended 1 Jan. 1972. South Hackensack, 1972
Rowat, D. C., *The Ombudsman: Citizen's Defender*. London, 1965
Råttsstatistisk årsbok. (Year Book of Legal Statistics). Stockholm, from 1975

The *Riksåklagaren* (a royal appointment) is the chief public prosecutor.

The kingdom has a Supreme Court of Judicature and is divided into 6 high-court districts and 100 district-court divisions (*tingsrätter*).

Of the district courts 28 also serve as real estate courts and 6 as water rights courts.

These district courts (or courts of first instance) deal with both civil and criminal cases. More serious criminal cases are generally tried by a judge and a jury (*nämnd*) of 4–5 members (lay judges); petty cases are tried by the judge alone. Civil cases are tried as a rule by 3 to 4 judges or in minor cases by 1 judge. Disputes of greater consequence relating to the Marriage Code and the Code relating to Parenthood and Guardianship are tried by a judge and a *nämnd*. When cases concerning real estate are being tried the court consists of 2 qualified lawyers, 1 specialist on technical matters and 2 lay assessors.

In trials by *nämnd* the judge decides the case except when the majority of the *nämnd* (at least 4 members of 5 or 3 members of 4) differs from him, in which case the decision of the *nämnd* prevails.

Those with low incomes can receive free legal aid out of public funds. In criminal cases a suspected person has the right to a defence counsel, paid out of public funds.

The Attorney-General (*Justitiekanslern*) and the Parliamentary Commissioner (*Justitieombudsmannen*) for the Judiciary and Civil Administration supervises the application in the public sector of acts of parliament and regulations. The Attorney-General is the Government's legal adviser and also the Public Prosecutor.

The holders of the office of Parliamentary Commissioner, now 3 in number, are appointed by Parliament.

There were 72 penal and correctional institutions for delinquents, with 3,153 male and 112 female inmates on 1 Aug. 1977. Besides, there were 18 institutions with 526 places for children and juveniles in need of care owing to viciousness, maladjustment or delinquency on 31 Dec. 1976.

Religion. The overwhelming majority of the population belong to the Evangelical Lutheran Church, which is the established national church. There were 13 bishoprics (Uppsala being the metropolitan see) and 2,570 parishes at the beginning of 1975. The clergy are chiefly supported from the parishes and the proceeds of the church lands. The nonconformists mostly still adhere to the national church. The largest denominations, on 1 Jan. 1975, were: Swedish Missionary Society, 83,178; Pentecost Movement, 94,500 (1974); Evangelical National Missionary Society, 26,109; Salvation Army, 36,450; Swedish Baptist Church, 23,391; Swedish Alliance Missionary Society, 13,759; Methodists, 6,540; Orebro Missionary Society, 19,836.

There were also 74,117 Roman Catholics (under a Bishop resident at Stockholm, about 35,000 Orthodox Catholics and about 15,000 Jews.

Parliament and Convocation (*Kyrkomötet*) decided in 1958 to admit women to ordination as priests.

Murray, R., *L'église Suédoise. Son Histoire et Son Organisation*. Stockholm, 1970

Education. In 1976–77 Sweden had 6 state universities, at Uppsala (founded in 1477) with 15,698 students, in the faculty of theology 425, law, 1,512, medicine 1,855, arts 4,442, pharmacy, 534, social sciences 5,028, natural sciences 2,389 and technology 380; Lund (founded in 1668), with 17,358 students, in the faculty of theology 301, law 1,820, medicine 1,375, odontology 498, arts 3,499, social sciences 5,809, natural sciences, 1,733 and technology 3,288; Göteborg (founded as a private university in 1889; state university in 1954) with 14,814 students, in the faculty of medicine 1,508, odontology 624, arts 4,367, social sciences 7,158 and natural sciences 1,685; Stockholm (founded as a private university in 1877; state university in 1960) with 24,063 students, in the faculty of law 2,439, arts 7,644, social sciences 12,342 and natural sciences 2,625 students; Umeå (founded in 1963) with 5,695 students, in the faculty of medicine 667, odontology 280, arts 1,454, social sciences 2,538 and natural sciences 983 students, and Linköping (founded in 1970) with 5,854 students, in the faculty of medicine 368, arts 739, social sciences 2,064, natural sciences 455 and technology 2,423 in autum term 1976. In 1976–77 there were established 3 affiliated universities: in Örebro, 1,685 students, in the faculty of arts, 436, social sciences 1,171 and natural sciences 106; in Vaxjö, 1,348 students, in the faculty of arts 304, social sciences 965 and natural sciences 114, and in Karlstad, 1,411 students, in the faculty of arts 297, social sciences 1,037 and natural sciences 111 in autumn term 1976. There is also in Stockholm an autonomous state institute of medicine (founded 1810) with 2,688 students at the faculty of medicine, 944 students at the faculty of odontology and a business school of economics with 1,280 students. The institute of technology in Stockholm had 5,504; that in Göteborg, 4,322, and that in Luleå, 756 students. The institute of agriculture in Uppsala had 1,111 students, the college of veterinary medicine had 370; the college of forestry in Stockholm, 232; 2 institutes of physical education in Stockholm and Örebro, 446; 4 institutes of physiotherapy in Stockholm, Uppsala, Lund and Göteborg, 549; in the 6 teachers' university colleges in Stockholm, Malmö, Göteborg, Uppsala, Umeå and Linköping, 884, and in the 7 colleges of social work and public administration in Stockholm (2), Göteborg, Lund, Umeå, Örebro and Östersund, 7,571 students. The 2 journalists' university colleges in Stockholm and Göteborg had 389 students. The state library in Borås had 696 students. There is one academy of fine arts and one academy of music. From 1 July 1977, the post-secondary education is reorganized in a new institutional structure. Only the two largest municipalities, Stockholm and Göteborg, from this date have more than one institution for third-level education. In other municipalities with education of this kind there is but one institution for all types of third-level education. Some of the objectives of the reform are to facilitate recurrent education and the inclusion of new groups of students. No formal basic degrees will exist, but the students will receive a diploma showing the courses they have passed.

In autumn term in the school year 1976–77 there were 709,000 pupils in primary education (grades 1–6 in compulsory comprehensive schools). Secondary education at the lower stage (grades 7–9 in compulsory comprehensive schools) comprised 324,000 pupils. In secondary education at the higher stage (the integrated upper secondary school), there were 221,000 pupils. The folk high schools had 12,800 pupils in courses of more than 30 weeks.

In municipal adult education there were 154,000 pupils and in state adult education there were about 10,500 pupils.

There are also teacher-training colleges with 12,600 students, schools of nursing, merchant navy officers' schools and other special schools; besides special schools for pupils with visual and hearing handicaps and those who are mentally retarded.

Educational Policy and Planning, Sweden. OECD, Paris, 1967

Higher Education in Sweden, A Guide for Foreign Students. Stockholm, 1972

Orring, J., *Schools in Sweden: A Survey of Primary, Middle and Secondary Education.* Stockholm, 1969

Paulston, R. G., *Educational Change in Sweden: Planning and Accepting the Comprehensive School Reforms.* New York, 1968

Stenholm, B., *Education in Sweden.* Stockholm, 1970

Social Welfare. The social security schemes are greatly expanding. Supported by a referendum, the Diet in 1958 and 1959 decided that the national pensions should be increased successively until 1968 and supplementary pensions paid from 1963. These pensions are of invariable value. In 1969 the Diet decided that as from 1 July 1969 an increment to the basic pension was to be paid to persons without supplementary pensions, and this amount is to be successively increased in a 10-year period. The basic and supplementary pensions consist of old-age and family pensions, as well as pensions paid to the disabled. The financing of the supplementary system is based on the current-cost method.

The most important social welfare schemes are described in the conspectus below.

Type of scheme	*Intro-duced*	*Scope*	*Principal benefits*
Sickness insurance (compulsory—current law, 1962)	1955	All residents	Hospital fees, most private doctors charge the insured person normally 25 kr., district physicians and doctors in hospitals charge the insured person only 15 kr. for full medical treatment, some reimbursement of cost of transportation as well as costs of physiotherapy, convalescent care, etc., medicines at reduced prices or free of charge. During sickness daily allowance 90% of the yearly income in between 4,500 and 80,250 kr. There is generally no maximum benefit period. Dental care is available to all residents from 17 years of age, the maximum payable by the patient being 50%.
Employment injury insurance (compulsory—current law, 1954)	1901	All employed persons	Medical treatment, medicine and medical appliances, hospital care, sickness benefit 90% of the yearly income in between 4,500 and 80,250 kr. (first 90 days covered by sickness insurance), disability annuities, funeral benefit and survivor's pensions.
Unemployment insurance (current law, 1973)	1935	Members of recognized unemployment insurance societies (about 70% of all employees)	50–160 kr. per day subject to tax.
Basic pensions (current law, 1962)			
Old-age	1914	All citizens	Payable from the age of 65 or, at a reduced rate, from the age of 60. 25,134 kr. per annum for married couples, 14,632 kr. for others (including the special increment of 6,844 kr. and 3,422 kr. respectively for those without supplementary pension); about half of them receive municipal housing supplement.
Disability	1914	All citizens	Payable before the age of 65. Full pension 18,054 kr. per annum (including the special increment of 6,844 kr.).
Survivors	1948	All citizens	Widow's pension is payable before the age of 65. The pension is 14,632 kr. (including the special increment of 3,422 kr.) but less for those who have become widows before the age of 50 and have no child below 16. Many of them receive municipal housing supplements.

Type of scheme	*Intro-duced*	*Scope*	*Principal benefits*
Survivors (contd.)	1948	All citizens	Child pension is payable before the age of 18. The pension amounts to 4,720 kr. (fatherless or motherless) and 7,080 kr. (orphans).
Supplementary pensions (current law, 1962)			
Old-age	1960	All gainfully occupied persons	Payable from the same age as the basic pension (*see above*). The pension is in principle 60% of the insured person's average annual earnings during the best 15 years except an amount corresponding to the basic pension and subject to a ceiling.
Disability	1960	All gainfully occupied persons	Payable before the age of 65. Full pension corresponds in principle to supplementary old-age pension.
Survivors	1960	All gainfully occupied persons	Payable to widow and children, before the age of 19, of a deceased person as a certain percentage of the deceased's supplementary pension.
Partial pensions (current law, 1975)	1976	All employees between 60–65 years of age	The pension is payable between 60–65 years of age. The insured must have reduced his working time by 5 hours on an average a week and the part-time work must thereafter comprise at least 17 hours per week. Furthermore the insured must have worked during at least 5 of the last 12 months and achieved a right to supplementary pension for 10 years after the age of 45. The partial pension is paid out by 65% of the loss of income in connection with the change-over to part-time work.
Parents benefit	1974	All resident parents in connection with confinement	Parents cash benefit of 25 kr. a day during 7 months (210 days). Employed parents entitled to daily parents cash benefit of 90% of the daily income (in between 4,500–72,750 kr. yearly) for 7 months. Maximum daily parents cash benefit 179 kr.
Children's allowances	1948	All children below 16	2,100 kr. per annum.
		Children at school 16–18	150 kr. per month during school-courses. Children at school (16–19 years) living more than 6 km from school may receive supplementary allowance of 85–195 kr. per month; other allowance (income- and means-tested) up to 110 kr. per month.

Total social expenditure, including also hygiene, care of the sick and social assistance, amounted to 71,238m. kr. in 1975, representing 24·8% of the GDP.

The Cost and Financing of the Social Services in Sweden, 1974. Stockholm, 1976
Modern Trends in Swedish Pension Systems. Stockholm, 1968
Socialnytt (Official Journal of the National Board of Health and Welfare). Stockholm, from 1968
Social Benefits in Sweden. Stockholm, 1974
Faramond, G. de, *La Suède et la qualité de la Vie*. Paris, 1975
Fors, Å., *Social Policy and How it Works*. Stockholm, 1972
Heclo, H., *Modern Social Politics in Britain and Sweden: From Relief to Income Maintenance*. New Haven, 1974
Michanek, E., *For and Against the Welfare State: Swedish Experiences*. Stockholm, 1964
Mollstedt, B., *Public Health in Sweden. Health Services, Environmental Hygiene and Health Education*. Stockholm, 1972
Rosenthal, A.-H., *The Social Programs of Sweden, A Search for Security in a Free Society*. Minneapolis, 1967

DIPLOMATIC REPRESENTATIVES

OF SWEDEN IN GREAT BRITAIN (23 North Row, London, W1R 2DN)

Ambassador: Olof Rydbeck (accredited 22 Feb. 1977).

OF GREAT BRITAIN IN SWEDEN (Skarpögatan 6–8, 115 27 Stockholm)

Ambassador: J. C. Petersen, CMG.

OF SWEDEN IN THE USA (600 New Hampshire Avenue, NW, Suite 1200, Washington, D.C., 20037)

Ambassador: Count W. H. F. Wachtmeister.

OF THE USA IN SWEDEN (Stradvagen 101, Stockholm)

Ambassador: Rodney Kennedy-Minott.

OF SWEDEN TO THE UNITED NATIONS

Ambassador: Anders I. Thunborg.

Books of Reference

Statistical Information: The National Central Bureau of Statistics (Statistiska, Centralbyrån, Fack, S-10250 Stockholm 27) was founded in 1858, in succession to the Kungl. Tabellkommissionen, which had been set up in 1756. *Director-General:* Dr Ingvar Ohlsson. Its publications include:

Levnadsförhållanden, årsbok (Living Conditions). Annual. From 1975.—*Rapport*. from 1976
Statistik årsbok för Sverige (Statistical Abstract of Sweden). From 1914
Siffror om Sverige (Sweden). From 1971. Also in English as *Sweden*
Historisk statistik för Sverige (Historical Statistics of Sweden). 1955 ff. (4 vols. to date)
Sveriges officiella statistik (Official Statistics of Sweden). From 1911. (With summary in French; from 1952 in English)
Allmän månadsstatistik (Monthly Digest of Swedish Statistics). From 1963
Statistiska meddelanden (Statistical Reports). From 1963

Ahlmann, H. W. (ed.), *Sverige, Land och Folk*. 3 vols. Stockholm, 1967
Andersson, I., *A History of Sweden*. Stockholm, 1962
Atlas över Sverige. Stockholm, 1953–71. [Publ. in separate parts dealing with population, economics, etc.]
Bastide, F.-R., *Suède*. Paris, 1969
Britten Austin, P., *The Swedes: How They Live and Work*. Newton Abbot, 1970
Courtier, E., *En Suède*. Montreal, 1970
Documentation on Sweden. Stockholm, 1976
Documents on Swedish Foreign Policy, 1973. Stockholm, 1976
Faramond, G. de, *Un Politique du Bien-Être*. Paris, 1972
Fleisher, F., *The New Sweden*. New York, 1967
Fullerton, B., and Williams, A. F., *Scandinavia*. London, 1972
Furer, H. B. (ed.), *The Scandinavians in America 986–1970. A Chronology and Fact Book*. Dobbs Ferry, 1972
Gullberg, I. E., *Swedish–English Dictionary of Technical Terms.—Svensk-Engelsk Fackordbok*. Stockholm, 2nd ed. 1977

Hancock, M. D., *Sweden. The Politics of Post-Industrial Change*. Hinsdale, Ill., 1972
Heilborn, A., *Travel, Study and Research in Sweden*. 6th ed. Stockholm, 1965
Mead, W. R., and Hall, W., *Scandinavia*. London, 1972
Nobel, The Man and His Prizes. Published by the Nobel Foundation. Stockholm, 1950
Nordic Council, *Yearbook of Nordic Statistics*. From 1962 (in English and one Nordic Language)
Nording, R., *Suède Socialiste et Libre Entreprise*. Paris, 1970
Parent, J., *Le Modèle Suédois*. Paris, 1970
Paul, W. W., *The Story of Scandanavia*. Cincinnati, 1971
Scobbie, I., *Sweden*. London, 1972
Stomberg, A. A., *A History of Sweden*. New York, 1970
Scott, F. D., *Sweden: The Nation's History*. Univ of Minnesota Press, 1977
Tomason, R. F., *Sweden: Prototype of Modern Society*. New York, 1970
Toyne, S. M., *The Scandanavians in History*. Freeport, 1970
Turner, B., *Sweden*. London, 1976
Sveriges statskalender. Published by Vetenskapsakademien. Annual, from 1813

National Library: Kungliga Biblioteket, Stockholm. *Directoror:* Lars Tynell.

SWITZERLAND

Schweiz—Suisse—Svizzera

Capital: Bern
Population: 6·35m. (1976)
GNP per capita: US$8,880 (1976)

HISTORY. On 1 Aug. 1291 the men of Uri, Schwyz and Unterwalden entered into a defensive league. In 1353 the league included 8 members and in 1513, 13. Various territories were acquired either by single cantons or by several in common, and in 1648 the league became formally independent of the Holy Roman Empire, but no addition was made to the number of cantons till 1798. In that year, under the influence of France, the unified Helvetic Republic was formed. This failed to satisfy the Swiss, and in 1803 Napoleon Bonaparte, in the Act of Mediation, gave a new constitution, and out of the lands formerly allied or subject increased the number of cantons to 19. In 1815 the perpetual neutrality of Switzerland and the inviolability of her territory were guaranteed by Austria, France, Great Britain, Portugal, Prussia, Russia, Spain and Sweden, and the Federal Pact, which included 3 new cantons, was accepted by the Congress of Vienna. In 1848 a new constitution was passed without foreign interference. The 22 cantons set up a Federal Government (consisting of a Federal Parliament and a Federal Council) and a Federal Tribunal. This constitution, in turn, was on 29 May 1874 superseded by the present constitution.

AREA AND POPULATION. Area and population, according to the census held on 1 Dec. 1960 and the census held on 1 Dec. 1970, are shown in the following table. The cantons are given in the official order and the year of the entrance of each into the league or confederation is stated:

Canton	*Area (sq. km)*	*Census population 1 Dec. 1960*	*Census population 1 Dec. 1970*	*Pop. per sq. km, 1970*
Zürich (Zurich) (1351)	1,729	952,304	1,107,788	641
Bern (Berne) (1553)	6,887	889,523	983,296	143
Luzern (Lucerne) (1332)	1,494	253,446	289,641	194
Uri (1291)	1,075	32,021	34,091	32
Schwyz (1291)	908	78,048	92,072	101
Obwalden (Obwald) (1291)	492	23,135	24,509	50
Nidwalden (Nidwald) (1291)	274	22,188	25,634	94
Glarus (Glaris) (1352)	684	40,148	38,155	56
Zug (Zoug) (1352)	239	52,489	67,996	285
Fribourg (Freiburg) (1481)	1,670	159,194	180,309	108
Solothurn (Soleure) (1481)	791	200,816	224,133	283
Basel-Stadt (Bâle-V.) (1501)	37	225,588	234,945	6,338
Basel-Land (Bâle-C.) (1501)	428	148,282	204,889	479
Schaffhausen (Schaffhouse) (1501)	298	65,981	72,854	244
Appenzell A.-Rh. (Rh.-Ext.) (1513)	243	48,920	49,023	202
Appenzell I.-Rh. (Rh.-Int) (1513)	172	12,943	13,124	76
St Gallen (St Gall) (1803)	2,016	339,489	384,475	191
Graubünden (Grisons) (1803)	7,109	147,458	162,086	23
Aargau (Argovie) (1803)	1,404	360,940	433,284	309
Thurgau (Thurgovie) (1803)	1,006	166,420	182,835	182
Ticino (Tessin) (1803)	2,811	195,566	245,458	87
Vaud (Waadt) (1803)	3,211	429,512	511,851	159
Valais (Wallis) (1815)	5,231	177,783	206,563	39
Neuchâtel (Neuenburg) (1815)	797	147,633	169,173	212
Genève (Genf) (1815)	282	259,234	331,599	1,175
Total	41,288[1]	5,429,061	6,269,783	152

[1] 15,941 sq. miles.

Population (1976 estimate) 6,346,000.

The German language is spoken by the majority of inhabitants in 19 of the 25 cantons above (French names given in brackets), the French in 5 (Fribourg, Vaud, Valais. Neuchâtel and Genève, for which the German names are given in brackets), the Italian in one (Ticino). In 1970, 64·9% spoke German, 18·1% French, 11·9% Italian, 0·8% Romansch and 1·4% other languages; counting only Swiss nationals, the percentages were 74·5, 20·1, 4, 1 and 0·4. On 8 July 1937 Romansch was made the fourth national language; it is spoken mostly in Graubünden.

At the end of 1976 the population figures of the principal towns (and their *'agglomérations'* or conurbations) were as follows: Zürich, 383,000 (708,200); Basel, 188,800 (368,900); Geneva, 152,600 (323,100); Bern, 146,800 (283,500); Lausanne, 132,800 (227,300); Winterthur, 87,900 (107,300); St Gallen, 76,300 (87,500); Luzern, 64,200 (156,200); Biel, 59,200 (88,600); La Chaux-de-Fonds, 39,500.

The number of foreigners resident in Switzerland at 31 Dec. 1976 was 958,599. The number of Swiss resident outside Switzerland on 31 Dec. 1974 was 161,511: in France, 29,938; Federal Republic of Germany, 24,428; USA, 16,223; Italy, 12,446; Canada, 9,440; UK, 8,464; South Africa, 4,672; Austria, 4,161; Argentina, 3,985; Brazil, 3,558.

Vital statistics for calendar years:

	Live births					
	Total	*Illegitimate*	*Marriages*	*Divorces*	*Still births*	*Deaths*
1974	84,507	3,088	38,499	8,193	603	56,403
1975	78,464	2,927	35,189	8,917	566	55,924
1976	74,199	2,810	32,058	9,582	586	57,095

The excess of emigrants over remigrants was: 1968, 3,065; 1969, 3,276; 1970, 2,618; 1971, 1,313; 1972, −18; 1973, 1,355; 1974, 1,755.

Historisch-Biographisches Lexikon der Schweiz. 7 vols. Neuenburg, 1919–34. (Also in French)

Früh, J., *Geographie der Schweiz*. 3 vols. St Gallen, 1930–38

Jacot, A., *Neues Schweizerisches Orts-Lexikon mit Verkehrs-Karte*. Lucerne, 1949

Leeman, Walter, *Landeskunde der Schweiz*. Zürich, 1939

Mayer, Kurt B., *The Population of Switzerland*. New York and London, 1952

CONSTITUTION AND GOVERNMENT. Switzerland is a republic. The highest authority is vested in the electorate, *i.e.*, all Swiss citizens of over 20. This electorate—besides electing its representatives to the Parliament—has the voting power on amendments to, or on the revision of, the constitution. It also takes decisions on laws and international treaties if requested by 30,000 voters or 8 cantons (facultative referendum), and it has the right of initiating constitutional amendments, the support required for such demands being 50,000 voters (popular initiative).

The Federal Government is supreme in matters of peace, war and treaties; it regulates the army, the railway, telecommunication systems, the coining of money, the issue and repayment of bank-notes and the weights and measures of the republic. It also legislates on matters of copyright, bankruptcy, patents, sanitary police in dangerous epidemics, and it may create and subsidize, besides the Polytechnic School at Zürich and at Lausanne, 2 federal universities and other educational institutions. There has also been entrusted to it the authority to decide concerning public works for the whole or great part of Switzerland, such as those relating to rivers, forests and the construction of national highways and railways. By referendum of 13 Nov. 1898 it is also the authority in the entire spheres of common law. In 1957 the Federation was empowered to legislate on atomic energy matters and in 1961 on the construction of pipelines of petroleum and gas.

National flag: Red with a white couped cross.

National anthem: Trittst im Morgenrot daher (words by Leonard Widmer, 1808–68; tune by Alberik Zwyssig, 1808–54); adopted by the Federal Council in 1962.

The legislative authority is vested in a parliament of 2 chambers, a *Ständerat*, or Council of States, and a *Nationalrat*, or National Council.

The *Ständerat* is composed of 44 members, chosen and paid by the 22 cantons of the Confederation, 2 for each canton. The mode of their election and the term of membership depend entirely on the canton. Three of the cantons are politically divided—Basel into Stadt and Land, Appenzell into Ausser-Rhoden and Inner-Rhoden, and Unterwalden into Obwalden and Nidwalden. Each of these 'half-cantons' sends one member to the State Council.

The *Nationalrat*—after the referendum taken on 4 Nov. 1962—consists of 200 National Councillors, directly elected for 4 years, in proportion to the population of the cantons, with the proviso that each canton or half-canton is represented by at least one member. The members are paid from federal funds at the rate of 150 francs for each day during the session and a nominal sum of 10,000 francs per annum.

In 1975 the 200 members were distributed among the cantons[1] as follows:

Zürich (Zurich)	35	Schaffhausen (Schaffhouse)	2
Bern (Berne)	31	Appenzell—Outer- and Inner-Rhoden	3
Luzern (Lucerne)	9	St Gallen (St Gall)	12
Uri	1	Graubünden (Grisons)	5
Schwyz	3	Aargau (Argovie)	14
Unterwalden—Upper and Lower	2	Thurgau (Thurgovie)	6
Glarus (Glaris)	1	Ticino (Tessin)	8
Zug (Zoug)	2	Vaud (Waadt)	16
Fribourg (Freiburg)	6	Valais (Wallis)	7
Solothurn (Soleure)	7	Neuchâtel (Neuenburg)	5
Basel (Bâle)—town and country	14	Genève (Genf)	11

[1] The name of the canton is given in German, French or Italian, according to the language most spoken in it, and alternative names are given in brackets.

At the elections held on 26 Oct. 1975 the following parties were returned to the National Council: Social Democrats, 55; Radicals, 47; Christian-Democratic People's Party, 46; Central Democrats, 46; Independents, 11; Protestant Party, 3; Liberal Democrats, 6; Communists, 4; Republicans, 4; Action Party, 4; Independent Socialists, 1.

Council of States (1975): Catholic Democrats, 17; Radicals, 15; Socialists, 5; Central Democrats, 5; Independents, 1; Liberals, 1.

A general election takes place by ballot every 4 years. Every citizen of the republic who has entered on his 20th year is entitled to a vote, and any voter, not a clergyman, may be elected a deputy. Laws passed by both chambers may be submitted to direct popular vote, when 30,000 citizens or 8 cantons demand it; the vote can be only 'Yes' or 'No'. This principle, called the *referendum*, is frequently acted on.

Women's suffrage, although advocated by the Federal Council and the Federal Assembly, was on 1 Feb. 1959 rejected, but in a subsequent *referendum*, held on 7 Feb. 1971, women's suffrage was carried.

The chief executive authority is deputed to the *Bundesrat*, or Federal Council, consisting of 7 members, elected from 7 different cantons for 4 years by the *Vereinigte Bundesversammlung*, *i.e.*, joint sessions of both chambers. The members of this council must not hold any other office in the Confederation or cantons, nor engage in any calling or business. In the Federal Parliament legislation may be introduced either by a member, or by either House, or by the Federal Council (but not by the people). Every citizen who has a vote for the National Council is eligible for becoming a member of the executive.

The President of the Federal Council (called President of the Confederation) and the Vice-President are the first magistrates of the Confederation. Both are elected by the Federal Assembly for one calendar year and are not immediately re-eligible to the same offices. The Vice-President, however, may be, and usually is, elected to succeed the outgoing President.

President of the Confederation for 1978: Willi Ritchard.

The 7 members of the Federal Council—each of whom has a salary of 203,000 francs per annum, while the President has 215,000 francs—act as ministers, or chiefs of the 7 administrative departments of the republic. The city of Berne is the seat of the Federal Council and the central administrative authorities.

The Federal Council is composed as follows (1 Dec. 1976):

Foreign Affairs: Pierre Aubert.
Interior: Hans Hurlimann.
Justice and Police: Kurt Furgler.
Military: Rudolf Gnägi.
Finance: Dr Georges-André Chevellaz.
Public Economy: Fritz Honegger.
Transport, Communications and Energy: Willi Ritchard.

Local Government. Each of the cantons and demi-cantons is sovereign, so far as its independence and legislative powers are not restricted by the federal constitution; all cantonal governments, though different in organization (membership varies from 5 to 11, and terms of office from 1 to 5 years), are based on the principle of sovereignty of the people.

In all cantons a body chosen by universal suffrage, usually called *der Grosse Rat*, or *Kantonsrat*, exercises the functions of a parliament. In all the cantonal constitutions, however, except those of the cantons which have a *Landsgemeinde*, the referendum has a place. By this principle, where it is most fully developed, as in Zürich, all laws and concordats, or agreements with other cantons, and the chief matters of finance, as well as all revisions of the constitution, must be submitted to the popular vote. In Appenzell, Glarus and Unterwalden the people exercise their powers direct in the *Landsgemeinde*, *i.e.*, the assembly in the open air of all male citizens of full age. In all the cantons the *popular initiative* for constitutional affairs, as well as for legislation, has been introduced, except in Lucerne, where the *initiative* exists only for constitutional affairs. In most cantons there are districts (*Amtsbezirke*) consisting of a number of communes grouped together, each district having a Prefect (*Regierungsstatthalter*) representing the cantonal government. In the larger communes, for local affairs, there is an Assembly (legislative) and a Council (executive) with a president, maire or syndic, and not less than 4 other members. In the smaller communes there is a council only, with its proper officials.

Basler Handelskammer, *La neutralité suisse*, 1962
Bonjour, E., *Swiss Neutrality*. London, 1946
Huber, H., *How Switzerland is Governed*. Zürich, 1947
Hughes, C., *The Federal Constitution of Switzerland. Translation and Commentary*. Oxford, 1954
Hughes, C. J., *The Parliament of Switzerland*. Hansard Society, 1962
Marx, Dr Paul, *Systematisches Register zu den geltenden Staatsverträgen der schweizerischen Eidgenossenschaft und der Kantone mit dem Auslande*. Zürich, 1918. *Appendix*, 1934
Rappard, W. E., *La Constitution fédérale de la Suisse*. Zürich, 1948.—*Collective Security in Swiss Experience*. London, 1948
Ruck, Erwin, *Schweizerisches Staatsrecht*. Zürich, 1933
Silbernagel-Caloyanni, Alfred, *Suisse: Organisation Politique, Administrative et Judiciaire de la Confédération Helvétique et de Chaque Canton*. Paris, 1936

DEFENCE. There are fortifications in all entrances to the Alps and on the important passes crossing the Alps and the Jura. Large-scale destructions of bridges, tunnels and defiles are prepared for an emergency.

Army. Switzerland depends for defence upon a *national militia*. Service in this force is compulsory and universal, with few exemptions except for physical disability. Those excused or rejected pay certain taxes in lieu. Liability extends from the 20th to the end of the 50th year for soldiers and of the 55th year for officers. The first 12 years are spent in the first line, called the *Auszug*, or *Élite*, the next 10 in the *Landwehr* and 8 in the *Landsturm*. The unarmed *Hilfsdienst* comprises all other males between 20 and 50 whose services can be made available for non-combatant duties of any description.

The initial training of the Swiss militia soldier is carried out in recruits' schools, and the periods are 118 days for infantry, engineers, artillery, etc. The subsequent trainings, called 'repetition courses', are 20 days annually; but after going through 8 courses further attendance is excused for all under the rank of sergeant. The *Landwehr* men are called up for training courses of 13 days every 2 years, and the *Landsturm* men have to undergo a refresher course of 13 days.

The Army is divided into 3 armoured divisions, 3 infantry divisions, 3 frontier divisions, 3 mountain divisions, and into frontier-, fortress- and territorial-brigades, organized in 4 army corps. Strength: 37,000, including 34,000 conscripts, and 578,000 reserves.

The administration of the Swiss Army is partly in the hands of the Cantonal authorities, who can promote officers up to the rank of captain. But the Federal Government is concerned with all general questions and makes all the higher appointments.

In peace-time the Swiss Army has no general; only in time of war the Federal Assembly in joint session of both Houses appoints a general.

The Swiss infantry are armed with the Swiss automatic rifle and with machine-guns, bazookas and mortars. The field artillery is armed with a Q.F. shielded 10·5 Bofors and field howitzers of 10·5 cm calibre. The heavy artillery is armed with guns of 10·5 cm and howitzers of 15 cm calibre. The armoured troops are equipped with the light French AMX, the British Centurion and a modern Swiss tank.

Air Force. The Air Force consists of 3 regiments, made up of 21 first-line squadrons with about 350 combat aircraft. The fighter squadrons are equipped with Mirage IIIS supersonic interceptor/ground-attack (2 squadrons), Mirage IIIRS fighter/reconnaissance (1 squadron), Venom ground-attack (9 squadrons) and Hunter interceptor/ground-attack (9 squadrons) aircraft. Four of the Venom squadrons will re-equip with F-5E Tiger IIs, beginning in 1978. Bloodhound surface-to-air missile batteries are operational. Training aircraft are Pilatus P-2 and P-3 and Vampire; there are also communications and transport aircraft and helicopters. Personnel numbers, 3,000 regulars, 6,000 conscripts and 40,000 reservists.

INTERNATIONAL RELATIONS

Membership. Switzerland is a member of OECD, EFTA and the Council of Europe.

ECONOMY

Budget. Revenue and expenditure of the Confederation, in 1m. francs, for calendar years:

	1971	*1972*	*1973*	*1974*	*1975*	*1976*
Revenue	8,517	10,366	11,625	13,052	13,541	14,287
Expenditure	8,609	10,119	10,846	12,012	12,232	15,863

The public debt, comprising consolidated debt and flowing debt, of the Confederation on 31 Dec. 1976 amounted to 13,804m. francs. The floating debt was 407·2m. francs.

Schweizerisches Finanz-Jahrbuch. Bern. Annual. From 1899
Staatsicchnung der Schweizerischen Eidgenossenschaft. Bern, 1976

Currency. The *franc* of 100 *Rappen* or *centimes* is the monetary unit. By law of 17 Dec. 1952, which came into force on 20 April 1953, the value of the franc was fixed at 0·20322 gramme of fine gold. On 10 May 1971 there was a revaluation to 0·21759 gramme of fine gold. The legal gold coins are 20- and 10-franc pieces; cupro-nickel coins are 5, 2, 1 and ½ franc, 20, 10 and 5 centimes; bronze, 2 and 1 centime. Notes are of 1,000, 500, 100, 50, 20, 10 and 5 *francs*.

On 31 Dec. 1971 the coin in circulation (of francs of nominal value) was as follows: 1,640,681 cupro-nickel coins of 713·6m. and 242,318 bronze coins of 3·1m.

Banking. The National Bank, with headquarters divided between Bern and Zürich, opened on 20 June 1907. It has the exclusive right to issue bank-notes. In 1976 the condition of the bank was as follows (in 1m. francs): Gold, 11,897·7; foreign exchange (currency), 13,371·8; foreign treasury bonds, 5,388·9; currency in circulation, 17,778·4; short-term liabilities, 10,062·8.

In 1976 there were 1,740 banking institutions with total assets of 347,710·5m. Swiss francs. They included 28 cantonal banks (79,376m. francs), 5 big banks (161,382m.), 225 regional banks (38,138m.), 185 other banks (43,267m.).

On 31 Dec. 1976 the total amount of savings deposits in Swiss banks was 73,903m. francs, with 11·2m. depositors.

National Bank: Bulletin mensuel.—Das schweizerische Bankwesen. Yearly. From 1920

Weights and Measures. The metric system of weights and measures was made compulsory by the federal law on 3 July 1875 and since 1 Jan. 1887 only metric units have been legal. By the federal law of 24 June 1909 the international electric units were also adopted.

ENERGY AND NATURAL RESOURCES

Electricity. In 1975 Switzerland had electrical power-plants with a capacity of 31,527m. kwh. The total production of energy amounted to 36,241m. kwh. in 1975–76 (Oct.–Sept.); 26,787m. kwh. were generated by hydro-electric plants. The production of gas in 1976 was 94m. cu. metres (total consumption, 646m. cu. metres).

Minerals. There are 2 salt-mining districts; that in Bex (Vaud) belongs to the canton, but is worked by a private company, and those at Schweizerhalle, Rheinfelden and Ryburg are worked by a joint-stock company formed by the cantons interested. The output of salt of all kinds in 1976 was 311,611 tonnes. At Sargans (St Gallen) and Herznach (Aargau) iron ore and manganese ore were mined; output (in 1,000 tonnes) 1960, 125; 1965, 113. Since 1966 the mine of Gonzen (at Sargans) and since 1967 Herznach are closed.

Agriculture. Of the total area of the country of 4,129,315 hectares, about 1,057,794 hectares (25·6%) are unproductive. Of the productive area of 3,071,521 hectares, 1,051,991 hectares are wooded. The agricultural area, in 1975, consisted of 274,093 hectares arable land (including vineyards), 102,634 hectares artificial meadows and 660,776 hectares permanent meadow. In 1975 there were 136,708 farms with a total area of 1,055,627 hectares. The gross value of agricultural products was estimated at 6,292m. in 1974 and 6,402·7m. in 1975.

In 1975, 177,804 hectares were planted with cereals, of which 86,225 hectares were wheat; rye, 6,196; barley, 44,697; potatoes, 23,811; sugar-beet, 10,641; vegetables, 6,214; tobacco, 713. Production, 1975 (in 1,000 tonnes): Wheat, 341; rye, 24; barley, 172; potatoes 908; sugar-beet, 479; tobacco, 2. Milk production (in 1,000 tonnes): 1960, 3,112; 1970, 3,204; 1974, 3,360; 1975, 3,396; 1976, 3,473.

The fruit production (in 1,000 tonnes) in 1975 was: Apples, 440; pears, 192; cherries, 49; plums, 44; nuts, 7.

Wine is produced in 18 of the cantons. In 1976 Swiss vineyards (13,583 hectares) yielded 1,193,858 hectolitres of wine, valued at 407,878,000 francs.

Livestock, 1977: 46,070 horses, 368,400 sheep, 2,004,800 cattle (including 896,900 milch cows), 2,065,200 pigs, 6,058,000 poultry.

Forestry. Of the forest area of 976,811 hectares, 53,672 were owned by the Federation or the cantons, 627,106 by communes and 296,033 by private persons or companies in 1976. The utilization of timber, in 1976, was 3,686,467 cu. metres, of which 279,056 in state-owned, 2,465,744 in communal and 891,667 in private forests.

INDUSTRY AND TRADE

Industry. The chief food producing industries, based on Swiss agriculture, are the manufacture of cheese, butter, sugar and meat. The production in 1975 was (in tonnes): Cheese, 103,500; butter, 34,500; sugar, 76,611; meat, 400,724. There are 46 breweries, producing in 1976, 4·3m. hectolitres of beer. Tobacco products in 1975: Cigars, 493m.; cigarettes, 27,788m.

Among the other industries, the manufacture of textiles, wearing apparel and footwear, chemicals and pharmaceutical products, bricks, glass and cement, the manufacture of basic iron and steel and of other metal products, the production of machinery (including electrical machinery and scientific and optical instruments) and watch and clock making are the most important. In 1976 there were 9,609 factories with 683,200 workers. Of these, 41,178 were working in textile industries, 41,054 in the manufacture of textile goods and footwear, 61,508 in chemical works, 19,155 in the manufacture of clay products, glass and glass products, cement and cement products, 91,976 in manufacture of metal products, 219,519 in the manufacture of machinery and 50,957 in watch and clock making and in the manufacture of jewellery.

Production in 1976 was: Woollen and blended yarn, 16,921 tonnes; woollen and blended cloth, 12,523 metres; footwear, 8·65m. pairs; cement, 3,546,000 tonnes; raw aluminium, 78,000 tonnes; chocolate, 60,968 tonnes. 42·14m. watches and clocks were exported.

Labour. According to the census of industries, 1975, the total working population was reduced to about 2·7m., of which 6·3% were active in agriculture and forestry, 44·7% in manufacture and construction and 48·9% in services. In all non-agricultural sectors there were 288,470 establishments (including 594 being shut down) with 2,537,738 occupied persons, divided in 159,289 occupants and 2,378,449 employees.

The main groups show the following numbers of gainfully occupied persons: Agriculture and forestry, 172,649; food processing, 103,306; textiles, 89,660; chemical industry, 68,975; metalwork, 175,983; engineering, 254,185; watchmaking, 61,058; construction 225,533; wholesale trade, 113,197; retail trade, 228,751; banking and insurance, 105,106; transport and postal services, 171,081; catering, 158,500.

The foreign labour force with permit of temporary residence was 342,026 in Aug. 1976. Of the number recorded 129,264 were Italians, 56,225 Spaniards, 42,994 Frenchmen, 31,048 Germans and 10,240 Austrians. 67,108 were construction workers, 56,474 metal-workers and mechanics and 43,128 housekeepers, hotel and restaurant workers.

The Swiss Federation of Trade Unions had, in 1976, a membership of 474,725. Other organizations of employees had about 427,350 members.

Commerce. The special commerce, excluding gold (bullion and coins) and silver (coins), was (in 1m. Swiss francs) as follows:

	1970	*1971*	*1972*	*1973*	*1974*	*1975*	*1976*
Imports	27,873	29,642	32,372	36,589	42,929	34,268	36,871
Exports	22,140	23,617	26,188	29,948	35,353	33,430	37,045

The following table, in 1m. francs, shows the distribution of the special trade of Switzerland among the principal countries:

	Imports from				*Exports to*			
Countries	*1973*	*1974*	*1975*	*1976*	*1973*	*1974*	*1975*	*1976*
Federal Rep. of Germany	11,062·7	12,478·7	9,552·9	10,470·0	4,200·5	4,842·6	4,944·2	5,761·2
France	5,117·1	5,886·1	4,753·8	4,891·1	2,646·9	3,108·6	2,964·8	3,365·9
Italy	3,416·7	3,929·8	3,386·2	3,564·0	2,495·2	2,822·6	2,306·0	2,758·0
Netherlands	1,448·5	1,760·1	1,375·8	1,362·9	765·0	920·6	890·7	992·0
Belgium–Luxembourg	1,288·8	1,459·5	1,109·8	1,311·8	658·9	793·6	794·5	1,007·8
UK	2,239·9	2,501·6	2,105·0	2,482·7	2,276·0	2,538·7	2,050·8	2,181·8
Denmark	474·2	483·4	371·0	372·2	554·3	494·2	507·1	545·6
Irish Republic	67·9	73·7	62·7	70·1	58·9	67·7	60·7	66·5
EEC Total	25,115·8	28,572·9	22,717·2	24,524·8	13,655·7	15,588·6	14,518·8	16,678·8
Austria	1,811·8	2,108·9	1,488·9	1,511·4	1,800·3	2,326·1	1,852·3	1,972·8
Norway	163·9	209·5	164·2	167·2	360·3	410·3	447·7	473·1
Sweden	1,098·9	1,190·1	933·7	876·6	850·2	1,055·7	1,095·5	1,054·5
Portugal	171·9	194·0	157·4	130·5	412·6	481·3	281·2	356·2
Finland	234·7	277·0	189·2	201·9	323·4	424·6	396·5	389·7
Iceland	40·0	60·4	10·6	29·1	12·7	12·5	11·8	10·4
EFTA	3,521·2	4,039·9	2,944·0	2,916·7	3,759·5	4,710·5	4,085·0	4,256·7
Spain	431·0	492·6	389·0	397·6	823·3	929·7	879·3	894·1
Gibraltar, Malta	3·8	2·2	1·3	2·3	9·3	14·5	14·5	14·0
German Dem. Republic	62·3	79·5	59·8	51·7	177·1	177·6	185·4	212·6
Poland	90·7	107·9	102·6	88·1	281·4	419·9	456·3	444·9
Czechoslovakia	176·8	218·6	170·3	152·0	198·0	241·2	270·2	259·3

Countries	Imports from 1973	1974	1975	1976	Exports to 1973	1974	1975	1976
Hungary	155·5	215·6	133·6	170·4	156·9	238·7	263·8	268·3
Yugoslavia	125·9	132·8	98·2	124·4	441·5	610·2	623·0	505·8
Greece	51·5	54·4	52·4	52·4	241·1	264·0	278·4	248·9
Bulgaria	25·0	27·5	23·5	26·0	60·5	93·8	98·1	129·1
Romania	65·3	73·1	84·9	111·6	164·7	176·1	169·4	163·8
USSR	201·7	360·0	312·1	644·5	305·0	419·9	468·2	504·2
Turkey	106·1	105·9	96·3	134·6	228·8	301·6	262·7	281·6
Other European countries	3·0	2·1	1·6	2·6	19·4	27·1	11·1	15·4
Europe Total	30,135·6	34,485·0	27,186·8	29,399·7	20,522·2	24,213·4	22,584·2	24,877·5
Egypt	38·8	41·6	19·1	35·2	63·4	100·4	165·3	190·2
Sudan	24·8	16·7	24·0	23·4	19·5	23·4	31·8	24·4
Libya	234·3	273·0	81·8	91·7	78·0	106·7	106·1	193·7
Tunisia	9·3	110·2	52·5	6·6	13·9	19·2	36·6	32·5
Algeria	102·1	151·6	35·4	124·7	99·6	107·2	146·8	191·5
Morocco	30·4	44·6	43·3	28·7	59·1	71·9	87·1	97·8
Ivory Coast	26·6	38·9	24·2	29·0	15·2	18·7	32·5	30·0
Guinea	15·0	17·7	24·9	7·0	10·8	7·5	14·9	10·7
Ghana	33·3	38·6	33·9	31·1	18·1	23·5	22·5	44·4
Nigeria	85·4	261·8	213·4	215·3	85·8	120·9	297·8	274·1
Zaïre	8·1	10·1	7·0	15·9	46·7	53·2	37·6	42·6
SW Africa	45·6	30·8	24·6	14·7	31·7	45·2	15·9	19·8
South Africa, Rep. of	65·7	79·7	73·3	69·0	342·5	507·0	504·5	371·1
Zambia	24·3	30·1	15·3	10·2	18·6	23·6	17·1	14·5
Rhodesia	24·4	21·9	18·8	19·1	12·1	13·4	7·1	5·0
Tanzania	7·7	5·5	6·3	3·9	18·9	17·9	17·7	15·5
Kenya	16·8	23·7	18·3	24·4	26·9	30·2	21·1	20·4
Other African countries	88·8	106·1	94·0	106·1	133·3	150·5	140·5	162·1
Africa Total	881·4	1,302·6	810·1	856·0	1,094·1	1,440·4	1,702·9	1,740·3
Syria	5·6	3·4	0·5	9·6	54·5	77·2	106·4	158·6
Lebanon	13·0	12·6	9·6	7·5	102·7	133·4	121·1	45·0
Israel	122·4	132·2	120·7	156·7	240·4	293·4	338·8	650·5
Iraq	16·3	6·2	0·3	0·2	38·5	101·7	171·3	146·7
Kuwait	53·0	177·9	138·9	25·0	51·0	78·9	85·8	103·6
Iran	103·4	100·4	100·0	192·3	321·9	454·8	628·4	761·3
Saudi Arabia	44·5	149·4	118·6	44·0	95·8	181·0	284·2	600·4
UAE	178·9	566·5	522·2	389·4	98·7	129·8	103·0	178·9
Pakistan	24·2	31·4	21·8	20·3	28·8	47·6	54·2	60·5
India	69·3	86·6	85·1	278·6	120·4	139·7	137·6	137·0
Thailand	32·3	50·5	39·6	47·3	81·3	76·9	83·9	59·5
Malaysia	22·1	18·6	16·3	21·0	34·0	47·9	35·6	28·5
Singapore	20·9	31·6	35·8	42·9	132·8	154·4	149·4	141·8
China	90·6	107·3	79·8	90·8	132·7	162·5	144·6	130·1
Hong Kong	203·0	261·2	257·0	323·6	543·5	629·6	478·2	567·8
Korea, Rep. of	23·3	44·6	54·2	100·0	50·0	58·8	60·0	97·5
Taiwan	64·2	94·5	84·0	74·8	133·5	136·8	73·8	73·2
Japan	927·6	1,027·1	832·3	971·4	1,156·9	1,237·7	925·8	1,010·2
Philippines	15·7	14·8	31·4	22·3	40·9	54·5	64·3	62·7
Indonesia	49·6	59·1	48·3	73·5	59·6	89·2	79·5	79·8
Other Asian countries	84·5	71·3	45·5	36·9	85·0	139·0	163·1	213·1
Asia Total	2,164·4	3,047·2	2,641·9	2,928·1	3,602·9	4,424·8	4,289·0	5,306·7
Canada	175·9	337·3	219·2	240·6	345·0	386·9	435·6	369·6
USA	2,333·0	2,806·3	2,587·1	2,520·2	2,444·5	2,501·4	2,134·6	2,521·2
Mexico	44·2	51·9	85·6	101·7	209·9	235·7	246·9	267·5
Guatemala	33·3	40·5	34·2	29·8	16·5	23·6	18·8	29·2
Honduras	16·0	18·0	8·6	21·2	7·1	6·7	4·5	5·8
Costa Rica	45·5	44·2	32·5	37·0	13·8	20·4	14·7	22·1

Countries	Imports from 1973	1974	1975	1976	Exports to 1973	1974	1975	1976
Panama	59·3	87·4	89·3	70·2	54·2	86·4	80·6	88·3
Cuba	11·6	15·4	10·5	12·4	37·2	48·2	71·4	24·4
Colombia	39·2	46·2	57·9	62·8	83·1	108·3	92·1	78·8
Venezuela	9·7	7·8	10·4	8·7	168·8	165·1	215·0	246·2
Brazil	185·1	178·9	181·5	166·1	493·5	558·0	566·8	538·7
Uruguay	18·1	24·7	23·4	21·4	16·2	19·5	21·4	19·8
Argentina	174·6	125·7	71·0	115·4	139·8	265·6	212·6	176·4
Chile	7·1	15·2	15·6	10·8	46·7	39·6	33·4	37·7
Bolivia	0·7	1·1	0·7	1·7	11·3	18·2	19·4	27·4
Peru	56·3	54·6	41·5	59·5	102·8	124·7	136·9	96·8
Ecuador	15·4	20·6	17·6	16·9	20·6	29·6	36·4	41·6
Other American countries	69·0	81·9	66·5	88·5	124·2	142·0	139·9	127·2
Australia and Oceania	113·2	136·9	75·9	102·5	393·9	494·6	372·6	401·6

Custom receipts (in 1,000 francs): 1973, 2,896,763; 1974, 2,802,789; 1975, 2,939,161; 1976, 2,833,305.

Total trade between Switzerland (including Liechtenstein from 1968) and UK for calendar years (British Department of Trade, in £1,000 sterling):

	1973	1974	1975	1976	1977
Imports to UK	591,582	717,143	711,338	962,877	1,319,281
Exports and re-exports from UK	520,873	600,450	710,046	1,000,360	1,421,382

Federal Customs Office, *Statistique mensuelle du commerce extérieur de la Suisse*. From 1925.—*Statistique annuelle du commerce extérieur de la Suisse*. 2 vols. From 1840.—*Rapport annuel de la statistique du commerce Suisse*. From 1889

Handbuch der schweizerischen Volkswirtschaft. 2 vols. Bern, 1955

Tourism. Tourism is an important industry. In 1976, 3,571,000 Swiss and 5,879,000 foreigners (including 341,000 British) visited Swiss holiday resorts. The tourist trade earned 5,500m. francs in 1976.

COMMUNICATIONS

Roads. There are (1975) 18,515 km of main roads, including 952 km of 'national roads' for motor cars only. There is a postal autobus service, which, in 1976, carried 53·7m. passengers. Motor vehicles, as at 30 Sept. 1976, numbered 2,138,011, including 1,863,615 private cars, 94,228 trucks, 93,689 motor cycles, 9,909 buses and 5,068 agricultural tractors and special cars.

Railways. Railway history in Switzerland begins in 1847. In 1976 the length of the Swiss Federal Railways was 2,920 km, nearly 2,904 km of it electrified. The operating receipts amounted to 2,322,132,000 francs; operating expenses, 2,333,458,000 francs. Traffic was 38·09m. tonnes and 208·35m. passengers. There are many privately-owned lines, the most important of which are the Bern–Lotschberg–Simplon (115 km) and Rhaetian (363 km) networks.

Aviation. In 1976 civil aviation on domestic and international routes carried 9,916,923 passengers, 275,532 tonnes of mail, freight and luggage, and flew 157·15m. km.

The air transport organization Swissair (founded in 1931) in 1976 flew 344·25m. ton-km, carrying 5,988,131 passengers. Swissair is a mixed enterprise with a capital of originally 14m. francs, raised to 422m. on 15 May 1977. Its fleet consisted of 48 aircraft on 31 May 1977.

Shipping. A merchant marine was created by a decree of the Swiss Government dated 9 April 1941, the place of registry of its vessels being Basel. On 31 Dec. 1976 it consisted of 28 vessels with a total of 253,408 GRT. In 1976, 7,979,728 tonnes of goods entered and 312,210 tonnes left the port of Basel.

Post and Broadcasting. In 1976 there were 3,968 post offices. On 1 Jan. 1977 there were 4,016,322 telephones, all integrated in one dial system.

Wireless communication is furnished by 3 main medium-wave stations and one short-wave station. There are 3 television studios and more than 100 transmitters. TV programmes are financed by licence fees and advertisements. Advertisements are limited to 15 minutes each day. All stations are operated by the Federal Post, Telephone and Telegraph (PTT) services. Radio-telegraph circuits are operated by Radio Suisse SA, radio-telephone circuits by the PTT. Radio licences, 1976, 2,107,900; television licences, 1,809,000 (200,000 colour sets).

The total expenditure of the PTT in 1976 was 4,959m. francs, the total gross receipts 5,119m. francs.

Cinemas (1976). There were 501 cinemas with a seating capacity of 182,599.

Newspapers (1970). The number of daily newspapers was estimated to be 118 with a combined circulation of 2·5m.

JUSTICE, RELIGION, EDUCATION AND WELFARE

Justice. The Federal Tribunal (*Bundes-Gericht*), which sits at Lausanne, consists of 26–28 members, with 11–13 supplementary judges, appointed by the Federal Assembly for 6 years and eligible for re-election; the President and Vice-President serve for 2 years and cannot be re-elected. The President has a salary of 170,000 francs a year, and the other members 158,000 francs. The Tribunal has original and final jurisdiction in suits between the Confederation and cantons; between cantons and cantons; between the Confederation or cantons and corporations or individuals, the value in dispute being not less than 8,000 francs; between parties who refer their case to it, the value in dispute being at least 20,000 francs; in such suits as the constitution or legislation of cantons places within its authority; and in many classes of railway suits. It is a court of appeal against decisions of other federal authorities, and of cantonal authorities applying federal laws. The Tribunal also tries persons accused of treason or other offences against the Confederation. For this purpose it is divided into 4 chambers: Chamber of Accusation, Criminal Chamber (*Cour d'Assises*), Federal Penal Court and Court of Cassation. The jurors who serve in the Assize Courts are elected by the people, and are paid 100 francs a day when serving.

On 3 July 1938 the Swiss electorate accepted a new federal penal code, to take the place of the separate cantonal penal codes. The new code, which abolished capital punishment, came into force on 1 Jan. 1942.

By federal law of 5 Oct. 1950 several articles of the penal code concerning crime against the independence of the state have been amended with a view to reinforcing the security of the state.

Thormann, P., and Overbeck, A. (ed.), *Das Schweizerische Strafgesetzbuch*. Zürich, 1939
Williams, Ivy, *The Swiss Civil Code*. English version. Oxford, 1925

Religion. There is complete and absolute liberty of conscience and of creed. No one is bound to pay taxes specially appropriated to defraying the expenses of a creed to which he does not belong. No bishoprics can be created on Swiss territory without the approbation of the Confederation. The Society of Jesus and its affiliated societies cannot be received in any part of Switzerland.

According to the census of 1 Dec. 1970 Roman Catholics numbered 3,097,000 (49·4%) of the population; Protestants, 2,992,000 (47·7%) and others, 181,000 (2·9%). In 1960 Protestants were in a majority in 10 of the cantons and Catholics in 12. Of the more populous cantons, Zürich, Bern, Vaud, Neuchâtel and Basel (town and land) were mainly Protestant, while Luzern, Fribourg, Ticino, Valais and the Forest Cantons are mainly Catholic. The Roman Catholics are under 6 Bishops, viz., of Basel (resident at Solothurn), Chur, St Gallen, Lugano, Lausanne–Geneva–Fribourg (resident at Fribourg) and Sitten (Sion), all of them immediately subject to the Holy See. The Old Catholics have a theological faculty at the university of Bern.

Lampert, U., *Kirche und Staat in der Schweiz*. 2 vols. Freiburg, 1937

Education. Education is administered by the cantons. Before the year 1848 most of the cantons had organized a system of primary schools, and since that year elementary education has steadily advanced. In 1874 it was made obligatory for the whole country (the school age varying in the different cantons) and placed under the civil authority. In some cantons the cost falls almost entirely on the communes, in others it is divided between the canton and communes. In all the cantons primary instruction is free.

In most cantons there are also secondary schools for youths of from 12 to 15, gymnasia, higher schools for girls, teachers' seminaries, commercial and administrative schools, trade schools, art schools, technical schools, schools for the instruction of girls in domestic economy and other subjects, agricultural schools, schools for horticulture, for viticulture, for arboriculture and for dairy management. There are also institutions for the blind, the deaf and dumb and feeble-minded.

There are 7 universities in Switzerland. These universities are organized on the model of those of Germany, governed by a rector and a senate, and divided into 4 faculties of theology, jurisprudence, philosophy and medicine. In 1976–77 the Federal Institute of Technology at Zürich (founded in 1855) had 626 teachers and 7,156 matriculated students; the Federal Institute of Technology at Lausanne, independent of the university since 1946, had 210 teachers and 1,857 students; the St Gall School of Economics and Social Sciences, founded in 1899, had 155 teachers and 1,696 matriculated students.

University statistics in the winter of 1976–77:

	Theology	*Law*	*Economics and Social Sciences*	*Medicine*	*Arts and Science*	*Others*	*Total*	*Teaching staff*
Basel (1460)	142	770	444	1,607	2,501	7	5,471	492
Zürich (1523 & 1833)	151	2,131	1,215	2,651	6,649	—	12,791	1,334
Bern (1528 & 1834)	135	1,249	561	1,638	3,194	86	6,863	640
Genève (1559[1] & 1873[1])	70	744	1,010	1,257	2,751	2,017	7,849	1,171
Lausanne (1537[1] & 1890[2])	84	715	813	1,137	1,623	259	4,631	459
Fribourg (1889)	306	597	621	269	2,176	—	3,969	302
Neuchâtel (1866 & 1909)	39	225	236	61	1,046	146	1,753	203

[1] Founded as an academy. [2] Reorganized as a university.

These numbers are exclusive of 'visitors', but inclusive of women students.

Social Security. The Federal Insurance Law against illness and accident, of 13 June 1911, entitles all Swiss citizens to insurance against illness; foreigners may be admitted to the benefits. Compulsory insurance against illness does not exist as yet, but cantons and communities are entitled to declare insurance obligatory for certain classes or to establish public benefit (sick fund) associations, and to make employers responsible for the payment of the premiums of their employees. In 1975 the 662 societies insuring against illness had 6,622,191 members.

Unemployment insurance is based since 13 June 1976 upon a Constitution amendment which stipulates unemployment insurance as compulsory for all wage-earners.

A federal law was in preparation in 1976. At 30 Sept. 1975 there existed 123 public and private unemployment insurance organizations with a total membership of 1,060,700 (39·5% of working population).

Insurance against accident is compulsory for all officials, employees and workmen of all the factories, trades, etc., which are under the federal liability law. The Swiss Accident Insurance Institution commenced operations on 1 April 1918.

On 6 July 1947 a federal law was accepted by a referendum, providing compulsory old age and widows and widowers insurance for the whole population, as from 1 Jan. 1948. In March 1976 the number of normal pensioners was 881,132, the number of interim pensioners, 50,780. On 1 Jan. 1960 the old-age insurance scheme was extended to cover invalidity. In March 1976, 146,258 invalids received a regular annuity and 18,641 invalids an interim annuity.

DIPLOMATIC REPRESENTATIVES

OF SWITZERLAND IN GREAT BRITAIN

(16–18 Montagu Place, London, W1H 2BQ)

Ambassador: Dr Ernesto Thalmann (accredited 18 Feb. 1976).

OF GREAT BRITAIN IN SWITZERLAND (Thunstrasse 50, 3005 Berne)
Ambassador: A. K. Rothnie, CMG.

OF SWITZERLAND IN THE USA (2900 Cathedral Ave., NW, Washington, D.C., 20008)
Ambassador: Raymond Probst.

OF THE USA IN SWITZERLAND (Jubilaeumstrasse 93, 3005, Bern)
Ambassador: Marvin Warner.

Books of Reference

Statistical Information: The Bureau fédéral de statistique (15 Hallwyl St, Bern) was established in 1860. *Director:* J.-J. Senglet. Its principal publications are:

Annuaire statistique de la Suisse. Bâle. From 1891
Statistique de la Suisse. From 1930
Contributions à la Statistique Suisse. From 1930
Bibliographie Suisse de statistique et d'economie politique. Annual, from 1937

Swiss Confederation
Annuaire; Budget; Message du Budget; Compte d'Etat (annual) *Feuille Fédérale; Recueil des Lois fédérales* (weekly)
Recueil systématique des lois et ordonnances, 1848–1947 (in German, French and Italian). Bern, 1951
Sammlung der Bundes- und Kantonsverfassungen (in German, French and Italian). Bern, 1937

Federal Department of Economics
La vie économique (and supplements). Monthly. From 1928
Législation sociale de la Suisse. Annual, from 1928

Behrendt, R. F. (ed.), *Strukturwandlugen der schweizerischen Wirtschaft und Gesellschaft.* Bern, 1962
Bonjour, E., Offler, H. S., and Potter, G. R., *A Short History of Switzerland.* Oxford, 1952
Dürrenmatt, P., *Schweizer Geschichte.* Zürich, 1963.—*Schweiz.* Zürich, 1962.—*Wir Schweizer und der totale Krieg.* Zürich, 1960
Imhof, E. (ed.), *Atlas der Schweiz.* Bern, 1965 ff.
Meyer, Alice, *Anpassung oder Widerstand. Die Schweiz zur Zeit des Nationalsozialismus*
Riklin, A., *et al, Handbuch der schweizerischen Aussenpolitik.* Bern, 1975
Sorell, W., *The Swiss: A Cultural Panorama of Switzerland.* Indianapolis, 1972. London, 1973
Tschäni, H., *Profil der Schweiz.* Zürich, 1967
Unser Schweizer Standpunkt 1914, 1939, 1964. Bern, 1964
Who's Who in Switzerland. Ed. H. and E. Girsberger. Zürich, 1952

National Library: Bibliothèque Nationale Suisse, 15 Hallwyl St, Bern. *Director:* F. G. Maier.

SYRIA

al-Jamhouriya al Arabia as-Souriya

Capital: Damascus
Population: 8·3m. (1976)
GNP per capita: US$780 (1976)

HISTORY. For the history of Syria from 1920 to 1946 *see* THE STATESMAN'S YEAR-BOOK, 1957, pp. 1408 f. For the union with Egypt concluded on 1 Feb. 1958, *see* THE STATESMAN'S YEAR-BOOK, 1961, pp. 1527 ff. On 28 Sept. 1961 a national revolution broke out, and on 5 Oct. President Nasser acknowledged the dissolution of the union. Syria was re-admitted to the United Nations (13 Oct.) and the Arab League.

AREA AND POPULATION. Syria is bounded by the Mediterranean and the Lebanese Republic on the west, by Israel and Jordan on the south, by Iraq on the east and by Turkey on the north. The frontier between Syria and Turkey (Nisibim-Jeziret ibn Omar) was settled by the Franco-Turkish agreement of 22 June 1929.

The administrative districts of Syria consist of the *mohafazets* of Damascus, the city of Damascus, Hama, Homs, Dera'a, Aleppo, Lattakia, Deir-ez-Zor, Sweida, Hassakeh, Raqqa, Idlib, Kunaitra and Tartous.

The area of Syria is 185,680 sq. km (71,772 sq. miles), of which 35,000 sq. km have been surveyed. The census of 17 Sept. 1970 gave a total population of 6,304,685, showing about 10% less than the estimates. Estimate (1976) 8·3m. The principal towns with population in 1970 (and estimate, 1975), are: City of Damascus, (1,042,000); Damascus, (732,000); Aleppo, 639,361 (1,523,000); Homs, 215,526 (629,000); Hama, 137,589 (601,000); Lattakia, 121,570 (444,000); Deir-ez-Zor, 66,143 (332,000); Idlib, (428,000); Hassakeh, 532,000; Raqqa, 281,000; Sweida, 162,000; Deràa, 282,000; Tartous, 348,000; Kunaitra, 19,000.

Arabic is the official language.

CONSTITUTION AND GOVERNMENT. On 8 March 1963 a National Council of Revolution seized power, probably in collusion with the revolutionary junta in Iraq and President Nasser of Egypt.

Lieut.-Gen. Hafez al Assad seized power on 16 Nov. 1970 and formed a cabinet on 21 Nov. A provisional Constitution was published and on 16 Feb. 1971 a People's Council of 173 members was nominated by presidential decree. Lieut.-Gen. Assad was sworn in as President on 14 March 1971. On 12 March 1973 a plebiscite was held to approve a new Constitution.

President: Lieut.-Gen. Hafez al Assad (re-elected for further 7-year term in 1978).

Prime Minister: Mohammed Ali Al-Halabi.

National flag: Three horizontal stripes of red, white, black, with the federal emblem in gold in the centre.

DEFENCE. The post of Commander-in-Chief of the Army and the Armed Forces, abolished on 12 Sept. 1965, was re-established on 23 Feb. 1966.

Army. The Army in 1976 was composed of about 200,000 trained men, the *gendarmerie* of 8,000, the Bedouin Control Force of about 1,500 and the civil police of 1,800. The USSR supplies technical advisers and equipment, which include over 2,000 tanks (700 T-62). The Army was organized (Oct. 1974) into 2 armoured and 3 mechanized infantry divisions, 3 armoured, 1 mechanized, 2 artillery brigades, 5 commando and 3 parachute battalions and about 24 surface-to-air missile batteries.

Navy. The Navy includes 2 small (*ex*-Soviet) frigates, 12 missile boats, 8 torpedo boats, 1 fleet minesweeper, 2 coastal minesweepers, 3 patrol vessels and 1 diving base ship. Personnel in 1978 totalled 2,500 officers and men.

Air Force. The Air Force is believed to have about 25,000 personnel and about 400 first-line jet combat aircraft, made up of about 250 MiG-21 supersonic interceptors, 50 MiG-23 and 60 Su-7 supersonic fighter-bombers and 50 MiG-17 fighter-bombers. Training units have Soviet Yak-18 piston-engined primary trainers and Czechoslovakian L-29 Delfin jet basic trainers. There are also transport units with An-12, Il-14 and other types, and helicopter units with Soviet-built Ka-25s, Mi-4s and Mi-8s, and French-built Gazelles and Super Frelon. 'Guideline', 'Goa' and 'Gainful' surface-to-air missiles are widely deployed in Syria.

INTERNATIONAL RELATIONS

Membership. Syria is a member of UN and the Arab League.

ECONOMY

Planning. A 5-year development plan for 1960/61–1964/65 incorporated many of the features in the 7-year expenditure development project of 1955 and the 10-year plan of 1958 (*see* THE STATESMAN'S YEAR-BOOK, 1958, p. 1426, and 1961, p. 1541). The total expenditure in the second 5-year plan was estimated at £Syr.4,955m. The expenditure in the third 5-year development plan for 1971–75 is estimated at £Syr.8,120m. 19% of the total spent on Euphrates project, 4·3% on irrigation and reclamation, 6·3% on communication and transportation, 6·3% on agriculture, 22·7% on industry and mining, 17·6% on power and fuel, 7·4% on public services and 12% on internal trade.

Budget. The ordinary budget for the calendar year 1977 gave revenue at £Syr.17,000m. and ordinary and development expenditure at £Syr.17,000m.

Currency. The monetary unit is the Syrian *pound*, divided into 100 *piastres*.

In 1975–76 total currency in circulation amounted to £Syr.6,965·8m.

Banking. The Central Bank has the sole right of issuing currency. Other banks were nationalized in March 1963, namely, the Omaya Bank and its subsidiary, the Popular Mortgage Bank; the Orient Arab Bank; the Bank of Syria and Overseas; the Agricultural Bank; the Arab World Bank. Number of branches, 1973: Central Bank of Syria, 9; Commercial Bank of Syria, 22; Industrial Bank, 3; Agricultural Co-operative Bank, 50; Real Estate Bank, 3; Bank of Popular Discount, 27.

Weights and Measures. A decree dated 22 Aug. 1935 makes the use of the metric system legal and obligatory throughout the whole of the country. In outlying districts the former weights and measures may still be in use. They are: 1 *okiya* = 0·47 lb.; 6 *okiyas* = 1 *oke* = 2·82 lb.; 2 *okes* = 1 *rottol* = 5·64 lb.; 200 *okes* = 1 *kantar*.

ENERGY AND NATURAL RESOURCES

Oil. A branch of the Iraq Petroleum Company's oil pipeline from Kirkuk crosses Syria between Makaleb in the east and Nahr el Kebir valley in the west. The Iraq Petroleum Company has constructed a new pipeline from Kirkuk to the small fishing port of Banias (south of Lattakia), which came into use in April 1952; the Trans-Arabian Pipeline Company's line to Sidon crosses southern Syria. Another pipeline is being constructed from the Karachouk oilfield *via* Homs to the port of Tartous.

On 8 Dec. 1955 the Syrian Parliament ratified a Supplemental Convention concluded with the Iraq Petroleum Company. By the terms of the Convention, Syria will receive an annual payment of approximately £6·5m. sterling as transit dues and a sum of £8·5m. in settlement of claims for back payment.

Search for petroleum in the Lattakia and Deir El Zor regions continues. Oil has been discovered in the Jezirah region. Crude oil production (1976), 11m. tonnes.

Minerals. Syria is poorer in minerals than in other resources, but this may be due to insufficient exploration.

Phosphate deposits have been discovered at two places near al-Shargiya and at Khneifis. Production, 1975, 857,000 tonnes; other minerals were salt, 34,000; natural asphalt, 31,000. There are indications of lead, copper, antimony, nickel, chrome and other minerals widely distributed. Manganese ore was mined before 1914. Sodium chloride and bitumen deposits are being worked. There is abundance of good calcareous building stone and basalt. Deposits of natural gas have been discovered in the Jezirah.

Agriculture. Syria is an agricultural country but is moving towards greater industrialization, the bulk of the population being engaged in the cultivation of the soil and in cattle breeding. In 1975 the cultivated area was 5,476,000 hectares, of which 516,000 are irrigated; in 1975, 1,692,000 hectares were under wheat, 2m. hectares under cotton and 1,011,000 hectares under barley. The total cultivable area was 5·95m. hectares, including 455,000 hectares of forest and 8,631,000 hectares of steppe and pasture.

The Agrarian Reform Law of 1958, as modified by 1963, allows proprietors a maximum of 15–50 hectares of irrigated land and 80 hectares of uncultivated land, taking into account irrigation possibilities, rainfall, size of families, etc.

Yield of principal crops, 1975 (in 1,000 tonnes): Wheat, 1,550; barley, 597; olives, 157; tobacco, 12; lentils, 66·6; millet, 14·5; sugar-beet, 14·5; cotton, 414 (ginned, 141·5).

INDUSTRY AND TRADE

Industry. The most important industries are flour, oils, soap, cement, tanning, tobacco, textiles, knitwear, glassware, spinning, sugar, margarine, hosiery, footwear and brassware. Limited nationalization of certain basic industries was decreed in March 1963. On 3 Jan. 1965, 22 companies were completely nationalized, the owners of 61 companies were allowed to keep a quarter share and those of 24 companies to retain a tenth of their property.

Industrial production in 1975 included (in 1,000 tonnes): Cement, 994; sugar, 117; cotton yarn, 31·6; vegetable oil, 22·1; woollen fabrics, 1,254; manufactured tobacco, 6·7; salt, 34; cottoncake, 103. In addition, 3·7m. pairs of shoes were manufactured and 50,040 refrigerators assembled.

Commerce. In April 1965 a state trading company (SIMEX) was set up to handle the nationalized imports and exports.

Trade in calendar years in £Syr.1m. was as follows:

	1973	*1974*	*1975*
Imports	2,342	4,571	6,173
Exports	1,341	2,914	3,441

Cotton is one of the chief exports (£Syr.502·4m., 1975). Others include oil, cereals, live animals and, since 1972, phosphates. Imports include industrial raw materials, machinery, chemicals and electrical equipment.

Total trade of Syria with UK (British Department of Trade returns, in £1,000 sterling):

	1973	*1974*	*1975*	*1976*	*1977*
Imports to UK	1,154	20,572	4,905	7,673	5,351
Exports and re-exports from UK	11,630	20,854	35,099	64,398	57,203

COMMUNICATIONS

Roads. In 1975 there were 10,740 km of asphalted roads, 1,500 km of paved non-asphalted road and 2,364 km of levelled roads. The first-class roads are capable of carrying all types of modern motor transport and are usable all the year round, while the second-class roads are usable during the dry season only, *i.e.*, for about 9 months. The Nairn Transport Company operate a trans-desert pullman motor coach service between Damascus and Baghdad. There are also two pullman transport companies (Elkarnak, Syrian, and Jett, Jordanian) operating a joint service between Damascus and Amman. The motor vehicles registered at the end of 1975 totalled 100,972, including 11,125 motor cycles, 4,192 buses, 49,674 cars and 19,184 goods vehicles.

Railways. In Syria the following railways are open (in addition to those listed under LEBANON (p. 777): Standard gauge from Aleppo to Meidan-Ekbes (Turkish frontier), 116 km; Aleppo to Tel-Kotchek (Iraq frontier), 523 km; narrow gauge from Damascus to El Hammé, 195 km; Damascus to Dera'a (Jordan frontier), 130 km. Two lines have recently been constructed: a standard gauge from Akari to Tartous, 42 km, and the 755-km Aleppo–Kamechli, opened to traffic in 1976. Work is in progress on the Mhein–Palmyra line, the Aleppo–Hama–Homs line, and the Akari–Homs–Damascus line; lines between Deir El Zor and Al-Boukamal, Palmyra and Deir El Zor, Lattakia and Tartous are planned.

Aviation. In 1975, 7,582 aircraft arrived at Damascus and Aleppo airports, disembarking 346,552 passengers and embarking 359,711. Syrian Air carried 480,000 passengers in 1976.

Shipping. The amount of cargo discharged in 1975 was 38,982,000 NRT and the amount loaded 38,532,000 NRT. A deep water harbour at Lattakia was built by a Yugoslav firm and in 1976 it was announced that further extensions would take place.

Tartous remains a fishing port and Banias is used as an oil terminal and loading port by the Iraq Petroleum Co. Ltd. Movement of vessels through Syrian ports in 1975:

	Cleared		*Entered*	
Harbours	*Sailing vessels*	*Steam vessels*	*Sailing vessels*	*Steam vessels*
Lattakia	44	2,043	47	2,062
Jableh	1	1	1	1
Banias	37	594	40	601
Tartous	25	1,278	26	1,338
Erwad	128	233	134	240

Post and Broadcasting. An automatic telephone system has been installed in Damascus, and most other towns. Number of telephones (1977), 176,930; of these, 72,176 were in Damascus and 33,506 in Aleppo. There are 1·6m. radio sets.

Newspapers. There were (1977) 3 national daily newspapers in Damascus; other dailies and periodicals appear in Hama, Homs, Aleppo and Lattakia.

RELIGION, EDUCATION AND WELFARE

Religion. The population is composed mainly of Sunni Moslems and there are also Shiites and Ismailis. There are also Druzes and Alawites. Christians include Greek Orthodox, Greek Catholics, Armenian Orthodox, Syrian Orthodox, Armenian Catholics, Protestants, Maronites, Syrian Catholics, Latins, Nestorians and Assyrians. There are also Jews and Yezides.

Education. The Syrian University was founded in 1924, although the faculties of law and of medicine had existed previously. In 1975 there were 3 universities comprised of 25 faculties with 61,156 students. In 1974–75 there were 42,204 students at the University of Damascus; 15,805 at the University of Aleppo; 3,147 at the University of Teshreen.

In 1975, 6,760 primary schools had 34,995 teachers and 1,211,570 pupils; 1,050 secondary and intermediate schools, 20,479 teachers and 314,272 pupils; 58 vocational schools, 2,304 teachers and 21,211 pupils; 23 teacher-training colleges, 506 teachers and 5,913 students; 95 various schools and mining institutes, 4,449 teachers and 15,719 students.

Health. In 1977 there were 7,479 hospital beds (1 per 983 persons) in 31 state hospitals, 69 private hospitals and 4 sanatoria.

DIPLOMATIC REPRESENTATIVES

OF SYRIA IN GREAT BRITAIN
(5 Eaton Terr., London, SW1W 8EX)

Ambassador: Adnan Omran (accredited 20 March 1974).

OF GREAT BRITAIN IN SYRIA (Quarter Malki, 11 Muhammed Kurd Ail St., Damascus)

Ambassador: A. J. M. Craig, CMG.

OF SYRIA IN THE USA (2215 Wyoming Ave., NW, Washington, D.C., 20008)

Ambassador: Dr Sabah Kabbani.

OF THE USA IN SYRIA (Abu Rumaneh, Al Monsur St., Damascus)

Ambassador: Richard W. Murphy.

OF SYRIA TO THE UNITED NATIONS

Ambassador: Mowaffak Medani

Books of Reference

Statistical Information: There is a Central Statistics Bureau affiliated to the Council of Ministers, Damascus. It publishes a monthly summary and an annual Statistical Abstract (in Arabic and English).

Census of Population 1960. 15 vols. Ministry of Planning, Damascus, 1961–65
The Economic Development of Syria. International Bank Report. Baltimore, 1955
Asfour, E. Y., *Syria: Development and Monetary Policy.* Harvard Univ. Press, 1959
Barthélemy, A., *Dictionnaire arabe-français. Dialectes de Syrie.* 4 vols. Paris, 1935–50
Hourani, A. H., *Syria and Lebanon.* 2nd ed. R. Inst. of Int. Affairs, 1954
Petran, T., *Syria.* London, 1972

UNITED REPUBLIC OF TANZANIA

Capital: Dar es Salaam
Population: 15m. (1975)
GNP per capita: US$180 (1976)

HISTORY. German East Africa was occupied by German colonialists from 1884 and placed under the protection of the German Empire in 1891. It was conquered in the First World War and subsequently divided between the British and Belgians. The latter received the territories of Ruanda and Urundi and the British the remainder, except for the Kionga triangle, which went to Portugal. The country was administered as a League of Nations mandate until 1946 and then as a UN trusteeship territory until 9 Dec. 1961.

Tanganyika achieved responsible government in Sept. 1960 and full self-government on 1 May 1961. On 9 Dec. 1961 Tanganyika became a sovereign independent member state of the Commonwealth of Nations. It adopted a republican form of government on 9 Dec. 1962.

At the end of the 17th century the inhabitants of Zanzibar drove out the Portuguese with the assistance of the Arabs of Oman. Thereafter an Arab governor from Oman was sent to Zanzibar, but the government of the interior remained in the hands of a local ruler. In 1832 Seyyid Said bin Sultan, ruler of Oman, established his capital at Zanzibar, and thereafter the whole of that island and the island of Pemba together with a large strip of the East African mainland coast came under his effective rule. Seyyid Said died in 1856. Five years later his former African possessions were, under an arbitration award made by Lord Canning (then Governor-General of India), declared to be independent of Oman. In 1887 the Sultan of Zanzibar handed over the administration of his possessions to the north of Vanga on the African continent to the British East Africa Association. These territories eventually passed to the British Government and are now part of Kenya. In 1888 a similar concession was granted to the German East Africa Association of the Sultan's mainland territories between the river Umba and Cape Delgado. In 1890 the German Government bought these territories outright for 4m. marks. In 1892 the administration of the Benadir Ports (which had in 1889 been conceded to the British East Africa Association) was, with the consent of the Sultan, transferred to the Italian Government in consideration of a quarterly payment of Rs 40,000. The Sultan renounced in 1886 in favour of Portugal all claims to the coast to the south of Cape Delgado.

In 1890 the islands of Zanzibar and Pemba were placed under British protection by the Sultan, Seyyid Ali bin Said.

On 24 June 1963 Zanzibar became an internal self-governing state and on 9 Dec. 1963 she became independent. On 24 June 1963 the Legislative Council was replaced by a National Assembly.

On 12 Jan. 1964 the sultanate was overthrown and the sultan sent into exile by a revolt of the Afro-Shirazi Party leaders who established the People's Republic of Zanzibar.

On 26 April 1964 Tanganyika, Zanzibar and Pemba combined to form the United Republic of Tanganyika and Zanzibar (named Tanzania on 29 Oct.).

AREA AND POPULATION. Tanzania is bounded north-east by Kenya, north by Lake Victoria and Uganda, north-west by Rwanda and Burundi, west by Lake Tanganyika, south-west by Zambia and Malawa and south by Mozambique. The census of Aug. 1967 gave 12,231,342 for the United Republic, of which 11,876,982 were counted in mainland Tanzania (density per sq. mile, 34·8) and 354,360 in Zanzibar (density per sq. mile, 347·1). Estimate (1975) 15m.

Dar es Salaam is the capital and chief port (population, 1973, 521,827). Other towns include Tanga, Arusta, Dodoma, Kigoma, Iringa, Morogoro and Lindi.

Swahili is generally spoken and understood throughout Tanzania.

CONSTITUTION AND GOVERNMENT. An 'interim constitution' was approved by parliament on 5 July 1965 and assented to by the President on 8 July 1965. A new Constitution was approved in April 1977.

The country is a one-party state. The Tanganyika African National Union and the Afro-Shirazi Party in Zanzibar merged into one revolutionary party, *Chama cha Mapinduzi*, in Jan. 1977.

The President of the United Republic is head of state, chairman of the party and commander-in-chief of the armed forces. The first vice-president is head of the executive in Zanzibar and vice-chairman of the party; the Prime Minister and the second vice-president is also the leader of the National Assembly.

The National Assembly is composed of 96 elected members from the mainland, 10 members appointed (from both Tanganyika and Zanzibar), 15 National Members (elected by the National Assembly after nomination by various national institutions), 20 Regional Commissioners, up to 32 members of the Zanzibar Revolutionary Council and up to 20 other Zanzibar members appointed by the president in agreement with the vice-president.

The Government was in June 1978 composed as follows:

President of the United Republic: Dr Julius K. Nyerere (re-elected for a further 5-year term in Oct. 1975).

First Vice-President: Aboud Jumbe. *Second Vice-President and Prime Minister:* Edward Sokoine.

Foreign Affairs: Ben Mkapa. *Home Affairs:* Ali Hassan Mwinyi. *Finance and Economic Planning:* Edwin Mtei. *Agriculture:* John S. Malecela. *Justice:* Julie Manning. *Industry:* Cleopa Msuya. *Land, Housing and Urban Development:* Tabitha Siwale. *Labour and Social Welfare:* Crispin Tungaraza. *Manpower Development:* Nicholas Kuhanga. *National Education:* Isael Elinawinga. *Commerce:* Alfred Rulegura. *Capital Development:* Hasnu Makame. *Water Resources, Energy and Minerals:* Dr Wilbert Chagula. *Communications and Transport:* Alfred Tandau. *Information and Broadcasting:* Daudi Mwakawago. *Works:* Samuel Sitta. *Defence and National Service:* Rashidi Mfaume Kawawa. *Culture and Youth:* Chidiel Mgonja. *Health:* Dr Leader Dominic Sterling. *Natural Resources and Tourism:* Solomon Ole Saibul. *Minister of State:* Hassan Shekilango (*Prime Minister's Office*); Hassan Nassor Moyo (*First Vice-President's Office*); Peter Siyovelwa (*President's Office*).

National flag: Divided diagonally green, black, blue, with the black strip edged in yellow.

DEFENCE

Army. The Army consists of 1 tank and 4 infantry battalions. Strength, 13,000.

Air Force. The Tanzanian People's Defence Force Air Wing was built up initially with the help of Canada, but combat equipment is now being acquired from China. Personnel totalled about 1,000 in 1977, with about 12 Shenyang F-8 (MiG-21), 15 F-6 (MiG-19) and 3 F-4 (MiG-17) jet fighters; 10 Canadian-built Caribou twin-engined STOL transports; 1 An-2 light transport; 2 Agusta-Bell JetRanger and 2 Bell 47G light helicopters; and Piper Cherokee, Cessna 310 and MiG-15UTI trainers.

INTERNATIONAL RELATIONS

Membership. Tanzania is a member of UN, OAU, the Commonwealth and is an ACP state of EEC.

ECONOMY

Planning. The first 5-year plan ran from 1964 to 1969. The second plan for economic and social development ran from 1969 to 1974. The third 5-year plan starting

1976 envisaged a small but actively growing industrial factories to manufacture small parts with the object of improving foreign exchange earnings.

Budget. Revenue and expenditure (in Tanzanian Sh. 1m.) for financial years ending 30 June:

	1971–72[1]	*1973–74*	*1974–75*[1]	*1975–76*	*1976–77*[1]	*1977–78*[1]
Revenue	1,875·0	2,613·5	3,661·5	4,390·2	7,883·0	9,556·2
Expenditure	1,824·0	2,613·1	3,661·5	5,888·9	7,228·0	9,556·0

[1] Estimate.

Import duties in 1975–76 amounted to Sh. 451·1m. and income tax to Sh. 1,067·5m. The main items of expenditure for the year 1969–70 were communications, transport and labour (Sh. 278·5m.), education (Sh. 56·2m.) and agriculture, food and co-operatives (Sh. 109·9m.).

Development expenditure, 1975–76, was Sh. 2,253m.

Total national debt on 30 June 1969 amounted to Sh. 1,412·44m.

Currency. The monetary unit is the Tanzanian shilling divided into 100 cents. Although it replaced the East African shilling on 14 June 1966, the latter remained legal tender until Oct. 1967. The Tanzanian coinage has denomination of 5, 20, 50 cents. 1 Sh. and 5 Sh.; 1 Sh. = 14 US cents. Notes and coins in circulation at the end of Nov. 1973 were Sh. 1,258·2m. In 1976 the country left the East African Currency Board, establishing its own national currency, the Tanzanian shilling.

Banking. On 14 June 1966 the central bank called the Bank of Tanzania, with a government-owned capital of Sh. 20m. began operations.

On 6 Feb. 1967 all commercial banks with the exception of National Co-operative Banks were nationalized and their interests vested in the National Bank of Commerce on the mainland and the Peoples' Bank in Zanzibar.

Weights. An important local unit of weight is the frasla (or frasila) = 35 lb. av.

ENERGY AND NATURAL RESOURCES

Electricity. A hydro-electric station on the Pangani River near Tanga has been built; £3m. of its estimated cost of £5·25m. is being provided by the Commonwealth Development Corporation. Kidatu power-station in Morogoro region is nearing completion. Kiwira River power project, estimated to cost Sh. 55m. was scheduled for completion in 1976. Electric power generated (1975) was 190·1mw.

Minerals. The value of mineral exports in 1975 was Sh. 149·3m. Principal exports, 1975, were (in Sh. 1m.): Diamonds, 130·6; gold, 0·1; tin, 0·2; salt, 14·3; gemstones, 1·9. New discoveries of coal and iron ore were made in the south while copper, cobalt, nickel and tin deposits have been found in Western Tanganyika. Gas, at shallow depths, has been found off the coast. Diamond sales (1973) Sh. 123·6m.; salt, Sh. 8·2m.; tin concentrates, Sh. 1·1m.

Agriculture. The target set for cotton in 1974 was 700,000 bales. Production of sisal has been declining since 1967. The Tanganyika Sisal Corporation has embarked on a diversification programme by introducing various new crops. Crops already planned are cardamon, beans, cashew nuts, citrus, cocoa, coconuts, cotton, maize and timber. Cattle ranching, dairying and twine spinning have also been introduced.

Zanzibar provides the greater part of the world's supply of cloves. There are about 80,000 acres under cloves with about 4m. trees; five-sixths of the clove output is produced on Pemba. Cloves and clove oil (distilled from the stems) form more than half Zanzibar's exports. In recent years cloves production has decreased from an average annual figure of 12,000 tons to 4,000 in 1974.

The coconut industry ranks next in importance. There are about 5·5m. bearing trees in both islands. Chillies, cocoa, limes, other tropical fruits and coil tobacco are also cultivated. The chief food crops are rice, bananas, cassava, pulses, maize and sorghum.

Livestock (1976, including Zanzibar): 14·4m. cattle, 2·9m. sheep, 4·6m. goats, 24,000 pigs.

Forestry. In 1973 work continued on planting new areas with hard-woods and soft-woods. Hard-woods could be planted in old sisal estates that are now reverting to bush.

Fisheries. A Fisheries Development Company, in which the Government has a financial interest, is catching sardines and tuna for export.

INDUSTRY AND TRADE

Industry. Industry is limited and is mainly textiles, food processing, tobacco and brewing.

Commerce. Total trade (in Tanzanian Sh. 1m.):

	1973	*1974*	*1975*	*1976*
Imports	3,140	5,258	5,710	5,350
Exports	2,238	2,681	2,764	4,108

Major export items 1976 (in Sh. 1m.): Coffee, 1,282; cotton, 627; tobacco, 188; sisal, 159; tea, 134.

Total trade with UK (British Department of Trade returns, in £1,000 sterling):

	1974	*1975*	*1976*	*1977*
Imports to UK	49,105	31,865	34,101	45,460
Exports and re-exports from UK	29,129	41,540	43,932	72,060

Tourism. In 1973 over 100,000 tourists visited Tanzania and spent Sh. 130m.

COMMUNICATIONS

Roads. Motor traffic is possible over 25,000 miles of road during dry season and at almost all times over 21,500 miles. In Zanzibar there were 279 miles of tarmac roads and 70 miles of all-weather unsealed roads; in Pemba there are 86 miles of tarmac roads and 184 miles of dry-weather earth roads.

Railways. On 23 Sept. 1977 the independent Tanzanian Railway Corporation was formed following the break-up of the East African Railways administration. The network totals 2,580 km (metre-gauge), excluding the Tan-Zam Railway 969 km in Tanzania (1,067 mm guage) operated by a separate administration.

Aviation. There are 53 aerodromes and landing strips maintained or licensed by Government; of these, 2 are of international standards category and 18 are suitable for Dakotas. The East African Airways Corporation provide regular and frequent services to all the more important towns within the territory and the neighbouring countries of Kenya and Uganda, together with a regular service to the UK, India and Pakistan, Zambia and Malawi. Charter services are operated by 2 companies. In 1973, 313,000 passengers and (1970) 2·6m. kg of freight were handled at Dar es Salaam airport. This airport and the one at Kilimanjaro can handle Jumbo-jets and 6 further airports are being modified to handle Fokker Friendship aircraft. In 1975 passengers for Dar es Salaam were 345,688 and for Kilimanjaro 92,335.

There is an all-weather landing-ground in Zanzibar and a smaller all-weather landing-ground in Pemba.

Shipping. In 1974 there were 1,500 ships of 5m. NRT.

Post and Broadcasting. On 1 Jan 1977 there were 68,413 telephones. There are 2 broadcasting stations and colour television operates in Zanzibar.

Newspapers (1976). There were 3 dailies and 1 Sunday newspaper.

EDUCATION. The educational system has been integrated on non-racial lines. Schools are maintained by the Government, local authorities and voluntary agencies, including missions; most of the latter are wholly or partly financed by government or local authorities.

In 1973, 1,106,000 children attended primary schools and 35,000 secondary schools.

Technical and vocational education is provided at 2 government trade schools and at the Dar es Salaam Technical College.

There were, in 1973, 23 teacher-training centres, including the college at Chang'ombe for secondary-school teachers. About 3,300 students were in training.

In 1973, 2,500 Tanzanian students attended the University of East Africa founded in 1963.

It is intended that all children of school age will attend school by 1977 which is free up to university standard. In the 4 years (1972–76) illiteracy has been reduced to about 31%. The University of Dar es Salaam, independent since 1970, has faculties of science, law, arts, social sciences, medicine, agriculture, engineering, veterinary science and forestry.

HEALTH. In 1973 there were 540 doctors and 18,000 hospital beds.

DIPLOMATIC REPRESENTATIVES

OF TANZANIA IN GREAT BRITAIN
(43 Hertford St., London, W1)

High Commissioner: Amon James Nsekela.

OF GREAT BRITAIN IN TANZANIA (Permanent Hse., Independence Ave., Dar es Salaam)

High Commissioner: M. Brown, CMG, OBE.

OF TANZANIA IN THE USA (139 R St., NW, Washington, D.C., 20008)

Ambassador: Paul Bomani.

OF THE USA IN TANZANIA
(National Bank of Commerce Bldg., Dar es Salaam)

Ambassador: James W. Spain.

OF TANZANIA TO THE UNITED NATIONS

Ambassador: Salim Ahmed Salim.

Books of Reference

Atlas of Tanganyika. 3rd ed. Dar es Salaam, 1956
Tanganyika Notes and Records. Tanganyika Society, Dar es Salaam. (Twice yearly, from 1936)
The Economic Development of Tanganyika. Report . . . by the International Bank. Johns Hopkins Univ. Press and OUP, 1961
Ingle, C. R., *From Village to State in Tanzania.* London, 1973
Lofchie, M. F., *Zanzibar: Background to Revolution.* Princeton Univ. Press, 1965
Nellis, J. R., *A Theory of Ideology: The Tanzanian Example.* New York, OUP, 1972
Ommanney, F. D., *Isle of Cloves.* London, 1955
Samoff, J., *Tanzania: Local Politics and the Structure of Power.* Univ. of Wisconsin Press, 1975
Taylor, J. C., *The Political Development of Tanganyika.* Stanford Univ. Press, 1963

THAILAND

Capital: Bangkok
Population: 44·2m. (1977)
GNP per capita: US$380 (1976)

Prathes Thai, or Muang-Thai

HISTORY. Until 24 June 1932 Siam was an absolute monarchy. On that date a *coup d'état* was effected and a Provisional Constitution Act was promulgated on 27 June. This was replaced by the Constitution of 10 Dec. 1932, which in turn was superseded by new Constitutions.

AREA AND POPULATION. The area of Thailand is 514,000 sq. km (198,250 sq. miles).

At the census taken in 1976 the registration gave a population of 44,272,693 (22,314,837 males, 21,957,856 females), of whom 30·4% lived in the Central region, 35·2% in the North-East region, 12·5% in the South region, 21·9% in the North region. Of the 1960 population, 1·6% were Chinese.

Bangkok Metropolis is the capital (population 1977, 4,742,774). Other towns (1970 census) are Chiang Mai (83,729), Nakhon Ratchasima (66,071), Udon Thani (56,218).

REIGNING KING. Bhumibol Adulyadej, born 5 Dec. 1927, younger brother of King Ananda Mahidol, who died on 9 June 1946. King Bhumibol married on 28 April 1950 Princess Sirikit, and was crowned 5 May 1950. Children: Princess Ubol Ratana (born 5 April 1951), Crown-Prince Vajiralongkorn (born 28 July 1952, married 3 Jan. 1977 Soamsawali Kitiyakra), Princess Sirindhorn (born 2 April 1955), Princess Chulabhorn (born 4 July 1957).

CONSTITUTION AND GOVERNMENT. The military government resigned on 14 Oct. 1973 and a new government was formed. New Constitutions were enacted on 7 Oct. 1974 and on 9 Nov 1977. However on 20 Oct. 1977 a further military *coup* took place in order to return more swiftly to democracy.

Prime Minister: Gen. Kriangsak Chammanard.

Foreign Minister: Upadit Pachari Yangkun.

National flag: Five horizontal stripes of red, white, blue, white, red, with the blue of double width.

Local Government. For purposes of administration Thailand is divided into 72 provinces (*changwads*), each under the control of a *changwad* governor. The *changwads* are subdivided into 650 districts (*amphurs*) and 51 sub-districts (*king amphurs*), 5,458 communes (*tambons*) and 48,715 villages (*moobans*). Local legislative and executive bodies with limited powers are being established with functions, procedure and method of election closely modelled on those of the central Assembly.

DEFENCE. Under the Ministry of Defence Organization Act of 1960 the Ministry of Defence has assumed the Supreme Command and the control of the Army, Navy and Air Force with the advice of the Defence Council headed by the Ministry of Defence. The National Defence College, the Armed Forces Staff College and the Military Preparatory School serve the education of officers. Each service has its own C.-in-C., service council, schools of arms and Command and General Staff College.

Under the Military Service Act of 1954 every able-bodied man between the ages of 21 and 30 is liable to serve 2 years with the colours; 7 years in the first reserve; 10 years in the second reserve; 6 years in the third reserve.

Army. The Army is organized in 6 infantry divisions (including 4 tank battalions) and 3 independent regimental combat teams. Equipment includes light American armoured vehicles. Peace-time strength is 141,000.

Navy. In 1977 the Navy included 4 frigates (1 new built in Britain, 2 old *ex*-US, and 1 old *ex*-US destroyer escort), 1 training ship (40-year-old *ex*-frigate), 2 corvettes (small frigates), 1 escort (training) minesweeper, 2 coastal minelayers, 4 coastal minesweepers, 3 new fast missile craft, 11 patrol vessels, 1 minesweeper support ship, 18 coastal gunboats, 18 coastal patrol boats, 8 landing ships, 9 landing craft, 32 minor landing craft, 10 minesweeping boats, 1 surveying ship, 3 surveying boats, 2 transports, 6 oilers, 1 training ship (*ex*-corvette), 18 coastguard vessels, 2 water carriers and 4 tugs.

Naval personnel totalled 20,000, including the Marine Corps of 7,000. There is a Royal Naval Academy at Paknam.

There was a small naval air arm, equipped with obsolescent piston-engined Firefly reconnaissance-fighters and Helldiver bombers.

At the mouth of the Chao Praya River are the Paknam forts. The naval dockyard was reconstructed; a large new graving dock was under consideration.

Air Force. The Royal Thai Air Force was reorganized with the assistance of a US Military Air Advisory Group. It has a strength of about 42,000 personnel, and is made up of a headquarters and Combat, Logistics Support, Training and Special Services Groups. The 3 squadrons of 1st Wing form the primary combat element, equipped from 37 F-5A/E supersonic fighter-bombers, some of the 38 OV-10C Bronco light reconnaissance/attack aircraft, and 24 T-33A/RT-33A and 4 RF-5A armed reconnaissance aircraft acquired from the USA. Six light attack squadrons in 2nd Wing operate the remaining OV-10Cs, about 60 T-6 and T-28 armed piston-engined trainers, 16 A-37B light jet attack aircraft and 25 AU-23A Peacemakers, for security duties. There are transport units equipped with about 70 HS 748, CASA Aviocar, C-123 Provider, C-47 and smaller aircraft; training units with Airtrainer CT/4 primary trainers built in New Zealand, Chipmunks, Italian-built SF.260MTs, T-37 intermediate and T-33A advanced trainers; and large numbers of helicopters for assault and rescue duties.

INTERNATIONAL RELATIONS

Membership. Thailand is a member of UN and the Colombo Plan.

ECONOMY

Budget. Ordinary expenditures in 1977–78 (in 1m. baht) provided 13,094·6 for defence; agriculture, 6,868·8; communications, 6,776·5; education, 14,731; public health, 8,011·5.

Revenue in 1976–77 derived from taxes and duties, sales and charges and government enterprises, 50,470m. baht.

In March 1976 the national internal debt was 44,852·9m. baht. External debt in March 1976 totalled 4,859·4m. baht, including US$5,646·4m. and DM 616·9m.

Currency. The unit of currency is the *baht*, formerly called in English the *tical*, which is divided into 100 *satang*. Silver coins have gone out of circulation. Only nickel, copper, tin and bronze coins are now minted, in denominations of 1, 5 *baht*, 50, 25, 10 and 5 *satang*. Currency notes, first issued in 1902, now comprise, 5, 10, 20, 100, 500 *baht* notes.

On 31 March 1976 the total amount of notes and coins in circulation was 30,280m. baht.

The currency law is based on the Currency Act of Aug., B.E. 2501 (1958).

Banking. In 1942 the Bank of Thailand was established under the Bank of Thailand Act, B.E. 2485 (1942) and began operations on 10 Dec. 1942, with the functions of a central bank. The Bank was organized on similar lines to the Bank of England, having its banking activities entirely separate from the management of the note issue. The Bank also took over the note issue previously performed by the Treasury Department of the Ministry of Finance. Although the entire capital is owned by the Government, the Bank is an independent body. Its gold and foreign-exchange reserves, at the end of Dec. 1973, amounted to US$1,082m.

In Jan. 1966 the Agricultural Bank and the Provincial Bank merged in the Krung Thai Bank (capital 105m. baht, of which 80% is owned by the Government).

Banks incorporated under Thai law include the Bangkok Bank Ltd, the Bangkok Bank of Commerce Ltd, the Bank of Asia for Industry & Commerce Ltd, the Bank of Ayudhya Ltd, Bangkok Metropolitan Bank Ltd, the Laem Thong Bank Ltd, the Siam City Bank Ltd, the Siam Commercial Bank Ltd, Thai Development Bank Ltd, the Thai Farmers Bank Ltd, Thai Danu Bank Ltd, the Thai Military Bank Ltd, the Union Bank of Bangkok Ltd and the Wang Lee Chan Bank Ltd. Foreign banks include the Chartered Bank, the Hongkong and Shanghai Banking Corporation, the Mercantile Bank Ltd, Banque de l'Indochine, Bank of Canton Ltd, Bank of China Ltd, Bank of America, N.T. & S.A., the Mitsui Bank Ltd, The Asia Trust Bank Ltd, Bharat Overseas Bank Ltd, The Chase Manhattan Bank, Krung Thai Bank Ltd, United Malayan Banking Corporation and the Bank of Tokyo Ltd.

The commercial Thai banks had, in 1973, 690 branches in Thailand and 11 abroad; only Mae Hongson province has no commercial bank services. The deposits held by commercial banks in Jan. 1972 amounted to 39,308·8m. baht.

The Government Savings Bank, which was established as an independent organization in 1947, originated in 1913 when the Government Savings Office was established.

Weights and Measures. The metric system was made compulsory by a law promulgated on 17 Dec. 1923. The actual weights and measures prescribed by law are: Units of weight: 1 *standard picul* = 60 kg; 1 *standard catty* ($\frac{1}{100}$ picul) = 600 grammes; 1 *standard carat* = 20 centigrammes. Units of length: 1 *sen* = 40 metres; 1 *wah* ($\frac{1}{20}$ sen) = 2 metres; 1 *sauk* ($\frac{1}{4}$ wah) = 0·50 metre; 1 *keup* ($\frac{1}{2}$ sawk) = 0·25 metre. Units of square measure: 1 *rai* (1 sq. sen) = 1,600 sq. metres; 1 *ngan* ($\frac{1}{4}$ rai = 400 sq. metres; 1 *sq. wah* ($\frac{1}{100}$ ngan) = 4 sq. metres. Units of capacity: 1 *standard kwien* = 2,000 litres; 1 *standard ban* ($\frac{1}{2}$ kwien = 1,000 litres; 1 *standard sat* ($\frac{1}{50}$ ban) = 20 litres; 1 *standard tanan* ($\frac{1}{20}$ sat) = 1 litre.

Legislation passed in 1940 provided that the calendar year shall coincide with the Christian Year, and that the year of the Buddhist era 2484 shall begin on 1 Jan. 1941. (The New Year's Day was previously 1 April.) The years B.E. 2514–2518 therefore correspond to A.D. 1974 and 1975.

NATURAL RESOURCES

Minerals. The mineral resources are extensive and varied, including cassiterite (tin ore), wolfram, scheelite, antimony, coal, copper, gold, iron, lead, manganese, molybdenum, rubies, sapphires, silver, zinc and zircons. By far the most important are tin and wolfram. Ore output in 1975 (in tonnes): Tin, 22,402; wolfram, 3,467; lead, 3,648; antimony, 7,707; manganese, 24,369; iron, 32,476; gypsum, 254,842; lignite, 462,320.

Agriculture. The chief produce of the country is rice, which forms the national food and the staple article of export. The area under paddy is about 18m. acres. With the completion of the Chao Phya dam located near Chai-nat in 1957 the irrigable area in the Central Plain had by 1962 been extended to about 8,409,000 rai (3,363,600 acres). Additional projects now under construction will bring the irrigable lands to the total of about 11,605,900 rai (4,642,360 acres). Tank irrigation projects which were designed to ensure water supply for upland crop cultivation, especially in the north-eastern part, irrigate 325,418 rai (130,167 acres).

Output of the major crops in 1975–76 was (in tonnes): Paddy, 15·1m.; maize, 5·3m.; sugar-cane, 13·4m.; kenaf, 250,000; tobacco, 36m. kg; tapioca-root, 7·2m.; soybeans, 180,000.

Livestock, 1973 (in 1,000): Elephants (1967), 11·5; horses, 168; buffaloes, 5,634; cattle, 4,571; swine, 4,573.

Forestry. About 60% of the land area of Thailand is under forest. In the north, mixed deciduous forests with teak (*Tectona grandis, Linn.*), growing in mixture with several other species, predominate. In the north-eastern section hardwood of the *Dipterocarpus* species, especially *Shorea obtusa* and *Pentacme Siamensis, Kurz* exist in most parts. In all other regions of the country tropical evergreen forests are found, with the well-known timber of commerce, Yang (*Dipterocarpus alatus, Roxb* and *Dipterocarpus* spp.) as the outstanding crops. Most of the teak timber exploited in northern Thailand is floated down to Bangkok. Some of them, however, are exported through the Salween into Burma.

About one-third of the teak-forest area is being exploited by the Forest Industry Organization, and the remaining two-thirds is to be worked by timber company lessees and other private enterprises.

Output of main forestry products in 1973 was (in 1,000 cu. metres): Teak, 133; yang, 720; other woods, 1,140; firewood, 1,400; charcoal, 500.

Rubber production (in 1,000 tonnes), 1955, 133·3; 1960, 170·8; 1965, 217; 1966, 220; 1967, 219; 1968, 259; 1969, 281·8; 1973, 384.

Fisheries. In 1973 the catch of sea fish was 1·8m. tonnes; of freshwater fish, 139,000 tonnes, and of marine prawns, shrimps and crabs, 150,000 tonnes.

INDUSTRY AND TRADE

Industry. Production of manufactured goods in 1973 included 3,705,849 tonnes of cement, 39,503 tonnes of white cement, 717,170 tonnes of sugar, 91·2m. gunny bags, 15,500 tonnes of paper, 19,422 tonnes of tobacco, 92,144 tonnes of sweetened condensed milk, 19,850 tonnes of evaporated milk, 21,200 tonnes glass sheets, 43·2m. litres of beer, 520m. sq. yd of cotton textiles, 265m. sq. yd of man-made textiles, 3,569,823 sheets of plywood and 509,964 sq. metres of vinyl tiles (1972).

GNP (1976) 174,048m. baht.

Trade Unions. The Thai National Trade Union Congress is a member of the International Confederation of Free Trade Unions.

Commerce. The foreign trade (in 1m. baht) was as follows:

	1971	*1972*	*1973*	*1974*	*1975*	*1976*
Imports (c.i.f.)	26,794	30,875	41,795	64,044	64,001	73,250
Exports (f.o.b.)	17,218	22,491	32,088	50,245	48,509	60,300

In 1973 the main items of imports were (in 1m. baht): Food, 1,371; beverages and tobacco, 415; crude materials, 3,547; mineral fuels and lubricants, 4,318; animal and vegetable oils and fats, 85; chemicals, 6,848; manufactured goods, 10,880; machinery, 13,708; miscellaneous commodities, 587.

In 1973 exports of rice were 847,870 tonnes (3,610m. baht); rubber, 390,714 tonnes (4,557m. baht); maize, 1,394,643 tonnes (2,936m. baht); tin, 22,346 tonnes (2,019m. baht); teak, 51,743 cu. metres (425m. baht); jute and kenaf, 263,850 tonnes (1,052m. baht); tapioca products, 1,813,099 tonnes (2,506m. baht); shrimps, 14,790 tonnes (798m. baht); tobacco leaves, 16,339 tonnes (307m. baht); sugar, 254,239 tonnes (1,067m. baht); mung beans, 96,524 tonnes (374m. baht); fluorite, 275,428 tonnes (225m. baht); sorghum, 123,888 tonnes (240m. baht); cement, 883,552 tonnes (303m. baht).

Total trade between Thailand and UK (British Department of Trade returns, in £1,000 sterling):

	1973	*1974*	*1975*	*1976*	*1977*
Imports to UK	11,663	18,340	13,603	25,461	34,904
Exports and re-exports from UK	36,094	50,415	55,781	59,142	82,448

Tourism. In 1975 about 1,180,075 foreigners visited Thailand, including 329,616 neighbouring visitors and 850,549 overseas visitors.

COMMUNICATIONS

Roads. In 1973 the length of highways and provincial roads open to traffic was 17,000 km, of which about 10,000 km were concrete or asphalt-surfaced. Motor vehicles registered in 1973 included 216,567 passenger cars, 25,870 buses, 151,185 lorries and 413,425 motor cycles.

Railways. In 1975 there were 3,765 km of state railways (metre gauge) open to traffic.

The northern line runs from Bangkok to Chieng Mai (741 km), the extreme northern terminus. The southern line (990 km) runs from Bangkok down the Peninsula to the frontier station of Padang Besar, where it connects with the Malayan railway from Penang, and to Singapore. Another line (214 km) branching off from Haad Yai on the southern line runs along the east coast of the peninsula to Su-gnai Kolok, where it connects with the Malayan railway line. There are branch lines (totalling 190 km) to Song Khla, Nakhon-Sithammarat, Kan Tang and Tha-Kanon. The extensions of the north-eastern line (264 km) from Nakhon Ratsima (Korat) to Nong Khai (360 km) and from Kaeng Koi to Buayai (250 km) have been completed. The Nakhon Ratsima–Ubol line (311 km) has been completed as far as Ubol Rat Thani. The eastern line (255 km) runs from Makkasan to Aran Pradet on the Cambodian frontier. The northern and southern railway systems are linked by a railway bridge over the Menam Chao Phya, and both systems terminate in Bangkok. All state railways are under one management.

Aviation. Thai Airways Co. Ltd (TAC), established in 1947, is the sole Thai air transport enterprise, with authorized capital of 300m. baht. The Company operates 11 domestic routes and 3 international routes. On 24 Aug. 1959 Thai Airways and the Scandinavian Airlines System set up a new company, Thai International Airways, to operate the international air services from Thailand.

Shipping. In 1969, 1,685 vessels of 6,986,571 NRT entered and 1,732 of 4,914,197 NRT cleared the port of Bangkok.

The port of Bangkok, about 30 km from the mouth of the Chao Phya River, is capable of berthing ocean-going vessels of 10,000 gross tons and 28 ft draught. Bangkok is now a port of entry for Laos, and goods arriving in transit are sent up by rail to Nong Khai and ferried across the river Mekhong to Vientiane.

In 1973 there were 3 Thai steamship companies: Thai Navigation Co. Ltd (7 vessels); Thai Maritime Navigation Co. Ltd (3 vessels); Thai Lines Ltd (10 vessels). There are also 40 foreign steamship lines serving the port.

Post and Broadcasting. In 1974 there were 555 post offices proper, 341 licensed and Amphur post offices and 545 railway-station post offices. In 1967, the length of telegraph lines was 21,203 km. On 1 Jan. 1977 there were 333,761 telephones, of which 260,394 were in Bangkok.

A ground satellite station at Sriracha, Chon Buri was completed in 1968. It provides a 24-hour service for telecommunications to all parts of the world and also receives and transmits live television programmes to and from other countries. The second station, at the same site, was opened in April 1970 and covers the Indian Ocean.

Cinemas (1970). There were 244 cinemas with a seating capacity of 202,798.

Newspapers (1977). There are 20 daily newspapers in Bangkok, including 4 in English and 4 in Chinese, with a combined circulation of more than 800,000.

JUSTICE, RELIGION, EDUCATION AND WELFARE

Justice. The judicial power is exercised in the name of the King, by (*a*) courts of first instance, (*b*) the court of appeal (*Uthorn*) and (*c*) the Supreme Court (*Dika*). The King appoints, transfers and dismisses judges, who are independent in conducting trials and giving judgment in accordance with the law.

Courts of first instance are subdivided into 20 magistrates' courts (*Kwaeng*) with limited civil and minor criminal jurisdiction; 85 provincial courts (*Changwad*) with unlimited civil and criminal jurisdiction; the criminal and civil courts with exclusive jurisdiction in Bangkok; the central juvenile courts for persons under 18 years of age in Bangkok.

The court of appeal exercises appellate jurisdiction in civil and criminal cases from all courts of first instance. From it appeals lie to Dika Court on any point of law and, in certain cases, on questions of fact.

The Supreme Court is the supreme tribunal of the land. Besides its normal appellate jurisdiction in civil and criminal matters, it has semi-original jurisdiction over general election petitions. The decisions of Dika Court are final. Every person has the right to present a petition to the Government who will deal with all matters of grievance.

Religion. About 94% of the population are Buddhists, 4% Moslems, 2% Christians, Hindus and others.

Education. Primary education is compulsory for children between the ages of 7–14 and free in local municipal schools. In 1973 there were 6,117,727 students enrolled in 29,016 government schools and 1,203,035 in 2,526 private schools. There were 40 teachers' training schools with 4,629 teachers and 135,074 students and 172 government vocational schools with 6,548 teachers and 91,294 students. In 1973 there were 12 universities: Chulalongkorn University (1917), Thammasat University (1934), Universities of Medical Science, Agriculture and Fine Arts; Ramkamhaeng University (1971)—all in Bangkok; Chiengmai University (1964), the Khon Kaen University (1966) in the North-East and Prince of Songkhla University (1968) in the South.

The literacy of the population 10 years of age and over was 70·8% in 1960 (53·7% in 1947).

Health. In 1971 there were 3,722 hospitals and health centres throughout the country. In 1973 there were 4,124 physicians, 748 dentists and 2,801 pharmacists.

DIPLOMATIC REPRESENTATIVES

OF THAILAND IN GREAT BRITAIN (30 Queen's Gate, London, SW7 5JB)

Ambassador: Phan Wannamethee (accredited 19 Dec. 1977).

OF GREAT BRITAIN IN THAILAND (Wireless Rd., Bangkok)

Ambassador: John Peter Tripp, CMG.

OF THAILAND IN THE USA (2300 Kalorama Rd., NW, Washington, D.C., 20008)

Chargé d'Affaires: Sukho Suwansiri.

OF THE USA IN THAILAND (95 Wireless Rd., Bangkok)

Ambassador: Charles S. Whitehouse.

OF THAILAND TO THE UNITED NATIONS

Ambassador: Dr Pracha Guna-Kasem.

Books of Reference

Thailand Statistical Yearbook 1978. National Statistical Office, Bangkok
Thailand Official Yearbook 1968. Government Printer, Bangkok
Bibliography of Materials About Thailand in Western Languages. Chulalongkorn University, Bangkok, 1960
Chu, V., *Thailand Today*. New York, 1968
Exell, F. K., *The Land and People of Thailand*. London, 1960
Haas, M. R., *Thai–English Student's Dictionary*. OUP, 1966
Kirkup, J., *Bangkok*. London, 1968
Muscat, R. J., *Development Strategy in Thailand: A Case Study of Economic Modernization*. London, 1966
Phloyphrom, P., *Modern Standard Thai–English Dictionary*. Bangkok, 1958
Silcock, T. H. (ed.), *Thailand: Social and Economic Studies*. Canberra, 1967

TOGO

République Togolaise

Capital: Lomé
Population: 2·2m. (1976)
GNP per capita: US$260 (1976)

HISTORY. The Republic of Togo became independent on 27 April 1960, after having been a German protectorate (1894–1914, subsequently divided between the French and the British), a mandate of the League of Nations (20 July 1922) and a trusteeship territory of the United Nations (14 Dec. 1946).

On 28 Oct. 1956 a plebiscite was held to determine the status of the territory. Out of 438,175 registered voters, 313,458 voted for an autonomous republic within the French Union and the end of the trusteeship system. The trusteeship was abolished on the achievement of independence on 27 April 1960.

On 13 Jan. 1963 the President Sylvanus Olympio was murdered by n.c.o.s. of the army. Nicolas Grunitzky, a former prime minister and Olympio's brother-in-law, was appointed President of the Republic and head of government. On 13 Jan. 1967 in a bloodless *coup* the army under Col. Etienne Eyadéma made President Grunitzky 'voluntarily withdraw'. On 14 April 1967 Col. Eyadéma assumed the offices of President and Defence Minister in a government of 4 officers and 8 civilians.

AREA AND POPULATION. Togo is bounded north by Upper Volta, east by Dahomey, south by the Bight of Benin and west by Ghana. Area, about 56,000 sq. km. The population of Togo in 1976 was 2,225,000. The capital is Lomé (population, 1974, 214,200). Lomé, Anécho, Palimé, Bassari, Atakpamé, Sokodé and Tsévié are *communes de plein exercise.*

The southern part of Togo is peopled by tribes using several different languages, of which the principal are Ewe and Mina; these may be regarded as an offshoot of the Bantu peoples. The northern half contains, ethnologically, a totally different population descended largely from Hamitic tribes and speaking a fairly large number of different languages, of which Dagomba, Tim and Cabrais are the most important.

CONSTITUTION AND GOVERNMENT. Administratively, Togo is divided into 19 districts: Lomé, Tsévié, Anécho, Atakpamé, Sokodé, Lama-Kara, Bassari, Mango, Dapango, Tabligbo, Akposso, Klouto, Nautja, Bafilo, Niamtougou, Pagouda, Kandé, Sotouboua, Vogan. A single party system was introduced in 1969.

President: Gen. Gnassingbe Eyadena.
Foreign Affairs: Edem Kudjo.
National flag: Five horizontal stripes of green and yellow, a red quarter with a white star.

DEFENCE

Army. The Army consists of 3 infantry battalions of 2,500 men.

Air Force. An Air Force, established with French assistance, has 3 Brazilian-built EMB-326 Xavante (Aermacchi MB.326) armed jet trainers; 1 twin-turbofan F-28 Fellowship, 2 turboprop Buffalo and 1 C-47 transport; 2 Cessna Skymaster communications aircraft; 5 Magister jet trainers; and 1 Puma and 2 Alouette helicopters.

INTERNATIONAL RELATIONS

Membership. Togo is a member of UN, OAU and is an ACP state of EEC.

ECONOMY

Planning. A first 5-year development plan (1966–70) was adopted by the National Assembly in 1965. A second 5-year development plan (1971–75) aimed at economic independence.

Budget. The ordinary budget for 1975 balanced at 30,515m. francs CFA.

Banking. In Dec. 1966 the Crédit du Togo was reorganized as a national development bank, named Banque Togolaise de Développement, with a capital of 300m. francs CFA (increased to 400m. in 1975), of which the government's share is 60%.

NATURAL RESOURCES

Minerals. A Mines Department was set up in 1953 after the discovery of very rich deposits of phosphate and bauxite; mining began in 1961. Output of phosphate rock (1,000 long tons): 1964, 801·4; 1965, 982; 1966, 1,111; 1968, 1,357. Other mineral deposits are limestone, estimated at 28m. tons; iron ore, estimated at 550m. tons with iron content varying between 40% and 55%, and 3 magnesian limestone deposits, estimated at about 170m. tons.

Agriculture. Inland the country is hilly, rising to 3,600 ft, with streams and waterfalls. There are long stretches of forest and brushwood, while dry plains alternate with arable land. Maize, yams, cassava, plantains, groundnuts, etc., are cultivated; oil palms and dye-woods grow in the forests; but the main commerce is based on coffee, cocoa, palm-oil, palm-kernels, copra, groundnuts, cotton, manioc. There are considerable plantations of oil and cocoa palms, coffee, cacao, kola, cassava and cotton.

Livestock (1976): Cattle, 235,000; sheep, 750,000; swine, 270,000; horses, 3,000; asses, 2,000; goats, 630,000.

INDUSTRY AND TRADE

Industry. Industry, although small, is developing and includes a cement works, oil refinery and food processing plants.

Trade (in 1m. francs CFA):

	1970	*1971*	*1972*	*1973*	*1974*
Imports	17,928	19,455	21,381	22,388	28,612
Exports	15,176	13,626	12,542	12,755	45,174

Exports in 1973 were (in tonnes): Cocoa, 17,666; cotton, 1,371; coffee, 10,816; palm-kernels, 6,458; palm-oil, 4·6; groundnuts (husked), 5,726; manioc starch, 488; copra, 70; phosphate, 2,196,826. In 1973 phosphates constituted 97·6% of the total tonnage and 45·6% of the total value of exports; coffee and cocoa, 39·7% of the total value.

Trade with UK (British Department of Trade returns, in £1,000 sterling):

	1973	*1974*	*1975*	*1976*	*1977*
Imports to UK	174	542	366	577	48
Exports and re-exports from UK	3,009	3,834	10,432	82,721	16,133

COMMUNICATIONS

Roads. There were, in 1972, 4,644 km of roads, of which 490 km were paved.

Railways. There are 3 metre-gauge railways connecting Lomé with Anécho, Palimé and Blitta; total, 443 km.

Aviation: Air services connect Lomé with Paris, Dakar, Abidjan, Douala, Accra, Lagos, Cotonou and Niamey. In 1972 aircraft disembarked 19,350 passengers and 477 tonnes of freight.

Shipping. In 1972, 549 vessels landed 328,436 tonnes and cleared 74,202 tonnes at Lomé.

Post and Broadcasting. There were (1972) 39 post offices and 16 postal agencies and 6,144 telephones. Togo is connected by telegraph and telephone with Ghana,

Dahomey, Abidjan and Dakar, and by wireless telegraphy with Europe and America.

RELIGION. In 1975 there were 521,185 Christians, of which 402,476 were Catholics and 118,709 Protestants. There were 226,186 Mohammedans.

EDUCATION. In 1974–75 there were 329,443 pupils in primary schools, 48,216 pupils in secondary and technical schools.

DIPLOMATIC REPRESENTATIVES

OF TOGO IN GREAT BRITAIN

Ambassador: Kodjovi Vinyo Dagadou (resides in Brussels).

OF GREAT BRITAIN IN TOGO

Ambassador: J. Mellon.

OF TOGO IN THE USA (2208 Massachusetts Ave., NW, Washington, D.C., 20008)

Ambassador: Kokou Kekeh.

OF THE USA IN TOGO (Rue Pelletier Caventou, Lomé)

Ambassador: Roland D. Palmer.

OF TOGO TO THE UNITED NATIONS

Ambassador: Akanyi-Awunyo Kodjovi.

Book of Reference

Cornevin, R., *Histoire du Togo*. Paris, 1959

TONGA

Capital: Nuku'alofa
Population: 90,128 (1976)

Friendly Islands

HISTORY. The kingdom of Tonga attained unity under Taufa'ahau Tupou (George I) who became ruler of his native Ha'apai in 1820, of Vava'u in 1833 and of Tongatapu in 1845. By 1960 the kingdom had become converted to Christianity (George himself having been baptized in 1831). In 1862 the king granted freedom to the people from arbitrary rule of minor chiefs and gave them the right to the allocation of land for their own needs. These institutional changes, together with the establishment of a parliament of chiefs, paved the way towards the democratic constitution under which the kingdom is now governed, and provided a background of stability against which Tonga was able to develop her agricultural economy.

The kingdom continued up to 1899 to be a neutral region in accordance with the Declaration of Berlin, 6 April 1886. By the Anglo-German Agreement of 14 Nov. 1899 subsequently accepted by the USA, the Tonga Islands were left under the Protectorate of Great Britain.

A protectorate was proclaimed on 18 May 1900, and a British Agent and Consul appointed.

AREA AND POPULATION. The kingdom consists of some 169 islands and islets with a total area of 270 sq. miles (700 sq. km; including inland waters), and lies between 15° and 23° 30′ S. lat and 173° and 177° W. long., its western boundary being the eastern boundary of Fiji. The islands are split up into the following groups reading from north to south: The Niuas, Vava'u, Ha'apai, Kotu, Nomuka, Otu Tolu and Tongatapu. The 3 main groups, both from historical and administrative significance, are Tongatapu in the south, Ha'apai in the centre and Vava'u in the north. The Tongatapu group was discovered by Tasman in 1643.

The capital is Nuku'alofa on Tongatapu.

The islands to the east, being mostly of limestone formation, are low lying and with but a few exceptions seldom exceed 100 ft above sea-level. The islands to the west are of a volcanic nature, approximately 11, average between 350 and 3,433 ft in height. After a violent volcanic eruption in Sept. 1946 on the island of Niuafo'ou (Tin Can Island to philatelists, so named because of the method that was used of collecting and delivering mail) the 1,300 inhabitants were evacuated, most of them to Tongatapu and 'Eua, but more than 600 have returned since 1958. It was thought that a new island had been born when an eruption took place on the Metis Shoal on 12 Dec. 1967; during the volcanic activity a small rocky mass reached a maximum elevation of about 50 ft, but by Feb. 1968 the area was once more awash.

The climate is mild and healthy, malaria being unknown. The temperature from May to Nov. rarely exceeds 84° F. in the shade, with a minimum temperature of 52° F. Census population (1976) 90,128.

CONSTITUTION AND GOVERNMENT. Relations between the UK and Tonga have been governed by the 1900 Treaty of Friendship and Protection and several subsequent revisions. For earlier history of this relationship *see* THE STATESMAN'S YEAR-BOOK, 1970–71. By exchange of letters on 19 May 1970 it was agreed that the UK Government should, as from 4 June 1970, cease to have any responsibility for the external relations of the Kingdom of Tonga.

King: HM King Taufa'ahau Tupou IV, GCVO, GCMG, KBE, born 4 July 1918, succeeded on 16 Dec. 1965 on the death of his mother, Queen Salote Tupou III; his coronation took place on 4 July 1967.

Prime Minister: HRH Prince Tu'ipelehake, KBE, younger brother of the King.

National flag: Red with a white quarter bearing a red couped cross.

The present constitution is almost identical with that granted in 1875 by King George Tupou I. There is a Privy Council, Cabinet, Legislative Assembly and Judiciary. The legislative assembly, which meets annually, is composed of 7 nobles elected by their peers, 7 elected representatives of the people and the Privy Councillors (numbering 8); the King appoints one of the 7 nobles to be the Speaker. The elections are held triennially. In 1960, women voted for the first time.

INTERNATIONAL RELATIONS

Membership. Tonga is a member of UN, the Commonwealth and is an ACP state of EEC.

ECONOMY

Planning. Since 1965 Tonga has organized its development effort around a 5-year development Plan. The Second Plan 1970–75 laid greater stress than its predecessor on developing the economic potential of the Kingdom with expenditure of T$4·4m. Urgent social needs were largely met in the First Plan 1965–70.

The Third Plan 1975–80 is the Kingdom's first attempt at formal, comprehensive indicative planning covering both the public and private sectors. The plan places considerable emphasis on investment in the productive sectors of the economy particularly agriculture, fisheries, manufacturing and tourism and on the development of supporting infrastructure and policies. Estimated expenditure for the public sector during the plan period amounts to T$31m. A Central Planning Office has been established to co-ordinate the implementation of the Third Plan and to formulate future development plans.

Budget. Revenue and expenditure in T$1,000:

	1970–71	*1971–72*	*1972–73*	*1973–74*	*1974–75*
Revenue	2,731	3,143	3,357	4,473	5,530
Expenditure	3,002	3,162	3,256	3,470	4,773

Currency. There is a government note issue of *pa'anga* (T$)10, 5, 2, 1 and ½ and coin issue of T$2, T$1 and *seniti* 50, 20, 10, 5, 2 and 1. The change-over to decimal currency took place on 3 April 1967. In Sept. 1974, following devaluation by Australia, the Australian dollar equalled 88 *seniti*. In April 1963 gold coins were issued in denominations of 1, ½ and ¼ *koula* (1 *koula* = T$20) and in July 1967, Coronation Palladium coins of 1, ½ and ¼ *hau* (1 *hau* = T$100). In Nov. 1975, gold coins (T$100, 75, 50 and 25) and silver coins (T$20, 10 and 5) were issued to commemorate the Centenary of the Constitution.

AGRICULTURE. Tongan produce consists almost entirely of copra (T$723,223 exported, 1971) and bananas (T$370,184 exported, 1971).

COMMERCE. Imports in 1971 were valued at T$6,305,000; exports, T$2·2m.

Trade with UK (British Department of Trade returns, in £1,000 sterling):

	1974	*1975*	*1976*	*1977*
Imports to UK	773	508	431	1,003
Exports and re-exports from UK	334	534	693	434

COMMUNICATIONS

Aviation. Air services to Tongatapu are provided by Air Pacific from Suva and Auckland and Polynesian Airlines from Apia, Western Samoa. There are 4 flights a week from Fiji and Auckland, N.Z. and 3 flights a week from Western Samoa. On the return journey from Tongatapu to Apia Polynesian Airlines flies *via* Niue twice a week. Air Pacific flies the BAC 111 jet and Polynesian Airlines the HS 748 turbo-prop.

The Tonga Internal Air Service operates a scheduled service between Tongatapu, 'Eua, Ha'apai and Vava'u.

Shipping. The Union Steamship Co. of New Zealand maintains a fortnightly service

New Zealand–Fiji–Samoa–Tonga, and cargo steamers visit the group from time to time for shipments of copra. Shipping cleared at all ports in 1975, 103 cargo vessels, 48 cruise vessels, 8 gas vessels and 10 tankers.

Cruise ships from the following lines call at Vava'u and Nuku'alofa: P & O, Chandris, Sitmar, Royal Viking, Shaw Savill, Pacific Far East Line. The Pacific Navigation Co. Ltd maintains a regular inter-island shipping services between 'Eua, Ha'apai and Vava'u.

Post. The kingdom has its own issue of postage stamps. Telephones numbered 552 in 1977.

JUSTICE, RELIGION AND EDUCATION

Justice. Now that British extra-territorial jurisdiction has lapsed and British and foreign nationals charged with an offence against the laws of Tonga (the enforcement of which is a responsibility of the Minister of Police) are fully subject to the jurisdiction of the Tongan courts to which they are already subject in all civil matters.

Religion. The Tongans are Christian, the vast majority being adherents of the Wesleyan Church.

Education. The Tongans enjoy free education, free medical attendance and dental treatment. In 1975 there were 82 government and 43 denominational primary schools, with a total of 19,115 pupils. There are 2 government and 39 mission schools and 1 private school at which post-primary education is provided for both boys and girls, with a total roll of 10,420. The Atenisi Institute University Division opened in 1975 and in 1977 there were 15 students with 11 staff.

DIPLOMATIC REPRESENTATIVES

OF TONGA IN GREAT BRITAIN (New Zealand House, Haymarket, London, SW1Y 4TE)

High Commissioner: 'I. F. Faletau.

OF GREAT BRITAIN IN TONGA (Nuku'alofa)

High Commissioner: H. A. Arthington-Davy, OBE.

OF THE USA IN TONGA

Ambassador: A. I. Selden, Jr (resides in Wellington).

Books of Reference

Tonga Government Departmental Reports, 1972
Biennial Report, 1962–63. HMSO, 1965
Bain, K. R., *Royal Visit to Tonga: Tonga Government Official Record.* London, 1954.—*The Friendly Islanders.* London, 1967
Churchward, C. M., *Tongan Dictionary.* London, 1959
Luke, Sir Harry, *Queen Salote and Her Kingdom.* London, 1954
Morrell, W. P., *Britain in the Pacific Islands.* OUP, 1960
Wood, A. H., *A History and Geography of Tonga.* Rev. ed. Nuku'alofa, 1963

TRINIDAD AND TOBAGO

Capital: Port-of-Spain
Population: 1·07m. (1974)
GNP per capita: US$2,240 (1976)

HISTORY. Trinidad was discovered by Columbus in 1498 and colonized by the Spaniards in the 16th century. During the French Revolution a large number of French families settled in the island. In 1797, Great Britain being at war with Spain, Trinidad was occupied by the British and ceded to Great Britain by the Treaty of Amiens in 1802. Trinidad and Tobago were joined in 1889.

Under the Bases Agreement concluded between the governments of the UK and the USA on 27 March 1941, and the concomitant Trinidad–US Bases Lease of 22 April 1941, defence bases were leased to the US Government for 99 years. On 8 Dec. 1960 the US agreed to abandon 21,000 acres of leased land and the US has since given up the remaining territory, except for a small tracking station.

AREA AND POPULATION. Area: Trinidad, 1,864 sq. miles (4,828 sq. km); Tobago, 116 sq. miles (300 sq. km). Population (census 7 April 1970): 931,071 (459,512 males and 471,559 females) (Trinidad, 892,317; Tobago, 38,754). Capital, Port-of-Spain, 62,680; other important towns, San Fernando (36,879) and Arima (11,636). The white population (1·22%) is chiefly composed of persons of English, French, Spanish and Portuguese descent. The majority are of African descent (42·83%), the balance being made up of Indians (40·11%), mixed races (14·17%), Syrian Lebanese (0·11%) and Chinese (0·86%). English is spoken generally.

Estimated population in mid-1974, 1,073,800 (549,050 males, 524,750 females).

Vital statistics (rate per 1,000), 1974: Births, 24·4; deaths, 6·2; infant deaths, 25·6. Proportion of population under 15 years (1974) 39·2%.

Tobago is situated about 21 miles north-east of Trinidad. Main town is Scarborough.

Principal goods shipped from Tobago to Trinidad are copra, cocoa, livestock and poultry, fresh vegetables, coconut oil and coconut fibre.

CONSTITUTION AND GOVERNMENT. On 31 Aug. 1962 Trinidad and Tobago became an independent member state of the British Commonwealth. A Republican Constitution was adopted on 26 Oct. 1976.

The constitution provides for a bicameral legislature of a Senate and a House of Representatives. The Senate consists of 31 members, 16 being appointed by the President on the advice of the Prime Minister, 6 on the advice of the Leader of the Opposition and 9 at the discretion of the President.

The voting age in the 1976 election was reduced from 21 to 18 years and ballot boxes were re-introduced in place of the voting machines used in previous elections.

The House of Representatives consists of 36 elected members and a Speaker elected from outside the House.

The Cabinet consists of the Prime Minister, appointed by the President, and other Ministers, including the Attorney-General (15 in 1974).

The general elections held on 13 Sept. 1976 gave the People's National Movement all the 36 seats.

President: Ellis Clarke.
Prime Minister: Dr Eric E. Williams, PC, CH.
National flag: Red with a diagonal black strip edged in white.

INTERNATIONAL RELATIONS

Membership. Trinidad and Tobago is a member of UN, the Commonwealth, Caricom and is an ACP state of EEC.

ECONOMY

Budget. Statistics of 5 calendar years (in TT$1,000):

	1969	*1970*	*1973*	*1974*	*1975*[1]
Revenue	348,900	348,334	591,300	1,397,700	1,769,000
Expenditure	325,330	291,116	573,500	1,301,400	1,768,800
Public debt[2]	370,493	392,600	625,900	628,700	634,800

[1] Provisional. [2] Revised.

The principal items of revenue during 1975 were: Customs and excise, $131m.; direct taxes, $1,218m.

Currency. The Trinidad and Tobago dollar of 100 cents equals £0·21. Total circulation of currency was TT$98,125,000 in 1973.

Banking. Banks operating: Barclays Bank of Trinidad and Tobago Ltd; Royal Bank of Trinidad and Tobago Ltd; Canadian Imperial Bank of Commerce; Bank of Nova Scotia; Chase Manhattan Bank; Citibank; National Commercial Bank of Trinidad and Tobago; Workers' Bank of Trinidad and Tobago. A Central Bank began operations in Dec. 1964.

Government savings banks are established in 62 offices, with a head office in Port-of-Spain, the amount of deposits at the end of 1973 being $8,316,739, and the total number of depositors, 137,349.

AGRICULTURE. Of the total area of 1,267,236 acres (Trinidad, 1,192,844 acres, and Tobago, 74,392 acres), about half has been alienated. Acres under cultivation and care include (1973): Forest, 685,604; sugar, 118,703; cocoa, 119,703; coconuts, 35,797; citrus, 13,667; tonca beans, 1,735. Sugar production in 1975 was 160,000 (1974: 183,400) tons. The territory is still largely dependent on imported food supplies, especially flour, dairy products, meat and rice. Areas have been irrigated for rice, and soil and forest conservation is practised.

Livestock (1976): Cattle, 73,000; sheep, 10,000; goats, 42,000; pigs, 55,000; poultry, 6·48m.

INDUSTRY AND TRADE

Industry. Oil production is one of Trinidad's leading industries and an important source of revenue. Commercial production began in 1909; production in 1974 was 122·5m. bbls; in 1975, 81m. bbls. Trinidad also possesses 3 refineries, with throughput capacity of 144·2m. bbls annually; crude oil is imported from Venezuela, Indonesia, Ecuador, Nigeria Brazil, and Saudi Arabia and refined in Trinidad. Besides oil, Trinidad's natural resources include the 'Pitch Lake', an important source of asphalt; production, 1972, 113,627 tons; 1973, 107,800 tons.

The working population in 1974 was 393,400 (114,900 women) and unemployment was 61,800 (25,300 women).

Commerce. Chief imports, 1975:

	TT$1,000		*TT$1,000*
Food	285,100	Machinery and transport equipment	196,800
Beverages and tobacco	17,500	Manufactured goods	207,400
Mineral fuels, lubricants, etc.	1,640,000		
Chemicals	150,000		

The principal domestic exports during 1973 were (in TT$1,000): Food, 81,500; petroleum products (including crude petroleum), 1,120,900; chemicals, 74,900; manufactured goods, 25,200.

The chief countries of origin of imports were: Saudi Arabia (23·9%), USA (15·7%), UK (11·1%), Indonesia (9·9%). Exports were shipped chiefly to USA (52·6%), CARICOM (11·3%), Sweden (6·2%), UK (4·7%).

Trade of Trinidad and Tobago with UK (British Department of Trade returns, in £1,000 sterling):

	1973	*1974*	*1975*	*1976*	*1977*
Imports to UK	16,257	15,312	34,546	48,255	29,500
Exports and re-exports from UK	32,859	37,169	52,270	73,834	97,308

Tourism. In 1975, 166,360 foreigners visited Trinidad and Tobago including 33,750 in transit.

COMMUNICATIONS

Roads. There are 2,630 miles of main and local roads. Motor vehicles registered in 1975 included 91,414 private cars, 9,911 hiring and rented cars, and 18,755 goods vehicles.

Aviation. The following airlines operate scheduled passenger, mail and freight services. British West Indian Airways, Ltd, Air Canada, PANAM, KLM, Linea Aeropostal Venezolana, Aerolinas Argentinas, Leeward Islands Air Transport, Air France, ASPA, Air India, Caribair and British Airways.

Shipping. In 1969, 6,539 vessels arrived at Port-of-Spain.

Post and Broadcasting. International communications to all parts of the world are provided by Trinidad and Tobago External Telecommunications Co. Ltd (TEXTEL) by means of a satellite earth station and various high quality radio circuits. The marine radio service is also maintained by TEXTEL. Number of post offices (1973), 179; number of telephones (1977), 70,304.

Four wireless stations are maintained by the Trinidad Government and 3 by airline companies. A meteorological station is maintained at Piarco airport.

Cinemas (1973). There are 72 cinemas and 4 drive-in cinemas.

Newspapers (1973). There are 2 daily newspapers with an average daily circulation of 90,000, 3 Sunday newspapers with an average circulation of 146,000, 1 evening paper and 5 weekly newspapers.

JUSTICE, RELIGION, EDUCATION AND WELFARE

Justice. The High Court consists of the Chief Justice and not fewer than 10 puisne judges. In criminal cases a judge of the High Court sits with a jury of 12 in cases of treason and murder, and with 9 jurors in other cases. The Court of Appeal consists of the Chief Justice and 3 Justices of Appeal; there is a limited right of appeal from it to the Privy Council. There are 10 High Courts and 28 magistrates' courts.

Police. At the end of 1970 the police force consisted of 63 officers, 72 inspectors and 2,446 other ranks.

Religion. In 1970, 18·1% of the population were Anglicans (under the Bishop of Trinidad and Tobago), 35·6% Roman Catholics (under the Archbishop of Port-of-Spain), 4·2% Presbyterians, 24·7% Hindus and 6·3% Moslems.

Education. In 1972–73 there were 476 primary and intermediate schools (government assisted) and (1971–72) 116 secondary schools (47 government and assisted and 69 private).

There were 222,928 pupils on roll in the primary and intermediate schools and 35,302 in the secondary schools (government and assisted). Education in government and assisted secondary schools was made free in 1960. There are also 5 training colleges. Technical and commercial education is provided by 4 government sponsored technical schools.

Health. State medical services are free and in 1972 a National Insurance Scheme was established.

DIPLOMATIC REPRESENTATIVES

OF TRINIDAD AND TOBAGO IN GREAT BRITAIN
(42 Belgrave Sq., London, SW1X 8NT)

High Commissioner: Eustace Seignoret.

OF GREAT BRITAIN IN TRINIDAD AND TOBAGO
(Furness Hse., 90 Independence Sq., Port of Spain)

High Commissioner: H. S. H. Stanley, C.M.G.

OF TRINIDAD AND TOBAGO IN THE USA
(1708 Massachusetts Ave., NW, Washington, D.C., 20036)

Ambassador: Victor C. McIntyre.

OF THE USA IN TRINIDAD AND TOBAGO
(15 Queen's Park West, Port of Spain)

Ambassador: Richard K. Fox, Jr.

OF TRINIDAD AND TOBAGO TO THE UNITED NATIONS

Ambassador: Frank Owen Abdulah.

Books of Reference

Statistical Information: The Central Statistical Office, Government of Trinidad and Tobago, 2 Edward St., Port-of-Spain. *Director:* J. Harewood. Publications include *Annual Statistical Digest*, *Quarterly Economic Report*, *Annual Overseas Trade Report*, *Population and Vital Statistics Annual Report*.

Report of the Trinidad and Tobago Independence Conference, 1962. (Cmnd. 1757.) HMSO, 1962
Development Plan for Tobago. HMSO, 1957
Economic Survey of Trinidad and Tobago, 1953–58. Government Printer, Port-of-Spain, 1959
Five Year Development Programme, 1958–1962. Government Printer, Port-of-Spain, 1958
Third Five Year Plan, 1969–73. Government Printer, Port-of-Spain, 1970
Trinidad and Tobago Year Book. Port-of-Spain. Annual (from 1865)
Trade Dictionary of Trinidad and Tobago. 2nd ed. London, 1966
Anthony, M., *Profile Trinidad: A Historical Survey from the Discovery to 1900.* London, 1975

Central Library: The Central Library of Trinidad and Tobago, Queen's Park East, Port-of-Spain. *Acting Librarian:* Mrs L. Hutchinson.

TUNISIA

Capital: Tunis
Population: 5·77m (1975)
GNP per capita: US$840 (1976)

Al-Djoumhouria Attunusia

HISTORY. Tunisia, was a French protectorate from 1883 and achieved independence on 20 March 1956. The Constituent Assembly, elected on 25 March 1956, abolished the monarchy (of the Bey of Tunis) on 25 July 1957 and proclaimed a Republic.

AREA AND POPULATION. The boundaries are on the north and east the Mediterranean Sea, on the west Algeria and on the south Libya. The area is about 164,150 sq. km (63,362 sq. miles), including that portion of the Sahara which is to the east of the Djerid, extending towards Ghadamès.

At the census of 3 May 1966 there were 4,457,862 inhabitants (2,267,915 males and 2,189,947 females). Estimate (1975) 5·77m.

The estimated populations of the *gouvernorats* were as follows as at 31 Dec. 1969 (in 1,000): Tunis and suburbs (944), Bizerta (359), Béja (343), Jendouba (273), Le Kef (335), Kassérine (226), Gafsa (357), Médénine (262), Gabès (221), Sfax (471), Kairouan (298), Sousse (576), Nabeul (362).

Tunis, the capital, had (estimate, 1976) 944,000 inhabitants: Sfax, 475,000; Sousse, 255,000; Bizerta, 62,000; Kairouan, a holy city of the Moslems, 54,000. Other towns (estimate 1966): Gabès, 76,356; Béja, 72,034; Djerba, 65,533; Médénine, 39,218; Hammam-Lif, 22,161.

Vital statistics (1971). Births, 182,749; deaths, 48,762; marriages, 37,642.

CONSTITUTION AND GOVERNMENT. The Constitution of the Republic was promulgated on 1 June 1959. The President and the National Assembly are elected simultaneously by direct universal suffrage for a period of 5 years. The President cannot be re-elected more than 3 times consecutively. An amendment to the constitution in 1969 gives the Prime Minister power to act as President in case of a sudden vacancy of the Presidency.

It was announced on 12 Jan. 1974 by the President that Tunisia and Libya would be merged into a single state eventually but this proposal collapsed in the same year.

President of the Republic and Head of Government: Habib Bourguiba (elected 25 July 1957, re-elected 8 Nov. 1959, 8 Nov. 1964, 2 Nov. 1969 and elected President for life in Nov. 1974).

Prime Minister: Hedi Nouira.

Special Adviser to the President: Habib Bourguiba, Jr. *Minister-Delegate attached to the Prime Minister:* Mohammed Sayah. *Minister-Delegate attached to the Prime Minister responsible for Planning:* Mustapha Zaanouni. *Foreign Affairs:* Mohamed Fitouri. *Defence:* Abdallah Farhat. *Industry, Mines and Energy:* Rashid Sfar. *Trade:* Slaheddine Mbarek. *Health:* Mongi Ben Hamida. *Cultural Affairs and Information:* Chedli Klibi. *Finance:* Abdelaziz Mathari. *Justice:* Salaheddine Bali. *Interior:* Dhaouri Hannablia. *Agriculture:* Hassan Belkhodja. *Education:* Mohammed M'Zali. *Transport and Communications:* Abdelhamid Saffi. *Supply:* Lassaad Ben Osman. *Social Affairs:* Mohamed Jomaa. *Youth and Sports:* Fouad M'Baza. *Relations with the National Assembly and Secretary-General of the Government:* Othman Kecherid. *Secretaries of State:* Larbi Mallakh (*Supply*), Ibrahim Turki (*Foreign Affairs*), Hedi Zeghala (*Education*), Mustapha Masmoudi (*Information, attached to the Prime Minister*), Noureddine Ktari (*Vocational Training, attached to the Minister of Social Affairs*).

By decree of 21 July 1959 the country was divided into *gouvernorats*, each subdivided into *délégations, communes* and *cheikhats*.

The official language is Arabic.

Flag: Red with a white circle in the middle, on which is a 5-pointed red star encircled by a red crescent.

DEFENCE. A Tunisian National Army was created in 1956. It consisted in 1978 of about 20,000 officers and men. Selective military service is 1 year. Officer-cadets are being trained in France. Defence expenditure in 1973 was 13·8m. dinars.

Army. The Army consists of 2 combined arms regiments, 1 commando, 1 desert, 1 artillery and 1 engineer battalion.

Navy. The Navy consists of 1 frigate (*ex*-US old destroyer-escort), 2 fast attack craft (British-built in 1977), 1 coastal minesweeper, 4 patrol vessels, 14 patrol boats and 3 tugs. A small frigate is under construction in France. In 1978 naval personnel totalled 2,100 officers and ratings.

Air Force. Equipment of the Air Force, acquired from various Western sources, includes single squadrons of Aermacchi M.B.326K jet light attack aircraft and SF.260W piston-engined light trainer/attack aircraft, 12 T-6 Texan advanced trainers, 12 M.B.326 armed jet trainers, 1 Puma and about 8 Alouette II and III helicopters and 3 Aeritalia G222 twin-turboprop transports. Personnel, about 1,800.

INTERNATIONAL RELATIONS

Membership. Tunisia is a member of UN, OAU and the Arab League.

ECONOMY

Planning. A fourth development plan (1973–76) envisaged investment of 1,194m. dinars.

Budget (in 1,000 dinars). Ordinary receipts and expenditure for calendar years balanced as follows: 1964, 68,300; 1965, 86,000. Budget estimates, 1966, revenue, 100,500; expenditure, 135,500. The budget for 1969 balanced at 130,000; 1970, 146,500; 1971, 154,000; 1972, 176,000; 1973, 208,100; 1974, 215,700.

Currency. On 1 Nov. 1958 a new currency, the *dinar*, divided into 1,000 *millimes*, was established. The Central Bank of Tunisia is the note-issuing agency. Note circulation, July 1974, was 374·56m. *dinars*.

The issue consists of coins of 1, 2, 10, 20, 50 and 100 *millimes*, and notes of 500 *millimes*, 1 *dinar*, 5 and 10 *dinars*.

Banking. In 1977 there were 14 banks operating in Tunisia, including 3 French and 1 British banks. Bank deposits amounted to 267·8m. dinars at 31 Dec. 1972.

Weights and Measures. The metric system of weights and measures has almost entirely taken the place of those of Tunisia, but corn is still sold in *kaffis* and *wibas*. The *kfiz* (of 16 *wiba*, each of 12 *sa'*) = 16 bushels. The *ounce* = 31·487 grammes; the multiples of the ounce are the various denominations of the *R'lal*, which contains from 16 to 42 oz.

The principal measure of length is the *pik*: the *pik Arbi* for linen = 0·5392 yd; the *pik Turki* for silk = 0·7058 yd; the *pik Andoulsi* for cloth = 0·7094 yd.

ENERGY AND NATURAL RESOURCES

Electricity. The electricity, gas and water services, formerly run by a French company, were nationalized on 26 Nov. 1959 and are now run by the Société Tunisienne d'Electricité et du Gaz.

Electrical energy generated was 1,125·1m. kwh. in 1973, of which 964m. was produced by STEG.

Minerals. Mineral production (in 1,000 tonnes) in 1973 (and 1971): Phosphate, 3,500 (3,200); iron ore, 814 (940); lead ore, 25·2 (33·7); zinc ore, 15·6 (20·7).

Processed minerals (in 1,000 tonnes) in 1976: Phosphates, 3,301; lead, 17; iron ore, 494.

Agriculture. Tunisia may be divided into 5 districts—the north, characterized by its mountainous formation, having large and fertile valleys (*e.g.*, the valley of the

Medjerdah and the plains of Mornag, Mateur and Béja); the north-east, with the peninsula of Cap Bon, the soil being specially suited for the cultivation of oranges, lemons and tangerines; the Sahel, where olive trees abound; the centre, the region of high table lands and pastures, and the desert of the south, famous for its oases and gardens, where dates grow in profusion.

Agriculture is the chief industry, and large estates predominate. Of the total area of 15,583,000 hectares, about 9m. hectares are productive, including 2m. under cereals, 3·6m. used as pasturage, 900,000 forests and 1·3m. uncultivated.

Products	*1971*	*1972*	*1973*
Wheat (in 1,000 tonnes)	60	81	90
Barley (in 1,000 tonnes)	140	180	210
Olive oil[1] (in 1,000 tonnes)	167	70	130
Oranges and lemons[1] (in 1,000 tonnes)	100	74	100
	...	...	...
Dates (in 1,000 tonnes)	25	22	52
Wine (in 1,000 hectolitres)	1,050	994	1,150

[1] Crop year 1971–72, etc.

Other products are apricots, pears, apples, peaches, plums, figs, pomegranates, almonds, shaddocks, pistachios, esparto grass, henna and cork. Agricultural tractors numbered 18,360 in 1966.

Livestock (1976): Horses, 106,000; asses, 195,000; mules, 66,000; cattle, 880,000; sheep, 3·5m.; goats, 900,000; camels, 195,000; pigs, 3,000.

Fisheries. In 1967, 7,000 boats with 20,000 men were engaged in fishing. In 1972 the catch amounted to 34,000 tonnes; 1974, 37,850.

INDUSTRY AND TRADE

Industry. Major modern plants include a sugar refinery in Béja (51,110 tonnes in 1973), a cellulose plant in Kassérine (19,033 tonnes in 1968), a petroleum refinery in Bizerta and a steel plant at Menzel Bourguiba which in 1966 turned out 92,000 tons of pig-iron, 25,000 tons of steel and 30,000 tons of finished products. There is a marble work plant and a tyre factory at Mégrine. In 1972 a phosphoric acid plant opened at Ghannouche with an annual capacity of 120,000 tonnes. The index of industrial production stood at 137 in 1976 (1970 = 100).

Trade Unions. The Union Générale des Travailleurs Tunisiens was placed under government control in Aug. 1965. There are 4 other unions.

Commerce. The imports and exports for calendar years (in 1,000 dinars) were as follows:

	1970	*1971*	*1972*	*1973*	*1974*	*1975*	*1976*
Imports	160,396	180,000	222,219	265,947	488,658	521,800	566,000
Exports	95,804	113,000	150,327	168,653	397,695	345,600	351,000

Exports to France in 1976 totalled 57·7m. dinars, and imports from France, 210·9m. dinars and exports to USA were valued at 46·5m. dinars and imports from USA were valued at 40·8m. dinars.

In 1976 exports of iron ore totalled 112,600 tonnes; lime phosphates and hyperphosphates, 1,961,800; crude petroleum, 3,686,800.

Total trade between Tunisia and UK (British Department of Trade returns, in £1,000 sterling):

	1973	*1974*	*1975*	*1976*	*1977*
Imports to UK	3,565	6,192	2,968	3,116	12,641
Exports and re-exports from UK	7,554	11,465	26,729	22,969	28,371

Tourism. In 1976, 977,818 tourists visited Tunisia, not counting ships' passengers in transit.

COMMUNICATIONS

Roads. In 1971 there were 18,267 km of roads (51·5% paved), of which 10,483 km were main roads.

Number of motor vehicles, 1973, included 74,627 private cars, 39,872 commercial cars, 9,808 motor cycles and 19,661 tractors.

Railways. In 1975 there were 2,257 km of railways, owned by the state Société Nationale des Chemins de Fer Tunisiens. Traffic in 1972 was 22·4m. passengers and 7·2m. tonnes of freight.

Aviation. The national airline is 'Tunis-Air'. The main airport is at Tunis-Carthage. In 1973, 615,356 passengers were carried.

Shipping. The main port is Tunis, and its outer port is Tunis-Goulette. These two ports and Sfax, Sousse and Bizerta are directly accessible to ocean going vessels. The port of La Skhirra, in the south, is used for the shipping of Algerian and Tunisian oil.

In 1973, 4,403 ships of 13·2m. tons entered Tunisian ports.

Post and Broadcasting. There were, in 1977, 71,309 telephones, of which 32,471 were in Tunis. There were, in 1966, 381 post offices, and a wireless transmitting station. Wireless sets in use in 1975 were 356,600. Television began in 1966 and in 1970 there were 93,000 sets.

Cinemas (1973). There were 105 cinemas with a seating capacity of 49,800.

Newspapers. There are 2 Arabic and 2 French daily newspapers.

JUSTICE, RELIGION, EDUCATION AND WELFARE

Justice. The Government has abolished the multiple jurisdictions of religious (shara'ic and rabbinic) tribunals. These have been integrated into the civil courts so as to form a single three-level jurisdiction (courts of primary jurisdiction, courts of appeal and the High Court).

A Personal Status Code was promulgated on 13 Aug. 1956 and applied to Tunisians from 1 Jan. 1957. This raised the status of women, made divorce subject to a court decision, abolished polygamy and decreed a minimum marriage age.

Religion. The constitution recognizes Islam as the state religion. There are about 13,000 Roman Catholics, under the Archbishop of Carthage. The Greek Church, the French Protestants and the English Church are also represented.

Education. All education was in 1956 made dependent on the Ministry of National Education. The 208 independent koranic schools have been nationalized and the distinction between religious and public schools has been abolished. All education is free from primary schools to university. A teachers' training college (*école normale supérieure*) was established in 1955. There are also a high school of law, a centre of economic studies, a school of engineering, 1 medical school, a faculty of agriculture and an institute of business administration.

In 1973–74 primary schools had 943,000 pupils; secondary, technical and vocational schools had 178,650 pupils; higher education mainly at the University of Tunis had 14,750 students.

Health. In 1972 there were 92 hospitals (13,550 beds). The registered medical personnel in Tunisia comprised 864 doctors (374 Tunisians and 490 foreigners), 233 pharmacists, 65 dentists and 42 veterinaries.

Social Security. A system of social security was set up in 1950 (amended 1963, 1964 and 1970).

DIPLOMATIC REPRESENTATIVES

OF TUNISIA IN GREAT BRITAIN (29 Prince's Gate, London, SW7 1QG)

Ambassador: Said Ben Ammar (accredited 21 Dec. 1976).

OF GREAT BRITAIN IN TUNISIA (5 Place de la Victoire, Tunis)

Ambassador and Consul-General: J. H. Lambert, CMG.

OF TUNISIA IN THE USA (2408 Massachussetts Ave., NW, Washington, D.C., 20008)

Ambassador: Ali Hedda.

OF THE USA IN TUNISIA (144 Ave. de la Liberté, Tunis)

Ambassador: Edward W. Mulcahy.

OF TUNISIA TO THE UNITED NATIONS

Ambassador: Mahmoud Mestiri.

Books of Reference

Statistical Information: Institut National de la Statistique (Dar-el-Bey, Tunis) was set up on 13 March 1947. Its main publications are: *Annuaire statistique de la Tunisie* (latest issue, 1969).

Journal Officiel de la République Tunisienne (in Arabic and French)
Tunisie, 1953. (*L'Encyclopédie d'outre-mer.*) Paris, 1953
Bannour, A. (ed.), *Economic Yearbook of Tunisia.* 2nd ed. Tunis, 1966
Garas, F., *Bourguiba et la Naissance d'une Nation.* Paris, 1956
Knapp, W., *Tunisia.* London, 1970
Ling, D. L., *Tunisia: From Protectorate to Republic.* Indiana Univ. Press, 1967
Rossi, P., *Bourguiba's Tunisia.* Tunis, 1967
Rudebeck, L., *The Tunisian Experience: Party and People.* London, 1970
Sylvester, A., *Tunisia.* London, 1969
Tlatli, S. E., *Tunisie Nouvelle: Problèmes et Perspectives.* Tunis, 1957
Vibert, J., *Tableau de l'Économie Tunisienne.* Tunis, 1955

TURKEY

Türkiye Cumhuriyet

Capital: Ankara
Population: 40·2m. (1975)
GNP per capita: US$990 (1976)

HISTORY. The Turkish War of Independence (1919–22), following the disintegration of the Ottoman Empire, was led and won by Mustafa Kemal (Atatürk) on behalf of the Grand National Assembly which first met in Ankara on 23 April 1920. On 20 Jan. 1921 the Grand National Assembly voted a constitution which declared that all sovereignty belonged to the people and vested all power, both executive and legislative, in the Grand National Assembly. The name 'Ottoman Empire' was later replaced by 'Turkey'. On 1 Nov. 1922 the Grand National Assembly abolished the office of Sultan and Turkey became a republic on 29 Oct. 1923.

On 27 May 1960 the Turkish Army, directed by a National Unity Committee under the leadership of Gen. Cemal Gürsel, overthrew the government of the Democratic Party. The Grand National Assembly was dissolved and party activities were suspended. Party activities were legally resumed on 12 Jan. 1961. A new constitution was approved in a referendum held on 9 July 1961 and general elections were held the same year.

AREA AND POPULATION. The Treaty of Peace between the Allied Powers and Turkey, which was signed at Lausanne on 24 July 1923, defined the European frontier of the new Turkey and to some extent her Asiatic frontiers. This treaty was ratified by the Grand National Assembly in Ankara on 23 Aug. 1923 and entered into force 6 Aug. 1924.

The Treaty of Lausanne and the conventions attached to it provided for the demilitarization of zones adjoining the European frontier, the Dardanelles and the Bosphorus, subject to the right to maintain a garrison at İstanbul, for the demilitarization of İmroz, Bozcaada (Tenedos) and Tavşan Islands, as well as the islands in the Sea of Marmara with one exception and for a special administrative regime in İmroz and Bozcaada.

On 10 July 1936 a new Straits Convention was signed at Montreux (ratified on 9 Nov. 1936) to take the place of the 1923 Convention, whereby Turkey obtained the right of re-militarizing the zone of the Straits, and this area was re-occupied by Turkish troops on 21 July 1936. The International Commission of the Straits ceased to function on 30 Sept. 1936.

By an agreement between the Turkish and French Governments concluded at Ankara on 23 June 1939, the Sanjak of Alexandretta (the Hatay) was incorporated in the Turkish Republic.

The area of Turkey (including lakes) is 779,452 sq. km (300,947 sq. miles). Area in Europe (Trakya), 23,764 sq. km. Area in Asia (Anadolu), 755,855 sq. km; population, 1970, 32,394,384; in 1975 estimated at 40,197,669.

The census population of Turkey is given as follows:

	Males	*Females*	*Total*	*Increase %*
1927	6,563,879	7,084,391	13,648,270	—
1935	7,936,770	8,221,248	16,158,018	21·2
1940	8,898,912	8,922,038	17,820,950	17·3
1945	9,446,580	9,343,594	18,790,174	10·5
1950	10,527,085	10,420,103	20,947,188	22·9
1955	12,233,421	11,831,342	24,064,763	29·7
1960	14,163,888	13,590,932	27.754,820	28·9
1965	15,996,964	15,394,457	31,391,421	24·9
1970	18,006,986	17,598,190	35,605,176	25·1

The population of the İls, at the census of 26 Oct. 1975, was as follows:

Adana	1,234,735	Erzincan	284,660	Maraş	620,246
Adıyaman	345,764	Erzurum	749,157	Mardin	529,260
Afyonkarahisar	576,860	Eskişehir	492,902	Muğla	401,413
Ağrı	337,606	Gaziantep	715,474	Muş	252,135
Amasya	318,082	Gireşun	462,449	Nevşehir	248,971
Ankara	2,572,562	Gümüsane	286,922	Niğde	460,928
Antalya	669,913	Hakkari	126,241	Ordu	661,679
Artvin	227,107	Hatay	744,318	Rize	334,952
Aydin	607,126	Isparta	710,728	Sakarya	495,771
Balıkesir	788,576	İçel	322,062	Samsun	904,774
Bilecik	136,011	İstanbul	3,864,493	Siirt	389,347
Bingöl	209,107	İzmir	1,660,529	Sinop	266,609
Bitlis	218,997	Kars	701,772	Sivas	739,073
Bolu	427,273	Kastamonu	436,946	Tekirdağ	318,704
Burdur	222,375	Kayseri	674,015	Tokat	592,612
Bursa	960,034	Kırklareli	268,224	Trabzon	716,168
Çanakkale	367,121	Kırşehir	231,973	Tunceli	163,273
Çankırı	266,450	Kocaeli	478,468	Urfa	598,238
Çorum	550,426	Konya	1,423,910	Uşak	228,715
Denizli	556,173	Kütahya	480,442	Van	386,059
Diyarbakir	649,796	Malatya	577,309	Yozgat	497,960
Edirne	337,898	Manisa	870,841	Zonguldak	829,204
Elâziğ	417,751				

The population of towns of over 70,000 inhabitants was as follows in 1970:

İstanbul	2,132,407	Erzurum	133,494	Antalya	95,616
Ankara	1,236,152	Samsun	134,081	Kırıkkale	91,658
İzmir	520,838	Sivas	133,979	Balıkesir	85,004
Adana	347,454	Malatya	128,891	Denizli	82,372
Bursa	275,953	Kocaeli	120,694	İskenderun	79,291
Eskişehir	216,373	İçel	112,982	Trabzon	80,795
Gaziantep	227,652	Elaziğ	107,368	Tarsus	74,510
Konya	200,444	Maraş	110,761	Zonguldak	77,135
Kayseri	160,958	Adapazarı	101,483	Manisa	72,276
Diyarbakir	149,566	Urfa	100,654		

The population of Turkey according to 'mother tongue' (1965 census) comprises 28,317,579 Turks, 2,180,721 Kurds, 365,971 Arabs, 57,337 Circassians, 48,143 Greeks, 32,484 Armenians, 32,334 Georgians, 23,715 Lazes and 9,124 Spanish-speaking Jews.

CONSTITUTION AND GOVERNMENT. The constitution of 9 July 1961 has consolidated the modernizing reforms: the abolition of the Caliphate and of old-style religious education (1924), the prohibition of oriental headgear (1925), the suppression of the dervish orders (1925), the introduction of the Western civil code, ending polygamy (1926), the substitution of the Latin for the Arabic alphabet (1928), the abolition of old-style titles (1934) and the prohibition of clerical garb (1934).

Religious courts were abolished in 1924, Islam ceased to be the official state religion in 1928, women were given the franchise and western-style surnames were adopted in 1934.

Thirty-five Articles of the 1961 Constitution were amended in Sept. 1971 and 9 temporary articles added. Five more articles were amended in 1973 and a further one in 1974.

Legislative power is vested in the Grand National Assembly, executive power in the President of the Republic and the Council of Ministers, judicial power in independent courts. The President of the Republic is elected by the National Assembly and the Senate in joint session for a 7-year term; he is not re-eligible.

Turkish men and women are entitled to vote at the age of 21 and to become deputies at the age of 30. Secret ballot was introduced by law on 10 July 1948.

Elections held on 5 June 1977 resulted in the following composition of the National Assembly: Republican People's Party, 213; Justice Party, 189; Republican Reliance Party, 3; National Salvation Party, 24; National Action Party, 16; Democratic Party, 1; Independents, 4; Total, 450.

The Senate (150 members elected by direct vote, 15 nominated by the President of the Republic, and 19 life senators, formerly members of the National Unity Committee) is composed of (after 5 June 1977 elections): Republican People's Party, 78; Justice Party, 64; National Salvation Party, 6; National Action Party, 1; Republican Reliance Party, 4; Independents, 1; Nominees of the President of the Republic, 11; former President of the Republic, 1.

National flag: A white crescent and star on red.

National anthem: Korkma! Sönmez bu şafaklarda yüzen al sancak (words by Mehmed Akif Ersoy; tune by Zeki Güngör; adopted 12 March 1921).

Past Presidents of the Republic: Mustafa Kemal Atatürk (29 Oct, 1923–10 Nov. 1938), İsmet İnönü (11 Nov. 1938–21 May 1950), Celâl Bayar (22 May 1950–27 May 1960), Cemal Gürsel (26 Oct. 1961–27 March 1966), Cevdet Sunay (29 March 1966–28 March 1973).

President of the Republic: Fahri Korutürk (elected 6 April 1973 by 365 out of 557 votes).

The Coalition Cabinet was in Jan. 1978 constituted as follows:

Prime Minister: Bülent Ecevit.

Deputy Prime Ministers: Orhan Eyüboğlu, Dr Turhan Feyzioğlu, Dr Faruk Sükan. *Ministers of State:* Hikmet Çetin, Enver Akova, Dr Lütfi Doğan, Salih Yıldız, Ali Rıza Septioğlu, Mustafa Kılıç, Ahmet Şener. *Justice:* Mehmet Can. *National Defence:* Hasan Esat Işık. *Interior:* İrfan Özaydınlı. *Foreign Affairs:* Gündüz Ökçün. *Finance:* Ziya Müezzinoğlu. *National Education:* Necdet Uğur. *Public Works:* Şerafettin Elçi. *Commerce:* Teoman Köprülüler. *Health and Social Welfare:* Dr Mete Tan. *Custom and Monopolies:* Tuncay Mataracı. *Communications:* Güneş Öngüt. *Food, Agriculture and Animal Husbandry:* Mehmet Yüceler. *Labour:* Bahir Ersoy. *Industry and Technology:* Orhan Alp. *Industrial State Enterprises:* Dr Kenan Bulutoğlu. *Energy and Natural Resources:* Dr Deniz Baykal. *Tourism and Information:* Alev Çoşkun. *Housing and Reconstruction:* Ahmet Karaaslan. *Rural Affairs and Co-operatives:* Ali Topuz. *Forestry:* Vecdi İlhan. *Youth and Sport:* Yüksel Çakmur. *Social Security:* Hilmi Işgüzar. *Culture:* Dr Ahmet Taner Kişlalı. *Local Administration:* Mahmut Özdemir.

Local Government. The constitution of 1921 provided for the administrative division of the country into *İl,* province (now 67 in number), divided into *Ilçe* (district), subdivided in their turn into *Bucak* (township or commune). At the head of each İl is a Vali representing the Government. Each İl has its own elective council.

The İlçe is regarded as a mere grouping of Bucaks for certain purposes of general administration. The Bucak or cummune is an autonomous entity and possesses an elective council charged with the administration of such matters as are not reserved to the State.

According to the municipal law passed in 1930, Turkish women have the right to be electors and to be elected at municipal elections.

DEFENCE. Several bills for the reorganization of the armed forces were passed in June 1961 by the Grand National Assembly. One of these placed all organizations connected with national defence under the authority of the Minister of National Defence. Another created a Supreme Council of National Security, under the chairmanship of the Prime Minister, with the object of co-ordinating the resources of the country in case of war. Besides the Minister of National Defence and the Chief of the General Staff, the heads of economic Ministries are members of this council

Military service in Army, Air Force and Navy is 18 months for officers and 20 months for other ranks. Men are called up when they reach the age of 20. The average number of men liable to be called up is 175,000 every year. The strength of the forces is about 514,000 officers and men. The total number that could be mobilized is estimated at over 2m.

Army. The land forces contain 14 infantry divisions (2 mechanized), 1 armoured division and 6 armoured brigades (M-48 tanks), 1 commando and 5 infantry brigades, 4 mechanized infantry brigades, 1 parachute brigade. The units are largely equipped with 10·5 cm, 15·5 cm and 20·3 cm howitzer guns. Ground forces have been assigned to the South-Eastern Command of NATO, of which İzmir is the headquarters. Total strength, 375,000; trained reservists, 800,000.

Navy. The Navy includes 15 diesel-powered submarines (3 new built in the Federal Republic of Germany and 12 old *ex*-US patrol submarines), 12 old *ex*-US destroyers, 2 new Turkish-built frigates, 3 minelayers, 6 coastal minelayers, 8 fast missile vessels, 21 coastal minesweepers, 8 patrol vessels, 13 torpedo boats 4 inshore minesweepers, 9 minehunting boats, 37 coastal patrol craft, 3 repair ships 2 submarine support ships, 1 large training ship (*ex*-yacht), 2 landing ships, 33 landing craft, 20 minor landing craft, 2 submarine rescue ships, 5 oilers, 8 transports, 2 survey ships, 2 survey boats, 4 boom defence vessels, 3 gate vessels, 11 auxiliary vessels, 8 tugs and 2 tenders. Five *ex*-US diesel-powered old patrol submarines were taken over as non-operational harbour training boats. Ships under construction include 3 patrol diesel-powered submarines being built in the Federal Republic of Germany.

The naval bases are at Gölcük in the Gulf of İzmut, at İskenderun, at Taskizak (İstanbul) and at İzmir. Personnel strength in 1978 was 3,400 officers and 41,600 ratings.

Air Force. The Air Force is under the control of the General Staff and, operationally, under 6 ATAF. It is organized as 2 tactical air forces, with F-5s equipping about 7 fighter-bomber/interceptor and 2 reconnaissance squadrons: F-100 Super Sabres in 3 fighter-bomber squadrons; F-104G and F-104S Starfighters in 4 squadrons; F-4E Phantoms in 2 squadrons; and 2 squadrons of *ex*-USAF Convair F-102A supersonic interceptors, plus Nike-Hercules surface-to-air missile batteries. The 4 or 5 transport squadrons are equipped with Transall C-160, C-130 Hercules, Viscount and C-47 aircraft. Training types include T-33A and T-37A advanced trainers and T-41 and T-34 Mentor primary trainers. Personnel strength is about 45,000, with 370 combat aircraft.

INTERNATIONAL RELATIONS

Membership. Turkey is a member of UN, OECD, NATO, Council of Europe and CENTO.

ECONOMY

Planning. The first 5-year development plan, 1963–67, provided for investments of TL68,000m. (at 1965 prices); TL64,000m. were invested, the gross national product increasing at the rate of 6·7% per annum. The second 5-year plan (1968–72) aimed at achieving an annual growth of 7%; external financing amounting to US$1,716m. The third 5-year plan (1973–78) sets out to achieve an annual growth of 7·9%.

Budget. Estimates of revenue and expenditure (in TL1,000) for financial years 1 March–28/29 Feb.:

	1974–75	*1975–76*	*1976–77*	*1977–78*
Revenue	75,657,576	97,888,231	139,719,980	203,449,003
Expenditure	82,411,411	106,888,231	153,637,351	222,949,003

Currency. The Turkish *Lira* (TL) is divided into 100 *kuruş* (*piastres*). Coins in general circulation are of the following values: 5, 10, 25 and 50 *kuruş*; 1, 2½ and 5 *Lira*. Bank-notes in circulation are as follows: 5, 10, 20, 50, 100 and 500 *Lira*.

Banking. The Turkish banking system is composed of the Central Bank of the Republic of Turkey (Merkez Bankası) and 45 other banks. Thirteen (including the Central Bank) are established by special laws.

The 13 banks established by special laws carry out specialized banking activities beside their general banking transactions. Five of them are state economic enterprises whose capital is owned wholly by the State. They include: Ziraat Bankası (rural credits, capital: TL1,500m.), Sümerbank (textiles, etc., capital: TL1,500m.), Etibank (mining, energy, capital: TL500m.), İller Bankası (urban works, capital: TL1,200m.), İstanbul Emniyet Sandığı (savings bank). Six of them are joint-stock companies; the majority of their share capital is owned by the public sector. They include: the Emlâk Kredi Bankası (housing, capital: TL1,000m.), Denizcilik Bankası (shipping, capital: TL1,500m.), Türkiye Vakıflar Bankası (investments of pious foundations, funds, capital: TL50m.), Türkiye Halk Bankası (small business, capital: TL50m.); Türkiye Öğretmenler Bankası (teachers' housing, capital: TL30m.), T. C. Turizm Bankası (tourism, capital: TL300m.).

The development banks are: Devlet Yatırım Bankası (investment credits to state economic enterprises, capital: TL1,000m.), Türkiye Sınaî Kalkınma Bankası (investment credit to the private sector, capital: TL 50m.), Sınaî Yatırım ve Kredi Bankası (industrial medium-term credit, capital: TL40m.).

Of the 31 commercial banks, 5 are foreign banks established in Turkey, and one is a bank whose capital is shared by a foreign bank.

The total deposits with banks at 31 Dec. 1972 amounted to TL62,994m.

Weights and Measures. The metric system came into force on 1 Jan. 1934. On 24 May 1928 the Grand National Assembly made European numerals obligatory as from 1 June 1929.

On 1 March 1917 the Gregorian calendar was introduced into Turkey, to be used side by side with the Hegira calendar, while as from 26 Dec. 1925 it was decided finally to adopt the Gregorian calendar alone, the Turkish civil year 1342 becoming 1926.

ENERGY AND NATURAL RESOURCES

Electricity. The potential hydro-electric power in Turkey is estimated at 56,000m. kwh. In 1976 the electrical power plants (hydro-electric or thermal) produced 18,500m. kwh.

Oil. Oil is being produced in Garzan and Raman by the Turkish Petroleum Company. Under the oil law of 14 Oct. 1954 private companies can explore and produce oil. Four private companies (2 of them foreign) produced 3,095,000 tons in 1975. The 3 refineries refined 12m. tons of crude oil in 1975. With a fourth refinery, introduced in 1973, total refining capacity now reaches 24m. tons a year. The oil pipeline Batman–İskenderun (494 km) was opened on 4 Jan. 1967. Imports (refined locally) in 1975 were 9·63m. tons.

Minerals. The Turkish provinces, especially those in Asia, are reported rich in minerals. Turkey is one of the four principal producers of chrome in the world.

Production of principal minerals (in 1,000 tonnes) was:

	1972	*1973*	*1974*	*1975*	*1976*
Coal (S and P)	7,871	7,851	8,554	8,365	4,632
Lignite (S and P)	10,260	10,665	11,161	11,851	7,440
Chrome (S and P)	690	574	726	946	830
Sulphur (S)	21	18	19	19	21
Manganese (P)	15	4	4	35	21
Iron ore (S and P)	2,005	2,570	2,285	2,296	3,081
Copper (Blister) (S)	17	15	19	16	28
Petroleum (S and P) (tons)	3,409	3,604	3,430	3,095	2,592

(S) State; (P) Private enterprise.

Of the Government organizations producing these ores, Zonguldak coal mines operate under the Turkish State Coal Exploitation; while the copper mines at Murgul and Ergani, the Eastern chromite mines, Keçiborlu sulphur, Emet colemanite, Küre pyrite and cupriferous pyrite, Keban argentiferous lead mines operate under the Etibank.

Agriculture. The number of people aged 15 and over engaged in agriculture in 1975 was 9,463,310.

In 1976, 240,570 sq. km were cultivated land, 163,100 sq. km of its own and 77,470 sq. km fallow; vineyards, fruit orchards and olive groves occupied 34,600 sq. km; forest occupied 201,700 sq. km.

The soil for the most part is very fertile; the principal products are cotton, tobacco, cereals (especially wheat), figs, silk, olives and olive oil, dried fruits, liquorice root, nuts, almonds, mohair, skins and hides, furs, wool, gums, canary seed, linseed and sesame. The principal tobacco districts are Samsun, Bafra, Çarsamba, İzmit and İzmir. Two-thirds of the exports of leaf tobacco goes to the USA. The principal centre for silk production is Bursa. The production of olive oil, mainly confined to the İls of Aydın and Balıkesir, is very important (178,000 tonnes in 1976). Sugar production (refined) in 1976 was 982,329 tonnes. Agricultural production (in tonnes) in 1976 included 3·08m. grapes, 884,000 oranges and lemons, 245,000 hazelnuts, 1m. apples, 1,097,000 olives, 760,000 onions, 2·85m. potatoes. Tea production (fresh leaves) was 301,000 tonnes.

Turkey produced 3,500 tonnes of flax fibre and 7,000 tonnes of hemp fibre in 1975. Cotton production was 480,000 tonnes. Agricultural tractors numbered 243,066 in 1975.

Yield (in 1,000 tonnes) of principal crops:

	1972	*1973*	*1974*	*1975*	*1976*
Wheat	12,200	10,000	11,167	14,750	16,500
Barley	3,750	2,900	3,330	4,500	4,916
Oats	396	380	380	390	400
Maize	1,030	1,100	1,200	1,200	1,310
Rye	755	690	560	750	740
Rice	122	159	150	150	158
Tobacco	173	149	203	193	315

On 7 June 1945 the Grand National Assembly passed the Land Reform Bill under which large tracts of agricultural land are being distributed to peasants without land or with insufficient for their subsistence.

Livestock, 1976, 41,504,000 sheep, 14,973,000 ordinary goats, 3,535,000 Angora goats, 14·1m. cattle, 1,465,000 asses, 853,000 horses, 1,056,000 buffaloes.

In 1975 Turkey produced 53,325 tonnes of wool and 5,590 tonnes of mohair.

Forestry. On 8 Feb. 1937 a new forest law was voted, providing for state control of all forests, including those under private ownership. It contains measures for planting, protection against fire, marauders and insects, and lays down penalties for infringements of its clauses. The most wooded İls are Kastamonu, Aydın, Bursa, Bolu, Trabzon, Konya and Balıkesir. Of the forest land, 10,417,560 hectares belonged to the State in 1951. In 1975 total forest land was 20·17m. hectares.

Fisheries. On 25 Aug. 1964 Turkey extended her waters in which she has exclusive fishing rights to 12 nautical miles.

INDUSTRY AND TRADE

Industry. Production in 1976 included 12·4m. tonnes of cement, 295,029 tonnes of paper. Industrial plants number about 30,000.

In 1976 Turkey produced 1·2m. tonnes of pig-iron, 1·46m. tonnes of steel ingots and 1·15m. tonnes of rolled products. There are steel works at Karabük, Ereğli and İskenderun.

Labour. On 27 June 1945 a Ministry of Labour was set up, superseding the Department of Labour under the control of the Ministry of Economic Affairs. According to the strikes and lock-outs law, which came into effect on 24 Aug. 1963, strikes and lock-outs may be declared only after due effort has been made to negotiate and after the local authorities as well as the Ministry of Labour have been informed.

Conditions of work are regulated by the Labour Act of 12 Aug. 1967, which covers all places of work, employing more than 3 persons, outside agriculture. Children under 16 must not be employed for more than 8 hours a day, and employment should not impede school attendance. The Act provides for annual paid holidays of 12–24 working days and regulates overtime payment.

The trade-union movement began in 1947. There are 4 national confederations (including Türk-İş and Disk) and 6 federations. There are 35 unions affiliated to Türk-İş and 17 employers' federations affiliated to Disk. In 1972, labour unions totalled 660 and employers' unions, 109.

Employment, 1975: Manufacturing, 1,243,567; construction, 447,342; transport, communications and warehousing, 512,327; mining, 108,506; services, 176,207. There were 157,466 manufacturing firms, 236,995 trading establishments and 580,635 service establishments.

Commerce. Imports and exports (in US$1m.) for calendar years:

	1974	*1975*	*1976*	*1977*
Imports	3,778	4,739	5,128	5,218
Exports	1,532	1,401	1,960	1,487

Imports and exports of chief commodities (in US$1m.):

Imports	*1974*	*1975*	*1976*	*Exports*	*1974*	*1975*	*1976*
Machinery	811·1	1,256·9	1,343·9	Tobacco	197·6	183·3	251·3
Iron and steel	530·6	679·1	545·7	Fruits	297·0	282·4	375·3
Oil, etc.	762·8	811·3	1,125·7	Cotton	250·7	230·0	428·0
Transport	245·9	332·2	517·8	Minerals	84·7	105·7	110·0
Fabrics and yarns	104·6	117·8	107·3	Cereals	25·3	33·2	37·6
Medicines and dyes	280·4	423·9	459·0				

Total trade between Turkey and UK (British Department of Trade returns, in £1,000 sterling):

	1973	*1974*	*1975*	*1976*	*1977*
Imports to UK	33,872	35,152	34,595	60,395	56,733
Exports and re-exports from UK	81,770	104,624	143,548	210,897	210,181

Tourism. A tourist industry is developing. The number of foreign tourists was over 1·6m. in 1976.

COMMUNICATIONS

Roads. Turkey had, in 1975, 59,069 km of national highways, of which 25,307 were hard surfaced. In 1974 there were registered 618,302 motor vehicles, including 303,845 passenger cars and 21,387 buses.

Railways. The total length of railway lines in 1975 was 8,138 km, all state-owned; 28 km are electrified. In 1975 Turkish railways carried 13·5m. tonnes.

Aviation. The State Airways Administration, formed in 1938, has been converted into the mixed company Turkish Airlines (Türk Havayollari Anonim Ortaklığı); British Airways became a partner in July 1957. It conducts foreign services to Athens, Beirut, Brussels, Amsterdam, Munich, Rome, Frankfurt, Vienna, London, Paris, Belgrade, Nicosia and Tel-Aviv. In 1972 Turkish Airlines carried 1,774,476 passengers, 1·39m. kg of mail and 144·5m. kg of freight. İstanbul or Ankara are connected with all the principal countries by 27 national airlines.

Shipping. In 1974 Turkish Maritime Lines and private companies had a gross tonnage of 1,252,000, of which 54 vessels were cargo and tankers, and 19 were passenger liners. The main ports in order of tonnage capacity are: İstanbul, İzmir, Samsun, Mersin, İskenderun and Trabzon.

Ports built or extended since 1950 are İskenderun, Ereğli, Trabzon, Samsun, Mersin, Zonguldak, Giresun, Hopa, Antalya and Bandirma. New facilities have been provided at Haydarpaşa, Salıpazari, Hopa, Yarımca and İzmir.

Post and Broadcasting. Number of telephones in 1977 was 1,130,978; İstanbul, 365,572; Ankara, 176,707.

In 1975 there were 4·12m. licensed (and over 1m. unlicensed) wireless sets. There were 639,348 television receivers.

Newspapers. In 1975 there were 2,362 daily newspapers and periodicals in the Turkish language, 2 in Greek, 1 in French and 1 in English. In 1976, 27 dailies were published in Ankara, 40 dailies in İstanbul, 6 dailies in İzmir, 5 dailies in Bursa and 4 dailies in Konya.

JUSTICE, RELIGION, EDUCATION AND WELFARE

Justice. The unified legal system consists of: (1) justices of the peace (single judges with limited but summary penal and civil jurisdiction); (2) courts of first instance (single judges, dealing with cases outside the jurisdiction of (3) and (4)); (3) central criminal courts (a president and 2 judges, dealing with cases where the crime is punishable by imprisonment over 5 years); (4) commercial courts (3 judges); (5) state security courts, to prosecute offences against the integrity of the state (a president and 4 judges, 2 of the latter being military).

The civil and military Courts of Cassation sit at Ankara.

The Council of State is the highest administration tribunal; it consists of 5 chambers. Its 31 judges are nominated from among high-ranking personalities in politics, economy, law, the army, etc.

The Military Court of Cassation in Ankara is the highest military tribunal. The Military Administrative Court deals with the judicial control of administrative acts and deeds concerning military personnel.

The Constitutional Court, set up under the constitution, can review and annul legislation and try the President of the Republic, Ministers and senior judges. It consists of 15 regular and 5 alternate members.

The Civil Code and the Code of Obligations have been adapted from the corresponding Swiss codes. The Penal Code is largely based upon the Italian Penal Code, and the Code of Civil Procedure closely resembles that of the Canton of Neuchâtel. The Commercial Code is based on the German.

Religion. Freedom of religion is guaranteed by the constitution. Although Islam is no longer the official state religion of Turkey, Moslems form 98·2% of the population. The administration of the Moslem religious organizations is in charge of the Presidency of Religious Affairs, attached to the Prime Minister's office. Under the imperial system the non-Moslem communities were recognized as organized communities or *millets*, the heads of which exercised spiritual as well as civil functions; their authority is now purely ecclesiastical. The Turkish Republic is a secular state.

Istanbul is the seat of the Œcumenical Patriarch, who is the head of the Orthodox Church in Turkey. The Armenian Church (Gregorian) is ruled by a Patriarch in İstanbul who is subordinate to the Katholikos of Etchmiadzin, the spiritual head of all Armenians. The Armenian Apostolic Church is ruled by the Patriarch of Cilicia. The Chaldeans (Nestorian Uniats) have a Bishop at Mardin. The Syrian Uniats have a See of Mardin and Amida, but it is united with their Patriarchate of Antioch (residence, Damascus). Greek Uniats (Byzantine Rite) have as their Ordinary in İstanbul, the Titular Bishop of Gratianopolis. The Latins have an Apostolic Delegate in İstanbul and an Archbishop in İzmir, but their Patriarch of İstanbul is titular and non-resident. There is a Grand Rabbi (Hahambaşı) in İstanbul for the Jews, who are nearly all Sephardim.

At the 1965 census there were in Turkey 31,391,421 Moslems, 73,725 Orthodox, 69,526 Gregorians, 25,833 Roman Catholics, 22,983 Protestants, 14,758 other Christians (unspecified), 18,267 Jews, 14,661 adherents of other religions, 1,212 without religion and 602 undeclared or unknown.

A law passed in Dec. 1934 forbids the wearing of clerical garb for those other than religious leaders except in places of worship and during divine service. The constitution forbids the political exploitation of religion or any impairment of the secular character of the republic.

In lieu of religious formulae, all citizens take oaths on their honour.

Education. Elementary education is compulsory and co-educational and, in state schools, free. All children from 7 to 12 are to receive primary instruction, which may be given in state schools, schools maintained by communities, or private schools, or, subject to certain tests, at home. The state schools are under the direct control of the Ministry of Education. They include primary schools, secondary or middle schools, and *lycées* or secondary schools of a superior kind. There are also training schools for male and female teachers, and technical schools. There are 3 universities in İstanbul, Robert College became Bosphorus University in 1971, 3 in Ankara (including the Middle East Technical University designed to meet the technical needs of the whole Middle East), the Aegean University in İzmir, Atatürk University in Erzurum (opened in Nov. 1957) and the Black Sea Technical University in Trabzon. A new university is being built at Sivas, Central Anatolia. The important non-Moslem communities in İstanbul maintain their own schools, which, like all 'private' schools, are subject to the supervision of the Ministry of Education.

Literacy of the population of 6 years and over was 10·6% in 1927, 19·2% in 1935, 29% in 1945, 40·9% in 1955, 39·5% in 1960, 48·7% in 1965, 49% in 1970.

Religious instruction in schools, hitherto prohibited, was made optional in elementary and middle schools in May 1948. There are many training schools for Moslem clergy as well as a Faculty of Theology in Ankara.

Statistics for 1974–75	*Number*	*Teachers*	*Students*
Primary schools (state and private)	42,209	160,584	5,381,000
Middle schools (state and private)	2,635	26,881	927,000
Lycées (state and private)	773	14,000	333,000
Professional and technical schools	1,020	18,000	300,000
Faculties (university and higher education)	195	13,812	264,000

On 1 Nov. 1928 the Grand National Assembly voted a law for the adoption of Latin characters as from 1 Dec. 1928. The publication of books in Arabic characters was forbidden after 1 Jan. 1929.

Health. Public health is the responsibility of the Ministry of Health and Social Welfare, established in 1920; social insurance for workers comes under the Workers' Insurance Institution attached to the Ministry of Labour. A law promulgated in 1961 and being implemented from 1963 provides for the nationalization of the health services within 15 years. In 1972, 1·52m. workers and employees were covered by social insurance, including free medical care.

In 1975 there were 21,714 doctors and nearly 85,872 beds in some 807 hospitals.

The counterpart of the Red Cross in Turkey is the Red Crescent Society founded in 1877.

DIPLOMATIC REPRESENTATIVES

OF TURKEY IN GREAT BRITAIN (43 Belgrave Sq., London, SW1X 8PA)

Ambassador: Turgut Menemencioğlu (accredited 14 Dec. 1972).

OF GREAT BRITAIN IN TURKEY (Sehit Ersan Caddesi 46/A, Canyaka, Ankara)

Ambassador: Sir Derek Dodson, KCMG, MC.

OF TURKEY IN THE USA (1606–23rd St., NW, Washington, D.C., 20008)

Ambassador: Melih Esenbel.

OF THE USA IN TURKEY (110 Ataturk Blvd., Ankara)

Ambassador: Ronald I. Spiers.

OF TURKEY TO THE UNITED NATIONS

Ambassador: Ilter Turkmen.

Books of Reference

Statistical Information: The State Institute of Statistics in Ankara consists of a research bureau and 10 sections dealing with agriculture, education, foreign trade, etc. It published an *Annuaire Statistique/İstatistik Yılığı* (1928–53) and *Aylık İstatistik Bülteni*, Monthly Bulletin of Statistics.

The Turkish Constitution, 1971. Ankara, 1972
Resmî Gazete, Official Gazette. Ankara
Konjonktür. Ministry of Commerce (three times a year, from 1940)
Banque Centrale de la République de Turquie. *Bulletin Mensuel* (from Jan. 1953)
Bulletins of the Chambers of Commerce of İstanbul and İzmir
Turkish Trade Directory, 1971–72. İstanbul, 1971
Ahmad, F., *The Turkish Experiment in Democracy*. London, 1977
Akurgal, E., *Ancient Civilizations and Ruins of Turkey*. Ankara, 1973
Aslanapa, O., *Turkish Art and Architecture*. London, 1971
Cenani, Rasim, *Foreign Capital Investments in Turkey*. 2nd ed. İstanbul, 1958
Dewdney, J. C., *Turkey*. London, 1971
Economic News Digest. Ankara, 1971
Frey, F. W., *The Turkish Political Elite*. M.I.T. Press, 1965
Goodwin, G., *A History of Ottoman Architecture*. London, 1971

Hotham, D., *The Turks*. London, 1973
Kinross, Lord, *Atatürk*. London, 1964
Koray, Enver, *Türkiye Tarih Yayınları Bibliografyası 1729–1950* (*Bibliography of Historical Works on Turkey*). Ankara, 1952
Kortepeter, C. M., *Ottoman Imperialism During Reformation: Europe and the Caucasus*. London, 1972
Landau, J. M., *Radical Politics in Modern Turkey*. Leiden, 1974
Lewis, B., *The Emergence of Modern Turkey*. OUP, 1961
Lewis, G., *Turkey*. 3rd ed. London, 1965
Lewis, R., *Everyday Life in Ottoman Turkey*. London, 1971
Mair, C., *A Time in Turkey*. London, 1973
Mango, A., *Discovering Turkey*. London, 1971
Newman, B., *Turkey and the Turks*. London, 1968
Price, M. P., *A History of Turkey*. London, 1968
Robinson, D. R., *The First Turkish Republic*. Harvard Univ. Press and OUP, 1964
Tamkoç, M., *The Warrior Diplomats*. Univ. of Utah Press, 1976
Weiker W., *Political Tutelage and Democracy in Turkey*. Leiden, 1972
Williams, G., *Turkey: A Traveller's Guide and History*. London, 1967

State Library: MilliKütüphane Müdürlüğü, Ankara. *Director-General:* Müjgân Cunbur.

THE TURKS AND CAICOS ISLANDS

Capital: Grand Turk
Population: 5,558 (1970)

AREA AND POPULATION. The Turks and Caicos Islands are geographically a portion of the Bahamas, of which they form the two south-eastern groups. There are upwards of 30 small cays; area 192 sq. miles (430 sq. km). Only 6 are inhabited; the largest, Grand Caicos, is 30 miles long by 2 to 3 miles broad. The seat of government is at Grand Turk, 7 miles long by 1·25 broad; 2,287 inhabitants. Population (1970 census), 5,558. South Caicos, 1,018; Middle Caicos, 362; North Caicos, 989; Providenciales, 558.

Vital statistics (1976): Births, 199; marriages, 39; deaths, 44.

CONSTITUTION AND GOVERNMENT. A new Constitution was introduced in Sept. 1976, providing for an Executive Council and a Legislative Council. The Governor retains responsibility for external affairs, internal security, defence and certain other matters. The Executive Council comprises 3 official members: the Financial Secretary, the Chief Secretary and the Attorney-General; a Chief Minister and 3 other ministers from among the elected members of the Legislative Council; and is presided over by the Governor. The Legislative Council consists of a Speaker, the 3 official members of the Executive Council, 11 elected members and 2 nominated members.

Governor: J. C. Strong.

Flag: British Blue Ensign with the shield of the Colony in the fly.

ECONOMY

Budget. 1976 revenue (revised) US$4,922,711 including $2,348,826 budgetary aid; expenditure (revised) $4,076,437.

1977 revenue (estimated) US$4,363,610 including $1·91m. budgetary aid; expenditure (estimated) $4,363,610.

Currency. The currency in circulation is US$.

Banking. The Government Savings Bank has 3 branches. Barclays Bank International and the Oxford International Bank and Trust Co. Ltd have offices in Grand Turk with branches in South Caicos, North Caicos and Providenciales.

COMMERCE (1976). Exports (estimated) US$1,608,548. Imports (estimated) $4,939,125. Principal imports, food, drink, tobacco and clothing. Exports, 1975–76 season, crawfish, US$473,093; conch, $370,525.

Trade with UK (British Department of Trade returns, in £1,000 sterling):

	1974	*1975*	*1976*	*1977*
Imports to UK	304	107	133	6
Exports and re-exports from UK	3,467	1,873	278	321

TOURISM. Number of hotels and guest houses, 15 (beds 219). Number of visitors, 1976, 7,055.

COMMUNICATIONS

Aviation. There is a 5,500 ft paved airfield on Grand Turk under the control of the US Air Force but open to civil aviation. On South Caicos there is a 6,000 ft paved airstrip. There are small unpaved airstrips on the other 4 inhabited islands. Southeast Airlines operate a twice or thrice weekly passenger service to Miami.

Bahamas Air operate a once weekly scheduled passenger service to the Bahamas. Trans Jamaica Airline operate a once fortnightly service between Kingston and Grand Turk. Air Turks and Caicos operate a twice daily service to the islands and 2 flights a week to Cap Haitien (Haiti). Turks Air Ltd operate a regular weekly cargo service to Miami.

Shipping. Registered shipping (1974), 148 sailing vessels of 1,874 tons and 22 motor vessels of 1,410 tons.

Post and Broadcasting. Air-mail is received and dispatched by Miami twice or thrice weekly. Surface mail from all parts of the world is routed *via* the US arriving at 3 weekly intervals from Miami, Florida. There is no regular outgoing surface mail. Cable & Wireless (West Indies) provide internal and international cable, telephone, telex and telegraph services and also operate telephone and telegraph services to ships at sea. A 600-line automatic exchange operates in Grand Turk, a 100-line automatic exchange in South Caicos and a 50-line automatic exchange on Providenciales. North Caicos and Salt Cay are linked with the Providenciales and Grand Turk exchanges respectively. The Government operates a radio broadcasting service from the Islands to Grand Turk, call sign VSI radio Turks and Caicos, for a total of 85 hours a week on 1,500 KHZ medium wave. Number of receivers approximately 5,000.

EDUCATION AND WELFARE

Education. Education is free and compulsory up to 15 years of age in the 14 government primary and 2 government secondary schools. There are also 2 private primary and 1 secondary schools. Number on rolls, 1 Jan. 1977, primary, 1,802 (including 130 private); secondary, 671 (including 133 private). Expenditure on education 1976 (revised) US$645,616 recurrent, $124,273 capital.

Health. In 1970 there were 2 doctors and 30 hospital beds.

TUVALU

Capital: Funafuti
Population: 5,887 (1973)

AREA AND POPULATION. Tuvalu (formerly the Ellice Islands) lie between 5° 30′ and 11° S. lat. and 176° and 180° E. long. and comprise Nanumea, Nanumanga, Niutao, Nui, Vaitupu, Nukufetau, Funafuti (administrative centre), Nukulaelae and Nurakita. Population (Dec. 1973) 5,887. Area approximately 9½ sq. miles (24 sq. km). The population is of a Polynesian race.

CONSTITUTION AND GOVERNMENT. On the recommendation of a Commissioner, appointed by the British Government, to consider requests that the island group be separated from the Gilbert Islands, a referendum was held in 1974, There was a large majority in favour of separation and this took place in Oct. 1975.

The Constitution provides for a Chief Minister and 2 other Ministers to be elected from among the 12 elected members of the House of Assembly, for which general elections took place on 29 Aug. 1977. The Cabinet, chaired by the Commissioner, consists of the 3 ministers and 2 *ex officio* members, the Attorney-General and the Financial Secretary, who are also *ex officio* members of the House of Assembly. Independence is envisaged for 1 Oct. 1978. Local Government services are provided by an elected Island Council on each of the 8 atolls.

Chief Minister: Toalipi Lauti.
Minister for Commerce and Natural Resources: Tumu Sione.
Minister for Social Services: Taui Finikaso.
Commissioner: Thomas Henry Layng.

Flag: The British Blue Ensign with the shield of the colony on a white disc in the fly.

INDUSTRY. Experiments and surveys were being undertaken in 1976 to see if the copra and fishing industries could be established.

COMMUNICATIONS. Tuvalu is linked to the outside world by Air Pacific HS748 which operates weekly, arriving on Wednesday and leaving on Thursday. Inter-island communication is undertaken by ship which takes cargo and passengers.

EDUCATION. In 1976 there was 1 secondary school jointly administered by the Government and the Church. In addition there were 8 primary schools run by Island Councils and subsidized by the central government.

HEALTH. In 1976 there was 1 central hospital with 36 beds situated at Funafuti. There were 3 doctors.

UGANDA

Capital: Kampala
Population: 11·2m. (1974)
GNP per capita: US$240 (1976)

AREA AND POPULATION. Uganda is bounded on the north by Sudan, on east by Kenya, on south by Tanzania and west by Zaïre. Total area 91,343 sq. miles (236,860 sq. km), including 15,217 sq. miles (39,459 sq. km) of swamp and water.

The population of Uganda is 11,171,900 (1974 estimate), including some 9,000 Europeans and 88,000 Asians. On 4 Aug. 1972 President Amin announced that he would ask the UK to take responsibility for Asians in Uganda holding British passports. Later that year 27,200 Asians had left Uganda for Britain. The majority of the Africans (1,044,000) are Baganda, the tribe from which the country takes its name. In 1966 some 68,000 Tutsi refugees from Rwanda, some 55,000 Sudanese refugees and some 33,000 refugees from the Congo were living in Uganda.

About 3m. Africans speak Bantu languages; there are a few Congo pygmies living near the Semliki River; the rest of the Africans belong to the Hamitic, Nilotic and Sudanese groups. Ki-Swahili is generally understood in trading centres. The capital is Kampala; the population of greater Kampala (1969), 330,700.

The official language is English.

CONSTITUTION AND GOVERNMENT. Uganda became a fully independent member of the Commonwealth on 9 Oct. 1962 after nearly 70 years of British rule. Full sovereign status was granted by the Uganda Independence Act, 1962, and the Constitution is embodied in the Uganda (Independence) Order in Council, 1962. The post of Governor-General was on 9 Oct. 1963 replaced by that of President as head of state, elected by the National Assembly for a 5-year term.

Uganda became a republic on 8 Sept. 1967. Under the 1967 Constitution, the executive authority is vested in the President. The President is assisted by a Cabinet of Ministers. Unlike the Presidential system in the USA and other countries, in Uganda the President is a Member of the National Assembly, and takes an active part in the Assembly's deliberations.

On 25 Jan. 1971, Dr A. Milton Obote was overthrown by troops led by Gen. Idi Amin.

Military Head of State: Gen. Idi Amin.

National flag: Six horizontal stripes of black, yellow, red, black, yellow, red, in the centre a small white disc bearing a representation of a Balearic Crested Crane.

For administrative purposes Uganda is divided into 10 provinces, subdivided into 38 districts. The provinces are: Busoga, Central, Eastern, Karamoja, Nile, North Buganda, Northern, South Buganda, Southern, Western.

DEFENCE

Army. The Army has a strength of 20,000 and is organized into 2 brigades, each of 4 infantry battalions, 2 mechanized, 1 commando and 1 border battalion.

Navy. A small lake patrol was being formed in 1977.

Air Force. The Air Force was formed in 1964 and later underwent rapid expansion with the assistance of Israeli and Czechoslovakian training missions. Current equipment includes about 10 MiG-21 and 12 MiG-17 jet fighter-bombers, 2 MiG-15 UTI two-seat trainers, about 5 L-29 Delfin armed jet trainers, 11 Super Cub liaison aircraft, 5 Piaggio P 149 piston-engined trainers, 6 Swiss-built Bravo primary trainers, 6 Agusta-Bell 205, 2 Agusta-Bell 206 JetRanger and some Mi-8 helicopters. Personnel number about 600. In addition the Police Air Wing has 1 Twin Otter and 1 Caribou twin-engined STOL transports, 1 Turbo-Beaver and 1 Piper Aztec light transports, and about 10 Bell 205, JetRanger Bell 212 and Scout helicopters.

INTERNATIONAL RELATIONS

Membership. Uganda is a member of UN, OAU, the Commonwealth and is an ACP state of EEC.

ECONOMY

Budget. The revenue and expenditure (exclusive of loan disbursements) for fiscal years (1 July–30 June) were (in Uganda Sh. 1m.):

	1971–72	*1972–73*
Revenue	1,436	1,525
Expenditure	1,374	1,430

Currency. East African Currency Board notes ceased to be legal tender from 14 Sept. 1967. The exchange rate is 17·14 Uganda shillings = £1.

Banking. The Bank of Uganda was set up on 16 May 1966; its external assets as at 31 Aug. 1967 were £9m. The Uganda Credit and Savings Bank, set up in 1950, was on 9 Oct. 1965 reconstituted as the Uganda Commercial Bank, with its capital fully owned by the Government.

Barclays Bank International has 11 branches and 7 agencies; National & Grindlays Bank Ltd has 12 branches and 12 agencies; the Standard Bank Ltd has 6 branches and 2 agencies; the Bank of Baroda Ltd has 3 branches; the Bank of India Ltd has 2 branches. Other banks operating in Uganda are the Algemene Bank Nederland NV and the Commercial Bank of Africa.

ENERGY AND NATURAL RESOURCES

Electricity. Industrial expansion is based on hydro-electric power provided by the Owen Falls scheme, which has a capacity of 150,000 kwh.

Minerals. With the opening of the Kilembe mine in 1956, copper has become Uganda's most valuable mineral export. In 1966 the principal minerals produced were: Blister copper, 16,041 long tons (£6,995,500) (1967: 14,392 long tons, £5,593,000); cement (1963), 54,282 long tons (£616,101); tin ore, 180·3 long tons (£171,982) (1967: 156·6 long tons, £143,325). Total value of mineral production in 1963 was £4,539,240.

Agriculture. Cotton and coffee are the principal exports, the former being grown entirely and the latter very largely by African farmers. Production of cotton in 1969–70 was 468,000 bales (of 400 lb.) which was a record. The 1965–66 coffee crop amounted to 160,000 tons, of which 145,000 tons was *robusta*. Other cash crops produced in 1965–66 were tea (24·7m. lb.), tobacco (6m. lb.), groundnuts (8,400 lb. exported), maize (42,000 lb. exported), castor seed (1,900 tons exported) sisal (320 tons) and sugar (1966, 125,700 tons; 1965, 115,696 tons).

Livestock (1976): Cattle, 4·9m.; asses, 16,000; sheep, 1·1m.; goats, 2·2m.; pigs, 190,000; poultry, 12m.

Forestry. Exploitable forests consist almost entirely of hardwoods. Internal consumption is rising. During 1964–65 approximately 28,000 tons of sawn timber were produced. About half of the timber exported goes to the UK and another quarter to Kenya and Tanganyika, from which in return the bulk of the softwood imports are obtained.

Fishery. With its 13,600 sq. miles of lakes and many rivers, Uganda possesses one of the largest fresh-water fisheries in the world. In 1966 fish production was 80,000 tons with a retail value of £6·5m. Fish farming (especially carp and tilapia) is a growing industry.

COMMERCE. In 1975 the 3 main exports (in Uganda Sh.) were: Coffee, 1,473m.; raw cotton, 211m.; tea, 121m.

Trade (in Uganda Sh. 1m.):

	1973	*1974*	*1975*
Imports	1,139	1,555	1,469
Exports	2,206	2,332	1,977

Total trade between Uganda and UK (British Department of Trade returns, in £1,000 sterling):

	1972	*1973*	*1974*	*1975*	*1976*	*1977*
Imports to UK	18,795	20,788	24,412	20,680	32,448	33,402
Exports and re-exports from UK	9,302	4,913	7,238	7,301	11,171	21,227

COMMUNICATIONS

Roads. There are 3,876 miles of all-weather roads maintained by the Ministry of Works, of which 796 miles are two-lane bitumenized highways, and some 11,230 miles of other roads, maintained by district governments.

Railways. On 26 Aug. 1977 Uganda Railways was formed following break-up of the East African Railways administration. The network totals 1,120 km (metre gauge).

Aviation. Entebbe has a first-class international airport and has direct flights to Europe, Rhodesia, Sudan, Kenya, Tanzania, Congo Republic, Burundi and Rwanda by British Airways, BUA, EAA, Sudan Airways, Air Congo, SABENA, SAS, Alitalia and many charter companies. Eleven other government airfields are used for internal communications.

Posts. There were 46,344 telephones in use at 1 Jan. 1977.

Cinemas. In 1971 there were 16 cinemas with a seating capacity of 8,000.

JUSTICE, EDUCATION AND WELFARE

Justice. The High Court of Uganda, presided over by the Chief Justice and 12 puisne judges, exercises original and appellate jurisdiction throughout Uganda. Subordinate courts, presided over by Chief Magistrates and Magistrates of the first, second- and third-grade Magistrates are trained to diploma level at the Law School, grade of Magistrate. Chief and first-grade Magistrates are professionally qualified; second- and third-grade Magistrates are trained to diploma level at the Law School, Entebbe.

Chief Magistrates exercise supervision over and hear appeals from second- and third-grade courts.

The Court of Appeal for Eastern Africa was re-established on 9 Dec. 1962 as the Court of Appeal for Uganda; it hears appeals from the High Court.

A law school has been established at Entebbe to train magistrates in civil and criminal law.

The African courts have been integrated with the Central Government Courts so that a unifed courts system has been established.

Education. Education is a joint undertaking by the Government, local authorities and, to some extent, voluntary agencies. The education system is divided into 3 sectors, primary, secondary and post-secondary. The primary course covers 7 years. There were 786,899 pupils in grant-aided primary schools in 1972. Education at secondary level falls into 4 categories, namely, secondary schools, which are the grammar type of schools with a course extending over 6 years to Higher School Certificate; technical schools; farm schools; and primary teacher-training colleges. Further education is provided at the Uganda Technical College, the National Teachers' College, the Uganda College of Commerce and Agricultural Colleges.

There are also several Departmental Training Schools for training staff for different departments.

The Medical Department alone has 8 such schools for training nurses, midwives, Medical Assistants, Health Inspectors, and other medical staff.

University level education is available at Makerere University College and the 2 other constituent Colleges of the University of East Africa; the University College, Nairobi, in Kenya, and the University College, Dar es Salaam, in Tanzania. Uganda students also go to universities and colleges outside East Africa for higher education.

Health. In 1973 there were 300 doctors and over 15,000 hospital beds.

DIPLOMATIC REPRESENTATIVES

OF UGANDA TO THE UNITED NATIONS

Ambassador: Khalid Younis Kinene.

Diplomatic relations between UK and Uganda were broken off on 28 July 1976.

The US embassy in Kampala was closed on 10 Nov. 1973. The Federal German Embassy has assumed protection of US interests in Uganda.

Books of Reference

Atlas of Uganda. Dept. of Lands and Surveys. Kampala, 1962
Faller, L. A. (ed.), *The King's Men.* OUP, 1964
Gukiina, P. M., *Uganda: A Case Study in African Political Development.* Univ. of Notre Dame Press, 1972
Hills, D., *The White Pumpkin.* New York, 1976
Ingham, K., *The Making of Modern Uganda.* London, 1957
Kendall, H., *Town Planning in Uganda.* London, 1955
Kitching, A. L., and Blackledge, G. R., *A Luganda–English and English–Luganda Dictionary.* Kampala, 1925
Larimore, A. E., *The Alien Town: Patterns of Settlement in Uganda.* Chicago, 1959
Listowel, J., *Amin.* Irish Univ. Press, 1973

UNION OF SOVIET SOCIALIST REPUBLICS

Soyuz Sovyetskikh Sotsialisticheskikh Respublik

Capital: Moscow
Population: 257·9m. (1977)

POST-REVOLUTION HISTORY. Up to 12 March 1917 the territory now forming the USSR, together with that of Finland, Poland and certain tracts ceded in 1918 to Turkey, but less the territories then forming part of the German, Austro-Hungarian and Japanese empires—East Prussia, Eastern Galicia, Transcarpathia, Bukovina, South Sakhalin and Kurile Islands—which were acquired during and after the Second World War, was constituted as the Russian Empire. It was governed as an autocracy under the Tsar, with the aid of Ministers responsible to himself and a State Duma with limited legislative powers, elected by provincial assemblies chosen by indirect elections on a restricted franchise.

On 12 March 1917 a revolution broke out. The Duma parties, the same day, set up a Provisional Committee of the State Duma, while the factory workmen and the insurgent garrison of Petrograd elected a Council (Soviet) of Workers' and Soldiers' Deputies. Soviets were also elected by the workmen in other towns, in the Army and Navy and, as time went on, by the peasantry. On 15 March 1917 the Tsar abdicated, and the Provisional Committee, by agreement with the Petrograd Soviet, appointed a Provisional Government and, on 14 Sept., proclaimed a republic. However, a political struggle went on between the supporters of the Provisional Government—the Mensheviks and the Socialist-Revolutionaries—and the Bolsheviks, who advocated the assumption of power by the Soviets. When they had won majorities in the Soviets of the principal cities and of the armed forces on several fronts, the Bolsheviks organized an insurrection through a Military-Revolutionary Committee of the Petrograd Soviet. On 7 Nov. 1917 the Committee arrested the Provisional Government and transferred power to the second All-Russian Congress of Soviets. This elected a new government, the Council of People's Commissars, headed by Lenin.

On 31 Jan. 1918 the third All Russian Congress of Soviets issued a Declaration of Rights of the Toiling and Exploited Masses, which proclaimed Russia a Republic of Soviets of Workers', Soldiers' and Peasants' Deputies; and on 10 July 1918 the fifth Congress adopted a Constitution for the Russian Socialist Federal Soviet Republic. In the course of the civil war other Soviet Republics were set up in the Ukraine, Belorussia and Transcaucasia. These first entered into treaty relations with the RSFSR and then, in 1922, joined with it in a closely integrated Union.

AREA AND POPULATION. The total area of the Soviet Union in April, 1965 was 22·4m. sq. km (8·65m. sq. miles). The census population on 15 Jan. 1959 was 208·8m. (94m. males and 114·8m. females; 99·8m. urban, 109m. rural). The census population on 15 Jan. 1970 was 241·7m. (111·3m. males, 130·4m. females; 136m. urban, 105·7 rural). The increase of 36m. in urban population between 1959 and 1970 was due to a natural increase of 19·6m., an influx of over 16m. from the countryside and the transformation of rural areas with a population of 5m. into urban areas. The natural increase in the rural areas exceeded 18m., but for the reasons stated the net rural population declined by 3m. Estimated population on 1 Jan. 1977, 257·9m. (119·9m. males, 138m. females; 159·6m. urban; 98·3m. rural).

Regions, towns, streets, factories, schools, etc., named after Stalin were renamed in Nov. 1961 when Stalin's body was removed from the Lenin–Stalin tomb in Red Square in Moscow. Similarly, in Jan. 1962 towns bearing the names of Molotov, Kaganovich and Malenkov were renamed.

The areas (in 1,000 sq. km) and population (in 1m., in Jan. 1977) of the constituent republics are as follows (capitals in brackets):

Constituent Republics	*Area*	*Population*
RSFSR (Moscow)	17,075	135·6
Ukraine (Kiev)	604	49·3
Kazakhstan (Alma-Ata)	2,717	14·5
Uzbekistan (Tashkent)	447	14·5
Belorussia (Minsk)	208	9·4
Azerbaijan (Baku)	87	5·8
Georgia (Tbilisi)	70	5·0
Moldavia (Kishinev)	34	3·9
Lithuania (Vilnius)	65	3·3
Kirgizia (Frunze)	198	3·5
Tadzhikistan (Dushanbe)	143	3·6
Latvia (Riga)	64	2·5
Armenia (Yerevan)	30	2·9
Turkmenistan (Ashkhabad)	488	2·7
Estonia (Tallin)	45	1·4

Nationalities. The most numerous nationalities at the 1970 census were: 129m. Russians, 40·8m. Ukrainians, 9·2m. Uzbeks, 9·1m. Belorussians, 5·9m. Tatars, 5·3m. Kazakhs, 4·4m. Azerbaijanians, 3·6m. Armenians, 3·2m. Georgians, 2·7m. Lithuanians, 2·7m. Moldavians, 2·2m. Jews, 2·1m. Tadzhiks, 1·8m. Germans, 1·7m. Chuvashes, 1·5m. Kirgiz, 1·5m. Turkmenians, 1·4m. Latvians, 1·3m. Mordovians, 1·2m. Bashkirs, 1·2m. Poles, 1m. Estonians. The great majority (in each case 84–99%) indicated the language of their nationality as their native tongue; exceptions were the Bashkirs (66%), Poles (33%) and Jews (17·7%).

Estimated losses of population in the Second World War, 20m., of which 7m. were military losses.

The following tables show the growth of the population in Russia:

1897 (Russian Empire)	126,900,000
1913 (Russian Empire)	170,900,000
1913 (present frontiers)	159,200,000
1939 (census)	170,600,000
1959 (census)	208,826,000
1970 (census)	241,748,000

The following was the population on 1 Jan. 1977 of the larger towns (in 1,000):

Aktyubinsk	184
Alma-Ata	871
Andizhan	224
Angarsk	233
Anjero-Sudjensk	105
Arkhangelsk	391
Armavir	158
Ashkhabad	302
Astrakhan	466
Baku	1,435
Barnaul	522
Belovo	112
Berezniki	176
Biisk	212
Blagoveshchensk	177
Bobruisk	192
Bryansk	385
Cheboksary	292
Chelyabinsk	1,007
Cherepovetz	246
Chernigov	233
Chernovtzy	214
Chimkent	303
Chita	294
Djambul	252
Dneprodzerzhinsk	257
Dnepropetrovsk	995
Donetsk	984
Dushanbe	460
Dzerzhinsk (Gorky region)	248
Elektrostal	135
Engels	163
Frunze	511
Gomel	360
Gorlovka	342
Gorky	1,319
Grozny	387
Habarovsk	524
Irkutsk	532
Ivanovo	461
Izhevsk	534
Kadievka	141
Kalinin	401
Kaliningrad	353
Kaluga	262
Kamensk-Uralski	187
Karaganda	576
Kaunas	359
Kazan	970
Kemerovo	454
Kertch	154
Kharkov	1,405
Kherson	324
Kiev	2,079
Kirov	381
Kirovabad (Azerbaijan)	216
Kirovograd	228
Kiselyovsk	124
Kishinev	489
Klaipeda	173
Kokand	155
Kolomna	145
Kommunarsk	129
Komsomolsk-on-Amur	252
Kopeisk	157
Kostroma	250
Kovrov	140
Kramatorsk	171
Krasnodar	552
Krasnoyarsk	769
Kremenchug	206
Krivoi Rog	641
Kuibyshev	1,204
Kurgan	304
Kursk	373
Kustanai	154
Kutaisi	182
Leninakan	192
Leningrad	4,425
Leninsk-Kuznetski	131
Lipetsk	375
Lvov	642
Lyubertsy	156
Magnitogorsk	398
Mahachkala	239
Makeyevka	437
Melitopol	157
Miass	146
Minsk	1,231
Mogilev	275
Moscow	7,819
Murmansk	374
Mytishchi	136
Naberezhnye Chelny	253
Nalchik	199
Namangan	224
Nikolayev	447
Nizhni Tagil	399
Norilsk	173

Novocherkassk	184
Novokuznetsk	537
Novomoskovsk	147
Novorossiisk	153
Novoshakhtinsk	101
Novosibirsk	1,304
Odessa	1,039
Omsk	1,026
Ordzhonikidze (Vladikavkaz)	281
Orehovo-Zuyevo	130
Orenburg	446
Orsk	244
Oryol	289
Pavlodar	258
Penza	443
Perm	972
Pervouralsk	126
Petropavlovsk-Kamchatski	207
Petropavlovsk (North Kazakhstan)	199
Petrozavodsk	220
Podolsk	193
Poltava	274
Prokopyevsk	267
Riga	876
Rostov-on-Don	921
Rubtsovsk	173
Ryazan	442
Rybinsk	237
Samarkand	312
Saransk	248
Saratov	856
Semipalatinsk	282
Serov	101
Serpukhov	132
Sevastopol	283
Shakhty	223
Simferopol	291
Smolensk	264
Sochi	255
Stavropol	245
Sterlitamak	211
Sumgait	174
Sumy	203
Sverdlovsk	1,187
Syzran	187
Taganrog	285
Tallin	415
Tambov	265
Tashkent	1,689
Tbilisi	1,042
Temirtau	202
Togliatti	479
Tomsk	423
Tselinograd	222
Tula	510
Tyumen	347
Ufa	942
Ulan-Ude	308
Ulyanovsk	447
Uralsk	162
Ussuriisk	147
Ust-Kamenogorsk	267
Vladimir	284
Vladivostok	536
Vilnius	458
Vinnitsa	297
Vitebsk	286
Volgograd	931
Vologda	224
Voroshilovgrad	445
Voronezh	779
Yaroslavl	584
Yerevan	956
Yoshkar-Ola	216
Zaporozhye	772
Zhdanov	474
Zhitomir	236
Zlatoust	197

Balzac, Vasyutin and Felgin, *Economic Geography of the USSR*. London, 1951
Baransky, N. N., *Economic Geography of the USSR*. Moscow, 1956 (in English)
Cole, J. P., and German, F. C., *A Geography of the USSR*. London, 1961
Leimbach, W., *Die Sowjet-Union*, Stuttgart, 1950
Narodnoye Hoziaistvo SSSR 1977. Moscow, 1977
The Oxford Regional Atlas of the USSR. Clarendon Press, Oxford, 1956
Yezhegodnik B.S.E., 1977

CONSTITUTION

Constituent Republics. The Union of Soviet Socialist Republics was formed by the union of the RSFSR, the Ukrainian Soviet Socialist Republic, the Belorussian Soviet Socialist Republic and the Transcaucasian Soviet Socialist Republic; the Treaty of Union was adopted by the first Soviet Congress of the USSR on 30 Dec. 1922. In May 1925 the Uzbek and Turkmen Autonomous Soviet Socialist Republics and in Dec. 1929 the Tadzhik Autonomous Soviet Socialist Republic were declared constituent members of the USSR, becoming Union Republics.

At the 8th Congress of the Soviets, on 5 Dec. 1936, a new constitution of the USSR was adopted. The Transcaucasian Republic was split up into the Armenian Soviet Socialist Republic, the Azerbaijan Soviet Socialist Republic and the Georgian Soviet Socialist Republic, each of which became constituent republics of the Union. At the same time the Kazakh Soviet Socialist Republic and the Kirghiz Soviet Socialist Republic, previously autonomous republics within the RSFSR, were proclaimed constituent republics of the USSR.

In Sept. 1939 Soviet troops occupied eastern Poland as far as the 'Curzon line', which in 1919 had been drawn on ethnographical grounds as the eastern frontier of Poland, and incorporated it into the Ukrainian and Belorussian Soviet Socialist Republics. In Feb. 1951 some districts of the Drogobych Region of the Ukraine and the Lublin Voivodship of Poland were exchanged.

On 31 March 1940 territory ceded by Finland was joined to that of the Autonomous Soviet Socialist Republic of Karelia to form the Karelo-Finnish Soviet Socialist Republic, which was admitted into the Union as the 12th Union Republic. On the 16 July 1956 the Supreme Soviet of the USSR adopted a law altering the status of the Karelo-Finnish Republic from that of a Union (constituent) Republic of the USSR to that of an Autonomous (Karelian) Republic within the RSFSR.

On 2 Aug. 1940 the Moldavian Soviet Socialist Republic was constituted as the 13th Union Republic. It comprised the former Moldavian Autonomous Soviet

Socialist Republic and Bessarabia (44,290 sq. km, ceded by Romania on 28 June 1940), except for the districts of Khotin, Akerman and Ismail, which, together with Northern Bukovina (10,440 sq. km), were incorporated in the Ukrainian Soviet Republic. The Soviet–Romanian frontier thus constituted was confirmed by the peace treaty with Romania, signed on 10 Feb. 1947. On 29 June 1945 Ruthenia (Sub-Carpathian Russia, 12,742 sq. km) was by treaty with Czechoslovakia embodied in the Ukrainian Soviet Socialist Republic.

On 3 Aug. 1940 Estonia, Latvia and Lithuania were incorporated in the Soviet Union as the 14th, 15th and 16th Union Republics. The change in the status of the Karelo-Finnish Republic has reduced the number of Union Republics to 15.

After the defeat of Germany it was agreed by the governments of the UK, the USA and the USSR (by the Potsdam declaration) that part of East Prussia should be embodied in the USSR. The area (11,655 sq. km), which includes the towns of Königsberg (renamed Kaliningrad), Tilsit (renamed Sovietsk) and Insterburg (renamed Chernyakhovsk) was joined to the Russian Soviet Federal Socialist Republic by decree of 7 April 1946.

By the peace treaty with Finland, signed on 10 Feb. 1947, the province of Petsamo (Pechenga), ceded to Finland on 14 Oct. 1920 and 12 March 1946, was returned to the Soviet Union. On 19 Sept. 1955 the Soviet Union renounced its treaty rights to the naval base of Porkkala-Udd and on 26 Jan. 1956 completed the withdrawal of the forces from Finnish territory.

In 1945, after the defeat of Japan, the southern half of Sakhalin (36,000 sq. km) and the Kurile Islands (10,200 sq. km) were, by agreement with the Allies, incorporated in the USSR.[1]

[1] However, Japan asks for the return of the Etorofu and Kunashiri Islands as not belonging to the Kurile Islands proper. The Soviet Government informed Japan on 27 Jan. 1960 that the Habomai Islands and Shikotan would be handed back to Japan on the withdrawal of the American troops from Japan.

GOVERNMENT. The Soviet Union is a socialist state of the whole people (1977 constitution), the political units of which are the Soviets of Working People's Deputies. All central and local authority is vested in these Soviets.

The economic foundation of the USSR is the socialist system of economy and the socialist ownership of the means of production. There are two forms of socialist property: (1) state property (property of the whole people); (2) co-operative and collective farm (*Kolhoz*) property (property of individual collective farms and property of co-operative associations). The land, mineral deposits, waters, forests, mills, factories, mines, railways, water and air transport, banks, means of communication, large state-organized agricultural enterprises, such as state farms (*Sovhozy*), machine-repair stations and the like, as well as municipal enterprises and the principal dwelling-house properties in the cities and industrial localities, are state property, but the land occupied by collective farmers is secured to them in perpetuity so long as they use it in accordance with the laws of the country. The members of the *Kolhozy* may have small plots of land attached to their dwellings for their own use. Peasants unwilling to enter a Kolhoz may retain their individual farms, but they are not allowed to employ hired labour. The right of personal property of citizens in their income from work and in their savings, in their dwelling-houses and auxiliary household economy, their domestic furniture and utensils and objects of personal use and comfort, as well as the right of inheritance of personal property of citizens, are protected by law. The constitution recognizes the right of all citizens to work, rest, leisure, education, health protection, housing and maintenance in old age, sickness or incapacity, without distinction of sex, race or nationality, and lays down that any direct or indirect restriction of the rights of, or conversely, the establishment of direct or indirect privileges for, citizens on account of their race or nationality, as well as the advocacy of racial or national exclusiveness or hatred and contempt, is punishable by law. The franchise is enjoyed by all citizens of the USSR, including members of the Armed Forces, who have reached the age of 18, irrespective of sex, with the exception of the insane and of persons convicted by court of law to sentences including deprivation of rights. Candidates for election to the Supreme Soviet of the USSR must be 21 years of age;

for all other authorities the minimum age for candidates is 18. A member of any Soviet may be recalled by a decision of a majority of his or her electors if he or she fails to give satisfaction (law on procedure for this, 30 Oct. 1959).

The USSR consists of 15 Union Republics, each inhabited by a major nationality which gives its name to the Republic. These are divided into 127 territories and regions, and these again into 3,117 districts and 2,040 towns and 3,784 urban settlements (1 Jan. 1977). Within the districts there are 41,249 rural districts (usually each including a number of villages). The territories and regions also include a number of smaller nationalities, forming their own self-governing units—20 Autonomous Republics, 8 Autonomous Regions and 10 National Areas.

The highest legislative organ is the Supreme Soviet of the USSR. It consists of 2 chambers with equal legislative rights, elected for a term of 4 years: the Soviet of the Union and the Soviet of Nationalities.

The Soviet of the Union is elected by the citizens of the USSR on the basis of 1 deputy for every 300,000 of the population. The Chamber elected on 16 June 1974 consists of 767 members (*Chairman*, A. P. Shitikov).

The Soviet of Nationalities is elected by the citizens of the USSR, voting by Union and Autonomous Republics, Autonomous Regions and National Areas on the basis of 32 (from June 1966) deputies from each Union Republic, 11 deputies from each Autonomous Republic, 5 deputies from each Autonomous Region and 1 deputy from each National Area. The Chamber elected on 16 June 1974 consists of 750 members (*Chairman*, V. P. Rubenis).

Each chamber has 14 standing committees: planning and budget; industry; transport and communications; building; agriculture; health and social welfare; education, science and culture; trade and services; draft legislation; foreign affairs; youth affairs; natural environment; credentials; consumer goods.

The highest executive and administrative organ is the Council of Ministers (called People's Commissars before 16 March 1946); they are appointed by the Supreme Soviet.

The Presidium of the Supreme Soviet of the USSR is elected at a joint session of both chambers of the Supreme Soviet and consists of the chairman, first vice-chairman, 15 vice-chairmen (1 from each of the Union republics), 19 members and the secretary. It acts as the supreme state authority between sessions of the Supreme Soviet and is accountable to the latter for all its activities.

Deputies are elected by the voters on the basis of universal, equal and direct suffrage by secret ballot. The only legal political party is the Communist Party; non-members are classed as non-party citizens. Candidates up to the present have been selected at a preliminary 'constituency electoral consultation' (selection conference), to which organizations which have put forward nominations send delegates, who discuss the various nominees. As a consequence, so far, a single candidate has been arrived at in each constituency, whose name has appeared on the ballot paper, to be struck out or approved by a cross as the voter desires. This procedure, however, is not laid down by the constitution, and may be altered. At the election held on 16 June 1974, 161,689,612 electors voted. The Supreme Soviet elected on that day consists of 1,096 Communist and 421 non-party deputies; 475 were women, 498 manual workers in industry and state farms, and 271 collective farmers.

On 1 Feb. 1944 each of the constituent republics of the Union was given the right to have separate Commissariats (now Ministries) for Defence and Foreign Affairs. After the death of Stalin, 5 March 1953, a number of Ministries comprising different branches of trade, engineering, transport and electricity were merged into single Ministries. In 1957 the number of Ministries in the central government was reduced from 52 to 19, and in Dec. 1959 to 15; but in Oct. 1964 it was again increased to 47, in Aug. 1966 to 48 and in 1968 to 56.

The Council of Ministers, in July 1976 included 13 vice-chairmen, the Premiers of the 15 Union Republics, the head of the Central Statistical Department, the chairmen of 8 commissions of the Presidium of the Council of Ministers (4 of them vice-chairmen of the Council), of the Committee for People's Control, State Planning Committee, the Agricultural Technique Organization and of 7 other State Committees; 62 Ministers; and the chairman of the State Bank.

Soon after the adoption of the 1936 constitution all the constituent republics of the Union held their Soviet congresses, at which they adopted their own constitutions based in all essentials on the constitution of the Union, but adapted where necessary to national and local requirements. Article 73 of the 1977 constitution reserves to the central government the spheres of war and peace, diplomatic relations, defence, foreign trade, state security, economic planning, education, criminal and civil codes, etc. The right of the constituent republics to withdraw from the Union is expressly recognized.

The 20 Autonomous Republics include 16 in the RSFSR, 1 in Azerbaijan, 2 in Georgia, 1 in Uzbekistan. Five Autonomous Regions are in the RSFSR, 1 each in Georgia, Azerbaijan, Tadzhikistan; all 10 National Areas are in the RSFSR.

The Autonomous Republics are governed by their own Supreme Soviet and Council of Ministers: the regions and territories, districts, towns and rural areas have their own Soviets, elected for a term of 2½ years. In June 1975, 9,259 deputies were elected to the Supreme Soviets of Union and of Autonomous Republics: 3,393 (36·6%) were women, 3,126 (33·8%) non-Party, 3,055 (33%) industrial workers and 1,604 (17·3%) collective farmers. To the regional, district and other local Soviets in June 1977, 2,229,641 deputies were elected, 1,093,235 of them women (42·3%), 1,266,949 non-Party (56·8%), 943,240 (42·3%) industrial workers and 582,373 (26·1%) collective farmers (June 1977).

In June 1977 there were 47,412 rural and urban Soviets with 1·96m. deputies, 1·7m. voluntary co-opted members participating in their standing committees and 43,000 women were chairmen or secretaries of Soviets.

State flag: Red, with sickle and hammer in gold in the upper corner near the staff, and above them a 5-pointed star bordered in gold.

National anthem: Soyuz nerushimy respublik svobodnykh (words by S. Mikhalkov and El-Registan; music by A. V. Alexandrov; 1944).

The Presidium of the Supreme Soviet may, within the framework of the constitution, issue edicts (*ukaz*) interpreting existing legislation or amending it, subject to ratification subsequently by the Supreme Soviet.

Legislation by decree and executive authority is vested in the Council of Ministers. The Council of Ministers is responsible to the Supreme Soviet of the USSR and in the intervals between sessions to the Presidium of the Supreme Soviet.

President of the Presidium of the Supreme Soviet of the USSR: Leonid Ilyich Brezhnev (June 1977).

First Vice-President: Victor Vasilievich Kuznetsov (Oct. 1977)

Secretary of the Presidium: M. P. Georgadze.

Chairman of the Council of Ministers: Alexei Nikolayevich Kosygin (Oct. 1964).

First Vice-Chairmen: K. T. Mazurov, N. A. Tckhorov (Sept. 1976).

Minister of Defence: Marshal D. F. Ustinov. *Minister of Foreign Trade:* N. S. Patolichev. *Minister for Foreign Affairs:* A. A. Gromyko.

Yezhegodnik BSE. Moscow (annual)
Denisov, A., and Kirichenko, M., *Soviet State Law.* Moscow, 1960
Hazard, J. N., *The Soviet System of Government.* Univ. of Chicago Press, 1957
Meyer, A. G., *The Soviet Political System: An Interpretation.* New York, 1965

Communist Party. According to the rules adopted by the 22nd Congress of the Party on 31 Oct. 1961, the Communist Party of the Soviet Union 'unites, on a voluntary basis, the more advanced, politically more conscious section of the working class, collective-farm peasantry and intelligentsia of the USSR', whose principal objects are to build a Communist society by means of gradual transition from Socialism to Communism, to raise the material and cultural level of the people, to organize the defence of the country and to strengthen ties with the workers of other countries.

The Party is built on the territorial-industrial principle. The supreme organ is the Party Congress. Ordinary congresses are convened not less than once in 4 years. The Congress elects a Central Committee which meets at least every 6 months, carries on the work of the Party between congresses, and guides the work of central Soviet and public organizations through Party groups within them.

The Central Committee forms a Political Bureau to direct the work of the Central Committee between plenary meetings, a Secretariat to direct current work and a Commission of Party Control to consider appeals against decisions about expulsion. Similar rules hold for the Regional, Territorial and Republican Party organizations.

Over 394,000 primary Party organizations exist in mills, factories, state machine and tractor stations and other economic establishments, in collective farms, units of the Soviet Army and Navy, in villages, offices, educational establishments, etc., where there are at least 3 Party members. On 1 July 1977 nearly 42% of the members were industrial workers, 14% were collective farmers and 45% office and professional workers. 24·7% were women.

The Central Committee elected by the 25th Congress in March 1976 consisted of 287 members and 139 candidate members.

On 1 Nov. 1977 the Political Bureau of the Central Committee consisted of the following members: Y. V. Andropov, L. I. Brezhnev, V. V. Grishin, A. A. Gromyko, A. P. Kirilenko, A. N. Kosygin, F. D. Kulakov, D. A. Kunayev, K. T. Mazurov, A. Y. Pelshe, G. V. Romanov, M. A. Suslov, D. F. Ustinov, V. V. Shcherbitsky; and the following alternate members: G. A. Aliev, P. N. Demichev, P. M. Masherov, B. N. Ponomaryov, S. R. Rashidov, M. S. Solomentsev.

Secretariat: L. I. Brezhnev (*General-Secretary*); K. U. Chernenko; V. I. Dolgikh; I. V. Kapitonov; A. P. Kirilenko; F. D. Kulakov; B. N. Ponomaryov; K. V. Rusakov; Y. P. Ryabov; M. A. Suslov; M. V. Zymianin.

Chairman of the Commission of Party Control: A. Y. Pelshe.
Vice-Chairman: Z. T. Serdyuk.

On 1 July 1977 the Communist Party had 16·2m. members. Membership of the Young Communist League was 37·8m. in April 1978.

The Communist International (The Comintern), founded on the initiative of the Russian Communist Party in 1919, was dissolved on 15 May 1943. In Oct. 1947 a Communist Information Bureau (Cominform) was set up in Belgrade to serve the Communist parties of Bulgaria, Czechoslovakia, France, Hungary, Italy, Poland, Romania, USSR and Yugoslavia. On 28 June 1948 Yugoslavia was expelled from the Cominform and the bureau was transferred to Bucharest. The Cominform was on 17 April 1956 declared dissolved.

Hammond, T. T. (ed.), *Soviet Foreign Relations and World Communism.* Princeton and OUP, 1965
Hunt, R. N. C., *Books on Communism* [in English]. London, 1960
Kassof, A., *The Soviet Youth Program.* Harvard and OUP, 1965
Schapiro, L., *The Communist Party of the Soviet Union.* New York, 1960.—*The Government and Politics of the Soviet Union.* New York, 1965
History of the Communist Party of the Soviet Union (English ed.). Moscow, 1960; rev. Russian ed., Moscow, 1965

DEFENCE. On 26 Feb. 1946 the control of the Soviet Armed Forces was unified under a single Ministry of the Armed Forces. On 25 Feb. 1950 the Defence Ministry was divided into a War Ministry and a Navy Ministry; on 15 March 1953 a single Ministry of Defence was reconstituted.

In 1955 the Air Defence Command and in 1960 the Strategic Rocket Forces were established as the 4th and 5th 'branches' of the armed forces beside the army, navy and air force.

The direction of Party and political work in the Armed Forces is exercised by the Central Committee of the Communist Party of the Soviet Union through the chief political directorate of the Ministry of Defence. The chiefs of the political departments of military commands, fleets and armies must be Party members of 5 years' standing and the chiefs of political departments of divisions and regiments Party members of 3 years' standing. Nearly 90% of the officers are members of the Communist Party or Young Communist League, and 45% have had an engineering and technical education.

Military service begins at the age of 19 (or 18 for graduates of secondary schools). Active service lasts 2 years for privates in the Army and M.V.D. troops, 3 years for n.c.o.s in the Army and M.V.D. troops and for privates and n.c.o.s in the Air

Force, 4 years for privates and n.c.o.s in the Coastal Defence, 5 years for ratings in the Navy. Reserve service lasts up to the ages of 35, 45 or 50 years according to fitness, family status and other considerations. Conscientious objection is treated as a criminal offence. Students in places of higher education are freed from military service, but receive military instruction. About half the service personnel have had higher, or 10-year, education and over 80% are members of the Communist Party.

In Jan. 1960 Prime Minister Khrushchov quoted the following figures of the armed forces of the Soviet Union: 1927, 586,000; 1937, 1,433,000; 1941, 4,207,000; May 1945, 11,365,000; 1948, 2,874,000; 1955, 5,763,000; 1959, 3,623,000; 1960, 2,423,000. The reduction, according to Khrushchov, was mainly due to the switch-over to rocket and nuclear weapons.

The estimated expenditure on defence (in 1m. new roubles) for 1961 was 9,255; 1968, 16,700; 1969, 17,702; 1970, 17,900; 1971, 17,900; 1972, 17,900; 1973, 17,900; 1974, 17,700; 1975, 17,400; 1976, 17,400; 1977, 17,200.

Eastern Security Treaty. On 14 May 1955 the USSR, Albania, Bulgaria, Czechoslovakia, the German Democratic Republic, Hungary, Poland and Romania signed in Warsaw a 20-year treaty of friendship and collaboration, after the USSR had (on 7 May) annulled the 20-year treaties of alliance with the UK (1942) and France (1944).

The main provisions of the treaty are as follows:

ARTICLE 4. In case of armed aggression in Europe against one or several States party to the pact by a State or group of States, each State member of the pact . . . will afford to the State or States which are the object of such aggression immediate assistance . . . with all means which appear necessary, including the use of armed force. . . . These measures will cease as soon as the Security Council takes measures necessary for establishing and preserving international peace and security.

ARTICLE 5. The contracting Powers agree to set up a joint command of their armed forces to be allotted by agreement between the Powers, at the disposal of this command and used on the basis of jointly established principles. They will also take over agreed measures necessary to strengthen their defences.

ARTICLE 9. The present treaty is open to other States, irrespective of their social or Government regime, who declare their readiness to abide by the terms of the treaty in order to safeguard peace and security of the peoples.

ARTICLE 11. In the event of a system of collective security being set up in Europe and a pact to this effect being signed—to which each party to this treaty will direct its efforts—the present treaty will lapse from the day such a collective security treaty comes into force.

It is estimated (1978) that the armed forces of the Warsaw pact countries total 3·83m., including 3·45m. Russians, compared with 4·82m. NATO forces.

Marshal Grechko was from July 1960 to April 1967 C.-in-C. of the united Armed Forces, with headquarters in Moscow. He was succeeded by Marshal I. I. Yakubovsky in 1967 and by Marshal V. G. Kulikov in Jan. 1977.

In 1962 Albania was no longer invited to the Warsaw Pact meetings, without being formally expelled.

Two Soviet divisions are stationed in Poland, 20 divisions in German Democratic Republic, 4 divisions in Hungary and 5 in Czechoslovakia.

Army. The Army was, in 1976, thought to consist of about 168 divisions, of which some 100 are of combat readiness, numbering about 2m. men.

The mechanized and tank divisions are equipped with the T54 medium tank, mounting an 85-mm gun, and with the Stalin III heavy tank, mounting a 122-mm gun. The T54 is being replaced by the T62 medium tank mounting a 115-mm gun. Rocket units are stated to be 'the main force' of the Army.

In addition to the Soviet Army, there are some 350,000 security and border troops.

Navy. The Soviet Fleet is steadily expanding and progressively modernizing under a continuity of policy and technology given by the two decades in office of Admiral of the Fleet of the Soviet Union Sergei Georgiyevich Gorshkov, C.-in-C. of the Soviet Navy and Deputy Minister of Defence. The overall picture is of an unprecedentedly powerful and well-balanced navy, the capacity of which is increasing annually by scientific application if not by numerical strength.

The principal surface ships of the Soviet Navy are as follows:

Completed	*Name*	*Standard displacement Tons*	*Armour Belt In.*	*Armour Guns In.*	*Principal armament*	*Shaft horse-power*	*Speed Knots*
			Aircraft Carriers[1]				
1977	Minsk	40,000	—	—	4 twin SS missile launchers; 4 twin SA missile launchers; 1 twin AS missile launcher; 20 fixed-wing aircraft; 25 helicopters; 4 76-mm AA guns	150,000	30
1976	Kiev						

[1] *See* Aircraft carriers under construction, successors of *Kiev* and *Minsk*, p. 1211.

Completed	*Name*	*Standard displacement Tons*	*Armour Belt In.*	*Armour Guns In.*	*Principal armament*	*Shaft horse-power*	*Speed Knots*
			Helicopter Carriers				
1968	Leningrad	15,000	5	4	2 twin SA missile launchers; 1 twin AS missile launcher; 2 twin 57-mm AA guns	100,000	30
1967	Moskva						
			Cruisers				
1978	Azov[3]	8,000	—	—	2 quadruppe SS missile launchers; 4 twin SA missile launchers; 4 76-mm AA guns	120,000	34
1976	Kerch						
1976	Ochakov						
1973	Nikolaiev						
1958	Admiral Senyavin[1]	15,450	5	4	12 6-in.; 12 3·9-in.	130,000	34
1957	Mikhail Kutuzov						
1956	Dimitri Pojarski						
1956	Oktyabrskaya Revolutsiya (*ex*-Molotovsk)						
1956	Admiral Lazarev						
1955	Alexandr Suvorov						
1954	Admiral Ushakov						
1954	Dzerzhinski[2]						
1953	Alexandr Nevski						
1953	Murmansk						
1953	Zhdanov[1]						
1953	Sverdlov						
1950	Komsomolets[4]	11,500	—	—	12 6-in.; 8 3·9-in.	113,000	35

[1] *Admiral Senyavin* now has a helicopter pad and hangar ('X' and 'Y' turrets removed) while *Zhdanov* has high deckhouse ('X' turret removed). Each carries twin surface-air missile launchers. Both latterly employed as command and communications ships.

[2] *Dzerzhinski* has only nine 6-in. guns in 3 triple turrets, 'X' turret having been replaced by a twin surface-air missile launcher.

[3] *Azov* and a fifth ship of this class are reported to be of a modified design.

[4] Of sister ships, *Kirov* and *Slava* (ex-*Molotov*) were deleted from the effective list in 1976–77 and *Zheleznyakov* in 1978.

There are also 145 nuclear-powered submarines, 255 diesel-electric powered submarines, 17 missile armed light cruisers, 54 missile armed destroyers, 58 gun armed destroyers, 42 missile armed escorts (corvettes), 108 gun armed escorts (small frigates), 124 coastal escorts, 165 fleet minesweepers, 130 coastal minesweepers, 112 inshore minesweepers, 120 missile patrol boats, 90 torpedo boats, 65 anti-submarine boats, 46 hydrofoil gunboats, 25 coastal patrol craft, 130 river patrol boats, 43 tank landing ships, 82 medium landing ships, 85 utility landing craft, 100 minor landing craft, 55 intelligence collecting ships, 65 major support ships, 23 space associated ships, 100 survey ships, 25 research ships, 4 nuclear powered icebreakers, 39 icebreakers, 27 training ships, 200 fishery protection and research ships, 6 fleet replenishment ships, 44 oilers, 21 salvage vessels, 20 transports, 15 rescue ships, 150 tenders, 15 lifting ships, 6 cable ships, 120 fleet tugs and thousands of auxiliaries, para-military ships and service craft.

The new construction programme includes several aircraft carriers (successors of *Kiev* and *Minsk*), 7 nuclear powered ballistic missile submarines, 4 nuclear powered cruise missile submarines, 8 nuclear powered torpedo-armed submarines and 3 guided missile cruisers ('Kara' class, sister ships of *Ochakov* and *Nikolaiev*, *see* p. 1210).

In the revised forward procurement programme at least 5 aircraft carriers of improved 'Kiev' class are envisaged and eventually 6 or more to fit into the Soviet global and strategic maritime pattern.

There are 5 shipyards in and near Leningrad; Black Sea yards are at Nikolaiev and Sevastopol, new shipyards are at Molotovsk in the White Sea region and at Komsomolsk on the Amur.

The completion of a through canal system between the Baltic and White Seas and the opening of regular traffic *via* the North-East Passage (during the ice-free season) have enabled the Soviet Government to transfer tonnage between the Baltic and Far East.

Estimated number of personnel in 1978 totalled 500,000 officers and men, including naval aviation, naval infantry, coastal defence, cadets, apprentices and central administration; but the weakness is that only about 30% are volunteers, *i.e.*, officers and petty officers, the remainder comprising national service men serving 3 years at sea and 2 if ashore.

Air Force. The Soviet Air Force (excluding PVO air defence force) is believed to consist, in 1978, of over 470,000 officers and men and some 9,000 first-line aircraft, excluding second-line and training types. To supplement long-range rocket missiles (limited by SALT I interim agreement to 1,618 ICBM, 600 MRBM/IRBM), the DA strategic bomber force is estimated to have still 105 Tupolev Tu-95 ('Bear')[1] 4-turboprop bombers, 80 Myasishchev M-4 4-jet bombers and flight-refuelling tankers ('Bison'), 425 Tupolev Tu-16 ('Badger'), and 150 supersonic Tupolev Tu-22 ('Blinder') twin-jet bombers, and a rapidly growing number of new Tupolev Tu-26 ('Backfire') swing-wing bombers, of which about 100 were operational in autumn 1977. All types are used also by the Naval Air Force for long-range maritime reconnaissance; the Tu-16, Tu-95, Tu-22 and 'Backfire' can carry air-to-surface guided self-propelled missiles and all 5 types have provision for flight refuelling.

The FA tactical air forces, under local army command in the field, have an estimated total of 4,500 ground attack and reconnaissance aircraft, including 850 MiG-23/27 ('Flogger') and 250 two-seat Sukhoi Su-19 ('Fencer') supersonic swing-wing aircraft, twin-jet Yakovlev Yak-28 ('Brewer') multi-purpose combat aircraft, 250 single-jet Sukhoi Su-7B ('Fitter-A'), 300 swing-wing Su-17 ('Fitter-C'), and 1,500 MiG-21 ('Fishbed') fighter-bombers, 250 MiG-21 and 100 MiG-25 ('Foxbat') reconnaissance aircraft, and diminishing numbers of older types such as the MiG-17 ('Fresco'), with strong interceptor, transport and helicopter support. In service in large numbers is the MiG-24 ('Hind') assault helicopter, in transport and gunship versions. The PVO defence forces, organized as a separate service, have an estimated total of 2,540 jet interceptors. A high proportion of the squadrons are equipped with the latest MiG-23 ('Flogger'), Su-15 ('Flagon') and MiG-25 ('Foxbat') all-weather interceptors, armed with air-to-air missiles. The single-seat single-engined Su-9 and Su-11 ('Fishpot') and twin-jet Yak-28P ('Firebar') and Tu-28P ('Fiddler') make up the balance of the force, with a few MiG-17s ('Fresco') in less critical areas. Early warning and fighter-control duties are performed by radar-carrying adaptations of the Tu-114 turboprop transport, redesignated Tu-126 ('Moss'). Very large numbers of surface-to-air guided missiles are operational, on some 10,000 launchers, including the 'Guild', 'Guideline', 'Goa', 'Gainful' and

[1] For convenience Soviet aircraft and missiles are usually referred to by invented English names in non-Soviet military writings.

'Ganef', the long-range 'Gammon' and the 'Galosh' which is deployed around Moscow on 64 launchers and has anti-missile capability.

Soviet Air Force transport squadrons have an estimated total of 1,500 aircraft, consisting primarily of An-12 ('Cub') 4 turboprop transports and An-24s ('Coke') and An-26s ('Curl'), with a few very large An-22s ('Cock'), a growing number of new Il-76 ('Candid') heavy four-jet freighters, a variety of older and smaller types and many helicopters, including the turbine-powered Mi-6, Mi-8 and Mi-10 flying crane. Training aircraft include the piston-engined Yak-18 primary trainer, the Czech-built L-29 Delfin and L-39 jet basic trainers and versions of operational types such as the MiG-21, MiG-23, MiG-25, MiG-15, Su-7, Su-9, Su-17, Yak-28 and Tu-22.

Naval Air Force. Operating 1,200 fixed-wing aircraft and helicopters, the Soviet Navy has the world's second largest naval air arm. Under the control of the various naval commands, *i.e.*, Baltic, Black Sea and Pacific, the Naval Air Arm has an estimated 550 land-based maritime patrol bombers and 100 flying-boats. Primary offensive aircraft are 360 Tu-16 ('Badger') twin-jet bombers, and 30 Tu-26 'Backfire' swing-wing bombers, able to carry air-to-surface missiles, 50 supersonic twin-jet Tu-22 ('Blinder') reconnaissance bombers and 100 Beriev M-12 ('Mail') maritime patrol amphibian. Some 60 Tu-95 ('Bear') and Myasishchev M-4 ('Bison') 4-engined bombers, as well as Tu-16s and Tu-26s and 50 Il-38 ('May'), are used for long-range over-water reconnaissance. The Tu-95 also has an important targeting role for ships fitted with anti-shipping missile launchers. Over 200 anti-submarine helicopters, notably the Ka-25 ('Hormone'), are carried in naval vessels, including 2 aircraft carriers (which also operate Yak-36 ('Forger') VTOL attack/reconnaissance aircraft) and 2 helicopter carriers. Several hundred transport, utility and training fixed-wing aircraft and helicopters are also under Navy control.

Berman, H. J., and Kerner, M. (ed.), *Soviet Military Law and Administration.* 2 vols. Harvard Univ. Press, 1955
Gouré, L., Kohler, F. D., and Harvey, M. L., *The Role of Nuclear Forces in Current Soviet Strategy.* Washington, 1974
Kilmarx, R. A., *A History of Soviet Air Power.* London, 1962
O'Ballance, E., *The Red Army.* London, 1964
Saunders, M. G. (ed.), *The Soviet Navy.* London, 1958

INTERNATIONAL RELATIONS

Membership. USSR is a member of UN, Comecon and the Warsaw Pact.

External Debt. The debts contracted by the tsarist regime, *i.e.*, before 1917, have been repudiated by the Soviet Government.

After the Second World War the USSR has become one of the biggest creditor countries in the world. Between 1945 and Jan. 1977 economic aid in the form of 2% or 2½% loans to be repaid, as a rule, over 12 years has been advanced for 2,541 industrial and agricultural enterprises in Socialist countries and 998 enterprises in developing countries; the latter including loans (in 1m. old roubles): India, 2,500m.; Egypt, 2,300m.; Iraq, 550m.; Afghánistán, 480m.; Indonesia, 443m.; Argentina, 400m.; Ethiopia, 400m.; Guinea, 140m.; Cuba, US$100m. 76% of aid is for industrial development and 14% for agriculture and transport. 1,368 industrial plants have been completed in these countries, and nearly as many are being completed; 340,000 native skilled workers have been trained by Soviet specialists in Africa and Asia alone, and many thousands more in the USSR. Agreements for economic co-operation operate with 45 developing countries in all.

ECONOMY

Planning. Planning is based on public ownership in industry and trade, and on mixed public and collective (co-operative) ownership in agriculture. The first plan drawn up by Gosplan (the State Planning Commission) was the 'Goelro' drawn up in 1920. This was to be the basis for the economic development of the country and for the construction of a system of electrical power plants with an aggregate capacity of 1·75m. kw., in the course of 15 years. By 1927–28 the capacity of the electrical stations in operation was already 1,792,000 kw. with an output of 5,160m. kwh.

In 1925 Gosplan started to draw up annual plans for the national economy, and in 1927–29 undertook to draw up the first 5-year plan, which was to have run from 1 Oct 1928 to 30 Sept. 1933. It was considered completed in Dec. 1932, when 93·7% of the planned industrial output for the 5 years had been carried out. Stress was laid on the development of the heavy industries, particularly in the outlying areas rich in natural resources and inhabited by the national minorities.

The second 5-year plan ran from 1933 to 1937. It aimed at strengthening the defensive capacity of the Soviet Union, and more stress was laid than in the first 5-year plan on increasing the output and improving the quality of consumer goods. About one-half of the total investments in new heavy industrial constructions was allocated to the eastern areas. By the end of 1937 the plan for large-scale industry was overfulfilled by 4%, but the target for the light industries and consumer goods was not reached.

The third 5-year plan, 1938–42, envisaged an average annual increase in output of 13·5%, but that of the means of production was to be 15·25% and the means of consumption 11%; stress was to be laid on war industry. During the first 3½ years, industrial output was increasing annually by an average of 13%. In the Urals, the Volga area, Siberia and Central Asia industrial output increased during 1938–40 by about 50%. One of the richest grain-growing areas of the Soviet Union was created in the eastern part of the country. Capital construction amounted in value to a total of 130,000m. roubles; more than one-third fell to the eastern areas. The plan was interrupted in June 1941, when Hitler attacked the USSR. The whole of the national economy was switched to help the war effort, and whole industries were shifted from the western areas to the east.

For details of the fourth 5-year plan, 1946–50, *see* THE STATESMAN'S YEAR-BOOK, 1952, pp. 1424 f. The 1950 target of the gross output of industry was exceeded by 2%.

On 10 Oct, 1952 the 19th Congress of the Communist Party issued directives for the fifth 5-year plan, 1951–55; for details, *see* THE STATESMAN'S YEAR-BOOK, 1953, pp. 1435–36. During Sept. and Oct. 1953 the Government issued a number of decrees to stimulate the development of agriculture, the output of consumer goods and the expansion of the home trade. For details of these decrees, *see* THE STATESMAN'S YEAR-BOOK, 1955, pp. 1448–50.

The directive for the sixth 5-year plan, 1956–60, was adopted by the 20th Congress of the Communist Party on 25 Feb. 1956; for details *see* THE STATESMAN'S YEAR-BOOK, 1958, p. 1472.

In May 1955 Gosplan was reorganized to consist of 2 state commissions for long-term planning (Gosplan) and for current planning (Goseconomcommissya); at the same time a committee was set up to improve the application to industry of advance science and technology (Gostekhnika).

Between 1954 and 1956 considerable changes were made in planning methods. In March 1954 collective farms were given greater authority over planning their own output, only the quantities required by the State in fixed deliveries being determined beforehand, and voluntary sales by contract. In 1955 they were authorized to make changes in their statutes, which had followed a fixed model since 1935. In 1955–57 over 15,000 industrial establishments in various basic industries, previously controlled by the Union Government, and later a number of entire light industries were turned over to the Constituent (Union) Republics. By 1962 they controlled from 95 to 100% of all industrial output.

In 1957 a comprehensive plan for decentralization of management of industry was initiated. Industrial establishments responsible for about 71% of all Soviet industrial output were turned over to Economic Councils set up in 104 (in 1963: 47) economic administrative areas. These in 1962 controlled 73% of all industrial production. The Ministries previously responsible for the industries concerned were either abolished or transformed into purely planning and supervisory bodies. The State Committee for current planning was abolished, and Gosplan was given wider powers.

In consequence of this change a 7-year plan for 1959–65 was adopted by the 21st Congress of the Communist Party in Feb. 1959. Industrial output was to increase by 80%; it was in fact, in 1965, 84% above that of 1959. Capital investments would roughly equal the total for 1917–58: special attention was to be given to mechanization of agriculture and arduous industrial labour, automation and new technological processes, and housing. Diesel or electric traction of railway freight was to rise to 85%. Real incomes were to rise 40%, the 7-hour day (6 hours for miners) became general in 1960 and the 40-hour week in 1961, and introduction of the 35-hour week (30 hours for miners) began in 1964.

In Oct. 1965 the regional and Republic Economic Councils were abolished and also 28 Ministries for various branches of industry (17 Union-Republican, *i.e.*, corresponding to similar Ministries in the Union Republics, and 11 all-Union).

A 20-year plan was adopted by the 22nd Congress of the Communist Party on 31 Oct. 1961. Compared with 1960, by 1980 the output was to be increased as follows: Electric power, ninefold; steel, fourfold; oil, fivefold; coal, double; machinery, tenfold; fertilizers, ninefold; cement, fivefold; textiles, treble; leather footwear, double; grain, double; milk, treble; meat, fourfold. Two new iron and steel centres were to be developed in Kazakhstan and in Kursk region. A single deepwater system was to link the main inland waterways in the European USSR. Some rivers in northern Asia are to be diverted south for irrigation purposes. A 6-hour day for a 6-day week or 35 hours for a 5-day week were to be achieved by 1970. Housing, water, gas, heating, public urban transport and school meals were to be free by 1980. These and cognate measures were to provide 'the material and technical basis of communism'.

The 23rd Congress of the Communist Party in April 1966 adopted 'directives' for a 5-year plan for 1966–70. Under these, power output was to reach 830,000–850,000m. kwh.; oil, 345–355m. tons; coal, 665–675m. tons; steel, 124–129m. tons; mineral fertilizers, 62–65m. tons; machine-tools, 220,000–230,000; cars, 700,000–800,000; tractors, 600,000–625,000; paper, 5–5·3m. tons; cement, 100–105m. tons; fabrics, 9·5–9·8m. sq. metres; leather footwear, 610–630m. pairs; meat, 5·9–6·2m. tons; butter, 1·2m. tons; sugar, 9·8–10m. tons. The average annual output of grain was to increase 30% over 1964–65. 7,000 km of new railway line, 63,000 km of new motor roads and 35–40 new airports were to be built; marine tonnage was to be increased by 50%.

The 9th Five-Year Plan adopted in 1971 provided for an increase in electric power output to 1,065,000m. kwh.; oil, 496m. tons; gas, 320,000m. cu. metres; steel, 146m. tons; coal, 695m. tons; mineral fertilizers, 90m. tons; tractors, 575,000; passenger cars, 1·26m., and lorries, 750,000. Grain output was to rise to 195m. in 1975; meat, approximately 16m. tons; milk, 100m. tons; textiles, 11,000m. sq. metres; leather footwear, 830m. pairs. Average wages were to increase by 22%, incomes of collective farmers 30–35%, and the average of real incomes by 31%. 3,400 miles of new railway tracks were to be built and 3,700 miles electrified, with 17,000 miles of new oil pipelines, and 40% more cargo carried by sea. 580m. sq. metres of new housing (over 16m. flats and houses) were to be built.

By July 1972, 43,000 industrial plants had been transferred to the new system of decentralized cost-accounting; they produced 94% of total output of Soviet industry and 95% of its total profit. All public establishments in trade and catering and all the state farms, have gone over to the new system.

On 29 Oct. 1976, the Supreme Soviet adopted the 10th Five-Year Plan (1976–80). This provided for an increase of industrial output from 104·3% of the 1975 level to 136%, an average annual increase of agricultural output by 16%, freight traffic (all forms) from 105·7% to 132%, state capital investments from 105·1% of the 1975 level in 1976 to 114·6% in 1980, real income per head from 103·7% to 121%, retail commodity turnover from 103·6% to 128·7%. 550m. sq. metres of new housing were to be built. Children in pre-school establishments would increase by 104·4% in 1976 and 125·5% in 1980, pupils in day schools from 108·9% to 148·8%, and students in higher education from 100·4% to 105·4%. Hospital beds were to increase from 102·2% in the first year to 109·7% in the final year.

A far-reaching plan for land improvement, increasing of agricultural, housing and road facilities and expansion of village amenities, from 1976 to 1980, in the 'Non-Black-Earth Zone' (northern and central European Russia), was begun in 1975–76, at a total cost of 35,000m. roubles.

The National Economy of the USSR in 1977. (Statistical annual in Russian.) Moscow, 1977
Directives of the 5-Year Economic Plan, 1971–1975. Moscow, 1971 (in English)

Bandera, U.N., and Melnyk, Z. L. (ed.), *The Soviet Economy in Regional Perspective*. New York, 1973
Conyngham, W. J., *Industrial Management in the Soviet Union*. Stanford, California, 1973
Dobb, M., *Soviet Economic Development Since 1917*. London, 1966

Budget. Revenue and expenditure in 1,000m. new roubles for calendar years:

	1972	*1973*	*1974*	*1975*	*1976*	*1977*
Revenue	175,100	188,000	201,300	218,800	232,200	242,200
Expenditure	173,200	185,400	197,400	214,500	226,700	241,800

The 1977 budget allotted 125,000m. roubles to the national economy, 17,200m. to defence and 85,100m. to social and cultural services.

The social insurance budget, which is controlled by the Central Council for Trade Unions and its affiliated bodies, was 19,900m. roubles in 1972, 21,057m. in 1973, 22,169m. in 1974, 26,100m. in 1975 and 27,992m. in 1976.

The national income was assessed (in 1,000m. roubles) at 152·9 in 1961, 193·5 in 1965, 207·4 in 1966, 225 in 1967, 261·9 in 1969, 289·9 in 1970, 305 in 1971, 313·6 in 1972, 337·8 in 1973, 353·7 in 1974, 363·3 in 1975, 385·7 in 1976 and 403 in 1977.

Income tax was abolished on 1 Oct. 1961 for earnings up to 60 roubles per month and reduced for earnings between 61 and 70 roubles; in Dec. 1967 further cuts of 25% were made for earnings from 61 to 80 roubles; in 1972 earnings up to 70 roubles were freed of income tax, and taxes on incomes up to 90 roubles were cut by about 33⅓%.

Capital investment (1977) was 121,900m. roubles, including 105,300m. by State and co-operative enterprises, 11,000m. by collective farms and 1,700m. by individuals (on housing). Taking 1913 as 100, the physical volume of industrial production within the present territory of the USSR was 769 in 1940 and 145,000 in 1977.

Currency. As from 1 Jan. 1961 the gold content of the *rouble* was raised from 0·222 168 to 0·987 412 gramme. The official exchange rates are 74·80 *kopeks* = US$1, and (from Dec. 1976) 1·23 *roubles* = £1.

The gold holdings of the USSR were, in Dec. 1955, estimated at about 200m. fine oz. (US$7,000m.), or about 20% of the world total of monetary gold.

The currency in circulation is: (1) State Bank notes in denominations of 10, 25, 50 and 100 *roubles*; (2) Treasury notes in denominations of 1, 3 and 5 *roubles*; (3) cupro-nickel coins in denominations of 10, 15, 20 and 50 *kopeks* and 1 *rouble*; (4) cupro-zinc coins in denominations of 1, 2, 3 and 5 *kopeks*.

Banking. The State Bank began operations on 16 Nov. 1921. By an edict of 7 April 1959 a number of specialized banks for planned long-term investments, which had existed since 1932, were abolished. The State Bank, in addition to short-term credits, effects long-term investments in agriculture and in individual rural house-building. The Bank for Financing Capital Investments (*Stroibank*) covers industry, transport, urban housing schemes and public utilities and individual house-building in towns.

Deposits in 80,400 savings banks were over 116,700m. new roubles to the credit of 120·5m. depositors at 1 Jan. 1978.

Weights and Measures. The metric system has been in use since 1 Jan. 1927.

The Gregorian Calendar was adopted as from 14 Feb. 1918.

ENERGY AND NATURAL RESOURCES

Electricity. Many hydro-electrical power stations are being constructed. The Irkutsk station (4,500m. kwh. output per annum) is in operation; Bratsk (4·5m. kw. capacity) was completed in 1967. Sayano-Shushenskaya, of 6·4m. kw. capacity (in Eastern Siberia) and Ust-Ilimskaya, of 4·4m. kw. capacity (Central Siberia) are under construction. Krasnoyarsk (6m. kw. capacity) was completed and began full production in July 1972.

The Kremenchug power station (625,000 kw. capacity) was completed in Nov. 1960, rendering the Dnieper navigable for large vessels from Kanev to the Black Sea (over 800 km). Two power stations in Central Asia are under construction: at Nurek on the Amu-Darya (2·7m. kw.) and at Toktogul in the Syr-Darya basin (1·2m. kw.). Their reservoirs will irrigate 1·5m hectares.

Total installed capacity of electrical plants in 1938 was 8·7m. kw. and 240m.

kw. in 1977. Industry consumes about 70% of the total electricity. Over 35,000 small rural power stations have been closed in recent years owing to supply from State stations becoming available, but there are still many operating in the countryside. 800 towns and urban settlements were heated by central thermal plants.

An atom-driven power station, with a capacity of 5,000 kw., was put into operation at Obninsk (Kaluga region) on 27 June 1954; the Novo-Voronezh station (now 1·5m. kw.) began operating in Dec. 1964, and Beloyarsk (1m. kw.) in 1965. The 2m. kw. station in the Leningrad Region was in full operation in 1978. 2m.–6m. kw. stations are being built at Kirovsk in the north; Novy Uzen, on the Caspian; Bilibino (in Chukotka), Shevchenko (Kazakhstan), Kursk, Smolensk and elsewhere. An experimental tidal energy station is working at Kislaya Guba (Murman coast). Atomic power capacity is to exceed 30m. kw. by 1980.

At 19 thermal power stations new generating sets of 300,000 kw. each were installed in 1970 and others begun with capacity of up to 1·2m. kw.

The integrated power grid for the whole country is to be completed by 1980. Power grids for Siberia, Central Asia and European Russia (700 stations) are already operating.

A unified power grid ('Mir') with all the Socialist countries of eastern Europe was built up between 1962 and 1967. Total capacity (1972) was 58m. kw.

Oil. In the 1930s practically all Soviet oil came from the Caucasian fields, of which the Baku fields yielded 75–80% and the Grozny and Maikop fields between them 15%. Since then, the distribution has considerably changed. The Ural–Volga area, the 'Second Baku', has 4 large centres in operation, at Samarska Luka (Kuibyshev), Tuimazy (Bashkiria), Ishimbaev (Bashkiria) and Perm. A large new oilfield has been developed in the Trans-Volga area of the Saratov region. The USSR is now the second-largest oil-producer in the world after the USA (*see* pp. xxiii f.).

The total length of pipeline on 1 Jan. 1939 was 4,212 km, divided as follows: Baku–Batumi, 1,717 km; Grozny–Mahach-Kala, 150 km; Grozny–Armavir–Tuapse, 618 km; Armavir–Trudovaya, 488 km; Guriev–Orsk, 845 km, and other, 394 km. One pipeline (1,700 km) was completed in 1955, connecting Tuimazy in Bashkiria with the refineries of Omsk. In 1957 the Almetyevsk–Gorky pipeline (580 km) and 479 km of the Stavropol–Moscow pipeline were completed. At the end of 1976 there were 58,600 km of pipeline, through which (in 1976) were conveyed 532m. tons of oil.

The construction of the 'Druzhba' pipeline of about 5,327 km from the oilfields near Kuibyshev to Poland and the German Democratic Republic (northern branch) and to Czechoslovakia and Hungary (southern branch)—separating in Belorussia—begun in 1960, was completed in 1965.

In 1976 the USSR exported 111m. tonnes of crude oil and oil products.

Minerals. Miners are trained in 6 mining, 3 oil and 1 peat institutes, the mining faculties of 17 higher educational establishments, oil faculties of 2 industrial institutes and a peat faculty at the Belorussian Polytechnical Institute.

The Soviet Union is rich in minerals. Soviet scientists claim that it contains 58% of the world's coal deposits, 58·7% of its oil, 41% of its iron ore, 76·7% of its apatite, 25% of all timber land, 88% of its manganese, 54% of its potassium salts and nearly one-third of its phosphates.

Estimated output (in tonnes) in 1962: Copper, 634,900; zinc, 399,000; lead, 363,000; tungsten, 10,500; antimony, 5,980; silver, 27m. fine oz. Output in 1963: Baryte, 199,500; magnesium, 31,745; aluminium, 961,400; manganese ore (1976), 8·6m.; graphite, 54,000; bauxite, 4·3m.; asbestos, 1·3m.; phosphate rock, 3·7m. (plus 7·4m. apatite); chromite, 1·23m.; gold, 12·5m. fine oz.; molybdenum, 12·5m. lb.; cadmium (1956), 160.

Output of iron and steel in the USSR (in 1m. tonnes):

	Pig-iron	*Ingot steel*	*Rolled steel*		*Pig-iron*	*Ingot steel*	*Rolled steel*
1913	4·2	4·2	3·5	1960	46·8	65·3	50·9
1928–29	4·0	4·8	3·9	1965	66·2	91·0	61·7
1932	6·2	5·9	4·4	1970	85·9	115·9	80·6
1940	14·9	18·3	13·1	1975	102·9	141·3	98·7
1946	10·0	13·4	9·6	1976	105·4	144·8	101·4
1950	19·2	27·3	20·9	1977	107·0	147·0	102·0

Coal production (in 1m. tonnes) was 29·1 in 1913, 64·4 in 1932, 165·9 in 1940, 261·1 in 1950, 513 in 1960, 608 in 1969, 624 in 1970, 641 in 1971, 655 in 1972, 668 in 1973, 685 in 1974, 701 in 1975, 711 in 1976, 722 in 1977.

The main centre of the atomic industry is at Ust-Kamenogorsk in the Altai Mountains. Uranium deposits are being worked near Taboshar (south-east of Tashkent), Adizhan (in the Tynya-Muyan Mountains), Slyudianka (near Lake Baikal), on the Kolyma River and in Southern Armenia.

Output of natural gas reached 346m. cu. metres in 1977; oil, 546m. tonnes.

Agriculture. The Soviet Union, up to about 1928 predominantly agricultural in character, has become an industrial–agricultural country. Of the gross social product, industry and transport accounted for 42·1% in 1913 and 79·4% in 1976; agriculture for 57·9% in 1913 and 14% in 1976. Of the total state land fund of 2,227·5m. hectares, agricultural land in use in 1976 amounted to 1,047·5m., state forests and state reserves to 1,118m. hectares. 23% of all gainfully employed in 1976 were engaged in agriculture (1913, 75%).

The total area under cultivation (including single-owner peasant farms, state farms and collective farms) was (in the same territory) 118·2m. hectares in 1913, 129·7m. in 1933, 146·3m. in 1950, 203m. in 1960, 206·7m. in 1970, 216·5m. in 1974, 225·5m. in 1975, 225·7 in 1976, 217·7m. in 1977.

Collective farms on 1 Nov. 1976 possessed 270·7m. hectares, of which 105m. were under crops of various kinds; state farms and other state agricultural undertakings possessed 772·9m. hectares, of which 118·1m. were under crops; manual and clerical workers held 3·9m. hectares as allotments.

In Nov. 1969 the Third Congress of collective farmers adopted a new model constitution, considerably enlarging the planning powers of collective farms and making payments to their members a priority.

Since 1969 conferences of collective farms have elected 2,417 district collective farm councils with 85,000 members, to study and co-ordinate local experience in methods and finance. Processing and other joint agricultural productive establishments in 1977 numbered 7,688.

Produce marketed (after consumption by collective farmers) was, in 1m. tonnes, for the present area of the USSR:

	1950	*1960*	*1970*	*1976*
Grain	38·2	54·1	80·8	101·5
Raw cotton[1]	3·5	4·3	6·9	8·3
Sugar-beet	19·7	52·2	71·4	85·3
Potatoes	14·0	13·7	18·1	20·6
Vegetables	4·3	8·0	13·8	18·4

	1950	*1960*	*1970*	*1976*
Meat[2] and fats	2·5	6·0	9·4	10·9
Milk and milk products	11·4	29·1	48·0	58·4
Wool	138·0	319·0	395·0	424·0
Eggs (1,000m.)	3·5	10·5	22·1	36·3

[1] Seed-cotton unginned. [2] Slaughter weight.

Since 1954 grain crops have been measured in 'barn crop' (*i.e.*, net quantities delivered to barns) and not in 'gross harvest' or 'biological yield' (*i.e.*, calculated as growing crops) as previously. Average annual crops (in 1m. tonnes): 1909–13, 72·5; 1946–50, 64·8; 1951–55, 88·5; 1956–60, 121·5; 1961–65, 130·3; 1966–70, 167·5; 1971–75, 181·6. Other produce (in 1m. tonnes) in 1977: Raw cotton, 8·8; sunflower, 5·8; meat (slaughter weight), 14·8; milk, 94·8; sugar-beet, 33; potatoes, 83·4; vegetables, 23; 55,600m. eggs.

In Dec. 1963 collective farms comprised 99·7% of all peasant holdings. In 1976 they produced 49% of all marketed grain, cotton 71%, sugar-beet 91%, potatoes 30%, vegetables 34%, meat 40%, milk 52%, eggs 13%.

Between 1953 and 1 Jan. 1978 the number of collective farms was reduced, mainly by amalgamation and partly by transformation into state farms, from 93,300 to 27,000, their cultivated area falling from 132m. hectares to 96·7m. The number of state farms rose in the same period from 4,857 to 20,006, their cultivated area from 15·2m. hectares to 111·9m.

State purchases in 1975 (in 1m. tonnes; 1976 figures in brackets): Grain, 50·2 (92·1); sugar-beet, 61·9 (85·3); cotton, 7·9 (8·3); meat, 16·8 (14·7); milk, 56·3 (56·2); eggs (1,000m.), 33·1 (32·9).

By 1971, in the collective farms 99% of the ploughing of the areas under grain, cotton and sugar-beet and 97–98% of the sowing under these crops were mechanized; 95% of their areas under grain and 79% under sugar-beet were harvested by combines. 85% of dairy farming in state and collective farms was using mechanical milking in 1976.

Rural electrical stations in 1940 had a capacity of 265,000 kw.; in 1976, 2·9m. kw. 99·9% of collective farms and 99·9% of state farms were using electric power in 1973. In 1977 agriculture consumed 91,000m. kwh. of electric power.

Investments in agriculture in 1976 were 19,500m. roubles by the state and 9,600m. by collective farms.

In 1913 the total of irrigated land was 4m. hectares; in 1953, 11m.; in 1976, 18·3m. The total of land drained was 8·4m. hectares in 1956 and 14·4m. in 1976. The Andizhan Reservoir covering 5,500 hectares, on the borders of Uzbekistan and Kirgizia, under construction since 1970, will irrigate over 400,000 hectares. The Krasnodar Reservoir (46,000 hectares, was completed and will irrigate over 200,000 hectares, mainly under rice. In 1975 nearly 85m. hectares were treated from the air against weed, pest and disease.

In 1913, 188,000 tonnes of mineral fertilizers were used; in 1950, 5·3m. tonnes, and in 1976, 77·7m. On 1 Jan. 1977 there were 2·4m. tractors, 685,000 grain combine harvesters and 1·44m. lorries in the countryside. Under the 5-year plan (1971–75) agriculture received 1·7m. tractors and 449,000 grain combines.

An All-Union Academy of Agricultural Sciences, founded in 1929, has regional branches in Siberia and Central Asia and 169 research institutes.

Livestock. Livestock (1 Jan. 1977), in 1m. heads: Cattle, 110·3 (including 42 milch cows); pigs, 63·1; sheep, 139·8. Since 1957 the enumeration of livestock is being made on 1 Jan. instead of 1 Oct., *i.e.*, after the winter sales and slaughter for the market. Percentage of farm production in 1976:

	All grain	*Cotton*	*Sugar-beet*	*Potatoes*	*Vegetables*	*Meat*	*Milk*	*Eggs*	*Wool*
State	47	29	9	15	43	33	31	54	45
Collective	52	71	91	23	30	36	39	9	35
Private[1]	1	0	0	62	27	31	30	37	20

[1] *I.e.*, household plots of collective farmers.

Forestry. On the 747m. hectares of forest land of the USSR, a large portion is administered and worked by the State, and the other, about 38m. hectares in extent, is granted for use to the peasantry free of charge.

The largest forest areas are 515m. hectares in the Asiatic part of USSR, 51·4m. along the northern seaboard, 25·4m. in the Urals and 17·95m. in the north-west.

On 24 Oct. 1948 a plan was published for planting crop-protecting forest belts, introducing crop rotation with grasses and building of ponds and water reservoirs in the steppe and forest-steppe areas of the European part of the USSR. By the middle of 1952 some 2·6m. hectares had been planted with shelter-belt trees and 13,500 ponds and reservoirs had been built. The planting of the shelter belts in the Kamyshin–Volgograd and Byelgorod–Don areas has in the main been completed. A Volga forest belt has been planted along 1,200 km of railway. Re-afforestation was completed in 1970 on an area of 2·3m. hectares. A further 1·3m. hectares were planted in 1971 and 1·2m. in 1972. A total of 12m. were planned for the period 1971–75.

Fisheries. The fishing catch including whaling (in 1,000 tons): 1913, 1,051; 1940, 1,422; 1960, 3,541; 1976, 10,478.

Belov, F., *The History of a Soviet Collective Farm.* New York, 1956
Simush, P., *The Soviet Collective Farm* (in English). Moscow, 1971
Symons, L., *Russian Agriculture: A Geographic Survey.* London, 1972
Vasiliev, P., and Kozlovsky, V. *Forest Wealth of the USSR* (in Russian). Moscow, 1959

INDUSTRY AND TRADE

Industry. The organization of industry in the USSR is based on state ownership and control, administered by a separate Ministry for each large industry.

Under the successive 5-year plans, large-scale modern industrial works have been constructed, namely: 1st, over 1,500; 2nd, 4,500; 3rd (up to June 1941), 3,000; war-time, 3,500 (apart from reconstruction of destroyed plants); 4th, 6,200; 5th, 3,200; 6th, 2,700; 7th (1959–65), 5,470; 8th (1966–70), 1,870; 9th (1971–75), 2,000.

Output of some heavy industries was as follows:

Industry	*1913*	*1940*	*1950*	*1960*	*1975*	*1976*
Iron ore (1m tonnes)	9·2	29·9	39·7	106·2	233·0	239·0
Oil (1m. tonnes)	9·2	31·1	37·9	148·0	491·0	520·0
Electric power (1,000m. kwh.)	1·9	48·3	91·2	292·0	1,039·0	1,111·0
Mineral fertilizers (1m. tonnes)	0·07	3·0	5·5	13·8	90·2	92·2
Machine tools (1,000)	1·5	58·4	70·6	154·0	231·0	233·0
Steam and gas turbines (1,000 kw.)	5·9	972·0	2,381·0	9,200·0	18,900·0	19,600·0
Oil industry equipment (1,000 tonnes)	—	15·5	47·9	92·8	171·0	164·0
Oil locomotives (1,000 h.p.)	—	5·0	125·0	1,303·0	1,375·0	1,455·0
Electric locomotives (no.)	—	9·0	102·0	396·0	395·0	425·0
Lorries and buses (1,000)	—	136·0	294·4	385·0	763·0	776·0
Tractors (1,000)	—	31·6	108·8	238·5	550·0	562·0
Looms (1,000)	4·6	1·8	8·7	16·4	31·3	30·9
Excavators (no.)	—	274·0	3,540·0	12,290·0	38,965·0	40,400·0
Timber (hauled, 1m. cu. metres)[1]	27·2	117·9	161·0	261·5	313·0	302·9
Cement (1m. tonnes)	1·8	5·7	10·2	45·5	122·0	124·2

[1] Excluding collective farm production.

The process of industrial mechanization and the installation of automatic remote control is being pushed ahead. About 90% of Soviet pig-iron and 87% of the steel is produced in fully automatic furnaces. All hydro-electric plants (in terms of capacity) are fully automatic. Coal production in open-cast mines has been completely mechanized; hydraulic mining is coming into general use. Coal-cutting and underground haulage had been over 99% mechanized by the end of 1962 (loading on inclined seams 56%); peat-cutting, 100%, and loading, nearly 80%; timber-cutting, 98%; haulage to loading centres, 93%, and despatch, 97%.

Output in some consumer industries was as follows:

Industry	*1913*	*1940*	*1950*	*1960*	*1975*	*1976*
Cotton fabrics (1m. linear metres)	2,672·0	3,954·0	3,899·2	6,387	7,810·0	7,899·0
Woollen fabrics (1m. linear metres)	107·7	119·7	155·5	342	552·0	567·0
Silk fabrics (1m. linear metres)	42·6	77·3	129·7	810	1,517·0	1,618·0
Leather footwear (1m. pairs)	60·0	211·0	203·4	419	698·0	724·0
Clocks and watches (1m.)	0·7	2·8	7·6	26	55·1	57·9
Radio and television sets (1,000)	—	161·0	1,083·0	5,900	15,336·0	15,519·0
Bicycles and mopeds (1,000)	4·9	255·0	649·3	2,800	5,007·0	5,072·0
Paper (1,000 tonnes)	269·0	812·0	1,193·0	2,334	5,215·0	5,389·0
Meat (abattoirs) (1,000 tonnes)[1]	1,042·0	1,501·0	1,556·0	4,400	9,862·0	8,368·0
Dairy butter (1,000 tonnes)[1]	104·0	226·0	336·0	737	1,231·0	1,263·0
Granulated sugar (1,000 tonnes)	1,363·0	2,165·0	2,523·0	6,360	10,382·0	9,249·0
Canned foods (1,000m. tins)	116·0	1,113·0	1,113·0	4,864	14,600·0	14,520·0

[1] Excluding collective farm and other home production, home-killed meat, etc.

Since 1945 the cotton industry has expanded, especially in the Urals, Central Asia and Siberia. Large mills have been built at Kamyshin, Kherson, Barnaul, Engels, Alma-Ata, Chernigov and Frunze.

In 1973 the eastern regions (Urals, Siberia, Far East and Central Asian Republics) accounted for 52% of the coal output, 37% of the oil, 39% of the pig-iron, 43% of the steel and 38% of electric power.

In 1974 the first power units at Ust-Ilimskaya, Chirkei (Dagestan) and Riga hydro-electrical stations, and the second units at the Dnieper station; the second power unit at the Kola atomic station and 500,000 kw. turbines at the Leningrad atomic station; new large units in the oil-refining, petrochemical and gas works at Angarsk, Grozny, Kremenchug, Novoufimsk, Omsk and several other places; a 2,500 km gas pipeline from Tyumen region (Siberia) to Central Russia; new mines in the Donetz coalfield; a new blast furnace of 4m. tonnes per year capacity at Krivoi Rog; many other metallurgical, non-ferrous metal and chemical works; new engineering units at the Sverdlovsk and Kharkov turbine works, and at the Glazov (Udmurtia) and Dzerzhinsk (Gorky region) chemical machine building works; with a number of cellulose, paper and cement factories, were built or under construction. Many light and food industry factories were expanded.

A natural-gas pipeline from Gazli, near Khiva, to Voskresensk, near Moscow (2,750 km), with a planned capacity of 100m. cu. metres per day, began operating in

Oct. 1967. Since then it has been extended to Czechoslovakia, where a 1,000-km extension, for transmission of Soviet gas to Austria, Italy, German Democratic Republic and Federal Republic of Germany, is under construction and another to Bulgaria. Another natural-gas pipeline, over 3,000 km from Medvezhye (Tyumen Region) to Moscow, began operating in Oct. 1974. A gas pipeline starting from Orenburg (Urals), passing across the Volga at Kamyshin, and continuing across the Ukraine *via* Kremenchug and Vinnitsa to Czechoslovakia (2,750 km), was under construction in July 1976. When completed, it is to supply Czechoslovakia, Poland, Bulgaria and Hungary with 14,000m. cu. metres annually and Romania with 1,500m. A unified gas-grid exceeding 99,000 km now exists.

Trade Unions and Labour. Trade unions are organized on an industrial basis, all workers, whether manual or brain, in every branch of a given industry being eligible for membership of the same union.

Since 1933 the trade unions have carried out the functions of the former Labour Commissariat; they control and supervise the application of labour laws, introduce new labour laws for approval by the Government and administer social insurance and factory inspection. Social insurace is non-contributory. The All-Union Congress has met at irregular intervals; the 14th Congress met in 1968, the 15th in 1972 and the 16th in 1977. Membership (1978) 121m.

In 1944 there were 176 unions. This number was reduced by amalgamation of unions to 22 in 1958, but increased to 25 in 1968; membership on 1 Dec 1976, 110m. (including wage-earners in collective farms). Contributions range from 0·5 to 6% of wages. There are 167 regional and Republican Trades Councils.

Chairman, Central Council of Trade Unions: A. I. Shibayev.

The average number of industrial and clerical workers engaged (1976) in the whole national economy of the Soviet Union was 104·2m., 51·5% of them women. The 7-hour day (6 hours for miners underground and other heavy trades) was generally in operation by the end of 1960. The average working week since 1970 has been 39·4 hours and the working day in industry 6·93 hours. The 5-day week (without reduction of total working hours) was introduced in 1967.

New 'Fundamentals of Labour Legislation', intended to codify and extend labour laws adopted in the last 40 years, were adopted by the Supreme Soviet in July 1970. They lay down, *inter alia,* the right to receive wages irrespective of the income of the enterprise concerned, the right to free vocational and advanced technical training; the right to form trade unions without state registration; the right of trade unions to participate in and supervise management and planning, labour legislation, safety regulation and housing, fixing of working conditions and wages, etc. Pensioners in Jan. 1977 numbered 45·9m., including 30m. old age; 11·7m. were collective farmers. In 1972 doctors and educational workers had an average 20% increase in pay; wages were also increased for industrial workers in some eastern regions, for night workers in light industry and for tractor drivers in agriculture and forestry. Students' grants were increased by 25% in higher education and 50% in technical colleges. Average monthly wages were 155·5 roubles in 1977.

The Trade Union Situation in the USSR. International Labour Office, 1960
From the 14th Congress to the 15th Congress of the Soviet Trade Unions (in Russian). Moscow, 1972

Commerce. Retail home trade takes three forms—state, co-operative and the free market, *i.e.*, sales by individual collective-farm members and by the collective farms of their surplus products, after having fulfilled their statutory deliveries and made their regular allocations to their members.

In 1977 the consumer co-operative societies had 64m. members and did 28·8% of the retail trade of the USSR. They were organized in 8,400 societies, employing about 3m. workers, with 371,100 rural shops, 88,400 catering establishments, 10,600 bakeries and 324 canneries. Their central union is affiliated to the International Co-operative Alliance. Retail trade by the State and co-operatives totalled 230,600m. roubles in 1976; by collective farm markets (agricultural produce), 5,700m. roubles. Total state and co-operative retail trade turnover represented (in comparable prices) an increase of 4·8% on 1977.

Foreign trade is organized as a state monopoly. Importation and exportation of goods are effected under licences issued by the Ministry for Foreign Trade and its respective departments in pursuance of a plan annually sanctioned by the Government. The right of purchasing goods for importation, and that of selling Soviet exports abroad, is vested in Trade Delegations and representatives of the appropriate state corporations in foreign countries.

There are 29 state import and export organizations, including chartering and tourist corporations (one, Vostokintorg, dealing with Mongolia, Sinkiang and Afghánistán). The Central Union of Consumers' Societies (Centrosoyuz) is also authorized to conduct foreign trade operations.

For foreign trade up to 1938 *see* THE STATESMAN'S YEAR-BOOK, 1951, p. 1465. The Central Statistical Department of the USSR estimates that, in comparable prices, the volume of foreign trade in 1938 was less than one-third that of 1913, but was in 1976, 25 times as large as in 1913. Exports in 1977 were valued at 28,731m. roubles (15,104m. to the Socialist countries), and imports at 28,731m. roubles (15,104m. from the Socialist countries).

Russia's imports of fuel and raw materials, between 1913 and 1976, declined from 43·5 to 22·8%, of machinery and equipment increased from 16·6 to 36·3%; imports of foodstuffs and manufactured consumer goods increased from 31·5% in 1913 to 35·4% in 1976.

Main items of exports in 1974:

Oil (1m. tonnes)	116·2	Cotton (1,000 tonnes)	739·0
Coal (1m. tonnes)	26·2	Vegetable oil (1,000 tonnes)	513·0
Iron ore (1m. tonnes)	43·3	Tractors (1,000)	40·1
Iron and rolled metal (1m. tonnes)	11·3	Motor cars and lorries (1,000)	327·4
Manganese ore (1,000 tonnes)	1,500·0	Clocks and watches (1,000)	15,700·0
Paper (1,000 tonnes)	650·0	Grain (1m. tonnes)	4·9

Total trade between the USSR and UK for calendar years (British Department of Trade returns, in £1,000 sterling):

	1974	*1975*	*1976*	*1977*
Imports to UK	395,457	408,421	666,946	780,572
Exports and re-exports from UK	110,016	210,297	240,425	347,432

Tourism. Pre-revolutionary Russia was never a country for any but the most hardy and better-off tourists, as the introductory pages of Baedeker's guide made clear. For her subjects, too, touring was no more inviting. Acute shortage of hotels and boarding-houses, poor roads, lack of ordinary services for visitors were among the least of their difficulties.

These have not by any means been fully overcome: but very great efforts to meet them have been made.

	1972	*1973*	*1974*	*1975*
Foreign visitors to the USSR	2,316,974	2,909,158	3,446,933	3,690,751
Of whom, from non-Socialist countries	875,395	1,309,979	1,558,522	1,582,741
Soviet visitors abroad	1,973,333	2,082,385	2,224,601	2,450,087
Of whom, to non-Socialist countries	854,792	868,725	893,059	932,119

Within the USSR, tourism by Soviet citizens has been much encouraged by the trade unions, which are developing an extensive network of facilities, particularly for hikers, campers and climbers. These facilities number more than 10,000 tourist camps, 650 tourist 'bases' (supply depots for hiring equipment), and over 4,000 huts for anglers, hunters and mountaineers. The Central Council of Trade Unions also owns or controls 137 river or seagoing ships, 120 trains and 8,000 motor coaches exclusively for tourist use.

Soviet tourists recorded by this network numbered 40,000 in 1950; 1,997,000 in 1965; 5,041,000 in 1970 and 16,591,000 in 1976.

COMMUNICATIONS

Roads. By 1941 there were over 1·5m. km of constructed roads, of which 143,000 km were suitable for motor traffic. The total length of motor roads in 1976 was 689,700 km. Road freights by lorry amounted to 859m. tons in 1940 and 21,500m. tons in 1976. Passengers carried were 590m. in 1940 and 37,867m. in 1976. In 1976, 20,700 inter-urban bus routes had a total length of 3,056,000 km. An asphalted highway from Chelyabinsk (Urals) to Lake Baikal, 5,000 km, was more than half completed in Dec. 1976.

Railways. The length of railways in Jan. 1977 was 138,500 km (1913: 58,500). By the end of 1976, 133,700 km of main-line railways had changed to electric and diesel traction, 39,700 km wholly electrified, and 99·6% of railway freight went by these means. In 1976, 60% of all goods traffic and 40% of passenger transport went by rail (in 1913, 57% and 91% respectively). The Moscow–Donetz, Leningrad–Leninakan (3,400 km) and western frontier–Baikal (7,500 km) lines have been electrified.

There are 43 main railway systems which may be grouped as follows:

In the west: Estonian (1,388 km), Latvian (3,100 km) and Lithuanian (2,100 km), Kalinin (2,064 km, Moscow–Orsha and Moscow–Zilupe, centre at Smolensk), Belorussian (5,800 km), October (Moscow–Leningrad, centre Leningrad, 3,857 km), Lvov (south-western Ukraine, 4,257 km), South-Western (centre Kiev–western Ukraine and southern Belorussia, 3,888 km), Moscow–Kiev (centre Kaluga–western Russia, eastern Belorussia, north-Ukraine, western 3,821 km).

In the north: Northern (Moscow and north European Russia, centre Yaroslavl, 3,750 km), Pechora (centre Kotlas: north-eastern European Russia, 1,953 km), Kirov (Murmansk–Petrozavodsk–Volhovstroi, centre Petrozavodsk, 3,587 km).

In the European south: Moscow–Kursk–Donbass (centre Moscow, 3,027 km), Southern (centre Kharkov: eastern Ukraine, south-eastern Russia, 3,304 km), South-Eastern (centre Voronezh: Ukraine–Urals, Rostov–Penza regions, 2,579 km), Odessa (south-eastern Ukraine–south-western Moldavia, centre Odessa, 3,839 km), Moldavian (Kishinev, 1,200 km), Stalin (centre Dnepropetrovsk, links this heavy-industry area with the Black Sea coast, 3,298 km), North Caucasus (centre Rostov-on-Don, 3,391 km), Ordzhonikidze (links northern Caucasus Autonomous Republics with Caspian coast, centre Ordzhonikidze, 1,708 km). Donetz (centre Donetsk, served the Donetz coalfield, 2,862 km). The entire route from Leningrad to Simferopol (Crimea) was electrified during 1970.

In eastern European Russia: Moscow–Ryazan (centre Moscow, 2,089 km), Kazan (centre Kazan, links Volga with Urals, 2,783 km), Gorky (Moscow–Ryazan–north-eastern Russia, centre Gorky, 1,543 km), Ufa (links Bashkir and Tartar Republics and northern Volga regions, centre Ufa, 1,866 km), Kuibyshev (centre Kuibyshev, links Volga regions with Urals, 2,012 km), Volga (centre Saratov, links it with Volgograd and Astrakhan, 3,149 km).

In the Urals and western Asia: Sverdlovsk (centre Sverdlovsk, links northern Urals with western Siberia, 4,000 km), South Urals (centre Chelyabinsk, links eastern regions of Russia in Europe with northern Kazakhstan, 2,875 km), Orenburg (centre Orenburg, links southern Urals with Siberia, 3,150 km), Omsk (centre Omsk, links western Siberia with northern Kazakhstan and Altai, 2,050 km), Tomsk (centre Novosibirsk, links western Siberia, Kemerovo coalfield and Altai, 3,039 km).

In south-western Asia: Transcaucasian (centre Tbilisi, links Black Sea coast with Yerevan, 1,887 km), Azerbaijan (centre Baku, 1,650 km).

In Central Asia: Tashkent (centre Tashkent, links Tadjik, Uzbek, Kirgiz and Kazakh republics with Orenburg, 2,420 km), Ashkhabad (centre Ashkhabad, links Caspian coast and Turkmen Republic with Uzbekistan, 2,647 km), Kazakh (centre Alma-Ata, 9,000 km). The 334-km Guriev–Astrakhan railway, across the Caspian desert, began operating on 1 Jan. 1971, shortening the route from Central Asia to the Caucasus by nearly 700 km. New lines, Kokchetav–Volodarskoye and Kustanai–Uritskoye, are under construction in Kazakhstan, and a Termez–Yavan line in Tadjikistan.

In central and eastern Siberia: Krasnoyarsk (centre Krasnoyarsk, a part of Trans-Siberian line but with new branches serving the Khakass and Tuva republics, 1,279 km), East Siberia (centre Irkutsk, serves Irkutsk region and Buryat Republic with link to Mongolian People's Republic, 1,696 km), Transbaikal (centre Chita, part of Trans-Siberian line but serving Buryatia and linked with China and Mongolia, 3,320 km). The Abakan–Taishet line, connecting the South-Siberian and main Trans-Siberian lines and linking the Bratsk and Kuznetzk industrial areas (640 km), began operating in 1964 with electric traction. A Tyumen–Surgat–Nizhnevartovsk (on the upper Ob) line, of nearly 1,000 km is under construction.

A line from Khrebtovaya, on the Taishet–Zena railway in East Siberia, to Ust-Ilimskaya on the Angara (215 km) has been opened, as the first section of a new North Siberian main line, skirting the northern shore of Lake Baikal, and stretching from Lena, on the Lena River, 3,145 km to Komsomolsk-on-Amur. This line, is scheduled for full electrification and operation in 1982. Electrification of the first 640 km began in June 1975.

The Baikal–Amur Magistral (BAM) will provide a more direct route to the Pacific ports of Nakhodka and Vladivostok than that offered by the Trans-Siberian railway and much of its route will lie several hundred km north of the Trans-Siberian railway, avoiding the latter's lengthy detour round Lake Baikal. It will give access to valuable raw materials such as coal, iron ore, copper, nickel and timber. The Baikal–Amur Magistral will ease the very heavy pressure on the Trans-Siberian route, which is only partially electrified and is not double-track throughout. Development of new port facilities on the east coast will create even greater strain on the existing facilities and the Baikal–Amur Magistral will become the principal route for export traffic to these ports. Oil from the Tyumen fields will be among the major commodities.

Construction of the Baikal–Amur Magistral is the most arduous railway-building project ever tackled by Soviet engineers and the greatest drawback to development of the region has been its severe climatic and geological conditions. There is permafrost throughout the area, and winter temperatures fall to −60° C. Severe danger exists in the mountains in winter from avalanches and in summer freak streams of mud fill river beds and valleys, hindering construction.

Work is being carried out from 7 major construction sites, each equipped with its own reinforced concrete plant, steel fabrication works and extensive engineering plant. When the line is completed in 1982 these sites will remain to form the nucleus of new heavy industry towns.

Over 3,200 bridges, tunnels and culverts are being built for the Baikal–Amur Magistral, including 140 major river crossings and a 1,200-metre bridge 40 metres high over the river Zeya reservoir. One of the first projects tackled was the 1,450-metre-long crossing of the river Amur near Komsomolsk. Extraordinary conditions here necessitated development of entirely new construction techniques. Large bridge spans are being used wherever possible to minimize the number of piles to be driven in permafrost conditions. Two tunnels are of particular note—a 15-km bore through the Severo-Muisky range, and one of 7 km through the Baikal ridge.

A 180-km link from the Trans-Siberian railway at Skovorodino to Tyndin, about midway between Ust-Kut and Komsomolsk, was opened in May 1975, and a northwards extension of this route, to Berkakit, was due to open in Nov. 1977. This line will reach the rich Chulman coalfields, allowing exploitation to begin well ahead of completion of the Baikal–Amur Magistral.

Many thousands of workers are involved in this major project, but despite the huge commitment of labour and equipment construction of at least a further 1,500 km of lines is due to begin during the next 5 years. Two major extensions of the Tyumen–Surgut line will exploit oil, natural gas and timber in Northern Siberia. One will serve Nizhne-Vartovskoye on the river Ob, while the other will reach Urengoi on the river Pur. Survey work has also been completed for a 400-km line in the Yamal Peninsula from Khal'mer-Yu to Cape Kharasavei. This will extend more than 73° North on the coast of the Kara Sea, making it the world's most northerly railway. Included is a 600-km crossing of the Baydaratskaya Gulf, which will be achieved by ice-breaking train ferries.

See map in THE STATEMAN'S YEAR-BOOK, 1977–78.

In the Far East: Far Eastern (centre Habarovsk, serves Maritime regions, 1,712 km), Amur (centre Blagoveshchensk, part of Trans-Siberian line, serves the Amur valley, 2,468 km), South Sahalin (centre Yuzhno-Sahalinsk, 752 km).

Underground railways have been built in Moscow, Leningrad, Kiev, Tbilisi, Kharkov and Baku. Line 1 of the Tashkent metro is scheduled to open by 1980, and surveys are in progress for lines in Minsk, Gorky, Novosibirsk, Kuibyshev and Sverdlovsk.

Aviation. In 1976 total length of internal airlines in the USSR was approximately 652,000 km; 100·9m. passengers were carried. The Central Asian Airways in some instances provide the only means of communication across the desert and mountainous regions of the local republics. An 8,500-km air service was opened in Feb. 1941 between Moscow and Anadyr (Eastern Siberia), through Archangel, Igarka, Khatanga, Tiksi Bay and Cape Schmidt, *i.e.*, along the entire course of the Northern Sea Route. There are also other Arctic airlines, *e.g.*, Igarka–Gulf of Kozhevnikov; Igarka–Dickson Island; Yakutsk–Tiksi Bay; Yakutsk–Viluisk; Yakutsk–Verkhoiansk.

Direct air services are maintained throughout the year between Moscow and the capitals of all Soviet republics as well as London, New York, Montreal, Tōkyō, Delhi, Rangoon, Belgrade, Peking, Pyongyang, Ulan Bator, Kábul, Tirana, Paris, Warsaw, Prague, Budapest, Bucharest, Sofia, Vienna, Berlin, Helsinki, Stockholm, Copenhagen, Jakarta and Dakar.

Soviet air services reach 64 countries, and 20 foreign lines have regular services to the USSR, including British Airways, KLM, SAS, Air France, SABENA, Air India, PANAM.

Hunter, H., *Soviet Transportation Policy.* Harvard Univ. Press, 1957
MacDonald, H., *Aeroflot: Soviet Air Transport since 1923.* London, 1975

Shipping. In 1977 the Soviet mercantile marine comprised 7,000 self-propelled vessels, of which 80% were built between 1957 and 1966. By May 1977 the gross cargo capacity was (including fishing vessels) 19·9m. registered tons.

Freights carried were: In 1913 (present frontiers), 15·1m. tonnes; in 1940, 31·2m. tonnes; in 1950, 33·7m. tonnes, and in 1977, 220m. tonnes; 49·9m. passengers were carried. The Soviet share in world marine tonnage was 2% in 1960 and 6·6% in 1971. Deep-sea ports are under construction at Vostochny (Far East) and Grigorevsky (Black Sea) with new deep-sea wharves at Ventspils (Latvia), Murmansk and Archangel (for Arctic traffic). Archangel is to be kept open by icebreakers all the year round from 1979.

The North Sea route affords convenient communication between the European USSR and the Far East along the Soviet coast, for the produce of the basins of the Obi, Yenissei, Lena and Kolyma rivers.

The length of navigable rivers and canals in exploitation was (1976) 146,400 km, of which the length of floatable rivers is 90,000 km. There are several thousand miles of canals and other artificial waterways; among them the Baltic and White Sea Canal (235 km), the Moscow–Volga Canal (130 km). Goods turnover on inland waterways was 28,900m. tonne-km in 1913, 35,900m. in 1940, 45,900m. in 1950 and 222,700m. in 1976; freight carried rose from 35·1m. tonnes in 1913 to 485m. tonnes in 1976.

The Volga–Don Shipping Canal was opened for traffic in 1952. The Volga–Don waterway from Volgograd to Rostov is 540 km long, of which the Volga–Don canal comprises 101 km. The canal has transformed the section of the river from Kalach, where the Don is joined by the Volga–Don canal, to Rostov into a deep-water highway suitable for big Volga shipping. The canal links the White, Baltic, Caspian, Azov and Black Seas into a single water transport system. In Oct. 1964 the 2,430-km Baltic–Volga waterway, linking Klaipeda on the Baltic to Kahovka at the mouth of the Dnieper and suitable for 5,000-tonne vessels, was begun. Reconstruction of the 18th-century Mariinsky canal system in north-west Russia was completed, providing a through waterway from Leningrad to Rybinsk (on the Upper Volga) and cutting the passage of freight from 18 to 2½ days.

In 1962 a canal was completed across the Kara-Kum desert in southern Turkmenistan (replacing an earlier project for a more costly scheme across the north of the republic). The canal, from Bussag on the river Amu-Darya to Archnan, north-west of Ashkhabad, through the Murgab oasis, 820 km long, supplies water to an area exceeding 200,000 hectares, suitable for cotton, fruit, vineyards and livestock. An extension to the Caspian (500 km) is under construction; the complete system will irrigate 1m. hectares.

An irrigation canal system (250 miles), bringing water from Kahovka on the Dnieper to North Crimea, is nearing completion. Work on diverting water from the Pechora and Vychegda rivers (flowing into the White Sea) south to the Volga is in progress. Work has begun on a 300-mile canal which will supply water from the Irtysh to Karaganda in Central Kazakhstan, irrigating over 150,000 acres; the first 37 miles were opened in 1965 and another 45 miles in Dec. 1967. Most of the 11 reservoirs required had been completed by 1 Jan. 1972. Other irrigation canals under construction are Kuibyshev (279 km long, to supply over 100,000 hectares) and Stavropol (481 km, irrigating 200,000 hectares); the second section of the latter went into commission in Nov. 1974, 14 months ahead of schedule. In Sept. 1972 the Saratov Canal (irrigating 1m. hectares) went into commission.

Post and Broadcasting. In Dec. 1976 the number of post, telegraph and telephone offices was 88,000 and of telephones 18·4m.

The international radio-telecommunications services are operated by the Ministry of Communications of the USSR. The Great Northern Telegraph Co., Ltd, of Denmark, operates cables connecting Denmark with Leningrad, whence connexion is made by means of a trans-Siberian landline with Vladivostok. From the latter place the Great Northern Telegraph Co. owns cables connecting with Japan, China and Hong Kong. Direct radio and telephone communication with India is provided for in an agreement concluded in 1955.

The State Committee for Broadcasting and Television produces 3 programmes in Moscow, broadcasting throughout the Union. In addition the Regional radio stations produce 1, 2 or 3 programmes for the republic as well as local programmes for a town or region. The foreign service from Moscow is beamed to all parts of the world, in 64 languages. Chinese is broadcast for 28½ hours a day. several republics have their own foreign services. English is broadcast from Moscow, Kiev, Tashkent, Vilnius and Yerevan. There are 130 TV centres in the USSR, several of them producing more than 1 programme. In Moscow there are 4 programmes. Colour programmes are broadcast by SECAM system.

Number of receivers: radio, 61·5m.; television, 57·6m.

Cinemas (Jan. 1977). There were 145,800 permanent and 8,400 mobile cinemas.

Newspapers. In 1976, 7,844 newspapers with a total circulation of 169m. copies were published in 57 languages of the USSR.

JUSTICE, RELIGION, EDUCATION AND WELFARE

Justice. The basis of the judiciary system is the same throughout the Soviet Union, but the constituent republics have the right to introduce modifications and to make their own rules for the application of the code of laws. The Supreme Court of the USSR is the chief court and supervising organ for all constituent republics and is elected by the Supreme Soviet of the USSR for 5 years. Supreme Courts of the Union and Autonomous Republics are elected by the Supreme Soviets of these republics, and Territorial, Regional and Area Courts by the respective Soviets, each for a term of 5 years.

Court proceedings are conducted in the local language with full interpreting facilities as required. All cases are heard in public, unless otherwise provided for by law, and the accused is guaranteed the right of defence.

Laws establishing common principles of criminal legislation, criminal responsibility for state and military crimes, judicial and criminal procedure and military tribunals were adopted by the Supreme Soviet on 25 Dec. 1958 for the courts both of the USSR and the constituent Republics.

The Law Courts are divided into People's Courts and higher courts. The People's Courts consist of the People's Judge and 2 Assessors, and their function is to examine, as the first instance, most of the civil and criminal cases, except the more important ones, some of which are tried at the Regional Court, and those of the highest importance at the Supreme Court. The Regional Courts supervise the activities of the People's Courts and also act as Courts of Appeal from the decisions of the People's Court. Special chambers of the higher courts deal with offences committed in the Army and the public transport services.

People's Judges and rota-lists of Assessors are elected directly by the citizens of each constituency: judges for 5 years, assessors for 2½. Should a judge be found not to perform his duties conscientiously and in accordance with the mandate of the people, he may be recalled by his electors.

The People's Assessors are called upon for duty for 2 weeks in a year. The People's Assessors for the Regional Court must have had at least 2 years' experience in public or trade-union work. The list of Assessors for the Supreme Court is drawn up by the Supreme Soviet of the republic.

The Labour Session of the People's Court supervises the regulations relating to the working conditions and the protection of labour and gives decisions on conflicts arising between managements and employees, or the violation of regulations.

Disputes between State institutions must be referred to an arbitration commission. Disputes between Soviet State institutions and foreign business firms may be referred by agreement to a Foreign Trade Arbitration Commission of the All-Union Chamber of Commerce.

The Procurator-General of the USSR is appointed for 5 years by the Supreme Soviet. All procurators of the republics, autonomous republics and autonomous regions are appointed by the Procurator-General of the USSR for a term of 5 years. The procurators supervise the correct application of the law by all state organs, and have special responsibility for the observance of the law in places of detention. The procurators of the Union republics are subordinate to the Procurator-General of the USSR, whose duty it is to see that acts of all institutions of the USSR are legal, that the law is correctly interpreted and uniformly applied; he has to participate in important cases in the capacity of State Prosecutor.

Capital punishment was abolished on 26 May 1947, but was restored on 12 Jan. 1950 for treason, espionage and sabotage, on 7 May 1954 for certain categories of murder, in Dec. 1958 for terrorism and banditry, on 7 May 1961 for embezzlement of public property, counterfeiting and attack on prison warders and, in particular circumstances, for attacks on the police and public order volunteers and for rape (15 Feb. 1962) and for accepting bribes (20 Feb. 1962).

In view of criminal abuses, extending over many years, discovered in the security system, the powers of administrative trial and exile previously vested in the security authorities (M.V.D.) were abolished in 1953; accelerated procedures for trial on charges of high treason, espionage, wrecking, etc., by the Supreme Court were abolished in 1955; and extensive powers of protection of persons under arrest or serving prison terms were vested in the Procurator-General's Office (1955). Supervisory commissions, composed of representatives of trade unions, youth organizations and local authorities, were set up in 1956 to inspect places of detention.

Further reforms of the civil and criminal codes were decreed on 25 Dec. 1958. Thereby the age of criminal responsibility has been raised from 14 to 16 years; deportation and banishment have been abolished; a presumption of innocence is not accepted, but the burden of proof of guilt has been placed upon the prosecutor; secret trials and the charge of 'enemy of the people' have been abolished.

Religion. With the Revolution the Orthodox Church lost its position as the dominant religion and all religions were placed on an equal footing. Article 124 of the 1936 constitution of the USSR reads as follows: 'With the aim of ensuring freedom of conscience for the citizens, the Church in the USSR is separated from the State and the school from the Church, and freedom of religious worship and anti-religious propaganda is permitted to all citizens.'

By decree of 23 Jan. 1918 the Orthodox Church was disestablished; its property, together with that of all other denominations, was nationalized. The congregations themselves have to maintain their churches and clergy, regardless of confession or denomination, and may organize a minimum of 20 persons, which may request and receive the use of a church building, free of charge, except for maintenance, insurance, land taxes, etc. About two-thirds of all the churches have been closed. Religious instruction may be given in private, but otherwise only in church classes. The income of religious communities is not subject to taxation. The state supplies paper and printing facilities to all denominations for producing the Bible, the Koran, prayer books, missals, etc.

Relations between the religious communities of all creeds and the Government are maintained through a Council for Religious Affairs (*Chairman*, V. A. Kuroyedov).

The Russian Orthodox Church, represented by the Patriarchate of Moscow, had, in 1967, 30m. regular worshippers. There are still many Old Believers, whose schism from the Orthodox Church dates from the 17th century. The Russian Church is headed by the Patriarch of Moscow and All Russia, assisted by the Holy Synod, which has 6 members—the Patriarch himself and the Metropolitans of Krutitsy (Moscow), Leningrad and Kiev *ex officio*, and 3 bishops alternating for 6 months in order of seniority from the 3 regions forming the Moscow Patriarchate. In 1967 there were 20,000 places of worship (54,000 before the Revolution). Religious instruction in classes for persons under 18 is forbidden. The Patriarchate of Moscow maintains jurisdiction over a few parishes of Russian Orthodox abroad, at Tehran, Jerusalem, German Democratic Republic, France (1 archbishop), England, North and South America (2 bishops).

After the Russian Orthodox Church the next Christian community in importance are the Armenians; their Catholicos (Patriarch), whose seat is at Etchmiadzin, is head of all the Armenian (Gregorian) communities throughout the world.

The Georgian Church has its own organization under a Catholicos (Patriarch).

Protestantism is represented chiefly by the Evangelical Christian Baptists, with over 512,000 baptized adult members and some 5,000 churches: the Lutheran (350,000 in Estonia, 600,000 in Latvia) are concentrated mainly in the Baltic States, the Reformed in the Transcarpathian Region of the Ukraine (70,000).

The Roman Catholics are most numerous in Lithuania and the western Ukraine. There are only 4 bishops now in office. In 1946 some 3·5m. Uniates in the USSR withdrew their allegiance to Rome and came under the jurisdiction of the Orthodox Patriarchate in Moscow.

The Moslems, mainly Sunnis, are divided into 4 administrative regions; 3 of them (Central Asia, European Russia and Siberia, Northern Caucasus) headed by a Mufti; the largest (Transcaucasia, with its centre at Baku) by a Shaikh-ul-Islam.

The Armenian-Gregorian and the Roman Catholic churches and the Moslems of Central Asia maintain theological colleges.

There are various Jewish communities, the chief being in Moscow and Kiev. Large synagogues maintain bakeries for producing unleavened bread. The Central Buddhist Council of the USSR is headed by a Lama with communities in Buryatia, Tuva, Kalmykia and in the national (minority) areas of the Chita and Irkutsk regions.

Bordeaux, M., *Opium of the People. The Christian Religion in the USSR*. London, 1965.—*Religious Ferment in Russia*. London, 1968
Braham, R. L., *Jews in the Communist World; a bibliography, 1945–1960*. New York, 1961
Conquest, R. (ed.), *Religion in the USSR*. London, 1968
Curtiss, J. S., *The Russian Church and the Soviet State, 1917–50*. New York, 1953
Fejtö, F., *Les Juifs et l'antisémitisme dans les pays communistes*. Paris, 1960
Fletcher, W. C., *A Study in Survival: The Church in Russia 1927–43*. New York, 1965
Goldberg, B. Z., *The Jewish Problem in the Soviet Union*. New York, 1961
Kolarz, W., *Religion in the Soviet Union*. London, 1961
Leneman, L., *La Tragédie des Juifs en URSS*. Bruges, 1959
Novosti Press Agency (ed.), *Soviet Jews: Fact and Fiction*. Moscow, 1970
Struve, N., *Les Chrétiens en URSS*. Paris, 1963

Education. Education is free and compulsory from 7 to 15/16. Co-education was reintroduced in all schools on 1 Sept. 1954. There are 3 types of schools—those with a 4-year, an 8-year and an 11-year curriculum; the school-leaving age was raised to 17 for 96% of children in 1975. Under a law of 24 Dec. 1958 general polytechnical education is to last 8 years (*i.e.*, until the age of 15 or 16) and thereafter is to be combined for 2 years with work in production (except for the specially artistically gifted who go to art schools). Instruction is given in more than 100 languages.

In 1976–77 there were 159,000 primary and secondary schools. Pupils in primary, secondary, technical, etc., schools numbered 48m. (10·9m. of them in the 16–18 age-groups) and the teachers 2·7m. There were 14,020 schools providing a 10-year secondary education for 4·9m. workers and peasants who had already begun earning their living.

At the end of 1940 labour reserve schools (both vocational and industrial) were organized, admitting applicants from 14 to 17 years of age. From 1959 onwards these and other technical schools were reorganized as town and rural professional and technical schools. Between 1940 and 1977 they trained 35m. skilled workers. In 1976, 2·1m. graduated from such schools, including 610,000 for agriculture; 600,000 agricultural mechanics were trained in state and collective farms. Over 6,450 vocational training schools existed in 1976, training 3·2m. boys and girls, about one-third providing full secondary education. In 1976, 8·9m. children of from 3 to 7 years of age attended kindergartens. Children in boarding schools numbered over 800,000 in 1972–73.

In 1976–77 there were 4,303 technical colleges with 4·6m. students, and 859 universities, institutes and other places of higher education, with 4·9m. students (including 2·24m. taking correspondence or evening courses). 68,000 students enrolled after work in factories, collective farms, or the armed forces were attending preparatory courses at 524 places of higher education (similar to the 'workers' faculties' of early Soviet years).

Among the 65 university towns are: Moscow, Leningrad, Kharkov, Odessa, Tartu, Kazan, Saratov, Tomsk, Kiev, Sverdlovsk, Tbilisi, Alma-Ata, Tashkent, Minsk, Gorky and Vladivostok. On 1 Jan. 1977 there were 1,253,500 scientific workers in places of higher education, research institutes and Academies of Sciences. There are 33,000 foreign students from 130 countries.

The Academy of Sciences of the USSR had 733 members and corresponding members. Total learned institutions under the USSR Academy of Sciences number 244, with 42,951 scientific staff. Fourteen of the Union Republics have their own Academies of Sciences, with scientific staff numbering 45,458. On 1 Jan. 1977 there were 95,657 post-graduate students.

An Academy of Pedagogical Sciences had 14 research institutes with 1,687 staff.

In Dec. 1976 there were employed in the national economy 10m. specialists with a completed higher education and 14m. with a completed secondary technical education.

In 1976–77 about 93·7m. people were studying at schools, colleges and training or correspondence courses. 90 per 1,000 of the employed population had a higher education (1939, 13; 1959, 33).

Health and Social Security. All health services are free of charge; but private practice exists. Health is administered by the Ministry of Health of the USSR, which supervises the work of the Health Ministries of the Union Republics and the Autonomous Republics.

In 1944 an Academy of Medical Sciences was formed; it has under its direct control 42 research institutes. In all, there were, in 1976, 393 medical research institutions with 70,000 research staff. Smallpox, trachoma and malaria have been virtually eliminated.

In 1976–77, 98 institutes and medical faculties had a total of 357,000 students taking a 6-year course.

In Dec. 1976 there were 23,900 civil hospitals with 3,076,000 beds. There were 1m. infants in day nurseries and another 2·2m. in the crèche-sections of kindergartens. 864,000 doctors (including dentists) were in the health service. All confinements in towns and 75% in the country were in hospital.

There were 35,700 clinics and dispensaries, and 4,260 sanitary epidemiological stations.

The death-rate in the USSR in 1976 was 9·5 per 1,000, and the birth rate 18·4 per 1,000. Infant death rate was 27·9 (per 1,000 live births) in 1974, compared with 273 in 1913, 184 in 1940 and 81 in 1950. Average expectation of life, 70 (1913, 32).

Social insurance is administered by the trade unions, through social insurance councils elected in places of work and social insurance sub-committees of factory committees: about 5m. volunteers are engaged in this work. 32m. people were sent to sanatoria or rest homes in 1976. There were nearly 46m. pensioners in Jan. 1977. 11·7m. collective farmers were receiving state-aided pensions.

Total number of sanatoria in 1976 was 2,345 with 509,800 beds; in addition, there were 2,277 'one-night' or 'one-day' sanatoria, with 174,800 beds. There were 1,170 rest homes with 354,100 beds.

State expenditure (in 1m. new roubles) on health services proper, 1960, 4,800; 1970, 9,300; 1973, 10,500; 1974, 11,000; 1975, 11,470; 1976, 11,800.

Between 1950 and 1976, 52,505,000 apartments (in towns) and houses (in rural areas) were built. In 1976, 2·1m. apartments and houses were built. By the end of 1976, 69% of all housing in urban settlements and 59% in villages, had gas supply installed.

DIPLOMATIC REPRESENTATIVES

OF THE USSR IN GREAT BRITAIN (13 Kensington Palace Gdns, London, W8 4QX)

Ambassador: Nikolai M. Lunkov.

OF GREAT BRITAIN IN THE USSR (Naberezhnaya Morisa Toreza 14, Moscow 72)

Ambassador: Sir Howard Smith, KCMG.

OF THE USSR IN THE USA (1125–16th St., NW, Washington, D.C., 20036)

Ambassador: Anatoly F. Dobrynin.

OF THE USA IN THE USSR (Ulitsa Chaykovskogo 19, Moscow)

Ambassador: Malcolm Toon.

OF THE USSR TO THE UNITED NATIONS

Ambassador: Vladimir N. Martinenko.

Books of Reference

Narodnoye Hozyaistvo SSSR 1922–1974 (National Economy of the USSR). Statistical Summary. 1975
SSSR v Tsifrakh. Central Statistical Department, 1975
Pravda [Truth]. Daily organ of the Central Committee of the Communist Party
Izvestia [News]. Daily organ of the Presidium of the Supreme Soviet of the USSR
Viedomosti Verkhovnovo Sovieta. Bulletin of the Supreme Soviet of the USSR, in the languages of the 16 republics
Sovietskaia Torgovlia. Thrice-weekly publication of the Ministry of Trade of the USSR
Planovoye Khoziaistvo. Monthly. Moscow
Voprosy Torgovli. A monthly journal published by the Ministry of Trade of the USSR
Vneshnaya Torgovlya. Published by the Ministry for Foreign Trade. Monthly. Moscow
Trud. The daily organ of the All-Union Central Council of Trade Unions
Professionalnye Soyuzy. A trade union fortnightly. Moscow
Kommunist. A fortnightly organ of the Communist Party of the Soviet Union
Finansy i Khoziaistvo. A weekly publication of the Ministry for Finance
Sotsialistitcheskoye Zemledelie. A daily publication of the Ministry of Agriculture
Soviet Foreign Policy During the Patriotic War; Documents and Materials. 2 vols (translated by A. Rothstein). London, 1946–47
History of the USSR. Published by the Soviet Academy of Sciences. 3 vols. Moscow, 1948–57. (In Russian.) German edition, *Geschichte der Völker der Sowjetunion.* Basle, 1945
Bolshaya Sovietskaya Entsiklopedia. 65 vols. Moscow, 1926–47; 2nd ed., 51 vols. Moscow, 1949–58; annual supplement (*Yezhegodnik*)
Soviet Union. A monthly pictorial. Moscow. (In English)
Soviet Import–Export Dictionary (in Russian, with English, etc., terms). Moscow, 1952
Velikaia Otechestvennaya Voina Sovetskogo Soyuza. Moscow, 1965
Soviet Studies; a Quarterly Review. Ed. J. Miller and R. J. A. Schlesinger. Oxford, 1949 ff.
The Current Digest of the Soviet Press. Published by Joint Committee on Slavic Studies. Weekly. Washington, D.C.
Beloff, M., *The Foreign Policy of Soviet Russia, 1929–41.* 2 vols. 1947–49.—*Soviet Policy in the Far East.* Oxford, 1953.—*Soviet Policy in Asia, 1944–52.* Oxford, 1953
Brown, A., and Kaser, M., *The Soviet Union Since the Fall of Krushchev.* London, 1975
Carr, E. H., *The Bolshevik Revolution.* 8 vols. London, 1950–64
Coates, W. P., and Coates, Zelda K., *A History of Anglo-Soviet Relations.* 2 vols. London, 1944–58

Degras, J. (compiler), *Soviet Documents on Foreign Policy, 1917–41*. 3 vols. London, 1948–52
Deutscher, K., *Trotsky*. 3 vols. OUP, 1954 ff.
Ellman, M., *Soviet Planning Today*. CUP, 1971
Fitzsimmons, T., and others, *USSR; Its People, Its Society, Its Culture*. New Haven, 1960
Galperin, I. R., *New English–Russian Dictionary*. 2 vols. Moscow, 1972
Horecky, P. L. (ed.), *Russia and the Soviet Union: A Bibliographical Guide to Western-Language Publications*. Univ. of Chicago Press, 1965
Hutchings, R., *Soviet Economic Development*. New York, 1971
Jones, D. L., *Books in English in the Soviet Union 1917–73: A Bibliography*. London and New York, 1975
Kirby, E. S., *The Soviet Far East*. London, 1971
Lenin, V. L., *Collected Works*. 45 vols. London, 1960–70
Lydolph, P. E., *Geography of the USSR*. New York, 1970
Maynard, J., *Russia in Flux*. London, 1941.—*The Russian Peasant: and Other Studies*. London, 1942.—*Russia in Flux* (abridged ed. of the two foregoing books). New York, 1948
Miller, W., *Who are the Russians? A History of the Russian People*. London, 1973
Moore, Harriet L., *Soviet Far Eastern Policy, 1931–45*. Princeton and Oxford, 1946
Müller, V. K., *Anglo-russkii slovar*. 13th ed. Moscow, 1967
Pares, Sir B., *A History of Russia*. London, 1962
Preobrazhensky, A. G., *Etymological Dictionary of the Russian Language*. Columbia Univ. Press, 1951
Riasanovsky, N. V., *A History of Russia*. 3rd ed. OUP, 1977
Rothstein, A., *A History of the USSR*. 2nd ed. London, 1951
Schlesinger, R., *The Spirit of Post-war Russia. Soviet Ideology, 1917–46*. London, 1947.—*Changing Attitude in Soviet Russia: The Family*. London, 1949
Shinkarev, L., *The Land Beyond the Mountains: Siberia and its People Today*. London, 1973
Slusser, R. M., and Triska, J. F., *A Calendar of Soviet Treaties, 1917–57*. Stanford Univ. Press, 1959
Smirnitzky, A. I. (ed.) *Rusko–angliiskii slovar*. 4th ed. Moscow 1959
Stalin, J. V., *Collected Works*. 13 vols. London, 1952–55
Utechin, S. V. (ed.), *Everyman's Concise Encyclopaedia of Russia*. London, 1961
Vernadsky, G., *A History of Russia*. 4th ed. Yale Univ. Press, 1954
Wheeler, M., *The Oxford Russian–English Dictionary*. OUP, 1972

RUSSIAN SOVIET FEDERAL SOCIALIST REPUBLIC (RSFSR)

Rossiskaya Sovietskaya Federativnaya Sotsialisticheskaya Respublika

AREA AND POPULATION. The RSFSR occupies over 76% of the total area of the USSR stretching from the Far North to the Black Sea in the south and from the Far East to Kaliningrad in the west. 82·8% of its population in Jan. 1970 were Russians, the rest being 38 national minorities such as the Tartars, Jews, Mordovians, Chuvashis, Bashkirs, Poles, Germans, Udmurts, Buryats, Mari, Yakuts and Ossetians. The 2 principal cities are Moscow, the capital, with a population (est. Jan. 1977) of 7·8m. (without suburbs, 7·6m.) and Leningrad, the second capital, 4·4m. (without suburbs, 3·96m.). Among other important large towns are Gorki, Rostov-on-Don, Volgograd, Sverdlovsk, Novosibirsk, Chelyabinsk, Kazan, Omsk and Kuibyshev.

The RSFSR has a variety of climates (ranging from arctic to sub-tropical) and of geographical conditions (tundra, forest lands, steppes and rich agricultural soil). It also contains great mineral resources: iron ore in the Urals, the Kerch Peninsula and Siberia; coal in the Kuznetz Basin, Eastern Siberia, Urals and the sub-Moscow Basin; oil in the Urals, Azov–Black Sea area and Bashkiria. It also has abundant deposits of gold, platinum, copper, zinc, lead, tin and rare metals.

The RSFSR produces about 70% of the total industrial and agricultural output of the Soviet Union. Industrial and office workers averaged 61·8m. in 1976.

CONSTITUTION AND GOVERNMENT. The RSFSR adopted its present constitution at the 17th Extraordinary All-Russian Congress of Soviets in Jan. 1937.

Since then slight alterations have been introduced in the constitution from time to time.

President, Presidium of the Supreme Soviet: M. A. Yasnov.
Chairman, Council of Ministers: M. S. Solomentsev.
Foreign Minister: F. E. Titov.

A special bureau of the Central Committee of the Communist Party of the USSR has been set up for the RSFSR.

The RSFSR consists of:

(1) *Territories:* Altai, Khabarovsk, Krasnodar, Krasnoyarsk, Primorye, Stavropol.

(2) *Regions:* Amur, Archangel, Astrakhan, Belgorod, Briansk, Chelyabinsk, Chita, Gorki, Irkutsk, Ivanovo, Kaluga, Kalinin, Kaliningrad, Kamchatka, Kemerovo, Kirov, Kostroma, Kuibyshev, Kurgan, Kursk, Leningrad, Lipetsk, Magadan, Moscow, Murmansk, Novgorod, Novosibirsk, Omsk, Orel, Orenburg, Penza, Perm, Pskov, Rostov, Ryazan, Sakhalin, Saratov, Smolensk, Sverdlovsk, Tambov, Tomsk, Tula, Tyumen, Ulyanovsk, Vladimir, Volgograd, Vologda, Voronezh, Yaroslavl.

(3) *Autonomous Soviet Socialist Republics:* Bashkir, Buryat, Checheno-Ingush, Chuvash, Daghestan, Kabardino-Balkar, Kalmyk, Karelian, Komi, Mari, Mordovian, North Ossetia, Tatar, Tuva, Udmurt, Yakut.

(4) *Autonomous Regions:* Adygei, Karachayevo-Cherkess, Gorno-Altai, Jewish, Khakass.

(5) *National Areas:* Aginsky-Buryat, Chukot, Evenki, Khanty-Mansi, Komi-Permyak, Koryak, Nenetz, Taimyr (Dolgano-Nenetz), Ust-Ordynsky-Buryat, Yamalo-Nenetz.

The Supreme Soviet, elected in June 1975, consisted of 904 deputies (1 per 150,000 population); 604 were Communists, 317 women, 454 workers and collective farmers.

On 19 June 1977, 1,116,025 deputies were elected to local authorities; 559,843 (50·2%) were women, 645,589 (57·8%) non-Party and 745,250 (66·8%) industrial workers and collective farmers.

FINANCE. Revenue and expenditure balanced as follows (in 1m. new roubles): 1970, 41,146; 1971, 44,113 (surplus 639m.); 1974, 47,865; 1975, 58,068 (surplus 1,337m.). These figures, and those for the other 14 Union Republics, include grants from the Union Budget.

Annual planned investments in the national economy rose from 14,762m. roubles in 1956 to 72,736m. in 1976 (excluding those by collective farms).

COMMUNICATIONS. Length of railways on 1 Jan. 1977 was 79,870 km, inland waterways, 126,000 km, hard-surface motor roads 306,500 km.

Newspapers. In 1976 there were 4,253 newspapers, 3,949 of them in Russian, with a circulation of 113·4m. and 110·4m. respectively.

EDUCATION. In 1976–77 there were 22·1m. pupils in 83,500 primary 7-year and secondary schools; 2,905,700 students in 484 higher educational establishments (including correspondence students) and 2,732,300 students in 2,482 technical colleges of all kinds (including correspondence students). There were 7m. children attending pre-school institutions. There were, on 1 Jan. 1977, 863,400 scientific staff in 3,009 learned and scientific institutions.

In 1957 a Siberian branch of the Academy of Sciences was organized, in charge of all scientific research institutions from the Urals to the Pacific.

There is an Academy of Municipal Economy (with 5 research institutions and a staff of 428).

HEALTH. Doctors at the end of 1976 numbered 485,500, and hospital beds 1·68m. (133,400 in 1913 and 482,000 in 1940); 2·96m. infants in crèches.

BASHKIR AUTONOMOUS SOVIET SOCIALIST REPUBLIC

Area 143,600 sq. km (55,430 sq. miles), population (Jan. 1977) 3,833,000. Capital, Ufa. Bashkiria was annexed to Russia in 1557. It was constituted as an Autonomous Soviet Republic on 23 March 1919. Population, on 5 Jan. 1970, included 23·5% Bashkirians, 40·5% Russians, 29% Tartars and Chuvashes.

255 deputies were elected on 15 June 1975, 97 of them women.

In 1976–77 there were over 5,000 schools with 841,000 pupils. There is a state university and a branch of the USSR Academy of Sciences with 8 learned institutions (501 research workers). There were 71,100 students in technical colleges and 50,500 receiving higher education.

In Jan. 1977 there were 9,194 doctors and 43,015 hospital beds.

There are expanding chemical, coal, steel, electrical engineering, timber and paper industries. There were 631 collective farms and 160 state farms in 1976. Crop area was 4,643,000 hectares. Bashkiria is the second largest oil producer in USSR.

BURIAT AUTONOMOUS SOVIET SOCIALIST REPUBLIC

The Buriat Republic, situated to the south of the Yakut Republic, adopted the Soviet system on 1 March 1920. This area was penetrated by the Russians in the 17th century and finally annexed from China by the treaties of Nerchinsk (1689) and Kyakhta (1727).

The area is 351,300 sq. km (135,650 sq. miles). The population (Jan. 1977) was 879,000. Capital, Ulan-Udé. The name of the Republic was changed from 'Buriat-Mongol' on 7 July 1958. The population includes 22% Buriats and 73·5% Russians.

150 deputies were elected on 15 June 1975, 50 of them women.

The main industries are coal, timber, building materials, fisheries, sheep and cattle farming. In 1976 there were 100 state and 59 collective farms. Crop area was 881,000 hectares. Gold, molybdenum and wolfram are mined.

In 1976–77 there were over 700 schools with 176,800 pupils, 16 technical colleges with 22,300 students and 2 higher educational institutions with 21,500 students. A branch of the Siberian Department of the Academy of Sciences had 4 learned institutions with 285 research workers.

At the end of 1976 there were 2,360 doctors and 11,102 hospital beds.

CHECHENO-INGUSH AUTONOMOUS SOVIET SOCIALIST REPUBLIC

Area, 19,300 sq. km (7,350 sq. miles); population (Jan. 1977), 1,159,000. Capital, Grozny. After 70 years of almost continuous fighting, the Chechens and Ingushes were conquered by Russia in the late 1850s. In 1918 each nationality separately established its 'National Soviet' within the Terek Autonomous Republic, and in 1920 (after the Civil War) were constituted areas within the Mountain Republic. The Chechens separated out as an Autonomous Region on 30 Nov. 1922 and the Ingushes on 7 July 1924. In Jan. 1934 the two regions were united, and on 5 Dec. 1936 constituted as an Autonomous Republic. This was dissolved in 1944, but re-constituted on 9 Jan. 1957: 232,000 Chechens and Ingushes returned to their homes in the next 2 years. The population includes 47·8% Chechens, 10·7% Ingushes, 34·5% Russians.

160 deputies were elected on 15 June 1975, 73 of them women.

The Republic has one of the major Soviet oilfields: also a number of large engineering works, chemical factories, building materials works and food canneries. There is an expanding timber, woodworking and furniture industry. In 1976–77 there were 100 state and 45 collective farms. Crop area was 468,000 hectares.

There were, in 1976–77, 534 schools with 288,100 pupils, 12 technical colleges with 15,000 students and 2 places of higher education with 11,700 students.

In 1976 there were 75 hospitals, 2,694 doctors and 11,210 hospital beds.

CHUVASH AUTONOMOUS SOVIET SOCIALIST REPUBLIC

Area, 18,300 sq. km (7,064 sq. miles); population (Jan. 1977), 1,281,000. Capital, Cheboksary. The territory was annexed by Russia in the middle of the 16th century. On 24 June 1920 it was constituted as an Autonomous Region, and on 21 April 1925 as an Autonomous Republic. The population includes Chuvashes (70%), Russians (24·5%), Tartars and Mordovians (4·7%).

165 deputies were elected on 15 June 1975, 62 of them women.

Like most of the Autonomous Republics, Chuvashia before 1914 was a region of primitive agriculture, with a certain development of the timber industry. Today it has several big railway repair works, an expanding electrical and other engineering industry, building materials, chemicals, textiles and food industries; timber felling and haulage are largely mechanized. In 1976 there were 210 collective farms and 96 state farms. Grain crops account for nearly two-thirds of all sowings and fodder crops for nearly a quarter. Fruit and wine-growing are a developing branch of agriculture.

In 1976–77 there were 820 schools attended by 283,100 children, 22 technical colleges with 23,200 students and 3 places of higher education with 15,200 students.

There were 2,901 doctors and 13,950 hospital beds.

DAGESTAN AUTONOMOUS SOVIET SOCIALIST REPUBLIC

Area, 50,300 sq. km (19,416 sq. miles); population (Jan. 1977), 1·59m. Capital, Mahachkala. Over 30 nationalities inhabit this republic apart from Russians (14·7%); the most numerous are the Avartsy (24·5%), Dargintsy (14·5%), Lezginy (11·4%), Kumyki (11·8%), Laki (5·1%), Tabasarany (3·7%) and Azerbaidjanis (3·8%). Annexed from Persia in 1723, Dagestan was constituted an Autonomous Republic on 20 Jan. 1921.

190 deputies were elected on 15 June 1975, 83 of them women.

There are large engineering, oil, chemical, woodworking, textile, food and other light industries. Agriculture is very varied, ranging from wheat to grapes, with sheep farming and cattle breeding; in 1976 there were 311 collective farms and 233 state farms. A chain of power stations is under construction in the Sulak River (total capacity 2·5m. kw.). Crop area was 425,400 hectares.

In 1976–77 there were 1,576 schools with 478,500 pupils, 26 technical colleges with 26,000 students and 4 higher educational establishments with 23,400 students; and a branch of the USSR Academy of Sciences with 4 learned institutions (363 research workers). Doctors numbered 4,395 and hospital beds 15,560.

On 14 May 1970 an earthquake rendered 35,668 families homeless, destroyed school buildings and hospitals. By 1 Nov. considerable progress had been made in rehousing and classes were restarted in 170 new and repaired schools.

KABARDINO-BALKAR AUTONOMOUS SOVIET SOCIALIST REPUBLIC

Area, 12,500 sq. km (4,825 sq. miles); population (Jan. 1977), 664,000. Capital, Nalchik. Kabarda was annexed to Russia in 1557. The Republic was constituted on 5 Dec. 1936. Population includes Kabardinians (45%), Balkars (8·7%), Russians (37·2%).

145 deputies were elected on 15 June 1975, 66 of them women.

Main industries are ore-mining, timber, engineering, coal, food processing, timber and light industries, building materials. Grain, livestock breeding, dairy farming and wine-growing are the principal branches of agriculture. There were, in 1976, 54 state and 74 collective farms.

In 1976–77 there were 250 schools with 143,300 pupils, 12,100 students in 11 technical colleges and 8,600 students receiving higher education; 2,319 doctors and 7,385 hospital beds.

KALMYK AUTONOMOUS SOVIET SOCIALIST REPUBLIC

The Kalmyks migrated from western China to Russia (Nogai Steppe) in the early 17th century. The territory was constituted an Autonomous Region on 4 Nov. 1920, and an Autonomous Republic on 22 Oct. 1935; this was dissolved in 1943. On 9 Jan. 1957 it was reconstituted as an Autonomous Region and on 29 July 1958 as an Autonomous Republic once more.

Area, 75,900 sq. km (29,300 sq. miles); population (Jan. 1977), 274,000. Capital, Elista (63,000). The population includes 41% Kalmyks, 45·8% Russians, 6·9% Kazakhs, Chechens and Dagestanis.

125 deputies were elected on 15 June 1975, 52 of them women.

Main industries are fishing, canning and building materials. Cattle breeding and irrigated farming (mainly fodder crops) are the principal branches of agriculture. In 1976 there were 90 state and 23 collective farms. Crop area was 815,500 hectares.

In 1976–77 there were 67,300 pupils in 242 schools, 6,300 students in technical colleges and 4,800 in higher education; 788 doctors and 4,080 hospital beds.

KARELIAN AUTONOMOUS SOVIET SOCIALIST REPUBLIC

HISTORY. Before 1917, Karelia (then known as the Olonetz Province) was noted chiefly as a place of exile for political and other prisoners.

After the November Revolution of 1917, Karelia formed part of the RSFSR. In June 1920 a Karelian Labour Commune was formed and in July 1923 this was transformed into the Karelian Autonomous Soviet Socialist Republic (one of the autonomous republics of the RSFSR). On 31 March 1940, after the Soviet–Finnish war, practically all the territory (with the exception of a small section in the neighbourhood of the Leningrad area) which had been ceded by Finland to the USSR was added to Karelia and the Karelian Autonomous Republic was transformed into the Karelo-Finnish Soviet Socialist Republic as the 12th republic of the USSR. In 1946, however, the southern part of the Republic, including its whole seaboard and the town of Viipuri (Vyborg) and Keksholm, was attached to the RSFSR. In 1956 the status of the Republic was changed (*see* p. 1204).

AREA AND POPULATION. The Karelian Autonomous Republic, capital Petrozavodsk, covers an area of 172,400 sq. km, with a population of 738,000 (Jan. 1977). Karelians represent 11·8% of the population, Russians 68·1%, Belorussians 9·3%, Finns 3·1%.

145 deputies were elected on 15 June 1975, 50 of them women.

NATURAL RESOURCES. Karelia is chiefly noted for its wealth of timber, some 70% of its territory being forest land. It is also rich in other natural resources, having large deposits of diabase, spar, quartz, marble, mica, granite, zinc, lead, silver, copper, molybdenum, tin, baryta, iron ore, etc. Karelia takes first place in the USSR for the production of mica. It has 43,643 lakes, which, as well as its rivers, are rich in fish.

Agriculture. There were 10 fishery collective farms and 60 state farms in 1976. Livestock on 1 Jan. 1977 included 104,000 cattle, 39,000 pigs, 56,000 sheep and goats.

INDUSTRY. The Republic has some 25 large-scale enterprises, such as timber-mills, paper-cellulose works, mica, chemical plants, electrical stations and furniture factories. Output, 1976: Timber, 12·8m. cu. metres; paper and cellulose, 1,643,000 tons; power, 2,690m. kwh.; canned fish, 12·3m. tins.

The construction of the White Sea–Baltic Canal had a powerful influence on the economic development of Karelia. New refrigerating plants, cellulose factories and timber industry equipment began working in 1970.

COMMUNICATIONS. A railway between Petrozavodsk and Suoyarvi connects the capital and the Murmansk Railway with the main railway line Sortavala–Vyborg. A railway line was also laid between Kandalaksha and Kuolayarvi. Length of track, 1,600 km.

EDUCATION. In 1976–77 there were 126,100 pupils in 747 schools. There were 9,900 students in 3 places of higher education and 16,300 in 10 technical colleges.

There are in Petrozavodsk a university (4,028 full-time students, 2,036 taking correspondence courses and 622 evening students in 1971), 2 other higher institutes and a teachers' training college. A branch of the Academy of Sciences was set up in 1949 with 8 learned institutions (360 research workers).

HEALTH. There were 2,930 doctors in 1976, and 10,995 hospital beds.

KOMI AUTONOMOUS SOVIET SOCIALIST REPUBLIC

Area, 415,900 sq. km (160,540 sq. miles); population (Jan. 1977), 1,067,000. Capital, Syktyvkar (161,000). Annexed by the princes of Moscow in the 14th century and occupied by British and American forces in 1918–19, the territory was constituted as an Autonomous Region on 22 Aug. 1921 and as an Autonomous Republic on 5 Dec. 1936. The population includes Komi (28·6%), Russians (53·1%), Ukrainians and Belorussians (11·2%).

170 deputies were elected on 15 June 1975, 54 of them women.

There are large coal, oil, timber, gas, asphalt and building materials industries; light industry is expanding. Livestock breeding (including dairy farming) is the main branch of agriculture. There were 51 state farms in 1976. Crop area 92,000 hectares.

In 1976–77 there were 214,000 pupils in 789 schools, 11,900 students receiving higher education, 17,300 students in 13 technical colleges; and a branch of the Academy of Sciences with 4 learned institutions (307 research workers).

There were 3,549 doctors and 15,800 hospital beds.

MARI AUTONOMOUS SOVIET SOCIALIST REPUBLIC

Area, 23,200 sq. km (8,955 sq. miles); population (Jan. 1977), 704,000. Capital, Yoshkar-Ola. The Mari people were annexed to Russia, with other peoples of the Kazan Tartar Khanate, when the latter was overthrown in 1552. On 25 Nov. 1920 the territory was constituted as an Autonomous Region, and on 5 Dec. 1936 as an Autonomous Republic. The population includes Mari (43·7%), Tartars (5·9%), Chuvashes (1·3%), Russians (46·9%).

130 deputies were elected on 15 June 1975, 44 of them women.

There are over 300 modern factories. The main industries are metalworking, timber, paper, woodworking and food processing. In 1976 there were 105 collective farms and 72 state farms. Over 69% of cultivated land is under grain, but flax, potatoes, fruit and vegetables are also expanding branches of agriculture, as is also livestock farming. 642,000 hectares were under crops.

Estimated reserves of the Pechora coalfield are 262,000m. tons.

In 1976–77 there were 714 schools with 142,100 pupils, 12 technical colleges and institutes with 12,200 students and 2 higher educational establishments with 16,300 students; also 1,817 doctors and 8,445 hospital beds.

MORDOVIAN AUTONOMOUS SOVIET SOCIALIST REPUBLIC

Area, 26,200 sq. km (10,110 sq. miles); population (Jan. 1977), 980,000. Capital, Saransk. By the 13th century the Mordovian tribes had been subjugated by the Russian princes of Ryazan and Nizhni-Novgorod. In 1928 the territory was constituted as a Mordovian Area within the Middle-Volga Territory, on 10 Jan. 1930 as an Autonomous Region and on 20 Dec. 1934 as an Autonomous Republic. The population includes Mordovians (35·4%), Russians (58·9%), Tartars (4·4%).

150 deputies were elected on 15 June 1975, 64 of them women.

The Republic has a wide range of industries: Electrical, timber, cable, building materials, furniture, textile, leather and other light industries. Agriculture is devoted chiefly to grain, sugar-beet, sheep and dairy farming. In 1976 there were 76 state and 275 collective farms.

There were 205,100 children at school, 17,500 students in technical colleges and 20,000 at the state university and institutes, in 1976–77. There were 2,446 doctors and 12,400 hospital beds.

NORTH OSSETIAN AUTONOMOUS SOVIET SOCIALIST REPUBLIC

Area, 8,000 sq. km (3,088 sq. miles); population (Jan. 1977), 597,000. Capital, Ordzhonikidze (formerly Vladikavkaz). The Ossetians, known to antiquity as Alani (who were also called by their immediate neighbours 'Ossi' or 'Yassi'), were annexed to Russia after the latter's treaty of Kuchuk-Kainardji with Turkey, and in 1784 the key fortress of Vladikavkaz was founded on their territory (given the name of Terek region in 1861). On 4 March 1918 the latter was proclaimed an Autonomous Soviet Republic, and after the Civil War this territory with others was set up as the Mountain Autonomous Republic (20 Jan. 1921), with North Ossetia as the Ossetian (Vladikavkaz) Area within it. On 7 July 1924 the latter was constituted as an Autonomous Region and on 5 Dec. 1936 as an Autonomous Republic. The population comprises chiefly Ossetians (48·7%), Russians (36·6%), Ingushi and other Caucasian nationalities (10%).

140 deputies were elected on 15 June 1975, 63 of them women.

The main industries are non-ferrous metals (mining and metallurgy), maize-processing (at the Beslan Works, the largest in Europe), timber and woodworking, textiles, building materials, distilleries and food processing. There is also a prosperous and varied agriculture. In 1976 there were 36 state and 44 collective farms.

There were in 1976–77, 111,600 children in 205 schools, 14,700 students in technical colleges and 17,900 students in 4 higher educational establishments (pedagogical, agriculture, medical and mining-metallurgical institutes). There were 3,081 doctors and 7,015 hospital beds.

TARTAR AUTONOMOUS SOVIET SOCIALIST REPUBLIC

Area, 68,000 sq. km (26,250 sq. miles); population (Jan. 1977), 3,359,000. Capital, Kazan. From the 10th to the 13th centuries this was the territory of the flourishing Volga-Kama Bulgar State; conquered by the Mongols, it became the seat of the

Kazan (Tartar) Khans when the Mongol Empire broke up in the 15th century, and in 1552 was conquered again by Russia. On 27 May 1920 it was constituted as an Autonomous Republic. The population includes Tartars (49·1%), Chuvashes, Mordovians and Udmurts (6·7%), Russians (42·4%).

220 deputies were elected on 15 June 1975, 83 of them women.

The Republic has highly developed engineering, oil and chemical industries, while timber, building materials, textiles, clothing and food industries are also expanding. The Kama works at Naberejnye Chelny plan to produce 400,000 vehicles annually. In 1976, 552 collective and 238 state farms served a total area under crops of 3·8m. hectares.

In 1976–77 there were 3,492 schools with 672,000 pupils, 39 technical colleges with 58,100 students and 12 higher educational establishments with 68,300 students (including a state university). There is a branch of the USSR Academy of Sciences with 5 learned institutions (517 research workers).

Doctors at the end of 1976 numbered 9,700 and hospital beds 37,925.

TUVA AUTONOMOUS SOVIET SOCIALIST REPUBLIC

Area, 170,500 sq. km (65,810 sq. miles); population (Jan. 1977), 258,000. Capital, Kizyl (59,000). Tuva was incorporated in the USSR as an autonomous region on 13 Oct. 1944 and elevated to an Autonomous Republic on 10 Oct. 1961. It is situated to the north-west of Mongolia, between 50° and 53° N. lat. and between 90° and 100° E. long. It is bounded to the east, west and north by Siberia, and to the south by the Republic of Mongolia. The Tuvans are a Turki people, formerly ruled by hereditary or elective tribal chiefs. (For the earlier history of the former Tannu-Tuva Republic, *see* THE STATESMAN'S YEAR-BOOK, 1946, p. 798.) The population includes Tuvans (58·6%) and Russians (38·3%).

125 deputies were elected to its Supreme Soviet on 15 June 1975, 52 of them women.

Tuva is well-watered and has much good pastoral land; 47 hydro-electric stations have been set into operation. The Tuvans are mainly herdsmen and cattle farmers, but, in 1976, 373,000 hectares were under crops. There are deposits of gold, cobalt and asbestos. The main exports are hair, hides and wool, and the imports manufactured goods and iron. There are 22 collective farms and 41 state farms. Mining, woodworking, garment, leather, food and other industries are rapidly developing.

In 1976–77 there were 194 schools with 66,400 pupils; 5 technical colleges with 4,400 students, and an Institute of Linguistics, Literature and History with 2,200 students; 11 newspapers (2 in Russian). There were 766 doctors and 4,040 hospital beds.

A Soviet steamer-service along the river Yenisei maintains communication with Minussinsk, in Central Siberia. Internal transport is chiefly by lorry and motor coach. There is an air service from Kizyl to Krasnoyarsk.

UDMURT AUTONOMOUS SOVIET SOCIALIST REPUBLIC

Area, 42,100 sq. km (16,250 sq. miles); population (Jan. 1977), 1·48m. Capital, Izhevsk. The Udmurts (formerly known as 'Votyaks') were annexed by the Russians in the 15th and 16th centuries. On 4 Nov. 1920 the Votyak Autonomous Region was constituted (the name was changed to Udmurt—used by the people themselves—in 1932), and on 28 Dec. 1934 it was raised to the status of an Autonomous Republic. The population includes Udmurts (34·2%), Tartars (6·1%), Russians (57·1%).

185 deputies were elected on 15 June 1975, 60 of them women.

Heavy industry includes the manufacture of locomotives, machine tools and other engineering products, timber and building materials. There are also light industries—clothing, leather, furniture, food, etc.

There were 95 state and 261 collective farms in 1976.

In 1976–77 there were 513 schools with 279,300 pupils, 25 technical colleges with 22,700 students and 5 places of higher education with 24,100 students.

There were 4,583 doctors and 15,745 hospital beds.

YAKUT AUTONOMOUS SOVIET SOCIALIST REPUBLIC

The area is 3,103,000 sq. km (1,197,760 sq. miles); population (Jan. 1977), 812,000. Capital, Yakutsk (149,000). The Yakuts were subjugated by the Russians in the 17th century. The territory was constituted an Autonomous Republic on 27 April 1922. The population includes Yakuts (43%), other northern peoples (3%), Russians (47·3%).

205 deputies were elected on 15 June 1975, 92 of them women.

The principal industries are mining (gold, tin, mica, coal) and livestock-breeding. The Soviet Soyuz-Zoloto Trust and a number of individual prospectors are working the fields. Silver- and lead-bearing ores and coal are worked; large diamond fields have been opened up. Timber and food industries are developing. There was 1 collective farm in 1975 with 82 state farms, with an area under crops of 90,000 hectares. Trapping and breeding of fur-bearing animals (sable, squirrel, silver fox, etc.) are an important source of income. A severe climate and lack of railways are serious obstacles to the economic development of the republic. There are, however, 10,000 km of roads and internal airlines totalling 10,000 km. There is an air service between Irkutsk and Yakutsk.

In 1976–77 there were 652 schools with 176,100 pupils; 70 were secondary schools. There are 18 technical colleges with 10,900 students, a state university and a pedagogical institute with 6,500 students and a branch of the Academy of Sciences with 16 research institutes and 511 scientific staff.

There were 2,833 doctors and 12,130 hospital beds.

ADYGEI AUTONOMOUS REGION

Part of Krasnodar Territory. Area, 7,600 sq. km (2,934 sq. miles); population (Jan. 1977), 406,000. Centre, Maikop (128,000). Established 27 July 1922.

Chief industries are timber, woodworking, food processing; but engineering is rapidly expanding. Cattle breeding predominates in agriculture. There were 39 collective and 26 state farms in 1976.

In 1976–77 there were 267 schools with 75,300 pupils, 6 technical colleges with 7,200 students and a pedagogical institute with 4,000 students. Regional newspapers are in Adygei and Russian. There were 1,054 doctors and 4,830 hospital beds.

GORNO-ALTAI AUTONOMOUS REGION

Part of Altai Territory. Area, 92,600 sq. km (35,740 sq. miles); population (Jan. 1977), 169,000. Capital, Gorno-Altaisk (39,000). Established 1 June 1922 as Oirot Autonomous Region; renamed 7 Jan. 1948.

Chief industries are gold, mercury and brown coal mining, timber, chemicals and dairying. Cattle breeding predominates; pasturages and hay meadows cover over 1m. hectares, but 145,500 hectares are under crops. There were 20 collective and 33 state farms in 1976.

In 1976–77 there were 239 primary and secondary schools with 32,500 pupils; technical colleges had 4,400 students and 3,600 students were receiving higher education. There were 410 doctors and 2,470 hospital beds.

JEWISH AUTONOMOUS REGION

Part of Habarovsk Territory. Area, 36,000 sq. km (13,895 sq. miles); population (Jan. 1977), 195,000 (Russians, 128,000; Ukrainians, 14,000; Jews, 15,000). Capital,

Birobidjan (67,000). Established as Jewish National District in 1928, became an autonomous region 7 May 1934.

Chief industries are non-ferrous metallurgy, building materials, timber, engineering, textiles, paper and food processing. There were in 1976, 50 factories, 154,500 hectares under crops, 79,700 cattle and 48,600 pigs. There were 35 state farms and 2 collective farms in 1976.

In 1976–77 there were 31,800 schoolchildren; students in technical colleges numbered 6,000. Students in higher education, 3,900. There are a Yiddish national theatre, a Yiddish newspaper and a Yiddish broadcasting service. Doctors numbered 457 and hospital beds 2,353.

KARACHAYEVO-CHERKESS AUTONOMOUS REGION

Part of Stavropol Territory. Area, 14,300 sq. km (5,442 sq. miles); population (Jan. 1977), 359,000. Capital, Cherkessk (89,000). A Karachai Autonomous Region was established on 26 April 1926 (out of a previously united Karachayevo–Cherkess Autonomous Region created in 1922), and dissolved in 1943. A Cherkess Autonomous Region was established on 30 April 1928. The present Autonomous Region was re-established on 9 Jan. 1957.

Ore-mining, engineering, chemical and woodworking industries have been built up since 1917. There are 70 large factories, and a copper works and sugar factory are under construction. A large irrigation scheme, Kuban–Kalaussi, is being developed, to irrigate 200,000 hectares. Livestock breeding and grain growing predominate in agriculture; crop area in 1976 was 199,100 hectares. There were 14 collective farms and 40 state farms in 1976.

In 1976–77 there were 78,800 pupils in 220 schools, 6 technical colleges with 6,600 students and 2 institutes with 3,600 students; 928 doctors and 3,720 hospital beds.

KHAKASS AUTONOMOUS REGION

Part of Krasnoyarsk Territory. Area, 61,900 sq. km (23,855 sq. miles); population (Jan. 1977), 483,000. Capital, Abakan (123,000). Established 20 Oct. 1930.

Coal- and ore-mining, timber and woodworking industries have been highly developed since 1917. The region is linked by rail with the Trans-Siberian line. Large textile and sugar factories are being built.

In 1976, 647,100 hectares were under crops. Livestock breeding, dairy and vegetable farming are developed. There are 58 state farms.

In 1976–77 there were 86,900 pupils in 363 schools, 7 technical colleges with 10,000 students and a pedagogical institute with 4,400 students; 1,042 doctors and 6,560 hospital beds. A Khakass alphabet was created after the Revolution.

Books of Reference

Armstrong, T., *Russian Settlement in the North.* CUP, 1965
Dallin, D. J., *The Rise of Russia in Asia.* New York, 1949.—*Soviet Russia and the Far East,* London, 1949
Kolarz, W., *The Peoples of the Soviet Far East.* London, 1954
Leprince-Ringuet, F., *L'Avenir de l'Asie russe.* Paris, 1951
Mikhailov, N. L., *Sibir.* Moscow, 1955
Thiel, E., *The Soviet Far East.* London, 1957
Wallace, H., *Soviet Asia Mission.* London, 1947
Yezhegodnik, B. S. E., *1922–1972.* Moscow, 1972

UKRAINE
Ukrainska Radyanska Sotsialistichna Respublika

HISTORY. The Ukrainian Soviet Socialist Republic was proclaimed on 27 Dec. 1917 and was finally established in Dec. 1919. In Dec. 1920 it concluded a military and economic alliance with the Russian Soviet Federal Socialist Republic and on 6 July 1923 formed, together with the other Soviet Socialist Republics, the Union of Soviet Socialist Republics. On 1 Nov. 1939 Western Ukraine (about 88,000 sq. km) was incorporated in the Ukrainian SSR. On 2 Aug. 1940 Northern Bukovina (about 6,000 sq. km) ceded to the USSR by Romania 28 June 1940, and the Khotin, Akkerman and Izmail provinces of Bessarabia were included in the Ukrainian SSR, and on 29 June 1945 Ruthenia (sub-Carpathian Russia), about 7,000 sq. km, was also incorporated. From the new territories 2 new regions (provinces) were formed, Chernovitz and Izmail.

AREA AND POPULATION. The Ukraine is in south-west USSR; it has a Black Sea coast and western frontiers with Romania, Hungary, Poland and Czechoslovakia. It is bounded north by Belorussia and otherwise by the RSFSR. In 1938 the Ukrainian SSR covered an area of 445,000 sq. km (171,770 sq. miles); it now covers 603,700 sq. km (231,990 sq. miles).

The population in Jan. 1959 was 41,869,000. Population, Jan. 1977, 49·3m. (in 1970, 75% Ukrainians, 19·4% Russians, 1·6% Jews, 0·8% Belorussians).

The principal towns are the capital Kiev, Kharkov, Donetsk, Odessa, Dniepropetrovsk, Lvov, Zaporozhye and Krivoi Rog.

The Ukrainian Soviet Socialist Republic consists of the following regions: Cherkassy, Chernigov, Chernovtzy, Crimea (transferred from the RSFSR on 19 Feb. 1954), Dniepropetrovsk, Donetsk, Ivan Franko, Khmelnitsky (formerly Kamenetz-Podolsk), Kharkov, Kherson, Kiev, Kirovograd, Lvov, Nikolaiev, Odessa, Poltava, Rovno, Sumy, Ternopol, Vinnitza, Volhynia, Voroshilovgrad, Zakarpatskaya (Transcarpathia), Zaporozhye, Zhitomir.

CONSTITUTION AND GOVERNMENT. The Supreme Soviet, elected in 1975, consists of 570 deputies (1 per 90,000 population); 394 are Communists and 201 women.

At elections to regional, district, urban and rural Soviets (19 June 1977), out of 521,984 deputies returned, 248,260 (47·6%) were women, 286,142 (54·8%) non-Party and 378,018 (72·4%) industrial workers and collective farmers.

President, Presidium of the Supreme Soviet: A. F. Vatchenko (June 1976).
Chairman, Council of Ministers: A. P. Lyashko.
Foreign Minister: G. G. Shevel.
First Secretary, Communist Party: V. V. Shcherbitsky.

FINANCE. Budget estimates (in 1m. new roubles), 1965, 10,223; 1970, 13,550; 1976, 16,845; 1977, 17,964.

AGRICULTURE. The Ukraine contains some of the richest land in the USSR. It raises wheat, buckwheat, beet, sunflower, cotton, flax, tobacco, soya, hops, the rubber plant kok-sagyz, fruit and vegetables, and in 1976 provided nearly 20% of the grain production in the USSR and over 62% of the sugar-beet. Nine-tenths of the grain exported from Russia came from the Ukraine. The area under cultivation was 27·9m. hectares in 1913, 27m. in 1939 before the new territories were added, and 33·5m. in 1976.

Output (in 1m. tons) in 1976 (1913 figures in brackets): Sugar-beet, 61·8 (9·3); sunflower seed, 2·1 (0·07); flax, 0·2 (0·004); potatoes, 23·7 (8·5); meat and fats, 3·1 (1·1); milk, 20·8 (4·7); wool, 0·025 (0·015); 11,751m. eggs (3,005m.).

On 1 Jan. 1977 there were 24·2m. cattle, 18·2m. pigs, 8·9m. sheep and goats. In 1949 silver-fox breeding farms were started.

On 1 Jan. 1977 there were 2,087 state farms and 7,235 collective farms.

Irrigation networks supplied 1·65m. hectares of land; 2·1m. hectares were drained.

Tractors numbered 382,900 in Jan. 1977 and combine harvesters, 81,700.

INDUSTRY. Coal in the Donetz field (25,900 sq. km stretching from Donetsk to Rostov), estimated to contain 60% of the bituminous and anthrhracite-coal reserves of the Union, yielded, in 1961, 186·1m. tonnes—about 36% of the Union production. Large new seams have been found near Novo-Moskovsk (Dniepropetrovsk region), Kharkov, Lugansk (beyond the Don) and on the left bank of the Dnieper. Within the present frontiers of the Ukraine, coal output was 22·8m. tons in 1913, 83·8m. tons in 1940, 78m. tons in 1950 and 218m. tons in 1976.

Combining coal from the Donetz field with the iron-ore from the mines in Krivoi Rog has made possible the development of a large ferrous metallurgical industry in the Ukraine. Output of iron ore was 6·9m. tons in 1913, 18·9m. tons in 1940 and 127m. tons in 1976.

Manganese is also available at Nikopol; output in 1976, 6·7m. tons.

Pig-iron output was 2·9m. tons in 1913, 9·6m. tons in 1940, 9·2m. tons in 1950 and 46·4m. tons in 1975. Steel output (in the present frontiers) was 2·4m. tons in 1913, 8·9m. in 1940, 8·4m. in 1950 and 53·1m. in 1976.

The Ukraine also contains oil, rich deposits of salt and various important chemicals. Oil output was 1m. tons in 1913 (in present frontiers), 353,000 tons in 1940 and 11·6m. tons in 1976; with 68·7m. cu. metres of natural gas.

The Ukraine has highly developed chemical and machine-construction industries producing one-fifth of the total output of machinery and chemicals in the Soviet Union. 146,100 tractors and 1,389 main-line diesel locomotives were produced in 1976.

In Northern Bukovina there are deposits of gypsum, oil, alabaster, brown coal and timber. Output of mineral fertilizers were 36,000 tons in 1913 and 19·4m. tons in 1976; cement output increased in the same years from 269,000 to 22·5m. tons (in present frontiers in both cases). Paper output in 1976 was 245,000 tons (1913: 26,900).

Consumer goods and food industries are important. Output of cotton fabrics was (in present frontiers) 4·7m. linear metres in 1913, 13·8m. in 1940, 20·6m. in 1950 and 429·4m. in 1975. Granulated sugar output in the same years was 1·1m. tons, 1·6m. tons, 1·8m. tons and 5m. tons. Leather footwear manufactured in 1940 totalled 40·8m. pairs; 1976, 170·2m.

The number of industrial and office workers at the end of 1950 was 6·9m., and the average in 1976, 18·7m. There were 1,816,000 specialists with a higher education.

During the first 5-year plan (1929–32) the Dnieper power-station was built; destroyed during the War, it was restored during the fourth plan (1946–50). Another large hydro-electric station at Kahovka began operations during the fifth plan (1951–55). Power output (in 1,000m. kwh.) increased as follows: 1913, 0·5; 1940, 12·4; 1950, 14·7; 1976, 209.

COMMUNICATIONS. The total length of railways of the Ukrainian SSR in 1976 was 22,240 km, and the navigable rivers, 3,900 km. Length of hard-surface motor roads was 120,800 km.

Airlines connect Kiev, Lvov, Chernovtsy and Odessa with Crimean and Caucasian spas, Kiev with Tbilisi, Odessa with Riga and Donetsk.

Newspapers (1976). Out of 1,840 newspapers, 1,392 were in Ukrainian, with a circulation of 24·1m. and 16·1m. respectively.

RELIGION. Several Christian Churches have their adherents in the Ukraine, the chief being the Orthodox Greek Church and the Catholic Church. The Western Ukraine Uniate Church, which in 1596 had been forced by the Poles to establish unity with the Roman Church, severed this connexion in March 1946 and joined the Orthodox Church. There are also some Protestants as well as Jews and others.

EDUCATION. In 1976–77 the number of pupils in 24,900 primary, secondary and special schools was 7·9m.; 143 higher educational establishments had 844,400 students, and 724 technical colleges 805,600 students; 2·2m. children were attending 17,400 pre-school institutions.

The Ukrainian Academy of Sciences was established in 1919; in 1977 it had 70 institutions with 12,250 scientific staff. There is an academy of building and architecture. Total scientific staff in 814 learned institutions numbered 173,700.

HEALTH. Doctors numbered 161,300 in 1976, and hospital beds, 589,700.

Books of Reference

Allen, W. E. D., *The Ukraine: A History*. London, 1940
Andrusyshen, C. H. (ed.), *Ukrainian–English Dictionary*. Toronto, 1955
Brégy, Pierre, and Obolensky, Prince S., *The Ukraine: A Russian Land*. London, 1940
Chamberlin, W. H., *The Ukraine*. New York, 1945
Chirovsky, N. L., *The Ukrainian Economy*. New York, Paris, Toronto, 1965
Doroshenko, D., *History of the Ukraine*. 2nd ed. Edmonton (Alberta), 1941
Holubnychy, V., *The Industrial Output of the Ukraine, 1913–56*. Munich, 1957
Hrushevsky, M., *A History of the Ukraine*. New Haven, 1941
Manning, C. A., *Twentieth-century Ukraine*. New York, 1951
Mirchuk, L. (ed.), *Ukraine and its People*. London, 1949
Soviet Ukraine. (English ed.) Ukrainian Soviet Encyclopaedia, 1970

BELORUSSIA
Belaruskaya Sovietskaya Sotsialistychnaya Respublika

HISTORY. The Belorussian Soviet Socialist Republic was set up on 1 Jan. 1919. It forms one of the constituent republics of the USSR.

AREA AND POPULATION. Belorussia is situated along the Western Dvina and Dnieper. It is bounded west by Poland, north by Latvia and Lithuania, east by the RSFSR and south by the Ukraine. The area is 207,600 sq. km (80,134 sq. miles). The capital is Minsk. Other important towns are Gomel, Vitebsk, Mogilev, Bobruisk, Grodno and Brest. On 2 Nov. 1939 western Belorussia was incorporated with an area of over 108,000 sq. km and a population of 4·8m. The population (Jan. 1977) was 9·4m. About 81% of this population in 1970 were Belorussians, 10·4% Poles, 2·1% Russians, 4·3% Ukrainians and 1·6% Jews.

Belorussia now comprises the following regions: Brest, Gomel, Grodno, Mogilev, Minsk, Vitebsk.

CONSTITUTION AND GOVERNMENT. The Supreme Soviet, elected in 1975, consists of 430 deputies (1 per 20,000 population); 301 are Communists and 159 women.

At elections to regional, district, urban and rural Soviets (19 June 1977), of 79,815 deputies returned, 38,233 (47·9%) were women, 45,096 (56·5%) non-Party and 54,001 (67·7%) industrial workers and collective farmers.

President, Presidium of the Supreme Soviet: I. E. Poliakov.
Chairman, Council of Ministers: T. Y. Kiselyov.
Foreign Minister: A. E. Gurinovich.
First Secretary, Communist Party: P. M. Masherov.

FINANCE. Budget estimates (in 1m. new roubles, 1965, 1,960; 1970, 3,506; 1976, 4,351; 1977, 4,578.

NATURAL RESOURCES. Belorussia is hilly, with a general slope towards the south. It contains large tracts of marsh land, particularly to the south-west, and valuable forest land wooded with oak, elm, maple and white beech: there are over 6,500 peat deposits.

AGRICULTURE. The area under cultivation (in hectares) was 4·5m. in 1913, 5·2m. in 1940 and 6·2m. in 1976. There were 6·5m. cattle, 4·2m. pigs and 554,000 sheep and goats on 1 Jan. 1977.

Output of main agricultural products (in 1,000 tons) in 1976 (1913 figures in brackets): Flax, 122 (33); sugar-beet, 1,063 (0); potatoes, 14,200 (4,024); meat, 804 (219); milk, 6,125 (1,429); wool, 1 (2·3); grain (7·4m.); 2,523m. eggs (413m.).

Agriculturally, Belorussia may be divided into three main sections—Northern:

growing flax, fodder, grasses and breeding cattle for meat and dairy produce; Central: potato growing and pig breeding; Southern: good natural pasture land, hemp cultivation and cattle breeding for meat and dairy produce.

At the end of 1976 there were 1,994 collective farms and 899 state farms. About 2·4m. hectares of marsh land had been drained for agricultural use, 788,100 of these for crops. This land has been found to be as rich as the soil of the Black Earth Zone, and yields good harvests of grain, fodder, potatoes, kok-sagyz and other crops. Another 840,000 hectares are to be drained or irrigated in 1976–80.

In Jan. 1977 there were 105,900 tractors and 30,000 grain combine harvesters.

INDUSTRY. Industry in this republic was almost completely destroyed during the years 1941–45. By 1956, aggregate industrial output was three times what it had been in 1940. Plants producing tip-lorries, machine-tools and agricultural machinery are prominent.

The republic also contains timber works; a match factory in Borisov; building materials, machine, pre-fabricated house construction, glass-blowing and other factories; canneries, creameries and other food industries; chemical, textiles, artificial-silk, flax-spinning and leather works.

The automobile and tractor industry produced 86,500 tractors and 37,100 lorries in 1976. Cement output, 33,000 tons in 1913, was 2·17m. tons in 1975. Leather footwear output, 9·8m. pairs in 1940, was 42·3m. pairs in 1976. Linen fabrics, 13,000 linear metres in 1913, 68·4m. in 1975; woollens, 37,000 linear metres in 1913, 29m. in 1975.

Particular attention has been paid to the development of the peat industry with a view to making Belorussia as far as possible self-supporting in fuel, and in 1939 local peat provided 67·5% of her total requirements of fuel. The average annual output is about 18m. tons.

There are also rich deposits of rock salt. In 1951 the first sugar refinery in Belorussia was opened in Grodno; sugar output in 1976 was 244,200 tons.

Output of electricity in 1976, 29,000m. kwh. (508m. in 1940). New power-plants have been built in Baranovichi, Grodno, Molodechno and Lida.

The number of industrial and office workers at the end of 1976 was 3·7m.

COMMUNICATIONS. In 1976 there were 5,470 km of railways, 71,100 km of motor roads (35,600 km hard-surface) and 3,900 km of navigable waterways.

Newspapers (1976). Of 180 newspapers published 128 were in Belorussian, with a circulation of 4·7m. and 1·7m. respectively.

EDUCATION. In 1976–77 there were 164,600 students in 31 places of higher education and 159,200 students in 133 technical colleges. There were 33,200 scientific personnel in 178 institutions, and 340,000 specialists with a higher education employed in the national economy. The Belorussian Academy of Sciences controlled 32 learned institutions with 4,736 scientific staff. The number of children in primary, secondary and special schools was 489,000 in 1914–15, and 1·7m. in 1976–77. 395,000 children were attending 2,523 pre-school institutions in 1976–77.

HEALTH. In 1976–77 there were 29,200 doctors (900 in 1913, within present frontiers), and 111,200 hospital beds (6,400 in 1913).

Books of Reference

Kovalevski, G. T., and Rakov, Y. G. (ed.), *Belorusskaya SSR, An Outline of Her Economic Geography*. Minsk, 1953

Vakar, N. P., *Belorussia*. Harvard Univ. Press, 1956.—*A Bibliographical Guide to Belorussia*. Harvard Univ. Press, 1956

AZERBAIJAN
Azarbaijchan Soviet Sotsialistik Respublikasy

HISTORY. The 'Mussavat' (Nationalist) party, which dominated the National Council or Constituent Assembly of the Tartars, declared the independence of Azerbaijan on 28 May 1918, with a capital, first at Ganja (Elizavetpol) and later at Baku. On 28 April 1920 Azerbaijan was proclaimed a Soviet Socialist Republic. With Georgia and Armenia it formed the Transcaucasian Soviet Federal Socialist Republic. In 1936 it assumed the status of one of the Union (constituent) republics of the USSR.

AREA AND POPULATION. Azerbaijan covers an area of 86,600 sq. km (33,430 sq. miles) and has a population (Jan. 1977) of 5,776,000. Its capital is Baku. Other important towns are Kirovabad and Sumgait. Nahichevan is the capital of the Autonomous Republic of the same name.

Azerbaijan includes the Nahichevan Autonomous Republic and the Nagorno-Karabagh Autonomous Region. Situated in the eastern area of Transcaucasia, it is protected by mountains in the west and north, washed by the Caspian Sea in the east and bounded by Iran in the south. Its climate is inclined to drought.

In 1970 about 74% of the population were Azerbaijan Tiurks. Other nationalities were Russians (10%), Armenians (9%) and Georgians (2·7%).

CONSTITUTION AND GOVERNMENT. The Supreme Soviet, elected in 1975, consists of 400 deputies (1 per 10,000 population); 277 are Communists and 151 women.

At elections to the Nagorno-Karabagh regional Soviet and the district, urban and rural Soviets (19 June 1977), of 48,911 deputies returned, 22,731 (46·5%) were women, 26,841 (54·9%) non-Party and 32,061 (65·6%) industrial workers and collective farmers.

President, Presidium of the Supreme Soviet: K. A. Halilov.
Chairman, Council of Ministers: A. I. Ibrahimov.
First Secretary, Communist Party: G. A. Aliev.

FINANCE (in 1m. new roubles). Estimate, 1965, 1,033; 1970, 1,520; 1974, 1,507; 1977, 1,729.

AGRICULTURE. The chief agricultural products are grain, cotton, rice, vine, fruit, vegetables, tobacco and silk. The Mexican rubber plant *grayule* has been acclimatized. A new kind of high-yielding winter wheat has been produced for use in mountainous parts of the republic.

Livestock on 1 Jan. 1977: Cattle, 1·6m.; pigs, 137,600; sheep and goats, 5·1m.

Output of main agricultural products (in 1,000 tons) in 1976 (1913 figures in brackets): Cotton, 532 (4); potatoes, 161 (38); tea, 14·1 (0); meat, 115 (40); milk, 667 (203); wool, 10 (4·1); grapes, 765; fruit, 200; 566m. eggs (97m.).

Azerbaijan has become an important cotton-growing and sub-tropical base. About 70% of cultivated land is irrigated. On the irrigated land crops of Egyptian and Sea-Island cotton are obtained. Here, too, rice and lucerne are cultivated, and in the mountain valleys there are also orchards, vineyards and silk cultures.

In the south along the coast of the Caspian, where the climate is more moist, there are tea plantations, and citrus fruits and other sub-tropical plants are grown.

In 1941 a scientific research institute for sub-tropical research was opened to develop the culture of sub-tropical plants in Azerbaijan and other parts of Transcaucasia. A forestry research institute was opened in 1949.

There were at the end of 1976, 779 collective farms, 546 state farms, 31,600 tractors and 4,400 grain combine harvesters.

INDUSTRY. The republic is rich in natural resources: oil, iron, aluminium, copper, lead, zinc, precious metals, sulphur pyrites, limestone and salt. Iron and steel and aluminium works have been built at Sumgait.

The most important industry is the oil industry, especially in the Baku region. The output of oil was 7·7m. tons in 1913, 22·2m. tons in 1940 and 16·5m. tons in 1976. The largest producing area lies along the western shore of the Caspian Sea, north and south of Baku, where the largest refineries are located. Other wells lie west of Baku, and some have been drilled in the Caspian itself, off the Apsheron Peninsula. Baku is connected by a double pipeline with Batum on the Black Sea. All the oilfields have been electrified and are connected with Baku.

Azerbaijan has also copper, chemical, cement and building material, food, timber, salt, textiles and fishing industries. 788,000 tons of steel were produced in 1976, 1·4m. tons of cement, 130·4m. linear metres of cotton fabrics, 15·2m. pairs leather footwear, 32·3m. linear metres of silk fabrics, 1·3m. tons of iron ore.

In addition to Baku, among the important industrial centres are Kirovabad, Nukha, Stepanakert, Nahichevan, Lenkoran.

In 1976 electric power output was 15·3m. kwh. Output of gas, which began in 1928 with 176m. cu. metres, was 10,989m. in 1976. Pipelines from Karadag to Baku and Sumgait supply gas fuel for all oil-cracking factories and most engineering works.

Synthetic rubber works (Sumgait), tyre works and a worsted combine (Baku) and a large textile combine (Mingechaur) have been built.

The number of industrial and office workers in 1976 (average for year) was 1·57m., and specialists with a higher education employed in the national economy numbered 193,000.

COMMUNICATIONS. Railway lines, apart from narrow gauge, 1,850 km. The first electrical railway (42 km) in the USSR was constructed in Azerbaijan in 1924; in 1949, 27 km was added, and the line now runs Baku–Surakhany–Sabunchi–Buzovny–Baku. The capital is also linked by rail with Tbilisi, Yerevan, Derbent, Julfa and Astara. There were, in 1976, 22,900 km of motor roads (15,900 km hard-surface) and 500 km of inland waterways.

Newspapers (1976). There were 118 newspapers, 93 of them in the Azerbaijani language, with a circulation of 2·7m. and 2·2m. respectively.

EDUCATION. In 1976–77 there were 1·6m. pupils in 4,500 elementary and secondary schools and 130,000 children attending 1,622 pre-school institutions. There were 78 technical colleges with 76,300 students, 17 higher educational institutions, including a state university at Baku, with 100,200 students (including correspondence students).

The Azerbaijan Academy of Sciences has 28 research institutions with 4,242 research workers. There are 142 learned and scientific institutions, with 22,000 research workers in all.

HEALTH. In 1976 there were 17,300 doctors and 55,800 hospital beds. There were also 451 maternity and infant welfare centres.

NAHICHEVAN AUTONOMOUS SOVIET SOCIALIST REPUBLIC

Area, 5,500 sq. km (2,120 sq. miles), population (Jan. 1977), 231,000. Capital, Nahichevan (37,000). This territory, on the borders of Turkey and Iran, forms part of the Azerbaijan SSR although separated from it by the territory of Soviet Armenia. Its population, mainly Azerbaijanis, had a chequered history for 1,500 years under the ancient Persians, Arabs, Seljuk Turks, Mongols, Ottoman Turks and modern Persians before being annexed by Russia in 1828. On 9 Feb. 1924 it was constituted as an Autonomous Republic within Azerbaijan. Its Supreme Soviet, elected 15 June 1975, has 100 members including 48 women.

The Republic has silk, clothing, cotton, canning, meat-packing and other factories. Nearly 70% of the people are engaged in agriculture, of which the main branches are cotton and tobacco growing. Fruit and grapes are also produced in increasing quantity. There are 47 collective and 26 state farms. Crop area 37,400 hectares.

In 1976–77 there were 225 primary, 8-year and 11-year schools with 70,800 pupils. There were 1,700 pupils in 4 technical colleges and a pedagogical institute with 2,400 students.

Doctors numbered 399, and hospital beds, 2,230.

NAGORNO-KARABAGH AUTONOMOUS REGION

Populated by Armenians and Azerbaijanis, a separate khanate in the 18th century, it was established on 7 July 1923 as an Autonomous Region within Azerbaijan. Area, 4,400 sq. km (1,700 sq. miles); population (Jan. 1977), 156,000. Capital, Stepanakert (33,000).

Main industries are silk, wine, dairying and building materials. Crop area is 67,200 hectares; cotton, grapes and winter wheat are grown. There are 53 collective and 21 state farms.

In 1976–77 there were 199 8-, 10- and 11-year schools and schools for working youth, with 40,600 pupils. There are a medical school, a teachers' training college and 2 agricultural schools with a total of 2,000 students and a higher education institute with 1,800 students; 335 doctors and 1,685 hospital beds.

Books of Reference

Baddeley, J. F., *The Rugged Flanks of Caucasus.* 2 vols. Oxford, 1941
Tutaeff, D., *The Soviet Caucasus.* London, 1942

GEORGIA
Sakartvelos Sabchota Sotsialisturi Respublica

HISTORY. The independence of the Georgian Social Democratic Republic was declared at Tiflis on 26 May 1918 by the National Council, elected by the National Assembly of Georgia on 22 Nov. 1917. The independence of Georgia was recognized by the Soviet Union on 7 May 1920. On 12 Feb. 1921 a rising broke out in Mingrelia, Abhazia and Adjaria, and Soviet troops invaded the country, which, on 25 Feb. 1921, was proclaimed the Georgian Soviet Socialist Republic. At the first Transcaucasian Soviet Congress, 15 Dec. 1922, Georgia, together with Armenia and Azerbaijan, united to form the Transcaucasian Soviet Federal Socialist Republic, and a federal constitution was adopted and published 10 Jan. 1923. In 1936 the Georgian Soviet Socialist Republic became one of the constituent republics of the USSR and, like other republics of the Union, adopted a new constitution.

AREA AND POPULATION. Georgia is bounded west by the Black Sea and south by Turkey, Armenia and Azerbaijan. It occupies the whole of the western part of Transcaucasia and covers an area of 69,700 sq. km (26,900 sq. miles). Its population on 1 Jan. 1977 was 5m. The capital is Tbilisi (Tiflis). Other important towns are Kutaisi, Sukhumi (120,000), Rustavi (131,000), Batumi (118,000), Poti (54,000), Gori (54,000).

Protected from the north by the Caucasian mountains, and receiving in the west the warm, moist winds from the Black Sea, into which most of its rivers flow, Georgia is outstanding for its fine, warm climate and its natural wealth, variety and beauty. It has the highest snow-capped peaks of the Caucasian mountains. Georgia contains valuable sulphur and other medicinal springs. Georgians, an ancient people, were (1970) 66·8% of the population; Armenians, 9·7%; Russians, 8·5%; Azerbaijanis, 4·6%; Ossetians, 3·2%; Abhazians, 1·7%.

CONSTITUTION AND GOVERNMENT. The Georgian Soviet Socialist Republic includes the Abhazian ASSR, the Adjarian ASSR and the South Ossetian Autonomous Region.

The Supreme Soviet, elected in 1975, consists of 400 deputies (1 per 10,000 population); 142 are women, 264 Communists.

At elections to the district, rural and urban Soviets, and that of the South Ossetian region (19 June 1977), of 49,371 deputies returned 23,903 (48·5%) were women, 28,064 (56·8%) non-Party and 33,303 (67·3%) industrial workers and collective farmers.

President, Presidium of the Supreme Soviet: P. G. Gilashvili.
Chairman, Council of Ministers: Z. A. Pataridze.
First Secretary, Communist Party: E. A. Shevardnadze.

FINANCE (in 1m. new roubles). Budget estimates, 1965, 1,049; 1970, 1,491; 1974, 1,626; 1976, 1,765.

AGRICULTURE. There are 3 main agricultural areas: (1) The moist sub-tropical area along the Black Sea coast, where are cultivated tea, citrus fruits (lemons, oranges, mandarins, etc.), the tung tree (which yields special industrial oils), eucalyptus, bamboo, high-quality tobacco; (2) Imeretia (the Kutais region), where the chief cultures are grapes and silk, and (3) Kakhetia, along the Alazani (a tributary of the Kura River), famed for its orchards and wines. Land (in hectares) under cultivation was 748,000 in 1913, 896,000 in 1940, 778,000 in 1961, 745,000 in 1976.

Output of main agricultural products (in 1,000 tons) in 1976 (1913 figures in brackets): Sugar-beet, 130 (0); fruit, 522; grapes, 388; tea in leaf, 356; meat, 139 (49); wool, 5·4 (3·4); milk, 576 (222); silk, 439; 564m. eggs (119m.); wine, 18·2m. decalitres.

On 1 Jan. 1977 there were 732 collective farms working over 66% of all agricultural land, 380 state farms working nearly 34% of such land. In the Colchis area 115,000 hectares of extremely rich land have been reclaimed. There are 380,000 hectares of irrigated land. 151,500 hectares of marsh land have been drained. Tractors numbered 22,900; grain combines, 1,600.

Livestock on 1 Jan. 1977: Cattle, 1·5m.; pigs, 731,000; sheep and goats, 2m.

Georgia is rich in forest lands where fine varieties of timber are grown. Area covered by forests, 2·4m. hectares.

INDUSTRY. The most important mining industry of Georgia is the exploitation of the manganese deposits, the richest of which lie in the Chiatura region, where 1·6m. tons of ore were produced in 1971. Manganese deposits in Georgia are calculated at 250m. tons, distributed over an area of 140 sq. km. The most important coal seams are at Tkvarcheli (deposits estimated at 250m. tons) and Tkibuli (deposits of 80m. tons). Other important minerals are baryta, the best in the USSR, fire-resisting and other clays, diatomite shale, oil, agate, marble, cement, alabaster, iron and other ores, building stone, arsenic, molybdenum, tungsten and mercury. In 1941 a goldfield was discovered. Output of coal in 1976 was 1·9m. tons (625,000 in 1940).

Since the Second World War the Transcaucasian Metallurgical Plant has been built at Rustavi (near Tbilisi) and a motor works at Kutaisi. There are modern factories for processing green tea-leaves, creameries and breweries; Georgia has also textile and silk industries.

In 1976, 784,000 tons of pig-iron, 1·5m. tons of steel, 1,334,000 tons of rolled metal were produced; also 1·7m. tons of cement, 713,000 tons of mineral fertilizer, 56·7m. linear metres of cotton fabrics, 43·8m. linear metres of silk fabrics, 14·1m. pairs of leather footwear and 42,600 tons of granulated sugar.

Georgia's fast flowing rivers form an abundant source of energy. One of the most powerful stations completed in recent years is Tbilisi (1m. kw.). Power output in 1976 was 12,100m. kwh. (742m. in 1940).

There were 1·8m. industrial and office workers in 1976, and 235,000 specialists with a higher education in the national economy.

COMMUNICATIONS. Length of railways in 1976 was 1,420 km. The trunk line leading from Batum through Tbilisi to Baku on the Caspian Sea has several narrow-gauge branches on Georgian territory to the coalmines of Tkibuli, to the port of Poti, to the manganese mines of Chiatura, to the mineral springs of Borjom and the health resort Bakuriani, to the towns Signakh and Telavi, in Kakhetia, and to the Armenian frontier, across the coalmine district of Alaverdi. The last branch divides in Armenia, going on the one side to Tabriz in Iran, and on the other to Erzerum in Anatolia. A railway line from Akhal-Senaki along the Black Sea coast, through Sukhum to Tuapse, was completed in 1946. All lines are electrified or work on diesel traction. In 1976 there were 21,600 km of motor roads, 18,000 km of them hard-surfaced.

Newspapers (1976). Out of 142 newspapers, 123 were in Georgian, with a circulation of 3·2m. and 3m. respectively.

EDUCATION. In 1976–77 there were 1m. pupils in 4,400 primary and secondary schools, 50,900 in 95 technical colleges and 84,200 students in 19 higher educational institutions. Tbilisi University has 16,300 students. In towns, 11 years' education is usual. In Abastuman there is an astro-physical observatory. In 1936 a branch of the Academy of Sciences of the USSR was formed in Tbilisi, and in Feb. 1941 a Georgian Academy of Sciences was opened, which in 1977 had 42 institutions with scientific staff totalling 5,626. There were in all 194 research institutions with 24,300 scientific staff.

In 1976, 150,000 children were attending 1,805 pre-school institutions.

HEALTH. There were 21,100 doctors and 49,600 hospital beds in 1976.

ABHAZIAN AUTONOMOUS SOVIET SOCIALIST REPUBLIC

Area, 8,600 km (3,320 sq. miles); population (Jan. 1977), 503,000. Capital Sukhumi. This area, the ancient Colchis, included Greek colonies from the 6th century B.C. onwards. From the 2nd century B.C. onwards, it was a prey to many invaders—Romans, Byzantines, Arabs, Ottoman Turks—before accepting a Russian protectorate in 1810. However, from the 4th century A.D. a West Georgian kingdom was established by the Lazi princes in the territory (known to the Romans as 'Lazica') and by the 8th century the prevailing language was Georgian and the name Abhazia.

On 4 March 1921 a congress of local Soviets proclaimed it a Soviet Republic, and its status as an Autonomous Republic, within Georgia, was confirmed on 17 April 1930.

130 deputies were elected on 15 June 1975, 50 of them women.

The Abhazian coast (along the Black Sea) possesses a famous chain of health resorts—Gagra, Sukhumi, Akhali-Antoni, Gulripsha and Gudauta—sheltered by thickly forested mountains.

The republic has coal, electric power, building materials and light industries. In 1976 there were 93 collective farms and 48 state farms; main crops are tobacco, tea, grapes, oranges, tangerines and lemons. Crop area 41,200 hectares.

Livestock, 1 Jan. 1977: 135,000 cattle, 69,000 pigs, 27,000 sheep and goats.

101,500 pupils were attending 460 schools in 1976–77. There were 7 technical colleges with 3,100 students; 6,100 students were receiving higher education (including correspondence courses).

There were 152,700 industrial and office workers, and 13,200 specialists with a higher education in the national economy. Doctors, 1,883; hospital beds, 5,800.

ADJARIAN AUTONOMOUS SOVIET SOCIALIST REPUBLIC

Area, 3,000 sq. km (1,160 sq. miles); population (Jan. 1977), 347,000. Capital, Batumi. After a history similar to that of Abhazia, it fell under Turkish rule in the 17th century, and was annexed to Russia (rejoining Georgia) after the Berlin Treaty of 1878. On 16 June 1921 the territory was constituted as an Autonomous Republic within the Georgian SSR.

100 deputies were elected on 15 June 1975, 38 of them women.

The republic specializes in sub-tropical agricultural products. These include tea, mandarines and lemons, grapes, bamboo, eucalyptus, etc. Livestock: 116,000 cattle, 10,000 sheep and goats. In 1976 there were 77 collective farms and 21 state farms.

There are shipyards at Batumi, modern oil-refining plant (the pipeline from the Baku oilfields ends at Batumi), food-processing and canning factories, clothing, building materials, drug factories, etc.

Health resorts are Kobuleti, Tsihis-Dari, Batumi on the coast and Beshumi in the hills. The sub-tropical climate and flora, and the combination of mountains and sea, make this republic (like Abhazia) a favourite holiday country.

In 1976 there were 426 schools with 75,900 pupils, several technical colleges with 3,500 students, a pedagogical institute and several research institutions. 2,300 students were receiving a higher education.

There were 92,700 industrial and office workers, and 10,500 specialists with a higher education in the national economy. Doctors, 1,097; hospital beds, 3,695.

SOUTH OSSETIAN AUTONOMOUS REGION

This area was populated by Ossetians from across the Caucasus (North Ossetia), driven out by the Mongols in the 13th century. The region was set up within the Georgian SSR on 20 April 1922. Area, 3,900 sq. km (1,505 sq. miles); population (Jan. 1977), 103,000. Capital, Tskhinvali (34,000).

Main industries are mining, timber, electrical engineering and building materials. Crop area, chiefly grains, was 21,600 hectares in 1976; other pursuits are sheep-farming (80,500 sheep and goats) and vine-growing. There were 14 collective farms and 13 state farms.

There are a pedagogical institute (2,345 students) and several technical colleges (700 students). In 1976 there were 24,000 pupils in elementary and secondary schools.

There were 34,900 industrial and office workers, and 3,800 specialists with a higher education in the national economy. Doctors, 401; hospital beds, 1,350.

Books of Reference

Avalishvill, Zourab, *The Independence of Georgia in International Politics, 1918–21.* London, 1940

Gvesiani, G. G., and Klopotovsky, B. A., *Gruzinskaya SSR.* Moscow, 1955

Lang, D. M., *A Modern History of Georgia.* London, 1962

Tutaeff, D., *The Soviet Caucasus.* London, 1942

ARMENIA
Haikakan Sovetakan Sotsialistakan Respublika

HISTORY. On 29 Nov. 1920 Armenia was proclaimed a Soviet Socialist Republic. The Armenian Soviet Government, with the Russian Soviet Government, was a party to the Treaty of Kars (March 1921), which confirmed the Turkish possession of the former Government of Kars and of the Surmali District of the Government of Yerevan. From 1922 to 1936 it formed part of the Transcaucasian Soviet Federal Socialist Republic. In 1936 Armenia was proclaimed a constituent republic of the USSR.

AREA AND POPULATION. Armenia covers an area of 29,800 sq. km (11,490 sq. miles). It is bounded in the north by Georgia, in the east by Azerbaijan and in the south and east by Turkey and Iran. It is a very mountainous country with but little forest land, has many turbulent rivers and a highly fertile soil, but subject to drought. In Jan. 1977 the population was 2,893,000. About 89% of the population are Armenians, the rest are Russians (2·7%), Kurds (1·5%), Azerbaijanians (5·9%) (1970 census). The capital is Yerevan. Other large towns are Leninakan and Kirovakan (133,000).

CONSTITUTION AND GOVERNMENT. The Supreme Soviet, elected in 1975, consists of 315 deputies (1 per 5,000 population); 111 are women, 202 Communists.

At elections to the district, urban and rural Soviets (19 June 1977), of 26,592 deputies returned 12,952 (48·7%) were women, 15,317 (57·6%) non-Party and 18,436 (69·3%) industrial workers and collective farmers.

President, Presidium of the Supreme Soviet: B. E. Sarkisov.
Chairman, Council of Ministers: F. T. Sarkisian.
First Secretary, Communist Party: K. S. Demirchian.

FINANCE. Budget estimates (in 1m. new roubles), 1965, 699; 1970, 1,130; 1974, 1,119; 1976, 1,187.

AGRICULTURE. The chief agricultural area is the valley of the Arax and the area around Yerevan. Here there are considerable cotton plantations as well as orchards and vineries. Sub-tropical plants, such as almonds and figs, are also grown. Olive groves and pomegranate plantations occupy large areas; experiments are being made to naturalize cork oak. In the mountainous areas the chief pursuit is livestock raising. In 1913 the total cultivated area of Armenia amounted to 346,000 hectares; in 1940, 434,000; in 1965, 400,000; in 1970, 409,000; in 1976, 419,000.

Output of main agricultural products (in 1,000 tons) in 1976 (1913 figures in brackets): Wheat, 186 (110); sugar-beet, 168 (0); potatoes, 207 (47); fruit, 145; grapes, 201; meat, 72 (19); milk, 434 (129); wool, 4·7 (2·3); and 373m. eggs (54m.).

Area of irrigated land in Armenia in 1976 was 285,000 hectares.

There were, on 1 Jan. 1976, 371 collective farms, and these together with the 384 state farms tilled 99·9% of the total cultivated area. Livestock included 166,000 pigs, 721,000 cattle and 2·3m. sheep and goats. All the state farms and collective farms had been electrified by the end of 1960. There were 12,000 tractors and 1,500 grain and cotton combines in Jan. 1977.

INDUSTRY. Armenia contains large deposits of copper, zinc, aluminium, molybdenum and other metals. It is also rich in marble, granite, cement and other building materials. The mining of these minerals is becoming more and more important. Among other industries are the chemical, producing chiefly synthetic rubber and fertilizers, and the extraction and processing of building materials such as cement, pumice-stone, tuffs, marble, volcanic basalt and fire-proof clay, ginning- and textile-mills, carpet weaving, food, including wine-making, fruit, meat-canning and creameries. Machine-tool and electrical engineering works have also been established. Among the industrial centres are Yerevan, Leninakan, Alaverdi, Kafan, Kirovakan, Daval, Megri and Oktemberyan. Output of electricity in 1976 was 9,700m. kwh. A chain ('cascade') of 8 hydro-electric stations on the river Razdan, as it falls about 3,300 ft from the mountain lake Sevan to its junction with the Arax, has been completed.

In 1976 there were produced 1,828,000 tons of cement, 385,000 tons of mineral fertilizers, 95·6m. linear metres of cotton fabrics, 18·5m. linear metres of silk fabrics, 11·2m. pairs of leather footwear, 11,900 tons of granulated sugar and 9·3m. decalitres of wine (excluding collective farm output).

There were 1,024,000 industrial and office workers and 121,000 specialists with a higher education working in the national economy.

COMMUNICATIONS. Length of railways in 1976, 710 km; motor roads, 8,600 km (hard surface, 6,100); airlines, 570 km.

Newspapers (1976). Out of 81 newspapers 71 appeared in Armenian, with a circulation of 1·52m. and 1·41m. respectively.

EDUCATION. In 1976–77 there were 668,000 pupils in 1,535 primary, secondary and special schools; 63 technical colleges with 53,700 students; 13 higher educational institutions with 55,500 students (including correspondence students). Erevan houses the Armenian Academy of Sciences, 43 scientific institutes, a medical institute and other technical colleges, and a state university. 31 learned institutions with 2,898 scientific staff are under the Academy of Sciences; scientific workers totalled 17,600 in 101 institutions in 1976.

In 1976 there were 933 pre-school institutions with 118,000 children.

HEALTH. In 1976 there were 10,200 doctors and 24,800 hospital beds.

Books of Reference

Aslanyan, A., Bagdasarian, A., *et al.*, *L'Arménie Sovietique.* Moscow, 1972
Baghdasarian, A. B. (ed.) *Atlas Armyanskov SSR.* Moscow, 1961
Kurkjian, V., *A History of Armenia.* New York, 1958
Missakian, J., *A Searchlight on the Armenian Question, 1878–1950.* Boston, Mass., 1950
Shaginyan, M., *A Journey Through Soviet Armenia.* Moscow (English ed., 1954)

MOLDAVIAN SOVIET SOCIALIST REPUBLIC
Respublika Sovietike Sochialiste Moldovenyaske

HISTORY. The Moldavian Soviet Socialist Republic, capital Kishinev, was formed by the union of part of the former Moldavian Autonomous Soviet Socialist Republic (organized 12 Oct. 1924), formerly included in the Ukrainian Soviet Socialist Republic, and the areas of Bessarabia (ceded by Romania to the USSR, 28 June 1940) with a mainly Moldavian population. As from 2 Aug. 1940 the MSSR includes the following regions of the former Moldavian Autonomous Soviet Socialist Republic: Grigoriopol, Dubossarsk, Kamensk, Rybnitz, Slobedzeisk and Tiraspol, and the following districts of Bessarabia: Beltsk, Bender, Kagulsk, Kishinev, Orgeev and Sorok. The republic, however, is divided not into regions but into 34 rural districts, 21 towns and 37 urban settlements.

AREA AND POPULATION. Moldavia forms an enclave on the Romanian border of the Ukraine. The area is 33,700 sq. km (13,000 sq. miles). In Jan. 1977 the population was 3·88m., of whom 65% are Moldavians. Others include Ukrainians (14%), Russians (11·6%), Gagauzi (3·5%), Jews (2·7%). Apart from Kishinev, larger towns are Tiraspol (142,000), Beltsy (123,000) and Bendery (100,000).

CONSTITUTION AND GOVERNMENT. The Supreme Soviet, elected in 1975, consists of 330 deputies (1 per 10,000 population); 119 are women, 220 Communists.

At elections to the district, urban and rural Soviets (19 June 1977), of 34,361 deputies returned, 16,994 (49·5%) were women, 18,759 (54·6%) non-Party and 23,840 (69·4%) industrial workers and collective farmers.

President, Presidium of the Supreme Soviet: K. F. Ilyashenko.
Chairman, Council of Ministers and Foreign Minister: S. K. Grossu.
First Secretary, Communist Party: I. I. Bodyul.

FINANCE. Budget estimates (in 1m. new roubles), 1965, 598; 1970, 967; 1974, 1,088; 1976, 1,264.

AGRICULTURE. On 1 Jan. 1977 there were 454 collective farms and 227 state farms. All ploughing and sowing is mechanized. Livestock included (1 Jan. 1977) 1·1m. cattle, 1·6m. pigs and 1·2m. sheep and goats. There were 47,300 tractors and 3,100 combine harvesters.

Output of main agricultural products (in 1,000 tons) in 1976 (1913 figures in brackets): Wheat, 964 (526); maize, 1,450 (639); sugar-beet, 4,205 (15), sunflower seeds, 227 (9); potatoes, 393 (119); vegetables, 1,109; fruit, 729; grapes, 1,581; meat, 227 (53); milk, 1,041 (210); wool, 2·4 (3); 679m. eggs (275m.).

Bessarabia has an equable climate and very fertile soil. It contains nearly one-quarter of the vineyards of the USSR. Bessarabia is also rich in fish in the south: sturgeon, mackerel, brill.

INDUSTRY. There are canning plants, wine-making plants, woodworking and metallurgical factories, a factory of ferro-concrete building materials, and footwear and textile plants. Moldavia takes third place in the USSR in the production of wine, tobacco and food-canning. Power output in 1976 was 13,700m. kwh. Production in 1976 included 28·9m. linear metres of silk fabrics, 15·5m. pairs of leather footwear, 339,400 tons of granulated sugar, 1,276m. tins of preserves and 24·5m. decalitres of wine. Meat and dairy produce are rapidly expanding food industries.

There are lignite, phosphorites, gypsum and valuable building materials.

In 1976 there were 1·3m. industrial and office workers and 119,000 specialists with higher education working in the national economy.

COMMUNICATIONS. Length of railways, 1,110 km. There is direct air communication with Leningrad, Moscow, Kiev, Lvov and across the Black Sea. There are 10,300 km of motor roads (8,400 hard surface), and 1,100 km of inland waterways.

Newspapers (1976). There were 147 newspapers, of which 63 were in the Moldavian language, with a circulation of 1·91m. and 1,161,000 respectively.

EDUCATION. In 1976–77 there were 814,000 pupils in 2,196 primary, secondary and special schools, 56,600 students in 48 technical colleges and 45,300 students in 8 higher educational institutions including the state university. A Moldavian Academy of Sciences was established in 1961: it had 19 research institutions and a staff of 895 in 1976. In all, there are 68 learned institutions with 7,300 scientific staff. In 1976 there were 188,000 children attending 1,123 pre-school institutions.

HEALTH. Moldavia has 800 medical centres, many district hospitals, a state medical institute and 9 medical schools with over 2,500 students. Doctors in 1976 numbered 10,700; hospital beds, 43,100.

Book of Reference

Zlatova, Y., and Kotelnikov, V., *Across Moldavia* [English ed.]. Moscow, 1959

ESTONIA
Eesti Nõukogude Sotsialistlik Vabariik

HISTORY. The workers' and soldiers' Soviets in Estonia took over power on 8 Nov. 1917, were overthrown by the German occupying forces in March 1918, and were restored to power as the Germans withdrew in Nov. 1918, establishing the 'Estland Labour Commune'. It was overthrown with the assistance of British naval forces in May 1919, and a democratic republic proclaimed.

The secret protocol of the Soviet–German agreement of 23 Aug. 1939 assigned Estonia to the Soviet sphere of interest. An ultimatum (16 June 1940) led to the formation of a government acceptable to the USSR; on 21 July the State Duma, elected by universal suffrage, proclaimed Soviet power and applied to join the USSR: on 6 Aug. the Supreme Soviet accepted the application. The incorporation has been accorded *de facto* recognition by the British Government, but not by the US Government, which continues to recognize an Estonian consul-general in New York.

AREA AND POPULATION. Estonia is bounded west and north by the Baltic, east by the RSFSR and south by Latvia. Area, 45,100 sq. km (17,410 sq. miles); population, 1,447,000 (Jan. 1977). 68·2% are Estonians, 24·7% Russians, 1·4% Finns. The capital is Tallin. Other large towns are Tartu (100,000). Pärnu, Narva (72,000). There are 15 districts, 33 towns and 26 urban settlements.

CONSTITUTION AND GOVERNMENT. The Supreme Soviet, elected in 1975, consists of 200 deputies (1 per 10,000 population); 69 are women, 135 Communists.

At elections to district, urban and rural Soviets (19 June 1977), out of 10,880 deputies returned 5,330 (49%) were women, 6,035 (55·5%) non-Party and 7,294 (67%) industrial workers and collective farmers.

President, Presidium of the Supreme Soviet: A. P. Vader (died June 1978).
Chairman, Council of Ministers: V. I. Klauson.
First Secretary, Communist Party: I. G. Kebin.

FINANCE. Budget estimates (in 1m. new roubles), 1965, 480; 1970, 708; 1974, 757; 1976, 854.

AGRICULTURE. Agriculture and dairy farming are the chief occupations. Area under cultivation was 697,000 hectares in 1913, 918,000 hectares in 1940 and 945,000 hectares in 1976. There were 151 agricultural and 8 fishery collectives and 163 state farms in 1976 using 19,500 tractors and 3,400 grain combines. 97% of state farms and 70% of collective farms were receiving electric power.

On 1 Jan. 1977 there were 826,000 head of cattle, 152,000 sheep and goats, 891,000 pigs and 5·2m. poultry.

Output of main agricultural products (in 1,000 tons) in 1976 (1913 figures in brackets): Potatoes, 1,181 (689); grains, 1,344 (428); vegetables, 74; meat (slaughter weight), 175 (60); milk, 1,203 (415); wool, 0·4 (0·7); 446m. eggs (67m.).

INDUSTRY. Some 22% of the territory is covered by forests which provide good material for its sawmills, furniture, match and pulp industries, as well as wood fuel. Since the end of the War, 80,000 hectares have been afforested. 903,500 hectares of marsh land had been reclaimed by 1976.

Estonia has rich high-quality shale deposits (particularly in the north-east) which are estimated at 3,700m. tons. Shale output was 1·9m. tons in 1940 and 29m. in 1976. A factory for the production of gas from shale and a pipeline (208 km long) from Kohtla-Järve supplies shale gas to Leningrad and Tallin. Estonian factories are now turning out agricultural and peat-digging machines, complex control and measuring instruments. The 'Volta' factory in Tallin produces electric motors.

In the neighbourhood of Tallin, phosphorites have been found, and in 1947 a plant for refining and for the production of superphosphates was started. Estonia also contains valuable peat deposits, and some of her electrical stations work on peat. A hydro-electric station was erected in 1955 on the Narva. There are 350 rural electric stations. Output of mineral fertilizers in 1976 was 1·4m. tons; cement, 1·26m. tons; paper, 104,000 tons; cotton fabrics, 196m. linear metres; linen fabrics, 6·1m. linear metres; sawn timber, 779,000 cu. metres; leather footwear, 5·6m. pairs; electric power, 18,700m. kwh.

In 1976 there were 665,000 industrial and office workers and 62,000 specialists with a higher education engaged in the national economy.

COMMUNICATIONS. Length of main railways 950 km, of secondary lines 730 km. Estonia has 20 ports, but Tallin handles four-fifths of the total sea-going transport. Inland waterways total 500 km; motor roads, 27,000 km (hard surface, 24,100 km). Airlines link Tallin with Moscow, Leningrad, Riga and the Estonian islands.

Newspapers (1976). There were 38 newspapers, 29 of them in Estonian, with a circulation of 1,166,000 and 1m. respectively.

EDUCATION. Estonia has retained an 11-year school curriculum, when it was reduced to 10 years elsewhere in the USSR. In 1976–77 pupils in 731 primary, secondary and special schools numbered 216,000. There were 24,100 students in 6 higher educational establishments, including Tartu (Dorpat) University, founded in 1632, and 24,600 students in 37 technical colleges.

The Estonia Academy of Sciences, founded in 1946, has 13 institutions with 984 scientific staff; in all, 5,500 scientists are working in 72 institutions.

In 1976 there were 77,000 children attending 661 pre-school institutions.

HEALTH. In 1976 there were 5,500 doctors and 16,300 hospital beds.

Books of Reference

Druzhinin, V., *Soviet Estonia.* Moscow, 1953 (in English)
Estonia. Basic Facts on Geography, History and Economy. Stockholm, 1948
Jackson, J. H., *Estonia.* London, 1948
Kareda, E., *Estonia in the Soviet Grip.* London, 1949
Pranspill, A., *Estonian Anthology.* Milford, Conn., 1957
Silvet, J., *Inglise–eesti sõraamat.* Vadstena, 1949
Varetz, E. F., and Tarmisto, V. Y., *Estonia.* Moscow, 1967 (in Russian)
Woods, E. G., *The Baltic Region: A Study in Physical and Human Geography.* London, 1945

LATVIA
Latvijas Padomju Socialistiska Republika

HISTORY. In the part of Latvia unoccupied by the Germans, the Bolsheviks won 72% of the votes in the Constituent Assembly elections (Nov. 1917). Soviet power was proclaimed in Dec. 1917, but was overthrown when the Germans occupied all Latvia (Feb. 1918). Restored when they withdrew (Dec. 1918), it was overthrown once more by combined British naval and German military forces (May–Dec. 1919), and a democratic government set up.

The secret protocol of the Soviet–German agreement of 23 Aug. 1939 assigned Latvia to the Soviet sphere of interest. An ultimatum (16 June 1940) led to the formation of a government acceptable to the USSR; on 21 July a People's Diet, elected by universal suffrage, established Soviet power and applied to join the USSR: the Supreme Soviet accepted the application on 5 Aug. The incorporation has been accorded *de facto* recognition by the British Government, but not by the US Government, which continues to recognize the *Chargé d'Affaires* in Washington D.C.

AREA AND POPULATION. Latvia is bounded north by Estonia and the Baltic Sea, west by the Baltic, south by Lithuania and Belorussia and east by the RSFSR. Lativa has a total area of 63,700 sq. km (25,590 sq. miles). Population, Jan. 1977, 2·5m., of whom 57% are Letts and 30% Russians. There are 26 districts, 56 towns and 36 urban settlements.

The chief town is Riga (the capital); other principal towns are Daugavpils (Dvinsk) (114,000), Liepāja (104,000), Jelgava (Mitau) (65,000) and Ventspils (Windau).

CONSTITUTION AND GOVERNMENT. The Supreme Soviet, elected in 1975, consists of 310 deputies (1 per 10,000 population); 106 are women, 202 Communists.

At elections to district, urban and rural Soviets (19 June 1977), of 23,081 deputies returned, 11,339 (49·1%) were women, 12,324 (53·4%) non-Party and 15,287 (63%) industrial workers and collective farmers.

President, Presidium of the Supreme Soviet: P. Y. Strautmanis.
Chairman, Council of Ministers: Y. Y. Ruben.
First Secretary, Communist Party: A. E. Voss.

FINANCE. Budget estimates (in 1m. new roubles), 1965, 678; 1970, 1,047; 1974, 1,199; 1976, 1,353.

AGRICULTURE. Latvia is now no longer mainly an agricultural country. The urban population, 35% of the total in 1939, was 66% in Jan. 1977.

Latvian forest lands, state and private (2·4m. hectares), produced in 1937–38, 3·4m. cu. metres of timber; 1976 output, 3·9m. cu. metres.

Area under cultivation was 1·4m. hectares in 1913, 2m. in 1940, 1·6m. in 1976. 1,626,800 hectares of marsh land have been drained.

Cattle breeding and dairy farming are the chief agricultural occupations. Oats, barley, rye, potatoes and flax are the main crops.

After the establishment of the Soviet regime about 960,000 hectares were distributed among the landless peasants or those with very small holdings. On 1 Jan. 1977 there were 250 state farms and 371 collective farms. There were 31,900 tractors and 6,900 grain combine harvesters. By 1 Jan. 1964, all state farms and collective farms were using electric power.

Livestock (1 Jan. 1977): Cattle, 1·4m. (1939: 1·3m.); sheep, 244,000 (1939: 1·5m.); pigs, 1·3m. (1939: 891,500).

Output of main agricultural products (in 1,000 tons) in 1976 (1913 figures in brackets): Sugar-beet, 194 (0); potatoes, 1,554 (645); all grains, 1,889 (880); vegetables, 155; fruit, 178; meat and fats, 241 (122); milk, 1,813 (673); wool, 0·6 (1·4); flax, 4·7 (21); 627m. eggs (136m.).

INDUSTRY. Latvia is the main producer of electric railway passenger cars and long-distance telephone exchanges in the USSR, fourth in output of paper and woollen goods, fifth of sawn timber, sixth of mineral fertilizers.

Industrial output in 1976 (in 1,000 tons) included: Steel, 502; rolled metal, 630; cement, 903; granulated sugar, 251; paper, 169; fish catch, 550; cotton fabrics, 62·8m. linear metres; linen fabrics, 21·3m. linear metres; woollens, 14m. linear metres; silks, 19·9m. linear metres; leather footwear, 10·3m. pairs; radio sets, 2·5m. Electric power output was 2,500m. kwh.

The peat deposits extend over 645,000 hectares or about 10% of the total area, and it is estimated that the total deposits of peat are 3,000–4,000m. tons; output, 1971, 2·3m. tons. There are also gypsum deposits; amber is frequently found in the coastal districts.

In 1976 industrial and office workers numbered 1·1m.; 101,000 specialists with a higher education were employed in the national economy.

COMMUNICATIONS. In 1976 the length of railways was 2,460 km, and motor roads, 24,200 km (hard surface, 14,000 km). Riga is the largest port in the Baltic after Leningrad.

Newspapers (1976). There were 87 newspapers (54 in Lettish), with a circulation of 1·5m. and 1·07m. respectively.

RELIGION. The Latvian Lutheran Church numbered 600,000 members in 1956.

EDUCATION. In 1976–77 there were 1,101 primary, continuation and secondary schools, with a total of 400,000 pupils: 97,000 children attended 764 preschool institutions. Ten places of higher education had 46,300 students, 54 technical colleges had 42,200 students; there were also 21 music and art schools, 3 teachers' training colleges and an agricultural academy. In 1946 an Academy of Sciences was opened which in 1976 had 16 research institutes with a staff of 1,688 scientific workers; there were over 12,000 scientific workers in 101 research institutions.

HEALTH. There were 10,100 doctors and 32,100 hospital beds in 1976.

Books of Reference

Latvian Academy of Sciences, *Istoria Latviiskoi SSR.* Riga, 1952–58
Central Statistical Department, Latvian Branch, *Latviiskaya SSR v Tsifrakh.* Riga
Bilmanis, A., *A History of Latvia.* Princeton Univ. Press, 1951
Roze, B. and K., *Latviska–Angliska Vānicā.* Göppingen, 1948
Skujenicks, M., *Atlas Statistique de la Lettnoie.* Riga, 1938
Spekke, A., *History of Latvia.* Stockholm, 1951
Turkina, E., *Angliski–Latviska Vānicā.* Riga, 1948

LITHUANIA
Lietuvas Taryu Socialistine Respublika

HISTORY. In 1914–15 the German army occupied the whole of Lithuania. On its withdrawal (Dec. 1918) Soviets were elected in all towns and a Soviet republic was proclaimed. In the summer of 1919 it was overthrown by Polish, German and nationalist Lithuanian forces, and a democratic republic established.

The secret protocol of the Soviet–German frontier treaty of 28 Sept. 1939 assigned the greater part of Lithuania to the Soviet sphere of influence. In Oct. 1939 the province and city of Vilnius (in Polish occupation 1920–39) were ceded by the USSR. An ultimatum (16 June 1940) led to the formation of a government acceptable to the USSR. A people's diet, elected on 14–15 July, applied for Lithuania's admission to the Soviet Union on 22 July, which was effected by decree of the Supreme Soviet on 3 Aug. and included also those parts of Lithuania which had been reserved for inclusion in Germany. This incorporation has been accorded *de facto* recognition by the British Government, but not by the US Government, which continues to recognize a Lithuanian *Chargé d'Affaires* in Washington, D.C.

AREA AND POPULATION. Lithuania is bounded north by Latvia, east and south by Belorussia, west by Poland, the Kaliningrad area of the RSFSR and the Baltic Sea. The total area of Lithuania is 65,200 sq. km (25,170 sq. miles) and the population (Jan. 1977) 3·3m., of whom 80% were Lithuanians, 8·6% Russians and 7·7% Poles.

The capital is Vilnius (Vilna). Other large towns are Kaunas (Kovno), Klaipéda (Memel), Šauliai (115,000) and Panevėžys (97,000). There are 44 rural districts, 92 towns and 20 urban settlements.

CONSTITUTION AND GOVERNMENT. The Supreme Soviet, elected in 1975, consists of 320 deputies (1 per 15,000 population); 109 are women, 216 Communists.

At elections to district, urban and rural Soviets (19 June 1977), of 28,276 deputies returned, 13,832 (48·9%) were women, 15,870 (56·1%) non-Party and 18,951 (67%) industrial workers and collective farmers.

President, Presidium of the Supreme Soviet: A. S. Barkauskas.
Chairman, Council of Ministers: J. A. Maniušis.
First Secretary, Communist Party: P. P. Griškevičius.

FINANCE. Budget estimates (in 1m. new roubles), 1965, 944; 1970, 1,665; 1976, 2,048; 1977, 2,073.

AGRICULTURE. Lithuania before 1940 was a mainly agricultural country, but has since been considerably industrialized. The urban population was 23% of the total in 1937 and 58% in Jan. 1977. The resources of the country consist of timber and agricultural produce. Of the total area, 49·1% is arable land, 22·2% meadow and pasture land, 16·3% forests and 12·4% unproductive lands.

Area under cultivation in 1913 was 1·9m.; in 1938, 2·7m.; in 1976, 2·4m. hectares. By 1976 over 2·31m. hectares of swamps had been drained.

Output of main agricultural products (in 1,000 tons) in 1976 (1913 figures in brackets): All grains, 3,220 (1,449); sugar-beet, 641 (0); flax, 20 (17); potatoes, 2,251

(1,375); vegetables, 228; fruit, 209; meat and fats, 442 (159); milk, 2,749 (832); wool, 0·2 (1·5); 831m. eggs (264m.).

On 1 Jan. 1977 there were 2·13m. cattle, 2·3m. pigs, 79,000 sheep and goats.

Forests cover 1,554,000 hectares; 70% of the forests consist of conifers, mostly pines. Peat reserves total 4,000m. cu. metres.

Between 1940 and 1947 about 575,500 hectares (about 1·4m. acres) were distributed among the landless and poor peasant farmers. In 1976 there were 48,800 tractors and 10,500 grain combines serving 837 collective farms and 343 state farms. Nearly all collective farms and all state farms received electric power in 1974.

INDUSTRY. Heavy engineering, shipbuilding and building material industries are developing. Industrial output included, in 1976: Cement, 2·99m. tons; granulated sugar, 198,100 tons; paper 122,000 tons; cotton fabrics, 86·3m. linear metres; linens, 19m. linear metres; woollens, 12·4m. linear metres; sawn timber, 1·1m. cu. metres; leather footwear, 9·5m. pairs; electric power, 9·7m. kwh.

In 1976 there were 1·4m. industrial and office workers and 117,000 specialists with a higher education employed in the national economy.

COMMUNICATIONS. Length of railways, 2,000 km. Vilnius has one of the largest airports of the USSR. There are 33,100 km of motor roads (18,900 km hard surface) and 600 km of inland waterways. Klaipéda, as a non-freezing harbour and fishery base, is of national importance.

Newspapers (1976). Of 113 newspapers, 89 were in Lithuanian, with a circulation of 2·06m. and 1,882,000 respectively.

RELIGION. In 1956, the Lithuanian Lutheran Church had 215,000 members; Roman Catholics, including those in Estonia and Latvia, numbered 2·5m.

EDUCATION. In 1976–77 there were 600,000 pupils in 2,700 primary, secondary and special schools. The University of Vytautas the Great, at Káunas, was opened on 16 Feb. 1922. On 15 Jan. 1940 certain faculties were transferred to Vilnius as an independent institution to form the University of Vilnius. There were 12 higher educational institutions with 64,900 students: in 76 technical colleges of all kinds there were 69,600 students. The Lithuanian Academy of Sciences, founded in 1941, had 11 institutions with a total scientific staff of 1,582; there were 88 scientific institutions with 13,000 research personnel. 125,000 children in 1976 were attending 813 pre-school institutions.

HEALTH. In 1976 there were 11,800 doctors and 37,700 hospital beds.

Books of Reference

Jurgéla, C. R., *History of the Lithuanian Nation*. New York, 1948
Metelsky, G., *Lithuania, Land of the Niemen*. Moscow, 1959
Peteraitis, V., *Lithuanian–English Dictionary*. 2 vols. Chicago, 1960

SOVIET CENTRAL ASIA

Soviet Central Asia embraces the Kazakh Soviet Socialist Republic, the Uzbek Soviet Socialist Republic, the Turkmen Soviet Socialist Republic, the Tadzhik Soviet Socialist Republic and the Kirghiz Soviet Socialist Republic.

Turkestan (by which name part of this territory was then known) was conquered by the Russians in the 1860s. In 1866 Tashkent was occupied and in 1868 Samarkand, and subsequently further territory was conquered and united with Russian Turkestan. In the 1870s Bokhara was subjugated, the emir, by the agreement of 1873, recognizing the suzerainty of Russia. In the same year Khiva became a vassal state to Russia. Until 1917 Russian Central Asia was divided politically into the Khanate of Khiva, the Emirate of Bokhara and the Governor-Generalship of Turkestan.

In the summer of 1919 the authority of the Soviet Government became definitely established in these regions. The Khan of Khiva was deposed in Feb. 1920, and a People's Soviet Republic was set up, the medieval name of Khorezm being revived. In Aug. 1920 the Emir of Bokhara suffered the same fate, and a similar regime was set up in Bokhara. The former Governor-Generalship of Turkestan was constituted an Autonomous Soviet Socialist Republic within the RSFSR on 11 April 1921.

In the autumn of 1924 the Soviets of the Turkestan, Bokhara and Khiva Republics decided to redistribute the territories of these republics on a nationality basis; at the same time Bokhara and Khiva became Socialist Republics. The redistribution was completed in May 1925, when the new states of Uzbekistan, Turkmenistan and Tadzhikistan and several autonomous regions were established. The remaining districts of Turkestan populated by Kazakhs were united with Kazakhstan. Kirghizia, until then part of the RSFSR, was established as a Union Republic in 1936.

Books of Reference

Nove, A. and Newth, J. A., *The Soviet Middle East.* London, 1967
Vaidyanathy, R., *The Formation of the Soviet Central Asian Republics.* New Delhi, 1967
Wheeler, G., *The Modern History of Soviet Central Asia.* London, 1964
Yuldashev, M. (ed.), *Oktiabrskaya Sotsialisticheskaya Revolutsia i Grajdanskaya Voina v Turkestane.* Tashkent, 1957
Zevelyov, A. (ed.), *Za Sovetski Turkestan.* Tashkent, 1963

KAZAKHSTAN
Kazak Soviettik Sotzialistik Respublikasy

HISTORY. On 26 Aug. 1920 Uralsk, Turgai, Akmolinsk and Semipalatinsk provinces formed the Kazakh Soviet Socialist Republic within the RSFSR. It was made a constituent republic of the USSR on 5 Dec. 1936. To this republic were added the parts of the former Governorship of Turkestan inhabited by a majority of Kazakhs. It consists of the following regions: Aktyubinsk, Alma-Ata, Chimkent, Dzhambul, Dzhezkazgan, East Kazakhstan, Guryev, Karaganda, Kokchetav, Kustanai, Kzyl-Orda, Mangyshlak, North Kazakhstan, Pavlodar, Semipalatinsk, Taldy-Kurgan, Tselinograd, Turgai, Uralsk.

AREA AND POPULATION. Kazakhstan is bounded on the west by the Caspian Sea and the RSFSR, on the east by China, on the north by the RSFSR and on the south by Uzbekistan and Kirghizia. The area of the republic is 2,717,300 sq. km (1,049,155 sq. miles). It is the next in size to the RSFSR, is far larger than all the other Central Asian Soviet Republics combined and stretches nearly 3,000 km from west to east and over 1,500 km from north to south. Population (Jan. 1977) 14·5m., of whom 54% live in urban areas. The Kazakhs form 32·6%, Russians 42% and Ukrainians 7·2% (owing to the industrialization of the country since 1941 and the opening of virgin lands since 1945). The population includes over 100 nationalities.

The capital is Alma-Ata, formerly Verny; other large towns are Karaganda, Semipalatinsk, Chimkent and Petropavlovsk. In all there are 82 towns, 189 urban settlements and 210 rural districts.

CONSTITUTION AND GOVERNMENT. The Supreme Soviet, elected in 1975, consists of 490 deputies (1 per 20,000 population); 174 are women, 324 Communists.

At elections to the regional, district, urban and rural Soviets (19 June 1977), out of 123,266 deputies returned, 59,341 (48·1%) were women, 73,554 (59·7%) non-Party and 83,725 (67·9%) industrial workers and collective farmers.

President, Presidium of the Supreme Soviet: S. B. Niyazbekov.
Chairman, Council of Ministers: B. A. Ashimov.
First Secretary, Communist Party: D. A. Kunayev.

FINANCE. The budget (in 1m. new roubles) balanced as follows: 1965, 4,689; 1970, 6,072; 1974, 5,971; 1976, 6,721.

AGRICULTURE. Kazakh agriculture has changed from primarily nomad cattle breeding to production of grain, cotton and other industrial crops. In 1976 the crop area was 35·6m. hectares—over 16% of the total cultivated area of the USSR (1913, 4·2m.; 1940, 6·8m.).

1,707,000 hectares of land have an irrigation network.

The 'Ukrainka' winter wheat has been transformed into a spring wheat suitable for cultivation in Kazakhstan. Tobacco, rubber plants and mustard are also cultivated. Kazakhstan has rich orchards and vineyards; 22,000 hectares were under vines and 105,000 under orchards in 1976. Between 1954 and 1959, over 23m. hectares of virgin and long fallow land were opened up, 544 new state grain farms being organized for the purpose. Grain deliveries to the state were 10·5m. tons in 1960; 2·4m. in 1965; 17m. in 1966; 8·2m. in 1967; 11·7m. in 1968; 11m. in 1969; 13·4m. in 1970; 17·4m. in 1972; 16·7m. in 1973; 9·9m. in 1974; 5·1m. in 1975; 19·6m. in 1976.

Kazakhstan is noted for its livestock, particularly its sheep, from which excellent quality wool is obtained. The Akharomerino is a newly developed crossbreed of merino sheep and the wild Akhar mountain ram. Livestock on 1 Jan. 1977 included 7·7m. cattle, 34·4m. sheep and goats and 2·2m. pigs.

There were, on 1 Jan. 1977, 421 collective farms and 1,984 state farms with 233,000 tractors and 113,600 grain combine harvesters. There were 5,293 rural power stations of 307,800 kwh. capacity.

Output of main agricultural products (in 1m. tons) in 1976 (1913 figures in brackets): All grains, 29·8 (2·2); cotton, 0·3 (0·015); sugar-beet, 2 (0); potatoes, 1·7 (0·18); vegetables, 0·89; meat, 0·9 (0·44); milk, 4 (0·85); 2,918m. eggs (233m.); wool, 0·1 (0·04).

INDUSTRY. Kazakhstan is extremely rich in mineral resources. Coal and tungsten in Karaganda (in the centre), oil along the river Emba (in the west), copper, lead and zinc—Kazakhstan contains about one-half of the total deposits of these three metals contained in the USSR—Iceland spar (in the south), nickel and chromium in the Kustanai and Semipalatinsk regions, molybdenum and other minerals.

In 1943 big deposits of manganese were found in Eastern Kazakhstan; new coal seams were also discovered there. In South Kazakhstan new copper and bauxite deposits have been found.

Coal, oil, non-ferrous metallurgy, heavy engineering and chemical industries have brought Kazakhstan to the third place among the industrial republics of the USSR.

Coal output in 1976 was 93·7m. tons; oil, 23·3m. tons; steel, 5·6m. tons; rolled metal, 4·4m. tons; cement, 6·8m. tons; mineral fertilizers, 5·8m. tons; cotton fabrics, 101·2m. linear metres; leather footwear, 31·1m. pairs; woollen fabrics, 16·7m. linear metres; granulated sugar, 154,400 tons. The Leninogorsk and Chimkent lead plants, the Balkhash, Irtysh and Karaskpai copper-smelting works and others supply the country with nonferrous metals. A meat-packing plant has been built in Semipalatinsk, a fish cannery in Guryev, a chemical plant in Aktyubinsk, a tractor works at Pavlodar, and a superphosphate plant in Dzhambul. The oil industry in Emba and Aktyubinsk yields high-quality aviation oil. Iron ore output in 1976 was 22·7m. tons.

Aviation plays an important part in agriculture. About 14m. hectares were in 1970 treated from the air (destruction of pests, surface feeding of sugar-beet plantations, pollination of orchards, etc.).

Among recent enterprises are a large textile combine at Kustanai, hosiery factories at Djezkazgan, Leninogorsk and Aktiubinsk, a sugar factory at Aksu, meat canneries at Djetygar and Kzyl-Orda.

Electric power output in 1976 was 55·800m. kwh.

There were, in 1976, 5·5m. (average for year) industrial and office workers in the national economy and 412,000 specialists with a higher education.

COMMUNICATIONS

Roads. In 1976 there were 96,900 km of motor roads (61,600 km hard surface).

Railways. A 430-km railway line between the settlements of Mointi and Chu in Kazakhstan to complete the Transkazakh trunk line, connecting Petropavlovsk, Akmolinsk, Karaganda and Balkhash, was opened in 1953. The new line links the Transkazakh trunk line with the Turkestan–Siberian railway carrying Karaganda coal to South Kazakhstan. The Akmolinsk–Pavlodar railway (438 km), a section of the South Siberian line, was opened in Dec. 1953. Other lines in operation are Dzhambul–Chalaktan, Akmolinsk–Kartaly, Uralsk–Iletsk, Guriev–Kandagach. In 1976 the total length of railways in operation was 14,140 km. Over 600 km of narrow-gauge line and 700 km of broad-gauge line were built in the virgin lands area in 1951–57.

Inland waterways. 5,500 km. A 500-km canal to bring water from the Irtysh at Yermak, below Pavlodar, along the Shiderta, Tuzda and Nura rivers to the new industrial centre of Karaganda was begun in 1960. It is to irrigate in all 60,000 hectares and provide water for a number of new industrial towns.

Newspapers (1976). Of 403 newspapers, 151 were in the Kazakh language, with a circulation of 5·16m. and 1·76m. respectively.

EDUCATION. Nearly the whole population is literate. In 1976–77 there were 3·3m. pupils at 9,800 elementary and secondary schools; 216 technical colleges with 240,800 students, 50 higher educational institutions with 225,000 students, and 207 research institutes with 33,000 scientific personnel. The Kazakh Academy of Sciences, founded in 1945, had, in 1976, 31 institutions, the scientific staff of which numbered 3,736. 743,000 children were attending 5,945 pre-school institutions.

HEALTH. In 1976 there were 41,100 doctors and 182,800 hospital beds.

Books of Reference

Central Statistical Dept. of Kazakh SSR., *Narodnoye Hoziaistrvo Kazakhstana.* Alma-Ata, 1968
Alampiev, P., *Soviet Kazakhstan.* Moscow, 1958.—*Where Economic Inequality is No More.* Moscow, 1959
Grauman, J., and others, *The Kazakhs under Changing Russian Regimes.* Washington, 1951
Lias, G., *Kazak Exodus.* London, 1956

TURKMENISTAN
Tiurkmenostan Soviet Sotsialistik Respublikasy

HISTORY. The Turkmen Soviet Socialist Republic was formed on 27 Oct. 1924 and covers the territory of the former Trans-Caspian Region of Turkestan, the Charjiui vilayet of Bokhara and a part of Khiva situated on the right bank of the Oxus. In May 1925 the Turkmen Republic entered the Soviet Union as one of its constituent republics.

AREA AND POPULATION. Turkmenistan is bounded on the north by the Autonomous Kara-Kalpak Republic, a constituent of Uzbekistan, by Iran and Afghánistán on the south, by the Uzbek Republic on the east and the Caspian Sea on the west. The principal Turkmen tribes are the Tekkés of Merv and the Tekkés of the Attok, the Ersaris, Yomuds and Goklans. All speak closely related varieties of a Turkoman language (of the south-western group of Turk languages); many are Sunni Mohammedans.

The country passed under Russian control in 1881, after the fall of the Turkoman stronghold of Gök-Tépé. 66% of the population are Turkmenians, most of whom were nomads before the First World War. 14·5% are Russians living mostly in urban areas, and 8·3% Uzbeks. There are also Kazakhs (3·2%), Tartars, Ukrainians, Armenians and others (1970 census).

The area of Turkmenistan is 488,100 sq. km (186,400 sq. miles), and its population in Jan. 1977 was 2·65m.

There are 5 regions: Chardzhou, Maruy, Ashkhabad, Tashauz and Krasnovodsk, comprising 40 rural districts, 15 towns and 73 urban settlements.

The capital is Ashkhabad (Poltoratsk); other large towns are Chardzhou (113,000), Maruy (Merv) (72,000), Nebit-Dag (67,000) and Krasnovodsk (55,000).

CONSTITUTION AND GOVERNMENT. The Supreme Soviet, elected in 1975, consists of 300 deputies (1 per 5,000 population); 106 are women, 203 Communists.

At elections to regional, district, urban and rural Soviets (19 June 1977), of 22,367 deputies returned, 10,506 (47%) were women, 12,708 (56·8%) non-Party and 15,425 (69%) industrial workers and collective farmers.

President, Presidium of the Supreme Soviet: A. M. Klychev.
Chairman, Council of Ministers and Foreign Minister: B. Yazkuliev.
First Secretary, Communist Party: M. G. Gapurov.

FINANCE. Budget estimates (in 1m. new roubles), 1965, 557; 1970, 724; 1974, 704; 1976, 821.

AGRICULTURE. The main occupation of the people is agriculture, based on irrigation. Turkmenistan produces cotton, wool, Astrakhan fur, etc. It is also famous for its carpets, and produces a special breed of Turkoman horses and the famous Karakul sheep.

There were 338 collective farms and 58 state farms in 1976, with 34,100 tractors and 1,000 grain combines. There were 608 rural power stations.

A considerable area is under Egyptian cotton, and from it has been evolved an original Soviet long-fibred cotton.

The main grain grown is maize. Sericulture, fruit and vegetable growing are also important; dates, olives, figs, sesame and other southern plants are grown. There is fishing in the Caspian. 845,000 hectares were under cultivation in 1976 (1913, 318,000; 1940, 411,000).

Between 1958 and 1970 the Kara-Kum Canal was extended to 860 km. In 1971 the fourth section, to reach the Caspian, was begun to reach 1,000 km. By 1977 over 250,000 hectares in the canal zone were irrigated, and 150 km through rocky western Turkmenia had been started.

Livestock on 1 Jan. 1977: Cattle, 548,000; pigs, 126,000; sheep and goats, 4·2m.

Output of main agricultural products (in 1,000 tons) in 1976 (1913 figures in brackets): Wheat, 53 (113); cotton, 1,046 (69); vegetables, 233; grapes, 40; fruit, 20; meat, 71 (58); milk, 260 (63); wool, 14·7 (9·7); 181m. eggs (18m.).

INDUSTRY. Turkmenistan is rich in minerals, such as ozocerite, oil, coal, sulphur and salt. Industry is being developed, and there are now chemical, tailoring, textile, light, food, agricultural implements, cement and other factories, oil refineries, as well as ore-mining.

In the Kara-Kum Desert deposits of magnesium, minerals and coal were discovered, as well as some 50 new saltmines. Here a new oil town, Nebit-Dag, has sprung up. On the Kara-Bogaz bay a sulphate industry has been developed. Industrial output in 1976 included 14·8m. tons of oil, 564,000 tons of cement, 23·1m. linear metres of cotton fabrics, 3·3m. pairs of leather footwear. Electric power output was 5,200m. kwh. (in 1940). 62,581m. cu. metres of natural gas were produced.

In 1976 there were 596,000 industrial and office workers in the national economy; specialists with a higher education numbered 67,000.

COMMUNICATIONS. Length of motor roads 9,600 km (7,000 km hard surface). Motor communication exists between Ashkhabad and Meshed (Iran).

Length of railways, 2,120 km. The line Chardzhou–Kungrad crosses the Chardzhou and Tashauz regions of Turkmenia and runs across Uzbekistan. Another line connects Chardzhou and Urgench. Inland waterways, 1,300 km.

Airlines connect Leninsk and Tashauz, and Ashkhabad and remote areas in the west, north and east.

Newspapers (1976). Of 26 newspapers, 14 were in the Turkmen language, with a circulation of 778,000 and 606,000 respectively.

EDUCATION. In 1976–77 there were 1,800 primary and secondary schools with 700,000 pupils, 6 higher educational institutions with 32,100 students, 31 technical colleges with 30,500 students, and 11 music and art schools. The Turkmen Academy of Sciences directs the work of 14 learned institutions with a staff of 883 scientists; there were 58 research institutions in all, with 4,600 research workers, in 1976. A Turkmenian State University was opened in 1951: in 1973 it had 10,124 students.

In 1976, 108,000 children were attending 840 pre-school institutions.

HEALTH. In 1976 there were 6,900 doctors and 26,400 hospital beds.

UZBEKISTAN
Ozbekiston Soviet Sotsialistik Respublikasy

HISTORY. In Oct. 1917 the Tashkent Soviet assumed authority, and in the following years established its power throughout Turkestan. The semi-independent Khanates of Khiva and Bokhara were first (1920) transformed into 'People's Republics', then (1923–24) into Soviet Socialist Republics and finally merged in the Uzbek SSR and other republics.

The Uzbek Soviet Socialist Republic was formed on 27 Oct. 1924 from lands formerly included in Turkestan. It includes a large part of the Samarkand region, the southern part of the Syr Darya, Western Ferghana, the western plains of Bukhara, the Kara-Kalpak ASSR and the Uzbek regions of Khorezm. In May 1925 Uzbekistan, by the decision of the Congress of Soviets of the USSR, was accepted as one of the constituent republics in the Soviet Union.

AREA AND POPULATION. Uzbekistan is bordered on the north by the Kazakh Soviet Socialist Republic, on the east by the Kirghiz Soviet Socialist Republic and the Tadzhik Soviet Socialist Republic, on the south by Afghánistán and on the west by the Turkmen Soviet Socialist Republic. The Uzbeks, who form 65% of the population, were the ruling race in Central Asia, until the arrival of the Russians during the third quarter of the 19th century. The several native states over which Uzbek dynasties formerly ruled were founded in the 15th century upon the ruins of Tamerlane's empire. The Uzbek speak Jagatai Turk, which is related to Osmanli and Azerbaijan Turk; many are Sunni Mohammedans. Russians number 12·5%, other Central Asians 10·7%, Tartars 4·9%.

The area of Uzbekistan is 447,400 sq. km (172,741 sq. miles). The population in Jan. 1977 was 14,474,000 (39% urban). The country comprises the following regions: Andijan, Bukhara, Dzhizak (formed 29 Dec. 1973), Ferghana, Kashkadar, Khorezm, Namangan, Samarkand, Surkhan-Darya, Syr-Darya (formed 16 Feb. 1963), Tashkent and the Autonomous Soviet Republic of Kara Kalpakia. The capital of the Republic is Tashkent; other large towns are Samarkand, Andizhan, Namangan. There are 82 towns, 84 urban settlements and 134 rural districts.

On 19 Sept. 1963 the Supreme Soviet of the USSR confirmed decisions of the Supreme Soviets of Kazakhstan and Uzbekistan, transferring over 40,000 sq. km from the former to the latter to ensure more efficient use of the 'Hungry Steppe'.

CONSTITUTION AND GOVERNMENT. The Supreme Soviet, elected in 1975, consists of 470 deputies (1 per 15,000 population); 164 are women, 321 Communists.

At elections to the regional, district, urban and rural Soviets (19 June 1977), of 93,430 deputies returned, 44,953 (48·1%) were women, 51,691 (55·3%) non-Party and 64,600 (69·1%) industrial workers and collective farmers.

President, Presidium of the Supreme Soviet: N. M. Matchanov.
Chairman, Council of Ministers: N. D. Hudaiberdyev.
First Secretary, Communist Party: S. R. Rashidov.

FINANCE. Budget estimates (in 1m. new roubles), 1965, 2,133; 1970, 3,228; 1971, 3,315; 1974, 3,798; 1976, 4,299.

AGRICULTURE. Uzbekistan is a land of intensive farming, based on artificial irrigation. It is the chief cotton-growing area in the USSR and the third in the world. About 3·1m. hectares of collective and state farmland have irrigation networks and all are in full use.

In 1939 the Ferghana Canal (270 km) was built. During 1940, among the irrigation canals completed were: the North Ferghana Canal (165 km), and Andreev South Ferghana Canal (108 km) and the first section of the Tashkent Canal (63 km). A canal from the Amu-Darya to Bokhara across the Kzil-Kum and Ust-Urt deserts (180 km) was completed in 1965. A 200-km canal joining the river Zeravshan with the Kashka Darya at the village of Paruz was completed in Aug. 1955; it is part of the Iski–Angara Canal. The first section (93 km) of a canal irrigating the southern 'Hungry Steppe' was opened in 1960; 500,000 hectares of this desert were under cultivation in 1967.

Agriculture flourishes, particularly in the well-watered, warm, rich oases areas, such as the Ferghana valley, Zeravshan, Tashkent and Khorezm, where cotton, fruit, silk and rice are cultivated. In the higher-lying plains grain is grown; the wide desert and semi-desert area of Western Uzbekistan is mainly given to pasture land and the breeding of the Karakul sheep; there is a Karakul institute at Samarkand.

Orchards occupied 194,000 hectares and the vineyards 66,000 hectares in 1976. The Central Asian Branch of the Scientific Research Institute of Viticulture in Tashkent has produced new frost resistant grapes by crossing the wild Amur grape with Central Asian and European types. In 1976 there were 947 collective farms and 626 state farms, with 149,500 tractors and 27,400 cotton picking and grain combines. Ploughing, cotton-sowing and cultivation are completely mechanized; cotton-picking over 46%.

Uzbekistan provides 67% of the total cotton, 50% of the total rice and 60% of the total lucerne grown in the USSR. The area under crops was 2,189,000 hectares in 1913, 3,036,000 hectares in 1940 and 3·7m. hectares in 1976.

Livestock on 1 Jan. 1977: 3·22m. cattle, 8m. sheep and goats and 317,000 pigs.

Output of main agricultural products (in 1,000 tons) in 1976 (1913 figures in brackets): Wheat, 123 (513); maize, 504 (39); cotton, 5,338 (517); potatoes, 190 (46); fruit, 595; grapes, 390; meat, 265 (89); milk, 1,785 (231); wool, 24·5 (5·3); 1,227m. eggs (87).

Afforestation over an area of 50,000 hectares has been carried out to protect the Bokhara and Karakul oases from the advancing Kzyl-Kum sands and to stop the sand-drifts in a number of districts of Central Ferghana.

INDUSTRY. Of its mineral resources, in addition to oil and coal, copper and building materials and ozocerite deposits are now also exploited. New very rich coal deposits were discovered in 1944 and 1947 near Tashkent.

There are nearly 1,600 factories and mills. They include a factory of agricultural machinery (in Tashkent), a cement factory, a sulphur-mine, an oxygen factory, a paper-mill, a leather factory, textile-mills, clothing factories, iron and steel works, the Chirchik electro-chemical plant, a superphosphate plant in Kokand and oil refineries, coalmines, etc. Output in 1976 included 5·4m. tons of coal, 411,000 tons of steel, 1·4m. tons of oil, 3·54m. tons of cement, 5·8m. tons of mineral fertilizers, 223·1m. linear metres of cotton fabrics, 96·5m. linear metres of silk fabrics, 26·2m. pairs of leather footwear, 784,000 hectolitres of wine (apart from collective farm output). Gold is being worked at Muruntau, Chadak and Kochbulak.

The Tashkent power station (2m. kw.) was completed in 1971. Power output in 1976 was 35,100m. kwh. (481m. kwh. in 1940). Two natural-gas pipelines (Djaikak–

Tashkent, Ferghana–Kokand) and a third from Bukhara to the Urals are operating. Natural gas output (1976) was 36,100m. cu. metres.

In 1976 there were 3·5m. industrial and office workers in the national economy and 389,000 specialists with a higher education.

COMMUNICATIONS. The total length of railway in 1976 was 3,380 km. Branches lead to Karshe-Kitab, Kerki-Termez, Jalal-Abad, Namangan, Andijan and other centres. In 1947–55 a new line was built from Chardzhou to Kungrad.

The Great Uzbek Highway was completed in April 1941. Total length of motor roads in 1976 was 30,700 km (hard surface, 28,300 km). Inland waterways, 1,100 km.

An airline, serving all of Central Asia, is most developed in Uzbekistan.

Newspapers (1976). There were 168 newspapers in the Uzbek and Kara-Kalpak languages out of a total of 256, with a circulation of 3·35m. and 4·5m. respectively.

EDUCATION. In 1976–77 there were 9,500 elementary and secondary schools with 3·8m. pupils, 42 higher educational establishments with 254,500 students and 189 technical colleges with 196,600 students. Uzbekistan has an Academy of Sciences and 188 research institutes with 31,300 scientific staff, 3,545 of them in 30 institutions of the Uzbek Academy of Sciences. There are universities and medical schools in Tashkent and Samarkand. In 1976, 598,000 children were attending 4,220 pre-school institutions.

The Uzbek Arabic script was in 1929 replaced by the Latin alphabet which in 1940 was superseded by one based on the Cyrillic alphabet.

HEALTH. In 1976 there were 37,500 doctors and 151,200 hospital beds.

Books of Reference

Istoria Uzbekskoi SSSR. 2 vols. Tashkent, 1955–57
Pobeda Oktiabrskoi Revolutsii v Uzbekistane. Vol. I. Tashkent, 1963

KARA-KALPAK AUTONOMOUS SOVIET SOCIALIST REPUBLIC

Area, 165,600 sq. km (63,920 sq. miles); population (Jan. 1977), 849,600. Capital, Nukus (100,000). The Karakalpaks are first mentioned in written records in the 16th century as tributary to Bokhara, and later to the Kazakh Khanate. In the second half of the 19th century, as a result of the Russian conquest of Central Asia, they came under Russian rule. On 11 May 1925 the territory was constituted within the then Kazakh Autonomous Republic (of the Russian Federation) as an Autonomous Region. On 20 March 1932 it became an Autonomous Republic within the Russian Federation, and on 5 Dec. 1936 it became part of the Uzbek SSR.

165 deputies were elected to its Supreme Soviet on 15 June 1975, of whom 57 are women and 108 Communists.

Its manufactures are in the field of light industry—bricks, leather goods, furniture, canning, wine. Output of cotton in 1976 was 371,000 tons (in 1913, 8,000 tons). There were 4,217 tractors. Cattle numbered 312,000 and sheep and goats 644,000. There were 46 collective and 81 state farms. 216,100 industrial and office workers, and 14,800 specialists with a higher education, were employed in the national economy.

In 1976–77 there were 239,000 pupils in 605 schools; there are also a State University (4,800 students) and technical and teachers' training colleges with 12,900 students.

There were 1,878 doctors and 8,920 hospital beds.

TADZHIKISTAN
Respublikai Sovieth Sotsialistii Tojikiston

HISTORY. The Tadzhik Soviet Socialist Republic was formed from those regions of Bokhara and Turkestan where the population consisted mainly of Tadzhiks. It was admitted as a constituent republic of the Soviet Union on 5 Dec. 1929.

AREA AND POPULATION. Tadzhikistan is situated between 39° 40′ and 36° 40′ N. lat. and 67° 20′ and 75° E. long., north of the Oxus (Amu-Darya). On the west and north it is bordered by Uzbekistan and by the Kirghiz Soviet Socialist Republic; on the east by Chinese Turkestan and on the south by Afghánistán. It includes two regions (Leninabad and Kulyab) and 35 rural districts, 18 towns and 49 urban settlements, together with the Gorno-Badakhshan Autonomous Region. Its highest mountains are Communism Peak (7,495 metres) and Lenin Peak (7,127 metres). Even the lowest valleys in the Pamirs are not below 3,500 metres above sea-level. The huge mountain glaciers are the source of many rapid rivers—the tributaries of the Amu-Darya, which flows from east to west along the southern border of Tadzhikistan. About 56% of the population are Tadzhiks. They speak an Iranian dialect, little different from Persian, and they are considered to be the descendants of the original Aryan population of Turkestan. Unlike the Persians, the Tadzhiks are mostly Sunnis. Of the rest, 23% are Uzbeks living in the north-west of the republic. Russians and Ukrainians number 13% (1970 census).

The area of the territory is 143,100 sq. km (55,240 sq. miles). Population (Jan. 1977), 3·6m. The capital is Dushanbe. Other large towns are Leninabad (123,000), Kurgan-Tyube, Kulyab.

CONSTITUTION AND GOVERNMENT. The Supreme Soviet, elected in 1975, consists of 325 deputies (1 per 5,000 population); 111 are women and 224 Communists.

At elections to the district, urban and rural Soviets and the regional Soviet of Gorno-Badakhshan (19 June 1977), out of 24,890 deputies returned, 11,813 (47·5%) were women, 13,817 (55·5%) non-Party and 17,239 (69·2%) industrial workers and collective farmers.

President, Presidium of the Supreme Soviet: Makhmadullo Kholov.
Chairman, Council of Ministers and Foreign Minister: R. Nabiev.
First Secretary, Communist Party: D. Rasulov.

FINANCE. Budget estimates (in 1m. new roubles), 1965, 553; 1970, 827; 1974, 913; 1976, 1,024.

AGRICULTURE. The occupations of the population are mainly farming, horticulture and cattle breeding. Area under crops in 1976 was 774,000 hectares (1913, 494,000; 1940, 807,000). Wine production, 1976, was 450,000 hectolitres.

There are 43,000 km of irrigation canals: the irrigation networks cover about 582,000 hectares of land.

Tadzhikistan grows many varieties of fruit, including apricots, figs, olives, pomegranates, a local variety of lemons and oranges, and in the south sugar-cane has been grown. Even on the highest mountain plateaux of the Pamirs, 'the roof of the world', the biological station of Tadzhikistan (3,860 metres above sea-level) has succeeded in raising crops of 60 varieties of barley, 10 varieties of oats, 4 of wheat, as well as vegetables. Eucalyptus and geranium are grown for the perfumery industry. Jute, rice and millet are also grown.

Tadzhikistan contains rich pasture lands, and cattle breeding is a very important branch of its agriculture. Livestock on 1 Jan. 1977: 1·1m. cattle, 2·9m. sheep and goats and 98,000 pigs.

The Gissar sheep is famous in the south for its meat and fat; the Karakul sheep is widely bred for its wool.

There were 209 collective farms (208 with electric power) and 168 state farms in 1976, with 29,200 tractors and 2,900 cotton and grain combine harvesters.

Output of main agricultural products (in 1,000 tons) in 1976 (1913 figures in brackets): Wheat, 96 (133); maize, 41 (2); cotton, 847 (32); potatoes, 110 (10); vegetables, 303; fruit, 201; grapes, 167; meat, 88 (48); milk, 394 (102); wool, 5·4 (2·1); 248m. eggs (20m.).

INDUSTRY. The original small-scale handicraft industries have been replaced by big industrial enterprises, including mining, engineering, food, textile, clothing and silk factories.

There are rich deposits of brown coal, lead, zinc and oil (in the north of the republic), rare elements, such as uranium, radium, arsenic and bismuth. Asbestos, mica, corundum and emery, lapis lazuli, potassium salts, sulphur and other minerals have been found in other parts of the republic.

Industrial output in 1976 included: 800,000 tons of coal, 274,000 tons of oil, 1·01m. tons of cement, 116m. linear metres of cotton fabrics, 58m. linear metres of silk fabrics; leather footwear, 7·1m. pairs; refrigerators, 126,400.

There are 80 big electrical stations. The hydro-electric Varzob station began to operate in 1954, that at Kairak-Kum on the Syr Darya River was completed in 1957 and 2 more at Murgab in 1964. Output in 1976 was 5,200m. kwh. (in 1940, 62m. kwh.).

Construction of an electro-chemical combine, the largest in the USSR, has begun in the Yavan steppe in south Tadjikistan, and of a 3·2m. kw. power station in the upper reaches of the Vakhsh River.

In 1976 there were 785,000 industrial and office workers in the national economy, and 85,000 specialists with a higher education.

COMMUNICATIONS

Roads. There are 13,300 km of motor roads. Of these, 9,900 km are hard surface, including the Osh–Khorog (700 km), Yasui–Bazar–Charm (107 km) and Dushanbe–Khorog in the Pamirs (557 km) roads.

Railways. A railway line between Termez and Dushanbe (258 km) connects the republic with the railway system of the USSR. The mountainous nature of the republic makes ordinary railway construction difficult; accordingly 345 km of narrow gauge railways have been constructed (Kurgan–Tyube–Piandzh and Dushanbe–Kurgan–Tyube, connecting Dushanbe with the cotton-growing Vakhsh valley and are particularly important).

Aviation. Dushanbe is connected by air with Moscow, Tashkent, Baku and the regional and district centres of the republic.

Shipping. A steamship line on the Amu-Darya runs between Termez, Sarava and Jilikulam on the river Vakhsh (200 km).

Newspapers. (1976). 58 newspapers had a total circulation of 1,168,000. Of these, 51 with 813,000 circulation, were in Tadzhik.

EDUCATION. In 1976–77 there were 3,100 primary and secondary schools with 900,000 pupils, 9 higher educational institutions with 51,900 students and 38 technical colleges with 38,500 students; the Tadzhik state university had 12,467 students. In 1976, 91,000 children were attending 496 pre-school institutions. In 1951 an Academy of Sciences was established; it has 17 institutions, the scientific staff of which numbers 1,262; there are 61 research institutions in all, with 6,800 scientific personnel. The Pamir research station is the highest altitude meteorological observatory in the world.

In 1940 a new alphabet based on Cyrillic was introduced.

HEALTH. There are 120 hospitals as well as maternity homes, clinics and special institutes to combat tropical diseases. There were 7,800 doctors in 1976 and 34,600 hospital beds.

GORNO-BADAKHSHAN AUTONOMOUS REGION

Comprising the Pamir massif along the borders of Afghánistán and China, the region was set up on 2 Jan. 1925. Area, 63,700 sq. km (24,590 sq. miles); population (est. Jan. 1977), 119,000 (83% Tadjiks, 11% Kirghiz). Capital, Khorog (14,800).

There were 35,900 pupils in 268 schools in 1976–77 and 170 students in technical colleges, 151 doctors and 1,005 hospital beds.

Mining industries are developed (gold, rock-crystal, mica, coal, salt). Wheat, fruit and fodder crops are grown and cattle and sheep are bred in the western parts. In 1976 there were 64,200 cattle, 340,800 sheep and goats.

In 1976 there were 17 collective farms and 15 state (livestock) farms.

Books of Reference

Academy of Science of Tadzhikistan, *Istoria Tadzhikskogo Naroda.* 3 vols. Moscow, 1963–65
Chumichev, D. A., *Tadzhikskaya SSR.* Moscow, 1954
Luknitsky, P., *Soviet Tajkistan* [In English]. Moscow, 1954

KIRGHIZIA
Kyrgyz Sovietik Sotsialistik Respublikasy

HISTORY. After the establishment of the Soviet regime in Russia, Kirghizia was part of Soviet Turkestan, which itself became an Autonomous Soviet Socialist Republic within the RSFSR in April 1921. In 1924, when Central Asia was reorganized territorially on a national basis, Kirghizia was separated from Turkestan and formed into an autonomous region within the RSFSR. On 1 Feb. 1926 the Government of the RSFSR transformed Kirghizia into an Autonomous Soviet Socialist Republic within the RSFSR, and finally in Dec. 1936 Kirghizia was proclaimed one of the constituent Soviet Socialist Republics of the USSR.

AREA AND POPULATION. The territory of Kirghizia covers 198,500 sq. km (76,460 sq. miles), and its population in Jan. 1977 was 3·4m. The republic comprises 3 regions: Issyk-Kul, Naryn and Osh. There are 18 towns, 31 urban settlements and 37 rural districts. Its capital is Frunze (formerly Pishpek). Other large towns are Osh (161,000), Przhevalsk (51,000), Kyzyl-Kia, Tokmak.

Kirghizia is situated on the Tian-Shan mountains and bordered on the east by China, on the west by Kazakhstan and Uzbekistan, on the north by Kazakhstan and in the south by Tadzhikistan. The Kirghizians are of Turkic origin and form 44% of the population; the rest are Russians (29%), Ukrainians (4%), Uzbeks (11·3%) and others (1970 census).

CONSTITUTION AND GOVERNMENT. The Supreme Soviet, elected in 1975, consists of 340 deputies (1 per 5,000 population); 119 are women, 232 Communists.

At elections to the regional, district, urban and rural Soviets (19 June 1977), of the 24,890 deputies returned, 11,813 (47·5%) were women, 13,817 (55·5%) non-Party and 17,239 (69·2%) industrial workers and collective farmers.

President, Presidium of the Supreme Soviet: Turabay Kulatov.
Chairman, Council of Ministers: A. S. Suyumbayev.
First Secretary, Communist Party: T. U. Usubaliev.

FINANCE. Budget estimates (in 1m. new roubles), 1965, 603; 1970, 886; 1974, 1,047; 1976, 1,155.

AGRICULTURE. Kirghizia is famed for its livestock breeding. On 1 Jan. 1977 there were 940,000 cattle, 220,000 pigs, 9·9m. sheep and goats. Yaks are bred as meat and dairy cattle, and graze on high altitudes unsuitable for other cattle.

Crossed with domestic cattle, hybrids are produced much heavier than ordinary Kirghiz cattle and giving twice the yield of milk. The Kirghizian horse is famed for its endurance, but it is of small stature; it has in recent years been crossed with Don, Arab and other breeds.

On 1 Jan. 1977 there were 213 collective and 183 state farms. Area under crops (1976), 1·28m. hectares (1913, 640,000; 1940, 1,056,000). There were 25,600 tractors and 4,000 grain combine harvesters and 1,600 cotton combines in 1976; nearly all collective and state farms received electric power.

Kirghizia raises wheat sufficient for its own use and other grains and fodder, particularly lucerne; also sugar-beet, hemp, kenaf, kendyr, tobacco, medicinal plants and rice. Sericulture, orchards, vineries, vegetables and apiary are also important branches of Kirghiz agriculture. Agriculture is highly mechanized; nearly all the area under crops is worked by tractors. In 1976 irrigation networks in collective and state farms covered 924,000 hectares; practically all were in use. A canal in the western Tien-Shan ranges and a reservoir in the Urto-Tokoi mountains are being constructed.

The health resorts of Jety-Oguz (7,200 ft) and Jalal-Abad are famous for their mild alpine climate and mineral springs.

Output of main agricultural products (in 1,000 tons) in 1976 (1913 figures in brackets): Wheat, 477 (250); maize, 191 (37); cotton, 208 (28); sugar-beet, 1,768 (0); potatoes, 268 (19); vegetables, 308; fruit, 182; grapes, 62; meat, 142 (39); milk, 616 (91); wool, 31·2 (4·7); 386m. eggs (19m.).

INDUSTRY. Kirghizia contains 500 large modern industrial enterprises, including sugar refineries, tanneries, cotton and wool-cleansing works, flour-mills, a tobacco factory, food, timber, textile, engineering, metallurgical, oil and mining enterprises.

The output of coal in 1976 was 4·3m. tons; oil, 230,000 tons; granulated sugar, 249,100 tons; silk fabrics, 9·7m. linear metres; cotton fabrics, 64m. linear metres; leather footwear, 10·6m. pairs.

Hydro-electric power stations are being built in the Central Tien-Shans and the cotton-growing districts in the Osh Region, the Chui valley and on the shore of Lake Issyk-Kul. Power output (1976) was 4,800m. kwh.

There were, in 1976, 965,000 industrial and office workers in the national economy, in which 96,000 specialists with a higher education were engaged.

COMMUNICATIONS. In the north a railway runs from Lugovaya through Frunze to Rybachi on Lake Issyk-Kul. Towns in the southern valleys are linked by short lines with the Ursatyevskaya–Andizhan railway in Uzbekistan. Total length of railway is 370 km. Most of the traffic is by road; there were 21,700 km of motor roads (14,600 hard surface) in 1975. A road tunnel through the Tien Shan mountains at an altitude of 9,600 ft, connecting Frunze and Osh, is being constructed. Inland waterways, 600 km. Airlines link Frunze with Moscow and Tashkent.

Newspapers (1976). Of 102 newspapers with 1,211,000 circulation, 56 with 741,000 circulation are in the Kirghiz language.

EDUCATION. Kirghizia had 1,803 primary, continuation (8-year) and secondary schools with 800,000 pupils in 1976–77; 127,000 children attended 853 pre-school institutions. There were also 9 higher educational institutions with 51,500 students, 39 technical and teachers' training colleges with 45,400 students, as well as music and art schools. The Kirghizian Academy of Sciences was established in 1954. In 1975 there were 65 research institutes, 18 of them, with 1,460 scientific staff, under the Kirghiz Academy of Sciences; the others have scientist staffs of 5,800. A university was opened in 1951. It has 13,370 students, 6,268 full-time, 1,054 evening and 6,048 correspondence students taking a full degree course. In Sept. 1940 a new alphabet, based on Cyrillic, was introduced.

HEALTH. In 1976 there were 8,600 doctors and 38,800 hospital beds.

Books of Reference

Istoria Kirgizii. Frunze, 1956
Ryazantsev, S. N., *Kirghizia.* Moscow, 1951

UNITED ARAB EMIRATES

Population: 652,846 (1976 estimate)
GNP per capita: US$13,990 (1976)

HISTORY. From Sha'am, 35 miles south-west of Ras Musam dam, for nearly 400 miles to Khor al Odeid at the south-eastern end of the peninsula of Qatar, the coast, formerly known as the Trucial Coast, of the Gulf (together with 50 miles of the coast of the Gulf of Oman) belongs to the rulers of the 7 Trucial States. In 1820 these rulers signed a treaty prescribing peace with the British Government. This treaty was followed by further agreements providing for the suppression of the slave trade and by a series of other engagements, of which the most important are the Perpetual Maritime Truce (May 1853) and the Exclusive Agreement (March 1892). Under the latter, the sheikhs, on behalf of themselves, their heirs and successors, undertook that they would on no account enter into any agreement or correspondence with any power other than the British Government, receive foreign agents, cede, sell or give for occupation any part of their territory save to the British Government.

British forces withdrew from the Gulf at the end of 1971 and the treaties whereby Britain had been responsible for the defence and foreign relations of the Trucial States were terminated, being replaced on 2 Dec. 1971 by a treaty of friendship between Britain and the United Arab Emirates. The United Arab Emirates (formed 2 Dec. 1971) consists of the former Trucial States: Abu Dhabi, Dubai, Sharjah, Ajman, Umm al Quawain, Ras al Khaimah (joined in Feb. 1972) and Fujairah. The small state of Kalba was merged with Sharjah in 1952. *See* map in THE STATESMAN'S YEAR-BOOK, 1972–73, The Gulf States of the Middle East.

AREA AND POPULATION. The Emirates are bounded north by the Persian Gulf, east by Oman, south and west by Saudi Arabia, north-west by Qatar. The area of these states is approximately 32,300 sq. miles (92,100 sq. km). The total population at census (1975), 655,937, against an estimate (1974), 350,000. About one-tenth are nomads.

Population (1976 estimate): Abu Dhabi, 235,662; Ajman, 21,566; Dubai, 206,861; Fujairah, 26,498; Ras al Khaimah, 57,282; Sharjah, 88,188; Umm al Quawain, 16,789.

GOVERNMENT. The Emirates are a federation, headed by a Supreme Council which is composed of the 7 rulers and which in turn appoints a Council of Ministers. The Council of Ministers drafts legislation and a federal budget; its proposals are submitted to a federal National Council of 40 elected members which may propose amendments but has no executive power.

President: HH Sheikh Zayed bin Sultan al Nahyan, Ruler of Abu Dhabi.

Members of the Supreme Council of Rulers:

HH Sheikh Rashid bin Saeed al-Maktoum, Vice-President and Ruler of Dubai.
HH Sheikh Sultan bin Mohammed al-Qasimi, Ruler of Sharjah.
HH Sheikh Saqr bin Mohammed al-Qasimi, Ruler of Ras al Khaimah.
HH Sheikh Ahmad bin Rashid al-Mualla, Ruler of Umm al Qaiwain.
HH Sheikh Hamad bin Mohammed al Sharqi, Ruler of Fujairah.
HH Sheikh Rashid bin Humaid al-Nuaimi, Ruler of Ajman.

The Cabinet in Jan. 1977 was:

Prime Minister: Sheikh Maktoum bin Rashid al-Maktoum.

Deputy Prime Minister: Sheikh Khalifa bin Zayed al-Nahyan. *Finance and Industry:* Sheikh Hamdan bin Rashid al-Maktoum. *Interior:* Sheikh Mounarak bin

Mohammed al-Nahyan. *Defence:* Sheikh Mohammed bin Rashid al-Maktoum. *Foreign Affairs:* Sayyed Ahmed Khalifa al-Suweidi. *Petroleum and Mineral Resources:* Sayyed Mana' Saeed al-Oteiba. *Agriculture and Fisheries:* Sheikh Hamad bin Mohammed al-Sharqi. *Health:* Sheikh Saif bin Mohammed al-Nahyan. *Information and Culture:* Sheikh Ahmed bin Hamad. *Justice:* Sheikh Ahmed bin Sultan al-Qasimi. *Employment and Labour:* Sheikh Mohammed bin Sultan al-Qasimi. *Social Affairs:* Sheikh Abdulaziz bin Rashid al-Nuaimi. *Public Works:* Sheikh Hamdan bin Mohammed al-Nahyan. *Electricity and Water:* Sheikh Abdullah bin Humaid al-Qasimi. *Economy and Trade:* Sheikh Sultan bin Ahmed al-Moualla. *Islamic Affairs:* Sheikh Thani bin Essa bin Harib. *Communications:* Sayyed Mohammed Saeed al-Mulla. *Education:* Sayyed Abdullah bin Omran Taryan. *Housing:* Sayyed Saeed bin Ali Salman. *Planning:* Sayyed Mohammed bin Khalifa al-Kindi. *Youth and Sports:* Sayyed Rashid bin Hamid.

National flag: Three horizontal stripes of green, white, black, with a vertical red strip in the hoist.

DEFENCE

Army. The Army consists of 1 Royal Guard brigade, 3 armoured, 7 infantry, 3 artillery and 3 air defence battalions. The strength was (1977) 23,500.

Navy. The Navy has 6 large and 9 small patrol craft and 14 coastal patrol craft and personnel number (1978) 800.

Air Force. Formation of an air wing in Abu Dhabi, to support land forces, began in 1968 with the purchase of 2 (since increased to 4) Britten-Norman Islander light STOL transports and 4 Agusta-Bell JetRanger light helicopters. Four larger Caribou STOL transports are now in service, together with 8 Hunter fighters and reconnaissance fighters and 2 Hunter 2-seat trainers. The JetRangers have been replaced with 5 Pumas and 7 Alouette IIIs. Other new equipment includes 26 Mirage 5 supersonic fighters, 3 Mirage 5R tactical reconnaissance aircraft, and 3 Mirage 5D 2-seat trainers from France, and 2 C-130 Hercules turboprop transports from the US. Initial personnel were mostly British but considerable assistance is now being received from Arab countries and from Pakistan. The air wing became the Air Force of Abu Dhabi in 1972, in which year the 3 remaining JetRanger helicopters were transferred to the air wing of the Union Defence Force, since augmented by 4 Bell 205A-1 and 1 Bell 212 helicopters. A small air wing has been formed to support the Dubai Defence Force. Initial equipment, bought mainly in Italy, comprises 3 Aermacchi MB 326K jet light attack aircraft, 2 Aeritalia G222 twin-turboprop transports, 1 piston-engined SF-260W armed basic trainer and 1MB 326L jet trainer, 4 Bell 205A-1, 3 Bell 212 and 6 JetRanger helicopters and 1 Cessna 182 liaison aircraft.

INTERNATIONAL RELATIONS

Membership. The UAE became a member of the Arab League on 6 Dec. and of the UN on 9 Dec. 1971.

External Debt. The UAE (mainly the government of Dubai) borrowed about $205m. on Eurocurrency markets in 1976 and about $850m. in 1977.

Aid. Abu Dhabi committed 25% of government oil revenues to external aid 1971–76; this included aid to other Arab countries and loans at concessionary rates through the Abu Dhabi Fund for Arab Economic Development. The government of Abu Dhabi has also committed funds to the IMF and the World Bank.

ECONOMY

Planning. Public projects completed include the 15-berth Port Rashid harbour opened 1972. A municipal sewerage scheme is under way and a police headquarters is planned. Further developments are expected to include reclamation of part of the sea front, improvement of the creek unloading facilities and a traffic tunnel or additional bridge over the creek. In Sharjah, Mina Khalid is now operational and ships are using the new jetty, while improvement of the creek entrance and additional wharfage are now being undertaken. There are plans for a cement works and a flour-mill in Dubai in the near future and a large deep-water harbour is being constructed in Abu Dhabi.

Budget. Revenue is principally derived from oil-concession payments. The federal budget (1977–78) UD 13,000m.

Currency. The UAE issued its own currency in 1972 based on the *dirham*. 1 UAE *dirham* = 10 *dinar* = 1,000 *fils*. There are notes of 1, 5, 10, 50, 100 and 1,000 *dirham* and coins of 1, 5, 10, 25, 50 and 100 *fils*. Rate of exchange, 1977: £1 = 6·71 *dirham*.

Banking. The British Bank of the Middle East has branches in Dubai, Abu Dhabi, Sharjah, Fujairah, Ajman and Ras al Khaimah; the Chartered Bank has branches in Dubai, Sharjah, Abu Dhabi and Al Ain; the National & Grindlays Bank (Ottoman Branch) has branches in Abu Dhabi and Sharjah. The Arab Bank has branches in Ajman, Ras al Khaimah, Sharjah, Abu Dhabi and Dubai; the Citibank has branches in Dubai, Sharjah and Abu Dhabi; the Habib Bank of Pakistan has branches in Abu Dhabi, Dubai and Sharjah and the United Bank Ltd of Pakistan branches in Dubai, Sharjah, Abu Dhabi and Al Ain. There is also the National Bank of Dubai, formed in 1963, which has a branch in Abu Dhabi and Umm al Qaiwain, and the Bank of Oman Ltd, formed in 1967, which has branches in Ajman, Abu Dhabi and Dubai. The Commercial Bank opened in Dubai in 1969. The Bank Sadarat of Iran has branches in Abu Dhabi, Dubai and Sharjah. The National Bank of Abu Dhabi, formed in 1967, has its head office in Abu Dhabi and a branch office in Dubai.

The UAE is to become the headquarters of the new Arab Monetary Fund, which will have an initial capital of 250m. Arab Dinar units of account, worth about US$900m., and is providing 15m. units of account as its contribution. It is also a shareholder in the International Gulf Bank, recently established by the UAE, Qatar, Bahrain, Saudi Arabia, Kuwait and Iraq.

ENERGY AND NATURAL RESOURCES

Oil. *Abu Dhabi.* Until the end of 1972 production was in the hands of 2 major companies, the Abu Dhabi Petroleum Co. and the Abu Dhabi Marine Area. The Government has acquired a 60% interest in both companies. Ownership in 1976 was as follows: *ADPC*, 60% Government; 9·5% BP; 9·5% Shell; 9·5% CFP; 4·75% Mobil; 2% Partex. *ADMA*, 60% Government; 26·7% BP/Japan Oil Development Co.; 13·3% CFP. A Japanese company, Abu Dhabi Oil Co. (ADOCO) began production from its Mubarraz field in 1973. There are other companies which have concessions in the state: Japan's Middle East Oil; a US consortium led by Pan Ocean Oil and Sunningdale Oils of Canada. A State Petroleum Co., the Abu Dhabi National Oil Co. (ADNOC), was formed in 1971 and began to set up its own tanker fleet known as the Abu Dhabi National Tankers Co. (ADNATCO). At the end of 1972 Abu Dhabi signed a participation agreement which would have given it an immediate 25% interest in the companies, rising to 51% by 1982. Oil production, 1976, 583m. bbls, value UD 19,000m.

Dubai. In July 1975 Dubai decided to take full control of all foreign oil and gas operations in the state. The companies were to remain however. A Dubai producing group was set up to comprise the foreign interests—US and continental companies. Dubai Petroleum Co. (DPC—a subsidiary of Continental Oil) has a 30% interest in this group; the other members are Dubai Marine Areas (*Compagnie Française des Pétroles*) with 50%; Deutsche Texaco with 10%; Dubai Sun Oil 5%; and Delfzee Dubai Petroleum (Wintershall) 5%. Oil production, 1976, 115m. bbls, value about UD 4,700m.

Sharjah. In Sharjah the concession is given to Crescent Oil, its shareholders are: Ashland Oil, Skelly Oil, Kerr-McGee, Cities Services and Juniper. Other oil concessions have recently been given to the Crystal Oil Co. of USA and the Reserves Oil and Gas Co. Oil production, 1976, about 13m. bbls, value about UD 200m.

Ajman. An oil concession was awarded to United Refining in 1974.

Umm al Quawain. The concession here was given to US Occidental Petroleum; another was awarded to a consortium led by the US company United Refinery.

Ras al Khaimah. The Dutch oil firm Vitol took over Union's concession in 1973. Shell began prospecting in 1969 but pulled out in 1971. A concession in the same area was awarded to Peninsula Petroleum, a subsidiary of the US California Time Group, in 1973.

Gas. Abu Dhabi has reserves of natural gas, nationalized in 1976. The Abu Dhabi Gas Liquefaction Plant at Das Island (51% ADNOC) has a capacity of 2m. tons LNG, 1m. tons LPG, 220,000 tons of light distillate and 230,000 tons of pelletized sulphur.

Agriculture. The fertile Buraimi Oasis, known as Al Ain, is largely in Abu Dhabi territory, but owing to lack of water and good soil there is little agriculture in the rest of UAE. However, since the establishment of an agricultural trials station and an agricultural school in Ras al Khaimah the number of gardens under cultivation has more than doubled and there have been remarkable increases in the variety of crops and the length of the agricultural season.

In 1970 a herd of dairy cattle was imported for the agricultural trials station. An experimental agricultural farm exists in Al Ain which produces vegetables for Abu Dhabi.

Fisheries. The industry is still a major employer. Sharjah exports shrimps and prawns; a fishmeal plant is operating in Ras al Khaimah and plants are planned for Ajman and Sharjah.

INDUSTRY. Main industries in Abu Dhabi relate to the construction industry and to oil and gas extraction; there is also a steel rolling mill. Dubai has a cement factory of 500,000 tons annual capacity, and a dry dock complex under construction. Work has also begun on a complex at Jabal Ali consisting of a liquefied petroleum gas plant, an aluminium smelter with power station and desalination plant, and a service harbour. Sharjah has a cement factory and various manufacturing estates. Ras al Khaimah also produces cement and crushed rock.

COMMERCE. Imports in 1976 for UAE were UD 13,150m. Exports and re-exports totalled UD 35,141m. Japan, UK and USA provided 50% of imports.

Total trade between the UAE (excluding Abu Dhabi) and UK (British Department of Trade returns, in £1,000 sterling):

	1973	*1974*	*1975*	*1976*	*1977*
Imports to UK	35,747	56,374	60,291	121,923	137,779
Exports and re-exports from UK	24,710	54,285	107,295	188,697	190,514

Total trade between Abu Dhabi and UK (British Department of Trade returns, in £1,000 sterling):

	1973	*1974*	*1975*	*1976*	*1977*
Imports to UK	33,462	149,529	98,870	77,752	121,276
Exports and re-exports from UK	24,714	42,626	91,330	125,692	264,463

COMMUNICATIONS

Aviation. International airports at Dubai and Abu Dhabi are served by a large number of major airlines, as well as by Gulf Air partially owned by the Government of the UAE. Plans are underway for the construction of a new Abu Dhabi airport. The country's first airport at Sharjah has been replaced by a new international airport. A Ras al Khaimah international airport was opened early in 1976 although it initially had only one scheduled service by Kuwait Airways. An airstrip exists at Al Ain, in the Buraimi Oasis, and in the oilfields, both onshore and offshore, on Das Island, while construction of a strip at Khor Fakkan is planned.

Abu Dhabi and Dubai are served by Alia, Air France, Air India, British Airways, Egyptair, Iran Air, Kuwait Airways, Middle East Airlines, PIA, KLM, Gulf Air, Iraqi Airways, Olympic, Sabena, Saudia, Syrian Arab Airlines and TMA. Lufthansa and Singapore Airlines initiated scheduled flights to Dubai in mid-1976, while Sharjah is served by Gulf Air and TMA. A number of cargo airlines also fly regularly to the country's major airports. An air-taxi service, Emirates Air Services, flying between Abu Dhabi and Dubai, began in June 1976.

Shipping. British and European shipping lines call at Dubai (30–40 vessels a month) and Abu Dhabi. In 1972 Port Rashid, equipped with 15 deep-water berths, was opened, making Dubai harbour the largest in the Middle East, and a new contract was granted to a British company in 1976 to build a further 22 berths. A major dry dock, capable of handling super-tankers has also been built. Abu Dhabi has also become an important port since the opening of the first stage of its artificial harbour, Port Zayed, which, when completed, will have 17 deep-water berths.

In 1976, the Government of the UAE joined with Qatar, Bahrain, Saudi Arabia, Kuwait and Iraq in forming the United Arab Shipping Company.

Post and Broadcasting. In 1977 there were 70,863 telephones, of which 23,868 were in Abu Dhabi. In Sharjah a new telephone company has been formed and the other Northern States are now linked by telephone. The new Cable and Wireless Station at Jebel Ali in the State of Dubai links the system with the international communication network.

Television stations are at Abu Dhabi and Dubai, with extension of the service well advanced to the rest of the Emirates. Stations for The Voice of the United Arab Emirates began broadcasting in 1972 at Abu Dhabi, Dubai, Ras al Khaimah and Sharjah. Estimated radios (1976) 50,000 and television sets over 16,000.

The UAE is a founder member of the New Arab Space Communications Organization, having one satellite ground station at Jebel Ali in Dubai connected to the Indian Ocean Satellite; another is building and a link with the Atlantic Ocean satellite is well underway.

Newspapers (1977). There are a number of daily and weekly publications mostly in Arabic, but some in English, notably *The Emirates News* of Abu Dhabi, and *The Gulf Mirror*, a weekly, published in Bahrain.

JUSTICE, RELIGION, EDUCATION AND WELFARE

Justice. UAE subjects and citizens of all Arab and Moslem states are subject to the jurisdiction of the local courts. In the local courts the rules of Islamic law prevail. A new code of law is being produced for Abu Dhabi. In Dubai there is a court run by a *qadi*, while in some of the other states all legal cases are referred immediately to the Ruler or a member of his family, who will refer to a *qadi* only if he cannot settle the matter himself. In Abu Dhabi a professional Jordanian judge presides over the Ruler's Court. The 95th article of the provisional constitution of 1971 provided for the setting up of a Union Supreme Court and Union Primary Tribunals.

Religion. Nearly all the inhabitants are Moslems of the Sunni and Shi'ite sects.

Education (1977). Primary and secondary education for boys and girls is available in the UAE, and there are now 185 schools with over 70,000 pupils, with 10 under construction. There are 4 junior colleges and 112 adult education centres, established in order to eliminate illiteracy. The education system is the same as that followed in Kuwait, and many of the teachers are supplied by the Kuwait, Qatar, Egypt, Jordan and Bahrain education departments. The oil companies in Abu Dhabi operate apprentice training schools and there is also a vocational training institute. A vocational training centre is under construction.

There are trade schools in Sharjah, Dubai and Ras al Khaimah. A university is at an advanced stage of planning.

Health. There are several hospitals in Dubai, including a 400-bed hospital opened in 1973. A hospital at Abu Dhabi, and 1 at Al Ain, were under construction in 1976. There are also hospitals in Ras al Khaimah and in Sharjah. Clinics have been built in Sharjah and other towns. Medical centres and polyclinics are opening in remote areas. A tuberculosis sanatorium is to be constructed by the State of Kuwait in Sharjah.

DIPLOMATIC REPRESENTATIVES

OF THE UAE IN GREAT BRITAIN
(30 Prince's Gate, London, SW7 1PT)

Ambassador: Sayed Mohamed Mahdi Al-Tajir.

OF GREAT BRITAIN IN THE UAE

Ambassador: David Roberts, CMG (at the British Embassy Abu Dhabi).

OF THE UAE IN THE USA (600 New Hampshire Ave., NW, Washington, D.C., 20037)

Ambassador: Mohammed Abdul Rahman Al Madfa.

OF THE USA IN THE UAE (Shaikh Khalid Bldg., Corniche Rd., Abu Dhabi)

Ambassador: François M. Dickman.

OF THE UAE TO THE UNITED NATIONS

Ambassador: Dr Ali Humaidan.

Books of Reference

Middle East Annual Review. London, 1978
Albaharna, H. M., *The Legal Status of the Arabian Gulf States.* Manchester, 1969
Busch, B. C., *Britain and the Persian Gulf 1894–1914.* California, 1967
Daniel, John, *Abu Dhabi: A Portrait.* London, 1974
Fact Sheet on Eastern Arabia. Vilvoorde, Belgium
Fenelon, K. G., *The United Arab Emirates: An Economic and Social Survey.* London, 1973
Hawley, D. F., *Courtesies in the Trucial States.* 1965.—*The Trucial States.* London, 1971
Hay, Sir Rupert, *The Persian Gulf States.* Washington, 1959
Hopwood, D., *The Arabian Peninsula.* London, 1972
Mann, C., *Abu Dhabi: Birth of an Oil Sheikhdom.* Beirut, 1964
Marlowe, J., *The Persian Gulf in the 20th Century.* London, 1962
Miles, S. B., *The Countries and Tribes of the Persian Gulf.* (3rd ed.) London, 1966
Sadiq, M. T. *with* W. P. Snavely, *Bahrain, Qatar and the UAE: Colonial Past, Present Problems and Future Prospects.* Lexington, Mass., 1972
Wilson, Sir A. T., *The Persian Gulf.* 1928

UNITED KINGDOM OF GREAT BRITAIN AND NORTHERN IRELAND

Capital: London
Population: 55·93m. (1976)
GNP per capita: US 4,020 (1976)

'Great Britain' is a geographical term describing the main island of the British Isles which comprises England, Scotland and Wales (so called to distinguish it from 'Little Britain' or Brittany). By the Act of Union, 1801 Great Britain and Ireland formed a legislative union as the United Kingdom of Great Britain and Ireland. Since the separation of Great Britain and Ireland in 1921 Northern Ireland remained within the Union which is now the United Kingdom of Great Britain and Northern Ireland. The United Kingdom does not include the Channel Islands or the Isle of Man which are direct dependencies of the Crown with their own legislative and taxation systems.

GREAT BRITAIN

AREA AND POPULATION. Area (in sq. miles) and population at the census taken 25 April 1971:

Divisions	*Area*	*Males*	*Females*	*Total*
England	50,331	22,299,460	23,580,210	46,019,000
Wales (incl. Monmouthshire)	8,016	1,324,205	1,400,070	2,731,000
Scotland	30,405	2,514,622	2,514,341	5,228,963
Isle of Man	211	26,461	29,828	56,289
Channel Islands	75	59,648	63,415	123,063
	89,038[1]	26,224,396	27,787,864	54,158,315

[1] 230,609 sq. km.

Population at the 4 previous decennial censuses:

Divisions	*1921*	*1931*	*1951*	*1961*
England	35,230,225	37,359,045	41,159,213	43,460,525
Wales	2,656,474	2,158,374	2,598,675	2,644,023
Scotland	4,882,497	4,842,980	5,096,415	5,178,490
Isle of Man	60,284	49,308	55,253	48,151
Channel Islands	90,230	93,205	102,806	104,378
Army, Navy and Merchant Seamen abroad	256,811	434,532	—	—
Total	43,176,521	44,937,444	50,383,283	52,867,716

In 1971 in Wales and Monmouthshire 32,725 persons 3 years of age and upwards were able to speak Welsh only, and 509,700 able to speak Welsh and English: these totals represent 20% of the total population. In Scotland in 1971, 338 persons could speak Gaelic only, and 88,415 could speak Gaelic and English, totalling 1·8% of the population.

At the census of 1971, in England and Wales, there were 16,509,905 private households; in Great Britain, 18,195,965.

The age distribution in 1971 of the population of England and Wales and Scotland was as follows (in 1,000):

Age-group	*England and Wales*	*Scotland*	*Great Britain*
Under 5	3,904	444	4,349
5 and under 10	4,044	468	4,512
10 ,, 15	3,627	442	4,069
15 ,, 20	3,313	392	3,705
20 ,, 25	3,731	390	4,121
25 ,, 35	6,062	616	6,676
35 ,, 45	5,721	611	6,333
45 ,, 55	6,022	617	6,651
55 ,, 65	5,815	598	6,414
65 ,, 70	2,399	247	2,647
70 ,, 75	1,778	179	1,957
75 ,, 85	1,892	180	2,072
85 and upwards	424	36	461
Total	48,749	5,228	53,978

At 30 June 1976 the estimated sex distribution of the population of England and Wales was: between 0 and 14, 5,722,800 males, 5,421,500 females; 15 and under 65, 15,488,100 males, 15,495,200 females; aged 65 and over, 2,742,400 males, 4,314,400 females.

Estimated total home population of Great Britain at 30 June:

	England and Wales[1]	*Scotland*[2]	*Total of Great Britain*
1973	49,174,600	5,211,700	54,386,000
1974	49,195,100	5,226,400	54,421,500
1975	42,219,000	5,206,000	54,425,000
1976	49,184,400	5,205,100	54,389,500

[1] The home population of England and Wales is the population of all types, actually in the country. [2] Excluding merchant seamen overseas.

England and Wales: The census population of England and Wales 1801 to 1961:

Date of enumeration	*Population*	*Pop. per sq. mile*	*Date of enumeration*	*Population*	*Pop. per sq. mile*
1801	8,892,536	152	1881	25,974,439	445
1811	10,164,256	174	1891	29,002,525	497
1821	12,000,236	206	1901	32,527,843	558
1831	13,896,797	238	1911	36,070,492	618
1841	15,914,148	273	1921	37,886,699	649
1851	17,927,609	307	1931	39,952,377	685
1861	20,066,224	344	1951	43,757,888	750
1871	22,712,266	389	1961	46,104,548	791

There is only one other major country in Europe, Netherlands (population density 893 persons per sq. mile), which is more crowded than England and Wales.

Population of the administrative counties and county boroughs in 1971 (for areas of administrative counties, etc., 1931, *see* THE STATESMAN'S YEAR-BOOK, 1950, p. 51):

ENGLAND	
Bedfordshire	463,493
Berkshire	633,457
Buckinghamshire	586,211
Cambridgeshire	302,507
Isle of Ely	—
Cheshire	1,542,624
Cornwall	379,892
Cumberland	292,009
Derbyshire	884,339
Devonshire	896,245
Dorsetshire	361,213
Durham	1,408,103
Essex	1,353,564
Gloucestershire	1,069,454
Hampshire	1,561,605
Isle of Wight	109,284
Herefordshire	138,425
Hertfordshire	922,188
Huntingdonshire	202,337[1]
Kent	1,396,030
Lancashire	5,106,123
Leicestershire	771,213
Lincolnshire—	
The parts of Holland	105,643
The parts of Kesteven	232,215
The parts of Lindsey	470,526
London	7,379,014[2]
Middlesex	—
Norfolk	616,427
Northamptonshire	467,843
Soke of Peterborough	—
Northumberland	794,975
Nottinghamshire	974,640

[1] Includes Peterborough. [2] Greater London.

England—*contd.*	
Oxfordshire	380,814
Rutlandshire	27,463
Shropshire	336,934
Somerset	681,974
Staffordshire	1,856,890
Suffolk, East	380,524
Suffolk, West	164,201
Surrey	999,588
Sussex, East	750,312
Sussex, West	491,020
Warwickshire	2,079,799
Westmorland	72,724
Wiltshire	486,048
Worcestershire	692,605
Yorkshire, East Riding	542,565
Yorkshire, North Riding	724,463
Yorkshire, West Riding	3,780,539
Total	45,870,062

Wales	
Anglesey	59,705
Breconshire	53,234
Caernarvonshire	122,852
Cardiganshire	54,844
Carmarthenshire	162,313
Denbighshire	184,824
Flintshire	175,396
Glamorganshire	1,255,374
Merionethshire	35,277
Monmouthshire	461,459
Montgomeryshire	42,761
Pembrokeshire	97,295
Radnorshire	18,262
Total Wales (13 counties)	2,723,596
Total—England and Wales	48,593,658

Local authority areas in being from April 1974. Area in sq. km and population estimate 1976:

England *Metropolitan counties*	*Area sq. km*	*Population*
Greater London	1,580	7,028,200
Greater Manchester	1,286	2,684,100
Merseyside	652	1,578,000
South Yorkshire	1,560	1,318,300
Tyne and Wear	540	1,182,900
West Midlands	899	2,743,300
West Yorkshire	2,039	2,072,500
Non-metropolitan counties		
Avon	1,338	920,200
Bedfordshire	1,235	491,700
Berkshire	1,256	659,000
Buckinghamshire	1,883	512,000
Cambridgeshire	3,409	563,000
Cheshire	2,322	916,400
Cleveland	583	567,900
Cornwall and Isles of Scilly	3,546	407,100
Cumbria	6,809	473,600
Derbyshire	2,631	887,600
Devon	6,715	942,100
Dorset	2,654	575,800
Durham	2,436	610,400
East Sussex	1,795	655,600
Essex	3,674	1,426,200
Gloucestershire	2,638	491,500
Hampshire	3,772	1,456,100
Hereford and Worcester	3,927	594,200
Hertfordshire	1,634	937,300
Humberside	3,512	848,600
Isle of Wight	381	111,300
Kent	3,732	1,448,100
Lancashire	3,043	1,375,500

Non-Metropolitan counties—contd.	*Area sq. km*	*Population*
Leicestershire	2,553	837,900
Lincolnshire	5,885	524,500
Norfolk	5,355	662,500
Northamptonshire	2,367	505,900
Northumberland	5,033	287,300
North Yorkshire	8,317	653,000
Nottinghamshire	2,164	977,500
Oxfordshire	2,611	541,800
Salop	3,490	359,000
Somerset	3,458	404,400
Staffordshire	2,716	997,600
Suffolk	3,800	577,600
Surrey	1,655	1,002,900
Warwickshire	1,981	471,000
West Sussex	2,016	623,400
Wiltshire	3,481	512,800
Total		46,417,600

Wales		
Clwyd	2,425	376,000
Dyfed	5,765	323,100
Gwent	1,376	439,600
Gwynedd	3,868	225,100
Mid-Glamorgan	1,019	540,400
Powys	5,077	101,500
South Glamorgan	416	389,200
West Glamorgan	815	371,900
Total Wales		2,766,800
Total—England and Wales		49,184,400

County districts with populations of over 90,000 (1976 estimates):

England	
Allerdale	94,900
Amber Valley	106,000
Arun	111,600
Ashfield	103,100
Aylesbury Vale	118,800
Barnsley	224,400
Basildon	141,700

ENGLAND—*contd.*

Basingstoke	120,800
Bassetlaw	100,300
Beverley	106,700
Birmingham	1,058,800
Blackburn	142,500
Blackpool	149,000
Bolton	261,000
Bournemouth	144,100
Bradford	458,900
Braintree	104,600
Brighton	156,500
Bristol	416,300
Broxtowe	102,600
Burnley	92,100
Bury	181,200
Calderdale	190,100
Cambridge	106,400
Canterbury	115,600
Carlisle	99,600
Charnwood	133,100
Chelmsford	130,000
Cherwell	104,700
Chester	117,200
Chesterfield	93,900
Chichester	93,200
Chiltern	90,100
Colchester	132,400
Coventry	336,800
Crewe and Nantwich	98,100
Dacorum	121,900
Darlington	96,900
Derby	213,700
Derwentside	90,400
Doncaster	286,500
Dover	101,000
Dudley	300,200
East Devon	104,100
East Hertfordshire	104,000
East Lindsey	100,100
East Staffordshire	96,500
Elmbridge	112,300
Epping Forest	116,200
Erewash	101,100
Exeter	93,300
Gateshead	222,000
Gedling	101,600
Gillingham	93,900
Gloucester	91,600
Gravesham	96,000
Grimsby	93,800
Guildford	121,000
Halton	113,100
Harrogate	135,500
Hartlepool	97,100
Havant	116,400
Hertsmere	87,400
Horsham	92,300
Huntingdon	118,100
Ipswich	121,500
Kingston upon Hull	276,600
Kirklees	372,500
Knowsley	189,700
Lancaster	126,300
Langbaurgh	151,500
Leeds	744,500
Leicester	289,400
Liverpool	539,700
Luton	

ENGLAND—*contd.*

Macclesfield	149,200
Maidstone	126,500
Manchester	490,000
Mansfield	97,200
Medway	144,500
Mid-Bedfordshire	97,600
Middlesbrough	153,900
Mid-Sussex	107,100
Newark	102,800
Newbury	115,300
Newcastle under Lyme	120,700
Newcastle upon Tyne	295,800
New Forest	139,200
Northampton	142,000
Northavon	116,400
North Bedfordshire	130,300
North-East Derbyshire	92,500
North Hertfordshire	104,600
North Tyneside	202,600
North Wiltshire	102,400
Norwich	119,200
Nottingham	280,300
Nuneaton	111,100
Oldham	227,500
Oxford	117,400
Peterborough	118,900
Plymouth	259,100
Poole	110,600
Portsmouth	198,500
Preston	131,200
Reading	131,200
Reigate and Banstead	112,400
Rochdale	210,200
Rotherham	249,400
St Albans	123,800
St Helens	194,400
Salford	261,100
Salisbury	105,300
Sandwell	312,900
Scarborough	99,000
Sedgefield	91,700
Sefton	306,000
Sevenoaks	102,200
Sheffield	558,000
Slough	99,700
Solihull	199,600
Southampton	213,700
South Bedfordshire	99,300
South Cambridgeshire	100,900
Southend on Sea	159,300
South Lakeland	94,000
South Oxfordshire	140,400
South Ribble	92,000
South Tyneside	166,800
Spelthorne	95,900
Stafford	114,700
Staffordshire Moorlands	94,300
Stockport	292,900
Stockton on Tees	165,400
Stoke on Trent	256,200
Stratford on Avon	100,100
Stroud	95,800
Suffolk Coastal	96,200
Sunderland	295,700
Swale	106,700
Tameside	222,100
Teignbridge	94,500
Tendring	109,100

ENGLAND—*contd.*		ENGLAND—*contd.*	
Thamesdown	142,700	Windsor and Maidenhead	128,400
Thanet	118,400	Wirral	348,200
Thurrock	127,700	Wokingham	112,600
Tonbridge and Malling	94,800	Wolverhampton	266,400
Torbay	109,900	Woodspring	151,100
Trafford	227,400	Wrekin	112,400
Tunbridge Wells	96,000	Wycombe	150,600
Vale of White Horse	97,800	Wyre	101,000
Vale Royal	109,900	Wyre Forest	93,000
Wakefield	306,500	Yeovil	124,100
Walsall	268,600	York	101,900
Warrington	166,200		
Warwick	113,100		
Waveney	96,200	WALES	
Waverley	108,900	Cardiff	281,500
Wealden	113,500	Newport	134,100
Welwyn Hatfield	91,300	Ogwr	128,400
West Lancashire	105,800	Rhymney Valley	106,600
West Norfolk	115,700	Swansea	190,800
West Wiltshire	94,500	Vale of Glamorgan	107,700
Wigan	310,700	Wrexham Maelor	108,100

The following table shows the distribution of the urban and rural population of England and Wales in 1951, 1961 and 1971.

		Population		*Percentage*	
	England and Wales	*Urban districts*[1]	*Rural districts*[1]	*Urban*[1]	*Rural*
1951	43,757,888	35,335,721	8,422,167	80·8	19·2
1961	46,071,604	36,838,442	9,233,162	80·0	20·0
1971	48,755,000	38,151,000	10,598,000	78·2	21·5

[1] As existing at each census.

Conurbations. These are aggregates of local-authority areas with high population densities. In April 1971 there were 7 in England and Wales, with a population of 16m. (33·2% of total population). Excluding the London conurbation, their populations were: Tyneside, 0·8m.; W. Yorks., 1·73m.; S.E. Lancs., 2·39m.; Merseyside, 1·26m.; W. Midlands, 2·37m.; S.E. Wales, 1·83m. The municipal and parliamentary City of London, coinciding with the registration City of London, has an area of 677 acres. The registration County of London (the London for purposes of the census, the registration of births, deaths and marriages, and for poor law purposes), coinciding with the former administrative county, has an area of 74,898 acres, and nearly coincides with the collective area of the London parliamentary boroughs. The population of registration London, of the 'Outer Ring', and of 'Greater London' (the area covered by the City and Metropolitan police) at the dates of the census, was:

	1931	*1941*	*1961*	*1971*
Registration London	4,397,003	3,347,982	3,200,484	2,145,185
'Outer Ring'	3,818,670	5,000,041	4,982,066	5,307,160
'Greater London'[1]	8,215,673	8,348,023	8,182,550	7,452,345

[1] Area 461,885 acres (1961).

Greater London Boroughs. Estimated population in June 1976:

Barking	153,800	Haringey	228,200	Merton	169,400
Barnet	305,200	Harrow	200,200	Newham	228,900
Bexley	213,500	Havering	239,200	Redbridge	231,600
Brent	256,500	Hillingdon	230,800	Richmond-on-Thames	166,800
Bromley	299,100	Hounslow	199,100	Southwark	224,900
Camden	185,800	Islington	171,600	Sutton	166,700
Croydon	330,600	Kensington and Chelsea	161,400	Tower Hamlets	146,100
Ealing	293,800	Kingston upon Thames	135,600	Waltham Forest	223,700
Enfield	260,900	Lambeth	290,300	Wandsworth	284,600
Greenwich	207,200	Lewisham	237,300	Westminster	216,100
Hackney	192,500				
Hammersmith	170,000				

Census of England and Wales, 1961. HMSO. 1961–65
Royal Commission on Local Government in Greater London, Report. HMSO, 1960 (Cmnd. 1164)

Census 1971, England and Wales, Preliminary Report. HMSO, 1971
Census 1971, Great Britain; Advance Analysis. HMSO, 1972

Scotland: Area 29,796 sq. miles, including its islands, 186 in number, but excluding inland water 609 sq. miles.

Population (including military in the barracks and seamen on board vessels in the harbours) at the dates of each census:

Date of enumeration	*Population*	*Pop. per sq. mile*	*Date of enumeration*	*Population*	*Pop. per sq. mile*
1811	1,805,864	60	1891	4,025,647	135
1821	2,091,521	70	1901	4,472,103	150
1831	2,364,386	79	1911	4,760,904	160
1841	2,620,184	88	1921	4,882,497	164
1851	2,888,742	97	1931	4,842,980	163
1861	3,062,294	100	1951	5,096,415	171
1871	3,360,018	113	1961	5,179,344	174
1881	3,735,573	125	1971	5,229,963	175

The 1971 population included 2,514,622 males, 2,714,341 females.

The 33 civil counties were as follows:

	Area in statute acres (1931)	*Census population* 1931	1951	1961	*Estimated population*[1] *June 1974*
1. Aberdeen	1,261,521	300,436	308,008	321,783	324,574
2. Angus	559,037	270,190	274,876	278,399	281,131
3. Argyll	1,999,472	63,050	63,361	59,390	59,926
4. Ayr	724,523	285,217	321,237	342,822	369,636
5. Banff	403,053	54,907	50,148	46,454	43,767
6. Berwick	292,535	26,612	25,086	22,437	21,224
7. Bute	139,658	18,823	19,283	15,170	12,743
8. Caithness	438,833	25,656	22,710	27,370	27,901
9. Clackmannan	34,927	31,948	37,532	41,394	46,611
10. Dumfries	686,302	81,220	85,660	88,440	88,540
11. Dunbarton	157,433	146,723	164,269	184,559	244,354
12. East Lothian	170,971	47,338	52,258	52,677	56,966
13. Fife	322,844	276,368	306,778	320,692	337,690
14. Inverness	2,695,094	82,108	84,930	83,480	91,698
15. Kincardine	244,482	39,865	47,403	48,810	27,188
16. Kinross	52,410	7,454	7,418	6,702	7,090
17. Kirkcudbright	575,832	30,168	30,725	28,870	27,761
18. Lanark	562,821	1,587,665	1,614,363	1,626,424	1,456,151
19. Midlothian	234,325	526,296	565,735	580,329	603,615
20. Moray	304,931	40,805	48,218	49,170	54,833
21. Nairn	104,252	8,294	8,719	8,423	8,906
22. Orkney	240,847	22,077	21,255	18,747	17,462
23. Peebles	222,240	15,051	15,232	14,156	13,584
24. Perth	1,595,802	120,793	128,029	127,056	128,692
25. Renfrew	153,332	287,991	324,660	338,872	366,485
26. Ross and Cromarty	1,977,248	62,799	60,508	57,642	61,464
27. Roxburgh	426,028	45,685	45,557	43,183	42,255
28. Selkirk	170,793	22,711	21,729	21,052	20,743
29. Shetland (Zetland)	352,319	21,421	19,352	17,812	18,445
30. Stirling	288,842	166,447	187,527	194,878	211,994
31. Sutherland	1,297,914	16,101	13,670	13,507	12,728
32. West Lothian (Linlithgow)	76,861	81,431	88,577	92,768	112,833
33. Wigtown	311,984	29,331	31,620	29,124	27,410
Total Scotland	19,070,466	4,842,980	5,096,415	5,179,344	5,226,400

[1] Home population.

Population (estimates, 1976 and area in sq. km) for Scottish regions: Borders, 99,917 (4,670); Central, 270,056 (2,621); Dumfries and Galloway, 143,585 (6,369); Fife, 338,734 (1,305); Grampian, 453,829 (8,702); Highland, 186,460 (25,141); Lothian, 755,293 (1,753); Strathclyde, 2,488,643 (13,849); Tayside, 408,180 (7,501). Island Authorities: Orkney, 17,748 (905); Shetland, 18,962 (1,429); Western Isles, 29,693 (2,898).

In 1971 the population of cities and large burghs was 2,669,000 (50·1% of the total).

Burghs	Census population 1951	1961	1971	Burghs	Census population 1951	1961	1971
Glasgow	1,079,000	1,055,017	893,790	Kircaldy	51,800	52,390	50,091
Edinburgh	470,800	468,361	543,025	Clydebank	44,638	49,651	48,170
Dundee	181,800	182,978	182,930	Dunfermline	44,719	47,151	51,738
Aberdeen	186,900	185,390	181,785	Kilmarnock	42,123	47,509	48,992
Paisley	97,200	95,750	95,067	Ayr	42,377	45,276	48,021
Motherwell	73,100	72,794	74,038	Hamilton	40,174	41,928	46,376
Greenock	78,400	74,560	69,171	Perth	40,487	41,196	42,438
Coatbridge	54,300	53,825	51,985	Falkirk	37,535	38,044	37,489

Population (estimate, 1976): Glasgow, 856,000; Edinburgh, 467,000; Aberdeen, 210,000; Renfrew, 209,476; Dundee, 194,000; Motherwell, 161,104.

The birthplaces of the 1971 population were: Scotland, 4,759,475; England, 279,340; Wales, 11,905; Northern Ireland, 32,790; Irish Republic 31,260; Commonwealth, 43,600; foreign countries, 51,345 (including 7,470 aliens).

The population of the Central Clydeside conurbation in 1971 was 1,731,048.

At 30 June 1976 the estimated sex distribution of the population in Scotland was: between 0 and 14, 644,100 males, 610,700 females; 15 and 65, 1,595,000 males, 1,657,200 females; 65 and over, 264,000 males, 433,500 females.

Isle of Man and Channel Islands:

Islands	Area in statute acres, 1951	Census population 1951	1961	1971
Isle of Man	141,263	55,253	48,151	56,289
Jersey	28,717	57,310	57,200	69,329
Guernsey, Herm and Jethou	16,068	45,496	47,178	53,734
Alderney	1,962			
Sark, Brechou and Lihou	1,386			
Total	189,396	158,059	152,529	179,352

Vital statistics for England and Wales:

	Estimated home population at 30 June[1]	Total live births	Illegitimate live births	Deaths	Marriages	Divorces, annulments and dissolutions
1970	48,660,100	784,486	64,744	575,194	415,487	58,239
1971	48,854,400	783,155	65,678	567,262	404,737	74,437
1972	49,025,600	725,440	62,511	591,889	426,241	119,025
1973	49,153,800	675,953	58,097	587,478	400,435	106,003
1974	49,158,900	639,885	56,486	585,292	384,389	113,500
1975	49,157,100	603,445	54,891	582,841	380,620	120,522
1976	49,142,400	584,270	53,766	598,516	358,567	126,694

[1] The population actually in England and Wales.

In 1976 the proportion of male to female births was 1,058 male to 1,000 female; the live birth rate was 11·3 and the death rate 12·2 per 1,000 of the population; infant mortality rate, 14·3 per 1,000 of live births. The average age at marriage (1976) was 29·2 years for males and 26·51 years for females.

Vital statistics for Scotland:

	Estimated home population at 30 June[1]	Total births	Illegitimate births	Deaths	Marriages	Divorces, annulments and dissolutions
1970	5,199,000	87,335	6,712	63,440	43,203	4,618
1971	5,217,400	86,728	7,029	61,614	42,500	4,812
1972	5,210,400	78,550	6,661	65,017	42,139	5,531
1973	5,211,700	74,392	6,520	64,545	42,018	7,135
1974	5,226,400	70,093	6,349	64,740	41,174	7,221
1975	5,206,200	67,943	6,314	63,125	39,191	8,319
1976	5,205,100	64,895	6,025	65,253	37,543	8,692

[1] Includes merchant navy at home and forces stationed in Scotland.

In 1976 the proportion of male to female births was 1,067 male to 1,000 female; the live birth rate was 12·5 and the death rate 12·5 per 1,000 of the population; infant mortality rate, 15 per 1,000 of live births. The average age of marriage was 27 years for males and 25 years for females.

Emigration and Immigration. The UK has traditionally been a net exporter of population. In the two 30-year periods 1871–1901 and 1901–31 there was a net loss of population due to emigration of 1·6m. and 2·4m. persons respectively. Since then there have been two periods when this trend was reversed. During the 1930s there was an inflow of refugees from Europe and during the decade centred on 1960 there was an inflow from the new Commonwealth countries. More recently there has been a return to the traditional pattern with a new outflow during the period 1965–75 of 700,000 persons.

The following table shows a summary of migration statistics for 1975 based on the International Passenger Survey which is conducted by the Office of Population Censuses and Surveys for the Department of Trade and Industry and covers all the principal air and sea routes to the UK except those to and from the Irish Republic.

UK migration 1976 (in 1,000):

By country of last or future intended residence		*Into UK*	*Out from UK*	*Balance*
All Countries		179·8	210·4	−41·2
Australia, New Zealand, Canada		40·1	63·4	−23·3
India, Bangladesh, Sri Lanka		9·3	3·6	+ 5·7
Other Commonwealth		39·0	24·4	+14·6
EEC		25·0	31·1	− 6·1
USA		16·4	20·9	− 4·5
South Africa		8·9	21·0	−12·1
Rest of World		41·0	46·3	− 5·2
	By sex/age			
Males	0–14	14·3	19·7	− 5·3
	15–24	31·8	26·4	+ 5·4
	25–44	43·3	59·3	−16·0
	45 and over	9·0	12·3	− 3·3
	All ages	98·5	117·6	−19·1
Females	0–14	15·2	20·6	− 5·4
	15–24	28·5	25·3	+ 3·2
	25–44	30·0	37·9	− 8·0
	45 and over	7·6	8·9	− 1·3
	All ages	81·3	92·8	−11·5

QUEEN, HEAD OF THE COMMONWEALTH. Elizabeth II Alexandra Mary, born 21 April 1926 daughter of King George VI and Queen Elizabeth; married on 20 Nov. 1947 Lieut. Philip Mountbatten (formerly Prince Philip of Greece), created Duke of Edinburgh, Earl of Merioneth and Baron Greenwich on the same day and created Prince Philip, Duke of Edinburgh, 22 Feb. 1957; succeeded to the crown on the death of her father, on 6 Feb. 1952. Offspring: *Charles* Philip Arthur George, Prince of Wales, born 14 Nov. 1948 (Heir Apparent); Princess *Anne* Elizabeth Alice Louise, born 15 Aug. 1950, married Mark Anthony Peter Phillips on 14 Nov. 1973. Offspring: *Peter* Mark Andrew, born 15 Nov. 1977. Prince *Andrew* Albert Christian Edward, born 19 Feb. 1960; Prince *Edward* Antony Richard Louis, born 10 March 1964.

The Queen Mother: Queen Elizabeth, born 4 Aug. 1900, daughter of the 14th Earl of Strathmore and Kinghorne; married the Duke of York, afterwards King George VI, on 26 April 1923.

Sister of the Queen: Princess Margaret Rose, born 12 Aug. 1930; married Antony Armstrong-Jones (created Earl of Snowdon, 3 Oct. 1961) on 6 May 1960; divorced, 1978. Offspring: *David* Albert Charles (Viscount Linley), born 3 Nov. 1961; Lady *Sarah* Frances Elizabeth Armstrong-Jones, born 1 May 1964.

Children of the late Duke of Gloucester (died 10 June 1974): William Henry Andrew Frederick, born 18 Dec. 1941, died 28 Aug. 1972; Richard Alexander Walter George, Duke of Gloucester, born 26 Aug. 1944, married Birgitte van Deurs on 8 July 1972 (offspring: Alexander Patrick Gregers Richard Windsor, Earl of Ulster, born 24 Oct. 1974; Davina Elizabeth Alice Benedikte Windsor, born 19 Nov. 1977).

Children of the late Duke of Kent (died 25 Aug. 1942): Edward George Nicholas Patrick, Duke of Kent, born 9 Oct. 1935; married Katharine Worsley on 8 June 1961 (offspring: George Philip Nicholas, Earl of St Andrews, born 26 June 1962; Lady Helen Windsor, born 28 April 1964; Lord Nicholas Charles Edward Jonathan Windsor, born 25 July 1970). Alexandra Helen Elizabeth Olga Christabel, born 25 Dec. 1936; married 24 April 1963, Angus Ogilvy (offspring: James Robert Bruce, born 29 Feb. 1964; Marina Victoria Alexandra, born 31 July 1966). Michael George Charles Franklin, born 4 July 1942; married Marie-Christine von Reibnitz on 30 June 1978.

Children of the late Princess Royal (died 28 March 1965): George Henry Hubert, 7th Earl of Harewood, born 7 Feb. 1923; married Marion Stein on 29 Sept. 1949; divorced on 6 April 1967; remarried Patricia Tuckwell on 31 July 1967 (offspring: David Henry George, Viscount Lascelles, born 21 Oct. 1950; James Edward Lascelles, born 5 Oct. 1953; Robert Jeremy Hugh Lascelles, born 14 Feb. 1955; Mark Hubert Lascelles, born 5 July 1964); Gerald David Lascelles, born 21 Aug. 1924; married Angela Dowding on 15 July 1952 (offspring: Henry Ulick Lascelles, born 19 May 1953).

The Queen's legal title rests on the statute of 12 and 13 Will. III, c. 3, by which the succession to the Crown of Great Britain and Ireland was settled on the Princess Sophia of Hanover and the 'heirs of her body being Protestants'. By proclamation of 17 July 1917 the royal family became known as the House and Family of Windsor. On 8 Feb. 1960 the Queen issued a declaration varying her confirmatory declaration of 9 April 1952 to the effect that while the Queen and her children should continue to be known as the House of Windsor, her descendants, other than descendants entitled to the style of Royal Highness and the title of Prince or Princess, and female descendants who marry and their descendants should bear the name of Mountbatten-Windsor. The Royal Style and Titles of Queen Elizabeth are: In *Australia*: 'Elizabeth the Second, by the Grace of God Queen of Australia and Her other Realms and Territories, Head of the Commonwealth'. In the *Bahamas*: 'Elizabeth the Second, by the Grace of God, Queen of the Commonwealth of the Bahamas and of Her other Realms and Territories, Head of the Commonwealth'. In *Barbados*: 'Elizabeth the Second, by the Grace of God, Queen of Barbados and of Her other Realms and Territories, Head of the Commonwealth'. In *Canada*: 'Elizabeth the Second, by the Grace of God of the United Kingdom, Canada and Her other Realms and Territories Queen, Head of the Commonwealth, Defender of the Faith'. In *Fiji*: 'Elizabeth the Second, by the Grace of God, Queen of Fiji and of Her other Realms and Territories, Head of the Commonwealth'. In *Grenada*: 'Elizabeth the Second, by the Grace of God, Queen of the United Kingdom of Great Britain and Northern Ireland and of Grenada and Her other Realms and Territories, Head of the Commonwealth'. In *Jamaica*: 'Elizabeth the Second, by the Grace of God of Jamaica and of Her other Realms and Territories Queen, Head of the Commonwealth'. In *Mauritius*: 'Elizabeth the Second, Queen of Mauritius and of Her other Realms and Territories, Head of the Commonwealth'. In *New Zealand*: 'Elizabeth the Second, by the Grace of God Queen of New Zealand and Her Other Realms and Territories, Head of the Commonwealth, Defender of the Faith'. In *Papua New Guinea*: 'Elizabeth the Second, Queen of Papua New Guinea and Her other Realms and Territories, Head of the Commonwealth'. In the *United Kingdom*: 'Elizabeth the Second, by the Grace of God of the United Kingdom of Great Britain and Northern Ireland and of Her other Realms and Territories Queen, Head of the Commonwealth, Defender of the Faith'.

By letters patent of 30 Nov. 1917 the titles of Royal Highness and Prince or Princess are restricted to the Sovereign's children, the children of the Sovereign's sons and the eldest living son of the eldest son of the Prince of Wales.

Provision is made for the support of the royal household by the settlement of the Civil List soon after the beginning of each reign. (For historical details, *see* THE STATESMAN'S YEAR-BOOK, 1908, p. 5, and 1935, p. 4.) According to the Civil List Act of 1 Jan. 1972 and the Civil List (Increase of Financial Provision) Order 1975, the Civil List of the Queen, after the usual surrender of hereditary revenues, was

(1978) £1·95m. These Acts also provide for £93,500 a year to the Duke of Edinburgh.

The Civil List Acts of 1978 provides for an annuity of £60,000 to the Princess Anne; £175,000 to Queen Elizabeth (the Queen Mother); £59,000 to the Princess Margaret.

Sovereigns of Great Britain, from the Restoration (with dates of accession):

House of Stewart	
Charles II	29 May 1660
James II	6 Feb. 1685
House of Stewart-Orange	
William and Mary	13 Feb. 1689
William III	28 Dec. 1694
House of Stewart	
Anne	19 March 1702
House of Hanover	
George I	1 Aug. 1714
George II	11 June 1727
George III	25 Oct. 1760
George IV	29 Jan. 1820
William IV	26 June 1830
Victoria	20 June 1837
House of Saxe-Coburg and Gotha	
Edward VII	22 Jan. 1901
House of Windsor	
George V	6 May 1910
Edward VIII	20 Jan. 1936
George VI	11 Dec. 1936
Elizabeth II	6 Feb. 1952

CONSTITUTION AND GOVERNMENT. The supreme legislative power is vested in Parliament, which in its present form, as divided into two Houses of Legislature, the Lords and the Commons, dates from the middle of the 14th century.

Parliament is summoned by the writ of the sovereign issued out of Chancery, by advice of the Privy Council, at least 20 days previous to its assembling. Every session must end with a prorogation, and all Bills which have not been passed during the session then lapse. A dissolution may occur by the will of the sovereign, or, as is most usual, during the recess, by proclamation, or finally by lapse of time, the statutory limit of the duration of any Parliament being 5 years.

Under the Parliament Acts 1911 (1 and 2 Geo. V, ch. 13) and 1949 (12, 13 and 14 Geo. VI, ch. 103), all Money Bills (so certified by the Speaker of the House of Commons), if not passed by the House of Lords without amendment, may become law without their concurrence on the royal assent being signified within 1 month. Public Bills, other than Money Bills or a Bill extending the maximum duration of Parliament, if passed by the House of Commons in 2 successive sessions, whether of the same Parliament or not, and rejected each time, or not passed, by the House of Lords, may become law without their concurrence on the royal assent being signified, provided that 1 year has elapsed between the second reading in the first session of the House of Commons and the third reading in the second session. All Bills coming under this Act must reach the House of Lords at least 1 month before the end of the session.

The House of Lords consists of: (1) hereditary peers and peeresses sitting by virtue of creation or descent, other than those who have disclaimed their titles for life under the provisions of the Peerage Act, 1963; (2) life peers being (*a*) 18 Lords of Appeal (active and retired), under the Appellate Jurisdiction Act, 1876, as amended; (*b*) (Jan. 1978) 282 life peers and peeresses under the Life Peerages Act, 1958: (3) 2 archbishops and 24 bishops of the Church of England (as long as they hold their sees). The full House consists of about 1,139, of whom about 89 are without a writ of summons, and the average attendance is about 281; in Jan. 1977 133 peers were on leave of absence.

The House of Commons consists of members representing county and borough constituencies. Persons under 21 years of age, Clergymen of the Church of England, Ministers of the Church of Scotland, Roman Catholic clergymen, civil servants, members of the regular armed forces, policemen and most judicial officers are disqualified from sitting in the House of Commons. No English or Scottish peer can be elected to the House of Commons unless he has disclaimed his title for life under the Peerage Act, 1963, but Irish peers and holders of courtesy titles, who are not members of the House of Lords, are eligible. Under the Parliament (Qualification of Women) Act, 1918, women are also eligible.

In Aug. 1911 provision was first made for the payment of a salary of £400 per annum to members, other than those already in receipt of salaries as officers of the House, as Ministers or as officers of Her Majesty's household. As from June 1975 the salaries of members are £5,750 per annum, with income-tax relief on expenses incurred in the course of parliamentary duties. There is a secretarial allowance of up to £3,200 per annum and a living allowance, for an additional home, of up to £1,814 per annum. Members of the House of Lords are only entitled to recover expenses incurred for the purpose of attendance at sittings of the House. From 24 March 1977 the limit was increased from £13·50 to £16·50 for those Lords who necessarily incur additional expenses away from their main residence. Certain travelling expenses can be re-imbursed in each House.

The Representation of the People Act, 1948, abolished the business premises and University franchises, and the only persons entitled to vote at Parliamentary elections are those registered as residents or as service voters. No person may vote in more than one constituency at a general election. Persons may apply on certain grounds to vote by post or by proxy.

All persons over 17 years old and not subject to any legal incapacity to vote and who are either British subjects or citizens of the Irish Republic are entitled to be included in the register of electors for the constituency containing the address at which they were residing on the qualifying date for the register and are entitled to vote at elections held during the period for which the register remains in force. The current register was published on 16 Feb. 1976.

Members of the armed forces, Crown servants employed abroad, and the wives accompanying their husbands, are entitled, if otherwise qualified, to be registered as 'service voters' provided they make a 'service declaration'. To be effective for a particular register, the declaration must be made on or before the qualifying date for that register.

The Representation of the People Act, 1969, abolished the occupier's qualification for voting in Local Government elections.

The House of Commons (Redistribution of Seats) Acts, 1944, 1949 and 1958, provided for the setting up of Boundary Commissions for England, Wales, Scotland and Northern Ireland. The Commissions are required to make general reports at intervals of not less than 3 and not more than 7 years and to submit reports from time to time with respect to the area comprised in any particular constituency or constituencies where some change appears necessary. Any changes giving effect to reports of the Commissions are to be made by Orders in Council laid before Parliament for approval by resolution of each House. The electorate of the United Kingdom and Northern Ireland in the register used at the election of 10 Oct. 1974 numbered 39,798,899, of whom 32,769,792 were in England, 1,997,571 in Wales, 3,666,325 in Scotland and 1,041,886 in Northern Ireland.

At the general election held in Oct. 1974, 635 members were returned, 516 from England, 71 from Scotland, 36 from Wales and 12 from Northern Ireland. Every constituency returns a single member.

The following is a table of the duration of Parliaments called since the accession of King Edward VII.

Reign	*When met*	*When dissolved*	*Duration (years and days)*	
Edward VII	13 Feb. 1906	10 Jan. 1910	3	328
Edward VII and George V	15 Feb. 1910	28 Nov. 1910	0	287
George V	31 Jan. 1911	25 Nov. 1918	7	301
,,	4 Feb. 1919	26 Oct. 1922	3	269
,,	20 Nov. 1922	16 Nov. 1923	0	362
,,	8 Jan. 1924	9 Oct. 1924	0	276
,,	2 Dec. 1924	10 May 1929	4	161
,,	25 June 1929	7 Oct. 1931	2	75
,,	3 Nov. 1931	25 Oct. 1935	3	358
George V, Edward VIII and George VI	26 Nov. 1935	15 June 1945	9	205
George VI	1 Aug. 1945	3 Feb. 1950	4	188
,,	1 Mar. 1950	5 Oct. 1951	1	219
George VI and Elizabeth II	31 Oct. 1951	6 May 1955	3	188
Elizabeth II	7 June 1955	18 Sept. 1959	4	105
,,	20 Oct. 1959	25 Sept. 1964	4	341

Reign	When met	When dissolved	Duration (years and days)	
Elizabeth II (*contd.*)	27 Oct. 1964	10 Mar. 1966	1	134
,,	18 Apr. 1966	29 May 1970	4	81
,,	29 June 1970	8 Feb. 1974	3	225
,,	12 Mar. 1974	20 Sept. 1974	0	224
,,	22 Oct. 1974	—	—	

The executive government is vested nominally in the Crown, but practically in a committee of Ministers, called the Cabinet, which is dependent on the support of a majority in the House of Commons.

The head of the Ministry is the Prime Minister, a position first constitutionally recognized, and special precedence accorded to the holder, in 1905. His colleagues in the Ministry are appointed on his recommendation, and he dispenses the greater portion of the patronage of the Crown.

Heads of the Administrations since 1908 (C. = Conservative, L = Liberal, Lab. = Lab, Nat. = National, Coal. = Coalition, Care. = Caretaker):

H. H. Asquith (L.)	8 Apr. 1908	W. S. Churchill (Coal.)	10 May 1940
H. H. Asquith (Coal.)	25 May 1915	W. S. Churchill (Care.)	23 May 1945
D. Lloyd George (Coal.)	7 Dec. 1916	C. R. Attlee (Lab.)	26 July 1945
A. Bonar Law (C.)	23 Oct. 1922	W. S. Churchill (C.)	26 Oct. 1951
S. Baldwin (C.)	22 May 1923	Sir Anthony Eden (C.)	6 Apr. 1955
J. R. MacDonald (Lab.)	22 Jan. 1924	H. Macmillan (C.)	10 Jan. 1957
S. Baldwin (C.)	4 Nov. 1924	Sir Alec Douglas-Home (C.)	18 Oct. 1963
J. R. MacDonald (Lab.)	5 June 1929	H. Wilson (Lab.)	16 Oct. 1964
J. R. MacDonald (Nat.)	25 Aug. 1931	E. Heath (C.)	19 June 1970
S. Baldwin (Nat.)	7 June 1935	H. Wilson (Lab.)	12 Mar. 1974
N. Chamberlain (Nat.)	28 May 1937	J. Callaghan (Lab.)	5 Apr. 1976

In April 1977 the Government consisted of the following members:

(*a*) Members of the Cabinet

1. *Prime Minister and First Lord of the Treasury and Minister for the Civil Service:* Rt Hon. James Callaghan, MP, born 1913. (Salary £20,000 per annum.)

2. *Lord President of the Council and Leader of the House of Commons:* Rt Hon. Michael Foot, MP, born 1914. (£13,000.)

3. *Lord High Chancellor of Great Britain:* Rt Hon. The Lord Elwyn Jones, CH, born 1910. (£20,000.)

4. *Chancellor of the Exchequer:* Rt Hon. Denis Healey, MBE, MP, born 1918. (£13,000.)

5. *Secretary of State for the Home Department:* Rt Hon. Merlyn Rees, MP, born 1921. (£13,000.)

6. *Secretary of State for Foreign and Commonwealth Affairs:* Rt Hon. David Owen, MP, born 1938. (£13,000.)

7. *Secretary of State for Education and Science and Paymaster-General:* Rt Hon. Shirley Williams, MP, born 1931. (£13,000.)

8. *Secretary of State for Energy:* Rt Hon. Anthony Wedgwood Benn, MP, born 1926. (£13,000.)

9. *Secretary of State for Industry:* Rt Hon. Eric Varley, MP, born 1933. (£13,000.)

10. *Secretary of State for the Environment:* Rt Hon. Peter Shore, MP, born 1925. (£13,000.)

11. *Secretary of State for Northern Ireland:* Rt Hon. Roy Mason, MC, MP, born 1925. (£13,000.)

12. *Secretary of State for Scotland:* Rt Hon. Bruce Millan, MBE, MP, born 1912. (£13,000.)

13. *Secretary of State for Wales:* Rt Hon. John Morris, QC, MP, born 1932. (£13,000.)

14. *Secretary of State for Defence:* Rt Hon. Frederick Mulley, MP, born 1919. (£13,000.)

15. *Secretary of State for Employment:* Rt Hon. Albert Booth, MP, born 1928. (£13,000.)

16. *Secretary of State for Social Services:* Rt Hon. David Ennals, MP, born 1923. (£13,000.)

17. *Secretary of State for Trade, President of the Board of Trade:* Rt Hon. Edmund Dell, MP, born 1922. (£13,000.)

18. *Lord Privy Seal and Leader of the House of Lords:* Rt Hon. The Lord Peart, born 1915. (£13,000.)

19. *Chief Secretary of the Treasury:* Rt Hon. Joel Barnett, MP, born 1924. (£9,500.)

20. *Minister of Agriculture, Fisheries and Food:* Rt Hon. John Silkin, MP, born 1924. (£13,000.)

21. *Secretary of State for Prices and Consumer Protection:* Rt Hon. Roy Hattersley, MP, born 1933. (£13,000.)

22. *Secretary of State for Transport:* Rt Hon. William Rodgers, MP, born 1929. (£13,000.)

23. *Minister for Social Security:* Rt Hon. Stanley Orme, MP, born 1924. (£13,000.)

24. *Chancellor of the Duchy of Lancaster:* Rt Hon. Harold Lever, MP, born 1914. (Unpaid.)

(*b*) Law Officers

25. *Attorney-General:* Rt Hon. Samuel Silkin, QC, MP, born 1918. (£14,500.)

26. *Lord Advocate:* Rt Hon. Ronald King Murray, QC, MP, born 1923. (£11,000.)

27. *Solicitor-General:* Peter Archer, QC, MP, born 1927. (£11,000.)

28. *Solicitor-General for Scotland:* Lord McCluskey, QC, born 1930. (£7,750.)

(*c*) Ministers not in the Cabinet

29. *Parliamentary Secretary, Treasury:* Michael Cocks, MP, born 1929 (£9,500.)

30. *Minister of State for Foreign and Commonwealth Affairs:* Rt Hon. Frank Judd, MP, born 1935. (£13,000.)

31. *Minister of State for Foreign and Commonwealth Affairs:* Rt Hon. The Lord Goronwy Roberts, born 1913. (£9,500.)

32. *Minister of State for Overseas Development:* Rt Hon. Judith Hart, MP, born 1925. (£9,500.)

33. *Financial Secretary, Treasury:* Robert Sheldon, MP, born 1924. (£9,500.)

34. *Minister of State, Treasury:* Denzil Davies, MP, born 1938. (£9,500.)

35. *Minister of State for Foreign and Commonwealth Affairs:* Edward Rowlands, MP, born 1940. (£7,500.)

36. *Minister of Housing and Construction:* Reginald Freeson, MP, born 1926. (£9,500.)

37. *Minister of State, Privy Council Office:* Rt Hon. John Smith, MP, born 1938. (£9,500.)

38. *Minister of State, Civil Service Department:* Charles Morris, MP, born 1927. (£7,500.)

39. *Minister of State, Department of the Environment:* Rt Hon. Denis Howell, MP, born 1924. (£7,500.)

40. *Minister of State, Home Office:* Rt Hon. The Lord Harris of Greenwich, born 1931. (£7,500.)

41. *Minister of State, Home Office:* Brynmor John, MP, born 1934. (£7,500.)

42. *Minister of State, Department of Energy:* Rt Hon. Dickson Mabon, MP, born 1925. (£7,500.)

43. *Minister of State, Ministry of Defence:* Dr John Gilbert, MP, born 1928. (£9,500.)

44. *Minister of State, Department of Industry:* Rt Hon. Alan Williams, OBE, MP, born 1930. (£9,500.)

45. *Minister of State, Department of Industry:* Rt Hon. Gerald Kaufman, MP, born 1930. (£9,500.)

46. *Minister of State, Northern Ireland Office:* Don Concannon, MP, born 1930. (£7,500.)

47. *Minister of State, Scottish Office:* Gregor Mackenzie, MP, born 1927. (£9,500.)

48. *Minister of State, Scottish Office:* The Lord Kirkhill, born 1930. (£7,500.)

49. *Minister of State for Agriculture, Fisheries and Food:* Edward Bishop, MP, born 1920. (£7,500.)

50. *Minister of State, Department of Employment:* Harold Walker, born 1927. (£7,500.)

51. *Minister of State, Department of Health and Social Security:* Rt Hon. Roland Moyle, MP, born 1928. (£7,500.)

52. *Minister of State, Department of Prices and Consumer Protection:* John Fraser, MP, born 1934. (£7,500.)

53. *Minister of State, Department of Education and Science:* The Lord Donaldson of Kingsbridge, born 1907. (£9,500.)

54. *Minister of State, Department of Education and Science:* Gordon Oakes, MP, born 1931. (£9,500.)

55. *Minister of State, Northern Ireland Office:* The Lord Melchett, born 1948. (£7,500.)

Leader of the Opposition in the House of Commons: Rt Hon. Margaret Thatcher, MP, born 1925. (£9,900.)

Leader of the Opposition in the House of Lords: The Rt Hon. Lord Carrington, born 1919. (£3,500.)

The constitution of the House of Commons after the general election held on 10 Oct. 1974 was as follows: Labour, 319; Conservative, 276; Liberal, 13; Scottish Nationalist, 11; United Ulster Unionist, 10; Others, 5; Speaker, 1; total, 635. The numbers of votes cast were: Labour, 11,468,136 (39·3% of poll); Conservative, 10,464,675 (35·8%); Liberals, 5,346,800 (18·3%); Others, 1,908,995 (6·6%).

Blake, R. N. W., *The Office of Prime Minister.* OUP, 1975
Butler, D. E., and Sloman A., *British Political Facts 1900–1975.* London 1975
Butler D. E., and Kavanagh, D., *The British General Election of February 1974.* London, 1975
Butler, D. E., and Kavanagh, D., *The British General Election of October 1974.* London, 1975
Butler D. E., and Stokes, D., *Political Change in Britain: The Evolution of Electoral Choice.* London, 1975
Butt, R., *The Power of Parliament.* 2nd ed. London, 1969
Cook, C., *A Short History of the Liberal Party.* London, 1976
Cook, C., and Ramsden, J., *By-Elections in British Politics.* London, 1973
Craig, F. W. S., *British Electoral Facts 1885–1975.* London, 1976.—*The Most Gracious Speeches to Parliament 1900–1974.* London, 1975
Ford, P. and G., *A Guide to Parliamentary Papers.* New ed. OUP, 1956
Herman, V., and Att, J. E., *Cabinet Studies.* London, 1976
Jennings, Sir I., *Cabinet Government.* 3rd. ed. CUP, 1959.—*The British Constitution.* 5th ed. CUP, 1966.—*Parliament.* 2nd ed. CUP, 1957.—*Party Politics.* 3 vols. CUP, 1960–62

Jones, J. M., *British Nationality Law*. Rev. ed. London, 1955
King, A. (ed.), *The British Prime Minister*. London, 1969.—*British Members of Parliament*. London, 1974
Laundy, P., *The Office of Speaker*. London, 1964
Lindsay, T. F., *The Conservative Party 1918–1970*. London, 1976
Mackintosh, J. P., *The British Cabinet*. 3rd ed. London, 1977.—*The Government and Politics of Britain*. 4th ed. London, 1977
May, Sir T. E., *Treatise on the Law, Privileges, Proceedings and Usage of Parliament*. 19th ed., London, 1976
Mitchell, B. R., and Boehm, K. H., *British Parliamentary Elections, 1950–64*. CUP, 1966
Pelling, H., *A Short History of the Labour Party*. London, 1976
Pulzer, P. G. J., *Political Representation and Elections in Britain*. London, 1972
Rush, M., and Shaw, M., *House of Commons*. London, 1974
Stacey, F., *British Government 1966–1975*. London, 1975
Taylor, E., *The House of Commons at Work*. 7th ed. London, 1967
Wilding, N., and Laundy, P., *An Encyclopaedia of Parliament*. 4th ed. London, 1972
Young, R., *The British Parliament*. London, 1962

Local Government. Local Administration is carried out by four different types of bodies, namely: (i) local branches of some central ministries, such as the Department of Health and Social Security; (ii) local sub-managements of nationalized industries (coal, electricity, gas, public transport and the post office); (iii) specialist authorities such as the police and water conservation; and (iv) the system of *local government* described below. The phrase 'local government' has come to mean that part of the local administration conducted by elected councils.

There are two separate systems: one for England and Wales and one for Scotland, but both systems are financed by a species of tax on property, levied locally, combined with government grants which, in the aggregate amount to more than the yield of the local tax. This local tax is called 'the rate'. The system of financing local government was the subject of a major review in 1975.

Local Government: England and Wales—*Outside London*. England and Wales have slightly differing systems. Each country has three types of councils namely, county, district and English parish or Welsh Community Councils. In addition, England has some metropolitan county and district councils.

Councillors are elected by their local electors for 4 years. The chairman of the council is one of the councillors elected by the rest. In a district with the status of city or borough his title is mayor, or in a few famous places Lord Mayor. Any parish council can by simple resolution adopt the style 'town council' and the status of town for the parish. The chairman will then be known as the town mayor.

Counties and Districts: There are 47 non-metropolitan counties (of which 8 are in Wales) and 6 metropolitan counties (Greater Manchester, Merseyside, South Yorkshire, Tyne and Wear, West Yorkshire and West Midlands). Within the counties there are 369 districts (36 metropolitan and 333 non-metropolitan, of which 37 are in Wales).

Parishes and Communities: There are some 10,000 parishes within the English districts, of which 7,000 or so of them have councils. About 300 are former small boroughs or urban districts which became successor parishes. Parishes generally, however, remain comparatively unaffected by reorganization.

County boundaries are laid down by the Local Government Act, 1972, and the district boundaries are settled by orders made in 1973 under that Act; community boundaries are undergoing a review which will probably be completed by 1978; parish boundaries will be reviewed later.

Permanent Local Government Commissions for England and for Wales advise the Secretary of State on boundaries and electoral arrangements.

A council has only those powers which have been conferred upon it expressly by Act of Parliament, and no more. The relationship between the different types of council is thus primarily one of specialization, not of hierarchy. The larger do not in principle supervise the smaller; each being, within its own sphere, entitled to make its own decisions. Government sanction, however, is required to borrow money and to sell land below its market value, and certain types of land use are subject to planning control.

Councils are kept within the law by a system of publicly regulated audit, and in the last resort they can be restrained from exceeding their powers by the courts.

Local government functions may be classified into county, district and parish or community functions, but whereas county and district functions are distinct, the parish and community functions are mostly concurrent with those of the districts. Arrangements may, however, be made so that any council may discharge functions of any other as its agent.

The following is the classification of powers suggested above: *Parish and Community Functions*. Allotments, burial and cremation, halls, meeting places and entertainments, facilities for exercise and recreation, public lavatories, street lighting, off-street vehicle parking, footpaths, the support of local arts and crafts, the encouragement of tourism and the right to be consulted by the district council on planning application and certain byelaws. *District Functions*. In addition to the Parish and Community functions, aerodromes, civic restaurants, housing, markets, refuse collection, the administration of planning control, the formulation of local plans, sewerage, on behalf of the water authority, museums, the licensing of places of entertainment and refreshment, and the constitutional oversight of parishes and communities. *County Functions*. The formulation of structure plans, traffic, transportation and roads, education, public libraries and museums, youth employment and social services.

There are, in addition, a number of special arrangements. For the inspection of food, drugs, weights and measures, the English authority outside London is the county council, but the Welsh authority is the district. The county councils also either separately or jointly appoint the fire and police authorities, and the bodies responsible for national parks. In Metropolitan counties the district not the county councils are responsible for education, social services and libraries.

The total number of local government electors in England and Wales was 35,974,998 in 1976.

Greater London. Since 1965 London has been governed by the Greater London Council covering the whole metropolitan area, and by 32 London Boroughs and the City of London, each with responsibilities in its own area. In the City and the 12 boroughs covering the inner part of Greater London education is the responsibility of the Inner London Education Authority, a special Committee of the GLC but independent of it, while in the 20 outer boroughs the London Borough Council is the education authority. Other functions are divided between the GLC and the boroughs. The main responsibilities of the GLC are housing, strategic planning, major roads, public transport (through the London Transport Executive, which is responsible to it), major parks and open spaces, the fire service, refuse disposal and Thames flood prevention. The boroughs also have housing functions limited to their own areas, while the GLC operates over the whole of London. The City has preserved a large measure of independence and has its own powers regarding police, justice, bridges, sanitation, etc. Except in the City the police authority covering the whole of Greater London is the Metropolitan Police, which is responsible direct to the Central Government.

Estimated population of Greater London in June 1976 was 7·03m., and rateable value at 1 April 1976 was £1,879,646,155. Estimated gross revenue expenditure of the GLC in 1976–77 was £1,492·7m. (including £453·4m. for the ILEA and £346·2m. for London Transport). Estimated gross capital expenditure was £448m. (including ILEA £25m., London Transport £73m.) and included £75m. for loans to housing associations and to individuals for house purchase.

Scotland. Under the system, which came into effect in 1975, the Scots mainland is divided into 9 regions, and in addition there are the 3 islands areas of Orkney, Shetland and the Western Isles. There is no equivalent to the English metropolitan county. The regions are divided into districts which total 53. All these units have a council consisting of councillors elected for 4 years and a chairman elected by the councillors for 4 years. Community councils have been established under schemes submitted by district and island councils. These community councils cannot claim public funds as of right, nor do they have powers directly conferred by Statute: consequently they are not local authorities in the sense that Welsh Community Councils are.

As in England and Wales a permanent Local Government Boundary Commission advises the Secretary of State on Local Authority Boundaries and electoral arrangements.

On the mainland, functions are allocated between regional and district authorities, in the same way (with minor exceptions) as they are allocated between English counties on the one hand and English districts and parishes on the other, but the councils of the islands areas, which have no districts, perform both sets of functions.

Despite differences of nomenclature the effect of the reforms of 1972 (England) and 1973 (Scotland) is to assimilate the systems of mainland Scotland and of England and Wales more closely than has been the case in the past.

The total number of local government electors in Scotland was 3,764,322 in 1976.

Complaints. Under both systems, complaints, by members of the public, of maladministration may be investigated by a Commissioner for Local Administration. Initially a complaint must be referred to him through a councillor, but a direct approach to him is possible if this fails. He can deal only with matters for which there is no other remedy; he reports to the council concerned and may publish his report.

For map of regions *see* THE STATESMAN'S YEAR-BOOK, 1974–75.

Our Changing Democracy: Devolution to Scotland and Wales. HMSO, 1975
Arnold-Baker, C., *The Local Government Act 1972.* London, 1973
Griffith, J. A. G., *Central Departments and Local Government.* London, 1966

DEFENCE. All important problems of defence policy are considered by the Defence and Oversea Policy Committee presided over by the Prime Minister, and consisting of certain Ministers of the Government, among whom are the Secretary of State for Defence, the Foreign and Commonwealth Secretary and the Home Secretary. The Secretary of State for Defence is responsible for carrying out this Committee's decisions relating to defence, after endorsement as necessary by the Cabinet.

The complete re-organization of the 3 Service Departments (Admiralty, War Office and Air Ministry) under the Secretary of State for Defence took place in 1964. A Defence Council was also established under the Secretary of State to exercise the powers of command and administrative control previously exercised by the separate service councils, which became subordinate to it. Further reorganization, on 6 Jan. 1967, reduced the status of the administrative heads of the 3 Services from Ministers to Under-Secretaries of State, while creating 2 new posts: Minister of Defence (Administration) and Minister of Defence (Equipment). Further reorganization of these 2 posts later reduced them to that of a single Minister of State for Defence. The present membership of the Defence Council consists of the Secretary of State for Defence, the Minister of State for Defence, the 3 Service Under-Secretaries of State, the Chiefs of Defence, Naval, General and Air Staffs, the Chief of Personnel and Logistics, the Chief Scientific Adviser, the Chief Executive of the Procurement Executive and the Permanent Under-Secretary of State.

Logistics Services. Since the inception of a unified Ministry of Defence in 1964, progress has been made in the rationalization of the logistics services of the Royal Navy, the Army and the Royal Air Force. Airfield construction for all Services is now the responsibility of the Army's Royal Engineers; the Air Force Department is responsible for accommodation stores for maintenance and for the initial furnishing of new buildings; the Army Department is the single management authority for the design, development, procurement and inspection of clothing other than certain specialized clothing; the Navy Department has for some time been responsible for ration policy provisioning, procurement, storing and distribution of food to main depots and to Army forward supply depots in BAOR and is responsible for water transport to its tri-service responsibilities. The supply of Naval air stores is now being integrated with those of the RAF. Considerable savings in money and in Service and civilian manpower have already been realized and are expected to continue.

The Procurement Executive. An important development in 1971 was the creation of a Procurement Executive to combine the Defence Procurement responsibilities of the Ministry of Defence and the former Ministry of Aviation Supply.

Service Strengths at 1 April 1977, all ranks, males and females: Royal Navy and Royal Marines, 76,000; Army, 167,000; Royal Air Force, 87,000; Total, 330,000.

Defence Budget Estimates: 1977–78, £6,298m. (out-turn, £6,754); 1978–79, £6,886m.

Army. Control of the British Army is vested in the Defence Council and is exercised through the Army Board, which consists of 6 civilian and 5 military members. The Secretary of State for Defence is Chairman of the Army Board. The other civilian members are the Minister of State for Defence and the Parliamentary Under-Secretary of State for Defence for the Army, the Chief Scientist (Army) and the Deputy Under-Secretary of State (Army) and the Second Permanent Under-Secretary of State (Administration) who attend meetings as appropriate.

The Military members of the Army Board are the Chief of the General Staff, the Adjutant-General, the Quartermaster-General, the Master-General of the Ordnance and the Vice-Chief of the General Staff. The Chief of the General Staff is the professional head of his Service and the professional adviser to Ministers on the Army aspects of military problems. He is responsible for the fighting efficiency of his Service; for the consideration of all Army aspects of policy planning; for Army advice on the conduct of operations; and for the issuing of such single Service operational orders as may be appropriate resulting from defence policy decisions. The Chief of the General Staff is a member of the Chiefs of Staff Committee which is collectively responsible to HM Government for professional advice on strategy and military operations and on the military implication of defence policy. This advice is tendered to the Secretary of State for Defence by the Chairman of the Chiefs of Staff Committee, the Chief of the Defence Staff. The Chief of the General Staff is also responsible for the Territorial and Army Volunteer Reserve, the Army Cadet Force and the Combined Cadet Force. In exercise of his General Staff responsibilities the Chief of the General Staff is assisted by the Vice-Chief of the General Staff. The Adjutant-General is responsible for Army manpower within the policy set by the General Staff; for recruiting and selection; for the administration and individual training of military personnel; for the discipline of the Army; for pay and allowances and pensions; for Army medical services; for dental and nursing services; for legal services; for the veterinary and remount services; for questions of Army welfare and education including school children overseas; and for resettlement and sports. The Quartermaster-General is responsible for logistic planning for the Army; for the storage, distribution, maintenance, repair and inspection of equipment, stores and ammunition; for development of stores; for supply, transport and accommodation; for the development, production and inspection of clothing; for military movements and transportation; for the Army postal, catering, salvage and fire services; and for questions connected with canteens, institutes and military labour. The Master General of the Ordnance is a member of both of the Army Board and of the Procurement Executive. He is responsible to the Chief Executive (Procurement Executive) for the financial and technical management of the approved programme for the procurement of land service equipment for the Armed Services, and to the Army Board for the co-ordination of the Army's total equipment programme. The Chief Scientist (Army) is responsible for providing scientific advice to the Army Board and its members and for ensuring that the Defence Research Programme properly reflects their needs. He is also a member of the Procurement Executive as Deputy Controller, Research and Development Establishments, and Research (B). The Deputy Under-Secretary of State (Army) is responsible for the general co-ordination of Army Board business and, under the Permanent Under-Secretary of State and the Second Permanent Under-Secretary of State (Administration), for providing the Board with financial and administrative guidance.

Headquarters United Kingdom Land Forces at Wilton commands all Army units in UK but the Ministry of Defence retains direct operational control of units in Northern Ireland. Command by HQ United Kingdom Land Forces will be exercised through 9 district headquarters and Headquarters 3 Division. There are 3 major overseas Commands: Near East Land Forces, Hong Kong and the British Army of the Rhine.

There are also garrisons in Gibraltar and Belize.

The strength of the Regular Army (less the Brigade of Gurkhas and locally enlisted personnel) on 1 April 1977 was 161,000 men and 6,000 women. The citizen force is the Territorial and Army Volunteer Reserve, formed on 1 April 1967 to replace the Territorial Army and the Army Emergency Reserve.

The Territorial and Army Volunteer Reserve has an establishment of about 74,000. Its role is to provide a national reserve for employment on specific tasks at home and overseas and to meet the unexpected when required; and, in particular, to complete the Army Order of Battle of NATO committed forces and to provide certain units for the support of NATO Headquarters, to assist in maintaining a secure UK base in support of forces deployed on the Continent of Europe and to provide a framework for any future expansion of the Reserves. In addition, men who have completed service in the Regular Army normally have some liability to serve in the Regular Reserve. All members of the TAVR and Regular Reserve may be called out by a Queen's Order in time of emergency or imminent national danger and most of the TAVR and a large proportion of the Regular Reserve may be called out by a Queen's Order when warlike operations are in preparation or in progress. There is a special reserve force in Northern Ireland, the Ulster Defence Regiment, 7,800 strong, which gives part-time support to the regular army.

Men, women and juniors enlist in the Army for 22 years' active and reserve service. However, under a scheme introduced in May 1972 they are entitled to give 18 months' notice to leave active service provided they serve for a minimum of 3 years. Alternatively, they can agree to serve for 6 or 9 years to receive the benefit of higher rates of pay. Those enlisting in certain technical trades must agree to serve for a minimum of 6 years. Recruits under the age of 17½ on reaching the age of 18 are entitled either to confirm their original engagement or to reduce their period of service to 3 years.

Women serve in both the Regular Army and the TAVR in the Queen Alexandra's Royal Army Nursing Corps, the Ulster Defence Regiment and the Women's Royal Army Corps, the latter's employments including communications, motor transport, clerical and catering duties. Some officers of the Women's Royal Army Corps are employed on the staffs of military headquarters.

Barnett, C., *Britain and her Army 1509–1970*. London, 1970
Blaxford, G., *The Regiments Depart: A History of the British Army 1945–70*. London, 1971
Fortescue, J. W., *History of the British Army*. 14 vols. London, 1899–1930
Sheppard, E. W., *Short History of the British Army*. 4th ed. London, 1950

Navy. The Royal Navy is a permanent establishment, governed by the Admiralty Board of the Defence Council. The Secretary of State for Defence is Chairman of the Admiralty Board; the Minister of State for Defence is Vice-Chairman. The members of the Admiralty Board and their responsibilities are as follows: The Parliamentary Under-Secretary of State for Defence for the Royal Navy; The Chief of the Naval Staff and First Sea Lord (professional head of the Royal Navy), assisted by the Vice-Chief of the Naval Staff, responsible for fighting efficiency, policy planning and operations advice; The Chief of Naval Personnel and Second Sea Lord, responsible for the manning of the Fleet, service conditions, training, discipline and welfare; The Controller of the Navy (formerly also Third Sea Lord), responsible for research and development, design, production, inspection, repair and maintenance of ships, their weapons and equipment; The Chief of Fleet Support, known until 1968 as Chief of Naval Supplies and Transport and Vice-Controller (formerly also Fourth Sea Lord), responsible for the provision of naval armament, victualling and medical stores and fuels, and for the movement of transport of persons and material, and superintending Dockyard organization and maintenance of the Fleet; and The Chief Scientist (Royal Navy), responsible for superintending the conduct of all research and development and the deployment of scientific effort. The post of Second Permanent Under-Secretary of State (Royal Navy) (formerly Permanent Secretary) lapsed in 1968 (he was Civil Service head, responsible for general co-ordination of the Admiralty Board business, the interior economy of the Navy department, Navy contracts and the administration of civil staff, and accounting officer for Navy Votes responsible for the control of expenditure and adviser to the Admiralty Board on financial questions). Thus the office of Samuel Pepys, of which the last holder was the 33rd, passed into history. The Deputy Under-Secretary of State (Navy) is the Board Member now responsible for some of these functions. Financial and staff control is vested in the Second Permanent Under-Secretary for Administration and the Second Permanent Under-Secretary for Equipment.

The following is a summary of the more important units:

	Completed by the end of								
Category	*1969*	*1970*	*1971*	*1972*	*1973*	*1974*	*1975*	*1976*	*1977*
Aircraft carriers	5[1]	5[2]	5[2]	4[2]	3[1]	3[1]	3[1]	3[3]	3[3]
Submarines	35	34	36	35	34	32	30	31	31
Cruisers	3	3	3	2	2	2	2	2	2
Destroyers	15	11	12	12	9	10	10	10	10
Frigates	64	64	65	65	62	60	58	56	56

[1] Included 2 commando carriers. [2] Included 3 commando carriers.
[3] Included 1 helicopter/VOSTOL carrier and 1 commando carrier in reserve.

There are also 2 assault ships, 3 depot, repair and maintenance ships, 1 ice patrol ship, 1 fast patrol craft, 3 fast training boats, 2 seaward defence boats, 13 surveying vessels, 5 coastal patrol vessels (*ex*-coastal minesweepers), 15 minehunters, 18 coastal minesweepers, 5 inshore minesweepers, 1 mine countermeasures support ship, 3 trial ships, 1 helicopter support ship, 1 submarine tender (ocean-going tug), 5 offshore patrol vessels (fishery protection), 4 inshore patrol boats, 12 mooring, salvage and boom vessels, 9 fleet support and supply ships, 17 fleet oilers, 60 other auxiliaries, 6 logistic landing ships, 1 tank landing ship, 59 landing craft, 18 fleet tugs, 53 other tugs, and 66 tenders. In the following table the principal surface warships are grouped in classes, in descending order of modernity.

Completed	*Name*	*Standard displacement Tons*	*Armour Belt In.*	*Armour Turrets In.*	*Principal armament*	*Shaft horse-power*	*Speed knots*
			Aircraft Carrier				
1955	Ark Royal	43,060	?	—	Fitted for 4 'Seacat'	152,000	31·5

Her sister ship *Eagle*, reconstructed Dec. 1959 to May 1964, was de-stored in 1972 but was still in reserve, for disposal in 1978.

The aircraft carrier *Victorious* was scheduled for disposal in Nov. 1967, decommissioned on 13 March 1968 to await disposal and left Portsmouth for breaking up at Faslane on 11 July 1969. The aircraft carrier *Centaur* used from 1965 to 1970 as an accommodation ship for aircraft carriers and commando carriers refitting, was officially declared for disposal in Feb. 1971 and broken up in 1973.

Commando A/S Support (Carriers)

1959	Hermes[2]	23,900	—	—	2 'Seacat'	78,000	28·0
1954	Bulwark[1]	23,300	—	—	Light AA	78,000	28·0

[1] Converted from fixed wing aircraft carrier to commando carrier 1959–60 and reduced to care and maintenance reserve in April 1976. Her sister ship *Albion*, converted in 1961–62, was decommissioned in May 1973 and towed away for disposal in Dec. 1973.

[2] Converted from fixed wing aircraft carrier to commando carrier 1971–73. Converted to anti-submarine and VOSTOL role in 1976.

Cruisers

1961 1959	Blake[1] Tiger[2]	9,550	4	2	2 6-in; 2 3-in.	80,000	31·5

[1] Converted into a helicopter carrier 1965–69.

[2] Converted into a helicopter carrier 1968–72. Sister ship *Lion* was not converted into a helicopter carrier (reconstruction rescinded in Oct. 1970). Scheduled for disposal in 1972, but still listed laid up in 1975.

The cruiser *Belfast* was reclassified as a harbour accommodation ship in June 1966 but ceased to act in this capacity in Feb. 1971, and on 21 Oct. 1971 became a museum ship on the Thames above Tower Bridge.

The cruisers *Ceylon* and *Newfoundland* were sold to Peru in Dec. and Nov. 1959 respectively. *Birmingham* was scrapped in 1960; *Jamaica* and *Superb* were scrapped in 1961; *Kenya* and *Swiftsure* in 1962; *Bermuda* and *Mauritius* in 1965. *Sheffield* was towed to the shipbreakers in Jan. 1967; *Gambia* in 1968.

Submarines are of the following classes: 'Resolution' (nuclear powered and Polaris missile armed), 4; 'Swiftsure' (nuclear powered), 3; 'Churchill' (nuclear powered), 3; 'Valiant' (nuclear powered), 2; 'Dreadnought' (nuclear powered), 1; 'Oberon', 13; 'Porpoise', 5. Surface displacements range from 2,030 to 7,500 tons.

The first nuclear-powered fleet submarine, *Dreadnought*, was commissioned on 17 April 1963; and the first nuclear powered ballistic missile submarine, *Resolution*, was accepted in Oct. 1967.

The destroyers of the Royal Navy are of the following classes: 'Sheffield', 2; 'Bristol', 1; 'County', 7. Standard displacements range from 3,150 to 6,100 tons.

Frigates are of the following classes: 'Amazon', 5; 'Leander', 26; 'Tribal', 7; 'Rothesay', 9; 'Leopard', 2; 'Salisbury', 3; 'Whitby', 2; 'Blackwood', 2. Displacements range from 1,180 to 2,500 tons.

Ships under construction or on order include 4 nuclear powered submarines, 6 guided missile armed destroyers, 6 frigates, 2 mine counter measures vessels and 2 offshore patrol vessels. A 'through-deck' (flat-top) 'anti-submarine cruiser' (small vertical aircraft/helicopter carrier) was ordered in April 1973, laid down in July 1973 and launched in May 1977, and a sister ship was ordered in 1976.

The 'Type 82' guided missile armed destroyer *Bristol*, larger than the 'County' class, was launched on 30 June 1969 and completed in 1973; and the second 'Type 42', *Birmingham*, was launched on 30 July 1973 and commissioned on 3 Dec. 1976.

The Navy estimates for 1970–71, £659,378,500; 1971–72, £690m.; 1972–73, £750m.; 1973–74, £810m.; 1974–75, £925m.; 1975–76, £1,064m.; 1976–77, £1,300m. Figures since 1972 are unofficial, as the Navy Estimates are now included in a total Defence Budget.

The total personnel of officers and ratings provided for was (in 1,000) 1974–75, 78·3; 1975–76, 77·4; 1976–77, 76·5; 1977–78, 76·1 (including 4,000 servicewomen).

Blackman, R. V. B., *The World's Warships*. London, 1969
Blackman R. V. B., *Ships of the Royal Navy*. London, 1975
Moore, J. E. (ed.), *Jane's Fighting Ships*, 80th ed. London, 1977–78

Air Force. In May 1912 the Royal Flying Corps first came into existence with military and naval wings, of which the latter became the independent Royal Naval Air Service in July 1914. On 2 Jan. 1918 an Air Ministry was formed, and on 1 April 1918 the Royal Flying Corps and the Royal Naval Air Service were amalgamated, under the Air Ministry, as the Royal Air Force. In 1937 the units based on aircraft carriers and naval shore stations again passed to the operational and administrative control of the Admiralty, as the Fleet Air Arm. In 1964 control of the Royal Air Force became a responsibility of the unified Ministry of Defence.

The Royal Air Force is administered by the Air Force Board, of which the Secretary of State for Defence is Chairman. The Minister of State for Defence is Vice-Chairman, as is the Under-Secretary of State for Defence for the Royal Air Force, who normally acts as Chairman on behalf of the Secretary of State. Other members of the Board are the Chief of the Air Staff, who is assisted by the Vice-Chief of the Air Staff, the Air Member for Personnel, the Air Member for Supply and Organization, the Controller of Aircraft, the Chief Scientist (Royal Air Force), the Deputy Under-Secretary of State (Air) and the Second Permanent Under-Secretary of State for Administration. The Royal Air Force is organized into commands:

Home Commands. Strike and Support Commands. The Air Training Corps and the Air Sections of the Combined Cadet Force are under the administrative control of Support Command and functionally controlled by the Ministry of Defence.

Overseas Commands. Royal Air Force Germany. Small units in Gibraltar, Malta, Cyprus and Hong Kong.

The RAF College, which trains general-duties, engineering, and supply and secretarial graduates for permanent commissions, is at Cranwell. The RAF staff College is at Bracknell. The Department of Air Warfare is at Cranwell. Estimated strength in April 1978, including WRAF and boys, was 84,600. There were 1,640 fixed-wing aircraft and 171 helicopters on establishment on 30 Sept. 1976.

There is a single multi-role operational command in the UK, known as Strike Command, made up of 5 Groups. No. 1 Group is responsible for control and training of the strike/attack, air-to-air refuelling and reconnaissance forces. There are home-based squadrons of Vulcan Mk. 2 medium bombers; Buccaneer low-level strike and maritime attack aircraft; Victor flight refuelling tankers; and reconnaissance squadrons of Vulcan SR. Mk. 2 and Canberra aircraft. No. 11 Group controls air defence squadrons of Lightning and Phantom supersonic all-weather fighters armed with air-to-air missiles, and their associated communications and ground environment radars, including the Ballistic Missile Early Warning System station at Fylingdales. No. 11 Group also has Shackleton AEW. Mk. 2 airborne early warning aircraft, and Bloodhound surface-to-air missiles. No. 18 Group has Nimrod MR. Mk. 1 maritime reconnaissance aircraft and Whirlwind and Wessex helicopters for search and rescue. The first long-range Sea King helicopters entered service in 1978. No. 38 Group is responsible for the UK ground attack force of Jaguars and V/STOL Harriers; reconnaissance Jaguars; VC10 jets, turboprop Hercules transports, and smaller communications aircraft; and the Queen's Flight, with 3 Andover and 2 Wessex helicopters; Wessex and Puma helicopters for tactical and logistic support in the battlefield area; RAF Regiment UK squadrons, equipped with Bofors L40/70 guns, Tiger-cat and Rapier missiles, and other weapons for airfield defence; and the Tactical Communications Wing. Strike Command has NATO commitments, but is available for overseas reinforcement. Its fifth Group is Military Air Traffic Operations. The training element of RAF Support Command utilizes Bulldog and Chipmunk primary trainers, Jet Provost basic trainers, Gnat and Hunter advanced trainers (being replaced progressively by Hawks), Jetstreams for multi-engine pilot training, twin-jet Dominies for training navigators and other non-pilot aircrew, and Sioux, Gazelle and Whirlwind helicopters.

Squadrons of RAF Germany, which forms part of NATO's 2nd Allied Tactical Air Force under SACEUR, have Harrier V/STOL and Jaguar attack aircraft, Phantom fighters, Buccaneer strike aircraft, Wessex helicopters, Pembroke communications aircraft and Bloodhound and Rapier surface-to-air missiles. Malta has one squadron each of Canberra reconnaissance aircraft (being withdrawn) and Nimrod maritime reconnaissance aircraft. A squadron of Wessex helicopters is based in Hong Kong. New types of aircraft under development for the RAF include the Tornado multirole combat aircraft and an AEW conversion of the Nimrod.

The Royal Air Force, 1939–45. Vol. I, II, III. HMSO, 1953–54
Taylor, J. W. R. *Pictorial History of the R.A.F.* Vols. I, II, III. London, 1968–70
Taylor J. W. R. (ed.), *Jane's All the World's Aircraft.* London. Annual from 1909
Taylor, J. W. R., *Military Aircraft of the World.* London 1975
Thetford, O., *Aircraft of the Royal Air Force since 1918.* London, 1971

INTERNATIONAL RELATIONS

Membership. The UK is a member of UN, the Commonwealth, EEC, OECD, the Council of Europe, NATO and the Colombo Plan.

ECONOMY

Budget. Revenue and expenditure for years ending 31 March, in £ sterling:

Revenue	*Estimated in the Budgets*	*Actual receipts into the Exchequer*	*More (+) or less (−) than estimates*
1974	17,451,000,000	18,050,000,000	+ 599,000,000
1975	23,188,000,000	23,570,000,000	+ 382,000,000
1976	28,110,000,000	29,417,000,000	+1,307,000,000
1977	33,197,000,000	33,797,000,000	+ 600,000,000
1978	37,742,000,000	38,773,000,000	+1,031,000,000

The Budget estimate of ordinary revenue for 1978–79 is £42,746m.

Expenditure	*Budget and supplememtary estimates*	*Actual payments out of the Exchequer*	*More (+) or less (−) than estimates*
1974	18,648,000,000	19,769,000,000	+1,121,000,000
1975	22,203,000,000	26,802,000,000	+4,599,000,000

Expenditure	*Budget and supplementary estimates*	*Actual payments out of the Exchequer*	*More (+) or less (−) than estimates*
1976	30,858,000,000	36,047,000,000	+5,189,000,000
1977	39,915,000,000	39,402,000,000	− 513,000,000
1978	43,489,000,000	43,989,000,000	+ 500,000,000

The Budget estimate of ordinary expenditure for 1978–79 is £51,378m.

The imperial revenue in detail for 1977–78 and the expenditure, are given below, as is the budget estimate for 1978–79 (in £1m.):

Sources of revenue	*Net receipts 1977–78*	*Budget estimate 1978–79*
Inland Revenue:		
Income	17,420	19,310
Surtax	30	15
Corporation tax	3,346	4,170
Petroleum revenue tax	—	170
Capital Gains tax	340	375
Development land tax	7	10
Estate duties	87	50
Capital transfer tax	312	320
Stamp duties	375	440
Total Inland Revenue	21,917	24,860
Customs and Excise:		
Value Added Tax	4,226	4,775
Tobacco	2,465	2,500
Oil	2,056	2,450
Spirits, beer and wine	2,062	2,400
Betting and gaming	320	350
Car tax	286	325
Other revenue duties	10	10
Protective duties	676	765
Agricultural levies	183	175
Total Customs and Excise	12,284	13,750
Motor Vehicle duties	1,072	1,120
National insurance surcharge	1,163	1,475
Total taxation	36,436	41,205
Miscellaneous receipts:		
Broadcasting receiving licences	294	317
Interest and dividends	240	264
Other	1,803	960
Total	38,773	42,746

The following are the branches of expenditure and the issues out of the Exchequer for year ended 31 March 1978 and the estimates for 1978–79 (in £1m.):

Supply Services

	Estimates 1977–78	*Estimates 1978–79*
Defence		
Defence	6,754	6,886
Civil supply:		
Overseas Services	1,065	1,062
Agriculture, Fisheries, Food and Forestry	653	535
Trade, Industry and Employment	2,683	3,039
Roads and Transport	1,261	1,266
Housing	2,489	2,618
Other Environmental Services	234	299

	Estimates 1977–78	Estimates 1978–79
Civil supply—contd.		
Law, Order and Protective Services	1,182	1,249
Education and Libraries, Science and Arts	1,645	1,740
Health and Personal Social Services	6,015	6,163
Social Security	5,227	6,683
Other Public Services	1,032	1,071
Common Services	1,023	1,157
Northern Ireland	884	592
Rate Support Grant, Financial Transactions, etc.	887	7,968
Total Civil Supply	40,043	42,328
Allowing for prices changes	—	2,400
Supplementary provision	—	1,450
Total Supply Services	40,043	46,178
Consolidated Fund Standing Services		
Payment to the National Loans Funds in respect of service of the National Debt	2,220	3,160
Northern Ireland—share of reserved taxes, etc.	689	786
Payments to European Communities	977	1,237
Contingencies fund	43	—
Other Services	17	17
Total	43,989	51,378

In 1971 the Chancellor of the Exchequer announced a single graduated income tax which came into operation on 6 April 1973, replacing the existing income tax and surtax.

The previous system income tax and surtax was constructed in terms of investment income with a complicated pattern of allowances for earned income (the earned income relief for income tax and surtax and the special earnings allowance for surtax).

After deducting earned income relief and personal allowances, a person's total income was charged to income tax at the standard rate (for 1972–73) of 38·75%: in practice, this rate applies primarily to investment income and the effective marginal rate on earned income (up to £4,005) was reduced to 30·14% by the earned income relief of two-ninths.

Surtax was an additional income tax charged where an individual's income from all sources, after deducting admissible charges on income and certain personal allowances and reliefs for earned income, exceeded £3,000 (for 1971–72). The tax was charged on the excess of the income over £2,000, a rising scale of rates being applied to successive slices of the excess. Surtax was assessed quite separately from standard rate income tax. It is not included in the amounts deducted from earnings under PAYE or from dividends or interest.

Rates of Personal Tax from 6 April 1978[1]	%
Income up to £750	25
£750–7,000	34
£7,000–8,000	40
£8,000–9,000	45
£9,000–10,000	50
£10,000–11,500	55
£11,500–13,000	60
£13,000–15,000	65
£15,000–17,500	70
£17,500–23,000	75
Over £23,000	83

[1] The Finance Act was still being debated as THE STATESMAN'S YEAR-BOOK went to press but two amendments have been made on the rates and bonds by end-May.

Rates of Personal Tax from 6 April 1978—contd.	%
Surcharge on investment income (under 65)	
Up to £1,700	—
£1,700–2,250	10
Over £2,250	15
Surcharge on investment income (over 65)	
Up to £2,500	—
£2,500–3,000	10
Over £3,000	15

Under the tax system, the amounts of the personal allowances are adjusted so that they retain their equivalent value in relation to earned income.

Personal Allowances	*1977–78* £	*1978–79* £
Single person / Wife's earned income		985
Married man	1,455	1,535
Children[1]: under 11	196	100
11–16	231	135
over 16	261	165
Dependent relative:		
Single woman claimant	145	145
Others	100	100
Housekeeper	100	100
Relative taking charge of younger brother or sister	100	100
Daughter's services	55	55
Blind person	180	180

[1] Child tax allowances are being replaced by child benefit. Transitional measures are proposed for certain students and children living abroad.

Deductions of tax under PAYE extend over the full range of unified tax rates and not merely the basic rate. Similarly, assessment on business profits and on other income which was directly assessed to tax, such as rents and interest on bank deposits, are made by reference to the full scale of rates, including where appropriate the investment income surcharge.

The standard rate of 34% is the rate at which tax is deducted from payments of interest, etc., and corresponds under the new corporation tax system, to the tax credit on dividends. Where an individual's total income is such that he is liable on this taxed investment income at rates exceeding 34%, or if his investment income is high enough to make him liable to the surcharge, the higher rate or surcharge liability on this taxed investment income will in general be assessed separately after the end of the tax year.

Corporation Tax. Corporation Tax applies, with certain exceptions, to trades or businesses carried on by bodies corporate or by unincorporated societies or other bodies and this tax came into force from April 1966 replacing Profits Tax. The rate of this tax for 1969–71, 45%; but in Oct. 1970 this was reduced to 42·5% for financial year 1969–70 and reduced again to 40% in 1970–71. There are reduced rates of Corporation Tax for small companies.

Capital Gains Tax. Gains resulting from the disposal of capital assets (other than British Government and Government guaranteed securities and certain exempted forms of property such as a private car and personal residences) are taxed under the Finance Act 1965. In 1978–79 exemption was granted for all gains made in a financial year which in total did not exceed £1,000 and a lower rate of 15% on the excess of gains up to £5,000 and a marginal relief for gains between £5,000–9,500.

Value Added Tax. Value Added Tax was introduced from 1 April 1973 at the rate of 10% on the supply of goods (with certain exceptions) and services. At the same time a tax of 10% on the wholesale value of new and imported cars was introduced. The rate was reduced to 8% on 29 July 1974. In the budget of April 1975 the rate was fixed at 25% for certain luxury items but reduced to 12% in April 1976.

Local Taxation. The rateable value on which rates were leviable in England and Wales on 1 April 1976 was £6,809m. In England and Wales, the average amount of the rates collected per £ of rateable value was £0·34 in 1913–14; and estimated to be 60·3p for 1976–77 and 39·7p for 1973–74. In Scotland the estimated average amounts per £ of rateable value of the rates, inclusive of water rates in 1977–78 was £1·96½ and exclusive of water rates £1·82.

Under the Local Government Act 1974, the Government gives general financial assistance to local authorities by means of rate support grants. These grants contain: (i) the needs element which is payable to non-metropolitan counties, metropolitan districts and London Boroughs. Its purpose is to compensate for differences between Local Authorities in their need to spend. The total needs element for England and Wales has been fixed at £3,946m. for 1978–79; (ii) the resources element which is payable to rating authorities. Its purpose is to compensate for differences between authorities in their rateable value per head of population. Total resources grant has been estimated at £1,901m. for 1978–79; (iii) the domestic element has been fixed at £674m. for 1978–79. This will provide relief of 18½p in the £ to domestic ratepayers in England (in 4 inner London areas the relief is higher than this) and 36p to domestic ratepayers in Wales. There is also provision in the Act for grants to be paid for particular purposes. National Parks supplementary grants are payable to county councils with all or part of a national park in their area. Total grants of £3·5m. have been prescribed for 1978–79. Transport supplementary grants totalling £275m. will be paid to county councils and the Greater London Council in 1978–79. These were paid for the first time in 1975–76 and replaced certain grants for specific items of expenditure.

Grants are also payable on revenue expenditure for specific services, including police and housing; and capital expenditure on certain services also attracts capital grant.

In Scotland, from 16 May 1967, under the Local Government (Scotland) Act 1966, rate support grants replaced General grant, Exchequer Equalization Grant and certain specific grants, in particular grants in aid of school milk and school meals, and some highway grants. The totals of the rate support grants and the amounts of the three component parts of the rate support grants for the local authority years 1977–78, as prescribed by the Rate Support Grant (Scotland) 1977 are as follows: £932·9m.; needs element, £705·9m.; resources element, £177·3m.; domestic element, £49·7m. The domestic element is given towards the cost of reducing the rates payable on domestic properties (27p in the £ in 1976–77 and 31p in 1977–78), and payments under Part V of the Local Government Act, 1948, amounted in 1977–78 to £12,074,000.

As in England and Wales, capital and revenue grants are also payable on expenditure for certain specific services.

Local authority loan debt at 31 March 1974 amounted to £19,391m.

The rateable value of the Greater London Council was £1,874,019,928 on 1 April 1977. The outstanding debt of the Greater London Council on 31 March 1977 was £1,435·8m. and the Inner London Education Authority, £173m.

Rates and Rateable Values, 1974–75. HMSO
Rates and Rateable Values in Scotland, 1974–75. HMSO
Estimates, 1977–78 GLC
Analysis of Rateable Values List. GLC, 1977
Report on Rate Support Grant Order 1976. HMSO

Gross National Product:

	1946	*1950*	*1960*	*1970*	*1976*
Expenditure (*£1m.*)					
Consumers' expenditure	7,273	9,400	16,939	31,696	73,656
Central government final consumption	2,282	2,123	4,206	8,964	26,562
Gross domestic fixed capital formation	925	1,700	4,190	9,453	23,427

	1946	1950	1960	1970	1976
Expenditure (£lm.)—contd.					
Value of physical increase in stocks and work in progress	−126	−210	562	444	359
Total domestic expenditure at market prices	10,354	13,013	25,897	50,557	124,004
Exports of goods and services	1,775	3,807	5,152	11,451	34,837
Less Imports of goods and services	−2,083	−3,492	−5,549	−11,101	−36,564
Less Taxes on expenditure	−1,573	−2,065	−3,378	−8,451	−16,660
Subsidies	384	474	493	876	3,463
Gross domestic product at factor cost	8,855	11,737	22,615	43,368	109,080
Factor incomes (£lm.)					
Income from employment	5,758	7,627	15,174	30,415	78,639
Income from self-employment [1]	1,126	1,389	2,008	3,774	10,208
Gross trading profits of companies [1]	1,476	2,126	3,730	5,930	12,445
Gross trading surplus of public corporations [1]	20	196	534	1,447	4,460
Gross trading surplus of other public enterprises [1]	86	139	189	151	120
Rent [2]	429	539	1,086	2,833	7,771
Total domestic income before providing for depreciation and stock appreciation	8,895	12,016	22,863	44,882	114,655
Less Stock appreciation	−125	−650	−122	−1,157	−6,557
Residual error	—	−25	−126	−357	982
Gross domestic product at factor cost	8,770	11,341	22,615	43,368	109,080
Net property income from abroad	85	396	233	556	1,179
Gross national product	8,855	11,737	22,848	43,924	110,259
Less Capital consumption	...	−953	−2,042	−4,437	−13,583
National income	...	10,784	20,806	39,487	96,676

[1] Before providing for depreciation and stock appreciation.
[2] Before providing for depreciation.

National Economic Development Council. The NEDC (Neddy), which first met in 1962, is the national forum for economic consultation between government, management and unions. It includes leading representatives of the government, CBI and TUC and also chairmen of nationalized industries and independent members. It meets usually under the chairmanship of the Chancellor of the Exchequer although the Prime Minister takes the chair from time to time. Discussions at the monthly council meetings are normally based on papers, presented by the participating parties, which deal primarily with questions of medium-term national economic performance and prospects, besides seeking to agree on ways of improving industrial efficiency. Council meetings are held in private to encourage the frank exchange of views between members, and discussions are summarized at a press conference taken by the Director-General of the National Economic Development Committee Office (NEDO) following each meeting. The Economic Development Committees (Little Neddies), like the NEDC, bring together representatives of management and unions and officials from government, who use this neutral meeting place to study the efficiency and prospects of individual industries. There are a number of sector working parties who look at problems of individual industries in greater depth. The National Economic Development Office (NEDO) provides the professional staff for the NEDC, the EDCs and the sector working parties.

Currency. The monetary unit of Great Britain is the pound sterling. A gold standard was adopted in 1816, the sovereign or twenty-shilling piece weighing 7·98805 grammes 0·916$\frac{2}{3}$ fine. Currency notes for £1 and 10*s*. were first issued by the Treasury in 1914, replacing the circulation of sovereigns. The issue of £1 and 10*s*. notes was taken over by the Bank of England in 1928. The issue of 10*s*. notes ceased on the issue of the 50p coin in 1969.

Following the post-war fluctuations in the value of the pound, Great Britain returned to the Gold Standard in 1925 with the pound fixed at the pre-war parity of US$4.8665. But the world financial crisis of 1931 forced the country off the Gold Standard again, and in the following year the Exchange Equalization Account was set up for the purpose of checking undue fluctuations in the exchange value of the pound. With the relative stability of the pound which followed, a 'Sterling Bloc' emerged consisting of most Empire countries and those others who voluntarily pegged their currencies to the pound.

The Bloc was superseded at the outbreak of the Second World War by the 'Sterling Area'. The pound was then fixed at $4.03 and remained at that rate until Sept. 1949, when it was devalued to $2.80. On 18 Nov. 1967 it was further devalued to $2.40. Following the general international currency re-alignment of Dec. 1971, the rate for the pound, in terms of the US$, was fixed at £1 = $2.6057 but in June 1972 the pound was allowed to float.

When the pound was floated in June 1972 measures were also introduced under the Exchange Control Act, 1947 to control payments between the 'Scheduled Territories', comprising the UK (including the Channel Islands and the Isle of Man) and the Irish Republic, and the rest of the Sterling Area as well as the rest of the world. The Scheduled Territories were subsequently increased, in Jan. 1973, by the addition of Gibraltar.

Coinage. The sovereign (£1) weighs 123·27447 grains, or 7·98805 grammes, 0·916$\frac{2}{3}$ (or eleven-twelfths) fine, and consequently it contains 113·00159 grains or 7·32238 grammes of fine gold. On 15 Feb. 1971 (Decimalization Day) a decimal currency system was introduced retaining the pound sterling as the major unit but now divided into 100 new pence instead of 240 old pence. The decimal coins are the 50p (equilateral curve heptagon, 30 mm diameter, 13·5 grammes weight); 10p (28·5 mm, 11·31 grammes); 5p (23·6 mm, 5·65 grammes); 2p (25·9 mm, 7·12 grammes); 1p (20·3 mm, 3·56 grammes) and p (17·1 mm, 1·78 grammes). The Decimal Currency Act, 1967 and the Proclamation of 27 Dec. 1968 required that the 50p, 10p and 5p be made of three-quarters copper and one-quarter nickel (75/25 cupro-nickel) and the 2p, 1p and $\frac{1}{2}$p of mixed metal: copper, tin and zinc (bronze). The Decimal Currency Act, 1969, provided that the coins of the Queen's Maundy Money should continue to be made in silver to a millesimal fineness of 925; and, if issued before Decimalization Day, should be treated as denominated in the same number of new pence in which they were denominated.

By Proclamation dated 28 July 1971, which came into force on 30 Aug. 1971, the crown, double-florin, the florin, the shilling and the sixpence are to be treated as coins of the new currency and as being of the denominations respectively of 25, 20, 10, 5 and 2$\frac{1}{2}$ new pence.

The Coinage Act, 1971, specified that the legal tender limits for coins were: Gold coins, for payment of any amount; coins of cupro-nickel and silver of denominations of more than 10p, for payment of any amount not exceeding £10; coins of cupro-nickel and silver of not more than 10p, for payment of any amount not exceeding £5; coins of bronze, for payment of any amount not exceeding 20p.

The value of money issued in the 12 months up to March 1976 was, cupro-nickel £35·4m. (plus re-issues of £300,000), and bronze £5·5m.

By the end of 1975 the transfer to Llantrisant of all of the functions of the London Mint had been completed.

UK coins produced in 1975–76 totalled 862·4m., as follows, in millions: Sovereigns 2·9, 50p 41·6, 10p 173·6, 5p 72·1, 2p 129·4, 1p 226·8, $\frac{1}{2}$p 216.

It is estimated that the following coins were in circulation in the UK at 31 March 1976, in millions: 50p 287·6, 25p 33·5, 10p 1,733·4, 5p 1,497·6, 2$\frac{1}{2}$p 179·6, 2p 1,375·5, 1p 2,030, $\frac{1}{2}$p 1,946 making a total of 9,082·2m. coins.

Bank-notes. The Bank of England issues notes in denominations of £1, £5, £10 and

£20 for the amount of the fiduciary note issue. Under the provisions of the Currency and Bank Notes Act, 1954, which came into force on 22 Feb. 1954, the amount of the fiduciary note issue was fixed at £1,575m., but this figure might be altered by direction of HM Treasury and after representations made by the Bank of England.

All Bank of England notes are legal tender in England and Wales, and notes of denominations less than £5 are legal tender in Scotland and Northern Ireland. The banks in Scotland and Northern Ireland have certain note-issuing powers. The average circulations of such notes were £363m. (Scotland—4 weeks ended 10 Dec. 1976) and £39m. (Northern Ireland—4 weeks ended 11 Dec. 1977); these notes are widely accepted in their area of origin but are not legal tender in any part of the UK.

The total amount of notes issued at 30 Dec. 1977 was £8,150m., of which £8,142m. were in the hands of other banks and the public and £8m. in the Banking Department of the Bank of England.

Banking. The Bank of England, Threadneedle Street, London, is the Government's banker and the 'banker's bank'. It has the sole right of note issue in England and Wales, manages the National Debt and administers the Exchange Control regulations. The Bank operates under royal charters of 1694 and 1946 and the Bank of England Act, 1946. The capital stock has, since 1 March 1946, been held by the Treasury.

The statutory return is published weekly. End-December figures for the past 5 years are as follows (in £1m.):

	Notes in circulation	*Notes and coin in Banking Department*	*Public deposits (government)*	*Other deposits*[1]
1973	4,989	12	25	2,127
1974	5,780	21	17	1,747
1975	6,341	10	22	1,818
1976	7,291	9	16	2,799
1977	8,302	23	30	2,219

[1] Including Special Deposits.

The fiduciary note issue was £8,325m. at 28 Dec. 1977. All the profits of the note issue are passed on to the National Loans Fund.

Official reserves of gold and convertible currencies, SDR and reserve position in the IMF at 31 Dec. 1977 were US$20,557m.

The value of debit bank clearings (excluding provincial clearings) for 1977, £2,599m.; 1976, £2,205m. Credit clearings for 1976, £27m.; 1977, £32m.

The following statistics relate to the 6 London clearing banks at mid-Dec. 1977. Total deposits (sterling and currency), £32,694m.; reserve assets, £3,067m.; sterling market loans (other than reserve assets), £4,116m.; advances (sterling and currency), £19,277m.; sterling investments, £2,512m.

Total net profits from the operations of clearing bank groups in 1977 amounted to £421m., of which £86m. in gross dividends, £313m. transferred to reserves.

Most commercial banking business in Britain is conducted by clearing banks. Industrial and overseas trading business is handled primarily by the merchant banks, who also deal with such matters as the issue of shares to the public for new companies and act as registrars for public companies.

Trustee Savings Banks. Trustee Savings Banks started in Scotland in 1810. They are managed by Boards of Trustees, under the terms of the Trustee Savings Bank Acts 1969 and 1976. There are 19 banks with a network of 1,655 branches throughout the UK and the Channel Islands. The banks are supervised by the TSB Central Board, a statutory body established by the TSB Act 1976.

On 20 Nov. 1977 the funds of all Trustee Savings Banks totalled £4,517·1m. The balances due being £224·6m. on current accounts, £1,669·5m. on savings accounts and £2,622·9m. on investment accounts. The total number of active accounts exceeded 14m.

All TSB customers are private individuals.

National Savings Bank. Statistics for 1975 and 1976:

	Ordinary accounts		*Investment accounts*	
	1975	*1976*	*1975*	*1976*
Accounts open at 31 Dec.	19,170,531[1]	19,456,881[1]	821,498	842,269
	£1,000	*£1,000*	*£1,000*	*£1,000*
Amounts—				
Received	545,257	544,788	101,699	112,304
Interest credited	57,720	58,838	50,027	55,487
Paid	593,361	594,006	108,119	118,442
Due to depositors at 31 Dec.	1,524,795	1,534,415	615,832	665,181
Average amount due to each depositor in active accounts	£79·26	£78·59	£749·65	£789·75

[1] Excluding accounts with balances of less than £1 which have been inactive for 3 years or more. The average balances of these accounts is £0·15.

The amount due to depositors in Ordinary Accounts on 1 Jan. 1978 was approximately £1,630,983,410 and in Investment Accounts £1,408,452,791.

Bank of England Quarterly Bulletin. Bank of England
Bank of England Annual Report. Bank of England
British Banking and Other Financial Institutions. HMSO, 1977
Central Statistical Office, Financial Statistics. HMSO (monthly)
Report of the Committee on the Working of the Monetary System. HMSO, 1959
Report of the Select Committee on Nationalised Industries—The Bank of England. HMSO, 1970
The Royal Mint. 6th ed. HMSO, 1977
Clapham, Sir J. H., *The Bank of England: A History.* 2 vols. CUP, 1944
Craig, J., *The Mint.* Cambridge, 1953
Horne, H. O., *History of Savings Banks.* London, 1947
Sayers, R. H., *The Bank of England 1891–1944.* CUP, 1976

Weights and Measures. Conversion to the metric system was in progress (1978) which will replace the imperial system at present in force.

ENERGY AND NATURAL RESOURCES

Electricity. The electricity industry was vested in the British Electricity Authority on 1 April 1948. Following the re-organization of the electricity supply industry after the passing of the Electricity Act, 1957, the statutory bodies comprising the electricity service in England and Wales are the Electricity Council, the Central Electricity Generating Board and the 12 Area Electricity Boards.

The Electricity Council has functioned from Jan. 1958 as the central council for the supply industry in England and Wales for consultation on, and formulation of, general policy; its main functions are to advise the Secretary of State for Energy on all matters affecting the supply industry, and to promote and assist the maintenance and development by the Central Electricity Generating Board and the Area Boards (known collectively as Electricity Boards) of an efficient, co-ordinated and economical system of electricity supply. The Council can also perform services for the Boards, and, in addition, has certain specific functions, particularly in matters of finance, research and industrial relations.

The Central Electricity Generating Board is responsible for the generation and bulk supply of electricity to the 12 Area Boards in England and Wales. It therefore plans the provision of new generating and transmission capacity, including the siting and construction of new generating stations, both conventional and nuclear, and is responsible for the operation and maintenance of generating stations and the main transmission system.

Area Electricity Boards. Each of the 12 Area Electricity Boards acquires bulk supplies of electricity from the Generating Board and is responsible for distribution networks and sales of electricity to its Area consumers. Thus distribution and utilization of electricity, and also the contracting and sale of appliances side of the industry, are their responsibilities.

The number of power stations owned by the Generating Board in England and Wales on 31 March 1977 was 137 with a total output capacity of 56,365 mw. Total number of consumers in England and Wales on 31 March 1977 was 19,767,869 (on 31 March 1976, 19,525,920).

Electricity sold in England and Wales in 1976–77 amounted to 191,960m. units. Revenue from sales of electricity in 1976–77 was £3,873m. Coal used for electricity generation in 1975–76 amounted to 67·3m. tonnes (70·3m. tonnes in 1976–77). Total fuel (coal equivalent) used in 1976–77 amounted to 97·4m. tonnes and in 1975–76 to 96·9m. tonnes. Nine nuclear stations of total output capacity 3,862 mw provided 12% of total units supplied in 1976–77. Eight of these are gas-cooled graphite-moderated reactors using natural uranium fuel canned in magnesium alloy (Magnox) and 1 is an advanced gas-cooled reactor (AGR). With 3 AGRs under construction capacity will reach 8,500 mw by 1981.

The number of persons employed by the Generating Board, the Electricity Council and Area Boards at the end of March 1977 was 160,873.

The North of Scotland Hydro-Electric Board, established under the Hydro-Electric Development (Scotland) Act 1943, are the nationalized authority responsible not only for generating and transmitting electricity but also for distributing and selling it to over 500,000 consumers.

The Board's district covers a quarter of the land mass of Great Britain and lies generally north and west of a line joining the firths of Clyde and Tay as well as all the island groups extending to the Outer Hebrides Orkney and Shetland. About 99% of potential consumers have now been provided with supply. On the mainland the Board operates generating stations with a total installed generating capacity of 1,990 mw consisting of 1,050 mw of hydro power and 700 mw of pumped storage supplied by Cruachan and Foyers Schemes, together with 240 mw of oil fired thermal plants at Carolina Port Dundee. Diesel power stations with a total installed capacity of 11 mw supply the principal island groups while a further 1,320 mw of oil gas fired thermal plant is nearing completion at Peterhead.

The main transmission system consists of 4,913 circuit km of 275 kv and 132 kv lines linking the power stations and the bulk supply points serving the distribution networks. The system control centre at Pitlochry co-ordinates the operation of the transmission system and power stations together with the continuous interchange of power with the South of Scotland Electricity Board. The number of staff at the end of the year was 3,796.

The South of Scotland Electricity Board was established in April 1955 by the Electricity Reorganisation (Scotland) Act 1954, replacing in South Scotland 2 Electricity Boards and 2 Divisions of the British Electricity Authority. The area of Scotland served by the Board lies south of a line from the Firth of Clyde to the Firth of Tay and extends to about 8,000 sq. miles, including the industrial belt of Scotland, with a population of 4m. By special arrangement a small part of North-East England is also supplied. The remainder of Scotland is served by the North of Scotland Hydro-Electric Board.

The Board differs from those established in England and Wales in that its responsibilities cover not only the distribution of electricity and retail sale of electrical appliances but also the generation and transmission of bulk power within South Scotland.

At 31 March 1977 the Board operated 19 generating stations (including 2 nuclear and 7 hydro-electric stations) with a total output capacity of 7,183 mw. In 1976–77 the Board sold 17,524m. units to 1·5m. consumers and had a total revenue of £356m. The number of staff employed at the end of the year was 13,700.

Oil. Production 1976, in 1,000 tons (1975 in brackets): Throughput of crude and process oils, 97,788 (93,576); output of refinery fuel, 7,500 (6,936); gases, 1,728 (1,608); naphtha, 4,584 (3,972); motor spirits, 15,228 (13,944); kerosine, 6,624 (6,264); diesel oil, 24,192 (22,328); fuel oil, 32,700 (32,712); lubricating oils, 1,308 (1,140); bitumen, 1,896 (2,100). Total output, 90,288 (86,640).

Gas. The British gas industry, nationalized in 1949, was reorganized as the British Gas Corporation on 1 Jan. 1973. Under the terms of the Gas Act 1972, the Corporation has the general duty 'to develop and maintain an efficient, co-ordinated and economical system of gas supply'. The chairman and members of the Corporation are appointed by the Secretary of State for Energy. British Gas explores for and produces natural gas, manufactures substitute natural gas, transmits, distributes and sells gas, and sells, installs and maintains gas appliances.

Gas Council (Exploration) Ltd and Hydrocarbons Great Britain Ltd, wholly owned subsidiaries of British Gas, have been involved in exploration for oil and gas in the Irish Sea and Celtic Sea and, in partnership with oil companies, in the North Sea and onshore. British Gas is a partner in gasfields in the southern North Sea, the Beryl and Montrose oilfields in the northern North Sea and the Wytch Farm oilfield in Dorset.

In 1976–77, British Gas sold 13,837m. therms of gas, over 97% of which was natural gas. By the end of 1976, all customers in England and Wales were using natural gas, and conversion was completed in Scotland in 1977. There were 13·65m. domestic customers, who used 6,183m. therms; 69,000 industrial customers, who used 6,107m. therms; and 489,000 commercial customers, who used 1,547m. therms.

The turnover of British Gas in 1976–77 was £1,957·5m. and the average capital employed was £2,346m. The surplus for the year was £31·5m. In March 1977, there were 99,926 employees.

Minerals. The number of National Coal Board mines producing coal on 27 March 1977 was 238. Statistics of the coalmining industry (including licensed mines) for recent years are as follows:

	1973–74[1]	*1974–75*[1]	*1975–76*[1]	*1976–77*[1]
Saleable output of coal:				
Total deep-mined (1m. tons)	98·2	116·1	113·6	107·7
Opencast (1m. tons)	8·9	9·1	10·2	11·2
Average weekly number of wage-earners on colliery books:				
All workers (NCB only)	252,000	246,000	247,100	242,000
Underground workers (NCB only)	198,900	193,400	195,500	192,200
Coal exports:				
Total (1m. tons)	2·14	2·06	1·40	1·44

[1] 12-month period ending March.

Total stocks of coal on 27 March 1977 amounted to 27·7m. tons (18·1m. tons distributed, 9·6m. tons undistributed). Trading profit made by the NCB for the year ended 27 March 1977 amounted to £109·8m. Interest payable was £79·6m., of which to the Secretary of State for Energy, £44·6m.

Production of coke (including coke breeze) amounted in 1976–77 to 5·9m. tons.

In 1976–77 inland consumption (1,000 tons) of coal at home is estimated to have been 122,706, some of the principal users being: Power stations, 77,750; coke ovens, 19,273; domestic, 10,393; other conversion industries, 3,124; collieries, 1,074; industry, 9,094.

The UK is the fifth largest steel producing country in the world. Output in recent years was as follows (in 1,000 tons):

	Iron ore	*Pig-iron*	*Crude steel*	*Home consumption*[1]
1971	10,228	15,416	24,174	22,400
1972	9,049	15,316	25,321	22,240
1973	7,105	16,850	26,649	24,190
1974	3,602	13,903	22,426	23,240
1975	4,490	12,131	20,198	21,539

[1] Finished steel (ingot equivalent).

In 1975 imports of iron ore amounted to 16·05m. tonnes. Exports of finished steel products were 2·67m. tonnes in 1975.

Iron Castings. Production of iron castings was 3m. tons in 1975 (3·18m. tons in 1974).

The industry is divided between the 'public sector' and the 'private sector'. The former consists of the British Steel Corporation which was established on 22 March

1967 under the Iron and Steel Act 1967. This Act brought into public ownership the 14 major steel producers who together accounted for over 90% of the UK output of crude steel. These companies, including nearly 200 subsidiaries, of which some 50 were overseas subsidiaries, vested in the Corporation on 28 July 1967. Following the transfer to the Corporation under the Iron and Steel Act 1969, of the assets and undertakings, as distinct from the shares, of the publicly owned companies and the subsequent dissolution of many of the companies, the Corporation is operated as a single business entity with 5 manufacturing divisions. The creation of the Corporation represented a massive merger, resulting in what is now the third largest steel business in the free world and one of the world's largest industrial undertakings. It produces and sells steel and other products with an annual value of £2,360m. and employs some 210,000 people. A substantial part of the British steel industry remains in private ownership and although responsible for only 15% of UK crude steel production, produces about half the UK requirements of engineering steels and much higher proportions of steel in finished form. For some products such as bright bars, wire, open-die forgings and high speed and tool steels, nearly all UK production is in the private sector. Because of the private sector involvement in higher value steels it accounts for over a third of the total turnover of the British steel industry but employs a smaller proportion of the total labour force at about 70,000 people. Private sector companies have been engaged in recent years in a heavy programme of investment, particularly in crude steel production, and a number of new companies, some with overseas ownership, have become established in the UK for this purpose.

The private sector of the steel industry has formed the British Independent Steel Producers Association (BISPA), over 100 members, to protect and represent its interests to the Corporation, the Government and any international body organization, and to ensure that liaison continues between the public and private sectors in areas of mutual interest, such as research, standards, statistics and European affairs.

Production of non-ferrous metals in 1976 (in 1,000 tonnes): Refined copper, 137·3 (151·5 in 1975); refined lead, 119·3 (123·4 in 1975); tin metal, 12·6 (15 in 1975); virgin aluminium, 334·5 (308·3 in 1975); slab zinc, 41·6 (53·4 in 1975).

Agriculture. General distribution of the surface, in acres (1970):

Divisions	*Total land surface*	*Rough grazing land*	*Permanent pasture*	*Arable land*
England	32,030,000	3,116,000	8,059,000	13,167,000
Wales and Monmouth	5,100,000	1,554,000	1,826,000	738,000
Scotland	19,071,000	11,328,000	1,018,000	3,140,000
Isle of Man	141,000	45,000	24,000	54,000

Distribution of the cultivated area in the UK (in hectares):

	1976
Corn crops[1]	3,684,000
Green crops[2]	1,136,000
Hops	6,000
Fruit	68,000
Bare fallow	65,000
Rotation grasses including lucerne	2,153,000
Permanent pasture	5,081,000

[1] Includes wheat, barley, oats, mixed corn and rye, for threshing.
[2] Green crops include beans, potatoes, turnips and swedes, mangolds, sugar-beet, cabbage, etc., for fodder, vegetables, and all other crops.

The number of workers employed in agriculture, forestry and fishing in the UK was, in June 1976, 395,000; 371,000 were solely engaged in agriculture; in 1977 there were also 256,400 farmers, partners and directors (192,200 full-time).

In 1976 there were 525,900 tractors, 59,400 combine harvesters and (1974) 52,700 drying machines in use.

Principal crops in the UK as at June in each year:

	Wheat	*Barley*	*Oats*	*Beans*	*Potatoes*	*Fodder crops*[2]	*Mangold*[1]	*Sugar-beet*
	Acreage (1,000 acres and 1,000 hectares from 1976)							
1972	2,786	5,653	777	130	584	240	20	468
1973	2,831	5,603	695	148	555	243	18	480
1974	3,046	5,471	624	164	532	251	18	482
1975	2,557	5,794	575	138	504	264	17	488
1976	1,231	2,182	235	62	222	103	6	206
	Total product (1,000 tons and 1,000 tonnes from 1976)							
1972	4,686	9,098	1,235	163	6,441	4,899	470	6,118
1973	4,932	8,846	1,084	184	6,501	5,542	499	7,957
1974	5,937	8,939	960	197	6,667	6,118	470	4,013
1975	4,368	8,309	789	226	4,445	5,940	404	4,787
1976	4,470	7,648	764	195	4,789	4,816	360	6,325

[1] Fodder crops. [2] Turnips and swedes for stock-feeding, including fodder beet.

Livestock in the UK as at June in each year (in 1,000):

	1973	*1974*	*1975*	*1976*	*1977*
Cattle	14,445	15,203	14,717	14,013	14,069
Sheep	27,943	28,498	28,270	28,184	28,265
Pigs	8,979	8,544	7,532	7,932	7,947
Poultry	144,079	139,672	136,572	116,673	142,222

Forestries. On 31 March 1977 the UK forest area was 2,057,000 hectares, of which 63,000 were in Northern Ireland. The Forestry Commission was responsible for 1,251,000 hectares, mainly softwood plantations.

Fisheries. Quantity (in 1,000 tons and 1,000 tonnes from 1976) and value (in £1,000) of fish of British taking landed in Great Britain (excluding salmon and sea-trout):

	1972	*1973*	*1974*	*1975*	*1976*
Quantity					
Wet fish	873·3	931·7	893·6	792·0	839·4
Shell fish	53·6	66·3	60·8	63·4	77·8
	926·9	998·0	954·4	855·4	917·2
Value					
Wet fish	98,613	138,495	141,036	136,642	184,950
Shell fish	8,972	11,871	10,881	12,707	21,539
	107,585	150,366	151,917	149,349	206,489

The fishing fleet of England and Wales comprised (1976) 3,822 vessels including 1,477 trawlers and 610 line fishing vessels; the Scottish fleet (1976) 2,616 vessels including 741 trawlers and 1,038 creel fishing vessels.

INDUSTRY AND TRADE

Industry. Statistics of a cross-section of industrial production are as follows (1,000 tonnes):

	1974	*1975*	*1976*
Sulphuric acid	3,855	3,166	3,271
Synthetic resins	2,335	2,044	2,501
Tractors (no.)	119,600	141,098	136,500
Commercial motor vehicles (no. 1,000)	403	380	372
Cotton single yarn	81	77	91
Wool tops (1m. kg)	99	91	104
Woollen yarn (1m. kg)	123	112	108
Man-made fibres (rayon, nylon, etc.)	628	563	618
Newsprint	382	315	326
Other paper and board	4,245	3,343	3,856

	1974	*1975*	*1976*
Fertilizers, nitrogen, phosphate and potash (1,000 tons)	1,639	1,756	1,625
Cement	17,781	16,891	15,780
Fabricated aluminium	555	469	523

Engineering. In 1976 the number (in 1,000) of passenger cars produced amounted to 1,333 (1975: 1,267); aircraft production was 341 (1975: 339); computers, value £627·9m.

Electrical Goods. Production (in £1m.) for 1976 (1975 in brackets): Radio and electronic components, 779·2 (640·3); broadcasting receiving and sound reproducing equipment, 418·5 (388·5); gramophone records and tape recordings, 112·5 (115·4); television sets, 2·1 (2·12); domestic electrical appliances, 513 (513·2).

Textile Manufacturers. Production for 1976 (1975 in brackets): Woven cloth, cotton (1m. metres), 375 (405); man-made fibres (1m. metres), 385·8 (398·8); woven woollen and mixture fabrics (1m. sq. metres), deliveries, 143·1 (151·4).

Construction. Total value (in £1m.) of constructional work by all agencies in 1976 was 12,527 (11,421 in 1975), including new housing, 3,588. Value of industrial buildings for private developers completed in 1976 was £1,211m. New work (other than housing) for public authorities was valued at £1,358m.

Census of Production. Reports for 1963. 130 parts. HMSO, 1968
Chester, Sir N., *The Nationalisation of British Industry, 1945–51.* HMSO, 1976
Kelf-Cohen, R., *British Nationalization: 1945–1973.* New York, 1973
Smith, Wilfred, *An Economic Geography of Great Britain.* 2nd ed. London, 1953
Stamp, L. D., *The Land of Britain: Its Use and Misuse.* 3rd ed. London, 1962
Statistical Summary of the Mineral Industry. HMSO, annual
Worswick, G. D. N., and Ady, P. H. (ed.), *The British Economy, 1945–50.* OUP, 1952.—*The British Economy in the Nineteen-Fifties.* OUP, 1962

Labour. The distribution of total manpower in Great Britain was in June 1976 (in 1,000): Total working population, 25,487 (15,846 males, 9,641 females). Total employed in armed forces and women's services, 336. Total engaged in civil employment, 22,048, including agriculture, 360; mining and quarrying, 346; metal manufacture, 469; national and local government service, 1,581; transport and communications, 1,453; construction, 1,269; distributive trades, 2,669; insurance, banking, business, professional and scientific services, 4,646.

The average monthly numbers (in 1,000) of registered unemployed in Great Britain were: 1971, 758·4 (males, 639·8; females, 118·6); 1972, 844·1 (males, 705·1; females, 139); 1973, 598 (males, 499; females, 99); 1974, 600 (males 501; females, 99); 1975, 936 (males, 747; females, 188).

Trade Unions. In Dec. 1977 there were 115 unions affiliated to the Trade Union Congress with a total membership of 11,515,920 (including (1976) 3,033,591 women). The unions affiliated to the TUC during 1977 ranged in size from the Transport and General Workers' Union, with 1,929,834 members, to the Cloth Pressers' Society with 70 members. Non-manual workers accounted for nearly a third of the total TUC membership.

The TUC's executive body, the General Council, is elected at the annual Congress. It is composed of 41 members elected from 18 industrial groupings of unions (railways, mining and quarrying, etc.), to ensure that the Council is broadly representative of the whole trade union movement. Two members are elected to represent women workers. The General Secretary is elected by the Congress but is not subject to annual re-election.

The TUC General Council appoints committees, which draw upon the services of specialist departments in preparing policies on economic, education, international, employment, industrial organization, production and social security questions.

The TUC is affiliated to the International Confederation of Free Trade Unions and the European Trade Union Confederation, provides a service of education for members of its affiliated unions, has sponsored an institute for the investigation of occupational health problems and provides members to serve, with representatives of employers, on joint committees advising the Government on issues of national importance (*e.g.*, National Economic Development Council and the Royal Commission on Income and Wealth) and on the managing boards of such bodies as the Health and Safety Commission; Advisory, Conciliation and Arbitration Service; and Manpower Services Commission.

The following table is a statistical summary relating to trade disputes for recent years:

	No. of stoppages	*No. of workers involved*	*Working days lost through stoppages*
1972	2,497	1,726,000	23,909,000
1973	2,854	1,513,000	7,173,000
1974	2,922	1,622,000	14,845,000
1975	2,282	789,000	6,012,000
1976	2,016	670,000	3,509,000

Lovell, J., and Robert, B. C., *A Short History of the T.U.C.* London, 1968
Pelling, H., *A History of British Trade Unionism.* 2nd ed. London, 1972

Commerce. Value of the imports and exports of merchandise (excluding bullion and specie and foreign merchandise transhipped under bond) of the UK for 6 recent years (in £1,000):

	Total imports	*Total exports*		*Total imports*	*Total exports*
1972	11,155,418	9,745,682	1975	24,028,143	19,762,403
1973	15,854,443	12,455,110	1976	31,212,619	25,777,537
1974	23,116,718	16,494,315	1977	36,493,152	32,951,476

The value of goods imported is generally taken to be that at the port and time of entry, including all incidental expenses (cost, insurance and freight) up to the landing on the quay. For goods consigned for sale, the market value in this country is required and recorded in the returns. For exports, the value at the port of shipment (including the charges of delivering the goods on board) is taken. Imports are entered as from the country whence the goods were consigned to the UK, which may, or may not, be the country whence the goods were last shipped. Exports are credited to the country of ultimate destination as declared by the exporters.

For details of imports and exports for 1976 and 1977, *see* pp. 1313–14.

Trade according to countries for 1976 and 1977 (in £1,000):

Countries	*Imports of merchandise from* 1976[1]	1977[1]	*Exports of merchandise to* 1976[1]	1977[1]
Foreign countries				
Europe and Overseas Possessions—				
Albania	40	61	127	222
Austria	232,436	268,630	212,352	251,923
Belgium and Luxembourg	1,300,229	1,682,511	1,401,243	1,837,119
Bulgaria	11,210	11,863	23,048	24,961
Czechoslovakia	70,286	86,179	60,080	65,183
Denmark and Faroe Islands	713,027	821,448	656,917	800,602
Finland	562,462	593,675	288,960	345,957
France	2,091,308	2,660,123	1,710,262	2,147,613
Germany (Demo. Rep.)	60,229	95,446	44,811	54,440
Germany (Fed. Rep.)	2,757,025	3,574,241	1,834,438	2,501,120
Greece	64,606	95,563	149,207	220,393
Hungary	30,771	43,203	49,515	61,894
Iceland	31,659	44,880	26,215	39,276
Italy	1,106,165	1,532,155	826,403	978,368
Netherlands	2,427,921	2,491,986	1,500,350	2,138,789
Netherlands Antilles	49,675	26,075	14,945	71,096
Norway	622,816	846,669	473,539	761,851
Poland	154,150	174,265	189,473	200,409
Portugal, Azores and Madeira	199,124	229,889	223,317	299,321
Romania	49,514	52,448	49,173	80,477
Spain	360,354	435,176	368,483	464,829
Canary Islands	54,200	52,601	39,504	45,367

[1] Provisional figures.

Countries	Imports of merchandise from 1976[1]	1977[1]	Exports of merchandise to 1976[1]	1977[1]
Europe and Overseas Possessions—contd.				
Sweden	1,187,887	1,259,859	1,045,046	1,196,773
Switzerland and Liechtenstein	962,877	1,319,281	1,000,360	1,421,382
Turkey	60,365	56,733	210,897	210,181
USSR	666,946	780,572	240,425	347,432
EEC	11,396,472	14,035,234	9,174,128	12,040,645
EFTA	3,799,261	4,562,884	3,269,790	4,316,483
Yugoslavia	33,502	40,487	128,456	175,011
Africa—				
Algeria	80,228	49,762	101,834	98,655
Angola	23,160	5,506	17,020	10,501
Burundi	993	1,817	844	1,645
Cameroon	8,991	12,237	8,089	20,702
Egypt	65,254	88,065	171,851	190,516
Ethiopia	14,913	4,689	12,584	19,111
Ivory Coast	45,105	79,541	17,848	25,173
Liberia	10,035	14,052	23,893	21,539
Libya	166,608	141,472	134,647	173,333
Mali	1,797	2,124	1,453	1,554
Mauritania	14,948	11,825	6,176	4,364
Morocco	56,784	46,268	60,498	67,971
Mozambique	5,464	41,650	7,306	18,163
Rwanda	3,924	6,115	844	1,085
Senegal	22,738	31,369	9,385	9,521
South Africa, Republic of	612,992	879,724	645,363	581,063
S.W. Africa	33,323	26,122	2,914	1,348
Sudan	14,209	13,164	91,975	86,834
Tunisia	3,116	12,641	22,969	28,371
Zaïre	38,393	59,246	16,851	18,234
Asia—				
Afghánistán	18,508	21,865	7,577	11,427
Bahrain	30,146	13,673	89,628	113,777
Burma	2,711	3,652	7,044	12,314
China	86,995	104,388	68,216	62,316
Indonesia	22,321	28,740	80,616	86,683
Iran	1,049,263	789,819	510,901	654,661
Iraq	279,530	331,714	149,853	166,940
Israel	127,796	159,025	249,398	273,925
Japan	796,259	1,065,355	359,126	469,308
Jordan	892	1,996	55,737	48,974
Korea (South)	135,723	178,693	63,125	75,855
Kuwait	587,067	541,262	144,343	243,341
Lebanon	6,065	8,365	10,052	48,591
Pakistan	40,421	48,790	92,723	121,051
Philippines	33,485	44,696	86,180	92,721
Qatar	248,813	100,761	86,696	116,611
Saudi Arabia	978,472	1,095,116	400,399	576,904
Syria	7,673	5,351	64,398	57,203
Thailand	25,461	34,904	59,142	82,448
America—				
Argentina	90,113	120,040	63,356	130,271
Bolivia	24,510	37,333	9,995	12,049
Brazil	239,491	300,576	174,286	245,405
Chile	80,673	76,890	36,295	39,432
Colombia	25,818	31,641	28,854	41,685
Costa Rica	496	1,378	8,614	10,647
Cuba	25,602	9,732	42,925	27,455
Dominican Republic	4,063	2,025	9,537	10,501
Ecuador	2,540	4,978	23,260	59,522
El Salvador	1,603	3,138	12,478	11,770
Guatemala	2,133	3,600	14,022	16,676

[1] Provisional figures.

Countries	*Imports of merchandise from* 1976[1]	1977[1]	*Exports of merchandise to* 1976[1]	1977[1]
America—contd.				
Haiti	882	1,063	2,697	3,394
Honduras (not British)	483	1,107	4,580	6,965
Mexico	23,432	40,312	119,889	79,006
Nicaragua	1,174	1,393	8,335	8,841
Panama	1,068	732	11,747	16,928
Paraguay	7,897	8,183	5,478	8,318
Peru	41,873	34,634	35,761	34,585
Puerto Rico	14,704	36,369	14,686	17,994
Uruguay	13,200	16,956	10,525	19,242
USA	3,044,259	3,662,505	2,448,751	3,087,279
Venezuela	117,636	67,017	128,794	175,035
Total (including those not specified above)	26,035,323	30,662,279	20,659,593	26,540,630
Commonwealth countries:				
In Europe—				
Cyprus	63,315	79,749	51,009	82,906
Gibraltar	2,171	2,650	13,252	18,149
Malta	25,528	34,041	49,187	64,339
In Africa				
West Africa:				
Gambia	6,761	8,503	10,865	12,362
Ghana	82,230	126,632	79,563	100,072
Nigeria, Federation of	316,967	219,286	774,179	1,068,707
Sierra Leone	35,531	40,053	17,935	19,669
South Africa:				
Botswana	24,935	39,843	1,133	3,017
Lesotho	331	188	755	807
Malawi	35,496	51,040	16,594	18,359
Rhodesia	211	208	1,205	1,057
Swaziland	30,188	13,340	710	559
Zambia	73,052	93,254	66,181	80,175
East Africa:				
Kenya	61,473	155,067	97,713	118,464
Mauritius	99,995	102,906	27,766	34,403
Uganda	32,448	33,402	11,171	21,227
Tanzania	34,101	45,460	43,932	72,060
Seychelles	177	160	5,734	6,021
St Helena	109	156	1,632	2,387
In Asia—				
Bangladesh	23,646	25,001	28,635	30,627
Hong Kong	439,605	454,056	204,430	271,194
India	355,074	383,462	206,918	278,098
Malaysia	157,150	223,558	118,175	147,450
Singapore	94,358	102,611	168,235	201,162
Sri Lanka	35,518	50,793	17,913	27,872
In Oceania—				
Australia	394,300	343,054	687,756	761,009
Fiji Islands	25,145	45,948	13,482	12,584
Nauru	2	4	367	484
New Zealand	320,824	383,163	251,199	286,891
Papua New Guinea	16,453	30,577	7,079	10,038
Western Samoa	201	776	449	609
In America—				
Bahamas	15,094	13,960	7,801	21,995
Barbados	1,639	5,239	19,141	24,713
Belize	9,156	13,300	7,346	8,129

[1] Provisional figures.

Countries	*Imports of merchandise from* 1976[1]	1977[1]	*Exports of merchandise to* 1976[1]	1977[1]
In America—contd.				
Bermuda	3,065	5,780	14,396	19,686
Canada	1,159,651	1,222,871	628,470	712,662
Falkland Islands	2,127	2,385	1,269	1,502
Guyana	46,414	46,447	37,977	33,441
Jamaica	63,193	78,229	50,605	39,650
Leeward Islands	3,286	4,547	19,004	14,152
Trinidad and Tobago	48,255	29,500	73,834	97,308
Windward Islands	25,454	24,338	15,921	15,635
Total, Commonwealth countries (including those not specified above)	4,168,862	4,548,313	3,871,369	4,770,535
Irish Republic	1,008,434	1,282,560	1,246,575	1,640,311
Grand Total	31,212,619	36,493,152	25,777,537	32,951,476

[1] Provisional figures.

Imports and exports for 1976 and 1977 (Great Britain and Northern Ireland) (in £1,000):

Import values c.i.f. *Export values f.o.b.*	*Total imports* 1976[1]	1977[1]	*Domestic exports* 1976[1]	1977[1]
0. *Food and Live Animals*				
Live animals (excluding zoo animals, dogs and cats)	83,974	98,456	62,416	109,303
Meat and meat preparations	838,586	974,314	182,247	250,504
Dairy products and eggs	504,601	460,105	115,410	98,127
Fish and fish preparations	191,021	210,292	81,266	107,325
Cereals and cereal preparations	747,906	820,714	134,489	210,684
Fruit and vegetables	948,354	1,114,151	84,263	110,384
Sugar, sugar preparations, honey	429,598	428,007	129,128	111,873
Coffee, tea, cocoa, spices	493,308	919,591	142,369	278,517
Feeding stuff for animals	172,363	209,883	45,180	60,410
Miscellaneous food preparations	94,371	147,231	59,163	80,997
Total of Section 0	4,504,082	5,382,744	1,035,931	1,418,125
1. *Beverages and Tobacco*				
Beverages	251,704	306,111	524,444	629,202
Tobacco and tobacco manufactures	236,909	256,247	133,781	169,696
Total of Section 1	488,613	562,358	658,225	798,898
2. *Crude Materials, Inedible, except Fuels*				
Hides, skins and furskins, undressed	171,623	210,573	157,800	160,789
Oil seeds, oil nuts and oil kernels	207,102	299,452	3,597	5,018
Crude rubber (including synthetic and reclaimed)	140,328	166,575	61,545	76,589
Wood and cork	585,103	632,947	8,806	12,256
Pulp and waste paper	464,070	439,715	9,245	8,483
Textile fibres and their waste	438,261	467,303	294,159	308,185
Crude fertilizers and crude minerals (excluding fuels)	195,221	208,083	107,068	128,757
Metalliferous ores and metal scrap	684,670	690,984	98,898	137,072
Crude animal and vegetable materials, not elsewhere specified	51,880	157,820	13,443	38,877
Total of Section 2	2,938,258	3,273,453	754,561	876,026

[1] Provisional figures.

Import values c.i.f. *Export values f.o.b.*	*Total imports* *1976*[1]	*1977*[1]	*Domestic exports* *1976*[1]	*1977*[1]
3. *Mineral Fuels, Lubricants and Related Materials*				
Coal, coke and briquettes	90,264	88,325	71,773	79,932
Petroleum and petroleum products	5,518,181	5,063,588	1,161,632	1,953,180
Gas, natural and manufactured; electric energy	43,435	76,558	21,378	33,552
Total of Section 3	5,651,880	5,228,471	1,254,783	2,066,664
4. *Animal and Vegetable Oils and Fats*	200,735	282,126	36,190	57,076
5. *Chemicals*				
Chemical elements and compounds	899,013	1,120,457	1,056,035	1,370,734
Dyeing, tanning and colouring materials	104,805	125,606	281,500	352,007
Medicinal and pharmaceutical products	139,350	173,707	452,522	554,620
Essential oils and perfume; toilet and cleansing preparations	97,088	125,988	235,867	326,081
Fertilizers, manufactured	60,760	69,810	51,134	60,578
Plastic materials	463,006	557,479	531,204	642,127
Total of Section 5	1,764,022	2,173,047	2,608,262	3,306,147
6. *Manufactured Goods Classified Chiefly by Material*				
Leather and dressed furs	107,576	134,122	148,457	176,793
Rubber	130,639	201,957	299,709	328,701
Wood and cork (excluding furniture)	290,339	311,123	53,436	72,685
Paper, paperboard	827,366	974,881	278,386	354,583
Textile yarn, fabrics	910,044	1,118,827	926,656	1,147,119
Non-metallic mineral manufactures	1,385,470	2,114,253	1,647,167	2,535,133
Iron and steel	965,650	985,568	824,635	1,016,401
Non-ferrous metals	1,039,063	1,147,667	722,181	838,250
Manufactures of metal, not elsewhere specified	415,296	499,506	800,300	1,012,046
Total of Section 6	6,071,442	7,487,904	5,700,927	7,481,711
7. *Machinery and Transport Equipment*				
Machinery, other than electric	3,253,970	3,966,194	5,058,039	6,078,520
Electrical machinery, apparatus	1,383,029	1,768,278	2,003,937	2,507,692
Transport equipment	1,751,895	2,592,594	3,064,186	3,748,812
Total of Section 7	6,388,894	8,327,066	10,126,162	12,335,024
8. *Miscellaneous Manufactured Articles*				
Sanitary, plumbing, heating and lighting fixtures	39,453	48,291	60,978	90,467
Furniture	122,525	139,450	142,309	211,039
Travel goods, handbags and similar articles	37,824	45,001	9,572	13,120
Clothing	683,802	766,615	412,334	598,031
Footwear	165,480	214,253	68,239	102,381
Scientific instruments; watches and clocks	567,048	728,863	609,983	777,198
Miscellaneous manufactured articles, not elsewhere specified	690,280	1,085,947	864,661	1,320,671
Total of Section 8	2,506,412	3,028,419	2,168,076	3,112,907

[1] Provisional figures.

Import values c.i.f. *Export values f.o.b.*	*Total imports* 1976[1]	1977[1]	*Domestic exports* 1976[1]	1977[1]
9. *Commodities and Transactions not Classified According to Kind*				
Post parcels	97,088	121,091	284,021	497,928
Continental shelf warehouse transactions	197,617	200,160	91,775	106,109
Total of Section 9	294,705	321,251	375,796	604,037
Total of all classes (including items not specified here)	31,212,619	36,493,152	25,777,537	32,951,476

[1] Provisional figures.

Tourism. There were 10,089,000 overseas visitors in 1976. Foreign exchange from tourism was £2,156m. including £528m. from fares to British air and shipping lines.

COMMUNICATIONS

Roads. Central Government responsibility for highways in England rests with the Secretary of State for the Environment. His responsibilities for roads are administered by the Department of the Environment through the Highways Directorate General at Headquarters, 8 Regional Controllers (Roads and Transportation) and 6 Road Construction Units. For Welsh and Scottish roads central Government responsibility rests with the Secretaries of State for Wales and Scotland respectively.

The Secretary of State is wholly responsible for trunk roads. Under the local government system introduced in 1974, the responsible authorities for principal roads are the County Councils. District Councils may claim maintenance powers for urban roads which are neither trunk roads nor classified roads. In London responsibility is shared between the Greater London Council and the London Boroughs.

The Secretary of State has powers to provide roads designed for limited classes of motor traffic, and to confirm schemes for the provision of such special roads by local authorities. The former have the status of trunk roads; the latter principal roads. They are generally referred to as motorways. There are now about 1,200 miles of motorways in England that are open to traffic and some 500 miles are under construction or in preparation.

The Road Construction Units are responsible for the design and supervision of construction of major trunk roads (including motorways). Regional Controllers (Roads and Transportation) are responsible for the smaller trunk road schemes (generally those costing under £1·5m.) and for the maintenance of all trunk roads (including motorways). Local authorities act as the Secretary of State's agents for construction and maintenance. The work being carried out by them or by contractors acting on their behalf. The Secretary of State bears the full cost.

On 1 April 1975 specific grants to local authorities for the construction or improvement of principal roads were abolished. All aid to local authorities for transport expenditure is now given through the rate support grant and through a transport supplementary grant is paid to County Councils whose expenditure for the year, as accepted by the Secretary of State, exceeds the level determined by a formula prescribed in the Rate Support Grant Order.

The public highways in Great Britain at 1 April 1976 (Scotland, 16 May 1976), excluding mileages of unsurfaced roads (green lanes), had a total length of 207,177 miles (England, 157,809 miles; Wales, 19,134; Scotland, 30,233). There were 8,381 miles of all-purpose trunk roads, 1,382 of motorways (both trunk and principal), 20,649 were principal roads and 176,824 were other roads. There were about 6,000 miles of unsurfaced roads (green lanes) in England and 2,000 in Wales.

Motor vehicles for which licences were current under the Vehicles (Excise) Act, 1971, numbered, at 30 Sept. 1976, 17·8m., including 14·07m. cars, 1·22m. mopeds, scooters and motor cycles, 113,000 public transport vehicles (including taxis) and 1·77m. goods vehicles. New vehicle registrations in 1977 numbered 1·86m.

Road casualties in Great Britain numbered in 1976, 339,673 (51,529 under 15) including 6,570 killed; in 1975, 324,950 (52,433 under 15) including 6,366 killed.

Railways. The nationalized railway system, known as 'British Rail', together with British Transport Hotels Ltd, British Rail Engineering Ltd, British Rail Hovercraft Ltd and Transportation Systems and Market Research Ltd (Transmark), the Shipping and International Services Division and the British Rail Property Board are owned and managed by a public authority, the British Railways Board. The Board is required to direct its affairs in such a way as to ensure that standards of public service and safety are maintained while at the same time keeping within specified financial constraints.

The role of the British Railways Board is to determine policies and objectives, establish the organization to carry them out, monitor performance and take major decisions.

The management of the railways, which forms the bulk of the Board's activity, is the responsibility of the Chief Executive (Railways). In this role he establishes plans and budgets for the achievement of objectives set by the Board, monitors and achieves results against those plans and budgets and directs the organization and deployment of manpower resources. He is assisted by Executive Board Members with functional responsibility for Engineering and Research, Finance and Planning, Marketing, Operating and Productivity, and Personnel.

He also directs the General Managers of the 5 operating Regions of the railways. The responsibilities of these managers are for the day-to-day operation of the passenger and freight railway systems throughout the country.

The management of each subsidiary activity is the responsibility of each Managing Director, directed by a Subsidiary Board.

The Transport Act, 1968, reduced the railways commencing debt from £1,562m. to £300m. The Act also enabled the Secretary of State for the Environment to make grants for the maintenance of unremunerative passenger services and, additionally, to make grants, until 1973, towards the cost of surplus track and signalling equipment. The Railways Act, 1974, introduced a new system of financial support in accordance with EEC Regulations 1191/69 and 1192/69. On 1 Jan. 1975, the Board's capital debt was reduced to £250m. and their borrowing limit, including commencing debt, was increased to £600m. extendable to £900m. The power to make grants for unremunerative passenger services is withdrawn. The Secretary of State is authorized to impose general obligations on the Board in respect of passenger services and is empowered to compensate the Board for providing adequate transport services. Aggregate compensation is limited to £900m., extendable to £1,500m. subject to Parliamentary approval.

In 1977 the total freight traffic amounted to 170m. tonnes, comprising coal and coke 97m. tonnes, iron and steel 25m. tonnes and other freight, excluding carryings for Freightliners Ltd and National Carriers Ltd, for which tonnage figures are not available, 50m. tonnes. Passenger journeys amounted to 702m. Rolling stock (standard gauge) at the end of 1977 included 3,686 locomotives (including 76 high speed power units), 17,044 passenger-carrying vehicles (including Pullman carriages), 4,838 luggage and parcel vans and 166,935 freight vehicles. At the end of the year 11,168 (standard gauge) route miles were open to traffic.

The London Transport Executive, in Jan. 1977, had 237 route miles of railway open for traffic and also operated over 17 miles of track owned by British Rail. Number of vehicles owned: Railways, 4,519 (including 3,118 electric motor vehicles); buses 6,946. Total number of miles run in passenger service (1976) was 395m. miles. The number of passengers carried in 1976 was: Railways, 546m.; buses, 1,423m. Average takings per passenger journey (1976) were: Railways, 22·3p; buses, 8·9p.

Under the provisions of the Transport Act, 1947, the 4 main-line railways, together with their associated lines, docks, steamships and hotels, the London Passenger Transport Board and the major canal undertakings, passed on 1 Jan. 1948 into the ownership of the British Transport Commission, as the instrument of the State.

The Transport Act, 1962, dissolved the Commission, and created in its stead separate Boards for British Railways, London Transport, British Transport Docks and

British Waterways. The new Boards assumed their responsibilities as from 1 Jan. 1963. Other main provisions of the Act reconstructed the finances of the Boards and gave them a greater measure of commercial freedom.

The Transport Act, 1968, set up 3 new state-owned transport organizations. The National Freight Corporation inherited the road haulage subsidiaries of the THC, British Rail sundries division, now National Carriers Ltd, and 51% of BR's freightliner company. The National Bus Company acquired the assets of 65 companies, mainly concerned with road passenger transport in England and Wales, including those companies operated by the THC. The Scottish Transport Group acquired the assets of the THC's road passenger transport companies in Scotland, and also certain ships, ferry services and British Railways domestic Scottish shipping services. These new organizations assumed their responsibilities on 1 Jan. 1969.

On 1 Jan. 1970, the responsibility for the London Transport Board was transferred to the Greater London Council and renamed London Transport Executive. The LTB Country Bus services and Green Line services were transferred at the same time to the National Bus Company and renamed London Country Buses.

Gross receipts in 1976 for these Boards were: British Railways Board, from 1975 the Railways Act 1974 introduced, *inter alia*, new arrangements for the financial support of the railway passenger system and provided for the reconstruction of the finances of the Board, £1,287m.; London Transport Executive, £369m.; British Transport Docks Board, £77m.; National Bus Company, £358·4m.; National Freight Corporation, £304m., and British Waterways Board, £8·5m.

Aviation. On 23 Jan. 1973 plans were announced to incorporate the 2 state-owned airlines (BOAC and BEA) as the British Airways divisions of a larger group to be known as the British Airways Group.

The British Overseas Airways Corporation (BOAC) was set up under the British Overseas Airways Act 1939 and British European Airways (BEA) was established under the Civil Aviation Act 1946. In addition to the nationalized corporation, there are about 20 independent air transport operators.

BOAC is engaged on long-haul operations. Its scheduled services link Britain with Europe, the Middle East, the Far East, Australasia, Africa and North and South America. It co-operates closely with airlines of several other Commonwealth countries and has financial interests in companies operating local and regional services adjacent to its main routes as well. BEA operates a network of short-haul services to over 100 places in Britain, Europe, North Africa and the Middle East. BEA also has a financial interest in several associated companies both in Britain and abroad, most of which collaborate in providing local services.

The 2 State Corporations had a statutory monopoly up to 1961, although there was an arrangement by which independent operators could provide services as private companies associated with the Corporations. The Civil Aviation (Licensing) Act 1960 established a new independent licensing authority, the Air Transport Licensing Board, and placed the independent airlines on an equal footing with the 2 Corporations for licensing purposes. There has since been a significant expansion by independent operators who have carried increasing numbers of passengers and volumes of freight on a network of scheduled and non-scheduled domestic and international services, in particular British Caledonian Airways has emerged as the principal independent scheduled airline.

Following the Civil Aviation Act 1971, the Civil Aviation Authority was established as an independent public body responsible for the economic and safety regulation of British civil aviation. It took over the responsibilities of the former Air Transport Licensing Board and Air Registration Board, and also runs the National Air Traffic Services.

In addition to the public transport operators there are a number of companies engaged in miscellaneous aviation activities such as crop-spraying, aerial survey and photography, and flying instruction.

The operating and traffic statistics of the UK airlines on scheduled services during the calendar year 1976 (and 1975) are as follows: Aircraft km flown, 301m.

(286,687,000); revenue passengers carried, 17·5m. (16·34m.); cargo (freight and mail) carried 247,686 (246,251) tonnes.

Traffic between the UK airports and places abroad in 1975 (and 1976) included 405,357 (424,345) air transport aircraft movements, and 30,276,272 (32,545,655) passengers were carried.

There were 4,953 civil aircraft registered in the UK at 31 Dec. 1976.

Shipping. The UK flag merchant fleet in July 1977 totalled 50·7m. DWT (dry cargo, 21·5m. DWT; tankers, 29·1m. DWT) representing 8% of the world fleet. The total number of UK flag ships was 1,939. The number of UK seafarers was about 79,000.

Capital investment in new tonnage and facilities by British shipping companies 1966–76 was over £4,100m. In 1976 capital expenditure was £393m., equal to nearly 10% of the investment by the whole of British manufacturing industry. The average age of UK owned and registered tonnage in mid-1976 was 6·3 years and about half was under 5 years old.

Total gross earnings by UK owned and registered ships in 1976 amounted to nearly £2,500m. The net direct foreign exchange earnings were £1,041m. and, in addition, there were gross import savings of £478m.

On 31 Jan. 1978, 38 UK flag ships (3·3m. DWT) were laid up out of a world total of 685 ships (45·6m. DWT).

British Shipping Statistics 1975. London, 1976
Committee of Inquiry into Shipping. Cmnd 4337. HMSO, 1970
Bird, J., *The Major Seaports of the United Kingdom.* London, 1963
Rees, H., *British Ports and Shipping.* London, 1958
Sturmey, S. G., *British Shipping and World Competition.* London, 1962
Thornton, R. H., *British Shipping*, 2nd ed. CUP, 1958

Inland Waterways. There are approximately 2,500 miles of navigable canals and locked river navigations in Great Britain. Of these, the British Waterways Board are responsible for some 300 miles of commercial waterways (maintained for freight traffic) and some 1,100 miles of cruising waterways (maintained for pleasure cruising, fishing and amenity). The Board is also responsible for a further 600 miles of canals, some of which are no longer navigable and whose future is being considered in conjunction with local authorities; a number of these lengths have been restored for cruising or as local amenities. The Board's gross receipts for the year 1976 were £9·9m. The total traffic on their waterways was 4·6m. tonnes.

The most important of the river navigations and canals under other authorities include the rivers Thames, Great Ouse, Nene and Yorkshire Ouse, the Norfolk Broads and the Manchester Ship Canal.

Manchester, one of the leading ports in the UK, was opened to maritime traffic in 1894 by the construction of the Manchester Ship Canal, which is 35¼ miles in length and owned and operated by the Manchester Ship Canal Company. The entrance lock is 80 ft (24·38 metres) wide and the maximum width of other locks within the canal is 65 ft (19·81 metres). Ships up to 28 ft 10 in. (8·78 metres) fresh-water draught can navigate to Ince Oil Berth; between Ince Oil Berth and Manchester the maximum draught is 26 ft 6 in. (8·07 metres) in fresh water.

The Port of Manchester includes the Queen Elizabeth II Oil Dock at Eastham (separate entrance lock 100 ft wide), the oil docks at Stanlow and a considerable number of public and private wharves and installations along the canal, as well as the terminal docks at Manchester. Total sea-borne and barge traffic in 1977 amounted to 14,505,973 tonnes; operating revenue, £23·34m.; operating surplus, £1,587,000. The total issued capital at 31 Dec. 1977 was £20,243,000.

British Waterways, Recreation and Amenity. (Cmd 3401.) HMSO, 1967
Edwards, L. A., *Inland Waterways of Great Britain and Northern Ireland.* 5th ed. St Ives, 1972
Hadfield, C., *British Canals.* Rev. ed. Newton Abbot, 1975
McKnight, H., *The Shell Book of Inland Waterways.* Newton Abbot, 1975
Nicholson's Guides to the Waterways. 5 vols. NE, NW, SE, SW, Midlands. British Waterways Board, 1971–75
The Last Ten Years. British Waterways Board, 1973

Posts and Telecommunications. Number of post offices at 31 March 1977 was 23,124; number of letter boxes including those at post offices, over 100,000; staff employed, 428,414 (including 21,043 sub-postmasters employed on an agency basis).

	1972–73 (*1m.*)	*1973–74* (*1m.*)	*1974–75* (*1m.*)	*1975–76* (*1m.*)	*1976–77* (*1m.*)
Correspondence (incl. registered items) posted	10,790	11,010	10,878	9,903	9,458
Parcels handled	194	195	201	170	152
Telegrams handled	27	27	25	21	19
Telex: Inland (units)	369	363	378	393	407
Overseas (minutes)	167	201	224	238	267

Weight (kg) of air-mail traffic (all services) dispatched abroad:

	1974	*1975*	*1976*	*1977*
Letters, printed paper, datapost, etc.	11,130,400	11,657,000	13,843,000	15,149,000
Parcels	5,401,200	6,166,000	6,434,000	7,312,000

In 1976–77 the total value of money orders, including COD trade charge orders, was £43m.; postal orders, £526m.

On 31 March 1977 the total number of telegraph acceptance offices was 9,209 and the London Telecommunications Region had 452 local exchanges, 64 auto-manual and automatic trunk exchanges, 11,149 call offices and 5,205,300 telephone stations. In the provinces there were 5,807 local exchanges, 325 auto-manual and automatic trunk exchanges, 66,376 call offices and 16,870,506 telephone stations. The accrued revenue derived in 1976–77 from private telephone wires amounted to £77m.

The approximate deficits of income over expenditure (after charging interest on capital) are as follows for years ended 31 March (in £1,000 sterling): 1973, 1974 and 1975 was £64·1m.; £128·1m. and £306·6m. respectively. However, compensation claimed by the Post Office under the Statutory Corporations (Financial Provisions) Act 1974 amounting to £133·3m. resulted in a net profit of £5·2m. for the year ended 31 March 1974; compensation claimed in respect of price restraint for year ended 31 March 1975 amounted to £307m. resulting in a net profit of £0·4m. 1976 and 1977 resulted in a surplus of income over expenditure of £147·5m. and £298·5m. respectively.

Broadcasting. Radio and television services in the UK are controlled by the British Broadcasting Corporation and (in the case of the commercial networks) by the Independent Broadcasting Authority. These are public corporations, the BBC is constituted by Royal Charter until 31 July 1979 and the Independent Broadcasting Authority by the IBA Act 1973 as extended by the IBA (No. 2) Act 1974 until 31 July 1979. Both organizations are independent of the Government in the conduct of their services. The BBC broadcasts 4 domestic sound radio services on long- and medium-wave and on VHF. There are local radio stations (BBC or IBA) in 30 centres broadcasting on medium-wave and VHF. The BBC commenced regular TV programmes in 1936 and broadcasts 2 programmes in colour. IBA broadcasts 1 commercial programme in colour.

The number of broadcast receiving licences in force at 30 Nov. 1977 was 18·09m., including 10·6m. for colour.

Cinemas. In 1974 there were 1,535 cinemas with a seating capacity of 973,000.

Newspapers. In 1978 there were 9 national dailies with a circulation of over 13m.

JUSTICE, RELIGION, EDUCATION AND WELFARE

Justice. *England and Wales.* The legal system of England and Wales, divided into civil and criminal courts has at the head of the superior courts, as the ultimate court of appeal, the House of Lords, which hears each year a number of appeals in civil matters, including a certain number from Scotland and Northern Ireland, as well as some appeals in criminal cases. In order that civil cases may go from the Court of Appeal to the House of Lords, it is necessary to obtain the leave of either the Court of Appeal or the House itself, although in certain cases an appeal may lie direct to the House of Lords from the decision of the High Court. An appeal can be brought from a decision of the Court of Appeal or the Divisional Court of the Queen's Bench Division of the High Court in a criminal case provided that the Court is satisfied that a point of law 'of general public importance' is involved, and either the Court or the House of Lords is of the opinion that it is desirable in the public interest that a further appeal should be brought. As a judicial body, the House of Lords consists of the Lord Chancellor, the Lords of Appeal in Ordinary, commonly called Law Lords, and such other members of the House as hold or have held high judicial office. The final court of appeal for certain of the Commonwealth countries is the Judicial Committee of the Privy Council which, in addition to Privy Counsellors who are or have held high judicial office in the UK, includes others who are or have been Chief Justices or Judges of the Superior Courts of Commonwealth countries.

Civil Law. The main courts of original civil jurisdiction are the county courts for less important cases, and the High Court for the more important ones.

There are about 313 county courts located throughout the country, grouped in districts, and each presided over by a circuit judge, sitting as a county court judge. They have a general jurisdiction (subject to certain rights of transfer to the High Court given to defendants) to determine all actions founded on contract or tort involving sums of not more than £2,000. Certain matters, such as actions of libel and slander, are entirely reserved for the High Court. In addition, certain designated county courts have jurisdiction in matrimonial proceedings. Divorce proceedings must now commence in these courts and, subject to being transferred to the High Court upon becoming defended, are determined in the County Court.

The High Court has both appellate and original jurisdiction, covering virtually all civil causes not determined in the county court. The judges of the High Court are attached to one of its 3 divisions: Chancery; Queen's Bench; and Family; each with its separate field of jurisdiction. There are 72 such judges, called puisne judges. For the hearing of cases at first instance, the High Court judges sit singly. Appellate jurisdiction is usually exercised by Divisional Courts consisting of 3 (sometimes 2) judges, though in certain circumstances a judge sitting alone may hear the appeal.

The Restrictive Practices Court was set up in 1956 under the Restrictive Trade Practices Act, and is responsible for deciding whether a restrictive trade agreement is in the public interest. It is presided over by a judge, but laymen sit on the bench also.

The Court of Appeal (Civil Division) hears appeals in civil actions from both the High Court and County Courts. It includes the Lord Chancellor, who is President of the Chancery Division, and the heads of the other 2 divisions (the Lord Chief Justice and the President) of the High Court, but effectively the head of the Civil Division is the Master of the Rolls, aided by 16 Lords Justices of Appeal sitting in 5 divisions.

Civil proceedings are instituted by the aggrieved person, but, as they are a private matter, they are frequently settled by the parties to a dispute through their lawyers before the matter actually comes to court. In some cases, at the instance of either party, a jury may sit to decide questions of fact and award of damages.

Criminal Law. At the base of the system of criminal courts are the lay justices who try the great proportion of minor offenders (over 98% of all criminal cases) as well as undertaking a small proportion of civil work. Magistrates' courts are comprised of 3 lay justices who are unpaid and need not possess legal qualifications (though they undergo a course of training), though they do have the assistance on points of law of a professional clerk to justices. In central London and large cities there exist stipendiary magistrates, paid for their duties. These are professional lawyers and usually sit alone. Exercising summary jurisdiction in petty sessions, justices have power to pass sentences of imprisonment up to, in general, 6 months, and to impose fines up to, in general, £400. One of their functions is to examine persons charged with indictable offences and to determine whether they should be committed for trial at the Crown Court. Justices deal each year with almost 2m. cases, including thefts, assaults, road traffic infringements, drug abuse, breaches of licensing laws, etc. There are some 23,500 justices who are appointed to the Commission of the Peace by the Lord Chancellor; he is assisted by advisory committees. Women are eligible to be appointed justices, and the number on the Commission of the Peace is about 8,850.

Specially qualified justices sit in juvenile courts to deal with cases involving persons under 17 years of age charged with criminal offences (other than homicide and other grave offences) or brought before the court as being in need of care or control. These courts normally sit with 3 justices, including 1 woman, and are accommodated separately from other courts.

Above the magistrates' courts is the Crown Court. This was set up by the Courts Act 1971 to replace quarter sessions and assizes. Unlike quarter sessions and assizes, which were individual courts, the Crown Court is a single court which is capable of sitting anywhere in England and Wales. It has power to deal with all trials on indictment and has inherited the jurisdiction of quarter sessions to hear appeals, proceedings on committal of persons for sentence, and certain original proceedings on civil matters under individual statutes.

The jurisdiction of the Crown Court is exercisable by a High Court judge, a Circuit judge or a Recorder (who is a part-time judge) sitting alone, or, in specified circumstances, with justices of the peace. The Lord Chief Justice has given directions as to the types of case to be allocated to High Court judges (the more serious cases) and to Circuit judges or Recorders respectively.

Appeals from magistrates' courts go either to a Divisional Court of the High Court (when a point of law alone is involved) or to the Crown Court which is empowered to deal with appeals against conviction and/or sentence. Appeals from the Crown Court lie to the Court of Appeal (Criminal Division). Appeals on questions of law go by right, and appeals on other matters by leave. The Lord Chief Justice and the other judges of the High Court may sit with the Master of the Rolls and the Lords Justices to constitute this court.

There remains as a last resort the invocation of the royal prerogative exercised on the advice of the Home Secretary. In 1965 the death penalty was abolished for murder.

All contested criminal trials, except those which come before the magistrates' courts, are tried by a judge and a jury consisting of 12 members. The defence may object, without showing cause, to up to 3 jurors. The prosecution may ask that any number may 'stand by' until the jury panel is exhausted, and only then need to show cause. When these peremptory challenges have been exhausted further challenges may only be made for cause and this rarely happens. The jury decides whether the accused is guilty or not. The judge is responsible for summing up on the facts and explaining the law; he sentences convicted offenders. If, after at least 2 hours of deliberation, a jury is unable to reach a unanimous verdict it may, provided that in a full jury of 12 at least 10 of its members are agreed, bring in a majority verdict. The failure of a jury to agree on a unanimous verdict or to bring in a majority verdict involves the retrial of the case before a new jury.

The Employment Appeal Tribunal. The Employment Appeal Tribunal which is a superior Court of Record with the like powers, rights, privileges and authority of the High Court, was set up in 1976 to hear appeals on questions of law against decisions of industrial tribunals and on questions of fact and law against decisions of the Certification Officer. The appeals are heard by a High Court Judge sitting with 2 members (in exceptional cases 4) appointed for their special knowledge or experience of industrial relations either on the employer or the trade union side, with always an equal number on each side. Industrial tribunals are responsible for deciding questions under a wide variety of jurisdictions, *e.g.*, Redundancy Payments Act 1965, Trade Union and Labour Relations Act 1974, Sex Discrimination Act 1975, Employment Protection Act 1975. The great bulk of their work is concerned with the problems which can arise between employees and their employers. The

Certification Officer is responsible for deciding questions under the Trade Union Act 1913, the Trade Union (Amalgamations, etc.) Act 1964, the Trade Union and Labour Relations Act 1974 and the Employment Protection Act 1975.

Military Courts. Offences by persons subject to service law against the system of military law created under the powers of the Army Act, Air Force Act or Naval Discipline Act are dealt with either summarily or by courts-martial. Petitions may be made to the Defence Council. Subsequent appeals lie to a Courts-Martial Appeals Court, and from that court an appeal may lie to the House of Lords.

The Personnel of the Law. All judicial officers except the Lord Chancellor (who is a member of the Cabinet) are independent of Parliament and the Executive. They are all appointed by the Crown on the advice of the Prime Minister or the Lord Chancellor and hold office until retiring age. The legal profession is divided; barristers, who advise on legal problems and conduct cases in court, usually act for the public only through solicitors, who deal directly with the legal business brought to them by the public. Most judicial appointments are made from barristers of long standing, though solicitors are eligible for appointment as Recorders, who may, after 3 years, be appointed Circuit Judges.

Aid is provided for persons who are unable through lack of means to pay for legal assistance in civil or criminal proceedings. Under the provisions of the Legal Aid and Advice Act, 1947, a person of poor or moderate means may be provided with the services of solicitor and counsel in most civil proceedings, and proceedings before the Lands Tribunal either without charge or, if his means allow, on payment of a contribution. In 1972–73 there were over 260,000 applications for legal aid under the Act. The cost of legal aid in civil cases is met from (*a*) contributions from convicted persons; (*b*) costs recovered from opposing parties; (*c*) a grant from the Exchequer. The cost of such legal aid to the State in the year 1972–73, including the cost of legal aid for criminal cases in magistrates' courts, was £17,953,068. Under Part IV of the Criminal Justice Act, 1967, which came into operation on 1 Oct. 1968, a court dealing with criminal proceedings has discretion to order legal aid to be given if it appears that the defendant (or appellant) requires financial assistance in meeting the costs of his legal representation, and that it is in the interests of justice for him to be granted legal aid. (Legal aid must be granted where a person is committed for trial on a charge of murder or where the prosecutor appeals or applies to appeal to the criminal division of the Court of Appeal or the Courts-Martial Appeal Court to the House of Lords.) The costs of legal aid in criminal proceedings are paid by the central government, but courts have the power to require legally aided persons to contribute towards the cost of legal aid given to them. The cost of legal aid in criminal proceedings in 1975–76 was £32,801,956, £18,430,543 of this was for legal aid in the higher courts which is paid for out of the Home Office vote, and £14,371,413 for legal aid in the magistrates' courts which is paid from the legal aid fund.

Under the Parliamentary Commissioner Act, passed 22 March 1967, M.P.s may refer to the Parliamentary Commissioner complaints received from the public regarding improper or inequitable administration in most spheres of central government affairs. Generally, other available remedies (such as legal action) must be exhausted before a complaint can be investigated. If a complaint is found to require a remedy the Parliamentary Commissioner makes a report to Parliament.

Commissions for Local Administration in England and Wales were set up under the Local Government Act 1974. The Commissioners carry out similar functions in relation to local government bodies to those the Parliamentary Commissioner discharges with regard to maladministration in central government.

Police. The authorized strength of the police force in England and Wales in Dec. 1977 was 118,279: the actual strength was 108,201 men and 7,866 women. In addition there were 19,252 special constables (including 2,329 women). Total police net expenditure (estimated) in England and Wales for 1976–77 was £972·2m.

Blom-Cooper, L. and Drewry, G., *Final Appeal: A Study of the House of Lords in its Judicial Capacity.* OUP, 1972

Critchley, T. A., *A History of Police in England and Wales.* Rev. ed. London, 1978

Scotland. The High Court of Justiciary is the supreme criminal court in Scotland and has jurisdiction in all cases of crime committed in any part of Scotland, unless expressly excluded by statute. It consists of the Lord Justice-General, the Lord Justice-Clerk and 18 other judges, who are the same judges as of the Court of Session, the Scottish supreme civil court. The Court, which is presided over by the Lord Justice-General, whom failing, the Lord Justice-Clerk, exercises an appellate jurisdiction as well as one of first instance, and sits as business requires in Edinburgh as a Court of Appeal (the *quorum* being 3 judges). The decisions of the Court in either case are not subject to review by the House of Lords. One judge sitting with a jury of 15 persons can, and usually does, try cases, but 2 or more (with a jury) may do so in important or complex cases. It has a privative jurisdiction over cases of treason, murder, rape, deforcement of messengers and breach of duty by magistrates. It also, in practice, is the only court which tries cases of incest, sodomy and other serious or aggravated crimes against person or property and generally those cases in which a sentence greater than imprisonment for 2 years may be imposed either under statute or common law. Moreover, the Court has inherent power to try and to punish all acts which are plainly criminal though previously unknown and not dealt with by any statute.

The appellate jurisdiction of the High Court of Justiciary extends to all cases tried on indictment, whether in the High Court or the Sheriff Court, and persons so convicted may appeal to the Court on any ground involving a question of law alone, or apply for leave to appeal, on any question of fact or of mixed law and fact, or on any other sufficient ground, and also against sentence unless it is one fixed by law. It is also a court of review from courts of summary criminal jurisdiction, and on the final determination of any summary prosecution either party may appeal to the Court by way of stated case on questions of law, procedure, etc., but not on questions of fact. A further or complementary form of process of review which can be resorted to by convicted persons in these courts is by Bill of Suspension (and Liberation), but it is of strictly limited application. A prosecutor in these courts may also bring under review a decision in law, prior to final judgment of the case, by way of Bill of Advocation, but this process is infrequently resorted to. The Court also hears appeals under the Courts-Martial (Appeals) Act 1951.

The Sheriff Court has an inherent universal criminal jurisdiction (as well as an extensive civil one) limited in general to crimes and offences committed within a sheriffdom (a specifically defined part of a local authority region), which has, however, been curtailed by statute or practice under which the High Court of Justiciary has exclusive jurisdiction in relation to the crimes above-mentioned. This Court is presided over by a Sheriff-Principal or a Sheriff, and when trying cases on indictment sits with a jury of 15 persons. His power of awarding punishment involving imprisonment is restricted to 2 years in the maximum, but he may under certain statutory powers remit the prisoner to the High Court for sentence. The Sheriff also exercises a wide summary criminal jurisdiction and when doing so sits without a jury; and he has concurrent jurisdiction with every other court within his sheriffdom in regard to all offences competent for trial in summary courts. The great majority of offences which come before the courts are of a minor nature and, as such, are disposed of in the Sheriff Courts. In cases indicated for trial in the High Court of Justiciary the Pleading, or First Diet, is always held in the Sheriff Court and, in these cases, the Sheriff may dispose of any objection of a preliminary nature, whether to the citation or relevancy or otherwise, or may refrain from doing so. In either case the Sheriff's decision can be reviewed by the High Court at the second, or trial, Diet.

District Courts in each local authority district have jurisdiction in minor offences occurring within the district. These courts are presided over by lay magistrates, known as justices, and have limited powers of fine and imprisonment.

The Court of Session, presided over by the Lord President (the Lord Justice-General in criminal cases), and divided into an Inner House comprising 2 divisions of 4 judges each, and an Outer House comprising 13 single judges, exercises the highest civil jurisdiction in Scotland, with the House of Lords as a court of appeal.

Police. The police forces in Scotland at the end of 1976 had an authorized establishment of 13,163; the strength was 11,577 men and 740 women. Whole-time 'additional' policemen numbered 138, and there were 3,424 part-time special constables. The total police net expenditure in Scotland was £76·3m. for 1975–76.

CIVIL JUDICIAL STATISTICS

ENGLAND AND WALES	1974	1975	1976
Appellate Courts	*Appeals*	*Appeals*	*Appeals*
Judicial Committee of the Privy Council	26	54	39
House of Lords	34	64	50
Court of Appeal	1,176	1,302	1,302
High Court of Justice (appeals and special cases from inferior courts)	784	901	988
Courts of First Instance			
High Court of Justice:			
Chancery Division[1]	17,256	15,917	15,677
Queen's Bench Division	233,474	243,456	214,063
Family Division	2,380	2,573	2,584
County courts: Divorce	131,662	140,091	146,415
Other	1,776,321	1,841,112	1,684,660
Other courts[2]	5,008	5,342	5,846
SCOTLAND			
House of Lords (Appeals from Court of Sessions)	8	6	3
Court of Session—General Department	18,248	19,228	21,047
Sheriff's Ordinary Court	59,950	66,470	68,614
Sheriff's Small Debt Court[3]	113,317	107,434	95,287
Summary Cause[4]	...	...	36,941

[1] Including contentious probate.

[2] From Jan. 1972 certain 'other' courts, namely, the Palatine Chancery Court of Lancaster and Durham were merged with the High Court; the Mayor's and City of London Court became a County Court; Borough Courts of Record were abolished. The figure 5,846 for 1976 represents: Court of Protection, 3,685; Restrictive Practices Court, 3; Transport Tribunal, 23; Patents Appeal Tribunal, 71; Lands Tribunal, 1,637; Employment Appeal Tribunal, 427.

[3] Small Debt Court record 31 Aug. 1976.

[4] Summary cause replaced Small Debt Court 1 Sept. 1976.

CRIMINAL STATISTICS

ENGLAND AND WALES	1974	1975	1976
Indictable offences—			
Number of persons proceeded against	406,277	439,191	456,693
Number of persons found guilty at Magistrates' Courts	328,128	349,894	359,267
Number of persons found guilty at the Crown Court	46,790	52,587	56,236
Non-indictable offences—			
Number of persons proceeded against	1,645,403	1,671,698	1,753,246
Number of persons found guilty	1,558,731	1,586,198	1,657,141
Juveniles (included above)[1]—			
Number of persons found guilty of indictable offences	92,879	91,126	90,667
Number of persons found guilty of non-indictable offences	35,290	35,696	38,949
Number of persons found guilty of indictable or non-indictable offences at Magistrates' Courts	126,911	125,443	128,251
Number of persons found guilty at Crown Court	1,258	1,379	1,365
SCOTLAND			
Crimes—			
Number of persons proceeded against in all courts	35,823	38,584	40,600
Number of persons proceeded against summarily	33,032	35,481	37,351
Miscellaneous offences—			
Proceedings taken	205,323	198,663	183,646
Children[2]—			
Proceeded against in court	2,900	2,262	2,094
Police warnings and referred to reporter	36,093	...	...

[1] Young persons under 17 years of age. [2] Young persons under 16 years of age.

Average population in prisons, borstals and detention centres (1976) in England and Wales was 41,443 (convicted 37,625; untried 3,303, and 515 non-criminal prisoners); in Scotland (1976), 4,884 (sentenced, 4,138; remanded, 746).

Religion. The Anglican Communion has originated from the Church of England and parallels in its fellowship of autonomous churches the evolution of British influence beyond the seas from colonies to dominions and independent nations. There is no terrestrial head of the Anglican Communion; the Archbishop of Canterbury presides as *primus inter pares* at the decennial meetings of the bishops of the Anglican Communion at the Lambeth Conference.

The Anglican churches, in addition to the Church of England, comprise the churches, councils, and provinces in communion with the see of Canterbury which are situated in Wales; Ireland; Scotland; United States of America; Canada; Australia; New Zealand; West Indies; Brazil; South Africa; Central Africa; West and East Africa; Jerusalem and the Middle East; South East Asia; Burma, Sri Lanka, Japan, South America, China.

In addition to the dioceses included within the Provinces of Canterbury and York, the Church of England includes a number of dioceses overseas over which the Archbishop of Canterbury exercises metropolitan jurisdiction, while Church of England chaplaincies in North and Central Europe are under the jurisdiction of the Bishop of London.

England and Wales. The established Church of England, which baptizes some two-thirds of the children born in England (*i.e.*, excluding Wales but including the Isle of Man and the Channel Islands), is Protestant Episcopal. Civil disabilities on account of religion do not attach to any class of British subject. Under the Welsh Church Acts, 1914 and 1919, the Church in Wales and Monmouthshire was disestablished as from 1 April 1920, and Wales was formed into a separate Province.

The Queen is, under God, the supreme governor of the Church of England, with the right, regulated by statute, to nominate to the vacant archbishoprics and bishoprics. The Queen, on the advice of the First Lord of the Treasury, also appoints to such deaneries, prebendaries and canonries as are in the gift of the Crown, while a large number of livings and also some canonries are in the gift of the Lord Chancellor.

There are 2 archbishops (at the head of the 2 Provinces of Canterbury and York), 41 diocesan bishops and 88 suffragan and assistant bishops in England. Each archbishop has also his own particular diocese, wherein he exercises episcopal, as in his Province he exercises metropolitan, jurisdiction. In the Church are 36 deans (including Westminster, Windsor and other Peculiars), 14 provosts of cathedrals and 110 archdeacons. There is an Assembly, called 'the General Synod', in England, consisting of a House of Bishops, a House of Clergy and a House of Laity, which has power to frame legislation regarding Church matters. The first two Houses consist of the members of the Convocations of Canterbury and York, each of which consists of the diocesan bishops and elected representatives of the suffragan bishops, 6 for Canterbury province and 3 for York (forming an Upper House), deans, provosts, and archdeacons, and a certain number of proctors elected as the representatives of the inferior clergy, together with, in the case of Canterbury Convocation, representatives of the Universities of Oxford, Cambridge and London and in the case of York a representative for the Universities of Durham and Newcastle; the chaplains in the Forces (forming the Lower House). They are elected by their fellow suffragans. The House of Laity is elected by the lay members of the Deanery Synods. Parochial affairs are managed by annual parochial church meetings and parochial church councils. Every Measure passed by the General Synod must be submitted to the Ecclesiastical Committee, consisting of 15 members of the House of Lords nominated by the Lord Chancellor and 15 members of the House of Commons nominated by the Speaker. This committee reports on each Measure to Parliament, and the Measure receives the Royal Assent and becomes law if each House of Parliament resolves that the Measure be presented to the Queen.

At 31 Dec. 1973 there were 14,113 ecclesiastical parishes, inclusive of the Isle of

Man and the Channel Islands. These parishes do not, in many cases, coincide with civil parishes. Owing to the pastoral re-organization, although most parishes have their own churches, not every parish nowadays can have its own incumbent or minister; so that in some areas one or more parishes may be served by a clergyman, who must be in priest's orders, and in these cases he holds the parishes in plurality. In 1976 there were 10,513 parochial incumbencies in which 1,805 benefices were under suspension of presentation. There were 8,271 beneficed clergymen, 1,019 other clergymen of incumbent status and 2,175 assistant curates working in the parishes.

Private persons possess the right of presentation to over 2,000 benefices; the patronage of the others belongs mainly to the Queen, the bishops and cathedrals, the Lord Chancellor, and the universities of Oxford and Cambridge. In addition to the 11,465 parochial incumbents and assistant curates, there were (1976) 357 dignitaries, 229 non-parochial clergymen working within the diocesan framework and approximately 2,000 non-parochial clergymen outside the framework.

The membership of the Church at 30 June 1976 was estimated to be 27,180,000 baptized members of whom 9·1m. were confirmed.

Of the 40,977 churches and chapels registered for the solemnization of marriages at 1 Jan. 1977, 16,699 belonged to the Established Church and the Church in Wales and 24,278 to other religious denominations. Of the 358,567 marriages celebrated in 1976 (380,620 in 1975), 33% were in the Established Church and the Church in Wales, 16·6% in churches or chapels of other denominations and 50% were civil marriages in a Register Office.

Roman Catholics in England and Wales were 4,190,550 in 1977. There were 5 archdioceses and 20 dioceses, 7,210 clergy and 2,590 parish churches and 1,116 other churches open to the public. Convents, 1,266.

The Unitarians have about 330 places of worship, the Catholic Apostolic Church over 80, the New Jerusalem Church about 75. The Salvation Army, a religious body with a quasi-military organization, carries on both spiritual and social work at home and abroad, and had, in British Territory, 1973, 2,100 officers, 1,035 corps, 31 Red Shield Centres and 51 Red Shield Mobile Units. There were also 38 eventide homes, 13 maternity homes, 2 maternity hospitals, 46 hostels for men, 14 hostels for women and girls, and 9 approved and training schools.

The following is a summary of statistics of certain churches in England and Wales, Channel Islands and Isle of Man:

Denomination	*Full members*	*Ministers in charge*	*Local and lay preachers*
Methodist	557,249	3,865	16,962
Independent Methodist	5,367	189	—
Wesleyan Reform Union	4,523	22	237
United Reform	187,408	1,837	—
Baptist	187,144	1,572	—
Calvinistic Methodist Church of Wales	99,288	290	—
Moravian	3,500	40	—
Society of Friends	20,242	—	—

There are about 410,000 Jews in the UK with about 240 synagogues.

Scotland. The Church of Scotland (established in 1560 at the Reformation and re-established in 1688 as part of the Revolution Settlement) is Presbyterian, the ministers all being of equal rank. There is in each parish a kirk session, consisting of the minister and of several laymen called elders. There are presbyteries (formed by groups of parishes), meeting frequently throughout the year, and these are again grouped in synods, which meet half-yearly and can be appealed to against the decisions of the presbyteries. The supreme court is the General Assembly, which now consists of some 1,300 members, half clerical and half lay, chosen by the different presbyteries. It meets annually in May (under the presidency of a Moderator appointed by the Assembly, the Sovereign being present or represented by a Lord High Commissioner, appointed by the Queen on the nomination of the Government of the day), and sits for 7 days. Any matters not decided during this period may be left to a Commission which sits at stated intervals until the meeting of the next General Assembly.

On 2 Oct. 1929 the Church of Scotland and the United Free Church of Scotland were reunited under the name of The Church of Scotland, and the two bodies met in General Assembly in Edinburgh as one. The united Church had, in Scotland, on 31 Dec. 1976, 1,964 congregations, 1,041,772 members; 23,817 teachers and 152,288 scholars in attendance in Sunday schools. The Church courts are the General Assembly, 12 synods, 47 presbyteries in Scotland, 1 in England and 2 on the Continent. Income in 1976 was £17,644,424. There are divinity faculties in 4 Scottish universities of Edinburgh, Glasgow, Aberdeen and St Andrews, with 60 professors and lecturers who are mostly ministers of the Church of Scotland.

The Episcopal Church of Scotland is a province of the Anglican Church and one of the historic Scottish churches. It consists of 7 dioceses. As at 31 Dec. 1977 it had 302 churches and missions, 225 clergy and 76,298 members, of whom 43,760 were communicants.

There are in Scotland some small outstanding Presbyterian bodies and also Baptists, Congregationalists, Methodists and Unitarians.

The Roman Catholic Church which celebrated the centenary of the restoration of the hierarchy in 1978, had in Scotland (1977) 1 cardinal, 1 archbishop and 9 bishops, 1,187 clergy, about 70 parishes, and 813,200 adherents.

The proportion of marriages in Scotland according to the rites of the various Churches in 1976 was: Church of Scotland, 41·8%; Roman Catholic, 15%; Episcopal, 1·5%; United Free, 0·5%; others, 3·8%; civil, 37·6%.

Bossy, J., *The English Catholic Community, 1570–1850*. London, 1975
Davies, H., *The English Free Churches*. 2nd ed. London, 1963
Mayfield, G., *The Church of England: Its Members and its Business*. 2nd ed. OUP, 1963
Moorman, J. R. H., *A History of the Church in England*. London, 1973

Education. *The Publicly Maintained System of Education in England and Wales:* Compulsory schooling begins at the age of 5 and the minimum leaving age for all pupils is 16.[1] No tuition fees are payable in any publicly maintained school (but it is open to parents, if they choose, to pay for their children to attend other schools). The post-school stage, which is voluntary, includes universities, polytechnics and other further education colleges, and colleges of education (for the training of teachers), as well as adult education and the youth service. Financial assistance is generally available to students on higher education courses in the university and non-university sectors and to many students on other courses in further education.

Nursery Education. Children under 5 may be provided for in nursery schools or in nursery classes attached to primary schools. In the public sector no fees are payable and there are 648 such nursery schools accommodating about 52,260 children while some 3,900 nursery classes accommodate about 157,600 children. Over 75% of all these children attend on a part-time basis. There are also nearly 269,000 children under the compulsory school age attending maintained primary schools.

Between 1968 and 1974 a continuing programme to help socially deprived urban areas has included provision for 24,000 additional full-time places in nursery schools and classes in these areas.

The Secretary of State for Education and Science and the Secretary of State for Wales (of the then administration) announced in Dec. 1972 in a White Paper (Cmnd. 5174) that they intended to expand nursery education at a rate which would enable provision to be made by 1981–82 for all the children whose parents want them to have it (as estimated by the Central Advisory Councils in 1967 in the Plowden and Gittins Reports). The aim was that by Jan. 1982 places would exist in nursery schools and classes for 90% of 4-year olds and 50% of 3-year olds. Half-day attendance would be the general rule. Since the programme began priority has been given to the provision of places in areas of greatest social need. The need for

[1] As a result of the Education (School Leaving Dates) Act 1976, one of the two former leaving dates was amended. This means that pupils whose dates of birth fall between 1 Feb. and 31 Aug. (inclusive) cease to be of compulsory school age on the Friday before the last Monday in May; but in 1977 only this date has had to be varied slightly because of HM The Queen's Silver Jubilee celebrations. Some of these pupils will leave school before their 16th birthdays. Pupils whose dates of birth fall between 1 Sept. and 31 Jan. (inclusive) remain of compulsory school age until the end of the Easter term following their 16th birthdays.

restraint in public expenditure has meant that the rate of expansion of nursery education provision has been slower than was hoped in 1972.

Nonetheless, since the start of the special building programme for nursery education in 1974, capital allocations of £50·2m. have been made to local education authorities. Allocations in each of these years have been weighted in favour of authorities proposing to carry out projects in areas of acute multiple deprivation.

To further assist the provision of nursery education in these areas authorities have been invited, for the first time since the present programme began, to make application for grant aid under the urban and inner cities programme.

Primary Schools. Children normally begin primary school when they are 5. Nearly half of the 22,679 primary schools take the complete age-range from 5 upwards. About 4,600 take infants only, up to about 7 years; the rest take juniors only, from 7 or 8 on. The great majority of primary schools take both boys and girls. Over 13,000 of these schools had between 100 and 300 pupils each; of the remainder, over half had less than 100 pupils.

A little under 2,000 of these primary schools are in Wales. In those primary schools (and some secondary schools) which are in the predominantly Welsh-speaking areas, the main language of instruction is Welsh. There are also 'Welsh', or, more accurately, bilingual schools in mainly English-speaking parts of Wales. Generally children transfer from primary to secondary schools at 11.

Middle Schools. In some areas middle schools are being developed. These cover the age-ranges 8 to 12, 9 to 12, 9 to 13, 10 to 13 or 10 to 14. In Jan. 1977 there were 1,249 middle schools (there were only 15 in 1969) and more are planned as local education authorities introduce a 3-tier system of compulsory education to replace the traditional 2-tier system.

Secondary Education. In some areas, pupils are selected at 11 for grammar schools on the basis of ability. The grammar schools, of which there were 407 at Jan. 1977, provide a mainly academic course from age 11 to 18. There were also a small number of so-called technical schools which are the academic equals of grammar schools but can specialize to a greater or lesser extent in technical studies. Modern schools provide a general education up to the minimum school leaving age, though some pupils can, and increasingly do, stay on beyond that age. At Jan. 1977 there were 837 of these schools. There are also a small number of other schools which are various combinations of grammar, technical and modern schools.

In a growing number of areas there is no selection for secondary education and comprehensive schools provide courses for pupils of all abilities. In Jan. 1977 there were 3,083 fully comprehensive schools with over 2·98m. pupils, in comparison with 262 such schools with almost 240,000 pupils in 1965. With the development of comprehensive education various patterns of secondary school organization have come into operation, of which the main ones are: all through schools with an age-range of 11–18 or 11–16 (with possible transfer to an 11–18 school or to a sixth form college (*i.e.*, 16–19) for further studies); 3-tier systems, which incorporate middle schools with a transfer age of 12, 13 or 14, and corresponding 12–18, 13–18 or 14–18 schools; or a system of junior and senior comprehensive schools, catering for the 11–18 age group with a transfer age of 13 or 14.

In Nov. 1976, a new Education Act became law which requires local education authorities to provide secondary education only in schools where admission arrangements are not based on selection by reference to ability or aptitude.

Direct Grant Grammar Schools. These schools receive grants direct from the Department of Education and Science for their secondary departments (or 'upper schools') and are independent of local education authorities. However in 1975 the Government decided to phase out direct grant and invited the schools to join the maintained sector as comprehensive schools. 51 out of the total of 170 schools in England and Wales decided to accept the invitation, the first 4 becoming voluntary aided comprehensive schools in Sept. 1977. The remaining 118 (one closed in July 1976) preferred to become independent, so that pupils entering these schools in Sept. 1976 or later will be charged full economic fees. Those in the schools before Sept. 1976 will continue to attract grants (and thereby pay lower fees), and also be eligible for fee remission (related to their parents' income) until they leave. In Jan. 1976 there were 31,161 pupils in Upper Departments of the 47 schools still to enter the maintained sector and 69,082 pupils in those which have opted to become independent.

Special Schools. Special education is provided for children who are deaf, partially hearing, blind, partially sighted, physically handicapped, educationally sub-normal, epileptic, delicate, maladjusted, autistic or suffering from speech defects not due to deafness. The educationally sub-normal are the largest category in this group. Some handicapped children attend ordinary schools. Others attend maintained special schools: there are at present 1,541 of these, catering (in Jan. 1977) for over 127,000 pupils, including about 8,580 pupils in schools in hospitals for children receiving medical treatment as in-patients. (Local education authorities also send pupils to 'non-maintained' special schools and independent schools and pay the fees.) Special education is intended to enable handicapped children to overcome their difficulties in order that they may, as far as possible, take their place in society. To this end these schools have a more generous staffing ratio and provide physiotherapy, speech therapy and other medical treatment as well as special teaching facilities. Over three-quarters of the maintained special schools are day schools. For children with severe handicaps, for whom day special schools cannot cater, and for children who live out of reach of a suitable day school, free boarding education is provided. Attendance is compulsory from 5 to 16. In addition, local authorities have a duty to provide special educational treatment from the age of 2 for those ascertained as being in need of it and until the age of 18 for those who want it (education from 16–18 may be provided either in a school or a college of further education). In addition to the provision in special schools, authorities make special arrangements for educating children at home, in small groups or in hospitals when there is no special school. In Jan. 1976 about 6,000 pupils were being educated in this way. There are also some establishments which provide further education, pre-vocational training and for assessment for employment purely for handicapped school leavers (these students are usually those who cannot attend ordinary establishments for further education).

Ancillary Services. Every local education authority is required to make dinners available to day pupils attending maintained schools as far as is reasonably practicable. Part of the cost is borne by the parent but a pupil may receive a dinner free if the parent's income after certain allowances is below a national scale laid down by the Department of Education and Science or if he is receiving supplementary benefit or family income supplement.

Every local education authority has a duty to provide, on every school day, $\frac{1}{3}$ pint of milk free of charge to all pupils in special schools; all pupils in other maintained schools up to the end of the summer term after they attain the age of 7; other pupils in maintained primary schools and junior pupils in all age and middle schools where a school medical officer certifies that the pupil's health requires that he should be provided with milk at school. Milk may also be provided for similar pupils at non-maintained schools at the discretion of local education authorities but this discretionary power does not extend to the provision of milk on grounds of health.

Local education authorities have the power to sell milk to all pupils in their maintained schools. This is one of the provisions of the Education (Milk) Act, 1971, and came into effect 1 Sept. 1971.

In primary and secondary schools in England (including nursery and special schools) maintained by local education authorities 61·7% of pupils present took dinners on a day in autumn 1977 and 93·4% of eligible pupils present took milk. For 1977–78 the estimated cost of school meals was £356m. and of milk £11m.

Further Education. In Nov. 1976 there were about 650 institutions in England and Wales providing courses of further education, ranging from shorthand instruction to degree-level, postgraduate work and courses of teacher-training. Students attending these colleges numbered just over 501,000 full-time (including 49,600 sandwich students) and 1,421,000 part-time and evening; students released by their employers numbered 532,000. There were in addition some 7,000 evening institutes, which provided mainly part-time courses of non-advanced general education and were attended by 1·8m. students. At the top end of this range are the 30 polytechnics, these are engaged almost entirely in higher education, offering degrees of a standard comparable to those of universities, professional qualifications and courses leading to Higher National Diplomas and Certificates in a wide range of disciplines. Many other colleges of further education are however involved to a greater or lesser extent in the higher education sector of further education; and all polytechnics and most further education colleges cater for full-time, part-time and sandwich students, whose periods of study at college alternate with periods of practical training in industry.

Courses were also provided by the Workers' Education Association (6,630), the University extramural departments (7,554) and the Welsh National Council of YMCAs (78). The total number of students registered at these courses was 285,902.

Education at institutions of further education is not free, but fees are generally low, and are remitted for most students under the age of 18 by the local authority.

The Youth Service. A wide range of facilities for the leisure-time recreation and informal special education of young people primarily in the 14–20 age range is provided by local education authorities and voluntary youth organizations. A duty is laid upon local education authorities by the provisions of the 1944 Education Act to secure the adequacy of such facilities for young people in their areas; to this end they either provide, maintain and staff youth clubs, centres and other facilities from their own resources or assist voluntary agencies to do so.

Grants to local voluntary agencies to help meet the cost of their capital projects and to national voluntary bodies towards their headquarters and training expenses are made by the Government.

Awards to Students. Local education authorities are responsible for making awards to practically all students taking first-degree and comparable courses at universities and further education establishments and to students taking initial teacher-training courses. These awards cover fees and maintenance but the maintenance grants are subject to parental or spouse's means. In addition the universities may provide scholarships of various kinds. The authorities also give discretionary awards, which are mainly for non-graduate study to students attending full-time and sandwich courses at universities and further education establishments.

In 1975–76 there were 157,496 full value awards current at universities and 115,648 at further education establishments. In 1975–76 there were 104,732 current initial teacher-training awards. These include awards to students at university departments of education for which responsibility was transferred to local authorities in 1975–76. Lesser value awards, for which the maximum rate of grant payable is below the full cost of the student's fees and maintenance, were also made by the authorities. There were 38,458 awards taken up in the calendar year 1975–76.

The Research Councils (generally in science and social science subjects) and the Department of Education and Science (generally in the arts and the humanities) make awards to students at postgraduate level. The Research Councils gave 7,165 new awards in 1977–78 and there were 13,518 current awards in that academic year. The Department gave 1,793 new awards (state studentships and state bursaries) in 1977–78 and current awards totalled about 3,000

Teachers. In order to qualify for work in maintained schools, most teachers take a course of professional training. Graduates and holders of some specialist qualifications obtained before 31 Dec. 1969 are regarded as qualified to teach without training, but anyone obtaining these qualifications after that date is obliged to take a training course before being appointed for the first time to a primary school, and since 1 Jan. 1974 before first appointment to a secondary school. For the time being, however, this requirement has been waived for graduates in science and mathematics because of the acute shortage of teachers in these subjects.

Until recently there were about 132 colleges (including 22 polytechnic departments of education) providing 3-year and other courses for intending teachers. The majority were general teacher education colleges and were concerned with most subjects taught in schools, but a few were concerned only with the training of specialist teachers of physical education or housecraft. About two-thirds of the colleges were maintained by local education authorities, and the remainder by voluntary bodies which are usually associated with a religious denomination. At Oct. 1977 there were about 84,100 students on teacher-training courses.

Following the White Paper *Education: A Framework for Expansion*, published in 1972, a major reorganization of higher education in the non-university sector is resulting in considerable change in the traditional pattern. Many colleges are merging with polytechnics and other further education colleges to create single institutions providing a wide range of courses. Others, while remaining separate, are broadening their provisions to include more general courses of higher education, while a few colleges will continue to be concerned mainly with teacher training. It is probable that by the early 1980s about 25 polytechnics and about 50 other colleges will be providing teacher-training courses. There will, of course, also be the university departments of education which provide training courses for graduates.

On 30 Sept. 1977, 436,838 full-time teachers (180,055 men and 256,783 women) were employed by local education authorities in maintained primary and secondary (excluding nursery) schools.

Finance. Total current and capital expenditure on education in England and Wales from public funds (excluding university education and loan charges) is estimated at £5,967m. for 1976–77 as compared with £5,347m. for 1975–76.

Scotland:

Nursery Education. In Sept. 1975 there were 376 nursery schools and departments (education authority and grant-aided), with a total enrolment of 22,750 pupils.

Primary Education. In Sept. 1975 there were 2,533 primary schools and departments and the number on the registers was 628,722.

In Sept. 1975, 28,094 qualified teachers were employed in primary schools and departments.

Secondary Education. In Sept. 1975 there were 467 secondary schools with 411,642 pupils. Of these, 325 were all-through comprehensive establishments providing the full range of Scottish Certificate of Education courses and also non-certificate courses. A further 94 schools were comprehensive in intake and provided both non-certificate and certificate courses, the latter however only up to Ordinary grade. Of the remaining 48 schools, these were selective in intake, 25 provided certificate courses only (Ordinary grade and Higher grade) and 23 non-certificate and certificate courses, the latter again not extending beyond Ordinary grade. Pupils who start their secondary education in schools which do not cater for courses beyond Ordinary grade may in the light of their performance, or for other reasons, be transferred at the end of their second or fourth year to schools providing Higher grade courses. There were 27,325 teachers in secondary schools at Sept. 1975.

Special Schools. In Sept. 1975 there were 264 special schools and departments. The total number of handicapped children under instruction was 13,064, of which 10,077 were mentally handicapped, 1,110 were physically handicapped, 353 were blind or paritially blind and 749 were deaf or partially deaf, and 775 were otherwise handicapped.

At Sept. 1975 there were 26 'List D' schools (these establishments correspond to Community Homes in England and Wales) with a total enrolment of 1,291.

Further Education. Centres and colleges for formal further education numbered 218 in 1975–76. The student population was 172,845, of whom 31,847 attended full-time—advanced courses, 15,268; non-advanced, 16,579—and 140,998 part-time—advanced courses, 12,844; non-advanced, 140,998.

Teacher-Training. In Nov. 1975 there were 11,315 students, including 2,502 graduates, in 10 colleges of education on pre-service courses of teacher-training.

Finance. Total expenditure on education during 1975–76 was £530·2m. (excluding university education and loan charges).

Independent Schools. Outside the state system of education there were in England

and Wales 2,302 independent schools in Jan. 1977, ranging from large 'public' schools to small local ones catering for a handful of children; there were 412,075 full-time and 10,907 part-time pupils in these schools. Fees are charged by all these schools, which receive no grant from central government sources. Recognized as efficient status has been discontinued but the requirement for the registration of all independent schools by the Department and their inspection by HM Inspectors, remains unchanged. The term 'public schools' refers to independent schools in membership of the Headmasters' Conference, Governing Bodies Association or the Governing Bodies of Girls' Schools Association. Qualifications under which a school may be represented at the Headmasters' Conference include the measure of independence enjoyed by the governing body and the amount of advanced courses undertaken. Some of these schools are for boarders only, but the majority include non-resident 'day-pupils'. In Scotland there were 98 independent schools, with a total of 18,825 pupils in 1976. A small number of the Scottish independent schools are of the 'public school' type but they are not known as 'public schools' since in Scotland this term is used to denote education authority (*i.e.*, state) schools.

The earliest of the schools were founded by, and attached to, the medieval churches. Many were founded as 'grammar' (classical) schools in the 16th century, receiving charters from the reigning sovereign. Reformed mainly in the middle of the 19th century, these schools now provide the highest form of English pre-university education. Among the most well-known independent schools are Eton College, founded in 1440 by Henry VI, with 1,233 boys; Winchester College, 1394, founded by William of Wykeham, Bishop of Winchester, 554 boys; Harrow School, founded in 1560 as a grammar school by John Lyon, a yeoman, 732 boys; Charterhouse, 1611, 691 boys. Among the earliest foundations are King's School, Canterbury, founded 600; King's School, Rochester, 604; St Peter's, York, 627.

Universities. In *England* there are 33 degree-giving universities. In addition there are the University of Manchester Institute of Science and Technology; and the London and Manchester Business Schools. Seven new universities have been established since 1961.

In *Wales* there is one university, the University of Wales, with colleges at Aberystwyth, Bangor, Cardiff, Lampeter and Swansea. The Welsh National School of Medicine is a school of the University, and the University of Wales Institute of Science and Technology became a constituent college in Nov. 1967.

In *Scotland* there are 8 universities, Aberdeen, Dundee, Edinburgh, Stirling, Strathclyde, Heriot-Watt, Glasgow and St Andrews. The Carnegie Trust, founded in 1901 with a capital of £7m., has an annual income of £450,000, of which half is devoted to the equipment and expansion of the Scottish universities and half to assisting students.

All these universities and colleges are independent, self-governing institutions, although they receive substantial aid from the state through the University Grants Committee. This is a committee appointed by the Secretary of State for Education and Science designed to advise the Government on the needs of the universities, and to prepare plans for future development. The members are drawn from education and industry. The Government receives advice on the universities' requirements for central computing facilities from the Computer Board for the Universities and Research Councils whose members are also drawn from the universities and industry.

The Royal College of Art and the Cranfield Institute of Technology are post-graduate institutions which award higher degrees under charters granted in 1967 and 1969 respectively. They receive grants direct from the Department of Education and Science.

The local education authorities have no responsibility for universities.

The Open University received its charter on 1 June 1969 and is an independent, self-governing institution, awarding its own degrees. It is financed by the Government through the Department of Education and Science and by the receipt of students' fees.

Tuition is by means of correspondence textbooks, radio and television broadcasts and summer schools. Students can also attend one of 260 local study centres. No formal qualifications are required for entry to undergraduate or associate student courses. Anyone resident in the UK aged 21 or over may apply. In the 1977 Feb.–Oct. teaching year there were 55,397 undergraduates and 6,021 students; 5,288 part-time tutors and counsellors; 288 full-time academic staff at the University's head-quarters in Milton Keynes and 168 full-time academic staff (*i.e.*, in tutorial and counselling posts) based in 13 regional offices.

The University College at Buckingham, a new independent institution of higher education, took its first students in Feb. 1976. It offers a first degree (licence) in 2 academic years of 40 weeks each (the academic year is Jan.–Dec. and has 4 terms) in the following schools of study: Law, economics, politics, economics and law, history, politics and English literature, accounting and financial management and European studies. The latter course takes 3 years. In 1978 there were 232 full-time students and 29 staff.

All universities charge fees, but financial help is available to students from several sources.

The universities themselves provide scholarships of various kinds, the Department of Education and Science offers a number of scholarships for mature students every year and all local education authorities have a system of awards to help suitable students to attend university. Most of the undergraduate awards to UK students made by local education authorities are offered on the results of the General Certificate of Education. The amount of aid given generally depends upon the parents' means. About 98% of the students at the English and Welsh universities are in receipt of some form of financial assistance.

Awards known as state studentships are offered on a competitive basis by the Department from among candidates considered by the universities to be qualified for post-graduate studies in the humanities; similar awards, tenable at universities or technical colleges, are offered by the Research Councils to students studying science, mathematics and technology at the post-graduate level.

The following table gives the approximate number of professors, lecturers, etc., and students (full-time and sandwich courses) for 1975–76.

University or college	*Students*	*Staff*
Aston	4,529	490
Bath	3,351	359
Birmingham	7,980	1,451
Bradford	4,175	520
Bristol	6,637	909
Brunel	2,375	320
Cambridge	10,849	1,179
City	2,202	329
Durham	4,192	484
East Anglia	3,472	328
Essex	2,294	307
Exeter	4,076	492
Hull	4,174	524
Keele	2,320	336
Kent	3,008	423
Lancaster	3,828	491
Leeds	9,480	1,364
Leicester	3,774	566
Liverpool	7,151	1,005
London Business School	194	66
London	35,941	6,963
Loughborough	3,684	455
Manchester Business School	132	60
Manchester University	10,381	1,704
Univ. of Manchester Inst. of Science and Technology	3,540	536
Newcastle	6,682	1,053
Nottingham	5,988	888
Oxford	11,591	1,777
Reading	5,329	703

University or college	*Student*	*Staff*
Salford	3,968	503
Sheffield	7,121	866
Southampton	5,437	657
Surrey	2,770	318
Sussex	4,191	641
Warwick	3,944	442
York	2,814	284
Wales—		
Aberystwyth U.C.	2,974	407
Bangor U.C.	2,720	365
Cardiff U.C.	4,568	590
St David's, Lampeter	536	64
Swansea U.C.	3,221	485
Welsh Nat. School of Medicine	587	143
Univ. of Wales Institute of Science and Technology	2,530	267
Scotland—		
Aberdeen	5,325	832
Dundee	2,758	492
Edinburgh	9,337	1,419
Glasgow	9,241	1,460
Heriot-Watt	2,792	273
St Andrews	3,037	358
Stirling	2,075	281
Strathclyde	5,983	838

Women students are admitted on equal terms with men. Number of women students: England, 66,382; Wales, 6,099; Scotland, 15,187. There are, however, colleges exclusively for female students at Oxford and Cambridge. Numbers of students at institutions receiving aid from the University Grants Committee: England, 203,574; Wales, 17,136; Scotland, 40,548; total, 261,258.

McIntosh, N. E., Calder, J. A. and Swift, B., *A Degree of Difference*. London, 1976
Perry, W., *Open University: A Personal Account*. Open Univ. Press, 1976
Tunstall, J., *The Open University*. London, 1974

The British Council. The British Council was established in Nov. 1934 and incorporated by Royal Charter in 1940, which defines its aims as the promotion of a wider knowledge of Britain and the English language abroad and the development of closer cultural relations between Britain and other countries.

The Council's expenditure in 1976–77 amounted to £67m. Funds were provided by a grant-in-aid of £21m. from the Overseas Information (Foreign and Commonwealth Office) vote and a contribution of £10m. from the Overseas Aid Vote. A further £26m. was provided by the Ministry of Overseas Development to cover the cost of administration of, and the reimbursement of sums expended on technical co-operation schemes. The balance of £10m. was derived from Council earnings and from international agencies, overseas governments, etc. for educational services.

The Council is governed by a board consisting of up to 30 members, 6 of whom are nominated by Ministers. There are advisory committees for Scotland and Wales, and also advisory committees or panels for the main branches of the Council's work. In Feb. 1978 the Council had staff in 79 countries.

The Council is normally the body designated by the British Government to carry out bilateral cultural agreements, including that with the Soviet Union. The Council's work broadly divides into English language teaching and other educational work, the promotion of wider use and availability of British books and periodicals, the development of personal contacts and the exchange of information, especially in the fields of education, medicine, science, technology and the arts.

The general policy in the field of English language teaching is to advise and assist education authorities overseas, particularly in curriculum and materials development and the training of local teachers of English; courses are provided in Britain and abroad for the further training of English language teaching experts from overseas. In many countries the Council runs its own direct English teaching centres. The English Teaching Information Centre in London provides advisory and informational services and produces a wide range of publications. The Council acts as a centre for the dissemination of information about British educational thought and practice at all levels and, through its complement of education specialists permanently working overseas, it has become closely involved with the administration of aid on behalf of the Ministry of Overseas Development. It assists in producing English teaching and other educational television and radio programmes overseas and arranges training courses in TV, radio and audio-visual aids both in Britain and overseas. A prominent aspect of the educational work is the assistance given in developing countries to the adoption of modern and locally relevant methods of science and mathematics teaching in schools, and for this work the Council maintains a growing group of science educationalists and administers the ODM funded Aid for Commonwealth Teaching of Science scheme. Over 700 lecturers etc., mainly in the field of English language, are working overseas, having been recruited by the British Council on behalf of universities, schools etc. in about 80 different countries. The Council is concerned to promote closer international academic collaboration through a variety of interchange and linking schemes, and through the provision of information and advice on educational institutions; it also administers the British Government's Technical Co-operation Training Programme and scholarship programmes on behalf of a large number of international organizations, notably UN and EEC. It administers examinations on behalf of a number of British examining boards; and it also circulates films for general educational purposes.

During recent years the Council has collaborated with British educational institutions and firms in designing and implementing a wide range of educational projects, for which overseas authorities or multilateral agencies pay the full cost.

The sciences, including medicine, technology and agriculture, form an increasingly important part of Council work. Contacts are built up and information collected and distributed through the specialist departments and libraries in London and the qualified scientists serving overseas, who also advise on training in Britain and the provision of experts abroad.

The importance of the arts as a medium for fostering cultural relations is reflected in the Council's encouragement of the appreciation of British achievements in the performing and the visual arts, both by supporting local activity and by sending theatre and ballet companies, orchestras and chamber groups, and exhibitions both of fine arts and photographs, from Britain on tours overseas. The Council also produces booklets, records and tapes on a wide range of literary and artistic subjects.

The Council runs, or is associated with, over 150 libraries in the countries in which it is represented. It arranges touring exhibitions of new British books and periodicals (some 85,500 books were exhibited in 233 exhibitions in 1976–77). Additional publicity for British books is provided by the publication *British Book News*, the distribution of specialized book lists and the operation of a review scheme. The Council also administers for ODM funds (approximately £2m. in 1976–77) for library development, the presentation of books and periodicals to educational institutions in developing countries and the subsidized publication of low-priced books for students under the imprint of the English Language Book Society.

The Council arranges short advisory tours overseas by British experts. In a number of countries it is also the overseas administrative arm of the British Volunteer Programme. It awards scholarships and bursaries and arranges study programmes for some 18,000 visitors a year in Britain. It administers central government funds for youth exchanges with other countries.

In Britain the Council administers the programmes of award schemes for overseas students, meets many students on arrival from overseas, and provides an accommodation service and a programme of educational and recreational courses and visits, mainly for students from overseas for whom it has a special responsibility. The Council runs 25 offices in Britain, mainly in university cities, for these purposes.

The Council is increasingly called on to administer training schemes and educational services financed by overseas authorities, or by multilateral agencies, on a contractual basis. The Council's specialist courses and summer schools provide advanced study in a number of fields, notably medicine, science, literature and the arts, English language and education. Payment is made by the student, or his parent organization, or by some other sponsor.

The Council publishes the following periodicals: *British Medical Bulletin*, *British Medicine*, *Educational Broadcasting International*, and *British Book News*. Other publications produced include the series *Writers and their Work*, a number of booklets such as *Poetry Today*, *Drama in Britain*, *Higher Education in the United Kingdom* and *How to Live in Britain*. The Council has sponsored two major series of literature recordings, *The Complete Works of Shakespeare* and *The English Poets from Chaucer to Yeats*.

Chairman: Sir Charles Troughton, CBE, MC, TD.
Director-General: Sir John Llewellyn, KCMG.
Headquarters: 10 Spring Gdns., London, SW1A 2BN.

Arts Council of Great Britain. The Arts Council is an independent organization established by Royal Charter in 1946, and is one of the principal channels for British Government aid to the arts. The Council's objects are to develop and improve the knowledge, understanding and practice of the arts, to increase their accessibility to the public, and to advise and co-operate with government departments, local authorities and other organizations.

The Council consists of a Chairman and not more than 19 other members who are appointed by the Secretary of State for Education and Science after consultation with the Secretaries of State for Scotland and Wales. The Council is advised by panels and committees concerned with different aspects of the arts. With the approval of the appropriate Secretary of State, the Council appoints committees for Scotland and Wales known respectively as the Scottish Arts Council and the Welsh Arts Council.

The Council receives a grant-in-aid from the Government voted annually by Parliament. The grant-in-aid for 1977–78 is £41·7m., with £500,000 for 'Housing the Arts' fund. Annual Reports are published giving details of the Council's work and the way in which the grant-in-aid is spent.

As well as giving financial help and advice to over 1,200 artistic organizations from the major opera, dance, drama companies, orchestras and festivals, to the smallest touring theatre and experimental group, the Council encourages such diverse interests as contemporary dance, photography, art films, and helps professional creative writers, dramatists, poets, musicians, composers, artists and photographers by means of bursary and award schemes. The Council provides funds for specialist training courses in the arts, and assists projects for the construction of new buildings, or improvements to existing ones under its 'Housing the Arts' scheme.

A growing proportion of the Council's funds is channelled to the network of regional arts associations which practically covers the whole of England and Wales. The regional arts associations are not branches of the Arts Council, but are autonomous bodies, financed by a combination of Arts Council, local authority and private funds.

The Council directly promotes and mounts art exhibitions at the Hayward and Serpentine and other Galleries in London and also in the regions. Other direct promotions include tours of opera and drama companies, of the Council's own films on art and of music groups under the Contemporary Music Network scheme. Writers are sent out on tour and to visit schools and the Council has a library of contemporary British poetry.

Chairman: Rt Hon. Kenneth Robinson, PC.

Secretary General: Roy Shaw.

Headquarters: 105 Piccadilly, London, W1V 0AU. *The Scottish Arts Council:* 19–20 Charlotte Sq., Edinburgh, EH2 4DF. *The Welsh Arts Council:* 9 Museum Place, Cardiff, CF1 3NX.

National Insurance. The National Insurance Act, 1946, came into operation on 5 July 1948, repealing the existing schemes of health, pensions and unemployment insurance. This Act, along with later legislation, was consolidated as the National Insurance Act, 1965.

The Social Security Act 1975 introduced, from 6 April 1975, a new system of national insurance contributions to replace the previous system of flat-rate and graduated contributions. Since 6 April 1975, Class 1 contributions have been related to the employee's earnings and are collected with PAYE income tax, instead of by affixing stamps to a card. Class 2 and Class 3 contributions remain flat-rate, but, in addition to Class 2 contributions, those who are self-employed may be liable to pay Class 4 contributions, which for the year 1978–79 will be at the rate of 5% on profits or gains between £2,000 and £6,250, which are assessable for income tax under Schedule D. The non-employment and others whose contribution record is not sufficient to give entitlement to benefits are able to pay a Class 3 contribution voluntarily to qualify for a limited range of benefits. Class 2 contributions for 1978–79 are £1·90 a week for men and women. Class 3 contributions are £1·80 a week.

From 6 April 1978 the Social Security Pensions Act 1975 introduced earnings-related retirement, invalidity and widows pensions. Employee's national insurance contribution liability depends on whether he is in contracted out or not contracted out employment. The not-contracted out employee pays 6½% on all earnings up to £120 a week. The employer's rate is 10% and a 2% surcharge of the same earnings. An employee's contracted-out contribution is 6½% of the first £17·50 a week of earnings and 4% of earnings between £17·50 and £120 a week. The employer's contribution is 10% (and the 2% surcharge) of the first £17·50 of weekly earnings and 5½% (and the 2% surcharge) of earnings up to £120 a week.

The State supplements the contributions paid by contributors and employers, from general taxation. Contributions (other than the surcharge) and supplement together with interest on investments form the income of the National Insurance Fund from which benefits are paid.

Benefits. The range of benefits will be unaffected by the new arrangements from 5 April 1975. The benefits are: (1) Unemployment benefit; (2) Sickness benefit; (3) Invalidity benefit; (4) Maternity benefit; (5) Widow's benefit; (6) Guardian's allowance; (7) Child's special allowance; (8) Retirement pension; (9) Death grant.

Employed persons may qualify for all the benefits; self-employed may qualify for all except unemployment; non-employed may qualify for all except unemployment, sickness, invalidity and maternity allowance. Qualification for any benefit depends upon the fulfilment of the appropriate contribution and other conditions.

Sickness and Unemployment Benefit. From 17 Nov. 1977 the normal rate is £14·70 (£10·50 for a married woman) a week plus £9·10 a week for an adult dependant, plus £3·50 for the first child and £3 for each subsequent child. From 3 April 1978 the rate for married women will be increased to £14·70, and the addition for each child will be reduced to £2·20 to allow for the increase in child benefit to £2·30 for all children. An earnings-related supplement may be paid from the 13th to 168th day of a period of interruption of employment to persons under minimum pension age (65 for men, 60 for women) who are entitled to flat-rate sickness benefits, unemployment benefit or maternity allowance and who have paid Class 1 (employee's) National Insurance contributions or an amount of more than 50 times the lower earnings limit for contributions in the relevant income-tax year.

Invalidity Benefit replaces sickness benefit after 168 days of entitlement. It comprises of an invalidity pension of £17·50 weekly and an invalidity allowance of £3·70 if incapacity began before age 35: £2·30 if incapacity began between 35 and 45 or £1·15 if it began between 45 and 60 (55 for women). Increases are: £10·50 for an adult dependant plus £6·10 for each child for whom child benefit is payable.

Maternity Benefit. For a confinement a woman may receive a maternity grant of £25 and, where 2 or more children are born at the confinement, a further grant of £25 for each additional child who is alive 12 hours after its birth. If the woman has been gainfully employed or self-employed, and has paid sufficient full-rate national insurance contributions in the relevant income tax year, she may receive a maternity allowance of £14·70 a week normally payable for 18 weeks commencing 11 weeks before the expected week of confinement, provided she does not work during this period. Maternity allowance may be increased in certain circumstances in respect of dependants in the same way as sickness and unemployment benefits and an earnings-related supplement may be payable.

Widow's Benefit. On her husband's death a widow normally qualifies for 26 weeks for an allowance of £24·50 a week for herself plus an allowance for each child for whom child benefit is payable at £6·10 a week. Allowances for children at the following rates: £7·40 for the first, £6·90 for each other child. From 4 April 1978 when child benefit increases to £2·30 (see below), the rates of increases will be £6·10 for each child. An earnings related addition based on the amount on which her late husband had paid Class 1 (employee's) contributions in the relevant tax year may also be paid. At the end of the 26 weeks she may qualify for a widowed mother's allowance of £17·50 for herself, and the allowances for the children for whom child benefit is payable continue at the same rate as for the first 26 weeks of widowhood. She may also receive her allowance at the personal rate of £17·50 a week if she has living with her a son or daughter who is under 19. The child increase for widow's allowance and widowed mother's allowance is, generally speaking, payable only in respect of a child for whom child benefit is payable.

A widow's pension may be paid to: (1) A widow after the termination of her widow's allowance, if she does not qualify for widowed mother's allowance and was over the age of 40 when her husband died. (ii) A widow after she ceases to be entitled to a widowed mother's allowance if she is then over the age of 40. The standard rate of this pension is £17·50 a week if the widow was over 50 when her husband died or when her entitlement to widowed mother's allowance ended. If she was between 40 and 50, however, the standard rates range in 7% steps from 93% of the full age-50 rate (*i.e.*, £16·28 a week) for the widow who was 49 at that time to 30% (*i.e.*,£5·25 a week) for the widow who was then 40.

Child's Special Allowance. An allowance may be payable for the children of divorced parents where the father has died. It is payable to the mother if she has not remarried and her former husband was contributing, or legally liable to contribute, at least 25p a week towards the children's support in cash or kind or if she took reasonable steps to enforce maintenance and she was entitled to child benefit for the child(ren) when her former husband died or it is her child by her former husband and he was entitled to child benefit for the child(ren) when he died. It is similar to the allowances for widow's children and is payable at the same rates.

Guardian's Allowance. A person who is responsible for an orphan child below the child benefit age limits may be entitled to a guardian's allowance of £6·10 a week in addition to the amount of child benefit payable in respect of that child. Normally both the child's parents must be dead but when the child is illegitimate, or the parents were divorced, or one parent is missing, or serving a long sentence of imprisonment, the allowance may, in certain circumstances, be paid on the death of one parent only.

Retirement Pension. In order to receive a retirement pension, men between 65 and 70, and women between 60 and 65 must have retired from regular employment. This does not apply to women who are widowed or divorced when over 60, who can receive this pension on the termination of their marriage. The standard rates are £17·50 a week for a man or a woman on his or her own contributions and £10·50 for a married woman through her husband's contributions. Proportionately reduced pensions are payable where contribution records are deficient. An increase of £10·50 a week may be payable for a dependent wife. If she resides with the beneficiary the increase is gradually reduced for earnings over £40 a week. If she does not reside with the beneficiary an increase is not payable if she earns more than £10·50 a week. In addition £6·10 a week may be payable for each child for whom child benefit is payable. In certain circumstances an increase of £10·50 a week may be payable for a woman having care of the pensioner's children. In addition, a man who had paid graduated contributions receives 2½p per week for every £7·50 of graduated contributions paid, and a woman 2½p per week for every £9 paid. Although no further graduated contributions have been paid after April 1975, pension already earned will be paid along with the flat-rate pension in the normal way. If, after being awarded a retirement pension, a man under 70 or a woman under 65 earns more than £40 in a calendar week the pension for the next pension week, including any increase for dependants, will be reduced by 5p for every 10p earned berween £40 and £44 and by 5p for every 5p earned over £44. If retirement is postponed after minimum pension age increments of flat-rate pension can be earned for periods of deferred retirement: after 5 April 1975 increments are earned at the rate of one-eighth penny per £1 of basic pension rate for every 6 days (excluding Sundays) for which the pension has been forgone. Any days for which another benefit has been paid will not count. There must be at least 48 days before increments can be earned unless one 6p increment has been earned before 6 April 1975. For period of deferred retirement before 6 April 1975 increments were based on the number of contributions paid as an employed or self-employed person. At age 70 (65) the pension for which a person has qualified may be paid in full whether a person continues in work or not irrespective of the amount of earnings. At the age of 80 an age addition of £0·25 a week is payable. In addition non-contributory pensions are now payable, subject to residence conditions, to persons aged 80 and over who do not qualify for a retirement pension or qualify for one at a low rate. The rates of these pensions, which are financed by Exchequer funds, are £10·20 a week for a single person and £6·30 for a married woman. These amounts do not include the £0·25 age addition.

Death Grant. This is a lump sum paid on the death of an insured person or his close relative. The normal amount of the payment is: For an adult, £30; for a child aged 6 but under 18, £22·50; for a child aged 3 but under 6, £15; for a child under 3, £9. For the death of a person who was within 10 years of pensionable age on 5 July 1948 (*i.e.*, a man over 55 and a woman over 50 on that date) only half the standard amount is payable. No grant is payable for the death of a person who was over the pensionable age on 5 July 1948.

Payment. Unemployment benefit is paid through the local unemployment benefit offices of the Department of Employment.

The Industrial Injuries Provisions of the Social Security Act, 1975. The Industrial Injuries Act, which also came into operation on 5 July 1948, with its later amending Acts, was consolidated as the National Insurance (Industrial Injuries) Act, 1965. This legislation was incorporated in the Social Security Act, 1975. The scheme provides a system of insurance against 'personal injury by accident arising out of and in the course of employment' and against certain prescribed diseases and injuries due to the nature of the employment. It takes the place of the Workmen's Compensation Acts and covers persons who are employed earners under the Social Security Act. There are no contribution conditions for the payment of benefit. Three types of benefit are provided:

(*1*) *Injury benefit*, payable for incapacity for work due to an industrial accident or a prescribed disease for a maximum of 26 weeks from the date of the accident or the development of the prescribed disease. The rate of this benefit is £17·45 a week, with increases of £9·10 for 1 adult dependant and £2·20 for each child for whom child benefit is payable. An earnings related supplement may be paid where there is an entitlement to sickness benefit or maternity allowance. If the employed earner is under 18 years of age and is not entitled to a dependant's increase benefit will be payable at a reduced rate—£14·70. For children under 16 years of age in part-time employment, the rate is £4·50.

(*2*) *Disablement benefit*. This is payable where, as the result of an industrial accident or prescribed disease, there is a loss of faculty after injury benefit ceases to be payable. The loss of faculty will be assessed at a percentage by comparison with a person of the same age and sex whose condition is normal. If the assessment is 20% or more, benefit will be a pension varying according to the assessment, from £5·72 a week to £28·60 a week. If the assessment is under 20% benefit will normally be a gratuity of an amount not exceeding £1,900. Unemployability supplement plus age additions similar to invalidity allowance, is payable to a disablement pensioner who, as a result of the relevant loss of faculty is incapable of work and likely to remain permanently so incapable. Increases for dependants at the same rates as for invalidity pension are also payable to a disablement pensioner who is entitled to unemployability supplement. The supplement cannot be paid at the same time as certain other benefits payable under the Social Security Act or out of public funds. Other increases of disablement benefit may be payable where the loss of faculty causes special hardship, *i.e.*, it prevents the beneficiary from undertaking his regular job or one of an equivalent standard; where there is a need for constant attendance; where there is exceptionally severe disablement and the need for constant attendance is likely to be permanent or where disablement is assessed at less than 100% and the beneficiary is in hospital for treatment for his injury or prescribed disease. Pensions for persons under 18 are reduced similarly to injury benefit.

(*3*) *Death Benefit*. On the death of a person as the result of an industrial accident or a prescribed disease, certain dependants may qualify for benefit. Benefit for a widow is a pension normally of £24·50 weekly for the first 26 weeks and thereafter £18·05, depending on such factors as age, entitlement to a child's allowance and permanent incapacity for self-support. If the conditions for pension at the higher rate are not satisfied the widow may receive a pension of £5·25 a week. Children's allowances are payable to the widow, or other person, entitled to child benefit for children of the deceased. For widows, these allowances are usually at the rate of £6·10 a week for each child; for other persons, the rate is £2·20 for each child. An allowance of £1 is payable to a woman having care of a child of the deceased. Benefit for widowers, parents and certain other relatives takes the form of pensions, allowances or gratuities according to the relationship to, and degree of maintenance by, the deceased.

War Pensions. The number of beneficiaries in receipt of war (1914–18) pensions or allowances as at 31 Dec. 1976 was 64,500. The number of beneficiaries in receipt of war (1939–45 and later) pensions or allowances in payment as at 31 Dec. 1976 was 348,000. The estimated expenditure for both wars for 1975–76 was £258m. The expenditure is exclusive of administration expenses.

National Insurance Fund. At 1 April 1976 the balance of the National Insurance Fund at market value amounted to £2,218,579,000. Income during the period 1 April 1976 to 31 March 1977, consisting of contributions from insured persons and employers, payments from the Exchequer and interest on investments, etc., was £9,397,616,000. Payments of benefit in respect of unemployment were £558,846,000; sickness, £496,142,000; invalidity, £562,808,000; maternity, £81m.; widows, £434m.; guardian's allowance and child's special allowance, £2·2m.; retirement pension, £5,651,329,000; death grants, £14,989,000; injury benefit, £45,651,000; disablement benefits, £167,222,000; death benefit, £25·5m. Included in those figures are the following estimated amounts of earnings-related supplement: unemployment benefit, £87m.; sickness benefit, £112m.; maternity allowance, £16m.; widow's benefit, £11m.; graduated retirement benefit, £68m. Administrative and other payments cost approximately £429,918,000. The balance at 31 March 1976 was £3,146·59m.

Industrial Injuries Fund. At 1 April 1974 there was a balance of £400,478,566. Income during the period 1 April 1974 to 31 March 1975, consisting of contributions from insured persons and employers, payments from the Exchequer and interest on investments, etc., amounted to £209,724,073. Benefits for injury totalled £34,998,785; for disablement, £110,096,727; for deaths, £17·2m. Administrative and other payments cost approximately £25·7m. There was a balance at 31 March 1975 of £422,186,863.

From 1 April 1975 the National Insurance Reserve Fund and the Industrial Injuries Fund were merged with the National Insurance Fund. All basic scheme contributions payable under the 1975 Social Security Act are paid into the single fund out of which the existing range of benefits will continue to be financed. The new national insurance fund will continue to receive a Treasury Supplement set at a level of 18% of total contribution income.

Child Benefit. Child benefit is a weekly tax-free cash allowance for all children. The weekly rates for each child is £2·30 a week. Child benefit is payable for all children under age 16 and, with certain exceptions, for those under age 19 receiving full-time education at a university, college or school or the like.

Family Income Supplement. Family income supplement is payable to families with at least 1 dependent child where the head of the household is in full-time, *i.e.*, 30 hours or more a week, remunerative work, and where the family's normal gross weekly income (but excluding child benefits) is below a prescribed amount. The prescribed amount for a 1-child family is £43·80, this amount being increased by £4 for each additional child in the family. The weekly rate of benefit payable is one-half of the difference between the prescribed amount and the family's normal income, subject to a maximum weekly payment of £9·50 for families with 1 child, increasing by £1 for each additional child. Benefit is usually payable for 52 weeks and is not affected by changes in circumstances. The prescribed amounts are the same for both 1- and 2-parent families.

Attendance allowance. This is a tax-free allowance for severely disabled people, including children aged 2 or over, who require a lot of help from another person. There are 2 rates, the higher rate of £14 a week for those who require attention or supervision by day and night, and the lower rate of £9·30 a week for those who need the attendance either by day or night. In addition to the medical requirements a simple test of residence and presence in Great Britain must also be satisfied.

Supplementary benefit. Under the Supplementary Benefits Act, 1976, the Supplementary Benefits Commission is responsible for the award of financial assistance to any persons in Great Britain aged 16 years or over (excluding persons at school or college or anyone directly involved in a trade dispute) who are not in full-time remunerative work and who are without resources, or whose resources including national insurance benefits) need to be supplemented in order to meet their requirements. A person who is excluded from benefit may, nevertheless, receive payments to meet urgent need. The general standards by reference to which supplementary benefit is granted are determined by statutory regulations approved by Parliament. Persons who are dissatisfied with the amount of benefit granted to them may appeal to an independent Appeal Tribunal established under the Act.

During the financial year 1975–76 net payments on supplementary benefit amounted to £1,187m.

Newman, T. S., *Digest of British Social Insurance.* London, 1947 (and supplements, to date)

National Health. The National Health Service in England and Wales started on 5 July 1948 under the National Health Service Act, 1946. There is a separate Act for Scotland and also one for Northern Ireland, where the Health Services are run on similar lines to those in England and Wales.

The National Health Service, which is available to every man, woman and child, is a charge on the national income in the same way as the armed forces and other facilities.

Every person normally resident in this country is entitled to use any complete part of the services, and no insurance qualification is necessary.

Most of the cost of running the service is met from the national exchequer, *i.e.*, from taxes.

Since Sept. 1957 a small weekly National Health Service contribution has been payable by contributors and where applicable by their employers. For convenience this contribution is collected with the National Insurance contribution and for 1976–77 is estimated to be £572m.

Organization. Under the provisions of the National Health Service Reorganization Act 1973, the administration of the National Health Service is organized under a system of regional and area health authorities. There are 90 area health authorities in England responsible for the administration and development of all the health services in their areas. Fourteen regional health authorities, each consisting of a number of complete health areas, are responsible for allocating resources between the area health authorities in their regions and for monitoring their performance. The regional health authorities are responsible for developing strategic plans and priorities and for carrying out certain executive functions.

Services. The National Health Service broadly consists of hospital and specialist services, general medical, dental and ophthalmic services, pharmaceutical services, community health services and school health services. All these services are free of charge except for such things as prescriptions, spectacles, dentures and dental treatment, amenity beds in hospitals and for some of the community services, for which charges are made with certain exemptions.

The total cost of the Health and Personal Social Services (England and Wales) is estimated at £7,027m. for 1977–78 and the estimated net expenditure by the Exchequer (except for the Local Authority and Personal Social Services, where the rates and the Exchequer grants amounted to £1,124m.) in 1977–78 is £6,166m.

The number of abortion notifications received in 1976 under the provisions of the Abortion Act, 1967, was 127,904, of which 101,003 related to England and Wales residents. Of these 101,003 notifications, 50,481 (50%) were to single women, 39,868 (39·5%) were to married women, and 10,654 (10·5%) were to widowed, divorced or separated women and to women who did not state their marital status.

In 1976 there were 26,418 general medical practitioners, 13,254 general dental practitioners and (1975) 202,464 qualified nurses and midwives. There were (1976) 479,359 allocated hospital beds.

The number of abortion notifications received in 1976 under the provisions of the Abortion Act 1967, was 7,205, of which 7,198 related to Scottish residents. Of these 7,198 notifications, 3,446 (47·9%) were to single women, 2,885 (40·1%) were to married women, and 867 (12%) were to widowed, divorced or separated women and to women who did not state their marital status.

Personal Social Services. Under the Local Authority Social Services Act 1970 and in Scotland the Social Work (Scotland) Act 1968 the welfare and social work services provided by local authorities were made the responsibility of a new local authority department—the Social Services Department in England and Wales, and Social Work Departments in Scotland headed by a Director of Social Work. The social services thus administered include: the fostering, care and adoption of children, welfare services and social workers for the mentally disordered, the disabled and the aged, accommodation for those needing residential care services. In Scotland the social work departments' functions also include the supervision of persons on probation, of adult offenders and of persons released from penal institutions or subject to fine supervision orders.

The number of persons in residential and temporary accommodation was as follows:

England and Wales (31 Dec.)	*Residential accommodation*[1] *Adults*	*Temporary accommodation Adults*	*Children*	*Total Adults and Children*
1973	123,718	8,352	13,036	145,106
1974	125,799	12,320	17,712	155,831
1975	127,937	...	...	...
1976[2]	134,000	...	...	...
1977[2]	135,000	...	...	...

[1] Year ending 31 March 1976.
[2] Provisional.

Scotland	*Adults and Children*	*Adults*	*Children*	*Adults and Children*
1973	11,329	118[2]	198[2]	11,645
1974[1]	11,729	164	220	12,113
1976[3]	11,926	114	176	12,216

[1] Provisional.
[2] Almost 600 places taken over by housing department.
[3] 12 months April 1975–March 1976.

England and Wales. Expenditure and income relating to the personal social services administered by local authorities (in £ sterling):

Year ended 31 March	*Expenditure (including loan charges)*	*Income (including payments by recipients of services)*	*Net Expenditure*
1973	390,534,000	66,514,000	324,020,000
1974	499,540,000	83,460,000	416,080,000
1975	715,394,000	107,348,000	608,046,000
1976	963,380,000	144,571,000	818,809,000
1977[1]	1,130,651,000	175,860,000	954,791,000

[1] Provisional.

Scotland. The total local authority expenditure for 1974–75 in respect of residential accommodation and welfare services under the Social Work (Scotland) Act, 1968, was £78·5m., of this sum £3·2m. was from the central government and £75·3m. from local authorities.

Social Security Statistics 1975. HMSO, 1977

DIPLOMATIC REPRESENTATIVES

OF THE USA IN GREAT BRITAIN (Grosvenor Sq., London, W1A 1AE)

Ambassador: Dr Kingman Brewster.

OF GREAT BRITAIN IN THE USA (3100 Massachusetts Ave., Washington, D.C., 20008)

Ambassador: Peter Jay.

OF GREAT BRITAIN TO THE UNITED NATIONS

Ambassador: Ivor Richard, QC.

Books of Reference

The annual and other publications of the various Public Departments, and the Reports, etc. of Royal Commissions and Parliamentary Committees. (These may be obtained from HM Stationery Office.)

Allen, G. C., *British Industries and their Organization.* 4th ed. London, 1959
Bickmore, D. P., and Shaw, M. A. (ed.), *The Atlas of Great Britain and Northern Ireland.* OUP, 1963
Burn, D., *The Structure of British Industry.* 2 vols. CUP, 1958
Central Statistical Office. *Annual Abstract of Statistics.* HMSO.—*Monthly Digest of Statistics.* HMSO
Central Office of Information. *Britain: An Official Handbook*. HMSO, 1978.—*Britain in Brief* 18th ed. HMSO, 1977
Demangeon, A., *The British Isles.* 3rd ed. London, 1952
Halsey, A. H., *Trends in British Society since 1900.* London, 1972
History of the Second World War. HMSO, 1949 ff.
Kendall, M. G. (ed.), *The Source and Nature of the Statistics of the United Kingdom.* 2 vols. London, 1952–1957
Mitchell, B. R., *Abstract of British Historical Statistics.* OUP, 1962
Mitchell, J. (ed.), *Great Britain: Geographical Essays.* CUP, 1962
Oxford History of England. 15 vols. OUP, 1936 ff.
Stamp, L. D., and Beaver, S. H., *The British Isles: A Geographic and Economic Survey.* 4th ed., London, 1954
Woodward, Sir E. L., and Butler, R., *Documents on British Foreign Policy, 1919–39.* HMSO, 1957 ff.

Scotland

Scottish Council (Development and Industry). *Inquiry into the Scottish Economy, 1900–61.* Edinburgh, 1961
Scottish Development Dept. *Scottish Economic Bulletin.* HMSO (annual).—*Scottish Abstract of Statistics.* HMSO (annual).
The New Scottish Local Authorities: Organisation and Management Structures. HMSO, 1973
Duncan, A. A. M., *Scotland: The Making of the Kingdom.* Edinburgh, 1975
Hanham, H. J., *Scottish Nationalism.* London, 1969
Hogg, A., and Hutcheson, A. MacG., *Scotland and Oil.* 2nd ed. Edinburgh, 1975
Johnston, T. L., *Structure and Growth in the Scottish Economy.* London, 1971
Kellas, J. G., *Modern Scotland: The Nation since 1870.* London, 1968.—*The Scottish Political System.* 2nd ed. CUP, 1975
Meikle, H. W. (ed.), *Scotland: A Description of Scotland and Scottish Life.* London, 1947
Oakley, C. A. (ed.), *Scottish Industry.* Edinburgh, 1953
Turnock, D., *Patterns of Highland Development.* London, 1970

Wales

Wales: The Way Ahead (Cmnd 3334.) HMSO, 1971
Wales: Employment and the Economy. Cardiff, 1972
Digest of Welsh Statistics. HMSO (annual)
Kohr, L., *Is Wales Viable?* London, 1971
Thomas, B. (ed.), *The Welsh Economy.* Cardiff, 1962
Williams, D., *A History of Modern Wales.* New ed. London, 1977

NORTHERN IRELAND

AREA AND POPULATION. Area (revised by the Ordnance Survey Department) and population at the census of 25 April 1971 were as follows:

Counties and county boroughs	*Area in hectares*	*Males*	*Females*	*Total*
Antrim	304,526	175,177	180,539	355,716
Armagh	132,697	66,917	67,052	133,969
Belfast C.B.	7,305	172,397	189,685	362,082
Down	246,624	152,622	159,254	311,876
Fermanagh	185,097	25,830	24,425	50,255
Londonderry	210,782	65,827	65,062	130,889
Londonderry C.B.	1,044	25,331	26,874	52,205
Tyrone	326,550	70,575	68,498	139,073
Northern Ireland	1,414,625	754,676	781,389	1,536,065

Vital statistics for calendar years:

	Marriages	*Divorces*	*Births*	*Deaths*
1971	12,152	341	31,765	16,202
1972	11,905	360	29,994	17,032
1973	11,212	395	29,200	17,669
1974	10,783	361	27,160[1]	17,327[1]
1975	10,867	434	26,130[1]	16,511[1]

[1] Provisional.

CONSTITUTION AND GOVERNMENT. The Northern Ireland Constitution Act 1973 as amended by the Northern Ireland Constitution (Amendment) Act 1973 provides for a Northern Ireland Executive of not more than 11 members (including the Chief Executive Member). The Secretary of State appointed this full number to take office from 1 Jan. 1974. He may also, under the Amendment Act, appoint others to carry out particular functions in the Administration up to a total (including members of the Executive) of 15. This additional number were appointed.

Devolution of legislative and executive responsibility to the Northern Ireland Assembly and the new Administration under Section 2 of the Constitution Act was given effect by the Northern Ireland Constitution (Devolution) Order 1973 from 1 Jan. 1974 ('the appointed day'). On that day, Section 1 of the Northern Ireland (Temporary Provisions) Act 1972 expired and, with it, the power to legislate for Northern Ireland by Order in Council under that Act.

Power to make laws (to be known as Measures) in respect of 'transferred' matters, that is on matters other than those listed in Schedules 2 and 3 to the Constitution Act was vested in the Assembly subject to the overriding power of the UK Parliament to legislate on such matters and subject to Section 17 of the Constitution Act which declares void any provision which discriminates against any person or class of persons on the ground of religious belief or political opinion. The procedure for Measures is set out in the Standing Orders of the Assembly. All Measures require the approval of the Queen in Council before they become law. The first election of Members to the 78 seats in the Northern Ireland Assembly was held in 1973. The state of the parties following the election was: Social Democratic and Labour Party 19; Democratic Unionist Loyalist Coalition 8; Official Unionist 24; Northern Ireland Labour 1; Other Unionist 8; Alliance 8; Vanguard Unionist Coalition 7; Other Loyalist Coalition 2; Other Loyalist 1. Northern Ireland also returns 12 members of the UK House of Commons.

On 28 May 1974 the Unionist members of the Administration resigned, as a result of which the Secretary of State terminated the appointments of members, and HM the Queen prorogued the Assembly for a period of 4 months (thus preventing it from legislating). Parliament subsequently enacted the Northern Ireland Act 1974 extending the prorogation of the Assembly and providing for its dissolution. The Act also reintroduced the power to legislate for Northern Ireland by Order in Council. The Assembly was dissolved on 27 March 1975, and an election, provided for under the 1974 Act, of a Constitutional Convention took place on 1 May 1975. The Convention had the purpose of considering what provision for the government of Northern Ireland is likely to command the most widespread acceptance throughout the community there. The Convention was dissolved on 5 March 1976 as there was no prospect of agreement.

What began ostensibly as a Civil Rights campaign in 1968, escalated in 1969–77 into a full-scale offensive designed to overthrow the State. This offensive was originally mounted by an illegal organization, the Irish Republican Army (not to be confused with the legitimate Army of the Republic of Ireland). At times countermeasures have required the services of over 20,000 regular troops, in addition to the Royal Ulster Constabulary, the RUC Reserve and the part-time Ulster Defence Regiment.

Secretary of State for Northern Ireland: Right Hon. Roy Mason, MP.

Flag: White with a red cross, charged in the centre with a 6-pointed star bearing a red hand and surmounted by a royal crown.

Local Government. Northern Ireland has a single-tier system of 26 district councils based on main centres of population.

The district councils are responsible for the provision of a wide range of local services including refuse collection and disposal, street cleansing, litter prevention, consumer protection, environmental health, miscellaneous licensing, the provision and management of recreational and cultural facilities, the promotion of tourist development schemes, the enforcement of building regulations and gas supply. They have in addition both a representative role in which they send forward representatives to sit as members of statutory bodies including the Northern Ireland Housing Executive, the Fire Authority and the Area Boards for health and personal social services and education and libraries; and a consultative role under which the Department of Environment (NI) and the Northern Ireland Housing Executive, among others, have an obligation to consult them regarding the provision of the regional services for which these bodies are responsible.

Regional development strategy in Northern Ireland throughout the late sixties and early seventies was based on the *Matthew Report* of 1963, which marked the beginning of a new era in regional planning in the Province. This in turn was endorsed by the economic plan prepared by Professor Wilson in 1965, which modified and up-dated a number of the original Matthew proposals. The Northern Ireland Development Programme 1970–75 extended the scope of the regional strategy and basically identified two categories of interest: (*i*) centres of accelerated growth consisting of the greater Belfast area (including the Belfast Urban Area, Craigavon, Antrim, Bangor, Carrickfergus and Newtownards), Londonderry and Ballymena. These were centres where a proportionately large expansion was deliberately planned and where population growth was to be actively encouraged. (*ii*) Eight key centres which were to be made as attractive as possible to potential new industry and where significant expansion was anticipated. The 8 centres were the provincial towns of Newry, Dungannon, Coleraine, Enniskillen, Omagh, Larne, Downpatrick and Strabane. This growth and key centre policy had a twofold purpose: to maintain a Development Stopline around Belfast and to encourage movement of population from the city and elsewhere to the major towns outside the Belfast Urban Area.

In 1975 the Development Programme of 1970 having run its full course, the Government published a discussion paper which outlined and evaluated 6 very broad options for the future development of the Province for the period 1975–95. Following comments from a wide variety of sources the Government announced its decision to adopt in principle the District Towns Strategy. Basically the strategy advocates that the growth and key centre strategy should be extended to embrace the major town in each local government district. A detailed exposition *Northern Ireland Regional Physical Development Strategy 1975–95* was published in May 1977.

While the physical strategy sets out the Government's aims and objectives on a regional basis, the details required to pursue these aims and objectives at local level are promulgated in Area Plans. These have been published for the Belfast Urban Area, the Coleraine–Portrush–Portstewart Triangle, North Down, Londonderry, West Tyrone, Newry, Limavady, Armagh and East Antrim. Plans for Fermanagh, East Tyrone, Magherafelt and the north-east of the Province which will incorporthe Coleraine–Portrush–Portstewart Plan are at an advanced stage of preparation. Work is continuing on the preparation of a plan for the Lisburn District.

Statements of the Department's conclusions and decisions have been published on the Belfast Urban, North Down, Londonderry and West Tyrone Plans following consideration of the Reports of Public Inquiries held into objections to the Plans, and the latter 3 Plans have been adopted as statutory development plans under Article 7(2) of the Planning (NI) Order 1972. Public Inquiries have been held into the Armagh, Newry and Limavady Area Plans. A major review of the Belfast Urban Area Transportation Strategy has been carried out and a public inquiry was being carried out (1977) to decide the future system of transport in Belfast.

Provisions in Part VII of the Planning (NI) Order 1972 enable the Department of the Environment (NI) to deal with areas requiring to be developed or redeveloped in overall schemes involving the participation of several agencies. Land when acquired is not normally developed by the Department itself but is disposed of to other agencies for the carrying out of their development. The Department is currently using these powers for two main purposes, the promotion of commercial redevelopment of certain town centre sites and the acquisition overall of large areas, principally in Belfast, which are in need of redevelopment and are proposed to be redeveloped for mainly other than housing purposes. Where land is to be developed by the private sector then disposal by the Department is invariably on the basis of a lease rather than by transfer of the freehold.

The legislative framework for planning in Northern Ireland is contained in the Planning (NI) Order 1972. Under the Order the Department of the Environment for Northern Ireland is the sole planning authority for Northern Ireland. The Order includes procedures for the preparation of plans and development control, establishes a Planning Appeals Commission, contains provisions for the protection of buildings of special architectural or historic merit and trees and gives powers for the carrying out of town-centre redevelopment.

FINANCE. There exists a separate Northern Ireland Consolidated Fund from which is met the expenditure of Northern Ireland Departments. Its main sources of revenue are: (*i*) The Northern Ireland attributed share of UK taxes; (*ii*) A non-specific grant in aid of Northern Ireland's revenue, payable by the Secretary of State for Northern Ireland; (*iii*) Rates and other receipts of Northern Ireland Departments.

The general principle underlying the financial arrangements is that Northern Ireland should have parity of taxation and services with Great Britain.

Since the financial year 1975–76 the income of the Northern Ireland Consolidated Fund has been as follows (in £ sterling):

	1975–76	*1976–77*	*1977–78*[3]
Attributed share of UK taxes	554,160,642[1]	637,673,107[2]	734,500,000
Payments by UK Government:			
Grant in Aid	351,000,000	360,000,000	341,400,000
Agriculture Acts	2,045,000	2,385,000	...
Refund of value added tax	5,639,000	5,468,000	5,500,000
Regional and district rates	69,000,000	76,270,000	88,500,000
Other receipts	101,871,952	125,728,593	126,600,000
Total	1,083,716,594	1,207,524,700	1,296,500,000

[1] Including final adjustment of 1973–74. [2] Including final adjustment of 1974–75. [3] Provisional.

The public debt at 31 March 1977 was as follows: Northern Ireland 6% Exchequer Stock 1977, £7m.; Northern Ireland 6½% Exchequer Stock 1979–80, £15m.; Northern Ireland 7% Exchequer Stock 1982–84, £20m.; Ulster Savings Certificates, £50,941,126; Ulster Development Bonds, £8,970,403; borrowing from UK Government, £649,320,456; borrowing from Northern Ireland Government Funds, £124,869,000; borrowing from bank, £2·6m.; sundry short-term borrowings, £11,238,000; total, £889,938,985.

The above amount of public debt is offset by equal assets in the form of loans from Government to public and local bodies and of cash balances.

ENERGY AND NATURAL RESOURCES

Electricity. The planning, generation and distribution of electricity supplies are the responsibility of the Northern Ireland Electricity Service.

The installed capacity of the system is 2,025 mw provided from 5 thermal power-stations. Work is in progress on the construction of an oil-fired power-station of 1,200 mw rating at Kilroot, Co. Antrim. This station is due for commissioning progressively between 1979 and 1982 in annual increments of 300 mw. Gas-turbine capacity has recently been added to the system.

The total sales of electricity in Northern Ireland in the year ended 31 March 1976 amounted to 4,641m. units (provisional) supplied to a total of 505,483 consumers.

Water Supplies and Sewerage. The Water Service Division of the Department of the Environment for Northern Ireland is responsible for water supply and sewerage. Over 130m. gallons of water a day are supplied throughout the Province. More than 90% of the population have a mains supply of water and about 85% live in property connected to public sewers.

Minerals. The output of minerals (in 1,000 tonnes) during 1975 was approximately: Basalt and igneous rock (other than granite), 8,642; chalk, 598; clay and shale, 265; grit and conglomerate, 3,442; limestone, 1,849; sand and gravel, 3,887; and other minerals (rocksalt, flint, sandstone, diatomite and granite), 237.

Agriculture. Estimated gross output in 1975–76:

		Quantity (1,000)	*Value (£1m.)*
Fat cattle	head	501	94·7
Calves	head	44	3·0
Store cattle	head	17	2·5
Exports of breeding livestock	head	7	1·2
Fat sheep and lambs	head	397	5·9
Fat pigs	head	813	36·7
Poultry (tonnes)		36·1	13·4
Eggs (1,000 dozen) for consumption		121,497	26·9
Wool (kg)		1,372	0·8
Milk (litres)		969,034	76·8
Potatoes	tonnes	189	19·8
Oats	tonnes	5	0·3
Barley	tonnes	65	4·0
Wheat	tonnes	1	0·1

		Quantity (1,000)	*Value (£1m.)*
Grass seed	tonnes	0·1	—
Hay and straw	tonnes	11	0·4
Fruit		29	3·2
Vegetables		36	2·7
Mushrooms		3	1·7
Flowers		—	1·5
Sundry		—	3·5
Total receipts			299·0
Value of changes in stocks due to volume			– 5·2
Gross output			293·8

Area (in 1,000 hectares) of crops at June census (preliminary for 1977):

	1976	*1977*		*1976*	*1977*
Oats	6·9	·7	Other crops	1·7	1·2
Barley	49·8	53·3	Fruit	2·7	2·6
Other cereals and pulses	2·1	1·8	Grass for mowing	266·7	248·9
Potatoes	14·2	17·6	Grass for grazing	489·1	509·5
Turnips, swedes, kale and cabbage[1]	0·8	0·8	Rough grazing (excluding common land)	210·3	213·3
Vegetables	1·2	1·3			

[1] Stock feeding only.

Livestock (1,000) at June census (1977 preliminary):

	1976	*1977*		*1976*	*1977*
Dairy cows	241·9	250·5	Total sheep	925·9	968·6
Beef cows	291·2	289·1	Breeding sows	76·8	70·8
Total cattle	1,547·6	1,592·1	Total pigs	698·1	668·0
Breeding ewes	477·1	492·7	Total poultry	12,109·0	11,384·0

INDUSTRY AND TRADE

Industry. Northern Ireland is an important industrial region where manufacturing output has been increasing at an average annual rate of 2·8% over the last 10 years. In 1975 employment in manufacturing and construction amounted to 194,000, some

40% of the total workforce. Of this number, 48,000 (25%) were engaged in the engineering and allied industries, which include shipbuilding and aircraft manufacture. The former predominance of shipbuilding has diminished, and the engineering sector now produces an impressive variety of goods: from textile machinery, air-conditioning plant and oilfield equipment to automobile and aero-engine components, data-processing and sound-reproduction equipment, and electronic components. The textile industry, with a work-force of 35,500, has traditionally been associated with linen, but man-made fibre production has brought diversification to the sector and now accounts for a third of the total output of synthetic and artificial fibres in the UK. The related clothing and footwear trades employ 20,000 people. Taken together, food, drink and tobacco account for 24,500 jobs, the remainder of the manufacturing sector comprising a multiplicity of trades, such as chemicals and oil-refining, rubber and plastic goods, and furniture. The construction industry employs 39,500 people.

The Government offers special encouragement towards the establishment of new and the expansion of existing industry, including substantial grants towards capital investment and the provision of government-built factories at a low rent or on repayment terms. By Oct. 1976 the establishment of 192 new firms and over 371 schemes of expansion by existing firms since 1945 had been assisted, giving employment to over 60,000 workers.

Labour. An annual census of employment provides industrial analyses of employees. The census held in June 1976 (provisional) showed that there were then 491,582 employees in Northern Ireland comprising 291,151 males and 200,431 females. The figures include 15,810 part-time male employees and 60,429 part-time female employees.

Statistics of persons registered as unemployed in Northern Ireland are compiled monthly. The average rate of unemployment in Northern Ireland in 1976 was 10·3% compared with 7·9% in 1975. The average number of males registered as unemployed in 1976 was 37,481 (11·7%) and the average number of females was 17,388 (8·2%). The Department of Manpower Services provides an all-age guidance and placement service through a network of Employment Service Offices and Employment Service Careers Offices situated in the principal towns of Northern Ireland. They maintain registers of persons seeking employment (either full- or part-time) and those already in employment who wish to change their job. In 1976 the number of vacancies filled in Northern Ireland by the Employment Service was 22,209 (adults and young persons). The number of men (18 and over) placed was 13,381.

Unemployed workers or those about to become redundant who transfer to employment beyond daily travelling distance of their homes in Northern Ireland or to Great Britain or Western Europe may qualify for free fares, temporary separation allowances and other facilities. In addition, workers who resettle permanently within Northern Ireland or Great Britain may be eligible for dependants' fares, household removal expenses, a grant for incidental expenses and an amount to assist with legal expenses and house agents fees incurred in the sale and purchase of housing. Assistance is also available to employers who transfer key workers temporarily or permanently to Northern Ireland from other countries or within Northern Ireland in connection with the establishment or expansion of an industrial undertaking. Free advice on manpower problems is available from the specially trained staff of the Department's Manpower Advisory Unit on the request of any employer.

The Department of Manpower Services maintains a register of disabled persons who are in the employment field and under the provisions of the Disabled Persons (Employment) Acts (NI) 1945 and 1960, makes efforts to find suitable work for those who are unemployed. Employment rehabilitation courses are provided at the Employment Rehabilitation Unit at Whitehouse to assist unemployed disabled persons to readjust themselves to working conditions and to enhance their prospects of obtaining suitable employment. Allowances are paid to persons attending these courses.

Enterprise Ulster is a direct labour organization with the main function of providing employment. Labour is recruited directly from the Unemployed Register and is offered a prospect of interesting and stable employment while at the same time employees are given every encouragement to seek better paid work in industry. Training is a vital element in its operations, and a wide range of training courses and facilities has been developed. Work is carried out mainly for public bodies and projects are of a community and amenity nature such as play areas, parks, playing fields, etc. At 31 Aug. 1977, 127 schemes were in operation providing employment for 1,750 men.

There are 14 Government Training Centres in Northern Ireland which now provide some 3,500 training places and are capable of an annual output of over 4,000 trainees. Two of the centres provide 100 training places in traditionally female occupations. Apprentice training accounts for approximately two-thirds of training places. Most of the remaining places are reserved for adults but there are also special courses for young people under 18 years who have been unable to obtain an apprenticeship.

In the sphere of industrial relations a new independent and statutory body entitled The Labour Relations Agency was established under the Industrial Relations (NI) Order 1976 with the general duty to promote the improvement of industrial relations and to encourage the extension, development and, where necessary, the reform of collective bargaining machinery. The Agency is empowered to undertake research and provide an advisory service on industrial relations matters and to act as a forum for discussion of matters of mutual concern to management and unions. It also has a range of specific functions in the industrial relations field, including the settlement of disputes concerning trade-union recognition. In addition, since Aug. 1977 the Agency has assumed the role previously performed by the Department in relation to the provision of conciliation and arbitration services. This means that, supplementing the procedures within industry for the prevention and settlement of disputes, the Agency plays an important part as an impartial third party in helping the sides to clarify issues in dispute and to settle their differences by agreement. Where conciliation fails, the Agency may arrange, if the parties agree, for independent arbitration by one or more persons appointed by the Agency or by the Industrial Court. Occasionally a settlement is promoted by the appointment of a Court of Inquiry. However, the great majority of industrial disputes are settled without stoppage of work, and Northern Ireland's record of days lost due to industrial disputes bears favourable comparison with that of the rest of the UK.

The Fair Employment Agency for Northern Ireland was established under the Fair Employment (NI) Act 1976, with a duty of promoting an equality of opportunity in Northern Ireland as between persons of different religious beliefs, and of working for the elimination of religious and political discrimination in employment which the Act makes unlawful.

The Equal Opportunities Commission for Northern Ireland was established under the Sex Discrimination (NI) Order 1976 with a duty of working towards the elimination of Sex Discrimination in the fields covered by the Order, the promotion of equality of opportunity between men and women generally and the review of the working of the Order and equal pay legislation.

The Department of Manpower Services is responsible, through the Factory Inspectorate, for the administration in Northern Ireland of services concerned with the safety, health and welfare of workers in factories, offices, shops and certain other industrial undertakings. These services are embodied mainly in the Factories Act (NI) 1965, the Office and Shop Premises Act (NI) 1966 and the Regulations and Orders made thereunder. The Factories Act, which sets out statutory requirements for securing minimum standards of safety, health and welfare in factories, docks, warehouses, electrical stations, institutions, building operations and works of engineering construction, applies to over 7,200 premises and sites. The Office and Shop Premises Act sets out similar standards which apply to over 17,000 premises. Over 3,000 of these premises are subject to enforcement by the Department of Manpower Services. The remainder are subject to enforcement by the District Councils or, in the case of offices and shops at quarries, by the Department of Commerce through its Quarries Inspector. The hours of employment in factories of women and of young persons under 18 years of age are limited by the Factories Act.

The hours of employment of adult male factory workers and of all office and shop workers is outside the scope of the above legislation. Any accident occurring to a person employed in premises subject to the above legislation, which causes death or which disables the person from earning full wages for more than 3 days, is reportable to the enforcing authority. During 1975, 13 fatal and 4,579 non-fatal accidents were reported under the Factories Act and 19 non-fatal accidents were reported under the Office and Shop Premises Act. The Department is also responsible for the enforcement of the Truck Acts which require that the wages of a manual worker be paid in the coin of the realm, unless the worker has requested a prescribed alternative form of payment and the employer has acceded to this request.

COMMERCE. Northern Ireland has a substantial export trade with countries overseas, but as a large part of it is routed through Great Britain, separate details are not available. The main markets outside the UK are Canada, USA, the Irish Republic, USSR, the EEC and EFTA. From 1975 no detailed trade figures of Northern Ireland were compiled.

Imports and exports, including trade with Great Britain (in £1m. sterling), for calendar years:

	1966	*1967*	*1968*	*1969*	*1970*	*1971*	*1972*	*1973*
Imports	523	552	660	728	829	892	937	1,304
Exports	478	507	596	669	745	843	917	1,175

In 1975, about 80% of the total trade came from or to Great Britain or from foreign countries *via* Great Britain.

Principal imports in 1973 (including imports from Great Britain) were valued at: Textiles, fibres, yarns and fabrics, £222m.; machinery, £162·7m.; transport equipment, £154·6m.; chemicals, £62m.; cereals and cereal preparations, £54m.; petroleum and petroleum products, £50·5m.; tobacco and manufactures, £44·6m.; fruit and vegetables, fresh and processed, £36·6m.

Principal exports in 1973 (including exports to Great Britain) were valued at: Textiles, fibres, yarns and fabrics, £402m.; machinery, £108·9m.; meat and meat preparations, £70m.; transport equipment, £69m.; dairy produce and eggs, £51·6m.

Tourism. Tourism earns a substantial amount of revenue for Northern Ireland and total spending by some 500,000 visitors in 1976 was estimated at £25m. Altogether tourism provides over 8,000 permanent jobs and some 3,000 temporary or seasonal jobs. The Northern Ireland Tourist Board plays a major role in promoting the development of tourist traffic in Northern Ireland.

The protection of scenic beauty, scientific and nature interest, and wildlife is fostered under the Amenity Lands Act (NI) 1965 and the Wild Birds Protection Acts (NI) 1931 to 1968 by the Department of the Environment for Northern Ireland, which is advised by the Ulster Countryside Committee, the Nature Reserves Committee and the Wild Birds Advisory Committee. Eight Areas of Outstanding Natural Beauty and 40 Areas of Scientific Interest have been designated, and in these areas special attention is given respectively to the amenity and scientific aspects of planning applications. Country Parks have been established at Crawfordsburn, Co. Down, and the Roe Valley and Ness Wood, Co. Londonderry, and land for further parks has been acquired at Scrabo and Redburn, Co. Down, Castle Archdale, Co. Fermanagh, and The Birches in N. Armagh. The Lagan Valley between Belfast and Lisburn is being administered as a Regional Park in which there will be collaboration between public and private amenity developments. Thirty-one National Nature Reserves have been declared, and steady progress is being made with the acquisition of further reserves. Nine areas have been designated as Bird Sanctuaries.

The Department is advised by the Historic Monuments Council on the exercise of its powers under the Historic Monuments Act (NI) 1971 in respect of the conservation of historic monuments and the preservation of objects of archaeological or historic interest. At present there are 140 monuments in State care, either in the Department's ownership or guardianship. The Department, advised by the Historic Buildings Council, is also responsible for listing buildings of special architectural or historic interest and for designating areas of similar interest the character or appearance of which it is desirable to preserve or enhance. To date some 2,500 buildings have been listed and 7 areas have been designated.

COMMUNICATIONS

Road and Rail. The Northern Ireland Transport Holding Company was established under the Transport Act (NI) 1967 with overall responsibility for the financing but not the operation of bus and train services. All train services are operated by the Northern Ireland Railways Co. Ltd which is a subsidiary of the Holding Company. In Jan. 1978 there were 357 km (1,600 mm gauge) of railway open. Most bus services are operated by two other subsidiaries, Ulsterbus Ltd and Citybus Ltd. Ulsterbus runs services outside the Belfast Area (except for a few services provided by privately owned bus undertakings in certain rural areas) while all the services within the Belfast Area are run by Citybus.

A mixed public sector/private enterprise system under licence is in operation for the carriage of goods by road for reward. Approximately 1,800 operators and 4,000 vehicles have been licensed; the biggest single operator is Northern Ireland Carriers Ltd.

The number of motor vehicles licensed at 30 Sept. 1976 was 403,219, comprising private cars, 325,766; motor cycles, 15,252; hackney vehicles, 2,317; goods vehicles, 11,544; agricultural tractors, 7,046. In addition, there were some 6,000 vehicles which were not subject to licence duty.

The Department of the Environment (NI) is responsible for the provision and maintenance of all public roads, bridges and street lighting in the Province and for the operation of the Strangford Lough Ferry. In addition to a Headquarters Unit this Roads Service of the Department operates through Divisional Offices in Ballymena, Belfast, Coleraine, Craigavon, Downpatrick and Omagh and smaller offices in other centres.

At 1 April 1977 the total mileage of roads was 14,477, graded for administrative purposes as follows: Motorway, 67 miles; all purpose trunk, 330 miles; Class I, 1,033 miles; Class II, 1,760 miles; Class III, 2,938 miles; unclassified, 8,349 miles.

Aviation. On 1 June 1971 ownership of Belfast Airport passed to the Northern Ireland Transport Holding Company and a subsidiary of the Holding Company, Northern Ireland Airports Ltd, is now responsible for the operation and development of the airport. Development, which will double the size of the terminal building was under construction in 1978. In 1977, 1·1m. passengers and 11,000 tonnes of freight and mail were handled.

Passenger services operate between Belfast and London, Birmingham, Blackpool, Bristol, Cardiff, East Midlands, Edinburgh, Exeter, Glasgow, Leeds/Bradford, Liverpool, Manchester, Newcastle upon Tyne and Southampton.

Shipping. Passenger services operate between Belfast and Liverpool and between Larne and (i) Cairnryan and (ii) Stranraer. In 1975 the net tonnage of shipping using these ports was about 12·5m. tons. Conventional cargo services have given way in many cases to container, unit load and drive on/drive off services. The latter type of service now operates between Belfast, Larne and Warrenpoint to various ports in UK.

JUSTICE, RELIGION, EDUCATION AND WELFARE

Justice. The superior courts in Northern Ireland comprise the Supreme Court of Judicature and the Court of Criminal Appeal. All matters relating to these courts are under the jurisdiction of the Parliament of the UK and the judges of the superior courts are appointed by the Crown on the advice of the Lord Chancellor.

The inferior courts comprise the County Courts and the Magistrates' Courts (Petty Sessions). The judiciary in these courts (County Court Judges and Resident Magistrates) are appointed by the Crown on the recommendation of the Lord Chancellor. The County Courts deal with criminal matters and with civil disputes, where the sum at issue does not exceed £1,000. But in criminal injury cases their jurisdiction is unlimited. County Court staff are also responsible for administering all the Assize and Belfast City Commission Courts for criminal trials on indictment. These trials are presided over by High Court Judges. The County Courts act as appellate courts from the decisions in Petty Sessions. The Petty Sessions are held regularly in 59 Petty Sessions districts and are presided over by Resident Magistrates, who are permanent legally qualified judicial officers and normally sit alone. In Juvenile Courts, however, the bench is composed of 1 Resident Magistrate and 2 lay members, 1 of whom must be a woman.

Police. The police force consists of the Royal Ulster Constabulary, supported by the Royal Ulster Constabulary Reserve, a mainly part-time force.

Religion. The religious professions at the census of 1971 were: Roman Catholics, 477,919; Presbyterians, 405,719; Church of Ireland, 334,318 (including Church of England and Episcopal Church of Scotland); Methodists, 71,235; others and not stated, 230,449.

Education. Education in Northern Ireland is administered centrally by the Department of Education and locally by 5 education and library boards. The Department is concerned with the whole range of education from nursery education through to higher education and continuing education; for sport and recreation; for youth services; for the arts and culture (including libraries) and for community relations and community development. District councils are the main providers of sport, recreation and community facilities and the Education and Library Boards have a responsibility where the facilities are intended primarily for education and youth service activities. The Department assists with grants as far as the district councils are concerned and meets the full cost in relation to Education and Library Boards.

The 5 Education and Library Boards which took over responsibility for the local administration of the education and library services on 1 Oct. 1973 are required to ensure that there are sufficient schools of all kinds to meet the needs of their area. They provide primary and secondary schools, special schools for handicapped pupils and institutions of further education. The Boards also make contributions towards the cost of maintaining voluntary schools; award grammar, university and other scholarships; provide milk and meals; free books and transport for pupils; enforce school attendance; regulate the employment of children and young people and secure the provision of recreational and youth service facilities. They are also required to develop a comprehensive and efficient library service for their areas. The following are the statistics for the 1976–77 academic year:

Universities. The Queen's University of Belfast (founded in 1849 as a college of the Queen's University of Ireland and reconstituted as a separate university in 1908) had 86 professors, 219 readers and senior lecturers, 445 lecturers and tutors and 5,754 full-time students.

The New University of Ulster at Coleraine, of which Magee University College, Londonderry, is now an integral part, had 31 professors, 30 readers and senior lecturers, 149 lecturers and demonstrators and 1,757 full-time students.

The Ulster College, the Northern Ireland Polytechnic, is a central institution providing higher education for the whole of Northern Ireland with a full-time academic staff of 495, 3,057 full-time and 2,599 part-time students on vocational courses of further education and 443 students on teacher-training courses.

Secondary Education. 79 grammar schools with 56,127 pupils and 3,198 full-time teachers; 183 secondary (intermediate) schools with 104,654 pupils and 6,314 full-time teachers: the last technical intermediate school closed in June 1974.

Primary Education. 1,089 primary schools with 207,574 pupils and 8,272 teachers; 45 nursery schools with 2,374 pupils and 78 teachers.

Further Education. 27 institutions of further education with 1,446 full-time and 1,791 part-time teachers and an enrolment of 10,924 full-time, 12,290 part-time day and 14,568 evening students on vocational courses; and over 34,300 students on non-vocational (mostly evening) courses.

Special Educational Treatment. 30 special schools, including hospital schools, with 2,613 pupils and 268 teachers.

Teachers. There were 19,645 full-time teachers (7,954 men and 11,691 women) in grant-aided schools and institutions of further education. The minimum general teacher-training course is of 3 years' duration and there were 3,413 students (1,073 men and 2,340 women) in training; these included students following teacher-training courses at university establishments and at Ulster College.

Expenditure. Expenditure by the Department of Education in 1976–77 was £260·9m.

Health and Personal Social Services. Under the provisions of the Health and Personal Social Services (NI) Order 1972, the Department of Health and Social Services is responsible for the provision of integrated health and personal social services in Northern Ireland, designed to promote the physical and mental health of the people of Northern Ireland through the prevention, diagnosis and treatment of illness, and also to promote their social welfare. Four Health and Social Services Boards, Eastern, Northern, Southern and Western, established under the above Order, administer health and personal social services, as the Department directs, within their designated areas.

Social Security. The social security schemes in Northern Ireland are similar to those in force in Great Britain.

The system of social security established by the Social Security Act 1975, and the corresponding system established by the Social Security (NI) Act 1975, operate, by virtue of a reciprocal agreement between Great Britain and Northern Ireland, as a single system throughout the United Kingdom. The National Insurance Joint Authority, consisting of the Secretary of State for Social Services and the Head of the Department of Health and Social Services for Northern Ireland is responsible under this reciprocal agreement for making any necessary financial adjustments between the National Insurance of the two countries and also has responsibility for determining the administrative procedures for the purpose of giving effect to the provisions of the reciprocal agreement. There are comprehensive reciprocal agreements with the Isle of Man, and agreements covering reciprocity in respect of most benefits have been made by the Government of the UK, applying to the schemes in both Great Britain and Northern Ireland, with Australia, Austria, Belgium, Canada, Cyprus, Denmark, Finland, France, Germany (Fed. Rep.), Gibraltar, Guernsey, Irish Republic, Israel, Italy, Jamaica, Jersey, Luxembourg, Malta, the Netherlands, New Zealand, Norway, Spain, Sweden, Switzerland, Turkey and Yugoslavia. There are also limited agreements with Bermuda and USA.

Since 1 April 1973 the reciprocal agreements between the UK and the other members of the EEC have been largely replaced by the Social Security Regulations of the Community.

National Insurance. The total number of contributions at the close of the former scheme in April 1975 was about 660,000. Statistics for the current scheme are not yet available. During the year ended 31 March 1977 the average number of persons in receipt of sickness benefit was over 19,000 and in receipt of unemployment benefit was 30,000. Widows' benefits were in payment to about 15,000 women and retirement pensions to about 181,000 persons. Persons in receipt of invalidity pension at 31 March 1977 numbered about 27,000, of whom about 24,000 were awarded invalidity allowance. Accidents in respect of which claims to benefit are made occur at the rate of approximately 290 a week. Receipts, including an item related to the financial adjustments mentioned above, of the Northern Ireland National Insurance Fund in the year ended 31 March 1977 were £265·6m. and payments, £235m.

Family Allowances. The number of families in receipt of allowances at 31 March 1977 was 146,795, and the cost of the allowances in the year ended 31 March 1977 was £22·9m. Family Allowances were replaced by Child Benefit from April 1977.

Supplementary Benefits. Persons in receipt of supplementary benefits numbered 109,778 at 22 Feb. 1977 at a cost of £59·2m. in the year ended 31 March 1977.

Family Income Supplement. Family income supplement at 31 March 1977 was in payment to 8,272 persons at a cost of £2·2m.

Books of Reference

The annual and other publications of the various Departments and the Reports, etc., of Parliamentary Committees may be obtained from HM Stationery Office, Belfast.

Ulster Year Book, 1977. Belfast, HMSO, 1977
Census of Population Reports, Northern Ireland. Belfast, HMSO
Digest of Statistics. Belfast, HMSO (bi-annual)
Northern Ireland Development 1970–75. Belfast, HMSO, 1970
Northern Ireland Economic Report. Belfast, HMSO (annual)
Who Makes What in Northern Ireland: A Trade Directory. Belfast, HMSO
Re-organization of Local Government. Belfast, HMSO, 1972
Reports on the Census of Production of Northern Ireland. Belfast, HMSO (annual)
Higher Education in Northern Ireland. Belfast, HMSO
The Education, Initial Training and Probation of Teachers in Northern Ireland Schools and Institutions of Further Education (Lelievre Report). Belfast, HMSO, 1973
Re-organization of Secondary Education in Northern Ireland. Belfast, HMSO, 1976
Economic Development in Northern Ireland. Belfast, HMSO, 1965
The Future of Northern Ireland: A Paper for Discussion. London, HMSO, 1972
Bell, G., *The Protestants of Ulster.* London, 1976
Biggs-Davison, J., *The Hand is Red.* London, 1974
Budge, I., and O'Leary, C., *Belfast: Approach to Crisis.* London, 1973
Farrell, M., *Northern Ireland: The Orange State.* London, 1976
Hull, R. H., *The Irish Triangle.* Princeton Univ. Press, 1976
Lawrence, R. J., *The Government of Northern Ireland: Public Finance and Public Services.* OUP, 1965
Mansergh, N., *The Government of Northern Ireland.* London, 1936
Quekett, Sir A. S., *The Constitution of Northern Ireland.* 3 pts. Belfast, 1928–47
Rose, R., *Northern Ireland: A Time of Choice.* London, 1976
Shearman, Hugh, *Northern Ireland. Its People, Resources, History and Government.* Belfast, HMSO, 1968
Winchester, S., *Northern Ireland in Crisis: Reporting the Ulster Troubles.* New York, 1975

ISLE OF MAN

AREA AND POPULATION. Area, 227 sq. miles (572 sq. km); resident population census April 1976, 60,496. The principal towns are Douglas (population, 19,897), Ramsey (5,372), Peel, (3,295), Castletown (2,788). Vital statistics, 1976: Births, 721; deaths, 977; marriages, 392. The number of Manx-speaking people was 284 in 1971 (165 in 1961 and 4,657 in 1901), all of whom are bilingual.

CONSTITUTION AND GOVERNMENT. The Isle of Man is administered in accordance with its own laws by the Court of Tynwald, consisting of the Governor, appointed by the Crown; the Legislative Council, composed of the Lord Bishop of Sodor and Man, the Attorney-General and 8 members selected by the House of Keys, total 11 members, including the Governor; and the House of Keys, a representative assembly of 24 members chosen on adult suffrage with 6 months' residence for 5 years by the 6 'sheadings' or local sub-divisions, and the 4 municipalities. The island is not bound by Acts of the Imperial Parliament unless specially mentioned in them.

A special relationship exists between the Isle of Man and the European Economic Community providing for free trade and adoption by the Isle of Man of the EEC's external trade policies with third countries. The Island remains free to levy its own system of rates and taxes.

Flag: Red, with 3 steel-coloured legs armoured and spurred (knees and spurs, yellow) in the centre.

The elections to the House of Keys, Nov. 1976, resulted in the return of 20 Independents, 3 Labour and 1 Manx Nationalist. Number of voters, 44,324.

An Executive Council to act with the Governor on all matters of government was set up under the Isle of Man Constitution Act, 1961. It consists at present of 5 members of the House of Keys and 2 of the Legislative Council.

Lieut.-Governor: Sir John Paul, GCMG, OBE, MC (term of office began Jan. 1974).

Government Secretary: T. Kelly.

Government Treasurer: W. Dawson.

ECONOMY

Budget. Revenue is derived from customs duties and from income tax. In 1977–78 the budget allowed for revenue and capital expenditure of £59,232,880. Income tax was 21·25p in the £. No death duties or surtaxes are levied. Company registration tax is levied at a flat rate of £200 on every company incorporated in the Isle of Man which trades and is controlled outside the island. A Land Speculation Tax has recently been introduced at the same rate as income tax.

The island makes an annual contribution to the UK Government of 5% of net 'common purse' receipts (share of customs and excise duties and VAT received by Treasury) towards cost of defence and other common services provided by the UK Government. That contribution currently amounts to about £500,000.

Currency. Notes to the value of £10, £5, £1 and 50p are issued by the Isle of Man Government. Both the UK and Irish Republic currency are accepted and used in the Island which is within the Sterling Area for Exchange Control purposes. Annual minting of decimal coinage takes place, and in 1973 and 1974 legal tender gold coins in half sovereign, sovereign, £2 and £5 pieces were issued. Commemorative crowns have also been issued since 1970, and silver and platinum decimal sets have been minted more recently.

AGRICULTURE. The principal agricultural produce of the island consists of oats, wheat, barley, potatoes, grasses, fatstock dairy products. The total area under crops in 1976 was 7,563 acres and of rough grazings (1976), 42,201 acres. The total area under cereals was 11,608 acres, including 3,257 under oats, 899 under wheat and 6,941 under barley or bere. There were also 1,482 acres under turnips and swedes, 900 under potatoes, 6,834 under hay and 61,443 of permanent grass for both grazing and silage. Livestock in 1976: 652 horses, 39,166 cattle, 100,794 sheep and 3,889 pigs.

COMMUNICATIONS

Roads. There are 500 miles of good roads. The International TT Motor Cycle Races and cycle races take place annually. Omnibus services operate to all parts of the island.

Number of vehicles (31 March 1976): 26,445 cars and commercial vehicles, 865 taxis and buses, 2,407 motor-cycles and scooters, 1,419 tractors.

Railways. The island retains several unique transportation systems, including 100-year-old horse-drawn trams, and the Manx Electric Railway, which links Douglas with Ramsey and has a spur line which makes the ascent of Snaefell Mountain (2,036 ft) in the summer season.

The Isle of Man Steam Railway still operates between Douglas and Port Erin.

Aviation. Ronaldsway Airport handles scheduled services operated by British Airways, Dan-Air, BIA and British Midland Airways to and from London, Manchester, Belfast, Dublin, Glasgow, Liverpool, Birmingham, Blackpool, Newcastle upon Tyne, etc. Air taxi services also operate.

Shipping. Car ferries of the Isle of Man Steam Packet Company link the Island with Fleetwood, Liverpool, Ardrossan, Dublin and Belfast, and Unit-load cargo and container services operate from Douglas, Castletown and Ramsey to many UK and foreign ports.

Broadcasting. The first constitutionally licensed commercial radio station in the British Isles, Manx Radio, is operated by Government on medium and VHF wave-lengths from Douglas.

Newspapers. In 1976 there were 5 weekly newspapers.

JUSTICE AND EDUCATION

Police. The police force numbered 147 all ranks and 8 cadets in 1977.

Education. In Jan. 1977 there were 37 primary schools. The enrolled pupils numbered 5,771. The net expenditure on education for 1974–75 amounted to £2·99m.; in addition, capital grants of £559,000 were made for school buildings. There are 6 secondary schools, 4 provided by the Education Board (3,935 registered pupils), 1 direct grant school for girls (362 registered pupils), 1 independent public school for boys (488 registered pupils), 1 college of further education (222 full- and 3,128 part-time and evening pupils).

Books of Reference

Isle of Man Digest of Economic and Social Statistics, 1977. Isle of Man Government, 1977
Birch, J. W., *The Isle of Man: A Study in Economic Geography.* CUP, 1963
Kinvig, R. H., *History of the Isle of Man.* Oxford, 1945.—*The Isle of Man: A Social, Cultural and Political History.* Liverpool Univ. Press, 1975
Mais, S. P. B., *Isle of Man.* London, 1954
Stenning, E. H., *Portrait of the Isle of Man.* London, 1958

CHANNEL ISLANDS

AREA. The Channel Islands are situated off the north-west coast of France and are the only portions of the 'Duchy of Normandy' now belonging to the Crown of England, to which they have been attached since the Conquest. They consist of Jersey (28,717 acres), Guernsey (15,654 acres) and the following dependencies of Guernsey—Alderney (1,962), Brechou (74), Great Sark (1,035), Little Sark (239), Herm (320), Jethou (44) and Lihou (38), a total of 48,083 acres, or 75 sq. miles (194 sq. km).

The climate is mild. Total rainfall (1976), Jersey, 669·2 mm; Guernsey, 682 mm. Temperature registered (1976): highest, Jersey, 33·3° C.; Guernsey, 30·8° C.; lowest, Jersey, −2·6° C.; Guernsey, 1·6° C.

CONSTITUTION. The Lieut.-Governors and Cs.-in-C. of Jersey and Guernsey are the personal representatives of the Sovereign, the Commanders of the Armed Forces of the Crown and the channel of communication between H.M. Government in the UK and the insular governments. They are appointed by the Crown and have an invoice but no vote in the Assemblies of the States (the insular legislatures). The Secretaries to the Lieut.-Governors are their staff officers.

The Bailiffs are appointed by the Crown and are Presidents both of the Assembly of the States and of the Royal Courts of Jersey and Guernsey. They have in the States a casting vote.

LANGUAGE. The official languages are French and English, but English is gradually supplanting French. The language commonly used is English, but in the country districts of Jersey and Guernsey and throughout Sark some people also speak a Norman-French dialect; that of Alderney has died out.

TRADE. From 1958 the trade of the Channel Islands with the UK has been regarded as internal trade.

COMMUNICATIONS

Road. Omnibus services operate in all parts of Jersey and Guernsey.

Aviation. Scheduled air services are maintained by British Airways, BIA, Aurigny Air Services, Caledonian and other companies between the islands and airports in the UK, Irish Republic, the Netherlands and France. During the summer months these services are greatly increased, both in the number of airports served and in the frequency of flights.

Shipping. Passenger and cargo steam services between Jersey, Guernsey and England are maintained by British Rail; between Guernsey, Jersey and England and St Malo by the Commodore Shipping Co.; between Guernsey, Jersey, Alderney and France by Condor Ltd (hydrofoil), and between Guernsey and Alderney and England and Guernsey and Sark by local companies.

Post and Broadcasting. Postal and overseas telephone and telegraph services are maintained by the respective Postal Administrations of each bailiwick. The local telephone services are maintained by the insular authorities. There were, in 1976, 25,637 subscribers in Jersey and 19,635 in Guernsey.

There is an independent television station in Jersey.

JUSTICE AND RELIGION

Justice. Justice is administered by the Royal Courts of Jersey and Guernsey, each of which consists of the Bailiff and 12 Jurats, the latter being elected by an electoral college. There is an appeal from the Royal Courts to the Courts of Appeal of Jersey and of Guernsey. A final appeal lies to the Privy Council in certain cases. A stipendiary magistrate in each, Jersey and Guernsey, deals with minor civil and criminal cases.

Church. Jersey and Guernsey each constitutes a deanery within the diocese of Winchester. The rectories (12 in Jersey; 10 in Guernsey) are in the gift of the Crown. The Roman Catholic and various Nonconformist Churches are represented.

Books of Reference

Ambrière, F., *Les Iles Anglo-Normandes*. Paris, 1971
Coysh, V., *The Channel Islands: A New Study*. Newton Abbot, 1977
Lempière, R., *Portrait of the Channel Islands*. London, 1970.—*History of the Channel Islands*. London, 1974
Lockley, R. M., *The Channel Islands*. London, 1968
Myhill, H., *Introducing the Channel Islands*. London, 1964
Uttley, J., *The Story of the Channel Islands*. London, 1966
Wood, J., *Herm, Our Island Home*. London, 1973

JERSEY

POPULATION (census, 1976), 74,470. In the year ended 31 Dec. 1976 there were 812 births and 900 deaths. The town is St Helier on the south coast.

CONSTITUTION. The States consist of 12 senators (elected for 6 years, 6 retiring every third year), 12 Constables (triennial) and 28 Deputies (triennial), all elected on universal suffrage by the people.

The island legislature is 'The States of Jersey'. The States comprises the Bailiff, the Lieut.-Governor, 12 Senators, the Constables of the 12 parishes of the island, 28 Deputies, the Dean of Jersey, the Attorney-General and the Solicitor-General. They all have the right to speak in the Assembly, but only the 52 elected members (the Senators, Constables and Deputies) have the right to vote; the Bailiff has a casting vote. General elections for Senators and Deputies are held every third year. Except in specific instances, enactments passed by the States require the sanction of The Queen-in-Council. The Lieut.-Governor has the power of veto on certain forms of legislation.

Flag: White with a red saltire.

Lieut.-Governor and C.-in-C. of Jersey: Gen. Sir Desmond Fitzpatrick, GCB, DSO, MBE, MC.

Secretary and ADC to the Lieut.-Governor: Lieut.-Cdr O. M. B. de Las Casas, OBE, RN (Retd).

Assistant Secretary to the Lieut.-Governor: Capt. J. Tessier-Yandell, OBE.

Bailiff of Jersey and President of the States: Sir Frank Ereaut.
Deputy Bailiff: P. L. Crill.

ECONOMY

Budget, (year ending 31 Dec. 1976). Revenue, £55,167,513; expenditure, £39,882,100; public debt, £4,138,690. The standard rate of income tax is 20p in the pound. No super-tax or death duties are levied. Parochial rates of moderate amount are payable by owners and occupiers.

Currency. The States issue bank-notes in denominations of £10, £5 and £1.

INDUSTRY AND TRADE

Industry. Principal activities: Tourism; total number of hotel and guesthouse beds (1976), 25,362; expenditure of tourists (1975), £61·3m. Agriculture; total output (1976), £16m. Light industry, mainly electrical goods, textiles and clothing. Total exports (1976), £15·5m. Banking and finance; total bank deposits (1976), £1,100m., and parent companies, £800m.

Commerce (1976). Principal imports: Food, £23,055,774; manufactured goods, classified by material, £21,360,899, and miscellaneous, £19,923,855; machinery and transport equipment, £26,115,086; mineral fuels, £10,083,890; chemicals, £7,770,847. Principal exports (1976): Food, £16,083,160; manufactured goods, classified by material, £23,241,297, and miscellaneous, £22,691,707; machinery and transport equipment, £9,976,667.

COMMUNICATIONS

Aviation. The Jersey airport is situated at St Peter. It covers approximately 375 acres. Number of aircraft movements (1976) 68,234; number of passenger arrivals, 1,401,038.

Shipping (1976). Number of commercial ships entering St Helier, 3,836; Gorey, 592. All vessels arriving in Jersey from outside Jersey waters report at St Helier or Gorey on first arrival. There is a harbour of minor importance at St Aubin. Ships registered in Jersey: Commercial, 32; fishing boats, 355; yachts, 1,193 (of 15 ft and over). Passengers arrived in 1976, 427,790.

EDUCATION (1977). There are 7 secondary schools and 30 primary schools (including fee-paying preparatory departments); 6,914 pupils attend the primary schools, 5,450 the secondary schools. Highlands College offers full- and part-time courses to Ordinary and National Certificate and Diploma levels or similar standards and, together with Les Quennevais Adult Community Centre, evening classes in technical and recreational subjects.

Books of Reference

Balleine, G. R., *Biographical Dictionary of Jersey*. London, 1948.—*A History of the Island of Jersey*. London, 1950.— *The Bailiwick of Jersey*. 3rd ed. London, 1970
Bois, F. de L., *The Constitutional History of Jersey*. Jersey, 1970
Carre, A. L., *English–Jersey Language Vocabulary*. Jersey, 1972
Le Maistre, F., *Dictionnaire Jersiais-Français*. Jersey, 1966
Powell, G. C., *Economic Survey of Jersey*. Jersey, 1971

States of Jersey Library: Royal Square, St. Helier. *Librarian:* J. K. Antill, FLA.

GUERNSEY

POPULATION. Census population, 1976, was 54,256 (1975 estimate, 51,620). Births during 1976 were 618; deaths, 632. The town is St Peter Port.

CONSTITUTION. The government of the island is conducted by committees appointed by the States.

The States of Deliberation, the Parliament of Guernsey, is composed of the following members: The Bailiff, who is President *ex officio*; 12 Conseillers; H.M. Procureur and H.M. Comptroller (Law Officers of the Crown), who have a voice but no vote; 33 People's Deputies elected by popular franchise; 10 Douzaine Representatives elected by their Parochial Douzaines; 2 representatives of the States of Alderney.

The States of Election, an electoral college, elects the Jurats and Conseillers. It is composed of the following members: The Bailiff (President *ex officio*); the 12 Jurats or 'Jurés-Justiciers'; the 12 Conseillers; the 10 Rectors; H.M. Procureur and H.M. Comptroller; the 33 People's Deputies; 34 Douzaine Representatives; and (for the election of Conseillers) 4 representatives of the States of Alderney.

Since Jan. 1949 all legislative powers and functions (with minor exceptions) formerly exercised by the Royal Court have been vested in the States of Deliberation. Projets de Loi (Bills) require the sanction of The Queen-in-Council.

Flag: White with a red cross.

Lieut.-Governor and C.-in-C. of Guernsey and its Dependencies: Vice-Adm. Sir John Martin, KCB, DSC, FNI.

Secretary and ADC to the Lieut.-Governor: Capt. M. H. T. Mellish, OBE.

Bailiff of Guernsey and President of the States: Sir John Loveridge, CBE.

Deputy Bailiff of Guernsey: C. K. Frossard.

FINANCE (year ending 31 Dec. 1976). Revenue, £21·5m. (including £702,796 for Alderney); expenditure, £18·5m. (including £651,206 for Alderney), States' funded debt less sinking fund provisions, £1,824,320; note and coin issue, £9,159,880. The standard rate of income tax is 20p in the pound. States and parochial rates are very moderate. No super-tax or death duties are levied.

COMMERCE (1976). Principal imports: Coal, 14,246 tons; petrol and oils, 44m. gallons. Principal exports: Tomatoes (1975), 45,906 tons net; flowers and fern, £8m.; sweet peppers, £167,698.

COMMUNICATIONS

Aviation. The airport in Guernsey, situated at La Villiaze, has a landing area of approximately 124 acres and a tarmac runway of 4,800 ft. In 1976, 190,072 passengers arrived from places outside the Channel Islands.

Shipping. The principal harbour is that of St Peter Port, and there is a harbour at St Sampson's (used mainly for commercial shipping). In 1976 the number of ship tons net entering and leaving Guernsey was 1,515,402. 105,723 passengers arrived from places outside the Channel Islands. Ships registered in Guernsey at 31 Dec. 1976 numbered 340 and 429 fishing vessels. Small craft registered, 3,509.

EDUCATION. There are 2 public schools in the island: Elizabeth College, founded by Queen Elizabeth in 1563, for boys, and the Ladies' College, for girls. The States grammar schools provide for education up to University entrance requirements, and there are numerous modern secondary and primary schools and a College of Further Education. The total number of school children is 9,860. Facilities are available for the study of art, domestic science and many other subjects of a technical nature. There is also a convent school with boarding facilities for girls.

ALDERNEY. Population (census, 1971), 1,686 (1975 estimate, 1,785). The island has an airport. The constitution of the island (reformed 1949) provides for its own popularly elected President and States (12 members), and its own Court. The town is St Anne's.

Flag: White with a red cross with the island badge in the centre.

President of the States: J. Kay-Mouat.

Clerk of the States: W. R. Jones, MA.
Clerk of the Court: K. K. Lacey, DSC.

SARK. Population (census, 1971), 584 (1975 estimate, 604). The constitution is a mixture of feudal and popular government with its Chief Pleas (parliament), consisting of 40 tenants and 12 popularly elected deputies, presided over by the Seneschal. The head of the island is the Seigneur. Sark has no income tax. Motor vehicles, except tractors, are not allowed.

Flag: White with a red cross and a red first quarter bearing two gold lions.

The Seigneur: J. M. Beaumont.
Seneschal: B. G. Jones.
Greffier: H. Carre, MBE.

Books of Reference

Carteret, A. R. de, *The Story of Sark.* London, 1956
Clark, L., *Sark Discovered.* London, 1956
Coysh, V., *Alderney.* Newton Abbot, 1974
Durand, R., *Guernsey, Present and Past.* Guernsey, 1933.—*Guernsey under German Rule.* London, 1946
A Short History of and Guide to Alderney. New ed. Guernsey, 1968
Hathaway, Sybil, *Dame of Sark: An Autobiography.* London, 1961
Le Huray, C. P., *The Bailiwick of Guernsey.* London, 1952
Robinson, G. W. S., *Guernsey.* Newton Abbot, 1977
Wood, A. and M. S., *Islands in Danger.* 2nd ed. London, 1957

UNITED STATES OF AMERICA

Capital: Washington, D.C.
Population: 216·82m. (1977)
GNP per capita: US$7,890 (1976)

HISTORY. The Declaration of Independence of the 13 states of which the American Union then consisted was adopted by Congress on 4 July 1776. On 30 Nov. 1782 Great Britain acknowledged the independence of the USA, and on 3 Sept. 1783 the treaty of peace was concluded and was ratified by the USA on 14 Jan. 1784.

AREA AND POPULATION. Population of conterminous USA at each census from 1790 to 1950, and for USA including Alaska and Hawaii, 1960 and 1970. Residents of Puerto Rico, the Philippine Islands, Guam, American Samoa, Virgin Islands of the USA and Panama Canal Zone, and persons in the military and naval service stationed abroad are not included in the figures of this table. Residents of Hawaii and Alaska are excluded prior to 1960. Residents of Indian reservations are excluded prior to 1890.

	White	*Negroes*[1]	*Other races*[2]	*Total*	*Decennial increase %*
1790	3,172,006[3]	757,208	—	3,929,214	—
1800	4,306,446	1,002,037	—	5,308,483	35·1
1810	5,862,073	1,377,808	—	7,239,881	36·4
1820	7,866,797	1,771,656	—	9,638,453	33·1
1830	10,537,378	2,328,642	—	12,866,020	33·5
1840	14,195,805	2,873,648	—	17,069,453	32·7
1850	19,553,068	3,638,808	—	23,191,876	35·9
1860	26,922,537	4,441,830	78,954[4]	31,443,321	35·6
1870[5]	33,589,377	4,880,009	88,985	38,558,371	22·6
1870[5]	*34,337,292*	*5,392,172*	*88,985*	*39,818,449*	*26·6*
1880	43,402,970	6,580,793	172,020	50,155,783	30·1
1890	55,101,258	7,488,676	357,780	62,947,714	25·5
1900	66,809,196	8,833,994	351,385	75,994,575	21·0
1910	81,731,957	9,827,763	412,546	91,972,266	21·0
1920	94,820,915	10,463,131	426,574	105,710,620	14·9[6]
1930	110,286,740[7]	11,891,143	597,163	122,775,046	16·1[6]
1940	118,214,870	12,865,518	588,887	131,669,275	7·3
1950	134,942,028	15,042,286	713,047	150,697,361	14·5
1960[8]	158,831,732	18,871,831	1,619,612	179,323,175	18·5
1970	177,748,975	22,580,289	2,882,662	203,211,926	13·3

[1] Seventeen southern states (including D.C.) in 1900 had 7,922,969 Negroes (89·7% of the total Negro population); in 1920, 8,912,231 (85·2%); in 1940, 9,904,619 (77%); in 1950, 10,225,407 (68%); in 1960, 11,311,607 (59·9%); in 1970, 11,969,961 (53%).

[2] 1870: 63,199 Chinese, 55 Japanese and 25,731 Indians; 1880, 105,465 Chinese, 148 Japanese and 66,407 Indians; 1890, 107,488 Chinese, 2,039 Japanese and 248,253 Indians; 1900, 89,863 Chinese, 24,326 Japanese and 237,196 Indians; 1910, 71,531 Chinese, 72,157 Japanese, 265,683 Indians and 3,175 other races; 1920, 61,639 Chinese, 111,010 Japanese, 244,437 Indians and 9,488 other races; 1930, 332,397 Indians, 74,954 Chinese, 138,834 Japanese and 50,978 other races; 1940, 333,969 Indians, 77,504 Chinese, 126,947 Japanese and 50,467 other races; 1950, 343,410 Indians, 141,768 Japanese, 117,629 Chinese, 110,240 other races; 1960, 523,591 Indians, 464,332 Japanese, 237,292 Chinese, 176,310 Filipino, 218,087 other races; 1970, 792,730 Indians, 591,290 Japanese, 435,062 Chinese, 343,060 Filipino, 720,520 other races.

[3] Made up of Anglo-Scottish, 89·1%; German, 5·6%; Dutch, 2·5%; Irish, 1·9%; French, 0·6%.

[4] 34,933 Chinese and 44,021 Indians.

[5] Enumeration in 1870 incomplete. Figures in italics represent estimated corrected population.

[*Footnotes continued on p. 1362.*]

Total population in 1970 at 203,211,926 comprised 98,912,192 males and 104,299,734 females; 149,324,930 were urban and 53,886,996 were rural. Negroes, 10,748,316 males and 11,831,973 females.

Estimated population, including Alaska and Hawaii, and armed forces overseas, on 1 July 1950, 152,271,000; 1955, 165,931,000; 1960, 180,671,000; 1965, 194,303,000; 1968, 200,706,000; 1969, 202,677,000; 1970, 204,878,000; 1971, 207,053,000; 1972, 208,846,000; 1973, 210,410,000; 1974, 211,901,000; 1975, 213,559,000; 1976, 215,142,000; 1977, 216,817,000.

The age distribution by sex of the total population of the US (excluding armed forces overseas, US population abroad and outlying areas) at the 1970 census was as follows:

Age-group	*Male*	*Female*	*Total*
Under 5	8,745,499	8,408,838	17,154,337
5–9	10,168,496	9,787,751	19,956,247
10–14	10,590,737	10,198,731	20,789,468
15–19	9,633,847	9,436,501	19,070,348
20–24	7,917,269	8,453,752	16,371,021
25–34	12,217,357	12,690,072	24,907,429
35–44	11,221,236	11,856,569	23,087,805
45–54	11,199,250	12,020,701	23,219,951
55–59	4,765,821	5,207,207	9,973,028
60–64	4,026,972	4,589,812	8,616,784
65–74	5,437,084	6,998,372	12,425,456
75 and over	2,978,624	4,651,422	7,630,046
Total	98,912,192	104,299,734	203,211,926

The following table includes population statistics, the year in which each of the original 13 states ratified the constitution, and the year when each of the other states was admitted into the Union. Postal abbreviations for the names of the states are shown in brackets. Land area includes land temporarily or partially covered by water, and lakes, etc., of less than 40 acres. (For census population by states and regions in 1940 and 1950 *see* THE STATESMAN'S YEAR-BOOK, 1952, pp. 552 and 553.)

Geographic divisions and states		*Land area: sq. miles, 1970*	*Census population 1 April 1960*	*Census population 1 April 1970*	*Pop. per sq. mile, 1970*
United States		3,536,855	179,323,175	203,235,298	57·5
New England		62,951	10,509,367	11,847,186	188·1
Maine (1820)	(*Me.*)	30,920	969,265	993,663	32·1
New Hampshire (1788)	(*N.H.*)	9,027	606,921	737,681	81·7
Vermont (1791)	(*Vt.*)	9,267	389,881	444,732	47·9
Massachusetts (1788)	(*Mass.*)	7,826	5,148,578	5,689,170	727·0
Rhode Island (1790)	(*R.I.*)	1,049	859,488	949,723	902·5
Connecticut (1788)	(*Conn.*)	4,862	2,535,234	3,032,217	623·6
Middle Atlantic		100,318	34,168,452	37,283,339	370·8
New York (1788)	(*N.Y.*)	47,831	16,782,304	18,241,266	380·3
New Jersey (1787)	(*N.J.*)	7,521	6,066,782	7,168,164	953·1
Pennsylvania (1787)	(*Pa.*)	44,966	11,319,366	11,793,909	262·3

[6] Between the 1910 census (15 April 1910) and the 1920 census (1 Jan. 1920), the period covered was 116 months (less than a full decade). Adjusting for this, the exact rate of increase for the decade was 15·4%. Similarly correcting for the 123 months between the 1920 and 1930 censuses, the true rate of increase was 15·7%.

[7] Figures for 1930 have been revised to include Mexicans (1,422,533), who were classified with 'Other Races' in the 1930 census reports.

[8] Figures for 1960 strictly comparable with those given for other years (*i.e.*, excluding Alaska and Hawaii) are: White, 158,454,956; Negroes, 18,860,117; other races, 1,149,163; total, 178,464,236; decennial increase, 18·4%.

Geographic divisions and states		*Land area: sq miles 1970*	*Census population 1 April 1960*	*Census population 1 April 1970*	*Pop. per sq. mile, 1970*
East North Central		244,101	36,225,024	40,252,678	164·9
Ohio (1803)	(*Oh.*)	40,975	9,706,397	10,652,017	260·0
Indiana (1816)	(*Ind.*)	36,097	4,662,498	5,193,669	143·9
Illinois (1818)	(*Ill.*)	55,748	10,081,158	11,113,976	199·4
Michigan (1837)	(*Mich.*)	56,817	7,823,194	8,875,083	156·2
Wisconsin (1848)	(*Wis.*)	54,464	3,951,777	4,417,933	81·1
West North Central		507,723	15,394,115	16,344,389	32·1
Minnesota (1858)	(*Minn.*)	79,289	3,413,864	3,805,069	48·0
Iowa (1846)	(*Ia.*)	55,941	2,757,537	2,825,041	50·5
Missouri (1821)	(*Mo.*)	68,995	4,319,813	4,677,399	67·8
North Dakota (1889)	(*N.D.*)	69,273	632,446	617,761	8·9
South Dakota (1889)	(*S.D.*)	75,955	680,514	666,257	8·8
Nebraska (1867)	(*Nebr.*)	76,483	1,411,330	1,483,791	19·4
Kansas (1861)	(*Kans.*)	81,787	2,178,611	2,249,071	27·5
South Atlantic		266,970	25,971,732	30,671,337	114·9
Delaware (1787)	(*Del.*)	1,982	446,292	548,104	276·5
Maryland (1788)	(*Md.*)	9,891	3,100,689	3,922,399	396·6
Dist. of Columbia (1791)	(*D.C.*)	61	763,956	756,510	12,401·8
Virginia (1788)	(*Va.*)	39,780	3,966,949	4,648,494	116·9
West Virginia (1863)	(*W. Va.*)	24,070	1,860,421	1,744,237	72·5
North Carolina (1789)	(*N.C.*)	48,798	4,556,155	5,082,059	104·1
South Carolina (1788)	(*S.C.*)	30,225	2,382,594	2,590,516	85·7
Georgia (1788)	(*Ga.*)	58,073	3,943,116	4,589,575	79·0
Florida (1845)	(*Fla.*)	54,090	4,951,560	6,789,443	125·5
East South Central		178,982	12,050,126	12,804,552	71·5
Kentucky (1792)	(*Ky.*)	39,650	3,038,156	3,219,311	81·2
Tennessee (1796)	(*Tenn.*)	41,328	3,567,089	3,924,164	94·9
Alabama (1819)	(*Al.*)	50,708	3,266,740	3,444,165	67·9
Mississippi (1817)	(*Miss.*)	47,296	2,178,141	2,216,912	46·9
West South Central		427,791	16,951,255	19,322,458	45·2
Arkansas (1836)	(*Ark.*)	51,945	1,786,272	1,923,295	37·0
Louisiana (1812)	(*La.*)	44,930	3,257,022	3,643,180	81·0
Oklahoma (1907)	(*Okla.*)	68,782	2,328,284	2,559,253	37·2
Texas (1845)	(*Tex.*)	262,134	9,579,677	11,196,730	42·7
Mountain		856,047	6,855,060	8,283,585	9·7
Montana (1889)	(*Mont.*)	145,587	674,767	694,409	4·8
Idaho (1890)	(*Id.*)	82,677	667,191	713,008	8·6
Wyoming (1890)	(*Wyo.*)	97,203	330,066	332,416	3·4
Colorado (1876)	(*Colo.*)	103,766	1,753,947	2,207,259	21·3
New Mexico (1912)	(*N. Mex.*)	121,412	951,023	1,016,000	8·4
Arizona (1912)	(*Ariz.*)	113,417	1,302,161	1,772,482	15·6
Utah (1896)	(*Ut.*)	82,096	890,627	1,059,273	12·9
Nevada (1864)	(*Nev.*)	109,889	285,278	488,738	4·4
Pacific		891,972	21,198,044	26,525,774	29·7
Washington (1889)	(*Wash.*)	66,570	2,853,214	3,409,169	51·2
Oregon (1859)	(*Oreg.*)	96,184	1,768,687	2,091,385	21·7
California (1850)	(*Calif.*)	156,361	15,717,204	19,953,134	127·6
Alaska (1959)	(*Ak.*)	566,432	226,167	302,173	0·5
Hawaii (1960)	(*Hi.*)	6,425	632,772	769,913	119·8

Geographic divisions and states	*Land area sq. miles, 1970*	*Census population 1 April 1960*	*Census population 1 April 1970*	*Pop. per sq. mile, 1970*
Outlying Territories, 1960	4,914 [1]	3,961,834	4,672,564	806·2
Puerto Rico (1898)	3,421	2,349,544	2,712,033	793
Virgin Islands (1917)	132	32,099	63,200	479
American Samoa (1900)	76	20,051	27,769	365
Guam (1898)	209	67,044	86,926	415
Panama Canal Zone (1903)	362	42,122	44,650	123
US population abroad	—	1,374,421	1,737,836	—

[1] Including Midway Islands (2 sq. miles), Wake Island (3 sq. miles), Canton and Enderbury Islands (27 sq. miles), Swan Islands (1 sq. mile), Corn Islands (4 sq. miles), Howland, Baker and Jarvis Islands (3 sq. miles), other islands (6 sq. miles), and Trust Territory of the Pacific Islands (687 sq. miles). Johnston and Sand Islands, Palmyra Island and Kingman Reef, less than 1 sq. mile. The sovereignty of 25 islands in the Pacific (including Canton and Enderbury Islands and Christmas Island) is disputed with the UK or New Zealand; that of 3 islands in the Caribbean with Colombia. Canton and Enderbury are controlled jointly by the USA and Great Britain. Corn Islands are leased from Nicaragua.

The 1970 census showed 8,733,770 foreign-born Whites. The 8 countries contributing the largest numbers who were foreign-born were Italy, 1,005,687; Germany, 830,498; Canada, 798,782; Mexico, 746,327; United Kingdom, 681,140; Poland, 547,010; USSR, 461,444; Irish Republic, 250,492.

Increase or decrease of native White, and foreign-born White, population from 1860 to 1970, by decades:

	Native White			*Foreign-born White*		
	Total	*Increase*	*Per cent. increase*	*Total*	*Increase or decrease (−)*	*Per cent. change*
1860	22,825,784	5,513,251	31·8	4,096,753	1,856,218	82·8
1870	28,095,665	5,269,881	23·1	5,493,712	1,396,959	34·1
1880	36,843,291	8,747,626	31·1	6,559,679	1,065,967	19·4
1890	45,979,391	9,018,732 [1]	24·5	9,121,867	2,562,188	39·1
1900	56,595,379	10,615,988	23·1	10,213,817	1,091,950	12·0
1910	68,386,412	11,791,033	20·8	13,345,545	3,131,728	30·7
1920	81,108,161	12,721,749	18·6	13,712,754	367,209	2·8
1930	96,303,335	15,195,174	18·7	13,983,405	270,651	2·0
1940	106,795,732	10,492,397	10·9	11,419,138	−2,564,267	−18·3
1950	124,780,860	17,985,128	16·8	10,161,168	−1,257,970	−11·0
1960	149,543,638	24,762,778	19·8	9,293,992	−867,176	−8·5
1970	169,385,451	19,841,813	13·3	8,773,770	−560,222	6·0

[1] Exclusive of population specially enumerated in 1890 in Indian Territory and on Indian reservations.

Principal cities in 1910, 1960 and 1970:

Cities with	*No. of cities* [1] 1910	1960	1970	*Combined population* [1] 1910	1960	1970
250,000 or more	19	51	56	15,461,680	39,360,931	42,177,800
100,000–250,000	31	81	100	4,840,458	11,652,426	14,286,033
50,000–100,000	60	201	240	4,213,098	13,835,902	16,723,878
25,000–50,000	119	432	520	4,023,397	14,950,612	17,848,297
25,000 or more	229	765	916	28,504,450	79,799,871	91,036,008

[1] Exclusive of Honolulu (Hawaii) in 1910 and 1950 and San Juan (Puerto Rico) in 1910, 1950 and 1970.

The population of leading cities (with over 100,000 inhabitants) at the censuses of 1960 and 1970 were as follows:

Cities	*1 April 1960*	*1 April 1970*	*Cities*	*1 April 1960*	*1 April 1970*
New York, N.Y.	7,781,984	7,895,563	Houston, Tex.	938,219	1,233,535
Chicago, Ill.	3,550,404	3,369,357	Baltimore, Md.	939,024	905,787
Los Angeles, Calif.	2,479,015	2,811,801	Dallas, Tex.	679,684	844,401
Philadelphia, Pa.	2,002,512	1,949,996	Washington, D.C.	763,956	756,668
Detroit, Mich.	1,670,144	1,514,063	Cleveland, Ohio	876,050	750,879

Cities	*1 April 1960*	*1 April 1970*
Indianapolis, Ind.	476,258	746,992
Milwaukee, Wisc.	741,324	717,372
San Francisco, Calif.	740,316	715,674
San Diego, Calif.	573,224	697,471
San Antonio, Tex.	587,718	654,153
Boston, Mass.	697,197	641,071
Memphis, Tenn.	497,524	623,988
St Louis, Mo.	750,026	622,236
New Orleans, La.	627,525	593,471
Phoenix, Ariz.	439,170	584,303
Columbus, Ohio	471,316	540,025
Seattle, Wash.	557,087	530,831
Jacksonville, Fla.	201,030	528,865
Pittsburgh, Pa.	604,332	520,089
Denver, Colo.	493,887	514,678
Kansas City, Mo.	475,539	507,330
Atlanta, Ga.	487,455	495,039
Buffalo, N.Y.	532,759	462,768
San Jose, Calif.	204,196	459,913
Cincinnati, Ohio	502,550	453,514
Nashville-Davidson, Tenn.	170,874	447,877
Minneapolis, Minn.	482,872	434,400
Ft Worth, Tex.	356,268	393,476
Toledo, Ohio	318,003	383,062
Newark, N.J.	405,220	381,930
Portland, Oregon	372,676	379,967
Oklahoma City, Okla.	324,253	368,164
Louisville, Ky.	390,639	361,706
Oakland, Calif.	367,548	361,561
Long Beach, Calif.	344,168	358,879
Omaha, Nebr.	301,598	346,929
Miami, Fla.	291,688	334,859
Tulsa, Okla.	261,685	330,350
Honolulu, Hawaii	294,194	324,871
El Paso, Tex.	276,687	322,261
St Paul, Minn.	313,411	309,866
Norfolk, Va.	304,869	307,951
Birmingham, Ala.	340,887	300,910
Rochester, N.Y.	318,611	295,011
Tampa, Fla.	274,970	277,714
Wichita, Kans.	254,698	276,554
Akron, Ohio	290,351	275,425
Tucson, Ariz.	212,892	262,933
Jersey City, N.J.	276,101	260,350
Sacramento, Calif.	191,667	257,105
Austin, Tex.	186,545	253,539
Richmond, Va.	219,958	249,431
Albuquerque, N. Mex.	201,189	243,751
Dayton, Ohio	262,332	242,917
Charlotte, N.C.	201,564	241,299
St Petersburg, Fla.	181,298	216,159
Corpus Christi, Tex.	167,690	204,525
Yonkers, N.Y.	190,634	204,297
Des Moines, Iowa	208,982	201,404
Grand Rapids, Mich.	177,313	197,649
Syracuse, N.Y.	216,038	197,297
Flint, Mich.	196,940	193,317
Mobile, Ala.	194,856	190,026
Shreveport, La.	164,372	182,064
Warren, Ohio	89,246	179,260
Worcester, Mass.	186,587	176,572
Salt Lake City, Utah	189,454	175,885
Gary, Indiana	178,320	175,415
Knoxville, Tenn.	111,827	174,587
Virginia Beach, Va.	8,091	172,106

Cities	*1 April 1960*	*1 April 1970*
Providence, R. I.	207,498	179,116
Ft Wayne, Ind.	161,776	178,021
Madison, Wisc.	126,706	171,809
Spokane, Wash.	181,608	170,516
Kansas City, Kans.	121,901	168,213
Anaheim, Calif.	104,184	166,408
Baton Rouge, La.	152,419	165,921
Fresno, Calif.	133,929	165,655
Springfield, Mass.	174,463	163,905
Hartford, Conn.	162,178	158,017
Bridgeport, Conn.	156,748	156,542
Santa Ana, Calif.	100,350	155,710
Columbus, Ga.	116,779	155,028
Tacoma, Wash.	147,979	154,407
Jackson, Miss.	144,422	153,968
Lincoln, Nebr.	128,521	149,518
Lubbock, Tex.	128,691	149,101
Rockford, Ill.	126,706	147,370
Paterson, N.J.	143,663	144,824
Greensboro, N.C.	119,574	144,076
Youngstown, Ohio	166,689	140,909
Riverside, Calif.	84,332	140,089
Ft Lauderdale, Fla.	83,648	139,590
Huntsville, Ala.	72,365	139,282
Evansville, Ind.	141,543	138,764
Newport News, Va.	113,662	138,177
New Haven, Conn.	152,048	137,707
Colorado Springs, Colo.	70,194	135,060
Torrance, Calif.	100,991	134,968
Winston-Salem, N.C.	111,135	133,683
Montgomery, Ala.	134,393	133,386
Glendale, Calif.	119,442	132,644
Little Rock, Ark.	107,813	132,483
Lansing, Mich.	107,807	131,403
Erie, Pa.	138,440	129,265
South Bend, Ind.	132,445	127,328
Amarillo, Tex.	137,969	127,010
Peoria, Ill.	103,162	126,963
Las Vegas, Nev.	64,405	125,787
Topeka, Kans.	119,484	125,011
Raleigh, N.C.	93,931	122,830
Macon, Ga.	69,764	122,423
Garden Grove, Calif.	84,238	121,155
Hampton, Va.	89,258	120,779
Springfield, Mo.	95,865	120,096
Chattanooga, Tenn.	130,009	119,923
Savannah, Ga.	149,245	118,349
Beaumont, Tex.	119,175	117,548
Huntington Beach, Calif.	11,492	115,960
Albany, N.Y.	129,726	115,781
Berkeley, Calif.	111,268	114,091
Columbia, S.C.	97,433	113,542
Pasadena, Calif.	116,407	112,951
Elizabeth, N.J.	107,698	112,654
Independence, Mo.	62,328	111,630
Portsmouth, Va.	114,773	110,963
Alexandria, Va.	91,023	110,927
Cedar Rapids, Iowa	92,035	110,642
Livonia, Mich.	66,702	110,109
Canton, Ohio	113,631	110,053
Stockton, Calif.	86,321	109,963
Allentown, Pa.	108,347	109,871
Stamford, Conn.	92,713	108,798
Lexington, Ky.	62,810	108,137

Cities	1 April 1960	1 April 1970	Cities	1 April 1960	1 April 1970
Waterbury, Conn.	107,130	108,033	Camden, N.J.	117,159	102,551
Hammond, Ind.	111,698	107,983	Hialeah, Fla.	66,972	102,452
Hollywood, Fla.	35,237	106,873	New Bedford, Mass.	102,477	101,777
San Bernardino, Calif.	91,922	106,869	Fremont, Calif.	43,790	100,869
Trenton, N.J.	114,167	104,786	Duluth, Minn.	106,884	100,578
Dearborn, Mich.	112,007	104,199	Cambridge, Mass.	107,716	100,361
Scranton, Pa.	111,443	102,696	Parma, Ohio	82,845	100,216

Vital Statistics: Vital statistics are based on records of births, deaths, fœtal deaths, marriages and divorces filed with registration officals of states and cities. Figures for the US include Alaska beginning with 1959 and Hawaii beginning with 1960.

Annual collection of mortality records from a national death-registration area was inaugurated in 1900. A national birth-registration area was established in 1915. These areas, which at their inception comprised 10 states and the District of Columbia, expanded gradually until 1933, when both the birth- and death-registration areas covered the entire continental US. Marriage and divorce statistics are compiled from reports furnished by state and local officials. Data on annulments are included in the divorce statistics. The marriage-registration area was established in 1957 with 29 states and 4 other areas. The divorce-registration area was established in 1958 with 14 states and 3 other areas. In Jan. 1972 the marriage-registration area included 41 states and 5 other areas, and the divorce-registration area included 29 states and one other area.

	Live births[1]	Deaths[2]	Marriages[3]	Divorces[4]	Maternal deaths[5]	Deaths under 1 year[6]
1900	—	343,217	709,000	56,000	—	—
1910	2,777,000	696,856	948,000	83,000	—	—
1920	2,950,000	1,118,070	1,274,476	170,505	16,320	170,911
1930	2,618,000	1,327,240	1,126,856	195,961	14,915	143,201
1940	2,559,000	1,417,269	1,595,874	264,000	8,876	110,984
1950	3,632,000	1,452,454	1,667,231	385,144	2,960	103,825
1960	4,257,850[7]	1,711,982	1,523,000	393,000	1,579	110,873
1970	3,731,386	1,921,031	2,158,802	708,000	803	74,667
1971	3,555,970	1,927,542	2,190,481	783,000	668	67,981
1972	3,258,411	1,963,944	2,282,154	845,000	612	60,182
1973	3,136,965	1,973,003	2,284,108	915,000	477	55,581
1974	3,159,958	1,934,388	2,229,667	977,000	462	52,776
1975[8]	3,149,000	1,910,000	2,126,000	1,026,000	340	51,000

[1] Figures through 1959 include adjustment for under-registration (the 1959 registered count was 4,244,796); beginning 1960 figures represent number registered.
[2] Excluding fœtal deaths and deaths among the armed forces overseas.
[3] Estimates for all years except 1970 and 1971.
[4] Includes reported annulments. Estimated for all years except 1930.
[5] Deaths for 1968–74 (Eighth Revision, International Classification of Diseases, adapted, 1965). Deaths from deliveries and complications of pregnancy, childbirth and the puerperium. Deaths for 1958–67 were classified according to the Seventh Revision of the International Lists of Diseases and Causes of Death, those for 1949–57 according to the Sixth Revision and those for 1939–48, according to the Fifth Revision.
[6] Excluding fœtal deaths. [7] Based on a 50% sample.
[8] Provisional.

The crude birth rate, based on total live-birth estimates per 1,000 total population, fell from 29·5 in 1915 to 18·4 in 1933; it rose to a peak of 26·6 in 1947—its highest for 25 years. This peak reflects demobilization (1945–46), the record number of marriages that followed, and the high levels of employment and income. The decrease in the following 3 years was moderate. In 1951 the rate moved upward and levelled off in 1957 at about 25 per 1,000 population. Since 1957 the crude birth rate has declined every year to 18·4 live births per 1,000 population in 1966. The crude birth rate for 1974 was 14·9. Estimated number of illegitimate births in 1973 was 407,300, a ratio of 129·8 illegitimate births per 1,000 registered live births.

Deaths, excluding fœtal deaths (per 1,000 population), declined from 17·2 in 1900 to 10 in 1946. The death rate has been below 10 per 1,000 since 1947, fluctuating slightly from year to year, mainly under the impact of occurrences of outbreaks of severe respiratory diseases. Since the record low of 9·2 in 1954 the rate has changed only between 9·3 and 9·7. The rate for 1968, 9·7; for 1969, 9·5; for 1970, 9·5; for 1971, 9·3; for 1972, 9·4; for 1973, 9·4; for 1974, 9·2.

Leading causes of death, 1975, per 100,000 population: Diseases of heart, 339; malignant neoplasms, 174·4; cerebrovascular diseases, 91·8; accidents, 47·6. Suicides in 1975 were 12·6 per 100,000 population; homicides, 10·2.

The marriage rate per 1,000 population for selected years are: 1920, 12; 1932, 7·9; 1946, 16·4; 1951, 10·4; 1961, 8·5; 1964, 9; 1965, 9·3; 1969, 10·6; 1970, 10·6; 1971, 10·6; 1972, 11; 1973, 10·9; 1974, 10·5. The divorce rates per 1,000 population for selected years are: 1920, 1·6; 1946, 4·3; 1951, 2·5; 1961, 2·3; 1965, 2·5; 1971, 3·7; 1972, 4·1; 1973, 4·4; 1974, 4·6.

Maternal mortality rates (deaths of mothers from conditions associated with deliveries and complications of pregnancy, childbirth and the puerperium) per 100,000 live births, were 1915–19, 727·9 and thereafter declined: 493·9 for 1935–39; 376 for 1940; 207·2 for 1945; 83·3 for 1950; 52·4 for 1954; 47 for 1955; 37·1 for 1960; 31·6 for 1965; 21·5 for 1970; 18·8 for 1972; 15·2 for 1973; 14·6 for 1974. The 1973 rate for white women was 10·7 and for all other women 34·6. By state, the average maternal mortality rate for 1971–73 was highest for Mississippi (38·1) and lowest for Rhode Island (4·9).

The infant mortality rates, per 1,000 live births were: 1915–19, 95·7; 1920–24, 76·7; 1925–29, 69; 1930–34, 60·4; 38·3 in 1945; 29·2 in 1950; 26·4 in 1955; 26 in 1960; 20·9 in 1969; 20 in 1970; 19·1 in 1971; 18·5 in 1972; 17·7 in 1973; 16·7 in 1974. In 1974 the rate for whites was 14·8; for all other, 24·9.

Immigration: The Immigration and Nationality Act, as amended by Public Law 89–236, establishes a numerical ceiling of 170,000 visas for the entire Eastern Hemisphere, with a maximum of 20,000 visas available for any one country. The visas are allocated under a system of 7 preference categories, 4 of which are designed to reunite close relatives of US citizens and resident aliens of the US, 2 for skilled and professional workers and 1 for refugees. Visa numbers not used in any of the preference categories are made available to qualified non-preference immigrants. The law also provides for a ceiling of 120,000 immigrant visas for natives of independent Western Hemisphere countries. Spouses, children and parents of US citizens from both hemispheres are exempt from the numerical limitations.

During the year ended 30 June 1976, 398,613 aliens became permanent residents of the US. Of the total immigrants admitted, 350,664 had obtained visas abroad and entered the US while 47,949 aliens who were already in the US had their status adjusted to that of permanent residents.

Immigrant aliens admitted to US for permanent residence, by country or region of birth, years ended 30 June:

Country or region of birth	*Immigrants admitted*			
	1973	*1974*	*1975*	*1976*
All countries	400,063	394,861	386,194	398,613
Europe	92,870	81,212	73,996	72,404
Germany (GDR and FRG)	6,600	6,320	5,154	5,836
Greece	10,751	10,824	9,984	8,417
Italy	22,151	15,884	11,552	8,380
Poland	4,914	4,033	3,941	3,805
Portugal	10,751	11,302	11,845	10,511
Spain	4,134	3,390	2,549	2,254
UK	10,638	10,710	10,807	11,392
Yugoslavia	7,582	5,817	3,524	2,820
Other Europe	15,349	12,932	14,640	18,989
Asia	124,160	130,662	132,469	149,881
China and Taiwan	17,297	18,056	18,536	18,823
Hong Kong	4,359	4,629	4,891	5,766
India	13,124	12,779	15,773	17,487
Japan	5,461	4,860	4,274	4,258
Korea (North and South)	22,930	28,028	28,362	30,803
Philippines	30,799	32,857	31,751	37,281

	Immigrants admitted			
Country or region of birth	*1973*	*1974*	*1975*	*1976*
Asia (*contd.*)				
Thailand	4,941	4,956	4,217	6,923
Other Asia	25,249	24,497	24,665	28,540
North America	152,788	151,444	146,668	142,307
Canada	8,951	7,654	7,308	7,638
Mexico	70,141	71,586	62,205	57,863
Cuba	24,147	18,929	25,955	29,233
Dominican Republic	13,921	15,680	14,066	12,526
Haiti	4,786	3,946	5,145	5,410
Jamaica	9,963	12,408	11,076	9,026
Trinidad and Tobago	7,035	6,516	5,982	4,839
Other West Indies	4,913	5,480	5,206	5,805
Central America	8,841	9,237	9,696	9,912
Other North America	90	8	29	55
South America	20,335	22,307	22,984	22,706
Colombia	5,230	5,837	6,434	5,742
Ecuador	4,139	4,795	4,727	4,504
Other South America	10,966	11,675	11,823	12,460
Africa	6,655	6,182	6,729	7,723
Australia and New Zealand	1,890	1,645	1,500	1,796
Other countries	1,365	1,409	1,848	1,796

The total number of immigrants admitted from 1820 up to 30 June 1976 was 47,497,532; this included 6,960,802 from Germany (GDR and FRG), 5,277,985 from Italy, 4,864,776 from UK, 4,721,389 from Irish Republic, 4,059,768 from Canada, 3,361,443 from USSR, 1,970,305 from Mexico.

Aliens coming to the US for temporary periods of time are classified as non-immigrants. In the year ending 30 June 1976, a total of 7,654,491 non-immigrants came to the US as tourists, students, exchange visitors, aliens in transit and representatives of foreign governments and foreign information media, temporary workers and their children, and intracompany transferees and their spouses and children. This is exclusive of multiple entries at land borders and of alien crewmen. Tourists, primarily from Mexico, Japan, the UK, the West Indies, Germany (GDR and FRG) and Canada numbered 1,225,656.

A total of 793,092 aliens were expelled from the US during the year ending 30 June 1976. Of this number, 27,998 were deported and 765,094 were required to depart without formal orders of deportation.

In accordance with the Immigration and Nationality Act, 4,775,559 aliens filed address reports during 1976: of the 4,265,034 permanent resident aliens who reported, 885,971 were nationals of Mexico, 319,325 of Cuba, 306,647 of Canada, 277,103 of the UK, 203,525 of Italy, 188,671 of the Philippines and 162,798 of Germany (GDR and FRG). 67% of the permanent resident aliens live in the following 8 states: California, 1,096,948; New York, 703,623; Texas, 324,601; Florida, 315,079; Illinois, 254,933; New Jersey, 236,450; Massachusetts, 158,436, and Michigan, 121,960.

In the year ended 30 June 1976, 142,504 persons became US citizens through naturalization; this includes 114,653 who were naturalized under the general provisions of 5-year residence in the US, 22,176 spouses and children of US citizens, 5,631 military and 44 who were naturalized under other provisions. Of the total, there were 15,138 former nationals of Cuba, 14,765 of the Philippines, 9,326 of China and Taiwan, 8,696 of Italy, 8,695 of UK, 6,595 of Greece, 5,602 of Mexico and 5,056 of Germany (GDR and FRG).

US Depart. of Commerce. *Population of the United States: Trends and Prospects, 1950–1990*. Washington, 1974

Coale, A. J., and Zelnik, M., *New Estimates of Fertility and Population in the United States*. Princeton Univ. Press, 1963

Divine, R. A., *American Immigration Policy, 1924–52*. Yale Univ. Press, 1957

Hutchinson, E. P., *Immigrants and Their Children, 1850–1950*. New York, 1956

Jones, M. A., *American Immigration*. Univ. of Chicago Press, 1960

Okun B., *Trends in Birth Rates in the US Since 1870*. Johns Hopkins Univ. Press, 1958

CONSTITUTION AND GOVERNMENT. The form of government of the USA is based on the constitution of 17 Sept. 1787.

By the constitution the government of the nation is composed of three co-ordinate branches, the executive, the legislative and the judicial.

The National Government has authority in matters of general taxation, treaties and other dealings with foreign Powers, foreign and inter-state commerce, bankruptcy, postal service, coinage, weights and measures, patents and copyright, the armed forces (including, to a certain extent, the militia), and crimes against the USA; it has sole legislative authority over the District of Columbia and the possessions of the US.

The 5th article of the constitution provides that Congress may, on a two-thirds vote of both houses, propose amendments to the constitution, or, on the application of the legislatures of two-thirds of all the states, call a convention for proposing amendments, which in either case shall be valid as part of the constitution when ratified by the legislatures of three-fourths of the several states, or by conventions in three-fourths thereof, whichever mode of ratification may be proposed by Congress. Ten amendments (called collectively 'the Bill of Rights') to the constitution were added 15 Dec. 1791; two in 1795 and 1804; a 13th amendment, 6 Dec. 1865, abolishing slavery; a 14th in 1868, including the important 'due process' clause; a 15th, 3 Feb. 1870, establishing equal voting rights for white and coloured; a 16th, 3 Feb. 1913, authorizing the income tax; a 17th, 8 April 1913, providing for popular election of senators; an 18th, 16 Jan. 1919, prohibiting alcoholic liquors; a 19th, 18 Aug. 1920, establishing woman suffrage; a 20th, 23 Jan. 1933, advancing the date of the President's and Vice-President's inauguration and abolishing the 'lame-duck' sessions of Congress; a 21st, 5 Dec. 1933, repealing the 18th amendment; a 22nd, 26 Feb. 1951, limiting a President's tenure of office to 2 terms, or to 2 terms plus 2 years in the case of a Vice-President who has succeeded to the office of a President; a 23rd, 30 March 1961, granting citizens of the District of Columbia the right to vote in national elections; a 24th, 4 Feb. 1964, banning the use of the poll-tax in federal elections; a 25th, 10 Feb. 1967, dealing with Presidential disability and succession; a 26th, 22 June 1970, establishing the right of citizens who are 18 years of age and older to vote.

National flag: Seven red and 6 white alternating stripes, horizontal; with a blue canton, extending down to the lower edge of the 4th red stripe from the top, and displaying 50 white 5-pointed stars, one for each state. The stars have one point directed vertically upward, and they are arranged in 6 rows of 5 each, alternating with 5 rows of 4 each. On the admission of additional states, stars are added, effective on 4 July following the date of admission. Congress, by law of 22 Dec. 1942, has codified 'existing rules and customs' pertaining to the display of the flag, for civilians.

National anthem: The Star-spangled Banner, 'Oh say, can you see by the dawn's early light' (words by F. S. Key, 1814; tune by J. S. Smith; formally adopted by Congress 3 March 1931).

National motto: 'In God we trust'; formally adopted by Congress 30 July 1956.

Presidency. The executive power is vested in a president, who holds office for 4 years, and is elected, together with a vice-president chosen for the same term, by electors from each state, equal to the whole number of senators and representatives to which the state may be entitled in the Congress. The President must be a natural-born citizen, resident in the country for 14 years, and at least 35 years old.

The presidential election is held every fourth (leap) year on the Tuesday after the first Monday in November. Technically, this is an election of presidential electors, not of a president directly; the electors thus chosen meet and give their votes (for the candidate to whom they are pledged, in some states by law, but in most states by custom and prudent politics) at their respective state capitals on the first Monday after the second Wednesday in December next following their election; and the votes of the electors of all the states are opened and counted in the presence of both Houses of Congress on the sixth day of January. The total electorate vote is one for each senator and representative.

If the successful candidate for President dies before taking office the Vice-President-elect becomes President; if no candidate has a majority or if the successful candidate fails to qualify, then, by the 20th amendment, the Vice-President acts as President until a president qualifies. The duties of the Presidency, in absence of the President and Vice-President by reason of death, resignation, removal, inability or failure to qualify, devolve upon the Speaker of the House under legislation enacted 18 July 1947. And in case of absence of a Speaker for like reason, the presidential duties devolve upon the President *pro tem.* of the Senate and successively upon those members of the Cabinet in order of precedence, who have the constitutional qualifications for President.

The presidential term, by the 20th amendment to the constitution, begins at noon on 20 Jan. of the inaugural year. This amendment also installs the newly elected Congress in office on 3 Jan. instead of—as formerly—in the following December. The President's salary is $200,000 per year, plus $50,000 to assist in defraying expenses resulting from official duties. Also $40,000 non-taxable for travel and official entertainment. The office of Vice-President carries a salary of $62,500, plus $10,000 allowance for travel.

The President is C.-in-C. of the Army, Navy and Air Force, and of the militia when in the service of the Union. The Vice-President is *ex-officio* President of the Senate, and in the case of 'the removal of the President, or of his death, resignation, or inability to discharge the powers and duties of his office', he becomes the President for the remainder of the term.

President of the United States: James Earl Carter, of Georgia, born at Plains, Georgia, in 1924; US Navy, 1946–53 (resigned his commission); Georgia State Senator, 1962; Governor of Georgia, 1970–74.

At the Presidential election on 2 Nov. 1976 total vote cast, including men and women in the armed services, was over 80m., of which James Earl Carter (D.) received 40,827,394 (50·5%) (297 electoral college votes), Gerald R. Ford (R.) 39,145,977 (48·3%) (241 electoral college votes) and Eugene McCarthy 745,042 (0·9%). Votes cast represented approximately 63% of the total registered vote.

PRESIDENTS OF THE USA

Name	*From state*	*Term of service*	*Born*	*Died*
George Washington	Virginia	1789–97	1732	1799
John Adams	Massachusetts	1797–1801	1735	1826
Thomas Jefferson	Virginia	1801–09	1743	1826
James Madison	Virginia	1809–17	1751	1836
James Monroe	Virginia	1817–25	1759	1831
John Quincy Adams	Massachusetts	1825–29	1767	1848
Andrew Jackson	Tennessee	1829–37	1767	1845
Martin Van Buren	New York	1837–41	1782	1862
William H. Harrison	Ohio	Mar.–Apr. 1841	1773	1841
John Tyler	Virginia	1841–45	1790	1862
James K. Polk	Tennessee	1845–49	1795	1849
Zachary Taylor	Louisiana	1849–July 1850	1784	1850
Millard Fillmore	New York	1850–53	1800	1874
Franklin Pierce	New Hampshire	1853–57	1804	1869
James Buchanan	Pennsylvania	1857–61	1791	1868
Abraham Lincoln	Illinois	1861–Apr. 1865	1809	1865
Andrew Johnson	Tennessee	1865–69	1808	1875
Ulysses S. Grant	Illinois	1869–77	1822	1885
Rutherford B. Hayes	Ohio	1877–81	1822	1893
James A. Garfield	Ohio	Mar.–Sept. 1881	1831	1881
Chester A. Arthur	New York	1881–85	1830	1886
Grover Cleveland	New York	1885–89	1837	1908
Benjamin Harrison	Indiana	1889–93	1833	1901
Grover Cleveland	New York	1893–97	1837	1908
William McKinley	Ohio	1897–Sept. 1901	1843	1901
Theodore Roosevelt	New York	1901–09	1858	1919

Name	*From state*	*Term of service*	*Born*	*Died*
William H. Taft	Ohio	1909–13	1857	1930
Woodrow Wilson	New Jersey	1913–21	1856	1924
Warren Gamaliel Harding	Ohio	1921–Aug.1923	1865	1923
Calvin Coolidge	Massachusetts	1923–29	1872	1933
Herbert C. Hoover	California	1929–33	1874	1964
Franklin D. Roosevelt	New York	1933–Apr. 1945	1882	1945
Harry S. Truman	Missouri	1945–53	1884	1972
Dwight D. Eisenhower	New York	1953–61	1890	1969
John F. Kennedy	Massachusetts	1961–Nov. 1963	1917	1963
Lyndon B. Johnson	Texas	1963–69	1908	1973
Richard M. Nixon	California	1969–74	1913	—
Gerald R. Ford	Michigan	1974–77	1913	—
James Earl Carter	Georgia	1977–	1924	—

Vice-Presidents of the USA

John Adams	Massachusetts	1789–97	1735	1826
Thomas Jefferson	Virginia	1797–1801	1743	1826
Aaron Burr	New York	1801–05	1756	1836
George Clinton	New York	1805–12[1]	1739	1812
Elbridge Gerry	Massachusetts	1813–14[1]	1744	1814
Daniel D. Tompkins	New York	1817–25	1774	1825
John C. Calhoun	South Carolina	1825–32[1]	1782	1850
Martin Van Buren	New York	1833–37	1782	1862
Richard M. Johnson	Kentucky	1837–41	1780	1850
John Tyler	Virginia	Mar.–Apr. 1841[1]	1790	1862
George M. Dallas	Pennsylvania	1845–49	1792	1864
Millard Fillmore	New York	1849–50[1]	1800	1874
William R. King	Alabama	Mar.–Apr. 1853[1]	1786	1853
John C. Breckinridge	Kentucky	1857–61	1821	1875
Hannibal Hamlin	Maine	1861–65	1809	1891
Andrew Johnson	Tennessee	Mar.–Apr. 1865[1]	1808	1875
Schuyler Colfax	Indiana	1869–73	1823	1885
Henry Wilson	Massachusetts	1873–75[1]	1812	1875
William A. Wheeler	New York	1877–81	1819	1887
Chester A. Arthur	New York	Mar.–Sept. 1881[1]	1830	1886
Thomas A. Hendricks	Indiana	Mar.–Nov. 1885[1]	1819	1885
Levi P. Morton	New York	1889–93	1824	1920
Adlai Stevenson	Illinois	1893–97	1835	1914
Garret A. Hobart	New Jersey	1897–99[1]	1844	1899
Theodore Roosevelt	New York	Mar.–Sept. 1901[1]	1858	1919
Charles W. Fairbanks	Indiana	1905–09	1855	1920
James S. Sherman	New York	1909–12[1]	1855	1912
Thomas R. Marshall	Indiana	1913–21	1854	1925
Calvin Coolidge	Massachusetts	1921–Aug. 1923[1]	1872	1933
Charles G. Dawes	Illinois	1925–29	1865	1951
Charles Curtis	Kansas	1929–33	1860	1935
John N. Garner	Texas	1933–41	1868	1967
Henry A. Wallace	Iowa	1941–45	1888	1965
Harry S. Truman	Missouri	1945–Apr. 1945[1]	1884	1972
Alben W. Barkley	Kentucky	1949–53	1877	1956
Richard M. Nixon	California	1953–61	1913	—
Lyndon B. Johnson	Texas	1961–Nov. 1963[1]	1908	1973
Hubert H. Humphrey	Minnesota	1965–69	1911	1978
Spiro T. Agnew	Maryland	1969–73	1918	—
Gerald R. Ford	Michigan	1973–74	1913	—
Nelson Rockefeller	New York	1974–77	1908	—
Walter Mondale	Minnesota	1977–	1928	—

[1] Position vacant thereafter until commencement of the next presidential term.

Cabinet. The administrative business of the nation has been traditionally vested in several executive departments, the heads of which, unofficially and *ex officio*, formed the President's Cabinet. Beginning with the Interstate Commerce Commission in 1887, however, an increasing amount of executive business has been entrusted to some 60 so-called independent agencies, such as the Veterans Administration, Housing and Home Finance Agency, Tariff Commission, etc.

All heads of departments and of the 60 or more administrative agencies are appointed by the President, but must be confirmed by the Senate.

The Cabinet consisted of the following (April 1978):

1. *Secretary of State* (created 1789). Cyrus Roberts Vance, of West Virginia; lawyer; diplomatic negotiator 1964–69; born 1917.

2. *Secretary of the Treasury* (1789). W. Michael Blumenthal, chairman, Bendix International; chief American trade negotiator to GATT, 1963–67; born 1926.

3. *Secretary of Defense* (1947). Harold Brown, President of the California Institute of Technology; Secretary of the Air Force 1965–69; born 1927.

4. *Attorney-General* (Department of Justice, 1870). Griffin B. Bell, of Georgia, federal judge 1961–76; born 1918.

5. *Secretary of the Interior* (1849). Cecil Andrus, Governor of Idaho; born 1931.

6. *Secretary of Agriculture* (1889). Robert Bergland, of Minnesota; farmer; Congressman since 1970; born 1928.

7. *Secretary of Commerce* (1903). Juanita M. Kreps, economist and company director; born 1921.

8. *Secretary of Labor* (1913). F. Ray Marshall, Professor of Economics, University of Texas; President of the National Rural Center; born 1928.

9. *Secretary of Health, Education and Welfare* (1953). Joseph A. Califano, Jr, lawyer; adviser to President Johnson 1964–68; born 1931.

10. *Secretary of Housing and Urban Development* (1966). Patricia R. Harris, lawyer and diplomat; born 1924.

11. *Secretary of Transportation* (1967). Brock Adams, Congressman for Washington since 1964; railway systems specialist; born 1927.

12. *Secretary of Energy* (1977). James Schlesinger, formerly White House adviser on energy; born 1928.

Each of the above Cabinet officers receives an annual salary of $60,000 and holds office during the pleasure of the President.

Congress: The legislative power is vested by the Constitution in a Congress, consisting of a Senate and House of Representatives.

Electorate: By amendments of the constitution, disqualification of voters on the ground of race, colour or sex is forbidden. Accordingly, the electorate consists theoretically of all citizens of both sexes over 18 years of age, but the franchise is not universal. There are requirement of residence varying in the several states as to length from 6 months to 2 years and differing requirements as to registration. In 20 states the ability to read (usually an extract from the constitution) is required—in Alaska the ability to read English; in Hawaii, English or Hawaiian; in Louisiana, English or one's native tongue. In Alabama the voter must take an 'anti-Communist oath' and fill out a questionnaire to the satisfaction of the registrars. In some southern states voters are required to give a reasonable explanation of what they read. Estimate of Negroes registered in the 11 southern states of Ala., Ark., Fla., La., Miss., N.C., Okla., S.C., Tex., Tenn. and Va.: 1947, 595,000; 1956, 1,238,000; 1960, 1,414,000; 1970, 3,324,000; 1972, 5,678,939. In 1972 there were about 14·2m. registered Negro voters in the USA. In most states convicts are excluded from the franchise, in some states duellists and fraudulent voters.

Legislation designed to discourage the rise of third parties has been adopted in a few states. In Illinois a new party must present a petition signed by at least 25,000 voters, including at least 200 in each of 50 of the 102 counties.

The method of balloting varies greatly. Seventeen states use different ballots for federal, state and local elections. In Delaware and South Carolina the various political parties furnish their own ballot-papers to the voters as he or she enters the polling-booth.

Senate: The Senate consists of 2 members from each state, chosen by popular vote for 6 years, one-third retiring or seeking re-election every 2 years. Senators must be no less than 30 years of age; must have been citizens of the USA for 9 years, and be residents in the states for which they are chosen. The Senate has complete freedom to initiate legislation, except revenue bills (which must originate in the House of Representatives); it may, however, amend or reject any legislation originating in the lower house. The Senate is also entrusted with the power of giving or withholding its 'advice and consent' to the ratification of all treaties initiated by the President with foreign Powers, a two-thirds majority of senators present being required for approval (However, it has no control over 'international executive agreements' made by the President with foreign governments; such 'agreements', representing an important but very recent development, cover a wide range and are actually more numerous than formal treaties.) It also has the power of confirming or rejecting major appointments to office made by the President, but it has no direct control over the appointment by the President of 'personal representatives' or 'personal envoys' on missions abroad. Members of the Senate constitute a High Court of Impeachment, with power, by a two-thirds vote, to remove from office and disqualify any civil officer of the USA impeached by the House of Representatives, which has the sole power of impeachment.

The Senate has 16 Standing Committees to which all bills are referred for study revision or rejection. The House of Representatives has 21 such committees. In both Houses each Standing Committee has a chairman and a majority representing the majority party of the whole House; each has numerous sub-committees. The jurisdictions of these Committees correspond largely to those of the appropriate executive departments and agencies. Both Houses also have a few special Committees with limited duration; there are some Joint Committees.

House of Representatives: The House of Representatives consists of 435 members elected every second year. The number of each state's representatives is determined by the decennial census, in the absence of specific Congressional legislation affecting the basis. The states, in 1976, had the following representatives:

Alabama	7	Indiana	11	Nebraska	3	South Carolina	6
Alaska	1	Iowa	6	Nevada	1	South Dakota	2
Arizona	4	Kansas	5	New Hampshire	2	Tennessee	8
Arkansas	4	Kentucky	7	New Jersey	15	Texas	24
California	43	Louisiana	8	New Mexico	2	Utah	2
Colorado	5	Maine	2	New York	39	Vermont	1
Connecticut	6	Maryland	8	North Carolina	11	Virginia	10
Delaware	1	Massachusetts	12	North Dakota	1	Washington	7
Florida	15	Michigan	19	Ohio	23	West Virginia	4
Georgia	10	Minnesota	8	Oklahoma	6	Wisconsin	9
Hawaii	2	Mississippi	5	Oregon	4	Wyoming	1
Idaho	2	Missouri	10	Pennsylvania	25		
Illinois	24	Montana	2	Rhode Island	2		

The Supreme Court decided on 17 Feb. 1964, that the federal constitution requires congressional districts within each state to be substantially equal in population. By almost invariable custom the representative lives in the district from which he is elected.

Representatives must be not less that 25 years of age, citizens of the USA for 7 years and residents in the states from which they are chosen. The District of Columbia, Guam and the Virgin Islands have one non-voting delegate each. The House also admits a 'resident commissioner' from Puerto Rico, who has the right to speak on any subject and to make motions, but not to vote; he is elected in the same manner as the representatives but for a 4-year term. Each of the two Houses of Congress is sole 'judge of the elections, returns and qualifications of its own members'; and each of the Houses may, with the concurrence of two-thirds, expel a member. The period usually termed 'a Congress' in legislative language continues for 2 years, terminating at noon on 3 Jan.

The salary of a senator or representative, also that of a resident commissioner in Congress, is $42,500 per annum, with tax-free expense allowance and allowances for travelling expenses and for clerical hire. The salary of the Speaker of the House of Representatives is $62,500 per annum, with a taxable allowance of $10,000.

No senator or representative can, during the time for which he is elected, be appointed to any *civil* office under authority of the USA which shall have been created or the emoluments of which shall have been increased during such time; and no person holding *any* office under the USA can be a member of either House during his continuance in office. No religious text may be required as a qualification to any office or public trust under the USA or in any state.

The 94th Congress (1977–79) was constituted (March 1978) as follows: Senate, 61 Democrats, 38 Republicans, 1 Independent; House of Representatives, 289 Democrats, 146 Republicans.

Indians: By an Act passed on 2 June 1924 full citizenship was granted to all Indians born in the USA, though those remaining in tribal units were still under special federal jurisdiction. Those remaining in tribal units constitute from one-half to three-fourths of the Indian population. The Indian Reorganization Act of 1934 gave the tribal Indians, at their own option, substantial opportunities to self-government and of self-controlled corporate enterprises empowered to borrow money, buy land, machinery and equipment; these corporations are controlled by democratically elected tribal councils; by 1945 roughly a third of the Indians had taken advantage of this Act. Recently a trend towards releasing Indians from federal supervision has resulted in legislation terminating supervision over specific tribes. Indian lands (1965) amounted to 55,319,000 acres, of which about 71% was tribally owned and 20% in trust allotments, with the remainder owned by the Government. Indian lands are held free of taxes. Indian population under jurisdiction of the Indian Bureau was about 343,000 in 1950; nearly one-half were in the three states of Oklahoma, Arizona and New Mexico. Total Indian population at the 1970 census was 791,839, of which Oklahoma, Arizona, California, North Carolina and New Mexico accounted for 53%.

State and Local Government: The Union comprises 13 original states, 7 states which were admitted without having been previously organized as territories, and 30 states which had been territories—50 states in all. Each state has its own constitution (which the USA guarantees shall be republican in form), deriving its authority, not from Congress, but from the people of the state. Admission of states into the Union has been granted by special Acts of Congress, either (1) in the form of 'enabling Acts' providing for the drafting and ratification of a state constitution by the people, in which case the territory becomes a state as soon as the conditions are fulfilled, or (2) accepting a constitution already framed, and at once granting admission.

Each state is provided with a legislature of two Houses (except Nebraska, which since 1937 has had a single-chamber legislature), a governor and other executive officials, and a judicial system. Both Houses of the legislature are elective, but the senators (having larger electoral districts usually covering 2 or 3 counties compared with the single county or, in some states, the town, which sends one representative to the Lower House) are less numerous than the representatives, while in 38 states their terms are 4 years; in 12 states the term is 2 years. Of the 4-year senates, Illinois, Montana, and New Jersey provide for two 4-year terms and one 2-year term in each decade. Terms of the lower houses are usually shorter; in 45 states, 2 years.

Members of both Houses are paid at the same rate, which varies from $200 per biennium (New Hampshire) to $64,140 per biennium (California). The trend is towards annual sessions of state legislatures; in 1976, 36 were constitutionally required to meet annually (in 1939, only 4), the other 14 holding biennial sessions, 12 in the odd-numbered and 2 in the even-numbered years. Of these 14, 6 met annually in practice by invoking flexible constitutional powers to reconvene at intervals during the biennium.

The Governor has power to summon an extraordinary session, but not to dissolve or adjourn. The duties of the two Houses are similar, but in many states money bills must be introduced first in the Lower House. The Senate sits as a court for the trial of officials impeached by the other House, and often has power to confirm or reject appointments made by the Governor.

State legislatures are competent to deal with all matters not reserved for the federal government by the federal constitution nor specifically prohibited by the federal or state constitutions. Among their powers are the determination of the qualifications for the right of suffrage, and the control of all elections to public office, including elections of members of Congress and electors of President and Vice-President; the criminal law, both in its enactment and in its execution, with unimportant exceptions, and the administration of prisons; the civil law, including all matters pertaining to the possession and transfer of, and succession to, property; marriage and divorce, and all other civil relations; the chartering and control of all manufacturing, trading, transportation and other corporations, subject only to the right of Congress to regulate commerce passing from one state to another; labour; education; charities; licensing; fisheries within state waters, and game laws (apart from the hunting of migratory birds, which is a federal concern under treaties with Canada and Mexico). Taxes on income were left to the states until 1913, when the 16th amendment authorized the imposition of federal taxes on income without regard to apportionment.

The Governor is chosen by direct vote of the people over the whole state. His term of office varies in the several states from 2 to 4 years, and his salary from $10,000 (Arkansas) to $85,000 (New York). His duty is to see to the faithful administration of the law, and he has command of the military forces of the state. He may recommend measures but does not present bills to the legislature. In some states he presents estimates. In all but one of the states (North Carolina) the Governor has a veto upon legislation, which may, however, be overridden by the two Houses, in some states by a simple majority, in others by a three-fifths or two-thirds majority. In some states the Governor, on his death or resignation, is succeeded by a Lieut.-Governor who was elected at the same time and has been presiding over the state Senate. In several states the Speaker of the Lower House succeeds the Governor.

The chief officials by whom the administration of state affairs is carried on (secretaries, treasurers, members of boards of commissioners, etc.) are usually chosen by the people at the general state elections for terms similar to those for which governors hold office. State employees, Oct. 1970, numbered 2,755,033, earning $1,612·1m. monthly; education accounted for 1·18m. employees (43%). Local government employees numbered 7,392,437, earning $4,294·2m. monthly.

Local Government: The chief unit of local government is the county, of which there were (1976) 3,088 with definite functions; in addition, Rhode Island has 5 'counties' which have no functions; Alaska does not have 'counties' as such and, since Oct. 1960, there has been no active county government in Connecticut. Louisiana has 64 'parishes'. The counties maintain public order through the sheriff and his deputies, who may, in a crisis, be drawn temporarily from willing citizens; in many states the counties maintain the smaller local highways; other functions are the granting of licences and the apportionment and collection of taxes. In a few states they also manage the schools.

The unit of local government in New England is the rural township, governed directly by the voters, who assemble annually or oftener if necessary, and legislate in local affairs, levy taxes, make appropriations and appoint and instruct the local officials (selectmen, clerk, school-committee, etc.). Townships are grouped to form counties. Where cities exist, the township government is superseded by the city government.

The **District of Columbia**, ceded by the State of Maryland for the purposes of government in 1791, is the seat of the US Government. It includes the city of Washington, and embraces a land area of 61 sq. miles, The Reorganization Plan No. 3 of 1967 instituted a Mayor Council form of government with appointed offices. In 1973 an elected Mayor and elected councillors were introduced; in 1974 they received power to legislate in local matters. Congress retains power to enact legislation and to veto or supersede the Council's acts. Since 1961 citizens have had the right to vote in national elections.

The **Commonwealth of Puerto Rico, Guam and the Virgin Islands** each have a local legislature, whose acts may be modified or annulled by Congress, though in practice this has seldom been done. The President appoints the Governor and Federal District Judge in Guam. Puerto Rico since its attainment of commonwealth status on 25 July 1952, enjoys practically complete self-government, including the election of its governor and other officials. The conduct of foreign relations, however, is still a federal function and federal bureaus and agencies still operate in the island.

General supervision of territorial administration is exercised by the Office of Territories in the Department of Interior.

The Book of the States 1976–77. Council of State Governments, Lexington, 1976
Constitution of the US, National and State. 2 vols. [with subsequent amendments]. Dobbs Ferry, 1962
Adrian, C. R., *State and Local Government.* 3rd ed. New York, 1971
Anderson, W., and others. *Government in the Fifty States.* Rev. ed. New York, 1960
Barber, J. D. (ed.), *The 44th American Assembly, New York 1973.—Choosing the President.* Englewood Cliffs, 1974
Barone, M. (ed.). *The Almanac of American Politics.* Rev. ed. New York and London, 1976
Bates, F. G., *State Government.* 3rd ed. by Field, Sikes and Stoner. New York, 1949
Beloff, M., and Vale, V. (eds.), *American Political Institutions in the 1970s.* London, 1975
Bell, J., *The Presidency. Office of Power.* Boston, 1967
Berger, M., *Equality by Statute; The Revolution in Civil Rights.* Rev. ed. Gordon City, N.Y., 1968
Binkley, W. E., *American Political Parties.* 4th ed. New York, 1963
Binkley, W. E., and Moos, M. C., *A Grammar of American Politics: The National, State and Local Governments.* 3rd ed. New York, 1957
Bone, H. A., *American Politics and the Party System.* 4th ed. New York, 1971
Cater, D., *Power in Washington.* London, 1964
Corwin, E. S., *The President: Office and Powers. History and Analysis of Practice and Opinion.* 4th ed. New York, 1957
Coyle, D. C., *The United States Political System and How it Works.* Rev. ed. New York, 1963; London, Hansard Society, 1957
Dumbauld, E., *The Constitution of the United States.* Univ. of Oklahoma Press, 1965
Egger, R. A., *The President of the United States.* 2nd ed. New York, 1972
Fisher, L., *Presidential Spending Power.* Princeton Univ. Press, 1975
Ferguson, J. H., and McHenry, D. E., *Elements of American Government.* 6th ed. New York, 1963
Hardin, C. M., *Presidential Power and Accountability: Towards a New Constitution.* Univ. of Chicago Press, 1974
Kelly, A. H., and Harbison, W. A., *The American Constitution, Its Origin and Development.* 4th ed. New York, 1970
Koenig, L. W., *The Chief Executive.* 3rd ed. New York, 1975
Levine, E. L., *An Introduction to American Government.* 2nd ed. New York, 1974
Maddox, R. W., and Fuquay, R. F., *State and Local Government.* New York, 1961; London, 1962
Mayer, G. H., *The Republican Party, 1854–1964.* OUP, 1964
Moe, R. C., *Congress and the President, Allies and Adversaries.* Pacific Palisades, 1971
Ogg, F. A., and Ray, P. O., *Introduction to American Government.* 12th ed. New York, 1962.—*Essentials of American National Government.* 9th ed. New York, 1964
Pritchett, C. H., *The American Constitution.* 2nd ed. New York, 1968
Redford, E. S., *Democracy in the Administrative State.* OUP, 1969
Ripley, R. B., *American National Government and Public Policy.* New York, 1974
Robinson, J. A., *State Legislative Innovation.* New York, 1973
Rossiter, C., *Parties and Politics in America.* Ithaca, 1964
Scammon, R. M. (ed.). *America Votes. Handbook of Contemporary Election Statistics.* Pittsburg, 1975
Scheer, R., *America after Nixon: The politics of the New World Order.* New York, 1975
Schlesinger, A. M., *Congress and the Presidency: Their Role in Modern Times.* Washington, 1967
Tugwell, R. G., *The Enlargement of the Presidency.* Garden City, N.Y., 1960
White, T. H., *The Making of the President.* New York, 1960.—*The Making of the President, 1964.* New York, 1965.—*The Making of the President, 1968.* New York, 1969

DEFENCE. The President is C.-in-C. of the Army, Navy and Air Force.

The National Security Act of 1947 provides for the unification of the Army,

Navy and Air Forces under a single Secretary of Defense with cabinet rank. The President is also advised by a National Security Council and the Office of Civil and Defense Mobilization.

The major components of the Department of Defense are the Office of the Secretary of Defense and the Joint Chiefs of Staff, who provide immediate staff assistance and advice to the Secretary; the departments of the Army, Navy and Air Force, each separately organized under a civilian head (not of cabinet rank); and the unified and specified commands.

Army. *Secretary of the Army:* Martin R. Hoffmann.

Central Administration. The Secretary of the Army is the head of the Department of the Army. Subject to the authority of the President as C.-in-C. and of the Secretary of Defense, he is responsible for all affairs of the Department.

The Secretary of the Army is assisted by the Under Secretary of the Army, 5 Assistant Secretaries of the Army (Financial Management; Installations Logistics; Research and Development; Manpower and Reserve Affairs, and Civil Works), the General Counsel, an Administrative Assistant, Chief of Legislative Liaison, Chief of Public Affairs and the Army Staff headed by the Chief of Staff, US Army. The office of the Under Secretary of the Army includes a Deputy Under Secretary (Operations Research).

The Chief of Staff is the principal military adviser of the Secretary of the Army, and performs his duties under the direction of the Secretary of the Army, except as otherwise prescribed by law, by the President or by the Secretary of Defense. He has supervision of all members and organizations of the Army. The Vice Chief of Staff assists and advises the Chief of Staff.

The Army General Staff is the principal element of the Army Staff and includes the offices of the Chief of Staff, Vice Chief of Staff, Director of Staff, the 4 Deputy Chiefs of Staff (Military Operations, Personnel, Logistics, and Research, Development and Acquisition), the Comptroller of the Army, the Assistant Chief of Staff for Intelligence, the Ballistic Missile Defense Program Manager and the Army Reserve Forces Policy Committee. Other elements of the Army Staff are the offices of the Judge Advocate General, Surgeon General, Adjutant General, Inspector General and Auditor General, Chief of Chaplains, Chief, Army Reserve, Chief, National Guard Bureau, and Chief of Engineers.

The Army consists of the Regular Army, the Army National Guard of the US, and the Army Reserve; and all persons appointed to or enlisted into the Army without component; and all persons serving under call or conscription, including members of the National Guard of the States, etc., when in the service of the US.

Department of the Army authorized strength, including cadets, was (1976) 782,000, including 48,650 women, comprised, in major combat units, or 16 divisions and several separate brigades and regiments.

The US Army Forces Command, with headquarters at Fort McPherson, Georgia, commands the continental US Armies and all assigned Active Army and US Army Reserve troop units in the continental US, Alaska, Hawaii, Panama, Guam, Johnston Island, the Commonwealth of Puerto Rico, and the Virgin Islands of the USA. The headquarters of the continental US Armies are: First US Army, Fort George G. Meade, Maryland; Fifth US Army, Fort Sam Houston, Texas; Sixth US Army, Presidio of San Francisco, California. The US Army Training and Doctrine Command, with headquarters at Fort Monroe, Virginia, co-ordinates and integrates the total combat development effort of the Army as well as developing, managing and supervising the training of individuals of the US Army and authorized foreign nationals. The US Army Health Services Command, with headquarters at Fort Sam Houston, Texas, provides health services in the continental US for the US Army and provides professional education and training for medical personnel of the US Army and authorized foreign national personnel. The US Army Material Development and Readiness Command, with headquarters in Alexandria, Virginia, is responsible for all US Army operations dealing with equipment development, procurement, delivery, supply and maintenance. The US Army Communications Command, with headquarters at Fort Huachuca, Arizona, provides worldwide communications to the Department of the Army and supports the Defense

Communications Systems. The US Army Military District of Washington, with headquarters at Fort McNair, Washington, D.C. provides support to the Department of the Army and the Department of Defense at the seat of Government.

Some 35% of the Army is deployed overseas. One division two-thirds of which is located in the USA keeps equipment in the Federal Republic of Germany and can be flown there in 48–72 hours. Headquarters of US Seventh and Eighth Armies are in Europe and Korea respectively.

Operational Commands and Weapons. The larger commands are the theater army and the corps. The typical theater army may consist of a variable number of corps; combat forces of armour and infantry; air defense artillery (*Nike-Hercules* and *Hawk* missile battalions); field artillery and Pershing missile battalions; combat support forces of aviation, engineer and signal elements; and combat service support forces. A typical corps consists of a variable number and mixture of infantry, mechanized infantry, armoured, airmobile, and airborne divisions; one or more separate infantry brigades; one or more armoured cavalry regiments; corps artillery (155-mm howitzer, 8-in. howitzer, 175-mm gun, *Lance* missile battalions); an air defense element of a size commensurate with the hostile air threat (*Nike-Hercules*, *Hawk* and *Chaparral/Vulcan* battalions), and a target acquisition unit; combat support and combat service support forces.

US Army Divisions have a common base (containing command, aviation divisional artillery, combat, combat support units and combat service support units) and a varying mixture of 'combat manoeuvre battalions' (usually 10 or 11 in number in 3 brigades) to make up airborne, infantry, armoured, mechanized infantry and airmobile divisions. Divisions can in this way be 'tailored' to fit a variety of strategic or tactical situations. An infantry division, with about 16,900 men, may have 8 infantry battalions, an armoured battalion and a mechanized infantry battalion; a mechanized infantry division, with about 16,600 men, may have 6 mechanized infantry battalions and 4 armoured battalions; and armoured division, with about 16,900 men, may have 5 mechanized infantry battalions and 6 armoured battalions; an airborne division, with 13,000 men, may have 9 infantry (airborne) battalions.

Small arms include the M-16, which fires a 5·56-mm cartridge. The standard general-purpose machine-gun is the M-60 (23 lb.; 550 rounds of 7·63-mm per minute). Infantry weapons also include M-203 grenade launcher attachment for the M16A1 rifle, which fire a 40-mm grenade up to 400 metres, the *Tow* and *Dragon* anti-tank missile system, and the M-72 rocket, a light anti-tank weapon.

Combat vehicles of the US Army are the tank, armoured personnel carrier, armoured reconnaissance airborne assault vehicle and the armoured command and reconnaissance vehicle. The first-line tank is the M-60A1 with 105-mm main armament. The M-60A2, a version of the M-60 series tank, fires both the *Shillelagh* missile and conventional ammunition. The standard armoured personnel carrier is the M-113A1; it carries a mechanized infantry squad. The M-113A1 is also being utilized as the ground scout vehicle in armoured cavalry regiments, squadrons and in scout platoons of armoured and mechanized infantry battalions. The M-551 'Sheridan' is an armoured reconnaissance airborne assault vehicle in armoured cavalry units and light armour battalions; it fires both *Shillelagh* missiles and conventional ammunition. Combat vehicles under development are mechanized infantry combat vehicle, armoured reconnaissance scout vehicle and XM1 Tank.

The approved calibres of artillery are: light, 105-mm howitzer, medium 155-mm howitzer; the heavy, 175-mm gun and 8-in. howitzer. The 4·2-in. mortars and the 81-mm mortar are used by combat manoeuvre elements. The 90-mm, 106-mm recoilless rifles are being replaced by the *Dragon* and *Tow* anti-tank missile systems which are the primary anti-tank weapons. *Chaparral* and *Vulcan*, forward-area air-defence weapons, provide the capability of low-altitude defence against high-performance aircraft.

The Army has two categories of missiles—surface-to-surface (field artillery) and surface-to-air (air defence artillery). Surface-to-surface missiles are: *Honest John*, free flight, rocket equivalent to long-range artillery, nuclear or high explosive warhead, highly mobile, operational; *Pershing*, ballistic, nuclear warhead, range about

400 miles operational; *Lance*, guided, nuclear warhead, storable, liqud propellant, operational. Surface-to-air missiles, for air defence, are: *Nike-Hercules*, guided, field or fixed installation, nuclear warhead, operational; *Hawk*, homing type, low-to-mid-altitude, field, operational (an improved system is now replacing the basic *Hawk* in the near future); *Chaparral*, infra-red homing, low-altitude, forward area, operational (improvements to the basic system are under development); *Redeye*, hand-held, infra-red homing, low-altitude, forward area, operational; *Patriot*, mid-to-high-altitude, replacement for *Hawk* and *Nike-Hercules*, under development; *Stinger*, hand-held infra-red homing, low-altitude, forward area, replacement for *Redeye* is under development. Anti-tank missiles are: *Tow*, tube launched, optically tracked, wire guided, anti-armour, forward area, operational; *Hellfire*, terminal homing under development.

The Army employs rotary- and fixed-wing aircraft as organic elements of its ground formations where their use is required on a full-time basis and their immediate and constant availability is essential. The front line commander exploits the benefits of aviation technology to perform traditional land battle tasks in the third dimension. This concept of airmobility for ground formation utilizes aerial vehicles as a highly integrated team to perform all five functions of land combat: reconnaissance, command and control, logistics and that inseparable combination, firepower and manoeuvre.

Enlistment, Terms of Service. Since 1974 the Army has operated a 'zero draft' system making it, in effect, an all-regular force. Terms of service may be 3, 4, 5 or 6 years.

All male citizens and all male aliens admitted for permanent residence are required to register at age 18. Men who enlist incur a 6-year obligation and must serve in the reserve any part of the period not served on active duty.

The Women's Army Corps is composed of volunteers in the Regular and Reserve components of the Army. They are eligible for military duties (other than of a combat nature) in all the Army's occupational areas.

The Army National Guard is a reserve military component with a dual status and role. Enlistment is voluntary. The members are recruited by each state, but are equipped and paid by the federal government. Training is supervised by the active Army (FORSCOM), and unit organization parallels that for the active army; training facilities are made available by the USA and each state. As the organized militia of the several states, the District of Columbia, Puerto Rico and the Territory of the Virgin Islands, the Guard may be called into service for local emergencies by the sovereigns in those jurisdictions; and may be called into federal service by the President to thwart invasion or rebellion or to enforce federal law. In its role as a reserve component of the Army, the Guard is subject to the order of the President in the event of national emergency. The Air Guard provide 100% of the air defence of Hawaii.

The Army Reserve is designed to supply qualified and experienced units and individuals in an emergency. US Army Forces Command is charged with the command, support and training supervision of US Army Reserve units. Members are assigned to one of 3 categories: the Ready, Standby or Retired Reserve. A limited number of Ready Reservists is subject to call by the President in case of national emergency without declaration of war by Congress. The Standby Reserve and the Retired Reserve may be called only after declaration of war or national emergency by Congress.

Army 1968 Green Book. Association of the U.S. Army, Washington, D.C.
The Army Almanac. Dept. of the Army, Washington, D.C.
Dupuy, R. E. and T. N., *Military Heritage of America*. New York, 1956
Forman, S., *West Point*. New York, 1950
ROTCM 145–20, Department of the Army ROTC Manual, *American Military History, 1607–1953*. Washington, 1956

Navy. *Secretary of the Navy:* W. Graham Claytor, Jr.

The Department of the Navy is administered under the Secretary of Defense by the Secretary of the Navy, assisted by an Under Secretary, 4 Assistant Secretaries, the Chief of Naval Operations, and the Commandant of the Marine Corps. The 3 divisions of the Department of the Navy are:

Central Executive Authority: comprising staff offices of the Secretary; those dealing with financial management, installations and logistics, man-power and reserves affairs, research and development; offices of administration, general counsel, programme appraisal, information, Judge Advocate General, and legislative affairs; the office of the Chief of Naval Operations (comprised of the Vice Chief, Assistant Vice Chief/Director of Naval Administration, 6 Deputy Chiefs, 8 Directors, and the Naval Inspector General); Headquarters, US Marine Corps; Headquarters, Naval Material Command; Bureau of Naval Personnel; and Bureau of Medicine and Surgery.

Operating Forces: comprising the US Naval Forces, Europe; Atlantic and Pacific Fleets, including Fleet Marine Forces; Military Sealift Command; other Navy and Marine Corps forces and commands not otherwise assigned.

Shore Establishment: comprising commands dealing with systems (air, electronic, facilities engineering, sea and supply) and naval telecommunications; intelligence; security group, oceanographer of the Navy, education and training, reserve, and 13 naval district headquarters; Marine Corps Reserve and supporting establishment and other designated shore activities.

Major shore activities include 8 shipyards, 35 air stations and facilities, 2 amphibious bases, 2 submarine bases and 15 naval stations and facilities. By agreement dated 2 Sept. 1940, Britain granted leases for naval and air bases in Newfoundland, Bermuda, Bahamas, Jamaica, St Lucia, Trinidad, Antigua and British Guiana (Guyana); but these are not all now active.

Naval appropriations in recent fiscal years: 1972, $24,048m.; 1973, $25,425m.; 1974, $26,860m.; 1975, $27,426m.; 1976, $28,752m.; 1977, $32,800m.; 1978, $34,700m.

The active personnel on duty on 31 July 1977 was 531,650 Navy officers and enlisted men, plus 192,000 Marine Corp officers and men.

The following is a tabulated statement of US vessels listed on 31 Dec.:

Category	*1970*	*1971*	*1972*	*1973*	*1974*	*1975*	*1976*	*1977*
Attack aircraft carriers	15	15	15	15	15	15	15	15
Support aircraft carriers	12	12	10	7	5[1]	5[1]	5[1]	5[1]
Helicopter carriers	7	7	7	7	7[2]	7[2]	9	9
Communications relay ships	2	2	2	2	2	2	1	—
Command ships	2	2	2	2	3[3]	3[3]	3[3]	3[3]
Nuclear powered submarines	93	100	103	106	107	107	108	109
Submarines (conventional)	62	56	39	33	18	15	15	15
Battleships	4	4	4	4	4	4	4	4
Cruisers	32	23	23	23	14	35[4]	35[4]	35[4]
Frigates (Destroyer leaders)	33	33	32	33	32	—	—	—
Destroyers	289	232	177	173	156	112[5]	101[5]	97[5]
Frigates (former Escort ships)	223	198	143	105	82	71[6]	65[6]	65[6]

[1] Includes 1 training carrier and 4 anti-submarine carriers in reserve.
[2] Includes 1 latterly rated as sea control ship and 6 amphibious assault ships.
[3] Includes 1 Middle East Flagship (converted amphibious transport dock).
[4] Includes 22 frigates reclassified as cruisers in 1975.
[5] Includes 10 frigates reclassified as destroyers in 1975.
[6] Reclassified as frigates from escort ships on 1 July 1975.

The table below shows principal surface ships, including those to be completed by 1 April 1978, guns under 3-in. calibre not given):

Completed	*Name*	*Standard displacement Tons*	*Armour Belt In.*	*Armour Guns In.*	*Principal armament*	*Shaft horsepower*	*Speed Knots*
		Attack Aircraft Carriers					
1977	Eisenhower	81,600	—	—	Guided missiles (95 aircraft)	260,000	33
1975	Nimitz	81,600	—	—			
1968	John F. Kennedy	61,000	—	—	Guided missiles (85 aircraft)	280,000	35
1965	America	60,300	—	—	Guided missiles (85 aircraft)	280,000	35
1962	Enterprise	75,700	—	—	85 aircraft	300,000 (nuclear power)	35

Completed	Name	Standard displacement Tons	Armour Belt In.	Armour Guns In.	Principal armament	Shaft horsepower	Speed Knots
1962	Constellation	61,000	—	—			35
1961	Kitty Hawk	61,000	—	—			35
1959	Independence	60,000	—	—	Guided missiles (85 aircraft)	280,000	35
1957	Ranger	60,000	—	—			35
1956	Saratoga	59,100	—	—			35
1955	Forrestal	59,100	—	—	Guided missiles (80 aircraft)	260,000	33
1950	Oriskany[1]	33,250	3	—	2 5-in. (70 aircraft)	150,000	33
1947	Coral Sea	52,500	—	—	3 5-in. (75 aircraft)	212,000	33
1945	F. D. Roosevelt	51,000	—	—	4 5-in. (75 aircraft)	212,000	33
	Midway				3 5-in. (75 aircraft)		
1944	Bon Homme Richard[1]	33,100	3	—	4 5-in. (70 aircraft)	150,000	33

[1] In reserve.

Anti-Submarine Aircraft Carriers[1]

Completed	Name	Standard displacement Tons	Armour Belt In.	Armour Guns In.	Principal armament	Shaft horsepower	Speed Knots
1944	Bennington	33,000	3	—	4 5-in. (45 aircraft—more or fewer, according to size and type	150,000	33
	Shangri-La						
1943	Hornet						
	Intrepid						

The 'Essex' class originally comprised 24 ships, the *Essex, Yorktown, Intrepid, Hornet, Franklin, Lexington, Bunker Hill, Wasp, Ticonderoga, Hancock, Randolph, Bennington, Bon Homme Richard, Shangri-La, Tarawa, Antietam, Boxer, Kearsarge, Lake Champlain, Leyte, Philippine Sea, Princeton, Valley Forge, Oriskany*. (Five were rated as attack aircraft carriers, 11 as anti-submarine warfare aircraft carriers, 5 as auxiliary aircraft transports and 3 as amphibious assault ships.)

Of the auxiliary aircraft transports, *ex*-support aircraft carriers of the 'Essex' class, *Franklin* was stricken in Oct. 1964, *Bunker Hill* in Nov. 1966, *Tarawa* in June 1967, *Leyte* in June 1969 and *Philippine Sea* in Dec. 1969.

[1] All in reserve. *Lake Champlain* was stricken from the Navy List in Dec. 1969, *Wasp* in July 1972, *Antietam* and *Kearsarge* in May 1973, *Essex, Randolph* and *Yorktown* in June 1973, *Ticonderoga* in Nov. 1973 and *Hancock* on 31 Jan. 1975.

Training Carrier

Completed	Name	Standard displacement Tons	Armour Belt In.	Armour Guns In.	Principal armament	Shaft horsepower	Speed Knots
1943	Lexington	32,800	3	—	Removed	150,000	33

Aircraft Ferry Ships (ex-*Escort Carriers*)[1]

[1] The 'Commencement Bay' class comprising the *Kula Gulf, Rabaul* and *Point Cruz*, and the 'Bogue' class comprising the *Breton, Card, Core* and *Croatan* were deleted in 1972–73.

Helicopter Carriers (*Amphibious Assault Ships*)

Completed	Name	Standard displacement Tons	Armour Belt In.	Armour Guns In.	Principal armament	Shaft horsepower	Speed Knots
1977	Saipan	39,300 (full load)	—	—	26 helicopters (or VOSTOL aircraft); 3 5-in. guns; 2 missile launchers	140,000	24
1976	Tarawa						
1970	Inchon	17,000	—	—	24 helicopters	23,000	20
1968	New Orleans						
1966	Tripoli						
1965	Guam[1]						
1963	Guadalcanal						
1962	Okinawa						
1961	Iwojima						

[1] *Guam* was modified in 1971–72 as 'interim' sea control ship but reverted to the amphibious role in 1974. (The Amphibious Assault ship *Thetis Bay*, former Escort Aircraft Carrier, was stricken in 1964 and *Valley Forge, Boxer* and *Princeton*, all of the 'Essex' class in 1969.)

Command Ships

Completed	Name	Standard displacement Tons	Armour Belt In.	Armour Guns In.	Principal armament	Shaft horsepower	Speed Knots
1953	Northampton[1]	14,700	6	—	1 5-in.	120,000	33
1947	Wright[2]	14,500	4	—	Light AA	120,000	33

[1] Originally designed as a heavy cruiser; redesigned as a tactical command ship; reclassified as a command ship in 1961.

[2] Originally built as light fleet aircraft carrier, reclassified as aircraft transport in 1959; reclassified and converted into Command Ship in 1962–63.

Major Communications Relay Ships (ex-*Carriers*)[1]

[1] The former Auxiliary Aircraft Transport *Saipan* (*ex*-Aircraft Carrier completed in 1946), converted to Major Communications Relay Ship (instead of Command Ship) and renamed *Arlington* in 1963–64 was stricken on 15 Aug. 1975.

The former Aircraft Ferry Ship *Gilbert Islands* (*ex*-Escort Carrier) converted to Major Communications Relay Ship 1962–64 and renamed *Annapolis* was stricken on 15 Oct. 1976.

Battleships

Completed	Name	Standard displacement Tons	Armour Belt In.	Armour Guns In.	Principal armament	Shaft horsepower	Speed Knots
1944	Missouri[1] Wisconsin[1]	45,000	19	18	9 16-in.; 20 5-in.	212,000	33
1943	Iowa[1] New Jersey[2]						

[1] All laid up in reserve since 1955–58. [2] Reactivated in 1968–69, reserve sincce.

Heavy Cruisers

Completed	Name	Standard displacement Tons	Armour Belt In.	Armour Guns In.	Principal armament	Shaft horsepower	Speed Knots
1961	Long Beach	14,200	—	—	1 twin 'Talos' and 2 twin 'Terrier'; guided missile launchers; 2 5-in.	80,000 (nuclear power)	35
1949	Newport News* Salem	17,000	8	3–5	9 8-in.; 12 5-in.; 20 3-in.	130,000	33
1948	Des Moines						
1946	Albany[1]	13,700	6	3–5	2 twin 'Talos'; 2 twin 'Terrier'; 2 5-in.	120,000	33
1945	Chicago	13,600	6	3–5	2 twin 'Talos'; 2 twin 'Terrier'; 2 5-in.	120,000	33
1945	Saint Paul[2]	13,600	6	3–5	9 8-in.; 12 5-in.; 14 3-in.	120,000	33
1943	Canberra	13,300	6	3–5	2 twin 'Terrier', 6 8-in.; 10 5-in.; 8 3-in.	120,000	33

*Centre gun of no. 2 turret removed after accidental explosion and turret not operable, only two 3-inch guns.

[1] Of two unconverted sisterships, *Oregon City* was stricken from the Navy List in Nov. 1970 and *Rochester* in 1974.

[2] Sole survivor of the 'Baltimore' class. Of 9 sister ships *Macon* was stricken in 1969, *Baltimore* and *Fall River* in 1971, *Bremerton*, *Pittsburg* and *Quincy* in 1973, and *Helena*, *Los Angeles* and *Toledo* in 1974.

The *Boston* and *Canberra* were reclassified as guided-missile cruisers in 1955 (*Boston* was stricken in Nov. 1973). The *Albany* was reclassed guided-missile cruiser in 1958 for conversion, completed by Nov. 1962. The *Chicago* and *Columbus* (stricken 1976) were reclassed guided-missile cruisers in 1958–59 for conversion, completed in 1964 and 1963, respectively.

Light Cruisers

Completed	Name	Standard displacement Tons	Armour Belt In.	Armour Guns In.	Principal armament	Shaft horsepower	Speed Knots
1945	Little Rock Providence	10,670	5	3–5	Twin 'Talos' of 'Terrier'; 3 or 6 6in.; 2 or 6 5-in.	100,000	33
1944	Oklahoma City Springfield						

These ships with *Galveston*, *Little Rock* and *Topeka* (all 6 originally of the 'Cleveland' class) converted into guided-missile cruisers in 1958–60. *Topeka* and *Galveston* were striken in Dec. 1973 and *Little Rock* on 22 Dec. 1976 to become museum ship at Boston Navy Yard.

Of the original 'Cleveland' class *Amsterdam*, *Pasadena*, *Portsmouth* and *Wilkes-Barr* were stricken from the Navy List in 1970–71, *Astoria* in 1969 and *Vincennes* in 1966. *Atlanta* of this class, was converted for support of Pacific experiments before being discarded as a target. *Fargo* was stricken from the Navy List in 1970.

Of the 'Juneau' class anti-aircraft light cruisers *San Diego*, *San Juan*, *Oakland*, *Reno* and *Juneau* were stricken in 1959, *Fresno* and *Flint* in 1965, and *Tucson* in 1966. The remaining ship, *Spokane*, was converted into a sonar test ship in 1967.

Cruisers, Former Frigates (*Destroyer Leaders*)

Completed	Name	Standard displacement Tons	Armour Belt In.	Armour Guns In.	Principal armament	Shaft horsepower	Speed Knots
1977 1976	Texas Virginia	9,000	—	—	2 twin 'Tartar/ASROC'; 2 5-in.	80,000 (nuclear power)	30
1974 1973	South Carolina California	9,000	—	—	2 single 'Tartar'; 2 5-in.;	70,000 (nuclear power)	30

Completed	*Name*	*Standard displacement Tons*	*Armour Belt In.*	*Armour Guns In.*	*Principal armament*	*Shaft horse-power*	*Speed Knots*
1967	Truxtun	8,200	—	—	1 twin 'Terrier'; 1 5-in.; 2 3-in.	Over 60,000 (nuclear power)	Over 30
1962	Bainbridge	7,600	—	—	2 twin 'Terrier'; 4 3-in.	Over 60,000 (nuclear power)	Over 30
1964–67	9 Belknap Class[1]	6,570	—	—	1 twin 'Terrier'; 1 5-in.; 2 3-in.	85,000	34
1962–64	9 Leahy Class[2]	5,670	—	—	2 twin 'Terrier'; 4 3-in.	85,000	34

[1] The 'Belknap' class comprises *Belknap, Biddle, Fox, Horne, Josephus, Daniels, Jouett, Sterett, Wainwright* and *William H. Standley*. The *Belknap* was severely damaged by collision with the aircraft carrier *John F. Kennedy* on 22 Nov. 1975 in the Mediterranean and towed to the United States for 2-year re-building.

[2] The 'Leahy' class comprises *Dale, England, Gridley, Halsey, Harry E. Yarnell, Leahy, Reeves, Richmond K. Turner* and *Worden*.

*Destroyers, Former Frigates (Destroyer Leaders)**

1959–62	10 Coontz Class[1]	4,700	—	—	1 twin 'Terrier'; 1 5-in.; 4 3-in.	85,000	34

[1] The 'Coontz' class comprises *Coontz, Dahlgren, Dewey, Farragut, King, Luce, Macdonough, Mahan, Preble* and *William V. Pratt*. They were reclassified from frigates (DLG) to destroyers (DDG) on 1 July 1975.

The *Norfolk*, designed as a special anti-submarine cruiser (*Cruiser, Hunter, Killer Ship*), reclassified as a destroyer leader in 1951 and as a frigate in 1955, was stricken in Nov. 1973.

* Of the original 4 'frigates' (DL—destroyer leaders) of the 'Mitschel' class, *John S. McCain* and *Mitscher*, converted into guided-missile destroyers in 1968–69, and *Wilkinson* and *Willis A. Lee*, both unconverted, were discarded in 1973–74.

In addition to the above named ships there are 109 nuclear-powered submarines, 15 conventional submarines, 97 destroyers, 65 frigates, 33 ocean minesweepers, 9 patrol vessels, 4 fast patrol boats, 83 amphibious warfare ships, 40 replenishment ships, 70 sealift ships, 90 fleet support ships and auxiliaries and 1,130 service craft.

Ships under construction include the *Ohio* of 18,700 tons submerged (the largest submarine ever built) with nuclear power and ballistic missiles (and 4 sister ships); 25 nuclear powered attack submarines; the giant nuclear powered aircraft carrier *Carl Vinson* of 93,400 tons war load; 2 nuclear powered guided missile cruisers of 10,000 tons full load; 25 destroyers; 10 guided missile frigates; and 3 very large amphibious assault ships (helicopter carriers) of 39,000 tons full load.

Projected new construction (1978–82 five-year programme plan) includes 8 more 'Ohio' class nuclear powered deterrent or 'strategic' submarines; 8 more nuclear powered fleet or 'attack' submarines; 2 vertical lift (CVV) aircraft carriers; 2 (tentative) nuclear powered strike (CSGN) cruisers of 17,210 tons full load; 10 guided missile destroyers of 9,055 tons full load; 58 guided missile frigates; 6 amphibious ships; 19 mine countermeasures ships and 44 support ships and auxiliaries.

The US Coast Guard operates under the Department of Transportation in time of peace and as a part of the Navy in time of war. The act of establishment stated the Coast Guard 'shall be a military service and branch of the armed forces of the United States at all times'. The Coast Guard did operate as part of the Navy during the First and Second World Wars. It comprises 259 ships including cutters or destroyers, frigate, corvette and patrol vessel types, powerful icebreakers, and paramilitary auxiliaries and tenders. Its peace-time duties embrace generally law enforcement upon the sea and navigable waters of US, the maintenance of navigational aids and the saving of life and property. In the new construction programme are 11 (minimum) cutters of frigate size and utility each carrying a helicopter. The strength of personnel at 30 Sept. 1977 was 6,000 officers and 31,640 enlisted men. Personnel was increased by some 1,000 in 1977 to man the greater cutter fleet to enforce the 200-mile fishery and conservation limits off the coasts of the USA.

Air Force. *Secretary of the Air Force:* John C. Stetson.

The Department of the Air Force was activated within the Department of Defense on 18 Sept. 1947, coequal with the Army and the Navy under the terms of the National Security Act of 1947. It is headed by a Secretary of the USAF, assisted by an Under Secretary and 4 Assistant Secretaries (Research, Development and Logistics; Financial Management; Manpower, Reserve Affairs and Installations; and International Affairs).

The USAF, under the administration of the Department of the Air Force, is commanded by a Chief of Staff, who is a member of the Joint Chiefs of Staff. He is assisted by a Vice Chief of Staff, Assistant Vice Chief of Staff, 5 Deputy Chiefs of Staff and a Comptroller.

The USAF consists of the Regular Air Force, the Air National Guard and the Air Force Reserve. For operational purposes the service is organized into 13 major commands and 13 separate operating agencies. The Aerospace Defense Command is responsible for the air defence of the USA. It is a major component of the North American Air Defense Command (NORAD), a combined command which employs US and Canadian Air Force, and US Army and Navy air defence units for air defence of North America. The Strategic Air Command, equipped with long-range bombers based both in the USA and overseas, and with intercontinental ballistic missiles, is maintained primarily for strategic air operations anywhere on the globe. The Tactical Air Command operates fighters, fighter-bombers and aircraft for photo-reconnaissance and special operations such as psychological warfare. The Military Airlift Command provides worldwide airlift for men and supplies, aero-medical evacuation, audio-visual products, weather services, and rescue and recovery activities.

The other functional commands are the Air Force Systems Command, Air Force Logistics Command, Air Force Communications Service, Air Training Command, Air University, and the USAF Security Service.

The overseas commands are the Pacific Air Forces, the US Air Forces in Europe and the Alaskan Air Command. These overseas commands are operationally responsible to joint theater commands normally headed by an officer of a service with primary interests.

There are also a number of separate operating agencies which include the Air Force Accounting and Finance Center, Air Force Audit Agency, Air Force Data Automation Agency, Air Force Inspection and Safety Center, Air Force Intelligence Service, Air Force Test and Evaluation Center, Air Force Military Personnel Center, Air Force Office of Special Investigations, Air Force Reserve, Air Reserve Personnel Center, US Air Force Academy, Air Force Management Engineering Agency and the Air Force Commissary Service.

Of the fighter-bomber and interceptor aircraft in service, the F-15 Eagle, F-105 Thunderchief, F-106 Delta Dart, F-111 and F-4 Phantom II fly faster than the speed of sound in level flight and can carry a variety of armament, including nuclear weapons. The subsonic A-7 Corsair II is an attack aircraft and the A-10 is a close-support aircraft; both are intended for non-nuclear warfare. Strategic bombers are the B-52 Stratofortress heavy bomber and the FB-111A 'swing-wing' supersonic bomber. The Strategic Air Command also operates the KC-135 Stratotanker jet tanker, used primarily for aerial refuelling, the SR-71 long-range supersonic reconnaissance aircraft. Current transport types include the C-141 Starlifter, the very large C-5 Galaxy jet transport and the turboprop-powered C-130 Hercules. Intercontinental ballistic missiles in USAF service are Titan II and Minuteman II and III.

In 1977, the Air Force had 828,000 military and civilian personnel. Total FY 1978 aircraft strength 9,253.

The total budget requested for the Air Force for the 1976 fiscal year is approximately $34,079m.

American Defense Policy. 3rd ed. Johns Hopkins Univ. Press, 1975
The Army Air Forces in World War II. 7 vols. Univ. of Chicago Press, 1948 ff.
Goldberg, A., *A History of the US Air Force, 1907–57*. New York, 1957

INTERNATIONAL RELATIONS

Membership. USA is a member of UN, OAS, NATO, OECD and the Colombo Plan.

ECONOMY

Budget. The budget covers virtually all the programmes of federal government, including those financed through trust funds, such as for social security, Medicare and highway construction. Receipts of the Government include all income from its sovereign or compulsory powers; income from business-type or market-orientated activities of the Government is offset against outlays. Budget receipts and outlays (in $1m.):

Year ending 30 June	*Receipts*	*Outlays*	*Surplus (+) or deficit (−)*
1945	45,216	92,690	−47,474
1950	39,485	42,597	− 3,112
1955	65,469	68,509	− 3,041
1960	92,492	92,223	+ 269
1970	193,743	196,588	+ 2,845
1975	280,997	324,601	−43,604
1976	299,197	365,657	−66,461
1977[1]	438,634	496,642	−68,008

[1] 1 July 1976–30 Sept. 1977.

Budget receipts, by source, for fiscal years (in $1m.):

Source	*1975*	*1976*	*1977*[1]
Individual income taxes	122,386	130,795	156,725
Corporation income taxes	40,621	41,409	54,892
Social insurance taxes and contributions	86,441	92,714	108,683
Excise taxes	16,551	16,963	17,548
Estate and gift taxes	4,611	5,216	7,327
Customs	3,676	4,074	5,150
Miscellaneous	6,711	8,026	6,536
Total	280,997	299,197	356,861

[1] In 1977, the fiscal year changed from a 1 July–30 June basis to a 1 Oct.–30 Sept. basis.

Budget outlays, by function, for fiscal years (in $1m.):

Source	*1975*	*1976*	*1977*[1]
National defence	86,585	89,996	96,721
International affairs	5,862	5,067	5,593
General science, space, and technology	3,989	4,370	4,677
Natural resources, environment and energy	9,537	11,282	14,335
Agriculture	1,660	2,502	5,330
Commerce and transportation	16,010	17,248	14,731
Community and regional development	4,431	5,300	7,394
Education, training, employment and social services	15,248	18,167	19,718
Health	27,647	33,448	38,838
Income security	108,605	126,598	137,151
Veterans benefits and services	16,597	18,432	18,040
Law enforcement and justice	2,942	3,320	3,589
General government	3,089	2,927	3,338
Revenue sharing and general purpose fiscal assistance	7,005	7,119	9,404
Interest	30,974	34,589	38,092
Undistributed offsetting receipts	−14,075	−14,704	−15,053
Total budget outlays	326,105	365,657	401,896

[1] In 1977, the fiscal year changed from a 1 July–30 June basis to a 1 Oct.–30 Sept. basis.

Budget outlays, by agency, for fiscal years (in $1m.):

Agency	*1975*	*1976*	*1977*[1]
Legislative branch	726	779	1,084
The judiciary	284	325	373
Executive Office of the President	93	79	73
Funds appropriated to the President	3,988	3,525	2,497
Agriculture	9,722	12,796	16,738
Commerce	1,583	2,020	2,607
Defence—Military	85,020	88,036	95,751
Defence—Civil	2,051	2,124	2,280
Health, Education and Welfare	112,411	128,785	147,455
Housing and Urban Development	7,488	7,079	5,832
Interior	2,139	2,293	3,085
Justice	2,067		2,350

Agency	*1975*	*1976*	*1977*[1]
Labour	17,649	25,742	22,374
State	829	1,062	1,132
Transportation	9,247	11,936	12,514
Treasury	41,177	45,143	49,560
Energy Research and Development Administration	3,165	3,759	5,020
Environmental Protection Agency	2,530	3,118	4,365
General Services Administration	−624	−92	−31
National Aeronautics and Space Administration	3,267	3,670	3,944
Veterans Administration	16,575	18,415	18,019
Other independent agencies:			
Civil Service Commission	7,036	8,320	9,620
Postal Service	1,877	1,720	2,267
Railroad Retirement Board	3,083	3,482	3,859
All other	6,799	4,022	4,181
Undistributed offsetting receipts	−14,075	−14,704	−15,053
Total budget outlays	326,105	365,657	401,896
Department of Defense—Military and military assistance	86,019	88,537	102,233

[1] In 1977 the fiscal year changed from a 1 July–30 June basis to 1 Oct.–30 Sept. basis.

National Debt: The gross public debt and guaranteed obligations on 30 June 1972 was $427,260m.

National direct debt excluding guaranteed obligations (in $1,000), and *per capita* debt (in $) on 30 June of the years shown:

	Public debt	*Per capita*[2]		*Public debt*	*Per capita*[2]
1919[1]	25,484,506	243	1966	320,369,000	1,662
1920	24,299,321	228	1967	326,220,938	1,638
1930[1]	16,185,310	132	1968	347,578,406	1,727
1940	48,496,602	367	1969	353,720,253	1,740
1950	257,376,855	1,697	1970	370,918,706	1,811
1960	286,470,603	1,585	1971	398,129,744	1,923

[1] On 31 Aug. 1919 gross debt reached its First World War (1914–18) peak of $26,596,702,000, which was the highest ever reached up to 1934; on 31 Dec. 1930 it had declined to $16,026m., the lowest it has been since the First World War. On the 30 Nov. 1941, just preceding Pearl Harbour, debt stood at $61,363,867,932. The highest Second World War debt was $279,764,369,348 on 28 Feb. 1946.

[2] *Per capita* figures, beginning with 1960, have been revised; they are based on the Census Bureau's estimates of the total population of the US, including Alaska and Hawaii.

State and Local Finance: Revenue of the 50 states and all local governments (78,269 in 1972) from their own sources amounted to $249,089m. in fiscal year 1975–76; in addition they received $55,589m. in revenue from fiscal aid, shared revenues and reimbursements from the federal government, bringing total revenue from all sources to $304,678m. Of the revenue from state and local sources, taxes provided $156,813m., of which property taxes (mainly imposed by local governments) yielded $57,001m. or 36% of all tax revenue; and sales taxes, both general sales taxes and selective excises, provided $54,547m. (35%).

State tax revenue totalled $89,256m. in fiscal year 1976. Largest sources of state tax revenue are general sales taxes (imposed during 1975 by 45 states), motor fuel sales taxes (all states), individual income (44 states), motor vehicle and operators' licences (49 states), corporation income (46 states), tobacco products (all states) and alcoholic beverage sales taxes (all states).

General revenue of local units from own sources in fiscal year 1975–76 totalled $93,186m. In addition they received $69,746m. from state and federal aids. Property taxes provided 34% of total general revenue.

Total expenditures of state and local governments were $305,268m. in 1975–76, of which approximately 67% was for current operation. Education took $97,216m. in current and capital expenditure; highways, $23,907m.; welfare (chiefly public assistance), $32,604m., and health and hospitals, $20,686m. Capital outlays (construction, equipment and land purchases) totalled $46,531m.

Gross debt of state and local governments totalled $240,086m. or $1,118 *per capita* at the close of their 1975–76 fiscal year. Total cash and investment assets of state and local governments were $242,154m., about 25% being in cash and deposits, and the remainder in investments, mainly non-governmental securities.

US Bureau of the Census, *Governmental Finances in 1975–76*. Washington, 1977
American Economic Association, *Readings in Fiscal Policy*. Homewood, Ill., 1955
Brookings Institute and National Bureau of Economic Research, *Role of Direct and Indirect Taxes in the Federal Revenue System*. Washington, D.C., 1964
National Bureau of Economic Research, *National Economic Accounts of the US; Review, Appraisal and Recommendations*. 1958
Burkhead, J., *Government Budgeting*. New York, 1956
Kimmell, L. H., *Federal Budget and Fiscal Policy, 1789–1958*. Washington and London, 1959
Lewis, W., *Federal Fiscal Policy in the Post-war Recessions*. New York, 1963

National Income. The Bureau of Economic Analysis of the Department of Commerce prepares detailed estimates on the national income and product of the United States. The principal estimates are published monthly in *Survey of Current Business*; the complete set of national income and production tables are published in the *Survey* regularly each July, showing data for recent years. *The National Income and Product Accounts of the United States, 1929–1974: Statistical Tables* (1976) contains a complete set of tables from 1929 through 1974. The conceptual framework and statistical methods, underlying the US accounts were described in *National Income, 1954*. Subsequent limited changes were described in *US Income and Output* (1958), and in *Survey of Current Business* (Aug. 1965 and Jan. 1976).

These latest figures[1] in $1,000m. for various years are as follows:

	1929[2]	*1933*[3]	*1950*	*1960*	*1970*	*1975*	*1976*
I. Gross National Product	103·4	55·8	286·2	506·0	982·4	1,528·8	1,706·5
(*a*) Personal consumption expenditures	77·3	45·8	192·0	324·9	618·8	980·4	1,094·0
(*b*) Gross private domestic investment	16·2	1·4	53·8	76·4	140·8	189·1	243·3
(*c*) Net exports of goods and services	1·1	0·4	1·9	4·4	3·9	20·4	7·8
(*d*) Government purchases of goods and services	8·8	8·2	38·5	100·3	218·9	338·9	361·4
1. GNP *less* capital consumption allowances with capital consumption adjustment, indirect business tax and non-tax liability, business transfer payments, statistical discrepancy, *plus* subsidies less current surplus of government enterprises, equals:							
2. National Income	84·8	39·9	236·2	412·0	798·4	1,217·0	1,364·1
which, *less* corporate profits and inventory valuation and capital consumption adjustments, contributions for social insurance, wage accruals less disbursements, *plus* government transfer payments to persons, interest paid by government to persons and business less interest received by government, interest paid by consumers, dividends, business transfer payments, equals:							
3. Personal income whereof	84·9	46·9	226·1	399·7	801·3	1,253·4	1,382·7
4. Personal tax and non-tax payments take leaving	2·6	1·4	20·6	50·4	115·3	169·0	196·9
5. Disposal personal income divided into	82·3	45·5	205·5	349·4	685·9	1,084·4	1,185·8
(*e*) Personal outlays[4]	79·1	46·5	194·7	332·3	635·4	1,004·2	1,119·9
(*f*) Personal saving	3·1	−1·0	10·8	17·1	50·6	80·2	65·9
IA. GNP in constant (1972) $s	314·7	222·1	533·5	736·8	1,075·3	1,202·1	1,274·7
(*a*) Personal consumption expenditures	215·6	170·7	338·1	453·0	668·9	775·1	821·3

[1] The inclusion of statistics for Alaska and Hawaii in 1960 does not significantly affect the comparability of the data.

[2] Peak year between First and Second World Wars. [3] Low point of the depression.

[4] Includes personal consumption expenditures, interest paid by consumers and personal transfer payments to foreigners (net).

	1929[1]	1933[2]	1950	1960	1970	1975	1976
(*b*) Gross private domestic investment	55·9	8·4	93·7	105·4	154·7	141·6	173·0
(*c*) Net exports of goods and services	2·2	0·2	4·0	5·5	1·4	22·5	16·0
(*d*) Government purchases of goods and services	40·9	42·8	97·7	172·9	250·2	263·0	264·4
II. National Income composed of	84·8	39·9	236·2	412·0	798·4	1,217·0	1,364·1
Compensation of employees	*51·1*	*29·5*	*154·8*	*294·9*	*609·2*	*930·3*	*1,036·3*
(*g*) Salaries and wages	50·5	29·0	147·0	271·9	546·5	805·7	891·8
(*h*) Supplements to wages and salaries	0·6	0·5	7·8	23·0	62·7	124·6	144·5
Proprietors' income	*14·9*	*5·8*	*38·4*	*47·0*	*65·1*	*86·0*	*88·0*
(*i*) Farm	6·2	2·6	13·5	11·4	13·9	23·2	18·6
(*j*) Business and professional	8·8	3·2	24·9	35·6	51·2	62·8	69·4
Personal income from rents	*4·9*	*2·2*	*7·1*	*13·8*	*18·6*	*22·3*	*23·3*
Net interest	*4·7*	*4·1*	*2·3*	*9·8*	*37·5*	*79·1*	*88·4*
Corporate profits and inventory valuation and capital consumption adjustments	*9·2*	*−1·7*	*33·7*	*46·6*	*67·9*	*99·3*	*128·1*
(*k*) Tax liabilities	1·4	0·5	17·9	22·7	34·5	50·2	64·7
(*l*) Inventory valuation adjustment	0·5	−2·1	−5·0	0·3	−5·1	−12·0	−14·1
(*m*) Capital consumption adjustment	−1·3	−0·5	−4·0	−2·3	1·5	−12·2	−14·7
(*n*) Dividends	5·8	2·0	8·8	12·9	22·9	32·4	35·8
(*o*) Undistributed profits	2·8	−1·6	15·9	13·0	14·1	41·0	56·4

[1] Peak year between First and Second World Wars.
[2] Low point of the depression.

Consumer Price Index: The Department of Labor compiles an index of retail prices of consumer goods and services bought by wage-earners and clerical workers in 56 cities and urban areas ranging in population from 2,500 upward.

Indexes shown below are published on the 1967 = 100 base. The index for 'housing' has several sub-groups; in the table below only that for rent is given.

Average for year or month	*All items*	*Food*	*Apparel & Upkeep*	*Total*[1]	*Housing Rent*	*Transport*	*Medical care*
1945	53·9	50·7	61·5	59·1	58·8	47·8	42·1
1960	88·7	88·0	89·6	90·2	91·7	89·6	79·1
1965	94·5	94·4	93·7	94·9	96·9	95·9	89·5
1970	116·3	114·9	116·1	118·9	110·1	112·7	120·6
1972	125·3	123·5	122·3	129·2	119·2	119·9	132·5
1973	133·1	141·4	126·8	135·0	124·3	123·8	137·7
1974	147·7	161·7	136·2	150·6	130·2	137·7	150·5
1975	161·2	175·4	142·3	166·8	137·3	150·6	168·6

[1] Includes shelter, rent, home ownership, home maintenance and repairs, and household furnishings and operation.

Currency. Prior to the banking crisis that occurred early in 1933, the monetary system had been on the gold standard for more than 50 years. An Act of 14 March 1900 required the Secretary of the Treasury to maintain at a parity with gold all forms of money issued by the USA. For a description of these, *see* THE STATESMAN'S YEAR-BOOK, 1934, p. 491.

The old gold dollar had a par value of 49·32*d*., or $4·8666 to the £ sterling; it contained 25·8 grains (or 1·6718 grammes) of gold 0·900 fine. By the act of 12 May 1933 the President of the USA was given authority to reduce the gold content of the dollar by not more than 50% and by the Gold Reserve Act of 30 Jan. 1934 the minimum reduction which he could made was fixed at 40%; on 31 Jan. 1934 he fixed its value at 59·06%, or $15\frac{5}{21}$ grains of gold 0·900 fine. This was equal to a price for gold of $35 a fine oz. (old price, $20·67183). The President's power to alter the gold content of the dollar to 50% of its value, which was extended by Congress in 1937, 1939 and 1941, was not again extended in 1943.

The Par Value Modification Act (Public Law 92–268), enacted on 31 March 1972, authorized and directed the Secretary of the Treasury to take the steps necessary to establish a new par value of the dollar of $1.00 = 0·818513 gramme of fine gold or $38 per fine troy oz. of gold. The Secretary of the Treasury, pursuant to the statutory directive, proposed the new par value for the US dollar to the International Monetary Fund, which par value became effective on 8 May 1972.

In Public Law 93–110, enacted on 21 Sept. 1973, Congress amended the Par Value Modification Act of 1972, and authorized and directed the Secretary of the Treasury to take the steps necessary to establish a new par value of $1 equals 0·828948 Special Drawing Right or $1/42\frac{9}{10}$ of a fine troy ounce of gold. Pursuant to the statutory directive, the Secretary of the Treasury notified the International Monetary Fund that, effective 18 Oct. 1973, the par value of the dollar would be changed from 1/38 to $1/42\frac{9}{10}$ a fine troy ounce of gold. Expressed in terms of gold, the new par value of the dollar is 0·736662 gramme of gold per dollar, or $42.222 per fine troy ounce of gold. Expressed in percentage, the change in the par value of the dollar amounted to a reduction of 10% in the former gold content of the dollar. This is the equivalent to an 11·1% increase in the former dollar price of gold.

The USA has accepted the proposed second amendment to the Articles of Agreement of the International Monetary Fund. The par value of the dollar will no longer be defined in terms of the Special Drawing Right and gold, and the USA will not be obliged to establish and maintain a par value for the dollar.

At the time of the banking crisis in March 1933 gold payments by banks and the Treasury were suspended by the Government, and an embargo was placed on gold exports. Steps were taken to withdraw from circulation all gold coin and gold certificates and to prohibit the private ownership of all gold coin except for numismatic purposes. Public Law 93–373, 14 Aug. 1974, amended the Par Value Modification Act so as to provide for the termination of all governmental restrictions on private ownership of gold, including gold coins, no later than 31 Dec. 1974.

Currency in the USA for many years has comprised several varieties. Prior to May 1933 the legal tender qualities of the classes varied, but in that month all types of currency were made equally legal tender. Under the Coinage Act of 1965, all coins and currencies of the USA, regardless of when coined or issued, are legal tender for all debts, public and private.

Only two of the eight kinds of notes outstanding are now significant: Federal Reserve notes in denominations of $1, $5, $10, $20, $50 and $100; and US notes in denominations of $100. The issue of (*a*) $500, $1,000, $5,000 and $10,000 Federal Reserve notes; of (*b*) silver certificates, and of (*c*) $5 and $2 US notes was discontinued recently, although they are still in general circulation. The following issues were stopped many years ago and are in process of retirement: (1) Federal Reserve Bank notes; (2) National Bank notes; (3) Treasury notes of 1890; (4) fractional currency.

Federal Reserve notes are obligations of the USA and a first lien on the assets of the Federal Reserve Banks, through which they are issued. Each of the 12 banks issues them against the security of an equal volume of collateral.

Gold coins (of the old weight and fineness) were $20, $10, $5 and $2½ pieces called *double eagles*, *eagles*, *half-eagles* and *quarter-eagles*. The old eagle weighed 258 grains or 16·7181 grammes 0·900 fine, and therefore contained 232·2 grains or 15·0463 grammes of fine gold. Except for collector's holdings, these are no longer in circulation. The stock of gold bullion held by the Treasury on 30 June 1977 was 276·1m. fine oz., valued at $11,700m.; stock of silver bullion was 40m. fine oz. (excluding 139·5m. fine oz. held for defence stockpile). Estimated stock of domestic coin was $10,477m., of which $482m. were standard silver dollars and the remainder silver and other subsidiary coin.

The silver dollar weighs 412·5 grains or 26·7296 grammes 0·900 fine, and contains 371·25 grains or 24·0566 grammes of fine silver. Subsidiary, 0·900 fine, silver coins contain 347·22 grains of fine silver per dollar. These are the half-dollar, quarter-dollar and dime (one-tenth). Minor coins currently issued are the cupro-nickel 5-cent piece and the bronze 1-cent piece. Pursuant to the Coinage Act of 1965, Congress authorized the minting and issuance of new silver clad half-dollars containing 40% silver and cupro-nickel quarter-dollars and dimes containing no silver. In an amendment to the Coinage Act enacted on 31 Dec. 1970, Congress provided that all coins minted thereafter, including dollar and half-dollar coins, be made of cupro-nickel composition. However, a provision in the 1970 law permitted the coining of 150m. dollar coins containing 40% silver. These dollar coins, which bear the likeness of the late President Eisenhower, are sold at premium price to coin collectors.

Banking. On 31 Dec. 1976 there were 15,145 domestic banks doing a general deposit business with the public and having aggregate deposits of $975,307m. Of these, 4,735 with deposits of $469,378m. were national banks operating under charters granted by the federal government; the remaining banks, including trust companies and savings banks, were organized under the laws of the various states. Of the total number, 5,759 were members of the Federal Reserve System, namely, all the 4,735 national banks and 1,023 state banks admitted to membership.

The Federal Reserve System, established under an Act of 1913, comprises the Board of 7 Governors, the 12 regional Federal Reserve Banks with their 25 branches, the Federal Open Market Committee and the Federal Advisory Council. The 7 members of the Board of Governors are appointed by the President by and with the consent of the Senate. Each Governor is appointed to a full term of 14 years or an unexpired portion of a term, one term expiring every 2 years. No two may come from the same Federal Reserve District. The Board supervises the Reserve Banks and the issue and retirement of Federal Reserve notes; it designates 3 of the 9 directors of each Reserve Bank one of whom is designated Chairman; it passes on the admission of state banks to the System and has power to correct unsound conditions in State member banks or violations of banking law by them, including, if necessary, disciplinary action to remove officers and directors for unsafe or unsound banking practices or for continuous violations of banking laws; it also authorizes State member bank branches and approves mergers and consolidations if the acquiring, assuming or resulting bank is to be a State member; and it has power to control the expansion of bank holding companies and to require divestment of certain non-banking interests. The 12 members of the Federal Open Market Committee include the 7 members of the Board of Governors and 5 of the 12 Federal Reserve Bank presidents. The latter serve 1-year terms on the Committee in rotation except for the President of the Federal Reserve Bank of New York, who is a permanent member. The Federal Open Market Committee influences credit market conditions, money and bank credit, by buying or selling US Government securities; and it also supervises System operations in foreign currencies for the purpose of helping to safeguard the value of the dollar in international exchange markets and facilitating co-operation and efficiency in the international monetary system. The Board also influences credit conditions through powers to set member-bank reserve requirements, to approve discount rates at Federal Reserve Banks, and to fix margin requirements on stock-market credit.

The 12 Reserve Banks (one for each district) implement Federal Reserve policies, chiefly through their dealings with member banks, which, although outnumbered by non-member banks, hold about 73% of the country's total commercial banking deposits. The Reserve Banks hold bank reserves, advance funds to member banks, issue Federal Reserve notes, which are the principal form of currency in the US, act as fiscal agent for the Government and afford nation-wide cheque-clearing and fund transfer arrangements. They may issue notes, fully secured; discount paper for member banks; increase or reduce the country's supply of reserve funds by buying or selling Government securities and other obligations at the direction of the Federal Open Market Committee. Their capital stock is held by the member banks, but it carries no voting rights except in the election of directors.

Every member bank is required to subscribe to stock in the Reserve Bank of its district in an amount equal to 6% of its paid-up capital and surplus. Only one-half of the par value of the stock is paid in, the other half remaining subject to call by the Board of Governors. However, no call has been made for the second half of the subscription. The reserve balances which member banks must carry with Reserve Banks are based on the volume of their net demand and time deposits. The Board of Governors has the power to alter these requirements within limits. The Board of Governors also has authority to limit the rate of interest payable by member banks on time and savings deposits. Under provisions of the Defense Production Act of

1950 the Board of Governors prescribes regulations under which the Federal Reserve Banks act as fiscal agents of certain Government departments and agencies in guaranteeing loans made by banks and other private financing institutions to finance contracts for the procurement of materials or services which the guaranteeing agencies consider necessary for the national defence.

Under the Credit Control Act of 1969 the President is empowered to authorize the Board of Governors to institute selective credit controls when necessary to curb inflation.

Beginning in 1968, the Congress passed a number of consumer credit protection acts, the first of which was the Truth in Lending Act (and including the Equal Credit Opportunity Act), Home Mortgage Disclosure Act, Consumer Leasing Act and the Fair Credit Billing Act, for which it has directed the Board to write implementing regulations and assume partial enforcement responsibility. To manage these responsibilities the Board has established a Consumers Affairs Division. To assist it, the Board consults with a Consumer Advisory Council, established by the Congress as a statutory part of the Federal Reserve System.

Another statutory body, the Federal Advisory Council, consists of 12 members (one from each district); it meets in Washington four times a year (or oftener) to advise the Board of Governors on general business and financial conditions.

Banks which participate in the federal deposit insurance fund have their deposits insured against loss up to $40,000 for each depositor. The fund is administered by the Federal Deposit Insurance Corporation established in 1933; it obtains resources through annual assessments on participating banks.

All members of the Federal Reserve System are required to insure their deposits through the Corporation, and non-member banks may apply and qualify for insurance. On 31 Dec. 1976, 14,671 commercial banks with deposits of $838,328,000m. were members of the insurance fund. This insurance also covered 329 mutual savings banks with deposits of $110,999m. There were 419 uninsured banks comprising 275 commercial banks and trust companies and 144 mutual savings banks with deposits of $25,980,639,000 (in 1975 this figure included mutual savings banks only).

There are also banks which operate solely in the field of agricultural credits under the Farm Credit Administration; Federal Home Loan Banks makes advances to financial associations and institutions upon the security of home mortgages.

US Board of Governors of the Federal Reserve System. *The Federal Reserve System Purposes and Functions.* 6th ed., 1974.—*Federal Reserve Bulletin.* Monthly.—*Annual Report.*—*The Federal Reserve Act, As Amended Through 1975*
Bach, G. L., *Making Monetary and Fiscal Policy.* Washington, 1971
Beckhart, B. B., *Federal Reserve System.* New York, 1972
Chandler, L. V., *Economics of Money and Banking.* 7th ed. New York, 1977
Clifford, A. J., *The Independence of the Federal Reserve System.* Philadelphia, 1965
Friedman and Swartz, *A Monetary History of the United States*, 1867–1960, National Bureau of Economic Research, New York, 1963
Maisel, S. J., *Managing the Dollar.* New York, 1973
Myers, M. G., *A Financial History of the United State.* Columbia Univ. Press, 1970
OECD, *Monetary Policy in the United States.* Paris, 1974
Young, R. A., *Instruments of Monetary Policy in the United States; the Role of the Federal Reserve System.* Washington, 1973

Weights and Measures. British weights and measures are usually employed, but the old Winchester bushel and wine gallon are used instead of the new or Imperial standards: *Wine gallon* = 0·83268 Imperial gallon; *Bushel* = 0·9690 Imperial bushel. Instead of the British cwt of 112 lb., one of 100 lb. is used; the *short* or *net ton* contains 2,000 lb.; the *long* or *gross ton*, 2,240 lb.

ENERGY AND NATURAL RESOURCES

Minerals. Total value of minerals produced in US (including Alaska and Hawaii) in 1976 was estimated at $69,189m. ($62,268m. in 1975). Details are given in the following tables.

Production statistics of metallic minerals (long tons, 2,240 lb.; short tons, 2,000 lb.):

Metallic minerals	1975 Quantity	1975 Value ($1,000)	1976 Quantity	1976 Value ($1,000)
Bauxite (dried equiv.) long tons	1,772,000	25,083	1,958,000	26,645
Copper (recoverable content), short tons	1,413,366	1,814,763	1,605,586	2,234,975
Gold (recoverable content), troy oz.	1,052,252	169,928	1,048,037	131,340
Iron ore (usable),[1] 1,000 long tons, gross	75,695	1,620,599	76,697	1,860,102
Lead (recoverable content), short tons	621,464	267,230	609,546	281,610
Molybdenum (content of concentrate), 1,000 lb.	105,170	259,328	114,527	333,494
Silver (recoverable content), 1,000 troy oz.	34,938	154,424	34,328	149,328
Zinc (recoverable content), short tons	469,355	366,097	484,513	358,541
Other metals	—	518,920	—	710,071
Total metals	—	5,191,000	—	6,086,000

[1] Excluding by-product iron sinter.

The two world wars and record levels of industrial production have hastened the depletion of once abundant supplies of metal and US is increasingly an importer. US is wholly or almost wholly dependent upon imports for industrial diamonds, bauxite, tin, chromite, nickel, strategic-grade mica and long-fibre asbestos; it imports the bulk of its tantalum, platinum, manganese, mercury, tungsten, cobalt and flake graphite, and substantial quantities of antimony, cadmium, arsenic, fluorspar, zinc, gypsum and bismuth.

In 1976 precious metals were mined mainly in Idaho, Arizona, Colorado, Utah, Montana and Missouri (in order of combined output of gold and silver). US output of gold (troy oz.), 1930–39, 31,453,370; 1940–49, 24,171,646; 1950–59, 18,817,241; total 1792–1970, 316,620,436. Output of silver (troy oz.), 1930–39, 466,412,499; 1940–49, 434,656,631; 1950–59, 374,055,521; total 1792–1970, 4,701,429,507.

Statistics of important non-metallic minerals and mineral fuels are:

Non-metallic minerals	1975 Quantity	1975 Value ($1,000)	1976 Quantity	1976 Value ($1,000)
Boron minerals, short tons	1,172,000	158,772	[1]	[1]
Cement:				
Portland, 1,000 short tons	65,215	2,015,625	69,163	2,330,402
Masonry, 1,000 short tons	2,868	111,801	3,267	139,564
Clays, 1,000 short tons	49,047	424,556	52,848	539,894
Gypsum, 1,000 short tons	9,751	44,654	11,980	59,888
Lime, 1,000 short tons	19,133	523,805	20,229	609,010
Phosphate rock, 1,000 short tons	48,816	1,122,184	49,241	949,365
Potassium salts, 1,000 short tons (K_2O equivalent)	2,501	223,098	2,541	213,478
Salt (common), 1,000 short tons	41,030	368,063	44,191	430,959
Sand and gravel, 1,000 short tons	789,436	1,416,346	885,156	1,774,030
Stone, 1,000 short tons	902,900	2,123,049	901,660	2,221,000
Sulphur (Frasch-process), 1,000 long tons	6,077	304,843	5,860	299,999
Other non-metallic minerals	—	680,893	—	990,298
Total non-metallic minerals	—	9,518,000	—	10,558,000
Mineral fuels				
Coal: Bitum. and lignite, 1,000 short tons	648,438	12,472,486	678,685	13,189,481
Pennsylv. anthracite,[2] 1,000 short tons	6,203	198,481	6,228	209,234
Gas: Natural gas,[3] 1m. cu. ft	20,108,661	8,945,062	19,952,438	11,571,776
Natural gasoline and cycle products, 1,000 bbls of 42 gallons	595,958	2,772,588	587,045	3,284,089
L.P. gases, 1,000 bbls of 42 gallons				
Petroleum (crude), 1,000 bbls of 42 gallons	3,056,779	23,166,059	2,976,180	24,229,540
Other mineral fuels	—	54,334	—	60,989
Total mineral fuels	—	47,559,000	—	52,545,000

[1] Included with other non-metallic minerals.
[2] Includes a small quantity of anthracite mined in states other than Pennsylvania.
[3] Value at wells.

Minerals Yearbook. Bureau of Mines. Washington, D.C. Annual from 1932–33; containing the *Mineral Resources of the United States* series (1866–1931); from 1963 in 3 vols. (*Metals, Minerals, Fuels; Area Reports, Domestic; and Area Reports, International*)

Agriculture. Agriculture in the USA is characterized by its ability to adapt to widely varying conditions, and still produce an abundance and variety of agricultural products. From colonial times to about 1920 the major increases in farm production were brought about by adding to the number of farms and the amount of land under cultivation. During this period nearly 320m. acres of virgin forest were converted to crop land or pasture, and extensive areas of grass lands were ploughed. Improvident use of soil and water resources was evident in many areas.

During the next 20 years the number of farms reached a plateau of about 6·5m., and the acreage planted to crops held relatively stable around 330m. acres. The major source of increase in farm output arose from the substitution of power-driven machines for horses and mules. Greater emphasis was placed on development and improvement of land, and the need for conservation of basic agricultural resources was recognized. A successful conservation programme, highly co-ordinated and on a national scale—to prevent further erosion, to restore the native fertility of damaged land and to adjust land uses to production capabilities and needs—has been in operation since early in the 1930s.

Following the Second World War the uptrend in farm output has been greatly accelerated by increased production per acre and per farm animal. These increases are associated with a higher degree of mechanization; greater use of lime and fertilizer; improved varieties, including hybrid maize and grain sorghums; more effective control of insects and disease; improved strains of livestock and poultry; and wider use of good husbandry practices, such as nutritionally balanced feeds, use of superior sites and better housing. During this period land included in farms decreased slowly, crop land harvested declined somewhat more rapidly, but the number of farms declined sharply.

Some significant changes during these transitions are:

All land in farms totalled less than 500m. acres in 1870, rose to a peak of over 1,200m. acres in the 1950s and declined to 1,088m. acres in 1974, even with the addition of the new States of Alaska and Hawaii in 1960. The number of farms declined from 6·35m. in 1940 to 2,830,490 in 1974, as the acreage size of farm doubled. The average size of farms in 1974 was 385 acres, but ranged from 3 to many thousand acres. In 1969, 162,111 farms (244,328 in 1959) were smaller than 10 acres; 473,465 (813,216), 10–49 acres; 459,942 (657,990), 50–99 acres; 706,973 (998,084), 100–219 acres; 561,154 (660,446), 200–499 acres; and 366,605 (336,439), 500 acres or larger. Nearly 60,000 farms contained at least 2,000 acres in 1969.

Farms operated by owners or part-owners, 1969, were 2,377,237 (87% of all farms), by all tenants, 352,923 (13%). The proportion of farms operated by tenants is declining, and currently is three-tenths of the peak recorded in 1930. The average size of farms in 1969 was 220 acres for full-owners, 820 acres for part-owners and 391 acres for tenants. Farms with white operators numbered 2,642,857, and non-white operators 87,393. A higher proportion of non-white operators were tenants and operated a significantly smaller acreage than white operators.

Farms also vary widely in degree of specialization and output. About 60% of all farms received over half their farm income from a single enterprise, such as dairying, or from a single crop, such as cotton, wheat, tobacco or fruit. In 1974 (with 1960 figures in parentheses) large-scale, highly mechanized farms with sales of agricultural products totalling over $20,000 per farm made up 37% (9%) of all farms and accounted for 90% (51%) of the value of farm products sold. Farms selling between $2,500 and $20,000 worth of products per farm were 38% (45%) of all farms and sold 9% (43%) of all sales. The remaining 25% (46%) of farms sold less than $2,500 worth of products per farm in 1974, 1% (6%) of total sales. Many farms in this lowest sales class are called part-time or part-retirement farms. Operators in every sales category received off-farm income, but operators selling less than $2,500 per year received 94% of their average income of $17,209 from non-farm sources.

A century ago three-quarters of the total US population was rural, and practically all rural people lived on farms. In April 1974 less than 30% of the population was rural, and the 9·3m. farm residents comprised less than 5% of the total population.

Hired farm workers in 1974 averaged about 1·3m., and farm family workers, including operators, about 3·1m. In 1950 there were nearly 10m. farm workers. At that time each farm worker supplied farm products for 15 people; today, over 48 people.

Cash receipts from farm marketings and government payments (in $1m.):

	Crops	*Livestock and livestock products*	*Government payments*	*Total*
1932	1,996	2,752	—	4,748
1945	9,655	12,008	742	22,405
1950	12,356	16,105	283	28,744
1960	15,259	18,989	702	34,950
1969	19,606	28,573	3,794	51,973
1970	20,976	29,563	3,717	54,256
1971	22,276	30,583	3,145	56,004
1972	25,520	35,670	3,961	65,151
1973	41,051	45,824	2,607	89,482
1974	52,097	41,424	530	94,051

Realized gross farm income (including government payments), in $1m., was 101,112 in 1974, compared with 95,311 in 1973; net income of farm operators, 27,240 (27,707). Farm-mortgage debt, on 1 Jan. 1975, was estimated at $47,236m.; increase in 1974 was about 14%.

US agricultural exports, fiscal year, totalled: 1964–65, $6,097m.; 1965–66, $6,676m.; 1966–67 $6,771m.; 1967–68, $6,311m.; 1968–69, $5,741m.; 1969–70, $6,721m.; 1970–71, $7,758m.; 1971–72, $8,049m.; 1972–73, $12,901m.; 1973–74, $21,321m.

Total area of farm land under irrigation in 1969 was 39,121,693 acres (257,147 farms); in 1959: 33,162,978 acres and 307,783 farms.

Federal income taxes paid by farm people was $15m. in 1941, $1,365m. in 1948, $1,182m. in 1967, $3,434m. in 1971, $5,309m. in 1972, $8,364m. in 1973 and $8,277m. in 1974. Total taxes levied on farm real estate in 1971 was $2,294m., $2,390m. in 1972, $2,450m. in 1973 and $2,520m. in 1974 (estimated).

According to census returns and estimates of the Economic Research Service, the acreage and specified values of farms has been as follows (area in 1,000 acres; value in $1,000):

	Farm area[1]	*Crop land available for crops*	*Value, land, bldgs, machinery, livestock*	*Value of products sold in preceding year*
1910	878,798	432,000	41,089,000	...
1930	986,771	480,000	57,815,000	9,609,924
1940	1,060,852	467,000	41,829,000	6,681,581
1950	1,158,566	478,000	99,366,000	22,051,129
1959	1,125,508	448,100	164,200,000	30,492,721
1964	1,110,185	434,236	192,000,000	34,003,733
1969	1,063,346	459,048	206,751,000	44,519,658

[1] Acreages are for the preceding year except for 1959.

The areas and production of the principal crops for 3 years were:

	1972			*1973*			*1974*		
	Harvested 1,000 acres	*Production 1,000 bu.*	*Yield per acre bu.*	*Harvested 1,000 acres*	*Production 1,000 bu.*	*Yield per acre bu.*	*Harvested 1,000 acres*	*Production 1,000 bu.*	*Yield per acre bu.*
Corn for grain	57,421	5,573,320	97·1	61,894	5,646,806	91·2	65,191	4,651,167	71·3
Oats	13,525	691,973	51·2	14,065	666,867	47·4	13,325	620,539	46·6
Barley	9,707	423,461	43·6	10,452	421,527	40·3	8,281	308,077	37·2
All wheat	47,284	1,544,936	32·7	53,869	1,705,167	31·7	65,459	1,793,322	27·4
Rice (cwt)	1,817·9	85,439	4,700	2,170·2	92,765	4,274	2,569	114,096	4,441
Soybeans for beans	45,698	1,270,630	27·8	55,796	1,547,165	27·7	52,460	1,233,425	23·5
Flaxseed	1,151	13,909	12·1	1,692	16,091	9·5	1,645	13,337	8·1
Cotton lint (bale)	12,983·8	13,704·1	507	11,970·2	12,974	520	12,669·8	11,701·8	443
Potatoes	1,253·8	295,955	236	1,304·6	299,410	230	1,380·7	340,116	246
Tobacco (lb.)	842·4	1,749,085	2,076	886·6	1,742,105	1,965	961·8	1,958,214	2,036

Wheat. The chief wheat-growing states (1974) were (estimated yield in 1,000 bu.): Kansas, 319,000; N. Dakota, 205,062; Oklahoma, 134,400; Washington, 122,200; Montana, 120,108; Nebraska, 98,600; Minnesota, 80,862; Colorado, 67,809; Ohio, 64,680; Idaho, 61,860.

Cotton. In 1974 the 6 western-most states producing cotton (Texas, New Mexico, Arizona, Oklahoma, Nevada and California) furnished 57% of the crop. Leading production, 1974, by state (in 1,000 bales, 480 lb. net weight) was: Texas, 2,647; California, 2,550; Mississippi, 1,640; Arizona, 1,013; Arkansas, 920; Louisiana, 570; Alabama, 530; Tennessee, 310; Oklahoma, 300; South Carolina, 280.

Tobacco. Output (1,000 lb.) of the chief tobacco-growing states (92% of the crop) was in 1974: N. Carolina, 789,395; Kentucky, 424,596; S. Carolina, 172,000; Georgia, 161,420; Virginia, 141,328; Tennessee, 114,305.

Livestock. Number of farm animals (in 1,000) on farms on 1 Jan.:

	1973	*1974*	*1975*
Cattle of all kinds	121,534	127,670	131,826
Milch cows	11,624	11,286	11,217
Sheep and lambs	17,724	16,394	14,538
Swine (hogs and pigs)[1]	61,106	55,062	...

[1] At 1 Dec.

The value (in $1,000) was:

	1973	*1974*	*1975*
Cattle of all kinds	30,582,529	40,976,795	20,963,981
Sheep and lambs	472,714	533,366	442,271
Hogs and pigs	3,691,416	2,481,644	...

Total value of livestock, excluding poultry and, from 1961, horses and mules (in $1m.) on farms in the USA on 1 Jan. was: 1930, 6,061; 1933 (low point of the agricultural depression), 2,733; 1969, 19,714; 1970, 22,886; 1971, 23,170; 1972, 23,904; 1973, 34,081; 1974, 45,836.

In 1974 the production of shorn wool was 132·9m. lb. from 16·1m. sheep (average 1970–74, 320m. lb. from 18·2m. sheep); of pulled wool, 5·7m. lb. (1970–74, 10·1m. lb.).

Fact Book of US Agriculture. US Dept. of Agriculture, 1976
Cochrane, W. W., *The City Man's Guide to the Farm Problem.* Minneapolis, 1965
Higbee, E. C., *American Agriculture: Geography, Resources, Conservation.* New York, 1958
Paarlberg, D., *American Farm Policy.* New York, 1964
Tweeton, L., *Foundations of Farm Policy.* Lincoln, 1970
Wilcox, W. W., *Economics of American Agriculture.* 2nd ed. New York, 1960

Forestry. In 1970 the US forest lands, including Alaska and Hawaii, capable of producing timber for commercial use, covered 499,697,200 acres (more than one-fifth of the land area), classified as follows: Saw-timber stands, 215,867,400 acres; pole timber stands, 126,693,400 acres; seedling and sapling stands, 131,368,000 acres; non-stocked and other areas, 20,721,600 acres. Ownership of commercial forest land is distributed as follows: Federal government, 107,108,800 acres; state, county and municipal, 29,011,700 acres; privately owned, 363,576,700 acres, including 131,134,900 acres on farms. Of the live saw-timber stand (2,420·77m. bd ft) Douglas fir constitutes 22%; Southern yellow pine, 10%; Western yellow (ponderosa and jeffrey) pine, 8%; other softwoods, 39%; hardwoods, 21%. In 1970 timber cut amounted to 14m. cu. ft compared to net annual growth of about 18·57m. cu. ft. Saw-timber cut amounted to 62·77m. bd ft against an annual growth of 59·92m. bd ft. The net area of the 154 national forests and other areas in USA and Puerto Rico administered by the US Forest Service, including commercial and non-commercial forest land, was on 30 June 1976, 187,639,754 acres.

Fire takes a heavy annual toll in the forest; total area burned over in 1976 was 5,109,926 acres, of which 28% was commercial forest; 1·42m. acres of land are now under organized fire-protection service. The area planted in the year ending 30 June 1976 was 1,892,309 acres, a decrease of 38,205 acres over the previous year.

The Outlook for Timber in the United States. Forest Service, US Dept. of Agriculture, 1974
National Forest System. Forest Service, US Dept. of Agriculture, 1976
Report of the Chief of the Forest Service, 1976

Fisheries. The main fishing industries are in California (anchovy, tuna and sole); Alaska (notably salmon); Washington (salmon and halibut); Florida (the main source of turtles and sponges); Massachusetts, Maine, North Carolina and Oregon. Total catch, 1975, 5,350m. lb. valued at $1,353m.

Tennessee Valley Authority. Established by Act of Congress, 1933, the TVA is a multiple-purpose federal agency which carries out its duties in an area embracing some 41,000 sq. miles, in 125 counties (aggregate population, about 4m.) in the 7 Tennessee River Valley states: Tennessee, Kentucky, Mississippi, Alabama, North Carolina, Georgia and Virginia. In addition, 76 counties outside the Valley are served by TVA power distributors. Its 3 directors are appointed by the President, with the consent of the Senate; headquarters are in Knoxville, Tenn. There were 37,947 employees at 30 Sept. 1977.

Under the Act its chief duties are flood control; the maintenance of navigation; generation, transmission and sale of electric power; the development and production of fertilizers and munitions; assistance in forestry development; and related activities in a single unified approach to resource development. There are now 33 major dams and reservoirs (23 built by TVA) controlling the flow of the river. A navigable channel 650 miles long, connecting with the American system of inland waterways, in 1975 carried 28·3m. tons of traffic in iron and steel products, grains, coal, petroleum, chemicals and other products. Flood damages averted by river control exceed $1,380m.

TVA supplies electric power to 160 local distribution systems serving 2·5m. customers in an area of 80,000 sq. miles. The TVA power system originated with the water-power development of the Tennessee River, but has become predominantly a coal-fired system as power requirements have outgrown the region's hydro-electric potential. In fiscal year 1977 the TVA system generated 122,805m. kwh.; the same region used 1,500m. kwh. in 1933 before TVA operations began. Installed capacity, 1977, was about 28·2m. kw., with another 19·6m. kw. under construction or authorized in nuclear, gas-turbine and pumped-storage installations. Residential consumers served by TVA power distributors used an average of 16,400 kwh. in fiscal year 1977 at an average rate of about 2·3 cents per kwh.; US averages were 9,000 kwh. and about 3·6 cents.

Another activity is experimentation in the development and manufacture of mineral fertilizers accompanied by programmes designed to encourage proper fertilizer use in all parts of the country. The TVA works closely with other federal agencies, and with state and local authorities in combating soil erosion, improving forest resources, improving agriculture and to the development of local industries based on natural resources. In the depression year, 1933, the average *per capita* income in the Valley region was $168 compared with the national average of $375; in 1975 the region's *per capita* income had multiplied over 25 times to $4,570 while the national average had increased 16 times.

Other TVA activities include participation in the first US large-scale fast breeder reactor demonstration project, demonstration of effective ways of reclaiming strip-mined areas, development of new and improved methods of controlling air and water pollution, and a leading role in the US programme of energy development and conservation.

Power operations are financially self-supporting from revenues. In fiscal year 1977 power revenues were $1,966·7m. and net income $149·8m. Power facilities are financed from revenues and the sale of revenue bonds and notes, and TVA is repaying appropriations previously invested in power facilities. In fiscal 1977 TVA paid the US Treasury $20m. as a capital repayment and $64m. in dividends on the remaining appropriation investment, making a total of $1,423m. to date paid to the Treasury from power revenues. Other TVA resource development programmes continue to be financed primarily from appropriations, which amounted to $126m. in fiscal year 1977.

Annual Report of the TVA. Knoxville, 1934 to date
Clapp, G. R., *The TVA; an Approach to the Development of a Region*. Univ. of Chicago Press, 1955
Lilienthal, D. E., *TVA; Democracy on the March*. 20th Anniversary ed. New York and London, 1953
Munger, M. E., *Valley of Vision: The TVA Years*. New York, 1969
Tennessee Valley Authority. *A Quality Environment in the Tennessee Valley*, 1973.—*Directory of TVA Environment Programs*, 1974.—*Short History of the TVA*. Knoxville, Tennessee, 1973.—*TVA: the First Twenty Years* (ed. R. C. Martin), Univ. of Tennessee Press, 1956

INDUSTRY AND TRADE

Industry. The following table presents general statistics of manufactures as reported at various censuses from 1909 to 1975 and from the Annual Survey of Manufactures for years in which no census was taken. The figures for 1958 to 1975 include data for some establishments previously classified as non-manufacturing. The figures for 1939, but not for earlier years, have been revised to exclude data for establishments classified as non-manufacturing in 1954. The figures for 1909–33 were previously revised by the deduction of data for industries excluded from manufacturing during that period.

The statistics for 1958, 1963, 1967 and 1972 relate to all establishments employing 1 or more persons anytime during the year; for 1950, 1956–57, 1959–62, 1964–66 and 1968–74 on a representative sample of manufacturing establishments of 1 or more employees; for 1929 through 1939, those reporting products valued at $5,000 or more; and for 1909 and 1919, those reporting products valued at $500 or more. These differences in the minimum size of establishments included in the census affect only very slightly the year-to-year comparability of the figures.

The annual Surveys of Manufactures carry forward the key measures of manufacturing activity which are covered in detail by the Census of Manufactures. The estimate for 1950 is based on reports for approximately 45,000 plants out of a total of more than 260,000 operating manufacturing establishments; those for 1956–57 on about 50,000, and those for 1959–62, 1964–66 and 1968–74 on about 60,000 out of about 300,000. Included are all large plants and representative samples of the much more numerous small plants. The large plants in the surveys account for approximately two-thirds of the total employment in operating manufacturing establishments in the US.

	Number of establishments	*Production workers (average for year)*	*Production workers' wages, total ($1,000)*	*Value added by manufacture*[1] *($1,000)*
1909	264,810	6,261,736	3,205,213	8,160,075
1919	270,231	8,464,916	9,664,009	23,841,624
1929	206,663	8,369,705	10,884,919	30,591,435
1933	139,325	5,787,611	4,940,146	14,007,540
1939	173,802	7,808,205	8,997,515	24,487,304
1947	240,807	11,917,884	30,243,971	75,366,527
1950	260,000	11,778,803	34,600,025	89,749,765
1959	...	12,272,622	54,714,135	161,535,816
1960	...	12,209,514	55,555,452	163,998,531
1961	...	11,778,518	54,764,619	164,291,080
1962	...	12,126,500	59,134,100	179,071,100
1963	306,617	12,232,041	62,093,601	192,103,102
1964	...	12,403,300	65,838,900	206,193,600
1965	...	13,076,000	71,361,500	226,939,900
1966	...	13,826,500	78,256,400	250,880,100
1967	305,680	13,955,300	81,393,600	261,983,800
1968	...	14,042,500	87,485,400	285,016,200
1969	...	14,359,600	93,459,600	304,308,200
1970	...	13,258,000	91,609,000	300,227,600
1971	...	12,874,900	93,063,200	314,151,700
1972	320,710	13,527,900	105,501,800	353,994,000
1973	...	14,223,100	118,224,100	404,376,200

See note at end of table at top of p. 1398.

	Number of establish ments	Production workers (average for year)	Production workers' wages, total ($1,000)	Value added by manufacture[1] ($1,000)
1974	...	13,979,900	124,983,200	452,477,600
1975	...	12,601,000	121,708,000	441,850,000

[1] For the period 1954–67 value added represents adjusted value added and for earlier years unadjusted value added. Unadjusted value is obtained by subtracting cost of materials, supplies and containers, fuel, electricity and contract work from the value of shipments for products manufactured plus receipts for services rendered. Adjusted value added also takes into account value added by merchandizing operations plus net change in finished goods and work-in-process inventories between the beginning and end of the year.

For comparison of broad types of manufacturing, the industries covered by the Census of Manufactures have been divided into 20 general groups according to the *Standard Industrial Classification*. This was revised in 1972; 1963 and 1967 figures are not therefore strictly comparable.

Code No. Industry group	Census year	Production workers (average for year)	Production workers' wages total ($1,000)	Value added by manufacture[1] ($1,000)
20. Food and kindred products	1963	1,098,116	5,159,376	21,825,516
	1967	1,121,700	6,062,600	26,620,900
	1972	1,085,400	8,007,400	35,616,600
21. Tobacco manufactures	1963	68,579	271,496	1,680,594
	1967	66,200	303,600	2,032,000
	1972	57,400	400,900	2,637,200
22. Textile mill products	1963	775,330	2,768,414	6,122,982
	1967	828,200	3,556,600	8,153,000
	1972	836,200	4,807,200	11,718,000
23. Apparel and related products	1963	1,132,859	3,482,286	7,861,011
	1967	1,200,000	4,340,600	10,064,400
	1972	1,198,300	5,461,100	13,487,500
24. Lumber and wood products	1963	497,409	1,943,287	4,020,600
	1967	495,700	2,290,600	4,973,400
	1972	601,100	3,932,900	10,309,400
25. Furniture and fixtures	1963	314,762	1,289,989	3,068,287
	1967	357,500	1,653,700	4,169,500
	1972	383,800	2,321,300	6,089,500
26. Paper and allied products	1963	467,795	2,551,148	7,395,677
	1967	507,700	3,205,500	9,756,300
	1972	498,800	4,320,200	13,064,100
27. Printing and publishing	1963	559,843	3,190,988	10,476,433
	1967	631,600	4,011,300	14,355,100
	1972	637,400	5,459,300	20,197,100
28. Chemical and allied products	1963	474,141	2,779,938	17,586,138
	1967	541,400	3,555,200	23,550,100
	1972	525,000	4,753,900	32,413,900
29. Petroleum and coal products	1963	109,448	745,123	3,713,231
	1967	99,400	786,400	5,425,800
	1972	97,900	1,064,000	5,793,100
30. Rubber and plastics products, not elsewhere classified[3]	1963	328,785	1,672,376	4,653,953
	1967	410,100	2,312,500	6,799,500
	1972	486,800	3,605,000	11,653,300
31. Leather and leather products	1963	290,339	932,096	2,078,572
	1967	293,300	1,147,000	2,626,500
	1972	240,400	1,230,800	2,917,200
32. Stone, clay and glass products	1963[2]	455,818	2,350,233	7,043,987
	1967	469,300	2,784,100	8,333,400
	1972	492,600	4,037,300	12,586,500
33. Primary and metal industries	1963	922,160	5,933,628	15,261,089
	1967	1,041,500	7,457,300	19,978,200
	1972	922,700	9,202,400	23,258,100

[1] Figures represent adjusted value added. For definitions see footnote to previous table above.
[2] Includes production of unhardened concrete omitted in previous years.
[3] Figures for 1963 and 1967 are not comparable to 1972 due to revisions in the Standard Industrial Classification System.

Code No.	Industry group	Census year	Production workers (average for year)	Production workers' wages, total ($1,000)	Value added by manufacture[1] ($1,000)
34.	Fabricated metal products[2]	1963	843,795	4,483,688	11,791,081
		1967	1,056,900	6,541,600	18,042,600
		1972	1,148,000	9,544,400	26,945,800
35.	Machinery (except electrical)	1963	1,045,075	6,209,341	17,310,599
		1967	1,349,000	9,236,100	27,836,400
		1972	1,266,900	11,358,600	37,562,900
36.	Electrical machinery[2]	1963	1,049,357	5,045,786	17,010,665
		1967	1,323,800	7,607,000	24,587,000
		1972	1,160,800	8,822,600	30,583,600
37.	Transportation equipment[2]	1963	1,150,082	7,731,192	22,765,674
		1967	1,336,500	9,918,200	28,173,900
		1972	1,246,200	12,848,600	39,799,400
38.	Instruments and related products[2]	1963	208,448	1,100,718	3,992,131
		1967	265,900	1,569,000	6,418,400
		1972	292,000	2,237,100	10,583,700
39.	Miscellaneous manufacturing	1963	315,017	1,253,518	3,992,131
		1967	344,400	1,552,500	4,599,400
		1972	350,200	2,086,700	6,777,000

[1] Figures represent adjusted value added. For definitions see footnote to previous table, p. 1398.

[2] Figures for 1963 and 1967 are not comparable to 1972 due to revisions in the Standard Industrial Classification System.

Iron and Steel: Output of the iron and steel industries (in net tons of 2,000 lb.), according to figures supplied by the American Iron and Steel Institute, was:

	Furnaces in blast 31 Dec.	Pig-iron (including ferro-alloys)	Raw steel	Steel by method of production[1]			
				Open hearth	Bessemer	Electric[2]	Basic Oxygen
1932[3]	44	9,835,227	15,322,901	13,336,210	1,715,925	270,044	...
1939	195	35,677,097	52,798,714	48,409,800	3,358,916	1,029,067	...
1944[4]	218	62,866,198	89,641,600	80,363,953	5,039,923	4,237,699	...
1950	234	66,400,311	96,336,075	86,262,509	4,534,558	6,039,008	...
1960	114	68,566,384	99,281,601	86,367,506	1,189,196	8,378,743	3,346,156
1970	152	87,933,000	131,514,000	48,022,000	—	20,162,000	63,330,000
1974	136	98,175,000	145,720,000	35,499,000	—	28,669,000	81,552,000
1975	119	82,060,000	116,642,000	22,161,000	—	22,680,000	71,801,000
1976	107	88,874,000	128,000,000	23,470,000	—	24,612,000	79,918,000

[1] The sum of these 4 items should equal the total in the preceding column; any difference appearing is due to the very small production of crucible steel, omitted prior to 1950.
[2] Includes crucible production beginning 1950.
[3] Low point of the depression
[4] Peak year of war production.

Wholesale price index of iron and steel (1967 = 100) was: 1950, 59·4; 1960, 96·4; 1970, 114·3; 1972, 130·4; 1973, 134·1; 1974, 170; 1975, 197·2; 1976, 209·8.

Leading producers of pig-iron in 1976 were: Pennsylvania, 18·02m. net tons; Indiana, 17·44m.; Ohio, 15·75m.; Illinois, 6·43m.

Consumption of ore, 1976, was 127,826,000 net tons, of which blast-furnaces took 101·4m. tons; steel producing furnaces, 1,152,000 tons, and agglomerating plants, 25,226,000 tons.

The iron and steel industry in 1976 employed 339,021 wage-earners (compared with 449,888 in 1960), who worked an average of 36·4 hours per week and earned an average of $9.132 per hour: total wages were $5,187m. and total salaries for 115,107 employees were $2,434m.

Annual Statistics Report. American Iron and Steel Institute
Adams, W. (ed.), *The Structure of American Industry.* 3rd ed. New York, 1961
Alderfer, E. B., and Michl, H. E., *Economics of American Industry.* 3rd ed. New York, 1957
Fuchs, V. R., *Changes in the Location of Manufacturing Since 1929.* Yale Univ. Press, 1962
Glover, J. G. (ed.), *The Development of American Industries.* 4th ed. New York, 1959
Resources for the Future. *Regions, Resources and Economic Growth.* Baltimore, 1960

Labour. The American trade unions comprise about 177 national and international unions plus a large number of small independent local or single-firm unions. In 1974 total membership was approximately 21m., including 1·6m. Canadian workers affiliated with American unions and under 90,000 others outside the USA. The American Federation of Labor (founded 1881 and taking its name in 1886) and the Congress of Industrial Organizations merged into one organization, named the AFL–CIO, in Dec. 1955, representing 16·6m. workers in 1976.

Unaffiliated or independent unions, interstate in scope, including those organizing coalminers, teamsters and government employees and railroad workers, had an estimated total membership of about 4·5m. In addition, unaffiliated, professional and state employee associations represent approximately 3m. members for collective bargaining purposes. Together, unions affiliated with the AFL–CIO, unaffiliated unions and professional and state employee associations represented 22·5m. workers or 23·2% of the labour force in 1976.

The Labor–Management Relations (Taft–Hartley) Act, 1947, applicable to industries affecting inter-state commerce, prohibits the closed shop, but permits union shop arrangements except where forbidden by state laws. Statutes regulating, restricting or prohibiting closed shop or other types of union security agreements are in effect in 20 states which ban all types of union security agreements (Alabama, Arizona, Arkansas, Florida, Georgia, Iowa, Kansas, Louisiana, Mississippi, Nebraska, Nevada, North Carolina, North Dakota, South Carolina, South Dakota, Tennessee, Texas, Utah, Virginia and Wyoming). Colorado and Wisconsin ban all-union agreements unless a certain percentage of employees have voted for them; in Hawaii an all-union agreement may be entered into unless a majority of employees votes against it. Thirteen states have acts to prevent industrial disputes between public utilities and their employees by means of compulsory arbitration or seizure; however, a number of these laws have been declared unconstitutional in so far as industries in inter-state commerce are concerned. Laws to restrict or regulate picketing or other strike activities have been enacted in over half the states. About one-half of the states also prohibit certain types of strikes, as 'sit down', jurisdictional or sympathy strikes.

The Employee Retirement Income Security Act of 1974 protects the interests of workers and their beneficiaries who are entitled to benefits from employee pension and welfare plans. The law requires disclosure of plan provisions and financial information and establishes standards of conduct for trustees and administrators of welfare and pension plans. It provides funding, participation and vesting requirements for pension plans and makes termination insurance available for most pension plans. The Department of Labor and the Internal Revenue Service share administration of the law. The pension plan termination insurance programme is administered by the Pension Benefit Guaranty Corporation.

The law does not require a company to establish a welfare or pension plan. But it does provide that any employee not covered by a pension plan, other than Social Security, may put aside a certain amount of his income, tax-free, to take care of his retirement needs.

Minimum wage laws governing private employers are in operation in 44 jurisdictions: 40 states, the District of Columbia, Guam, Puerto Rico and the Virgin Islands have minimum wage laws and minimum wage rates. As of 1 June 1976, the laws of 38 states and of the 4 jurisdictions cover men, women and, usually, minors; in the remaining 2 states the laws cover only women and minors. The minimum wage rate under federal law is $2.30 per hour for non-farm employees who are engaged in commerce, in the production of goods for commerce or in certain enterprises which are engaged in commerce. For hired farm workers on large farms the minimum wage is $2.00 per hour.

A total of 5,648 strikes and lockouts occurred in 1976, involving 2·4m. workers and 37·9m. idle days; the number of idle days was 0·19% of the year's total working time of all workers.

There are 3 federal agencies which provide formal machinery for the adjustment of labour disputes: (1) The Federal Mediation and Conciliation Service, now an independent agency, whose mediation services are available 'in any labor dispute in any industry affecting commerce'; under Executive Order 11491, as amended, to federal agencies and organizations of federal employees involved in negotiation disputes; and in state and local government collective bargaining disputes when adequate dispute resolution machinery is not available to the parties. Its aim is to prevent and minimize work stoppages. (2) The National Mediation Board (1934) provides much the same facilities for the railroad and air-transport industries pursuant to the Railway Labor Act. (3) The National Railroad Adjustment Board (1934) acts as a board of final appeal for grievances arising over the interpretation of existing collective agreements under the Railway Labor Act; its decisions are binding upon both sides and enforceable by the courts.

The National Labor Relations Act, as amended by the Labor–Management Relations (Taft–Hartley) Act, 1947 (*see* THE STATESMAN'S YEAR-BOOK, 1955, p. 617), was again amended by the Labor–Management Reporting and Disclosure Act, 1959. This requires extensive reporting and disclosure of certain financial and administrative practices of labour organizations, employers and labour relations consultants. In addition, certain powers are vested in the Secretary of Labor to prevent abuses in the administration of trusteeships by labour organizations, to provide minimum standards and procedures for the election of union officers and to establish rules prescribing minimum standards for determining the adequacy of union procedures for the removal of officers. Other provisions impose a fiduciary responsibility upon union officers and provide for the exclusion of those convicted of certain named felonies from office for specified periods; more stringently regulate secondary boycotts and banning of 'hot' cargo agreements; put limitations upon organizational and recognition picketing and permit States to assert jurisdiction over labour disputes where the National Labor Relations Board declines to act. The Act also contains a 'Bill of Rights' for union members (enforceable directly by them) dealing with such things as equal rights in the nomination and election of union officers, freedom of speech and assembly subject to reasonable union rules, and safeguards against improper disciplinary action.

The Census of Population (1 April 1970) showed that the total labour force was 82,048,781 (58·2% of those 16 years and over); the armed forces accounted for 1,997,735 and the civilian labour force for 80,051,046, of whom 76,553,599 were employed and 3,497,447—or 4·4%—were unemployed. The following table shows employment by industry group and sex and percentage distribution of the total:

Industry Group	*Male*	*Female*	*Total*	*Percentage distribution*
Employed (1,000 persons):	47,624	28,930	76,554	100·0
Agriculture, forestry and fisheries	2,521	320	2,841	3·7
Mining } Construction }	4,885	318	631	0·8
			4,572	6·0
Manufacturing:				
Durable goods	9,248	2,493	11,741	15·3
Non-durable (including not specified)	4,925	3,171	8,096	10·6
Transportation, communication and other public utilities	4,072	1,114	5,186	6·8
Wholesale and retail trade	9,039	6,334	15,373	20·1
Finance, insurance and real estate	1,925	1,913	3,838	5·0
Business and repair services	1,719	676	2,395	3·1
Personal services	1,007	2,530	3,537	4·6
Entertainment and recreation services	407	224	631	0·8
Professional and related services	4,954	8,557	13,511	17·6
Public administration	2,921	1,281	4,202	5·5

The Bureau of Labor Statistics estimated the average total labour force (including armed forces) during 1976 at 96·92m., of the civilian labour force (96,917,000), 7·3m. persons (7·7%) were unemployed; 3·3m. were working in agriculture and 84·2m. in non-agricultural industries. The Bureau estimated that an average of 18·96m. persons were employed in manufacturing, 17,694,000 in trade and 14·95m. in civilian government services.

Bureau of Labor Statistics, US Dept. of Labor. *Directory of National Unions and Employee Associations in the US.* 1975.—*Brief History of the American Labor Movement.* 1976.—*Handbook of Labor Statistics.* 1975

Commons, J. R. (ed.), *History of Labor in the United States.* 4 vols. New York, 1918–36

Hardman, J. B. S., and Neufeld, M. S. (ed.), *The House of Labor: Internal Operation of American Unions*. New York, 1951
Lebergott, S., *Manpower in Economic Growth: The American Record Since 1800*. New York and London, 1963
Millis, H. A., and Brown, E. C., *From the Wagner Act to Taft–Hartley*. Chicago, 1950
Raybeck, J. G., *A History of American Labor*. New York, 1959
Peterson, F., *American Labor Unions*. Rev. ed. New York and London, 1963
Taft, P., *The Structure and Government of Labor Unions*. Harvard Univ. Press, 1954.—*Organized Labor in American History*. New York, 1964

Commerce. The subjoined table gives the total value of the imports and exports of merchandise by yearly average or by year (in $1m.):

	Exports		*General*		*Exports*		*General*
	Total	*US mdse.*[1]	*imports*		*Total*	*US mdse.*[1]	*imports*
1946–50	11,829	11,673	6,659	1972	49,759	48,959	55,583
1951–55	15,333	15,196	10,832	1973	71,339	70,246	69,475
1956–60	19,204	19,029	13,650	1974	98,507	97,144	100,977
1961–65	24,006	24,707	17,659	1975	107,652	106,157	96,940
1970	43,224	42,590	39,952	1976	114,997	113,323	121,793

[1] Re-exports.

For a description of how imports and exports are valued by the US Customs, see *Explanation of Statistics of Report FT990, Highlights of US Export and Import Trade*, Bureau of the Census, US Department of Commerce, Washington, D.C., 1946.

The 'most favoured nation' treatment in commerce between Great Britain and US was agreed to for 4 years by the treaty of 1815, was extended for 10 years by the treaty of 1818, and indefinitely (subject to 12 months' notice) by that of 1827.

Imports and exports of gold and silver bullion and specie in calendar years (in $1,000):

	Gold		*Silver*	
	Exports	*Imports*	*Exports*	*Imports*
1932	809,528	363,315	13,850	19,650
1940	4,995	4,749,467	3,674	58,434
1944	959,228	113,836	126,915	23,373
1955	7,257	104,592	8,331	72,932
1960	1,647	335,032	25,789	57,438
1965	1,285,097	101,669	54,061	64,769
1970	36,887	227,472	53,003	58,838
1971	27,779	276,683	13,634	33,979
1972	48,522	343,666	44,361	41,579
1973	116,273	336,762	20,315	216,153
1974	179,070	350,706	27,694	432,864
1975	429,278	406,583	104,086	274,106

The domestic exports of US produce, including military, and the imports for consumption by economic classes for 2 calendar years were (in $1m.):

	Exports (US merchandise)			*Imports for consumption*		
	1974	*1975*	*1976*	*1974*	*1975*	*1976*
Food and live animals	13,986	15,484	15,710	9,380	8,492	10,223
Crude materials	10,934	9,784	10,891	5,915	5,340	6,722
Machinery and transport equipment	38,189	45,668	49,510	24,713	24,163	30,681
Chemicals	8,819	8,691	9,958	3,991	3,668	4,788
Total	71,928	79,686	86,069	43,999	41,663	52,414

Leading exports of US merchandise are listed below for the calendar year 1976: Special category merchandise is included. Data for major subdivisions of certain classes are also given:

Commodity	*$1m.*	*Commodity*	*$1m.*
Machinery, total	49,510	Automobiles (and parts)	10,949
Power generating machinery	3,662	Aircraft (and parts)	
Metalworking machinery	949	Soybean	6,116
Agricultural machines and tractors	2,108	Cotton	3,315
Office machines	2,937	Textiles and apparel	1,049

Commodity	*$1m.*	*Commodity*	*$1m.*
Electrical apparatus	9,278	Tobacco and manufactures	2,480
Telecommunications apparatus	1,997	Iron and steel-mill products	1,457
Electrical power machinery and		Nonferrous base metals and alloys	1,833
switchgear	2,138	Pulp, paper and products	1,088
Grains and preparations		Coal	1,004
Wheat (and flour)	4,041	Fruits, nuts and vegetables	2,988
Maize	5,224	Petroleum and products	1,535
Chemicals	9,958	Firearms of war and ammunition	998
Chemical elements and compounds	4,408		1,261
Plastic materials and resins	1,672		

Chief imports for 28 commodity classes for consumption for the calendar year 1976:

Commodity	*$1m.*	*Commodity*	*$1m.*
Petroleum and products	31,755	Fertilizers	588
Petroleum	25,446	Sugar	1,148
Petroleum products	6,309	Iron and steel-mill products	3,978
Nonferrous base metals	3,494	Cattle, meat and preparations	1,603
Copper	777	Automobiles and parts	13,757
Aluminium	550	Fish (and shellfish)	
Nickel	526	Fruit, nuts and vegetables	1,854
Bauxite, crude	—	Alcoholic beverages	1,186
Tin	330	Wool and other hair	1,172
Pulp, paper and products	—	Metal manufactures	123
Newsprint	1,742	Diamonds (excl. industrial)	2,058
Wood pulp	1,191	Rubber	1,019
Textiles and apparel	5,266	Plywood	520
Clothing	3,613	Oils and oilseeds	538
Cotton fabrics, woven	394	Cocoa (and cacao beans)	514
Machinery, total	15,438	Glass and pottery	358
Electrical apparatus	7,484	Footwear	644
Agricultural machines and tractors	853	Toys and sports goods	1,725
Office machines	1,353	Furs, undressed	910
Coffee	2,633	Scientific/Photographic apparatus	101
Chemicals	4,829	Artworks and antiques	983
Chemical elements and compounds	2,899	Grains and animal feeds	580
Uranium oxide	204		247

Total trade between the USA and the UK for 5 years (British Department of Trade returns, in £1,000 sterling):

	1973	*1974*	*1975*	*1976*	*1977*
Imports to UK	1,610,331	2,241,066	2,319,118	3,044,259	3,662,505
Exports and re-exports from UK	1,512,947	1,757,082	1,755,518	2,448,751	3,087,279

Imports and exports by continents, areas and selected countries for calendar years (in $1m.):

Area and country	*General imports*		*Exports, incl. re-exports*[1]	
	1975	*1976*	*1975*	*1976*
Canada	22,151	26,827	21,744[2]	24,109[2]
20 American Republics	11,847	13,243	15,655[2]	15,492[2]
Western Europe	20,891	23,045	29,945[2]	32,401[2]
	54,926	...	67,368	...
Western Hemisphere	38,209	43,962	38,843	41,082
Canada	22,151	26,827	21,744	24,109
20 American Republics[3]	11,847	13,243	15,655	15,492
Central American Common Market	811	1,207	968	1,153
Costa Rica	179	235	212	255
El Salvador	182	287	194	232
Guatemala	173	288	255	334
Honduras	145	216	151	162
Nicaragua	131	181	156	169

[1] Data include exports of commodities classed for security reasons as 'special category' except as indicated.

[2] 'Special category' exports are included in these totals.

[3] Except Cuba.

Area and country	General imports 1975	General imports 1976	Exports, incl. re-exports[1] 1975	Exports, incl. re-exports[1] 1976
Western Hemisphere (*contd.*)				
Panama	196	142	317	358
Latin American FTA	10,100	11,225	13,773	13,399
Argentina	215	310	628	544
Brazil	1,467	1,740	3,056	2,809
Chile	138	222	533	508
Columbia	596	657	643	703
Ecuador	463	539	414	416
Mexico	3,066	3,606	5,144	4,990
Paraguay	19	20	33	38
Peru	398	378	896	573
Uruguay	24	62	51	58
Dominican Republic	634	520	453	432
Haiti	107	149	144	150
Bolivia	89	113	138	133
Venezuela	3,625	3,576	2,243	2,628
Bahamas	880	670	208	199
Netherlands Antilles	1,559	1,170	228	248
Jamaica	307	312	381	285
Trinidad and Tobago	1,171	1,501	256	309
Europe				
Western Europe	20,891	23,045	29,945	32,401
OECD Countries	20,626	22,651	29,575	32,052
European Economic Community	16,732	18,070	22,862	25,406
Belgium and Luxembourg	1,199	1,131	2,417	2,991
Denmark	464	565	445	444
France	2,164	2,541	3,031	3,449
Germany (Fed. Rep.)	5,409	5,700	5,194	5,730
Irish Republic	178	206	190	280
Italy	2,457	2,544	2,867	3,068
Netherlands	1,089	1,094	4,194	4,645
UK	3,773	4,289	4,525	4,799
Greece	110	146	450	591
Turkey	145	223	608	451
EFTA countries	7,040	8,148	8,458	8,827
Austria	243	242	181	197
Norway	403	647	510	500
Portugal	157	128	427	400
Sweden	887	926	925	1,036
Switzerland	879	1,041	1,153	1,173
Finland	149	190	261	243
Iceland	85	120	32	35
Spain	836	919	2,161	2,021
Yugoslavia	261	387	328	298
Soviet bloc	734	867	2,788	3,502
Poland	243	319	583	623
USSR	254	221	1,836	2,308
Asia[2, 3]	27,325	39,665	28,813	30,257
Near East	5,401	9,010	8,263	9,237
Egypt	28	93	683	810
Iran	1,398	1,480	3,242	2,776
Iraq	19	110	310	382
Israel	314	424	1,551	1,409
Kuwait	111	38	366	472
Lebanon	33	5	369	49
Saudi Arabia	2,623	5,213	1,502	2,774
Japan	11,425	15,683	9,565	10,144
Other Asia	15,667	23,716	18,356	19,452
Bangladesh	54	64	382	117
Hong Kong	1,573	2,409	808	1,165
India	549	710	1,290	1,135

[1] See note on previous page. [2] Includes Egypt.
[3] Excludes Yemen (Aden) (formerly Southern Yemen), and Bahrain.

Area and country	*General imports* 1975	1976	*Exports, incl. re-exports*[1] 1975	1976
Other Asia (*contd.*)				
Indonesia	2,222	3,007	810	1,036
Korea, Republic of	1,442	2,440	1,761	2,015
Malaysia	772	943	395	536
Singapore	534	697	994	965
Pakistan	49	70	372	394
Philippines	757	888	832	819
Sri Lanka	40	43	38	37
Thailand	217	277	357	347
Taiwan (Formosa)	1,946	2,999	1,660	1,635
Vietnam	6	1	213	1
China[2]	158	202	304	135
Oceania	1,508	1,675	2,339	2,690
Australia	1,147	1,214	1,816	2,185
New Zealand and W. Samoa	245	331	414	417
Africa[3]	8,271	12,544	4,267	4,396
Algeria	1,359	2,210	632	487
Ethiopia	49	94	70	78
Libya	1,045	2,241	232	277
Morocco	10	17	200	297
Ghana	151	155	100	133
Liberia	96	98	90	85
Nigeria	3,281	4,931	536	770
Kenya	36	60	49	43
Zaïre	67	190	188	99
South Africa, Republic of[4]	874	931	1,310	1,360

[1] See note on p. 1403.
[2] Imports from China (including Manchuria) and North Korea, rigidly controlled by the US Treasury, were 1962, $241,000; 1963, $268,000; 1964, $0·5m.; 1965, $0·5m.; 1966, $0·1m.; exports are embargoed.
[3] Excludes Egypt.
[4] Includes also South-West Africa (Namibia).

US Department of Commerce. Bureau of Census. Report FT 990, Highlights of US Export and Import Trade
US Department of Commerce. Bureau of International Commerce. Overseas Business Reports

Tourism. In 1975, 15,698,000 tourists visited the USA and spent $4,875m. They came mainly from Canada (9·9m.), Mexico (2·15m.), Japan (746,000), the UK (438,000) and the Federal Republic of Germany (298,000).

COMMUNICATIONS

Roads. On 31 Dec. 1975 the total US highway mileage, including rural and urban roads, amounted to 3,838,146 miles, of which, 3,100,704 miles were surfaced roads. The total mileage cited includes 710,797 miles of rural roads under control of the states, 2,260,544 miles of local roads, 227,255 miles of federal park and forest roads, and 639,550 miles of municipal roads and streets. Preliminary estimate of expenditures for construction and maintenance amounted to $20,210m. in 1975.

By the end of 1975, toll roads, financed by private capital through bond issues and administered by state toll authorities, totalled, 4,751 miles (including some under construction) compared with 344 miles in 1940. Additional toll-road programmes contemplated at present will add approximately 1,592 miles to the toll-road network.

Motor vehicles registered in the calendar year 1975 were (Federal Highways Administration) 132,950,410, including 106,712,551 automobiles, 462,144 buses and 25,775,715 trucks.

Road haulage of goods by motor lorries and trucks in 1975 used 25,775,715 vehicles (250,048 in 1916). The industry (1975) employed 9·05m. workers, or 1 out of every 10 employed in the USA.

Inter-city trucks (private and for hire) averaged 441,000m. revenue net ton-miles in 1975. Of the 462,144 buses in service in 1975, 365,982 were school buses. Inter-city service operated a total of 1,120m. bus-miles and earned a total of $1,165·4m. in 1975.

There were 46,000 deaths in road accidents in 1975.

Railways. Railway history in the USA commences in 1828, but the first railway to convey both freight and passengers in regular service (between Baltimore and Ellicott's Mills, Md., 13 miles) dates from 24 May 1830. Mileage rose to 52,922 miles in 1870; to 167,191 miles in 1890, and to a peak of 266,381 miles in 1916, falling thereafter to 261,871 in 1925; 246,739 in 1940 and 222,164 in 1969 (these include some duplication under trackage rights and some mileage operated in Canada by US companies). The ordinary gauge is 4 ft 8½ in. (about 99·6% of total mileage). The USA has about 29% of the world's railway mileage.

In addition to the independent railroad companies, railway service is provided by two federally-assisted organizations, the National Railroad Passenger Corporation (Amtrak), and the Consolidated Rail Corporation (Conrail).

Amtrak was set up on 1 May 1971 to maintain a basis network of inter-city passenger trains with government assistance, and is responsible for almost all non-commuter services.

Conrail is the organization established on 1 April 1976 to run freight services in the industrial north-east formerly operated by the bankrupt Penn Central, Reading, Lehigh Valley, Central of New Jersey. Erie Lackawanna, and Lehigh & Hudson railroads.

The following table, based on the figures of the Interstate Commerce Commission, shows some railway statistics for 4 calendar years:

	1960	*1970*	*1974*	*1975*[1]
Classes I and II Railroads				
Mileage owned (first main tracks)	223,779	204,621	199,215	172,428
Revenue freight originated (1m. short tons)	1,421	1,572	1,619	1,395
Freight ton-mileage (1m. ton-miles)	591,550	771,012	852,262	754,580
Passengers carried (1,000)	488,019	289,469	275,185	269,394
Passenger-miles (1m.)	31,790	10,786	10,349	9,935
Operating revenues ($1m.)	9,587	12,209	17,458	16,683
Operating expenses ($1m.)	7,135	9,806	13,758	13,792
Net railway operating income ($1m.)	1,055	506	539	21
Net income after fixed charges ($1m.)	855	126	558	−73
Class I Railroads:				
Locomotives in service	40,949	27,086	28,377	28,395
Steam locomotives	25,640	—	—	—
Freight-train cars (excluding caboose cars)	1,721,269	1,423,921	1,339,286	1,313,888
Passenger-train cars	57,146	11,177	6,908	6,471
Average number of employees	1,220,784	566,282	533,277	494,348
Average wage per week ($1)	72.59	188.71	273.21	294.20

[1] Class I railroads only.

Aviation. In civil aviation there were, on 31 Dec. 1975, 728,187 certified pilots (305,863 private) and 196,342 registered civil aircraft (171,156 active).

Airports on 31 Dec. 1975: Air carrier, 649; general aviation, 12,602. Of these airports, 11,224 were conventional land-based, while 468 were seaplane bases, 1,524 were heliports and 35 stolports (STOL—Short Take-Off and Landing).

Statistics from the Civil Aeronautics Board indicate that for 12 months ended June 1977 on US flag carriers in scheduled international service there were 17·3m. enplanements with 268m. aircraft miles (excluding all-cargo) for a total of 34,730m. revenue passenger-miles. The non-scheduled airlines had a total of 8,291m. revenue passenger-miles internationally. Domestically US scheduled airlines in 1976 had 212·1m. enplanements with a total of 1,991m. miles for 149,042m. revenue passenger-miles. Non-scheduled airlines in the US recorded 988m. revenue passenger-miles in 1975. (A revenue passenger-mile is one paying passenger carried per mile.)

Shipping. On 1 Aug. 1977 the US merchant marine included 842 sea-going vessels of 1,000 gross tons or over, with aggregate dead-weight tonnage of 19·1m. This included 272 tankers of 11·3m. DWT.

On 1 Aug. 1977 US merchant ocean-going vessels were employed as follows: Active, 558 of 15·1m. DWT, of which 286 of 8m. tons were foreign trade, 208 of

6m. tons in domestic trade and 64 of 1·1m. tons in other US agency operations. Inactive vessels totalled 4·01m. DWT; 20 of 0·8m. DWT privately owned were laid up and 243 of 2·4m. tons were in the National Defense reserve fleet. Of the total vessels in the US fleet, 577 of 16·6m. DWT were privately owned.

US exports and imports carried on dry cargo and tanker vessels in the year 1976 totalled 698·8m. long tons, of which 33·5m. long tons or 4·8% were carried in US flag vessels.

Post and Broadcasting. The telephone business is largely in the hands of the American Telephone and Telegraph Company and its telephone operating subsidiaries, which together are known as the Bell Telephone System. There are, however, many hundreds of smaller telephone companies having no common ownership affiliation with the Bell companies, but which connect with them for universal service, countrywide and worldwide. The message telegraph and telex services are in the hands of The Western Union Telegraph Company, but it competes with the telephone industry in providing private leased lines.

The number of telephones in service in the USA has increased in the period since the close of the Second World War much more proportionately than has the population. Among principal reasons there may be cited the facts that an increasingly high percentage of families have telephones installed in their homes, and extension phones associated with the main home telephones have become increasingly common. In marked contrast, the number of public telegrams has decreased by more than 80%. Telegrams have lost favour due to shifts in user preference to the air-mail and to the telephone. The telex services of the telegraph company have also found broad acceptance in place of telegrams for business purposes. The following table contains key data items on a comparative basis for the domestic telephone and message telegram services:

	1950	*1960*	*1970*	*1976*
All telephone systems:				
Total telephones	43,131,000	74,342,000	120,218,000	155,173,000
Bell Telephone System:				
Total telephones	35,343,400	60,735,100	96,561,000	123,131,000
Average daily telephone calls	140,782,000	219,093,000	368,363,000	485,439,000
Local	134,870,000	209,373,000	346,505,000	450,174,000
Long distance	5,912,000	9,720,000	21,858,000	35,265,000
Total plant in service ($1,000)	10,101,522	24,072,499	54,813,202	93,626,174
Total operating revenues ($1,000)	3,271,029	7,958,125	17,094,846	33,014,157
Employees, number	523,251	580,405	772,980	760,040
Western Union Telegraph System:				
Public telegrams for year	153,054,000	102,931,000	46,083,860	28,586,000
Total plant ($1,000)	294,451	398,023	1,029,149	1,680,554
Revenue from public telegrams ($1,000)	132,281	160,746	126,739	75,413
Total operating revenues ($1,000)	177,994	262,365	402,456	527,530
Employees, number	40,482	32,655	24,293	11,996

International communication services, providing overseas connexions with all parts of the world, are furnished principally by the American Telephone and Telegraph Company and three telegraph companies. The old-type telegraph-only-transmission-capability ocean cables have all been abandoned in favour of using telegraph circuits derived from voice channels in the newer telephone ocean cables which have also made inroads on the use of high-frequency radio. More recently, satellite communications facilities have been utilized not only for telephone and telegraph services but for television transmission as well.

International overseas telegrams, inbound to and outbound from the continental US, numbered 13·2m. in 1976 (13·8m. in 1975). This service has tended to decline in volume in recent years. It has lost ground to the air-mail and, in addition, in more recent years to the telex and telephone services. For the US and its possessions the volume of international overseas telephone calls has grown enormously with the availability of the excellent voice-transmission qualities provided in the telephone ocean cables and in the satellite radio relays. Whereas, international telephone calls were 990,000 in 1955, the last year in which there was no cable service available, there were 54·9m. such calls in 1976.

Postal business for the years ended 30 Sept. included the following items:

	1974	*1975*	*1976*	*1977*
Number of post offices, on 30 June[1]	31,000	30,754	30,528	30,521
Postal revenue ($1,000)[2]	9,008,314	10,015,170	11,199,211	12,997,873
Postal expenses ($1,000)[3]	11,295,339	12,574,205	13,922,736	15,310,169

[1] The US Postal Service was established 1 July 1971. Financial statements prior to that date are those of the Post Office Department. Such statements for 1969–71 have been restated to be in a format and on an accounting principle basis generally consistent with 1972.

[2] Operating revenue excludes government appropriations, operating reimbursements and other income.

[3] Operating expenses are stated net of operating reimbursements and exclude certain costs financed by revenue.

On 1 Jan. 1975 there were in the USA and Territories, 7,068 authorized commercial radio stations, 711 commercial television stations: of non-commercial stations 717 were for radio, 241 for television.

Cinemas. Cinemas increased from 17,003 in 1940 to 20,239 in 1950 and decreased to 12,187 in 1967.

Newspapers. Of the daily newspapers being published in the USA in 1971, 339 were morning papers with a circulation of 26,116,000, and 1,425 were evening papers with a circulation of 36,115,000. The 590 Sunday papers had a total circulation of 49·7m.

JUSTICE, RELIGION, EDUCATION AND WELFARE

Justice. Legal controversies may be decided in two systems of courts: the federal courts, with jurisdiction confined to certain matters enumerated in Article III of the Constitution, and the state courts, with jurisdiction in all other proceedings. The federal courts have jurisdiction exclusive of the state courts in criminal prosecutions for the violation of federal statutes, in civil cases involving the government, in bankruptcy cases and in admiralty proceedings, and have jurisdiction concurrent with the state courts over suits between parties from different states, and certain suits involving questions of federal law.

The highest court is the Supreme Court of the US, which reviews cases from the lower federal courts and certain cases originating in state courts involving questions of federal law. It is the final arbiter of all questions involving federal statutes and the Constitution; and it has the power to invalidate any federal or state law or executive action which it finds repugnant to the Constitution. This court, consisting of 9 justices who receive salaries of $60,000 a year (the Chief Justice, $62,500), meets from Oct. until June every year and disposes of about 3,380 cases, deciding about 380 on their merits. In the remainder of cases it either summarily affirms lower court decisions or declines to review. A few suits, usually brought by state governments, originate in the Supreme Court, but issues of fact are mostly referred to a master.

The US courts of appeals number 11 (in 10 circuits composed of 3 or more states and 1 circuit for the District of Columbia); the 97 circuit judges receive salaries of $42,500 a year. Any party to a suit in a lower federal court usually has a right of appeal to one of these courts. In addition, there are direct appeals to these courts from many federal administrative agencies. In the year ending 30 June 1976 more than 18,400 appeals were filed in the courts of appeals.

The trial courts in the federal system are the US district courts, of which there are 89 in the 50 states, 1 in the District of Columbia and 1 each in the territories of Puerto Rico, Virgin Islands, Canal Zone and Guam. Each state has at least 1 US district court, and 3 states have 4 apiece. Each district court has from 1 to 27 judgeships. There are 400 US district judges ($40,000 a year), who handle about 130,600 civil cases and 55,000 criminal defendants every year.

In addition to these courts of general jurisdiction, there are special federal courts of limited jurisdiction. The Court of Claims (7 judges at $42,500 a year) decides claims for money damages against the federal government in a wide variety of matters; the Customs Court (9 judges at $40,000 a year) determines controversies concerning the classification and valuation of imported merchandise; and the Court of

Customs and Patent Appeals (5 judges at $42,500 a year) hears appeals from the Customs Court, the Tariff Commission and the Patent Office.

The judges of all these courts are appointed by the President with the approval of the Senate; to assure their independence, they hold office during good behaviour and cannot have their salaries reduced. This does not apply to the territorial judges, who hold their offices for a term of years. The judges may retire with full pay at the age of 70 years if they have served a period of 10 years, or at 65 if they have 15 years of service, but they are subject to call for such judicial duties as they are willing to undertake. Only 9 US judges up to 1974 have been involved in impeachment proceedings, of whom 3 district judges and 1 commerce judge were convicted and removed from office.

Of the 130,597 civil cases filed in the district courts in the year ending 30 June 1976, about 70,372 arose under various federal statutes (such as labour, social security, tax, patent, securities, antitrust and civil rights laws); 25,736 involved personal injury or property damage claims; 23,998 dealt with contracts; and 8,475 were actions concerning real property.

Of the 37,667 criminal cases filed in the district courts in the year ending 30 June 1974, about 1,900 were charged with alleged infractions of the immigration laws; 3,000, the transport of stolen motor vehicles; about 3,225 larceny and theft; 4,700, embezzlement and fraud; about 650, liquor laws, and 7,400 narcotics laws.

Persons convicted of federal crimes are either fined, released on probation under the supervision of the probation officers of the federal courts, confined in prison for a period of up to 6 months and then put on probation (known as split sentencing) or confined in one of the following institutions: 3 for juvenile and youths; 7 for young adults; 7 for intermediate term adults; 7 for short-term adults; 2 for females; 1 hospital and 15 community service centres. In addition, prisoners are confined in centres operated by the National Institutes of Mental Health. In addition, prisoner drug addicts may be committed to US Public Health Service hospitals for treatment. In 1972–73 about 1,500 of the federal prison population were placed on work release, that is, they were confined in community treatment centre at night and permitted to work at gainful employment during the weekdays. Prisoners confined in institutions operated by the US Bureau of Prisons for the year ending 30 June 1973, numbered 23,336.

The state courts have jurisdiction over all civil and criminal cases arising under state laws, but decisions of the state courts of last resort as to the validity of treaties or of laws of the United States, or on other questions arising under the Constitution, are subject to review by the Supreme Court of the US. The state court systems are generally similar to the federal system, to the extent that they generally have a number of trial courts and intermediate appellate courts, and a single court of last resort. The highest court in each state is usually called the Supreme Court or Court of Appeals with a Chief Justice and Associate Justices, usually elected but sometimes appointed by the Governor with the advice and consent of the State Senate or other advisory body; they usually hold office for a term of years, but in some instances for life or during good behaviour. Their salaries range from $14,000 to $40,000 a year. The lowest tribunals are usually those of Justices of the Peace; many towns and cities have municipal and police courts, with power to commit for trial in criminal matters and to determine misdemeanours for violation of the municipal ordinances; they frequently try civil cases involving limited amounts.

The Federal Bureau of Investigation estimates the number of major crimes in the US and its possessions as follows:

Crime index classification	*1959–61 average*	*1975*
Murder	8,670	20,510
Forcible rape	15,860	56,090
Robbery	87,570	464,970
Aggravated assault	129,400	484,710
Burglary	789,300	3,252,100
Larceny over $50	464,300	5,977,700
Motor car theft	312,000	1,000,500
Total	1,807,100	11,256,600

The death penalty is illegal in Alaska, Hawaii, Iowa, Maine, Minnesota, Oregon, West Virgina, Wisconsin and Michigan; in North Dakota it is legal only for treason and first-degree murder committed by a prisoner serving a life sentence for first-degree murder, in Rhode Island only for murder committed by a prisoner serving a life sentence and in Vermont and New York for the murder of a peace officer in the line of duty and for first-degree murder by those who kill while serving a life sentence for murder. The death penalty, although still legal in most states, has fallen into disuse and has been abolished *de facto* in many states. The US Supreme Court has held the death penalty, as applied in general criminal statutes, to contravene the eighth and fourteenth amendments of the US constitution, as a cruel and unusual punishment when used so irregularly and rarely as to destroy its deterrent value.

In 1967 only 2 persons were executed under civil authority; both for murder. There were no executions 1968–76. In 1977 a convicted murderer requested that he should be executed and after a lengthy legal dispute the sentence was carried out at Utah state prison. In Jan. 1977, 350 prisoners were reported under sentence of death.

The total number of civilian executions carried out in the US from 1930 to 1967 was 3,859, including 1,751 white persons (20 women), 2,066 Negroes (12 women) and 42 persons of other races.

Federal 'Political' Crimes. Prosecutions for what may be loosely described as 'political' offences, or crimes directed towards the overthrow by violence of the federal government, which were somewhat numerous in the early 1950s, have declined sharply over the last 15 years and are now exceedingly rare. During the fiscal year 1975–76 the following number of defendants appeared in federal courts: Espionage, none; Subversive Activities Control Act, 1950, none; contempt of Congress, none.

A Guide to Court Systems. Institute of Judicial Administration. New York, 1960
The United States Courts (88th Congress, 1st Session, House Document No. 180). US Government Printing Office, 1975
The Challenge of Crime in a Free Society. Report of the President's Commission on Law Enforcement and Administration of Justice. US Government Printing Office, 1967
Hart and Wechsler, *The Federal Courts and the Federal System.* Brooklyn, N.Y., 1953
Hurst, J. Willard, *The Growth of American Law.* New York, 1950
Huston, L. A., *The Department of Justice.* New York, 1967
Huston, L. A., and others. *Roles of the Attorney General of the United States.* New York, 1968
McCloskey, R. G., *The Modern Supreme Court.* Harvard Univ. Press, 1972
Mayers, L., *The American Legal System.* Rev. ed. New York, 1964
Murphy, W. F., *Congress and the Court.* Univ. of Chicago Press, 1962
Smith, B., *Police Systems in the US.* Rev. ed. New York, 1960
Vanderbilt, A. T., *Minimum Standards of Judicial Administration.* New York, 1949
Warren, Charles, *The Supreme Court in United States History.* 2 vols. Rev. ed. Boston, Mass, 1960

Religion. *The Yearbook of American and Canadian Churches for 1977*, published by the National Council of the Churches of Christ in the USA, New York, presents the latest figures available from official statisticians of church bodies. The large majority of reports are for the calendar year 1975, or a fiscal year ending 1975. The 1975 reports indicated that there were 129,713,735 members with 333,114 local churches. There were 261,550 clergymen having local congregations. The principal religious bodies (numerically or historically) or groups of religious bodies are shown below:

Denominations	*Local churches*	*Total membership*
Summary:		
Protestant bodies	300,563	69,743,302
Roman Catholic Church	24,135	48,881,872
Jewish Congregations[1]	5,000	6,115,000
Eastern Churches	1,505	3,695,860
Old Catholic, Polish National Catholic and Armenian	420	845,922
Buddhists	60	60,000
Miscellaneous[2]	1,431	371,799
1977 totals	333,114	129,713,735[3]

[1] Includes Orthodox, Conservative and Reformed bodies.
[2] Includes non-Christian bodies such as Spiritualists, Ethical Culture, Unitarian-Universalists.
[3] Care should be taken in interpreting membership statistics for the US Churches. Some statistics are accurately compiled and others are estimates. Also statistics are not always comparable.

Protestant Church Membership	*Total membership*
Baptist bodies	
Southern Baptist Convention	12,733,124
National Baptist Convention, USA	5,500,000
National Baptist Convention of America	2,668,799
National Primitive Baptist Convention	250,000
American Baptist Churches in the USA	1,603,033
American Baptist Association	1,071,000
Progressive National Baptist Convention	521,692
Conservative Baptist Association of America	300,000
Regular Baptist Churches	250,000
Free Will Baptists	227,434
Baptist Missionary Association of America	215,788
Christian Church (Disciples of Christ)	1,302,164
Christian Churches and Churches of Christ	1,048,816
Church of the Nazarene	441,093
Churches of Christ	2,400,000
The Episcopal Church	2,857,513
Latter-Day Saints:	
Church of Jesus Christ of Latter-day Saints	2,336,715
Reorganized Church of Jesus Christ of Latter Day Saints	157,762
Lutheran Bodies:	
Lutheran Church in America	2,986,078
The Lutheran Church-Missouri Synod	2,763,542
The American Lutheran Church	2,415,810
Wisconsin Evangelical Lutheran Synod	395,440
Methodist Bodies:	
United Methodist Church	9,957,710
African Methodist Episcopal Church	1,166,301
African Methodist Episcopal Zion Church	1,024,974
Christian Methodist Episcopal Church	466,718
Pentecostal Bodies:	
Assemblies of God	1,239,197
Church of God in Christ, International	501,000
Church of God in Christ	425,000
Church of God (Cleveland, Tenn.)	343,249
United Pentecostal Church, International, Inc.	300,000
Presbyterian Bodies:	
United Presbyterian Church in the USA	2,657,699
Presbyterian Church in the US	878,126
Reformed Churches:	
Reformed Church in America	355,052
Christian Reformed Church	287,503
The Salvation Army	384,817
Seventh-day Adventists	495,699
United Church of Christ	1,818,762

Yearbook of American and Canadian Churches. Annual, from 1951. New York
Clarke, E. T., *The Small Sects in America*. Rev. ed. New York, 1949
Johnson, A. W., and Yost, F. H., *Separation of Church and State in the United States*. Minneapolis and London, 1949
Mead, F. S., *Handbook of Denominations in the US*. 4th ed. New York, 1965
Moehiman, C. H., *The Wall of Separation between Church and State*. Boston, 1951
Roemer, T., *The Catholic Church in the United States*. Rev. ed. New York, 1961
Sperry, W. L., *Religion in America*. London, 1945
Stokes, A. P., and Pfeffer, L., *Church and State in the US*. New York. 1964
Sweet, W. W., *The Story of Religion in America*. 2nd ed. New York, 1950

Education. Under the system of government in the USA, elementary and secondary education is committed in the main to the several states. Each of the 50 states has a system of free public schools, established by law, with courses covering 12 years plus kindergarten. There are 3 structural patterns in common use: the K8–4 plan, meaning kindergarten plus 8 elementary grades followed by 4 high school grades; the K6–3–3 plan, or kindergarten plus 6 elementary grades followed by a 3-year junior high school and a 3-year senior high school; and the K6–6 plan, kindergarten plus 6 elementary grades followed by a 6-year high school. All plans lead to high-school graduation, usually at age 17 or 18. Vocational education is an integral part of secondary education. In addition, some states have 2-year junior colleges as part of the free public school system. Each state has delegated a large degree of control of the educational programme to local school districts (numbering 16,376 in autumn 1975), each with a board of education (usually 3 to 9 members) elected locally and serving mostly without pay. The school policies of the local districts must be in accord with the laws and the regulations of their state Departments of Education. Forty-nine states have compulsory school attendance laws; in 36 states and the District of Columbia children are required to attend school until the age of 16 years; in 7 states until 17 and 6 states until 18.

The Census Bureau estimates that in Nov. 1969 only 1,433,000 or 1% of the 143m. persons who were 14 years of age or older were unable to read and write; in 1930 the percentage was 4·8. In 1940 a new category was established—the 'functionally illiterate', meaning those who had completed fewer than 5 years of elementary schooling; for persons 25 years of age or over this percentage was 3·9 in March 1976 (for the non-white population alone it was 10·7%); it was 0·8 for white and 0·9% for non-whites in the 25–29-year-old group. The Bureau reported that in March 1976 the median years of school completed by all persons 25 years old and over was 12·4, and that 14·7% had completed 4 or more years of college. For the 25–29-year-old group, the median school years completed was 12·9 and 23·7% had completed 4 or more years of college.

In the autumn of 1975, 9·7m. students (5·3m. men and 4·4m. women) were enrolled in 2,765 colleges and universities; 1·9m. were first-time students. Total enrolment represents a number equal to 35 per 100 persons between the ages of 18 and 24.

Public elementary and secondary school revenue is supplied from the county and other local sources (48·4% in 1975–76), state sources (43·7%) and federal sources (8%). In 1975–76 the estimated amount, including interest, expended on public elementary and secondary schools was $61,120m., representing an annual cost per pupil of $1,436. In addition, $5,983m., or $145 per pupil, was expended for capital outlay. Estimated total expenditures, for private elementary and secondary schools in 1975–76 were $7,900m. In 1975–76 the 2,765 universities and colleges expended an estimated $39,700m. from current funds, of which $26,800m. was spent by institutions under public control. The federal government contributed 15·6% of total current-fund revenue; state governments, 29·9%; student tuition and fees, 20·3%; and all other sources, 34·2%.

Vocational education below college grade, including the training of teachers to conduct such education, has been federally aided since 1918. During the school year 1974–75 enrolments in the vocational classes were: Agriculture, 1,012,595; distributive occupations, 873,224; health occupations, 616,638; home economics, 3,746,540; trade and industry, 3,016,509; technical education, 447,336; office occupations, 2,951,065; other programmes, 2,821,921. Federal support funds were $536m.

Summary of statistics of schools (public and non-public), teachers and pupils in autumn 1975 (compiled by the US National Center for Education Statistics):

Schools by level	*Number of schools 1974–75*	*Teachers autumn 1975*	*Enrolment autumn 1975*
Elementary schools:			
Public	63,619	1,195,000	25,865,000
Non-public	14,372	173,000	3,925,000
Secondary schools:			
Public	25,697	1,023,000	19,211,000
Non-public	3,770	93,000	1,435,000
Higher education:			
Public	1,214	484,000	7,426,000
Non-public	1,533	186,000	2,306,000
Total	110,205	3,154,000	60,168,000

Most of the non-public elementary and secondary schools are affiliated with religious denominations. Of the children attending non-public schools in 1970–71 81%

were enrolled in Roman Catholic schools, 10% in other church-related schools and 9% in schools which were not affiliated to a religious denomination.

During the school year 1974–75 high-school graduates numbered 3·14m. (1·54m. boys and 1·6m. girls). Institutions of higher education conferred an estimated 978,849 bachelor's and first professional degrees for the academic year 1974–75, 553,797 to men and 425,052 to women; 292,450 master's degrees, 161,570 to men and 130,880 to women; and 34,083 doctorates, 26,817 to men and 7,266 to women.

During the academic year, 1974–75, 154,580 foreign students were enrolled in American colleges and universities. The percentages of students coming from various areas were: Asia, 53·3; Latin America, 17; Africa, 11·9; Europe, 8·9; North America, 5·6; Oceania, 1·7; Country unknown, 1·5; Stateless, 0·1.

School enrolment, Oct. 1976, embraced 87% of the children who were 5 years old; 99% of the children aged 6–13 years; 94% of those aged 14–17, and 30% of those aged 18–24 years.

The US National Center for Education Statistics estimates the total enrolment in the autumn of 1976 at all the country's educational institutions (public and non-public) at 60·1m. (60·2m. in the autumn of 1975); this was 28% of the total population of the USA as of 1 Sept. 1976.

Enrolment at the elementary school level is expected to be down by more than 1% in autumn 1976, to rise by less than 1% at the secondary level (grades 9 to 12), and to rise by 3% for students pursuing degree-credit programmes in colleges and universities.

The number of teachers in the public and non-public elementary and secondary schools in the autumn of 1976 is expected to remain at 2·5m. The average annual salary of the public school teachers was about $12,524 in 1975–76.

All states require at least a bachelor's degree, and 3 states require completion of 5 years of college work for secondary school teachers; 47 states require a bachelor's degree for elementary school teachers, and the other states at least 2 years of college work. Thirty states, the District of Columbia and Puerto Rico require that the applicant for a teaching certificate be a citizen of the US or that he must have filed a declaration of intent. Twenty-five states, the District of Columbia and Puerto Rico require that the applicant subscribe to an oath of allegiance or loyalty to the US and the state.

Digest of Educational Statistics. Annual. Office of Education, Washington 25, D.C. (from 1962)
American Junior Colleges. 6th ed. American Council of Education. Washington, 1963
American Universities and Colleges. 9th ed. American Council of Education. Washington, 1964
Ayer's Directory of Newspapers and Periodicals. Annual, from 1880. Philadelphia
Berelson, B., *Graduate Education in the United States*. New York, 1960
De Young, C. A., and Wynn, D. R., *American Education*. 5th ed. New York, 1964
Douglass, H. R., *Secondary Education in the US*. 2nd ed. New York, 1964
French, W. M. *America's Educational Tradition*. Boston, 1964
Good, H. G., *History of American Education*. 2nd ed. New York and London, 1962
Hofstadter, R., and Smith, W. *American Higher Education: A Documentary History*. 2 vols. Univ. of Chicago Press, 1962

Health and Welfare. Admission to the practice of medicine (for both doctors of medicine and doctors of osteopathic medicine) is controlled in each state by examining boards directly representing the profession and acting with authority conferred by state law. Although there are an increasing number of variations, the usual time now required to complete basic training is 8 years beyond the secondary school with an additional year of graduate training. Certification as a specialist may require as much as 5 more years of graduate training plus experience in practice. In academic year 1974–75 the 123 US schools (including 7 osteopathic, 2 developing osteopathic, 107 medical, 5 developing and 2 basic science with medical 2-year programmes after which the students complete their training in a medical school) graduated 13,370 physicians. About 18% of the total students were women. In Dec. 1974 the total estimated number of physicians (MD and DO—in all forms of practice and retired from medical practice) in the US, Puerto Rico and outlying US areas was 395,000. The distribution of physicians throughout the country is uneven, both by state and by urban–rural areas.

In 1974–75 the 58 dental schools graduated 4,970 dentists. Active dentists in Dec. 1974 numbered 109,430. New York state had 1 active civilian dentist to 1,351 population and Mississippi, 1 to 3,846.

In 1974–75 schools of professional nursing numbered 1,372 with 74,500 graduates that year. In Jan. 1976 there were an estimated 961,000 professional nurses employed full- or part-time (1 to 223 inhabitants), ranging (in 1972) from 1 per 154 in Massachusetts to 1 per 526 in Arkansas.

Number of hospitals listed by the American Hospital Association in 1974 was 7,174, with 1,512,684 beds and 35,506,190 admissions during the year; average daily census was 1,167,353. Of the total, 387 hospitals with 135,634 beds were operated by the federal government; 2,298 with 625,655 beds by state and local government; 3,425 with 653,078 beds by non-profit organizations (including church groups); 841 with 73,769 beds are proprietary. The categories of non-federal hospitals are 5,977 short-term general and special hospitals with 931,172 beds; 221 non-federal long-term general and special hospitals with 54,236 beds; 543 psychiatric hospitals with 383,480 beds; 46 tuberculosis hospitals with 8,162 beds. Hospital beds in short-term general facilities range from 2·6 (Alaska) to 6·7 (District of Columbia) hospital beds per 1,000 population; the national average is 4·5. It was estimated that, on 1 Jan. 1975, more than 42,165 additional beds in general hospitals and 127,429 additional long-term care beds (nursing homes and chronic disease hospitals) were needed. Also 150,566 general hospital beds and 226,762 long-term care beds are in need of modernization.

Social welfare legislation was chiefly the province of the various states until the adoption of the Social Security Act of 14 Aug. 1935. This as amended provides for a federal system of old-age, survivors and disability insurance; health insurance for the aged and disabled; supplemental security income for the aged, blind and disabled; federal state unemployment insurance; and federal grants to states for public assistance (medical assistance for the aged and aid to families with dependent children generally) and for maternal and child-health and child-welfare services. The Social Security Administration of the Department of Health, Education and Welfare has responsibility for the only completely federal programmes under the Act—old-age, survivors and disability insurance, health insurance for the aged and disabled, and supplemental security income. The Social and Rehabilitation Service, an agency of the same Department, has federal responsibility for all other programmes except unemployment insurance, which is the responsibility of the Department of Labor, and maternal and child health services which is the responsibility of Public Health Service.

The Social Security Act provides for protection against the cost of medical care through the two-part programme of health insurance for people 65 and over and for certain disabled people who receive disability insurance payments (Medicare). During 1975, 9·7m. in-patient hospital claims were recorded under the hospital part of the programme. Hospitals were paid $10,355m. for this in-patient care. Under the voluntary medical insurance part of Medicare, $3,765m. was paid on 83·1m. claims for services during 1976.

In 1976 about 99m. persons were in employment covered by old-age survivors and disability insurance (including about 620,000 covered jointly by that programme and railroad retirement).

In Jan. 1976, 32·1m. beneficiaries were on the rolls, and the average benefit paid to a retired worker (not counting any paid to his dependants) was about $207 per month.

Benefits paid during 1975 totalled $66,585m., including $8,414m. paid to disabled workers and their dependants.

Total expenditures for public assistance (including $5·5m. medical assistance) during the fiscal year 1971 amounted to $16,300m. By Jan. 1970 all states, plus Washington, D.C., Guam, Puerto Rico and the Virgin Islands were making payments under the programme of medical assistance (Medicaid) authorized by 1965 legislation. By June 1971 about 10·28m. persons (adults and children) were receiving payments under aid to families with dependent children (average, $49.40). In Jan. 1976, 4·3m. persons received supplemental security income payments, including 2·3m. persons aged 65 or over; 75,110 blind persons, and 1·96m. disabled persons.

Payments, including supplemental amounts from the various states, totalled $497m.

During the fiscal year 1970–71 federal appropriations for grants to states were made for maternal and child health services amounting to $59·2m.; for crippled children's services, $58·6m., and for child welfare services, $46m. Additional appropriations for grants for research projects relating to maternal and child health and crippled children's services were $5·7m.; research, training and demonstration projects in the field of child welfare, $10·2m.; maternity and infant care projects, $38·6m.; projects to provide comprehensive health care for school and pre-school children, $43·8m.; and training personnel for health care of mothers and children, $11·2m.

Burns, E. M., *Social Security and Public Policy*. New York, 1956
Friedlander, W. A., *Introduction to Social Welfare*. 2nd ed. New York, 1961
De Groot, L. J. et al., *Medical Care, Social and Organizational Aspects*. Springfield, 1966
Gagliardo, D., *American Social Insurance*. Rev. ed. New York, 1955
Grod, F. P., *Public Health Law Manual*. New York, 1965
Schottland, C. A., *The Social Security Program in the US*. New York, 1963
Smillie, W. G., *Public Health Administration in the US*. 3rd ed. New York, 1947

DIPLOMATIC REPRESENTATIVES

OF THE UNITED STATES IN GREAT BRITAIN (Grosvenor Sq., London, W1A 1AE)

Ambassador: Dr Kingman Brewster.

OF GREAT BRITAIN IN THE USA (3100 Massachusetts Ave., Washington, D.C., 20008)

Ambassador: Peter Jay.

OF THE UNITED STATES TO THE UNITED NATIONS

Ambassador: Andrew Young.

Books of Reference

I. Statistical Information

Within the federal government of the USA, responsibilities for the collection, compilation, analysis and publication of statistics are decentralized among a number of agencies, with specified responsibilities for general-purpose statistics in particular areas. In addition, most agencies of the Government collect statistical data as a by-product of their administrative or operating responsibilities in specific fields. Responsibility for co-ordinating the decentralized statistical activities rests in the Office of Statistical Standards, Bureau of the Budget, Washington 25, D.C., as a part of the Executive Office of the President. This Office reviews all proposed collections of statistical data to avoid duplication or overlapping; promotes the use of improved statistical techniques; develops standard definitions and classifications so that the data collected by different agencies are comparable; serves as liaison between federal agencies and international organizations and as an information centre on government statistical programmes. The Division does not itself collect or publish statistics.

The major general-purpose statistical agencies and their principal areas of responsibility are:

(1) Bureau of the Census in the Department of Commerce (A. Ross Eckler, Director). Decennial censuses of population and housing and quinquennial censuses of agriculture, manufactures and business; current statistics on population and the labour force, manufacturing activity and commodity production, retail and wholesale trade and services, foreign trade, and state and local government finances and operations.

(2) Bureau of Labor Statistics in the Department of Labor (Geoffrey H. Moore, Commissioner). Current statistics on employment, earnings, man-hours, labour turnover, industrial accidents, work stoppages, wage rates; collective bargaining agreements; construction; industrial productivity; wholesale prices, retail prices and urban consumers' price indexes; income and expenditures of urban families.

(3) Statistical Reporting Service and Economic Research Service in the Department of Agriculture. Statistics on crop and livestock production and inventories; crop forecasts; food processing and food consumption; farm population, labour and wages; farm management; farm ownership values, transfers; taxation and finance; prices farmers pay and receive; farm income; accidents; studies of land and water uses.

(4) National Center for Health Statistics in the Public Health Service, Department of Health, Education and Welfare (Theodore D. Woolsey, Chief). Current statistics on births, deaths, marriages and divorce.

(5) Bureau of Mines in the Department of the Interior (John F. O'Leary, Director). Statistics on production, consumption and stocks of metals and minerals, and on injuries in mineral industries.

Other agencies in which statistics are an important by-product of regulatory or other administrative functions include: Social Security Administration in the Department of Health, Education and Welfare; Internal Revenue Service in the Treasury Department; Federal Power Commission; Federal Trade Commission; Interstate Commerce Commission, and the Securities and Exchange Commission.

Among the more important statistical publications of a fairly general nature are:

Statistical Abstract of the United States, published by the Bureau of the Census, Department of Commerce. Annual. Important summary statistics on the industrial, social, political and economic organization of the USA, with a representative selection from most of the important statistical publications. *Survey of Current Business*, published by the Office of Business Economics, Department of Commerce. Monthly. Interpretative text and charts reviewing business trends, etc.; official estimates of national income. *Economic Indicators*, prepared by the Council of Economic Advisers and published by the Congressional Joint Committee on the Economic Report. Monthly. Tables and charts presenting current data on the total output of the economy; prices; employment and wages; production and business activity; purchasing power; money, banking and federal finance. *Monthly Labor Review*, published by the Bureau of Labor Statistics, Department of Labor. *Federal Reserve Bulletin*, published by the Board of Governors of the Federal Reserve System. Monthly. Current data on money and banking and selected other economic series. Federal Reserve indexes of industrial production, etc.; international financial statistics. *Treasury Bulletin*, published by the Office of the Secretary, Department of the Treasury. Monthly. Current coverage of federal fiscal statistics; international capital movements. *Minerals Yearbook*, published by the Bureau of Mines, Department of the Interior. Annual. *Agricultural Statistics*, published by the Department of Agriculture. Annual. *Crops and Markets*, published by the Bureau of Agricultural Economics in the Department of Agriculture. Monthly. Crop report and market statistics. *Foreign Agriculture*, published by the Office of Foreign Agriculture Service, Department of Agriculture. Monthly. Foreign agricultural production, foreign government policies relating to agriculture and international trade in agricultural products. *Vital Statistics of the United States*, published by the Public Health Service, US Department of Health, Education and Welfare. Monthly and Annual. Natality and mortality data tabulated by place of occurrence, with supplemental tables for Puerto Rico and the Virgin Islands; and tabulated by place of residence.

An annotated bibliography of about 100 periodical statistical publications is included in *Statistical Services of the United States Government*, a pamphlet issued by the Division of Statistical Standards, Bureau of the Budget, describing the general organization of the statistical system of the USA and the principal types of economic statistics.

II. Other Official Publications

Guide to the Study of the United States of America. General Reference and Bibliography Division, Library of Congress. 1960.

Historical Statistics of the United States, Colonial Times to 1957: A Statistical Abstract Supplement. Washington, 1960.—*Continuation to 1962 and Revisions*. 1965.

United States Government Manual. Washington. Annual.

The official publications of the USA are issued by the US Government Printing Office and are distributed by the Superintendent of Documents, who issued in 1940 a cumulative *Catalog of the Public Documents of the . . . Congress and of All the Departments of the Government of the United States*. This *Catalog* is kept up to date by *United States Government Publications, Monthly Catalog* with annual index and supplemented by *Price Lists*. Each *Price List* is devoted to a special subject or type of material, *e.g.*, *American History* or *Census*. Useful guides are Schmeckebier, L. F., and Eastin, R. B. (eds.), *Government Publications and Their Use*. 2nd ed., Washington, D.C., 1961; Boyd, A. M., *United States Government Publications*. 3rd ed. New York, 1949, and Leidy, W. P., *Popular Guide to Government Publications*. 2nd ed. New York and London, 1963.

Treaties and other International Acts of the United States of America (Edited by Hunter Miller), 8 vols. Washington, 1929–48. This edition stops in 1863. It may be supplemented by *Treaties, Conventions . . . Between the US and Other Powers, 1776–1937* (Edited by William M. Malloy and others). 4 vols. 1909–38. A new Treaty Series, *US Treaties and Other International Agreements* was started in 1950.

Writings on American History. Washington, annual from 1902 (except 1904–5 and 1941–47).

III. Non-Official Publications

A. Handbooks

National Historical Publications Commission. *Guide to Archives and Manuscripts in the United States*, ed. P. M. Hamer. Yale Univ. Press, 1961

Adams, J. T. (ed.), *Dictionary of American History*. 2nd ed. 7 vols. New York, 1942
Dictionary of American Biography, ed. A. Johnson and D. Malone. 23 vols. New York, 1929–64.—*Concise Dictionary of American Biography*. New York, 1964
Current Biography. New York, annual from 1940; monthly supplements
Alsberg, H. G. (ed.), *The American Guide*. New York, 1955
Handlin, O., and others. *Harvard Guide to American History*. Cambridge, Mass., 1954
Kreutz, B., and Fleming, E., *Introducing America*. London, 1963
Lord, C. L. and E. H., *Historical Atlas of the US*. Rev. ed. New York, 1953
Who's Who in America. Chicago, 1899–1900 to date; monthly Supplement. 1940 to date

B. General History

Barck, Jr, O. T., and Blake, N. M., *Since 1900: A History of the United States*. 4th ed. New York, 1965
Bellot, H. H., *America History and American Historians*. London, 1952
Billington, R. A., *Westward Expansion*. 2nd ed. New York, 1960
Carman, H. J., and others, *A History of the American People*. Rev. ed. 2 vols. New York, 1961
Clark, T. D., *Frontier America: The Story of the Westward Movement*. New York, 1959
Commager, H. S. (ed.). *Documents of American History*. 8th ed. New York, 1966
Divine, R. A., *Since 1945: Politics and Diplomacy in Recent American History*. New York, 1975
Faulkner, H. U., *American Political and Social History*. 7th ed. New York, 1957
Hicks, J. D., *The American Nation, A History of the United States from 1865*. 4th ed. Boston 1963
Link, A. S., and Catton, W. B., *American Epoch: A History of the United States Since the 1890s*. 3rd ed. New York, 1967
Morison, S. E., *The Oxford History of the American People*. OUP, 1968
Morison, S. E., with H. S. Commager, *The Growth of the American Republic*. 2 vols. 5th ed. OUP, 1962–63
Parkes, H. B., *The United States of America, a History*. 3rd ed. New York, 1968
Savelle, M., *A Short History of American Civilization*. New York, 1957
Scammon, R. N. (ed.), *American Votes: A Handbook of Contemporary American Election Statistics*. Washington, D.C., 1956 to date (biennial)
Schlesinger, A. M., *The Rise of Modern America, 1865–1951*. 4th ed. New York, 1951.—*The Age of Roosevelt*. 4 vols. New York and London, 1957–62.—*A Thousand Days: John F. Kennedy in the White House*. New York and London, 1965
Thistlewaite, F., *The Great Experiment: An Introduction to the History of the American People*. CUP, 1955
Watson, R. A., *The Promise and Performance of American Democracy*. 2nd ed. New York, 1975
Wish, H., *Society and Thought in America*. 2 vols. OUP, 1962

C. Minorities

Bennett, M. T., *American Immigration Policies: A History*. Washington, D.C., 1963
Brown, F. J. (ed.), *One America: The History, Contributions and Present Problems of Our Racial and National Minorities*. 3rd ed. New York, 1952
Burma, J. J., *Spanish-speaking Groups in the US*. Duke University Press, 1954
Burns, W. H., *The Voices of Negro Protest in America*. OUP, 1963
Frazier, E. F., *The Negro in the United States*. Rev. ed. New York, 1957
McNickle, D., *The Indian Tribes of the United States*. OUP, 1962
McWilliams, Carey, *Brothers Under the Skin: A Study of the Position of Racial Minorities in Continental United States and the Possessions*. Rev. ed. New York, 1951
Rose, A. and C., *America Divided: Minority Group Relations in the United States*. New York, 1949
Sklare, M., *The Jews: Social Patterns of an American Group*. Glencoe, Ill., 1958
Wissler, Clark, *Indians of the United States*. New York, 1946

D. Economic History

The Economic History of the United States. 9 vols. New York, 1946 ff.
Bining, A. C., and Cochran, T. C., *The Rise of American Economic Life*. 4th ed. New York, 1963
Dorfman, J., *The Economic Mind in American Civilization*. 5 vols. New York, 1946–59
Fainsod, M., and Gordon L., *Government and the American Economy*. 3rd ed. New York, 1959
Faulkner, H. U., *American Economic History*. 8th ed. New York, 1960
Friedman, M., and Schwartz, A. J., *A Monetary History of the United States, 1867–1960*. New York, 1963
Jones, P. d'A., *America's Wealth*. London, 1963
Landsberg, H. H., and others, *Resources in America's Future: Patterns of Requirements and Availabilities, 1960–2000*. Washington, D.C., 1963
Mund, V. A., *Government and Business*. 4th ed. New York, 1965

E. Foreign Relations

American Foreign Policy Library, ed. Sumner Wells (Harvard Univ. Press); E. A. Speiser, *The US and the Near East* (rev. ed. 1950); C. Brinton, *The US and Britain* (rev. ed. 1948); J. K. Fairbank, *The US and China* (rev. ed. 1958); V. M. Dean, *The US and Russia* (1948); D. Perkins, *The US and the Caribbean* (rev. ed., 1967); A. P. Whitaker, *The US and South America* (1948); D. C. McKay, *The US and France* (1951); E. O. Reischauer, *The US and Japan* (rev. ed., 1957); W. N. Brown, *The US and India and Pakistan* (1953); H. S. Hughes, *The US and Italy* (1953); H. F. Cline, *The US and Mexico* (1953); L. V. Thomas and R. N. Frye, *The US and Turkey and Iran* (1951); F. D. Scott, *The US and Scandinavia* (1950); A. P. Whitaker, *The US and Argentina* (1954); R. L. Wolff, *The Balkans in Our Time* (1956); C. H. Grattan, *The US and the SW Pacific* (1961)

Documents on American Foreign Relations. Princeton, from 1948. Annual

The United States in World Affairs. 1931 ff. Council on Foreign Relations. New York, from 1932. Annual

Allison, G., and Szanton, P., *Remaking Foreign Policy: The Organizational Connection*. New York, 1976

Bartlett, R. (ed.), *The Record of American Diplomacy; Documents and Readings in the History of American Foreign Relations*. 4th ed. New York, 1964

Beloff, M., *The United States and the Unity of Europe*. London, 1963

Bemis, S. F., *Diplomatic History of the US*. 4th ed. New York, 1955.—*Short History of American Foreign Policy and Diplomacy*. Rev. ed. New York, 1959.—*The United States as a World Power: A Diplomatic History*. Rev. ed. New York, 1955

Connell-Smith, G., *The United States and Latin America*. London, 1975

DeConde, A., *The American Secretary of State*. London, 1963

Graebner, N. A. (ed.). *An Uncertain Tradition: American Secretaries of State in the 20th Century*. New York, 1961.—*Cold War Diplomacy: American Foreign Policy, 1945–60* Princeton, 1962

Hyde, L. K., *The United States and the United Nations*. New York, 1960

Lary, H. B., *Problems of the United States as World Trader and Banker*. New York, 1963

Leopold, R. W., *The Growth of American Foreign Policy: A History*. New York, 1962

McCamy, J. L., *Conduct of the New Diplomacy*. New York, 1964

Morgan, R., *The United States and West Germany, 1945–73*. OUP, 1975

Pratt, J. W., *A History of United States Foreign Policy*. New York, 1955

Rostow, W. W., *The United States in the World Arena: An Essay in Recent History*. New York, 1960

Smith, R. F., *The United States and Cuba: Business and Diplomacy, 1917–1960*. New York, 1962

Spanier, J. W., *American Foreign Policy Since World War II*. 2nd ed. London, 1962.

Stebbins, R. P., and Adam, E. A., *Documents of American Foreign Relations, 1968–69*. New York, 1972

Stuart, Graham H., *American Diplomatic and Consular Practice*. 2nd ed. New York, 1952.—*Latin America and the United States*. 5th ed. New York, 1955

Wilcox, F. C., and Kalijarvi, T. V., *Recent American Foreign Policy: Basic Documents, 1941–51*. New York, 1952

Williams, W. A. (ed.), *The Shaping of American Diplomacy: Readings and Documents in American Foreign Relations, 1750–1955*. 2 vols. Chicago, 1956

F. National Character

Brogan, D. W., *USA: An Outline of the Country, Its People and Institutions*. 2nd ed. Oxford, 1947

Coan, O. W., *America in Fiction, An Annotated List of Novels*. 5th ed. Stanford Univ. Press, 1967

Commager, H. S., *The American Mind*. Yale Univ. Press, 1950

Curti, M. B., *The Growth of American Thought*. 3rd ed. New York, 1964

Degler, C. N., *Out of Our Past: The Forces That Shaped Modern America*. New York, 1959

Gabriel, R. H., *The Course of American Democratic Thought*. 2nd ed. New York, 1956

Hertzler, J. O., *American Social Institutions: A Sociological Analysis*. Boston, 1961

Lerner, M., *America as a Civilization: Life and Thought in the United States Today*. 2 vols. New York, 1961

Riesman, D., with R. Denny and N. Glazer, *The Lonely Crowd: A Study of the Changing American Character*. New York, 1950

Rossiter, C. L., *Conservation in America*. 2nd ed. New York, 1962

Wish, H., *Society and Thought in America*. 2nd ed. 2 vols. New York [1962].—*Contemporary America*. 3rd ed. New York, 1961

National Library: The Library of Congress. Washington 25, D.C. *Librarian:* Lawrence Quincy Mumford, AB, MA, BS.

STATES AND TERRITORIES

For information as to State and Local Government, see under United States, *p.* 1374

Against the names of the Governors and the Secretaries of State, (D.) *stands for Democrat and* (R.) *for Republican.*

Figures for the revenues and expenditures of the various states are those of the Federal Bureau of the Census unless otherwise stated, which takes the original state figures and arranges them on a common pattern so that those of one state can be compared with those of any other.

Official publications of the various states and insular possessions are listed in the *Monthly Check-List of State Publications*, issued by the Library of Congress since 1910. Their character and contents are discussed in J. K. Wilcox's *Manual on the Use of State Publications* (1940). Of great importance bibliographically are the publications of the Historical Records Survey and the American Imprints Inventory, which record local archives, official publications and state imprints. These publications supplement those of state historical societies which usually publish journals and monographs on state and local history. An outstanding source of statistical data is the material issued by the various state planning boards and commissions, to which should be added the annual *Governmental Finances* issued by the US Bureau of the Census.

The Book of the States. Biennial. Chicago, Council of State Governments, 1953 ff.
County and City Data Book. Dept of Commerce, 1967
State Government Finances. Annual. Dept. of Commerce, 1966 ff.

Regionalism

Bogue, D. J., and Beale, C. L., *Economic Areas of the United States*. New York, 1961
Odum, H. W., *American Regionalism, A Cultural–Historical Approach to National Integration*. New York, 1938
Jensen, M. (ed.), *Regionalism in America*. Univ. of Wisconsin Press, 1965
Visher, S. X., *Climatic Atlas of the USA*. Harvard Univ. Press., 1954

A. North-East

Gottman, J., *Megalopolis, the Urbanized North-eastern Seaboard of the US*. New York, 1964
Harris, S. E., *The Economics of New England*. Harvard Univ. Press, 1952

B. The South

Cash, W. J., *The Mind of the South*. New York, 1960
Clark, T. D., *The Emerging South*. New York, 1961
Clement, E., *A History of the Old South*. New York, 1949
Ezell, J. S., *The South Since 1865*. New York and London, 1963
Heseltine, W. B., and Smiley, D. L., *The South in American History*. 2nd ed. Englewood Cliffs, 1960
Sindler, A. P. (ed.), *Change in the Contemporary South*. Duke Univ. Press, 1963
Stephenson, W. H., and Coulter, E. M. (ed.), *A History of the South*. 10 vols. Louisiana State Univ. Press, 1947–67

C. The Middle West

Atherton, L. E., *Main Street on the Middle Border*. Indiana Univ. Press, 1954
Lynd, R. S. and H. M., *Middletown: A Study in Contemporary American Culture*. New York and London, 1929.—*Middletown in Transition: A Study in Cultural Conflicts*. New York and London, 1937
Nye, R. B., *Midwestern Progressive Politics, 1870–1938*. Michigan State Univ. Press, 1959

D. The West

Fogelson, R. U., *The Fragmented Metropolis: Los Angeles, 1850–1930*. Harvard Univ. Press, 1967
Freeman, O. W., and Martin, H. H., *The Pacific Northwest: An Overall Appreciation*. 2nd ed. 1954
Fuller, G. W., *History of the Pacific Northwest*. 2nd ed. New York, 1938
Hafen, L. R. R., and Rister, C. C., *Western America . . . Beyond the Mississippi*. 2nd ed. New York, 1950
Johansen, D. O., and Gates, C. M., *Empire of the Columbia: A History of the Pacific North-West*. New York, 1957
Parrish, P. H., *Before the Covered Wagon*. Portland, Oreg., 1931
Quiett, G. C., *They Built the West, An Epic of Rails and Cities*. New York and London, 1934
Scott, H. W., *History of the Oregon Country*. 6 vols. Cambridge, Mass, 1924
Winther, O. O., *The Great Northwest: A History*. 2nd ed., rev. New York, 1950

ALABAMA

HISTORY. Alabama, settled in 1702 as part of the French Province of Louisiana, and ceded to the British in 1763, was organized as a Territory, 1817, and admitted into the Union on 14 Dec. 1819.

AREA AND POPULATION. Alabama is bounded north by Tennessee, east by Georgia, south by Florida and the Gulf of Mexico and west by Mississippi. Area, 51,609 sq. miles, including 901 sq. miles of inland water. Census population, 1 April 1970, 3,444,165, an increase of 5·4% over that of 1960. Estimate, 1976, 3,555,000. Births, 1976, 57,974 (15·8 per 1,000 population); deaths, 34,220 (9·6); infant deaths (under 28 days), 1,156 (20 per 1,000 live births); marriages, 46,515 (13·1); divorces, 24,056 (6·8).

Population in 5 census years (with distribution by sex, 1970) was:

	White	*Negro*	*Indian*	*Asiatic*	*Total*	*Per sq. mile*
1910	1,228,832	908,282	909	70	2,138,093	41·4
1930	1,700,844	944,834	465	105	2,646,248	51·3
1950	2,079,591	979,617	928	669	3,061,743	59·9
1960	2,283,609	980,271	1,726	915	3,266,740	64·0
			All others			
1970	2,533,831	903,469	6,867		3,444,165	66·7
Male	1,235,489	423,083	3,369		1,661,941	—
Female	1,298,342	480,384	3,498		1,782,224	—

Of the total population in 1970, 2,011,941 (58·4%) were urban (54·8% in 1960). Those 21 years or older numbered 2,020,959; 65 years or older, 325,961. Foreign-born whites numbered 15,988 in 1970. In 10 of the 67 counties Negroes constitute 50% or more of the population.

The large cities (1970) were: Birmingham, 300,910 (urbanized area, 558,099); Mobile, 190,026 (257,816); Huntsville, 137,802 (146,565); Montgomery (capital), 133,386 (138,983); Tuscaloosa, 65,773 (85,875); Gadsden, 53,928 (67,706).

CONSTITUTION AND GOVERNMENT. The present constitution dates from 1901; it has had 370 amendments. The legislature consists of a Senate of 35 members and a House of Representatives of 105 members, all elected for 4 years. The Governor and Lieut.-Governor are elected for 4 years.

The state is represented in Congress by 2 senators and 7 representatives. Applicants for registration must take an 'anti-communist oath' and fill out a questionnaire to the satisfaction of the registrars. In the 1976 presidential election Carter polled 659,170 votes, Ford, 504,070.

Montgomery is the capital.

Governor: George C. Wallace (D.), 1975–79 ($28,955).
Lieut.-Governor: Jere Beasley.
Secretary of State: Agnes Baggett (D.) ($22,500).

BUDGET. The general revenue for the fiscal year ending 30 Sept. 1976 was $3,446m.; general expenditure was $2,987m.

The net long-term debt on 30 Sept. 1976 amounted to $1,079m.

Estimated *per capita* income (1976) was $5,106.

ENERGY AND NATURAL RESOURCES

Minerals. Production of principal minerals (1975): Coal, 21·42m. short tons; Portland cement, 2·5m. short tons. Total mineral output (1972) was valued at $365m.

Agriculture. Alabama is largely an agricultural state; the number of farms in 1974 was 56,678, covering 11,852,946 acres; average farm had 209 acres and was valued at $76,049.

Area of national forest lands on 30 June 1974, 638,000 acres.

Cash receipts from farm marketings, 1975: Crops, $406·3m.; livestock, $699·4m.;

and total, $1,122·5m. Principal crops: soybeans, cotton, corn and peanuts; potatoes, tomatoes, hay and wheat are also important. In 1974, poultry accounted for the largest percentage of cash receipts from farm marketings; hogs were second, cattle and calves third, dairy products fourth. Soybeans are the most valuable crop.

INDUSTRY. In 1976, 5,200 manufacturing establishments employed 340,355 production workers, earning $3,466,722,431. Pig-iron, 1976, amounted to 3·3m. short tons.

TOURISM is rapidly expanding and during 1974 became the largest single industry. Total receipts of tourism amounted to $993m. in 1976.

COMMUNICATIONS

Roads. Paved roads of all classes in 1971 totalled 38,950 miles; total highways, 68,118 miles.

Railways. In 1972 the railways had a length of 4,566 miles.

Aviation. In 1971 the state had 174 airports.

Shipping. The only port is Mobile, with a large ocean-going trade; imports (1971), 528,346,000 tons; exports (1971), 9,765,617 tons. The 9-ft channel of the Tennessee River traverses North Alabama for 200 miles; the Warrier–Tombigbee Waterway (476 miles) connects the Birmingham industrial area with Mobile and also with the Gulf Intracoastal Waterway; the Chattahoochee River 9-ft channel extends from the Gulf to Phenix City (Alabama). In 1971 a 9-ft channel was completed which connects Montgomery and Mobile through the Alabama River System. The Alabama State Docks also operates a system of 16 inland docks.

JUSTICE, RELIGION, EDUCATION AND WELFARE

Justice. The prison population on 11 Sept. 1972 was 3,997.

From 1927 to 1965 there were 153 executions (electrocution): 121 for murder, 25 for rape, 5 for armed robbery, 1 for burglary and 1 for carnal knowledge.

The transport system is now integrated.

In 37 counties the state controls the sale of alcoholic beverage, while 30 counties remain 'bone dry'.

Religion. Chief religious bodies (in 1968) are: Negro Baptists (500,000), Southern Baptists (802,793), Methodist (North Alabama Conference, 199,855 in 1967); West Florida Conference, 129,175), Roman Catholic (140,000), Presbyterian (41,780), Episcopalian (33,393 in 1967).

Education. In 1975–76 the 1,331 public elementary and high schools required 36,659 teachers to teach 783,218 pupils enrolled in grades 1–12. The 11 senior or 4-year universities had 47,756 students and 4,032 faculty members. The 20 junior colleges had 29,315 students and 2,259 teachers, 29 vocational technical schools 15,319 students and 782 teachers. During the regular session (1975–76) only, University of Montevallo, Auburn University, the University of Alabama, Alabama Agricultural and Mechanical University enrolled 32,884 resident students; the state universities at Florence, Jacksonville and Livingston, 8,062 resident students.

Health. In 1974 there were 134 hospitals (18,214 beds) licensed by the State Board of Health. In 1974 hospitals for mental diseases had approximately 4,281 beds.

Social Security. In August 1977 there were 16,441 recipients of state old-age assistance, receiving an average of $48·23 a month; 55,863 families with dependent children, $111·49 per family; 3,305 permanently and totally disabled, $69·36; 178 blind, $47·01.

Books of Reference

Alabama Official and Statistical Register. Montgomery. Quadrennial
Alabama Encyclopædia. Vol. I. Northport, 1965

Economic Abstract of Alabama. Centre for Business and Economic Research, Univ. of Alabama, 1975
The Deep South in Transformation: A Symposium. Univ. of Alabama Press, 1964
Farmer, H., *The Legislative Process in Alabama.* Univ. of Alabama, 1949

ALASKA

HISTORY. Discovered in 1741 by Vitus Bering, its first settlement, on Kodiak Island, was in 1784. The area known as Russian America with its capital (1806) at Sitka was ruled by a Russo-American fur company and vaguely claimed as a Russian colony. Alaska was purchased by the United States from Russia under the treaty of 30 March 1867 for $7·2m. It was not organized until 1884, when it became a 'district' governed by the code of the state of Oregon. By Act of Congress approved 24 Aug. 1912 Alaska became an incorporated Territory; its first legislature in 1913 granted votes to women, 7 years in advance of the Constitutional Amendment.

Alaska officially became the 49th state of the Union on 3 Jan. 1959.

AREA AND POPULATION. Alaska is bounded north by the Beaufort Sea, west and south by the Pacific and east by Canada. It has the largest area of any state, being more than twice the size of Texas. The gross area (land and water) is 586,400 sq. miles; the land area is 571,065 sq. miles, of which 96·4% was in federal ownership in 1975. Census population, 1 April 1970, was 302,173, including military personnel, an increase of 33·6% over 1960. Estimate (1976) 413,289. Births, 1975, were 7,350 (20·9 per 1,000 population); deaths, 1,587 (4·5); infant deaths, 99 (13·5 per 1,000 live births); marriages, 4,789 (13·6); divorces, 2,890 (8·2).

Census population: 1880, 33,426; 1900, 63,592; 1910, 64,356; 1940, 72,526; 1950, 128,643; 1960, 226,167; 1970, 302,173.

The white population in 1970 numbered 236,767 (163,258 males and 137,124 females); Indians, Aleuts, Eskimos and others, 54,704; Negroes, 8,911.

The largest town is Anchorage, which had a 1970 census population of 48,029; Fairbanks had 14,771; Metropolitan area populations (1976), Anchorage, 185,200; Fairbanks, 51,500; Juneau, 18,800; Ketchikan, 11,400. There are 11 major incorporated boroughs. The total assessed valuation of cities and boroughs was $8,607·2m. in 1977. There were 11 home-rule cities, 20 first-class cities and about 110 second-class cities in Jan. 1976.

CONSTITUTION AND GOVERNMENT. An important provision of the Enabling Act is that the state has the right to select 103·55m. acres of vacant and unappropriated public lands in order to establish 'a tax basis'; it can open these lands to prospectors for minerals, and the state is to derive the principal advantage in all gains resulting from the discovery of minerals. In addition, certain federally administered lands reserved for conservation of fisheries and wild life have been transferred to the state. Special provision is made for federal control of land for defence in areas of high strategic importance.

The constitution of Alaska was adopted by public vote, 24 April 1956. The state legislature consists of a Senate of 20 members (elected for 4 years) and a House of Representatives of 40 members (elected for 2 years). The state sends 2 senators and 1 representative to Congress. The franchise may be exercised by all citizens over 18 years of age.

The capital is Juneau. A new capital site near Anchorage was chosen in 1976.

In the 1976 presidential election Ford polled 39,008 votes, Carter 22,994.

Governor: Jay S. Hammond (R.), 1974– ($50,000).
Lieut.-Governor: Lowell Thomas, Jr (R.) ($44,000).

ECONOMY

Budget. Total state government revenue for the year ended 30 June 1977 (Bureau of the Census figures) was $1,200m. ($754·7m. from taxation, $316·7m. from federal sources). Total expenditure was $1,055·4m. (including $358m. for education, $278m. for transport and $152m. for health and social services).

Net bonded debt on 30 June 1973 was $274m.

Per capita income (1976) was $9,775.

Banking. Total assets at 30 Sept. 1977 were $1,956·3m., total deposits $1,676·6m.

ENERGY AND NATURAL RESOURCES

Oil and Gas. Commercial production of crude petroleum began in 1959 and by 1961 had become the most important mineral by value. Production: 1961, 6,327,000 bbls (of 42 gallons); 1965, 11m. bbls; 1976, 67m. bbls, value $353m. Oil comes mainly from the McArthur River field, Prudhoe Bay and several Cook Inlet fields. Natural gas production, 1976, 153·5m. cu. ft, value $53·7m. Alaska receives 90% of all royalties (12·5%) from oil, gas and coal production on federal lands and the full 12·5% royalty for oil and gas production in state lands (coal royalties are being negotiated). Revenue to the state from oil and gas production tax in 1977 was $23·9m. and from reserves tax $270·6m. In 1969, the state conducted a major competitive lease sale for the arctic coastal region where reserves are estimated to be as large as 50,000m. bbls.

Oil from the Prudhoe Bay arctic field is now carried by the Trans-Alaska pipeline to Prince William Sound on the south coast, where a tanker terminal has been built at Valdez.

Minerals. Value of production, 1976. Sand and gravel (45m. short tons), $24·3m.; gold (22,887 troy oz.), $2·87m.; others, including silver, gemstones, lead, copper, tin, barite and platinum group minerals, $37m.

Agriculture. In some parts of the state the climate during the brief spring and summer (about 100 days in major areas and 152 days in the south-eastern coastal area) is suitable for agricultural operations, thanks to the long hours of sunlight, but Alaska is a food-importing area. In 1964, 1,959,440 acres were classified as agricultural land, 90% of this was unimproved pasture primarily government leases for grazing of sheep and beef cattle in south-west Alaska. In 1977 about 20,000 acres was cultivated. In 1969 there were 3,000 milch cows, 1,100 hogs and 27,000 sheep and lambs.

Farm production in 1976: Milk, $2·9m.; eggs, $570,000; silage, $391,000; potatoes, $1m.; hay, $2·32.; beef and veal, $608,000; barley, $261,000; lettuce, $261,000. Total, $8·67m.

There were about 31,000 reindeer in western Alaska in 1969, owned by individual Eskimo herders except for 750 at Nome owned by the government.

Forestry. In south-eastern Alaska timber fringes the shore of the mainland and all the islands extending inland to a depth of 5 miles. The state's enormous forests could produce an estimated annual sustained yield of 1,500m. bd ft of lumber, nearly twice Alaska's record 1973 cut. Alaska has 2 national forests: the Tongass of 16·8m. acres and the Chugach of 4·8m. acres. A total of 529·8m. bd ft was cut in 1976, of which 472·2m. came from national forests and 41·5m. from state forests. Alaska has 2 large pulp-mills at Ketchikan and Sitka.

Fisheries. The catch for 1975 was 442·4m. lb. of fish and shellfish having a value to fishermen of $129·4m. This compares with 471m. lb. in 1971 with a value of $85·5m. Salmon remains the highest per unit value species, with a catch in 1975 of 137·6m. lb. valued to the fishermen at $55·3m.

INDUSTRY. Main industries with employment, 1976: Government, 47,900; contract construction, 30,200; services, 27,700; trade, 27,600; manufacturing, 10,300; oil and gas, 3,600.

The major manufacturing industry was food processing, followed by timber industries. Total employment outside agriculture, 171,700. Total wages and salaries, $3,972,427,000.

TOURISM. About 270,000 tourists visited the state in 1976.

COMMUNICATIONS

Roads. Alaska's highway and road system, 1974, totalled 9,848 miles, including marine highway systems, local service roads, borough and city streets, national park, forest and reservation roads and military roads, of which 4,692 miles were surfaced primary roads; unsurfaced secondary roads totalled 3,654 miles. Registered motor vehicles, 1976, 295,373.

The Alaska Highway extends 1,523 miles from Dawson Creek, British Columbia, to Fairbanks, Alaska. It was built by the US Army in 1942, at a cost of $138m. The greater portion of it, because it lies in Canada, is maintained by the Canadian Government.

Railways. There is a railway of 111 miles from Skagway to the town of Whitehorse, in the Canadian Yukon region. The government-owned Alaska Railroad runs from Seward to Fairbanks, a distance of 471 miles.

Aviation. In 1974 the state had about 766 airports, of which about 545 were publicly owned. Passengers by air to and from Alaska's international airports Anchorage and Fairbanks (1976) numbered 2·6m.; freight handled, 228,786 short tons. General aviation aircraft in the state totalled 3,669, 11 per 1,000 population and ten times the US average.

Shipping. Regular shipping services to and from the US are furnished by 2 steamship lines and several barge lines operating out of Seattle and other Pacific coast ports. Two Canadian companies also furnish a regular service from Vancouver, B.C. Freight handled at the Port of Anchorage, 1976 (short tons): Bulk petroleum, 1·69m.; vans, flats and containers, 978,610; cement and drilling mud, 40,360; vehicles, 36,676; total 2·76m.

A 490-mile ferry system for motor cars and passengers (the 'Marine Highway') operates from Seattle, Washington and Prince Rupert (British Columbia) to Juneau, Haines (for access to the Alaska Highway) and Skagway. A second system extends throughout the south-central region of Alaska linking the Cook Inlet area with Kodiak Island and Prince William Sound.

JUSTICE, RELIGION, EDUCATION AND WELFARE

Justice. There is no death penalty in Alaska.

Religion. In Alaska are many religious missions representing the Russian Orthodox, Roman Catholic, Episcopalian, Presbyterian, Methodist and other denominations.

Education. During 1976–77 there were 87,129 pupils at public schools, 2,708 at private schools. The Bureau of Indian Affairs schools had 3,189 pupils attending schools in the state. The University of Alaska (founded in 1922) had (1974) 2,928 students on the main campus and 10,381 in community colleges. Sheldon Jackson Junior College had 324 students in 1974.

Welfare. Old-age assistance was established under the Federal Social Security Act; in 1976 aid to dependent children funds covered a monthly average of 13,299 persons; dependent children received an average of $76 per month; adult public assistance (including old age assistance, aid to the blind and to the disabled) was given to a monthly average of 3,469 persons receiving on average $109 per month.

Health. In 1974 there were 26 civilian hospitals with 1,600 beds, of which 11 were federal public health hospitals; there were 2 mental hospitals and 3 regional mental health clinics.

Books of Reference

Statistical Information: Department of Commerce and Economic Development, Division of Economic Enterprise, Pouch EE, Juneau.

Alaska Economic Information. Reporting Service, Division of Economic Enterprise, Juneau 99811. Quarterly

Alaska Economy, The,. Division of Economic Enterprise, Juneau. Annual

Alaskan Earthquake, preliminary report. Civil Defense Office (Army), Washington, 1964

Establishing a Business in Alaska. Division of Economic Enterprise, Juneau, 1976

Look North. Department of Economic Development, Juneau, 1970
Adams, B., *The Last Frontier.* New York, 1961
Gardey, J., *Alaska: The Sophisticated Wilderness.* London, 1976
Hulley, Clarence C., *Alaska Past and Present.* Portland, Oregon, 1970
Rogers, G. W., *Alaska in Transition: the south-east region.* Johns Hopkins Univ. Press, 1960.—*The Future of Alaska.* Johns Hopkins Univ. Press, 1962

State Library: Pouch G, Juneau. *Librarian:* Richard Engen.—Alaska Historical Library, Pouch G, Juneau. *Librarian:* Phyllis Nottingham.

ARIZONA

HISTORY. Arizona was settled in 1752, organized as a Territory in 1863 and became a state on 14 Feb. 1912.

AREA AND POPULATION. Arizona is bounded north by Utah, east by New Mexico, south by Mexico, west by California and Nevada. Area, 113,909 sq. miles, including 346·6 sq. miles of inland water. Of the total area (72,680,320 acres) 32,336,577 were owned by the federal government in 1970, including 19,623,000 acres held by the Office of Indian Affairs. Census population on 1 April 1970 was 1,772,482, an increase of 36% over 1960. Estimate, 1975, 2,245,000. Births, 1976, 39,969; deaths, 17,302; infant deaths, 614; marriages, 26,534; divorces, 19,029.

Population in 5 census years (with distribution by sex, 1970):

	White	*Negro*	*Indian*	*Chinese*	*Japanese*	*Total*	*Per sq. mile*
1910	171,468	2,009	29,201	1,305	371	204,354	1·8
1930	378,551	10,749	43,726	1,110	879	435,573	3·8
1950	654,511	25,974	65,761	1,951	780	749,587	6·6
1960	1,169,517	43,403	83,387	2,937	1,501	1,302,161	11·3
				All others			
1970	1,604,498	53,344	95,812	16,640		1,772,482	15·6
			All others				
Male	587,872	22,252	44,804			654,928	—
Female	581,645	21,151	44,437			647,233	—

Of the total population in 1970, 1,408,864 (79·6%) were urban (74·5% in 1960).

The 1970 census population of Phoenix was 581,562 (urbanized area, 863,357); Tucson, 262,933 (294,184); Scottsdale, 67,823; Tempe, 62,907; Mesa, 62,853; Glendale, 36,228; Yuma, 29,007; Flagstaff, 26,117.

CONSTITUTION AND GOVERNMENT. The state constitution (1910, with now 70 amendments) placed the government under direct control of the people through the Initiative, Referendum and the Recall. The state Senate consists of 30 members, and the House of Representatives of 60, all elected for 2 years. Arizona sends to Congress 2 senators and 4 representatives. In the 1976 presidential election Ford polled 418,642 votes, Carter 295,602, McCarthy 19,229 and MacBride 7,647.

The state capital is Phoenix. The state is divided into 14 counties.

Governor: Wesley Bolin (D.), 1977– ($35,000).

BUDGET. General revenues, year ending 30 June 1975 (US Census Bureau figures), were $1,419m. (taxation, $579·6m. and federal aid, $302·9m.); general expenditures, $1,459·7m. (education, $736·8m.; highways, $217·7m., and public welfare, $83·6m.).

Per capita income (1975) was $5,127.

NATURAL RESOURCES

Minerals. The mining industries of the state are important, but less so than agriculture and manufacturing. By value the most important mineral produced is copper.

Production (1976): Copper (1,012,660 short tons); gold (92,790 troy oz.) and silver (7,297,000 troy oz.) are both largely recovered from copper ore. Other minerals include sand and gravel (16,016,000 short tons), zinc (8,650 short tons) and lead (310 short tons). Total value of minerals mined in 1976 was $1,693,992,000.

Agriculture. Arizona, despite its dry climate, is well suited for agriculture along the water-courses and where irrigation is practised on a large scale from great reservoirs constructed by the US as well as by the state government and private interests. Irrigated area, 1976, 1·6m. acres. The wide pasture lands are favourable for the rearing of cattle and sheep, but numbers are either stationary or declining compared with 1920.

In 1976 Arizona contained 5,900 farms and ranches with 1·6m. acres (estimate) of crop land, out of a total farm and pastoral area of 37·2m. acres. The average farm (1977) was estimated at 6,640 acres. Farming is highly commercialized and mechanized and concentrated largely on cotton (1,500 cotton farms 1976) picked by machines and by Indian, Mexican and migratory workers.

Areas under cotton (1977), 516,000 acres, 834,000 bales (of 500 lb.) of short staple and 50,300 bales of American Pima cotton were harvested in 1976.

Cash income, 1976, from crops, $808m.; from livestock, $503·9m. Most important cereals are grain sorghums and barley; other crops include oranges, grapefruit and lettuce. On 1 Jan. 1976 there were 1·09m. all cattle, 72,000 milch cows, 464,000 sheep and 99,000 swine. The wool clip in 1976 amounted to 3·12m. lb.

Forestry. The national forests in the state had an area (1976) of 11·36m. acres.

INDUSTRY. Manufacturing establishments (numbering 1,460 in 1974, Census Bureau figures) had (1975) 96,700 production workers, earning $1,149·8m.; value of output $1,950m.

TOURISM. In 1976 total estimated tourist business in the state was $2,260m.

COMMUNICATIONS

Roads. There were (1977) 8,067·2 miles of municipal roads and 22,687·9 miles of rural roads, of which 6,024·3 miles were surfaced.

Aviation. Airports, 1977, numbered 211.

JUSTICE, RELIGION, EDUCATION AND WELFARE

Justice. Marriage is forbidden between white and coloured persons.

A 'right-to-work' amendment to the constitution, adopted 5 Nov. 1946, makes illegal any concessions to trade-union demands for a 'closed shop'.

The Arizona state prison 30 June 1977 held 2,015 men and 140 women. There have been no executions since 1968; from 1930 to 1968 there were 38 executions (lethal gas) all for murder, and all men (28 whites, 10 Negro).

Religion. The leading religious bodies are Roman Catholics and Mormons (Latter Day Saints); others include Methodists, Presbyterians, Baptists and Episcopalians. No recent statistics of membership are available.

Education. School attendance is compulsory between the ages of 8 and 16 years, and instruction is free for pupils from 6 to 21 years of age. The enrolled pupils in 1975–76 in the elementary schools were 378,510 and public high schools had 162,298 pupils. Teachers for both elementary and high schools totalled 22,041 in 1976. The total expenditure for public schools, 1975–76, was $23,117,581. In 1975–76 teachers' salaries averaged $12,497. The state maintains 3 universities at Tucson, Tempe and Flagstaff and 15 junior colleges.

Health. In 1977 there were 88 hospitals reported by the State Department of Health; capacity 11,839 beds. Resident patients in mental hospitals on 30 June 1976 numbered 696.

Social Security. Old-age assistance (maximum depending on the programme) is given, with federal aid, to needy citizens 65 years of age or older. In June 1977,

2,616 people were receiving general assistance at an average of $97.9 a month; 18,808 families, $47.22 per family in aid to dependent children; in the supplemental payment programme 978 old persons received $86.48 per month; 7 blind, $33; 68 totally disabled, $31.47.

Books of Reference

Arizona Statistical Review. 32nd ed. Valley National Bank, Phoenix, 1976
Federal Writers' Project. *Arizona: The Grand Canyon State*. 4th ed. New York, 1966
Cross, J. L., ed., *Arizona, its People and Resources*. Tucson, 1960
Goff, J. S., *Arizona Civilization*. 2nd ed. Cave Creek, 1970
Mason, B. B., and Hink, H., *Constitutional Government of Arizona*. 4th ed. Tempe, 1972
Morey, R. D., *Politics and Legislation: The Office of Governor in Arizona*. Tucson, 1965
Wyllys, R. K., *Arizona: The History of a Frontier State*. Phoenix, 1951

State Library: Department of Library, Archives and Public Records, Capitol, Phoenix 85007. *Director:* Mrs Marguerite B. Cooley.

ARKANSAS

HISTORY. Arkansas was settled in 1686, made a Territory in 1819 and admitted into the Union on 15 June 1836. The name originated with the Quapaw Indian tribe. The constitution, which dates from 1874, has been amended 57 times.

AREA AND POPULATION. Arkansas is bounded north by Missouri, east by Tennessee and Mississippi, south by Louisiana, south-west by Texas and west by Oklahoma. Area, 53,104 sq. miles (1,159 sq. miles being inland water). Census population on 1 April 1970 was 1,923,295, an increase of 7·7% from that of 1960. Estimate, 1976, 2,109,000. Births, 1976 (provisional), were 34,162 (16·2 per 1,000 population); deaths, 21,215 (10·1); infant deaths, 598 (18 per 1,000 live births); marriages, 22,630 (10·7); divorces (1975), 15,562 (7·4).

Population in 5 census years (with distribution by sex, 1970) was:

	White	*Negro*	*Indian*	*Asiatic*	*Total*	*Per sq. mile*
1910	1,131,026	442,891	460	72	1,574,449	30·0
1930	1,375,315	478,463	408	296	1,854,482	35·2
1950	1,481,507	426,639	533	832	1,909,511	36·3
1960	1,466,084	482,578	580	996	1,786,272	34·0
			All others			
1970	1,565,915	352,445	4,935		1,923,295	37·0
Male	762,982	167,019	2,309		932,301	—
Female	802,933	185,426	2,626		990,985	—

Of the total population in 1970, 960,865 persons (50%) were urban (43% in 1960); 1,169,498 were 21 years of age or older. Foreign-born numbered 8,287.

Little Rock (capital) had a population of 132,483 in 1970; Fort Smith, 62,802; North Little Rock, 60,040; Pine Bluff, 57,389; Hot Springs, 35,631; Fayetteville, 30,729; Jonesboro, 27,050; West Memphis, 26,070. The population of the standard metropolitan statistical areas: Little Rock–North Little Rock, 323,296; Fort Smith, 160,421; Pine Bluff, 85,329; Fayetteville–Springdale, 127,846.

GOVERNMENT. The General Assembly consists of a Senate of 35 members elected for 4 years, partially renewed every 2 years, and a House of Representatives of 100 members elected for 2 years. The sessions are biennial and usually limited to 60 days. The Governor and Lieut.-Governor are elected for 2 years. The state is represented in Congress by 2 senators and 4 representatives.

In the 1976 presidential election Carter polled 498,604 votes, Ford 267,903.

The state is divided into 75 counties; the capital is Little Rock.

Governor: David Pryor (D.), 1977–78 ($35,000).

Lieut.-Governor: Joe Purcell (D.) ($14,000).
Secretary of State: Winston Bryant (D.) ($22,500).

FINANCE

Budget. The state's general revenue for the fiscal year 1975 was $1,138·9m., of which taxation furnished $652·6m. and federal aid, $379·7m. General expenditure was $1,135·6m., of which education took $457·2m.; highways, $233·2m., and public welfare, $169·3m.

Net long-term debt on 30 June 1975 was $122·4m.

Per capita income (1975) was $4,617.

Banking. At 30 June 1976 total bank deposits were $6,173m.

ENERGY AND NATURAL RESOURCES

Minerals. In 1975 crude petroleum amounted to 16·1m. bbls; natural gas, 122·2m. cu. ft. Arkansas produces about 90% of the country's supply of bauxite for aluminium; production 1975, 2·1m. long tons dried bauxite equivalent. The state has a large coal area; 454,000 short tons were mined in 1975. Total mineral output in 1975 was valued at $315·5m.

Agriculture. Arkansas is an agricultural state. In 1974 (Federal Census, preliminary), 53,497 farms had a total area of 14·7m. acres; average farm was of 276 acres; 6·59m. acres were harvested cropland; 940,107 acres were irrigated.

The largest source of income in 1976 was soybeans ($622·7m.), then chickens including broilers ($442·8m.), rice ($303m.), cattle and calves ($278·4m.) and cotton ($236m.). Cash farm income (1976) was $2,417·2m.; from crops, $1,325m., and from livestock, $1,092m.

Livestock on 1 Jan. 1976 included 2·4m. all cattle, 890,000 milch cows, 5,300 sheep and 302,000 swine.

INDUSTRY. In July 1977 total employment averaged 863,900 (75,000 agricultural, 212,900 manufacturing, 150,000 wholesale and retail trade, 118,400 government). The Arkansas Department of Labor estimated that 176,300 factory production workers earned an average $172.03 per week (40·1 hours). The most important manufacturing group was food and kindred products employing 31,300, followed by electric and electronic equipment (22,800) and lumber and wood products (21,200). Construction employed 37,800.

COMMUNICATIONS

Roads. State-maintained highways (1976) total 15,821 miles; local county highways, 47,463 miles; municipal roads, 8,225 miles. In 1976 there were 1,369,625 registered motor vehicles.

Railways. In 1976 there were in the state 3,728 miles of commercial railway.

Aviation. Seven commercial airlines serve the state; there were, in 1976, 230 airports (79 publicly-owned and 151 private).

Waterways. There are 1,126 miles of navigable streams including the Kerr-McClellan Channel which bisects the state and gives access to the sea *via* the Mississippi River.

EDUCATION, RELIGION AND WELFARE

Education. In the school year 1974–75 elementary schools had 229,406 enrolled pupils and 9,135 classroom teachers; secondary schools, 223,795 pupils and 10,286 teachers. Average salaries of teachers in elementary and secondary schools was $8,489. Expenditure on public schools was $335·7m.

An educational TV network began operating in 1966 with a full 12-hour-day telecasting.

Higher education is provided at 31 institutions: 9 state universities, 1 medical college, 12 private or church colleges, 9 community and junior colleges. Total enrolment in institutions of higher education, 1975–76, was 65,547. Total expenditure, 1975–76, $125m.

There are 23 vocational-technical schools with 44,374 students, including night students. Total expenditure, 1975–76, $9·7m.

Religion. The most numerous religious bodies in the state are Baptist (601,199 members in 1974), Methodist (211,991), Roman Catholic (53,555) and Assembly of God (26,910). Total known membership, all denominations, 973,996.

Social Welfare. In Feb. 1976, 59,904 persons were drawing old-age assistance at an average amount of $74.96 per month; 34,657 families (80,330 children), $117.71 per family; 1,706 blind persons, $113.72; 28,922 totally and permanently disabled, $104.09.

There were 100 licensed hospitals (with 11,779 beds) in 1976, and 215 licensed nursing homes (19,889 beds); resident patients in mental hospitals, 1976, numbered 410.

State prisons in Aug. 1976 had 2,375 inmates (11·2 per 100,000 population).

Books of Reference

State and County Economic Data for Arkansas. Industrial Research and Extension Center, Little Rock

Ferguson and Atkinson, *Historic Arkansas.* Little Rock, 1966

Fletcher, J. G., *Arkansas.* Univ. of N. Carolina, Chapel Hill, 1947

CALIFORNIA

HISTORY. California, first settled in July 1769, was from its discovery down to 1846 politically associated with Mexico. On 7 July 1846 the American flag was hoisted at Monterey, and a proclamation was issued declaring California to be a portion of the US, and on 2 Feb. 1848, by the treaty of Guadalupe–Hidalgo, the territory was formally ceded by Mexico to the US, and was admitted to the Union 9 Sept. 1850 as the thirty-first state, with boundaries as at present.

AREA AND POPULATION. Area, 158,693 sq. miles (2,120 sq. miles being inland water). In 1974 the federal government owned 45m. acres (45·03% of the land area); in 1975, 546,000 acres were under jurisdiction of the Bureau of Indian Affairs, of which 472,000 acres were tribal. Public lands, vacant in 1975, totalled 15,607,125 acres, practically all either mountains or deserts.

Census population, 1 April 1970, 19,953,134, an increase of 27% over 1960, making California the most populous state of the USA (New York: 18,190,740). Estimated population (1977), 21·89m. Births in 1975, 317,318 (15 per 1,000 population); deaths, 170,797 (8·1); infant deaths, 4,257 (13·4 per 1,000 live births); marriages, 154,803 (7·3); divorces, 128,489 (6·1).

Population in 5 census years (with distribution by sex, 1970) was:

	White	*Negro*	*Japanese*	*Chinese*	*Total (incl. all others)*	*Per sq. mile*
1910	2,259,672	21,645	41,356	36,248	2,377,549	15·3
1930	5,408,260	81,048	97,456	37,361	5,677,251	36·2
1950	9,915,173	462,172	84,956	58,324	10,586,223	67·5
1960	14,455,230	883,861	157,317	95,600	15,717,204	100·4
1970	17,761,032	1,400,143	213,280	170,131	19,953,134	125·7
Male	8,731,367	683,026	99,567	87,835	9,816,685	—
Female	9,029,665	717,117	113,713	82,296	10,136,449	—

On the 1970 population 90·9% were urban (86·4% in 1960). The largest county, Los Angeles, had (1 July 1976) 6,970,100. Those 21 years old or older numbered 12·25m.; foreign-born whites were 1,512,435.

The largest cities with 1970 census population are:

Los Angeles	2,816,061	Anaheim	166,701	Berkeley	116,716
San Francisco	715,674	Fresno	165,972	Huntington Beach	115,960
San Diego	696,769	Santa Ana	156,601	Pasadena	113,327
San José	445,779	Riverside	140,089	Stockton	107,644
Oakland	361,561	Torrance	134,584	East Los Angeles	105,038
Long Beach	358,633	Glendale	132,752	San Bernardino	104,251
Sacramento	254,413	Garden Grove	122,524	Fremont	100,869

Urbanized areas (1970 census): Los Angeles–Long Beach, 8,351,266; San Francisco–Oakland, 2,987,850; San Diego, 1,198,323; San José, 1,025,273; Sacramento, 633,732; San Bernardino–Riverside, 583,597; Fresno, 262,908.

CONSTITUTION AND GOVERNMENT. The present constitution became effective from 4 July 1879; it has had numerous amendments since 1962. The Senate is composed of 40 members elected for 4 years—half being elected each 2 years—and the Assembly, of 80 members, elected for 2 years. Two-year regular sessions convene in Dec. of each even-numbered year. The Governor and Lieut.-Governor are elected for 4 years.

California is represented in Congress by 2 senators and 43 representatives.

In the 1976 presidential election Ford polled 3,882,244 votes and Carter 3,742,284 votes.

The capital is Sacramento. The state is divided into 58 counties.

Governor: Edmund G. Brown, Jr (D.), 1974 ($49,100).

Lieut.-Governor: Mervyn M. Dymally (D.) ($35,000); ($42,500 from 1 Jan. 1979).

Secretary of State: March Fong Eu (D.) ($35,000); ($42,500 from 1 Jan. 1979).

BUDGET. For the year ending 30 June 1977 (estimates) general revenues were $12,322m. (taxation, $12,107m., and federal aid, $215m.); general expenditures were $12,327m. ($3,232m. for education, $2,980m. for health and welfare).

The net long-term state debt was $3,546m. on 30 June 1975.

Per capita personal income (1976) was $7,180.

ENERGY AND NATURAL RESOURCES

Minerals. California is one of the three most important petroleum-producing states of the US (Texas and Louisiana being the other two); crude oil output was 321,043,000 bbls in 1975. Output of natural gas was 320,615m. cu. ft; of natural gas liquids, 5,117,000 bbls. Gold output was 8m. troy oz.; gypsum, 1·29m. short tons; lead, zinc, copper and iron ore are also produced. The estimated value of all the minerals produced was $2,964,593,000, of which petroleum accounted for $1,859,553,000.

Agriculture. Extending 700 miles from north to south, and intersected by several ranges of mountains, California has almost every variety of climate, from the very wet to the very dry, and from the temperate to the semi-tropical. Of the total surface area (100,313,600 acres), estimates (1971) show 5·9m. acres to be seriously eroded, 35·4m. acres moderately affected and 58·8m. with little or no erosion.

In 1974 there were 63,000 farms, comprising 36·2m. acres; average farm, 574 acres. The state ranks first in value of farm products, cotton, fruit, poultry and vegetables being particularly important. Cash income, 1974, from crops, $5,444m.; from livestock and poultry, $2,788m. Cattle, dairy produce, cotton, grapes, hay, tomatoes (in that order) are the main sources of farm income.

Production of cotton, 1975, was 1,954,100 bales (480 lb. gross); other field crops included sugar-beet (8·5m. short tons, leading all states). Cereal crops include barley, 60·4m. bu; wheat, 62·2m. bu., and rice, 30·1m. cwt in 1975. Principle tree crops (1975) include wine, table and raisin grapes (3,924,000 tons—90·5% of US total); peaches (920,000 tons); pears (300,350 tons); apricots (152,000 tons); prunes (150,000 tons); plums, nectarines, avocados, olives and cherries. Citrus fruit crops were: Oranges, 55·1m. boxes; lemons, 22·2m. boxes; grapefruit, 6·7m. boxes.

On 1 Jan. 1975 the farm animals were: 800,000 milch cows, 5·2m. all cattle, 910,000 sheep and 124,000 swine.

Forestry. Total forest area in 1973 was 42,416,000 acres, of which 17,345,000 acres was commercial forest. California ranks third to Oregon and Washington in volume of standing timber (278,000m. bd ft); total annual cut is about 4,703·6m. bd ft (1974). National forest service land in 1973 was 20,074,000 acres.

Fishery. California ranks first as a fishing state (by value of fish caught). The catch in 1976 was 1,370m. lb.; leading species were anchovy, tuna and sole.

INDUSTRY. In 1973, 33,363 manufacturing establishments employed 1,097,200 production workers earning $9,413·9m.; value added by manufacture $36,727·6m. The petroleum products industry ranks second to Texas. Transport equipment (200,292 employees, annual average 1975) and food products (170,075) are leading industries. Aircraft, electrical machinery and equipment, and missile engineering are important.

COMMUNICATIONS

Roads. In 1975 California had 47,909 miles of roads inside cities and 123,191 miles outside. In 1975 there were 11,119,563 registered motor cars and 2,588,025 trucks, buses and public vehicles, leading all states in all items by a wide margin.

Railways. Total mileage of railways, 1 Jan. 1977, was 7,600 miles.

Aviation. Airports, 1977, numbered 1,035, including 822 privately owned. There were 350 heliports (127 publicly owned).

Shipping. The chief ports are San Francisco and Los Angeles.

JUSTICE, RELIGION, EDUCATION AND WELFARE

Justice. State prisons, 31 Dec. 1976, had 21,088 inmates (98 per 100,000 population). From 1893 to 1942, 307 inmates were executed by hanging. From 1938 to 1976, 194 inmates were executed by lethal gas.

Religion. The Roman Catholic Church, with 2,483,411 adherents in 1954, is much stronger than any other single church; next are the Jewish congregations with an estimated 431,471 members, Methodists, Presbyterians and Baptists. There were 210,000 Episcopalians in 1973.

Education. Full-time attendance at school is compulsory for children from 6 to 16 years of age for a minimum of 175 days per annum, and part-time attendance is required from 16 to 18 years. In autumn 1974 there were 3,027,936 pupils enrolled in elementary schools and 1,399,507 pupils in secondary schools. Elementary schools (1974–75) had 111,500 classroom teachers (average salary, $14,700) and secondary schools, 75,800 teachers ($16,000). Estimated expenditure on public schools, 1976–77, was $2,759m.

Community Colleges had 1,234,407 students in autumn 1975.

California has two publicly supported higher education systems: the University of California (1868) and the California State University and Colleges. In 1974–75, the University of California with campuses for resident instruction and research at Berkeley, Los Angeles, San Francisco and 6 other centres, had 119,646 full-time students, 7,084 full-time faculty members and 1,520 teaching assistants. California State University and Colleges with campuses at Sacramento, Long Beach, Los Angeles, San Francisco and 15 other cities had 183,007 full-time students in autumn 1976, and full-time faculty of 11,287. In addition to the 28 publicly supported institutions for higher education there are 266 private colleges and universities which had a total estimated enrolment of 191,000 in the autumn of 1977. State expenditure on education totalled about $3,231m.

Health. In 1976 there were 571 general hospitals; capacity, 107,293 beds. On 30 June 1976 state hospitals for the mentally disabled had 6,114 patients and state hospitals for the developmentally disabled had 10,050 patients. There were 515 clinics.

Social Security. On 1 Jan. 1974 the federal government (Social Security Administration) assumed responsibility for the Supplemental Security Income/State Supplemental Program which replaced the State Old-Age Security. The SSI/SSP provides financial assistance for needy aged (65 years or older), blind or disabled persons. An individual recipient may own assets up to $1,500; a couple up to $2,250, subject to specific exclusions. There are federal, state and county programmes assisting the aged, the blind, the disabled and needy children. In 1975, 422,562 families with one or more children were receiving an average of $230.89 per month per family.

Books of Reference

California Statistical Abstract. 17th ed. Dept. of Finance, Sacramento, 1976
Economic Report of the Governor. Annual. Governor's Office, Sacramento
Arnold, R. K. (ed.), *The California Economy 1947–1980.* Menlo Park, 1961
Crouch, W. E., and others, *California Government and Politics.* 2nd ed. New York, 1960
Turner, H. A., and Veig, J. A., *The Government and Politics of California.* 2nd ed. New York, 1964

State Library: The California State Library, Library-Courts Bldg, Sacramento 95814.

COLORADO

HISTORY. Colorado was first settled in 1858, made a Territory in 1861 and admitted into the Union on 1 Aug. 1876.

AREA AND POPULATION. Colorado is bounded north by Wyoming, north-east by Nebraska, east by Kansas, south-east by Oklahoma, south by New Mexico and west by Utah. Area, 104,247 sq. miles (450 sq. miles being inland water). Federal lands, 1974, 23,974,000 acres (36% of the land area).

Census population, 1 April 1970, was 2,207,259, an increase of 453,312 or 25·8% since 1960. Estimated population, 1977, 2·63m. Births, 1976, were 41,003 (15·6 per 1,000 population); deaths, 17,966 (6·8); infant deaths, 531 (13 per 1,000 live births); marriages, 28,601 (10·9); dissolutions, 17,520 (6·7).

Population in 5 census years (with distribution by sex, 1970) was:

	White	*Negro*	*Indian*	*Asiatic*	*Total*	*Per sq. mile*
1910	783,415	11,453	1,482	2,674	799,024	7·7
1930	1,018,793	11,828	1,395	3,775	1,035,791	10·0
1950	1,296,653	20,177	1,567	5,870	1,325,089	12·7
1960	1,700,700	39,992	4,288	8,967	1,753,947	16·7
1970	2,112,352	66,411	8,836	10,388	2,207,259	21·3
Male	1,041,364	34,047	4,513	4,861	1,089,377	—
Female	1,070,988	32,364	4,323	5,527	1,117,882	—

Of the total population in 1970, 1,581,739 (71·7%) were urban (73·7% in 1960); those 21 years or older were 1,301,577. Denver, the capital, had a 1975 population of 487,000 (urbanized area, 1,413,000). Other cities with 1975 population: Colorado Springs, 180,000; Pueblo, 105,000; Lakewood, 120,000; Aurora, 118,000; Boulder, 79,000; Arvada, 74,000; Fort Collins, 56,000; Greeley, 47,000; Englewood, 36,000; Grand Junction, 28,000.

GOVERNMENT AND CONSTITUTION. The constitution adopted in 1876 is still in effect with (1970) 78 amendments. The General Assembly consists of a Senate of 35 members elected for 4 years, one-half retiring every 2 years, and of a House of Representatives of 65 members elected for 2 years. Sessions are annual, beginning 1951. The Governor, Lieut.-Governor, Attorney-General and Secretary of State are elected for 4 years. Qualified as electors are all citizens, male and female (except criminals and insane), 18 years of age, who have resided in the state for 32 days immediately preceding the election. The state is divided into 63 counties. The state sends to Congress 2 senators and 5 representatives.

In the 1976 presidential election Ford polled 584,456 votes, Carter 460,801 and McCarthy 27,047.

The capital is Denver.

Governor: Richard D. Lamm (D.), 1975 ($40,000).
Lieut.-Governor: George L. Brown (D.) ($20,000).
Secretary of State: Mary E. Buchanan (R.) ($20,000).

BUDGET. The state's total budget, 1976–77, is $1,985m., of which taxation and other revenue furnish $979·7m. and federal grants $551·6m. Education takes $956·7m.; health, welfare and rehabilitation, $481·4m., and highways, $198·1m. Total state and local taxes *per capita* (1973–74) were $587.

The state has no general debt. The net long-term debt (in revenue bond) on 30 June 1974 was $126·7m.

Per capita personal income (1976) was $6,440.

ENERGY AND NATURAL RESOURCES

Minerals. Colorado has a variety of mineral resources. Among the most important are crude oil, coal and molybdenum. The world's largest molybdenum mine is at Climax; output since 1914 has been about 72% of the country's cumulative total. Mineral production, 1975, was: Gold, 50,300 oz. ($5·5m.); silver, 3·91m. oz. ($14·3m.); coal, 9·46m. tons ($143·5m.); lead, 25,270 tons ($9·3m.); zinc, 48,475 tons ($24·6m.); petroleum, 39m. bbls ($183·7m.); natural gas, 174,300m. cu. ft ($111·9m.); molybdenum, 63·7m. lb. ($183·4m.); uranium ore, 779,000 lb. ($13m.). Total mineral output in 1976 was valued at $982m.

Agriculture. Farms number about 29,500, with a total area of 39·9m. acres in 1976 (58·4% of the land area); 5,662,000 acres (1976) were harvested crop land; average farm, 1,353 acres (1975). Cash income, 1976, from crops, $531m.; from livestock, $1,446m. In 1974 there were 2,874,000 acres under irrigation.

Production of principal crops in 1976: Maize, 62·4m. bu. (from 600,000 acres); wheat, 48m. bu. (2·22m.); hay, 2·82m. tons (1·4m.); dry beans, 1·7m. cwt (185,000); potatoes, 11m. cwt (44,000); sugar-beet, 2·3m. tons (121,000); oats, rye, sorghums and broomcorn are grown, as well as fruit.

On 1 Jan. 1977 the number of farm animals was: 71,000 milch cows, 3·03m. all cattle, 830,000 sheep, 280,000 swine. The wool clip in 1976 yielded 8·54m. lb. of wool.

INDUSTRY. The 2,842 manufacturers (1972 census) had 132,600 employees, who earned $1,298·2m., value added by manufacture was $2,509·6m. Wholesale trade (1972) had 4,757 establishments with 49,435 employees, who earned $435·7m.; total value of wholesale sales was $8,030m. Retail trade (1972) had 24,335 establishments with 146,202 employees, who earned $709·9m.; total value of retail sales was $5,869m. Service industries had 24,011 establishments with 74,083 employees, who earned $398·6m.; total value of receipts of service industries was $1,234m. Distribution of employment in 1976 was: Government, 214,200; services, 194,200; retail trade, 193,600; manufacturing, 142,600; transport and utilities, 60,300.

TOURISM. During 1976 visitors to Colorado totalled 9·1m., including 3·65m. for ski-ing; there are 54 mountain peaks over 14,000 ft high, 27 of which rank among the 50 highest in the US. Tourist expenditures, $772m.

COMMUNICATIONS

Roads. The state highway system (1974) included 9,318 miles of highway. County roads totalled 67,572, and city streets, 7,634 miles. Total road mileage, 84,524, of which 9,892 miles are unmaintained county and city roads.

Railways. In 1973 there were in the state 3,492 miles of main-track and branch railway.

Aviation. There were (1973) 62 public airports and 42 private airports for general use.

JUSTICE, RELIGION, EDUCATION AND WELFARE

Justice. State prisons during 1974 had 1,350 inmates in the State Penitentiary and 685 in the State Reformatory. In 1967 there was 1 execution; since 1930 executions (by lethal gas) numbered 47, including 41 whites, 5 Negroes and 1 other; all were for murder.

Colorado has a Civil Rights Act (1935) forbidding places of public accommodation to discriminate against any persons on the grounds of race, religion, sex, colour or nationality. No religious test may be applied to teachers or students in the public schools, 'nor shall any distinction or classification of pupils be made on account of race or colour'. In 1957 the General Assembly prohibited discrimination in employment of persons in private industry and in 1959 adopted the Fair Housing Act to discourage discrimination in housing. A 1957 Act permits marriages between white persons and Negroes or mulattoes.

Religion. In 1970 the Roman Catholic Church had 412,000 members; the 100 Protestant and independent Churches totalled 404,000 members; the Jewish community had 26,000 members. Buddhism is among other religions represented.

Education. In autumn 1975 the public elementary and secondary schools had 568,900 pupils and 34,571 teachers and administrators; total instructional salaries averaged $11,927. Enrolments in universities and larger colleges, 1977, were: US Air Force Academy (Colorado Springs), 4,572 students; University of Colorado (Boulder), 21,767; University of Colorado (Denver), 8,832; University of Colorado (Colorado Springs), 4,127; University of Colorado (Medical Centre), 1,477; Colorado State University (Fort Collins), 17,812; University of Denver (Denver), 7,753; Colorado School of Mines (Golden), 2,584; University of Northern Colorado (Greeley), 11,048; University of Southern Colorado (Pueblo), 5,166; Western State College (Gunnison), 3,152; Adams State College (Alamosa), 2,345; Metropolitan State College (Denver), 12,587; Colorado College (Colorado Springs), 1,928; Fort Lewis College (Durango), 2,787; Mesa College, 3,068.

Health. Approved hospitals, 1976, numbered 93 with 12,691 beds. In 1976, there were 26 public mental health centres, clinics and hospitals with 28,436 patients (1,102 per 100,000 population).

Social Security. A constitutional amendment, adopted 1956, provides for minimum old age pensions of $100 per month, which may be raised on a cost-of-living basis ($201 for 1976); for a $5m. stabilization fund and for a $10m. medical and health fund for pensioners. Old-age assistance is available to citizens 60 years of age and resident for stated periods, with assets not exceeding $1,000 (excluding home ownership). In 1975–76 an average of 21,754 persons were drawing an average of $36.46 per month. There were 150,032 recipients of medical assistance and 160,673 recipients of food stamp assistance.

Books of Reference

Directory of Colorado Manufacturers, 1977. Business Research Division, School of Business, University of Colorado, Boulder, 1977

Economic Outlook Forum, 1978. Colorado Division of Commerce and Development, and the College of Business, University of Colorado, Denver, 1977

State Library: Colorado State Library, State Capitol, Denver, 80203. *State Librarian:* Gordon Bennett.

CONNECTICUT

HISTORY. Connecticut was first settled in 1635 and has been an organized commonwealth since 1637. In 1629 a written constitution was adopted which, it is claimed, was the first in the history of the world formed under the concept of a social compact. This constitution was confirmed by a charter from Charles II in 1662, and replaced in 1818 by a state constitution, framed that year by a constitutional convention.

AREA AND POPULATION. Connecticut is bounded north and east by Massachusetts, south by the Atlantic and west by New York. Area, 4,862 sq. miles (110 sq. miles being inland water). Census population, 1 April 1970, 3,031,709, an increase of 496,475 or 19·6% since 1960. Births (1975) were 35,166 (11·4 per 1,000 population); deaths, 25,921 (8·4); infant deaths, 530 (15·1 per 1,000 live births); marriages, 22,887 (7·4); divorces, 11,957 (3·9).

Population in 5 census years (with distribution by sex, 1970) was:

	White	*Negro*	*Indian*	*Asiatic*	*Total*	*Per sq. mile*
1910	1,098,897	15,174	152	533	1,114,756	231·3
1930	1,576,700	29,354	162	687	1,606,903	328·0
1950	1,952,329	53,472	333	1,146	2,007,280	409·7
1960	2,423,816	107,449	923	3,046	2,535,234	517·5
			All others			
1970	2,838,690	181,474	10,545		3,031,709	629·0
Male	1,378,771	85,975	5,772		1,470,518	—
Female	1,459,919	95,499	4,773		1,561,191	—

In 1970 foreign-born whites numbered 251,844. Of the total population, 2,343,578 persons (74%) were urban (78·3% in 1960). Those 21 years old or older numbered 1,866,908.

The chief cities and towns, with census population 1 April 1970, are:

Hartford	158,017	East Hartford	57,583	Manchester	47,994
Bridgeport	156,542	Fairfield	56,487	Enfield	46,189
New Haven	137,707	Meriden	55,959	Norwich	41,433
Stamford	108,798	Bristol	55,487	Groton	38,523
Waterbury	108,033	West Haven	52,851	Wallingford	36,924
New Britain	83,441	Milford	50,858	New London	35,714
Norwalk	79,113	Danbury	50,781	Torrington	31,952
West Hartford	68,031	Stratford	49,775	Middletown	31,630
Greenwich	59,755	Hamden	49,357		

Larger urbanized areas, 1970 census: Hartford, 657,104; Bridgeport, 385,746; New Haven, 348,424; Stamford, 204,888; Waterbury, 206,625.

CONSTITUTION AND GOVERNMENT. The 1818 Constitution was revised in June 1953 effective 1 Jan. 1955. On 30 Dec. 1965 a new constitution went into effect, having been framed by a constitutional convention in the summer of 1965 and approved by the voters in Dec. 1965.

The 1965 Constitution provides for 30 to 50 members of the Senate (instead of 24 to 36) and for 125 to 225 members of the House of Representatives, to be elected from assembly districts, rather than 2 or 1 from each town, as in the former constitution. The convention has added a new provision for a 3-day session following each regular or special session, solely to reconsider bills vetoed by the Governor.

The General Assembly consists of a Senate of 36 members and a House of Representatives of 177 members. Members of each House are elected for the term of 2 years (annual salary $6,500 first year, $4,500 second year; expenses $1,000 and travel expenses). Legislative sessions are annual. The Governor and Lieut.-Governor are elected for 4 years. All citizens (with necessary exceptions and the usual residential requirements) have the right of suffrage.

Connecticut is one of the original 13 states of the Union. The state is represented in Congress by 2 senators and 6 representatives.

In the 1976 presidential election Ford polled 712,414 votes, Carter 641,010. The state capital is Hartford.

Governor: Mrs Ella Grasso (D.), 1975–79 ($42,000).

Lieut.-Governor: Robert Killian (D.) ($18,000).
Secretary of State: Mrs Gloria Schaeffer (D.) ($20,000).

BUDGET. For the year ending 30 June 1974 (state government figures) general revenues were $1,421,876,633 (taxation, $916·1m., and federal aid, $151·5m.); general expenditures were $1,252,929,660 (education, $4,759,983, highways, $260,449,380, and public welfare, $296,643,097).

The total net long term debt on 30 June 1976 was $1,850,315,000.

Per capita income, 1973, was $5,889.

NATURAL RESOURCES

Minerals. The state has some mineral resources: sheet mica, sand, gravel, clays and stone; total production in 1972 was valued at $33,123,000.

Agriculture. In 1975 the state had 4,400 farms with a total area of 540,000 acres; average farm was of 123 acres, valued at $1,737 per acre. Of the farms, 2,795 were commercial in 1974 (4,500 in 1971) and 1,505 were residential or part-time. Total cash income, 1973, was $188·6m., including $62·1m. from crops and $124·6m. from livestock and products (mainly from dairy products and poultry). Principal crops are tobacco, hay, oats, maize, potatoes, apples, peaches, pears, vegetables and small fruit.

Livestock (1 Jan. 1973): 113,000 all cattle (value $38·9m.), 4,800 sheep ($134,000), 6,800 swine ($270,000) and 5m. poultry ($10m.).

Forestry. The state had (1975) 170,000 acres of state forest land, which is about 4·3% of the total land area.

INDUSTRY. Manufacturing establishments employed 420,800 production workers in Dec. 1974 who earned average weekly wages of $185.76; value added by manufacture (1973), $3·6m. Total non-agricultural employment in Dec. 1974 was 1,221,100.

COMMUNICATIONS

Roads. The state (1974) maintains 3,994 miles of highways, all surfaced. Motor vehicles registered 1 July 1973 numbered 2,103,813 (licences issued 1973, 1,213,141).

Railways. On 30 June 1974 there were 664 miles of railway track.

Aviation. In 1974 there were 68 airports (28 commercial including 5 state-owned, and 22 heliports).

JUSTICE, RELIGION, EDUCATION AND WELFARE

Justice. In 1970 there were no executions; since 1930 there have been 22 executions (19 by electrocution, 3 by hanging), including 19 whites and 3 Negroes, all for murder. The 6 community correctional centres, 1974, had 1,508 inmates; 5 correctional institutions had 1,136 inmates.

The Civil Rights Act makes it a punishable offence to discriminate against any person or persons 'on account of alienage, colour or race' and to hold up to ridicule any persons 'on account of creed, religion, colour, denomination, nationality or race'. Places of public resort are forbidden to discriminate. Insurance companies are forbidden to charge higher premiums to persons 'wholly or partially of African descent'. Schools must be open to all 'without discrimination on account of race or colour'.

Religion. The leading religious denominations (1974) in the state are the Roman Catholic (1,372,712 members), United Churches of Christ (124,042), Protestant Episcopal (111,489), Jewish (110,000), Greek Orthodox (60,000), Methodist (53,892), Baptist (42,270), Presbyterian (10,200).

Education. Elementary instruction is free for all children between the ages of 4 and 16 years, and compulsory for all children between the ages of 7 and 16 years. In

1974–75 the 847 public elementary schools had 449,407 enrolled pupils; the 146 high schools had 189,973 pupils; the 15 vocational technical state schools, 8,907 pupils. Expenditure of the state Board of Education for grants-in-aid, 1973–74, was $143,169,480; local expenditure, 1973–74, $549,047,011. Average salary of teachers in public schools, 1973–74, $12,061.

Connecticut has 47 colleges, 4 state teachers' colleges and 8 regional community colleges. The University of Connecticut at Storrs, founded 1881, had 1,078 faculty and 20,048 students in 1974. Yale University, New Haven, founded in 1701, had 1,395 faculty and 8,665 students. Wesleyan University, Middletown, founded 1831, had 278 faculty and 1,530 students. Trinity College, Hartford, founded 1823, had 152 faculty and 1,525 students. Connecticut College for Women, New London, founded 1915, had 186 faculty and 1,500 students. The University of Hartford had 186 faculty and 2,323 students. The regional community colleges (2-year course) had 857 staff and 21,500 students.

Health. Hospitals listed by the American Hospital Association, 1974, numbered 67 (including 5 federal), with 20,874 beds, and an average daily census of 343 persons per hospital. Average daily census of the 11 state psychiatric hospitals was 902 per hospital. In July 1970 the state controlled 4 hospitals for the mentally retarded, 1 institution for the deaf and 3 chronic disease hospitals.

Social Security. Disbursements during the year ending 30 June 1974 amounted to $5,096,756 for old-age assistance, and medical aid to the aged, $66,068,000. In June 1974, 3,671 old people were receiving $68.60 monthly; 35,975 families were receiving $257.18 per family on aid to dependent children; 6,466 totally disabled, $69.26.

Books of Reference

Connecticut in Focus. League of Women Voters of Connecticut. 2nd ed. Hamden, 1974
The Register and Manual of Connecticut. Secretary of State. Hartford. Annual
The Structure of Connecticut's State Government. Connecticut Public Expenditure Council. Hartford, 1973
Adams, V. Q., *Connecticut: The Story of Your State Government.* Chester, 1973
Hoyt, J. R., *The Connecticut Story.* New Haven, 1961
Smith, Allen R., *Connecticut, a Thematic Atlas.* Newington, 1974

State Library: Connecticut State Library, Capitol Avenue, Hartford, 06015. *State Librarian:* Charles E. Funk.

DELAWARE

HISTORY. Delaware, permanently settled in 1638, is one of the original 13 states of the Union, and the first one to ratify the Federal Constitution.

AREA AND POPULATION. Delaware is bounded north by Pennsylvania, north-east by New Jersey, east by Delaware Bay, south and west by Maryland. Area 2,399 sq. miles (437 sq. miles being inland water). Census population, 1 April 1970, was 584,104, an increase of 101,812 or 22·7% since 1960. Births in 1977, 8,771; deaths, 4,884; infant deaths, 103; marriages, 3,999; divorces, 3,044.

Population in 5 census years (with distribution by sex, 1970) was:

	White	*Negro*	*Indian*	*Asiatic*	*Total*	*Per sq. mile*
1910	171,102	31,181	5	34	202,322	103·0
1930	205,718	32,602	5	55	238,380	120·5
1950	273,878	43,598	—	87	266,505	134·7
1960	384,327	60,688	597	410	446,292	224·0
			All others			
1970	466,459	78,276	3,369		548,104	276·5
Male	227,978	37,646	1,708		267,332	—
Female	238,481	40,630	1,661		280,772	—

Of the total population in 1960, 292,994 (65·7%) were urban (62·6% in 1950); households, 158,582. Those 18 years old or older numbered 283,253; foreign-born whites, 14,307.

The 1970 census figures show Wilmington, with population of 80,386; Newark, 21,078; Dover, 17,488; Wilmington Manor, 10,134; Elsmere, 8,415; Dover Air Force Base, 8,106.

CONSTITUTION AND GOVERNMENT. The present constitution (the fourth) dates from 1897, and has had 51 amendments; it was not ratified by the electorate but promulgated by the Constitutional Convention. The General Assembly consists of a Senate of 19 members elected for 4 years and a House of Representatives of 39 members elected for 2 years. The Governor and Lieut.-Governor are elected for 4 years.

With necessary exceptions, all adult citizens, registered as voters, who have resided in the state 1 year, and complied with local residential requirements, have the right to vote; those who have attained the age of 18 since 1900 must be able to read English and to write their names. Citizens resident for 3 months or over may vote for President and Vice-President only.

Delaware is represented in Congress by 2 senators and 1 representative, elected by the voters of the whole state.

In the 1976 presidential election Carter polled 122,610 votes, Ford 109,926.

The state capital is Dover. Delaware is divided into 3 counties.

Governor: Pierre S. du Pont (R.), 1977–81 ($35,000).

Lieut.-Governor: James D. McGinnis (D.) ($9,000).

Secretary of State: Glenn C. Kenton (R.) ($18,000) (appointed by the Governor).

FINANCE. For the year ending 30 June 1974 general receipts were $680·98m., of which taxes furnished $359·56m. and federal grants $138·2m. General expenditure was $668m. (education, $249·9m.; highways, $70·8m.; health and public welfare, $100·7m.).

On 30 June 1973 the operating cash deficit was $6,023,690.

Per capita income (1975) was $6,748.

NATURAL RESOURCES

Minerals. The mineral resources of Delaware are not extensive, consisting chiefly of clay products, stone, sand and gravel. Value of mineral production in 1974 (preliminary) was $3·3m.

Agriculture. Delaware is mainly an industrial state, but about 54% of the land area is in farms (698,000 acres), which in 1974 numbered 3,600; average farm (1969) was of 181·6 acres and valued (land and buildings) at $90,632.

Cash income, 1974, from crops and livestock, $272·2m.; net income per farm was $23,189. The chief crops are maize and soybeans.

INDUSTRY. In 1973–74 manufacturing establishments (numbering 573) employed 74,500 people, earning $948m.

COMMUNICATIONS

Roads. The state in 1974 maintained 4,602 miles of roads and streets and 2,111 miles of federally-aided highways. Vehicles registered in 1974, 351,283.

Railways. In 1974 the state had 291 miles of railway.

Aviation. Delaware had 23 airports, of which 11 were for general use in 1970.

JUSTICE, RELIGION, EDUCATION AND WELFARE

Justice. State prisons, June 1972–June 1973, had daily average of 682 inmates. The death penalty was illegal from 2 April 1958 to 18 Dec. 1961. Executions since 1930 (by hanging) have totalled 12 (none since 1946).

Religion. Membership, 1973–74: Methodists, 101,239; Roman Catholics, 98,637; Episcopalians, 19,935; Presbyterians, 17,191; Lutherans, 10,000.

Education. The state has free public schools and compulsory school attendance. In Sept. 1974 the elementary and secondary public schools had an estimated number of 130,609 enrolled pupils and 6,290 classroom teachers. Appropriation for public schools (financial year 1974) was $151,733,762. Average salary of classroom teachers (financial year 1974), $11,304. The state supports the University of Delaware at Newark (1834) which had 738 professors and 18,511 students in Sept. 1974, and State College, Dover (1892), with 116 full-time instructors and 2,038 students.

Health. In 1973 there were 15 hospitals (5,002 beds) listed by the American Hospital Association. In Oct. 1973 patients in mental hospitals numbered 1,734.

Social Security. In 1974 the federal Supplemental Security Income programme lessened state responsibility for the aged, blind and disabled. Provisions are also made for the care of dependent children in (1975) 10,087 cases totalling 31,742 recipients ($52.34 per person); general assistance, families in 2,107 cases totalling 4,081 persons ($31.64 per person). The total programme assisted 42,555 persons, at a cost of $2·4m.

Books of Reference

Information: Division of Historical and Cultural Affairs, Hall of Records, Dover.

State Manual, Containing Official List of Officers, Commissions and County Officers. Secretary of State, Dover. Annual

The Delaware Economy, 1939–58. Bureau of Economic & Business Research, Univ. of Delaware, 1961

Topical History of Delaware. Division of Historical and Cultural Affairs. Dover, 1977

Dolan, P., *The Government and Administration of Delaware.* New York, 1956

Federal Writers' Project. *Delaware: A Guide to the First State.* Rev. ed. New York, 1955

DISTRICT OF COLUMBIA

HISTORY. The District of Columbia, organized in 1790, is the seat of the Government of the US, for which the land was ceded by the state of Maryland to the US as a site for the national capital. It was established under Acts of Congress in 1790 and 1791. Congress first met in it in 1800 and federal authority over it became vested in 1801.

AREA AND POPULATION. The District forms an enclave on the Potomac River, where the river forms the south-west boundary of Maryland. The area of the District of Columbia is 69·245 sq. miles, 8 sq. miles being inland water. The federal government on 30 June 1968 owned 13,314 acres (43·3% of the land area).

Census population, 1 April 1970, was 756,510, a decrease of 4·1% from that of 1960. Population of the metropolitan statistical area of Washington, D.C.–Md–Va. (1968 estimate), 2·8m. Births, 1975, in the District were 19,438 (27·1 per 1,000 population); resident deaths, 9,522 (13·3); infant deaths, 490 (25·2 per 1,000 live births); marriages, 5,033 (7); divorces, 2,508 (3·5).

Population in 5 census years (with distribution by sex, 1960) was:

	White	*Negro*	*Indian*	*Chinese and Japanese*	*Total*	*Per sq. mile*
1910	236,128	94,446	68	427	331,069	5,517·8
1930	353,981	132,068	40	780	486,869	7,981·5
1950	517,865	280,803	330	2,178	802,178	13,150·5
1960	345,263	411,737	587	3,532	763,956	12,523·9
			All others			
1970	209,272	537,712	9,526		756,510	12,321·0
Male	158,124	196,257	3,790		358,171	—
Female	187,139	215,480	3,166		405,785	—

GOVERNMENT. Local government, from 1 July 1878 until Aug. 1967, was that of a municipal corporation administered by a board of 3 commissioners, of whom 2 were appointed from civil life by the President, and confirmed by the Senate, for a term of 3 years each. The other commissioner was detailed by the President from the Engineer Corps of the Army. Reorganization Plan No. 3 of 1967 submitted by the President to Congress on 1 June 1967 abolished the Commission form of government and instituted a new Mayor Council form of government with officers appointed by the President with the advice and consent of the Senate. On 24 Dec. 1973 the appointed officers were replaced by an elected Mayor and councillors, with full legislative powers in local matters as from 1974. Congress retains the right to legislate, to veto or supersede the Council's acts. The 23rd amendment to the federal constitution (1961) conferred the right to vote in national elections; in the 1976 presidential election Carter polled 127,562 votes, Ford, 25,184.

BUDGET. The District's revenues are derived from a tax on real and personal property, sales taxes, taxes on corporations and companies, licences for conducting various businesses and from federal payments.

The District of Columbia has no bonded debt not covered by its accumulated sinking fund.

INDUSTRY. The District has few industries, with products mainly for local consumption.

COMMUNICATIONS

Roads. Within the District are 340 miles of bus routes.

Railways. There is a rapid rail transit system including a town subway system.

Aviation. The District is served by 2 general airports; across the Potomac River in Arlington, Va., is National Airport, and in Chantilly, Va., is Dulles International Airport.

JUSTICE, RELIGION, EDUCATION AND WELFARE

Justice. Since 1958 there have been no executions; from 1930 to 1957 there were 40 executions (electrocution) including 3 whites for murder and 35 Negroes for murder and 2 for rape.

Religion. The largest churches are the Protestant and Roman Catholic Christian churches; there are also Jewish, Eastern Orthodox and Islamic congregations.

Education. In 1966, 145 public elementary, junior and senior high, and special schools had 145,460 pupils; teachers numbered 5,784. Segregation was abolished in 1954. Higher education is given in Georgetown University, founded in 1795 by the Jesuit Order, with (1964) 1,392 faculty and 7,461 students; George Washington University, non-sectarian, founded in 1821, 500 faculty and 11,965 students; Howard University, founded in 1867, 855 faculty and 9,401 students; Catholic University of America, founded in 1884, with 739 faculty and 6,050 students; American University (Methodist) with 270 faculty and 11,243 students.

Social Security. In Jan. 1968 old-age assistance was being paid to 2,346 persons, receiving an average of $74.45 per month; aid to 198 blind persons $89.04, aid to 5,515 families ($38.23 per 25,527 recipients per month) for dependent children, and aid to 4,299 permanently and totally disabled, $88.74. In 1967 over $18m. was spent on public assistance payments, an increase of 23% on 1966.

Books of Reference

Reports of the Commissioners of the District of Columbia. Annual. Washington

Federal Writers' Project. *Washington, D.C.: A Guide to the Nation's Capital.* New York, 1942

National Capital Park and Planning Commission. *Monographs on Washington, Present and Future.* Washington, D.C., 1950

Rutherford, G. W., *Administration Problems in a Metropolitan Area: The National Capital Region.* Chicago, 1952

FLORIDA

HISTORY. White men, probably Spaniards but possibly English, saw Florida for the first time in the period 1497–1512. Juan Ponce de Leon sighted Florida on 27 March 1513. Going ashore between 2 and 8 April in the vicinity of what is now St Augustine, he named the land 'Pasqua de Flores' because his landing was 'in the time of the Feast of Flowers'. The first permanent settlement in the entire US was made at St Augustine, 8 Sept. 1565. It was claimed by Spain until 1763, then ceded to England; back to Spain in 1783, and to the US in 1821. Florida became a Territory in 1821 and was admitted into the Union on 3 March 1845.

AREA AND POPULATION. Florida is a peninsula bounded west by the Gulf of Mexico, south by the Straits of Florida, east by the Atlantic, north by Georgia and north-west by Alabama. Area, 58,560 sq. miles, including 4,298 sq. miles of inland water. Census population, 1 April 1970, was 6,789,443, an increase of 37·1% since 1960—second largest increase of any state. Estimate, July 1975, 8,485,230. Births in 1975 were 106,031 (12·7 per 1,000 population); deaths, 88,859 (10·6); infant deaths, 1,868 (17·6 per 1,000 live births); marriages, 86,152 (10·3); divorces, 63,267 (7·6).

Population in 5 federal census years (with distribution by sex, 1970) was:

	White	*Negro*	*Indian*	*Asiatic*	*Total*	*Per sq. mile*
1910	443,634	308,669	74	242	752,619	13·7
1930	1,035,390	431,828	587	406	1,468,211	27·1
1950	2,166,051	603,101	1,011	1,142	2,771,305	51·1
1960	4,063,881	880,186	2,504	4,990	4,951,560	84·6
			All others			
1970	5,711,411	1,049,578	28,454		6,789,443	115·9
Male	2,762,779	498,695	14,097		3,275,571	—
Female	2,956,564	542,956	14,352		3,513,872	—

Of the population in 1970, 80% were urban (73·9% in 1960); 3,962,178 were 21 years of age or over; in 1960, 255,071 were foreign-born whites.

The largest cities in the state (1970 census) are: Jacksonville, 528,865; Miami, 334,859 (urbanized area, 1972, 1,340,700); Tampa, 277,767; St Petersburg, 216,232; Fort Lauderdale, 139,590; Hollywood, 106,873; Hialeah, 102,976; Orlando, 99,006; Miami Beach, 87,072; Tallahassee, 71,897; Pensacola, 59,507; West Palm Beach, 57,375; Clearwater, 52,074; Daytona Beach, 45,327; Coral Gables, 42,494; Lakeland, 41,550; Sarasota, 40,237; Melbourne, 40,236.

CONSTITUTION AND GOVERNMENT. The 1968 Legislature revised the constitution of 1885. The state legislature consists of a Senate of 40 members, elected for 4 years, and House of Representatives with 120 members elected for 2 years. Sessions are held annually, and are limited to 60 days. The Governor is elected for 4 years, and can hold two terms in office. Two senators and 15 representatives are elected to Congress.

In the 1976 presidential election Carter polled 1,561,383 votes and Ford 1,375,296.

The state capital is Tallahassee. The state is divided into 67 counties.

Governor: Reubin Askew (D.), 1975–79 ($50,000).
Lieut.-Governor: Jim Williams (D.), 1975–79 ($36,000).
Secretary of State: Bruce Smathers (D.) ($40,000).

FINANCE. There is no state income tax on individuals. For the year ending 30 June 1974 the state had a general revenue of $4,326·52m., of which taxation furnished $2,786,602,000. General expenditure was $4,084,511,000, of which education took $1,659,184,000; public welfare, $376,633,000; and highways, $665,177,000.

Net long-term debt, 30 June 1974, amounted to $1,234m.

Per capita personal income (1975) was $53,642.

NATURAL RESOURCES

Minerals. Chief mineral is phosphate rock, of which marketable production in 1968 was 27·5m. long tons, leading all states (Florida still leads in production, but figures are no longer made available). Total value of mineral production, 1973, $309·7m.

Agriculture. In 1974, 34,000 farms had a total acreage of 14·5m.; net income per farm was $25,249. Total cash receipts from crops and livestock (1976), $2,532m., of which crops provided $1,840m. The state ranks first in citrus fruit production, farm value $705·6m., and melons and vegetables provided $551m. Other crops are maize ($48·7m.); soybeans ($47·2m.); sugar-cane ($192m.); tobacco and peanuts. On 1 Jan. 1974 the state had 2·88m. cattle, including 204,000 milch cows and 304,000 swine.

The national forests area in June 1967 was 1,076,000 acres.

Fisheries. Florida has extensive fisheries for oysters, shrimp, red snapper, crabs, mackerel and mullet. Catch (1975), 114m. lb. valued at $62m.

INDUSTRY. In 1975 there were 9,294 manufacturers. They employed 327,700 persons with value added by manufacture, about $5,000m. The metal-working, lumber, chemical, woodpulp, food-processing and instruments industries are important.

TOURISM. During 1975 over 27m. tourists visited Florida. They spent over $8·8m., making tourism one of the biggest industries in the state. There are 74 state parks, 4 state forests, 1 national park and 9 national forests. The state parks were visited by 10·2m. people in 1973, 1·5m. of them campers.

COMMUNICATIONS

Roads. The state (1975) had over 16,000 miles of road and streets and 20,190 miles of federally-aided highways.

In 1974, 5·8m. vehicle licence plates were issued.

Railways. In 1975 there were 4,500 miles of railway.

Aviation. In 1975 Florida had 330 airports, including 6 seaplane bases.

JUSTICE, RELIGION, EDUCATION AND WELFARE

Justice. Since 1968 there have been no executions; from 1930 to 1968 there were 168 executions (electrocution), including 57 whites and 73 Negroes for murder, 1 white and 36 Negroes for rape and 1 white for kidnapping. State prisons, 18 Aug. 1968, had 8,412 inmates (133 per 100,000 population).

Religion. In 1960, 30·3% of the population were members of 6 churches: Baptists (455,175), Roman Catholics (466,028), Methodists (223,151), Presbyterians (105,834) and Episcopalians (83,656). Jews numbered 159,337.

Education. Attendance at school is compulsory between 7 and 16.

In 1974 the public elementary and secondary schools had 1,570,850 enrolled pupils. State expenditure on public schools (1970) was $344·2m. The state maintains 28 community colleges (1976). There were 332,872 students in higher education in 1975.

There are 9 universities in the state system, namely the University of Florida at Gainesville (founded 1853) with 27,797 students in 1975; the Florida State University (founded at Tallahassee in 1857) with 21,524 students; the University of South Florida at Tampa (founded 1960) with 23,034 students; Florida A. & M. University at Tallahassee (founded 1887) with 5,463 students; Florida Atlantic University (founded 1964) at Boca Raton with 7,250 students; the University of West Florida at Pensacola with 5,225 students; the Florida Technological University at Orlando with 10,451 students; the University of North Florida at Jacksonville with 4,300 students; Florida International University at Miami with 10,540 students.

Health. Hospitals listed by the American Hospital Association, 1971, numbered 578 with 70,432 beds; there were 191 general, 12 long-term and 3 tuberculosis hospitals;

state and county mental hospitals had an average daily census of 10,023 patients in 1966.

Social Security. From 1974 aid to the aged, blind and disabled became a federal responsibility. The state continued to give aid to families with dependent children and general assistance. Monthly payments 1975: aid to 2,374 blind averaged $122; aid to 192,837 dependent children averaged $38; aid to 54,610 disabled averaged $115; aid to 92,217 aged averaged $88.

Books of Reference

1973 Legislative Economic Bulletin. Comptroller's Office, Tallahassee, 1973
Florida Statistical Abstract. Univ. of Florida Press, 1973
Florida Tourist Study. Florida Department of Commerce, Tallahassee. Annual
Report. Florida Secretary of State. Tallahassee. Biennial
Report of the Comptroller. Tallahassee. Annual
Dimensions. Bureau of Business and Economic Research, Univ. of Florida, Gainesville. Monthly
Cowles, F., *What to Look for in Florida.* Tampa, 1964
Morris, Allen, *The Florida Handbook.* Tallahassee, 1973–74. Biennial
Raisz, E. J., and others, *Atlas of Florida.* Univ. of Florida Press, 1974
State Library: Supreme Court Building, Tallahassee. *Librarian:* Cecil P. Beach.

GEORGIA

HISTORY. Georgia (so named from George II) was founded in 1733 as the 13th original colony; she became the 4th original state.

AREA AND POPULATION. Georgia is bounded north by Tennessee and North Carolina, north-east by South Carolina, east by the Atlantic, south by Florida and west by Alabama. Area, 58,876 sq. miles, of which 602 sq. miles are inland water. Census population, 1 April 1970, was 4,589,575. Births, 1975, were 79,951 (16·2 per 1,000 population); deaths, 41,314 (8·4); infant deaths, 1,466 (18·3 per 1,000 live births); marriages, 63,245 (12·8); divorces and annulments, 29,478 (6).

Population in 5 census years (with distribution by sex, 1960) was:

	White	*Negro*	*Indian*	*Asiatic*	*Total*	*Per sq. mile*
1910	1,431,802	1,176,987	95	237	2,609,121	44·4
1930	1,837,021	1,071,125	43	317	2,908,506	49·7
1950	2,380,577	1,062,762	333	—	3,444,578	58·9
1960	2,817,223	1,122,596	749	2,004	3,943,116	67·7
			All others			
1970	3,391,242	1,187,149	11,184		4,589,575	79·0
Male	1,391,735	532,509	1,669		1,925,913	—
Female	1,425,488	590,087	1,628		2,017,203	—

Of the 1970 population, 2,759,255 (60%) were urban (55·3% in 1960); those 21 years of age and over numbered 2,685,290; foreign-born whites, 32,988.

The largest cities are: Atlanta (capital), with population, 1970 census, of 496,953 (urbanized area, 1,370,164); Columbus, 154,168 (193,190); Savannah, 118,349 (187,767); Macon, 122,423 (206,423); Augusta, 59,864 (164,437); Albany, 72,623 (89,369).

CONSTITUTION AND GOVERNMENT. A new constitution was ratified in the general election of 2 Nov. 1976, proclaimed on 22 Dec. 1976 and became effective 1 Jan. 1977. The General Assembly consists of a Senate of 56 members and a House of Representatives of 180 members, both elected for 2 years. The Governor and Lieut.-Governor are elected for 4 years. Legislative sessions are annual, beginning the 2nd Monday in January and lasting for 40 days.

Georgia was the first state to extend the franchise to all citizens 18 years old and above. The state is represented in Congress by 2 senators and 10 representatives.

Registered voters, 1976, numbered 2,178,623. At the 1976 presidential election Carter polled 979,409 votes, Ford 483,743.

The state capital is Atlanta. Georgia is divided into 159 counties.

Governor: George Busbee (D.), 1975–78 ($50,000)
Lieut.-Governor: Zell Miller (D.) ($25,000).
Secretary of State: Ben W. Fortson, Jr (D.) ($35,000).

BUDGET. For the fiscal year ending 30 June 1976 general revenue was $2,796,628,651 ($1,685,039,494 from taxes and $827,095,069 in federal aid); general expenditure was $2,766,605,213 out of total available funds of $3,214,678,810.

On 30 June 1976 net long-term debt, reserves, balances and surplus was $3,250,939,753.

Estimated *per capita* personal income (1976), was $5,571.

NATURAL RESOURCES

Minerals. Georgia is the leading producer of kaolin; production 1975 had a value of $177·6m. The state ranks first in production of crushed and dimensional granite, second in production of fuller's earth and marble (crushed and dimensional).

Mineral products, 1976, had a record value of $389·2m.

Agriculture. In 1977, 70,000 farms had an area of 17m. acres; average farm was of 243 acres. For 1976 cotton output was 199,000 bales (of 480 lb.) (valued at $59·3m.). Other crops, 1976, included tobacco, 123·8m. lb ($138·3m.); corn, 133·9m. bu. ($176·2m.); peanuts, 1,554m. lb. ($311·5m.); pecans, 52m. lb. ($40m.). Cash income, 1976, $2,279m: from crops, $1,103·3m.; from livestock, $1,165·7m.

On 1 Jan. 1977 farm animals included 2·3m. all cattle, including 129,000 milch cows, 3,600 sheep, 34m. chickens and 1·6m. swine.

Forestry. The national forest area in 1974 was 855,000 acres.

INDUSTRY. In 1976 the state had approximately 7,489 manufacturing establishments employing 461,907 workers; the value added by manufacture was $9,785·3m. in 1975.

COMMUNICATIONS

Roads. Total road mileage (1976) was 101,656 (city, county and state); paved mileage totalled 55,976. Motor vehicles registered, 1976, numbered 3,706,288.

Railways. In 1976 there were 5,417 miles of railways.

Aviation. Airports numbered 140 (107 publicly owned, 33 privately owned but open to the public) in 1977.

Shipping. The principal port is Savannah.

JUSTICE, RELIGION, EDUCATION AND WELFARE

Justice. State prisons, 1 Sept. 1977, had 11,800 inmates. Since 1964 there have been no executions. From 1924 to 1964 there were 415 executions (electrocution), including 75 whites and 268 Negroes for murder, 3 whites and 63 Negroes for rape and 6 Negroes for armed robbery.

Under a Local Option Act, the sale of alcoholic beverages (not including malt beverages and light wines) is prohibited in more than half the counties.

Religion. An estimated 78% of the population are church members. Of the total population, 74·3% are Protestant, 3·2% are Roman Catholic and 1·5% Jewish.

Education. Since 1945 education has been compulsory; tuition is free for pupils between the ages of 6 and 18 years. At the end of the 1975–76 school year the 346 high schools, 33 junior high schools, 1,287 elementary schools and 104 combination junior high and elementary schools had 1,192,129 pupils and 54,673 teachers and principals. Teachers' salaries averaged $10,729. Integration in public schools is now an accepted practice.

The University of Georgia (Athens) was founded in 1785 and was the first chartered State University in the US. Other institutions of higher learning include Georgia Institute of Technology (Atlanta), Emory University (Atlanta), Agnes Scott College (Decatur), Georgia College (Milledgeville), Georgia State University (Atlanta) and Mercer University (Macon). The Atlanta University Center, devoted primarily to Negro education, includes Clark College and Morris Brown College, co-educational, Morehouse, a liberal arts college for men, Interdenominational Theological Center, a co-educational theological school, and Spelman College, the first liberal arts college for Negro women in the US. Atlanta University serves as the graduate school centre for the complex. Wesleyan College near Macon is the oldest chartered women's college in the US. Total enrolment, 1976–77, was 166,756 in 61 institutions of higher education.

Health. Hospitals licensed by the Department of Human Resources, 1 July 1977, numbered 222 with 38,941 beds.

Social Security. In Aug. 1977, 85,235 persons were receiving old-age assistance of an average $84.77 per month; 83,413 families were receiving as aid to dependent children an average of $105.61 per family; aid to the blind went to 2,733 persons (averaging $131.33 monthly); aid to 73,678 disabled persons was $121.70 monthly.

Books of Reference

Georgia Statistical Abstract. Univ. of Georgia, Athens. Annual

Official Register. Dept. of Archives and History. Atlanta. Irregular

Gosnell, C. B., and Anderson, C. D., *The Government and Administration of Georgia*. New York, 1956

Range, W., *A Century of Georgia Agriculture*. Univ. of Georgia, Athens, 1954

Rowland, A. R., *A Bibliography of the Writings on Georgia History*. Hamden, Conn., 1966

Saye, A. B., *A Constitutional History of Georgia, 1732–1945*. Univ. of Georgia, Athens 1948

State Library: Judicial Building, Capital Sq., Atlanta. *State Librarian:* John D. M. Folger.

HAWAII

HISTORY. The Hawaiian Islands, formerly known as the Sandwich Islands, were discovered by Capt. James Cook in Aug. 1778. During the greater part of the 19th century the islands formed an independent kingdom, but in 1893 the reigning Queen, Liliuokalani (died 11 Nov. 1917), was deposed and a provisional government formed; in 1894 a Republic was proclaimed, and in accordance with the request of the people of Hawaii expressed through the Legislature of the Republic, and a resolution of the US Congress of 6 July 1898 (signed 7 July by President McKinley), the islands were on 12 Aug. 1898 formally annexed to the US. On 14 June 1900 the islands were constituted as a Territory of Hawaii.

Statehood was granted to Hawaii on 18 March 1959.

AREA AND POPULATION. The Hawaiian Islands lie in the North Pacific Ocean, between 18° 50′ and 28° 15′ N. lat. and 154° 40′ and 178° 15′ W. long., about 2,090 nautical miles south-west of San Francisco. There are more than 20 islands in the group, of which 7 are inhabited. The land and inland water area of the state is 6,424 sq. miles, with census population, 1 April 1970, of 769,913, an increase of 137,141 or 21·7% since 1960; density was 119·8 per sq. mile. Estimated population (1974) 846,900.

The principal islands are Hawaii, 4,038 sq. miles (population, 1970, 63,468); Manui, 729 (38,961); Oahu, 608 (630,528); Kauai, 553 (29,524); Molokai, 261 (5,261); Lanai, 140 (2,204); Niihau, 73 (237); Kahoolawe, 45 (0). The capital

Honolulu, on the island of Oahu, had a population in 1970 of 324,871 and Hilo on the island of Hawaii, 27,072.

Figures for racial groups, 1970, are: 298,160 Caucasians, 7,573 Negroes, 1,126 Indians, 217,307 Japanese, 52,039 Chinese, 93,915 Filipinos, 98,441 all others. Of the total, approximately 89% were citizens of the US.

Inter-marriage between the races is popular. Of the 9,647 persons married in the calendar year 1974, 40·1% married a wife or husband of a different race. Births, 1977, were 17,024; deaths, 4,723; infant deaths, 208; marriages, 10,274; divorces and annulments, 4,653.

CONSTITUTION AND GOVERNMENT. The constitution took effect on 21 Aug. 1959.

The Legislature consists of a Senate of 25 members elected for 4 years, and a House of Representatives of 51 members elected for 2 years. The constitution provides for annual meetings of the legislature with 60-day regular sessions. The Governor and Lieut.-Governor are elected for 4 years. The registered voters, 1974, numbered 343,404.

The state sends to Congress 2 senators and 2 representatives.

In the 1976 presidential election Carter polled 147,375 votes, Ford 140,003.

Governor: George R. Ariyoshi (D.), 1975–78 ($50,000).

BUDGET. Revenue is derived mainly from taxation of sales and gross receipts, real property, corporate and personal income, and inheritance taxes, licences, public land sales and leases. For the year ending 30 June 1974 state general fund receipts amounted to $687m.; special fund receipts, $208,383,000, and federal grants, $224·8m. State expenditures were $898,884,000 (education, $306,376,000; highways, $16,166,000; public welfare, $118,154,000; figures include both special and general funds).

Net long-term debt, 31 Dec. 1974, amounted to $1,274·4m.

Estimated *per capita* personal income (1974) was $8,494.

NATURAL RESOURCES

Minerals. Total value of mineral production, 1974, amounted to $42·7m. Cement shipped from plants amounted to 490,000 short tons (valued at $16·6m.); stone, 8·09m. short tons (value $23·3m.).

Agriculture. Farming is highly commercialized, aiming at export to the American market, and highly mechanized. In 1974 there were 4,300 farms with an acreage of 2·3m. Of the total farms (1964), 88 were under managers, 3,659 were farmed by their owners and 1,117 by tenants; the average farm was of 484·1 acres.

Sugar and pineapples are the staple crops. Income from crop sales, 1974, was $516m., and from livestock, $58m. The sugar crop was valued at $442m.; pineapple, $41m.; vegetables and melons, $10m.; flowers and foliage, $5·3m. Coffee and rice production have declined sharply, but macadamia nuts have increased in importance. For the local market (1974) Hawaii produced 42·4% of fresh vegetable needs, 34·3% of fresh fruit, 100% of milk, 35·2% of meat, 18·4% of poultry meat and 91·4% of eggs.

Forestry. Commercial forests totalled 1·1m. acres (1975); state lands, 1·5m. acres. Land held by the federal government totalled 355,769 acres in 1968.

INDUSTRY AND TRADE

Industry. In 1974 manufacturing establishments employed 22,790 production workers who earned an estimated $190·2m.; in 1972 value added by manufacture was estimated at $412·3m.

Commerce. In 1973 imports of newsprint, fertilizer, lumber, feed, crude oil and other products from foreign countries such as Saudi Arabia, Indonesia and Japan exceeded $272·6m. In 1973 exports, primarily food and manufactures, amounted to $438·7m. About 87% of Hawaii's overseas trade is with the mainland USA.

Tourism. Tourism is an outstanding factor in Hawaii's economy. Tourist arrivals numbered 109,798 in 1955, and reached 2,786,000 in 1974. Tourist expenditures, totalling $55m. in 1955, contributed $1,100m. to the state's economy in 1974.

COMMUNICATIONS

Roads. In Dec. 1974 there were 484,448 passenger motor cars, and a total of 3,600 miles of highways (including 1,085 miles of federally assisted highways and federal highways in national parks).

Aviation. Ten scheduled and 2 non-scheduled airlines connect Hawaii with US, British Columbia, the Antipodes and the Orient. In 1974 passengers overseas numbered 6·9m., and there were 5·2m. passengers between the islands. Overseas cargoes amounted to 44,000 tons. Five scheduled and 2 irregular air carriers operated between the islands. There are 14 commercial airports.

Shipping. Several lines of steamers connect the islands with the mainland USA, Canada, Australia, the Philippines, China and Japan. In 1974, 1,587 overseas vessels entered and cleared the port of Honolulu; cargoes carried, 8·2m. tons. A barge navigation company provides communication between the islands.

Post. There were 567,685 telephones at 1 Jan. 1976.

JUSTICE, RELIGION, EDUCATION AND WELFARE

Justice. There is no capital punishment in Hawaii.

Religion. The residents of Hawaii are mainly Christians, though there are many Buddhists. There were (1972) about 834 churches in the state, 69 of which are Roman Catholic. Roman Catholics number about 220,000, Mormons about 30,000, Congregationalists about 12,000.

Education. Education is free, and compulsory for children between the ages of 6 and 18. The language in the schools is English. In 1974–75 there were 225 public schools (176,844 pupils with 7,711 teachers) and 120 private schools (34,858 pupils) ranging from kindergarten through the 12th grade. The expenditure for public instruction in 1974 was $221,923,654. The University of Hawaii, founded in 1907, had 21,526 day students in 1975; total university and college attendance, 45,600.

Social Security. During 1974 the state spent $111,627,000 (excluding administrative costs); the federal government met 41% of this fund. In 1973 there were 30 non-military hospitals (4,304 beds in 1973) listed by the Department of Health. During 1974 there were 21,713 recipients of assistance given by the state. Welfare costs in 1974 were $111·6m. with an average payment to each case of $238.

Books of Reference

Government in Hawaii. Tax Foundation of Hawaii. Honolulu, 1971
Guide to Government in Hawaii. 5th ed. Legislative Reference Bureau. University of Hawaii, Honolulu, 1972
All About Hawaii: Thrum's Hawaiian Annual and Standard Guide. Honolulu, 1875 to date
Current Hawaiiana (quarterly bibliography). Hawaii Library Association, Honolulu
The State of Hawaii Data Book 1974: A Statistical Abstract. Dept. of Planning and Economic Development, Honolulu, 1974
Allen, G. E., *Hawaii's War Years.* 2 vols. Hawaii Univ. Press, 1950–52
Catton, M. M. L., *Social Service in Hawaii.* Palo Alto, 1959
Day, A. Grove, *Hawaii and Its People.* New York, 1955.—and Stroven, C., *A Hawaiian Reader.* New York, 1961
Fodor, E., ed., *Hawaii, 1965.* New York, 1965
Fuchs, L. E., *Hawaii Pono: A Social History.* New York, 1961
Kamins, Robert M., *Hawaii's Revised Tax System.* Honolulu, 1957
Kuykendall, R. S., and Day, A. G., *Hawaii, A History.* Rev. ed. New Jersey, 1961
Lind, A. W., *Hawaii's People.* Honolulu, 1955
Mann, A. F., *Hawaii: The Fiftieth State: Government and Economy.* Honolulu, 1960
Pukui, M. K., and Elbert, S. H., *Hawaiian–English Dictionary.* Honolulu, 1957
Smith, Branford, *Yankees in Paradise: The New England Impact on Hawaii.* Philadelphia, 1956

IDAHO

HISTORY. Idaho was first permanently settled in 1860, although there was a mission for Indians in 1836 and a Mormon settlement in 1855. It was organized as a Territory in 1863 and admitted into the Union as a state on 3 July 1890.

AREA AND POPULATION. Idaho is bounded north by Canada, east by the Rocky Mountains of Montana and Wyoming, south by Nevada and Utah, west by Oregon and Washington. Area, 83,557 sq. miles, of which 849 sq. miles are inland water. In 1970 the federal government owned 33,979,389 acres (64% of the state area). Census population, 1 April 1970, 713,008, an increase of 6·8% since 1960. Estimate (1976), 821,000.

Births, 1975, 16,242 (19·8 per 1,000 population); deaths, 6,505 (7·9); infant deaths, 214 (13·2 per 1,000 live births); marriages, 12,688 (15·5); divorces, 5,203 (6·2).

Population in 5 census years (with distribution by sex, 1970) was:

	White	*Negro*	*Indian*	*Asiatic*	*Total*	*Per sq. mile*
1910	319,221	651	3,488	2,234	325,594	3·9
1930	438,840	668	3,638	1,886	445,032	5·4
1950	581,395	1,050	3,800	2,392	588,637	7·1
1960	657,383	1,502	5,231	2,958	667,191	8·1
1970	693,375	3,655	5,413	2,526	713,008	8·5
			All others			
Male	350,613		5,123		355,736	—
Female	352,146		4,685		356,831	—

Of the total 1970 population, 588,387 (80%) were urban (57·5% in 1960). Those 20 years of age or older were 431,343, foreign-born whites numbered 12,572.

The largest cities are Boise (capital) with 1970 census population of 85,142; Pocatello, 40,036; Idaho Falls, 35,776; Twin Falls, 21,914; Nampa, 20,768.

CONSTITUTION AND GOVERNMENT. The constitution adopted in 1890 is still in force; it has had 79 amendments. A new constitutional study is under revision. The Legislature consists of a Senate of 35 members and a House of Representatives of 70 members, all the legislators being elected for 2 years. Annual sessions last for 60 days and 30 days for extraordinary sessions. The Governor, Lieut.-Governor and Secretary of State are elected for 4 years. Voters are citizens, over the age of 18 years. The state is represented in Congress by 2 senators and 2 representatives.

In the 1976 presidential election Ford polled 204,151 votes, Carter 126,549.

The state is divided into 44 counties. The capital is Boise.

Governor: John V. Evans (D.), 1977–78 ($33,000).
Lieut.-Governor: William J. Murphy (D.), 1977–78 ($8,000).
Secretary of State: Pete Cenarrusa (R.), 1967–78 ($21,500).

BUDGET. For the year ending 30 June 1976 (State Treasurer's Office) general revenues were $227·3m. and general expenditures included education, $104m., highways, $93·67m., and public welfare, $108·8m.

Per capita personal income (1975) was $5,159.

NATURAL RESOURCES

Minerals. Production of the most important minerals (1976): Lead, 52,870 short tons, ranking second in US; silver, 11·55m. troy oz.; zinc, 46,640 short tons, ranking fifth in US. Other minerals produced included phosphate rock, cobalt and antimony, columbium–tantalum, copper, gold, mercury, nickel, rare-earth metals, tungsten, thorium barite and clays. Beryllium ore has recently been discovered. Value of total mineral output was $219m.

Agriculture. Agriculture is the leading industry, although a great part of the state is naturally arid. Extensive irrigation works have been carried out, bringing an estimated 2·9m. acres under irrigation; 83 reservoirs have a total capacity of 10·4m. acre-ft, 7·3m. acre-ft of which is primarily used for irrigation.

In 1977 there were 26,900 farms with a total area of 15·6m. acres (32% of the land area); average farm had 580 acres with land and buildings valued at approximately $130,012,000.

On 30 June 1976 there were 57 soil conservation districts, managed by local farmers and ranchers, embracing 52·69m. acres.

Cash income, 1975, from major crops and livestock $1,323m. The most important crop is potatoes—leading all states; in 1976 the production amounted to 85·2m. cwt. Other crops are wheat, sugar-beet, alfalfa, oats, barley, field peas, dry beans, apples, prunes and hops. On 1 Jan. 1976 the number of sheep was 520,000; milch cows, 149,000; all cattle, 1·9m.; swine, 90,000.

Forestry. In 1976 a total of 21,815,000 acres (almost 41% of the state's area) was in forests; 73% of this was in commercial production. The volume of sawtimber in commercial forests was 126,801m. bd ft; of growing stock, 26,514 cu. ft. The value of forest products is about $247·7m. per annum, and an additional $112m. is added by process. Ownership of commercial forests is 75% federal, 6% state, 19% private. Some 14,800 workers are involved in forestry.

INDUSTRY. In 1977 there were about 1,265 manufacturing establishments and they employed 53,000 production workers; value added by manufacture (1976) was $821m.

COMMUNICATIONS

Roads. The state maintained in 1975, 4,985 miles of roads of the total of 57,498 miles of public roads. On 31 Dec. 1975, 548,757 passenger vehicles were registered.

Railways. The state had (1970) 3,073 miles of railways operated by 3 companies.

Aviation. There were, 1976, 138 airports.

Shipping. Water transport is provided from the Pacific to Lewiston, by way of the Columbia and Snake rivers, a distance of 480 miles.

JUSTICE, RELIGION, EDUCATION AND WELFARE

Justice. The death penalty is mandatory for first degree murder, but has been used sparingly. Since 1926 only 3 men (white) have been executed, by hanging (2 in 1951 and 1 in 1957).

The state prison, 1 Aug. 1976, had 679 inmates.

Religion. The leading religious denomination is the Church of Jesus Christ of Latter Day Saints (Mormon Church), with 191,286 adherents; Roman Catholics had 53,104; Methodists, 19,017; Presbyterians, 14,130, Episcopalians, 5,000, and Lutherans, 4,602.

Education. In 1975–76 public elementary schools (grades 1 to 6) had 99,922 pupils and 4,354 classroom teachers; secondary schools had 96,694 pupils and 4,776 classroom teachers.

Average salary, 1975–76, of elementary and secondary classroom teachers, $10,255. The University of Idaho, founded at Moscow in 1889, had 342 professors in 1976 and 8,476 students. There are 10 other institutions of higher education; 6 of them are public institutions with a total enrolment (1975–76) of 23,686 (excluding vocational-technical colleges).

Social Welfare. Old-age assistance is granted to needy persons 65 years of age. In June 1976, 1,366 persons were drawing an average of $53.75 per month; 6,517 families with 13,425 children were drawing an average of $243.51; 24 blind persons, $49.58; 1,595 persons permanently and totally disabled, $54.69.

Health. In 1975, 37 hospitals (2,543 beds) were listed by the American Hospitals Association. In 1975 there were 158 patients in mental hospitals and 747 in institutions for the mentally retarded.

Books of Reference

Biennial Report. Secretary of State. Boise
Idaho. Idaho First National Bank
Idaho's Yesterdays. State Historical Society. Quarterly
Incredible Idaho. Division of Tourism and Industrial Development. Quarterly
Prospectus: Idaho. Division of Tourism and Industrial Development, 1976
Martin and Barber, *Idaho in the Pacific Northwest*. Boise, 1956

ILLINOIS

HISTORY. Illinois was first discovered by Joliet and Marquette, two French explorers, in 1673, and settled in 1720. In 1763 the country was ceded by the French to the British. In 1783 Great Britain recognized the title of the US to Illinois, which was organized as a Territory in 1809 and admitted into the Union on 3 Dec. 1818.

AREA AND POPULATION. Illinois is bounded north by Wisconsin, north-east by Lake Michigan, east by Indiana, south-east by the Ohio River (forming the boundary with Kentucky), west by the Mississippi River (forming the boundary with Missouri and Iowa). Area, 56,400 sq. miles, of which 470 sq. miles are inland water. Census population, 1970, 11,113,976, an increase of 10·21% since 1960. Estimate, July 1975, 11,206,393. Births in 1976 were 170,257; deaths, 101,417; infant deaths, 2,731; marriages, 11,261; divorces, 50,043.

Population in 5 census years (with distribution by sex, 1970) was:

	White	*Negro*	*Indian*	*All others*	*Total*	*Per sq. mile*
1910	5,526,962	109,049	188	2,392	5,638,591	100·6
1930	7,295,267	328,972	469	5,946	7,630,654	136·4
1950	8,064,058	645,980	1,443	18,695	8,712,176	155·8
1960	9,010,252	1,037,470	4,704	28,732	10,081,158	180·3
			All others			
1970	9,600,381	1,425,674	87,921		11,113,976	199·4
Male	4,674,899	673,097	5,463	38,377	5,391,836	—
Female	4,925,482	752,577	5,950	38,131	5,722,140	—

Of the total population in 1970, 9,229,321 persons (83%) were urban (80·7% in 1960); 6,756,755 were 21 years of age or older; foreign-born whites numbered 2,139,784 in 1970.

The most populous cities with population (1970 census), are:

Chicago	3,366,957	Cicero	67,058	Moline	46,237
Rockford	147,370	Waukegan	65,269	Quincy	45,288
Peoria	126,963	Oak Park	62,511	Danville	42,570
Springfield (cap.)	91,753	Oaklawn	60,305	Park Ridge	42,466
Decatur	90,397	Des Plaines	57,239	Belleville	41,699
Joliet	80,378	Champaign	56,532	Chicago Heights	40,900
Evanston	79,808	Elgin	55,691	Granite City	40,440
Aurora	74,182	Berwyn	52,502	Alton	39,700
East St Louis	69,996	Elmhurst	50,547	Bloomington (1965)	39,992
Skokie (1964)	68,627	Rock Island	50,166	Galesburg	36,290

Standard Metropolitan Statistical Area population (1970 census): Chicago, 6,979,000; St Louis, Mo.–Ill., 2,363,000; Davenport–Rock Island–Moline, Iowa–Ill., 363,000; Peoria, 342,000; Rockford, 272,000.

CONSTITUTION AND GOVERNMENT. The present constitution became effective 1 July 1971. The General Assembly consists of a House of Representatives of 177 members, elected for 2 years and a Senate of 59 members who serve 2 terms of 4 years and 1 of 2 years during a decade. Sessions are annual. The Governor and Lieut.-Governor are elected as a team for 4 years; the Comptroller and Secretary of State are elected for 4 years. Electors are citizens 18 years of age, having the usual residential qualifications.

The state is divided into legislative districts, in each of which 1 senator and 3 representatives are chosen; for the election of the latter each elector has 3 votes, of which he may cast 3 for 1 candidate or distribute them equally among no more than 3 candidates.

Illinois is represented in Congress by 2 senators and 24 representatives.

In the 1976 presidential election Ford polled 2,384,269 votes, Carter 2,271,295.

The capital is Springfield. The state has 102 counties.

Governor: James R. Thompson (R.), 1977–79 ($50,000).
Lieut.-Governor: Dave O'Neal (R.), 1977–79 ($37,500).
Secretary of State: Alan J. Dixon (D.), 1977–79 ($42,000).

BUDGET. For the year ending 30 June 1976 general revenues were $13,715m. and general expenditures were $13,550m.

Total net long-term debt, 1 July 1977, was $2,870·3m.

Per capita personal income (1974) was $5,107.

ENERGY AND NATURAL RESOURCES

Minerals. Chief mineral product is coal; 55 operative mines had an output (1975) of 59·5m. tons. Mineral production also included: Crude petroleum, 26·1m. bbls; fluorspar, 99,898 short tons. Total value of mineral products, 1974, was $988·1m.

Agriculture. In 1976, 122,000 farms had an area of 29·1m. acres; the average farm was 239 acres.

Cash receipts, 1975, from crops, $3,513·4m.; from livestock and livestock products, $1,891·5m. Illinois is a large producer of soybeans, the state's leading cash commodity. Output, 1976, was 291·8m. bu. Other crops were, in 1975–76, maize, 1,194·8m. bu.; wheat, 70·3m. bu; potatoes, hay, barley, rye and buckwheat are also grown. In Jan. 1976 there were 244,000 milch cows, 3·4m. all cattle, 180,000 sheep and 5·6m. swine. The wool clip in 1977 (estimate) was 1·32m. lb.

Forestry. National forest area under the US Forest Service administration, 1976, was 255,320 acres.

INDUSTRY AND TRADE

Industry. In 1974, 18,638 manufacturing establishments employed 1,306,000 workers, earning $12,780·4m.; value added by manufacture was $25,863·7m. Largest industry was machinery (excluding electrical). Pig-iron production in 1974 was 7·17m. short tons; steel, 12,939,000 net tons.

Labour. In 1974, 57,031 retail establishments had total sales of $5,663m. and 711,456 employees; 20,208 wholesale establishments had total sales of $11,498m. and 291,454 employees; 54,326 selected service establishments with total receipts of $10,703m. employed 726,894 persons. In May 1975 there were 4,311,400 employees on non-agricultural payrolls. In 1973 there were 945,400 production workers in manufacturing earning $8,657,400.

In 1974 the seaport of Chicago handled exports of 594,291 short tons and imports of 1·23m. short tons. Overseas grain exports were 481,424 short tons.

COMMUNICATIONS

Roads. In 1976 there were 10·9m. passenger vehicles, 15,840 trucks and buses, 924,372 trailers and 688,992 motor cycles registered in the state. In 1976 there were 20,769 miles of state administered main roads, 18,114 miles of state administered rural roads and 416,618 miles of locally administered roads. There were 4,652 miles of interstate or freeway roads.

Railways. There were 1975, 13,868 miles of main line railway.

Aviation. There were (1976) 510 certified airports, 125 heliports and 569 restricted landing areas.

Post. In 1976 there were 9,110,273 telephones in the state.

JUSTICE, RELIGION, EDUCATION AND WELFARE

Justice. In 1970 there were no executions; since 1930 there have been 90 executions (electrocution), including 58 white men, 1 white woman and 31 Negro men, all for murder. In 1976 the total average daily prison population was 9,500.

A Civil Rights Act (1941), as amended, bans all forms of discrimination by places of public accommodation, including inns, restaurants, retail stores, railroads, aeroplanes, buses, etc., against persons on account of 'race, religion, colour, national ancestry or physical or mental handicap'; another section similarly mentions 'race or colour'.

The Fair Employment Practices Act of 1961, as amended, prohibits discrimination in employment based on race, colour, sex, religion, national origin or ancestry, by employers, employment agencies, labour organizations and others. These principles are embodied in the 1971 constitution.

Religion. Among the larger religious denominations (1976) are: Roman Catholic, 9,051,153; Jewish, 6,115,000; United Presbyterian Church, USA, 1,040,444; Lutheran Church in America, 782,558; Lutheran Church Missouri Synod, 723,787; American Baptist, 500,000; Disciples of Christ, 124,120; Methodist, 114,007.

Education. Education is free and compulsory for children between 7 and 16 years of age. In 1976 there were 1,025 school districts. Public school elementary enrolments (1976–77) were 1,506,052 pupils and 65,368 teachers; secondary enrolments, 732,077 pupils and 34,326 teachers. Enrolment (1976–77) in non-public schools was 274,038 elementary and 98,717 secondary. Teachers' salaries, 1976–77, averaged $13,100 (elementary) and $13,800 (secondary). Total expenditure on public schools, 1976–77, $1,808m. Total enrolment in institutions of higher education (autumn 1976) was 665,997.

Colleges and universities with over 3,000 students:

Founded	*Name*	*Place*	*Control*	*Autumn 1976 Enrolment*
1851	Northwestern University	Evanston	Methodist	15,225
1857	Illinois State University	Normal	Public	20,443
1867	University of Illinois	Urbana	Public	62,015
1869	Chicago State University[1]	Chicago	Public	6,880
1869	Southern Illinois University	Carbondale	Public	34,626
1870	Loyola University	Chicago	Roman Catholic	14,380
1890	University of Chicago	Chicago	Non-Sect.	9,310
1895	Eastern Illinois University	Charleston	Public	9,923
1895	Northern Illinois University	DeKalb	Public	25,586
1897	Bradley University	Peoria	Non-Sect.	4,820
1898	DePaul University	Chicago	Roman Catholic	11,052
1899	Western Illinois University	Macomb	Public	14,768
1940	Illinois Institute of Technology[2]	Chicago	Non-Sect.	6,737
1945	Roosevelt University	Chicago	Non-Sect.	7,413
1961	Northeastern Illinois University[3]	Chicago	Public	10,040
1970	Sangamon State University	Springfield	Public	3,792

[1] Formerly Illinois Teachers College (South).
[2] Illinois Institute of Technology formed in 1940 by merger of two older technical schools.
[3] Formerly Illinois Teachers College (North).

Health. In 1975–76 hospitals listed by the American Hospital Association numbered 469, with 99,781 beds. In 1976 state institutions for the mentally retarded had 6,653 residents and state hospitals for the mentally ill, 5,474.

Social Security. In June 1975, 27,280 persons were drawing old age assistance totally $3·3m., 804,865 were drawing aid to dependent children totalling $89·9m., 1,434 persons blind assistance totalling $0·2m. and 73,021 persons assistance to the disabled totalling $13·3m.

Books of Reference

Blue Book of the State of Illinois. Edited by Secretary of State. Springfield. Biennial
Federal Writers' Project. *Illinois: A Descriptive and Historical Guide.* Rev. ed. Chicago, 1947

Angle, P. M., and Beyer, R. L., *A Handbook of Illinois History*. Illinois State Historical Society. Springfield, 1943
Pease, T. C., *The Story of Illinois*. 3rd ed. Chicago, 1965

The Illinois State Library: Centennial Building, Springfield. *Librarian:* Michael J. Howlett.

INDIANA

HISTORY. Indiana, first settled in 1732–33, was made a Territory in 1800 and admitted into the Union on 11 Dec. 1816.

AREA AND POPULATION. Indiana is bounded west by Illinois, north by Michigan and Lake Michigan, east by Ohio and south by Kentucky across the Ohio River. Area, 36,291 sq. miles, of which 194 sq. miles are inland water. Census population, 1 April 1970, was 5,193,669, an increase of 531,171 or 11·4% since 1960. Estimated population (1977), 5·33m. In 1976 (provisional figures) births were 80,260 (15·1 per 1,000 population); deaths, 46,712 (8·8); infant deaths, 1,143 (14·2 per 1,000 live births); marriages, 53,359 (10·6).

Population in 5 census years (with distribution by sex, 1970) was:

	White	*Negro*	*Indian*	*Asiatic*	*Total*	*Per sq. mile*
1910	2,639,961	60,320	279	316	2,700,876	74·9
1930	3,125,778	111,982	285	458	3,238,503	89·4
1950	3,758,512	174,168	438	1,106	3,934,224	108·7
1960	4,388,554	269,275	948	2,447	4,662,498	128·9
			All others			
1970	4,820,324	357,464	15,881		5,193,669	143·9
Male	2,351,540	171,942	7,688		2,531,170	—
Female	2,468,784	185,522	8,193		2,662,499	—

Of the total in 1970, 3,372,060 (65%) were urban (62·4% in 1960); in 1970, 3,072,025 were 21 years of age or older; foreign-born whites numbered 78,232.

The largest cities with population (census 1970, revised) are: Indianapolis (capital), 744,624; Fort Wayne, 177,671; Gary, 175,415; Evansville, 138,764; South Bend, 125,580; Hammond, 107,790; Anderson, 70,787; Terre Haute, 70,286; Muncie, 69,080; East Chicago, 46,982; Lafayette, 44,955; Kokomo, 44,042; Richmond, 43,999; Elkhart, 43,152.

CONSTITUTION AND GOVERNMENT. The present constitution (the second) dates from 1851; it has had (as of 1977) 33 amendments. The General Assembly consists of a Senate of 50 members elected for 4 years, and a House of Representatives of 100 members elected for 2 years.

A constitutional amendment of 1970 allows the legislators to set the length and frequency of sessions, which are currently held annually. The Governor and Lieut.-Governor are elected for 4 years. The state is represented in Congress by 2 senators and 11 representatives.

In the 1976 presidential election Ford polled 1,183,958 votes, Carter 1,014,714.

The state capital is Indianapolis. The state is divided into 92 counties and 1,008 townships.

Governor: Otis Bowen (R.), 1977–81 ($36,000 plus $6,000 expenses).
Lieut.-Governor: Robert D. Orr (R.), 1977–81 ($23,500).
Secretary of State: Larry Conrad (D.), 1974–78 ($23,500).

BUDGET. In the fiscal year 1975–76 (US Census Bureau figures) general revenues were $3,117m. ($726m. from federal government, $1,915·55m. from taxes), general expenditures were $3,096m. ($1·35m. for education, $360·6m. for public welfare and $498·2m. for highways).

Total long-term debt, on 30 June 1976, was $585·5m.

Per capita personal income (1976) was $6,222.

ENERGY AND NATURAL RESOURCES

Minerals. The state provided 47% of all limestone and dolomite (building stone) used or shipped by producers in the US in 1974. In 1974 the output of coal was 23,726,000 short tons; petroleum, 4·92m. bbls (of 42 gallons); stone, 31·03m. short tons. The total mineral output in 1974 was valued at $440·7m.

Agriculture. Indiana is largely agricultural, about 75% of its total area being in farms. In 1976, 104,000 farms had 17·4m. acres (average, 167 acres). Cash income, 1976, from crops, $1,996m.; from livestock and products, $1,334·8m.

The chief crops (1976) were maize (693m. bu.), winter wheat (57·6m. bu.), oats (10·6m. bu.), soybeans (108·2m. bu.), popcorn (127·4m. lb.); rye, barley, hay (alfalfa, clover, timothy), lespedeza seed, mint, clover seed, apples, strawberries, tomatoes, water-melons and tobacco.

The livestock on 1 Jan. 1977 included 2·13m. all cattle, 213,000 milch cows, 187,000 sheep and lambs, 4m. swine, 16·9m. chickens. In 1976 the wool clip yielded 1·38m. lb. of wool from 182,000 sheep.

Forestry. The national forests area, 30 Sept. 1976, was 180,077 acres; 13 state forests totalled 140,548 acres in Dec. 1976.

INDUSTRY. Manufacturing establishments employed, in 1975, 469,500 workers, earning $5,154·4m.; value added by manufacture was $13,289·6m. The steel industry is the third largest in the country. Production of pig-iron, 1974, was 17m. short tons. Refinery production, 1974, included 80m. bbls of petrol.

COMMUNICATIONS

Roads. In 1976 there were 963 miles of interstate highways; 157 miles, toll road; 9,853 miles, other state highways; 80,518 miles, county roads and city streets. Motor vehicles registered, 1975, 3,772,173.

Railways. In 1975 there were 6,357 miles of railway.

Aviation. Of airports, 1977, 140 were for public use and 1 was military.

JUSTICE, RELIGION, EDUCATION AND WELFARE

Justice. In 1963–75 there were no executions; since 1930 there were 41 executions (electrocution), namely, 31 whites and 10 Negroes for murder. State correctional institutions, 1976–77, had daily average of 5,521 inmates.

The Civil Rights Act of 1885 forbids places of public accommodation to bar any persons on grounds not applicable to all citizens alike; no citizen may be disqualified for jury service 'on account of race or colour'. An Act of 1947 makes it an offence to spread religious or racial hatred.

A 1961 Act provided 'all . . . citizens equal opportunity for education, employment and access to public conveniences and accommodations' and created a Civil Rights Commission.

Religion. Religious denominations include Methodists, Roman Catholic, Disciples of Christ, Baptists, Evangelical United Brethren, Presbyterian churches, Society of Friends.

Education. School attendance is compulsory from 7 to 16 years of age. In 1976–77 public elementary schools, nursery school to grade 6, had 581,135 pupils and 24,157 teachers; public secondary schools, grades 7 to 12, had 554,177 pupils and 24,397 teachers. Teachers' salaries, 1976–77, averaged $12,666. Total expenditure for public schools, 1975–76, $609m.

The principal institutions for higher education are (1976):

Founded	*Institution*	*Control*	*Teachers*	*Students (full-time)*
1824	Indiana University, Bloomington	State	2,878	76,905
1837	De Pauw University, Greencastle	Methodist	170	2,412
1942	University of Notre Dame	R.C.	660	6,847
1850	Butler University, Indianapolis	—	235	4,300

Founded	Institution	Control	Teachers	Students (full-time)
1859	Valparaiso University, Valparaiso	Evangelical Lutheran Church	339	3,517
1870	Indiana State University, Terre Haute	State	750	11,012
1874	Purdue University, Lafayette	State	2,475	40,284
1898	Ball State University, Muncie	State	889	18,972

Health. Hospitals listed by the Indiana State Board of Health (1977) numbered 121 (24,094 beds). On 30 June 1977, 12 state mental hospitals had 9,877 patients enrolled (6,250 present).

Social Security. Old-age assistance, assistance to the blind and to the disabled were transferred from state to federal programmes in June 1974. In July–Dec. 1976, state supplemental assistance and/or Federal Supplemental Security Insurance was paid to an average of 21,273 elderly persons per month (total \$8·1m.), 1,078 blind (\$675,303) and 19,567 disabled (\$11m.). Assistance was given to 57,209 families with 172,880 dependent children, at an average of \$70.98 per family per month.

Books of Reference

Indiana State Chamber of Commerce. *Here is Your Indiana Government.* 18th ed. Indianapolis, 1977

Martin, J. B., *Indiana: An Interpretation.* New York, 1947

State Library: Indiana State Library, 140 North Senate, Indianapolis 46204. *Acting Director:* Miss Jean Jose.

IOWA

HISTORY. Iowa, first settled in 1788, was made a Territory in 1838 and admitted into the Union on 28 Dec. 1846.

AREA AND POPULATION. Iowa is bounded east by the Mississippi River (forming the boundary with Wisconsin and Illinois), south by Missouri, west by the Missouri River (forming the boundary with Nebraska), north-west by the Big Sioux River (forming the boundary with South Dakota) and north by Minnesota. Area, 56,290 sq. miles, including 247 sq. miles of inland water. Census population, 1 April 1970, 2,825,041, an increase of 2·4% since 1960. Population (1975 estimate), 2·86m. Births, 1977, were 45,270; deaths, 26,355; infant deaths, 5·43; marriages, 26,422; dissolutions, 10,938.

Population in 5 census years (with distribution by sex, 1960) was:

	White	Negro	Indian	Asiatic	Total	Per sq. mile
1870	1,188,207	5,762	48	3	1,194,020	21·5
1930	2,452,677	17,380	660	222	2,470,939	44·1
1950	2,599,546	19,692	1,084	620	2,621,073	46·8
1960	2,729,286	25,354	1,708	1,022	2,757,537	49·2
			All others			
1970	2,782,762[1]	32,596[1]	9,018[1]		2,825,041	50·5
Male	1,344,933	12,373	1,741		1,359,047	—
Female	1,383,776	12,981	1,733		1,398,490	—

[1] Preliminary figure.

At the census of 1970, 1,616,405 persons (57·2%) were urban (53% in 1960).

The largest cities in the state, with their census population in 1970 (and estimated population, 1975), are: Des Moines (capital), 200,587 (194,168); Cedar Rapids,

110,642 (108,998); Davenport, 98,469 (99,941); Sioux City, 85,925 (85,719); Waterloo, 75,533 (77,681); Dubuque, 62,309 (61,754); Council Bluffs, 60,348 (58,660); Iowa City, 46,850 (47,899); Ames, 39,505 (43,412); Clinton, 34,719 (33,794); Burlington, 32,366 (29,806); Fort Dodge, 31,263 (30,173); Mason City, 30,491 (30,556); Ottumwa, 29,610 (26,601).

CONSTITUTION AND GOVERNMENT. The constitution of 1857 still exists; it has had 34 amendments. The General Assembly comprises a Senate of 50 and a House of Representatives of 100 members, meeting annually for an unlimited session. Senators are elected for 4 years, half retiring every second year: representatives for 2 years. The Governor and Lieut.-Governor are elected for 4 years. The state is represented in Congress by 2 senators and 6 representatives. Iowa is divided into 99 counties; the capital is Des Moines.

In the 1976 presidential election Ford polled 631,667 votes, Carter 618,898.

Governor: Robert Ray (R.), 1975–78 ($55,000).
Lieut.-Governor: Arthur Neu (R.) ($18,000).
Secretary of State: Melvin D. Synhorst (R.) ($30,000).

BUDGET. For fiscal year 1976 state tax revenue was $1,062m. General expenditures were $1,771m. (education, $774·7m.; highways, $248·7m.; public welfare, $236·1m.; health and hospitals, $96·4m.).

On 30 June 1974 the net long-term debt was $129·2m.

Per capita personal income (1976) was $6,245.

ENERGY AND NATURAL RESOURCES

Minerals. The leading products by value are cement (2·23m. tons in 1975) and stone (30·36m. tons in 1975). Coalfields produced 622,000 tons in 1975. The value of mineral products, 1974, was $165·9m.

Agriculture. Iowa is the wealthiest of the agricultural states, partly because nearly the whole area (95·5%) is arable and included in farms. It has escaped large-scale commercial farming. The average farm (in 1977) was 261 acres.

In 1977, 131,000 farms had 34·2m. acres of farm land.

The national forest area in 1970 was 360 acres.

Cash farm income (1976) was $7,009m. (ranks second); from livestock, $4,042m. (leading all states), and from crops, $2,968m. Production of maize in 1975 was 1,092m. bu. (ranks first). Commercial meat production in 1974 totalled 6,019·3m. lb. On 1 Jan. 1976 livestock included swine, 12·6m. (leading all states); milch cows, 392,000; all cattle, 7·5m. (second only to Texas), and sheep and lambs, 320,000. The wool clip (1974) yielded 3·88m. lb. of wool from 516,000 sheep.

INDUSTRY. In 1975 manufacturing establishments employed 229,600 people with average weekly earnings of $214.38, value added by manufacture was $7,018·2m. in 1975.

COMMUNICATIONS

Roads. On 1 Jan. 1975 the number of miles of state park and institutional roads was 273·63 miles; rural road, 98,763·56 miles, and municipal road, 13,967·18 miles.

Railways. The state, 1975, had 11,286·85 miles of Class I railway, 428·42 miles of Class II railway and 34 miles of electric railway.

Aviation. Airports (1975), numbered 233, including 123 municipal and 110 private and commercial.

JUSTICE, RELIGION, EDUCATION AND WELFARE

Justice. There is now no capital punishment in Iowa. State prisons, 30 June 1976, had 1,913 inmates.

Religion. Chief religious bodies in 1975 were: Roman Catholic (528,244 members); United Methodists, 296,500; American Lutheran, 200,992 baptised members; United Presbyterians, 100,891; United Church of Christ, 54,900.

Education. School attendance is compulsory for 24 consecutive weeks annually during school age (7–16). In 1975–76 of the 809,817 persons between the ages of 5 and 21 years, 603,919 were attending public schools; 59,989 pupils were enrolled in private and parochial schools. In 449 high school districts there were 358,566 elementary and 305,342 secondary pupils. Classroom teachers (1975–76) numbered 33,237 with average salary of $11,570. Total expenditure on public schools in 1975–76 was $879,416,000. Leading institutions for higher education (1975–76) were:

Founded	*Institution*	*Control*	*Professors and instructors*	*Students (full-time)*
1847	University of Iowa, Iowa City	State	1,007	22,512
1847	Grinnell College, Grinnell	Congregational	106	1,150
1852	Wartburg College, Waverly	—	75	1,453
1853	Cornell College, Mount Vernon	Methodist	77	893
1858	Iowa State University, Ames	State	1,151	21,105
1876	Univ. of Northern Iowa, Cedar Falls	State	528	9,287
1881	Drake University, Des Moines	Private	290	6,836
1881	Coe College, Cedar Rapids	Presbyterian	68	1,213
1894	Morningside College, Sioux City	Methodist	73	1,502

Health. In 1970, the state had 146 hospitals (21,862 beds). On 30 June 1976 hospitals for mental diseases had 1,017 patients.

Social Security. Iowa has a Civil Rights Act (1939) which makes it a misdemeanour for any place of public accommodation to deprive any person of 'full and equal enjoyment' of the facilities it offers the public.

Old-age assistance was established in 1934 for citizens 65 years of age or older; in Aug. 1976, 16,062 persons were drawing an average of $70.90 per month. Aid to dependent children, established 1944, was received by 30,496 families ($272.69 per family) representing 96,080 persons; aid to disabled was paid to 12,347 persons (average, $98.80); 963 recipients of aid to the blind averaged $117.69.

Books of Reference

Statistical Information: State Departments of Health, Public Instruction and Social Services; State Aeronautics, Commerce and Development Commissions; Crop and Livestock Reporting Services, Des Moines; State Highway Commission, Ames; Geological Survey, Iowa City.

Official Register. Secretary of State. Des Moines. Biennial
Petersen, W. J., *Iowa History Reference Guide*. Iowa City, 1952

Iowa State Library: Des Moines 50319. *Librarian:* Frances Desmond.

KANSAS

HISTORY. Kansas, first settled in 1727, was made a Territory (along with part of Colorado) in 1854, and was admitted into the Union with its present area on 29 Jan. 1861.

AREA AND POPULATION. Kansas is bounded north by Nebraska, east by Missouri, with the Missouri River as boundary in the north-east, south by Oklahoma and west by Colorado. Area, 82,264 sq. miles, including 216 sq. miles of inland water. Census population, 1 April 1970, 2,249,071, an increase of 3·23% since 1930. Vital statistics, 1975: Births, 32,386 (14·3 per 1,000 population); deaths, 21,176 (9·3); infant deaths, 405 (12·5 per 1,000 live births); marriages, 23,887 (10·5); divorces 12,565 (5·5).

Population in 5 federal census years (with distribution by sex, 1960) was:

	White	*Negro*	*Indian*	*Asiatic*	*Total*	*Per sq. mile*
1870	346,377	17,108	914	—	364,399	4·5
1930	1,811,997	66,344	2,454	204	1,880,999	22·9
1950	1,828,961	73,158	2,381	431	1,905,299	23·2
1960	2,078,666	91,445	5,069	2,271	2,178,611	26·3
			All others			
1970	2,122,068	106,977	17,533		2,249,071	27·5
Male	1,031,409	45,743	4,225		1,081,377	—
Female	1,047,257	45,702	4,275		1,097,234	—

Of the total population in 1960, 1,328,741 were urban (61% compared with 52·1% in 1950). Households were 672,907. Those 21 years of age or older numbered 1,321,835; foreign-born whites numbered 31,098.

Cities, with 1970 census population, are Wichita, 276,554; Kansas City, 168,213; Topeka (capital), 125,011; Overland Park, 79,034; Lawrence, 45,698; Salina, 37,714; Hutchinson, 36,885.

CONSTITUTION AND GOVERNMENT. The year 1861 saw the adoption of the present constitution; it has had 54 amendments. The Legislature includes a Senate of 40 members, elected for 4 years, and a House of Representatives of 125 members, elected for 2 years. Sessions are annual. The Governor and Lieut.-Governor are elected for 2 years. The right to vote (with the usual exceptions) is possessed by all citizens. The state is represented in Congress by 2 senators and 5 representatives.

The state was the first (of 42 states) to establish in 1933 a Legislative Council of 10 senators and 15 representatives to sit continuously between sessions for the study of legislative problems.

In the 1976 presidential election Ford polled 501,759 votes, Carter 429,003.

The capital is Topeka. The state is divided into 105 counties.

Governor: Robert F. Bennett (R.), 1975–78 ($35,000).
Lieut.-Governor: Shelby Smith (R.) ($12,275).
Secretary of State: Elwill M. Shanahan (R.) ($18,500).

BUDGET. For the year ending 30 June 1974 (US Census Bureau figures) general revenue was $1,234,503,000, of which taxation furnished $702,709,000. General expenditures were $1,112,219,000 ($439m. for education, $182,529,000 for highways and $160,696,000 for public welfare).

Total net long-term debt, 30 June 1974, amounted to $174·57m.

Per capita personal income (1969) was $3,488.

ENERGY AND NATURAL RESOURCES

Minerals. Important minerals are coal, petroleum, natural gas, lead and zinc.

Agriculture. Kansas is pre-eminently agricultural, but sometimes suffers from lack of rainfall in the west. In 1974, 83,000 farms had an area of 49·9m. acres; average farm (1969) was 568 acres, value of lands and buildings (1959) $48,084; in 1959, 10,070 farms had 1,000 acres or more and 10,562 farms had 49 acres or less. The national grassland area, 30 June 1968, was 107,708 acres.

Cash income, 1974, from crops was $2,140m.; from livestock and products, $1,835.

Kansas is a great wheat-producing state. Its output in 1969 was 305·3m. bu. Other crops in 1969 (in bushels) were maize, 91·5m.; grain sorghums, 182·9m.; soybeans, 19·6m.; oats, 6·08m.; barley, 6·11m.; rye, 1·12m. The state has an extensive livestock industry, comprising, on 1 Jan. 1970, 224,000 milch cows, 6,016,000 all cattle, 378,000 sheep and lambs and 1,643,000 swine. Wool clip (1969), 2,944,000 lb. from 352,000 sheep.

INDUSTRY. In 1967 there were 2,564 manufacturing establishments, 107,000 production workers earned $655m.; value added by manufacture was $2,108m. The slaughtering industry, manufacture of transport equipment and petroleum refining are important.

COMMUNICATIONS

Roads. The state in 1974 had 10,891 miles of roads and streets and 32,329 miles of federally-aided highways.

Railways. There were 7,621 miles of railway in 1974.

Aviation. There were 272 airports in 1969, of which 119 were public and 163 were private.

JUSTICE, RELIGION, EDUCATION AND WELFARE

Justice. There were 2,042 sentenced prisoners in state institutions, Dec. 1969. The death penalty (by hanging) for murder was abolished in 1907 and restored in 1935; there were no executions in 1968; total executions 1934 to 1968 have been 15 (all for murder).

For the various Civil Rights Acts forbidding racial or political discrimination, *see* THE STATESMAN'S YEAR-BOOK, 1955, p. 666. The 1965 Kansas Act against Discrimination declared that it is the policy of the state to eliminate and prevent discrimination in all employment relations, and to eliminate and prevent discrimination, segregation or separation in all places of public accommodations covered by the Act.

Religion. The most numerous religious bodies are Roman Catholic, with 157,292 adherents in 1936, Methodists (140,792), and Disciples of Christ (65,740). Total membership, all denominations, was 691,438.

Education. In 1974–75 organized school districts had 449,564 enrolled pupils in elementary and secondary schools. There were 113,352 students in higher education.

Kansas has 6 state supported institutions of higher education: the University of Kansas, Lawrence, founded in 1865; Kansas State University of Agriculture and Applied Science, Manhattan (1863); Kansas State Teachers' College, Emporia (1865); Kansas State College of Pittsburg, Pittsburg (1903); Fort Hays State College, Hays (1901) and Wichita State University (1964), an associate of the University of Kansas. There is one municipal university, Washburn University, Topeka (1944).

Health. In 1969 the state had 165 hospitals (19,900 beds) listed by the American Hospital Association; psychiatric hospitals had an average daily census of 4,317.

Social Security. In June 1975, 103,142 persons received state and federal aid under programmes of aid to the aged, blind or disabled, aid to dependent children, general assistance, and medical assistance. Total payments amounted to $7,386,396.

Books of Reference

Annual Economic Report of the Governor. Topeka

Directory of State Officers, Boards and Commissioners and Interesting Facts Concerning Kansas. Topeka. Biennial

Drury, J. W., *The Government of Kansas.* Lawrence, Univ. of Kansas, 1970

Hornbaker, Allison L., *The Kansas Mineral Industry, 1967.* Lawrence, Univ. of Kansas, State Geological Survey, 1968

Howes, C. C., *This Place Called Kansas.* Univ. of Oklahoma, Norman, Okla., 1952

Zornow, W. F., *Kansas: A History of the Jayhawk State.* Norman, Okla., 1957

State Library: Kansas State Library, Topeka. *State Librarian:* Denny Stephens.

KENTUCKY

HISTORY. Kentucky, first settled in 1765, was originally part of Virginia; it was admitted into the Union on 1 June 1792 and its first legislature met on 4 June.

AREA AND POPULATION. Kentucky is bounded north by the Ohio River (forming the boundary with Illinois, Indiana and Ohio), north-east by the Sandy River (forming the boundary with West Virginia), east by Virginia, south by Tennessee and west by the Mississippi River (forming the boundary with Missouri). Area, 39,655 sq. miles, of which 544 sq. miles are water. Census population, 1970, 3,219,311, an increase of 6% since 1960. Births in 1976, 55,198 (16·3 per 1,000 population); deaths, 32,267 (9·5); infant deaths, 810 (14·7 per 1,000 live births); marriages, 32,931 (9·7); divorces, 16,051 (4·7).

Population in 4 census years (with distribution by sex, 1970) was:

	White	*Negro*	*All others*	*Total*	*Per sq. mile*
1930	2,388,452	226,040	97	2,614,589	65·2
1950	2,742,090	201,921	195	2,944,806	73·9
1960	2,820,083	215,949	1,689	3,038,156	75·6
1970	2,971,425	241,448	6,438	3,219,311	79·7
Male	1,464,399	111,642	2,995	1,579,036	—
Female	1,517,367	119,151	3,152	1,639,670	—

Of the total population in 1970, 1,684,053 (52·3%) were urban (44·5% in 1960). Those 21 years old or older numbered 1,918,642; foreign-born whites numbered 16,096.

The principal cities with census population in 1970 are: Louisville, 361,706 (urbanized area, 695,055); Lexington, 108,137 (urbanized area, 174,323); Covington, 52,535; Owensboro, 50,329; Bowling Green, 36,705; Paducha, 31,627; Ashland, 30,386; Frankfort (capital), 21,902.

CONSTITUTION AND GOVERNMENT. The constitution dates from 1891; there had been 3 preceding it. The 1891 constitution was promulgated by convention and provides that amendments be submitted to the electorate for ratification. The General Assembly consists of a Senate of 38 members elected for 4 years, one-half retiring every 2 years, and a House of Representatives of 100 members elected for 2 years. Sessions are biennial. The Governor and Lieut.-Governor are elected for 4 years. All citizens are (with necessary exceptions) qualified as electors; the voting age was in 1955 reduced from 21 to 18 years. Registered votes, Oct. 1977: 1,847,960. In the presidential election of 1976: Carter polled 615,717 votes, Ford 531,852.

The state is represented in Congress by 2 senators and 7 representatives.

The capital is Frankfort. The state is divided into 120 counties.

Governor: Julian M. Carroll (D.), 1975–79 ($35,000).
Lieut.-Governor: Thelma Stovall (D.) ($29,294).
Secretary of State: Drexall Davis (D.) ($29,294).

BUDGET. For the fiscal year ending 30 June 1975 general revenues were $2,073m. (federal grants, $469·4m., and taxes, $1,270·9m.). General expenditures for the year ending 30 June 1974, $1,522·4m. (education, $696·5m.; public welfare, $413·4m.; highways, $412·5m.).

The total net long-term debt on 30 June 1974 was $1,678·5m.

Per capita personal income (1973) was $3,967.

ENERGY AND NATURAL RESOURCES

Minerals. The principal mineral product of Kentucky is coal, 143·6m. tons mined in 1975. Output of petroleum, 7·6m. bbls (of 42 gallons); natural gas, 60·5m. cu. ft; stone, 31·7m. short tons; clay 778,000 short tons in 1975. Total value of mineral products in 1975 was $2,738·9m. Other minerals include fluorspar, ball clay, lead, zinc, cement, natural gas liquids and quartzite.

Agriculture. In 1976, 124,000 farms had an area of 16m. acres. The average farm was 129 acres.

Cash income, 1976, from crops, $896,536,000, and from livestock $729,592,000. The chief crop is tobacco: production, in 1976, 425·1m. lb., ranking second to N. Carolina in US. Other principal crops include corn, hay, soybeans, wheat, sorghum grain, rye, barley, popcorn and oats.

Stock-raising is important in Kentucky, which has long been famous for its horses. The livestock on 1 Jan. 1976 included 287,000 milch cows, 3·45m. all cattle, 33,000 sheep, 1m. swine.

Forestry. National forests area, 1975, 648,000 acres. Total commercial forest land, 1975, 11,763,000 acres; almost 93% is privately owned.

INDUSTRY. In 1976 the state's 3,150 manufacturing plants had 273,508 production workers earning $3,100m.; value added by manufacture in 1975 was $7,400m. The leading manufacturing industries are electrical equipment, apparel and other fabric products, non-electrical machinery and foods.

COMMUNICATIONS

Roads. In 1977 the state had over 70,000 miles of federal, state and local roads. There were, 1974, 2,273,036 motor vehicle registrations.

Railways. In 1976 there were 4,669 miles of railway.

Aviation. There were 69 certified airports in 1977, of which 57 were public owned and public used, 8 were commercial, 6 privately owned and for public use, 6 privately owned for private use and 2 military. There were 2 heliports.

Shipping. There is an increasing amount of barge traffic on 1,300 miles of navigable rivers.

JUSTICE, RELIGION, EDUCATION AND WELFARE

Justice. There are 5 correctional institutions and 2 camps for adults. Juvenile offenders are placed in custody of the Bureau for Social Services, Department for Human Resources, which maintains 20 institutions.

In 1974–75 the prisons had an average of 3,049 inmates. There has been no execution since 1962. Total executions, 1911–62, were 162, including 76 whites and 86 Negroes; 144 were for murder, 13 for rape, 5 for armed robbery.

Religion. The chief religious denominations in 1971 were: Baptists (Southern and General), with 844,933 members, Roman Catholic (339,375), Methodists (214,322), Christian Church and Disciples of Christ (72,276). Total, all denominations, about 1,764,374.

Education. Attendance at school between the ages of 7 and 15 years (inclusive) is compulsory, the normal term being 9½ months. In 1976–77, 17,840 teachers were employed in public elementary and 10,948 in secondary schools, in which 438,085 and 255,876 pupils enrolled respectively. Expenditure on elementary and secondary day schools in 1976–77 was $734m.; public school classroom teachers' salaries (1976–77) averaged $10,950. There were also 3,788 teachers working in private elementary and secondary schools with 76,465 students.

The state has 23 universities and senior colleges, 7 junior colleges and 14 community colleges, with a total (autumn 1976) of 124,984 students. Of these universities and colleges, 22 are state-supported, and the remainder are supported privately. The largest of the institutions of higher learning are (autumn 1976): University of Kentucky, with 22,887 students; University of Louisville, 16,300 students; Western Kentucky University, 13,336 students; Eastern Kentucky University, 13,510 students; Murray State University, 8,030 students; Morehead State University, 7,572 students; Northern Kentucky University, 6,407 students. Four of the several privately endowed colleges of standing are Berea College, Berea; Centre College, Danville, Transylvania University, Lexington, and Bellarmine College, Louisville.

Health. In 1977 the state had 109 general hospitals (14,136 beds), 25 hospitals for mental diseases (2,641 beds), 4 respiratory disease hospitals (313 beds) and 2 children's hospitals (164 beds).

There are 4 rehabilitation hospitals with 213 beds.

Welfare. In June 1977 there were 306,887 persons receiving financial assistance; 100,810 of these persons received the Federal Supplemental Security Income (SSI);

54,317 of them were aged, 2,187 blind, 44,306 disabled. The average monthly SSI payment in each group is as follows: $91 to aged, $147 to blind and $129 to disabled. Also, in the all state funded Supplementation programme payments were made to 8,988 persons, of which 7,541 received SSI, the rest being all State Supplementation. Among the SSI category 1,177 were aged, 104 blind, and 261 disabled. The average State Supplementation payment is $97.54 to aged, $72.10 to blind and $104.73 to disabled.

In the Aid to Families with Dependent Children Programme as of June 1977, aid was given to 204,630 persons in 67,522 families. The average payment per person was $56.15. (Included in this figure are the 6,236 cases receiving under the Unemployment Father segment of the AFDC Programme which was discontinued in July 1977 when employment rates improved.)

In addition to money payments, medical care services are available to all grant recipients as well as an additional 51,313 persons eligible for medical care only. The average monthly cost for those receiving services is approximately $90.43.

Books of Reference

Deskbook of Kentucky Economic Statistics. 11th ed. Department of Commerce, Frankfort, 1974

Directory for the Use of Courts, State and County Officials and General Assembly of the State of Kentucky. Frankfort. Biennial

Vital Statistics. Kentucky Department for Human Resources, 66th Annual Report, 1973

Federal Writers' Project. *Kentucky: A Guide to the Bluegrass State.* Rev. ed. New York, 1954

Coleman, J. W., *A Bibliography of Kentucky History.* Univ. of Kentucky, Lexington, 1949

Schwendeman, J. R., *Geography of Kentucky.* Oklahoma City, 1958

LOUISIANA

HISTORY. Louisiana was first settled in 1699. That part lying east of the Mississippi River was organized in 1804 as the Territory of New Orleans, and admitted into the Union on 30 April 1812. The section west of the river was added very shortly thereafter.

AREA AND POPULATION. Louisiana is bounded north by Arkansas, east by Mississippi, with the Mississippi River forming the boundary in the north-east, south by the Gulf of Mexico and west by Texas, with the Sabine River forming most of the boundary. Area, 48,523 sq. miles, including 3,417 sq. miles of inland water. Census population, 1 April 1970, 3,641,306, an increase of 11·8% since 1960. Births, 1975, 67,394 (17·8 per 1,000 population); deaths, 33,597 (8·9); infant deaths, 1,198 (17·8 per 1,000 live births); marriages, 36,789; divorces (1972), 10,771.

Population in 5 census years (with distribution by sex, 1970) was:

	White	*Negro*	*Indian*	*Asiatic*	*Total*	*Per sq. mile*
1910	941,086	713,874	780	648	1,656,388	36·5
1930	1,322,712	776,326	1,536	1,019	2,101,593	46·5
1950	1,796,683	882,428	409	3,996	2,683,516	59·4
1960	2,211,715	1,039,207	3,587	2,004	3,257,022	72·2
			All others			
1970	2,541,498	1,086,832	12,976		3,641,306	81·1
Male	1,249,632	515,231	6,621		1,771,484	—
Female	1,291,866	571,601	6,355		1,869,822	—

Of the 1970 total, 2,406,150 (66·1%) were urban (63·3% in 1960); those 21 years of age or older were 2,040,776; foreign-born whites numbered 36,146.

The largest cities with their 1970 census population are: New Orleans, 593,471 (urban area, 1,045,809); Shreveport, 182,064 (294,703); Baton Rouge (capital), 165,963 (285,167); Lake Charles, 77,998; Lafayette, 68,908; Monroe, 56,374; Bossier City, 41,595; Alexandria, 41,557.

CONSTITUTION AND GOVERNMENT. The present constitution dates from 1974.

The Legislature consists of a Senate of 39 members and a House of Representatives of 105 members, both chosen for 4 years. Sessions are annual; a fiscal session is held in odd years. The Governor and Lieut.-Governor are elected for 4 years. A Governor may serve a second consecutive term. Qualified electors are (with the usual exceptions) all registered citizens with the usual residential qualifications.

In the 1976 presidential election Carter polled 683,512 votes, Ford 606,204.

The state sends to Congress 2 senators and 8 representatives. Louisiana is divided into 64 parishes (corresponding with the counties of other states).

The capital is Baton Rouge.

Governor: Edwin W. Edwards (D.), 1975–78 ($50,000).
Lieut.-Governor: James Fitzmorris (D.), 1975–78 ($40,000).
Secretary of State: Paul Hardy (D.), 1975–78 ($35,000).

BUDGET. For the fiscal year ending 30 June 1974 (Louisiana Division Administration figures) general revenues were $2,302,164,349, of which $517,613,350 were federal funds; general expenditures were $2,157,676,820 (education, $812,354,952; transport and public works, $358,728,169; health, hospitals and public welfare, $534,663,320).

Per capita personal income (1973) was $3,931.

ENERGY AND NATURAL RESOURCES

Minerals. Louisiana is second only to Texas as a petroleum-producing state. The yield in 1971 of crude petroleum was 935m. bbls; natural gas, 8m. cu. ft. Rich sulphur mines are found in the state, and wells for the extraction of sulphur by means of hot water and compressed air are in operation; output, 1970, 3·6m. long tons. Output of salt (1970) was 13·58m. short tons. Total mineral output in 1971 was valued at $5,553m. ranking second in the US.

Agriculture. The state is divided into two parts, the uplands and the alluvial and swamp regions of the coast. A delta occupies about one-third of the total area. Manufacturing is the leading industry, but agriculture is important. In 1974 there were 48,000 farms covering 11·8m. acres; average farm, 246 acres.

Cash income, 1974, from crops $1,045·2m.; from livestock, $335·5m. Production of sugar-cane was 7m. tons; rice, 24·7m. cwt; grain, 4·7m. bu.; sweet potatoes, 3·7m. cwt; soybeans, 44·9m. bu.; pecans, 3m. lb.; cotton, 560,000 bales (of 500 lb.); strawberries, 5·5m. lb. On 1 Jan. 1974 the state contained 137,000 milch cows, 1·7m. all cattle, 18,000 sheep and 175,000 swine.

Forestry. Forests, 14·5m. acres, represent 47% of the state's area. Income from manufactured products exceeds $1,300m. annually. In 1974 pulpwood cut, 3,754,240 cords; sawtimber cut, 1,193·5m. bd ft.

INDUSTRY. The manufacturing industries are chiefly those associated with petroleum, chemicals, lumber, food, paper. In 1970 manufacturing establishments employed 173,107 workers, who earned $1,351,473,466.

COMMUNICATIONS

Roads. The state has more than 52,000 miles of public roads. In 1975, 1,607,866 automobiles were registered in the state.

Railways. In 1974 the railways in the state had a length of about 3,700 miles.

Aviation. There were, 1972, 240 commercial and private airports.

Shipping. New Orleans is the second largest seaport of the US handling some 10% of the national total. The Mississippi and other waterways provide 7,500 miles of navigable water.

JUSTICE, RELIGION, EDUCATION AND WELFARE

Justice. Prisons, Oct. 1975, had 5,082 inmates.

Since 1961 there have been no executions; total executions by electrocution since 1930 were 135 (30 whites and 105 Negroes—including 17 Negroes for rape).

Whites and Negroes are no longer segregated in educational institutions, mental hospitals and penal institutions. Interracial marriages and adoptions are legal.

Religion. The Roman Catholic Church is the largest denomination in Louisiana, with 1,231,378 white and Negro members in 1964. The leading Protestant Churches are Baptist, with 430,557 white members; Methodist, 123,155; Episcopal, 28,095, and Presbyterian, 32,123.

Education. Attendance in elementary schools was, until 1956, compulsory between the ages of 7 and 15, both inclusive; but in 1956 the Legislature exempted any school faced with racial desegregation by court order, and the constitution was amended, giving the Legislature sole control over segregation. In 1960 token integration was enforced in 2 New Orleans primary schools. More than 4 times as much desegregation occurred since 1970 than in all prior history in Louisiana. In 1970–71, two-thirds of all Louisiana public school students were enrolled in schools with at least 10% of both races. More than one-fourth of all Louisiana public school students in 1970–71 were enrolled in schools with at least 30% of both races. Compulsory school attendance was restored in 1966. In 1973–74 there were 1,438 public elementary and high schools which had 870,468 pupils. In 1973–74 instructional staff had an average salary of $9,165. There are 15 four-year-endowed colleges and universities and 34 state trade schools. Total expenditure on elementary and secondary schools (1973–74), $756,007,161. Superior instruction is given in the Louisiana State University (founded 1860), with 42,650 students (1974). Tulane University (1835) in New Orleans had 9,100 students (1974). This university has state support to the extent of the remission of certain taxes. The Roman Catholic Loyola University (1911) at New Orleans had 4,474 students (1974). Dillard University in New Orleans (1,118 students in 1974) and Southern University in Baton Rouge (8,685 students in 1974) were formerly for Negroes.

Health. In 1972 the state had 83 accredited hospitals (16,386,beds); 3 mental hospitals cared for 15,372 patients.

Social Security. In June 1975, 97,569 persons were receiving old-age assistance to the average of $84 per month; 67,675 families with dependent children were receiving an average of $117.61 per month; 2,133 blind persons, $120 per month; 48,971 totally disabled persons, $111.6. Aid was from state and federal sources.

Books of Reference

Louisiana Almanac. 9th ed. 1975–76
Louisiana: History and Government. Legislative Council, Baton Rouge, 1964
Statistical Abstract of Louisiana. Division of Business and Economic Research. University of New Orleans, 1974
Havard, W. C., *Government of Louisiana*. Baton Rouge, 1959
Smith, T. L., and Hitt, H. L., *The People of Louisiana*. Baton Rouge, 1952

MAINE

HISTORY. After a first attempt in 1607, Maine was settled in 1623. From 1652 to 1820 it was part of Massachusetts and was admitted into the Union on 15 March 1820.

AREA AND POPULATION. Maine is bounded west, north and east by Canada, south-east by the Atlantic, south and south-west by New Hampshire. Area, 33,215 sq. miles, of which 2,282 are inland waters. Of the state's total area, about 17·2m. acres (87%) are in timber and wood lots. Census population, 1 April 1970, 993,663, an increase of 2·45% since 1960. Estimate (1974), 1,049,395. In 1977 live births numbered 15,695; deaths, 10,176; infant deaths, 135; marriages, 11,526; divorces, 5,751.

Population for 5 census years (with distribution by sex, 1970):

	White	*Negro*	*Indian*	*Asiatic*	*Total*	*Per sq. mile*
1910	739,995	1,363	892	121	742,371	24·8
1930	795,185	1,096	1,012	130	797,423	25·7
1950	910,846	1,221	1,522	185	913,774	29·4
1960	963,291	3,318	1,879	597	969,265	31·3
			All others			
1970	985,276[1]	2,800[1]	3,972		993,663	32·1
Male	479,241	1,618	2,006		482,865	—
Female	506,035	1,182	1,966		509,183	—

[1] Preliminary.

The urban population was 504,157 or 53·9% of the total (51·3% in 1960); those 21 years or older numbered 595,938.

The largest city in the state is Portland with a census population of 65,120 in 1970. Other cities (with population in 1970) are: Lewiston, 41,780; Bangor, 33,170; Auburn, 24,150; South Portland, 23,270; Augusta (capital), 21,950; Biddeford, 19,980; Waterville, 18,190.

CONSTITUTION AND GOVERNMENT. The constitution of 1820 is still in force, but it has been amended 131 times. In 1951 and 1965 the Legislature approved recodifications of the constitution as arranged by the Chief Justice under special authority.

The Legislature consists of the Senate with 33 members and the House of Representatives with 151 members, both Houses being elected simultaneously for 2 years. Apart from these legislators and the Governor (elected for 4 years), no other state officers are elected. The Justices of the Supreme Judicial Court give their opinion upon important questions of law and upon solemn occasions when required by the Governor, Council, Senate or House of Representatives. The suffrage is possessed by all citizens, 18 years of age; persons under guardianship for reasons of mental illness have no vote. Indians residing on tribal reservations and otherwise qualified have the vote in all county, state and national elections, but retain the right to elect their own tribal representative to the legislature.

In the 1976 presidential election Ford polled 236,320 votes, Carter 232,279, McCarthy 10,874 and Buber 3,495.

The state sends to Congress 2 senators and 2 representatives.

The capital is Augusta. The state is divided into 16 counties.

Governor: James Longley (Ind.), 1975–79 ($35,000).
Secretary of State: Mark Gartley (D.), 1975–79 ($20,000).

BUDGET. For the financial year ending 30 June 1977 total general revenue was $823,361,589 and expenditure was $822,560,923.

Total net long-term debt on 30 June 1977 was $274·8m.

Per capita personal income (1974) was $4,592.

NATURAL RESOURCES

Minerals. Minerals include sand and gravel, 13,583,000 short tons in 1973; stone, lead, clay, copper, peat, silver and zinc. Mineral output, 1973, was valued at $33·5m.

Agriculture. In 1976, 7,600 farms occupied 1·7m. acres; the average farm was 225 acres.

Cash receipts, 1976, $443·1m., of which $138·3m. came from potatoes; Maine is the fourth largest producer of potatoes (about 8% of the country's total); production in 1976 was 27·4m. cwt. Other important items include broilers ($81·6m.), eggs ($105·6m.) and dairy products ($67·4m.); these with potatoes provide 89% of receipts. Sweet corn, peas and beans, oats, hay, apples and blueberries are also grown. On 1 Jan. 1976 the farm animals included 60,000 milch cows, 141,000 all cattle, 12,000 sheep, 7,500 swine.

Forestry. Lumber, wood turnings and pulp are important. In 1976 the cut of softwood was 816,302m. bd ft; hardwood, 164,028m. bd ft, and pulpwood, 2,802,496 cords. Spruce and fir, white pine, hemlock, white and yellow birch, sugar maple, northern white cedar, beech and red oak are the most important species cut. There were (1974) 16,894,300 acres of commercial forest (98% in private ownership). National forests comprise 37,500 acres; other federal, 35,800 acres; state forests, 163,000 acres; municipal, 75,200 acres.

Wood products industries are of great economic importance; in 1972 the paper, lumber and wood industries' production was valued at $943·4m. (38% of total industrial production). There were (1974) 340 primary manufacturers and over 200 secondary.

Fisheries. In 1975, 138,359,242 lb. of fish and shellfish (valued at $48,498,843 were landed; the catch included 17,017,411 lb. of lobsters (valued at $27,478,773). 27m. lb. of sardines were packed in 1975 valued at $27m.

INDUSTRY. In 1975, 2,451 manufacturing establishments reported 99,080 production workers, earning $816·4m., gross value of production, $3,694·5m. (decrease of 2·9% from 1974). Leading industry is paper with 48 plants, 15,358 workers and output valued at $1,195·6m. (32·4% of the state's total manufactures).

COMMUNICATIONS

Roads. In 1975 there were 21,108 miles of roads, of which 3,925 miles were state highways and 7,649 miles were state-aided. In 1975, 1,275,167 motor vehicles were registered, including 465,037 automobiles.

Railways. In 1975 there were 2,357 miles of railway tracks.

Aviation. Commercially licensed airports, 1975, numbered 45, including 3 international, 2 county and 1 state; there were 2 military airports, 90 private landing strips (1 being state-owned), 26 licensed commercial seaplane bases and 45 registered non-commercial seaplane bases.

JUSTICE, RELIGION, EDUCATION AND WELFARE

Justice. The state's penal system in Oct. 1977 held 452 adults in the state prison, 196 in the Correctional Institute and 297 juveniles in the Youth Centre. There is no capital punishment. Inmates serving life sentences are eligible for parole consideration after 15 years, less remission for good conduct, provided they were imprisoned before the passage of a new Criminal Code by the 107th Maine Legislature, which abolished the parole system.

Religion. The largest religious bodies are: Roman Catholic (270,283 members), Baptists (36,808 members) and Congregationalists (40,750 members), and other Christian Churches (34,066 members).

Education. Education is free for pupils from 5 to 21 years of age, and compulsory from 7 to 17. In 1975–76 the 698 public elementary schools had 7,007 teachers and 171,742 enrolled pupils. The 141 public secondary schools had 4,628 teachers and 73,687 pupils. In 1975–76 there were 53 private elementary schools with 417 teachers and 9,144 pupils, and 48 private secondary schools with 414 teachers and 7,666 pupils. Public school teachers' salaries, 1975–76, averaged $10,963. Total public expenditure on public elementary and secondary education in 1975–76, $272,770,505.

The State University of Maine, founded in 1865, had (1973–74) 961 professors, 38 teachers and 17,092 students at 8 locations; Bowdoin College, founded in 1794 at Brunswick, had 112 professors and 1,250 students; Bates College at Lewiston, 100 professors and 1,258 students; Colby College at Waterville, 153 professors and 1,577 students; Nasson College at Springvale, 58 professors and 830 students; Husson College, 50 professors and 900 students; Ricker, 39 professors and 415 students; St Francis, 30 professors and 486 students; Thomas College, 33 professors and 500 students, and Westbrook College at Westbrook, 34 professors and 501 students.

Health. In Dec. 1977 the state had 52 general hospitals including 9 non-accredited,

(4,607 beds); 3 hospitals for mental diseases, acute care (62 beds); 165 nursing homes and units (659 beds).

Social Security. Supplemental Security Income (SSI) (maximum payment for single person, $177.80 per month) is administered by the Social Security Administration. It became effective on 1 Jan. 1974 and replaces former aid to the aged, blind and disabled, administered by the state with state and federal funds. SSI is supplemented by Medicaid for nursing home patients or hospital patients. Payments for SSI recipients for July 1977 totalled $432,227, covering 22,710 cases. Aid to families with dependent children is granted where one or both parents are disabled or absent and income is insufficient; aid was being granted in July 1977 to 18,662 families (39,865 children) with an average payment per family of $210.22 per month. Total aid under the programme, July 1977, $3·7m. Payments under Medical Assistance Programme July 1977 totalled $7,589,893. There is a programme of assistance for catastrophic illness. Child welfare services include basic child protective services, foster home placements, adoptions; services in divorce cases and licensing of foster homes, day care and residential treatment services, and public guardianship.

The Work Incentive Programme served about 6,000 persons through the Employment Security Commission and the Bureau of Social Welfare.

Books of Reference

Maine Register, State Year-Book and Legislative Manual. Tower Publishing, Portland. Annual
Federal Writers' Project. *Maine, a Guide 'Down East'.* Courier Gazette, 1970
Banks, R., ed., *A History of Maine: a Collection of Readings on the History of Maine 1600–1970.* Kendall/Hunt, 1969
Banks, R., *Maine Becomes A State.* Wesleyan U.P., 1970
Day, C. A., *Farming in Maine, 1060–1940.* Univ. Maine Press, 1963
Rowe, W. H., *Maritime History of Maine.* Norton, New York, 1948

MARYLAND

HISTORY. Maryland, first settled in 1634, was one of the 13 original states.

AREA AND POPULATION. Maryland is bounded north by Pennsylvania, east by Delaware and the Atlantic, south by Virginia and West Virginia, with the Potomac River forming most of the boundary, and west by West Virginia. Chesapeake Bay almost cuts off the eastern end of the state from the rest. Area, 12,303 sq. miles, of which 703 sq. miles are inland water; in addition, water area under Maryland jurisdiction in Chesapeake Bay amounts to 1,726 sq. miles. Census population, 1 April 1970, 3,922,399, an increase since 1960 of 821,710 or 26·5%. In 1975 births were 45,501 (11·1 per 1,000 population); deaths, 31,203 (7·6); infant deaths, 573 (12·6 per 1,000 live births); marriages, 44,667 (10·9); divorces, 14,909 (3·6).

Population for 5 federal censuses (with distribution by sex, 1970) was:

	White	*Negro*	*Indian*	*Asiatic*	*Total*	*per sq. mile*
1920	1,204,737	244,479	32	413	1,449,661	145·8
1930	1,354,226	276,379	50	871	1,631,526	165·0
1950	1,954,975	385,972	314	1,084	2,343,001	237·1
1960	2,573,919	518,410	1,538	5,700	3,100,689	314·0
			All others			
1970	3,194,888	499,479	28,032		3,922,399	396·6
Male	1,565,481	336,950	13,890		1,916,321	—
Female	1,629,407	362,529	14,142		2,006,078	—

Of the total population in 1970, 3,003,935 persons (76·6%) were urban (72·7% in 1960); those 21 years old or older numbered 2,342,854; foreign-born whites, 89,977 in 1960.

The largest city in the state (containing 23·1% of the population of the state) is Baltimore, with 905,759 in 1970; population of metropolitan areas around Baltimore and Washington, D.C., was 4,931,793. Maryland residents in the Washington, D.C., metropolitan area total more than 1m.; other cities are Dundalk (85,377); Towson (77,799); Silver Spring (77,496); Bethesda (71,621), Annapolis (capital), 29,592.

CONSTITUTION AND GOVERNMENT. The present constitution dates from 1867; it has had 125 amendments. The General Assembly consists of a Senate of 43, and a House of Delegates of 142 members, both elected for 4 years. Voters are citizens who have the usual residential qualifications.

At the 1976 presidential election Carter polled 735,618 votes, Ford 648,980.

Maryland sends to Congress 2 senators and 8 representatives.

The state capital is Annapolis. The state is divided into 23 counties and Baltimore City.

Governor: Blair Lee, III (D.), 1971 ($24,000).

Secretary of State: Fred L. Wineland ($12,000).

BUDGET. For the fiscal year ending 30 June 1973 general revenues were $1,116,449,704 ($1,067,921,416 from taxation). General expenditures, $1,187,513,626, including $508·2m. for education and $98·9m. for public welfare; special fund expenditures, $569,356,773, including (federal funds) $230,603,744 for highways.

Total authorized long-term state debt, 30 June 1973 was $2,274,823,236. (Issued and outstanding, $1,018,664,000; authorized but not issued, $1,256,159,236.)

Per capita personal income (1972) was $4,897.

ENERGY AND NATURAL RESOURCES

Minerals. Value of mineral production, 1972, was $115·5m. Sand and gravel (12·6m. short tons) and stone (19·4m. short tons) account for over 59% of the total value. Stone is the leading mineral commodity by value followed by Portland cement, sand and gravel and coal. Output of coal was 1·6m. short tons, valued at $8·9m. Natural gas is produced from 2 fields in Garrett County; 244m. cu. ft in 1972. A third gas field in the same county is used for natural gas storage.

Agriculture. Agriculture is an important industry in the state. In 1972 there were approximately 18,000 farms with an area of 3·01m. acres (48% of the land area).

Farm animals, 1 Jan. 1972, were: Milch cows, 149,000; all cattle, 400,000; swine, 206,000; sheep and lambs, 20,000; chickens (not broilers), 2·04m. The most important crops, 1971, were: maize, 37·15m. bu.; soybeans, 6·6m. bu.; tobacco, 28·08m. lb., and hay, 578,000 tons.

Cash receipts from farm marketings, 1970, were $394m.; from livestock and livestock products, $268m., and crops, $126m. Dairy products and broilers accounted for 52% of cash receipts in 1970.

INDUSTRY. In 1971 manufactories had 173,000 production workers earning $1,311m.; value added by manufacture, $4,279·4m. Chief industries are food and kindred products, primary metal products, transport equipment, electrical and other machinery, chemicals and products, printing and publishing.

TOURISM. Tourism is one of the state's leading industries. In 1972 tourists spent over $300m.

COMMUNICATIONS

Roads. The state highway department maintained, 1 Jan. 1973, 5,224 miles of highways, of which 71 miles were toll roads. The 23 counties maintained 15,885 miles of highways, and the 159 municipalities (including the city of Baltimore) maintained 3,719 miles of streets and alleys. Total mileage, 1 Jan. 1973, of public highways, streets and alleys, 24,829 miles. In 1971, 2m. automobiles were registered.

Railways. Railways, in 1970, had 1,110 miles of line.

Aviation. There were, 1972, 41 commercially licensed airports.

Shipping. In 1972 Baltimore was the fourth largest US seaport in foreign waterborne trade.

JUSTICE, RELIGION, EDUCATION AND WELFARE

Justice. Prisons on 30 June 1973 had 5,693 men and 176 women; the total equalled 138 per 100,000 population, a high rate, which may be explained by the fact that Maryland incarcerates domestic relations law violators in state prisons; state prisons also receive a considerable number of persons committed for misdemeanours by magistrates' courts of the counties as well as from Baltimore's court system.

Since 1930 there have been 68 executions (by lethal gas since 1957; earlier by hanging)—7 whites and 37 Negroes for murder, and 6 whites and 18 Negroes for rape. Last execution was June 1961.

Maryland's prison system has conducted a work-release programme for selected prisoners since 1963. All institutions have academic and vocational training programmes.

In accordance with the 1950 Supreme Court decisions declaring segregation unconstitutional, the University of Maryland and other public and private colleges admitted Negro students in Sept. 1956. Elementary and secondary schools accept the ruling, and gradual integration is under way in all counties under different methods.

Religion. Maryland was the first US state to give religious freedom to all who came within its borders. Present religious affiliations of the population are approximately: Protestant, 32%; Roman Catholic, 24%; Jewish, 10%; remaining 34% is non-related and other faiths.

Education. Education is compulsory from 6 to 16 years of age. In Sept. 1972 the public elementary schools (including kindergartens and secondary schools) had 920,896 pupils. Teachers and principals in the elementary schools numbered 23,277; secondary schools had 23,267 teachers. Average salary of principals and teachers in elementary and secondary schools (1971–72) was $10,881. Current expenditure by local school boards on education, 1971–72, was $930·8m., of which the state's contribution was $311·8m.

In 1972 there were 32 degree-granting 4-year institutions and 20 2-year colleges. The largest two were the University of Maryland system, with 55,351 students (Oct. 1972) and Towson State College with 11,391 students (Oct. 1972).

Health. In Jan. 1973, 70 hospitals (25,037 beds) were licensed by the State Department of Health and Mental Hygiene.

The Maryland State Department of Health, organized in 1874, was in 1969 made part of the Department of Health and Mental Hygiene which performs its functions through its central office, 23 county health departments and the Baltimore City Health Department. For the financial year 1973 the department's budget was $335,733,174, of which $294,807,371 were general funds and $18,487,530 special funds appropriated by the General Assembly. The balance of the budget, $22,438,273, derives from federal funds.

During 1973 Maryland's programme of medical care for indigent and medically indigent patients covered an average of 393,974 persons. The programme, which covers inpatient and outpatient hospital services, laboratory services, skilled nursing home care, physician services, pharmacy services, dental services and home health services, cost approximately $130m.

Social Security. Under the supervision of the Department of Employment and Social Services, local social service departments administer public assistance for needy persons. In June 1973, 9,789 persons were receiving old age assistance, with an average of $67.17 per month; 14,369 families were receiving general public assistance, with an average of $99.31; 414 needy blind, $103.05; 19,544 persons permanently and totally disabled, $92.65; 342 employable persons were receiving general public assistance, average $94.93; 62,455 families, $150.20 per family, in respect of 157,671 dependent children and foster care of 9,145 children, average $107.5353.

Books of Reference

Statistical Information: Maryland Department of Economic and Community Development, Annapolis, 21401. *Secretary:* Joseph C. Anastasi.

Maryland Manual: A Compendium of Legal, Historical and Statistical Information Relating to the State of Maryland. Annapolis. Biennial

State Library: Maryland State Library, Annapolis. *Director:* Nelson J. Molter.

MASSACHUSETTS

HISTORY. The first permanent settlement within the borders of the present state was made at Plymouth in Dec. 1620, by the Pilgrims from Holland, who were separatists from the English Church, and formed the nucleus of the Plymouth Colony. In 1628 another company of Puritans settled at Salem, forming eventually the Massachusetts Bay Colony. In 1630 Boston was settled. In the struggle which ended in the separation of the American colonies from the mother country, Massachusetts took the foremost part, and on 6 Feb. 1788 became the sixth state to ratify the US constitution.

AREA AND POPULATION. Massachusetts is bounded north by Vermont and New Hampshire, east by the Atlantic, south by Connecticut and Rhode Island and west by New York. Area, 8,257 sq. miles, 190 sq. miles being inland water (the state government puts the area at 8,093 sq. miles, including 254 sq. miles of water). The census population 1 April 1970 was 5,689,170, an increase of 539,336 or 10·5% since 1960. Births, 1976 were 66,012 (11·4 per 1,000 population); deaths, 53,980 (9·3 per 1,000); infant deaths, 799 (12·1 per 1,000 live births); marriages, 41,501 (7·2); divorces, 16,938 (2·9).

Population at 4 federal census years (with distribution by sex, 1970):

	White	*Negro*	*Other*	*Total*	*Per sq. mile*
1940	4,257,596	55,391	3,734	4,316,721	550·7
1950	4,611,503	73,171	5,840	4,690,514	598·4
1960	5,023,144	111,842	13,592	5,148,578	656·8
1970	5,477,624	175,817	35,729	5,689,170	725·8
Male	2,618,930	82,573	17,895	2,719,398	—
Female	2,858,694	93,244	17,834	2,969,772	—

Of the total population in 1970, 4,810,449 persons (84·6%) were urban (83·6% in 1960); those 18 years old or older numbered 3,813,406.

In 1970 the population of the principal towns and cities was:

Boston	641,071	Lowell	94,239	Lawrence	66,915
Worcester	176,572	Newton	91,263	Chicopee	66,676
Springfield	163,905	Lynn	90,294	Medford	64,397
New Bedford	101,777	Brockton	89,040	Framingham	64,048
Cambridge	100,361	Somerville	88,779	Waltham	61,582
Fall River	96,898	Quincy	87,966	Brookline	58,689

The largest of 10 standard metropolitan statistical areas, 1970 census were: Boston, 2,753,700; Springfield–Chicopee–Holyoke, 529,922; Worcester, 344,320.

CONSTITUTION AND GOVERNMENT. The constitution dates from 1780 and has had 106 amendments. The legislative body, styled the General Court of the Commonwealth of Massachusetts, meets annually, and consists of the Senate with 40 members, elected biennially, and the House of Representatives of 240 (160 from 1979) members, elected for 2 years. The Governor and Lieut.-Governor are elected for 4 years. The state sends 2 senators and 12 representatives to Congress.

At the 1976 presidential election Carter polled 1,391,201 votes, Ford 1,004,598.

Electors are all citizens 18 years of age or older.

The capital is Boston. The state has 14 counties, 39 cities and 312 towns.

Governor: Michael S. Dukakis (D.), 1975–78 ($40,000).
Secretary of the Commonwealth: Paul H. Guzzi (D.) ($30,000).

BUDGET. For the fiscal year ending 30 June 1976 the total revenue of the state was $5,459,703,540 ($2,652·5m. from taxes and $1,316·2m. from federal aid); general expenditures, $4,693,615,522 ($1,243m. for education, $347·5m. for highway and transport construction and $1,260·3m. for public welfare).

The net long-term debt on 30 June 1976 amounted to $2,852·7m.

Per capita personal income (1976) was $6,588.

NATURAL RESOURCES

Minerals. There is little mining within the state. Total mineral output in 1974 was valued at $62m., of which most came from sand, gravel and stone.

Agriculture. On 1 Jan. 1975 there were 5,800 farms (11,179 in 1959) with an area of 710,000 acres. Commercial farms (1974) numbered 4,970, of which 4,347 had gross sales of over $10,000.

Cash income, 1975, totalled $202·2m.; dairy, $58·8m.; greenhouse and nursery, $35·1m.; poultry, $34·4m.; vegetables, $19·7m.; tobacco, $12·8m.; cranberries, $8·7m.; other fruit, $11·2m.; potatoes, $4·2m.; all other, $17·6m.

Principal 1975 crops include cranberries, 810,000 bbls; apples, 2·1m. (42-lb. units); potatoes, 718,000 cwt, and tobacco, 2m. lb. On 1 Jan. 1975 farms in the state had 55,000 milch cows, 107,000 all cattle, 55,000 swine (Dec. 1975), 125,000 turkeys and 2·8m. chickens.

Forestry. State forests cover about 270,000 acres. Commercially important hardwoods are sugar maple, northern red oak and white ash; softwoods are white pine and hemlock. About 100m. bd ft of timber are cut annually.

Fisheries. The 1975 catch amounted to 245·6m. lb. of finfish valued at $51m.; 12·4m. lb. of shellfish ($14·8m.); 1·9m. lb. lobster ($3·3m.).

INDUSTRY. In 1976, 10,043 manufacturing establishments employed an average of 595,425 workers, who earned an annual $7,035·8m.; value added by manufacture (1973) was $11,717·6m. The 5 most important manufacturing groups, based on employment, were electric and electronic equipment, machinery (except electrical), fabricated metal products, instruments and related products, apparel and finished goods.

LABOUR. In July 1977 the work force was 2,751,900. Local unions numbered 2,279 with a combined membership of 583,886; city and state employees forming the largest group. Changes in the industrial pattern have caused the loss of jobs in the shoe and textile industries.

In 1976 there were 129 work stoppages involving 61,200 workers which resulted in 741,600 man-days idle.

COMMUNICATIONS

Roads. In Sept. 1977 the state had 32,867 miles of roads and streets and registered 3·4m. motor vehicles.

Railways. In 1977 there were 1;874 miles of mainline railway.

Aviation. There were, in 1977, 54 aircraft landing areas for commercial operation, of which 25 were publicly owned.

Shipping. The state had 3 deep-water harbours, the largest of which is Boston (port trade (1976), 26,172,442 short tons). Other ports are Fall River and New Bedford.

JUSTICE, RELIGION, EDUCATION AND WELFARE

Justice. On 13 Sept. 1977 state penal institutions held 3,487 inmates. There have been no executions since 1947.

Religion. The principal religious bodies are the Roman Catholics with 2,864,332 members in 1966; Jewish Congregations, 226,000; Methodists, 94,810;

Episcopalians, 102,822; Unitarians, 35,931. Total membership, all denominations, was 3,639,198.

Education. A regulation effective from 1 Sept. 1972 makes school attendance compulsory for ages 6–16. In 1976–77 expenditure by cities and towns on public schools was $2,300m., including $220m. debt retirement and service payments. In 1975–76 there were 61,439 classroom teachers (of whom 2,277 were part-time) and 1,189,160 pupils.

Within the state there were (1976–77) 125 degree-granting institutions of higher learning (including 87 colleges and universities) with about 22,000 full-time staff members and 380,938 students. Some leading institutions are:

Year opened	*Name and location of universities and colleges*	*Students 1976*
1636	Harvard University, Cambridge [1]	20,498
1793	Williams College, Williamstown [1]	1,932
1821	Amherst College, Amherst [1]	1,320
1837	Mount Holyoke College, South Hadley [2]	1,964
1843	College of the Holy Cross, Worcester [1]	2,680
1852	Tufts University, Medford [1, 3]	6,232
1861	Mass, Institute of Technology, Cambridge [1]	8,474
1863	University of Massachusetts, Amherst [1]	26,116
1863	Boston College (RC), Chestnut Hill [1]	13,544
1865	Worcester Polytechnic Institute, Worcester [1]	2,831
1869	Boston University, Boston [1]	24,292
1870	Wellesley College, Wellesley [2]	2,045
1875	Smith College, Northampton [1]	2,559
1879	Radcliffe College, Cambridge [1]	
1885	Springfield College, Springfield [1]	2,842
1887	Clark University, Worcester [1]	2,983
1894	University of Lowell [1]	11,536
1898	Northeastern University, Boston [1, 4]	35,970
1899	Simmons College, Boston [2]	2,625
1948	Brandeis University, Waltham [1]	3,537

[1] Co-educational.
[2] For women only.
[3] Includes Jackson College for women.
[4] Includes Forsyth Dental Center School.

Health. In 1975 the state had 197 hospitals (with 49,171 beds); average daily census, 40,066, of which 11,712 patients were in public and private mental hospitals and 9,742 patients were in institutions for the mentally retarded.

Social Security. The Department of Public Welfare had an appropriation of $1,379m. in 1976 and paid $422m. in aid to families with dependent children (average 111,000 families per month); other main items were general relief (average 28,805 cases), Supplemental Security Income (average 127,000 cases) and Medical Assistance (average 349,000 cases).

Books of Reference

Annual Reports. Massachusetts and US Boards, Commissions, Departments and Divisions, Boston, 1977

Manual for the General Court. By Clerk of the Senate and Clerk of the House of Representatives, Boston, Mass. Biennial

Mariner, E. C., and Levitan, D., *Your Massachusetts Government.* Arlington, Mass., 1977

New England Board of Higher Education. *Facts.* Wellesley, Mass., 1976–77

MICHIGAN

HISTORY. Michigan, first settled by Marquette at Sault Ste Marie in 1668, became the Territory of Michigan in 1805, with its boundaries greatly enlarged in 1818 and 1834; it was admitted into the Union with its present boundaries on 26 Jan. 1837.

AREA AND POPULATION. Michigan is divided into two by Lake Michigan. The northern part is bounded south by the lake and by Wisconsin, west and north by Lake Superior, east by the North Channel of Lake Huron; between the two latter lakes the Canadian border runs through straits at Sault Ste Marie. The southern part is bounded west and north by Lake Michigan, east by Lake Huron, Ontario and Lake Erie, south by Ohio and Indiana. Area, 58,216 sq. miles, of which 56,818 sq. miles are land area, 1,398 sq. miles are inland water; in addition the Great Lakes area amounts to 38,459 sq. miles. Census population, 1 April 1970, 8,875,083, an increase of 1,051,889 or 13·4% since 1960. Estimate (1976), 9,151,000. In 1976 births were 131,370; deaths, 75,801; infant deaths, 1,978; marriages, 82,753; divorces, 43,101.

Population of 5 federal census years (with distribution by sex, 1970):

	White	*Negro*	*Indian*	*Asiatic*	*Total*	*Per sq. mile*
1910	2,785,247	17,115	7,519	292	2,810,173	48·9
1930	4,663,507	169,453	7,080	2,285	4,842,325	84·9
1950	5,917,825	442,296	7,000	4,645	6,371,766	111·7
1960	7,085,865	717,581	9,701	10,047	7,823,194	137·2
			All others			
1970	7,833,474	991,066	50,543		8,875,083	156·2
Male	3,520,422	352,142	4,898	5,406	3,882,868	—
Female	3,565,443	365,439	4,803	4,641	3,940,326	—

Of the total population in 1970, 6,553,773 persons (73·8%) were urban (73·4% in 1960). Those 21 years old or older numbered 5,090,126.

Population of the chief cities (census of 1 April 1970) was:

Detroit	1,492,507	St Clair Shores	86,378	Wyoming	56,196
Grand Rapids	193,878	Westland	86,291	Sterling Heights	55,721
Flint	193,574	Pontiac	84,951	Lincoln Park	52,979
Warren	179,196	Kalamazoo	84,444	Bay City	49,051
Lansing (capital)	129,021	Royal Oak	84,081	Jackson	45,721
Dearborn	112,007	Dearborn Heights	80,040	Muskegon	44,377
Livonia	109,746	Taylor	69,668	Battle Creek	38,454
Ann Arbor	98,414	Southfield	68,844		
Saginaw	90,603	Roseville	60,505		

Larger standard metropolitan areas, 1970 census: Detroit, 4,163,517; Grand Rapids, 535,702; Flint, 493,402; Lansing, 373,474.

CONSTITUTION AND GOVERNMENT. The present constitution was adopted in April 1963 and became effective on 1 Jan. 1964. The Senate consists of 38 members, elected for 4 years, and the House of Representatives of 110 members, elected for 2 years. The Governor and Lieut.-Governor are elected for 4 years. Electors are all citizens over 18 years of age meeting the usual residential requirements. The state sends to Congress 2 senators and 19 representatives.

At the 1976 presidential election Ford polled 1,893,742 votes, Carter 1,696,714. The capital is Lansing. The state is organized in 83 counties.

Governor: William G. Milliken (R.), 1975–78 ($58,000).
Lieut.-Governor: James J. Damman (R.), 1975–78 ($40,000).
Secretary of State: Richard H. Austin (D.), ($45,000).

BUDGET. Because of the recession and state constitutional limits on deficit spending the financial year beginning on 1 July 1975 was extended to a fifteen-month period ending on 30 Sept. 1976. For this period the general revenue was $7,888,417m. (taxation, $4,907·9m., and federal aid, $2,144,561m.); general expenditures including special revenue funds, $7,139,422m. (education, $2,967,237m.; social services, $2,391,461m.

Per capita personal income (1976) was $6,975.

ENERGY AND NATURAL RESOURCES

Minerals. Most important minerals by value of production are iron ore, petroleum and cement. Output (1976, preliminary): Iron ore, 15·22m. long tons ($392·6m.);

Portland cement, 5,264,000 short tons ($160·2m.); petroleum, 28,493,000 bbls ($325·1m.); copper, 45·23m. short tons ($63·3m.); sand and gravel, 48m. short tons ($74·8m.); salt, 3,992,000 short tons ($69·1m.); stone, 42,369,000 short tons ($80m.); lime, 1,434,000 short tons ($36·7m.); natural gas, 123m. cu. ft ($110·7m.); natural gas liquids, 3,704,000 bbls (of 42 gallons) of gasoline ($19·1m.) and 1,215m. bbls of LP gases ($5·3m.). Total value of natural salines, $114,535m. Mineral output in 1976 was valued at $1,500m.

Agriculture. The state, formerly agricultural, is now chiefly industrial. In 1977 it contained 78,000 farms with a total area of 12·3m. acres; the average farm was 158 acres.

Cash income, 1975, from crops, $943,417,000; from livestock and products, $712,801,000. Principal crops are maize (production, 1976, 141·5m. bu.), oats (20·7m. bu.), wheat (37·6m. bu.), sugar-beet (1,536m. tons); soybeans (11·6m. bu.), hay 3,010m. tons, dry beans 4,883m. cwt. On 1 Jan. 1977 there were in the state 149,000 sheep, 405,000 milch cows, 1·65m. all cattle, 720,000 swine, 6·73m. chickens and 55m. turkey breeder hens. In 1976 the wool clip yielded 1·15m. lb. of wool from 115,000 sheep.

Forestry. The forests of Michigan consist of 19,373,400 acres, about 52% of total state land area. About 18·9m. acres of this total is commercial forest, 67% of which is privately owned, 19% state forest, 13% national forest and 1% in various public ownerships. Three-fourths of the timber volume is hardwoods, principally hard and soft maples, aspen, oak and elm. Christmas trees are another important forest crop.

Michigan leads in the number of state parks and public campsites. There are 83 state parks and recreation areas, 33 state forests, 5 national forests and 3 national parks. There are 180 state forest campgrounds and 66 state game and wildlife areas.

INDUSTRY. Transport equipment and non-electrical machinery are the most important manufactures. The state ranks first in 19 manufacturing categories; among principal products are motor vehicles and trucks, cement, chemicals, furniture, paper, cereal, baby food and pharmaceuticals. Total labour force, 1976, 3,879,900, of which 1,040,700 are in manufacturing.

COMMUNICATIONS

Roads. State trunk-line mileage (31 July 1977) totalled, 9,439, all hard surfaced. Passenger car registrations, 30 June 1976, 4,681,236.

Railways. On 1 Jan. 1975 there were 6,200 miles of railway.

Aviation. Airports (1975) numbered 205 licensed airports, 106 emergency airports, 5 licensed seaplane bases, 4 emergency seaplane bases and 4 licensed heliports.

JUSTICE, RELIGION, EDUCATION AND WELFARE

Justice. The 1963 Constitution provides that no person shall be denied the equal protection of the law; nor shall any person be denied the enjoyment of his civil or political rights or be discriminated against in the exercise thereof because of religion, race, colour or national origin. A Civil Rights Commission was established, and its powers and duties were implemented by legislation in the extra session of 1963. Earlier statutory enactments guaranteeing civil rights in specific areas are as follows. An Act of 1885, last amended in 1956, orders all places of public accommodation and resort, etc., to furnish equal accommodations without discrimination. An Act of 1941, as last amended, forbids the Civil Service in counties with population exceeding 1m. to discriminate against employees or applicants on the ground of political, racial or religious opinions or affiliations. An Act of 1881 incorporated into the school code of 1955 forbids any discrimination in school facilities. An Act of 1893 incorporated in the insurance code of 1956 prohibits insurance companies from discriminating between white and coloured persons.

In 1951 the legislature restored the unique one-man grand jury system abandoned in 1949.

Religion. There were 2,345,558 Roman Catholics in 1973; largest Protestant denominations, Lutherans, 500,000; United Methodists, 278,245; United Presbyterians, 155,864; Episcopalians, 63,873.

Education. Education is compulsory for children from 6 to 16 years of age. The operating expenditure for graded and ungraded public schools for the fiscal year ending 30 June 1976, was $2,772,531,003; total, including capital and debt expenditures, $3,448,942,939. In 1976 there were 587 school districts (elementary and secondary schools) with 2,127,197 pupils and 92,677 teachers. Teachers' salaries in 1976 averaged $15,064.

In the autumn of 1976 the 13 public 4-year institutions reported 238,831 students and the 54 non-public institutions reported 60,372 students. During fiscal year 1976–77 the public colleges had operating budgets financed by tuition and $484·8m. by State appropriations. The community colleges had an autumn enrolment (1976) of 187,622 students.

Universities and students (1976):

Founded	*Name*	*Students*
1817	University of Michigan	45,742
1849	Eastern Michigan University	18,175
1855	Michigan State University	47,796
1884	Ferris State College	9,934
1885	Michigan Technological University	6,387
1868	Wayne State University	34,818
1892	Central Michigan University	18,041
1889	Northern Michigan University	9,268
1903	Western Michigan University	23,058
1946	Lake Superior State College	2,457
1959	Oakland University	10,457
1960	Grand Valley State College	7,376
1965	Saginaw Valley College	3,322

Social Welfare. Old-age assistance is provided for persons 65 years of age or older who have resided in Michigan for one year before application; assets must not exceed various limits. In 1974 federal Supplementary Security Income replaced the adults' programme. In 1976 aid was supplied to a monthly average of 463,353 dependent children in 201,676 families at $284.72 per family.

Health. In 1977 the state had 229 hospitals (41,994 beds) licensed by the state and 21 psychiatric hospitals.

In 1957 a programme came into force which provided for free medical care and hospital treatment for certain categories of persons. On 1 Oct. 1966 this programme was superseded by a more comprehensive programme called 'Medicaid' which, with federal support, disbursed in 1975–76, $704·8m. to an estimated 978,959 persons.

Books of Reference

Michigan Department of Economic Development. *Publications.* Lansing
Michigan Manual. Dept of State. Lansing. Biennial
Bureau of Business and Economic Research, Michigan State University. *Michigan Statistical Abstract.* East Lansing, 1977
Bald, F. C., *Michigan in Four Centuries.* 2nd ed. New York, 1961
Catton. B., *Michigan—a Bicentennial History.* Norton, New York. 1976
Lewis, F. E., *State and Local Government in Michigan.* Lansing, 1974
Davis, C. M. (ed.), *Readings in the Geography of Michigan.* Ann Arbor, 1964
Dunbar, W. F., *Michigan: A History of the Wolverine State.* Grand Rapids, 1972
Milliken, W. G., *Economic Report of the Governor 1975.* Lansing, 1977

State Library Services: Michigan Department of Education, Lansing 48909. *State Librarian:* Francis X. Scannell.

MINNESOTA

HISTORY. Minnesota, first explored in the 17th century and first settled in the 20 years following the establishment of Fort Snelling (1819), was made a Territory in 1849 (with parts of North and South Dakota), and was admitted into the Union, with its present boundaries, on 11 May 1858.

AREA AND POPULATION. Minnesota is bounded north by Canada, east by Lake Superior and Wisconsin, with the Mississippi River forming the boundary in the south-east, south by Iowa, west by South and North Dakota, with the Red River forming the boundary in the north-west. Area, 84,068 sq. miles, of which 4,059 sq. miles are inland water. Census population, 1 April 1970, 3,805,069, an increase of 11·4% since 1960. Estimate (1975) 3,926,000. Births in 1975, 56,983 (14·5 per 1,000 population); deaths, 33,701 (8·6); infant deaths, 800 (14 per 1,000 live births); marriages, 30,457 (7·8); divorces, 12,473 (3·2).

Population in 5 census years (with distribution by sex, 1970) was:

	White	*Negro*	*Indian*	*Asiatic*	*Total*	*Per sq. mile*
1910	2,059,227	7,084	9,053	344	2,075,708	25·7
1930	2,542,599	9,445	11,077	832	2,563,953	32·0
1950	2,953,697	14,022	12,533	2,231	2,982,483	37·3
1960	3,371,603	22,263	15,496	3,642	3,413,864	42·7
			All others			
1970	3,805,069	34,868	34,065		3,805,069	47·6
Male	1,863,810	17,641	—		1,863,810	—
Female	1,941,161	17,227	—		1,941,161	—

Of the 1970 population, 2,527,308 persons (64·4%) were urban (62·2% in 1960); those 21 years of age or older numbered 2,219,785; foreign-born whites, 141,655 in 1960.

The largest cities are Minneapolis, 434,400; St Paul (capital), 309,980 (Minneapolis–St Paul standard metropolitan statistical area, 1,813,647); Duluth, 100,578; Bloomington, 81,970; Rochester, 53,776; St Louis Park, 48,883; Richfield, 47,231; Edina, 44,046.

CONSTITUTION AND GOVERNMENT. The present constitution dates from 1858; it has had 94 amendments. The Legislature consists of a Senate of 67 members, elected for 4 years, and a House of Representatives of 134 members, elected for 2 years. The Governor and Lieut.-Governor are elected for 4 years. The state sends to Congress 2 senators and 8 representatives.

In the 1976 presidential election Carter polled 1,067,536 votes, Ford 817,349.

The capital is St Paul. There are 87 counties, few containing less than 400 sq. miles, the largest being 6,092 sq. miles.

Governor: Wendell R. Anderson (DFL), 1975–79 ($27,500).
Lieut.-Governor: Rudolf G. Perpich (DFL), 1975–79 ($9,600).
Secretary of State: Joan Anderson Growe (DFL), 1975–79 ($20,500).

BUDGET. General revenues for the year ending 30 June 1974 were $3,043·5m. (taxation, $1,843m.); general expenditures, $2,780·1m. (education, $1,163·8m.; public welfare, $350·9m.; highways, $338·5m.).

The state's four principal trust funds (derived from royalties from state-owned iron-mines, special tax on iron ore, and sales of land and of timber) on 30 June 1972 totalled $252,293,253.

Net long-term debt, 30 June 1974, was $766,378,000.

Per capita personal income (1971) was $4,032.

NATURAL RESOURCES

Minerals. The mining of iron ores on the Mesabi, Vermilion and Cuyuna ranges has changed dramatically since the passage of a Taconite Amendment in 1964. Since then new capital investment in taconite facilities has reached approximately $1,574m., bringing the total investment in the taconite industry to over $2,074m. Taconite made up 68·4% of Minnesota's iron-ore shipments in 1974. Shipments of usable iron ore from mines came to 57·9m. long tons and was valued at $857m. Total mineral output in 1974 was valued at $920m.

Agriculture. Agriculture, including processing, is the leading industry. In 1975 there were 118,000 farms with a total area of 30·6m. acres (63% of the land area); the average farm was of 259 acres. Average value of land and buildings (1969) $58,804. Commercial farms in 1969 numbered 110,874; 15·5% of the farms were operated by tenant-farmers. Cash income, 1974, from crops, $2,773·1m.; from livestock, $1,980·9m. In 1974 Minnesota ranked first in creamery butter, oats, non-fat dried milk, sweetcorn for processing, turkeys and timothy seed, and second in American cheese and sunflower seed. Other important products are flaxseed, milch cows, milk, corn, barley, swine, cattle for market, rye, sugar-beet, soybeans, honey, hay, red-clover seed, potatoes, wheat and green peas. Of livestock, cattle represents 18% of total farm income, swine 12% and dairy products 13·8%. Of crops, corn represent 15·4% and soybeans 15·8%. On 1 Jan. 1975 the farm animals included 4·43m. all cattle, 886,000 milch cows, 390,000 sheep, 3·7m. swine, 12·82m. chickens and 479,000 breeder hen turkeys. Turkey production, 1974, 21·93m. In 1974 the wool clip amounted to 2,734,000 lb. of wool from 367,000 sheep.

Forestry. Forests of commercial timber cover 17·1m. acres, of which the national forest area, 1974, was 2·8m. acres and state forest area 3·3m. acres; value of forest products, 1974, was $576·8m.

INDUSTRY. In 1974 there were about 5,900 manufacturing establishments; they employed 220,053 production workers who earned $2,088·2m.; value added by manufacture was (1972), $5,523·8m.

TOURISM. Estimates for 1974 give approximately 6m. tourists (55% from outside the state), with a total expenditure of $996m.

COMMUNICATIONS

Roads. The state highway system covered 11,514 miles state rural trunk highways in 1972; total highway mileage, 127,742. In 1972, 1,769,518 passenger automobiles were registered.

Railways. There are 11 Class I railroads operating, with mainline mileage of 8,031 (total track miles, 11,992).

Aviation. Airports in 1972 numbered 223 (139 municipal, 51 privately owned for public use, 33 public seaplane bases).

JUSTICE, RELIGION, EDUCATION AND WELFARE

Justice. A Civil Rights Act (1927) forbids places of public resort to exclude persons 'on account of race or colour' and another section forbids insurance companies to discriminate 'between persons of the same class on account of race'. Contractors on public works may have their contracts cancelled if 'in the hiring of common or skilled labour' they are found to have discriminated on the grounds of 'race, creed or colour'. The state's penal reformatory system on 31 June 1971 held 2,144 men and women. There is no death penalty in Minnesota.

Religion. The chief religious bodies are: Lutheran with 1,112,495 members in 1970; Roman Catholic, 1,061,614; Methodist, 213,084. Total membership of all denominations, 3,044,055.

Education. In 1975, 1,120 public elementary schools had 22,503 teachers and 457,753 enrolled pupils; 624 public secondary schools had 27,538 teachers and 467,200 pupils. In 1975 the 53,184 teachers had an average salary of $12,926. The total public school expenditure (1973–74) was $959,857,966, of which $631,289,810 came from state funds. The University of Minnesota at Minneapolis–St Paul, chartered in 1851 and opened in 1869, had a total enrolment in 1975 of 55,114 students and 9,597 academic staff. The 18 state junior colleges had a total enrolment of 26,314. Seven state colleges (4-year) had a 1975 enrolment of 46,360, State colleges are at Bemidji, Mankato, Marshall, Moorhead, St Cloud, Winona, Minneapolis and St Paul.

Health. In 1975 the state had 179 general acute hospitals with 19,869 beds. Patients resident in institutions under the Department of Public Welfare included 1,640 mentally ill, 3,409 mentally retarded and 560 chemically dependent. In 1957 a Community Mental Health Act authorized mental health centres in local communities with grants from the state to be matched by local funds; in 1974, 26 centres served about 21,000 persons.

Social Security. On 1 Jan. 1974 the state administered programmes of old age assistance, aid to the disabled, and aid to the blind were given over to federal administration under the Supplemental Security Income (SSI) Programme. For some states, the new maintenance grants were less than under the state administered programmes. These states could establish a supplemental programme to correct the deficiency. The Minnesota Supplemental Aid (MSA) programme was later expanded to cover individuals who were not receiving SSI and to provide one-time payment for certain special needs such as major home repair, replacement of essential basic furniture or appliances, moving expenses and fuel and utility adjustments.

Books of Reference

Statistical Information: Current information is obtainable from the Department of Economic Development (State Capital, St Paul 55101); non-current material from the Reference Library, Minnesota Historical Society, St Paul 55101).

Legislative Manual. Secretary of State. St Paul. Biennial
Minnesota Statistical Profile. Dept of Econ. Dev., 1974
Blegen, T. C., *Minnesota: A History of the State.* Minnesota Univ. Press, 1963
Minnesota Agriculture Statistics. Dept. of Agric., St Paul. Annual
Manufacturers' Directory, 1975–76. Dept. of Econ. Dev. 1975
Atlas of Minnesota Resources and Settlement. State Planning Agency. Rev. ed. 1969
Minnesota Pocket Data Book. State Planning Agency, 1974

MISSISSIPPI

HISTORY. Mississippi, settled in 1716, was organized as a Territory in 1798 and admitted into the Union on 10 Dec. 1817. In 1804 and in 1812 its boundaries were extended, but in March 1817 a part was taken to form the new Territory of Alabama, leaving the boundaries substantially as at present.

AREA AND POPULATION. Mississippi is bounded north by Tennessee, east by Alabama, south by the Gulf of Mexico and Louisiana, west by the Mississippi River forming the boundary with Louisiana and Arkansas. Area, 47,716 sq. miles, 493 sq. miles being inland water. Census (preliminary) population, 1 April 1970, 2,216,912, an increase of 1·79% since 1960. Births occurring in the state, 1975, were 42,861; births to residents, 43,336; deaths, 22,391; infant deaths, 949; marriages, 26,269; divorces, 12,303.

Population of 5 federal census years (with distribution by sex, 1970):

	White	*Negro*	*Indian*	*Asiatic*	*Total*	*Per sq. mile*
1910	786,111	1,009,487	1,253	263	1,797,114	38·8
1930	998,077	1,009,718	1,458	568	2,009,821	42·4
1950	1,188,632	986,494	2,502	1,286	2,178,914	46·1
1960	1,257,546	915,743	3,119	1,481	2,178,141	46·1
			All others			
1970	1,393,283	815,770	7,859		2,216,912	46·9
Male	683,747	386,580	3,890		1,074,217	—
Female	709,536	429,190	3,069		1,142,695	—

Of the population in 1970, 986,642 persons (49·3%) were urban (10·8% in 1940). Those 21 years old or older numbered 1,242,965; foreign-born whites, 6,741. In 1960 in 31 of the 82 counties Negroes constituted 49% or more of the population; Tunica County, with 79% Negro, had the highest percentage of any county in the US.

The largest cities (1970) are Jackson, 153,968 (urbanized area, 190,060); Biloxi, 48,486; Meridian, 45,083; Gulfport, 40,791; Greenville, 39,648; Hattiesburg, 38,277; Columbus, 25,795; Vicksburg, 25,478; Laurel, 24,145; Natchez, 19,704.

CONSTITUTION AND GOVERNMENT. The present constitution was adopted in 1890 without ratification by the electorate; it has since had 48 amendments.

The Legislature consists of a Senate (52 members) and a House of Representatives (122 members), both elected for 4 years, as are also the Governor and Lieut.-Governor. Electors are all citizens who have resided in the state 1 year, in the county 1 year, in the election district 6 months next before the election and have been registered according to law. In the 1976 presidential election Carter polled 381,309 votes, Ford 366,846.

The state is represented in Congress by 2 senators and 5 representatives.

The capital is Jackson; there are 82 counties.

Governor: Charles Clifford Finch (D.), 1976–80 ($43,000).
Lieut.-Governor: Evelyn Gandy (D.) ($15,000).
Secretary of State: Heber Ladner (D.) ($16,500).

BUDGET. For the fiscal year ending 30 June 1977 the general revenues were $1,579,396,591 (taxation, $972,670,613; federal aid, $534,264,708; other state resources, $72,461,269), and general expenditures were $1,665,376,649 ($604,645,624 for education, $282,117,080 for highways and $256,117,080 for public welfare).

On 30 June 1977 the total net long-term debt was $779,472,000.

Per capita personal income (1970) was $2,575 (lowest in US).

ENERGY AND NATURAL RESOURCES

Minerals. Petroleum and natural gas account for about 90% (by value) of mineral production. Output of petroleum, 1976, was 46,072,466 bbls and of natural gas 88,148,669m. cu. ft. There are 5 oil refineries. Value of oil and gas products sold 1976 was $391,651,092.

Agriculture. Agriculture is the leading industry of the state because of the semi-tropical climate and a rich productive soil. In 1977 farms in the state numbered 83,000 with an area of 17m. acres. Average size of farm was 205 acres (valued at $84,255). This compares with an average farm size of 138 acres (valued at $13,597) in 1960.

Cash income from all crops and livestock during 1976, including $28·5m. in government payments, was $1,700·36m. Cash income from crops was $989·5m. and from livestock and products, $682·2m. The chief product is soybeans, cash income $421·9m. from 3·3m. acres. In cotton, 1·15m. bales (480 lb.) were produced, with cash receipts from cotton lint and cotton-seed totalling $441·69m. As a source of farm income, rice, corn, hay, wheat, peanuts, pecans, sweet potatoes, peaches, other vegetables, nursery and forest products continue to contribute.

On 1 Jan. 1977 there were 2·67m. head of cattle and calves on Mississippi farms (seventeenth nationally). Milch cows and heifers which had calved totalled 115,000, beef cows and heifers that had calved, 1,325,000 (eleventh nationally); sheep and lambs, 5,400 head, and hogs and pigs, 405,000 head (Dec. 1976), chickens (excluding broilers), 10·9m. In 1976 cash income from livestock and products was 41% of total cash receipts. Of this total, $203·2m. was credited to cattle and calves. Cash income from poultry and eggs totalled $327·35m.; dairy products, $86·1m.; swine, $31·7m.

In 1977 there were 87 soil-conservation districts covering 26,342,406 acres.

Forestry. In 1976 income from forestry amounted to over $1,000m.; output of logs, lumber, etc., was 1,413·7m. bd ft; pulpwood, 4·2m. cords; distillate wood, 20,539 tons; turpentine gum, 2,954 bbls. There are about 16·7m. acres of forest (55% of the state's area). National forests area, 1977, 1,137,200 acres.

INDUSTRY. In 1976 the 3,028 manufacturing establishments employed 219,559 workers, earning $1,922,427,614.

COMMUNICATIONS

Roads. The state in 1977 maintained 10,113·68 miles of highways, of which 9,915·38 miles were paved. In 1976, 1,087,230 cars were registered.

Railways. The state in 1977 had 3,584 miles of railway.

Aviation. There were 78 public airports in 1977, 68 of them general. There were also 4 privately owned airports.

JUSTICE, RELIGION, EDUCATION AND WELFARE

Justice. In 1977 there were no executions; from 1955 to 1976 executions (by gas-chamber) totalled 31 (7 whites and 14 Negroes for murder, 9 Negroes for rape and 1 Negro for armed robbery). On 30 Sept. 1977 the state prisons had 1,757 inmates.

Religion. Southern Baptists in Mississippi (1976), 595,010 members; Methodists (1977), 204,265; Roman Catholics (1977), 88,406. Negro Baptists (1976 estimate), 400,000.

The number of churches relative to the population is the highest in the US (one church per 289 persons; national average, 814).

Education. Attendance at school was compulsory until this was repealed by the Legislature in 1956. The elementary and secondary schools in 1976–77 had 496,053 pupils and 24,335 classroom teachers; private elementary and high schools had 52,772 pupils (1976). In 1976–77, teachers' average salary was $9,399. The expenditure per pupil in average daily attendance, 1976–77, was $1,096.78.

There are 17 universities and senior colleges, of which 8 are state-supported. The University of Mississippi, at Oxford (1844), had, 1977–78, 456 instructors and 9,570 students; Mississippi State University, Starkville, 543 instructors and 11,385 students; Mississippi University for Women, at Columbus, 156 instructors and 2,862 students; University of Southern Mississippi, Hattiesburg, 528 instructors and 9,806 students; Jackson State University, Jackson, 323 instructors and 7,797 students; Delta State University, Cleveland, 182 instructors and 2,819 students; Alcorn State University, Lorman, 133 instructors and 2,776 students; Mississippi Valley State University, Itta Bena, 140 instructors and 2,950 students. State operational expenditure, 1977–78, for higher education was $85·39m.

Junior colleges had (1976–77) 46,810 students and 1,716 instructors. The state appropriation for junior colleges, 1977–78, was $24·7m.

Health. In 1977 the state had 120 acute general hospitals (11,669 beds) listed by the Mississippi Commission on Hospital Care. In 1977, 8 hospitals with facilities for care of the mentally ill had 4,151 beds.

Social Security. Department of Public Welfare figures show (June 1977) 767 persons receiving Aged State Mandatory Supplementation payments amounting to an average of $17.47 per month; 14 persons receiving Blind State Mandatory Supplementation payments amounting to an average of $16 per month; 137 persons receiving Disabled State Mandatory Supplementation payments amounting to an average of $20.39 per month. The state Medicaid commission paid (1976–77) $134m. for medical services, including $18m. for drugs, $37·14m. for skilled nursing home care, $39m. for hospital services. There were 52,457 families with 131,138 dependent children receiving $2,397,903 in the Aid to Dependent Children's programme. This amounted to an average payment of $45.71 per family for the month of June 1977. There were 80,598 persons eligible for Aged Medicaid, 1,740 persons eligible for Blind Medicaid and 27,220 persons eligible for Disabled Medicaid benefits in June 1977.

Books of Reference

Mississippi Official and Statistical Register. Secretary of State. Jackson. Biennial
Bettersworth, J. K., *Mississippi: A History*. Rev. ed. Austin, Tex., 1964
Highsaw, R. B., and Fortenberry, C. N., *The Government and Administration of Mississippi*. New York, 1954
Silver, J. W., *Mississippi: The Closed Society*. New York, 1964
Wilber, G. L., and Bryant, E. S., *Illustrative Projections of Mississippi Population, 1960 to 1985*. State College, 1964

Mississippi Library Commission: PO Box 3260 Jackson, Ms. 39207. *Head of Information Services:* Dennis Read.

MISSOURI

HISTORY. Missouri, first settled in 1735 at Ste Genevieve, was made a Territory on 1 Oct. 1812, and admitted to the Union on 10 Aug. 1821. In 1837 its boundaries were extended to their present limits.

AREA AND POPULATION. Missouri is bounded north by Iowa, east by the Mississippi River forming the boundary with Illinois and Kentucky, south by Arkansas, south-west by Oklahoma, west by Kansas and Nebraska, with the Missouri River forming the boundary in the north-west. Area, 69,686 sq. miles, 640 sq. miles being water. Census population, 1 April 1970, 4,677,399, an increase since 1960 of 7·6%. Estimate (1975), 4,769,816. Births, 1975, were 71,701 (15·1 per 1,000 population); deaths, 50,558 (10·6); infant deaths, 1,255 (17·5 per 1,000 live births); marriages, 45,618 (9·6); divorces, 25,455 (5·3).

Population of 5 federal census years (with distribution by sex, 1970):

	White	*Negro*	*Indian*	*Asiatic*	*Total*	*Per sq. mile*
1910	3,134,932	157,452	313	638	3,293,335	47·9
1930	3,403,876	223,840	578	1,073	3,629,367	52·4
1950	3,655,593	297,088	547	1,046	3,954,653	57·1
1960	3,922,967	390,853	1,723	3,146	4,319,813	62·5
			All others			
1970	4,177,495	480,172	18,834		4,677,399	67·0
Male	2,029,656	226,296	—		2,255,952	—
Female	2,167,672	253,871	—		2,421,549	—

Of the total population in 1970, 3,278,857 persons (70·1%) were urban (66·6% in 1960). Those 21 years of age or older numbered 2,880,159.

Cities with 20,000 or more people (1970 census) are:

St Louis	622,236	University City	46,309	Cape Girardeau	31,282
Kansas City	507,087	Joplin	39,256	Ferguson	28,915
Springfield	120,096	Raytown	33,632	Webster Groves	26,995
Independence	101,662	Jefferson City	32,407	Overland	24,949
St Joseph	72,691	Kirkwood	31,890	Sedalia	22,847
Florissant	65,908	St Charles	31,834	Gladstone	23,128
Columbia	58,804				

Metropolitan areas, 1970 census: St Louis, 1,826,907; Kansas City, 849,409.

CONSTITUTION AND GOVERNMENT. A new constitution, the fourth, was adopted on 27 Feb. 1945; it has been amended 26 times. The General Assembly consists of a Senate of 34 members elected for 4 years (half for re-election every 2 years), and a House of Representatives of 163 members elected for 2 years. The Governor and Lieut.-Governor are elected for 4 years. Missouri sends to Congress 2 senators and 10 representatives.

Voters (with the usual exceptions) are all citizens and those adult aliens who, within a prescribed period, have applied for citizenship. In the 1976 presidential election Carter polled 984,413, Ford 916,903.

Jefferson City is the state capital. The state is divided into 114 counties and the city of St Louis.

Governor: Joseph Teasdale (D.), 1977–81 ($37,500).
Lieut.-Governor: William C. Phelps (R.), 1977–81 ($16,000).
Secretary of State: James C. Kirkpatrick (D.) ($20,000).

BUDGET. For the year 1975 state and local general revenues were $3,996·2m. (taxes, $2,490·5m.); general expenditures were $3,947·3m.

Total net long-term debt, 30 June, 1975, was $242·5m.

Per capita personal income (1970) was $3,704.

NATURAL RESOURCES

Minerals. Principal minerals are lead, clays, coal, zinc, iron ore, and between 40m. and 50m. tons of stone annually for cement and lime manufacture.

Agriculture. In 1977 there were 137,000 farms in Missouri covering 32·6m. acres. The average size of farms is 238 acres. The 1976 acreage of corn harvested for grain was 2·8m. acres; soybeans for beans, 4·2m. acres, and wheat, 1·6m. acres. Production of principal crops, 1976: Corn, 174m. bu.; soybeans, 84m. bu.; wheat, 54·4m. bu.; sorghum grain, 36m. bu.; oats, 6·8m. bu. Number of pigs raised, 6m.; calves raised, 2·7m. Cash receipts from farming, 1976, $2,760m.; crops $1,050m.; livestock, $1,710m.

Forestry. Forest land area, 1974, 12·9m. acres. Timber resources (sawtimber), 128,108·5m. bd ft.

INDUSTRY. The largest employer in 1973 was the transport equipment industry employing 75,450 workers. Other large industries are food and kindred products, electrical equipment and supplies, apparel and related products and non-electrical machinery, leather products, chemicals, paper, metal industries, stone, clay and glass. In 1973 there were 454,500 production workers employed; value added by manufacture was $8,178·3m. in 1972. Growth figures for 1973: New manufacturing plants, 178; expansions, 164; jobs created, 6,383 by new manufacturers and 7,776 by expansions; investments, $51m. by new manufacturers and $133·2m. through expansion.

LABOUR. The State Board of Mediation has jurisdiction in labour disputes involving only public utilities. The Prevailing Wage Law (1959) provides that no less than the local hourly rate of wages for work of a similar character shall be paid to any workmen engaged in public works. The Industrial Commission has authority to inspect records and to institute actions for penalties described in the Act. There is a state programme for industrial safety in hand, under the Federal Occupational and Health Act.

COMMUNICATIONS

Roads. Federal and state highways, July 1976, totalled 33,668 miles. In 1974 there were 3·2m. vehicles licensed in the state. In 1974 there were 31 bus companies and about 1,200 internal truck lines.

Railways. The state has 16 Class I railroads, operating approximately 3,820 miles of main-line track and 1,810 miles of branch-line track.

Aviation. In July 1974 there were 304 airports, of which 97 were publicly owned. There were 10 heliports and 4 seaplane bases.

Shipping. Ten carrier barge lines operate on 1,900 miles of navigable waterways, including the Missouri and Mississippi Rivers. Boat shipping seasons: Missouri River, March–end Nov.; Mississippi River, early March–mid-Dec.

Post and Broadcasting. There are 175 commercial radio stations and 21 television stations. The number of telephones in autumn 1974 was 3·2m.

Newspapers. Newspapers numbered 375 in 1976.

JUSTICE, RELIGION, EDUCATION AND WELFARE

Justice. State prisons in 1977 had an average of 4,800 inmates. Of those committed, 60% are aged 17–28. There have been no executions since 1965; since 1930 executions (by lethal gas) have totalled 40, including 31 for murder, 6 for rape and 3 for kidnapping. There are about 7,470 law enforcement officers. The Missouri Law Enforcement Assistance Council was created in 1969 for law reform.

Religion. Chief religious bodies are Catholic, with 759,503 members, Southern Baptists (515,383), United Methodists (253,627), Christian Churches (121,827), Lutheran (107,763), Presbyterian (100,056). Total membership, all denominations, about 2·2m. in 1970.

Education. School attendance is compulsory for children from 7 to 16 years for the full term. In the 1975–76 school year, public schools (kindergarten through grade 12) had 1,042,881 pupils. Total expenditure for public schools in 1975–76, $1,325m. Salaries for 52,697 teachers (kindergarten through grade 12), 1975–76, averaged $10,813. Institutions for higher education include the University of Missouri, founded in 1839 with campuses at Columbia, Rolla, St Louis and Kansas City, with 2,847 accredited teachers and 47,640 students in 1976. Washington University at St Louis, founded in 1857, and St Louis University (1818), are both private universities. Nine state colleges had 42,879 students in 1975. Two of these are former junior colleges now 4-year colleges with the local junior college district financing the first 2 years and the state financing the third and fourth years. Private liberal arts colleges had (1975) 25,602 students. Public junior colleges had 58,426 students. There are about 60 vocational, professional and technical schools. There were 218,667 students in higher education in autumn 1975.

Health. The state department of Mental Health has 22 hospitals and other centres; costs of operation (together with related community programmes) amount to about $100m.

Social Security. In June 1974 the state was providing medical benefits and welfare payments to 341,359 persons; 41,000 others received only medical benefits. The largest programme was in aid to dependent children, average monthly receipt, $38.57. In Jan. 1975, 82,441 families including 257,842 persons received payments which averaged $120.44 per family.

Books of Reference

Official Manual, Secretary of State, Jefferson City. Biennial
Annual Survey of Manufactures, U.S. Dept of Commerce, Bureau of the Census
General Population Characteristics, Office of Comptroller and Budget Director, Jefferson City
Missouri Final Production Count, Office of Comptroller and Budget Director, Jefferson City
Missouri Corporate Planner, Division of Commerce and Industrial Development, Jefferson City

MONTANA

HISTORY. Montana, first settled in 1809, was made a Territory (out of portions of Idaho and Dakota Territories) in 1864 and was admitted into the Union on 8 Nov. 1889.

AREA AND POPULATION. Montana is bounded north by Canada, east by North and South Dakota, south by Wyoming and west by Idaho and the Bitterroot Range of the Rocky Mountains. Area, 147,138 sq. miles, including 1,551 sq. miles of water, of which the federal government, 1975, owned 27,666,000 acres or 29·7%. US Bureau of Indian Affairs administered 5,282,000 acres, of which 1·98m. were allotted to tribes. Census population, 1 April 1970, 694,409, an increase of 2·9% since 1960. Births, 1975, were 11,781 (15·8 per 1,000 population); deaths, 6,493 (8·7); infant deaths, 173 (14·7 per 1,000 live births); marriages, 7,318 (9·8); divorces 4,307 (5·8).

Population in 5 census years (with distribution by sex, 1970) was:

	White	*Negro*	*Indian*	*Asiatic*	*Total*	*Per sq. mile*
1910	360,580	1,834	10,745	2,870	376,053	2·6
1930	519,898	1,256	14,798	1,239	537,606	3·7
1950	572,038	1,232	16,606	—	591,024	4·1
1960	650,738	1,467	21,181	1,082	674,767	4·6
1970	663,043	1,995	27,130	1,302	694,409	4·7
			All others			
Male	331,211	1,254	14,540		347,005	—
Female	331,832	741	14,831		347,404	—

Of the total population in 1970, 370,676 persons (53·4%) were urban (50·2% in 1960). There were 347,005 male and 347,404 females (national average, 95·2 males to every 100 females). Persons 18 years of age or older numbered 441,284. Households, 1970, 217,304.

The largest cities (1970) are Billings, 61,581; Great Falls, 60,091; Missoula, 29,497; Butte, 23,368; Helena (capital), 22,730; Bozeman, 18,670; Havre, 10,558; Kalispell, 10,526; Anaconda, 9,771.

CONSTITUTION AND GOVERNMENT. A new constitution was ratified by the voters on 6 June 1972, and fully implemented on 1 July 1973; the Senate to consist of 50 senators, elected for 4 years, one half at each biennial election. The 100 members of the House of Representatives are elected for 2 years.

The Governor and Lieut.-Governor are elected for 4 years. Montana sends to Congress 2 senators and 2 representatives.

In the 1976 presidential election Ford polled 173,703 votes, Carter 149,259.

The capital is Helena. The state is divided into 56 counties.

Governor: Thomas L. Judge (D.), 1977–81 ($35,000).
Lieut.-Governor: Ted Schwinden (D.), 1977–81 ($25,000).
Secretary of State: Frank Murray (D.), 1977–81 ($22,500).

BUDGET. Total state revenues for the year ending 30 June 1976 were $737,101,000 ($277·7m. from taxes); total expenditures were $687,758,000 ($221·3m. for education, $123·8m. for highways and $58·2m. for public welfare).

Total net long-term debt on 30 June 1976 was $85,055,000.

Per capita personal income (1975) was $5,422.

ENERGY AND NATURAL RESOURCES

Electricity. Electric power generated in Aug. 1976 was 1,293·37m. kwh., of which 1,069·54m. was hydro-electric.

Minerals (1974). Output of crude petroleum, 34·55m. bbls; copper, 131,131 short tons, sand and gravel, 4·2m. short tons; phosphate rock, undisclosed; silver, 3·5m. troy oz.; gold, 28,268,000 troy oz.; zinc, 136 short tons; manganese ore, 239 short tons (1973); natural gas, 54,873m. cu. ft; coal, 14·1m. short tons. Value of total mineral production (1974), $574,801,000, with petroleum ($229,802,000) the first and copper ($202,728,000) the second most important commodity.

Agriculture. In 1976 there were 22,500 farms and ranches (50,564 in 1935) with an area of 62·4m. acres (47,511,868 acres in 1935). Large-scale farming predominates; in 1976 the average size per farm was 2,773 acres. Income from all farm marketings was $1,078,329,000 in 1975 (crops, $657·6m.; livestock, $420·6m.). Irrigated area of total crop land harvested in 1975 was 1,736,490 acres or 19%; value of irrigated crops, $224·27m.

The chief crops are wheat, amounting in 1975 to 155·9m. bu., ranking fourth in US; barley, 50·7m. bu.; oats, 10·75m. bu.; sugar-beet, hay, potatoes, alfalfa, dry beans, flax and cherries. In 1975 there were 26,000 milch cows, 3·15m. all cattle; 145,000 swine. The wool clip in 1975 was 5,795,000 lb. from 635,000 head of sheep.

Forestry. Total forest area (1974), 28m. acres. In 1975 there were 16·7m. acres within 11 national forests.

INDUSTRY. In 1976 manufacturing establishments numbering 774 had 17,403 production workers; value added by manufacture was (1973) $515·2m.

LABOUR (1977). Work force, 365,700; total employed, 342,900; total non-agricultural workers, 299,400; agricultural workers, 43,500. Workers employed by major industry group: Mining, 5,800 (average net weekly earnings, $333.17); contract construction, 14,000 ($352.47); manufacturing, 25,100 ($270.26); transport and public utilities, 20,000 ($322.09); wholesale/retail trade, 68,400 ($149.63); finance/insurance/real estate, 11,300 ($128.43); services, 51,400 ($109.96); government, 70,900 (no income figures available). Average weekly earnings for all workers in private non-agricultural industries $185.26. Total unemployed 22,800 (6·2% of the work force in June as compared to 7·5% nationally for that month).

There were 30 work stoppages in 1975 involving 5,600 workers, with a total of 84,800 man days idle during the year.

COMMUNICATIONS

Roads. In 1976 the state had 69,094 miles of public roads and streets including 11,278 miles of federally-aided highway. There were 432,456 passenger vehicles registered, 259,971 trucks and 43,974 motor-cycles in July 1977.

Railways. In 1977 there were 4,862 miles of railway in the state.

Aviation. There were 117 airports open for public use in 1977, of which 111 were publicly owned.

JUSTICE, RELIGION, EDUCATION AND WELFARE

Justice. In June 1977 the Montana state prison held 547 inmates. Since 1943 there have been no executions; total since 1930 (all by hanging) was 6; 4 whites and 2 Negroes, for murder.

Religion. The leading religious bodies are (1970): Roman Catholic with 140,000 members (Diocesan estimate); Lutheran, 73,944; Methodist, 28,140.

Education. In autumn 1976 public elementary and secondary schools had 170,343 pupils. In addition there were 8,117 in schools not run by public school districts. Pupils of at least one quarter Indian blood, in 1970, numbered 7,943. In autumn 1976 public elementary school teachers (5,176) had an average salary of $11,265; secondary school teachers (4,252), $12,318. Total estimated expenditure on public school education (1975–76) was $243·3m.; expenditure per pupil was $1,555. The Montana University system consists of the Montana State University, at Bozeman (1976: 8,514 full-time students), the University of Montana, at Missoula, founded in 1895 (7,054), the College of Mineral Science and Technology at Butte (869 students), Northern Montana College at Havre (992), Eastern Montana College at Billings (2,563) and Western Montana College at Dillon (483).

Social Security. In June 1977, 4,784 persons over age 65 were receiving in medical assistance an average of $324.90 per month; 181 blind person, $188.41; 3,817 totally disabled, $380.41; 6,108 families (12,147 dependent children) receiving in aid-to-dependent children assistance an average of $165.38 per month. Aid was from state and federal sources.

Health. In 1977 the state had 63 hospitals (3,529 beds) listed by the Montana Board of Health. Four centres for mental disease and development disorders had 1,254 beds and 975 patients.

Books of Reference

Montana Agricultural Statistics. Dept. of Agriculture, Labor and Industry, Helena. Biennial from 1946

Montana Business Quarterly. Montana State Univ. From 1963

Montana Data Book. Dept. of Planning and Economic Development, Helena, 1970

The Montana Study (13 parts). Bureau of Business and Economic Research, Univ. of Mont., Missoula, 1969–70
Hamilton, J. McL., *From Wilderness to Statehood: A History of Montana, 1805–1900*. Portland, Ore., 1957
Toole, K. R., *Montana, An Uncommon Land*. Univ. of Oklahoma Press, 1959
Toole, K. Ross, *Twentieth Century Montana*. Univ. of Oklahoma Press, 1972

NEBRASKA

HISTORY. The Nebraska region was first reached by white men from Mexico under the Spanish general Coronado in 1541. It was ceded by France to Spain in 1763, retroceded to France in 1801, and sold by Napoleon to the US as part of the Louisiana Purchase in 1803. Its first settlement was in 1847, and on 30 May 1854 it became a Territory and on 1 March 1867 a state. In 1882 it annexed a small part of Dakota Territory, and in 1908 it received another small tract from South Dakota.

AREA AND POPULATION. Nebraska is bounded north by South Dakota, with the Missouri River forming the boundary in the north-east and the boundary with Iowa and Missouri to the east; south by Kansas, south-west by Colorado and west by Wyoming. Area, 77,227 sq. miles, of which 744 sq. miles are water. Census population, 1 April 1970, 1,483,791, an increase of 5·1% since 1960. Estimated population, 1976: 1,553,000. Births, 1976, were 23,767 (15·3 per 1,000 population); deaths, 14,536 (9·4); infant deaths, 337 (14·2 per 1,000 live births); marriages, 13,431 (8·6): divorces, 5,788 (3·7).

Population in 5 census years (with distribution by sex, 1970) was:

	White	*Negro*	*Indian*	*Asiatic*	*Total*	*Per sq. mile*
1910	1,180,293	7,689	3,502	730	1,192,214	15·5
1920	1,279,219	13,242	2,888	1,023	1,296,372	16·9
1950	1,301,328	19,234	3,954	821	1,325,510	17·3
1960	1,374,764	29,262	5,545	1,195	1,411,330	18·3
1970	1,432,867	39,911	6,624	4,091	1,483,791	19·4
Male	699,842	19,291	3,322	2,000	724,455	—
Female	733,025	20,620	3,302	2,091	759,038	—

Of the total population in 1970, 914,139 persons (61·6%) were urban (53·6% in 1960); 894,145 were 21 years of age or older. The largest cities in the state are: Omaha, with a census population, 1970, of 346,929; Lincoln (capital), 149,518; Grand Island, 31,269; Hastings, 23,580; Fremont, 22,962; Bellevue, 21,953; North Platte, 19,447; Kearney, 19,181; Norfolk, 16,607.

The Bureau of Indian Affairs, as of 30 June 1975, administered 61,000 acres, of which 18,000 acres were allotted to tribal control.

CONSTITUTION AND GOVERNMENT. The present constitution was adopted in 1875; it has been amended 167 times. By an amendment adopted in Nov. 1934 Nebraska has a single-chambered legislature (elected for 4 years) of 49 members—the only state in the Union to have one. The Governor and Lieut.-Governor are elected for 4 years. Amendments adopted in 1912 and 1920 provide for legislation through the initiative and referendum and permit cities of more than 5,000 inhabitants to frame their own charters. A 'right-to-work' amendment adopted 5 Nov. 1946 makes illegal the 'closed shop' demands of trade unions. Nebraska is represented in Congress by 2 senators and 3 representatives.

In the 1976 presidential election Ford polled 359,219 votes, Carter 233,293.

The capital is Lincoln. The state has 93 counties.

Governor: James Exon (D.), 1975–78 ($25,000).
Lieut.-Governor: Gerald Whelan (D.) ($25,000).
Secretary of State: Allen Beerman (R.) ($25,000).

BUDGET. For the fiscal year ending 30 June 1975 (US Census Bureau figures) the state's revenues were $790·6m. (taxation, $424·8m. and federal aid, $228·1m.); general expenditures were $595·2m. ($184·9m. for education, $125·9m. for highways and $121·4m. for public welfare).

The state has a bonded indebtedness limit of $100,000.

Per capita personal income (1976) was $6,086.

ENERGY AND NATURAL RESOURCES

Minerals. The total output of minerals, 1976, was valued at $126·5m., petroleum (5·9m. bbls) and sand and gravel (13·5m. tons) being the most important.

Agriculture. Nebraska is one of the most important agricultural states. In 1976 it contained approximately 68,000 farms, with a total area of 48m. acres. The average farm was 706 acres.

In 1976, 5·9m. acres were irrigated and 55,078 irrigation wells were registered.

Cash income from crops (1976), $1,690·7m., and from livestock, $2,176·9m. Principal crops, with estimated 1976 yield: Maize, 514·6m. bu. (ranking fourth in US); wheat, 94·4m. bu.; sorghums for grain, 119·7m. bu.; oats, 26·9m. bu.; soybeans, 20·6m. bu. About 1,250 farms grow sugar-beet for 5 factories; output, 1976, 1·7m. short tons. On 1 Jan. 1977 the state contained 6·45m. all cattle (ranking third in US), 138,000 milch cows, 210,000 sheep and 3·1m. swine.

Forestry. The area of national forest, 1974, was 351,000 acres.

INDUSTRY. In 1973, 1,703 manufacturing establishments had 66,300 production workers, earning $516·5m.; value added by manufacturing (1973), $1,989·8m. The chief industry is meat-packing, employing (1973), 11,300 (9,500 production workers) and value added was $294·8m.

COMMUNICATIONS

Roads. The state-maintained highway system embraced 9,866 miles in 1975; local roads, 87,440 miles. In 1976, 810,933 automobiles were registered.

Railways. In 1976 there were 7,589 miles of railway.

Aviation. Airports (1975) numbered 341, of which 122 were publicly owned.

JUSTICE, RELIGION, EDUCATION AND WELFARE

Justice. A 'Civil Rights Act' revised in 1969 provides that all people are entitled to a 'full and equal enjoyment of the accommodations, advantages, facilities and privileges' of hotels, restaurants, public conveyances, amusement places and other places. The state university is forbidden to discriminate between students 'because of age, sex, color or nationality'. An Act of 1941 declares it to be 'the policy of this state' that no trade union should discriminate, in collective bargaining, 'against any person because of his race or color'.

The state's prisons had, 30 Sept, 1976, 1,392 inmates (90 per 100.000 population). From 1930 to 1962 there were 4 executions (electrocution), 3 white men and 1 American Indian, all for murder, and none since.

Religion. The Roman Catholics had 313,100 members in 1973; Protestant Churches, 475,200; Jews, 8,000 members. Total, all denominations, 796,300 (unofficial figures).

Education. School attendance is compulsory for children from 7 to 16 years of age. Public elementary schools, autumn 1976, had 163,951 enrolled pupils; secondary schools, 148,066 pupils. Teachers' salaries, 1975, averaged $9,945 in elementary and $10,926 in secondary schools. Estimated public school expenditure for year ending 30 June 1975 was $336·8m. Total enrolment in 31 institutions of higher education, autumn 1976, was 77,921 students. The largest institutions were (1975):

Opened	*Institution*	*Students*
1867	Peru State College, Peru (State)	805
1869	Univ. of Nebraska, Lincoln (State)	23,927
1878	Creighton Univ., Omaha (RC)	4,797
1883	Midland Lutheran College, Fremont (CA)	1,125
1887	Nebraska Wesleyan Univ. (Methodist)	1,152
1891	Union College, Lincoln (Seventh Day Adventist)	907
1894	Concordia Teachers College, Seward (Lutheran)	1,125

Opened	*Institution*	*Students*
1905	Kearney State College, Kearney (State)	5,642
1908	Univ. of Nebraska, Omaha (State)	14,993
1910	Wayne State College, Wayne (State)	2,135
1911	Chadron State College, Chadron (State)	1,907
1966	Bellevue College, Bellevue (Private)	1,543

The state holds 1·52m. acres of land as a permanent endowment of her schools; permanent public school endowment fund in June 1976 was $49·6m.

Health. In 1976 the state had 118 hospitals and 510 patients in mental hospitals.

Social Security. The administration of public welfare is the responsibility of the County Divisions of Welfare with policy-forming, regulatory, advisory and supervisory functions performed by the State Department of Public Welfare. In 1976 public welfare provided financial aid and/or services as follows: for 12,172 individuals who were aged, blind or disabled, with an average state supplement of $43.09; for 11,830 families with dependent children, with an average payment of $204.13 per family; for 71,464 individuals who had medical needs, $816.09 per individual; for 849 children in need of child welfare services; for 3,386 children who were in need of crippled children's services and medical care. The amount of aid is based on need in accordance with State assistance standards; the programme of aid to families with dependent children is limited to a maximum maintenance payment of $210 for 1 child plus $42 for each additional child.

Books of Reference

Nebraska Statistical Handbook, 1978–79. Nebraska Dept. of Econ. Development, Lincoln
Nebraska Blue-Book. Legislative Council. Lincoln. Biennial
Olson, J. C., *History of Nebraska.* Univ. of Nebraska Press, 1955

State Library: State Law Library, State House, Lincoln. *Librarian:* Larry D. Donelson.

NEVADA

HISTORY. Nevada, first settled in 1851, when it was a part of the Territory of Utah (created 1850), was made a Territory in 1861, enlarged in 1862 by an addition from Utah Territory and admitted into the Union on 31 Oct. 1864 as the 36th state. In 1866 and 1867 the area of the state was significantly enlarged at the expense of the Territories of Utah and Arizona.

AREA AND POPULATION. Nevada is bounded north by Oregon and Idaho, east by Utah, south-east by Arizona, with the Colorado River forming most of the boundary, south and west by California. Area 110,540 sq. miles, 752 sq. miles being water. The federal government in 1973 owned 60,908,872 acres, or 86·5% of the land area. Vacant public lands, 48,340,876 acres. The Bureau of Indian Affairs controlled 1·35m. acres in 1975, of which 1,062,047 acres have been assigned to Indian tribes.

Census population on 1 April 1970, 488,738, an increase of 203,460 or 71·3% since 1960. Estimate, 1976, 630,530. Births, 1976, were 9,631 (15·2 per 1,000 population); deaths, 4,543 (7·2); infant deaths, 142 (30·9 per 1,000 live births); marriages, 101,400 (166·3 per 1,000 population, largest of any state); divorces, 10,300 (16·4).

Population in 5 census years (with distribution by sex, 1970) was:

	White	*Negro*	*Indian*	*Asiatic and all others*	*Total*	*Per sq. mile*
1910	74,276	513	5,240	1,846	81,875	0·7
1930	84,515	516	4,871	1,156	91,058	0·8
1950	149,908	4,302	5,025	848	160,083	1·5
1960	263,443	13,484	6,681	1,670	285,278	2·6
1970	449,850	27,579	7,329	3,980	488,738	4·4
Male	228,416	13,754	3,516	1,948	247,697	—
Female	221,371	13,825	3,813	2,032	241,041	—

Of the total population in 1970, 395,336 persons (80·9%) were urban (70·4% in 1960). In 1970 native born numbered 470,559; foreign-born, 18,179; those 18 years of age or older, 318,151.

The largest cities are Las Vegas, with population (1970 census) of 125,787 (urbanized area, 236,681); Reno, 72,863 (99,687); North Las Vegas, 36,216; Sparks, 24,187; Henderson, 16,395, and Carson City, 15,468. Clark County (Las Vegas, North Las Vegas and Henderson) and Washoe County (Reno and Sparks) together had 80% of the total state population in 1970.

CONSTITUTION AND GOVERNMENT. The constitution adopted in 1864 is still in force, with over 60 amendments. The Legislature meets biennially (and in special sessions) and consists of a Senate of 20 members elected for 4 years, half their number retiring every 2 years, and an Assembly of 40 members elected for 2 years. The Governor, Lieut.-Governor and Attorney-General are elected for 4 years. Qualified electors are all citizens with the usual residential qualification. Nevada is represented in Congress by 2 senators and 1 representative. A Supreme Court of 5 members is elected for 4 years on a non-partisan ballot.

In the 1976 presidential election Ford polled 100,786 votes and Carter 92,023.

The state capital is Carson City (population, 15,468 in 1970). There are 16 counties, 16 incorporated cities and towns and 1 city-county (Carson City).

Governor: Mike O'Callaghan (D.), 1975–78 ($40,000).
Lieut.-Governor: Robert Rose (D.) ($6,000).
Secretary of State: William D. Swackhammer (D.) ($25,000).

BUDGET. For the fiscal year ending 30 June 1976 estimated state general fund revenues were $179m., including federal receipts; general expenditures were $180·6m. Highways and education followed by health and welfare received the largest appropriations.

State bonded indebtedness on 30 June 1975, was $14·6m. The state has no franchise tax, capital stock tax, special intangibles tax, chain stores tax, stock transfer tax, admissions tax, estate tax, gift tax, income taxes or inheritance tax. The sales and use tax and gaming taxes are the largest revenue producers.

Per capita personal income (1975) was $6,673.

ENERGY AND NATURAL RESOURCES

Electricity. Electricity power stations supplied 13,950m. kwh. in 1974. There were 182,000 consumers in 1970. There are 8 suppliers of natural gas and there were 88,000 consumers in 1972; 1972 sales revenue, $46m.

Minerals. Production, 1975, in order of value was copper, gold, sand and gravel, barium. Other minerals are gypsum, iron ore, mercury, lime, lithium, silver, antimony, gemstones, lead, molybdenum, petroleum, fluorspar, perlite, pumice, clays, talc, salt, tungsten and zinc. Value of mineral output for 1975, $258m.

Agriculture. In 1974, 2,000 farms had a farm area of 9m. acres (9·2m. in 1960). Farms averaged (1974) 4,500 acres. Area under irrigation (1969 census figure) was 752,696 acres compared with 542,976 acres in 1959.

Gross income, 1974, from crops, livestock and government payments, $153·6m. Cattle, dairy products, hay and sheep are the principal commodities in order of cash receipts. Average income per farm, $25,636 (estimate). Total value of crops produced, $77·9m., of which hay accounted for 67·4%. On 1 Jan. 1975 there were 20,000 milch cows, 637,000 beef cattle, 151,000 sheep and 10,000 swine. In 1975 the wool clip yielded 1·3m. lb. of wool.

Forestry. The area of national forests (1975) under US Forest Service administration was 5,051,938 acres.

INDUSTRY. The principal industries are the service industry, especially tourism and legalized gambling, mining and smelting, livestock and irrigated agriculture, chemical manufacturing, and lumber processing. In 1973 there were 383 establishments with 10,367 production workers, earning (1974) $94m.; value added by manufacture (1974) was $216m.; value of shipments, $433m.

Gaming industry gross revenue for financial year ending 30 June 1976, $1,186m. There were at the same time 1,236 licences in force.

LABOUR. In July 1977 unemployment was at 6·5% of the work force. All industries, employed 307,900 workers. Main industries and employees, 1976: Mining, 4,100; contract construction, 11,300; manufacturing, 12,600; transport (except railways), public works and utilities, 17,200; interstate railways, 1,600; hotels, gaming and recreation, 72,300; other service industries, 36,000; retail trade, 43,200; government, 45,800.

COMMUNICATIONS

Roads. Highway mileage (federal, state and local) totalled 49,659 in 1973, of which 16,464 miles were surfaced; motor vehicle registrations at 1 Jan. 1975 numbered 510,627.

Railways. In 1973 there were 1,553 miles of main-line railway. Nevada is served by Southern Pacific, Union Pacific and Western Pacific railways, and Amtrak passenger service for Carlin, Elko, Reno and Sparks.

Aviation. There were (1974) 114 civil airports and heliports (1,307 civil aircraft registered); 7 scheduled airlines operated: Air West, Delta, Frontier, National, TWA, United and Western. During 1976 McCarren International Airport and Reno International Airport handled 8·9m. passengers.

Post. In 1976 there were 11 telephone exchanges with 549,087 telephones in service.

JUSTICE, RELIGION, EDUCATION AND WELFARE

Justice. Prohibition of marriage between persons of different race was repealed by statute in 1959.

A 1965 Civil Rights Act makes it illegal for persons operating public accommodations, employers of 15 or more employees, labour unions, and employment agencies to discriminate on the basis of race, colour, religion or national origin; a 1971 law makes racial discrimination in the sale or renting of houses illegal. A Commission on Equal Rights of Citizens is charged with enforcing these laws.

Between 1924 and 1967 executions (by lethal gas—the first state to adopt this method, in 1921), have numbered 31. Capital punishment was abolished in 1972.

Prison population, 1976, was 953; men 902, women 51.

Religion. Roman Catholics are the most numerous religious group, followed by members of the Church of Jesus Christ of Latter-day Saints (Mormons) and various Protestant churches.

Education. School attendance is compulsory for children from 7 to 17 years of age. In Oct. 1976 the 170 public elementary schools, including kindergartens, had 69,647 pupils; there were 83 secondary public schools, including junior and high schools. There were 2,788 elementary teachers (average salary $13,175), 2,539 secondary teachers with an average salary of $13,236 and 523 special education teachers (for handicapped pupils) earning an average of $12,438. There were 41 parochial and private schools. The University of Nevada, Reno, had, in 1976, 370 full-time instructors and 7,525 students, and University of Nevada, Las Vegas, 285 instructors and 6,507 students. Two-year community colleges operate as part of the University of Nevada in Carson City, Elko and Las Vegas. There were (1976) 221 full-time instructors in community colleges and 14,300 students.

Health. In 1976 the state had 24 hospitals (3,064 beds) and 19 skilled nursing units (1,158 beds).

Social Security. Old-age assistance is granted to all 65 years of age or older who are in need, and have assets not over $750 ($1,500 for married couples); end of fiscal year 1974–75, total expenditure was $6,179,040 at an average of $140 each person per month, for 3,678 people. Families with dependent children received $7,613,458 at $45.52 monthly average per person. The blind received $328,440 at $170 for 161 people. Nevada is the only state without aid to the permanently and totally disabled.

Books of Reference

Information: Bureau of Business and Economic Research (Univ. of Nevada).

Handbook of the Nevada Legislature, 55th Session, 1969. Legislative Counsel Bureau. Carson City

Legislative Manual, State of Nevada, 55th Cession, 1969. Legislative Counsel Bureau. Carson City

Political History of Nevada. Secretary of State. Carson City, 1965

Financing State and Local Government in Nevada. Legislative Counsel Bureau. Carson City, 1960

Study of General Fund Revenues of the State of Nevada. Legislative Counsel Bureau. Carson City, 1966

Education, Manpower and Economic Data for Nevada. Nevada Employment Security Dept., Carson City, 1971

Bushnell, E., *The Nevada Constitution: Origin and Growth.* Univ. of Nevada Press, 2nd ed., 1968

Hulse, James W., *The Nevada Adventure, A History.* Univ. of Nevada Press, 2nd ed., 1969

Mack, E. M., and Sawyer, B. W., *Here is Nevada: A History of the State.* Sparks, Nevada, 1965

State Library: Nevada State Library, Carson City. *State Librarian:* Mildred J. Heyer.

NEW HAMPSHIRE

HISTORY. New Hampshire, first settled in 1623, is one of the 13 original states of the Union.

AREA AND POPULATION. New Hampshire is bounded north by Canada, east by Maine and the Atlantic, south by Massachusetts and west by Vermont. Area, 9,304 sq. miles, of which 312 sq. miles are inland water. Census population, 1 April 1970, 737,681, an increase of 21·5% since 1960. Births, 1975, were 12,064; deaths, 7,147; infant deaths, 147; marriages, 8,992; divorces, 4,256.

Population at 5 federal censuses (with distribution by sex, 1970) was:

	White	*Negro*	*Indian*	*Asiatic*	*Total*	*Per sq. mile*
1910	429,906	564	34	68	430,572	47·7
1930	464,351	790	64	88	465,293	51·6
1950	532,275	731	74	162	533,242	59·1
1960	604,334	1,903	135	549	606,921	65·2
			All others			
1970	733,106	2,505	2,070		737,681	81·7
Male	358,261	1,418	993		360,672	—
Female	374,845	1,087	1,007		377,009	—

Native whites, 1970, were 697,396; foreign-born whites, 36,422. 416,040 (60·1%) were urban (58·3% in 1960); those 21 years of age or older numbered 443,312.

The largest city of the state is Manchester, with a 1970 census population of 87,754. Other cities are: Nashua, 55,820; Concord (capital), 30,022; Dover, 20,850; Portsmouth, 25,717; Keene, 20,467; Rochester, 17,938; Berlin, 15,256; Claremont, 14,221; Laconia, 14,888; Lebanon, 9,725; Somersworth, 9,026; Franklin, 7,292.

CONSTITUTION AND GOVERNMENT. While the present constitution dates from 1784, it was extensively revised in 1792 when the state joined the Union. Since 1775 there have been 16 state conventions with 49 amendments adopted to amend the constitution.

The Legislature consists of a Senate of 30 members, elected for 2 years, and a House of Representatives, restricted to between 375 and 400 members, elected for 2 years. The Governor and 5 administrative officers called 'Councillors' are also elected for 2 years.

Electors must be adult citizens, able to read and write, duly registered and not paupers or under sentence for crime. New Hampshire sends to the Federal Congress 2 senators and 2 representatives.

In the 1976 presidential election Ford polled 185,472 votes, Carter 147,618.

The capital is Concord. The state is divided into 10 counties.

Governor: Meldrim Thomson (R.), 1977–79 ($30,000).
Secretary of State: Robert L. Stark (R.).

BUDGET. The state government's general revenue for the fiscal year ending 30 June 1975 (US Census Bureau figures) was $170m.; general expenditures, $140·3m. ($48·3m. for education and $29·9m. for public welfare).

Net long-term debt of state, 30 June 1975, was $138·6m.

Per capita personal income (1970) was $4,570.

NATURAL RESOURCES

Minerals. Minerals are little worked; they consist mainly of sand and gravel, stone, and clay for building and highway construction.

Agriculture. In 1975, 2,600 farms had a total acreage of 540,000 acres; average farm was 211 acres with average land value at $261 per acre. Commercial farms in 1968 numbered about 1,500 with 600,000 acres of crop land. The US Soil Survey estimates that the state has 164,167 acres of excellent soil, 486,615 acres of fair soil, 530,630 of poor soil and 3,843,798 of non-arable soil. Only 636,195 acres (11% of the total area) show moderate erosion.

Cash income, 1974, from dairy products, crops and livestock, $91m. The chief field crops are hay and vegetables; the chief fruit crop is apples. On 1 Jan. 1975 animals on farms were 40,000 milch cows, 69,000 all cattle, 4,800 sheep, 8,700 swine, 1·8m. poultry, 28,000 turkeys and about 36,225 horses.

Forestry. In 1975 commercial forest land totalled 4,907,400 acres; national forest, 591,909 acres; state forests and parks, 72,353 acres; forest industry ownership, 793,400 acres.

INDUSTRY. In 1968, 1,191 manufacturing establishments employed 99,074 persons who earned $586m.; 47% of manufacturing employment is accounted for in durable goods.

Principal industries are leather products, electrical machinery, non-electrical machinery and textiles. In 1968, 794 wholesale establishments had gross sales of $505·3m.; 7,045 retail establishments had gross sales of $881·8m.

COMMUNICATIONS

Roads. On 1 Jan. 1975 the length of state highways was 4,373 miles, of which the state maintained 4,155 miles and municipalities 218 miles. The length of town roads, urban and rural, totalled 7,918 miles. Motor vehicles registered, 1975, numbered 558,252.

Railways. In 1975 the length of railway in the state was 826 miles.

Aviation. There were 47 airports of which 14 were public.

JUSTICE, RELIGION, EDUCATION AND WELFARE

Justice. The state prison held 262 persons on 1 Aug. 1975. Since 1930 there has been only one execution (by hanging)—a white man, for murder, in 1939.

Religion. The Roman Catholic Church is the largest single body. The largest Protestant churches are Congregational, Episcopal, Methodist and United Baptist Convention of N.H.

Education. School attendance is compulsory for children from 6 to 14 years of age during the whole school term, or to 16 if their district provides a high school. Employed illiterate minors between 16 and 21 years of age must attend evening or special classes, if provided by the district.

In 1975 the 362 public elementary schools enrolled 102,760 pupils and the 97 public secondary schools 69,353 pupils. In 1975, 70 private and parochial elementary schools had 11,817 registered pupils and 20 secondary schools, 6,057. Public school salaries, 1973–74, averaged $9,841. Total expenditure on public schools in 1973–74 was estimated at $195,924,155.

Total enrolment, 1973–74, in 29 institutions of higher education was 27,415 students. Dartmouth College, at Hanover, founded in 1769, had 292 instructors and 3,370 students; the University of New Hampshire, at Durham, founded in 1866, had 615 instructors and 10,297 students.

Health. In 1975 the state had 28 hospitals (3,246 beds). In 1975 mental hospitals had 1,260 patients, and there were 724 persons in institutions for the mentally retarded.

Social Security. The Division of Welfare handles public assistance for (1) aged citizens 65 years or over, (2) needy aged aliens, (3) needy blind persons, (4) needy citizens between 18 and 64 years inclusive, who are permanently and totally disabled, (5) needy children under 21 years, (6) Medicaid and the medically needy not eligible for a monthly grant.

In Sept. 1975, 1,804 persons were receiving old-age assistance of an average $394 per month; 143 blind, $627 annually; 937 permanently and totally disabled, $725 annually; 455 mentally disabled, $850 annually.

Books of Reference

Morrison, L. S. *The Government of New Hampshire.* Concord, 1952
N.H. Register. State Year Book and Legislative Manual. Portland, Maine, 1965
Squires, J. D., *Granite State of the United States.* New York, 1956

NEW JERSEY

HISTORY. New Jersey, first settled in the early 1600s, is one of the 13 original states in the Union.

AREA AND POPULATION. New Jersey is bounded north by New York, east by the Atlantic with Long Island and New York City to the north-east, south by Delaware Bay and west by Pennsylvania. Area (US Bureau of Census), 7,836 sq. miles (304 sq. miles being inland water). Census population, 1 April 1970, 7,168,164, an increase of 18·2% since 1960. Estimate, 1975, 7,414,700. Births, 1976, were 90,549 (12·2 per 1,000 population); deaths, 65,276 (8·8); infant deaths, 1,366 (15·1 per 1,000 live births); marriages, 51,291 (6·9); divorces, 22,331 in 1975–76.

Population at 5 federal censuses (with distribution by sex, 1970) was:

	White	*Negro*	*Indian*	*Asiatic*	*All others*	*Total*	*Per sq. mile*
1910	2,445,894	89,760	168	1,345	—	2,537,167	337·7
1930	3,829,663	208,828	213	2,630	122	4,041,334	537·3
1950	4,511,585	318,565	621	3,601	956	4,835,329	642·8
1960	5,539,003	514,875	1,699	8,778	2,427	6,066,782	739·5
1970	6,349,908	770,292	4,706	20,537	22,721	7,168,164	953·1
Male	3,080,215	363,756	2,163	9,831	11,408	3,467,373	—
Female	3,269,693	406,536	2,543	10,706	11,313	3,700,791	—

Of the population in 1970, 6,373,405 persons (88·9%, the highest percentage of any state) were urban (88·6% in 1960); 4,564,050 were 20 years of age or older.

Census population of the larger cities and towns in 1970 was:

Newark	381,930	Irvington	59,743	Woodbridge[1]	98,944
Jersey City	260,545	Union City	58,537	Hamilton[1]	79,609
Paterson	144,824	Passaic	55,124	Edison[1]	67,120
Elizabeth	112,654	Bloomfield	52,029	Cherry Hill[1]	64,395
Trenton (capital)	104,638	Atlantic City	47,859	Parsippany-Troy Hills[1]	55,112
Camden	102,551	Vineland	47,399	Middleton[1]	54,623
Clifton	82,437	Plainfield	46,862	Union[1]	53,077
East Orange	75,471	Hoboken	45,380		
Bayonne	72,743	Montclair	44,043		

[1] Urban townships.

Largest urbanized areas (1970) were: New York NY–NE New Jersey, 16,206,841 (including Newark, Jersey City, Paterson, Clifton and Passaic); Philadelphia (Pa.–NJ), 744,045; Trenton (NJ–Pa.), 242,673. State population estimates for several of the larger cities and towns in 1975 were: Newark, 375,125; Jersey City, 257,485; Paterson, 147,720; Elizabeth, 114,485; Trenton, 106,465; Woodbridge, 101,690; Camden, 101,485.

CONSTITUTION AND GOVERNMENT. The legislative power is vested in a Senate and a General Assembly, the members of which are chosen by the people, all citizens (with necessary exceptions) 18 years of age, with the usual residential qualifications, having the right of suffrage. The present constitution, ratified by the registered voters on 4 Nov. 1947, has been amended 17 times. In 1966 the Constitutional Convention proposed, and the people adopted, a new plan providing for a 40-member Senate and an 80-member General Assembly. This plan, as certified by the Apportionment Commission and modified by the courts, provides for 40 legislative districts, with 1 senator and 2 assemblymen elected for each. Assemblymen serve 2 years, senators 4 years, except those elected at the election following each census, who serve for 2 years. The Governor is elected for 4 years.

The state sends to Congress 2 senators and 15 representatives.

In the 1976 presidential election Ford polled 1,477,858 votes, Carter 1,420,668.

The capital is Trenton. The state is divided into 21 counties, which are subdivided into 567 municipalities—cities, towns, boroughs, villages and townships.

Governor: Brendan T. Byrne (D.), 1978–81 ($65,000).
Secretary of State: Donald Lan ($43,000).

BUDGET. For the year ending 30 June 1976 (US Census Bureau figures) general revenues were $4,116·91m. (taxation, $2,292,438,000 and federal aid, $1,139·6m.; general expenditures were $5,853·4m. (education, $1,360·4m., highways, $357·4m., and public welfare, $1,059·49m.).

Total net long-term debt, 30 June 1976, was $3,121,189,000.

Per capita personal income (1976) was $7,269.

NATURAL RESOURCES

Minerals. The chief minerals are stone ($45·58m. 1973) and sand and gravel ($43m.); others are zinc ($13·6m.), clay products ($666,000), peat and gemstones. New Jersey is a leading producer of glass sand, moulding sand, trap rock and of green sand, used in water-softening. Total value of mineral products, 1973, was $114m.

Agriculture. Livestock raising, market-gardening, fruit-growing, horticulture and forestry are pursued. In 1976, 7,900 farms had a total area of 1,025,000 acres; average farm had 130 acres valued (1976) land and buildings, at $2,852 per acre, highest in US. In 1974 full owners had 5,593 farms; part-owners 1,672; tenant-farmers, 790.

Cash income, 1976, from crops, $196·7m., and livestock, $111·47m.

Leading crops are tomatoes (value, $20·47m., 1976), maize ($41·69m.), peaches ($12·1m.), potatoes ($8·87m.), blueberries ($11·97m.), soybeans ($18·36m.).

Farm animals on 1 Jan. 1977 included 60,000 milch cows, 114,000 all cattle, 8,300 sheep and 85,000 swine.

INDUSTRY. In 1975 manufacturing establishments employed 470,900 production workers, receiving $4,605·7m. in wages; value added by manufacture, $17,878·4m. The principal industries by value (1975) are: Chemicals and allied products, $4,826·9m.; food and kindred products, $1,852·7m.; electrical equipment and supplies, $1,462·3m.; machinery (except electrical), $1,389·3m.

COMMUNICATIONS

Roads. In 1976 there were 33,027 miles of roads (municipal, 23,159 miles; state, 2,208 miles; county, 6,795 miles; others, 865 miles).

Railways. In 1977, the state had 1,404 route miles of railway.

Aviation. There were (1975) 222 airports, of which 26 were publicly owned.

JUSTICE, RELIGION, EDUCATION AND WELFARE

Justice. State prisons in 1976 had a daily average of 6,396 inmates. Since 1930 executions (by electrocution) have totalled 74, including 47 whites, 25 Negroes and 2 other races, all for murder. There have been none since 1966.

The constitution of New Jersey forbids discrimination against any person on account of 'religious principles, race, color, ancestry or national origin'. The state has had, since 1945, a 'fair employment act', *i.e.*, a Civil Rights statute forbidding any employer, public or private (with 6 or more employees), to discriminate against any applicant for work (or to discharge any employee) on the grounds of 'race, creed, color, national origin or ancestry'. Trade unions may not bar Negroes from membership.

Religion. The Roman Catholic population of New Jersey in 1976 was 2,840,483. No official Protestant figures are available; estimates place Jewish population at 429,850 (1975).

Education. Elementary instruction is compulsory for all from 6 to 16 years of age and free to all from 5 to 20 years of age. In autumn 1976 public elementary schools had 894,505 and secondary schools had 526,843 enrolled pupils; public colleges had 225,511 students and independent colleges 63,387. The total cost of public schools, 1975–76, $2,686m. Average salary of all elementary and secondary classroom teachers in public schools 1976–77 was $14,537.

Rutgers, the State University (founded as Queen's College in 1766) had, in 1976, an opening autumn enrolment of 33,870 full- and part-time students. Princeton (founded in 1746) had 4,494 students. Fairleigh Dickinson (1941) had 12,183; Kean College, 10,107; Montclair State College, 11,156; Glassboro State College, 8,898; Trenton State College, 8,333.

Health. In 1976 the state had 144 hospitals (47,645 beds), listed by the American Hospital Association.

Social Security. The Assistance for Dependent Children Programme had (1976) 1,612,748 cases, average cost per case, $275.88. The Assistance to the Families of the Working Poor Programme had 95,055 cases, average cost per case, $211.64. The Food Stamp Programme had 6,356,801 persons participating.

The state's welfare system (Oct. 1976) cared for 15,422 in institutions for the mentally retarded and diseased, 576 in veterans' homes and 441 in training schools for delinquents.

Books of Reference

Manual of the Legislature of New Jersey. Trenton. Annual

Boyd, J. P. (ed.), *Fundamentals and Constitutions of New Jersey, 1664–1954*. Princeton, 1964

Cunningham, J. T., *This is New Jersey*. 2nd ed. Rutgers Univ. Press, 1968

Rich, B. M., *The Government and Administration of New Jersey*. New York, 1957

League of Women Voters of New Jersey. *New Jersey: Spotlight on Government*. Rutgers Univ. Press, 1972

State Library: 185 W. State Street, Trenton, N.J. 08625. *Acting Director:* David C. Palmer.

NEW MEXICO

HISTORY. The first settlement was established in 1598. Until 1771 New Mexico was the Spanish kings' 'Kingdom of New Mexico'. In 1771 it was annexed to the northern provinces of New Spain. When New Spain won its independence in 1821, it took the name of Republic of Mexico and established New Mexico as its northernmost department. When the war between the US and Mexico was concluded on 2 Feb. 1848 New Mexico was recognized as belonging to the US, and on 9 Sept. 1850 it was made a Territory. Part of the Territory was assigned to Texas; later Utah was formed into a separate Territory; in 1861 another part was transferred to Colorado, and in 1863 Arizona was disjoined, leaving to New Mexico its present area. New Mexico became a state in Jan. 1912.

AREA AND POPULATION. New Mexico is bounded north by Colorado, north-east by Oklahoma, east by Texas, south by Texas and Mexico and west by Arizona. Land area 121,412 sq. miles (221 sq. miles water). Public lands, administered by federal agencies (1974) amounted to 25·7m. acres of 33% of the total area. The Bureau of Indian Affairs held 7·3m. acres; the State of New Mexico held 9·4m. acres; 35·4m. acres were privately owned.

Census population, 1 April 1970, 1,016,000, an increase of 64,977 or 6·8% since 1960. Mid-year estimate 1975, 1,147,000. Vital statistics, 1975: Births, 20,413 (17·8 per 1,000 population); deaths, 7,877 (6·9); infant deaths, 334 (16·4 per 1,000 live births); marriages, 13,505 (11·8); divorces, 7,223 (6·3).

The population in 5 census years (with distribution by sex, 1970) was:

	White	*Negro*	*Indian*	*Asiatic*	*Total*	*Per sq. mile*
1910	304,594	1,628	20,573	506	327,301	2·7
1940	492,312	4,672	34,510	324	531,818	4·4
1950	630,211	8,408	41,901	667	681,187	5·6
1960	875,763	17,063	56,255	1,942	951,023	7·8
1970	915,815	19,555	72,788	7,842[1]	1,016,000	8·4
Male	452,120	9,833	35,035	3,836	500,824	—
Female	463,695	9,722	37,753	4,006	515,176	—

[1] Includes unspecified races, 1970.

Native whites, 1970, were 901,740; foreign-born whites, 21,512. Of the 1970 total, 711,334 persons (70%) were urban (65·6% in 1960); 609,784 were 18 years of age or older.

Before 1930 New Mexico was largely a Spanish-speaking state, but since 1945 an influx of population from other states has reduced the percentage of white persons of Spanish origin or descent to an estimated 30%.

The largest cities are Albuquerque, with population (July 1974) 286,300; Santa Fé (capital), 44,800; Las Cruces, 41,600; Roswell, 40,100; Clovis, 33,100; Hobbs, 28,300.

CONSTITUTION AND GOVERNMENT. The constitution of 1912 is still in force with 73 amendments. The state Legislature, which meets annually, consists of 42 members of the Senate, elected for 4 years, and 70 members of the House of Representatives, elected for 2 years. The Governor and Lieut.-Governor are elected for 4 years. The state sends to Congress 2 senators and 2 representatives.

In the 1976 presidential election Ford polled 207,718 votes, Carter 199,225.

The state capital is Santa Fé. For local government the state is divided into 32 counties.

Governor: Jerry Apodaca (D.), 1975 ($35,000).
Lieut.-Governor: Robert Ferguson (D.), 1975 ($7.21 hourly rate).
Secretary of State: Ernestine Evans (D.), 1975 ($24,000).

BUDGET. For the year ending 30 June 1975 (US Census Bureau figures) general revenues were $1,264·3m. ($628·6m. from taxation and $342·5m. from federal government); general expenditures, $1,144·5m. (education, $519·7m.; highways, $150·9m., and public welfare, $89·5m.).

Long-term debt on 30 June 1975 was $642m.
Per capita personal income (1975) was $4,775.

ENERGY AND NATURAL RESOURCES

Minerals. New Mexico is the country's largest domestic source of uranium, perlite and potassium salts. Production of recoverable U_3O_8 was 9·9m. lb. in 1975; perlite, 419,000 short tons; potassium salts, 2,099,000 short tons; petroleum, 94,553,000 bbls of 42 gallons); natural gas, 1,203,302,000 cu. ft; natural gas liquids, 9,048,000 bbls (of 42 gallons); copper, 140,535 short tons; zinc, 11,515 short tons; coal, 9m. short tons. The value of the total mineral output was $2,159·8m. An average of 20,100 persons were employed monthly in the mining industry in 1975.

Agriculture. New Mexico produces cereals, vegetables, fruit, livestock and cotton. Dry farming and irrigation have proved profitable in periods of high prices. There were 11,800 farms and ranches covering 47·2m. acres in 1975, average farm (or ranch) was valued (land and buildings) at $168,336 in the 1969 US Census of Agriculture; 3,584 farms and ranches were of 1,000 acres and over.

Cash income, 1975, from crops, $177·4m., and from livestock products, $636·3m. Principal crops are cotton (73,000 bales from 97,500 acres in 1975), hay (963,000 tons from 272,000 acres) and grain sorghums (15·5m. bu. from 310,000 acres). The farm animals on 1 Jan. 1976 included 31,000 milch cows, 1·65m. all cattle, 590,000 sheep and 53,000 swine (1975). National forest area (1974) covered 9·2m. acres.

INDUSTRY. Average monthly non-agricultural employment during 1975 was 364,800: 27,200 were employed in manufacturing, 105,000 in government. In 1972, 17,200 production workers earned $98·7m. during the year; value added by manufacture was $366·2m.

COMMUNICATIONS

Roads. The state, 1975, had 70,198 miles of road, of which the state maintained 12,704 miles. Motor vehicle registrations, 1975, 915,852.

Railways. In 1974 there were 2,057 miles of railway.

Aviation. There were 141 airports in April 1976.

JUSTICE, RELIGION, EDUCATION AND WELFARE

Justice. The number of state penitentiary prisoners, average population 1975–76, was 1,160. The death penalty (by electrocution) has been imposed on 8 persons since 1933, 6 whites and 2 Negroes, all for murder. The last execution was in 1960.

Since 1949 the denial of employment by reason of race, colour, religion, national origin or ancestry has been forbidden. A law of 1955 prohibits discrimination in public places because of race or colour.

Religion. There were (1975) approximately 315,470 Protestant Church members and 356,530 Roman Catholics.

Education. Elementary education is free, and compulsory between 6 and 17 years or high-school graduation age. In 1974–75 the 88 school districts had an estimated enrolment of 273,294 students in public elementary and secondary schools. Private and parochial schools had 13,029 pupils. There were 12,382 teachers receiving an average salary of $10,005. Public education expenditure (excluding inter-government transfers) for 1974–75 was $519·7m.

The state-supported 4-year institutes of higher education are (1976):

	Faculty	*Students*
University of New Mexico, Albuquerque	783	21,529
New Mexico State University, Las Cruces	511	11,184
Eastern New Mexico University, Portales	172	3,872
New Mexico Highlands University, Las Vegas	145	2,055
Western New Mexico University, Silver City	60	1,916
New Mexico Institute of Mining and Technology, Sorocco	70	1,016

Health. In 1976 the state had 53 hospitals (5,027 beds).

Social Security. In April 1976, 13,811 persons were receiving aid to the disabled (average $119.10 per month); 12,600 persons were receiving old-age assistance (average $77.14 per month); 417 persons were receiving aid to the blind (average $119.90 per month); 59,940 people (Feb. 1976) received aid to families with dependent children (average $43.69 per month). Total expenditure for 1974 fiscal year: Old-age assistance, $10,836,000; aid to blind, $570,000; aid to disabled, $15,787,000; aid for dependent children, $28,857,000.

Books of Reference

Writers' Program. *New Mexico: A Guide to the Colorful State.* Rev. ed. New York, 1953
New Mexico Business (monthly; annual review in Jan.–Feb. issue). Bureau of Business and Economic Research, University of N.M., Albuquerque
New Mexico Statistical Abstract: 1975. Bureau of Business and Economic Research, Univ. of N.M., Albuquerque, 1975
Donnelly, T. C., *The Government of New Mexico.* Univ. of N.M. Press, Albuquerque, 1953
Holmes, Jack, *Politics in New Mexico,* Univ. of N.M. Press, Albuquerque, 1966
Muench, D., and Hillerman, T., *New Mexico.* Belding, Portland, Oregon, 1974

NEW YORK STATE

HISTORY. From 1609 to 1664 the region now called New York was claimed by the Dutch; then it came under the rule of the English, who governed the country till the outbreak of the War of Independence. On 20 April 1777 New York adopted a constitution which transformed the colony into an independent state; on 26 July 1788 it ratified the constitution of the US, becoming one of the 13 original states. New York dropped its claim to Vermont after the latter was admitted to the Union in 1791. With the annexation of a small area from Massachusetts in 1853, New York assumed its present boundaries.

AREA AND POPULATION. New York is bounded west and north by Canada with Lake Erie, Lake Ontario and the St Lawrence River forming the boundary; east by Vermont, Massachusetts and Connecticut, south-east by the Atlantic, south by New Jersey and Pennsylvania. Area, 49,576 sq. miles (1,745 sq. miles being water). Census population, 1 April 1970, 18,241,266, an increase of 8·7% since 1960: 1975 estimate, 18,122,116. Births in 1975 were 235,803; deaths, 168,739; infant deaths, 3,764; marriages, 142,752; divorces, 55,612 (includes all dissolutions).

Population in 5 census years (with distribution be sex, 1970) was:

	White	*Negro*	*Indian*	*Asiatic*	*Total*	*Per sq. mile*
1910	8,966,845	134,191	6,046	6,532	9,113,614	191·2
1930	12,143,191	412,814	6,973	15,088	12,588,066	262·6
1950	13,872,095	918,191	10,640	29,266	14,830,192	309·3
1960	15,287,071	1,417,511	16,491	51,678	16,782,304	350·1
			All others			
1970	15,834,090	2,168,949	233,828		18,236,967	380·3
Male	—	1,001,996	—	—	8,715,339	—
Female	—	1,166,953	—	—	9,521,628	—

Of the Asiatics in 1970, 81,378 were Chinese and 20,351 Japanese. 15,602,486 or 85·6% were urban (85·4% in 1960); those 21 years of age or older numbered 11,510,452; foreign-born whites numbered 1,847,926 in 1970. Aliens registered in Jan. 1972 numbered 811,039.

The population of New York City, by boroughs, census of 1 April 1970 was: Manhattan, 1,539,233; Bronx, 1,471,701; Brooklyn, 2,602,012; Queens, 1,987,174; Richmond, 295,443; total, 7,895,563. The New York metropolitan statistical area had, in 1970 11,571,899 while the larger New York–NE New Jersey urbanized area had 16,206,841.

Population of other large cities and unincorporated places, estimate, July 1974 was:

Buffalo	438,620	Binghamton	57,630	*Unincorporated towns*	
Rochester	284,670	White Plains	49,850	Freeport	41,750
Yonkers	204,000	Rome	45,800	Valley Stream	41,350
Syracuse	184,920	Jamestown	38,650	Hempstead	40,450
Albany (capital)	107,690	Elmira	36,700	Lindenhurst	31,850
Utica	87,600	N. Tonawanda	35,700	Rockville Center	28,150
Niagara Falls	81,150	Auburn	35,700	Garden City	25,950
Schenectady	76,350	Watertown	29,050	Massapequa Park	21,900
New Rochelle	74,600	Poughkeepsie	28,750		
Mount Vernon	71,950	Newburgh	24,900		
Troy	60,900				

Other large urbanized areas, July 1974; Buffalo, 1·13m.; Rochester, 764,050; Albany–Schenectady–Troy, 660,490.

CONSTITUTION AND GOVERNMENT. The present constitution dates from 1894; a later constitutional convention, 1938, is now legally considered merely to have amended the 1894 constitution, which has now had 93 amendments. The Constitutional Convention of 1967 (4 April through 26 Sept.) was composed of 186 delegates who proposed a new state constitution; however this was rejected by the registered voters on 7 Nov. 1967. The Senate consists of 60 members, and the Assembly of 150 members, both elected every 2 years. The Governor and Lieut.-Governor are elected for 4 years. The right of suffrage resides in every adult who has been a citizen for 90 days, and has the usual residential qualifications; new voters must establish, by certificates or test, that they have had at least an elementary education.

The state is represented in Congress by 2 senators and 39 representatives.

In the 1976 presidential election Carter polled 3,336,665 votes, Ford 3,060,695.

The state capital is Albany. For local government the state is divided into 62 counties, 5 of which constitute the city of New York. New York leads in state parks and recreation areas, covering 248,277 acres in 1976.

Cities are in 3 classes, the first class having each 175,000 or more inhabitants and the third under 50,000. Each is incorporated by charter, under special legislation. The government of New York City is vested in the mayor (Edward Koch), elected for 4 years, and a city council, whose president and members are elected for 4 years. The council has a President and 37 members, each elected from a state senatorial district wholly within the city. The mayor appoints all the heads of departments, except the comptroller, who is elected. Each of the 5 city boroughs (Manhattan, Bronx, Brooklyn, Queens and Richmond) has a president, elected for 4 years. Each of these boroughs is also a county, bearing the same name except Manhattan borough, which, as a county, is called New York, and Brooklyn, which is Kings County.

Governor: Hugh Carey (D.), 1975 ($85,000).
Lieut.-Governor: Mary Anne Krupsack (D.) ($50,000).
Secretary of State: Mario Cuomo (D.) ($44,175).

BUDGET. The state's general revenues for the financial year ending 31 March 1976 (preliminary) were $10,019·33m. ($9,480·98m. from taxes, $234·9m. from federal revenue sharing); general expenditures were $10,651m. ($3,267m. for education, $3,311·4m. for public welfare, $1,031·1m. for hospitals).

Per capita personal income was $6,564 in 1975.

The assessed valuation in 1975–76 of taxable real property in New York City was $39,656m. The assessed valuation of the state was $75,465m.

ENERGY AND NATURAL RESOURCES

Minerals (1973). Production of principal minerals: Sand and gravel (29·5m. short tons), salt (5·6m. short tons), zinc (81,455 short tons), petroleum (967,000 bbls), natural gas (4,539m. cu. ft.). The state is a leading producer of titanium concentrate, talc, abrasive garnet, wollastonite and emery. Quarry products include trap rock, slate, marble, limestone and sandstone. The value of mineral ouptut in 1973 was \$375·8m.

Agriculture. New York has large agricultural interests. On 1 Jan. 1976 it had 58,000 farms, with a total area of 11·4m. acres; average farm was 197 acres (1974).

Cash income, 1975, from crops and livestock, \$1,545m. Dairying, with 21,500 farms, 1975, is an important type of farming (39%) with produce at a market value of \$851·6m. Field crops comprise maize, winter wheat, oats and hay. New York (1975) ranks second in US in the production of apples, grapes, tart cherries and first for maple syrup. Other products are peaches, pears, plums, strawberries, raspberries, cabbages, onions, potatoes, maple sugar. Estimated farm animals, 1976, included 1,915,000 all cattle, 916,000 milch cows, 70,000 sheep, 90,000 swine and 10·65m. chickens.

INDUSTRY. In 1975 manufacturing establishments numbering 35,000 employed 1,424,327 production workers. The 1975 weekly earnings of workers engaged in industry and manufacturing averaged \$241. Leading industries were food and allied products, clothing and other textile products, printing and publishing, chemical and allied products, electrical equipment, transport equipment, instruments.

COMMUNICATIONS

Roads. There were (1975) 108,637 miles of municipal and rural roads. The New York State Thruway extends 559 miles from New York City to Buffalo and thence to the Pennsylvania State line; in 1975 receipts from tolls amounted to \$123,198,930. The Northway, a 176-mile toll-free highway, has been completed as a connecting road from the Thruway at Albany to the Canadian border at Champlain, Quebec.

Motor vehicle registrations in 1975 were 8,204,116, most of which (6,672,646) were private passenger vehicles.

Railways. There were in 1976, 5,015 miles of railways.

Aviation. There were 539 airports in 1976.

Shipping. The canals of the state, combined in 1918 in what is called the Improved Canal System, have a length of 524 miles, of which the Erie or Barge canal has 340 miles. In 1975 the canals carried 2m. tons of freight.

JUSTICE, RELIGION, EDUCATION AND WELFARE

Justice. The State Human Rights Law was approved 12 March 1945, effective 1 July, 1945. The State Division of Human Rights is charged with the responsibility of enforcing this law. The division may request and utilize the services of all governmental departments and agencies; adopt and promulgate suitable rules and regulations; test, investigate and pass upon complaints alleging discrimination in employment, in places of public accommodation, resort or amusement, education, and in housing, land and commercial space; hold hearings, subpoena witnesses and require the production for examination of papers relating to matters under investigation; grant compensatory damages and require repayment of profits in certain housing cases among other provisions; apply for court injunctions to prevent frustration of orders of the Commissioner.

On 30 Aug. 1976, 17,400 persons were in state prisons.

In 1963–75 there were no executions. Total executions (by electrocution) from 1930 to 1962 were 329 (234 whites, 90 Negroes, 5 other races; all for murder except 2 for kidnapping).

In 1975 murders reported in New York were 1,981; total violent crimes, 1,009,632. Police strength in Jan. 1976 was 66,880 (33,401 New York City; 4,806 county; 3,991 state police and 24,682 others).

Religion. The chief churches are Roman Catholic, with 6,348,132 members in 1975, Jewish congregations (2,150,385 in 1973) and Protestant Episcopal (482,095 in 1975).

Education. Education is compulsory between the ages of 7 and 16. In autumn 1975 the public elementary schools (grades kindergarten to 6) enrolled 1,748,419 children, public secondary schools (grades 7 to 12) had 1,657,596 pupils; classroom teachers numbered 182,772 in public schools. Total expenditure on public schools in 1974–75 was $7,394,850,184. Teachers' salaries, 1975–76, averaged $16,300.

The state's educational system, including public and private schools and secondary institutions, universities, colleges, libraries, museums, etc., constitutes (by legislative act) the 'University of the State of New York', which is governed by a Board of Regents consisting of 15 members appointed by the Legislature. Within the framework of this 'University' was established in 1948 a 'State University' which controls 66 colleges and educational centres, 36 of which are locally operated community colleges. The 'State University' is governed by a board of 15 Trustees, appointed by the Governor with the consent and advice of the Senate.

Higher education in the state is conducted in 249 institutions (613,046 full-time students), of which 163 are under private control and 86 under public control.

In 1975–76 the 249 institutions of higher education in the state had a total of approximately 1,077,000 degree and non-degree credit students. Among them were:

Founded	*Name and place*	*Teachers*	*Students*
1754	Columbia University, New York	3,467	24,177
1795	Union University, Schenectady and Albany	1,061	5,012
1824	Rensselaer Polytechnic Institute, Troy	862	5,117
1831	New York University, New York	3,380	40,813
1846	Colgate University, New York	193	2,514
1846	Fordham University, New York	1,058	14,266
1847	University of the City of New York, New York	16,534	262,731
1848	University of Rochester, Rochester	1,433	8,652
1849	Syracuse University, Syracuse	2,176	26,761
1854	Polytechnic Institute of New York	415	4,606
1856	St Lawrence University, Canton	158	2,601
1857	Cooper Union Institute of Technology, New York	126	1,627
1861	Vassar College, Poughkeepsie	229	2,314
1863	Manhattan College, New York	294	4,590
1865	Cornell University, Ithaca	1,861	11,482
1948	State University of New York	25,311	394,461

The Saratoga Performing Arts Centre (5,100 seats), a non-profit, tax-exempt organization, which opened in 1966, is the summer residence of the New York City Ballet and the Philadelphia Orchestra—two groups which present special educational programmes for students and teachers.

Health. In 1976 the state had 332 hospitals (82,137 beds), 549 nursing homes (67,750 beds) and 232 other institutions (26,865 beds). On 30 Sept. 1976 mental hospitals and institutions for the mentally retarded had 49,300 patients.

Social Security. The federal Supplemental Security Income programme covered aid to the needy aged, blind and disabled from 1 Jan. 1975. In the state programme there were 1·46m. welfare recipients in 1975; average benefit, $100 per month; medical assistance went to 1,151,619 persons, average $261; aid to dependent children in 1975 went to 1,217,265 recipients, average benefits $99 per month.

Books of Reference

Basic Statistics for Counties and Metropolitan Areas of New York State. Dept. of Commerce, Albany, 1967

Manual for the Use of the Legislature. Secretary of State. Albany

New York State Statistical Yearbook, 1974. Albany

Division of the Budget. Office of Statistical Co-ordinarion.

Caldwell, L. K. *The Government and Administration of New York.* New York, 1954

Ellis, D. M., *Short History of New York State.* Cornell Univ. Press, 1958

Hepburn, A., *Complete Guide to New York City.* New York, 1964

Nevins, A., and Krout, J. A. (ed.), *The Greater City: New York, 1898–1948.* New York and London, 1949

Rosenwhike, I., *Population History of New York City.* Syracuse Univ. Press, 1972

Thompson, J. H. (ed.), *Geography of New York State.* Syracuse Univ. Press, 1966

Vernon, R., *Metropolis 1985: An Interpretation of the New York Metropolitan Region Study.* Harvard Univ. Press, 1960

Wheeler, Alfred H., and Kolevzow, Edward R., *New York State: Its History and Constitution.* New York, 1950

State Library: The New York State Library, Albany 12234. *State Librarian and Assistant Commissioner for Libraries:* John A. Humphry.

NORTH CAROLINA

HISTORY. North Carolina, first settled in 1585 by Sir Walter Raleigh and permanently settled in 1663, was one of the 13 original states of the Union.

AREA AND POPULATION. North Carolina is bounded north by Virginia, east by the Atlantic, south by South Carolina, south-west by Georgia and west by Tennessee. Area, 52,712 sq. miles, of which 3,645 sq. miles are inland water. Census population, 1 April 1970, 5,082,059, an increase of 11·5% since 1960.

Births, 1976, were 84,722; marriages, 43,400; deaths, 46,213; infant deaths, 1,701; divorces and annulments, 25,065.

Population in 5 census years (with distribution by sex, 1970):

	White	*Negro*	*Indian*	*Asiatic*	*Total*	*Per sq. mile*
1910	1,500,511	697,843	7,851	82	2,206,287	45·3
1930	2,234,958	918,647	16,579	92	3,170,276	64·5
1950	2,983,121	1,047,353	3,742	—	4,061,929	82·7
1960	3,399,285	1,116,021	38,129	2,012	4,556,155	92·2
			All others			
1970	3,901,767	1,126,478	53,814		5,082,059	104·1
Male	1,920,842	540,718	26,807		2,488,367	—
Female	1,980,925	585,760	27,007		2,593,692	—

Of the total population in 1970, 2,285,168 persons (44·9%) were urban (39·5% in 1960); 65·3% were 18 years old or older; 23·2% were Negro.

Cities (with census population in 1970) are: Charlotte, 271,178; Greensboro, 144,076; Winston-Salem, 132,913; Raleigh (capital), 121,577; Durham, 95,438; High Point, 63,204; Asheville, 57,681; Fayetteville, 53,510; Gastonia, 47,142; Wilmington, 46,169.

CONSTITUTION AND GOVERNMENT. The present constitution dates from 1876 (though largely based on that of 1868); it has had 134 amendments. The General Assembly consists of a Senate of 50 members and a House of Representatives of 120 members; all are elected by districts for 2 years. The Governor and Lieut.-Governor are elected for 4 years. The Governor may not succeed himself and has no veto. There are 17 other executive heads of department, 8 elected by the people and 7 appointed by the Governor. All registered citizens with the usual residential qualifications have a vote.

The state is represented in Congress by 2 senators and 11 representatives.

In the presidential election of 1976 Carter polled 921,110 votes, Ford 736,602.

The capital is Raleigh, established in 1792.

Governor: James B. Hunt, Jr (D.) 1977–81 ($37,500).
Lieut.-Governor: James C. Green.
Secretary of State: Thad Eure (D.) ($29,500).

BUDGET. General revenue for the year ending 30 June 1974 (US Census Bureau figures) was $3,126m. ($1,806·4m. from taxation). General expenditure was $2,721·6m. (education, $1,351·2m.; highways, $354·3m.; public welfare, $263·4m.).

On 30 June 1974 the net total long-term debt amounted to $459·6m.

Per capita personal income (1973) was $4,258.

NATURAL RESOURCES

Minerals. Mining production in 1973 was valued at $129·5m. Principal minerals were stone, sand and gravel, phosphate rock, feldspar, clay, mica, lithium minerals, kaolin and talc. North Carolina ranked first in the production of mica, feldspar and lithium minerals. It is also the leading producer of bricks. In 1972 North Carolina manufactured 1,200m. bricks valued at over $62m. or 14% of the total US production.

Agriculture. In 1974 there were 135,000 farms in North Carolina covering 14m. acres; average size of farms was 104 acres (lowest of any state) and average value (1964), $22,800.

Income is primarily from tobacco, poultry, cattle, swine, maize, cotton, peanuts and soybeans. Cash income, 1973, from crops, was $1,409m. and from livestock and products, $971m.

North Carolina leads in production of tobacco (812m. lb., 1973). Production of maize, 1973, was 115m. bu.; cotton, 164,000 bales (of 500 lb.); peanuts, 466m. lb.; soybeans, 36m. bu. Also grown extensively are wheat, oats, barley, sweet potatoes, hay, peaches and apples. On 1 Jan. 1974 farms had 155,000 milch cows, 1·07m. all cattle, 1·95m. swine and 12,000 sheep. Production of commercial broilers amounted to 290·4m. in 1973 (fourth highest in US).

Forestry. North Carolina is the largest lumber-producing state in the South and the fifth largest in the US. Timber, covering 21m. acres in 1973 (66% of land area), provided approximately $2,000m. income in forest industries and products. The area of forest lands in public ownership in 1973 was 1·8m. acres.

Fisheries. Fish catch, 1974, amounted to 196m. lb.; value approximately $17·5m. Total annual value of commercial fisheries, about $175m.

INDUSTRY. North Carolina's 9,000 industrial establishments in 1973 had 770,000 production workers. Value added by manufacture (1972 estimate) was $11,000m. The leading industries are textile goods (leading all states), manufacture of cigarettes (about 55% of the US production, leading all states), chemicals, electrical machinery, processing of food crops and the manufacture of furniture and bricks (leading all states in both). Total receipts of all travel-serving industries, $954m. in 1973. In 1974 new investment in 85 new industries and 147 expanding industries was over $872m. and created 18,778 jobs.

COMMUNICATIONS

Roads. The state was the first to undertake the maintenance of all highways, and maintained, 1974, nearly 75,000 miles of highways, more than any other state. In 1974, 2,752,313 automobiles and 718,957 trucks were registered.

Railways. The state in 1974 contained 4,336 miles of railway, almost wholly diesel-powered.

Aviation. Airports in 1974 numbered 186, of which 58 are publicly owned, and are served by 5 airlines.

Shipping. There are 2 ocean ports, Wilmington and Morehead City.

JUSTICE, RELIGION, EDUCATION AND WELFARE

Justice. Total executions (by lethal gas) since 1930 were 263, including 59 whites, 199 Negroes and 5 other races.

Prison population, 7 Nov. 1973, was 11,431.

Religion. Leading denominations are the Baptists (48·9% of church membership in 1974), Methodists (20·7%), Presbyterians (7·7%), Lutherans (3%) and Roman Catholics (2·7%). Total estimate of all denominations in 1974 was 2·58m.

Education. School attendance is compulsory between 7 and 16. Integration of Negro pupils and teachers into formerly all-white schools is being carried out under freedom of choice plans in compliance with the federal Civil Rights Act 1965 and in nearly all school units.

Public school enrolment, 1974–75, was 1,159,913; elementary and secondary schools numbered 2,031. Instructional staff consisted of 73,843 classroom teachers and administrators. Estimated total current expenditure for public schools, 1973–74, \$985·3m., including \$677·3m. from state, \$183·7m. from local and \$124·2m. from federal sources.

In autumn 1973 state-supported colleges and universities included 15 two-year community colleges with 27,330 students; 16 four-year colleges with 84,893 students and 19 technical institutes with 30,550 students. The 16 senior universities are all part of the University of North Carolina System, the largest campus being the University of North Carolina at Chapel Hill. This university was founded in 1789 and first opened in 1792. Its 1974–75 enrolment was 19,952 with a faculty of 1,720. The next three largest campuses are North Carolina University in Raleigh (1887) with an enrolment of 15,751 and a faculty of 1,076, East Carolina University in Greenville (1907) with an enrolment of 11,341 and a faculty of 679; and the University of North Carolina at Greensboro (1891) with an enrolment of 8,759 and a faculty of 512. The total enrolment of public institutions of higher learning in 1974–75 was 108,638.

In addition to the state-supported institutions there were 10 private junior colleges with an enrolment of 6,060 and 29 senior institutions with a total enrolment of 41,637. The largest of these are Duke University (1924) in Durham, a Methodist affiliated school with 8,902 students, and Wake Forest University (1834) in Winston-Salem, a Baptist school with 4,195 students. There were also 1,343 students enrolled in Bible or theological schools. The total enrolment in private institutions for 1974–75 was 49,040.

Health. In March 1973 the state had 156 hospitals (34,300 beds).

Social Security. Old-age assistance was being received in Feb. 1975 by 5,972 persons receiving an average (not including medical care) of \$113.03 per month; and to families with dependent children received by 176,792 recipients averaged \$53.68 per person monthly; 4,086 totally disabled, \$117.12.

Books of Reference

North Carolina Manual. Secretary of State. Raleigh. Biennial
North Carolina: A Guide to the Old North State. Univ. of N.C., Chapel Hill, 1955
North Carolina Report. First Union National Bank, Charlotte, 1967
Corbitt, D. L., *The Formation of the North Carolina Counties.* Raleigh, 1969
Hobbs, S. H., *North Carolina: An Economic and Social Profile.* Univ. of N.C., Chapel Hill, 1958
Lefler, H. T., and Newsome, A. R., *North Carolina: The History of a Southern State.* Univ. of N.C., Chapel Hill, 1963
Powell, W. S., *The North Carolina Gazetteer.* Univ. of N.C., Chapel Hill, 1968
Thornton, M. L., *Bibliography of North Carolina, 1589–1956.* Univ. of N.C., Chapel Hill, 1958
Lonsdale, R. E., *Atlas of North Carolina.* Univ. of N.C., Chapel Hill and OUP, 1967

State Library: North Carolina State Library, Raleigh. *State Librarian:* Philip S. Ogilvie.

NORTH DAKOTA

HISTORY. North Dakota was admitted into the Union, with boundaries as at present, on 2 Nov. 1889; previously it had formed part of the Dakota Territory, established 2 March 1861.

AREA AND POPULATION. North Dakota is bounded north by Canada, east by the Red River (forming a boundary with Minnesota), south by South Dakota and west by Montana. Land area, 69,457 sq. miles, and 1,208 sq. miles of water. The Federal Bureau of Indian Affairs administered (1971) 850,000 acres, of which 153,000 acres were assigned to tribes. Census population, 1 April 1970, 617,761, a decrease of 14,685 or 2·3% since 1960. Estimated population, 1976,

643,000. Births in 1976 were 10,726 (16·7 per 1,000 population); deaths, 5,523 (8·6); infant deaths, 149; marriages, 5,649; divorces, 1,852.

Population at 5 census years (with distribution by sex, 1970) was:

	White	*Negro*	*Indian*	*Asiatic*	*Total*	*Per sq. mile*
1910	569,855	617	6,486	98	577,056	8·2
1930	671,851	377	8,617	194	680,845	9·7
1950	608,448	257	10,766	143	619,636	8·8
1960	619,538	777	11,736	274	632,446	9·1
			All others			
1970	599,485	2,494	15,782		617,761	8·9
Male	302,338	1,536	7,725		311,609	—
Female	297,147	958	8,047		306,152	—

Of the total population in 1970, 273,442 (44·3%) were urban (35·1% in 1960); those 21 years old or older numbered 355,763.

The largest cities are Fargo with population (census), 1970, of 53,365; Grand Forks, 39,008; Bismarck (capital), 34,703, and Minot, 32,290.

CONSTITUTION AND GOVERNMENT. The present constitution dates from 1889; it has had 95 amendments. The Legislative Assembly consists of a Senate of 50 members elected for 4 years, and a House of Representatives of 100 members elected for 2 years. The Governor and Lieut.-Governor are elected for 4 years. Qualified electors are (with necessary exceptions) all citizens and civilized Indians. The state sends to Congress 2 senators elected by the voters of the entire state and 1 representative.

In the 1976 presidential election Ford polled 153,470 votes, Carter 136,078 and Anderson 3,698.

The capital is Bismarck. The state has 53 organized counties.

Governor: Arthur A. Link (D.), 1977–78 ($18,000 plus $4,000 expenses).
Lieut.-Governor: Wayne Sanstad (D.), 1977–78 ($2,000 plus $2,000 expenses).
Secretary of State: Ben Meier (R.), 1977–78 ($11,000 plus $3,000 expenses).

FINANCE. General revenue of state and local government for the year ending 30 June 1975 was $578m. and general expenditures, $515m., taxation provided $300m. and federal aid, $143m.; education took $213m.; highways, $100m., and public welfare, $40m.

Total net long-term debt (state and local government) on 30 June 1975, $260m.

Per capita personal income (1976) was $5,400.

ENERGY AND NATURAL RESOURCES

Minerals. The mineral resources of North Dakota consist chiefly of oil which was discovered in 1951. Production of crude petroleum in 1976 was 22m. bbls; of natural gas, 31,470m. cu. ft. Output (1976) of lignite coal was 11·1m. short tons. Total value of mineral output, 1976, $244·1m.

Agriculture. Agriculture is the chief pursuit of the North Dakota population. In 1977 there were 40,000 farms (61,963 in 1954) with an area of 42m. acres (41,876,924 in 1954); the average farm was of 1,040 acres. The greater number of farms are cash-grain or livestock farms with annual sales of $20,000–$39,999.

Cash income, 1976, from crops, $1,005·2m., and from livestock, $538·7m. North Dakota leads in the production of barley, rye, flaxseed, durum and spring wheat. Other important products are sugar-beet, beans, potatoes, hay, oats, sunflowers and maize.

The state has also an active livestock industry, chiefly cattle raising. On 1 Jan. 1977 the farm animals were: 113,000 milch cows, 2·23m. all cattle, 262,000 sheep and 330,000 swine. The wool clip yielded (1976), 2·2m. lb. of wool from 236,000 sheep.

Forestry. National forest area, 1976, 1·15m. acres.

INDUSTRY. From 1970 to 1976 agricultural employment declined from 51,920 to 51,250; non-agricultural jobs rose from 148,910 to 228,730. Between 1970 and 1974, employment in manufacturing rose from 9,910 to 16,060, in trade from 43,890 to 60,750 and in government from 49,240 to 56,190.

COMMUNICATIONS

Roads. The state highway department maintained, in 1976, 6,993 miles of highway; local authorities, 95,382 miles, and municipal, 2,741 miles.

Car and truck registrations in 1976 numbered 540,671.

Railways. In 1976 there were 5,262 miles of railway.

Aviation. Airports in 1976 numbered 262, of which 107 were publicly owned.

JUSTICE, RELIGION, EDUCATION AND WELFARE

Justice. The state penitentiary, on 1 Oct. 1977, held 265 inmates. Of these, 30 were incarcerated at the North Dakota State Farm. There is no death penalty.

Religion. The leading religious denominations are the Roman Catholics, with 171,185 members in 1975; Combined Lutherans, 216,579; Methodists, 28,880; Presbyterians, 18,636.

Education. School attendance is compulsory between the ages of 7 and 16, or until the 17th birthday if the eighth grade has not been completed. In Sept. 1975 the public elementary schools had 4,696 classroom teachers and 86,640 pupils; secondary schools, 3,111 teachers and 48,642 pupils. Average salary of teachers, 1970, was $6,375 in elementary and $7,263 in secondary schools. State expenditure on public schools, 1970, $122·7m. Private schools had 8,243 elementary pupils and 410 teachers, 3,106 secondary pupils and 168 teachers in 1975.

The university at Grand Forks, founded in 1883, had 8,858 students in 1976; the state university of agriculture and applied science, at Fargo, 7,159 students. Total enrolment in the 8 public institutions of higher education, 1976, 24,658, and in private institutions (1975) 1,169.

Health. In 1977 the state had 53 hospitals (4,051 beds), 53 nursing homes (3,908) and 27 institutions for intermediate care (1,680).

Social Security. In 1974 aid to the aged, blind and disabled was taken out of state programmes and included in federal programmes as Supplemental Security Income (SSI). In 1975–76 grants were made to 13,791 cases, including 4,491 families with dependent children, 9,388 cases for medical aid and 121 cases for general assistance. At 30 June 1977, 5,898 people received SSI assistance.

Books of Reference

North Dakota Growth Indicators, 1978. 17th ed. Business and Industrial Development Dept., Bismarck, 1978

North Dakota Industrial Location Facts. Business and Industrial Development Dept., Bismarck, 1977

North Dakota Blue Book. Secretary of State, Bismarck, 1973

Federal Writers' Project. *North Dakota: A Guide to the Northern State.* 2nd ed. OUP, New York, 1950

Goodey, R. B. (ed.), *Readings in the Geography of North Dakota.* North Dakota Studies, 1968

Robinson, E. B., *History of North Dakota.* Univ. of Nebraska Press, 1966

OHIO

HISTORY. Ohio, first settled in 1788, unofficially entered the Union on 19 Feb. 1803; entrance was made official, retroactive to 1 March 1803, on 8 Aug. 1953.

AREA AND POPULATION. Ohio is bounded north by Michigan and Lake Erie, east by Pennsylvania, south-east and south by the Ohio River (forming a boundary with West Virginia and Kentucky) and west by Indiana. Area, 40,975 sq. miles, of which 204 sq. miles are inland water. Census population, 1 April 1970, 10,652,017, an increase of 945,620 or 9·7% since 1960. In 1976 births numbered 155,215 (14·6 per 1,000 population); deaths, 96,000; infant deaths, 2,315 (9·1 per 1,000 live births); marriages, 96,776 (9·1); divorces and annulments, 59,521 (5·6).

Population at 5 census years (with distribution by sex, 1970) was:

	White	*Negro*	*Indian*	*Asiatic*	*Total*	*Per sq. mile*
1910	4,654,897	111,452	127	645	4,767,121	117·0
1930	6,335,173	309,304	435	1,785	6,646,697	161·6
1950	7,428,222	513,072	1,146	0,000	7,946,627	193·8
1960	8,909,698	786,097	1,910	8,692	9,706,397	236·9
			All others			
1970	9,646,997	970,477	34,543		10,652,017	260·0
Male	4,685,685	461,274	3,144	13,265	5,163,373	—
Female	4,961,312	509,203	3,505	14,624	5,488,644	—

Of the total population in 1970, 8,025,697 persons (75·3%) lived in urban areas (73·4% in 1960). Those 21 years old or older numbered 6,431,709; 65 years or over, 998,094.

Estimated population of chief cities on 1 April 1970 was:

Cleveland	750,879	Kettering	71,864	Newark	41,836
Columbus	540,025	Euclid	71,552	Garfield Heights	41,417
Cincinnati	451,455	Lakewood	70,173	East Cleveland	39,600
Toledo	383,105	Hamilton	67,865	Upper Arlington	38,727
Akron	275,425	Warren	63,494	Marion	38,646
Dayton	242,917	Cleveland Heights	60,767	Mentor	36,912
Youngstown	140,909	Mansfield	55,047	Shaker Heights	36,306
Canton	110,053	Lima	53,734	Findlay	35,800
Parma	100,216	Elyria	53,427	North Olmsted	34,861
Springfield	91,941	Cuyahoga Falls	49,678	Maple Heights	34,093
Lorain	78,185	Middletown	48,767		

Urbanized areas, 1970 census: Cleveland, 2,064,194; Cincinnati, 1,104,668; Columbus (the capital), 916,228; Dayton, 850,266; Akron, 679,239; Toledo, 574,092; Youngstown-Warren, 536,003; Canton, 372,210.

CONSTITUTION AND GOVERNMENT. The question of a general revision of the constitution drafted by an elected convention is submitted to the people every 20 years. The constitution of 1851 had 99 amendments by 1973.

In the 111th General Assembly the Senate consisted of 33 members and the House of Representatives of 99 members. The Senate is elected for 4 years, half each 2 years; the House is elected for 2 years; the Governor, Lieut.-Governor and Secretary of State for 4 years. Qualified as electors are (with necessary exceptions) all citizens 18 years of age who have the usual residential qualifications. Ohio sends 2 senators and 23 representatives to Congress.

In the 1976 presidential election Carter polled 2m. votes, Ford, 1,992,400.

The capital (since 1816) is Columbus. Ohio is divided into 88 counties.

Governor: James A. Rhodes (R.), 1975–79 ($50,000).
Lieut.-Governor: Richard F. Celeste (D.), 1975–79 ($30,000).
Secretary of State: Ted W. Brown (R.), 1975–79 ($38,000).

BUDGET. For the 2 years ending 30 June 1977 (Budget of the State of Ohio) total general revenue was $5,831·8m. and general expenditure was $5,925·6m.

The net long-term debt of the state on 30 June 1977 was $2,109·3m.

Per capita personal income (1976) was $6,432.

ENERGY AND NATURAL RESOURCES

Minerals. Ohio has extensive mineral resources, of which coal is the most important by value: output (1975) 46·7m. short tons, value $736·9m. Production of other minerals, 1975: Sand and gravel, 36·4m. short tons ($59·4m.); limestone, 44·6m. short tons ($93·3m.); sandstone, 2·2m. short tons ($11·9m.); crude petroleum, 9·58m. bbls ($113·9m.); natural gas, 85·81m. cu. ft ($60·6m.); clay, 2·77m. short tons ($6·4m.) in 1974; salt, 4·6m. short tons ($37·2m.).

Agriculture. Ohio is extensively devoted to agriculture. In 1977, 115,000 farms covered 17·2m. acres; average farm was valued at $169,000. Commercial farms (1974 census) with over $2,500 gross sales numbered 70,283. Owners operated 55·2%, part-owners 31·6%, tenant-farmers 13·2% of these farms.

Cash income 1976, from crops and livestock and products, $2,782m. The most important crops in 1976 were: Maize (395·9m. bu., value $910·6m.), wheat (66m. bu., value $194·7m.), oats (27·5m. bu., value $42·6m.), soybeans (93·6m. bu., value $631·8m.). The wool clip in 1976 yielded 3·35m. lb. from 423,000 sheep. On 1 Jan. 1977 there were 1m. swine and 11m. chickens, 2·25m. all cattle and 445,000 sheep.

Forestry. State forest area, 1977, 165,052 acres; reclamation area, 5,911 acres.

INDUSTRY. During Jan.–April 1974, 16,546 manufacturing employers employed 1·36m. workers. The value added by manufacture in 1973 was $31,174m. The largest industry was manufacturing of non-electrical machinery with 228,846 workers.

COMMUNICATIONS

Roads. The state (1976) maintained 19,436 miles of highway, including 1,300 miles of interstate highways and 241 miles on the Ohio Turnpike; there were 91,184 miles of country, township, city, park and forest development roads. Total miles of highway maintained by all government agencies (1976) 110,620.

Railways. The railroads had 7,400 route miles of track in 1977.

Aviation. Ohio had (1977) 719 airports and airfields, of which 222 are commercial and 497 private, 130 heliports and 5 seaplane bases. There were 5,983 licensed aeroplanes.

JUSTICE, RELIGION, EDUCATION AND WELFARE

Justice. A Civil Rights Act (1933) forbids inns, restaurants, theatres, retail stores and all other places of public resort to discriminate against citizens on grounds of 'colour or race'; none may be denied the right to serve on juries on the grounds of 'colour or race'; insurance companies are forbidden to discriminate between 'white persons and coloured, wholly or partially of African descent'.

A state Civil Rights Commission (created 1959) has general administrative powers to prevent discrimination because of race, colour, religion, national origin or ancestry in employment, labour organization membership, use of public accommodations and in obtaining 'commercial housing' or 'personal residence'. Ohio has no *de jure* segregation in the public schools.

The state's adult correctional institutions, 15 Sept. 1975, held 10,988 inmates average daily count). Total executions (by electrocution) since 1930 were 170, all for murder. There have been no executions since 1963. The Department of Rehabilitation and Correction was created in July 1972, and has established probation services in 42 counties where services would otherwise be inadequate or non-existent.

Religion. Many religious faiths are represented, including (but not limited to) the Baptist, Jewish, Lutheran, Methodist, Presbyterian and Roman Catholic.

Education. School attendance during full term is compulsory for children from 6 to 18 years of age. In 1974–75, public schools had 2,323,286 enrolled pupils; elementary schools had 49,931 teachers and 1,029,142 enrolled pupils; secondary schools had 45,764 teachers and 1,128,540 pupils. There were 6,068 special education teachers. Teachers' salaries averaged $10,730. Operating expenditure on elementary and secondary schools for 1974–75 was $2,516m., total state tax support, $1,104m. The state's universities and colleges had a total enrolment (1976) of 419,925 students; the following had 7,000 or more students, autumn 1976:

Founded	*Institutions*	*Enrolments*
1804	Ohio University, Athens (State)	13,045
1809	Miami University, Oxford (State)	14,715
1826	Case Western Reserve University, Cleveland	8,178
1850	University of Dayton (R.C.)	7,280
1870	University of Akron (State)	22,017
1872	Ohio State University, Columbus (State)	49,846
1872	University of Toledo (State)	16,640
1874	University of Cincinnati (State-affiliated)	33,199
1887	Sinclair Community College, Dayton	12,514
1908	Youngstown University (State)	15,898
1910	Bowling Green State University (State)	16,345
1912	Kent State University (State)	20,406
1962	Cuyahoga Community College (Municipal)	27,250
1964	Cleveland State University (State)	17,627
1964	Wright State University (State)	13,067

Health. In 1976 the state had 212 hospitals (47,288 beds) listed by the American Hospital Association. State hospitals for mental diseases and retardation had 7,177 patients on 31 Aug. 1977, and the state psychiatric hospitals had 697 patients.

Social Security. Public assistance is administered through 4 basic programmes: aid to dependent children, emergency assistance, Medicaid and general relief. Total public assistance expenditures during the year ending 30 June 1977 were $1,246·9m. In 1976–77 the number of persons receiving public assistance averaged 626,100 per month. Under the aid to dependent children programme $456·5m. provided assistance to an average of 572,935 recipients per month. Payments for Medicaid were $556·2m.; for social services, $133m.; for general relief and emergency assistance, $101·2m.

Books of Reference

Official Roster: Federal State, County Officers and Department Information. Secretary of State, Columbus. Biennial

Statistical Abstract of Ohio, 1960. Dept. of Industrial and Economic Development. Columbus, 1960

Aumann, F. R., and Walker, H., *The Government and Administration of Ohio.* New York, 1956

Rose, A. H., *Ohio Government, State and Local.* Saint Louis, 1953

Rosebloom, E. H., and Weisenburger, F. P., *A History of Ohio.* State Arch. and Hist. Soc., Columbus, 1953

OKLAHOMA

HISTORY. An unorganized area in the centre of the present state was thrown open to white settlers on 22 April 1889. The Territory of Oklahoma, organized in 1890 to include this area and other sections, was opened to white settlements by runs or lotteries during the next decade. In 1893 the Territory was enlarged by the addition of the Cherokee Outlet, which fixed part of the present northern boundary. On 16 Nov. 1907 Oklahoma was combined with the remaining part of the Indian Territory and admitted as a state with boundaries substantially as now.

AREA AND POPULATION. Oklahoma is bounded north by Kansas, northeast by Missouri, east by Arkansas, south by Texas (the Red River forming part of the boundary) and, at the western extremity of the 'panhandle', by New Mexico and Colorado. Area 69,919 sq. miles, of which 1,281 sq. miles are water. Census population, 1 April 1970, 2,559,253, an increase of 230,945 or 9·9% since 1960. Estimate, 1975, 2,712,000. Births, 1976, were 43,819; deaths, 26,606; infant deaths (1975), 688; marriages, 40,983; divorces, including annulments, 21,487.

The population at 5 federal censuses (with distribution by sex, 1970) was:

	White	Negro	Indian	Asiatic	Total	Per sq. mile
1910	1,444,531	137,612	74,825	187	1,657,155	23·9
1930	2,130,778	172,198	92,725	339	2,396,040	34·6
1950	2,032,526	145,503	53,769	534	2,233,351	32·4
1960	2,107,900	153,084	68,689	1,414	2,328,284	33·8
			All others			
1970	2,275,104	177,907	106,218		2,559,253	37·2
Male	1,113,345	81,299	51,711		1,246,355	—
Female	1,167,017	90,593	55,264		1,312,874	—

In 1970, 1,740,137 (68%) were urban (62·9% in 1960). Those 21 years of age or older numbered 1,584,292; 65 years or older, 299,756. Foreign-born whites numbered 20,160. In 1975 the US Bureau of Indian Affairs administered 1,327,105 acres, of which 63,757 acres were allotted to tribes.

The most important cities with population, 1970 (and estimated population 1975) are Oklahoma City (capital), 368,856 (370,800), Tulsa, 330,350 (348,800); Lawton, 74,447 (81,000); Norman, 52,117 (63,600); Midwest City, 48,212 (56,500).

CONSTITUTION AND GOVERNMENT. The present constitution, dating from 1907, provides for amendment by initiative petition and legislative referendum; it has had 87 amendments.

The Legislature consists of a Senate of 48 members, who are elected for 4 years, and a House of Representatives elected for 2 years and consisting of 101 members. The Governor and Lieut.-Governor are elected for 4-year terms; the Governor can only be elected for two terms in succession. Electors are (with necessary exceptions) all citizens 18 years or older, with the usual qualifications. Indians are qualified as voters.

The state is represented in Congress by 2 senators and 6 representatives.

In the 1976 presidential election Ford polled 539,948 votes, Carter 528,761.

The capital is Oklahoma City. The state has 77 counties.

Governor: David L. Boren (D.), 1975–79 ($42,500).
Lieut.-Governor: George Nigh (D.) ($24,000).
Secretary of State: Jerome W. Byrd (D.) ($18,500).

BUDGET. Total revenue for the year ending 30 June 1977 (State Budget Office figures) was $2,200m. General revenue was $582·7m.

Total net long-term debt, 30 June 1977, was $548·29m.

Per capita personal income (1974) was $4,586.

ENERGY AND NATURAL RESOURCES

Minerals. Resources include petroleum, helium, natural gas, coal (bituminous), copper and silver. Production in 1974 was: Petroleum, 172,608,181 bbls; natural gas, 1,424,304,973m. cu. ft. In 1977 there were 73,298 oilwells and 11,112 natural gaswells in production.

Agriculture. Agriculture is the largest industry. In 1976 the state had 86,000 farms with a total area of 36·8m. acres; average farm was 428 acres with a value, land and buildings, of $150,000; there were (1969) 51,675 commercial farms. Owners and part owners operated 71,325 farms and tenants 11,712 farms. Large-scale commercial farming is predominant; 5,907 farms exceeded 1,000 acres; 10,479 farms sold products valued at $20,000 or more. On the other hand, small-scale farming also exists; 10,931 farms were of less than 50 acres, and, of the commercial farms, 5,702 sold products valued at less than $2,500.

Soil erosion is serious. The conservation and development of the renewable natural resources of the state has received close attention by local, county and state governments during the past 40 years. All of the land in the state is within the boundaries of one of the 88 conservation districts. Of the total surface (44·5m. acres), 32·26m. acres are being operated under a basic conservation plan prepared by the conservation district with assistance from the Soil Conservation Service. There are a little over 100,000 district co-operators. At Feb. 1976, 524,000 acres had suffered damage from wind erosion, mainly in Western Oklahoma. This was mainly because of drought, but also because land in permanent cover and susceptible to wind erosion had been ploughed and sown with grain when grain prices began rising. One-fourth of all the upstream flood prevention reservoirs built in the US have been built in Oklahoma. In addition to these, 1,067 reservoirs have been built on the Washita River Watershed: 16·7m. acres are within the boundaries of 175 watersheds and 6 Resource Conservation and Development Projects which have asked for assistance under this programme.

The largest change in land use in 1973 was the conversion of 170,284 acres of cropland to grass. This is a continuation of a trend of the last 40 years; cattle and calves rank first in agricultural products, valued, 1974, at $914m., wheat is second, valued, 1974, at $560m.

Cash income from crops, 1974, was $830m. and from livestock products, $117·5m. The most valuable crop, by value, is wheat; output, 1975, 160·8m. bu. Other crops included cotton (170,000 bales of 500 lb.), grain sorghums (25m. bu.) and peanuts (232·3m. lb.). On 1 Jan. 1976 the stock included 117,000 milch cows, 6·4m. all cattle, 79,000 sheep and lambs and 300,000 swine.

Forestry. National forest lands, 1974, 243,072 acres; 23,321 acres were state owned. Commercial timber lands, 5·5m. acres.

INDUSTRY. Petroleum refining is the chief industry; production, 1973, included 213,313,000 bbls of petrol. Tourism and food processing are growing in importance. In 1977, 50,087 employers had 778,270 employees covered by workmen's compensation.

COMMUNICATIONS

Roads. The state, 1 Jan. 1976, maintained 12,320 miles of highway; the counties, 85,718 miles; municipalities, 9,309 miles. In 1976, 486 miles of turnpikes were maintained by the Oklahoma Turnpike Authority. Motor car registrations, 1976, 2,474,624.

Railways. In 1976 Oklahoma had 5,187 miles of railway.

Aviation. Airports, 1976, numbered 280, of which 124 were publicly owned.

Shipping. The Arkansas–Verdigris Navigation System connects all the navigable inland waterways in the state with the Arkansas and Mississippi rivers, and provides a direct route from Tulsa to New Orleans.

JUSTICE, RELIGION, EDUCATION AND WELFARE

Justice. Penal institutions, 1977, held 4,210 inmates.

The death penalty was suspended in 1966 and re-imposed in 1974. Since 1915 there have been 83 (52 whites, 27 Negroes, 4 other races) executions by electrocution, replaced (1977) by lethal injection.

Religion. The chief religious bodies in 1976 were Southern Baptists, 610,687; United Methodists, 257,603; Churches of Christ, 150,000; Roman Catholics, 106,266; Disciples of Christ, 51,000; Presbyterian, 37,680; Episcopal, 16,759.

Education. In 1976–77 there were 300,070 pupils enrolled in elementary schools (kindergarten through grade 6) and 294,283 pupils in secondary schools; in June 1976, 33,738 teachers at elementary schools and secondary schools had average salaries of $10,105. Total expenditure on public schools (1976–77), $546·3m.

Approximately 100,000 of the 650,000 school age children are handicapped and in need of special education. In 1975–76, there were 1,838 special education units with 48,541 students in class and an estimated 78,000 in need of such classes.

The University of Oklahoma (founded at Norman in 1899) had 691 full-time faculty and 20,010 enrolled students in autumn 1976; Oklahoma State University of Agriculture and Applied Science (founded in 1890 at Stillwater) had 669 full-time faculty and 21,129 students; Central State University (founded at Edmond in 1971) had 317 faculty and 13,000 students. There are 14 other institutions of higher learning in the state system at the senior level and 14 junior colleges. Total enrolment in institutions of higher education, autumn 1976, 152,663.

Health. In 1976 there were 128 hospitals (14,162 beds). In 1977 institutions for mentally retarded had 1,977 inmates; the schools for deaf and blind had 271 children, 3 schools for delinquents, 1,008 children and 2 children's homes 1,279 children.

Social Security. Public assistance, June 1977, was being drawn by 158,101 persons, receiving an average of $51. This includes old age assistance, aid to families with dependent children, AFDC emergency, AFDC foster home care, aid to the blind and aid to the disabled. Medical payments were made for 49,486 persons, totalled $7·54m. and averaged $152.47 per person. Nursing-home service was provided for 18,461 persons at an average of $481.48 per person. Non-technical medical care was provided for 4,290 persons at an average of $159.61 per person. A total of $1,791,088 was spent for vocational rehabilitation.

Books of Reference

Directory of Oklahoma Airports. Oklahoma Aeronautics Commission
Directory, State of Oklahoma. State Election Board, Oklahoma City
Chronicles of Oklahoma. State Historical Society, Oklahoma City (from 1921)
Statistical Abstract of Oklahoma, 1975. Center for Economic and Management Research, Univ. of Oklahoma, Norman, 1975
Dale, E. E., and Wardell, M. L., *History of Oklahoma.* New York, 1948
Debo, Angie, *Oklahoma.* Norman, 1950
McReynolds, Edwin C., *Oklahoma: A History of the Sooner State.* Univ. of Oklahoma, Norman, 1954
Strain, J. E., *Outline of Oklahoma Government.* Norman, 1976

State Library: Oklahoma Dept. of Libraries, 200 N.E. 18th Street, Oklahoma City 73105.
State Librarian and State Archivist: Robert L. Clark, Jr.

OREGON

HISTORY. Oregon was first settled in 1811 by the Pacific Fur Company at Astoria, a provisional government was formed on 5 July 1834; a Territorial government was organized, 14 Aug. 1848, and on 14 Feb. 1859 Oregon was admitted to the Union.

AREA AND POPULATION. Oregon is bounded north by Washington, with the Columbia River forming most of the boundary, east by Idaho, with the Snake River forming most of the boundary, south by Nevada and California and west by the Pacific. Area, 96,981 sq. miles, 797 sq. miles being inland water. The federal government owned (1975) 32,234,309 acres (52·3% of the state area). Census population, 1 April 1970, 2,091,385, an increase of 322,698 or 18·2% since 1960. Estimate, 1976, 2,341,750. In 1975 resident births numbered 33,352 (14·5 per 1,000 population); deaths, 20,142 (8·8); infant deaths (deaths within the first year of life), 502 (15·1 per 1,000 live births); marriages, 19,322 (8·4), and divorces, 15,526 (6·8). Three maternal deaths took place in 1975.

Population at 5 federal censuses (with distribution by sex, 1970) was:

	White	*Negro*	*Indian*	*Asiatic*	*Total*	*Per sq. mile*
1910	655,090	1,492	5,090	11,093	672,765	7·0
1930	938,598	2,234	4,776	8,179	953,786	9·9
1950	1,497,128	11,529	5,820	6,864	1,521,341	15·8
1960	1,732,037	18,133	8,026	9,120	1,768,687	18·4
1970	2,032,079	26,308	13,510	13,290	2,091,385	—
Male	994,500	13,188	6,576	6,581	1,023,952	—
Female	1,037,579	13,120	6,934	6,709	1,067,433	—

Of the total population in 1970, 1,402,704 persons (67·1%) were urban (62·2% in 1960). Those 21 years and older were 1,284,174; 65 years and older, 226,799.

The US Bureau of Indian Affairs (area headquarters in Portland) administers (1976) 742,151·74 acres, of which 597,222·94 acres are held by the US in trust for Indian tribes, and 144,928·8 acres for individual Indians.

The largest towns, according to 1970 census figures (and 1976 estimates), are: Portland, 372,200 (382,000); Eugene, 76,346 (96,600); Salem (the capital), 68,296 (80,000); Corvallis, 35,153 (40,180); Medford, 28,454 (34,900); Springfield, 27,047 (35,580); Beaverton, 18,577 (23,300); Albany, 18,181 (22,800).

CONSTITUTION AND GOVERNMENT. The present constitution dates from 1859; some 80 items in it have been amended. The Legislative Assembly consists of a Senate of 30 members, elected for 4 years (half their number retiring every 2 years), and a House of 60 representatives, elected for 2 years. The Governor is elected for 4 years. The constitution reserves to the voters the rights of initiative and referendum and recall. In Nov. 1912 suffrage was extended to women.

The state sends to Congress 2 senators and 4 representatives.

In the 1976 presidential election Ford polled 491,055 votes, Carter 488,808 and McCarthy 40,465.

The capital is Salem. There are 36 counties in the state.

Governor: Robert W. Straub (D.) 1975–79 ($42,350 plus $1,000 monthly for expenses).

Secretary of State: Norma Paulus (R.), 1977–81 ($35,090).

BUDGET. General revenues for the fiscal year ending 30 June 1976 were $2,673,099,236 (taxation, $836,578,607 and federal aid, $559,173,515); general expenditures, $2,514,593,661 (education, $595,727,076; highways, $211,493,969; public welfare, $270,935,102).

On 30 June 1976 the outstanding bonded debt was $2,353,027,627.

Per capita personal income (1976) was $5,769.

ENERGY AND NATURAL RESOURCES

Electricity. Four privately owned utilities, 11 municipally owned utilities, 16 co-operatives and 4 utility districts provide electricity in the state. The privately owned companies serve 78% of the electricity. Private utilities sold 24,140,775,000 kwh. of hydro-electric power in 1975.

A federal agency, the Bonneville Power Administration, also markets electric power from 29 federal dams in the Pacific Northwest to 158 public and private utilities and large industrial plants. The dams, which are operated by the Army Corps of Engineers or the Bureau of Reclamation, had on 30 June 1976 a total generating capacity of 13,617,780 kw. One more dam and additions to existing dams are under construction, with a total capacity of 5,721,000 kw. The Bonneville transmission network now covers the states of Oregon, Washington, Idaho, Western Montana, and parts of California, Nevada, Utah and Wyoming.

Minerals. Oregon's mineral resources include gold, silver, copper, lead, mercury, chromite, sand and gravel, stone, clays, lime, silica, diatomite, expansible shale, scoria, pumice and uranium. Oregon is the only state producing nickel in the US. Value of mineral products, 1974, was $90·7m.

Agriculture. Oregon, which has an area of 61,557,184 acres, is divided by the Cascade Range into two distinct zones as to climate. West of the Cascade Range there is a good rainfall and almost every variety of crop common to the temperate zone is grown; east of the Range stock-raising and wheat-growing are the principal industries and irrigation is needed for row crops and fruits. There are numerous irrigation districts and in 1973 some 22,000 farms, covering 2m. acres, used irrigation water.

Oregon farms are decreasing in number and increasing in size. There were, in 1975, 32,500 farms with an acreage of 19·5m. (31·6% of the land area), including 5·2m. acres of total crop land; average farm size in 1974 was 600 acres; commercial farms numbered 20,000.

There were 426 farming corporations in Oregon in 1970; 2·5% of all commercial farms. The average corporation farm was 5,982 acres, over 4 times the average commercial farm.

Cash receipts from crops in 1975 amounted to $1,051·3m., and from livestock and livestock products, $324·65m. Principal crops are hay, wheat, potatoes, barley, snap beans, ryegrass, strawberries, pears, peppermint, onions, apples.

Livestock, 1 Jan. 1976: Milch cows, 90,000; all cattle, 1·44m.; sheep and lambs, 410,000; swine, 90,000.

Federal and state land for grazing cattle and sheep, 19·2m. acres. In 1975 the wool clip yielded 3·4m. lb. from 450,000 sheep.

Forestry. Forest products manufacturing is Oregon's leading industry, and provides for 20% of the country's softwood lumber needs, 50% of its plywood and more than 25% of the hardboard. Increased productivity of the forest land, greater diversity of wood products and more efficient use of the log have been factors in developing a more stable economic base. Some 30m. acres of forest land provide an annual harvest of 8,360m. bd ft plus recreational areas, watersheds and grazing. The $2,963m. value of finished wood fibre production in Oregon in 1975 means that every 1,000 bd ft of timber earned $300. Employment in that year reached 83,541, and accounted for 46% of all manufacturing employment. Payrolls were over $1m. The forest industry and public forestry agencies are active in forest conservation.

Fisheries. All food and shellfish landings in the calendar year 1975 amounted to 86,045,735 lb., including salmon, 12,364,168 lb.; tuna, 23,584,409 lb.; crabs, 4,026,937 lb.; bottom fish, 21,032,886 lb.; shrimp, 24,083,568 lb.; shad, 456,758 lb.

INDUSTRY. During Oct.–Dec. 1975, 5,184 manufacturing establishments reported to the Employment Division, average annual employment, 1975, 183,207 with pay of $2,154m.; value added by manufacture (1973), $3,489·1m.

TOURISM. In 1975, 10,598,000 out-of-state cars visited Oregon; the total 1975 income from tourism was estimated to be $689m.

COMMUNICATIONS

Roads. The state maintains (1976) 7,586 miles of primary and secondary highways, almost all surfaced; counties maintain 28,939 miles, and cities 5,718 miles; there were 53,635 miles in national parks and federal reservations. Registered motor vehicles, 1 Jan. 1976, totalled 2·25m.

Railways. The state had (1975) 20 common carrier railways with a total mileage of 4,073·53.

Aviation. There were 334 airports and heliports in 1976; 73 are heliports; 130 personal-use airports; 131 public-use airports.

Shipping. Portland is a major seaport for large ocean-going vessels and is 101 miles inland from the mouth of the Columbia River.

Post and Broadcasting. In 1976 there were 118 commercial radio stations and 13 educational radio stations. There were 13 commercial television stations and 2 educational television stations.

Newspapers. In 1976 there were 21 daily newspapers with a circulation of 664,994 and 89 other newspapers with a circulation of 314,322.

JUSTICE, RELIGION, EDUCATION AND WELFARE

Justice. There are 3 correctional institutions in Oregon, all in Salem. The Oregon State Penitentiary, in Oct. 1976, held an average of 1,732 males; the Women's Correctional Center had a resident population of 85; and the Oregon Correctional Institution, which is for first offenders, had a population of 725.

The sterilization law, originally passed in 1917, was amended in 1967. The amendments changed the number of persons on the Board of Social Protection from 15 to 7 and provided that the Public Defender would automatically represent all persons examined. In 1973 the State Board of Health was abolished and its physician no longer sat on the Board. The bases on which a person would be subject to examination by the Board are: (*a*) if such person would be likely to procreate children having an inherited tendency to mental retardation or mental illness, or (*b*) if such person would be likely to procreate children who would become neglected or dependent because of the person's inability by reason of mental illness or mental retardation to provide adequate care. Up to 1 July 1976, 941 men and 1,740 women have been sterilized.

Religion. The chief religious bodies are Catholic, Baptist, Lutheran, Methodists, Presbyterian and Mormon. Total membership, all denominations, 691,085 in 1971.

Education. School attendance is compulsory from 7 to 18 years of age if the twelfth year of school has not been completed; those between the ages of 16 and 18 years, if legally employed, must attend part-time or evening schools. On 30 June 1976 the 949 public elementary schools, 100 junior high schools and 233 standard senior high schools had 28,539 administrators and teachers; net enrolment was 499,151 (excluding transfers between districts), of whom 161,721 were high school pupils. Average salary for all classroom teachers, 1975–76, was $12,280. Total expenditure on elementary and secondary education (1975–76) was $900m.

Leading state-supported institutions of higher education (1976–77) included:

	Teachers	*Students*
University of Oregon, Eugene	893	16,750
University of Oregon Health Sciences Center:		
Medical School, Portland	216	1,165
Dental School, Portland	90	403
Oregon State University, Corvallis	910	16,250
Portland State University, Portland	556	15,300
Oregon College of Education, Monmouth	183	3,500
Southern Oregon College, Ashland	218	4,450
Eastern Oregon College, La Grande	92	1,450
Oregon Institute of Technology, Klamath Falls	156	2,350

Largest of the privately endowed universities are Lewis and Clark College, Portland, with 1976–77, 2,976 students; University of Portland, 2,289 students; Willamette University, Salem, 1,753 students; Reed College, Portland, 1,212 students, and Linfield College, McMinnville, 1,053 students. There are 13 community colleges with an estimated enrolment of 100,000 students in 1976–77.

Health. In 1976 there were 99 licensed hospitals (11,702 beds) and 190 nursing homes with 13,438 beds. In Oct. 1976 there were 5 state hospitals for mentally ill and mentally retarded (2 for mentally ill, 2 for mentally retarded and 1 with both programmes). The daily average for the mentally ill on 1 Oct. 1976 was 1,150 and the daily average for the mentally retarded was 1,906.

Social Security. Old-age assistance is provided for all needy persons 65 years or older who meet certain eligibility requirements. As of June 1976, 3,787 persons were drawing an average of $60.54 per month.

The July 1976 average payment, apart from medical care, was $88.71 for the 116,270 persons in 38,760 families with dependent children; $68.65 for the 572 blind persons; $55.62 for 7,323 disabled persons, and $106.62 for 3,696 general assistance cases.

Total medical care cost $8,253,493 in July 1976.

A system of unemployment benefit payments, financed by employers, with administrative allotments made through a federal agency, started 2 Jan. 1938, and covers about 55,000 employers with average employment in 1975 of 791,806. By June 1976, $989·7m. in taxes had been paid into the trust fund plus $201·3m. in interest and reimbursed benefits. About $1,164·3m. has been paid in benefits which from July 1976 range from $28 to $102 weekly and up to $2,652 per year with $1,326 extended benefits and $2,652 in federal supplements. About 35,191 state employees, 44,400 school employees and 14,665 political subdivision employees are participants in the public employees retirement programme. The same employees are covered under the federal old-age, survivors and disability insurance programme. Approximately 24,457 retired public employees are receiving monthly benefit cheques.

Books of Reference

Oregon Blue Book. Issued by the Secretary of State. Salem. Biennial
Oregon State University. *Atlas of the Pacific Northwest Resources and Development*, ed. by R. M. Highsmith. 4th ed. Corvallis, 1968
Oregon University, Bureau of Business and Economic Research. *Oregon Economic Statistics*. Eugene. Annual
Atkeson, R., *Oregon*. Portland, 1968.—*Oregon Coast*. Portland, 1972
Federal Writers' Project. *Oregon: End of the Trail*. Rev. ed. Portland, 1972
Baldwin, E., *Geology of Oregon*. 2nd ed. Eugene, 1964
Berry, J., *Profile of Oregon Churches*. Portland, 1963
Brooks, J. E., *Oregon Almanac and Book of Facts*. Portland, 1961
Corning, H. M. (ed.), *Dictionary of Oregon History*. New York, 1956
Dicken, S. N., *Oregon Geography*. 5th ed. Eugene, 1973
Friedman, R., *Oregon for the Curious*. 3rd ed. Portland, 1972
McArthur, L. A., *Oregon Geographic Names*. 4th ed., rev. and enlarged. Portland, 1974
Patton, Clyde P., *Atlas of Oregon*. Univ. Oregon Press, Eugene, 1976

State Library: The Oregon State Library, Salem. *Librarian:* Marcia Lowell.

PENNSYLVANIA

HISTORY. Pennsylvania, first settled in 1682, is one of the 13 original states in the Union.

AREA AND POPULATION. Pennsylvania is bounded north by New York, east by New Jersey, south by Delaware and Maryland, south-west by West Virginia, west by Ohio and north-west by Lake Erie. Area, 45,333 sq. miles, of which 399 sq. miles are inland water. Census population, 1 April 1970, 11,793,909, an increase of 474,543 or 4·2% since 1960. Births, 1977, 153,654; deaths, 119,689; infant deaths, 2,136; marriages, 91,382; divorces, 37,675.

Population at 5 census years (with distribution by sex, 1970) was:

	White	*Negro*	*Indian*	*All others*	*Total*	*Per sq. mile*
1910	7,467,713	193,919	1,503	1,976	7,665,111	171·0
1930	9,196,007	431,257	523	3,563	9,631,350	213·8
1950	9,853,848	638,485	1,141	4,538	10,498,012	233·1
1960	10,454,004	852,750	2,122	10,490	11,319,366	251·5
			All others			
1970	10,744,515	1,016,561	32,843		11,793,909	262·3
Male	5,172,655	475,986	15,405		5,664,046	—
Female	5,591,860	540,565	17,438		6,129,863	—

Of the total population in 1970, 8,430,410 persons (71·5%) were urban (71·6% in 1960); 7,358,942 were 21 years of age or older.

The population of the larger cities and townships, 1970 census, was:

Philadelphia	1,950,098	Bethlehem	72,686	Wilkes-Barre	58,856
Pittsburgh	520,117	Harrisburg	68,061	Lancaster	57,690
Erie	129,231	Bristol	67,498	Chester	56,331
Allentown	109,527	Lower Merion	63,490	Haverford	55,132
Scranton	103,564	Altoona	63,115	York	50,335
Upper Darby	95,910	Abington	62,899		
Reading	87,643	Penn Hills	62,886		

Larger urbanized areas, 1976 estimate: Philadelphia (in Pennsylvania), 3,802,100; Pittsburgh, 2,500,300; Wilkes-Barre-Scranton, 579,200, Allentown-Bethlehem-Easton (in Pennsylvania), 489,900; Harrisburg, 428,500.

CONSTITUTION AND GOVERNMENT. The present constitution dates from 1968. The General Assembly consists of a Senate of 50 members chosen for 4 years, one-half being elected biennially, and a House of Representatives of 203 members chosen for 2 years. The Governor and Lieut.-Governor are elected for 4 years. Every citizen 18 years of age, with the usual residential qualifications, may vote. The state sends to Congress 2 senators and 25 representatives.

In the 1976 presidential election Carter polled 2,328,677 votes, Ford 2,205,604 and Maddox 23,344.

The state capital is Harrisburg. The state is organized in counties (numbering 67), cities, boroughs, townships and school districts.

Governor: Milton J. Shapp (D.), 1975–79 ($60,000).
Lieut.-Governor: Ernest P. Kline (D.) ($45,000).

BUDGET. Total revenues for the year ending 30 June 1976 were $7,743·7m.; general expenditure, $8,238·2m. (education, $2,567·8m.; transport, $1,550·9m.; public welfare, $2,641·9m.; environment, $174·9m.).

On 30 June 1976 total net long-term debt amounted to $4,538·5m.

Per capita personal income (1974) was estimated at $5,490.

ENERGY AND NATURAL RESOURCES

Minerals. Pennsylvania is almost the sole producer of anthracite coal; its output reached a peak of 100,445,299 short tons in 1917 with a labour-force of 156,148 men. Production in 1975: Anthracite, 5·6m. tons, with 3,877 men; bituminous coal, 84·5m. tons, with 34,170 men; crude petroleum, 3·3m. bbls; natural gas (1973), 78,514m. cu. ft. Total value of other minerals produced (1973), $437·2m., including $168·4m. for cement.

Agriculture. Agriculture, market-gardening, fruit-growing, horticulture and forestry are pursued within the state. In 1975 there were 72,000 farms with a total farm area of 10m. acres (4·45m. acres in crops); the average farm was 139 acres with average value of production, $23,440. Cash income, 1974, from crops, $504·5m., and from livestock and products, $1,103·6m.

Pennsylvania ranks high in the production of cigar leaf tobacco (26m. lb., 1974) and mushrooms (164m. lb., value $63·8m.). Other crops are winter wheat (12·6m. bu.), oats (20·1m. bu.), maize (95·7m. bu.), barley (8·7m. bu.) and potatoes (7·4m. cwt). On 1 Dec. 1974 there were on farms: 1·96m. cattle and calves, including 686,000 milch cows, 125,000 sheep, 633,000 swine. Milk production, 1974, was 6,971m. lb. valued at $622·5m., and eggs numbered 3,492m. valued at $157·1m. Pennsylvania is also a major fruit producing state; in 1974 apples totalled 470m. lb.; peaches, 120m. lb.; cherries, 7,300 tons, and grapes, 53,000 tons. Other important items are soybeans (1·1m. bu.), vegetables for processing (142,650 tons), fresh vegetables (1·4m. cwt) and broiler-chickens (63·6m.).

Forestry. In 1974 national forest lands totalled 636,682 acres; state forests, 1,887,665 acres; state parks, 279,344 acres; state game land, 1,138,969 acres; game land leased but not owned by the state, 5,065,404 acres (co-operative and safety-zone programmes).

INDUSTRY. Pennsylvania leads in the production of iron and steel. Output of steel, 1975, 25·8m. net tons and of pig-iron, 17·6m. net tons.

In 1975, 16,242 manufacturing establishments employed 1,237,022 workers (wages, $13,725m.); value added by manufacture was $28,739m.

COMMUNICATIONS

Roads. Highways and roads in the state (federal, local and state combined) totalled (1975) 114,945 miles. Registered motor vehicles for 1975 numbered 8,691,926 (including 6,649,163 passenger cars, 1,572,804 trucks, truck-tractors and trailers).

Railways. In 1975, 32 railways operated within the state with a line mileage of 8,583.

Aviation. There were (1975) 166 commercial airports, 3 public landing strips, 136 heliports and 363 airports for personal use.

Shipping. Trade at Delaware river ports (1975, short tons) imports, 70·8m., exports, 5·9m.

Post and Broadcasting. Broadcasting stations comprised (1975) 33 television stations and 281 radio stations.

Newspapers. There were (1975) 108 daily and 342 weekly newspapers.

JUSTICE, RELIGION, EDUCATION AND WELFARE

Justice. No executions took place in 1963–77; since 1930 there have been 149 executions (electrocution), all for murder.

Prison population, on 31 Dec. 1975, was 12,930.

Religion. The chief religious bodies in 1977 were the Roman Catholic, with 3,717,667 members; Protestant, 3,150,920 (1971), and Jewish, 469,070. The 5 largest Protestant denominations (by communicants) were: Lutheran Church in America. 766,276; United Methodist, 728,915 (1971); United Presbyterian Church in the USA, 573,905 (1971); United Church of Christ, 257,138; Episcopal, 193,399 (1971).

Education. School attendance is compulsory for children 8–17 years of age. In 1975–76 the public kindergartens and elementary schools had 1,129,451 pupils; secondary schools had 1,116,606 pupils. Non-public schools had 306,037 elementary pupils and 121,932 secondary pupils. Average salary, public school professional personnel, men $14,197; women $12,516.

Leading senior academic institutions (autumn, 1975) included:

Founded	*Institutions*	*Faculty*[1]	*Students*[2]
1740	University of Pennsylvania (non-sect.)	6,043	20,380
1787	University of Pittsburgh	6,935	34,949
1832	Lafayette College, Easton (Presbyterian)	229	2,308
1842	Villanova University (R.C.)	801	9,612
1846	Bucknell University (Baptist)	345	3,248
1851	St Joseph's College, Philadelphia (RC)	433	5,716
1852	California State College	373	5,163
1855	Pennsylvania State University	9,491	68,223
1855	Millersville State College	367	6,258
1863	LaSalle College, Philadelphia (R.C.)	543	5,995
1866	Lehigh University, Bethlehem (non-sect.)	896	6,251
1871	West Chester State College	563	9,295
1875	Indiana University of Pennsylvania	659	11,119
1878	Duquesne University, Pittsburgh (R.C.)	765	7,795
1884	Temple University, Philadelphia	4,571	34,950
1885	Bryn Mawr College	321	1,592
1888	University of Scranton (R.C.)	242	4,124
1891	Drexel University, Philadelphia	990	9,082
1900	Carnegie–Mellon University, Pittsburgh	1,044	4,842

[1] Includes full- and part-time. [2] Total enrolments.

Health. In Jan. 1976 the state had 247 hospitals (55,109 beds) listed by the American Hospital Association, excluding federal hospitals and mental institutions. In June 1976 mental hospital hospitals had 13,866 patients (117 per 100,000 population); institutions for the mentally retarded, 11,818 (100).

Social Security. During the year ending 30 June 1976 the monthly average number of cases receiving public assistance was: Old-age assistance entirely taken over by federal government together with aid to the disabled and some aid to the blind; aid to dependent children, 625,242; blind persons, 6,001; general assistance, 136,148.

Payments for medical assistance for the year ending 30 June 1976 totalled $811·1m. Under the medical assistance programme payments are made for inpatient hospital care ($259·3m.); nursing care in home ($2m.); care in public institutions (nursing homes, mental institutions and geriatric centres) ($266·5m.); private nursing home care ($97·4m.); other medical care ($132·4m.).

Books of Reference

Pennsylvania Manual. Dept. of Property and Supplies, Division of Documents. Harrisburg. Biennial

Pennsylvania's Regions, A Survey of the Commonwealth. State Planning Board. Harrisburg, 1967
Pennsylvania Statistical Abstract. Dept. of Commerce, Harrisburg. Annual
Pennsylvania State Industrial Directory. New York. Annual
Carstens, A. H., *What to See in Pennsylvania.* 2nd ed. Cresco, 1965
Klein, P. S., and Hoogenboom, A., *A History of Pennsylvania.* New York, 1973
League of Women Voters of Pennsylvania, *Key to the Keystone State.* Philadelphia, 1972
Pennsylvania Chamber of Commerce, *Pennsylvania Government Today.* State College, Pa., 1973
Stevens, S. K., *Pennsylvania: Birthplace of a Nation.* New York, 1964.—*Exploring Pennsylvania: Geography History, Civics.* 3rd ed. New York, 1968
Wallace, P. A. W., *Pennsylvania: Seed of a Nation.* New York, 1962
Wilkinson, N. B., *Bibliography of Pennsylvania History.* Pa. Historical & Museum Commission. Harrisburg, 1957

RHODE ISLAND

HISTORY. The earliest settlers in the region which now forms the state of Rhode Island were colonists from Massachusetts who had been driven forth on account of their non-acceptance of the prevailing religious beliefs. The first of the settlements was made in 1636, settlers of every creed being welcomed. In 1647 a patent was granted for the government of the settlements, and on 8 July 1663 a charter was executed recognizing the settlers as forming a body corporate and politic by the name of the 'English Colony of Rhode Island and Providence Plantations, in New England, in America'. On 29 May 1790 the state accepted the federal constitution and entered the Union as the last of the 13 original states.

AREA AND POPULATION. Rhode Island is bounded north and east by Massachusetts, south by the Atlantic and west by Connecticut. Area, 1,214 sq. miles, of which 165 sq. miles are inland water. Census population, 1 April 1970, 949,723, an increase of 10·5% since 1960. Population estimate, July 1975, 952,200.

Births, 1977, were 11,932; deaths (excluding foetal deaths), 9,208; infant deaths, 175; marriages, 7,096; divorces, 3,414.

Population of 5 census years was:

	White	*Negro*	*Indian*	*Asiatic*	*Total*	*Per sq. mile*
1910	532,492	9,529	284	305	542,610	508·5
1930	677,026	9,913	318	240	687,497	649·3
1950	777,015	13,903	978		791,896	748·5
1960	838,712	18,332	932	1,190	859,488	812·4
1970	914,757	25,338	1,390	5,240	949,723[1]	905·0

[1] Through tabulation errors there were 2,998 people unaccounted for, as to race and sex, in 1970.

Of the total population in 1970, 824,930 persons (86·9%) were urban (86·4% in 1960); 590,876 were 21 years of age or older.

The chief cities and their population (census, 1970) are Providence, 179,116; Warwick, 83,694; Pawtucket, 76,984; Cranston, 74,287; East Providence, 48,207; Woonsocket, 46,820; Newport, 34,562; North Kingstown (town), 29,793; Middletown (town), 29,290; Cumberland (town), 26,605. The Providence–Pawtucket–Warwick Standard Metropolitan Statistical Area had a population of 914,110 in 1970.

CONSTITUTION AND GOVERNMENT. The present constitution dates from 1843; it has had 36 amendments. The General Assembly consists (1975) of a Senate of 50 members and a House of Representatives of 100 members, both elected for 2 years, as are also the Governor and Lieut.-Governor. Every citizen, 18 years of age, who has resided in the state for 30 days, and is duly registered, is qualified to vote.

Rhode Island sends to Congress 2 senators and 2 representatives.

At the 1976 presidential election Carter polled 216,991 votes, Ford, 172,138.

The capital is Providence. The state has 5 counties (unique in having no political functions) and 39 cities and towns.

Governor: J. Joseph Garrahy (D.), 1977–79 ($42,500).
Lieut.-Governor: (Vacant).
Secretary of State: Robert F. Burns (D.), 1977–79 ($25,500).

BUDGET. For the fiscal year ending 30 June 1975 (Office of the State Controller) general revenues were $560·2m. (taxation, $342·3m., and federal aid, $139·9m.); general expenditures were $576·5m. (education, $178·1m.; highways, $36·2m.; and public welfare, $181·4m.).

Total net long-term debt on 30 June 1975 was $225m.

Per capita personal income (1974) was $5,376.

NATURAL RESOURCES

Minerals. The small mineral output, mostly stone, sand and gravel, was valued (1974) at $6m.

Agriculture. While Rhode Island is predominantly a manufacturing state, agriculture contributed $26m. to the general cash income in 1974. In 1969 it had 700 farms with an area of 68,720 acres (10·2% of the total land area), of which 31,840 acres were crop land; the average farm was 98·1 acres, valued (land and buildings) at $72,033.

Fisheries. The number of commercial fishermen in the state in 1970 (US census) was 310; value of all fish landed in 1974, $15·9m.

INDUSTRY. Total civilian employment in 1974 was 395,900, of which 125,800 were manufacturing, 241,900 non-manufacturing and 28,200 farm, household and self-employed. Manufacturing firms totalled 3,070 with payroll of $1,076m.; average weekly earnings for production workers in manufacturing, $142.28; value added by manufacture (1973), $1,764·4m. Principal industries are metals and machinery, textile and jewellery–silverware.

COMMUNICATIONS

Roads. The state had (1 Jan. 1975) 5,231 miles of road, of which 1,313 were state-owned. In 1975, 617,678 motor vehicles were registered.

Railways. In 1975, 6 railways operated 135 line-miles.

Aviation. Of the 12 airports in 1975, 7 were state-owned and 5 privately owned. Theodore Francis Green airport at Warwick, near Providence, is served by 5 airlines, and handled 805,650 passengers and 20m. lb. of freight in 1974.

Shipping. Waterborne freight through the Port of Providence (1974) totalled 9m. tons.

Broadcasting. There are 22 radio stations and 4 television stations in the state.

JUSTICE, RELIGION, EDUCATION AND WELFARE

Justice. The state's penal institutions, Oct. 1975, had 671 inmates (70 per 100,000 population).

The death penalty is illegal, except that it is mandatory in the case of murder committed by a prisoner serving a life sentence.

Religion. Chief religious bodies are (estimated figures Sept. 1975): Roman Catholic with 597,000 members; Protestant Episcopal (baptized persons), 50,000; Baptist, 22,500; Congregational, 12,000; Methodist, 10,000; Jewish, 24,000.

Education. The school census of 1974 showed 302,155 persons under 20 years of age; at the 1970 US census approximately 70% were attending school. In 1973–74 the 347 public elementary schools had 6,175 teachers and total enrolment of 103,385 pupils; about 30,639 pupils were enrolled in private and parochial schools. The 44 senior and vocational high schools had 4,632 teachers and 61,427 pupils. Teachers' salaries (1974–75) averaged $10,975. Local expenditure, for schools (including evening schools) in 1973–74 totalled $203·3m.

There are 11 institutions of higher learning in the state, including 1 junior college. The state maintains Rhode Island College, at Providence, with 469 faculty members, and 4,000 full-time students (1975), and the University of Rhode Island, at South Kingstown, with over 717 faculty members and over 11,000 students (including graduate students). Brown University, at Providence, founded in 1764, is now non-sectarian; in 1975 it had over 500 full-time faculty members and 6,700 full-time students. Providence College, at Providence, founded in 1917 by the Order of Preachers (Dominican), had (1975) 218 professors and 3,300 students. The largest of the other colleges are Bryant College, at Smithfield, with 125 faculty and over 2,600 students, and the Rhode Island School of Design, in Providence, with about 100 faculty and 1,400 students.

Health. In 1975 the state had 24 hospitals (over 10,000 beds), including 4 mental hospitals.

Social Security. In July 1975 aid to dependent children was being granted to 36,829 children in 16,147 families (52,472 persons), $71.95 per month, and general assistance to 12,718 persons at an average of $70.25 per month. (All other aid programmes were taken over by the federal government.)

Books of Reference

Rhode Island Manual. Prepared by the Secretary of State. Providence

An Introduction to the Economy of Rhode Island. Issue by the Rhode Island Development Council. Providence, 1953

Providence Journal Almanac: A Reference Book for Rhode Islanders. Providence. Annual

Rhode Island Basic Economic Statistics. Rhode Island Dept. of Economic Development. Providence, 1972

State Library: Rhode Island State Library, State House, Providence 02908. *State Librarian:* Elliott E. Andrews.

SOUTH CAROLINA

HISTORY. South Carolina, first settled permanently in 1670, was one of the 13 original states of the Union.

AREA AND POPULATION. South Carolina is bounded in the north by North Carolina, east and south-east by the Atlantic, south-west and west by Georgia. Area, 31,055 sq. miles. Census population, 1 April 1970, 2,590,516, an increase of 8·7% since 1960. Estimate, July 1976, 2,848,000. Births, 1975, were 46,665 (16·6 per 1,000 population); deaths, 23,343 (8·3); infant deaths, 897 (19·2 per 1,000 live births); marriages, 50,249 (17·8); divorces and annulments, 9,671 (3·4).

The population in 5 census years (with distribution by sex, 1970) was:

	White	*Negro*	*Indian*	*Asiatic*	*Total*	*Per sq. mile*
1910	679,161	835,843	331	65	1,515,400	49·7
1930	944,049	793,681	959	76	1,738,765	56·8
1950	1,293,405	822,077	554	—	2,117,927	69·9
1960	1,551,022	829,291	1,098	946	2,382,594	78·7
			All others			
1970	1,794,430	789,040	3,588		2,590,516	85·7
Male	891,573	376,912	3,602		1,272,087	—
Female	775,268	412,129	3,443		1,318,429	—

Of the total population in 1970, 1,232,195 persons (47·6%) were urban (41·2% in 1960); those 21 years old or older numbered 1,467,299.

Populations of large towns at the 1970 census (with those of associated metropolitan areas): Columbia (capital), 113,542 (322,880); Charleston, 66,945 (303,849); Greenville, 61,208 (299,502); Spartanburg, 44,546; Rock Hill, 33,846; Anderson, 27,556. Estimated population of the metropolitan areas, July 1976: Charleston, 377,300; Columbia, 372,700; Greenville–Spartanburg, 529,200.

CONSTITUTION AND GOVERNMENT. The present constitution dates from 1895, when it went into force without ratification by the electorate. The General Assembly consists of a Senate of 46 members, elected for 4 years (half retiring biennially), and a House of Representatives of 124 members, elected for 2 years. The Governor and Lieut.-Governor are elected for 4 years. Only registered citizens have the right to vote. South Carolina sends to Congress 2 senators and 6 representatives.

At the 1976 presidential election Ford polled 346,149 votes, Carter 450,807, Anderson 2,996 and Maddox 1,905.

The capital is Columbia.

Governor: James B. Edwards (R.), 1975–79 ($35,000).

Secretary of State: O. Frank Thornton (D.) ($30,000).

BUDGET. For the fiscal year ending 30 June 1975 (US Census Bureau figures) general revenues were $1,705m.; general expenditures were $1,855m.

On 30 June 1975 the net long-term debt was $927m.

Per capita personal income (1976) was $5,126.

NATURAL RESOURCES

Minerals. Non-metallic minerals are of chief importance: value of mineral ouput in 1976 was $126·7m., chiefly from cement, kaolin, clay, stone, sand and gravel, and vermiculite. South Carolina ranks second nationally in the production of kaolin and vermiculite. Commodities of minor importance produced include scrap mica, lime pyrite, feldspar, dimension stone and peat. Potentially economic reserves of phosphate and heavy minerals exist.

Agriculture. In 1977 there were 47,000 farms covering a farm area of 7·8m. acres. The average farm was of 166 acres. Of the 29,275 commercial farms of the 1974 census, there were 1,059 of 1,000 acres or more, average farm 211 acres; owners operated 18,589 farms; tenants 2,802. There were 1,502 farms with $100,000 or more in value of sales.

Cash receipts from farm marketing in 1976 amounted to $557m. for crops and $285m. for livestock. Chief crops are tobacco ($172m.), soybeans ($144m.), and maize ($90m.). Production, 1976: Cotton 145,000 lb.; peaches, 255m. lb.; soybeans 21·4m. bu.; tobacco, 153·4m. lb.; maize, 46·7m. bu. Value of production, 1976, $613m. Livestock on farms, 1 Jan. 1977: 750,000 all cattle, 510,000 swine, 7·1m. poultry.

Forestry. The forest industry is important; state and private forest land (1976), 12m. acres. National forests amounted to 592,319 acres.

Industry. About 370,500 workers were employed in manufacturing industries in 1976, earning $3m; value added by manufacture (1974) was $6,374m.

COMMUNICATIONS

Roads. Total highway mileage in the combined highway system in 1975 was 38,161 miles. Motor vehicle registration numbered 1·7m. in 1975.

Railways. In 1973 the length of railway in the state was 3,003 miles.

Aviation. There were, 1976, 72 major airports and numerous others. There were 1,400 registered aircraft.

Shipping. The state has 3 deep-water ports.

JUSTICE, RELIGION, EDUCATION AND WELFARE

Justice. In 1976 penal institutions held 6,840 inmates.

Education. In 1975–76 the total public-school enrolment was 620,003; there were 364,497 white pupils and 255,506 Negro pupils. The total number of teachers was 28,050; average salary was $9,959.

For higher education the state operates the University of South Carolina, founded at Columbia in 1801, with, 1975–76, 31,288 enrolled students; Clemson University, founded in 1889, with 11,213 students; Citadel College, at Charleston, with 3,352 students; Winthrop College, Rock Hill, with 3,957 students; Medical University of S. Carolina, at Charleston, with 1,868 students; S. Carolina State College, at Orangeburg, with 3,519 students, and Francis Marion College, at Florence, with 2,681 students.

There are also 374 private kindergartens, elementary and high schools with total enrolment of 51,669 pupils, and 25 private and denominational colleges and junior colleges with enrolment of 116,408 students.

Health. In 1977 the state had 88 hospitals (11,811 beds), 87 nursing homes (5,531) and 66 intermediate care institutions (3,674) listed by the South Carolina Department of Health and Environmental Control.

Social Security. Old-age assistance was being granted in Dec. 1975 to 389,683 persons, who received an average of $153.31 per month; 173,944 retired received $181.82 monthly; 41,602 disabled, $205.01.

Books of Reference

Reports of the South Carolina State Development Board. Columbia. Annual
South Carolina Legislative Manual. Columbia. Annual
South Carolina Statistical Abstract, 1976. South Carolina Budget and Control Board, Columbia, 1976

State Library: South Carolina State Library, Columbia.

SOUTH DAKOTA

HISTORY. South Dakota was first visited by Europeans in 1743 when Verendrye planted a lead plate (discovered in 1913) on the site of Fort Pierre, claiming the region for the French crown. Beginning with a trading post in 1794, it was settled from 1857 to 1861 when Dakota Territory was organized. It was admitted into the Union on 2 Nov. 1889.

AREA AND POPULATION. South Dakota is bounded north by North Dakota, east by Minnesota, south-east by the Big Sioux River (forming the boundary with Iowa), south by Nebraska (with the Missouri River forming part of the boundary) and west by Wyoming and Montana. Area, 77,047 sq. miles, of which 1,092 sq. miles are water. Area administered by the Bureau of Indian Affairs, 1972, covered 4·96m. acres (10% of the state), of which 2,085,000 acres were held by tribes. The federal government, 1975, owned 3,296,012 acres or 6·743% of the total.

Census population, 1 April 1970, 666,257, a decrease of 2·1% since 1960. Provisional estimate, July 1976, 685,993. Births, 1976, were 11,655 (17 per 1,000 population); deaths, 6,727 (9·8); infant deaths, 199 (17·1 per 1,000 live births); marriages, 10,781 (15·7); divorces, 2,350 (3·4).

Population in 5 federal censuses (with distribution by sex, 1970) was:

	White	*Negro*	*Indian*	*Asiatic*	*Total*	*Per sq. mile*
1910	563,771	817	19,137	163	583,888	7·6
1930	669,453	646	21,833	101	692,849	9·0
1950	628,504	727	23,344	165	652,720	8·5
1960	653,098	1,114	25,794	336	680,514	8·9
			All others			
1970	630,333	1,627	33,547		666,257	8·8
Male	312,588	994	16,801		330,383	—
Female	317,745	633	17,496		335,874	—

Of the total population in 1970, 297,030 persons (43·4%) were urban (39·3% in 1960); 386,371 were 21 years of age or older; foreign-born whites numbered 18,333, in 1960.

Population of the chief cities (census of 1970) was: Sioux Falls, 72,488; Rapid City, 43,836; Aberdeen, 26,476; Huron, 14,299; Brookings, 13,717; Mitchell, 13,425; Watertown, 13,388.

CONSTITUTION AND GOVERNMENT. Voters are all citizens 18 years of age or older who have complied with certain residential qualifications. The people reserve the right of the initiative and referendum. The Senate has 35 members, and the House of Representatives 70 members, all elected for 2 years; the Governor and Lieut.-Governor are elected for 4 years. The state sends 2 senators and 2 representatives to Congress.

In the 1976 presidential election Ford polled 151,619 votes, Carter 146,153.

The capital is Pierre (population, 1970, 9,700). The state is divided into 64 organized counties and 3 unorganized, *i.e.*, with no local functions.

Governor: Richard Kneip (D.), 1975–79 ($27,500).
Lieut.-Governor: Harvey Wollman (D.), 1975–79 ($4,500).
Secretary of State: Lorna Herseth (D.), 1975–79 ($17,500).

On 1 Jan. 1979 salaries will be: Governor, $32,000; Lieut.-Governor, $4,500 for every 30 day legislative session (even years) and $7,500 for every 45 day session (odd years); Secretary of State, $22,500.

BUDGET. For the fiscal year ending 30 June 1975 general revenues were $481·6m. and general expenditures, $414·6m. Taxes and fees from state sources furnished $334·7m. and federal receipts $146·8m.

Per capita personal income (1976) was $5,120.

NATURAL RESOURCES

Minerals. The mineral products include gold (343,800 troy oz. in 1974, second largest yield of all states), sand and gravel (14·7m. short tons), silver (64,000 troy oz.) and gypsum (29,000 short tons). Mineral products, 1974, were valued at $117·5m., of which gold accounts for $55·4m.

Agriculture. In 1974, 42,825 farms had an acreage of 46m.; the average farm had 1,074 acres. Farm units are large; at the 1974 census there were only 3,329 farms of 50 acres or less, compared with 10,533 exceeding 1,000 acres. 12,384 farms sold produce valued at $40,000 or over.

Cash income, 1974, from crops, $816m. and from livestock and products, $1,279m. South Dakota ranks first in the US as producer of rye, second in flaxseed and third in durum wheat. The leading crops (1974) are oats (79m. bu.), maize (77m. bu.), wheat (58m. bu.) and barley (13m. bu.). The farm livestock on 1 Jan. 1975 included 4·95m. cattle, 792,000 sheep, 1·7m. swine. There are 148,000 bee colonies. Milk production, 1974, was 164m. lb. and egg production, 770m. The wool clip in 1974 amounted to 8·4m. lb.

Forestry. National forest area, 1975, 1,995,000 acres.

INDUSTRY. Food processing is by far the largest industry with an annual value of $116·9m., dairy, lumber and wood products, printing and publishing and non-electrical machinery are other major industries with the electronic components industry rapidly growing. On 1 Oct. 1975, manufacturing establishments numbered 874 and had 20,100 workers who earned $158·5m.; value added by manufacture was $272·5m.

COMMUNICATIONS

Roads. Total road mileage was 73,751. Registered passenger cars numbered 328,324 in 1974; trucks, 162,492.

Railways. In 1975 the railways were 3,342 miles in length.

Aviation. Approved airports, 1975, numbered 84; approved private landing strips, 13.

JUSTICE, RELIGION, EDUCATION AND WELFARE

Justice. State prisons had, in 1976, 480 inmates. The death penalty was illegal from 1915 to 1938; since 1938, one person has been executed, in 1949 (by electrocution), for murder.

Religion. The chief religious bodies are (1970): Lutherans with 162,243 members, Roman Catholics (138,250), Methodist (45,795), Disciples of Christ (22,374), Presbyterian (19,494), Baptist (16,055) and Episcopal (17,268).

Education. Elementary and secondary education are free from 6 to 21 years of age. Between the ages of 8 and 16, attendance is compulsory. In 1976 159,101 pupils were attending elementary and high (including parochial) schools (8,134 full-time equivalent classroom teachers). Teachers' salaries (1975–76) averaged an estimated $9,314. Total expenditure on public schools (1975–76), $162m.

The School of Mines at Rapid City, established 1885, had, spring 1975, 108 instructors and 1,440 students; the State University at Brookings, 569 instructors and 6,217 students; the University of South Dakota, founded at Vermillion in 1882, 350 instructors and 5,154 students; Northern State College, 114 instructors and 2,195 students; Black Hills State College, 87 instructors and 1,736 students; Dakota State College, 56 instructors and 713 students; University of South Dakota, Springfield, 64 instructors and 805 students. Seven public colleges had 1,041 instructors and 19,572 students. The Government maintains Indian schools on its reservations and 2 outside at Flandreau and Pierre.

Health. In 1977 the state Health Department listed 61 licensed hospitals (3,669 beds).

Social Security. In financial year 1976, 5,539 persons received as old-age assistance $4,391,082 in Supplemental Security Income; 112 blind persons received $159,573; 3,245 disabled, $3,729,071; 24,663 recipients, $19,536,947 in aid for dependent children.

State supplements to federal SSI payments were $108,265 to 291 aged; $7,915 to 19 blind; $112,858 to 266 disabled. Medical payments to the aged were $12,286,336; to the blind $81,457; to the disabled, $5,588,969. Food stamps (federal funds) were sold to 10,010 households monthly: total value, $13,924,383; bonus value, $8,219,784.

Books of Reference

Digest of Annual Reports, 1970–71 et seq. South Dakota Department of Administration. Annual
Governor's Budget Report. South Dakota Bureau of Finance and Management. Annual
South Dakota Facts: An Abstract of Statistics and Graphics Concerning the People and Resources of South Dakota. South Dakota State Planning Bureau, 1977
South Dakota Historical Collections. 1902–72
South Dakota Economic and Business Abstract, 1972. Business Research Bureau, University of S. Dakota. Vermillion, 1972
South Dakota Legislative Manual. Department of Finance, Pierre, S.D. Biennial
Karolevitz, Robert F., *Challenge: the South Dakota Story.* Sioux Falls, 1975
Milton, John R. *South Dakota; a Bicentennial History.* New York, W. W. Norton, 1977
Schell, H. S., *History of South Dakota.* 3rd ed. Lincoln, Neb., 1975
White, H. L. and B., *Who's Who for South Dakota.* Pierre, S.D., 1961

State Library: South Dakota State Library, State Library Building, Pierre, S.D., 57501. *State Librarian:* Herschel V. Anderson.

TENNESSEE

HISTORY. Tennessee, first settled in 1757, was admitted into the Union on 1 June 1796.

AREA AND POPULATION. Tennessee is bounded north by Kentucky and Virginia, east by North Carolina, south by Georgia, Alabama and Mississippi and west by the Mississippi River (forming the boundary with Arkansas and Missouri). Area, 42,244 sq. miles (482 sq. miles water). Census population, 1 April 1970, 3,923,687, an increase of 356,598 or 10% since 1960. Estimate, July 1975, 4,188,000.

Vital statistics, 1976: Births, 65,284; deaths, 41,475; infant deaths (1975), 1,008 (16·2 per 1,000 live births); marriages, 53,365; divorces, 27,801.

Population in 5 census years (with distribution by sex, 1970) was:

	White	Negro	Indian	Asiatic	Total	Per sq. mile
1910	1,711,432	473,088	216	53	2,184,789	52·4
1930	2,138,644	477,646	161	105	2,616,556	62·4
1950	2,760,257	530,603	339	334	3,291,718	78·8
1960	2,977,753	586,876	638	1,243	3,567,089	85·4
			All others			
1970	3,283,432	631,696	8,559		3,923,687	95·0
Male	1,596,572	296,221	4,142		1,896,935	—
Female	1,686,860	335,475	4,417		2,026,752	—

Of the population in 1970, 2,305,181 persons (58·7%) were urban (52·3% in 1960); those 20 years of age or older numbered 2,446,770.

The cities, with population, 1970 (and estimated population, 1973), are Memphis, 623,530 (658,868); Nashville (capital), 447,877 (427,064); Knoxville, 174,587 (182,276); Chattanooga, 119,082 (137,957); Jackson, 39,996 (42,724); Kingsport, 31,938 (31,382); Oak Ridge, 28,319 (26,182). Standard metropolitan areas: Memphis, 770,120 (1974 estimate, 853,100); Nashville, 540,982 (853,100); Knoxville, 400,337 (427,700); Chattanooga, 304,927 (390,300).

CONSTITUTION AND GOVERNMENT. The state has operated under 3 constitutions, the last of which was adopted in 1870 and has been since amended 10 times (first in 1953). Voters at an election may authorize the calling of a convention limited to altering or abolishing one or more specified sections of the constitution. The General Assembly consists of a Senate of 33 members and a House of Representatives of 99 members, senators elected for 4 years and representatives for 2 years. No clergyman of any denomination is eligible to either House. Qualified as electors are all citizens (with the usual residential and age (18) qualifications). Tennessee sends to Congress 2 senators and 8 representatives.

In the 1976 presidential election Carter polled 821,594 votes, Ford 632,731.

For the Tennessee Valley Authority *see* p. 1396.

The capital is Nashville. The state is divided into 95 counties.

Governor: Ray Blanton (D.), 1975–79 ($30,000).

Secretary of State: Gentry Crowell (D.), ($20,000).

BUDGET. For 1976 total revenue was $2,300m. (taxation, $1,273·2m.; federal aid, $769·9m.), general expenditure, $2,807m., included education, $1,013m.; highways, $369m.; public welfare, $365m.; hospitals, $132·6m.

Total net long-term debt on 30 June 1974 amounted to $522·9m.

Per capita personal income (1976) was $4,895.

ENERGY AND NATURAL RESOURCES

Minerals. Coalfields cover about 5,000 sq. miles; output in 1975 was 8·1m. short tons. In 1973 Tennessee led the states in the production of ball clay (487,625 tons valued at $7·7m., 64% of US total) and pyrite and was the third largest producer of phosphate rock (2,511,853 tons). Other mineral products are zinc (83,000 short tons in 1975), copper, mica, cement, sand and gravel, limestone. Total value of mineral products in 1974 was $396m.

Agriculture. In 1976, 124,000 farms coverd 15·3m. acres. The average farm (1969) was of 124 acres (only a few states had a smaller average) valued land and buildings, at $24,178.

Cash income (1975) from crops was $514m.; from livestock, $581m. Main crops were cotton and tobacco.

On 1 Jan. 1976 the domestic animals included 212,000 milch cows, 3·1m. all cattle, 17,000 sheep, 920,000 swine.

Forestry. Forests occupy 13,695,000 acres (52% of total land area). The forest industry and industries dependent on it employ about 40,000 workers, earning $150m. per year. Wood products are valued at over $500m. per year. National forest system land (1975) 619,000 acres.

INDUSTRY. The manufacturing industries include iron and steel working, but the most important products are chemicals, including synthetic fibres and allied products, electrical equipment and food. In 1972, 5,647 manufacturing establishments employed 467,000 workers, who received wages of $3,352,000; value added by manufactures in 1973 was $7,662,000.

TOURISM. 45m. out-of-state tourists spent $1,295m. in 1976. 930m. people travelled through the state in 1976. 8% of retail business is generated by tourists and travellers. There are 20,430 retail sales and service enterprises based on the tourist business. There are 132,000 people employed in industries directly connected with tourism.

COMMUNICATIONS

Roads. In 1974 there were 81,042 miles of municipal and rural roads, 67,085 miles of surfaced rural roads and 1,671 miles of unsurfaced rural roads. The state is served by 115 intrastate bus companies.

Motor-vehicle registrations, 1975, totalled 2,655,000.

Railways. The state had (1975) 3,500 miles of track on 11 railways.

Aviation. The state is served by 11 major airlines. Airports, 1970, numbered 101.

JUSTICE, RELIGION, EDUCATION AND WELFARE

Justice. There has been no execution since 1960; since 1930 there have been 22 whites and 44 Negroes executed (by electrocution) for murder and 5 whites and 22 Negroes for rape. A US Supreme Court ruling prohibits the use of capital punishment under present Tennessee law, except for first degree murder.

Prison population, 30 June 1974, 3,771.

The law prohibiting the inter-marriage of white and Negro was declared unconstitutional by the US Supreme Court in June 1967.

Religion. The leading religious bodies are the Southern Baptists, Methodists and Negro Baptists.

Education. School attendance has been compulsory since 1925 and the employment of children under 16 years of age in workshops, factories or mines is illegal.

In 1974 there were 1,789 public schools with a net enrolment of 914,867 pupils. In 1976 39,600 teachers earned an average salary of $10,300. Total expenditure for operating county and city public schools (kindergarten to Grade 12) in 1973–74, $735m. Tennessee has 49 accredited colleges and universities, 18 2-year colleges and 28 vocational schools. The universities include the University of Tennessee, Knoxville (founded 1794), with 1,516 faculty and 22,438 students in 1974; Vanderbilt University, Nashville (1873), Tennessee State University (1912), the University of Tennessee at Chattanooga (1886) and Fisk University (1866).

Health. In 1974 the state had 157 hospitals. In 1973 7,096 patients were in mental hospitals. There were 233 nursing homes with 14,200 beds.

Social Security. Old-age assistance was granted (1975) to 79,506 persons, who received an average of $74.5 per person; 1,825 blind persons, $127.09 per person; 57,342 disabled persons, $113.39 per person; 68,978 families with dependent children, $105,25 per family.

Books of Reference

Tennessee Dept. of Finance and Administration, Annual Report, 1971
Dept. of Education Annual Report for Tennessee, 1972
Survey of Current Business, 1972

Tennessee Blue Book. Secretary of State, Nashville
Tennessee Statistical Abstract, 1971. Knoxville, 1971

State Library: State Library and Archives, Nashville. *Librarian:* Miss K. Culbertson. *State Historian:* Dr S. Horn.
Statistics: Tennessee Dept. of Public Welfare, 1972.

TEXAS

HISTORY. In 1836 Texas declared its independence of Mexico, and after maintaining an independent existence, as the Republic of Texas, for 10 years, it was on 29 Dec. 1845 received as a state into the American Union. The state's first settlement dates from 1686.

AREA AND POPULATION. Texas is bounded north by Oklahoma, north-east by Arkansas, east by Louisiana, south-east by the Gulf of Mexico, south by Mexico and west by New Mexico. Area, 267,339 sq. miles (including 4,369 sq. miles of inland water). Census population, 1 Jan. 1970, 11,196,730, an increase of 16·9% since 1960. Vital statistics for 1975: Births, 222,988 (18·2 per 1,000 population); deaths, 100,324 (8·2); infant deaths, 3,655 (16·4 per 1,000 live births); marriages, 153,826 (12·6); divorces, 77,438 (6·3).

Population for 5 census years (with distribution by sex, 1970) was:

	White	*Negro*	*Indian*	*Asiatic*	*Total*	*Per sq. mile*
1910	3,204,848	690,049	702	943	3,896,542	14·8
1930	4,967,172	854,964	1,001	1,578	5,824,715	22·1
1950	6,726,534	977,458	2,736	3,392	7,711,194	29·3
1960	8,374,831	1,187,125	5,750	9,848	9,579,677	36·5
			All others			
1970	9,717,128	1,399,005	80,597		11,196,730	42·7
Male	4,767,630	672,901	40,638		5,481,169	—
Female	4,949,498	726,104	39,959		5,715,561	—

Of the population in 1970, 8,921,000 persons (79·7%) were urban (75% in 1960); households numbered 3,432,000. Those 21 years old and older were 6,567,000. A census report, 1970, showed, 1,723,531 persons with Spanish surnames, of whom 1,533,460 were natives of the state.

The largest cities, with census population in 1970, are:

Houston	1,232,802	Amarillo	127,010	Odessa	81,437
Dallas	844,401	Beaumont	115,919	Garland	78,380
San Antonio	654,153	Wichita Falls	97,564	Laredo	69,024
Fort Worth	393,476	Irving	97,262	San Angelo	63,884
El Paso	322,261	Waco	95,326	Galveston	61,809
Austin (capital)	251,808	Arlington	90,643	Midland	59,463
Corpus Christi	204,525	Abilene	89,653	Tyler	57,770
Lubbock	149,101	Pasadena	89,277	Port Arthur	57,371

Larger urbanized areas, 1970: Houston, 1·98m.; Dallas, 1·55m.; San Antonio, 864,014; Fort Worth, 762,086.

CONSTITUTION AND GOVERNMENT. The present constitution dates from 1876; it has been amended 212 times. The Legislature consists of a Senate of 31 members elected for 4 years (half their number retiring every 2 years), and a House of Representatives of 150 members elected for 2 years.

The Governor and Lieut.-Governor are elected for 4 years. Qualified electors are all citizens with the usual residential qualifications. Texas sends to Congress 2 senators and 24 representatives.

In the 1976 presidential election Carter polled 2,031,562 votes, Ford 1,876,316.

The capital is Austin. The state has 254 counties.

Governor: Dolph Briscoe (D.), 1975–79 ($65,000).

Lieut.-Governor: William P. Hobby (D.), 1975–79 ($7,200).
Secretary of State: Mark W. White Jr.

BUDGET. In the fiscal year ending 31 Aug. 1974 general revenues were $5,014,755,658; general expenditures, $4,492,958,989 (education, $1,951,567,413; welfare, $859,672,000; highways, $649,448,272).

Texas is unique in the large revenue derived from the severance tax (*i.e.*, tax on the removal of oil, natural gas and sulphur from the soil or waters of the state) which in the 1973–74 fiscal year yielded $526,368,768; tax on motor fuels yielded $398,556,049; cigarette and tobacco taxes and licences $248,476,145; sales tax, $1,128,532,563.

Net long-term debt, 31 Aug. 1974, was $869,060,042.

Per capita personal income (1974) was $4,952.

ENERGY AND NATURAL RESOURCES

Minerals. Texas leads all states by a wide margin in the production of crude petroleum and related minerals. In 1972 Texas had 34·22% of proved US petroleum reserves. Production, 1972: Crude petroleum, 1,301,685,000 bbls; natural gas, 8,657,840m. cu. ft; natural gasoline, 92,437,000 bbls; butane and propane gases, 131,793,909 bbls in 1971; cement, 8m. short tons; salt, 9·7m. short tons. Other minerals include helium (1,106m. cu. ft), crude gypsum (1,542m. short tons), granite and sandstone.

Total value of mineral products in 1972, $7,200m., leading all states.

Agriculture. Texas is one of the most important agricultural states of the Union. In 1969 (census) it had 213,550 farms covering 142,567,000 acres; average farm was of 668 acres valued, land and buildings, at $99,000. Large-scale commercial farms, highly mechanized, dominate in Texas; farms of 1,000 acres or more numbered 23,005, a number far exceeding that of any other state; 29,601 farms sold produce valued at $20,000 or more. But small-scale farming persists; 38,105 farms were under 50 acres.

Soil erosion is serious in some parts. For some 97,297,000 acres drastic curative treatment has been indicated and for 51,164,000 acres, preventive treatment. In 1970 there were 188 soil-conservation districts embracing an area of 166·57m. acres, of which 144,366,000 acres were in farms and ranches.

Production, 1974: Cotton, 2,462,000 bales from 5·2m. acres; yield was 269 lb. per acre compared with the average of 461 lb. for all cotton states; pecans, 38m. lb.; grain sorghum, 312m. bu. Other important crops were maize (73m. bu.), wheat, (53m. bu.), oats and barley (30m. bu. in 1973), rough rice (25·2m. cwt), peanuts (413m. lb.), oranges (6·6m. boxes), grapefruit (10·7m. boxes), and peaches, potatoes, sweet potatoes.

Cash income, 1974, from crops was $2,848m.; from livestock, $2,972m.

The state has a very great livestock industry, leading in the number of all cattle, 16·6m. on 1 Jan. 1975, and sheep, 2·68m.; it also had 350,000 milch cows, and 800,000 swine. The wool clip in 1974 amounted to 23·9m. lb.; mohair, 8·4m. lb.

Forestry. National forests area under forest service administration (1974) 1,755,028 acres (gross area).

INDUSTRY. The 1971 survey of manufactures showed manufacturing establishments numbering 13,336 employing 694,000 production workers earning $3,300m.; value added by manufactures was $3,793,900. Chemical industries along the Gulf Coast, such as the production of synthetic rubber and of primary magnesium (from sea-water), are increasingly important.

COMMUNICATIONS

Roads. The state maintained (31 Aug. 1974) 69,268 miles of roads. Motor registration in 1974, 9·5m.

Railways. The railways (1974) had a total mileage of 19,134 miles, of which 13,303 miles were main lines.

Aviation. Public airports, 1975, numbered 496, in addition, there were 725 private airports.

Shipping. The port of Houston, connected by the Houston Ship Channel (50 miles long) with the Gulf of Mexico, is the largest inland cotton market in the world.

JUSTICE, RELIGION, EDUCATION AND WELFARE

Justice. The prison system, Dec. 1974, held 16,833 men and women. Since 1968 there have been no executions. Total executions from 1930 through 1968 have been 297, of which 210 were for murder, 84 (including 71 Negroes) for rape and 3 for armed robbery.

Texas has adopted 11 laws governing the activities of trade unions. An Act of 1955 forbids the state's payment of unemployment compensation to workers engaged in certain types of strikes.

Religion. The largest religious bodies are Roman Catholics, Baptists, Methodists, Churches of Christ, Lutherans, Presbyterians and Episcopalians.

Education. In 1970 persons 25 years of age or older who reported no school years completed numbered 176,675 (3% of that age group), of whom 154,147 were whites and 21,079 were non-whites; of persons between 5 and 24, 3,101,020 (70·8%) were attending school. School attendance is compulsory from 7 to 17 years of age. In 1965–66 all public schools had completed or begun desegregation. The estimated total enrolment in 1973 was 2,821,202.

In autumn 1973 public elementary schools (kindergarten through grade 6) had 1,515,956 enrolled pupils and 54,550 classroom teachers; secondary schools, 1,305,246 enrolled pupils and 53,915 classroom teachers. Teachers' salaries, 1972, estimate, averaged $8,376. Total public school expenditure, 1973, $2,700m.

The state maintains 127 institutions of higher learning with an estimated enrolment, Sept. 1974, of 578,414 students. The largest institutions, with faculty numbers and student enrolment, were:

Founded	*Institutions*	*Control*	*Students*
1845	Baylor University, Waco	Baptist	8,130
1852	St Mary's University, San Antonio	R.C.	3,564
1869	Trinity University, San Antonio	Presb.	3,412
1873	Texas Christian University, Fort Worth	Christian	6,537
1876	Texas A. and M. Univ., College Station	State	21,245
1876	Prairie View Agr. and Mech. Coll., Prairie View	State	4,870
1879	Sam Houston State University	State	10,144
1883	University of Texas, Austin	State	41,840
1890	North Texas State University	State	15,875
1891	Hardin-Simmons University, Abilene	Baptist	1,630
1895	University of Texas, Arlington	State	15,434
1899	East Texas State University	State	9,241
1899	South West Texas State University	State	12,894
1901	North Texas State University, Denton	State	15,875
1903	Texas Woman's University, Denton	State	7,190
1906	Abilene Christian College, Abilene	Church of Christ	3,647
1911	Southern Methodist University, Dallas	Methodist	10,079
1912	William Marsh Rice University, Houston	—	3,525
1913	University of Texas, El Paso	State	11,418
1923	Stephen F. Austin State University	State	10,881
1923	Texas Technical University, Lubbock	State	21,927
1924	College of Arts and Industries, Kingsville	State	6,796
1934	University of Houston, Houston	State	29,389
1947	Texas Southern University, Houston	State	7,125
1951	Lamar University	State	11,080

Health. In 1973, the state had 566 hospitals (77,402 beds) listed by the American Hospital Association; on 31 Dec. 1974 mental hospitals had 8,588 resident patients and institutions for the mentally retarded, 13,309 resident patients.

Social Security. Aid is from state and federal sources. Old-age assistance was being granted in Dec. 1973 to 171,275 persons, who received an average of $54.44 per month; aid was given to 3,734 blind persons ($82.40 per month), to 122,209 families with 322,441 dependent children (average per family, $109.75), and to 31,468 permanently and totally disabled persons ($75.42).

Books of Reference

Texas Almanac. Dallas. Biennial
MacCorkle, S. A., and Smith, D., *Texas Government.* 7th ed. New York, 1974
Richardson, R. N., *Texas, the Lone Star State.* 3rd ed. New York, 1970
Webb, W. P. (ed.), *The Handbook of Texas.* State Hist. Ass., Austin, 1952

Legislative Reference Library: Box 12488, Capitol Station, Austin, Texas 78811. *Director:* James R. Sanders.

UTAH

HISTORY. Utah, which had been acquired by the US during the Mexican war, was settled by Mormons in 1847, and organized as a Territory on 9 Sept. 1850. It was admitted as a state into the Union on 4 Jan. 1896 with boundaries as at present.

AREA AND POPULATION. Utah is bounded north by Idaho and Wyoming, east by Colorado, south by Arizona and west by Nevada. Area, 82,096 sq. miles, of which 2,577 sq. miles are water. The federal government (1967) owned 35,397,274 acres or 67·1% of the area of the state. The area of unappropriated and unreserved lands was 23,268,250 acres in 1974. The Bureau of Indian Affairs in 1974 administered 3,035,190 acres, all of which were allotted to Indian tribes.

Census population, 1 April 1970, 1,059,273, an increase of 18·9% since 1960. Estimated population, 1974, 1,173,000. Births in 1975 were 32,641 (27·1 per 1,000 population); deaths, 7,871 (6·5); infant deaths, 467 (14·3 per 1,000 live births); marriages, 13,899 (11·5); divorces, 6,160 (5·1).

Population at 5 federal censuses (with distribution by sex, 1970) was:

	White	*Negro*	*Indian*	*Asiatic*	*Total*	*Per sq. mile*
1910	366,583	1,144	3,123	2,501	373,851	4·5
1930	499,967	1,108	2,869	3,903	507,847	6·2
1950	676,909	2,729	4,201	—	688,862	8·4
1960	873,828	4,148	6,961	5,207	890,627	10·8
1970	1,031,926	6,617	11,273	6,230	1,059,273	12·9
Male	508,997	3,987	5,492	3,089	523,265	6·4
Female	522,929	2,630	5,781	3,141	536,008	6·5

Of the total in 1970, 851,472 persons (80·4%) were urban (74·9% in 1960); 570,349 were 21 years of age or older.

The largest cities are Salt Lake City (capital), with a population (census, 1970) of 175,885 (urbanized area, 557,635); Ogden, 169,478; Provo, 53,131; Bountiful, 27,853; Orem, 25,25,729; and Logan, 22,333.

CONSTITUTION AND GOVERNMENT. Utah adopted its present constitution in 1896 (now with 61 amendments). It sends to Congress 2 senators and 2 representatives.

The Legislature consists of a Senate (in part renewed every 2 years) of 30 members, elected for 4 years, and of a House of Representatives of 75 members elected for 2 years. The Governor is elected for 4 years. The constitution provides for the initiative and referendum. Electors are all citizens, who, not being insane or criminal, have the usual residential qualifications.

The capital is Salt Lake City. There are 29 counties in the state.

In the 1976 presidential election Ford polled 335,144 votes, Carter 180,974.

Governor: Scott Matheson (D.), 1977–81 ($35,000).
Lieut.-Governor: Clyde L. Miller (D.), 1977–81 ($22,000).
Attorney-General: Vernon B. Romney (R.), 1977–81 ($25,000).

BUDGET. For the year ending 30 June 1974 general revenue was $654·1m. while general expenditures were $638·9m. ($289·3m. for education, $113m. for highways and $236m. for social services).

The net long-term debt on 30 June 1974 was about $30m.

Per capita personal income (1974) was $4,450.

ENERGY AND NATURAL RESOURCES

Minerals (1971). Production of principal minerals: Copper, 270,300 short tons; gold, 374,400 troy oz.; petroleum (1970), 27·4m. bbls; lead, 38·7m. lb.; silver, 5,251,000 troy oz.; zinc, 26·3m. lb. Total value of mineral production, 1970, $601·9m.

Agriculture. In 1975 Utah had 12,600 farms with a total area of 13m. acres (25% of the total land area), of which about 2m. acres were crop land and about 300,000 acres pasture. About 1m. acres had irrigation; the average farm was of 1,030 acres.

Of the total surface area (52,721,500 acres, including 2,577 sq. miles of water), 9% is severely eroded and only 9·4% is free from erosion; the balance is moderately eroded.

Cash income, 1974, from crops, $100·9m. and from livestock, $219·7m. The principal crops are: Barley (threshed), 7·2m. bu.; wheat (spring and winter, threshed), 8·81m. bu.; oats (threshed), 636,000 bu.; potatoes (100 lb. bags), 1·48m.; sugar-beet, 296,000 tons; hay (alfalfa, sweet clover and lespedeza), 1·69m. tons; alfalfa seed, 4·8m. lb.; corn, 1·68m. tons; apples, 18,500 tons; cherries (sweet and tart), 10,800 tons; peaches, 8,000 tons; pears, 3,200 tons; vegetables for processing, 20,400 tons. In 1975 there were 660,000 sheep; 79,000 milch cows; 900,000 all cattle; 41,000 swine. The 1974 wool clip yielded 7·4m. lb. of wool; 922m. lb. of milk were produced; and 1·79m. chickens produced 311m. eggs and 1·2m. broilers.

Forestry. Area of national forests, 1970, was 9,088,986 acres, of which 8·01m. acres were under forest service administration.

INDUSTRY. In 1973 the 1,469 manufacturing establishments had 64,128 workers, who earned $549m.; value added by manufacture was (1970) $783·5m. Leading manufactures by value added (1970): primary metals, ordinances and transport, food, fabricated metals and machinery, petroleum products.

COMMUNICATIONS

Roads. The state has about 58,000 miles of highway. In 1974 there were 861,690 motors registered.

Railways. On 1 July 1974 the state had 1,734 miles of railways.

Aviation. There were (1971) 89 airports (51 municipal, 32 private, 6 commercial).

JUSTICE, RELIGION, EDUCATION AND WELFARE

Justice. The number of inmates of the state prison on 13 Oct. 1975 was 659. Since 1930 total executions have been 14 (13 by shooting, 1 by hanging—the condemned man has choice), all whites, and all for murder.

Religion. Latter-day Saints (Mormons) form about 73% of the church membership of the state, with approximately 829,990 members in 1974; their church is a substantial property-owner. There were (1970) about 50,483 Catholics. Most Protestant denominations are represented.

Education. School attendance is compulsory for children from 6 to 18 years of age. There are 40 school districts. Teachers' salaries, 1973, averaged $9,150. There were (autumn 1974) 316,592 pupils in public elementary and secondary schools. In 1970–71 estimated public school expenditure was $137·2m.

The University of Utah (1850) (21,364 students in 1975) is in Salt Lake City; the Utah State University (1890) (8,805 students) in Logan has 2 branch colleges. The Mormon Church maintains the Brigham Young University at Provo (1875) with

26,515 students. Other colleges include: Westminster College, Salt Lake City, 933 students; Weber State College, Ogden, 8,574; Southern Utah State College, Cedar City, 1,811; College of Eastern Utah, Price, 626; Snow College, Ephraim, 842; Dixie College, St George, 1,203; Utah Technical College, Salt Lake City, 5,644; Utah Technical College, Provo, 3,138; L.D.S. Business College, Salt Lake City, 1,035. Total college students, June 1975, 80,490. A state bond of $70m. was approved in July 1975 for the University of Utah medical centre.

Health. In 1974, the state had 43 hospitals (5,061 beds) listed by the Utah Department of Social Services.

Social Security. The state department of public welfare provided assistance to an average of 44,987 persons per month during the financial year 1974; 34,124 persons received aid to dependent children at an average $74.57 per month; aid to the aged, the blind and disabled is provided from federal funds. Total expenditure of the department for assistance, welfare and administration, 1974–75, was $70,417,582 (state and federal aid).

Books of Reference

Compiled Digest of Administrative Reports. Secretary of State, Salt Lake City. Annual
Statistical Abstract of Government in Utah. Utah Foundation, Salt Lake City. Annual
A Statistical Abstract of Utah's Economy. Bureau of Economic and Business Research, Univ. of Utah, 1964
Utah Agricultural Statistics. Dept. of Agriculture, Salt Lake City. Annual
Utah: Facts. Bureau of Economic and Business Research, Univ. of Utah, 1975
Writers' Program. *A Guide to the State.* New York, 1954
Arrington, L., *Great Basin Kingdom: An Economic History of the Latter-Day Saints, 1830–1900.* Cambridge, Mass., 1958
Nelson, E., *Utah's Economic Patterns.* Salt Lake City, 1956

VERMONT

HISTORY. Vermont, first settled in 1724, was admitted into the Union as the fourteenth state on 4 March 1791. The first constitution was adopted by convention at Windsor, 2 July 1777, and established an independent state government.

AREA AND POPULATION. Vermont is bounded north by Canada, east by New Hampshire, south by Massachusetts and west by New York. Area, 9,267 sq. miles, of which 333 sq. miles are inland water. Census population, 1 April 1970, 444,732, an increase of 14% since 1960. Births, 1975, were 5,999 (12·7 per 1,000 population); deaths, 4,080 (8·7); infant deaths, 77 (12·8 per 1,000 live births); marriages, 4,351 (9·2); divorces, 1,866 (4).

Population at 5 census years (with distribution by sex, 1970) was:

	White	*Negro*	*Indian*	*Asiatic*	*Total*	*Per sq. mile*
1910	354,298	1,621	26	11	355,956	39·0
1930	358,966	568	36	41	359,611	38·8
1950	377,188	443	30	48	377,747	40·7
1960	389,092	519	57	172	389,881	42·0
1970	442,553	761	229	787	444,732	48·0
Male	216,230	443	112	381	217,166	—
Female	226,323	318	117	406	227,164	—

Of the population in 1970, 142,889 persons (32·2%) were urban (38·5% in 1960); those 21 years of age or older (1970), 252,809; there were (1960) 23,218 foreign-born whites. Households (1973) numbered 145,000. The largest cities are Burlington, with a population in 1970 of 38,633; Rutland, 19,293; Barre, 10,209.

CONSTITUTION AND GOVERNMENT. The constitution was adopted in 1793 and has since been amended. Amendments are proposed by two-thirds vote of the Senate every 4 years, and must be accepted by two sessions of the legislature; they are then submitted to popular vote. The state Legislature, consisting of a Senate of 30 members and a House of Representatives of 150 members (both elected for 2 years), meets in Jan. in odd-numbered years. The Governor and Lieut.-Governor are elected for 2 years. Electors are all citizens who possess certain residential qualifications and have taken the freeman's oath set forth in the constitution.

The state is divided into 14 counties; there are 251 towns and cities and other minor civil divisions. The state sends to Congress 2 senators and 1 representative, who are elected by the voters of the entire state.

In the 1976 presidential election Ford polled 98,982 votes, Carter 77,746.

The capital is Montpelier (8,609, census of 1970).

Governor: Richard Snelling (R.) 1977–78 ($36,100).
Lieut.-Governor: Brian Burns (D.) ($15,500).
Secretary of State: Richard C. Thomas (R.) ($19,600).

BUDGET. The general revenue for the year ending 30 June 1974 was $143·5m. (excluding federal aid); highway fund revenue, $70·3m.; general expenditure was $145·9m. (education, $62·8m.; highways, $73·4m., and public welfare, $45.6m.).

Total net long-term debt, 1 July 1974, was $339,035,275.

Per capita personal income (1973) was $4,011.

NATURAL RESOURCES

Minerals. Stone, chiefly granite, marble and slate, is the leading mineral produced in Vermont, contributing about 60% of the total value of mineral products. Other products include asbestos, talc, peat, sand and gravel. Total value of mineral products, 1974, $31·2m.

Agriculture. Agriculture is the most important industry. In 1973 the state had about 6,600 farms with a total area of 1·86m. acres, of which 566,000 acres were crop land; the average farm was of 282 acres valued, land and buildings, at $110,200. Cash income, 1973, from livestock and products, $187·5m.; from crops, $15·9m. The 3,385 dairy farms produce 1,958m. lb. of milk annually. The chief agricultural crops are hay, apples and maple syrup. In 1974 Vermont had 293,884 milch cows, 5,364 sheep, 3,595 swine, 342,310 laying hens and 10,220 horses.

Forestry. In 1973 there was cut 98m. bd ft hardwood and 87m. bd ft softwood. In addition, 142,139 cords of pulpwood and boltwood and 185m. bd ft of logs were produced.

National forests area (1972), 242,309 acres. In 1975 there were 34 state forests, and 41 state parks; total acreage 132,329.

INDUSTRY. In 1972, 850 manufacturing establishments employed 37,900 production workers who earned $320·9m.; value added by manufacture was $578·9m.

COMMUNICATIONS

Roads. The state maintained (1974) 2,551 miles of paved and gravelled highways. Total highways, 13,594 miles. Motor vehicle registrations, 1974, 307,045.

Railways. There were, in 1973, 724 miles of main line railway, 277 of which was leased by the state to private operators.

Aviation. There were 23 airports, of which 10 were state operated, 3 municipally owned and 10 privately owned but open to public use.

Post and Broadcasting. In 1973 there were 280,212 telephones in use. There were (1975) 2 commercial television stations, 35 cable television companies franchised to serve 96 communities and 35 radio broadcasting stations.

JUSTICE, RELIGION, EDUCATION AND WELFARE

Justice. During 1972–73 there was an average of 2,444 people under the supervision or in the custody of the Department of Corrections. There is no capital punishment in Vermont. The Vermont State Prison was closed in Aug. 1975 and prisoners transferred to federal prisons and community correction centres.

Religion. The principal denominations (1975) are Roman Catholic (with about 50,000 adult confirmed and 130,000 baptized), United Church of Christ (22,748), United Methodist (about 22,000), Protestant Episcopal (about 7,500), Baptist (about 7,000) and Unitarian-Universalist (2,054 in 1970).

Education. School attendance during the full school term is compulsory for children from 7 to 16 years of age, or to have completed the 10th grade. In 1973–74 the 346 public elementary schools had 64,608 enrolled pupils; the 71 public secondary schools had 41,628 pupils; the 64 private schools had 10,125 pupils. Full-time teachers for public elementary and secondary schools numbered 6,537. Teachers' salaries for 1973–74 averaged $8,573 (elementary) and $9,202 (secondary). The University of Vermont (1791) had 8,500 full-time students in 1973–74; Middlebury College (1800), 1,941 students; Norwich University (1834), 997 students; St Michael's College, 1,543 students; the 4 state colleges, 3,585 students. Total expenditure for education, 1971–72, was an estimated $104m., exclusive of capital outlay.

Health. In July 1972 the state had 18 general hospitals (2,252 beds), 2 mental hospitals (1,474 beds) and 1 T.B. hospital (50 beds). There was 1 federal general hospital with 175 beds.

Social Security. Old-age assistance was being granted in 1974 to 3,423 persons, drawing an average of $64.19 per month; aid to dependent children was being granted to 22,014 persons, drawing an average of $71.64 per month; aid to the blind was being granted to 74 persons, drawing an average of $92.20; and aid to the permanently and totally disabled was being granted to 2,505 persons, drawing an average of $96.43.

Books of Reference

Legislative Directory. Secretary of State, Montpelier. Biennial
Vermont Facts and Figures. Office of Statistical Co-ordination, Montpelier. 3rd ed. 1975
Vermont Year-Book, formerly *Walton's Register.* Chester. Annual

State Library: Vermont Dept. of Libraries, Montpelier. *State Librarian:* John A. McCrossan.

VIRGINIA

HISTORY. The first English Charter for settlements in America was that granted by James I in 1606 for the planting of colonies in Virginia. The state was one of the 13 original states in the Union. Virginia lost just over one-third of its area when West Virginia was admitted into the Union (1863).

AREA AND POPULATION. Virginia is bounded north-west by West Virginia, north-east by Maryland, east by the Atlantic, south by North Carolina and Tennessee and west by Kentucky. Area, 40,817 sq. miles, including 1,037 sq. miles of inland water. Census population, 1 April 1970, 4,648,484, an increase of 681,545 or 17·2% since 1960. In 1975 there were 70,032 births (14·1 per 1,000 population); 39,543 deaths (8); 1,233 infant deaths (17·6 per 1,000 live births); 54,688 marriages (11), and 19,361 divorces (3·9).

Population for 5 federal census years (with distribution by sex, 1970) was:

	White	*Negro*	*Indian*	*Asiatic*	*Total*	*Per sq. mile*
1910	1,389,809	671,096	539	168	2,061,612	51·2
1930	1,770,441	650,165	779	466	2,421,851	60·7
1950	2,581,555	734,211	1,056	758	3,318,680	83·2
1960	3,142,443	816,258	2,155	4,725	3,966,949	99·3
			All others			
1970	3,761,514	861,368	25,612		4,648,484	116·9
Male	1,864,716	419,248	13,157		2,297,121	—
Female	1,896,798	442,120	12,455		2,351,373	—

Of the total population in 1970, 2,934,841 persons (63·1%) were urban (55·6% in 1960); those 21 years of age or older numbered 2·79m.

The population (census of 1970) of the principal cities was: Norfolk, 307,951 (urbanized area, Norfolk–Portsmouth, 680,600); Richmond, 249,430; Newport News, 138,177 (Newport News–Hampton, 292,159); Hampton, 120,779; Alexandria, 110,938; Portsmouth, 110,963; Roanoke, 92,115; Lynchburg, 54,083; Danville, 46,391; Charlottesville, 38,880; Petersburg, 36,103.

CONSTITUTION AND GOVERNMENT. The present constitution dates from 1971.

The General Assembly consists of a Senate of 40 members, elected for 4 years, and a House of Delegates of 100 members, elected for 2 years. The Governor and Lieut.-Governor are elected for 4 years. Qualified as electors are (with few exceptions) all citizens 18 years of age, fulfilling certain residential qualifications, who have registered. The state sends to Congress 2 senators and 10 representatives.

In the 1976 presidential election Ford polled 836,554 votes, Carter 813,896, Camejo 17,802, Anderson 16,686, La Rouche 7,508 and MacBride 4,648.

The state capital is Richmond; the state contains 95 counties and 35 independent cities.

Governor: John N. Dalton (R.), 1978–82 ($55,000).
Lieut.-Governor: Charles S. Robb (D.) ($13,265).
Secretary of the Commonwealth: Stanford E. Parris (R.) ($17,400).

BUDGET. General revenue for the year ending 30 June 1976 was $3,563,416,817 (taxation, $1,734,106,433, and federal aid, $849,864,702); general expenditures, $3,512,065,088 ($1,328,904,305 for education, $118,418,589 for transport and $224,648,909 for public welfare).

Total net long-term debt, 30 June 1975, amounted to $197,527,279.

Per capita personal income (1975) was $5,785.

ENERGY AND NATURAL RESOURCES

Minerals (1976). Coal is the most important mineral, with output of 39,995,546 short tons. Lead and zinc ores (25,103 short tons), stone, sand and gravel, lime and titanium ore are also produced. Total mineral output was 52·8m. tons.

Agriculture. In 1969 there were 65,000 farms with an area of 10·65m. acres; average farm had 165 acres and was valued at $47,000.

Income, 1975, from crops, $483m., and from livestock and livestock products, $525m. The chief crops (1976) are tobacco (153·8m. lb.), corn, wheat, oats, potatoes, sweet potatoes, peanuts (304·8m. lb.) and apples.

Animals on farms on 1 Jan. 1976 included 165,000 milch cows, 1·62m. all cattle, 164,000 sheep and 650,000 swine.

Forestry. National forests, 1975, covered 1,598,000 acres.

INDUSTRY. The manufacture of cigars and cigarettes and of rayon and allied products and the building of ships lead in value of products. In 1972, 4,837 manufacturing establishments employed 375,000 workers; valued added by manufacture was $6,178m.

COMMUNICATIONS

Roads. The state highways system, 30 June 1976, had 52,000 miles of highways, of which 8,976 miles were primary roads. Motor registrations, 1975, 3·325m.

Railways. In 1976 there were 4,301 miles of state-owned railways.

Aviation. There were, in 1974, 227 airports, of which 54 were publicly owned.

JUSTICE, RELIGION, EDUCATION AND WELFARE

Justice. Executions (by electrocution) since 1930 totalled 95, including 17 whites and 58 Negroes for murder and 20 Negroes for rape. Prison population, 31 Dec. 1974, 5,032 in federal and state prisons.

Religion. The principal churches are the Baptists, Methodists, Protestant, Episcopal and Presbyterian.

Education. Elementary and secondary instruction is free, and for ages 6–17 attendance is compulsory. No child under 12 may be employed in any mining or manufacturing work.

In 1974–75 the 140 school districts had, in primary schools, 703,573 pupils and 33,107 teachers and in public high schools, 467,956 pupils and 24,666 teachers. Teachers' salaries (1975) averaged $10,671. Total expenditure on education, 1974–75, was $1,486m. The more important institutions for higher education (1976) were:

Founded	*Name and place of college*	*Staff*	*Students*
1693	William and Mary College, Williamsburg (State)	458	5,947
1749	Washington and Lee University, Lexington	126	1,600
1776	Hampden-Sydney College, Hampden-Sydney (Pres.)	55	746
1819	University of Virginia, Charlottesville (State)	1,532	15,179
1832	Randolph-Macon College, Ashland (Methodist)	72	811
1832	University of Richmond, Richmond (Baptist)	292	6,176
1838	Virginia Commonwealth University, Richmond	1,727	18,053
1839	Virginia Military Institute, Lexington (State)	106	1,298
1865	Virginia Union University, Richmond	123	1,318
1872	Virginia Polytechnic Institute, Blacksburg (State)	1,493	18,477
1882	Virginia State College, Petersburg	226	4,559
1930	Old Dominion University, Norfolk	617	13,160

Health. In 1975 the state had 129 hospitals (32,314 beds) listed by the American Hospital Association.

Social Security. In 1938 Virginia established a system of old-age assistance under the Federal Security Act; in Dec. 1976, 1,134 persons were drawing an average grant of $56.18; aid to permanently and totally disabled, 803 persons, average grant $58.06; aid to dependent children, 57,336 persons, average grant $64.37; general relief, 8,181 cases, average grant $108.88.

Books of Reference

Statistical Abstract of Virginia. 2 vols. Charlottesville, 1967–70
Dabney, V., *Virginia, the new Dominion.* 1971
Gottmann, J., *Virginia in our Century.* Charlotteville, 1969

State Library: Virginia State Library, Richmond 23219. *State Librarian:* Donald R. Haynes.

WASHINGTON

HISTORY. Washington, formerly part of Oregon, was created a Territory in 1853, and was admitted into the Union as a state on 11 Nov. 1889. Its settlement dates from 1811.

AREA AND POPULATION. Washington is bounded north by Canada, east by Idaho, south by Oregon with the Columbia River forming most of the boundary, and west by the Pacific. Area, 68,192 sq. miles, of which 1,622 sq. miles are inland water. Lands owned by the federal government, 1975, were 12·6m. acres or 29·5% of the total area. Census population, 1 April 1970, 3,409,169, an increase of 555,955 or 19·5% since 1960. Births, 1975 were 50,821 (14·5 per 1,000 population); deaths, 29,778 (8·5); infant deaths, 798 (15·7 per 1,000 live births); marriages, 41,767; divorces and annulments, 25,540.

Population in 5 federal census years (with distribution by sex, 1970) was:

	White	*Negro*	*Indian*	*Asiatic and others*	*Total*	*Per sq. mile*
1910	1,109,111	6,058	10,997	15,824	1,141,990	17·1
1930	1,521,661	6,840	11,253	23,642	1,563,396	23·3
1950	2,316,496	30,691	13,816	17,960	2,378,963	35·6
1960	2,751,675	48,738	21,076	31,725	2,853,214	42·8
1970	2,351,055	71,308	33,386	53,420	3,409,169	51·2
Male	1,612,802	37,837	16,678	26,430	1,693,747	—
Female	1,638,253	33,471	16,708	26,990	1,715,422	—

Of the total population in 1970, 2,476,468 persons (72·6%) were urban (68·1% in 1960); 2,057,714 were 21 years of age or older; foreign-born, 156,020.

There are 22 Indian reservations, the largest being Yakima, which contains 1,367,405 acres. Indian reservation acreage includes (1973) 2,483,708 acres, of which 2,046,274 acres are owned by the various tribes, and 437,434 acres by individual Indians. Indians living in or near reservation in 1973, 20,708.

Leading cities are Seattle, with a population (1977 estimate) of 500,000; Spokane, 174,500; Tacoma, 156,000; Bellevue, 68,500; Everett, 51,700; Yakima, 51,100; Vancouver, 46,500; Bellingham, 43,160; Bremerton, 39,350; Richland, 31,050; Longview, 29,830; Renton, 27,150; Edmonds, 26,115; Walla Walla, 24,300. Urbanized areas (1970 census): Seattle–Everett, 1,238,107; Tacoma, 332,521; Spokane, 229,620.

CONSTITUTION AND GOVERNMENT. The constitution, adopted in 1889, has had 63 amendments. The Legislature consists of a Senate of 49 members elected for 4 years, half their number retiring every 2 years, and a House of Representatives of 98 members, elected for 2 years. The Governor and Lieut.-Governor are elected for 4 years. The state sends 2 senators and 7 representatives to Congress.

Qualified as voters are (with some exceptions) all citizens 18 years of age, having the usual residential qualifications.

In the 1976 presidential election Ford polled 777,732 votes, Carter 717,323 and other candidates 60,479.

The capital is Olympia (population, 1970, 23,111; estimate, 1977, 25,520). The state contains 39 counties.

Governor: Dixy Lee Ray (D.), 1977–81 ($55,000).
Lieut.-Governor: John A. Cherberg (D.), 1977–81 ($25,000).
Secretary of State: Bruce Chapman (R.), 1977–81 ($27,000).

BUDGET. For the year ending 30 June 1976 the state's total revenue was $3,976·09m. ($1,848·05m. from taxes and $730·49m. from federal aid); general expenditure was $2,852·15m. (education, $1,434·04m.; highways, $201·72m., and public welfare, $418·75m.).

Total net long-term debt on 30 June 1976 was $1,227,331,000.

Per capita personal income (1976) was $6,772.

ENERGY AND NATURAL RESOURCES

Minerals (1976, preliminary). Production of principal minerals: Sand and gravel, 17·1m. short tons; cement, 1·4m. short tons; stone, 7·7m. short tons; coal, 3·9m. short tons; clays, 307,000 short tons. Uranium ore is also mined but production figures are not disclosed. Total mineral output in 1976 was valued at $176·56m.

Agriculture. Agriculture is constantly growing in value because of more intensive and diversified farming and will be further aided as the 1m.-acre Columbia Basin Irrigation Project proceeds. Irrigated land in farms (1974) amounted to 1,286,412 acres.

In 1974 there were 32,514 farms with an acreage of 16,683,976, of which 4,931,851 acres were harvested crop land; average farm was of 513 acres with a value of $183,659; 4,493 farms had less than 10 acres and 3,344 farms had 1,000 acres and over. Realized net income per farm in 1974 was $21,798 compared with a national average of $9,611.

Agriculture is diversified, with 40 commodities, all except one, worth over $1m. in 1975. Value of farm production, 1976, was $1,933·4m. (from crops, $977·3m.; from speciality products, including flowers, bulbs, Christmas trees, $122m., and from livestock, $483·1m.). Wheat, the leading farm commodity, was valued at $417·7m. Cattle and calves were valued at $144·5m. Other major commodities are milk ($244·7m.), apples ($184·8m.), hay, potatoes and eggs. Washington was the leading state in production of apples, hops, dry peas and sweet cherries in 1975, and second in potatoes, Bartlett pears, green peas, asparagus and mint oil.

On 1 Jan. 1976 animals on farms included 179,000 milch cows, 1·37m. all cattle, 78,000 sheep and 71,000 swine. The wool clip in 1975 amounted to 817,000 lb.

Forestry. From the early 1900s to about 1940 the state ranked first in annual bd ft of lumber, but is now third to Oregon and California, producing 10% of the nation's lumber (3,566m. bd ft in 1976). The state is second to Georgia as a producer of woodpulp (3,127,000 short tons in 1975) and second to Oregon in production of plywood (12% of national total, 1,894m. sq. ft in 1976). Timber harvested in 1975 was 6,185,051 bd ft. The national forest lands of the state had (1977) an area of 8,785,934 acres.

Fisheries. Washington ranks second only to Alaska in the catch of salmon and halibut, and in the production of canned salmon. Value of sea products in 1975 was $62,685,142 catch value, $153,035,715 processed value. Total weight of fish caught, 149,611,106 lb., including salmon, 45,180,715 lb.; halibut, 1,458,323 lb.; oysters, 4,819,592 lb.; other shellfish, 22,134,274 lb.; bottom fish, 38,233,187 lb.; and other foodfish, 37,785,015 lb.

INDUSTRY. In 1972, 223,200 workers earned $2,281·9m.; value added by manufacture was $4,570·5m. Aircraft and aerospace manufacture, lumber and wood products, pulp and paper, plywood, food processing, machinery, metals, shipbuilding and chemicals are the major manufacturing industries.

With about 20% of potential water-power resources of US, the state is first in developed and potential hydro-electricity. Abundance of electric power has made Washington the leading producer of primary aluminium; production, 1975, was 1,075,000 short tons, 27% of the national total.

COMMUNICATIONS

Roads. The state (1975) maintained 6,906 miles of highway; the counties, 40,200 miles; municipalities, 9,773 miles. Motor vehicle registrations (1976), 3,181,648.

Railways. The railways had, in 1974, 4,676 miles.

Aviation. There were in 1975, 307 airports (112 publicly owned).

JUSTICE, RELIGION, EDUCATION AND WELFARE

Justice. The average daily adult population in state prisons for 1977–78 was 3,848. Since 1963 there have been no executions; total 1930–63 (by hanging) was 47, including 40 whites, 5 Negroes and 2 other races, all for murder, except 1 white for kidnapping.

Religion. Chief religious bodies (1971) are the Roman Catholic (366,087), United Methodist (116,723), Lutheran (98,815), Presbyterian (75,818), Latter-day Saints (66,109), Episcopalian (56,319).

Education. Education is given free to all children between the ages of 6 and 21 years, and is compulsory for children from 8 to 16 years of age. In Oct. 1976 the 1,018 elementary schools had 16,256 classroom teachers and 391,511 pupils, 185 junior high schools, 72 middle schools and 294 high schools had 15,096 classroom teachers and 389,534 pupils. In 1976–77 the average salary of teaching staff was $14,921. There were 2,289 teachers of handicapped children. The total expenditure on public elementary and secondary schools for the school year 1975–76 was $1,088·5m. In

Oct. 1976 an estimated 307 private and parochial elementary and secondary schools had 49,354 elementary and high school pupils.

The University of Washington, founded 1861, at Seattle, had, autumn 1976, 35,277 students, and Washington State University at Pullman, founded 1890, for science and agriculture, had 16,693 students. The 4 state colleges had 26,430 students. Twenty-seven community colleges had (1976) a total enrolment of 154,564 students (83,993 full-time equivalent).

Health. In 1976 the 2 state hospitals for mental illness had a daily average of 1,227 patients; schools for handicapped children, 2,896 residents.

In 1977 the state had 112 licensed general hospitals (13,082 beds) and 6 licensed psychiatric hospitals (318 beds).

Social Security. Old-age assistance is provided for persons 65 years of age or older without adequate resources (and not in need of continuing home care) who are residents of the state. In May 1977, 18,505 old people were drawing an average of $91.11 per month; aid to 91,108 children in 47,933 families averaged $249.34 per family monthly; to 504 blind persons, $157.68 per person monthly; to 30,005 totally disabled, $152.10 monthly. 7,546 persons, under foster care, received payments of $236.03 per person. Total unemployment in 1976 averaged 137,000 (8·6% of the labour force). In 1976 unemployment insurance system covered 79,048 employers with average employment of 1,052,788. Benefits to 176,856 beneficiaries ranged from $17 to $102 per week and averaged (1975–76) $73.69.

Books of Reference

Washington State Research Council. *Handbook: A Compendium of Statistical and Explanatory Information about State and Local Government in Washington.* 4th ed. Olympia, 1973

Avery, M. W., *Washington, a History of the Evergreen State.* Univ. of Wash. Press, 1965.—*Government of Washington State.* Univ. of Wash. Press, revised ed. 1973

Ogden, Jr, D. M., and Bone, H. A., *Washington Politics.* New York Univ. Press, 1960

Webster, D. H., and others, *Washington State Government: Administrative Organization and Functions.* Univ. of Wash. Press, 1962.—Supplement No. 1, by Barbara B. Howard, 1968

State Library: Washington State Library, Olympia. *State Librarian:* Roderick Swartz.

WEST VIRGINIA

HISTORY. In 1862, after the state of Virginia had seceded from the Union, the electors of the western portion ratified an ordinance providing for the formation of a new state, which was admitted into the Union by presidential proclamation on 20 June 1863, under the name of West Virginia. Its constitution was adopted by the voters almost unanimously on 26 March 1863.

AREA AND POPULATION. West Virginia is bounded north by Pennsylvania and Maryland, east and south by Virginia, southwest by the Sandy River (forming the boundary with Kentucky) and west by the Ohio River (forming the boundary with Ohio). Area, 24,282 sq. miles, of which 102 sq. miles are water. Census population, 1 April 1970, 1,744,237, a decrease of 6·3% since 1960. Estimate (1975) 1,803,000. Births, 1977, 30,118; deaths, 19,349; infant deaths, 438; marriages, 17,522; divorces, 9,552.

Population in 5 federal census years (with distribution by sex, 1970) was:

	White	*Negro*	*Indian*	*Asiatic*	*Total*	*Per sq. mile*
1910	1,156,817	64,173	36	93	1,221,119	50·8
1940	1,614,191	114,893	18	103	1,729,205	71·8
1950	1,890,282	114,867	160	243	2,005,552	83·3
1960	1,770,133	89,378	181	419	1,860,421	77·3
1970	673,480	67,342	751	1,463	1,744,237	71·8
Male	811,409	31,634	338	707	844,669	—
Female	862,071	35,705	413	766	899,568	—

Of the total population in 1970, 679,491 (39%) were urban (38·2% in 1960); those 21 years of age or older numbered 1,069,033. Foreign-born whites, 1960, were 23,483.

The 1970 census population of the principal cities was: Huntington, 74,315 (urbanized area, 167,583); Charleston, 71,505 (urbanized area, 157,662); Wheeling, 48,188; Parkersburg, 44,208; Morgantown, 29,431; Weirton, 27,131; Fairmont, 26,093; Clarksburg, 24,864.

CONSTITUTION AND GOVERNMENT. The present constitution was adopted in 1872; it has had 51 amendments.

The Legislature consists of the Senate of 34 members elected for a term of 4 years, one-half being elected biennially, and the House of Delegates of 100 members, elected biennially. The Governor is elected for 4 years and may succeed himself once. Voters are all citizens (with the usual exceptions) 18 years of age and meeting certain residential requirements. The state sends to Congress 2 senators and 4 representatives.

In the 1976 presidential election Carter polled 430,404 votes, Ford 311,012.

The state capital is Charleston. There are 55 counties.

Governor: John D. Rockefeller IV (D.), 1977–80 ($50,000).
Secretary of State: A. James Manchin (D.) ($30,000).

FINANCE. Total revenues for the year ending 30 June 1976 were $2,396,397,100 ($676·1m. from general revenue fund, $500m. from federal funds, $295·9m. from state road fund, $161m. from special revenue fund); general expenditures were $2,368,495,296 (education, $476·1m.; highways, $495·9m.; public welfare, $324·6m.; other governmental costs, $229·4m.).

Bonds outstanding were $929,907,500 on 30 June 1976.

Estimated *per capita* personal income (1976) was $5,460.

ENERGY AND NATURAL RESOURCES

Minerals. 55% of the state is underlain with mineable coal; 108,793,594 short tons of coal were produced in 1976; coke (oven and bee-hive), 79,497,628 short tons. Petroleum output, 2,921,000 bbls; natural gas production was 154,484m. cu. ft. Lime salt, sand and gravel, sandstone and limestone are also produced. The total value of mineral output in 1976 was $3,494,298m.

Agriculture. In 1976 the state had 26,500 farms with an area of 4·75m. acres; average size of farm was 179 acres and valued at $401 per acre. Livestock farming predominates.

Cash income, 1976, from crops was $37·2m.; from government payments, $2·6m., and from livestock and products, $103·4m. Total area of major crops harvested was 741,000 acres, chief crop being hay (595,000 acres); all corn, 104,000 acres. Apples (200m. lb.) and peaches (15m. lb.) are important fruit crops. Livestock on farms, 1976, included 549,000 cattle, of which 38,000 were milch cows; sheep, 120,000; hogs, 55,000; chickens, 1·13m. excluding broilers. Production, 1976, included 15·1m. broilers, 230m. eggs; 1·8m. turkeys.

Forestry. State forests, 1977, covered 79,308 acres; national forests, 1,647,146 gross acres; 75% of the state is woodland.

INDUSTRY. In 1976 average employment was 651,600 who earned an average of $207.65 a week.

West Virginia University has pioneered research in wood plastic combinations (WPC). This is a process in which wood is impregnated with a monomer (liquid plastic) and bombarded with gamma-rays to polymerize the plastic; thereby creating a 'super hard wood'.

COMMUNICATIONS

Roads. Total highways in 1976, 36,543 miles (state maintained, 32,231 miles; interstate, 368 miles; national parks and other roads, 3,855 miles; West Virginia

Turnpike, 87 miles). Registered motor vehicles, fiscal year ending 30 June 1976, numbered 1,114,175.

Railways. In 1976 the state had 3,510 miles of railway, all operated by diesel or electric trains.

Aviation. There were 55 licensed airports in 1976.

Post and Broadcasting. There are 61 AM radio stations, 31 FM radio stations. Television channels number 9 VHF and 3 UHF.

Newspapers. Daily newspapers number 28; weekly newspapers 82.

JUSTICE, RELIGION, EDUCATION AND WELFARE

Justice. All statutes requiring racial segregation in West Virginia have been eliminated. After a United States Supreme Court decision in June 1967 voided all state and local anti-miscegenation laws, West Virginia's Attorney-General issued a formal opinion that West Virginia's anti-miscegenation law is unconstitutional and invalid. Effective on 1 July 1967, the West Virginia Human Rights Act prohibits discrimination in employment and places of public accommodations based on race, religion, colour, national origin or ancestry.

There are 8 penal and correctional institutions which had, on 30 June 1976, 1,685 inmates. In 1965 the State Legislature abolished capital punishment.

Religion. Chief denominations in 1976 were United Methodist (185,000 members, estimated); Baptists (125,000 members, estimated); and Roman Catholics (95,000).

Education. Public school education is free for all from 5 to 21 years of age, and school attendance is compulsory for all between the ages of 7 and 16 (school term, 200 days—180–185 days of actual teaching). The public schools are non-sectarian. During school year 1975–76 elementary schools had 11,186 instructional personnel and 228,542 pupils enrolled; secondary schools, 10,108 and 169,885 respectively. Average minimum salary of instructional personnel (1976) was $11,058. Total 1975–76 expenditures for public schools, $528,170,961.

Leading institutions of higher education in 1976:

Founded		*Full-time students*
1837	Marshall University, Huntington	11,166
1837	West Liberty State College, West Liberty	2,686
1867	Fairmont State College, Fairmont	5,145
1868	West Virginia University, Morgantown	19,640
	School of Medicine	1,477
1872	Concord College, Athens	1,675
1872	Glenville State College, Glenville	1,606
1872	Shepherd College, Shepherdstown	2,605
1891	West Virginia State College	4,009
1895	West Virginia Institute of Technology, Montgomery	3,236
1895	Bluefield State College, Bluefield	1,739
1901	Potomac State College of West Virginia Univ., Keyser	1,013
1972	West Virginia College of Graduate Studies	2,450

In addition to the universities and state-supported schools, there are 3 community colleges (12,777 students in 1976), 13 denominational and private institutions of higher education and 20 business colleges.

Health. In 1975–76 the state had 74 hospitals (10,378 beds) and 29 intermediate-care facilities, 31 skilled-nursing homes and 9 mental hospitals (3,514 beds).

Social Security. The Department of Welfare, originating in the 1930s as the Department of Public Assistance, is both state and federally financed. In the year ending 30 June 1976 day care for 5,844 children per month was provided; aid was given to 20,498 families with dependent children (average award, $165.58 per month); crippled children's services conducted 19,103 examinations; 59,128 families per month received food stamps.

On 1 Jan. 1974 all blind, aged and disabled services were converted to the Federal Supplemental Security Income Programme.

Books of Reference

West Virginia Blue Book. Legislature, Charleston. Annual, since 1916

West Virginia Statistical Handbook, 1974. Bureau of Business Research, W. Va. Univ., Morgantown, 1974

Bibliography of West Virginia. 2 parts. Dept. of Archives and History, Charleston, 1939

West Virginia History. Dept. of Archives and History. Charleston. Quarterly, from 1939

Writers' Program. *West Virginia: A Guide to the Mountain State*. New York, 1948

Ambler, Charles H. and Summers, F. P., *West Virginia: the Mountain State*, Prentice-Hall, 1958

Cometti, Elizabeth, and Summers, F. P., *The Thirty-Fifth State*. Morgantown, 1966

Conley, P., and Doherty, W. T., *West Virginia History*. Charleston, 1974

Davis, C. J., and others, *West Virginia State and Local Government*. West Virginia Univ. Bureau for Government Research, 1963

Rice, Otis K., *The Allegheny Frontier*. Lexington, 1970; *West Virginia, the State and its People*. Parsons, 1972

Shetler, C., *Guide to the Study of West Virginia History*. Morgantown, 1960; *West Virginia Civil War Literature*. Morgantown, 1963

Williams, J. W., *West Virginia: A Bicentennial History*. New York, 1976

State Library: Division of Archives and History, Dept. of Culture and History, Charleston.

WISCONSIN

HISTORY. Wisconsin was settled in 1670 by French traders and missionaries. Originally a part of New France, it was surrendered to the British in 1763 and in 1783, when ceded to the US, became part of the North-west Territory. It was then contained successively in the Territories of Indiana, Illinois and Michigan. In 1836 it became part of the Territory of Wisconsin, which also included the present states of Iowa, Minnesota and parts of the Dakotas. It was admitted into the Union with its present boundaries on 29 May 1848.

AREA AND POPULATION. Wisconsin is bounded north by Lake Superior and Michigan, east by Lake Michigan, south by Illinois, west by Iowa and Minnesota, with the Mississippi River forming most of the boundary. Area, 56,154 sq. miles, including 1,439 sq. miles of inland water, but excluding any part of the Great Lakes. Revised census population, 1 April 1970, 4,417,933, an increase of 11·8% since 1960. Births in 1976 (provisional) were 64,945 (14 per 1,000 population); deaths, 40,191 (8); infant deaths, 818 (13·4 per 1,000 live births); marriages, 36,024 (7); divorces and annulments 14,579 (3).

Population in 5 census years (with distribution by sex, 1970) was:

	White	*Negro*	*Indian*	*Asiatic*	*Total*	*Per sq. mile*
1910	2,320,555	2,900	10,142	263	2,333,860	42·2
1930	2,916,255	10,739	11,548	464	2,939,006	53·7
1950	3,392,690	28,182	12,196	1,507	3,434,575	62·8
1960	3,858,903	74,546	14,297	4,031	3,951,777	72·2
1970	4,258,959	128,224	18,924	11,624	4,417,933	80·8
			All others			
Male	2,090,226	62,116	15,031		2,167,373	—
Female	2,168,733	66,108	15,517		2,250,358	—

Of the total population in 1970, 2,910,877 persons (65·9%) were urban (63·8% in 1960); 2,593,018 were 21 years old or older. Foreign-born whites (1960) numbered 170,609.

Population of the larger cities, 1970 census, was as follows:

Milwaukee	717,372	Appleton	57,143	Beloit	35,729
Madison	172,007	Oshkosh	53,221	Fond du Lac	35,515
Racine	95,162	La Crosse	51,153	Manitowoc	33,430
Green Bay	87,809	Sheboygan	48,484	Wausau	32,806
Kenosha	78,805	Janesville	46,426	Superior	32,237
West Allis	71,649	Eau Claire	44,619	Brookfield	32,140
Wauwatosa	58,676	Waukesha	40,274	Menominee Falls	31,697

Population of larger urbanized areas, 1970 census: Milwaukee, 1,403,688; Madison, 290,272; Duluth–Superior (Minn.–Wis.), 265,350; Racine, 170,838; Green Bay, 158,244.

CONSTITUTION AND GOVERNMENT. The constitution, which dates from 1848, has 99 amendments. The legislative power is vested in a Senate of 33 members (1975 term: 22 Democrats, 11 Republicans), elected for 4 years, one-half elected alternately, and an Assembly of 99 members (1977 term: 66 Democrats, 33 Republicans) all elected simultaneously for 2 years. The Governor and Lieut.-Governor are elected for 4 years. All 6 constitutional officers serve 4-year terms.

Wisconsin has universal suffrage for all citizens over 18 years of age; but, as there is no official list of voters, the size of the electorate is unknown; 1,227,685 voted for Governor in 1974.

Wisconsin is represented in Congress by 2 senators and 9 representatives.

In the 1976 presidential election Carter polled 1,037,056 votes, Ford 1,003,039.

The capital is Madison. The state has 72 counties.

Lieut.-Governor: Martin J. Schreiber (D.), 1975–79 ($28,668).
Secretary of State: Douglas J. La Follette (D.), 1975–79 ($13,500).

BUDGET. For the year ending 30 June 1977 (Wisconsin Bureau of Financial Services figures) total revenue for all funds was $5,694,897,754 ($2,591,056,105 from taxation and $1,074,750,091 from federal aid). General expenditure from all funds was $5,089,321,662 ($1,529,171,008 for education, $391,171,305 for highways).

Per capita personal income (Aug. 1977) was $6,117.

ENERGY AND NATURAL RESOURCES

Electricity. There were, Dec. 1975, 88 hydro-electric power plants (15 of them municipal, 58 private in Wisconsin; 15 private outside the state) operated by public utilities with a total installed capacity of 409,103 kw.; output, 1975, was 1,861,026m. kwh.

Fossil fuel and nuclear plants numbered 25 (4 municipal); total installed capacity, 6,707,911 kw.; total output (1975), 27,942,510m. kwh.

Minerals. Sand and gravel, stone and zinc are the chief mineral products. Mineral production (except for taconite pellets) in 1975 was valued at $132·3m. This value included $40·6m. for sand and gravel and $40·2m. for stone. Production of zinc ore (1974) was valued at $6·3m., and lead ore worth approximately $578,000 was recovered as a by-product. Iron-ore mining (1975) produced 791,000 long tons of taconite pellets from a mine in Jackson County. Exploration for base metal sulphides is taking place in northern Wisconsin.

Three copper deposits have been found; in Rusk County significant deposits have been located (estimated at 6m. tons of 4% grade); in Oneida County (estimated 2·3m. tons of 4·5% zinc, 1% copper) and in Forest County (70m. tons of 5% zinc, 1% copper, minor deposits of lead, silver and gold). The Forest County ore body is 5,000 ft long, about 200 ft wide and over 1,500 ft deep and almost vertical.

Agriculture. The total number of farms has declined in the last 39 years, but farms have become larger and more productive. There was 100,000 farms with a total acreage of 19·1m. acres and an average size of 191 acres in 1977, compared with 142,000 farms with a total acreage of 22·4 acres and an average of 158 acres in 1959.

Cash income from products sold by Wisconsin farms in 1975 of $2,665·7m. was the highest on record, and included $2,112,795 from livestock and livestock products and $538,860,000 from crops.

Wisconsin ranked first among the states in 1976 in the number of milch cows, milk production, output of American, both Brick and Munster, Italian and Blue Mold Cheese. Production of all cheese accounted for 37·2% of the nation's total. The state also ranked first in bulk sweetened whole milk and bulk skim condensed milk sweetened. In crops the state ranked first for sweet corn for processing, snap beans for processing, all hay, green peas for processing, beets for canning and cranberries. Production of the principal field crops in 1976 included: Corn for grain, 148·24m. bu.; corn for silage, 11·3m. tons; oats, 55m. bu.; all hay, 8·1m. tons. Other crops of importance were more than 15m. cwt of potatoes, 20·2m. lb. of tobacco, 825,000 bbls of cranberries, 2m. cwt of cabbage, 1·2m. cwt of carrots and the processing crops of 543,850 tons of sweet corn, 119,600 tons of green peas and 170,250 tons of snap beans.

Forestry. In July 1973 national forests comprised 1·5m. acres; state forests, 430,000 acres; the county forests, 2·25m. acres. Wisconsin has an estimated 14·9m. acres of forest land (about 43% of land area). The production and remanufacture of wood and products is one of the state's most important industries.

INDUSTRY. Wisconsin has much heavy industry, particularly in the Milwaukee area. In 1977 the state ranked twelfth in manufactured exports, non-electrical machinery was the major industrial group (22% of all employed persons), followed by food processing, electrical machinery, transport equipment, fabricated metals, paper and products, primary metals and printing. Manufacturing establishments in 1972 provided 25·9% of all employment, 36% of all earnings and exports of over $1,000m. annually. The total number of establishments is over 8,000; the biggest concentration is in the southeast.

TOURISM. The tourist-vacation industry ranks among the first three in economic importance. Approximately $4,223m. is spent annually by tourists, at least 47% of this amount by non-residents. The decline of lumbering and mining in the northern section of the state has increased dependency on the recreation industry. The Division of Tourism of the Department of Business Development spends $400,000 annually to promote tourism, and up to $196,618 on tourist information centres.

COMMUNICATIONS

Roads. The state had on 1 Jan 1977, 105,520 miles of highway. 69% of all roads in the state have a bituminous (or similar) surface. There are 11,958 miles of state trunk roads and 19,685 miles of county trunk roads.

In the year ending 30 June 1977 Wisconsin registered 2,159,456 private motor cars.

Railways. On 1 Jan. 1977 the state had 5,740 road-miles of railway.

Aviation. There were, in 1977, 101 publicly operated airports. Ten airports were served by 5 certificated air carriers and 12 by commuter air carriers.

Shipping. With the opening of the St Lawrence Seaway in 1959, 14 Wisconsin ports became accessible to ocean-going vessels. Green Bay, Kenosha, Manitowoc, Marinette, Milwaukee, Sheboygan, Sturgeon Bay and Superior (one of the world's largest iron-ore and grain ports) have developed foreign waterborne commerce.

JUSTICE, RELIGION, EDUCATION AND WELFARE

Justice. The state's penal, reformatory and correctional system on 1 Sept. 1976 held 3,694 men and 200 women in the 8 institutions for adult and juvenile offenders; the probation and parole system was supervising 16,542 men and 2,762 women. Wisconsin does not impose the death penalty.

Religion. Wisconsin church affiliation, as a percentage of the 1976 population, was estimated in Jan. 1977 at 33% Catholic, 34% Protestant, 33% unaffiliated and others.

Education. All children between the ages of 7 and 16 are required to attend school full-time to the end of the school term in which they become 16 years of age. Children living in a district with a vocational school must attend until 18. In 1976–77 the public elementary schools had 588,348 pupils and 28,976 teachers; secondary schools had 256,337 pupils and 25,401 teachers. Elementary school teachers' salaries, 1976–77, averaged $12,894; secondary school teachers, $13,653. Total cost per pupil was $1,582 in 1976–77.

In 1975–76 vocational, technical and adult schools had a total enrolment of

355,681, and there were 6,427 faculty members. There is a school for the visually handicapped and a school for the deaf.

The University of Wisconsin, established in 1848, was joined by law in 1971 with the Wisconsin State Universities System to become the University of Wisconsin System with 13 degree granting campuses, 14 two-year campuses in the Center System, and the University Extension. The 27 campuses had, in 1976–77, 6,941 full-time professors and instructors, 690 part-time teachers, and 2,197 (full-time equivalent) teaching and research graduate assistants. There were, during the first half-year, 143,282 students enrolled (9,974 at Eau Claire, 3,612 at Green Bay, 7,755 at La Crosse, 37,924 at Madison, 24,686 at Milwaukee, 10,082 at Oshkosh, 4,984 at Parkside, 4,447 at Platteville, 4,873 at River Falls, 8,542 at Stevens Point, 6,002 at Stout, 2,450 at Superior, 9,387 at Whitewater and 8,564 in the Center System freshman-sophomore centres).

The total expenditure, 1975–76, for all public education (except capital outlay and debt service) was $2,362m.

The state maintains an educational broadcasting and television service.

Health. In 1976 the state had 147 general and allied special hospitals (23,013 bed), 28 mental hospitals (3,430 beds), 2 tuberculosis sanatoria (52 beds), 6 treatment centres for alcoholism (242 beds), 1 rehabilitation centre (64 beds). Patients in state and county mental hospitals and institutions for the mentally retarded on 1 July 1976 numbered 3,766.

Social Security. On 1 Jan. 1974 the US Social Security administration assumed responsibility for financial aid (Supplemental Security Income) to persons 65 years old and over, blind persons and totally disabled persons, who satisfy requirements as to need. Recipients receive a federal payment plus a federally administered state supplementary payment, except for those who reside in a medical institution. In Sept. 1977, there were 65,151 SSI recipients in the state. In June 1977 payment levels increased to $254 for a single individual, $297 for an eligible individual with an ineligible spouse, and $386 for an eligible couple. A special payment level of $350 may be paid with special approval for an SSI recipient who is developmentally disabled, living in a non-medical living arrangement not his own home. All SSI recipients receive state medical assistance coverage.

Under the Aid to Families with Dependent Children programme, 65,680 families constituting 196,644 persons received an average of $396.28 per family in June 1977; 5,295 children in 3,661 foster homes received an average of $181.09. Medicaid in financial year 1977 cost $485·5m.

Books of Reference

Wisconsin Statistical Abstract. Wis. Dept. of Administration, State Bureau of Planning and Budget, Madison, 1974

Dictionary of Wisconsin Biography. Wis. Historical Society, Madison, 1960

Wisconsin Blue Book. Wis. Legislative Reference Bureau, Madison. Biennial

The Natural Resources of Wisconsin. Wis. Natural Resources Committee of State Agencies, Madison, 1964

Austin, H. R., *The Wisconsin Story.* 5th ed. Milwaukee, 1964

Smith, Alice E., *The History of Wisconsin,* Vol. 1. State Historical Society of Wisconsin, Madison, 1973

State Information Agency: Legislative Reference Bureau, State Capitol, Madison, Wis. 53702. *Chief:* Dr. H. Rupert Theobald.

WYOMING

HISTORY. Wyoming, first settled in 1834, was admitted into the Union on 10 July 1890. The name originated with the Delaware Indians.

AREA AND POPULATION. Wyoming is bounded north by Montana, east by South Dakota and Nebraska, south by Colorado, south-west by Utah and west by Idaho. Area 97,914 sq. miles, of which 711 sq. miles are water. The Yellowstone National Park occupies about 2,221,773 acres; the Grand Teton National Park has 310,350 acres. The federal government in 1972 owned 29,986,128 acres (48·1% of the total area of the state). The Federal Bureau of Indian Affairs in 1971 administered 1,886,329 acres.

Census population, 1 April 1970, 332,416, an increase of 0·7% since 1960. Estimate, July 1976, 390,000. Births in 1976 were 6,890 (17·7 per 1,000 population); deaths, 3,109 (8); infant deaths (1974), 79 (12·2 per 1,000 live births); marriages, 5,885 (15·1); divorces, 2,850 (7·3).

Population in 5 census years (with distribution by sex, 1970) was:

	White	*Negro*	*Indian*	*Asiatic*	*Total*	*Per sq. mile*
1910	140,318	2,235	1,486	1,926	145,965	1·5
1930	221,241	1,250	1,845	1,229	225,565	2·3
1950	284,009	2,557	3,237	726	290,529	3·0
1960	322,922	2,183	4,020	805	330,066	3·4
			All others			
1970	323,024	2,568	6,824		332,416	3·4
Male	161,961	1,369	3,445		166,775	—
Female	161,063	1,199	3,379		165,641	—

Of the total population in 1970, 201,111 persons (60·5%) were urban (56·8% in 1960). Persons over 21 years of age numbered 195,077; foreign-born, 9,896.

The largest towns are Cheyenne (capital), with census population in 1970 of 40,914 (1975 estimate, 46,677); Caspar, 39,361 (41,192); Laramie, 23,143 (23,421); Rock Springs, 11,657 (17,773) and Sheridan, 10,856 (11,617).

CONSTITUTION AND GOVERNMENT. The constitution, drafted in 1890, has since had 43 amendments. The Legislature consists of a Senate of 30 members elected for 4 years, and a House of Representatives of 62 members elected for 2 years. The Governor is elected for 4 years.

The state sends to Congress 2 senators and 1 representative, elected by the voters of the entire state.

The suffrage extends to all citizens, male and female, who have the usual residential qualifications.

In the 1976 presidential election Ford polled 92,717 votes and Carter 62,239.

The capital is Cheyenne. The state contains 23 counties.

Governor: Ed Herschler (D.), 1974–78 ($45,000).
Secretary of State: Mrs Thyra Thomson (R.), 1974–78 ($28,000).

BUDGET. In the fiscal year ending 1 July 1975 (State Auditor figures) general revenues were $403,640,973; general expenditures were $137,006,252. Revenue Sharing Funds from federal government, $3·3m.

Total net long-term debt, 30 June 1974, was $76·2m.

Per capita personal income (calendar year 1975) was $6,079.

ENERGY AND NATURAL RESOURCES

Minerals. Wyoming is largely an oil-producing state. In 1977 the output of petroleum was valued at $894m.; natural gas, $88·9m. Other mining (1975): Coal, $124·7m.; trona, $44·3.; uranium, $20·8m.; iron ore, $15m.; other minerals mined include feldspar, gypsum, limestone, phosphate, sand, gravel and marble, taconite, bentonite and hematite.

Value of mineral products in 1975 was $1,198·9m.

Agriculture. Wyoming is semi-arid, and agriculture is carried on by irrigation and by dry farming. In 1977 there were 7,900 farms and ranches. Total land area 35·4m. acres.

Cash receipts, 1975, from crops was $96·2m.; from livestock and products, $250·3m. Principal commodities are wheat ($25·3m.), cattle and calves ($209·6m.), lambs and sheep ($18m.) sugar-beet ($28·9m.) and wool ($5·3m.). Animals on farms on 1 Jan. 1977 included 11,000 milch cows, 1·55m. all cattle, 1·2m. sheep and lambs and 26,000 swine (1976).

INDUSTRY AND TRADE

Industry. In 1975 there were 633 manufacturing establishments. There were 460 mining establishments. A large portion of the manufacturing in the state is based on natural resources, mainly oil and farm products. Leading industries are food, wood products (except furniture) and machinery (except electrical). Casper is the most industrialized city, with 92 manufacturers and 257 mining companies. There were 1,704 new business incorporations in 1976. The Wyoming Industrial Development Corporation assists in the development of small industries by providing credit. Available capital, $3m.

Labour. Government is the largest employer in the state with 34,600 workers in 1976. The total civilian labour force for 1976 was 179,000; non-agricultural, 156,900. The average unemployment rate was 4·1% and average weekly earnings were $223.11 for private non-farm production workers. The average weekly hours in manufacturing for 1976 were 40·2.

Tourism. There are over 5m. tourists annually, mainly sportsmen. The state has the largest elk and pronghorn antelope herds in the world, 11 fish hatcheries and numerous wild game. Receipts from hunters and fishermen in 1975, $8,333,216.

COMMUNICATIONS

Roads. The roads in 1976 comprised 3,768 miles of primary roads, 1,959 miles of secondary roads and 929 miles of multi-lane roads. There were (1975) 356,884 registered motor vehicles and 25 bus companies, 12 regular route and 13 charter.

Railways. The railways, 1974, had a length of 2,405 mainline miles (Union Pacific, 1,198).

Aviation. There were 36 airports and 3 towns on jet routes in 1974.

JUSTICE, RELIGION, EDUCATION AND WELFARE

Justice. The state penitentiary in July 1976 held 234 inmates. There have been 14 executions in Wyoming, 8 by hanging and 6 by lethal gas. There were 10 other state institutions, 2 of which were correctional; daily population of state institutions was 1,438.

Religion. Chief religious bodies are the Roman Catholic (with 45,917 members in 1974), Mormon (28,954 in 1971) and Protestant churches (83,327 in 1974). There were 5,000 members of the Eastern Orthodox Church in 1972.

Education. In 1976–77 public elementary and secondary schools had 90,587 pupils. Enrolment in the parochial elementary and secondary schools (1975–76) was 2,418. Approximately 5,283 public school teachers earned an average (1975–76) of $12,024. The average total expenditure per pupil for 1976–77 was $1,558.

The University of Wyoming, founded at Laramie in 1887, had in 1976–77, 8,726 students. There are 2-year colleges at Casper, Riverton, Torrington, Cheyenne, Powell, Rock Springs and Sheridan with 15,158 students.

Social Welfare. In Jan. 1974 the federal government assumed many of the previous state programmes including old age assistance, aid to the blind and disabled. The state continues to administer over $5m. annually in emergency aid and aid to families with dependent children. In 1975–76, $4,475,996 was distributed in food stamps. Total state expenditure on public assistance and social services programmes, financial year 1976, $20,543,723.

Health. In 1976 the state had 28 hospitals (2,035 beds). There are 33 nursing homes.

Books of Reference

News of Big Wyoming. Cheyenne, 1975
Official Directory. Secretary of State. Cheyenne. Biennial

1977 Wyoming Data Handbook. Dept. of Administration and Fiscal Control. Division of Research and Statistics, Cheyenne, 1977
Davis, T. S., *A Study of Wyoming People*. Laramie, 1965
Larsen, T. A., *History of Wyoming*. Denver, 1965
Trachsel, H. H., and Wase, R. M., *The Government and Administration of Wyoming*. New York, 1953

OUTLYING TERRITORIES

Non-Self-Governing Territories: Summaries of Information Transmitted to the Secretary-General of the United Nations. Annual
Coulter, J. W., *The Pacific Dependencies of the United States*. New York, 1957
Perkins, W. T., *The United States and its Dependencies*. Leiden, 1962
Pratt, J. W., *America's Colonial Experiment: How the United States Gained, Governed and in Part Gave Away a Colonial Empire*. New York, 1950
Wiens, H. J., *Pacific Island Bastions of the US*. New York and London, 1962

GUAM

HISTORY. Magellan is said to have discovered the island in 1521; it was ceded by Spain to the US by the Treaty of Paris (10 Dec. 1898). The island was captured by the Japanese on 10 Dec. 1941, and retaken by American forces from 21 July 1944. Guam is of great strategic importance; substantial numbers of naval and air force personnel occupy about one-third of the usable land.

AREA AND POPULATION. Guam is the largest and most southern island of the Marianas Archipelago, in 13° 26′ N. lat., 144° 43′ E. long. The length is 30 miles, the breadth from 4 to 10 miles, and there are about 210 sq. miles (450 sq. km). Agaña, the seat of government is about 8 miles from the anchorage in Apra Harbour. The census on 1 April 1970 showed a population of 84,996, an increase of 17,952 or 26·8% since 1960; those of Guamanian ancestry numbered about 52,000; foreign-born, 13,484; density was 321 per sq. mile. On 1 Jan. 1970 transient residents connected with the military were estimated at 19,307. Estimated population, 1975, 105,400. The Malay strain is predominant. The native language is Chamorro; English is the official language and is taught in all schools.

CONSTITUTION AND GOVERNMENT. Guam's constitutional status is that of an 'unincorporated territory' of the US. Entry of US citizens is unrestricted; foreign nationals are subject to normal regulations. In 1949 the President transferred the administration of the island from the Navy Department (who held it from 1899) to the Interior Department. The transfer was completed by 1 Aug. 1950, on the passage of the Organic Act, which conferred full citizenship on the Guamanians, who had previously been 'nationals' of the US.

The Governor and his staff constitute the executive arm of the government. He is advised by a Cabinet, and a Sub-Cabinet composed of elected representatives of the 19 municipalities. The Legislature is unicameral; its powers are similar to those of an American state legislature. At the general election of Nov. 1976, the Democratic Party won 8 seats and the Republicans 13. All adults 18 years of age or over are enfranchised. Guam returns one non-voting delegate to the House of Representatives.

Governor: Ricardo Jerome Bordallo (D.), 1974–78.

Lieut.-Governor: Rudolph G. Sablan, 1974–78.

ECONOMY

Budget. At 30 June 1976 total assets were $43m.; federal grants-in-aid, $23·4m., taxes, $15m.: total liabilities were $59·4m.

Banking. Recent changes in banking law make it possible for foreign banks to operate in Guam; the first to obtain a licence was the First Commercial Bank of Taiwan.

ENERGY AND NATURAL RESOURCES

Water. Supplies are from springs, reservoirs and groundwater; 65% comes from water-bearing limestone in the north. The Navy and Air Force conserve water in reservoirs. The Water Resources Research Centre is at Guam University.

Agriculture. The major products of the island are maize, sweet potatoes, taro, cassava, bananas, and citrus and truck crops, including breadfruit, coconuts and sugar-cane. In 1970–71, 569 full-time and part-time farmers each held 500 acres under cultivation. Livestock (1975) included 2,502 cattle, 11,726 hogs, and 142,537 poultry. Commercial production (1976) amounted to 1·19m. lb. of fruit and vegetables ($329,835), 2m. doz. eggs ($1·97m.), 513,000 lb. of pork ($428,098), 120,600 lb. of chicken meat ($57,406), 78,795 lb. of beef ($61,775). There is an agricultural experimental station at Inarajan.

Fisheries. Fresh fish caught in 1976 was valued at $187,318. About 16,000 people are active in inshore fishing, with a catch of 208,131 lb. Off-shore fishing produced 26,224 lb., including 16,200 lb. of mackerel. Shrimp farming is being developed.

INDUSTRY AND TRADE

Industry. Guam Economic Development Authority controls three industrial estates: Cabras Island (32 acres); Calvo estate at Tamuning (26 acres); Harmon estate (16 acres). Industries include textile manufacture, cement and petroleum distribution, warehousing, printing, plastics and ship-repair.

Labour. In May 1976 the labour force was 27,300, of which 3,600 were unemployed.

Trade. Guam is the only American territory which is complete 'free trade'; excise duties are levied only upon imports of tobacco, liquid fuel and liquor. In the year ending 30 June 1976 imports were valued at $266·3m. and accounted for 91% of trade.

Tourism. Tourism is developing; there were 1,900 visitors in 1964 and 205,436 in 1976. 150,119 of them from Japan.

COMMUNICATIONS

Roads. There are 183 miles of paved and 63 miles of improved roads.

In 1976 there were 54,156 motor vehicles registered.

Aviation. Four commercial airlines (PANAM, Air Nauru, Island Air and Continental Air Micronesia) serve Guam.

Post and Broadcasting. Overseas telephone and radio dispatch facilities are available. On 30 June 1975 there were 22,055 telephones.

There are 3 commercial radio stations, a commercial television station, a public broadcasting station and a cable television station with 6 channels.

Newspapers. There is 1 daily newspaper and 4 weekly publications (all of which are of military or religious interest only).

JUSTICE, RELIGION, EDUCATION AND WELFARE

Justice. The Organic Act established a District Court with jurisdiction in matters arising under both federal and territorial law; the judge is appointed by the President subject to Senate approval. There is also a Supreme Court and a Superior Court; all judges are locally appointed except the Federal District judge. Misdemeanours are under the jurisdiction of the police court. The Spanish law was superseded in 1933 by 5 civil codes based upon California law.

Religion. About 96% of the Guamanians are Roman Catholics; others are Baptists, Episcopalians, Bahais, Lutherans, Mormons, Presbyterians, Jehovah's Witnesses and members of the Church of Christ and Seventh Day Adventists.

Education. Elementary education is compulsory. There are Chamorro Studies courses and bi-lingual teaching programmes to integrate the Chamorro language and culture into elementary and secondary school courses. There were, 1976–77, 15,888 elementary school pupils, 6,142 junior high and 5,242 senior high school pupils. Department of Education staff, 2,416, including 1,107 teachers. The Catholic school system also operates 3 senior high schools, 3 junior high and 5 elementary schools. The Seventh Day Adventist Guam Mission Academy operates a school from grades 1 through 12, serving over 100 students. St John's Episcopal Preparatory School provides education for 200 students between kindergarten and the 9th grade. The University of Guam (an accredited institution) had 10,285 students, 1975–76. There is a vocational technical school for high school pupils and adults.

Health. There is a hospital, 8 nutrition centres, a school health programme and an extensive immunization programme. Emphasis is on disease prevention, health education and nutrition.

Books of Reference

Report (Annual) of the Governor of Guam to the US Department of Interior
Beardsley, C., *Guam past and present.* Rutland, Vt, 1964
Carano, P., and Sanchez, P. C., *Complete history of Guam.* Rutland, Vt, 1964
Thompson, Laura, *Guam and its People.* 3rd ed. New York, 1947

COMMONWEALTH OF PUERTO RICO

HISTORY. Puerto Rico, by the treaty of 10 Dec. 1898 (ratified 11 April 1899), was ceded by Spain to the US. The name was changed from Porto Rico to Puerto Rico by an Act of Congress approved 17 May 1932. Its territorial constitution was determined by the 'Organic Act' of Congress (2 March 1917) known as the 'Jones Act', which ruled until 25 July 1952, when the present constitution of the Commonwealth of Puerto Rico was proclaimed.

AREA AND POPULATION. Puerto Rico is the most easterly of the Greater Antilles and lies between the Dominican Republic and the U.S. Virgin Islands. The island has a land area of 3,435 sq. miles (8,891 sq. km) and a population, according to the census of 1970, of 2,712,033, an increase of 362,489 or 15% over 1960; estimated population (1976), 3,213,000, density 939 per sq. mile. Males (1976) numbered 1,567,700; females, 1,645,300. Of the population in 1970 about 529,000 were bilingual, Spanish being the mother tongue and (with English) one of the two official languages. Rural population (1970), 1,180,391 (43·6%).

Vital statistics (1976): Births, 75,798 (23·6 per 1,000 population); deaths, 19,893 (6·2%); deaths under 1 year, 1,472 (19·4 per 1,000 live births).

Chief towns (1976) are: San Juan, 514,500; Bayamón, 204,100; Ponce, 187,000; Carolina, 161,400; Caguas, 106,600; Mayaguez, 99,000.

The Puerto Rican island of Vieques, 10 miles to the east, has an area of 51·7 sq. miles and 7,372 inhabitants. The island of Culebra, with 1,000 inhabitants, between Puerto Rico and St Thomas, has a good harbour.

CONSTITUTION AND GOVERNMENT. Puerto Rico has representative government, the franchise being restricted to citizens 18 years of age or over, residence (1 year) and such additional qualifications as may be prescribed by the Legislature of Puerto Rico, but no property qualification may be imposed. Women were enfranchised in 1932 (with a literacy test) and fully in 1936. Puerto Ricans do not vote in the US presidential elections, though individuals living on the mainland are free to do so subject to the local electoral laws. The executive power resides in a Governor, elected directly by the people every 4 years. Fourteen heads of departments form the Governor's advisory council, also designated as his Council of Secretaries. The legislative functions are vested in a Senate, composed of 27 members (2 from each of the 8 senatorial districts and 11 senators at large), and the House of Representatives, composed of 51 members (1 from each of the 40 representative districts and 11 elected at large). Puerto Rico sends to Congress a Resident Commissioner to the US, elected by the people for a term of 4 years, but he has no vote in Congress. Puerto Rican men are subject to conscription in US services.

On 27 Nov. 1953 President Eisenhower sent a message to the General Assembly of the UN stating 'if at any time the Legislative Assembly of Puerto Rico adopts a resolution in favour of more complete or even absolute independence' he 'will immediately thereafter recommend to Congress that such independence be granted'.

For an account of the constitutional developments prior to 1952, *see* THE STATESMAN'S YEAR-BOOK, 1952, p. 742. The new constitution was drafted by a Puerto Rican Constituent Assembly and approved by the electorate at a referendum on 3 March 1952. It was then submitted to Congress, which struck out Section 20 of Article 11 covering the 'right to work' and the 'right to an adequate standard of living'; the remainder was passed and proclaimed by the Governor on 25 July 1952.

At the election on 7 Nov. 1976 the New Progressive Party (advocates of statehood), headed by Carlos Romero Barceló, polled 682,607 votes (46·6% of the total); the Popular Democratic Party, headed by Rafael Hernández Colon, polled 634,941 votes (43·3% of the total); the Independence Party (full independence by constitutional means), 58,556 (4% of the total); Partido Socialista Puertorriqueño (full independence), 9,761 votes (0·7% of the total).

Governor: Carlos Romero Barceló (New Progressive Party), 1977–80 ($35,000).

ECONOMY

Budget. Receipts and disbursements (US$) in central government fund for the year ending 30 June 1976 were:

Balance, 1 July 1976	41,844,608	Disbursements	2,481,121,911
Receipts	2,582,798,002	Balance, 1 July 1977	59,831,483
Total	2,540,953,394	Total	2,540,953,394

Assessed value of property, 30 June 1976, was $6,154m., and bonded indebtedness, $972m.

The US administers and finances the postal service and maintains air and naval bases. US payments in Puerto Rico, including direct expenditures (mainly military), grants-in-aid and other payments to individuals and to business totalled: 1971–72, $715·7m.; 1972–73, $854·9m.; 1973–74, $908·1m.; 1974–75, $1,384·8m.; 1975–76, $1,989·5m.

Banking. Nineteen banks on 30 June 1977 had total deposits of $5,531m. and debits of $8,237m. Bank loans were $4,831m.

NATURAL RESOURCES

Minerals. Production (1976): Cement, 1·7m. short tons, value, $68·8m.; stone, 14m. short tons, value $47·4m. Total value of mineral production in 1976 was $119·8m.

Agriculture. In 1974 there were 47 'proportional profit' farms of 22,051 cords (about 22,704 acres) (mostly sugar-cane). The land had been bought from the big corporations by the Land Authority.

Production of raw sugar, 96 degrees basis, for the 1975 crop year, was 298,960 short tons.

COMMERCE. In 1976–77 imports amounted to $6,108·1m., of which $3,669·5m. came from US; exports were valued at $4,479·5m., of which $3,863·3m. went to US.

In 1976–77, the US took: Sugar, 239,534,750 lb. ($32,706,383); tobacco and products, 9,791,879 lb.; rum, 15,561,262 proof gallons ($59,654,646).

Puerto Rico is not permitted to levy taxes on imports.

Trade between Puerto Rico and UK (British Department of Trade returns, in £1,000 sterling):

	1973	*1974*	*1975*	*1976*	*1977*
Imports to UK	11,634	12,789	22,113	14,704	36,369
Exports and re-exports from UK	7,004	8,548	9,464	14,686	17,994

COMMUNICATIONS

Roads. The Department of Public Works had under maintenance in June 1976, 6,640 miles of paved road. Motor vehicles registered 30 June 1976, 814,373.

Shipping. In fiscal year 1975–76, 7,731 American and foreign vessels of 45,738,700 gross tons entered and cleared Puerto Rico.

Post and Broadcasting. In 1975 there were 96 broadcasting stations and 16 television companies. There were (1976) 474,333 telephones.

Cinemas (1975). Cinemas numbered 110, with annual attendance of 6·84m.

Newspapers (1977). There are 4 newspapers; 2 have a circulation of 100,000.

JUSTICE AND EDUCATION

Justice. The Commonwealth judiciary system is headed by a Supreme Court of 7 members, appointed by the Governor, and consists of a Superior Tribunal with 11 sections and 89 superior judges, a District Tribunal with 38 sections and 98 district judges, and 37 municipal judges all appointed by the Governor. The police force (1977) consisted of 9,032 men and women.

Education. Education was made compulsory in 1899, but in 1975–76, 3% of the children still had no access to schooling. The percentage of illiteracy in 1976 was 8·7% of those 10 years of age or older. Total enrolment in public schools, 1977, was 711,155. Accredited private schools had 91,510 pupils. All instruction below senior high school standard is given in Spanish only.

The University of Puerto Rico, in Río Piedras, 7 miles from San Juan, had 50,225 students in 1976–77 and 9,175 in 5 Regional Colleges. Higher education is also available in the Inter-American University of Puerto Rico (26,379 students in 1976–77), the Catholic University of Puerto Rico (10,804), the Sacred Heart College (3,934) and the Puerto Rico Junior College (10,560). These and other private colleges and universities had 51,911 students in 1976–77.

Books of Reference

Statistical Information: The Bureau of Economics and Research of the Puerto Rico Planning Board publishes: (*a*) annual *Economic Report to the Governor*; (*b*) *Statistical Yearbook* (since 1940–41); (*c*) *External Trade Statistics* (annual report); (*d*) *Economics Indicators* monthly); (*e*) *Historical Series* (since 1958); (*f*) Reports on national income and balance of payments. In addition there are annual reports by various Departments.

Annual Reports. Governor of Puerto Rico. Washington

Bird, A., *Bibliografia Puertorriqueña, 1930–45.* Social Science Research Centre, Univ. of Puerto Rico. 2 vols. 1946–47

Crampsey, R. A., *Puerto Rico.* Newton Abbot, 1973

Hill, R. (ed.), *Family and Population Control: A Puerto Rican Experiment.* Univ. of N. Carolina Press, 1959

Jones, C. F., and Pico, R. (ed.), *Symposium on the Geography of Puerto Rico.* Univ. of P.R. Press, 1955

Tumin, M. M., and Feldman, A. S., *Social Class and Social Change in Puerto Rico.* Princeton Univ. Press, 1961

Commonwealth Library: Univ. of Puerto Rico Library, Rio Piedras. *Librarian:* José Lázaro.

AMERICAN SAMOA

HISTORY. The Samoan Islands were first visited by Europeans in the 18th century; the first recorded visit was in 1722. On 14 July 1889 a treaty between the USA,

Germany and Great Britain proclaimed the Samoan islands neutral territory, under a 4-power government consisting of the 3 treaty powers and the local native government. By the Tripartite Treaty of 7 Nov. 1899, ratified 19 Feb. 1900, Great Britain and Germany renounced in favour of the US all rights over the islands of the Samoan group east of 171° long. west of Greenwich, the islands to the west of that meridian being assigned to Germany (now the Independent State of Western Samoa, *see* p. 1588). The islands of Tutuila and Aunu'u were ceded to the US by their High Chiefs on 17 April 1900, and the islands of the Manu'a group on 16 July 1904. Congress accepted the islands under a Joint Resolution approved 20 Feb. 1929. Swain's Island, 210 miles north-north-west of the Samoan Islands, was annexed in 1925 and is administered as an integral part of American Samoa.

AREA AND POPULATION. The islands are approximately 650 miles north-east of Fiji. The total area of American Samoa is 76·1 sq. miles (197 sq. km); population, 1970, 27,159, nearly all Polynesians or part-Polynesians. 1977 population estimate, 30,600. The Island of Tutuila, 80 miles from Apia, has an area of 53 sq. miles, with a population (1970) of 24,973 (28,669 in 1977) (including the island of Aunu'u). Ta'u has an area of 17 sq. miles, and the other islands (Ofu and Olosega) of the Manu'a group have an area of about 5 sq. miles with a population of 2,112 in 1970 (1,700 in 1976). Swain's Island, circular in shape, has an area of 1·9 sq. miles and a population, 1970, of 74 (31 in 1977). Rose Island (uninhabited) is 0·4 sq. mile in area. In 1975 there were 1,154 births and 160 deaths.

CONSTITUTION AND GOVERNMENT. American Samoa is constitutionally an unorganized unincorporated territory of the US administered under the Department of the Interior. Its indigenous inhabitants are US nationals and are classified locally as citizens of American Samoa with certain privileges under local laws not granted to non-indigenous persons. Polynesian customs (not inconsistent with US laws) are respected.

Fagatogo is the seat of the Government.

The islands are organized in 14 counties grouped in 3 districts; these counties and districts correspond to the traditional political units. On 25 Feb. 1948 a bicameral legislature was established, at the request of the Samoans, to have advisory legislative functions. With the adoption of the Revised Constitution of American Samoa, effective 1 July 1967, the legislature was vested with limited law-making authority. The lower house, or House of Representatives, is composed of 20 members elected by universal adult suffrage and 1 non-voting member for Swain's Island. The upper house, or Senate, is composed of 18 members elected, in the traditional Samoan manner, in meetings of the chiefs.

Governor: Frank Barnet (election pending 1978).

Lieut.-Governor: (Vacant).

ECONOMY

Planning. The first formal Economic Development and Planning Office completed its first year in 1971. Much has been done to promote economic expansion within the Territory and a large amount of outside investment interest has been stimulated.

The Office initiated the first Territorial Comprehensive Plan. This plan when completed will, with periodic updating, provide a guideline to territorial development for the next 20 years. The planning programme was made possible under a Housing and Urban Development '701' grant programme.

The focus will be on physical development and the problems of a rapidly increasing population with severely limited land resources.

Budget. The chief sources of revenue are annual federal grants from the US, and local revenues from individual and corporate income taxes, import duties, sale of utilities, rents and leases and liquor sales. During the fiscal year 1976 the government had a revenue of $45·4m. including local appropriation of $3·9m. and federal appropriations of $41m.

Banking. The American Samoa branch of the Bank of Hawaii offers all commercial banking services. The Development Bank of American Samoa, government owned, is concerned primarily through loans and guarantees with the economic advancement of the Territory. The American Savings and Loan Bank has a branch in American Samoa.

ENERGY AND NATURAL RESOURCES

Electricity. Net power generated (1976) was 62·6m. kwh., of which 31·6m. kwh. was supplied to large power users and 16m. kwh. to householders. All the Manu'a islands have electricity.

Agriculture. There are virtually no public lands in American Samoa. Nearly all the land is owned by Samoans and, with a few exceptions, cannot be sold except to persons having at least one-half Samoan blood. Of the 48,640 acres of land area, 11,000 acres are suitable for tropical crops, 1,000 acres for most temperate vegetables, 8,000 acres only to such crops as coconut and cacao with good conservation practice, 5,000 acres to controlled forestation and about 22,500 to indigenous and introduced forest with strict conservation measures; 1,000 acres are roads, building sites and villages. Principal crops are taro, bread-fruit, yams, bananas, coconuts, arrowroot and papayas. Principal livestock are poultry, swine and cattle.

INDUSTRY AND TRADE

Industry. Fish canning is important, employing the second largest number of people (after government). Attempts are being made to provide a variety of light industries. Tuna fishing and local inshore fishing are both expanding.

Commerce. In 1976 American Samoa exported goods valued at $50,180,042 and imported goods valued at $37,953,154. Chief exports are canned tuna, watches, pet foods and handicrafts. Chief imports are cement, lumber, rice, flour, fish, meat, fuel oil, sugar.

COMMUNICATIONS

Roads. There are about 45·2 miles of paved roads, 30·8 miles of unpaved and 5·4 miles of secondary roads. There are 12·7 miles of secondary unpaved roads maintained mainly on Tutuila. Motor vehicles registered, 1976, 3,424.

Aviation. PANAM operates between Western America, Honolulu, New Zealand, American Samoa and Tahiti. South Pacific Island Airways and Polynesian Airlines operate daily services between American Samoa and Western Samoa. The islands are also served by Air New Zealand and UTA. Total landings at Pago Pago, 1975, 6,616.

Shipping. The harbour at Pago Pago, which nearly bisects the island of Tutuila, is the only good harbour for large vessels in Samoa. By sea, there is a twice-monthly service between Western America, New Zealand and Australia and regular service between US, South Pacific ports and Japan. In 1976, 640 vessels entered and 645 cleared Pago Pago harbour.

Post and Broadcasting. A commercial radiogram service is available to all parts of the world through 3 principal trunks, Hawaii, Fiji and Western Samoa. Commercial phone services are operated to all parts of the world on a 24-hour service. Number of telephones (June 1976), 3,500.

JUSTICE, EDUCATION AND WELFARE

Justice. Judicial power is vested in a High Court. Fifty-nine district courts, traffic courts and small claims courts are heard without record and appeals therefrom are tried, *de novo*, in the trial division of the High Court. The trial division also has original jurisdiction of all criminal and civil cases. The probate division has jurisdiction of estates, guardianships, trusts and other matters. The land and title division decides cases relating to disputes involving communal land and Matai title court rules on questions and controversy over family titles. The appellate division hears appeals from trial, land and title and probate divisions as well as having original jurisdiction in selected matters. The appellate court is the court of last resort. Two American judges sit with 5 Samoan judges permanently. In addition there are 8 temporary judges or assessors who sit occasionally on cases involving Samoan customs.

Education. Education is compulsory between the ages of 6 and 18. The Government (1977) maintains 27 consolidated elementary schools, 4 senior high schools with technical departments, 1 community college and 160 village schools for small children. Total elementary and secondary enrolment (1976), 7,994; in schools for small children, 1,916; total elementary and secondary classroom teachers, 355. Six private schools had 1,855 students. The community college had 599 full-time students and 30 full-time instructors. Learning is by a variety of media including television.

Health. The Department of Health provides the only medical and dental care in American Samoa. It operates a general hospital (181 beds including 31 bassinets), 3 dispensaries on Tutuila, 4 dispensaries in the Manu'a group and 1 on Swain's Island. A $3·5m. tropical medical centre was completed and placed in service in 1968.

VIRGIN ISLANDS OF THE UNITED STATES

HISTORY. The Virgin Islands of the United States, formerly known as the Danish West Indies, were named and claimed for Spain by Columbus in 1493. They were later settled by Dutch and English planters, invaded by France in the mid-seventeenth century and abandoned by the French *c.* 1700, by which time Danish influence had been established.

They were purchased by the United States from Denmark for $25m. in a treaty ratified by both nations and proclaimed 31 March 1917. Their value was wholly strategic, inasmuch as they commanded the Anegada Passage from the Atlantic ocean to the Caribbean sea and the approach to the Panama Canal. Although the inhabitants were made US citizens in 1927, the islands are, constitutionally, an 'unincorporated territory'.

AREA AND POPULATION. The Virgin Islands group, lying about 40 miles due east of Puerto Rico, comprises the islands of St Thomas (28 sq. miles), St Croix (84 sq. miles), St John (20 sq. miles) and about 50 small islets or cays, mostly uninhabited. The total area of the 3 principal islands is 132 sq. miles, of which the US Government owns 9,599 acres as National Park.

The population, according to the census of 1 April 1970, was 62,800, an increase of 30,701 or 96% since 1960; density was 475 per sq. mile. The 1970 population of St Thomas was 29,565; St Croix, 31,892; St John, 1,743. Population had slowly declined since 1835, when it stood at 43,000, but began to recover in the 1940s. Estimated population, 1976, was 100,000: St Croix, 49,000; St Thomas, 48,000; St John, 3,000. About 20–25% are native-born, 35–40% from other Caribbean islands, 10% from mainland USA and 5% from Europe. St Croix has about 40% of Puerto Rican origin or extraction, Spanish speaking. Births, 1970, were 2,921 (46·8 per 1,000 population); deaths, 466 (7·5); infant deaths, 72 (24·6 per 1,000 live births); marriages, 1,089 (17·4 per 1,000 population); divorces (1966), 293 (5·8).

The capital and only city, Charlotte Amalie, on St Thomas, had a population (1970) of 12,372; there are two towns on St Croix. Christiansted with 2,966 and Frederiksted with 1,548.

CONSTITUTION AND GOVERNMENT The Organic Act of 22 July 1954 gives the US Department of the Interior full jurisdiction; some limited legislative powers are given to a single-chambered legislature, composed of 15 senators elected for 2 years representing the two legislative districts of St Croix and St Thomas St John.

The Governor was formerly appointed by the President, with the consent of the Senate, for an indefinite term. In 1970 the islanders elected a Governor for the first time; the term is 4 years.

For administration, there are 13 executive departments, 12 of which are under commissioners and the other, the Department of Law, under an Attorney-General. The US Department of the Interior appoints a Federal Comptroller of government revenue and expenditure.

The franchise is vested in residents who are citizens of the United States, 18 years of age or over. In 1974 there were 22,000 voters, of whom 73% participated in the local elections that year. They do not participate in the US presidential election but they have a non-voting representative in Congress.

The capital is Charlotte Amalie, on St Thomas Island.

Governor: Cyril E. King ($35,890).

Lieut.-Governor: Juan Luis ($28,804).

ECONOMY

Budget. Under the 1954 Organic Act finances are provided partly from local revenues—customs, federal income tax, real and personal property tax, trade tax, excise tax, pilotage fees, etc.—and partly from Federal Matching Funds, being the excise taxes collected by the federal government on such Virgin Islands products transported to the mainland as are liable. Revenue for fiscal year ending 30 June 1976, $114,126,889, and expenditure totalled $116,925,842.

Currency and Banking. United States currency became legal tender on 1 July 1934. Banks are the Chase Manhattan Bank; the Bank of Nova Scotia; the First Federal Savings and Loan Association of Puerto Rico; Barclays Bank International; Bank of America; Citibank; Deposit Insurance National Bank; First Pennsylvania Bank, and the Royal Bank of Canada.

ENERGY AND NATURAL RESOURCES

Electricity. The Virgin Islands Water and Power Authority provides electric power from generating plants on St Croix and St Thomas; St John is served by power cable and emergency generator.

Water. There is a shortage of pure water, of which rain-water is the most reliable source. Every building must have a cistern to provide rain-water for drinking, even in areas served by mains (10 gallons capacity per sq. ft of roof for a single-storey house). There are 6 desalinization plants producing 8·7m. gallons of fresh water per day.

Agriculture. With the phasing out of the sugar-cane industry in St Croix, and the accelerated construction activities carried on in all three islands, the number of farms decreased, but there has recently been a revival of interest in growing food crops. Land for fruit, vegetables and animal feed is available on St Croix, and there are tax incentives for development. Sugar has been terminated as a commercial crop and over 4,000 acres of prime land will be utilized for food crops.

Fisheries. There is a fishermen's co-operative with a market at Christiansted. There is a shellfish-farming project at Rust-op-Twist.

INDUSTRY AND TRADE

Industry. The main occupations on St Thomas are tourism and government service; on St Croix manufacturing is more important. Manufactures include watches, textiles, pharmaceuticals, rum and fragrances. The Martin Marietta Alumina plant processes bauxite from Africa for refining in mainland USA. The Amerada Hess oil refinery has a capacity of 700,000 bbls per day.

The Virgin Islands offer liberal tax exemptions to persons, firms or companies prepared to invest $15,000 in new industries or in the promotion of tourism.

Commerce. Exports, 1976, totalled $2,010m. and imports $2,678m.

Trade between the US Virgin Islands and UK (British Department of Trade returns, in £1,000 sterling):

	1973	*1974*	*1975*	*1976*	*1977*
Imports to UK	26	521	1,162	15	11
Exports and re-exports from UK	1,866	4,387	2,629	3,010	3,155

Tourism. St Thomas, once an important commercial shipping centre, is now an important port of call for pleasure cruises. There were about 900,000 visitors in 1976. Annual income from tourists is about $100m.

Tourism is the most important business in St John, where the Virgin Islands National Park covers more than half the island.

COMMUNICATIONS

Roads. The Virgin Islands have approximately 455 miles of roads, and 33,587 motor vehicles were registered in 1974.

Aviation. There is a daily air-mail and passenger service between St Thomas and St Croix. Hamilton Airport on St Croix can take 707-class aircraft and is being extended to take 747s. Harry S. Truman Airport on St Thomas takes 727-class aircraft. There are air connexions to mainland USA, other Caribbean islands, Latin America and Europe.

Shipping. St Thomas is a free port. There is an hourly boat service between St Thomas and St John.

Post and Broadcasting. All three Virgin Islands have a dial telephone system. In Jan. 1976 there were 35,796 telephones. Direct dialling to Puerto Rico and the mainland is now possible. Worldwide radio telegraph service is also available.

The islands are served by 5 radio stations, 2 television stations and 6 newspapers, 2 of them dailies.

RELIGION AND EDUCATION

Religion. There are churches of the Protestant, Roman Catholic and Jewish faiths in St Thomas and St Croix.

Education. Education is compulsory between the ages of $5\frac{1}{2}$ and 16 years, inclusive. In 1977 there were 32 public schools (ranging from kindergarten to high schools); enrolment was 25,036; other schools had 6,694 pupils; the school budget was $29·2m. In 1974 the College of the Virgin Islands had 539 full-time and over 1,379 part-time students.

Books of Reference

Evans, L. H., *The Virgin Islands: From Naval Base to New Deal.* Ann Arbor, Mich., 1945
Jarvis, J. A., *The Virgin Islands and Their People.* Philadelphia, 1944
McGuire, J. W., *Geographic Dictionary of the Virgin Islands of the United States.* US Coast and Geodetic Survey. Special Publication No. 103. Washington, 1925
Reid, C. F., *Bibliography of the Virgin Islands of the United States.* New York, 1941

TRUST TERRITORY OF THE PACIFIC ISLANDS

HISTORY. Under the Treaty of Versailles (1919) Japan was appointed mandatory to the former German possessions north of the Equator. In 1946 the US agreed to administer the former Japanese-mandated islands of the Caroline, Marshall and Mariana groups (except Guam) as a Trusteeship for the United Nations; the trusteeship agreement was approved by the Security Council 27 April 1947 and came into effect on 18 July 1947. In 1951 all the islands passed under the care of the US Department of the Interior, but in 1953 responsibility for civil administration of the Northern Marianas (except Rota) was transferred back to the Department of the

Navy. On 7 May 1962 Saipan and the islands of the Northern Marianas were transferred back to the Secretary of the Interior. In June 1975 the Northern Marianas voted to become a 'commonwealth' of USA. The new status was approved by USA on 21 July 1975, pending the agreement of the UN to the dissolution of the trusteeship agreement. The area is now separated as the Government of the Northern Marianas.

AREA AND POPULATION. The Trust Territory extends from 1° to 22° N. lat. and from 130° to 172° E. long. The area is generally known as Micronesia, or 'land of the small islands'; 2,141 atolls and islands (of which 96 are inhabited) cover less than 700 sq. miles (1,813 sq. km) in some 3m. sq. miles (8m. sq. km) of ocean.

The estimated population of the 6 administrative districts as of Oct. 1977 was: Truk, 35,220; Ponape, 21,187; Marshall Islands, 27,096; Palau, 13,519; Yap, 8,482; Kosrae, 4,471. The former Mariana Islands District has been separated administratively from the Trust Territory; its estimated population is 15,000. The administrative centre is Saipan, Mariana Islands. Nine different languages are spoken, each with variations; English is used in the schools and is the official language.

CONSTITUTION AND GOVERNMENT. Elected legislatures function in all districts. Membership in some of these includes hereditary leaders as well as elected representatives, although the trend is towards all-elective bodies.

The bicameral Congress of Micronesia, a Senate and House of Representatives, was established in 1965. Regular sessions of 50 days begin annually in January.

High Commissioner: Adrian P. Winkel.

ECONOMY. Living standards are being improved through the introduction of higher standards of subsistence and exportable agricultural and marine products.

TRADE (1976). Major imports were food, $14·6m.; beverages, $5·2m.; and building materials, $3·09m. Total imports were an estimated $38·3m., of which $24·38m. (estimate) were from US and $8·09m. from Japan. Major exports were copra, fish, handicraft, meat, vegetables and fruits. Total exports were estimated at $6·5m.

COMMUNICATIONS

Aviation. The island groups are served by Continental Air Micronesia. There are connexions to international routes at Guam and Hawaii.

JUSTICE, EDUCATION AND WELFARE

Justice. Law and order is maintained by the armed, uniformed and trained Micronesia Police in each district; the local district community court judges, sheriffs and deputy sheriffs are all Micronesians. Local customs are respected in law and practice.

Education. In 1975–76 there were 248 public and private elementary schools (30,285 pupils), 31 public and private high schools (7,951 pupils), 1,091 students were attending institutions of higher education abroad.

Health. The public health system, which includes 6 district and 3 large field hospitals and 154 dispensaries, is carried on by a staff consisting chiefly of trained Micronesian medical and dental officers and assistants under senior US medical officers. There is a school of nursing in the Mariana Islands.

Books of Reference

Report on the Administration of the Trust Territory of the Pacific Islands by the United States to the United Nations. Annual
Basic Information. High Commissioner's Office, Saipan, Mariana Islands

UPPER VOLTA

République de Haute-Volta

Capital: Ouagadougou
Population: 6·1m. (1975)
GNP per capita: US$110 (1976)

HISTORY. A separate colony of Upper Volta was in 1919 carved out of the colony of Upper Senegal and Niger, which had been established in 1904. It was suppressed in 1932 and its territory divided between Ivory Coast, Sudan and Niger. On 4 Sept. 1947 the Territory of Upper Volta was re-established, comprising the area of the old colony of Upper Volta as at 5 Sept. 1932. The Republic of Upper Volta became independent on 5 Aug. 1960 and was admitted to the UN on 20 Sept. 1960.

AREA AND POPULATION. Upper Volta is bounded north and west by Mali, east by Niger, south by Dahomey, Togo, Ghana and the Ivory Coast. The Republic covers an area of 274,200 sq. km; population (census, 1975) 6,147,363. Ouagadougou, the capital (168,607 inhabitants, of whom 1,000 Europeans) and Bobo-Dioulasso (112,572 inhabitants, of whom 1,500 Europeans), are *communes de plein exercice.* The principal autochthonous tribes are the Mossi (48%), Peul (10%), Lobi-Dagari (7%), Mande (7%), Bobo (7%), Senoufo (6%), Gourounsi (5%), Bisa (5%), Gourantché (5%).

CONSTITUTION AND GOVERNMENT. The 1970 Constitution was suspended in Feb. 1974 and the National Assembly dissolved. In 1977 a referendum produced a vote for a new constitution and return to civilian rule which was achieved in May 1978.

Administratively there are 10 departments.

President: Gen. Sangoulé Lamizana.

National flag: Three horizontal stripes of black, white, red.

DEFENCE

Army. The Army consists of 5 infantry battalions, 1 reconnaisance squadron and support units; total strength (1978), 5,505.

Air Force. Creation of a small air arm to support the land forces began, with French assistance, in 1964. Equipment now comprises 1 HS.748 twin-turbo prop freighter, 2 C-47s, 2 twin-turboprop Frégates, an Aero Commander 500, 3 Broussards and 2 Cessna Super Skymasters for transport and liaison duties.

INTERNATIONAL RELATIONS

Membership. Upper Volta is a member of UN, OAU and is an ACP state.

ECONOMY

Planning. The Second Development Plan 1972–76 aimed at a 4% average annual real growth in GDP but this was not realized. The Third Development Plan 1977–81 was at a preliminary stage in 1978.

Budget. Government revenue in 1975 was 19·6m. francs CFA, of which taxes accounted for about 87%. Expenditure was 20·63m. francs CFA.

Banking. In 1968 the savings banks had 18,733 depositors with 777,606,000 francs CFA to their credit.

ENERGY AND NATURAL RESOURCES

Electricity. Production of electricity (1973) was 42m. kwh.

Minerals. There are deposits of manganese but exploitation is limited by existing transport facilities. Magnetite, bauxite, zinc, lead, nickel and phosphates have been found in the same area.

Agriculture. Production (1974, in tonnes): Millet and sorghum, 742,100; maize, 129,521; rice, 30,300; groundnuts, 75,100; cotton, 29,268. Rice and groundnuts are of increasing importance.

Livestock (1976): 1·9m. cattle, 3·6m. sheep and goats, 100,000 horses, 180,000 donkeys.

INDUSTRY AND TRADE

Industry. In 1970 gross manufacturing output (including energy) was 8·9m. francs CFA, of which foodstuffs (4m. francs CFA), textiles (2·6m. francs CFA) and metal products (1·8m. francs CFA). In 1972 there were 91 industrial units.

Commerce. In 1974 imports totalled 34,664m. francs CFA and exports 8,702m. francs CFA. The principal exports (francs CFA) were livestock (3m.), groundnuts (1·7m.) and cotton (1·5m.).

Trade with the UK (British Department of Trade returns, in £1,000 sterling):

	1973	*1974*	*1975*	*1976*	*1977*
Imports to UK	19	336	718	5,855	2,970
Exports and re-exports from UK	167	417	299	536	3,687

COMMUNICATIONS

Roads. The road system comprises 16,662 km, of which 2,614 km are all-weather roads.

Railway. Ouagadougou is the terminus of the Abidjan–Niger railway. An extension to Tambao is proposed.

Aviation. Ouagadougou and Bobo-Dioulasso are regularly served by UTA and Air Afrique and in 1973 dealt with 43,341 passengers and 2,328 tonnes of freight.

Post. There were, in 1970, 66 post offices and 1,504 telephones.

EDUCATION. There were, in 1974, 160,962 pupils in 1,429 schools.

HEALTH (1971). There were 5 hospitals, 308 dispensaries and 78 maternity units with a total 2,799 beds. There were 74 doctors, 5 dentists and 1,291 nurses. Government expenditure on health was 781m. francs CFA.

DIPLOMATIC REPRESENTATIVES

OF UPPER VOLTA IN GREAT BRITAIN

Ambassador: (Vacant).

OF GREAT BRITAIN IN UPPER VOLTA

Ambassador: J. B. Wright (resides in Abidjan).

OF UPPER VOLTA IN THE USA (5500 16th St, NW, Washington, D.C., 20011)

Ambassador: Telesphore Yaguibou.

OF THE USA IN UPPER VOLTA (P.O. Box 35, Ouagadougou)

Ambassador: Pierre R. Graham.

OF UPPER VOLTA TO THE UNITED NATIONS

Ambassador: Aissé Mensah.

URUGUAY

República Oriental del Uruguay

Capital: Montevideo
Population: 2·76m. (1975)
GNP per capita: US$1,390 (1976)

HISTORY. The Republic of Uruguay, formerly a part of the Spanish Vice-royalty of Río de la Plata and subsequently a province of Brazil, declared its independence 25 Aug. 1825 which was recognized by the treaty between Argentina and Brazil signed at Rio de Janeiro 27 Aug. 1828. The first constitution was adopted 18 July 1830.

AREA AND POPULATION. Uruguay is bounded on the north-east by Brazil, on the south-east by the Atlantic, on the south by the Rio de la Plata and on the west by Argentina. The area is 186,926 sq. km (72,172 sq. miles). The following table shows the area and the population of the 19 departments (capitals in brackets) as estimated in May 1975:

Departments	*Area, sq. km*	*Population*	*Pop. per sq. km*
Artigas (Artigas)	11,378	57,528	4·6
Canelones (Canelones)	4,752	313,858	54·3
Cerro-Largo (Melo)	14,929	73,204	4·8
Colonia (Colonia)	5,682	110,820	18·5
Durazno (Durazno)	14,315	54,990	3·7
Flores (Trinidad)	4,519	24,684	5·2
Florida (Florida)	12,107	66,092	5·3
Lavalleja (Minas)	12,485	65,240	5·3
Maldonado (Maldonado)	4,111	75,607	14·9
Montevideo (Montevideo City)	664	1,229,748	2,072·6
Paysandú (Paysandú)	13,252	98,735	6·6
Río Negro (Fray Bentos)	8,471	49,816	5·5
Rivera (Rivera)	9,829	79,330	7·8
Rocha (Rocha)	11,089	59,952	5·0
Salto (Salto)	12,603	100,407	7·3
San José (San José)	6,963	88,281	11·4
Soriano (Mercedes)	9,223	80,114	8·4
Tacuarembó (Tacuarembó)	21,015	84,829	3·7
Treinta y Tres (Treinta y Tres)	9,539	45,680	4·5
Total	186,926	2,763,964	14·7

Estimated population in 1975 was 2,763,964. In 1975 Montevideo (the capital) had an estimated population of 1,229,748. Other cities (1975): Salto, 80,000; Paysandú, 80,000; Mercedes, 53,000.

CONSTITUTION AND GOVERNMENT. Since 1900 Uruguay has been unique in her constitutional innovations, all designed to protect her from the emergence of a dictatorship. The favourite device of the group known as the 'Batllistas' (a *Colorado* faction) which, until defeated at the 1958 elections, held the majority for over 90 years, has been the collegiate system of government, in which the two largest political parties were represented.

One such pattern lasted from 1917 to 1933, when it was abolished by a dictator who re-established the system of an individual President. Until 1951 Presidents were elected every 4 years and they selected their own Cabinet Ministers (*see* list of Presidents in THE STATESMAN'S YEAR-BOOK, 1956, p. 1493). In 1951, on the initiative of the 'Batllistas', the Constitution was amended: the individual presidency was abolished and the executive power vested in a National Council of Government of 9 members (6 from the majority and 3 from the minority parties).

As a result of a referendum held in conjunction with the elections on 27 Nov. 1966, which gave the Colorado party a majority, Uruguay returned to the presidential system. The President appoints a council of 11 Ministers; the Vice-President presides over the Senate and the General Assembly when this takes place.

President: Dr Aparicio Méndez (sworn in for a 5-year term on 1 Sept. 1976).

The Cabinet in June 1978 was as follows:

Interior: Gen. Hugo Linares Brum. *Foreign Affairs:* Alejandro Rovira. *Justice:* Dr Fernando Bayardo Bengoa. *Economy and Finance:* Dr Valentín Arismendi. *Transport and Public Works:* Eduardo Sampson. *Public Health:* Dr Antonio Cañellas. *Industry and Energy:* Luis H. Meyer. *National Defence:* Dr Walter Ravenna. *Agriculture and Fisheries:* Luis H. Meyer. *Education:* Daniel Darracq. *Labour and Social Security:* Dr José Enrique Etcheverry Stirling. *Secretary to Presidency:* Luis Vargas Garmendia.

Parliament was dissolved by Presidential decree on 27 June 1973 but a return to democratic government has been promised by 1981.

The electorate in 1971 numbered 1·7m.; women constituted 50%.

The Colorado party favours 'statism' and social-welfare legislation. Most banking and all forms of insurance are government monopolies, as are also the railways and all the public utilities. The Government controls cement, fuel, petroleum and alcohol, including the manufacture of *caña*, a cheap rum-like drink which is the national beverage.

National flag: Nine horizontal stripes of white and blue, a white canton with the 'Sun of May' in gold.

National anthem: Orientales, la patria ó la tumba (words by Francisco Acuña de Figueroa; music by Francisco José Deballi).

DEFENCE

Army. The Army is composed of the active army and its reserves. The active army is formed of volunteers, who contract for 1 year or 2 years' service. In 1977 there were 3 armoured regiments, 6 regiments of cavalry, 4 artillery groups, 13 infantry battalions, 5 engineer battalions. Peace-time strength 20,000 men.

The reserve is formed by elements who, for some reason or other, retire from the active army. It is reckoned that about 120,000 men could be mobilized in case of war.

Navy. The Navy consists of 3 frigates (*ex*-US old destroyer escorts), 2 escorts (*ex*-US fleet minesweepers), 1 patrol vessel (*ex*-coastal minesweeper), 6 patrol craft, 2 survey ships, 1 salvage vessel, 2 minor amphibious craft, 2 oilers and 2 tenders. Personnel in 1978: 3,500 officers and ratings.

There is a small US-equipped naval air service of 18 aircraft and helicopters with 3 bases on the river Plate estuary.

Air Force. Organized with US aid, the Air Force has about 3,000 personnel and 100 aircraft, including 1 fighter-bomber squadron with 12 F-86F Sabres and 6 AT-33 armed jet trainers, 8 A-37B light strike aircraft, 2 transport squadrons with 4 turboprop FH-227/F.27 Friendships, 4 Brazilian-built EMB-110 Bandeirantes, 10 C-47s and 2 Queen Airs, a search and rescue squadron with light helicopters, and a number of Cessna U-17A/182, Super Cub and T-6 aircraft for liaison and reconnaissance duties. Basic training types are the T-41 and T-6.

INTERNATIONAL RELATIONS

Membership. Uruguay is a member of UN, OAS and LAFTA.

ECONOMY

Budget. The receipts and expenditure of the national accounts as approved by the National Council of Government (UR$1m.):

	1971	*1972*	*1973*	*1974*	*1975*	*1976*
Revenue	99,429	167,500	370,200	587,900	892,000	495,200
Expenditure	116,736	196,500	406,500	789,100	1,096,000	561,400

Now covering a 5-year period the budget is presented during the year following election of each new government; differences in actual annual income and expenditure and amendments to the budget (including new taxes) must be approved by Parliament each year-end; these usually come forward in July each year.

Expenditures in 1975 (in 1m. nuevo pesos) included 19,463 for education and welfare, 219,237 for defence, 82,757 for health, 152,632 for interior, 43,608 for finance and public works, 7,991 for agriculture and 22,497 for transport and tourism. Expenditure on public works is separately financed from specific revenues (*e.g.*, fuel tax). A law inaugurating income tax came into operation on 1 July 1961, but was repealed on 1 Jan. 1974.

Public debt outstanding on 30 June 1976 was US$1,034·8m. Total reserves of the Banco Central on 30 June 1976 were US$579,200.

Currency. There is no gold in circulation, but the monetary standard is gold, the theoretical gold coin being the *peso oro*, gold content of which was fixed, Dec. 1964, at 0·05924 gramme. It is equal to 100 *pesos*. The unit of currency is the *Nuevo Peso* (1,000 old pesos) of 100 *centésimos*. The actual circulating medium consists of paper notes issued by the Central Bank in denominations of 10,000, 5,000, 1,000, 500 and 100 old *pesos*. (Some notes have been restamped N$5 and N$10.) New notes in *Nuevo Peso* denominations of 50 and 100 are also in circulation, as is a *Nuevo Peso* 5 coin. There are bronze and aluminium coins of 50, 20 and 10 old *pesos*.

In Sept. 1977 there were N$5.04 to the US$; N$8.77 = £1.

Banking. The Bank of the Republic (founded 1896), whose president and directors are appointed by the Government, has a paid-up capital of UR$1,852m. The Banco Central was inaugurated on 16 May 1967. Note circulation on 31 Dec. 1973 was UR$200,600m.

A state-owned National Insurance Bank (*Banco de Seguros del Estado*) has a monopoly of new insurance business of all kinds. The Bank re-insures much of its business in London.

Of the 36 banks in Uruguay the Bank of London and South America (British) has a main office and 10 branch agencies.

Weights and Measures. The metric system was adopted in 1862.

ENERGY AND NATURAL RESOURCES

Electricity. The supply of electricity for light, power and traction has been a State monopoly since 1897. In Jan. 1949 the first hydro-electric plant at the site of the dam of Rincón del Bonete was completed with an installed capacity of 128 megawatts. Another plant at Rincón de Baygorria on the Río Negro came into operation in 1960, with a capacity of 108 megawatts. Power output in 1973 was 2,430m. kwh.

Oil. An extension of the ANCAP refining plant, opened at Montevideo on 6 Dec. 1961, gives a capacity of 7,500 cu. metres daily of high-octane petrol and high-grade gas for domestic and industrial use.

Agriculture. Uruguay is primarily a pastoral country. Of the total land area of 46m. acres some 41m. are devoted to farming, of which 90% to livestock and 10% to crops. Some large *estancias* have been divided up into family farms; rural landlordism is much less than elsewhere. Uruguay is said to be the only Latin American country in which agricultural workers have the protection of a minimum-wage law. Animals and animal products constitute 71% of the exports. The 1966 census reported on 79,101 farms of all kinds, totalling 16·5m. hectares.

There were (1977) 11,362,000 cattle, 15m. sheep, 420,972 horses, 418,709 pigs and 10,461 goats.

Wool production in 1975 exceeded 55,000 tonnes. Exports in 1975 totalled US$383·8m. Imports, US$556·5m.

Agricultural products are raised chiefly in the departments of Paysandú, Río Negro, Colonia, San José, Soriano and Florida. The average farm is about 250 acres. The principal crops and their estimated yield (in tonnes) in 2 crop years were as follows:

	1973–74	1974–75		1973–74	1974–75
Wheat	296,800	526,500	Barley	3,080	28,000
Linseed	26,272	39,300	Maize	225,300	157,000
Oats	55,300	46,600	Rice	157,900	188,500

Uruguay is self-sufficient in rice, with usually a small surplus for export. Three sugar refineries handle cane and (mainly) beet, their total production being approximately 70,000 tonnes, and approaching self-sufficiency.

Wine is produced chiefly in the departments of Montevideo, Canelones and Colonia, about enough for domestic consumption (918,000 hectolitres in 1974). The country has some 6m. fruit trees, principally peaches, oranges, tangerines and pears.

Forestry. In 1974 roundwood removals were 1,077,000 cu. metres of which 1,001,000 cu. metres was softwood.

Fisheries. The 1974 catch was 16,000 tonnes live weight.

In 1978 a Swiss bank granted a loan of US$28m. to the Government to finance development of the fishing industry.

INDUSTRY AND TRADE

Industry. In 1968 there were 72,646 registered enterprises with 341,000 employees. These cover basic activities such as meat packing, lumbering, oil refining, cement manufacture and also many branches of light industry, including one rolling mill for steel and one for aluminium, light engineering and electrical, chemical and textile production. There are 136 textile mills, but with the exception of half a dozen large plants, these are on the whole small.

Total capital invested in industry is UR$340·2m.: there are some 147,500 cotton, woollen and rayon spindles, 1,300 looms for woollen fabric and 1,000 looms for cotton rayon goods.

A number of public works programmes are under consideration, including the Carrasco and internal airport modernization, port of Montevideo modernization and bridges and ferry boats to link with Argentina across the river Uruguay; in addition to contracts issued for Highways 5 and 26 with IBRD loans.

Trade Unions. Trade unions number about 150,000 members. About 1,036,000 (40%) of the population are classed as gainfully occupied.

Commerce. The Latin American Free Trade Association came into being as a result of a conference in Montevideo in 1961. The foreign trade (officially stated in US$, with the figure for imports based on the clearance permits granted and that for exports on export licences utilized) was as follows (in US$1,000):

	1971	1972	1973	1974	1975	1976	1977
Imports	222·1	186·6	284·8	486·7	516·9	587·2	721·0
Exports	205·6	196·8	321·5	382·2	381·2	546·5	607·5

Of the imports in 1975 (in US$1m.) EEC furnished 109·8; Middle East, 98·1; Brazil, 66·9; USA and Canada, 65·8; Argentina, 46·7 and Federal Republic of Germany, 41·4; of the exports in 1975 Brazil took 65·7; Federal Republic of Germany, 45·2; UK, 18·1; Italy 13·1; France, 9·8; Netherlands, 8·7.

Principal imports and exports (in US$1,000):

Imports	1974	1975	*Exports*	1974	1975
Raw materials	207,213	189,132	Meat and meat products	144,727	88,622
Kits and tractors	18,199	36,684	Wool	66,887	73,626
Fuel and lubricants	160,624	125,605	Textiles	34,822	8,957
Machinery and accessories	23,053	60,387			

Total trade between Uruguay and UK (British Department of Trade returns, in £1,000 sterling):

	1973	1974	1975	1976	1977
Imports to UK	10,150	9,211	7,226	13,200	16,956
Exports and re-exports from UK	4,562	6,694	9,489	10,525	19,242

Tourism. There were 590,000 tourists in 1974 spending an estimated US$45m.

COMMUNICATIONS

Roads. The main highways, linking Montevideo with the interior, have a total length of 7,820 km, of which about 5,000 km are paved. Other roads, unpaved, are about 33,800 km. Considerable improvements, financed both internally and by international loans, have been carried out in the last few years.

Registered motor vehicles, 31 Dec. 1970, are estimated at 202,000 passenger cars and 84,196 trucks and buses.

Railways. The 4 principal railway systems, embracing 2,398 km, were all built by British capital amounting to £14,513,000. The Uruguayan Government in 1948 bought these railways for £7·15m., assuming control in that year. The East Coast Railway (125·5 km) and 3 minor lines were already controlled by the State under a separate administration. In Oct. 1952 the railways were brought under a single administration and a major programme of track upgrading and rolling stock rehabilitation was in progress in 1977. The total railway system open for traffic was (1976) 2,975 km of 1,435 mm gauge. In 1974 it carried 5·8m. passengers, 1m. tonnes of freight.

Aviation. Carrasco, 22·5 km from Montevideo, is the most important airport. US, Argentine, Brazilian, Chilean, Dutch, French, Fed. German, Italian, Scandinavian and Paraguayan airlines fly to and from Uruguay. The state-operated civil airline PLUNA runs services in the interior of the country and to Brazil, Paraguay and Argentina.

Shipping. On 31 Dec. 1975 the 8 merchant vessels and 4 tankers under the Uruguayan flag had a GRT of 103,336. In 1974, 759 vessels cleared Montevideo, 56 being British. River transport (1,270 km) is extensive; its main importance being to link Montevideo with Paysandú and Salto.

Post and Broadcasting. The telegraph lines in operation have a total length of 12,083 km. The telephone system in Montevideo is controlled by the State; small companies operate in the interior. Telephone instruments, 1977, numbered 257,624. There are 1,277 post offices. Uruguay has 54 long-wave and 17 short-wave broadcasting stations. There are about 1m. wireless sets and 200,000 television receivers. There are 4 television stations. The State itself operates one of the most powerful sound broadcasting stations in South America. Four cable companies connect Montevideo with the US and Europe.

Cinemas (1971). Cinemas numbered 150 with seating capacity of 83,000.

Newspapers (1977). There were 5 daily newspapers in Montevideo with aggregate daily circulation of about 210,000; most of the 25–30 provincial newspapers appear bi-weekly.

JUSTICE, RELIGION, EDUCATION AND WELFARE

Justice. The Ministry of Justice was created in 1977 to be responsible for relations between the Executive Power and the Judiciary and other jurisdictional entities. The Court of Justice is made up by 5 members appointed by the Council of the Nation at the suggestion of the Executive Power, for a period of 5 years. This court has original jurisdiction in constitutional, international and admiralty cases, and hears appeals from the appellate courts, of which there are 4, each with 3 judges.

In Montevideo there are also 8 courts for ordinary civil cases, 3 for government (*Juzgado de Hacienda*), as well as criminal and correctional courts. Each departmental capital has a departmental court; each of the 224 judicial divisions has a justice of peace court. In Sept. 1907 the death penalty was abolished, replaced by penal servitude for a period of 30–40 years.

Religion. State and Church are separated, and there is complete religious liberty. The religion professed by the majority of the inhabitants is Roman Catholic. The archbishopric of Montevideo has 9 suffragan bishops in Salto, Melo, Florida, Minas, San José, Canelones, Tacuarembó, Mercedes and Maldonado.

Protestants numbered about 10,500 in 1957.

Education. Primary education is obligatory; both primary and superior education are free.

In 1971 there were 1,950 primary public schools with 331,754 pupils and approximately 10,300 teachers; in 1968, 249 secondary schools had 189,204 pupils. There are also evening courses for adults. Illiteracy is now confined largely to the older age groups.

The University of the Republic at Montevideo, inaugurated in 1849, has about 16,200 students; tuition is free to both native-born and foreign students; there are 10 faculties. There are 43 normal schools for males and females, and a college of arts and trades with about 26,909 students. There are also many religious seminaries throughout the Republic with a considerable number of pupils, a school for the blind, 2 for deaf and dumb and a school of domestic science.

Health. Hospital beds, 1971, numbered 15,250; physicians numbered 4,434.

DIPLOMATIC REPRESENTATIVES

OF URUGUAY IN GREAT BRITAIN (48 Lennox Gdns, London, SW1X 0DL)

Ambassador: Edgardo Héctor Abellá (accredited 20 Oct. 1977).

OF GREAT BRITAIN IN URUGUAY (Marco Bruto 1073, Montevideo)

Ambassador: William Peters, MVO, MBE.

OF URUGUAY IN THE USA (1918 F St, NW, Washington, D.C., 20006)

Ambassador: José Perez Caldas.

OF THE USA IN URUGUAY (Calle Lauro Muller 1776, Montevideo)

Ambassador: Lawrence H. Pezzullo.

OF URUGUAY TO THE UNITED NATIONS

Ambassador: Dr Carlos Giambruno.

Books of Reference

The official gazette is the *Diario Oficial*
Statistical Reports of the Government. Montevideo. Annual and biennial
Anales de Instruccion Primaria. Montevideo. Quarterly

Arcas, J. A., *Historia del siglo XX uruguayo, 1897–1943.* Montevideo, 1950
De Carlos, M., *La escuela púplica uruguaya.* Montevideo, 1949
Fernández Saldaña, J. M., *Diccionario Uruguayo de Biografias.* Montevideo, 1945
Fitzgibbon, R. H., *Uruguay, Portrait of a Democracy.* New Brunswick, NJ, 1954; London, 1956
Montañés, M. T., *Desarrollo de la agricultura en el Uruguay.* Montevideo, 1948
Pendle, G., *Uruguay.* 3rd ed. R. Inst. of Int. Affairs, 1963
Porzecanski, A. C., *Uruguay's Tupamaros.* London and New York, 1973
Salgado, José, *Historia de la Republica O. del Uruguay.* 8 vols. Montevideo, 1943

National Library: Biblioteca Nacional del Uruguay, Guayabo 1793, Montevideo. It publishes *Anuario Bibliográfico Uruguayo.*

VATICAN CITY STATE

Stato della Città del Vaticano

HISTORY. For many centuries the Popes bore temporal sway over a territory stretching across mid-Italy from sea to sea and comprising some 17,000 sq. miles, with a population finally of over 3m. In 1859–60 and 1870 the Papal States were incorporated with the Italian Kingdom. The consequent dispute between Italy and successive Popes was only settled on 11 Feb. 1929 by three treaties between the Italian Government and the Vatican: (1) A Political Treaty, which recognized the full and independent sovereignty of the Holy See in the city of the Vatican; (2) a Concordat, to regulate the condition of religion and of the Church in Italy; and (3) a Financial Convention, in accordance with which the Holy See received 750m. lire in cash and 1,000m. lire in Italian 5% state bonds. This sum was to be a definitive settlement of all the financial claims of the Holy See against Italy in consequence of the loss of its temporal power in 1870. The treaty and concordat were ratified on 7 June 1929. The treaty has been embodied in the Constitution of the Italian Republic of 1947.

The Vatican City State is governed by a Commission appointed by the Pope. The reason for its existence is to provide an extra-territorial, independent base for the Holy See, the government of the Roman Catholic Church.

In 1930 the issue of Papal coinage was resumed, after a lapse of 60 years. In virtue of a special convention between the Vatican City and the Italian Government (last renewed in 1962), each state allows the currency of the other to circulate in its territory. The Vatican City has, however, given an undertaking that the total value of its coins issued in ordinary years will not exceed 100m. lire, 200m. lire in years of 'Sede vacante' or holy years, or 300m. in the year of the opening of a Council.

AREA AND POPULATION. The area of the Vatican City is 44 hectares (108·7 acres). It includes the Piazza di San Pietro (St Peter's Square), which is to remain normally open to the public and subject to the powers of the Italian police. It has its own railway station (opened Nov. 1932), postal facilities, coins and radio. Twelve buildings in and outside Rome enjoy extra-territorial rights, including the Basilicas of St John Lateran, St Mary Major, St Paul without the Walls and the Pope's summer villa at Castel Gandolfo. On 8 Oct. 1951 extra-territorial rights were also granted to a new Vatican radio station on Italian soil. *Radio Vaticana* is broadcasting an extensive service in 31 languages from transmitters in the Vatican City and in Italy.

The Vatican City has about 1,000 inhabitants.

CONSTITUTION. The Pope exercises the sovereignty and has absolute legislative, executive and judicial powers. The judicial power is delegated to a tribunal in the first instance, to the Sacred Roman Rota in appeal and to the Supreme Tribunal of the Signature in final appeal.

The Pope is elected by the College of Cardinals, meeting in secret conclave. The election is by scrutiny and requires a two-thirds majority.

From the accession of Clement VII in 1523 all Popes have been Italians.

Name and family	*Election*	*Name and family*	*Election*
Benedict XIV (*Lambertini*)	1740	Pius VI (*Braschi*)	1775
Clement XIII (*Rezzonico*)	1758	Pius VII (*Chiaramonti*)	1800
Clement XIV (*Ganganelli*)	1769	Leo XII (*della Genga*)	1823

Name and family	*Election*	*Name and family*	*Election*
Pius VIII (*Castiglioni*)	1829	Benedict XV (*della Chiesa*)	1914
Gregory XVI (*Cappellari*)	1831	Pius XI (*Ratti*)	1922
Pius IX (*Mastai-Ferretti*)	1846	Pius XII (*Pacelli*)	1939
Leo XIII (*Pecci*)	1878	John XXIII (*Roncalli*)	1958
Pius X (*Sarto*)	1903	Paul VI (*Montini*)	1963

Supreme Pontiff: **Paul VI** (Giovanni Battista Montini), born at Concesio near Brescia, 26 Sept. 1897; Secretariat of State 1923–54; Archbishop of Milan 1954–63; elected Pope 21 June 1963; coronation 30 June 1963; died 6 Aug. 1978.

Secretary of State: Cardinal Jean Villot (appointed 5 May 1969).

Flag: Vertically yellow and white, with on the white the crossed keys and tiara of the Papacy.

ROMAN CATHOLIC CHURCH. The Roman Pontiff (in orders a Bishop, but in jurisdiction held to be by divine right the centre of all Catholic unity, and consequently Pastor and Teacher of all Christians) has for advisers and coadjutors the Sacred College of Cardinals, consisting in Jan. 1977 of 134 Cardinals appointed by him from senior ecclesiastics who are either the bishops of important Sees or the heads of departments at the Holy See. In addition to the College of Cardinals, the Pope has created a 'Synod of Bishops'. This consists of the Patriarchs and certain Metropolitans of the Catholic Church of Oriental Rite, of elected representatives of the national episcopal conferences and religious orders of the world, of the Cardinals in charge of the Roman Congregations and of other persons nominated by the Pope. The Synod meets as and when decided by the Pope; its first session was held in the autumn of 1967 and its third session in Oct. 1974.

The central administration of the Roman Catholic Church is carried on by a number of permanent committees called Sacred Congregations, each composed of a number of Cardinals and diocesan bishops (both appointed for 5-year periods), with Consultors and Officials. Besides the Secretariat of State and the Council for Public Affairs of the Church (which deals with external relations) there are now 9 Sacred Congregations, viz.: Doctrine, Oriental Churches, Bishops, the Sacraments and Divine Worship, Clergy, Religious, Catholic Education, Evangelization of the Peoples and Causes of the Saints. There are also 3 Secretariats: for Christian Unity, Non-Christians and Non-Believers; a Prefecture of Economic Affairs, a Prefecture of the Pontifical Household and a Statistical Office. Furthermore, the Roman Curia contains 3 tribunals, the Apostolic Penitentiary, the Supreme Tribunal of the Apostolic Signature and the Sacred Roman Rota; and, lastly, various other councils and commissions dealing with the Laity, Justice and Peace, Women, the Family, the Revision of Canon Law, Social Communications, Migration and Tourism. The Pontifical Academy of Sciences was revived by Pius XI in 1936 with 70 members.

More than 2,500 Roman Catholic prelates and 99 observer-delegates from 27 other Christian Churches attended the Second Vatican Council which met 11 Oct. 1962 and 8 Dec. 1965. Sixteen Constitutions and Decrees were approved at the Council, and 7 commissions were set up to implement these decisions.

DIPLOMATIC REPRESENTATIVES

In its diplomatic relations with foreign countries the Holy See is represented by the Council for Public Affairs of the Church. It maintains permanent observers to the UN in New York and Geneva and to UNESCO and FAO. The Holy See is a member of IAEA and the Vatican City State is a member of UPU and ITU. It therefore attends as a member those international conferences open to State members of the UN and specialized agencies.

Envoy and Minister to the Holy See: G. A. Crossley, CMG. *First Secretary:* M. A. Cafferty.

Apostolic Delegate[1] *for Great Britain, Bermuda and Gibraltar:* Mgr Bruno Heim, Titular Archbishop of Xanto.

[1] Apostolic delegate is a representative of the Holy See without diplomatic status or privileges.

Books of Reference

Acta Apostolicæ Sedis Romanæ. Rome
Annuario Pontificio. Rome. Annual
L'Attività della Santa Sede. Rome. Annual
The Catholic Directory. London. Annual
Codex Juris Canonici. Latest ed., 1948
Atlas Missionum. Vatican City, 1958
Bilan du Monde: Encyclopédie catholique du monde chrétien. Tournai, 1964
Cardinale, Mgr. Igino, *Le Saint-Siège et la diplomatie*. Paris and Rome, 1962
Hales, E. E., *The Catholic Church and the Modern World*. London, 1958
Kerr, W. S., *A Handbook on the Papacy*. London, 1950
Nichols, P. *The Politics of the Vatican*. London, 1968
Pallenborg, C., *Vatican Finances*. Harmondsworth, 1971
Purdy, W., *The Church on the Move*. London, 1966

VENEZUELA

Republica de Venezuela

Capital: Caracas
Population: 12·4m. (1976)
GNP per capita: US$2,570 (1976)

AREA AND POPULATION. Venezuela is bounded north by the Caribbean, east by Guyana, south by Brazil, south-west and west by Colombia. The official estimate of the area is 912,050 sq. km (352,143 sq. miles); the frontiers with Colombia, Brazil and Guyana extend for 2,972 miles. Over half the population live in the valleys of Caracas and Valencia (once the capital). There are 20 states, 2 territories, the federal district and the federal dependencies (*i.e.*, 72 islands in the Antilles); further states may be created from the territories. Bolívar, the largest state, has an area of 91,868 sq. miles; the other states are far smaller. The federal district embraces 745 sq. miles.

The language of the country is Spanish.

Population according to the 1971 census (estimate (1976) 12·4m.):

State	*Capital*	*Population*	*State*	*Capital*	*Population*
Anzoátegui	Barcelona	506,297	Portuguesa	Guanare	297,044
Apure	San Fernando	164,705	Sucre	Cumaná	469,006
Aragua	Maracay	543,170	Táchira	San Cristóbal	511,344
Barinas	Barinas	231,046	Trujillo	Trujillo	381,335
Bolívar	Ciudad Bolívar	391,665	Yaracuy	San Felipe	223,540
Carabobo	Valencia	659,339	Zulia	Maracaibo	1,229,037
Cojedes	San Carlos	94,351	Ter. Amazonas	Puerto Ayacucho	21,696
Falcón	Coro	407,957	Ter. Delta		
Guárico	San Juan	318,905	Amacuro	Tucupita	48,139
Lara	Barquisimeto	671,410	Federal District	Caracas	1,860,637
Mérida	Mérida	347,095	Federal Depen-		
Miranda	Los Teques	856,272	dencies	—	463
Monagas	Maturin	298,239			
Nueva Esparta	La Asunción	118,830		Total	10,721,522

The 1971 census excluded tribal Indians estimated at 31,800, of whom 20,000 are in Ter. Amazonas and 4,000 in Zulia.

Of the working population of 3·2m. more than 82,000 were between 10 and 14 years and 429,000 were between 15 and 19 years.

The 1971 population of Caracas was 1,035,499; Maracaibo, 651,574; Barquisimeto, 330,815; Valencia, 367,154; Maracay, 255,134; San Cristóbal, 152,239; Ciudad Guyana, 143,540; Cabimas, 122,239; Baruta, 121,066; Cumaná, 119,751; Ciudad Bolívar, 103,728.

Vital statistics, 1968: 405,964 births, 66,044 marriages, 70,478 deaths.

CONSTITUTION AND GOVERNMENT. The constitution of 1958 provides for popular election for a term of 5 years of a President, a National Congress, and State and Municipal legislative assemblies, and guarantees the freedom of labour, industry and commerce. Aliens are assured of treatment equal to that extended to nationals.

Congress consists of a Senate and a Chamber of Deputies. At least 2 Senators are elected for each State and for the Federal District. Senators must be Venezuelans by birth and over 30 years of age. Deputies must be native Venezuelans over 21 years of age; there is 1 for every 50,000 inhabitants. The territories, on reaching the population fixed by law, also elect deputies. Voting (by proportional representation) is compulsory for men and women over 18. Owing to the high rate of illiteracy, voting is by coloured ballot cards.

The President must be a Venezuelan by birth and over 30 years of age; he has a qualified power of veto.

The following is a list of presidents since 1941:

	Took Office		Took Office
Gen. Isaias Medina Angarita	6 May 1941	Rear-Adm. Wolfgang Larrazábal Ugueto	23 Jan. 1958[2,3]
Rómulo Betancourt	20 Oct. 1945	Dr Edgard Sanabria	14 Nov. 1958[3]
Rómulo Gallegos	15 Feb. 1948	Rómulo Betancourt	13 Feb. 1959
Lieut.-Col. Carlos Delgado Chalbaud	24 Nov. 1948[4]	Raul Leoni	11 March 1964
Dr G. Suárez Flamerich	27 Nov. 1950[2]	Rafael Caldera	11 March 1969
Col. Marcos Pérez Jiménez.	3 Dec. 1952[1]		

[1] Deposed. [2] Resigned. [3] Provisional. [4] Assassinated 13 Nov. 1950.

President: Carlos Andrés Pérez, elected 9 Dec. 1973 with 2,006,214 out of 4,308,703 votes, assumed office on 11 March 1974.

Foreign Minister: Dr Ramón Escovar Salom.

The city of Caracas is the capital. The 20 states, autonomous and politically equal, have each a legislative assembly and an elected governor. The states are divided into 156 districts and 613 municipalities. There are also 2 federal territories with 7 departments, and a federal district with 2 departments and 2 parishes. Each district has a municipal council, and each municipio a communal junta. The federal district and the 2 territories are administered by the President of the Republic.

National flag: Three horizontal stripes of yellow, blue, red, with an arc of 7 white stars in the centre, and the national arms in the canton.

National anthem: Gloria al bravo pueblo (1811; words by Vicente Salias, tune by Juan Landaeta).

DEFENCE. In 1958 a Joint Staff Organization was established under the Minister of Defence for the closer integration of defence policy and administration of the three Services and the National Guard.

Army. All Venezuelans on reaching 18 years of age are liable for 2 years in the Armed Forces. They can opt for the Air Force or the Navy instead of the Army, but their allocation is finally dependent upon current requirements. The Army's established strength of approximately 28,000 all ranks furnishes a cavalry regiment, 11 infantry battalions, 13 ranger battalions, 3 tank battalions and supporting engineering, artillery, anti-aircraft and supply services. There is a military academy for cadets, a school for staff studies and other technical training schools. Women can also be conscripted, as nurses, clerks, etc.

Navy. Strength includes 5 diesel-powered patrol submarines (2 new built in Federal Republic of Germany and 3 old *ex*-US submarines), 2 large destroyers built in Great Britain in 1953–56, 2 old *ex*-US destroyers, 5 small fast frigates built in Italy in 1956–57, 6 new fast missile-armed patrol craft built in Britain by Vosper–Thornycroft in 1974–75, 10 patrol vessels, 5 landing ships, 1 transport landing ship (*ex*-repair ship), 1 survey ship, 2 survey launches, 39 coastal patrol boats, 3 transports and 14 tugs. Sixteen of the coastal patrol boats are operated by the National Guard.

New construction includes 6 frigates, armed with guided missiles and equipped with helicopter, hangar and flight deck, ordered from Italy.

There is a naval academy for the training of officer cadets and a school of staff studies and various technical training schools. Personnel in 1978: 7,500 officers and men including 4,000 of the Marine Corps.

Air Force. Formed in 1920, the Air Force of some 8,000 officers and men is a small, but well-equipped service with a total of about 240 aircraft. There are 5 combat squadrons. One is equipped with 9 Mirage IIIE and 4 Mirage 5 supersonic fighters and 2 Mirage 5D trainers. Two others have a total of 15 Canadair CF-5A fighter-bombers and 2 two-seat CF-5Bs. Two bomber squadrons are equipped respectively with 26 modernized Canberra jet-bombers and 16 OV-10E Bronco twin-turboprop counter-insurgency aircraft, supported by 2 Canberra reconnaissance aircraft. A helicopter force consists of more than 40 Bell JetRangers, H-19s, UH-1B/D/H Iroquois and Alouette IIIs. Transport units are equipped with 12 C-123 Providers, 6 C-130H Hercules, 1 HS.748, 2 C-54s and 15 C-47s. Communications aircraft are Queen Airs and other types. T-34 Mentors and Jet Provosts are used for training, together with 24 T-2D Buckeye advanced jet trainers, which have a secondary attack role. A battalion of paratroops comes within Air Force responsibility. There is a staff college and a cadet academy.

National Guard, a volunteer force of some 10,000 under the Ministry of Defence, is broadly responsible for internal security. It includes customs and forestry duties among its tasks.

INTERNATIONAL RELATIONS

Membership. Venezuela is a member of UN, OAS and LAFTA.

Aid. Venezuela has lent about US$500m. to the World Bank, SDR 650m. to the IMF and US$100m. to the UN Emergency Fund. A trust fund administered by the Inter-American Development Bank is to distribute US$500m. during 1975–80, and there are separate agreements with a number of Central and Southern American states.

ECONOMY

Planning. The fifth 5-year plan (1976–80) aims at an average annual growth rate in GDP of 8%; total investment, about Bs.223,000m., of which Bs.119,000m. is for the public sector. The plan aims to lessen dependence on the oil industry by stimulating manufacturing and construction, but at the same time it is investing in further exploration for oil, mainly on the continental shelf and in the Orinoco heavy oil belt. Power-generating capacity is being increased.

Budget. The revenue and expenditure for calendar years were, in Bs.1m., as follows:

	1972	*1973*	*1974*	*1975*	*1976*	*1977*
Revenue	16,500	16,433	42,799	41,270	41,926	35,836
Expenditure	12,842	15,042	40,059	40,266	43,888	35,636

The oil industry contributes about 70% of ordinary revenue in the form of royalties and income-tax, the government share of oil companies' profit amounts to about 66%.

The 1977 estimates include receipts of Bs.25,904m. from the oil industry, and expenditures of Bs.9,201m. for developments and Bs.21,348m. for current expenditure.

The public debt on 31 May 1972 was Bs.6,957m.

Currency. The official monetary unit is the *bolívar*. As a result of exchange reforms of Jan. 1964 the selling rate to the public was changed to Bs.4·50 = US$1. The selling rate applicable to iron and petroleum companies is Bs.4·30 = US$1. Cocoa and coffee exporters may sell exchange to the Central Bank at Bs.4·485. Importers of wheat and powdered milk are eligible for subsidies amounting to the difference between the previous selling rate of Bs.3·35 and the current sellers' Bs.4·30 = US$1. The exchange rate of the £ sterling (Jan. 1977) is Bs.7·73; 4·29 Bs. to US$.

The *bolívar* (Bs.) is divided into 100 *céntimos*. Gold coins, 100 (*pachanos*), 20 and 10 *bolívars* have been minted but are no longer in circulation; silver coins are 5 (*fuerte*), 2, 1 *bolívars*; nickel, 50 (*real*), 25 (*medio*) and 12·5 *céntimos* (*locha*), copper-nickel, 5 *céntimos* (*puya*).

The bank-notes in circulation are 500, 100, 50, 20 and 10 bolívars. The circulation of foreign bank-notes is forbidden.

Banking. In Oct. 1939 a Central Bank was established, with a capital of 10m. bolívars (one-half by the Government and one-half by the public) to regulate the currency and to act as fiscal agent for the Government. This was opened on 1 Jan. 1941 with a gold stock equal to US$29m., which rose to US$503m. in Oct. 1956.

In Nov. 1974 it was announced that the Central Bank would be nationalized over a period of 2 years.

Before 1939 the Bank of Venezuela, with (now) a capital of Bs.105m. was the sole depository of government funds and controlled the circulation of the currency. There are 36 commercial banks, of which 32 are Venezuelan (including the Banco Nacional de Descuento, with an authorized capital of Bs.120m.), Banco Unión (100m.), Banco Mercantil y Agrícola (60m.), Banco Venezolano de Crédito (42m.),

Banco de Maracaibo (40m.); and 4 are foreign (1 Canadian, 1 American, 1 Dutch and 1 French–Italian). Banco Obrero, with capital and reserves of Bs.1,038m, and Banco Agricola y Pecuario (176m.) are important instruments of official policy.

On 1 June 1965 the British Bank of London and South America merged with the Venezuelan Banco de La Guaira under the name of Banco La Guaira Internacional. In 1976 bank demand deposits were Bs.19,086m., time deposits and foreign currency deposits were Bs.17,386m. and money supply was Bs.25,548m.

Weights and Measures. Decrees of 1875 and 1917 introduced the metric system.

ENERGY AND NATURAL RESOURCES

Oil. Venezuela is the largest petroleum exporting country in the world and the fifth largest producer; production began in 1917 with 18,000 cu. metres. The oil-producing region around Maracaibo, covering some 30,000 sq. miles, produces about three-quarters of Venezuelan petroleum, and the country is likely to remain a major producer of oil well into 21st century. Deposits in the Orinoco region are likely to prove one of the largest heavy oil reserves in the world.

Powerful foreign oil groups used to own all the concessions. The companies were nationalized on 1 Jan. 1976. CVP (the state oil company) has a 'wells to petrol pumps' operation. On takeover, the new state holding became known as Petroven. A policy of conservation and a decline in demand has resulted in a 1975 production of 2·4m. bbls per day; in 1976 production was stabilized at 2·2m. bbls daily.

A largely state-run petrochemical complex is being developed at Morón and in the state of Zulia, and private investment in this and the chemical industry is being encouraged.

Minerals. There are important goldmines in the region south-east of Bolívar State, and new deposits have been discovered near El Callao (1959) and Sosa Méndez (1961) in the Guayana region. Output, 1974, amounted to 528 kg. Imports of 7,000 kg per annum are necessary for industrial purposes. Diamond output, from Amazonas territory, was 1,249,000 carats in 1974. Manganese deposits, estimated at several million tons, were discovered in 1954. Phosphate-rock deposits (yielding from 64 to 82% tricalcium phosphate) are found in the state of Falcón; reserves of 15m. tons of high-quality rock have been established. The state of Sucre has large sulphur deposits. Coal is worked in the states of Táchira, Aragua and Anzoátegui, production in 1974 being 57,000 tonnes. An important nickel deposit (at Loma de Hierro near Tejerías) is estimated to equal 600,000 tons of pure nickel. Saltmines are now worked by the Government on the Araya peninsula; output, 1964, 202,000 tonnes. Asbestos and copper pyrite are being exploited.

Iron ore is exploited in Bolívar State by the Orinoco Mining Co. and Iron Mines of Venezuela, subsidiaries respectively of the US Steel Corp. and the Bethlehem Steel Co. Proven reserves at the end of 1963 were 1,513m. tonnes. National output of iron ore, 1976, 48·7m. tonnes.

Agriculture. Venezuela is divided into 3 distinct zones—the agricultural, the pastoral and the forest zone. In the first are grown coffee, cocoa, sugar-cane, maize, rice, wheat (grown in the Andes), tobacco, cotton, beans, sisal, etc.; the second affords grazing for more than 6m. cattle and numerous horses; and in the third, which covers a very large portion of the country, tropical products, such as caoutchouc, balatá (a gum resembling rubber), tonka beans, dividivi, copaiba, vanilla, growing wild, are worked by the inhabitants. The 1950 census showed 40% of the population engaged in agriculture; the 1976 livestock estimate showed cattle, 9·4m.; pigs, 1·9m.; goats, 1·5m.; sheep, 103,000; poultry, 29·4m. Area under cultivation is 5,530,898 acres.

Production in tonnes in 1976: Coffee, 50,000; maize, 432,000; rice, 277,000, sugar, 5·4m. (1975).

The coffee plantations number 62,673, covering 543,400 acres with 135m. bushes. The Venezuelan cocoa, from 13,000 plantations, is considered to be of high quality; it is grown chiefly in the states of Sucre and Miranda. The sugar industry has 6 government and 20 privately owned mills.

Under the Agrarian Reform Law of 1960, the Instituto Agrario Nacional establishes agricultural colonies where farmers are settled on small-holdings. Since the Agrarian Reform Act of early 1960 to the end of 1966, 119,384 families received about 6·5m. acres of land. In 1966 two-thirds of the rural population had a *per capita* annual income of less than Bs.800. The ultimate envisaged is 300,000 farmers possessing 74m. acres.

Between 1975 and 1977 the banks advanced Bs.4,000m. to agriculture, agricultural investment was exempted from income tax and support prices were raised.

Forestry. Resources have been barely tapped; 600 species of wood have been identified. Output of timber, two-thirds being soft wood, 1972, 560,454 cu. metres.

Fisheries. The total catch for 1972 consisted of 133,461,548 kg of freshwater and 6,241,969 kg of salt-water fish.

INDUSTRY AND TRADE

Industry. Within the last 30 years Venezuela has been transformed from a largely agricultural country to a leading producer of oil. Since 1960 the government has encouraged the diversification of the economy by industrialization to avoid over-dependence upon oil. In 1974 the gross national product amounted to Bs.58,989m. (at 1968 prices), principal items being: Oil and natural gas production, 12·7%; manufactures, 14%; agriculture, 6·8%; commerce, 11%; services, 6·6%; construction, 4·8%; transport and communications, 11·2%. The cost of living has remained fairly stable for a number of years, and in 1974 was 126 (1968 = 100).

Venezuela is not yet highly industrialized, but the government are encouraging the establishment of local industries both by offering financial assistance and by establishing and equipping factories, which are then leased out to manufacturers. The development of local industries is fostered either in the form of high import duties or by the virtual elimination of imports through licensing restrictions. In 1946–72 the State Development Corporation (CVF) advanced credit and authorized financial decrees amounting to Bs.6,609m.

The government-owned steel corporation (SIDOR) has a capacity of 1·25m. tons a year; the ALCASA aluminium plant has a capacity of 54,000 tons a year.

Well-established industries include food processing, textiles, shoes, chemicals (195,140 tons in 1966, of which 240,236 tons is fertilizers), wood, finished metal goods and assembly of cars and trucks.

Labour. The first trade unions were those of the workers in the oilfields (36,897 in all) formed in 1935. Members of trade unions and peasant leagues now number 1·8m. The important Venezuelan Workers' Confederation has 600,000 members in 14 industrial and 21 regional federations and a peasant membership of 700,000. By 1963 over 500,000 workers were covered by long-term collective agreements.

Ministry of Development figures reported 3,029,184 people 'economically active' in 1969. These were (in 1,000): Agriculture, 661; services, 710; manufactures, 458; commerce and finance, 520; building, 152; transport, 177, extractive, including oil, 59; public utilities, 44; unemployed, 244.

In mid-1964 the Instituto Nacional de Cooperación Educativa estimated that about 90,000 enter the labour market each year, but there are new openings only for about 35,000.

Commerce. The UN give the values of Venezuela's exports and imports (in US$1m.):

	1972	*1973*	*1974*	*1975*
Exports	3,151	5,628	15,207	11,150
Imports	2,403	2,626	3,841	5,377

The principal foreign imports in 1973 came, by value in £1m., from USA, 421·1; Federal Republic of Germany, 117·9; Japan, 79·4; Italy, 53·2; France, 42·2; Canada, 42·1; UK, 39·2. The value of main exports in 1973 was, in US$1m.: Petroleum, 14,327; iron ore, 133; coffee, 20.

Total trade between UK and Venezuela (British Department of Trade returns, in £1,000 sterling):

	1973	*1974*	*1975*	*1976*	*1977*
Imports to UK	58,804	135,226	165,425	117,636	67,017
Exports and re-exports from UK	39,242	50,311	91,630	128,794	175,035

Tourism. 144,085 tourists visited Venezuela in 1971.

COMMUNICATIONS

Roads. There were, 1971, 43,238 km of road fit for traffic the year round; of these, 13,728 km are paved, 11,358 km are gravel. There are 10,097 km of high-speed 4-lane motorway type. The motorway system runs from Caracas to Puerto Cabello *via* Valencia and will shortly be linked direct with one from La Guaira to Caracas. Venezuela has received two World Bank loans for US$45m. and 30m. in connexion with this programme, for improvements of the express-ways in Caracas and for 2 roads in the south-west of the country. Motor vehicles, 1971, totalled 809,287 and included 601,098 private cars, 18,083 buses and 190,106 lorries. The 1,678-metre Angostura bridge linking the Orinoco cities of Ciudad Bolívar and Soledad was opened in Jan. 1967.

Railways. Construction started early in 1976 of a 3,697-km national railway network, and work is also in progress on Line 1 of the Caracas metro.

Aviation. The chief Venezuelan airlines are LAV (Líneas Aéreas Venezolanas), a government-owned concern, and AVENSA (Aerovías Venezolanas). Both operate numerous internal services. VIASA operates international routes in conjunction with KLM. There are also 3 specialist air freight companies. In all there are over 100 commercial aircraft in operation. In addition to Venezuelan international services, a number of US and Latin American and European lines operate services to Venezuela. British Airways operates twice-weekly flights between London and Caracas.

Shipping. Foreign vessels are not permitted to engage in the coasting trade, except by special concessions or by contract with the Government. La Guaira, Maracaibo, Puerto Cabello, Puerto Ordaz and Guanta are the chief ports. In Dec. 1974 the merchant fleet—with a total of 313 ships of 100 tons and over—had an aggregate gross tonnage of 488,704; this included 16 tankers of 266,844 gross tons.

The principal navigable rivers are the Orinoco and its tributaries Apure and Arauca, from San Fernando to Tucupita through Ciudad Bolívar, Puerto Ordaz and San Félix; San Juan from Carípito to the Gulf of Paria; and Esculante in Lake Maracaibo.

Post and Broadcasting. The telegraph system had a network, 1975, of 45,000 km with 600 telegraph offices. It is supplemented by wireless telegraphy, with 72 stations, and by wireless telephony. There are telephone systems in the principal towns (nationalized in 1954). There were 742,050 instruments in 1977; 416,358 were in Caracas. The telephone network is to be extended by 100,000 additional lines over the next 3 years. An international telex service operates in the Caracas metropolitan zone. There is a submarine telephone link with USA.

There are 77 radio stations at Caracas, Maracaibo, Maracay and other towns. There are 3 television stations in Caracas, of which 2 cover, with relays, most of the country. In Oct. 1963 a new station with transmitter located in Valencia but relaying programmes to Caracas began operations.

Cinemas (1973). There were 431 cinemas.

Newspapers (1972). There were 48 daily newspapers and 44 weeklies out of a total of 354 periodicals. In 1961 Caracas had 9 daily and 14 weekly newspapers with a total circulation of about 445,000.

JUSTICE, RELIGION AND EDUCATION

Justice. The Supreme Court, which operates in Divisions, each with 5 members, is elected by Congress for 5 years. The country is divided into 20 legal districts. They select their own President and Vice-President. The Federal Procurator-General is appointed for 5 years. There are lower federal courts.

Each state has a Supreme Court with 3 members, a superior court, or superior tribunal, courts of first instance, district courts and municipal courts. In the territories there are civil and military judges of first instance, and also judges in the municipios. Finally, there is an income-tax claims tribunal.

Religion. The Roman Catholic is the prevailing religion, but there is toleration of all others. There are 4 archbishops, 1 at Caracas, who is Primate of Venezuela, 2 at Mérida and 1 at Ciudad Bolívar. There are 19 bishops. In the state primary schools instruction is given only to those children whose parents expressly request it. Protestants number about 20,000.

Education. Elementary instruction is free and, from the age of 7 to the completion of the primary grade, compulsory. In 1971 Venezuela had 10,509 primary schools with (1971) 46,736 teachers and a total enrolment of 1,819,839 pupils; there were 1,120 secondary and technical schools, of which 528 were private, with a total of 288,100 pupils in secondary and 77,000 pupils in technical schools. For superior education (1970–71) there are the University of Los Andes at Mérida (8,365 students), the Central University in Caracas (300 years old, rebuilt and modernized in 1944) with 30,028 students, the University of Zulia at Maracaibo (16,299 students), the University of Carabobo (3,949 students), the University of Oriente (5,770 students) and the Instituto Pedagógico (3,116 students). The first 3 universities were granted autonomy on 28 Sept. 1946. Bs.535m. from the yearly national revenue was assigned to the national universities in 1966. A Workers' University in Caracas was set up by law in 1947. Two private universities in Caracas (Universidad Católica 'Andrés Bello', 6,400 students and Universidad Santa Maria, 5,333 students) were authorized by the Government in 1953. The census of 1950 showed that 48·7% of those 10 years of age and older were unable to read and write; this figure was (1965) less than 20%.

DIPLOMATIC REPRESENTATIVES

OF VENEZUELA IN GREAT BRITAIN
(1 Cromwell Rd., London, SW7)

Ambassador: Juan Manuel Sucre-Trías.

OF GREAT BRITAIN IN VENEZUELA (Edificio La Estancia, Avenida La Estancia 10, Caracas)

Ambassador: J. L. Taylor, CMG.

OF VENEZUELA IN THE USA (2445 Massachusetts Ave., NW, Washington, D.C., 20008)

Ambassador: Ignacio Iribarren.

OF THE USA IN VENEZUELA (Avenida Francisco de Miranda and Avenida Principal de la Floresta, Caracas)

Ambassador: Viton P. Vaky.

OF VENEZUELA TO THE UNITED NATIONS

Ambassador: (Vacant).

Books of Reference

Statistical Information: The following are some of the principal publications:

Dirección General de Estadistica, Ministerio de Fomento, *Boletin Mensual de Estadistica.—Annuario Estadistico de Venezuela, 1971.* Caracas, 1973

Banco Central, *Memoria Annual* and *Boletin Mensual*

Ministerio de Sanidad y Asistencia Social, Dirreción de Salud Pública, *Anuario de Epidemiologia y Asistencia Social*

Buitrón, A., *Causas y Efectos del Exodo Rural en Venezuela.—Efectos Económicos y Sociales de las Inmigraciones en Venezuela.—Las Inmigraciones en Venezuela.* Pan American Union, Washington, D.C., 1956

Lieuwen, E., *Venezuela.* 2nd ed. OUP, 1965

Luzardo, R., *Venezuela Business and Finances*. Englewood Cliffs, N.J., 1957
Martz, J. D., *Acción Democratica . . . in Venezuela*. Princeton Univ. Press, 1966
Morón, G., *A History of Venezuela* (ed. J. Street). London, 1964
Perales, P., *Manual de Geografía Económica de Venezuela*. Caracas, 1955
Tugwell, F., *The Politics of Oil in Venezuela*. Stanford Univ. Press, 1975
Ward, E., *The New El Dorado, Venezuela*.. London, 1957

VIETNAM

Capital: Hanoi
Population: 47·15m. (1976)

Cộng Hòa Xã Hội Chu Nghĩa Việt Nam—The Socialist Republic of Vietnam

HISTORY. The recorded history of Vietnam can be traced to Tonkin (now known as the northern part of Vietnam) at the beginning of the Christian era. Conquered by the Chinese (Han dynasty) in A.D. 111, the kingdom of Nam-Viet, as it was then called, broke free of Chinese domination in 939, though at many subsequent periods it again became a nominal vassal of the Chinese emperors.

By the end of the 15th century the Vietnamese had conquered most of the kingdom of Champa (in Annam, now known as the central part of Vietnam) and by the end of the 18th had acquired Cochin-China (now known as the southern part of Vietnam), formerly Cambodian territory.

French interest in Vietnam started in the late 16th century with the arrival of French and Portuguese missionaries. The most notable of these was Alexander of Rhodes, who, in the following century, romanized Vietnamese writing. At the end of the 18th century a French bishop and several soldiers of fortune helped to establish the Emperor Gia-Long (with whom Louis XVI had signed a treaty in 1787) as ruler of a unified Vietnam, known then as the Empire of Annam.

An expedition sent by Napoleon III in 1858 to avenge the death of some French missionaries led in 1862 to the cession to France of part of Cochin-China, and thence, by a series of treaties between 1874 and 1884, to the establishment of French protectorates over Tonkin and Annam, and to the formation of the French colony of Cochin-China. By a Sino-French treaty of 1885 the Empire of Annam (including Tonkin) ceased to be tributary to China. Cambodia had become a French protectorate in 1863, and in 1899, after the extension of French protection to Laos in 1893, the Indo-Chinese Union was proclaimed.

In 1940 Vietnam was occupied by the Japanese and used as a military base for the invasion of Malaya. During the occupation there was considerable underground activity among nationalist, revolutionary and Communist organizations. In 1941 a nominally nationalist coalition of such organizations, known as the Vietminh League, was founded by the Communists.

On 9 March 1945 the Japanese interned the French authorities and proclaimed the 'independence' of Indo-China. In Aug. 1945 they allowed the Vietminh movement to seize power, dethrone Bao Dai, the Emperor of Annam, and establish a republic known as Vietnam, including Tonkin, Annam and Cochin-China, with Hanoi as capital. In Sept. 1945 the French re-established themselves in Cochin-China and on 6 March 1946, after a cease-fire in the sporadic fighting between the French forces and the Vietminh had been arranged, a preliminary convention was signed in Hanoi between the French High Commissioner and President Ho Chi Minh by which France recognized 'the Democratic Republic of Vietnam' as a 'Free State within the Indo-Chinese Federation'. Subsequent conferences convened in the same year at Dalat and Fontainebleau to draft a definitive agreement broke down chiefly over the question of whether or not Cochin-China should be included in the new republic. On 19 Dec. 1946 Vietminh forces made a surprise attack on Hanoi, the signal for hostilities which were to last for nearly 8 years.

An agreement signed by the Emperor Bao Dai on behalf of Vietnam on 8 March 1949 recognized the independence of Vietnam within the French Union, and certain sovereign powers were forthwith transferred to Vietnam. The Paris agreements of 29 Dec. 1954 completed the transfer of sovereignty to Vietnam. Supreme authority in the military field remained with the French until the departure of the last French C.-in-C. in April 1956. Treaties of independence and association were initialled by representatives of the French and Vietnamese governments on 4 June 1954.

An agreement on the cessation of hostilities in Vietnam was reached on 20 July 1954 at the Geneva conference. The agreement was signed on behalf of the C.-in-C. of the French Forces in Indo-China and on behalf of the C.-in-C. of the People's Army of Vietnam. The Government of Vietnam did not sign the agreement.

The final declaration of the Geneva conference (21 July 1954) declared that general elections should take place in July 1956. These did not take place, and Vietnam remained divided until 1976.

In Paris on 27 Jan. 1973 an agreement was signed ending the war in Vietnam. After the US withdrawal, however, hostilities continued between the North and the South until the spring of 1975, when North Vietnamese forces opened a successful offensive in the Central Highlands which rapidly spread to the rest of the country, bringing about the complete military defeat of the South Vietnamese forces. President Thieu resigned on 21 April. He was replaced by the Vice-President, Tran Van Huong, who was in turn replaced by Gen. Duong Van Minh who surrendered to the Communist forces on 30 April. 150,000–200,000 South Vietnamese fled the country, including the former President Thieu. By 30 April Saigon had fallen.

For details of the constitution and government of the former Republic of Vietnam (South Vietnam), *see* THE STATESMAN'S YEAR-BOOK, 1975–76. After the collapse of President Thieu's regime the Provisional Revolutionary Government established an administration in Saigon on 6 June 1975 under the presidency of Huynh Tan Phat. A North–South conference on the reunification of Vietnam was held 15–21 Nov. 1975 at which it was announced that agreement on 'the basic problems posed by reunification' had been reached. On 21 Jan. 1976 Saigon reverted from military to civil rule. A general election was held on 25 April 1976 for a new National Assembly representing the whole country. Voting was by universal suffrage of all citizens of 18 or over, except former functionaries of South Vietnam undergoing 're-education' in special camps. The number of these was between 200,000 and 300,000. The unification of North and South Vietnam into the Socialist Republic of Vietnam took place formally on 2 July 1976. After previous US vetoes the new administration of President Carter indicated that it was not opposed to Vietnam's application to join the UN, and Vietnam was admitted to membership unanimously and without a vote on 20 Sept. 1977. Relations with China deteriorated in 1978 following the alleged persecution and exodus of Chinese residents.

AREA AND POPULATION. The country has a total area of 329,566 sq. km.

Following reorganization, the country is now divided administratively into 35 provinces and 3 cities. Areas and populations (in 1,000) at the census of 5 Feb. 1976 are as follows:

Province	*Sq. km*	*Population*	*Province*	*Sq. km*	*Population*
Lai Chau	17,408	265·6	Phu Khanh	9,620	1,066·2
Son La	14,656	410·1	Lam Dong	10,000	343·1
Hoang Lien Son	14,125	677·2	Thuan Hai	11,000	836·9
Ha Tuyen	13,519	686·4	Dong Nai	12,130	1,260·3
Cao Bang	13,731	843·9	Song Be	9,500	561·4
Bac Thai	8,615	752·9	Tay Ninh	4,100	625·9
Quang Ninh	7,076	701·8	Long An	5,100	828·8
Vinh Phu	5,187	1,579·5	Dong Thap	3,120	991·3
Ha Bac	4,708	1,466·2	Tien Giang	2,350	1,137·2
Ha Son Binh	6,860	2,041·6	Ben Tre	2,400	932·0
Hai Hung	2,526	1,929·9	Cuu Long	4,200	1,319·1
Thai Binh	1,344	1,416·2	An Giang	4,140	1,361·7
Ha Nam Ninh	3,522	2,574·6	Hau Giang	5,100	1,870·4
Thanh Hoa	11,138	2,262·1	Kien Giang	6,000	834·0
Nghe Tinh	22,380	2,704·6	Minh Hai	8,000	981·1
Binh Tri Thien	19,048	1,751·8	Hanoi[1]	597	1,443·5
Quang Nam – Da Nang	11,376	1,414·4	Ho Chi Minh[1]	1,845	3,460·5
Nghia Binh	14,700	1,789·1	Haiphong[1]	1,515	1,190·9
Gia Lai – Kontum	18,480	465·0			
Dac Lac	18,300	372·7		329,466	47,150·0

[1] Cities.

Vital statistics (North Vietnam): Death rate (1973), 7 per 1,000; infant mortality (1968), 28 per 1,000; growth rate (since 1960) 2·9% per annum.

84% of the population are Vietnamese (Kinh). There are also over 60 minority groups thinly spread in the extensive mountainous regions. The largest minorities are (1976 figures in 1,000): Tay (742); Khmer (651); Thai (631); Muong (618); Nung (472); Meo (349); Dao (294). (Several of these groups have been collectively referred to as 'Montagnards'.)

Following the suppression of private commerce in 1978 more than 100,000 Chinese fled or were evacuated to China.

CONSTITUTION AND GOVERNMENT. In June 1976 a Commission was set up to draft a new constitution for reunified Vietnam. The former, second, North Vietnamese Constitution dated from 1960 (the first was promulgated in 1946). It consisted of a preamble and 112 articles grouped into 12 chapters. It stated that North Vietnam was a 'people's democratic state based on the alliance between the workers and peasants and led by the working class', and that the 'DRV is advancing step by step from people's democracy to socialism'.

At the elections for the new National Assembly held on 25 April 1976 turnout was 98·77%. 605 candidates stood and 492 were elected (243 from the South), including 132 women, 67 representatives of ethnic minorities and 13 representatives of religious organizations.

Local government authorities are the people's councils, which appoint executive committees. Local elections were held in Ho Chi Minh City and the 38 provinces of the former South Vietnam on 5 May 1977. A special form of autonomous administration has been established in the regions inhabited by the ethnic minorities.

President: Ton Duc Thang (elected 2 July 1976).
Vice-Presidents: Nguyen Luong Bang, Nguyen Huu Tho.
Chairman of the Standing Committee of the National Assembly: Truong Chinh.

All political power stems from the Communist Party of Vietnam (until Dec. 1976 known as the Workers' Party of Vietnam), founded in 1930; it had 1·2m. members in 1973. In June 1978 the Politburo consisted of 14 full and 3 alternate members: Le Duan (*First Secretary*); Truong Chinh (*Chairman of the National Assembly*); Pham Van Dong (*Prime Minister*); Pham Hung (*Deputy Prime Minister*); Le Duc Tho; Vo Nguyen Giap (*Deputy Prime Minister and Minister of Defence*); Nguyen Duy Trinh (*Deputy Prime Minister and Foreign Minister*); Le Thanh Nghi (*Deputy Prime Minister and Chairman, State Planning Commission*); Tran Quoc Hoan (*Minister of the Interior*); Gen. Van Tien Dung (*Chief of General Staff*); Le Van Luong; Nguyen Van Linh; Vo Chi Cong (*Deputy Prime Minister and Minister of Agriculture*); Chu Huy Man; (alternate): To Huu; Vo Van Kiet; Do Muoi (*Deputy Prime Minister*). Ministers not in the Politburo include: Huynh Tan Phat (*Deputy Prime Minister*); Hoang Anh (*Finance*); Dang Viet Chau (*Foreign Trade*); Tran Van Hien (*Home Trade*); Phan Trong Tue (*Transport*); Nguyen Thi Binh (*Education*).

There are 2 puppet parties, the Democratic (founded 1944) and the Socialist (1946), which are unified with the trade and youth unions in the Fatherland Front.

National flag: Red, with a yellow 5-pointed star in the centre.
National anthem: 'Tien quan ca' ('The troops are advancing').

DEFENCE. Conscription is for 3 years at age 18.

Army. Estimated strength in 1976, 600,000, of whom over 200,000 were serving in South Vietnam, the Laos and Kampuchea border areas. The Army is organized in 18 infantry divisions (plus 2 training divisions), 1 artillery division, 3 armoured regiments and about 15 independent infantry regiments. There are also 20 SAM regiments and 40 AA artillery regiments.

Navy. The naval forces are being reorganized, culled and modernized. Before the North Vietnamese victory in 1975 the Navy comprised 3 old coastal escorts, 2 fast missile boats, 28 fast torpedo boats, 22 fast motor gunboats, 34 small patrol boats, 24 landing craft, 4 minesweeping boats, 10 tenders, 100 auxiliaries and 200 armed junks. It also had 10 Mi-4 SAR helicopters. Personnel numbered more than 4,000 officers and men.

At least 1 frigate, several other major warships and a considerable number of auxiliaries were captured while many small craft which had been abandoned were taken over. Thus the Navy, even taking into account heavy losses in action, is larger than before the South Vietnamese surrender.

The fleet reportedly includes 2 frigates, 2 corvettes (*ex*-US fleet minesweepers), 2 fast missile boats, 12 fast torpedo boats, 22 fast gunboats, 80 patrol craft, 8 landing ships, 24 landing craft, 690 riverine craft, 15 auxiliaries and 230 armed junks; but it is difficult to accurately assess the operational availability, fitness for sea or steaming capacity of this heterogeneous collection and few of these vessels can be ready for action in view of the fuel shortage.

Air Force. The Air Force, built up with Soviet and Chinese assistance, has 1 squadron (probably inactive) of Il-28 twin-jet tactical bombers, about 70 MiG-21 and 80 Chinese F-6 (MiG-19) supersonic fighters, 100 MiG-17 and 30 Su-7 jet fighter-bombers, about 20 helicopters, including 8 large Mi-6s, and some 30 training and 50 transport aircraft. Fighter pilots are trained in the USSR. 'Guideline', 'Goa' and 'Gainful' surface-to-air missiles are operational in large numbers. Personnel, about 12,000 with 300 first-line aircraft.

INTERNATIONAL RELATIONS

Membership. Vietnam is a member of UN.

ECONOMY

Planning. Long-term forward planning envisages the creation of local industry geared to agriculture manned by surplus peasant labour as a first step towards the development of a heavy industrial base. The current 5-year plan (1976–80) envisages the development of agriculture, light industry and heavy industry in that order. (For previous plans *see* THE STATESMAN'S YEAR-BOOK, 1976–77, p. 1473.)

Currency. The monetary unit is the *dong* = 100 *hao*. There are coins of 1, 2 and 5 *hao*, and notes of 1, 2, 5 and 10 *dong*. The *dong* has been reported to stand at an official commercial rate of 0·0306 roubles = 1 *dong*. Using the value of the US dollar and sterling in terms of roubles as at 15 Sept. 1975, the following cross-rates can be calculated: £1 = 5·10 *dong*; US$1 = 2·42 *dong*. In May 1978 the currency system was unified. The northern *dong* and the southern *piastre* were replaced by a 'unified *dong*' which has the same exchange rate as the old northern *dong*.

Banking. The bank of issue is the National Bank of Vietnam (founded in 1951). There is also a Bank for Foreign Trade (Vietcombank). All banks in the South have been nationalized.

NATURAL RESOURCES

Electricity. In 1964, 548·7m. kwh. of electricity were produced in the North and in 1972, 1,482m. kwh. were produced in the South.

Minerals. North Vietnam is rich in anthracite, lignite and hard coal: total reserves are estimated at 20,000m. tonnes. Anthracite production in 1975 was 5m. tonnes. Coal production is estimated at 5m. tonnes per year. There are deposits of iron ore, manganese, titanium, chromite, bauxite and a little gold. Chromite production in 1962 was 35,000 tons. Reserves of apatite are some of the biggest in the world. Estimated production of phosphates in 1971, 1·1m. tonnes; salt, 150,000 tonnes. In 1973 and 1974 the former Vietnamese Government awarded concessions for off-shore oil exploration. Oil and natural gas have been found. There are large limestone deposits in Kien Giang, Chau Doc and Thua Thien provinces. A recent geological survey reported on the prospects of valuable bauxite deposits. There is a small coal-bearing region at Nong-Son.

Agriculture. In 1977, 90% of the population was engaged in agriculture. Rice production for all Vietnam was 12·5m. tonnes in 1976. In the North in 1975 agricultural co-operatives were reorganized into larger units. (Previously there had been about 18,000 co-operatives, each comprising 200–400 households and averaging 200 hectares of land each.) In 1977 there were 15,200 co-operatives in the North averaging 300–500 hectares (less than 100 hectares in mountain regions) and a workforce of 1,000–2,000. There were 105 state farms employing in all 70,000 workers and with 55,000 hectares arable and 50,000 hectares of pasture. Other crops include maize, sugar-cane, sweet potatoes and cotton. The cultivated area in 1973 was 3·4m. hectares; in 1964, 2·4m. hectares were irrigated.

In the South to redress the disproportionate urbanization of the southern population during the war (40% of the population were living in Ho Chi Minh City by April 1975) resettlement of family units in rural areas began after the Communist take-over. Each family was allotted an average of 5,000 sq. metres of land, a dwelling and agricultural equipment. 1,000 sq. metres of this total are for private plots. Families are grouped by twenties in 'mutual aid and labour cells'. Rice is the main crop cultivated. In 1972, 2·7m. hectares yielded 6·3m. tonnes of paddy; in 1972, 83,300 hectares produced 20,000 tonnes of rubber. In 1977 there were 74 state farms and a few experimental co-operatives. Co-operativization is expected to be complete by 1980.

The production figures of other crops, 1972, were as follows: Maize (41,700 tons from 35,500 hectares), sugar-cane (331,000 tons from 12,400 hectares), tobacco (8,800 tons from 9,400 hectares), sweet potatoes (240,500 tons from 38,000 hectares), manioc (247,300 tons from 32,100 hectares), peanuts (38,900 tons from 35,200 hectares), tea (5,100 tons), coffee (3,900 tons), timber (660,345 cu. metres).

Livestock, 1973: Cattle 2·5m.; pigs, 4·5m.; poultry, 30m.

Forestry. 50% of the North is forested; 10·95m. cu. metres of timber were produced in 1964.

Fisheries. Fishing is important, especially in Halong Bay. In 1976, 6m. tonnes of sea fish and 180,000 tonnes of freshwater fish were caught (representing only 83% of the planned target.)

INDUSTRY AND TRADE

Industry. In the North next to mining, food processing and textiles are the most important industries; there is also some machine building. Older industries include cement, cotton and silk manufacture. Local industries and handicrafts account for 50% of production.

Production in 1964 (in 1,000 tonnes): Coal, 3,410; steel, 50; cement, 595; paper, 19·4; sugar, 26·7; mineral fertilizers, 177; cotton fabrics, 105·2m. metres; irrigation pumps, 2,064 units.

In the South 5 types of enterprise exist: state-owned, co-operative, mixed co-operative, national capitalist and private, the latter tending to be grouped in 'production cells'. Foreign firms, principally French, are continuing to function, but all US property has been nationalized. There is little heavy industry. Most industry is concentrated in the Ho Chi Minh area and comprised, under the former Government, rice-milling, brewing, distilling, ice-making, cotton spinning and weaving, the manufacture of gunny bags, cement, paper and tyres, the assembly of radios, motor scooters, sewing-machines and bicycles, the manufacture of tobacco products and matches, the production of oxygen, acetylene and carbonic acid gases, and the processing of duck feathers. There are also small factories making soap, paint, ballpoint pens, pencils, articles in plastic, ceramic tiles, aluminium hollow-ware, dry-cell batteries, fruit and fish conserves, etc.

The following are some figures of production in 1972: Beer, 143·1m. litres; soft drinks, 115·6m. litres; rice alcohol, 12·3m. litres; ice, 309,000 tonnes; acetylene gas, 211,000 cu. metres; carbon dioxide, 102 tonnes.

The textile industry was developed with the active help of Chinese technicians and some American investment. A total of 170,000 spindles and 24,000 looms had been installed by Dec. 1971.

Kenaf yarn production was severely affected by the war. From a peak of 3,185 tons in 1965, production fell to 1,615 tons in 1972.

Total production of paper products reached 46,376 tons in 1972.

In 1967 trade unions had 1·1m. members.

Commerce. USSR and China are Vietnam's main trading partners; others are Japan, Singapore and Hong Kong. Main exports are coal, farm produce, sea produce and livestock. Imports: technical equipment, industrial raw materials, foodstuffs and medical supplies. The Vietnamese Government recognizes a need for foreign aid and credit for the development of an industrial base. The USSR has given substantial aid, and aid agreements were concluded in 1976 with Japan and in 1976 and 1977 with France. On 14 Oct. 1977 the UN ratified a recommendation of its Economic Commission that international aid should be given for the reconstruction of Vietnam's economy. Foreign investments are encouraged and guaranteed for 15 years. Profits may be transferred and indemnities paid in the event of nationalization. In the case of foreign firms installed in Vietnam all capital may remain in foreign hands if goods are produced for export only; otherwise the Vietnamese Government will retain 51% of shares.

Trade between Vietnam and UK (British Department of Trade returns, in £1,000 sterling):

		1973	*1974*	*1975*	*1976*	*1977*[1]
(*North*)	Imports to UK	58	299	286	1,168	4,859
	Exports and re-exports from UK	83	215	146	566	261
(*South*)	Imports to UK	229	303	122	58	—
	Exports and re-exports from UK	2,182	1,592	491	358	—

[1] Unified Vietnam.

COMMUNICATIONS

Roads. In 1973 there were about 9,500 km of roads in the North. In 1970 there were 20,905 km of roads in the South. Of these, 5,908 km were asphalted.

Railways. 'Project Reunification', the rebuilding of the Hanoi–Ho Chi Minh City railway, is a major part of the new authorities' programme to repair and extend all communications systems and link them with the North. The Da Nang–Hue railway was reopened in 1975. Important sections of railway have been reconstructed rapidly since the cessation of hostilities in 1975, and through trains commenced running again between Hanoi and Ho Chi Minh City in Jan. 1977.

Aviation. Civil Aviation of Vietnam operates internal services from Hanoi to Ho Chi Minh City, Cao Bang, Na Son and Dien Bien, Vinh and Hue, and from Ho Chi Minh City to Ban Me Thuot and Da Nang, Can Tho, Con Son Island and Quan Long.

The Civil Aviation Administration of China maintains scheduled services to Hanoi (Gia Lam airport) from Peking and Nanning. Aeroflot (USSR) operate regular services from Hanoi to Moscow, Rangoon and Vientiane, Interflug (German Dem. Rep.) to Berlin, Moscow and Dacca and Air France to Paris.

Shipping. The major ports are Haiphong, which can handle ships of 10,000 tons, Ho Chi Minh City and Da Nang, and there are ports at Hong Gai and Haiphong Ben Thuy. There are regular services to Hong Kong, Singapore, Democratic Kampuchea and Japan. In 1953 there were 830 km of navigable waterways in the North and, in 1971, 4,783 km in the South.

Cargo is handled by the Vietnam Ocean Shipping Agency; other matters by the Vietnam Foreign Trade Transport Corporation.

Post and Broadcasting. Postal and telegraphic communications with China were opened in 1955; and international mail for the UK is now carried by this route. In 1966 there were 1·4m. radios. There were 46,509 telephones in the South in 1974.

Cinemas. There were 41 cinemas in North Vietnam in 1961.

Newspapers. The Communist Party daily is *Nhan Dan* ('The People'). The official daily in the South is *Giai Phong*. Two unofficial dailies, *Cong Giao Va Dan Toc* (Catholic) and *Tin Sang* (independent) are also published.

JUSTICE, RELIGION, EDUCATION AND WELFARE

Justice. There are the Supreme People's Court, local people's courts and military courts. The president of the Supreme Court is responsible to the National Assembly, as is the Procurator-General, who heads the Supreme People's Office of Supervision and Control.

Religion. Taoism is the traditional religion but Buddhism is widespread. The Hoa Hao sect, associated with Buddhism, claimed 1·5m. adherents in 1976. Caodaism, a synthesis of Christianity, Buddhism and Confucianism founded in 1926, has some 2m. followers. There are some 3·5m. Roman Catholics headed by the Archbishop of Hanoi, Cardinal Trinh Nhu Khue.

Education. Primary education consists of a 10-year course divided into 3 levels of 4, 3 and 3 years respectively. In 1977–78 in Vietnam as a whole there were 13m. pupils and students including 1m. at kindergartens and 1m. attending part-time instruction. In North Vietnam in 1973–74 there were 11,563 general education schools, and 237 colleges and vocational middle schools. In 1974–75 there were 161,200 all-level general education teachers.

In the South the former education system is being reorganized and all private and church schools have been placed under state control. At the start of the academic year 1975–76 there were 10,360 schools. There are also 're-education' programmes (*hoc tap*) for adults and anti-illiteracy drives.

In 1977–78 there were 47 institutions of higher education (including 3 universities (Hanoi, Ho Chi Minh City, Central Highlands University at Ban Me Thuot), 13 industrial colleges, 7 agricultural colleges, 5 economics colleges, 9 teacher-training colleges, 7 medical schools and 3 art schools. In 1974 there were 3,000 Vietnamese studying in the USSR.

Health. In 1965 there were over 2,000 doctors and 480 hospitals.

DIPLOMATIC REPRESENTATIVES

OF VIETNAM IN GREAT BRITAIN (12–14 Victoria Rd, London, W8)

Ambassador: Tran Hoan (accredited 19 May 1978).

OF GREAT BRITAIN IN VIETNAM

Ambassador: J. W. D. Margetson.

Books of Reference

Buttinger, J., *Vietnam: A Political History*. London, 1969
Chen, J. H.-M., *Vietnam: A Comprehensive Bibliography*. London, 1973
Gallucci, R. L., *Neither Peace Nor Honor*. Johns Hopkins Univ. Press, 1975
Ho Chi Minh, *On Revolution: Selected Writings, 1920–66*. London, 1967
Le Thanh Khoi, *Socialisme et Développement au Vietnam*. Paris, 1978
Le Van Hung, *Vietnamese–English Dictionary*. Paris, 1955
Phan Thien Chau, *Vietnamese Communism: A Research Bibliography*. Westport (Conn.), 1975
Pic, R., *Le Vietnam d'Ho Chi Minh*. Paris, 1976

BRITISH VIRGIN ISLANDS

Capital: Tortola
Population: 10,030 (1975)

HISTORY. The Virgin Islands were discovered by Colombus on his second voyage in 1493. The British Virgin Islands were first settled by the Dutch in 1648 and taken over in 1666 by a group of English planters.

AREA AND POPULATION. The British Virgin Islands form the eastern extremity of the Greater Antilles and, exclusive of small rocks and reefs, number 36, of which 16 are inhabited. The largest are Tortola (1970 population, 8,866), Virgin Gorda (904), Anegada (269) and Jost Van Dyke (123). Other islands in the group have a total population of 68. Total area about 59 sq. miles (130 sq. km); population (1975), 10,030. Road Town, on the south-east of Tortola, is a port of entry; population, approximately 3,500.

CONSTITUTION AND GOVERNMENT. The Governor is responsible for defence and internal security, external affairs, the public service, and the courts. The Executive Council consists of the Governor, 1 *ex-officio* member and 3 ministers from the Legislature. The Legislative Council consists of 1 *ex-officio* member, as the Financial Secretary has been replaced by the Minister of Finance who is the Chief Minister, 1 nominated member and 7 elected members; the Speaker is elected from outside the Council.

Governor: W. W. Wallace, CBE, DSC.
Flag: The British Blue Ensign with the arms of the Colony in the fly.

ECONOMY

Planning. The Government's capital programme in 1975–78 continues to concentrate on improvements to roads, further primary school rebuilding; the first phase of the new hospital as an extension to the present building was already in progress in 1977.

Budget. In 1976 revenue was US$5,926,800; expenditure US$6,660,948. Capital expenditure was US$2,027,044, most of it provided by Development Aid Grants.

Currency. The unit of currency is the US dollar.

Banking. Barclays Bank International, the First Pennsylvania Bank, the Bank of Nova Scotia, the Chase Manhattan Bank and the Commercial Bank of Tortola have branches in the islands.

INDUSTRY AND TRADE

Industry. Agricultural production is now very limited with the chief products being livestock (including poultry) fish, fruit and vegetables. The export trade is carried on almost entirely with the Virgin Islands of the USA. The main industry is tourism and related activities, notably construction.

Trade. In 1975 imports were US$13·7m. and exports US$39,807.

EDUCATION AND WELFARE

Education. Primary education is provided in 14 government schools, 3 private primary schools and 5 private infant schools. Total number of pupils (Dec. 1976) 1,906.

Secondary education to the GCE level is provided at the B.V.I. High School. Total pupils in Dec. 1976, 821.

In 1976 the total number of teachers in all the schools was 162.

Health. In 1974 there were 7 doctors and 42 hospital beds.

Books of Reference

Biennial Report 1971. HMSO
Report of Constitutional Commissioner, 1965. HMSO, 1965
Dookhan, I., *A History of the British Virgin Islands.* Epping, 1975

Library: Public Library, Road Town. *Librarian:* Miss Verna Penn, ALA.

WESTERN SAMOA

Capital: Apia
Population: 151,275 (1976)
GNP per capita: US$350 (1976)

Samoa i Sisifo

HISTORY. Western Samoa, a former German protectorate (1900 to the First World War), was administered by New Zealand from 1920 to 1961, at first under a League of Nations Mandate and since 1946 under a United Nations Trusteeship Agreement. In May 1961 a plebiscite held under the supervision of the United Nations on the basis of universal adult suffrage voted overwhelmingly in favour of independence as from 1 Jan. 1962, on the basis of the Constitution, which a Constitutional Convention had adopted in Aug. 1960. In Oct. 1961 the General Assembly of the United Nations passed a resolution to terminate the trusteeship agreement as from 1 Jan. 1962, on which date Western Samoa became an independent sovereign state.

Under a treaty of friendship signed on 1 Aug. 1962 New Zealand acts, at the request of Western Samoa, as the official channel of communication between the Samoan Government and other governments and international organizations outside the Pacific islands area. Liaison is maintained by the New Zealand High Commissioner in Apia, who is the only diplomatic representative accredited to the Government of Western Samoa.

AREA AND POPULATION. Western Samoa lies between 13° and 15° S. lat. and 171° and 173° W. long. It comprises the two large islands of Savai'i and Upolu, the small islands of Manono and Apolima, and several uninhabited islets lying off the coast. The total land area is 1,097 sq. miles (2,842 sq. km), of which 662 sq. miles are in Savai'i, and 433 sq. miles in Upolu. The islands are of volcanic origin, and the coasts are surrounded by coral reefs. Rugged mountain ranges form the core of both main islands and rise to 3,608 ft in Upolu and 6,094 ft in Savai'i. The large area laid waste by lava-flows in Savai'i is a primary cause of that island supporting less than one-third of the population of the islands despite its greater size than Upolu.

The population at the 1976 census (provisional) was 151,275, of whom 109,787 were in Upolu (including Manono and Apolima) and 41,488 in Savai'i. The capital and chief port is Apia in Upolu (population approximately 30,000 in 1976).

CONSTITUTION AND GOVERNMENT. The Constitution provides for a Head of State known as 'Ao o le Malo', which position from 1 Jan. 1962 was held jointly by the representatives of the two royal lines of Tuiaana/Tuiatua and Malietoa. On the death of HH Tupua Tamasese Mea'ole, CBE, on 5 April 1963, HH Malietoa Tanumafili II, CBE, became, as provided by the constitution, the sole Head of State for life.

Future Heads of State will be elected by the Legislative Assembly and hold office for 5-year terms.

The executive power is vested in the Head of State, who appoints the Prime Minister and, on the Prime Minister's advice, the 8 Ministers to form the Cabinet which has general direction and control of the executive Government.

Parliament comprises the Head of State and the Legislative Assembly. The Legislative Assembly has 45 members elected from territorial constituencies on a franchise confined to matais or chiefs (of whom there are about 11,000) and 2 members elected on universal adult suffrage from the individual voters roll, which has replaced the old European roll (approximately 1,350 in 1971).

The official languages are English and Samoan.

Head of State: HH Malietoa Tanumafili II, CBE.
Prime Minister: Tupuola Efi.
National flag: Red with a blue quarter bearing 5 white stars of the Southern Cross.

INTERNATIONAL RELATIONS

Membership. Western Samoa is a member of UN, the Commonwealth and is an ACP state of EEC.

ECONOMY

Budget. In 1978 budgeted revenue was $WS22·3m.; expenditure, $WS17·7m.; statutary expenditure, $WS1·6m.

Currency. On 10 July 1966 Western Samoa changed over to decimal currency. The Western Samoa *talā* (dollar) is at parity with the NZ dollar, equally £0·50. Currency in circulation consists of Samoan Treasury notes and coins.

Banking. In 1959 the Bank of Western Samoa was established with a capital of $WS500,000, of which $WS275,000 was subscribed by the Bank of New Zealand and $WS225,000 by the Government of Western Samoa. In 1977 the Pacific Commercial Bank was established jointly by Australia's Bank of New South Wales and the Bank of Hawaii.

COMMERCE. In 1977, imports were valued at $WS28m. (estimated) and exports at $WS8·5m. Principal exports were copra (11,921 tons; $WS1,893,800), taro and ta'amu (77,450 tons; $WS363,400) and timber (446,700 ft; $WS63,000). Chief imports in 1976 included meat ($WS1,647,000), petroleum ($WS1,894,000) and machinery and transport equipment ($WS5·16m.).

Total trade between Western Samoa and UK (British Department of Trade returns, in £1,000 sterling):

	1972	*1973*	*1974*	*1975*	*1976*	*1977*
Imports to UK	124	372	322	911	201	776
Exports and re-exports from UK	1,116	987	387	507	449	609

COMMUNICATIONS

Roads (1976). Western Samoa has over 244 miles of main roads, 101 miles of municipal secondary and village roads and 195 miles of plantation roads fit for light traffic. A major road development programme has been under way including an all-weather coastal road and a cross-island road, both for Upolu. A rural access roads programme to improve access to plantations is also underway. In 1976 there were 2,525 passenger cars and 955 commercial vehicles.

Aviation. Western Samoa is linked by daily air service with American Samoa, which is on the route of the weekly New Zealand–Tahiti and New Zealand–Honolulu air services, with connexions to Fiji, Australia, USA and Europe. There are also services throughout the week to and from Tonga, Fiji, Nauru, the Cook Islands and New Zealand. Internal services link Upolu and Savai'i.

Shipping. Western Samoa is linked to Japan, USA, Europe, Fiji, Australia and New Zealand by regular shipping services. The newly established Pacific Forum Shipping Line has its headquarters in Apia.

Post and Broadcasting. There is a radio communication station at Apia. Radio telephone service connects Western Samoa with American Samoa, Fiji, New Zealand, Australia, Canada, USA and UK. Telephone subscribers numbered 3,300 in 1977.

Cinemas. In 1974 there were 10 cinemas with a seating capacity of 1,600.

EDUCATION. In 1976 there were 160 primary, 40 intermediate and 15 secondary schools with a total of 48,736 pupils. There is also a trades training institute, a teacher-training college, a broadcasting training centre and a college of agriculture.

DIPLOMATIC REPRESENTATIVE

OF THE UK IN WESTERN SAMOA

High Commissioner: H. Smedley, CMG, MBE (resides in Wellington, New Zealand).

OF WESTERN SAMOA IN THE USA AND ALSO TO THE UNITED NATIONS

Ambassador: Maiava Iulai Toma.

Books of Reference

Statistical Year-Book. 1976
Economic Prospects 1978
The Economy of Western Samoa. 1968
Clare, B. L., *A Review of Social. Labour and Economic Conditions in Western Samoa*. Apia, 1962, reprinted 1963.—*The Parliament of Western Samoa*. Rev. ed. Apia, 1964
Fox, J. W. (ed.), *Western Samoa*. Univ. of Auckland, 1963
Milner, G. B., *Samoan–English, English–Samoan Dictionary*. OUP, 1965

WEST INDIES

HISTORY. The West Indies Federation, established on 3 Jan. 1958, was dissolved in Feb. 1962 after Jamaica and Trinidad had opted out of it.

In 1967 new constitutional arrangements were made for the 'West Indies Associated States', Antigua, St Kitts–Nevis–Anguilla (on 27 Feb.), Dominica, St Lucia (on 1 March), Grenada (on 3 March) and St Vincent (on 1 June) were given self-government in association with Britain which retains powers and responsibilities for defence and external affairs. Grenada became independent in Feb. 1974.

DEFENCE. The responsibility for defence rests with the British Government. International relationships and defence policy are conducted in close consultation with the Associated States by the British Government Representative (J. S. Arthur).

CURRENCY. After Trinidad and British Guiana had withdrawn from the British Caribbean Currency Board, Barbados, the Leeward Islands (Antigua, St Kitts–Nevis–Anguilla, Montserrat), and the Windward Islands (St Vincent, St Lucia, Dominica) united under the East Caribbean Currency Authority to issue new currency notes of $1, 5, 20 and 100, with effect from 6 Oct. 1965. Barbados subsequently withdrew from ECCA and has established its own central bank.

On 1 April 1965, $69,860,809 notes and $5,824,343 coins were in circulation; demonetized government notes outstanding totalled $292,550. The liability for Trinidad and Tobago Government demonetized notes outstanding at 14 Dec. 1964 has been assumed by the Central Bank of Trinidad and Tobago and is therefore not included in the circulation for which the British Caribbean Currency Board is liable.

TRADE. The Caribbean Free Trade Area (CARIFTA now CARICOM) was established between Antigua, Barbados, Guyana, and Trinidad and Tobago on 1 May 1968; it was joined by Dominica, Grenada, St Kitts–Nevis–Anguilla, St Lucia and St Vincent on 1 July 1968, by Jamaica and Montserrat on 1 Aug. 1968 by the Bahamas and Belize. *See* International Organizations section in this edition.

SHIPPING. The West Indies Shipping Corporation continues to provide a regular shipping service for passengers and cargo, the West Indies Shipping Corporation Act 1961 continuing with adaptation to be part of the law of the territories, including Jamaica and Trinidad and Tobago.

The West Indies Meteorological Service continues on a completely reorganized basis. It also serves Guyana, British Honduras and British Virgin Islands.

TELECOMMUNICATIONS. The territories are linked by cable, radio-telegraph and radio-telephone. Cable & Wireless (W.I.) Ltd have installed a multi-channel tropospheric scatter-link between Trinidad and Barbados and a network of VHF circuits covering the other territories.

JUSTICE. The British Caribbean Court of Appeal has replaced the West Indies Associated States Court of Appeal, serving the Associated States. In each of the independent countries there is a Court of Appeal.

EDUCATION. The University College of the West Indies, situated at Mona, Jamaica, was affiliated to London University, but became independent in April 1962. It received a Royal Charter in 1949 and has faculties of Medicine, Arts, Natural Sciences and a Department of Education. The former Imperial College of Tropical Agriculture in Trinidad is the faculty of Agriculture and Engineering; a

College of Arts and Science has been added. Barbados also has a campus of the University of the West Indies where training is offered in Arts, Natural Science, the Social Science, and Law.

Books of Reference

A Survey of Economic Potential and Capital Needs of the Leeward Islands, Windward Islands and Barbados. HMSO, 1963
The West Indies and Caribbean Year Book. London, annual
Aspinall, Sir Algernon, *The Pocket Guide to the West Indies.* 10th ed. London, 1954
Aycarst, X., *The British West Indies: The Search for Self-government.* London, 1960
Burns, Sir Alan, *History of the British West Indies.* 2nd ed. London, 1965
Mordecai, J., *The West Indies.* London, 1968
Parry, J. H., and Sherlock, P. M., *A Short History of the West Indies.* London, 1956
Phillips, Sir F., *Freedom in the Caribbean.* New York, 1977
Proudfoot, M., *Britain and the United States in the Caribbean.* London, 1954

Leeward and Windward Islands

HISTORY. A new Constitution was introduced for the Leeward and Windward Islands in 1967, called Statehood in Association. For earlier constitutions *see* THE STATESMAN'S YEAR-BOOK, 1972–73, p. 506. This is really a quasi-independent status whereby each State is responsible for its own internal affairs while Britain retains responsibility for external affairs and defence. Montserrat, though, did not opt for this improved constitution and so remains a Crown Colony.

For the new Associated States, this Legislature is bicameral in Antigua, Grenada, Dominica and St Vincent, while in St Kitts and St Lucia it is unicameral.

Administrators have been replaced by Governors representing the Queen, who can only act on the advice of the Premiers.

Each State has its own police force and its own police Service Commission.

Reports by the Leeward and Windward Islands Constitutional Conference, 1961. (Cmd 1434)

Leeward Islands. The group, which lies to the north of the Windward group, and south-east of Puerto Rico, consists of Antigua (with Barbuda and Redonda) and St Christopher–Nevis and Anguilla is administered by a Commissioner in consultation with the Anguilla Council.

The chief products are sugar and molasses (St Kitts), cotton (Antigua, Montserrat, St Kitts–Nevis), limes and fruits, vegetables, cotton seed (Montserrat), salt (Anguilla and St Kitts) and livestock, fish, vegetables, fruit and charcoal (Virgin Islands).

ANTIGUA

Area and population, 108 sq. miles (280 sq. km); the islands of Barbuda (62 sq. miles, 160 sq. km) and Redonda (1 sq. mile) are dependencies; population in 1975 was 69,700. Chief town, St John's, 13,000. In 1974 the birth rate per 1,000 was 18·3, the death rate 7·1; there were (1963) 203 marriages.

In Nov. 1940 sites near Parham were leased to the USA as military and naval bases; in Dec. 1960, 900 acres including Coolidge airfield were released; 300 acres are being retained for 17 years.

Governor: Sir Wilfred Jacobs, QC.

Premier: Hon. Vere C. Bird, Sen.

Flag: Red, with a triangle based on the top edge, divided horizontally black, blue, white, with a rising sun in gold on the black portion.

Finance and Trade. The budget for 1976 was $52,052,526. Imports (1974), $143,749,504; exports, $66,468,288. The chief product is cotton, 178,804 lb. in 1976. Tourism is of increasing importance (1976, 62,971 visitors).

Total trade of Antigua, St Christopher and Montserrat with UK (British Department of Trade returns, in £1,000 sterling):

	1973	*1974*	*1975*	*1976*	*1977*
Imports to UK	1,415	2,532	4,483	3,286	4,547
Exports and re-exports from UK	6,627	6,303	9,283	19,004	14,152

Banking. In government savings bank, 4,917 depositors on 31 Dec. 1971, $432,277 deposits. Barclays Bank International, Royal Bank of Canada, Canadian Imperial Bank of Commerce, the Virgin Islands National Bank, the Antilles International Trust Co. and the Bank of Nova Scotia have branches at St John's. The Antigua Co-operative Bank was opened in Jan. 1965.

Shipping. The main harbour is the St John's deep water harbour. There are 2 tugs for the berthing of ships and all modern and efficient general cargo handling equipment. The harbour can also accommodate 3 large cruise ships simultaneously.

Post. Telephone lines, 720 miles; 3,104 telephones. There are air-mail service connexions with the rest of the world.

Education. In 1974 there were 67 schools with 484 teachers and 22,000 pupils.

Library: Public Library, St John's. *Librarian:* Mrs Phyllis Meyers.

DOMINICA

Area and Population, 289·5 sq. miles (728 sq. km). Census population, 1970, 70,302 (males, 33,550, females, 36,752), estimate, 1976, 78,000. Chief town, Roseau (population, about 10,157). Dominica contains a Carib settlement with a population of about 500, nearly all of whom are of mixed blood.

Constitution and Government. On 1 March 1967 Dominica received a new constitution. A Constitutional Conference to prepare the way for independence will be held in 1977.

The House of Assembly has 21 elected and 3 nominated members, 1 nominated on the advice of the Leader of the Opposition. The Speaker is elected from among the members of the House or from outside. The Cabinet is presided over by the Premier and consists of 5 other Ministers and the Attorney-General (official member). The Premier is appointed by the Governor from the elected members of the House of Assembly. The other Ministers are appointed by the Governor on the advice of the Premier.

Governor: Sir Louis Cools-Lartigue, OBE.
Premier: Patrick Roland John.
Flag: The British Blue Ensign with the arms of Dominica in the fly.

Finance. Revenue, 1973, $18,590,695 (including $4,108,566 from British development aid fund, and $1,932,038 loan funds); expenditure, $21,226,643; public debt, $7,710,750.

Banking. Savings bank (1974), 2,954 depositors, with $571,794 deposits. There are branches of Barclays Bank International, Royal Bank of Canada and Dominica Co-operative Bank in Roseau, a branch of Barclays at Portsmouth and agencies of Barclays at Marigot and Grand Bay. The National Commercial and Development Bank was opened in 1977.

Trade (1975). Imports, $45,036,389 c.i.f.; exports, $24,646,717. Chief products: Bananas, soap, fruit juices, essential oils, cocoa, coconuts, vegetables, fruit and fruit preparations, and alcoholic drinks. Exports (1975) of cocoa, 60 long tons ($226,366); bananas, 27,917 tons ($14,407,117); coconut oil, 16,272 lb. ($172,728); essential oils, 36,284 lb. ($672,394); citrus fruits, 7,990,486 lb. ($3,154,236); soap, 404 tons ($574,628); fruit juices, 115,796 gallons ($1,017,197); vegetables, 702 tons ($487,870).

Tourism. Tourists (1974) totalled 18,996.

Post. Telephone lines, 272·5 route miles; number of telephones, 2,679 (1975).

Cinemas. In 1970 there were 3 cinemas with a seating capacity of 1,500.

Justice. There are 4 magistrates' courts. They dealt with 11 civil and 3,274 criminal cases in 1973. The police force consists of 10 officers and 247 other ranks.

Library: Public Library, Roseau. *Librarian:* Miss C. Henry.

ST CHRISTOPHER (ST KITTS), NEVIS AND ANGUILLA

Area and Population. The area is 136 sq. miles (272 sq. km): St Kitts, 65; Nevis, 36; Anguilla, 35. Population, 1976: St Kitts, 36,100; Nevis, 11,900; Anguilla, 6,500. Chief town of St Kitts, Basseterre (population, 15,897); of Nevis, Charlestown (population, 1,530).

Constitution and Government. In Feb. 1967 the colonial status was replaced by an 'association' with Britain, giving the islands full internal self-government, while Britain remains responsible for defence and foreign affairs. There is an elected House of Assembly and a Cabinet system of Government. The Premier is the head of the Government and presides at Cabinet meetings.

Governor: Sir Probyn Inniss, MBE.

Flag: Three vertical strips of green, yellow, blue with black palm tree in centre.

Finance. The 1977 budget balanced at EC$29·6m. Grant for airport improvement from UK in 1974–75, £1·1m. (1973–74, £1·1m.). Grant aid from UK, 1974–5, £400,000 (1973–74, £400,000).

Banking. There is a branch of Barclays Bank International, of the Royal Bank of Canada and of the Bank of America at Basseterre, a sub-branch of Barclays Bank at Charlestown and a branch of the Swiss bank in Anguilla. Local banks are the St Kitts–Nevis–Anguilla National Bank in Basseterre and the Nevis Co-operative Banking Co. Ltd in Nevis.

Trade. Imports, 1966, $15,817,508; exports, $8,614,875. Chief exports were: Sugar ($7,599,641), molasses ($207,791), cotton ($178,328) and salt ($168,170).

Post. There were 2,242 telephones on 1 Jan. 1977 in St Kitts.

Education (1977). There were 29 government primary and senior schools and 6 denominational; 6 government and 2 private secondary schools. A teachers' college prepares approximately 30 teachers annually in a 2-year course.

Library: Public Library, Basseterre. *Librarian:* Miss V. Archibald.

Anguilla, although technically part of the Associated State of St Kitts–Nevis–Anguilla, is administered as a dependent territory and now has its own Constitution and Ministerial form of Government. The Anguilla (Constitution) Order 1976 (made under the Anguilla Act 1971) came into operation on 10 Feb. 1976. Provision is made in the Constitution for a Legislative Assembly, comprising 7 elected members, 2 nominated members and 3 *ex-officio* members, and for an Executive Council comprising the Chief Minister, 2 other Ministers and 2 *ex-officio* members. The Constitution provides for the Executive authority of Anguilla to be exercised by HM Commissioner. The Constitution of St Kitts–Nevis–Anguilla now no longer applies in and in relation to Anguilla.

British Commissioner: C. H. Godden.

Sombrero is a small island in the Leeward Islands group, attached to the Colony of St Kitts–Nevis–Anguilla; area, 2 sq. miles. Phosphate of lime exists in limited quantities. There is a Board of Trade lighthouse.

Windward Islands. The group consists of Grenada, St Vincent, the Grenadines (half under St Vincent, half under Grenada), St Lucia and Dominica, and form the eastern barrier to the Caribbean Sea between Martinique and Trinidad.

Total trade with UK (British Department of Trade returns, in £1,000 sterling):

	1972	*1973*	*1974*	*1975*	*1976*	*1977*
Imports to UK	9,894	11,581	18,300	19,580	21,672	24,338
Exports and re-exports from UK	10,013	10,361	12,251	15,289	13,318	15,635

ST LUCIA

Area and Population, 238 sq. miles (616 sq. km); population (1975) 114,000. The capital is Castries (population, 45,000). Vital statistics (1974): Births, 3,909; deaths, 829.

Governor: Sir Allen Lewis.
Prime Minister: J. G. M. Compton.
Flag: Blue with a design of a black triangle edged in white, bearing a smaller yellow triangle, in the centre.

Finance. Estimated revenue in 1974 (including Colonial Development and Welfare schemes and overseas aid scheme) was $37·1m.; estimated expenditure, $36·7m.
Public debt, 31 Dec. 1974, $2·5m.

Banking. There are Barclays Bank International with 2 branches and 4 agencies, the Royal Bank of Canada, the Bank of Nova Scotia and the Canadian Imperial Bank of Commerce (all of which have 1 branch each), the Chase Manhattan Bank, the St Lucia Co-operative Bank and the Government Savings Bank. The Government Savings Bank (end of 1974), 8,400 depositors, $359,086 deposits.

Agriculture. Bananas, cocoa, copra and coconut oil are the chief products.

Trade. Value of imports (1974), $91,114,926; of exports, $32,908,783, including coconut oil, cocoa beans, copra and bananas. Main items of imports were artificial silk and cotton piece-goods, cement, plastic goods, iron and steel products, hardware, motor vehicles, agricultural machinery, fertilizers, wheat flour, codfish and rice, meat and meat preparation.

Tourism. The total number of visitors during 1974 was 51,816; their estimated expenditure was $9,874,030.

Roads. The island has 500 miles of main and secondary roads.

Aviation. The island is served on a scheduled basis by Leeward Islands Air Transport, British West Indian Airways and Eastern Airline. There are 2 airfields—Hewanorra International Airport, with 9,000 ft runway, and Vigie.

Shipping. Registered fleet (31 Dec. 1974): 3 motor vessels (94 gross tons). In 1974, 2,798 vessels of 3·5m. gross tons entered Castries and Vieux Fort.

Post. There are 104 miles of telephone trunk lines, plus 300 miles of local lines. There are 6,630 telephone instruments coupled to 3,423 exchange lines. They operate through 12 automatic exchanges.

Cinemas. There were 9 cinemas in 1970 with a seating capacity of 9,500.

Justice. The island is divided into 2 judicial districts, and there are 9 magistrates' courts. Appeals lie with the Court of Appeal of the Windward and Leeward Islands, subject to exceptions and conditions as may be enacted by the St Lucia legislature.
In 1974 the Supreme Court dealt with 91 civil and 33 criminal cases.
Police establishment in 1974 was 11 officers, 11 inspectors and 267 others.

Education (31 Dec. 1974). 74 primary schools (51 Roman Catholic, 3 Anglican, 3 Methodist, 17 government), with 30,000 pupils on roll; government expenditure, 1974, $5,526,945. Primary education is free and compulsory by law, but the legislation is not enforced. There are 12 secondary schools (2 Roman Catholic, 1 Seventh Day Adventist, 9 government) with 4,600 pupils. There is 1 technical college with 250 students.

Library: The Central Library, Castries. *Librarian:* Mrs Mary Prescod.

ST VINCENT

Area and Population, 150·3 sq. miles (389 sq. km); population, estimate, 1976, 109,743. Capital, Kingstown, population, 22,000. Vital statistics (1976): Live births, 3,783; still births, 59; deaths, 772.

Governor: Sir Sydney Gun-Munro.
Premier: R. Milton Cato.
Flag: The British Blue Ensign with the badge of St Vincent in the fly.

Finance. Revenue (estimate), 1977–78, $28,613,288, including budgetary assistance, $1,555,988; development aid, $7,802,354, and other sources, $11,103,068; expenditure, $28,613,288, including $7,802,354 on colonial development and welfare schemes and $11,103,068 on other schemes. Public debt at the end of the financial year 1976–77 was $10,253,874.

Banking. There are branches of Barclays Bank International, the Royal Bank of Canada and the Canadian Imperial Bank of Commerce at Kingstown.

Production. The estimated alienated area is about 47,000 of the total acreage of 85,120. 34,000 acres are under forest and woodland; of these about 5,000 acres are used for grazing; 3,000 are considered potentially productive for agriculture and 5,000 for forestry. About 14,000 acres are considered unsuitable for either agriculture or forestry and approximately 6,000 acres are built on roads, rivers, etc. Of the total alienated area, 34,000 acres are considered arable land, of which 20,000 acres are under temporary crops, 4,000 acres under temporary meadows, 300 acres devoted to market-garden crops with temporary fallow and all other arable land making up a further 9,700 acres. About 2,000 acres are under permanent meadow, of which 750 are cultivated.

Bananas, arrowroot flour, copra, carrots, sweet potatoes, yams, tannias and other starchy roots, nutmegs and mace and small amounts of peanuts are produced. The Territory is largely self-supporting in vegetables. St Vincent is renowned for its arrowroot starch.

Land ownership: Crown, 38,000 acres; planters, 17,000 acres; small farmers, 25,500 acres; settlements, 6,000 acres.

The electricity system is owned and operated by the St Vincent Electricity Services (CDC). The system consists of 3 power stations: Colonarie Hydro (716 kw.); Kingstown Diesel (1,460 kw.) and Richmond Hydro (1,100 kw.), which are linked by 11,000-volt transmission lines covering the island from Richmond through Kingstown to Georgetown. Current is supplied at 400 volts 3-phase, 50 cycles for industrial purposes and 230 volts single phase for domestic purposes. There are 6,250 consumers.

Labour (1975). The Department of Labour serves both workers 'and employers' organizations as a conciliatory body in case of dispute. Conciliatory meetings are held on dispute matters such as delay in the recognition of a union as collective bargaining agent for the workers, dismissals, overtime pay, delay in finalizing collective agreement and other conditions of work. There are 5 registered trade unions: Federated Industrial and Agricultural Workers Union, the St Vincent Union of Teachers, the Civil Service Association, the Commercial, Technical and Allied Workers' Union, and the St Vincent Workers' Union. The St Vincent Employers Federation continued to render services on behalf of the employers.

Trade (1975). Imports, $53,834,730; exports, $15,517,218. Value of imports from the UK, $14,440,919; of exports to the UK, $8,805,735 (plus bullion and specie).

Principal exports, 1974:

		$EC			*$EC*
Arrowroot starch	2,332,237 lb.	868,874	Sweet potatoes	3,876,009 lb.	642,195
Carrots	1,385,355 lb.	642,195	Nutmegs	267,472 lb.	539,297
Bananas	48,564,488 lb.	7,986,691	Mace	47,159 lb.	68,746

Tourism. There were 19,242 visitors in 1975.

Communication. There are 200 miles of all-weather roads, 260 miles of rough motorable roads and 250 miles of tracks.

There is a General Post Office at Kingstown and 40 district post offices. There is a telephone system with 1,200 miles of line and 4,875 subscribers, and a radio telephone service to Bequia in the Grenadines.

Shipping (1966): (*a*) 316 sailing vessels and schooners of 10,217 NRT entered, while 312 of 9,674 NRT cleared. (*b*) 398 steamships of 729,228 NRT entered the territory; of these 185 of 242,515 tons were British. (*c*) 379 steamships of 687,516 NRT cleared, 167 of 290,826 tons being British. (*d*) 34 tankers of 19,089 NRT entered and 39 of 23,230 NRT cleared. A deep-water harbour at Kingstown was completed in 1964.

Scheduled services are operated daily by LIAT and thrice weekly by Caribair. Passengers are able to travel daily through the chain of islands stretching as far north as San Juan, Puerto Rico and south to Trinidad. Connexions to the USA, Canada, South America and Europe are possible *via* Barbados, Antigua and Trinidad.

Cinemas. There were 3 cinemas in 1970 with a seating capacity of 2,400.

Justice (1975). There were 2,066 convictions in the 3 magistrates' courts. Strength of police force, 378 (including 9 officers).

Education (1976). Sixty primary schools; pupils on roll, 26,016, average attendance, 19,205. Expenditure on primary education, $2,918,805. There is also a secondary school for boys (556 pupils) and one for girls (749 pupils) as well as 11 assisted secondary schools (2,560 pupils) and 4 junior secondary schools with 820 pupils. Expenditure on secondary education, $644,230.

Biennial Report, 1964–65. HMSO, 1966

Library: St Vincent Public Library, Kingstown. *Librarian:* Mrs Lorna Small.

YEMEN ARAB REPUBLIC

Capital: San'a
Population: 5·24m. (1975)
GNP per capita: US$250 (1976)

al Jamhuriya al Arabiya al Yamaniya

HISTORY. On the death of the Iman Ahmad on 18 Sept. 1962, army officers seized power on 26–27 Sept., declared his son, Saif Al-Islam Al-Badr (Iman Mansur Billah Muhammad), deposed and proclaimed a republic. The republican regime was supported by Egyptian troops, whereas the royalist tribes received aid from Saudi Arabia. On 24 Aug. 1965 President Nasser and King Faisal signed an agreement according to which the two powers are to support a plebiscite to determine the future of the Yemen; a conference of republican and royalist delegates met at Haradh on 23 Nov. 1965, but no plebiscite was agreed upon. At a meeting of the Arab heads of state in Aug. 1967 the President and the King agreed upon disengaging themselves from the civil war in Yemen. At the time there were still about 50,000 Egyptian troops in the country, holding San'a, Ta'iz, Hodeida and the plains, whereas the mountains are in the hands of the royalist tribes. By the end of 1967 the Egyptians had withdrawn.

The British Government recognized the Yemen Arab Republic in 1970.

AREA AND POPULATION. In the north the boundary between the Yemen and Saudi Arabia has been defined by the Treaty of Taif concluded in June 1934. This frontier starts from the sea at a point some 5 or 10 miles north of Maidi and runs due east inland until it reaches the hills some 30 miles from the coast, whence it runs northwards for approximately 50 miles so as to leave the Sa'da Basin within the Yemen. Thence it runs in an easterly and south-easterly direction until it reaches the desert area near Nejran. The area is about 73,300 sq. miles (195,000 sq. km) with a population of 5,237,893, census, 1975. The capital is San'a with a population of about 125,000.

The most important towns are the port of Hodeida (population, 100,000), San'a (150,000) and Ta'iz (100,000); other towns are Ibb, Yerim, Dhamar and the ports of Mokha and Loheiya.

There are nearly 1m. Yemenis abroad.

CONSTITUTION AND GOVERNMENT. On 31 Oct. 1962, 13 April 1963, 17 April 1964, 9 May 1965 the revolutionary council issued 'interim' constitutions and on 28 Dec. 1970 a first permanent constitution was announced with provision for a Council of 179 members (20 members would be chosen by the President and the remainder by general franchise).

On 11 Oct. 1977 the Head of State was assassinated. The Command Council appointed a Presidential Council, consisting of 3 members. The Command Council was dissolved in early 1978.

On 6 Feb. 1978 a 99-man People's Constituent Assembly was established.

President: Lieut.-Col. Ahmed Hussein Al-Ghashmi.

National flag: Three horizontal stripes of red, white, black, with a green star in the centre.

DEFENCE

Army. The Army consists of 10 infantry, 1 parachute and 3 commando brigades, 2 armoured battalions and supports. Strength: 37,000.

Navy. The Navy consists of 5 large patrol craft and 3 torpedo-boats. Personnel (1977) 750.

Air Force. Built up with Egyptian, Soviet and Czech aid, the Air Force has 12 MiG-21 and 12 MiG-17 jet fighters, 14 Il-28 light jet bombers, Il-14, C-47, An-24 and 2 Skyvan transports, Mi-4, Mi-8 and Agusta-Bell 204B helicopters and Yak-11 armed trainers. Some aircraft are believed to be in storage.

INTERNATIONAL RELATIONS

Membership. The Yemen Arab Republic is a member of UN and the Arab League.

ECONOMY

Planning. A development plan (1976–81) envisages expenditure of 16,500m. riyals. The largest allocations are for infrastructure development.

Budget. The budget for 1974–75 had estimated revenue, 366m. riyal; estimated expenditure, 510m. riyal, of which education and health, 266m.

Currency. The currency is the paper *riyal* of 100 *rial.* In May 1976, 8·12 *riyal* = £ and 4·51 *riyal* = US$1.

ENERGY AND NATURAL RESOURCES

Oil. In 1977 there were plans to build a refinery.

Minerals. The only commercial mineral being exploited is salt and (1974) production was 1m. tonnes. Reserves (estimate) 25m. tonnes.

Agriculture. Wherever water-supply allows, and in general throughout the south-western part of the country, millet (*dhurra*) is grown as a subsistence crop. The traditional cultivation of coffee (no longer exported through Mokha) continues but is giving place to that of *qat* (*cathula edulis*), a narcotic shrub. Cotton (production, 1971–72 15,000 tonnes) is grown in the Tihama, the coastal belt, round Bait al Faqih and Zabid (seat of a medieval university). Fruit is plentiful, especially fine grapes from the San'a district. There were 10·6m. sheep and goats in 1976.

INDUSTRY AND TRADE

Industry. There is very little industry. In 1970 there were over 60 industrial enterprises employing 4,750. The largest is a textile factory at San'a. A cement factory with a capacity of 100,000 tonnes a year exists.

Commerce. Imports totalled 1,163·4m. riyals in 1974–75 (204·43m. in 1971–72) the largest item being food and live animals. Exports totalled 58·5m. in 1974–75 (24·7m. in 1971–72). Japan provided 14·6% of the imports and China took 46·3% of the exports.

Trade with the UK (British Department of Trade returns, in £1,000 sterling):

	1973	*1974*	*1975*	*1976*	*1977*
Imports to UK	428	1,412	226	1,465	455
Exports and re-exports from UK	3,159	6,021	8,986	19,661	28,356

COMMUNICATIONS

Roads. There were (1974) 1,650 km of roads. An Anglo-Federal German consortium completed the surfacing of the San'a–Ta'iz road in 1975 and the same consortium was working on the Ta'iz–Mokha stretch in 1977.

Aviation. There are 3 international airports: San'a, Ta'iz (under construction) and Hodeida (which is to be extended).

Shipping. Hodeida, Mokha Salif and Loheiya are the 4 main ports.

Post. There were about 20,000 telephones in 1978.

DIPLOMATIC REPRESENTATIVES

OF YEMEN ARAB REPUBLIC IN GREAT BRITAIN
(41 Mount St., London, W1Y 5PD)

Ambassador: Mohamed A. Alerhani.

OF GREAT BRITAIN IN YEMEN ARAB REPUBLIC
(11/13 Qasr al Jumhuri St., San'a)

Ambassador: B. L. Strachan.

OF YEMEN ARAB REPUBLIC IN THE USA
(600 New Hampshire Ave., NW, Washington, D.C., 20037)

Ambassador: Yahya M. Al-Mutawakel.

OF THE USA IN YEMEN ARAB REPUBLIC (PO Box 33, San'a)

Ambassador: Thomas J. Scotes.

OF YEMEN ARAB REPUBLIC TO THE UNITED NATIONS

Ambassador: Ahmed Al-Haddad.

Books of Reference

Heyworth-Dunne, G. E., *Al-Yemen. Social, Political and Economic Survey.* Cairo, 1952
Ingrams, H., *The Yemen.* London, 1963
Macro, E., *Yemen and the Western World, 1571–1964.* London, 1967
Stookey, R. W., *Yemen: The Politics of the Yemen Arab Republic.* Boulder, 1978

THE PEOPLE'S DEMOCRATIC REPUBLIC OF YEMEN

Capital: Aden
Population: 1·6m. (1975)
GNP per capita: US$280 (1976)

Jumhurijah al-Yemen al Dimuqratiyah al Sha'abijah—Southern Yemen

HISTORY. Between Aug. and Oct. 1967 the 17 sultanates of the Federation of South Arabia (*see* MAP in the STATESMAN'S YEAR-BOOK, 1965–66) were overrun by the forces of the National Liberation Front (NLF). The rulers were deposed, resigned or fled. At the same time the rival organization of FLOSY (Front for the Liberation of Occupied South Yemen) fought a civil war against NLF and harassed the British forces and civilians in Aden. In November the UAR withdrew its support from FLOSY, and with the backing of the Army the NLF took over throughout the country.

The last British troops left Aden on 29 Nov., and on 30 Nov. the Southern Yemen People's Republic was proclaimed and the name subsequently changed to the People's Democratic Republic of Yemen. An agreement for eventual unification with the Yemeni Arab Republic was signed in Cairo on 28 Oct. 1972.

AREA AND POPULATION. The People's Democratic Republic of Yemen is bounded north by Saudi Arabia, east by Oman, south by the Gulf of Aden and west by the Yemeni Arab Republic. The Republic covers an area of approximately 61,890 sq. miles (160,300 sq. km). The population was (estimate, 1975) 1,663,170. The capital is Aden. The main towns are Aden (population, 250,000), Shaikh Othman (30,000) and Mukalla (25,000).

The island of **Kamaran** in the Red Sea (area 70 sq. miles) was in British occupation from 1915 to 1967, when the inhabitants opted in favour of remaining with the Republic but Yeman Arab Republic occupied it in 1972.

The island of **Perim** was first occupied by the French in 1738. In 1799 the British took formal possession but evacuated the island the same year. It was re-occupied by the British in Jan. 1851 and was later used as a coaling station. In Nov. 1967 the inhabitants opted in favour of remaining with the Republic.

GOVERNMENT

Chairman of Presidential Council: Salim Robai'a Ali.
Prime Minister: Ali Nasser Mohamed.

Foreign Affairs: Mohamed Salih Yafai Muti. *Interior:* Saleh Musleh. *Defence:* Lieut.-Col. Ali Ahmad Nasser Antar. *Justice and Waafs:* Abdullah Mohammed Ghanem. *Health:* Dr Abdullah Ahmad Bukir. *Local Administration:* Ali Salem al Baid. *Education:* Said Abdel Khair an Noban. *Communications:* Mahmud Abdullah Osheish. *Labour and Civil Service:* Ali Assad Mutanna. *Finance:* Fadl Muhsin Abdullah. *Agriculture and Agrarian Reform:* Mohammed Sulaiman Nasser. *Installations:* Haidar Abu Bakr al Attas. *Fishery Resources:* Mohammed Salim Akosh. *Culture and Tourism:* Ali Abdel Razzaq Badib. *Information:* Ahmad Salim Obeid. *Trade and Supply:* Mahmud Said Mahdi. *Industry and Acting Minister of Planning:* Abdel Aziz Abdel Wali. *State Security:* Mohammed Said Abdullah Muhsin.

National flag. Three horizontal stripes of red, white, black, with a blue triangle based on the hoist bearing a red star.

DEFENCE

Army. The Army, about 19,000 strong, and consists of 10 infantry and 1 artillery brigades, and 2 armoured battalions.

Navy. The Navy comprises 2 old patrol vessels, 2 motor torpedo-boats, 2 medium landing ships and 3 minor landing craft, all transferred from the Soviet Navy, 3 inshore minesweepers and 1 landing craft given by Britain and 4 small patrol boats purchased in Britain. Naval personnel in 1978 totalled 250 officers and men.

Air Force. Formed in 1967, the Air Force is now equipped mainly with aircraft of Soviet design. It has a squadron of 12 MiG-21 fighters, a squadron of 15 MiG-17 fighter-bombers, a few Il-28 twin-jet bombers, 3 An-24 twin-turboprop transports, 4 C-47s and about 8 Mi-8 and 6 Mi-4 helicopters. Personnel about 2,000.

INTERNATIONAL RELATIONS

Membership. The People's Democratic Republic of Yemen is a member of UN and the Arab League.

ECONOMY

Budget. The budget of the Republic (in £ sterling) for financial years ending 31 March was as follows:

	1970–71[1]	*1971–72*	*1972–73*	*1973–74*	*1974–75*
Revenue	13,000,000	14,519,230	13,890,502	13,545,295	13,810,662
Expenditure	18,000,000	22,557,152	25,060,255	23,524,154	29,353,764

[1] Estimates.

Currency. The currency is the South Yemen *dinar* and is divided into 1,000 *fils*. Coins: 50, 25, 5, 1 *fils*; notes: 10, 5 and 1 *dinar*, 500 and 250 *fils*.

Banking. The leading bank is the National Bank of Yemen. All foreign banks have been nationalized.

AGRICULTURE. Agriculture is the main occupation of the people. This is largely of a subsistence nature, sorghum, sesame and millet being the chief crops, and wheat and barley widely grown at the higher elevations. Of increasing importance, however, are the cash crops which have been developed since the Second World War, by far the most important of which is the Abyan long-staple cotton, now the country's major export.

Owing to paucity of rainfall, cultivation is largely confined to fertile valleys and flood plains on silt, built up and irrigated in the traditional manner. These traditional methods are being augmented and replaced by the use of modern earth-moving machinery and pumps. Irrigation schemes with permanent installations are in progress. Production (1972–73 in 1,000 tonnes): Sorghum and millet, 69; wheat, 16·8; cotton lint and seed, 11·7; sesame, 3·5; barley, 2.

Livestock (1976): Cattle, 102,000; sheep, 930,000; goats, 1·2m.; poultry, 1·4m.

FISHERIES. There is a thriving fisheries industry, fish being the Republic's major export after cotton.

COMMERCE. Trade is mainly transhipment and entrepôt, the port serving as a centre of distribution to and from neighbouring territories. Transit trade is mainly in cotton piece-goods, grains, coffee, hides and skins, and cheap consumer goods.

In 1974 imports totalled US$187m.; exports and re-exports, US$203m.

Total trade between Republic of Yemen and UK (British Department of Trade returns, in £1,000 sterling):

	1973	*1974*	*1975*	*1976*	*1977*
Imports to UK	3,445	8,118	3,630	781	187
Exports and re-exports from UK	4,470	5,968	8,394	12,325	22,613

COMMUNICATIONS

Roads. There are 1,150 miles of roads. Registered motor vehicles in 1972 numbered 19,373.

Aviation. Eleven airlines operate scheduled services: Alyemda, Air-India, Ethiopian Airlines, Middle East Airlines, Sudan Airways, Yemen Airlines, Aeroflot, Somali Air, Saudi Airlines, Kuwait Airways, Air Djibouti and Egyptair.

Shipping. Because of its favourable geographical position and its efficient service to ships, Aden used to be one of the busiest oil-bunkering ports in the world, handling some 550 ships a month.

Post. The automatic telephone system provided service to about 9,876 subscribers in 1973.

Radio telephone services are available with London (with extensions to Europe and America), Kenya (with extensions to Tanzania and Uganda), Bombay, Djibouti, Bahrain and Addis Ababa.

Cinemas (1971). There were 19 cinemas with a seating capacity of about 20,000.

EDUCATION. There were 961 schools in 1970–71.

DIPLOMATIC REPRESENTATIVES

OF THE PEOPLE'S DEMOCRATIC REPUBLIC OF YEMEN IN GREAT BRITAIN (57 Cromwell Rd, London, SW7 2ED)

Ambassador: Muhammad Hadi Awad.

OF GREAT BRITAIN IN THE PEOPLE'S DEMOCRATIC REPUBLIC OF YEMEN (28 Shara Ho Chi Minh, Khormaksor, Aden)

Chargé d'Affaires: J. S. M. Roberts.

The US Embassy in Aden was closed on 26 Oct. 1969.

OF THE PEOPLE'S DEMOCRATIC REPUBLIC OF YEMEN TO THE UNITED NATIONS

Ambassador: Abdalla Saleh Ashtal.

Books of Reference

Hickinbotham, Sir T., *Aden.* London, 1959
Ingrams, H., *Arabia and the Isles.* London
Thesiger, W., *Arabian Sands.* London, 1959
Trevaskis, K., *Shades of Amber.* London

YUGOSLAVIA

Capital: Belgrade
Population: 21·56m. (1976)
GNP per capita: US$1,680 (1976)

Socijalistička Federativna Republika Jugoslavija—Socialist Federal Republic of Yugoslavia

On 29 Nov. 1945 Yugoslavia was proclaimed a republic. On 8 March 1947 King Peter II and the other members of the dynasty were deprived of their nationality and their property was confiscated.

The peace treaty with Italy, signed in Paris on 10 Feb. 1947, stipulated the cession to Yugoslavia of the greater part of the Italian province of Venezia Giulia, the commune of Zara and the island of Pelagosa and the adjacent islets.

By an agreement of 10 Nov. 1975 the city of Trieste ('Zone A') was recognized as Italian and the Adriatic coastal portion of the former Free Territory of Trieste ('Zone B') as Yugoslav. A free industrial zone was set up in the Fernetici–Sezana region on both sides of the frontier.

AREA AND POPULATION. Yugoslavia is bounded in the north by Austria and Hungary, north-east by Romania, east by Bulgaria, south by Greece and west by Albania, the Adriatic Sea and Italy. According to the census taken 31 March 1971 the area and population of Yugoslavia are shown as follows:

Federal units	*Area in sq. km*	*Population*	*Pop. per sq.km*
Bosnia and Herzegovina	51,129	3,746,000	73
Montenegro (Crna Gora)	13,812	530,000	38
Croatia	56,538	4,426,000	78
Macedonia	25,713	1,647,000	64
Slovenia	20,251	1,727,000	85
Serbia with Vojvodina and Kosovo	88,361	8,447,000[1]	96
	255,804[2]	20,523,000	80

[1] Serbia proper, 5·25m.; Vojvodina, 1,953,000; Kosovo, 1,244,000. [2] 98,725 sq. miles.

Population (estimate) 1976: 21·56m.

The federal capital is Belgrade (Beograd).

The population of the principal towns and their conurbations (census, 31 March 1971) are as follows:

	Town	*Conurbation*
Serbia		
Belgrade (capital)	746,000	1,204,271
Niš	128,000	193,320
Kragujevac	71,180	130,396
Leskovac	45,000	147,248
Vojvodina		
Novi Sad (capital)	141,712	214,048
Subotica	88,787	146,755
Zrenjanin	59,580	129,846
Pančevo	54,269	110,433
Sombor	43,971	97,905
Kikinda	38,000	68,800
Vršac	34,231	50,503
Senta	24,714	31,407
Bečej	27,000	44,571
Kosovo		
Priština (capital)	77,000	152,733
Croatia		
Zagreb (capital)	566,084	602,058
Rijeka-Sušak	132,933	160,630
Split	153,000	183,912
Osijek	95,000	143,109
Karlovac	47,532	73,842
Pula	47,414	69,755
Slovenia		
Ljubljana (capital)	173,530	257,640
Maribor	97,167	172,155
Kranj	27,209	56,324
Bosnia and Herzegovina		
Sarajevo (capital)	244,045	292,241
Tuzla	53,825	107,124
Banja Luka	91,000	157,515
Mostar	47,606	89,405

	Town	Conurbation		Town	Conurbation
Macedonia			*Montenegro*		
Skopje (capital)	313,000	387,889	Titograd (formerly Podgorica) (capital)	54,509	98,437
Bitolj	65,851	124,648			
Prilep	48,242	96,521			

The working population at the 1971 census was (in 1,000) 8,890; broken down as follows: Agriculture and forestry, 3,903; industry and mining, 1,575; building, 398; government and administration, 289; crafts, 434; commerce, 524; transport, 324.

Vital statistics for calendar years:

	Live births	*Still-born*	*Deaths*	*Infantile deaths*	*Marriages*	*Divorces*
1973	379,051	3,162	180,997	16,692	183,665	23,221
1974	382,947	3,074	177,691	15,666	181,192	24,717
1975	386,721	2,923	184,924	15.413	181,165	25,101
1976	390,487	2,730	182,966	14,488	177,388	24,784

The Yugoslav (*i.e.*, South Slav) languages proper are Slovene, Macedonian and Serbo-Croat, the latter having 2 variants (Serbian and Croatian) which are regarded as constituting one language. There are claims, largely politically-motivated, that Croatian is a separate language and Macedonian a dialect of Bulgarian. Macedonian is and Serbian may be written in the Cyrillic alphabet. There are also substantial Albanian and Hungarian-speaking minorities. Art. 246 of the Constitution lays down that 'The languages of the nations and nationalities and their alphabets shall be equal throughout the territory of Yugoslavia'. In practice Serbo-Croat serves as a *lingua franca* throughout the country.

CONSTITUTION AND GOVERNMENT. The Constitution passed on 31 Jan. 1946 declared the Federal Republic to be composed of 6 republics: Serbia, Croatia, Slovenia, Bosnia and Herzegovina, Macedonia and Montenegro.

On 13 Jan. 1953 a new Constitution (Fundamental Law) confirmed the management of all public affairs by the workers and their representatives (which was introduced in 1950) as the basis of the entire social, economic and political system of Yugoslavia.

The Constitution promulgated on 7 April 1963 changed the name of the country into the Socialist Federal Republic of Yugoslavia, composed of the socialist republics of Bosnia and Herzegovina, Crna Gora (Montenegro), Croatia, Macedonia, Serbia and Slovenia (*i.e.*, now ranking in alphabetical order), and the 2 socialist autonomous provinces of Kosovo and Vojvodina within the framework of Serbia.

Under this Constitution, social self-government was exercised by the representative bodies of communes, districts, autonomous provinces, republics and the Federation and the rights to self-government and distribution of income proclaimed in 1953 were extended to those employed in public services. The former Council of Producers, in which only workers and employees engaged in economic production were represented, was replaced by Councils of Working Communities representing the working people employed in every field of social activity.

All the means of production and all natural resources are social property. Exceptions are peasants' holdings (up to 10 hectares of arable land) and handicrafts. Citizens may be owners of houses and dwellings for their personal and family needs.

A new Constitution was proclaimed on 21 Feb. 1974. The political principle of this Constitution is the direct transfer of economic and political decision making power to the working people through the 'assembly system'. An assembly is defined (Art. 132) as 'a body of social self-management and the supreme organ of power within the framework of the rights and duties of its socio-political community'. Assemblies are based upon the work-place or community and take various forms depending upon the nature of employment. Art. 133 states, 'Working people in basic self-managing organizations and communities and in socio-political organizations shall form delegations for the purpose of the direct exercise of their rights, duties and responsibilities and of organized participation in the performance of the functions of the assemblies of the socio-political communities', and Art. 135,

'Candidates for members of delegations of basic self-managing organizations and communities shall be proposed and determined by the working people in these organizations and communities in the Socialist Alliance of the Working People . . . or in trade union organizations'. At the apex of the assembly system is the federal legislature, the Assembly of the Socialist Federal Republic of Yugoslavia which has 2 Chambers: the Federal Chamber and the Chamber of Republics and Provinces.

The Federal Chamber consists of 30 delegates of self-managing organizations, communities and socio-political organizations from each Republic, and 20 delegates from each Autonomous Province. The Chamber of Republics and Provinces consists of 12 delegates from each Republican Assembly and of 8 delegates from each Provincial Assembly.

The Federal Executive Council consists of a President and several members, and of Federal Secretaries and Chairman of Federal Committees. Members of the Federal Executive Council are elected in conformity with the principle of equal representation of the Republics with corresponding representation of Autonomous Provinces.

The President of the Federal Executive Council is elected by the Chambers of the Assembly of the SFRY at the proposal of the Presidency; Members of the Council, at the proposal of the candidate President of the Federal Executive Council.

At the federal level there exist side by side two institutions which have the character of the head of state: the President and the Presidency of the Republic.

Every citizen over the age of 18 has the suffrage (16 if employed). At the general election of March–May 1978 turn-out was over 96% of the electorate.

President of the Republic: Josip Broz-Tito (elected 14 Jan. 1953; re-elected 30 Jan. 1954, 19 April 1958, 30 June 1963, 17 May 1967 and 29 July 1971. In 1974 he was re-elected for an unlimited term). *Vice-President:* Fadilj Hodža.

The membership of the collective Presidency (of which Marshal Tito is President by virtue of his office as President of Yugoslavia) was (1978) as follows:

Serbia: Peter Stambolić. *Croatia:* Vladimir Bakarić. *Slovenia:* Edvard Kardelj. *Montenegro:* Vidoje Zarković. *Bosnia–Herzegovina:* Cvijetin Mijatović. *Macedonia:* Lazar Kolićevski. *Kosovo:* Fadilj Hodža. *Vojvodina:* Stevan Doronjski.

President of the Assembly of the SFRY: Dragoslav Marković (elected May 1978).

President of the Federal Executive Council (Prime Minister): Veselin Djuranović. *Vice-Presidents:* Branislav Ikonić, Ivo Margan, Andrej Marinc, Dragoljub Stavrej, Gojko Ubiparić.

Federal Secretary for Foreign Affairs: Josip Vrhovec.

The Communist League of Yugoslavia had 1·7m. members in June 1978. In June 1978 its Praesidium had 24 members led by President Tito; *Secretary:* Stane Dolanc.

National flag: Three horizontal stripes of blue, white, red, with a large red, yellow-bordered star in the centre.

National anthem: Hej, Slaveni, jošte živi reč naših dedova—O Slavs, our ancestors' words still live.

DEFENCE

Army. The Yugoslav Army comprises 9 infantry divisions, 7 armoured, 11 infantry and 3 mountain brigades and 1 airborne battalion. Military service is for 15 months. Peace-time strength, 193,000.

Navy. The Navy comprises 5 submarines, 2 midget submarines, 1 destroyer, 10 fast missile boats, 14 fast torpedo boats, 20 fast gunboats (*ex*-torpedo boats), 1 minelayer (training ship), 3 patrol vessels, 4 coastal minesweepers, 23 patrol boats, 10 inshore minesweepers, 14 river minesweepers, 30 landing craft, 1 training ship (schooner), 1 survey ship, 1 salvage vessel, 1 yacht, 1 headquarters ship, 11 transports, 9 oilers, 8 water carriers and 21 tugs. Ten larger fast missile boats are under construction, and 2 submarines, 1 frigate, 1 tank landing ship and 12 assault landing craft are projected. Personnel in 1978: 2,500 officers and 24,500 ratings.

Air Force. The Air Force has about 350 combat aircraft and is organized in 2 Air

Corps, with HQ at Zagreb and Zemun. There are 2 fighter divisions equipped primarily with more than 100 Russian-built MiG-21s, 2 ground-attack divisions of locally-built Jastreb light jet attack aircraft, and 2 squadrons of RT-33A and Jastreb jet reconnaissance aircraft. Transport units fly Il-14 and C-47 twin-engined aircraft, 4-turboprop An-12s, and a few other types in small numbers. Training types are the nationally-designed Galeb jet basic trainer and the T-33A jet advanced trainer. A large number of Alouette III, Whirlwind, Ka-25, Mi-4 and Mi-8 helicopters are in service, with more than 100 locally-built Gazelles entering service as replacements. 'Guideline' surface-to-air missiles have been supplied by the USSR. Personnel numbers 30,000.

INTERNATIONAL RELATIONS

Membership. Yugoslavia is a member of UN and has special relationships with Comecon and OECD.

ECONOMY

Planning. A 5-year plan of economic development for 1976–80 envisages that industrial production should increase annually by 8%, and that of agriculture by 4%. A Danube–Tisa canal system is under construction.

Budget. Revenue and expenditure (Federal, Republican, Provincial and Communal) for calendar years (in 1m. dinars):

	1970	*1971*	*1972*	*1973*	*1974*	*1975*
Revenue	28,540	37,277	50,173	59,314	82,302	107,191
Expenditure	27,072	31,679	49,591	58,743	81,492	106,545

The revenue, 1975 (and 1974), was composed of 59,944m. (48,600m.) dinars in the federal budget, 21,590m. (15,124m.) dinars in the republican budgets, 7,210m. in the budgets of the autonomous provinces and 28,447m. (15,571m.) dinars in other budgets.

Main items of distributed resources in 1975 (in 1m. dinars): Defence, 28,815; government, 18,329; investments in economy, 19,342; non-economic investments, 3,649.

Currency. On 26 July 1965 the value of 1 *dinar*, divided into 100 *para*, was fixed at 0·710937 milligrammes of fine gold instead of 2·96224 milligrammes.

A new *dinar*, equivalent of 100 old dinars, was introduced on 1 Jan. 1966.

On 22 Jan. 1972 the dinar was devalued.

The National Bank issues coins of 0·05, 0·1, 0·2, 0·5 and 1, 2, 5 and 10 dinars, and notes of 5, 10, 50, 100, 500 and 1,000 dinars.

Circulation of notes and coins, as of 31 Dec. 1974, was 32,521m. dinars.

Banking. Banking was nationalized immediately after the War. The main bank is the National Bank. At 30 Sept. 1975 total credits for working assets amounted to 160,536m. dinars. Savings deposits totalled 63,073 dinars in 1976.

Weights and Measures. The metric weights and measures have been in use since 1883. The *wagon* of 10 tonnes is used as a unit of measure for coal, roots and corn. The Gregorian calendar was adopted in 1919.

ENERGY AND NATURAL RESOURCES

Electricity. Generation of electricity in 1976 (and 1975) was 43,573m. kwh. (40,004m.), of which 20,555m. kwh. (19,817m.) was hydro-electric.

Minerals. Yugoslavia has considerable mineral resources, including coal (chiefly brown coal), iron, copper ore, gold, lead, chrome, antimony and cement. The most important iron mines are at Vareš and Ljubija in Bosnia, and there are also considerable siderite and limonite iron ores between Prijedor, Sanski Most and Topusko. Copper ore is exploited chiefly at Bor (Serbia). The principal lead mines are at Trepča and Mežice. Chrome mines are in southern Serbia (Kosovo) and Macedonia (Skopje, Kumanovo). There are 2 antimony mines in western Serbia (Podrinje).

Mining output, in 1,000 tonnes, in 1976 (and 1975): Coal, 587 (598); lignite,

27,148 (25,509); bauxite, 2,033 (2,306); mercury, 0·4 (0·6); salt, 289 (295); manganese ore, 19 (17); iron ore, 4,259 (5,239); copper ore, 17,377 (14,576); lead and zinc ore, 3,806 (3,606); chrome ore, 2 (2); antimony ore, 71 (83); crude petroleum, 3,880 (3,692); pyrite concentrates, 440 (346); magnesite, 391 (485). In 1971, gold output was 3,850 kg; silver output in 1976, 144,000 kg.

Agriculture. Yugoslavia, with a total area of 25,580,400 hectares, had a cultivated area of 9·9m. hectares in 1977. Agriculture is not collectivized, though private holdings are limited to 10 hectares.

Area (in hectares) and yield (in 1,000 tonnes) in 1976: Maize, 2·37m. (9,106); wheat, 1·72m. (5,979); barley, 0·3m. (643); rye, 76,000 (105); tobacco, 69,000 (75); hemp, 7,500 (56); sunflower, 174,500 (319); potatoes, 308,000 (2,828).

Livestock. Jan. 1977: 812,000 horses, 5·6m. cattle, 7·4m. sheep, 7·3m. pigs.

The 1976 yield of fruit was as follows (in 1,000 tonnes): Apples, 486; pears, 105; grapes, 1,204; plums, 562; olives, 11; walnuts, 33; 6·4m. hectolitres of wine were produced.

There were, in 1976, 2,599,552 individual holdings and 2,362 peasant co-operatives. Total agricultural work force, 5·4m.; tractors, 225,524.

Forestry. The forest areas of Yugoslavia consist largely of beech, oak and fir. Forest area in 1976: 9,040,000 hectares (2,833,000 in private hands). The gross timber cut in 1976 was 18·42m. cu. metres.

Fisheries. In 1976 the landings of fish were (in tonnes): salt-water, 34,848; freshwater, 23,891. The number of fishing craft was 202 motor vessels (7,428 GRT) and 1,734 sailing and rowing vessels.

INDUSTRY AND TRADE

Employment. In Sept. 1977 there were 5·13m. employed in the social sector (i.e. excluding armed forces and self-employed) of whom 1·9m. were in manufacturing and mining, and 867,000 in the social services. There were some 700,000 unemployed. There were (1978) 4·5m. trade union members.

Industry. The majority of industries are situated in the north-west part of the country.

Industrial output (in 1,000 tonnes) in 1976 (and 1975): Pig-iron, 1,920 (2,100); steel, 2,740 (2,916); cement, 7,600 (7,066); sulphuric acid, 910 (936); fertilizers, 2,000 (2,195); plastics, 206 (160). Fabrics (in 1 sq. metres); Cotton, 381 (376); woollen, 67 (66). Sugar (1,000 tonnes), 535 (534). Motor cars (in 1,000s), 166 (183).

Commerce. Foreign trade, in 1m. dinars, for calendar years:

	1971	*1972*	*1973*	*1974*	*1975*
Imports	48,781	54,957	76,689	127,837	130,844
Exports	27,217	38,033	48,494	64,678	69,228

Imports to Yugoslavia, 1976, in 1m. dinars, from: Federal Republic of Germany, 20,858; Italy, 14,761; USSR, 17,526; USA, 6,450; Czechoslovakia, 4,826; UK, 45,344. Exports from Yugoslavia, 1976, in 1m. dinars, to: USSR, 19,646; Italy, 10,072; Federal Republic of Germany, 7,257; Czechoslovakia, 3,778; German Democratic Republic, 3,224.

The main imports (by value) in 1974 were (in 1m. dinars): Chemicals, 17,156; machinery and metal products, 15,049·5; textiles, 9,728; iron and steel, 9,506; electro industry, 5,449. The main exports: Non-ferrous metals, 9,595; machinery and metal products, 8,910; timber, 5,476; textiles, 4,944; shipbuilding, 3,438.

Total trade between Yugoslavia and UK (British Department of Trade returns, in £1,000 sterling):

	1973	*1974*	*1975*	*1976*	*1977*
Imports to UK	24,495	30,576	24,362	33,502	40,487
Exports and re-exports from UK	56,208	83,087	94,207	128,456	175,011

Tourism. In 1976, 5,590,000 (1975: 5,835,000) tourists visited Yugoslavia.

COMMUNICATIONS

Roads (1975). There were 36,836 km of asphalted roads and 36,531 km of macadamized roads. There were 1·53m. passenger motor cars and 160,000 trucks and buses. The north–south highway is being converted to 6-lane motorway.

Railways. In 1976 Yugoslavia had 9,967 km of railway, of which 2,649 km are electrified, carrying 126m. passengers, and, 74m. tonnes of freight. In 1976 the new railway linking Belgrade and the Adriatic coast port of Bar was completed.

Aviation. The national airline, Jugoslovenski Aero Transport (Adria-aviopromet, Pan-adria and Aviogenex) in 1976 flew on its home services, 9,838,000 km and carried 1·69m. passengers and 3·8m. ton-km of freight; international services (without Pan-adria), 21·9m. km, 1,117,000 passengers and 18·1m. ton-km of freight. The chief airfields are Belgrade, Zagreb, Ljubljana, Sarajevo, Skopje, Dubrovnik, Split, Titograd, Pula and Zadar.

Shipping. In 1976 Yugoslavia possessed a total of 432 vessels of 2m. gross tons.

In 1976 vessles of 41m. net tons entered the ports of Yugoslavia.

In 1971 Yugoslavia had 1,413 river craft. The length of the navigable rivers amounted to 1,844 km, that of canals to 191 km. There are 2 navigable lakes: Skadar (391 sq. km, of which 243 in Yugoslavia) and Ohrid (348 sq. km, of which 230 in Yugoslavia).

Post and Broadcasting. There were 3,438 post offices and 1,402,000 telephone subscribers in 1975. *Jugoslovenska Radiotelevizija* consists of almost 250 main, relay and local stations operating on medium-waves and FM. *Radio Koper* also broadcasts commercial programmes in Italian for northern parts of Italy. National and regional TV programmes are broadcast. Advertisements are broadcast for maximum 170 minutes each week. Number of receivers in 1976: radio, 4·4m.; television, 6·5m.

Cinemas (1976). 1,414, seating 459,000

Theatres (1976). 251, seating 76,000.

Newspapers (1976). There are 27 dailies, 1,912 other newspapers and 1,229 journals. There are no party newspapers but *Borba* and *Politika* enjoy semi-official status.

JUSTICE, RELIGION, EDUCATION AND WELFARE

Justice. There are county tribunals, district courts, supreme courts of the constituent republics and the supreme court of the Socialist Federal Republic of Yugoslavia. In county tribunals and district courts the judicial functions are exercised by professional judges and by lay assessors constituted into collegia. There are no assessors at the supreme courts.

All judges are elected by the socio-political communities in their jurisdiction. The judges exercise their functions in accordance with the legal provisions enacted since the liberation of the country.

The constituent republics enact their own criminal legislation, but offences concerning state security and the administration are dealt with at federal level.

Religion. Religious communities are separate from the State and are free to perform religious affairs. All religious communities recognized by law enjoy the same rights.

Serbia has been traditionally Orthodox and Croatia Roman Catholic. Moslems are found in the south as a result of the Turkish occupation. The 1953 percentage of the denominations was: Orthodox, 41·2%; Roman Catholic, 31·7%; Moslems, 12·3%; Protestants, 0·9%; without religion, 12·6%.

The Serbian Orthodox Church with its seat in Belgrade has 20 bishoprics within the country and 4 abroad, 3 in US and Canada and 1 in Hungary. The Serbian Orthodox Church numbers about 2,000 priests.

The Macedonian Orthodox Church with the Archbishop of Ohrid and Macedonia as its head in Skopje, has 4 bishoprics in the country and 1 abroad (American–Canadian–Australian). The Macedonian Orthodox Church numbers about 300 priests.

The Roman Catholic Church is divided into two provinces: Zagreb with 4 suffragan sees, and Sarajevo with 2 suffragan sees. In addition, the Roman Catholic

Church has 4 archbishoprics, 10 independent bishoprics directly connected with the Vatican and 3 Apostolic Administrators. There is a National Conference of Bishops with the Archbishop of Zagreb, at its head. The Roman Catholic Church has about 4,000 priests.

The Moslem Religious Union has 4 republic Superiorates in Sarajevo, Skopje, Titograd and Priština. The highest authority is the supreme synod of the Islamic Religious Community, which elects the Reis-ul-Ulema and the Supreme Islamic Superiorate.

The Moslem religious community has about 2,000 priests.

The Protestant churches covering 4 independent Lutheran Churches, numbering about 150,000 believers, the Reformed Christian Church, numbering about 60,000 believers, include also several much smaller churches of Baptists, Methodists, Adventists, Nazarenes, etc., numbering together about 100,000 believers. The Protestant churches have about 450 priests.

Also there are independent Old Catholic Churches with Synodal Council at Zagreb.

The Jewish religious community has about 35 communities making up a common league of Jewish Communities with its seat in Belgrade.

Education. Compulsory general education lasts 8 years, secondary 3–4 years. In 1976–7 there were 13,389 primary schools with 131,596 teachers and 2,861,985 pupils, 2,534 secondary schools with 50,380 teachers and 904,452 pupils, 460 primary schools for adults with 3,519 teachers and 56,586 pupils, 585 secondary schools for adults with 58,915 pupils (1975–6), 796 technical schools with 283,138 pupils and 5,877 teachers, 37 teacher training schools with 9,039 students and 768 teachers.

Schools and teacher training colleges of ethnic minorities (1976–7): Albanian, 1,131, 151; Hungarian, 179, 89; Bulgarian, 78, nil; Czech, 13, 2; Slovak, 26, 6; Italian, 30, 14; Romanian, 30, 10; Turkish, 64, 9; Ukrainian, 4, 2.

For higher and specialized education there were (1972–73) 256 faculties, academies and high schools with 16,783 professors and instructors and 261,302 students.

The national minorities have been provided with elementary, secondary and teachers' training schools of their own, namely: Albanian (1,114, 49, 125), Hungarian (178, 12, 70), Bulgarian (78, 0, 0), Czech (13, 1, 0), Slovak (27, 1, 4), Italian (30, 5, 5), Romanian (30, 2, 2), Turkish (64, 7, 3), Ukrainian (4, 1, 1).

Social Welfare. In 1975 there were 31,059 doctors and dentists, and 127,646 hospital beds (11,022 psychiatric).

Health insurance benefits totalled 19,325m. dinars and pensions 27,452m. dinars in 1974.

DIPLOMATIC REPRESENTATIVES

OF YUGOSLAVIA IN GREAT BRITAIN
(5 Lexham Gdns, London, W8 5JJ)

Ambassador: Živan Berisavljević (accredited 18 March 1977).

OF GREAT BRITAIN IN YUGOSLAVIA (46 Generala Ždanova, Belgrade)

Ambassador: R. A. Farguharson, CMG.

OF YUGOSLAVIA IN THE USA (2410 California St., NW, Washington, D.C., 20008)

Ambassador: Dimce Belovski.

OF THE USA IN YUGOSLAVIA (50 Kneza Miloša, Belgrade)

Ambassador: Lawrence S. Eagleburger.

OF YUGOSLAVIA TO THE UNITED NATIONS

Ambassador: Jakša Petric.

Books of Reference

Statistical Information: The Federal Institute for Statistics (Savezni Zavod za Statistiku; Kneza Miloša 20, Belgrade) was founded in Dec. 1944. *Director:* Ibrahim Latifić. It publishes: *Indeks* (from April 1952, with English and French translations); *Statistički bilten* (1950 ff., with English or French translations); *Statistical Yearbook* (from 1954, with English, Russian and French translations); *Statistics of Foreign Trade of the SFR Yugoslavia* (annual, from 1946; half-yearly, from 1951); *Statistical Pocket-book* (from 1955; in 5 eds.: Yugoslav, English, French, Russian, German).

The Assembly of the SFR of Yugoslavia. Belgrade, 1974
The Constitution of the Socialist Federal Republic of Yugoslavia. Belgrade, 1974
Auty, P., *Yugoslavia*. New York, 1965.—*Tito: A Biography*. London, 1970
Bogadek, F. A., *English–Croatian, Croatian–English Dictionary*. London, 1950
Clissold, S., *A Short History of Yugoslavia*. CUP, 1966
Dedijer, V., *et al.*, *History of Yugoslavia*. New York, 1974
Denitch, B. D., *The Legitimation of a Revolution: The Yugoslav Case*. Yale Univ. Press, 1976
Djilas, M., *Memoir of a Revolutionary*. New York, 1973
Horvat, B., *The Yugoslav Economic System*. White Plains, 1976
Hunter, B., *Soviet–Yugoslav Relations, 1948–72: A Bibliography*. New York, 1976
Jambrek, P., *Development and Social Change in Yugoslavia*. Farnborough, Hants., 1975
Kotnik, J., *Slovensko–angleski slovar*. 4th ed. Ljubljana, 1959
Nord, L., *Nonalignment and Socialism: Yugoslavia's Foreign Policy in Theory and Practice*. Uppsala, 1974
Pavlowitch, S. K., *Yugoslavia*. New York, 1971
Rusinow, D. I., *The Yugoslav Experiment, 1948–1974*. London, 1977
Ristić, Simić, Popović: *An English–Serbocroatian Dictionary*. 2 vols. Belgrade, 1956
Singleton, F., *Twentieth Century Yugoslavia*. London, 1976
Skerlj, R., *English–Slovene Dictionary*. 4th ed. Ljubljana, 1957
Tito, J. B., *The Essential Tito*. New York, 1970

National Library: Narodna biblioteka, 56 Kneza Mihailova, Belgrade. *Director:* Svetislav Djurić.

ZAÏRE

République du Zaïre

Capital: Kinshasa
Population: 25·6m. (1976)
GNP per capita: US$140 (1976)

HISTORY. Until the middle of the 19th century the territory drained by the Congo River was practically unknown. When Stanley reached the mouth of the Congo in 1877, King Leopold II of the Belgians recognized the immense possibilities of the Congo Basin and took the lead in exploring and exploiting it. The Berlin Conference of 1884–85 recognized King Leopold II as the sovereign head of the Congo Free State.

The annexation of the state to Belgium was provided for by treaty of 28 Nov. 1907, which was approved by the chambers of the Belgian Legislature in Aug. and Sept. and by the King on 18 Oct. 1908. The law of 18 Oct. 1908, called the Colonial Charter (last amended in 1959), provided for the government of the Belgian Congo, until the country became independent on 30 June 1960.

The departure of large numbers of the Belgian administrators, teachers, doctors, etc., on the day of independence left a vacuum which speedily resulted in complete chaos. Neither Joseph Kasavubu, the leader of the Abako Party, who on 24 June 1960 had been elected head of state, nor Patrice Lumumba, leader of the Congo National Movement, who was the prime minister of an all-party coalition government, could establish his authority. Lumumba found his main support in the Oriental and Kivu provinces. Personal, tribal and regional rivalries led to the breakaway of Katanga province under premier Moïse Tshombe. Early in July the Force Publique mutinied and removed all Belgian officers. Lumumba and Kasavubu called for intervention by the United Nations as well as the USSR. The Secretary-General dispatched a military force of about 20,000, composed of contingents of African and Asian countries. Lumumba was kidnapped by Katanga tribesmen and, in early Feb. 1961, murdered; his place was taken by Antoine Gizenga, who set up a government in Stanleyville.

On 15 Aug. 1961 the United Nations recognized the government of Cyrille Adoula as the central government. United Nations forces, chiefly Irish and Ethiopians, in mid-September invaded Katanga.

On 15 Jan. 1962 the forces of Gizenga in Stanleyville surrendered to those of the central government, and on 16 Jan. Adoula dismissed Gizenga. United Nations forces, chiefly Ethiopians and Indians, again invaded Katanga in Dec. 1962 and by the end of Jan. 1963 had occupied all key towns; Tshombe left the country. The UN troops left the Congo by 30 June 1964.

The Gizenga faction started a fresh rebellion and after the capture of Albertville (19 June) and Stanleyville (5 Aug.) proclaimed a People's Republic on 7 Sept. 1964. Government troops, Belgian paratroopers and a mercenary contingent captured Stanleyville on 24 Nov. after the rebels had massacred thousands of black and white civilians. The last rebel strongholds were captured at the end of April 1965.

In 1977 an Angolan-based invasion of Shaba (formerly Katanga) province was reported and in 1978 a full-scale conflict developed.

AREA AND POPULATION. Zaïre is bounded north by the Central African Empire, north-east by Sudan, east by Uganda, Rwanda, Burundi and Lake Tanganyika, south by Zambia, south-west by Angola, north-west by Congo. There is a short Atlantic coastline between the two last-named. The boundaries of the Congo colony were defined by the neutrality declarations of Aug. 1885 and Dec. 1894, and by treaties with Germany, Great Britain, France and Portugal.

On 22 July 1927 Belgium ceded to Portugal territory in the extreme south-west portion of the Belgian Congo, having an area of 3,500 sq. km, in return for a cession by Portugal of an area in the estuary of the Congo, near Matadi, of 3 sq. km. Belgium further undertook the construction of a railway to link up with the Portuguese railway, starting at Lobito; this railway was opened on 1 July 1931.

The area of the republic is estimated at 2,345,409 sq. km (895,348 sq. miles). The population is composed of 3 ethnical groups: Negroes (Bantu, Sudanese, Nilotics), Pygmies and Hamites (in the east). In the census (1970) the population was 21,637,876. Estimate (1976) 25·6m. Rate of growth 1970–75 was 2·85%.

In 1974 over 1·5m. refugees were living in Zaïre. Over 1m. of these were from Angola, others were mainly from Rwanda and Burundi.

On 2 May 1966 the main cities were renamed, population 1974: Kinshasa (Leopoldville), 1,990,717; Kananga (Luluabourg), 595,954; Lubumbashi (Elisabethville), 401,612; Mbuji-Mayi (Bakwanga), 334,725; Kisangani (Stanleyville), 297,829; Bukavu, 180,633; Likasi (Jadotville), 150,000; Kikwit, 149,324; Matadi, 142,808; Mbandaka (Coquilhatville), 136,877. The capital is Kinshasa.

The country and the river were named 'Zaïre' in 1971.

The country is divided into the following regions (with population at Dec. 1975): Kinshasa city (2·2m.), Bandundu (2·91m.), Equateur (2·68m.), Kasai West (3·15m.), Kasai East (2·75m.), Kivu (3·8m.), Bas-Zaïre (1·69m.), Shaba (2·04m.), Haut-Zaïre (3·58m.). (*See* map in THE STATESMAN'S YEAR-BOOK, 1966–67.)

The most important languages are: Kiswahili in the east, Tshiluba in the south, Kikongo in the area between Kinshasa and the coast, while Lingala is spoken widely in and around Kinshasa and along the river; Lingala has become the *lingua franca* after French.

CONSTITUTION AND GOVERNMENT. A Constitution, approved in a national referendum by over 90% of the voters in June 1967, established a Presidential regime. In 1971, 1974 and 1977 it was revised to establish: a single-chamber Parliament, the National Legislative Council, directly elected with 268 deputies, 1 for every 100,000 inhabitants; there is an equal number of substitute deputies who are known as 'suppléants'; a President directly elected for 7 years. The supreme institution is the sole political party, the *Mouvement Populaire de la Révolution* (MPR); its President is President of the Republic; its chief organ is the *Bureau Politique* consisting of the President of the Republic, the President of the National Legislative Council, the State Commissioners of Political Affairs, Justice, and leading members of the MPR. For details of earlier constitutions and governments *see* THE STATESMAN'S YEAR-BOOK, 1976–77, p. 1487.

The *Bureau Politique* of the MPR had 18 members in 1977 and nominates the Presidential candidate and appoints a permanent committee of 12 to assist him. The President appoints and leads the cabinet, the National Executive Council, comprising the State Commissioners with departmental responsibilities.

In July 1977 a series of constitutional and administrative reforms were introduced in order to decentralize government: they included elections by universal suffrage and secret ballot to the Urban Zone Councils, the Legislative Council and the *Bureau Politique* of the MPR.

The regions are each administered by a Commissioner, except for Kinshasa which has a Governor.

President: Mobuto Sese Seko (elected for a third term on 5 Dec. 1977).
Prime Minister: Mpinga Kasanga (re-appointed 12 Dec. 1977).
Foreign Affairs: Umba Di Lutete.

National flag: Green, with a yellow disc bearing an arm holding a flaming torch.

DEFENCE

Army. The country is divided in 9 military regions. Total strength approximately 30,000. Major units comprise 1 infantry division, 1 airborne division, 2 armoured battalions and 14 infantry battalions. Supporting units include engineer, signal, transport and military police companies.

The *Gendarmerie Nationale* is a separate service with responsibility for security. Estimated strength (1976) 35,000.

Navy. River and lake squadrons total 30 patrol craft of 7 different types, of French, US, North Korean and Chinese origin, of which less than half are in commission. Personnel in 1978 numbered 200 officers and men.

Air Force. The Air Force has been built up with training assistance from Italy. In 1977 it had a few Mirage 5 supersonic fighters, 20 Reims-Cessna Milirole observation and light attack aircraft, 13 Aermacchi MB.326GB armed jet trainers, 6 C-130 Hercules and 4 DHC-5 Buffalo turboprop transports, 18 Alouette and SA 330 Puma helicopters, 23 SIAI-Marchetti SF.260MC basic trainers and a variety of other transport and training aircraft. Personnel, approximately 1,500.

INTERNATIONAL RELATIONS

Membership. Zaïre is a member of UN, OAU and is an ACP state of EEC.

ECONOMY

Budget. Estimated revenue and expenditure (in 1m. zaïres) for calendar years:

	1970	*1971*	*1972*	*1973*	*1974*	*1975*	*1976*[1]
Revenue	215	289	299	383	447	556	615
Expenditure	300	273	274	364	650	...	471

[1] Provisional.

Currency. The currency unit, introduced on 23 June 1967, is the *zaïre*, divided into 100 *makuta*. Each *likuta* (plural *makuta*) is divided into 100 *sengi*. Bank-notes are issued in the following denominations: 10, 5 and 1 *zaïre*, 50, 20, 10 *makuta*. In Oct. 1976, £1 sterling = 1·46 *zaïre*.

Banking. The national bank is Banque du Zaïre. A development bank with state backing is the Société pour Finance et Développement (SOFIDE). Commercial banks operating in Zaïre are Banque de Paris et des Pays-Bas, Banque de Kinshasa, National & Grindlays Bank, Barclay's Bank SZPRL, First National City Bank, Union Zaïroise de Banques, Banque Commerciale Zaïroise, Bank du Peuple, Caisse Nationale d'Epargne et de Crédit Immobilier and Banque Internationale pour L'Afrique au Zaïre.

Weights and Measures. The metric system was introduced by law on 17 Aug. 1910.

ENERGY AND NATURAL RESOURCES

Electricity. The installed generating capacity (1974) was hydro, 1,054 mw; thermal, 79 mw.

Minerals. In 1975 most of Zaïre's foreign exchange was derived from mining of copper (461,000 tonnes), zinc concentrates (141,490), zinc (79,238), gold (2,439 kg), cobalt (12,104), cadmium (264), silver (84,487). The most important mining area is in the region of Shaba (formerly Katanga).

The principal mining companies are the State-owned Gecamines which took over the interests of Union Minière du Haut Katanga in 1967; the Belgian Société Générale des Minerais; the Zaïre-Japanese Sodimiza; the international Société Minière de Tenke-Fungurume which started production in 1976; and 2 diamond companies, MIBA and British Zaïre Diamond Distributors. Offshore oil production began in Nov. 1975.

Agriculture. Production has fallen greatly in the last few years and agriculture is now named *Priorité des Priorités* in the country's revival programme. A new Ministry of Rural Development was established in 1977 to stimulate output. Six projects have been inaugurated, using overseas aid, with the aim of increasing production of palm-oil, cocoa, tea, tobacco, cotton and sugar, and there are also continuing efforts towards improving strains and yields of maize, rice and manioc.

Production (1973, in tonnes): Palm-oil, 176,000; coffee, 71,000; rubber, 35,000; cacao, 14,360; tea, 8,000; rice (paddy), 227,000; sugar-cane, 451,960; ivory, 91; bananas, 70,321; plantains, 1,005,000; fish, 80,000. Chief imports were maize (125,000), rice (52,000), wheat (129,300), meats (16,000). Chief exports (1975) were palm-oil (53,000), coffee (59,000), rubber (24,000), tea (4,600) and timber (49,000 cu. metres).

Livestock (1976): Cattle, 1m.; sheep, 711,000; goats, 2·3m.; poultry, 11m.

COMMERCE. Imports in 1975 totalled 349m. zaïres, exports totalled 289m. zaïres. In 1975, 65% of the exports (by value) consisted of copper.

Total trade between Zaïre and UK (British Department of Trade returns, in £1,000 sterling):

	1972	*1973*	*1974*	*1975*	*1976*	*1977*
Imports to UK	19,081	22,214	36,496	29,933	38,393	59,246
Exports and re-exports from UK	13,600	11,568	20,428	23,609	16,853	18,234

COMMUNICATIONS

Roads. Of 150,000 km of roads only 20,600 km are of national importance and all roads are earth-surfaced. There were 177,931 motor vehicles registered in Dec. 1975. Of these, 95,978 were cars, 33,505 trucks, 2,989 buses, 9,153 motor cycles, and other types, 36,306.

Railways. The total length of public railways in Sept. 1975 was 5,230 km, 858 km being electrified.

Aviation. There are 2 international and 40 principal airports, and over 150 other landing strips.

Ten international airlines, including British Caledonian Airways, operate in and out of Kinshasa from Europe, Africa and the USA. The national airline Air Zaïre, with a fleet of 25 planes (Nov. 1975), operates on all the main internal routes as well as on international routes to Europe and other African cities. Internal feeder services are assured by the private charter company AMAZ. PANAM act as technical and managerial advisers to Air Zaïre.

Shipping. The Zaïre River and its tributaries are navigable for about 14,000 km. Regular traffic has been established between Kinshasa and Kisangani as well as Ilebo, on the Lualaba (*i.e.*, the river above Kinsangani), on some tributaries and on the lakes. Zaïre has only 30 km. of sea coast.

At the port of Matadi, the most important harbour, the imports in 1974 amounted to 655,000 tonnes and the exports to 540,000 tonnes.

Post and Broadcasting. In 1970 there were 351 post offices. Zaïre is included in the Universal Postal Union and in the African Postal Union. Length of telegraph lines, 2,459 km. There were 15 broadcasting stations, 161 stations of wireless telegraphy and 206 telegraph offices; telephones numbered 26,274 in 1975. There is a ground satellite communications station outside Kinshasa.

Cinemas (1974): 91 cinemas had a seating capacity of 23,300.

JUSTICE, RELIGION AND EDUCATION

Justice. In 1976 there was a supreme court in Kinshasa, 2 courts of appeal (Kinshasa and Lubumbashi) and 8 courts of first instance. An Appeal Court sits in Kisangani.

Religion. There were, on 31 Dec. 1975, 2,637 foreign Catholic missionaries and 3,375 Catholic nuns. Numerous missionaries were massacred in 1964.

Roman Catholics in 1975 numbered 9m.; Protestants, 1·1m.; Moslems, about 115,000, and Jews, 1,520.

Education. In the state and state-inspected primary schools in 1972–73 there were 2·99m. pupils while the secondary school students numbered 308,000. In 1971 all Institutes of Higher Education combined to form the National University of Zaïre. In the 1976 academic year there was a total of 26,000 students attending the National University.

DIPLOMATIC REPRESENTATIVES

OF ZAÏRE IN GREAT BRITAIN (26 Chesham Place, London, SW1X 8HH)

Ambassador: Kaninda Mpumbua Tshingomba, GCVO.

OF GREAT BRITAIN IN ZAÏRE (Ave. de l'Equateur, Kinshasa)

Ambassador: A. E. Donald.

OF ZAÏRE IN THE USA (1800 New Hampshire Ave., NW, Washington, D.C., 20009)

Ambassador: Kasongo Mutuale.

OF THE USA IN ZAÏRE (310 Ave. des Aviateurs, Kinshasa)

Ambassador: Walter L. Cutler.

OF ZAÏRE TO THE UNITED NATIONS

Ambassador: Kabeya wa Mukeba.

Books of Reference

Anstey, R., *King Leopold's Legacy: The Congo under Belgian Rule 1908–1960*. OUP, 1960
Area Handbook for the Democratic Republic of the Congo (Kinshasa). US Government Printing Office, Washington, 1971
Atlas Général du Congo. Académie Royale, Brussels
Cornevin, R., *Histoire de Congo*. Paris, 1963
Ganshof van de Meersch, W. J., *Fin de la souveraineté Belge au Congo*. Brussels and The Hague, 1965
Lefever, Ernest W., *Uncertain Mandate: Politics of the UN Congo Operation*. Johns Hopkins Press, 1967
Martelli, G., *Experiment in World Government: The UN Operation in the Congo 1960–64*. London, 1967
Slade, R. M., *King Leopold's Congo: Aspects of the Development of Race Relations in the Congo's Independent State*. OUP, 1962
Young, C., *Politics in the Congo: Decolonization and Independence*. Princeton UP and OUP, 1965
Zaïre, Republic of. *Profits du Zaïre*, Kinshasa, 1972

ZAMBIA

Capital: Lusaka
Population: 5·14m. (1976)
GNP per capita: US$440 (1976)

HISTORY. The independent Republic of Zambia (formerly Northern Rhodesia) came into being on 24 Oct. 1964 after 9 months of internal self-government following the dissolution of the Federation of Rhodesia and Nyasaland on 31 Dec. 1963.

By an Order in Council dated 4 May 1911 the two provinces of North-eastern and North-western Rhodesia were amalgamated under the name of Northern Rhodesia, with effect from 17 Aug. 1911.

By an Order in Council dated 20 Feb. 1924, the office of Governor was created, an executive council constituted and provision made for the institution of a legislative council which, since 1945, had an unofficial majority. On 1 April 1924 the British South Africa Company was relieved of the administration of the territory by the Crown.

AREA AND POPULATION. Zambia is bounded by Tanzania in the north, Malawi in the east, Mozambique in the south-east and by Rhodesia and South West Africa (Namibia) in the south. The area is 290,586 sq. miles (752,620 sq. km). Population (1976), 5,138,000. Capital, Lusaka, 401,000; Kitwe, 251,000; Ndola, 229,000; Mufulira, 134,000; Chingola, 136,000; Luanshya, 121,000; Kabwe, 98,000; Livingstone, 58,000.

CONSTITUTION AND GOVERNMENT. The Constitution provides for a President, elected in the first instance by the Legislative Assembly, but subsequently at each general election by the electorate. On 13 Dec. 1972 President Kaunda signed a new Constitution based on one-party rule.

The single political party is the United National Independence Party. Its full-time executive organ (headed by a Secretary-General) is the Central Committee, whose 24 members are elected by the National Council of the Party. The Central Committee has precedence over the legislative body, the National Assembly, which is led by the Prime Minister and consists of 125 elected members and up to 10 nominated members, including a cabinet of 24 ministers.

The Cabinet, as of April 1978, was composed as follows:

President: Dr Kenneth David Kaunda.

Secretary-General to the Party: A. G. Zulu. *Prime Minister:* E. H. Mudenda. *Foreign Minister:* Dr S. G. Mwale. *Home Affairs:* A. Milner. *Finance:* J. Mwanakatwe. *Development and Planning:* Peter Matoka. *Rural Development:* P. Lusaka. *Power, Transport and Communications:* J. C. Mapoma. *Labour and Social Services:* H. D. Banda. *Education:* Prof. L. Goma. *Mines and Industry:* A. J. Soko. *Commerce:* Dr M. M. Bull. *Health:* C. Mwananshiku. *Lands, Natural Resources and Tourism:* Dr N. S. Mulenga. *Legal Affairs and Attorney-General:* M. Chona. *Information and Broadcasting:* U. G. Mwila. *Local Government and Housing:* A. B. Chikwanda. *Lusaka Province;* R. Kunda. *Central Province:* J. B. A. Siyomunji. *Copperbelt Province:* J. B. Mutale. *Eastern Province:* S. M. Chisembele. *Luapula Province:* W. R. Mwondela. *Northern Province:* M. Ngalande. *North-Western Province:* N. Mundia. *Southern Province:* S. K. Tembo. *Western Province:* W. Nkanza.

Flag: Green, with in the fly a panel of 13 vertical strips of dark red, black and orange, and above these a soaring eagle in gold.

Provincial Administration. The Republic is divided into 9 provinces. Their names, headquarters, area (in sq. miles) and estimated population in 1974 were as follows:

Province	*Headquarters*	*Area*	*Population*	*Province*	*Headquarters*	*Area*	*Population*
Lusaka	Lusaka	139	415,000	Eastern	Chipata	26,682	557,000
Copperbelt	Ndola	12,096	1,072,000	Southern	Livingstone	32,928	543,000
Luapula	Mansa	19,524	355,000	N.-Western	Solwezi	48,582	259,000
Northern	Kasama	51,076	577,000	Western	Mongu	48,798	471,000
Central	Kabwe	44,900	917,000				

The provinces are administered by Central Committee Members for the provinces who are responsible for the overall government and Party administration of their respective areas. The Members are assisted by a Cabinet Minister, a Political Secretary and a Permanent Secretary. Each district in all provinces is headed by a District Governor, and these are directly responsible to their respective provincial Cabinet Ministers.

The seat of Government is at Lusaka. The other important centres are Livingstone, the old capital, Ndola, Luanshya, Mufulira, Kitwe, Chililabombwe, Kalulushi and Chingola on the Copperbelt; Kabwe, the oldest mining township; Chipata, centre of a tobacco farming area.

DEFENCE

Army. The Army consists of 3 infantry battalions, 1 armoured car squadron, 2 artillery batteries and supporting units. Strength, 5,000.

Air Force. Creation of the Zambian Air Force was assisted initially by an RAF mission. Equipment acquired in this period and still in use includes 5 twin-engined Caribou and 4 single-engined Beaver transports built in Canada. Training and expansion of the Air Force was next taken over by Italy, with the purchase of 20 Aermacchi M.B.326G jet basic trainers, 8 SIAI-Marchetti SF.260M piston-engined trainers and 28 Agusta-Bell 205/212 helicopters. Four SOKO Jastreb jet light attack aircraft and 2 Galeb jet trainers have since been acquired from Yugoslavia, 6 DHC-5 Buffalo twin-turboprop transports from Canada and 20 Supporter armed light trainers from Sweden.

INTERNATIONAL RELATIONS

Membership. Zambia is a member of UN, the Commonwealth, OAU and is an ACP state of EEC.

ECONOMY

Planning. A second 5-year development plan (1972–76) envisaged investment of K2,609m. and an economic growth rate of 6·8% per annum. The emphasis has been on rural development and an important goal is to achieve self-sufficiency in staple foodstuffs, particularly maize. The third development plan has been postponed from Jan. 1977 to Jan. 1978.

To promote industrial growth and to ensure greater Zambian participation in the economy the Government has, since 1968, taken a controlling interest in several companies, including the mines. Government's control of those companies in which it has a majority shareholding is exercised *via* the Zambian Industrial and Mining Corporation (ZIMCO) the holding company for the Industrial Development Corporation (INDECO) which controls all industrial and distributive concerns; the Mining Development Corporation (MINDECO) which holds the Government's 51% share in the mines.

Budget. Revenue and expenditure for calendar years (in K1,000):

	1972	*1973*	*1974*	*1975*
Revenue: Current	315,226	385,180	647,523	448,338
Capital fund	138,477	290,295	150,160	169,792
Expenditure: Current	363,122	394,111	440,913	580,991
Capital fund	160,367	388,152	193,772	245,560

Currency. Decimal currency was introduced on 16 Jan. 1968. The *Kwacha* (K) is divided into 100 *ngwee* (n). Notes of K20, K10, K5, K2, K1 and 50 *ngwee* are in use. Money circulation at 31 Dec. 1975 was K317,096,000.

Banking. Barclays Bank International has 25 branches, 6 sub-branches and 17 agencies; Standard Bank has 18 branches and 17 agencies; National & Grindlays, 10 branches and 1 sub-branch; National Commercial Bank, 10 branches and 1 in London; the post office saving bank has branches throughout the Republic.

The Finance Development Corporation (FINDECO) controls the building societies, all insurance companies, one commercial bank and has shares in a second one. The Agricultural Finance Corporation provides loans to farmers, co-operatives, farmers' associations, agricultural societies and such bodies as will further the agricultural industry.

ENERGY AND NATURAL RESOURCES

Electricity. The total installed capacity of hydro and thermal power stations, excluding Zambia's share of Kariba South, amounts to 855 mw and the energy consumption during 1975 amounted to some 5,539·4m. kwh., including imports from Zaïre.

The hydro stations are located at Mbala, Mansa, Kasama, Mulungushi, Lunsemfwa and Victoria Falls, Lusiwasi and Kafue Gorge. Work has started on the Kariba North Project. The thermal stations are located on the Copperbelt. A number of diesel power stations have been installed, mostly in the North-Western and Northern Provinces.

Minerals. The total value of minerals produced in 1975 was:

	Output (1,000 tonnes)	*Value (K1,000)*		*Output (1,000 tonnes)*	*Value (K1,000)*
Copper (blister)	21·1	12,712	Lead	19·1	3,551
Copper (electrolytic)	619·2	442,540	Coal	813·9	9,613
Zinc	46·8	19,559	Cobalt	1·8	9,666

Agriculture. Although 70% of the population is dependent on agriculture only 10% of GDP is provided by the industry. Principal agricultural products (1973) were maize, 386,016 tonnes; tobacco, 6,694 tonnes; groundnuts, 2,784 tonnes; cotton, 4,090 tonnes; sugar, 446,350 tonnes.

Livestock (1976): 2·3m. cattle; 100,000 pigs; 50,000 sheep and 300,000 goats. Poultry (1976): 13·3m. day-old chicks; 250m. eggs; 11·46m. live and dressed birds.

INDUSTRY AND TRADE

Industry. In Dec. 1974 there were 31,700 persons employed in agriculture, forestry and fisheries; 63,630 in mining and quarrying; 40,820 in manufacturing; 68,630 in construction and 24,650 in transport and communications.

Commerce. In 1975 imports totalled K597,610,596, exports K518,043,534 and re-exports K4,129,132. The principal imports were machinery and transport equipment (K211,300,485), electricity and mineral fuels (K81,115,484), chemicals (K77,292,528), manufactured articles (K140,211,165). Principal exports were metals (K505,077,000) and tobacco (K4,969,000).

Principal trade areas were: Other African countries: imports K1,264,000, exports K9,015,000; EEC: imports K108,181,000, exports K204,707,000; EFTA (excluding UK): imports K36,127,000, exports K26,631,000; other European countries: imports K7,721,000, exports K31,833,000; Soviet bloc: imports K2,413,000, exports K388,000; dollar area: imports K90,415,000, exports K139,000; non-dollar Latin America: imports K1,326,000, exports K11,521,000; Middle East countries: imports K76,044,000, exports K761,000; other Asian countries: imports K73,204,000, exports K104,891,000.

Total trade between Zambia and UK (British Department of Trade returns, in £1,000 sterling):

	1974	*1975*	*1976*	*1977*
Imports	75,261	91,964	73,052	93,254
Exports and re-exports from UK	63,623	79,938	66,181	80,175

COMMUNICATIONS

Roads. There were (1978) over 4,500 km of tarred roads.

Railways. Zambia Railways are that part of the old Rhodesia Railways north of the Victoria Falls. Route-miles open for traffic, 649 (3 ft 6 in. gauge). Construction of the 1,100-mile Tan–Zam railway, giving Zambia access to Dar es Salaam, began in 1970.

The line, connecting with Zambia Railways at Kapiri Mposhi, was opened for traffic in Oct. 1975.

Aviation. There were (1978) 130 airports in Zambia (51 government owned). Lusaka is the principal international airport. Seven foreign airlines use Lusaka.

Post. There were (1978) 13 head post offices and 219 other post offices. On 1 Jan. 1977 there were 55,403 telephones.

Cinemas. In 1971 there were 28 cinemas with a seating capacity of 13,400.

Newspapers. There are 2 national daily papers: *The Times of Zambia* (circulation, 65,000) and *Zambia Daily Mail* (45,000).

JUSTICE, RELIGION, EDUCATION AND WELFARE

Justice. The Judiciary consists of the Supreme Court, the High Court and 4 classes of magistrates' courts; all have civil and criminal jurisdiction.

The Supreme Court hears and determines appeals from the High Court. Its seat is at Lusaka.

The High Court exercises the powers vested in the High Court in England, subject to the High Court ordinance of Zambia. Its sessions are held where occasion requires, mostly at Lusaka and Ndola.

All criminal cases tried by subordinate courts are subject to revision by the High Court.

Religion. Freedom of worship is one of the constitutional rights of Zambian citizens. Minority groups, such as the Asian community, are free to practise the religions of Hinduism and Islam, and the views of the leaders of these communities are respected by the Government. The Lumpa Church was banned in 1965 for security reasons, following considerable loss of life, but the Jehovah's Witnesses are allowed to continue their way of life despite the conflict of authority in their views and the views of politicians.

The Christian faith has largely replaced traditional African religion, and the Christian Churches number about 500,000 members and adherents. The Churches, founded mainly from the Western world, are slowly finding their autonomy—as illustrated by the United Church of Zambia (formerly British and French missions) and the Reformed Church of Zambia (formerly South African mission).

There is close co-operation between Catholic and Protestant churches, and the Protestant churches themselves work in the fields of radio, television, education, medicine, refugee aid, etc., through the Christian Council of Zambia. The United Church and the Anglican Church are holding union discussions, and Roman Catholic, Anglican and United Church leaders meet together for consultation, and together they discuss matters of common concern with the President of Zambia, Dr Kaunda.

Education. In 1974 the primary school enrolments were 858,191 and secondary school enrolments were 65,764. In 1974 the University of Zambia had 2,612 full-time students. Government expenditure on education in 1974 was K91·36m.

Health. In 1978 there were 80 hospitals and over 1,000 children's clinics served by 423 doctors.

DIPLOMATIC REPRESENTATIVES

OF ZAMBIA IN GREAT BRITAIN (7–11 Cavendish Pl., London, W1N 0HB)

High Commissioner: Lombe Phyllis Chibesakunda (accredited 11 Oct. 1977).

OF GREAT BRITAIN IN ZAMBIA (Independence Ave., Lusaka)

High Commissioner: W. L. Allinson.

OF ZAMBIA IN THE USA (2419 Massachusetts Ave., NW, Washington, D.C., 20008)

Ambassador: Putteho M. Ngonda.

OF THE USA IN ZAMBIA (P.O. Box 1617, Lusaka)

Ambassador: Stephen Low.

OF ZAMBIA TO THE UNITED NATIONS

Ambassador: Gwendoline C. Konie.

Books of Reference

General Information: The Director, Zambia Information Services, P.O. Box RW 20, Lusaka.

Office of National Development and Planning, *First National Development Plan 1966–70*
Central Statistical Office, Lusaka, *Statistical Year-Book, 1973*
Laws of Zambia. 13 vols. Govt. Printer, Lusaka
Bond, G. C., *The Politics of Change in a Zambian Community.* Univ. of Chicago Press, 1976
Gann, L. H., *History of Northern Rhodesia to 1953.* London, 1964
Hall, R., *Kaunda, Founder of Zambia.* London, 1964
Kaunda, Kenneth D., *Zambia Shall be Free.* London, 1962.–*Humanism in Zambia.* Lusaka. 2 vols. 1967 and 1974.—*Zambia's Economic Revolution.* Lusaka, 1968.—*Zambia's Guidelines for the Next Decade.* Lusaka, 1968.—*Letter to my Children.* Lusaka, 1973
Kay, G., *A Social Geography of Zambia.* London, 1967
Legum, C., *Zambia Independence and Beyond.* London, 1966
Mebeelo, H., *Reaction to Colonialism.* London, 1971
Mulford, D. C., *The Northern Rhodesia General Election 1962.* OUP, 1964.—*Zambia, the Politics of Independence 1957–64.* OUP, 1968
Mwanakatwe, J., *The Growth of Education in Zambia.* London, 1968
Roberts, A., *A History of Zambia.* London, 1977
Sklar, R. L., *Corporate Power in an African State.* Univ. of California Press, 1976
Schultz, J., *Land Use in Zambia.* Munich, 1976
Tordoff, W., *Politics in Zambia.* Manchester Univ. Press, 1974

INDEX

PLACE AND INTERNATIONAL ORGANIZATIONS INDEX

PRODUCT INDEX